HANDBOOK ON NEUROSYMBOLIC AI AND KNOWLEDGE GRAPHS

Frontiers in Artificial Intelligence and Applications

The book series Frontiers in Artificial Intelligence and Applications (FAIA) covers all aspects of theoretical and applied Artificial Intelligence research in the form of monographs, selected doctoral dissertations, handbooks and proceedings volumes. The FAIA series contains several sub-series, including 'Information Modelling and Knowledge Bases' and 'Knowledge-Based Intelligent Engineering Systems'. It also includes the biennial European Conference on Artificial Intelligence (ECAI) proceedings volumes, and other EurAI (European Association for Artificial Intelligence, formerly ECCAI) sponsored publications. The series has become a highly visible platform for the publication and dissemination of original research in this field. Volumes are selected for inclusion by an international editorial board of well-known scholars in the field of AI. All contributions to the volumes in the series have been peer reviewed.
The FAIA series is indexed in ACM Digital Library; DBLP; EI Compendex; Google Scholar; Scopus; Web of Science: Conference Proceedings Citation Index – Science (CPCI-S) and Book Citation Index – Science (BKCI-S); Zentralblatt MATH.

Volume 400

Recently published in this series

Vol. 399. Y. Kiyoki, V. Sornlertlamvanich, M. Tropmann-Frick, H. Jaakkola and N. Yoshida (Eds.), Information Modelling and Knowledge Bases XXXVI
Vol. 398. A.J. Tallón-Ballesteros (Ed.), Fuzzy Systems and Data Mining X – Proceedings of FSDM 2024, Matsue, Japan, 5–8 November 2024
Vol. 397. J. Seibt, P. Fazekas and O.S. Quick (Eds.), Social Robots with AI: Prospects, Risks, and Responsible Methods – Proceedings of Robophilosophy 2024 – 19–23 August 2024, Aarhus University, Denmark, and online
Vol. 396. A.J. Tallón-Ballesteros (Ed.), Electronics, Communications and Networks – Proceedings of the 14th International Conference (CECNet 2024), Matsue, Japan, 5–8 November 2024
Vol. 395. J. Savelka, J. Harasta, T. Novotna and J. Misek (Eds.), Legal Knowledge and Information Systems – JURIX 2024: The Thirty-seventh Annual Conference, Brno, Czech Republic, 11–13 December 2024
Vol. 394. C. Trojahn, D. Porello, P.P.F. Barcelos (Eds.), Formal Ontology in Information Systems – Proceedings of the 14th International Conference (FOIS 2024)
Vol. 393. J.-L. Kim (Ed.), Machine Learning and Intelligent Systems – Proceedings of MLIS 2024, Kampar, Perak, Malaysia, 17-20 November 2024

ISSN 0922-6389 (print)
ISSN 1879-8314 (online)

Handbook on Neurosymbolic AI and Knowledge Graphs

Edited by

Pascal Hitzler

Department of Computer Science, Kansas State University

Abhilekha Dalal

Department of Computer Science, Kansas State University

Mohammad Saeid Mahdavinejad

Department of Computer Science, Kansas State University

and

Sanaz Saki Norouzi

Department of Computer Science, Kansas State University

Sage | IOS Press

ISBN 978-1-64368-578-6 (print)
ISBN 978-1-64368-579-3 (online)
Library of Congress Control Number: 2025933046
doi: 10.3233/FAIA400

IOS Press

A Sage company
Nieuwe Hemweg 6B
1013 BG Amsterdam

Sage
1 Oliver's Yard
55 City Road
London EC1Y 1SP

Sage
2455 Teller Road
Thousand Oaks
California 91320

Sage
Unit No 323-333, Third Floor, F-Block
International Trade Tower
Nehru Place, New Delhi – 110 019

Sage
8 Marina View Suite 43-053
Asia Square Tower 1
Singapore 018960

Printed in Germany
Libri Plureos GmbH
Friedensallee 273
22763 Hamburg

Preface

Neurosymbolic integration has emerged as a very active subfield of artificial intelligence research. Historically, neural approaches have excelled at perceptual tasks—such as pattern recognition in images and natural language—while symbolic frameworks have offered powerful methods for knowledge representation, logical inference, and interpretability. Today's AI landscape is increasingly defined by hybrid systems that blend these complementary paradigms, enabling both sophisticated pattern recognition and robust reasoning grounded in explicit knowledge. This confluence is particularly relevant in the context of knowledge graphs (KGs), which provide a structured, machine-readable representation of relational data and domain ontologies. KGs serve as a bridge between symbolic logic and the subsymbolic world of deep learning, bringing forward a new era of data-driven discovery and explainable AI.

This book was conceived to capture and organize state-of-the-art neurosymbolic and knowledge graph-based AI. It reflects an ecosystem in which large language models, deep neural networks, and symbolic representations converge. The chapters collected here illustrate the progress that has been made in bridging data-driven machine learning with the semantic richness of KGs, while also uncovering emerging challenges in trustworthiness, interpretability, and scalability. The primary aim is to provide researchers, practitioners, and students with a comprehensive overview of these intersecting fields—unifying theoretical foundations with practical insights and real-world applications.

We have intentionally designed this volume's structure to move from Foundations and Representation to Construction, Reasoning, Interpretability, and, ultimately, Applications. After setting the conceptual stage in Foundations of Neural and Symbolic AI, the book explores the nuances of Knowledge Graph Representation and Embeddings, where readers gain insight into the cutting-edge methods of turning symbolic knowledge into continuous vector spaces. We then move on to Knowledge Graph Construction, Integration, and Quality, covering key challenges such as entity alignment, canonicalization, fusion, and the critical aspect of uncertainty management. Next, in Neurosymbolic Reasoning and Hybrid Architectures, readers will find an anthology of solutions that seamlessly combine symbolic logic with deep learning pipelines—spanning question answering, program synthesis, dynamic KG methods, and beyond. The subsequent section, Explainable and Interpretable AI, addresses one of the most pressing needs in modern AI: ensuring transparency, accountability, and trust in systems that operate on increasingly complex data. Finally, Interdisciplinary Perspectives and Real-World Applications showcase how these methods tackle domain-specific problems across news analytics, literary studies, life sciences, food computing, social media, and more—demonstrating the far-reaching impact of knowledge-infused neural AI.

Our hope is that this book not only advances the conversation in neurosymbolic integration and knowledge graphs but also serves as a practical guide for building AI systems that are robust, transparent, and ethically grounded. We see this volume as a starting point for researchers and developers who wish to create applications that meaningfully combine data-driven models with explicit symbolic reasoning. By tying together fundamental concepts, advanced methods, and real-world scenarios, we strive to offer a well-rounded perspective suitable for graduate students, academic researchers, and industrial practitioners alike.

We extend our sincere gratitude to the authors and contributors whose expertise, vision, and dedication made this volume possible. Their chapters reflect a remarkable diversity of approaches, each reinforcing the notion that the synergy between symbolic and neural methodologies is indispensable for the future of AI. We also thank our readers for embarking on this journey. May these pages spark your curiosity, inform your practice, and inspire breakthroughs at the vibrant intersection of knowledge graphs, deep learning, and symbolic reasoning.

Pascal Hitzler
Abhilekha Dalal
Mohammad Saeid Mahdavinejad
Sanaz Saki Norouzi

Manhattan, Kansas, December 2024

Contents

Part III. Knowledge Graph Construction, Integration, and Quality

Part IV. Neurosymbolic Reasoning and Hybrid Architectures

Part I

Foundations of Neural and Symbolic AI

Handbook on Neurosymbolic AI and Knowledge Graphs
P. Hitzler et al. (Eds.)
IOS Press, 2025

doi:10.3233/FAIA250199

Primer on Deep Learning Models

Sanaz SAKI NOROUZI [a,1], Mohammad MASJEDI [b], Hossein SHOLEHRASA [a], Samira ALKAEE TALEGHAN [c] and Ali ARASTEHFARD [d]
[a] *Kansas State University, USA*
[b] *Providence Health & Services, USA*
[c] *University of Colorado Denver, USA*
[d] *University of Connecticut, USA*
ORCiD ID: Sanaz Saki Norouzi https://orcid.org/0009-0003-4441-108X, Mohammad Masjedi https://orcid.org/0009-0000-0510-2821, Hossein Sholehrasa https://orcid.org/0009-0000-9952-9841, Samira Alkaee Taleghan https://orcid.org/0009-0009-2928-8144, Ali Arastehfard https://orcid.org/0009-0009-3811-3960

Abstract. This chapter offers a detailed overview of key concepts in deep learning. In addition to traditional Neural Networks, several deep learning models such as Convolutional Neural Networks, Recurrent Neural Networks, Transformers, Generative Adversarial Networks, Graph Neural Networks, and Autoencoders are reviewed. Each model is described in terms of its architecture, functionality, and primary applications. The chapter also highlights the significance of popular deep learning frameworks in facilitating model implementation and deployment.

Keywords. Deep Learning, CNN, RNN, Generative models, GNN, Transformer

1. Introduction

Deep Learning has made a revolution in Artificial Intelligence (AI) and Machine Learning (ML) in the past decade. Although Neural Networks (NN) were first proposed in the mid-20th century, today's deep learning is much more sophisticated. It can automatically learn complex patterns from vast amounts of data, enabled by access to large datasets, faster computers, and new neural network-building methods [1,2]. Deep learning traces its origins to the work of Warren McCulloch and Walter Pitts in the 1940s, who introduced the concept of artificial neurons [3]. But it wasn't until the 1980s, when David Rumelhart, Geoffrey Hinton, and Ronald Williams introduced the Backpropagation algorithm, that neural networks began to take off [4]. Nevertheless, early models were still unable to train deep networks, mainly due to limited computing power.

The 2000s saw a remarkable resurgence of interest in deep learning, especially with major advances in computer vision and speech recognition. Yann LeCun's work on Convolutional Neural Networks (CNNs) showed impressive results in classifying images. At the same time, Recurrent Neural Networks (RNNs), especially those with long short-term memory (LSTM) units, demonstrated strong performance on sequential data like

[1]Corresponding Author: Sanaz Saki Norouzi, sanazsn@ksu.edu.

language. More recently, the introduction of Transformers has made a profound impact on the field of Natural Language Processing (NLP), yielding significant advancements in machine translation, text summarization, and a range of other tasks. [1,5,6]. Additionally, they serve as the foundation for Large Language Models (LLMs) such as GPT and BERT, which have transformed NLP by enabling more accurate language understanding and generation at scale.

A significant advantage of deep learning is that it can automatically find valuable patterns in raw data, therefore there is no need to manually create features [7]. This is helpful in areas like image processing, where CNNs are great at recognizing spatial patterns, and in NLP, where LLMs help understand complex language. Despite this, deep learning has its own challenges. For instance, it requires large amounts of labeled data, is computationally expensive to run, and can be difficult to interpret due to the complexity of the models.

Researchers are continuously working to build, improve, and explain deep learning models as the field progresses. One promising idea is Neuro-symbolic AI, which integrates the strengths of neural networks with symbolic (logic and rules-based) reasoning. This approach enables AI systems to learn from data and comprehend abstract concepts and relationships, thereby facilitating the development of more interpretable and efficient models.Among the aspects of neuro-symbolic AI is the utilization of Knowledge Graphs, a structured representation of information that organizes data into entities, attributes, and their relationships. This forms a network of interconnected facts that can be leveraged for reasoning and insights, making deep learning more understandable by bridging the gap between data-driven and knowledge-driven AI.

The applications of deep learning have expanded significantly beyond the academic domains, with widespread applications across various industries such as healthcare, finance, autonomous vehicles, and entertainment. As scholars explore different deep learning models, their designs, and the challenges they face, it is also essential for them to learn about the historical context and the seminal works that have made today's AI systems possible. In this chapter, a comprehensive overview of various deep learning architectures is provided, detailing their advantages and challenges.

2. Fundamentals of Deep Learning

The fundamentals of deep learning include a set of key concepts and techniques that form the backbone of this powerful machine learning approach. At its core, deep learning is based on artificial neural networks composed of multiple layers, inspired by the structure of the human brain [1]. One of the fundamental principles of deep learning is the idea of hierarchical feature learning. As data passes through the layers of a neural network, each layer extracts increasingly abstract features, allowing the model to capture complex relationships in the data. This ability to automatically learn representations is what sets deep learning apart from traditional machine learning approaches [8]. Another crucial aspect of deep learning is the use of various activation functions that introduce non-linearity into the network and enable it to model complex, non-linear relationships [9]. The process of training these networks involves optimizing a large number of parameters using techniques like backpropagation and gradient descent, which are fundamental to the learning process [4]. Regularization techniques are also fundamental to deep learning, as they help prevent overfitting and improve the generalization capability of models [10].

Deep learning also relies heavily on large datasets and significant computational power. The availability of big data and advances in GPU technology have been key drivers in the recent success of deep learning. The depth of neural networks—referring to the number of hidden layers—has been a key factor in the recent success of deep learning. These fundamentals collectively enable deep learning models to achieve state-of-the-art performance in areas like computer vision, natural language processing, and graph representation, revolutionizing numerous fields and applications.

2.1. Basics of NNs

Neural Networks (NNs) are inspired by the structure and functioning of the human brain, designed to identify patterns and solve complex problems by learning from data. A neural network consists of artificial neurons, organized into layers: an input layer, one or more hidden layers, and an output layer. Each neuron in a layer is connected to neurons in the next layer with associated weights. The input layer receives the data, which is then processed through the hidden layers by performing weighted sums and applying activation functions. The output layer produces the final result, which could be a classification, a regression value, or a more complex structure depending on the task [1]. The power of neural networks lies in their ability to learn from data training. During training, the network adjusts its weights and biases to minimize a loss function, typically using optimization algorithms like gradient descent and backpropagation. This allows the network to improve its performance on the given task over time.

2.1.1. Perceptron

The simplest form of a neural network is the perceptron, introduced by Frank Rosenblatt in 1958 [11]. The key innovation in Rosenblatt's model is the combination of inputs in a weighted sum, which, when exceeding a predefined threshold, causes the neuron to fire and produce an output. This threshold serves as the activation function, typically outputting 1 if the weighted sum is positive, and 0 otherwise. Mathematically, the output of a perceptron can be expressed as:

$$y = f\left(\sum_{i=1}^{n} w_i x_i + b\right) \tag{1}$$

where x_i are the inputs, w_i are the weights, b is a bias term, and f is an activation function. The perceptron uses a simple learning algorithm to adjust its weights based on the difference between the predicted and actual outputs. While limited to linearly separable problems, the perceptron forms the basis for more complex neural architectures and played a key role in the early development of artificial neural networks.

2.1.2. MLP

The Multilayer Perceptron (MLP) is a type of feedforward neural network that extends the concept of the single perceptron to multiple layers of neurons. It typically consists of an input layer, one or more hidden layers, and an output layer [9]. MLPs can learn non-linear relationships in data and are capable of approximating any continuous function [12]. In an MLP, each neuron in a hidden layer receives inputs from all neurons in the previous layer, computes a weighted sum, applies an activation function, and sends the result to all neurons in the next layer. This feedforward structure allows MLPs to map inputs to outputs effectively. MLPs are trained using the backpropagation algorithm, which efficiently computes the gradient of the loss function with respect to each weight in the network. This allows the network to learn complex, non-linear decision boundaries, making MLPs capable of solving a wide range of problems.

2.2. Activation Functions

The power of NNs lies in their ability to learn complex, non-linear relationships in data. This is achieved through the use of activation functions, which allow neural networks to capture and represent complex patterns that would otherwise be impossible with purely linear functions. Activation functions are applied to the weighted sum of inputs at each neuron, determining whether and to what extent the signal should propagates through the network's subsequent layers [13,14]. Mathematically, for a neuron receiving inputs $x_1, x_2, \ldots, x_n$ with corresponding weights $w_1, w_2, \ldots, w_n$ and bias b, the output y is computed as $y = f\left(\sum_{i=1}^{n} w_i x_i + b\right)$, where f is the activation function. This non-linear transformation is crucial for the network's ability to approximate complex functions and make non-linear decisions.

Common activation functions are sigmoid, hyperbolic tangent (tanh), and Rectified Linear Unit (ReLU) [9]. The choice of activation function can greatly affect the network's performance and training dynamics. The sigmoid function, defined as $f(x) = \frac{1}{1+e^{-x}}$, maps inputs to a value between 0 and 1. While historically popular, it can suffer from vanishing gradient problems for very large or small inputs. The tanh function, $f(x) = \frac{e^x - e^{-x}}{e^x + e^{-x}}$, maps inputs to a value between -1 and 1 and often performs better than sigmoid in practice due to its zero-centered nature. However, it is still susceptible to vanishing gradients for extreme inputs. ReLU, defined as $f(x) = \max(0, x)$, has become the most widely used activation function in recent years [15]. It helps alleviate the vanishing gradient problem for positive inputs and allows for sparse activation, as it outputs zero for all negative inputs. The computational efficiency of ReLU (simply requiring a max operation) also contributes to its popularity, especially in deep networks with many layers. However, ReLU can suffer from the "dying ReLU" problem, where neurons can get stuck in a state where they always output zero. Leaky ReLU, defined as $f(x) = \max(\alpha x, x)$ where α is a small constant, addresses the "dying ReLU" problem by allowing a small gradient when the unit is not active [16]. For the output layer, the choice of activation function depends on the specific task. In multi-class classification problems, the softmax function is often used as it normalizes the output to a probability distribution over predicted output classes. This ensures that the outputs are positive and sum to 1, which can be interpreted as probabilities.

2.3. Backpropagation

Backpropagation is a fundamental algorithm in training neural networks, serving as the backbone for efficiently computing gradients of the loss function with respect to the network's parameters. Introduced by Rumelhart, Hinton, and Williams in 1986, backpropagation has become an indispensable tool in the field of deep learning [4]. The core idea of backpropagation is to efficiently calculate the gradient of the loss function with respect to each weight in the network by applying the chain rule of calculus. This process occurs in two main phases: a forward pass and a backward pass. In the forward pass, input data propagates through the network layer by layer, with each neuron computing its output based on its inputs, weights, and activation function. This culminates in the network's final output and the calculation of the loss. The backward pass then begins at the output layer, where the gradient of the loss with respect to the output is computed. This gradient is then propagated backwards through the network, layer by layer. At each layer, the algorithm computes two key quantities: The gradient of the loss with respect to the layer's inputs (to be passed to the previous layer) and the gradient of the loss with respect to the layer's weights and biases (used for updating the parameters). Mathematically, for a loss function L and a weight $w_{ij}^{(l)}$ connecting neuron j in layer $l-1$ to neuron i in layer l, the gradient is computed as:

$$\frac{\partial L}{\partial w_{ij}^{(l)}} = \frac{\partial L}{\partial a_i^{(l)}} \cdot \frac{\partial a_i^{(l)}}{\partial z_i^{(l)}} \cdot \frac{\partial z_i^{(l)}}{\partial w_{ij}^{(l)}} \tag{2}$$

where $a_i^{(l)}$ is the activation of neuron i in layer l, and $z_i^{(l)}$ is its weighted input [17]. Despite its effectiveness, backpropagation can face challenges in very deep networks, such as the vanishing or exploding gradient problem. This occurs when gradients become extremely small or large as they are propagated back through many layers, making it difficult for early layers to learn effectively. Various techniques have been developed to address these challenges, including careful weight initialization (e.g., Xavier/Glorot initialization), the use of effective activation functions like ReLU to mitigate gradient issues, and architectural innovations such as skip connections in residual networks and normalization techniques like batch normalization [18,15].

2.4. Loss Functions and Optimization

Optimization is a fundamental concept in machine learning and deep learning, involving the adjustment of model parameters to either minimize or maximize an objective function $f(x)$. In the context of neural networks, we typically aim to minimize a function, often referred to as the cost function, loss function, or error function. Loss functions measure the difference between predicted and actual outputs. The formula of a generic loss function $\mathscr{L}$ can be represented as: $\mathscr{L}(\hat{y}, y)$ where $\hat{y}$ represents the predicted output from the model, and y represents the actual target or ground truth. It provides a measure of how well the model is performing and guides the optimization process. Common loss functions include Mean Squared Error (MSE) for regression tasks and Cross-Entropy Loss for classification problems [19].

At the core of neural network training is the optimization process, with gradient descent being the primary algorithm. The optimization process in neural networks involves determining the parameters θ (weights and biases) that minimize a cost function J(θ). Gradient descent iteratively refines the model parameters to minimize the loss function by following the gradient of the loss with respect to these parameters. The core idea of gradient descent can be expressed mathematically as:

$$\theta_{t+1} = \theta_t - \eta \nabla_\theta J(\theta) \tag{3}$$

where θ_t represents the current parameter values, η is the learning rate, and $\nabla_\theta J(\theta)$ is the gradient of the cost function J with respect to the parameters θ [20]. The backpropagation algorithm provides an efficient method for computing the gradients necessary for optimization by applying the chain rule to calculate the gradient of the loss function with respect to each parameter in the network. Optimization algorithms can be broadly categorized into batch (or deterministic) methods and stochastic methods. **Batch Gradient Descent**: This method computes the gradient using the entire training dataset in each iteration. While it provides a stable estimate of the gradient, it can be computationally expensive for large datasets. **Stochastic Gradient Descent (SGD)**: This approach updates the parameters using only one randomly selected example at each iteration. SGD is computationally efficient and can help escape local minima, but it introduces more noise in the optimization process [21]. **Mini-batch Gradient Descent**: A compromise between batch and stochastic methods, mini-batch gradient descent computes the gradient on small random subsets of the training data. This approach balances the benefits of both batch and stochastic methods.

The effectiveness of gradient descent is heavily influenced by the learning rate η. A learning rate that is too high may cause the algorithm to overshoot the minimum, while one that is too low can result in slow convergence. Adaptive methods like AdaGrad, RMSprop, and Adam adjust learning rates dynamically during training, optimizing performance by adapting to the gradients' characteristics.

The choice of an optimization algorithm can significantly impact both the speed of training and the final performance of neural networks.

2.5. Overfitting and Regularization

Overfitting is a common challenge in deep learning, where a model becomes overly complex and starts to memorize noise and random variations in the training data rather than learning underlying patterns. This often leads to high performance on the training set but poor generalization to new, unseen data [22]. Overfitting can be influenced by several factors such as limited training data or an overly complex model compared to the problem at hand. Recognizing overfitting is crucial for developing robust models, often identified by a growing gap between training and validation performance as training progresses [23].

To combat overfitting, various regularization techniques have been developed. Regularization includes any adjustments made to a learning algorithm aimed at decreasing its generalization error without necessarily reducing its training error.[24] Common regularization approaches include L1 and L2 regularization (also known as weight decay), which add penalties to the loss function based on the magnitude of the model weights [25]. Dropout is another powerful technique that randomly deactivates a portion of neurons during training, forcing the network to learn more robust features [10]. The choice of regularization techniques varies among different problems, datasets, and model architectures, often requiring empirical tuning to achieve optimal results.

3. Convolutional Neural Networks

Convolutional Neural Networks (CNNs) were introduced by LeCun in 1989 for recognizing hand-written digits [26]. It is, also known as ConvNet, is a deep learning algorithm for processing data with a known grid-like topology, such as images, signals, and sequences. For instance, a color image can be represented as three 2D arrays, each corresponding to the intensity values of red, green, and blue channels. This multi-array structure is common across various types of data: 1D arrays for time-series or text sequences, 2D arrays for grayscale images or audio spectrograms, and 3D arrays for video frames or medical imaging scans. CNNs are adept at processing diverse data formats, making them versatile tools in machine learning applications. Four main ideas behind the CNNs allow them to take advantage of the properties of natural signals: local connections, shared weights, pooling, and the use of multiple layers [1].

CNNs are inspired by the biological visual cortex, where the structure of the visual area is composed of small regions of cells that are sensitive to specific areas of the visual field [27]. This biological model helps CNNs in recognizing patterns and spatial hierarchies within the data. The core idea is to use convolution operations, which apply filters to the input data, allowing the network to detect various features like edges, textures, and more complex patterns as the network depth increases [28].

CNNs are similar to traditional neural networks in that they are composed of neurons that are optimized through the learning process. Each neuron receives input and performs operations such as scalar products followed by non-linear functions. The network, from the input to the output, represents a single perceptive score function, with the final layer containing loss functions associated with the classes. Although mainly utilized in image pattern recognition tasks, traditional neural networks' techniques and tricks still apply to the CNNs. This focus allows CNNs to incorporate image-specific features into their architecture, making them more suitable for such tasks [29]. CNNs have revolutionized the fields of computer vision and pattern recognition by leveraging local connectivity and parameter sharing, enabling significant advancements in tasks like image classification (e.g. ImageNet, Inception and VGGNet), object detection (e.g. YOLO), and segmentation. While traditional neural networks can handle small datasets like the MNIST database (28x28 pixels), larger images (e.g., 64x64 pixels or more) can significantly increase their number of weights per neuron, thus making them impractical for such large-scale image tasks. CNNs address these challenges by efficiently managing the complexity and the scale of image data.

CNNs are structured using three primary types of layers: convolutional, pooling, and fully-connected layers. Each layer type serves a specific purpose: convolutional layers extract features, pooling layers reduce spatial dimensions, and fully-connected layers integrate information for the final decision-making. This combination allows CNNs to progressively learn hierarchical representations of input data.

3.1. Convolution Layer

Convolution layers are the fundamental building block of CNNs. They process and extract features from the input data by applying a set of learnable filters, or kernels, across the input volume. This mechanism is crucial in various tasks, including image recognition and object detection, as it enables the network to identify diverse patterns and structures within the data. In a convolution layer, each filter slides (or convolves) over the input data, performing element-wise multiplications and summations. The result of this operation is a feature map, which highlights the presence of specific features detected by the filter at different spatial locations. This process is repeated across multiple layers, enabling the network to learn increasingly complex and abstract representations of the input data. While each filter is spatially compact (in terms of width and height), it extends through the entire depth of the input volume. The convolution layer's primary components include Convolution Operation, Stride and Padding, and Activation Function.

3.1.1. Convolution Operation

This involves sliding the filter over the input and performing element-wise multiplications followed by summation. The result of this operation is known as the feature map. Mathematically, if I represents the input and K represents the kernel, the convolution operation can be expressed as [20]:

$$(I * K)(i,j) = \sum_m \sum_n I(i+m, j+n)K(m,n) \tag{4}$$

where i and j are spatial coordinates and m, n are filter coordinates.

3.1.2. Stride and Padding

Stride defines the step size with which the filter moves across the input. Padding is used to control the output size by adding borders to the input. Common padding strategies include 'valid' (no padding) and 'same' (the output has the same dimensions as the input). The output height (H_{out}) and width (W_{out}) with stride S are given by [30]:

$$H_{out} = \left\lfloor \frac{H_{in} - F}{S} \right\rfloor + 1 \tag{5}$$

$$W_{out} = \left\lfloor \frac{W_{in} - F}{S} \right\rfloor + 1 \tag{6}$$

The output height (H_{out}) and width (W_{out}) with padding P are given by [30]:

$$H_{out} = \left\lfloor \frac{H_{in} - F + 2P}{S} \right\rfloor + 1 \tag{7}$$

$$W_{out} = \left\lfloor \frac{W_{in} - F + 2P}{S} \right\rfloor + 1 \tag{8}$$

3.1.3. Activation Function

Activation functions are essential components in CNNs, applied after each convolution operation to introduce non-linearity, normalize the output, and enable feature selection. They allow the network to learn complex patterns beyond simple linear combinations. Common activation functions such as ReLU, Leaky ReLU, and Tanh are applied element-wise to the convolution output, enabling the network to progressively learn more abstract features as data flows through the layers.

3.1.4. 1D, 2D and 3D Convolutional Layer

1D convolutional layers operate on one-dimensional sequences of data. The operation slides along a single axis, making them ideal for data with a clear sequential structure. Some of their applications includes time-series prediction, audio signal processing, and NLP tasks like text classification and sentiment analysis.

2D convolutional layer are the most common type which operate on two-dimensional grids of data, such as image pixels. The operation slides over both height and width dimensions of the input. The key applications include image classification, face recognition, and object detection.

3D convolutional layer extend the concept to three-dimensional data, particularly useful for volumetric data or sequences of 2D data like videos. The operation slides along three axes: height, width, and depth (or time in the case of videos). Some applications are video analysis, medical imaging (CT scans, MRI), and 3D object recognition.

While the complexity in terms of computational requirements and parameter count increases from 1D to 3D, the fundamental principles of CNNs (local connectivity, weight sharing, and hierarchical feature learning) remain the same.

3.1.5. Other Convolutional Layers

There are several other convolution layers developed to address specific challenges or to enhance the performance of CNNs.

Dilated Convolution is an advanced technique that expands the receptive field of the network without increasing the number of parameters. This method modifies the standard operation by introducing "holes" or "dilation" in the kernel, where the dilation factor in the filter expands the receptive field. Some applications include semantic segmentation, audio generation, and tasks requiring context aggregation over a larger field [31].

Transpose Convolution (Deconvolution) performs upsampling, essentially the reverse operation of the standard convolution, with the filter sliding over the input data to increase the spatial dimensions. This method is popular in Image generation, super-resolution, and semantic segmentation tasks [32].

Depthwise Separable Convolutions decompose the standard method into a depthwise followed by a pointwise convolution. The depthwise operation applies a single filter per input channel, while the pointwise (1x1) operation combines the output channels. This significantly reduces the number of parameters and the computational cost. The key applications are lightweight text models and Natural Language Processing (NLP) [33].

3.2. Pooling Layer

Pooling layers are typically inserted after the convolutional layers, with the primary function of downsampling. This, while retaining the most important information, reduces the spatial dimensions of the feature maps. While the convolutional layers detect local features, pooling layers merge the similar ones. Pooling, typically max or average, creates invariance to small shifts and distortions in the input. This mean that small movements in the feature's position will have less impact on the output, making the model more robust. This combination allows CNNs to progressively build complex representations of data. [1]. Decreasing the number of parameters in the network results in faster training times and lower computational costs. Multiple stages of convolution, non-linearity, and

pooling are usually stacked, followed by additional convolutional and fully-connected layers. Despite their complex structure, CNNs can be trained efficiently using standard backpropagation techniques. There are several types of pooling available:
Max Pooling: It is the most common type of pooling which operates by dividing the input into non-overlapping rectangular regions and taking the maximum value from each. This, while reducing the dimensionality, will retain the most prominent features.
Min Pooling: It works by taking the minimum value from each pooling window. This is less common but can be useful in applications where the smallest values in the feature map are of interest.
Average Pooling: It calculates the mean value of the elements in each region. It is beneficial in scenarios where the average presence of the features is more important than their strongest activation, and is often used in applications requiring smoother outputs and more generalized feature representations.
Global Average Pooling: This method reduces all channels of the input feature map to a single value by taking the average over the entire spatial dimensions. This effectively summarizes the feature map by generating a vector with a length equal to the number of channels. This is commonly used at the end of the CNN architecture, before the fully connected layers, or directly before the output layer. It lowers the spatial dimensions to a vector of class scores, making it suitable for classification tasks. This technique also reduces the number of parameters in the network, helping to prevent overfitting.

3.3. Fully Connected Layer

Fully connected (FC) layers are crucial in high-level reasoning and final decision-making. Found towards the end of the CNN architecture, they integrate all learned features from previous layers by connecting each input to all the neurons. This enables the network to transform high-dimensional feature maps into actionable outputs such as class scores. FC layers excel at learning complex patterns and dependencies, making them indispensable for accurate predictions in classification and regression tasks. They are also pivotal in transfer learning and multimodal data integration tasks, contributing to versatility and robustness [20].

4. Recurrent Neural Networks

A Recurrent neural network (RNN) is another type of deep learning model designed to work with sequential data like texts, genomes, sensors, and stock market data. Intuitively, they try to simulate people's behavior in understanding a context; for example, as they read further into a text, they memorize and recall related words, which help them grasp the overall meaning. In other words, they capture the dependencies of data points in time-series data using memory mechanism. Thus, RNNs have applications in areas like language modeling and generating text, speech recognition, image descriptions, and video tagging [34,35].

4.1. RNN

The concept of the RNN was first proposed by Rumelhart et al [4]. A feed-forward NN lacks loops, whereas an RNN has a feedback loop that enables it to feed information back to itself. This loop helps to take into account the previous inputs $X_{0:t-1}$ beside the current input X_t for time t. A simple RNN consists of an input layer, a hidden layer, and an output layer which is illustrated in Figure 1.

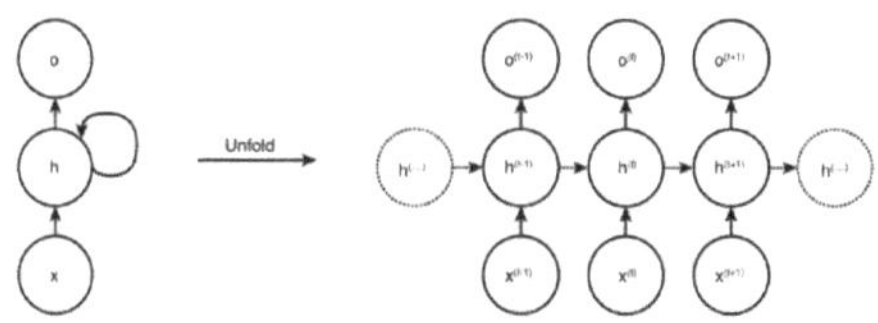

Figure 1. A simple recurrent neural network [36]

At time t, let's consider H_t and X_t as the hidden state and the input, respectively. Also, there is a weight matrix from the input to the hidden state W_{xh}, and a weight matrix for hidden state to hidden state W_{hh}, the bias b_h, and the activation function Φ which is usually a sigmoid or a tanh function. Thus, the hidden and output variables are:

$$H_t = \varphi_h(X_t W_{xh} + H_{t-1} W_{hh} + b_h) \tag{9}$$

$$O_t = \varphi_o(H_t W_{ho} + b_o) \tag{10}$$

Another important aspect of RNNs is that they use Backpropagation Through Time (BPTT) to update their weights during training. BPTT is an extension of the standard backpropagation algorithm that accounts for the temporal nature of sequences [34,37].

As stated before, deep neural network architectures are much more efficient than shallow ones. One such architecture is the Deep Recurrent Neural Network (DRNN). To construct a DRNN with L hidden layers, RNNs of any type are simply stacked on top of each other. In this structure, the hidden state of the initial layer is calculated like the Eq.(9) and Eq.(10), but for the subsequent layers, the hidden state from the preceding layer is used as input. [34].

Bidirectional RNN (BRNN) is another type of RNN, which processes the input in forward and backward directions (Figure 2). Thus, To calculate the forward and backward hidden states, Eq.(9) is used for each direction. Then, after concatenating the results, it is fed to the output layer.[38].

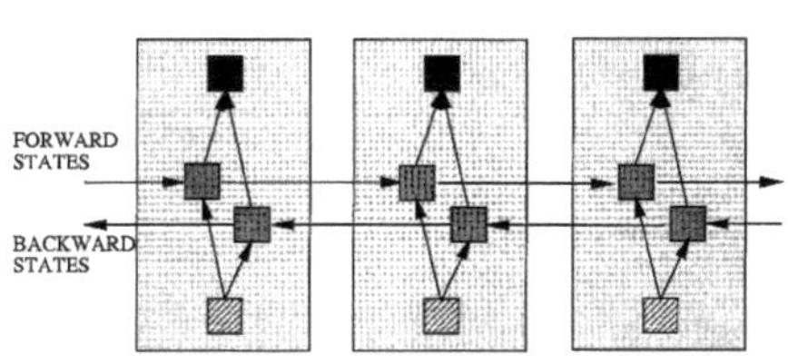

Figure 2. Bidirectional recurrent neural network architecture [38].

Recurrent connections enhance the performance of neural networks by capturing sequential dependencies. Nevertheless, the memory efficiency of these connections is constrained by the employed training algorithms. One major challenge in training deep neural networks is the vanishing gradient problem. It refers to the process where, during the training of deep neural networks with gradient-based optimization methods, the gradients of the loss function for the weights progressively diminish as they backpropagate through each layer. This is known as the "vanishing gradients" problem, which leads to extremely small updates to the weights of the earlier layers. As a result, these initial layers learn very slowly or stop learning altogether, making it challenging to train deep networks effectively. This problem can be mitigated by approaches like using different activation functions such as ReLU and other variants such as Leaky ReLU, Parametric ReLU, and Exponential Linear Units (ELUs) [39], using Residual Networks (ResNets) [40], using different techniques for weight initialization such as Xavier [18], batch normalization [41], and gradient clipping [42]. Besides such approaches, several studies have been done to change the architecture of the network. For instance, adding gates to control the information flow introduces two well-known RNN structures called Long Short-Term Memory (LSTM) [5] and Gated Recurrent Unit (GRU) [43] networks that are elaborated in the following.

4.2. LSTM

LSTM is a type of RNN designed to address the limitations of traditional RNNs. These networks are effective in dealing with long-range dependencies, and are able to mitigate the vanishing gradient problem. The memory cell is the core of the LSTM, maintaining the cell state during the time. It is regulated by three gates to control the information flow such that the information should be kept or forgotten [5]. Figure 3 shows the LSTM structure, and these three gates are as follows:

- Input Gate: determines how much of the input should be considered.
- Forget Gate: decides which information should be forgotten.
- Output Gate: decides which information should be passed to the next hidden state.

The information computation of these gates is as below [34]:

$$I_t = \sigma(X_t W_{xi} + H_{t-1} W_{hi} + b_i) \tag{11}$$

$$F_t = \sigma(X_t W_{xf} + H_{t-1} W_{hf} + b_f) \tag{12}$$

$$O_t = \sigma(X_t W_{xo} + H_{t-1} W_{ho} + b_o) \tag{13}$$

The memory cell, memory content, and hidden state computation are as follows, where $\tilde{C}_t$, uses tanh as the activation function: $\tilde{C}_t = \tanh(X_t W_{xc} + H_{t-1} W_{hc} + b_c)$. The new memory content is computed by considering the previous time memory content, and the mentioned gates: $C_t = F_t \circ C_{t-1} + I_t \circ \tilde{C}_t$, and finally $H_t = O_t \circ \tanh(C_t)$ [34].

Bi-LSTM (Bidirectional LSTM) is the extended version of the LSTM that takes into account both past and future context in sequence modeling tasks. Its information processing is similar to that of BiRNN, described previously [45].

4.3. GRU

Gated Recurrent Unit (GRU) is another type of RNN that is designed to alleviate the vanishing gradient problem. It is a simplified version of LSTM, which makes it efficient

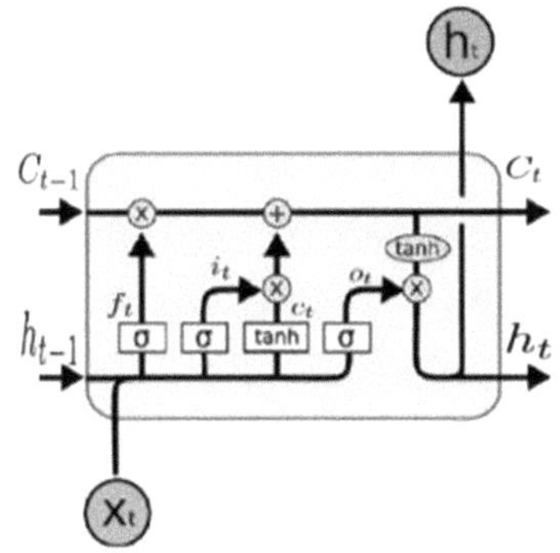

Figure 3. LSTM structure [44]

in terms of fewer learning parameters. GRU also uses gated mechanisms, but unlike LSTM, it does not have a separate memory cell state, and it controls the information flow using update (z) and reset (r) gates, and the current memory content [46]. In the following, the gates computations are as follows [47]:

$$\text{Update Gate:} \quad z_t = \sigma(W_z \cdot [h_{t-1}, x_t]) \tag{14}$$

$$\text{Reset Gate:} \quad r_t = \sigma(W_r \cdot [h_{t-1}, x_t]) \tag{15}$$

$$\text{Candidate Activation:} \quad \tilde{h}_t = \tanh(W_h \cdot [r_t \circ h_{t-1}, x_t]) \tag{16}$$

$$\text{New Memory:} \quad h_t = (1 - z_t) \circ h_{t-1} + z_t \circ \tilde{h}_t \tag{17}$$

$$\text{Output:} \quad o_t = \sigma_o(W_o h_t + b_o) \tag{18}$$

The update and reset gates control which part of the information should be considered and forgotten, respectively. The candidate activation is computed based on the previous hidden state and the reset gate while concatenating with the current input. Finally, the new memory is calculated based on the candidate activation and the previous hidden state.

4.4. Encoder-Decoder Architecture

The encoder and decoder are the two primary components in the encoder-decoder architecture. The encoder transforms the input into a latent vector which is a compressed representation of the input. A simple RNN or any other type of RNN can be used for implementing the encoder. Conversely, the decoder produces output based on the latent vector as its input. The decoder model can also be a simple RNN or other RNN variants. Sequence-to-Sequence (Seq2seq) is a specific implementation of the Encoder-Decoder architecture which converts one sequence to another. Its working mechanism is to map the input sequence to the output. Figure 4, is an example of a seq2seq model; the encoder consists of an RNN that processes individual elements of the input (the hidden state for each RNN is calculated based on the previously mentioned formula), and the latent vector is derived from the final hidden state of the encoder network and encapsulates all information from the preceding input elements. The latent vector serves as the initial hidden state for the decoder network, and the decoder model (also an RNN-based one) predicts the output for each time step [34].

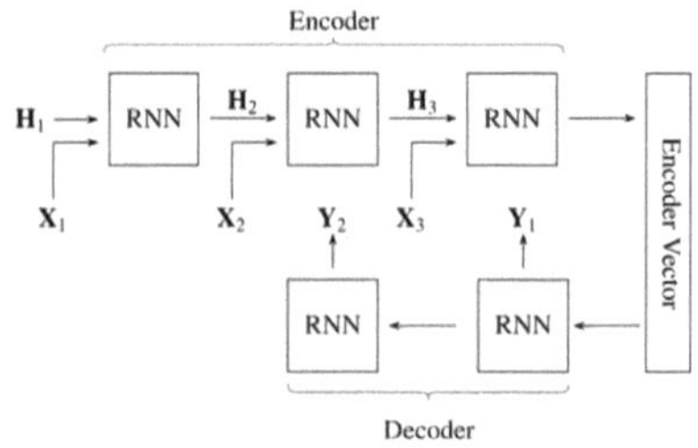

Figure 4. Encoder-Decoder architecture [34]

5. Transformer Neural Networks

Transformer is developed by Vaswani et al [6] to address the limitations of traditional sequence models like RNNs and their variants like LSTM networks. While these models show good performance in different sequential data tasks, they struggle with challenges like vanishing gradient and limited parallel processing due to their sequential structure. Additionally, their lack of scalability to large datasets and their computational inefficiencies slowed progress in tasks such as machine translation, text generation, and summarization. Unlike RNNs, which process input sequentially, the input is passed through transformer models only once, and the calculation is performed in a single step. The self-attention mechanism (the attention is generated from the model's input) in transformers allows them to process multiple data points simultaneously by distributing attention across different parts of the input, allowing for parallel processing instead of sequential steps [6,48]. Transformers are a type of encoder-decoder model and have shown significant success in different NLP tasks, such as machine translation, summarization, and text generation [49]. After the success in NLP, transformer-based models have been applied to other domains such as computer vision, protein folding, and more. This demonstrates the versatility of the transformers beyond textual data [50,51]. The transformer architecture is shown in Figure 5. Its main components are attention, positional encoding, feed-forward neural network that helps transform the representation learned by the self-attention mechanism, and layer normalization and residual connection. The attention and positional encoding components are elaborated on in the following section.

5.1. Attention and Self-Attention Mechanisms

The attention mechanism is a concept in deep learning that allows the model to pay more attention to some parts of the input when generating the output. The efficiency of using encoder-decoder models for processing sequential data was discussed in the previous section. However, it is worth noting that they may overlook important information from distant parts of the input sequence. The attention mechanism overcomes this limitation by enabling the decoder to focus on specific parts of the input sequence while generating

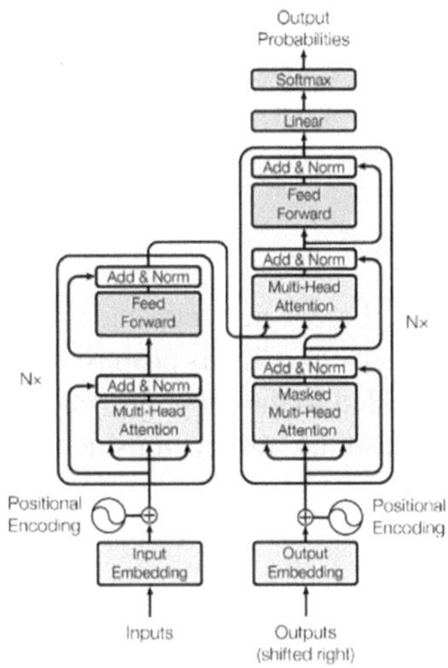

Figure 5. Transformer architecture [6]

each word. The attention score is derived from the Query (Q) and Key (K) vectors, while the Value (V) vector is not involved in this scoring process. The Value vector is used to generate the final output after the attention weights have been applied. Different methods can be used to calculate the attention score, such as additive and dot-product [43]. Also, there is another way known as self-attention, where all the Q, K, and V vectors are computed from the input. The self-attention mechanism is the core part of the transformer networks, which enables transformers to capture relationships between tokens, regardless of their position in the sequence [6]. The attention score equation (Eq.(19)) is as follows, with d_k as the dimension of the key vectors:

$$\text{Attention}(Q,K,V) = \text{softmax}\left(\frac{QK^T}{\sqrt{d_k}}\right)V \tag{19}$$

Transformers employ multi-head attention to capture various types of relationships between words within a sequence. Rather than relying on a single attention mechanism, multiple attention heads are employed, while each one learns to focus on different parts of the input. These heads function in parallel, with their outputs being concatenated and linearly transformed. Multi-head attention enhances the model's capability to simultaneously focus on information from different representation subspaces. The multi-head attention equation is as follows (Eq.(20)), where Q, K, and V are linearly projected to have different representations [6]:

$$\text{MultiHead}(Q,K,V) = \text{Concat}(\text{head}_1, \ldots, \text{head}_h)W_O \tag{20}$$

$$\text{head}_i = \text{Attention}(QW_i^Q, KW_i^K, VW_i^V) \tag{21}$$

There are two differences between the encoder and the decoder parts of the transformer. In the decoder, there is a masked multi-head attention, which is used for self-attention to avoid considering future words for prediction. This is also in line with the process at the testing time when the model is predicting the next words. The other difference refers to the encoder-decoder attention (the multi-head attention in the decoder), where K and V are the encoded representations from the encoder, and Q is from the decoder self-attention output [6].

5.2. Positional Encoding

As mentioned, in transformers, there is no recurrence (like RNNs) to handle the sequential structure of data, so positional encoding is proposed to provide information about the positions of tokens, and it is added to the input embeddings. In the seminal transformer paper [6], this is based on sinusoidal and cosinusoidal functions (with i and pos indicating dimension and position, respectively), ensuring that tokens at different positions receive unique encoding values.

$$\mathrm{PE}(\mathrm{pos}, 2i) = \sin\left(\frac{\mathrm{pos}}{10000^{\frac{2i}{d_{\mathrm{model}}}}}\right) \tag{22}$$

$$\mathrm{PE}(\mathrm{pos}, 2i+1) = \cos\left(\frac{\mathrm{pos}}{10000^{\frac{2i}{d_{\mathrm{model}}}}}\right) \tag{23}$$

5.3. Popular Transformer Models

The transformer architecture has paved the way for the creation of numerous influential models, each designed for specific tasks and domains. Below are some of the most prominent and widely used transformer-based models.

5.3.1. Bidirectional Encoder Representations from Transformers (BERT)

BERT is a pre-trained encoder-based language model developed by Google [52]. It is one of the pioneers of LLMs, where the model considers both the left and right contexts when learning word representations. In general, there are several objectives for training language models. One such objective for training BERT is Masked Language Modeling (MLM), where words are masked randomly, and the model predicts the masked word based on the rest of the input sentence. BERT is also trained for next-sentence prediction, which involves predicting whether two sentences are related and can follow each other. The pre-trained BERT model is fine-tuned on many downstream tasks, such as question answering and knowledge graph completion. Several variants of BERT with different parameters, as well as some quantized versions, are also available. The original BERT came in two versions, known as Base and Large, with 110 million and 340 million parameters, respectively [52,53,54].

5.3.2. Generative Pretrained Transformer (GPT)

GPT is a collection of language models developed by OpenAI [55]. They are decoder-based LLMS with the objective of predicting the next word based on the previous ones, known as autoregressive language modeling. There are various variants of GPT with different parameters; GPT, GPT-2, GPT-3, and GPT-4 are OpenAI language models as of now. The recent models show significant enhancement in many NLP tasks. These advancements are primarily attributed to the increase in the model's scale, in terms of the number of parameters and the volume of training data. The newer models, such as GPT-3 and GPT-4, have demonstrated improved contextual understanding, coherence in long-form text generation, and the ability to handle diverse tasks with minimal fine-tuning, making them highly versatile in various text-related applications. It should be noted that GPT-4, as a multimodal language model, can handle text and image input, which makes it more flexible than the other ones [55,56].

5.3.3. Text-to-Text Transfer Transformer (T5)

T5 is a text-to-text framework developed by Google. T5 formulates every task in NLP as text-to-text, such as summarization and sentiment analysis. Span corruption is used to pre-train this model, which modifies masked language modeling so that continuous spans of tokens are masked, making it more generalized. T5 is available in variant types: T5-small, T5-Base, T5-Large, T5-3B, and T5-11B, ranging from 60 million to 11 billion parameters [57].

5.3.4. Vision Transformer (ViT)

ViT is a Google-developed method for applying transformer models to image classification. It processes images as sequences of patches, like transformers process tokens in text. To do so, the image is divided into patches of size 16*16, each considered a token in NLP tasks. Applying the self-attention mechanism to patches captures local and global dependencies across the image, outperforming traditional CNN-based models. ViT is available in two variants of ViT-Base and ViT-Large, with 86 million and 307 million parameters, respectively, that can be fine-tuned for downstream tasks [58].

6. Graph Neural Networks

Graph Neural Networks (GNNs) are a powerful class of deep learning models designed to work with graph-structured data to learn representations of nodes and edges, capturing relational information effectively [59,60]. They are particularly well-suited for tasks involving KGs and graph-structured data. GNNs learn node representations (embeddings) by aggregating information from neighboring nodes within the graph, capturing both local and global structural patterns [60]. Attention mechanisms are also employed to help models focus on relevant parts of the graph during reasoning tasks [61]. Common GNN variants include Graph Convolutional Networks (GCN), Graph Attention Networks (GAT), and GraphSAGE [62].

6.1. Core Components of GNNs

The core components of GNNs include message passing, aggregation, update mechanisms, and readout layer. Each of them plays a critical role in how these networks learn from and process graph data [59].

6.1.1. Message Passing

The core process in GNNs is message passing. This is how information moves between connected points in a graph. Message passing happens in two main steps: 1- Creating Messages: Each point in the graph creates and send a message to its connected points. This message contains information about the point itself, such as its features or what it has learned so far. 2- Combining Messages: Each point then collects all the messages it received from the connected neighbors. It combines these messages into one piece of information. There are different ways to do this combination: adding all the messages together, taking the average of the messages, picking the largest value, or using more complex methods that give different importance to different messages [62]. By repeating these two steps, information can spread across the entire graph. This allows each point to learn from both nearby and far-away parts of the graph.

6.1.2. Aggregation

The way messages are combined is a key part of how GNNs work. This step decides how information from nearby points is put together. Different types of GNNs use different methods to combine messages. One simple way is to add up all the received messages, or to find their average. This method is often used in GCNs. It treats all nearby points as equally important. Another way is to pick the largest value from each type of information in the messages. This is called max pooling which is helpful when the strongest signal from the neighborhood is of interest. More advanced networks use a method called attention. This method gives different weights to different messages before combining them. It is like deciding which neighbors to listen to more carefully. The network learns how to assign these weights as it trains on data. This allows the network to focus on the most important connections, leading to better results in some tasks.

Each of the above methods has its strengths, and the choice depends on the specific problem the network aims to solve. By carefully selecting how to combine messages, better GNNs at understanding and working with complex graph structures are built [63].

6.1.3. Update Mechanism

After aggregating the messages from the neighbors, each node updates its own feature vector. This update is generally performed using a neural network layer, such as a feed-forward layer, which combines the aggregated information with the node's current state to produce a new embedding. The update function can be expressed as [62]:

$$\mathbf{h}_v^{(k+1)} = \sigma\left(\mathbf{W} \cdot \text{AGGREGATE}\left(\left\{\mathbf{h}_u^{(k)} : u \in \mathcal{N}(v)\right\}\right)\right) \tag{24}$$

Where $\mathbf{h}_v^{(k+1)}$ is the updated feature vector of node v at layer $k+1$, $\mathbf{W}$ is a weight matrix learned during training, AGGREGATE represents the aggregation function, σ is an activation function (e.g., ReLU), and $\mathcal{N}(v)$ is the set of neighbors of node v.

6.1.4. Readout Layer

After a GNN has processed information across the graph, it needs to use this information to make predictions. The method used depends on the type of prediction being made. Sometimes, a prediction about the entire graph is desired; for example, classifying the entire graph into a category. In such cases, a method is needed to combine all the information from every point in the graph into a single piece of information. This process is called "readout." One simple way to do readout is to add up the final information from all points in the graph, which gives one set of numbers representing the entire graph. Sometimes, a more complex methods called "graph pooling" is employed to combine the information. This method tries to capture the most important features of the graph structure. Other times, predictions about specific points in the graph is desired, for instance, classifying each point into a category. In such cases, the final information at each point is directly used to make predictions, without the need to combine information from the whole graph.

The choice between the discussed methods depends on whether one is interested in the properties of the entire graph or individual points within it. By selecting the right method, Graph Neural Networks are capable of solving a wide range of problems involving graph-structured data [64].

6.2. GCN

GCNs represent a significant advancement in the field of machine learning for graph-structured data. The concept of 'convolution' in GCNs bears similarities to the convolution layers in traditional CNNs. In CNNs, filters or kernels slide across an image, multiplying input values by weights to extract features. This process allows CNNs to learn from nearby pixels, capturing local patterns effectively. GCNs perform an analogous operation on graphs, learning from neighboring nodes instead of nearby pixels [65].

The main idea behind GCNs is to process information in a way that respects the graph structure. For each point in the graph, a GCN looks at all the neighboring points it is connected to, and collects information from them. It then combines the information of the point with that of the neighborhood. Finally, this mixed information is used to update what is known about the point. This process occurs for all points in the graph at the same time, and can be repeated several times, which spreads the information further across the graph [62]. Each layer in a GCN performs two main steps, convolution and aggregation. The convolution step, similar to CNNs, applies learned filters to the node features. The aggregation step then combines the processed features from the neighboring nodes. Through multiple layers, GCNs can capture complex patterns and relationships within the graph structure [65].

GCNs have some significant advantages over other types of GNNs. They can efficiently handle very large graphs, as the processing time grows in proportion to the number of connections, but not the number of points. They can learn to represent complex relationships in the graph. This means they can understand both what each point is like and how it relates to other points [66].

6.3. GAT

GATs represent an advanced evolution in the GNN architecture, specifically designed to address the limitations of earlier models by integrating attention mechanisms, a concept adapted from NLP. GATs enhance the processing of graph-structured data by allowing the model to assign varying levels of importance to different nodes within a neighborhood, all without the need for complex matrix operations or prior knowledge of the graph's structure.

The core of the GAT architecture involves initializing each node in the graph with a feature vector that captures its characteristics. The model then applies self-attention, where it calculates attention scores between a central node and its neighbors. These scores, which are based on the features of both the central node and its neighbors, dictate how much influence each neighbor's information will have on the central node's updated representation. The features of the neighboring nodes are then aggregated in a weighted manner according to these attention scores, resulting in a new, contextually informed feature vector for the central node [67].

GATs often use multi-head attention, where several attention mechanisms operate in parallel, each capturing different aspects of the graph's relationships. The results from these heads are combined to form the final feature vectors, allowing the model to capture more complex and abstract patterns. GATs can also be stacked in layers, with each successive layer refining the node representations based on increasingly abstracted neighborhood information [62,67].

One key advantage of GATs is their flexibility, as they can assign different levels of importance to nodes within a neighborhood, making them more adaptable than models with fixed aggregation methods like GCNs. Additionally, GATs are effective in both transductive and inductive learning scenarios, enabling them to generalize beyond the nodes and structures seen during training. This makes them particularly useful in dynamic graphs where the structure may evolve over time [62,67].

In comparison to GCNs, which rely heavily on the structure of the graph for aggregation, GATs offer a more flexible approach by using attention to focus on the most relevant parts of a node's neighborhood. This attention-based flexibility allows GATs to achieve better performance in various graph-based tasks and adapt to different types of graph structures and feature distributions [62].

6.4. GraphSAGE

GraphSAGE, short for Graph SAmple and aggreGatE, represents a significant advancement in graph-based machine learning. This model introduces an inductive learning framework, allowing it to generate embeddings for nodes it has not seen during training. This capability makes GraphSAGE particularly useful for dynamic graphs where new nodes frequently appear [68].

The GraphSAGE algorithm operates through a series of interconnected steps. It begins by initializing feature vectors for all nodes in the input graph. Then, for each node, it samples a set of neighboring nodes. This sampling step is crucial, as it allows the model to efficiently process large graphs by considering only a subset of each node's neighbors. Once the neighbors are sampled, GraphSAGE employs an aggregation function to combine the information from these neighboring nodes. This aggregated information is then combined with the node's own features and passed through a non-linear transformation, typically implemented as a fully connected layer with an activation function. This process updates the node's embedding, capturing both its own characteristics and those of its local graph neighborhood [68,62].

At its core, GraphSAGE revolves around two primary operations which are sampling and aggregation. The sampling step determines how to select a manageable number of neighbors for each node, especially important in large graphs. The aggregation step defines how to combine the embeddings of these sampled neighbors [68].

One of GraphSAGE's strengths lies in its flexibility regarding the choice of aggregator function. Unlike some earlier models that simply sum or average neighbor information, GraphSAGE allows for more sophisticated aggregation methods. These include element-wise mean operations, max-pooling layers, or even more complex functions like LSTM networks. A key feature of GraphSAGE is its inductive learning capability. By learning a set of aggregation functions rather than specific node embeddings, GraphSAGE can generate embeddings for new, unseen nodes. This is achieved by applying the learned aggregation functions to the new node's features and neighborhood, without requiring a full retraining of the model. This inductive approach allows GraphSAGE to generalize to dynamic graphs where the structure may change over time or to entirely new graphs with similar characteristics. This makes it particularly useful in real-world scenarios where graphs often evolve, such as social networks gaining new users or citation networks incorporating new papers [62].

6.5. Applications of GNNs

Node Classification: GNNs are widely used for node classification tasks, where the goal is to determine the labels of nodes within a graph based on the labels of their neighbors. This approach is crucial in applications like social network analysis and fraud detection, where the label of a node (e.g., user classification) can often be inferred from the labels of its connections [66].
Graph Classification: In graph classification, GNNs are used to categorize entire graphs into predefined categories. This method is particularly useful in bioinformatics for classifying molecular structures, in document categorization, and in analyzing social networks where the overall structure of a graph provides meaningful insights [62,66].
Link Prediction: GNNs excel in link prediction, which involves predicting the likelihood of a connection (or edge) between two nodes in a graph. This application is crucial in social networks for suggesting new connections, and in recommender systems for predicting user-item interactions [62,66].
Graph Clustering: GNNs are also applied in graph clustering, where nodes or entire graphs are grouped based on similarity. This application is valuable in understanding community structures within social networks or grouping similar proteins in bioinformatics [62,66].
Social Network Analysis: GNNs are heavily used in social network analysis for tasks like link prediction, community detection, and node classification. These tasks help in understanding and predicting social interactions, detecting groups within networks, and classifying users [62,66].
Knowledge Graphs: GNNs are increasingly applied in KGs to enhance various tasks by leveraging the graph structure's inherent relationships. GNNs are particularly effective for KG completion, where they predict missing links or entities by learning embeddings that infer new facts, thereby completing the graph [60]. Additionally, GNNs facilitate the extraction of entities and relations from unstructured text, automating the process of populating KGs. Furthermore, they improve reasoning over KGs by enabling complex logical reasoning and efficient traversal of the graph structure, enhancing the ability to answer queries and derive new knowledge [61].

Furthermore, GNNs have made significant strides in computer vision tasks like scene graph generation, where they create graphs representing objects and their relationships in a scene, image segmentation to divide images into meaningful segments, object detection to identify and classify objects, and scene understanding to comprehend context and relationships between objects. In NLP, GNNs are increasingly used for document classification, text generation, question answering, and sentiment analysis. In bioinformatics, they are applied to protein-protein interaction prediction, genomic sequence analysis, and drug discovery, where they predict molecular properties and potential drug candidates [62,66]

7. Generative Adversarial Networks

7.1. Introduction to GANs

Generative Adversarial Networks (GANs) are a type of machine learning framework designed by Ian Goodfellow et al. in 2014 [69]. GANs have revolutionized the field of artificial intelligence by enabling machines to generate data that closely mimics real-world data. The core idea behind GANs is that there are two neural networks against each other in a game-theoretic scenario, leading to the generation of highly realistic data. This technique has found applications in a wide range of areas, from creating realistic photo images to enhancing the quality of audio signals.

GANs consist of two key components [20]: 1- Generator Network, responsible for generating new data instances resembling the training data. It takes random noise as input and transforms it into plausible data samples. 2- Discriminator Network, to distinguish between real data (from the training set) and fake data (produced by the generator). The discriminator provides feedback to the generator on how to improve its data generation. The generator and discriminator are trained simultaneously in a zero-sum game, where the generator aims to fool the discriminator, and the discriminator strives to become better at identifying fake data. For instance, GANs can be used to generate art paintings in the style of famous artists like Van Gogh. The generator creates paintings while the discriminator evaluates and provides feedback on them. Through a game-like process, the Generator refines its skills to produce paintings that are remarkably similar to Van Gogh's style, but with its own unique twist. The result is a new, original painting that captures the essence of Van Gogh's artistic style.

The architecture of GANs is illusted in Figure 6. The training process of GANs involves an adversarial process, where the generator and discriminator improve through iterative feedback loops [69]:

- Adversarial Training: Initially, the generator produces random data, which the discriminator evaluates. The discriminator's feedback helps the generator to refine its output to make it more realistic.
- Loss Functions: The generator's loss function measures how well it can fool the discriminator, while the discriminator's loss function measures its ability to distinguish real data from generated data.
- Iterative Improvement: Through multiple iterations, both networks continuously enhance their performance. The generator becomes better at creating realistic data, and the discriminator becomes more proficient at detecting fake data.

GANs are versatile tools with a wide range of applications across multiple domains. In image processing, they can generate photorealistic images [71], perform image-to-

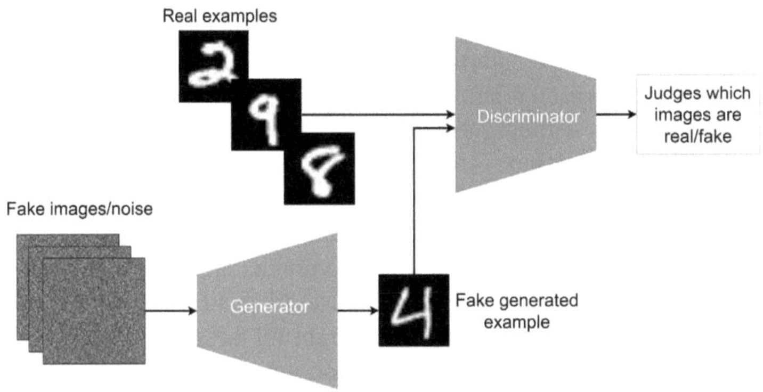

Figure 6. GANs architecture [70]

image translation [72], and enhance image resolution [73]. GANs are also used for video prediction [74] and 3D model creation [75]. They are additionally valuable for generating synthetic training data, text and audio applications, and domain-specific areas. Overall, GANs are powerful tools for generating high-quality synthetic data, with applications that span creative, analytical, and practical fields such as art, healthcare, and scientific research.

7.2. Applications of GANs in Knowledge Graphs

Improving Knowledge Graph Embeddings: KBGAN [76] introduces an innovative adversarial learning framework aimed at enhancing the performance of KG embedding models by utilizing the principles of GANs. Central to this framework is the use of one KG embedding model as a negative sample generator. This model plays a pivotal role in the training process of the target model by generating negative samples that are highly informative and challenging to classify correctly. The negative sample generator's primary function is to produce samples that are difficult to distinguish from positive facts, thereby increasing the complexity of the learning task for the target model. By introducing these high-quality negative samples, the generator compels the target model, which acts as the discriminator within this adversarial framework, to improve its ability to learn accurate and robust embeddings. This process ultimately leads to better discrimination between true and false information within the KG. Importantly, KBGAN is designed with versatility in mind, allowing it to be applied to a wide range of existing KG embedding models. This flexibility makes KBGAN a valuable tool in advancing the development and refinement of KG embedding across different domains and applications.

Zero-Shot Relational Learning: GANs have effectively been employed to facilitate zero-shot learning for novel relations in KGs. This approach addresses the challenge of reasoning over relations that lack direct training examples by leveraging the capabilities of GANs in a unique and innovative manner. In this framework, the generator is tasked with learning to produce plausible relation embeddings derived from textual descriptions of new, unseen relations. By capturing the essential characteristics of these new relations through text-based embeddings, the generator enables the system to reason about relations not present in the training data. This process effectively converts the problem of zero-shot learning into a supervised classification task, where the model can classify and reason over these new relations as if they had been part of the original training set. This methodology represents a significant advancement in the ability to generalize KG embeddings to new and unseen relations, making it possible to extend the capabilities of knowledge-based systems without the need for exhaustive training data [77].

Knowledge Graph Completion: GAN-based reinforcement learning models, such as the Generative Reinforcement Learning (GRL) framework, have been proposed as powerful tools for the task of KG completion. This approach leverages the combined strengths of GANs and reinforcement learning to predict and infer missing facts within KGs, thereby addressing gaps in the available data. In this framework, the generator is responsible for producing candidate facts that might fill the gaps in the KG. These candidate facts are then evaluated by the discriminator, which assesses their plausibility and accuracy. Through this adversarial process, the model iteratively improves its ability to generate and validate missing information, leading to more accurate and complete KGs. The integration of reinforcement learning further enhances this process by guiding the generator towards producing higher-quality candidate facts based on feedback from the discriminator. This synergy between GANs and reinforcement learning enables the GRL framework to effectively complete KGs, even in the presence of significant missing information [78].

Supporting Design Creativity: An innovative application of GANs involves interleaving them with KGs to enhance the creative design process for book covers. This approach offers a novel solution to the challenge of generating diverse and creative book cover designs by incorporating the structured information contained within KGs. In this application, KGs are utilized to generate multiple variations of book titles, which are then used as augmented inputs for the GAN. By providing a richer and more varied set of inputs, the KG enhances the GAN's ability to generate a wide array of book cover designs. This process allows for the exploration of a broader range of design possibilities, offering authors and editors more creative options than would be possible using GANs alone. The interleaving of KGs with GANs not only enriches the input data but also introduces a level of semantic understanding that guides the GAN in producing designs that are not only visually appealing but also contextually relevant to the book's content. This approach represents a significant advancement in the use of AI for creative design, particularly in the publishing industry [79].

8. AutoEncoder

8.1. Introduction to Autoencoders

Autoencoders are a class of neural networks introduced by Hinton et al [80]. They are designed primarily for unsupervised learning tasks, including dimensionality reduction, feature extraction, and data compression. These networks function by encoding input data into a lower-dimensional representation, known as the latent space or code, and then decoding this representation to reconstruct the original input as accurately as possible [81]. The architecture of an autoencoder (Figure 7) comprises three essential components. The encoder is responsible for compressing the input data into a lower-dimensional representation. This compression is achieved through a series of neural network layers that progressively reduce the dimensionality of the input data. The most compressed form of the data is located in the bottleneck layer, which represents the latent space or code. This layer has the lowest dimensionality in the network and contains the most critical features of the input data. The decoder, which typically mirrors the encoder's architecture, attempts to reconstruct the original input from the latent space representation. The goal is for the decoder to generate an output that closely matches the original input data [20].

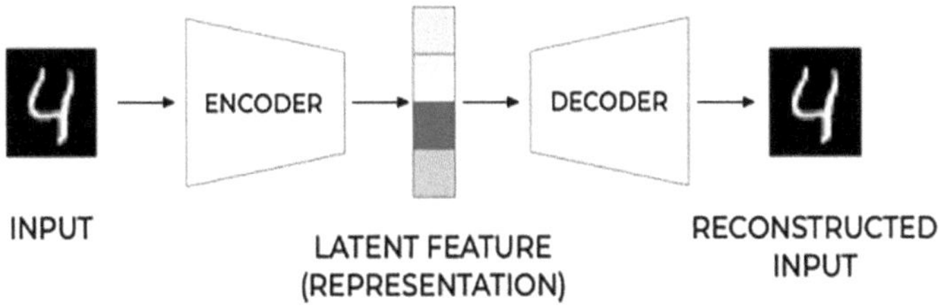

Figure 7. AutoEncoder structure [82]

Training an autoencoder involves reducing the reconstruction error. The process begins by passing the input data through the encoder to generate a compressed representation. This representation is then passed through the decoder to reconstruct the input. A loss function, such as Mean Squared Error, is used to calculate the reconstruction error, and the network's parameters are updated via backpropagation to minimize this error [82].

There are various types of autoencoders, each tailored for specific tasks. The vanilla autoencoder is the most basic form, utilizing fully connected layers. Convolutional Autoencoders (CAE) use convolutional layers, making them particularly effective for handling image data [81]. Denoising autoencoders are designed to reconstruct clean data from noisy inputs, making them useful for tasks involving noise reduction . Sparse autoencoders encourage sparsity in the latent representation, promoting more efficient and interpretable representations [20]. Variational Autoencoders (VAE) extend the basic architecture by learning a probabilistic mapping to the latent space, which is particularly useful for generative modeling [81].

Autoencoders have found applications in a wide array of domains. They are commonly used for dimensionality reduction, enabling more efficient data visualization and analysis. In feature learning, autoencoders help in extracting important features from data that can be used in subsequent machine learning tasks. They are also effective in anomaly detection, identifying data points that deviate significantly from the norm. In the realm of image processing, autoencoders are employed for tasks such as image denoising and inpainting. Additionally, they are used in generative modeling to create new data samples, in recommender systems to predict user preferences, and in sequence-to-sequence learning for tasks like language translation [81].

8.2. AutoEncoder and GANs Differences

Autoencoders consist of an encoder that compresses input data into a lower-dimensional latent representation and a decoder that reconstructs the original input from this representation. In contrast, GANs comprise a generator that creates fake samples from random noise and a discriminator that distinguishes between real and fake samples. Autoencoders are trained to minimize the reconstruction error between the input and output using backpropagation. GANs, on the other hand, employ adversarial training, where the generator tries to fool the discriminator, and the discriminator attempts to correctly classify real versus fake samples, creating a competitive minimax game between the two [81].

Autoencoders are typically used for tasks such as dimensionality reduction, feature learning, data compression, denoising, and anomaly detection. GANs excel in generating new, realistic samples, such as images or text, and are known for producing diverse and high-quality synthetic data. The outputs of autoencoders tend to be smoother and more continuous, focusing on accurately reconstructing the input data. GANs can generate more realistic and varied examples, though they may encounter issues like mode collapse, where only a limited variety of samples are produced. Autoencoders can operate effectively on smaller datasets and are primarily used in unsupervised learning without requiring labeled data. GANs typically require larger, more diverse datasets for stable training and to generate high-quality outputs [81].

In summary, while both autoencoders and GANs are valuable generative models, autoencoders are better suited for tasks involving data representation and reconstruction, whereas GANs are ideal for creating realistic new data through adversarial training. The choice between the two depends on the specific application and the desired outcome.

8.3. Applications of Autoencoders in Knowledge Graphs

Autoencoders have been successfully applied in various aspects of knowledge graph processing. Their ability to learn compact, low-dimensional representations and reconstruct data makes them particularly useful for tasks such as feature learning, knowledge graph completion, explainable recommendations, noise reduction, and knowledge graph refinement.

Feature Learning and Dimensionality Reduction: Autoencoders are instrumental in learning compact, low-dimensional representations of entities and relations within knowledge graphs. This capability is particularly valuable for reducing the dimensionality of large-scale knowledge graphs, thereby facilitating more efficient storage and computation. Additionally, autoencoders enable the learning of latent features that encapsulate the semantic information inherent in the graph's structure. These latent features enhance the performance of downstream tasks, such as link prediction, by providing a more abstract and meaningful representation of the graph's entities and relations [83].

Knowledge Graph Completion: In the realm of knowledge graph completion, autoencoders play a significant role in predicting missing links and relations. Graph autoencoder models, such as Graph Autoencoder with Attention (GAEAT) [84], employ attention mechanisms to simultaneously learn embeddings for both entities and relations, improving the accuracy of link prediction tasks. Similarly, variational autoencoders, like the Graph Convolutional Network Variational Autoencoder (GCN-VAE) [85], leverage the information from graph neighborhoods to encode and reconstruct knowledge graphs, effectively filling in missing information and completing the graph.

Explainable Recommendations: Autoencoders that are aware of knowledge graph structures can be utilized to generate explainable recommendations. This is achieved by attaching semantic labels to neurons within the hidden layer of the autoencoder, based on concepts from the knowledge graph [83]. As a result, the model can provide interpretable explanations for its recommendations, using the knowledge graph's structure to elucidate the reasoning behind each suggestion. This approach not only improves the transparency of recommendation systems, but also enhances user trust by offering clear and understandable explanations.

Knowledge Graph Refinement: Autoencoders also contribute to the refinement and improvement of existing knowledge graphs. By learning to reconstruct the graph, autoencoders can identify missing information and inconsistencies within the graph's structure. This capability allows for the automatic filling in of gaps and correction of errors, leading to a more complete and accurate knowledge graph. This process of refinement ensures that the knowledge graph remains up-to-date and reliable, which is essential for its effective use in various applications.

9. Training and Evaluation

The training and evaluation phases are crucial in machine learning, as they determine how well a model learns from data and performs on unseen examples. Training adjusts the model's parameters by minimizing a loss function, while evaluation measures its generalization using performance metrics. This section discusses data preparation, augmentation, training strategies, and evaluation metrics, all essential for effective model development [20].

9.1. Data Preparation and Augmentation

Good data preparation and augmentation are essential for improving model performance in machine learning. Data preparation transforms raw data into a format suitable for modeling, while augmentation adds diversity by generating variations of existing data. These steps work together to improve training, prevent overfitting, and boost generalization [20].

9.1.1. Data Preparation

Data preparation involves converting raw data into a format suitable for predictive modeling, addressing issues like data types, errors, and complexity. Key techniques include data cleaning, feature selection, transformation, feature engineering, and dimensionality reduction. Each step tackles specific challenges, from fixing errors to enhancing the model's ability to understand data relationships [20].

Data cleaning involves identifying and fixing errors, inconsistencies, or noise in the dataset. This includes dealing with missing values, removing outliers, and correcting invalid entries to ensure the data is accurate and reliable for model training.

Feature selection focuses on choosing the most important variables for the task. By reducing the number of features, it helps make the model simpler, prevents overfitting, and improves performance. Techniques like correlation analysis or model-based methods are often used to filter out irrelevant features.

Data transformation adjusts the scale or format of variables to make them suitable for machine learning algorithms. This can involve normalizing or standardizing numerical data and encoding categorical data, making it easier for models to interpret and compare different variables.

Feature engineering is about creating new variables from existing ones to help the model recognize patterns more effectively. This often requires domain expertise to combine features or generate new interaction terms that add value to the model.

Dimensionality reduction simplifies the dataset by reducing the number of input variables while keeping as much useful information as possible. Methods like Principal Component Analysis (PCA) or t-SNE are used to condense the data, making models faster and often more accurate.

The goal of data preparation is to reveal the underlying structure of the problem to machine learning algorithms. This process can be complex and must be adapted to both the data and the algorithm being used. As part of the broader machine learning workflow, its effectiveness directly impacts model performance. A practitioner needs to understand various data preparation techniques and know when to apply them, making it a crucial yet challenging aspect of predictive modeling [86].

9.1.2. Data Augmentation

Data augmentation involves applying transformations to existing data to artificially increase the size of the training dataset. In deep learning, where large datasets are crucial for good performance, augmentation enhances model generalization and reduces the risk of overfitting by creating more diverse training examples. In computer vision, common methods include rotations, translations, flips, and scaling to simulate real-world variations, while in natural language processing (NLP), techniques like adding noise, removing words, or replacing them with synonyms are used to diversify input samples. The key benefit of data augmentation is that it improves model performance without additional data collection, making models more robust to changes and better at handling unseen data. Augmentation techniques are often customized to the specific data types and tasks [20].

9.2. Training Techniques

Effective training techniques are crucial for improving model performance and reducing the risk of overfitting, which occurs when a model learns the training data too well but struggles to generalize to new data. One commonly used approach is **early stopping**, where the model's performance on a validation set is continuously monitored during training. If performance stops improving, training is halted to prevent the model from overfitting. Another important technique is **learning rate scheduling**, which dynamically adjusts the learning rate throughout training. Starting with a higher learning rate can speed up learning, while reducing it later helps fine-tune the model for better convergence [20].

Regularization methods like **dropout** and **weight decay** are also key strategies to prevent overfitting. Dropout works by randomly deactivating neurons during training, forcing the model to rely on various subsets of neurons and learn more generalized features. Weight decay, on the other hand, penalizes large weights, pushing the model toward simpler, more generalizable solutions. These techniques are fundamental to effective training and are widely applied in modern deep learning models [20].

9.3. Evaluation Metrics

In deep learning, evaluating a model's performance is key to identifying its strengths, weaknesses, and areas for improvement. Different metrics are used to measure how well the model handles new data. These metrics help assess its accuracy, ability to correctly classify positives, and ability to minimize errors. This section covers three important metrics: accuracy, precision, and recall, each providing a different view of the model's classification performance [20].

9.3.1. Accuracy, Precision, Recall

Accuracy, precision, and recall are key metrics for evaluating classification models. The definitions are outlined below:

Accuracy is a metric that quantifies the overall performance of a model by determining the ratio of correct predictions to the total number of predictions. It is particularly effective for datasets with balanced class distributions, but may provide unreliable results when the class distribution is imbalanced.

$$\text{Accuracy} = \frac{\text{Number of correct predictions}}{\text{Total number of predictions}} \tag{25}$$

Precision measures the proportion of correct predictions for a specific class, referred to as the positive class. In this context, true positives are instances correctly identified as belonging to the positive class, while false positives are instances incorrectly classified as belonging to this class. Precision is particularly important when minimizing false positives is crucial, as it evaluates the accuracy of positive predictions.

$$\text{Precision} = \frac{\text{True Positives}}{\text{True Positives} + \text{False Positives}} \tag{26}$$

Recall, or sensitivity, measures how well a model identifies positive instances from all actual positives. Positive refers to the class of interest, while negative represents instances not in this class. This metric is important when minimizing false negatives is critical, as it shows how effectively the model captures relevant positive instances.

$$\text{Recall} = \frac{\text{True Positives}}{\text{True Positives} + \text{False Negatives}} \tag{27}$$

These metrics are often used alongside the *confusion matrix* to give a full picture of the classification performance. The *F1 score*, a balance between precision and recall, is particularly useful when both metrics are important. Additionally, *ROC curves* and *AUC* provide insights into the model's performance across various thresholds. For a more detailed explanation of these metrics and their role in deep learning, the reader is referred to *Deep Learning* by Goodfellow et al. [20], which also covers topics such as cross-validation and bias-variance tradeoff.

9.3.2. Mean Reciprocal Rank (MRR)

Mean Reciprocal Rank (MRR) is a statistical measure used to evaluate the effectiveness of information retrieval systems, particularly in tasks like search engine ranking, question answering, and recommendation systems. It assesses the rank position of the first relevant item in the list of results for a given set of queries [87].

Definition. The Reciprocal Rank (RR) for a single query is defined as the reciprocal of the rank position of the first relevant result. If the first relevant result appears at position k, the Reciprocal Rank is given by:

$$\mathrm{RR} = \frac{1}{k} \tag{28}$$

Mean Reciprocal Rank is the average of the Reciprocal Ranks for a set of queries. Formally, for a set of queries Q, MRR is calculated as:

$$\mathrm{MRR} = \frac{1}{|Q|} \sum_{i=1}^{|Q|} RR_i \tag{29}$$

where $|Q|$ is the number of queries, and RR_i is the Reciprocal Rank of the first relevant result for the i-th query.

9.3.3. Hits@N

Hits@N is a metric used in ranking and information retrieval tasks to determine if the correct result appears within the top N predictions. It calculates the proportion of queries where at least one relevant result is found in the top N. This is especially useful in recommendation systems and search engines, where showing relevant results early is crucial for user satisfaction. For example, Hits@5 measures the percentage of times the correct result is in the top 5 predictions, making it a simple and effective metric for ranking systems [87].

$$\mathrm{Hits@N} = \frac{\text{Number of queries with a relevant result in the top } N}{\text{Total number of queries}} \tag{30}$$

10. Tools and Frameworks

Deep learning models have revolutionized a variety of fields such as computer vision and natural language processing, and this is not only related to developing algorithms but also the availability of robust and user-friendly tools and frameworks. The most widely used frameworks are Tensorflow, Pytorch, and Keras. In the following, a brief overview of them is explained.

TensorFlow: TensorFlow, which was developed by Google Brain, allows developers to build deep learning models for a variety of tasks. It supports running on both CPU and GPU and also supports distributed computing. TensorFlow hub is a repository of pre-trained models that can be fine-tuned or integrated into other projects. Also, TensorFlow Serving helps deploy machine learning models in production, and TensorFlow

Ecosystem includes tools like TensorFlow Lite for mobile devices and TensorFlow.js for running models in browsers [88].

PyTorch: PyTorch was created by the AI Research Lab at Facebook. It allows the developer to change the structure of the model during runtime. Other features include Autograd, an automatic differentiation engine for easy backpropagation, and TorchScript for transition from research to production via converting PyTorch models into static graphic versions [89].

Keras: Keras can be regarded as one of the frameworks that was first developed to work with TensorFlow, but later expanded to support others. It is designed for simplicity and rapid experimentation, making it ideal for both beginners and advanced users [90].

11. Closure

This chapter provides an overview of foundational deep learning models. These models are designed to perform a range of different tasks, such as processing images and sequences or generating new data, highlighting the versatility and broad applicability of deep learning. It also demonstrates how powerful tools have simplified the process of building and training models.

Despite remarkable advancements in deep learning, significant challenges still persist. Scaling up is a major issue, as training large models demands a significant amount of computing power. This makes it difficult for smaller organizations or researchers with limited infrastructure to exploit the technology entirely. Another challenge is understanding how these models make decisions, as they often act like black boxes and are difficult to interpret. Finally, issues arise when integrating these models into current systems, as they need to work smoothly with other technologies while still performing quickly in real-time. To fully take advantage of deep learning, the field needs to keep finding new ways to overcome these challenges, ensuring that the technology is solid and easy to scale, understand, and use in real-world applications.

Acknowledgment This work is supported in part by Kansas State University through the Game-changing Research Initiation Program (GRIP), as part of the 'Towards a Global Food Systems Data Hub: Seeding the Center for Sustainable Wheat Production' project.

References

[1] LeCun Y, Bengio Y, Hinton G. Deep learning. Nature. 2015;521(7553):436-44.

[2] Schmidhuber J. Deep learning in neural networks: An overview. Neural networks. 2015;61:85-117.

[3] McCulloch WS, Pitts W. A logical calculus of the ideas immanent in nervous activity. The bulletin of mathematical biophysics. 1943;5:115-33.

[4] Rumelhart DE, Hinton GE, Williams RJ. Learning representations by back-propagating errors. Nature. 1986;323(6088):533-6.

[5] Hochreiter S, Schmidhuber J. Long short-term memory. Neural computation. 1997;9(8):1735-80.

[6] Vaswani A. Attention is all you need. Advances in Neural Information Processing Systems. 2017.

[7] Bengio Y. Learning Deep Architectures for AI. Now Publishers Inc; 2009.

[8] Bengio Y, Courville A, Vincent P. Representation Learning: A Review and New Perspectives. vol. 35. IEEE; 2013.

[9] Nair V, Hinton GE. Rectified linear units improve restricted Boltzmann machines. In: Proceedings of the 27th International Conference on Machine Learning (ICML-10); 2010. p. 807-14.

[10] Srivastava N, Hinton G, Krizhevsky A, Sutskever I, Salakhutdinov R. Dropout: A Simple Way to Prevent Neural Networks from Overfitting. The Journal of Machine Learning Research. 2014;15(1):1929-58.
[11] Rosenblatt F. The perceptron: a probabilistic model for information storage and organization in the brain. Psychological Review. 1958;65(6):386-408.
[12] Haykin S. Neural Networks: A Comprehensive Foundation. Prentice Hall PTR; 1998.
[13] Maas AL, Hannun AY, Ng AY. Rectifier nonlinearities improve neural network acoustic models. In: Proceedings of the 30th International Conference on Machine Learning (ICML-13). vol. 30; 2013. p. 3.
[14] He K, Zhang X, Ren S, Sun J. Delving deep into rectifiers: Surpassing human-level performance on imagenet classification. In: Proceedings of the IEEE International Conference on Computer Vision; 2015. p. 1026-34.
[15] Glorot X, Bordes A, Bengio Y. Deep sparse rectifier neural networks. In: Proceedings of the Fourteenth International Conference on Artificial Intelligence and Statistics. JMLR Workshop and Conference Proceedings; 2011. p. 315-23.
[16] Clevert DA, Unterthiner T, Hochreiter S. Fast and accurate deep network learning by exponential linear units (ELUs). arXiv preprint arXiv:151107289. 2015.
[17] LeCun Y, Bottou L, Orr GB, Müller KR. Efficient backprop. In: Neural networks: Tricks of the trade. Berlin, Heidelberg: Springer Berlin Heidelberg; 2002. p. 9-50.
[18] Glorot X, Bengio Y. Understanding the difficulty of training deep feedforward neural networks. In: Proceedings of the thirteenth international conference on artificial intelligence and statistics. JMLR Workshop and Conference Proceedings; 2010. p. 249-56.
[19] Zhang Z, Sabuncu MR. Generalized cross entropy loss for training deep neural networks with noisy labels. In: Advances in Neural Information Processing Systems. vol. 31; 2018. .
[20] Goodfellow I, Bengio Y, Courville A. Deep Learning. MIT Press; 2016.
[21] Bottou L. Large-scale machine learning with stochastic gradient descent. In: Proceedings of COMPSTAT'2010: 19th International Conference on Computational Statistics Paris France, August 22-27, 2010 Keynote, Invited and Contributed Papers. Physica-Verlag HD; 2010. p. 177-86.
[22] Caruana R, Lawrence S, Giles CL. Overfitting in Neural Nets: Backpropagation, Conjugate Gradient, and Early Stopping. In: Advances in Neural Information Processing Systems. vol. 13; 2000. .
[23] Yao Y, Rosasco L, Caponnetto A. On early stopping in gradient descent learning. In: Constructive Approximation. vol. 26. Springer; 2007. p. 289-315.
[24] Ng AY. Feature selection, L1 vs. L2 regularization, and rotational invariance. In: Proceedings of the Twenty-First International Conference on Machine Learning; 2004. p. 78.
[25] Hastie T, Tibshirani R, Friedman JH. The Elements of Statistical Learning: Data Mining, Inference, and Prediction. vol. 2. New York: Springer; 2009.
[26] LeCun Y, Boser B, Denker JS, Henderson D, Howard RE, Hubbard W, et al. Backpropagation Applied to Handwritten Zip Code Recognition. Neural Computation. 1989;1(4):541-51.
[27] Hubel TN D H & Wiesel. Receptive fields, binocular interaction, and functional architecture in the cat's visual cortex; 1962. p. 106–154.
[28] Felleman DCV D J & Essen. Distributed hierarchical processing in the primate cerebral cortex. Cereb. Cortex; 1991. p. 1-47.
[29] O'Shea R Keiron & Nash. An Introduction to Convolutional Neural Networks. ArXiv e-prints; 2015. .
[30] Dumoulin V, Visin F. A guide to convolution arithmetic for deep learning. vol. abs/1603.07285; 2016. Available from: `https://api.semanticscholar.org/CorpusID:6662846`.
[31] Yu F, Koltun V. Multi-Scale Context Aggregation by Dilated Convolutions. vol. abs/1511.07122; 2015. Available from: `https://api.semanticscholar.org/CorpusID:17127188`.
[32] Blumberg SB, Rav'i D, Xu M, Figini M, Kokkinos I, Alexander DC. Deformably-Scaled Transposed Convolution. vol. abs/2210.09446; 2022. Available from: `https://api.semanticscholar.org/CorpusID:252968239`.
[33] Chollet F. Xception: Deep Learning with Depthwise Separable Convolutions. In: 2017 IEEE Conference on Computer Vision and Pattern Recognition (CVPR); 2017. p. 1800-7.
[34] Schmidt RM. Recurrent neural networks (rnns): A gentle introduction and overview. arXiv preprint arXiv:191205911. 2019.
[35] Chung J, Gulcehre C, Cho K, Bengio Y. Gated feedback recurrent neural networks. In: International conference on machine learning. PMLR; 2015. p. 2067-75.
[36] Das S, Tariq A, Santos T, Kantareddy SS, Banerjee I. Recurrent neural networks (RNNs): architectures, training tricks, and introduction to influential research. Machine Learning for Brain Disorders.

2023:117-38.
[37] Werbos PJ. Backpropagation through time: what it does and how to do it. Proceedings of the IEEE. 1990;78(10):1550-60.
[38] Schuster M, Paliwal KK. Bidirectional recurrent neural networks. IEEE transactions on Signal Processing. 1997;45(11):2673-81.
[39] Ravikumar A, Sriraman H. Mitigating Vanishing Gradient in SGD Optimization in Neural Networks. In: Ranganathan G, Papakostas GA, Rocha Á, editors. Inventive Communication and Computational Technologies. Singapore: Springer Nature Singapore; 2023. p. 1-11.
[40] He K, Zhang X, Ren S, Sun J. Deep residual learning for image recognition. In: Proceedings of the IEEE conference on computer vision and pattern recognition; 2016. p. 770-8.
[41] Ioffe S, Szegedy C. Batch normalization: Accelerating deep network training by reducing internal covariate shift. In: International conference on machine learning. pmlr; 2015. p. 448-56.
[42] Pascanu R, Mikolov T, Bengio Y. On the difficulty of training recurrent neural networks. In: International conference on machine learning. Pmlr; 2013. p. 1310-8.
[43] Bahdanau D, Cho K, Bengio Y. Neural machine translation by jointly learning to align and translate. arXiv preprint arXiv:14090473. 2014.
[44] Fang W, Chen Y, Xue Q. Survey on research of RNN-based spatio-temporal sequence prediction algorithms. Journal on Big Data. 2021;3(3):97.
[45] Graves A, Schmidhuber J. Framewise phoneme classification with bidirectional LSTM and other neural network architectures. Neural networks. 2005;18(5-6):602-10.
[46] Cho K, Van Merriënboer B, Bahdanau D, Bengio Y. On the properties of neural machine translation: Encoder-decoder approaches. arXiv preprint arXiv:14091259. 2014.
[47] Chung J, Gulcehre C, Cho K, Bengio Y. Empirical evaluation of gated recurrent neural networks on sequence modeling. arXiv preprint arXiv:14123555. 2014.
[48] Sutskever I, Vinyals O, Le QV. Sequence to sequence learning with neural networks. Advances in neural information processing systems. 2014;27.
[49] Radford A, Wu J, Child R, Luan D, Amodei D, Sutskever I, et al. Language models are unsupervised multitask learners.
[50] Alexey D. An image is worth 16x16 words: Transformers for image recognition at scale. arXiv preprint arXiv: 201011929. 2020.
[51] Jumper J, Evans R, Pritzel A, Green T, Figurnov M, Ronneberger O, et al. Highly accurate protein structure prediction with AlphaFold. nature. 2021;596(7873):583-9.
[52] Devlin J. Bert: Pre-training of deep bidirectional transformers for language understanding. arXiv preprint arXiv:181004805. 2018.
[53] Mohamed Hassan HA, Marengo E, Nutt W. A BERT-Based Model for Question Answering on Construction Incident Reports. In: International Conference on Applications of Natural Language to Information Systems. Springer; 2022. p. 215-23.
[54] Yao L, Mao C, Luo Y. KG-BERT: BERT for knowledge graph completion. arXiv preprint arXiv:190903193. 2019.
[55] Radford A. Improving language understanding by generative pre-training. 2018.
[56] Brown TB. Language models are few-shot learners. arXiv preprint arXiv:200514165. 2020.
[57] Raffel C, Shazeer N, Roberts A, Lee K, Narang S, Matena M, et al. Exploring the limits of transfer learning with a unified text-to-text transformer. Journal of machine learning research. 2020;21(140):1-67.
[58] Dosovitskiy A. An image is worth 16x16 words: Transformers for image recognition at scale. arXiv preprint arXiv:201011929. 2020.
[59] Scarselli F, Gori M, Tsoi AC, Hagenbuchner M, Monfardini G. The Graph Neural Network Model. IEEE Transactions on Neural Networks. 2009;20(1):61-80.
[60] Bacciu D, Errica F, Micheli A, Podda M. A gentle introduction to deep learning for graphs. Neural Networks. 2020;129:203-21. Available from: `https://www.sciencedirect.com/science/article/pii/S0893608020302197`.
[61] Amayuelas A, Zhang S, Rao XS, Zhang C. Neural Methods for Logical Reasoning over Knowledge Graphs. In: International Conference on Learning Representations; 2022. .
[62] Khemani B, Patil S, Kotecha K, et al. A review of graph neural networks: concepts, architectures, techniques, challenges, datasets, applications, and future directions. Journal of Big Data. Available from: `https://doi.org/10.1186/s40537-023-00876-4`.

[63] Wang B, Jiang B, Tang J, Luo B. Generalizing Aggregation Functions in GNNs: Building High Capacity and Robust GNNs via Nonlinear Aggregation. IEEE Transactions on Pattern Analysis and Machine Intelligence. 2023;45(11):13454-66.

[64] Wu Z, Pan S, Chen F, Long G, Zhang C, Yu PS. A Comprehensive Survey on Graph Neural Networks. IEEE Transactions on Neural Networks and Learning Systems. 2021;32(1):4-24.

[65] Kipf T, Welling M. Semi-Supervised Classification with Graph Convolutional Networks. ArXiv. 2016;abs/1609.02907. Available from: https://api.semanticscholar.org/CorpusID:3144218.

[66] Zhou J, Cui G, Hu S, Zhang Z, Yang C, Liu Z, et al. Graph neural networks: A review of methods and applications. AI Open. 2020;1:57-81. Available from: https://www.sciencedirect.com/science/article/pii/S2666651021000012.

[67] Veličković P, Cucurull G, Casanova A, Romero A, Liò P, Bengio Y. Graph Attention Networks; 2018. Available from: https://arxiv.org/abs/1710.10903.

[68] Hamilton WL, Ying R, Leskovec J. Inductive representation learning on large graphs. In: Proceedings of the 31st International Conference on Neural Information Processing Systems. NIPS'17. Red Hook, NY, USA: Curran Associates Inc.; 2017. p. 1025–1035.

[69] Goodfellow IJ, Pouget-Abadie J, Mirza M, Xu B, Warde-Farley D, Ozair S, et al.. Generative Adversarial Networks; 2014. Available from: https://arxiv.org/abs/1406.2661.

[70] Developer I. Generative Adversarial Networks Explained; 2020. Accessed: 2024-08-25. Available from: https://developer.ibm.com/articles/generative-adversarial-networks-explained/.

[71] Karras T, Aila T, Laine S, Lehtinen J. Progressive Growing of GANs for Improved Quality, Stability, and Variation; 2018. Available from: https://arxiv.org/abs/1710.10196.

[72] Isola P, Zhu JY, Zhou T, Efros AA. Image-to-Image Translation with Conditional Adversarial Networks; 2018. Available from: https://arxiv.org/abs/1611.07004.

[73] Ledig C, Theis L, Huszar F, Caballero J, Cunningham A, Acosta A, et al.. Photo-Realistic Single Image Super-Resolution Using a Generative Adversarial Network; 2017. Available from: https://arxiv.org/abs/1609.04802.

[74] Vondrick C, Pirsiavash H, Torralba A. Generating Videos with Scene Dynamics; 2016. Available from: https://arxiv.org/abs/1609.02612.

[75] Wu J, Zhang C, Xue T, Freeman WT, Tenenbaum JB. Learning a Probabilistic Latent Space of Object Shapes via 3D Generative-Adversarial Modeling; 2017. Available from: https://arxiv.org/abs/1610.07584.

[76] Cai L, Wang WY. KBGAN: Adversarial Learning for Knowledge Graph Embeddings. In: Walker M, Ji H, Stent A, editors. Proceedings of the 2018 Conference of the North American Chapter of the Association for Computational Linguistics: Human Language Technologies, Volume 1 (Long Papers). New Orleans, Louisiana: Association for Computational Linguistics; 2018. p. 1470-80. Available from: https://aclanthology.org/N18-1133.

[77] Qin P, Wang XE, Chen W, Zhang C, Xu W, Wang WY. Generative Adversarial Zero-Shot Relational Learning for Knowledge Graphs. In: AAAI Conference on Artificial Intelligence; 2020. Available from: https://api.semanticscholar.org/CorpusID:210064470.

[78] Wang Q, Ji Y, Hao Y, Cao J. GRL: Knowledge graph completion with GAN-based reinforcement learning. Knowledge-Based Systems. 2020;209:106421. Available from: https://www.sciencedirect.com/science/article/pii/S0950705120305505.

[79] Motogna A, Groza A. Interleaving GANs with knowledge graphs to support design creativity for book covers; 2023. Available from: https://arxiv.org/abs/2308.01626.

[80] Hinton GE, Zemel RS. Autoencoders, Minimum Description Length, and Helmholtz Free Energy. In: Advances in Neural Information Processing Systems. vol. 6; 1993. p. 3-10.

[81] Sharma A. Introduction to Autoencoders. In: Chugh P, Gosthipaty AR, Huot S, Kidriavsteva K, Raha R, editors. PyImageSearch; 2023. Available from: https://pyimg.co/ehnlf.

[82] Michelucci U. An Introduction to Autoencoders; 2022. Available from: https://arxiv.org/abs/2201.03898.

[83] Bellini V, Schiavone A, Noia TD, Ragone A, Sciascio ED. Computing Recommendations via a Knowledge Graph-aware Autoencoder. ArXiv. 2018;abs/1807.05006. Available from: https://api.semanticscholar.org/CorpusID:49740983.

[84] Han Y, Fang Q, Hu J, Qian S, Xu C. GAEAT: Graph Auto-Encoder Attention Networks for Knowledge Graph Completion. New York, NY, USA: Association for Computing Machinery; 2020. p. 2053–2056.

Available from: https://doi.org/10.1145/3340531.3412148.
[85] Yang K. GCN-VAE for Knowledge Graph Completion; 2019. Available from: https://api.semanticscholar.org/CorpusID:218537728.
[86] Brownlee J. Data preparation for machine learning: data cleaning, feature selection, and data transforms in Python. Machine Learning Mastery; 2020.
[87] Schütze H, Manning CD, Raghavan P. Introduction to information retrieval. vol. 39. Cambridge University Press Cambridge; 2008.
[88] Abadi M, Barham P, Chen J, Chen Z, Davis A, Dean J, et al. {TensorFlow}: a system for {Large-Scale} machine learning. In: 12th USENIX symposium on operating systems design and implementation (OSDI 16); 2016. p. 265-83.
[89] Paszke A, Gross S, Massa F, Lerer A, Bradbury J, Chanan G, et al. Pytorch: An imperative style, high-performance deep learning library. Advances in neural information processing systems. 2019;32.
[90] Chollet F, et al.. Keras; 2015. https://keras.io.

Handbook on Neurosymbolic AI and Knowledge Graphs
P. Hitzler et al. (Eds.)
IOS Press, 2025

doi:10.3233/FAIA250200

How the (Tensor-) Brain Uses Embeddings and Embodiment to Encode Senses and Symbols

Volker TRESP [a,1] and Hang LI [a]
[a] *LMU Munich*

Abstract.
The Tensor Brain (TB) has been introduced as a computational model for perception and memory. This paper provides an overview of the TB model, incorporating recent developments and insights into its functionality. The TB is composed of two primary layers: the representation layer and the index layer. The representation layer serves as a model for the subsymbolic global workspace, a concept derived from consciousness research. Its state represents the cognitive brain state, capturing the dynamic interplay of sensory and cognitive processes. The index layer, in contrast, contains symbolic representations for concepts, time instances, and predicates. In a bottom-up operation, sensory input activates the representation layer, which then triggers associated symbolic labels in the index layer. Conversely, in a top-down operation, symbols in the index layer activate the representation layer, which in turn influences earlier processing layers through embodiment. This top-down mechanism underpins semantic memory, enabling the integration of abstract knowledge into perceptual and cognitive processes. A key feature of the TB is its use of concept embeddings, which function as connection weights linking the index layer to the representation layer. As a concept's "DNA," these embeddings consolidate knowledge from diverse experiences, sensory modalities, and symbolic representations, providing a unified framework for learning and memory. Although the TB is primarily a computational model, it has been hypothesized to reflect certain aspects of actual brain function. Notably, the sequential generation of symbols in the TB may represent a precursor to the development of natural language. The model incorporates an attention mechanism and supports multitasking through multiplexing, simulating the brain's ability to rapidly switch between mental states. Additionally, the TB emphasizes multimodality, with the representation layer integrating inputs across multiple sensory and cognitive dimensions.

Keywords. Symbolic Representation, Embeddings, Index Layer, Representation Layer, Perception, Episodic Memory, Semantic Memory, Reasoning

1. Introduction

The debate between symbolic and subsymbolic processing in intelligent systems remains a central topic in cognitive science and artificial intelligence. The perspective presented here posits that symbols are the outcomes of measurement devices. These devices may be

[1] Corresponding Author: Volker Tresp, Ludwig-Maximilians-Universität München, Oettingenstr. 67, D-80538 Muenchen, Volker.Tresp@lmu.de.

technical in nature or, as in this case, biological—representing the brain itself. Through the sensory system, the real world provides inputs to these measurement devices, with symbols serving as the resulting outputs. Importantly, these outputs can feed back into the processing pipeline, influencing subsequent operations. When the measurement device is an actor, such as a robot or a human, it can also actively modify the real world.

The Tensor Brain (TB), reviewed in this paper, builds upon these ideas. It suggests that while much of the brain's processing is subsymbolic, symbols play a crucial role at the highest levels of cognition.

A key component of the TB is the subsymbolic representation layer, which acts as a central communication hub akin to the "global workspace" in consciousness research. This layer functions as a "mental canvas" or "theater of the brain," comparable to the blackboard concept in multi-agent systems. Brain modules can write to and read from this representation layer, making it a cognitive hub. Its activation state defines the cognitive brain state, encompassing the information that reaches conscious awareness and propagates throughout the system.

The second major component is the symbolic index layer, where each symbol or index has a localized representation. For example, when the brain perceives a scene and identifies an entity as a dog, it acts as a bottom-up measurement device, producing the symbol *Dog* as the output. Symbols and subsymbolic representations interact, creating complementary descriptions of the world. Every symbol activation is associated with subsymbolic activity, while subsymbolic representations are continuously annotated with symbolic labels.

The connection weights between the symbolic index and the representation layer form the embedding vector of the symbol. This embedding, in a way a symbol's "DNA," integrates perceptual inputs, experiences, and embodied knowledge. When a symbol like *Dog* is activated—whether due to sensory input or deliberate focus—it triggers activity in the representation layer via its embedding, propagating this information to other brain regions through grounding and embodiment. Symbols also interact with other symbols, forming networks of relationships. The embedding vectors are optimized to fulfill their roles in this network.

Figure 1 illustrates the TB architecture, showing how the representation layer integrates sensory inputs and interacts with symbols through the index layer. The activation state of the representation layer serves as a distributed code, providing a latent representation for both sensory input and symbolic indices.

In the TB framework, symbols represent concepts such as entities, classes, attributes, predicates, and episodic instances. This enables the formation of episodic memories, where symbolic similarity contributes to memory recall. The similarity between two scenes, for instance, depends not only on sensory input but also on their symbolic representations. This dynamic interplay between perception and memory reflects Goethe's adage: "You only see what you know!" Figure 2 demonstrates how episodic and semantic memory support perception.

Symbolic decoding—essential for perception and memory—is conceptualized as a serial process, akin to an "inner thought language." Humans excel at articulating perceptions and memories with minimal effort, suggesting that spoken language evolved from an earlier, internal symbolic language. While much reasoning and communication rely on symbols, the cognitive brain state encompasses more than just symbolic activity. It is reflected in embodiment and grounding, manifested through intonation, gestures, body language, and facial expressions.

The TB framework aligns with the notion of the brain as a prediction machine, a view supported by substantial evidence at the level of implicit memories, such as perceptual and motor skills. However, to make predictions over longer timescales—such as planning an evening—the mind must relate the present to both past experiences and future possibilities. This requires explicit understanding, explicit memory, and imagination.

The remainder of the paper is organized as follows. Section 2 summarizes the literature on the Tensor Brain. Section 3 introduces the representation layer as a model for the global workspace and defines the cognitive brain state, illustrating its progression over time as a recurrent neural network. Section 4 provides a probabilistic interpretation of the cognitive brain state. Section 5 discusses symbolic decoding as bottom-up inference, covering symbolic indices for concepts, predicates, and episodic time instances. Section 6 explains symbolic encoding as top-down inference, introducing an attention mechanism and discussing embodiment as an encoder in an autoencoder framework. Section 7 describes the Tensor Brain's operational modes, including perception, episodic memory, and semantic memory. It elaborates on the generation of triple statements and language understanding. Section 8 details how self-supervised learning adapts embedding vectors. Section 9 examines multitasking via multiplexing and cognitive control. Section 10 explores multimodality and various forms of reasoning, including embedded reasoning, symbolic reasoning, and embedded symbolic reasoning. Section 11 concludes with a summary of key findings and implications.

Glossary and notation:

- The **agent** represents an **individual** and serves as the actor, with its **mind** executing cognitive functions through its neurobiological foundation—the **brain**.
- The **representation layer** is a model for the brain's **global workspace**. Its activation is the **cognitive brain state** (CBS). The probabilistic interpretation of the CBS is the **probabilistic cognitive brain state** (pCBS).
- The **index layer** encodes indices which can be concepts, predicates, and episodic indices. Each index is realized by an *ensemble of neurons*. An ensemble is referred to as an **index**, a **symbol**, or a **label**.
- The synaptic weights linking an index with the representation layer form the **embedding** vector of that index. An embedding vector is the signature or "DNA" of the associated index.
- $\vec{\gamma}$ is the vector of post-activations of the ensembles in the representation layer, and $\mathbf{q}$ is the vector of pre-activations. $\mathbf{a}_k$ is the embedding vector of index k. Components are γ_i, q_i, and $a_{i,k}$, with $i = 1, \ldots n$.

2. The Development of the Tensor Brain

This section provides an overview of the key milestones in the development of the Tensor Brain (TB) model, tracing its evolution and contributions to the fields of perception, memory, and cognitive modeling.

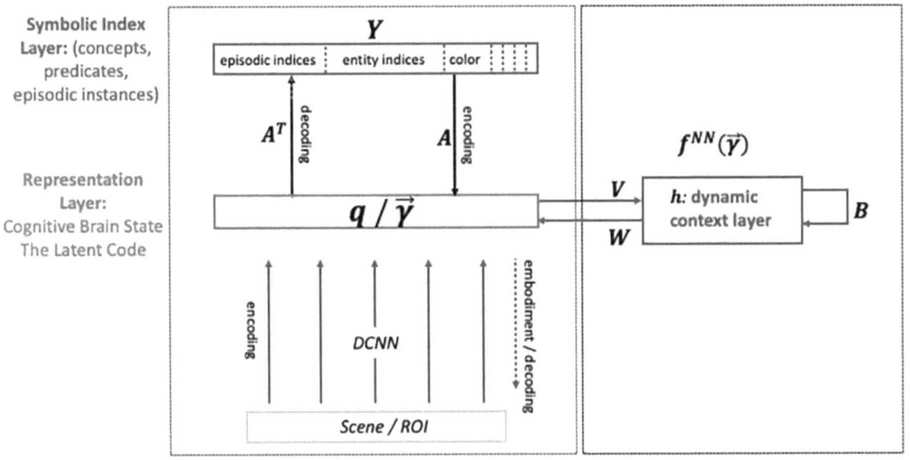

Figure 1. The Tensor Brain (TB) Architecture: The architecture processes scene input (illustrated at the bottom) through the layers of a deep convolutional network, mapping it to the representation layer, which serves as a mathematical model of the global workspace. On the right, the evolution neural network, featuring one hidden layer, provides recurrence. Within the TB framework, this recurrent component is referred to as the dynamic context layer. The representation layer connects to the index layer, which in turn feeds back into the representation layer. The embedding vectors are represented by the columns of matrix **A**. Through bottom-up and top-down processing, the system can generate multiple labels for a given scene or region of interest (ROI).

The first foundational paper on the TB model was published in 2015 [42]. It explored the interaction between symbolic representations, subsymbolic representations, and concept embeddings in brain function. The paper introduced the Tucker tensor decomposition—a mathematical approach for reducing the complexity of multi-dimensional data—as a generative model for perception and memory processes. Central components of the TB model, including the representation layer and the index layer, were introduced.

The work connected semantic memory to knowledge graph factorization and episodic memory to the factorization of temporal knowledge graphs, pioneering the field of temporal knowledge graph embedding models. Additionally, it proposed the analysis of visual scenes through factorized graph models, which later evolved into the scene graph embedding models widely used today. The paper also renewed interest in index-based approaches to memory, echoing the work of Teyler and colleagues [41].

The vision component of the TB model was extended in [2] by incorporating bounding boxes as regions of interest (ROIs) for identifying entities within a scene. This extension included experimental validation using annotated image data from [18]. Concurrently, the concept of temporal knowledge graphs received further exploration in works such as [44] and [27], solidifying its role in the model's development.

In 2020, [45] introduced a probabilistic generative model for the TB, enriching its theoretical underpinnings. Meanwhile, [38] focused on integrating an attention mechanism and emphasized the role of prior knowledge and grounding in the model.

The TB model underwent further refinement in [46], which integrated extensive experimental evidence and provided a robust mathematical framework. This work estab-

Figure 2. Johann Wolfgang von Goethe gazes upon a picturesque landscape, with mountains forming the distant backdrop (perception). As his eyes sweep across the scene, he identifies the Frauenkirche (symbolic labeling) and deduces that the city before him must be Munich (semantic memory). Observing the mountains, he further concludes they must be the Alps (semantic memory). This view triggers memories of his last visit to Munich (episodic memory), particularly a delightful dinner at the Flaucher. Reflecting on the weather forecast, which promises a pleasant evening, Goethe contemplates whether to revisit the Flaucher for another memorable meal (decision support through future episodic memory and imagination).

lished critical connections between the TB approach and cognitive neuroscience, enhancing its relevance for both theoretical and applied research. The most recent development, [43], derived a probabilistic Tensor Brain model inspired by the Heisenberg measurement process, drawing parallels to concepts in decoherent quantum theory.

3. The Subsymbolic Representation Layer

3.1. The Representation Layer and the Cognitive Brain State (CBS)

The brain is composed of thousands, potentially millions, of interconnected modules that must coordinate and exchange information effectively. To support higher-order processing, including conscious awareness, an integrative mechanism is essential for organizing and relaying information across these modules.

In the tensor brain (TB) model, the representation layer serves as an integrative, high-dimensional workspace where modules can exchange information by writing to and reading from shared representations. This layer facilitates the coordination of neural activities and synthesizes the cognitive brain state (CBS).

The CBS is defined by the activation pattern of all ensembles in the representation layer. Specific ensembles may represent concrete features, such as the color 'red,' while others encode abstract latent factors. Experimental findings suggest that the CBS exhibits a well-organized clustering structure, reflecting meaningful groupings of cognitive and perceptual representations [46].

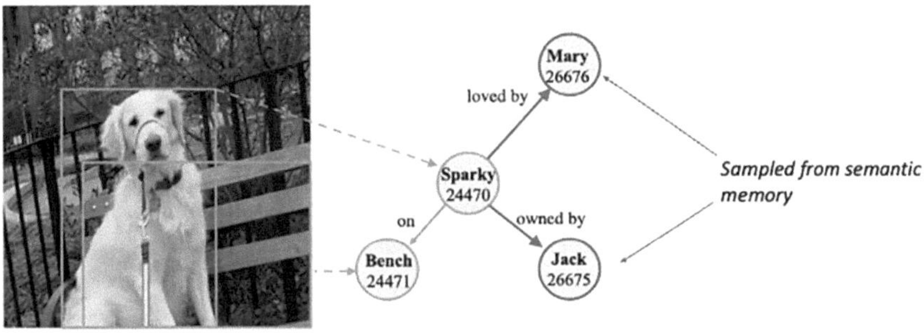

Figure 3. Experimental results from the Tensor Brain (TB) for perception, enhanced by semantic memory, are shown in [46]. In the first region of interest (ROI), the left bounding box is identified as *Sparky*. The top-ranked labels for this ROI include: *Dog*, *Mammal*, *LivingBeing*, *Young*, *White*, and *OtherActivity*. For the second ROI, the top-ranked labels are: *Bench*, *Furniture*, *NonLivingBeing*, *Old*, *OtherColor*, and *OtherActivity*. The sampled binary statements are: *(Dog, sit on, Bench)*, *(LivingBeing, on, Furniture)*, *(Mammal, sit on, Old)*, *(White, sit on, Bench)*. Additionally, semantic memory enhances perception by providing binary statements related to entities not present in the scene, such as: *(Sparky, ownedBy, Jack)* and *(Sparky, lovedBy, Mary)*, where *Jack* and *Mary* are part of the agent's semantic memory, but not visible in the scene.

Let n represent the total number of neuron ensembles in the representation layer. The activation γ_i of each ensemble i is calculated as a function of its pre-activation input q_i as

$$\gamma_i \leftarrow \text{sig}(q_i). \tag{1}$$

Here, $\gamma_i \in [0, 1]$ denotes the post-activation value, where $\gamma_i = 1$ indicates maximal firing intensity, and $\gamma_i = 0$ corresponds to basal or no firing. The function $\text{sig}(q_i) = (1 + \exp(-q_i))^{-1}$ is the standard logistic activation function.

In this framework, q_i represents the cumulative input signals received by ensemble i, while γ_i represents the corresponding output activation. This dynamic ensures that the representation layer accurately reflects ongoing cognitive states. The CBS, represented by the activation vector $\vec{\gamma}$ of the representation layer, encapsulates the brain's distributed coding of sensory inputs and higher-order representations. This framework enables the TB model to simulate cognitive processes such as perception, memory integration, and decision-making.

3.2. The Representation Layer, the Global Workspace Theory, and the Blackboard

Baars and his colleagues introduced the concept of a global workspace [1], which serves as the foundation for several theories of consciousness [1,8]. The global workspace functions as a central hub for broadcasting and integrating information, enabling its dissemination across various brain modules. Often referred to as the "theater of the brain" or the "mental canvas," the global workspace has been likened to a blackboard in a multi-agent system, where computational modules collaborate by sharing information [1].

The global workspace facilitates communication and interaction, particularly among modules that handle higher levels of abstraction, where direct, module-to-module interactions may be insufficient or impractical.

Consider the example of vision. Visual inputs are processed through visual pathways, contributing to the pre-activations of neural ensembles within the global workspace. These inputs are "written" into the representation layer, forming part of the cognitive brain state (CBS). In turn, the CBS can feed back into the visual pathways. This feedback, often associated with embodiment, acts as an input to the early visual processing layers, modulating their activity. Thus, the global workspace enables a bidirectional exchange of information: visual input informs the global workspace, and the global workspace influences early visual processing.

Beyond vision, the global workspace integrates signals from a wide array of brain modules, each corresponding to different sensory modalities, such as vision, hearing, taste, smell, touch, proprioception, and pain. Crucially, the global workspace is not merely a passive integrator. Brain modules can also be affected by the state of the global workspace, creating a dynamic feedback loop.

This process extends to states of consciousness. It has been proposed that all brain states capable of reaching consciousness—such as inner feelings, emotional states, and even pain after injury—contribute to the global workspace. In turn, these states can be influenced by the global workspace's current configuration. However, not all brain modules have a direct impact on the global workspace. Consequently, some processes or information may never reach conscious awareness.

While sensory input plays a dominant role in shaping the global workspace, other factors—such as emotions tied to memories or physical pain—also contribute significantly. For example, the discomfort from an injury or the emotional resonance of a recalled memory can profoundly affect the global workspace's state.

In the tensor brain (TB) model, the global workspace is hypothesized to be implemented by the representation layer. This representation layer is conceptually related to the hidden layer of a recurrent neural network (RNN), but with critical modifications to accommodate the unique requirements of the TB architecture. These modifications are explored in greater detail in the following discussion.

3.3. Evolution Neural Network and Recurrency

The representation layer in the tensor brain (TB) model incorporates feedback connections, creating dependencies between the activations of neural ensembles and an internal memory. This feedback mechanism is modeled as follows, for $i = 1, \ldots, n$

$$q_i^{(\tau)} \leftarrow q_i^{(\tau-1)} + g_i(\mathbf{v}^{(\tau)}) + f_i^{NN}(\vec{\gamma}^{(\tau-1)}). \qquad (2)$$

Here, τ denotes a discrete-time step, representing sequential operations of the brain. All computations performed during a specific τ are linked to the same concept or episodic index.

THen, $f_i^{NN}(\vec{\gamma}^{(\tau-1)})$ is the i-th output of a neural network with linear output units This component, known as the evolution neural network, models interactions among ensembles and their evolution over time. $\mathbf{v}^{(\tau)}$ represents an external input (e.g., from a visual scene). This input is processed by a deep convolutional neural network, $\mathbf{g}(\mathbf{v}^{(\tau)})$, which maps sensory input to the representation layer using linear output units. Recall that $\gamma_i^{(\tau)} \leftarrow \text{sig}(q_i^{(\tau)})$ (Equation1).

In this framework, a specific $q_i^{(\tau)}$ can depend on only a subset of ensembles, promoting modularity in the system. The term $q_i^{(\tau-1)}$, representing the state of the ensemble at the previous time step, introduces a skip connection (a common feature in deep learning models like ResNets [15] and LSTMs [17]).[2] This dependency implements self-memory, allowing the system to maintain continuity across time steps.

The evolution neural network enables the prediction of future cognitive brain states (CBS), a critical capability for tasks involving sequential reasoning or anticipating future events. By modeling relationships in both semantic memory (knowledge about the world) and episodic memory (personal experiences), the network supports the integration of knowledge and experience into the CBS. This dual functionality is central to the TB model's ability to handle complex cognitive tasks.

4. The Probabilistic Cognitive Brain State (pCBS)

The post-activation γ_i can be interpreted as the parameter of a Bernoulli distribution, where

$$P(X_i = 1) = \gamma_i. \tag{3}$$

Here, $X_i = 1$ represents the ensemble i being "on," while $X_i = 0$ represents it being "off." Assuming mutual independence among ensembles, the probabilistic cognitive brain state (pCBS) can be defined as a joint probability distribution

$$P(X_1 = i_1, \ldots, X_n = i_n) = \prod_{j=1}^{n} (\gamma_j)^{i_j} (1 - \gamma_j)^{1-i_j}$$

where $i_j \in \{0, 1\}$. This probabilistic formulation of the CBS introduces a new layer of interpretability and flexibility, as extensively discussed in [43]. It supports top-down inference and extends the model to account for uncertainty and variability in neural activation patterns.[3]

Equation 2 now has two interpretations. First, one can assume that the dynamics of the neural activations is the basic deterministic dynamic equation, and Equation 3 describes a noisy measurement. Alternatively, one can consider the states of the random variables X_i to be the fundamental quantity and we need to consider the evolution of a multivariate probability distribution. In [43], it is demonstrated that the evolution neural network can be derived from the latter probabilistic perspective, assuming certain ap-

[2] The skip connection was not used in [46]

[3] A distribution with maximum entropy corresponds to $\gamma_j = 1/2, \forall j$, which implies that, in the absence of input, all neurons fire with half intensity. While this may not be physiologically plausible for real neurons (e.g., neurons with ReLU activation functions remain inactive without input), it reflects the statistical nature of the pCBS.

proximations and independence constraints. Specifically, the pCBS is approximated at each instance by n independent Bernoulli distributions. While the brain's physical reality is represented by the firing rates γ_i, the random variables X_i serve as mathematical constructs for modeling purposes and are not directly observed.

5. The Symbolic Index Layer

5.1. The Index Layer

The symbolic index layer is a cognitively significant module that interacts dynamically with the representation layer. It not only receives input from the representation layer but also provides feedback, establishing a bidirectional connection.

In the brain, an index (or pointer) may be represented by an ensemble of neurons, similar to other neural ensembles. However, a distinguishing feature of the index layer is its ability to enforce a sample-take-all mechanism—a variation of the well-known winner-take-all concept.

Each index corresponds to a distinct symbol, and we categorize these symbols into three types: concept indices, predicate indices, and episodic indices. Importantly, we propose that an episodic index can also be treated as a symbol. In perceptual tasks, the term label is used interchangeably with symbol.

5.2. Concept Indices

Indices associated with concepts are inherently symbolic. These concepts can represent a wide range of entities, such as objects, classes, attributes, locations, inner emotional states, actions, or decisions. Concept indices enable the recognition and encoding of stable patterns within the Cognitive Brain State (CBS). For example, a cluster analysis of the CBS could allow the brain to detect recurring patterns corresponding to concepts like *Dog*, a specific dog named *Sparky*, or attributes such as *Black* and *Happy*.

In perception, concept indices may be used to label scenes or define regions of interest (ROIs) within a visual field. This labeling mechanism is essential for identifying areas that are contextually or semantically significant.

Assuming the CBS is represented by the activation vector $\vec{\gamma}$, an index k in the index layer receives input from the representation layer, with its activation governed by

$$P(Y = k|\vec{\gamma}) = \text{softmax}_{dom}(a_{0,k} + \sum_{i=1}^{n} a_{i,k}\gamma_i). \quad (4)$$

Here, $Y = k$ indicates that the index layer is in state k, i.e., only index k is active, while all other indices remain inactive. The vector $\mathbf{a}_k = (a_{1,k}, \ldots, a_{n,k})^\top$ is the typically sparse embedding vector of concept k, representing its connection weights to the representation layer. $a_{0,k}$ is a bias term to concept k. In the architecture, $a_{i,k}$ is the weight on the link from ensemble i in the representation layer to ensemble k in the index layer. The softmax function is defined as

$$\text{softmax}_{dom}(a_{0,k} + \sum_{i=1}^{n} a_{i,k}\gamma_i) = \frac{\exp(a_{0,k} + \sum_{i=1}^{n} a_{i,k}\gamma_i)}{\sum_{k' \in dom} \exp(a_{0,k'} + \sum_{l=1}^{n} a_{l,k'}\gamma_l)}.$$

It normalizes over a domain (*dom*) such as the set of all entities, predicates, classes, or colors. Each domain defines a mutually exclusive and collectively exhaustive set of labels, although in practice, violations such as assigning multiple labels (e.g., two colors) to the same entity might occur. See Section 7.4.3 for further discussion.[4]

Concept indices capture repeated patterns within the CBS and are identified through their embeddings or potentially their location within a topographic map. While these indices in animals do not correspond to explicit names like *Dog*, *Sparky*, *Black* and *Happy*, in humans, they directly reflect concepts encoded in natural language.

5.3. Predicate Indices

The second type of indices refers to predicates. Imagine an agent analyzing a scene. The CBS first identifies a region of interest (ROI) that, for instance, contains *Sparky*, a *Dog* in the scene. Next, it identifies a second ROI, which, for example, contains *Jack*, a *Person*, in the scene. A third ROI is then formed that encompasses both of the previous ROIs. Within the context of these two ROIs, the third one may be labeled according to their relationship, such as *looksAt*. Therefore, the brain not only considers the labels of individual ROIs, but also the labels of the relationships between them. In this context, $\mathbf{a}_k$ represents the embedding vector of predicate k.

5.4. Episodic Indices Refer to Time Instances

The third type of indices pertains to episodic indices and relates to time instances. In the TB, an episodic index is introduced for each relevant time instance. In its simplest form, the embedding vector of index t corresponds to the vector of pre-activations from the representation layer at that specific instance, i.e., $\mathbf{a}_t \leftarrow \mathbf{q}^{(t)}$. If the representation layer is primarily influenced by visual input from a scene, it will store the resulting pre-activations of the CBS, which may include information such as the emotional state at that time. Later, we will explore how $\mathbf{a}_t$ is optimized.

6. Symbolic Encoding

The indices or symbols in the index layer can be encoded into subsymbolic representations, a process that embodies top-down inference. The primary purpose of top-down inference is to inform the representation layer—and, by extension, the entire brain—about which concept has been detected in vision, or more generally, which concept the brain is currently focusing on. For instance, if the concept of *Sparky* is detected, this information should be communicated to the representation layer and, ultimately, to the brain. This is particularly important for integrating memory with perception. With the current hypothesis that *Sparky* is present in the image, the brain can augment this perception with background knowledge, such as that *Sparky* is *Friendly*, *ownedBy Jack*, and *lovedBy Mary* (see Figure 3). We will discuss four variants of this process.

First, we explore the deterministic model without top-down inference. Second, we examine how a sampled concept label feeds back into the representation layer. Third, we address the generation of multiple sampled concepts. Finally, we discuss the attention approximation.

[4]For the pCBS, Equation 4 approximates $P(Y=k|context) = \mathbb{E}_{P(X_1,\ldots,X_n|context)} P(Y=k|X_1,\ldots,X_n)$ [43].

6.1. A Deterministic Model without Top-down Inference

In a deterministic CBS interpretation, Equation 4 describes the system's output. Suppose the labels for *Sparky*, *Dog*, *Black*, and *Happy* show substantial activation. The agent might select the label with the highest probability, such as *Sparky*. Alternatively, the agent could consider other likely labels, such as *Dog*, *Black*, and *Happy*. In either case, there is no feedback to the representation layer, and the rest of the brain remains uninformed about the likely labels. This setup reflects the standard RNN model, where all labels are treated as independent. However, this is not the approach used in the TB.

6.2. A Single Sampled Label

Assume that the labels for *Sparky*, *Dog*, and *Black* exhibit substantial activation. In sampling mode, the TB samples from the distribution in Equation 4 and may generate the label *Sparky*. Generally, when index k is sampled, it is assumed that concept k is represented in the representation layer.

The index layer operates in a "sample-take-all" mode, meaning only one index fires at a time, suppressing the firing of all other indices. In the example, the index *Sparky* would be the active one. Technically, after sampling, the state of the index layer is represented as a one-hot vector.

When index $Y = k$ fires, it activates the global workspace in a top-down manner according to the following update rule

$$\mathbf{q} \leftarrow \alpha \mathbf{q} + \beta \mathbf{a}_k. \tag{5}$$

Here, $\mathbf{a}_k$ represents the embedding vector for concept k. The term $a_{i,k}$ can be interpreted as the synaptic weight connecting ensemble k in the index layer to ensemble i in the representation layer. In the pCBS interpretation, we obtain independent Bernoulli distributions. This update equation was derived in [43].

The factor α, where $0 \leq \alpha \leq 1$, controls how much of $\mathbf{q}$ is preserved during the update. With $\beta = 0$ and $\alpha = 1$, we recover an RNN update, where the CBS is unaffected by the sample. With $\beta = 1$ and $\alpha = 0$, we obtain the Heisenberg approximation, where the CBS is entirely overwritten by the sample's embedding vector. Finally, with $\beta = 1$ and $\alpha = 1$, we have the Heisenberg approximation with an "added prior." This latter version is used in the TB.

As reflected in the last equation and in Equation 4, the connections are bipartite and symmetrical. Strict symmetry is implied by some theoretical considerations [43], though it is not a strict requirement and is likely to be violated biologically. Note that when $\alpha = 1$, the previous pre-activation is not eliminated but rather added to the embedding vector, acting as a skip connection.

6.3. Multiple Sampled Labels

The process can be repeated multiple times by continuously sampling from Equation 4 and updating Equation 5. With $\alpha > 0$, each sample is always conditioned on the previous ones. Each sample represents a specific interpretation of the CBS, framed within the context of prior samples. For instance, the first sample might correspond to the label *Sparky*, followed by *Dog*, then *Black*, *Happy*, and so on.

Finally (with $\beta = 1$ and $\alpha = 1$, as in the TB), we have the following update rule

$$\mathbf{q} \leftarrow \mathbf{q} + \sum_{k \in Sample} \mathbf{a}_k. \tag{6}$$

Thus, the index layer functions as part of a labeling engine. This clearly contrasts with a standard RNN, where the last equation would not include the summation term—meaning there is no feedback from the samples to the state. In the TB, the representation layer is explicitly informed about all generated samples, and subsequent samples are generated with consideration of all previously generated labels.

The activation of an index is an internal brain measurement that feeds back into the system, allowing all modules in the brain to learn about what has been detected. Equation 7 illustrates the additive combination of embedding vectors, a concept found in models like word2vec [29] and TransE [4].

6.4. Probabilistic Averaging: Attention

Consider the case where there is no sampling, and the CBS is updated by taking into account all possible labels, weighted by their probabilities. In [43, 46], the following equation is introduced

$$\mathbf{q} = \mathbf{q} + \sum_k \mathbf{a}_k \text{softmax}_{dom}(a_{0,k} + \sum_{l=1}^{n} a_{l,k} \gamma_l). \tag{7}$$

This equation provides an update to the CBS, not through sampling, but by considering the probabilities of the labels. It can be interpreted as a form of attention mechanism with a skip connection, commonly found in generative AI models. In this context, the CBS vector $\vec{\gamma}$ acts as the query vector, while the embedding vectors $\mathbf{a}_k$ (for all k) serve as both the key and value vectors.

6.5. Attention versus Sampling

Attention does not yield a symbolic interpretation because no single index is active in isolation. However, a key advantage of the attention mechanism is its speed, parallelism, and holistic consideration of all possible interpretations. The attention equation links indices to related indices, facilitating the sharing of statistical strength across them.

In [43], it is shown that the attention mechanism can be derived from a Heisenberg framework rather than a Bayesian one. In a Bayesian scenario, only the indices that are actually sampled would influence the CBS, while in the Heisenberg scenario, all indices are considered together.

Sampling commits the brain to a specific interpretation. For instance, if the black object in a scene is sampled as *Sparky*, the brain can incorporate a wealth of background information about *Sparky*. However, if the object is sampled as a *Puma*, the brain adds different background knowledge, and the agent's response may differ significantly. Sampling allows both possibilities to be explored in separate sampling rounds, enabling the exploration of joint dependencies between labels. This process of sampling and top-down inference forms the foundation of semantic memory, as illustrated in Figure 4.

The sampling of indices is a fundamental feature of the TB. But what triggers the sampling? Sampling appears to share many similarities with the collapse of the wave function in quantum mechanics. Does this suggest that the brain functions as a decoherent quantum computer? These questions are explored in [43]. Additionally, [48] discusses sequential Monte Carlo (SMC) as a sampling method. In contrast to SMC, the TB does not require the filtering step because the labels are self-generated and do not depend on external measurements. Sensory data provides deterministic inputs and are "given."

6.6. Attention, Autoencoding and Embodiment

We examine two types of autoencoders where the representation layer functions as the latent code or bottleneck layer.

In the first autoencoder, indices represent the visible data points, while the cognitive brain state (CBS) serves as the latent code. The decoder maps the CBS to the index layer activation (Equation 4), where an index is sampled. The sample forms the data point. The encoder operates in the reverse direction, mapping an index to the representation layer via Equation 5, with parameters $\beta = 1$ and $\alpha = 0$.

In the second autoencoder, sensory inputs constitute the visible representation. The encoder maps visual input $\mathbf{v}$ to the index layer using a visual processing function $\mathbf{g}(\mathbf{v})$. The decoder reconstructs the visual input from the CBS by approximating the inverse of the visual processing function, i.e., $\hat{\mathbf{v}} = \mathbf{g}^{\text{inv}}(\vec{\gamma})$. This top-down processing reflects a form of grounding or embodiment: it not only updates the representation layer but also propagates changes through all visual processing layers to reflect the consideration of the concept *Sparky* in the index layer.

In brain circuits, connections are typically bi-directional—if one module connects to another, there is usually a reciprocal connection. Consistently, the TB model assumes bi-directional connections between the representation layer and the index layer, as well as within the perceptual processing pipeline. However, the inverse perceptual pipeline often lacks precision. For example, while observing *Sparky* in a scene provides a vivid and detailed image, a mental reconstruction of *Sparky* is generally less clear and detailed.

7. Operational Modes

One of the strengths of the TB approach is its ability to model different operational modes of the brain within a single architecture. Specifically, we explore how the TB can represent perception, episodic memory, and semantic memory.

7.1. Pseudocode

The pseudocode is described in Algorithm 1, Algorithm 2, and Algorithm 3.

Algorithm 1. Evolution Neural Network

```
Input: q^in                                   ▷ The CBS is the input
q_i ← q_i^in + f_i^NN(sig(q^in)), ∀i           ▷ Evolution NN with skip connection
Output: q
```

Algorithm 2. Input and Attention

1: Input: $\mathbf{q}, \mathbf{v}$ ▷ The CBS is the input
2: $\mathbf{q} \leftarrow \mathbf{q} + \mathbf{g}(\mathbf{v})$ ▷ $\mathbf{v}$ from scene or bounding box
3: $\mathbf{q} \leftarrow \mathbf{q} + \sum_k \mathbf{a}_k \mathrm{softmax}_{dom}(a_{0,k} + \sum_{l=1}^{n} a_{l,k} \mathrm{sig}(q_l))$ ▷ Attention
4: Output: $\mathbf{q}$

Algorithm 3. Decoding (bottom-up) and encoding (top-down); the Heisenberg approximation with an added prior (used in the TB) uses $\alpha = 1$ and $\beta = 1$

1: Input: $\mathbf{q}$, α, β ▷ The CBS is the input
2: Sample $k \sim \mathrm{softmax}_{dom}(a_{0,k} + \sum_{l=1}^{n} a_{l,k} \mathrm{sig}(q_l))$ ▷ Bottom-up: k is sampled
3: $\mathbf{q} \leftarrow \alpha \mathbf{q} + \beta \mathbf{a}_k$ ▷ Top-down inference
4: Output: $\mathbf{q}, k$

7.2. Visual Perception

7.2.1. Visual Scene

Assume the agent is analyzing a visual scene. Algorithm 2 begins with an initial neutral input, such as $\mathbf{q} = 0$. The visual input, $\mathbf{v} \leftarrow \mathbf{v}^{scene}$, is then processed (Line 2). Next, the attention mechanism is applied to extract relevant information from past episodic memories (Line 3).

Algorithm 3 describes the decoding and encoding process. A label is sampled from the scene (bottom-up), and the sampled label is fed back to the representation layer (top-down). Algorithm 3 may be called multiple times, with each iteration generating a label k. These labels might, for instance, indicate the agent's location (e.g., *EnglishGarden*) or the weather condition (e.g., *Sunny*). Additionally, a generated label could represent a past time-index, suggesting a similarity to a previous scene.

7.2.2. A First ROI in a Visual Scene

The agent may then focus on the properties of an entity, which are typically defined by a specific region of interest (ROI) in the scene. The TB applies the evolution neural network from Algorithm 1. Its input, $\mathbf{q}_i^{in}$, is the output from Algorithm 2, as previously applied. Algorithm 2 is then called again.

The ROI, $\mathbf{v} \leftarrow \mathbf{v}^{ROI}$, serves as the visual input (Line 2). Attention is computed with respect to entities that have already been identified. Algorithm 3 governs the decoding and encoding process, which may be called multiple times. Each time, a new label k is generated. These labels could include entities such as *Sparky*, *Dog*, *Black*, and *Happy*.

Due to top-down inference, labels become interdependent. For example, the probability of labeling *Dog* will be influenced by the prior labeling of *Sparky*. In a given scene, multiple labels are generated for each ROI, and the sampling process is repeated over several rounds.

7.2.3. A Second ROI in a Visual Scene

Next, the agent may analyze a second ROI within the context of the scene and the first bounding box. The same sequence of steps—Algorithm 1, Algorithm 2, and Algorithm 3—is applied again. The second ROI might correspond to the entity *Jack*, with additional labels such as *Person*, *Tall*, and *ContentLooking*.

7.2.4. A Third ROI in a Visual Scene

Finally, a third ROI may be defined, encompassing both of the previous bounding boxes. This third ROI could label the relationship between the two entities with a predicate label like *looksAt*, once again utilizing Algorithm 1, Algorithm 2, and Algorithm 3.

7.2.5. Forming Episodic Indices

For each perceptual event, an episodic index t is introduced (see Section 5.4), which can be indexed as an episodic event. Its embedding vector, $\mathbf{a}_t$, is optimized not only to reconstruct the labels of the scene but also to reconstruct the labels for the ROIs, even when the visual inputs are missing. Therefore, the goal is to achieve both symbolic and subsymbolic reconstruction. For further details, see Section 8.

7.2.6. From Labels to Triples

An ROI and an episodic time index serve as unique identifiers (keys) for the other labels associated with an ROI. Assuming that entities are mutually exclusive, one can replace the ROI with the entity it represents, e.g., *Sparky*. The generated labels at time t can then be described as follows *(Sparky, type, ClassDog)*, *(Sparky, type, ColorBlack)*, *(Sparky, type, MoodHappy)*, or more succinctly *(Sparky, type, Dog)*, *(Sparky, type, Black)*, and *(Sparky, type, Happy)*.[5] These are triple statements, and the first entry is the subject, the second is the predicate, and the third is the object. Thus, a logical triple statement describes the relationship between concept labels. In the context of perception, triples describe currently generated labels, and in the context of episodic memory, past generated labels. If an entity's index does not yet exist it can be introduced.

One can conceptualize an entity as the object on which a measurement is executed, the predicate describing the type of measurement, and the object representing the outcome of the measurement. Importantly, for reasoning purposes, triples can also be generated with subjects that are not entities, such as *(Dog, type, Happy)*, *(Black, type, Sparky)*. These are referred to as generalized statements in the TB and are useful for embedded symbolic reasoning (see Section 10.2).

By involving two ROIs (for the subject and object) and an enclosing ROI (for the predicate), triples can also take the form *(Sparky, looksAt, Jack)*.

7.3. Episodic Memory

According to Tulving, who introduced the term episodic memory [47], it stores information about both general and personal events, essentially capturing the information we "remember." It pertains to past observations. In the context of vision, this would involve the reconstruction and decoding of a past scene.

[5]The relations would be *dog(Sparky)*, *black(Sparky)*, *happy(Sparky)*.

7.3.1. Episodic Engram

In the TB framework, an episodic memory engram consists of the episodic index and its associated embedding. When an episodic index is activated, its embedding vector defines the CBS, which then propagates to earlier visual processing layers through embodiment. This process enables the brain to form a subsymbolic understanding of the past event. In the case of vision, this would result in an approximate reconstruction of the past scene. The TB proposes that episodic indices are symbolic in nature, similar to concept indices.

7.3.2. Encoding and Decoding of Episodic Memory

In the TB approach, episodic memory is realized through the activation of the episodic index corresponding to a past memory. This activation approximately restores the CBS of a past instance.

We begin with Algorithm 3, using a neutral input ($\mathbf{q} = 0$) and setting $k \leftarrow t$ (without sampling). Then, Algorithm 3 is reapplied to generate labels for the past scene, such as *EnglishGarden* and *Sunny*. Note that if the CBS of the original scene is perfectly restored during episodic recall, the label probabilities will be identical to those at the time of perception.

Next, we consider an ROI from the past scene. The computational evolution neural network of Algorithm 1 is applied, followed by the application of Algorithm 3, which generates labels via sampling. The first label might correspond to the episodic index associated with an ROI in the scene. Labels such as *Sparky*, *Dog*, *Black*, and *Happy* might then be generated. By reapplying Algorithm 1 and Algorithm 3, we can also generate labels for objects and predicates from the past scene.

Essentially, the process of labeling and relationship prediction in episodic memory is similar to that of perception, except that visual inputs are replaced by stored episodic embedding vectors, and attention is not applied. This allows past scenes to be embodied and partially reconstructed. Thus, one can recover not only past memories but also emotions associated with those memories.

As with perception, episodic memory involves exploring different interpretations of a memory. The initiation of an episodic memory and its decoding into symbols, along with the embodiment process, may activate substantial parts of the brain. Based on the generated labels, triple statements can be created.

Episodic memories are not limited to visual events alone. The CBS at any given moment can be stored as an episodic memory with its own unique episodic index. This capability allows for the restoration of previous thoughts, for instance. We will explore this further in Section 9.

7.3.3. Recent Episodic Memory

Recent episodic memory enhances perception by retrieving past perceptual experiences, providing the agent with a sense of the present moment—its current context. To understand its own state and the state of the world, the agent needs to recall recent events, including scenes it has perceived and entities it has encountered. This state information cannot be derived solely from perceptual input.

For example, the agent must remember that, even though current perception offers no indication, it is still in hiding because a bear had been chasing it and might still be lurking outside. In this way, recent episodic memory influences behavior and supports decision-making.

Notably, patients who are unable to form new episodic memories often experience severe deficits in personal orientation and understanding of context. These deficits are commonly linked to significant bilateral damage to the medial temporal lobe (MTL), including the hippocampus [12]. Age also plays a role in the decline of episodic memory.

7.3.4. Remote Episodic Memory

Remote episodic memory refers to events that are memorable but occurred further in the past. These memories provide valuable decision support by informing the agent about the outcomes of similar past experiences, guiding its behavior based on prior knowledge of what worked or failed. For example, the agent might remember past encounters with bears and the dangerous situations that followed, helping it avoid similar risks in the future.

Recall of remote episodic memories is triggered by the similarity between the episodic representation and the current scene representation.

Remote episodic memories can persist for a long time and are associated with brain retraining, which occurs both during conscious activity and sleep [28].

Consider the vast number of movies, TV shows, comic strips, and other media you can recall or at least recognize as either novel or familiar. This illustrates the numerous episodic indices present in the brain, especially if you follow the indexing approach of the TB model.

7.3.5. Future Episodic Memories and Imagination

A future episodic memory is a predicted event that, at some point, is expected to become a regular episodic memory. This concept is closely related to prospective memory in cognition.

For example, imagine the agent knows there will be a football game in town this evening, and that the weather will be bad. By creating a future episodic index with labels such as *FootballGame* and *RainyWeather*, the agent might predict bad traffic conditions. This prediction, associated with a future event, is a form of imagination. Importantly, this imagination is grounded and embodied.

Thus, memory guides future behavior through future episodic memories [37]. Duncan et al. (2016) describe this process as the integration of relational events by imagining possible future rewards. The value associated with a memory (e.g., reward or threat) is a key aspect of episodic memory. Empirical evidence now strongly supports the role of episodic memory in decision-making tasks [9].

Consider that the brain has one or more modules evaluating the CBS, which could categorize states as *PersonallyRewarding*, *ImprovesSocialStatus*, or *Undesirable*. Each state might have an associated index. By imagining different future scenarios based on the agent's potential decisions (e.g., drive to a friend's house and face bad traffic, or stay home), the agent can assess which decision leads to the maximum expected reward. This facilitates decision support by selecting the action that might lead to the best imagined future scenario.

Imagining future scenarios allows the agent to reason about what is likely to happen under certain conditions, much like logical reasoning.

Perhaps, as many have suggested [7, 11, 14, 20, 21, 34, 40], the brain functions as a predictive machine. This predictive system may operate as part of the brain's fast-reactive system, also known as implicit memory. For example, it could explain improvements in skills like tennis playing. However, to make predictions over longer time scales, the brain needs to understand the present and relate it to the past—it requires explicit understanding and memory. This is where future episodic memory and imagination play essential roles.

7.3.6. Temperature Scaling, Simulation, and Bayes Probabilities

To decide on the scenario with the most expected reward, the mind needs to consider the plausibility or likelihood of each scenario. In the TB, only samples are visible, not probabilities. So, how does the brain manage probabilities?

For instance, consider this statement: "From what I know and from my gut feeling, I bet that *Sparky* will win the race." *Sparky* may now be identified as a *RacingDog*. Betting behavior is often cited as evidence that people behave in a Bayes-optimal way, requiring the careful comparison and integration of probabilities. We can introduce temperature scaling in the softmax_{dom} function ($\text{softmax}_{dom}(x)$ becomes $\text{softmax}_{dom}(x/T)$ with temperature T). By lowering the temperature, we can shift from a "sample-take-all" approach to a "winner-take-all" approach, where only the most likely outcome is chosen—in this case, *Sparky* wins the race. Even if the brain cannot always obtain precise probabilities, this method enables optimal decision-making.

Alternatively, as suggested by Sanborn et al. (2016) [36], the brain may function as a Bayesian sampler. The authors note that "only with infinite samples does a Bayesian sampler conform to the laws of probability; with finite samples, it systematically generates classic probabilistic reasoning errors, such as the unpacking effect, base-rate neglect, and the conjunction fallacy."

Statements in semantic memory may also be associated with probabilities (see Section 7.4.3), and sampling could be used as a strategy to estimate these probabilities as well.

7.4. Semantic Memory

In cognitive literature, semantic memory refers to the representation of factual knowledge that we know, but cannot recall the specific time or context in which we learned it. It involves statements that are either true, false, or probabilistic in nature. These logical or probabilistic statements are typically time-invariant or change only slowly or infrequently over time.

For example, imagine a friend describes a dog you have never met before. While your episodic memory might provide insights from previous encounters with dogs, your semantic memory likely holds a general understanding of the concept *Dog*—even in the absence of specific episodic recollections.

7.4.1. Semantic Engram

In the TB framework, a semantic memory engram consists of the concept index s and its corresponding embedding vector $\mathbf{a}_s$. When the embedding of a concept is activated in the representation layer and propagates to earlier layers through embodiment, the brain gains a subsymbolic understanding of that concept.

The embedding vector $\mathbf{a}_s$ can be thought of as a prototype vector, but it exists in the abstract embedding space. In Section 10.7, we argue that $\mathbf{a}_s$ acts as the "signature" or "DNA" of the symbolic index s, providing a unique representation of the concept.

7.4.2. Embedded Semantic Memory

Consider the recall of a symbol s, such as *Sparky*, from semantic memory. We begin by applying Algorithm 3 with a neutral input $\mathbf{q} = 0$, where we set $k \leftarrow \bar{t}$ and do not sample. Here, $\bar{t}$ represents the index for a time-independent constant embedding vector $\bar{\mathbf{a}}$.

Next, we apply the computational evolution neural network from Algorithm 1, followed by another application of Algorithm 3, setting $k \leftarrow s$ and again avoiding sampling. For example, s might be *Sparky*. Repeated applications of Algorithm 3 might yield labels such as *Dog*, Black, and *Happy*. By reapplying both Algorithm 1 and Algorithm 3, we can also recall relationships, such as *Sparky* is *ownedBy Jack*.

Semantic memory recall thus mirrors episodic recall, with the key difference being that $t \leftarrow \bar{t}$ and s is explicitly set rather than sampled. Importantly, we can use the same (brain) architecture for both semantic and episodic memory retrieval.[6]

Substituting the expression from Equation 6 into Equations 1 and 4, we observe that the sample probability depends on all previous samples. The brain could implement an AND operation across multiple arguments. However, the dependencies are not fully general, which is why the computational evolution neural network, as discussed in Section 10.6, must be applied to handle more complex dependencies.

7.4.3. Triple-Facts and Conditional Probabilities

Perception and episodic memory involve observations. In contrast, semantic memory is concerned with facts. But what exactly constitutes a fact? Consider the perceptual analysis discussed in Section 7.2.6. Suppose each time an ROI is identified as *Sparky* and, if the domain color is determined, it is classified as *Black*. In this case, the statement *(Sparky, type, Black)* is not merely an observation; it is also a fact, independent of any specific episodic instance.

The TB framework can also attach probabilities to facts. For example, assume that whenever *Sparky* appears in a scene, his mood is determined. If *Sparky* is found to be *Happy* 60% of the time, we can express this fact with the conditional probability: $P(Happy|Sparky) = 0.6$. Thus, facts and their associated probabilities can be derived from observational statistics of the generated labels.

(Sparky, type, Black) can be interpreted not only as a statement about the color of *Sparky* but also as a rule: "If an entity is identified as *Sparky*, then it is *Black*." This interpretation allows the TB framework to define conditional probabilities for generalized statements like $P(Black|Dog)$. Specifically, the associated probability is determined by the number of times the color is classified as *Black* for an ROI labeled as *Dog*. More explicitly, $P(Black|Sparky)$ can be written as $P(Color = Black|Entity = Sparky)$ where *Color* and *Entity* are treated as random variables.

[6]Consider the pCBS. For semantic memory, we need to average over potential visual inputs, i.e., define a prior distribution for the pCBS. We again assume that the prior distribution can be described by independent Bernoulli distributions with pre-activation vector $\bar{\mathbf{a}}$ with index $\bar{t}$. This approximates the distribution $P^{prior}(X_1,..,X_n) = \int P(X_1,...,X_n|\mathbf{v})P(\mathbf{v})d\mathbf{v}$.

It is important to note that a triple does not necessarily have to be derived from visual perception. For instance, the observation *(Sparky, type, Purebred)* could come from another modality, such as language. In this case, $P(Purebred|Sparky) = 1$ means that whenever anyone makes a statement about *Sparky*'s pedigree, it is always stated that he is purebred.

Probabilities, however, are complex, especially for the brain. The brain must account for challenges like non-IID (independent and identically distributed) labels, limited sample sizes, and the reliability or uncertainty of the source of the information.

Another issue arises with the mutual exclusivity implied by the softmax normalization over a domain. Consider that *Sparky* is both *Black* and *White* (checkered). One possible solution would be to introduce a new color category, *BlackWhite*, with $P(BlackWhite|Sparky) = 1$. Alternatively, perception could label *Sparky* as *Black* 50% of the time and *White* 50% of the time, so we would have $P(Black|Sparky) = P(White|Sparky) = 0.5$. A third option would be to define separate domains for *Black* and *White*, with labels *Black* and *NotBlack* for the first domain, and *White* and *NotWhite* for the second. In this case, we would get $P(Black|Sparky) = P(White|Sparky) = 1$.

This normalization issue may not be as critical for the brain. First, the brain is primarily concerned with generating samples, rather than directly calculating probabilities. Second, the brain may leverage the subsymbolic aspects of semantic or episodic memory recall to conclude that *Sparky* is both *Black* and *White*, without needing to resolve the exact probabilistic distribution. As discussed in Sections 7.3.5 and 7.3.6, the brain may handle probabilities in decision-making scenarios by sampling from potential outcomes.

7.4.4. Symbolic Semantic Memory

It is also possible to model semantic memory directly through symbolic methods. Consider the equation for symbolic decoding of semantic memory

$$P(Y = k|s) = \text{softmax}_{dom}(b_{0,k} + b_{s,k}). \tag{8}$$

where $b_{s,k}$ represents the link between concept s and concept k, and $b_{0,k}$ is an offset. In this case, the embeddings of the concepts are not involved. This approach is known as symbolic decoding of semantic memory.

Symbolic decoding is particularly useful for modeling relationships such as successor relations between time indices or *partOf* relationships. For example, it can model the connection between a time index for a scene and the associated ROI, enabling the framework to reason about symbolic relationships between concepts and events.

7.5. Knowledge Graphs

Triples form a knowledge graph (KG), where concepts are represented as nodes and predicates serve as the links between labels. Some of these triples are certain, in the probabilistic sense described earlier, while others are associated with conditional probabilities. The concept of episodic memory can be linked to a temporal knowledge graph (tKG), capturing the dynamic, time-dependent nature of events and experiences. Generative models for embedded knowledge graphs have also been explored by [24].

7.6. Serial Processing as a Prerequisite for Language

As previously discussed, symbolic and subsymbolic representations are tightly interconnected. For example, one cannot think of *Sparky* without simultaneously activating its subsymbolic embedding and engaging in an embodiment process that might trigger earlier visual and other processing layers in a top-down manner. Similarly, anything represented in the representation layer is constantly decoded into labels (e.g., *Sparky*) through a bottom-up process.

Different brain modules often process information in parallel, particularly during the processing of perceptual pathways. However, symbolic decoding itself follows a serial process, as discussed in Dehaene's work [8], where it is described as a "serial bottleneck" in consciousness. The importance of sampling in conscious perception is also emphasized, with Dehaene stating that "consciousness is a slow sampler."

The sequential nature of symbol generation in the TB may have been a key prerequisite for the development of natural language. The natural "outer" language likely stems from an inner, triple-oriented thought language. Individuals largely share common concepts (within the "inner" language), even if they do not share a common spoken language (the "outer language"). While embeddings may be unique to each individual brain, recent research suggests they may also be shared to some degree [13, 39].

Natural language, particularly in its factual aspects, can be seen as a reflection of this inner thought language. For instance, some managers might simply ask, "Just give me the facts." It has been speculated that even more sophisticated language consists of facts that are connected by fillers—a characteristic observed in certain texts generated by large language models.

Natural (outer) language can also serve as an input to the system. It feeds into the representation layer, where a sentence or paragraph becomes analogous to an episode that is decoded into the inner thought language. Just like any episodic memory with an embedding vector, an input sentence becomes part of the memory system, allowing for recall of both the sentence and its meaning.

Upon completing this manuscript, we noticed interesting parallels with the discussion in [48]. Our inner thought language can be linked to their concept of a probabilistic language of thought (PLoT), which is rooted in probabilistic programming and includes domain knowledge that can be learned from language by large language models. We agree with the paper's argument that PLoT (and our inner thought language) likely preceded natural language, both in child development and in evolution, with natural language evolving on this foundation. While the paper focuses on System 2 functionalities, most operations in the TB align with the effortless, intuitive processes of System 1.

8. Self-supervised Learning

8.1. Associative Learning?

Consider simple associations between indices and embeddings: an episodic memory embedding can be formed by storing the CBS at the time of perception. Similarly, the embedding vector for a concept could be the average of all CBSs where the concept appeared. This approach might have served as the foundation of biological evolution. The

TB, however, employs self-supervised learning, which is described in the following sections and leads to improved performance.

8.2. Self-generated Labels

In this model, no external agent provides training data or symbolic labels. Instead, perception itself generates labels through stochastic sampling, which the brain then treats as actual labels for training. This is a form of bootstrap learning, where the model's predictions are used as targets for further learning. See the bootstrap Widrow-Hoff rule [16] and learning with pseudo labels [23] for related concepts. Self-generated labels are incorporated into various cost functions, as discussed in [3], which outlines different principled methods for self-supervised adaptation in deep learning.

8.3. Embedding Learning with Self-generated Labels

Let's assume that a scene, $\mathbf{v}^{scene}$, has been observed, and the focus shifts to a region of interest (ROI) with $\mathbf{v}^{ROI}$. For simplicity, we exclude attention mechanisms. Assume that the labels $s = Sparky$ and $k = Dog$ are generated.

For perception, the contribution to the log-likelihood (negative cost function) is $\log P(s|\mathbf{v}^{ROI}, \mathbf{v}^{scene}) + \log P(k|s, \mathbf{v}^{ROI}, \mathbf{v}^{scene})$ which becomes

$$\log \mathrm{softmax}_{dom}(\mathbf{a}_s^\top \mathrm{sig}(\mathbf{h}_1)) + \log \mathrm{softmax}_{dom}(\mathbf{a}_k^\top \mathrm{sig}(\mathbf{a}_s + \mathbf{h}_1)).$$

where $\mathbf{h}_1 = \mathbf{g}(\mathbf{v}^{ROI}) + \mathbf{g}(\mathbf{v}^{scene}) + \mathbf{f}^{NN}(\mathbf{g}(\mathbf{v}^{scene}))$.

Let's assume this is the first time the label $s = Sparky$ has been observed. The first term in the cost function will attempt to align the embedding $\mathbf{a}_s$ with the visual input. The second cost term will attempt to align $\mathbf{a}_s$ with the embedding for *Dog*, thereby integrating the "dogginess" into *Sparky*'s embedding.

For the episodic memory at time t, the contribution to the log-likelihood is $\log P(s|t) + \log P(k|s,t)$ which becomes

$$\log \mathrm{softmax}_{dom}(\mathbf{a}_s^\top \mathrm{sig}(\mathbf{h}_2)) + \log \mathrm{softmax}_{dom}(\mathbf{a}_k^\top \mathrm{sig}(\mathbf{a}_s + \mathbf{h}_2)).$$

where $\mathbf{h}_2 = \mathbf{a}_t + \mathbf{f}^{NN}(\mathbf{a}_t)$.[7]

For semantic memory related to entity s, the contribution to the log-likelihood is:

$$\log P(k|s) = \log \mathrm{softmax}_{dom}(\mathbf{a}_k^\top \mathrm{sig}(\mathbf{a}_s + \mathbf{h}_3))$$

where $\mathbf{h}_3 = \bar{\mathbf{a}} + \mathbf{f}^{NN}(\bar{\mathbf{a}})$. This cost term aims to align the embedding of *Sparky* with the embedding of *Dog*. As a result, when semantic memory recalls *Sparky*, it is likely that *Dog* will be sampled next. The embedding of the index *Sparky* will integrate all labels generated in context with *Sparky*.

We can also derive cost terms for triples with predicates other than *type*, such as *(Sparky, looksAt, Jack)*.[8]

---

[7] If the embedding vector for the ROI, $\mathbf{a}_{t_{roi}}$, is available, $\mathbf{h}_2$ can be updated to $\mathbf{h}_2 = \mathbf{a}_{t_{roi}} + \mathbf{a}_t + \mathbf{f}^{NN}(\mathbf{a}_t)$.

[8] Note that the equations are not commutative: Sampling s first and then k results in a different cost compared to sampling k first and then s.

A consolidated episodic memory recall is more consistent with the agent's worldview. Past memories are slightly adjusted to better fit the agent's expectations. Memories that align with the agent's understanding are more easily recalled than those from unfamiliar or foreign contexts. As discussed in [6, 19], humans can only effectively report past scenes when they align with the agent's worldview.

The adaptation of embedding vectors and the formation of semantic memory likely occur during the memory consolidation process, which is believed to take place during sleep.

8.4. Autoencoder Learning

In Section 6.6, we discussed how scene input can be used to train an autoencoder, a key component in realizing embodiment. The cost functions derived from a perceptual autoencoder can help regularize and stabilize the learning process.

8.5. Memory Recall Changes Memories

As previously mentioned, the recall of episodic or semantic memories involves the complex decoding of embedding vectors, during which samples are generated. The brain may then decide to train on these samples, providing an explanation for the well-documented phenomenon that memory traces can change upon retrieval. In fact, memories can even be manipulated, as demonstrated in the work of Loftus [25, 26].

8.6. New Indices

For existing indices, predicted labels can be used to adapt their embeddings. However, the brain also needs to create new indices. A new perceptual experience is represented by a newly formed episodic index and its corresponding learned embedding. At a slower rate, new entity indices are introduced, and even more slowly, new indices for classes and attributes are required. The neurobiological aspects of forming new indices are extensively discussed in [46].

9. Multitasking, Cognitive Control, and Working Memory

9.1. Multitasking by Multiplexing

Consider the scenario where an agent is planning a friend's visit while simultaneously driving a car. Suddenly, the traffic situation demands full attention for a few seconds, after which the agent resumes planning the visit. How can the brain manage this?

One leading hypothesis suggests that it only appears as if the mind can think of several things at once. In reality, at the conscious level, we rapidly switch between mental states. This implies that cognitive attention may represent a serial bottleneck in the brain. An extreme example of this phenomenon is multitasking, where humans seem to manage two tasks at once, such as driving and conversing. However, cognitive multitasking is an illusion—the brain performs multiplexing, rather than truly multitasking [30].

The TB model supports the concept of multitasking via multiplexing. In the example provided, the evening-planning CBS is stored as the embedding vector of an episodic index. After the traffic situation is resolved, this CBS is retrieved by activating the corresponding episodic index.

However, multitasking by multiplexing might have a capacity limit. The capacity of working memory is often estimated to be seven items or fewer [5, 10, 31], meaning the mind can switch between seven or fewer mental states. In the context of the TB, cognitive control likely involves managing up to seven episodic or concept indices and their embeddings for problem-solving.

A specific example of multitasking is the use of episodic and semantic memory during perception. If time allows, the brain can activate these memory systems to supplement ongoing perceptual activity with background information, such as recent episodic memory (providing state information) or remote episodic memory (guiding decision-making). See Figure 3. The multitasking between perception and memory is easily supported by the TB model but may be more challenging for other technical models.

Samples generated by semantic memory can be considered as prior samples, while samples generated from perception or episodic memory can be seen as data. In [46], this relationship was explored in the context of Dirichlet fusion.

9.2. Cognitive Control and Working Memory

Many mental tasks appear to require some form of cognitive control. Multitasking is an obvious example: How does the brain decide which mental or physical task to prioritize at any given moment?

Another example is the navigation of semantic memory. Imagine the agent is thinking about *Sparky*. Should the mind remain focused on *Sparky*, or should it digress? For instance, thinking of *Sparky* might lead to recalling *Jack* (his owner), who recently married *Mary*, who lives in *Munich*. This might trigger thoughts of the *English Garden* in Munich, known for its charming *BeerGardens*, which in turn reminds the agent to buy some beer on the way home.[9]

A third example involves the sequential selection of regions of interest (ROIs) in visual processing, as explored in [35].

Cognitive control appears to be a central faculty of consciousness and conscious decision-making. But who—or what—is ultimately in charge? Technically, the module governing cognitive control may be optimized through reinforcement learning, guiding decisions and actions based on learned priorities and rewards.

10. Multimodality, Generalization, Reasoning, and Semantics

Is the TB merely a large database, as might be inferred from its focus on past observations and statistical patterns? Certainly not. While concept labels sampled from past experiences are not stored explicitly, they serve to refine perception and enable generalization in memory through the learning and fine-tuning of embedding vectors, as we discuss in this section. The TB clearly generalizes to new perceptual inputs, such as novel scenes. Since labels are self-generated, there is no traditional training data to overfit to—another indication of its capacity for generalization. Let us now explore reasoning, which can be best understood through the lens of multimodality.

[9]This type of digression is humorously depicted in the character J.D. from the sitcom Scrubs.

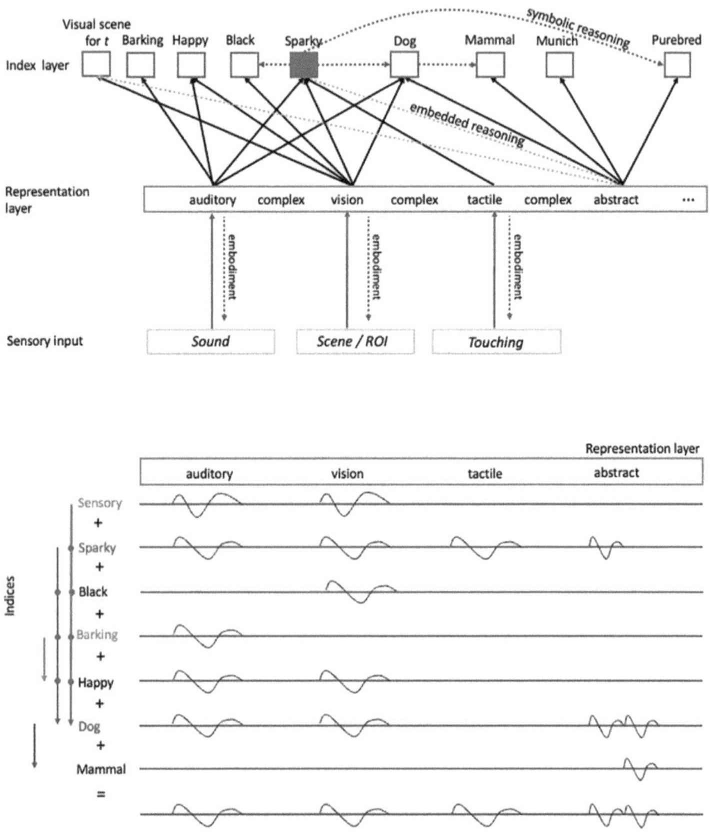

Figure 4. Multimodality and Reasoning. Top: Some dimensions in the representation layer are visual, some auditory, some tactile, and some abstract. Different dimensions communicate with different perceptual paths and symbolic indices. The horizontal dotted lines between the indices indicate symbolic semantic memory and reasoning. Bottom: Sequential operations in perception. Indices are sampled and added from top to bottom. The first line indicates that sensory input activates auditory and visual dimensions of the representation layer. Then the index *Sparky* fires which adds information on auditory and visual dimensions and in addition on tactile and abstract dimensions. The decoding continues with *Black*, *Barking*, *Happy*, *Dog* and *Mammal*. *Mammal* fires because *Dog* has fired; there is no direct overlap in the representation layer with *Sparky*. This can be achieved by an adaptation of *Sparky*'s embedding (embedded reasoning). In an episodic memory, the first line is represented by an embedding vector. In semantic memory, the first line is missing, and the process starts by activating the index for *Sparky*.

10.1. Multimodality: More Dimensions

The TB is inherently multimodal by design. Multiple modules communicate with the representation layer, especially sensory modalities. Each modality contributes to specific dimensions of the representation layer. For example, some dimensions may predominantly process visual inputs, while others are auditory, tactile, or abstract, as illustrated in Figure 4.

Embeddings may also be sparse. For instance, the index *Black* primarily interacts with visual dimensions, while *Loud* or *Barking* interacts with auditory dimensions. However, concepts sometimes transcend modalities—for example, one might describe an image as "loud."

Consider the entity *Sparky*. Visual dimensions provide information about his appearance, such as color and shape. Auditory dimensions describe his bark and other sounds, tactile dimensions represent how he feels, and abstract dimensions capture higher-level associations. This rich, multimodal inference process enables the TB to construct a holistic understanding of *Sparky*, as depicted in Figure 4.

10.2. Embedded Symbolic Reasoning and Chaining

Consider the example in Figure 4, where sensory input activates both visual and auditory dimensions of the representation layer. This bottom-up inference might sample the index *Sparky*, activating all regions of the representation layer associated with him, including visual, auditory, tactile, and abstract dimensions.

The activation of *Sparky* supports the activation of *Dog*. Once *Dog* is activated, *Mammal* is triggered, demonstrating symbolic chaining. Notably, *Mammal* does not directly connect to the visual dimensions of *Sparky*, but rather through its association with *Dog*. This process illustrates the brain's capacity for symbolic embedded reasoning—concluding that *Sparky* is a *Mammal* without directly modifying his embedding.

10.3. Embedded Reasoning and Materialization

Now consider the same scenario, but assume the embedding for *Sparky* has been updated to integrate the label *Mammal*. In this case, activating *Sparky*'s index might directly sample *Mammal*, bypassing the intermediate step of activating *Dog*.

This form of reasoning, akin to that used in recommendation systems [22], resembles the process of materialization in logic and database theory, where precomputed relationships facilitate faster, direct retrieval.

10.4. Embedded Reasoning Creates Episodic Similarities

Imagine the agent has stored two scenes: one from the *English Garden* at time t_1, labeled with *Sunny*, and another from *Marienplatz* at time t_2, labeled with *Rainy*. Initially, their episodic embeddings and visual labels may share little similarity.

However, a location module in the brain might associate both scenes with *Munich*. This location-generated label can be shared across both episodes. As the episodic embeddings are updated, they begin to integrate the embedding for *Munich*. For instance, the embedding vector for t_1 is adapted to generate the label *Munich*, as is the embedding for t_2.

As a result, the two engrams become similar in their embeddings. Recalling one episodic memory may activate the other, and recalling the semantic concept *Munich* could now activate both episodic memories.

This is a powerful example of how perceptual and symbolic embedding adaptation can enrich memory and reasoning.

10.5. Symbolic Reasoning

Symbolic reasoning refers to reasoning processes that do not explicitly utilize the embeddings of symbolic indices. As discussed in Section 7.4.4, symbolic decoding in semantic memory relies solely on symbolic indices, independent of their embeddings.

This type of reasoning can represent binary relationships, such as the association between *Dog* and *Black*, and supports chaining operations. For example, if *Sparky* is sampled in a scene, triggering the activation of *Dog*, which in turn activates *Mammal*, the mind can infer that *Sparky* is a *Mammal*.

Chaining can be materialized by introducing a direct excitatory connection from *Sparky* to *Mammal*, bypassing intermediate steps. More complex forms of reasoning—such as those based on relational Bayesian networks—are also conceivable within the framework of symbolic indices. Symbolic reasoning has been implemented as probabilistic programming, as demonstrated in [48].

10.6. Universal Approximation Property

In Section 7.4.2, we noted that a sample can depend nonlinearly on prior samples, though this dependency is not fully general. To achieve complete generality, the involvement of the evolution neural network is necessary.

Consider an example where an entity serves as both a subject and an object, such as *Sparky*. Sampling the entity in its role as a subject might yield attributes like *Dog* and *Black*, while sampling it as an object might result in *Cute*. The latter typically exhibits a nonlinear dependency on the former because the evolution neural network governs the transition from subject to object roles.

This process enables the brain to leverage the evolution neural network for general mappings, thereby achieving a universal approximation capability.

10.7. The Embedding is the "DNA"

What encapsulates the semantics of a concept like *Sparky*? The embedding of *Sparky* serves as its unique signature or "DNA." Decoding this "DNA" involves activating the representation layer with *Sparky*'s embedding, which informs various brain modules about his sensory and other properties.

For instance, decoding conveys how *Sparky* looks, sounds, and feels. Semantic memory further provides information about *Sparky*'s attributes, such as being *Black*, as well as his relationships, like being owned by *Jack* and loved by *Mary*. Past episodic memories involving *Sparky* may also be recalled, contributing additional context.

Through this process, substantial regions of the brain's sensory and memory systems collaboratively "decode" *Sparky*'s embedding. This adaptable signature is unique to the individual brain interpreting it. Consequently, thinking intensely about *Sparky* triggers a "firework" of neural activity—a phenomenon mirrored during perception and episodic memory recall.

10.8. Working Memory and Cognitive Control

Working memory and cognitive control are often seen as hallmarks of intelligence. As discussed in Section 9, working memory may function by manipulating a limited number of symbolic indices to guide decision-making.

While perception and memory provide foundational inputs, reasoning also relies on model-based inference, as elaborated in [48]. Human intelligence, however, is multifaceted and depends on a diverse array of functional modules working in concert.

11. Summary and Conclusions

Perception and memory recall are processes that engage substantial regions of the brain. The Tensor Brain (TB) framework proposes that symbolic indices are activated through a bottom-up process in both functions. In turn, these activated indices communicate with the representation layer and earlier processing layers in a top-down manner. During perception and memory recall, multiple indices are sequentially activated, creating a dynamic interaction. This interplay can be likened to a"dance," where symbolic indices activate subsymbolic representation layers and are themselves influenced in return.

A key innovation of the TB is learning through self-generated labels, a concept that has shown promising initial results. However, it carries inherent risks. As discussed, not only does the formation of new memories generate labels, but so does memory retrieval. The brain may use these labels for adaptation, which could lead to potential falsification or alteration of past memories.

The brain has often been described as a prediction machine. Over shorter time scales, this predictive mechanism may integrate with the brain's fast, reactive systems and implicit memory. However, making predictions on the longer time scales relevant to the TB requires more than reactivity; it necessitates explicit understanding and explicit memory. To predict effectively, the mind must connect the present to both the past and the future. This includes imagining future possibilities—a process requiring memory-based imagination, supplemented by model-based imagination.

The TB framework demonstrated embedded and symbolic reasoning, and explored their relationship with semantic memory. It also examined the roles of working memory and cognitive control. While perception and memory may provide the foundation for these functions, more complex forms of reasoning appear to be uniquely human. It has been speculated that language plays a crucial role, as both reasoning and language rely on distinct but interacting brain regions.

Despite these advancements, it is important to remember that the brain operates as a multitasking system. Most of its activities occur outside conscious awareness, employing diverse strategies to address specific problems concurrently.

The debate over localized versus distributed representations in the brain remains active. Evidence supports the existence of concept-specific representations. In particular, concept cells have been identified in the medial temporal lobe (MTL). These neurons exhibit remarkable selectivity, responding to a wide range of representations for specific individuals, landmarks, or objects—and even to textual representations such as letter strings corresponding to their names [32, 33]. This lends support to index-specific "symbolic" representations.

A distinctive feature of the TB is its reliance on the sampling of indices. But what initiates this sampling process? The nature of this initiation bears intriguing parallels to the collapse of the wave function in quantum mechanics, triggered by measurement. These questions are explored further in [43].

References

[1] Bernard J Baars. *In the theater of consciousness: The workspace of the mind.* Oxford University Press, USA, 1997.

[2] Stephan Baier, Yunpu Ma, and Volker Tresp. Improving visual relationship detection using semantic modeling. In *ISWC*, volume 16. Springer, 2017.

[3] Yoshua Bengio, Dong-Hyun Lee, Jorg Bornschein, Thomas Mesnard, and Zhouhan Lin. Towards biologically plausible deep learning. *arXiv preprint arXiv:1502.04156*, 2015.

[4] Antoine Bordes, Nicolas Usunier, Alberto Garcia-Duran, Jason Weston, and Oksana Yakhnenko. Translating Embeddings for Modeling Multi-relational Data. In *Advances in Neural Information Processing Systems 26*, 2013.

[5] Nelson Cowan. The magical mystery four: How is working memory capacity limited, and why? *Current directions in psychological science*, 19(1):51–57, 2010.

[6] Fergus IM Craik and Endel Tulving. Depth of processing and the retention of words in episodic memory. *Journal of experimental Psychology: general*, 104(3):268, 1975.

[7] Peter Dayan, Geoffrey E Hinton, Radford M Neal, and Richard S Zemel. The Helmholtz machine. *Neural computation*, 7(5):889–904, 1995.

[8] Stanislas Dehaene. *Consciousness and the brain: Deciphering how the brain codes our thoughts.* Penguin, 2014.

[9] Katherine D Duncan and Daphna Shohamy. Memory states influence value-based decisions. *Journal of Experimental Psychology: General*, 145(11):1420, 2016.

[10] Randall W Engle. What is working memory capacity? In H. L. Roediger, III, I. Neath J. S. Nairne, and A. M. Surprenant, editors, *The nature of remembering: Essays in honor of Robert G. Crowder*. American Psychological Association Press, 2001.

[11] Karl Friston. The free-energy principle: a unified brain theory? *Nature Reviews Neuroscience*, 11(2):127–138, 2010.

[12] Mark A Gluck, Eduardo Mercado, and Catherine E Myers. *Learning and memory: From brain to behavior.* Palgrave, 2013.

[13] Ariel Goldstein, Zaid Zada, Eliav Buchnik, Mariano Schain, Amy Price, Bobbi Aubrey, Samuel A Nastase, Amir Feder, Dotan Emanuel, Alon Cohen, et al. Shared computational principles for language processing in humans and deep language models. *Nature neuroscience*, 25(3):369–380, 2022.

[14] Thomas L Griffiths, Charles Kemp, and Joshua B Tenenbaum. Bayesian models of cognition. In *The Cambridge Handbook of Computational Psychology*. Cambridge University Press, 2008.

[15] Kaiming He, Xiangyu Zhang, Shaoqing Ren, and Jian Sun. Deep residual learning for image recognition. In *Proceedings of the IEEE conference on computer vision and pattern recognition*, 2016.

[16] Geoffrey E Hinton and Steven J Nowlan. The bootstrap Widrow-Hoff rule as a cluster-formation algorithm. *Neural Computation*, 2(3):355–362, 1990.

[17] Sepp Hochreiter and Jürgen Schmidhuber. Long short-term memory. *Neural computation*, 9(8):1735–1780, 1997.

[18] Justin Johnson, Ranjay Krishna, Michael Stark, Li-Jia Li, David Shamma, Michael Bernstein, and Li Fei-Fei. Image retrieval using scene graphs. In *CVPR*, 2015.

[19] Alex Kafkas and Daniela Montaldi. Expectation affects learning and modulates memory experience at retrieval. *Cognition*, 180:123–134, 2018.

[20] David C Knill and Alexandre Pouget. The Bayesian brain: the role of uncertainty in neural coding and computation. *Trends in Neurosciences*, 27(12):712–719, 2004.

[21] Konrad P Körding, Shih-pi Ku, and Daniel M Wolpert. Bayesian integration in force estimation. *Journal of Neurophysiology*, 92(5):3161–3165, 2004.

[22] Yehuda Koren, Robert Bell, and Chris Volinsky. Matrix factorization techniques for recommender systems. *Computer*, 42(8):30–37, 2009.

[23] Dong-Hyun Lee et al. Pseudo-label: The simple and efficient semi-supervised learning method for deep neural networks. In *Workshop on challenges in representation learning, ICML*, 2013.

[24] Lorenzo Loconte, Nicola Di Mauro, Robert Peharz, and Antonio Vergari. How to turn your knowledge graph embeddings into generative models. *Advances in Neural Information Processing Systems*, 36, 2024.

[25] Elizabeth F Loftus and Katherine Ketcham. *Witness for the defense: The accused, the eyewitness, and the expert who puts memory on trial.* Macmillan, 1991.

[26] Geoffrey R Loftus and Elizabeth F Loftus. *Human memory: The processing of information*. Psychology Press, 2019.

[27] Yunpu Ma, Volker Tresp, and Erik A Daxberger. Embedding models for episodic knowledge graphs. *Journal of Web Semantics*, 2018.

[28] James L McClelland, Bruce L McNaughton, and Randall C O'Reilly. Why there are complementary learning systems in the hippocampus and neocortex: insights from the successes and failures of connectionist models of learning and memory. *Psychological review*, 102(3):419, 1995.

[29] Tomas Mikolov, Ilya Sutskever, Kai Chen, Greg S Corrado, and Jeff Dean. Distributed representations of words and phrases and their compositionality. *Advances in neural information processing systems*, 26, 2013.

[30] Earl K Miller and Timothy J Buschman. Working memory capacity: Limits on the bandwidth of cognition. *Daedalus*, 144(1):112–122, 2015.

[31] George A Miller. The magical number seven, plus or minus two: Some limits on our capacity for processing information. *Psychological review*, 63(2):81, 1956.

[32] R Quian Quiroga, Leila Reddy, Gabriel Kreiman, Christof Koch, and Itzhak Fried. Invariant visual representation by single neurons in the human brain. *Nature*, 435(7045):1102–1107, 2005.

[33] Rodrigo Quian Quiroga. Concept cells: the building blocks of declarative memory functions. *Nat Rev Neurosci*, 13(8), 2012.

[34] Rajesh PN Rao and Dana H Ballard. Predictive coding in the visual cortex: a functional interpretation of some extra-classical receptive-field effects. *Nature neuroscience*, 2(1):79–87, 1999.

[35] D Sabatinelli, DW Frank, TJ Wanger, M Dhamala, BM Adhikari, and X Li. The timing and directional connectivity of human frontoparietal and ventral visual attention networks in emotional scene perception. *Neuroscience*, 277:229–238, 2014.

[36] Adam N Sanborn and Nick Chater. Bayesian brains without probabilities. *Trends in cognitive sciences*, 20(12):883–893, 2016.

[37] Daniel L Schacter, Donna Rose Addis, Demis Hassabis, Victoria C Martin, R Nathan Spreng, and Karl K Szpunar. The future of memory: remembering, imagining, and the brain. *Neuron*, 76(4):677–694, 2012.

[38] Sahand Sharifzadeh, Sina Moayed Baharlou, and Volker Tresp. Classification by attention: Scene graph classification with prior knowledge. In *AAAI*, volume 35, 2021.

[39] Ilia Sucholutsky, Lukas Muttenthaler, Adrian Weller, Andi Peng, Andreea Bobu, Been Kim, Bradley C Love, Erin Grant, Jascha Achterberg, Joshua B Tenenbaum, et al. Getting aligned on representational alignment. *arXiv preprint arXiv:2310.13018*, 2023.

[40] Joshua B Tenenbaum, Thomas L Griffiths, and Charles Kemp. Theory-based Bayesian models of inductive learning and reasoning. *Trends in cognitive sciences*, 10(7):309–318, 2006.

[41] Timothy J Teyler and Pascal DiScenna. The hippocampal memory indexing theory. *Behavioral neuroscience*, 1986.

[42] Volker Tresp, Cristóbal Esteban, Yinchong Yang, Stephan Baier, and Denis Krompaß. Learning with memory embeddings. *arXiv preprint arXiv:1511.07972*, 2015.

[43] Volker Tresp and Hang Li. Bayes or Heisenberg: Who(se) rules? *arXiv preprint*, 2024.

[44] Volker Tresp, Yunpu Ma, Stephan Baier, and Yinchong Yang. Embedding learning for declarative memories. In *European Semantic Web Conference*, volume 14. Springer, 2017.

[45] Volker Tresp, Sahand Sharifzadeh, Dario Konopatzki, and Yunpu Ma. The tensor brain: Semantic decoding for perception and memory. *arXiv preprint arXiv:2001.11027*, 2020.

[46] Volker Tresp, Sahand Sharifzadeh, Hang Li, Dario Konopatzki, and Yunpu Ma. The tensor brain: A unified theory of perception, memory, and semantic decoding. *Neural Computation*, 35(2):156–227, 2023.

[47] Endel Tulving. *Elements of episodic memory*. Oxford University Press, 1985.

[48] Lionel Wong, Gabriel Grand, Alexander K Lew, Noah D Goodman, Vikash K Mansinghka, Jacob Andreas, and Joshua B Tenenbaum. From word models to world models: Translating from natural language to the probabilistic language of thought. *arXiv preprint arXiv:2306.12672*, 2023.

Handbook on Neurosymbolic AI and Knowledge Graphs
P. Hitzler et al. (Eds.)
IOS Press, 2025

doi:10.3233/FAIA250201

Logical Expressiveness of Graph Neural Networks on Knowledge Graphs

Xingyue HUANG [a,1], Miguel ROMERO [b,d], İsmail İlkan CEYLAN [a], Pablo BARCELÓ [c,d]
[a] *Department of Computer Science, University of Oxford*
[b] *Department of Computer Science, Universidad Católica de Chile*
[c] *Inst. for Math. and Comp. Eng., Universidad Católica de Chile & IMFD Chile*
[d] *CENIA Chile*
ORCiD ID: Xingyue Huang https://orcid.org/0009-0008-6533-6599, Miguel Romero https://orcid.org/0000-0002-2615-6455, İsmail İlkan Ceylan https://orcid.org/0000-0003-4118-4689, Pablo Barceló https://orcid.org/0000-0003-2293-2653

Abstract. Graph neural networks are prominent models for representation learning over graph-structured data. While the capabilities and limitations of these models are well-understood for simple graphs, our understanding remains incomplete in the context of knowledge graphs. Our goal is to provide a systematic understanding of the landscape of graph neural networks for knowledge graphs pertaining to the prominent task of link prediction. Our analysis entails a unifying perspective on seemingly unrelated models and unlocks a series of other models. The expressive power of various models is characterized via a precise logical characterization of the class of functions captured by a class of graph neural networks. The theoretical findings presented in this paper explain the benefits of some widely employed practical design choices, which are validated empirically.

Keywords. graph neural networks, knowledge graphs, logical characterization

1. Introduction

Graph neural networks (GNNs) [1, 2] are prominent models for representation learning over graph-structured data, where the idea is to iteratively compute vector representations of nodes of an input graph through a series of invariant (resp., equivariant) transformations. While the landscape of GNNs is overwhelmingly rich, the vast majority of such models are instances of *message passing neural networks* [3] which are well-studied, leading to a theoretical understanding of their capabilities and limitations [4, 5]. In turn, our understanding is rather limited for GNN models dedicated to learning over *knowledge graphs*, which are applied in a wide range of domains.

To make our context precise, we first consider an extension of message passing neural networks[2] with relation-specific message functions, which we call *relational* message

[1]Corresponding Author
[2]All the presented results first appeared in Huang et al. [6].

passing neural networks. Two prominent examples of this framework are RGCN [7] and CompGCN [8], and their expressive power has recently been characterized through a dedicated relational Weisfeiler-Leman test [9].

While offering principled means for learning over knowledge graphs, the standard relational message passing framework is tailored for computing *unary* node representations and therefore models of this class are better suited for node-level tasks (e.g., node/entity classification). Actually, it is well-known that even a good node-level representation might not necessarily induce a good edge representation, hindering the applicability of such models for the crucial task of link prediction [10]. This has led to the design of GNN architectures specifically tailored for link prediction over knowledge graphs [11, 12, 13, 14], for which our understanding remains limited.

The goal of this paper is to offer a theory of the capabilities and limitations of a class of relational GNN architectures which compute *pairwise* node representations to be utilized for link prediction. Although most such architectures can be seen to be subsumed by *higher-order* message passing neural networks that compute pairwise representations on nodes, the inherently quadratic behavior of the latter justifies local approximations which align better with models used in practice. Of particular interest to us is Neural Bellman-Ford Networks (NBFNets) [12], which define a message passing approach inspired by the Bellman-Ford algorithm. We argue in salient detail that the crucial insight of this approach is in leveraging the idea of computing *conditional* pairwise-node representations, which leads to more expressive models at a more reasonable computational cost, given its local nature.

Building on this fundamental aspect, we define *conditional* message passing neural networks, which extend traditional ones by a conditional message passing paradigm: every node representation is conditional on a source node and a query relation, which allows for computing pairwise node representations. This framework strictly contains NBFNets and allows for a systematic treatment of various other models. Through a careful study of this framework, we can explain the conceptual differences between different models along with their respective expressive power.

Our contributions can be summarized as follows:

- We extend the theoretical results from Barceló et al. [9] and present a logical characterization of *relational* message passing neural networks that encode unary representations, based on a variant of *graded modal logic* [15, 16].
- We introduce *conditional* message passing neural networks which encode representations of nodes v conditioned on a (source) node u and a query relation q, yielding pairwise node representations.
- Viewing *conditional* message passing neural networks (with or without global readouts) as classifiers over pairs of nodes, we give logical characterizations of their expressive power based on formulas definable in some *binary* variants of *graded modal logic* [15, 16].
- We conduct an experimental analysis to verify the impact of various model choices, particularly pertaining to initialization and global readout functions. We also conduct both inductive and transductive experiments on various real-world datasets, empirically validating our theoretical findings.

2. Related Work and Motivation

Early GNNs for knowledge graphs are relational variations of message passing neural networks. A prototypical example is the RGCN architecture [7], which extends graph convolutional networks (GCNs) [17] with relation-specific message functions. CompGCN [8] and several other architectures [18] follow this line of work with differences in their aggregate, update, and message functions. These architectures encode *unary* node representations and typically rely on a *pairwise decoder* function to predict the likelihood of a link which is known to be suboptimal for link prediction [10]. There is a good understanding of the expressive power of these architectures [9]: we generalize these results in Section 3, since they form the basis for the rest of our results.

A different approach is given for single-relational graphs by SEAL [19], where the idea is to encode (labeled) subgraphs (instead of nodes). GraIL [11] extends this idea to knowledge graphs, and one important virtue of these models is that they are *inductive* even if there are no node features in the input graph. The idea is to use a form of labeling trick [10] based on pairwise shortest path distances in sampled subgraphs, but these architectures suffer from scalability issues. More recent inductive architectures integrate ideas from earlier path-based link prediction approaches [20, 21] into modern GNN architectures, resulting in proposals such as PathCon [13], Geodesic GNNs [14], and NBFNets [12]. Our study is very closely related to NBFNets which is inspired by the generalized version of the Bellman-Ford algorithm for finding shortest paths. These architectures aggregate over relational paths by keeping track of conditional pairwise-node representations. While NBFNets can be intuitively seen as the neural counterpart of the *generalized* Bellman-Ford algorithm, they do *not* provably align with this algorithm since the "semiring assumption" is invalidated through the use of non-linearities (which is explicit in Zhu et al. [12]). This leaves open many questions regarding the capabilities and limitations of these architectures.

In this paper, we argue that the key insight behind architectures such as NBFNets is in locally computing *pairwise representations through conditioning* on a source node, and this has roots in earlier works, such as ID-GNNs [22]. To formally study this, we introduce conditional message passing neural networks as a strict generalization of NBFNets [12] and related models such as NeuralLP [23], or DRUM [24]. Through this abstraction, we theoretically study the properties of a large class of models in relation to logical characterizations. It was shown in Barceló et al. [25] that a logical classifier is captured by a message passing neural network over single-relational graphs if and only if it can be expressed in *graded modal logic* [15, 16]. Our study first generalizes this logical characterization result to relational message-passing neural networks [9], and then extends this analysis towards conditional message-passing neural networks. We believe these results to be conceptually relevant as they allow us to understand the capabilities of these models in terms of simple logical formalisms.

3. Background

Knowledge Graphs. A *knowledge graph* is a tuple $G = (V, E, R, c)$, where V is a set of nodes, $E \subseteq R \times V \times V$ is a set of labeled edges, or facts, R is a fix set of relation types and $c : V \to D$ is a node coloring. When $D = \mathbb{R}^d$, we also say that c is a d-dimensional *feature map*, and typically use $\boldsymbol{x}$ instead of c. We write $r(u,v)$ to denote a labeled edge, or a fact, where $r \in R$ and $u,v \in V$. The *neighborhood* of a node $v \in V$ relative to a relation $r \in R$ is defined as $\mathcal{N}_r(v) := \{u \mid r(u,v) \in E\}$.

Graph Invariants. We define *k-ary graph invariants* following the terminology of Grohe [26], for which we first define isomorphism over knowledge graphs. An *isomorphism* from a knowledge graph $G = (V,E,R,c)$ to a knowledge graph $G' = (V',E',R,c')$ is a bijection $f : V \to V'$ such that $c(v) = c'(f(v))$ for all $v \in V$, and $r(u,v) \in E$ if and only if $r(f(u), f(v)) \in E'$, for all $r \in R$ and $u,v \in V$. If there exists an isomorphism from G to G', we say that G and G' are *isomorphic*. A *0-ary graph invariant* is a function ξ defined on knowledge graphs such that $\xi(G) = \xi(G')$ for all isomorphic knowledge graphs G and G'. For $k \geq 1$, a *k-ary graph invariant* is a function ξ that associates with each knowledge graph $G = (V,E,R,c)$ a function $\xi(G)$ defined on V^k such that for all knowledge graphs G and G', all isomorphisms f from G to G', and all k-tuples of nodes $\boldsymbol{v} \in V^k$, it holds that $\xi(G)(\boldsymbol{v}) = \xi(G')(f(\boldsymbol{v}))$. If $k = 1$, this defines a *node invariant*, or *unary invariant*, and if $k = 2$, this defines a *binary invariant*, which is central to our study.

4. Relational Message Passing Neural Networks

We introduce *relational message passing neural networks (R-MPNNs)*, which encompass several known models such as RGCN [7] and CompGCN [8]. The idea is to iteratively update the feature of a node v based on the different relation types $r \in R$ and the features of the corresponding neighbors in $\mathcal{N}_r(v)$. In our most general model, we also allow readout functions, that allow further updates to the feature of v by aggregating over the features of all nodes in the graph. Let $G = (V,E,R,\boldsymbol{x})$ be a knowledge graph, where $\boldsymbol{x}$ is a feature map. An *R-MPNN* computes a sequence of feature maps $\boldsymbol{h}^{(t)} : V \to \mathbb{R}^{d(t)}$, for $t \geq 0$. For simplicity, we write $\boldsymbol{h}_v^{(t)}$ instead of $\boldsymbol{h}^{(t)}(v)$. For each node $v \in V$, the representations $\boldsymbol{h}_v^{(t)}$ are iteratively computed as:

$$\boldsymbol{h}_v^{(0)} = \boldsymbol{x}_v$$

$$\boldsymbol{h}_v^{(t+1)} = \textsc{Upd}\left(\boldsymbol{h}_v^{(t)}, \textsc{Agg}(\{\{\textsc{Msg}_r(\boldsymbol{h}_w^{(t)}) \mid w \in \mathcal{N}_r(v), r \in R\}\}), \textsc{Read}(\{\{\boldsymbol{h}_w^{(t)} \mid w \in V\}\})\right),$$

where $\textsc{Upd}$, $\textsc{Agg}$, $\textsc{Read}$, and $\textsc{Msg}_r$ are differentiable *update*, *aggregation*, *global readout*, and relation-specific *message* functions, respectively. An R-MPNN has a fixed number of layers $T \geq 0$, and then, the final node representations are given by the map $\boldsymbol{h}^{(T)} : V \to \mathbb{R}^{d(T)}$. We sometimes write R-MPNNs *without global readout* to refer to the class of models which do not use a readout component.

The use of a readout component in message passing is well-known [27] but its effect is not well-explored in a relational context. It is of interest to us since it has been shown that standard GNNs can capture a larger class of functions with global readout [25].

An R-MPNN can be viewed as an encoder function enc that associates with each knowledge graph G a function $\mathsf{enc}(G) : V \to \mathbb{R}^{d(T)}$, which defines a node invariant corresponding to $\boldsymbol{h}^{(T)}$. The final representations can be used for node-level predictions. For link-level tasks, we use a binary decoder $\mathsf{dec}_q : \mathbb{R}^{d(T)} \times \mathbb{R}^{d(T)} \to \mathbb{R}$, which produces a score for the likelihood of the fact $q(u,v)$, for $q \in R$.

4.1. Logical Characterization of R-MPNNs

We turn our focus to studying the expressive power of R-MPNNs, which aims to answer the following question: *which (node) classifiers can be expressed as R-MPNNs?* That is, we look at R-MPNNs that classify each node in a knowledge graph as true or false.

Following Barceló et al. [25], we study *logical* (node) classifiers, i.e., those that can be defined in the formalism of first-order logic (FO). Briefly, a first-order formula $\phi(x)$ with one free variable x defines a logical classifier that assigns value true to the node u in knowledge graph G whenever $G \models \phi(u)$, i.e., ϕ holds in G when x is interpreted as u. A logical classifier $\phi(x)$ is *captured* by a R-MPNN $\mathscr{A}$ if over *every* knowledge graph G the nodes u that are classified as true by ϕ and $\mathscr{A}$ are the same. A natural problem then is to understand what are the logical classifiers captured by R-MPNNs. This is a *uniform* analysis in the sense that R-MPNNs are analyzed uniformly over *all* knowledge graphs with the same relational vocabulary.

4.1.1. R-MPNNs Without Global Readout

Fix a set of relation types R and a set of node colors $\mathscr{C}$. We consider knowledge graphs of the form $G = (V, E, R, c)$ where c is a node coloring assigning colors from $\mathscr{C}$. In this context, logical formulas can refer to relation types from R and node colors from $\mathscr{C}$. We define the fragment $\mathsf{rFO}^2_{\mathrm{cnt}}$ of FO as follows. A $\mathsf{rFO}^2_{\mathrm{cnt}}$ formula is either $a(x)$ for $a \in \mathscr{C}$, or one of the following, where φ and ψ are $\mathsf{rFO}^2_{\mathrm{cnt}}$ formulas, $N \geq 1$ is a positive integer and $r \in R$:

$$\neg\varphi(x), \quad \varphi(x) \wedge \psi(x), \quad \exists^{\geq N} y\,(\varphi(y) \wedge r(y,x)).$$

As expected, $a(x)$ expresses that node x has color a, and the quantifier $\exists^{\geq N}$ expresses the existence of at least N nodes satisfying the desired property. We remark that $\mathsf{rFO}^2_{\mathrm{cnt}}$ is actually the fragment of FO used in Barceló et al. [25] to characterize GNNs, adapted to multiple relations. It is well-known that $\mathsf{rFO}^2_{\mathrm{cnt}}$ is equivalent to *graded modal logic* [15]. We have the following characterization:

Theorem 4.1. *A logical classifier is captured by R-MPNNs without global readout if and only if it can be expressed in* $\mathsf{rFO}^2_{\mathrm{cnt}}$.

Proof. The proof follows the same strategy as the proof of Theorem 4.2 in Barceló et al. [25], adapted to knowledge graphs. For completeness, we provide all the details here.

We start with the backward direction. Let $\varphi(x)$ be a formula in $\mathsf{rFO}^2_{\mathrm{cnt}}$ for relation types R and node colors $\mathscr{C}$. Let $\varphi_1, \ldots, \varphi_L$ be an enumeration of the subformulas of φ such that if φ_i is a subformula of φ_j, then $i \leq j$. In particular, $\varphi_L = \varphi$. We shall define an R-MPNN without global readout $\mathscr{B}_\varphi$ with L layers computing L-dimensional features in each layer. The idea is that at layer $\ell \in \{1, \ldots, L\}$, the ℓ-th component of the feature $\boldsymbol{h}_v^{(\ell)}$ is computed correctly and corresponds to 1 if φ_ℓ is satisfied in node v, and 0 otherwise. We add an additional final layer that simply outputs the last component of the feature vector, so $\mathscr{B}_\varphi$ actually captures φ.

We use models of R-MPNNs of the following form:

$$\boldsymbol{h}_v^{(t+1)} = \sigma\Big(\boldsymbol{W}\boldsymbol{h}_v^{(t)} + \sum_{r \in R} \sum_{w \in \mathcal{N}_r(v)} \boldsymbol{W}_r \boldsymbol{h}_w^{(t)} + \boldsymbol{b}\Big),$$

where $\boldsymbol{W} \in \mathbb{R}^{L \times L}$ is a parameter matrix and $\boldsymbol{b} \in \mathbb{R}^L$ is the bias term. As message function MSG_r we use $\text{MSG}_r(\boldsymbol{h}) = \boldsymbol{W}_r \boldsymbol{h}$, where $\boldsymbol{W}_r \in \mathbb{R}^{L \times L}$ is a parameter matrix . For the non-linearity σ we use the truncated ReLU function $\sigma(x) = \min(\max(0,x),1)$. The ℓ-th row of $\boldsymbol{W}$ and $\boldsymbol{W}_r$, and the ℓ-th entry of $\boldsymbol{b}$ are defined as follows (omitted entries are 0):

1. If $\varphi_\ell(x) = a(x)$ for a color $a \in \mathscr{C}$, then $\boldsymbol{W}_{\ell\ell} = 1$.
2. If $\varphi_\ell(x) = \neg\varphi_k(x)$ then $\boldsymbol{W}_{\ell k} = -1$, and $b_\ell = 1$.
3. If $\varphi_\ell(x) = \varphi_j(x) \wedge \varphi_k(x)$ then $\boldsymbol{W}_{\ell j} = 1$, $\boldsymbol{W}_{\ell k} = 1$ and $b_\ell = -1$.
4. If $\varphi_\ell(x) = \exists^{\geq N} y\, (\varphi_k(y) \wedge r(y,x))$ then $(\boldsymbol{W}_r)_{\ell k} = 1$ and $b_\ell = -N+1$.

Let $G = (V,E,R,c)$ be a knowledge graph with node colors from $\mathscr{C}$. In order to apply $\mathscr{B}_\varphi$ to G, we choose initial L-dimensional features $\boldsymbol{h}_v^{(0)}$ such that $(\boldsymbol{h}_v^{(0)})_\ell = 1$ if $\varphi_\ell = a(x)$ and a is the color of v, and $(\boldsymbol{h}_v^{(0)})_\ell = 0$ otherwise. In other words, the L-dimensional initial feature $\boldsymbol{h}_v^{(0)}$ is a one-hot encoding of the color of v. It follows from the same arguments than Proposition 4.1 in Barceló et al. [25] that for all $\ell \in \{1,\dots,L\}$ we have $(\boldsymbol{h}_v^{(t)})_\ell = 1$ if $G \models \varphi_\ell(v)$ and $(\boldsymbol{h}_v^{(t)})_\ell = 0$ otherwise, for all $v \in V$ and $t \in \{\ell,\dots,L\}$. In particular, after L layers, $\mathscr{B}_\varphi$ calculates $\boldsymbol{h}_v^{(L)}$ such that $(\boldsymbol{h}_v^{(L)})_L = 1$ if $G \models \varphi(v)$ and $(\boldsymbol{h}_v^{(L)})_L = 0$ otherwise. As layer $L+1$ extracts the L-th component of the feature vector, we are done.

Now we turn to the forward direction. Given a knowledge graph $G = (V,E,R,c)$ and a number $L \in \mathbb{N}$, we define the *unravelling* of $v \in V$ at depth L, denoted $\mathsf{Unr}_G^L(v)$, as the knowledge graph having:

- A node $(v,u_1,\dots,u_i)$ for each directed path $u_i,\dots,u_1,v$ in G of length $i \leq L$.
- For each $r \in R$, a fact $r((v,u_1,\dots,u_i),(v,u_1,\dots,u_{i-1}))$ whenever $r(u_i,u_{i-1}) \in E$ (here $u_0 := v$).
- Each node $(v,u_1,\dots,u_i)$ is colored with $c(u_i)$, that is, the same color as u_i.

Note that the notion of directed path is defined in the obvious way, as for directed graphs but ignoring relation types. Note also that $\mathsf{Unr}_G^L(v)$ is a tree in the sense that the underlying undirected graph is a tree.

We write $\mathsf{Unr}_G^L(v) \simeq \mathsf{Unr}_{G'}^L(v')$ if there exists an isomorphism f from $\mathsf{Unr}_G^L(v)$ to $\mathsf{Unr}_{G'}^L(v')$ such that $f(v) = v'$. The following proposition is a direct translation of Proposition C.4 from Barceló et al. [25] to the case of multiple relations, and it is based on the so-called *relational Weisfeiler-Leman test.* (For more details, see Huang et al. [6].)

Proposition 4.2. *Let G and G' be two knowledge graphs and v and v' be nodes in G and G', respectively, such that $\mathsf{Unr}_G^L(v) \simeq \mathsf{Unr}_{G'}^L(v')$ for all $L \in \mathbb{N}$. Then for any R-MPNN without global readout with T layers, we have that $\boldsymbol{h}_v^{(T)}$ on G coincides with $\boldsymbol{h}_{v'}^{(T)}$ on G'.*

Finally, the following theorem follows from Theorem C.5 in Barceló et al. [25], which in turn follows from Theorem 2.2 in Otto [28]. The key observation here is that the results from Otto [28] are actually presented for multi-modal logics, that is, multiple relation types.

Theorem 4.3. *[28] Let α be a unary FO formula over knowledge graphs. If α is not equivalent to a $\mathsf{rFO}^2_{\mathrm{cnt}}$ formula, then there exist two knowledge graphs G and G', and two nodes v in G and v' in G' such that $\mathsf{Unr}_G^L(v) \simeq \mathsf{Unr}_{G'}^L(v')$ for all $L \in \mathbb{N}$ and such that $G \models \alpha(v)$ but $G' \not\models \alpha(v')$.*

Now we are ready to obtain the forward direction of the theorem. Suppose that a logical classifier α is captured by an R-MPNN without global readout $\mathcal{B}$ with T layers, and assume by contradiction that α is not equivalent to a $\mathsf{rFO}^2_{\text{cnt}}$ formula. Then we can apply Theorem 4.3 and obtain two knowledge graphs G and G', and two nodes v in G and v' in G' such that $\mathsf{Unr}^L_G(v) \simeq \mathsf{Unr}^L_{G'}(v')$ for all $L \in \mathbb{N}$ and such that $G \models \alpha(v)$ but $G' \not\models \alpha(v')$. Applying Proposition 4.2, we have that $\boldsymbol{h}_v^{(T)}$ on G coincides with $\boldsymbol{h}_{v'}^{(T)}$ on G', and hence $\mathcal{B}$ classifies either both v and v' as true over G and G', respectively, or both as false. This is a contradiction. □

4.1.2. R-MPNNs with Global Readout

Interestingly, arbitrary R-MPNNs (with global readout) are strictly more powerful than R-MPNNs without global readout in capturing logical classifiers: they can at least capture a strict extension of $\mathsf{rFO}^2_{\text{cnt}}$, denoted by $\mathsf{erFO}^2_{\text{cnt}}$, which is a simple extension of $\mathsf{rFO}^2_{\text{cnt}}$ from Section 4.1.1 with *negated modalities*, that is, one can check for non-neighbors of a node. Fix a set of relation types R and a set of node colors $\mathcal{C}$. Recall we consider knowledge graphs of the form $G = (V, E, R, c)$ where c is a node coloring assigning colors from $\mathcal{C}$. The logic $\mathsf{erFO}^2_{\text{cnt}}$ contains only unary formulas and it is defined inductively as follows: First, $a(x)$ for $a \in \mathcal{C}$, is in $\mathsf{erFO}^2_{\text{cnt}}$. Second, if φ and ψ are in $\mathsf{erFO}^2_{\text{cnt}}$, $N \geq 1$ is a positive integer, and $r \in R$, then the formulas

$$\neg\varphi(x), \quad \varphi(x) \wedge \psi(x), \quad \exists^{\geq N} y\,(\varphi(y) \wedge r(y,x)), \quad \exists^{\geq N} y\,(\varphi(y) \wedge \neg r(y,x))$$

are also in $\mathsf{erFO}^2_{\text{cnt}}$. It is easy to see that $\mathsf{erFO}^2_{\text{cnt}}$ is strictly more expressive than $\mathsf{rFO}^2_{\text{cnt}}$. For completeness, we show this below.

Proposition 4.4. *There is a formula in* $\mathsf{erFO}^2_{\text{cnt}}$ *that cannot be expressed by any formula in* $\mathsf{rFO}^2_{\text{cnt}}$.

Proof. Consider the following two knowledge graphs G_1 and G_2 over $R = \{r\}$ and colors $\mathcal{C} = \{\text{Green}\}$. The graph G_1 has two nodes u and v and one edge $r(u, v)$. The graph G_2 has three nodes u, v and w and one edge $r(u, v)$ (hence w is an isolated node). In both graphs, all nodes are colored Green.

We show first that for every formula $\varphi(x)$ in $\mathsf{rFO}^2_{\text{cnt}}$, it is the case that $G_1 \models \varphi(n)$ iff $G_2 \models \varphi(n)$, for $n \in \{u, v\}$. We proceed by induction on the formula. For $\varphi(x) = \text{Green}(x)$, we have that $G_1 \models \varphi(n)$ and $G_2 \models \varphi(n)$ and hence we are done. Suppose now that $\varphi(x) = \neg\psi(x)$. Assume $G_1 \models \varphi(n)$ for $n \in \{u, v\}$. Then $G_1 \not\models \psi(n)$, and by inductive hypothesis, we have $G_2 \not\models \psi(n)$ and then $G_2 \models \varphi(n)$. The other direction is analogous. Assume now that $\varphi(x) = \psi_1(x) \wedge \psi_2(x)$. Suppose $G_1 \models \varphi(n)$ for $n \in \{u, v\}$. Then $G_1 \models \psi_1(n)$ and $G_1 \models \psi_2(n)$, and by inductive hypothesis, $G_2 \models \psi_1(n)$ and $G_2 \models \psi_2(n)$. Then $G_2 \models \varphi(n)$. The other direction is analogous. Finally, suppose that $\varphi(x) = \exists^{\geq N} y(\psi(y) \wedge r(y,x))$. Assume that $G_1 \models \varphi(n)$ for $n \in \{u, v\}$. Then there exist at least N nodes $z \in \mathcal{N}_r(n)$ in G_1 such that $G_1 \models \psi(z)$. Since $\mathcal{N}_r(u) = \emptyset$, we have $n = v$. As $\mathcal{N}_r(v) = \{u\}$, we have $z = u$. Since the neighborhood $\mathcal{N}_r(v)$ is the same in G_1 and G_2, and by the inductive hypothesis, we have that there are at least N nodes $z \in \mathcal{N}_r(v)$ in G_2 such that $G_2 \models \psi(z)$. This implies that $G_2 \models \varphi(v)$. The other direction is analogous.

Now consider the $\mathsf{erFO}^2_{\text{cnt}}$ formula $\varphi(x) = \exists^{\geq 2} y(\text{Green}(y) \wedge \neg r(y,x))$. We claim that there is no $\mathsf{rFO}^2_{\text{cnt}}$ formula equivalent to $\varphi(x)$. By contradiction, suppose we have such an equivalent formula φ'. As shown above, we have $G_1 \models \varphi'(v)$ iff $G_2 \models \varphi'(v)$. On the other hand, by definition, we have that $G_1 \not\models \varphi(v)$ and $G_2 \models \varphi(v)$. This is a contradiction. $\square$

Now we are ready to prove that R-MPNN can at least capture $\mathsf{erFO}^2_{\mathrm{cnt}}$. We follow the same strategy as in the proof of the backward direction of Theorem 4.1.

Theorem 4.5. *Each classifier expressible in* $\mathsf{erFO}^2_{\mathrm{cnt}}$ *can be captured by an R-MPNN.*

Proof. Let $\varphi(x)$ be a formula in $\mathsf{erFO}^2_{\mathrm{cnt}}$, for relation types R and node colors $\mathscr{C}$. Let $\varphi_1, \dots, \varphi_L$ be an enumeration of the subformulas of φ such that if φ_i is a subformula of φ_j, then $i \leq j$. In particular, $\varphi_L = \varphi$. We will construct an R-MPNN $\mathscr{A}_\varphi$ with L layers computing L-dimensional features in each layer. At layer $\ell \in \{1, \dots, L\}$, the ℓ-th component of the feature $\boldsymbol{h}_v^{(\ell)}$ will correspond to 1 if φ_ℓ is satisfied on v, and 0 otherwise. We add an additional final layer that simply outputs the last component of the feature vector.

We use models of R-MPNNs of the following form:

$$\boldsymbol{h}_v^{(t+1)} = \sigma\Big(\boldsymbol{W}_0 \boldsymbol{h}_v^{(t)} + \sum_{r \in R} \sum_{w \in \mathscr{N}_r(v)} \boldsymbol{W}_r \boldsymbol{h}_w^{(t)} + \boldsymbol{W}_1 \sum_{w \in V} \boldsymbol{h}_w^{(t)} + \boldsymbol{b}\Big),$$

where $\boldsymbol{W}_0, \boldsymbol{W}_1 \in \mathbb{R}^{L \times L}$ are parameter matrices and $\boldsymbol{b} \in \mathbb{R}^L$ is the bias term. As message function $\textsc{Msg}_r$ we use $\textsc{Msg}_r(\boldsymbol{h}) = \boldsymbol{W}_r \boldsymbol{h}$, where $\boldsymbol{W}_r \in \mathbb{R}^{L \times L}$ is a parameter matrix . For the non-linearity σ we use the truncated ReLU function $\sigma(x) = \min(\max(0,x),1)$. The ℓ-th row of $\boldsymbol{W}_0$, $\boldsymbol{W}_1$ and $\boldsymbol{W}_r$, and the ℓ-th entry of $\boldsymbol{b}$ are defined as follows (omitted entries are 0):

1. If $\varphi_\ell(x) = a(x)$ for a color $a \in \mathscr{C}$, then $(\boldsymbol{W}_0)_{\ell\ell} = 1$.
2. If $\varphi_\ell(x) = \neg\varphi_k(x)$ then $(\boldsymbol{W}_0)_{\ell k} = -1$, and $b_\ell = 1$.
3. If $\varphi_\ell(x) = \varphi_j(x) \wedge \varphi_k(x)$ then $(\boldsymbol{W}_0)_{\ell j} = 1$, $(\boldsymbol{W}_0)_{\ell k} = 1$ and $b_\ell = -1$.
4. If $\varphi_\ell(x) = \exists^{\geq N} y\,(\varphi_k(y) \wedge r(y,x))$ then $(\boldsymbol{W}_r)_{\ell k} = 1$ and $b_\ell = -N+1$.
5. If $\varphi_\ell(x) = \exists^{\geq N} y\,(\varphi_k(y) \wedge \neg r(y,x))$ then $(\boldsymbol{W}_r)_{\ell k} = -1$, $(\boldsymbol{W}_1)_{\ell k} = 1$ and $b_\ell = -N+1$.

Let $G = (V,E,R,c)$ be a knowledge graph with node colors from $\mathscr{C}$. In order to apply $\mathscr{A}_\varphi$ to G, we choose initial L-dimensional features $\boldsymbol{h}_v^{(0)}$ such that $(\boldsymbol{h}_v^{(0)})_\ell = 1$ if $\varphi_\ell = a(x)$ and a is the color of v, and $(\boldsymbol{h}_v^{(0)})_\ell = 0$ otherwise. In other words, the L-dimensional initial feature $\boldsymbol{h}_v^{(0)}$ is a one-hot encoding of the color of v. Using the same arguments as in the proof of Theorem 4.1, we have $(\boldsymbol{h}_v^{(t)})_\ell = 1$ if $G \models \varphi_\ell(v)$ and $(\boldsymbol{h}_v^{(t)})_\ell = 0$ otherwise, for all $v \in V$ and $t \in \{\ell, \dots, L\}$. In particular, after L layers, $\mathscr{A}_\varphi$ calculates $\boldsymbol{h}_v^{(L)}$ such that $(\boldsymbol{h}_v^{(L)})_L = 1$ if $G \models \varphi(v)$ and $(\boldsymbol{h}_v^{(L)})_L = 0$ otherwise. As layer $L+1$ extracts the L-th component of the feature vector, the result follows. $\square$

Remark 4.6. We note that in Barceló et al. [25], it is shown that a more expressive graded modal logic (with more expressive modalities) can be captured by GNNs with global readout in the context of single-relation graphs. It is by no means obvious that an adaption of this logic to the multi-relational case is captured by our R-MPNNs. We leave as an open problem to find more expressive logics that can be captured by R-MPNNs (with global readout).

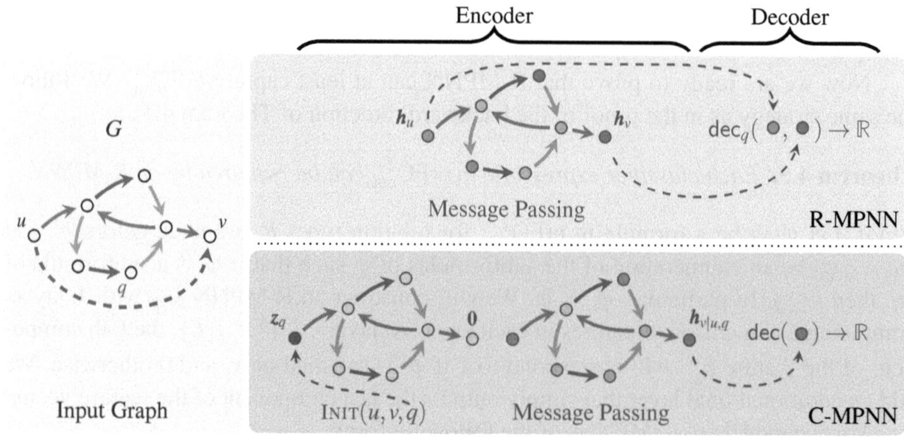

Figure 1. Visualization of R-MPNN and C-MPNN. The dashed arrow is the target query $q(u, v)$. Arrow colors indicate distinct relation types, while node colors indicate varying hidden states. R-MPNN considers a unary encoder and relies on a binary decoder, while C-MPNN first initializes binary representation based on the target query $q(u, v)$, and then uses a unary decoder.

5. Conditional Message Passing Neural Networks

R-MPNNs have serious limitations for the task of link prediction [10], which has led to several proposals that compute pairwise representations directly. In contrast to the case of R-MPNNs, our understanding of these architectures is limited. In this section, we introduce the framework of conditional MPNNs that offers a natural framework for the systematic study of these architectures.

Let $G = (V, E, R, \boldsymbol{x})$ be a knowledge graph, where $\boldsymbol{x}$ is a feature map. A *conditional message passing neural network* (C-MPNN) iteratively computes pairwise representations, relative to a fixed query $q \in R$ and a fixed node $u \in V$, as follows:

$$\boldsymbol{h}_{v|u,q}^{(0)} = \textsc{Init}(u, v, q)$$

$$\boldsymbol{h}_{v|u,q}^{(t+1)} = \textsc{Upd}(\boldsymbol{h}_{v|u,q}^{(t)}, \textsc{Agg}(\{\{\textsc{Msg}_r(\boldsymbol{h}_{w|u,q}^{(t)}, \boldsymbol{z}_q) \mid w \in \mathcal{N}_r(v), r \in R\}\}), \textsc{Read}(\{\{\boldsymbol{h}_{w|u,q}^{(t)} \mid w \in V\}\})),$$

where $\textsc{Init}$, $\textsc{Upd}$, $\textsc{Agg}$, $\textsc{Read}$, and $\textsc{Msg}_r$ are differentiable *initialization*, *update*, *aggregation*, *global readout*, and relation-specific *message* functions, respectively. The vector $\boldsymbol{z}_q$ is a learnable vector representing the query $q \in R$. We denote by $\boldsymbol{h}_q^{(t)} : V \times V \to \mathbb{R}^{d(t)}$ the function $\boldsymbol{h}_q^{(t)}(u, v) := \boldsymbol{h}_{v|u,q}^{(t)}$. A C-MPNN has a fixed number of layers $T \geq 0$, and the final pair representations are given by $\boldsymbol{h}_q^{(T)}$. We sometimes write C-MPNNs *without global readout* to refer to the class of models which do not use a readout component.

Intuitively, C-MPNNs condition on a source node u in order to compute representations of (u, v) for all target nodes v. To further explain, we show a visualization of C-MPNNs and R-MPNNs in Figure 1 to demonstrate the differences in the forward pass. Contrary to the R-MPNN model where we carry out relational message passing first and rely on the binary decoder to compute a query fact $q(u, v)$, the C-MPNN model first initializes all node representations with the zero vector except the representation of the node u which is assigned a vector with non-zero entry. Following the initialization, we carry out relational message passing and decode the hidden state of the target node v to obtain the output, which yields the representation of v conditioned on u.

Observe that C-MPNNs compute binary invariants, provided that the initialization $\textsc{Init}$ is a binary invariant. To ensure that the resulting model computes pairwise representations, we require $\textsc{Init}(u,v,q)$ to be a nontrivial function in the sense that it needs to satisfy *target node distinguishability*: for all $q \in R$ and $v \neq u \in V$, it holds that $\textsc{Init}(u,u,q) \neq \textsc{Init}(u,v,q)$.

This is very closely related to the *Labeling Trick* proposed by Zhang et al. [10], which is an initialization method aiming to differentiate a set $\{u,v\}$ of target nodes from the remaining nodes in a graph. However, the *Labeling Trick* only applies when both the source u and target nodes v are labeled. Recent state-of-the-art models such as ID-GNN [22] and NBFNet [12] utilize a similar method, but only with the source node u labeled differently in initialization. Our definition captures precisely this, and we offer a theoretical analysis of the capabilities of the aforementioned architectures accordingly.

One alternative is to directly learn pairwise representations following similar ideas to those of higher-order GNNs, but these algorithms are not scalable. Architectures such as NBFNets represent a trade-off between computational complexity and expressivity. The advantage of learning conditional representations $\boldsymbol{h}_{v|u,q}$ is to be able to learn such representations in parallel for all $v \in V$, amortizing the computational overhead; see Zhu et al. [12] for a discussion. We have also carried out a runtime analysis comparison among different classes of models in Section 5.3.

5.1. Design Space and Basic Model Architectures

To specify a C-MPNN architecture, we need to specify the functions $\textsc{Init}$, $\textsc{Agg}$, $\textsc{Msg}_r$, and $\textsc{Read}$. In the following, we consider three initialization functions $\{\textsc{Init}^1, \textsc{Init}^2, \textsc{Init}^3\}$, two aggregation functions $\{\text{sum}, \text{PNA}\}$, three message functions $\{\textsc{Msg}_r^1, \textsc{Msg}_r^2, \textsc{Msg}_r^3\}$, and either *sum global readout* or no readout term.

Initialization. We consider the following natural variants for initialization:

$$\textsc{Init}^1(u,v,q) = \mathbb{1}_{u=v} * \mathbf{1},$$

$$\textsc{Init}^2(u,v,q) = \mathbb{1}_{u=v} * \mathbf{z}_q,$$

$$\textsc{Init}^3(u,v,q) = \mathbb{1}_{u=v} * (\mathbf{z}_q + \varepsilon_u),$$

where $*$ represents element-wise multiplication, the function $\mathbb{1}_{u=v}(v)$ is the indicator function which returns the all-ones vector $\mathbf{1}$ if $u = v$ and the all-zeros vector $\mathbf{0}$ otherwise with corresponding size.

Clearly, both $\textsc{Init}^1$ and $\textsc{Init}^2$ satisfy the *target node distinguishability* assumption if we assume $\mathbf{z}_q$ has no zero entry, where $\textsc{Init}^2$, in addition, allows query-specific initialization to be considered. Suppose we further relax the condition to be *target node distinguishability in expectation*. Then, $\textsc{Init}^3$ can also distinguish between each conditioned node u given the same query vector $\mathbf{z}_q$ by adding an error vector ε_u sampled from $\mathcal{N}(0,1)$ to the conditioned node's initialization.

Aggregation. We consider sum aggregation and Principal Neighborhood Aggregation (PNA) [29].

Message. We consider the following variations of *message* functions:

$$\text{MSG}_r^1(\boldsymbol{h}_{w|u,q}^{(t)}, \boldsymbol{z}_q) = \boldsymbol{h}_{w|u,q}^{(t)} * \boldsymbol{W}_r^{(t)} \boldsymbol{z}_q,$$

$$\text{MSG}_r^2(\boldsymbol{h}_{w|u,q}^{(t)}, \boldsymbol{z}_q) = \boldsymbol{h}_{w|u,q}^{(t)} * \boldsymbol{b}_r^{(t)},$$

$$\text{MSG}_r^3(\boldsymbol{h}_{w|u,q}^{(t)}, \boldsymbol{z}_q) = \boldsymbol{W}_r^{(t)} \boldsymbol{h}_{w|u,q}^{(t)},$$

where $\boldsymbol{W}_r^{(t)}$ are relation-specific transformations. MSG_r^1 computes a query-dependent message, whereas MSG_r^2 and MSG_r^3 are analogous to message functions of CompGCN and RGCN, respectively.

Readout. We consider a standard readout which sums the representations and applies a linear transformation on the resulting representations. Alternatively, we consider the special case, where we omit this component (we discuss a dedicated readout operation in our empirical analysis later).

A simple architecture. Consider a *basic* C-MPNN architecture with global readout, which, for a query relation $q \in R$ and a fixed node u, updates the representations as:

$$\boldsymbol{h}_{v|u,q}^{(0)} = \mathbb{1}_{u=v} * \boldsymbol{z}_q$$

$$\boldsymbol{h}_{v|u,q}^{(t+1)} = \sigma\left(\boldsymbol{W}_0^{(t)}\left(\boldsymbol{h}_{v|u,q}^{(t)} + \sum_{r\in R}\sum_{w\in\mathcal{N}_r(v)} \text{MSG}_r^1(\boldsymbol{h}_{w|u,q}^{(t)}, \boldsymbol{z}_q)\right) + \boldsymbol{W}_1^{(t)} \sum_{w\in V} \boldsymbol{h}_{w|u,q}^{(t)}\right),$$

where $\boldsymbol{W}_0^{(t)}, \boldsymbol{W}_1^{(t)}$ are linear transformations followed by a non-linearity σ.

5.2. Logical Characterization of C-MPNNs

We now turn to the problem of which *binary classifiers* can be expressed as C-MPNNs. That is, we look at C-MPNNs that classify each *pair of nodes* in a knowledge graph as true or false. Following Section 4.1, we consider *logical* binary classifiers, i.e., those that can be defined in the formalism of first-order logic (FO). In this case, we need to consider first-order formulas $\phi(x,y)$ with two free variables. As expected, a logical binary classifier $\phi(x,y)$ is *captured* by a C-MPNN $\mathcal{A}$ if over every knowledge graph G the pairs (u,v) of nodes that are classified as true by ϕ and $\mathcal{A}$ are the same. A natural problem then is to understand what are the logical binary classifiers captured by C-MPNNs.

5.2.1. C-MPNNs without Global Readout

Fix a set of relation types R and a set of pair colors $\mathcal{C}$. We consider knowledge graphs of the form $G = (V,E,R,\eta)$ where η is a mapping assigning colors from $\mathcal{C}$ to pairs of nodes from V. In this context, FO formulas can refer to the different relation types in R and the different pair colors in $\mathcal{C}$. Our first characterization is established in terms of a simple fragment of FO, which we call $\mathsf{rFO}^3_{\text{cnt}}$, and is inductively defined as follows: First,

$a(x,y)$ for $a \in \mathscr{C}$, is in $\mathsf{rFO}^3_{\mathrm{cnt}}$. Second, if $\varphi(x,y)$ and $\psi(x,y)$ are in $\mathsf{rFO}^3_{\mathrm{cnt}}$, $N \geq 1$ is a positive integer, and $r \in R$, then the formulas

$$\neg\varphi(x,y), \quad \varphi(x,y) \wedge \psi(x,y), \quad \exists^{\geq N} z(\varphi(x,z) \wedge r(z,y))$$

are also in $\mathsf{rFO}^3_{\mathrm{cnt}}$. As expected, $a(x,y)$ expresses that node pair (x,y) has color a, and the quantifier $\exists^{\geq N}$ expresses the existence of at least N nodes satisfying the desired property. We use the acronym $\mathsf{rFO}^3_{\mathrm{cnt}}$ as this logic corresponds to a restriction of FO with three variables and counting. We can show the following result which is the first of its kind in the context of knowledge graphs:

Theorem 5.1. *A logical binary classifier is captured by C-MPNNs without global readout if and only if it can be expressed in* $\mathsf{rFO}^3_{\mathrm{cnt}}$.

The idea of the proof of Theorem 5.1 is to reduce the problem from C-MPNNs to R-MPNNs, and then apply Theorem 4.1. In order to achieve this, we need to define suitable translations between C-MPNNs and R-MPNNs, and also between the logics $\mathsf{rFO}^2_{\mathrm{cnt}}$ and $\mathsf{rFO}^3_{\mathrm{cnt}}$. Before giving the proof of Theorem 5.1, we present these auxiliary translations.

Let $G = (V,E,R,c,\eta)$ be a knowledge graph where c is a node coloring and η is a coloring for pairs of nodes. We denote by G^2 the knowledge graph $G^2 = (V \times V, E', R, c_\eta)$ where $E' = \{r((u,w),(u,v)) \mid r(w,v) \in E, r \in R\}$ and c_η is the node coloring $c_\eta((u,v)) = \eta(u,v)$. Note that the coloring c is irrelevant in the construction. Intuitively, G^2 encodes the adjacency relation between pairs of nodes of G used in C-MPNNs. We stress that G and G^2 have the same relation type set R. If $\mathscr{A}$ is a C-MPNN and $\mathscr{B}$ is an R-MPNN, we write $\boldsymbol{h}^{(t)}_{\mathscr{A},G}(u,v) := \boldsymbol{h}^{(t)}_q(u,v)$ and $\boldsymbol{h}^{(t)}_{\mathscr{B},G^2}((u,v)) := \boldsymbol{h}^{(t)}((u,v))$ for the features computed by $\mathscr{A}$ and $\mathscr{B}$ over G and G^2, respectively. We sometimes write $\mathscr{N}_r^H(v)$ to emphasize that the neighborhood is taken over the knowledge graph H. Finally, we say that an initial feature map $\mathbf{y}$ for G^2 satisfies target node distinguishability if $\mathbf{y}((u,u)) \neq \mathbf{y}((u,v))$ for all $u \neq v$.

We have the following equivalence between C-MPNNs and R-MPNNs without global readout:

Proposition 5.2. *Let* $G = (V,E,R,\mathbf{x},\eta)$ *be a knowledge graph where* $\mathbf{x}$ *is a feature map, and* η *is a pairwise coloring*[3]*. Let* $q \in R$ *be any query relation. Then:*

1. *For every C-MPNN without global readout* $\mathscr{A}$ *with* T *layers, there is an initial feature map* $\mathbf{y}$ *for* G^2 *and an R-MPNN without global readout* $\mathscr{B}$ *with* T *layers such that for all* $0 \leq t \leq T$ *and* $u,v \in V$*, we have* $\boldsymbol{h}^{(t)}_{\mathscr{A},G}(u,v) = \boldsymbol{h}^{(t)}_{\mathscr{B},G^2}((u,v))$.
2. *For every initial feature map* $\mathbf{y}$ *for* G^2 *satisfying target node distinguishability and every R-MPNN without global readout* $\mathscr{B}$ *with* T *layers, there is a C-MPNN without global readout* $\mathscr{A}$ *with* T *layers such that for all* $0 \leq t \leq T$ *and* $u,v \in V$*, we have* $\boldsymbol{h}^{(t)}_{\mathscr{A},G}(u,v) = \boldsymbol{h}^{(t)}_{\mathscr{B},G^2}((u,v))$.

Proof. We start with item (1). The sought R-MPNN $\mathscr{B}$ has the same aggregation and update functions as $\mathscr{A}$ for all the T layers. For each layer, the message function of $\mathscr{B}$ is defined as $\textsc{Msg}_r(\cdot) = \textsc{Msg}_r(\cdot, z_q)$, where the latter is the message function of $\mathscr{A}$ for

[3]The pairwise coloring η does not play any role in the proposition.

the corresponding layer. The initial feature map $\mathbf{y}$ is defined as $\mathbf{y}((u,v)) = \textsc{Init}(u,v,q)$, where $\textsc{Init}$ is the initialization function of $\mathscr{A}$.

We show the equivalence by induction on t. For $t=0$, we have $\boldsymbol{h}_{\mathscr{A}}^{(0)}(u,v) = \textsc{Init}(u,v,q) = \mathbf{y}((u,v)) = \boldsymbol{h}_{\mathscr{B}}^{(0)}((u,v))$. For the inductive case, take $u,v \in V$. We have

$$\begin{aligned}
\boldsymbol{h}_{\mathscr{A}}^{(t+1)}(u,v) &= \textsc{Upd}(\boldsymbol{h}_{\mathscr{A}}^{(t)}(u,v), \textsc{Agg}(\{\{\textsc{Msg}_r(\boldsymbol{h}_{\mathscr{A}}^{(t)}(u,w),\mathbf{z}_q) \mid w \in \mathscr{N}_r^G(v), r \in R\}\})) \\
&= \textsc{Upd}(\boldsymbol{h}_{\mathscr{B}}^{(t)}((u,v)), \textsc{Agg}(\{\{\textsc{Msg}_r(\boldsymbol{h}_{\mathscr{B}}^{(t)}((u,w))) \mid (u,w) \in \mathscr{N}_r^{G^2}((u,v)), r \in R\}\})) \\
&= \boldsymbol{h}_{\mathscr{B}}^{(t+1)}((u,v)).
\end{aligned}$$

For item (2), we take $\mathscr{A}$ to have the same aggregation and update functions than $\mathscr{B}$, for all the T layers. For each layer, the message function of $\mathscr{A}$ is $\textsc{Msg}_r(\cdot,\mathbf{z}_q) = \textsc{Msg}_r(\cdot)$, where the latter is the message function of $\mathscr{B}$ for the corresponding layer. The parameter vector $\mathbf{z}_q$ can be defined arbitrarily, for instance, we can take the all-ones vector $\mathbf{1}$. The initialization function $\textsc{Init}$ is defined as $\textsc{Init}(u,v,q) = \mathbf{y}((u,v))$. The argument for the equivalence is the same as item (1). □

We now provide useful translations from $\mathsf{rFO}^2_{\mathrm{cnt}}$ to $\mathsf{rFO}^3_{\mathrm{cnt}}$ and vice versa.

Proposition 5.3. *We have the following:*

1. *For all $\mathsf{rFO}^3_{\mathrm{cnt}}$ formula $\varphi(x,y)$, there is a formula $\widetilde{\varphi}(x)$ in $\mathsf{rFO}^2_{\mathrm{cnt}}$ such that for all knowledge graph $G=(V,E,R,\eta)$ and all nodes $u,v \in V$, we have $G \models \varphi(u,v)$ if and only if $G^2 \models \widetilde{\varphi}((u,v))$.*
2. *For all formula $\varphi(x)$ in $\mathsf{rFO}^2_{\mathrm{cnt}}$, there is an $\mathsf{rFO}^3_{\mathrm{cnt}}$ formula $\widetilde{\varphi}(x,y)$ such that for all knowledge graph $G=(V,E,R,\eta)$ and all nodes $u,v \in V$, we have $G \models \widetilde{\varphi}(u,v)$ if and only if $G^2 \models \varphi((u,v))$.*

Proof. We start with item (1). We define $\widetilde{\varphi}(x)$ by induction on the formula $\varphi(x,y)$:

1. If $\varphi(x,y) = a(x,y)$ for color a, then $\widetilde{\varphi}(x) = a(x)$.
2. If $\varphi(x,y) = \neg\psi(x,y)$, then $\widetilde{\varphi}(x) = \neg\widetilde{\psi}(x)$.
3. If $\varphi(x,y) = \varphi_1(x,y) \wedge \varphi_2(x,y)$, then $\widetilde{\varphi}(x) = \widetilde{\varphi}_1(x) \wedge \widetilde{\varphi}_2(x)$.
4. If $\varphi(x,y) = \exists^{\geq N} z\,(\psi(x,z) \wedge r(z,y))$ then $\widetilde{\varphi}(x) = \exists^{\geq N} y\,(\widetilde{\psi}(y) \wedge r(y,x))$.

Fix $G=(V,E,R,\eta)$ and $G^2 = (V \times V, E', R, c_\eta)$. We show by induction on the formula φ that $G \models \varphi(u,v)$ if and only if $G^2 \models \widetilde{\varphi}((u,v))$, for all nodes $u,v \in V$.

For the base case, that is, case (1) above, we have that $\varphi(x,y) = a(x,y)$ and hence, for all $u,v \in V$, we have $G \models \varphi(u,v)$ iff $\eta(u,v) = a$ iff $c_\eta((u,v)) = a$ iff $G^2 \models \widetilde{\varphi}((u,v))$.

Now we consider the inductive cases. For case (2) above, we have $\varphi(x,y) = \neg\psi(x,y)$. Then, for all $u,v \in V$, we have $G \models \varphi(u,v)$ iff $G \not\models \psi(u,v)$ iff $G^2 \not\models \widetilde{\psi}((u,v))$ iff $G^2 \models \widetilde{\varphi}((u,v))$.

For case (3), we have $\varphi(x,y) = \varphi_1(x,y) \wedge \varphi_2(x,y)$. Then, for all $u,v \in V$, we have $G \models \varphi(u,v)$ iff $G \models \varphi_1(u,v)$ and $G \models \varphi_2(u,v)$ iff $G^2 \models \widetilde{\varphi_1}((u,v))$ and $G^2 \models \widetilde{\varphi_2}((u,v))$ iff $G^2 \models \widetilde{\varphi}((u,v))$.

Finally, for case (4), we have $\varphi(x,y) = \exists^{\geq N} z\,(\psi(x,z) \wedge r(z,y))$. Take $u,v \in V$. Assume $G \models \varphi(u,v)$, then there exist at least N nodes $w \in V$ such that $G \models \psi(u,w)$ and $r(w,v) \in E$. By the definition of G^2, there exist at least N nodes in G^2 of the form (u,w)

such that $G^2 \models \widetilde{\psi}((u,w))$ and $r((u,w),(u,v)) \in E'$. It follows that $G^2 \models \widetilde{\varphi}((u,v))$. On the other hand, suppose $G^2 \models \widetilde{\varphi}((u,v))$. Then there exist at least N nodes (o,o') in G^2 such that $G^2 \models \widetilde{\psi}((o,o'))$ and $r((o,o'),(u,v)) \in E'$. By definition of G^2, each (o,o') must be of the form $(o,o') = (u,w)$ for some $w \in V$ such that $r(w,v) \in E$. Then there are at least N nodes $w \in V$ such that $G \models \psi(u,w)$ and $r(w,v) \in E$. It follows that $G \models \varphi(u,v)$.

Item (2) is similar. We define $\widetilde{\varphi}(x,y)$ by induction on the formula $\varphi(x)$:

1. If $\varphi(x) = a(x)$ for color a, then $\widetilde{\varphi}(x,y) = a(x,y)$.
2. If $\varphi(x) = \neg\psi(x)$, then $\widetilde{\varphi}(x,y) = \neg\widetilde{\psi}(x,y)$.
3. If $\varphi(x) = \varphi_1(x) \wedge \varphi_2(x)$, then $\widetilde{\varphi}(x,y) = \widetilde{\varphi}_1(x,y) \wedge \widetilde{\varphi}_2(x,y)$.
4. If $\varphi(x) = \exists^{\geq N} y\,(\psi(y) \wedge r(y,x))$ then $\widetilde{\varphi}(x,y) = \exists^{\geq N} z\,(\widetilde{\psi}(x,z) \wedge r(z,y))$.

Following the same inductive argument from item (1), we obtain that $G \models \widetilde{\varphi}(u,v)$ if and only if $G^2 \models \varphi((u,v))$, for all nodes u,v in G. □

Now we are ready to present the proof of Theorem 5.1.

Proof of Theorem 5.1. Let α be a logical binary classifier and suppose it is captured by a C-MPNN without global readout $\mathscr{A}$. By Proposition 5.2, item (1), we know that $\mathscr{A}$ can be simulated by a R-MPNN without global readout $\mathscr{B}$ over G^2. In turn, we can apply Theorem 4.1 and obtain a formula φ in $\mathsf{rFO}^2_{\mathrm{cnt}}$ equivalent to $\mathscr{B}$. Finally, we can apply the translation in Proposition 5.3, item (2), and obtain a corresponding formula $\widetilde{\varphi}$ in $\mathsf{rFO}^3_{\mathrm{cnt}}$. We claim that $\widetilde{\varphi}$ captures $\mathscr{A}$. Let G be a knowledge graph and u,v two nodes. We have that $G \models \widetilde{\varphi}(u,v)$ iff $G^2 \models \varphi((u,v))$ iff $\mathscr{B}$ classifies (u,v) as true over G^2 iff $\mathscr{A}$ classifies (u,v) as true over G.

The other direction is obtained analogously following the reverse translations. □

5.2.2. C-MPNNs with Global Readout

As in the case of R-MPNNs, we have that arbitrary C-MPNNs (with global readout) are strictly more powerful than C-MPNNs without global readout, as they can at least capture a strict extension of $\mathsf{rFO}^3_{\mathrm{cnt}}$, denoted by $\mathsf{erFO}^3_{\mathrm{cnt}}$. The extension $\mathsf{erFO}^3_{\mathrm{cnt}}$ is analogous to $\mathsf{erFO}^2_{\mathrm{cnt}}$ from Section 4.1.2, that is, it incorporates negated modalities checking for non-neighbors of a node. Formally, fix a set of relation types R and a set of pair colors $\mathscr{C}$. The logic $\mathsf{erFO}^3_{\mathrm{cnt}}$ contains only binary formulas and it is defined inductively as follows: First, $a(x,y)$ for $a \in \mathscr{C}$, is in $\mathsf{erFO}^3_{\mathrm{cnt}}$. Second, if $\varphi(x,y)$ and $\psi(x,y)$ are in $\mathsf{erFO}^3_{\mathrm{cnt}}$, $N \geq 1$ is a positive integer, and $r \in R$, then the formulas

$$\neg\varphi(x,y), \quad \varphi(x,y) \wedge \psi(x,y), \quad \exists^{\geq N} z\,(\varphi(x,z) \wedge r(z,y)), \quad \exists^{\geq N} z\,(\varphi(x,z) \wedge \neg r(z,y))$$

are also in $\mathsf{erFO}^3_{\mathrm{cnt}}$. As expected, $\mathsf{erFO}^3_{\mathrm{cnt}}$ is strictly more expressive than $\mathsf{rFO}^3_{\mathrm{cnt}}$, which follows from the following proposition:

Proposition 5.4. *There is a formula in* $\mathsf{erFO}^3_{\mathrm{cnt}}$ *that cannot be expressed by any formula in* $\mathsf{rFO}^3_{\mathrm{cnt}}$.

Proof. The proof is similar to the proof of Proposition 4.4. We consider two knowledge graphs G_1 and G_2 over $R = \{r\}$ and colors $\mathscr{C} = \{\text{Green}\}$. The graph G_1 has two nodes u and v and one edge $r(u,v)$. The graph G_2 has three nodes u, v and w and one edge $r(u,v)$ (hence w is an isolated node). In both graphs, all pairs are colored Green.

Using the same inductive argument as in Proposition 4.4, we obtain that for every formula $\varphi(x,y)$ in $\mathsf{rFO}^3_{\mathrm{cnt}}$, it is the case that $G_1 \models \varphi(u,n)$ iff $G_2 \models \varphi(u,n)$, for $n \in \{u,v\}$.

Now consider the $\mathsf{erFO}^3_{\mathrm{cnt}}$ formula $\varphi(x,y) = \exists^{\geq 2} z(\mathrm{Green}(x,z) \wedge \neg r(z,y))$. There is no $\mathsf{rFO}^3_{\mathrm{cnt}}$ formula equivalent to $\varphi(x,y)$. By contradiction, take an equivalent formula φ'. As shown above, we have $G_1 \models \varphi'(u,v)$ iff $G_2 \models \varphi'(u,v)$. However, by definition, we have that $G_1 \not\models \varphi(u,v)$ and $G_2 \models \varphi(u,v)$, which is a contradiction. □

We conclude this section by showing that C-MPNNs can at least capture $\mathsf{erFO}^3_{\mathrm{cnt}}$.

Theorem 5.5. *Each logical binary classifier expressible in* $\mathsf{erFO}^3_{\mathrm{cnt}}$ *can be captured by a C-MPNN.*

Proof. We can mimic the proof of Theorem 4.5 for R-MPNNs. For completeness, we give more details here. Let $\varphi(x,y)$ be a formula in $\mathsf{erFO}^3_{\mathrm{cnt}}$, for relation types R and pair colors $\mathscr{C}$. Let $\varphi_1, \ldots, \varphi_L$ be an enumeration of the subformulas of φ such that if φ_i is a subformula of φ_j, then $i \leq j$ (so $\varphi_L = \varphi$). We construct a C-MPNN $\mathscr{A}_\varphi$ with L layers computing L-dimensional features in each layer. At layer $\ell \in \{1, \ldots, L\}$, the ℓ-th component of the feature $\boldsymbol{h}^{(\ell)}_{v|u,q}$ will correspond to 1 if φ_ℓ is satisfied on (u,v), and 0 otherwise. The query relation q plays no role in the construction, that is, for any possible $q \in R$ the output of $\mathscr{A}_\varphi$ is the same. Hence, for simplicity, in the remaining of the proof we shall write $\boldsymbol{h}^{(t)}_{v|u}$ instead of $\boldsymbol{h}^{(t)}_{v|u,q}$. We add an additional final layer that simply outputs the last component of the feature vector.

We use models of C-MPNNs of the following form:

$$\boldsymbol{h}^{(t+1)}_{v|u} = \sigma\Big(\boldsymbol{W}_0 \boldsymbol{h}^{(t)}_{v|u} + \sum_{r \in R} \sum_{w \in \mathcal{N}_r(v)} \boldsymbol{W}_r \boldsymbol{h}^{(t)}_{w|u} + \boldsymbol{W}_1 \sum_{w \in V} \boldsymbol{h}^{(t)}_{w|u} + \boldsymbol{b}\Big),$$

where $\boldsymbol{W}_0, \boldsymbol{W}_1 \in \mathbb{R}^{L \times L}$ are parameter matrices and $\boldsymbol{b} \in \mathbb{R}^L$ is the bias term. As message function $\textsc{Msg}_r$ we use $\textsc{Msg}_r(\boldsymbol{h}) = \boldsymbol{W}_r \boldsymbol{h}$, where $\boldsymbol{W}_r \in \mathbb{R}^{L \times L}$ is a parameter matrix . For the non-linearity σ we use the truncated ReLU function $\sigma(x) = \min(\max(0,x),1)$. The ℓ-th row of $\boldsymbol{W}_0$, $\boldsymbol{W}_1$ and $\boldsymbol{W}_r$, and the ℓ-th entry of $\boldsymbol{b}$ are defined as follows (omitted entries are 0):

1. If $\varphi_\ell(x,y) = a(x,y)$ for a color $a \in \mathscr{C}$, then $(\boldsymbol{W}_0)_{\ell\ell} = 1$.
2. If $\varphi_\ell(x,y) = \neg\varphi_k(x,y)$ then $(\boldsymbol{W}_0)_{\ell k} = -1$, and $b_\ell = 1$.
3. If $\varphi_\ell(x,y) = \varphi_j(x,y) \wedge \varphi_k(x,y)$ then $(\boldsymbol{W}_0)_{\ell j} = 1$, $(\boldsymbol{W}_0)_{\ell k} = 1$ and $b_\ell = -1$.
4. If $\varphi_\ell(x,y) = \exists^{\geq N} z\,(\varphi_k(x,z) \wedge r(z,y))$ then $(\boldsymbol{W}_r)_{\ell k} = 1$ and $b_\ell = -N+1$.
5. If $\varphi_\ell(x,y) = \exists^{\geq N} z\,(\varphi_k(x,z) \wedge \neg r(z,y))$ then $(\boldsymbol{W}_r)_{\ell k} = -1$, $(\boldsymbol{W}_1)_{\ell k} = 1$ and $b_\ell = -N+1$.

The correctness of the construction follows from the same arguments as in the proof of Theorem 4.5. □

5.3. Runtime Analysis

We present the asymptotic time complexity of R-MPNN, C-MPNN, and a labeling-trick-based relation prediction model GraIL [11] in Table 1, taken from Zhu et al. [12]. We also consider 2-RN, the neural architecture from Barceló et al. [9] corresponding to rwl_2

Table 1. Model asymptotic runtime complexities. Observe that the amortized complexity of 2-RN becomes obsolete by the fact that its forward pass being prohibitive in practice (quadratic in $|V|$).

Model	Complexity of a forward pass	Amortized complexity of a query
R-MPNNs	$\mathcal{O}(T(\|E\|d+\|V\|d^2))$	$\mathcal{O}(T(\frac{\|E\|d}{\|R\|\|V\|^2}+\frac{d^2}{\|R\|\|V\|}+d))$
C-MPNNs	$\mathcal{O}(T(\|E\|d+\|V\|d^2))$	$\mathcal{O}(T(\frac{\|E\|d}{\|V\|}+d^2))$
GraIL	$\mathcal{O}(T(\|E\|d^2+\|V\|d^2))$	$\mathcal{O}(T(\|E\|d^2+\|V\|d^2))$
2-RN	$\mathcal{O}(T(\|V\|\|E\|d+\|V\|^2d^2))$	$\mathcal{O}(T(\frac{\|E\|d}{\|R\|\|V\|}+\frac{d^2}{\|R\|}+d))$

to showcase an example of higher-order GNNs. We present both the complexity of a single forward pass of the model as well as the amortized complexity of a single query to better reflect the practical use cases and the advantages stemming from parallelizability. To avoid confusion, we take CompGCN [8] as the example of R-MPNN, and *basic* C-MPNN, since specific architecture choices will impact the asymptotic complexity of the model.

Notation. Given a knowledge graph $G = (V, E, R, c)$, we have that $|V|, |E|, |R|$ represents the size of vertices, edges, and relation types, respectively. d is the hidden dimension of the model, and T is the number of layers in the model.

Runtime of C-MPNNs. Let us note that C-MPNNs subsume NBFNets. Indeed, if we consider C-MPNNs without readout and set the self-transformation to be applied on $\boldsymbol{h}^{(0)}$, we obtain (a slight generalization of) NBFNets. In terms of the runtime, C-MPNNs and NBFNets are comparable: even though the readout component of C-MPNNs incurs a linear overhead, this is dominated by other factors. Thus, as shown in Lemma 2 of Zhu et al. [12], the total complexity for a forward pass is $\mathcal{O}(T(|E|d+|V|d^2))$ to compute $|V|$ queries at the same time, resulting an amortized complexity of $\mathcal{O}(T(\frac{|E|d}{|V|}+d^2))$. See Zhu et al. [12] for detailed discussion and proof.

Comparison with R-MPNNs. As directly carrying out relational message passing in R-MPNN for each triplet is costly, a common way to carry out link prediction task is to first compute all node representations and then use a binary decoder to perform link prediction. This would result in $\mathcal{O}(T(|E|d+|V|d^2))$ for a complete forward pass. Consequently, we obtain $|R||V|^2$ triplets, and since passing through binary decoder has a complexity of $\mathcal{O}(d)$, we have that the amortized complexity for each query is $\mathcal{O}(T(\frac{|E|d}{|R||V|^2}+\frac{d^2}{|R||V|}+d))$. Although the complexity of a forward pass for R-MPNN and C-MPNN are the same, we compute $|R||V|^2$ queries with R-MPNN but only $|V|$ queries with C-MPNN, resulting difference in amortized complexity of a single query. However, as discussed in Section 5, this comes at the cost of expressivity.

Comparison with the architectures using labeling trick. GraIL is an architecture using labeling trick and we focus on this to make the comparison concrete. In terms of runtime, architectures that rely on the labeling trick are typically slower, since they need to label both the source and the target node, as we state in Section 5. This yields worse runtime complexity for these models, and particularly for GraIL[4], with an amortized complexity of a query being the same as the one for a forward pass, that is, $\mathcal{O}(T(|E|d^2+|V|d^2))$.

[4]Comparing to C-MPNN, the complexity for $\textsc{Msg}_r$ is different because GraIL utilizes RGCN as relational message passing model, which needs $\mathcal{O}(d^2)$ for linear transformation in its $\textsc{Msg}_r$.

In C-MPNNs, we only label the source node u, which allows parallel comparison for all queries in the form $q(u,?)$: a single forward pass would compute all hidden representations of these queries. With the labeling trick, $|V|$ forward passes need to be carried out as each time, both source u and target v need to be specified. See Zhu et al. [12] for detailed discussion and proof.

Comparison with higher-order GNNs. Regarding higher-order GNNs, we take 2-RN, the neural architecture from Barceló et al. [9] corresponding to rwl_2. These higher-order models require $\mathcal{O}((|V||E|d + |V|^2d^2))$ in each layer (assuming each message function takes $\mathcal{O}(d)$ as before) to update all pairwise representations in a single forward pass, which is computationally prohibitive in practice. This makes the study of the amortized complexity obselete, but we provide an analysis for the sake of completeness. Similar to R-MPNN, we need an additional query-specific unary decoder for the task of link prediction on knowledge graphs, resulting in $\mathcal{O}(d)$ complexity overhead. The amortized complexity of a single query is thus $\mathcal{O}(T(\frac{|E|d}{|R||V|} + \frac{d^2}{|R|} + d))$.

6. Experimental Evaluation

We experiment on existing benchmarks to answer the following questions:

Q1. Are C-MPNNs empirically strong? More specifically, do C-MPNNs outperform R-MPNNs empirically?
Q2. Does the use of a global readout, or a relational version affect the performance?
Q3. What is the impact of the initialization function on the performance? What happens when the target identifiability property does not hold?

To answer these questions, we evaluate C-MPNNs on a broad range of experiments:

- **Inductive experiments (Q1)**: We evaluate C-MPNNs on inductive link prediction tasks and reported state-of-the-art results.
- **Transductive experiments (Q1)**: We evaluate C-MPNNs on transductive link prediction tasks to showcase strong empirical performances of C-MPNNs compared to R-MPNNs.
- **Evaluating the effect of readout (Q2)**: We evaluate different readout components and observe their empirical performances.
- **Synthetic experiments on global readout (Q2)**: We conduct a synthetic experiment on TRI-SQR to evaluate the power of global readout.
- **Ablation on initialization (Q3)**: We carry out experiment to evaluate the effect of initialization functions.

6.1. Experiments on Inductive Link Prediction (Q1)

Datasets. We use the datasets WN18RR [30] and FB15k-237 [31], for inductive relation prediction tasks, following a standardized train-test split given in four versions [11]. We augment each fact $r(u,v)$ with an inverse fact $r^{-1}(v,u)$. There are no node features for either of the datasets, and the initialization is given by the respective initialization function INIT. This allows all the proposed GNN models to be applied in the inductive setup. The statistics of the datasets are reported in Table 2. All hyperparameter details are reported in Table 3.

Table 2. Dataset statistics for the inductive relation prediction experiments. **#Query*** is the number of queries used in the validation set. In the training set, all triplets are used as queries.

Dataset		#Relation	Train & Validation #Nodes	#Triplet	#Query*	Test #Nodes	#Triplet	#Query
WN18RR	v_1	9	2,746	5,410	630	922	1,618	188
	v_2	10	6,954	15,262	1,838	2,757	4,011	441
	v_3	11	12,078	25,901	3,097	5,084	6,327	605
	v_4	9	3,861	7,940	934	7,084	12,334	1,429
FB15k-237	v_1	180	1,594	4,245	489	1,093	1,993	205
	v_2	200	2,608	9,739	1,166	1,660	4,145	478
	v_3	215	3,668	17,986	2,194	2,501	7,406	865
	v_4	219	4,707	27,203	3,352	3,051	11,714	1,424

Table 3. Hyperparameters for inductive experiments with C-MPNN.

Hyperparameter		WN18RR	FB15k-237
GNN Layer	Depth(T)	6	6
	Hidden Dimension	32	32
Decoder Layer	Depth	2	2
	Hidden Dimension	64	64
Optimization	Optimizer	Adam	Adam
	Learning Rate	5e-3	5e-3
Learning	Batch size	8	8
	#Negative Samples	32	32
	Epoch	20	20
	Adversarial Temperature	1	1

Implementation. All models use 6 layers, each with 32 hidden dimensions. The decoder function parameterizes the probability of a fact $q(u,v)$ as $p(v \mid u,q) = \sigma(f(\boldsymbol{h}_{v|u,q}^{(T)}))$, where σ is the sigmoid function, and f is a 2-layer MLP with 64 hidden dimensions. We adopted layer-normalization [32] and short-cut connection after each aggregation and before applying ReLU. We ran the experiments for 20 epochs on 1 Tesla T4 GPU. with mild modifications to accommodate all architectures studied in this paper. We discard the edges that directly connect query node pairs to prevent overfitting. The best checkpoint for each model instance is selected based on its performance on the validation set. The code for experiments is reported in `https://github.com/HxyScotthuang/CMPNN`.

Evaluation. All of the model variations minimize the negative log-likelihood of positive and negative facts. We follow the *partial completeness assumption* [33] and consider *filtered ranking protocol* [34] by randomly corrupting the head entity or the tail entity to generate 50 negative samples. We report Hits@10, the rate of correctly predicted entities appearing in the top 10 entries for each instance list prediction. We also report averaged results of *five* independent runs for all experiments. We adopt *self-adversarial negative sampling* [35] by sampling negative triples from the following distribution with α as the *adversarial temperature*: $\mathscr{L}(v \mid u,q) = -\log p(v \mid u,q) - \sum_{i=1}^{k} w_{i,\alpha} \log(1 - p(v_i' \mid u_i', q))$

Table 4. Inductive relation prediction results. We use *basic* C-MPNN architecture with $\text{AGG} = \text{sum}$, $\text{MSG} = \text{MSG}_r^1$, and $\text{INIT} = \text{INIT}^2$ with no readout component. All the baselines are taken from the respective works.

Model	**WN18RR**				**FB15k-237**			
	v1	v2	v3	v4	v1	v2	v3	v4
NeuralLP[23]	0.744	0.689	0.462	0.671	0.529	0.589	0.529	0.559
DRUM [24]	0.744	0.689	0.462	0.671	0.529	0.587	0.529	0.559
RuleN [36]	0.809	0.782	0.534	0.716	0.498	0.778	0.877	0.856
GraIL [11]	0.825	0.787	0.584	0.734	0.642	0.818	0.828	0.893
C-MPNN	**0.932**	**0.896**	**0.900**	**0.881**	**0.794**	**0.906**	**0.947**	**0.933**

where k is the number of negative samples for one positive sample and (u_i', q, v_i') is the i-th negative sample. Finally, w_i is the weight for the i-th negative sample, given by $w_{i,\alpha} := \text{Softmax}\left(\frac{\log(1-p(v_i'|u_i',q))}{\alpha}\right)$.

Results. We report inductive link prediction results for different C-MPNN architectures in Table 4, all initialized with INIT^2. Notice that C-MPNN significantly outperforms the existing baselines by a large margin, proven to be state-of-the-art in the task of inductive link prediction.

6.2. Experiments on Transductive Link Prediction (*Q1*)

We further conducted transductive link prediction experiments to empirically validate that C-MPNNs are more expressive than R-MPNNs via the logical characterization given by $\mathsf{rFO}^3_{\text{cnt}}$ and $\mathsf{rFO}^2_{\text{cnt}}$, respectively.

6.2.1. Experiments on knowledge graph completion benchmarks

Datasets. We use two benchmark datasets for transductive link prediction experiments, namely WN18RR [30] and FB15k-237 [31], with the provided standardized train-test split. Similar to the inductive relation prediction experiments, we augment the fact $r(u,v)$ with its inverse fact $r^{-1}(v,u)$. The detailed data statistics are shown in Table 5.

Implementation. For *basic* C-MPNN without readout (denoted as C-MPNN-*basic* in Table 7), all hyper-parameters used are reported in Table 6, and we adopt layer-normalization [32] and short-cut connection after each aggregation and before applying ReLU. We also discard the edges that directly connect query node pairs to prevent over-fitting. For RGCN, we use two layers, each with a hidden dimension of 100. We consider the same basis-decomposition trick with a basis number equal to 30. In addition, we train the model with a learning rate of 0.1 and a dropout rate of 0.2, using Adam optimizer for 10,000 epochs. For CompGCN, we use three layers, each with hidden dimension 200, and adopt *distmult* scoring function as well as element-wise multiplication as a composition function. During the training process, we consider a learning rate of 0.001 and a dropout rate of 0.1, using Adam optimizer for 500 epochs. Additionally, since there are no node features for both of the datasets, we initialize node representations using learnable embeddings with Xavier initialization for RGCN and CompGCN. We take the results of NeuralLP from Yang et al. [23], and the results of DRUM from Sadeghian et al. [24], respectively. The best checkpoint for each model instance is selected based on its performance on the validation set. All experiments are performed on one NVIDIA V100 32GB GPU.

Table 5. Dataset statistics for transductive experiments on WN18RR and FB15k-237.

Dataset	#Nodes	#Relation	#Triplet		
			#Train	#Valid	#Test
WN18RR	40,943	11	86,835	3,034	3,134
FB15k-237	14,541	237	272,115	17,535	20,466

Table 6. Hyperparameters for transductive experiments on FB15k-237 and WN18RR with C-MPNN.

Hyperparameter		WN18RR	FB15k-237
GNN Layer	Depth(T)	6	6
	Hidden Dimension	32	32
Decoder Layer	Depth	2	2
	Hidden Dimension	64	64
Optimization	Optimizer	Adam	Adam
	Learning Rate	5e-3	5e-3
Learning	Batch size	8	8
	#Negative Sample	32	32
	Epoch	20	20
	Adversarial Temperature	1	1

Table 7. Transductive knowledge graph completion task of C-MPNNs and R-MPNNs on WN18RR and FB15k-237. Here, C-MPNN-*basic* refers to *basic* C-MPNN model without readout.

Model class	Architectures	WN18RR			FB15k-237		
		MR	MRR	Hits@10	MR	MRR	Hits@10
R-MPNNs	RGCN	3069	0.367	0.405	210	0.205	0.387
	CompGCN	3590	0.433	0.519	217	0.334	0.514
C-MPNNs	NeuralLP	–	0.435	0.566	–	0.240	0.362
	DRUM	–	0.486	0.586	–	0.343	0.516
	C-MPNN-*basic*	**687**	**0.534**	**0.643**	**121**	**0.400**	**0.583**

Evaluation. We consider *filtered ranking protocol* [34] with 1 negative sample per positive triplet, and report Mean Rank(MR), Mean Reciprocal Rank(MRR), and Hits@10 for each model. We also report averaged results of *five* independent runs for all experiments.

Results. From Table 7, it is evident that models under the class of C-MPNN consistently outperform R-MPNN models across both datasets and all evaluation metrics, with only one exception on FB15k-237 with NeuralLP. This aligns with our theoretical understanding, as C-MPNN models are inherently more expressive than R-MPNNs. In particular, the C-MPNN-*basic* model stands out by achieving the lowest MR and the highest values for both MRR and Hits@10, surpassing all other models by a significant margin, underscoring its efficiency and robustness in transductive knowledge graph completion tasks.

Table 8. Dataset statistics for transductive biomedical knowledge graph completion.

Dataset	#Nodes	#Node Type	#Relation	#Triplet		
				#Train	#Valid	#Test
Hetionet	47,031	11	24	1,800,157	225,020	225,020
ogbl-biokg	93,773	5	51	4,762,677	162,886	162,870

Table 9. Hyperparameters for the transductive experiments on biomedical knowledge graphs with C-MPNN.

Hyperparameter		Hetionet	ogbl-biokg
GNN Layer	Depth(T)	4	6
	Hidden Dimension	32	32
Decoder Layer	Depth	2	2
	Hidden Dimension	32	32
Optimization	Optimizer	Adam	Adam
	Learning Rate	2e-3	2e-4
Learning	Batch size	64	8
	#Negative Sample	32	32
	Epoch	1	1
	Adversarial Temperature	1	0.5

6.2.2. *Experiments on Biomedical Knowledge Graphs (**Q1**)*

To compare R-MPNNs and C-MPNNs on large-scale graphs, we carried out additional transductive knowledge graph completion experiments on biomedical datasets: Hetionet [37] and ogbl-biokg [38].

Datasets. Hetionet [37] is a large biomedical knowledge graph that integrates data from 29 different public databases, representing various biological connections and associations, and ogbl-biokg is a large-scale biomedical knowledge graph dataset, developed as a part of the Open Graph Benchmark (OGB) [38] suite. We have used the provided standardized train-test split for both datasets and similarly augmented every fact $r(u,v)$ with its inverse relation $r^{-1}(u,v)$. We present the detailed dataset statistics in Table 8.

Implementation. We study the *basic* C-MPNN without readout, referred to as C-MPNN in the Table 10, the epoch number is set to 1 due to the datasets being larger and denser, leading to longer execution times for C-MPNN. All hyperparameters used for C-MPNN are reported in Table 9, and we adopt layer-normalization [32] and short-cut connection after each aggregation and before applying ReLU. We also discard the edges that directly connect query node pairs. For RGCN, we consider a batch size of 65536, a learning rate of 0.001, and 100 epochs for both datasets. On Hetionet, we use a hidden dimension size of 200, and a learning rate of 0.001 across 4 layers. On ogbl-biokg, we consider a dimension size of 500, and a dropout rate of 0.2 across 2 layers. For CompGCN on Hetionet, the parameters include a batch size of 65536, 100 epochs, a dimension size of 200, a learning rate of 0.01, and a single layer. We adopt *distmult* scoring function and element-wise multiplication as a composition function. On ogbl-biokg, CompGCN results cannot be reproduced to the best of our effort due to an out-of-memory (OOM)

Table 10. Transductive experiments on biomedical knowledge graphs. We use *basic* C-MPNN architecture with $\text{AGG} = \text{sum}$, $\text{MSG} = \text{MSG}_r^1$, and $\text{INIT} = \text{INIT}^2$ with no readout component. OOM stands for out of memory.

Model	Hetionet			ogbl-biokg		
	MRR	**Hits@1**	**Hits@10**	**MRR**	**Hits@1**	**Hits@10**
RGCN	0.120	0.067	0.228	0.636	0.511	0.884
CompGCN	0.152	0.083	0.292	OOM	OOM	OOM
C-MPNN	**0.479**	**0.394**	**0.649**	**0.790**	**0.718**	**0.927**

error. The best checkpoint for each model instance is selected based on its performance on the validation set. All experiments are performed on one NVIDIA V100 32GB GPU. In addition, since there are no node features for both of the datasets, we initialize node representations using learnable embeddings with Xavier initialization for RGCN and CompGCN.

Evaluation. We consider *filtered ranking protocol* [34], but restrict our ranking to entities of the same type. With each positive triplet, we use 32 number of negative samples and report the averaged results of Mean Reciprocal Rank(MRR), Hits@1, and Hits@10 over *five* independent runs for each model.

Results. From Table 10, it is evident that C-MPNN outperforms R-MPNN on both datasets by a large margin, despite the challenges posed by the large and dense nature of biomedical knowledge graphs. These results are reassuring as they have further consolidated our theory, showing that the expressivity gain of C-MPNNs compared to R-MPNNs has a significant impact on real-world biomedical datasets.

6.3. Empirically Evaluating the Effect of Readout (Q2)

To understand the effect of readout, we experiment with C-MPNNs using INIT^2, PNA, MSG_r^1, and $t = t$. We consider three architectures: (i) no readout component, (ii) global readout component (as defined earlier), and finally (iii) relation-specific readout. The idea behind the relation-specific readout is natural: instead of summing over all node representations, we sum over the features of nodes w which have an incoming q-edge ($w \in V_q^+$) or an outgoing q-edge ($w \in V_q^-$), where q is the query relation, as:

$$\text{READ}(\{\{\boldsymbol{h}_{w|u,q}^{(t)} \mid w \in V_q^+\}\}, \{\{\boldsymbol{h}_{w|u,q}^{(t)} \mid w \in V_q^-\}\}) = \mathbf{W}_1^{(t)} \sum_{w \in V_q^+} \boldsymbol{h}_{w|u,q}^{(t)} + \mathbf{W}_2^{(t)} \sum_{w \in V_q^-} \boldsymbol{h}_{w|u,q}^{(t)}.$$

Table 11. Results for inductive relation prediction on WN18RR and FB15k-237 using *no readout, global readout* and *relation-specific readout, respectively*. We use C-MPNN architecture with $\text{AGG} = \text{PNA}$, $\text{MSG} = \text{MSG}_r^1$, and $\text{INIT} = \text{INIT}^2$.

Model architectures	**WN18RR**				**FB15k-237**			
READ	**v1**	**v2**	**v3**	**v4**	**v1**	**v2**	**v3**	**v4**
no readout	0.941	**0.895**	**0.904**	**0.886**	0.804	0.949	0.945	0.954
global readout	**0.946**	0.890	0.881	0.872	0.799	0.897	0.942	0.864
relation-specific	0.932	0.885	0.882	0.874	**0.835**	**0.959**	**0.953**	**0.960**

We report all results in Table 11. First, we observe that the addition of global readout does not lead to significant differences on WN18RR, but it degrades the model performance on FB15k-237 in two splits (v2 and v4). We attribute this to having more relation types in FB15k-237, so a readout over all nodes does not necessarily inform us about a relation-specific prediction. This is the motivation behind the relation-specific readout: we observe that it leads to significant improvements compared to using no readout (or a global readout) over all splits, leading to state-of-the-art results. In contrast, relation-specific readout does not yield improvements on the relationally sparse WN18RR. These findings suggest that the global information can be very useful in practice, assuming the graph is rich in relation types.

6.4. Evaluating the Power of Global Readout on a Synthetic Dataset (Q2)

We constructed a synthetic experiment to showcase the power of global readout: architectures without global readout cannot exceed random performance, while those using a global readout can solve the synthetic link prediction task.

Dataset. We proposed a synthetic dataset TRI-SQR, which consists of multiple pairs of knowledge graphs in form (G_1, G_2) s.t. $G_1 = (V_1, E_1, R, c_1)$, $G_2 = (V_2, E_2, R, c_2)$ where $R = \{r_0, r_1, r_2\}$. For each pair, we constructed as follows:

1. Generate an Erdős–Rényi graph G_{init} with 5 nodes and a random probability p. We randomly select one of the nodes as the source node u.
2. G_1 is constructed by disjoint union G_{init} with two triangles, one with edges relation of r_1, and the other with r_2. The target query is $r_3(u,v)$ for all v in a triangle with an edge relation of r_1.
3. Similarly, G_2 is constructed by disjoint union another copy of G_{init} with two squares, one with edges relation of r_1, and the other with r_2. The target query is $r_3(u,v)$ for all v in a square with an edge relation of r_2.

One example of such a pair can be shown in Figure 2. We generate 100 graph pairs and assign 70 pairs as the training set and the remaining 30 pairs as the testing set (140 training graphs and 60 testing graphs). In total, there are 490 training triplets and 210 testing triplets.

Objective. For all node $v \notin G_{\text{init}}$, we want a higher score for all the links $r_0(u,v)$ if either v is in a triangle consists of r_1 relation or v is in a square consists of r_2 relation, and a lower score otherwise. For negative sampling, we choose counterpart triplets for each graph, that is, we take $r_0(u,v)$ for all v in a triangle with an edge relation of r_2 in G_1 and in a square with an edge relation of r_1 in G_2.

Model architectures. To evaluate the effect of global readout, we consider two model architectures. Specifically, we consider C-MPNNs with $\text{INIT} = \text{INIT}^2$, $\text{AGG} = \text{sum}$, $\text{MSG} = \text{MSG}_r^2$, and $t = t$ without sum global readout:

$$\boldsymbol{h}_{v|u,q}^{(0)} = \mathbb{1}_{u=v} * \mathbf{z}_q,$$

$$\boldsymbol{h}_{v|u,q}^{(t+1)} = \sigma\Big(\mathbf{W}_0^{(t)}\big(\mathbf{h}_{v|u,q}^{(t)} + \sum_{r\in R}\sum_{w\in\mathcal{N}_r(v)} \text{MSG}_r^2(\mathbf{h}_{w|u,q}^{(t)}, \mathbf{z}_q)\big)\Big).$$

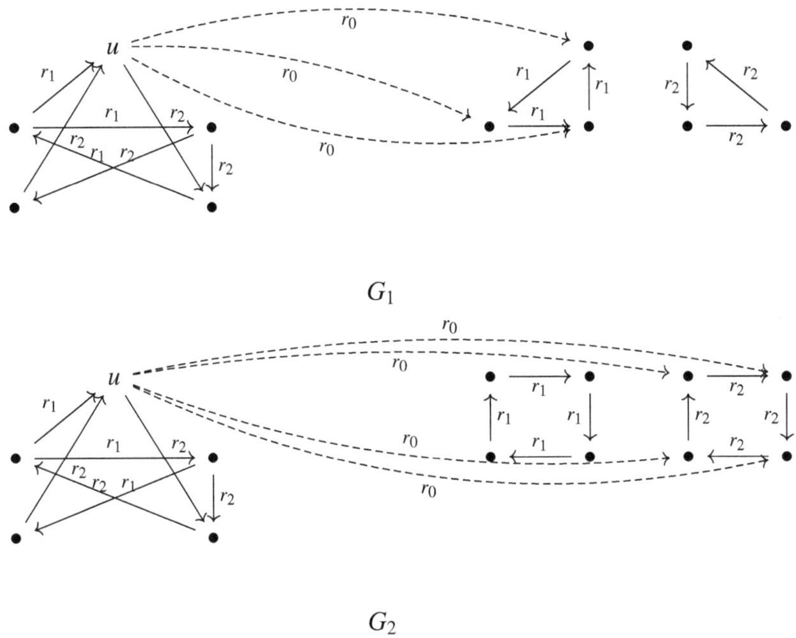

Figure 2. Construction of graph pair in TRI-SQR for global readout.

Furthermore, we consider the same C-MPNN architecture with sum global readout:

$$\boldsymbol{h}_{v|u,q}^{(0)} = \mathbb{1}_{u=v} * \mathbf{z}_q,$$

$$\boldsymbol{h}_{v|u,q}^{(t+1)} = \sigma\Big(\mathbf{W}_0^{(t)}\big(\mathbf{h}_{v|u,q}^{(t)} + \sum_{r\in R}\sum_{w\in\mathcal{N}_r(v)} \textsc{Msg}_r^2(\mathbf{h}_{w|u,q}^{(t)}, \mathbf{z}_q)\big) + \mathbf{W}_1^{(t)} \sum_{w\in V} \boldsymbol{h}_{w|u,q}^{(t)}\Big).$$

Design. We claim that C-MPNNs with sum readout can correctly predict all testing triplets, whereas C-MPNNs without sum readout will fail to learn this pattern and achieve 50% as random guessing. TRI-SQR is designed in such a way that any R-MPNN model assigns identical node representations to nodes in triangles and squares with the same relation type. Consequently, any C-MPNN model without global readout cannot determine which graph between G_1 and G_2 in the graph pair is being predicted, making it challenging to learn the conditional representation $\boldsymbol{h}_{u|v,q}$. However, we anticipate that a C-MPNN model with sum readout can differentiate between G_1 and G_2 in each pair, as it can access global information such as the total number of nodes in the graph. This allows it to accurately identify the graph being predicted in the graph pair, even when the representations of the triangle and square with the same relation are identical.

Experimental details. We configure each model variant with four layers and 32 hidden dimensions per layer. We set a learning rate of 1e-4 for both models and train them for 500 epochs. Empirically, we find that C-MPNN with global sum readout achieves 100% accuracy, while C-MPNN without global sum readout reaches 50% accuracy as random guesses, which is consistent with our theoretical expectations.

Table 12. Inductive relation prediction of C-MPNN using $\text{AGG} = \text{sum}$, $\text{MSG}_r = \text{MSG}_r^1$, $t = t$ and different initialization methods.

Initialization	**WN18RR**				**FB15k-237**			
$\text{INIT}(u,v,q)$	**v1**	**v2**	**v3**	**v4**	**v1**	**v2**	**v3**	**v4**
$\text{INIT}^0(u,v,q)$	0.615	0.715	0.811	0.654	0.777	0.903	0.894	0.910
$\text{INIT}^1(u,v,q)$	0.932	0.894	**0.902**	**0.883**	**0.809**	**0.927**	0.944	0.911
$\text{INIT}^2(u,v,q)$	0.932	**0.896**	0.900	0.881	0.794	0.906	**0.947**	0.933
$\text{INIT}^3(u,v,q)$	**0.934**	0.890	0.894	0.877	0.804	0.924	0.941	**0.944**

6.5. Experiments for Evaluating the Effect of Initialization Functions (Q3)

We argued that the initialization function $\text{INIT}(u,v,q)$ needs to satisfy the property of *target node distinguishability* to compute binary invariants. To validate the impact of different initialization regimes, we conduct a further experiment which is reported in Table 12, with the same experiment settings as in Section 6. In addition to the initialization functions $\text{INIT}^1, \text{INIT}^2, \text{INIT}^3$ defined in Section 5.1, we also experiment with a simple function INIT^0 which assigns $\mathbf{0}$ to all nodes.

Results. As expected, using INIT^0 initialization, results in a very sharp decrease in model performance in WN18RR, but less so in FB15k-237. Intuitively, the model suffers more in WN18RR since there are much fewer relations, and it is harder to distinguish node pairs without an initialization designed to achieve this. Perhaps one of the simplest functions satisfying target node distinguishability criteria is $\text{INIT}^1 = \mathbb{1}_{u=v} * \mathbf{1}$, which pays no respect to the target query relation. Empirically, INIT^1 achieves strong results, showing that even the simplest function ensuring this property could boost the model performance. Interestingly, the performance of models using INIT^1 match or exceed models using INIT^2, even though the latter additionally has a relation-specific learnable query vector. Note, however, that this shall not undermine the role of the learnable query relation: integrating the learnable query vector either in the initialization function *or* in the message computation function seems to suffice.

Random initialization. The idea of random node initialization is known to lead to more expressive models [39, 40]. Inspired by this, we can incorporate varying degrees of randomization to the initialization, satisfying the target node distinguishability property in expectation. The key advantage is that the resulting models are still inductive and achieve a nontrivial expressiveness gain over alternatives. In this case, the models with INIT^3 perform closer to the models with INIT^2, but we do not see a particular advantage on these benchmarks.

7. Outlook and Limitations

We studied a broad general class of GNNs designed for link prediction over knowledge graphs with a focus on formally characterizing their expressive power. Our study shows that recent state-of-the-art models are at a 'sweet spot': while they compute binary invariants, they do so through some local variations of higher-dimensional WL tests. This is precisely characterized within our framework. To capture global properties, we propose readout components and show that their relational variant is useful on datasets with many relation types. This study paints a more complete picture for our overall understanding of existing models and informs future work on possible directions.

In terms of limitations, it is important to note that the presented approach has certain restrictions. For instance, it is limited to binary tasks, such as link prediction. Thus, this approach does not directly extend to higher arity tasks, e.g., link prediction on relational hypergraphs [41] or predicting the existence of substructures of size k in a knowledge graph. When considering local or conditional variations of the k-WL algorithm, computational demands can become a significant challenge. Further research is needed to explore potential optimizations for higher-order MPNNs that can enhance their performance while preserving their expressive power.

Acknowledgement

The authors would like to acknowledge the use of the University of Oxford Advanced Research Computing (ARC)[5] facility in carrying out this work. We would also like to thank Google Cloud for kindly providing computational resources. Barceló is funded by ANID–Millennium Science Initiative Program - CodeICN17002. Romero is funded by Fondecyt grant 11200956. Barceló and Romero are funded by the National Center for Artificial Intelligence CENIA FB210017, BasalANID.

References

[1] Franco Scarselli, Marco Gori, Ah Chung Tsoi, Markus Hagenbuchner, and Gabriele Monfardini. The graph neural network model. *IEEE Transactions on Neural Networks*, 2009.

[2] Marco Gori, Gabriele Monfardini, and Franco Scarselli. A new model for learning in graph domains. In *IJCNN*, 2005.

[3] Justin Gilmer, Samuel S. Schoenholz, Patrick F. Riley, Oriol Vinyals, and George E. Dahl. Neural message passing for quantum chemistry. In *ICML*, 2017.

[4] Keyulu Xu, Weihua Hu, Jure Leskovec, and Stefanie Jegelka. How powerful are graph neural networks? In *ICLR*, 2019.

[5] Christopher Morris, Martin Ritzert, Matthias Fey, William L. Hamilton, Jan Eric Lenssen, Gaurav Rattan, and Martin Grohe. Weisfeiler and Leman go neural: Higher-order graph neural networks. In *AAAI*, 2019.

[6] Xingyue Huang, Miguel Romero Orth, İsmail İlkan Ceylan, and Pablo Barceló. A theory of link prediction via relational weisfeiler-leman on knowledge graphs. In *Thirty-seventh Conference on Neural Information Processing Systems*, 2023.

[7] Michael Sejr Schlichtkrull, Thomas N. Kipf, Peter Bloem, Rianne van den Berg, Ivan Titov, and Max Welling. Modeling relational data with graph convolutional networks. In *ESWC*, 2018.

[8] Shikhar Vashishth, Soumya Sanyal, Vikram Nitin, and Partha Talukdar. Composition-based multi-relational graph convolutional networks. In *ICLR*, 2020.

[5]http://dx.doi.org/10.5281/zenodo.22558

[9] Pablo Barceló, Mikhail Galkin, Christopher Morris, and Miguel Romero. Weisfeiler and leman go relational. In *LoG*, 2022.

[10] Muhan Zhang, Pan Li, Yinglong Xia, Kai Wang, and Long Jin. Labeling trick: A theory of using graph neural networks for multi-node representation learning. In *NeurIPS*, 2021.

[11] Komal K. Teru, Etienne G. Denis, and William L. Hamilton. Inductive relation prediction by subgraph reasoning. In *ICML*, 2020.

[12] Zhaocheng Zhu, Zuobai Zhang, Louis-Pascal Xhonneux, and Jian Tang. Neural bellman-ford networks: A general graph neural network framework for link prediction. In *NeurIPS*, 2021.

[13] Hongwei Wang, Hongyu Ren, and Jure Leskovec. Relational message passing for knowledge graph completion. In *KDD*, 2021.

[14] Lecheng Kong, Yixin Chen, and Muhan Zhang. Geodesic graph neural network for efficient graph representation learning. In *NeurIPS*, 2022.

[15] Maarten de Rijke. A note on Graded Modal Logic. In *Stud Logica*, 2000.

[16] Carsten Lutz, Ulrike Sattler, and Frank Wolter. Modal logic and the two-variable fragment. In *CSL*, 2001.

[17] Thomas Kipf and Max Welling. Semi-supervised classification with graph convolutional networks. In *ICLR*, 2017.

[18] Donghan Yu, Yiming Yang, Ruohong Zhang, and Yuexin Wu. Generalized multi-relational graph convolution network. In *ICML Workshop on Graph Representation Learning and Beyond*, 2020.

[19] Muhan Zhang and Yixin Chen. Link prediction based on graph neural networks. In *NeurIPS*, 2018.

[20] Bryan Perozzi, Rami Al-Rfou, and Steven Skiena. Deepwalk: online learning of social representations. In *KDD*, 2014.

[21] Aditya Grover and Jure Leskovec. Node2vec: Scalable feature learning for networks. In *KDD*, 2016.

[22] Jiaxuan You, Jonathan M. Gomes-Selman, Rex Ying, and Jure Leskovec. Identity-aware graph neural networks. In *AAAI*, 2021.

[23] Fan Yang, Zhilin Yang, and William W Cohen. Differentiable learning of logical rules for knowledge base reasoning. In *NeurIPS*, 2017.

[24] Ali Sadeghian, Mohammadreza Armandpour, Patrick Ding, and Daisy Zhe Wang. Drum: End-to-end differentiable rule mining on knowledge graphs. In *NIPS*, 2019.

[25] Pablo Barceló, Egor V. Kostylev, Mikaël Monet, Jorge Pérez, Juan L. Reutter, and Juan Pablo Silva. The logical expressiveness of graph neural networks. In *ICLR*, 2020.

[26] Martin Grohe. The logic of graph neural networks. In *LICS*, 2021.

[27] Peter W. Battaglia, Razvan Pascanu, Matthew Lai, Danilo Jimenez Rezende, and Koray Kavukcuoglu. Interaction networks for learning about objects, relations and physics. In *NIPS*, 2016.

[28] Martin Otto. Graded modal logic and counting bisimulation. In *arXiv*, 2019.

[29] Gabriele Corso, Luca Cavalleri, Dominique Beaini, Pietro Liò, and Petar Veličković. Principal neighbourhood aggregation for graph nets. In *NeurIPS*, 2020.

[30] Kristina Toutanova and Danqi Chen. Observed versus latent features for knowledge base and text inference. In *CVSC*, 2015.

[31] Tim Dettmers, Minervini Pasquale, Stenetorp Pontus, and Sebastian Riedel. Convolutional 2D knowledge graph embeddings. In *AAAI*, 2018.

[32] Lei Jimmy Ba, Jamie Ryan Kiros, and Geoffrey E. Hinton. Layer normalization. In *CoRR*, 2016.

[33] Luis Antonio Galárraga, Christina Teflioudi, Katja Hose, and Fabian Suchanek. AMIE: Association rule mining under incomplete evidence in ontological knowledge bases. In *WWW*, 2013.

[34] Antoine Bordes, Nicolas Usunier, Alberto Garcia-Duran, Jason Weston, and Oksana Yakhnenko. Translating embeddings for modeling multi-relational data. In *NIPS*, 2013.

[35] Zhiqing Sun, Zhi-Hong Deng, Jian-Yun Nie, and Jian Tang. Rotate: Knowledge graph embedding by relational rotation in complex space. In *ICLR*, 2019.

[36] Christian Meilicke, Manuel Fink, Yanjie Wang, Daniel Ruffinelli, Rainer Gemulla, and Heiner Stuckenschmidt. Fine-grained evaluation of rule- and embedding-based systems for knowledge graph completion. In *IWSW*, 2018.

[37] Daniel Scott Himmelstein, Antoine Lizee, Christine Hessler, Leo Brueggeman, Sabrina L Chen, Dexter Hadley, Ari Green, Pouya Khankhanian, and Sergio E Baranzini. Systematic integration of biomedical knowledge prioritizes drugs for repurposing. In *eLife*, 2017.

[38] Weihua Hu, Matthias Fey, Marinka Zitnik, Yuxiao Dong, Hongyu Ren, Bowen Liu, Michele Catasta, and Jure Leskovec. Open graph benchmark: Datasets for machine learning on graphs. In *NeurIPS*, 2020.

[39] Ryoma Sato, Makoto Yamada, and Hisashi Kashima. Random features strengthen graph neural networks. In *SDM*, 2021.

[40] Ralph Abboud, İsmail İlkan Ceylan, Martin Grohe, and Thomas Lukasiewicz. The surprising power of graph neural networks with random node initialization. In *IJCAI*, 2021.

[41] Xingyue Huang, Miguel Romero Orth, Pablo Barceló, Michael M. Bronstein, and İsmail İlkan Ceylan. Link prediction with relational hypergraphs. In *arXiv*, 2024.

Handbook on Neurosymbolic AI and Knowledge Graphs
P. Hitzler et al. (Eds.)
IOS Press, 2025

doi:10.3233/FAIA250202

Few-Shot Learning on Graphs

Chuxu ZHANG [a], Kaize DING [b] and Jundong LI [c]
[a] *University of Connecticut, Storrs, Connecticut, USA*
[b] *Northwestern University, Evanston, Illinois, USA*
[c] *University of Virginia, Charlottesville, Virginia, USA*
ORCiD ID: Chuxu Zhang https://orcid.org/0000-0002-8349-7926, Kaize Ding https://orcid.org/0000-0001-6684-6752, Jundong Li https://orcid.org/0000-0002-1878-817X

Abstract. Graph representation learning has garnered significant attention due to its outstanding performance across numerous real-world applications, such as social network analysis, bioinformatics, and recommendation systems. However, supervised graph representation learning models often struggle with label sparsity, as data labeling is time-consuming and resource-intensive. To address this, few-shot learning on graphs (FSLG) has been proposed, combining the strengths of graph representation learning and few-shot learning to mitigate performance issues caused by limited annotated data. This chapter comprehensively presents the body of work in FSLG. It begins by introducing the challenges and foundational concepts of FSLG. The chapter categorizes and summarizes existing FSLG research into three major graph mining tasks at different granularity levels: node, edge, and graph. Node-level tasks involve predicting labels for individual nodes, edge-level tasks focus on predicting relationships between nodes, and graph-level tasks involve predicting properties of entire graphs. This organization provides a clear overview of various methodologies and applications in FSLG. Finally, the chapter discusses potential future research directions in FSLG, which aims to inspire further investigation and innovation in FSLG, advancing its development and application to create more effective AI solutions.

Keywords. Graph Representation Learning, Graph Neural Networks, Few-Shot Learning, Knowledge Graph

1. Introduction

Many real-world systems can be effectively modeled as knowledge graphs, where nodes represent various entities and edges symbolize the relationships connecting these entities. Additionally, both nodes and edges can possess attributes that provide further information about their characteristics and properties. Traditional graph mining and learning algorithms often require a combination of domain understanding and exploratory search during the feature engineering process for a specific task. This approach necessitates a deep understanding of the domain to identify relevant features, along with an iterative process of exploration and refinement to optimize the feature set for the task at hand.

To address these challenges, graph representation learning (GRL) techniques have been developed. These techniques, particularly graph neural networks (GNNs), aim to automatically generate graph representations for various downstream applications across diverse domains. GRL methods eliminate the need for manual feature engineering by learning to represent nodes, edges, and subgraphs in a way that captures their structural and attribute information, which is essential for various tasks. These methods have been applied successfully in multiple domains, demonstrating their versatility and efficacy. In social networks, for instance, techniques like DeepWalk [1], node2vec [2], and Graph Convolutional Networks (GCNs) [3] have been used to predict user behavior, identify communities, and detect anomalies. In bioinformatics, GNNs have been employed to predict protein functions, model molecular interactions, and classify biological sequences, as seen in studies likes [4,5]. Similarly, in recommender systems, GRL techniques have enhanced recommendation accuracy by modeling user-item interactions more effectively, as demonstrated by [6,7].

Developing an effective GRL model for a specific downstream task often requires a substantial amount of annotated samples. However, in real-world scenarios, obtaining labeled data is usually challenging due to the high costs associated with data labeling [8]. For instance, testing molecular properties for therapeutic activity incurs significant expenses related to human labor and experimental resources [9]. Similarly, recommender systems encounter the cold-start problem when new users or items enter the system, making it difficult to gather sufficient labeled data for accurate recommendations [10]. These challenges highlight the need for a new GRL paradigm capable of effectively learning graph representations for various graph mining tasks despite the constraint of limited labeled data. Fortunately, few-shot learning (FSL) [11] has emerged as a solution to reduce the reliance on labeled data and to learn effective data representations. FSL has shown promising results across different domains, such as computer vision, natural language processing, and robotics, by using only a small number of labeled examples. In computer vision, techniques like matching networks and prototypical networks have enabled models to classify images with minimal labeled data [12,13]. In natural language processing, FSL approaches have been used to train models for text classification and sentiment analysis with few annotated examples [14,15]. In robotics, FSL has facilitated the learning of new tasks with limited demonstrations, enabling robots to adapt quickly to new environments and tasks [16,17].

Therefore, few-shot learning on graphs (FSLG), which combines the advantages of graph representation learning (GRL) and few-shot learning (FSL), has emerged as a promising research topic. This approach has garnered increasing attention from the AI community due to its potential to address the challenges posed by limited labeled data in graph mining tasks. Consequently, numerous FSLG studies spanning a variety of methods and applications have been conducted in recent years. This chapter provides a comprehensive and systematic review of FSLG. Figure 1 illustrates the framework of this chapter. Specifically, the chapter begins by analyzing the key challenges inherent in FSLG. Understanding these challenges is crucial for advancing the field and developing effective FSLG models. The chapter then delves into the foundational aspects of FSLG, which combine two collaborative machine learning techniques: GRL and FSL. By integrating these techniques, FSLG aims to improve the performance of graph-based models in scenarios with limited annotated data. Following this, the chapter introduces three typical FSLG problems to set the stage for further discussion: node-level FSL, edge-level FSL, and graph-level FSL. This categorization helps to systematically organize the existing body of FSLG research. Next, the chapter summarizes existing FSLG methods and applications, categorizing them into three parts corresponding to the three typical

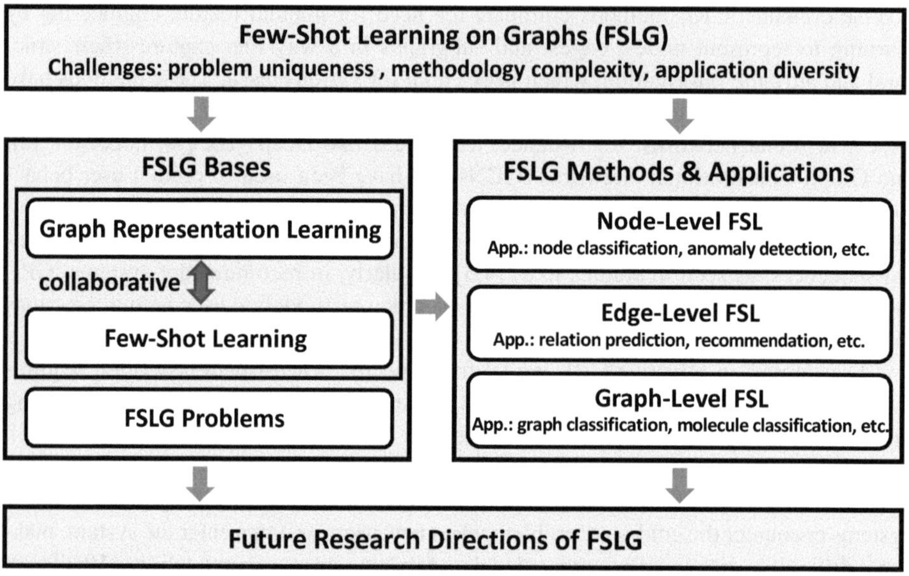

Figure 1. The framework of this chapter.

graph mining tasks. For each part, two major lines of work — metric-based methods and optimization-based methods — are explored. Related applications in each category are further discussed, highlighting the practical implications of FSLG in various domains. Additionally, the chapter provides summary tables that list representative FSLG work for each part, offering a clear overview of the field. These tables serve as a valuable reference for researchers and practitioners, enabling them to quickly identify key studies and methodologies in FSLG. Finally, the chapter discusses open problems and pressing issues in FSLG, highlighting future research directions. By providing a thorough understanding of the current state of FSLG research, its applications, and its ahead challenges, this chapter aims to serve as a comprehensive guide for readers. It seeks to inspire further investigation and innovation in the field of FSLG, ultimately contributing to the development of more effective and impactful AI solutions for graph-based tasks.

2. FSLG Challenges and Bases

FSLG, as a new and promising research topic within the AI community, presents several significant challenges that researchers are actively addressing. These challenges are crucial to understanding the complexity and potential of FSLG in various applications.

- **Unique Challenges of FSLG.** Unlike traditional graph representation learning (GRL) problems, FSLG encounters distinct hurdles primarily due to limited labeled data. Unlike images or text, graphs inhabit non-Euclidean spaces characterized by complex structures such as irregular connectivity, varying node degrees, and heterogeneous node types. These complexities make it challenging to apply conventional machine learning methods directly to graph data. Moreover, in few-shot learning scenarios, FSLG models must generalize from limited labeled examples to new, unseen tasks. This task is particularly complex in graph contexts where models need to learn not only the representations of individual nodes or subgraphs but also understand the intricate relationships and dependencies among them. The diverse structural characteristics of graphs across different tasks further necessitate adaptive learning algorithms capable of effectively transferring knowledge.

- **Methodological Complexity.** Before FSLG emerged, research was primarily focused separately on GRL, aimed at capturing and modeling complex graph structures, and FSL, designed to generalize from sparse labeled examples to new tasks. Integrating these methodologies into FSLG represents a significant advancement but introduces complexities due to the unique features of graph data and the specific requirements of few-shot learning tasks. Successfully merging GRL and FSL requires innovative approaches that can effectively navigate the complexities of graph data while harnessing the adaptability of few-shot learning.
- **Diverse Applications of Graph Mining.** Graph mining tasks encompass a wide range of analyses, including node-level, edge-level, and graph-level tasks, each presenting unique challenges that necessitate tailored approaches within FSLG. These tasks demand models capable of adapting to diverse data structures, handling scenarios with sparse labeled data, and meeting specific domain-specific requirements effectively. Developing customized FSLG methods that address these diverse complexities and application domains requires a deep understanding of graph structures and the nuanced demands of various real-world applications. Effective FSLG methods leverage advanced graph representation learning techniques and integrate robust few-shot learning strategies to generalize across different graph mining tasks and adapt seamlessly to new challenges within specific domains.

In summary, while FSLG holds promise for advancing AI applications across various domains, addressing its unique challenges requires interdisciplinary efforts and innovative methodologies to fully exploit its capabilities in complex graph-based learning scenarios. Section 3 presents FSLG methods and applications designed to address the above key challenges. The following of this section introduces foundational FSLG bases that include GRL and FSL, collaboratively used in FSLG. Additionally, three core FSLG problems that share common settings and objectives are outlined, emphasizing their applicability across various domains and tasks.

2.1. Graph Representation Learning

Graph representation learning (GRL) [18] aims to automatically generate meaningful vector representations for nodes, edges, or entire graphs, facilitating a wide range of downstream graph mining applications. The field of GRL encompasses several approaches that can be categorized into three primary categories: (1) **Network Embedding Models.** These models focus on capturing graph structure information by preserving the proximities among contextual nodes. Examples include DeepWalk [1], Node2Vec [2], and MetaPath2Vec [19], which employ techniques to embed nodes based on their network neighborhood. (2) **Graph Neural Networks (GNNs).** GNNs learn node embeddings by iteratively aggregating feature information from neighboring nodes. They update each node's representation based on the features of its neighbors, enabling them to capture complex relationships and dependencies within graphs. Notable models include GraphSAGE [20], GCN [3], GAT [21], and Heterogeneous GNNs (HetGNN) [22]. (3) **Knowledge Graph Embedding Methods.** These methods treat knowledge graphs as collections of fact triplets (entities and relations) and learn embeddings for both nodes and edges (entities and relations) by modeling the acceptability scores of each triplet. Examples include TransE [23], ConvE [24], and models based on tensor factorization and neural network architectures [25].

GNNs, as the current state-of-the-art in GRL, are most commonly employed to construct the GRL backbone of a FSLG method. Specifically, a graph can be represented as $G = (V, E, X)$, where V is the set of nodes, and $E \subseteq V \times V$ is the set of edges connecting pairs of nodes. The set X includes the attributes associated with both nodes and edges, providing additional information that characterizes the graph's elements and their relationships. GNNs learn node embedding through the message-passing framework:

$$h_v^{(l+1)} = \mathrm{COM}\left(h_v^{(l)}, \left[\mathrm{AGG}\left(\left\{h_u^{(l)} \mid \forall u \in N(v)\right\}\right)\right]\right), \tag{1}$$

where $h_v^{(l)}$ denotes the embedding of node v at the l-th layer of the GNN; $N(v)$ represents the set of neighbors of node v; $\mathrm{AGG}(\cdot)$ and $\mathrm{COM}(\cdot)$ are the neighbor aggregation and combination functions, respectively; and $h_v^{(0)}$ is initialized using the node attribute X_v. Additionally, the embedding for the entire graph can be computed as follows:

$$h_G^{(l)} = \mathrm{READOUT}\left\{h_v^{(l)} \mid \forall v \in V\right\}, \tag{2}$$

where the READOUT function can be a simple permutation-invariant function such as summation or a more sophisticated graph-level pooling function [26].

2.2. Few-Shot Learning

Few-shot learning (FSL) [11] aims to learn generalized experiences from existing tasks to establish transferable prior knowledge for new tasks with limited labeled data. It typically adopts a meta-learning framework [27] which performs episodic learning to train and optimize the model. Specifically, given a set of tasks T and their associated data, in the meta-training phase, the objective is to learn parameters θ^* that can effectively generalize across all tasks in T:

$$\theta^* = \arg\min_{\theta} \sum_{T_i \sim p(T)} \mathscr{L}\left(D_{T_i}, \theta\right), \tag{3}$$

where $p(T)$ represents the task distribution, D_{T_i} denotes the data for task T_i, and $\mathscr{L}$ denotes the loss function used for a downstream application. During the meta-testing phase, θ^* serves as the initialized parameters (meta-knowledge) that are quickly adapted to a new task T_j:

$$\theta^{**} = \mathscr{L}\left(D_{T_j}, \theta^*\right). \tag{4}$$

Note that D_{T_j} only contains limited labeled data. Notable FSL methods used in FSLG models generally fall into two categories: (1) **Metric-based Methods** [12,13,28]. These methods learn task-specific similarity metrics between query data and support set data. They aim to find embeddings or prototypes that facilitate efficient inference for new tasks by measuring the similarity of new examples to prototypes. (2) **Optimization-based Methods** [29,16,30]. These methods focus on learning well-initialized base learners that can quickly adapt to new tasks through gradient-based computation. They involve training meta-learners that provide a good starting point for model parameters, allowing rapid adaptation to new tasks with limited labeled data.

2.3. FSLG Problems

Different FSLG problems share a common setting in the realm of FSL. In specific, let C represent the entire set of classes in the dataset. This set can be divided into two categories: base classes set C_{base} for training data and the novel classes set C_{novel} for testing data, where $C = C_{base} \cup C_{novel}$ and $C_{base} \cap C_{novel} = \emptyset$. Typically, the number of labels is abundant in C_{base} but scarce in C_{novel}. Here, we introduce three typical FSLG problems corresponding to three distinct graph mining tasks.

Problem 1. ***Few-Shot Node Classification.*** *Given a graph, the objective is to develop a machine learning model that, after being trained on labeled nodes in C_{base}, can accurately predict labels for nodes in C_{novel} using only a limited number of labeled nodes from the support set.*

Problem 2. ***Few-Shot Relation Prediction.*** *Given a graph, the problem is to develop a machine learning model that, after being trained on node pairs representing relations in C_{base}, can accurately predict unknown node pairs for relations in C_{novel} using only a limited number of known node pairs from the support set.*

Problem 3. ***Few-Shot Graph Classification.*** *Given a set of graphs, the target is to develop a machine learning model that, after being trained on labeled graphs in C_{base}, can accurately predict labels for graphs in C_{novel} using only a limited number of labeled graphs from the support set.*

The FSL setting is applied to various FSLG problems by defining the meaning of a class. Specifically, each class corresponds to a node label in the node classification problem, a relation type in the relation prediction problem, and a graph label in the graph classification problem. If the support set contains exactly K nodes for each of N classes from C_{novel} and the query set is sampled from these N classes, the problem is referred to as an N-way K-shot problem. This approach is highly versatile and extends beyond these three typical problems to include other FSLG challenges, such as few-shot anomaly detection, where the goal is to identify unusual patterns or outliers in graphs, and few-shot recommendation on graphs, which aims to make personalized recommendations with limited interaction data. These diverse applications highlight the adaptability and wide-reaching potential of FSLG methods in addressing various graph-based tasks with minimal labeled data.

3. FSLG Methods and Applications

In general, FSLG combines the strengths of GRL (as detailed in Section 2.1) and FSL (as detailed in Section 2.2), for a wide range of applications. This section aims to comprehensively review the current methods and applications of FSLG by systematically categorizing them into three main parts, corresponding to the three problem areas discussed in Section 2.3: node-level FSL, edge-level FSL, and graph-level FSL. Most methods within FSLG adopt two typical FSL techniques: metric-based methods, which focus on learning a distance metric or prototype of each class, and optimization-based methods, which emphasize learning an optimal generalized model with limited data. Accordingly, the methods in each part are further summarized into two groups, depending on which FSL technique they rely on. This classification is followed by an in-depth discussion of related applications, highlighting how these methods are utilized in various practical scenarios. To provide a more detailed overview, each subsection concludes with a list of representative FSLG studies. This list includes key works that exemplify the approaches and advancements within the respective categories, offering readers a clear understanding of the state-of-the-art in FSLG.

3.1. Node-level FSL

Node is the fundamental unit from which graphs are constructed. Node-level learning not only facilitates a variety of node-based applications, such as node classification and anomaly detection, but also lays the groundwork for more complex edge-level and graph-level applications. However, collecting node labels in real-world scenarios often presents significant challenges. For instance, obtaining functional labels for proteins within the interactome (i.e., the protein-protein network) is a time-consuming and labor-intensive task, even for experienced experts [31]. Similarly, a substantial number of research venues (labels) in the DBLP database (i.e., academic network) have few labeled publications, complicating the task of obtaining comprehensive datasets [32]. Due to these challenges, many methods have been proposed to address node-level problems with limited labeled data. These approaches aim to leverage the available data effectively to build models capable of generalizing from a few labeled examples. This part of our review focuses on existing studies of node-level FSL. The summary of representative node-level FSL studies is reported in Table 1.

3.1.1. Metric-based Method

Metric-based Node-level Few-Shot Learning (MN-FSL) leverages the concept of the Prototypical Network (ProNet) [13], a straightforward yet effective framework for few-shot learning. In MN-FSL, a Graph Neural Network (GNN) encoder is first used to learn node embeddings. The prototype for each node class is then generated by averaging the embeddings of the support nodes. Finally, query nodes are classified by calculating the Euclidean distances between their embeddings and the different class prototypes. By integrating node embeddings generated by GNN into ProNet, MN-FSL effectively addresses the challenges of few-shot node classification. This integration allows MN-FSL to benefit from the powerful representation learning capabilities of GNNs, which can capture complex patterns and relationships within graph-structured data. Building on the basic MN-FSL model, several variants have been proposed to enhance its performance and adapt it to different scenarios. Graph Few-shot Learning (GFL) [33] introduces graph-structured prototypes to capture the relational structure of support samples, using a graph representation gate to incorporate whole graph information. This approach allows the model to better understand and leverage the intricate connections between nodes within a graph. Graph Prototype Network (GPN) [32] acknowledges the varying significance of nodes within a graph by using a self-attention mechanism to introduce node importance. It then computes a weighted summation of support nodes' embeddings for a refined class prototype, enhancing the model's ability to discriminate between different classes based on the importance of individual nodes. MetaTNE [34] employs an embedding transformation function to map task-agnostic node representations to task-specific ones, thus exploiting the complex and multifaceted relationships between nodes. HAG-Meta [35] enhances class prototype computation by utilizing both node-level and task-level attention. This dual-attention mechanism allows the model to focus on the most relevant information at different levels, improving the accuracy of the generated prototypes. HAG-Meta is further trained using an incremental learning paradigm. More recently, FSNC [36] has developed two knowledge distillation methods—local representation distillation and global representation distillation. These methods transfer information from the base set to the novel set, thereby improving few-shot node classification performance. By distilling knowledge from a larger, more diverse set of examples, FSNC enhances the model's ability to perform well on new, unseen tasks with limited examples.

3.1.2. Optimization-based Method

Optimization-based Node-level Few-Shot Learning (ON-FSL) is developed based on the model-agnostic meta-learning (MAML) framework [16]. ON-FSL employs a Graph Neural Network (GNN) encoder to learn node embeddings for classification tasks. During the optimization phase, ON-FSL first updates task-specific parameters for each node class and then aggregates all task-specific classification losses to refine task-agnostic parameters. These optimized task-agnostic parameters, shared by base classes, are subsequently adapted to predict the labels of nodes in new classes through gradient updates using a few labeled nodes. By integrating GNN with MAML, ON-FSL leverages prior experiences (meta-knowledge) across base classes to enable rapid adaptation to new classes, effectively addressing the few-shot node classification challenge. Meta-GNN [37] is the pioneering work that combines GNN and MAML for node classification. Since its introduction, several enhancements have been developed. For instance, considering the variability in feature distribution across different sampled tasks, AMM-GNN [31] introduces an attribute-level attention mechanism to better capture the unique properties of each meta-learning task. This allows the model to adapt more effectively to the specific characteristics of various tasks. G-META [38] provides theoretical justification that evidence for a prediction can be found in the local subgraph surrounding the target node. It utilizes these subgraphs to learn node embeddings and integrates both ProNet and MAML for model optimization. RALE [39] captures both task-level and graph-level dependencies to enhance the meta-knowledge transfer process by assigning node locations on the graph. This method ensures efficient knowledge transfer across different tasks and graph structures. TENT [40] introduces three modules to perform node-level, class-level, and task-level adaptations within each meta-task. By conducting adaptations at multiple levels, TENT enhances the model's generalization performance on meta-test tasks, making it more robust to data variations. GLITTER [41] learns task-specific structures based on node influence and mutual information, further refining node representations with these task-specific structures for each meta-task. More recently, ProMC [42] generates proxy subgraphs to calibrate the smoothness of the manifold, thereby obtaining generalizable and transferable prior knowledge. CGFL [43] introduces graph contrastive learning to improve the initialization of the GNN meta-learner, facilitating better adaptation to novel tasks. By employing contrastive learning, CGFL enhances the quality of initial embeddings, leading to more accurate and efficient learning in new contexts. In addition to the above-mentioned works, several other studies have contributed to the field of node-level FSL. For example, HG-Meta [44] addresses few-shot node classification on heterogeneous graphs by modeling both graph structure heterogeneity and task diversity. Unlike the aforementioned works that focus on predicting labels of nodes in new classes using few labeled samples, some models target classifying nodes with few links (tail nodes). For instance, methods developed by Liu et al. [45] specifically address this issue, ensuring accurate classification even for nodes with limited connections. To further advance research in this area, Zhuang et al. [46] created a large-scale dataset called HIN-FShot, designed to attract more attention to node-level FSL on heterogeneous graphs. This dataset provides a valuable resource for testing and developing new methods in this challenging domain.

3.1.3. Application

Besides node classification on various types of graphs (e.g., social network, academic graph, and biological network), node-level FSL has been applied to some other applications. Due to the scarcity of outlier data, it is natural to develop FSLG methods to detect anomalies on graphs. In particular, Meta-GDN [47] detects network anomaly through the FSL framework augmented with a graph deviation network. Furthermore, FSLG models that incorporate domain knowledge to solve domain-specific anomaly detection problems have also been proposed. For example, Meta-AHIN [48] incorporates malware-related attributes and information into GNN and MAML for malicious repository detection on social coding platforms (e.g., Github). Similarly, MetaHG [49] leverages drug-related features and knowledge to the joint model of GNN and MAML for illicit drug trafficker detection on social media (e.g., Instagram). Moreover, LHML [50] introduces a learnable hypersphere which is a changing boundary that can be used to identify anomalies in an unbalanced binary-classification setting and quickly adapt to a new subgraph by a few gradient updating steps of MAML.

3.2. Edge-level FSL

Edges explicitly interconnect nodes on a graph, and many applications such as relation prediction and recommendation rely heavily on edge-level graph learning. However, the scarcity of labeled data for relations is a prevalent issue in various real-world situations. For instance, in knowledge bases, a large portion of semantic relations appear only a few times [52]; E-commerce platforms face the cold-start problem from both user and item sides [10]; and relationships in biological interaction networks can be noisy and sparse [53]. These challenges have motivated researchers to propose extensive work to solve edge-level problems with limited labels. This part summarizes the existing studies on edge-level few-shot learning on graphs, with a particular emphasis on relation prediction in knowledge graphs. We explore how these studies have approached the problem, the methodologies they have employed, and the results they have achieved. The summary of representative edge-level FSL studies is reported in Table 2.

Table 1. A list of representative node-level FSLG methods.

Method	Learning Task	Learning Approach	Characteristic	Venue
GFL [33]	Node classification	ProNet	Graph structured prototype	AAAI'20
GPN [32]	Node classification	ProNet	Node importance	CIKM'20
MetaTNE [34]	Node classification	ProNet	Embedding transformation	NeurIPS'20
HAG-Meta [35]	Node classification	ProNet	Task attention	WSDM'21
FSNC [36]	Node classification	ProNet	Knowledge distillation	AAAI'24
G-META [38]	Node classification	ProNet+MAML	Local subgraph	NeurIPS'20
Meta-GPS [51]	Node classification	ProNet+MAML	Scaling and shifting transformation	SIGIR'22
Meta-GNN [37]	Node classification	MAML	Basic model	CIKM'19
RALE [39]	Node classification	MAML	Task dependency	AAAI'21
TENT [40]	Node classification	MAML	Task adaptation	KDD'22
GLITTER [41]	Node classification	MAML	Task-specific structure	NeurIPS'22
Pro-MC [42]	Node classification	MAML	Manifold calibration	AAAI'23
CGFL [43]	Node classification	MAML	Contrastive Learning	TMLR'23
Meta-GDN [47]	Anomaly detection	MAML	Graph deviation network	WWW'21
Meta-AHIN [48]	Anomaly detection	MAML	Task information	IJCAI'21
MetaHG [49]	Anomaly detection	MAML	Domain knowledge	NeurIPS'21
LHML [50]	Anomaly detection	MAML	Learnable hypersphere	CIKM'22

3.2.1. Metric-based Method

In general, existing Metric-based Edge-level Few-Shot Learning (ME-FSL) models rely on either Matching Network (MatchNet) [12], a popular framework in FSL, or Translation Network (TransNet) [23], a typical knowledge graph embedding method. ME-FSL models built on MatchNet first apply a GNN encoder to learn node (entity) embeddings. Then, they compute the aggregated embedding of each relation by aggregating the embeddings of node pairs in the reference data (support set). Finally, the matching score between the embeddings of relations and the query data is used to determine the acceptability of each query sample. Based on this idea, GMatching [52] was initially proposed to solve the one-shot relation prediction problem on knowledge graphs. Later, FSRL [54] extended GMatching to a few-shot scenario by attentively aggregating all support samples of each relation and improving node embedding formulation with a heterogeneous neighbor aggregator. FAAN [55] further improved upon FSRL by designing an adaptive attentional network to learn adaptive node and reference representations. This adaptive approach allows the model to better capture the varying importance of different nodes and references, leading to more accurate relation predictions. Additionally, GEN [56] addressed a more challenging out-of-graph scenario for relation prediction between unseen nodes or between seen and unseen nodes. This approach enables the model to generalize to new entities that were not present in the training data. More recently, REFORM [57] introduced an error mitigation module to alleviate the negative impact of errors incorporated into knowledge graph construction. This enhancement helps improve the robustness of the model by reducing the influence of noisy or incorrect data. Unlike node pair matching, P-INT [58] calculates the interactions of paths for relation prediction on knowledge graphs. This method leverages the structural information of paths connecting node pairs, providing a different perspective for relation prediction. Moreover, a recent study by Jambor et al. [59] explores the limits of existing models for few-shot link prediction on knowledge graphs, providing insights into the strengths and weaknesses of current approaches. For ME-FSL models built on TransNet, the process begins with computing relation meta by aggregating the embeddings of support node pairs. The relation meta is then used to model the correlation of query pairs using the objective loss of TransE [23]. Two recent models adopting this idea are MetaR [60] and GANA [61]. MetaR computes relation meta by averaging all node pair-specific relation metas and performs rapid updates on them for relation prediction on knowledge graphs. This averaging approach ensures that the relation meta captures a broad understanding of the relationships represented in the support set. Furthermore, GANA extends MetaR by refining node embedding and relation meta computation with an attention mechanism and an LSTM aggregator, respectively. The attention mechanism allows the model to focus on the most relevant nodes and relations, while the LSTM aggregator helps in capturing sequential dependencies within the data.

3.2.2. Optimization-based Method

Similar to ON-FSL, Optimization-based Edge-level Few-Shot Learning (OE-FSL) relies on MAML for model optimization. OE-FSL addresses the challenge of few-shot relation prediction by optimizing GNNs with MAML. In particular, Meta-KGR [62] is the first work to tackle few-shot multi-hop relation prediction on knowledge graphs. Meta-KGR introduces a reinforcement learning framework to model the multi-hop reasoning process, where the search path is encoded by a recurrent neural network. It then adopts MAML to learn effective meta-parameters from high-frequency relations, enabling quick adaptation to few-shot relations. Later, FIRE [54] extends Meta-KGR by incorporating a heterogeneous neighbor aggregator and a search space pruning strategy, enhancing the efficiency and accuracy of the multi-hop reasoning process. More recently, ADK-KG [63] further improves upon FIRE by enhancing the neighbor aggregator with node text content and augmenting MAML with task weights. This allows the model to better utilize textual information and adapt to varying task difficulties, resulting in more accurate relation predictions. Additionally, HMLS [64] leverages a hardness-aware reinforcement learning approach to conduct multi-hop reasoning. By training with hardness-aware batches and reducing noise, HMLS enhances the robustness of the learning process. Furthermore, it applies a knowledge-sharing meta-learning strategy that adapts to few-shot relations by exploiting common features within the hierarchical relation structure. In addition to these studies, there have been considerable advancements in edge-level FSL [65,66,59,67]. For instance, MetaDyGNN [68] proposes a meta-learner with hierarchical time interval-wise and node-wise adaptations to extract general knowledge for few-shot link prediction on dynamic networks. This approach allows the model to handle temporal variations and evolving network structures effectively. ZSGAN [66] explores zero-shot relation prediction by establishing connections between text and knowledge graphs using generative adversarial networks. This method enables the prediction of relations even when there are no direct examples in the training data, expanding the model's applicability to more scenarios.

Table 2. A list of representative edge-level FSLG methods.

Method	Learning Task	Learning Approach	Characteristic	Venue
GMatching [52]	Relation prediction	MatchNet	LSTM matching processor	EMNLP'18
FSRL [54]	Relation prediction	MatchNet	Support data aggregation	AAAI'20
FAAN [55]	Relation prediction	MatchNet	Adaptive matching	EMNLP'20
GEN [56]	Relation prediction	MatchNet	Inductive prediction	NeurIPS'20
REFORM [57]	Relation prediction	MatchNet	Error mitigation	CIKM'21
ZSGAN [66]	Relation prediction	MatchNet	Adversarial Networks	AAAI'20
P-INT [58]	Relation prediction	MatchNet	Path-based Matching	EMNLP'21
MetaR [60]	Relation prediction	TransNet	Relation meta	EMNLP'19
GANA [61]	Relation prediction	TransNet	Refined relation meta	SIGIR'21
MetaDyGNN [68]	Dynamic Link prediction	MAML	Adaptive meta-Learner	WSDM'22
Meta-KGR [62]	Multi-hop relation prediction	MAML	Basic model	EMNLP'19
FIRE [72]	Multi-hop relation prediction	MAML	Space pruning	EMNLP'20
ADK-KG [63]	Multi-hop relation prediction	MAML	Text-enhanced embedding	SDM'22
HMLS [64]	Multi-hop relation prediction	MAML	Hardness-aware learning	TKDE'23

3.2.3. Application

Edge-level few-shot learning (FSL) methods have been applied to a variety of problems beyond relation prediction on knowledge graphs, extending to numerous other applications. For instance, Meta-Graph [53] explores few-shot link prediction across different networks, including biological networks. This approach demonstrates the flexibility of FSL methods in handling diverse network structures and complexities. In the domain of recommendation systems, SEATLE [69] and MetaHIN [10] are designed to address the cold-start problem, which occurs when new users or items have limited interaction data. These models leverage the structure of the graph to make accurate recommendations despite the scarcity of labeled data. Furthermore, the creation of the FewRel dataset [70] has facilitated the development of models like MLMAN [71], which introduces a multi-level matching and aggregation network for few-shot relation classification. This dataset and model combination highlights the potential of FSL methods in improving the accuracy and robustness of relation classification tasks.

3.3. Graph-level FSL

Besides node-level and edge-level mining, graph-level learning is also significant in various application domains such as bioinformatics and social networks. Graph-level learning involves tasks where the entire graph is considered a single data point, such as classifying graphs based on their structures and attributes. Similar to the challenges faced in node-level and edge-level problems, generating labeled graph samples often encounters issues of scarcity and difficulty. For instance, in bioinformatics, collecting molecular graph labels for therapeutic activity requires substantial financial and resource investment [9]. The process of experimentally validating the properties of molecules is costly and time-consuming, resulting in a limited number of labeled samples. Similarly, in social networks, certain communities, such as those on Reddit, have only a limited number of sub-communities, making comprehensive labeling difficult. This scarcity of labeled data poses significant challenges for traditional supervised learning methods, which rely on large amounts of annotated data. This part focuses on summarizing the latest developments in graph-level FSLG. We will explore the methodologies proposed to overcome the challenges of limited labeled data and highlight the innovative solutions that have been developed. The summary of representative edge-level FSL studies is reported in Table 3.

3.3.1. Metric-based Method

Similar to MN-FSL, Metric-based Graph-level Few-Shot Learning (MG-FSL) focuses on computing the distance between a graph class prototype and a query graph to predict the labels of query graphs. MG-FSL addresses the challenges of few-shot graph classification by combining graph-level GNNs with ProNet. The first significant work in MG-FSL for few-shot graph classification is SuperClass [73]. Unlike the general ProNet, which computes the average of support samples' embeddings as the class prototype, SuperClass employs a graph-level GNN, specifically the Graph Isomorphism Network (GIN) [74], to learn graph embeddings. SuperClass then clusters graphs into different super-classes by computing prototype graphs for each class and further clusters these prototype graphs based on their spectral properties. The model is optimized using joint classification losses for both graph labels and super-class labels, which helps to capture the hierarchical structure of graph classes and improve classification accuracy. FAITH [75] advances the field by capturing task correlations through the construction of a hierarchical task graph at different granularities. FAITH designs a loss-based sampling strategy to select tasks with more correlated classes and employs a task-specific classifier that utilizes the learned task correlations for few-shot graph classification. This approach ensures that the model effectively leverages the relationships between tasks, leading to better generalization to new tasks. SPNP [76] introduces a structure-aware prototypical neural process for improving classification performance. Specifically, it incorporates encoded graph structural information as priors and uses a new prototypical decoder to define a metric space where unseen graphs can be predicted effectively. By leveraging structural information, SPNP enhances the model's ability to distinguish between different graph classes, even with limited examples. More recently, Temp-GFSM [77] proposes to learn a robust metric that can accurately classify different temporal graphs and adapt to discover new subspaces for unseen classes. Temp-GFSM addresses the unique challenges of temporal graph classification, where the graph structure can change over time, by focusing on learning metrics that are sensitive to temporal dynamics. This approach allows the model to handle the complexity of evolving graphs and make accurate predictions for unseen temporal graph classes.

3.3.2. Optimization-based Method

Similar to ON-FSL and OE-FSL, Optimization-based Graph-level Few-Shot Learning (OG-FSL) leverages MAML to optimize few-shot graph classification models. By doing so, OG-FSL effectively addresses the challenges associated with few-shot graph classification. Several studies have explored OG-FSL. Specifically, AS-MAML [78] generates graph embeddings by concatenating the mean and max-pooling of all node embeddings encoded by a GNN. It then employs a reinforcement learning-based controller to adaptively control MAML for model optimization. This adaptive approach ensures that the model can dynamically adjust to various few-shot learning tasks. More recently, MVG-Meta [79] has advanced the field by developing a multi-view enhanced Graph Isomorphism Network (GIN) to learn graph embeddings for cross-domain few-shot graph classification. Unlike typical few-shot graph classification tasks, which are usually performed on single-domain data, MVG-Meta transfers meta-knowledge learned from one domain to another. This cross-domain capability enables more robust and versatile graph classification, expanding the applicability of OG-FSL to diverse datasets and domains. Beyond MVG-Meta, CDTC [80] leverages a small set of labeled target domain data as prompt tasks. It models the association and discovers the relevance between meta-tasks from the source domain and the prompt tasks. Based on the discovered relevance, CDTC achieves adaptive task selection and optimizes a graph learner using the selected fine-grained meta-tasks. This approach ensures that the model can effectively utilize the available labeled data to enhance its performance on new tasks. In addition to graph classification tasks, several studies have focused on molecular property prediction, which can be viewed as a type of molecular graph classification. Meta-MGNN [9] takes each molecule as a graph and learns its embedding with a graph-level GNN. It further introduces task weights to make MAML aware of molecular property differences for better model optimization. By considering the unique properties of each molecule, Meta-MGNN can provide more accurate predictions. Furthermore, Pre-PAR [81] improves upon Meta-MGNN by modeling the relational structure among different molecular properties. This allows limited labels to be effectively propagated among similar molecules, enhancing the model's performance even with sparse data. HSL-RG [82] further improves performance by exploring the structural semantics of a molecule from both global and local granularities. HSL-RG first leverages graph kernels to construct relation graphs, facilitating global communication of molecular structural knowledge from neighboring molecules. It then designs self-supervised learning signals for structure optimization to locally learn transformation-invariant representations from the molecules themselves. MTA [83] conducts task augmentations by generating new labeled samples through retrieving highly relevant motifs from a predefined motif vocabulary as an external memory. This approach further improves few-shot molecular property prediction performance by enriching the training data with relevant examples. Different from the molecular classification problem, MPNN [84] targets few-shot molecular property regression tasks, such as chemical prediction. MPNN integrates the meta-learning algorithm into graph neural networks to tackle these regression tasks, ensuring accurate predictions with limited labeled data.

3.3.3. Application

As discussed above, besides general graph classification on different types of graphs (e.g., social networks and biological networks), existing graph-level FSL models have been applied to various other applications. One prominent application is molecular property prediction [9,81], where graph-level FSL models are employed to predict properties such as toxicity, solubility, and biological activity of molecules. For example, in drug discovery, predicting the therapeutic activity of molecules based on their structural properties is crucial. Traditional methods require extensive experimental validation, which is both costly and time-consuming. Graph-level FSL models can leverage the structural

Table 3. A list of representative graph-level FSLG methods.

Method	Learning Task	Learning Approach	Characteristic	Venue
SuperClass [73]	Graph classification	ProNet	Super classes	ICLR'20
FAITH [75]	Graph classification	ProNet	Task correlations	IJCAI'22
SPNP [76]	Graph classification	ProNet	Prototypical Neural Process	TNNLS'22
Temp-GFSM [77]	Temporal graph classification	ProNet	Temporal metric learning	KDD'22
AS-MAML [78]	Graph classification	MAML	Adaptation Controller	CIKM'20
MVG-Meta [79]	Cross-domain graph classification	MAML	Attention-based encoder	AAAI'22
CDTC [80]	Cross-domain graph classification	MAML	Cross Task Coordinator	AAAI'23
Meta-MGNN [9]	Molecule classification	MAML	Task weight	WWW'21
Pre-PAR [81]	Molecule classification	MAML	Property-aware embedding	NeurIPS'21
HSL-RG [82]	Molecule classification	MAML	Structured learning	Neural Nets'23
MTA [83]	Molecule classification	MAML	Motif task augmentation	SDM'23
MPNN [84]	Molecule regression	MAML	GNN ensembles	LoG'22

information from a few labeled molecular graphs to predict the properties of new, unseen molecules, significantly reducing the need for extensive lab experiments. Another application area is material science, where researchers use graph-level FSL models to predict the properties of new materials. This involves modeling the atomic structure of materials as graphs and using these models to predict properties such as conductivity, strength, and thermal stability. By applying FSL techniques, researchers can make accurate predictions with only a limited number of labeled examples, accelerating the discovery of new materials.

4. FSLG Future Research Directions

FSLG is an emerging and fast-developing research topic that has garnered significant attention in recent years. Despite the substantial progress that has been made, numerous challenges and open questions remain, highlighting the complexity and breadth of this field. These challenges present exciting opportunities for future research and innovation. In this section, we identify and briefly discuss some of these potential research directions, aiming to provide a roadmap for continued advancement and exploration in FSLG.

4.1. Generalization and Transferability

Most FSLG models excessively rely on labeled data and attempt to inherit a strong inductive bias for new tasks during the test phase. However, a distribution shift often exists between non-overlapping meta-training data and meta-testing data, which presents a significant challenge. Without supervision signals from ground-truth labels, the model may struggle to learn an effective GNN for new classes of test data. This gap severely limits the generalization and transferability of the meta-trained GNN.

Fortunately, contrastive learning has emerged as a promising approach to alleviate the dependence on labeled data. By leveraging unsupervised pretext tasks, contrastive learning can help the model learn label-irrelevant but transferable representations. Studies such as [85,86] have demonstrated the efficacy of contrastive learning in various contexts. By incorporating contrastive learning techniques, we can potentially improve the generalization and transferability capabilities of current FSLG methods, making them more robust to distribution shifts and better suited for practical applications. This approach opens up new avenues for enhancing FSLG models, ultimately contributing to more effective and reliable performance in real-world scenarios.

4.2. *Explainability*

Previous FSLG studies have primarily focused on developing models that excel in performance metrics. However, none of these studies have sufficiently addressed the critical aspect of model explanation. Developing FSLG models with explainability is essential to enhance model reliability and foster end-user trust. For instance, it is important to investigate and explain which components of the FSLG framework, such as GNN, meta-training processes, or meta-adaptation strategies, have the most significant impact on model performance. Understanding these elements can provide valuable insights and guidance for more effective model design.

Additionally, we can explore the development of information-based methods [87] to quantitatively explain the capabilities of FSLG models. These methods can help in systematically analyzing and interpreting the decision-making processes of the models, thereby making them more transparent and understandable to users. By prioritizing explainability in FSLG research, we not only improve the robustness and reliability of the models but also contribute to building greater confidence and trust among end-users, ultimately facilitating broader adoption and application of FSLG technologies.

4.3. *Graph Models for FSLG*

Though FSLG has been widely studied for certain types of graphs, such as plain graphs and attributed graphs, many other types of graphs remain largely understudied in this field. For instance, signed graphs, which involve positive and negative edges to represent different kinds of relationships, and multiplex graphs, which consist of multiple layers of graphs representing different types of connections, have not received as much attention in FSLG research. These types of graphs present unique challenges and opportunities that have yet to be fully explored. Moreover, the underlying GNN models adopted by existing FSLG work commonly follow the homophily principle, which assumes that connected nodes are similar. This assumption does not hold for heterophily graphs, where connected nodes may be dissimilar. GNN models based on homophily struggle to adapt to these heterophily graphs, limiting their applicability and effectiveness in such contexts.

Therefore, designing principled graph models that can handle graphs with different properties, including heterophily, is a promising research direction in the field of FSLG. This involves developing new algorithms and methodologies that can effectively capture and leverage the unique characteristics of various types of graphs. By doing so, we can enhance the versatility and robustness of FSLG models, making them more applicable to a broader range of real-world scenarios.

4.4. Theoretical Analysis of FSLG

A recent work [59] has empirically explored the limits of existing FSLG methods in relation prediction over knowledge graphs. This study has challenged the implicit assumptions and inductive biases of prior work, highlighting the need for a deeper understanding of the foundational aspects of FSLG methods.

To take a step further and unveil the profound theoretical underpinnings, conducting a thorough theoretical analysis of FSLG is necessary and important. Such an analysis has not been extensively explored before, yet it is crucial for advancing our understanding of how FSLG methods function and where their limitations lie. By developing a solid theoretical framework, researchers can identify the fundamental principles that govern FSLG, guiding the design of more effective and robust models. n particular, several recent works related to the theory of FSL could serve as valuable bases for this research direction. For instance, the theoretical insights provided by [88,89,90] offer a foundation upon which to build a comprehensive theoretical framework for FSLG. These studies have laid the groundwork in understanding the mathematical properties and theoretical bounds of FSL, and similar approaches could be adapted and extended to the specific context of FSLG.

By leveraging these theoretical insights, researchers can develop new methodologies that not only address the empirical limitations observed in current FSLG methods but also provide a more rigorous basis for evaluating and improving these models.

4.5. Broader Applications

As discussed in this chapeter, FSLG has been applied to not only general graph mining tasks at different granularity levels on various types of graphs but also to domain-specific applications such as malware detection and illicit drug trafficker detection. These applications demonstrate the versatility and effectiveness of FSLG in addressing complex problems in different fields.

In addition to these studies, it is worth exploring the potential of FSLG in other application domains, such as healthcare and social good, as suggested by Mandal et al. [91]. For instance, in the healthcare sector, we could develop FSLG models to analyze patients' drug refill behavior using prescription dispensing and refill data modeled as a graph. Given that labels in this context are often limited, FSLG's ability to work with few labeled examples makes it an ideal approach. By capturing patterns in patients' drug refill behavior, these models could help in identifying abnormal behaviors, such as opioid overdose risks, at an early stage. Early intervention in such cases is crucial for preventing adverse health outcomes and ensuring patient safety. The ability of FSLG to generalize from limited labeled data to new, unseen scenarios can significantly enhance the accuracy and timeliness of these interventions, thereby improving overall healthcare outcomes.

Overall, the potential applications of FSLG are vast and varied, encompassing numerous domains where data is abundant but labeled examples are scarce. By continuing to explore and expand the use of FSLG in these areas, we can harness its capabilities to address critical challenges and drive positive change across multiple sectors. This ongoing research will not only contribute to the advancement of FSLG technology but also to the betterment of society through innovative and impactful solutions.

5. Conclusion

As two popular research topics in the current AI community, graph representation learning and few-shot learning have laid the groundwork for a new and promising research direction: few-shot learning on graphs (FSLG). This emerging field holds significant potential for a variety of application domains, from social network analysis to bioinformatics and beyond.

In this chapter, we first introduce the major challenges and foundational concepts of FSLG. Understanding these challenges is crucial for advancing the field, as they highlight the inherent difficulties in applying few-shot learning techniques to graph-structured data. These challenges include the uniqueness of FSLG problem, the complexity of FSLG methods, and the diversity of graph mining applications.

We then comprehensively review existing studies of FSLG, systematically categorizing them into three parts: node-level, edge-level, and graph-level problems. Node-level problems involve predicting labels for individual nodes within a graph, such as classifying users in a social network. Edge-level problems focus on predicting the existence or type of relationships between nodes, which is essential for tasks like link prediction and recommender systems. Graph-level problems involve predicting properties of entire graphs, such as determining the function of a protein based on its molecular structure. By organizing the literature in this manner, we provide a clear overview of the current state of FSLG research and highlight the specific contributions and methodologies employed in each area.

Finally, we discuss several critical issues that remain unsolved in the field of FSLG. These issues include the need for more generalized and transferable models, the challenge of dealing with heterogeneous or multiplex graphs, and the importance of incorporating theoretical insights. We also share our thoughts on future research directions, suggesting areas where further investigation could yield substantial advancements. For example, integrating contrastive learning techniques, developing more interpretable models, and exploring new application domains such as healthcare for future research.

We hope this chapter will serve as a useful reference for researchers and practitioners, providing a comprehensive overview of the current landscape of FSLG and offering insights into the challenges and opportunities that lie ahead. By synthesizing the existing body of knowledge and identifying key areas for future work, we aim to advance the development and application of FSLG, ultimately contributing to more effective and impactful AI solutions.

References

[1] Perozzi B, Al-Rfou R, Skiena S. Deepwalk: Online learning of social representations. In: Proceedings of the ACM SIGKDD International Conference on Knowledge Discovery and Data Mining; 2014. .

[2] Grover A, Leskovec J. node2vec: Scalable feature learning for networks. In: Proceedings of the ACM SIGKDD International Conference on Knowledge Discovery and Data Mining; 2016. .

[3] Kipf TN, Welling M. Semi-supervised classification with graph convolutional networks. In: Proceedings of the International Conference on Learning Representations; 2017. .

[4] Jin W, Coley CW, Barzilay R, Jaakkola T. Predicting organic reaction outcomes with Weisfeiler-Lehman network. In: Proceedings of the Advances in Neural Information Processing Systems; 2017. .

[5] Hao Z, Lu C, Huang Z, Wang H, Hu Z, Liu Q, et al. ASGN: An active semi-supervised graph neural network for molecular property prediction. In: Proceedings of the ACM SIGKDD International Conference on Knowledge Discovery and Data Mining; 2020. .

[6] Ying R, He R, Chen K, Eksombatchai P, Hamilton WL, Leskovec J. Graph convolutional neural networks for web-scale recommender systems. In: Proceedings of the ACM SIGKDD International Conference on Knowledge Discovery and Data Mining; 2018. .
[7] Fan W, Ma Y, Li Q, He Y, Zhao E, Tang J, et al. Graph neural networks for social recommendation. In: Proceedings of the ACM Web Conference; 2019. .
[8] Ding K, Wang J, Caverlee J, Liu H. Meta Propagation Networks for Graph Few-shot Semi-supervised Learning. In: Proceedings of the AAAI Conference on Artificial Intelligence; 2022. .
[9] Guo Z, Zhang C, Yu W, Herr J, Wiest O, Jiang M, et al. Few-Shot Graph Learning for Molecular Property Prediction. In: Proceedings of the ACM Web Conference; 2021. .
[10] Lu Y, Fang Y, Shi C. Meta-learning on heterogeneous information networks for cold-start recommendation. In: Proceedings of the ACM SIGKDD International Conference on Knowledge Discovery and Data Mining; 2020. .
[11] Wang Y, Yao Q, Kwok JT, Ni LM. Generalizing from a few examples: A survey on few-shot learning. ACM Computing Surveys. 2020.
[12] Vinyals O, Blundell C, Lillicrap T, Wierstra D, et al. Matching networks for one shot learning. In: Proceedings of the Advances in Neural Information Processing Systems; 2016. .
[13] Snell J, Swersky K, Zemel R. Prototypical networks for few-shot learning. In: Proceedings of the Advances in Neural Information Processing Systems; 2017. .
[14] Yu M, Guo X, Yi J, Chang S, Potdar S, Cheng Y, et al. Diverse few-shot text classification with multiple metrics. In: Proceedings of the Annual Conference of the North American Chapter of the Association for Computational Linguistics; 2018. .
[15] Hu Z, Chen T, Chang KW, Sun Y. Few-Shot Representation Learning for Out-Of-Vocabulary Words. In: Proceedings of the Annual Meeting of the Association for Computational Linguistics; 2019. .
[16] Finn C, Abbeel P, Levine S. Model-agnostic meta-learning for fast adaptation of deep networks. In: Proceedings of the International Conference on Machine Learning; 2017. .
[17] Duan Y, Andrychowicz M, Stadie B, Jonathan Ho O, Schneider J, Sutskever I, et al. One-shot imitation learning. In: Proceedings of the Advances in Neural Information Processing Systems; 2017. .
[18] Zhang Z, Cui P, Zhu W. Deep learning on graphs: A survey. IEEE Transactions on Knowledge and Data Engineering.
[19] Dong Y, Chawla NV, Swami A. metapath2vec: Scalable representation learning for heterogeneous networks. In: Proceedings of the ACM SIGKDD International Conference on Knowledge Discovery and Data Mining; 2017. .
[20] Hamilton WL, Ying R, Leskovec J. Inductive representation learning on large graphs. In: Proceedings of the Advances in Neural Information Processing Systems; 2017. .
[21] Veličković P, Cucurull G, Casanova A, Romero A, Liò P, Bengio Y. Graph Attention Networks. In: Proceedings of the International Conference on Learning Representations; 2018. .
[22] Zhang C, Song D, Huang C, Swami A, Chawla NV. Heterogeneous Graph Neural Network. In: Proceedings of the ACM SIGKDD International Conference on Knowledge Discovery and Data Mining; 2019. .
[23] Bordes A, Usunier N, Garcia-Duran A, Weston J, Yakhnenko O. Translating embeddings for modeling multi-relational data. In: Proceedings of the Advances in Neural Information Processing Systems; 2013. .
[24] Dettmers T, Minervini P, Stenetorp P, Riedel S. Convolutional 2d knowledge graph embeddings. In: Proceedings of the AAAI Conference on Artificial Intelligence; 2018. .
[25] Socher R, Chen D, Manning CD, Ng A. Reasoning with neural tensor networks for knowledge base completion. In: Proceedings of the Advances in Neural Information Processing Systems; 2013. .
[26] Ying Z, You J, Morris C, Ren X, Hamilton W, Leskovec J. Hierarchical graph representation learning with differentiable pooling. In: Proceedings of the Advances in Neural Information Processing Systems; 2018. .
[27] Hospedales T, Antoniou A, Micaelli P, Storkey A. Meta-learning in neural networks: A survey. arXiv preprint arXiv:200405439. 2020.
[28] Sung F, Yang Y, Zhang L, Xiang T, Torr PH, Hospedales TM. Learning to compare: Relation network for few-shot learning. In: Proceedings of the IEEE/CVF Computer Vision and Pattern Recognition Conference; 2018. .
[29] Ravi S, Larochelle H. Optimization as a Model for Few-Shot Learning. In: Proceedings of the International Conference on Learning Representations; 2016. .

[30] Finn C, Xu K, Levine S. Probabilistic Model-Agnostic Meta-Learning. In: Proceedings of the Advances in Neural Information Processing Systems; 2018. .
[31] Wang N, Luo M, Ding K, Zhang L, Li J, Zheng Q. Graph few-shot learning with attribute matching. In: Proceedings of the ACM International Conference on Information and Knowledge Management; 2020. .
[32] Ding K, Wang J, Li J, Shu K, Liu C, Liu H. Graph prototypical networks for few-shot learning on attributed networks. In: Proceedings of the ACM International Conference on Information and Knowledge Management; 2020. .
[33] Yao H, Zhang C, Wei Y, Jiang M, Wang S, Huang J, et al. Graph few-shot learning via knowledge transfer. In: Proceedings of the AAAI Conference on Artificial Intelligence; 2020. .
[34] Lan L, Wang P, Du X, Song K, Tao J, Guan X. Node classification on graphs with few-shot novel labels via meta transformed network embedding. In: Proceedings of the Advances in Neural Information Processing Systems; 2020. .
[35] Tan Z, Ding K, Guo R, Liu H. Graph Few-shot Class-incremental Learning. In: Proceedings of the ACM international Conference on Web Search and Data Mining; 2021. .
[36] Wu Z, Mo Y, Zhou P, Yuan S, Zhu X. Self-Training Based Few-Shot Node Classification by Knowledge Distillation. In: Proceedings of the AAAI Conference on Artificial Intelligence; 2024. .
[37] Zhou F, Cao C, Zhang K, Trajcevski G, Zhong T, Geng J. Meta-gnn: On few-shot node classification in graph meta-learning. In: Proceedings of the ACM International Conference on Information and Knowledge Management; 2019. .
[38] Huang K, Zitnik M. Graph meta learning via local subgraphs. In: Proceedings of the Advances in Neural Information Processing Systems; 2020. .
[39] Liu Z, Fang Y, Liu C, Hoi SC. Relative and absolute location embedding for few-shot node classification on graph. In: Proceedings of the AAAI Conference on Artificial Intelligence; 2021. .
[40] Wang S, Ding K, Zhang C, Chen C, Li J. Task-adaptive few-shot node classification. In: Proceedings of the ACM SIGKDD Conference on Knowledge Discovery and Data Mining; 2022. .
[41] Wang S, Chen C, Li J. Graph few-shot learning with task-specific structures. In: Proceedings of the Advances in Neural Information Processing Systems; 2022. .
[42] Wang Z, Cao L, Lin W, Jiang M, Tan KC. Robust graph meta-learning via manifold calibration with proxy subgraphs. In: Proceedings of the AAAI Conference on Artificial Intelligence; 2023. .
[43] Zhang C, Liu H, Li J, Ye Y, Zhang C. Mind the gap: Mitigating the distribution gap in graph few-shot learning. Transactions on Machine Learning Research. 2023.
[44] Zhang Q, Wu X, Yang Q, Zhang C, Zhang X. Graph Meta-learning over Heterogeneous Graphs. In: Proceedings of the SIAM International Conference on Data Mining; 2022. .
[45] Liu Z, Nguyen TK, Fang Y. Tail-GNN: Tail-Node Graph Neural Networks. In: Proceedings of the ACM SIGKDD International Conference on Knowledge Discovery and Data Mining; 2021. .
[46] Zhuang Z, Xiang X, Huang S, Wang D. HINFShot: A Challenge Dataset for Few-Shot Node Classification in Heterogeneous Information Network. In: Proceedings of the Annual ACM International Conference on Multimedia Retrieval; 2021. .
[47] Ding K, Zhou Q, Tong H, Liu H. Few-shot network anomaly detection via cross-network meta-learning. In: Proceedings of the ACM Web Conference; 2021. .
[48] Qian Y, Zhang Y, Ye Y, Zhang C. Adapting Meta Knowledge with Heterogeneous Information Network for COVID-19 Themed Malicious Repository Detection. In: Proceedings of the International Joint Conference on Artificial Intelligence; 2021. .
[49] Qian Y, Zhang Y, Ye Y, Zhang C. Distilling Meta Knowledge on Heterogeneous Graph for Illicit Drug Trafficker Detection on Social Media. In: Proceedings of the Advances in Neural Information Processing Systems; 2021. .
[50] Guo Q, Zhao X, Fang Y, Yang S, Lin X, Ouyang D. Learning hypersphere for few-shot anomaly detection on attributed networks. In: Proceedings of the ACM International Conference on Information and Knowledge Management; 2022. .
[51] Liu Y, Li M, Li X, Giunchiglia F, Feng X, Guan R. Few-shot node classification on attributed networks with graph meta-learning. In: Proceedings of the International ACM SIGIR Conference on Research and Development in Information Retrieval; 2022. .
[52] Xiong W, Yu M, Chang S, Guo X, Wang WY. One-Shot Relational Learning for Knowledge Graphs. In: Proceedings of the Conference on Empirical Methods in Natural Language Processing; 2018. .
[53] Bose AJ, Jain A, Molino P, Hamilton WL. Meta-graph: Few shot link prediction via meta learning.

arXiv preprint arXiv:191209867. 2019.
[54] Zhang C, Yao H, Huang C, Jiang M, Li Z, Chawla NV. Few-shot knowledge graph completion. In: Proceedings of the AAAI Conference on Artificial Intelligence; 2020. .
[55] Sheng J, Guo S, Chen Z, Yue J, Wang L, Liu T, et al. Adaptive Attentional Network for Few-Shot Knowledge Graph Completion. In: Proceedings of the Conference on Empirical Methods in Natural Language Processing; 2020. .
[56] Baek J, Lee DB, Hwang SJ. Learning to extrapolate knowledge: Transductive few-shot out-of-graph link prediction. In: Proceedings of the Advances in Neural Information Processing Systems; 2020. .
[57] Wang S, Huang X, Chen C, Wu L, Li J. REFORM: Error-Aware Few-Shot Knowledge Graph Completion. In: Proceedings of the ACM International Conference on Information and Knowledge Management; 2021. .
[58] Xu J, Zhang J, Ke X, Dong Y, Chen H, Li C, et al. P-INT: A Path-based Interaction Model for Few-shot Knowledge Graph Completion. In: Proceedings of the Conference on Empirical Methods in Natural Language Processing (Findings); 2021. .
[59] Jambor D, Teru K, Pineau J, Hamilton WL. Exploring the Limits of Few-Shot Link Prediction in Knowledge Graphs. In: Proceedings of the Conference of the European Chapter of the Association for Computational Linguistics; 2021. .
[60] Chen M, Zhang W, Zhang W, Chen Q, Chen H. Meta Relational Learning for Few-Shot Link Prediction in Knowledge Graphs. In: Proceedings of the Conference on Empirical Methods in Natural Language Processing; 2019. .
[61] Niu G, Li Y, Tang C, Geng R, Dai J, Liu Q, et al. Relational Learning with Gated and Attentive Neighbor Aggregator for Few-Shot Knowledge Graph Completion. In: Proceedings of the International ACM SIGIR Conference on Research and Development in Information Retrieval; 2021. .
[62] Lv X, Gu Y, Han X, Hou L, Li J, Liu Z. Adapting Meta Knowledge Graph Information for Multi-Hop Reasoning over Few-Shot Relations. In: Proceedings of the Conference on Empirical Methods in Natural Language Processing; 2019. .
[63] Zhang Y, Qian Y, Ye Y, Zhang C. Adapting Distilled Knowledge for Few-shot Relation Reasoning over Knowledge Graphs. In: Proceedings of the SIAM International Conference on Data Mining; 2022. .
[64] Zheng S, Chen W, Wang W, Zhao P, Yin H, Zhao L. Multi-hop knowledge graph reasoning in few-shot scenarios. IEEE Transactions on Knowledge and Data Engineering. 2023.
[65] Mirtaheri M, Rostami M, Ren X, Morstatter F, Galstyan A. One-shot Learning for Temporal Knowledge Graphs. In: Proceedings of the Conference on Automated Knowledge Base Construction; 2021. .
[66] Qin P, Wang X, Chen W, Zhang C, Xu W, Wang WY. Generative adversarial zero-shot relational learning for knowledge graphs. In: Proceedings of the AAAI Conference on Artificial Intelligence; 2020. .
[67] Jiang Z, Gao J, Lv X. MetaP: Meta Pattern Learning for One-Shot Knowledge Graph Completion. In: Proceedings of the International ACM SIGIR Conference on Research and Development in Information Retrieval; 2021. .
[68] Yang C, Wang C, Lu Y, Gong X, Shi C, Wang W, et al. Few-shot link prediction in dynamic networks. In: Proceedings of the ACM International Conference on Web Search and Data Mining; 2022. .
[69] Li R, Wu X, Wu X, Wang W. Few-shot learning for new user recommendation in location-based social networks. In: Proceedings of the ACM Web Conference; 2020. .
[70] Han X, Zhu H, Yu P, Wang Z, Yao Y, Liu Z, et al. FewRel: A Large-Scale Supervised Few-Shot Relation Classification Dataset with State-of-the-Art Evaluation. In: Proceedings of the Conference on Empirical Methods in Natural Language Processing; 2018. .
[71] Ye ZX, Ling ZH. Multi-Level Matching and Aggregation Network for Few-Shot Relation Classification. In: Proceedings of the Annual Meeting of the Association for Computational Linguistics; 2019. .
[72] Zhang C, Yu L, Saebi M, Jiang M, Chawla N. Few-shot multi-hop relation reasoning over knowledge bases. In: Proceedings of the Conference on Empirical Methods in Natural Language Processing (Findings); 2020. .
[73] Chauhan J, Nathani D, Kaul M. Few-Shot Learning on Graphs via Super-Classes based on Graph Spectral Measures. In: Proceedings of the International Conference on Learning Representations; 2019. .
[74] Xu K, Hu W, Leskovec J, Jegelka S. How Powerful are Graph Neural Networks? In: Proceedings of the International Conference on Learning Representations; 2018. .
[75] Wang S, Dong Y, Huang X, Chen C, Li J. FAITH: Few-Shot Graph Classification with Hierarchical Task Graphs. In: Proceedings of the International Joint Conference on Artificial Intelligence; 2022. .

[76] Lin X, Li Z, Zhang P, Liu L, Zhou C, Wang B, et al. Structure-aware prototypical neural process for few-shot graph classification. IEEE Transactions on Neural Networks and Learning Systems. 2022.
[77] Fu D, Fang L, Maciejewski R, Torvik VI, He J. Meta-learned metrics over multi-evolution temporal graphs. In: Proceedings of the ACM SIGKDD Conference on Knowledge Discovery and Data Mining; 2022. .
[78] Ma N, Bu J, Yang J, Zhang Z, Yao C, Yu Z, et al. Adaptive-step graph meta-learner for few-shot graph classification. In: Proceedings of the ACM International Conference on Information and Knowledge Management; 2020. .
[79] Hassani K. Cross-Domain Few-Shot Graph Classification. In: Proceedings of the AAAI Conference on Artificial Intelligence; 2022. .
[80] Zhang Q, Pei S, Yang Q, Zhang C, Chawla NV, Zhang X. Cross-domain few-shot graph classification with a reinforced task coordinator. In: Proceedings of the AAAI Conference on Artificial Intelligence; 2023. .
[81] Wang Y, Abuduweili A, Yao Q, Dou D. Property-aware relation networks for few-shot molecular property prediction. In: Proceedings of the Advances in Neural Information Processing Systems; 2021. .
[82] Ju W, Liu Z, Qin Y, Feng B, Wang C, Guo Z, et al. Few-shot molecular property prediction via hierarchically structured learning on relation graphs. Neural Networks. 2023.
[83] Meng Z, Li Y, Zhao P, Yu Y, King I. Meta-learning with motif-based task augmentation for few-shot molecular property prediction. In: Proceedings of the SIAM International Conference on Data Mining; 2023. .
[84] de Ocáriz Borde HS, Barbero F. Graph neural network expressivity and meta-learning for molecular property regression. In: Proceedings of the Learning on Graphs Conference; 2022. .
[85] Chen T, Kornblith S, Norouzi M, Hinton G. A simple framework for contrastive learning of visual representations. In: Proceedings of the International Conference on Machine Learning; 2020. .
[86] You Y, Chen T, Sui Y, Chen T, Wang Z, Shen Y. Graph contrastive learning with augmentations. In: Proceedings of the Advances in Neural Information Processing Systems; 2020. .
[87] Guan C, Wang X, Zhang Q, Chen R, He D, Xie X. Towards a deep and unified understanding of deep neural models in nlp. In: Proceedings of the International Conference on Machine Learning; 2019. .
[88] Cao T, Law MT, Fidler S. A Theoretical Analysis of the Number of Shots in Few-Shot Learning. In: Proceedings of the International Conference on Learning Representations; 2019. .
[89] Du SS, Hu W, Kakade SM, Lee JD, Lei Q. Few-Shot Learning via Learning the Representation, Provably. In: Proceedings of the International Conference on Learning Representations; 2020. .
[90] Tripuraneni N, Jin C, Jordan M. Provable meta-learning of linear representations. In: Proceedings of the International Conference on Machine Learning; 2021. .
[91] Mandal D, Medya S, Uzzi B, Aggarwal C. Meta Learning with Graph Neural Networks: Methods and Applications. ACM SIGKDD Explorations Newsletter. 2022.

Part II

Knowledge Graph Representation and Embeddings

Handbook on Neurosymbolic AI and Knowledge Graphs
P. Hitzler et al. (Eds.)
IOS Press, 2025

doi:10.3233/FAIA250204

Vector Space Transformations to Uncover Knowledge Graphs in Neural Language Models

Giacomo MUNDA [a,1], Dagmar GROMANN [a] and Tobias HEINZLE [a]
[a] *University of Vienna, Gymnasiumstrasse 50, 1190 Vienna, Austria*

Abstract. Transformer-based language models are known to encode factual information in their hidden representations, however, an open question is how to explicate this implicitly encoded knowledge. Approaches to unveil encoded factual associations relate to prompt-based methods, techniques to localize or edit specific model weights, and to trace the information flow during inference. Inspired by evidence of entire dependency graphs in embedding (sub-)spaces of these models, this chapter presents an approach to utilize linear transformation of a model's vector representation space to uncover the properties of knowledge graphs. Subjects and objects of factual knowledge graph triples, i.e., from Wikidata, are expected to be near neighbors, a proximity of knowledge entity embeddings that can be measured with simple cosine similarity and approximated by training a transformation matrix in a supervised manner on minimizing the distance between the actual and predicted similarity scores. The obtained results are promising in terms of Pearson and Spearman correlations as well as mean squared error rates, indicating that there is a specific vector sub-space that encodes factual associations in the last layer of neural language models.

Keywords. knowledge graphs, vector space, linear transformation, neural language models

1. Introduction

The advent of self-supervised learning has enabled the development of robust Pre-trained Language Models (PLMs). These models excel in acquiring nuanced hidden representations, demonstrating remarkable efficacy across various Natural Language Processing (NLP) tasks. Thus, understanding what PLMs learn from textual data and encode in these representations is increasingly important. One popular method to uncover specific features in embedding spaces is to specify a probe [1], a supervised model trained to detect specific features in these spaces. Probing has been used to detect linguistic features encoded in language models, such as syntax [2,3], morphology [4,5] and discourse [6]. Coenen et al. [3] even suggest that specific linguistic features are represented in separate vector subspaces. In this chapter, we are particularly interested in whether PLMs' representations encode factual associations as found in Knowledge Graphs (KG).

[1]Corresponding Author: University of Vienna, Gymnasiumstrasse 50, 1190 Vienna, Austria; E-mail: a01614021@unet.univie.ac.at.

Analyzing whether hidden representations of language models implicitly encode factual information is of particular interest for knowledge-specific downstream tasks, neurosymbolic methods for better integration of existing knowledge, and in general for building better models. Methods to uncover factual information in PLMs range from prompt-based [7,8,9] over localization [10,11] to information flow analysis at inference time [12]. For instance, Cohen et al. [9] directly extract entire knowledge graphs from PLMs by means of few-shot prompting. Localization or tracing methods seek to uncover exactly where facts are stored in the embedding spaces, which, however, have been shown to be unreliable [11]. Approaches to analyze how these facts are composed at inference time [12] show evidence for interesting interactions between attention matrices on different layers in subject-predicate compositions to predict objects.

Despite existing approaches on the exploration of linguistic and factual knowledge in PLMs, it is still unclear to what extent factual knowledge is directly encoded in PLMs' vector spaces, how it can be successfully inspected and if it is encoded in a similar way as in KGs. We believe that such an exploration of facts in a vector space can shed light on the mechanisms by which PLMs encode and retrieve factual knowledge, potentially leading to improvements in model architecture, training techniques, and neurosymbolic approaches.

This chapter provides a general overview on how neural methods can be used to encode linguistic and factual information and how transformations of vector spaces can be achieved to what end (in Section 2) as well as existing approaches to explore facts in hidden representations (in Section 3). To address the open question on how to uncover a latent vector space specific to factual information, Section 4 details the KG and KG embeddings applied to a method (Section 5) that utilizes linear transformation to approximate the cosine distance between related KG entities. The hypothesis is that factual knowledge is encoded in the PLM's vector space if the transformation is able to approximate the true similarity scores provided in the KGs using only the contextual embeddings. The utilized KG is Wikidata, for which the cosine similarity of KG embedding object-subject pairs are utilized. PLMs with different architectures, including encoder-only BERT [13] and decoder-only GPT-2 [14], are chosen to test their performance and to potentially identify the best architecture and model size for factual information encoding. The resulting latent vector space is compared to the original vector space for its ability to approximate KG entity distances. Its exploration in downstream tasks is left to interesting future work.

In terms of positioning the proposed approach within the context of neurosymbolic approaches, this chapter relies on the typology proposed by Hamilton et al. [15] ranging from simple encoding of symbolic representations, even words, in vector space (Sequential) and interactions between a reasoner and a neural model (Cooperative) to approaches where knowledge is compiled into the network weights or loss function (Compiled). The final type is a vision of a not yet achieved ultimate neurosymbolic system. While the proposed approach seeks to explore factual associations in hidden representations, this objective is achieved by compiling knowledge from knowledge graphs into the loss function, thereby addressing the compiled objective of neurosymbolic systems. Nevertheless, this chapter does not seek to make the argument that learned representations of PLMs are equivalent to knowledge graphs or knowledge bases, but instead seeks to identify the vector subspace in which factual associations are encoded.

2. Preliminaries

This section provides a theoretical basis for neural language models, knowledge graphs, knowledge graph representation methods, as well as transformation of embedding spaces.

2.1. Neural Language Models

Neural language models build on neural networks, which with a deep architecture of several interconnected layers, have achieved groundbreaking results in a large number of tasks. Such models are trained on large collections of text in natural language by means of self-supervision, which means the supervision signal is learned directly from the data without the need of annotations or labels [16], resulting in models called PLMs. Based on the nature of the training data, a solid performance on NLP tasks can be expected. However, such PLMs have been shown to also perform remarkably well on tasks related to knowledge representation, e.g. generating SPARQL queries [17]. One of the first attempts to learn vector representations with a language modeling objective was conducted by Bengio et al. [18] with a simple multilayer perceptron.

One of the simpler architectures is the feedforward neural network in which layers are connected without any cycles or convolution. The outputs from one layer are passed to the next layer and the parameters of each layer are represented as a single weight matrix and bias. The input vector is multiplied with the weight matrix, the bias is added and the result is passed through a non-linear activation function. The final output of the layer represents the input to the next layer. Feedforward Neural Networks (FNN), despite their very simple architecture, have been widely used to create dense vector representations of words, as is the case of word2vec [19]. Word2vec proposes two models to either predict the center word or the context words and with these tasks to learn global word embeddings from textual data in a simple FNN. Many other types of neural architectures, such as Recurrent Neural Networks [20] and Convolutional Neural Networks [21], exist. The current state-of-the-art is the Transformer [22] architecture, which draws most of its success from multi-head attention in combination with feedforward and linear layers. This architecture allows for faster training, better accuracy, and improved representations [13,23]. These different architectures can be build to learn contextual embeddings, which means a vector representation of a single word differs depending on its meaning in context. Contextual embeddings, the hidden representations of neural language models, have been proven to capture extensive linguistics features from text data as well as facts. One interesting line of research is the exploration of the contribution of the specific layers to specific tasks or encoding of features. Conventionally, the averaged parameters of the last two layers of a neural language model are expected to contain most and most complete information.

Neural language models might differ based on the architecture they utilize, the languages they are trained on but also in terms of the training objective. Two main classes of models in terms of training objective are discriminative and generative pre-trained transformers. Discriminative models are generally trained to separate input data into specific classes. In the case of recent neural discriminative models, the training objective involves so-called masking, where a specific percentage of words in input sentences is randomly replaced by the [MASK] token that has to be filled by the model during training. BERT

[13] additionally introduced the task of predicting the next sentence as a second training objective. Generative models are trained to continue a sequences building on a given sequence. The joined encoder-decoder architecture was not only proposed for the Transformer, but for many sequence-to-sequence model. The encoder takes the input sequence and generates a compressed representation that is then passed to the decoder in order to generate the output sequence based on the compressed input sequence. It has become common to experiment with using only the encoder, e.g. BERT, or only the decoder, e.g. GPT-2.

2.2. Knowledge Graphs

Mathematically, a knowledge graph G is a set of triples (s,r,o), where s is the subject, o is the object, and r the relation or predicate to connect them. In case of directed graphs, the notation (h,r,t) is conventionally used to describe the head entity h, relation r, and tail entity t. These triples, often referred to as facts or factual associations, collectively construct a graph. Subjects and objects are referred to as entities and represent the primary objects of the graph, such as people, places, organizations, or events. They are typically depicted as nodes. Relations or predicates, which might be directed or undirected, are represented as edges that connect pairs of nodes.

Although there is no universally accepted formal definition of a knowledge graph beyond the mathematical description, Paulheim [24] suggests that a knowledge graph should meet several criteria to be considered as such:

- **Coverage across different domains**: It should span a variety of topics or fields.
- **Description of real-world entities and their interconnections**: It should accurately reflect complex real-world networks organized in a graph structure.
- **Structured schema**: It should include a schema defining classes of entities and types of relationships.
- **Interrelationships among entities**: It should demonstrate the interconnected nature of entities through explicit links.

2.3. Knowledge Graph Embeddings

Knowledge Graph Embeddings (KGEs) aim at representing entities and relations in a low-dimensional continuous vector space, while maintaining the original semantics. Given a fact represented as a triple $(h,r,t) \in D$, where D is the set of all triples in the KG, the objective is to embed all head and tail entities $h,t \in E$ and relations $r \in R$ in a vector $e \in \mathbb{R}^d$. E denotes the set of entities, whereas R is the set of relations. This section focuses on specific knowledge graph embeddings as required for the proposed factual probe. There are more refined neural network-based approaches to encode knowledge, e.g. graph neural networks or logic tensor networks, that provide interesting methods to encode knowledge. However, the main focus on the presented factual probe is factual associations as derived from KG embeddings.

Translational Distance Models. One of the most significant translational distance models is **TransE** [25]. TransE relies on a simple model architecture to compute embeddings of both entities and relations by considering relations as translations operating on the vectors $\mathbf{h}$ and $\mathbf{t}$ of the head and tail entities respectively. Similar to word2vec [19], TransE aims to approximate $\mathbf{t}$ by computing $\mathbf{h}+\mathbf{r} \approx \mathbf{t}$, meaning that when the fact holds, $\mathbf{r}$ can be seen as a vector connecting $\mathbf{h}$ and $\mathbf{t}$. Given a triple (`AlfredHitchcok`, `DirectorOf`, `Psycho`), the trained vectors should have the following property: $\mathbf{h}$(`AlfredHitchcok`) $+$ $\mathbf{r}$(`DirectorOf`) $\approx$ $\mathbf{t}$(`Psycho`) [26]. This property is achieved by maximizing the scoring function $f_r(h,t)$ depicted by Eq. (1).

$$f_r(h,t) = -\|\mathbf{h}+\mathbf{r}-\mathbf{t}\|_{1/2} \tag{1}$$

Eq. (1) should yield a large score if the fact holds and a small score otherwise, because the negative distance is computed. More intuitively, $\mathbf{t}$ should be as near as possible to $\mathbf{h}+\mathbf{r}$ for correct facts and further away for incorrect facts. Nevertheless, operating on a single vector space forces TransE to have problems when dealing with 1-to-N and N-to-1 relations. Given a relation $\mathbf{r}$ and a set of tail entities $\mathbf{t}_1,\ldots,\mathbf{t}_n$, $\mathbf{h}+\mathbf{r} \approx \mathbf{t}_1$, and $\mathbf{t}_1 \approx \ldots \approx \mathbf{t}_n$.

TransH [27] partly solves this issue by introducing translations on relation-specific hyperplanes. This model projects $\mathbf{h}$ and $\mathbf{t}$ onto a hyperplane defined by the normal vector $\mathbf{w}_r$, for each relation $\mathbf{r}$. The projection is computed as depicted in Eq. (2).

$$\mathbf{h}_\perp = \mathbf{h} - \mathbf{w}_r^T \mathbf{h} \mathbf{w}_r, \quad \mathbf{t}_\perp = \mathbf{t} - \mathbf{w}_r^T \mathbf{t} \mathbf{w}_r, \tag{2}$$

where $\mathbf{h}_\perp$ and $\mathbf{t}_\perp$ are the projections of $\mathbf{h}$ and $\mathbf{t}$ onto the hyperplane. The scoring function of TransE is modified in TransH to:

$$f_r(h,t) = -\|\mathbf{h}_\perp + \mathbf{r} - \mathbf{t}_\perp\|_2^2. \tag{3}$$

This enables TransH to introduce a sort of contextualized mechanism, allowing different vector representations of an entity depending on the specific relation involved.

Alternatively, **TransR** [28] models relations in specific spaces instead of hyperplanes. The model does so by projecting $\mathbf{h}$ and $\mathbf{t}$ onto a space, which is specific to the relation, using a projection matrix $M_r \in \mathbb{R}^{k\times d}$ as depicted in Eq. (4).

$$\mathbf{h}_\perp = M_r \mathbf{h}, \quad \mathbf{t}_\perp = M_r \mathbf{t}. \tag{4}$$

The scoring function remains the same as Eq. (3).

Semantic Matching Models. Semantic matching models differ from distance-based models in that they use operations like dot product and cosine similarity to compute scores that consider the latent semantic properties of head and tail entities. **RESCAL** [29] is one of the early examples of semantic matching models, representing entities as vectors and each relation as a matrix M_r, tasked with modeling pairwise interactions between latent features. Each element $w_{i,j}$ of the matrix M_r denotes the amount of interaction between the i-th latent factor of $\mathbf{h}$ and the j-th latent factor of $\mathbf{t}$. Therefore, the plausibility of a fact is given by Eq. (5).

$$f_r(h,t) = \mathbf{h}^T M_r \mathbf{t} = \sum_{i=1}^{d} \sum_{j=1}^{d} w_{ij}^{(r)} \mathbf{h}_i \mathbf{t}_j \tag{5}$$

In Eq. (5), d represents the dimension of the latent space. However, because RESCAL captures interactions between every pair of components in $\mathbf{h}$ and $\mathbf{t}$, it requires a significant number of parameters, specifically, $\mathcal{O}(d^2)$ parameters per relation.

DistMult [30] solves this issue by representing $\mathbf{M}_r$ as a diagonal matrix, such that the interactions between **h** and **t** are only captured along the same dimension. It embeds h,t and r in the same real dimensional space and uses a scoring function that relies on the dot product to determine the plausibility of a given triple. The scoring function is described by Eq. (6).

$$f_r(h,t) = \mathbf{h}^T \operatorname{diag}(\mathbf{r})\mathbf{t} = \sum_{i=0}^{d-1} \mathbf{r}_i \mathbf{h}_i \mathbf{t}_i \tag{6}$$

Here, $\operatorname{diag}(\mathbf{r})$ is a diagonal matrix derived from the relation vector **r**. The goal of this scoring function is to multiply **h** with $\operatorname{diag}(\mathbf{r})$, which outputs another vector $\mathbf{t}'$. The dot product is then computed between **t** and $\mathbf{t}'$. The resulting score ideally maximizes the alignment between the true tail entity **t** and the predicted tail entity $\mathbf{t}' = \mathbf{h}^T \cdot \operatorname{diag}(\mathbf{r})$, such that if the fact is correct, the dot product is as high as possible.

Combining the rich interactions of RESCAL with the efficiency of DistMult results in the Holographic Embeddings (**HolE**) model [31]. HolE introduces the circular correlation operator to combine the head and tail entity representations into $\mathbf{h} \star \mathbf{t} \in \mathbb{R}^d$, where the circular correlation $\star : \mathbb{R}^d \times \mathbb{R}^d \to \mathbb{R}^d$ is defined as:

$$[\mathbf{h} \star \mathbf{t}]_i = \sum_{k=0}^{d-1} \mathbf{h}_k \cdot \mathbf{t}_{(i+k) \bmod d}. \tag{7}$$

This way, each component $[\mathbf{h} \star \mathbf{t}]_i$ represents a summation over a fixed partition of pairwise interactions. This design enables HolE to group semantically similar interactions into a shared partition, allowing weights to be shared through the relation vector **r**. The scoring function for HolE is described by Eq. (8).

$$f_r(h,t) = \mathbf{r}^T\,(\mathbf{h} \star \mathbf{t}) = \sum_{i=0}^{d-1} \mathbf{r}_i \sum_{k=0}^{d-1} \mathbf{h}_k \cdot \mathbf{t}_{(i+k) \bmod d} \tag{8}$$

The inner sum represents the circular correlation between the head and tail embeddings, while the outer sum represents the dot product with the relation vector **r**.

Semantic matching models can also be implemented using neural networks. For instance, the Neural Tensor Network (**NTN**) [32] initially projects entities into their vector embeddings **h** and **t** in the first layer. It then combines these embeddings with a relation-specific tensor $\underline{M}_r \in \mathbb{R}^{d \times d \times k}$, integrating them into a non-linear hidden layer. The model proceeds to compute the score through a relation-specific linear layer as follows:

$$f_r(h,t) = \mathbf{r}^T \tanh\left(\mathbf{h}^T \underline{M}_r \mathbf{t} + M_r^1 \mathbf{h} + M_r^2 \mathbf{t} + \mathbf{b}_r\right), \tag{9}$$

where M_r^1 and M_r^2 are matrices in $\mathbb{R}^{k \times d}$ and $\mathbf{b}_r$ is a bias vector in $\mathbb{R}^k$, all of which are specific to each relation. The bilinear tensor product $\mathbf{h}^T \underline{M}_r \mathbf{t}$ yields a vector whose i-th entry is calculated as $\mathbf{h}^T \underline{M}_r^{[1:i]} \mathbf{t}$.

RDF2Vec. The idea to replicate the success of word embeddings for factual knowledge has lead to useful and still being used KG embedding methods, such as **RDF2Vec** [33]. The main idea is to treat RDF graphs like documents in which RDF triples, consisting of a subject, relation, and object, are analogous to words in text. RDF2Vec first involves walking through the RDF graph to generate sequences of nodes similar to sentences in natural language. These walks can be either random or deterministic. In random walks, the algorithm chooses the next node randomly among the connected nodes, while deterministic walks might use specific patterns or strategies for node selection.

To enrich the context captured by the embeddings, it is beneficial to extend these sequences beyond single triples. Paulheim et al. [34] describes how to construct two-hop sequences S_{2hop} from the set of all triples $T \subseteq V \times R \times V$ with Eq. (10).

$$S_{2hop} := \{(v_1, r_1, v_2, r_2, v_3) : (v_1, r_1, v_2) \in T \wedge (v_2, r_2, v_3) \in T\} \tag{10}$$

By incorporating more hops and therefore combining more triples, the sequence can capture more extensive contextual relationships, potentially leading to embeddings with a richer semantic understanding of the graph's structure. The hops are then inserted into the word2vec model.

2.4. Linear Maps and Transformations

This section presents the basis for the linear transformation utilized in existing approaches as presented in Section 3 as well as the factual probe proposed in this chapter.

2.4.1. Linear Maps

A linear map between two vector spaces U and V is a function $T : U \to V$ with the properties

$$T(\mathbf{u}+\mathbf{w}) = T(\mathbf{u}) + T(\mathbf{w}), \tag{11}$$

$$T(\lambda \mathbf{u}) = \lambda T(\mathbf{u}) \tag{12}$$

where $\mathbf{u}$ and $\mathbf{w}$ are two vectors in the domain U and λ is a scalar. An important fact about linear maps is that they are uniquely determined by knowing the values they take on a basis. More precisely, let the vectors $\mathbf{b_1}, \mathbf{b_2}, \ldots, \mathbf{b_n}$ be a basis of U. This means every vector $\mathbf{u} \in U$ can be expressed as a unique linear combination of basis vectors as depicted in Eq. (13), where the α_i are the unique coefficients of the basis representation of $\mathbf{u}$ with respect to the basis $\mathbf{b_1}, \mathbf{b_2}, \ldots, \mathbf{b_n}$.

$$\mathbf{u} = \alpha_1 \mathbf{b_1} + \alpha_2 \mathbf{b_2} + \ldots + \alpha_n \mathbf{b_n} \tag{13}$$

To fully determine T, it is enough to know its values for all the $\mathbf{b_i}$, since

$$T(\mathbf{u}) = T(\alpha_1 \mathbf{b_1} + \alpha_2 \mathbf{b_2} + \ldots + \alpha_n \mathbf{b_n}) \tag{14}$$

$$= \alpha_1 T(\mathbf{b_1}) + \alpha_2 T(\mathbf{b_2}) + \ldots + \alpha_n T(\mathbf{b_n}) \tag{15}$$

The vector $T(\mathbf{u}) \in V$ is called the image of $\mathbf{u}$ with respect to T. From now on, consider $U = \mathbb{R}^n$ and $V = \mathbb{R}^m$. Of particular importance in this case is the canonical basis $\mathbf{e_1}, \mathbf{e_2}, \ldots, \mathbf{e_n}$, where for each $\mathbf{e_i}$ the i-th component is one and all others are zero as exemplified in Eq. (16).

$$\mathbf{e_1} = \begin{pmatrix} 1 \\ 0 \\ \vdots \\ 0 \end{pmatrix}, \quad \mathbf{e_2} = \begin{pmatrix} 0 \\ 1 \\ 0 \\ \vdots \\ 0 \end{pmatrix}, \quad \ldots \quad , \mathbf{e_n} = \begin{pmatrix} 0 \\ \vdots \\ 0 \\ 1 \end{pmatrix} \tag{16}$$

Taking this basis as a starting point, the linear map T can be represented by an $m \times n$ matrix A represented in Eq. (17) such that the columns are the images of the basis vectors.

$$A := \begin{pmatrix} \vdots & \vdots & & \vdots \\ T(\mathbf{e_1}) & T(\mathbf{e_2}) & \ldots & T(\mathbf{e_n}) \\ \vdots & \vdots & & \vdots \end{pmatrix}. \tag{17}$$

This allows for T to be written as represented in Eq. (18).

$$T(\mathbf{u}) := A\mathbf{u}. \tag{18}$$

Example: Let $U = V = \mathbb{R}^2$, and T be the linear map that rotates all vectors counter clockwise by 45 degrees while simultaneously stretching them by a factor of $\sqrt{2}$. Step one is to compute the images of the basis vectors depicted in Eq. (19).

$$T(\mathbf{e_1}) = T\left(\begin{pmatrix} 1 \\ 0 \end{pmatrix}\right) = \begin{pmatrix} 1 \\ 1 \end{pmatrix}, \quad T(\mathbf{e_2}) = T\left(\begin{pmatrix} 0 \\ 1 \end{pmatrix}\right) = \begin{pmatrix} -1 \\ 1 \end{pmatrix}. \tag{19}$$

This leads to the matrix representation as shown in Eq. (20).

$$A = \left(T(\mathbf{e_1})\ T(\mathbf{e_2})\right) = \begin{pmatrix} 1 & -1 \\ 1 & 1 \end{pmatrix} \tag{20}$$

The effect of this transformation is visualized in Figure 1.

2.4.2. Linear Transformations

If one chooses $U = V = \mathbb{R}^n$, a linear map $T : U \to U$ can be interpreted as a linear coordinate transformation, if the images of $\mathbf{e_1}, \mathbf{e_2}, \ldots, \mathbf{e_n}$ again form a basis of U. In particular, every vector in U must have a unique representation as a linear combination of the images $T(\mathbf{e_1}), T(\mathbf{e_2}), \ldots, T(\mathbf{e_n})$. This condition implies that the matrix representation A of T is non singular, i.e., $\det A \neq 0$. The action of a linear transformation T is in general a combination of rotation, reflection and scaling. In practice, these transformations can be

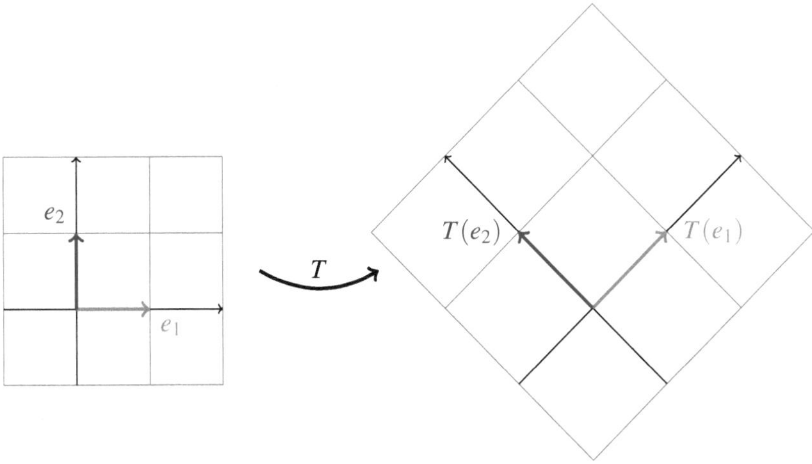

Figure 1. The space U before (left) and after (right) applying the transformation T.

useful to switch into a more suitable system of coordinates without loss of information, as the transformation can always be reversed. On the flip side, every non singular $n \times n$ matrix A defines a transformation from the space spanned by its columns $A_1, \ldots, A_n$ into the canonical basis. Of notable importance are orthogonal transformations corresponding to only rotations and reflections. An orthogonal transformation of $\mathbb{R}^n$ can be characterized via its matrix representation Q. It holds that $Q^T Q = QQ^T = I$, where I denotes the identity matrix. It also preserves the dot product of two vectors as Eq. (21) shows.

$$Q\mathbf{u} \cdot Q\mathbf{v} = (Q\mathbf{u})^T Q\mathbf{v} = \mathbf{u}^T Q^T Q\mathbf{v} = \mathbf{u}^T I\mathbf{v} = \mathbf{u} \cdot \mathbf{v}. \tag{21}$$

As a consequence, orthogonal transformations preserve angles and distances. Also, because of $1 = \det I = \det Q^T Q = (\det Q)^2$, it can be concluded that $\det Q \in \{-1, 1\}$.

2.4.3. Applications in Deep Learning

Because of their simplicity and convenient mathematical properties, linear functions are used extensively in practice. Numerical operations such as matrix vector products can be efficiently computed in parallel, hence linear functions also form one of the core building blocks of modern machine learning and deep learning. When training neural networks, including those used in language models, linear maps are applied at various layers to project input data into spaces that the model can more effectively learn from. For instance, the output vector $\hat{\mathbf{y}}$ of the first layer of a fully connected neural network is computed as the product of the input vector $\mathbf{x}$ with a weight matrix W, adding a bias term $\mathbf{b}$ and passing the result through a non-linear activation function f, as described by Eq. (22).

$$\hat{\mathbf{y}} = f(W\mathbf{x} + \mathbf{b}). \tag{22}$$

The term $W\mathbf{x} + \mathbf{b}$ is called an affine linear function, it consists of the strictly linear matrix vector product $W\mathbf{x}$ and an additional translation $\mathbf{b}$. Intuitively, an affine linear function acts by rotating, scaling, mirroring a vector and afterwards shifting the result by **b**. Note that W is in general not a square matrix, in practice it is common to have different input and output dimensions. In deep learning, linear functions also play a crucial role in data representation and manipulation across various tasks and model architectures. For instance in NLP, linear transformations can be employed to convert embeddings from one space to another, facilitating the processing of textual data in a way that captures semantic and syntactic relationships. In addition, tools such as singular value decomposition or analysis of eigenvalues can reveal further insights about models and embeddings. Moreover, linear transformation can be used as stand-alone machine learning models to unveil properties from hidden representations. Their simplicity and ability to preserve many structural aspects of a vector space can lead to robust and interpretable results. One can train linear transformations with supervised data to transform neural networks' vector spaces in a way that they can encode the property of interest [35,36,2]. Such models are often referred to as *probes*, as introduced in Section 1. If the transformation is orthogonal, the vector space maintains the dot product operations between vectors as well as their lengths and it is even more safe to assume that the properties are encoded and only need to be linearly transformed to become explicit.

3. Existing Approaches

A broad range of approaches address the question on how and where knowledge is encoded in neural language models. This section provides an overview of methods using linear transformations to identify specific, mostly linguistic features. Furthermore, it discusses prompt-based approaches to explicate knowledge and methods for localizing facts in vector spaces or tracing knowledge-related predictions. In contrast to these transformations to uncover linguistic features and other approaches to uncover knowledge, the proposed approach utilizes linear transformations to directly unveil factual associations in hidden vector spaces of PLMs.

3.1. Linear Transformations and Probing

Linear transformations of hidden representations of pre-trained language models have provided evidence of encoded implicit linguistic features, such as syntax trees [2] and discourse relations [6]. Within the context of this chapter, graph-based approaches, such as dependency graphs, are of most interest. One approach that inspired much of this work is the structural probe proposed by Hewitt and Manning [2], which evaluates whether a dependency parse tree is embedded in a linear transformation of BERT's [13] and ELMo's [37] vector space. The objective of showing that a tree structure is implicitly embedded in the vector spaces is considered achieved when the squared L2 distance in the transformed vector space represents the distance between words in the parse tree and the squared L2 norm encodes the depth in the parse tree. The transformation matrix is trained in a supervised manner with gradient descent in order to best approximate these properties. Coenen et al. [3] extend this idea to an attention probe, for which they form a model-wide attention vector by concatenating the entries of two tokens across all attention matrices in all layers. To test if this attention vector encodes the tokens' syntactic relation, the accuracy of L2 regularized linear classifiers is utilized. Apart from providing evidence that syntax trees are indeed implicitly encoded in hidden representations, both approaches suggest that the information might be encoded in a lower-dimensional subspace.

A different kind of probe on hidden representations is presented by Michael et al. [38], who introduce latent subclass learning by inducing latent categorizations on hidden representations of BERT and ELMo in order to identify linguistic features, e.g. named entity or dependency types. The probe is designed as a weakly supervised clustering task to identify latent classes related to specific class types, e.g. personhood, in the vector space.

Recently, Yom Din et al. [39] propose to bypass the multi-layer hidden representations of a Transformer model and use linear tranformations to cast the hidden representations as final representation with the objective to investigate the utility of these intermediate layers exemplified with BERT and GPT-2 [14]. The idea is that this type of approximation might provide further insights into the decision-making process of this type of architecture and that, similar to other uses of linear transformations, the direct use of these hidden representations for predictions might reduce computational costs. The resulting representations showed a higher prediction accuracy on the next token and mask prediction tasks than direct model inferences. Interestingly, this successful linear mapping of representations from one layer to another suggest more linearity involved in transformer inference than previously assumed.

3.2. Prompt-based Methods

A prompt within the context of generative neural language models represents an instruction on the task to be performed by the model. Prompt-based methods have been utilized to explicate facts present in the model's representations [7,8]. Recently, Cohen et al. [9] proposed a few-shot prompting method to directly obtain complete knowledge graphs from such models. Starting from a seed entity, the proposed approach utilizes prompts to recursively expand a knowledge graph around it. This task is split into the subtasks of relation generation, paraphrasing, and object generation, which are designed as few-shot prompts utilizing fact associations from Wikidata [40] as examples.

3.3. Localization and Tracing

One highly related line of research seeks to identify specific model weights that encode factual information, e.g. by means of a layer-wise localization technique called Causal Tracing [10]. However, Hase et al. [11] show evidence for a substantially low correlation of tracing results and model weight edit success and thus, how little is known about the encoding of factual information. Rather than focusing on where information is stored, Geva et al. [12] focus on how factual associations are retrieved during inference. To trace the information flow given a subject and a predicate to the prediction of the next token, i.e., the object, specific model parts are blocked to evaluate their importance during inference. Interestingly, this work shows that attention head parameters encode subject-object mappings, where the importance of early layers to enrich and encode subject-relation information is highlighted. In contrast, this chapter focuses on strengths of subject-object mappings in PLMs' hidden representations as opposed to linearly transformed representations, with the objective to unveil the factual associations present in hidden vector spaces.

4. Dataset

The dataset of knowledge base triples used for the presented approach is a subset from the Wikidata5m dataset [41] with more than 20 m triples from the Wikidata knowledge graph [40]. Instead of randomly sampling *n* triples from the original dataset, proportional sampling is used to reduce the dataset size while maintaining the original distribution of relations as much as possible. This approach ensures that the reduced dataset reflects the relational diversity and proportions of the original dataset. The algorithm calculates the proportion of each relation in the original dataset and uses these proportions to determine how many triples to sample for each relation, based on the target size of the reduced dataset. It also ensures that each selected relation has a minimum number of samples to avoid losing rare relations. The final numbers of the subset of Wikidata5m are presented in Table 1.

Table 1. Sampled subset of the Wikidata5m dataset

Type	Training	Validation	Test	Total
Triples	33,937	4,242	4,243	42,422
Entities	45,343	6,883	6,874	55,344
Relations	190	146	156	191

Based on the IDs in this dataset, the actual labels for entities and relations are obtained in English by means of the Wikidata API[2]. The proposed approach requires the calculation of similarities between entities. To this end, existing Wikidata KG embeddings provided by Nielsen [42] as the Wembedder[3] service are utilized. These embeddings have been derived using a streamlined adaptation of the RDF2Vec algorithm explained in Section 2.3. While any other KG embedding method could have been used here, we opted for the one openly available. In future experiments, a more comprehensive testing of available KG embedding methods would be desirable. The cosine similarity of these KG entity embeddings is utilized to represent relational and factual proximity.

5. Method

Inspired by the unveiling of a full dependency graph in PLMs' hidden representations [2,3], a similar approach utilizing linear transformation is described in this section to uncover factual associations in these representations. An approximation of the relation based on the two entities is utilized as input to the probe as depicted in Figure2.

5.1. Pre-trained Language Models and Vector Spaces

The choice of PLM to be utilized for the proposed approach required openly accessible models as well as vector spaces. For comparability with previous approaches that investigate specific properties of hidden representations [3,2,6], the first selected model is BERT [13], specifically the uncased base version[4]. Additionally, BERT is chosen for

[2]`https://www.wikidata.org/w/api.php`
[3]`https://wembedder.toolforge.org`
[4]`https://huggingface.co/google-bert/bert-base-uncased`

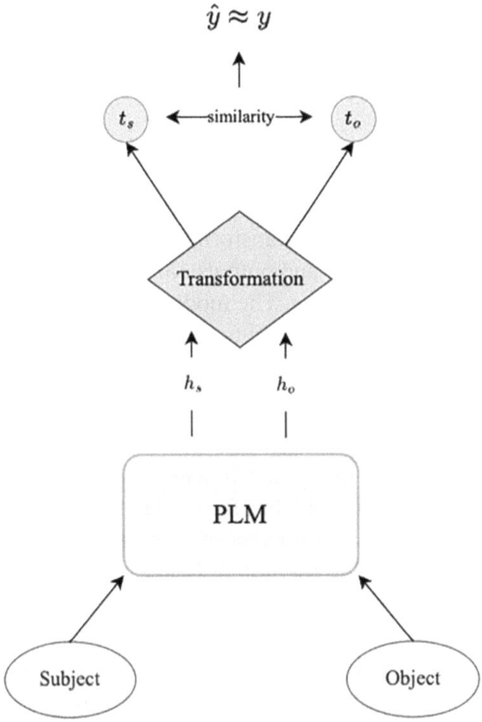

Figure 2. Method overview.

its robust contextual bidirectional representations and the extensive body of comparative research available. As BERT is an encoder-only Transformer model, the second architecture should be based on a different architecture. GPT-2, the open-source model from OpenAI's GPT family, offers interesting generative capabilities and it represents the choice for a decoder-only model. Nevertheless, because of its generative architecture, the model is trained in an auto-regressive manner and the hidden representations can therefore lack bidirectional context.

The contextual embeddings of the chosen language models are extracted from the last layers' hidden states. Since many of the entities present in the dataset are composed of multiple words, the embeddings of all tokens in the sequence are averaged and L2 normalization is applied to ensure that each embedding vector has a unit length in the vector space. Combining the operations of averaging and normalizing the hidden states, the complete process of extracting embeddings $\mathbf{h}' \in X$ for the set of knowledge graph entities X in the dataset can be described by Eq. 23.

$$\mathbf{h}' = \frac{\mathbf{h}_{\text{mean}}}{\|\mathbf{h}_{\text{mean}}\|_2} = \frac{\frac{1}{n}\sum_{i=1}^{n}\mathbf{h}_i}{\left\|\frac{1}{n}\sum_{i=1}^{n}\mathbf{h}_i\right\|_2} \tag{23}$$

For BERT, we also experiment with a different strategy, i.e., using the CLS token to represent the embedding of the sequence. The two training objectives of BERT consisted of masking specific words of a sequence to be predicted by the model as well as the prediction of the next sentence. For this sentence-level classification task, the [CLS] token was introduced in order to better capture the entire input sequence. The advantage of this special token is that during pre-training, the representation of the CLS token is optimized to aggregate the entire semantic content of the input sequence.

5.2. Factual Probe

Given the definition of linear maps and linear transformations in Sections 2.4.1 and 2.4.2, the factual probe is designed as a linear transformation $T : \mathbb{R}^n \to \mathbb{R}^n$ that takes as input n-dimensional contextual embeddings and outputs embeddings with the same dimensionality, but in a transformed vector space. The model itself consists of the transformation matrix B, which is multiplied with the input vector $\mathbf{h}$ to output a transformed vector $\mathbf{t}$, therefore, $\mathbf{t} = B\mathbf{h}$. Each element t_i of the output vector $\mathbf{t}$ is a linear combination of the columns of B weighted by the elements of $\mathbf{h}$. The parameters of the matrix B are initialized using a uniform distribution $U\left(-\frac{1}{\sqrt{n}}, \frac{1}{\sqrt{n}}\right)$, where n is the size of the input features, which in our case corresponds to the vector dimensionality of 768.

Since the objective is to probe whether factual knowledge as represented in knowledge graphs is encoded in PLMs' vector spaces, it is essential to ensure the integrity of the vector geometry by maintaining the initial dimensionality. In other words, no additional information should be added. The underlying assumption is that such knowledge is represented in the original vector space, which is evaluated by a linear transformation of the learned vector space. Hewitt and Manning [2] proposed a so-called structural probe by means of a linear transformation to show that entire syntax trees are encoded in the vector spaces of BERT and ELMo. In this chapter, we propose to apply linear transformation to evaluate factual knowledge in the vector space of BERT and GPT-2.

The corresponding model $\mathscr{M}$ seeks to learn a transformation matrix $B \in \mathbb{R}^{n\times n}$ under which the similarity scores between knowledge graph embeddings depicted in the training dataset can be approximated. The matrix B has a dimensionality of $\mathbb{R}^{n\times n}$, where n is the size of the input embeddings, resulting in a square matrix with 768×768 trainable parameters. The parameters of the transformation matrix are trained in a supervised manner by means of gradient descent, where the difference between the similarity scores of the KG entity embeddings and the entity embeddings of the transformed vector space are calculated. The similarity is measured in terms of cosine similarity. The hypothesis is that factual associations are embedded in the language model if the linear transformation is able to reproduce the similarity scores of the KG embeddings using only the contextual embeddings $\mathbf{h}_s$ and $\mathbf{h}_o$, which undergo a transformation by matrix B to become $\mathbf{t}_s$ and $\mathbf{t}_o$. Thus, the function that is approximated is $s_B(\mathbf{t}_s, \mathbf{t}_o) \approx s_T(e_s, e_o)$. The similarity function $s_B(\mathbf{t}_s, \mathbf{t}_o)$ is defined as cosine similarity:

$$s_B(\mathbf{t}_s, \mathbf{t}_o) = \frac{\mathbf{t}_s \cdot \mathbf{t}_o}{\|\mathbf{t}_s\| \|\mathbf{t}_o\|} = \frac{\sum_{i=1}^{n} (\mathbf{t}_s)_i (\mathbf{t}_o)_i}{\sqrt{\sum_{i=1}^{n} (\mathbf{t}_s)_i^2} \cdot \sqrt{\sum_{i=1}^{n} (\mathbf{t}_o)_i^2}}. \tag{24}$$

The approximation can be achieved by minimizing the loss function $\mathscr{L}$ using a mean-squared error regression objective and by training the parameters of the transformation matrix B using gradient descent in a supervised setting, as described by Eq. (25).

$$\mathscr{L} = \min_B \frac{1}{N} \sum_{\ell=1}^{N} |s_T(e_s^\ell, e_o^\ell) - s_B(\mathbf{t}_s^\ell, \mathbf{t}_o^\ell)|^2 \tag{25}$$

Here s_T is also defined as the goldstandard cosine similarity between knowledge graph embeddings of subject e_s and object e_o from the dataset. Then, s_B represents the predicted similarity scores between the transformed subject entity vector $\mathbf{t}_s$ and transformed object entity vector $\mathbf{t}_o$. ℓ indexes the different subject-object pairs in the dataset and N is the total number of subject-object pairs.

5.3. Training and Optimization

The models are trained for 100 epochs using an initial learning rate between 1e-3 and 5e-3, depending on the PLM used. The utilized optimizer is AdamW [43]. A regularization term R in form of a weight decay given by the AdamW optimizer is added to the objective function described by Eq. (25) to prevent overfitting by penalizing large weights. The updated loss function is described by Eq. (26).

$$\mathscr{L} = \min_B \frac{1}{N} \sum_{\ell=1}^{N} |s_T(e_s^\ell, e_o^\ell) - s_B(\mathbf{t}_s^\ell, \mathbf{t}_o^\ell)|^2 + R(\theta) \tag{26}$$

In Eq. (26), θ are the parameters of the transformation matrix B. During training, R is set to 5e-3 as weight decay factor. The hyperparameter patience describes the maximum number of epochs without improvements, which is here set to 5, before the learning rate is reduced by scheduler factor 0.1. Additionally, an early stopping mechanism is implemented to avoid overfitting. The early stopping hyperparameter is set to 10, which means that the model will wait for 10 epochs of no improvement before stopping the training process. All chosen hyperparameters are summarized in Table 2 and the algorithm is presented as pseudocode in Algorithm 1.

Table 2. Training hyperparameters with corresponding values.

	Value		
Hyperparameter	BERT-cls	BERT-avg	GPT2-avg
Nr. of epochs	100	100	100
Weight decay	5e-3	5e-3	5e-3
Learning rate	1e-3	1e-3	4e-3
Learning rate scheduler factor	1e-1	1e-1	1e-1
Learning rate patience	5	5	5
Early stopping	10	10	10

5.4. Evaluation

In order to assess the performance of the factual probe, the results are quantified, qualitatively analyzed and the difference between the original and transformed vector spaces are visualized. For a numeric evaluation, correlation coefficients and error rates are chosen, while the qualitative analysis entails manual inspections on specific relation types that resulted in particularly low improvements.

Algorithm 1 Training Algorithm

Given training data $D_t = \{X, Y\}$
Given validation data $D_v = \{X, Y\}$
Initialize transformation matrix B with $U\left(\frac{1}{\sqrt{n}}, \frac{1}{\sqrt{n}}\right)$
Define $\mathscr{L}$ as in Equation 26
epoch $\leftarrow 0$
best_loss $\leftarrow \infty$
early_stopping $\leftarrow 0$
while epoch < 100 and early_stopping < 10 **do**
    for each pair ℓ in D_t **do**
        Compute $\mathbf{t}_s^\ell = B\mathbf{h}_s^\ell$ and $\mathbf{t}_o^\ell = B\mathbf{h}_o^\ell$
        Calculate similarity $s_B(\mathbf{t}_s^\ell, \mathbf{t}_o^\ell) = \frac{\mathbf{t}_s \cdot \mathbf{t}_o}{\|\mathbf{t}_s\|\|\mathbf{t}_o\|}$
        Compute loss $\mathscr{L}$ for the pair ℓ given $s_B(\mathbf{t}_s^\ell, \mathbf{t}_o^\ell)$ and true score Y
        Perform backpropagation to update B
    end for
    Evaluate on validation data D_v using val_loss
    if learning_rate_patience $\leftarrow 5$ **then**
        Apply learning rate scheduler
    end if
    if val_loss $<$ best_loss **then**
        best_loss $\leftarrow$ val_loss
        early_stopping $\leftarrow 0$
    else
        early_stopping $\leftarrow$ early_stopping $+ 1$
    end if
    epoch $\leftarrow$ epoch $+ 1$
end while

Quantitative Evaluation. The output of the transformation process is a numerical value that corresponds to the cosine similarity, i.e., relational proximity, of two entities in the transformed vector spaces as compared to the same proximity in the KG entity embeddings. To effectively quantify the accuracy of the predictions, established metrics to evaluate regression models are used. Since the presented approach represents a linear transformation, it is reasonable to utilize the Pearson Correlation Coefficient (PCC), since it measures the linear correlation between two sets. The Spearman's Rank Correlation Coefficient (SRCC) is reported for comparison with other approaches and completeness. In addition, the Mean Squared Error (MSE), which assesses the average squared difference between observed and predicted values, and the Root Mean Squared Error (RMSE) are reported.

Visualization. One additional method to inspect the effect of the linear transformation on the hidden representations consists in a visual comparison between original and transformed vector spaces, which allows to potentially identify anomalies, outliers and clusters. To this end, the 768-dimensional embeddings need to be reduced to two dimensions. Several dimensionality reduction algorithms exist, such as Principal Component Analysis (PCA) [44], t-distributed Stochastic Neighbor Embedding (t-SNE) [45], and Uniform Manifold Approximation and Projection (UMAP) [46].

The unsupervised t-SNE algorithm is chosen because of its non-linear nature, its ability to preserve the local structure of the data and the better performance compared to PCA or UMAP [47]. t-SNE can be described by the following equations [48]:

$$p_{j|i} = \frac{\exp\left(-\left\|\mathbf{x}_i - \mathbf{x}_j\right\|^2 / 2\sigma_i^2\right)}{\sum_{k \neq i} \exp\left(-\left\|\mathbf{x}_i - \mathbf{x}_k\right\|^2 / 2\sigma_i^2\right)} \tag{27}$$

$$p_{ij} = \frac{p_{j|i} + p_{i|j}}{2N} \tag{28}$$

$$q_{ij} = \frac{\left(1 + \left\|\mathbf{y}_i - \mathbf{y}_j\right\|^2\right)^{-1}}{\sum_{k \neq l} \left(1 + \left\|\mathbf{y}_k - \mathbf{y}_l\right\|^2\right)^{-1}} \tag{29}$$

$$D_{KL}(P \| Q) = \sum_{i \neq j} p_{ij} \log \frac{p_{ij}}{q_{ij}} \tag{30}$$

where $p_{j|i}$ is the conditional probability modeling the similarity of datapoint $\mathbf{x}_j$ to datapoint $\mathbf{x}_i$ and σ_i is the variance of the Gaussian distribution centered on datapoint $\mathbf{x}_i$. The variance is adapted for each point differently and is chosen in a way that the perplexity of the conditional distribution equals a specified hyperparameter, which is set to 30. p_{ij} are the symmetrized joint probabilities used to capture the pairwise similarity between datapoints in the high-dimensional space, with N specifying the number of datapoints. q_{ij} measures the similarity between $\mathbf{y}_i$ and $\mathbf{y}_j$, which are the low-dimensional embeddings of the datapoints $\mathbf{x}_i$ and $\mathbf{x}_j$. D_{KL} is the Kullback-Leibler divergence [49], which is minimized during several iterations of gradient descent set to 1,000. The `TSNE` class of the Scikit-learn library encapsulates the learning process described by Eqs. 27, 28, 29 and 30 and was utilized to compare the visualization of the original and transformed vector space.

To provide more insight into the changes with the factual probe, one randomly selected set of related entity embeddings is traced before and after the transformation. The expectation is that the distance between the entities is reduced in the transformed vector space measured by cosine similarity.

Qualitative Analysis. To provide a more detailed analysis of the performance of the transformed vector spaces on factual associations, specific types of relations were analyzed. To this end, once the quantitative metrics have been computed on the entire test set, the subject-object pairs with the lowest scores and the biggest discrepancy between actual and predicted similarity value can be analyzed. Such an analysis aims to identify potential relation or entity types, for which the linear transformation is unable to approximate the true similarity scores, indicating potential differences of factual associations in the PLMs' hidden representations.

6. Results

The results are presented in form of quantified measures, visualized vector spaces and qualitative analysis assess the effect of the factual probe.

6.1. Quantitative Results

The four selected metrics to numerically analyze the effect are the Pearson Correlation Coefficient (PCC), Spearman Rank Correlation Coefficient (SRCC), Mean Squared Error (MSE) and Root Mean Squared Error (RMSE). Table 3 compares the results of these four metrics on the original hidden representations of CLS-token of BERT (BERT-cls), the averaged hidden representations of the final layer of BERT (BERT-avg), as well as the averaged hidden representations of the final layer of GPT-2 (GPT-avg). When solely retrieving contextual embeddings based on entity names, the factual associations do not correlate well with those in the KG as shown by the results of the original embeddings. As can be seen from the results, GPT-2 embeddings initially already encode stronger factual associations than BERT embeddings.

Table 3. Results of the original (top) and transformed (bottom) vector spaces in terms of Pearson Correlation Coefficient (PCC), Spearman Rank Correlation Coefficient (SRCC), Mean-Squared Error (MSE), and Root Mean-Squared Error (RMSE).

Original	**↑PCC**	**↑SRCC**	**↓MSE**	**↓RMSE**
BERT-cls	0.0289	0.0478	0.1254	0.3542
BERT-avg	0.2428	0.1917	**0.0520**	**0.2281**
GPT-2-avg	**0.4186**	**0.4231**	0.2283	0.4778
Transformed	**↑PCC**	**↑SRCC**	**↓MSE**	**↓RMSE**
BERT-cls	**0.8839**	**0.8696**	**0.0103**	**0.1013**
BERT-avg	0.8796	0.8674	0.0106	0.1030
GPT-2-avg	0.7988	0.7882	0.0185	0.1427

The semantics and relation between the entities s and o in the vector space might be latent, when no additional information beside their names is given. The task of the linear transformation is to make these properties explicit and to transform the embeddings in a way that they align with the geometric properties of the knowledge graph embedding space. After the transformation, as reported at the bottom of Table 3, BERT-cls achieves the highest PCC and SRCC scores as well as lowest error rates, providing the most successful factual probe. This is particularly interesting since the CLS token contains most contextual information and shows the strongest effect of the linear transformation. Nevertheless, high improvements for BERT-avg and GPT-2-avg can equally be observed, indicating a surprisingly robust encoding of factual associations according to the proposed factual probe.

Due to the comparatively lower change from original to transformed vector space for GPT-2 averaged embeddings, the optimization process was analyzed as depicted in Figure 3. While the loss curve represents expected and desired behaviour, the PCC calculation per epoch indicates a rather turbulent process. The progression of the PCC score throughout the epochs is inconsistent, displaying fluctuations rather than a steady increase. This volatility persists until around epoch 60, after which a distinct divergence between training and validation performance becomes apparent.

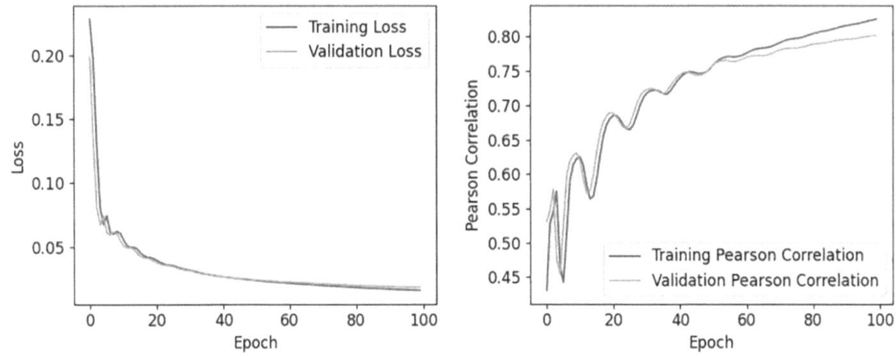

Figure 3. Loss curve (left) and Pearson correlation coefficient (right) for the GPT-2-avg vector space.

6.2. *Visualization*

By means of the t-SNE method, the embeddings of the test sets are visualized before and after the transformation. Due to space constraints, the focus of this visualization is on the best performing BERT-cls vector spaces, which are displayed as original and transformed in Figure 4. The initial vector space prior to the factual probe appears more compact, with few discernible clusters and some outliers at the lower part of the plane. In this visualization, orange data points represent the subjects in the knowledge graph, while blue points represent the objects. In contrast, the transformed vector space exhibits a less compact arrangement with a more distinct separation between subjects and objects, alongside enhanced clustering of objects in the peripheral areas. The magnitudes of the vectors also seem to increase compared to the original vector space, with several vectors approaching -100 and $+100$.

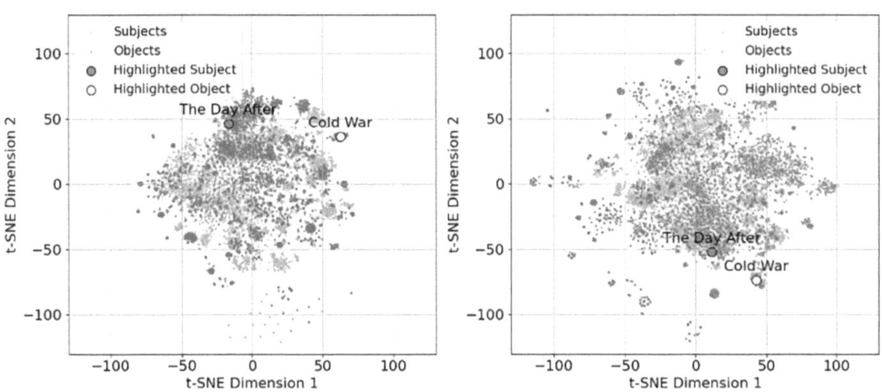

Figure 4. Original (left) and transformed (right) vector spaces of BERT-cls.

To gain more insights into how the transformation matrix B has transformed the vector space and moved the embeddings, two related entities are highlighted. The randomly selected entities are 'The Day After" (subject) and "Cold War" (object), which are related by "main subject". Their respective positions in the vector space are depicted in Figure 4, where the subject is displayed with a red dot and the object with a yellow dot. In contrast to their position in the original vector space, they jointly move to the bottom of the plane and considerably closer together as confirmed by a higher cosine similarity.

6.3. Qualitative Analysis

In order to provide more insights into the factual associations explicated in hidden representations of PLMs, the 30 triples that showed the biggest discrepancy between KG embedding similarity and predicted similarity in the transformed vector space. The higher the discrepancy, the lower the factual association in the hidden representations after the transformation.

It is particularly interesting to evaluate whether these triples with the highest discrepancy and thus, lowest factual association in vector space, share specific relations. As a result, both variants of BERT, that is, BERT-cls and BERT-avg, show low associations for geographic relations, in particular "shares border with". For BERT-cls, in total 8 of the analyzed triples (26%) shared this relation and two additional triples have geographic relations, i.e., "located in the administrative territorial entity" and "territorial entity". For BERT-avg, 10 triples with relation "shares border with" (33%) showed the lowest associations, as well as other geographic relations, such as"located in the administrative territorial entity", "twinned administrative body", "country", and "capital". These issues may be attributable to several factors. First, it is a prevalent relation within the dataset, increasing the likelihood of erroneous predictions due to its large volume. Second, many entities within this relation category have non-English names, which presents a challenge for BERT, primarily trained on English data. This can potentially hinder its ability to accurately encode these specific facts. Finally, this type of relation tends to encode and require substantial background knowledge. For instance, in the triple `(Pozzo d'Adda, shares border with, Basiano)` a detailed understanding of Italian geography, particularly the municipalities in the Lombardy region, is needed. This begs the question of how (much of) this knowledge is and can be encoded in and learned from exclusively textual data.

GPT-2 shares similarities with BERT, with the "shares border with" relation showing the weakest result with 11 erroneous predictions (36%), that might be attributed to similar reasons. Additional difficulties for GPT-2 are observed with familial and historical relationships. For instance, the model struggles with triples like `(Marcus Aurelius, child, Fadilla)`, or `(Elizabeth of Austria, spouse, Sigismund II Augustus)`, indicating a challenge in accurately encoding the nature of personal relationships between subjects and objects. Other problematic relations in this category include "father" and "sibling". One potential explanation for these difficulties might be attributed to the fact that these relations tend to contain named entities that consist of multiple words and are frequently in a language other than English, such as "Sigismund II Augustus" or "Germanicus".

7. Discussion

The proposed factual probe on two PLMs indicates a strong presence of factual associations in hidden representations. By means of a linear transformation to align the vector spaces with the properties of KG embeddings, a latent subspace in which these properties are primarily encoded could be uncovered. Even though other methods propose the use of more complex models involving non-linear transformation [50,51,6], this chapter focused on linearly transforming the original space to make the desired properties explicit. The factual probe, that is, to analyze whether hidden representations represent factual associations as found in knowledge graphs, results in strong improvements of correlation coefficients and error rates, suggesting that PLMs' hidden representations indeed implicitly encode factual knowledge.

Some relation types seem to be less successfully encoded than others, where, in particular, geographical relations seem to be problematic. This might be attributed to the fact that this type of relation requires substantial background knowledge, but it can also be partially explained by the fact that it conventionally relates named entities. Named entities can be problematic for language models due to the fact that they tend to be multi-word sequences and frequently contain words in a language other than English.

The proposed factual probe can be used to compare differences in a models' ability to encode factual associations, which means it equally allows for comparisons of different training objectives and neural architectures of these models. In this chapter, two different training objectives and architectures were compared. BERT is a discriminative language model that is trained on the masked learning objective, i.e., randomly masking a certain percentage of words during training, and has an encoder-only architecture. GPT-2 is a generative language model which is trained to predict the next word given a sequence of previous words and has a decoder-only architecture. The discriminative encoder-only model showed stronger factual associations in the probe, both when using the CLS token with more contextual information and when averaging the hidden states of token embeddings. Nevertheless, the improved correlation coefficients and reduced error rates for the generative decoder-only model still indicate a substantial presence of facts in its hidden representations. It could be that the bidirectional encoder in the BERT model, where training sequences are analyzed from both directions, might be beneficial to encoding facts. Furthermore, the training dataset might be taken into account, which was much more targeted for the smaller BERT model, including Wikipedia as the basis for Wikidata, than for the larger GPT-2 model, which relied on Wikipedia but also the much larger Common Crawl corpus.

Even though this factual probe provides promising results, there are a number of limitations that should be addressed. Firstly, the approach takes mostly triples rather than entire knowledge graphs into account. It would be interesting to extend the proposed probe to also consider the distance between entities in a knowledge graph instead of treating them in the form of individual triples that are either related or not. Secondly, cosine similarity is a valuable metric to evaluate the relatedness between vectors, however, it may not capture the factual relations in their entirety and it is sensitive to how the KG embeddings are trained and what their scoring functions are. Thirdly, the evaluation was limited to numeric, visual and manual inspections, however, it would be interesting to test the actual effect of the uncovered factual subspace in downstream tasks, such as question answering and textual entailment. We leave these experiments to interesting future work. Finally, the models utilized within the presented experiments were all exclusively trained on English, however, it would be interesting to not only compare the obtained results with novel ones on multilingual models, but also to consider the utilization of multilinual representations of knowledge graphs, as, for instance, proposed within the context of Linguistic Linked Open Data (LLOD).

While the integration of neural models and symbolic knowledge graphs in this chapter relates to the use of the latter to investigate properties of learned representations of the former, the factual probe still promises some benefits to neurosymbolic approaches. Being able to explicate and analyze factual associations in hidden representations of neural language models holds the promise of a more selective and better guided integration of knowledge, since it becomes evident which types of relations, e.g. geographical relations, show lowest associations and should be reinforced in particular in the neural model. Furthermore, it might permit approaches in neurosymbolic AI to select one model, architecture, and training objective on the neural side over another given the results of the factual probe. This might lead to better neural models but also better neurosymbolic approaches. Moreover, extending the proposed factual probe to include entire knowledge graphs rather than factual associations as presented by triples holds the promise to inspire novel ideas on how to fully integrate symbolic KGs with neural hidden representations, as we hope to some degree the proposed factual probe might do.

8. Conclusion

Recent methods to localize factual knowledge in neural language models have shown varied results. This chapter seeks to create a factual subspace rather than to explain where exactly in the original hidden representations knowledge is encoded. To this end, factual associations represented in knowledge graphs are directly integrated into the supervised training process of a matrix that is ultimately applied to transform the vector space into the factual subspace. This type of factual probe can be used to show that hidden representations of neural language models indeed encode factual associations and which types of associations are more problematic than others. On the neural side, such an approach is beneficial since a linear transformation is computationally less expensive than retraining or fine-tuning a model and requires fewer data points to achieve a stronger fact representation. From the neurosymbolic perspective, the proposed factual probe allows for better model selection on the neural part and more informed integration methods to unite both neural and symbolic approaches. With this first factual probe and overview of existing ideas on how to integrate knowledge graphs and neural language models, we hope to inspire interesting future work, such as evaluating the performance of different layers, inspecting attention parameters for their ability to encode factual knowledge, and experiment with knowledge as well as models across multiple languages.

References

[1] Conneau A, Kruszewski G, Lample G, Barrault L, Baroni M. What you can cram into a single $&!#* vector: Probing sentence embeddings for linguistic properties. In: Gurevych I, Miyao Y, editors. Proceedings of the 56th Annual Meeting of the Association for Computational Linguistics (Volume 1: Long Papers). Melbourne, Australia: Association for Computational Linguistics; 2018. p. 2126-36. Available from: `https://aclanthology.org/P18-1198`.

[2] Hewitt J, Manning CD. A Structural Probe for Finding Syntax in Word Representations. In: Burstein J, Doran C, Solorio T, editors. Proceedings of the 2019 Conference of the North American Chapter of the Association for Computational Linguistics: Human Language Technologies, Volume 1 (Long and Short Papers). Minneapolis, Minnesota: Association for Computational Linguistics; 2019. p. 4129-38. Available from: https://aclanthology.org/N19-1419.

[3] Coenen A, Reif E, Yuan A, Wattenberg M, Viegas FB, , et al. Visualizing and Measuring the Geometry of BERT. In: Wallach H, Larochelle H, Beygelzimer A, d'Alché-Buc F, Fox E, Garnett R, editors. Advances in Neural Information Processing Systems. vol. 32. Curran Associates, Inc.; 2019. p. 8594-603. Available from: https://proceedings.neurips.cc/paper_files/paper/2019/file/159c1ffe5b61b41b3c4d8f4c2150f6c4-Paper.pdf.

[4] Peters ME, Neumann M, Zettlemoyer L, Yih Wt. Dissecting Contextual Word Embeddings: Architecture and Representation. In: Riloff E, Chiang D, Hockenmaier J, Tsujii J, editors. Proceedings of the 2018 Conference on Empirical Methods in Natural Language Processing. Brussels, Belgium: Association for Computational Linguistics; 2018. p. 1499-509. Available from: https://aclanthology.org/D18-1179.

[5] Belinkov Y, Durrani N, Dalvi F, Sajjad H, Glass J. What do Neural Machine Translation Models Learn about Morphology? In: Barzilay R, Kan MY, editors. Proceedings of the 55th Annual Meeting of the Association for Computational Linguistics (Volume 1: Long Papers). Vancouver, Canada: Association for Computational Linguistics; 2017. p. 861-72. Available from: https://aclanthology.org/P17-1080.

[6] Koto F, Lau JH, Baldwin T. Discourse Probing of Pretrained Language Models. In: Toutanova K, Rumshisky A, Zettlemoyer L, Hakkani-Tur D, Beltagy I, Bethard S, et al., editors. Proceedings of the 2021 Conference of the North American Chapter of the Association for Computational Linguistics: Human Language Technologies. Online: Association for Computational Linguistics; 2021. p. 3849-64. Available from: https://aclanthology.org/2021.naacl-main.301.

[7] Jiang Z, Xu FF, Araki J, Neubig G. How Can We Know What Language Models Know? Transactions of the Association for Computational Linguistics. 2020;8:423-38. Available from: https://aclanthology.org/2020.tacl-1.28.

[8] Shin T, Razeghi Y, Logan IV RL, Wallace E, Singh S. Autoprompt: Eliciting knowledge from language models with automatically generated prompts. In: Proceedings of the 2020 Conference on Empirical Methods in Natural Language Processing. Association for Computational Linguistics; 2020. p. 4222-35.

[9] Cohen R, Geva M, Berant J, Globerson A. Crawling The Internal Knowledge-Base of Language Models. In: Vlachos A, Augenstein I, editors. Findings of the Association for Computational Linguistics: EACL 2023. Dubrovnik, Croatia: Association for Computational Linguistics; 2023. p. 1856-69. Available from: https://aclanthology.org/2023.findings-eacl.139.

[10] Meng K, Bau D, Andonian A, Belinkov Y. Locating and Editing Factual Associations in GPT. In: Koyejo S, Mohamed S, Agarwal A, Belgrave D, Cho K, Oh A, editors. Advances in Neural Information Processing Systems. vol. 35. Curran Associates, Inc.; 2022. p. 17359-72. Available from: https://proceedings.neurips.cc/paper_files/paper/2022/file/6f1d43d5a82a37e89b0665b33bf3a182-Paper-Conference.pdf.

[11] Hase P, Bansal M, Kim B, Ghandeharioun A. Does Localization Inform Editing? Surprising Differences in Causality-Based Localization vs. Knowledge Editing in Language Models. In: Oh A, Naumann T, Globerson A, Saenko K, Hardt M, Levine S, editors. Advances in Neural Information Processing Systems. vol. 36. Curran Associates, Inc.; 2023. p. 17643-68. Available from: https://proceedings.neurips.cc/paper_files/paper/2023/file/3927bbdcf0e8d1fa8aa23c26f358a281-Paper-Conference.pdf.

[12] Geva M, Bastings J, Filippova K, Globerson A. Dissecting Recall of Factual Associations in Auto-Regressive Language Models. In: Bouamor H, Pino J, Bali K, editors. Proceedings of the 2023 Conference on Empirical Methods in Natural Language Processing. Singapore: Association for Computational Linguistics; 2023. p. 12216-35. Available from: https://aclanthology.org/2023.emnlp-main.751.

[13] Devlin J, Chang MW, Lee K, Toutanova K. BERT: Pre-training of Deep Bidirectional Transformers for Language Understanding. In: Burstein J, Doran C, Solorio T, editors. Proceedings of the 2019 Conference of the North American Chapter of the Association for Computational Linguistics: Human Language Technologies, Volume 1 (Long and Short Papers). Minneapolis, Minnesota: Association for Computational Linguistics; 2019. p. 4171-86. Available from: https://aclanthology.org/N19-1423.

[14] Radford A, Wu J, Child R, Luan D, Amodei D, Sutskever I. Language Models are Unsupervised Multitask Learners. OpenAI blog; 2019. Available from: https://api.semanticscholar.org/CorpusID:160025533.

[15] Hamilton K, Nayak A, Božić B, Longo L. Is neuro-symbolic ai meeting its promises in natural language processing? a structured review. Semantic Web. 2022;Pre-press(Pre-press):1-42.

[16] Jurafsky D, Martin JH. Speech and Language Processing: An Introduction to Natural Language Processing, Computational Linguistics, and Speech Recognition. Upper Saddle River, N.J.: Pearson Prentice Hall; 2023. Available from: https://web.stanford.edu/~jurafsky/slp3/.

[17] Perevalov A, Gashkov A, Eltsova M, Both A. Language Models as SPARQL Query Filtering forImproving the Quality of Multilingual Question Answering overKnowledge Graphs. In: Stefanidis K, Systä K, Matera M, Heil S, Kondylakis H, Quintarelli E, editors. Web Engineering. Cham: Springer Nature Switzerland; 2024. p. 3-18.

[18] Bengio Y, Ducharme R, Vincent P, Janvin C. A neural probabilistic language model. J Mach Learn Res. 2003 mar;3(null):1137–1155.

[19] Mikolov T, Chen K, Corrado G, Dean J. Efficient estimation of word representations in vector space. arXiv preprint arXiv:13013781. 2013.

[20] Rumelhart DE, Hinton GE, Williams RJ. Learning representations by back-propagating errors. Nature. 1986;323(6088):533-6.

[21] LeCun Y, et al. Generalization and network design strategies. Connectionism in perspective. 1989;19(143-155):18.

[22] Vaswani A, Shazeer N, Parmar N, Uszkoreit J, Jones L, Gomez AN, et al. Attention is All you Need. In: Guyon I, Luxburg UV, Bengio S, Wallach H, Fergus R, Vishwanathan S, et al., editors. Advances in Neural Information Processing Systems. vol. 30. Curran Associates, Inc.; 2017. p. 5998-6008. Available from: https://proceedings.neurips.cc/paper_files/paper/2017/file/3f5ee243547dee91fbd053c1c4a845aa-Paper.pdf.

[23] Brown T, Mann B, Ryder N, Subbiah M, Kaplan JD, Dhariwal P, et al. Language Models are Few-Shot Learners. In: Larochelle H, Ranzato M, Hadsell R, Balcan MF, Lin H, editors. Advances in Neural Information Processing Systems. vol. 33. Curran Associates, Inc.; 2020. p. 1877-901. Available from: https://proceedings.neurips.cc/paper_files/paper/2020/file/1457c0d6bfcb4967418bfb8ac142f64a-Paper.pdf.

[24] Paulheim H. Knowledge graph refinement: A survey of approaches and evaluation methods. Semantic web. 2017;8(3):489-508.

[25] Bordes A, Usunier N, Garcia-Duran A, Weston J, Yakhnenko O. Translating Embeddings for Modeling Multi-relational Data. In: Burges CJ, Bottou L, Welling M, Ghahramani Z, Weinberger KQ, editors. Advances in Neural Information Processing Systems. vol. 26. Curran Associates, Inc.; 2013. p. 2787-95. Available from: https://proceedings.neurips.cc/paper_files/paper/2013/file/1cecc7a77928ca8133fa24680a88d2f9-Paper.pdf.

[26] Wang Q, Mao Z, Wang B, Guo L. Knowledge Graph Embedding: A Survey of Approaches and Applications. IEEE Transactions on Knowledge and Data Engineering. 2017;29(12):2724-43.

[27] Wang Z, Zhang J, Feng J, Chen Z. Knowledge graph embedding by translating on hyperplanes. Proceedings of the AAAI conference on artificial intelligence. 2014;28(1).

[28] Lin Y, Liu Z, Sun M, Liu Y, Zhu X. Learning entity and relation embeddings for knowledge graph completion. Proceedings of the AAAI conference on artificial intelligence. 2015;29(1).

[29] Nickel M, Tresp V, Kriegel HP, et al. A three-way model for collective learning on multi-relational data. In: Proceedings of the 28th International Conference on International Conference on Machine Learning. Madison, WI, USA: Omnipress; 2011. p. 809–816.

[30] Yang B, Yih Wt, He X, Gao J, Deng L. Embedding entities and relations for learning and inference in knowledge bases. arXiv preprint arXiv:14126575. 2014.

[31] Nickel M, Rosasco L, Poggio T. Holographic embeddings of knowledge graphs. Proceedings of the AAAI conference on artificial intelligence. 2016;30(1).

[32] Socher R, Chen D, Manning CD, Ng A. Reasoning with neural tensor networks for knowledge base completion. Advances in neural information processing systems. 2013;26.

[33] Ristoski P, Paulheim H. Rdf2vec: Rdf graph embeddings for data mining. In: The Semantic Web–ISWC 2016: 15th International Semantic Web Conference, Kobe, Japan, October 17–21, 2016, Proceedings, Part I 15. Springer; 2016. p. 498-514.

[34] Paulheim H, Ristoski P, Portisch J. Embedding Knowledge Graphs with RDF2vec. Synthesis Lectures

on Data, Semantics, and Knowledge. Springer Cham; 2023.
[35] Rothe S, Schütze H. Word Embedding Calculus in Meaningful Ultradense Subspaces. In: Erk K, Smith NA, editors. Proceedings of the 54th Annual Meeting of the Association for Computational Linguistics (Volume 2: Short Papers). Berlin, Germany: Association for Computational Linguistics; 2016. p. 512-7. Available from: https://aclanthology.org/P16-2083.
[36] Park S, Bak J, Oh A. Rotated Word Vector Representations and their Interpretability. In: Palmer M, Hwa R, Riedel S, editors. Proceedings of the 2017 Conference on Empirical Methods in Natural Language Processing. Copenhagen, Denmark: Association for Computational Linguistics; 2017. p. 401-11. Available from: https://aclanthology.org/D17-1041.
[37] Peters ME, Neumann M, Iyyer M, Gardner M, Clark C, Lee K, et al. Deep Contextualized Word Representations. In: Walker M, Ji H, Stent A, editors. Proceedings of the 2018 Conference of the North American Chapter of the Association for Computational Linguistics: Human Language Technologies, Volume 1 (Long Papers). New Orleans, Louisiana: Association for Computational Linguistics; 2018. p. 2227-37. Available from: https://aclanthology.org/N18-1202.
[38] Michael J, Botha JA, Tenney I. Asking without Telling: Exploring Latent Ontologies in Contextual Representations. In: Webber B, Cohn T, He Y, Liu Y, editors. Proceedings of the 2020 Conference on Empirical Methods in Natural Language Processing (EMNLP). Online: Association for Computational Linguistics; 2020. p. 6792-812. Available from: https://aclanthology.org/2020.emnlp-main.552.
[39] Yom Din A, Karidi T, Choshen L, Geva M. Jump to Conclusions: Short-Cutting Transformers with Linear Transformations. In: Calzolari N, Kan MY, Hoste V, Lenci A, Sakti S, Xue N, editors. Proceedings of the 2024 Joint International Conference on Computational Linguistics, Language Resources and Evaluation (LREC-COLING 2024). Torino, Italia: ELRA and ICCL; 2024. p. 9615-25. Available from: https://aclanthology.org/2024.lrec-main.840.
[40] Vrandečić D, Krötzsch M. Wikidata: a free collaborative knowledgebase. Commun ACM. 2014 sep;57(10):78–85. Available from: https://doi.org/10.1145/2629489.
[41] Wang X, Gao T, Zhu Z, Zhang Z, Liu Z, Li J, et al. KEPLER: A unified model for knowledge embedding and pre-trained language representation. Transactions of the Association for Computational Linguistics. 2021;9:176-94.
[42] Nielsen FÅ. Wembedder: Wikidata entity embedding web service. arXiv preprint arXiv:171004099. 2017.
[43] Loshchilov I, Hutter F. Decoupled weight decay regularization. arXiv preprint arXiv:171105101. 2017.
[44] Hotelling H. Analysis of a complex of statistical variables into principal components. Journal of Educational Psychology. 1933;6(23):417-41. Available from: https://doi.org/10.1037/h0071325.
[45] Hinton GE, Roweis S. Stochastic Neighbor Embedding. In: Becker S, Thrun S, Obermayer K, editors. Advances in Neural Information Processing Systems. vol. 15. MIT Press; 2002. p. 857-64. Available from: https://proceedings.neurips.cc/paper_files/paper/2002/file/6150ccc6069bea6b5716254057a194ef-Paper.pdf.
[46] McInnes L, Healy J, Saul N, Großberger L. UMAP: Uniform Manifold Approximation and Projection. Journal of Open Source Software. 2018;3(29):861. Available from: https://doi.org/10.21105/joss.00861.
[47] Arora S, Hu W, Kothari PK. An analysis of the t-sne algorithm for data visualization. In: Conference on learning theory. PMLR; 2018. p. 1455-62.
[48] Van der Maaten L, Hinton G. Visualizing data using t-SNE. Journal of machine learning research. 2008;9(11).
[49] Kullback S, Leibler RA. On information and sufficiency. The annals of mathematical statistics. 1951;22(1):79-86.
[50] White JC, Pimentel T, Saphra N, Cotterell R. A Non-Linear Structural Probe. In: Toutanova K, Rumshisky A, Zettlemoyer L, Hakkani-Tur D, Beltagy I, Bethard S, et al., editors. Proceedings of the 2021 Conference of the North American Chapter of the Association for Computational Linguistics: Human Language Technologies. Online: Association for Computational Linguistics; 2021. p. 132-8. Available from: https://aclanthology.org/2021.naacl-main.12.
[51] Sorodoc IT, Gulordava K, Boleda G. Probing for Referential Information in Language Models. In: Jurafsky D, Chai J, Schluter N, Tetreault J, editors. Proceedings of the 58th Annual Meeting of the Association for Computational Linguistics. Online: Association for Computational Linguistics; 2020. p. 4177-89. Available from: https://aclanthology.org/2020.acl-main.384.

Handbook on Neurosymbolic AI and Knowledge Graphs
P. Hitzler et al. (Eds.)
IOS Press, 2025

doi:10.3233/FAIA250205

How to Embed Large but Incomplete Knowledge Graphs in the Culture Heritage Sector

Lessons Learned from Odeuropa

Pasquale LISENA [1], Thibault EHRHART and Raphaël TRONCY
EURECOM, Sophia Antipolis, France
ORCiD ID: Pasquale Lisena https://orcid.org/0000-0003-3094-5585, Thibault Ehrhart https://orcid.org/0000-0003-1377-8279, Raphaël Troncy https://orcid.org/0000-0003-0457-1436

Abstract. Classic machine learning tasks, such as clustering and link prediction, can be applied to Knowledge Graphs making used of the so-called graph embeddings, mathematical vector representations of the nodes present within the graph structure. Often, the data structure of Knowledge Graphs in Digital Humanities is at the same time versatile and complex, challenging the machine learning tasks. In this work, we compare algorithms on two different subgraphs extracted from a large knowledge graph developed in the cultural heritage domain: one is randomly selected while the other is built to maximise the triple density. Using the European Olfactory Knowledge Graph (EOKG) as use-case, we show that embedding dense subgraph can improve the performances of state-of-art algorithms.

Keywords. Knowledge Graphs, Embeddings, Semantic Web, Machine Learning, Clustering, Link Prediction

1. Introduction

Methods for machine learning have gained significant attention in recent years in the semantic web research community. In the context of Knowledge Graphs (KG), machine learning can either be used for refining the knowledge graph itself (which involves predicting new edges and/or identifying erroneous edges) or for downstream tasks: training models on the KG data are then used for classification, recommendation, regression, etc. in an application domain [1]. For feeding machine learning algorithms, the data in the graph must be encoded in a suitable vectorial format, commonly called *graph embedding* [2]. A number of techniques have been proposed: translational models that interpret edge labels as transformations from subject nodes to object nodes [3], tensor decomposition models [4], neural models and language models [5,6]. These techniques have shown good performances on several machine learning tasks, involving both general knowledge and domain-specific datasets.

[1]Corresponding Author: pasquale.lisena@eurecom.fr.

When applied to fields such Digital Humanities and Cultural Heritage, multiple challenges arise [7]. In particular, the domain intrinsically exhibits knowledge that can be structurally complex [8,9], imprecise and uncertain [10], interpretable and subjective [11]. These qualities may lead to hypothesis that, in the Digital Humanities field, the attention to the data should be higher. Notably, data sparsity plays a role in the generation of graph embeddings, with several works demonstrating an high correlation between the graph density and the embedding performances [12,13,14]. We aim to study if an optimal selection of a cultural knowledge graph exists for training successful graph-based machine learning tasks.

We will use the European Olfactory Knowledge Graph (EOKG) [15] as a use case for this research. The EOKG has been realised in the context of the Odeuropa project[2] for representing smells and olfactory experiences. Using the EOKG as source knowledge graph, we want to use graph-based AI technologies – specifically, graph embeddings – to infer and extract new knowledge from the existing graph. We target two specific tasks:

- We investigate strategies for grouping related odours, measuring the similarity between two intangible items. Machine learning approaches relying on graph embeddings are implemented to cluster items;
- We try to predict missing links in the graph. More precisely, we train the machine to predict the smell source given the description of the smell experience and its surrounding context, or vice-versa, to generate context-specific descriptions for a given odour.

Our experiments demonstrate that the use of a dense graph entail an improvement of the performances for both tasks, making it a useful strategy in real-world applications in the Cultural Heritage domain.

The remainder of this paper is organised as follows. We outline some related work in Section 2. We provide an overview of the EOKG we use in Section 3. We describe our method in Section 4, which is then used in the two tasks: clustering (Section 5) and link prediction (Section 6). Finally, we conclude and outline some future work in Section 7.

2. Related Work

2.1. Graph Embeddings

Research about graph embeddings is quite vast: several methods have been proposed, which have been grouped into different taxonomies, with some overlap [2,16,17].

Random-walk based methods are particularly suitable for approximating properties such as proximity, similarity, and various structural characteristics of nodes and subgraphs [18]. The core idea of this family of techniques consists in the simulation of the movement of a "walker" through the graph structure. At each step, the algorithm randomly chooses one of the outgoing links of the current node, and follows it to the next node. The full path (walk) consists on a series of nodes. These walks serve as analogous structures to sentences in a corpus. Next, *word2vec*) is often used on these walks yielding a number of methods such as *rdf2vec* [5], *node2vec* [19], or *entity2vec* [6]. Entities (or words in the word embedding scenario) that appear in the same random walks (or

[2]`https://odeuropa.eu/`

sentences) are considered semantically close, and so have higher possibilities to appear close also in the embedding space.

TransE [3] is the most representative method of the translation-based family. This algorithm assigns vectors to both entities (nodes) and predicates (edges), with the idea that for each triple (*subject*, *predicate*, *object*), the object vector O corresponds to the translation of the subject vector S along the predicate vector P, that is $O = S + P$. In the training phase, the algorithm tries to minimise the distance between O and the translation $T = S + P$. This algorithm is widely used in heterogeneous graphs [17], in particular when the number of different properties is important.

Tensor-factorisation based models include techniques such as ComplEx [20] and DistMult [21]. Similarly to the translation models, these methods embeds nodes and edges in the same real dimensional space. What is different is the translating function of the object, being the dot product of the subject and the predicate.

Finally, rotation-based models replace the translation of TransE with a rotation in the space. RotatE is a well known example [22] of this family.

2.2. Embeddings in Cultural Heritage

There are several application of KG embedding in the specific field of Digital Humanities and Cultural Heritage. In [23,24], embeddings are trained on cultural KGs, demonstrating their suitability for link prediction and similarity computation. In [25], missing *Place* nodes are inferred from the entities in the graphs in which the information was missing, using a learning function over KG embeddings.

The quality of clusters is used as a measure of the embeddings quality in [9,26], while the graph embedding clustering is used for other tasks in [27], where a similarity metric is used for entity alignment in the history domain.

3. Dataset Overview

3.1. The European Olfactory Knowledge Graph (EOKG)

Odeuropa is a European project (2021-2023) which integrates expertise in sensory mining, knowledge representation, computational linguistics, (art) history and heritage science with the objectives of contributing to the topic of olfactory heritage. One of the project goals is to develop novel methods to collect, model and publish and disseminate information about smells from digital text and image collections, while also working with the material presence of odours.

The European Olfactory Knowledge Graph (EOKG) that results from these efforts is one of the main outcomes of Odeuropa. It consist of a large dataset of olfactory experience information extracted from textual and figurative resources using domain-specific techniques [28,29] and organised according to the Odeuropa Ontology [15] which makes use of semantic web technologies. This ontology represents a Smell as an entity that exists at a precise time and space, connected to a Smell Emission and an Olfactory Experience. These are linked respectively to objective (smell source, odor carrier, place, etc.) and subjective characteristics (quality, emotion, gestures, etc.), as depicted in Figure 1. These characteristics are normally represented by terms or *Concepts* from controlled vocabularies.

One of the strong points of the EOKG is the harmonisation in a single dataset of 21 data sources covering several centuries from 1600 to 1920, involving both images and textual resources in 6 European languages, as reported in Table 1. Figure 2 shows a visual representation of an excerpt of the EOKG. The KG can be accessed in multiple ways, namely querying a SPARQL endpoint[3], calling the grlc-based API[4] [30] or accessing the dumps on the open-source repository[5].

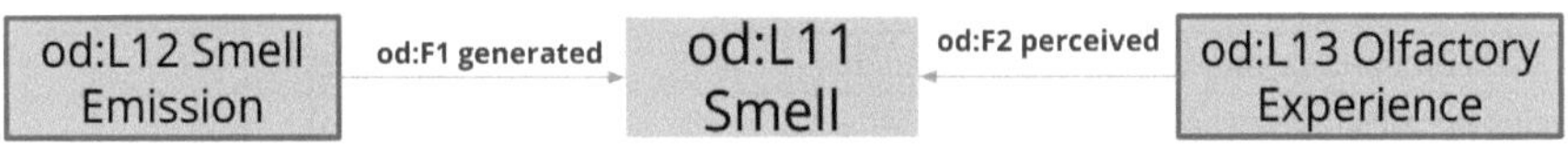

Figure 1. The core of the Odeuropa ontology

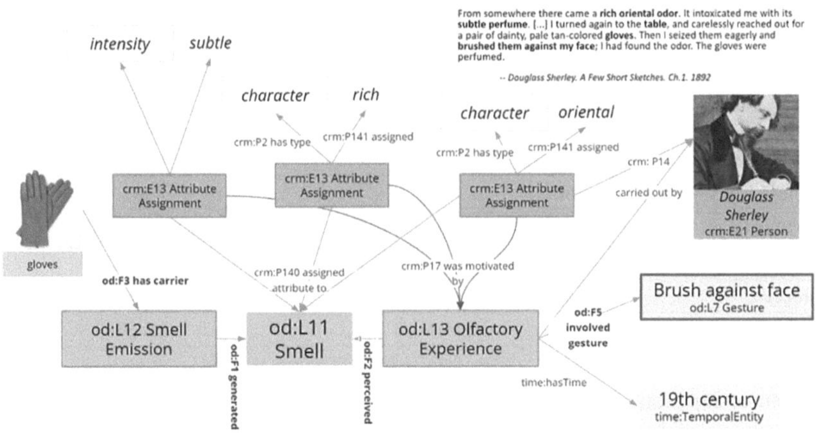

Figure 2. A visual representation of the EOKG. In this example, *Douglass Sherley* is the person who experiences a smell emitted by *gloves* and assigned characteristics such as being *intense*, *rich* and *oriental* in the 19th century.

The EOKG contains over 400 million statements (or triples), referring to over 2 million unique smells. For each of these smells, the dataset may contain a set of characteristics which are interlinked, whenever possible, with controlled vocabularies. The data population involved also some post-processing including parsing of time, parsing and interlinking of places to GeoNames, the interlinking of several entities with the controlled vocabularies.

3.2. The Role of Controlled Vocabularies

Together with a set of multi-language alternative labels which allow to disambiguate terms towards the same identifier (URI), the Odeuropa controlled vocabularies are organized as a hierarchical structure formalized in SKOS [32]. In addition, some links between vocabularies are instantiated for:

[3]`http://data.odeuropa.eu`
[4]`https://grlc.eurecom.fr/api/Odeuropa/kg-api/`
[5]`https://github.com/Odeuropa/knowledge-graph`

Table 1. Count of smell instances per data source

Graph	N. of smell instances	Type	Language
Odeuropa Benchmark [31]	7,125	Text	All
British Library	328,828	Text	EN
Medical Heritage	898,458	Text	EN
Gallica	811,633	Text	FR
Gutenberg	36,766	Text	EN, IT
Digitale Bibliotheek voor de Nederlandse Letteren	39,642	Text	NL
Digitalna knjižnica Slovenije (Dlib)	22,270	Text	SL
LiberLiber	30,228	Text	IT
Deutsches Textarchiv (DTA)	14,776	Text	DE
Wikisource	110,917	Text	EN, IT
Eighteenth Century Collections Online (ECCO)	8,435	Text	EN
Early English Books Online (EEBO)	81,038	Text	EN
London's Pulse: Medical Officer of Health reports	6,562	Text	EN
Royal Society Corpus	3,627	Text	EN
Old Bayley Corpus	1,170	Text	EN
Bibliothèque Bleue de Troyes	495	Text	FR
Grimm's Correspondance littéraire	64	Text	FR
ODOR dataset [29]	24,351	Image	-
Rijksmuseum	46	Image	-
Europeana	17,530	Image	-
NUK	1,752	Image	-

- connecting elements which refer to the same thing, linked using `skos:exactMatch`;
- connecting elements which are somehow related, linked using `skos:related`. For example, *tobacco* is related to *pipe*, *stable* is related to *cow*, etc.

To better appreciate the represented hierarchy, for the *olfactory objects* vocabulary, we present in Table 2 the top-level concepts with the relative number of narrower concepts. The full list of olfactory objects can be extracted from the EOKG using the following SPARQL query:[6]

```
PREFIX skos: <http://www.w3.org/2004/02/skos/core#>
SELECT DISTINCT ?top ?top_label ?concept ?concept_label
WHERE {
    ?top skos:prefLabel ?top_label;
       skos:topConceptOf
          <http://data.odeuropa.eu/vocabulary/olfactory-objects> ;
       skos:narrower* ?concept.
    ?concept skos:prefLabel ?concept_label .
    FILTER (lang(?concept_label) = "en")
    FILTER (lang(?top_label) = "en")
}
ORDER BY ?top ?top_label
```

[6]Quickly accessible at `https://tinyurl.com/bdft538n`

Table 2. The top concepts of the olfactory objects vocabulary, with the number of relative narrower concepts (at any depth). The sum of each individual count of narrower concepts may differ from the total dimension of the vocabulary, since some concepts belonging to two different categories are counted twice. The namespace `olfactory-objects:` is equivalent to `http://data.odeuropa.eu/vocabulary/olfactory-objects/`.

URI	label	# narrower concepts
olfactory-objects:560	Flora	178
olfactory-objects:405	Food	176
olfactory-objects:554	Artefact	148
olfactory-objects:555	Being	84
olfactory-objects:558	Fragrance / Cosmetic	56
olfactory-objects:533	Body	38
olfactory-objects:562	Element	32
olfactory-objects:559	Nature	27
olfactory-objects:563	Abstract	19
olfactory-objects:616	Matter	8
olfactory-objects:564	Religion	6
olfactory-objects:631	Product	4
olfactory-objects:615	Fumes	2

These vocabularies can be easily browsed at `https://vocab.odeuropa.eu/`. In Table 3, we report on the number of terms successfully interlinked with the controlled vocabularies. This gives an idea of the size, complexity and density of the graph.

Table 3. Statistics of the interlinking of controlled vocabularies for the most important properties in the EOKG

Graph element	**Nb. of disambiguated mentions**	**Relevant vocabularies**	**Nb. of concepts**
Gestures	3,066	Olfactory Gestures	36
Agents	8,868	Noses	14
Places	79,106	Fragrant Spaces	137
Evoked odorants	64,671		
Carriers	86,707	Olfactory Objects	682
Odor Sources	678,249		
Qualities	509,886	Smell Classifications, Hedonic, Intensity	1,824
Emotions	158,005	Plutchik + Odeuropa extension	32

4. Methodology

4.1. Pre-processing Steps

To generate embeddings from the EOKG, we collected a list of relevant properties, consisting of all the connections between the smell objects and the vocabularies in Table 3. We collected all pairs of instances involving these properties locally, in the edgelist format.

We decided to include only the data extracted by textual resources and exclude those coming from the annotation of images. The reason for this choice stems from the nature of those images: for example, still life paintings are widely represented and depict together a series of objects – from pipes to fruits, from fishes to wine – without having a clear meaning of their olfactory similarity or relatedness.

Given the size of the graph, any embedding strategy involving the totality of the data would be expensive and would require a computation time of several weeks or months to be completed. This effort may be repeated if the graph evolves over the time. For this reason, we decided to use a subset of the graph for training our machine learning models. However, following the research question mentioned in Section 1, we aim to investigate for an optimal subgraph, rather than randomly sampling a number N of entities. Considering the considerable effect of data sparsity in graph-based methods [33,34], we aim to to identify a dense subgraph for our purposes.

Given a directed graph $G(V,E)$ consisting of the vertex set V and the edge set E, we apply the *density* definition for directed graph from [35]:

$$d_G = \frac{|E|}{|V|(|V|-1)} \tag{1}$$

In addition to the density, we include a more *specific completeness* metric, which is measuring how much the studied entities (in our case, the smells) are interconnected with the rest of the properties in the graph. Getting freely inspired by the definition of completeness from graph theory[7], we consider our graph complete for the domain if all studied entities are the subject of the object for all relevant properties. For a specific entity type T, the relevant properties set P_T consists of all properties which have that specific entity type as property range or property domain. We define the relevant statement S_T a triple (s,p,o) in which $p \in P_T$. This *specific completeness* is measured as:

$$c_T = \frac{|S_T|}{|V| * |P_T|} \tag{2}$$

Please note that if the *density* measure is agnostic with respect to the schema, for computing the *completeness* one should have the knowledge of the relation between classes and properties present in the data model.

Given the particular structure of the schema, the relevant information is not directly linked to the Smell entity, but to its Smell Emission and Olfactory Experience. This ensures high flexibility in representation, allowing to have multiple Olfactory Experiences for the same Smell. However, looking at the real data of the EOKG, each Smell is linked to a single Experience, creating an unnecessary hop in the connection between the entity and the relevant informative values. Because of this, we made a series of selection of the graph, with the progression of changes tracked in Table 4, together with the main metrics. We created a new version of the KG called *Cleaned Graph* in which the core composed of Smell, Smell Emission, and Olfactory Experience is represented as a single atomic entity, which we will call *Smell* for simplicity. In addition, all edges not linked to a smell are removed from the graph, with the exception of the vocabulary hierarchy which is always kept in all subgraphs. As a consequence, the number of involved predicates slightly decrease.

Starting from this *Cleaned Graph*, we realise the *Dense Graph* by selecting only the smell entities having at least 4 links (ingoing or outgoing). Respect to the original graph,

---

[7] *"A simple graph in which every pair of two vertices is adjacent is called a complete graph"* [36]

this operation multiplied the density of the graph by over 17 times, and increased the specific completeness of 0.14.

From both the *Original Graph* and the *Dense Graph*, we extract a selection of 10,000 smells to reduce the computational complexity of the link prediction task. These two selections have density metrics quite similar and very different completeness, as it is possible to see in Table 4. The distribution of smells with different numbers of connections changes between graph, with the dense graph having the 47% of smells with 4 connections. The distribution is reported in Figure 3.

Table 4. The composition of each version of the dataset following the different preprocessing steps

Graph Version	Nb entities	Nb predicates	Nb edges	Density	Completeness
Original Graph	5,182,119	23	8,434,414	$0.31e^{-6}$	0.24
Original Graph 10k	9,071	22	10,795	$131.21e^{-6}$	0.048
Cleaned Graph	2,232,870	15	8,179,561	$1.64e^{-6}$	0.27
Dense Graph	823,265	15	3,752,435	$5.54e^{-6}$	0.37
Dense Graph 10k	18,208	13	61,343	$185.04e^{-6}$	0.50

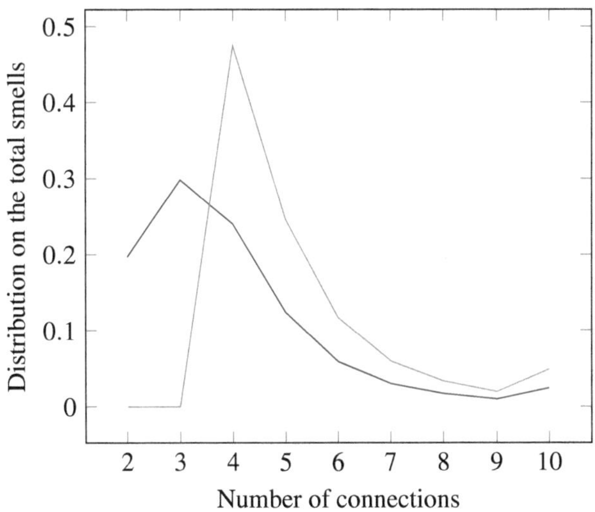

Figure 3. Distribution of connections (incoming or outgoing) for the cleaned (blue) and the dense (red) graphs, relatively to the total number of smells. The reduced version of 10k smells follows similar distributions.

4.2. *Embedding Strategies*

We experiment with three embedding algorithms:

- RDF2vec [5], that applies Random Walks [18] and Word2Vec [37] to the graph;
- TransE [3], as a representative of a geometric embedding strategy [38];
- DistMult [21], as a representative of a semantic embedding strategy (it quantifies the likelihood of a triple to belong to the KG through a multiplicative score function).

For RDF2vec, we use the PyRDF2vec implementation [39], while for TransE and DistMult, we use the PyKEEN library [40]. The resulting embeddings include in the same embedding space both the concepts coming from the vocabularies and the smell entities, even if the experiments reported later in this paper will focus on particular subset of them. The generated embeddings have been tested in two different tasks, clustering and link prediction, that we detail in the next sections.

5. Clustering

In this section, we investigate strategies for clustering related odours. The clustering targets two kinds of entities, namely, either the over 600 olfactory object concepts, or the smell instances. These targets have been studied separately, isolating the relevant embeddings from the rest.

We assess the clustering performances using three common metrics in the literature [41]:

- *Homogeneity*: a clustering output is considered homogeneous if all elements assigned to each cluster belong to the same ground-truth label;
- *Completeness*: a clustering output is considered complete if all elements from one ground-truth label fall into the same cluster;
- *V-Measure*: the harmonic mean of Homogeneity and Completeness. The V-Measure of 1.0 corresponds to a perfect alignment between clusters and ground truth labels.

For both targets, we compared the performances of the 3 embedding algorithms (Section 4.2) using the same K-means clustering algorithm, which is an iterative algorithm that tries to partition the dataset into K pre-defined distinct non-overlapping subgroups (clusters) where each data point belongs to only one group. Table 5 provides our evaluation for the 3 algorithms, with respectively 10, 20 and 100 clusters of olfactory objects. Each algorithm has been trained on both the original graph and the dense graph.[8] For each concept, we consider as ground truth class the `skos:broader` term which is also `skos:topConceptOf` the SKOS schema. In other words, we use as classes the 13 top categories of the vocabulary which are reported in Table 2. Given that an olfactory object may belong to multiple top categories – e.g. a *herb* belongs to both *Flora* (being a plant) and *Food* (being a seasoning) – we consider in the computation of the metrics the most popular class in the clustering itself, in order to not penalise meaningful aggregations.

From the results, the benefit of the dense graph is quite obvious: the embeddings trained on the dense graph have better scores regardless of the considered metric, incrementing in some cases of over 0.10 points.

Table 6 presents the same scores computed on smells clustering. In this case, we used the smell sources as the ground truth classes. Again, when a smell has multiple sources, we select the most popular source in the cluster. In addition, when computing the metrics, we also use the top categories of these smells as classes, e.g. *food* for *meat*, *seafood* or *fruit*.

[8]Please note that for DistMult and TransE, which have a longer training time, the 10k version of the graphs has been employed for training.

Table 5. **H**omogeneity, **C**ompleteness and **V**-measure computed on 10, 20 and 100 clusters of **olfactory objects**. In **bold**, the best results for each number of cluster, while underlined the best values in absolute

	# clusters →	10			20			100		
	trained on ↓	H	C	V	H	C	V	H	C	V
RDF2vec	original	0.80	0.69	0.74	0.87	0.59	0.70	0.95	0.44	0.59
	dense	**0.89**	**0.78**	**0.83**	0.94	0.61	0.74	**0.98**	**0.44**	**0.61**
DistMult	original	0.70	0.62	0.66	0.80	0.55	0.65	0.89	0.42	0.57
	dense	0.88	0.76	0.81	**0.96**	**0.66**	**0.78**	0.97	0.44	0.61
TransE	original	0.10	0.09	0.10	0.18	0.12	0.14	0.36	0.17	0.23
	dense	0.83	0.73	0.77	0.87	0.58	0.70	0.95	0.42	0.58

Table 6. **H**omogeneity, **C**ompleteness and **V**-measure computed on 10, 20 and 100 clusters of **smells**. In **bold**, the best results for each number of cluster, while underlined the best values in absolute

	# clusters →	10			20			100		
		H	C	V	H	C	V	H	C	V
	trained on ↓	**Smell Source**								
RDF2vec	original	0.04	0.12	0.06	0.05	0.12	0.07	0.08	0.15	0.10
	dense	0.24	0.51	0.33	0.57	0.59	0.58	0.55	0.57	0.56
DistMult	original	0.06	0.14	0.08	0.08	0.14	0.10	0.14	0.15	0.14
	dense	**0.25**	**0.51**	**0.34**	**0.59**	**0.60**	**0.60**	**0.59**	**0.59**	**0.59**
TransE	original	0.05	0.13	0.07	0.06	0.11	0.08	0.22	0.11	0.11
	dense	0.24	0.48	0.32	0.58	0.58	0.58	0.58	0.58	0.58
	trained on ↓	**Top Category**								
RDF2vec	original	0.03	0.03	0.03	0.04	0.03	0.03	0.06	0.04	0.04
	dense	**0.62**	**0.52**	**0.57**	**0.83**	**0.33**	**0.47**	**0.84**	**0.33**	**0.48**
DistMult	original	0.04	0.03	0.04	0.06	0.03	0.04	0.08	0.03	0.05
	dense	0.34	0.27	0.30	0.59	0.23	0.33	0.57	0.23	0.32
TransE	original	0.04	0.03	0.03	0.05	0.03	0.04	0.06	0.02	0.03
	dense	0.22	0.16	0.19	0.43	0.17	0.24	0.45	0.17	0.24

In this scenario, the embeddings trained on the original graph gave low scores, never surpassing 0.22. Moreover, the values are unexpectedly lower for the top category because the metrics are also taking into account the ground truth entropy. Hence, even if the clusters may result more homogeneous in absolute terms, their scores are lower when comparing with the original ground truth homogeneity. These factors make even more evident the increment of scores for the embeddings trained on the dense graph, for which we obtained scores almost always above 0.50, with the scores for top categories definitely better than those referring to fine-grained smell sources.

To provide a qualitative assessment, we computed the most similar entities to the centroid using the cosine similarity, for each cluster obtained by K-means using one of our embedding strategy (RDF2vec, TransE, DistMult), in the 20 clusters scenario. We present the results in Tables 9 to 14, to which we manually added – where possible – a meaningful label for each cluster. Apart from some miscellaneous clusters, the top concepts are quite homogeneous, making easy to manually assign a label to the cluster. Please note that there are some repeated entries (e.g. *sachet* in clusters 2 and 9) because it can happen that two centroids are quite close. Even if DistMult has better scores, qualitatively, the clusters generated on RDF2vec embeddings are easier to manually classify.

It is possible that the two algorithms capture different kind of knowledge. We observe that the clusters are relatively coherent also in the embeddings computed on the original graph.

Overall, we observe that both RDF2Vec and DistMult provide good embeddings of the EOKG for the clustering task, both according the quantitative and qualitative assessment. TransE embeddings yield, in contrast, hard to understand clusters, with lower performance scores.

6. Link Prediction

In this section, we investigate which method among our embedding strategies enables to best enrich the European Olfactory Knowledge Graph. We cast this problem as a link prediction task. More precisely, we aim to predict a possible smell source given a description of a smell experience. For example, looking at the example depicted in Figure 2, the task amounts to predict that the *gloves* are the olfactory object responsible for this smell experience, given the other attributes that describe it such as its characteristics (*subtle, rich, oriental*) and other circumstances (*19th century, Douglas Sherley*, etc.).

We employ two different ground truths: the 565 precise smell sources (a very fine-grained classification task), and their 13 top categories (a coarse-grained classification task) as shown in Table 2. The precise smell source represents the specific class responsible to a particular smell, while its top category represents the broader class to which the smell source class belongs. In the example depicted in Figure 2, the precise smell source is *gloves* while the broader class is *body*.

We take the two subgraph of 10,000 smells and randomly split them into 8,000 training samples and 2,000 test samples. We train TransE and DistMult on the training set. Table 7 provides the uneven distribution of the smell sources in the training dataset while the test dataset follows a similar distribution since the split was stratified.

Table 7. Distribution of the smell sources with their number of occurrences in the datasets. We present only the top 10 smell sources, to which a long tail distribution follows with more than 200 sources having less than 5 occurrences.

Original Graph 10k			Dense Graph 10k		
URI	**label**	**count**	**URI**	**label**	**count**
olfactory-objects:72	Flower	1,449	olfactory-objects:72	Flower	1,839
olfactory-objects:138	Rose	387	olfactory-objects:138	Rose	453
olfactory-objects:269	Incense	330	olfactory-objects:78	Plant	288
olfactory-objects:227	Tobacco	199	olfactory-objects:75	Fruit	246
olfactory-objects:270	Musk	187	olfactory-objects:193	Sheep	223
olfactory-objects:258	Jasmine	142	olfactory-objects:126	Water	218
olfactory-objects:223	Violet	111	olfactory-objects:531	Leaf	175
olfactory-objects:108	Odor of sanctity	101	olfactory-objects:460	Carcass	156
olfactory-objects:23	Cadaver	99	olfactory-objects:109	Oil	148
olfactory-objects:17	Blood	99	olfactory-objects:169	Grape	146

The model was trained for 200 epochs, with a batch size of 32. For each triple in the dataset, we attempted to predict the correct smell source by applying the `predict_triples` function from PyKEEN, which calculates a score for each given triple. We computed the accuracy by extracting the top-scoring entity from the predicted scores and comparing it to the actual smell source from the ground truth.

The results reported in Table 8 demonstrate that even if the task is complex, choosing the right sub-graph can have beneficial results: under any configuration, the accuracy of the prediction is almost doubled for the fine-grained smell source and more than doubled for the top category. Among the two studied methods, DistMult exhibited significantly better performances, achieving an average accuracy of 73% on the top category. However, the accuracy of 42% suggests that the current approach is not yet sufficient to precisely infer the fine-grained smell sources.

Table 8. Accuracy of link prediction for guessing the smell source using graph embeddings

Dataset →	**Original Graph 10k**		**Dense Graph 10k**	
Ground Truth	**Smell source**	**Top Category**	**Smell source**	**Top Category**
TransE	0.18	0.25	0.38	0.69
DistMult	0.28	0.31	**0.42**	**0.73**

7. Conclusions

In this paper, we applied state-of-art graph embedding techniques to the cultural heritage domain, namely on the EOKG, which represents olfactory heritage information. We used them on two different tasks: clustering and link prediction. Given the complexity of the involved Knowledge Graph, we applied a strategy for selecting smaller but curated subsets that are more homogeneous to train our embedding models. This effectively improved the performance of the predictions. In particular, we discovered that a more dense subset improved the accuracy of the models in all metrics. The obtained results can be directly used into the EOKG and support the research on it in the Cultural Heritage domain. The code for computing the embeddings, clustering and link predicting is available at `https://github.com/Odeuropa/kg-embeddings`.

Our future work will focus on using the clustering algorithm to select part of the graph which are more homogeneous in content, in order to refine the link prediction step to a specific graph area. In other words, we would create link prediction models that are specialised alternatively in floral smells, malodors, etc. As alternative, we may substitute the clustering with community detection approaches [42,43]. In addition, we aim to experiment with other graph embeddings methods such as RotatE [22] or GCN to better understand their capabilities in these scenarios where graphs can be sparse but where nodes and properties have well-defined semantics.

Acknowledgements

The authors would like to thank Inger Leemans, Marieke van Erp, Cecilia Bembibre and William Tullett for supporting the interpretation of the results. This work has been partially supported by European Union's Horizon 2020 research and innovation programme within the Odeuropa project (grant agreement No. 101004469).

Table 9. The most similar concept for each cluster centroid using the **RDF2vec** embeddings (20 clusters), clustered on the **original** graph

CLUSTER 1	**CLUSTER 2**	**CLUSTER 3**	**CLUSTER 4**	**CLUSTER 5**
Fruit	*Cosmetics and artefacts*	*Fruit*	*Flowers*	*Bodily fluids*
Melon Mandarin Durian Lemongrass Watermelon	Talc Scent box Earring Pomander ship Sachet	Lemon Pineapple Raspberry Currant Coconut	Petunia Raflessia Delphinium Chamomile Passion flower	Semen Slurry Breath Liquid manure Sweat
CLUSTER 6	**CLUSTER 7**	**CLUSTER 8**	**CLUSTER 9**	**CLUSTER 10**
Malodours	*Spices*	*Fuel*	*Artefacts*	*Balms*
Air pollution Filth Pollution Malodor Fumigation	Saffron Allspice Vanilla Anise Cinnamon cassia	Kerosene Petroleum Sea Peat Diesel fuel	Powder Box Scent box Pomander ship Feather Sachet	Opoponax Tolu balm Peru balm Spikenard Balm
CLUSTER 11	**CLUSTER 12**	**CLUSTER 13**	**CLUSTER 14**	**CLUSTER 15**
Beings	*Tobacco*	*Vegetables*	*Carriers*	*Animals*
Being Woman Person Man Bird	Cigar-box Snuff Box Match Tobacco packag. Plague mask	Cucumber Corn Cress Asparagus Aubergine	Incense ship Tobacco grater Beaver hat Beer stein Jan Steen jug	Monkey Tiger Rabbit Guinea pig Camel
CLUSTER 16	**CLUSTER 17**	**CLUSTER 18**	**CLUSTER 19**	**CLUSTER 20**
Interior	*Plants*	*Perfumes*	*Miscellaneous*	*Food*
Bath Head cone Fireplace Ciborium Distillation eq.	Furze Stapelia Sassafras Organic waste Rapeseed	Floral water Geosmin Lemon balm Eau de Luce Chypre	Bonfire Pigeon manure Candle Alchemy Equip. Chimney	Curry Yeast Chili Cream Liquorice

Table 10. The most similar concept for each cluster centroid using the **RDF2vec** embeddings (20 clusters), clustered on the **dense** graph

CLUSTER 1	**CLUSTER 2**	**CLUSTER 3**	**CLUSTER 4**	**CLUSTER 5**
Vessels	*Spices*	*Artefacts*	*Mammals*	*Flowers*
Barrel	Cinnamon cassia	Hand	Lion	Daffodil
Milk Jug	Allspice	Posy	Wolf	Jasmine
Beer stein	Pepper	Scent	Guinea pig	Violet
Chatelaine flask	Fennel	Perfume	Donkey	Raflessia
Betrothal Ring	Anise	Rosary	Camel	Acacia
CLUSTER 6	**CLUSTER 7**	**CLUSTER 8**	**CLUSTER 9**	**CLUSTER 10**
Resins	*Malodors*	*Fruits*	*Breakfast*	*Secretions*
Styrax	Air pollution	Apple	Butter	Breath
Opoponax	Filth	Rhubarb	Sausage	Semen
Benzoin	Halitosis	Pineapple	Yoghurt	Cat urine
Labdanum	Fumigation	Mandarin	Pie	Sweat
Tolu balm	Malodor	Blackcurrant	Ham	Vomit
CLUSTER 11	**CLUSTER 12**	**CLUSTER 13**	**CLUSTER 14**	**CLUSTER 15**
Vegetable	*Flowers*	*Liquids*	*Fresh flowers*	*Holders*
Horse radish	Garland	Mildew	Bouquet	Scent box
Celery	Violet	Lake	Heliotropium	Pomander ship
Cabbage	Neroli	Diesel fuel	Furze	Pomander Watch
Bellpepper	Hyacinth	Sea	Acacia farnesiana	Tobacco packaging
Pea	Lily-of-the-valley	Wet earth	Water mint	Medicine Jar
CLUSTER 16	**CLUSTER 17**	**CLUSTER 18**	**CLUSTER 19**	**CLUSTER 20**
Tobacco	*Animal-based perfumery*	*Equipments*	*Oils*	*Invertebrates*
Cigarette	Musk Rat	Distillation eq.	Geosmin	Butterfly
Cigar-holder	Musk Deer	Candle	Essential oil	Ant
Cigar-box	Civet (mammal)	Cassolette	Eau de Luce	Prawn
Cigar-case	Skunk	Alchemy equip.	Eau de Hungary	Onycha
Pipe	Beaver	Apothecary eq.	Ointment	Dragonfly

Table 11. The most similar concept for each cluster centroid using the **DistMult** embeddings (20 clusters), clustered on the **original** graph

CLUSTER 1	**CLUSTER 2**	**CLUSTER 3**	**CLUSTER 4**	**CLUSTER 5**
Perfumes	*Trees*	*Malodour*	*Carriers*	*Miscellaneous*
Eau de Lice	Flora	Abstract	Artefact	Nature
Boldoot	Tree	Malodor	Pomander watch	Miasma
Perfume	Pine needle	Halitosis	Pomander ship	Iso-butyl-quinoline
Acqua della Regina	Conifer	Theriaca	Cashmere	Artefact
Peau d'Espagne	Raflessia	Pollution	Posy holder	Cashmere
CLUSTER 6	**CLUSTER 7**	**CLUSTER 8**	**CLUSTER 9**	**CLUSTER 10**
Vegetable/Fruits	*Bodily Fluids*	*Jewelry*	*Flowers*	*Seasonings*
Strawberry	Body	Flacon ring	Neroli	Food
Salad	Grangreen	Bracelet vinaigrette	Columbine	Lemongrass
Cauliflower	Cat urine	Artefact	Heliotropium	Sage
Vegetable	Liquid manure	Jewelry	Carnation	Besamin
Fruit	Slurry	Berothal Ring	Cornflower	Coriander leaf
CLUSTER 11	**CLUSTER 12**	**CLUSTER 13**	**CLUSTER 14**	**CLUSTER 15**
Flora	*Mammals*	*Balms*	*Flowers*	*Vessels*
Flora	Pig	Styrax	Flower	Glass without stem
Pine needle	Tiger	Resin	Matthiola	Vessel
Coriander leaf	Mammal	Animal raw material	Orchid	Cup
Raflessia	Deer	Tolu balm	Raflessia	Ashtray
Beetroot	Guinea pig	Galbanum	Rosehip	Glass with stem
CLUSTER 16	**CLUSTER 17**	**CLUSTER 18**	**CLUSTER 19**	**CLUSTER 20**
Chemical	*Tobacco*	*Animal*	*Artefact*	*Animal*
Chemical Element	Match	Mammal	Jewelry	Invertebrate
Iso-butyl-quinoline	Musical snuff box	Being	Artefact	Reptile
Element	Smoking equipment	Deer	Posy holder	Vertebrate
Vinegar	Blueberry	Sperm whale	Dairy	Being
Ozone	Snuff box	Wolf	Earring	Butterfly

Table 12. The most similar concept for each cluster centroid using the **DistMult** embeddings (20 clusters), clustered on the **dense** graph

CLUSTER 1	**CLUSTER 2**	**CLUSTER 3**	**CLUSTER 4**	**CLUSTER 5**
	Flowers	*Vegetables*	*Fossils*	*Mammals*
Fireplace	Dahlia	Avocado	Peat	Civet (mammal)
Amulet	Woodruff	Parsnip	Mould	Guinea pig
Ink	Dandelion	Passion fruit	Petrichor	Bear
Flacon	Garland	Chives	Mildew	Donkey
Cigar	Mimosa	Radish	Diesel fuel	Beaver
CLUSTER 6	**CLUSTER 7**	**CLUSTER 8**	**CLUSTER 9**	**CLUSTER 10**
Resins			*Herbs*	*Chemicals*
Myrrh	Anatomical Lessons	Avocado	Thyme	Aceltene
Wax	Burnt offering	Curry	Rosemary	Carbolic acid
Rubber	Blossom	Cress	Musk mallow	Ozone
Resin	Soot	Passion fruit	Mint	Coumarin
Balm	various	Schalg	Basilic	Acetic acid
CLUSTER 11	**CLUSTER 12**	**CLUSTER 13**	**CLUSTER 14**	**CLUSTER 15**
Fruits	*Fishy*	*House products*	*Animal categories*	*Holders*
Peach	Slurry	Cashmere	Vertebrate	Cashmere
Plum	Cod liver oil	Bouquet Holder	Being	Posy holder
Mandarin	Liquid manure	Ammonia soap	Reptile/Amphibia	Chatelaine flask
Grape	Whale oil	Smelling Box	Amphibia	Cigar-case
Pear	Spermaceti	Cigar-case	Insect	Rope tobacco
CLUSTER 16	**CLUSTER 17**	**CLUSTER 18**	**CLUSTER 19**	**CLUSTER 20**
Trees	*Scented waters*	*Artefacts*	*Flowers*	*Malodors*
Tagetes	Boldoot	Jewelry	Petunia	Halitosis
Fir needle	Aqua mirabilis	Ring	Dandelion	Filth
Cedar (Lebanon)	Florida Water	Bracelet vinaigrette	Tulip	Sillage
Rapeseed	Reukwerk	Wine Bottle	Dahlia	Malodor
Oud	Peau d'Espagne	Oil lamp	Carnation	Fumigation

Table 13. The most similar concept for each cluster centroid using the *TransE* embeddings (20 clusters), clustered on the **original** graph

CLUSTER 1	CLUSTER 2	CLUSTER 3	CLUSTER 4	CLUSTER 5
Lether Perfume Vegetable Lily of the valley Fruit	Sulphur Asa foetida Man Lime blossom tree Geranium	Fumigation Pidgeon manure Powdered wig Asa foetida Geranium	Allspice Geranium Turmeric Currant Tulip	Worm Geranium Ambergris Turpentine Wet earth
CLUSTER 6	**CLUSTER 7**	**CLUSTER 8**	**CLUSTER 9**	**CLUSTER 10**
		Artefacts		
Watermelon Pineapple Physalis Sausage Geranium	Fish Pipe Oil Fruit Geranium	Drinking Glass Bracelet Ashtray Smelling Bottle Wine bottle	Lavender Geranium Hyacinth Water Saffron	Ointment Pipe Smoking equipment Bread Tobacco packaging
CLUSTER 11	**CLUSTER 12**	**CLUSTER 13**	**CLUSTER 14**	**CLUSTER 15**
Geranium Jonquil Passion flower Frog Butterfly	Acacia Geranium Hazelnut Asa foetida Mustard	Fur Man Iris Herb Geranium	Vial Butterfly Asa Foetida Geranium Calamus	Smoke Religion Vegetable Wine Garlic
CLUSTER 16	**CLUSTER 17**	**CLUSTER 18**	**CLUSTER 19**	**CLUSTER 20**
Matthiola Musk Deer Inro Dairy Pineapple	Egg Lignum aquilae Tallow Geranium Smelling box	Ink Raspberry Vinegar Geranium Myrtle	Being Food Flora Element Animal raw material	Patchouli Gunpowder Geranium Egg Sulphuric acid

Table 14. The most similar concept for each cluster centroid using the *TransE* embeddings (20 clusters), clustered on the **dense** graph

CLUSTER 1	CLUSTER 2	CLUSTER 3	CLUSTER 4	CLUSTER 5
Fruits	*Artefacts*	*Food*	*Malodors*	
Pineapple Watermelon Halitosis Peanut Apricot	Head cone Pomander Chamber pot Perfume flacon Lodereindoos	Oil Coffee Blueberry Spice Vegetable	Malodor Odor of sanctity Fumigation Abstract Pollution	Lodereindoos Leather Tapestry Cigar-box Diaper Perfume box
CLUSTER 6	**CLUSTER 7**	**CLUSTER 8**	**CLUSTER 9**	**CLUSTER 10**
	Trees	*Plants*	*Plants*	
Snuff Myrrh Sulphur Grass Blackcurrant leaf	Sassafras Cedar (Lebanon) Cedar (Virginia) Stapelia Acacia farnesiana	Rosehip Elm tree Passion flower Heliotropium Quince	Elderflower Rapeseed Quince Acacia farnesiana Dahlia	Spirit (alcohol) Carrot Grapefruit Broth Schalg
CLUSTER 11	**CLUSTER 12**	**CLUSTER 13**	**CLUSTER 14**	**CLUSTER 15**
Mammals	*Vegetables*	*Animal products*	*Scented waters*	*Flowers*
Wolf Beaver Lion Bull Man	Pea Radish Carrot Cress Spring onion	Body Tallow Liquid manure Whale oil Ambergris	Florida Water Eau de cologne Floral water Fougère Boldoot	Dahlia Geranium Furze Columbine Anemone
CLUSTER 16	**CLUSTER 17**	**CLUSTER 18**	**CLUSTER 19**	**CLUSTER 20**
Vessels	*Nature*	*Summer Fruits*	*Artefacts*	*Chemicals*
Vessel Drinking glass Teapot Bottle Pot	Nature Peat Wet earth Wind Lake	Fig Spring onion Plum Peach Coconut	Powdered Wig Necklace Vial Smelling Bottle Lodereindoos	Carbolic acid Aceltene Chemical Element Element Iso-butyl-quinoline

References

[1] Hogan A, Blomqvist E, Cochez M, d'Amato C, Melo GD, Gutierrez C, et al. Knowledge Graphs. ACM Computing Surveys. 2021;54(4).
[2] Cai H, Zheng VW, Chang KCC. A Comprehensive Survey of Graph Embedding: Problems, Techniques, and Applications. IEEE Transactions on Knowledge & Data Engineering. 2018;30(09):1616-37.
[3] Bordes A, Usunier N, Garcia-Duran A, Weston J, Yakhnenko O. Translating embeddings for modeling multi-relational data. Advances in neural information processing systems. 2013;26.
[4] Nickel M, Murphy K, Tresp V, Gabrilovich E. A Review of Relational Machine Learning for Knowledge Graphs. Proceedings of the IEEE. 2016;104(1):11-33.
[5] Ristoski P, Rosati J, Di Noia T, De Leone R, Paulheim H. RDF2Vec: RDF graph embeddings and their applications. Semantic Web. 2019;10(4):721-52.
[6] Palumbo E, Monti D, Rizzo G, Troncy R, Baralis E. entity2rec: Property-specific knowledge graph embeddings for item recommendation. Expert Systems with Applications. 2020;151.
[7] Fekete M, Bjerva J, Beinborn L. Typological Challenges for the Application of Multilingual Language Models in the Digital Humanities. In: Multilingual Digital Humanities. Digital Research in the Arts and Humanities. Routledge; 2023. .
[8] Lisena P, Troncy R. Representing Complex Knowledge for Exploration and Recommendation: The Case of Classical Music Information. In: Cota G, Daquino M, Pozzato GL, editors. Applications and Practices in Ontology Design, Extraction, and Reasoning. vol. 49 of Studies on the Semantic Web Series (SSWS). IOSPress; 2020. p. 107-23.
[9] El-Hajj H, Valleriani M. CIDOC2VEC: Extracting Information from Atomized CIDOC-CRM Humanities Knowledge Graphs. Information. 2021;12(12).
[10] Martin-Rodilla P, Gonzalez-Perez C. Representing Imprecise and Uncertain Knowledge in Digital Humanities: A Theoretical Framework and ConML Implementation with a Real Case Study. In: Proceedings of the Sixth International Conference on Technological Ecosystems for Enhancing Multiculturality. TEEM'18. Association for Computing Machinery; 2018. p. 863–871.
[11] Lisena P, van Erp M, Bembibre C, Leemans I. Data Mining and Knowledge Graphs as a Backbone for Advanced Olfactory Experiences. In: STT21: Smell, Taste, and Temperature Interfaces workshop. Yokohama, Japan; 2021. .
[12] Pujara J, Augustine E, Getoor L. Sparsity and Noise: Where Knowledge Graph Embeddings Fall Short. In: Conference on Empirical Methods in Natural Language Processing. Copenhagen, Denmark: Association for Computational Linguistics; 2017. p. 1751-6.
[13] Portisch J, Hladik M, Paulheim H. RDF2Vec Light – A Lightweight Approach for Knowledge Graph Embeddings. In: International Semantic Web Conference, Posters and Demos; 2020. .
[14] Fanourakis N, Efthymiou V, Kotzinos D, Christophides V. Knowledge graph embedding methods for entity alignment: experimental review. Data Mining and Knowledge Discovery. 2023;37(5):2070-137.
[15] Lisena P, Schwabe D, van Erp M, Troncy R, Tullett W, Leemans I, et al. Capturing the Semantics of Smell: The Odeuropa Data Model for Olfactory Heritage Information. In: 19th European Conference on the Semantic Web (ESWC); 2022. p. 387-405.
[16] Goyal P, Ferrara E. Graph embedding techniques, applications, and performance: A survey. Knowledge-Based Systems. 2018;151:78-94.
[17] Wang X, Bo D, Shi C, Fan S, Ye Y, Yu PS. A Survey on Heterogeneous Graph Embedding: Methods, Techniques, Applications and Sources. IEEE Transactions on Big Data. 2023;9(2):415-36.
[18] Spitzer F. Principles of random walk. vol. 34. Springer Science & Business Media; 2001.
[19] Grover A, Leskovec J. node2vec: Scalable Feature Learning for Networks. In: 22nd ACM SIGKDD International Conference on Knowledge Discovery and Data Mining. Association for Computing Machinery; 2016. p. 855–864.
[20] Trouillon T, Welbl J, Riedel S, Gaussier E, Bouchard G. Complex Embeddings for Simple Link Prediction. In: 33rd International Conference on Machine Learning. vol. 48 of Proceedings of Machine Learning Research. PMLR; 2016. p. 2071-80.
[21] Yang B, Yih W, He X, Gao J, Deng L. Embedding Entities and Relations for Learning and Inference in Knowledge Bases. In: International Conference on Learning Representations ICLR; 2015. .
[22] Sun Z, Deng ZH, Nie JY, Tang J. RotatE: Knowledge Graph Embedding by Relational Rotation in Complex Space. In: International Conference on Learning Representations; 2019. .
[23] Hou W, Bai B, Cai C. CR-TransR: A Knowledge Graph Embedding Model for Cultural Domain. Journal on Computing and Cultural Heritage. 2024;17(1).

[24] Han M, Wang Q, Chen H, Chen W, Zhang J, Wang G. Representing the Intangible Cultural Heritage Knowledge Graph with Vector Embedding. In: 2023 IEEE International Conference on High Performance Computing & Communications, Data Science & Systems, Smart City & Dependability in Sensor, Cloud & Big Data Systems & Application (HPCC/DSS/SmartCity/DependSys); 2023. p. 718-25.
[25] Mohamed HA, Vascon S, Hibraj F, James S, Pilutti D, Del Bue A, et al. Geolocation of Cultural Heritage Using Multi-view Knowledge Graph Embedding. In: Rousseau JJ, Kapralos B, editors. Pattern Recognition, Computer Vision, and Image Processing. ICPR 2022 International Workshops and Challenges. Springer Nature Switzerland; 2023. p. 142-54.
[26] El-Hajj H, Zamani M, Büttner J, Martinetz J, Eberle O, Shlomi N, et al. An Ever-Expanding Humanities Knowledge Graph: The Sphaera Corpus at the Intersection of Humanities, Data Management, and Machine Learning. Datenbank-Spektrum. 2022;22(2):153-62.
[27] Baas J, Dastani M, Feelders A. Tailored Graph Embeddings for Entity Alignment on Historical Data. In: 22nd International Conference on Information Integration and Web-Based Applications & Services. iiWAS '20. Association for Computing Machinery; 2021. p. 125–133.
[28] Menini S. Semantic Frame Extraction in Multilingual Olfactory Events. In: Joint International Conference on Computational Linguistics, Language Resources and Evaluation (LREC-COLING 2024). Torino, Italia: ELRA and ICCL; 2024. p. 14622-7. Available from: `https://aclanthology.org/2024.lrec-main.1273`.
[29] Zinnen M, Madhu P, Leemans I, Bell P, Hussian A, Tran H, et al. Smelly, dense, and spreaded: The Object Detection for Olfactory References (ODOR) dataset. Expert Systems with Applications. 2024;255:124576.
[30] Lisena P, Meroño-Peñuela A, Kuhn T, Troncy R. Easy Web API Development with SPARQL Transformer. In: 18th International Semantic Web Conference (ISWC), In-Use Track. Auckland, New Zealand; 2019. .
[31] Menini S, Paccosi T, Tonelli S, Van Erp M, Leemans I, Lisena P, et al. A Multilingual Benchmark to Capture Olfactory Situations over Time. In: 3rd Workshop on Computational Approaches to Historical Language Change. Dublin, Ireland: Association for Computational Linguistics; 2022. p. 1-10.
[32] Miles A, Pérez-Agüera JR. SKOS: Simple knowledge organisation for the web. Cataloging & Classification Quarterly. 2007;43(3-4):69-83.
[33] Chen Y, Sanghavi S, Xu H. Clustering Sparse Graphs. In: Advances in Neural Information Processing Systems. vol. 25. Curran Associates, Inc.; 2012. Available from: `https://proceedings.neurips.cc/paper_files/paper/2012/file/1e6e0a04d20f50967c64dac2d639a577-Paper.pdf`.
[34] Wang S, Zhu W. Sparse Graph Embedding Unsupervised Feature Selection. IEEE Transactions on Systems, Man, and Cybernetics: Systems. 2018;48(3):329-41.
[35] Chen J, Saad Y. Finding dense subgraphs for sparse undirected, directed, and bipartite graphs. Minnesota: University of Minnesota Twin Cities. 2009.
[36] Attenborough M. 19 - Graph theory. In: Attenborough M, editor. Mathematics for Electrical Engineering and Computing. Oxford: Newnes; 2003. p. 461-78.
[37] Mikolov T, Chen K, Corrado G, Dean J. Efficient Estimation of Word Representations in Vector Space. In: International Conference on Learning Representations (ICLR); 2013. .
[38] Chandrahas, Sharma A, Talukdar P. Towards Understanding the Geometry of Knowledge Graph Embeddings. In: 56th Annual Meeting of the Association for Computational Linguistics (ACL). Melbourne, Australia: Association for Computational Linguistics; 2018. p. 122-31.
[39] Steenwinckel B, Vandewiele G, Agozzino T, Ongenae F. pyRDF2Vec: A Python Implementation and Extension of RDF2Vec. In: European Semantic Web Conference (ESWC); 2023. p. 471-83.
[40] Ali M, Berrendorf M, Hoyt CT, Vermue L, Sharifzadeh S, Tresp V, et al. PyKEEN 1.0: A Python Library for Training and Evaluating Knowledge Graph Embeddings. Journal of Machine Learning Research. 2021;22(82):1-6. Available from: `http://jmlr.org/papers/v22/20-825.html`.
[41] Rosenberg A, Hirschberg J. V-Measure: A Conditional Entropy-Based External Cluster Evaluation Measure. In: Eisner J, editor. Joint Conference on Empirical Methods in Natural Language Processing and Computational Natural Language Learning (EMNLP-CoNLL). Prague, Czech Republic: Association for Computational Linguistics; 2007. p. 410-20. Available from: `https://aclanthology.org/D07-1043`.
[42] Fortunato S. Community detection in graphs. Physics Reports. 2010;486(3):75-174.
[43] Chen J, Saad Y. Dense Subgraph Extraction with Application to Community Detection. IEEE Transactions on Knowledge and Data Engineering. 2012;24(7):1216-30.

Handbook on Neurosymbolic AI and Knowledge Graphs
P. Hitzler et al. (Eds.)
IOS Press, 2025

doi:10.3233/FAIA250206

What Do Knowledge Graph Embeddings Learn to Represent?

Heiko PAULHEIM [a,1], Nicolas HUBERT [b], and Jan PORTISCH [c]
[a] *University of Mannheim, Data and Web Science Group, Germany*
[b] *Zalando SE, Berlin, Germany*
[c] *SAP SE, Walldorf, Germany*
ORCiD ID: Heiko Paulheim https://orcid.org/0000-0003-4386-8195, Nicolas Hubert https://orcid.org/0000-0002-4682-422X, Jan Portisch https://orcid.org/0000-0001-5420-0663

Abstract. Knowledge Graph Embeddings (KGEs) are widely used in many tasks beyond link prediction, such as node classification, analogical reasoning, or as background knowledge, e.g., for recommender systems. While they exhibit good results, little work has been done in understanding what different knowledge graph embedding methods actually learn. In this chapter, we present two studies: the first one analyzes which ontological patterns KGEs are capable of capturing and which they are not. The second one takes a closer look at the similarity relation in different embedding spaces, analyzing how reliable the common *KGE entity similarity assumption* – stating that similar entities are projected close to one another in the embedding space – actually is.

Keywords. Knowledge Graph Embedding, Node Classification, Entity Similarity, Embedding Space, Semantic Similarity, Representation Learning

1. Introduction

Knowledge Graphs (KGs) such as DBpedia [1], YAGO [2], and Wikidata [3] represent facts as triples (s, p, o) consisting of a subject s and an object o connected by a predicate p defining their relationship. [4,5] Common learning tasks with KGs include entity clustering, node classification, and link prediction. These tasks are predominantly tackled using Knowledge Graph Embedding Models (KGEMs), which generate dense vector representations for entities and relations of a KG, a.k.a. Knowledge Graph Embeddings (KGEs). The dense numerical vectors that are learnt for entities and relations are expected to preserve the intrinsic semantics of the KG [6].

As KGEMs take into account the semantic relationship between two entities to learn embeddings, it is often taken for granted that the resulting embeddings capture both the semantics and attributes of entities and their relationships in the KG. Embeddings are thus widely used to measure the semantic similarity between entities and relations, facilitating data integration through entity or relation alignments [7,8]. They are also used in various similarity-based tasks including entity similarity [9] and conceptual cluster-

[1]Corresponding Author: Heiko Paulheim, heiko@informatik.uni-mannheim.de

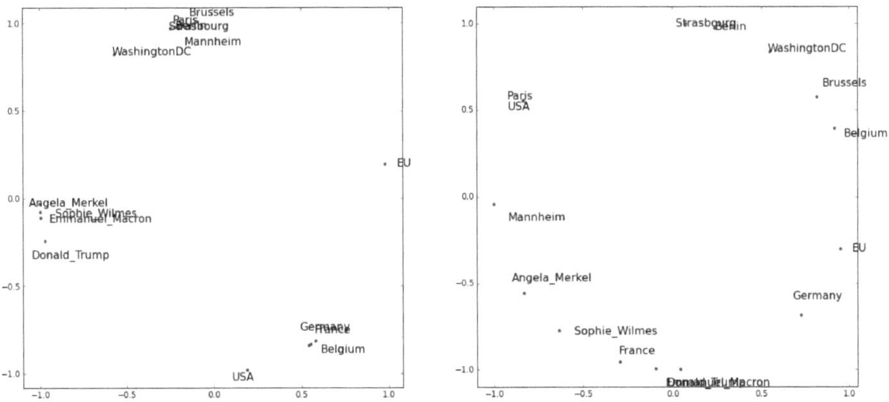

(a) Good class separation

(b) Bad class separation

Figure 1. Two Example Embeddings. The left-hand side embedding shows a good class separation of persons, countries, and cities, whereas the right-hand side one does not. [11]

ing [10]. All those downstream tasks make two central assumptions about how entities are embedded in a latent feature space:

1. Entities from different classes are embedded such that the classes can be separated by a classifier trained on the embedding space (see Figure 1).
2. Similar entities are assigned similar vectors, i.e., they are embedded close to one another in the embedding space.

The two assumptions can be seen as two sides of the same coin: entities that are dissimilar fall into different classes and should thus be embedded further away from one another than similar entities, i.e., entities that fall into the same class.

One issue with the first assumption is that it does not clearly define what a class is. Classes could be formed along ontological classes (e.g., all people), using constraints (e.g., all people born in New York City) or even across ontological classes (e.g., all things related to New York City). Depending on which notion of a class is used, one may find different KGE approaches fulfilling the assumption to a larger or lesser extent.

In order to analyze this problem at a finer scale, we have proposed the DLCC (for *Description Logic Class Constructors*) dataset and an evaluation framework that helps to better analyze and understand embedding approaches for specific DL constructors. In this chapter, we discuss (1) a framework for the DLCC gold standard creation, (2) two concrete gold standards – a real graph-based gold standard and one based on synthetic KGs, (3) an evaluation framework to easily evaluate and compare the class separation capabilities of embeddings, and (4) an analysis for different state-of-the-art embedding approaches.

As far as the second assumption goes, which we call the *KGE entity similarity assumption* [12], it has been challenged recently [13]. Jain *et al.* [13] demonstrate that entity embeddings learnt with KGEMs are not well-suited to identify the concepts or classes for a vast majority of KG entities, while simple statistical approaches provide comparable or better performance. Concerned with word embeddings, Ilievski *et al.* [14] also point out that KGEMs are consistently outperformed by simpler heuristics for similarity-based tasks. The authors argue that many properties on which KGEMs heavily rely are not useful for determining similarity, which introduces noise and subsequently decreases performance.

Similarly to the notion of classes, there is no universally accepted definition for entity similarity. Hence, we follow a straightforward approach: two entities in a KG are similar if we make similar statements about them. This aligns with the assumption of distributional semantics: words appearing in similar contexts are semantically similar [15].

In this chapter, we show that different KGEMs fulfill the *KGE entity similarity assumption* only to a limited extent. Notably, even for a given KGEM, results can vary substantially on a per-class basis. Moreover, the semantics of classes is inequally captured by different KGEMs, thereby highlighting that different KGEMs expose different notions of similarity. Moreover, we show that, in most cases, performance in link prediction does not correlate with a model's adherence to the KGE entity similarity assumption. This demonstrates that rank-based metrics cannot be used as a reliable proxy for assessing the semantic consistency of the embedding space. Finally, we analyze if different KGEMs turn their attention to different predicate subsets for learning similar embeddings for related entities.

The rest of this chapter is structured as follows. Section 2 reviews related works. In section 3, we present a series of experiments to understand which patterns can be captured by KGEMs, whereas in section 4, we take a closer look at the notion of similarity in embedding spaces. We conclude the paper with a summary and a few key takeaways.

2. Related Work

A lot of work has been done on benchmarking KGEMs with respect to different aspects. In the area of link prediction (or knowledge base completion), the two well-known evaluation datasets FB15k and WN18 [16] are both based on real datasets: FB15k is based on the Freebase dataset, and WN18 is based on WordNet [17]. They were presented in the context of link prediction: Given a triple in the form *(**h**ead, **r**elation, **t**ail)*, two prediction tasks *(head, relation, ?)* and *(?, relation, tail)* are created. The evaluation is performed by calculating the Mean Rank (MR), Mean Reciprocal Rank (MRR), or Hits@K for a list of proposals. Since it has been remarked that those datasets contain too many simple inferences due to inverse relations, the more challenging variants FB15k-237 [18] and WN18RR [19] have been proposed. More recently, evaluation sets based on larger KGs, such as YAGO3-10 [19] and DBpedia50k/DBpedia500k [20], have been introduced.

With respect to node classification, Bloem et al. [21] introduce *kgbench*, a node classification benchmark for KGs, which is based on real-world tasks and comes with datasets in different sizes and predefined train/test splits. Alshagari et al. [22] present a framework for ontological concepts covering three aspects: (i) categorization, (ii) hierarchy, and (iii) logic validation. The framework can be used for language models and for KGEs. The evaluation of this paper is, therefore, of analytical rather than descriptive nature. Ristoski et al. [23] provide a collection of benchmarking datasets for machine learning, including classification, clustering, and regression tasks. Later, the GEval framework [24,25] was introduced to provide a standardized evaluation protocol for this dataset. The evaluation datasets are based on DBpedia. Internally, the embeddings are processed by different downstream classification, regression, or clustering algorithms.

A slightly different angle is taken by the KGrEaT evaluation framework [26]. Instead of comparing the performance of different KGEMs on downstream tasks while fixing the KG at hand, the authors aim at investigating the performance of a fixed KGEM using different KGs. This framework could also reveal differences regarding which KGEM works better or worse given a particular KG, and help identifying relations between characteristics of a KG and the performance of particular KGEMs, however, to the best of our knowledge, such an analysis has not yet been performed.

While all of those frameworks measure performance metrics, i.e., how good a KGEM works for a particular task, they do not zoom into the representional capabilities of KGEMs. Likewise, the notion of similarity and the KGE entity similarity assupmtion have not been formally investigated.

Interestingly, many works *implicity* rely on the KGE entity similarity assumption to hold, but there are only few works actually *explicitly* validating this assumption: if a classifier is trained to solve a binary or multi-class entity classification task based on the entities' embeddings, it is assumed that class separation is possible in the embedding space. In [27], we have shown some anecdotic examples for a few embedding approaches, also suggesting that the underlying notions of similarity might differ, but not conducted any formal evaluation. Jain *et al.* [13] analyze KGEMs on the basis of class assignments, showing that the original class assignments can only be reconstructed to a limited extent with classification and clustering methods, which rather questions the assumption of similar entities being close in the vector space. A similar study is conducted by Alshargi *et al.* [28], also concluding that "the current quality of the embeddings for ontological concepts is not in a satisfactory state".

In this chapter, we present two studies that aim at closing those research gaps. First, the experiments using the DLCC gold standard analyze the representational capabalities of KGEMs with respect to different ontology class constructs in depth, and we conduct a series of experiments to empirically challenge the KGE similarity assumption.

3. Classification Patterns Learned by Knowledge Graph Embeddings

To analyze the representational capabilities of KGEMs, we first introduce a number of constructs to consider. From there on, we present two gold standards for experimentation, one based on DBpedia [1], the other based on synthetic KGs. Furthermore, we present and discuss experimental findings with a number of KGEMs.

3.1. Covered Patterns

To answer the question which patterns can be represented by different KGEMs, we define class labels using different Description Logics (DL) constructors. Later on, we apply classification algorithms to analyze how well the differently labeled classes can be separated using different embedding algorithms.

In order to describe the patterns, we use the following notation (see [29] for more details):

- $\top$ denotes the generic top class (i.e., `owl:Thing` in OWL)
- T denotes a specific class
- R denotes any relation
- r denotes a specific relation
- R^{-1} and r^{-1} denote the inverse of a relation
- e denotes a specific individual

Ingoing and Outgoing Relations All entities that have a particular outgoing or ingoing relations (e.g., *everything that has a location*).

$$\exists r.\top \tag{1}$$

$$\exists r^{-1}.\top \tag{2}$$

$$\exists r.\top \sqcup \exists r^{-1}.\top \tag{3}$$

where r is bound to a particular relation.

Relations to Particular Individuals All entities that have a relation (in any direction) to a particular individual (e.g., *everything that is related to New York City*).

$$\exists R.\{e\} \sqcup \exists R^{-1}.\{e\} \tag{4}$$

where R is *not* bound to a particular relation. Those relations can also span two (or more[1] hops):

$$\exists R_1.(\exists R_2.\{e\}) \sqcup \exists R_1^{-1}.(\exists R_2^{-1}\{e\}) \tag{5}$$

Particular Relations to Particular Individuals All entities that have a particular relation to a particular individual (e.g., *movies directed by Steven Spielberg*).

$$\exists r.\{e\} \tag{6}$$

Qualified Restrictions All entities that have a particular relation to an individual of a given type (e.g., *all people married to soccer players*).

$$\exists r.T \tag{7}$$

$$\exists r^{-1}.T \tag{8}$$

If types are modeled as a normal relation in the graph (i.e., `rdf:type` is yet another relation), we can reformulate Eqs. (7) and (8) to

$$\exists r.(\exists \texttt{rdf:type}.T) \tag{7a}$$

$$\exists r^{-1}.(\exists \texttt{rdf:type}.T) \tag{8a}$$

In that case, it behaves equally to a chained variant of Eq. (6).

Cardinality Restrictions of Relations All entities that have at least or at most n relations of a particular kind (e.g., *people who have at least two citizenships*). Here, we depict only the *lower bound* variant because the corresponding decision problem is between the two variants (entities that fall below the bound, i.e., adhere to the upper bound, are in the negative example set).[2]

$$\geq 2r.\top \tag{9}$$

$$\geq 2r^{-1}.\top \tag{10}$$

Qualified Cardinality Restrictions Qualified cardinality restrictions combine qualified restrictions with cardinalities (e.g., people who have published at least two science fiction novels).

$$\geq 2r.T \tag{11}$$

$$\geq 2r^{-1}.T \tag{12}$$

Table 1 summarizes the DL constructors for which test cases were built.

3.2. The DLCC Benchmark

For the twelve test cases in Table 1, we create positive examples (i.e., those which fall into the respective class) and those which do not (under closed-world semantics). For example, for tc01, we would generate a set of positive instances for which $\exists r.\top$ holds and a set of negative instances for which $\nexists r.\top$ holds, where the number is a configurable parameter in the benchmark. We then evaluate how well these two classes can be separated, given the embedding vectors of the positive and negative instances. For that, we split the examples into a training and testing partition, we train binary classifiers on the training subset of the examples, and evaluate their performance on the test subset.

The approach is visualized in Figure 2: A gold standard generator generates a set of positive and negative URIs, as well as a fixed train/test split. The approach presented in this paper allows to generate custom gold standards – however, a contribution of this paper is also to provide a pre-calculated gold standard. This pre-calculated gold standard can be used to guarantee reproducibility. Officially published gold standards are versioned to allow for future improvements. In this paper, we present version `v1` of the gold standard.

A user provides embeddings in a simple textual format and provides them together with the training data as input to the evaluator. The evaluator trains multiple classifiers and evaluates them on the selected gold standard using the provided vectors as classification input. The program then calculates multiple statistics in the form of CSV files that can be further analyzed in a spreadsheet program or through data analysis frameworks such as pandas[3]. These analyses help the user to understand how well the provided vectors are performing on a particular DL constructor.

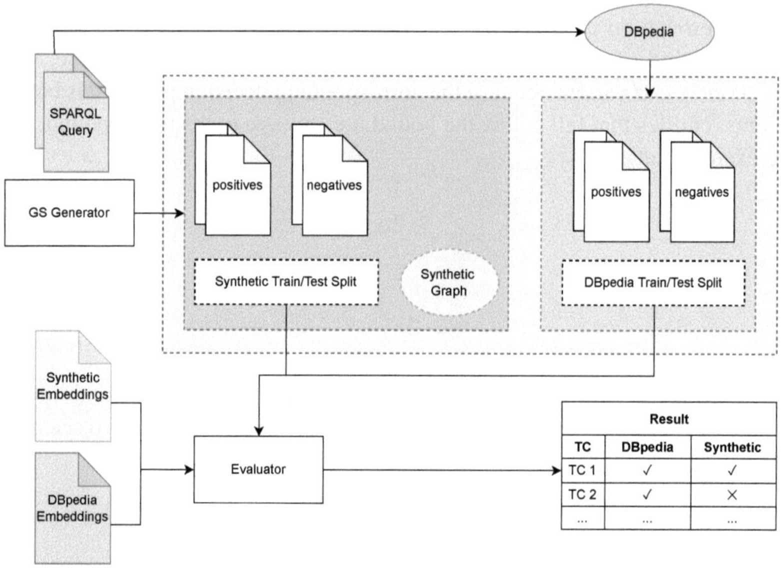

Figure 2. Overview of the DLCC generation pipeline [11]. The approach can generate both problems based on DBpedia and synthetic problems. In both cases, binary classification problems are created. Different classifiers are trained and tested for the embeddings of either DBpedia or the synthetic problem datasets, allowing to assess the representational capabilities of those embeddings.

Table 1. Overview of the Test Cases

Test Case	DL Expression
tc01	$\exists r.\top$
tc02	$\exists r^{-1}.\top$
tc03	$\exists r.\top \sqcup \exists r^{-1}.\top$
tc04	$\exists R.\{e\} \sqcup \exists R^{-1}.\{e\}$
tc05	$\exists R_1.(\exists R_2.\{e\}) \sqcup \exists R_1^{-1}.(\exists R_2^{-1}\{e\})$
tc06	$\exists r.\{e\}$
tc07	$\exists r.T$
tc08	$\exists r^{-1}.T$
tc09	$\geq 2r.\top$
tc10	$\geq 2r^{-1}.\top$
tc11	$\geq 2r.T$
tc12	$\geq 2r^{-1}.T$

3.2.1. Gold Standard Generator

The gold standard generator is publicly available[4]. It is implemented as a Java maven project. The generator can generate either a DBpedia benchmark (see Subsection 3.2.3) or a synthetic one (see Subsection 3.2.4). Any DBpedia version can be used; the user merely needs to provide a SPARQL endpoint. A comprehensive set of unit tests ensures a high code quality. The generator automatically generates a fixed train-test split for the evaluation framework or any other downstream application. The split is configurable; for the pre-generated gold standards, an 80-20 split is used. The resulting gold standard is balanced – i.e., the number of positives equals the number of negatives – and the train and test partitions are stratified. Hence, any classifier which achieves an accuracy significantly above 50% is capable of learning the test case's problem type from the vectors to some extent.

It is important to note that the generator only needs to be run by users who want to build their own gold standards. The typical user would merely download[5] the official gold standard files online. We recommend using the pre-calculated gold standards to ensure comparability across publications.

3.2.2. Evaluation Framework

The evaluator is publicly available[6] as well together with usage examples. It is implemented in Python and can be easily used in a Jupyter notebook. A comprehensive set of unit tests ensures a high code quality.

The standard user can directly download the gold standard and use the evaluation framework. To test class separability, the evaluation framework currently runs six machine learning classifiers:[7] (1) decision trees, (2) naïve Bayes, (3) KNN, (4) SVM, (5) random forest, and (6) a multilayer perceptron network. The framework uses the default configurations of the sklearn library[8].

After training and evaluation, the framework persists multiple CSV files per test case as well as higher-level aggregate CSV files. Examples of such CSV files are a file listing the accuracy per classifier and per test case or a file listing the accuracy of the best classifier per test case. In the case of DBpedia, test cases are created for multiple domains, and the results can be analyzed on the level of each domain separately or in an aggregated manner on the level of the test case.

3.2.3. The DLCC DBpedia Benchmark

We use the DBpedia knowledge graph to create test cases.[9] We created SPARQL queries for each test case (see Table 1) to generate positives, negatives, and hard negatives. The latter are meant to be less easily distinguishable from the positives and are created by variations such as softening the constraints in the class constructor or switching subject and object in the constraint. For example, for qualified relations, a positive example would be a person playing in a team which is a basketball team. A simple negative example would be any person not playing in a basketball team, whereas a hard negative example would be any person playing in a team that is not a basketball team.

In total, we used six different domains: people (P), books (B), cities (C), music albums (A), movies (M), and species (S). This setup yields more than 200 hand-written SPARQL queries, which are used to obtain positives, negatives, and hard negatives; they are available online[10] and can be easily extended, e.g., to add an additional domain. For each test case, we created differently sized (50, 500, 5000) balanced test sets.[11]

Query examples for every test case in the people domain are provided in Table 2. The framework uses slightly more involved queries to vary the size of the result set and to better randomize results.

3.2.4. The DLCC Synthetic Benchmark

The previous benchmark is realistic and well suited to compare approaches on differently typed DL constructors.

Table 2. Exemplary SPARQL Queries for Class Person [11]

TC	Query Positive	Query Negative	Query Negative (hard)

tc01	SELECT DISTINCT(?x) WHERE {
	?x a dbo:Person .
	?x dbo:child ?y . }
		SELECT DISTINCT(?x) WHERE {
		?x a dbo:Person .
		FILTER(NOT EXISTS {
		?x dbo:child ?z})}
			SELECT DISTINCT(?x) WHERE {
			?x a dbo:Person .
			?y dbo:child ?x.
			FILTER(NOT EXISTS {
			?x dbo:child ?z})}

tc02	Analogous to tc01 (inverse case).		

tc03	SELECT DISTINCT(?x) WHERE {
	{ ?x a dbo:Person .
	?x dbo:child ?y} UNION
	{ ?x a dbo:Person .
	?y dbo:child ?x}}
		SELECT COUNT(?x) WHERE {
		?x a dbo:Person .
		FILTER(NOT EXISTS{
		?x dbo:child ?y}
		AND NOT EXISTS {
		?z dbo:child ?x})}
			–

tc04	SELECT DISTINCT(?x) WHERE {
	{ ?x a dbo:Person .
	?x ?y dbr:New_York_City}
	UNION
	{ ?x a dbo:Person .
	dbr:New_York_City ?y ?x}}
		SELECT DISTINCT(?x) WHERE {
		?x a dbo:Person .
		FILTER(NOT EXISTS{
		?x ?y dbr:New_York_City}
		AND NOT EXISTS {
		dbr:New_York_City ?y
		?x})}
			SELECT DISTINCT(?x) WHERE {{
			?x a dbo:Person .
			?x ?y1 ?z .
			?z ?y2 dbr:New_York_City }
			UNION {
			?x a dbo:Person .
			?z ?y1 ?x .
			dbr:New_York_City ?y2 ?z }
			FILTER(NOT EXISTS
			{?x ?r dbr:New_York_City}
			AND NOT EXISTS
			{dbr:New_York_City ?s ?x})}

tc05	Analogous to tc04 (inverse case).		

tc06	SELECT DISTINCT(?x) WHERE {
	?x a dbo:Person .
	?x dbo:birthPlace
	dbr:New_York_City }
		SELECT DISTINCT(?x) WHERE {
		?x a dbo:Person .
		FILTER(NOT EXISTS{
		?x dbo:birthPlace
		dbr:New_York_City })}
			SELECT DISTINCT(?x) ?r WHERE {{
			?x a dbo:Person .
			?x dbo:birthPlace ?y .
			dbr:New_York_City ?r ?x .
			FILTER(?y!=dbr:New_York_City)}
			UNION {
			?x a dbo:Person .
			?x dbo:birthPlace ?y .
			?x ?r dbr:New_York_City .
			FILTER(?y!=dbr:New_York_City)}}

tc07	SELECT DISTINCT(?x) WHERE {
	?x a dbo:Person .
	?x dbo:team ?y .
	?y a dbo:BasketballTeam }
		SELECT DISTINCT(?x) WHERE {
		?x a dbo:Person .
		FILTER(NOT EXISTS{
		?x dbo:team ?y .
		?y a
		dbo:BasketballTeam})}
			SELECT DISTINCT(?x) WHERE {
			?x a dbo:Person .
			?x dbo:team ?z1 .
			?x ?r ?z2 .
			?z2 a dbo:BaseballTeam
			FILTER(NOT EXISTS{
			?x dbo:team ?y .
			?y a dbo:BasketballTeam })}

tc08	Analogous to tc07 (inverse case).		

tc09	SELECT DISTINCT(?x) WHERE {
	?x a dbo:Person .
	?x dbo:award ?y1.
	?x dbo:award ?y2.
	FILTER(?y1!=?y2)}
		SELECT DISTINCT(?x) WHERE {
		?x a dbo:Person .
		FILTER(NOT EXISTS{
		?x dbo:award ?y1.
		?x dbo:award ?y2.
		FILTER(?y1!=?y2)})}
			SELECT DISTINCT(?x) WHERE {
			?x a dbo:Person .
			?x dbo:award ?y .
			FILTER(NOT EXISTS{
			?x dbo:award ?z.
			FILTER(?y!=?z)})}

tc10	Analogous to tc09 (inverse case).		

tc11	SELECT DISTINCT(?x) WHERE {
	?x a dbo:Person .
	?x dbo:recordLabel ?y1 .
	?y1 a dbo:RecordLabel .
	?x dbo:recordLabel ?y2 .
	?y2 a dbo:RecordLabel .
	FILTER(?y1!=?y2)}
		SELECT DISTINCT(?x) WHERE {
		?x a dbo:Person .
		FILTER(NOT EXISTS{
		?x dbo:recordLabel ?y1 .
		?y1 a dbo:RecordLabel .
		?x dbo:recordLabel ?y2 .
		?y2 a dbo:RecordLabel .
		FILTER(?y1!=?y2)})}
			SELECT DISTINCT(?x) WHERE {
			?x a dbo:Person .
			?x dbo:recordLabel ?y1 .
			?y1 a dbo:RecordLabel .
			FILTER(NOT EXISTS{
			?x dbo:recordLabel ?y2 .
			?y2 a dbo:RecordLabel .
			FILTER(?y1!=?y2)})}

tc12	Analogous to tc11 (inverse case).		

However, the following aspects have to be considered: (1) DBpedia is a large KG; not every embedding approach can be used to learn an embedding for it (or not every researcher has the computational means to do so, respectively). (2) Depending on the DL constructor and the domain, not enough examples can be found on DBpedia. (3) It cannot be precluded that patterns correlate; therefore, the fact that an embedding approach can learn a particular class can only be an indicator that it *might* learn the underlying constructor pattern, but the results are not conclusive. Correlating properties, type biases for entities, etc., may lead to surprising results in some domains (see Section 3.3.3).

Therefore, we complement the DBpedia-based gold standard with a synthetic benchmark. The idea is to generate a graph that contains the DL constructors (positive and negative) of interest. The graph can be constructed to resemble the DBpedia graph statistically but can be significantly smaller (and contain a sufficient number of positives and negatives), and, by construction, side effects and correlations which exist in DBpedia can be mitigated to a large extent.

The configurable parameters are `numClasses`, `numProperties`, `numInstances`, `branchingFactor`, `maxTriplesPerNode`, and `numNodesInterest` (all parameters are integers). First, a class tree with `numClasses` classes is constructed in a way that each class has at most `branchingFactor` children. Then, `numproperties` properties are generated. Each property is assigned to a range and domain from the class tree, whereby the first property has the root node as domain and range type so that every node can be involved in at least one triple statement. A skew can be introduced so that domain and range refer with a higher probability to a more general class than to a specific one. Lastly, we generate instances and assign them to a class as their type.

Once the ontology is created, `numNodesInterest` positives and negatives are generated (adhering to domain/range restrictions). Each class constructor is first initialized explicitly for the positive examples. Then, for each entity *e* in the graph (i.e., positive and negative examples), $rand(n) \in [1, maxTriplesPerNode]$ random triples are generated, which have *e* as a subject and adhere to the domain and range definitions, whereby it is checked that no additional positives are created, and no negatives are turned into positives accidentally. Details on the algorithm can be found in [11].

For version `v1` of the gold standard, `numClasses = 760`, `numProperties = 1,355`, `numInstances = 10,000`, `branchingFactor = 5`, `maxTriplesPerNode = 11`, and `numNodesInterest = 1,000` were chosen. The parameters were chosen to form graphs which are smaller than DBpedia but resemble the DBpedia graph statistically. Therefore, the statistical properties of the DBpedia ontology calculated by Heist et al. [4] were used.

3.3. Comparison of KGEMs on DLCC

In this section, we present results using eleven different embedding models. Those encompass:

- RDF2vec CBOW [30]
- RDF2vec Skip-Gram [30]
- RDF2vec order-aware CBOW [31]
- RDF2vec order-aware Skip-Gram [31]
- TransE [16] with L1 norm
- TransE [16] with L2 norm
- TransR [32]
- ComplEx [33]
- DistMult [33]
- RESCAL [34]
- RotatE [35]

For the DBpedia benchmarks, we use version 2021-09. For the RDF2vec variants, we generated 500 walks per entity, with a depth of 4, a window size of 5, 5 epochs, and a dimension of 200. We used the same parameters for the synthetic gold standard with the exception of $dimension = 100$ and $walks = 100$ to account for the smaller gold standard size. The embeddings were trained using the jRDF2vec[12] framework [36]. The embedding files are publicly available[13] via KGvec2go [37] and can also be used for other downstream tasks. The remaining models were trained using the DGL-KE framework[14] [38], using the respective default parameters, with 200 dimensions for DBpedia and 100 for the synthetic datasets, as for RDF2vec. The models are publicly available and can also be used for other downstream tasks.[15]

As outlined in subsection 3.2.1, the DLCC benchmarks are balanced. That means that a performance significantly above 50% indicates that the model learns the constructor to some extent. It is important to highlight that tables 3 and 4 state the best results out of six classifiers (see subsection 3.2.2). In order to determine whether the stated result for an embedding configuration for a particular test case is significant, we performed an approximated one-sided binomial significance test with $\alpha = 0.05$. Since multiple classifiers were trained for each test case, we applied the conservative Bonferroni correction [39] of α to account for the multiple testing problem. The hypothesis underlying each significance test is that in the embedding space spanned by a given approach, positive and negative examples can be separated by a classifier. Therefore, we test whether the classification results yield an accuracy significantly greater than 0.5, since all classification problems are fully balanced. The null hypothesis is that the classes cannot be separated, i.e., the classification accuracy does not significantly exceed 0.5.

3.3.1. Results on the DLCC DBpedia Benchmark

The results on the DLCC DBpedia benchmark (class size 5,000) are reported in Table 3. For each model, six classifiers were trained resulting in more than 2,000 classification results. At first sight, it is quickly observable that all models can learn all tasks comparatively well; all results are statistically significant. It is, furthermore, visible that the hard test cases are indeed harder.

It can be seen that for most cases, the best results are obtained with RDF2vec SG_{oa} and TransE (L2). Moreover, we can observe that it seems easier to predict patterns involving outgoing edges than those involving ingoing edges (cf. tc02 vs. tc01, tc08 vs. tc07, tc10 vs. tc09, tc12 vs. tc11). Even though the tasks are very related, this can be explained by the learning process which often emphasizes outgoing directions: In RDF2vec, random walks are performed in forward direction; similarly, TransE is directed in its training process.

3.3.2. Results on the DLCC Synthetic Benchmark

The results on the synthetic benchmark (class size 1,000) are reported in Table 4. Again, for each model, six classifiers were trained whereby only the best performing classifiers' results are discussed. RDF2vec configurations are performing very well on this gold standard being the best performing embedding model in 10 out of 12 cases. In terms of the best RDF2vec configuration, the classic CBOW variant achieves the best results in five cases.

The best model from the link prediction family is RESCAL. RotatE produces insignificant results than significant results more often – the model outperforms pure guessing in only a third of the cases.

Table 3.: Results on the DLCC DBpedia Gold Standard (Accuracy). The best results are printed in bold. All results are significantly larger than the random baseline.

TC	RDF2vec SG	RDF2vec SG_{oa}	RDF2vec CBOW	RDF2vec $CBOW_{oa}$	TransE (L1)	TransE (L2)	TransR	DistMult	ComplEx	RESCAL	RotatE
tc01	0.915	0.937	0.778	0.870	0.842	0.947	0.858	0.874	0.862	**0.966**	0.768
tc01 hard	0.681	0.891	0.637	0.891	0.799	**0.916**	0.744	0.646	0.651	0.830	0.618
tc02	0.953	0.961	0.865	0.956	0.852	**0.970**	0.832	0.859	0.853	0.908	0.737
tc02 hard	0.637	0.780	0.618	0.774	0.780	**0.849**	0.693	0.622	0.608	0.729	0.649
tc03	0.949	**0.958**	0.846	0.905	0.821	0.933	0.856	0.894	0.874	0.943	0.780
tc04	0.960	0.968	0.705	0.872	0.934	0.986	0.973	0.984	**0.990**	0.990	0.862
tc04 hard	0.963	0.984	0.674	**0.992**	0.814	0.912	0.855	0.917	0.935	0.918	0.789
tc05	0.986	**0.992**	0.772	0.906	0.867	0.948	0.881	0.907	0.905	0.908	0.802
tc06	0.957	0.963	0.698	0.850	0.929	0.985	0.976	0.985	**0.991**	0.990	0.866
tc06 hard	0.863	0.936	0.604	0.908	0.823	0.779	**0.964**	0.882	0.933	0.964	0.819
tc07	0.938	0.955	0.742	0.785	0.930	**0.987**	0.978	0.929	0.966	0.945	0.847
tc08	0.961	**0.966**	0.891	0.896	0.898	0.964	0.870	0.856	0.888	0.875	0.831
tc09	0.902	0.901	0.773	0.858	0.884	**0.938**	0.879	0.877	0.883	0.929	0.780
tc09 hard	0.785	0.793	0.659	0.751	0.749	**0.848**	0.758	0.774	0.776	0.820	0.676
tc10	0.947	0.958	0.918	0.905	0.957	**0.984**	0.898	0.918	0.931	0.927	0.878
tc10 hard	0.740	0.737	0.716	0.711	**0.775**	0.774	0.656	0.743	0.739	0.713	0.665
tc11	0.932	0.897	0.865	0.780	0.917	0.960	0.930	0.889	0.946	0.954	0.838
tc11 hard	0.725	0.737	0.687	0.676	0.712	**0.806**	0.753	0.666	0.723	0.726	0.638
tc12	0.955	0.938	0.888	0.909	0.961	**0.984**	0.879	0.912	0.894	0.927	0.834
tc12 hard	0.714	0.717	0.712	0.699	0.762	**0.765**	0.659	0.714	0.710	0.701	0.652

The overall most complicating test case is tc07. Similarly, more than half of the models are not significantly able to learn tc08. This is remarkable since the constructors can be almost perfectly predicted on the corresponding DBpedia gold standards. Hence, we can reason that handling qualified restrictions is a very intricate task. The second hardest group of tasks is those involving cardinalities (tc10-tc12).

3.3.3. Comparison of the Two Benchmarks

The comparison of the DBpedia and the synthetic benchmark is particularly intriguing. We can see that the synthetic benchmark is much harder to solve since the results are drastically lower in most cases. While there are no insignificant results on the DBpedia gold standard, there are many for the synthetic one – particularly when it comes to the benchmark models. Many class constructors that are easily learnable on the DBpedia gold standard are hard on the synthetic one. Moreover, the previously reported superiority of RDF2vec$_{oa}$ over standard RDF2vec [40,31] cannot be observed on the synthetic data.

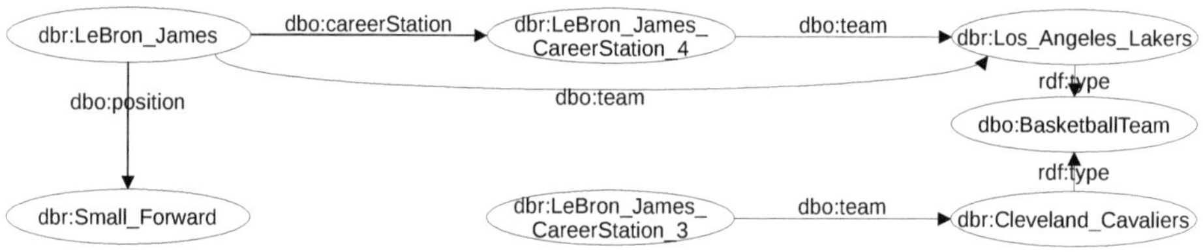

Figure 3. Excerpt of DBpedia [41]

Figure 3 shows an excerpt of DBpedia, which we will use to illustrate these deviations. The instance `dbr:LeBron_James` is a positive example for task tc07 (i.e., ∃`team.BasketballTeam`) for the Person case in the DBpedia benchmark. At the same time, 95.6% of all entities in DBpedia fulfilling the positive query for positive examples also fall in the class ∃`dbo:position`.⊤ (which is a tc01 problem), but only 13.6% of all entities fulfilling the query for trivial negatives. Hence, on a balanced dataset, this class can be learned with an accuracy of 0.91 by any approach than can learn classes of type tc01. As a comparison to the synthetic dataset shows, the results on the DBpedia test set for tc07 actually overestimate the capability of many embedding approaches to learn classes constructed with a tc07 class constructor. Such correlations are quite frequent in DBpedia but vastly absent in the synthetic dataset.

The example can also explain the advantage of RDF2vec$_{oa}$ on DBpedia. Unlike standard RDF2vec, this approach would distinguish the appearance of `dbo:team` as a direct edge of `dbr:LeBron_James` as well as an indirect edge connected to `dbr:LeBron_James_CareerStation_`*`N`*, where the former denotes the current team, whereas the latter also denote all previous teams. Those subtle semantic differences of different usages of the same property in different contexts also do not exist in the synthetic gold standard. Hence, the order-aware variant of RDF2vec does not have an advantage here. In the cases where a DLCC can be learned on the DBpedia dataset, but not on the synthetic dataset, we have to assume that the downstream learning algorithm cannot learn the DLCC per se, but some other pattern which appears in correlation with the DLCC at hand, since such correlations exist in the DBpedia dataset, but not in the synthetic dataset. The comparison between DBpedia and synthetic test cases reveals that most models are not *actually* learning the description logic constructor but instead are picking up cross-correlations very well.

Table 4.: Results on the Synthetic Gold Standard (Accuracy). The best result for each test case is printed in bold, statistically insignificant scores (w.r.t. a random baseline) are stated in italics. Listed are the results of the best classifier for each task and model.

TC	RDF2vec SG	RDF2vec SG_{oa}	RDF2vec CBOW	RDF2vec $CBOW_{oa}$	TransE (L1)	TransE (L2)	TransR	DistMult	ComplEx	RESCAL	RotatE
tc01	0.882	0.867	0.566	0.877	0.767	0.752	0.712	0.837	0.789	**0.895**	0.769
tc02	0.742	0.737	**0.769**	0.732	0.677	0.677	*0.531*	0.584	*0.549*	0.689	*0.546*
tc03	0.797	0.812	**0.927**	0.774	*0.531*	0.581	*0.554*	*0.556*	*0.536*	0.634	*0.541*
tc04	**1.000**	0.998	0.990	0.998	0.790	0.898	0.685	0.588	*0.553*	*0.528*	0.728
tc05	**0.892**	0.819	0.889	0.819	0.691	0.774	0.631	0.658	0.726	0.608	0.646
tc06	0.978	0.963	0.898	0.965	0.898	0.978	0.888	**1.000**	**1.000**	**1.000**	0.955
tc07	0.583	0.583	0.575	*0.555*	*0.540*	0.615	**0.673**	0.565	*0.518*	*0.550*	*0.508*
tc08	0.563	0.585	*0.555*	0.583	0.585	**0.613**	*0.540*	*0.535*	*0.523*	*0.533*	*0.535*
tc09	0.610	0.628	**0.648**	0.605	0.588	*0.543*	*0.525*	*0.525*	*0.545*	0.638	*0.538*
tc10	0.638	0.623	**0.665**	0.600	0.588	0.573	*0.518*	*0.525*	*0.510*	0.580	*0.533*
tc11	0.633	0.580	**0.668**	0.575	0.583	0.590	0.573	*0.518*	0.590	0.625	*0.538*
tc12	0.644	0.614	**0.657**	0.638	0.618	*0.550*	*0.513*	*0.553*	*0.540*	0.578	*0.533*

4. The KGE Entity Similarity Assumption

In this section, we detail our proposal for quantifying the KGE entity similarity assumption. While similarity in embedding spaces is usually measured using cosine similarity, there is no uniform definition of entity similarity in KGs. We first elaborate on the metrics used to capture the notion of similarity between entities in the KG, and discuss how the aforementioned notions of similarity can be compared. Afterwards, we present an extensive experimental evaluation analyzing the relation between the two notions of similarity.

4.1. Towards a Graph-based Notion of Similarity

There is no universally accepted definition of entity similarity in KGs. Multiple metrics and approaches can be used, and the choice between one or another largely depends on the particular aspect to be measured, but also on the complexity of computation. In what follows, we intend to explain the rationale behind our modeling choices, and briefly mention alternatives that we ultimately discarded.

To measure the similarity between two entities e_1 and e_2 in one KG, we (1) determine the set of common statements about e_1 and e_2, *i.e.*, relations to other entities that e_1 and e_2 have in common. While many entities will have such relations in common with central entities (*i.e.*, those with many ingoing and outgoing edges), we also (2) need to make sure that centrality does not skew our similarity measure. Finally, (3) since an entity cannot be fully described by its immediate neighbors, indirect dependencies also need to be captured.

To satisfy our first desideratum (1), we compare the subgraphs around e_1 and e_2. We experiment with the 1-hop only vs. 2-hop subgraph neighborhood. The latter option addresses desideratum (3), as we also consider indirect dependencies. In Figure 4, we give a concrete example of the 1-hop and 2-hop subgraphs for entities `Bob` (e_1) and `Julie` (e_2).[16] The similarity of e_1 and e_2 can now be measured by the similarity of their respective subgraphs. Graph Edit Distance (GED) [42] has been used for this intent. However, GED is NP-hard and thus computationally demanding, it comes with the need for arbitrarily defining weights for vertex and edge insertion/deletion/substitution, and we experimentally found it was sensitive to subgraphs' sizes, which is dentrimental to desideratum (2). The common neighbors metric (either absolute or as a Jaccard formulation [43]) does not consider predicates and is only suited for unlabeled graphs.[17]

In our experiments, we use the Jaccard coefficient to measure the overlap in the 1-hop and 2-hop subgraphs of entities. In particular, its value denotes how similar the respective subgraphs of two entities are, which gives us insight into how much two entities are related based on graph-based information. The central entity (e_1 or e_2) is replaced by a unique token, *e.g.* `:dummy`. Triples forming the 1-hop neighborhood are extracted as is, while for the 2-hop paths the intermediate entity is ignored (written as $\square$ below).

More formally: let $\mathcal{T}_1(A)$ be the set of all triples $\{(A,p,o) \cup (s,p,A)\}$, where A is replaced by a dummy identifier. Then, $J_1(e_1,e_2)$ is the Jaccard overlap of $\mathcal{T}_1(e_1)$ and $\mathcal{T}_1(e_2)$, *i.e.*, $\frac{|\mathcal{T}_1(e_1) \cap \mathcal{T}_1(e_2)|}{|\mathcal{T}_1(e_1) \cup \mathcal{T}_1(e_2)|}$.

Let $\mathcal{T}_2(A)$ be the set of all paths $\{(A,p1,\square,p2,o) \cup (s,p1,\square,p2,A)\}$, where A is replaced by a dummy identifier. Then $J_2(e_1,e_2)$ is the Jaccard overlap of $\mathcal{T}_2(e_1)$ and $\mathcal{T}_2(e_2)$, *i.e.*, $\frac{|\mathcal{T}_2(e_1) \cap \mathcal{T}_2(e_2)|}{|\mathcal{T}_2(e_1) \cup \mathcal{T}_2(e_2)|}$.

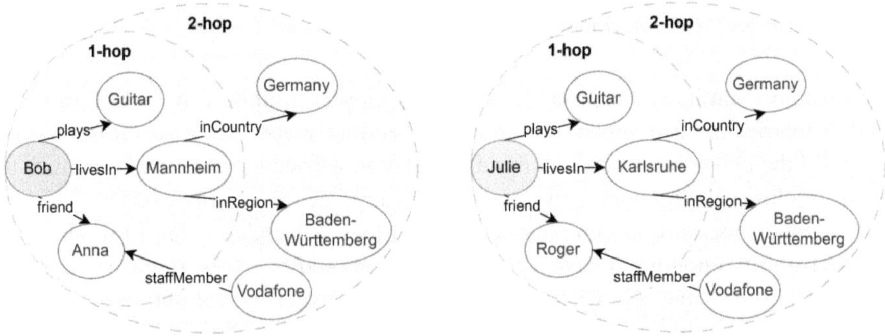

Figure 4. 1-hop and 2-hop subgraphs for `Bob` and `Julie`.

Following Figure 4, triples in the two 1-hop subgraphs are:

Bob	Julie
`(:dummy, plays, Guitar)`	`(:dummy, plays, Guitar)`
`(:dummy, livesIn, Mannheim)`	`(:dummy, livesIn, Karlsruhe)`
`(:dummy, friend, Anna)`	`(:dummy, friend, Roger)`

When considering 2-hop information, we also consider the following paths which are shared between Bob's and Julie's subgraphs (reverse edges included):

`(:dummy, livesIn, □, inCountry, Germany)`

`(:dummy, livesIn, □, inRegion, Baden-Württemberg)`

`(:dummy, friend, □,` $\texttt{staffMember}^{-1}$`, Vodafone)`

When considering the 1-hop subgraphs only, the similarity of `Bob` and `Julie` is $J_1(Bob, Julie) = 0.2$ (since they share one out of five triples). Considering the 2-hop neighborhood graphs, we obtain $J_2(Bob, Julie) = 0.5$ (since they share three out of six two-hop paths). For instance, we consider `(:dummy, livesIn, □, inCountry, Germany)` as the full path. This allows for capturing indirect dependencies, such as *both Julie and Bob live in a city in Germany*, or *both Julie and Bob know someone who works for Vodafone*. This approach better fits the general and commonsense idea that two entities should already be similar if they share relations to entities which are similar themselves according to their respecitve 1-hop subgraphs. Moreover, keeping the intermediate entity in the path would overweigh information already counted as part of the 1-hop subgraph, especially if the intermediate entity were a high degree entity (desideratum (3)). For any entity in the 1-hop neighborhood of a central entity, its own 1-hop neighborhood is known and fixed. Consequently, whenever there is a match between triples in the 1-hop neighborhood of two central entities being compared, there would be as many matches in their respective 2-hop subgraphs as there are relations connecting their shared 1-hop neighbors. For example, if `Bob` and `Julie` were living in the same city, *e.g.* Mannheim, this information would be counted multiple times – in `(:dummy, livesIn, Mannheim, inCountry, Germany)`, `(:dummy, livesIn, Mannheim, inRegion, Baden-Württemberg)`, etc.. The resulting relatedness between `Bob` and `Julie` would thus be overly influenced by that single fact. Similarly, if they were living in distinct cities – which is the case in our example – their relatedness score would be unduly penalized.

4.2. Embedding vs. Graph: a Different Notion of Similarity?

Based on a given entity e, it is possible to get its N closest neighbors in the KG (using the J_1 and J_2 metrics defined above) and in the embedding space (using cosine similarity). To assess if the two notions of similarity are different, we need to measure how much the two lists of closests neighbors between these two approaches actually overlap.

A common measure to compare two ranked lists is Kendall's Tau [44]. However, it suffers from two important caveats: the two lists should be of the same size and they should contain the same set of items. Considering our experimental purposes, the latter limitation is undesirable, as there is no reason why these two lists (of the top N similar entities according to J_1 or J_2, and in the embedding space) should share the same set of entities.

Consequently, we use the Rank-Biased Overlap (RBO) [45] to compare the similarity of two ranked lists. Unlike Kendall's Tau which is correlation-based, RBO is intersection-based. Most importantly, RBO can handle lists containing different items. It also allows for the weighting of rankings, giving higher importance to items at the top of the lists through tweaking the *persistence* parameter p. A small value for p will only consider the first few items, whereas a larger value will encompass more items. In a preliminary study, we found that results are very sensitive to the choice of p. Besides, when comparing two ranked lists, we want to consider all of their items. Consequently, we stick to the default parameter strategy $p = 1$ as proposed in an open-source implementation of RBO[18] that we used in our experiments. Formally, RBO is expressed as follows.

Let S and T be two ranking lists, and let S_i (resp. T_i) be the element at rank i in list S (resp. T). Then, $S_{c:d}$ (resp. $T_{c:d}$) denotes the set of the elements from position c to position d in list S (resp. T). At each depth d, the intersection of lists S and T to depth d is defined as $I_{S,T,d} = S_{1:d} \cap T_{1:d}$, and their overlap up to depth d is the size of the intersection, *i.e.* $|I_{S,T,d}|$. RBO relies on the notion of *agreement* between S and T to depth d:

$$A_{S,T,d} = \frac{|I_{S,T,d}|}{d} \tag{13}$$

In the case whre the persistence parameter $p = 1$, the RBO formula is expressed as follows:

$$RBO(S,T,k) = \frac{1}{k} \sum_{d=1}^{k} A_{S,T,d} \tag{14}$$

where k is the size of the two lists S and T being compared. For the case where $p \neq 1$, we refer the reader to [45].

In Figure 5, we illustrate how RBO@5 is calculated for two lists of top-5 neighbors, where one relies on similarity in the embedding space whereas the other one depends on the Jaccard overlap between entities' subgraphs. We see that (i) RBO can be calculated on lists with different sets of entities, (ii) RBO weighs more matches that occur at the top of the lists, and (iii) RBO is sensitive to the order of matching entities in the respective lists.

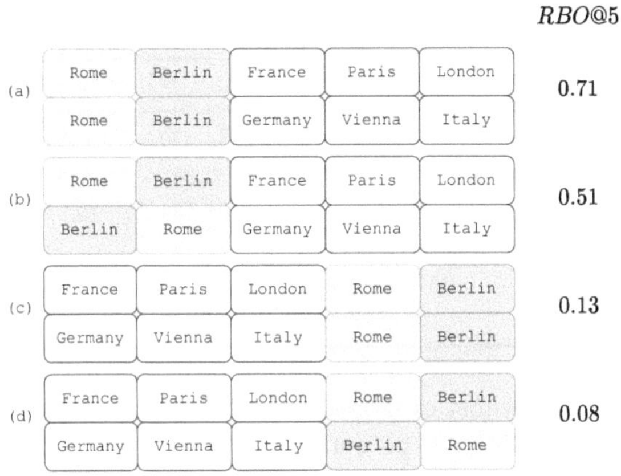

Figure 5. Illustration of RBO@5 values in four cases.

4.3. Experiments

In this section, we detail our experimental setting, *i.e.* the KGEMs (Section 4.3.1) and datasets (Section 4.3.2) used in the experiments.

4.3.1. Knowledge Graph Embedding Models

In our experiments, we use seven popular KGEMs from different families of models: geometric-based (TransE [46], TransD [47], BoxE [48]), multiplicative (RESCAL [49], DistMult [50], TuckER [51]), and convolutional-based (ConvE [52]) models. Other models have been considered, *e.g.* ComplEx [53] and RotatE [54]. However, these models generate complex-valued embeddings, which requires a different approach than using simple cosine similarity. We trained these KGEMs using PyKEEN [55] with the provided configuration files, when available. For those datasets with no reported best hyperparameters, we used the hyperparameters reported in the original paper (*e.g.* for YAGO4-19k, with best hyperparameters found in [56]) or performed manual hyperparameter search and kept the sets of hyperparameters leading to the best results on the validation sets (*e.g.* for AIFB). We also trained RDF2vec [30,57], which is a versatile embedding approach that can be adapted for different downstream applications and that relies on path-based information to encode entities (only). Even though RDF2vec is not specifically designed to handle the link prediction task and is not evaluated w.r.t. it, its entity embeddings are expected to reflect their similarity or relatedness in the KG to some extent [27]. We used the implementation provided by pyRDF2vec [58] with the default hyperparameters reported in [27]: embeddings of dimension 200, with 2,000 walks maximum, a depth of 4, a window size of 5, and 25 epochs for training word2vec [59] with the continuous skip-gram architecture.

4.3.2. Datasets

Since we also want to analyze results on a per-class basis, we consider only benchmark datasets which also come with a schema of multiple classes and relations. We use the following datasets in our evaluation: AIFB [60], Codex-S and Codex-M [61], DBpedia50 [62], FB15K-237 [63], and YAGO4-19k [56]. Entity types are not directly

Table 5. Datasets used in the experiments. Column header from left to right: number of entities, relations (predicates), classes, train triples, validation triples, and test triples.

Dataset	$\|\mathcal{E}\|$	$\|\mathcal{R}\|$	$\|\mathcal{C}\|$	$\|\mathcal{T}_{train}\|$	$\|\mathcal{T}_{valid}\|$	$\|\mathcal{T}_{test}\|$
AIFB	2,389	16	18	14,170	745	785
Codex-S	2,034	42	502	32,888	1,827	1,827
Codex-M	17,050	51	1,503	185,584	10,310	10,311
DBpedia50	24,624	351	285	32,388	123	2,098
FB15k237	14,541	237	643	272,115	17,535	20,466
YAGO4-19k	18,960	74	1,232	27,447	485	463

available in the original repository of DBpedia50[19] and FB15k-237[20]. However, we ran SPARQL queries against DBpedia to get entity types for DBpedia50. The resulting class hierarchy is a subset of the DBpedia ontology, with a maximum depth of 8, an average fan-out (branching factor) of 3.40, and each entity being typed with an average of 4.55 classes. For FB15K-237, we reused the entity-typed version presented in [56]. Table 5 provides finer-grained statistics for these datasets.

4.4. Results and Discussion

4.4.1. Different Notions of Similarity

Table 6 reports results w.r.t. rank-based metrics (MRR, Hits@K) and RBO@K for all the KGEMs and datasets considered in this work. Similar to MRR and Hits@K, RBO is computed for all entities in a KG and the average is reported.

When retaining 1-hop subgraphs (from R1@3 to R1@100 in Table 6), in most cases TuckER has the highest RBO values. In other words, it appears to fulfill the KGE entity similarity assumption best, having the highest tendency to position similar entities closer in the vector space. When moving to 2-hop subgraphs, DistMult and TuckER are the models with the best alignment capabilities (Table 6). BoxE, RDF2Vec, RESCAL, and TransD fare worse than other models. The substantially lower RBO values for RDF2Vec can be related to the fact that the vector distance in RDF2vec space (at least for the variant considered in this experiment) mixes similarity and relatedness, where the latter does not show a strong overlap in common paths [27]. For example, it will position *USA* close to *Washington D.C.*, but they have only few common paths starting/ending in the respective entities.

A crucial observation from our study is that the behavior of KGEMs varies not only across datasets but also across different classes within these datasets. Table 7 illustrates this insight on classes that were selected to provide a more intuitive understanding of how different KGEMs are differently able to capture similarities between instances of the same class. In particular, we clearly see that on YAGO4-19k, TransE captures the notion of `SpanishMunicipality` quite well compared to other models, but does not do well for `MusicPlaylist` entities (highlighted in blue). This means that different models are better suited for capturing the nuances of specific classes. Jain *et al.* [13] demonstrated that semantic representation in embeddings is not consistent across all KG entities, but is restricted to a small subset of them. Our results point in the same direction and suggest that KGEMs are not equipped with consistent capabilities to learn similar embeddings for entities within the same class. This problem appears at two different levels: First,

Table 6. Rank-based and RBO results. As RDF2Vec is not designed for link prediction, it is not evaluated w.r.t. rank-based metrics. H@3 and H@10 stand for Hits@3 and Hits@10, respectively. RBO is abbreviated as R, while the number directly following it denotes whether 1-hop subgraphs or 2-hop subgraphs are considered. Bold fonts indicate which KGEM performs best for a given configuration (dataset-metric). Underlined results denote the second-best performing model.

	FB15K-237									YAGO4-19k								
	MRR	H@3	H@10	R1@3	R1@10	R1@100	R2@3	R2@10	R2@100	MRR	H@3	H@10	R1@3	R1@10	R1@100	R2@3	R2@10	R2@100
RDF2Vec	–	–	–	0.023	0.033	0.063	0.014	0.021	0.054	–	–	–	0.126	0.154	0.177	0.164	0.170	0.183
TransE	0.240	0.264	0.404	0.132	0.178	0.228	0.035	0.050	0.108	0.762	0.836	0.895	0.247	0.301	0.360	0.368	0.362	**0.260**
TransD	0.184	0.205	0.378	0.176	0.220	0.259	0.065	0.083	0.135	0.763	0.895	0.915	0.197	0.252	0.365	0.181	0.237	0.137
DistMult	0.226	0.247	0.392	0.194	0.245	0.343	**0.103**	**0.131**	**0.222**	0.809	0.838	0.870	0.310	0.350	0.407	0.378	**0.372**	0.225
RESCAL	0.279	0.305	0.447	0.239	0.269	0.284	0.064	0.081	0.138	0.676	0.692	0.754	0.176	0.215	0.176	0.298	0.271	0.103
TuckER	**0.341**	**0.373**	**0.516**	0.321	0.364	**0.411**	0.099	0.121	0.205	0.897	0.901	0.910	**0.362**	**0.461**	**0.498**	**0.385**	0.362	0.228
ConvE	0.300	0.327	0.474	**0.341**	**0.370**	0.357	0.083	0.102	0.153	**0.905**	**0.907**	**0.916**	0.328	0.368	0.365	0.336	0.313	0.168
BoxE	0.299	0.326	0.477	0.221	0.261	0.313	0.060	0.081	0.166	0.895	0.902	0.914	0.136	0.146	0.113	0.244	0.231	0.096

	Codex-S									Codex-M								
	MRR	H@3	H@10	R1@3	R1@10	R1@100	R2@3	R2@10	R2@100	MRR	H@3	H@10	R1@3	R1@10	R1@100	R2@3	R2@10	R2@100
RDF2Vec	–	–	–	0.030	0.043	0.096	0.021	0.036	0.099	–	–	–	0.013	0.019	0.042	0.011	0.017	0.041
TransE	0.293	0.331	0.526	0.201	0.266	0.451	0.154	**0.210**	**0.345**	0.227	0.260	0.371	0.082	0.101	0.153	0.058	0.076	0.105
TransD	0.226	0.294	0.515	0.252	0.322	0.462	0.136	0.178	0.297	0.215	0.281	0.420	0.155	0.188	0.263	0.055	0.070	0.117
DistMult	0.261	0.298	0.409	0.452	**0.511**	**0.616**	**0.163**	0.205	0.339	0.209	0.233	0.356	0.173	0.212	0.312	**0.144**	**0.178**	**0.256**
RESCAL	0.283	0.307	0.475	0.135	0.193	0.336	0.132	0.176	0.274	0.149	0.159	0.253	0.067	0.084	0.115	0.025	0.036	0.057
TuckER	0.393	0.442	0.618	**0.461**	**0.511**	0.615	0.154	0.209	0.339	0.282	0.310	0.424	0.198	0.239	0.328	0.120	0.153	0.222
ConvE	**0.414**	**0.466**	0.611	0.450	0.495	0.574	0.146	0.195	0.306	**0.290**	**0.319**	0.425	**0.315**	**0.343**	**0.384**	0.098	0.119	0.158
BoxE	0.398	0.453	**0.622**	0.312	0.366	0.486	0.118	0.179	0.291	0.290	0.318	**0.431**	0.241	0.272	0.334	0.084	0.106	0.152

	AIFB									DBpedia50								
	MRR	H@3	H@10	R1@3	R1@10	R1@100	R2@3	R2@10	R2@100	MRR	H@3	H@10	R1@3	R1@10	R1@100	R2@3	R2@10	R2@100
RDF2Vec	–	–	–	0.089	0.131	0.223	0.137	0.174	0.210	–	–	–	0.04	0.053	0.179	0.059	0.082	0.189
TransE	0.469	0.524	0.699	0.413	0.456	0.571	0.304	0.349	0.455	0.397	**0.490**	**0.567**	0.109	0.123	0.297	0.214	0.246	0.282
TransD	0.472	0.689	0.817	0.472	0.507	0.617	0.305	0.330	0.382	0.260	0.376	0.442	0.111	0.136	0.318	0.126	0.187	0.244
DistMult	0.500	0.568	0.763	0.423	0.463	0.588	0.358	**0.406**	**0.495**	0.384	0.423	0.478	0.131	0.144	0.348	**0.241**	**0.275**	0.299
RESCAL	0.440	0.486	0.628	0.345	0.387	0.454	0.245	0.273	0.322	0.225	0.240	0.295	0.063	0.079	0.276	0.142	0.171	0.197
TuckER	0.797	0.824	0.888	**0.693**	**0.712**	**0.726**	**0.375**	0.380	0.394	0.424	0.442	0.502	**0.151**	**0.166**	**0.418**	0.235	0.271	**0.305**
ConvE	0.779	0.799	0.870	0.454	0.505	0.567	0.263	0.292	0.321	0.434	0.456	0.536	0.137	0.146	0.324	0.201	0.228	0.253
BoxE	**0.806**	**0.841**	**0.904**	0.570	0.587	0.614	0.343	0.374	0.437	**0.456**	0.480	0.556	0.137	0.147	0.351	0.214	0.247	0.278

we noted a general misalignment in the representation of certain classes across various datasets, regardless of the KGEM used. Second, there is noticeable inconsistency within specific classes, where entities might align well with their graph-based proximity in one KGEM but not in another.

To generalize this observation, we computed correlation matrices for RBO values across models and datasets, focusing on class-specific performance. Our analysis, averaging these matrices, gives us a broader view of how different KGEMs perceive similarity on a per-class basis. Figure 7 shows the rank correlations between models when considering 2-hop subgraphs, averaged over all datasets and RBO values. Notably, RDF2Vec stands out as it seems to capture a distinct notion of similarity compared to other KGEMs (cf. [27]). It demonstrates that RDF2Vec fares better on different classes than other KGEMs. We also observe a high degree of variation between models of the same family: TransE and TransD expose a different notion of similarity (0.64), as RESCAL and

Table 7. RBO@10 values per model for selected classes. Numbers in parenthesis indicate the rank of a class for a given model.

Dataset	Class	RDF2Vec	TransE	TransD	BoxE	RESCAL	DistMult	Tucker	ConvE
AIFB	`Book`	0.383 (1)	0.560 (1)	0.314 (7)	0.551 (1)	0.613 (1)	0.621 (1)	0.374 (5)	0.214 (13)
	`inProceedings`	0.048 (13)	0.419 (3)	0.227 (11)	0.461 (3)	0.412 (2)	0.453 (3)	0.332 (11)	0.326 (3)
Codex-S	`Republic`	0.000 (26)	0.556 (3)	0.236 (12)	0.463 (5)	0.363 (3)	0.339 (10)	0.399 (9)	0.311 (12)
	`NationalAcademy`	0.000 (27)	0.558 (2)	0.217 (14)	0.446 (8)	0.383 (2)	0.323 (11)	0.366 (12)	0.301 (14)
Codex-M	`UrbanDistrict`	0.002 (66)	0.538 (9)	0.178 (40)	0.482 (11)	0.057 (66)	0.494 (14)	0.504 (8)	0.327 (12)
	`CollegeTown`	0.000 (88)	0.615 (2)	0.205 (30)	0.653 (2)	0.133 (30)	0.670 (1)	0.640 (2)	0.337 (27)
DBpedia50	`Album`	0.134 (52)	0.336 (33)	0.270 (23)	0.351 (30)	0.300 (9)	0.310 (42)	0.387 (27)	0.315 (29)
	`EthnicGroup`	0.028 (136)	0.469 (9)	0.227 (36)	0.452 (9)	0.400 (1)	0.458 (9)	0.434 (16)	0.388 (12)
FB15k237	`Periodicals`	0.002 (414)	0.115 (109)	0.255 (64)	0.150 (163)	0.124 (181)	0.139 (280)	0.590 (11)	0.638 (3)
	`BaseballPlayer`	0.001 (420)	0.146 (78)	0.336 (31)	0.236 (93)	0.143 (160)	0.277 (104)	0.631 (4)	0.598 (12)
YAGO-19k	`MusicPlaylist`	0.233 (35)	**0.325 (94)**	0.322 (37)	0.411 (10)	0.350 (41)	0.366 (83)	0.627 (4)	0.554 (7)
	`SpanishMunicipality`	0.226 (40)	**0.636 (1)**	0.460 (4)	0.327 (33)	0.236 (95)	0.531 (20)	0.551 (20)	0.505 (17)

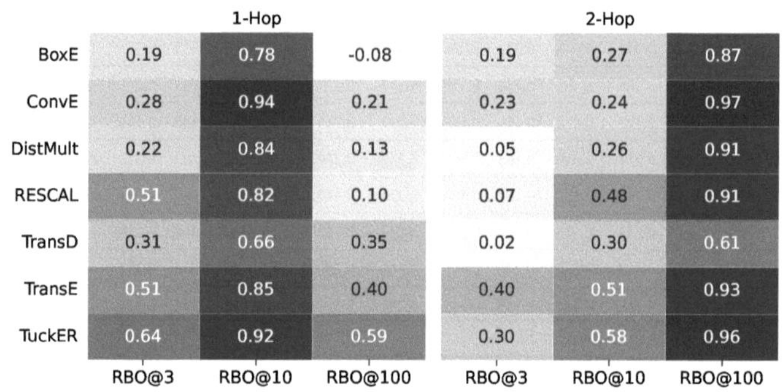

Figure 6. Correlations between MRR and RBO values with 1-hop and 2-hop subgraphs.

TuckER do (0.6). Strong rank correlations are observed between DistMult and BoxE (0.85), DistMult and TransE (0.84), and BoxE and TransE (0.84) (Figure 7). This demonstrates that while some KGEMs exhibit a close conceptualization of entity similarity, this is not universally the case. Therefore, we can conclude that proximity in the embedding space does *not* consistently align with the notion of entity similarity in the KG, since this property substantially differs between models and datasets. Consequently, careful consideration is necessary when using KGEs for drawing conclusions about similar entities (*e.g.* for recommending items to similar users).

4.4.2. Correlation between Rank-based Metrics and RBO

As previously mentioned, some KGEMs fare better than others in terms of RBO values, *e.g.* DistMult and TuckER. It is important to note that RBO values are designed to measure how well a KGEM entity embedding aligns with the concept of proximity within the original KG. This goal is distinct from the aim of rank-based metrics, which assess how effectively a KGEM assigns higher plausibility scores to ground-truth triples. In what follows, we aim study the relationship between these two types of metrics: how does KGEM performance in rank-based metrics correlate with RBO values?

We analyzed this using Pearson's correlation coefficient, comparing MRR and RBO values for 1-hop and 2-hop subgraphs across our 6 datasets, as depicted in Figure 6. The

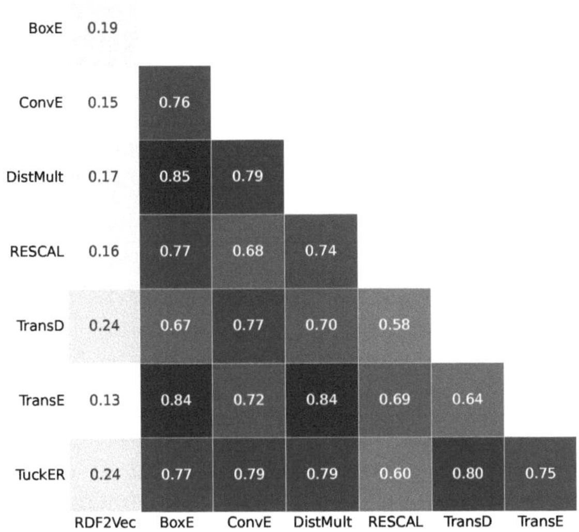

Figure 7. Rank correlations between KGEMs averaged over all datasets and all RBO metrics ($K = 3, 10, 100$).

results revealed notable disparities among the models. For instance, TransE and TuckER consistently show moderate to high correlation between MRR and RBO values. This implies that for these models, higher plausibility scoring of triples often aligns with better representation of entity proximity in the KG. However, this trend is not uniform across all models, and we do not observe general trends across families of models: while TransE and TransD are both translational models, correlation results are quite different.

From a coarse-grained viewpoint, we note that MRR *generally* does not correlate well with RBO values. Two specific cases are that MRR is heavily (and positively) correlated with RBO@10 (1-hop) and RBO@100 (2-hop), which means that MRR can be seen as a reliable proxy measure for those two metrics (and vice versa). However, it still remains to be explained why the correlation between MRR and RBO@10 (1-hop) is so high, while a substantial drop in correlation between MRR and RBO@100 (1-hop) is observed. Another result to be assessed is why MRR correlates more with RBO@K with lower K values when considering 1-hop subgraph and higher K values when considering 2-hop subgraphs.

The findings are mixed. While in the general case, the correlation between performance in grouping similar entities and link prediction performance is moderate at best, some metrics show a higher correlation. This has a severe practical implication: the commonly observed practice to pick a KGE model which is good at link prediction for a task heavily relying on entity similarity has to be considered a suboptimal strategy.

4.4.3. Analyzing Predicate Importance

We previously highlighted that different KGEMs are equipped with different notions of similarity in their respective embedding spaces. We also demonstrated that the adherence to the KGE entity similarity assumption can vary a lot between classes: for a given

Table 8. Top 5 predicates for entities of classes `MusicComposition` and `MusicGroup` on YAGO4-19k, along with their importance score.

	MusicComposition		MusicGroup	
	K=3	K=10	K=3	K=10
RDF2Vec	isPartOf (0.52)	isPartOf (0.46)	**genre (0.53)**	**genre (0.60)**
	inLanguage (0.18)	inLanguage (0.30)	**foundingLocation (0.38)**	**foundingLocation (0.32)**
	hasPart (0.17)	hasPart (0.15)	**award (0.10)**	**award (0.07)**
	composer (0.09)	composer (0.07)	memberOf (0.00)	memberOf (0.01)
	lyricist (0.02)	lyricist (0.02)	byArtist (0.00)	byArtist (0.00)
TransE	isPartOf (0.40)	isPartOf (0.36)	genre (0.79)	genre (0.85)
	hasPart (0.28)	hasPart (0.27)	foundingLocation (0.17)	foundingLocation (0.12)
	inLanguage (0.16)	inLanguage (0.26)	award (0.04)	award (0.02)
	composer (0.09)	composer (0.06)	memberOf (0.00)	memberOf (0.00)
	citation (0.05)	citation (0.04)	byArtist (0.00)	knowsLanguage (0.00)
TransD	isPartOf (0.40)	inLanguage (0.37)	genre (0.84)	genre (0.87)
	inLanguage (0.24)	isPartOf (0.31)	foundingLocation (0.13)	foundingLocation (0.11)
	hasPart (0.23)	hasPart (0.23)	award (0.03)	award (0.02)
	composer (0.08)	composer (0.06)	memberOf (0.00)	memberOf (0.00)
	citation (0.03)	citation (0.03)	byArtist (0.00)	knowsLanguage (0.00)
RESCAL	isPartOf (0.42)	inLanguage (0.33)	genre (0.74)	genre (0.81)
	inLanguage (0.23)	isPartOf (0.33)	foundingLocation (0.22)	foundingLocation (0.16)
	hasPart (0.21)	hasPart (0.25)	award (0.03)	award (0.02)
	composer (0.09)	composer (0.06)	memberOf (0.01)	memberOf (0.00)
	citation (0.04)	citation (0.02)	knowsLanguage (0.00)	knowsLanguage (0.00)
DistMult	isPartOf (0.38)	inLanguage (0.39)	genre (0.81)	genre (0.86)
	hasPart (0.26)	isPartOf (0.29)	foundingLocation (0.14)	foundingLocation (0.11)
	inLanguage (0.22)	hasPart (0.22)	award (0.04)	award (0.02)
	composer (0.08)	composer (0.05)	memberOf (0.00)	memberOf (0.00)
	citation (0.05)	citation (0.03)	knowsLanguage (0.00)	knowsLanguage (0.00)
TuckER	isPartOf (0.38)	inLanguage (0.37)	genre (0.85)	genre (0.90)
	hasPart (0.25)	isPartOf (0.30)	foundingLocation (0.11)	foundingLocation (0.08)
	inLanguage (0.24)	hasPart (0.23)	award (0.04)	award (0.02)
	composer (0.08)	composer (0.05)	memberOf (0.01)	memberOf (0.00)
	citation (0.04)	citation (0.03)	byArtist (0.00)	byArtist (0.00)
BoxE	isPartOf (0.48)	isPartOf (0.40)	genre (0.73)	genre (0.83)
	hasPart (0.29)	hasPart (0.30)	foundingLocation (0.23)	foundingLocation (0.15)
	inLanguage (0.11)	**inLanguage (0.19)**	award (0.04)	award (0.02)
	composer (0.10)	composer (0.07)	byArtist (0.00)	byArtist (0.00)
	lyricist (0.02)	citation (0.02)	memberOf (0.00)	memberOf (0.00)
ConvE	isPartOf (0.39)	isPartOf (0.33)	genre (0.83)	genre (0.86)
	hasPart (0.25)	inLanguage (0.31)	foundingLocation (0.14)	foundingLocation (0.12)
	inLanguage (0.22)	hasPart (0.25)	award (0.02)	award (0.02)
	composer (0.08)	composer (0.06)	memberOf (0.01)	memberOf (0.00)
	citation (0.04)	citation (0.04)	byArtist (0.00)	byArtist (0.00)

combination of dataset and model, how much the top-K neighbors of an entity in the embedding space align with its top-K neighbors in the graph largely depends on which class this entity belongs to.

To examine this behavior further, we pick random classes and count the predicates in the common triples of the top-K neighbors (in the embedding space) for entities of this class differs between models.

Results for two picked classes are reported in Table 8, where each predicate is weighted in accordance to its frequency in the set of common triples between the 2-hop subgraphs of top-K neighbors in the embedding space (for $K = 3$ and $K = 10$) and a given entity of class `MusicComposition` and `MusicGroup` (YAGO4-19k). A class-based analysis reveals that predicates are differently ranked, *i.e.* different KGEMs *may* rely on different sets of predicates. For example, for $K = 10$ and entities of the class `MusicComposition`, either `isPartOf` or `inLanguage` appears as the most frequent predicate depending on the KGEM considered.

We additionally observe that even when the ranking is the same between KGEMs – especially since the predicate distribution can be severely skewed towards one or few predicates – the relative importance of predicates can still differ. For instance, although `genre` is consistently ranked as the most frequent predicate for `MusicGroup` entities, results for RDF2Vec suggest a more balanced predicate distribution and a lesser emphasis put on this single predicate (highlighted in blue in Table 8). It is the only model to put a signficant emphasis on `award` (i.e., considers two `MusicGroups` as similar if they have won the same (1-hop) or similar (2-hop) awards). In some cases, a few KGEMs seem to assign a lower relevance to specific predicates. For instance, under BoxE the top-3 and top-10 neighbors of entities that are `MusicCompositions` contain the predicate `inLanguage` at a much lesser frequency in their subgraphs' intersection (highlighted in brown in Table 8), compared to other models. Overall, we observe that the different notions of entity similarity reflected by different KGEMs are comparable, as most of them put a focus on the same set of predicates when determining entity similarity.

5. Conclusion

In this chapter, we have taken a look at the semantic properties of knowledge graph embedding spaces, approaching from two angles. The first angle was looking which kinds of classes can be separated in embedding spaces. The second angle was a close look at the property of the similarity function in knowledge graph embedding spaces.

The outcomes of the first study can provide some guidance on which embedding method to use for which downstream task. For example, for identifying related items (e.g., for knowledge-based recommender systems [64] or collective entity disambiguation [65]), approaches performing well on tc04 and tc05, standard RDF2vec [41], are preferable, while for entity classification based on structural features [5], approaches performing well on tc01-tc03, tc07, and tc08, other methods may be preferable. With such considerations, users of KGE embeddings can make more informed decisions on which embedding model to choose. Therefore, they allow informed decisions beyond experimentations, involving the time-consuming training of multiple models just for the sake of selecting one.

Furthermore, we have shown that many patterns using DL class constructors on DBpedia are actually learned by recognizing patterns with other constructors correlating with the pattern to be learned, thus yielding misleading results. This effect is less prominent in the synthetic gold standard. We showed that certain DL class constructors, especially qualified restrictions and cardinality constraints, are particularly hard to learn. Such insights open an interesting way to new developments in knowledge graph embeddings, since they point to conceptual shortcomings of methods instead of using pure leaderboard-based methods for assessing embedding methods.

The second study delved into the intricate relationship between entity similarity in KGs and their respective embeddings in KGEMs, questioning the widespread *KGE entity similarity assumption*. Contrary to this belief, we showed that the choice of KGEM significantly influences the notion of entity similarity encoded in the resulting vector space. This finding has profound implications for a variety of downstream tasks where accurate entity similarity is crucial, *e.g.* recommender systems and semantic searches. For instance, if the proximity of graph embeddings does not align with our proposed metric for measuring entity similarity, the tacit assumption of downstream systems exploiting embeddings for recommender systems does not hold and caution is needed when deploying such systems.

In many research papers in which KGEMs are utilized for some downstream task other than link prediction, a general method can be observed: first, different embedding models (most often those built for link prediction) are trained on the KG at hand, and the one performing best according to the link prediction scoring metric is used for the considered downstream task. A critical takeaway from the second study is that this practice might not yield the best results in terms of capturing true entity similarity. Instead, our results advocate for cautiousness. Moreover, in scenarios where the similarity of specific classes of entities is of paramount importance, a per-class analysis becomes essential. This approach allows for a tailored selection of KGEMs that are more adept at capturing the nuances and semantics of particular classes, thereby ensuring a more accurate and meaningful representation of entity similarity.

In summary, this chapter has shown that, while KGEMs are well studied in terms of quantitative, empirical results on standard benchmark (and, as a downside, maybe overtuned to those benchmarks), qualitative studies of their representational capabilities are still rare. However, to leverage their full potential in downstream applications beyond link prediction benchmarks, it is paramount to understand their capabilities at a deeper level. The two studies in this chapter pave the way towards such an understanding.

Notes

1. For reasons of scalability, we restrict the provided gold standard to two hops.
2. The fact that most KGs follow the open-world assumption is neglected here since we test for the presence/absence of patterns.
3. `https://pandas.pydata.org/`
4. `https://github.com/janothan/DL-TC-Generator`
5. DOI: `10.5281/zenodo.6509715`; GitHub link for the latest version. `https://github.com/janothan/DL-TC-Generator/tree/master/results`
6. `https://github.com/janothan/dl-evaluation-framework`

7. The evaluation framework is not restricted to the set of classifiers listed here. New classifiers can be easily added if desired.
8. https://scikit-learn.org/stable/index.html. The exact parameter settings can be found at the respective documentation pages of scikit-learn, i.e.: https://scikit-learn.org/stable/modules/generated/sklearn.tree.DecisionTreeClassifier.html, https://scikit-learn.org/stable/modules/generated/sklearn.naive_bayes.GaussianNB.html, https://scikit-learn.org/stable/modules/generated/sklearn.neighbors.KNeighborsClassifier.html, https://scikit-learn.org/stable/modules/generated/sklearn.svm.LinearSVC.html, https://scikit-learn.org/stable/modules/generated/sklearn.ensemble.RandomForestClassifier.html, and https://scikit-learn.org/stable/modules/generated/sklearn.neural_network.MLPClassifier.html.
9. We used DBpedia version 2021-09. The generator can be configured to use any DBpedia SPARQL endpoint if desired.
10. https://github.com/janothan/DL-TC-Generator/tree/master/src/main/resources/queries
11. The desired size classes can be configured in the framework.
12. https://github.com/dwslab/jRDF2Vec
13. http://data.dws.informatik.uni-mannheim.de/kgvec2go/dbpedia/2021-09/
14. https://github.com/awslabs/dgl-ke
15. http://data.dws.informatik.uni-mannheim.de/kgvec2go/dbpedia/2021-09/non-rdf2vec/
16. We consider both ingoing and outgoing edges to define those neighborhoods.
17. Given, e.g., (SAP, headquarter, Germany), (BOSCH, headquarter, Germany), (Berlin, capitalOf, Germany), with common neighbors, SAP, BOSCH, and Berlin would be equally similar.
18. https://github.com/changyaochen/rbo/
19. https://github.com/bxshi/ConMask/
20. https://www.microsoft.com/en-us/download/details.aspx?id=52312/

References

[1] Auer S, Bizer C, Kobilarov G, Lehmann J, Cyganiak R, Ives ZG. DBpedia: A Nucleus for a Web of Open Data. In: The Semantic Web, 6th International Semantic Web Conference, 2nd Asian Semantic Web Conference, ISWC + ASWC. vol. 4825 of Lecture Notes in Computer Science. Springer; 2007. p. 722-35.

[2] Suchanek FM, Kasneci G, Weikum G. Yago: a core of semantic knowledge. In: Proc. of the 16th International Conference on World Wide Web, WWW. ACM; 2007. p. 697-706.

[3] Vrandecic D, Krötzsch M. Wikidata: a free collaborative knowledgebase. Commun ACM. 2014;57(10):78-85.

[4] Heist N, Hertling S, Ringler D, Paulheim H. Knowledge Graphs on the Web - An Overview. In: Tiddi I, Lécué F, Hitzler P, editors. Knowledge Graphs for eXplainable Artificial Intelligence: Foundations, Applications and Challenges. vol. 47 of Studies on the Semantic Web. IOS Press; 2020. p. 3-22. Available from: https://doi.org/10.3233/SSW200009.

[5] Paulheim H. Knowledge graph refinement: A survey of approaches and evaluation methods. Semantic web. 2017;8(3):489-508. Available from: https://doi.org/10.3233/SW-160218.

[6] Wang M, Qiu L, Wang X. A Survey on Knowledge Graph Embeddings for Link Prediction. Symmetry. 2021;13(3):485.

[7] Chen W, Zhu H, Han X, Liu Z, Sun M. Quantifying Similarity between Relations with Fact Distribution. In: Proceedings of the 57th Conference of the Association for Computational Linguistics, ACL

2019, Florence, Italy, July 28- August 2, 2019, Volume 1: Long Papers. Association for Computational Linguistics; 2019. p. 2882-94.

[8] Kalo J, Ehler P, Balke W. Knowledge Graph Consolidation by Unifying Synonymous Relationships. In: The Semantic Web - ISWC 2019 - 18th International Semantic Web Conference, Auckland, New Zealand, October 26-30, 2019, Proceedings, Part I. vol. 11778 of Lecture Notes in Computer Science. Springer; 2019. p. 276-92.

[9] Sun Z, Zhang Q, Hu W, Wang C, Chen M, Akrami F, et al. A Benchmarking Study of Embedding-based Entity Alignment for Knowledge Graphs. Proc VLDB Endow. 2020;13(11):2326-40.

[10] Gad-Elrab MH, Stepanova D, Tran T, Adel H, Weikum G. ExCut: Explainable Embedding-Based Clustering over Knowledge Graphs. In: The Semantic Web - ISWC 2020 - 19th International Semantic Web Conference, Athens, Greece, November 2-6, 2020, Proceedings, Part I. vol. 12506 of Lecture Notes in Computer Science. Springer; 2020. p. 218-37.

[11] Portisch J, Paulheim H. The DLCC Node Classification Benchmark for Analyzing Knowledge Graph Embeddings. In: International Semantic Web Conference. Springer; 2022. p. 592-609. Available from: https://doi.org/10.1007/978-3-031-19433-7_34.

[12] Hubert N, Paulheim H, Brun A, Monticolo D. Do Similar Entities have Similar Embeddings? In: Extended Semantic Web Conference; 2024. .

[13] Jain N, Kalo JC, Balke WT, Krestel R. Do embeddings actually capture knowledge graph semantics? In: The Semantic Web: 18th International Conference, ESWC 2021, Virtual Event, June 6–10, 2021, Proceedings 18. Springer; 2021. p. 143-59.

[14] Ilievski F, Shenoy K, Chalupsky H, Klein N, Szekely P. A Study of Concept Similarity in Wikidata. Semantic Web Journal. 2023.

[15] Boleda G. Distributional semantics and linguistic theory. Annual Review of Linguistics. 2020;6:213-34.

[16] Bordes A, Usunier N, García-Durán A, Weston J, Yakhnenko O. Translating Embeddings for Modeling Multi-relational Data. In: Burges CJC, Bottou L, Ghahramani Z, Weinberger KQ, editors. Advances in Neural Information Processing Systems 26: 27th Annual Conference on Neural Information Processing Systems 2013. Proceedings of a meeting held December 5-8, 2013, Lake Tahoe, Nevada, United States; 2013. p. 2787-95. Available from: https://proceedings.neurips.cc/paper/2013/hash/1cecc7a77928ca8133fa24680a88d2f9-Abstract.html.

[17] Fellbaum C, editor. WordNet: An Electronic Lexical Database. Language, Speech, and Communication. Cambridge, Massachusetts: MIT Press; 1998. Available from: https://doi.org/10.7551/mitpress/7287.001.0001.

[18] Toutanova K, Chen D. Observed versus latent features for knowledge base and text inference. In: Proceedings of the 3rd workshop on continuous vector space models and their compositionality; 2015. p. 57-66. Available from: https://www.doi.org/10.18653/v1/W15-4007.

[19] Dettmers T, Minervini P, Stenetorp P, Riedel S. Convolutional 2D Knowledge Graph Embeddings. In: McIlraith SA, Weinberger KQ, editors. Proceedings of the Thirty-Second AAAI Conference on Artificial Intelligence, (AAAI-18), the 30th innovative Applications of Artificial Intelligence (IAAI-18), and the 8th AAAI Symposium on Educational Advances in Artificial Intelligence (EAAI-18), New Orleans, Louisiana, USA, February 2-7, 2018. AAAI Press; 2018. p. 1811-8. Available from: https://www.aaai.org/ocs/index.php/AAAI/AAAI18/paper/view/17366.

[20] Shi B, Weninger T. Open-World Knowledge Graph Completion. In: McIlraith SA, Weinberger KQ, editors. Proceedings of the Thirty-Second AAAI Conference on Artificial Intelligence, (AAAI-18), the 30th innovative Applications of Artificial Intelligence (IAAI-18), and the 8th AAAI Symposium on Educational Advances in Artificial Intelligence (EAAI-18), New Orleans, Louisiana, USA, February 2-7, 2018. AAAI Press; 2018. p. 1957-64. Available from: https://www.aaai.org/ocs/index.php/AAAI/AAAI18/paper/view/16055.

[21] Bloem P, Wilcke X, van Berkel L, de Boer V. kgbench: A Collection of Knowledge Graph Datasets for Evaluating Relational and Multimodal Machine Learning. In: Verborgh R, Hose K, Paulheim H, Champin P, Maleshkova M, Corcho Ó, et al., editors. The Semantic Web - 18th International Conference, ESWC 2021, Virtual Event, June 6-10, 2021, Proceedings. vol. 12731 of Lecture Notes in Computer Science. Springer; 2021. p. 614-30. Available from: https://doi.org/10.1007/978-3-030-77385-4_37.

[22] Alshargi F, Shekarpour S, Soru T, Sheth AP. Metrics for Evaluating Quality of Embeddings for Ontological Concepts. In: Martin A, Hinkelmann K, Gerber A, Lenat D, van Harmelen F, Clark P, editors. Proceedings of the AAAI 2019 Spring Symposium on Combining Machine Learning with Knowledge En-

gineering (AAAI-MAKE 2019) Stanford University, Palo Alto, California, USA, March 25-27, 2019., Stanford University, Palo Alto, California, USA, March 25-27, 2019. vol. 2350 of CEUR Workshop Proceedings. CEUR-WS.org; 2019. Available from: http://ceur-ws.org/Vol-2350/paper26.pdf.

[23] Ristoski P, de Vries GKD, Paulheim H. A Collection of Benchmark Datasets for Systematic Evaluations of Machine Learning on the Semantic Web. In: Groth P, Simperl E, Gray AJG, Sabou M, Krötzsch M, Lécué F, et al., editors. The Semantic Web - ISWC 2016 - 15th International Semantic Web Conference, Kobe, Japan, October 17-21, 2016, Proceedings, Part II. vol. 9982 of Lecture Notes in Computer Science; 2016. p. 186-94. Available from: https://doi.org/10.1007/978-3-319-46547-0_20.

[24] Pellegrino MA, Altabba A, Garofalo M, Ristoski P, Cochez M. GEval: A Modular and Extensible Evaluation Framework for Graph Embedding Techniques. In: Harth A, Kirrane S, Ngomo AN, Paulheim H, Rula A, Gentile AL, et al., editors. The Semantic Web - 17th International Conference, ESWC 2020, Heraklion, Crete, Greece, May 31-June 4, 2020, Proceedings. vol. 12123 of Lecture Notes in Computer Science. Springer; 2020. p. 565-82. Available from: https://doi.org/10.1007/978-3-030-49461-2_33.

[25] Pellegrino MA, Cochez M, Garofalo M, Ristoski P. A Configurable Evaluation Framework for Node Embedding Techniques. In: Hitzler P, Kirrane S, Hartig O, de Boer V, Vidal M, Maleshkova M, et al., editors. The Semantic Web: ESWC 2019 Satellite Events - ESWC 2019 Satellite Events, Portorož, Slovenia, June 2-6, 2019, Revised Selected Papers. vol. 11762 of Lecture Notes in Computer Science. Springer; 2019. p. 156-60. Available from: https://doi.org/10.1007/978-3-030-32327-1_31.

[26] Heist N, Hertling S, Paulheim H. KGrEaT: a framework to evaluate knowledge graphs via downstream tasks. In: Proceedings of the 32nd ACM International Conference on Information and Knowledge Management; 2023. p. 3938-42.

[27] Portisch J, Heist N, Paulheim H. Knowledge graph embedding for data mining vs. knowledge graph embedding for link prediction–two sides of the same coin? Semantic Web. 2022;13(3):399-422.

[28] Alshargi F, Shekarpour S, Soru T, Sheth A. Concept2vec: Metrics for evaluating quality of embeddings for ontological concepts. arXiv preprint arXiv:180304488. 2018.

[29] Krötzsch M, Simancik F, Horrocks I. A description logic primer. arXiv preprint arXiv:12014089. 2012.

[30] Ristoski P, Paulheim H. RDF2Vec: RDF Graph Embeddings for Data Mining. In: The Semantic Web - ISWC 2016 - 15th International Semantic Web Conference, Kobe, Japan, October 17-21, 2016, Proceedings, Part I. vol. 9981 of Lecture Notes in Computer Science; 2016. p. 498-514.

[31] Portisch J, Paulheim H. Putting RDF2vec in Order. In: Seneviratne O, Pesquita C, Sequeda J, Etcheverry L, editors. Proceedings of the ISWC 2021 Posters, Demos and Industry Tracks: From Novel Ideas to Industrial Practice co-located with 20th International Semantic Web Conference (ISWC 2021), Virtual Conference, October 24-28, 2021. vol. 2980 of CEUR Workshop Proceedings. CEUR-WS.org; 2021. Available from: http://ceur-ws.org/Vol-2980/paper352.pdf.

[32] Lin Y, Liu Z, Sun M, Liu Y, Zhu X. Learning Entity and Relation Embeddings for Knowledge Graph Completion. In: Bonet B, Koenig S, editors. Proceedings of the Twenty-Ninth AAAI Conference on Artificial Intelligence, January 25-30, 2015, Austin, Texas, USA. AAAI Press; 2015. p. 2181-7. Available from: http://www.aaai.org/ocs/index.php/AAAI/AAAI15/paper/view/9571.

[33] Trouillon T, Welbl J, Riedel S, Gaussier É, Bouchard G. Complex Embeddings for Simple Link Prediction. In: Balcan M, Weinberger KQ, editors. Proceedings of the 33nd International Conference on Machine Learning, ICML 2016, New York City, NY, USA, June 19-24, 2016. vol. 48 of JMLR Workshop and Conference Proceedings. JMLR.org; 2016. p. 2071-80. Available from: http://proceedings.mlr.press/v48/trouillon16.html.

[34] Nickel M, Tresp V, Kriegel H. A Three-Way Model for Collective Learning on Multi-Relational Data. In: Getoor L, Scheffer T, editors. Proceedings of the 28th International Conference on Machine Learning, ICML 2011, Bellevue, Washington, USA, June 28 - July 2, 2011. Omnipress; 2011. p. 809-16. Available from: https://icml.cc/2011/papers/438_icmlpaper.pdf.

[35] Sun Z, Deng Z, Nie J, Tang J. RotatE: Knowledge Graph Embedding by Relational Rotation in Complex Space. In: 7th International Conference on Learning Representations, ICLR 2019, New Orleans, LA, USA, May 6-9, 2019. OpenReview.net; 2019. Available from: https://openreview.net/forum?id=HkgEQnRqYQ.

[36] Portisch J, Hladik M, Paulheim H. RDF2Vec Light - A Lightweight Approachfor Knowledge Graph Embeddings. In: Taylor KL, Gonçalves RS, Lécué F, Yan J, editors. Proceedings of the ISWC 2020 Demos and Industry Tracks: From Novel Ideas to Industrial Practice co-located with 19th International Semantic Web Conference (ISWC 2020), Globally online, November 1-6, 2020 (UTC). vol. 2721 of

CEUR Workshop Proceedings. CEUR-WS.org; 2020. p. 79-84. Available from: http://ceur-ws.org/Vol-2721/paper520.pdf.

[37] Portisch J, Hladik M, Paulheim H. KGvec2go - Knowledge Graph Embeddings as a Service. In: Calzolari N, Béchet F, Blache P, Choukri K, Cieri C, Declerck T, et al., editors. Proceedings of The 12th Language Resources and Evaluation Conference, LREC 2020, Marseille, France, May 11-16, 2020. European Language Resources Association; 2020. p. 5641-7. Available from: https://aclanthology.org/2020.lrec-1.692/.

[38] Zheng D, Song X, Ma C, Tan Z, Ye Z, Dong J, et al. DGL-KE: Training Knowledge Graph Embeddings at Scale. In: Huang J, Chang Y, Cheng X, Kamps J, Murdock V, Wen J, et al., editors. Proceedings of the 43rd International ACM SIGIR conference on research and development in Information Retrieval, SIGIR 2020, Virtual Event, China, July 25-30, 2020. ACM; 2020. p. 739-48. Available from: https://doi.org/10.1145/3397271.3401172.

[39] Salzberg S. On Comparing Classifiers: Pitfalls to Avoid and a Recommended Approach. Data Min Knowl Discov. 1997;1(3):317-28. Available from: https://doi.org/10.1023/A:1009752403260.

[40] Portisch J, Heist N, Paulheim H. Knowledge graph embedding for data mining vs. knowledge graph embedding for link prediction - two sides of the same coin? Semantic Web. 2022;13(3):399-422. Available from: https://doi.org/10.3233/SW-212892.

[41] Portisch J, Paulheim H. The RDF2vec family of knowledge graph embedding methods. Semantic Web;(Preprint):1-32.

[42] Sanfeliu A, Fu K. A distance measure between attributed relational graphs for pattern recognition. IEEE Trans Syst Man Cybern. 1983;13(3):353-62.

[43] Liben-Nowell D, Kleinberg J. The link prediction problem for social networks. In: Proceedings of the twelfth international conference on Information and knowledge management; 2003. p. 556-9.

[44] Kendall MG. A New Measure of Rank Correlation. Biometrika. 1938;30(1/2):81-93.

[45] Webber W, Moffat A, Zobel J. A similarity measure for indefinite rankings. ACM Trans Inf Syst. 2010;28(4):20:1-20:38.

[46] Bordes A, Usunier N, García-Durán A, Weston J, Yakhnenko O. Translating Embeddings for Modeling Multi-relational Data. In: Conference on Neural Information Processing Systems (NeurIPS); 2013. p. 2787-95.

[47] Ji G, He S, Xu L, Liu K, Zhao J. Knowledge Graph Embedding via Dynamic Mapping Matrix. In: Proceedings of the 53rd Annual Meeting of the Association for Computational Linguistics and the 7th International Joint Conference on Natural Language Processing of the Asian Federation of Natural Language Processing, ACL 2015, July 26-31, 2015, Beijing, China, Volume 1: Long Papers. The Association for Computer Linguistics; 2015. p. 687-96.

[48] Abboud R, Ceylan İİ, Lukasiewicz T, Salvatori T. BoxE: A Box Embedding Model for Knowledge Base Completion. In: Advances in Neural Information Processing Systems 33: Annual Conference on Neural Information Processing Systems 2020, NeurIPS 2020, December 6-12, 2020, virtual; 2020. .

[49] Nickel M, Tresp V, Kriegel H. A Three-Way Model for Collective Learning on Multi-Relational Data. In: Proc. of the 28th International Conference on Machine Learning, ICML; 2011. p. 809-16.

[50] Yang B, Yih W, He X, Gao J, Deng L. Embedding Entities and Relations for Learning and Inference in Knowledge Bases. In: 3rd International Conference on Learning Representations, ICLR; 2015. .

[51] Balazevic I, Allen C, Hospedales TM. TuckER: Tensor Factorization for Knowledge Graph Completion. In: Proceedings of the 2019 Conference on Empirical Methods in Natural Language Processing and the 9th International Joint Conference on Natural Language Processing, EMNLP-IJCNLP 2019, Hong Kong, China, November 3-7, 2019. Association for Computational Linguistics; 2019. p. 5184-93.

[52] Dettmers T, Minervini P, Stenetorp P, Riedel S. Convolutional 2D Knowledge Graph Embeddings. In: Proceedings of the Thirty-Second AAAI Conference on Artificial Intelligence, (AAAI-18), the 30th innovative Applications of Artificial Intelligence (IAAI-18), and the 8th AAAI Symposium on Educational Advances in Artificial Intelligence (EAAI-18), New Orleans, Louisiana, USA, February 2-7, 2018. AAAI Press; 2018. p. 1811-8.

[53] Trouillon T, Welbl J, Riedel S, Gaussier É, Bouchard G. Complex Embeddings for Simple Link Prediction. In: Proceedings of the 33rd International Conference on Machine Learning, ICML. vol. 48; 2016. p. 2071-80.

[54] Sun Z, Deng Z, Nie J, Tang J. RotatE: Knowledge Graph Embedding by Relational Rotation in Complex Space. In: 7th International Conference on Learning Representations, ICLR; 2019. .

[55] Ali M, Berrendorf M, Hoyt CT, Vermue L, Sharifzadeh S, Tresp V, et al. PyKEEN 1.0: a python li-

brary for training and evaluating knowledge graph embeddings. Journal of Machine Learning Research. 2021;22(82):1-6.

[56] Hubert N, Monnin P, Brun A, Monticolo D. Sem@K: Is my knowledge graph embedding model semantic-aware? Semantic Web. 2023 12;14:1-37.

[57] Paulheim H, Portisch J, Ristoski P. Embedding Knowledge Graphs with RDF2vec. Springer; 2023. Available from: `https://doi.org/10.1007/978-3-031-30387-6`.

[58] Steenwinckel B, Vandewiele G, Agozzino T, Ongenae F. pyRDF2Vec: a python implementation and extension of RDF2Vec. In: European Semantic Web Conference. Springer; 2023. p. 471-83.

[59] Mikolov T, Chen K, Corrado G, Dean J. Efficient Estimation of Word Representations in Vector Space. In: 1st International Conference on Learning Representations, ICLR 2013, Scottsdale, Arizona, USA, May 2-4, 2013, Workshop Track Proceedings; 2013. .

[60] Bloehdorn S, Sure Y. Kernel Methods for Mining Instance Data in Ontologies. In: The Semantic Web, 6th International Semantic Web Conference, 2nd Asian Semantic Web Conference, ISWC 2007 + ASWC 2007, Busan, Korea, November 11-15, 2007. vol. 4825 of Lecture Notes in Computer Science. Springer; 2007. p. 58-71.

[61] Safavi T, Koutra D. CoDEx: A Comprehensive Knowledge Graph Completion Benchmark. In: Proceedings of the 2020 Conference on Empirical Methods in Natural Language Processing, EMNLP 2020, Online, November 16-20, 2020. Association for Computational Linguistics; 2020. p. 8328-50.

[62] Shi B, Weninger T. Open-World Knowledge Graph Completion. In: Proceedings of the Thirty-Second AAAI Conference on Artificial Intelligence, (AAAI-18), the 30th innovative Applications of Artificial Intelligence (IAAI-18), and the 8th AAAI Symposium on Educational Advances in Artificial Intelligence (EAAI-18), New Orleans, Louisiana, USA, February 2-7, 2018. AAAI Press; 2018. p. 1957-64.

[63] Toutanova K, Chen D. Observed versus latent features for knowledge base and text inference. In: Proc. of the 3rd Workshop on Continuous Vector Space Models and their Compositionality. Association for Computational Linguistics; 2015. p. 57-66.

[64] Iana A, Alam M, Paulheim H. A survey on knowledge-aware news recommender systems. Semantic Web. 2022;(to appear). 10.3233/SW-222991.

[65] Oliveira IL, Fileto R, Speck R, Garcia LP, Moussallem D, Lehmann J. Towards holistic entity linking: Survey and directions. Information Systems. 2021;95:101624.

Handbook on Neurosymbolic AI and Knowledge Graphs
P. Hitzler et al. (Eds.)
IOS Press, 2025

doi:10.3233/FAIA250207

Instance Retrieval for Class Expression Learning Using SPARQL

Nikolaos KARALIS [a] Alexander BIGERL [a] Caglar DEMIR [a] Liss HEIDRICH [a]
Axel-Cyrille NGONGA NGOMO [a]

[a] *Paderborn University, DICE Research Group, Warburgerstrasse 100, 33098 Paderborn*

Abstract. Over 100 billions RDF assertions are available on the Web. With this high availability of knowledge expressed in RDF knowledge bases comes the need to make them amenable to Web-scale machine learning. Knowledge graph embeddings cater for enabling the use of knowledge bases in neural settings. However, they do so by discarding the explicit semantics that underpin knowledge bases. In contrast, class expression learning makes explicit use of the semantics of RDF knowledge bases expressed in description logics. In contrast to neural approaches, this form of machine learning generates models that can be translated into natural language and can thus be understood by domain experts. However, most implementations of this paradigm fail to scale to the large knowledge bases found on the Web and in real-life applications. The corresponding literature suggests that one common bottleneck of these approaches is the instance retrieval function. We address this drawback by introducing an approach based on worst-case optimal multi-way joins for the evaluation of SPARQL queries that correspond to $\mathcal{ALC}$ class expressions. We implement our algorithm into a tensor-based triple store and use this triple store as backend to efficiently answer retrieval queries in $\mathcal{ALC}$ under the closed-world assumption. We evaluate the implementation of our approach on five benchmark datasets against four state-of-the-art graph storage solutions for RDF knowledge graphs. The results of our extensive evaluation show that our approach outperforms its competition across all datasets and that it is the only one able to scale to large datasets. With our approach, class expression learning can now be used on Web-scale knowledge bases.

Keywords. knowledge graphs, class expression learning, multi-way join algorithms

1. Introduction

RDF knowledge bases are now first-class citizens of the Web. Ca. 100 billion RDF assertions are found in the 2023 crawl of the Web Data Commons.[1] RDF data dumps on the Web cover a similar order of magnitude.[2] Learning on RDF data at this scale is hence crucial for the deployment of machine learning on the Web—the world's largest shared information source with over 5.4 billion users.[3] The large proportion of the human popu-

[1] `http://webdatacommons.org/structureddata/#results-2023-1`
[2] `http://lod-a-lot.lod.labs.vu.nl/`
[3] `https://www.statista.com/statistics/617136/digital-population-worldwide`

lation impacted by machine learning on the Web entails the need for explainable machine learning because of its known societal advantages [1].

A popular family of ante-hoc explainable approaches for supervised learning on RDF knowledge graphs are class expression learning algorithms based on refinement operators [2,3,4]. Given a set of positive and negative examples, these approaches generate a class expression in a predefined description logic, which ideally describes the positive and not the negative examples. While these approaches were mostly symbolic in the past, recent approaches are neuro-symbolic in nature, and combine embeddings (see [5] for a recent survey) with classical reasoners–e.g., DRILL [6] uses Deep Q learning to improve the traversal of refinement trees. However, a large body of literature on learning class expressions [7,8,4] suggests that approaches to class expression learning based on refinement operators do not scale to the size of datasets found on the Web. This is mostly due to their instance retrieval function–which computes the instances of given class expressions [2,3,4]–being unable to retrieve instances in a time-efficient manner [3,4]. The authors of [9] suggest that this weakness can be addressed by converting class expressions into SPARQL queries.

SPARQL[4] is the designated language for querying RDF knowledge graphs. A recent advancement in querying processing is the introduction of worst-case optimal multi-way join algorithms [10]. Worst-case optimal multi-way join algorithms have been adopted by the semantic web community [11] and are now being used by state-of-the-art knowledge graph storage solutions (e.g., triple stores) for the efficient evaluation of SPARQL queries [12,13]. However, the use of multi-way joins for SPARQL is mostly limited to conjunctive queries. As shown in Section 3, class expression learning with SPARQL does not only deal with conjunctive queries. In particular, it requires the efficient evaluation of queries containing *negation*.

This work builds upon the hypothesis formulated in [9]. Our hypothesis is that we can exploit multi-way joins to implement a time-efficient retrieval function for class expression learning. To this end, as in previous works (e.g., [7,8]), we set our focus on the description logic $\mathcal{ALC}$ and present a multi-way join algorithm for the efficient evaluation of SPARQL queries generated by $\mathcal{ALC}$ class expressions. Such SPARQL queries include union graph patterns and negation, which is captured by `FILTER NOT EXISTS` patterns. To the best of our knowledge, there have not been any works for SPARQL that considered the evaluation of negation in multi-way join plans.

The main contributions of this work are the following: (i) Inspired by worst-case-optimal multi-way join algorithms and their efficiency in evaluating conjunctive queries, we present a multi-way join algorithm for the evaluation of SPARQL queries generated from $\mathcal{ALC}$ class expressions. Our approach relies on theoretical foundations of SPARQL to enable the use of multi-way joins in queries involving negation. (ii) We identify and fix an issue in the formulation of the mapping of class expressions to SPARQL queries presented in [9]. (iii) We implement the proposed algorithm in a state-of-the-art triple store and present the results of an extensive comparison of our implementation on multiple benchmark datasets of varying sizes with multiple state-of-the-art triple stores using SPARQL queries that correspond to $\mathcal{ALC}$ class expressions. In our evaluation, we use four datasets, ranging from 96K to 2.1M triples, that are commonly used to evaluate learning algorithms. To evaluate the scalabilty of our approach, we also use a dataset

[4]`https://www.w3.org/TR/2013/REC-sparql11-query-20130321/`

consisting of more than 40M triples. The results of our experimental evaluation show that our approach outperforms its competition across all datasets and that it is the only one that efficiently handles query workloads in the largest dataset.

The rest of this work is structured as follows: In Section 2, we provide background knowledge on the topics that are covered in this paper. In Section 3, we cover the translation of $\mathcal{ALC}$ class expressions to SPARQL queries. We present the proposed multi-way join algorithm for SPARQL queries generated from $\mathcal{ALC}$ class expressions in Section 4. Our experimental results are presented in Section 5. We discuss related works in Section 6 and conclude in Section 7.

2. Preliminaries

We begin first with a brief overview of the description logic $\mathcal{ALC}$. Second, we describe the problem of class expression learning. Third, we cover definitions and properties of SPARQL queries that are required in this work. Last, we briefly summarize worst-case optimal multi-way join algorithms. This chapter is an extension of the work [14].

2.1. The Description Logic $\mathcal{ALC}$

A description logic is a decidable fragment of first-order logic that uses only unary and binary predicates [15]. The set of unary predicates, binary predicates and constants correspond to the set of named concepts N_C, roles N_R, and individuals N_I of a description logic, respectively. Like in recent works on class expression learning (e.g., [7,8]), we focus on the description logic $\mathcal{ALC}$ [16]. Its syntax and semantics are provided in Table 1. In this paper, $\mathcal{C}$ denotes the set of all valid $\mathcal{ALC}$ concepts C under the construction rules: $C ::= A \mid \neg C \mid C \sqcap C \mid C \sqcup C \mid \exists r.C \mid \forall r.C$, where $A \in N_C$ and $r \in N_R$.

Knowledge bases in $\mathcal{ALC}$ are often defined as $\mathcal{K} = (Tbox, Abox)$. All axioms in *Tbox* are of the form $A \sqsubseteq B$ or $A \equiv B$. *Abox* contains the relationships between individuals $a, b \in N_I$ via roles $r \in N_R$ and membership relationships between N_I and $\mathcal{C}$. Following previous works on class expression learning [7,8,3], we adopt closed-world semantics. Hence, checking whether an instance belongs to a particular concept or retrieving the individuals of a particular concept is similar to querying in classical databases [9,17].

Table 1. Syntax and semantics of $\mathcal{ALC}$. $\mathcal{I}$ denotes an interpretation and $\Delta^{\mathcal{I}}$ its domain.

Construct	Syntax	Semantics
Top concept	$\top$	$\Delta^{\mathcal{I}}$
Bottom concept	$\bot$	$\emptyset$
Atomic concept	A	$A^{\mathcal{I}} \subseteq \Delta^{\mathcal{I}}$
Role	r	$r^{\mathcal{I}} \subseteq \Delta^{\mathcal{I}} \times \Delta^{\mathcal{I}}$
Conjunction	$C \sqcap D$	$C^{\mathcal{I}} \cap D^{\mathcal{I}}$
Disjunction	$C \sqcup D$	$C^{\mathcal{I}} \cup D^{\mathcal{I}}$
Negation	$\neg C$	$\Delta^{\mathcal{I}} \setminus C^{\mathcal{I}}$
Existential restriction	$\exists\, r.C$	$\{x \mid \exists\, (x^{\mathcal{I}}, y^{\mathcal{I}}) \in r^{\mathcal{I}} \land y^{\mathcal{I}} \in C^{\mathcal{I}}\}$
Universal restriction	$\forall\, r.C$	$\{x \mid \forall\, (x^{\mathcal{I}}, y^{\mathcal{I}}) \in r^{\mathcal{I}} \implies y^{\mathcal{I}} \in C^{\mathcal{I}}\}$

2.2. Class Expression Learning

Class expression learning approaches are a family of supervised machine learning algorithms. Given a knowledge base $\mathcal{K} = (Tbox, Abox)$, a set of positive examples E^+, and a set of negative examples E^- with $E^+ \cup E^- \subseteq N_I$ and $E^+ \cap E^- = \emptyset$, class expression learning algorithms aim to learn a class expression H that ideally describes all of the individuals of E^+ and not any of the individuals of E^-:

$$\forall e^+ \in E^+ (\mathcal{K} \models H(e^+))), \tag{1}$$

$$\forall e^- \in E^- (\mathcal{K} \not\models H(e^-)). \tag{2}$$

To find the most appropriate H for a particular pair (E^+, E^-), a class expression learning problem is often transformed into a search problem within a quasi-ordered space $(\mathcal{C}, \preceq)$ [18,3,19], where the quasi-ordering $\preceq$ over $\mathcal{C}$ is often the subsumption relation $\sqsubseteq$ between concepts [8]. The traversal of the search problem's space is usually conducted using a downward refinement operator $\rho : \mathcal{C} \to 2^{\mathcal{C}}$ such that

$$\rho(C) \subseteq \{C' \in \mathcal{C} \mid C' \sqsubseteq C, C' \neq C\}, \tag{3}$$

for all $C \in \mathcal{C}$ [8]. State-of-the-art class expression learning algorithms begin their search towards an H with a search tree that is initialized with the most general concept ($\top$) as root node. This search tree is iteratively built by selecting a node containing a quasi-ordered concept with the highest heuristic value and adding its qualifying refinements as its children into the search tree [20]. A heuristic function (e.g., [20,19]) is the key to an efficient search in $\mathcal{C}$ towards an H [20]. For instance, the heuristic function of a state-of-the-art algorithm, namely CELOE, is defined as

$$\phi_{\text{CELOE}}(A, B) = F_1(B) + \lambda \cdot \left[F_1(B) - \mathrm{Q}(A)\right] - \beta \cdot |B|, \tag{4}$$

where $A \in \mathcal{C}$, $B \in \rho(A)$, $\beta > \lambda \geq 0$, and $\mathrm{Q}(\cdot)$ denoting a quality function (e.g., F_1 score or accuracy). Through $\mathrm{Q}(\cdot)$ and $|\cdot|$, the search is steered based solely on A and B towards more accurate and syntactically shorter concepts. $F_1(\cdot)$ is defined as

$$F_1(A) = \frac{|E^+ \cap \mathcal{R}(A)|}{|E^+ \cap \mathcal{R}(A)| + 0.5(|E^- \cap \mathcal{R}(A)| + |E^+ \setminus \mathcal{R}(A)|)}. \tag{5}$$

To compute the quality of a class expression H, heuristic functions, such as CELOE's (Eq. (5)), use a retrieval function $\mathcal{R} : \mathcal{C} \to 2^{N_I}$, which returns all individuals in N_I that are instances of the provided class expression H. As discussed in Section 2.1, we assume that retrieval operations are carried out under closed world semantics. As the size of an input knowledge base grows, executing retrieval operations against reasoners becomes one of the main computational bottlenecks [9,3,4] of learning algorithms. The goal of this work is to accelerate class expression learning by reducing the runtimes of retrieval operations.

2.3. Semantics and Properties of SPARQL

Here, we provide the semantics and the properties of SPARQL queries that use those features of the language that are used in queries generated by $\mathcal{ALC}$ class expressions (Section 3). In particular, our focus is on SPARQL queries consisting of *triple patterns*, *basic graph patterns*, *union graph patterns*, and *negation* in the form of *FILTER NOT EXISTS* patterns. Note that SPARQL queries are defined under bag semantics. In this work, we adopt set semantics (i.e., the queries contain DISTINCT), which are in line with the semantics of $\mathcal{ALC}$. Let **I** be an infinite set of IRIs, **B** an infinite set of blank nodes, and **L** an infinite set of literals. The sets **I**, **B** and **L** are pairwise disjoint and their union, denoted as $\mathbf{T} = \mathbf{I} \cup \mathbf{B} \cup \mathbf{L}$, is the set of all terms. Furthermore, let **V** be an infinite set of variables. An RDF graph is a set of triples and is defined as $G = \{(s,p,o) \mid s \in (\mathbf{I} \cup \mathbf{B}), p \in \mathbf{I}, o \in \mathbf{T}\}$, where s, p, and o stand for *subject*, *predicate*, and *object*, respectively.

2.3.1. Triple, Basic and Union Graph Patterns

The following is based on [11,21]. A triple pattern *tp* is a triple (s,p,o), where $s \in (\mathbf{I} \cup \mathbf{L} \cup \mathbf{V})$, $p \in (\mathbf{I} \cup \mathbf{V})$, and $o \in (\mathbf{I} \cup \mathbf{L} \cup \mathbf{V})$. The set of variables of a triple pattern is denoted as $var(tp)$. Since blank nodes behave as variables, we do not consider them in triple patterns [11,21]. A basic graph pattern (BGP) is a set of triple patterns. The semantics of SPARQL queries are defined using mappings, which are partial functions assigning terms to variables. A mapping is formally defined as $\mu : \mathbf{V} \rightarrow \mathbf{T}$ and its domain is denoted as $dom(\mu)$. With $\mu(tp)$, we denote the RDF triple obtained by replacing the variables of $var(tp)$ with their corresponding values in μ. Two mappings μ_1 and μ_2 are compatible ($\mu_1 \sim \mu_2$), iff $\mu_1(?v) = \mu_2(?v)$ for every variable $?v \in dom(\mu_1) \cap dom(\mu_2)$. Two mappings μ_1 and μ_2 are not compatible ($\mu_1 \nsim \mu_2$), if for any $?v \in dom(\mu_1) \cap dom(\mu_2)$, $\mu_1(?v) \neq \mu_2(?v)$. Given two sets of mappings Ω_1 and Ω_2 the join operation is defined as $\Omega_1 \bowtie \Omega_2 = \{\mu_1 \cup \mu_2 \mid \mu_1 \in \Omega_1, \mu_2 \in \Omega_2 \text{ and } \mu_1 \sim \mu_2\}$ and the union operation is defined as $\Omega_1 \cup \Omega_2 = \{\mu \mid \mu \in \Omega_1 \text{ or } \mu \in \Omega_2\}$. The evaluation of a triple pattern *tp* and a BGP P over an RDF graph G is denoted as $[\![tp]\!]_G = \{\mu \mid dom(\mu) = var(tp) \text{ and } \mu(tp) \in G\}$ and $[\![P]\!]_G = [\![tp_1,\ldots,tp_n]\!]_G = [\![tp_1]\!]_G \bowtie \ldots \bowtie [\![tp_n]\!]_G$, respectively. In SPARQL, graph patterns are constructed recursively. Triple patterns and BGPs are graph patterns. The set of variables of a graph pattern P is denoted as $var(P)$. The conjunction and union between two graph patterns P_1 and P_2 are also graph patterns and are evaluated over G as $[\![P_1 \ AND \ P_2]\!]_G = [\![P_1]\!]_G \bowtie [\![P_2]\!]_G$ and $[\![P_1 \ UNION \ P_2]\!]_G = [\![P_1]\!]_G \cup [\![P_2]\!]_G$, respectively.

2.3.2. Negation

The following definitions are based on [22]. In SPARQL, there are multiple ways to express negation [22]. Here, we focus on patterns of negation that are expressed using FILTER NOT EXISTS patterns, which are used for converting $\mathcal{ALC}$ class expressions to SPARQL queries (Section 3). FILTER NOT EXISTS can be provided with either a subquery or a graph pattern. In this work, we are interested only in the latter case (Section 3). Given a graph pattern $P = (P_1 \ FNE \ P_2)$, where *FNE* stands for FILTER NOT EXISTS, the set of correlated variables $corVars(P)$ is defined as $corVars(P) = var(P_1) \cap var(P_2)$; P_1 and P_2 are correlated if $corVars(P) \neq \emptyset$. In this work, we focus only on queries for which P_1 and P_2 are always correlated (Section 3). If P_1 and P_2 are correlated, P_1 is evaluated before P_2 and P_2 is evaluated after each correlated variable in P_2 is replaced with

Algorithm 1 Generic Join

// Execution is resumed after a **yield** operation
function GENERICJOIN(P, G, X) ▷ P: BGP, G: RDF Graph, X: Mapping
  if $var(P) = \emptyset$ **then yield** X and **return** ▷ All variables are evaluated
  $?x \leftarrow$ a variable from $var(P)$ ▷ Select a variable to be evaluated
  $K \leftarrow \bigcap_{tp \in P \mid ?x \in var(tp)} \{\mu(?x) \mid \mu \in [\![tp]\!]_G\}$ ▷ All possible values of $?x$
  for all $k \in K$ **do** ▷ Iterate over the possible values of $?x$
    $X(?x) \leftarrow k$ ▷ Store k in the solution mapping
    $P' \leftarrow$ assign k to all occurrences of $?x$ in P
    yield all GENERICJOIN(P', G, X) ▷ proceeds with the next k afterwards

its corresponding value obtained in the evaluation of P_1 [22]. The set of certain variables of a graph pattern P, denoted as $cVars(P)$, consists of the variables that are always bound in the solution mapping of P [23]. The set of certain variables of a graph pattern P is defined recursively [22,23]: (i) if P is a triple pattern tp, then $cVars(P) = var(tp)$, (ii) if $P = (P_1\ AND\ P_2)$, then $cVars(P) = cVars(P_1) \cup cVars(P_2)$, (iii) if $P = (P_1\ UNION\ P_2)$, then $cVars(P) = cVars(P_1) \cap cVars(P_2)$, (iv) if $P = (P_1\ FILTER\ R)$, then $cVars(P) = cVars(P_1)$ with R being a built-in condition (e.g., integer addition), and (v) if $P = (P_1\ FNE\ P_2)$, then $cVars(P) = cVars(P_1)$. A graph pattern is *fne-safe*, if for every subpattern $P = (P_1\ FNE\ P_2)$ holds that $corVars(P) \subseteq cVars(P_2)$. Given two sets of mappings Ω_1 and Ω_2 the difference operation is defined as $\Omega_1 \setminus \Omega_2 = \{\mu_1 \in \Omega_1 \mid \forall \mu_2 \in \Omega_2, \mu_1 \nsim \mu_2\}$. For fne-safe patterns, the negation is defined as $[\![P_1\ FNE\ P_2]\!]_G = [\![P_1]\!]_G \setminus [\![P_2]\!]_G$. The notion of fne-safety ensures that nested *FNE* patterns can be evaluated using the difference operation [22].

2.3.3. *Filter Rewriting Rule and Union Normal Form*

A graph pattern $((P_1\ FILTER\ R)\ AND\ P_2)$ can be rewritten to a pattern $((P_1\ AND\ P_2)\ FILTER\ R)$, if every variable of R is also a certain variable of P_1 or if R and P_2 do not share any variables [23]. A graph pattern P is in *UNION normal form* if it is in the form $(P_1\ UNION\ P_2\ UNION\ \ldots\ UNION\ P_n)$ and each P_i, for $1 \leq i \leq n$, is UNION-free [21]. Every *AND-UNION-FILTER* graph pattern P is equivalent to a graph pattern P', which is in UNION normal form [21].

2.4. *Worst-case Optimal Multi-way Join Algorithms*

In recent years, worst-case optimal multi-way join algorithms [10] have been the subject of many research works in the database literature. This is due to their runtime complexity being bounded by the worst-case size of the result of the input query [24] and their ability to achieve state-of-the-art performance in the evaluation of conjunctive queries (e.g., [12,13,11]). Their main characteristic is that, contrary to conventional binary joins that carry out joins on two operands at a time, their evaluation follows a variable elimination process. This evaluation process resembles a backtracking search, does not store any intermediate results and enables the incremental output of solution mappings. A worst-case optimal multi-way join algorithm for the evaluation of BGPs (conjunctive queries) based on Generic Join [25] is shown in Algorithm 1.

Table 2. Our mapping of $\mathcal{ALC}$ expressions to SPARQL queries built upon the mapping in [9].

$\mathcal{ALC}$ Class Expression C_i	SPARQL Graph Pattern $\tau(C_i, ?var)$
A	{ $?var$ `rdf:type` A . }
$\neg C$	{ $?var$ $?p$ $?o$. `FILTER NOT EXISTS` { $\tau(C, ?var)$ } }
$C_1 \sqcap \cdots \sqcap C_n$	{ $\tau(C_1, ?var)$. $\tau(C_2, ?var)$ . .... $\tau(C_n, ?var)$ }
$C_1 \sqcup \cdots \sqcup C_n$	{ { $\tau(C_1, ?var)$ } `UNION` ... `UNION` { $\tau(C_n, ?var)$ } }
$\exists r.C$	{ $?var$ r $?s$. $\tau(C, ?s)$ }
$\forall r.C$	{ $?var$ $?p$ $?o$. `FILTER NOT EXISTS` { $?var$ r $?s$. `FILTER NOT EXISTS` { $\tau(C, ?s)$ } } }

3. Mapping $\mathcal{ALC}$ Class Expressions to SPARQL Queries

As discussed in Section 2.2, one of the main computational bottlenecks for class expression learning algorithms is the execution of retrieval operations against reasoners. To alleviate this issue, Bin et al. [9] propose a mapping for the conversion of class expressions to SPARQL queries. This mapping is shown in the first six entries of Table 2—including the struck through text. These conversions enable learning algorithms to carry out retrieval operations against a triple store instead of a reasoner.

During the development of our multi-way join algorithm for class expression learning (Section 4), we identified an issue with the mapping presented in [9]. In particular, the SPARQL queries corresponding to class expressions of the type $\forall r.C$ did not return the expected results. As per the semantics of $\mathcal{ALC}$, the set of instances corresponding to a class expression $\forall r.C$ should also contain those individuals that do not have any r-successors [26, Remark 18]. For example, assuming a knowledge base capturing the concepts of family members, the set of individuals corresponding to the concept $\forall hasChild.Male$ should also contain those individuals that do not have any children. However, this was not the case with the SPARQL queries corresponding to such class expressions, as they did not take individuals not having any r-successors into account [9, Section 3 of the corresponding technical report]. To alleviate this issue we propose a new mapping for $\forall r.C$ expressions, which is presented in the last entry of Table 2. The proposed graph pattern for $\forall r.C$ class expressions is constructed using the concept equivalence rule $\forall r.C \equiv \neg\exists r.\neg C$ [26, Section 5.1]. For individuals that do not have any r-successors, the first `FILTER NOT EXISTS` is always evaluated to true. For individuals that have at least one r-successor, the first `FILTER NOT EXISTS` is evaluated to true, if all of their r-successors belong to C, which is tested by the seconds `FILTER NOT EXISTS`. Note that applying a combination of the transformation rules corresponding to $\neg C$ and $\exists r.C$ would yield a query that is semantically equivalent to the updated query.

The SPARQL queries shown in Table 2 use only those features of SPARQL that were discussed in Section 2.3. Furthermore, all of the queries that involve patterns of negation (`FILTER NOT EXISTS`) are fne-safe and hence, can be evaluated using the difference operator for sets of mappings. To prove that the newly proposed mapping for $\forall r.C$ follows the semantics of $\mathcal{ALC}$, the existing proofs for $\neg C$ and $\exists r.C$, which are provided in the technical report of [9], can be used.

4. Negation in Multi-way Joins

The efficiency of worst-case optimal multi-way join algorithms in evaluating basic graph pattern queries has been demonstrated in recent works (e.g., [12,13,11]). However, to the best of our knowledge, there have not been any efforts for SPARQL that include patterns of negation in multi-way join plans. In this section, we present our algorithm for the efficient evaluation of SPARQL queries corresponding to $\mathcal{ALC}$ class expressions. Our algorithm follows the sketch provided in [27] for the evaluation of Datalog rules containing negation and incorporates the evaluation of `FILTER NOT EXISTS` patterns in multi-way join plans. The two main ideas behind the proposed algorithm are the following. First, the evaluation of union graph patterns should take advantage of multi-way joins and their efficiency in evaluating basic graph patterns [28]. To this end, we rely on the definitions provided in Section 2.3 to rewrite each query generated by $\mathcal{ALC}$ class expressions to a semantically equivalent query that is in UNION normal form. Second, instead of waiting for a graph pattern to be fully evaluated, `FILTER NOT EXISTS` patterns should be evaluated as soon as their correlated variables (Section 2.3) are bound to a particular term.

4.1. Rewriting Rule for Negation and UNION Normal Form

As discussed in Section 2.3, a graph pattern $((P_1\ \mathit{FILTER}\ R)\ \ \mathit{AND}\ P_2)$ can be rewritten to a semantically equivalent graph pattern $((P_1\ \mathit{AND}\ P_2)\ \mathit{FILTER}\ R)$, if every variable of R is also a certain variable of P_1 or R and P_2 do not share any variables [23]. The above rewriting rule is also applicable to `FILTER NOT EXISTS` patterns. Note that the SPARQL standard treats `FILTER NOT EXISTS` patterns as filter expressions.

Proposition 4.1 *Let $P = ((P_1\ \mathit{FNE}\ P_3)\ \ \mathit{AND}\ P_2)$ and $P' = ((P_1\ \mathit{AND}\ P_2)\ \mathit{FNE}\ P_3)$ be fne-safe graph patterns. P and P' are semantically equivalent, if corVars$(P_1\ \mathit{FNE}\ P_3)$ = corVars$((P_1\ \mathit{AND}\ P_2)\ \mathit{FNE}\ P_3)$.*

Proof 4.1 *For $[\![P]\!]_G = [\![P']\!]_G$, we need $(([\![P_1]\!]_G \setminus [\![P_3]\!]_G) \bowtie [\![P_2]\!]_G) = (([\![P_1]\!]_G \bowtie [\![P_2]\!]_G) \setminus [\![P_3]\!]_G)$. As per the semantics (Section 2.3), for the equality to hold, we need $(dom([\![P_1]\!]_G) \cap dom([\![P_3]\!]_G)) = (dom([\![P_1]\!]_G \bowtie [\![P_2]\!]_G) \cap dom([\![P_3]\!]_G))$, which holds because corVars$(P_1$ $\mathit{FNE}\ P_3)$ = corVars$((P_1\ \mathit{AND}\ P_2)\ \mathit{FNE}\ P_3)$.*

Intuitively, for the equivalence to hold, any variable of P_2 that does not appear in P_1 should also not appear in P_3. To enable the rewriting of $P = ((P_1\ \mathit{FNE}\ P_3)\ \mathit{AND}\ P_2)$ to a semantically equivalent pattern $P' = ((P_1\ \mathit{AND}\ P_2)\ \mathit{FNE}\ P_3)$, we propose the replacement of each variable of P_3 that is not in *corVars*$(P_1\ \mathit{FNE}\ P_3)$ with a unique variable that is not used in P. This way, we ensure that P_2 and P_3 do not share any variables that do not appear in P_1.

By following the SPARQL standard and treating `FILTER NOT EXISTS` patterns as `FILTER` expressions, we can apply the UNION normal form provided for *AND-UNION-FILTER* graph patterns (Section 2.3) to SPARQL queries generated by $\mathcal{ALC}$ class expressions. By applying the UNION normal form and the rewriting rule proposed above to the queries of Table 2, we end up dealing with queries that are disjunctions of graph patterns, where each graph pattern is either a BGP or a set of triple patterns alongside patterns of negation. Our proposed algorithm, which is presented below, is able to evaluate the resulting queries by carrying out a series of multi-way joins.

Algorithm 2 Multi-Way Join for Class Expression Learning in $\mathcal{ALC}$

1: **function** MWJ(P, G, X) ▷ P: Graph Pattern, G: RDF Graph, X: Mapping
2: // P is a single graph pattern or a *UNION* of *UNION*-free graph patterns
3: **for all** UNION-free patterns P_i of P **do**
4: **if** P_i is a BGP **then yield all** GENERICJOIN(P_i, G, X) ▷ Algorithm 1
5: **else yield all** MWJFNE(P_i, G, X) ▷ P_i contains negation
6: **function** MWJFNE(P, G, X) ▷ P: Graph Pattern, G: RDF Graph, X: Mapping
7: $P' \leftarrow P$ ▷ Copy pattern to preserve original
8: **for all** *FNE* patterns P_i of P **do**
9: Let $P_i = P_l$ *FNE* P_r ▷ P_l is a set of triple patterns
10: **if** $corVars(P_i) = \emptyset$ **then** ▷ Correlated variables are evaluated (fne-safety)
11: **if** EVALFNE(P_r, G, X) is **false then**
12: **return** ▷ The current mapping X does not yield a solution mapping
13: **else** remove (FNE P_r) from P' ▷ successfully evaluated
14: // All *FNE* patterns that were evaluated returned **true** and were removed
15: **if** there are no more *FNE* patterns in P' **then**
16: **yield all** GENERICJOIN(P', G, X) and **return**
17: $?x \leftarrow$ a variable from $cVars(P')$ ▷ Select a certain variable to be evaluated
18: // Evaluate the selected variable $?x$ using the triple patterns of P'
19: $K \leftarrow \bigcap_{tp \in P' \mid ?x \in var(tp)} \{\mu(?x) \mid \mu \in [\![tp]\!]_G\}$
20: **for all** $k \in K$ **do** ▷ Iterate over the possible values of $?x$
21: $X(?x) \leftarrow k$ ▷ Store k in the solution mapping
22: $P'' \leftarrow$ assign k to all occurrences of $?x$ in the triple patterns of P'
23: **yield all** MWJFNE(P'', G, X) ▷ after yielding proceeds with the next k
24: **function** EVALFNE(P, G, X)
25: // Uses the values assigned to the correlated variables to evaluate P
26: $P' \leftarrow \forall ?v \in var(P) \cap dom(X)$, assign $X(?v)$ to $?v$ in the triple patterns of P
27: $X' \leftarrow$ new empty mapping ; $X'(?v) \leftarrow X(?v)$
28: **if** MWJ(P', G, X') yields a solution **then return false**
29: **else return true**

4.2. Multi-way Join Algorithm

The proposed algorithm for the evaluation of SPARQL queries generated by $\mathcal{ALC}$ class expressions is shown in Algorithm 2. The algorithm's entry point is the function `MWJ` (lines 1–5), which takes a graph pattern that is already in UNION normal form as input. `MWJ` iterates over all UNION-free graph patterns P_i of the input graph pattern P and for each P_i calls the appropriate function for its evaluation. If P_i is a BGP, it is evaluated by Generic Join (line 4), otherwise it is evaluated by the function `MWJFNE` (line 5), which is responsible for the evaluation of graph patterns containing `FILTER NOT EXISTS` patterns.

The function `MWJFNE` (lines 6–23) iterates first over the `FILTER NOT EXISTS` patterns ($P_i = P_l$ *FNE* P_r) of the provided graph pattern P (lines 8–13). For each P_i having its correlated variables evaluated (lines 11–13), the function `EvalFNE` is called (line 11). `EvalFNE` (lines 24–29) checks whether the current solution mapping X is a solution of P_i. This is done by evaluating P_r (line 28) after all the occurrences of the correlated variables of P_i are replaced with their corresponding term in the triple patterns of P_r (line 26). If the evaluation of P_r yields at least one solution, `EvalFNE` is evaluated to false, which leads to the active solution mapping in `MWJFNE` to be discarded (line 13). Recall that the mappings of P_l and P_r should not be compatible (Section 2.3). If all `FILTER NOT EXISTS` patterns are successfully evaluated, `MWJFNE` proceeds with the evaluation of P' (lines 15–23). Note that successfully evaluated `FILTER NOT EXISTS` patterns are removed from P' (line 13) and hence, are not evaluated multiple times. If P' is a BGP, it is evaluated by Generic Join (line 16). Otherwise, the evaluation proceeds in a similar fashion to Generic Join (lines 17-23). If there are remaining `FILTER NOT EXISTS` patterns in P', the evaluation focuses on the certain variables of P', i.e., on the variables appearing only in triple patterns (line 19). For each possible value of the selected certain variable (lines 20–23), `MWJFNE` is called recursively.

The proposed algorithm integrates negation in multi-way join plans by calling `MWJ` within `EvalFNE` (line 28). In addition, provided a solution mapping, it does not completely evaluate the right hand side of `FILTER NOT EXISTS` patterns. Instead, it terminates its evaluation once a solution mapping is found, thus avoiding storing intermediate results. The use of the UNION normal form may result in a larger number of joins. However, this can be beneficial, as the joins may limit the intermediate mappings generated by the original union patterns.

4.3. Implementation

We have implemented the proposed algorithm within the tensor-based triple store Tentris [13]. We chose Tentris because it supports multi-way joins [13] and achieves state-of-the-art performance in the evaluation of basic graph patterns [29]. However, Tentris is not able to evaluate SPARQL queries generated by $\mathcal{ALC}$ class expressions, due to its missing support for `FILTER NOT EXISTS` patterns. By implementing our proposed algorithm within Tentris, we further improve the state of the art, as demonstrated by the experimental results (Section 5). The performance of multi-way joins is affected by the order in which variables are evaluated [11]. Tentris dynamically selects a variable at each recursive step of the algorithm using cardinality estimations. We modified its selection process to take the number of `FILTER NOT EXISTS` patterns a particular variable appears into account to break ties (i.e., provided two variables with the same cardinality estimation, the one that appears in a `FILTER NOT EXISTS` pattern is selected). Last, we apply the UNION normal form to the provided queries while parsing them. Henceforth, we refer to our implementation as TentrisALC.

5. Experimental Results

We evaluated the performance of our implementation using SPARQL queries corresponding to $\mathcal{ALC}$ class expressions on five datasets of varying sizes. The experiments that are presented below were carried out on a Debian 10 server with an AMD EPYC 7282 CPU, 256GB RAM and a 2TB Samsung 970 EVO Plus SSD. Supplementary material—including datasets, binaries, queries, scripts, and configurations—is available online.[5]

[5] `https://github.com/dice-group/alc2sparql-bench`

5.1. Systems, Setup and Execution

As the learning of class expressions using SPARQL is carried out over HTTP [9], we compared the performance of TentrisALC against the performance of the following triple stores that provide a SPARQL compliant HTTP endpoint: (i) Blazegraph 2.1.6.RC, (ii) Fuseki 4.10.0, (iii) GraphDB 10.3.3, and (iv) Virtuoso 7.2.10. In our experiments, we also wanted to include MilleniumDB[6], commit: 442e650 [30], which uses multi-way joins for the evaluation of basic graph patterns. However, we did not include it, as it does not evaluate queries having union graph patterns within `FILTER NOT EXISTS` patterns correctly. Each triple store was configured following its respective documentation. The experiemnts were executed over HTTP using the benchmark execution framework IGUANA 3.3.3 [31]. For each dataset, each query was executed once during the warmup phase. After the warmup phase, the sets of queries were executed three consecutive times. The query timeout was set to three minutes. As in [29], we measured the performance of the triple stores using the following metrics: (i) QPS, i.e., the number of queries executed per second, (ii) pAvgQPS, i.e., the penalized average QPS and (iii) QMPH, i.e., the number of query mixes executed per hour. A query mix is a set or a multiset of queries. The metric QMPH captures the number of times a particular query mix is evaluated in an hour. This means that the lower the runtimes of individual queries are, the higher the QMPH value is. Queries that failed (e.g., timed out or returned an error code) are penalized with a runtime of three minutes.

5.2. Datasets and Queries

Our evaluation comprises five datasets (i.e., knowledge graphs). Four of these datasets, namely Carcinogenesis, Mutagenesis, Premier League and Vicodi, are frequently used to evaluate class expression learning algorithms (e.g., [7,8]) and are available in [8,32]. The largest of these datasets, namely Premier League, contains 2.1M triples. To evaluate the scalability of our approach, we used a subset of the English version of YAGO4 [33], which contains more than 40M triples. As in previous works that follow closed-world semantics (e.g., [9,7]), we first materialized the inferences of the knowledge graphs. Table 3 reports the statistics of the knowledge bases after the materialization process. For the class expression learning datasets, we generated 300 unique $\mathcal{ALC}$ class expressions using a slightly modified version of the learning problem generator of [8]. This modified version does not prioritize simple class expressions. For YAGO4English, due to the generator not scaling to its size, we randomly created 300 unique class expressions by recursively applying the construction rules of $\mathcal{ALC}$. During the generation of class expressions for YAGO4English, we focused only on the properties of the dataset that come from schemas.org (i.e., we did not consider properties coming from bioschemas.org or the RDF/S vocabulary). Schema.org has a richer taxonomy than bioschemas.org, which resulted in $\forall r.C$ and $\exists r.C$ class expressions being more diverse. All class expressions were mapped to SPARQL queries using the mapping of Table 2. For YAGO4English, we ended up having to remove eight queries, as IGUANA was not able to handle them properly (non-escaped characters in IRIs). The last column of Table 3 shows the number of queries having at least one `FILTER NOT EXISTS` pattern.

[6]`https://github.com/MillenniumDB/MillenniumDB`

Table 3. The statistics of the datasets used in the evaluation

	#Triples	#Distinct Subjects	#Distinct Predicates	#Distinct Objects	# Queries \w Negation
Carcinogenesis	157K	22.5K	25	23.2K	169
Mutagenesis	96K	14.2K	16	15K	208
Premier League	2.1M	11.5K	217	12.5K	209
Vicodi	405K	33.4K	14	35.2K	137
YAGO4English	40.2M	7.2M	104	3M	209

Table 4. The results on class expression learning datasets (cold run). The column failed reports the number of queries for which the corresponding system failed (e.g., timed out) at least once.

	Carcinogenesis			Mutagenesis		
	QMPH	pAvgQPS	failed	QMPH	pAvgQPS	failed
Blazegraph	68.122	49.221	0	40.911	31.637	0
Fuseki	43.426	96.789	0	28.580	58.097	0
GraphDB	28.003	139.800	0	21.156	102.190	0
TentrisALC (ours)	**1410.674**	**792.274**	**0**	**1128.076**	**545.604**	**0**
Virtuoso	148.622	372.766	0	113.312	268.588	0
	Premier League			**Vicodi**		
	QMPH	pAvgQPS	failed	QMPH	pAvgQPS	failed
Blazegraph	16.832	44.261	0	2.508	48.152	0
Fuseki	3.254	85.898	2	1.399	101.890	9
GraphDB	5.708	139.975	0	1.756	128.904	5
TentrisALC (ours)	**2463.874**	**902.343**	**0**	**715.107**	**773.800**	**0**
Virtuoso	82.245	390.305	0	6.227	411.529	0

5.3. Results and Discussion

The results of our evaluation on the datasets for class expression learning are shown in Tables 4 and 5. The results on YAGO4English are shown in Table 6. Figure 1 captures the performance of the systems w.r.t their penalized QPS across all datasets. Many queries of YAGO4English return more than 7M results, due to their corresponding class expression covering the whole set of individuals. As Virtuoso has a limit of 2^{20} results [13], we did not evaluate it on YAGO4English.

The results show that TentrisALC achieves the highest pAvgQPS, median penalized QPS, and QMPH values across all datasets. To ensure the that difference in the performance is statistically significant, we performed the Wilcoxon signed-rank test using the penalized QPS values achieved by each system in each query. The null hypothesis (i.e., the performances of TentrisALC and the baseline systems come from the same distribution) was rejected for all systems in all datasets (p-value $p < 0.001$).

The scalabality of our approach can already be observed in the datasets for class expression learning. Table 5 shows that, in the smaller datasets for class expression learning, TentrisALC achieves a value of QMPH that is 10 times higher than the sec-

Table 5. The results on class expression learning datasets (warm runs). The column failed reports the number of queries for which the corresponding system failed (e.g., timed out) at least once.

	Carcinogenesis			Mutagenesis		
	QMPH	pAvgQPS	failed	QMPH	pAvgQPS	failed
Blazegraph	72.920	58.134	0	42.615	37.090	0
Fuseki	45.509	133.754	0	28.940	82.716	0
GraphDB	31.263	246.155	0	22.802	162.238	0
TentrisALC (ours)	**1605.557**	**1571.377**	**0**	**1224.473**	**1015.727**	**0**
Virtuoso	149.928	734.093	0	114.822	532.871	0
	Premier League			Vicodi		
	QMPH	pAvgQPS	failed	QMPH	pAvgQPS	failed
Blazegraph	17.303	51.415	0	2.524	58.075	0
Fuseki	3.237	110.457	2	1.381	144.729	14
GraphDB	5.823	257.314	0	1.763	220.353	5
TentrisALC (ours)	**3176.005**	**1984.633**	**0**	**761.052**	**1554.764**	**0**
Virtuoso	84.486	1150.088	0	5.991	762.763	0

Table 6. The results on the largest dataset, namely YAGO4English. The column failed reports the number of queries for which the corresponding system failed (e.g., timed out) at least once. Virtuoso is not included due to its hard limit of 2^{20} results.

	YAGO4English (cold run)			YAGO4English (warm runs)		
	QMPH	pAvgQPS	failed	QMPH	pAvgQPS	failed
Blazegraph	0.131	18.275	58	0.131	25.985	66
Fuseki	0.116	36.425	168	0.116	66.201	168
GraphDB	0.123	46.120	161	0.123	100.297	161
TentrisALC (ours)	**1.342**	**207.281**	**0**	**1.351**	**435.361**	**0**

ond best system, namely Virtuoso. In Premier League and Vicodi, TentrisALC performs 37 and 126 times better than Virtuoso in terms of QMPH, respectively. This is due to TentrisALC being able to efficiently evaluate queries having `FILTER NOT EXISTS` patterns. More specifically, in Vicodi, TentrisALC achieves a QMPH value that is 7.6 times higher than the second best system (Virtuoso) in the set of queries that do not have any `FILTER NOT EXISTS` patterns. In the set of queries that contain negation, TentrisALC achieves a QMPH value that is 128 times higher than the second best value (Virtuoso). This shows that the overall results are mostly affected by the systems' ability to efficiently evaluate queries with `FILTER NOT EXISTS` patterns. This observation becomes more evident in YAGO4English (Table 6), where all systems apart from TentrisALC timed out in multiple queries. In particular, Fuseki and GraphDB timed out in more than half of the queries. More importantly, the timeouts occurred only in queries that contain `FILTER NOT EXISTS` patterns. As mentioned earlier, many queries in YAGO4English return more than 7M results. In queries with large result sets, the runtime can be heavily impacted by the results' enumeration. An example of a class expression that captures the efficiency of our approach is $\neg(\forall exampleOfWork.Prueba\_Villafranca\_de\_Ordizia)$. The corresponding SPARQL query includes three nested `FILTER NOT EXISTS` patterns and

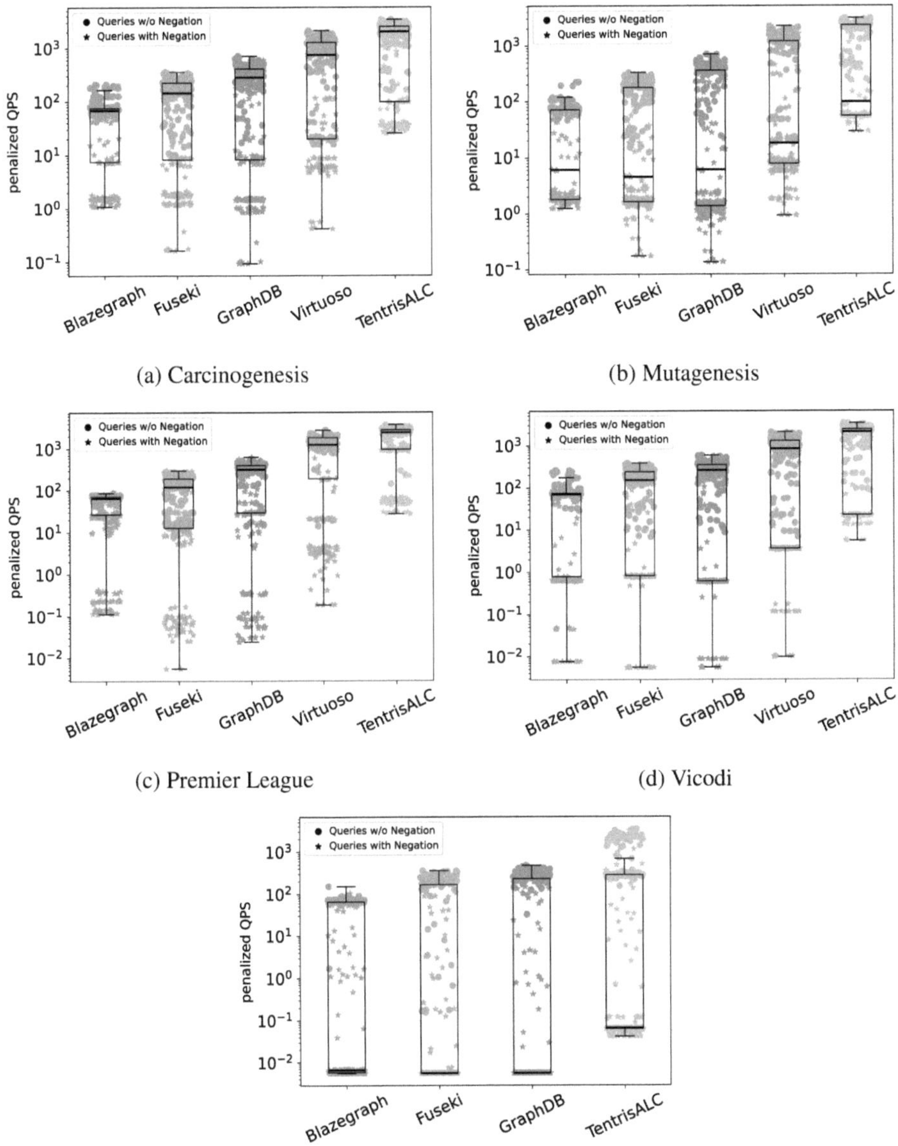

(a) Carcinogenesis

(b) Mutagenesis

(c) Premier League

(d) Vicodi

(e) YAGO4English

Figure 1. Performance of triple stores in terms of penalized QPS (warm runs).

returns only 161 solutions (i.e., the results' enumeration did not impact the query's execution time). TentrisALC required 8.3 seconds on average to evaluate this query, whereas all other systems timed out.

The efficiency of our approach lies in its ability to evaluate `FILTER NOT EXISTS` patterns without having to materialize intermediate results and its ability to terminate the evaluation of such patterns once a single mapping is found. Regarding the size of the datasets, to the best of our knowledge, recent works on class expression learning have focused only on small scale datasets that contain up to a few million triples (e.g., Premier League). As demonstrated above, our approach is able to scale to large datasets and we believe that it will enable learning algorithms to be deployed on large scale knowledge graphs.

6. Related Work

Class expression learning has been extensively investigated (e.g., [34,3,35]). In recent years, several works have focused on accelerating the process of learning class expressions. For instance, Westphal et al. [19] accelerate class expression learning by introducing a heuristic function that is based on simulated annealing. With their meta-heuristics, they are able to reduce the number of instance retrieval operations that are required to reach a goal concept. Kouagou et al. [8] accelerate class expression learning by accurately predicting lengths of possible goal concepts. By this, they avoid instance retrieval operations on lengthy concepts. In [18], the authors employ deep reinforcement learning to learn non-myopic heuristic functions, i.e., heuristic functions that take future rewards into account. These non-myopic heuristic functions accelerate class expression learning, as they are able to efficiently steer the search process towards goal states. Our work builds upon [9] that showed that class expression learning can be accelerated by converting class expressions to SPARQL queries. Our work focuses on improving the runtimes of retrieval operations and hence can be used in combination with the approaches described above.

Hogan et al. [11] were the first to formalize worst-case optimal join algorithms for the evaluation of basic graph pattern SPARQL queries. Several works have employed such algorithms for the evaluation of conjunctive queries [12,13,11] and demonstrated their efficiency. Recently, a multi-way join algorithm for the evaluation of conjunctive regular path queries based on the evaluation process of worst-case optimal join algorithms was proposed in [28]. This algorithm also makes use of the UNION normal form for AND-UNION patterns (i.e., it does not consider filters). One of the first worst-case optimal multi-way join algorithms was presented in [27]. As mentioned in Section 4, a sketch for the evaluation of Datalog rules containing negation is provided in [27]. However, to the best of our knowledge, there have not been any works for SPARQL that integrate the evaluation of negation in multi-way join plans.

7. Conclusion And Future Work

We presented a multi-way join algorithm for the evaluation of SPARQL queries corresponding to $\mathcal{ALC}$ class expressions. The main characteristic of our algorithm is the inclusion of `FILTER NOT EXISTS` patterns (i.e., negation) in multi-way join plans. Its purpose is to accelerate class expression learning in $\mathcal{ALC}$ by reducing the runtimes of instance retrieval operations. The experimental results on five datasets show that our implementation outperforms its competition across all datasets and that it is the only one scaling to the largest dataset, which contains more than 40M triples. In the future, we will extend our approach to support more expressive description logics (e.g., $\mathcal{SROIQ}$).

References

[1] Burnett M. Explaining AI: fairly? well? In: Proceedings of the 25th International Conference on Intelligent User Interfaces; 2020. p. 1-2.

[2] d'Amato C. Machine Learning for the Semantic Web: Lessons learnt and next research directions. Semantic Web. 2020;11(1):195-203.

[3] Lehmann J. Learning OWL Class Expressions. vol. 6 of Studies on the Semantic Web. IOS Press; 2010.

[4] Sarker MK, Hitzler P. Efficient Concept Induction for Description Logics. In: The Thirty-Third AAAI Conference on Artificial Intelligence, AAAI 2019, The Thirty-First Innovative Applications of Artificial Intelligence Conference, IAAI 2019, The Ninth AAAI Symposium on Educational Advances in Artificial Intelligence, EAAI 2019, Honolulu, Hawaii, USA, January 27 - February 1, 2019; 2019. p. 3036-43.

[5] Cao J, Fang J, Meng Z, Liang S. Knowledge Graph Embedding: A Survey from the Perspective of Representation Spaces. ACM Comput Surv. 2024;56(6):159:1-159:42. Available from: `https://doi.org/10.1145/3643806`.

[6] Demir C, Ngomo ACN. Neuro-symbolic class expression learning. In: Proceedings of the Thirty-Second International Joint Conference on Artificial Intelligence; 2023. p. 3624-32.

[7] Heindorf S, Blübaum L, Düsterhus N, Werner T, Golani VN, Demir C, et al. EvoLearner: Learning Description Logics with Evolutionary Algorithms. In: WWW '22: The ACM Web Conference 2022, Virtual Event, Lyon, France, April 25 - 29, 2022. ACM; 2022. p. 818-28.

[8] Kouagou NJ, Heindorf S, Demir C, Ngomo AN. Learning Concept Lengths Accelerates Concept Learning in ALC. In: The Semantic Web - 19th International Conference, ESWC 2022, Hersonissos, Crete, Greece, May 29 - June 2, 2022, Proceedings. vol. 13261 of Lecture Notes in Computer Science; 2022. p. 236-52.

[9] Bin S, Bühmann L, Lehmann J, Ngomo AN. Towards SPARQL-Based Induction for Large-Scale RDF Data Sets. In: ECAI 2016 - 22nd European Conference on Artificial Intelligence, 29 August-2 September 2016, The Hague, The Netherlands - Including Prestigious Applications of Artificial Intelligence (PAIS 2016). vol. 285 of Frontiers in Artificial Intelligence and Applications; 2016. p. 1551-2.

[10] Ngo HQ, Porat E, Ré C, Rudra A. Worst-case Optimal Join Algorithms. J ACM. 2018:16:1-16:40.

[11] Hogan A, Riveros C, Rojas C, Soto A. A Worst-Case Optimal Join Algorithm for SPARQL. In: The Semantic Web - ISWC 2019 - 18th International Semantic Web Conference, Auckland, New Zealand, October 26-30, 2019, Proceedings, Part I. vol. 11778 of Lecture Notes in Computer Science. Springer; 2019. p. 258-75.

[12] Arroyuelo D, Hogan A, Navarro G, Reutter JL, Rojas-Ledesma J, Soto A. Worst-Case Optimal Graph Joins in Almost No Space. In: SIGMOD '21: International Conference on Management of Data, Virtual Event, China, June 20-25, 2021; 2021. p. 102-14.

[13] Bigerl A, Conrads F, Behning C, Sherif MA, Saleem M, Ngomo AN. Tentris - A Tensor-Based Triple Store. In: The Semantic Web - ISWC 2020 - 19th International Semantic Web Conference, Athens, Greece, November 2-6, 2020, Proceedings, Part I. vol. 12506 of Lecture Notes in Computer Science; 2020. p. 56-73.

[14] Karalis N, Bigerl A, Demir C, Heidrich L, Ngonga Ngomo AC. Evaluating Negation with Multi-way Joins Accelerates Class Expression Learning. In: Machine Learning and Knowledge Discovery in Databases. Research Track. Springer Nature Switzerland; 2024. p. 199-216.

[15] Baader F, Calvanese D, McGuinness DL, Nardi D, Patel-Schneider PF, editors. The Description Logic Handbook: Theory, Implementation, and Applications. Cambridge University Press; 2003.

[16] Schmidt-Schauß M, Smolka G. Attributive concept descriptions with complements. Artificial intelligence. 1991;48(1):1-26.

[17] Hogan A, Blomqvist E, Cochez M, d'Amato C, de Melo G, Gutiérrez C, et al. Knowledge Graphs. ACM Comput Surv. 2021:71:1-71:37.

[18] Demir C, Ngomo AN. Neuro-Symbolic Class Expression Learning. In: Proceedings of the Thirty-Second International Joint Conference on Artificial Intelligence, IJCAI 2023, 19th-25th August 2023, Macao, SAR, China; 2023. p. 3624-32.

[19] Westphal P, Vahdati S, Lehmann J. A Simulated Annealing Meta-heuristic for Concept Learning in Description Logics. In: International Conference on Inductive Logic Programming. Springer; 2021. p. 266-81.

[20] Lehmann J, Auer S, Bühmann L, Tramp S. Class expression learning for ontology engineering. J Web Semant. 2011;9(1):71-81.

[21] Pérez J, Arenas M, Gutierrez C. Semantics and complexity of SPARQL. ACM Trans Database Syst. 2009;34(3):16:1-16:45.

[22] Angles R, Gutierrez C. Negation in SPARQL. In: Proceedings of the 10th Alberto Mendelzon International Workshop on Foundations of Data Management, Panama City, Panama, May 8-10, 2016. vol. 1644 of CEUR Workshop Proceedings; 2016. .

[23] Schmidt M, Meier M, Lausen G. Foundations of SPARQL query optimization. In: Segoufin L, editor. Database Theory - ICDT 2010, 13th International Conference, Lausanne, Switzerland, March 23-25, 2010, Proceedings. ACM International Conference Proceeding Series. ACM; 2010. p. 4-33.

[24] Atserias A, Grohe M, Marx D. Size Bounds and Query Plans for Relational Joins. In: 49th Annual IEEE Symposium on Foundations of Computer Science, FOCS 2008, October 25-28, 2008, Philadelphia, PA, USA; 2008. p. 739-48.

[25] Ngo HQ, Ré C, Rudra A. Skew strikes back: new developments in the theory of join algorithms. SIGMOD Rec. 2013;42(4):5-16.

[26] Rudolph S. Foundations of Description Logics. In: Reasoning Web. Semantic Technologies for the Web of Data - 7th International Summer School 2011, Galway, Ireland, August 23-27, 2011, Tutorial Lectures. vol. 6848 of Lecture Notes in Computer Science. Springer; 2011. p. 76-136.

[27] Veldhuizen TL. Triejoin: A Simple, Worst-Case Optimal Join Algorithm. In: Proc. 17th International Conference on Database Theory (ICDT), Athens, Greece, March 24-28, 2014. OpenProceedings.org; 2014. p. 96-106.

[28] Karalis N, Bigerl A, Heidrich L, Sherif MA, Ngomo AN. Efficient Evaluation of Conjunctive Regular Path Queries Using Multi-way Joins. In: The Semantic Web - 21st International Conference, ESWC 2024, Hersonissos, Crete, Greece, May 26-30, 2024, Proceedings, Part I. vol. 14664 of Lecture Notes in Computer Science. Springer; 2024. p. 218-35.

[29] Bigerl A, Conrads L, Behning C, Saleem M, Ngomo AN. Hashing the Hypertrie: Space- and Time-Efficient Indexing for SPARQL in Tensors. In: The Semantic Web - ISWC 2022 - 21st International Semantic Web Conference, Virtual Event, October 23-27, 2022, Proceedings. vol. 13489 of Lecture Notes in Computer Science. Springer; 2022. p. 57-73.

[30] Vrgoč D, Rojas C, Angles R, Arenas M, Arroyuelo D, Buil-Aranda C, et al. MillenniumDB: An Open-Source Graph Database System. Data Intelligence. 2023:1-39.

[31] Conrads F, Lehmann J, Saleem M, Morsey M, Ngomo AN. Iguana: A Generic Framework for Benchmarking the Read-Write Performance of Triple Stores. In: The Semantic Web - ISWC 2017 - 16th International Semantic Web Conference, Vienna, Austria, October 21-25, 2017, Proceedings, Part II. vol. 10588 of Lecture Notes in Computer Science. Springer; 2017. p. 48-65.

[32] Westphal P, Bühmann L, Bin S, Jabeen H, Lehmann J. SML-Bench - A benchmarking framework for structured machine learning. Semantic Web. 2019;10(2):231-45.

[33] Tanon TP, Weikum G, Suchanek FM. YAGO 4: A Reason-able Knowledge Base. In: The Semantic Web - 17th International Conference, ESWC 2020, Heraklion, Crete, Greece, May 31-June 4, 2020, Proceedings. vol. 12123 of Lecture Notes in Computer Science. Springer; 2020. p. 583-96.

[34] Fanizzi N, d'Amato C, Esposito F. DL-FOIL Concept Learning in Description Logics. In: Inductive Logic Programming, 18th International Conference, ILP 2008, Prague, Czech Republic, September 10-12, 2008, Proceedings. vol. 5194 of Lecture Notes in Computer Science. Springer; 2008. p. 107-21.

[35] Tran AC, Dietrich J, Guesgen HW, Marsland S. Parallel Symmetric Class Expression Learning. J Mach Learn Res. 2017;18:64:1-64:34.

Handbook on Neurosymbolic AI and Knowledge Graphs
P. Hitzler et al. (Eds.)
IOS Press, 2025

doi:10.3233/FAIA250208

Geometric Relational Embeddings: Progress and Prospects

Bo XIONG [1], Mojtaba NAYYERI [2], Ming JIN [3], Yunjie HE [4], Michael COCHEZ [5], Shirui PAN [6], Steffen STAAB [7]

Abstract. Geometric relational embeddings map relational data as geometric objects that combine vector information suitable for machine learning and structured/symbolic information suitable for symbolic reasoning, typically in low dimensions. Their preservation of relational structures and their appealing properties and interpretability have led to their uptake for multiple neuro-symbolic reasoning tasks such as knowledge graph completion, ontology and hierarchy reasoning, logical query answering, and hierarchical multi-label classification. We survey methods that underly geometric relational embeddings and categorize them based on (i) the embedding geometries that are used to represent the data; and (ii) the relational reasoning tasks that they aim to improve. We identify the desired properties (i.e., inductive biases) of each kind of embedding and discuss some potential future work.

Keywords. Relational Embeddings, Neuro-Symbolic AI, Relational Reasoning, Knowledge Representation and Reasoning, Geometric Embeddings

1. Introduction

Vector embeddings map objects to a low-dimensional vector space. Vector embeddings have been developed to learn representations of objects that allow for distinguishing relevant differences and ignoring irrelevant variations between objects. When vector embeddings are used to embed structural/relational data, they fail to represent key properties of relational data that cannot be easily modeled in a plain, low-dimensional vector space. For example, relational data may have been defined by applying set operators such as set inclusion and exclusion [1], logical operations such as negation [2], or they may exhibit relational patterns like the symmetry of relations [3] and structural patterns (e.g., trees and cycles) [4, 5]. These types of data are rather "symbolic" and cannot be vectorized in a plain vector space without losing the symbolic information.

Going beyond plain vector embeddings, *geometric relational embeddings* replace the vector representations with more advanced geometric objects, such as convex regions [6, 7, 1], density functions [8, 2], elements of hyperbolic manifolds [4, 5, 9], and their

[1] Bo Xiong is with University of Stuttgart, Germany. Email: bo.xiong@ki.uni-stuttgart.de.
[2] Mojtaba Nayyeri is with University of Stuttgart, Germany.
[3] Ming Jin is with Griffith University, Australia
[4] Yunjie He is with Bosch Center for AI and University of Stuttgart, Germany.
[5] Michael Cochez is with VU Amsterdam, The Netherlands.
[6] Shirui Pan is with Griffith University, Australia.
[7] Steffen Staab is with University of Stuttgart, Germany and University of Southampton, UK.

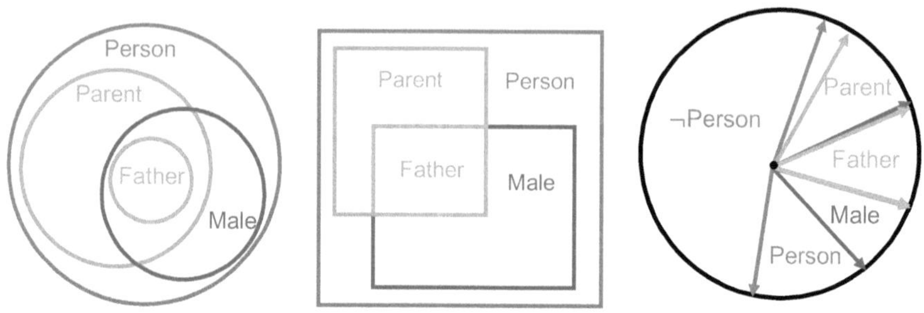

Figure 1. An illustration of region-based embeddings. (a) Ball embedding represents concepts as n-ball allowing for modeling set inclusion; (b) Box embedding represents concepts as boxes that further support intersectional closure; (c) Cone embedding represents concepts as cones that support intersectional and negation closures.

combinations [10]. Geometric relational embeddings provide a rich geometric inductive bias for modeling relational/structured data. For example, embedding objects as convex regions allows for modeling not only similarity but also set-based and logical operators such as set inclusion, set intersection [1] and logical negation [11] (cf. Figure 1) while representing data on non-Euclidean manifolds allows for capturing complex structural patterns, such as representing hierarchies in hyperbolic space [4].

Geometric relational embeddings have been successfully applied in many relational reasoning tasks including but not limited to knowledge graph (KG) completion [3, 5], ontology/hierarchy reasoning [12, 1], hierarchical multi-label classification (HMC) [13, 14], and logical query answering [2]. Different downstream applications require varying capabilities from underlying embeddings and, hence, appropriate choice requires a sufficiently precise understanding of embeddings' characteristics and task requirements.

In this paper, we identify the desired capabilities of geometric relational embeddings on different relational reasoning tasks. We conduct a comprehensive survey on the methods of geometric relational embeddings. The methods are classified based on the underlying geometries used to represent objects as well as the targeted relational reasoning tasks. Figure 2 shows a taxonomy of these methods. We systematically discuss and compare the inductive biases of different embeddings and discuss the applications in four relational reasoning tasks: KG completion, ontology and hierarchy completion, hierarchical multi-label classification, and logical query answering.

2. Preliminaries and Problem Definition

Relational reasoning aims to infer missing relationships among different objects, e.g., links over entities in KGs (i.e., KG completion), subsumption relations between classes (i.e., ontology completion), category relations between instances and classes in a taxonomy (i.e., HMC), links between entities and queries (i.e., logical query answering), and so on. These tasks take relational data as input and output the missing relationships. We describe input relational data as a directed edge-labeled graph or multi-relational graph [15].

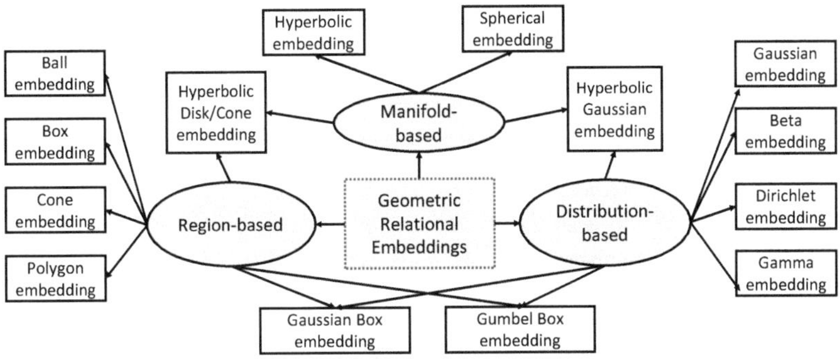

Figure 2. A systematic categorization of geometric relational embeddings. The methods for geometric relational embeddings can be classified into distribution-based, region-based, and manifold-based. Each two of them can be combined and form a hybrid method, e.g., the hyperbolic cone is a combination of hyperbolic (manifold-based) and cone embedding (region-based).

Definition 1 (directed edge-labeled graph)**.** *A directed edge-labeled graph is a tuple $G = (V, E, L)$, where $V \subseteq$ **Con** is a set of nodes, $L \subseteq$ **Con** is a set of edge labels, and $E \subseteq V \times L \times V$ is a set of edges, where **Con** denote a countably infinite set of constants.*

Such data structures can be used to represent a knowledge graph. For example, in a KG about proteins, nodes represent proteins and edges represent (binary) interactions between proteins. Using reserved keywords, such as defined for RDFS or OWL [16], directed edge-labeled graphs can also be used to define ontologies. E.g., in the gene ontology, nodes represent gene functional concepts and edges represent (binary) relations between them. Ontology-based KGs comprise facts about entities and complex concepts definitions.

Classical logical reasoning on structured knowledge remains unchallenged when it comes to sound and complete deduction of new facts from given, consistent relational data. Geometric relational embeddings operate on the premise that relational data is incomplete and some missing facts must be derived by induction or transduction. To this end, all geometric relational embeddings establish principles of analogy. Embeddings of relations are sought such that all the pairs of nodes in a relation are located in analogous manner to each other in geometric space. Then, key functional capabilities of geometric relational embeddings include the querying for similar nodes and the completion of triple patterns in the absence of directly matching triples. If a triple $(h, r, t) \notin E$ is plausible, then queries in form of the triple patterns $(h, r, ?t)$ or $(h, ?r, t)$ should bind the query variable $?t$ to t or the query variable $?r$ to r, respectively.

Desiderata. The key functional capability of a geometric relational embedding model is based on the proper judgement of plausibility, whose quality benefits if relational properties and patterns can be represented geometrically in the embedding space as follows: 1) **similarity:** an embedding model should produce similar embeddings for similar entities/relations; 2) **uncertainty:** an embedding model should capture the *degree of truthfulness*; 3) **set theory:** an embedding model should capture set-theoretical semantics including set inclusion, set exclusion, set overlap, and set difference; 4) **logical operations:** an embedding model should capture logical connectives such as logical conjunction, negation, and union. 5) **relational patterns:** an embedding model should

Table 1. The desiderata of different relational reasoning tasks.

	properties	hierarchy	KG	ontology	HMC	query
similarity		✓	✓	✓	✓	✓
uncertainty		✓	✓	✓	✓	✓
set theory	inclusion	×	×	✓	✓	✓
	exclusion	×	×	✓	✓	✓
	overlap	×	×	✓	✓	✓
	difference	×	×	✓	✓	✓
logical	intersection	×	×	✓	×	✓
	union	×	×	✓	×	✓
	negation	×	×	✓	×	✓
relational	symmetry	×	✓	✓	×	✓
	inversion	×	✓	✓	×	✓
	composition	×	✓	✓	×	✓
	transitivity	✓	✓	✓	✓	✓
structural	cycles	×	✓	×	×	✓
	trees	✓	✓	✓	✓	✓
	tree-cycle	✓	✓	✓	×	✓

capture some relational patterns like symmetry, inversion, composition, and transitivity; and 6) **structural patterns:** an embedding model should capture structural/topological patterns such as trees, cycles, and their combination. The desiderata differ w.r.t different relational reasoning tasks. For example, logical operations only matter when dealing with ontologies, and queries with conjunction and negation might exist. Table 1 summarizes the desiderata of each relational reasoning task.

3. Geometric Relational Embeddings

As Table 2 summarizes, the methodologies can be divided into four categories based on the underlying geometries.

3.1. Distribution-based Embeddings

Probability distributions provide a rich geometry of the latent space. Their density can be interpreted as soft regions and it allows us to model uncertainty, asymmetry, set inclusion/exclusion, entailment, and so on.

Gaussian embeddings. Word2Gauss [49] maps words to multi-dimensional Gaussian distributions over a latent embedding space such that the linguistic properties of the words are captured by the relationships between the distributions. A Gaussian $\mathcal{N}(\mu,\Sigma)$ is parameterized by a mean vector μ and a covariance matrix Σ (usually a diagonal matrix for the sake of computing efficiency). The model can be optimized by an energy function $-E\left(\mathcal{N}_i,\mathcal{N}_j\right)$ that is equivalent to the KL-divergence $D_{\mathrm{KL}}\left(\mathcal{N}_j \| \mathcal{N}_i\right)$ defined as

$$D_{\mathrm{KL}}\left(\mathcal{N}_j \| \mathcal{N}_i\right) = \int_{x \in \mathbb{R}^n} \mathcal{N}\left(x;\mu_i,\Sigma_i\right) \log \frac{\mathcal{N}\left(x;\mu_j,\Sigma_j\right)}{\mathcal{N}\left(x;\mu_i,\Sigma_i\right)} dx. \quad (1)$$

Table 2. Summary of the geometric relational embedding methods.

Category	Method	Embedding	Task	Institute	Venue	Year
Distribution-based	KG2E [17]	Gauss	KG	CAS	CIKM	2015
	TransG [18]	Gauss	KG	Tsinghua	ACL	2016
	HCGE [19]	Gauss	HMC	Sorbonne	ECML PKDD	2016
	PERM [20]	Gauss	query	Virginia Tec	NeurIPS	2021
	BetaE [2]	Beta	query	Stanford	NeurIPS	2020
	DiriE [8]	Dirichlet	KG	BUPT	WWW	2022
	GammE [21]	Gamma	query	OPPO	EMNLP	2022
Region-based	ELEm [6]	Ball	ontology	KAUST	IJCAI	2019
	[22]	Ball	hierarchy	U. Bonn	ICLR	2019
	Box Lattice [12]	Box	hierarchy	UMass	ACL	2018
	Joint Box [23]	Box	hierarchy	UMass	AKBC	2020
	BEUrRE [24]	Box	KG	UCLA	NAACL-HLT	2021
	BoxE [3]	Box	KG	Oxford	NeurIPS	2021
	Box4Type [25]	Box	HMC	UT Austin	ACL	2021
	Quer2Box [7]	Box	query	Stanford	ICLR	2019
	MBM [13]	Box	HMC	UMass	ICLR	2022
	BoxEL [1]	Box	ontology	USTUTT	ISWC	2022
	BC-BOX [26]	Box	hierarchy	UMass	NeurIPS	2022
	ShrinkE [27]	Box	KGs	USTUTT	ACL	2023
	OE [28]	Cone	hierarchy	U. Toronto	ICLR	2016
	Cone Semmantic [29]	Cone	ontology	U. Lubeck	IJCAI	2021
	ConE [11]	Cone	query	CAS	NeurIPS	2021
	ExpressE [30]	Polygons	KGs	TU Vienna	ICLR	2023
Manifold-based	5∗E [31]	Spherical	KG	U. Bonn	AAAI	2020
	MuRS [32]	Spherical	KG	UIUC	WWW	2021
	MuRP [33]	Hyperbolic	KG	Edinburgh	NeurIPS	2019
	AttH [4]	Hyperbolic	KG	Stanford	ACL	2020
	HyperIM [34]	Hyperbolic	HMC	BJTU	AAAI	2020
	HBE [35]	Hyperbolic	KG	Southeast	EMNLP	2021
	HyboNet [36]	Hyperbolic	KG	Tsinghua	ACL	2022
	HMI [14]	Hyperbolic	HMC	USTUTT	NeurIPS	2022
	MuRMP [32]	Mixed	KG	UIUC	WWW	2021
	GIE [37]	Mixed	KG	CAS	EMNLP	2022
	UltraE [5]	Mixed	KG	USTUTT	KDD	2022
	DGS [38]	Mixed	KG	UCLA	KDD	2022
	NestE [39]	Mixed	KG	USTUTT	AAAI	2024
Hybrid	Smooth Box [40]	Gauss+Box	hierarchy	UMass	ICLR	2019
	Gumbel Box [41]	Gumbel+Box	hierarchy	UMass	NeurIPS	2020
	HWN [42]	Hyperbolic+Gauss	hierarchy	U. Tokyo	ICML	2019
	ROWN [43]	Hyperbolic+Gauss	hierarchy	POSTECH	NeurIPS	2022
	HypDisk [10]	Hyperbolic+Ball	hierarchy	LAPRA	ICML	2019
	HypE [44]	Hyperbolic+Box	query	Virginia Tech	WWW	2021
	HypCone [45]	Hyperbolic+Cone	hierarchy	ETH	ICML	2018
	ConeE [46]	Hyperbolic+Cone	KG	Tsinghua	NeurIPS	2021
	[47]	Hyperbolic+Cone	HMC	ETH	CVPR	2020
	PolygonE [48]	Hyperbolic+Polygon	KG	CAS	AAAI	2022

KG2E [17] extends this idea to KG embedding by mapping entities and relations as Gaussians. Given a fact (h,r,t), the scoring function is defined as $f(h,r,t) = \frac{1}{2}\left(\mathscr{D}_{\mathrm{KL}}(\mathscr{N}_h, \mathscr{N}_r) + \mathscr{D}_{\mathrm{KL}}(\mathscr{N}_r, \mathscr{N}_t)\right)$. The covariances of entity and relation embeddings allow us to model uncertainties in KGs. While modeling the scores of triples as KL-divergence allows us to capture asymmetry. TransG [18] generalizes KG2E to a Gaussian mixture distribution to deal with multiple relation semantics revealed by the entity pairs.

For example, the relation HasPart has at least two latent semantics: composition-related as (*Table, HasPart, Leg*) and location-related as (*Atlantics, HasPart, NewYorkBay*).

Dirichlet embeddings. DiriE [8] embeds entities as Dirichlet distributions $f(x|\alpha) = \frac{1}{\mathrm{B}(\alpha)}\prod_{i=1}^{d} x_i^{\alpha_i - 1}$ where $\alpha = (\alpha_1, \alpha_2, \cdots, \alpha_d) > 0$ is the distribution parameter, $\mathrm{B}(\alpha) = \frac{\prod_{i=1}^{d}\Gamma(\alpha_i)}{\Gamma(\sum_{i=1}^{d}\alpha_i)}$ and $\Gamma(\alpha) = \int_0^\infty t^{\alpha-1}e^{-t}dt$ are the multivariate beta function and Gamma function, respectively. DiriE embeds relations as multinomial distributions $f(x|\mu) = \frac{\Gamma(\sum_i \mu_i + 1)}{\prod_i \Gamma(\mu_i + 1)}\prod_{i=1}^{k} x_i^{\mu_i}$ where $\mu_i \in \mathbb{R}^+$is the distribution parameter. Given a triple (h, r, t), since the Dirichlet distribution is a conjugate prior of the multinomial distribution and according to Bayesian inference, DiriE views the head entity as a prior distribution, the tail entity as a posterior distribution and the relation as a likelihood function that transforms the prior to the posterior distribution, i.e., $q_t \propto b_r p_h$ and $q_h \propto b_{r^{-1}} p_t$, where p and q are PDFs of Dirichlet distributions, and b is PMF of the multinomial distribution. Due to the flexibility of the multinomial distributions of relation modeling, DiriE is able to model various relational patterns, including symmetry, inversion and composition, e.g., a symmetric relation can be modeled by learning b_r as $b_{r^{-1}}$.

Beta embeddings. Logical query answering includes logical connectives such as negation which can be properly modeled by distributions. BetaE [2] embeds entities and queries as multivariate beta distributions $f(\mathbf{x}|\alpha, \beta) = \frac{\mathbf{x}^{\alpha-1}(1-\mathbf{x}^{\beta-1})}{\mathbf{B}(\alpha,\beta)}$ and models the negation by taking the reciprocal of the parameters α and β. By doing so, BetaE converts the regions with high density into low-density areas and vice versa, which resembles the desired property of negation. In addition, a conjunction of entity sets $S_1, \ldots, S_n$ can be modeled as a weighted product of involved Beta distributions,i.e., $f_{\text{inter}} = \frac{1}{Z}\prod f_{S_i}^{w_i}$, where Z is a normalization constant and $w_1, \ldots, w_n$ are the attention weights summing to 1. Such weighted product of Beta distribution follows the intuition of conjunction, namely the regions of high density in the intersection set should also have high density in all input distributions.

Gamma embeddings. GammaE [21] improves BetaE by embedding entities and queries as Gamma distributions defined as $f(x|\alpha, \beta) = \frac{x^{\alpha-1}e^{-\beta x}\beta^{\alpha}}{\Gamma(\alpha)}$, where $x > 0, \alpha > 0$ is the shape, $\beta > 0$ is the rate, and $\Gamma(*)$ is the Gamma function. GammaE models intersection as product of Gamma distributions $P_{S_{\text{Inter}}} = \frac{1}{Z}\prod_{i=1}^{k} P_{S_i}^{w_i}$ and union as Gamma mixture models $P_{S_{\text{Union}}} = \sum_{i=1}^{k}\theta_i P_{S_i}$ where $\theta_i = \frac{\exp((P_{S_i}))}{\sum_j \exp(P_{S_i})}$, and $P_{S_i} = f(x|\alpha_i, \beta_i)$. Similar to BetaE, GammaE models negation by reversing the shape of the density function $N_{P_S} = f\left(x|\frac{1}{\alpha}, \beta\right) + \varepsilon$ where $P_S = f(x|\alpha, \beta)$ and $\varepsilon \in (0, 1)$ is the elasticity.

3.2. Region-based Embeddings

Mapping data as convex regions is inspired by the Venn diagram. Region-based embeddings nicely model the set theory that can be used to capture uncertainty [24], logical rules [3], transitive closure [12], logical operations [7], etc. Several convex regions have been explored including balls, boxes, and cones. Figure 1 shows examples of the three embeddings.

Ball embeddings Ball embedding associates each object w with an n-dimensional ball $\mathbb{B}_w(\mathbf{c}_w, r_w)$, where $\mathbf{c}_w$ and r_w are the central point and its radius of the ball, respectively. A ball is defined as the set of vectors whose Euclidean distance to $\mathbf{c}_w$ is less than r_w: $\mathbb{B}(\mathbf{c}_w, r_w) = \{\mathbf{p} | \|\mathbf{c}_w - \mathbf{p}\| < r_w\}$. In ElEm [6], each concept in $\mathcal{EL}^{++}$ ontologies is represented as an open n-ball, and subsumption relations between concepts are modeled as ball containment. This explicit modeling of subsumption structure leads to significant improvements in predicting human protein-protein interactions. [22] represents categories with n-balls while considering tree-structured category information. By embedding subordinate relations between categories as ball containment, it shows promising results on NLP tasks compared to conventional word embeddings.

Box embeddings Box embeddings represent objects with d-dimensional rectangles, i.e., a Cartesian product of d closed intervals denoted by $\prod_{i=1}^{d} \left[x_i^{\mathrm{m}}, x_i^{\mathrm{M}}\right]$, where $x_i^{\mathrm{m}} < x_i^{\mathrm{M}}$ and x_i^{m} and x_i^{M} are lower-left and top-right coordinates of boxes [12]. Box embeddings capture anticorrelation and disjoint concepts better than order embeddings. Joint Box [23] improves box embeddings' ability to express multiple hierarchical relations (e.g., hypernymy and meronymy) and proposes joint embedding of these relations in the same subspace to enhance entity characterization, resulting in improved performance. BoxE [3] proposes embedding entities and relations as points and boxes in knowledge bases, improving expressivity by modeling rich logic hierarchies in higher-arity relations. BEUrRE [24] is similar to BoxE but it differs in embedding entities and relations as boxes and affine transformations, respectively, which enables better modeling marginal and joint entity probabilities. Query2Box [7] shares BoxE's idea, embedding queries as boxes, with answer entities inside, to support a range of querying operations, including disjunctions, in large-scale knowledge graphs. BoxEL [1], ELBE [50] and Box^{2}EL [51] propose to capture concept-level knowledge in the description logic $\mathcal{EL}^{++}$ or its extension to statistical $\mathcal{EL}$ [52] by modeling concepts and/or roles as axis-aligned boxes such that concept and role inclusions can be geometrically captured. ShrinkE [27] considers hyper-relational facts and model qualifiers as "shrinking" of box embeddings.

Cone embeddings Cone embedding was first proposed in Order embedding (OE) [28] to represent a partial ordered set (poset). However, this method is restricted to axis-parallel cones and it only captures positive correlations as any two axis-parallel cones intersect at infinite. Recent cone embeddings formulate cones with additional angle parameters. As one of the main advantages, angular cone embedding has been used to model the negation operator since the angular cone is closed under negation. For example, negation can be modeled as the polarity of a cone as used in ALC ontology [29] or the complement of a cone as used in ConE for logical queries [11].

Polygon embeddings PolygonE [48] models n-ary relational data as gyro-polygons in hyperbolic space, where entities in facts are represented as vertexes of gyro-polygons and relations as entity translocation operations. ExpressivE [30] embeds pairs of entities as points and relations as hyper-parallelograms in the virtual triple space $\mathbb{R}^{2d}$. Such more flexible modeling allows for not only capturing a rich set of relational patterns jointly but additionally to display any supported relational pattern through the spatial relation of hyper-parallelograms.

3.3. Manifold-based Embeddings

The ability of embedding models to capture complex structural patterns intrinsically bounded by the volume of the embedding space. This consequently leads to distortion issues during the embedding of relational data with complex structural patterns. A thread of work tries to mitigate this problem for a certain class of patterns e.g., hierarchy by embedding on a non-Euclidean manifold which is a smooth geometric object $\mathcal{M}$ (e.g., Poincare ball) which is locally Euclidean, but not globally. A Riemannian manifold is a pair $(\mathcal{M}, g)$ where g is a metric tensor used to define the distance between any two points on the manifold. Several methods have been proposed to embed relational data on non-Euclidean manifolds such as Poincare balls and Sphere [53] to model hierarchical and loop structures, respectively.

Hyperbolic embeddings The Poincaré ball has been used for modeling hierarchical structures [53]. MuRP [33] models multi-relational data by transforming entity embeddings by Möbius matrix-vector multiplication and addition. To capture both hierarchy and logical patterns e.g., symmetry and composition, AttH [4] models relation transformation by rotation/reflection and also embeds entities on the Poincaré ball. FieldH and FieldP [54] embed entities on trajectories that lie on hyperbolic manifolds namely Hyperboloid and Poincaré ball to capture heterogeneous patterns formed by a single relation (e.g., a combination of loop and path) besides hierarchy and logical patterns. [35] embeds nodes on the extended Poincaré Ball and polar coordinate system to address numerical issues when dealing with the embedding of neighboring nodes on the boundary of the ball on previous models. HyboNet [36] proposes a fully hyperbolic method that uses Lorentz transformations to overcome the incapability of previous hyperbolic methods of fully exploiting the advantages of hyperbolic space. Poincaré Glove [55] adapts the GloVe algorithm to learn unsupervised embedding in a Cartesian product of hyperbolic spaces which is theoretically connected to the Gaussian word embeddings and their Fisher geometry. The application of hyperbolic geometry in entity alignment has been done in [56] where HypKA embeds two graphs on a Poincaré ball and then aligns the corresponding node pairs in two graphs. HMI [14] targets the problem of structured multi-label classification where the labels are organized under implication and mutual exclusion constraints, and are encoded as Poincaré hyperplanes that work as linear decision boundaries. In addition to the mentioned works, the application of hyperbolic manifolds in temporal knowledge graph embedding has been done in [57] which is an extension of AttH [4] with time-dependent curvature.

Spherical embeddings A spherical manifold $\mathcal{M} = \{x \in \mathbb{R}^d | \ \|x\| = 1\}$ has been used as embedding space in several works to model loops in graphs. MuRS [32] models relations as linear transformations on the tangent space of spherical manifold, together with spherical distance in score formulation. A more sophisticated approach is FiledP [54] in which entity spaces are trajectories on a sphere based on relations to model more complex patterns compared to MuRS. 5*E [31] embeds entities on flows on the product space of a complex projective line which is called the Riemann sphere. The projective transformation then covers translating, rotation, homothety, reflection, and inversion which are powerful for modeling various structures and patterns such as combination of loop and loop, loop and path, and two connected path structures.

Mixed manifold embeddings Relational data exhibit heterogeneous structures and patterns where each class of patterns and structures can be modeled efficiently by a particular manifold. Therefore, combining several manifolds for embedding is beneficial and addressed in the literature. MuRMP [32] extends MuRP [33] to a product space of spherical, Euclidean, and hyperbolic manifolds. GIE [37] improves the previous mixed models by computing the geometric interaction on tangent space of Euclidean, spherical and hyperbolic manifolds via an attention mechanism to emphasize on the most relevant geometry and then projects back the obtained vector to the hyperbolic manifold for score calculation. DGS [38] targets the same problem of heterogeneity of structures and utilizes the hyperbolic space, spherical space, and intersecting space in a unified framework for learning embeddings of different portions of two-view KGs (ontology and instance levels) in different geometric space. While the reviewed works provide separate spherical, Euclidean, and hyperbolic manifolds and act on Riemannian manifolds, UltraE [5] embeds graphs on the Ultrahyperbolic manifold which is a semi-Riemannian manifold that seamlessly interleaves Euclidean, hyperbolic and spherical manifolds. In this model, relations are modeled by the pseudo orthogonal transformation which is decomposed into cosine-sine forms covering hyperbolic/circular rotation and reflection. This model can capture heterogeneous structures and logical patterns.

3.4. Hybrid Embeddings

Many methods try to combine the advantages of using distributions/regions and the advantages of using manifolds. Classical box embeddings use a hard volume in the objective function, leading to gradient issues. Soft volume-based methods like smoothed box [40] and Gumbel box [41] alleviate this problem by modeling the box via a Gaussian process and Gumbel process, respectively. To simultaneously model hierarchies and set-theoretic semantics, Hyperbolic disk embedding [10] embeds relational objects as disks defined in hyperbolic space. HypE [44], on the other hand, simulates the box in hyperbolic space, but, this is no longer closed under intersection. A successful combination of manifolds and region-based methods is the hyperbolic cone embedding [45] that models relational objects as angular cones in hyperbolic space. ConE[46] further extends it to logical queries on KGs. To combine the advantages of distribution-based methods and manifolds, HWN [42] and RoHWN [43] generalize Gaussian distributions to hyperbolic space, namely hyperbolic wrapped Gaussian.

4. Applications in Relational Reasoning

4.1. Knowledge Graph Completion.

To perform KG completion, a KGE model takes a triple pattern $(h,r,?)$ as a query, and replaces "?" by an entities in the KG to generate a new triple (h,r,e). Table 3 summarizes the characteristics of some prominent geometric KG embeddings.

To capture the uncertainty in a KG, KG2E [17] embeds each entity and relation as a Gaussian distribution parameterized by a mean vector and diagonal covariance matrix. KG2E measures the plausibility of the triple by $\mathcal{D}_{\mathcal{KL}}(\mathcal{P}_e,\mathcal{P}_r)$, where $\mathcal{P}_e \sim \mathcal{N}(\mu_h-\mu_t,\Sigma_h+\Sigma_t)$ and $\mathcal{D}_{\mathcal{KL}}$ is the KL divergence. TransG [18] generalizes the idea of KG2E to a mixture of Gaussian distribution to deal with the issue of multiple relation semantics. DiriE models entities as Dirichlet distributions and relations as multinomial distributions, which is able to model relational patterns.

BEUrRE [24] models uncertainty of KGs by using box embedding, where entities are mapped as boxes (axis-parallel rectangulars) and relations are modeled as affine transformations involving a translation of the position of boxes and a scaling of the size of boxes. BoxE, on the other hand, embeds entities as points, and relations as a set of boxes with the number of boxes depending on the arity of the relation. Hence, BoxE is able to model n-ary relations. Besides, the relational boxes spatially characterize the basic logical properties of relations and BoxE is proven to be fully expressive. However, BoxE is not able to capture composition. To further support composition, ExpressE [30] embeds relations as hyper-parallelograms in the virtual triple space $\mathbb{R}^{2d}$ where the relational patterns are characterized through the spatial relationship of hyper-parallelograms. To embed hierarchical structure in KGs, HAKE [58] maps entities into the polar coordinate system to model semantic hierarchies. On the other hand, MuRP [33] embeds KGs into hyperbolic space and significantly reduces the dimensionality. To further embed relational patterns such as symmetry, inversion and composition, AttH [4] represents relations as hyperbolic isometries including hyperbolic rotations and reflections parameterized by Givens matrices. HyboNet [36] formulates the relational transformation matrices by a Lorentz transformation that is decomposed into a Lorentz rotation and a Lorentz boost. HBE [35] proposes a KGE model with an extended Poincare Ball where the hierarchy-specific parameters are optimized on the polar coordinate system. Recently, some works [37, 32, 5] argue that embedding KGs in a single homogeneous curvature space, no matter the zero-curvature Euclidean space, negatively curved hyperbolic space or positively curved hyperspheric space, cannot faithfully model the complex structures of KGs. MuRMP [32] proposes to embed KGs into a mixed curvature space, namely a product of Euclidean, spherical and hyperbolic space. However, they do not explicitly model the possible interactions between these spaces. GIE [37] combines Euclidean, hyperbolic and hyperspherical spaces and models their interactions by learning these complex spatial structures interactively between these different spaces. DGS [38] further distinguishes the representations of the instance-view entities and the ontology-view concepts as they have inherently quite different structures (i.e., instance-view entities are organized more cyclically while ontology-view concepts are organized more hierarchically). UltraE [5], on the other hand, considers a pseudo-Riemannian space, namely, pseudo-hyperboloid equipped with a pseudo-Riemannian metric. This is inspired by the fact that pseudo-hyperboloid generalizes hyperbolic and spherical spaces. Besides, UltraE models relations by hyperbolic and spherical rotation, allowing the inference of complex relation patterns.

4.2. Ontology/Hierarchy Completion.

Ontology completion aims to predict subsumption relations between classes in ontologies whose logical structure is expressed in the ontology axioms. Ontology embedding aims at embedding classes and relations such that the logical structure and the deductive closure can be preserved [6]. ELEm [6] proposes to embed each class and instance as a n-ball with a learnable radius and models each relation as a translation of the n-ball. This method is not able to represent intersectional closure because that n-ball is not closed under

Table 3. Characteristics of different geometric embeddings for KGs. ⋆ means "partially", – means not available.

Method	uncertainty	relational	set theory	structural
KG2E	✓	⋆	⋆	×
DiriE	✓	⋆	×	×
BEUrRE	✓	⋆	⋆	×
BoxE	✓	⋆	✓	×
ExpressE	✓	✓	✓	×
MuRP	×	⋆	×	⋆
AttH	×	⋆	×	⋆
MuRMP	×	-	-	✓
GIE	×	⋆	×	✓
UltraE	×	⋆	×	✓
DGS	×	⋆	×	✓

intersection, and the translational relation modeling suffers from a key issue, namely, not able to model relations between classes with different sizes. BoxEL [1] and ELBE [50] both consider boxes as the class embedding due to their advantages of modeling intersectional closure. One major difference is that ELBE still uses translation as relation embeddings while BoxEL replaces it with affine transformation similar to BEUrRE [24]. Furthermore, different from ELEm and ELBE which do not distinguish classes and instances, BoxEL embeds entities as points while classes as boxes, which is consistent with the classical conceptual space model where points denote objects, and regions denote concepts [59]. Box^{2}EL[51] further improves BoxEL and ELBE by embedding roles as boxes, in a similar way like BoxE [3]. BoxSEL [60] generalizes BoxEL into statistical EL ontologies by modeling the explicit uncertainty of EL axioms.

All these methods are limited to the embedding of ontology expressed by the lightweight Description Logics EL++, where full concept negation is not expressible. For the embeddings of ontologies expressed by $\mathscr{ALC}$ description logic where full negation is of interest, [29] embeds each class as an angular convex cone and models the negation as the polarity of cone, which is inspired by the Farkas' Lemma [61]. However, [29] is limited in modeling relations. [62] embeds $\mathscr{SROI}^-$ concept as a cone in complex vector space, and each $\mathscr{SROI}^-$ relation is embedded as a transformation that rotates and scales cones.

Hierarchy completion can be viewed as a special case of ontology completion where only one hierarchical relation (e.g., *is_a*) exists and the graph can be viewed as a hierarchy, partial order set/lattice or directed acyclic graph (DAG). Hence, the modeling of transitivity is an essential part of hierarchy completion. Order embedding [28] represents entities as axis-parallel cones. Probabilistic box embedding [12, 41] extends it to axis-parallel boxes while [26] further extend it to deal with directed graphs with cycles. Hyperbolic semantic cone [45] combines the advantages of hyperbolic space and cones.

4.3. Hierarchical Multi-label Classification.

HMC aims to associate each instance with multiple labels that are hierarchically organized in a directed acyclic graph. HCGE, the first geometric embedding model for HMC, models the uncertainty of node representations using Gaussian embeddings and shows improvement on multi-label node classification. Recent works [63] demonstrate that enforcing the output of an HMC model to respect the hierarchy constraint can boost the performance of HMC. To this end, MBM [13] embeds instances and labels as boxes so that the logical structure can be respected, i.e., if an instance has a label then it also has all of the parent labels. Similar to MBM, Box2Type [25] considers an instance of HMC, fine-grained entity typing, and embed entity types as boxes. Some methods [34, 64] propose to do HMC in hyperbolic space but they do not consider regions as type embeddings and hence cannot preserve logical structures. HMI [14], on the other hand, embed each label as a curved hyperbolic hyperplane that corresponds to an enclosing n-ball and model the relationships between labels as geometric relations between the corresponding n-balls. HMI is able to preserve logical structure including both implication and exclusion. [47] leverage hyperbolic cones as label embeddings that aims to preserve label hierarchy. LogicR [65] further applies HMI into recommendation systems by modeling tag hierarchy in hyperbolic space and improves the predictive consistency.

4.4. Logical Query Answering.

Answering complex logical queries, for example, *"list the countries that have hosted the Olympic Games but not the World Cup"*, is an important yet challenging task due to KGs incompleteness and the difficulty in properly modeling logic operations. Geometric and probabilistic query embedding methods provide a way to tractably handle logic operators in queries and equip excellent computing efficiency. Essentially, existing query embedding models represent logical queries by either geometry shapes or distributions. Logical operations, such as conjunction, disjunction, and negation, are performed as geometric or algebraic manipulations on them. Query2Box [7] is the earliest work that maps each entity as a point and each query as a box. By doing so, this method models the conjunction of two query embeddings as the intersection of two boxes and evaluates the plausibility of each candidate answer based on the distance between the query box embedding and each entity point. Query2Box is limited in modeling negation due to the non-closure property of negation set in Euclidean space, i.e. the negation of a box embedding in Euclidean space is not a box. BetaE [2] remedies this problem by modeling queries as Beta distributions. It models the conjunction by computing the weighted product of beta distributions, and the negation by taking the reciprocal of the shape parameters α and β. Alternatively, ConE [11] and its follow-up work [66] model conjunction and negation by representing queries as cones, i.e. the conjunction is the intersection of cones and the negation is the closure-complement. All of the above methods are not able to directly handle disjunctions, but can only transform the entire query into Disjunctive Normal Form (DNF) and perform the disjunction in the last step. GammaE [21] and PERM [20] enclose all logical operations in distributional (Gamma and Gaussian) spaces and allow them to be handled independently. Specifically, PERM encodes entities as Multivariate Gaussian distributions and queries as a mixture of Gaussian distributions. GammaE represents entities and queries using Gamma distributions. Similar to BetaE, these two methods also model the conjunction of query embeddings by the product of input distributions. However, both GammaE and PERM get rid of the DNF technique and model disjunction as the weighted mixture of Gamma and Gaussian distributions respectively.

5. Summary and Future Work

This paper conducts a comprehensive survey on geometric embedding methods for modeling relational data. Methods are systematically classified, discussed, and compared according to the proposed taxonomy. As we discussed, different geometric embeddings provide different inductive biases that are suitable for different tasks. We believe our comparison and analysis will shed light on more applications of geometric embeddings on more relational reasoning tasks.

Despite its success, there are still challenges to be solved in this research field. We, therefore, suggest some promising directions for future research as follows

Heterogeneous hierarchies Most current geometric embedding methods can only encode one hierarchy relation (e.g., *is_a*). However, a real-world KG might simultaneously contain multiple hierarchical relations (e.g., *is_a* and *has_part*) [23]. An embedding model should be able to distinguish these different hierarchical relations, especially when they are intertwined with each other.

Deep geometric embeddings Most current geometric relational embeddings are non-parametric models that do not require neural network parameterization. Developing deep architectures for current geometric relational embeddings is an exciting topic of future research.

Learning with symbolic knowledge Incorporating symbolic knowledge, e.g., logical constraints over labels, into machine learning is in general a very promising direction as it enhances the robustness and interpretability of machine learning models. Geometric embeddings provide rich inductive biases for representing such logical constraints and have great potential for doing this. Besides modeling hierarchical constraints as in HMC, more kinds of logical constraints such as exclusion and intersection equivalence are worth exploring.

References

[1] Bo Xiong, Nico Potyka, Trung-Kien Tran, Mojtaba Nayyeri, and Steffen Staab. Faithful embeddings for EL++ knowledge bases. In *ISWC*, pages 22–38. Springer, 2022.

[2] Hongyu Ren and Jure Leskovec. Beta embeddings for multi-hop logical reasoning in knowledge graphs. *NeurIPS*, 33:19716–19726, 2020.

[3] Ralph Abboud, Ismail Ceylan, Thomas Lukasiewicz, and Tommaso Salvatori. BoxE: A box embedding model for knowledge base completion. *NeurIPS*, 33:9649–9661, 2020.

[4] Ines Chami, Adva Wolf, Da-Cheng Juan, Frederic Sala, Sujith Ravi, and Christopher Ré. Low-dimensional hyperbolic knowledge graph embeddings. In *ACL*, pages 6901–6914, 2020.

[5] Bo Xiong, Shichao Zhu, Mojtaba Nayyeri, Chengjin Xu, Shirui Pan, Chuan Zhou, and Steffen Staab. Ultrahyperbolic knowledge graph embeddings. *SIGKDD*, 2022.

[6] Maxat Kulmanov, Wang Liu-Wei, Yuan Yan, and Robert Hoehndorf. EL embeddings: Geometric construction of models for the description logic EL++. In *IJCAI*, pages 6103–6109. ijcai.org, 2019.

[7] Hongyu Ren, Weihua Hu, and Jure Leskovec. Query2box: Reasoning over knowledge graphs in vector space using box embeddings. In *ICLR*, 2019.

[8] Feiyang Wang, Zhongbao Zhang, Li Sun, Junda Ye, and Yang Yan. Dirie: Knowledge graph embedding with Dirichlet distribution. In *WWW*, pages 3082–3091, 2022.

[9] Dongzhuoran Zhou, Hui Yang, Bo Xiong, Yue Ma, and Evgeny Kharlamov. Alleviating over-smoothing via aggregation over compact manifolds. In *Pacific-Asia Conference on Knowledge Discovery and Data Mining*, pages 390–404. Springer, 2024.

[10] Ryota Suzuki, Ryusuke Takahama, and Shun Onoda. Hyperbolic disk embeddings for directed acyclic graphs. In *ICML*, pages 6066–6075. PMLR, 2019.

[11] Zhanqiu Zhang, Jie Wang, Jiajun Chen, Shuiwang Ji, and Feng Wu. ConE: Cone embeddings for multi-hop reasoning over knowledge graphs. *NeurIPS*, 34, 2021.

[12] Luke Vilnis, Xiang Li, Shikhar Murty, and Andrew McCallum. Probabilistic embedding of knowledge graphs with box lattice measures. In *ACL*, pages 263–272, 2018.

[13] Dhruvesh Patel, Pavitra Dangati, Jay-Yoon Lee, Michael Boratko, and Andrew McCallum. Modeling label space interactions in multi-label classification using box embeddings. In *ICLR*, 2021.

[14] Bo Xiong, Michael Cochez, Mojtaba Nayyeri, and Steffen Staab. Hyperbolic embedding inference for structured multi-label prediction. In *NeurIPS*, 2022.

[15] Aidan Hogan, Eva Blomqvist, Michael Cochez, Claudia d'Amato, Gerard de Melo, Claudio Gutierrez, Sabrina Kirrane, José Emilio Labra Gayo, Roberto Navigli, Sebastian Neumaier, et al. Knowledge graphs. *ACM Computing Surveys*, 54(4):1–37, 2021.

[16] Pascal Hitzler, Markus Krotzsch, and Sebastian Rudolph. *Foundations of semantic web technologies*. Chapman and Hall/CRC, 2009.

[17] Shizhu He, Kang Liu, Guoliang Ji, and Jun Zhao. Learning to represent knowledge graphs with Gaussian embedding. In *CIKM*, pages 623–632, 2015.

[18] Han Xiao, Minlie Huang, and Xiaoyan Zhu. Transg: A generative model for knowledge graph embedding. In *ACL*, pages 2316–2325, 2016.

[19] Ludovic Dos Santos, Benjamin Piwowarski, and Patrick Gallinari. Multilabel classification on heterogeneous graphs with Gaussian embeddings. In *ECML-PKDD*, pages 606–622. Springer, 2016.

[20] Nurendra Choudhary, Nikhil Rao, Sumeet Katariya, Karthik Subbian, and Chandan Reddy. Probabilistic entity representation model for reasoning over knowledge graphs. *NeurIPS*, 34:23440–23451, 2021.

[21] Dong Yang, Peijun Qing, Yang Li, Haonan Lu, and Xiaodong Lin. Gammae: Gamma embeddings for logical queries on knowledge graphs. *EMNLP*, 2022.

[22] Tiansi Dong, Christian Bauckhage, Hailong Jin, Juanzi Li, Olaf Cremers, Daniel Speicher, Armin B. Cremers, and Jörg Zimmermann. Imposing category trees onto word-embeddings using A geometric construction. In *ICLR (Poster)*. OpenReview.net, 2019.

[23] Dhruvesh Patel and Shib Sankar. Representing joint hierarchies with box embeddings. *AKBC*, 2020.

[24] Xuelu Chen, Michael Boratko, Muhao Chen, Shib Sankar Dasgupta, Xiang Lorraine Li, and Andrew McCallum. Probabilistic box embeddings for uncertain knowledge graph reasoning. In *NAACL-HLT*, pages 882–893. ACL, 2021.

[25] Yasumasa Onoe, Michael Boratko, Andrew McCallum, and Greg Durrett. Modeling fine-grained entity types with box embeddings. In *ACL/IJCNLP (1)*, pages 2051–2064. ACL, 2021.
[26] Dongxu Zhang, Michael Boratko, Cameron N Musco, and Andrew McCallum. Modeling transitivity and cyclicity in directed graphs via binary code box embeddings. In *NeurIPS*, 2022.
[27] Bo Xiong, Mojtaba Nayyeri, Shirui Pan, and Steffen Staab. Shrinking embeddings for hyper-relational knowledge graphs. *The 61st Annual Meeting of the Association for Computational Linguistics*, 2023.
[28] Ivan Vendrov, Ryan Kiros, Sanja Fidler, and Raquel Urtasun. Order-embeddings of images and language. *ICLR*, 2016.
[29] Özgü r Lü tfü Özçep, Mena Leemhuis, and Diedrich Wolter. Cone semantics for logics with negation. In *IJCAI*, pages 1820–1826, 2021.
[30] Aleksandar Pavlovic and Emanuel Sallinger. ExpressivE: A spatio-functional embedding for knowledge graph completion. *ICLR*, 2023.
[31] Mojtaba Nayyeri, Sahar Vahdati, Can Aykul, and Jens Lehmann. 5* knowledge graph embeddings with projective transformations. In *AAAI*, volume 35, pages 9064–9072, 2021.
[32] Shen Wang, Xiaokai Wei, Cicero Nogueira Nogueira dos Santos, Zhiguo Wang, Ramesh Nallapati, Andrew Arnold, Bing Xiang, Philip S Yu, and Isabel F Cruz. Mixed-curvature multi-relational graph neural network for knowledge graph completion. In *WWW*, pages 1761–1771, 2021.
[33] Ivana Balazevic, Carl Allen, and Timothy Hospedales. Multi-relational poincaré graph embeddings. *NeurIPS*, 32, 2019.
[34] Boli Chen, Xin Huang, Lin Xiao, Zixin Cai, and Liping Jing. Hyperbolic interaction model for hierarchical multi-label classification. In *AAAI*, pages 7496–7503. AAAI Press, 2020.
[35] Zhe Pan and Peng Wang. Hyperbolic hierarchy-aware knowledge graph embedding for link prediction. In *EMNLP*, pages 2941–2948, 2021.
[36] Weize Chen, Xu Han, Yankai Lin, Hexu Zhao, Zhiyuan Liu, Peng Li, Maosong Sun, and Jie Zhou. Fully hyperbolic neural networks. *ACL*, 2022.
[37] Zongsheng Cao, Qianqian Xu, Zhiyong Yang, Xiaochun Cao, and Qingming Huang. Geometry interaction knowledge graph embeddings. In *AAAI*, 2022.
[38] Roshni G Iyer, Yunsheng Bai, Wei Wang, and Yizhou Sun. Dual-geometric space embedding model for two-view knowledge graphs. In *SIGKDD*, 2022.
[39] Bo Xiong, Mojtaba Nayyeri, Linhao Luo, Zihao Wang, Shirui Pan, and Steffen Staab. Neste: Modeling nested relational structures for knowledge graph reasoning. *The 38th Annual AAAI Conference on Artificial Intelligence*, 2024.
[40] Xiang Li, Luke Vilnis, Dongxu Zhang, Michael Boratko, and Andrew McCallum. Smoothing the geometry of probabilistic box embeddings. In *ICLR*. OpenReview.net, 2019.
[41] Shib Dasgupta, Michael Boratko, Dongxu Zhang, Luke Vilnis, Xiang Li, and Andrew McCallum. Improving local identifiability in probabilistic box embeddings. *NeurIPS*, 33:182–192, 2020.
[42] Yoshihiro Nagano, Shoichiro Yamaguchi, Yasuhiro Fujita, and Masanori Koyama. A wrapped normal distribution on hyperbolic space for gradient-based learning. In *ICML*, pages 4693–4702. PMLR, 2019.

[43] Seunghyuk Cho, Juyong Lee, Jaesik Park, and Dongwoo Kim. A rotated hyperbolic wrapped normal distribution for hierarchical representation learning. *NeurIPS*, 2022.

[44] Nurendra Choudhary, Nikhil Rao, Sumeet Katariya, Karthik Subbian, and Chandan K. Reddy. Self-supervised hyperboloid representations from logical queries over knowledge graphs. In *WWW*, pages 1373–1384. ACM / IW3C2, 2021.

[45] Octavian Ganea, Gary Bécigneul, and Thomas Hofmann. Hyperbolic entailment cones for learning hierarchical embeddings. In *ICML*, pages 1646–1655. PMLR, 2018.

[46] Yushi Bai, Zhitao Ying, Hongyu Ren, and Jure Leskovec. Modeling heterogeneous hierarchies with relation-specific hyperbolic cones. *NeurIPS*, 34, 2021.

[47] Ankit Dhall, Anastasia Makarova, Octavian Ganea, Dario Pavllo, Michael Greeff, and Andreas Krause. Hierarchical image classification using entailment cone embeddings. In *CVPRW*, pages 836–837, 2020.

[48] Shiyao Yan, Zequn Zhang, Xian Sun, Guangluan Xu, Shuchao Li, Qing Liu, Nayu Liu, and Shensi Wang. Polygone: Modeling n-ary relational data as gyro-polygons in hyperbolic space. In *AAAI*, pages 4308–4317. AAAI Press, 2022.

[49] Luke Vilnis and Andrew McCallum. Word representations via Gaussian embedding. In *ICLR*, 2015.

[50] Xi Peng, Zhenwei Tang, Maxat Kulmanov, Kexin Niu, and Robert Hoehndorf. Description logic EL++ embeddings with intersectional closure. *CoRR*, abs/2202.14018, 2022.

[51] Mathias Jackermeier, Jiaoyan Chen, and Ian Horrocks. Box^{2}EL: Concept and role box embeddings for the description logic EL++. *CoRL*, 2023.

[52] Yuqicheng Zhu, Nico Potyka, Bo Xiong, Trung-Kien Tran, Mojtaba Nayyeri, Evgeny Kharlamov, and Steffen Staab. Approximating probabilistic inference in statistical el with knowledge graph embeddings. *arXiv preprint arXiv:2407.11821*, 2024.

[53] Melanie Weber and Maximilian Nickel. Curvature and representation learning: Identifying embedding spaces for relational data. *NeurIPS*, 2018.

[54] Mojtaba Nayyeri, Chengjin Xu, Franca Hoffmann, Mirza Mohtashim Alam, Jens Lehmann, and Sahar Vahdati. Knowledge graph representation learning using ordinary differential equations. In *EMNLP*, pages 9529–9548, 2021.

[55] Alexandru Tifrea, Gary Becigneul, and Octavian-Eugen Ganea. Poincaré GloVe: Hyperbolic word embeddings. In *ICLR*, 2019.

[56] Zequn Sun, Muhao Chen, Wei Hu, Chengming Wang, Jian Dai, and Wei Zhang. Knowledge association with hyperbolic knowledge graph embeddings. In *EMNLP*, pages 5704–5716, 2020.

[57] Sebastien Montella, Lina M Rojas Barahona, and Johannes Heinecke. Hyperbolic temporal knowledge graph embeddings with relational and time curvatures. In *Findings of ACL-IJCNLP*, 2021.

[58] Zhanqiu Zhang, Jianyu Cai, Yongdong Zhang, and Jie Wang. Learning hierarchy-aware knowledge graph embeddings for link prediction. In *AAAI*, pages 3065–3072. AAAI Press, 2020.

[59] Peter Gärdenfors. *Conceptual spaces - the geometry of thought*. MIT Press, 2000.

[60] Yuqicheng Zhu, Nico Potyka, Bo Xiong, Trung-Kien Tran, Mojtaba Nayyeri, Steffen Staab, and Evgeny Kharlamov. Towards statistical reasoning with ontology embeddings. *The 21st International Semantic Web Conference (Poster & Demo Track)*, 2023.

[61] Achiya Dax. Classroom note: An elementary proof of farkas' lemma. *SIAM review*, 39(3):503–507, 1997.

[62] Yunjie He, Daniel Hernandez, Mojtaba Nayyeri, Bo Xiong, Yuqicheng Zhu, Evgeny Kharlamov, and Steffen Staab. Generating $sroi^-$ ontologies via knowledge graph query embedding learning, 2024.

[63] Eleonora Giunchiglia and Thomas Lukasiewicz. Coherent hierarchical multi-label classification networks. In *NeurIPS*, 2020.

[64] Boli Chen, Xin Huang, Lin Xiao, and Liping Jing. Hyperbolic capsule networks for multi-label classification. In *ACL*, pages 3115–3124. ACL, 2020.

[65] Yanchao Tan, Hang Lv, Zihao Zhou, Wenzhong Guo, Bo Xiong, Weiming Liu, Chaochao Chen, Shiping Wang, and Carl Yang. Logical relation modeling and mining in hyperbolic space for recommendation. *The 40th IEEE International Conference on Data Engineering*, 2024.

[66] Yunjie He, Mojtaba Nayyeri, Bo Xiong, Evgeny Kharlamov, and Steffen Staab. Can pattern learning enhance complex logical query answering? *The 21st International Semantic Web Conference (Poster & Demo Track)*, 2023.

Handbook on Neurosymbolic AI and Knowledge Graphs
P. Hitzler et al. (Eds.)
IOS Press, 2025

doi:10.3233/FAIA250209

Knowledge Internalized in LLMs

Yushi SUN [a], Kai SUN [b], Xiao YANG [b] and Nan TANG [c]
[a] *Hong Kong University of Science and Technology*
[b] *Meta Reality Labs*
[c] *Hong Kong University of Science and Technology (Guangzhou)*
ORCiD ID: Yushi Sun https://orcid.org/0000-0003-3853-6364, Kai Sun https://orcid.org/0000-0001-8262-4906, Xiao Yang https://orcid.org/0000-0001-7992-8546, Nan Tang https://orcid.org/0000-0003-2832-0295

Abstract. LLMs, trained on a diverse range of resources, internalize a substantial amount of knowledge. Understanding this internalized knowledge is crucial for assessing the accuracy and reliability of their outputs, guiding improvements in model design, and addressing potential biases. In this chapter, we explore two primary forms of knowledge within LLMs: taxonomy and factual knowledge. We delve into the nature of internalized knowledge, examining how these models store and utilize information. Additionally, we introduce CRAG, a comprehensive benchmark for evaluating both the internalized knowledge of LLMs and their performance in retrieved-augmented generation tasks.

Keywords. large language models, internalized knowledge, ontology, factual knowledge, retrieval-augmented generation, benchmark

1. Introduction

Large Language Models (LLMs) represent a breakthrough in AI, achieving remarkable success across various natural language processing tasks. Trained on vast and diverse datasets, these models internalize a substantial amount of knowledge, ranging from common facts to nuanced domain-specific information and meta-knowledge e.g., ontology.

Understanding the knowledge internalized by LLMs is essential for multiple reasons. First, it enables us to assess the accuracy and reliability of the model's outputs. Second, the study of internalized knowledge informs model design improvements.

This chapter focuses on two primary forms of knowledge embedded within LLMs: taxonomy and factual knowledge. Taxonomy knowledge refers to the model's understanding of hierarchical relationships between entities, concepts, and categories, enabling it to reason about the world in structured ways. Factual knowledge, on the other hand, involves concrete pieces of information—such as historical dates, scientific facts, or geographic data—that LLMs internalize during training.

Furthermore, while LLMs demonstrate an impressive capacity for internalizing knowledge, their performance often benefits from external assistance, especially retrieval-augmented generation (RAG) methods. In this context, we introduce CRAG [1], a comprehensive benchmark designed to evaluate LLMs' internalized knowledge and ability to integrate retrieved information for enhanced performance effectively.

By examining the nature of internalized knowledge and the efficacy of retrieval-augmented generation, this chapter aims to provide a holistic understanding of the current capabilities and limitations of LLMs. Ultimately, this exploration will pave the way for future research aimed at building more reliable, efficient, and transparent AI systems.

2. Taxonomy Internalized in LLMs

The research landscape has been significantly reshaped by the rapid and remarkable advancements in LLMs such as GPTs [2] and Llamas [3] recently. Powerful language models [2,3,4] have demonstrated remarkable versatility, excelling across a diverse array of applications including question answering [5], text summarization [6], information retrieval [7], entity relation extraction [8], entity matching [9,10,11,12], table learning [13], data visualization [14,15,16], data preparation [17,18,19,20], and NL2SQL translation [21,22,23]. Such impressive capabilities have undoubtedly disrupted and redefined the development trajectories of these research domains.

While LLMs have shown impressive performance on various tasks, several previous studies have highlighted their limitations in domain-specific knowledge nuance [24,25]. Specifically, the studies have shown that despite their overall strong performance, LLMs often struggle to maintain the same level of knowledge depth and specificity as compared to more traditional knowledge representation approaches, such as curated knowledge graphs. This has raised questions about the suitability of LLMs for applications that heavily rely on comprehensive and accurate domain-specific knowledge, rather than just broad, general knowledge [5,25,26,27].

2.1. The Foundational Structure of Knowledge Organization: Taxonomy or LLM?

Taxonomies, as the foundational structures underpinning knowledge graphs, have long served as a systematic approach to organizing knowledge. Traditionally, taxonomies have followed a tree-like structure, where entities and concepts are classified based on their inherent characteristics. The root-level category denotes the broadest classification, while the leaf-level categories are specific. This hierarchical organization has facilitated efficient entity searching, category display, and knowledge reasoning, which rely on the fundamental "Is-A" relations between parent and child concepts.

However, the recent advancements in LLMs have brought into question the longevity of these conventional taxonomic structures. LLMs have demonstrated remarkable capabilities in learning and representing complex semantic relationships, potentially rendering the rigid, manually curated taxonomic hierarchies obsolete [25,28,29,30]. Introducing LLMs to fully/partially replace the traditional taxonomy structures in the symbolic reasoning process reduces the overall construction and maintenance cost of taxonomies. As these powerful language models continue to evolve, the role of taxonomies and the necessity of expert-driven curation may need to be re-evaluated to align with the emerging paradigm of knowledge representation.

2.2. Our Treasure Hunting: Are Large Language Models a Good Replacement of Taxonomies?

To provide a systematic view of whether traditional taxonomy structures are made obsolete by LLMs, we launched a *"treasure hunting"* in which our goal is to explore whether the knowledge internalized in LLMs is sufficient for the replacement of traditional explicit tree-like structures in taxonomies [30]. The treasure hunting considered the applicability of LLMs on taxonomic structures from two dimensions: 1) the domain coverage of the taxonomies; and 2) the granularity of the concepts in taxonomies. Specifically, we analyzed the performance of LLMs on eight taxonomies covering six different domains from common to specialized. We also evaluated the LLMs on the different granularities of the taxonomies from root to leaf levels.

Our treasure hunting is important for the community in the following ways: 1) Industrial enterprises can carefully consider the costs and benefits before investing resources into developing and sustaining conventional taxonomic systems; 2) LLM developers can obtain rigorous assessments of their models' capabilities and limitations within taxonomic applications, based on which they can systematically refine their systems to optimize support for users conducting taxonomy-related tasks. This iterative process of model evaluation and improvement is crucial for ensuring LLMs can reliably and effectively assist end-users in taxonomic workflows; 3) Database researchers can boldly innovate on novel taxonomic architectures and structures, while also pioneering the exploration of emerging application domains that can meaningfully enhance the reasoning capabilities of LLMs. By pushing the boundaries of taxonomic innovation and identifying high-impact use cases, these researchers can unlock new opportunities for LLMs to deliver transformative value across diverse industries and workflows.

2.3. Obstacles: Challenges

There are three major obstacles in our treasure hunting of discovering LLMs' level of mastery in terms of internalizing taxonomy knowledge. Firstly, The LLMs do not provide explicit theoretical guarantees for their output on taxonomy data, which implies a comprehensive benchmark is required for a detailed evaluation. However, there is a lack of comprehensive benchmarking studies on the LLMs' performance on taxonomy data. To the best of our knowledge, there are no studies that have extensively examined taxonomies across domains, prevalence, and complexity. Moreover, the hierarchical nature of taxonomies presents a unique challenge in developing comprehensive detection strategies to assess LLM intelligibility across all levels, from the broadest categorizations to the most granular details. Last but not least, the rapidly advancing LLM landscape offers a diverse array of base models and an ever-expanding range of configurations, including model sizes and prompting techniques. To navigate this dynamic field effectively, a comprehensive and systematic research approach is challenging.

To address these challenges, we developed the TaxoGlimpse benchmark [30], which casts a wide net across taxonomies spanning a diverse array of domains - from popular to highly specialized. The selected taxonomies were carefully curated to be representative of their respective fields. Furthermore, we meticulously crafted a comprehensive set of questions targeting each taxonomic level, enabling a granular assessment of LLM capabilities, from the broadest thematic categorizations down to the most nuanced details. Besides, we conducted a comprehensive evaluation of eighteen state-of-the-art LLMs. This was done to ensure a thorough assessment of the knowledge capabilities of the latest LLM advancements and their different variants. Furthermore, we examined the models' performance across a range of common prompt engineering settings. This systematic evaluation allowed us to gain deeper insights into the breadth and depth of knowledge embodied by these advanced language models.

Table 1. Statistics of taxonomies.

Domain	Taxonomy	# of entities	# of levels	# of entities in each level
Shopping	Google	5595	5	21-192-1349-2203-1830
Shopping	Amazon	43814	5	41-507-3910-13579-25777
Shopping	eBay	595	3	13-110-472
General	Schema	1346	6	3-17-215-403-436-272
CS	ACM-CCS	2113	5	13-84-543-1087-386
Geography	GeoNames	689	2	9-680
Language	Glottolog	11969	6	245-712-1048-1205-1366-7393
Biology	NCBI	2190125	7	53-309-514-1859-10215-107615-2069560

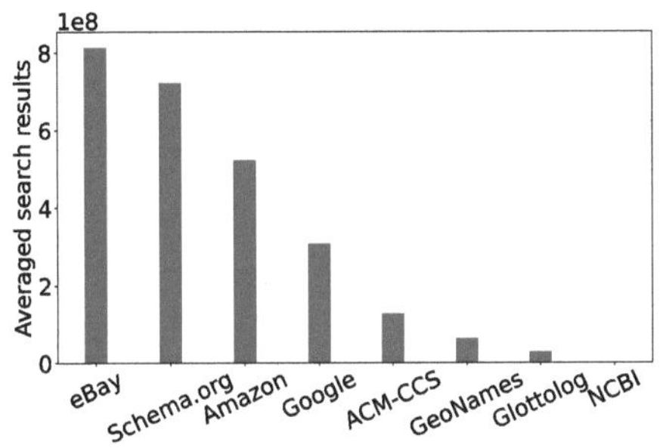

Figure 1. The popularity of different taxonomies.

2.4. Mine, Mining lamp, and Pickaxe: Datasets, Metrics, and Question Templates

In this treasure-hunting journey, we focus on eight different taxonomies, which are the mines that we aim to explore. We comprehensively considered the following factors when selecting the taxonomy datasets: 1) the taxonomies are publicly used and accessible; 2) the taxonomies cover a range of domains with different levels of popularities; 3) the taxonomies have distinct characteristics; 4) the taxonomies are representatives in their respective domains.

Based on these factors, we selected the following taxonomies: Google Product Category [31], Amazon Product Category [32], eBay Categories [33] from the shopping domain, Schema.org [34] from the general domain, ACM Computing Classification System [35] from the computer science domain, GeoNames [36] from the geography domain, Glottolog [37] from the language domain, and the NCBI Taxonomy Database [38] from the biology domain.

We preprocess the taxonomies collected and present their statistics in Table 1. Different taxonomies have different characteristics in terms of number of entities (size) and levels (depth). We measure the popularity of these taxonomies by searching the names of 100 randomly sampled entities from each taxonomy on Google.com and calculating the average number of results, as shown in Figure 1. Specifically, we consider eBay Categories, Schema.org, Amazon Product Category, and Google Product Category as common taxonomies, while the ACM-CCS, GeoNames, Glottolog, and NCBI taxonomies are considered specialized taxonomies.

Table 2. Question templates (True/False).

Domains	Question Templates
Shopping	Are [child] products a type of [parent] products? answer with (Yes/No/I don't know)
General	Is [child] entity type a type of [parent] entity type? answer with (Yes/No/I don't know)
CS	Is [child] computer science research concept a type of [parent] computer science research concept? answer with (Yes/No/I don't know)
Geography	Is [child] geographical concept a type of [parent] geographical concept? answer with (Yes/No/I don't know)
Language	Is [child] language a type of [parent] language? answer with (Yes/No/I don't know)
Biology	Is [child] a type of [parent]? answer with (Yes/No/I don't know)

Table 3. Statistics of datasets.

	eBay	Amazon	Google	Schema	ACM-CCS	GeoNames	Glottolog	NCBI
Level 1-root	176	438	258	34	138	492	500	344
Level 2-1	430	700	597	276	450	n/a	564	439
Level 3-2	n/a	748	653	394	567	n/a	584	636
Level 4-3	n/a	758	626	410	370	n/a	600	741
Level 5-4	n/a	n/a	n/a	320	n/a	n/a	732	766
Level 6-5	n/a	n/a	n/a	n/a	n/a	n/a	n/a	770
Total	606	2644	2134	1434	1525	492	2980	3696

In order to assess the quality of the answers produced by large language models (LLMs), we selected a set of evaluation metrics, drawing inspiration from prior work [25]. Specifically, we measured:

- **Accuracy** (A): The ratio of questions where LLMs respond correctly.
- **Miss Rate** (M): The ratio of questions where LLMs respond "I don't know".

We consider an LLM a good-performing model if it achieves both a high accuracy score and a low miss rate. These two metrics serve as mining lamps in our treasure hunting to provide a balanced view of the model's capabilities - its ability to answer questions correctly and its self-awareness in admitting when it is uncertain of the answer.

To uncover large language models' (LLMs') capability in internalizing hierarchical relationships within taxonomies, and to account for the distinctive characteristics of different taxonomies, as shown in Table 2, we designed a set of simple True/False question templates for each domain as the pickaxes for our treasure hunting. Given the question templates, we generate the questions based on the levels of the child entities in the taxonomies. Specifically, we randomly sample entities from each level except the root level of each taxonomy. The positive questions are formulated by getting the lowest parent entity of each sampled child entity, while the negative questions are obtained by randomly sampling an uncle entity that shares the same grand-parent entity of the lowest parent entity of the child entity. We present the detailed sizes of the generated question sets in each level for each taxonomy in Table 3.

2.5. Mined Gems: Our Key Findings

We consider eighteen state-of-the-art LLMs: GPTs [2] (GPT-3.5 (2023-05-15 version) and GPT-4 (2023-11-06-preview version)), Claude-3 [39] (Opus version), Llama-2s [3] (7B, 13B, 70B), Llama-3s [40] (8B, 70B), Flan-T5s [41] (3B, 11B), Falcons [42] (7B, 40B), Vicunas [43] (7B, 13B, 33B), Mistral and Mixtral [44,45] (7B, 8*7B), and LLMs4OL [28]. Among these models, GPTs and Claude-3 are close-sourced and accessed through API, the rest are open-sourced. LLMs4OL is fine-tuned on ontology learning tasks. We discuss the mined gems (our key findings) from our experiments.

Gem 1: LLMs capture the common domain taxonomy knowledge well while performing poorly on specialized taxonomies.

Our first important observation is that LLMs' performance declines as we go from common to specialized taxonomies. For instance, as shown in Table 4, the annotation accuracy of GPT-4 downgrades from over 90% to around 60% as we go from the common taxonomy eBay Categories to specialized taxonomies such as GeoNames, Glottolog, and NCBI. Interestingly, we note a slight increase in the miss rate (i.e., the rate of incorrect responses) for models such as GPT-3.5, GPT-4, Vicuna-13B, and Vicuna-33B when evaluated on the Glottolog and NCBI taxonomies - two specialized taxonomic domains that pose significant challenges for most large language models (LLMs). We consider this increased miss rate to be a positive outcome, as it suggests these models have learned to exercise appropriate caution when faced with taxonomic knowledge domains where their underlying training data and domain understanding are limited. We attribute these observations to the fact that the domain knowledge of common taxonomies is typically covered in the pre-training data of LLMs. In contrast, the knowledge of more specialized taxonomies is often scarce on the internet and therefore less likely to be included in the pre-training data. Consequently, accurately recovering the full hierarchical structures embedded within these specialized taxonomic domains remains a challenge that requires integrating more traditional taxonomy learning methods, in addition to the capabilities of large language models alone.

Gem 2: The performance of LLMs tends to degrade as we go from root to leaf taxonomy levels.

We present the annotation accuracy of representative LLMs in different levels of the taxonomies in Figure 2. A key observation is that the performance of LLMs tends to decline as we go from the root to leaf levels on most taxonomies, which matches with our intuition that the specific, nuanced knowledge is not likely to be well covered by the LLMs. Notably, the performance of GPT-4 drops by 30% on the Glottolog taxonomy. We surprisingly find that the root-to-leaf decline does not apply to the NCBI taxonomy as shown in Figure 2(g): most LLMs exhibit a sudden performance uplift at the last level of the taxonomy. We believe this might be due to the similar forms of the level 6 and level 5 entities. or instance, the ancestor chain of the level 6 entity *Verbascum chaixii* is *Eukaryota-Strepyophyta-Magnoliopsida-Scrophulariaceae-Verbascum-Verbascum chaixii*, where the names between the entity and its parent have very similar forms. As a result, LLMs may utilize the similarity between the level 6 and level 5 entities and perform well. Despite the fluctuation of the performance near the leaf levels of the NCBI taxonomy, the overall trend of LLMs' annotation performance

Table 4. Overall experimental results.

		eBay	Amazon	Google	Schema	ACM.	Geo.	Glot.	NCBI
GPT-3.5	*A*	0.891	0.724	0.814	0.591	0.617	0.598	0.510	0.495
	M	0.021	0.138	0.042	0.324	0.150	0.057	0.298	0.301
GPT-4	*A*	0.921	0.806	0.857	0.734	0.708	0.652	0.626	0.653
	M	0.003	0.051	0.011	0.193	0.017	0.002	0.154	0.132
Claude-3	*A*	0.901	0.668	0.781	0.315	0.624	0.679	0.244	0.449
	M	0.033	0.231	0.090	0.663	0.111	0.138	0.714	0.456
Llama-2-7B	*A*	0.201	0.052	0.092	0.000	0.032	0.006	0.001	0.000
	M	0.789	0.946	0.903	1.000	0.963	0.994	0.999	1.000
Llama-2-13B	*A*	0.898	0.766	0.822	0.712	0.658	0.543	0.192	0.457
	M	0.000	0.002	0.003	0.010	0.011	0.006	0.681	0.252
Llama-2-70B	*A*	0.899	0.806	0.836	0.616	0.687	0.553	0.305	0.535
	M	0.000	0.000	0.000	0.000	0.003	0.000	0.467	0.130
Llama-3-8B	*A*	0.880	0.789	0.774	0.788	0.664	0.663	0.608	0.691
	M	0.000	0.000	0.000	0.000	0.000	0.000	0.078	0.011
Llama-3-70B	*A*	0.904	0.770	0.824	0.419	0.705	0.693	0.388	0.551
	M	0.000	0.050	0.011	0.531	0.048	0.073	0.474	0.231
Flan-T5-3B	*A*	0.899	0.781	0.835	0.743	0.672	0.539	0.584	0.593
	M	0.000	0.000	0.000	0.000	0.000	0.000	0.000	0.000
Flan-T5-11B	*A*	0.919	0.793	0.864	0.786	0.698	0.520	0.589	0.633
	M	0.000	0.000	0.000	0.000	0.000	0.000	0.000	0.000
Falcon-7B	*A*	0.597	0.547	0.556	0.501	0.550	0.537	0.503	0.587
	M	0.000	0.000	0.000	0.000	0.000	0.000	0.000	0.000
Falcon-40B	*A*	0.434	0.253	0.348	0.013	0.043	0.108	0.021	0.013
	M	0.515	0.711	0.591	0.987	0.950	0.858	0.975	0.986
Vicuna-7B	*A*	0.827	0.725	0.728	0.699	0.599	0.705	0.637	0.609
	M	0.000	0.000	0.000	0.000	0.000	0.000	0.000	0.002
Vicuna-13B	*A*	0.690	0.625	0.601	0.581	0.527	0.492	0.301	0.350
	M	0.007	0.037	0.022	0.093	0.023	0.114	0.557	0.460
Vicuna-33B	*A*	0.759	0.713	0.682	0.728	0.591	0.728	0.496	0.522
	M	0.000	0.000	0.000	0.020	0.000	0.000	0.277	0.187
Mistral	*A*	0.583	0.474	0.532	0.214	0.433	0.240	0.146	0.176
	M	0.262	0.361	0.230	0.750	0.308	0.691	0.818	0.772
Mixtral	*A*	0.805	0.739	0.738	0.707	0.618	0.604	0.394	0.482
	M	0.000	0.000	0.000	0.017	0.111	0.041	0.450	0.313
LLMs4OL	*A*	0.904	0.849	0.860	0.912	0.753	0.677	0.711	0.725
	M	0.000	0.000	0.000	0.000	0.000	0.000	0.000	0.000

tends to degrade as we go from root to leaf taxonomy levels. Providing additional support to enhance LLMs' performance on leaf-level entities within taxonomic structures represents a promising direction for taxonomy.

Gem 3: Increasing sizes of LLMs does not necessarily lead to performance gain.

Jointly comparing the performance of multiple LLM series with different model sizes leads to the third observation that increasing the model sizes does not necessarily

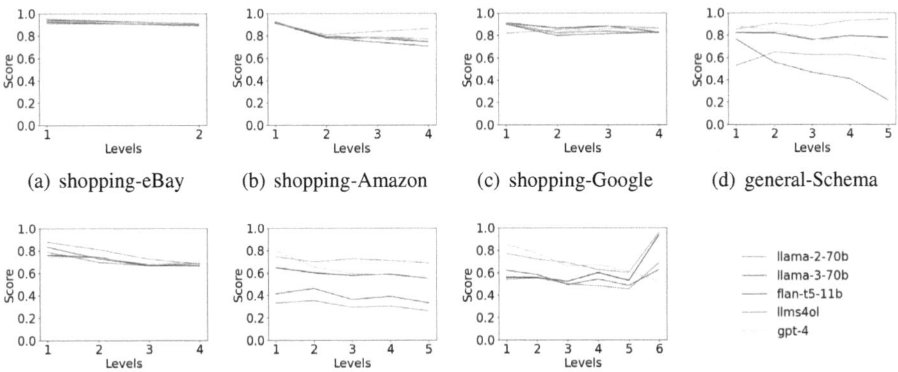

(a) shopping-eBay (b) shopping-Amazon (c) shopping-Google (d) general-Schema

(e) CS-ACM (f) language-Glottolog (g) biology-NCBI

Figure 2. Accuracies for different levels of questions of different taxonomies under the zero-shot setting.

uplift the annotation performance. Specifically, as shown in Table 4, the performance of Llama-2s, Flan-T5s, Mistral & Mixtral tends to improve as we opt for a larger LLM size, while the performance of Llama-3s, Falcons, and Vicunas does not exhibit a similar phenomenon. Once the LLM is sufficiently large, the performance of answering questions about taxonomy structures is heavily influenced by the differences in its pre-training data (e.g., coverage of data) and strategies (e.g., alignment), rather than the model size.

Gem 4: The performance improvements of top-performing LLMs when using few-shot and Chain-of-Thought prompting techniques are minimal.

We further conduct experiments on two additional prompting settings that claim to be helpful for the performance of LLMs and present the representative results in Figure 3. Specifically, in addition to zero-shot, we consider few-shot and Chain-of-thought settings. The zero-shot is the setting used in our main experiments. We provide five randomly sampled examples for the few-shot setting. In the CoT setting, we add a prompt "Let's think step by step" [46] in addition to the questions used in the zero-shot setting. We first identify that the few-shot setting largely reduces the miss rate and improves the annotation accuracy of the Llama-2-7B model as shown in Figures 3(d) and 3(c). However, the annotation accuracy of GPT-4 and Flan-T5-11B does not improve significantly under the few-shot setting (as shown in Figures 3(a) and 3(b)). The use of few-shot prompting appears to decrease miss rates, as it supplies the LLMs with concrete question-answer pairs that they can closely emulate to generate their predictions. This prompting approach seems to boost the models' confidence and the accuracy of their guesses. However, as for top-performing LLMs whose miss rates are already low, the performance uplift is not substantial. In conclusion, while few-shot prompting can enhance the performance of certain LLMs whose miss rates are high, it is unable to substantially improve the performance of the top-performing language models in this task. As for the CoT setting, we observe a significant miss rate increase for Llama-2-7B (Figure 3(d)). However, such influence is not significant for top-performing LLMs such as GPT-4 and Flan-T5-11B (as shown in Figures 3(a) and 3(b)). We attribute this observation to the fact that the taxonomy structure QA is relatively straightforward, not requiring complex reasoning. As a result, the Chain-of-Thought (CoT) approach may not

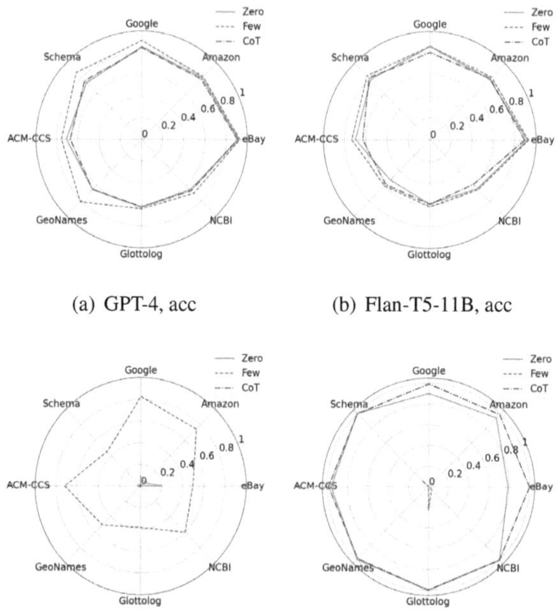

(a) GPT-4, acc (b) Flan-T5-11B, acc

(c) Llama-2-7B, acc (d) Llama-2-7B, miss

Figure 3. Radar charts for representative LLMs under different prompting settings in hard datasets.

be particularly helpful for this specific question-answering task, which aligns with the observation in [47]. In summary, we believe that the use of few-shot and CoT prompting settings cannot significantly improve the performance of LLMs.

2.6. The Future Foundational Structure of Knowledge Organization: Taxonomy and LLM!

After the treasure hunting in terms of taxonomy knowledge internalized in LLMs, we have a clearer vision of the future foundational structure of knowledge organization, which should be a harmonious combination of traditional taxonomy structures and LLM parameters. Our comprehensive experiments show that despite the internalization of knowledge in LLMs' parameters, their performance on specialized domains and leaf levels remains poor. Specifically, although LLMs showcase their mastery of common taxonomy content in shopping and general domains and at the root levels in most taxonomies, their performance remains satisfactory in specialized domains such as Geography, Language, and Biology as well as near the leaf levels of many taxonomies.

Our vision for the next-generation taxonomy is to fuse LLMs with traditional tree-structured taxonomies, forging a novel hybrid approach. This would combine the implicit hierarchical knowledge encoded within the LLM parameters with the explicit "Is-A" parent-child structure of classical taxonomies. The harmonious integration of these two modalities, harnessing the advancements of LLMs and the reliability of tree-based taxonomies, represents a captivating and promising research direction.

In the near future, the common domain taxonomies, which are likely to be well-covered by the massive training data of LLMs, tend to be internalized completely by the LLMs. While the traditional taxonomic structure may still have utility in certain use cases, such as relation display or safety-critical applications, the majority of common taxonomy use cases, including entity searching and knowledge reasoning, can be effectively handled by large language models (LLMs). We present a detailed case study in our paper for the replacement of traditional taxonomy structures with LLMs in the Shopping domain [30]. Specialized taxonomies such as Geography, Language, and Biology taxonomies tend to remain in their current explicit tree form or transform into a taxonomy-LLM-combined form. Current LLMs have not yet internalized these specialized taxonomies, especially near the leaf levels. We, therefore, suggest that industry practitioners should persist with the existing tree-structured taxonomies in specialized domains to ensure reliability and consistency. In parallel, the research community should begin exploring the possibilities of hybrid taxonomy architectures that seamlessly integrate LLMs with traditional tree-based structures to reduce the overall construction and maintenance costs of taxonomies while preserving high accuracy. In this envisioned approach, the entities situated near the upper levels of the taxonomy hierarchy would be represented within the weights of the LLM component, while the entities closer to the leaf nodes would continue to be expressed through the conventional tree-structured form. This harmonious fusion could unlock the benefits of both high accuracy and reduced construction/maintenance costs for taxonomy applications.

2.7. Summary

In this section, we introduce our treasure-hunting journey with TaxoGlimpse, a novel benchmark designed to comprehensively evaluate the performance of LLMs across different taxonomies, ranging from common to specialized domains, and from root to leaf levels. We systematically assessed the performances of eighteen state-of-the-art LLMs under three popular prompting settings: zero-shot, few-shot, and Chain-of-Thought, at varying levels of eight representative taxonomies. Our study provided valuable insights into future research opportunities for industry practitioners, LLM developers, and database researchers. The comprehensive evaluation reveals that even the best-performing LLMs perform poorly when applied to specialized taxonomies and entities near the leaf levels. In response to these findings, we suggest future research directions focused on combining LLMs with traditional taxonomies to create novel neural-symbolic taxonomy architectures that leverage the strengths of both approaches.

3. Knowledge Facts Internalized in LLMs

LLMs have gained significant attention in recent years, with two contrasting perspectives emerging: one that views LLMs as highly knowledgeable and the next generation of question-answering systems due to their impressive capabilities in internalizing knowledge, and another that sees them as prone to hallucinations [48] and therefore untrustworthy sources of factual information. To reconcile these opposing views, we must address a fundamental question: how many knowledge facts are internalized in LLMs? In this section, we discuss the approaches proposed to answer this question and present experimental results and insights from recent studies.

3.1. How to Evaluate the Factuality of LLMs?

Benchmarks. While most research on LLM factuality has utilized existing QA benchmarks, recent efforts have been developing new QA benchmarks specifically designed to evaluate how well LLMs incorporate knowledge facts, focusing on dimensions such as dynamism of facts and entity popularity [49,25]. We will primarily use two benchmarks in this chapter for discussion: FreshQA [49] in Section 3.2 and Head-to-Tail [25] in Section 3.3.

Metrics. *Accuracy* (**A**), measured as the percentage of questions that an LLM gives the correct answer, is the most widely used metric to evaluate the factuality of an LLM. Besides, we want to consider the conservativeness of the model in presenting non-confident answers and distinguish between hallucinated answers and missing answers. Therefore, *hallucination rate* (**H**) and *missing rate* (**M**) are two additional common metrics measuring the percentage of questions for which an LLM gives a wrong or partially incorrect answer, or admits it cannot answer, respectively. By definition, $\mathbf{A} + \mathbf{H} + \mathbf{M} = 100\%$.

Human Evaluation and Automatic Evaluation. Many studies rely on human evaluation to assess model responses due to the diverse range of responses generated by LLMs [50,49,1]. Recent studies have employed LLMs with few-shot in-context learning to evaluate model responses and have achieved a notable level of agreement with human evaluation [25,49,1]. To accomplish this, it is not only essential to establish a clear evaluation protocol but also beneficial to instruct LLMs to provide concise answers and acknowledge "unsure" when their confidence is low [25].

3.2. New and Rapidly Changing Facts Challenge LLMs to Internalize Knowledge

LLMs do not possess knowledge beyond their knowledge cutoff date, which means that new and rapidly changing facts can be challenging for LLMs to internalize. This limitation of LLMs has been quantitatively demonstrated through a recent study [49]. The study introduces a question answering benchmark FreshQA, which divides questions into four categories: never-changing, slow-changing (the answer typically changes with a frequency over a year), fast-changing (the answer typically changes within a year), and false premise (the question's premises are factually incorrect). Table 5 compares the accuracy of GPT-3.5 [51] and GPT-4 [52] with Google Search (using the answer in the answer box when available or the top-1 text snippet in the search result).

Table 5. (From Table 1 [49].) Comparison of the accuracy of GPT-3.5, GPT-4, and Google Search on FreshQA [49]. All numbers are in percentage (%).

Model	All	Never-Changing	Slow-Changing	Fast-Changing	False-Premise
Google Search	39.6	68.3	46.4	32.0	11.3
GPT-3.5	26.0	58.7	15.2	4.0	25.8
GPT-4	28.6	64.3	4.0	12.0	33.9

Not surprisingly, the performance of GPT-3.5/4 is much better for never-changing facts (59%/64%) compared to slow-changing (15%/4%) and fast-changing facts (4%/12%). There are a few interesting observations to note. Firstly, while GPT-4 cannot beat Google

Search in general, it can compete with Google Search for never-changing facts (64% vs. 68%). Secondly, GPTs do not perform significantly better on slow-changing facts than fast-changing facts, even though they may have already seen slow-changing facts in the training data before the cut-off date. Finally, GPTs perform relatively well on false-premise questions, significantly outperforming Google Search.

FreshQA consists of 500 questions contributed by NLP researchers and online freelancers, which may be biased towards popular facts. This potential bias will be discussed soon in this chapter.

3.3. LLMs Lack Torso-to-Tail Knowledge Compared to Head Knowledge

The study [49] discussed earlier in this chapter demonstrates GPT-4 can correctly answer 64% of questions about never-changing facts from FreshQA. However, a recent study [25] has shown that even for such facts, LLMs do not internalize them equally. The study considers factual information from Knowledge Graphs (KGs) that is mostly available before the cut-off time of the training data for their benchmarked LLMs. The study categorizes entities based on their popularity, which is approximated by either *traffic* (e.g., the count of ratings the entity has received) or *density* (e.g., the number of facts about the entity), into three groups: head entities (cumulatively contributing to top-33% traffic or density), torso entities (mid-33%), and tail entities (bottom-33%). By asking simple questions about entities randomly sampled from each group, the study approximates the amount of knowledge in an LLM based on its accuracy in answering these questions, without bias towards either popular or unpopular facts. The study reveals that the accuracy of LLMs in answering simple questions decreases from head to torso to tail entities, and similarly, decreases from popular to tail domains. Notably, even for popular entities from open domains, where training data is expected to be abundant, GPT-4 can only answer around half of the questions (Figure 4; Table 6). In addition to this study, there are other papers that demonstrate the struggles of LLMs with less popular factual knowledge [53], and there is a causal relationship between LLM accuracy and relevant document count [54].

Table 6. (From Table 3 [25].) Accuracy (**A**) and hallucination rate (**H**) of major LLMs on different domains. All numbers are in percentage (%).

Model	All		Open		Movie		Book		Academics	
	A	H	A	H	A	H	A	H	A	H
GPT-4	30.9	19.7	37.1	25.3	41.7	15.5	21.3	19.4	10.0	6.8
ChatGPT	20.3	14.1	22.1	14.8	34.7	13.3	16.9	24.9	3.0	1.9
Llama 2 (70B)	11.8	34.0	7.5	24.8	27.9	34.3	10.3	54.5	9.8	41.0
LLaMA (33B)	18.2	80.0	19.0	79.1	28.7	70.1	15.8	82.9	7.1	90.3

The study makes another contribution by distinguishing between hallucinations and missing answers and demonstrating that even when two models have the same accuracy, they may exhibit vastly different hallucination rates (e.g., ChatGPT vs. LLaMA in Table 6). Furthermore, the study reveals that an increase in accuracy often comes at the cost of a higher hallucination rate (GPT-4 vs. ChatGPT).

The study also compares LLMs in different sizes and with or without instruction tuning (Table 7). There are two notable observations. First, an increased model size does

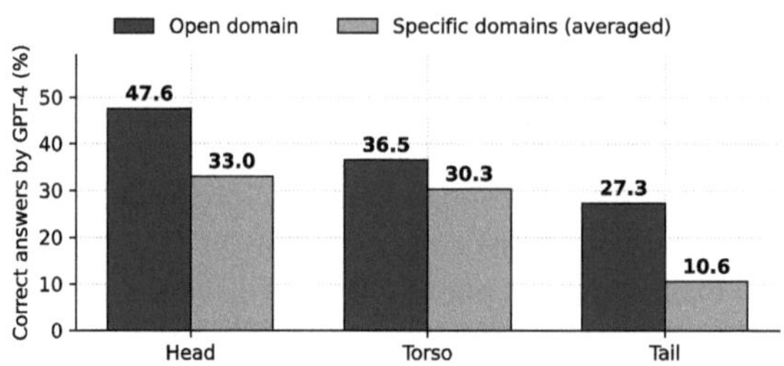

(a) Accuracy of GPT-4 for head, torso, and tail entities from specific domains (Movie, Book, Academia) and open domain.

Movie

Question: What profession does Tj Singh (known for John Carter (2012)) have?
Ground Truth: Visual effects
GPT-4: Actor

Book

Question: Who authored Choke (published in 1996)?
Ground Truth: Stuart Woods
GPT-4: Chuck Palahniuk

Academics

Question: Where did Josef Kittler receive the Ph.D. (thesis: Development and application of pattern recognition techniques.)?
Ground Truth: University of Cambridge, UK
GPT-4: University of Surrey

Open

Question: What college is the sister college of Trinity College, Oxford?
Ground Truth: Churchill College, Cambridge
GPT-4: Balliol College

(b) Example questions where GPT-4 gives incorrect answers.

Figure 4. (From Figure 1 [25].) The accuracy of GPT-4 decreases in the order of head, torso, and tail entities on the Head-to-Tail benchmark [25], and is only 31% on average.

not automatically translate to a better grasp of factual knowledge. For instance, LLaMA-33B marginally outperforms LLaMA-65B (+0.4% in accuracy and -1.9% in hallucination rate on average), despite sharing the same training dataset and hyperparameters. Second, compared with LLaMA and Falcon, the instruction-tuned counterparts (i.e., Vicuna and Falcon-Instruct) have lower accuracy, as they learned to be more conservative in providing factual answers. These observations show that normal methods that improve LLMs do not necessarily help LLMs to be more knowledgeable.

Finally, the study demonstrates that different prompts can lead to varying absolute performance. In particular, including in-domain examples in the prompt increases the number of correct answers but also results in more hallucinations. Despite these vari-

Table 7. (From Table 7 [25].) Accuracy (**A**) and hallucination rate (**H**) of different LLMs with different sizes. All numbers are in percentage (%).

Model	Head-to-Tail			Head		Torso		Tail	
	A	H	M	A	H	A	H	A	H
LLaMA (7B)	12.1	80.0	7.9	19.0	74.4	11.7	81.0	5.4	84.8
LLaMA (13B)	14.4	84.3	1.3	22.0	77.2	14.8	83.8	6.3	91.9
LLaMA (33B)	18.2	80.0	1.8	26.0	72.8	19.8	78.7	8.8	88.6
LLaMA (65B)	17.8	81.9	0.3	25.9	73.8	18.7	81.0	8.7	90.9
Vicuna (7B)	10.1	79.2	10.8	16.2	72.7	9.6	79.8	4.3	85.0
Vicuna (13B)	9.2	62.6	28.2	14.0	55.0	8.8	62.8	4.7	70.0
Flan-T5 (3B)	2.3	17.4	80.3	3.9	19.7	1.5	17.1	1.3	15.5
Flan-T5 (11B)	4.2	20.0	75.7	7.6	23.7	3.2	19.9	2.0	16.5
Falcon (7B)	9.5	57.9	32.6	14.5	53.8	9.2	57.9	4.8	62.0
Falcon (40B)	10.8	41.0	48.2	16.2	36.4	11.2	40.0	4.9	46.6
Falcon-Instruct (7B)	6.8	56.7	36.5	11.5	56.0	5.6	57.2	3.4	56.7
Falcon-Instruct (40B)	10.8	32.2	57.0	16.7	30.5	11.5	31.1	4.3	34.8

ations, the *relative* performance among the head, torso, and tail remains stable across different prompts. The conclusion remains unchanged: existing LLMs are still far from perfect in their grasp of factual knowledge, especially for facts related to torso-to-tail entities.

3.4. Summary

Although LLMs have incorporated factual knowledge within their parameters, the amount of this encoded knowledge remains limited as shown by the above studies. For head, never-changing knowledge, ideally, LLMs could be taught such knowledge for efficient retrieval, and a critical research area is to infuse head, never-changing knowledge into LLMs through model training. For torso-to-tail and recent knowledge, we need to leverage external sources to augment LLMs as training data are sparse. How to effectively decide when external knowledge is essential, efficiently retrieve the relevant knowledge, and seamlessly integrate it into the answers are directions that remain to be continued explored. We will discuss more about knowledge-augmented LLMs in the next section.

4. CRAG—A Comprehensive Benchmark for Retrieval Augmented Generation

Despite the advancements of Large Language Models (LLMs) achieved in Natural Language Processing (NLP) tasks, especially Question Answering (QA) [55,56,57], LLMs still lack knowledge in specialized taxonomy and torso-to-tail knowledge, as we saw in Section 2 and Section 3. Studies also show that GPT-4's accuracy in answering questions referring to slow-changing or fast-changing facts is below 15% [49]. Consequently, LLMs may generate answers that lack factual accuracy (hallucination) or

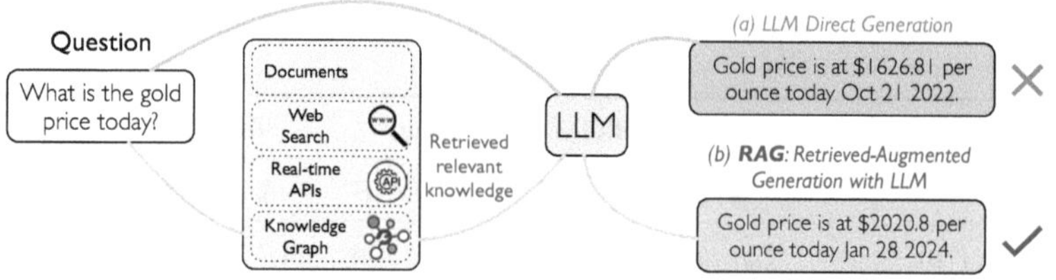

Figure 5. QA using LLMs (a) without RAG vs. (b) with RAG.

grounding [58,59], resulting in low trustworthiness of LLM applications. Overcoming hallucinations thus becomes a priority in building reliable QA systems [59,60].

Retrieval-Augmented Generation (RAG) [61,62,63,64] has recently emerged as a promising solution to alleviate LLM's deficiency in lack of knowledge and attracted a lot of attention from both academia research and industry. Given a question, a RAG system searches external sources to retrieve relevant information (as opposed to relying solely on LLMs' internalized knowledge) and then use them as additional context to provide generated answers [61,62,65] (see Figure 5 for an illustration). Despite its potential, RAG still faces many challenges, such as selecting the most relevant information, reducing question answering latency, and synthesizing information to answer complex questions.

4.1. Why Do We Need a Comprehensive Benchmark for RAG?

As RAG becomes a popular research area, a natural question is how do we benchmark RAG systems, reliably and efficiently? Existing RAG research [66,67] still relies on traditional QA benchmarks such as Natural Questions [68], TriviaQA [69], etc, which do *not* adequately represent the diverse and dynamic challenges RAG is facing. New benchmarks focusing on LLM or RAG have been proposed recently, but they usually target certain capabilities of LLMs [49,63,70,71] and lack a holistic view of the important factors for RAG. Concretely, existing benchmarks for RAG consider the following four design recipes.

First, whether the retrieval contents are provided and how to obtain the retrieval contents. Open-domain QA provides the knowledge source, usually a Wikipedia snapshot, instead of specific retrieval content for each question, which requires the system to be able to retrieve from large knowledge sources for answering the question. Benchmarks using knowledge sources beyond Wikipedia or standard knowledge bases provide certain number of web pages collected from search engines such as Google [68] and Bing [72], which relaxed the requirement for retrieval, but raised the requirement to process noisy data from the web. Benchmarks for Knowledge Base (KG) Question Answering provides knowledge graphs and usually also the querying method [73], which results in methods specific to QA over KB. There was no existing benchmark that considers both structured and unstructured search simultaneously for multiple domains, which is the scenario that RAG faces.

Second, whether the questions focus on simple knowledge questions or complex questions that require reasoning. Researchers design benchmarks with simple knowledge questions to learn how knowledgeable LLMs are on certain aspect. These data are usually constructed based on templates and sampled entities from KB [25,30,74]. Some recent benchmarks focus on more advanced capability of RAG such integrating information from multiple documents or robustness to noise [63,75]. But the questions were usually written by researchers, crowd workers or generated by models, and lack connection with real world applications, and the data size is around a few hundred.

Third, whether the data can explicitly support drawing insights on important slices such as dynamism, popularity, etc. QA benchmarks constructed from real user queries or built upon a collection of existing dataset contain large amounts of question-answering pairs [68,72,76]. However, they do not explicitly label the dynamism or popularity, and may not sufficiently represent these dimensions. Meanwhile, benchmarks focusing on these particular dimensions provide some of these information [49,25,30,53], but there was no benchmark that provides a holistic view of all the dimensions of importance.

Last, whether the evaluation uses matching-based metrics or model-based evaluators. Traditional QA benchmarks generally use matching based metrics such as ROUGE or F1 to evaluate the accuracy of the responses[68,69]. These metrics, although working well for extractive methods, are known to not work very effectively for LLMs that generate free-form responses[77]. Recent research built model-based auto-evaluators which show high agreement rate with manual evaluation[78,49].

4.2. What Is a Good Benchmark for QA over LLMs?

There are five critical features.

1. **Realism:** First and foremost, a good benchmark shall best reflect real use cases. In other words, a solution that achieves high metrics in the benchmark shall also perform very well in real scenarios. For example, the questions in a RAG benchmark shall be similar to questions people ask in real-world QA scenarios.
2. **Richness:** The benchmark shall contain a diverse set of instance types, covering both common use cases and some complex and advanced use cases, to represent real-world challenges and reveal possible limitations of existing solutions.
3. **Insightfulness:** The benchmark shall allow for an easy understanding of performance on different slices of the data, reflecting the capability of the solution in addressing different types of challenges.
4. **Reliability:** The benchmark shall allow reliable assessment of metrics: the ground truths shall be accurate; the metrics shall well capture the performance of the model; the evaluation shall be easy and reliable, and the computed metrics shall hold statistical significance.
5. **Longevity:** Finally, to enable research and experimental comparison in a long term, the scenarios and the data in the benchmark shall not quickly expire and ideally shall be refreshed and improved over time.

4.3. CRAG – Comprehensive Benchmark for RAG

CRAG – Comprehensive benchmark for RAG [1] is a benchmark created following the above principles, and designed to incorporate all the aforementioned factors for evaluating RAG.

4.3.1. Dataset

Diverse questions. CRAG contains a *rich* set of 4,409 QA pairs from five domains: *Finance, Sport, Music, Movie,* and *Open domain*. Besides simple-fact questions (asking for an attribute of an entity), CRAG contains seven types of complex questions to cover real user queries: questions with *Conditions*, *Comparison* questions, *Aggregation* questions, *Multi-hop* questions, *Set queries*, *Post-processing-heavy* questions, and *False-premise* questions (See Table 9). Moreover, CRAG reflects varied entity popularity from popular to long-tail and temporal spans ranging from seconds to years, allowing easy deep dives for *insights*.

Besides *richness* of questions, the authors referred to smart assistant use cases when generating the questions and made sure the questions are *realistic*, paraphrased the questions to increase the *diversity* of expressions, and manually verified ground truths to ensure *reliability*. Tables 10 and 11 summarize the distribution of the questions across different dimensions.

Rich retrieval information. CRAG provides both web search results and mock APIs to simulate retrieval from a diverse range of available information. It includes up to 50 full HTML pages for each question returned from a real-world search engine—the Brave Search API [79]. It also contains mock KGs with 2.6 million entities and 38 mock APIs to simulate real world KG search. The **Mock KGs** contain publicly available data used to generate the questions, randomly selected entities of the same type, and also "hard negative" entities with similar names (e.g., *"phantom"* for *"phantom of the opera"*). The **Mock APIs** are designed with pre-defined parameters to support structured search in the mock KGs. For example, for queries asking for stock prices, the mock API is in the form of `get_price_history(ticker)`.

4.3.2. Metrics Distinguish Missing and Hallucinated Answers.

CRAG uses a scoring method to assess the performance of RAG systems. Each response was first labeled with **perfect, acceptable, missing,** or **incorrect**, according to the following criteria.

- **Perfect.** The response correctly answers the user's question and contains no hallucinated content.
- **Acceptable.** The response provides a useful answer to the user's question but may contain minor errors that do not harm the usefulness of the answer.
- **Missing.** The response is "I don't know", "I'm sorry I can't find ...", a system error such as an empty response, or a request from the system to clarify the original question.
- **Incorrect.** The response provides wrong or irrelevant information to answer the user's question.

Then a scoring method $\textbf{Score}_h$ assigns score 1, 0.5, 0, and -1 to each *perfect, acceptable, missing*, and *incorrect* answer, respectively, which penalizes hallucinated answers since it can be more harmful to ruin user trust. For a given RAG system, the average score from all examples in the evaluation set is used as the final score.

4.3.3. Comprehensive and Reliable Evaluation

CRAG includes an evaluation mechanism to allow for *reliable* comparisons. It contains 3 tasks to test different components in RAG solutions: web retrieval, structured querying, and summarization. In addition, CRAG also contains an effective automatic evaluation method to support fast evaluation and development.

Similar to previous work [80], the authors employed both human evaluation **(human-eval)** and model-based automatic evaluation **(auto-eval)**. The automatic evalu-

Table 8. Comparing CRAG to existing benchmarks for factual question answering.

Benchmark	Web retrieval	KG search	Mock API	Dynamic question	Torso and tail facts	Beyond Wikipedia
QALD-10 [73]	✗	✓	✗	✗	✗	✗
MS MARCO [72]	✓	✗	✗	not explicitly	not explicitly	✓
NQ [68]	✓	✗	✗	not explicitly	not explicitly	✗
RGB [63]	✓	✗	✗	✗	✗	✓
FreshLLM [49]	✗	✗	✗	✓	✗	✓
CRAG	✓	✓	✓	✓	✓	✓

ation was used during the competition to provide fast update for the leaderboard, and to select top teams to do human-evaluation in the final competition. The human-evaluation was used to grade the selected top teams to determine the final winners. In the manual-eval, the authors used manual grading to judge *perfect, acceptable, missing*, and *incorrect* for each answer. In the auto-eval, they merged *perfect* and *acceptable*, called it **accurate**, and used a three-way scoring **Score**$_a$ with $1, -1, 0$ for *accurate*, *incorrect*, and *missing* answers.

They designed a two-step method for automatic evaluation: if the answer matches the ground truth exactly, it is considered *accurate*; otherwise, LLMs is used to determine whether the response is *accurate, incorrect*, or *missing*. To avoid the *self-preference* problem [81], they used two LLM evaluators: ChatGPT (`gpt-3.5-turbo`) [82] and Llama 3 (`llama-3-70B-instruct`) [40] and reported the average *accurate, hallucination, missing* rates, and scores from the two models for each RAG system. Their offline experiment showed that this two-step method yielded an average F1 score of 94.7% for ChatGPT and 98.9% for Llama 3 compared to human-eval.

The CRAG benchmark laid the groundwork for a KDD Cup 2024 challenge[1], which attracted thousands of participants and submissions.

Comparison with existing benchmarks. Table 8 compares CRAG with existing benchmarks for factual question answering, which illustrates several advantages of the CRAG benchmark: comprehensive coverage, realistic testing with mock APIs, dynamic question handling, diverse fact popularity, and extensive knowledge sources beyond Wikipedia.

These features make CRAG a robust and versatile benchmark for testing RAG systems and broadly QA systems, providing a shared testbed in evaluating how these systems handle real-world, dynamic, and diverse information retrieval and synthesis challenges for reliable LLM-based question answering.

4.4. Benchmarking State-of-the-Art LLMs and RAG Systems Using CRAG

The most advanced LLMs achieve $\leq 34\%$ accuracy on CRAG, while adding RAG in a straightforward manner improves the accuracy only to 44%. State-of-the-art industry RAG solutions answer only 63% questions without any hallucination, still having much lower accuracy in answering questions regarding facts with higher dynamism, lower popularity, or higher complexity.

[1]`https://www.aicrowd.com/challenges/meta-comprehensive-rag-benchmark-kdd-cup-2024`

Table 9. Definition of CRAG question types.

Question type	Definition
Simple	Questions asking for simple facts that are unlikely to change overtime, such as the birth date of a person and the authors of a book.
Simple w. Condition	Questions asking for simple facts with some given conditions, such as stock prices on a certain date and a director's recent movies in a certain genre.
Set	Questions that expect a set of entities or objects as the answer (e.g., "*what are the continents in the southern hemisphere?*").
Comparison	Questions that compare two entities (e.g., "*who started performing earlier, Adele or Ed Sheeran?*").
Aggregation	Questions that require aggregation of retrieval results to answer (e.g., "*how many Oscar awards did Meryl Streep win?*").
Multi-hop	Questions that require chaining multiple pieces of information to compose the answer (e.g., "*who acted in Ang Lee's latest movie?*").
Post-processing heavy	Questions that need reasoning or processing of the retrieved information to obtain the answer (e.g., "*how many days did Thurgood Marshall serve as a Supreme Court justice?*").
False Premise	Questions that have a false preposition or assumption (e.g., "*What's the name of Taylor Swift's rap album before she transitioned to pop?*" (Taylor Swift has not yet released any rap album)).

Table 10. The numbers and percentages (%, in parenthesis) of questions for each category of dynamism, decided manually. Finance and Sports domain have the most Real-time and Fast-changing questions.

Dynamism	Finance	Sports	Music	Movie	Open	Total
Real-time	434 (42)	0 (0)	2 (0)	0 (0)	1 (0)	437 (10)
Fast-changing	204 (20)	275 (33)	40 (6)	17 (2)	28 (4)	564 (13)
Slow-changing	183 (18)	215 (26)	152 (24)	253 (22)	204 (26)	1,007 (23)
Static	218 (21)	343 (41)	430 (69)	855 (76)	555 (70)	2,401 (54)
All	1,039	833	624	1,125	788	4,409

4.4.1. Straightforward RAG Solutions Achieve 44% Accuracy on CRAG

The straightforward RAG solution used Llama 2 Chat (`llama-2-7b-chat` and `llama-2-70b-chat`) [3], Llama 3 Instruct (`llama-3-8B-instruct` and `llama-3-70B-instruct`) [40], and GPT-4 Turbo [2]. The web-only RAG solutions (Task 1) used a fixed-length web context window (2K tokens for Llama 2 Chat and 4K for Llama 3 Instruct and GPT-4 Turbo); webpage snippets were concatenated using the original order from the data as the reference text, until filling up the window (similar to [49,54, 83]). The KG-based solutions (Tasks 2, 3) additionally used a fixed-length KG context window (1K tokens for Llama 2 Chat and 2K for Llama 3 Instruct and GPT-4 Turbo) to include the results from the Mock APIs; CRAG extracted relevant query entities using

Table 11. The number and percentages (%, in parenthesis) of questions for each question type, decided manually. Simple and simple with condition questions constitute 43% of all questions.

Question type	Finance	Sports	Music	Movie	Open	Total
Simple	466 (45)	23 (3)	112 (18)	519 (46)	85 (11)	1,205 (27)
Simple w. cond.	113 (11)	250 (30)	92 (15)	112 (10)	122 (15)	689 (16)
Set	48 (5)	93 (11)	72 (12)	104 (9)	86 (11)	403 (9)
Comparison	146 (14)	85 (10)	102 (16)	105 (9)	98 (12)	536 (12)
Aggregation	69 (7)	137 (16)	96 (15)	71 (6)	116 (15)	489 (11)
Multi-hop	86 (8)	64 (8)	55 (9)	90 (8)	87 (11)	382 (9)
Post-processing	26 (3)	24 (3)	26 (4)	28 (2)	76 (10)	180 (4)
False Premise	85 (8)	157 (19)	69 (11)	96 (9)	118 (15)	525 (12)
All	1,039	833	624	1,125	788	4,409

Table 12. Performance of straightforward RAG solutions. All numbers are in percentage. LLM-only solutions has up to 34% accuracy and straightforward RAG solutions has up to 44% accuracy.

	Model	Accuracy	Hallucination	Missing	Score_a
LLM only	Llama 3 70B Instruct	32.3	28.9	38.8	3.4
	GPT-4 Turbo	**33.5**	**13.5**	53.0	**20.0**
Task 1	Llama 3 70B Instruct	35.6	31.1	33.3	4.5
	GPT-4 Turbo	**35.9**	**28.2**	35.9	**7.7**
Task 2	Llama 3 70B Instruct	37.5	29.2	33.3	8.3
	GPT-4 Turbo	**41.3**	**25.1**	33.6	**16.2**
Task 3	Llama 3 70B Instruct	40.6	31.6	27.8	9.1
	GPT-4 Turbo	**43.6**	**30.1**	26.3	**13.4**

`llama-3-8B-instruct` with in-context learning (similar to [84]) and concatenated the results returned from all applicable mock APIs (based on the extracted entities), until filling up the window.

Table 12 shows the average evaluation scores from the two auto-evaluators (ChatGPT and Llama 3) and reveals gaps of the straightforward RAG solutions. First, the best LLM-only solutions (GPT-4 Turbo) obtained an accuracy of only 34%, with a score of 20%, showing a big room for improvement. Second, straightforward RAG solutions obtained up to 44% accuracy, showing that extra information *does* help answer more questions reliably. Interestingly, none of the RAG solutions obtain a score higher than 20%; this is because all RAG solutions introduce more hallucinations generated from irrelevant retrieval results, showing a big challenge in RAG—*How to judiciously use retrieval results without being distracted by retrieval noise?* Third, Task 2 scores are higher than Task 1, showing that the KG knowledge helps improve accuracy, with a similar or even lower hallucination rate, because the KG knowledge is typically brief but precise. Unfortunately, the improvement is mediocre, showing a second challenge in RAG—*How to best leverage the power of KG data?* Finally, the scores for Task 3 are also higher than Task 2, because of better search ranking (recall that Task 1 and 2 provide five pages

Table 13. Benchmarking CRAG questions with industry SOTA RAG systems. Perfect, acceptable (Acc.), hallucination (Hall.), missing (Miss.) rates, and score$_h$ are in percentages. The best system achieves a score of 51% and provides perfect answers for up to 63% of questions.

	System	Perfect	Acc.	Hall.	Miss.	Score$_h$	Latency (ms)
Equal weighted	Copilot Pro	**62.6**	11.7	17.9	7.8	**50.6**	11,596
	Gemini Advanced	60.8	10.1	**16.6**	12.5	49.3	5,246
	ChatGPT Plus	59.8	**13.1**	25.2	1.9	41.2	6,195
	Perplexity.ai	55.8	8.8	25.3	10.1	34.9	**2,455**
Traffic weighted	Copilot Pro	**60.7**	**14.2**	18.5	6.7	**49.3**	-
	Gemini Advanced	59.1	10.9	**16.6**	13.4	48.0	-
	ChatGPT Plus	59.7	13.3	25.1	1.9	41.3	-
	Perplexity.ai	55.8	9.7	25.2	9.3	35.5	-

randomly selected from the top-10 search results) and better search recall. This shows *the importance of search ranking* in RAG.

4.4.2. State-of-the-art Industry Solutions Only Answers 63% CRAG Questions Without any Hallucination

The authors also queried four RAG systems built upon SOTA LLMs and search engines with CRAG questions, collected the responses, and applied manual grading.

In addition, traffic weights were applied to the questions to understand the solutions in real-world use cases. The traffic weights come from a real QA use case and are generated as follows. Within each domain, questions were first clustered into sub-domains (e.g., current game points, sports teams), and then derived the sub-domain weights from aggregated data reflective of user interactions. The sub-domain weight was applied to each CRAG question to bridge the result to reflect user experience, and reported the macro average scores across all domains (i.e., giving the same weight to all domains) in Table 13.

Table 13 and Figure 6 show the overall performance of the SOTA systems and their performance across different dimensions. The evaluation results confirm that the CRAG benchmark *reveals interesting insights and shows room for improvement for existing RAG solutions.* First, the scores from SOTA solutions achieve much better scores (highest 51%) compared to the straightforward solutions. However, the weighted hallucination rate ranges from 17% to 25%, so the answers are still *not* trustworthy. Note that the scores between the SOTA solutions and the straightforward solutions are not completely comparable, as they have different accesses to retrieval contents, and the former used auto-eval, while the latter used human-eval; however, the trend is valid. Second, most difficult slices we see in the straightforward solutions remain to be difficult for SOTA solutions: *real-time* and *fast-changing* queries, and questions regarding *torso* and *tail* entities, showing the improvement needed for handling retrieval noise when the system relies on retrieval results to answer the question; as another example, we see lower scores for queries requiring *multi-hop reasoning* or *post-processing*, showing the improvement space for reasoning in question answering. Third, the third SOTA system has slightly higher weighted accuracy (perfect + acceptable) compared to the second system (73% and 70%), but much higher *hallucination* (25.1% and 16.6%), indicating the needs for

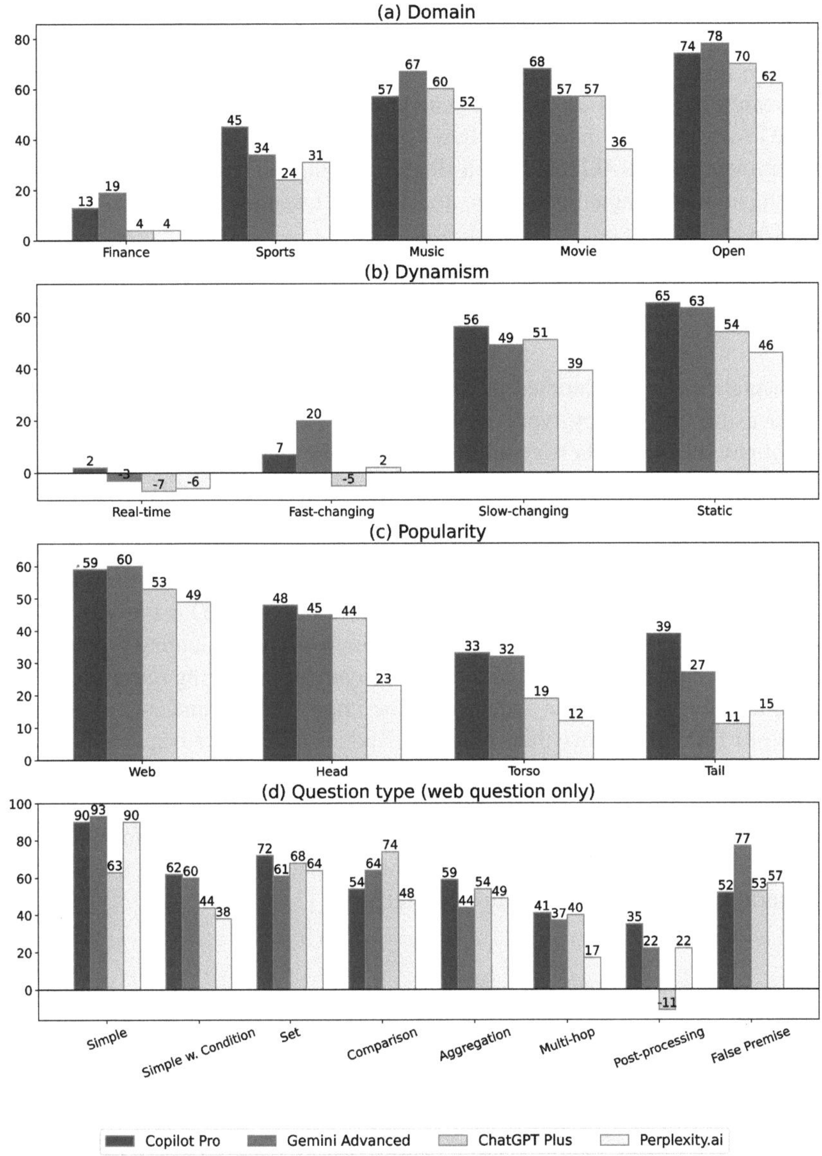

Figure 6. SOTA systems human-eval scores (in percentage) across different dimensions.

building RAG systems to wisely answer "I don't know" when confident answers cannot be found. Last, scores on *set* and *false premise* questions improved significantly in the SOTA solutions compared to the straightforward solutions, showing advancement in RAG systems in providing accurate and complete set answers and detecting *false premises*. Finally, we observed very different latency, ranging from 2.5s to 11.6s, reflecting the different design options in trading off latency and quality. Note that the latency results come from interacting with the API for Perplexity.ai and the web interfaces for the other systems.

4.5. Summary

This section discussed CRAG, a rich and comprehensive benchmark designed to advance research in retrieval-augmented generation (RAG). With detailed empirical studies, CRAG reviewed gaps in existing RAG solutions and provided valuable insights for future improvement. CRAG focused on single-turn English text queries. Future research can investigate multi-lingual questions, multi-modal questions, multi-turn conversations to push RAG research.

5. Conclusion

In this chapter, we have examined the crucial aspects of internalized knowledge within LLMs, focusing on two key types: taxonomy knowledge and factual knowledge. We have highlighted how LLMs store and utilize these forms of knowledge, demonstrating their strengths in recognizing patterns and relationships while identifying the challenges posed by incomplete or outdated internalized data.

Additionally, we discussed retrieval-augmented generation (RAG) in complementing LLMs' internal knowledge, offering external resources to enhance model performance in tasks that require current and accurate information. Our introduction of the CRAG benchmark provided a comprehensive framework for evaluating both the internal knowledge capabilities of LLMs and their proficiency in leveraging retrieval systems.

In conclusion, this chapter underscores the importance of understanding the inner workings of LLMs to improve their reliability and accuracy. By advancing both internal knowledge mechanisms and retrieval-augmented techniques, researchers can enhance the capacity of LLMs to deliver trustworthy, informed responses across a wide range of applications. The insights gleaned from this chapter lay the foundation for future work in building more advanced and reliable AI systems, capable of navigating the complexities of real-world knowledge representation and retrieval.

References

[1] Yang X, Sun K, Xin H, Sun Y, Bhalla N, Chen X, et al. CRAG – Comprehensive RAG Benchmark. arXiv preprint arXiv:240604744. 2024. Available from: https://arxiv.org/abs/2406.04744.

[2] Achiam J, Adler S, Agarwal S, Ahmad L, Akkaya I, Aleman FL, et al. GPT-4 Technical Report. arXiv preprint arXiv:230308774. 2023.

[3] Touvron H, Martin L, Stone K, Albert P, Almahairi A, Babaei Y, et al. Llama 2: Open foundation and fine-tuned chat models. arXiv preprint arXiv:230709288. 2023.

[4] Devlin J, Chang MW, Lee K, Toutanova K. BERT: Pre-training of Deep Bidirectional Transformers for Language Understanding. In: Proceedings of the 2019 Conference of the North American Chapter of the Association for Computational Linguistics: Human Language Technologies, Volume 1 (Long and Short Papers); 2019. p. 4171-86.

[5] Tan Y, Min D, Li Y, Li W, Hu N, Chen Y, et al. Can ChatGPT replace traditional KBQA models? An in-depth analysis of the question answering performance of the GPT LLM family. In: International Semantic Web Conference. Springer; 2023. p. 348-67.

[6] Zhang T, Ladhak F, Durmus E, Liang P, McKeown K, Hashimoto TB. Benchmarking large language models for news summarization. Transactions of the Association for Computational Linguistics. 2024;12:39-57.

[7] Zhu Y, Yuan H, Wang S, Liu J, Liu W, Deng C, et al. Large language models for information retrieval: A survey. arXiv preprint arXiv:230807107. 2023.

[8] Wadhwa S, Amir S, Wallace BC. Revisiting relation extraction in the era of large language models. In: Proceedings of the conference. Association for Computational Linguistics. Meeting. vol. 2023. NIH Public Access; 2023. p. 15566.
[9] Tu J, Fan J, Tang N, Wang P, Li G, Du X, et al. Unicorn: A Unified Multi-tasking Model for Supporting Matching Tasks in Data Integration. Proc ACM Manag Data. 2023;1(1):84:1-84:26.
[10] Fan M, Han X, Fan J, Chai C, Tang N, Li G, et al. Cost-Effective In-Context Learning for Entity Resolution: A Design Space Exploration. In: ICDE. IEEE; 2024. p. 3696-709.
[11] Fan J, Tu J, Li G, Wang P, Du X, Jia X, et al. Unicorn: A Unified Multi-Tasking Matching Model. SIGMOD Rec. 2024;53(1):44-53.
[12] Ebraheem M, Thirumuruganathan S, Joty SR, Ouzzani M, Tang N. Distributed Representations of Tuples for Entity Resolution. Proc VLDB Endow. 2018;11(11):1454-67.
[13] Tang N, Fan J, Li F, Tu J, Du X, Li G, et al. RPT: Relational Pre-trained Transformer Is Almost All You Need towards Democratizing Data Preparation. Proc VLDB Endow. 2021;14(8):1254-61.
[14] Luo Y, Tang N, Li G, Tang J, Chai C, Qin X. Natural Language to Visualization by Neural Machine Translation. IEEE Trans Vis Comput Graph. 2022;28(1):217-26.
[15] Luo Y, Zhou Y, Tang N, Li G, Chai C, Shen L. Learned Data-aware Image Representations of Line Charts for Similarity Search. Proc ACM Manag Data. 2023;1(1):88:1-88:29.
[16] Luo Y, Tang N, Li G, Chai C, Li W, Qin X. Synthesizing Natural Language to Visualization (NL2VIS) Benchmarks from NL2SQL Benchmarks. In: SIGMOD; 2021. p. 1235-47.
[17] Sun Y, Xin H, Chen L. Reca: Related tables enhanced column semantic type annotation framework. Proceedings of the VLDB Endowment. 2023;16(6):1319-31.
[18] Deng Y, Chai C, Cao L, Yuan Q, Chen S, Yu Y, et al. LakeBench: A Benchmark for Discovering Joinable and Unionable Tables in Data Lakes. Proc VLDB Endow. 2024;17(8):1925-38.
[19] Chen Z, Cao L, Madden S, Fan J, Tang N, Gu Z, et al. SEED: Simple, Efficient, and Effective Data Management via Large Language Models. CoRR. 2023;abs/2310.00749.
[20] Sun Y, Wang J, Cheng P, Zheng L, Chen L, Yin J. Cross-Domain-Aware Worker Selection with Training for Crowdsourced Annotation. In: 2024 IEEE 40th International Conference on Data Engineering (ICDE); 2024. p. 249-62.
[21] Gu Z, Fan J, Tang N, Cao L, Jia B, Madden S, et al. Few-shot Text-to-SQL Translation using Structure and Content Prompt Learning. Proc ACM Manag Data. 2023;1(2):147:1-147:28.
[22] Gu Z, Fan J, Tang N, Nakov P, Zhao X, Du X. PASTA: Table-Operations Aware Fact Verification via Sentence-Table Cloze Pre-training. In: EMNLP; 2022. p. 4971-83.
[23] Li B, Luo Y, Chai C, Li G, Tang N. The Dawn of Natural Language to SQL: Are We Fully Ready? CoRR. 2024;abs/2406.01265.
[24] Bang Y, Cahyawijaya S, Lee N, Dai W, Su D, Wilie B, et al. A multitask, multilingual, multimodal evaluation of chatgpt on reasoning, hallucination, and interactivity. arXiv preprint arXiv:230204023. 2023.
[25] Sun K, Xu Y, Zha H, Liu Y, Dong XL. Head-to-Tail: How Knowledgeable are Large Language Models (LLMs)? AKA Will LLMs Replace Knowledge Graphs? In: Proceedings of the 2024 Conference of the North American Chapter of the Association for Computational Linguistics: Human Language Technologies (Volume 1: Long Papers); 2024. p. 311-25.
[26] Choi Y. Common Sense: The Dark Matter of Language and Intelligence. In: Proceedings of the 2023 International Conference on Autonomous Agents and Multiagent Systems; 2023. p. 2-2.
[27] Chu X, Morcos J, Ilyas IF, Ouzzani M, Papotti P, Tang N, et al. KATARA: A Data Cleaning System Powered by Knowledge Bases and Crowdsourcing. In: SIGMOD. ACM; 2015. p. 1247-61.
[28] Babaei Giglou H, D'Souza J, Auer S. LLMs4OL: Large language models for ontology learning. In: International Semantic Web Conference. Springer; 2023. p. 408-27.
[29] Neuhaus F. Ontologies in the era of large language models–a perspective. Applied Ontology. 2023;18(4):399-407.
[30] Sun Y, Xin H, Sun K, Xu YE, Yang X, Dong XL, et al. Are Large Language Models a Good Replacement of Taxonomies? arXiv preprint arXiv:240611131. 2024.
[31] Google Product Category; 2021. Available from: `https://www.google.com/basepages/producttype/taxonomy.en-US.txt`.
[32] Amazon's Product Category; 2019. Available from: `https://www.browsenodes.com/`.
[33] eBay; 2024. Available from: `https://www.ebay.com/n/all-categories`.
[34] Guha RV, Brickley D, Macbeth S. Schema. org: evolution of structured data on the web. Communica-

tions of the ACM. 2016;59(2):44-51.
[35] ACM Computing Classification System; 2012. Available from: https://dl.acm.org/ccs.
[36] Geonames Website; 2024. Available from: https://www.geonames.org/export/codes.html.
[37] Glottolog-4.8; 2023. Available from: https://glottolog.org/meta/downloads.
[38] NCBI data download; 2023. Available from: https://ftp.ncbi.nlm.nih.gov/pub/taxonomy/.
[39] Claude-v3-documentation; 2024. Available from: https://www.anthropic.com/news/claude-3-family.
[40] Llama 3 Model Card; 2024. Available from: https://github.com/meta-llama/llama3/blob/main/MODEL_CARD.md.
[41] Chung HW, Hou L, Longpre S, Zoph B, Tay Y, Fedus W, et al. Scaling instruction-finetuned language models. arXiv preprint arXiv:221011416. 2022.
[42] Almazrouei E, Alobeidli H, Alshamsi A, Cappelli A, Cojocaru R, Debbah M, et al. The falcon series of open language models. arXiv preprint arXiv:231116867. 2023.
[43] Chiang WL, Li Z, Lin Z, Sheng Y, Wu Z, Zhang H, et al. Vicuna: An open-source chatbot impressing gpt-4 with 90%* chatgpt quality. See https://vicuna lmsys org (accessed 14 Apr 2023). 2023.
[44] Jiang AQ, Sablayrolles A, Mensch A, Bamford C, Chaplot DS, Casas Ddl, et al. Mistral 7B. arXiv preprint arXiv:231006825. 2023.
[45] Jiang AQ, Sablayrolles A, Roux A, Mensch A, Savary B, Bamford C, et al. Mixtral of experts. arXiv preprint arXiv:240104088. 2024.
[46] Kojima T, Gu SS, Reid M, Matsuo Y, Iwasawa Y. Large language models are zero-shot reasoners. Advances in neural information processing systems. 2022;35:22199-213.
[47] Wei J, Wang X, Schuurmans D, Bosma M, Xia F, Chi E, et al. Chain-of-thought prompting elicits reasoning in large language models. Advances in Neural Information Processing Systems. 2022;35:24824-37.
[48] Tang N, Yang C, Fan J, Cao L, Luo Y, Halevy AY. VerifAI: Verified Generative AI. In: CIDR; 2024. .
[49] Vu T, Iyyer M, Wang X, Constant N, Wei J, Wei J, et al.. FreshLLMs: Refreshing Large Language Models with Search Engine Augmentation; 2023.
[50] Omar R, Mangukiya O, Kalnis P, Mansour E. ChatGPT versus Traditional Question Answering for Knowledge Graphs: Current Status and Future Directions Towards Knowledge Graph Chatbots; 2023.
[51] Ouyang L, Wu J, Jiang X, Almeida D, Wainwright C, Mishkin P, et al. Training language models to follow instructions with human feedback. Advances in Neural Information Processing Systems. 2022;35:27730-44.
[52] OpenAI. GPT-4 Technical Report; 2023.
[53] Mallen A, Asai A, Zhong V, Das R, Khashabi D, Hajishirzi H. When Not to Trust Language Models: Investigating Effectiveness of Parametric and Non-Parametric Memories. In: Proceedings of the 61st Annual Meeting of the Association for Computational Linguistics (Volume 1: Long Papers). Toronto, Canada: Association for Computational Linguistics; 2023. p. 9802-22. Available from: https://aclanthology.org/2023.acl-long.546.
[54] Kandpal N, Deng H, Roberts A, Wallace E, Raffel C. Large language models struggle to learn long-tail knowledge. In: International Conference on Machine Learning. PMLR; 2023. p. 15696-707.
[55] Yasunaga M, Ren H, Bosselut A, Liang P, Leskovec J. QA-GNN: Reasoning with Language Models and Knowledge Graphs for Question Answering. Association for Computational Linguistics; 2021. .
[56] Liu P, Yuan W, Fu J, Jiang Z, Hayashi H, Neubig G. Pre-train, prompt, and predict: A systematic survey of prompting methods in natural language processing. ACM Computing Surveys. 2023;55(9):1-35.
[57] Liévin V, Hother CE, Motzfeldt AG, Winther O. Can large language models reason about medical questions? Patterns. 2024;5(3).
[58] Rawte V, Chakraborty S, Pathak A, Sarkar A, Tonmoy S, Chadha A, et al. The Troubling Emergence of Hallucination in Large Language Models–An Extensive Definition, Quantification, and Prescriptive Remediations. arXiv preprint arXiv:231004988. 2023.
[59] Ji Z, Lee N, Frieske R, Yu T, Su D, Xu Y, et al. Survey of Hallucination in Natural Language Generation. ACM Comput Surv. 2023 mar;55(12).
[60] Huang L, Yu W, Ma W, Zhong W, Feng Z, Wang H, et al. A survey on hallucination in large language models: Principles, taxonomy, challenges, and open questions. arXiv preprint arXiv:231105232. 2023.
[61] Gao Y, Xiong Y, Gao X, Jia K, Pan J, Bi Y, et al. Retrieval-Augmented Generation for Large Language Models: A Survey. arXiv preprint arXiv:231210997. 2024.
[62] Lewis P, Perez E, Piktus A, Petroni F, Karpukhin V, Goyal N, et al.. Retrieval-Augmented Generation

for Knowledge-Intensive NLP Tasks; 2021.
[63] Chen J, Lin H, Han X, Sun L. Benchmarking large language models in retrieval-augmented generation. arXiv preprint arXiv:230901431. 2023.
[64] Chen Z, Gu Z, Cao L, Fan J, Madden S, Tang N. Symphony: Towards Natural Language Query Answering over Multi-modal Data Lakes. In: CIDR; 2023. .
[65] Chen W, Hu H, Chen X, Verga P, Cohen W. MuRAG: Multimodal Retrieval-Augmented Generator for Open Question Answering over Images and Text. In: Proceedings of the 2022 Conference on Empirical Methods in Natural Language Processing; 2022. .
[66] Asai A, Wu Z, Wang Y, Sil A, Hajishirzi H. Self-rag: Learning to retrieve, generate, and critique through self-reflection. arXiv preprint arXiv:231011511. 2023.
[67] Li X, Zhao R, Chia YK, Ding B, Joty S, Poria S, et al. Chain-of-Knowledge: Grounding Large Language Models via Dynamic Knowledge Adapting over Heterogeneous Sources. In: The Twelfth International Conference on Learning Representations; 2023. .
[68] Kwiatkowski T, Palomaki J, Redfield O, Collins M, Parikh A, Alberti C, et al. Natural Questions: a Benchmark for Question Answering Research. Transactions of the Association of Computational Linguistics. 2019.
[69] Joshi M, Choi E, Weld D, Zettlemoyer L. TriviaQA: A Large Scale Distantly Supervised Challenge Dataset for Reading Comprehension. Association for Computational Linguistics; 2017. .
[70] Wu Y, Zhu J, Xu S, Shum K, Niu C, Zhong R, et al. Ragtruth: A hallucination corpus for developing trustworthy retrieval-augmented language models. arXiv preprint arXiv:240100396. 2023.
[71] Li M, Zhao Y, Yu B, Song F, Li H, Yu H, et al. Api-bank: A comprehensive benchmark for tool-augmented llms. arXiv preprint arXiv:230408244. 2023.
[72] Bajaj P, Campos D, Craswell N, Deng L, Gao J, Liu X, et al.. MS MARCO: A Human Generated MAchine Reading COmprehension Dataset; 2018.
[73] Usbeck R, Yan X, Perevalov A, Jiang L, Schulz J, Kraft A, et al. QALD-10–The 10th challenge on question answering over linked data. Semantic Web. 2023;(Preprint):1-15.
[74] Mallen A, Asai A, Zhong V, Das R, Khashabi D, Hajishirzi H. When not to trust language models: Investigating effectiveness of parametric and non-parametric memories. arXiv preprint arXiv:221210511. 2022.
[75] Tang Y, Yang Y. Multihop-rag: Benchmarking retrieval-augmented generation for multi-hop queries. arXiv preprint arXiv:240115391. 2024.
[76] Friel R, Belyi M, Sanyal A. RAGBench: Explainable Benchmark for Retrieval-Augmented Generation Systems. arXiv preprint arXiv:240711005. 2024.
[77] Gao M, Hu X, Ruan J, Pu X, Wan X. Llm-based nlg evaluation: Current status and challenges. arXiv preprint arXiv:240201383. 2024.
[78] Adlakha V, BehnamGhader P, Lu XH, Meade N, Reddy S. Evaluating correctness and faithfulness of instruction-following models for question answering. arXiv preprint arXiv:230716877. 2023.
[79] Brave Software. Brave Search API;. Available from: `https://search.brave.com/`.
[80] Xu F, Song Y, Iyyer M, Choi E. A Critical Evaluation of Evaluations for Long-form Question Answering. In: Association of Computational Linguistics; 2023. .
[81] Panickssery A, Bowman SR, Feng S. Llm evaluators recognize and favor their own generations. arXiv preprint arXiv:240413076. 2024.
[82] OpenAI. ChatGPT; 2023. Accessed: 2024-06-04. `https://openai.com/index/chatgpt/`.
[83] Mallen A, Asai A, Zhong V, Das R, Khashabi D, Hajishirzi H. When not to trust language models: Investigating effectiveness of parametric and non-parametric memories. In: ACL; 2023. .
[84] Schick T, Dwivedi-Yu J, Dessi R, Raileanu R, Lomeli M, Zettlemoyer L, et al. Toolformer: Language Models Can Teach Themselves to Use Tools. arXiv. 2023.

Part III

Knowledge Graph Construction, Integration, and Quality

Handbook on Neurosymbolic AI and Knowledge Graphs
P. Hitzler et al. (Eds.)
IOS Press, 2025

doi:10.3233/FAIA250211

Unsupervised Entity Alignment of Knowledge Graphs

Weishan CAI [a], and Yuncheng JIANG* [b,c]

[a] *School of Computer Science, Guangdong University of Education, GuangZhou 510303, China*

[b] *School of Computer Science, South China Normal University, GuangZhou 510631, China*

[c] *School of Artificial Intelligence and School of Software, South China Normal University, Foshan 528225, China*

ORCiD ID: Weishan Cai https://orcid.org/0000-0003-2416-6841, Yuncheng Jiang https://orcid.org/0000-0002-0402-5382

Abstract. In recent years, Knowledge Graphs (KGs) have sprung up in various fields to support a variety of applications, like question answering, recommendations, etc. When integrating knowledge from different KGs, a common task is to identify some equivalent entities from multiple KGs describing real-world objects, which is called the entity Alignment (EA) task. In recent years, unsupervised EA methods have attracted the interest of many researchers and achieved many research results. However, there are few literatures that comprehensively compare and analyze the modeling frameworks, research ideas and techniques of these methods. This chapter focuses on the research ideas and status of this field in order to provide practical insights. We summarize and analyze 22 unsupervised EA methods that have emerged in recent years, and propose a general framework for unsupervised EA methods. Then the related methods are divided into two categories: EA methods with training and EA methods without training, and the characteristics and implementation techniques of the related methods are analyzed. In addition, the current research challenges in this field are summarized and future research directions are prospected.

Keywords. Unsupervised Entity Alignment, Entity Alignment, Unsupervised Learning, Knowledge Graph

1. Introduction

With the development of graph construction technology, more and more knowledge graphs (KGs) have emerged, covering common sense knowledge, vocabulary knowledge, encyclopedic knowledge, taxonomy knowledge and geographical knowledge [1]. KGs play a huge role in a wide range of real-world applications such as text understanding, recommender systems, and natural language question answering, as they provide accurate explicit knowledge [2].

One of the core goals of artificial intelligence is to build a large-scale knowledge base that supports human-like reasoning and natural language understanding. However,

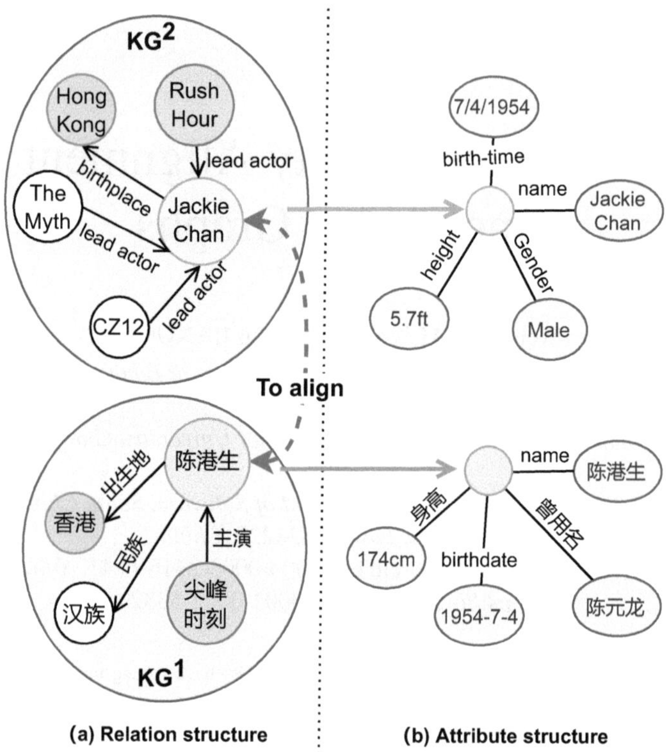

Figure 1. An example for entity alignment between two KGs.

due to the complexity, openness, diversity and huge scale of human knowledge, there is currently no large-scale knowledge base that meets the above requirements. Pure graph construction methods[3,4] are not enough to handle the incompleteness and dynamics of KGs in the real world, and it is difficult to construct KGs with comprehensive knowledge coverage.

An effective way to solve this problem is to integrate multiple KGs into a unified KG, which can not only expand the knowledge coverage, but also help refine the KG by discovering potential defects. The *Entity Alignment* (EA) task discussed in this chapter is one of the core tasks of KG integration. EA task aims to identify equivalent entity pairs from multiple KGs that describe real-world objects, thereby bridging heterogeneous information sources and promoting knowledge integration. Equivalent entity pairs refer to two entities that describe the same thing in the objective world but come from different knowledge graphs. Figure 1 shows the structural relationship of the entity "*Jackie Chan*" in two different KGs, including the relation structure and attribute structure.

As we all know, machine learning methods can be divided into three categories: supervised, semi-supervised, and unsupervised methods, distinguished by the percentage of available labeled data. Supervised methods rely on labeled data for model training. When only a small portion of the data is labeled, semi-supervised methods become a sub-optimal choice. It can use both labeled and unlabeled data during training. Since 2016, EA method has attracted the attention of many researchers and achieved excellent performance improvement. Earlier EA methods are supervised learning methods and state-of-the-art solutions. But their success depends heavily on the regulatory information provided by labels. Considering the cost of annotating data, in most practical scenarios, it is impossible to obtain enough training corpora to handle different fields, texts with different styles (standard, non-standard), and different languages (Chinese, English, and "Belt and Road" minority languages, etc.). Unsupervised technology without large training corpora, automatic resource construction technology, and transfer learning technology are the core research issues to solve the above problems.

Many books and special issues have also been devoted to this topic, although it is not possible for us to cover EA in full depth in this chapter. In this section, we try to provide practical insights by focusing on the current state of research ideas and techniques in the field of unsupervised EA methods. Although this research direction is developing rapidly, there are still some open questions about the underlying assumptions of the methods, the efficiency and effectiveness of EA in the real world. This chapter will discuss the following insights missing from the literature:

- Q1. **Method architecture**. What is the difference between unsupervised and supervised EA methods? What is the implementation of unsupervised methods?
- Q2. **Method family**. In addition to the relation structure of KGs, what other information can be considered in EA tasks? What are the common implementation techniques?
- Q3:**Method characteristics**. What are the differences and connections between different methods? What improvements can be made to the effectiveness of unsupervised alignment methods?
- Q4:**Research prospects**. What are the shortcomings of unsupervised EA methods? What are the future research directions of unsupervised EA methods?

Roadmap. The rest of this chapter is organized as follows: we first formalize the relevant problems in Section 2 and propose a general framework for unsupervised EA methods in Section 3, then report and analyze two categories of unsupervised EA methods in Sections 4 and 5, respectively. Finally, we summarize and look forward to existing research in Section 6.

2. Problem Formulation

In this section, we give some formal definitions relevant to this study before discussing related unsupervised EA methods.

Knowledge Graph (KG) stores knowledge edges or real-world facts in the form of triples, and is a structured and deterministic representation of knowledge. A triple is composed of three elements in the form *(head, predicate, tail)*, where *head* represents an entity, *tail* represents another entity or a literal (attribute value), and *predicate* represents the relationship between the former two. Here, if *tail* is an entity, the triple is called a *relation triple* and the *predicate* is called a *relation predicate*; If *tail* is a literal, the triple is called an *attribute triple* and the *predicate* is called an *attribute predicate*. The formal definitions of KG and EA task are given below.

Knowledge Graph (KG). Let E, R, A and V be the sets of entities, relations, attributes, and attribute values, respectively. A KG can be formulated as $G = (E,R,A,V,T_R,T_A)$, where T^R, T^A are the relation structure and attribute structure, respectively. Specifically, T_R and T_A are formalized as

$$T_R = \{(h,r,t)|h,t \in E, r \in R\} \subseteq E \times R \times E,$$
$$T_A = \{(h,a,v)|h \in E, a \in A, v \in V\} \subseteq E \times A \times V. \tag{1}$$

Obviously, a relation triple represents the relationship between two entities, and a attribute triple represents the attributes of an entity.

Entity Alignment (EA). The task of EA aims to find the set of equivalent entity pairs across two KGs, $G^1 = (E^1, R^1, A^1, V^1, T_R^1, T_A^1)$ and $G^2 = (E^2, R^2, A^2, V^2, T_R^2, T_A^2)$, denotes as

$$Y = \{(e^1, e^2)|e^1 \equiv e^2, e^1 \in E^1, e^2 \in E^2\}, \tag{2}$$

where the equivalence $\equiv$ indicates that two entities refer tothe same real-world object. In many cases, there will exist a small subset of equivalent entity pairs known in advance, called *seed alignments* and used as training data. However, no *seed alignments* are observed during EA model training in the unsupervised setting.

For convenience, sometimes we put G^1 and G^2 together as a primal graph $G = (E, R, A, V, T_R, T_A)$, where $E = E^1 \cup E^2$, $R = R^1 \cup R^2$, $A = A^1 \cup A^2$, $V = V^1 \cup V^2$, $T_R = T_R^1 \cup T_R^2$ and $T_A = T_A^1 \cup T_A^2$. Formally, we use capital calligraphic letters for sets and boldface letters for vectors and matrices.

3. General Framework for Unsupervised EA

In this section, we study unsupervised EA methods from the perspective of model framework, and then introduce their related works respectively.

To further explore the learning mode of unsupervised EA methods, we propose a general framework of unsupervised EA. Based on the analysis and summary of existing related works, unsupervised EA methods are divided into two categories according to the training method: EA methods with training and EA methods without training. Figure 2 (a) describes the four components of unsupervised EA methods with training:

1. **Input Module.** In addition to the basic relation structure, KGs also contains a large amount of auxiliary information. So far, the auxiliary information introduced in various works includes attribute structure, surface form (i.e., entity name, entity description, image, etc.), side information (relation, attribute, etc.).
2. **Alignment Estimate Module.** This module mainly estimates the similarity between the unaligned embedding obtained from external resources and the model encoder, and generates an alignment result (or called pseudo-label set). This module focuses on the design of similarity measurement functions and alignment inference strategies.
3. **Encoder Module.** EA methods based on representation learning [5,6,7] have become the mainstream solution for entity alignment due to their superior flexibility and accuracy. This module encodes node and side information such as relations and entities of KGs. The most commonly used encoders are based on translation models (e.g., TransE [8]) or Graph Neural Networks (e.g., GCN [9], GAT [10]).
4. **Alignment Learning Module.** This module first computes the similarity of unaligned aligned entities, just as *similarity calculation module.* does. Then a loss function is designed to train the embeddings output by the encoder module.

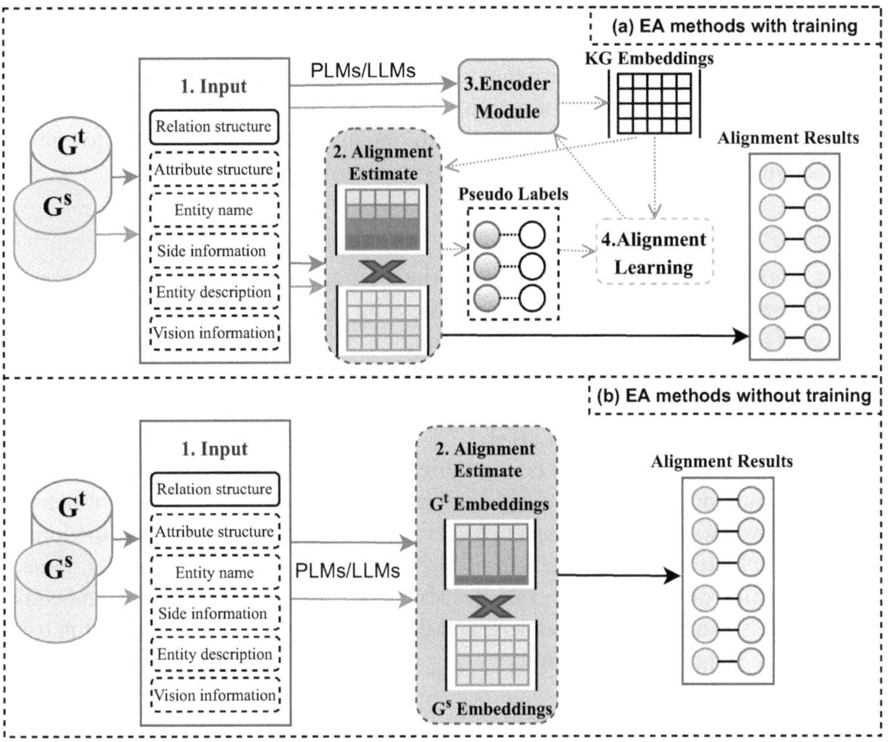

Figure 2. A general framework for unsupervised EA, where the data or modules contained by the dashed lines are optional (i.e., not all methods contain them) and the red virtual edges represent the training process.

Margin-based ranking function [8], Noise Contrastive Estimation (NCE) and so no are the most common choices.

Since the unsupervised EA methods without training has no training process, it only contains *Input*, *Alignment Estimate*, as shown in Figure 2(b). In the next two sections, we will discuss the related works of these two classification methods in detail.

4. EA Methods with Training

In this section, we will introduce the popular methods for implementing unsupervised EA methods with training in detail based on four modules.

4.1. Input Module

According to the input data for the model, unsupervised EA methods can be divided into three categories: relation structure-based methods, auxiliary text-based methods, and multimodal-based methods.

The most common input of EA task is the relation structures of KGs, which represents the external relationships between entities. Some works (e.g., SEU [11], UEA [12], SelfKG [13], UPLR [14], UED [15], SS-AGA [16], etc) primarily mine the similarity of aligned entities from their relation neighborhood structure. However, as an unsupervised method, it is difficult to obtain sufficient supervised information solely from the relation structures. Some researchers believe that unsupervised methods are best to maximize the exploration of more auxiliary information to eliminate the need for labeled data in EA. Therefore, they use some external resources to obtain semantic embeddings to enhance the extraction and alignment learning of entity name information.

4.1.1. External Resources

The first popular external resources are various language models, which have made significant progress in natural language processing (NLP). The language models are mainly used to convert a variety of text information into embedded vectors to obtain the text semantic information. Common language models include Word embedding models (e.g.,N-gram [17], GloVe [18], fastText [19], etc), pre-trained language models (PLMs) (e.g.,BERT [20], RoBERTa [21], LaBSE [22], etc) and large language models (LLMs).

Word embedding models can be used directly by looking for "dictionary" from the word embedding model, which is simple and easy to use. Since all textual information is composed of words or character sequences, it can be used directly by finding "dictionary" from PLMs, which is easy to use. Let $n_e = (w_1, w_2, ..., w_k)$ denote the entity name of enity e, consisting of k words. For example, **MultiKE** [23] queries each word embedding in n_e from the word embedding models, and then uses average pooling operation to get the final entity embedding as follows:

$$\mathbf{e}^n = ||Mean_{w_j \in n_e}(encode(w_j))||, \tag{3}$$

where $encode()$ returns the queried word embeddings.

Nevertheless, word embedding models only contain the pure word meaning of the text itself, but words have different meanings in different contexts. That is, the vector representations of words in two pieces of text in different contexts are the same. PLMs such as BERT [20], RoBERTa [21] can capture deep bidirectional representations of language through pre-training on large-scale text data. They allow downstream tasks to fine-tuning the results of pre-training to better understand the context and semantic relations of language. For example, **ICLEA** [24] and **SelfKG** [13] fully input entity names and relation names into PLMs to obtain the corresponding embeddings. Next, the average pooling operation is applied to the embedding of each token, followed by $L2$ normalization:

$$\mathbf{e}^n = ||f_{\theta_{PLMs}}(n_e)||, \tag{4}$$

where $f_{\theta_{PLMs}}()$ returns the name embeddings from PLMs.

Another external resource is the machine translation engine, such as Google Translator. Since most experimental data are cross-lingual datasets, some methods (e.g., UED [15], SEU [11], LightEA [25], etc.) first translate non-English entities into English, then encode them as text embeddings. Later, Liu et al. [13] suggest that these two-steps of machine translation and encoding can be replaced by a single pre-trained multilingual sentence-BERT model. LaBSE [22] is a SOTA language-agnostic sentence embedding PLM, which is trained on 109 different languages and widely used in EA tasks (e.g., ICLEA [24], SelfKG [13], FGWEA [26]). In addition, some methods (such as AutoAlign [27]) use large-scale language models (LLMs) to obtain more effective text information.

4.1.2. Auxiliary Text-based Methods

To compensate for the supervisory signal in alignment learning, other recent works obtain auxiliary text from side information of entities. Such information includes relations, attributes and entity descriptions. Attribute-based methods exploit relation and attribute information, and add them to the entity encoding process, such as IMUSE [28], MultiKE [23], PRASE [29], ICLEA [24], AutoAlign [27], FGWEA [26], UDCEA [30], etc.

In addition, entity descriptions contain rich semantics and can also be used to obtain more contextual information for entity storage. Each entity description usually consists of one or more sentences containing multifaceted features related to the entity. so **ICLEA** chose Sentence transformer to encode entity descriptions to further enhance information extraction of aligned entities. Sentence transformer [31] is a Python framework for SOTA sentence, text, and image embedding.

4.1.3. Multimodal-based Methods

Since most entities have unique visual features (e.g., people, objects, or animals) or have unique identification tags (e.g., companies, organizations, or associations), this is very beneficial for alignment judgment. Unsupervised multimodal-based entity alignment (MMEA) is first proposed by Liu et al.[32], which uses the visual similarity of entities to construct a set of pseudo labels and eliminates the dependence on labels. Previous MMEA works have shown that incorporating visual modalities in modeling can help improve the performance of EA. As text-based methods do, some of these works also use pre-trained visual models (PVMs) (e.g., ResNet-152 [33]) to learn image embeddings.

In fact, the mutual influence of different modal information plays an important role in multimodal representation and fusion [34,35]. Therefore, it is very important to exploit the effects between modalities to enrich entity representation. The ideal goal is to avoid the overwhelming influence of weak modalities and achieve enhanced fusion between modalities. Here we list some related research works.

EVA [36] is an unsupervised method that combines images with structures, relations, and attributes to align entities in different KGSs. EVA proposes different multimodal fusion modules to integrate entity representations from multiple modalities into a joint embedding:

$$\mathbf{F}_J = \bigoplus_{i=1}^{n} \left[\frac{e^{w_i}}{\sum_{j=1}^{n} e^{w_j}} \cdot \mathbf{F}_i \right], \tag{5}$$

where n is the number of modalities, and w_i is the attention weight of the i$-i$th modality. In addition, EVA uses visual similarity to create an initial seed dictionary and applies iterative learning to expand the set of alignment seeds. However, EVA only explores using different multimodal representations to enhance the contextual embedding of entities, while ignoring the interactions between modalities in modeling.

MCLEA [16] is another MMEA method that proposes a multimodal contrastive learning method, to effectively integrate multimodal information into the joint representation of EA. It applies KL divergence on the output distribution between the joint and unimodal entity embeddings to reduce the modality gap. Specifically, MCLEA first designs an intra-modality contrastive loss (ICL) and an inter-modality alignment loss

(IAL). ICL allows MCLEA to distinguish the embeddings of the same entity in different KGs from the embeddings of other entities in each modality as follows:

$$J_m^{\mathrm{ICL}} = -\mathbb{E}_{i \in B} \log \left[\frac{1}{2} (q_m(\mathbf{e}_i^1, \mathbf{e}_i^2) + q_m(\mathbf{e}_i^2, \mathbf{e}_i^1)) \right]. \tag{6}$$

where $q_m(\mathbf{e}_i^1, \mathbf{e}_i^2)$ is the alignment probability distribution of the modality of m for each positive pair (e_i^1, e_i^2). The goal of IAL is to reduce the gap between the output distributions on different modalities so that MCLEA can model inter-modality interactions and obtain a more meaningful representation. For IAL, MCLEA minimizes the bidirectional KL divergence of the output distribution between joint and unimodal embeddings as follows:

$$J_m^{IAL} = \mathbb{E}_{i \in B} \frac{1}{2} [\mathbf{KL}(q_o'(\mathbf{e}_i^1, \mathbf{e}_i^1) \parallel q_m'(\mathbf{e}_i^1, \mathbf{e}_i^1)) + \mathbf{KL}(q_o'(\mathbf{e}_i^1, \mathbf{e}_i^1) \parallel q_m'(\mathbf{e}_i^1, \mathbf{e}_i^1))], \tag{7}$$

where $q_o'(\mathbf{e}_i^1, \mathbf{e}_i^1)$, $q_m'(\mathbf{e}_i^1, \mathbf{e}_i^1)$, $q_o'(\mathbf{e}_i^1, \mathbf{e}_i^1)$ and $q_m'(\mathbf{e}_i^1, \mathbf{e}_i^1)$ represent the output predictions with two directions of joint embedding and the unimodal embedding of modality m, respectively. Finally, MCLEA adjusts the relative weight of each task in the loss function by deriving a multi-task loss function based on maximizing the Gaussian likelihood as follows:

$$J = J_o^{ICL} + \sum_{m \in M} \left(\frac{1}{\alpha_m^2} J_m^{ICL} + \frac{1}{\beta_m^2} J_m^{IAL} + \log \alpha_m + \log \beta_m \right) \tag{8}$$

where α_m and β_m are automatically learned during training.

4.2. Alignment Estimate Module

Unsupervised methods need to leverage external resources (as described in Section 4.1.1) to generate pseudo-labels, eliminating the need for annotated data in EA. The purpose of *similarity estimation* module is to estimate the similarity of unaligned entity embeddings retrieved from external resources to generate alignment results or a set of pseudo labels. Pseudo labels are used as a training set for alignment learning, just like in supervised learning methods. This module is mainly divided into two steps, measuring the similarity and alignment inference of entity pairs. The former calculates the similarity of unaligned aligned entities, and the latter is responsible for inferring the final alignment results.

4.2.1. Similarity Measure

Cosine distance, Euclidean distance and Manhattan distance are the most common similarity measures. Of course, there are more efficient similarity measures proposed by some unsupervised EA methods.

SS-AGA [16] utilizes the cross-domain similarity local scaling (CSLS) metric [37] to compute the entity similarity as follows:

$$\begin{gathered} CSLS(e_s, e_t) = 2sim(e_s, e_t) - s(e_s) - s(e_t) \\ s(e_s) = \frac{1}{K} \sum_{e_{s'} \in N(e_s)} sim(e_s, e_{s'}), s(e_t) = \frac{1}{K} \sum_{e_{t'} \in N(e_t)} sim(e_t, e_{t'}), \end{gathered} \tag{9}$$

where $N(e_s) = \{e_t | (e_s, r, e_t) \in T \ or \ (e_t, r, e_s) \in T \}$ denotes the set of two-party neighbors of entity e_s, K is the number of each node's k-nearest neighbors, and $sim(e_s, e_t)$ is the similarity score between two entities, by calculating cosine similarity maximum of their structure embeddings and text embeddings:

$$sim(e_s, e_t) = \max\left(\cos\left(\mathbf{e}_s^a, \mathbf{e}_t^a\right), \cos\left(\mathbf{e}_s^{\text{text}}, \mathbf{e}_t^{\text{text}}\right)\right) \tag{10}$$

SS-AGA argues that CSLS can better capture the structural similarity between entity pairs.

PRASE[29] combines probabilistic reasoning and semantic embedding through an iterative algorithm, in which PARIS [38] is introduced to infer the mapping relationship between entities and relations through an iterative strategy. PARIS is a typical traditional system that uses probabilistic reasoning and vocabulary matching. Specifically, PARIS measures the function of each relation in the following way:

$$\begin{aligned} F(r) &:= \frac{|\{e|(e,r,t) \in T^+\}|}{|\{(e,t)|(e,r,t) \in T^+\}|}, r \in R^+, \\ F^{-1}(r) &:= \frac{|\{t|(e,r,t) \in T^+\}|}{|\{(e,t)|(e,r,t) \in T^+\}|}, r \in R^+, \end{aligned} \tag{11}$$

where $R^+ = R \cup A$, $|\cdot|$ represents the set cardinality. Then PRASE designs a PARIS-based PR module to discover entity mappings $\tilde{Y}^P$ with their probabilities $P(e \equiv e')$:

$$\begin{aligned} P(e \equiv e') = 1 - &\prod_{(e,r,t) \in T^+, (e',r',t') \in T'^+} (1 - P(r' \subseteq r) F^{-1}(r) P(t \equiv t')\ ) \\ &\times (1 - P(r \subseteq r') F^{-1}(r') P(t \equiv t')\ ), \\ P(r' \subseteq r) = &\frac{\sum_{e,t} (1 - \prod_{(h',r',t') \in T'^+} (1 - P(h \equiv h') P(t \equiv t')\ )\ )}{\sum_{e,t} (1 - \prod_{h',t' \in E'^+} (1 - P(h \equiv h') P(t \equiv t')\ )\ )}, \end{aligned} \tag{12}$$

where $T^+ = T_R \cup T_A$, $(e,r,t) \in T^+ = T_R$, and $P(r' \subseteq r)$ represents the probability that r is a subrelation of r'. After several self-iterations, the PR module converges and outputs a new round of alignment results $\tilde{Y}_{P(k-1)}$, which is refined to generate reliable alignment seeds S_k for training. Moreover, a threshold $\delta \in [0,1]$ is set to obtain S_k:

$$S_k = \{(e,e') | (e,e') \in \tilde{Y}_{k-1}^P, P_{k-1}(e \equiv e') > \delta\}. \tag{13}$$

UPLR[14] proposes a graph interaction divergence to evaluate the similarity of a pair of entities. Specifically, it calculates the similarity of two entities based on neighboring entities:

$$GID(e_s^1, e_t^1) = D(e_s^1, e_t^2) - \alpha \overline{\sum_{p \in N(e_t^2)} D(e_s^1, p)} + \overline{\sum_{q \in N(e_s^1)} D(e_t^2, q)}, \tag{14}$$

where $D(\cdot) = cos(e_s^1, e_t^2)$ denotes the divergence between two entities, α represents a hyper-parameters, $N(\cdot)$ is a set of entity neighbor nodes.

4.2.2. Alignment Inference

The alignment inference aims to predict the EA result between two KGs. Early EA methods mainly implement local alignment, which calculates the cross-KGs similarity of entities and selects the most similar entity as alignment result (i.e., Nearest Neighbor Search).

In detail, based on the embedding of an unaligned entity e_s^1 of G^1 given, the most similar entity to e_s^1 is searched from the unaligned entities of G^2 to become the nearest neighbor entity of e_s^1. If a pair of unaligned entities (e_s^1, e_t^2) is the mutual nearest neighbors, it will be added to the pseudo-labels set in the next training round. To reduce the error rate of pseudo-labels, a similarity threshold or decision algorithm is also used to generate pseudo-labels. For example, UEA [12] proposes a thresholded bi-directional nearest neighbor search (TBNNS). Algorithm 1 is the implementation process of TBNNS.

Algorithm 1 Procedure of TBNNS [12]

Input: G^1 and G^2: the two KGs to be aligned; E^1 and E^2: the entity sets in G^1 and G^2; θ a given threshold; $\mathbf{M}$: a distance matrix.
Output: $\mathbf{S}$: Alignment results.

for each $e_i^1 \in E^1$ **do**
  $e_j^2 \leftarrow \arg\min_{\hat{e}_j^2 \in E_2} \mathbf{M}(e_i^1, \hat{e}_j^2)$;
  if $\arg\min_{\hat{e}_i^1 \in E_1} \mathbf{M}(e_j^2, \hat{e}_i^1) = u$ and $\mathbf{M}(e_i^1, e_j^2) < \theta$ **then**
    $\mathbf{S} \leftarrow \mathbf{S} + \{(u, v)\}$
Return $\mathbf{S}$;

However, local alignment ignores the fact that alignments are correlated with each other, leading to incorrect alignments and illegal many-to-one and many-to-many alignments [39,6]. Therefore, some existing global EA methods have been proposed to alleviate these problems. Some supervised methods propose approximate global alignments by adding additional constraints to reduce the complexity. CEA [6] requires entity pairs to be stably matched and uses a delayed acceptance algorithm (DAA) to find alignments. GM-EHD-JEA [39] decomposes the entire search space into many isolated subspaces, thereby restricting the alignment between subspaces.

Other global EA methods regard the task as an optimal transportation problem (OTP) (or assignment problem), which seeks the optimal global alignment by minimizing the total transportation distance. They usually use optimization algorithms such as the Hungarian algorithm [11], delayed acceptance algorithm [40] or Sinkhorn algorithm [11,25] to process the similarity matrix for alignment. While in the unsupervised domain, there are also some methods (e.g., UED [15], SEU [11], FGWEA [26], UDCEA [30], etc.) that adopt similar global alignment solutions.

In addition, the unsupervised method UDCEA [30] regards the alignment task as a binary matching problem and proposes a re-exchange method to complete the alignment. As shown in the Figure 3, (e_{11}, e_{21}) and (e_{12}, e_{22}) are first aligned entity pairs with a total similarity of $s_1 + s_2$. Then the two entity pairs are exchanged to obtain a new similarity value of $s_{12} + s_{21}$, and the value of $(s_{12} + s_{21}) - (s_1 + s_2)$ is calculated as the loss of the exchange operation. The larger the value of the loss, the higher efficiency of the exchange.

UDCEA repeats the above exchange process until all aligned entities in the preliminary alignment result are exchanged. UDCEA provides greater flexibility by accommodating two different types of optimization (i.e., Min and Max) in the binary matching process.

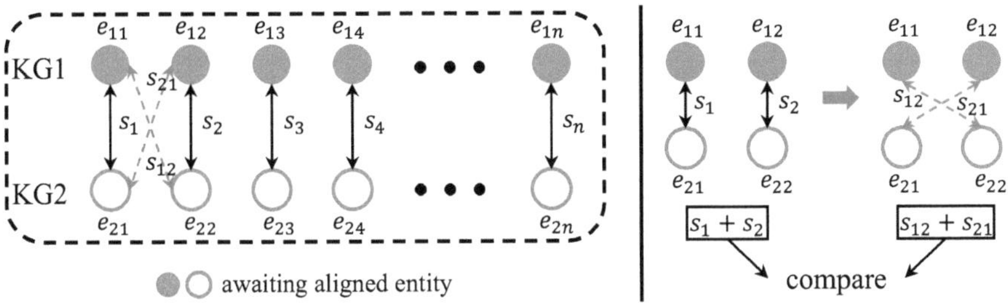

Figure 3. Re-exchange method of UDCEA method [30].

4.3. Encoder Module

Like most supervised EA methods, translation-based methods (e.g., TransE [8]) and Graph Neural Networks (e.g., GCN [9], GAT [10]) are common encoders for unsupervised EA methods. Below, we introduce these two categories respectively.

4.3.1. TransE-based Methods

TransE is the most widely used translation-based KG embedding method, which learns the embedding space of each knowledge graph separately, and then learns a transformation matrix to map the embedding space from one knowledge graph to another. In this method, both entities and relations are represented in the same vector space. The relation $\mathbf{r}$ is equivalent to translate the vector from the head entity $\mathbf{h}$ to the tail entity $\mathbf{t}$. If $(h,r,t) \in T$, then the embedding $\mathbf{t}$ of should be close to $\mathbf{h}$ plus $\mathbf{r}$, i.e., $\mathbf{h}+\mathbf{r} \approx \mathbf{t}$.

The TransE-based EA method uses the relation triples and attribute triples of KGs as translation relations. Figure 4 is a framework for AutoAlign [27] and shows AutoAlign using TransE as the encoders for relation structures, attribute structures, and predicate (relation) of KGs. Other unsupervised EA methods, such as IMUSE [28], KAGAN [41], MultiKE [23], PRASE [29], FGWEA [26], also use similar encoders.

4.3.2. GNNs-based Methods

Since aligned entities may have similar neighborhood structures in different KGSs, GNNs become the most popular solution for EA. GNNs-based EA methods use GCN [9], GAT [10] and their variants to compute entity embeddings by aggregating entity neighborhoods with graph structures. Unsupervised EA methods DFMKE [42] and EVA [36] both use GCN as the encoder of relation structure, while MCLEA [16] and MEAformer [43] both use GAT as the encoder. Taking GAT [10] as an example, GAT can be understood as performing the propagation and update of attention messages on nodes. It aggregates all neighboring entity embeddings of the central node to model the importance of different entities and treats all relations equally in form:

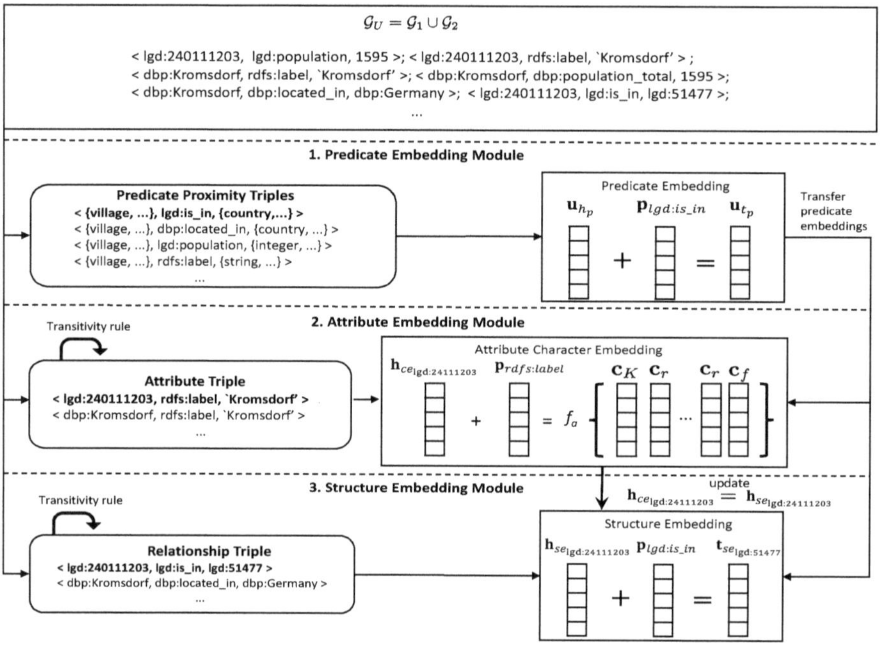

Figure 4. The framework of **AutoAlign** [27] method for unsupervised EA.

$$\mathbf{e}_i = \|_{k=1}^{K} \sigma\left(\sum_{j\in N_i\cup\{e_i\}} \alpha_{ij}^k \mathbf{W}^k \mathbf{e}_j\right), \tag{15}$$

$$\alpha_{ij} = \frac{\exp(\sigma(\overrightarrow{\mathbf{a}}^T[\mathbf{W}\mathbf{e}_i \oplus \mathbf{W}\mathbf{e}_j]))}{\sum_{k\in N_i\cup\{e_i\}} \exp(\sigma(\overrightarrow{\mathbf{a}}^T[\mathbf{W}\mathbf{e}_i \oplus \mathbf{W}\mathbf{e}_k]))}, \tag{16}$$

where $\mathbf{W}$ denotes the weight matrix, $\overrightarrow{\mathbf{a}}$ is a learnable parameter, $\oplus$ is the concatenation operation, K is the multi-head attention number, and σ is the LeakyReLU nonlinearity.

However, to improve the effect of graph modeling, some methods propose some improved GNNs methods as encoders of KGs. **ICLEA** [24] and **SS-AGA** [16] apply relation-aware GNNs as encoders. ICLEA uses an extended GAT to model the importance of different adjacency relations, which uses relation-specific attention heads as relational gates to control the information flow from neighbors. Its attention coefficient is calculated as follows:

$$\alpha_{ij} = \sigma\left(\sigma\left(\overrightarrow{\mathbf{r}}_{ij}\mathbf{W}_{r_{ij}^1} + \mathbf{B}_{r_{ij}^1}\right)\mathbf{W}_{r_{ij}^2} + \mathbf{B}_{r_{ij}^2}\right), \tag{17}$$

where $\overrightarrow{\mathbf{r}}_{ij}$ is trainable relation specific embedding between entity e_i and its neighbor e_i, $\mathbf{W}_{r_{ij}}$ and $\mathbf{B}_{r_{ij}}$ are the transformation and bias weight matrix of relation r_{ij}. While the attention coefficient in SS-AGA is calculated as follows:

$$\alpha_{ij}^r = \left(\mathbf{W}_k\mathbf{h}_{i(r)}\right)^T \cdot (\mathbf{W}_q\mathbf{h}_j) \cdot \frac{1}{\sqrt{d}} \cdot \beta_r, \tag{18}$$

where d is the dimension of the entity embeddings, $\mathbf{W}_k, \mathbf{W}_q$ are two transformation matrices, and β_r is a learnable relation factor. Different from GAT, SS-AGA introduce β_r to characterize the general significance of each relation r.

In addition, **UPLR** [14] introduces gate into the GAT, known as the Gate Graph Attention Network (GateGAT), enabling the EA encoder to effectively model the relationships between widely separated spatial regions.

4.4. Alignment Learning Module

Alignment Learning (AL) module is the key to model training, which guides the model to optimize the trainable parameters of the encoder according to the training objective through one or more loss functions. The different choice of encoder often determines the design of AL module. In the following, we focus on three common alignment learning methods, among which contrastive learning is a more common learning strategy for unsupervised EA methods.

4.4.1. TransE-based Learning

In the case of AutoAlign [27], whose encoder is TransE [8]. AutoAlign first employs TransE's margin-based ranking function(MRF) to learn embeddings by minimizing the following loss:

$$J_{SE} = \sum_{t_r \in T_r} \sum_{t_r' \in T_r'} \max\left(0, \alpha\left(f(t_r) - f(t_r')\right) + \gamma\right), \tag{19}$$

where T_r denotes the set of relation triples, T_r' denotes the set of corrupted relation triples, $\alpha = count(r)/|T|$, $count(r)$ is the occurrence count of relation r, and $|T|$ is the total number of triples. And $f(t) == ||\mathbf{e}+\mathbf{r}-\mathbf{t}||$ is the triple scoring function built according to the transE encoder.

AutoAlign [27] uses TransE to simultaneously learn relation structure, predicate structure, and attribute structure of KGs. So AutoAlign obtains the optimization objectives J_{PE} and J_{CE} for predicate embedding and attribute embedding in a similar way. To ensure that different entity embeddings can be transformed into the same vector space, TransE-based methods also embed into the same vector space through the strategies of parameter sharing, parameter exchange, embedding transformation or embedding calibration. AutoAlign adopts the following embedding calibration strategy to transfer the structure embedding $\mathbf{e}^{se}$ and attribute embedding $\mathbf{e}^{ce}$ into the same vector space:

$$J_{SIM} = \sum_{e \in G^1 \cup G^2} [1 - \cos(\mathbf{e}^{se}, \mathbf{e}^{ce})], \tag{20}$$

Finally, the overall objective function of the joint learning is:

$$J = J_{SE} + J_{PE} + J_{CE} + J_{SIM}. \tag{21}$$

4.4.2. GNNs-based Learning

The GNNs-based EA methods also use margin-based ranking function as the loss function:

$$J = \sum_{t_r \in T_r} \sum_{t'_r \in T'_r} \max\left(0, \left(d(t_r) - d(t'_r)\right) + \gamma\right), \tag{22}$$

where $d(\cdot)$ function directly uses standard similarity functions such as cosine distance, Euclidean distance, Manhattan distance, or dot product, unlike the scoring function $f(t) = ||\mathbf{e}+\mathbf{r}-\mathbf{t}||$ in Eq.(19). In addition, since GNN-based methods usually merge two KGs into one graph and then put them into the encoder for learning, there is no need for embedding transformation, embedding calibration, etc.

4.4.3. Contrastive Learning

Inspired by the recent excellent progress in contrastive learning (CL), several works adopt unsupervised contrastive loss to contrast different views of entity representation and enhance limited supervision signals by leveraging a large amount of unlabeled data.

For example, **ICLEA** [24] adopts info noise contrastive estimation (InfoNCE) loss [44] for contrastive learning. InfoNCE loss is often used in self-supervised learning by maximizing the similarity between positive pairs and minimizing the similarity between positive pairs and negative pairs:

$$J_{NCE} = -\sum_{e_i \in E^1 \cup E^2} \log \frac{\delta(e_i, e'_i)}{\delta(e_i, e'_i) + \sum_{k \neq i} \delta(e_i, e'_k)}, \tag{23}$$

where $\delta(e_i, e'_i) = \exp(\mathbf{e}_i \cdot \mathbf{e}'_i / \tau)$, (e_i, e'_i) is a positive pairs for entity e_i and their embedding can be obtained from the online encoder f_θ and momentum encoder $f_{\theta'}$, e'_k is the negative samples of e_i, and τ is a temperature hyperparameter. ICLEA also uses the momentum contrastive learning mechanism of MoCo, which is a very popular model for unsupervised training in the way of contrastive learning. The parameter θ of online encoder is instantly updated with the backpropagation, and the parameter $f_{\theta'}$ of momentum encoder is a moving average of θ:

$$\theta' \leftarrow m \times \theta' + (1-m) \times \theta, \tag{24}$$

where $m \in [0, 1)$ is a momentum coefficient.

SelfKG [13], based on InfoNCE loss, proposes a concept of relative similarity metric (RSM). Instead of directly pulling aligned entities closer in the embedding space, SelfKG tries to push unaligned negatives further away, thereby avoiding the supervision of using positive pairs.

$$J_{RSM} = -\frac{1}{\tau} + log(e^{1/\tau} + \sum_{k}^{M} \delta(e_i, e'_k)), \tag{25}$$

where M is the number of sampled negative samples.

RAC employs the graph contrastive learning with adaptive augmentation (GCA) [45], which is a fine-tuned InfoNCE objective. The goal of GAC is to better distinguish between embeddings of the same entity in two views and embeddings of other entities, thus exploiting the supervision signal in unlabeled data:

$$J_{GAC} = -\sum_{e_i \in E^1 \cup E^2} \log \frac{\delta(e_i, e_i')}{\underbrace{\delta(e_i, e_i')}_{\text{positive pair}} + \underbrace{\sum_{k \neq i} \delta(e_i, e_k')}_{\text{inter-view negative pairs}} + \underbrace{\sum_{k \neq i} \delta(e_i, e_k)}_{\text{intra-view negative pairs}}}. \tag{26}$$

Clearly, GAC defines two kinds of negative samples from all other nodes in the two views (inter-view and intra-view), respectively.

In addition, the multimodal-based methods (e.g., MCLEA [16] and MEAformer [43], etc) propose new modal-adaptive InfoNCE. We illustrated MCLEA's InfoNCE for multimodal fusion in Eqs.(6-8), in which the definition of $q_m(\mathbf{e}_i^1, \mathbf{e}_i^2)$ similar to the formulation of Eq.(26):

$$q_m(e_i^1, e_i^2) = \frac{\delta_m(e_i^1, e_i^2)}{\delta_m(e_i^1, e_i^2) + \sum_{e_j^1 \in E_1, j \neq i} \delta_m(e_i^1, e_j^1) + \sum_{e_j^2 \in E_2, j \neq i} \delta_m(e_i^1, e_j^2)}. \tag{27}$$

Finally, we summarize the basic features and techniques of such methods, covering five main categories:*Input*, *External Resources*, *Alignment Estimate*, *Encoder*, and *Alignment Learning*, as described in Table 1.

5. EA Methods without Training

In this section, we discuss the implementation of unsupervised EA methods without training and introduce related research methods.

Unsupervised EA method without training is a zero-training EA method, so its implementation framework generally does not have the modules of *Input*, *Encoder* and *Alignment Learning*, as shown in Figure 2(b). Most unsupervised methods with training improve the alignment effect by increasing the input data or optimizing the encoder method. More complex and efficient encoders lead to higher model complexity and greater model training. Therefore, unsupervised method without training is more advantageous in terms of model complexity and training amount.

However, unsupervised EA methods without training require high-quality external resources and multi-source data to support their unsupervised learning. Their core work is focused on designing more reasonable similarity measures and global Alignment strategies, which is the core of *Alignment Estimate* module. SEU [11], UDCEA [30], and FGWEA [26] all design their own global alignment strategies, which have been described in the Section 4.2.2. Here, we mainly describe their design of similarity measures.

Equal probability random walk matrix and the symmetric normalized Laplacian matrix is the common neighborhood matrix of GNNs-based method and similarity measure method. **SEU** [11] argues that the above matrix ignores the relation types in KGs and gives equal importance to all relation types. Following this intuition, SEU give higher weights to relations with lower frequencies, because they contain more unique informa-

Table 1. Categories of unsupervised EA with training

Methods	Input	External Resources	Alignment Estimate	Encoder	Alignment Learning
IMUSE [28]	Name;Rel.;Attr.	-	levenshtein	TransE	Mean squared error
KAGAN [41]	Rel.	-	-	TransE	MRF;GAN
MultiKE [23]	Name;Rel.;Attr.	PLMs; skip-Gram	-	TransE;CNN	MRF
EVA [36]	Rel.;Attr; Image	RESNET-152	-	GCN	Neighbourhood component analysis; Iterative learning
PRASE [29]	Rel.;Attr	-	PARIS	TransE	MRF
RAC [46]	Rel.	-	Reinforced active learning	GCN	InfoNCE
UEA [12]	Name;Rel.	fastText	cosine; Levenshtein	GCN	MRF
UPLR [14]	Name;Rel.	GloVe	Graph interactive divergence	GateGAT	MRF
MCLEA [16]	Name;Rel.; Attr;Image	ResNet-152; GloVe	cosine	GAT	InfoNCE
SelfKG [13]	Name;Rel.	LaBSE	dot product	GAT	InfoNCE
ICLEA [24]	Name;Rel.; Attr;Desc.	LaBSE	dot product	Relation-aware GAT; Sentence transformers	InfoNCE
MEAformer [43]	Name;Rel.; Attr;Image	GloVe	dot product	GAT;Transformer	InfoNCE; Iterative learning
DFMKE [42]	Rel.;Attr; Image	ResNet-152	-	GCN;TransE;	-
AutoAlign [27]	Rel.;Attr.	claude; WordNet	cosine	TransE	MRF

tion. Therefore, SEU adopts a simple strategy to generate the relational adjacency matrix A_{rel}, for $a_{ij} \in A_{rel}$:

$$a_{ij} = \frac{\sum\limits_{r_j \in R_{i,j}} \ln(|T|/|T_{r_j}|)}{\sum\limits_{k \in N_i} \sum\limits_{r_k \in R_{i,k}} \ln(|T|/|T_{r_k}|)} \tag{28}$$

where N_i denotes the neighboring set of entity e_i, $R_{i,j}$ denotes the relation set between e_i and e_k, and $|T|$ and $|T_r|$ are the total number of all relation triples and the triples containing relation r, respectively. Finally, A_{rel} is used in SEU's subsequent global alignment strategy.

FGWEA [26] optimizes global alignment by combining four cost matrices that represent differences between KGs at different angles. The four cost matrices are name similarity-based cost matrix C^{name}, attribute similarity-based cost matrix C^{attr}, relation similarity-based cost matrix C^{rel} and structure similarity-based cost matrix C^{stru}, which are defined as follows:

$$\begin{aligned} C^{name} &= \sum_{(e_i,e_j)\in M^k} (1-\cos(\mathbf{e}_i^{name},\mathbf{e}_j^{name})), \\ C^{attr} &= \sum_{(e_i,e_j)\in M^k} (1-\cos(\mathbf{e}_i^{attr},\mathbf{e}_j^{attr})), \\ C^{rel} &= 1-c\mathbf{S}^{rel}, \\ C^{stru} &= 1-c\mathbf{S}^{stru}, \end{aligned} \tag{29}$$

where M^k represents anchor set in round k, $\mathbf{e}_i^{name}, \mathbf{e}_i^{attr}$ represent the name and attribute embeddings of entity e_i, $c = 1/max(m,n)$, $\mathbf{S}^{rel}$ and $\mathbf{S}^{stru}$ respectively represent the number of alignment relations, and the number of aligned neighbors in each anchor in anchor set M^k.

Finally, we summarize the basic features and techniques of such methods, covering three main categories:*Input*, *External Resources* and *Alignment Estimate*, as described in Table 2.

Table 2. Categories of unsupervised EA without training

Methods	Input	External Resources	Alignment Estimate
SEU [11]	Name;Rel.	char-CNN or name-BERT	Hungarian; Sinkhorn
UDCEA [30]	Rel.;Attr	Sentence-BERT	-
FGWEA [26]	Rel.;Attr.	ResNet-152;LaBSE	cosine;Sinkhorn
ZeroEA [47]	Name;Rel.	PLMs	cosine

6. Challenges and Opportunities

Finally, we summarize the current challenges and opportunities of this problem based on the analysis of the above unsupervised EA method research.

Compared with supervised EA methods, unsupervised EA methods mainly seek breakthroughs on the two modules *Alignment Estimation* and *Alignment Learning*, while the other two modules are much the same as the supervised method. From the Sections 4 and 5 above, it can be seen that unsupervised EA methods have made some progress in recent years. However, we believe that those works still face the following challenges, which are also the future direction of the field:

- **Ambiguity and diversity of KGs auxiliary information**. Unsupervised EA methods are highly dependent on auxiliary information of KGs (e.g., entity name, attribute, entity description, entity image, etc). But the ambiguity and variety are inherent properties of natural language, and also characteristics of actual KGs. Therefore, how to eliminate interference and improve the utilization of these auxiliary information without increasing the model complexity, is still the core problem of unsupervised EA methods.

- **Trade-off between effectiveness and efficiency**. To eliminate the dependence on training set, the unsupervised EA methods explores the utilization of various auxiliary information and even external resources (such as PLMs, LLMs). However, not all KGs can find this auxiliary information, these methods will be much less useful in real-world scenarios. Furthermore, the complexity of modeling will inevitably increase after the introduction of such information and resources, especially PLMs. Whether the runtime overhead of each method is worth paying for in terms of the effectiveness achieved is a big question to consider.
- **Methods to improve results**. Currently, most unsupervised EA follow the encoders proposed by some supervised EA method, and do not seek new encoders that are more suitable for unsupervised learning. However, for unsupervised EA methods, studying effective encoders is the most valuable effort to improve alignment, and any other effort will reduce the effectiveness of method in practical scenarios.
- **Openness problem of KGs**. The openness of KGs means that the entities within KGs are not a closed set, that is, entities can increase, evolve, or fail over time. Openness is a common feature of practical KGs. Due to the limitations of experimental datasets, most current methods work in closed domain settings, making them unable to handle mismatched entities. In particular, GNNs-based methods are based on the fact that aligned KGs has a very similar graph structure.

Acknowledgment

This work was supported by the National Natural Science Foundation of China (Grant No. 62306079), the Education Science Planning Project of Guangdong Province (Specialized higher education) in China (Grant No. 2023GXJK422), the Key Research and Development Program of Guangdong in China (Grant No. 2023B0303010004), the Innovation Team Project for Universities in Guangdong Province in China (Grant No. 2023KCXTD011).

References

[1] Zhu X, Li Z, Wang X, Jiang X, Sun P, Wang X, et al. Multi-Modal Knowledge Graph Construction and Application: A Survey. IEEE Transactions on Knowledge and Data Engineering. 2024;36(2):715-35.
[2] Ji S, Pan S, Cambria E, Marttinen P, Yu PS. A Survey on Knowledge Graphs: Representation, Acquisition, and Applications. IEEE Transactions on Neural Networks and Learning Systems. 2022;33(2):494-514.
[3] Wan G, Pan S, Gong C, Zhou C, Haffari G. Reasoning like human: hierarchical reinforcement learning for knowledge graph reasoning. In: Proceedings of the Twenty-Ninth International Joint Conference on Artificial Intelligence; 2021. p. 1926-32.
[4] Luo L, Li YF, Haffari G, Pan S. Normalizing Flow-based Neural Process for Few-Shot Knowledge Graph Completion. In: Proceedings of the 46th International ACM SIGIR Conference on Research and Development in Information Retrieval. Association for Computing Machinery; 2023. p. 900-10.

[5] Chen M, Tian Y, Yang M, Zaniolo C. Multilingual Knowledge Graph Embeddings for Cross-lingual Knowledge Alignment. In: Proceedings of the 26th International Joint Conference on Artificial Intelligence (IJCAI). Melbourne, Australia: Morgan Kaufmann; 2017. p. 1511-7.
[6] Zeng W, Zhao X, Tang J, Lin X. Collective Entity Alignment via Adaptive Features. In: 36th IEEE International Conference on Data Engineering (ICDE). Online: IEEE; 2020. p. 1870-3.
[7] Wang H, Wang Y, Li J, Luo T. Degree Aware based Adversarial Graph Convolutional Networks for Entity Alignment in Heterogeneous Knowledge Graph. Neurocomputing. 2022;487:99-109.
[8] Bordes A, Usunier N, García-Durán A, Weston J, Yakhnenko O. Translating Embeddings for Modeling Multi-relational Data. In: Proceedings of the 26th International Conference on Neural Information Processing Systems (NeurIPS). Lake Tahoe, USA: MIT Press; 2013. p. 2787-95.
[9] Kipf TN, Welling M. Semi-supervised Classification with Graph Convolutional Networks. In: Proceedings of the 5th International Conference on Learning Representations (ICLR). Toulon, France; 2017. p. 1-14.
[10] Veličković P, Cucurull G, Casanova A, Romero A, Liò P, Bengio Y. Graph Attention Networks. In: Proceedings of the 6th International Conference on Learning Representations(ICLR). Vancouver, BC, Canada; 2018. p. 1-12.
[11] Mao X, Wang W, Wu Y, Lan M. From Alignment to Assignment: Frustratingly Simple Unsupervised Entity Alignment. In: Proceedings of the 2021 Conference on Empirical Methods in Natural Language Processing (EMNLP). Association for Computational Linguistics; 2021. p. 2843-53.
[12] Zeng W, Zhao X, Tang J, Li X, Luo M, Zheng Q. Towards Entity Alignment in the Open World: An Unsupervised Approach. In: Proceedings of the 26th International Conference on Database Systems for Advanced Applications (DASFAA); 2021. .
[13] Liu X, Hong H, Wang X, Chen Z, Kharlamov E, Dong Y, et al. SelfKG: Self-Supervised Entity Alignment in Knowledge Graphs. In: Proceedings of the 2022 World Wide Web Conference (WWW). Association for Computing Machinery; 2022. p. 860-70.
[14] Li J, Song D. Uncertainty-aware Pseudo Label Refinery for Entity Alignment. In: Proceedings of the ACM Web Conference 2022. Association for Computing Machinery; 2022. p. 829-37.
[15] Luo S, Yu S. An Accurate Unsupervised Method for Joint Entity Alignment and Dangling Entity Detection. In: Findings of the Association for Computational Linguistics: ACL 2022. Association for Computational Linguistics; 2022. p. 2330-9.
[16] Huang Z, Li Z, Jiang H, Cao T, Lu H, Yin B, et al. Multilingual Knowledge Graph Completion with Self-Supervised Adaptive Graph Alignment. In: Proceedings of the 60th Annual Meeting of the Association for Computational Linguistics (ACL). Association for Computational Linguistics; 2022. p. 474-85.
[17] Kondrak G. N-Gram Similarity and Distance. In: Proceedings of the 12th international conference on String Processing and Information Retrieval. Springer-Verlag; 2005. p. 115-26.
[18] Pennington J, Socher R, Manning C. Glove: Global Vectors for Word Representation. In: Proceedings of the 2014 Conference on Empirical Methods in Natural Language Processing (EMNLP). Association for Computational Linguistics; 2014. p. 1532-43.
[19] Joulin A, Grave E, Bojanowski P, Mikolov T. Bag of Tricks for Efficient Text Classification. In: Proceedings of the 15th Conference of the European Chapter of the Association for Computational Linguistics. Association for Computational Linguistics; 2017. p. 427-31.
[20] Devlin J, Chang MW, Lee K, Toutanova K. BERT: Pre-training of Deep Bidirectional Transformers for Language Understanding. In: Proceedings of the 2019 Conference of the North American Chapter of the Association for Computational Linguistics: Human Language Technologies(NAACL). Association for Computational Linguistics; 2019. p. 4171-86.
[21] Liu Y, Ott M, Goyal N, Du J, Joshi M, Chen D, et al. RoBERTa: A Robustly Optimized BERT Pretraining Approach. In: International Conference on Learning Representations; 2020. .
[22] Feng F, Yang Y, Cer D, Arivazhagan N, Wang W. Language-agnostic Bert Sentence Embedding. arXiv:200701852. 2020.
[23] Zhang Q, Sun Z, Hu W, Chen M, Guo L, Qu Y. Multi-view Knowledge Graph Embedding for Entity Alignment. In: Proceedings of the 28th International Joint Conference on Artificial Intelligence(IJCAI). Morgan Kaufmann; 2019. p. 5429-35.
[24] Zeng K, Dong Z, Hou L, Cao Y, Hu M, Yu J, et al. Interactive Contrastive Learning for Self-supervised Entity Alignment. In: Proceedings of the 31st ACM International Conference on Information and Knowledge Management (CIKM). Atlanta, GA, USA: Association for Computing Machinery; 2022. p. 2465-75.

[25] Mao X, Wang W, Wu Y, Lan M. LightEA: A Scalable, Robust, and Interpretable Entity Alignment Framework via Three-view Label Propagation. In: Proceedings of the 2022 Conference on Empirical Methods in Natural Language Processing. Association for Computational Linguistics; 2022-12. p. 825-38.
[26] Tang J, Zhao K, Li J. A Fused Gromov-Wasserstein Framework for Unsupervised Knowledge Graph Entity Alignment. In: Findings of the Association for Computational Linguistics: ACL 2023. Association for Computational Linguistics; 2023. p. 3320-34.
[27] Zhang R, Su Y, Trisedya BD, Zhao X, Yang M, Cheng H, et al. AutoAlign: Fully Automatic and Effective Knowledge Graph Alignment Enabled by Large Language Models. IEEE Transactions on Knowledge and Data Engineering (TKDE). 2023:1-14.
[28] He F, Li Z, Qiang Y, Liu A, Liu G, Zhao P, et al. Unsupervised Entity Alignment Using Attribute Triples and Relation Triples. In: Proceedings of the 24th International Conference on Database Systems for Advanced Applications (DASFAA). Springer, Cham; 2019. p. 367-82.
[29] Qi Z, Zhang Z, Chen J, Chen X, Xiang Y, Zhang N, et al. Unsupervised Knowledge Graph Alignment by Probabilistic Reasoning and Semantic Embedding. In: Proceedings of the 30th International Joint Conference on Artificial Intelligence(IJCAI). Morgan Kaufmann; 2021. p. 2019-25.
[30] Jiang C, Qian Y, Chen L, Gu Y, Xie X. Unsupervised Deep Cross-Language Entity Alignment. In: Machine Learning and Knowledge Discovery in Databases: Research Track: European Conference (ECML PKDD). Springer-Verlag; 2023. p. 3-19.
[31] Reimers N, Gurevych I. Making Monolingual Sentence Embeddings Multilingual using Knowledge Distillation. In: Proceedings of the 2020 Conference on Empirical Methods in Natural Language Processing (EMNLP). Association for Computational Linguistics; 2020. p. 4512-25.
[32] Liu Y, Li H, Garcia-Duran A, Niepert M, Onoro-Rubio D, Rosenblum DS. MMKG: Multi-modal Knowledge Graphs. In: Proceedings of the European Semantic Web Conference. Springer, Cham; 2019. p. 459-74.
[33] He K, Zhang X, Ren S, Sun J. Deep Residual Learning for Image Recognition. In: 2016 IEEE Conference on Computer Vision and Pattern Recognition (CVPR); 2016. p. 770-8.
[34] Wang Y, Huang W, Sun F, Xu T, Rong Y, Huang J. Deep Multimodal Fusion by Channel Exchanging. In: Advances in Neural Information Processing Systems. vol. 33. Curran Associates, Inc.; 2020. p. 4835-45.
[35] He W, Li Z, Lu D, Chen E, Xu T, Huai B, et al. Multimodal Dialogue Systems via Capturing Context-aware Dependencies of Semantic Elements. In: Proceedings of the 28th ACM International Conference on Multimedia. MM '20. Association for Computing Machinery; 2020. p. 2755-64.
[36] Liu F, Chen M, Roth D, Collier N. Visual Pivoting for (Unsupervised) Entity Alignment. In: Proceedings of the 34th AAAI Conference on Artificial Intelligence(AAAI). vol. 35; 2021. p. 4257-66.
[37] Lample G, Conneau A, Ranzato M, Denoyer L, Jégou H. Word Translation without Parallel Data. In: International Conference on Learning Representations; 2018. .
[38] Suchanek FM, Abiteboul S, Senellart P. PARIS: Probabilistic Alignment of Relations, Instances, and Schema. Proceedings of the VLDB Endowment. 2011;5(3):157-68.
[39] Xu K, Song L, Feng Y, Song Y, Yu D. Coordinated Reasoning for Cross-Lingual Knowledge Graph Alignment. In: Proceedings of the 34th AAAI Conference on Artificial Intelligence (AAAI). vol. 34(05). New York, USA: AAAI; 2020. p. 9354-61.
[40] Zhu R, Ma M, Wang P. RAGA: Relation-Aware Graph Attention Networks for Global Entity Alignment. In: Proceedings of the 25th Pacific-Asia Conference on Knowledge Discovery and Data Mining (PAKDD). Cham: Springer; 2021. p. 501-13.
[41] Qu M, Tang J, Bengio Y. Weakly-supervised Knowledge Graph Alignment with Adversarial Learning. In: Proceedings of the International Conference on Learning Representations (ICLR); 2019. .
[42] Zhu J, Huang C, De Meo P. DFMKE: A dual fusion multi-modal knowledge graph embedding framework for entity alignment. Information Fusion. 2023;90:111-9.
[43] Chen Z, Chen J, Zhang W, Guo L, Fang Y, Huang Y, et al. MEAformer: Multi-modal Entity Alignment Transformer for Meta Modality Hybrid. In: Proceedings of the 31st ACM International Conference on Multimedia. Association for Computing Machinery; 2023. p. 3317-27.
[44] Oord Avd, Li Y, Vinyals O. Representation Learning with Contrastive Predictive Coding. arXiv180703748. 2018.
[45] Zhu Y, Xu Y, Yu F, Liu Q, Wu S, Wang L. Graph Contrastive Learning with Adaptive Augmentation. In: Proceedings of the World Wide Web Conferences (WWW). Association for Computing Machinery; 2021. p. 2069-80.

[46] Zeng W, Zhao X, Tang J, Fan C. Reinforced Active Entity Alignment. In: Proceedings of the 30th ACM International Conference on Information & Knowledge Management(CIKM). Association for Computing Machinery; 2021. p. 2477-86.
[47] Huo N, Cheng R, Kao B, Ning W, Haldar NAH, Li X, et al. ZeroEA: A Zero-Training Entity Alignment Framework via Pre-Trained Language Model. Proceedings of the VLDB Endowment. 2024;17(7):1765-74.

Handbook on Neurosymbolic AI and Knowledge Graphs
P. Hitzler et al. (Eds.)
IOS Press, 2025

doi:10.3233/FAIA250212

Neuro-Symbolic Techniques in Open Knowledge Graph Canonicalization

Yang YANG, and Edward CURRY [1]
Insight Research Ireland Centre for Data Analytics, University of Galway
ORCiD ID: Yang Yang https://orcid.org/0000-0001-8190-8683, Edward Curry https://orcid.org/0000-0001-8236-6433

Abstract. Curated knowledge graphs (CKGs) play a fundamental role in both academia and industry. They require significant human involvement to pre-define the ontology and cannot quickly adapt to new domains and new data. To solve this problem, open information extraction (OIE) methods are leveraged to automatically extract structure information in the form of non-canonicalized triples <noun phrase, relation phrase, noun phrase> from unstructured text. OIE can be used to create large open knowledge graphs (OKGs). However, noun phrases and relation phrases in such OKGs are not canonicalized, which results in scattered and redundant facts. In order to disambiguate and eliminate redundancy in such OKGs, the task of OKG canonicalization is proposed to cluster synonymous noun phrases and relation phrases into the same group and assign them unique identifiers. Nevertheless, this task is challenging due to the high sparsity and limited information of OKGs. This chapter provides an overview and analysis of the neuro-symbolic techniques used in this task.

Keywords. Neuro-Symbolic Techniques, Open Knowledge Graph Canonicalization, Knowledge Graph Embedding

1. Introduction

Neural-symbolic computing has now become the subject of interest in both academic and industry research laboratories. As discrete symbolic representations of knowledge, Curated Knowledge Graphs (CKGs), such as YAGO [1], Freebase [2], DBpedia [3], and Wikidata [4], are a type of multi-relational graphs that store factual knowledge in the real world. CKGs have a widespread application in knowledge reasoning [5,6,7,8], question answering [9,10,11,12], recommendation systems [13,14,15,16], and other scientific domains. Normally, in CKGs, nodes represent real-world entities (e.g., names and products) and edges represent the relationships between entities. A large-scale CKG contains millions of entities and hundreds of millions of relational facts about them, which can be efficiently stored in the form of triples (i.e.,<*head entity, relation, tail entity*>), where each triple consists of two entities and one relation between them. For example, in the triple<*Windows95, is a trademark of, Microsoft Corporation*>, *Windows95* and *Microsoft Corporation* are real-world entities and *is a trademark of* represents the relation between *Windows95* and *Microsoft Corporation.*

[1]Corresponding Author: Edward Curry, Email: edward.curry@universityofgalway.ie

The construction of CKG is difficult to automate and usually suffers from two inevitable defects: 1) human supervision. CKG construction usually requires manual supervision to pre-define the ontology; 2) weak adaptability. This construction method makes it unable to quickly adapt to new domains and new data. For example, *dataspace* is a new data management abstraction proposed in 2005 by Michael Franklin [17]. After more than ten years of development [18,19,20,21], even though we can search about 7.09 million web page results in Google, we still cannot find useful information in CKGs. Here we take Wikidata [4] and YAGO [1] as of June 2024 as an example: in Wikidata, we can only find 1 label (*data space*), 1 description (*ecosystem comprised of rules, common standards and practices, infrastructures and a governance framework*), 4 alias (*dataspace, data-space, data-spaces, and dataspaces*), 1 statement (*<dataspace, subclass of, data integration>*), and 4 identifiers for the entity *dataspace* ("Q370685" for Wikidata, "/m/0bmf1y3" for Freebase, "2776136371" for Microsoft Academic, and "C2988382989" for OpenAlex); and the *dataspace* entity does not exist in YAGO.

To solve this problem, Open Information Extraction (OIE) techniques have been proposed to improve the efficiency of knowledge graph construction without any pre-defined ontology. Given an unstructured text corpus, OIE methods can be used to automatically extract non-canonicalized triples in the form *<noun phrase, relation phrase, noun phrase>* without requiring a pre-defined ontology schema. For example, from the sentence "3/3/2002 Windows 95 is no longer being supported by Microsoft.", the OIE method could extract the triple *<Windows 95, is no longer being supported by, Microsoft>*. This makes them suitable for quickly extracting and updating factual knowledge from rapidly growing web data, and highly adaptable to new domains and new data. Several prominent instances include TextRunner [22], OLLIE [23,24,25], ClausIE [26], Standford OIE [27], and MinIE [28]. Furthermore, the advent of the OIE method directly promotes the development of large-scale Open Knowledge Graphs (OKGs), such as ReVerb [29], OPIEC [30], and Open-CyKG [31]. Without human supervision, this automated OIE paradigm enables OKGs to easily grow to a very large scale. Therefore, in general, the coverage and diversity of OKGs are much higher than CKGs.

Different from CKG, the basic elements in OKG are non-canonicalized triples composed of Noun Phrases (NPs) and Relation Phrases (RPs). This is because the output of OIE methods typically inherits noise from unstructured text sources and the extraction process, which is usually not the case for CKGs with a pre-defined ontology. Due to this difference, one major challenge of OKGs is that NPs and RPs in OKGs are not canonicalized and lack unique identifiers. In such OKGs, an entity (or relation) may be denoted by multiple NPs (or RPs) and an NP (or RP) could refer to several different entities (or relations). Intuitively, this leads to two issues in such OKGs: 1) two NPs (or RPs) that have different surface forms but refer to the same entity (or relation) will be treated differently; 2) two NPs (or RPs) with the same surface form but referring to different entities (or relations) will be considered the same. Moreover, these problems also lead to the dispersion and redundancy of fact storage, making OKGs extremely sparse and far from being directly usable for downstream tasks.

This problem is still unsolved after ten years of development, mainly due to three difficulties: 1) It is difficult to mine and utilize useful information from new types, new views, and new modalities for this problem; 2) The available tools are limited, including neural tools, symbolic tools and neuro-symbolic tools; 3) Data infrastructure suitable for OKG is missing, including large-scale data sharing platforms such as dataspace [32].

To tackle these crucial problems, the task of OKG canonicalization [33] was proposed in 2014, to convert non-canonicalized triples in OKGs to their canonicalized form. In recent years, several methods [33,34,35,36,37,38,39,40] have been proposed, via treating this problem as a clustering task. More precisely, OKG canonicalization methods assign synonymous NPs (or RPs) to one cluster and then select one NP (or RP) to represent others in the cluster. The canonicalized OKG is the output of the OKG canonicalization task, which allows downstream applications such as link prediction, reasoning, and entity alignment to operate on top of OKG without ambiguity, thereby significantly improving their performance. As a consequence, the OKG canonicalization task helps to disambiguate, eliminate redundancy and integrate the highly diverse knowledge in OKGs, which can benefit downstream tasks.

Many comprehensive surveys have provided an overview of CKGs, in particular their construction, representation, and applications. For example, [41] provides an encyclopedic survey for CKGs, and [42,43,44] review the development in CKG construction. Other surveys summarize methods for refinement, completeness and quality management. [45,46] looks into methods that refine CKGs, and [47] focus on the quality management of CKGs, while [48] discusses completeness, recall, and negation in Open-World KGs. Knowledge graph embedding models is a popular topic and have been reviewed in [49,50,51,52,53,54]. Unlike other works that only focus on CKGs, in this chapter, we present an overview and analysis of the neuro-symbolic techniques used in the OKG canonicalization task.

We organize our chapter as follows. Section 2 gives the background for OKG canonicalization, including definitions and instances. In Section 3, we briefly introduce several existing methods in the OKG canonicalization task. Neural and symbolic techniques leveraged in existing methods are described in Section 4.1 and Section 4.2 respectively. Then, in Section 4.3, we introduce how existing methods integrate neural techniques and symbolic techniques to improve their performance. Finally, this chapter is concluded in Section 5.

2. Background

In this section, we start from some basic concepts of CKG, OKG and OKG canonicalization, adapted from [55], then describe an instance and a fundamental assumption commonly used in the OKG canonicalization task.

2.1. Definitions

Definition 1 (Curated Knowledge Graph) *A Curated Knowledge Graph (CKG) is defined as a finite set of triples which are generated by human effort following the pre-defined ontology.*

Entities and relations in CKGs are well canonicalized and pre-defined with unique identifiers. For example, the entity *Windows 95 (personal computer operating system by Microsoft)* has unique identifiers "/m/086n_" and "Q83370" in Freebase [2] and Wikidata [4] respectively.

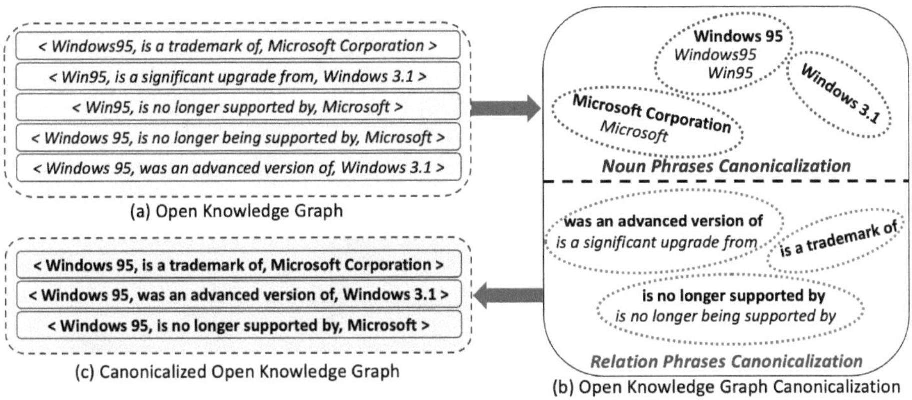

Figure 1. An illustration of the OKG Canonicalization task, adapted from [55]. (a) shows an open knowledge graph in which neither NPs nor RPs are canonicalized, thus storing ambiguous and redundant knowledge. (b) illustrates the process of the open knowledge graph canonicalization task, assigning NPs (or RPs) that refer to the same entity (or relation) into the same cluster, and selecting one (**bold**) to represent other elements in the cluster. (c) demonstrates a canonicalized open knowledge graph without ambiguity and redundancy.

Definition 2 (Open Knowledge Graph) *An Open Knowledge Graph (OKG) is a finite set of non-canonicalized triples which are automatically extracted from unstructured text without any pre-defined ontology via open information extraction methods.*

It is noted that the definition of an open knowledge graph in this chapter is different from [41]. In [41], they classify knowledge graphs into open knowledge graphs and enterprise knowledge graphs, based on the organisation or community. Specifically, open knowledge graph in [41] are published online and their content accessible for the public good, such as YAGO [1], Freebase [2], DBpedia [3], and Wikidata [4]. In contrast, enterprise knowledge graphs are typically internal to a company and applied for commercial use-cases [56]. However, following our definitions of CKG and OKG, both the definitions of open knowledge graphs and enterprise knowledge graphs in [41] are under the concept of CKGs in this chapter, since they all require human effort to pre-define the ontology but not constructed automatically from unstructured text. Following our definition, notable instances of OKGs include ReVerb [29], OPIEC [30], and Open-CyKG [31].

To be more specific, we give an example as shown in Figure 1 (a). If we search an NP *Windows 95* in a question-answering system which is built on top of the open knowledge graph in Figure 1 (a), we can only obtain answers related to *Windows 95* but other information hid behind *Windows95* and *Win95* is missed, because it is unknown for machines that *Windows 95*, *Windows95*, and *Win95* all refer to the same entity. Moreover, it can be seen that the two non-canonicalized triples *<Win95, is no longer supported by, Microsoft>* and *<Windows 95, is no longer being supported by, Microsoft>* are redundant facts, only one of which needs to be stored in practice.

Definition 3 (Open Knowledge Graph Canonicalization) *Given an Open Knowledge Graph consisting of a set of non-canonicalized triples, the goal of Open Knowledge Graph canonicalization is to cluster synonymous NPs referring to the same entity and synonymous RPs having the same semantic meaning into a group, which converts these*

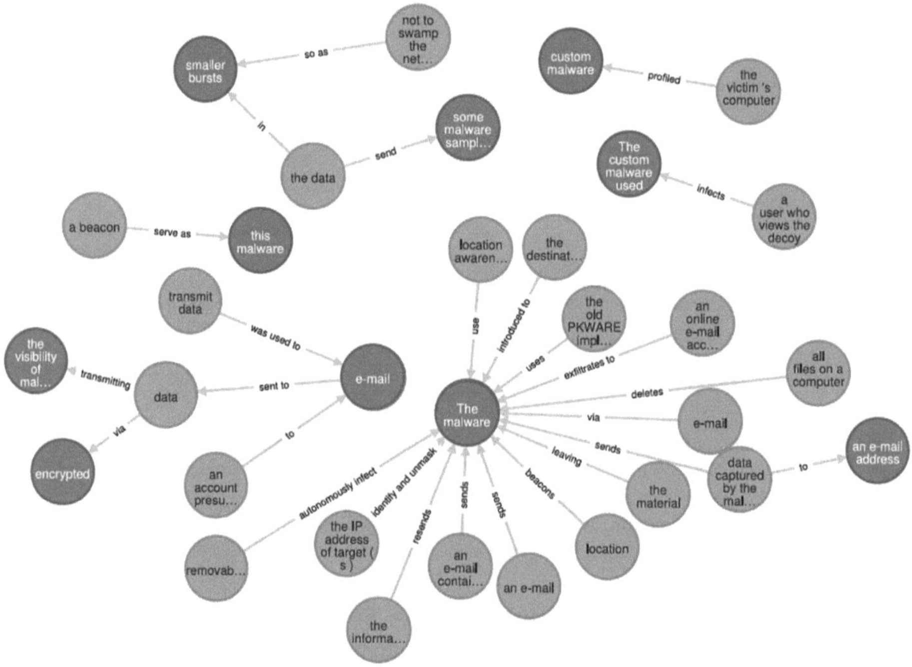

Figure 2. An uncanonicalized sample of Open-CyKG using Neo4J [57]. Courtesy of [31].

non-canonicalized triples to their canonicalized forms. Then, one element is selected to represent all others in the same group.

As shown in Figure 1 (b), the OKG canonicalization task can be divided into two subtasks: NP canonicalization (shown in blue at the top) and RP canonicalization (shown in green at the bottom). For NP canonicalization, the model should recognize that *Windows 95*, *Windows95*, and *Win95* all refer to the same entity, and assign all of them to one cluster. Additionally, the model should assign *Windows 3.1* separately to another cluster. Moreover, in each cluster, one NP should be selected to represent others in this cluster, such as *Windows 95* and *Microsoft Corporation*. Similarly, for RP canonicalization, the model needs to assign *is no longer supported by* and *is no longer being supported by* into one cluster and select one (*is no longer supported by*) as the representative.

Definition 4 (Canonicalized Open Knowledge Graph) *A canonicalized open knowledge graph is a finite set of canonicalized triples.*

As shown in Figure 1 (c), all of *Windows95*, *Win95* and *Windows 95* are represented by *Windows 95*. As a result, the number of triples in this Figure reduces from 5 to 3 after the OKG canonicalization.

2.2. Instance

In this chapter, we will introduce one important instance in the cybersecurity domain, called Open-CyKG [31]. In general, Open-CyKG defines a methodology for constructing threat intelligence knowledge graphs from unstructured advanced persistent threat

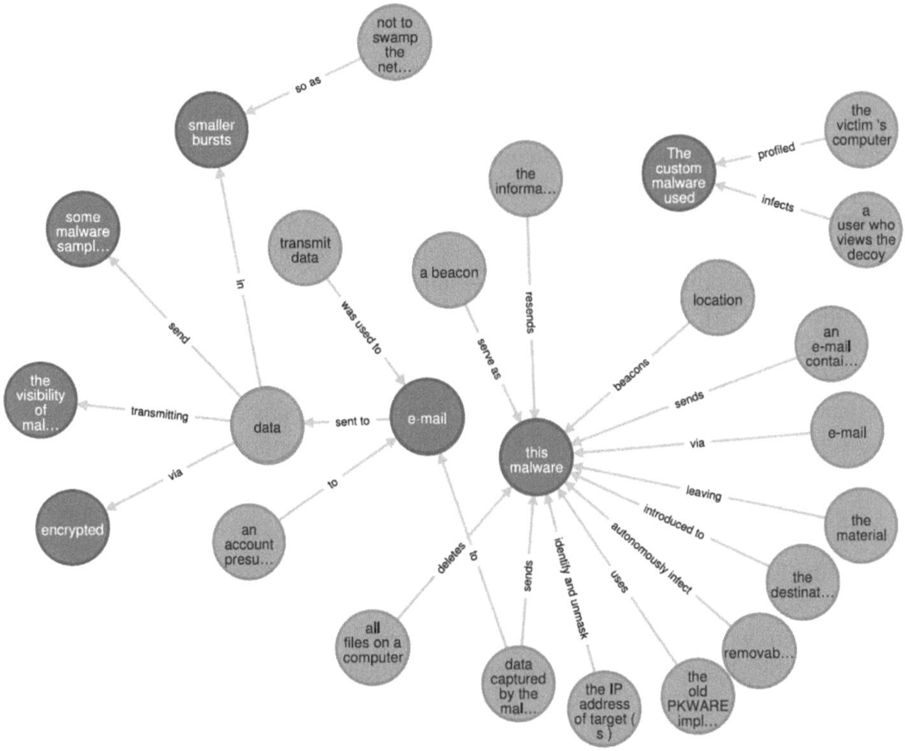

Figure 3. The canonicalized sample of Open-CyKG using Neo4J [57]. Courtesy of [31].

reports in an automated fashion. This is the first OKG in the cybersecurity domain that does not require pre-defined information extraction sets. OIE methods enable it to effectively extract valuable information from unstructured Advanced Persistent Threat (APT) reports and represent the retrieved data in an OKG, thereby providing efficient query and retrieval of threat-related information.

Open-CyKG is made up of three primary building blocks: an attention-based neural OIE architecture for extracting domain-independent relational triples from unstructured data, an NER module for automatic labelling of cybersecurity entities, and the canonicalization of the OKG. The process starts with an initial parsing of a text document, where embeddings corresponding to words, parts of speech (POS), and predicates are inputted into Bi-GRU to perform sequence labelling. The output is then passed to an additional attention layer, followed by a softmax layer to output separate probability distributions covering different labels. The NER module further employs Bi-GRU followed by dense layers and conditional random fields (CRF) to label each entity in the cybersecurity corpus. Based on the above steps, an OKG is created using non-canonicalized triples, with each node augmented with named entity labels. An uncanonicalized sample of Open-CyKG is shown in Figure 2. Finally, in the canonicalization of OKGs, they cluster the NPs and RPs by first averaging the pre-trained word embeddings and then performing hierarchical aggregation clustering (HAC) by using cosine similarity as the metric. Figure 3 illustrates the canonicalized version of Open-CyKG, where nodes are merged after the clustering process.

2.3. Assumption

Given an OKG, the goal of the OKG canonicalization task is to canonicalize its NPs and RPs. It is noted that the same string can have different meanings if it appears on two different web pages. For example, *<Michael Jordan, won, an award>* can refer to Michael Jeffrey Jordan (American basketball player and businessman who was born in 1963, with a unique identifier “Q41421” in Wikidata) or Michael Irwin Jordan (American computer scientist, University of California, Berkeley, with a unique identifier “Q3308285” in Wikidata), depending on where the triple appears.

Following [33], we assume, that the same NP on the same web page will always refer to the same entity. Similarly, the same RP on the same web page will always refer to the same relation. For example, a news article that uses “Michael Jordan” to refer to an American basketball player may not use that word (without other qualifications) to refer to the American computer scientist. This is a common assumption in linguistics [58] and data mining.

3. Existing Methods in Open Knowledge Graph Canonicalization

In this section, we briefly introduce several existing methods in the OKG canonicalization task. Table 1 summarizes OKG canonicalization models according to their techniques.

3.1. Full ML

Full ML [33] is the first OKG canonicalization method proposed in 2014. Specifically, they perform NP canonicalization by performing the HAC algorithm [59] over manually defined feature spaces and subsequently perform RP clustering by using the AMIE algorithm [60].

First, they define a mention as a triple $m = (n, u, A_n)$ where n is a subject NP such as Michael Jordan, u is the URL of a web document such as *bbc.com* where the mention is extracted by the OIE tools, and A_n is the set of attributes about n that are extracted from u. The HAC algorithm requires a similarity function for clustering the input data. Then, with the goal of determining which similarity function works best under which conditions, they defined different similarities, such as attribute overlap, string similarity, string identity, IDF token overlap, word overlap, entity overlap and type overlap. Many of the functions use the Jaccard coefficient:

$$Jaccard(S,S') = \left|\frac{S \cap S'}{S \cup S'}\right|, \tag{1}$$

where S and S' are two sets as the input. As an example, the attribute overlap is the Jaccard coefficient of the set of attributes:

$$f_{attr}(m,m') = Jaccard(A_m, A_m{}'), \tag{2}$$

where $f_{attr}(\cdot)$ is the attribute overlap score , m and m' are two input mentions, A_m and $A_m{}'$ are their attribute sets respectively.

Finally, they also study a combinatorial similarity that integrates all individual similarities according to a logistic function:

$$f_{ml}(m,m') = \frac{1}{1+e^{-f_{sim}(m,m')}}, \tag{3}$$

where $f_{sim}(m,m')$ is a linear combination of the individual similarities:

$$f_{sim}(m,m') = c_0 + \sum_{i=1}^{N} c_i f_i(m,m'), \tag{4}$$

Here, c_0 is the term for regularization, and $f_1,...,f_N$ are the individual similarities proposed in [33], like attribute overlap, string similarity, string identity and IDF token overlap.

After the NP canonicalization, they can obtain a semi-canonicalized OKG and use it as the input to the task of RP canonicalization. To deal with this RP canonicalization task, they apply AMIE [60] to the semi-canonicalized OKG to mine subsumption rules of the form $r(x,y) \Rightarrow r'(x,y)$. Following this AMIE algorithm, the infer equivalence rules of the form $r(x,y) \Leftrightarrow r'(x,y)$ are generated by merging subsumptions in both directions. Therefore, the output of the AMIE algorithm is a set of equivalent RPs, such as $be-named-after(x,y) \Leftrightarrow take-its-name-from(x,y)$. They can get a set of weighted equivalence relations between RPs via the rule-mining process. Additionally, they iteratively merge equivalence mappings with at least one RP in common since the equivalence relation is transitive. For example, given the equivalence mappings as follows:

$stand-for(x,y) \Leftrightarrow be-an-acronym-for(x,y)$
$be-short-for(x,y) \Leftrightarrow be-an-acronym-for(x,y)$
$refer-to(x,y) \Leftrightarrow be-short-for(x,y)$

They merge the RPs $stand-for(x,y)$, $be-an-acronym-for(x,y)$, $be-short-for(x,y)$ and $refer-to(x,y)$ into the same cluster.

3.2. CESI

Proposed in 2018, CESI [34] is the first OKG canonicalization method which leverages the knowledge graph embedding model. The input to CESI is a non-canonicalized OKG with source information for each triple, and the output is a list of canonicalized NPs and RPs. To be specific, CESI[2] achieves this target through its three-step procedure:

(1) Side Information Acquisition: The goal of this step is to gather various NP and RP side information for each triple in the given OKG by running several standard tools on the source text of the triples. For NP side information, they use Stanford CoreNLP Entity Linker [61] for entity linking, PPDB 2.0 [62] for identifying equivalence between NPs, WordNet [63] with word-sense disambiguation [64] to identify possible synsets for a given NP, IDF token overlap [33] to search if two NPs are sharing infrequent terms, and morph normalization [29] (like tense removal, pluralization, and capitalization) for finding out equivalent NPs. On the other hand, for RP side information, they utilize the AMIE algorithm [60] to learn implication rules between two relations r and r', and the

[2]https://github.com/malllabiisc/cesi

Table 1. Summary of OKG canonicalization models according to our proposed taxonomy. Courtesy of [55]. "KGE" refers to the knowledge graph embedding model, "PWE" refers to the pre-trained word embeddings, and "CI" refers to the context information.

Model	Side Information		KGE	PWE	CI	Supervised Manner
	NP	RP				
Full ML [33]	Attribute Overlap, String Similarity, String Identity, IDF Token Overlap, Word Overlap, Entity Overlap, Type Overlap	AMIE	-	-	-	Semi-supervised
CESI [34]	Entity Linking, PPDB, WordNet, IDF Token Overlap, Morph Normalization	AMIE, KBP	HolE	GloVe	-	Semi-supervised
SIST [35]	Jaro-Winkler Similarity, IDF Token Overlap, Entity Linking	PATTY, IDF Token Overlap	-	-	Domain Vector	Unsupervised
CUVA [36]	Entity Linking, PPDB, IDF Token Overlap, Morph Normalization	AMIE, KBP	HolE	GloVe	-	Semi-supervised
JOCL [37]	IDF token overlap, PPDB, Entity Linking	IDF token overlap, PPDB, AMIE, KBP, Relation Linking	-	FastText	-	Semi-supervised
CMVC [38]	Entity Linking, Web Url	AMIE, Web Url	TransE	FastText	BERT	Unsupervised

Stanford Knowledge Base Population (KBP) system [65] to check if two RPs fall in the same category.

(2) Embedding NP and RPs: In this step, leveraging a neural technique (knowledge graph embedding model), CESI learns specialized embeddings for all NPs and RPs in the OKG by making principled use of side information available from step (1). For learning embeddings of NPs and RPs in a given OKG, CESI utilizes the score function of HolE [66] along with terms for penalizing violation of equivalence conditions from the NP and RP side information, and uses the logistic function as the loss function. Specifically, given a triple $< h, r, t >$, they are represented as embeddings **h**, **r**, and **t**, respectively. The scoring function of HolE [66] captures the semantic relevance correlation between **h** and **t** using a circular correlation operator, namely

$$f_r(h,t) = \mathbf{r}^T (\mathbf{h} \star \mathbf{t}), \tag{5}$$

where $f_r(h,t)$ is the score of triple $< h,r,t >$, and $\star : R^d \times R^d \rightarrow R^d$ is the circular correlation operator defined as follows:

$$[\mathbf{h} \star \mathbf{t}]_k = \sum_{i=0}^{d-1} \mathbf{h}_i \mathbf{t}_{(k+i) \ mod \ d}, \tag{6}$$

The first index of $[\mathbf{h} \star \mathbf{t}]$ measures the similarity between **h** and **t**, while other indices capture the interaction of features from **h** and **t**, in a particular order. HolE can model asymmetric relations, since the circular correlation operator is not commutative, i.e., $\mathbf{h} \star \mathbf{t} \neq \mathbf{h} \star \mathbf{t}$. For more details, please refer to [66].

(3) Clustering Embeddings and Canonicalization: The goal of this step is to cluster the NPs and RPs based on their distance in the embedding space. Each cluster represents

a specific entity or relation. Based on certain relevant heuristics, they assign a representative to each NP and RP cluster. For clustering, CESI clusters NPs and RPs by performing the HAC algorithm using cosine similarity over the embeddings learned in step (2). The HAC algorithm is preferred over other clustering methods because the number of clusters is not known beforehand. However, the threshold value for HAC is chosen based on the validation dataset. Thus, CESI is a semi-supervised method, which is the same as Full ML [33]. For canonicalization, among each cluster, they compute a mean of all elements' embeddings weighted by the frequency of occurrence of each element in the input OKG. NP or RP which lies closest to the weighted cluster mean is chosen as the representative of the cluster.

Note that both Full ML [33] and CESI [34] use AMIE, a famous symbolic technique which can learn Horn rules on OKGs, to produce high-quality clusters of semantically equivalent relations in the given OKG. However, AMIE requires semi-canonicalized OKG as input and can only be applied to connected rules. Furthermore, CESI models the problem of NP and RP canonicalization jointly using relevant side information in a principled manner. This is different from Full ML [33] where NP and RP canonicalization were performed sequentially.

3.3. SIST

SIST [35] proposes an approach, which performs canonicalization by leveraging the side information of the original data sources, including the entity linking knowledge, the types of the candidate entities detected, as well as the domain knowledge of the source text. Specifically, they propose to learn the domain knowledge of a given source text based on the types of candidate entities detected in it efficiently. Note that SIST[3] is the first unsupervised method in the OKG canonicalization task.

First, they model the canonicalization problem of NPs and RPs in the given OKG jointly, leveraging the side information in the source text. Second, they propose an efficient graph-based solution to the HAC-based method to cluster non-canonicalized triples. Third, to assist in the clustering process of non-canonicalized triples from the OKG, they utilize the domain knowledge of the source text. The assumption behind this method is that triples extracted from source text that share similar domain knowledge have a higher probability of representing similar semantic meaning.

3.4. CUVA

CUVA [36] is a neural network architecture that learns unique embeddings for NPs and RPs as well as cluster assignments in a joint fashion. This framework consists of 3 key components: the Variational Deep Embedding (VaDE) framework [67], a knowledge graph embedding model, and side information. Previously, the CESI architecture [34] models the OKG canonicalization task in a two-step pipeline approach. In the first step, it uses a knowledge graph embedding model (i.e., HolE [66]) to learn embeddings for NPs and RPs. Then in the independent second step, based on these learned embeddings it generates clusters by using the HAC algorithm. Unlike CESI, CUVA[4] learns the embed-

[3]https://heathersherry.github.io
[4]https://github.com/IBM/Open-KG-canonicalization

ding representations and the cluster assignments of both NPs and RPs in an end-to-end manner.

VaDE is a generative clustering model that implements a Mixture of Gaussians within the latent space of a variational autoencoder (VAE). They prove such a deep clustering model is suited to cluster NPs (or RPs) because its soft-clustering ability can account for different meanings (i.e., ambiguity) of a given NP (or RP). Such behaviour is superior to hard-clustering methods such as the HAC algorithm that assigns each NP (or RP) to exactly one cluster. Furthermore, the high-dimensional input space of VaDE is more suitable for encoding the observed surface form variations of different NPs and RPs.

The motivation behind using a knowledge graph embedding module is to encode the structural knowledge within the OKG. This module is responsible for the joint learning between the latent representations of NPs and RPs. Similar to CESI [34], CUVA also employs HolE [66] as the encoder module to learn embeddings of NPs and RPs. In addition, CUVA uses additional side information obtained from the documents used to build the OKG. This is because NPs and RPs within an OKG can be often tagged with relevant side information extracted from the context sentence in which the triple appears. To be specific, side information pairs are obtained from CESI [34], including 4 strategies: entity linking [61], PPDB 2.0 [62], IDF token overlap [33], and morph normalization [29].

3.5. JOCL

With the same goal of eliminating redundant and ambiguous facts, the OKG canonicalization task (i.e., convert NPs and RPs to canonicalized form) and OKG linking (i.e., link NPs and RPs with their corresponding entities and relations in a CKG) are tightly coupled, and one task can benefit significantly from the other. Following this observation, JOCL [37] is proposed to explore the task of joint OKG canonicalization and linking for the first time. To tackle these two tasks, the JOCL framework[5] is based on a factor graph model to make them reinforce each other. It is noted that due to the intrinsic characteristics of the factor graph model, the JOCL framework is flexible enough to combine different signals from both tasks and able to extend to fit new signals via adding suitable factor nodes.

Given a set of non-canonicalized triples in an OKG as well as a CKG, JOCL first constructs a factor graph for each task. With respect to the task of OKG canonicalization, JOCL generates a variable node for each pair of NPs (or RPs) to represent whether they have the same semantic meaning and adds OKG canonicalization signals and transitive relation signals as factor nodes. Concerning the task of OKG linking, JOCL generates a variable node for each NP (or RP) to represent its corresponding entity (or relation) in a CKG and adds OKG linking signals and fact inclusion signals as factor nodes. Furthermore, in order to make these two tasks reinforce each other, consistency signals are added as factor nodes to perform the interaction between the two tasks. Subsequently, a reasonable working procedure (i.e., the interaction between two tasks after resolving them alone) is elaborately designed to pass messages among different types of nodes on the factor graph and learn the parameters among this framework. With the final messages, JOCL could compute the marginal probability for each node according to the learned

[5]https://github.com/JOCL-repo/JOCL

weights, infer the corresponding entity (or relation) for each NP (or RP) and generate canonicalization groups of NP (or RP) jointly.

Besides the factor graph model, another important module is factor signals. In JOCL, they employ 4 kinds of signals: 1) NP canonicalization signals (i.e., IDF token overlap [33], pre-trained word embedding [68], and PPDB 2.0 [62]); 2) RP canonicalization signals (AMIE [60], KBP [65] and all signals used in NP canonicalization); 3) OKG entity linking signals (i.e., entity popularity [69], pre-trained word embedding [68], and PPDB 2.0 [62]); 4) OKG relation linking signals (i.e., Ngram [70], Levenshtein distance, pre-trained word embedding [68], and PPDB 2.0 [62]). Overall, both neural techniques (such as pre-trained word embedding) and symbolic techniques (like AMIE) are leveraged in this framework.

3.6. CMVC

The authors of [38] find that two views of knowledge (i.e., a fact view based on the non-canonicalized triple and a context view based on the non-canonicalized triple's source context) provide complementary information that is vital to the task of OKG canonicalization. Based on this observation, they propose CMVC[6], an unsupervised framework that leverages these two views of knowledge jointly for canonicalizing OKGs without the need for manually annotated labels.

To achieve this goal, the proposed CMVC framework consists of 4 modules: 1) fact view: they leverage the knowledge graph embedding model (i.e., TransE [71]) to capture the relational structural information in the given OKG, and then propose a data augmentation operator to improve the quality of embeddings by making the OKG dense. 2) context view: they use BERT [72] as a context encoder to transform sentences into embeddings. To refine the learned embeddings, they proposed the iterative clustering procedure to transfer the prior knowledge from limited seed pairs to other pairs iteratively. 3) multi-view CH K-Means clustering algorithm: this algorithm is proposed to mutually reinforce the clustering of view-specific embeddings learned from each view by considering their different clustering qualities. Therefore, the input is the embeddings from each view and the output is the clustering result. 4) Log-Jump algorithm: the number of clusters (i.e., K) is the most important factor of the K-Means algorithm. However, in the OKG canonicalization task, we cannot know the exact K of the input data due to the lack of artificial labels. To deal with this problem, they propose a Log-Jump algorithm to predict the optimal number of clusters in a data-driven way without requiring any labels.

4. Neuro-Symbolic Techniques

In this section, we describe some important neural, symbolic, and neuro-symbolic integration techniques used by existing methods in the task of OKG canonicalization. Table 2 summarizes the leverage of these techniques for the OKG canonicalization models.

[6]https://github.com/Yang233666/cmvc

4.1. Neural Techniques

Neural techniques, such as deep learning models, are capable of modelling the implicit correlations inside data. However, the neural techniques cannot provide explicit inference evidence to explain the results, making them look like black boxes [73]. Overall, neural techniques are easy to use and perform well, but lack interpretability and are difficult to train due to the requirement for powerful GPUs.

4.1.1. Pre-Trained Word Embedding

GloVe [74] and FastText [68] are two commonly used models implementing the static word embedding methodology. Both models learn embeddings based on the co-occurrence information of words in text documents.

For obtaining static representations for words, GloVe [74] adopts a log-bilinear regression model with a weighted least-squares objective, which is performed on aggregated global word-word co-occurrence statistics from a corpus. The training objective of GloVe is to learn distributional word embeddings such that their dot product equals the logarithm of the words' probability of co-occurrence. In CESI [34] and CUVA [36], to initialize the input embeddings of the knowledge graph embedding model (i.e., HolE), the GloVe embeddings are used. To be specific, each NP and RP is represented by a 300-dimensional GloVe embedding. Furthermore, for multi-word phrases, phrase embeddings are averaged together to get embeddings.

By providing distinct static representations for the words in the vocabulary, pre-trained word embedding techniques, like word2Vec [75] and GloVe [74] have been widely used in many domains. However, this leads to ignorance of the internal structure of language and results in a limitation of morphologically rich language due to the neglect of syntactic relationships of words. Since many word formations follow rules in morphologically rich languages, character-level information can be used to improve vector representations for these languages.

To improve the pre-trained word embeddings for morphologically rich languages, FastText [68] provides embeddings of character n-grams, representing words as the average of these embeddings. FastText is an extension of the word2vec model. Similar to the word2vec model, FastText also uses CBOW and Skip-gram to compute the embeddings. One difference between word2vec and GloVe is that FastText can also handle out-of-vocabulary (OOV) words, i.e., it can find the word embeddings that do not occur while training the data and are not present in the model's vocabulary. This is because FastText provides embedding for that OOV word by embedding its character n-gram. In addition, to speed up computation, FastText uses hierarchical softmax, capitalizing on the imbalanced distribution of classes. All these techniques offer users scalable solutions for pre-trained word embeddings.

FastText is used by JOCL [37] as canonicalization signals and linking signals for both NP and RP. In CMVC, the pre-trained word embeddings of FastText are leveraged as input embeddings to the knowledge graph embedding model for initialization. This is helpful for the OKG canonicalization task because if the similarity scores (computed by their pre-trained word embeddings) of two NPs (or RPs) are high, they are likely to refer to the same entity. For instance, as reported JOCL [37], the similarity score of "Barack

Obama" and "President Obama" is 0.873 using FastText [68] embeddings trained on the Common Crawl[7].

4.1.2. BERT

Early pre-trained word embedding is a static technique, such as GloVe [74] and FastText [68], but they are difficult to adapt to different semantic contexts and domains. BERT [72] is proposed to solve this problem, which builds a deep bidirectional neural network based on the Transformer block [76]. The idea of BERT is to pre-train a general language model with large amounts of training data. After the pre-training, the model can then be effectively fine-tuned for different downstream tasks and applications, resulting in a deep-learning model that effectively produces sentence embeddings. CMVC extracts sentence embeddings resorting to BERT, to exploit the semantic distributional information of the source context where the triple occurs.

4.1.3. Knowledge Graph Embedding Models

The knowledge graph embedding model (KGEM) is a popular neural technique that aims to represent entities and relations of knowledge graphs into low-dimensional semantic spaces for a wide spectrum of applications such as knowledge graph completion, link prediction, and knowledge reasoning. The essential idea of KGEM is to represent entities and relations of a KG in a low-dimensional space where the embeddings should preserve the structure of the input KG. We will briefly introduce two KGEMs used in the OKG canonicalization task, i.e., TransE [71] and HolE [66].

In order to capture the translational relationships between entities, TransE [71] is proposed to embed KGs into Euclidean Space and represent relations between entities as translation embeddings between entity embeddings in the low-dimensional semantic space. Given a triple $< h, r, t >$, the relation is interpreted as a translation of the embedding $\mathbf{r}$ so that the entity embeddings $\mathbf{h}$ and $\mathbf{t}$ can be connected by $\mathbf{r}$ with low error, i.e., $\mathbf{h}+\mathbf{r} \approx \mathbf{t}$ when (h,r,t) holds ($\mathbf{t}$ should be a nearest neighbour of $\mathbf{h}+\mathbf{r}$), while $\mathbf{h}+\mathbf{r}$ should be away from $\mathbf{t}$ otherwise. The score function is defined as the distance between $\mathbf{h}+\mathbf{r}$ and $\mathbf{t}$, i.e.,

$$f_r(h,t) = \|\mathbf{h}+\mathbf{r}-\mathbf{t}\|_{1/2}, \tag{7}$$

where $f_r(h,t)$ is the score of triple $t_i = <h,r,t>$, $\mathbf{h}$, $\mathbf{r}$ and $\mathbf{t}$ are the embedding of h, r and t respectively. To capture the relational structural information of triples in an OKG, CMVC [38] learns structure embeddings in the fact view via TransE.

Semantic matching models use score functions in the form of products to measure the semantic relevance correlation of entities and relations. HolE [66] is one of the most representative semantic matching models. CESI [34] and CUVA [36] utilize the score function of HolE [66] along with regularization terms from the NP and RP side information, to learn NPs and RPs embeddings, as described in Section 3.2 and Section 3.4.

[7] https://commoncrawl.org/2017/06

Table 2. Summary of neuro-symbolic techniques leveraged in OKG canonicalization. "PWE" refers to the pre-trained word embeddings, "KGE" refers to the knowledge graph embedding model, "RPI" refers to the regularization perspective integration, and "FPI" refers to the regularization perspective integration.

Model		Full ML [33]	CESI [34]	SIST [35]	CUVA [36]	JOCL [37]	CMVC [38]
Neural Techniques	PWE	×	✓	×	✓	✓	✓
	BERT	×	×	×	×	×	✓
	KGE	×	✓	×	✓	×	✓
Symbolic Techniques	AMIE	✓	✓	×	✓	✓	✓
	PATTY	×	×	✓	×	×	×
Neuro-Symbolic Integration	RPI	×	✓	×	✓	×	×
	FPI	×	×	×	×	✓	✓

4.2. Symbolic Techniques

Generally, symbolism techniques have sound readability and interpretability and are another widely used technique in the OKG canonicalization task. In general, they are efficient, trustworthy and consume less energy than the neural techniques mentioned in Section 4.1. Two symbolic techniques are used in this task: AMIE [60] and PATTY [77], as described in Section 4.2.1 and Section 4.2.2, respectively.

4.2.1. AMIE

An important feature of the OKG canonicalization task is the side information. To obtain side information, most existing methods usually employ logic-based reasoning techniques. AMIE algorithm [60] is widely used by existing methods, which can determine whether two RPs represent the same semantics by learning Horn rules. Previous studies [33,34,36,37,38] usually take morphologically normalized triples as input to AMIE. After reasoning based on statistical rules and logic mining, the output of AMIE is a set of implication rules between two RPs p_i and p_j (e.g., $p_i \Rightarrow p_j$). Following this strategy, if both $p_i \Rightarrow p_j$ and $p_i \Leftarrow p_j$ satisfy the support and confidence thresholds, it means that p_i and p_j have the same semantics and should be grouped into one cluster.

AMIE+ [78] improves the efficiency of AMIE [60]. To speed it up, AMIE+ proposes an approximate metric based on pre-computed statistics, such as the size of the joins between two relations. In the implementation process, the SPARQL queries which are used to search rules are also simplified. As a result, AMIE+ achieves 100 speedup compared with the original AMIE.

4.2.2. PATTY

SIST [35] utilizes PATTY [77] to assist the canonization of RPs but with additional knowledge from NPs and side information from the source text. PATTY focuses on the subsumption rules between syntactic patterns using frequent itemset mining with the help of existing CKGs. Specifically, in SIST, the pattern repository in the PATTY dictionary is used to discover whether the RPs shared by two triples have the same semantic meaning. The two triples are labelled as equal, only if their NPs are linked to the same entity, and their RPs are in the same synset in the PATTY dictionary.

4.3. Neuro-Symbolic Integration

Integrating the neural techniques (described in Section 4.1) and symbolic techniques (described in Section 4.2) is important to achieve better performance in the OKG canonicalization task since the performance of using only one of the techniques is limited. This section discusses two representative methods to integrate neural and symbolic techniques at the regularization perspective and feature perspective, respectively.

4.3.1. Regularization Perspective Integration

In CESI [34], they employ a neural technique (i.e., knowledge graph embedding model) to learn the embeddings of NPs and RPs from an OKG. However, the performance using only neural techniques is limited (i.e., the average F1 of HolE initialized with GloVe embeddings on three datasets is 70.4, as shown in Table 2 in [34]). To deal with this problem, they integrate symbolic techniques in this framework, such as AMIE as regularization terms. The results of CESI show that through this regularization perspective strategy, they have improved the average F1 performance on three datasets from 70.4 to 86.3 by a staggering amount. This integration method is also used by CUVA [36].

4.3.2. Feature Perspective Integration

Besides the regularization perspective integration, another significant manner is to integrate the knowledge from neural and symbolic techniques from a feature perspective. As described in Section 3.5, the JOCL framework [37] is based on a factor graph model to make two tasks (i.e., OKG canonicalization task and OKG linking) reinforce each other. Due to the intrinsic characteristics of the factor graph model, the JOCL framework is flexible enough to combine different signals from both tasks and able to extend to fit new signals.

Neural techniques are used in this framework as signals, such as pre-trained word embedding. On the other hand, symbolic techniques, like AMIE, are signals for RPs to represent whether they have the same semantic meaning. The interaction between two tasks after resolving them alone is elaborately designed to pass messages among different types of nodes on the factor graph and learn the parameters of this framework. In this process, knowledge from neural and symbolic techniques is also transmitted, shared, and integrated along with the messages. Therefore, the neuro-symbolic integration of JOCL is achieved from a feature perspective via passing messages. With the final messages, JOCL could compute the marginal probability for each node according to the learned parameters, infer the corresponding entity (or relation) for each NP (or RP) and generate canonicalization groups of NP (or RP) jointly.

Different from the explicit feature perspective integration method of JOCL [37], CMVC [38] utilizes embeddings to perform implicit feature perspective integration. Specifically, they use particular encoders from different views to mine the knowledge hidden in neural and symbolic features and then employ the multi-view clustering framework to obtain the clustering result.

5. Conclusion and Future Work

Canonicalizing Open Knowledge Graphs (OKGs) is an important problem in modelling knowledge from unstructured text, but has not been fully explored. In this chapter, we provide an overview of the neuro-symbolic techniques used by existing methods in this task. Necessary background knowledge, such as definitions, instances and assumptions are introduced at first. Then we give a brief description and several existing methods and an analysis of neural and symbolic techniques leveraged among them. Finally, we summarize two manners of neuro-symbolic integration in the OKG canonicalization, i.e., regularization perspective integration and feature perspective integration.

To solve the OKG canonicalization problem, the use of neural technologies has proven to be effective so far, and there are many different models available, such as pre-trained word embeddings, BERT, and knowledge graph embedding models. However, they usually have a black-box nature and require powerful GPU machines during training. On the other hand, methods based on symbolic techniques are usually fast, low-energy and reliable, but there are few examples of existing methods applied to the OKG canonicalization task, like AMIE [60] and PATTY [77].

For future research, the three most important challenges can be summarized as follows: 1) How to develop more effective symbolic techniques for this task; 2) How to explore more effective and efficient neuro-symbolic integration techniques to achieve better performance; 3) How to mine and utilize more types of knowledge, such as more side information tools, and knowledge from different views and modalities.

Acknowledgments

This publication has emanated from research conducted with the financial support of Taighde Éireann – Research Ireland under Grant number SFI/12/RC/2289 P2.

References

[1] Suchanek FM, Kasneci G, Weikum G. Yago: a core of semantic knowledge. In: WWW; 2007. p. 697-706.
[2] Bollacker K, Evans C, Paritosh P, Sturge T, Taylor J. Freebase: a collaboratively created graph database for structuring human knowledge. In: SIGMOD; 2008. p. 1247-50.
[3] Lehmann J, Isele R, Jakob M, Jentzsch A, Kontokostas D, Mendes P, et al. DBpedia - a large-scale, multilingual knowledge base extracted from wikipedia. Semantic Web Journal. 2015;6(2):167-95.
[4] Vrandečić D, Krötzsch M. Wikidata: a free collaborative knowledgebase. Communications of the ACM. 2014;57(10):78-85.
[5] Chen X, Jia S, Xiang Y. A review: Knowledge reasoning over knowledge graph. Expert Systems with Applications. 2020;141:112948.
[6] Ji H, Ke P, Huang S, Wei F, Zhu X, Huang M. Language Generation with Multi-Hop Reasoning on Commonsense Knowledge Graph. In: EMNLP; 2020. p. 725-36.
[7] Liu L, Du B, Fung YR, Ji H, Xu J, Tong H. KompaRe: a knowledge graph comparative reasoning system. In: KDD; 2021. p. 3308-18.
[8] Li Z, Jin X, Li W, Guan S, Guo J, Shen H, et al. Temporal knowledge graph reasoning based on evolutional representation learning. In: SIGIR; 2021. p. 408-17.
[9] Dai Z, Li L, Xu W. CFO: Conditional Focused Neural Question Answering with Large-scale Knowledge Bases. In: ACL; 2016. p. 800-10.
[10] Bauer L, Wang Y, Bansal M. Commonsense for Generative Multi-Hop Question Answering Tasks. In: EMNLP; 2018. p. 4220-30.
[11] Zhang Y, Dai H, Kozareva Z, Smola A, Song L. Variational reasoning for question answering with knowledge graph. In: AAAI. vol. 32; 2018. .
[12] Jia Z, Pramanik S, Saha Roy R, Weikum G. Complex temporal question answering on knowledge graphs. In: CIKM; 2021. p. 792-802.
[13] Zhang F, Yuan NJ, Lian D, Xie X, Ma WY. Collaborative knowledge base embedding for recommender systems. In: KDD; 2016. p. 353-62.

[14] Wang X, He X, Cao Y, Liu M, Chua TS. Kgat: Knowledge graph attention network for recommendation. In: KDD; 2019. p. 950-8.
[15] Wang X, Huang T, Wang D, Yuan Y, Liu Z, He X, et al. Learning intents behind interactions with knowledge graph for recommendation. In: WWW; 2021. p. 878-87.
[16] Guo Q, Zhuang F, Qin C, Zhu H, Xie X, Xiong H, et al. A survey on knowledge graph-based recommender systems. IEEE Transactions on Knowledge and Data Engineering. 2020;34(8):3549-68.
[17] Franklin M, Halevy A, Maier D. From databases to dataspaces: a new abstraction for information management. ACM Sigmod Record. 2005;34(4):27-33.
[18] Halevy A, Franklin M, Maier D. Principles of dataspace systems. In: Proceedings of the twenty-fifth ACM SIGMOD-SIGACT-SIGART symposium on Principles of database systems; 2006. p. 1-9.
[19] Jeffery SR, Franklin MJ, Halevy AY. Pay-as-you-go user feedback for dataspace systems. In: SIGMOD; 2008. p. 847-60.
[20] Curry E. Real-time linked dataspaces: Enabling data ecosystems for intelligent systems. Springer Nature; 2020.
[21] Timilsina M, Buosi S, Song P, Yang Y, Haque R, Curry E. Enabling Dataspaces Using Foundation Models: Technical, Legal and Ethical Considerations and Future Trends. In: 2023 IEEE International Conference on Big Data (BigData). IEEE; 2023. p. 4712-21.
[22] Banko M, Cafarella MJ, Soderland S, Broadhead M, Etzioni O. Open information extraction from the web. In: IJCAI; 2007. p. 2670-6.
[23] Christensen J, Soderland S, Etzioni O. An analysis of open information extraction based on semantic role labeling. In: K-CAP; 2011. p. 113-20.
[24] Mausam M. Open information extraction systems and downstream applications. In: IJCAI; 2016. p. 4074-7.
[25] Saha S, Pal H, Mausam. Bootstrapping for numerical open ie. In: ACL; 2017. p. 317-23.
[26] Del Corro L, Gemulla R. ClausIE: clause-based open information extraction. In: WWW; 2013. p. 355-66.
[27] Angeli G, Johnson Premkumar MJ, Manning CD. Leveraging linguistic structure for open domain information extraction. In: ACL; 2015. p. 344-54.
[28] Gashteovski K, Gemulla R, Del Corro L. MinIE: minimizing facts in open information extraction. In: EMNLP; 2017. p. 2620-30.
[29] Fader A, Soderland S, Etzioni O. Identifying relations for open information extraction. In: EMNLP; 2011. p. 1535-45.
[30] Gashteovski K, Wanner S, Hertling S, Broscheit S, Gemulla R. OPIEC: an open information extraction corpus. In: AKBC; 2019. .
[31] Sarhan I, Spruit M. Open-cykg: An open cyber threat intelligence knowledge graph. Knowledge-Based Systems. 2021;233:107524.
[32] Curry E, Zaarour T, Yang Y, Timilsina M, Al-Qatf M, Haque R. Foundation Data Space Models: Bridging the Artificial Intelligence and Data Ecosystems (Vision Paper). In: 2023 IEEE International Conference on Big Data (BigData). IEEE; 2023. p. 190-5.
[33] Galárraga L, Heitz G, Murphy K, Suchanek FM. Canonicalizing open knowledge bases. In: CIKM; 2014. p. 1679-88.
[34] Vashishth S, Jain P, Talukdar P. Cesi: canonicalizing open knowledge bases using embeddings and side information. In: WWW; 2018. p. 1317-27.
[35] Lin X, Chen L. Canonicalization of open knowledge bases with side information from the source text. In: ICDE; 2019. p. 950-61.
[36] Dash S, Rossiello G, Mihindukulasooriya N, Bagchi S, Gliozzo A. Open knowledge graphs canonicalization using variational autoencoders. In: EMNLP; 2021. p. 10379-94.
[37] Liu Y, Shen W, Wang Y, Wang J, Yang Z, Yuan X. Joint open knowledge base canonicalization and linking. In: SIGMOD; 2021. p. 2253-61.
[38] Shen W, Yang Y, Liu Y. Multi-View Clustering for Open Knowledge Base Canonicalization. In: KDD; 2022. p. 1578-88.
[39] Viswanathan V, Gashteovski K, Gashteovski K, Lawrence C, Wu T, Neubig G. Large language models enable few-shot clustering. Transactions of the Association for Computational Linguistics. 2024;12:321-33.
[40] Shen W, Yang B, Liu Y. Jointly Canonicalizing and Linking Open Knowledge Base via Unified Embedding Learning. In: WWW; 2024. p. 2304-14.

[41] Hogan A, Blomqvist E, Cochez M, d'Amato C, Melo GD, Gutierrez C, et al. Knowledge graphs. ACM Computing Surveys. 2021;54(4):1-37.
[42] Weikum G, Dong XL, Razniewski S, Suchanek F, et al. Machine knowledge: Creation and curation of comprehensive knowledge bases. Foundations and Trends® in Databases. 2021;10(2-4):108-490.
[43] Chen X, Xie H, Li Z, Cheng G. Topic analysis and development in knowledge graph research: A bibliometric review on three decades. Neurocomputing. 2021;461:497-515.
[44] Zhong L, Wu J, Li Q, Peng H, Wu X. A comprehensive survey on automatic knowledge graph construction. arXiv preprint arXiv:230205019. 2023.
[45] Paulheim H. Knowledge graph refinement: A survey of approaches and evaluation methods. Semantic web. 2017;8(3):489-508.
[46] Subagdja B, Wang Z, Tan AH. Machine Learning for Refining Knowledge Graphs: A Survey. ACM Computing Surveys. 2023.
[47] Xue B, Zou L. Knowledge graph quality management: a comprehensive survey. IEEE Transactions on Knowledge and Data Engineering. 2022.
[48] Razniewski S, Arnaout H, Ghosh S, Suchanek FM. Completeness, Recall, and Negation in Open-World Knowledge Bases: A Survey. ACM Computing Surveys. 2024.
[49] Ji S, Pan S, Cambria E, Marttinen P, Philip SY. A survey on knowledge graphs: Representation, acquisition, and applications. IEEE Transactions on Neural Networks and Learning Systems. 2021;33(2):494-514.
[50] Cao J, Fang J, Meng Z, Liang S. Knowledge Graph Embedding: A Survey from the Perspective of Representation Spaces. arXiv preprint arXiv:221103536. 2022.
[51] Gesese GA, Biswas R, Sack H. A Comprehensive Survey of Knowledge Graph Embeddings with Literals: Techniques and Applications. DL4KG@ ESWC. 2019;2377:31-40.
[52] Gesese GA, Biswas R, Alam M, Sack H. A survey on knowledge graph embeddings with literals: Which model links better literal-ly? Semantic Web. 2021;12(4):617-47.
[53] Rossi A, Barbosa D, Firmani D, Matinata A, Merialdo P. Knowledge graph embedding for link prediction: A comparative analysis. ACM Transactions on Knowledge Discovery from Data. 2021;15(2):1-49.
[54] Wang Q, Mao Z, Wang B, Guo L. Knowledge graph embedding: A survey of approaches and applications. IEEE Transactions on Knowledge and Data Engineering. 2017;29(12):2724-43.
[55] Yang Y, Curry E. Open Knowledge Base Canonicalization: Techniques and Challenges. In: Text2KG 2024: International Workshop on Knowledge Graph Generation from Text, Co-located with the ESWC; 2024. p. 10.
[56] Nonaka I, Takeuchi H. The knowledge-creating company. Harvard business review. 2007;85(7/8):162.
[57] Miller JJ. Graph database applications and concepts with Neo4j. In: SAIS. vol. 2324; 2013. p. 141-7.
[58] Gale WA, Church K, Yarowsky D. One sense per discourse. In: Speech and Natural Language: Proceedings of a Workshop Held at Harriman, New York, February 23-26, 1992; 1992. .
[59] Tan PN, Steinbach M, Kumar V. Introduction to Data Mining. Addison-Wesley Longman Publishing. 2006.
[60] Galárraga LA, Teflioudi C, Hose K, Suchanek F. AMIE: association rule mining under incomplete evidence in ontological knowledge bases. In: WWW; 2013. p. 413-22.
[61] Spitkovsky VI, Chang AX. A cross-lingual dictionary for english wikipedia concepts. In: LREC; 2012. .
[62] Pavlick E, Rastogi P, Ganitkevitch J, Van Durme B, Callison-Burch C. PPDB 2.0: better paraphrase ranking, fine-grained entailment relations, word embeddings, and style classification. In: ACL; 2015. p. 425-30.
[63] Miller GA. WordNet: a lexical database for English. Communications of the ACM. 1995;38(11):39-41.
[64] Banerjee S, Pedersen T. An adapted Lesk algorithm for word sense disambiguation using WordNet. In: International conference on intelligent text processing and computational linguistics. Springer; 2002. p. 136-45.
[65] Surdeanu M, Tibshirani J, Nallapati R, Manning CD. Multi-instance multi-label learning for relation extraction. In: EMNLP; 2012. p. 455-65.
[66] Nickel M, Rosasco L, Poggio TA. Holographic embeddings of knowledge graphs. In: AAAI; 2016. p. 1955-61.
[67] Jiang Z, Zheng Y, Tan H, Tang B, Zhou H. Variational deep embedding: an unsupervised and generative approach to clustering. In: Proceedings of the 26th International Joint Conference on Artificial Intelligence; 2017. p. 1965-72.

[68] Bojanowski P, Grave E, Joulin A, Mikolov T. Enriching word vectors with subword information. Transactions of the Association for Computational Linguistics. 2017;5:135-46.
[69] Shen W, Wang J, Luo P, Wang M. LINDEN: linking named entities with knowledge base via semantic knowledge. In: WWW; 2012. p. 449-58.
[70] Nakashole N, Tylenda T, Weikum G. Fine-grained semantic typing of emerging entities. In: ACL; 2013. p. 1488-97.
[71] Bordes A, Usunier N, Garcia-Durán A, Weston J, Yakhnenko O. Translating embeddings for modeling multi-relational data. In: NIPS; 2013. p. 2787-95.
[72] Kenton JDMWC, Toutanova LK. Bert: pre-training of deep bidirectional transformers for language understanding. In: NAACL-HLT; 2019. p. 4171-86.
[73] Zhang J, Chen B, Zhang L, Ke X, Ding H. Neural, symbolic and neural-symbolic reasoning on knowledge graphs. AI Open. 2021;2:14-35.
[74] Pennington J, Socher R, Manning CD. Glove: Global vectors for word representation. In: EMNLP; 2014. p. 1532-43.
[75] Mikolov T, Chen K, Corrado G, Dean J. Efficient estimation of word representations in vector space. arXiv preprint arXiv:13013781. 2013.
[76] Vaswani A, Shazeer N, Parmar N, Uszkoreit J, Jones L, Gomez AN, et al. Attention is all you need. NIPS. 2017;30.
[77] Nakashole N, Weikum G, Suchanek F. PATTY: a taxonomy of relational patterns with semantic types. In: EMNLP; 2012. p. 1135-45.
[78] Galárraga L, Teflioudi C, Hose K, Suchanek FM. Fast rule mining in ontological knowledge bases with AMIE +. The VLDB Journal. 2015;24(6):707-30.

Handbook on Neurosymbolic AI and Knowledge Graphs
P. Hitzler et al. (Eds.)
IOS Press, 2025

doi:10.3233/FAIA250213

Knowledge Fusion

Wei HU [a,b] and Zequn SUN [a]
[a] *State Key Laboratory for Novel Software Technology, Nanjing University, Nanjing 210023, China*
[b] *National Institute of Healthcare Data Science, Nanjing University, Nanjing 210093, China*
ORCiD ID: Wei Hu https://orcid.org/0000-0003-3635-6335,
Zequn Sun https://orcid.org/0000-0003-4177-9199

Abstract. Knowledge fusion aims to integrate different knowledge graphs into a unified, consistent, and concise format, thereby establishing interoperability for applications that leverage multi-source knowledge. In this chapter, we introduce the research process of knowledge fusion. We begin with an exploration of the fundamental principles of multi-source knowledge fusion, followed by a survey of the technical advancements in knowledge fusion. Subsequently, we outline potential future research directions and conclude with a summary. We believe that the combination and mutual promotion of knowledge fusion and other knowledge graph technologies will make a big difference.

Keywords. Knowledge fusion, entity alignment, ontology matching, truth discovery, entity linking

1. Introduction

Knowledge graphs describe real-world entities as well as their relations and attributes, and organize them into a structure of triples. Today, knowledge graphs have become a valuable resource for various knowledge-driven AI applications, spanning domains such as social networking, biomedicine, geography, e-commerce, film, and music. They are extensively used in semantic search, question answering, recommender systems, and big data analysis.

Knowledge graphs can be constructed by diverse organizations and individuals, drawing data from various sources, which introduces diversity and heterogeneity across different knowledge graphs. For instance, within different domains (or even within the same domain), multiple entities may refer to the same real-world object.

The objective of knowledge fusion is to integrate different knowledge graphs into a unified, consistent, and concise format, thereby establishing interoperability for applications that leverage multi-source knowledge. Key research areas in knowledge fusion include ontology matching (a.k.a. ontology mapping), entity alignment (a.k.a. instance matching, entity resolution), truth discovery (a.k.a. truth inference), and entity linking. Major challenges involve addressing the issues of scale, heterogeneity, and resource scarcity.

Knowledge fusion is a fundamental task in knowledge graph research. Advances in knowledge fusion research can enhance the intelligence and effectiveness of information services based on knowledge graphs, driving technological progress in the fields such as artificial intelligence, natural language processing, semantic web, and databases. This area holds significant theoretical value and promising applications, potentially yielding substantial social and economic benefits.

Figure 1 illustrates a general process of knowledge fusion, including:

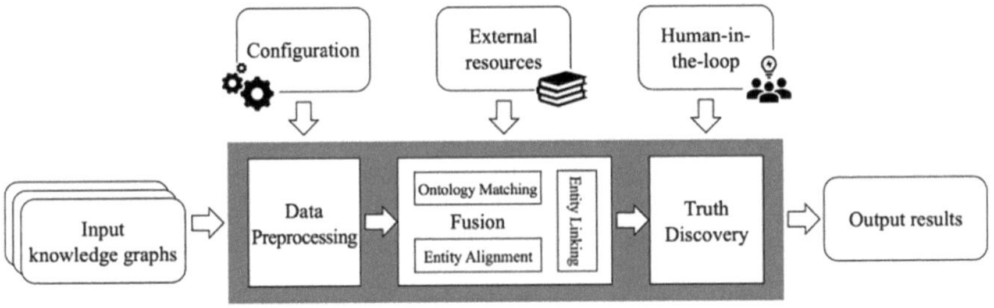

Figure 1. A general process of knowledge fusion

- Preprocessing focuses on cleaning the input knowledge graphs to rectify quality issues and preparing them for subsequent steps. Cleaning aims to enhance input quality, while preparation commonly uses blocking techniques to reduce the quadratic complexity of matching large knowledge graphs through index design. A key consideration involves optimizing the trade-off between block size and quantity to minimize blocks without compromising potential outcomes.
- Matching is categorized into ontology matching, entity alignment, and entity linking based on the objects being matched. Ontology matching identifies equivalent or similar classes, attributes, or relations in the schemata of knowledge graphs. Entity alignment identifies instances that refer to identical objects in the real world. Entity linking connects entity mentions in natural language text to entities in knowledge graph. Resolving semantic heterogeneity between these objects represents a critical scientific challenge in the matching process.
- Building upon matching, the primary objective of truth inference is to deduce the truth value from inconsistent data. This facilitates the integration and consolidation of heterogeneous knowledge from multiple sources, culminating in a cohesive outcome. The key of this research lies in effectively assessing the reliability of data sources and the credibility of data values.

The following is a survey of the main research content and recent trends.

2. Technical Methods and Research Trends

This section provides an overview of research progress and representative methods for knowledge fusion.

2.1. Ontology Matching

The objective of ontology matching is to establish semantic mappings between different ontology concepts. In the past few years, there has been limited research progress in this field. Some early works include RiMOM[1] and Falcon-AO[2]. Notably, LogMap[3] was awarded the 2021 SWSA (Semantic Web Science Association) Ten-year Award. LogMap is a highly scalable ontology matching system, as illustrated in Figure 2. Initially, it constructs a vocabulary index for each ontology using class labels and lexical variations, and calculates potential matches based on this index. Matches are initially selected based on high confidence levels, with adjustments made as necessary. The system then employs structural heuristics to further evaluate and identify new matches among the remaining candidates. Finally, LogMap aggregates all identified matches. This method efficiently handles ontologies containing tens of thousands (or even hundreds of thousands) of classes, employing ontology reasoning and repair techniques to minimize logical inconsistencies. It also supports user intervention through visual tools during the matching process. In recent years, LogMap has incorporated representation learning techniques to enhance ontology matching tasks.

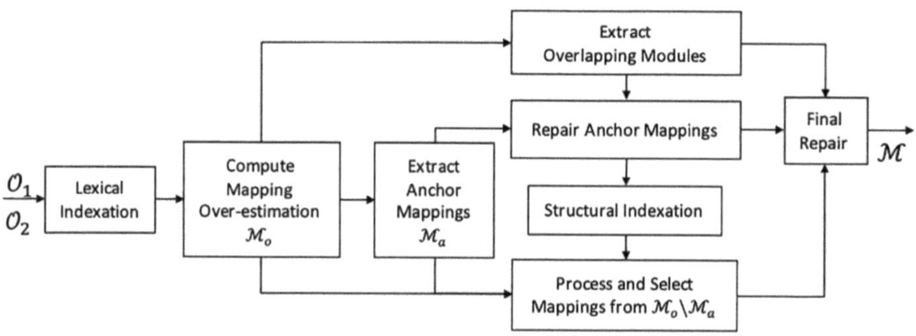

Figure 2. Pipeline of the ontology matching method LogMap

2.2. Entity Alignment

2.2.1. Entity Alignment Based on Representation Learning

In recent years, entity alignment methods leveraging knowledge graph representation learning have gained prominence. As depicted in Figure 3, the framework for entity alignment based on representation learning primarily consists of two core modules: The representation learning module embeds each individual knowledge graph into a vector space. Most methods employ geometric embedding models, while some leverage graph neural networks. The alignment module is trained on a limited set of prior alignment (i.e., training data) derived from prior knowledge or manual annotation. It aligns the vector representations of identical entities in the prior alignment. Additionally, iterative approaches are used to continually incorporate newly discovered entity alignment into the training data. This framework highlights two typical interaction methods between the representation learning and alignment modules: embedding different knowledge graphs into a unified vector space, and learning the mapping relationship between the vector spaces of different knowledge graphs.

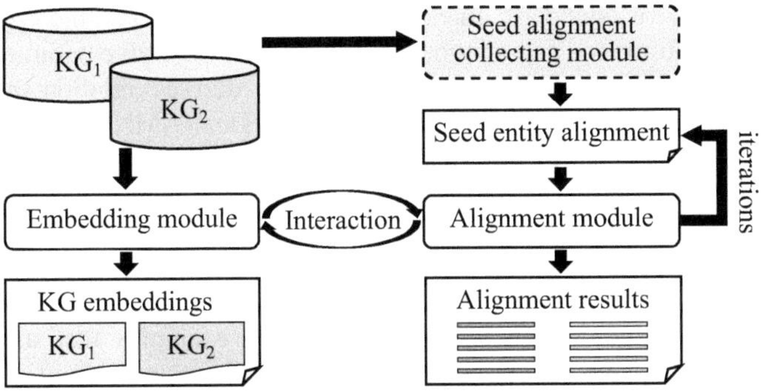

Figure 3. Entity alignment framework based on representation learning

MTransE[4] is an early pioneering work on entity alignment, which successfully extended the idea of TransE[5] to multi-source knowledge graph representation learning and alignment. TransE defines an energy function $f(\tau) = ||\vec{v}(h) + \vec{v}(r) - \vec{v}(t)||_2^2$ to measure the plausibility of a triple $\tau = (h, r, t)$, where $|| \cdot ||_2$ is the L2 vector norm, and $\vec{v}(\cdot)$ denotes the vector representation of an entity or relation. The lower the energy, the more reliable the triple is. TransE optimizes the marginal ranking loss to make the energy of positive triples lower than that of negative triples. As shown in Figure 4, in addition to modeling the triples within the knowledge graph using the relation translation assumption in TransE, such as <China, Capital, Beijing>, MTransE also models the alignment of identical entities from different knowledge graphs, such as <中国, China>. In terms of alignment learning, MTransE has experimented with methods such as distance-based axis calibration and linear transformations. Specifically, the axis calibration method minimizes the vector representation distance of identical entities, which can be regarded as representing and aligning identical entities in the same vector space. The linear transformation method introduces a learnable matrix to map the entity representations of the source knowledge graph to the vector space of the target knowledge graph, and then minimizes the embedding distance of identical entities, such as minimizing $||\mathbf{M}\vec{v}(\text{中国}) - \vec{v}(\text{China})||_2^2$.

Figure 4. An example of entity alignment in MTransE

Dual-AMN[6] is a recent notable method that uses advanced graph neural networks to model the information within and between knowledge graphs. Specifically, within a single knowledge graph, it employs a convolutional layer based on relational attention to capture structural information. This layer leverages learnable entity embeddings without employing a standard linear transformation matrix, thereby mitigating overfitting and performance degradation associated with excessive parameters. Instead, the proposed simplified relational attention layer derives relation-specific entity representations. To incorporate global information, Dual-AMN combines multi-hop neighbor representations from different layers to derive the final result. For aligning entities, Dual-AMN employs a group of proxy vectors to implicitly represent alignment relations between two knowledge graphs. It assumes that aligned entities exhibit similar similarity distributions relative to proxy vectors. To address the time-consuming problem of truncated uniform negative sampling in ranking candidate entities for alignment learning, Dual-AMN generates challenging negative examples that are difficult to distinguish from positive examples and employs normalization to stabilize sample loss mean and variance. This reduces reliance on hyperparameters, further enhancing computational efficiency.

In addition to the above entity alignment approaches, some research endeavors have explored more challenging scenarios. DiNGAL[7], for instance, introduced a dynamic entity alignment task, departing from the assumption of static knowledge graphs. DiNGAL posits that triples in knowledge graphs are changed dynamically, necessitating updates to entity representations in response to changing graph structures. To address this challenge, DiNGAL initially derives static entity representations using a topology-invariant mask gating mechanism. Subsequently, it employs a local updating strategy to adjust affected entity representations during dynamic processes. As new alignments emerge dynamically during this process, DiNGAL incorporates these alignments as positive examples, facilitating updates to all entity representations without the overhead of training from scratch.

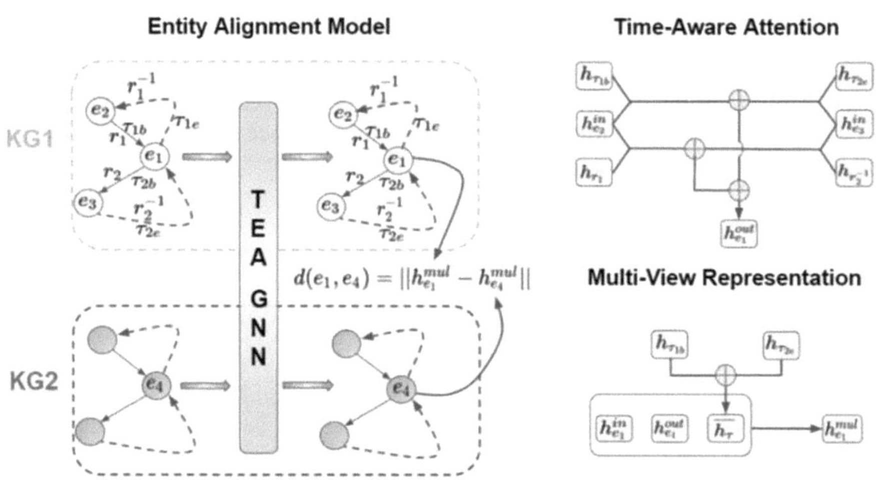

Figure 5. Overview of TEA-GNN, an entity alignment method for temporal knowledge graphs

The facts within knowledge graphs are time-sensitive, yet existing entity alignment methods typically overlook temporal information. To address this issue, TEA-GNN[8] introduces an entity alignment task tailored for temporal knowledge graphs. This approach utilizes start and end timestamps to encode temporal information and integrates entities, relations, and timestamps from diverse knowledge graphs into a unified vector space using graph neural networks, as depicted in Figure 5. TEA-GNN begins by generating inverse relations and appending start timestamps to original quadruples, while recording end timestamps in inverse relation quadruples. It then computes an orthogonal transformation matrix based on normalized relation and timestamp representations to ensure entity representations maintain norm and relative distance. For a central entity receiving incoming edges, TEA-GNN derives relation-specific and time-specific representations from these orthogonal matrices generated by neighboring entities. It employs a time-aware attention mechanism to distinguish the importance of different neighbors during aggregation. Specifically, it concatenates the central entity's representation, time-specific neighbor representations, and temporal representations into a vector. Subsequently, it designs a temporal attention vector, performs multiplication, and computes weights for temporal information from neighboring entities to the central entity. A similar process is applied for relation weights. Next, the model aggregates and combines both types of information, obtaining layer-wise perceived temporal outputs through activation functions. To capture multi-hop information, TEA-GNN concatenates outputs from each layer to achieve globally aware entity representations. Finally, to further integrate temporal information, TEA-GNN combines the entity and connected time representations to form final entity representations for alignment learning.

2.2.2. Entity Alignment Based on Human-Machine Collaboration

The entity alignment method leveraging human-machine collaboration enhances model performance by acquiring rich annotation data at reduced manual cost. Traditionally, these methods construct inference structures for labels of entity pairs, where users annotate unknown pairs for optimal utility inference. For instance, Power[9] computes entity pair similarities across different attributes, concatenates them into similarity vectors, and constructs a partial order structure. Users label entity pairs with the most predecessors and successors in this partial order.

Remp[10] improved the matching efficiency of human-in-the-loop from the aspects of matching graph construction and multiple question selection. As illustrated in Figure 6, given two knowledge graphs as inputs, Remp returns a matching set between them as output after iterating over four processing steps:

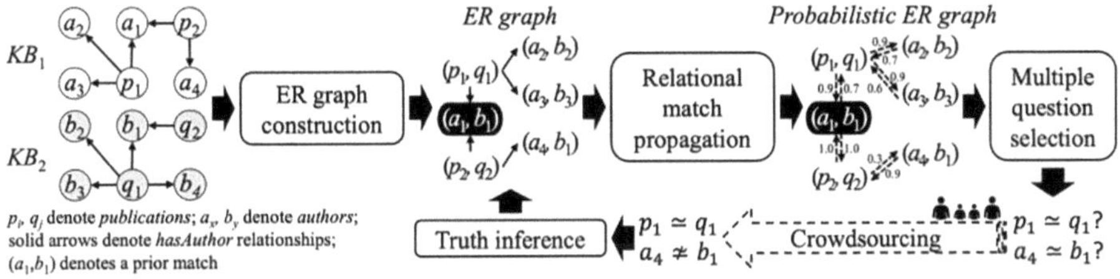

Figure 6. Pipeline the Remp method

- Entity Resolution (ER) graph construction aims to build a small entity matching graph by reducing the number of entity pairs. First, the similarity between attributes is calculated by using seed matching to find attribute matches. Then, some obviously mismatched entity pairs are filtered out based on the similarity of entity attributes.
- Relational match propagation models how to use existing alignment labels to infer the matching probability of an unlabeled entity pair in each connected component of an entity resolution graph. First, the consistency of the relationship is measured based on the seed matching and maximum likelihood estimation methods. Then, the conditional matching probability of the unlabeled entity pairs is calculated after a given match.
- Multi-question selection picks a set of unresolved entity pairs in the entity resolution graph as the questions to ask human workers. It models the discovery of the inferred matching set for each problem as the shortest path problem between all pairs of entities and solves it using a graph-based algorithm.
- Truth inference calculates matches based on the results labeled by the workers. It first calculates the posterior matching probabilities of questions based on the quality of the workers, and then uses these posterior probabilities to update the entity resolution graph.

Recent advancements integrate deep neural networks with human-machine collaboration methods. DTAL[11] initializes model parameters via transfer learning and selects candidate alignments for annotation based on the entropy given by the deep model. ActiveEA[12] introduces a structure-aware uncertainty sampling strategy to model alignment uncertainty and its impact on neighboring entities. Addressing isolated entities without potential alignments in corresponding knowledge graphs, ActiveEA designs a bachelor recognizer to mitigate sampling bias.

RAC[13] further explores the combination of deep reinforcement learning and active learning techniques, and the overall framework is shown in Figure 7. RAC designs three query strategies based on the degree of entities in the knowledge graph, the PageRank value, and the information density. Considering that the importance of different query strategies is different in different iteration rounds, and that a single query strategy cannot meet the needs of all datasets, RAC uses the multi-armed bandit mechanism to adaptively mix the three query strategies, and selects the optimal query for manual annotation. Considering the annotation cost, usually only a small amount of training data can be obtained for reinforcement active learning, so RAC designs a contrastive entity representation learning method to augment the training data by using unlabeled entities. RAC encodes entities using two encoders, a graph convolutional network and an approximate personalized propagation, to capture the features of a different view of each entity. Based on the idea of contrastive learning, the representation of each entity in the same view should be as consistent as possible, and the representations of different entities should be quite different.

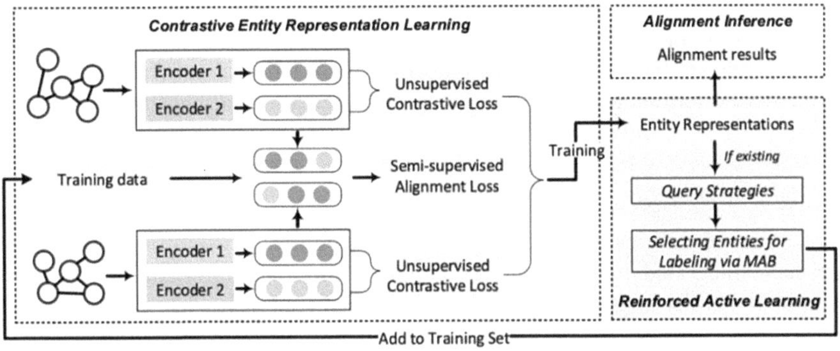

Figure 7. Entity alignment method RAC based on human-machine collaboration

DAAKG[14] is a recent active knowledge fusion method based on deep contrastive learning, which solves both entity alignment and ontology matching problems. Figure 8 illustrates the workflow for DAAKG, which takes two knowledge graphs as inputs and obtains entity alignment and ontology matching results through three main modules:

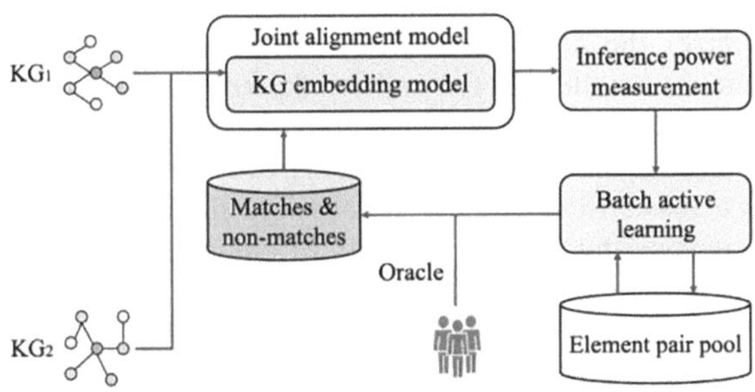

Figure 8. Pipeline the DAAKG method

- Embedded-based joint alignment. This module contains a knowledge graph embedding model and a joint alignment model. The embedding model not only encodes the entity-relation semantics, but also embeds the entity-class structure. The alignment model is trained by contrastive learning, and semi-supervised learning to match entities, relations and classes jointly.
- Inference power measurement. This module builds an alignment graph to represent the correlation between pairs of elements. For entity pairs, it searches for the target path in the alignment graph and estimates the inference power based on the similarity introduced by the embedding model. For relation pairs and class pairs, the inference power is measured based on the gradient of the alignment model.
- Batch active learning. This module pairs each entity with its top-k nearest neighbors based on schema signatures, and combines these entity pairs with all relation/class pairs as a sample pool. The element pair selection problem is defined to maximize the overall inference power of the expectation, and an

algorithm based on graph partitioning is proposed to find a batch of element pairs in the pool for manual annotation. It then uses the newly annotated element pairs to fine-tune the embedded-based joint alignment model.

The process terminates when the annotation budget is exhausted and returns matches of entities, relations, and classes as output.

2.2.3. Multimodal Entity Alignment

Given that image features can aid in disambiguating entities to a significant extent, recent studies have integrated image modalities and fused information from multiple modalities. Consequently, entity alignment based on multimodal approaches has emerged as a new research focus. MMEA[15] considers the image feature space in solid alignment earlier. The overall framework is shown in Figure 9, which mainly includes two modules: multimodal knowledge embedding and fusion. Multimodal knowledge embedding involves obtaining vector representations of entities across different modalities, specifically considering three modalities: relational structures, image information, and numerical attributes. MMEA uses TransE to learn entity vector representations within a graph structure. It employs VGG16 to encode image features, minimizing the distance between entity vectors and corresponding image vectors to integrate image features into entity representations. Addressing the sparse and discrete nature of numerical attributes, MMEA utilizes a radial basis function network to generate vector representations for this modality. It minimizes the distance between entity vectors and attribute vectors to incorporate attribute information. In the multimodal knowledge fusion module, MMEA posits that despite entities having representations from different feature spaces, all these representations signify the same entity. Thus, a shared feature space is established where entity embeddings across different modalities strive to align closely with representations in this shared space, ensuring complementarity of modal information. Finally, MMEA aligns entities in this common representation space that captures multimodal information. It achieves similarity among entities from different knowledge graphs by minimizing vector distances between entities that are pre-aligned.

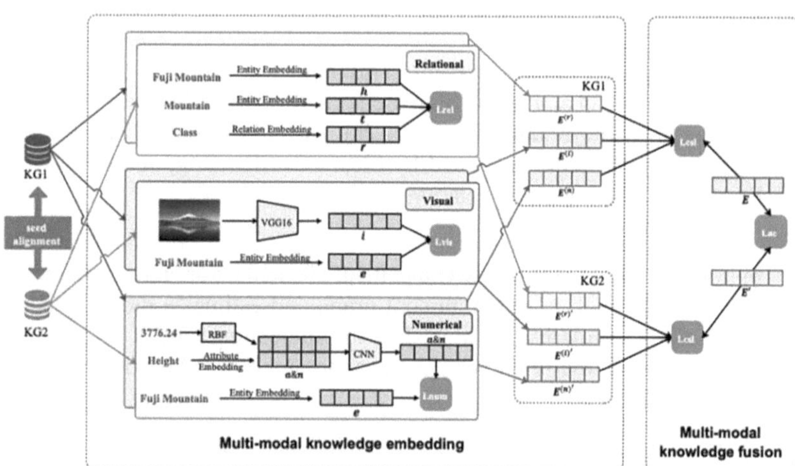

Figure 9. Multimodal-based entity alignment method MMEA

EVA[16] adopts a similar modeling approach by initializing image features with ResNet-152 and leveraging HMAN[17] to obtain embeddings of relations and attributes. Additionally, EVA introduces a multimodal weighting strategy based on attention mechanisms to fuse multimodal information effectively. For optimizing entity alignment, EVA employs the neighborhood component analysis (NCA) loss function. This function measures the importance of training samples and negative samples based on local and global statistics, addressing common issues like the hubness problem in representation learning and alignment tasks. Furthermore, EVA explores the application of multimodal technology in unsupervised entity alignment scenarios. It proposes a robust alignment pivot calculation method based on image features. Initially, EVA computes a similarity matrix between entities using their image representations. It then extracts and stores entity pairs represented by the largest elements in the matrix, discarding all elements in the corresponding rows or columns. This process continues until a predetermined number of entity pairs is obtained, which serve as pivots connecting two knowledge graphs for training an entity alignment model. Experimental results demonstrate that using image similarity alone to generate initial entity pairs can achieve similar performance in supervised settings.

2.2.4. Post-hoc Explanations for Entity Alignment

Entity alignment models, like other machine learning models, are often black-box models, which makes it challenging for people to understand how they make decisions. This lack of transparency reduces trust in their outputs. Consequently, efforts have been focused on explaining the results of entity alignment models. This allows decision-makers to gain a deeper understanding of the model's characteristics and limitations, which is crucial for extracting actionable insights to refine results. Recently, ExEA[18] conducted a comprehensive study in this area. Their framework, depicted in Figure 10, comprises three main modules: Explanation Generation, Alignment Dependency Graph (ADG) Construction, and Entity Alignment Repair.

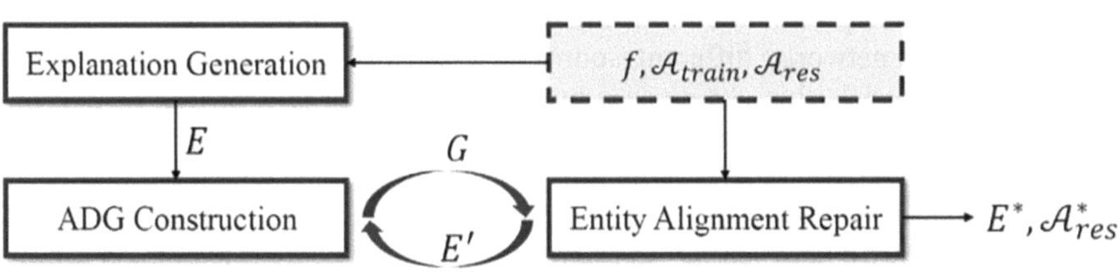

Figure 10. Post-hoc explanation generation for entity alignment

The Explanation Generation module builds on a profound understanding of entity alignment tasks: the alignment between two entities stems from semantically similar triples associated with them. This module models the generation of explanations as a search for semantic matching subgraphs between entities. To analyze explanation results further, ExEA designs the ADG structure, using matching outcomes to compute explanation confidence. This method supports refining results using explanations effectively. In the ADG, the matched entities constitute nodes and the embedding similarity between them serves as the influence of the node in the explanation. Based on ADG, ExEA resolves three types of conflicts to repair results: relation alignment conflicts, one-to-many alignment conflicts, and low-confidence conflicts. Through these three resolution methods, repaired and reliable alignment can ultimately be obtained.

2.3. Truth Discovery

Truth discovery typically employs conflict detection, truth inference, and other techniques to resolve conflicts during the knowledge fusion process. These methods correlate and merge disparate pieces of knowledge to ultimately produce a coherent and consistent result. How to deal with conflicts in multi-source data is the main research problem of truth discovery. For example, various data sources may provide different descriptions of the height of Mount Everest, some of which may be inaccurate and require inference to determine the most accurate value. There are three types of common approaches. The first is the iterative approach, such as TruthFinder[19], Investment[20], and ACCU[21]. These methods consider data sources, and iteratively evaluate the reliability of the data sources and the trustworthiness of the data values until they converge on a consistent result. The second type is the optimization method, which minimizes the weighted overall inference error. This approach ensures that the true value aligns more closely with the value proposed by highly reliable data sources, and the distant data source will be assigned a smaller weight as its reliability during the optimization process. The last type is the probabilistic graph model, such as SimpleLCA[22] and OKELE[23]. These approaches make assumptions about the underlying factors influencing the reliability of data sources and use models such as Bayesian networks to model random variables and their dependencies. Due to the series of calculation rules in iterative and optimization methods, as well as the various influencing factors in probabilistic graph models that need to be set manually, these approaches often fail to accurately reflect the potential data distribution and impact in different scenarios.

In recent years, some research has employed deep learning to explore truth inference problems. CASE[24] constructs a heterogeneous network (as shown in Figure 11) based on the correlation between source-claim, source-source and truth-claim. It models truth value discovery as a representation learning problem within this heterogeneous network. In a source-claim network, different sources choose different claims for the same problem. CASE models this choice as a multi-classification problem, using the inner product of the vector representation of the source and the claim to calculate the relevance, and calculates the source's preference for the claim. When dealing with the source-source network, the number of the same and different claims for each pair of sources is counted to reflect the similarity between the sources. The similarity of their claims on different targets is fitted according to the representations of the sources, and the Beta prior distribution is employed to address the problem of data sparsity. When ground truth is available as supervised data, a global truth is introduced to model the association through the representations of the global truth and the claim. Finally, CASE employs the known truth for semi-supervised learning to obtain the representation of network elements, and selects the claim closest to the representation of the global truth as the truth.

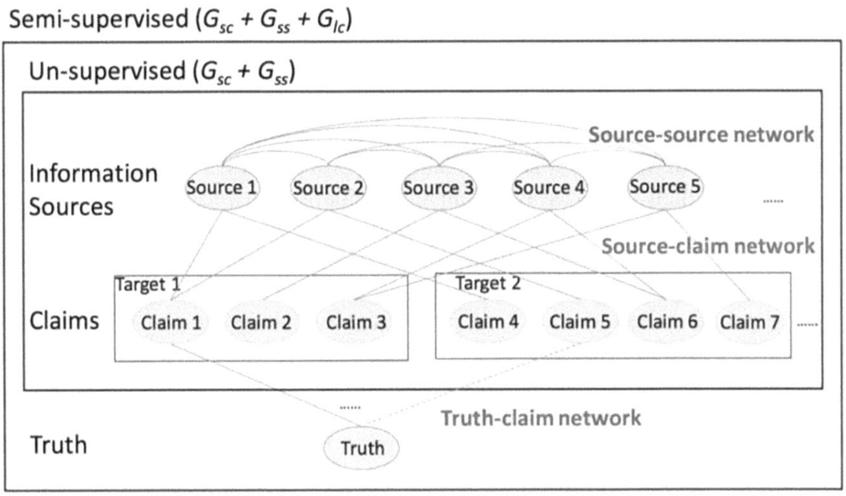

Figure 11. Heterogeneous network constructed based on CASE

BAT[25] models the data source, the inferred target, and the associations between them as a bipartite graph. It derives the initial features of a source based on the correlation between the graph autoencoder and the source, and obtains the initial features of an inferred target using a pre-trained text or image information encoder. BAT first calculates the correlation between nodes using the attention mechanism. It then employs a bipartite graph neural network to simultaneously aggregate the information, obtaining the representations of the data source, inference target, and associations. Finally, the truth of the target is predicted and inferred based on the information aggregated by the graph neural network, and the truth is used for training.

In addition, there is work to investigate ways to quickly update the reliability of data sources and the truth of entities for batch or streaming data. EvolveT[26] notes the correlation between the truth of the same inferred target at different points in time, and introduces the hidden Markov framework, which states that the truth at the next moment can be determined by the current truth and a fixed transition matrix. Based on the Kalman filter and smoother, EvolveT has designed an online estimation algorithm to achieve fast and efficient ground truth estimation.

2.4. Entity Linking

Entity linking is typically based on the entity recognition task, which first identifies the mention text of named entities within the text. It then enumerates possible candidate entities from the knowledge graph according to these mentions and uses ranking methods to select the entity that best fits the current context as the link result. Due to the diversity and ambiguity of natural language, entity representations often exhibit a high degree of ambiguity. This requires entity linking methods to address the challenges of "Polysemy" and "Pseudonymity". "Polysemy" refers to the case where the same entity name can represent multiple entities. For example, given the natural language text "Apple released the latest mobile phone product, the iPhone 13.", the entity linking method needs to link "Apple" to the entity "Apple (business)" rather than "Apple (fruit)". "Pseudonymity" refers to the case where an entity can be represented by more than one name. For example, "natural language processing" and "NLP" can both be used to refer to the entity "natural language processing (domain)".

A complete entity linking method usually includes three steps: (1) Candidate entity generation, that is, selecting a limited number of candidate entities from a vast collection based on identified entity mentions. This process can be categorized into three methods: string matching, external alias matching, and prior probability calculation. (2) Candidate entity ranking, which involves assessing the similarity between entity mentions and candidate entities within the context and ranking them based on the similarity scores. This process can be categorized into statistics-based methods and deep learning-based methods. (3) Unlinkable mention prediction. Due to the incompleteness of the knowledge graph, some entities do not exist in the knowledge graph, so it is necessary to determine whether the entity mention is linked to a non-existent entity. Here are some of the most representative methods in the recent past:

CHOLAN[27] employs a Transformer encoder for end-to-end entity linking. The architecture of CHOLAN is illustrated in Figure 12. CHOLAN believes that while existing pretrained models (e.g., BERT) are trained on extensive corpora, they are still account for additional contextual information specific to individual tasks. CHOLAN first employs BERT to identify mentions within input sentences. Subsequently, it utilizes the tools Falcon[28] and DCA[29] to generate entity candidates for each mention. Finally, CHOLAN concatenates entity mentions, sentences, entity candidates, and information about the entity in Wikipedia and feeds it into another BERT to predict the linked entity.

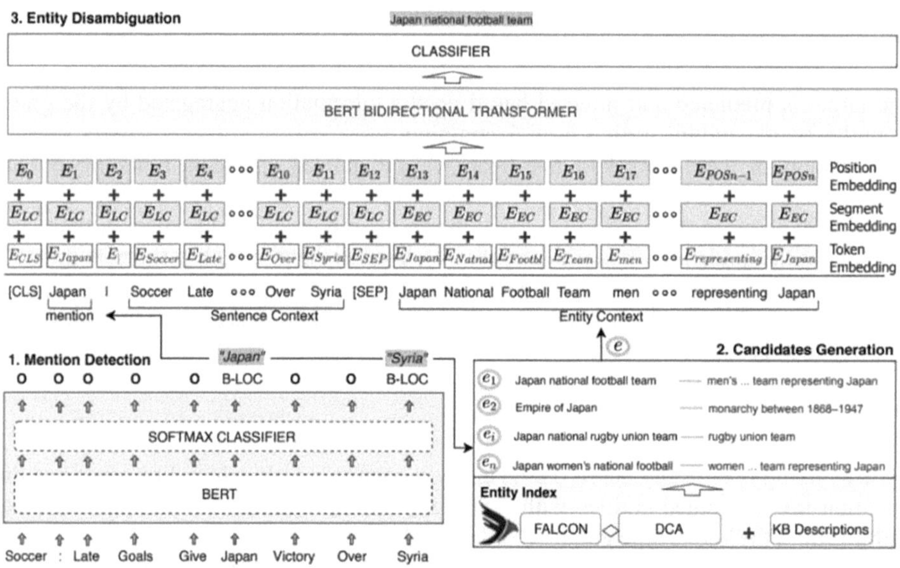

Figure 12. The end-to-end entity linking method CHOLAN

REL[30] uses an advanced named entity recognition model, Flair[31], to identify entity mentions. For candidate generation, REL first uses the number of hyperlinks in Wikipedia and CrossWikis to estimate the prior probability of each mention-entity pair, and then selects the top-ranked entity as a candidate based on that probability. Next, the similarity metric function is used to select the most similar entities from the nearby words mentioned as candidate entities. Finally, all candidate entities are ranked and disambiguated based on their prior importance, contextual similarity, and consistency of links to other entities in the document. EntQA[32] reverses the order of the two subtasks, mentioning detection and entity disambiguation, and modeled the entire linking task as an open-domain question answering task. EntQA uses the Retriever-Reader framework to model entities using the titles and descriptions of entities in the knowledge graph. The Retriever module calculates the similarity score between the text fragment and the entity, and quickly generates multiple candidate entities. The Reader module takes documents, text fragments, and candidate entities as inputs. It models both the probability that a candidate entity corresponds to the mention and the probability that the candidate entity is the correct entity, ultimately predicting the entity linking result.

2.5. Tools, Software, and Benchmark Datasets

Regarding ontology matching, some common ontology matching tools and systems can be downloaded from OAEI[1] (Ontology Alignment Evaluation Initiative) website. As far as entity alignment, OpenE[2] is a popular open-source software library for representation learning-based entity alignment. The overall framework is shown in Figure 13. Developed using Python and TensorFlow, OpenEA integrates several representative embedding-based entity alignment methods. It features a flexible architecture, facilitating integration with a wide range of existing models. The embedding module in OpenEA attempts to embed a knowledge graph into a low-dimensional space. Depending on the types of triples, embedding models can be divided into two categories: relational embeddings and attribute embeddings. The former uses relational learning techniques to capture the structure of the knowledge graph, and the latter leverages the attribute information of entities. The alignment module uses seed entity pairs as training data to capture the relevance of entity embedding representations. The interaction module contains four typical combination modes for adjusting the knowledge graph embedding for entity alignment. Furthermore, OpenEA provides two ways to use Python-based calls and command-line calls, and allows users to configure the system integration model in detail through JSON files. Another similar open-source software library is EAkit[3]. For truth discovery, CrowdTruthInference[4] integrates 17 kinds of truth inference algorithms and supports the truth inference of three types of tasks, namely decision-making, single-choice, and numeric tasks.[5]

---

[1] http://oaei.ontologymatching.org/
[2] https://github.com/nju-websoft/OpenEA
[3] https://github.com/THU-KEG/EAkit
[4] https://zhydhkcws.github.io/crowd_truth_inference

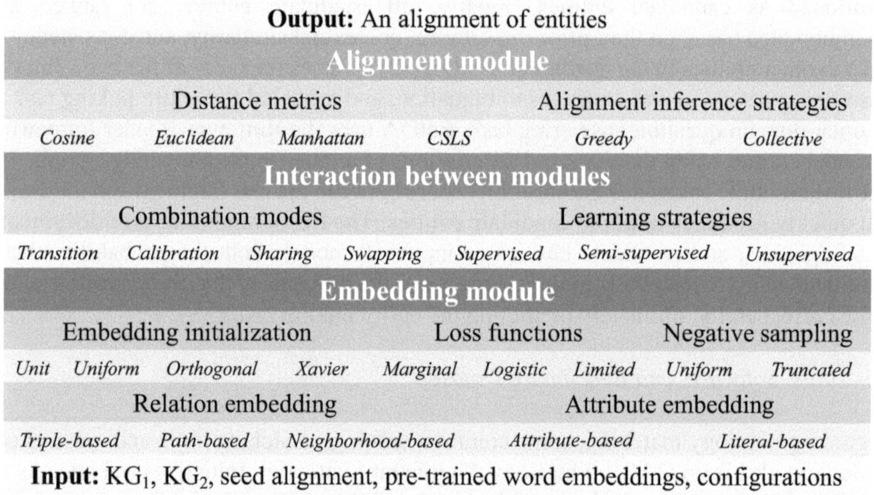

Figure 13. Framework of OpenEA

Benchmark datasets are also important for knowledge fusion, as they provide a platform to compare the performance of various methods side-by-side. With the vigorous development of knowledge fusion research, in addition to the traditional OAEI evaluation datasets, some new datasets have also been created, which are briefly introduced as follows:

- For entity alignment, the DBP15K[33] dataset includes three cross-language datasets derived from the multilingual version of DBpedia. These datasets cover Chinese to English, Japanese to English, and French to English alignment, each comprising 150,000 entity pairs. Table 1 provides specific statistics of the dataset, including the numbers of entities, relations, attributes, relation triples, and attribute triples. The number of entities involved in each language is well over 15,000, and the number of attributes is much higher than the number of relations. The numbers of relation triples and attribute triples in the dataset are at the level of 100,000, and the attribute triples form the main part of the dataset. DYW100K[34] contains two large-scale datasets, DBP-WD and DBP-YG, extracted from DBpedia, Wikidata, and YAGO3. Due to the lack of dangling entities in these datasets, a new entity alignment dataset DBP 2.0[35] based on the multilingual version of DBpedia has been constructed.

Table 1. Statistics for the DBP15k dataset

Datasets		Entities	Relations	Attributes	Relationship triples	Attribute triples
ZH-EN	ZH	66,469	2,830	8,113	153,929	379,684
	EN	98,125	2,317	7,173	237,674	567,755
JA-EN	JA	65,744	2,043	5,882	164,373	354,619
	EN	95,680	2,096	6,066	233,319	497,230
FR-EN	FR	66,858	1,379	4,547	192,191	528,665
	EN	105,889	2,209	6,422	278,590	576,543

- The importance and practicability of entity linking technology have received extensive attention from industry and academia. Datasets such as AIDA

CoNLL-YAGO and TAC KBP have been constructed through evaluation competitions such as AIDA, AQUAINT, ACE, etc. These competitions have facilitated the development of frameworks like TagMe[36], Dexter[37], AGDISTIS[38], and other open-source entity linking frameworks.

- In addition, a number of publicly available truth discovery datasets for different domains and task types, such as images, text, and numeric values, can be accessed from the following website: http://dbgroup.cs.tsinghua.edu.cn/ligl/crowddata.

3. Technique Outlook

In the last few years, representation learning has been widely used in knowledge fusion related research. Possible research directions in the future include:

- Pretrained language models have achieved great success in the field of natural language processing. Inspired by this, pretraining for large-scale knowledge graphs has become a potential research direction in the future, and the knowledge obtained from pretraining can also be transferred to many downstream tasks. For example, in entity alignment, the representation learning of large-scale knowledge graphs can obtain the general knowledge information of entities. This alleviates the problem of insufficient knowledge in downstream entity alignment, such as the lack of partial modal information in entities. Similarly, in multilingual entity linking, the pretrained knowledge of high-resource languages can indirectly help entity linking in low-resource languages. However, there are also some challenges in the exploration of related technologies, such as how to use knowledge fusion techniques in fusing heterogeneous knowledge graphs to carry out pretraining on larger knowledge graphs.
- In recent years, the research problem of knowledge fusion has also had some new settings. For instance, knowledge evolves over time, and future efforts may explore dynamic entity alignment and truth discovery techniques tailored for streaming data. This approach aims to capture more accurate facts that can dynamically supplement evolving knowledge graphs. For another example, the dynamic knowledge graph representation learning techniques can also be considered to provide a priori knowledge of truth for dynamic truth discovery, so as to improve the accuracy of truth value discovery.
- In terms of evaluation, the existing research work is mainly based on some small-scale datasets, such as the entity-alignment DBP15K dataset and the entity-linking TAC KBP dataset. However, the construction of these datasets has been around for some time and shown a certain lag. At the same time, the small dataset size and narrow coverage may introduce certain discrepancies from real-world scenarios. Therefore, in the future, it is important to explore ways to integrate current research advancements to develop larger-scale, higher-quality benchmark datasets for emerging tasks such as multimodal entity alignment, complex truth inference, cross-language entity linking, etc. This will

enable a more professional and comprehensive evaluation of work in the field of knowledge fusion.

4. Conclusion

With the widespread application of knowledge graphs, their representations have become increasingly diverse. They range from monolingual and symbolic knowledge graphs to multilingual and multimodal knowledge graphs. Knowledge fusion integrates different knowledge graphs into a unified, consistent, and concise form, promoting knowledge-driven AI to a broader range of application scenarios. Knowledge fusion techniques based on representation learning have taken over the mainstream, involving multiple tasks such as ontology matching, entity alignment, truth discovery, and entity linking. Besides, a number of available tools, software, and benchmark datasets have emerged. In the future, the combination and mutual promotion of knowledge fusion and other knowledge graph technologies will make a big difference.

References

[1] Li J, Tang J, Li Y, Luo Q. RiMOM: A dynamic multistrategy ontology alignment framework. IEEE Trans Knowl Data Eng. 2009 Sep;21(8):1218-32, doi: 10.1109/TKDE.2008.202
[2] Hu W, Qu Y. Falcon-AO: A pratical ontology matching system. Journal of Web Semantics. 2008 Sep;6(3):237-239, doi: 10.1016/j.websem.2008.02.006
[3] Jiménez-Ruiz E, Grau BC. LogMap: Logic-based and scalable ontology matching. In: Aroyo L, Welty C, Alani H, Taylor J, Bernstein A, Kagal L, et al., editors. Proceedings of the 10th International Semantic Web Conference; 2011 Oct 23-27; Bonn, Germany. Berlin (Germany): Springer; 2011. p. 273-88, doi: 10.1007/978-3-642-25073-6_18
[4] Chen M, Tian Y, Yang M, Zaniolo C. Multilingual knowledge graph embeddings for cross-lingual knowledge alignment. In: Sierra C, editor. Proceedings of the 26th International Joint Conference on Artificial Intelligence; 2017 August 19-25; Melbourne, Australia. San Francisco (CA): Morgan Kaufmann; 2017. p. 1511-7, doi: 10.5220/0010646400003064
[5] Bordes A, Usunier N, García-Durán A, Weston J, Yakhnenko O. Translating embeddings for modeling multi-relational data. In: Burges CJC, Bottou L, Ghahramani Z, Weinberger KQ, editors. Proceedings of the 27th Annual Conference on Neural Information Processing Systems; 2013 Dec 5-8; Lake Tahoe, NV. New York (NY): Curran Associates; 2013. p. 2787-95, doi: 10.5555/2999792.2999923
[6] Mao X, Wang W, Wu Y, Lan M. Boosting the Speed of Entity Alignment 10 ×: Dual Attention Matching Network with Normalized Hard Sample Mining. In: Leskovec J, Grobelnik M, Najork M, Tang J, Zia L, editors. Proceedings of the 30th International Conference on World Wide Web; 2021 Apr 19-23. New York (NY): ACM; 2021. p. 821-32, doi: 10.1145/3442381.3449897
[7] Yan Y, Liu L, Ban Y, Jing B, Tong H. Dynamic knowledge graph alignment. In: Proceedings of the 35th AAAI Conference on Artificial Intelligence; 2021 Feb 2-9. Menlo Park (CA): AAAI Press; 2021. p. 4564-72, doi: 10.1609/AAAI.V35I5.16585
[8] Xu C, Su F, Lehmann J. Time-aware graph neural network for entity alignment between temporal knowledge graphs. In: Moens M, Huang X, Specia L, Yih SW, editors. Proceedings of the 2021 Conference on Empirical Methods in Natural Language Processing; 2021 Nov 7-11; Punta Cana, Dominican Republic. Stroudsburg (PA): ACL; 2021. p. 8999-9010, doi: 10.18653/v1/2021.emnlp-main.709
[9] Chai C, Li G, Li J, Deng D, Feng J. A partial-order-based framework for cost-effective crowdsourced entity resolution. Proc VLDB Endow. 2018 Jun;27(6):745-70, doi: 10.1007/S00778-018-0509-6
[10] Huang J, Hu W, Bao Z, Qu Y. Crowdsourced collective entity resolution with relational match propagation. In: Proceedings of the 36th IEEE International Conference on Data Engineering; 2020 Apr 20-24; Dallas, TX. Piscataway (NJ): IEEE; 2020. p. 37-48, doi: 10.1109/ICDE48307.2020.00011
[11] Kasai J, Qian K, Gurajada S, Li Y, Popa L. Low-resource deep entity resolution with transfer and active learning. In: Korhonen A, Traum DR, Màrquez L, editors. Proceedings of the 57th Conference of the

Association for Computational Linguistics; 2019 Jul 28-Aug 2; Florence, Italy. Stroudsburg (PA): ACL; 2019. p. 5851-61, doi: 10.18653/v1/p19-1586
[12] Liu B, Scells H, Zuccon G, Hua W, Zhao G. ActiveEA: Active learning for neural entity alignment. In: Moens M, Huang X, Specia L, Yih SW, editors. Proceedings of the 2021 Conference on Empirical Methods in Natural Language Processing; 2021 Nov 7-11; Punta Cana, Dominican Republic. Stroudsburg (PA): ACL; 2021. p. 3364-74, doi:10.18653/V1/2021.EMNLP-MAIN.270
[13] Zeng W, Zhao X, Tang J, Fan C. Reinforced active entity alignment. In: Demartini G, Zuccon G, Culpepper JS, Huang Z, Tong H, editors. Proceedings of the 30th ACM International Conference on Information and Knowledge Management; 2021 Nov 1-5; Queensland, Australia. New York (NY): ACM; 2021. p. 2477-86, doi: 10.1145/3459637.3482472
[14] Huang J, Sun Z, Chen Q, Xu X, Ren W, Hu W. Deep active alignment of knowledge graph entities and schemata. Proc ACM Manag Data. 2023 Jun;1(2):159:1-159:26, doi: 10.1145/3589304
[15] Chen L, Li Z, Wang Y, Xu T, Wang Z, Chen E. MMEA: Entity alignment for multi-modal knowledge graph. In: Li G, Shen HT, Yuan Y, Wang X, Liu H, Zhao X, editors. Knowledge Science, Engineering and Management 13th International Conference, KSEM; 2020 Aug 28-30; Hangzhou, China. Switzerland: Springer; 2020. p. 134-47, doi: 10.1007/978-3-030-55130-8_12
[16] Liu F, Chen M, Roth D, Collier N. Visual pivoting for (unsupervised) entity alignment. In: Proceedings of the 35th AAAI Conference on Artificial Intelligence; 2021 Feb 2-9. Menlo Park (CA): AAAI Press; 2021. p. 4257-66, doi: 10.1609/AAAI.V35I5.16550
[17] Yang H, Zou Y, Shi P, Lu W, Lin J, Sun X. Aligning cross-lingual entities with multi-aspect information. In: Inui K, Jiang J, Ng V, Wan X, editors. Proceedings of the 2019 Conference on Empirical Methods in Natural Language Processing; 2019 Nov 3-7; Hong Kong, China. Stroudsburg (PA): ACL; 2019. p. 4430-40, doi: 10.18653/V1/D19-1451
[18] Tian X, Sun Z, Hu W. Generating explanations to understand and repair embedding-based entity alignment. In: Proceedings of the 40th IEEE International Conference on Data Engineering; 2024 May 13-16; Utrecht, The Netherlands. Piscataway (NJ): IEEE; 2024. p. 2205-17, doi: 10.1109/ICDE60146.2024.00175
[19] Yin X, Han J, Yu PS. Truth discovery with multiple conflicting information providers on the Web. IEEE Trans Knowl Data Eng. 2008 Apr;20(6):796-808, doi: 10.1109/TKDE.2007.190745
[20] Pasternack J, Roth D. Knowing what to believe (when you already know something). In: Huang C, Jurafsky D, editors. Proceedings of the 23rd International Conference on mputational Linguistics; 2010 Aug 23-27; Beijing, China. Beijing (China): Tsinghua University Press; 2010. p. 877-85, doi: 10.5555/1873781.1873880
[21] Dong XL, Berti-Equille L, Srivastava D. Integrating conflicting data: The role of source dependence. Proc VLDB Endow. 2009 Aug;2(1):550-61, doi: 10.14778/1687627.1687690
[22] Pasternack J, Roth D. Latent credibility analysis. In: Schwabe D, Almeida VAF, Glaser H, Baeza-Yates R, Moon SB, editors. Proceedings of the 22rd International Conference on World Wide Web; 2013 May 13-17; Rio de Janeiro, Brazil. New York (NY): ACM; 2013. p. 1009-20, doi: 10.1145/2488388.2488476
[23] Cao E, Wang D, Huang J, Hu W. Open knowledge enrichment for long-tail entities. In: Huang Y, King I, Liu T, van Steen M, editors. Proceedings of the 29th International Conference on World Wide Web; 2020 Apr 20-24; Taipei, Taiwan. New York (NY): ACM; 2020. p. 384-94, doi: 10.1145/3366423.3380123
[24] Lyu S, Ouyang W, Wang Y, Shen H, Cheng X. Truth discovery by claim and source embedding. IEEE Trans Knowl Data Eng. 2019 Nov;33(3):1264-75, doi: 10.1109/TKDE.2019.2936189
[25] Liu J, Tang F, Huang J. Truth inference with bipartite attention graph neural network from a comprehensive view. In: Proceedings of the 2021 IEEE International Conference on Multimedia and Expo; 2021 Jul 5-9; Shenzhenm, China. Piscataway (NJ): IEEE; 2021. p. 1-6, doi: 10.1109/ICME51207.2021.9428269
[26] Zhi S, Yang F, Zhu Z, Li Q, Wang Z, Han J. Dynamic truth discovery on numerical data. In: Proceedings of the 2018 IEEE International Conference on Data Mining; 2018 Nov 17-20; Singapore. New York (NY): IEEE Computer Society; 2018. p. 817-26, doi: 10.1109/ICDM.2018.00097
[27] Ravi MPK, Singh K, Mulang' IO, Shekarpour S, Hoffart J, Lehmann J. CHOLAN: A modular approach for neural entity linking on Wikipedia and Wikidata. In: Merlo P, Tiedemann J, Tsarfaty R, editors. Proceedings of the 16th Conference of the European Chapter of the Association for Computational Linguistics; 2021 Apr 19-23. Stroudsburg (PA): ACL; 2021. p. 504-14, doi: 10.18653/V1/2021.EACL-MAIN.40
[28] Sakor A, Mulang' IO, Singh K, Shekarpour S, Vidal M, Lehmann J, et al. Old is gold: Linguistic driven approach for entity and relation linking of short text. In: Burstein J, Doran C, Solorio T, editors. Proceedings of the 2019 Conference of the North American Chapter of the Association for Computational Linguistics; 2019 Jun 2-7; Minneapolis, MN. Stroudsburg (PA): ACL; 2019. p. 2336-46, doi: 10.18653/V1/N19-1243

[29] Yang X, Gu X, Lin S, Tang S, Zhuang Y, Wu F, et al. Learning dynamic context augmentation for global entity linking. In: Inui K, Jiang J, Ng V, Wan X, editors. Proceedings of the 2019 Conference on Empirical Methods in Natural Language Processing and the 9th International Joint Conference on Natural Language Processing; 2019 Nov 3-7; Hong Kong, China. Stroudsburg (PA): ACL; 2019. p. 271-81, doi: 10.18653/V1/D19-1026

[30] Hulst JMV, Hasibi F, Dercksen K, Balog K, de Vries AP. REL: An entity linker standing on the shoulders of giants. In: Huang JX, Chang Y, Cheng X, Kamps J, Murdock V, Wen J, et al., editors. Proceedings of the 43rd International ACM SIGIR conference on research and development in Information Retrieval; 2020 Jul 25-30. New York (NY): ACM; 2020. p. 2197-200, doi: 10.1145/3397271.340141

[31] Akbik A, Blythe D, Vollgraf R. Contextual string embeddings for sequence labeling. In: Bender EM, Derczynski L, Isabelle P, editors. Proceedings of the 27th International Conference on Computational Linguistics; 2018 Aug 20-26; Santa Fe, NM. Stroudsburg (PA): ACL; 2018. p. 1638-49.

[32] Zhang W, Hua W, Stratos K. EntQA: Entity linking as question answering. In: Proceedings of the 10th International Conference on Learning Representations; 2022 Apr 25-29. San Diego (CA): OpenReview.net; 2022. p. 1-13, doi: 10.48550/arXiv.2110.02369

[33] Sun Z, Hu W, Li C. Cross-lingual entity alignment via joint attribute-preserving embedding. In: d'Amato C, Fernández M, Tamma VAM, Lécué F, Cudré-Mauroux P, Sequeda JF, et al., editors. Proceedings of the 16th International Semantic Web Conference; 2017 Oct 21-25; Vienna, Austria. Switzerland: Springer; 2017. p. 628-44, doi: 10.1007/978-3-319-68288-4_37

[34] Sun Z, Hu W, Zhang Q, Qu Y. Bootstrapping entity alignment with knowledge graph embedding. In: Lang J, editor. Proceedings of the 27th International Joint Conference on Artificial Intelligence; 2018 Jul 13-19; Stockholm, Sweden. San Francisco (CA): Morgan Kaufmann; 2018. p. 4396-402, doi: 10.24963/IJCAI.2018/611

[35] Sun Z, Chen M, Hu W. Knowing the no-match: Entity alignment with dangling cases. In: Zong C, Xia F, Li W, Navigli R, editors. Proceedings of the 59th Annual Meeting of the Association for Computational Linguistics; 2021 Aug 1-6. Stroudsburg (PA): ACL; 2021. p. 3582-93, doi: 10.18653/V1/2021.ACL-LONG.278

[36] Ferragina P, Scaiella U. TAGME: On-the-fly annotation of short text fragments (by wikipedia Entities). In: Huang JX, Koudas N, Jones GJF, Wu X, Collins-Thompson K, An A, editors. Proceedings of the 19th ACM Conference on Information and Knowledge Management; 2010 Oct 26-30; Toronto, Ontario, Canada. New York (NY): ACM; 2010. p. 1625-8, doi: 10.1145/1871437.1871689

[37] Ceccarelli D, Lucchese C, Orlando S, Perego R, Trani S. Dexter: An open source framework for entity linking. In: Bennett PN, Gabrilovich E, Kamps J, Karlgren J, editors. Proceedings of the 6th International Workshop on Exploiting Semantic Annotations in Information Retrieval; 2013 Oct 28; San Francisco, CA. New York (NY): ACM; 2013. p. 17-20, doi: 10.1145/2513204.2513212

[38] Usbeck R, Ngomo AN, Röder M, Gerber D, Coelho SA, Auer S, et al. AGDISTIS - Graph-based disambiguation of named entities using linked data. In: Mika P, Tudorache T, Bernstein A, Welty C, Knoblock CA, Vrandecic D, et al., editors. Proceedings of the 13th International Semantic Web Conference; 2014 Oct 19-23; Riva del Garda, Italy. Switzerland: Springer; 2014. p. 457-71, doi: 10.1007/978-3-319-11964-9_29

Handbook on Neurosymbolic AI and Knowledge Graphs
P. Hitzler et al. (Eds.)
IOS Press, 2025

doi:10.3233/FAIA250214

From Certainty to Uncertainty in Knowledge: Exploring Modeling, Extraction, Representation, and Applications

Shumin DENG [a,1], Ningyu ZHANG [b] and Tianxing WU [c]
[a] *National University of Singapore*
[b] *Zhejiang University*
[c] *Southeast University*
ORCiD ID: Shumin Deng https://orcid.org/0000-0002-4049-8478, Ningyu Zhang https://orcid.org/0000-0002-1970-0678, Tianxing Wu https://orcid.org/0000-0003-4669-3570

Abstract. This chapter traverses the evolution of Artificial Intelligence (AI) from structured, deterministic systems to those proficient in managing ambiguity and uncertainty. It begins by detailing methods of knowledge modeling using ontologies, rules, and texts to establish a foundation of certain knowledge. The discourse progresses to explain how knowledge is symbolically and parametrically represented, notably through advanced language models, enhancing the depth and utility of AI systems. Further, the chapter explores the dynamic processes of knowledge acquisition, emphasizing the extraction of intricate data patterns and probing the embedded knowledge within pre-trained language models. It highlights techniques like Retrieval-Augmented Generation (RAG) and symbol-guided parametric knowledge editing to enhance AI capabilities. Concluding with the handling of uncertain knowledge, the chapter underscores strategies enabling AI to operate effectively amidst incomplete and ambiguous information, illustrating the shift towards systems that can robustly navigate the complexities of real-world applications. This concise overview encapsulates the core advancements in AI knowledge processes, marking a critical evolution from certainty to the proficient management of uncertainty.

Keywords. Certainty, Uncertainty, Symbolic, Parametric, Language Models

1. Introduction

The realm of Artificial Intelligence (AI) has dramatically evolved, moving from the confines of deterministic and structured knowledge to grappling with the fluid and often ambiguous nature of real-world information [1]. This evolution marks a pivotal shift in how AI systems are designed and utilized, transitioning from rigid frameworks of certainty [2]

[1] Corresponding Author: Shumin Deng, shumin@nus.edu.sg; 231sm@zju.edu.cn.

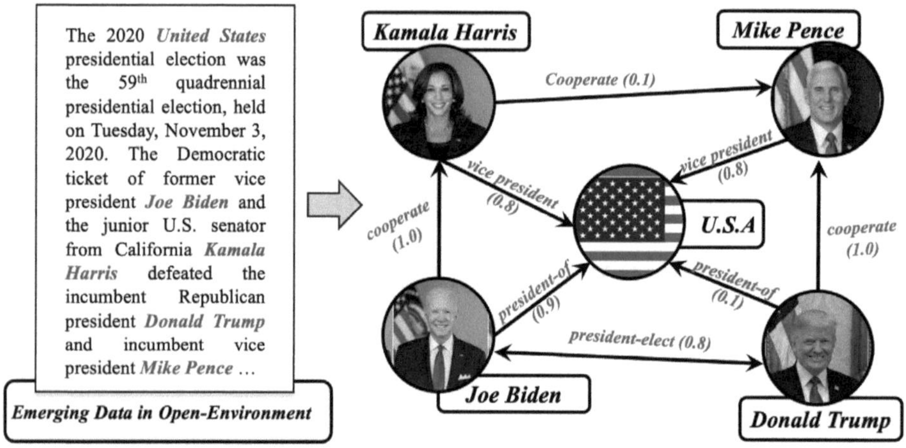

Figure 1. Certain and uncertain knowledge for AI.

to dynamic paradigms capable of handling uncertainty [3]. Concretely, AI relies on various types of knowledge, including certain facts, commonsense, rules, and various forms of uncertain knowledge as shown in Figure 1. This chapter delves into the foundational aspects and practical implications of this transition.

As we venture through this chapter, we will explore the multifaceted process of how knowledge is modeled, extracted, represented, and applied within AI systems. Starting with "Certain Knowledge", we examine traditional methodologies such as ontology-based knowledge modeling, where precise rules and structured data reign supreme. Techniques involving triples and rule-based logic as well as many off-the-shelf tools illustrate how structured knowledge is meticulously organized and manipulated to serve specific purposes for AI applications.

Progressing into knowledge representation, we delve into how symbols and neural-symbolic approaches, alongside advanced Language Models (LMs), play crucial roles in how knowledge is encapsulated and conveyed within AI systems. These representations are not just static but are dynamic, evolving with new data and interactions, leading to more sophisticated and context-aware AI applications.

In the sphere of knowledge acquisition, we address how modern AI systems, particularly through the capabilities of Large Language Models (LLMs) [4,5,6], extract and refine knowledge. We would highlight the innovative techniques of probing from LLMs and the extensive pretraining that these models undergo to assimilate vast amounts of information across various domains. Further enhancing our discussion, we also investigate how AI systems refine and utilize their knowledge bases. Here, methods like the Retrieval-Augmented Generation (RAG) [7,8] and symbol-guided parameter editing [9,10,11,12] are examined to demonstrate how AI models can enhance their functionality and accuracy in real-time applications, making them more adaptable and efficient.

Lastly, as we acknowledge the inherent uncertainties of real-world scenarios, the chapter will explore "Uncertain Knowledge", highlighting the challenges and strategies AI systems employ to interpret, manage, and utilize uncertain and incomplete information effectively.

This chapter aims to provide a comprehensive understanding of the current landscape of AI knowledge processes and their applications, illustrating the critical shift from certainty to uncertainty. This exploration not only enhances our grasp of the theoretical underpinnings of AI but also illuminates the practical challenges and innovations that define the field today.

This chapter is structured as follows: §2 explores *certain knowledge* in knowledge modeling (§2.1), knowledge representation (§2.2), knowledge acquisition (§2.3), and knowledge augmentation (§2.4) with symbols (§2.4.1) as well as neural networks parameters (§2.4.2). We also study *uncertain knowledge* in §3, mainly exploring uncertain knowledge computation (§3.1) and representation learning (§3.2). Finally, we outlook some promising applications in §4.

2. Certain Knowledge

2.1. Knowledge Modeling

Knowledge modeling is a crucial component of AI that focuses on representing knowledge in a structured and understandable format. Typically, knowledge can be modeled as ontology or rule. Ontological knowledge serves to represent the semantic hierarchy of entities and their interrelationships, providing a structured framework for modeling conceptual models within a specific domain. It captures the essential concepts and their connections, enabling a deeper understanding of the domain's structure. In contrast, rule-based knowledge focuses on the inferential rules governing the interactions between entities and relations, offering a more abstract and generalized form of knowledge. This type of knowledge is crucial for reasoning and decision-making processes, as it defines the logical pathways through which conclusions can be drawn from given data or facts. Generally, these two forms of knowledge representation complement each other, with ontological knowledge laying the groundwork for understanding, and rule-based knowledge enabling dynamic reasoning and inference.

Ontology. Ontology in knowledge modeling is a formal representation of a set of concepts within a domain and the relationships between those concepts [13]. It is a crucial aspect of knowledge engineering, AI, and semantic web technologies, serving as a framework for organizing information and enabling machines to understand, process, and utilize human knowledge in a structured way.

In the context of knowledge modeling, an ontology is often described as a "shared vocabulary" that includes definitions of classes, relations, functions, and other entities within a particular domain. Ontologies provide a structured way to represent knowledge, making it easier to share and reuse across different systems and applications. The concept of ontology originates from philosophy, where it refers to the study of being and existence, but in computer science, it has been adapted to represent knowledge about specific domains in a way that can be processed by computers. A well-defined ontology typically consists of the following components:

Classes (Concepts): These are the fundamental building blocks of an ontology, representing categories or types of objects within a domain. For instance, in a medical ontology, classes might include "Patient", "Doctor", "Disease", and "Treatment".

Individuals (Instances): These are the actual objects or entities within a domain that belong to a particular class. For example, "John Smith" might be an instance of the "Patient" class.

Attributes (Properties): These are characteristics or features of classes and individuals. In the medical ontology example, a "Patient" class might have attributes like "age", "gender", and "medical history".

Relationships (Relations): These define how classes and individuals are related to each other. For example, a "Doctor" might be related to a "Patient" through a "treats" relation.

Axioms: These are statements or rules that define constraints and relationships within the ontology. Axioms ensure consistency and logical coherence within the ontology. For instance, an axiom might state that a "Patient" must have at least one "Disease".

Functions: These represent mappings or operations that can be applied to classes or individuals within the ontology. For example, a function might calculate the "body mass index (BMI)" of a patient based on their "weight" and "height" attributes.

Ontology plays a pivotal role in knowledge modeling by providing a standardized way to represent and organize information. They enable different systems and applications to share and integrate knowledge, making it possible to build complex, interoperable systems. Common ontology description languages, ranging from simpler to more complex, include XML, RDF, RDFS, and OWL [14,15]. Each language serves different purposes, from data storage and exchange to providing robust frameworks for semantic descriptions and logical reasoning. Additionally, various ontology modeling tools, such as Protégé, are used to facilitate the creation, editing, and management of ontology, with Protégé being one of the most widely recognized for its versatility and support for the OWL language.

Rule. Another core component of knowledge modeling is rule-based knowledge, which plays a crucial role in various AI applications, such as expert systems and decision support systems. Rule-based knowledge modeling involves the use of explicit, formalized rules to represent knowledge and make inferences.

Specifically, rule-based knowledge refers to a formalized way of encoding knowledge using rules, which are essentially conditional statements that define how certain pieces of information relate to one another. These rules are often expressed in the form of "if-then" statements, where the "if" part represents a condition or a set of conditions, and the "then" part specifies an action or conclusion that follows if the conditions are met. For example, in a medical expert system, a rule might state, "If a patient has a fever and a sore throat, then the patient may have strep throat". This rule helps the system to make a diagnosis based on the symptoms presented.

Rules in knowledge modeling typically consist of three main components: the antecedent, the consequent, and the operator. The antecedent is the condition or set of conditions that must be satisfied for the rule to be applied. The consequent is the outcome or action that results when the antecedent conditions are met. The operator (often represented as "if-then" or "when-then") connects the antecedent and consequent.

Usually, a rule antecedent (head) is composed of a single binary atom, whereas the rule consequent (body) consists of one or more unary or binary atoms. An atom, which includes variables, can be either positive or negative. When the body of the rule contains only positive atoms, the rule is known as a Horn rule [16]. Rules play a crucial role in traditional reasoning. When a reasoning engine operates based on rule-based knowledge, it is referred to as a "rule engine".

Rule engines typically use a descriptive language to define rules, making the choice of rule modeling language a critical aspect. There is no widely accepted standard for rule modeling languages, with most being proprietary and falling into two main categories: structured languages and markup-based languages, often using XML. Several common logic rule programming languages include Prolog [17], Datalog [18], Rule Markup Language (RuleML) [19], and Semantic Web Rule Language (SWRL) [20]. Prolog [17] is widely used in AI for constructing expert systems and intelligent knowledge bases. Datalog [18], a subset of Prolog, is used for data querying with different execution semantics. RuleML [19] provides a standardized syntax for web documents, facilitating interoperability between various rule languages. SWRL [20] integrates RuleML concepts with OWL ontologies to allow semantic rule representation and is recognized as a W3C standard.

There are many tools for modeling rule-based knowledge. Cyc [21] is an AI project focused on integrating ontologies and common-sense knowledge for human-like reasoning in AI. OpenCyc provides APIs and datasets under an open-source license. KAON2 is an infrastructure for managing OWL-DL, SWRL, and F-Logic ontologies, improving upon KAON1 [22]. Drools [23] is a business rules management system with a fast, efficient rules engine based on the Rete algorithm. Flora-2 [24] is an open-source, rule-based engine with an object-oriented syntax derived from F-logic, HiLog, and Transaction logic. Prova [25] is a rule-based scripting system that combines imperative and declarative programming, allowing Java function calls for enhanced integration.

Other Knowledge Modeling. Textual and multimodal approaches extend the richness of knowledge modeling. Textual knowledge modeling focuses on extracting and structuring information from written content. This includes everything from simple facts to complex narratives, scientific theories, legal documents, and more. In contrast, multimodal knowledge modeling integrates multiple forms of data, such as text, images, and video, to create a more comprehensive representation of knowledge that reflects real-world complexity and nuances. In knowledge modeling, multimodal knowledge is essential for creating AI systems that can process and understand complex information from diverse sources, reflecting the way humans perceive and interact with the world.

2.2. Knowledge Representation

Knowledge representation involves the techniques and methodologies used to symbolize and organize information so that a computer system can utilize it to solve complex problems. Typically, it includes two types of representation: symbolic knowledge and neural network (parametric) knowledge.

Symbols are the fundamental elements of knowledge representation, serving as the building blocks for constructing meaning and encoding information. Since the early days of AI in the 1950s, many symbolic representation methods have been proposed. Based on the form and manner of knowledge presentation, knowledge can be classified into different types, including ontology knowledge and rule-based knowledge. Ontology knowledge represents the semantic hierarchy of entities and relationships and is used to model conceptual frameworks within a domain. Rule-based knowledge, on the other hand, represents the inferential relationships between entities and relationships and is more abstract in nature.

Neural networks can also serve as a form of knowledge representation, where a major challenge lies in capturing complex knowledge structures and relations within continuous vectors that machines can process. Currently, representations of complex knowledge are mainly divided into three categories: direct text-to-embedding mapping, knowledge graph (KG) embedding and pre-trained language models.

Direct Text-to-Embedding Mapping. Early researchers treat entities and relations in KGs as words and use embedding methods like GloVe [26] to convert them into continuous vector spaces. To obtain fixed-length vector representations, researchers employed techniques such as Recurrent Neural Networks (RNNs) and mean pooling, which encode KGs into fixed-size vectors suitable for subsequent computational tasks. For handling complex queries, such as long texts returned by SPARQL queries, [27] extract semantic information from variable-length texts using Doc2Vec [28] to construct fixed-length feature vectors, effectively capturing the deep semantics of the text. To further improve the quality of knowledge representation, researchers have also used techniques from Word2Vec to remove stop words, reducing noise from irrelevant words during mean pooling [29]. Additionally, some studies have attempted to convert fact sets from KGs into natural language sentences [30,31,32], making the facts easier to understand and enabling pre-trained language models to encode them directly into fixed-length vectors.

Knowledge Graph Embedding (KGE). This is an effective method for mapping entities and relationships into abstract vector spaces, revealing the semantic relationships between triples in a KG [33]. KGE is particularly important for initializing fact representations and integrating multimodal information [34,35,36]. Through self-supervised learning, KGE can encode information from neighboring entities into the central entity, aiding in the identification and integration of key entities. This process allows for effective feature extraction from specific sub-KGs without direct retrieval. Various KGE techniques have been proposed to extract and integrate features from different data sources. For example, [36] train the RotatE model to extract entity and relations features and combine these embeddings with image and question features to enhance model understanding. [37] present ConvE, a multi-layer convolutional network model designed for link prediction. Additionally, the work of RVL [38] and KVQAmeta [39] utilize PyTorch-BigGraph [40] and Wikipedia2Vec to embed Wikidata KG and Wikipedia entities, respectively, demonstrating the adaptability and versatility of KGE in integrating multi-source knowledge representations. KGE offers powerful knowledge representation capabilities and robust support for reasoning.

Pre-trained Language Models. Pre-trained LMs are represented as a new paradigm in knowledge representation. These models process and generate human-like text based on the patterns and structures they learn from massive datasets. [41] have proposed that pre-trained language models can serve as a form of parameterized knowledge base. However, we still know very little about how this knowledge is specifically organized within pre-trained language models. A key research area focuses on identifying where knowledge is stored in the model. [42] propose that the Feed-Forward Network (FFN) layers in language models function similarly to a key-value store, and they discovered that value vectors often reflect interpretable concepts and knowledge, which can be reinforced or diminished through specific manipulations. [43] further introduce the concept of "knowledge neurons", suggesting that knowledge is limited to a small subset of FFN neurons in the uppermost layers of the language model. Similarly, [44] use a method called "causal tracing" to assess the indirect effects of hidden states or activations, revealing that factual knowledge may primarily reside in the FFN layers of these models' earlier layers. Additionally, [45] find that large models contain neurons that express multilingual knowledge and degenerate neurons that represent redundant information. [46] propose that knowledge exists in a region of the weight space of pre-trained language models after fine-tuning. They found that models fine-tuned on similar datasets are close to each other in weight space. However, [47] argue that while MLP neurons might exhibit some so-called knowledge patterns, they merely reflect data correlations rather than representing true intrinsic knowledge mechanisms in large models. [48] delve into the computation graph of the language model to uncover the knowledge circuits that are instrumental in articulating specific knowledge.

To conclude, symbolic and neural networks are both forms of knowledge representation, and neural-symbolic knowledge representation can be a sophisticated blend where symbolic representations (capturing discrete, categorical knowledge) are combined with parametric models (such as those found in machine learning). This hybrid approach leverages the clarity of symbolic reasoning along with the adaptability and learning capabilities of parametric models.

2.3. Knowledge Acquisition

Knowledge acquisition is the process through which systems gain knowledge, a critical step in enhancing the capabilities of AI applications. Knowledge extraction is a primary method for knowledge acquisition, involving the automated discovery of knowledge from vast datasets. We will introduce two major techniques, namely data to knowledge with named entity extraction, relation extraction, event extraction as shown in Figure 2, as well as model to knowledge by probing pre-trained language models.

2.3.1. Data to Knowledge

Named Entity Extraction. The current dominant methods [49,50,51] treat NER as a sequence tagging problem with label-specific classifiers or CRF. Nevertheless, these works still need to modify the model architecture when facing new entity classes; the inability to solve the challenge of class transfer limits its efficiency and transferability, which is not suitable for low-resource scenarios. Meanwhile, one crucial research line of low-resource NER is prototype-based methods, which involve meta-learning and have recently become popular few-shot learning approaches in the NER area. Most of the approaches [52,53,54,55,56,57,58,59] utilize the nearest-neighbor criterion to assign the entity type, which depends on similar patterns of entity between the source domain and the target domain without fully exploiting the potential of PLMs, behaving unsatisfactorily for cross-domain instances. Recently, [60] propose template-based BART for few-shot NER, which enumerates all $\hat{\mathbf{n}}$-gram possible spans in the sentence and fills them in the hand-crafted templates, classifying each candidate span based on the corresponding template scores. [61] propose a lightweight tuning paradigm for low-resource NER via pluggable prompting (LightNER), which does not need template engineering and is more friendly with computation complexity. [62] propose GPT-NER by transforming the sequence labeling to a language generation task with LLMs.

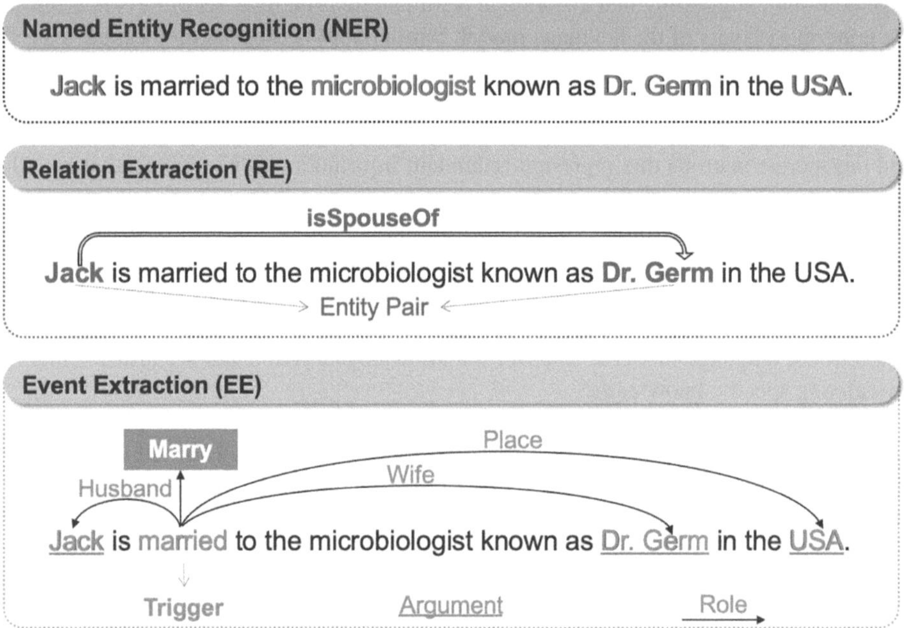

Figure 2. Knowledge acquisition with information extraction from data.

Relation Extraction. Relation extraction aims to identify the relation between entity pairs based on a given contextual text [63,64]. In order to reduce the cost of labeling, previous studies utilize distant supervision based on the KG to generate labeled examples automatically [65]. More recent few-shot relation extraction approaches leverage prototype network, multi-level matching and aggregation, relational twin network and meta-learning [66,67,68]. [69] propose prompt tuning with rules for text classification. [70] propose a Knowledge-aware Prompt-tuning approach with synergistic optimization (KnowPrompt) which is integrated in the open-sourced knowledge extraction tool DeepKE [71]. Specifically, they inject latent knowledge contained in relation labels into prompt construction with learnable virtual type words and answer words, then synergistically optimize their representation with structured constraints. [72] create a benchmark with 8 relation extraction (RE) datasets covering different languages, domains and contexts and perform extensive comparisons over the proposed schemes with combinations. [73] investigate principal methodologies, in-context learning and data generation, for few-shot relation extraction with LLMs.

Event Extraction. Event extraction aims to identify event triggers with arguments from text, which is generally formulated as a classification or structured prediction problem [74]. Many works focus on few-shot event extraction, for example, [75] utilize external knowledge from frame net and propose a global inference approach to improve the event detection performance. More recently, [76,77] reformulate the event extraction task as machine reading comprehension (MRC), which can achieve better performance in few-shot setting than vanilla fine-tuning. [78] propose Structured Prediction with Energybased Event-Centric Hyperspheres (SPEECH), which models complex dependency among event structured components with energy-based modeling, and represents event classes with simple but effective hyperspheres.

2.3.2. *Model to Knowledge*

Pre-trained language models represent a new paradigm in knowledge representation, and [41] suggest that these models can function as a parameterized knowledge base. Intuitively, we can use prompts to probe those knowledge as "model to knowledge" for knowledge acquisition. This technique involves querying LLMs to uncover embedded knowledge within their parameters, gained through extensive pretraining. By probing these models, researchers can extract sophisticated insights and understandings that are implicitly stored within the model's layers.

Concretely, language model pretraining itself is a foundational process for knowledge acquisition. During pretraining, language models are exposed to diverse and expansive text corpora, allowing them to learn a wide range of linguistic patterns, relationships, and factual information. This pretraining sets the stage for further fine-tuning and specific knowledge acquisition tasks, enabling the models to perform well across various domains and applications.

2.4. *Knowledge Augmentation*

Knowledge augmentation in AI refers to the methods and processes that improve the utility, accuracy, and relevance of knowledge within various systems. This enhancement is particularly critical as AI models become increasingly complex and are expected to perform with higher levels of sophistication across different domains. We will introduce knowledge augmentation including symbolic knowledge augmentation and parametric knowledge editing with symbol guidance.

2.4.1. *Symbolic Knowledge Augmentation*

One innovative approach to knowledge enhancement involves the use of symbols to enhance parameters within AI models. For instance, in Retrieval-Augmented Generation (RAG) models, symbolic knowledge (like entities, facts, and relationships stored in a knowledge base) is dynamically retrieved to augment the generation process of a neural network. We will mainly introduce symbolic knowledge augmentation via prompting.

Prompt Engineering is the process of guiding generative large models to produce the desired output. Leveraging rich knowledge can enhance the model's understanding of specific domains and tasks, and by incorporating knowledge into prompt engineering, the model's ability to solve complex problems can be significantly improved. Knowledge-enhanced prompt engineering can be divided into two categories: internal reasoning path-enhanced prompt engineering and external knowledge-enhanced prompt engineering. The internal reasoning path method focuses on improving the model's logical reasoning capabilities, while the external knowledge enhancement method aims to expand the model's knowledge base.

(1) Reasoning Path-Enhanced Prompt Engineering: A reasoning path refers to an internal reasoning mechanism, typically involving step-by-step reasoning within the model to achieve a deeper understanding of the problem and provide more accurate answers. Below are some representative works:

Chain-of-Thought Prompting (CoT) [79] helps the model better understand and solve complex reasoning problems by introducing chain-of-thought prompts that break down the reasoning process into multiple steps. One of the key ideas of CoT is to utilize natural language to express the knowledge reasoning path, thereby improving the model's performance in tasks such as complex reasoning.

The Tree of Thoughts (ToT) [80] framework further allows for thoughtful decision-making and problem-solving by considering multiple reasoning paths. One of the key advantages of the ToT framework is the introduction of "Thought Units," which represent coherent units of text as intermediate steps in problem-solving. By allowing the language model to explore and evaluate these Thought Units, ToT enables the model to make better global decisions, consider multiple possible reasoning paths, and engage in foresight or backtracking when necessary to make more informed choices.

The Graph of Thoughts (GoT) [81] framework introduces an innovative thinking concept by structuring the model's reasoning process into a graph. In this framework, the thought process is viewed as nodes, and the logical dependencies between nodes form connecting edges. This design simulates the thinking patterns of the human brain, enabling the model to solve problems more efficiently using a similar mechanism.

(2) External Knowledge-Enhanced Prompt Engineering: The knowledge reserves of large models are not exhaustive, and sometimes it is necessary to provide additional external knowledge when posing questions to enhance the model's knowledge capabilities. External knowledge enhancement refers to integrating the model with external knowledge sources (such as databases, KGs, the internet, etc.), allowing it to utilize this additional information when generating prompts.

Chain-of-Knowledge (CoK) [82] effectively reduces the occurrence of false content during the generation of thought chains by integrating multi-source knowledge information and significantly improves the accuracy of responses. The core advantage of CoK lies in its dynamic adaptation to different heterogeneous knowledge sources, such as web documents, databases, and other knowledge bases.

Chain-of-Note (CON) [83] aims to enhance the robustness of retrieval-augmented language models when dealing with noisy, irrelevant documents and unknown situations. This method generates sequential reading notes for retrieved documents, comprehensively assessing their relevance to the given question, and ultimately producing more accurate answers. From the perspective of enhanced prompt engineering, CON offers a significant contribution.

Retrieval-Augmented Generation (RAG) [7,8] refers to the process in which a model first retrieves relevant information from a large corpus of documents when answering questions or generating text. It then uses this retrieved information to generate responses or text, thereby improving the quality of predictions [84]. The RAG approach allows developers to avoid retraining an entire large model for each specific task. Instead, they can attach a knowledge base to provide additional input to the model, enhancing the accuracy of its responses. As a knowledge-intensive task, RAG employs different technical approaches during the pre-training, fine-tuning, and inference stages of language model training.

(1) Retrieval-Augmented Pre-training: REALM [85] introduced a more modular and interpretable knowledge embedding method, viewing the pre-training and fine-tuning processes as a retrieval-prediction process. RETRO [86] utilizes a retrieval-augmented method to pre-train an autoregressive language model, retrieving data from large-scale labeled datasets and conducting large-scale pre-training from scratch. RETRO also enables updating the knowledge stored in the language model without retraining the model. RETRO++ [87], an extended version of RETRO, increases the model's parameter scale. Research has shown that RETRO++ consistently improves text generation quality, factual accuracy, low toxicity, and downstream task accuracy, especially in knowledge-intensive open-domain question-answering tasks. Similarly, Atlas [88] introduces a retrieval mechanism during pre-training and fine-tuning using the T5 architecture and periodically refreshes the asynchronous index during pre-training. Overall, enhanced pre-training methods offer significant advantages and limitations: while they excel in handling knowledge-intensive tasks and can create domain-specific models by training on domain-specific corpora, they require large amounts of pre-training data and resources and tend to have slower update speeds.

(2) Retrieval-Augmented Fine-tuning: REPLUG [89] treats the large model as a black box and enhances it with an adjustable retrieval model. By receiving feedback from the black-box language model's supervision signals, REPLUG improves the initial retrieval model. UPRISE [90] fine-tunes on a diversified set of tasks to create a lightweight and versatile retriever capable of automatically providing retrieval prompts for zero-shot tasks, demonstrating its generality and improved performance across tasks. Meanwhile, fine-tuning methods for generators include Self-Mem [91], which fine-tunes the generator using a memory pool of examples, and Self-RAG [92], which meets active retrieval needs by generating feedback labels. In summary, retrieval-enhanced methods during the fine-tuning stage are flexible and customizable, but they also require specially prepared datasets for RAG fine-tuning and some degree of computational resources.

(3) Retrieval-Augmented Inference: The DSP [93] framework relies on a sophisticated knowledge retrieval enhancement framework to provide a more informative context to the large model, thereby improving generation quality. RECITE [94], on the other hand, samples one or more paragraphs from the large model to form the context during inference. Optimizing the RAG process during the inference stage can help adapt to more challenging tasks. For example, ITRG [95] enhances adaptability to multi-step reasoning tasks by iteratively retrieving and searching for the correct reasoning path. ITER-RETGEN [155] combines retrieval and generation using an iterative method, achieving an alternating process of "retrieval-augmented generation" and "generation-augmented retrieval". On the other hand, IRCOT [96] integrates the concepts of RAG and Chain-of-Thought (CoT), using alternating CoT to guide retrieval and utilizing the retrieval results to enhance CoT. This approach significantly improves GPT-3's performance on various question-answering tasks, highlighting the potential advantages of integrating retrieval and generation. In general, retrieval-enhanced methods during the inference stage are lightweight, cost-effective, require no additional training, and leverage powerful pre-trained models. However, this technique typically requires additional data processing and process optimization, while also being constrained by the capabilities of the base model.

2.4.2. Parametric Knowledge Editing with Symbol Guidance

Further, the parameters of neural networks can be edited or fine-tuned under the guidance of symbolic knowledge [97,12]. This process involves adjusting the neural network's parameters so that they align more closely with the structured knowledge represented by symbols. By guiding parameter adjustments with symbols, the models can better adhere to logical constraints and domain-specific rules, thus enhancing the reliability and credi-

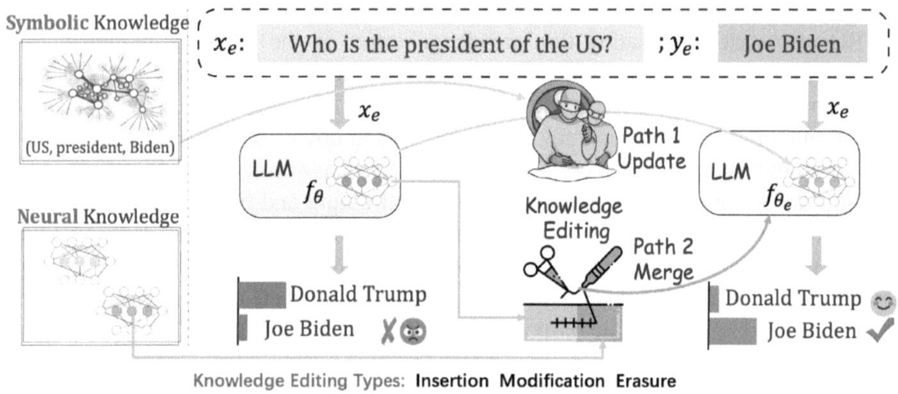

Figure 3. Knowledge editing to fix and update knowledge in LLMs.

bility of the model outputs. Ideally, as the world's state evolves, we aim to update LLMs in a way that sidesteps the computational burden associated with training a wholly new model. As shown in Figure 3, to address this issue, the concept of **knowledge editing** (or model editing) has been proposed in [98,99], enabling data-efficient alterations to the behavior of models, specifically within a designated realm of interest, while ensuring no adverse impact on other inputs. This method ensures that the learned patterns and predictions are not only data-driven but also conceptually sound and contextually appropriate.

Currently, numerous works on knowledge editing for LLMs [99,44,100,98,101,12] have made strides in various editing tasks and settings. As illustrated in Figure 4, these works manipulate the model's output for specific cases by either integrating an auxiliary network with the original unchanged model or altering the model parameters responsible for the undesirable output. The current methods for knowledge editing are categorized into two main groups, those centered on preserving existing parameters and those entailing modification. The preservative methods incorporate explicit memory and prompting techniques to rectify model predictions. Examples include SERAC [102], MemPrompt [103] and IKE [104]. Some modify the Feed-forward Neural Network (FFN) layer, as exemplified by CaliNET [105],T-Patcher [106], GRACE [107] and WISE [108]. Alternatively, the locate-and-edit approaches need to first locate the relevant neurons, followed by the adjustment of corresponding target parameters. Representative studies are KN [109], ROME [44], and MEMIT [100]. Conversely, meta-learning utilizes a hypernetwork, a smaller network that generates the weights for layers in the main network, including KE [110], MALMEN [111] and MEND [112]. Despite the wide range of model editing techniques present in the literature, a comprehensive comparative analysis, assessing these methods in uniform experimental conditions, is notably lacking. This absence of direct comparison impairs our ability to discern the relative merits and demerits of each approach, consequently hindering our comprehension of their adaptability across different problem domains.

To confront this issue, [9] endeavor to establish a standard problem definition accompanied by a meticulous appraisal of these methods. [9] conduct experiments under regulated conditions, fostering an impartial comparison of their respective strengths and weaknesses with the open-sourced framework EasyEdit [113]. [9] initially use two pop-

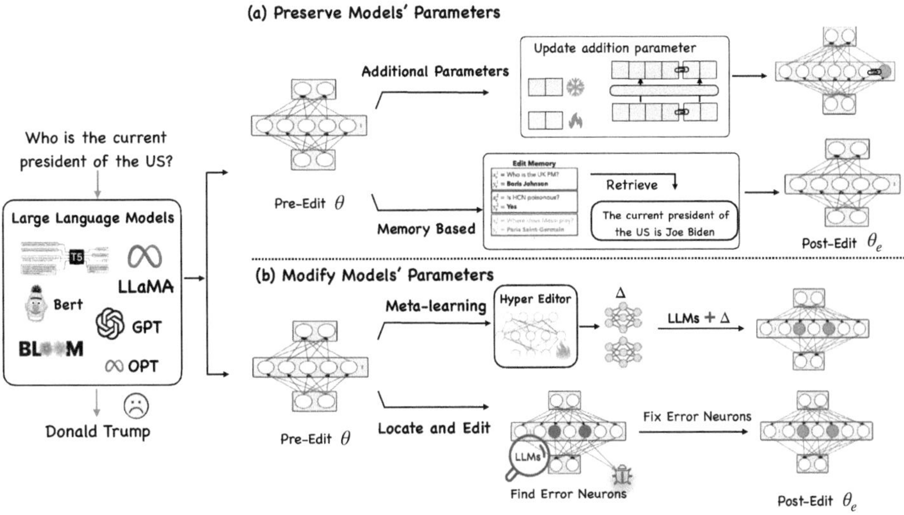

Figure 4. An overview of two paradigms of knowledge editing for LLMs.

ular datasets, ZsRE [114] and COUNTERFACT [44], and two structurally different language models, T5 [115] (encoder-decoder) and GPT-J [116] (decoder only), as our base models. Beyond basic edit settings, [9] assess performance for **batch** and **sequential** editing. While [9] observe that current methods have demonstrated considerable capacity in factual model editing tasks, [9] reconsider the current evaluation and create a more encompassing evaluation dataset: **portability** (robust generalization capabilities), **locality** (side effect), and **efficiency** (time and memory usage). [9] find current model editing methods are somewhat limited on these levels, thereby constraining their practical application, and deserve more research in the future. Recently, [117] critiques the standard formulation of the model editing problem and introduce a formal testbed.

Note that parameters edited by symbol guidance are grounded in the exploration of principles that guide the encapsulation of knowledge within pre-trained language models, drawing upon a range of pivotal studies such as those by [42,43,45,45,46,47,118]. These works provide foundational insights into how language models store and process information. The practice of knowledge editing, which includes the manipulation of a model's external knowledge, shares commonalities with knowledge augmentation techniques. This is because updating a model's stored knowledge essentially involves infusing it with new, relevant information. Additionally, we view knowledge editing as a nuanced form of lifelong learning [119] and unlearning [120,121,122], where models are designed to dynamically incorporate and adjust new knowledge, while also shedding outdated or incorrect data. This approach is crucial for enhancing the model's relevance and accuracy over time. Moreover, by enabling models to discard harmful or toxic information, knowledge editing presents a viable strategy for addressing the security and privacy challenges that accompany the use of LLMs [123].

3. Uncertain Knowledge

3.1. Uncertain Knowledge Computation

With the rapid rise of AI, KGs have been constructed across various domains, playing a critical role in applications such as semantic search and intelligent question-answering systems. In the early stages of KG development, the information within these graphs was typically assumed to be completely accurate. However, as automated methods have become more prevalent in the construction of KGs, the inevitable introduction of noise and errors has posed new challenges. Additionally, in fields such as medicine and law, much of the knowledge is heavily experiential and probabilistic, making it difficult to represent this information using deterministic approaches.

To address these challenges, researchers have proposed various methods to calculate the uncertainty (*i.e.*, confidence) of triples within KGs. These methods aim to assess the confidence of each triple, thereby enhancing the reliability of KGs in real-world applications. Notable examples include CKRL [124] and KGTtm [125], which employ different mechanisms to evaluate and improve the confidence of triples within a graph.

It is important to note that, while external KGs can aid in increasing the confidence of triples in a target KG, this section focuses on methods that compute uncertainty using internal information rather than those that rely on external KGs for confidence computation.

3.1.1. Explicit Contextual Evidence-Based Uncertainty Estimation

Uncertainty computation methods based on explicit contextual evidence utilize all explicit triples of the KG, to obtain contextual evidence and aid in confidence assessment of the particular triple. Explicit contextual evidence refers to structured information in the KG that can be directly associated with the particular triple, which usually includes entities, relationships, and their connection patterns in the graph structure. Specifically, this type of approach represents explicit contextual evidence in the form of paths (*e.g.*, meta paths and anchored predicate paths) or subgraphs, and combines techniques such as graph traversal, path extraction, and inductive summarization algorithms to construct models that achieve confidence prediction of triples.

Path-Based Representation. In KGs, the connections generated by typed nodes and edges are referred to as meta paths, describing how two entities are related by their type labels. The redundant entity types are further streamlined, *i.e.*, type labels are provided only for entities at the endpoints of the paths, and the meta paths are transformed into anchored predicate paths. These paths describe the connectivity patterns of the graph and can be used to capture the explicit context associated with the target triple. [126] proposed a method for fact-checking using predicate paths in the KG. The method verifies the truthfulness of factual statements, *i.e.*, the accuracy of triples, by mining discriminative predicate paths in the graph and using these paths to train models.

Specifically, the method can be presented through a fact-checking framework. Meta paths or predicate paths are first extracted from the graph using graph traversal mining. Then filtering selection is performed on the extraction results to determine the most discriminative paths by giving the importance of each path through principles such as information gain. Finally, the selected paths are used as features to construct feature vectors for training the prediction model, which in turn achieves the prediction of triple confidence. This article takes this method as an example to introduce the process from path extraction, path selection, and feature construction to model prediction. Here is the overview of the fact-checking framework in Figure 5.

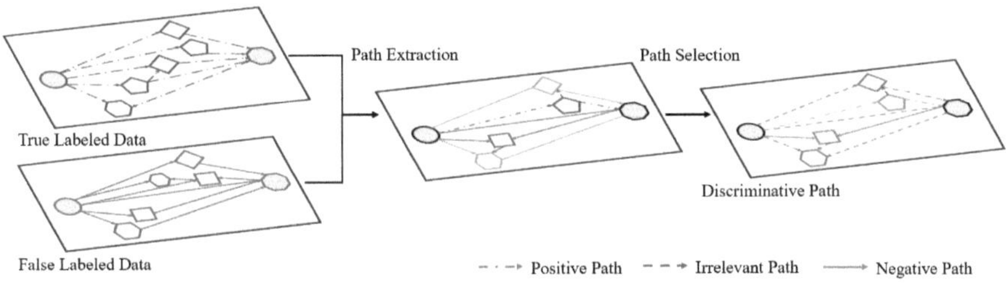

Figure 5. Overview of the proposed fact-checking framework.

Given a KG $\mathscr{G} = (\mathscr{V}, \mathscr{E}, \mathscr{R}, \mathscr{O}, \psi, \phi)$, where $\mathscr{V}$, $\mathscr{E}$, $\mathscr{R}$, and $\mathscr{O}$ respectively denote the set of entities, inter-entity directed edges, predicate labels, and ontologies. The ontology mapping function $\psi(v) = \mathbf{o}$ links entities to ontologies and the predicate mapping function $\phi(e) = p$ maps edges to predicate types. A meta path Π^k is the sequence $\mathbf{o}_1 \xrightarrow{p_1} \mathbf{o}_2 \xrightarrow{p_2} \dots \xrightarrow{p_{k-1}} \mathbf{o}_k$, where $\mathbf{o}_i$ denotes the set of ontology labels of vertex i and p_i denotes the predicate connecting vertex i and $i+1$. The sequence removing nodes outside the non-endpoint ones degenerates into an anchored predicate path $P^k = \boldsymbol{o}_1 \xrightarrow{p_1} \xrightarrow{p_2} \dots \xrightarrow{p_{k-1}} \boldsymbol{o}_k$. Discriminative paths $\mathbf{D}^k_{(\mathbf{o}_u, \mathbf{o}_v)}$ are then the set of anchored predicate paths, capable of alternately describing a given factual statement $\mathbf{o}_u \xrightarrow{p} \mathbf{o}_v$.

- **Path Extraction.** The method first proposes a fast discriminative path discovery algorithm using a constraint graph traversal process to mine all possible paths by traversing the graph starting from a given subject-entity to the end of a given object-entity. The traversal process is defined as a closure function $\mathbb{C}$. $\mathbb{C}_p(v)$ denotes finding all nodes reachable from an entity node v via predicate p (positive path) or p^{-1} (negative path).

$$\mathbb{C}_p(v) = \{(p, v') \mid (v, p, v') \in \mathscr{G}\} \cup \{(p^{-1}, v') \mid (v', p, v) \in \mathscr{G}\} \tag{1}$$

Then define a transition function $\mathscr{T}(v_i)$ containing all possible next nodes that can be visited from $\mathbb{C}_p(v)$, which in turn yields the path set $\mathscr{P}$ with length $\leq k$.

$$\mathscr{T}(v_i) = \{\cup_{p \in \mathscr{R}} \mathbb{C}_p(v_i) \setminus \cup_{j=1}^{i} \{v_j\}\} \tag{2}$$

$$\begin{aligned} \mathscr{P}^k = \{ & s, \mathscr{T}(v_1), \mathscr{T}(v_2), \dots, \mathscr{T}(v_{k-2}), t \mid \\ & (s,t) \in \mathbf{T}, v_1 = s, v_i \in \mathscr{T}(v_{i-1}), t \in \mathscr{T}(v_{k-1})\} \end{aligned} \tag{3}$$

- **Path Selection.** The path set $\mathbf{P}$ is further filtered to complete the feature construction by judging the importance of paths through information gain. For this purpose, $\mathbf{P}$ is transformed into an $n \times m$ matrix $\mathbf{X}$ of training instances, where the ith row denotes instances from the anchored pair (u, v) and the cell $\mathbf{X}_{i,j}$ is the number of paths P_j anchored by u and v. A new $n \times m'$ matrix $\mathbf{X}'$ is created by a feature selection function f, where m' contains only the most discriminative paths. And $\mathbf{w}$ is the m-dimensional feature importance vector, with $w_j \in \mathbf{w}$ determined by the information gain I of $\mathbf{X}_{:,j}$ and $\mathbf{y}$.

$$\mathbf{X}' = f(\mathbf{X}, \mathbf{w}, \delta) = \mathbf{X}_{1:n, \left\{ j | j \in 1:m, w_j \geq \delta \right\}} \tag{4}$$

$$I(\mathbf{X}_{:,j} : \mathbf{y}) = \sum_{x_{i,j} \in \mathbf{X}_{:,j}} \sum_{y_i \in \mathbf{y}} p(x_{i,j}) \, p(y_i) \log \left(\frac{p(x_{i,j}, y_i)}{p(x_{i,j}) \, p(y_i)} \right) \tag{5}$$

where $\mathbf{X}_{:,j}$ denotes the column vector of feature j, $\mathbf{y}$ denotes the corresponding label vector, and $x_{i,j}$ is the data value of the cell at $\mathbf{X}_{i,j}$.
- **Model Prediction.** The constructed feature vectors are then used to train a prediction model (*e.g.*, standard logistic regression model) for predicting the correctness of the triples, which in turn is factually verified.

Subgraph-Based Representation. Subgraphs contain the topology of other entities and relationships associated with the target triple, and its shape and connection patterns can be used to assess the position and role of the triple in the whole KG. Based on this property of subgraphs, the problem of finding missing or incorrect information on the large graphs is transformed into a KG summarization with a set of inductive rules to identify anomalous content. For example, for a given KG, KG_{IST} [127] generates succinct sets of inductive rules (defined as labeled, rooted graphs) via the Minimum Description Length (MDL) principle. These rules are used to describe what is normal and can be generalized to parts not covered by the graph. Finally, anomaly detection is performed separately for nodes and edges, including nodes that violate many rules, edges that are not explained by the model, and edges with more anomalous endpoints.

KG_{IST} provides a detailed explanation of various definitions, MDL models, and encoding methods for rules and assertions. KG_{IST} uses anomaly scores to determine which triples in the model have anomalies. This article mainly focuses on the part of confidence computation of triples and does not provide a detailed introduction to other contents of the paper except for necessary parameter explanations.

In KG_{IST}, a model M of KG is defined as a set of inductive rules, where a rule is represented as g. A specific example of a rule is 'Books have fictional family characters and are written by authors who are born in countries' and the rule is formally defined in KG_{IST}. The assertion $a(g)$ is the instantiation of the edges and labels of the rule around a specific node in KG, and the set of all assertions of rule g is defined as $\mathscr{A}(g)$. $\mathscr{A}(g)$ can be further divided into $\mathscr{A}_c^{(g)}$ and $\mathscr{A}_e^{(g)}$, where the former represents the correct assertion of g and the latter represents the assertion of anomalies (referred to as exceptions in the original paper). Here is the schematic of this specific example in Figure 6.

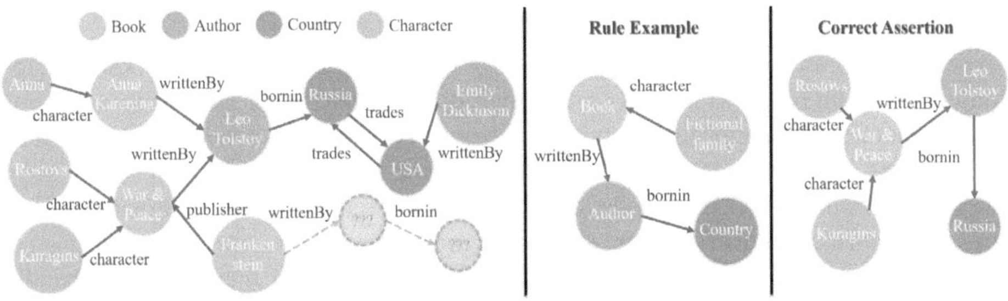

Figure 6. An example rule and one of its correct assertions.

- **Entity Anomalies.** The anomaly scores of a triple are composed of nodes and edges. For each node ε, its anomaly score is:

$$\eta(v) = \sum_{g \in r(v)} \sum_{v \in \mathscr{A}_{\xi}^{(g)}} \frac{1}{|\mathscr{A}_{\xi}^{(g)}|} \log\left(\frac{|\mathscr{A}^{(g)}|}{|\mathscr{A}_{\xi}^{(g)}|}\right) \tag{6}$$

where $r: \mathscr{V} \rightarrow \mathscr{P}(M)$ is the set of all rules applied to a node.

- **Relationship Anomalies.** KG_{IST} uses an adjacency tensor A of $|\mathscr{V}| \times |\mathscr{V}| \times |\mathscr{L}_{\mathscr{E}}|$ to represent the connectivity of KG, where $\mathscr{V}$ is the set of nodes and $\mathscr{L}_{\mathscr{E}}$ is the set of relationship types. $\mathbf{A}_M$ is the edges modeled by M, while the unmodeled edges are represented as $\mathbf{A}^- = \mathbf{A} - \mathbf{A}_M$. The edge that is not explained by M is abnormal, and its anomaly score is defined as the number of bits describing it as negative error:

$$\eta^{(r)}(h,r,t) = \begin{cases} \frac{1}{|\mathbf{A}^-|} \log\left(\frac{|\mathscr{V}|^2 * |\mathscr{L}_{\mathscr{E}}| - |\mathbf{A}_M|}{|\mathbf{A}^-|}\right) & \text{if } \mathrm{A}^-_{h,t,r} = 1 \\ 0 & \text{otherwise} \end{cases} \tag{7}$$

where $|.|$ denotes set cardinality and the number of 1s in a tensor/matrix.

- **Anomaly Scores.** The anomaly score of an abnormal tiple is ultimately represented as the sum of the anomaly scores of node and edge:

$$\eta(h,r,t) = \eta(h) + \eta(t) + \eta^{(r)}(h,r,t) \tag{8}$$

Explicit contextual evidence plays a crucial role in uncertainty computation, rich and consistent contextual evidence can enhance the model of confidence in triples, thus reducing uncertainty. Therefore, the accuracy of triple confidence assessment can be effectively improved by optimizing the extraction and weight assignment of contextual evidence. In conclusion, uncertainty computation based on explicit contextual evidence can improve the overall quality and reliability of KGs and has important application value in scenarios such as automated construction of KGs, knowledge verification, and error correction.

3.1.2. Embedding-Based Uncertainty Estimation

Uncertainty computation based on embedding representation evidence works by mapping entities and relations in a KG into a high-dimensional vector space, capturing implicit semantic information and complex nonlinear relations. These methods rely on neural networks or other fundamental embedding models, such as TransE [128], which learn latent patterns in the KG. The model estimates the uncertainty of triples through similarities, differences, and distributional states between the vectors.

The strength of embedding representation methods lies in their ability to handle large-scale, complex graph data, especially when explicit evidence is scarce. They can capture deep relations and latent patterns that are difficult to describe through explicit rules, making them effective in processing semantic associations, inferring implicit relations, and detecting anomalies. However, a significant challenge with these methods is their weak interpretability. Embedding representation methods are often difficult to explain through direct rules or paths, making it a challenge in practical applications to translate embedding results into intuitive reasoning processes.

Uncertainty computation methods based on embedding representation evidence can be further divided into two categories: one relies solely on the structural information of the KG, while the other integrates both structural and textual information to enhance the accuracy of uncertainty computation. The first category leverages only the structural information within the KG, such as the neighboring relations of entities or the paths between entity pairs. This approach is particularly suitable for scenarios lacking rich textual descriptions or external knowledge. However, as it solely relies on the graph structure, it may overlook external semantic information, thus failing to fully capture implicit semantic associations in certain complex situations. KGTtm [125] and CAGED [129] are representative methods in this category, effectively evaluating the confidence of triples through the structural information of the graph. The second category, in contrast, not only utilizes the structural information of the KG but also incorporates external textual information (*e.g.*, descriptions of entities) to further improve the accuracy of uncertainty estimation. These methods combine textual embeddings with structural embeddings, enhancing the model's capacity by integrating semantic information. CCA [130] is a typical example of this approach, which enhances the accuracy of triple confidence computation by integrating both structural and textual information.

KGTtm Overview. KGTtm (Knowledge Graph Triple Trustworthiness Measurement) is a model designed to measure the trustworthiness (or confidence) of triples within a KG. A KG typically represents facts using triples (head entity, relation, tail entity), which are susceptible to noise and errors during construction. KGTtm addresses this issue by quantifying the degree of correctness of these triples through a crisscrossing neural network architecture. The model synthesizes semantic information and global inference data from the KG to compute a confidence score for each triple. This score is used to identify and filter out erroneous triples, ensuring that only trustworthy information is retained in the KG.

Estimator Design. The KGTtm model contains three different estimators, each focusing on different aspects of triple trustworthiness.

- **Entity-Level Estimator:** The first estimator assesses whether a potential relationship exists between two entities, (h,t). This is achieved using the *ResourceRank* algorithm, which evaluates the association strength between the head and tail entities based on the resource allocation method. The amount of resource $R(t|h)$ passed from entity h to entity t is calculated as:

$$R(t|h) = (1-\theta) \sum_{e_i \in M_t} \frac{R(e_i|h) \cdot BW_{e_i t}}{OD(e_i)} + \frac{\theta}{N}, \tag{9}$$

where M_t represents the set of nodes with outgoing links to t, $OD(e_i)$ is the out-degree of node e_i, $BW_{e_i t}$ is the bandwidth of the edge from e_i to t, and N is the total number of nodes in the graph. The resulting feature vector $\mathbf{V}$ is transformed into a probability $RR(h,t)$ using a non-linear activation function α, as follows:

$$u = \alpha(W_1 \mathbf{V} + b_1), \quad RR(h,t) = W_2 u + b_2. \tag{10}$$

- **Relationship-Level Estimator:** The second estimator, based on the *Translation-based Energy Function* (TEF) algorithm, evaluates whether the specified relation r can plausibly occur between the entity pair (h,t). The triple's energy is defined as TransE [128]:

$$E(h,r,t) = \|h + r - t\|, \tag{11}$$

where h, r, and t are the embeddings of the head entity, relation, and tail entity, respectively. The probability $P(E(h,r,t))$ of the triple being trustworthy is derived from the energy function:

$$P(E(h,r,t)) = \frac{1}{1 + e^{-\lambda(\delta_r - E(h,r,t))}}, \tag{12}$$

where δ_r is a relationship-specific threshold, and λ is a hyperparameter controlling the smoothing.

- **Global-Level Estimator:** The third estimator uses the *Reachable Paths Inference* (RPI) algorithm to determine whether the triple (h,r,t) is supported by the global KG structure. The estimator evaluates the semantic relevance of paths between h and t by calculating the semantic distance $\mathrm{SD}(p_i, r)$ between the relation r and the relations in path p_i:

$$\mathrm{SD}(p_i(l), r) = \frac{1}{n} \sum_{l_j \in p_i(l)} \frac{r \cdot l_j}{\|r\| \|l_j\|}, \tag{13}$$

where n is the number of relations in the path. A Recurrent Neural Network (RNN) is used to learn a low-dimensional representation of the paths, which is then transformed into a recognition value $RP(h,r,t)$.

Estimator Fusion. The final trustworthiness score is generated by combining the outputs of the three estimators using a multi-layer perceptron (MLP). The feature vector $\mathbf{f}(s)$ for each triple $s = (h,r,t)$ is constructed as:

$$\mathbf{f}(s) = [RR(h,t), P(E(h,r,t)), RP(h,r,t)]. \tag{14}$$

This feature vector is passed through multiple hidden layers, with each layer computed as:

$$h_i = \sigma(W_{hi}\mathbf{f}(s) + b_{hi}), \tag{15}$$

where σ is the non-linear activation function, and W_{hi} and b_{hi} are trainable parameters. The final output layer produces a probability score for the trustworthiness of the triple:

$$p(y = 1|\mathbf{f}(s)) = \phi(W_o h + b_o), \tag{16}$$

where ϕ is the logistic sigmoid function and W_o, b_o are the parameters of the output layer.

CAGED Overview. In traditional KG representation learning, KGs are typically modeled as heterogeneous graphs where entities serve as nodes and relations are treated as semantic edges. However, this approach struggles to effectively capture the intricate correlations across triples. CAGED is designed to efficiently detect errors in large-scale KGs. The key idea is to reframe the KG into various hyper-views (*i.e.*, triple graphs), by treating each relational triple as a node, and then compute the confidence of each triple based on the consistency between its representations learned from these different views. The framework of CAGED is shown in Figure 7.

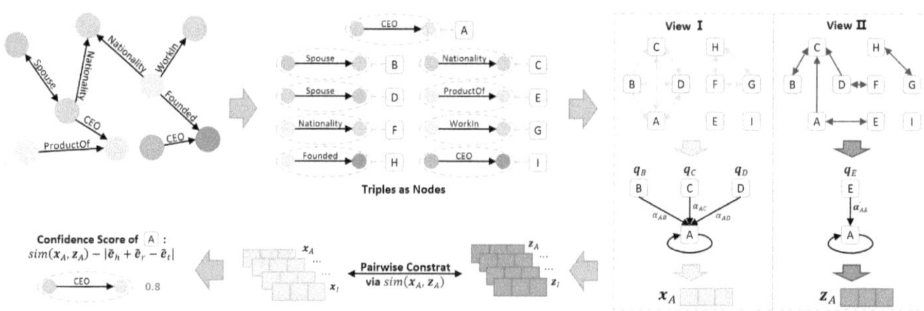

Figure 7. The framework of CAGED.

Knowledge Graph Augmentation. CAGED achieves KG augmentation by generating different views of KG at triple level, which avoids undermining the distribution of potential errors. Specifically, two triple graphs $T_1 = (h_1, r_1, t_1)$ and $T_2 = (h_2, r_2, t_2)$ are created, by regarding each relational triple as nodes and connect them based on two linking patterns: sharing head entity (*i.e.*, $h_1 = h_2 \oplus h_1 = t_2$) and sharing tail entity (*i.e.*, $t_1 = h_2 \oplus t_1 = t_2$). Then two triple graphs with these two linking patterns are constructed, which can be regarded as congruent views of the target KG. Concretely, T_1 models the correlation between relational triples from the perspective of head entity, while T_2 represents the distribution of relational triples from the perspective of tail entities. For normal triples in KGs, it is easy to find enough relevant neighboring triples in T_1, *i.e.*, View *I*, to reconstruct its semantics learned from T_2, *i.e.*, View *II*. Therefore, modeling and measuring the consistency between its representations learned from these two views can help compute the confidence of each triple in the original KG.

Error-aware Encoder - EaGNN. The tailored error-aware KG neural network (EaGNN) is designed as the encoder to capture the rich semantics and structure information of triples in each view, which tightly integrates a local information modeling layer and a global error-aware attention layer that works jointly to get the reliable KG embeddings. Specifically, after randomly initializing the embedding of entities and relations in the original KG, a local information modeling layer *i.e.*, a set of Bi-LSTM units) is adopted to learn the local relational structure within each triple. For the triple (h,r,t), the local information modeling layer is formulated as follows.

$$\tilde{\mathbf{e}}_h, \tilde{\mathbf{e}}_r, \tilde{\mathbf{e}}_t = Bi-LSTM(\mathbf{e}_h, \mathbf{e}_r, \mathbf{e}_t) \tag{17}$$

$$\mathbf{q}_i = [\tilde{\mathbf{e}}_h; \tilde{\mathbf{e}}_r; \tilde{\mathbf{e}}_t] \tag{18}$$

Because the output triple embeddings $\mathbf{q}_i$ could well capture the relational structure within the input triple, they are used as the initial triple embeddings in triple graphs.

Additionally, global contextual information also provides crucial hints for evaluating the trustworthiness of a triple. To reduce the adverse effect of potential errors, a novel triple-level attention mechanism is adopted to learn global triple representations for each view. Concretely, given an anchor triple $\mathbf{q}_i \in \mathbb{R}^d$ in View I, its embedding representation is updated based on the weighted aggregation of its neighbor triples. The weight between the anchor triple i and its neighbor triple j is calculated as:

$$\hat{\alpha}_{ij} = \mathscr{F}(\mathbf{W}\mathbf{q}_i, \mathbf{W}\mathbf{q}_j) \tag{19}$$

where $\hat{\alpha}_{ij}$ indicates the importance of triple j to triple i, $\mathbf{W} \in \mathbb{R}^{n\times d}$ is a learnable linear augmentation matrix to project the initial triple representations into the same vector space, $\mathscr{F}$ is the attentional function: $\mathbb{R}^n \times \mathbb{R}^n \to \mathbb{R}$. Attention coefficients are normalized by applying a softmax function to make them easily comparable across different triples:

$$\bar{\alpha}_{ij} = \frac{\exp(\hat{\alpha}_{ij})}{\sum_{k=1}^{m} \exp(\hat{\alpha}_{ik})} \tag{20}$$

Note that a hyperparameter $\mu \in \mathbb{R}$ is introduced as the threshold to block information that comes from potential anomalous triples, because erroneous triples are relatively irrelevant from their neighbors.

$$\alpha_{ij} = \begin{cases} \mu, & \text{if } \alpha_{ij} > \mu \\ 0, & \text{otherwise} \end{cases} \tag{21}$$

The final error-aware triple representation in View I can be calculated with a sigmoid function, which is depicted as:

$$\mathbf{x}_i = \sigma(\sum_{j=1}^{m} \alpha_{ij}\mathbf{W}\mathbf{q}_j) \tag{22}$$

Similarly, given an anchor triple $\mathbf{q}_i \in \mathbb{R}^d$ in View II, its embedding representation is updated by attending over its neighborhoods' features through:

$$\mathbf{z}_i = \sigma(\sum_{j=1}^{m} \alpha'_{ij}\mathbf{W}\mathbf{q}_j) \tag{23}$$

Joint Confidence Estimation. CAGED integrates KG embedding loss and standard contrastive learning loss to jointly train the model. The KG embedding loss is as follows:

$$\mathcal{L}_{kge} = \sum_{(h,r,t)\in\mathcal{G}} \sum_{(\hat{h},\hat{r},\hat{t})\in\hat{\mathcal{G}}} \max\left(0, \gamma + E(h,r,t) - E(\hat{h},\hat{r},\hat{t})\right) \tag{24}$$

where $E(h,r,t) = ||e_h + e_r - e_t||_2$ is the traditional energy score for translational embedding models following translation assumption. $\gamma > 0$ is the hyperparameter of margin, and $\mathcal{G}$ represents the sampled positive triple set, $\hat{\mathcal{G}}$ represents the negative triple set generated by replacing the head or tail entity randomly.

Normalized temperature-scaled cross entropy loss is employed as the contrastive learning objective to jointly train the model. The loss function is defined as follows:

$$\mathcal{L}_{con}(\mathbf{x}_i, \mathbf{z}_i) = -\log \frac{\exp\left(sim(\mathbf{x}_i, \mathbf{z}_i)/\tau\right)}{\sum_{j\in\{1,2,\ldots,n\}\setminus\{i\}} \exp\left(sim(\mathbf{x}_i, \mathbf{z}_j)/\tau\right)} \tag{25}$$

where $sim(\mathbf{x}_i, \mathbf{z}_i)$ denotes the cosine similarity of multi-view triple representations, *i.e.*, $\mathbf{x}_i$ and $\mathbf{z}_i$.

Upon the features learned, the final confidence score function is defined as follows:

$$C(h,r,t) = \sigma(sim(\mathbf{x}_i, \mathbf{z}_i) - \lambda \cdot E(h,r,t)) \tag{26}$$

where λ is a trade-off parameter to balance the contribution of these two learning signals for error detection, σ is a sigmoid function to map the score into the range of [0, 1].

CCA Overview. Previous works on detecting errors in KGs mainly rely on triple embedding from graph structure, which struggle to discriminate noise from semantically-similar correct triples. CCA integrates both textual and graph structural information from triple reconstruction for better distinguishing semantics. Additionally, interactive contrastive learning is designed to capture the differences between textual and structural patterns. It combines the reconstruction and contrastive learning output and generates pseudo-labels to represent triple confidence. This adaptive confidence guides model training by alleviating noise interference and transferring knowledge between reconstruction and contrastive learning.

Feature Extraction. CCA utilizes text encoder and structure encoder to extract textual features and structural features respectively.

- **Text Encoder.** CCA encodes entity text using pre-trained language models (PLMs) like BERT. It begins by adding the representation of a new entity to the model's vocabulary, leveraging the entity's description D_e and human-readable name N_e to learn its textual representation. Pre-trained prompts are then used to construct new token embeddings, such as through the sentence "*The description of [MASK] is $D_{e'}$* ", where [MASK] represents the entity to be predicted. When encoding a triple (h,r,t), the head and tail entities are masked and reconstructed via the encoder, with textual descriptions of the entities being incorporated to enhance the reconstruction. If the tail entity t is anomalous, it becomes difficult to reconstruct it based on its text description, so the reconstruction loss can be used to evaluate the likelihood of errors in the triple from the textual perspective.

- **Structure Encoder.** To make full use of the graph structure in KGs, CCA builds an entity's subgraph by random sampling and uses Transformer to encode it. Given a triple (h,r,t), it creates two input sequences by masking h and t, according to in-neighbor-set and out-neighbor-set, respectively. Then structure encoder learns the differences between t and the subgraph of h and reconstructs entities from the subgraphs, so errors can be distinguished.

Reconstruction Classifier. Given a triple (h,r,t), the text encoder outputs the representation $\mathbf{e}_h^T$ of the masked head entity. Then the prediction logits against all candidate entities are calculated, and the cross-entropy loss is defined as:

$$\mathscr{L}_h^T = CE(softmax(MLP(\mathbf{e}_h^T), \mathbf{E}^T), \mathbf{y}_h) \tag{27}$$

where $\mathbf{E}^T$ is the matrix of all entity embeddings and $\mathbf{y}_h$ is the corresponding labels. $\mathbf{e}_h^T$ is transferred by a multi-layer perceptron and used to calculate the prediction logits with all embeddings in $\mathbf{E}^T$. Note that the tail entity is reconstructed, and $\mathbf{e}_t^T$ and $\mathscr{L}_t^T$ are calculated in the same way. Additionally, adaptive confidence is introduced to the reconstruction loss and the final text reconstruction loss is as follows:

$$\mathscr{L}_{text} = \sum_{(h,r,t)\in\Gamma} c(h,r,t)(\mathscr{L}_h^T + \mathscr{L}_t^T) \tag{28}$$

where $c(h,r,t)$ is the triple confidence. In the same way, the masked entity losses $\mathscr{L}_h^S$ and $\mathscr{L}_t^S$ and the overall reconstruction loss $\mathscr{L}_{struct}$ are calculated. The final reconstruction loss is as follows:

$$\mathscr{L}_{reconstruction} = \alpha\mathscr{L}_{text} + (1-\alpha)\mathscr{L}_{struct} \tag{29}$$

where α is a hyperparameter to balance the training process. Finally, the scores of the triple (h,r,t) is computed:

$$score_{text} = \mathscr{L}_h^T + \mathscr{L}_t^T \tag{30}$$

$$score_{struct} = \mathscr{L}_h^S + \mathscr{L}_t^S \tag{31}$$

where $score_{text}$ and $score_{struct}$ are the confidence scores from text and structure reconstruction, respectively.

Interactive Contrastive Learning. For a triple (h, r, t), $\mathbf{v}_i^h$ and $\mathbf{v}_i^t$ represent the token embeddings generated from text encoder, $\mathbf{u}_i^h$ and $\mathbf{u}_i^t$ represent the token embeddings generated from structure encoder. $\mathbf{u}_i^t$ has the structural information of$h$ and the reconstruction of t from Transformer. Intuitively, $\mathbf{v}_i^h$ and $\mathbf{u}_i^t$ should be aligned, so that the prediction of h can match its structural information and the prediction of t can match its textual information. Therefore, $\mathbf{v}_i^h$ and $\mathbf{u}_i^t$ are used as one anchor pair and $\mathbf{v}_i^t$ and $\mathbf{u}_i^h$ as the other pair for contrastive learning. Figure 8 shows the overview of interactive contrastive learning.

CCA uses two negative sampling policies to support stable training. First, for the anchor sample from one encoder, a sample randomly selected from the other encoder is taken as one of the negative samples. Second, after randomly replacing the head or tail

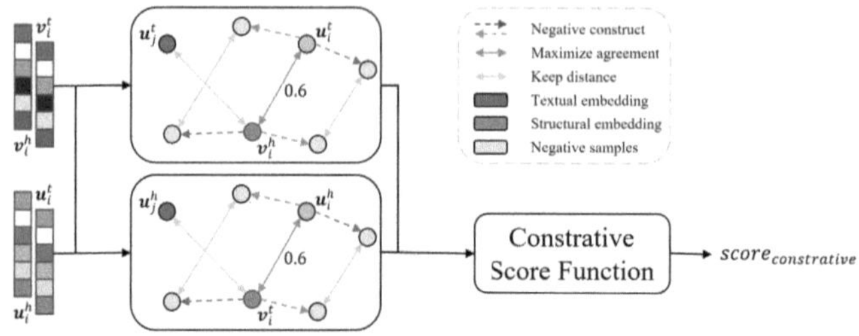

Figure 8. An overview of interactive contrastive learning.

entity of a triple, it is input to two encoders to generate its representation as negative samples.

After generating negative samples, the InfoNCE loss is employed to train interactive contrastive learning. For the anchor pair $\mathbf{v}_i^h$ and $\mathbf{u}_i^t$, the loss is:

$$\mathscr{L}_{ICL}^1(h,r,t) = -log\frac{exp(sim(\mathbf{v}_i^h,\mathbf{u}_i^t))}{exp(sim(\mathbf{v}_i^h,\mathbf{u}_i^t)) + neg\_sim(h,r,t)} \tag{32}$$

where $neg\_sim(h,r,t)$ is the similarity of negative samples. For the other anchor pair $\mathbf{v}_i^t$ and $\mathbf{u}_i^h$, $\mathscr{L}_{ICL}^2(h,r,t)$ is obtained in the same way. Therefore, the final contrastive training loss is:

$$\mathscr{L}_{contr} = \sum_{(h,r,t)\in\Gamma} c(h,r,t)(\mathscr{L}_{ICL}^1(h,r,t) + \mathscr{L}_{ICL}^2(h,r,t)) \tag{33}$$

where $c(h,r,t)$ is the adaptive confidence of the triple (h,r,t). The score function of contrastive learning of (h,r,t) is:

$$score_{constrative} = sim(\mathbf{v}_i^h,\mathbf{u}_j^t) \tag{34}$$

Knowledge Fusion. The reconstruction score $score_{reconstruction}$ is obtained by directly adding $score_{text}$ and $score_{struct}$. Then ranking is used to combine the scores from reconstruction and contrastive learning. The error ranks $R_1(h,r,t)$ and $R_2(h,r,t)$ of each triple is obtained By ranking the error scores $score_{reconstruct}$ and $score_{contrastive}$, and then the final score is:

$$score(h,r,t) = \frac{1}{\left\lceil\frac{R_1(h,r,t)}{\gamma}\right\rceil} + \frac{1}{\left\lceil\frac{R_2(h,r,t)}{\gamma}\right\rceil\beta} \tag{35}$$

where γ is the hyperparameter to control the number of triples with the same score, β is used to balance the scores. A pseudo label set $Z = normalize([z_1,\dots,z_n])$ is generated from the final score, where $z_i \sim N(\mu,\rho)$ and Z is sorted in ascending order. And the final adaptive confidence $c(h,r,t)$ of (h,r,t) is equal to $z_{R(h,r,t)}$, where $R(h,r,t)$ is the rank of $score(h,r,t)$.

3.2. Uncertain Knowledge Representation Learning

Uncertain knowledge representation learning is the process of embedding entities and relations from uncertain KGs into a continuous low-dimensional space while preserving both structural and semantic information. Unlike deterministic KGs, uncertain knowledge graphs (UKGs) associate triples with confidence scores, and thus the embeddings capture not only the relations between entities but also the associated uncertainty information.

The representation learning of UKG can be divided into two types based on application scenarios: learning in normal scenarios and learning in few-shot scenarios. Normal models aim to learn the embeddings of entities and relations in UKGs and represent structure and uncertainty information through these embeddings. And few-shot models apply metric-based learning frameworks under the assumption that each relation only provides a small number of fact samples, which enables these models to better represent situations in the real world where relations have long-tail distributions.

3.2.1. Learning in Normal Scenarios

UKGE [131] and PASSLEAF [132] are two UKG representation learning models that perform well in normal scenarios. We will introduce these two models in detail in this section.

UKGE is the most classic model for UKG representation learning. It mainly consists of embedding-based modeling of fact confidence scores and confidence reasoning for unseen facts using probabilistic soft logic (PSL), the latter essentially serves as a form of data augmentation. The detailed methods used in UKGE are as follows:

Confidence Score of Facts. Given a relation fact triple $l = (h, r, t)$ and their embeddings $\boldsymbol{h}, \boldsymbol{r}, \boldsymbol{t}$, the plausibility of l can be computed as follows:

$$g(l) = \boldsymbol{r} \cdot (\boldsymbol{h} \circ \boldsymbol{t}) \tag{36}$$

where $\circ$ is the element-wise product, and $\cdot$ is the inner product. The function is first adopted by DistMult[133].

To convert plausibility scores into confidence scores, the plausibility scores need to be mapped to a range of 0 to 1. For triple l, its confidence score $f(l)$ can be computed as:

$$f(l) = h(g(l)), h : \mathbb{R} \to [0, 1] \tag{37}$$

where $h(\cdot)$is the transformation function used to map $g(l)$ to $f(l)$. There are two options to compute $h(\cdot)$. The first one is the logistic function:

$$h(x) = \frac{1}{1 + e^{-(\mathbf{w}x + \mathbf{b})}} \tag{38}$$

the other option is the bounded rectifier:

$$h(x) = \min(\max(\mathbf{w}x + \mathbf{b}, 0), 1) \tag{39}$$

where **w** is a weight **b** is a bias. Both of the functions can map plausibility to the range of 0-1. The function (38) is more commonly used, and PASSLEAF is also improved based on function (38).

Using these methods, we can get the confidence score $f(l)$ for each triple l in the UKG.

Optimization Objective. Beyond the existing triples in the KG, UKGE further considers unseen relation facts. One way to deal with unseen relationship facts is to directly treat them as negative samples, that is, to set the ground truth confidence score of these facts directly to 0. The loss of UKGE aims to minimize the mean squared error (MSE) between the ground truth confidence score s_l and the prediction $f(l)$ for each triple. In this case, the loss function of UKGE is:

$$\mathcal{L} = \sum_{l \in D^+} |f(l) - s_l|^2 + \sum_{l \in D^-} |f(l)|^2 \tag{40}$$

where D^+ is the set of observed relation facts, s_l is the ground truth confidence score of fact l, and D^- is the set of unseen facts.

PSL-based Confidence Score Reasoning for Unseen Relation Facts. In the loss function described in Eq. (40), we directly treat the confidence scores of unseen relation facts as 0. However, this approach has limitations in the real world, as it fails to capture the uncertainty of unseen relation facts, which can lead to potential information loss.

To address this issue, UKGE further employs probabilistic soft logic (PSL) to infer the confidence scores of unseen relation facts. This approach enables the propagation of confidence from existing facts to unseen relation facts.

A PSL program consists of a set of first-order logic rules that describe logical dependencies between facts (atoms). PSL associates every atom, *i.e.*, a fact l, with a soft truth value from the interval [0, 1], which corresponds to the confidence score in and enables fuzzy reasoning. The assignment process of soft truth values is called an interpretation. The soft truth value of an atom l is defined as $I(l)$.

The assignment for observed relation facts is their observed confidence scores; for unseen facts, the embedding-based estimated confidence scores will be assigned as the soft truth value, *i.e.*, $f(l)$:

$$\begin{aligned} I(l) &= s_l, l \in D^+ \\ I(l) &= f(l), l \in D^- \end{aligned} \tag{41}$$

In PSL, Lukasiewicz t-norm is used to define the basic logical operations, including logical conjunction ($\wedge$), disjunction ($\vee$), and negation ($\neg$), as follows:

$$l_1 \wedge l_2 = \max\{0, I(l_1) + I(l_2) - 1\} \tag{42}$$

$$l_1 \vee l_2 = \min\{1, I(l_1) + I(l_2)\} \tag{43}$$

$$\neg l_1 = 1 - I(l_1) \tag{44}$$

For a rule $\gamma \equiv \gamma_{bodu} \rightarrow \gamma_{head}$, as it can be written as $\neg\gamma_{body} \vee \gamma_{head}$, thus its value p_γ can be computed as:

$$p_{\gamma_{body} \rightarrow \gamma_{head}} = \min\{1, 1 - I(\gamma_{body}) + I(\gamma_{head})\} \tag{45}$$

therefore, the distance to satisfaction of the ground rule is computed as:

$$d_\gamma = 1 - p_\gamma = \max\{0, I(\gamma_{body}) - I(\gamma_{head})\} \tag{46}$$

this distance will be used as one of the optimization objectives in the loss function. We will illustrate the computation process of PSL rule distance through an example.

Assuming that we have the following two weighted triples in UKG:

1. (college, synonym, university): 0.99

2. (university, synonym, institute): 0.86

Simultaneously, define a logic rule that reflects the transitivity of the "synonym" relationship.

(A,synonym,B) $\wedge$ (B,synonym,C) $\rightarrow$ (A,synonym,C)

By replacing the placeholders in a logical rule with concrete entities and relations, we can get rule instances, which are called ground rules. In this example, substituting the weighted triples into the rule yields the following ground rule:

(college, synonym, university) $\wedge$ (university, synonym, institute) $\rightarrow$ (college, synonym, institute)

Let (college, synonym, university) be l_1, (university, synonym, institute) be l_2, and (college, synonym, institute) be l_3. Note that l_3 is the unseen fact. according to Eqs. (41), (42), and (46), the distance to satisfaction of this ground rule is computed as:

$$\begin{aligned} d_\gamma &= \max\{0, I(l_1 \wedge l_2) - I(l_3)\} \\ &= \max\{0, s_{l_1} + s_{l_2} - 1 - f(l_3)\} \\ &= \max\{0, 0.85 - f(l_3)\} \end{aligned} \tag{47}$$

where s_{l_1} and s_{l_2} are the ground truth confidence scores of corresponding relation facts in the UKG.

As observed, when $f(l_3)$ is greater than or equal to 0.85, the rule distance d_γ is 0, indicating that the ground rule is satisfied. Since $f(l_3)$ is computed through embeddings, incorporating d_γ into the loss function allows for the optimization of $f(l_3)$ to better support the predefined PSL rule. We aim to minimize the rule distance, which means we hope that $f(l_3)$ should be as large as possible within the threshold range.

Compared to methods without PSL, the loss function for unseen facts changes when PSL rules are incorporated:

$$\mathcal{L}^- = \sum_{l \in D^-} \sum_{\gamma \in \Gamma_l} |\psi_\gamma(f(l))|^2 \tag{48}$$

where Γ_l is the set of ground rules with l as the rule head, $\psi_\gamma(f(l))$ denotes the weighted distance to satisfaction $w_\gamma d_\gamma$ of the rule γ, it is a function of $f(l)$ where w_γ is a handcrafted weight for the rule γ.

Note that when l is only covered by $\gamma_0 : \neg l$, we have $\sum_{\gamma \in \Gamma_l} |\psi_\gamma(f(l))|^2 = |f(l)|^2$, this is identical to the unseen facts part in Eq. (40), directly setting the confidence score of unseen facts to 0.

Therefore, the final loss function after incorporating the PSL rule is:

$$\mathscr{L} = \sum_{l \in D^+} |f(l) - s_l|^2 + \sum_{l \in D^-} \sum_{\gamma \in \Gamma_l} \left|\psi_\gamma(f(l))\right|^2 \tag{49}$$

PASSLEAF (Pool-bAsed Semi-Supervised LEArning Framework) is an enhancement built on the UKGE model, addressing two significant issues in UKGE. The first issue is that UKGE is limited by only supporting the DistMult scoring function for computing triple scores. To address this limitation, PASSLEAF introduces a generalized framework that allows the model to handle both semantic-based and translational distance-based confidence scoring functions. The second issue is that UKGE relies on PSL to address false negatives in unseen facts, which requires additional manual labor to define the rules. To overcome this, PASSLEAF proposes a pool-based semi-supervised learning algorithm to resolve the issue of false negatives in unseen facts, thus eliminating the need for extra manual effort. The overview of the PASSLEAF process is shown in Figure 9.

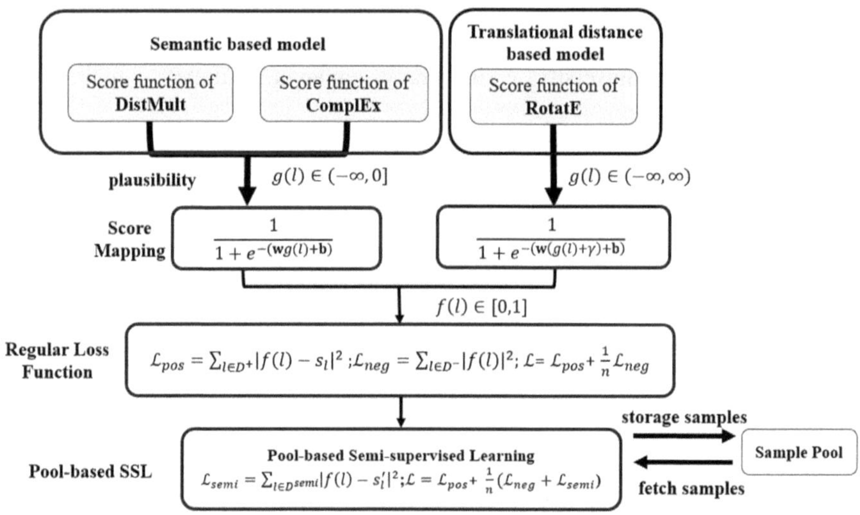

Figure 9. Overview of PASSLEAF

The Framework for Multiple Scoring Functions. As demonstrated in Eq. (36), UKGE utilizes the same score function as DistMult when calculating the confidence score of facts. While semantic-based scoring functions such as DistMult and ComplEx[134] are prevalent, there also exist translational distance-based scoring functions like RotatE[36]. For such scoring functions, directly applying the mapping function in Eq. (38) may work poorly because the plausibility values are negative. To concentrate the range of scores and mitigate this issue, PASSLEAF introduces a hyperparameter γ into the formulation based on Eq. (38):

$$h(x) = \frac{1}{1 + e^{-(\mathbf{w}(x+\gamma)+\mathbf{b})}} \tag{50}$$

Therefore, given a score function, depending on whether the score function is semantic-based or translational distance based, the score function will be mapped by the mapping function in Eqs. (38), and (50) accordingly.

Pool-Based Semi-Supervised Learning. To address the issue of false negatives for unseen facts, PASSLEAF employs a pool-based semi-supervised algorithm. The sample pool enables PASSLEAF to better exploit the benefits of training with past experiences.

The selection of semi-supervised samples in PASSLEAF follows a similar approach to that of randomly sampled negative examples, which involves disrupting the head or tail entities of triples from the training set. Unlike negative samples, the confidence score of semi-supervised samples is generated by the model, rather than being directly set to 0. Specifically, this algorithm works according to the following process:

PASSLEAF maintains a sample pool to keep C latest semi-supervised samples. For each epoch i there are two steps to take.

- First, $N_{new}(i)$ samples and their confidence scores should be generated and stored into the sample pool, where $N_{new}(i)$ is defined as below:

$$N_{new}(i) = \begin{cases} N_{gen}, & \text{if } i \geq T_{\text{NEW SEMI}} \\ 0, & \text{otherwise} \end{cases} \tag{51}$$

  where N_{gen} is the total number of generated samples per training step. The amount of generated samples per positive sample is a hyper-parameter, which is represented as n, N_{gen} is then computed by $n \times$batch size. $T_{\text{NEW SEMI}}$ is the epoch to start generating semi-supervised sample. When the epoch is less than $T_{\text{NEW SEMI}}$, the model does not add samples to the sample pool. In this way, the model will not generate semi-supervised samples until it reaches a relatively stable state.
- Second, we need to select $N_{semi}(i)$ samples from the pool as semi-supervised samples. Correspondingly, the remaining $N_{gen} - N_{semi}(i)$ samples are treated as negative samples. N_{semi} is a clipped linear function, which starts from zero and linearly increments until a given maximum. As the training epochs progress, the weight of semi-supervised samples in the overall training set will gradually increase. N_{semi} is defined as:

$$N_{semi}(i) = \begin{cases} \max\left(M_{\text{SEMI}}, \lfloor \alpha(i - T_{\text{SEMI TRAIN}}) \rfloor\right), & \text{if } i \geq T_{\text{SEMI TRAIN}} \\ 0, & \text{otherwise} \end{cases} \tag{52}$$

  where $T_{\text{SEMI TRAIN}}$ is the epoch to begin fetching samples from the pool, M_{SEMI} sets the upper limit on the number of semi-supervised samples in each batch. α represents the growth rate of the number of semi-supervised samples during the training process, before reaching its maximum value, the number of semi-supervised samples increases gradually with each epoch as the training progresses.

In summary, the process of pool-based semi-supervised learning can be outlined as follows, assuming that the current is the i-th epoch of the training process:

- When i is less than a certain threshold (*i.e.*, $T_{\text{NEW SEMI}}$), the training process remains consistent with UKGE, without generating or introducing any semi-supervised samples. All unseen facts are directly regarded as negative samples.

- when $T_{\text{NEW SEMI}} < i < T_{\text{SEMI TRAIN}}$, the model samples and generates N_{gen} new samples at each step, adding them to the sample pool.
- When i exceeds $T_{\text{NEW SEMI}}$, the model continues to add samples to the pool at each step (until the sample pool reaches its maximum capacity C). Additionally, it fetches $N_{semi}(i)$ semi-supervised samples from the pool at each step for inclusion in the training process, while reducing the number of negative samples to $N_{gen} - N_{semi}(i)$.

Optimization Objective. The loss function for the semi-supervised samples is defined as:

$$\mathscr{L}_{semi} = \sum_{l \in D^{semi}} \left| f(l) - s_l' \right|^2 \tag{53}$$

where D^{semi} represents the set of semi-supervised samples, s_l' is the confidence score of the semi-supervised samples generated by the model.

The overall loss function is the addition of $\mathscr{L}_{semi}$ based on the loss of positive and negative samples:

$$\mathscr{L} = \sum_{l \in D^{+}} |f(l) - s_l|^2 + \frac{1}{n}\Big(\sum_{l \in D^{-}} |f(l)|^2 + \sum_{l \in D^{semi}} \left| f(l) - s_l' \right|^2\Big) \tag{54}$$

3.2.2. Learning in Few-Shot Scenarios

Few-shot uncertain knowledge representation learning is a specialized method designed to handle situations where only a small number of examples are available for learning the relations in UKGs. Unlike standard scenarios that have ample data, few-shot settings necessitate specialized learning strategies that effectively generalize from sparse factual instances. This approach integrates structural, semantic, and uncertainty information, often utilizing metric-based frameworks to enable robust representation learning in scenarios where knowledge exhibits long-tail distributions and relations are underrepresented in the training data.

One of the most influential contributions is GMUC (Gaussian Metric Learning for Few-Shot Uncertain Knowledge Graph Completion) [135]. It first considers the long-tail distribution of relations in UKG completion tasks and formulates the problem as few-shot UKG completion, addressing the problem of internal uncertainty of entities and relations in KGs. In light of the success of GMUC, GMUC+ [136] introduces element-level uncertainty by quantifying the semantic uncertainty of entities and relations, which allows the model to more accurately capture uncertainty information, thereby improving performance in confidence prediction and link prediction tasks.

GMUC Overview. In few-shot settings, the already limited number of samples presents significant challenges. However, a more difficult problem is the substantial uncertainty inherent in these samples, resulting in highly ambiguous semantics for both entities and relations. This ambiguity prevents the model from learning accurate semantic representations of entities and relations effectively. To address the challenges mentioned above, compared to UKGE [131], which simultaneously embeds semantic information and confidence information into the same semantic space, GMUC separates the semantic representation and uncertainty representation into two distinct spaces, as shown in

Figure 10. This avoids confusion and interference between the two types of information, making it easier to combine different features for triple reasoning and confidence prediction respectively.

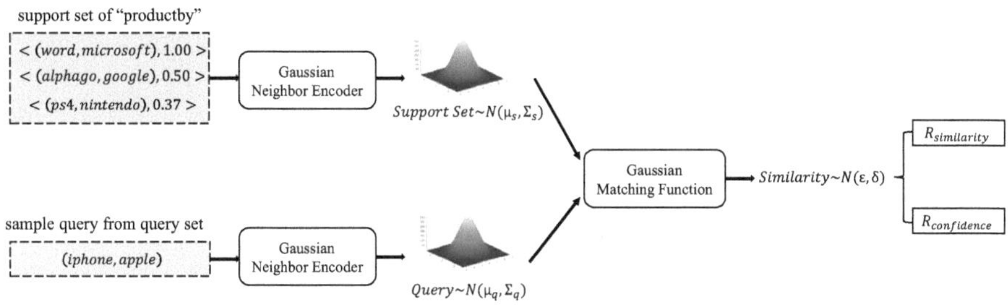

Figure 10. The framework of GMUC

Gaussian Neighbor Encoder. GMUC first encodes each triple in the query set and support set into a multi-dimensional Gaussian distribution using a Gaussian neighbor encoder. The Gaussian Neighbor Encoder is designed to enhance the representation of each entity using its local structure. GMUC leverages two heterogeneous neighbor encoders NE_μ and NE_Σ to learn enhanced mean embeddings μ and variance embeddings Σ of triples respectively. The neighbors of entity h are represented by $N_h = \{(r_i, t_i), s_i\}$, where s_i is the confidence score, and the attention module computes the impact of each neighbor on the overall representation. The calculation of a heterogeneous neighbor encoder is expressed as:

$$NE_*(h) = \tanh\left(\sum_i s_i \alpha_i e^*_{t_i}\right) \tag{55}$$

$$\alpha_i = \frac{\exp\left(u^T_{rt}\left(W_{rt}\left(e^*_{r_i} \oplus e^*_{t_i}\right) + b_{rt}\right)\right)}{\sum_j \exp\left(u^T_{rt}\left(W_{rt}\left(e^*_{r_j} \oplus e^*_{t_j}\right) + b_{rt}\right)\right)} \tag{56}$$

where $*$ could be μ or Σ, $e^\mu_{t_i}$ and $e^\mu_{r_i}$ are mean embeddings of t_i and r_i, $e^\Sigma_{t_i}$ and $e^\Sigma_{r_i}$ are variance embeddings of t_i and r_i. Moreover, $u_{rt} \in \mathbb{R}^{d\times 1}$, $W_{rt} \in \mathbb{R}^{d\times 2d}$ and $b_{rt} \in \mathbb{R}^{d\times 1}$ are learnable parameters, $\oplus$ is a concatenation operator.

Each triple in the support set and query is modeled as a Gaussian distribution with mean μ and variance Σ, calculated as:

$$\mu = \left[NE_\mu(h_k) \oplus NE_\mu(t_k)\right] \tag{57}$$

$$\Sigma = \left[NE_\Sigma(h_k) \oplus NE_\Sigma(t_k)\right] \tag{58}$$

To aggregate information from the support set, max-pooling is applied over the neighbors' distributions to obtain the final Gaussian distribution for each support set:

$$\mu_s = \text{pool}_{\max}(s_i \cdot \mu_i) \tag{59}$$

$$\Sigma_s = \text{pool}_{\max}(s_i \cdot \Sigma_i) \tag{60}$$

The Gaussian neighbor encoder captures both structural and uncertainty information for entities and relations, which is essential for UKG representation learning, particularly in few-shot scenarios.

Gaussian Matching Function. The Gaussian matching function is designed to measure the similarity between a query triple and triples in the support set. GMUC defines the matching similarity *Similarity* as a one-dimensional Gaussian distribution $\mathcal{N}(\varepsilon, \delta)$, where ε is the most likely similarity value, and $\delta \in [0,1]$ represents the variance (uncertainty) of the similarity.

To compute the *Similarity*, GMUC employs LSTM-based matching networks. Let x and y be the embeddings of the entities to be matched. The similarity score is calculated by iterating over the embeddings using the LSTM cell:

$$MN(x,y) = g_t \cdot x \tag{61}$$

$$g_t = g'_t + y \tag{62}$$

$$g'_t, c_t = \text{LSTM}(y, [g_{t-1} \oplus x, c_{t-1}]) \tag{63}$$

where g_t and c_t are the hidden and cell states of the LSTM at time step t, and $\oplus$ denotes the concatenation operator. The outputs of two distinct matching networks, MN_ε and MN_δ, are used to compute the mean value ε and variance δ of the similarity:

$$\varepsilon = MN_\varepsilon(\mu_s, \mu_q) \tag{64}$$

$$\delta = \text{sigmoid}(W \cdot MN_\delta(\Sigma_s, \Sigma_q) + b) \tag{65}$$

where W and b are learnable parameters, and sigmoid is the activation function that bounds δ between 0 and 1. The final similarity and confidence scores are calculated as:

$$R_{\text{similarity}} = \varepsilon + \lambda(1 - \delta) \tag{66}$$

$$R_{\text{confidence}} = 1 - \delta \tag{67}$$

Here, λ is a hyper-parameter, controlling the influence of uncertainty on the final similarity score. These scores are used to rank and predict missing triples and their corresponding confidence values.

The training process involves learning to minimize a joint loss function that balances the ranking of triples with their respective confidence scores. Given the few-shot nature of the task, GMUC's training is performed over a meta-training task set, where each relation is treated as a task. Through iterative updates, the model learns to generalize across relations, allowing for more accurate prediction of missing triples and their confidence scores, even with limited examples.

GMUC+ Overview. GMUC+ extends the core ideas of GMUC by incorporating element-level uncertainty for more refined UKG embeddings. While GMUC successfully separates semantic and uncertainty representations into distinct spaces, GMUC+ goes further by introducing specific metrics to quantify the uncertainty of both entities and relations. This approach leads to more accurate modeling of the inherent imprecision present in few-shot UKGs. By measuring uncertainty through intrinsic information content (IIC) for entities and utilizing domain and range metrics for relations, GMUC+ provides a more precise and structured way to handle the uncertainty embedded in UKGs. The innovations in GMUC+ compared to GMUC are summarized as follows:

- **Element-Level Uncertainty:** GMUC+ incorporates uncertainty at the semantic level, quantifying the imprecision of entities and relations using metrics such as intrinsic information content for entities and domain/range-based uncertainty for relations.
- **Improved Uncertainty Modeling:** By adding a constraint between the measured uncertainty and the variance in the Gaussian distribution, GMUC+ ensures a more accurate representation of uncertainty. This leads to enhanced predictions in tasks such as tail entity prediction and confidence score estimation.
- **Enhanced Metric-Based Learning:** GMUC+ leverages a more refined metric-based learning framework that combines both semantic and uncertainty information, resulting in better few-shot predictions for missing triples and their corresponding confidence scores.

Uncertainty Quantification. To measure the uncertainty of entities, GMUC+ utilizes *Intrinsic Information Content* (IIC), which assesses the degree of semantic abstraction of an entity. Entities that are closer to the root of a taxonomy have lower IIC values, indicating higher uncertainty due to their broader and more abstract nature. The formula for calculating IIC is:

$$\mathrm{IIC}(c) = 1 - \frac{\log(\mathrm{hypo}(c)+1)}{\log(N)} \tag{68}$$

where c is an entity in the taxonomy, N is the total number of concepts in the taxonomy, and $\mathrm{hypo}(c)$ denotes the number of hyponyms for entity c.

The uncertainty of relations is measured based on their domain and range, representing the diversity of entities a relation connects. GMUC+ defines the relation uncertainty as follows:

$$UCr(r) = |Dr| \times |Rr| \tag{69}$$

where $|Dr|$ and $|Rr|$ are the sizes of the domain and range sets for relation r, respectively. This approach ensures that relations connecting a broader range of entities are assigned higher uncertainty.

Gaussian Representation and Learning Framework. GMUC+ models each entity and relation as a multi-dimensional Gaussian distribution $N(\mu,\sigma)$, where μ denotes the mean embedding and σ denotes the variance (uncertainty) embedding. The norm of the variance vector is constrained to reflect the measured uncertainty and a loss function is introduced to optimize this relationship:

$$\mathscr{L}_{\text{unc}} = \sum_{i \in E \cup R} w \cdot \|\sigma_i\|^2 + b - UC(i) \tag{70}$$

where w and b are learnable parameters, $\|\sigma_i\|^2$ is the l_2 norm of the variance vector, and $UC(i)$ represents the uncertainty of entity or relation i.

This uncertainty-aware framework allows GMUC+ to improve performance in few-shot settings by capturing both the semantic and uncertainty information of entities and relations more effectively than previous methods.

3.2.3. Uncertain Knowledge Reasoning with unKR

unKR [137] is an open-source Python library designed specifically for UKG reasoning via representation learning. unKR allows users to conduct confidence prediction and link prediction tasks efficiently using a unified framework that supports both normal and few-shot scenarios.

unKR supports the reproduction of nine well-known UKG representation learning models, as well as the customization of new models for specific research needs. The library standardizes evaluation metrics for UKG reasoning, facilitating fair comparisons across different models. The core functionality of unKR is its ability to estimate the confidence of triples and predict missing relations in UKGs. With its comprehensive implementation, unKR empowers researchers to efficiently perform UKG completion, error detection, and confidence reasoning tasks. Examples of specific tasks include:

- **Confidence Prediction:** Estimating the confidence score of a given triple (h,r,t).
- **Link Prediction:** Predicting the missing entity in a triple when given a head entity and relation, or a tail entity and relation.

4. Applications

The exploration of knowledge from certainty to uncertainty within the context of AI offers profound implications across various domains, revealing the dynamic interplay between structured knowledge and the inherent unpredictability of real-world scenarios [138,139,140,141]. This transition not only emphasizes the technological strides in modeling, extracting, and representing knowledge but also highlights the critical applications of these concepts in practical settings.

Decision Support Systems. Decision support systems (DSS) are quintessential applications of AI where certain knowledge is leveraged to make informed decisions. By utilizing ontologies, knowledge bases, and enhanced parameters, these systems can provide expert advice in fields such as healthcare [142,143], finance [144,145], and urban planning [146,147]. For instance, in healthcare, a DSS can use knowledge extracted and enhanced through AI models to suggest treatment plans based on patient data, clinical guidelines, and published research, navigating through both certain knowledge (*e.g.*, diagnosed conditions) and uncertainties (*e.g.*, patient responses to treatments).

Intelligent Search Engines. The application of certain and uncertain knowledge is also pivotal in the development of intelligent search engines. These platforms go beyond keyword matching, employing language models and multimodal data to understand and predict user intent, enhancing the relevance of search results. For example, search engines can use symbol-parametric methods and knowledge modeling techniques to interpret queries in a more nuanced manner, handling ambiguity and personalization with greater finesse.

Autonomous Systems. Autonomous systems, such as self-driving cars and automated manufacturing robots, rely heavily on a mixture of certain and uncertain knowledge. These systems utilize ontologies and enhanced neural network parameters to navigate and operate in complex environments. They must process and react to uncertain situations on the road or in the factory by integrating real-time sensor data with pre-trained models, showcasing the critical role of adaptive knowledge systems in handling unpredictable elements.

Personalized Learning Environments. In education, personalized learning environments use AI to adapt content and teaching strategies to individual needs. By extracting knowledge from LLMs pre-trained on diverse educational materials and student interactions, these systems can offer tailored educational experiences that adjust to the learning pace and style of each student, managing the certainty of subject matter expertise with the uncertainty of individual learning trajectories.

Smart Home Assistants. Finally, smart home assistants represent a blend of certain and uncertain knowledge applications. These devices use voice commands and NLP to perform tasks ranging from setting reminders to controlling home automation systems. They must understand and predict user preferences and behaviors, often dealing with ambiguous or incomplete commands, to provide effective and personalized assistance.

Each of these applications demonstrates how AI, through the frameworks of knowledge modeling, representation, acquisition, and enhancement, can navigate the continuum from certainty to uncertainty, driving innovation and effectiveness in real-world applications. This exploration is vital for developing AI systems that are not only intelligent but also robust and adaptable in the face of the complex, often uncertain realities they are designed to manage.

5. Conclusion

This chapter explores the evolution from structured, deterministic AI systems to those proficient in managing uncertainty. We examined traditional knowledge modeling with ontologies and rules, progressing to dynamic knowledge representation through symbols and language models. Key discussions included advanced techniques for knowledge acquirement and augmentation, such as probing LLMs and employing RAG. Further, we address uncertain knowledge, emphasizing computational and learning strategies for handling ambiguity in AI applications. This exploration underlines the necessity for AI systems to navigate between certain and uncertain knowledge, highlighting the ongoing advancements that enhance their adaptability and effectiveness in real-world scenarios.

In summary, this exploration from certainty to uncertainty in knowledge has highlighted not only the theoretical advancements and methodological innovations in AI but also underscored the practical implications of these developments in real-world applications. As AI continues to advance, the ability to seamlessly navigate between certainty and uncertainty will become increasingly crucial in enhancing the robustness, adaptability, and effectiveness of AI systems across various domains. This shift is not merely technical but philosophical, urging us to rethink how knowledge is perceived, processed, and utilized in the age of intelligent machines.

Acknowledgments

We would like to express gratitude to the coauthors of this handbook for their kind and helpful comments. This work was supported by the National Natural Science Foundation of China (No. 62206246, 62376058), the Fundamental Research Funds for the Central Universities (226-2023-00138, 2242022R40045), Zhejiang Provincial Natural Science Foundation of China (No. LGG22F030011), Yongjiang Talent Introduction Programme (2021A-156-G), Zhejiang University, NUS-NCS Joint Laboratory (A-0008542-00-00), and ZhiShan Young Scholar Program of Southeast University.

References

[1] Chen H, Deng S, Zhang W, Xu Z, Li J, Kharlamov E. Neural symbolic reasoning with knowledge graphs: Knowledge extraction, relational reasoning, and inconsistency checking. Fundamental Research. 2021;1(5):565-73. Available from: https://www.sciencedirect.com/science/article/pii/S266732582100159X.

[2] Stanley J. Knowledge and certainty. Philosophical Issues. 2008;18:35-57. Available from: https://www.jstor.org/stable/27749898.

[3] Townsend DM, Hunt RA, McMullen JS, Sarasvathy SD. Uncertainty, knowledge problems, and entrepreneurial action. Academy of Management Annals. 2018;12(2):659-87. Available from: https://journals.aom.org/doi/abs/10.5465/annals.2016.0109.

[4] Zhao WX, Zhou K, Li J, Tang T, Wang X, Hou Y, et al. A Survey of Large Language Models. arXiv preprint. 2023;abs/2303.18223. Available from: https://doi.org/10.48550/arXiv.2303.18223.

[5] Yin S, Fu C, Zhao S, Li K, Sun X, Xu T, et al. A Survey on Multimodal Large Language Models. arXiv preprint. 2023;abs/2306.13549. Available from: https://doi.org/10.48550/arXiv.2306.13549.

[6] Zhu Y, Wang X, Chen J, Qiao S, Ou Y, Yao Y, et al. LLMs for Knowledge Graph Construction and Reasoning: Recent Capabilities and Future Opportunities. CoRR. 2023;abs/2305.13168. Available from: https://doi.org/10.48550/arXiv.2305.13168.

[7] Gao Y, Xiong Y, Gao X, Jia K, Pan J, Bi Y, et al. Retrieval-Augmented Generation for Large Language Models: A Survey. CoRR. 2023;abs/2312.10997. Available from: https://doi.org/10.48550/arXiv.2312.10997.

[8] Huang Y, Huang J. A Survey on Retrieval-Augmented Text Generation for Large Language Models. CoRR. 2024;abs/2404.10981. Available from: https://doi.org/10.48550/arXiv.2404.10981.

[9] Yao Y, Wang P, Tian B, Cheng S, Li Z, Deng S, et al. Editing Large Language Models: Problems, Methods, and Opportunities. In: EMNLP. Association for Computational Linguistics; 2023. p. 10222-40.

[10] Wang S, Zhu Y, Liu H, Zheng Z, Chen C, Li J. Knowledge Editing for Large Language Models: A Survey. CoRR. 2023;abs/2310.16218. Available from: https://doi.org/10.48550/arXiv.2310.16218.

[11] Mazzia V, Pedrani A, Caciolai A, Rottmann K, Bernardi D. A Survey on Knowledge Editing of Neural Networks. CoRR. 2023;abs/2310.19704. Available from: https://doi.org/10.48550/arXiv.2310.19704.

[12] Zhang N, Yao Y, Tian B, Wang P, Deng S, Wang M, et al. A Comprehensive Study of Knowledge Editing for Large Language Models. CoRR. 2024;abs/2401.01286. Available from: https://doi.org/10.48550/arXiv.2401.01286.

[13] Guarino N, Oberle D, Staab S. What Is an Ontology? In: Handbook on Ontologies. International Handbooks on Information Systems. Springer; 2009. p. 1-17. Available from: https://doi.org/10.1007/978-3-540-92673-3_0.

[14] Decker S, Melnik S, van Harmelen F, Fensel D, Klein MCA, Broekstra J, et al. The Semantic Web: The Roles of XML and RDF. IEEE Internet Comput. 2000;4(5):63-74. Available from: https://doi.org/10.1109/4236.877487.

[15] McBride B. The Resource Description Framework (RDF) and its Vocabulary Description Language RDFS. In: Handbook on Ontologies. International Handbooks on Information Systems. Springer; 2004. p. 51-66.

[16] Grosof BN, Horrocks I, Volz R, Decker S. Description logic programs: combining logic programs with description logic. In: WWW. ACM; 2003. p. 48-57. Available from: https://doi.org/10.1145/775152.775160.

[17] Clocksin WF, Mellish CS. Programming in PROLOG. Springer Science & Business Media; 2003. Available from: https://athena.ecs.csus.edu/~mei/logicp/Programming_in_Prolog.pdf.

[18] Ceri S, Gottlob G, Tanca L. What you Always Wanted to Know About Datalog (And Never Dared to Ask). IEEE Trans Knowl Data Eng. 1989;1(1):146-66. Available from: https://doi.org/10.1109/69.43410.

[19] Boley H, Tabet S, Wagner G. Design Rationale for RuleML: A Markup Language for Semantic Web Rules. In: SWWS; 2001. p. 381-401. Available from: http://www.semanticweb.org/SWWS/program/full/paper20.pdf.

[20] Horrocks I, Patel-Schneider PF, Boley H, Tabet S, Grosof B, Dean M, et al. SWRL: A semantic web rule language combining OWL and RuleML. W3C Member submission. 2004;21(79):1-31. Available from: https://www.w3.org/submissions/SWRL/.

[21] Lenat DB. CYC: A Large-Scale Investment in Knowledge Infrastructure. Commun ACM. 1995;38(11):32-8. Available from: https://doi.org/10.1145/219717.219745.

[22] Bozsak E, Ehrig M, Handschuh S, Hotho A, Maedche A, Motik B, et al. KAON - Towards a Large Scale Semantic Web. In: EC-Web. vol. 2455 of Lecture Notes in Computer Science. Springer; 2002. p. 304-13. Available from: https://doi.org/10.1007/3-540-45705-4_32.

[23] Proctor M. Drools: A Rule Engine for Complex Event Processing. In: Schürr A, Varró D, Varró G, editors. AGTIVE. vol. 7233 of Lecture Notes in Computer Science. Springer; 2011. p. 2. Available from: https://doi.org/10.1007/978-3-642-34176-2_2.

[24] Yang G, Kifer M, Zhao C, Chowdhary V. Flora-2: User's manual. Department of Computer Science, Stony Brook University, Stony Brook. 2002:49. Available from: https://www.cin.ufpe.br/~if684/refs/FloraManual.pdf.

[25] Kozlenkov A, Schroeder M. PROVA: Rule-Based Java-Scripting for a Bioinformatics Semantic Web. In: DILS. vol. 2994 of Lecture Notes in Computer Science. Springer; 2004. p. 17-30. Available from: https://doi.org/10.1007/978-3-540-24745-6_2.

[26] Pennington J, Socher R, Manning CD. Glove: Global vectors for word representation. In: Proceedings of the 2014 conference on empirical methods in natural language processing (EMNLP); 2014. p. 1532-43.

[27] Wu Q, Wang P, Shen C, Dick A, Van Den Hengel A. Ask me anything: Free-form visual question answering based on knowledge from external sources. In: Proceedings of the IEEE conference on computer vision and pattern recognition; 2016. p. 4622-30.

[28] Le Q, Mikolov T. Distributed representations of sentences and documents. In: International conference on machine learning. PMLR; 2014. p. 1188-96.

[29] Narasimhan M, Lazebnik S, Schwing A. Out of the box: Reasoning with graph convolution nets for factual visual question answering. Advances in neural information processing systems. 2018;31.

[30] Zhang L, Liu S, Liu D, Zeng P, Li X, Song J, et al. Rich visual knowledge-based augmentation network for visual question answering. IEEE Transactions on Neural Networks and Learning Systems. 2020;32(10):4362-73.

[31] Xie X, Zhang N, Li Z, Deng S, Chen H, Xiong F, et al. From discrimination to generation: Knowledge graph completion with generative transformer. In: Companion Proceedings of the Web Conference 2022; 2022. p. 162-5.

[32] Saxena A, Kochsiek A, Gemulla R. Sequence-to-Sequence Knowledge Graph Completion and Question Answering. In: Proceedings of the 60th Annual Meeting of the Association for Computational Linguistics (Volume 1: Long Papers); 2022. p. 2814-28.

[33] Wang Q, Mao Z, Wang B, Guo L. Knowledge graph embedding: A survey of approaches and applications. IEEE transactions on knowledge and data engineering. 2017;29(12):2724-43.

[34] Bordes A, Usunier N, Garcia-Duran A, Weston J, Yakhnenko O. Translating embeddings for modeling multi-relational data. Advances in neural information processing systems. 2013;26.

[35] Wang Z, Zhang J, Feng J, Chen Z. Knowledge Graph Embedding by Translating on Hyperplanes. In: AAAI. AAAI Press; 2014. p. 1112-9. Available from: https://doi.org/10.1609/aaai.v28i1.8870.

[36] Sun Z, Deng Z, Nie J, Tang J. RotatE: Knowledge Graph Embedding by Relational Rotation in Complex Space. In: ICLR (Poster). OpenReview.net; 2019. Available from: https://openreview.net/forum?id=HkgEQnRqYQ.

[37] Dettmers T, Minervini P, Stenetorp P, Riedel S. Convolutional 2D Knowledge Graph Embeddings. In: AAAI. AAAI Press; 2018. p. 1811-8. Available from: https://doi.org/10.1609/aaai.v32i1.11573.

[38] Shevchenko V, Teney D, Dick A, van den Hengel A. Reasoning over Vision and Language: Exploring the Benefits of Supplemental Knowledge. In: Proceedings of the Third Workshop on Beyond Vision and LANguage: inTEgrating Real-world kNowledge (LANTERN); 2021. p. 1-18.

[39] Garcia-Olano D, Onoe Y, Ghosh J. Improving and diagnosing knowledge-based visual question answering via entity enhanced knowledge injection. In: Companion Proceedings of the Web Conference 2022; 2022. p. 705-15.

[40] Lerer A, Wu L, Shen J, Lacroix T, Wehrstedt L, Bose A, et al. Pytorch-biggraph: A large scale graph embedding system. Proceedings of Machine Learning and Systems. 2019;1:120-31.

[41] Petroni F, Rocktäschel T, Riedel S, Lewis P, Bakhtin A, Wu Y, et al. Language Models as Knowledge Bases? In: Proceedings of the 2019 Conference on Empirical Methods in Natural Language Processing and the 9th International Joint Conference on Natural Language Processing (EMNLP-IJCNLP); 2019. p. 2463-73.

[42] Geva M, Schuster R, Berant J, Levy O. Transformer Feed-Forward Layers Are Key-Value Memories. In: Proceedings of the 2021 Conference on Empirical Methods in Natural Language Processing; 2021. p. 5484-95.

[43] Dai D, Dong L, Hao Y, Sui Z, Chang B, Wei F. Knowledge Neurons in Pretrained Transformers. In: Proceedings of the 60th Annual Meeting of the Association for Computational Linguistics (Volume 1: Long Papers); 2022. p. 8493-502.

[44] Meng K, Bau D, Andonian A, Belinkov Y. Locating and editing factual associations in GPT. Advances in Neural Information Processing Systems. 2022;35:17359-72.

[45] Chen Y, Cao P, Chen Y, Liu K, Zhao J. Journey to the Center of the Knowledge Neurons: Discoveries of Language-Independent Knowledge Neurons and Degenerate Knowledge Neurons. In: AAAI. AAAI Press; 2024. p. 17817-25. Available from: https://doi.org/10.1609/aaai.v38i16.29735.

[46] Gueta A, Venezian E, Raffel C, Slonim N, Katz Y, Choshen L. Knowledge is a Region in Weight Space for Fine-tuned Language Models. In: Findings of the Association for Computational Linguistics: EMNLP 2023; 2023. p. 1350-70.

[47] Niu J, Liu A, Zhu Z, Penn G. What does the Knowledge Neuron Thesis Have to do with Knowledge? In: The Twelfth International Conference on Learning Representations; 2024. .

[48] Yao Y, Zhang N, Xi Z, Wang M, Xu Z, Deng S, et al. Knowledge Circuits in Pretrained Transformers. arXiv preprint arXiv:240517969. 2024.

[49] Ma X, Hovy EH. End-to-end Sequence Labeling via Bi-directional LSTM-CNNs-CRF. In: Proceedings of the 54th Annual Meeting of the Association for Computational Linguistics, ACL 2016, August 7-12, 2016, Berlin, Germany, Volume 1: Long Papers. The Association for Computer Linguistics; 2016. Available from: https://doi.org/10.18653/v1/p16-1101.

[50] Liu Y, Meng F, Zhang J, Xu J, Chen Y, Zhou J. GCDT: A Global Context Enhanced Deep Transition Architecture for Sequence Labeling. In: Korhonen A, Traum DR, Màrquez L, editors. Proceedings of the 57th Conference of the Association for Computational Linguistics, ACL 2019, Florence, Italy, July 28- August 2, 2019, Volume 1: Long Papers. Association for Computational Linguistics; 2019. p. 2431-41. Available from: https://doi.org/10.18653/v1/p19-1233.

[51] Liu K, Fu Y, Tan C, Chen M, Zhang N, Huang S, et al. Noisy-Labeled NER with Confidence Estimation. In: Proceedings of NAACL. Association for Computational Linguistics; 2021. p. 3437-45. Available from: https://doi.org/10.18653/v1/2021.naacl-main.269.

[52] Fritzler A, Logacheva V, Kretov M. Few-shot classification in named entity recognition task. In: Hung C, Papadopoulos GA, editors. Proceedings of the 34th ACM/SIGAPP Symposium on Applied Computing, SAC 2019, Limassol, Cyprus, April 8-12, 2019. ACM; 2019. p. 993-1000. Available from: https://doi.org/10.1145/3297280.3297378.

[53] Wiseman S, Stratos K. Label-Agnostic Sequence Labeling by Copying Nearest Neighbors. In: Korhonen A, Traum DR, Màrquez L, editors. Proceedings of the 57th Conference of the Association for Computational Linguistics, ACL 2019, Florence, Italy, July 28- August 2, 2019, Volume 1: Long Papers. Association for Computational Linguistics; 2019. p. 5363-9. Available from: https://doi.org/10.18653/v1/p19-1533.

[54] Yang Y, Katiyar A. Simple and Effective Few-Shot Named Entity Recognition with Structured Nearest Neighbor Learning. In: Webber B, Cohn T, He Y, Liu Y, editors. Proceedings of the 2020 Conference on Empirical Methods in Natural Language Processing, EMNLP 2020, Online, November 16-20, 2020. Association for Computational Linguistics; 2020. p. 6365-75. Available from: https://doi.org/10.18653/v1/2020.emnlp-main.516.

[55] Ziyadi M, Sun Y, Goswami A, Huang J, Chen W. Example-Based Named Entity Recognition. CoRR. 2020;abs/2008.10570. Available from: https://arxiv.org/abs/2008.10570.

[56] Henderson M, Vulic I. ConVEx: Data-Efficient and Few-Shot Slot Labeling. In: Toutanova K, Rumshisky A, Zettlemoyer L, Hakkani-Tür D, Beltagy I, Bethard S, et al., editors. Proceedings of the 2021 Conference of the North American Chapter of the Association for Computational Linguistics: Human Language Technologies, NAACL-HLT 2021, Online, June 6-11, 2021. Association for Computational Linguistics; 2021. p. 3375-89. Available from: https://doi.org/10.18653/v1/2021.naacl-main.264.

[57] Hou Y, Che W, Lai Y, Zhou Z, Liu Y, Liu H, et al. Few-shot Slot Tagging with Collapsed Dependency Transfer and Label-enhanced Task-adaptive Projection Network. In: Jurafsky D, Chai J, Schluter N, Tetreault JR, editors. Proceedings of the 58th Annual Meeting of the Association for Computational Linguistics, ACL 2020, Online, July 5-10, 2020. Association for Computational Linguistics; 2020. p. 1381-93. Available from: https://doi.org/10.18653/v1/2020.acl-main.128.

[58] Lin H, Lu Y, Han X, Sun L. Sequence-to-Nuggets: Nested Entity Mention Detection via Anchor-Region Networks. In: Korhonen A, Traum DR, Màrquez L, editors. Proceedings of the 57th Conference of the Association for Computational Linguistics, ACL 2019, Florence, Italy, July 28- August 2, 2019, Volume 1: Long Papers. Association for Computational Linguistics; 2019. p. 5182-92. Available from: https://doi.org/10.18653/v1/p19-1511.

[59] Ding N, Xu G, Chen Y, Wang X, Han X, Xie P, et al. Few-NERD: A Few-shot Named Entity Recognition Dataset. In: Zong C, Xia F, Li W, Navigli R, editors. Proceedings of the 59th Annual Meeting of the Association for Computational Linguistics and the 11th International Joint Conference on Natural Language Processing, ACL/IJCNLP 2021, (Volume 1: Long Papers), Virtual Event, August 1-6, 2021. Association for Computational Linguistics; 2021. p. 3198-213. Available from: https://doi.org/10.18653/v1/2021.acl-long.248.

[60] Cui L, Wu Y, Liu J, Yang S, Zhang Y. Template-Based Named Entity Recognition Using BART. In: Zong C, Xia F, Li W, Navigli R, editors. Findings of the Association for Computational Linguistics: ACL/IJCNLP 2021, Online Event, August 1-6, 2021. vol. ACL/IJCNLP 2021 of Findings of ACL. Association for Computational Linguistics; 2021. p. 1835-45. Available from: https://doi.org/10.18653/v1/2021.findings-acl.161.

[61] Chen X, Li L, Deng S, Tan C, Xu C, Huang F, et al. LightNER: A Lightweight Tuning Paradigm for Low-resource NER via Pluggable Prompting. In: Proceedings of the 29th International Conference on Computational Linguistics; 2022. p. 2374-87.

[62] Wang S, Sun X, Li X, Ouyang R, Wu F, Zhang T, et al. Gpt-ner: Named entity recognition via large language models. arXiv preprint arXiv:230410428. 2023.

[63] Zhang N, Chen X, Xie X, Deng S, Tan C, Chen M, et al. Document-level Relation Extraction as Semantic Segmentation. In: Proceedings of IJCAI 2021; 2021. .

[64] Zhang N, Ye H, Deng S, Tan C, Chen M, Huang S, et al. Contrastive Information Extraction With Generative Transformer. IEEE ACM Trans Audio Speech Lang Process. 2021.

[65] Mintz M, Bills S, Snow R, Jurafsky D. Distant supervision for relation extraction without labeled data. In: Proceedings of the Joint Conference of the 47th Annual Meeting of the ACL and the 4th International Joint Conference on Natural Language Processing of the AFNLP; 2009. p. 1003-11.

[66] Gao T, Han X, Liu Z, Sun M. Hybrid Attention-Based Prototypical Networks for Noisy Few-Shot

Relation Classification. In: AAAI. AAAI Press; 2019. p. 6407-14. Available from: https://doi.org/10.1609/aaai.v33i01.33016407.
[67] Dong B, Yao Y, Xie R, Gao T, Han X, Liu Z, et al. Meta-Information Guided Meta-Learning for Few-Shot Relation Classification. In: Proceedings of COLING 2020; 2020. .
[68] Qu M, Gao T, Xhonneux LP, Tang J. Few-shot relation extraction via bayesian meta-learning on relation graphs. In: International conference on machine learning. PMLR; 2020. p. 7867-76.
[69] Han X, Zhao W, Ding N, Liu Z, Sun M. Ptr: Prompt tuning with rules for text classification. AI Open. 2022;3:182-92.
[70] Chen X, Zhang N, Xie X, Deng S, Yao Y, Tan C, et al. Knowprompt: Knowledge-aware prompt-tuning with synergistic optimization for relation extraction. In: Proceedings of the ACM Web conference 2022; 2022. p. 2778-88.
[71] Zhang N, Xu X, Tao L, Yu H, Ye H, Qiao S, et al. DeepKE: A Deep Learning Based Knowledge Extraction Toolkit for Knowledge Base Population. In: Proceedings of the 2022 Conference on Empirical Methods in Natural Language Processing: System Demonstrations; 2022. p. 98-108.
[72] Xu X, Chen X, Zhang N, Xie X, Chen X, Chen H. Towards Realistic Low-resource Relation Extraction: A Benchmark with Empirical Baseline Study. In: Findings of the Association for Computational Linguistics: EMNLP 2022; 2022. p. 413-27.
[73] Xu X, Zhu Y, Wang X, Zhang N. How to Unleash the Power of Large Language Models for Few-shot Relation Extraction? In: Proceedings of The Fourth Workshop on Simple and Efficient Natural Language Processing (SustaiNLP); 2023. p. 190-200.
[74] Lou D, Liao Z, Deng S, Zhang N, Chen H. MLBiNet: A Cross-Sentence Collective Event Detection Network. In: Proceedings of the 59th Annual Meeting of the Association for Computational Linguistics and the 11th International Joint Conference on Natural Language Processing (Volume 1: Long Papers); 2021. p. 4829-39.
[75] Chen Y, Liu S, Zhang X, Liu K, Zhao J. Automatically labeled data generation for large scale event extraction. In: Proceedings of the 55th Annual Meeting of the Association for Computational Linguistics (Volume 1: Long Papers); 2017. p. 409-19.
[76] Liu J, Chen Y, Liu K, Bi W, Liu X. Event Extraction as Machine Reading Comprehension. In: Proceedings of EMNLP 2020; 2020. .
[77] Wang XD, Weber L, Leser U. Biomedical Event Extraction as Multi-turn Question Answering. In: Proceedings of LOUHI@EMNLP 2020; 2020. .
[78] Deng S, Mao S, Zhang N, Hooi B. SPEECH: Structured Prediction with Energy-Based Event-Centric Hyperspheres. In: Proceedings of the 61st Annual Meeting of the Association for Computational Linguistics (Volume 1: Long Papers); 2023. p. 351-63.
[79] Wei J, Wang X, Schuurmans D, Bosma M, Ichter B, Xia F, et al. Chain-of-Thought Prompting Elicits Reasoning in Large Language Models. In: NeurIPS; 2022. Available from: http://papers.nips.cc/paper_files/paper/2022/hash/8bb0d291acd4acf06ef112099c16f326-Abstract-Conference.html.
[80] Yao S, Yu D, Zhao J, Shafran I, Griffiths TL, Cao Y, et al. Tree of Thoughts: Deliberate Problem Solving with Large Language Models. In: NeurIPS; 2023. Available from: https://doi.org/10.48550/arXiv.2305.10601.
[81] Besta M, Blach N, Kubicek A, Gerstenberger R, Gianinazzi L, Gajda J, et al. Graph of Thoughts: Solving Elaborate Problems with Large Language Models. CoRR. 2023;abs/2308.09687. Available from: https://doi.org/10.48550/arXiv.2308.09687.
[82] Li X, Zhao R, Chia YK, Ding B, Bing L, Joty SR, et al. Chain of Knowledge: A Framework for Grounding Large Language Models with Structured Knowledge Bases. In: ICLR. OpenReview.net; 2024. Available from: https://openreview.net/forum?id=cPgh4gWZlz.
[83] Yu W, Zhang H, Pan X, Ma K, Wang H, Yu D. Chain-of-note: Enhancing robustness in retrieval-augmented language models. arXiv preprint arXiv:231109210. 2023.
[84] Gao Y, Xiong Y, Gao X, Jia K, Pan J, Bi Y, et al. Retrieval-augmented generation for large language models: A survey. arXiv preprint arXiv:231210997. 2023.
[85] Guu K, Lee K, Tung Z, Pasupat P, Chang M. Retrieval augmented language model pre-training. In: International conference on machine learning. PMLR; 2020. p. 3929-38.
[86] Borgeaud S, Mensch A, Hoffmann J, Cai T, Rutherford E, Millican K, et al. Improving language models by retrieving from trillions of tokens. In: International conference on machine learning. PMLR; 2022. p. 2206-40.
[87] Wang B, Ping W, Xu P, McAfee L, Liu Z, Shoeybi M, et al. Shall we pretrain autoregressive language

models with retrieval? a comprehensive study. arXiv preprint arXiv:230406762. 2023.
[88] Izacard G, Lewis P, Lomeli M, Hosseini L, Petroni F, Schick T, et al. Atlas: Few-shot learning with retrieval augmented language models. Journal of Machine Learning Research. 2023;24(251):1-43.
[89] Shi W, Min S, Yasunaga M, Seo M, James R, Lewis M, et al. Replug: Retrieval-augmented black-box language models. arXiv preprint arXiv:230112652. 2023.
[90] Cheng D, Huang S, Bi J, Zhan Y, Liu J, Wang Y, et al. Uprise: Universal prompt retrieval for improving zero-shot evaluation. arXiv preprint arXiv:230308518. 2023.
[91] Cheng X, Luo D, Chen X, Liu L, Zhao D, Yan R. Lift yourself up: Retrieval-augmented text generation with self-memory. Advances in Neural Information Processing Systems. 2024;36.
[92] Asai A, Wu Z, Wang Y, Sil A, Hajishirzi H. Self-RAG: Learning to Retrieve, Generate, and Critique through Self-Reflection. In: The Twelfth International Conference on Learning Representations; 2024. .
[93] Khattab O, Santhanam K, Li XL, Hall D, Liang P, Potts C, et al. Demonstrate-search-predict: Composing retrieval and language models for knowledge-intensive nlp. arXiv preprint arXiv:221214024. 2022.
[94] Sun Z, Wang X, Tay Y, Yang Y, Zhou D. Recitation-Augmented Language Models. In: The Eleventh International Conference on Learning Representations; 2023. .
[95] Feng Z, Feng X, Zhao D, Yang M, Qin B. Retrieval-generation synergy augmented large language models. In: ICASSP 2024-2024 IEEE International Conference on Acoustics, Speech and Signal Processing (ICASSP). IEEE; 2024. p. 11661-5.
[96] Trivedi H, Balasubramanian N, Khot T, Sabharwal A. Interleaving retrieval with chain-of-thought reasoning for knowledge-intensive multi-step questions. arXiv preprint arXiv:221210509. 2022.
[97] Zou A, Phan L, Chen S, Campbell J, Guo P, Ren R, et al. Representation engineering: A top-down approach to ai transparency. arXiv preprint arXiv:231001405. 2023.
[98] Sinitsin A, Plokhotnyuk V, Pyrkin DV, Popov S, Babenko A. Editable Neural Networks. In: ICLR. OpenReview.net; 2020. Available from: https://openreview.net/forum?id=HJedXaEtvS.
[99] Cao ND, Aziz W, Titov I. Editing Factual Knowledge in Language Models. In: EMNLP (1). Association for Computational Linguistics; 2021. p. 6491-506. Available from: https://doi.org/10.18653/v1/2021.emnlp-main.522.
[100] Meng K, Sharma AS, Andonian AJ, Belinkov Y, Bau D. Mass-Editing Memory in a Transformer. In: The Eleventh International Conference on Learning Representations, ICLR 2023, Kigali, Rwanda, May 1-5, 2023. OpenReview.net; 2023. Available from: https://openreview.net/pdf?id=MkbcAHIYgyS.
[101] Huang Z, Shen Y, Zhang X, Zhou J, Rong W, Xiong Z. Transformer-Patcher: One Mistake Worth One Neuron. In: ICLR. OpenReview.net; 2023. Available from: https://openreview.net/forum?id=4oYUGeGBPm.
[102] Mitchell E, Lin C, Bosselut A, Manning CD, Finn C. Memory-Based Model Editing at Scale. In: Chaudhuri K, Jegelka S, Song L, Szepesvári C, Niu G, Sabato S, editors. International Conference on Machine Learning, ICML 2022, 17-23 July 2022, Baltimore, Maryland, USA. vol. 162 of Proceedings of Machine Learning Research. PMLR; 2022. p. 15817-31. Available from: https://proceedings.mlr.press/v162/mitchell22a.html.
[103] Madaan A, Tandon N, Clark P, Yang Y. Memory-assisted prompt editing to improve GPT-3 after deployment. In: Goldberg Y, Kozareva Z, Zhang Y, editors. Proceedings of the 2022 Conference on Empirical Methods in Natural Language Processing, EMNLP 2022, Abu Dhabi, United Arab Emirates, December 7-11, 2022. Association for Computational Linguistics; 2022. p. 2833-61. Available from: https://doi.org/10.18653/v1/2022.emnlp-main.183.
[104] Zheng C, Li L, Dong Q, Fan Y, Wu Z, Xu J, et al. Can We Edit Factual Knowledge by In-Context Learning? In: Bouamor H, Pino J, Bali K, editors. Proceedings of the 2023 Conference on Empirical Methods in Natural Language Processing, EMNLP 2023, Singapore, December 6-10, 2023. Association for Computational Linguistics; 2023. p. 4862-76. Available from: https://aclanthology.org/2023.emnlp-main.296.
[105] Dong Q, Dai D, Song Y, Xu J, Sui Z, Li L. Calibrating Factual Knowledge in Pretrained Language Models. In: Goldberg Y, Kozareva Z, Zhang Y, editors. Findings of the Association for Computational Linguistics: EMNLP 2022, Abu Dhabi, United Arab Emirates, December 7-11, 2022. Association for Computational Linguistics; 2022. p. 5937-47. Available from: https://doi.org/10.18653/v1/2022.findings-emnlp.438.
[106] Huang Z, Shen Y, Zhang X, Zhou J, Rong W, Xiong Z. Transformer-Patcher: One Mistake Worth

One Neuron. In: The Eleventh International Conference on Learning Representations, ICLR 2023, Kigali, Rwanda, May 1-5, 2023. OpenReview.net; 2023. Available from: https://openreview.net/pdf?id=4oYUGeGBPm.

[107] Hartvigsen T, Sankaranarayanan S, Palangi H, Kim Y, Ghassemi M. Aging with GRACE: Lifelong Model Editing with Discrete Key-Value Adaptors. In: Advances in Neural Information Processing Systems; 2023. Available from: http://papers.nips.cc/paper_files/paper/2023/hash/95b6e2ff961580e03c0a662a63a71812-Abstract-Conference.html.

[108] Wang P, Li Z, Zhang N, Xu Z, Yao Y, Jiang Y, et al. WISE: Rethinking the Knowledge Memory for Lifelong Model Editing of Large Language Models. arXiv preprint arXiv:240514768. 2024.

[109] Dai D, Dong L, Hao Y, Sui Z, Chang B, Wei F. Knowledge Neurons in Pretrained Transformers. In: Muresan S, Nakov P, Villavicencio A, editors. Proceedings of the 60th Annual Meeting of the Association for Computational Linguistics (Volume 1: Long Papers), ACL 2022, Dublin, Ireland, May 22-27, 2022. Association for Computational Linguistics; 2022. p. 8493-502. Available from: https://doi.org/10.18653/v1/2022.acl-long.581.

[110] Cao ND, Aziz W, Titov I. Editing Factual Knowledge in Language Models. In: Moens M, Huang X, Specia L, Yih SW, editors. Proceedings of the 2021 Conference on Empirical Methods in Natural Language Processing, EMNLP 2021, Virtual Event / Punta Cana, Dominican Republic, 7-11 November, 2021. Association for Computational Linguistics; 2021. p. 6491-506. Available from: https://doi.org/10.18653/v1/2021.emnlp-main.522.

[111] Tan C, Zhang G, Fu J. Massive Editing for Large Language Models via Meta Learning. CoRR. 2023;abs/2311.04661. Available from: https://doi.org/10.48550/arXiv.2311.04661.

[112] Mitchell E, Lin C, Bosselut A, Finn C, Manning CD. Fast Model Editing at Scale. In: The Tenth International Conference on Learning Representations, ICLR 2022, Virtual Event, April 25-29, 2022. OpenReview.net; 2022. Available from: https://openreview.net/forum?id=0DcZxeWfOPt.

[113] Wang P, Zhang N, Tian B, Xi Z, Yao Y, Xu Z, et al. EasyEdit: An Easy-to-use Knowledge Editing Framework for Large Language Models. In: Proceedings of the 62nd Annual Meeting of the Association for Computational Linguistics (Volume 3: System Demonstrations). Association for Computational Linguistics; 2024. p. 82-93. Available from: https://aclanthology.org/2024.acl-demos.9.

[114] Levy O, Seo M, Choi E, Zettlemoyer L. Zero-Shot Relation Extraction via Reading Comprehension. In: CoNLL. Association for Computational Linguistics; 2017. p. 333-42. Available from: https://doi.org/10.18653/v1/K17-1034.

[115] Raffel C, Shazeer N, Roberts A, Lee K, Narang S, Matena M, et al. Exploring the Limits of Transfer Learning with a Unified Text-to-Text Transformer. J Mach Learn Res. 2020;21:140:1-140:67. Available from: http://jmlr.org/papers/v21/20-074.html.

[116] Wang B, Komatsuzaki A. GPT-J-6B: A 6 billion parameter autoregressive language model. Software; 2021.

[117] Hase P, Hofweber T, Zhou X, Stengel-Eskin E, Bansal M. Fundamental Problems With Model Editing: How Should Rational Belief Revision Work in LLMs? arXiv preprint arXiv:240619354. 2024.

[118] Wang M, Yao Y, Xu Z, Qiao S, Deng S, Wang P, et al. Knowledge mechanisms in large language models: A survey and perspective. arXiv preprint arXiv:240715017. 2024.

[119] Biesialska M, Biesialska K, Costa-jussà MR. Continual Lifelong Learning in Natural Language Processing: A Survey. In: COLING. International Committee on Computational Linguistics; 2020. p. 6523-41. Available from: https://doi.org/10.18653/v1/2020.coling-main.574.

[120] Wu G, Hashemi M, Srinivasa C. PUMA: Performance Unchanged Model Augmentation for Training Data Removal. In: AAAI Conference on Artificial Intelligence; 2022. Available from: https://ojs.aaai.org/index.php/AAAI/article/view/20846.

[121] Tarun AK, Chundawat VS, Mandal M, Kankanhalli MS. Fast Yet Effective Machine Unlearning. IEEE transactions on neural networks and learning systems. 2021;PP. Available from: https://ieeexplore.ieee.org/abstract/document/10113700.

[122] Tian B, Liang X, Cheng S, Liu Q, Wang M, Sui D, et al. To Forget or Not? Towards Practical Knowledge Unlearning for Large Language Models. arXiv preprint arXiv:240701920. 2024.

[123] Wang M, Zhang N, Xu Z, Xi Z, Deng S, Yao Y, et al. Detoxifying Large Language Models via Knowledge Editing. arXiv preprint arXiv:240314472. 2024.

[124] Xie R, Liu Z, Lin F, Lin L. Does William Shakespeare Really Write Hamlet? Knowledge Representation Learning with Confidence. In: AAAI. vol. 32; 2018. .

[125] Jia S, Xiang Y, Chen X, Wang K. Triple Trustworthiness Measurement for Knowledge Graph. In: The

World Wide Web Conference; 2019. p. 2865-71.

[126] Shi B, Weninger T. Discriminative Predicate Path Mining for Fact Checking in Knowledge Graphs. In: Knowledge-Based Systems. vol. 104; 2016. p. 123-33.

[127] Belth C, Zheng X, Vreeken J, Koutra D. What is Normal, What is Strange, and What is Missing in a Knowledge Graph: Unified Characterization via Inductive Summarization. In: The Web Conference; 2020. p. 1115-26.

[128] Bordes A, Usunier N, Garcia-Duran A, Weston J, Yakhnenko O. Translating embeddings for modeling multi-relational data. Advances in neural information processing systems. 2013;26.

[129] Zhang Q, Dong J, Duan K, Huang X, Liu Y, Xu L. Contrastive Knowledge Graph Error Detection. In: CIKM; 2022. p. 2590-9.

[130] Liu X, Liu Y, Hu W. Knowledge Graph Error Detection with Contrastive Confidence Adaption. In: AAAI. vol. 38; 2024. p. 8824-31.

[131] Chen X, Chen M, Shi W, Sun Y, Zaniolo C. Embedding Uncertain Knowledge Graphs. In: AAAI. vol. 33; 2019. p. 3363-70.

[132] Chen ZM, Yeh MY, Kuo TW. PASSLEAF: A Pool-bAsed Semi-Supervised Learning Framework for Uncertain Knowledge Graph Embedding. In: AAAI. vol. 35; 2021. p. 4019-26.

[133] Yang B, Yih Wt, He X, Gao J, Deng L. Embedding entities and relations for learning and inference in knowledge bases. arXiv preprint arXiv:14126575. 2014.

[134] Trouillon T, Welbl J, Riedel S, Gaussier É, Bouchard G. Complex Embeddings for Simple Link Prediction. In: ICML; 2016. p. 2071-80.

[135] Zhang J, Wu T, Qi G. Gaussian Metric Learning for Few-Shot Uncertain Knowledge Graph Completion. In: DASFAA; 2021. p. 256-71.

[136] Wang J, Wu T, Zhang J. Incorporating Uncertainty of Entities and Relations into Few-Shot Uncertain Knowledge Graph Embedding. In: CCKS; 2022. p. 16-28.

[137] Wang J, Wu T, Chen S, Liu Y, Zhu S, Li W, et al. unKR: A Python Library for Uncertain Knowledge Graph Reasoning by Representation Learning. In: SIGIR; 2024. p. 2822-6.

[138] Pan JZ, Vetere G, Gomez-Perez JM, Wu H. Exploiting linked data and knowledge graphs in large organisations. Springer; 2017. Available from: https://doi.org/10.1007/978-3-319-45654-6.

[139] Wen B, Deng S, Chen H. Knowledge-Enhanced Collaborative Meta Learner for Long-Tail Recommendation. In: CCKS. vol. 1356 of Communications in Computer and Information Science. Springer; 2020. p. 322-33. Available from: https://doi.org/10.1007/978-981-16-1964-9_26.

[140] Guo Q, Zhuang F, Qin C, Zhu H, Xie X, Xiong H, et al. A Survey on Knowledge Graph-Based Recommender Systems. IEEE Transactions on Knowledge and Data Engineering. 2020. Available from: https://doi.org/10.1109/TKDE.2020.3028705.

[141] Li Y, Huang C, Deng S, Lock ML, Cao T, Oo N, et al. KnowPhish: Large Language Models Meet Multimodal Knowledge Graphs for Enhancing Reference-Based Phishing Detection. In: USENIX Security Symposium. USENIX Association; 2024. Available from: https://www.usenix.org/conference/usenixsecurity24/presentation/li-yuexin.

[142] Liu F, You C, Wu X, Ge S, Wang S, Sun X. Auto-Encoding Knowledge Graph for Unsupervised Medical Report Generation. In: NeurIPS; 2021. p. 16266-79. Available from: https://proceedings.neurips.cc/paper/2021/hash/876e1c59023b1a0e95808168e1a8ff89-Abstract.html.

[143] Fang Y, Zhang Q, Yang H, Zhuang X, Deng S, Zhang W, et al. Molecular Contrastive Learning with Chemical Element Knowledge Graph. In: Thirty-Sixth AAAI Conference on Artificial Intelligence, AAAI 2022, Thirty-Fourth Conference on Innovative Applications of Artificial Intelligence, IAAI 2022, The Twelveth Symposium on Educational Advances in Artificial Intelligence, EAAI 2022 Virtual Event, February 22 - March 1, 2022. AAAI Press; 2022. p. 3968-76. Available from: https://ojs.aaai.org/index.php/AAAI/article/view/20313.

[144] Ding X, Zhang Y, Liu T, Duan J. Knowledge-Driven Event Embedding for Stock Prediction. In: COLING 2016, 26th International Conference on Computational Linguistics, Proceedings of the Conference: Technical Papers, December 11-16, 2016, Osaka, Japan. ACL; 2016. p. 2133-42. Available from: https://aclanthology.org/C16-1201/.

[145] Deng S, Zhang N, Zhang W, Chen J, Pan JZ, Chen H. Knowledge-Driven Stock Trend Prediction and Explanation via Temporal Convolutional Network. In: WWW (Companion Volume). ACM; 2019. p. 678-85. Available from: https://doi.org/10.1145/3308560.3317701.

[146] Celino A, Concilio G, Liddo AD. Managing Knowledge in Urban Planning: Can Memory Support Systems Help? In: Knowledge Management In Action. vol. 270 of IFIP. Springer; 2008. p. 51-65.

Available from: https://doi.org/10.1007/978-0-387-09659-9_5.
[147] Yigitcanlar T. Planning for knowledge-based urban development: global perspectives. J Knowl Manag. 2009;13(5):228-42. Available from: https://doi.org/10.1108/13673270910988079.

Handbook on Neurosymbolic AI and Knowledge Graphs
P. Hitzler et al. (Eds.)
IOS Press, 2025

doi:10.3233/FAIA250215

Trustworthy Knowledge Graphs: Practices and Approaches

Bohui ZHANG [a], Elisavet KOUTSIANA [a], Yihang ZHAO [a], Albert MEROÑO-PEÑUELA [a] and Elena SIMPERL [a,1]
[a] *King's College London, London, UK*
ORCiD ID: Bohui Zhang https://orcid.org/0000-0001-5430-1624, Elisavet Koutsiana https://orcid.org/0000-0001-6544-0435, Yihang Zhao https://orcid.org/0009-0009-2436-8145, Albert Meroño-Peñuela https://orcid.org/0000-0003-4646-5842, Elena Simperl https://orcid.org/0000-0003-1722-947X

Abstract. Knowledge graphs (KGs) are essential in human-centered AI by reducing the need for extensive labeled machine-learning datasets, enhancing retrieval-augmented generation, and facilitating explanations. However, modern KG construction has evolved into a complex, semi-automated process, increasingly reliant on opaque deep-learning models and a multitude of heterogeneous data sources to achieve the scale and meet the requirements of downstream applications. As such, the KG lifecycle poses the same risks as any other AI context; designing AI assistants for KG construction requires a deeper understanding of emerging knowledge engineering practices, with a greater focus on automation with human oversight, as well as bespoke solutions to ensure transparency, accountability, fairness, and other trustworthy AI concerns. This chapter undertakes a comprehensive exploration of trustworthy KG construction through a systematic literature review combined with a series of use cases and user studies. It highlights tasks in the KG lifecycle where automation is underexplored, introduces new AI assistants for such KG tasks, and discusses gaps in research, datasets, and capabilities to use AI responsibly.

Keywords. Knowledge graphs, Trustworthy AI, AI assistants, Knowledge graph construction, Explainable AI

1. Introduction

To reach its potential, AI needs data and context. Without the right (amounts of) data, machine learning (ML) cannot identify patterns or make predictions. Without a deeper understanding of context, AI applications cannot engage people in a meaningful way. Knowledge graphs (KGs) [1], a term coined by Google in 2012 to refer to its general-purpose knowledge base, are critical to both: they reduce the need for large labeled ML datasets [2], enhance pre-trained language models (PLMs) [3,4], and generate explanations [5]. KGs are routinely used alongside ML in many applications, including search, question answering, recommendation [1] and, in industry contexts, enterprise data management, digital twins, supply chain management, procurement, and regulatory compli-

[1] Corresponding Author: Elena Simperl, E-mail: `elena.simperl@kcl.ac.uk`.

ance [6]. Moreover, with the rise of large language models (LLMs) such as GPT [7,8] and Llama series [9,10,11], KGs and LLMs have influenced each other in both ways: LLMs for KGs (using LLMs for KG construction and maintenance) and KGs for LLMs (using KGs to train, prompt, augment, and evaluate LLMs) [12].

As AI applications produce and consume more data, engineering KGs has evolved into a complex, semi-automatic process that increasingly relies on opaque deep-learning models and vast collections of heterogeneous data sources to scale to graphs with millions of entities and billions of statements [13,14]. The KG lifecycle is not transparent [15], accountability is limited, and accounts of how biased a KG is [16] or how fair the downstream applications that use it [17] are patchy. KGs are thus at odds with AI regulation, for instance UK's AI regulation[2], the EU's AI Act[3], and the US's AI Risk Management Framework (AI RMF 1.0)[4] with ongoing efforts elsewhere in AI to systematically audit and debias data and algorithms and to enhance AI trustworthiness [18,19,20,21,22]. Most regulators take a risk-based approach to the use of AI, prescribing, among other things, transparency and accountability obligations for different classes of AI applications. Organizations using KGs, either directly as data infrastructure, or as graph embeddings in ML models, need to document and attest that their KGs are compliant with the law. Furthermore, when a KG is part of an AI application that counts as high-risk, that application will have to undergo conformity assessments both at design and at run time. KGs themselves are meant to make ML models explainable [5] and hence facilitate such compliance tasks, but that would imply that the KG lifecycle abides by the same rules.

As referred to our previous work [23,24], questions regarding the user-centric aspects of knowledge engineering are yet not to be fully answered, such as users' tasks and goals, the way that they interact with KGs, KG construction tools, and KG-related applications. Up-to-date comparative surveys regarding the scale, complexity, and degree of automation of knowledge graph construction systems nowadays are needed. User-centric design and empirical methods should be established for trustworthy knowledge graph construction to ensure that human-centric challenges are not overlooked.

In this chapter, we would like to advance the field of **trustworthy knowledge graphs** to allow KG stakeholders to rely appropriately on AI algorithms and use KGs with confidence [25]. We explore the user-centric challenges in the KG lifecycle and practices. We aim to understand how AI technologies can be used to automate knowledge engineering (KE) and identify gaps in transparency, accountability, fairness, and explainability. The following sections start with a user study to investigate how knowledge engineers and AI researchers use generative AI, aiming to understand the changes in KE practices and the researchers' needs (Section 2). Our findings highlight several challenges, the need for researchers' support at different interaction levels with generative AI, and significant gaps in awareness and application of safety issues. Based on our findings, we introduce the OntoChat framework, an AI assistant designed to support ontology engineering tasks (Section 3). We conduct the second user study to evaluate the effectiveness and trustworthiness of generative AI-assisted user story writing. Finally, we present the second use case, focusing on schema generation and potential explainable solutions (Section 4). Additionally, we provide a literature review of state-of-the-art

[2]`https://www.gov.uk/government/publications/ai-regulation-a-pro-innovation-approach`
[3]`https://artificialintelligenceact.eu`
[4]`https://doi.org/10.6028/NIST.AI.100-1`

explainable AI methods in KE and introduce the third user study, which aims to offer a blueprint for designing explainable solutions tailored to KE tasks.

2. Generative AI for Knowledge Engineering Tasks: The User View

The emergence of generative AI and the development of LLMs have transformed the way researchers work in various fields, including KE. While knowledge engineers have been utilizing natural language processing (NLP) methods and tools to automate tasks, the impact of LLMs on these practices is not yet fully understood. As previously mentioned, we believe that the user-centric aspects of knowledge engineering remain unexplored, especially with the use of generative AI. To delve deeper into this topic, we conducted a user study.

During August 2023, we organized a four-day research hackathon for knowledge engineers and AI researchers to investigate KE with prompt engineering[5]. The hackathon format offered a tool to explore emerging practices as KE processes and approaches are disrupted by generative AI. The hackathon hosted 39 participants from 15 different institutes and various environments from academia and industry. The hackathon attendees were selected based on their background and experience with KE. During the hackathon, participants were split into 7 groups of 5 to 7 members, based on their research background and prior experience in KE. Participants received high-level descriptions of the projects but were free to choose which tools, methodologies, domains, and LLM techniques they focused on. Details can be found on [26].

Data Collection In this study, data was collected during and after the hackathon using three approaches to ensure both depth and comprehensiveness.

1. **Ethnographic observation** Two researchers performed an ethnographic observation study, using the 'observer as participant' technique for ethnographic research [27]. The technique moves the observer into the study environment and closer to the activity of interest. The participants are aware of the observer, but the observer is not engaging with the participants and does not ask or interact with anyone. The researchers observed the various groups and kept detailed notes of the 7 groups' interactions and decisions. We collected two sets of observation notes.
2. **Documents collected from the hackathon** Research output in the form of reports and documentation from the hackathon was collected. Hackathon groups produced reports regarding their experience answering specific questions and slide presentations with their strategies and results. This resulted in 7 presentations and reports. These two data collection activities were conducted contemporaneously with the hackathon.
3. **Semi-structured interviews** After the hackathon, we contacted 14 participants who had volunteered to participate in follow-up interviews to talk about their opinions and experiences interacting with LLMs for KE tasks. Interviewees had backgrounds in KG construction, KG explainability, ontologies, and machine learning, as well as biology and bioinformatics, data management, FAIR data [28], and digital humanities. We conducted these interviews virtually between

[5] `https://king-s-knowledge-graph-lab.github.io/knowledge-prompting-hackathon/`

Table 1. Themes identified through the inductive analysis.

Themes	Description
Challenges	Challenges that participants face while using LLMs for KE tasks
Skills	The skills and qualities participants have or need to gain to interact with LLMs
Safety issues	Participants opinions related to AI safety testing

August 17, 2023, and September 6, 2023 using Microsoft Teams. The interview guide can be found in [26].

Data Analysis To address our research questions, we conducted thematic analysis across all the data. We first used an inductive method to search for key themes from the interview topic guide. Table 1 shows three of the main themes identified. We then used a deductive method. We read the data corpus again for grounded themes that emerged in the data.

Ethics The ethnographic and documentary studies were approved by King's College London's Ethical Advisory Committee. The documentary data were collected as an output of the hackathon [26].

2.1. Main Challenges of LLMs for KE

Testing the use of LLMs for KE tasks has been challenging for all participants. Our observations during the hackathon revealed that the main concerns were identifying the appropriate dataset to use, prompting LLMs efficiently, and evaluating the LLM outputs. We asked interviewees which of these they considered important.

Dataset Interviewees (1), (14), and (12) emphasized the importance of datasets as a starting point, and groups used prompting as a means to create a dataset (Observer 1). Without a dataset, they felt they could not continue with prompting and evaluation (14). "There are many codes online to interact with language models that wasn't any problem at all. And the evaluation, given that you possess the ground truth, was not too difficult. So, the most challenging case work for us was finding a dataset" (8). Finding a dataset was challenging for specific group tasks, mainly because of the time pressure (14) and fast planning (1) needed to find and set domain knowledge for the task. On the other hand, an interviewee noted that LLMs should support establishing datasets. "The dataset is not what concerns me because, if anything, I'm pretty impressed with what large language models could potentially do in terms of extracting, like I was saying, concepts, relationships, maybe even constraints or parameters or universal restrictions or existential restrictions, from unstructured data" (13).

Prompting Many participants noted the time-consuming phase of iteratively testing prompts to receive desirable outcomes (3) (Observer 1). Some suggested the usefulness of possible "templates for prompting" (Observer 1), (Observer 2), (3), and (13). In addition, "once we settled on a specific prompt, it seems like it works well enough; the most tricky part of it was to make the language model consistent in its responses" (3). This was particularly problematic when the process was automated with thousands of prompting iterations. Furthermore, syntactical errors also break the scripts and prevent automation (3). In contrast, an interviewee pointed out that prompting engineering is "less scientific" and models "with billions of parameters are not controllable, resulting in an output that you cannot reproduce one hour later, two days later, this might be a problem" (9).

Evaluation Participants believed that evaluation is challenging mostly due to the lack of benchmarks for specific KE activities, which depend on manual intervention, "so there are papers doing auto-prompting. I'm a little biased towards evaluation simply because in my tasks, evaluation pretty much boils down to a manual evaluation; there's no other way to do it. It's not that we have solved the dataset problem, but we can synthesize some datasets, or create them artificially somehow. Evaluation still remains a challenge because. it has to be done manually" (5). In the case of using a specific controlled dataset for KG construction, the accuracy and coverage of the KG can be automatically evaluated (2), (10). However, in tasks such as designing competency questions or an ontology, there is not always a gold standard to compare with, and manual work from an expert is needed to evaluate the output. "There is no automatic way to assess how well the ontology represents the domain knowledge" (11). Nevertheless, exploring the use of holistic LLM benchmarks such as HELM [29] was suggested (5).

The interviewees suggested possible alternatives for sufficient evaluation. Some focused on the ontology design (2), (5), suggesting the development of a set of ontologies to be used as gold standards (observer 1). Others suggested the creation of toolkits (1) for LLMs to review ontology errors similar to existing ontology toolkits, like OntoClean [30] and Oops! [31]. However, they acknowledged that this cannot be applied to large-scale KGs like Wikidata, and manual work will still be required. Humans could be more efficient in evaluation if they had the information that the prompt was related to the results (Observer 1). In addition, some interviewees were more specific, suggesting the use of techniques used in other fields, like fact-checking (10), adversarial algorithms (13), and self-play from reinforcement learning (12).

2.2. Essential Skills Needed to Use LLMs for KE

Knowledge Engineering Skills Having skills in building ontologies was found to be useful in adding context to the prompts (10), (6). For example, using the knowledge structure of a dataset, such as Wikidata (6), and information on how to form triples (10): "adding context as part of the prompt actually helped with the result" (6). In contrast, one interviewee found that the added context did not make a difference, so despite having this skill, they did not consider it important (3). Building ontologies was also found to be useful in defining the overall goals for the task (5), (9): "I could contextualize the tasks defined by the hackathon. Also, from a more practical point of view, I knew before starting coding, how the final output would have looked like" (9). Many of the interviewees who lacked skills in ontology design and engineering stated its importance (2), (12), (13) specifically for the evaluation of the outputs of the LLM (1), (7). They felt that without this, it would be difficult to know what a desired output would look like.

Prompting Skills It was found to be important to have prompting skills and understand how prompts can be composed and revised to achieve a desired outcome (10), (12), (8). In turn, these participants were able to streamline their approach and prompt more efficiently due to their understanding of the different components of prompts. Even just limited experience was found to be useful for forming prompts, with one interviewee describing their skill as "not scientific" but finding this helped in "understanding how these models respond to small changes" (12). Interviewees acknowledged that rules are needed to prompt efficiently. There is a sweet spot in how much information is given to

LLMs in order to get a desirable output, with too much information being as problematic as too little.

For those who did not have prior prompting experience, there were two main distinctions in how they viewed this skill. The first way was that some interviewees did not see prompting as a skill and felt that it was too simple of a task with multiple participants, restricting it to a trial-and-error exercise and not acknowledging the possibility to go beyond this. They deemed prompting as requiring no expertise, whereas KE and ML were categorized as more skilled (7), (13). One interviewee who described themselves as being familiar with LLMs did not deem prompting a specialist skill in the KE process as they believed any developer could do it (11).

On the other hand, some interviewees were interested in gaining more experience to go beyond trial-and-error (4), (3), (1), (14). One interviewee acknowledged that prompting can be an intricate process. Some interviewees felt that time for experimentation with LLMs is important to build an understanding of prompting, and this familiarity with LLMs can improve performance (5). This can also allow for quicker execution of prompting to streamline the workflow, with one interviewee noting, "I'm pretty sure that there are a lot of tricks or tips that I don't know about" (6).

Coding Skills Coding was the main technical skill that many interviewees mentioned as being important (2), (3), (8), (9). It was found to be useful in interacting with LLMs through respective APIs (Application Programming Interfaces) and not the user interfaces, which was important in querying large batches of prompts. Furthermore, one interviewee mentioned learning to use computer clusters to fine-tune LLMs (10), which requires experience and very high computational resources. Along with this, knowledge in using repositories of models like Hugging Face[6] and PyTorch[7] and version control systems like Git[8].

2.3. The Perception of Safety Issues by Knowledge Engineers

Our question on responsible AI was initially framed in terms of "safety", offering the respondents the opportunity to engage with any aspect of AI safety they felt relevant. However, although two respondents raised data security (1) and insufficient data (13) as safety concerns, the majority were not clear on what concerns they might be considering. In these cases, we suggested they focus on bias, as most people are familiar with this concept. However, this familiarity may also breed contempt. The authors of this paper observed, "when asked about harms, they said it wasn't discussed – assumes humans are biased anyway, so there will be bias anyway, which to me sounds like implying that there is no need to consider bias" (Observer 2). One respondent noted that they felt it would be "interesting and helpful" to apply safety testing to LLMs and, so far, had read papers on it (9).

Bias Awareness When asked to consider bias, interviewees made comments such as that they had only fleetingly interacted with the issues. "I'm familiar with the terms, but I haven't worked on them directly" (10). They described themselves as having experienced limited exposure (2), possessing a lack of knowledge (12), and interpreting safety as a

[6]`https://huggingface.co/`
[7]`https://pytorch.org/`
[8]`https://git-scm.com/`

risk to researchers rather than other publics (14). One respondent had previously worked as an engineer on a bias detection algorithm but felt this was purely a "theoretical thing".

One reason for this lack of engagement appeared to be the perception that safety was seen as a siloed activity rather than integrated with engineering: "that's not my field" (4). This was not necessarily due to a lack of interest, but perhaps also to a lack of opportunity: participants had been interested in safety work but "haven't been able to get to it" (5).

The many variants of bias mean that this is a number of problems, not one (6). There was some awareness that understanding the type of bias is key to addressing it (4). In terms of specific types of bias, a few interviewees had an awareness of what these might be, such as provenance (13), selectivity (5), and gender (6). These had also been brought up with one group in the hackathon, with the observer noting, "Organizer [told the group] – make sure you don't bias against gender, race, or geographical concepts – if competency questions are biased, then ontology is biased" (Observer 2). It is therefore difficult to tell whether this knowledge was something the interviewees had applied to previous work or gained in the relatively recent past of the hackathon.

Correspondingly, there was variation in awareness of bias mitigation: "[I have] no idea how many safety checking solutions have already been provided" (1); "I have some doubts on how these tests are carried out" (9). One interviewee felt that bias mitigation was more important in commercial products than in the lab (12). There was awareness that addressing bias may change relationships in KG (4).

Bias and LLMs Particular issues related to LLMs were noted, for instance, "there are so many confounding issues in the training of an LLM that even if you address bias in a prompt, you can't see the resources it is using to make a decision" (6). This respondent suggested that there could be ways to mitigate this by mapping the results of repeated prompting. One noted that harm can arise from use, even in a well-tested model. "So even though [LLMs] pass [bias] tests, I think there's still risk if you prompt them in a hateful or discriminative way" (10).

Respondents concerns about difficulties with addressing bias included a lack of knowledge of LLM training data and processes (13), a fear that tests for bias would be ineffective (9), and concern that tests alone are insufficient if appropriate action is not subsequently taken (10). There was also concern about a lack of consensus around safety issues (13) and a feeling that other problems in the model (e.g., accuracy) may be more pressing (2).

Mitigating Bias One interviewee suggested that, given the difficulties of mitigating bias, we should at a minimum "put an array [of] practices in place to monitor what's coming out [and] how unbiased and ethical it is" (5). The idea of 'co-creating' bias mitigation with users was suggested, with one interviewee suggesting not only reviewing the model for bias before use but also asking users for feedback on perceived bias as they used it (7) and another suggesting that "either we fix the data, or maybe we fix the tools somehow that [users] can detect this bias and root it out during their working" (5).

Some interviewees felt there might be a tension between attempting to reduce bias and model efficacy (2), (12) "There is evidence that if you debias a language model, it usually downgrades in performance" (8). Whereas most respondents felt bias was found in the data, a few perceived biases might also lie in both the LLM (7) and KGs, specifically in the semantics (9). One respondent felt that safety was not a concern in KGs (14).

2.4. The Use of Generative AI by Knowledge Engineers

The user study revealed the challenges knowledge engineers encounter when using LLMs, the essential skills required, and safety concerns. Participants felt that aspects of requirement engineering, such as elicitation, analysis, documentation, and validation, were challenging when using LLMs and required additional skills. They highlighted the challenges of producing consistent datasets using LLMs and suggested that templates may support prompting. They emphasized the difficulty of using LLMs to design competency questions and ontologies, stressing the need for constant manual intervention and evaluation to ensure accuracy and consistency. Participants with limited knowledge engineering skills expressed a need for guidance in designing knowledge engineering tasks, while those with little LLM experience felt they required training to fully utilize LLM capabilities. Based on the challenges and skills required, some participants suggested the development of tools to guide their steps and facilitate the efficient use of LLMs.

In addition to these challenges, the user study also uncovered important concerns related to safety issues. Participants expressed that they had little previous concern about safety issues, especially bias, and that some distinct knowledge engineering tasks and bias testing were different assignments for different researchers. They also emphasized the black box in the LLM training process and the intentional or unintentional manipulation of LLMs that can raise serious safety issues that may not be solved. The uncertainty about whether knowledge engineers should be involved in safety issues and how they should be involved may raise essential concerns about trustworthy knowledge engineering. To address these issues, participants recommended practices on LLM output or even the 'co-creation' of LLMs and knowledge engineers for bias mitigation. Nevertheless, further investigation is crucial to explore the explainability of KE tasks using LLMs.

Following the discussion, we introduce OntoChat [32], a conversational framework for ontology engineering, and Wikidata Ontology Evaluation Framework (WOEF) for knowledge graph evaluation and curation, as examples to address the above highlighted challenges that knowledge engineers face when using LLMs.

3. LLMs for Conversational Ontology Engineering: The Use Case

Ontology Engineering (OE) encompasses a number of activities defining a collaborative effort to design, evaluate, and reuse ontologies of general or domain-specific purposes [33,34]. Depending on the intended reuse by one or more stakeholders, the process starts with ontology designers eliciting requirements from the former, while interacting with experts to validate their formal understanding of the domain. Although the way OE activities are organized may vary depending on the methodology adopted [35,36], these interactions are frequent and iterative throughout the development cycle. In large projects, ontology designers engage in a number of manual activities and interact with multiple parties to make sure requirements are collected consistently and comprehensively, seeking clarification from domain experts to formalize and test them [37].

Various OE methodologies have been proposed over the years, with their focus shifting towards collaborative approaches [34]. Early works include METHONTOLOGY [38], based on requirements elicitation from [39] and providing support for conceptualization, implementation, and maintenance steps; and DILIGENT [40] which also ac-

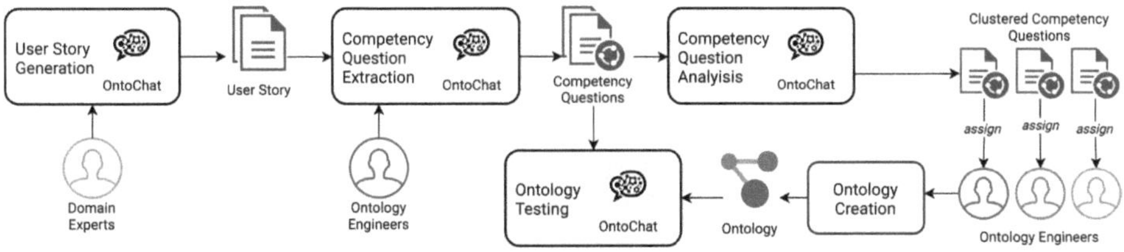

Figure 1. Illustration of the workflow alongside the main features in OntoChat.

count for the involvement of different stakeholders. More recent work incorporated Agile principles to support iterative ontology development, such as NEON [36], SAMOD [41], and *eXtreme Design* (XD) [35,42]. The latter also provides guidelines for requirement elicitation and is strongly test-based.

OE has long faced arguments about its technical challenges and costs. Despite the development of collaborative methodologies, the field still faces concerns about positively impacting the liveliness, evolution, and reusability of ontologies [43]. Meanwhile, LLMs have received increasing attention in the Semantic Web due to their language understanding capabilities. These provide generalization across various tasks (e.g., question answering, text summarization), making it possible to effectively generate, process, and annotate text to address knowledge engineering tasks [44,45].

Here, we hypothesize that LLMs can assist and facilitate OE activities to implement conversational workflows and prompt-driven functionalities that can reduce the complex interactions between domain experts and ontology designers, while accelerating the analysis and formalization of requirements. To confirm our motivations and collect insights for the design of such a framework, we put forth the following research questions:

- **RQ1**: Which ontology engineering activities are the most in need of computational support?
- **RQ2**: How can LLMs enable a conversational ontology engineering framework to support these activities?

To address RQ1 and inform the design of our framework, we conducted an online survey asking $N = 23$ participants with various levels of experience and familiarity with OE methodologies to rank OE activities for complexity and need of computational support. Given the size of our sample, we decided to rely on strong evidence ($\geq 75\%$ positive responses using 4-5 scores), finding that the most demanding OE tasks in need of computational support are: the collection of ontology requirements (86.4%), the extraction of CQs from textual ontology requirements (81.8%), the analysis of ontology requirements (77.3%), and ontology testing (81.8%). For more details and background information, one can refer to Appendix A in [32].

Based on these findings and building upon the IDEA approach [46], we designed OntoChat to support such OE activities. The workflow, illustrated in Figure 1, leverages LLMs as knowledge elicitators to reduce the demand and complexity of the multi-party interactions with ontology designers, and aims at accelerating OE tasks. To collect requirements, the process starts with stakeholders and domain experts co-creating user stories by interacting with our conversational agent. Ontology engineers can then extract CQs by iteratively refining the model's recommendations; reduce redundant requirements, and analyze the resulting CQs via clustering. Finally, OntoChat also allows testing preliminary versions of ontologies via verbalization and unit prompting.

3.1. OntoChat: Conversational Ontology Engineering

Assisted Persona and Story Creation To enable the collaborative user story generation, OntoChat follows the steps below.

Step 1: LLM role definition (back-end). The LLM behavior is primed to emulate a knowledge elicitator aiming to gather information from the user about each user story component – the persona definition, specification of concrete goals & addressed scenario, and the provision of data examples.

Step 2: Knowledge elicitation (user involvement). The user is guided through a series of questions focusing on a particular story aspect. For instance, to gather insights about the persona's background, OntoChat asks *"What are the name, occupations, skills, and interests of the user?"* Whenever the user does not provide enough details or gives partial answers, the LLM continues to elicit additional insights until all necessary information is gathered.

Step 3: User story generation (back-end) The initial user story draft is created following a one-shot learning approach [47]. The LLM is supplied with a user story example, and is prompted to follow the same structure for generating a *user story draft* summarizing the information extracted in the elicitation step.

Step 4: Refinement (user involvement). The user is presented with the user story draft and is encouraged to provide feedback. The refinement stage is iterative and continues until the user no longer requests further changes. Possible refinements include the correction of factual inconsistencies, additions to the user stories, removal of irrelevant details, etc.

Competency Question Extraction The main objective of this module is to assist ontology engineers in extracting CQs from user stories. The procedure is organized as follows:

Step 1: Instructing the LLM for CQ extraction (back-end). The model is provided with examples of pairs of user story fragments and expected CQs, to align its outputs to the expectations of ontology engineers.

Step 2: First extraction of CQs (user involvement). The ontology engineer is asked to provide a user story for CQ extraction. The user story may be manually crafted, or obtained from the previous step. As output, OntoChat provides an initial list of CQs.

Step 3: Competency question refinement (back-end). The LLM is provided with a series of prompts (hidden from the user) to perform two *refinement steps*.

- *Step 3.1: Split not atomic CQs.* If the example data is complex, users may get non-atomic questions from a single example. As these usually entail nested requirements, complex CQs need to be split. Following a few-shot learning approach, the LLM is asked whether each CQ has a complex form, hence triggering the simplification. For example, from the data "*The musical work Penny Lane has genre/style baroque pop and psychedelic pop.*", the LLM generated "*What genres/styles are associated with Penny Lane?*". After this step, the LLM replaces it with two distinct CQs: "*What genres are associated with Penny Lane?*" and "*What styles are associated with Penny Lane?*".
- *Step 3.2: Named entities abstraction.* As an example, the previous CQs replaced the specific genres with the interrogative pronoun "what" (genres/styles). However, it did not remove the real-world entity "Penny Lane". Within this step, LLMs

are prompted to check again the CQs, and, guided by examples, remove possible named entities. This yields abstract CQs like "*What genres are associated with the musical work?*" and "*What styles are associated with the musical work?*".

Step 4: User confirmation (user involvement). Finally, OntoChat asks the user whether the number of CQs and their formulation are sound. If not, by leveraging knowledge acquired from previous prompts (see Step 3), the model repeats the refinement steps until the user is satisfied.

Competency Question Filtration and Analysis As some CQs may be redundant or show negligible semantic variations that are of little interest to ontology engineers, OntoChat provides support for their filtration and analysis. This is achieved through: *paraphrase identification*, to remove equivalent CQs; and *CQ clustering*, to identify groups of similar requirements. In [48], the former was found to have two benefits: (i) it mitigates the noise and the artifacts introduced in the previous steps; (ii) it reduces the number of CQs that will be presented to ontology engineers.

In contrast to [48,46], which both rely on sentence embeddings and specialized models, this functionality is entirely supported by LLMs, which is motivated by recent findings demonstrating that LLMs possess clustering capabilities [49,50,51]. Given a list of CQs, the LLM is asked to remove redundant questions and find meaningful groups of CQs sharing the same thematic focus and intent. The latter is expected to support ontology designers in understanding requirements and possibly organizing their Agile teams (e.g., a team receiving a CQ cluster based on their familiarity with the sub-domain). In the current version, this step does not require user supervision.

Ontology Testing Support While the previous functionalities focus on requirement elicitation and analysis, this component provides support for testing preliminary or iterative versions of an ontology. Ontology testing efforts are often categorized into three methodologies: CQ verification, inference verification, and error provocation. The first two are concerned with verifying the correct implementation of a requirement, whereas the latter is needed to find cases where the ontology should fail [52]. These are typically done by formalizing CQs into SPARQL queries.

To test preliminary versions of an ontology, we aim for a SPARQL-free approach to achieve fast CQ verification and inference, while supporting error provocation. This is achieved in two steps: *ontology verbalization* and prompt-driven *CQ unit testing*. Our verbalization converts an OWL ontology into plain text by documenting classes, properties, named entities, and their relationships in a descriptive manner. The method follows a simple algorithmic procedure and assumes that the ontology is well commented to produce an expressive verbalization. Then, using the verbalization, the LLM is prompted to assess the coverage of each CQ by replying *Yes/No*. To prevent prompt leakage and ensure independence in the model's predictions, this is done separately for each CQ.

3.2. Evaluation

We performed a component-based evaluation of OntoChat to measure the effectiveness of each functionality and collect user feedback based on their experiences. The evaluation was organized to replicate the OE activities of the Music Meta ontology [53]. It was chosen as a benchmark/testbed for three reasons: it required considerable OE efforts and was already the source of ambiguities in the Polifonia project [54]; it was complemented by high-quality material (user stories, CQs, documentation, queries, etc.) from [46] to use as ground truth; the authors had access to a pool of domain experts for evaluation. To ensure each component is evaluated individually by the intended target users, we evaluate the more generative components by collecting feedback on their use from domain experts and ontology engineers through questionnaires.

Feedback collected from domain experts confirmed that the user stories generated with OntoChat captured the intended goal and requirements and always provided relevant information. More than 80% of participants enjoyed using the tool and found the final stories well-structured and easily understandable. While users acknowledged the model's ability to improve intermediate drafts through their feedback, only 50% were satisfied with the example data generated. Overall, 4/6 experts recognized the tool's potential to accelerate this task (2 neutral response), and 5 of them would prefer it over manual curation.

From the evaluation with ontology engineers, OntoChat was found to generate CQs that are comprehensive, reflective of the intended ontology scope, and easy to understand. However, 2/8 participants noted the extraction of entities outside the story's scope; and only 50% observed the potential to reduce possible author bias. While 6/8 participants expressed satisfaction with OntoChat and recognized its time-saving benefits, all agreed it holds promise for streamlining CQ generation, indicating a preference over fully manual creation.

The clustering feature proved advantageous for understanding and organizing ontology requirements when compared to full manual inspection. Participants found the interaction intuitive (62.5%) and the resulting clusters expressed meaningful groupings of CQs (87.5%). While the feature offers time-saving benefits by providing an aggregated view of ontology requirements, there were indications that it may not fully support comprehensive analysis on its own.

For more information on OntoChat, including survey results, implementation details, evaluation results, etc., one can refer to the original paper [32]. We maintain an online space on Hugging Face for research convinience[9].

3.3. Integrating User Needs into OntoChat: A Participatory Prompting Study

To improve the user experience and develop pre-defined prompt templates tailored to user queries for the current OntoChat user story creation workflow, we conducted a three-step participatory prompting process [55]: (1) *story description*: participants wrote stories based on their ontological needs; (2) *prompt development*: participants posed queries to request LLM support in writing user stories. Researchers refined these queries using pre-identified prompting strategies, then asked the LLM for answers, with participants evaluating the LLM-generated responses and providing feedback for further refinement; (3) *story evaluation*: participants assessed the stories for usefulness, clarity, and inspiration, resulting in more detailed and practical user stories.

The study involved 10 participants, including MuseIT[10] practitioners aiming to build an ontology for multi-sensory representation in cultural heritage and PhD researchers working on knowledge engineering. They have expertise in areas including machine learning, human resources, mixed reality, implantable medical devices, multimodal rep-

[9]https://huggingface.co/spaces/b289zhan/OntoChat

[10]https://www.muse-it.eu

resentation learning, and responsible AI. Ethical clearance was obtained from the Department of Informatics at King's College London, ensuring that no personal data was collected throughout the experiment.

After coding and analyzing the collected data, we identified a list of user queries and related prompts that can be used for enhancing the effectiveness of user story generation and refinement during the human-LLM interaction. Here we provide two examples. One is on *persona*, for the user query "detail the persona trait", the suggested prompt can be "Could you improve the persona by detailing [this specific trait] that is necessary for helping in writing an ontology user story? Explain why (this specific trait) are important." Another example is on *scenario*, where users have a query on "narrative story for the scenario", and the prompt is provided as "Could you narrate a detailed story about how the persona currently performs tasks related to their goal and how the system will enhance this process? Please include practical insights and a step-by-step sequence of actions.". We documented the complete list also in the OntoChat repository[11]. The identified prompts are integrated into OntoChat for future work.

4. LLMs for Schema-based Knowledge Graph Validation: The Use Case

In this section, we examine the second use case of LLMs in trustworthy knowledge In this section, we explore the second use case of LLMs in trustworthy knowledge engineering: schema-based knowledge graph validation. Schema validation, typically defined using shapes, is essential for ensuring that a given KG adheres to specified constraints [56]. While KGs and ontologies represented in RDF and OWL are governed by the open world assumption, related schemas, which rely on the closed world assumption, are often underdeveloped. The construction of validating schemas requires explicit definitions and input from domain experts, making the process labor-intensive and challenging to automate. For existing KGs, this manual effort can be time-consuming and difficult to scale. Considering recent advancements in the knowledge storage and expressive capabilities of LLMs [57,45], the potential application of LLMs in automating schema generation is promising and warrants further investigation. Thus, we propose the following research question: How can LLMs support schema generation?

Taking into account the practical requirements of collaborative knowledge engineering, we have chosen Wikidata [58] as the context for this work for two main reasons. First, a survey conducted by Wikimedia Deutschland[12] identified conceptual ambiguity and inconsistent modeling as the two most critical issues in Wikidata ontology. To address these challenges, the Wikidata community has adopted ShEx schemas (also known as EntitySchemas) as the primary method for defining the structure of data stored in Wikidata[13]. However, despite the community's efforts to construct these schemas, the process remains heavily reliant on manual work, resulting in inefficiencies and a lack of adequate tool support. Second, the Wikidata editors community provides a valuable resource for discussing and generating high-quality ShEx schemas, which can be used for evaluation. This collaborative environment offers a strong foundation for the development and refinement of schema-based validation approaches in KE. In this section,

[11] https://github.com/King-s-Knowledge-Graph-Lab/OntoChat
[12] https://www.wikidata.org/wiki/Wikidata:Ontology_issues_prioritization
[13] https://www.wikidata.org/wiki/Wikidata:Schemas

we primarily investigate the potential of using LLMs to create validating schemas represented in ShEx, which are used to validate items in KGs.

4.1. Task Definition

We propose the following tasks to evaluate a model's ability to generate validating schemas. ShEx schemas consist of constraints with elements including the focus node, predicate, cardinality, value constraint, etc [59]. For the purposes of this study, we simplify ShEx as used in Wikidata by grouping triple constraints with similar structures into shapes, where each shape targets a main node representing class c and specifies a list of constraints on that node. To initially assess the capability of LLMs in schema generation, we decompose this task into multiple sub-tasks, each focusing on different elements of the triple constraints.

In this section, we concentrate on one particular sub-task: cardinality prediction. Here, LLMs are tasked with determining whether a given predicate (i.e., property in Wikidata) is necessary for the items in a class. For a shape ϕ associated with nodes in class c, LLMs predict the cardinality $\xrightarrow{p} \phi\{\min, \max\}$ for each candidate property p. There are four possible outcomes: (1) "yes" or "required", indicating that the property is mandatory for all items within the class, resulting in a triple constraint with cardinality $\xrightarrow{p} \phi\{1, *\}$ (i.e., one or more matching statements); (2) "optional", indicating the property is used in some items, leading to a triple constraint with $\xrightarrow{p} \phi\{0, *\}$ (i.e., zero or more matching statements); (3) "no", indicating the property should not be used, which assigns the cardinality $\xrightarrow{p} \phi\{0, 0\}$ (i.e., no matching statements); and (4) "unknown", when the LLM is unable to make a decision based on the available information. In binary settings, only the first two options, "required" and "optional", are considered.

This task aims to assess the model's capability in determining the necessity of properties for classes in KGs. Additional sub-tasks can further evaluate the ability of LLMs, such as predicting detailed value sets or value shapes for shapes. For instance, if values for the triple constraint are generally identified as IRIs, LLMs can generate more detailed value sets or shapes. Another sub-task includes predicting allowed qualifiers for properties. For example, the property "educated at (P69)" may have qualifiers such as start time and end time, which can vary for different subject classes.

4.2. WOEF: Wikidata Ontology Evaluation Framework

We propose the framework, Wikidata Ontology Evaluation Framework (WOEF), designed to address ontology issues in knowledge graphs (KGs), with a particular focus on schema-based solutions for Wikidata. The workflow of WOEF, illustrated in Figure 3, consists of three main components: EntitySchema generation, knowledge graph validation, and knowledge graph curation.

The first component, **EntitySchema generation**, involves a three-step process. Initially, the framework queries items within a user-specified topic or domain class and filters out a list of relevant properties. This list, which includes example triples and property descriptions, is then provided to LLMs. In the second step, the LLMs process the domain class and property list to generate triple constraints. In the prompt engineering setting that we evaluated, the input information is formatted as prompt messages, including few-shot examples that consist of triples with their IDs. Figure 2 shows the prompt template

```
{
  "question": "Instances within the class '{class_label} (ID: {class_id})' use
  the property '{property_label} (ID: {property_id}) (description: {property_
  description})'. Here are examples: - {example_1}; - {example_2}; - {example_3}.
  Do you think the property is properly used for all instances within the class?
  - If you think the property is required for all items in the class, answer
  'Yes'. - If you think the property is only used on some items in the class,
  answer 'Optional'. - If you think the property should not be used on any items
  in the class, answer 'No'. - If you can't decide, answer 'Unknown'.",
  "answer": "Yes"
}
```

Figure 2. Prompt template for a question-answering pair used in the full setting. In the binary setting, only the first two options, "Yes" and "Optional", are provided when prompting LLMs.

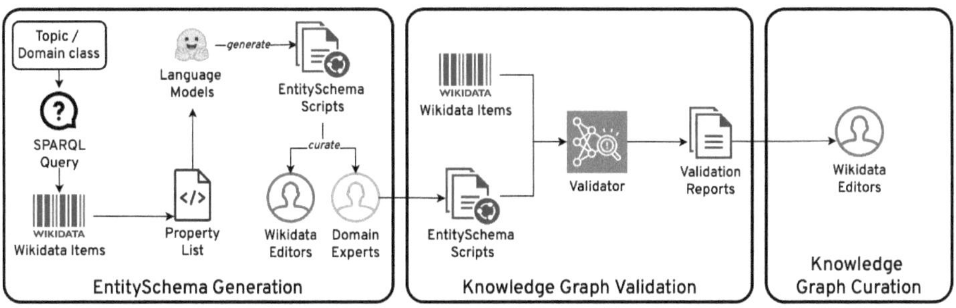

Figure 3. The human-in-the-loop WOEF workflow of EntitySchema generation and knowledge graph validation.

for these few-shot examples. The generated triple constraints are then combined into a complete ShEx schema. In the third step, users—including Wikidata editors, knowledge engineers, and domain experts—can review and revise the generated schema based on their expertise.

The second component of the framework focuses on **knowledge graph validation**. The schema generated in the previous step is used to validate items within its scope. The validation results identify ontology issues and suggest potential solutions. These results are compiled into reports for Wikidata editors and users, which include natural language descriptions and tables highlighting data that do not conform to the schema. The third component, **knowledge graph curation**, involves using these validation reports to improve the quality of Wikidata. Currently, Wikidata editors are responsible for curating the items based on these reports. However, there is potential for future enhancements where LLMs could assist by providing curation options.

4.3. Evaluation

Dataset Construction We constructed the dataset based on the EntitySchemas provided by the Wikidata community[14]. The dataset consists of 53 EntitySchemas and 909 triple constraints. For each EntitySchema, we extracted triple constraints from the main ShEx

[14] `https://www.wikidata.org/wiki/Wikidata:Database_reports/EntitySchema_directory`

shape. Each property in a constraint is classified as either "required" or "optional", which can be used for evaluating the task of cardinality prediction. In theory, triple constraints could also include a "No" option to explicitly reject certain properties. Therefore, we evaluate LLMs using two settings for the sub-task on the 909 triple constraints.

One issue with the current version of the dataset is that most of the EntitySchemas were manually created and may vary in quality. This variability implies that not all schemas may accurately represent the collaborative consensus on modeling the Wikidata ontology. Efforts are ongoing to improve the dataset's quality, drawing from two main sources. The first involves collecting existing ShEx resources, including ShEx schemas from other ontologies, such as schema.org, which could enhance the models' ability to generalize from Wikidata to other large KGs. The second source involves recruiting editors familiar with ShEx schemas to enrich a set of schemas for various Wikidata classes.

To facilitate the construction of this benchmark, we developed a human-in-the-loop tool, EntitySchema Generator (ESGen). This tool is hosted on Hugging Face[15]. For more information on the code and dataset, please refer to the repository[16].

Evaluation Metrics For the binary setting in the cardinality prediction task, we use Accuracy, Precision, Recall, F1-score, and confusion matrix as the primary evaluation metrics. In the full setting, since the output classes "No" and "Unknown" are currently absent from the dataset, Recall and F1-score cannot be effectively calculated. In this case, we rely on the confusion matrix to provide a basic understanding of the model's performance.

We also propose two methods for evaluating generated EntitySchemas, which can be utilized in future work. The first method is the passing rate. Given a complete ShEx schema as the ground truth and a large set of N items from Wikidata, the passing rate measures the proportion of these items that conform to the LLM-generated schema ϕ. If n items from this set match the results using schema ϕ, the passing rate can be calculated as $p(\phi) = n/N$.

The second evaluation metric, ShExBLEU, is derived from CodeBLEU [60], which is used for code generation. Similar to CodeBLEU, we transform the ShEx schema into a ShEx abstract syntax tree (AST) and calculate the syntactic AST match score as follows:

$$\text{Match}_{\text{ast}} = \text{Count}_{\text{clip}}(T_{\text{cand}})/\text{Count}(T_{\text{ref}}) \tag{1}$$

Here, $\text{Count}(T_{\text{ref}})$ represents the total number of sub-trees in the reference ShEx AST, and $\text{Count}_{\text{clip}}(T_{\text{cand}})$ denotes the number of sub-trees in the candidate ShEx AST that match sub-trees from the reference AST. For ShExBLEU, we replace the syntactic AST match and semantic data-flow match terms used in CodeBLEU with the ShEx AST match score. The ShExBLEU metric is calculated as follows:

$$\text{ShExBLEU} = \alpha \cdot \text{BLEU} + \beta \cdot \text{BLEU}_w + \gamma \cdot \text{Match}_{\text{ast}} \tag{2}$$

where BLEU is the original BLEU metric, and BLEU_w is the weighted n-gram match, where keywords may be assigned higher weights.

[15]`https://huggingface.co/spaces/b289zhan/ESGen`
[16]`https://github.com/bohuizhang/WOEF`

Table 2. Cardinality prediction (binary settings) test results on the constructed dataset, comparing different LLMs.

Model	Accuracy	Precision	Recall	F1-score
gpt-turbo-3.5-0125	0.557	0.614	0.653	0.543
Meta-Llama-3-8B-Instruct	0.705	0.643	0.686	0.648
Meta-Llama-3.1-8B-Instruct	0.696	0.638	0.682	0.641

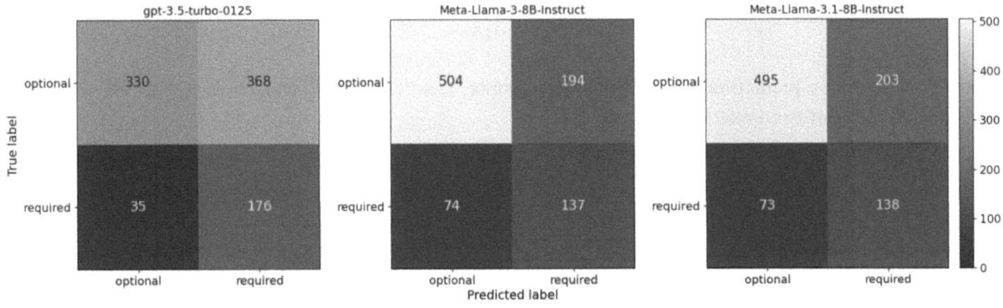

Figure 4. Cardinality prediction (binary settings) test results. Subtitles represent names of LLMs (`gpt-3.5-turbo-0125`, Meta-Llama-3-8B-Instruct, Meta-Llama-3.1-8B-Instruct).

Results We first present the results of the sub-task that tests the ability of LLMs to predict cardinality (i.e., necessity in the dataset) across the 909 triple constraints, as shown in Table 2. We selected Meta-Llama-3.1-8B-Instruct and Meta-Llama-3-8B-Instruct from Meta [11], as well as `gpt-3.5-turbo-0125` from OpenAI, to compare their performance in this cardinality prediction task. The Meta-Llama-3-8B-Instruct model outperforms the other two models in the binary setting, achieving an F1-score of 0.648. The performance of the two Llama models is closely matched, with Meta-Llama-3-8B-Instruct marginally outperforming Meta-Llama-3.1-8B-Instruct.

Analysis of the confusion matrices reveals that `gpt-3.5-turbo-0125` has a tendency to classify optional properties as required ones, which accounts for most of the observed performance difference (Figure 4). Further visualization of results in the full setting is shown in Figure 5. When two examples demonstrating the "No" option are added to the prompt message, a significant number of LLMs' predictions shift to "No" and "Unknown". In this scenario, Meta-Llama-3.1-8B-Instruct outperforms the other two models.

These findings underscore the importance of a more comprehensive dataset with better coverage of topics and a broader diversity of triple constraints. Such a dataset is crucial for thoroughly assessing the capabilities of LLMs in schema generation tasks and for optimizing prompt design and fine-tuning processes.

4.4. Integrating Explainability into LLM-assisted KE

Preliminaries As a crucial factor supporting Trustworthy AI, explainability in knowledge engineering has not been systematically investigated. To bridge this gap, we intend to propose an effective paradigm for designing XAI solutions for knowledge engineering tasks, taking user-centric factors into account. We analyze the KG lifecycle to identify tasks that are commonly automated with AI and those that still require human input and oversight and could potentially benefit from AI assistance [23]. In parallel, we survey

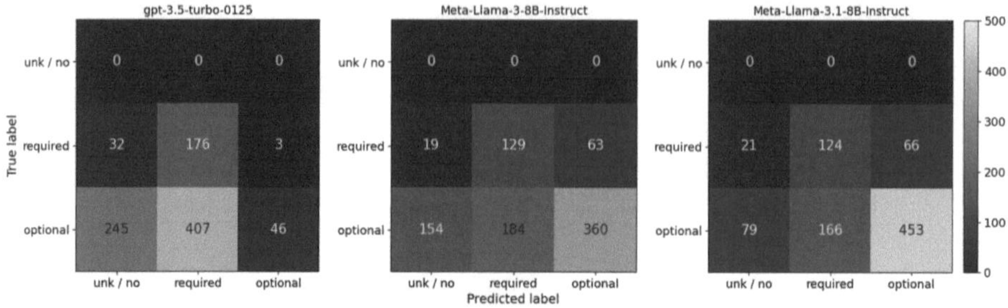

Figure 5. Cardinality prediction (full settings) test results. The "Unknown" and "No" options are combined when calculating confusion matrices.

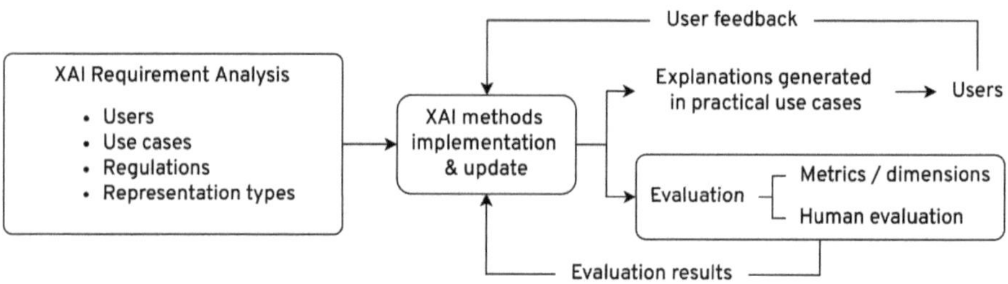

Figure 6. The XAI methods design blueprint.

the state-of-the-art in explainable AI (XAI) to inform the design of XAI approaches that are genuinely useful for KG stakeholders such as knowledge engineers, subject domain experts, and users. We maintain a public repository including the survey to enhance research convenience[17]. Then we conduct an interview study involving 13 knowledge engineers and researchers from the knowledge engineering community [61]. The interviews further allow us to directly explore the role of explainable AI in broader contexts, understand the needs of knowledge engineering and KG stakeholders for explanations, identify potential gaps and challenges in this field, and provide valuable insights for further research.

Explanation Design In [61], we propose several guidelines and combine them into blueprints for designing explainable solutions in knowledge engineering tasks that are usable and trustworthy to target users, as shown in Figure 6. We further apply the blueprint in this work for designing explainable solutions for schema generation and knowledge graph validation.

The first step in designing explainable models involves XAI requirement analysis, which collects design insights and creates goals for explanations. Several factors must be carefully considered and investigated to capture the scope and objectives of explainable models.

The most important factor is the **users** who consume the explanations. From the interview study, it is evident that the design of explanations should consider the users' level of understanding and interest in the technical details. Therefore, user analysis should include investigating their background, particularly their technical expertise and domain

[17] `https://github.com/bohuizhang/XKGC`

knowledge, and their expectations for the explanations, including the level of technical detail they require. Furthermore, if the consumers of explanations are involved in collaborative work with machines, understanding how they consume explanations and interact with models is crucial. In this context, the users include Wikidata editors, data re-users, and knowledge engineers.

The second part of XAI requirement analysis focuses on the **use cases** of explanations. Six use cases are identified in [61]: (1) modeling selecting and building, (2) model debugging, (3) understanding performance and contributing factors, (4) managing updates, (5) enhancing human-machine interactions, and (6) uncovering new and previously unnoticed insights. In our context, the explanations for schema generation and knowledge graph validation address questions such as "Why should property P not be used in class C?" and "Why do LLM A and LLM B conflict on the triple constraint T?". The scope of these explanations overlaps with use cases (1), (3), (5), and (6).

The third factor is the **representation** of explanations, which primarily depends on the task and its related input and output (datatype, modality, or property) and user needs. For example, in knowledge extraction tasks where the input modality is text, the context of the original input might be useful (though not necessarily sufficient) as supporting evidence to show the relevance of the output. This needs to be combined with user analysis to determine what "language" the user speaks, such as description logic, natural language, images, etc. In our scenario, the most effective representations are natural language explanations and tables.

Other factors, such as AI regulations mentioned in the Introduction, may also need to be considered in the requirement analysis. Moreover, this list of factors can be expanded based on actual scenarios. Such requirement analysis guides the selection and implementation of XAI methods, ensuring they meet the requirements of practical use cases. After implementing XAI methods, the workflow involves iterative loops for maintaining and continuously improving the methods. One loop focuses on the evaluation and assessment of explanations [62]. Evaluation methods should go beyond anecdotal evidence, selecting appropriate metrics or designing evaluation paradigms. Another iterative loop aims to improve explainable models and explanations in practical scenarios. Users who consume the explanations provide feedback and example explanations, which can be used in various ways to enhance the XAI model. This includes creating datasets of explanations for training and fine-tuning XAI models, providing few-shot examples, or even abstracting improvement directions for architecture-level adjustments.

5. Conclusion

In this chapter, we have explored the essential aspects of creating trustworthy knowledge graphs (KGs) and the practices and approaches necessary for their development, particularly those that leverage large language models (LLMs). We emphasized the importance of transparency, explainability, and reliability in KGs, given their increasing role in supporting human-centered AI applications.

Our user study, conducted within the context of knowledge engineering (KE) and LLMs, highlighted the main challenges faced by knowledge engineers in the era of LLMs and identified the essential skills needed to efficiently leverage LLMs for KE. Based on our discussion, we presented two practices focusing on ontology requirement elicitation and knowledge graph validation, offering insights into developing trustworthy tools for KE.

In summary, the development of trustworthy knowledge graphs is a multidisciplinary endeavor that necessitates careful consideration of data quality, transparency, and explainability. These elements are crucial for creating KGs that not only support advanced AI applications but also uphold the principles of trust and reliability.

References

[1] Hogan A, Blomqvist E, Cochez M, d'Amato C, de Melo G, Gutierrez C, et al. Knowledge Graphs. Synthesis Lectures on Data, Semantics, and Knowledge. Morgan & Claypool Publishers; 2021. Available from: https://books.google.co.uk/books?id=hJ1NEAAAQBAJ.

[2] Chen J, Geng Y, Chen Z, Pan JZ, He Y, Zhang W, et al. Zero-shot and Few-shot Learning with Knowledge Graphs: A Comprehensive Survey. CoRR. 2021;abs/2112.10006. Available from: https://arxiv.org/abs/2112.10006.

[3] Lewis PSH, Perez E, Piktus A, Petroni F, Karpukhin V, Goyal N, et al. Retrieval-Augmented Generation for Knowledge-Intensive NLP Tasks. CoRR. 2020;abs/2005.11401. Available from: https://arxiv.org/abs/2005.11401.

[4] Yang L, Chen H, Li Z, Ding X, Wu X. Give Us the Facts: Enhancing Large Language Models with Knowledge Graphs for Fact-aware Language Modeling; 2024.

[5] Tiddi I, Schlobach S. Knowledge graphs as tools for explainable machine learning: A survey. Artificial Intelligence. 2022;302:103627. Available from: https://www.sciencedirect.com/science/article/pii/S0004370221001788.

[6] Sequeda J, Lassila O. Designing and Building Enterprise Knowledge Graphs. Springer International Publishing; 2021. Available from: http://dx.doi.org/10.1007/978-3-031-01916-6.

[7] Brown TB, Mann B, Ryder N, Subbiah M, Kaplan J, Dhariwal P, et al. Language Models are Few-Shot Learners. CoRR. 2020;abs/2005.14165. Available from: https://arxiv.org/abs/2005.14165.

[8] OpenAI. GPT-4 Technical Report. arXiv preprint arXiv:230308774. 2023.

[9] Touvron H, Lavril T, Izacard G, Martinet X, Lachaux MA, Lacroix T, et al.. LLaMA: Open and Efficient Foundation Language Models; 2023.

[10] Touvron H, Martin L, Stone K, Albert P, Almahairi A, Babaei Y, et al.. Llama 2: Open Foundation and Fine-Tuned Chat Models; 2023.

[11] Dubey A, Jauhri A, Pandey A, Kadian A, Al-Dahle A, Letman A, et al. The llama 3 herd of models. arXiv preprint arXiv:240721783. 2024.

[12] Pan JZ, Razniewski S, Kalo JC, Singhania S, Chen J, Dietze S, et al. Large Language Models and Knowledge Graphs: Opportunities and Challenges. Transactions on Graph Data and Knowledge. 2023;1(1):2:1-2:38. Available from: https://drops.dagstuhl.de/entities/document/10.4230/TGDK.1.1.2.

[13] Tamašauskait˙ e Ge, Groth P. Defining a Knowledge Graph Development Process Through a Systematic Review. ACM Trans Softw Eng Methodol. 2023 feb;32(1). Available from: https://doi.org/10.1145/3522586.

[14] Weikum G, Dong L, Razniewski S, Suchanek FM. Machine Knowledge: Creation and Curation of Comprehensive Knowledge Bases. CoRR. 2020;abs/2009.11564. Available from: https://arxiv.org/abs/2009.11564.

[15] Wolf CT. From Knowledge Graphs to Knowledge Practices: On the Need for Transparency and Explainability in Enterprise Knowledge Graph Applications. In: Knowledge Graph Bias Workshop; 2020.
.

[16] Abián D, Meroño-Peñuela A, Simperl E. An Analysis of Content Gaps Versus User Needs in the Wikidata Knowledge Graph. In: The Semantic Web–ISWC 2022: 21st International Semantic Web Conference, Virtual Event, October 23–27, 2022, Proceedings. Springer; 2022. p. 354-74.

[17] Fisher J, Mittal A, Palfrey D, Christodoulopoulos C. Debiasing knowledge graph embeddings. In: Proceedings of the 2020 Conference on Empirical Methods in Natural Language Processing (EMNLP); 2020. p. 7332-45.

[18] Beyer L, Hénaff OJ, Kolesnikov A, Zhai X, Oord Avd. Are we done with imagenet? arXiv preprint arXiv:200607159. 2020.
[19] Danks D, London AJ. Algorithmic Bias in Autonomous Systems. In: Ijcai. vol. 17; 2017. p. 4691-7.
[20] Hooker S. Moving beyond "algorithmic bias is a data problem". Patterns. 2021;2(4):100241.
[21] Panch T, Mattie H, Atun R. Artificial intelligence and algorithmic bias: implications for health systems. Journal of global health. 2019;9(2).
[22] Ribeiro MT, Wu T, Guestrin C, Singh S. Beyond accuracy: Behavioral testing of NLP models with CheckList. arXiv preprint arXiv:200504118. 2020.
[23] Zhang B, Meroño Peñuela A, Simperl E. Towards Explainable Automatic Knowledge Graph Construction with Human-in-the- Loop. In: HHAI 2023: Augmenting Human Intellect. IOS Press; 2023. p. 274-89.
[24] Groth P, Simperl E, van Erp M, Vrandečić D. Knowledge Graphs and their Role in the Knowledge Engineering of the 21st Century (Dagstuhl Seminar 22372). Dagstuhl Reports. 2023;12(9):60-120. Available from: https://drops.dagstuhl.de/opus/volltexte/2023/17810.
[25] Lee JD, See KA. Trust in Automation: Designing for Appropriate Reliance. Human Factors. 2004;46(1):50-80. PMID: 15151155. Available from: https://doi.org/10.1518/hfes.46.1.50_30392.
[26] Koutsiana E, Walker J, Nwachukwu M, Meroño-Peñuela A, Simperl E. Knowledge Prompting: How Knowledge Engineers Use Large Language Models; 2024.
[27] emerald publishing limited. Ethnography techniques; 2023. Accessed on January, 2024. Available from: https://www.emeraldgrouppublishing.com/how-to/observation/use-ethnographic-methods-participant-observation,.
[28] Dodds L. FAIR, fairer, fairest?; 2020. Available from: https://blog.ldodds.com/2020/07/30/fair-fairer-fairest/.
[29] Bommasani R, Liang P, Lee T. Holistic Evaluation of Language Models. Annals of the New York Academy of Sciences. 2023.
[30] Guarino N, Welty CA. An overview of OntoClean. Handbook on ontologies. 2009:201-20.
[31] Poveda-Villalón M, Gómez-Pérez A, Suárez-Figueroa MC. Oops!(ontology pitfall scanner!): An on-line tool for ontology evaluation. International Journal on Semantic Web and Information Systems (IJSWIS). 2014;10(2):7-34.
[32] Zhang B, Carriero VA, Schreiberhuber K, Tsaneva S, González LS, Kim J, et al. OntoChat: a Framework for Conversational Ontology Engineering using Language Models. arXiv preprint arXiv:240305921. 2024.
[33] Kendall EF, McGuinness DL. Ontology engineering. Morgan & Claypool Publishers; 2019.
[34] Simperl E, Luczak-Rösch M. Collaborative ontology engineering: a survey. The Knowledge Engineering Review. 2014;29(1):101-31.
[35] Blomqvist E, Presutti V, Daga E, Gangemi A. Experimenting with eXtreme Design. In: Knowledge Engineering and Management by the Masses. EKAW 2010. vol. 6317. Springer, Berlin, Heidelberg; 2010. p. 120-34.
[36] Suárez-Figueroa MC, Gómez-Pérez A, Fernández-López M. The NeOn methodology for ontology engineering. In: Ontology engineering in a networked world. Springer; 2012. p. 9-34.
[37] Bottini T, Carriero VA, Carvalho J, Cathé P, Ciroku F, Daga E, et al. D1.1 Roadmap and pilot requirements 1st version. EU Commission, The Polifonia consortium; 2021.
[38] Fernández-López M, Gómez-Pérez A, Juristo N. METHONTOLOGY: From Ontological Art Towards Ontological Engineering. In: AAAI Conference on Artificial Intelligence; 1997. .
[39] Uschold M, King M. Towards a methodology for building ontologies. Citeseer; 1995.
[40] Pinto HS, Staab S, Tempich C. DILIGENT: Towards a fine-grained methodology for DIstributed, Loosely-controlled and evolvInG Engineering of oNTologies. In: ECAI. vol. 16. Citeseer; 2004. p. 393.
[41] Peroni S. A simplified agile methodology for ontology development. In: OWL: Experiences and Directions–Reasoner Evaluation. Springer; 2016. p. 55-69.
[42] Blomqvist E, Hammar K, Presutti V. Engineering Ontologies with Patterns - The eXtreme Design Methodology. In: Ontology Engineering with Ontology Design Patterns - Foundations and Applications. vol. 25 of Studies on the Semantic Web. Amsterdam: IOS Press; 2016. .
[43] Mateiu P, Groza A. Ontology engineering with large language models. arXiv preprint arXiv:230716699. 2023.
[44] Allen BP, Stork L, Groth P. Knowledge Engineering using Large Language Models. arXiv preprint

arXiv:231000637. 2023.

[45] Zhang B, Reklos I, Jain N, Peñuela AM, Simperl E. Using Large Language Models for Knowledge Engineering (LLMKE): A Case Study on Wikidata. arXiv preprint arXiv:230908491. 2023.

[46] de Berardinis J, Carriero VA, Jain N, Lazzari N, Meroño-Peñuela A, Poltronieri A, et al. The Polifonia Ontology Network: Building a Semantic Backbone for Musical Heritage. In: Proceedings of the 22nd International Semantic Web Conference (ISWC); 2023. .

[47] Brown T, Mann B, Ryder N, Subbiah M, Kaplan JD, Dhariwal P, et al. Language models are few-shot learners. Advances in neural information processing systems. 2020;33:1877-901.

[48] Ciroku F, de Berardinis J, Kim J, Meroño-Peñuela A, Presutti V, Simperl E. RevOnt: Reverse Engineering of Competency Questions from Knowledge Graphs via Language Models. Manuscript under review. 2024.

[49] Aharoni R, Goldberg Y. Unsupervised Domain Clusters in Pretrained Language Models. In: Jurafsky D, Chai J, Schluter N, Tetreault J, editors. Proceedings of the 58th Annual Meeting of the Association for Computational Linguistics. Online: Association for Computational Linguistics; 2020. p. 7747-63.

[50] Zhang Y, Wang Z, Shang J. ClusterLLM: Large Language Models as a Guide for Text Clustering. In: Bouamor H, Pino J, Bali K, editors. Proceedings of the 2023 Conference on Empirical Methods in Natural Language Processing. Singapore: Association for Computational Linguistics; 2023. p. 13903-20.

[51] Viswanathan V, Gashteovski K, Lawrence C, Wu T, Neubig G. Large Language Models Enable Few-Shot Clustering. arXiv preprint arXiv:230700524. 2023.

[52] Blomqvist E, Seil Sepour A, Presutti V. Ontology testing-methodology and tool. In: Knowledge Engineering and Knowledge Management: 18th International Conference, EKAW 2012, Galway City, Ireland, October 8-12, 2012. Proceedings 18. Springer; 2012. p. 216-26.

[53] de Berardinis J, Carriero VA, Meroño-Peñuela A, Poltronieri A, Presutti V. The Music Meta Ontology: a flexible semantic model for the interoperability of music metadata. In: Proceedings of the the 24th International Society for Music Information Retrieval Conference; 2023. .

[54] de Berardinis J, Peñuela AM, Jain N, Poltronieri A, Lazzari N, Presutti V, et al. Ontologies and knowledge graphs of music objects, patterns, and software package – 2nd version. European Commission, The Polifonia consortium; 2023.

[55] Sarkar A, Drosos I, Deline R, Gordon AD, Negreanu C, Rintel S, et al.. Participatory prompting: a user-centric research method for eliciting AI assistance opportunities in knowledge workflows; 2023. Available from: https://arxiv.org/abs/2312.16633.

[56] Gayo JEL, Prud'hommeaux E, Boneva I. Validating RDF Data. Morgan & Claypool Publishers; 2017.

[57] Alivanistos D, Santamaría SB, Cochez M, Kalo JC, van Krieken E, Thanapalasingam T. Prompting as Probing: Using Language Models for Knowledge Base Construction; 2023. Available from: https://arxiv.org/abs/2208.11057.

[58] Vrandečić D, Krötzsch M. Wikidata: a free collaborative knowledgebase. Communications of the ACM. 2014;57(10):78-85.

[59] Prud'hommeaux E, Labra Gayo JE, Solbrig H. Shape expressions: an RDF validation and transformation language. In: Proceedings of the 10th International Conference on Semantic Systems. SEM '14. New York, NY, USA: Association for Computing Machinery; 2014. p. 32–40. Available from: https://doi.org/10.1145/2660517.2660523.

[60] Ren S, Guo D, Lu S, Zhou L, Liu S, Tang D, et al. CodeBLEU: a Method for Automatic Evaluation of Code Synthesis. CoRR. 2020;abs/2009.10297. Available from: https://arxiv.org/abs/2009.10297.

[61] Zhang B, Meroño-Peñuela A, Simperl E. Towards Explainable Automated Knowledge Engineering with Human-in-the-loop; 2024. Submitted to Semantic Web Journal. Available from: https://www.semantic-web-journal.net/system/files/swj3732.pdf.

[62] Bonaventura CD, Siciliani L, Basile P, Meroño-Peñuela A, McGillivray B. Is Explanation All You Need? An Expert Survey on LLM-generated Explanations for Abusive Language Detection; 2024. Submitted to CLiC-it 2024: Tenth Italian Conference on Computational Linguistics.

Handbook on Neurosymbolic AI and Knowledge Graphs
P. Hitzler et al. (Eds.)
IOS Press, 2025

doi:10.3233/FAIA250216

Open Research Knowledge Graph: A Large-Scale Neuro-Symbolic Knowledge Organization System

Sören AUER [a,b,1], Jennifer D'SOUZA [a], Kheir Eddine FARFAR [a], Mohamad Yaser JARADEH [b], Azanzi JIOMEKONG [c], Oliver KARRAS [a], Allard OELEN [a], Lauren SNYDER [b], Markus STOCKER [a,b] and Lars VOGT [a]

[a] *TIB Leibniz Information Centre for Science and Technology*
[b] *L3S Research Center, Leibniz University of Hannover*
[c] *Department of Computer Science, University of Yaounde I, Yaounde, Cameroon*

ORCiD ID: Sören Auer https://orcid.org/0000-0002-0698-2864, Jennifer D'Souza https://orcid.org/0000-0002-6616-9509, Kheir Eddine Farfar https://orcid.org/0000-0002-0366-4596, Mohamad Yaser Jaradeh https://orcid.org/0000-0001-8777-2780, Azanzi Jiomekong https://orcid.org/0000-0002-8005-2067, Oliver Karras https://orcid.org/0000-0001-5336-6899, Allard Oelen https://orcid.org/0000-0001-9924-9153, Lauren Snyder https://orcid.org/0000-0001-6543-9565, Markus Stocker https://orcid.org/0000-0001-5492-3212, Lars Vogt https://orcid.org/0000-0002-8280-0487

Abstract. This article presents the implementation of a neuro-symbolic system within the Open Research Knowledge Graph (ORKG), a platform designed to collect and organize scientific knowledge in a structured, machine-readable format. Our approach leverages the strengths of symbolic knowledge representation to encode complex relationships and domain-specific rules, combined with the pattern recognition capabilities of neural networks to process large volumes of unstructured data, in particular scientific articles in the form of narrative text documents. With the ORKG, we developed a hybrid system that integrates a knowledge graph (symbolic system) with neural networks (subsymbolic system), enabling the machine-assisted extraction of scientific knowledge from research papers and symbolic knowledge representation, curation, organisation, and reuse. The implementation involves constructing a symbolic knowledge representation of the ORKG, training neural models on annotated datasets, and designing algorithms to synergize the two systems. Our findings suggest that neuro-symbolic integration enhances the ORKG's ability to support complex queries, infer new relationships, and provide more robust and explainable AI-driven insights. This research contributes to the broader field of AI by showcasing the practical benefits of combining neural and symbolic methodologies in knowledge management systems.

Keywords. Neuro-symbolic AI, scholarly communication, knowledge graphs, large language models

---

[1]Corresponding Author: Sören Auer, TIB, Welfengarten 1b, 30167 Hannover, Germany, auer@tib.eu.
The authors are listed in alphabetical order by last name.

1. Introduction

In the rapidly evolving landscape of scientific research and scholarship, the dissemination and utilization of knowledge are paramount. Traditional methods of publishing and sharing scientific knowledge, while valuable, silo knowledge within dense, static documents that challenge integration, comparison, and reuse across disciplines. The Open Research Knowledge Graph [1] (ORKG, orkg.org) presented in this chapter is a pioneering initiative that reimagines the future of scholarly communication. By leveraging neuro-symbolic technology integration, the ORKG transforms scholarly articles into a structured, interconnected web of research findings, making scientific knowledge more accessible, discoverable, and actionable. As such, the ORKG is an infrastructure that aims to support the production, curation, publication, and use of FAIR scientific knowledge with a mission to shape future scholarly publishing and communication where the contents of scholarly articles are FAIR research data [2].

The inception of the ORKG is rooted in recognizing the vast, untapped potential of digital scholarship. As researchers around the globe generate vast quantities of data and insights, the imperative to harness this wealth of knowledge in a machine-assisted manner becomes increasingly critical. The ORKG represents a paradigm shift, moving beyond the limitations of traditional research artifacts to a dynamic, open knowledge network. This network not only facilitates the seamless integration, comparison, reproducibility, and machine-based reuse of research findings, but also fosters new collaborations, innovations, and a deeper understanding of complex scientific questions.

Neuro-symbolic integration in the ORKG is a pivotal advancement in achieving these goals because it combines the strengths of symbolic knowledge representation and reasoning with neural networks, creating a synergistic system that enhances the capabilities of the ORKG. The hybrid system leverages the interpretability and rule-based nature of symbolic AI to manage and reason over the structured knowledge graph, while utilizing the pattern recognition and learning capabilities of neural networks to handle unstructured data and improve the extraction and classification of information from scientific articles.

In practice, neuro-symbolic integration in the ORKG involves several key components:

1. *Information Production:* Scientific knowledge is produced symbolically from the outset by integrating symbolic techniques in phases of the research lifecycle, in particular data analysis and manuscript authoring. This reduces the burying of scientific knowledge into narrative text documents [3] and, thus, reliance on information extraction.
2. *Information Extraction:* Neural networks are employed to extract relevant information from scientific articles. These networks are trained on large datasets to recognize and classify various entities and relationships within the text, such as research topics, methods, results, and conclusions.
3. *Expert Curation and Semantic Enrichment:* Once created, the symbolic information is further semantically enriched using symbolic AI techniques and curation by experts. This involves mapping the extracted information to a predefined ontology or schema within the ORKG, ensuring that the information is meaningfully structured and interconnected.

4. *Querying, Reasoning, and Inference:* Symbolic querying and reasoning are used to perform complex queries and infer new knowledge from the existing data in the ORKG. This allows researchers to discover hidden connections, generate hypotheses, and derive insights that would be difficult to achieve through manual analysis alone.
5. *ORKG ASK:* The ORKG Assistant for Scientific Knowledge (ASK, ask.orkg.org) is an advanced interface that utilizes neuro-symbolic integration to provide researchers with intuitive and powerful tools for interacting with the ORKG. It supports natural language queries, allowing users to ask complex questions and receive answers derived from a vast corpus of scientific literature and the integrated knowledge graph. This enhances the usability and accessibility of the ORKG, making it easier for researchers to find and use relevant information.

The integration of these neuro-symbolic technologies transforms the ORKG into a dynamic and intelligent platform, capable of continuously evolving and adapting to the growing body of scientific knowledge. This not only enhances the immediate utility of the ORKG for current research but also lays the foundation for future advancements in scholarly communication and knowledge management. Through neuro-symbolic integration, the ORKG is positioned at the forefront of the transition toward a more interconnected, accessible, and actionable scientific knowledge ecosystem.

Scientific Knowledge Organization (SKO) has undergone significant advancements in recent years, driven by the exponential growth of scientific literature and the need for more efficient methods of managing and accessing this vast body of knowledge. The integration of machine learning and artificial intelligence techniques has started to impact SKO. Recent work demonstrates the effectiveness of deep learning models in automatically classifying and organizing scientific knowledge across multiple disciplines [4]. Approaches using transformer-based architectures have shown promising results in accurately categorizing papers based on content, methodology, and research area [5]. Ontologies continue to play a crucial role in SKO [6] and have reached fields as diverse as behavioral sciences [7], chemistry [8] or bio-diversity and agiculture [9]. Recognizing the collective expertise of the scientific community, there has been a shift towards more collaborative approaches or even crowdsourcing to SKO [10]. Recent efforts have also focused on integrating SKO systems more seamlessly into researchers' workflows, e.g. via workflow management aud reuse [11], holistic data management for semantic interoperability e.g. in humanities [12] or life-sciences [13]. Advancements in data visualization have led to new ways of representing and navigating scientific knowledge [14]. SKO is also impacted by the evolution from basic keyword-based search (such as Google Scholar) to more advanced AI-driven research assistance, progressing through improved metadata utilization (e.g. Semantic Scholar [15]), semantic understanding (e.g. Elicit [16]), and context-aware recommendations. This development pathway represents a beginning shift from simple document retrieval to intelligent, personalized research support systems that understand and anticipate researchers' needs as pursued by the ORKG.

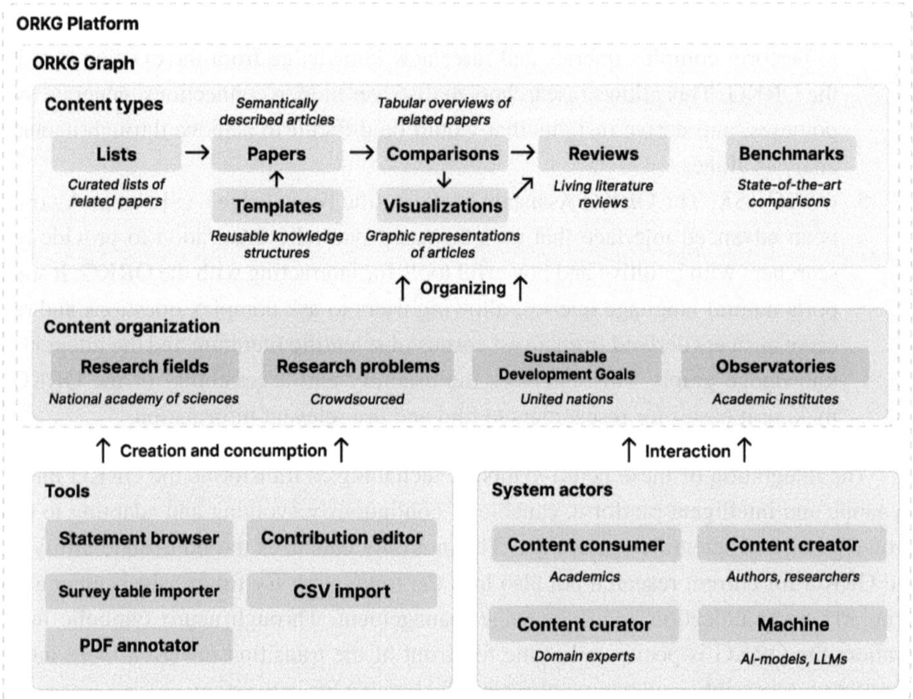

Figure 1. Diagram showing the main ORKG content types. Arrows between content types indicate a workflow for creating literature reviews with the ORKG. Content organization types are used to organize individual content types. Tools are part of the ORKG platform and support data creation and curation. System actors display different actors that are part of ORKG workflows.

2. ORKG Overview

We provide an overview of the core concepts and functionalities of the ORKG, including Benchmarks, Comparisons, Reviews, Observatories, Lists, Content Curation, and Data Use with tools such as Jupyter [17].

Content curation is a critical aspect of the ORKG, ensuring the knowledge graph remains accurate, relevant, and up-to-date. The ORKG supports both manual and automated curation processes. Researchers can contribute by adding, editing, and validating information, while automated tools help extract and update data from various sources. Effective content curation enhances the quality and reliability of the ORKG.

Semantic research contribution descriptions play a crucial role in structuring and standardizing the way research findings are represented. By using predefined templates, the ORKG ensures key elements of research contributions, such as hypotheses, methodologies, results, and conclusions are captured in a consistent and machine-readable format. These templates facilitate the research problem and field-specific annotation of research articles, enabling precise extraction and integration of data. This semantic structuring enhances the discoverability and comparability of research contributions, but also supports automated reasoning and advanced queries.

Lists are curated collections of related research items, such as articles, datasets, benchmarks, or software tools. They serve as an organizational tool to group and categorize information based on specific criteria or themes. Lists can be created and maintained by researchers or automatically generated based on predefined rules and algorithms.

Comparisons are a fundamental feature of the ORKG, allowing researchers to systematically compare research findings in a machine-assisted manner. The ORKG supports the creation of comparative tables and visualizations that highlight similarities and differences between studies. This capability is essential for synthesizing knowledge, identifying trends, and making informed decisions based on comprehensive data.

Reviews facilitate aggregating and structuring information from multiple sources. Researchers can use the ORKG to support systematic reviews and meta-analyses, providing a comprehensive overview of the current state of knowledge on a specific topic. The structured format of the ORKG ensures that reviews are detailed, transparent, and easily editable as new research emerges.

Benchmarks refer to standardized datasets and metrics used to evaluate and compare the performance of various methods and algorithms. The ORKG enables researchers to publish, share, discover, and reuse benchmarks, facilitating the validation and comparison of scientific results across different studies. By providing a common framework for benchmarking, the ORKG promotes transparency and reproducibility in scientific research.

Observatories are specialized knowledge hubs focused on specific research areas or themes. They are domain-specific entry points to the ORKG, providing a centralized platform for monitoring and analyzing trends, advancements, and gaps in research. Observatories are valuable for researchers, policymakers, and other stakeholders seeking to stay informed about developments in specific fields.

Data Use with Jupyter provides robust support for data use and analysis. Researchers can access ORKG data programmatically, enabling them to perform sophisticated analyses, create advanced visualizations, and develop interactive dashboards. Researchers can leverage the extensive ecosystem of Python, R, or comparable packages to enhance their data analysis workflows. The integration with the ORKG allows for seamless data retrieval, manipulation, and visualization, thus supporting the productive use of the ORKG in research.

These functionalities are enabled by the ORKG's robust architecture and modern technologies, which are designed to facilitate efficient knowledge management, data integration, and advanced analysis. A high-level overview of ORKG-related concepts is displayed in Figure 1. The previously discussed content types are part of the ORKG graph itself. In addition, there are content organization types, including research fields, research problems, Sustainable Development Goals (SDGs), and observatories. The content organization entities can be assigned to content types, as a means to organize the content types. Consequently, content types are searchable by their respective fields, addresses, problems, SDGs, and the observatory they belong to. The listed tools in the figure provide user interfaces to consume and curate the ORKG content. Finally, the system actors show the stakeholders of the system and their user interaction roles.

2.1. Architecture and Technology

The ORKG has been developed on top of a modern and scalable architecture while taking advantage of both mature and state-of-the-art technologies integrated in a microservice architecture. The ORKG is based on a knowledge graph – a powerful data model to structure, interconnect, and semantically enrich information. The way scientific knowledge is modeled in the knowledge graph is similar to RDF [18], in that it is based around the notion of a statement, consisting of two nodes (entities) linked by a directed edge (see Section 3.1). Similar to, but different from RDF, the ORKG uses a Labeled Property Graph (LPG) that is natively more suitable for identifying statements uniquely, and for qualifying these instances through annotating edges/statements. Provenance information is a particular application of such annotations and one of the metadata fields that has been identified as necessary to be connected with statements.

The ORKG ecosystem is designed along two concepts: first, it consists of a microservice architecture, and, second, it follows a classical layered architecture for all its components. This approach enables components and services to scale horizontally while keeping concerns separate. Also, it supports the rapid prototyping and deployment of new features by a larger development/research community, without affecting the performance of the ORKG as a service. Figure 2 gives an overview of the architecture of the ORKG and shows the main components of the platform and their dependencies. This figure also shows that we can add new features driven by real-world use cases while working within the existing functions and services. Furthermore, the microservices paradigm enables the decoupling of services so that they can be developed, deployed, and scaled independently of each other. A modular architecture ensures flexibility and maintainability, so that problems in one service do not affect the entire system.

In addition, each ORKG component follows a layered architecture (data access, business logic, and presentation), thus adhering to the separation of concerns. This architectural pattern helps developers achieve code organization and testability, and enables the reuse of different components or services. By following these software engineering principles, the ORKG system can evolve with changing requirements, adapt to new technologies, and scale to cope with increasing workloads and data volumes. The use of a microservice architecture combined with the layered architecture for each component provides a robust, extensible, and sustainable system capable of meeting the requirements of the research community.

In the realization of this architecture, the ORKG uses a very heterogeneous technology stack. At the core, the backend is implemented in Java, with the Spring Boot framework, guaranteeing good support for REST APIs and component communication, along with the smooth integration of external services. Additional REST APIs are exposed in Python, which is used for functionality that either requires higher flexibility or needs specialized libraries. At the center of the ORKG is a Neo4J-based[2] knowledge graph that enables both effective storage and querying for complex scholarly relationships. The Qdrant[3] vector store enriches the graph structure with advanced search functionality, such as similarity search and semantic matching. Furthermore, the frontend is powered by modern web technologies that guarantee good user experience across devices: ReactJS[4] for dynamic user interfaces, NextJS[5] for server-side rendering, and Tailwind CSS[6] for responsive design and styling web pages.

[2]https://neo4j.com/

[3]https://qdrant.tech/

[4]https://react.dev/

[5]https://nextjs.org/

[6]https://tailwindcss.com/

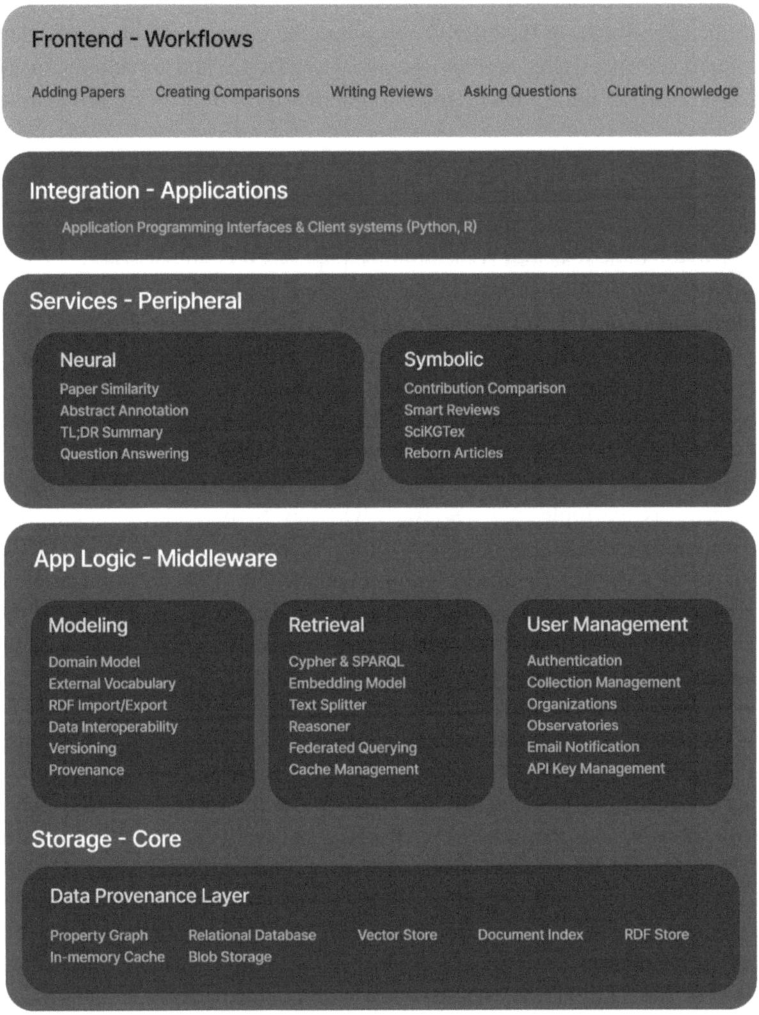

Figure 2. The ORKG technological architecture. The diagram highlights the main components of the ORKG ecosystem and the layered dependencies between the various components.

The ORKG promotes open science and transparency; hence, the codebase is completely open source. Such commitment furthers collaboration, innovation, and gives researchers and developers around the world the opportunity to audit, improve, and further adapt the platform. With open source development, the ORKG stands for a community-driven platform that evolves to meet the demands of the research community.

3. Symbolic Sub-system

The symbolic sub-system of the ORKG comprises the generic knowledge model, a templating system for specifying domain-specific knowledge, and a method for symbolic knowledge production tightly integrated into the phases of the research life-cycle.

3.1. Symbolic Knowledge Model

We briefly describe the main types that constitute ORKG's symbolic knowledge model, specifically statements, research contributions, papers, and comparisons.

Inspired by the RDF data model, the *Statement* is the basic type of the symbolic knowledge model in the ORKG. A Statement s_t is a triple $s_t = (s, p, o)$ for the statement's subject s and object o related by a predicate p. In terms of graph data model, s, o are KG nodes and p is a directed KG edge relating s with o. Logically, subjects s are ORKG Resources (i.e., instances, named individuals), predicates p are ORKG Predicates (aka Properties), and objects o may be ORKG Resources or ORKG Literals.

Building on statements, the ORKG symbolic knowledge model defines the *Research Contribution* r_c as the tuple $r_c = (\mathbf{S_t}, \mathbf{R_m})$, whereby $\mathbf{S_t}$ is a set of statements $s_t \in \mathbf{S_t}$ and $\mathbf{R_m}$ is a set of metadata associated with the research contribution r_c. ORKG does not further specify the set $\mathbf{S_t}$ of a research contribution. The general guideline is for a set $\mathbf{S_t}$ to describe a research finding originally published in an article, including the addressed research problem and the utilized materials and methods. Users may specify sets $\mathbf{S_t}$ using ORKG Templates (see Section 3.2). In the ORKG, the metadata set $\mathbf{R_m}$ consists of classic bibliographic metadata elements such as title, authors, and identifiers as well as provenance metadata elements including creation time and contributing user.

Building on research contributions, the ORKG symbolic knowledge model defines two primary derivative types: the ORKG *Paper* p_r as the tuple $p_r = (\mathbf{R_c}, \mathbf{R_m})$ and the ORKG *Comparison* c_r as the tuple $c_r = (\mathbf{R_c}, \mathbf{R_m})$, whereby $\mathbf{R_c}$ is a set of research contributions $r_c \in \mathbf{R_c}$ and $\mathbf{R_m}$ is a set of metadata associated with the paper p_r or the comparison c_r, respectively. ORKG papers and comparisons are thus both aggregations of research contributions. The main difference is that for papers p_r the aggregation consists of research contributions as originally published in a *single* research article while for comparisons c_r the aggregation consists of research contributions that share a common dimension (typically the research problem), but are originally published in *multiple* research articles[7]. ORKG papers are thus descriptions of the research findings originally published in the corresponding articles while ORKG comparisons juxtapose research findings to enable overviews of the state-of-the-art.

Describing the research findings originally published in an article in the ORKG involves the task of semantic parsing, i.e., determining how to model the semantic content of specific natural language statements into a graph representation by choosing appropriate ontology terms and graph patterns (i.e., semantic data schemata). Such graph patterns can be specified using constraint languages such as the Shapes Constraint Language (SHACL; see also Section 3.2).

Due to the high expressivity of the underlying triple structure (s, p, o) of the graph, any given natural language statement can be modelled in numerous and fundamentally

[7] As a corner case, it is possible to compare two or more research contributions originally published in a single research article, but in practice this is uncommon.

different ways. If a knowledge graph allowed more than one semantic pattern for modelling the same type of information and if it did not restrict the choice of ontology terms to be used in such a pattern, it would encounter substantial semantic interoperability issues regarding terminological and propositional interoperability, resulting in lack of overall findability, interoperability, and reusability of information within the graph [19].

Knowledge graphs typically attempt to model a mind-independent reality, with nodes representing real-world entities or concepts and the edges representing the relationships or associations between them. Many knowledge graphs apply this modelling paradigm and restrict their content to a specific scope, thereby typically employing a *static information extraction approach* in which they model a fixed set of statement types using a fixed set of associated graph patterns and ontologies. This *static knowledge graph construction approach* allows for the pre-definition of all necessary graph patterns and ontology terms, ensuring a logically consistent and semantically interoperable structure, resulting in a truly FAIR knowledge graph that supports reasoning. For ontology engineers closely collaborating with respective domain experts it is feasible to specify the limited set of graph patterns required for modelling all relevant information that is in the scope of the knowledge graph and to agree on the ontology terms being used with these patterns.

With its open, cross-domain scope, the ORKG, however, cannot adhere to the conventional static information extraction approach. Instead, it follows a *community-driven dynamic knowledge graph construction (DKGC) approach*, where the graph's information and knowledge are continuously evolving. DKGC approaches present unique challenges, as it is not feasible to pre-define all graph patterns and ontology terms required for modelling the information and knowledge that ORKG users might want to add. Consequently, the task of semantic parsing is imposed on the user, usually without support from an ontology engineer. This shift represents a significant barrier to data entry into the ORKG and is likely to lead into semantic ambiguities, logical inconsistencies across the knowledge graph, general data quality issues, and a lack of semantic interoperability and FAIRness of its data, resulting in limited findability of knowledge within the graph. Additionally, DKGC approaches usually require versioning of the graph's contents, as users may modify them at any time. Ideally, this versioning would include a detailed editing history to provide transparency and build trust among users.

Another consequence of applying the DKGC approach in cross-domain knowledge graphs is that reasoning over the entire graph is out of scope for both practical and theoretical reasons. Practically, it is not feasible to develop graph patterns across all domains that are logically consistent using ontology terms. Theoretically, constructing a set of ontologies that are both logically consistent and meet domain-specific requirements is impossible. For instance, Newtonian physics and quantum physics are ontologically inconsistent, yet physicists rely on both. However, when achieving reasoning capability is no longer a viable goal, tuples need not necessarily reflect the underlying semantics of a mind-independent reality. This opens new possibilities for modelling the information and knowledge in the graph.

To address the challenges of applying the DKGC approach, we developed and are currently implementing the *Rosetta Statement (RS) Approach* [20] for modelling natural language statements. The core idea is that statements are the smallest units of information that are semantically meaningful to a human. By adopting the RDF reification approach and applying it to simple natural language statements instead of triples, we defined a very general model that can be applied to any natural language statement comprising a subject phrase, a predicate/verb, and one or more object phrases. Each statement is represented in the graph by its own ORKG Resource, to which respective subject and object resources—instantiating appropriate ontology classes—are linked, enabling straightforward modelling of n-ary relations. The statement resource instantiates a corresponding RS class, defined based on the underlying predicate/verb. To each RS class, a graph pattern in the form of an ORKG template is associated. Since all RSs follow the same general underlying graph pattern, users can specify new types of RS classes and accompanying graph patterns by answering a set of simple questions, requiring no background in formal semantics and no support by ontology engineers. For each Rosetta template, we also specify a dynamic label that provides a human-readable sentence, with the subject and objects being variables identified by parsing the labels of the corresponding subject and object resources and literals of a given RS. Consequently, all content in the ORKG that has been modelled using RSs will be human-readable. Moreover, the approach supports versioning and provides a detailed editing history for each RS.

Modelling natural language statements instead of a mind-independent reality offers several advantages. It simplifies the semantic parsing task, lowering the barrier for adding content to the ORKG. It also provides a universal and generally applicable graph data structure against which functions can be programmed without having to consider the various peculiarities of domain-specific graph patterns, as it would be the case when modelling a mind-independent reality. Furthermore, the structural proximity of RSs to natural language statements facilitates the involvement of Large Language Models (LLMs) in developing services and functions to support users in any task that involves interacting with the graph. And although graphs based on the Rosetta approach are not capable of reasoning, reasoning capability can still be achieved for subgraphs within the ORKG by defining schema crosswalks between selected RS templates and graph patterns that support reasoning.

3.2. Specifying Domain-specific Symbolic Knowledge with Templates

Building on the Shapes Constraint Language (SHACL) [21] to define and enforce data structures, ORKG templates enable the definition of domain-specific knowledge types and support data consistency and quality.

While the ORKG does not implement SHACL in its entirety, it utilizes SHACL's vocabulary to guide the setup of input forms and validate data. This approach maintains data quality and structure without the need for full SHACL implementation on the graph and by adopting SHACL, the ORKG ensures that data adheres to specific formats and constraints, facilitating interoperability and enhancing the reliability of scientific knowledge integration. This approach allows machines to effectively understand and compare knowledge originally published in different articles.

The overall template system function is illustrated in Figure 3. Domain experts create templates that define the knowledge type of research contributions, integrating these templates with ontologies through the TIB Terminology Service[8]. This integration enriches the templates with standardized vocabularies, ensuring that the data captured is consistent with broader semantic frameworks.

[8] `https://terminology.tib.eu/ts`

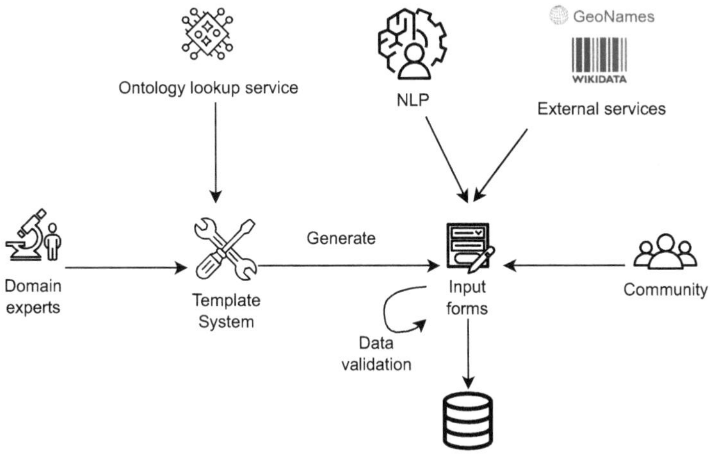

Figure 3. Schematic overview of the ORKG template system.

Once a template is created, the ORKG's Statement Browser component (Section 3.3) parses it, setting up the appropriate properties and constraints to generate specialized input forms. These forms ensure that data entered by researchers adheres to the template's specifications. Additionally, the system assists users by providing suggestions from the ORKG NLP service and offering autocomplete functionality that suggests values from well-established knowledge graphs such as Wikidata[9] or Geonames[10] for location values.

Before storing any new data, the Statement Browser validates it against the template's constraints, ensuring that it meets the expected data types, formats, and relationships. This validation process is crucial for maintaining the integrity of the data within the ORKG. Furthermore, it assists users by providing suggestions from the large language model (Section 5.2), ensuring that the introduced values accord with guidelines[11], especially when no restrictions have been set by the domain expert while creating the template.

The ORKG template system incorporates the ORKG NLP system, which assists users in selecting the most appropriate template for their research. When a researcher adds a paper, the system suggests a template based on the paper's research field, title, and abstract. This feature streamlines the data entry process and ensures that the data is organized in a manner that aligns with the article's content.

The template visualization diagram is an integral part of the template editor. This feature offers a UML-like representation to visually map the structure and relationships of templates. The diagram aids in comprehending complex template designs, allowing users to grasp the overall schema and connections more intuitively. Figure 4 presents the different components of the diagram. Each entity in the diagram represents a template in the ORKG. The header displays the template name and its associated target class, while the property relationships are presented visually through edges linking the properties to their respective template entities. The template visualization diagram is a powerful

[9]https://www.wikidata.org
[10]https://www.geonames.org/
[11]https://orkg.org/help-center/article/42/Modeling_best_practices_for_resources_and_properties

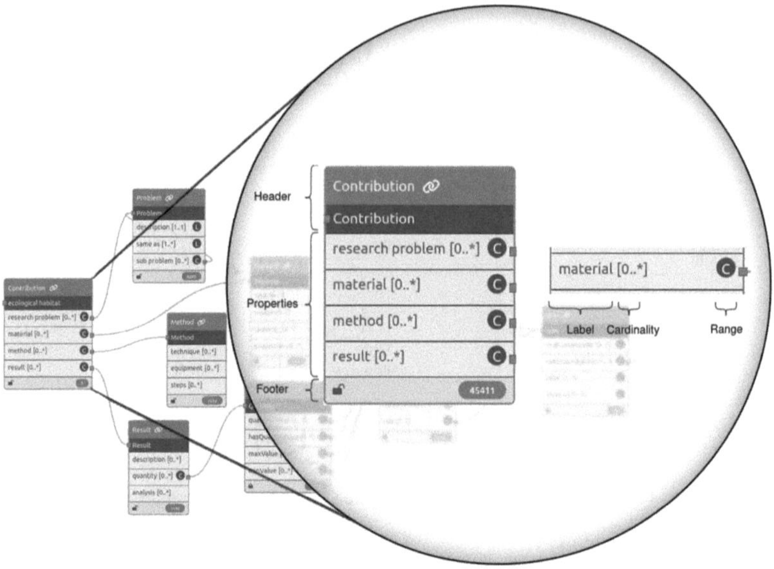

Figure 4. ORKG template diagram with a zoom in on one of the entities.

tool for quickly understanding the structure of templates, making it more accessible and efficient for users to analyze, create, and modify templates.

3.3. Symbolic Knowledge Production During Phases of the Research Life-cycle

Since scientific knowledge is generally available in unstructured form, producing structured symbolic knowledge is a key challenge for the ORKG. We have pursued related techniques falling into two broad categories: (1) expert-driven structuring, including author-driven at the time of knowledge production (i.e. pre-publication during phases of the research life-cycle) and (2) machine-driven structuring via knowledge extraction from articles (post-publication). Knowledge extraction is powered by ORKG's neural sub-system presented in Section 4. In this section, we present the expert-driven category of techniques, namely the statement browser in ORKG's frontend, SciKGTeX supporting annotations in LaTeXmanuscripts, and reborn articles enabling symbolic knowledge production in data analysis and final data production.

Statement Browser. The ORKG statement browser is a component of the Web-based frontend supporting the expert-driven manual description of research contributions as symbolic scientific knowledge. Knowledge is described as sets of statements, each consisting of a subject, property, and object. The frontend displays the subject in the header of the statement browser, and the property and object as columns. This simplifies user input, as data input is similar to providing key-value pairs, for the property and object positions, respectively. To further simplify user input, the statement browser integrates the ORKG template system presented in Section 3.2 to assist user input with user-defined knowledge types that specify properties and their constraints, presented by the frontend to users as forms. Furthermore, the statement browser integrates different data viewers, depending on the data type. This includes the display of data tables, images, videos, expressions in LaTeX, maps, etc. To reflect state-of-the-art user interaction patterns, properties and resources are selected via an autocomplete input, guiding users into reusing existing terms when available. To enable suggestions and improve interoperability, the autocomplete input integrates with external terminologies, in particular Wikidata, GeoNames, and ontologies from the EBI Ontology Lookup Service (OLS). It is thus possible to discover and select required terms without leaving the ORKG frontend. As an additional feature, the data type selector supports specifying the data type of objects. This includes resources (via the autocomplete) and literals (i.e., text, decimal, boolean, date, etc.). Additionally, special data types such as `Empty` and `List` allow for indicating that certain data are not reported in an article or support creating ordered lists. Finally, the statement browser also includes Smart Suggestions, as discussed in Section 5.1. These suggestions provide guidance to users while interacting with the statement browser. The statement browser is a reusable component, integrated at various locations in the ORKG frontend.

SciKGTeX. Similar to systems such as dokieli [22], SciKGTeX [23] supports symbolic knowledge production at the time of manuscript authoring during the scholarly communication phase of the research lifecycle. It is a LaTeXpackage for annotating research contributions directly in LaTeXsource code [24], based on the idea of "FAIR-by-Design" artifacts [25]. Authors can describe their manuscript with annotations and thereby create symbolic scientific knowledge that describes their research contributions at the time of writing. SciKGTeX embeds the annotations into the PDF's XMP metadata so that the symbolic knowledge persists with the manuscript. From the perspective of the research lifecycle, SciKGTeX anchors symbolic knowledge production in the scholarly communication phase and supports authors in creating "FAIR-by-Design" manuscripts [25]. These "FAIR-by-Design" manuscripts simplify the storage of the symbolic knowledge produced, which leads to better access to the knowledge of the manuscripts and thus lays the foundation for their effective (re-)use. The ORKG offers an upload function for SciKGTeX-annotated PDFs so that authors can easily add symbolic knowledge to the ORKG. Thus, the ORKG demonstrates how infrastructure providers can leverage such "FAIR-by-Design" manuscripts to automatically ingest symbolic knowledge in their systems and support dissemination, discoverability, and (re-)use of symbolic scientific knowledge.

Reborn Articles. The mainstream approach to scientific knowledge graph construction, i.e. symbolic scientific knowledge production, relies on knowledge extraction from published articles, either manually or supported by machines using NLP/LLM neural techniques (see Section 4). By enabling the structuring of knowledge at the time of knowledge production, specifically final data production in data analysis, reborn (born-reusable) articles [26] also fall into the category of expert-driven techniques that do not rely on knowledge extraction from articles. The primary intuition is that ORKG templates and, more generally, user-defined and well-specified data types accessible via Data Type Registries [27] including Schema.org, can be leveraged in any phase of the research lifecycle to ensure the efficient production of accurate and rich symbolic scientific knowledge. In addition to data analysis and manuscript authoring, this notion of "FAIR-by-Design" is applicable also earlier in the research lifecycle, e.g. in experiment and data management planning or in electronic lab notebooks that document experiment execution.

4. Neural Sub-system

Previous sections explored human curation methods for representing symbolic knowledge in the ORKG. This section transitions to discussing the automation goals against the backdrop of the ORKG, specifically those achieved using neural-network-based systems.

4.1. Generic Knowledge Extraction

As a start to the discussion on automation goals, this section highlights the importance of automated research field classification for scientific articles in the digital libraries generally as well as for the ORKG that are achieved using neural-network-based methods. Research field classification, which involves categorizing academic publications, represents a highly structured and specialized application within the broader context of generic knowledge extraction [4]. While generic knowledge extraction covers a wide range of techniques and applications across various data types and domains, research field classification focuses specifically on the academic domain, using similar techniques to achieve specialized goals in organizing and understanding scientific literature. As a subdomain of generic knowledge extraction, research field classification extracts textual features indicative of specific research fields by identifying relevant keywords, phrases, and contexts characteristic of certain disciplines [28,29,30,31]. This task enhances academic search engines and digital libraries [32,33,34,35,36] by enabling precise and relevant searches based on specific research fields. Furthermore, it supports bibliometric analysis, trend identification in research, and interdisciplinary studies by providing detailed classifications of scientific articles [37].

Recent advancements in neural systems for research field classification have significantly improved the precision and efficiency of categorizing scientific articles. One notable study introduces SCINOBO, a novel system that uses neural topic modeling [38] and community detection to dynamically construct a hierarchical Field-of-Science taxonomy, enhancing the classification of scientific papers across various domains [39]. This approach extends the taxonomy up to five levels, incorporating OECD fields [40] and demonstrating robust performance in classifying publications within the knowledge domains of Energy and AI. Additionally, a hierarchical classification system using deep learning, detailed by Rao et al. [41], categorizes research into a three-tier system, achieving high accuracy in distinguishing disciplines, fields, and subfields across 160 million abstracts. This system is designed to support both single-label and multi-label classification settings, showing over 90% accuracy in numerous experiments.

Language models, advanced systems using neural network architectures like transformers [42], are at the forefront of AI research and widely used for research field classification. Trained on vast amounts of text, they are specifically designed to generate and understand natural language, crucial for accurate text processing. These models utilize word embeddings, which are vector representations of words that capture their meanings, syntactic roles, and relationships with other words, enabling deeper semantic understanding. E.g., BERT (Bidirectional Encoder Representations from Transformers) [43] and its scientific variants [44,45,46], or the GPT series (Generative Pre-trained Transformer) [47,48,49]. Language models possess several key features in support of research field classification: 1) contextual understanding, which allows them to distinguish between different fields using similar terminology based on surrounding text; 2) semantic similarity, enabling accurate grouping of papers by understanding underlying topics and themes despite variations in vocabulary; 3) adaptability to new terminology, ensuring classifications remain current with evolving language use by training on diverse and recent datasets; 4) handling ambiguity and polysemy by using contextual clues to disambiguate terms with multiple meanings; 5) interdisciplinary insights, facilitating the classification of cross-disciplinary research by recognizing connections between different fields; and 6) scalability and efficiency, allowing rapid and comprehensive analysis of large volumes of research papers, crucial for managing the exponential growth of scientific literature. By leveraging these capabilities, language models can significantly enhance the accuracy and reliability of research field classification, supporting better organization and retrieval of scientific knowledge.

Building on these capabilities, the study by Wolff et al. [50] illustrates a practical application of language models for research field classification against the ORKG fields taxonomy. They employ a method using enriched BERT embeddings to classify articles into one of 123 predefined and representative fields from the ORKG taxonomy of over 700 research fields. Utilizing English scientific articles sourced from ORKG and arXiv, the team enhanced the dataset with metadata from bibliographic databases such as OpenAlex, Semantic Scholar, and Crossref. By leveraging various pre-trained language models, particularly BERT and its scientific variants like SciBERT, SciNCL, and SPECTER2 [51], the study focused on fine-tuned transfer learning approaches. The inclusion of additional metadata significantly improved classification accuracy, with the SPECTER2 model achieving the highest performance with a weighted F1-score of 0.7415. This approach demonstrates how combining pre-trained models with strategic data enrichment can further harness the inherent capabilities of language models, enhancing the precision and utility of automated scientific article classification systems.

4.2. Domain-specific Knowledge Extraction

Essential to support the automated construction of KGs such as the ORKG are also research-domain-specific automated KG extraction methods.

The emergence of the “deep learning tsunami” [52] revolutionized KG construction pipelines, which led to the adoption of neural learning techniques. Traditionally, this resulted in hybrid architectures that blended neural and symbolic methods, utilizing a sequence of complementary deep learning and rule-based strategies across different stages of the knowledge composition process to finally arrive at a KG. The CS-KG system [53] or AI-KG system [54] serves as a notable example of neural-symbolic scientific KG construction. It incorporated the DyGIEpp deep learning module [55], which operated within the transformers architecture [43] to extract predefined entities and relations. Additionally, it employed the Computer Science Ontology classifier (CSO-C) [56] for enhanced entity extraction. The system utilized the Stanford Core NLP suite’s OpenIE [57] to identify open domain relations, and the Stanford POS Tagger [58] to pinpoint verbs between entity pairs as potential relation candidates.

In general using the pipelined approach For KG construction, standard components include named entity recognition (NER) and relation extraction (RE) tasks, which can be efficiently handled by fine-tuning transformer models based on the BERT architecture [43] on specific datasets. BERT utilizes pretrained parameters from large-scale corpora like Wikipedia or Books, trained with a masked language model objective, enabling robust natural language understanding. The fine-tuning procedure involves initializing the desired language model with these pretrained parameters and then tuning the probabilistic parameters within task-specific architectures for downstream extraction tasks such as NER or RE using task-specific datasets. In the scientific domain, widely used transformer models include SciBERT [44], PubMedBERT [59], SemMedDB [60], BioBERT [61], BioClinicalBERT [62], and BlueBERT [63].

Additionally, in scientific KG construction, it is common to leverage external ontologies and knowledge bases for entity and relation extraction and linking, a practice often observed in biomedicine. Ontologies facilitate standardized representations and ensure interoperability between KGs, thereby enhancing their effectiveness and utility in complex research settings. For instance, the iASiS KG [64], which extracts knowledge from biomedical scientific articles on lung cancer and dementia, utilizes NLP techniques and standardized biomedical ontologies such as UMLS [65] to annotate entities and relations. This particular KG focuses on capturing knowledge about drug interactions in treatments for lung cancer, which also defines its scope for knowledge extraction. Another example is OpenBioDiv [66] in the domain of biodiversity science, where the knowledge extraction objective is guided by the OpenBiodiv-O ontology [67]. Consequently, the focus of knowledge extraction for KG construction varies by domain, ranging from diseases in biomedicine to plant treatments in biodiversity.

As introduced earlier, the ORKG aims to capture the contributions or structured salient facets of research. In this vein, showcased in the next sections 4.2.1 and 4.2.2 are two different domain-specific knowledge extraction objectives that have been explored for the ORKG.

4.2.1. Leaderboards Extraction

In the field or domain of artificial intelligence (AI), researchers commonly develop new models aimed at achieving state-of-the-art (SOTA) performance, reported through four key elements: Task, Dataset, Metric, and Score (T, D, M, S). Recently, it has become standard to compile these details into community-managed leaderboards, which function like scoreboards, showcasing the scores of various AI models for specific tasks, datasets, and metrics. The ORKG platform exemplifies this with its benchmarks feature. Figure 5 highlights the shift from traditional article-based reporting of (T, D, M, S) to recording them in the ORKG leaderboards. Moving away from the traditional community-curated approach, automated text mining techniques are now prevalent. The goal of such automation is to develop systems that can analyze the full text of AI research papers, determine if they report model performance on benchmark datasets, and extract all relevant (T, D, M, S) tuples [68,69].

Language model based neural systems have been shown to be efficacious for the (T, D, M, S) knowledge extraction task. The focus of these automated tasks has shifted from entailment testing [71,70,72] to generation tasks [73,74,75], driven by advancements in large language models (LLMs). Knowledge extraction systems developed by Kabongo et al. [73,74] are notable advancements. Their recent approach involved leveraging the FLAN-T5 strategy [76], which encompassed fine-tuning a pre-trained LLM with a standard set of instructions to better equip it for various tasks. Using the applicable instructions from the FLAN-T5 collection, they fine-tuned LLMs such as Mistral-7B [77] and LLaMA 2 [78], to improve their suitability for the (T, D, M, S) extraction task. For this fine-tuning, they employed the QLoRA (Quantized Low-Rank Adaptation) technique

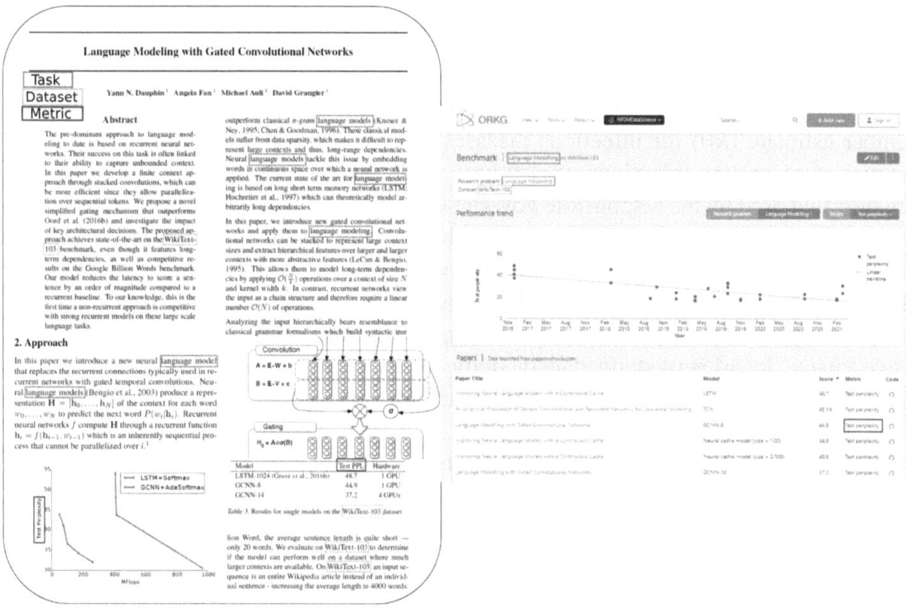

Figure 5. This figure presents a side-by-side comparison: on the left, it shows task, dataset, and metric information published in the traditional PDF format as non-machine-actionable data; on the right, the same information is displayed as machine-actionable data, recorded within the leaderboard of the ORKG benchmarks feature. This figure is reproduced from the original manuscript [70].

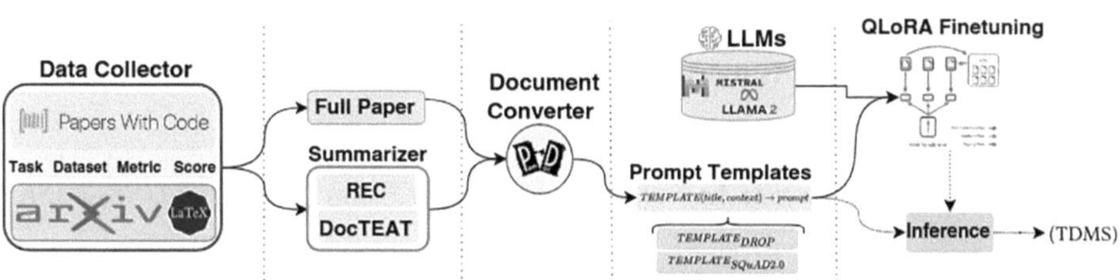

Figure 6. The automated (Task, Dataset, Metric, Score) knowledge extraction task workflow with large language model (LLM)-based neural systems. This figure is reproduced from the original manuscript [73].

[79], which reduces the computational cost and memory footprint by efficiently adapting the model using quantization and low-rank approximation techniques. Figure 6 illustrates the overall workflow of the approach. To identify the optimal context for (T, D, M, S) knowledge extraction, they tested heuristic-based methods focusing on parts of the article most likely to contain this information. They experimented with DocTAET (title, abstract, experimental setup, and tabular information), DocREC (results, experiments, and conclusions), and DocFULL (entire text). Among these, DocTAET proved to be the most effective. For additional experimental insights, we refer the reader to the original paper [73].

4.2.2. Basic Reproduction Number Estimate (R0) Extraction

As a second showcase, we address domain-specific knowledge extraction for the ORKG, focusing on a key research problem in Epidemics and Virology: the basic reproduction number estimate (*R*0) for infectious diseases. The *R*0 estimate represents the average number of secondary infections caused by a single infected individual [80] and was a key informat used by the responsible government organizations during the Covid 19 pandemic. The extraction objective was to develop an automated system to extract the *R*0 estimate values including its other relevant properties to add to the ORKG. Following the (T, D, M, S) extraction objective discussed earlier, and based on a preliminary research comparison[81], the comprehensive knowledge extraction target included six properties: disease name, location of study, date of study, *R*0 estimate value, %CI (confidence interval) values, and the method used to estimate the *R*0.

Despite current advancements in LLMs, they are noted to still struggle with specialised domains like science [82,83]. Efforts to align LLMs with scientific demands for knowledge extraction are in early stages, focusing on domain-specific fine-tuning [84]. To address the *R*0 estimates knowledge extraction task highlighted in this section, Shamsabadi et al. [85] instruction-finetuned an LLM, specifically the 780M parameter Flan-T5 variant [76], to align it with the extraction objective. They subsequently created a queryable knowledge graph (KG) as part of the ORKG for virologists [86]. Some of the representative infectious diseases extracted were covid-19, dengue, influenza, HIV, SARS, MERS-COV, cholera etc. Based on evaluations of the model's extraction performance on a gold-standard corpus of 1,500 annotated abstracts [87], their model (ORKG-FLAN-$T5_{R0}$) outperformed the vanilla variants of the finetuned models, i.e., T5 [88] and FLAN-T5, as well as a state-of-the-art GPT model with over a billion parameters, despite having significantly fewer parameters than GPT. This work, along with similar studies in biomedicine [89] and materials science [90], suggests that domain-specific instruction-finetuning of LLMs supports transfer learning and enhances knowledge extraction performance.

4.3. Neuro-symbolic Question Answering on Millions of Publications with ORKG ASK

The ORKG offers innovative approaches for interacting with scientific knowledge. Among these, the ORKG Assistant for Scientific Knowledge (ASK, ask.orkg.org) stands out as a modern tool for researchers and academics. ASK provides an intuitive natural language interface that enables users to search through millions of indexed and cataloged scientific items with ease and precision.

Embedding-based Scientific Literature Search. Traditional search engines generally only leverage keyword matching whereas the technology behind ASK permits input of full research questions and by leveraging document embeddings in turn greatly improves the relevance and accuracy of search results. This approach minimizes time and effort spent on locating relevant information, helping researchers to focus on their primary work instead of sorting among tons of irrelevant documents. ORKG ASK is not limited to classic search engine constraints, it actively helps to filter through the massive corpus of scientific literature and in practice, produces a set of documents that are directly relevant to a researcher's inquiry. In addition, it automatically generates important information based on these documents to assist researchers in their knowledge discovery.

ASK Overview. ASK is built upon three fundamental components, each playing a crucial role in its functionality:

- *Semantic Search:* Utilizes advanced natural language processing techniques to understand the context and meaning behind user queries.
- *Large Language Model (LLM):* Employs state-of-the-art AI to process and analyze scientific texts.
- *Knowledge Graphs (KGs):* Organizes and interconnects scientific information in a structured, easily navigable format.

The typical ASK service interaction can be summarized as follows:

1. *Query Input:* The researcher starts by formulating a research question.
2. *Semantic Parsing:* A semantic search component parses the question and represents it in a dense numerical vector capturing its essence.
3. *Corpus Comparison:* The resulting vector representation is then compared with a vast corpus of indexed documents, which have been similarly embedded.
4. *Relevant Article Retrieval:* Using Approximate Nearest Neighbor (ANN) algorithms [91], ASK identifies the most relevant articles within the corpus.
5. *Information Extraction:* Once relevant articles are found, a series of tailored prompts guide the generation of important details based on the articles' content.
6. *Retrieval Augmented Generation (RAG):* Built on top of open-source LLMs (e.g., Mistral [77]), the RAG [92] process ensures that the generated information comes only from the retrieved articles, minimizing the hallucinations of content. RAG does not ensure verbatim generation from the text, rather it limits the model to use in-context learning compared to parametric knowledge.
7. *Results Presentation:* Items of interest and extracted information are presented in tables that display item-specific formats, similar to traditional literature review tables.
8. *Knowledge Graph Integration:* The knowledge graph can be used for additional processing to refine results or filter the search space. It also acts as a core, linking the generated content to third-party knowledge graphs through Linked Open Data entities such as DBpedia [93].

Figure 7 shows a high-level depiction of a question answering workflow that invokes multiple components of the system in order to find relevant documents and answer the posed research question with citable claims.

Functionalities Beyond Search. Though various steps and components are involved from the moment a research question is presented to the system and the relevant documents are retrieved and augmented with relevant extracted information, ASK is a user-functionality-rich tool. Figure 8 shows the design of the ASK user interface. The interface is designed to be simple and accessible to all users but still capable of a wide array of functionalities.

We tag the figure with multiple nodes to highlight the actions that users can perform. *Node 1* (Question Answering) displays the input field for the research question. The answers to the question are presented in two ways. *Node 2* offers a synthesized response based on the top five resulting documents from the semantic search, while *Node 3* displays answers (if available) based on the individual papers. *Node 4* highlights the information extraction aspect of the workflow. Beyond answering the research question,

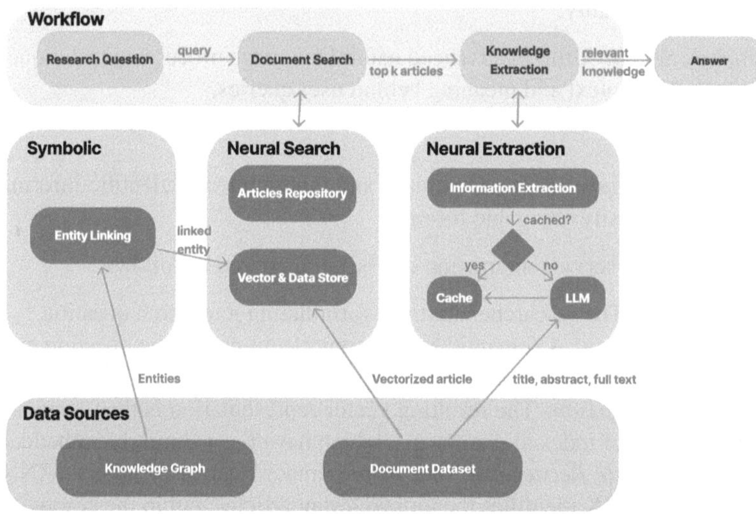

Figure 7. High-level sketch of the ORKG ASK workflow. The workflow shows how the system invokes both symbolic and neural subsystems to answer natural language questions from its internal document index.

additional information is extracted from relevant papers and displayed in tabular format (columns) next to the answer *Node 3*. A researcher is able to use this functionality to extract particular pieces of information that are more relevant to their search (e.g., dataset, participant count, etc.).

Given the large number of research articles out there and the sizable subset indexed within ASK, the use of filters is necessary to further narrow down the search space. *Node 5* exposes a fine-grained filtering system that enables users to refine their search based on various criteria such as language, year, citation count, and author names. This functionality can be used in conjunction with the bibliography manager that is integrated in the user interface *Node 8*. The manager empowers users to store and organize articles in collections under "My Library". As such articles can be added via the bookmark icon in the interface *Node 8*. Furthermore, it is possible for user to incorporate articles into My library by using DOI, title, or BibTeX import. These manually added articles are visually distinguished (by color) in the interface to provide feedback to the user.

To facilitate data reuse, articles are represented in CLS-Json format, providing standardized bibliographic metadata. With *Node 7* users can cite data items in various styles such as APA, Harvard, etc., and export citations in multiple formats including BibTeX and CLS-Json. Additionally, the entire search result table can be exported to CSV and ORKG CSV formats as highlighted with *Node 6*. To further enrich the data, an Entity Linking pipeline continuously applied to abstracts enables filtering articles based on semantically identical concepts that are mentioned in the relevant items.

In this section, we presented the details of ORKG ASK, a neuro-symbolic question answering tool. ASK with the integration of semantic search, large language models, and knowledge graphs, provides a novel solution for researchers to process vast amounts of scientific literature. In addition to saving time, ASK expands the scale of analysis in lit-

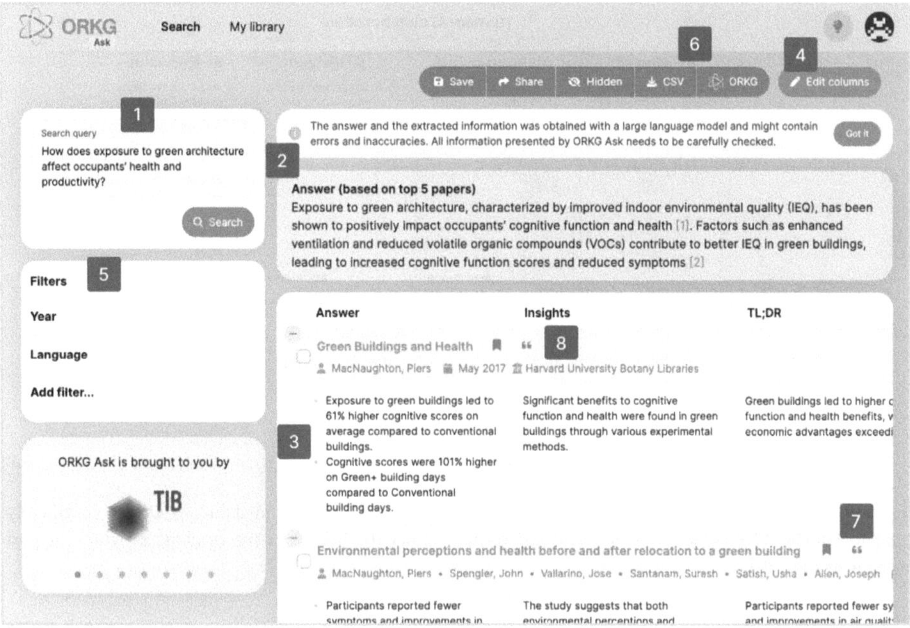

Figure 8. Design of the search result page of the ORKG ASK system. Different interaction opportunities for users are highlighted on the interface in numbered blue nodes.

erature reviews, potentially leading to new findings and connections in various fields of study. With the increasing volume of published scientific articles, tools such as ORKG ASK are necessary to ensure relevant research is easily found. By streamlining the literature review process, ASK enables researchers to advance scientific discovery.

5. Human-AI Collaboration

The ORKG takes an expert-sourced approach to describe knowledge in a structured form. This means that human intelligence plays a key role. However, we leverage AI to provide user assistance where possible. Broadly, ORKG user interactions can be divided into knowledge *consumers* and knowledge *creators*. AI assistance mainly targets knowledge creators, helping them to 1) simplify tasks, 2) reduce workload, and 3) improve data quality. Creating knowledge includes both generating new knowledge and curating and validating existing knowledge. The main task for ORKG content creators can be described as transforming unstructured scholarly knowledge (i.e., for scholarly articles) to structured scholarly knowledge. This is a multifaceted task that includes both data modeling and knowledge extraction.

5.1. Classification of Human-AI Collaboration

In the ORKG interface, different types of Human-AI interaction take place. Figure 9 displays a classification of these interactions. The AI-Absent approach is a traditional approach where users transform the data manually, without any AI assistance. In the ORKG, it is possible to use the system in such a way that no AI interaction happens. This

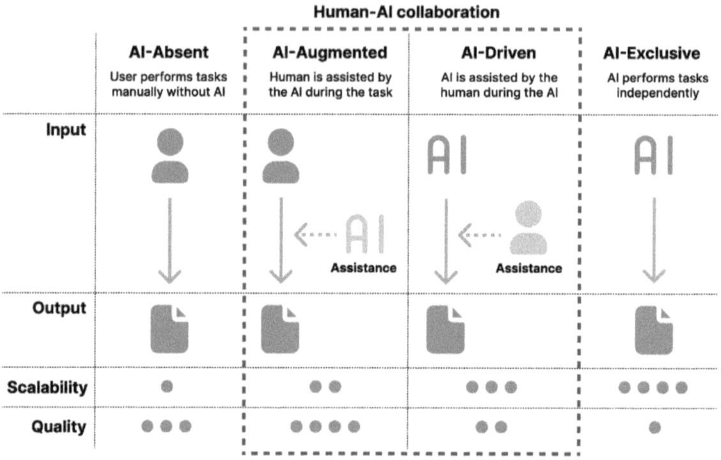

Figure 9. A classification of Human-AI interaction styles, where AI-Augmented and AI-Driven specifically relate to Human-AI collaboration. In these approaches, either the human or the machine provides support during a specific task.

means knowledge can be structured fully in a manual way. Scalability is a challenge with this approach, as you need more manual labor, to transform more knowledge. However, the reliability of the data transformation is generally high compared to the other methods.

Human-AI collaboration takes place in the AI-Augmented approach. As in the AI-Absent approach, the human still takes the initiative of describing the content in a structured form. Concretely, that means that a user decides which papers to describe and how to do this. However, during the process, the user is assisted with AI support. In the ORKG, this type of user interaction underlies numerous features, such as Smart Suggestions, PDF Annotator, and general recommendations in the User Interface (UI). Compared to the fully manual approach, scalability is improving as efficiency improves. Depending on the use case, the reliability could be the highest of all methods, given that the AI can point users towards mistakes and thus help them to improve the output quality.

Another type of Human-AI collaboration takes place in the AI-Driven interaction approach. Here the AI takes the initiative instead of the human. The human helps the AI in specific stages, for example, to verify, improve, and complete data. This means that the AI automatically processes articles and the user at a later point in time can validate the knowledge. In the ORKG, we experimented with the TinyGenius [94] approach, which follows this workflow of automatic extraction and manual verification. This approach is more scalable as machines are able to transform large quantities of scholarly knowledge. However, the reliability, or quality, of the extractions is lower compared to methods where human intelligence is involved.

Finally, the AI-Exclusive approach does not include human intelligence, meaning that no Human-AI collaboration takes place. The scalability of this approach is highest, as no manual labor is required, and scaling will only depend on machine resources. The reliability of such knowledge transformations is lowest compared to the other methods. This approach is currently not implemented in the ORKG, as data quality is an important aim for the ORKG.

5.2. Implementations in the ORKG

We will now discuss implementations of Human-AI collaboration in the ORKG, specifically focusing on AI-Augmented and AI-Driven interactions. To ensure ORKG users are aware of AI support in the ORKG, we use the same recognizable color scheme (green-blue, as displayed in Figure 10) throughout the UI. Additionally, we use the term "Smart" to indicate that a UI component is supported by AI.

ORKG **Smart Suggestions** uses an AI-Augmented interaction, where users are assisted by AI while performing a specific task. They provide a non-intrusive way of integrating (for instance) LLMs into the information transformation task [95]. This is done by placing a small button with a lightbulb icon at multiple locations in the UI (see Figure 10). Smart Suggestions have been integrated for approximately six tasks, including recommendation of properties, value recommendation for specific properties, assessing descriptiveness of metadata, providing guidance for creating reusable property labels, and more. These tasks are identified by considering previous user interaction by ORKG team members and are therefore meant to partially replace human assistance while using the ORKG. By positioning Smart Suggestion as optional guidance for users, existing workflows are not disturbed, simplifying LLM integration into an existing UI. Feedback is collected to ensure the performance of different LLM tasks can be tracked. Depending on the task, relevant context is inserted into the LLM prompt to provide more accurate suggestions.

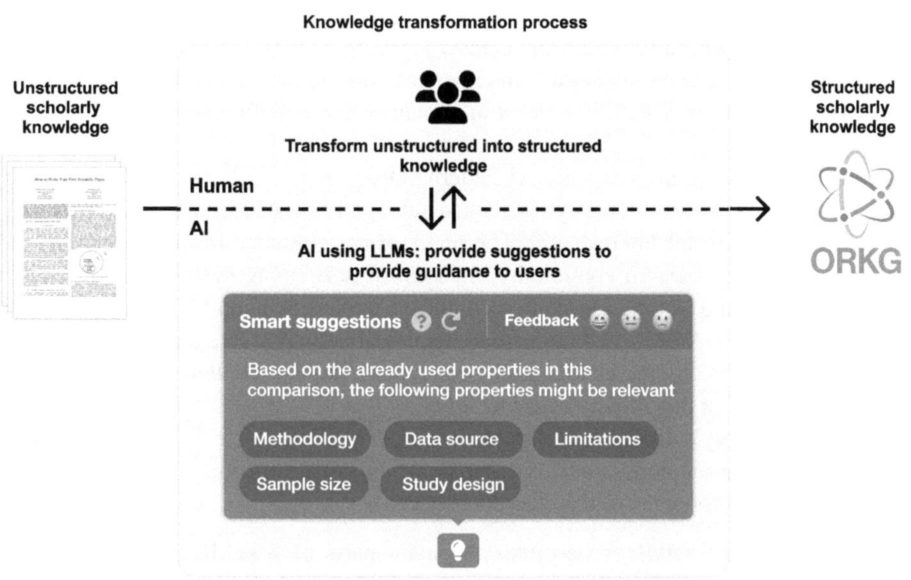

Figure 10. Smart Suggestions as implemented in the ORKG UI displayed by clicking the light bulb button. [96]

The **PDF Annotator** tool enables users to annotate key sentences in a paper with a list of predefined discourse classes [96]. This tool also takes an AI-Augmented approach; while users annotate sentences in PDF articles, they are supported by AI. Key sentences are highlighted in the interface by means of extractive summarization. Users can annotate them by simply clicking on highlighted sentences. When a sentence is selected for annotation, a zero-shot classifier tries to find the set of most relevant classes based on the selected sentence and the complete set of classes.

Finally, we developed an AI-Driven approach by means of crowdsourcing microtasks for validating AI-extracted knowledge [94]. The approach, called TinyGenius, processes the articles offline with a set of NLP tools. Therefore, the AI takes the initiative in this case. Among others, the NLP tasks included Named Entity Recognition (NER), Named Entity Linking (NEL), and summarization. After the data was extracted for a corpus of scientific articles, users were asked to verify the knowledge using microtasks. The task changed depending on which data was being evaluated, but most cases included buttons to indicate that the result was correct, incorrect, or that the evaluator was unsure.

6. Use Cases

This section presents three complementary use cases of the ORKG: 1) an observatory organizing neuro-symbolic AI research according to system composition patterns, 2) agroecological synthesis research, and 3) the organization of food composition information for Cameroon.

6.1. Neuro-symbolic AI Patterns Observatory

The role of an observatory within the ORKG is to organize research in a specific field and ensure a high-quality standard. This involves curating and semantically representing contributions from scientific articles in a manner that is both machine- and human-readable.

Maintaining a Neuro-symbolic AI Patterns Observatory[12] plays an important role in understanding and advancing symbolic and sub-symbolic AI techniques, an area that has garnered significant interest [97]. The observatory, grounded in important ways in the Semantic Web research community, focuses on developing systems that combine Semantic Web and Machine Learning technology, termed Semantic Web and Machine Learning Systems (SWeMLS). It aims to systematically analyze and characterize trends in SWeMLS, addressing the challenges of conducting large-scale, data-driven, and representative studies in this rapidly evolving area.

The observatory's data source is published in [98]. This article conducts a comprehensive systematic mapping study, encompassing information from 470 SWeMLS papers. The main components of this data source are:

- The *SWeMLS ontology* describes the main parts of SWeMLS, including their workflows using boxology patterns. The ontology schema, capturing important SWeMLS characteristics (e.g., StatisticalModel) and relevant instances (e.g., Convolutional neural network), were systematically derived during the scoping and analysis phases of the Systematic Mapping Study (SMS).
- The *SWeMLS-KG knowledge graph* comprises machine-actionable descriptions of almost 500 systems in terms of the SWeMLS ontology.

[12]`https://orkg.org/observatory/Neurosymbolic_artificial_intelligence`

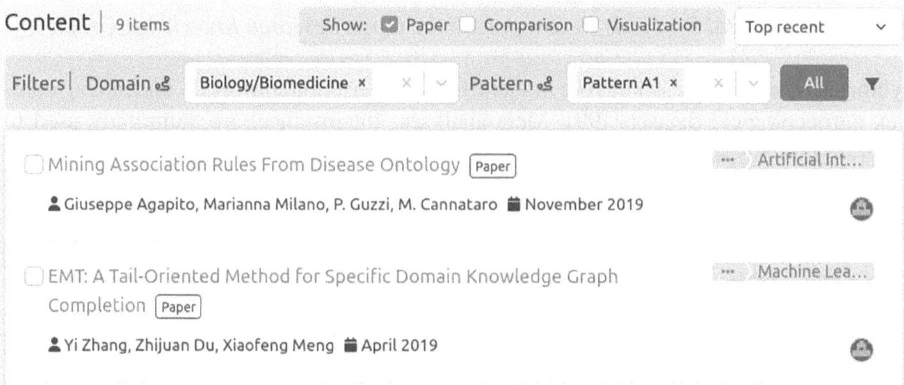

Figure 11. Neuro-symbolic AI Observatory filters.

- The *SWeMLS Pattern Library* contains machine-actionable descriptions of 45 SWeMLS patterns.

This source data was carefully transformed and imported into the ORKG. It is now maintained in the SWeMLS-KG observatory, which offers several functionalities that enhance the utility and impact of the data:

- *Browsing and Visualization:* Users can browse patterns and their instantiations, providing an intuitive understanding of common workflows in SWeMLS.
- *Search and Filter:* The observatory offers robust search and filtering capabilities, allowing users to find contributions based on specific characteristics, such as pattern types or application domains. For example, Figure 11 illustrates the filters on the observatory page, where the user searches for papers that use Pattern A1 in Biology/Biomedicine.
- *Data-Driven Analysis:* Researchers can perform data-driven analyses to uncover trends and best practices within the field of SWeMLS. This is particularly valuable for identifying frequent system patterns used in specific tasks, such as graph completion in the medical domain.
- *FAIR Principles:* The resource adheres to the FAIR principles, ensuring that the data is not only available, but also usable in a variety of research contexts.

To support source data import and new data production, we created ORKG templates[13] (Section 3.2) using the ontology. Users can now add additional related papers to the observatory following the same model and reuse the existing defined patterns. The observatory offers a powerful set of filters to facilitate the accessibility to SWeMLS data, providing researchers with comprehensive insights into the field.

In conclusion, the Neuro-symbolic AI Patterns Observatory in the ORKG demonstrates the potential of neuro-symbolic systems to transform the organization and accessibility of scientific knowledge. By leveraging both Semantic Web and Machine Learning components, this resource offers a platform for understanding and advancing the field of SWeMLS.

[13] `https://orkg.org/template/R575738`

6.2. Agroecological Synthesis Research with the Open Research Knowledge Graph

Synthesis research plays a key role in identifying patterns and processes underlying complex agroecological datasets [99]. Meta-analyses, for instance, are commonly used to integrate findings from multiple studies, generating insights and cross-disciplinary connections that can guide conservation policies and practices [100,101,99]. Despite its usefulness in addressing pressing challenges like climate change and biodiversity loss, conducting synthesis research is increasingly challenging due to the overwhelming volume of academic publications. Even in relatively narrow fields like agroecology, researchers must contend with hundreds of new publications annually [102]. Navigating this publication flood is a major hurdle to staying up-to-date on the latest research and identifying relevant new studies that should be included in a synthesis.

Compounding this problem is the mainstream approach of producing and formally communicating scientific knowledge in unstructured PDF articles [102]. Scientific findings produced in this format are inaccessible to many digital support tools like intelligent search, filter, or other knowledge processing approaches that could make the research life cycle more efficient [1,2]. Rather, most data extraction (from articles) and subsequent database development must be done by hand, which slows the pace and accuracy of research. For example, conducting a meta-analysis or systematic review typically requires researchers to manually extract data from tens or even hundreds of articles and organise this data into a new database, an inaccurate activity that can easily consume three to six months of full-time work [103].

There is a critical need for tools and standards that reduce these points of friction, and facilitate sharing, synthesising, and reproducing complex agroecological research for a range of stakeholders [101]. Here, we briefly present a use case in the ORKG to evaluate how the platform can support these goals in the field of agroecology and outline opportunities for continued development. For a more in-depth discussion of this case study and the ORKG's role in addressing challenges associated with transferring ecological knowledge, we refer readers to Snyder et al. [104].

6.2.1. Research Question

In this use case, we evaluated how the ORKG can support agroecological synthesis research with manually curated data extracted from peer-reviewed articles in the form of an ORKG comparison. Our comparison focused on the yield effects of intercropping cereals and legumes—plants that make atmospheric nitrogen available to other plants—in European agroecosystems. This research question is particularly timely in the context of ongoing efforts to meet global food security needs amidst growing constraints on the availability of arable land [105]. Studies included in the comparison were identified through a Web of Science search, which is described in the ORKG comparison. As our goal was to evaluate the capabilities of the ORKG in scoping articles for a synthesis rather than to conduct a robust synthesis, we did not conduct an exhaustive literature search.

6.2.2. ORKG Comparison

Our interactive comparison [106] can be viewed in full form on the ORKG[14]. We built the comparison using ORKG properties that describe key information published in each

[14]https://doi.org/10.48366/R655553

original contribution such as the study location, experimental methods, quantitative measurements, etc. The process of creating the ORKG comparison was analogous to compiling and coding primary data for a meta-analysis or systematic review. One motivation for organising this data directly in the ORKG rather than in an Excel or CSV file is the ability to leverage ORKG templates. However, as none of the existing templates were suitable for the complex agroecological data we wanted to describe, we had to first develop the required templates. A robust library of templates will be key for attracting and retaining new ORKG users, particularly those unfamiliar with conceptual modelling or unable to perform this task.

Since this comparison exists in a dynamic, open-access environment, other researchers can build upon the search criteria we used to generate the original comparison and integrate additional studies and properties. This dynamic approach to scientific knowledge curation addresses many of the challenges associated with publishing static PDF articles by providing a comprehensive, living resource that can be regularly updated with new and relevant research findings. This is one of the most powerful features of the ORKG.

6.2.3. Visualisations

Once information was coded in the ORKG, we used the ORKG visualisation tool to create a bar chart comparing grain yields across studies (see ORKG comparison). This task was completed in a matter of minutes, which suggests that users with even a low-level of scientific expertise could create meaningful visualisations from existing ORKG comparisons. Comparisons can be visualised in a number of simple formats (e.g., tables, bar charts, etc.) without having to recode the data, allowing users to quickly explore patterns and trends within a dataset.

While ORKG visualisations do not support statistical analyses, they allow researchers to quickly scope trends and patterns. This is particularly useful for systematic mapping in preparation for a review [107]. Moreover, once data is coded into the ORKG, it exists in a machine-reusable format. This means that users can bypass manual data extraction from articles and instead directly download data as a CSV file or import it into a computational environment like R studio. Once in a computational environment, users can use programming languages with enhanced visualisation capabilities (e.g., R or Python) to create custom-made plots and conduct statistical analyses.

6.2.4. Takeaways

Once extracted data are curated in a machine-reusable format in the ORKG, researchers can easily visualise trends and identify knowledge gaps that could be addressed with future research. Given the ease of reusing ORKG data, we can envision a well-populated ORKG drastically accelerating the process of conducting synthesis research. To increase the rigour of ORKG comparisons and their utility as a synthesis scoping tool, a formal literature search must be part of this practice. As in classical meta-analyses and systematic reviews, clearly documenting the literature search process underlying a comparison is a foundational step in creating a robust comparison and should be implemented as standard practice in the ORKG.

Extracting data from PDF articles and organising them in the ORKG was the most time consuming process associated with building our ORKG comparison. Developing templates to structure data related to common ecology methods and analyses will be key to streamlining this process. Recent ORKG initiatives such as reborn articles [26] or SciKGTeX [23] that allow researchers to produce machine-reusable findings from the outset will also be key in addressing this hurdle. These approaches ensure new research findings can be automatically collected by the ORKG and other knowledge bases, thereby eliminating the need for post-publication data extraction and organisation. Widespread adoption of these tools would facilitate seamless integration of new research into ORKG comparisons that could effectively function as living resources for research, policy, and management decisions.

6.3. Cameroon Food Composition Knowledge Graph

Fair access to food data is an essential catalyst for achieving Sustainable Development Goals, specifically Goal 2 "Zero Hunger", Goal 3 "Ensure healthy lives and promote well-being for all at all ages", and Goal 4 "Quality education". Quality education on food composition is particularly important because it allows people to have a healthy diet and avoid health problems such as malnutrition, obesity, diabetes, some cancers, etc. However, quality education is not a given in developing countries such as Cameroon. Indeed, the most recent versions of the Cameroonian Food Composition Tables (FCT) were published in 1957 [108] and 1966 [109]. These resources are outdated given the current evolution of the country in terms of food habits. However, many Cameroonian foods are described in scientific articles[15]. These resources, mostly in PDF format, are static, not harmonized, difficult to process by machines and difficult to access by different stakeholders.

This section presents how Cameroonian food, their ingredients and their components are being extracted from scientific articles, organized to build the Cameroonian food composition knowledge graph using the neuro-symbolic ORKG [110]. This task is accomplished by an extensive work of semi-automatic collection, extraction and curation of food data stored in scientific articles. Unlike the current FCT which is a static PDF document [109,108], the ORKG provides dynamic resources stored in a KG, which are machine-accessible and easy to continuously update.

The methodology used in this work is based on an iterative and incremental process during which a domain ontology is built, continuously refined, and populated with new food knowledge extracted from scientific articles to construct the food composition KG [111].

6.3.1. TSOTSAGraph: Cameroon Food Composition Knowledge Graph

The Cameroon Food Composition Knowledge Graph (also called TSOTSAGraph for "my food graph" in a local tongue in Cameroon) aims to organize and structure Cameroonian food so as to improve stakeholder access to this knowledge. To construct the KG, one of the most important activities is the development of the food composition ontology (also called TSOTSAOntology - "my food ontology"). This ontology aims to add an expressive layer to food information by introducing the semantic relationships between food, food components, and food ingredients. Thereafter, this ontology is enriched and populated to form the TSOTSAGraph.

[15] https://orkg.org/list/R693365

TSOTSAOntology To construct the food composition ontology, extracted information was organized into classes and properties with the help of an expert in food science and nutrition.

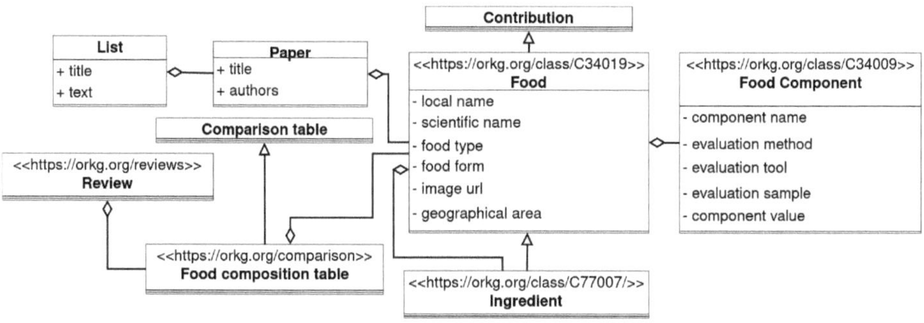

Figure 12. The main classes of the TSOTSAOntology.

The TSOTSAOntology is implemented using the ORKG template editor. This editor allows us to create classes and link these classes to templates (or form) allowing us to describe data properties and object properties. To reuse the large quantity of scientific knowledge already ingested in the ORKG, we employ semantic typing with suggestions based on the entered verbalization of the concept using ChatGPT. Figure 12 presents the main classes.

- *Food, Ingredient*: these classes are used to describe foods and their ingredients;
- *Food component*: this class is used to describe the different components (iron, fat, carbohydrate, etc.) contained in foods;
- *Food Composition Tables*: this class inherits the ORKG comparison table resource. It aims to compare the different ingredients (or) components contained in foods. It is generally associated with a visualization presenting, for instance, which ingredient or component is in small/large quantities in a food;
- Review: the class review aims to provide a food review described as food composition tables.

The *Food*, *Food ingredient* and *Food component* classes are linked to food, food ingredient, and food component templates respectively. They are used as conceptual models for populating the TSOTSAOntology with food data extracted from scientific articles.

TSOTSAGraph Stored in the ORKG, the TSOTSAGraph is obtained by populating the TSOTSAOntology with instances. To this end, the ORKG provides a wizard for adding and annotating papers using templates. Using the paper DOI or title, the ORKG automatically fetches the paper metadata and allows us to identify and import the corresponding template. Language Models are also used during this activity for resource suggestion and recommendation. To easily navigate the TSOTSAGraph, one may use food, food composition, food composition tables and reviews:

- *Food and food composition instances:* we use the ORKG contribution editor to describe food and their components. Each food described in a paper corresponds to one research contribution. More than 500 instances are already ingested in the TSOTSAGraph.

- *Food composition tables instances*[16] correspond to the different ORKG comparisons tables used to compare food, food ingredients, and food components. So far, we have created ten ORKG comparisons.
- *Food composition review:* so far, we have published one review of Cameroon food composition table[17]. This review will be updated as more food data are stored and organized and more food composition tables are created.

7. Conclusions and Future Work

The Open Research Knowledge Graph (ORKG) represents a transformative approach to scholarly communication, making scientific knowledge more accessible, discoverable, and actionable. By leveraging the power of neuro-symbolic technologies and providing robust tools for content production, curation, and use, the ORKG is poised to shape the future of research and knowledge management.

We see the current state of the ORKG as described in this chapter only as the first step in a larger research and development agenda. Our long-term aim is to develop an advanced neuro-symbolic AI system designed to support all phases of scientific research. Building on the ORKG, a Neuro-Symbolic Research Co-Pilot can assist researchers in hypothesis generation, literature review, experimental design, data analysis, and dissemination of findings. The ultimate goal is to create a versatile, intelligent assistant that augments researchers' capabilities, accelerates scientific discovery, and fosters interdisciplinary collaboration. One critical area in this journey is the expansion and refinement of semantic templates to cover a broader range of research domains, ensuring a comprehensive and accurate representation of diverse scientific contributions. Additionally, integrating more advanced neuro-symbolic AI techniques (e.g. models fine-tuned for the scholarly knowledge organization tasks) will improve the system's ability to process and understand complex scientific texts, leading to even richer and more precise knowledge graphs. Another promising direction involves enhancing user interfaces and developing more intuitive tools for researchers to interact with the ORKG, including advanced visualizations, dashboards and natural language assistance capabilities. Expanding collaborations with academic publishers, research institutions, funders, and other stakeholders will also be essential to drive widespread adoption and contribute to the continuous curation and updating of the knowledge graph. Lastly, efforts to ensure the ethical use and transparency of the ORKG, addressing issues such as data privacy and bias, will be paramount in maintaining trust and integrity within the scientific community. By pursuing these future directions, the ORKG aims to solidify its role as a cornerstone of the next generation of scholarly communication.

Acknowledgements

In addition to the authors of this article, there are many further researchers, software developers, content curators and community members, whose contributions to the ORKG we would like to acknowledge. In particular, we would like to thank Manuel

[16]Example: `https://orkg.org/comparison/R689520`
[17]`https://orkg.org/review/R700894`

Prinz, Anna-Lena Lorenz, Christof Bless, Gollam Rabby, Haşsan Hussein, Julia Evans, Mahsa Shamsabadi, Marcel Konrad, Muhammad Haris, Olga Lezhina, Qurat ain Aftab, Salomon Kabongo Kabenamualu, Sanju Tiwari, Vinodh Ilangovan, Vald Nechakhin, Hamed Babaei Giglou. We greatly appreciate the contributions and support provided by Ricardo Perez-Alvarez and Emily A. Martin, co-authors of the in-depth case study evaluation described in Snyder et al. [104].

Data and Code Availability

The ORKG promotes open science and transparency. The codebase is open source, MIT licensed, and made available to the community at gitlab.com/TIBHannover/orkg. The data is licensed under CC0 1.0 Universal except data sourced from named third-party sources, which are republished with permission under the original license. The license statements are available at orkg.org/page/license.

References

[1] Auer S, Oelen A, Haris M, Stocker M, D'Souza J, Farfar KE, et al. Improving Access to Scientific Literature with Knowledge Graphs. Bibliothek Forschung und Praxis. 2020;44(3):516-29. Available from: https://doi.org/10.1515/bfp-2020-2042 [cited 2024-06-19].

[2] Stocker M, Oelen A, Jaradeh MY, Haris M, Oghli OA, Heidari G, et al. FAIR scientific information with the Open Research Knowledge Graph. FAIR Connect. 2023;1(1):19-21. Publisher: IOS Press. Available from: https://doi.org/10.3233/FC-221513.

[3] Mons B. Which gene did you mean? BMC Bioinformatics. 2005 Jun;6(1). Available from: https://doi.org/10.1186/1471-2105-6-142.

[4] Hoppe F, Dessì D, Sack H. Deep Learning meets Knowledge Graphs for Scholarly Data Classification. In: Web Conference 2021 (WWW '21). USA: ACM; 2021. p. 417-21.

[5] Kozlowski D, Dusdal J, Pang J, et al. Semantic and relational spaces in science of science: deep learning models for article vectorisation. Scientometrics. 2021;126:5881-910.

[6] Guizzardi G. Ontology, ontologies and the "I" of FAIR. Data Intelligence. 2020;2(1-2):181-91.

[7] Michie S, Hastings J, Johnston M, Hankonen N, Wright AJ, West R. Developing and using ontologies in behavioural science: addressing issues raised. Wellcome Open Research. 2022.

[8] Pascazio L, Rihm SD, Naseri A, Mosbach S, Akroyd J, Kraft M. Chemical Species Ontology for Data Integration and Knowledge Discovery. Journal of Chemical Information and Modeling. 2023.

[9] Dumschott K, Dörpholz H, Laporte MA, Brilhaus D, Schrader A, Usadel B, et al. Ontologies for increasing the FAIRness of plant research data. Frontiers in Plant Science. 2023.

[10] Uhlmann EL, Ebersole CR, Chartier CR, Errington TM, Kidwell MC, Lai CK, et al. Scientific Utopia III: Crowdsourcing Science. Perspectives on Psychological Science. 2019;14(5):711-33.

[11] Skvortsov NA, Stupnikov SA. A Semantic Approach to Workflow Management and Reuse for Research Problem Solving. Data Intelligence. 2022.

[12] Fafalios P, Marketakis Y, Axaridou A, Tzitzikas Y, Doerr M. A Workflow Model for Holistic Data Management and Semantic Interoperability in Quantitative Archival Research. Digital Scholarship in the Humanities. 2023.

[13] Wegner P, Schaaf S, Uebachs M, Domingo-Fernández D, Salimi Y, Gebel S, et al. Integrative data semantics through a model-enabled data stewardship. Bioinformatics. 2022;38(15):3850-2.

[14] Luo Z, Chen Y, Li H, Li Y, Guo Y. TreeMerge: a visual comparative analysis method for food classification tree in pesticide residue maximum limit standards. Agronomy. 2022;12(12):3148.

[15] Kinney R, Anastasiades C, Authur R, Beltagy I, Bragg J, Buraczynski A, et al. The semantic scholar open data platform. arXiv preprint arXiv:230110140. 2023.

[16] Byun J, Stuhlmüller A. Elicit: Language models as research tools. In: Artificial Intelligence in Science: Challenges, Opportunities and the Future of Research. Paris: OECD Publishing; 2023. .

[17] Granger BE, Perez F. Jupyter: Thinking and Storytelling With Code and Data. Computing in Science & Engineering. 2021 Mar;23(2):7–14. Available from: https://doi.org/10.1109/MCSE.2021.3059263.

[18] Bizer, Christian, Vidal, Maria-Esther, Weiss, Michael. Resource Description Framework. Encyclopedia of Database Systems. 2018 1. Available from: https://doi.org/10.1007/978-1-4614-8265-9_905.

[19] Vogt L, Strömert P, Matentzoglu N, Karam N, Konrad M, Prinz M, et al.. FAIR 2.0: Extending the FAIR Guiding Principles to Address Semantic Interoperability; 2024. Available from: https://doi.org/10.48550/arXiv.2405.03345.

[20] Vogt L, Konrad M, Prinz M. Towards a Rosetta Stone for (meta)data: Learning from natural language to improve semantic and cognitive interoperability; 2023. Available from: https://arxiv.org/abs/2307.09605.

[21] Knublauch H, Kontokostas D. Shapes Constraint Language (SHACL); 2017. Available from: https://www.w3.org/TR/shacl/.

[22] Capadisli S, Guy A, Verborgh R, Lange C, Auer S, Berners-Lee T. Decentralised Authoring, Annotations and Notifications for a Read-Write Web with dokieli. Lecture Notes in Computer Science. 2017:469–481. Available from: https://doi.org/10.1007/978-3-319-60131-1_33.

[23] Bless C, Baimuratov I, Karras O. SciKGTeX - A LaTeX Package to Semantically Annotate Contributions in Scientific Publications. In: 2023 ACM/IEEE Joint Conference on Digital Libraries (JCDL). IEEE; 2023. Available from: https://doi.org/10.1109/JCDL57899.2023.00030.

[24] Bless C, Baimuratov I, Karras O. SciKGTeX - Scientific Knowledge Graph TeX; 2022. Available from: https://github.com/Christof93/SciKGTeX.

[25] Karras O, Kuckertz P, Göpfert J, Pelser T, Pueblas R, Weinand JM, et al. "FAIR-by-Design" Artifacts: Enriching Publications and Software with FAIR Scientific Information at the Time of Creation. In: Proceedings of the NFDI4Ing Conference 2023 - Innovation in Research Data Management: Bridging the gaps between disciplines and opening new perspectives for research in engineering science. NFDI4Ing. Zenodo; 2023. p. 34-5. Available from: https://doi.org/10.5281/zenodo.10036957.

[26] Stocker M, Snyder L, Anfuso M, Ludwig O, Thießen F, Farfar KE, et al.. Rethinking the production and publication of machine-reusable expressions of research findings. arXiv; 2024. Available from: https://doi.org/10.48550/ARXIV.2405.13129.

[27] Lannom L, Broeder D, Manepalli G. Data Type Registries working group output. Research Data Alliance; 2015. Available from: https://doi.org/10.15497/A5BCD108-ECC4-41BE-91A7-20112FF77458.

[28] Waltman L, Van Eck NJ. A new methodology for constructing a publication-level classification system of science. Journal of the American Society for Information Science and Technology. 2012;63(12):2378-92.

[29] Eykens J, Guns R, Engels TC. Fine-grained classification of social science journal articles using textual data: A comparison of supervised machine learning approaches. Quantitative Science Studies. 2021;2(1):89-110.

[30] Kandimalla B, Rohatgi S, Wu J, Giles CL. Large scale subject category classification of scholarly papers with Deep Attentive Neural Networks. Frontiers in research metrics and analytics. 2021;5:600382.

[31] Rivest M, Vignola-Gagné E, Archambault É. level classification of scientific publications: A comparison of deep learning, direct citation and bibliographic coupling. PloS one. 2021;16(5):e0251493.

[32] Burnham JF. Scopus database: a review. Biomedical digital libraries. 2006;3:1-8.

[33] Manghi P, Manola N, Horstmann W, Peters D. An Infrastructure for Managing EC Funded Research Output: The OpenAIRE Project. Grey Journal (TGJ). 2010;6(1).

[34] Lu Z. PubMed and beyond: a survey of web tools for searching biomedical literature. Database. 2011;2011:baq036.

[35] Herzog C, Hook D, Konkiel S. Dimensions: Bringing down barriers between scientometricians and data. Quantitative science studies. 2020;1(1):387-95.

[36] Ammar W, Groeneveld D, Bhagavatula C, Beltagy I, Crawford M, Downey D, et al. Construction of the literature graph in semantic scholar. arXiv preprint arXiv:180502262. 2018.

[37] Katz JS, Hicks D. The classification of interdisciplinary journals: a new approach. In: Proceedings of the fifth biennial conference of the International Society for Scientometrics and Informetrics. Learned Information Medford; 1995. p. 245-54.

[38] Grootendorst M. BERTopic: Neural topic modeling with a class-based TF-IDF procedure. arXiv

preprint arXiv:220305794. 2022.

[39] Kotitsas S, Pappas D, Manola N, Papageorgiou H. SCINOBO: a novel system classifying scholarly communication in a dynamically constructed hierarchical Field-of-Science taxonomy. Frontiers in Research Metrics and Analytics. 2023;8:1149834.

[40] Frascati M. Guidelines for collecting and reporting data on research and experimental development. The Measurement of Scientific, Technological and Innovation Activities. 2015.

[41] Rao SX, Egger PH, Zhang C. Hierarchical classification of research fields in the" web of science" using deep learning. arXiv preprint arXiv:230200390. 2023.

[42] Vaswani A, Shazeer N, Parmar N, Uszkoreit J, Jones L, Gomez AN, et al. Attention is all you need. Advances in neural information processing systems. 2017;30.

[43] Kenton JDMWC, Toutanova LK. Bert: Pre-training of deep bidirectional transformers for language understanding. In: Proceedings of naacL-HLT. vol. 1; 2019. p. 2.

[44] Beltagy I, Lo K, Cohan A. SciBERT: A Pretrained Language Model for Scientific Text. In: Proceedings of the 2019 Conference on Empirical Methods in Natural Language Processing and the 9th International Joint Conference on Natural Language Processing (EMNLP-IJCNLP); 2019. p. 3615-20.

[45] Cohan A, Feldman S, Beltagy I, Downey D, Weld DS. SPECTER: Document-level Representation Learning using Citation-informed Transformers. In: Proceedings of the 58th Annual Meeting of the Association for Computational Linguistics; 2020. p. 2270-82.

[46] Ostendorff M, Rethmeier N, Augenstein I, Gipp B, Rehm G. Neighborhood Contrastive Learning for Scientific Document Representations with Citation Embeddings. In: Proceedings of the 2022 Conference on Empirical Methods in Natural Language Processing; 2022. p. 11670-88.

[47] Radford A, Narasimhan K, Salimans T, Sutskever I, et al.. Improving language understanding by generative pre-training. OpenAI; 2018.

[48] Radford A, Wu J, Child R, Luan D, Amodei D, Sutskever I, et al. Language models are unsupervised multitask learners. OpenAI blog. 2019;1(8):9.

[49] Brown T, Mann B, Ryder N, Subbiah M, Kaplan JD, Dhariwal P, et al. Language models are few-shot learners. Advances in neural information processing systems. 2020;33:1877-901.

[50] Wolff B, Seidlmayer E, Förstner KU. Enriched BERT Embeddings for Scholarly Publication Classification. In: Proceedings of the 1st International Workshop on Natural Scientific Language Processing and Research Knowledge Graphs (NSLP 2024). Hersonissos, Crete, Greece; 2024. Submitted.

[51] Singh A, D'Arcy M, Cohan A, Downey D, Feldman S. SciRepEval: A Multi-Format Benchmark for Scientific Document Representations. In: Conference on Empirical Methods in Natural Language Processing; 2022. Available from: `https://api.semanticscholar.org/CorpusID:254018137`.

[52] Manning CD. Computational linguistics and deep learning. Computational Linguistics. 2015;41(4):701-7.

[53] Dessí D, Osborne F, Reforgiato Recupero D, Buscaldi D, Motta E. CS-KG: A large-scale knowledge graph of research entities and claims in computer science. In: International Semantic Web Conference. Springer; 2022. p. 678-96.

[54] Dessì D, Osborne F, Reforgiato Recupero D, Buscaldi D, Motta E, Sack H. AI-KG: an automatically generated knowledge graph of artificial intelligence. In: The Semantic Web–ISWC 2020: 19th International Semantic Web Conference, Athens, Greece, November 2–6, 2020, Proceedings, Part II 19. Springer; 2020. p. 127-43.

[55] Wadden D, Wennberg U, Luan Y, Hajishirzi H. Entity, Relation, and Event Extraction with Contextualized Span Representations. In: Proceedings of the 2019 Conference on Empirical Methods in Natural Language Processing and the 9th International Joint Conference on Natural Language Processing (EMNLP-IJCNLP); 2019. p. 5784-9.

[56] Salatino A, Osborne F, Motta E. CSO Classifier 3.0: a scalable unsupervised method for classifying documents in terms of research topics. International Journal on Digital Libraries. 2022;23(1):91-110.

[57] Angeli G, Premkumar MJJ, Manning CD. Leveraging linguistic structure for open domain information extraction. In: Proceedings of the 53rd Annual Meeting of the Association for Computational Linguistics and the 7th International Joint Conference on Natural Language Processing (Volume 1: Long Papers); 2015. p. 344-54.

[58] Manning CD, Surdeanu M, Bauer J, Finkel JR, Bethard S, McClosky D. The Stanford CoreNLP natural language processing toolkit. In: Proceedings of 52nd annual meeting of the association for computational linguistics: system demonstrations; 2014. p. 55-60.

[59] Gu Y, Tinn R, Cheng H, Lucas M, Usuyama N, Liu X, et al. Domain-specific language model pre-

training for biomedical natural language processing. ACM Transactions on Computing for Healthcare (HEALTH). 2021;3(1):1-23.
[60] Kilicoglu H, Shin D, Fiszman M, Rosemblat G, Rindflesch TC. SemMedDB: a PubMed-scale repository of biomedical semantic predications. Bioinformatics. 2012;28(23):3158-60.
[61] Lee J, Yoon W, Kim S, Kim D, Kim S, So CH, et al. BioBERT: a pre-trained biomedical language representation model for biomedical text mining. Bioinformatics. 2020;36(4):1234-40.
[62] Alsentzer E, Murphy JR, Boag W, Weng WH, Jin D, Naumann T, et al. Publicly Available Clinical BERT Embeddings. NAACL HLT 2019. 2019:72.
[63] Peng Y, Yan S, Lu Z. Transfer Learning in Biomedical Natural Language Processing: An Evaluation of BERT and ELMo on Ten Benchmarking Datasets. In: Proceedings of the 18th BioNLP Workshop and Shared Task; 2019. p. 58-65.
[64] Vidal ME, Endris KM, Jazashoori S, Sakor A, Rivas A. Transforming Heterogeneous Data into Knowledge for Personalized Treatments—A Use Case. Datenbank-Spektrum. 2019;19:95-106.
[65] Bodenreider O. The unified medical language system (UMLS): integrating biomedical terminology. Nucleic acids research. 2004;32(suppl_1):D267-70.
[66] Penev L, Dimitrova M, Senderov V, Zhelezov G, Georgiev T, Stoev P, et al. OpenBiodiv: A Knowledge Graph for Literature-Extracted Linked Open Data in Biodiversity Science. Publications. 2019;7(2):38.
[67] Senderov V, Simov K, Franz N, Stoev P, Catapano T, Agosti D, et al. OpenBiodiv-O: ontology of the OpenBiodiv knowledge management system. Journal of biomedical semantics. 2018;9(1):5.
[68] D'Souza J, Kabongo S, Prinz M, Jaradeh MY, Farfar KE. ORKG Benchmarks. In: Auer S, Ilangovan V, Stocker M, Tiwari S, Vogt L, editors. Open Research Knowledge Graph. Göttingen, Germany: Cuvillier; 2024. p. 49-56.
[69] D'Souza J, Kabongo S, Giglou HB, Zhang Y. Overview of the CLEF 2024 SimpleText Task 4: SOTA? Tracking the State-of-the-Art in Scholarly Publications. In: Faggioli G, Ferro N, Galuščáková P, de Herrera AGS, editors. Working Notes of CLEF 2024 - Conference and Labs of the Evaluation Forum. CEUR Workshop Proceedings. Online: CEUR-WS; 2024. .
[70] Kabongo S, D'Souza J, Auer S. ORKG-Leaderboards: a systematic workflow for mining leaderboards as a knowledge graph. International Journal on Digital Libraries. 2024;25(1):41-54.
[71] Hou Y, Jochim C, Gleize M, Bonin F, Ganguly D. Identification of Tasks, Datasets, Evaluation Metrics, and Numeric Scores for Scientific Leaderboards Construction. In: Proceedings of the 57th Annual Meeting of the Association for Computational Linguistics; 2019. p. 5203-13.
[72] Kabongo S, D'Souza J, Auer S. Zero-shot entailment of leaderboards for empirical ai research. In: 2023 ACM/IEEE Joint Conference on Digital Libraries (JCDL). IEEE; 2023. p. 237-41.
[73] Kabongo Kabenamualu S, D'Souza J, Auer S. Effective Context Selection in LLM-based Leaderboard Generation: An Empirical Study. In: Proceedings of the 29th International Conference on Natural Language & Information Systems; 2024. Available from: `https://nldb2024.di.unito.it/`.
[74] Kabongo Kabenamualu S, D'Souza J, Auer S. Exploring the Latest LLMs for Leaderboard Extraction. In: Faggioli G, Ferro N, Galuščáková P, de Herrera AGS, editors. Working Notes of CLEF 2024 - Conference and Labs of the Evaluation Forum. CEUR Workshop Proceedings. Online: CEUR-WS; 2024. .
[75] Staudinger M, El-Ebshihy A, Ningtyas AM, Piroi F, Hanbury A. AMATU@Simpletext2024: Are LLM alone any good for Scientific Entity Extraction? In: Faggioli G, Ferro N, Galuščáková P, de Herrera AGS, editors. Working Notes of CLEF 2024 - Conference and Labs of the Evaluation Forum. CEUR Workshop Proceedings. Online: CEUR-WS; 2024. .
[76] Chung HW, Hou L, Longpre S, Zoph B, Tay Y, Fedus W, et al. Scaling instruction-finetuned language models. Journal of Machine Learning Research. 2024;25(70):1-53.
[77] Jiang AQ, Sablayrolles A, Mensch A, Bamford C, Chaplot DS, de las Casas D, et al.. Mistral 7B; 2023. Available from: `https://arxiv.org/abs/2310.06825`.
[78] Touvron H, Martin L, Stone K, Albert P, Almahairi A, Babaei Y, et al. Llama 2: Open foundation and fine-tuned chat models. arXiv preprint arXiv:230709288. 2023.
[79] Dettmers T, Pagnoni A, Holtzman A, Zettlemoyer L. Qlora: Efficient Finetuning of Quantized LLMs. Advances in Neural Information Processing Systems. 2024;36.
[80] Foppa IM. 7 - O. Diekmann, J. Heesterbeek, and J.A. Metz (1991) and P. Van den Driessche and J. Watmough (2002): The spread of infectious diseases in heterogeneous populations. In: Foppa IM, editor. A Historical Introduction to Mathematical Modeling of Infectious Diseases. Boston: Academic Press; 2017. p. 157-94. Available from: `https://www.sciencedirect.com/science/article/`

pii/B9780128022603000079.

[81] Oelen A, D'Souza J, Stocker M, Vogt L, Farfar KE, Haris M, et al.. COVID-19 Reproductive Number Estimates. Open Research Knowledge Graph; 2020. Available from: https://www.orkg.org/orkg/comparison/R44930.

[82] Kamalloo E, Dziri N, Clarke C, Rafiei D. Evaluating Open-Domain Question Answering in the Era of Large Language Models. In: Proceedings of the 61st Annual Meeting of the Association for Computational Linguistics (Volume 1: Long Papers); 2023. p. 5591-606.

[83] Babaei Giglou H, D'Souza J, Auer S. LLMs4OL: Large language models for ontology learning. In: International Semantic Web Conference. Springer; 2023. p. 408-27.

[84] Kazemi M, Mittal S, Ramachandran D. Understanding finetuning for factual knowledge extraction from language models. arXiv preprint arXiv:230111293. 2023.

[85] Shamsabadi M, D'Souza J, Auer S. Large Language Models for Scientific Information Extraction: An Empirical Study for Virology. In: Graham Y, Purver M, editors. Findings of the Association for Computational Linguistics: EACL 2024. St. Julian's, Malta: Association for Computational Linguistics; 2024. p. 374-92. Available from: https://aclanthology.org/2024.findings-eacl.26.

[86] Shamsabadi M, D'Souza J. From Keywords to Structured Summaries: Streamlining Scholarly Knowledge Access. arXiv preprint arXiv:240214622. 2024.

[87] Shamsabadi M, D'Souza J. orkg-R0: A Dataset of Structured Summaries for the R0 estimate of Infectious Diseases from Complex Scientific Abstracts. Zenodo; 2023. Data set. Available from: https://doi.org/10.5281/zenodo.10003640.

[88] Raffel C, Shazeer N, Roberts A, Lee K, Narang S, Matena M, et al. Exploring the limits of transfer learning with a unified text-to-text transformer. The Journal of Machine Learning Research. 2020;21(1):5485-551.

[89] Crema C, Buonocore TM, Fostinelli S, Parimbelli E, Verde F, Fundarò C, et al. Advancing Italian biomedical information extraction with transformers-based models: Methodological insights and multicenter practical application. Journal of Biomedical Informatics. 2023;148:104557.

[90] Ai Q, Meng F, Shi J, Pelkie B, Coley CW. Extracting Structured Data from Organic Synthesis Procedures Using a Fine-Tuned Large Language Model; 2024.

[91] Malkov YA, Yashunin DA. Efficient and robust approximate nearest neighbor search using Hierarchical Navigable Small World graphs; 2018. Available from: https://doi.org/10.48550/arXiv.1603.09320.

[92] Lewis P, Perez E, Piktus A, Petroni F, Karpukhin V, Goyal N, et al. Retrieval-augmented generation for knowledge-intensive NLP tasks. In: Proceedings of the 34th International Conference on Neural Information Processing Systems. NIPS '20. Red Hook, NY, USA: Curran Associates Inc.; 2020. Available from: https://dl.acm.org/doi/abs/10.5555/3495724.3496517.

[93] Auer S, Bizer C, Kobilarov G, Lehmann J, Cyganiak R, Ives Z. DBpedia: A Nucleus for a Web of Open Data. In: Aberer K, Choi KS, Noy N, Allemang D, Lee KI, Nixon L, et al., editors. The Semantic Web. Berlin, Heidelberg: Springer Berlin Heidelberg; 2007. p. 722-35. Available from: https://doi.org/10.1007/978-3-540-76298-0_52.

[94] Oelen A, Stocker M, Auer S. Creating and validating a scholarly knowledge graph using natural language processing and microtask crowdsourcing. International Journal on Digital Libraries. 2023:1-13. Available from: https://doi.org/10.1007/s00799-023-00360-7.

[95] Oelen A, Auer S. Leveraging Large Language Models for Realizing Truly Intelligent User Interfaces. In: Extended Abstracts of the CHI Conference on Human Factors in Computing Systems (CHI EA '24), May 11–16, 2024, Honolulu, HI, USA. Honolulu, HI, USA; 2024. Available from: https://doi.org/10.1145/3613905.3650949.

[96] Oelen A, Stocker M, Auer S. Crowdsourcing scholarly discourse annotations. In: 26th International Conference on Intelligent User Interfaces; 2021. p. 464-74. Available from: https://doi.org/10.1145/3397481.3450685.

[97] Yu D, Yang B, Liu D, Wang H, Pan S. A survey on neural-symbolic learning systems. Neural Networks. 2023;166:105-26. Available from: https://www.sciencedirect.com/science/article/pii/S0893608023003398.

[98] Ekaputra FJ, Llugiqi M, Sabou M, Ekelhart A, Paulheim H, Breit A, et al. Describing and organizing semantic web and machine learning systems in the swemls-kg. In: European Semantic Web Conference. Springer; 2023. p. 372-89. Available from: https://doi.org/10.1007/978-3-031-33455-9_22.

[99] Halpern BS, Berlow E, Williams R, Borer ET, Davis FW, Dobson A, et al. Ecological Synthesis and Its Role in Advancing Knowledge. BioScience. 2020 Sep. Available from: https://doi.org/10.1093/biosci/biaa105.

[100] Díaz S, Demissew S, Carabias J, Joly C, Lonsdale M, Ash N, et al. The IPBES Conceptual Framework — connecting nature and people. Current Opinion in Environmental Sustainability. 2015 Jun;14:1–16. Available from: https://doi.org/10.1016/j.cosust.2014.11.002.

[101] Dicks LV, Walsh JC, Sutherland WJ. Organising evidence for environmental management decisions: a '4S' hierarchy. Trends in Ecology & Evolution. 2014 Nov;29(11):607–613. Available from: https://doi.org/10.1016/j.tree.2014.09.004.

[102] Mason RE, White A, Bucini G, Anderzén J, Méndez VE, Merrill SC. The evolving landscape of agroecological research. Agroecology and Sustainable Food Systems. 2020 Nov;45(4):551–591. Available from: https://doi.org/10.1080/21683565.2020.1845275.

[103] Li T, Higgins JPT, Deeks JJ. Chapter 5: Collecting data. Cochrane; 2023. Available from: https://training.cochrane.org/handbook/current/chapter-05.

[104] Snyder LD, Perez-Alvarez R, Martin EA. Harnessing the potential of the ORKG for synthesis reseaech in agroecology. In: Open Research Knowledge Graph. Cuvillier Verlag; 2024. p. 93–103. Available from: https://cuvillier.de/de/shop/publications/9037.

[105] Pérez-Escamilla R. Food Security and the 2015–2030 Sustainable Development Goals: From Human to Planetary Health. Current Developments in Nutrition. 2017 Jul;1(7):e000513. Available from: https://doi.org/10.3945/cdn.117.000513.

[106] Snyder L. An Agroecology Use Case in the ORKG: A mini-review on how legume intercrops affect cereal grain yields. Open Research Knowledge Graph; 2024. Available from: https://doi.org/10.48366/R655553.

[107] James KL, Randall NP, Haddaway NR. A methodology for systematic mapping in environmental sciences. Environmental Evidence. 2016 Apr;5(1). Available from: https://doi.org/10.1186/s13750-016-0059-6.

[108] B Bergeret RM. Table Provisoire de Composition des Aliments du Sud-Cameroun; 1957. Available from: https://horizon.documentation.ird.fr/exl-doc/pleins_textes/pleins_textes_5/b_fdi_14-15/20430.pdf.

[109] Pele J, Berre SL. Les aliments d'origine vegetale au Cameroun; 1967. Available from: https://horizon.documentation.ird.fr/exl-doc/pleins_textes/divers13-01/09986.pdf.

[110] Jiomekong A, Auer S, Oelen A. Linked Open Literature Review using the Neuro-symbolic Open Research Knowledge Graph. In: Companion Proceedings of the ACM on Web Conference 2024. WWW '24. New York, NY, USA: Association for Computing Machinery; 2024. p. 1015–1018. Available from: https://doi.org/10.1145/3589335.3651238.

[111] Jiomekong A, Tiwari S. An approach based on open research knowledge graph for knowledge acquisition from scientific papers. The Electronic Library. 2024. Available from: https://doi.org/10.1108/EL-06-2023-0154.

Handbook on Neurosymbolic AI and Knowledge Graphs
P. Hitzler et al. (Eds.)
IOS Press, 2025

doi:10.3233/FAIA250217

Ontology Population Using LLMs

Sanaz SAKI NOROUZI [a,1], Adrita BARUA [a], Antrea CHRISTOU [b], Nikita GAUTAM [a], Andrew EELLS [a], Pascal HITZLER [a], Cogan SHIMIZU [b,2]

[a] *Kansas State University, Manhattan, Kansas, USA*
[b] *Wright State University, Dayton, Ohio, USA*

ORCiD ID: Sanaz Saki Norouzi https://orcid.org/0009-0003-4441-108X, Adrita Barua https://orcid.org/0000-0002-3287-7443, Antrea Christou https://orcid.org/0009-0003-0428-2439, Nikita Gautam https://orcid.org/0000-0002-1572-5405, Andrew Eells https://orcid.org/0000-0001-6357-6646, Pascal Hitzler https://orcid.org/0000-0001-6192-3472, Cogan Shimizu https://orcid.org/0000-0003-4283-8701

Abstract. Knowledge graphs (KGs) are increasingly utilized for data integration, representation, and visualization. While KG population is critical, it is often costly, especially when data must be extracted from unstructured text in natural language, which presents challenges, such as ambiguity and complex interpretations. Large Language Models (LLMs) offer promising capabilities for such tasks, excelling in natural language understanding and content generation. However, their tendency to "hallucinate" can produce inaccurate outputs. Despite these limitations, LLMs offer rapid and scalable processing of natural language data, and with prompt engineering and fine-tuning, they can approximate human-level performance in extracting and structuring data for KGs. This study investigates LLM effectiveness for the KG population, focusing on the Enslaved.org Hub Ontology. In this paper, we report that compared to the ground truth, LLM's can extract ≈ 90% of triples, when provided a modular ontology as guidance in the prompts.

Keywords. knowledge graph population, large language models, modular ontology modeling

1. Introduction

Knowledge graphs (KGs) have quickly become a major paradigm supported [1,2] by a broad set of methods and tools for the creation, extraction, integration, representation, and visualization of data, and supported by long-established W3C standards and recommendations [3,4,5,6]. Unfortunately, many aspects of knowledge engineering are quite expensive: from the knowledge model (i.e., ontology) development to the actual population (and validation) of the resulting KG [7]. Population is, in some sense perhaps the easiest component, yet this is only true if the data is already in a machine-parseable format (as many tools provide such a service, e.g., OpenRefine [8]). However, when the

[1] The first three named authors share first authorship.
[2] Corresponding Author: Cogan Shimizu, `cogan.shimizu@wright.edu`

text is in natural language, this becomes problematic. Given the various complexities of interpreting sense, sentiment, frames, or anaphora, translating to facts or knowledge can be quite difficult. There are many natural language processing (NLP) techniques for tackling these problems, yet at the forefront – in terms of both popularity and broad applicability – are large language models (LLMs).

LLMs have rapidly emerged as powerful tools in various domains, showcasing remarkable proficiency in tasks such as natural language understanding, translation, and content generation [9,10]. Their ability to process – and interpret – vast amounts of text data allows them to generate coherent and contextually relevant responses, often surpassing traditional models in creativity and nuance.

However, LLMs are prone to an effect called confabulation, also referred to hallucination. This phenomenon occurs when the model produces responses that may *seem* coherent and contextually relevant but are factually inaccurate or entirely fabricated. There is no strict guarantee that any particular response does not have confabulation, but they are more likely to occur in certain scenarios, such as when the query is ambiguous, the topic in question is particularly niche (and thus not present in the original training data), or if the query requires a certain level of complexity or creativity to accomplish.

Even with these caveats, LLMs are much faster than humans at certain knowledge extraction tasks (e.g., ingesting, translating, and extracting from natural language), and especially at volume.

With appropriate guidance (e.g., through prompt engineering, retrieval augmented generation [11], or fine-tuning [12]) LLMs can approach human-level performance on such tasks. Therefore, we wish to explore how effective LLMs can be in specifically populating a KG. In particular, we take this to mean, how well can an LLM extract or otherwise transform unstructured natural language into an output constrained by the ontology (i.e., the schema) for the KG. Succinctly, these research questions are as follows.

RQ1 Are LLMs capable of *effective* KG population?
RQ2 What factors contribute to that effectiveness?
RQ3 Of the available LLMs, which perform best for the KG population task?

To answer these questions, we have selected a KG where we are aware of multiple – significantly different – schemas and data sources for the same data. In particular, we have chosen the Enslaved.Org Hub Ontology, which seeks to (re)construct the narratives of historically enslaved peoples [13] irrespective of their notability or infamy. Much of this data is manually curated from primary or secondary sources [14]. However, in many cases, there is overlap between public data sources (e.g., Wikipedia [15] and Wikidata [16]). Due to the variety of structured and unstructured (i.e., natural language) methods for representing the same data, this provides an opportunity to reasonably assess the ability of LLMs to extract the data and evaluate whether or not that the extracted data is valid for the purposes of populating our manually curated ontology.

The rest of this chapter is organized as follows. Section 2 introduces our case study: the Enslaved.Org Ontology and knowledge graph, as well as how we prepare the data for our experiments. Section 3 provides an overview of our methodology. In Section 4 we present our results and an evaluation thereof. Finally, we discuss related work in Section 6 before concluding in Section 7.

2. Background & Case Study

In this section, we briefly present some preliminary background knowledge that will be useful for understanding the rest of the chapter. In particular, we present definitions for terms and notational and graphical conventions for our figures. We also provide a brief description of the case study that drives our experiment and evaluation.

2.1. Schema Diagrams

From the Modular Ontology Modeling (MOMo) methodology [17], which was used in the development of the Enslaved.org Hub ontology – as appears in our case study, we use a (visual) graphical structure called a schema diagram as our primary method for communicating ontological structure. This diagram carries a reduced semantics; it is meant to be intuitive and easily understood, rather than explicitly and visually conveying the exact, underlying logical axioms. We use a consistent visual syntax across all diagrams.

Boxes of any non-gray color indicate a class. Goldenrod boxes are atomic classes. Purple boxes indicate a class that strictly consists of a controlled set of individuals. Blue boxes (with dashed borders) indicate *hidden complexity* — i.e., that there are additional relations, but which have been removed from view for clarity. Frequently, this means that it represents a class that is drawn from outside of the KWG namespaces (e.g., OWL Time [18]). Large gray boxes that encapsulate many arrows and boxes indicate a module, meaning that they are conceptually related. Yellow ellipses indicate a datatype. These are generally prefixed with the appropriate namespace, for clarity. Filled arrows indicate a binary relation. If one points to a box, then it is an object property. If one points to an ellipse, it is a data property. Open-face arrows indicate a subclass relation.

2.2. Ontology Design Patterns & Modules

Ontology design patterns (ODPs) are tiny, self-contained ontologies that are focused on solving specific modeling problems [19]. They are inspired by software engineering design patterns, and can be applied architecturally (i.e., a way to structure data) or exist on a spectrum from abstract to content-driven applications. ODPs, especially through the MOMo methodology, are *modularized* through a process called *template-based instantiation* [20], which is then followed by *systematic axiomatization* to produce a formalized model from the ODP using a series of 17 frequently used axioms for each node-edge-node construction in the schema diagram for the ODP or module [21]. The use of patterns, by moving from top-level or abstract concepts and subsequently customizing for a specific (narrower) use-case is meant to mimic the human conceptualization process, which in some sense can be viewed as an analogy-driven process [22].

By now, have a healthy ecosystem of various interactions, including libraries of ODPs (e.g., [23,24]), an annotation language for describing pattern-based and modular structure [25,26], and a tool ecosystem for creating pattern-based or modular ontologies [7,27].

Indeed, modular ontologies have a young, but rich history. Examples span many years, from more bespoke project-focused ontologies (e.g., [28]) to the largest public geospatial KG in the world [29,30,31]. Most pertinent for this chapter, is the Enslave.org Hub's modular ontology, which we describe in the next section.

2.3. The Enslaved.org Hub & Ontology

The scourge of African enslavement was fundamental to the making of Europe, Africa, the Americas, and Middle East and parts of the Asian subcontinent. The enduring legacies of black bondage shape the moral questions of humanity in our times. We have seen in the past decade a growth in interest in the subject in film, on television, and in historical fiction. Historians have spilled much ink writing monographs aimed primarily at other scholars. At the same time, however, it is a worthy goal to expand the production of scholarly output and to bring what historians do to the general public.

Recently, there has been a significant shift in perceptions about what we can know about Enslaved Africans, their descendants, and those who asserted ownership over them throughout the world. As a result, a growing number of collections of scanned original manuscript documents, digitized material culture, and databases, that organize and make sense of records of enslavement, are free and readily accessible for scholarly and public consumption. Although this data is available through individual data silos, this proliferation of different projects and databases presents scholars, students, and the interested public with a number of challenges: **(a)** hyper-focused data for individual projects, **(b)** little-to-no consistent disambiguation across projects, **(c)** no data clearinghouse for this sort of data, **(d)** query federation is not supported, **(e)** no established best practices, and **(f)** lack of incentive to publish data.

The Enslaved.Org project introduces a new collaborative model for humanities scholarship by bringing together various professionals to share and expand knowledge about slavery [32,33]. This approach encourages scholars to rethink the way research is produced and shared, aiming to transform both academic practices and historical perspectives on slavery. The technical goal of Enslaved.Org established the Enslaved.Org Hub,a website that provides one-stop querying and inspection capabilities for integrated historic data on the slave trade, originating from a diverse set of data sources and contributors, thereby allowing students, researchers and the general public to search over numerous databases to understand and reconstruct the lives of individuals who were part of the historical slave trade [14].

To address the underlying data integration issues, Enslaved.Org opted to follow the state of the art by establishing a KG equipped with an ontology as a schema. The Enslaved Ontology serves as the underlying schema and data organization paradigm for the Enslaved Hub. It is not used for reasoning or inference, but as a guide for organizing and integrating the data, and understanding the knowledge base as a whole. For additional detail on the modeling approach see [34], and for a thorough examination of the ontology and its core concepts are detailed in [13,35].

2.4. Wikidata & Patterns

Recently, *community-driven KG plaforms* have grown in interest. These are software that hosts a KG that accepts community data from community sources (i.e., data that comes from outside the original development team) and, in general, have a focus on modeling and presenting provenance and lineage of the constituent data. With the growth of the use of KGs, some communities and larger constituencies are being left behind because many of the human-machine interfaces for KGs require more advance technical skills. To address this, the platform, Wikibase, can be deployed to mitigate issues of access for less technically practiced community members. Wikidata is the pre-eminent public Wikibase installation hosted by the Wikimedia Foundation [16].

Using the Wikibase platform has many advantages: an out of the box software for de-referencing, a convenient user interface for the less technically practiced, a consistent way to track and record provenance and lineage of data, and the option to execute SPARQL queries against an RDF representation of the knowledge graph. However, the provenance mechanism and the exact nature of the structure of the Wikibase representation can complicate developing a principled schema for KGs, as well as the approach to the materialization of the data for upload to the platform.

Indeed, other institutions, such as the European Union (EU), have also come to the conclusion that utilizing Wikibase can serve as the foundation for a community-driven knowledge graph. For instance, the EU Knowledge Graph[3] [36] is deployed on a Wikibase installation, as is the Disability Wiki that serves as an metadata knowledge graph for community documents [37].

Recently, we have created a library of design patterns for Wikibase [38] that allow for facilitated transition from traditional ontology modeling, to the structure that would be expected so as to conform with Wikibase's underlying semantic structure.

3. Knowledge Graph Population Methodology

Our methodology consists of three stages: **(a)** Data Pre-processing, **(b)** Text Retrieval, and **(c)** KG Population. This is followed by an evaluation, which we describe in Section 4.

3.1. Data Pre-processing

This step consists of two sub-steps. First, the data needs to be collected, collated, and curated. Specifically, this means we needed to find relevant natural language text, such as from Wikipedia [15], that covered enslaved persons such that they could be found in Enslaved.org and Wikidata.

These articles needed to be cleaned for formatting. This included removal of headers and citations. Additionally the text taken from Wikipedia had the infobox removed, as exactly that information would be found in Wikidata.

3.1.1. Dataset Collection, Collation, & Curation

This step essentially prepares quality data for our experiments. We took the following actions.

1. First, a list of those individuals that exist on both Wikidata and Enslaved.org needed to be identified.
2. Next, we used string matching between sources to help narrow possible matches before having to manually choose.
3. Then, for each individual where we had data from both sources, we: individual:
   (a) downloaded the Wikitext from Wikidata[4]
   (b) downloaded the TTL file from Enslaved.org[5]

[3] `https://linkedopendata.eu/wiki/The_EU_Knowledge_Graph`
[4] `https://wikidata.org/`
[5] `https://lod.enslaved.org/`

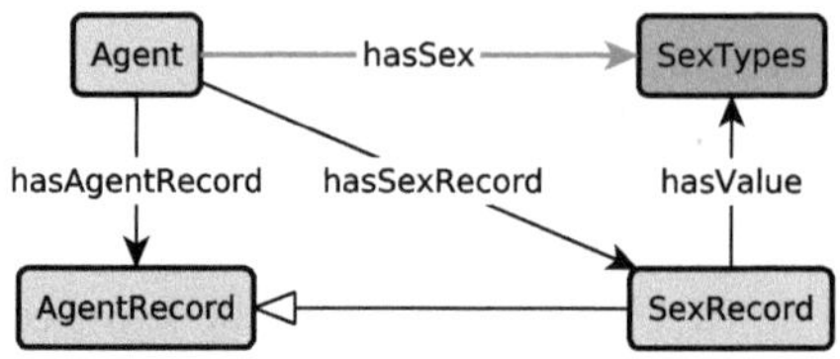

Figure 1. A graphical demonstration of how role chains in the Enslaved Ontology were "collapsed" into simpler shortcuts to generally improve data extraction performance.

(c) read the TTL file into a graph using RDFlib[6]
(d) all triples where individual was the subject were written to a tab-separated value (TSV) file

As we knew that we would be eventually sourcing data from a natural language driven process (i.e., the LLM), we opted for a simpler output structure: the TSV. Specifically, this allowed us to have a minimal syntax mechanism by which we could compare two outputs, without worrying about small errors in syntax.

3.1.2. Module Preparation

For both of the two different schemas, we generated and filtered ontology modules based on schema relationships presented in both the Wikibase [38] and Enslaved [17] ontologies. We focused on extracting and utilizing module information and attributes relevant to the content available in the Wikipedia text files. Modules and attributes that did not provide useful information from the text files were skipped, ensuring that only the relevant data was included during the ontology population process.

For example, in the Wikibase schema, we chose to skip the relation `isDirectlyBasedOn(Agent_Information, Reference)`, which typically provides information about the source from which the particular agent information was populated. Since we used Wikidata as the source to populate the ontology, this relation did not necessarily provide meaningful information about the actual source of the data, as it might not point to the original reference material. Similarly, for the Enslaved Ontology, we simplified chained relations to make them easier for the LLMs to capture. For instance, in the Sex Record Module, the original structure is `Agent` has `AgentRecord`, `SexRecord` is-a `AgentRecord`, and `SexRecord` `hasValue` `SexTypes`. We simplified this to a single relation: `hasSex(Agent, Sex_Type)`, as shown in Figure 1. Similar simplifications were made for other modules to enhance clarity and usability, ensuring the LLMs could effectively process and understand the relations. These shortcuts are included in our online documentation[7].

3.2. Relevant Text Retrieval

Given the large size of the text files crawled from Wikipedia, which often exceeds the context window (and thus token limit) of LLMs, it was necessary to determine methods for passing only maximally relevant information to the LLM for populating the ontology.

[6] `https://rdflib.readthedocs.io/en/stable/`
[7] `https://github.com/Data-Semantics-Laboratory/LLMDrivenOntologyDev`

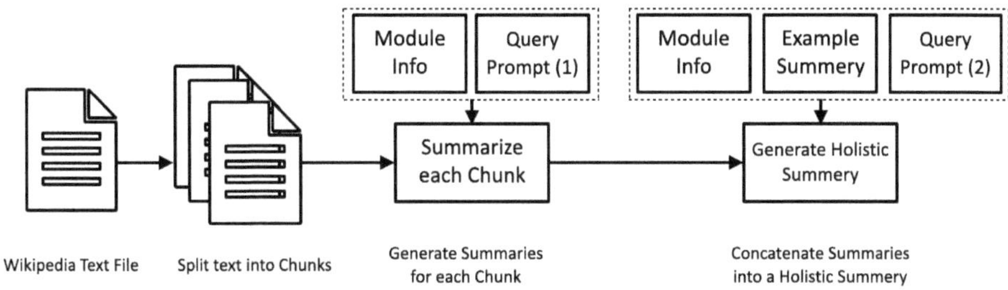

Figure 2. Summarizing the text files using few shot prompting

We used two methods for this purpose: text summarization and RAG, and we tested them both on GPT-4 and Llama-3 with temperature set to zero.

3.2.1. Text Summarization

In the summarization method, LLMs are used to generate concise summaries of the relevant texts from the dataset. These summaries serve as a condensed form of information that can be used in the subsequent ontology population step. We employ a few-shot prompting technique with LLMs to generate summaries that are specifically relevant to the ontology modules, a task that traditional summarization tools cannot accomplish. Figure 2 shows the steps for the summarization process.
Text Chunking: The text files are first split into manageable chunks, ensuring that each chunk stays within the model's token limit. This step involves reading the text file, splitting it into paragraphs, and then concatenating these paragraphs into chunks.
Module Integration: A predefined module file containing relevant schema relationships was used to guide the summarization process. This file was read and incorporated into the prompts fed to the LLM, ensuring that the summaries generated were aligned with the desired ontology structure.
Summary Generation: For each chunk, a query prompt was created that included both the text chunk and the relevant module content. The LLM model was then used to generate a summary that focused on extracting and retaining the most pertinent information based on the predefined modules. We provide our query prompt for the summarization.

> Summarize the following text, by keeping the relevant information from these modules (if any): {module_content}. The birth and death dates are mentioned in parenthesis after the agent name. For example : Joseph Vance Lewis (December 25, 1853 – April 24, 1925), was a slave who was freed. Here the Birth date is December 25, 1853 and Death date is April 24, 1925. So keep those information in the summary. The given text to summarize: {text_chunk}

Holistic Summary Creation with Few-Shot Learning: After generating individual summaries for each chunk, these were concatenated to form a complete context. To ensure consistency and relevance, an example summary was provided as part of the prompt for holistic summary generation, employing few-shot learning. A final holistic summary was then generated, which synthesized the key points from all chunks, ensuring that the summary adhered to the structure and details outlined in the modules and the example summary. We also explicitly mention additional information about certain modules (e.g., the Interagent Relationship Record Module) to help guide the LLM in understanding the module contents in relation to the ontology, which may not be as straightforward in other cases (e.g., the Sex Record Module). We provide our query prompt for this process.

> Query Prompt: "Here is an example summary that highlights the key points from a text file based on the given modules. The text file discusses a single agent or person who is introduced initially. So, the summary should focus solely on that particular agent. The birth and death dates are mentioned in parenthesis after the agent name. For example : Joseph Vance Lewis (December 25, 1853 – April 24, 1925), was a slave who was freed. Here the Birth date is December 25, 1853 and Death date is April 24, 1925. The Interagent Relationship Record Module describes whether the agent has a relationship with another Enslaver or Owner. The Person Status Module indicates whether the agent is an enslaved person and mentions any status-generating events.
> Example summary: {example_summary}
> Please provide a holistic summary from the given text that follows the format of the example summary and keeps the relevant information from these modules (if any): {module_content}.
> The given text is: {concatenation of summaries from each chunks}"

3.2.2. Retrieval-Augmented Generation

Retrieval Augmented Generation (RAG) is a machine learning approach used in NLP that integrates a retrieval system to improve the performance of a generative model [11].

The core idea is to leverage the strengths of retrieval-based methods and generative models to produce more precise results. In this setup, the relevant information is retrieved based on the user's query from an external knowledge source, such as a database or a knowledge graph. Thus, to implement the RAG mechanism, all extracted text files from Wikipedia are first divided into smaller chunks to ensure efficient processing and then embedded into a vector database. This chunking process helps manage large documents by breaking them into manageable sections, each of which can be individually compared for relevance. Two distinct prompt models are employed during the process: the first model explicitly instructs the system to populate the ontology for the agent, indicating that the document begins with a specific name and that the content is primarily about that entity. The second model, in contrast, omits this specific instruction, allowing for a more general approach to content retrieval.

In the RAG mechanism, the input prompt (query) is also transformed into an embedding, which is then compared against the pre-embedded document chunks. The similarity between the prompt embedding and the document chunk embeddings determines which chunks are most relevant. These selected chunks, based on their high similarity scores, are retrieved and used in conjunction with the original query as input to the language models. This approach enhances the system's ability to generate informed and context-rich responses by integrating relevant document content directly into the model's output generation.

For the implementation of the RAG mechanism, LangChain [8] was employed as the framework to handle the retrieval and augmentation processes. The embeddings used for both the documents and queries are generated using Hugging Face's pre-trained model, specifically the sentence-transformers/all-MiniLM-L6-v2, which is designed to efficiently capture semantic similarities between text chunks. This combination of tools

[8]https://www.langchain.com/

ensures accurate retrieval and seamless integration of relevant information into the language model's output. Besides using GPT-4 (temperature set to zero), we use the open-source LLM "Meta-Llama-3-8B-Instruct" so as to ensure reproducibility, with the temperature set to zero to obtain deterministic results in this approach.

3.3. Populating Ontology Modules

After extracting the relevant texts from each text file, we implemented a systematic approach to populate ontology modules using the extracted information. A predefined module file containing schema relationships guided the ontology population process. This module file was read and integrated into the system, serving as the foundation for structuring the ontology.

A detailed query prompt was then constructed, which included an example format demonstrating how the ontology should be populated based on the information available in the text files, utilizing a few-shot learning approach. The query prompt was explicitly designed, specifying the structure and terminology to be used for each ontology module. For instance, the example format used in the prompt for Age record module would be, hasAgeValue(Agent, xsd:double): hasAgeValue(Absalom Jones, 71).

In general, ontology modules were populated according to the schema relationships for each module and attributes described for that relation in the text files. The prompt also included instructions to skip any relations for which no information was provided in the text files, ensuring that only relevant data was captured.

The LLM was then prompted with the query, the content of the retrieved text files, and the schema modules. This combination allowed the model to accurately extract and structure the information according to the predefined ontology format, ensuring consistency and alignment with the specified schema. Both the Llama-3 and GPT-4 models were employed with a temperature setting of 0 for the prompts to populate the ontologies.

4. Evaluation

4.1. Dataset used

We aim to evaluate the triple generation accuracy of a Large Language Model (LLM) against reference data from Tab-Separated Values (TSV) files. These TSV files are our reference data and include information in triple format (subject, predicate, value) about every individual from the Enslaved ontology.

We organize the data for simpler comparison by first converting the generated text (TXT) files into tab-separated values (TSV) files in order to evaluate the language model's (LLM) performance. The quality of the data produced can be evaluated by comparing it to the truth data that is already in TSV format after the text of the TXT files has been parsed to extract relevant triples. By using a variety of string similarity variables, this comparison allows us to measure the degree to which the produced triples match the reference data.

4.2. Similarity Metrics

To make sure that both typographical errors and semantic differences are properly taken into account when assessing the alignment of characteristics and values between our generated files, we conduct a reconciliation step using a number of string similarity measures identified using guidance from [39].

Cosine Similarity – which calculates the cosine of the angle between two term frequency-inverse document frequency (TF-IDF) vectors – becomes useful [39]. It should be noted that cosine similarity can fail to accurately represent the subtle differences in very short texts or texts with similar structure but different contents. Short texts frequently produce less informative similarity scores and less discriminative TF-IDF vectors.

Fuzzy Matching: Creates similarity ratios that take into consideration possible typos and incomplete matches by using the `rapidfuzz` package [40]. These two ratios are employed:

- **FuzzyWuzzy Ratio:** compares two strings' overall similarity.
- **FuzzyWuzzy Token Set Ratio:** allows for the comparison of strings that have different word ordering by taking into account the token sets of two strings.

Jaro-Winkler Similarity: Calculates the similarity between strings by taking into account shared prefixes and small typographical changes, for the purpose of aligning attributes or values with comparable roots [39].

4.3. Evaluation Methodology

From the original text (TXT) files, we first focus on creating tab-separated values (TSV) files to start the evaluation process. The purpose of this transformation is to organize the data in a way that makes comparison and analysis easier. The output produced by the language model (LLM) is contained in the TXT files, which are our target data—the values we want to match the reference data with. This is to essentially make the evaluation process more accurate since now we will compare pair of files with similar structure.

The relevant triples, which usually consist of predicates and objects that point to the relationships within the data, are first extracted by parsing the text of each TXT file. We arrange the triples in an organized way when they have been detected, making sure that a tab character separates every element. We can preserve data readability with this setup.

In order to compare the truth data with the generated triples, pairs of files—one storing the reference data and the other containing the language model (LLM) output—are evaluated. To evaluate the degree of similarity between related entries in the truth and created datasets, we use a variety of string similarity measures for each pair, including fuzzy matching and cosine similarity. Iteratively going over each triple in the truth file and comparing it to the matching triple in the produced file, scores are determined based on how closely they match.

After that, we define a set of similarity thresholds to determine whether triples that are produced match the truth data sufficiently. Checking to see if any of the similarity metrics for both predicates and objects—exceed these predetermined thresholds is part of the evaluation process. Identifying unique truth predicates and objects enables us to calculate the total number of unique comparisons. The percentage of good matches in comparison to the total number of unique triples is subsequently calculated by counting the unique good matches that reach or exceed the specified thresholds.

Table 1. Similarity matching between triples extracted by the LLM models plus prompting strategy, reporting the average and total coverage for each module and in aggregate (columns with subscript A). The #F column indicates the number of modules for which triple extraction entirely failed (i.e., a coverage of 0).

LLM Model	Avg %	Ttl %	#F	Avg_A %	Ttl_A %
GPT4_RAG_Enslaved_MainAgent	82.30	81.60	14	88.55	88.09
GPT4_RAG_Enslaved_NotRestrictedToMainAgent	87.87	86.82	4	89.11	88.69
GPT4_RAG_WB_MainAgent	77.08	76.10	25	88.02	87.63
GPT4_RAG_WB_NotRestrictedToMainAgent	85.03	84.12	7	87.69	87.34
GPT-4_Summarization_Enslaved	81.16	80.86	0	81.16	80.86
GPT-4_Summarization_WB	82.60	82.03	0	82.60	82.03
Llama3_RAG_WB_MainAgent	71.17	70.88	6	73.64	73.20
Llama3_RAG_WB_NotRestrictedToMainAgent	71.25	70.63	2	71.92	71.41

The performance of our produced outputs was then assessed by determining the average, minimum, and maximum percentages of good matches for each llm-output comparison. This analysis helped us assess the overall quality of our results by revealing how well the created triples aligned with the reference data.

Furthermore, from every file and model, we extracted the highest values of the similarity metric.Understanding the top-performing data allowed us to identify the areas in which our models performed really well while also looking into weaknesses.

5. Results and Discussion

The LLM evaluation results are displayed in Table 1. For each LLM model and prompting strategy, extraction strategy, and source data, we evaluate how well the extracted triples match our ground truth. This is reported as *coverage* per module and overall. A triple is considered to be covered if an extracted triple has a similarity 80% in any of the metrics reported in Section 3.[9] This covers small typos in the text, but also small variants in naming. The most common example is the inclusion of a middle initial, but the rest of the extracted triple matches the ground truth.

Each LLM model had at least one module with 100% coverage, except for Llama3_RAG_WB_NotRestrictedToMainAgent, which had only a maximum of 90.1%. In this case, 100% indicates that all triples had an appropriate match. However, each experiment that did not use the summarization technique had modules where the model failed to extract any relevant triples, the LLM model refused to complete the task, or for some other inscrutable reason did not provide a list of triples appropriate for extraction and mapping.

Overall, we see the best performance from GPT-4, basically irrespective of the prompting strategy utilized.

For example, GPT-4_Summarization_Enslaved has the lowest average and total coverage and performs better than either of the experiments conducted with Llama models. Interestingly, extraction of triples according to the Wikibase model had highest fail rate, but still overall had higher coverage than the Llama models.

[9] It is generally considered to be a "good" match if a similarity metric returns 70% or better. We tend to a stricter threshold.

Generally, we see that the extraction of triples according to a schema is generally effective, approaching 90% coverage when the model performs the task.

6. Related Work

We have selected the below related research since it is consistent with our goal of automating ontology engineering tasks by utilizing large language models and solving issues like inaccurate development of concepts. The research articles brought light on the current issues surrounding ontology building, particularly those related to scalability and domain-specific accuracy. These publications also point to limitations in ontology population methods that we hope to fill with more accurate and organized data extraction techniques.

6.1. Ontology Engineering and Construction

Ontology Engineering with Large Language Models (2023): Large language models (LLMs) are investigated here as a potential tool for automating ontology engineering activities including relationship detection and entity extraction. Although LLMs have the potential to reduce manual tasks, they frequently provide concepts that are inaccurate or too broad, which can lead to errors in complicated domains [41].

We overcome these weaknesses in our approach by using module-guided summarization and few-shot prompting to make sure that the output is properly designed to meet the requirements and structure of the ontology. We give the model appropriate examples and schema-driven prompts, which guide it to focus on important relationships and entities, in contrast to general LLM approaches that might produce ambiguous notions. We reduce the possibility of excessive generalization and unimportant information through incorporating the predefined modules into the summary process and making sure that it is in line with the ontology's schema. This makes the results that are produced more accurate and appropriate for demanding ontology tasks.

Towards Ontology Construction with Language Models (2023): The goal of this work is to expedite the process of ontology generation by exploring the use of language models to automatically generate ontologies from text. Although the method works well, it has trouble guaranteeing that the generated ontologies are accurate and complete as well as catching details unique to a given domain [42].

On the other hand, our method focuses on carefully populating particular areas of the ontology by extracting relevant information and providing module-guided summaries, instead of automatically creating full ontologies. We maintain the accuracy and contextual relevance of the populated ontology by including the ontology schema into the summarization process and using structured prompts to target relevant content. This approach provides domain-specific relevance and minimizes errors in difficult domains by prioritizing exact text retrieval and alignment with the predetermined structure, so avoiding the frequent issues associated with broad or partial ontology development.

OLAF: An Ontology Learning Applied Framework (2023): With a focus on collecting and organizing information from massive datasets, OLAF presents a system for automating ontology learning. Although the system has its advantages, its scalability issues and potential for poor performance when dealing with noisy or unstructured data restrict its use in a variety of real-world situations [43].

By combining retrieval-based techniques with text chunking, our strategy, on the other hand, directly addresses the problem of large-scale data and the potential noisiness that might occur. To make sure the LLM uses important, organized content, we divide large data sets into manageable portions that fit within the token constraints of language models. Retrieval-Augmented Generation (RAG) and summarization are two other techniques that let us restrict our focus to the most important data. Targeted retrieval handles capacity concerns that systems like OLAF have by guaranteeing that, even when processing massive or unstructured data, the content used for ontology population remains accurate, relevant, and in line with the particular ontology structure.

6.2. Ontology Evaluation and Alignment

Automated Ontology Evaluation: Evaluating Coverage and Correctness using a Domain Corpus (2023): Using domain-specific databases, this research suggests an automated approach to assess the reliability and scope of ontologies. The method may not fully capture contextual significance or domain-specific details, and it is constrained by the quality of the input data, although offering a robust review [44].

Instead, in order to guarantee accuracy and relevance, our method concentrates on the ontology population. We prioritize domain-specific details to be directly included into the ontology during development by utilizing module-guided summarization and few-shot prompting. Our methodology involves domain-specific details during the population phase, resulting in a more contextually correct and relevant ontology, whereas this paper's method focuses on evaluating an ontology's scope and trustworthiness after it has been produced, frequently missing key details.

String Similarity Metrics for Ontology Alignment (2022): The paper addresses ontology alignment using string similarity metrics, which is essential for connecting different ontologies. These measures increase alignment accuracy, but their use in tricky alignments is limited since they may have difficulty with semantic mismatches and lack taking context for words into account [39].

6.3. Knowledge Graphs and Language Models

Large Language Models and Knowledge Graphs: Opportunities and Challenges (2023): With the goal of enhancing knowledge extraction and reasoning, this research investigates possibilities for collaboration between large language models and knowledge graphs. It does, however, draw attention to issues with scalability, model interpretability, and the requirement for high-quality data in order to avoid mistakes in knowledge graphs [45].

We address data quality and interpretability issues early by organizing the ontology population process with precise, domain-specific summaries, guaranteeing that the ontology is provided with relevant and accurate content right from the start.

TEXT2KGBENCH: A Benchmark for Ontology-Driven Knowledge Graph Generation from Text (2023): TEXT2KGBENCH presents a benchmark for assessing ontology-driven methods for text-to-knowledge graph generation. Though its reliance on particular ontologies restricts its applicability to other domains and methods of knowledge representation, the benchmark standardizes evaluation measures [46].

RAG is useful in our situation because it facilitates the extraction of relevant information from huge data sets, which is subsequently used to produce content that is directly related to the ontology. This method minimizes problems associated with large-scale data processing and maintains high-quality information by ensuring that only the most pertinent data is used.

6.4. Knowledge Extraction and Prompt Engineering

SPIRES: Structured Prompt Interrogation and Recursive Extraction of Semantics (2023): Using structured prompts for recursive semantic extraction, SPIRES offers a zero-shot learning approach for knowledge base population. The method works well, but it is constrained by the prompt design's quality and the model's comprehension of complicated or difficult ideas [47].

Testing Prompt Engineering Methods for Knowledge Extraction from Text (2023): This research uses language models to assess different prompt engineering techniques for knowledge extraction from text. The study highlights the benefit of different prompts but also points out their inconsistent aspects and the need for domain knowledge in order to create well-designed queries [48].

6.5. Evaluation Metrics for Text and Knowledge Extraction

BERTScore: Evaluating Text Generation with BERT (2019): A more sophisticated evaluation than previous techniques, BERTScore presents a metric for text output quality using BERT embeddings. However, the measure is susceptible to the selection of pre-trained BERT models and might not completely encompass semantic variations in produced text, particularly in synthetic or non-literal settings [49].

7. Conclusion

Knowledge graphs, are by now, utilized across many domains and across enterprise and academia [1]. They are supported by a healthy and mature ecosystem of W3C standards [3,4,5,6] and tool ecosystems (e.g., Protégé or GraphDB). They excel at the integration of heterogeneous datasets and perspective by allowing for semantic harmonization. Yet, when encountering new data, mapping into an existing ontology can be quite expensive. This might be due to the sheer volume of data to be interpreted.

In this chapter, we have presented a mechanism for examining the efficacy of utilizing large language models to do the semi-automated population of a modular ontology. This pipeline uses both LLM-powered text summarization and retrieval-augmented generation processes for conducting ontology-guided information distillation from natural language into forms more amenable to limited context windows and translation into triples to be loaded into a KG.

In our evaluation, we have shown that extraction of appropriate triples, as guided by a schema (and specifically in the case of our experiments: a modular ontology) is effective, approaching 90% coverage when the LLM performs the task. Performance is similarly high agnostic to the prompting strategy or mechanism to fit the text into the models' context windows. As such, we conclude that LLMs are a sufficient tool for the extraction of triples from text when guided by a (modular) schema via prompting.

Future Work. These experiments are preliminary, insofar that they demonstrate feasibility. The evaluation is comparatively shallow, demonstrating coverage in a naive way. Since we are comparing text to ground truth, which was manually curated not necessarily from the text at hand (e.g., other sources), it is not known if failure to extract a triple at a high enough similarity is due to the fact that that information was missing in the first place, or if the LLM somehow missed a particular fact.

As such, further experiments must be conducted. We envision some next steps to answer the following questions.

- Does this LLM triple extraction process perform better than a human? We know that it is certainly *faster*, but does the increase in speed outweigh missing or incorrect facts?
- What graph structures (i.e., data organized in which ontological formalisms) are most easily extracted to from textual data? Experiments demonstrate that the modular ontology originally developed for The Enslaved.org Hub performs better, but what exact characteristics facilitate that increase in coverage?

Acknowledgements The authors acknowledge partial funding under National Science Foundation grants 2333532 and 2333782, and from Kansas State University's Game Changing Research Initiative (GRIP) program.

References

[1] Hitzler P. A review of the semantic web field. Commun ACM. 2021;64(2):76-83. Available from: https://doi.org/10.1145/3397512.

[2] Noy NF, Gao Y, Jain A, Narayanan A, Patterson A, Taylor J. Industry-scale knowledge graphs: lessons and challenges. Commun ACM. 2019;62(8):36-43. Available from: https://doi.org/10.1145/3331166.

[3] Hitzler P, Krötzsch M, Parsia B, Patel-Schneider PF, Rudolph S, editors. OWL 2 Web Ontology Language: Primer (Second Edition). W3C Recommendation 11 December 2012; 2012. Available from http://www.w3.org/TR/owl2-primer/.

[4] Cyganiak R, Wood D, Lanthaler M, editors. RDF 1.1 Concepts and Abstract Syntax. W3C Recommendation 25 February 2014; 2014. Available from http://www.w3.org/TR/rdf11-concepts/.

[5] Baker T, Prud'hommeaux E, editors. Shape Expressions (ShEx) 2.1 Primer. Final Community Group Report 09 October 2019; 2019. Http://shex.io/shex-primer/index.html.

[6] Knublauch H, Kontokostas D, editors. Shapes Constraint Language (SHACL). W3C Recommendation 20 July 2017; 2017. Https://www.w3.org/TR/shacl/.

[7] Shimizu C, Hammar K, Hitzler P. Modular Graphical Ontology Engineering Evaluated. In: Harth A, Kirrane S, Ngomo AN, Paulheim H, Rula A, Gentile AL, et al., editors. The Semantic Web - 17th International Conference, ESWC 2020, Heraklion, Crete, Greece, May 31-June 4, 2020, Proceedings. vol. 12123 of Lecture Notes in Computer Science. Springer; 2020. p. 20-35. Available from: https://doi.org/10.1007/978-3-030-49461-2_2.

[8] Ham K. OpenRefine (version 2.5). Journal of the Medical Library Association. 2013 Jul;101(3):233-4. Copyright: © 2013, Authors. Available from: http://openrefine.org.

[9] Yang J, Jin H, Tang R, Han X, Feng Q, Jiang H, et al. Harnessing the Power of LLMs in Practice: A Survey on ChatGPT and Beyond. ACM Trans Knowl Discov Data. 2024 apr;18(6). Available from: https://doi.org/10.1145/3649506.

[10] Vaswani A, Shazeer N, Parmar N, Uszkoreit J, Jones L, Gomez AN, et al. Attention is All you Need. In: Guyon I, von Luxburg U, Bengio S, Wallach HM, Fergus R, Vishwanathan

SVN, et al., editors. Advances in Neural Information Processing Systems 30: Annual Conference on Neural Information Processing Systems 2017, December 4-9, 2017, Long Beach, CA, USA; 2017. p. 5998-6008. Available from: https://proceedings.neurips.cc/paper/2017/hash/3f5ee243547dee91fbd053c1c4a845aa-Abstract.html.

[11] Lewis P, Perez E, Piktus A, Petroni F, Karpukhin V, Goyal N, et al. Retrieval-augmented generation for knowledge-intensive nlp tasks. Advances in Neural Information Processing Systems. 2020;33:9459-74.

[12] Hu EJ, Shen Y, Wallis P, Allen-Zhu Z, Li Y, Wang S, et al. LoRA: Low-Rank Adaptation of Large Language Models. CoRR. 2021;abs/2106.09685. Available from: https://arxiv.org/abs/2106.09685.

[13] Shimizu C, Hitzler P, Hirt Q, Rehberger D, Estrecha SG, Foley C, et al. The enslaved ontology: Peoples of the historic slave trade. J Web Semant. 2020;63:100567. Available from: https://doi.org/10.1016/j.websem.2020.100567.

[14] Enslaved.org Hub;. https://enslaved.org/.

[15] Wikipedia;. https://wikipedia.org/.

[16] Wikidata;. https://wikidata.org/.

[17] Shimizu C, Hammar K, Hitzler P. Modular ontology modeling. Semantic Web. 2023;14(3):459-89. Available from: https://doi.org/10.3233/SW-222886.

[18] Little C, Cox S. Time Ontology in OWL. W3C; 2017. Https://www.w3.org/TR/2017/REC-owl-time-20171019/.

[19] Gangemi A, Presutti V. Ontology Design Patterns. In: Staab S, Studer R, editors. Handbook on Ontologies. International Handbooks on Information Systems. Springer; 2009. p. 221-43. Available from: https://doi.org/10.1007/978-3-540-92673-3_10.

[20] Hammar K, Presutti V. Template-Based Content ODP Instantiation. In: Hammar K, Hitzler P, Krisnadhi A, Lawrynowicz A, Nuzzolese AG, Solanki M, editors. Advances in Ontology Design and Patterns [revised and extended versions of the papers presented at the 7th edition of the Workshop on Ontology and Semantic Web Patterns, WOP@ISWC 2016, Kobe, Japan, 18th October 2016]. vol. 32 of Studies on the Semantic Web. IOS Press; 2016. p. 1-13. Available from: https://doi.org/10.3233/978-1-61499-826-6-1.

[21] Eberhart A, Shimizu C, Chowdhury S, Sarker MK, Hitzler P. Expressibility of OWL Axioms with Patterns. In: Verborgh R, Hose K, Paulheim H, Champin P, Maleshkova M, Corcho Ó, et al., editors. The Semantic Web - 18th International Conference, ESWC 2021, Virtual Event, June 6-10, 2021, Proceedings. vol. 12731 of Lecture Notes in Computer Science. Springer; 2021. p. 230-45. Available from: https://doi.org/10.1007/978-3-030-77385-4_14.

[22] Hitzler P, Shimizu C. Modular Ontologies as a Bridge Between Human Conceptualization and Data. In: Chapman P, Endres D, Pernelle N, editors. Graph-Based Representation and Reasoning - 23rd International Conference on Conceptual Structures, ICCS 2018, Edinburgh, UK, June 20-22, 2018, Proceedings. vol. 10872 of Lecture Notes in Computer Science. Springer; 2018. p. 3-6. Available from: https://doi.org/10.1007/978-3-319-91379-7_1.

[23] Shimizu C, Hirt Q, Hitzler P. MODL: A Modular Ontology Design Library. In: Janowicz K, Krisnadhi AA, Villalón MP, Hammar K, Shimizu C, editors. Proceedings of the 10th Workshop on Ontology Design and Patterns (WOP 2019) co-located with 18th International Semantic Web Conference (ISWC 2019), Auckland, New Zealand, October 27, 2019. vol. 2459 of CEUR Workshop Proceedings. CEUR-WS.org; 2019. p. 47-58.

[24] Eells A, Dave B, Hitzler P, Shimizu C. Commonsense Ontology Micropatterns. In: Besold TR, d'Avila Garcez A, Jiménez-Ruiz E, Confalonieri R, Madhyastha P, Wagner B, editors. Neural-Symbolic Learning and Reasoning - 18th International Conference, NeSy 2024, Barcelona, Spain, September 9-12, 2024, Proceedings, Part II. vol. 14980 of Lecture Notes in Computer Science. Springer; 2024. p. 51-9. Available from: https://doi.org/10.1007/978-3-031-71170-1_6.

[25] Hitzler P, Gangemi A, Janowicz K, Krisnadhi AA, Presutti V. Towards a Simple but Useful Ontology Design Pattern Representation Language. In: Blomqvist E, Corcho Ó, Horridge M, Carral D, Hoekstra R, editors. Proceedings of the 8th Workshop on Ontology Design and Patterns (WOP 2017) co-located with the 16th International Semantic Web Conference (ISWC 2017), Vienna, Austria, October 21, 2017.. vol. 2043 of CEUR Workshop Proceedings. CEUR-WS.org; 2017. Available from: http://ceur-ws.org/Vol-2043/paper-09.pdf.

[26] Hirt Q, Shimizu C, Hitzler P. Extensions to the Ontology Design Pattern Representation Language. In: Janowicz K, Krisnadhi AA, Poveda-Villalón M, Hammar K, Shimizu C, editors. Proceedings of the 10th

Workshop on Ontology Design and Patterns (WOP 2019) co-located with 18th International Semantic Web Conference (ISWC 2019), Auckland, New Zealand, October 27, 2019. vol. 2459 of CEUR Workshop Proceedings. CEUR-WS.org; 2019. p. 76-5. Available from: http://ceur-ws.org/Vol-2459/short2.pdf.

[27] Shimizu C, Hirt Q, Hitzler P. A Protégé Plug-In for Annotating OWL Ontologies with OPLa. In: Gangemi A, Gentile AL, Nuzzolese AG, Rudolph S, Maleshkova M, Paulheim H, et al., editors. The Semantic Web: ESWC 2018 Satellite Events - ESWC 2018 Satellite Events, Heraklion, Crete, Greece, June 3-7, 2018, Revised Selected Papers. vol. 11155 of Lecture Notes in Computer Science. Springer; 2018. p. 23-7. Available from: https://doi.org/10.1007/978-3-319-98192-5_5.

[28] Eberhart A, Shimizu C, Stevens CA, Hitzler P, Myers CW, Maruyama B. A Domain Ontology for Task Instructions. In: Villazón-Terrazas B, Ortiz-Rodríguez F, Tiwari SM, Shandilya SK, editors. Knowledge Graphs and Semantic Web - Second Iberoamerican Conference and First Indo-American Conference, KGSWC 2020, Mérida, Mexico, November 26-27, 2020, Proceedings. vol. 1232 of Communications in Computer and Information Science. Springer; 2020. p. 1-13. Available from: https://doi.org/10.1007/978-3-030-65384-2_1.

[29] Janowicz K, Hitzler P, Li W, Rehberger D, Schildhauer M, Zhu R, et al. Know, Know Where, Knowwheregraph: A Densely Connected, Cross-Domain Knowledge Graph and Geo-Enrichment Service Stack for Applications in Environmental Intelligence. AI Mag. 2022;43(1):30-9. Available from: https://doi.org/10.1609/aimag.v43i1.19120.

[30] Shimizu C, Stephen S, Barua A, Cai L, Christou A, Currier K, et al. The KnowWhereGraph Ontology. Journal of Web Semantics. 2023. Under review.

[31] Shimizu C, Stephen S, Zhu R, Currier K, Schildhauer M, Rehberger D, et al. The KnowWhereGraph Ontology: A Showcase. In: Toyoshima F, Katsumi M, Righetti G, Giorgis SD, Hedblom MM, Kutz O, et al., editors. Proceedings of the Joint Ontology Workshops 2023 Episode IX: The Quebec Summer of Ontology co-located with the 13th International Conference on Formal Ontology in Information Systems (FOIS 2023), Sherbrooke, Québec, Canada, July 19-20, 2023. vol. 3637 of CEUR Workshop Proceedings. CEUR-WS.org; 2023. Available from: https://ceur-ws.org/Vol-3637/paper46.pdf.

[32] A massive new effort to name millions sold into bondage during the transatlantic slave trade;. https://www.washingtonpost.com/history/2020/12/01/slavery-database-family-genealogy/.

[33] Computer Science Professor, Postdoc Launch Online Database on History of Slavery;. https://cacm.acm.org/news/249167-computer-science-professor-postdoc-launch-online-database-on-history-of-slavery/fulltext?mobile=false.

[34] Shimizu C, Hitzler P, Estrecha SG, Goeke-Smith J, Rehberger D, Foley C, et al. The Wikibase Approach to the Enslaved.Org Hub Knowledge Graph. In: Payne TR, Presutti V, Qi G, Poveda-Villalón M, Stoilos G, Hollink L, et al., editors. The Semantic Web - ISWC 2023 - 22nd International Semantic Web Conference, Athens, Greece, November 6-10, 2023, Proceedings, Part II. vol. 14266 of Lecture Notes in Computer Science. Springer; 2023. p. 419-34. Available from: https://doi.org/10.1007/978-3-031-47243-5_23.

[35] Shimizu C, Hitzler P, Hirt Q, Sheill A, Gonzalez S, Foley C, et al.. The Enslaved Ontology 1.0: People of the Historic Slave Trade; 2019. Available from https://daselab.cs.ksu.edu/projects/ontology-modeling-slave-trade.

[36] Diefenbach D, Wilde MD, Alipio S. Wikibase as an Infrastructure for Knowledge Graphs: The EU Knowledge Graph. In: Hotho A, Blomqvist E, Dietze S, Fokoue A, Ding Y, Barnaghi PM, et al., editors. The Semantic Web – ISWC 2021 - 20th International Semantic Web Conference, ISWC 2021, Virtual Event, October 24-28, 2021, Proceedings. vol. 12922 of Lecture Notes in Computer Science. Springer; 2021. p. 631-47.

[37] Bisen KS, Alemayehu SA, Maret P, Creighton A, Gorman R, Kundi B, et al. Wikibase as an Infrastructure for Community Documents: The example of the Disability Wiki Platform. In: Simsek U, Chaves-Fraga D, Pellegrini T, Vahdat S, editors. Proceedings of Poster and Demo Track and Workshop Track of the 18th International Conference on Semantic Systems co-located with 18th International Conference on Semantic Systems (SEMANTiCS 2022), Vienna, Austria, September 13th to 15th, 2022. vol. 3235 of CEUR Workshop Proceedings. CEUR-WS.org; 2022. Available from: http://ceur-ws.org/Vol-3235/paper14.pdf.

[38] Shimizu C, Eells A, Gonzalez S, Zhou L, Hitzler P, Sheill A, et al. Ontology design facilitating Wikibase integration — and a worked example for historical data. Journal of Web Semantics. 2024;82:100823. Available from: https://www.sciencedirect.com/science/article/pii/

S157082682400009X.

[39] Cheatham M, Hitzler P. String Similarity Metrics for Ontology Alignment. In: Alani H, Kagal L, Fokoue A, Groth P, Biemann C, Parreira JX, et al., editors. The Semantic Web – ISWC 2013. Berlin, Heidelberg: Springer Berlin Heidelberg; 2013. p. 294-309.

[40] Bosker HR. Using fuzzy string matching for automated assessment of listener transcripts in speech intelligibility studies. Behavior Research Methods. 2021 October;53(5):1945-53. Epub 2021 Mar 10. Available from: https://tokensortratio.netlify.app.

[41] Mateiu P, Groza A. Ontology engineering with Large Language Models; 2023. p. 226-9.

[42] Funk M, Hosemann S, Jung JC, Lutz C. Towards Ontology Construction with Language Models; 2023. Available from: https://arxiv.org/abs/2309.09898.

[43] Schaeffer M, Sesboüé M, Kotowicz JP, Delestre N, Zanni-Merk C. OLAF: An Ontology Learning Applied Framework. Procedia Computer Science. 2023;225:2106-15. 27th International Conference on Knowledge Based and Intelligent Information and Engineering Sytems (KES 2023). Available from: https://www.sciencedirect.com/science/article/pii/S1877050923013595.

[44] Zaitoun A, Sagi T, Hose K. Automated Ontology Evaluation: Evaluating Coverage and Correctness using a Domain Corpus. In: Companion Proceedings of the ACM Web Conference 2023. WWW '23 Companion. New York, NY, USA: Association for Computing Machinery; 2023. p. 1127–1137. Available from: https://doi.org/10.1145/3543873.3587617.

[45] Pan JZ, Razniewski S, Kalo JC, Singhania S, Chen J, Dietze S, et al.. Large Language Models and Knowledge Graphs: Opportunities and Challenges; 2023. Available from: https://arxiv.org/abs/2308.06374.

[46] Mihindukulasooriya N, Tiwari S, Enguix CF, Lata K. Text2KGBench: A Benchmark for Ontology-Driven Knowledge Graph Generation from Text; 2023. Available from: https://arxiv.org/abs/2308.02357.

[47] Caufield JH, Hegde H, Emonet V, Harris NL, Joachimiak MP, Matentzoglu N, et al.. Structured prompt interrogation and recursive extraction of semantics (SPIRES): A method for populating knowledge bases using zero-shot learning; 2023. Available from: https://arxiv.org/abs/2304.02711.

[48] Polat F, Tiddi I, Groth P. Testing Prompt Engineering Methods for Knowledge Extraction from Text. Submission type: Full Paper. 2024. Tracking #: 3719-4933. Available from: https://www.semantic-web-journal.net/system/files/swj3719.pdf.

[49] Zhang T, Kishore V, Wu F, Weinberger KQ, Artzi Y. BERTScore: Evaluating Text Generation with BERT; 2020. Available from: https://arxiv.org/abs/1904.09675.

Part IV

Neurosymbolic Reasoning and Hybrid Architectures

Handbook on Neurosymbolic AI and Knowledge Graphs
P. Hitzler et al. (Eds.)
IOS Press, 2025

doi:10.3233/FAIA250219

Knowledge Graph-Based Reasoning in Large Language Models

Teodoro BALDAZZI [a,1], Luigi BELLOMARINI [b] and Emanuel SALLINGER [c,d,2]
[a] *Università Roma Tre, Italy*
[b] *Banca d'Italia, Italy*
[c] *TU Wien, Austria*
[d] *University of Oxford, UK*
ORCiD ID: Teodoro Baldazzi https://orcid.org/0000-0002-1762-1431, Luigi Bellomarini https://orcid.org/0000-0001-6863-0162, Emanuel Sallinger https://orcid.org/0000-0001-7441-129X

Abstract. The integration of Large Language Models (LLMs) with logic-based Knowledge Graphs (KGs) and more generally with Knowledge Representation and Reasoning (KRR) methodologies has rapidly emerged as a pivotal area of research. Such a synergy is aimed at enhancing transparency and accountability in AI-driven applications, which is paramount for big data processing and robust decision-making over high-stakes domains such as finance and biomedicine. Indeed, despite the adaptability and human-centric understanding that LLMs bring, they inherently lack systematic reasoning capabilities, often operating opaquely with limited factuality and common sense. On the other hand, ontological reasoning with knowledge graphs offers robust and scalable reasoning, enriched with the step-by-step explainability of the inferred insights, but is often restricted by the rigidity of its structured rule-based formalism and falls short in providing the semantic understanding required in today's human-data interaction. In this chapter, we address the intrinsic limitations affecting the above paradigms individually and introduce KGLM, a novel neurosymbolic framework that synergistically combines state-of-the-art LLMs with powerful KRR approaches to perform complex reasoning tasks over large knowledge graphs. Through KGLM, language models such as Llama 3 are enhanced with domain awareness and transparency, enabling them to act as natural language interfaces to KGs. Conversely, ontological reasoning systems such as our Vadalog engine are augmented with human-like flexibility to capture semantic nuances in the data. The framework can be seamlessly integrated into existing data processing pipelines and tools to power data-intensive decision-making processes in complex real-world domains.

Keywords. knowledge graphs, ontological reasoning, large language models, explainability, neurosymbolic AI

[1]Corresponding Authors: Teodoro Baldazzi, teodoro.baldazzi@uniroma3.it,
[2]Emanuel Sallinger, sallinger@dbai.tuwien.ac.at

1. Introduction

The recent surge of AI-based chatbots has marked a significant turning point in the field of Natural Language Processing (NLP) [1]. Large Language Models (LLMs) have transcended traditional academic and industrial applications, capturing the general public's attention with their generative capabilities and human-like semantic understanding and revolutionizing the way users interact with data towards more natural language-based and higher-level paradigms. Today, models such as OpenAI's GPT [2] and Meta's Llama [3] are effectively adopted for a plethora of tasks across multiple domains [4], from enhancing language translation [5] to generating and analyzing multimedia content [6].

The primary driver of current interest is the search for novel solutions that employ LLMs to perform complex data analysis and multi-step reasoning [7,8], leveraging recently developed techniques such as *chain-of-thought* (CoT) prompting [9]. However, while these models excel in handling semantic relationships from natural language, concerns persist due to their intrinsic opacity and unpredictability [10], being unable to provide systematic, explainable outcomes necessary for big data processing and robust decision-making [11]. Indeed, adhering to the principles of Fairness, Accountability, Transparency, and Ethics (FATE) has become paramount in today's data-driven industrial landscape, particularly over high-stakes domains such as finance and bio-medicine [12]. Moreover, LLMs have been found to lack factual knowledge and common sense [13,14], often hallucinating with inaccurate or nonsensical outputs even when techniques such as *fine-tuning* or *Retrieval-Augmented Generation* (RAG) [15] are employed.

In this context, traditional *Knowledge Representation and Reasoning* (KRR) [16] approaches offer a robust alternative, being inherently domain-aware and FATE-ful [16]. Indeed, logic-based reasoning, often referred to as *ontological reasoning* [17], excels in powering systematic, scalable, and transparent decision-making by providing factual conclusions and the logically consequential steps that led to their inference [18,19]. Moreover, the database and the AI communities have recently developed increasingly mature, efficient, and scalable *intelligent systems with reasoning capabilities*, backed by expressive logic-based KRR formalisms. Among them, database query languages based on logic programming, such as Datalog and its extensions [20,17,21,22], have been successfully adopted [23], thanks to their effective balance between expressive power and computational complexity [24,25,16]. These reasoning systems are able to capture domain-specific knowledge by combining factual database information (the *extensional knowledge*) and formally specified business awareness, for instance in the form of ontologies (the *intensional knowledge*). Such a combination, further augmented by reasoning over it, can be suitably modeled with logic-based *knowledge graphs* (KGs) [26].

Despite their powerful capabilities, ontological reasoning systems face significant limitations as well, due to the rigid nature of KRR formalisms, which restrict their adaptability to the complexities of real-world data. Indeed, these systems typically rely on query-based interactions, operating at a low level and often proving challenging for non-specialists to use effectively. Moreover, the inputs and outputs are confined to structured formats such as facts, n-tuples, or triples, and the generation of new knowledge through rule activation is limited to what can be syntactically captured by predefined logical predicates. This rigidity fundamentally clashes with the inherent ambiguity and data quality issues of unstructured and raw data, inhibiting the applicability of KRR in scenarios where the semantic understanding of information is crucial [27].

Given the challenges and limits that affect both paradigms, the *neurosymbolic* direction has recently garnered significant attention in both the academic and industrial realm. In this context, it aims to seamlessly integrate the domain awareness and transparency of KRR solutions and the semantic understanding and flexibility of LLMs into more intelligent, adaptable, and explainable AI applications for decision-making processes [28].

This paper strives to contribute to the synergistic integration of LLMs and KRR over knowledge graphs. We operate in the context of the VADALOG [29,30] system, a Datalog-based reasoning engine, that finds many industrial applications [31,23,32,33,34,35,36, 37]. We employ VADALOG and the well-known CHASE procedure [38] at its foundation to enrich LLAMA 3 models with context and awareness of the domain of interest. In turn, such LLMs are leveraged to augment the ontological reasoning process with real-world semantics, injecting flexibility into rule activations. The combined use of VADALOG and LLAMA 3 enables us to perform complex reasoning tasks from natural language-based requests. The resulting KG, enriched with the explanation of the inferred conclusions, is accessible to the LLM via RAG-based mechanisms.
More in detail, our **contributions** can be summarized as follows.

- We provide a **high-level overview** of the intrinsic limitations of Large Language Models, to be addressed with neurosymbolic approaches.
- We delve into this paradigm in the context of LLMs and logic-based KGs, and we present **novel hybrid methodologies** to enhance the domain expertise and explanation capabilities of LLMs while increasing the flexibility of KRR formalisms.
- We unify such methodologies into KGLM, a **novel neuro-symbolic framework** to perform scalable and explainable reasoning tasks by combining the power of LLMs like LLAMA 3 with CHASE-based reasoners such as the VADALOG system.
- We provide a **practical application** of KGLM by integrating it within KG-ROAR [39], a web-based environment developed for the navigation and analysis of large enterprise KGs in the financial domain.

Related work. Current LLMs proved to be very effective for general tasks, but often struggle when it comes to specific domains [13]. For example, it has been shown that FinBert [40] and BloombergGPT [41], two fine-tuned models on financial textual data, outperform generic LLMs on question-answering tasks. This reason, paired with their lack of explainability and reasoning capabilities led neurosymbolic methodologies [42] to be today at the forefront of academic and industrial interest. Specifically, the integration of logic-based KGs and KRR approaches with LLMs shows particular promise [43,44]. Among the distinct forms of hybrid interactions between the two paradigms, current research mainly focuses on enriching LLMs with domain knowledge encapsulated in KGs [13] and with foundational reasoning skills [45], as well as on employing such models for KG construction from unstructured text [46] and exploration [47].
Overview. The remainder of this paper is organized as follows. In Section 2 we discuss the inherent limitations of LLMs. In Section 3 we provide essential background notions on KRR and introduce the VADALOG system. In Section 4 we present the KGLM framework. Section 5 delves into the application of KGLM within KG-ROAR and includes preliminary experimental evaluations. Our conclusions are drawn in Section 6.

2. An Overview of the Limitations of Large Language Models

Large Language Models (LLMs) have revolutionized natural language processing and various applications in artificial intelligence. However, despite their impressive capabilities, these Machine Learning-based technologies have major limitations in what we can call their "*data truthfulness*" [48,49,50,13]. In this section, we provide a high-level crackdown of data truthfulness, in the form of the crucial lacks of LLMs, which we will then address with our neurosymbolic proposal.

- **Lack of context.** LLMs can often misinterpret concepts that feature different meanings in distinct contexts. For instance, the word "bank" in English can refer to a financial institution or the side of a river. If the sentence "*He sat near the bank and watched the boats*" is provided to a model, it might incorrectly interpret "*bank*" as a financial institution, depending on the preceding context. This can lead to confusion and errors in understanding or generating text.
- **Lack of explanation.** LLMs operate as black-box models, as they do not provide a real explanation of how they generated a certain conclusion. This lack of transparency is particularly problematic in high-stakes domains such as finance and biomedicine. For instance, if an LLM suggests a treatment plan for a patient but cannot explain the rationale behind its suggestion, it would raise concerns about the reliability and safety of the recommendation.
- **Lack of knowledge.** LLMs learn from specific instances to generalize knowledge, which can lead to biases. For example, if an LLM is trained on data showing that women earn less than men in many jobs, it might incorrectly generalize this as a rule. This issue arises due to the fact that LLMs do not distinguish between empirically observed data and general knowledge or rules.
- **Lack of logic.** LLMs may struggle with logical constructs, such as giving the appropriate weight to a negation in a sentence. For instance, if asked to generate an image of a large room with no elephants inside, an LLM like DALL-E might incorrectly include an elephant in the image, as it may not process the negation "*no*" correctly. Such a limitation can result in outputs that are logically inconsistent or even plain incorrect.
- **Lack of common sense.** LLMs often lack common sense. For instance, if asked to list five Italian regions starting with "*L*", an LLM might incorrectly include "*Le Marche*" even though it should not be considered in the list based on strict criteria as "*Le*" actually corresponds to the definite article "*the*" in English.
- **Lack of factuality.** LLMs are prone to hallucinations, generating content that can be completely false. For example, when asked a question such as "*What was the Federal Reserve's interest rate decision in its latest meeting?*", an LLM might fabricate an answer like "*The Federal Reserve raised interest rates by 0.5% in its most recent meeting to combat rising inflation*" even if no such meeting or decision had actually occurred at all.
- **Lack of reasoning.** LLMs often fail to perform complex reasoning tasks. For example, when asked to solve a multi-step problem such as calculating the total interest on a loan over multiple periods with varying interest rates, an LLM might provide incorrect calculations as it inherently lacks the systematic and structured reasoning abilities required for such tasks.

3. Ontological Reasoning over Knowledge Graphs in the Vadalog System

To guide the rest of our discussion, we lay out some preliminary notions on ontological reasoning over knowledge graphs, with a specific focus on the VADALOG system and the CHASE procedure at its foundation.

Relational foundations. Let **C** and **V** be disjoint countably infinite sets of *constants* and *variables*, respectively. A (*relational*) *schema* **S** is a finite set of relation symbols (or *predicates*) with associated arity. A *term* is either a constant or a variable. An atom over **S** is an expression of the form $R(\bar{v})$, where $R \in \mathbf{S}$ is of arity $n > 0$ and $\bar{v}$ is an n-tuple of terms. A *database* (*instance*) over **S** associates to each symbol in **S** a relation of the respective arity over the domain of constants. The members of the relations are called *tuples* or *facts*. Given two conjunctions of atoms ς_1 and ς_2, we define a *homomorphism* from ς_1 to ς_2 as a mapping $h : \mathbf{C} \cup \mathbf{V} \rightarrow \mathbf{C} \cup \mathbf{V}$ s.t. $h(t) = t$ if $t \in \mathbf{C}$ and for each atom $a(t_1,\ldots,t_n) \in \varsigma_1$, then $h(a(t_1,\ldots,t_n)) = a(h(t_1),\ldots,h(t_n)) \in \varsigma_2$.

Vadalog syntax. VADALOG is a declarative language for ontological reasoning. It is based on *Warded Datalog*$^{\pm}$, a member of the Datalog family that, at the price of very mild syntactic restrictions, extends Datalog with existential quantifiers and guarantees PTIME data complexity for query answering [51]. A Warded Datalog$^{\pm}$ program consists of a set of *tuples* (or *facts*) and *tuple-generating dependencies* (TGDs) of the form $\forall\bar{x}\forall\bar{y}(\varphi(\bar{x},\bar{y}) \rightarrow \exists\bar{z}\ \psi(\bar{x},\bar{z}))$, where $\varphi(\bar{x},\bar{y})$ (the *body*) and $\psi(\bar{x},\bar{z})$ (the *head*) are conjunctions of atoms over the respective predicates, $\bar{x},\bar{y}$ are vectors of universally quantified variables and constants, and $\bar{z}$ is a vector of existentially quantified variables. Quantifiers can be omitted and conjunction is denoted by comma. In this context, VADALOG extends the Warded fragment with features of practical utility to address real-world scenarios. Support for aggregate functions, namely *sum*, *prod*, *min*, *max* and *count*, is achieved by means of *monotonic aggregations* [52]. Other relevant extensions include *negations* and negative constraints of the form $\varphi(\bar{x},\bar{y}) \rightarrow \bot$, where $\varphi(\bar{x},\bar{y})$ is a conjunction of atoms and $\bot$ denotes the truth constant false to model disjointness or non-membership, as well as *expressions* in rule bodies, modelled with comparison $(>,<,\geq,\leq,\neq)$ and algebraic $(+,-,*,/,$ etc.) operators.

Reasoning over knowledge graphs. KRR approaches model KGs as the combination of an *extensional component*, essentially the ground business data in a database, and an *intensional component*, which formally describes the business knowledge as a set of rules in a declarative language such as VADALOG. Performing ontological reasoning over the KG augments it with new inferred knowledge derived from the application of the rules over the business data. More formally, given a database D and the query $Q = (\Sigma, Ans)$, where Σ is the set of rules and Ans an n-ary predicate, a reasoning task consists of finding an instance J such that a tuple $\bar{t} \in J$ if and only if $\bar{t} \in Q(D)$ and for every other instance J' such that $\bar{t} \in J'$ if and only if $\bar{t} \in Q(D)$, there is a homomorphism h from J to J'.

Chase procedure. The semantics of a VADALOG program can be defined in an operational way with the CHASE *procedure* [53,38]. It enforces the satisfaction of a set Σ of rules over a database D, incrementally augmenting D with facts entailed via the application of the rules over D, until fixpoint. While VADALOG guarantees that such fixpoint exists when only the core features are used [29], the joint presence of algebraic operations and recursion must be carefully handled, as even simple Datalog programs can be in general non-terminating [20]. A TGD $\sigma : \varphi(\bar{x},\bar{y}) \rightarrow \psi(\bar{x},\bar{z})$ is applicable to D if: (i) there exists a homomorphism θ (technically known as *binding*) such that $\theta(\varphi(\bar{x},\bar{y}))$

$\subseteq D$, that is, if there exists a set of *mappings* from the terms of $\varphi(\bar{x},\bar{y})$ to the constants of facts in D such that each term maps to exactly one constant, and (ii) $\theta(\psi(\bar{x},\bar{z}))$ is a fact not already present in D. Then, a *chase step* adds the fact $\theta(\psi(\bar{x},\bar{z}))$ to D. The *chase graph* $\mathcal{G}(D,\Sigma)$ is the directed acyclic graph with the facts from the chase $\Sigma(D)$ as nodes and an edge from a node n to a node m if m derives from n (and possibly other facts) via a CHASE step [21]. A comprehensive examination of reasoning termination in VADALOG has been explored in dedicated works [54,55].

Example 1 *(Trading Activity) Let us consider a simple trading activity managed with a smart contract. Here, D contains a log over time of buy/sell orders from the traders who invest in it as well as market information, e.g., asset prices (Price), or market shutdowns (MarketClosed). The following set Σ contains the* VADALOG *rules governing the basic functioning of the market, i.e., under which conditions the orders are accepted and how profits and losses are computed.*

$$Open(x,y,t_1), \neg MarketClosed(t_1) \rightarrow Accepted(x,y,t_1) \qquad (\sigma_1)$$

$$Accepted(x,y,t_1), Price(p_1,t_1), k = y * p_1 \rightarrow Position(x,y,k,t_1) \qquad (\sigma_2)$$

$$Close(x,t_2), Price(p_2,t_2), Position(x,y,k,t_1), t_2 > t_1, pl = y * p_2 - k \rightarrow Return(x,pl) \qquad (\sigma_3)$$

If a trader x wants to open a position (buy) on a certain asset of size y at time t_1 and the market is open at t_1, the order is accepted (rule σ_1). If the order by x is accepted and the asset price at t_1 is p_1, then x holds a position on the market at time t_1 of size y and of notional (total value) k equal to $y * p_1$ (rule σ_2). If, later at t_2, trader x decides to close its position (sell) and the price at t_2 is p_2, then x gets returns (profits or losses) from its trading activity as $y * p_2 - k$ (rule σ_3).

Let us also consider an excerpt of database D = {*Open*(*EGTech*,0.3,1), *Price*(124,1), *Price*(147,9), *Close*(*EGTech*,9), *MarketClosed*(5)}. Figure 1 illustrates the CHASE graph derived from the activation of Σ over D. Specifically, rule σ_1 generates the fact *Accepted(EGTech*,0.3,1), as the market is not closed at time 1. Then, the fact *Position(EGTech*,0.3, 37.2,1) is derived via rule σ_2. Finally, as trader *EGTech* closes the position, i.e., sells the asset, at time 9 and the price goes up to 147$, then *EGTech* gets a profit of 6.9$ as return via rule σ_3.

The Vadalog system. The VADALOG system is a state-of-the-art ontological reasoning engine that leverages the theoretical underpinnings of the CHASE procedure and the vast experience of the database community on provenance to power efficient, scalable, and explainable reasoning tasks over critical business domains and large KGs [30]. To achieve this, it adopts a *streaming* data processing architecture based on the *pipes and filters* style [29,56]. Here, the set of logic rules Σ and the queries are translated into active *data scans* (linear scans for linear TGDs, join scans for join TGDs, and an output scan for the query), connected by intermediate buffers in a processing pipeline. The reasoning process is performed as a data stream along the pipeline, where each filter (i.e., scan) reads tuples from the respective parent, from the output scan down to the external data stores that inject ground facts into the pipeline. Since, for each filter, multiple parent filters may be available, VADALOG selects which one to invoke (via *next()* call)

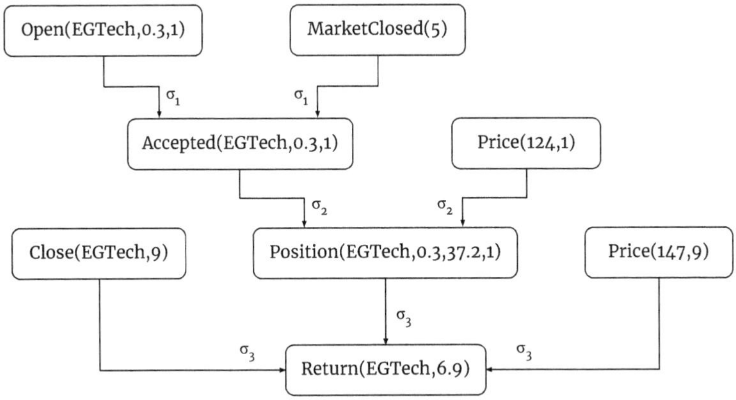

Figure 1. Instance of CHASE graph for Example 1.

by employing specific *routing strategies* (*round-robin*, *shortest path*, etc.) that manage a priority queue of the sources. This methodology allows VADALOG to keep track of the provenance of each result, derived from one or more CHASE steps. Unlike traditional *semi-naive* approaches [20], VADALOG generalizes the *volcano iterator model* [57], operating in a *pull-based query-driven* fashion in which, ideally, facts are materialized only at the end of the CHASE procedure and if they contributed to the reasoning task. Figure 2 illustrates VADALOG processing pipeline for the scenario in Example 1 given, as ontological reasoning task, the query *q* of finding the returns for the trader *EGTech*. Here the output filter *o* sends a *next()* message to the query processor, which propagates it to the TGDs scans. Note that each filter in the figure is labelled with the corresponding rule number from the above scenario.

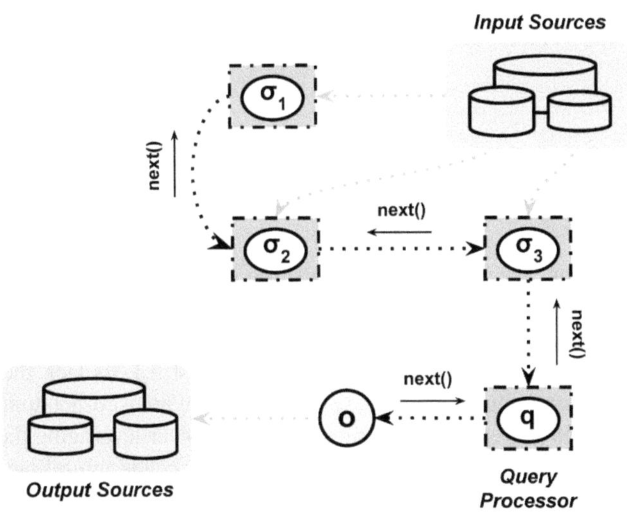

Figure 2. Processing pipeline of VADALOG for Example 1.

4. The KGLM Neurosymbolic Framework

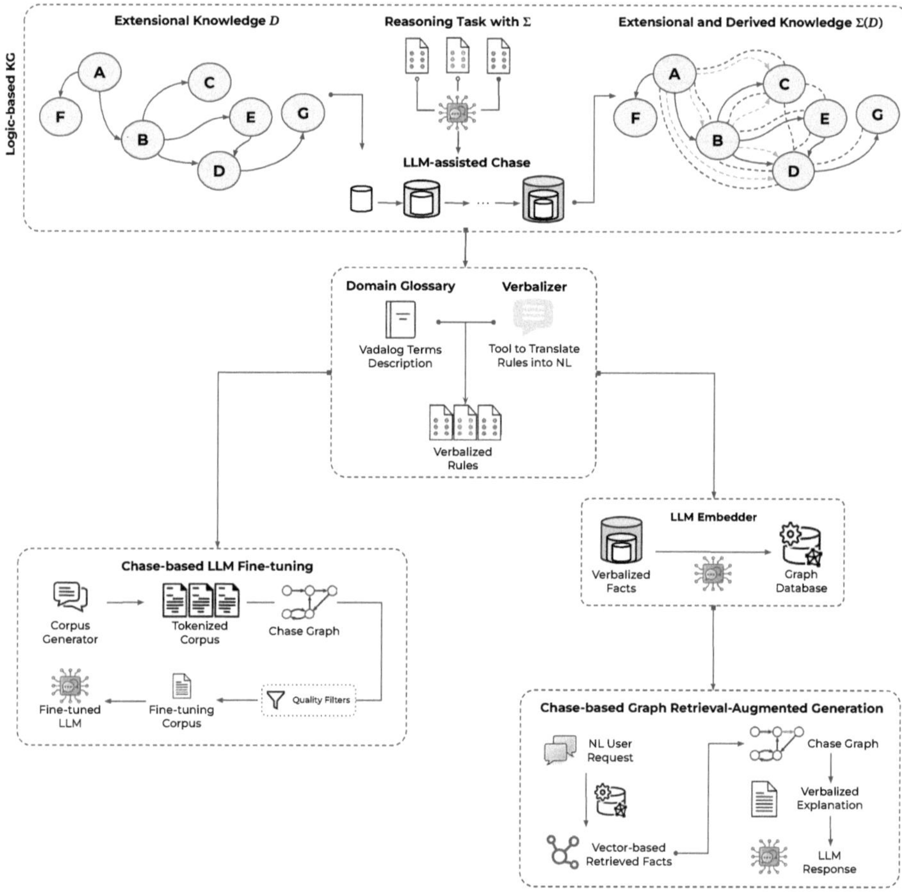

Figure 3. Visual overview of the KGLM neurosymbolic framework.

In the previous sections we pointed out the intrinsic limitations and challenges of AI applications that leverage LLMs or KRR methodologies individually. In fact, KRR systems require queries to be formulated in their specific formalisms, with knowledge generation restricted to what reasoning rules can capture. In contrast, LLMs lack the comprehensive domain awareness, robustness, and explainability that are a cornerstone of KRR approaches. To cope with this, one promising approach involves leveraging the strengths of both paradigms in a synergistic fashion. Indeed, LLMs excel at natural language understanding and generation. KRR-powered KGs, in turn, provide LLMs with a foundation of factual knowledge, provenance, and ontological reasoning, thus mitigating the risk of inconsistencies and biases often present in their outputs.

With the goal of contributing to such a pivotal line of research, in this section we introduce KGLM, the first, to the best of our knowledge, neuro-symbolic framework that combines LLMs such as LLAMA 3 and our VADALOG reasoner in meaningful ways to power real-world data-intensive and decision-making tasks in complex domains. In fact, KGLM can be interpreted as a toolkit that provides synergistic interactions between LLMs and KRR, which, as further showcased later in this section and in Section 5 are highly complementary and enable a proper neurosymbolic reasoning behavior by combining unstructured information with internal logic rules to derive novel knowledge. Specifically, KGLM offers three main synergies:

- leveraging the CHASE, which enriches the output of the reasoning with the explanation of each conclusion, to inject task- and domain-specific awareness into the LLM via fine-tuning (Section 4.1);
- employing the LLM to support the reasoning process, enriching VADALOG with real-world semantic flexibility, thus enabling rule activation on unstructured data affected by quality issue or that in general may not fit into the predefined logic predicates (Section 4.2);
- exploiting the text manipulation capabilities of LLMs and RAG-based mechanisms to enable a natural language navigation of the KG, presenting its inferred edges and explanation in a human-like fashion (Section 4.3).

4.1. Chase-based Domain-specific LLM Fine-tuning

The first KGLM task synthesizes question-answering fine-tuning corpora that cover the entire "reasoning space" of the use case of interest, conveying context awareness to the LLM. Note that here we are interested in the domain the use case belongs to (so, for instance, the trading and market world), not on a specific data and reasoning instance of that domain. The goal of the task is to enrich the model with domain specificity, preventing misinterpretation of potentially ambiguous concepts and teaching the LLM to recognize the reasoning task from a user request. To achieve this, we leverage the CHASE and perform a reasoning process over a representative set of synthetic data [58]. Algorithm 1 and Algorithm 2 provide the pseudo-code describing the task, corresponding to the left path of the pipeline in Figure 3.

Algorithm 1 Reasoning and plan verbalization in KGLM.

```
function ReasoningAndPlanVerbalization(D, Σ, glossary)
  chase ← Vadalog.reason(D, Σ)                                  ▷ chase generation
  aggrChase ← ∅
  for each step in chase do                                      ▷ chase aggregation
    stepAggrContrib ← ∅
    if hasAggregate(step.getRule()) then
      stepAggrContrib ← collectAggrContributors(step, chase)
    aggrStep ← aggregateStep(step, stepAggrContrib)
    aggrChase ← verbChase ∪ {aggrStep}
  verbRules ← verbalizeRules(Σ, glossary)                        ▷ rules verbalization
  verbPlan ← verbalizePlan(Σ.getLogicPlan(), verbRules)
  return (aggrChase, verbPlan)
```

The first step consists in the execution of the ontological reasoning task of interest with the VADALOG system. Given the extensional knowledge D and the set Σ of VADALOG rules encoding the domain knowledge as the intensional component, the KG is built by augmenting D with the new inferred edges. Consequently, the corresponding CHASE graph is generated (line 2 Algorithm 1). In the presence of results deriving from the application of aggregation functions, the CHASE is further processed to collect all the contributors that led to the resulting aggregated value by *unfolding* the corresponding path of CHASE steps altogether [59,55] (line 9 Algorithm 1).

Now, KGLM employs a *verbalizer* component to transform Σ into a set of natural language sentences via a deterministic transformation. To achieve this, we make use of a *domain glossary*, containing descriptions of the predicates and their terms involved in the rules (line 10 Algorithm 1). In the case of the *trading activity* scenario introduced in Example 1, the glossary in Figure 4 could be employed.

Predicate	**Description**
$Open(x,y,t)$	$<x>$ is a trader sending an order to open a position of size $<y>$ at time $<t>$
$MarketClosed(t)$	$<t>$ is a time in which the market is closed
$Accepted(x,y,t)$	The order by the trader $<x>$ of size $<y>$ is accepted at time $<t>$
$Price(p,t)$	$<p>$ is the price of the market at time $<t>$
$Position(x,y,k,t)$	The trader $<x>$ has a position at time $<t>$ of size $<y>$ and notional $<k>$
$Close(x,t)$	$<x>$ is a trader sending an order to close a position at time $<t_2>$
$Return(x,pl)$	The trader $<x>$ has returns amounting to $<pl>$

Figure 4. Domain glossary for the *trading activity* scenario in Example 1.

The NL translation of the rules leverages the *select-project-join* semantics, rewriting logic-based rules into textual "*since-then* closures". All VADALOG syntactic elements are converted into their textual counterparts. Conjunctions are rendered as "*and*" tokens, built-in operators are represented with specific keywords, e.g., $>$ becomes "*is higher than*", and the same occurs for aggregations, e.g., $x = count(y)$ becomes "*x is the total number of y*", etc. Moreover, rule variables are converted into tokens acting as placeholders. For instance, with respect to Example 1, the rule $Open(x,y,t_1), \neg MarketClosed(t_1) \rightarrow Accepted(x,y,t_1)$ (rule σ_1) is verbalized as: "*Since $<x>$ is a trader sending an order to open a position of size $<y>$ at time $<t_1>$, and the market is not closed at $<t_1>$, then the order is accepted at time $<t_1>$*".

Then, with the verbalization of the rules available, we can generate a fine-tuning corpus to teach an LLM the domain of interest and its intricacies. To generate the fine-tuning corpus, we exploit the effectiveness of powerful pre-trained LLMs [60], such as GPT-4, in text understanding and manipulation capabilities. In fact, we can ask it to act as a human agent and synthesize a set of possible prompt-response pairs based on an input text. In order to minimize the number of "calls" to the LLM, for cost- and time-efficiency reasons, we leverage the regularity of logical languages and resort to a *lifting technique* based on the creation of a *logic plan* out of Σ (line 11 Algorithm 1). Intuitively, a plan is the equivalent in our context of a database execution plan and can be seen as the dependency graph of the rules of Σ, where nodes represent rules and edges stand for head-body dependencies (similarly, at a high level, to VADALOG's processing pipeline introduced in Section 3). By sending natural language excerpts of the plan, obtained from the aggregation of the verbalized rules, we can automatically generate a corpus of tokenized question-answers, which capture the knowledge encoded in the rules and their interconnections (line 2 Algorithm 2). With such an approach, we achieve a corpus generation pipeline that is cost- and time-effective. The tokenized set of prompt-response pairs is then passed on to *filters*, which discard low-quality pairs. For instance, pairs in which the LLM generates new tokens are discarded. Such a step could also resort to a human-in-the-loop approach: in fact, as the pairs are a finite and relatively small set of *templates*, a validator could be hired to discard non-informative ones.

Algorithm 2 Chase-based LLM fine-tuning task in KGLM.

```
1:  function ChaseBasedFineTuning(aggrChase, verbPlan, model, threshold)
2:    tokenizedCorpus ← filter(generate(verbPlan))          ▷ tokenized corpus generation
3:    chaseCorpus ← ∅
4:    for each aggrStep in aggrChase do                     ▷ chase corpus generation
5:      chasePromptResp ← map(tokenizedCorpus, aggrStep)
6:      chaseCorpus ← chaseCorpus ∪ {chasePromptResp}
7:    for each pair ⟨prompt, resp⟩ in chaseCorpus do        ▷ quality-driven optimization
8:      qualityScore ← checkQuality(⟨prompt, resp⟩)
9:      if qualityScore ≤ threshold then
10:       chaseCorpus ← chaseCorpus \ {⟨prompt, resp⟩}
11:     else
12:       chaseCorpus ← chaseCorpus ∪ paraphrase(⟨prompt, resp⟩)
13:   fineTuningCorpus ← postprocess(chaseCorpus)
14:   fineTunedModel ← fineTune(model, fineTuningCorpus)    ▷ model fine-tuning
15:   return fineTunedModel
```

Finally, we materialize the actual fine-tuning corpus via the CHASE graph. For each new fact derived from CHASE procedure, we look up the corresponding verbalized portion of the plan and the tokenized corpus pairs. Each pair is instantiated by mapping the tokens to the corresponding constant arguments of the fact (line 4 Algorithm 2). In Figure 5, we provide some examples of tokenized corpora and their instantiations over artificial data for our running example. The corpus undergoes a more thorough quality check where each pair is filtered according to a BERT-score-based scoring model that returns a so-called *R-score*, to evaluate generated text on coherence and factual consistency with the input text [61] (line 7 Algorithm 2). The threshold under which a pair is dropped can be selected by the user. The filtered-in pairs are enhanced via *NLP paraphrasing* to improve generalization, cleansed with additional post-processing procedures, and finally injected into the LLM (line 14 Algorithm 2).

Plan Parts	Verbalized Plan	Tokenized Corpus	Fine-Tuning Corpus
$Open(x, y, t_1)$, $\neg\, MarketClosed(t_1)$ $\rightarrow Accepted(x, y, t_1)$	*Since the trader <x> at time <t_1> sends an order to open a position of size <y> and it is not true that <t_1> is a time when the market is closed, then the order of size <y> by <x> is accepted at time <t_1>.*	Q1: What is the size of the order accepted sent by trader <x>? A1: The size is <y>	Q1: What is the size of the order accepted sent by trader EGTech? A1: The size is 0.3
		Q2: Why was the order sent by trader <x> at time <t_1> accepted? A2: Because at time <t_1> the market was open	Q2: Why was the order sent by trader EGTech at time 1 accepted? A2: Because at time 1 the market was open
$Open(x, y, t_1)$, $\neg\, MarketClosed(t_1)$ $\rightarrow Accepted(x, y, t_1)$ ↓ $Accepted(x, y, t_1)$, $Price(p_1, t_1)$, $k = y * p_1$ $\rightarrow Position(x, y, k, t_1)$	*Since the trader <x> at time <t_1> sends an order to open a position of size <y> and it is not true that <t_1> is a time when the market is closed, then the order of size <y> by <x> is accepted at time <t_1>. Since the order of size <y> by <x> is accepted and the price is <p_1> at time <t_1>, then <x> holds a position of size <y> and notional <k> at time <t_1>.*	Q1: When did <x> send an order to open a position with notional <k>? A1: The order to open that position was sent at time <t_1>	Q1: When did EGTech send an order to open a position with notional 37.2? A1: The order to open that position was sent at time 1
		Q2: Why was the order sent by trader <x> at time <t_1> accepted? A2: Because at time <t_1> the market was open	Q2: Why was the order sent by trader EGTech at time 1 accepted? A2: Because at time 1 the market was open
...		...	...

Figure 5. Generation of domain-specific corpora for *trading activity* scenario in Example 1 for LLM fine-tuning. Parts of interest of the plan are extracted, verbalized and passed to an LLM for generating the Q&A pair. Then, based on the actual CHASE graph, the final corpus is generated.

4.2. LLM-powered Soft Chase with Vadalog

The second KGLM task consists in leveraging the semantic understanding of LLMs to inject flexibility in the reasoning process and handle the activation of the logic rules in the presence of data in raw formats or that would not bind to the rules if the purely syntactic activation were to be applied [27]. Indeed, as introduced in Section 3, in pure KRR settings, the set $\Sigma(D)$ is computed via the standard CHASE [38]: starting from $\Sigma(D) = D$, the CHASE augments $\Sigma(D)$ with facts derived from the application of the rules in Σ up to fixpoint. A rule is applicable if there exists a *binding*, that is, a set of variable-to-constant *mappings* from the body of the rule to facts in $\Sigma(D)$.

Now, let us extend Example 1 by taking into account an additional source of information apart from the input database D. For instance, let us assume the following raw data: $D' = \{$"EGTech also bought a high-risk asset of size 0.5 at time 1"$\}$. In this instance, relevant information would be lost due to the absence of syntactic bindings from the rule bodies to NL knowledge in D'. Thus, we can extend bindings by introducing an LLM that acts as a *semantic unifier* between rule bodies and D'. Specifically, the model operates on three phases of the CHASE, discussed below for our running scenario with the aid of Algorithm 3 and Figure 6. We name such an approach *soft* CHASE, as it "softens" the restrictions on rule activations.

As in a standard CHASE procedure, we begin by initializing the set I of CHASE facts to the ground ones in the database (line 2, in the algorithm). Next, we consider the data from I to activate the rules in Σ and generate new knowledge. For each rule σ and fact $i \in I$, we employ our verbalization module and the glossary to translate them (if required) from their VADALOG form into pure text.

Now, for each atom in the body of the rule, the model verifies whether there exists a semantic binding from the verbalized atom to the fact, in which case it generates the

Algorithm 3 Soft Chase Procedure.

1: **function** SOFT_CHASE($D, \Sigma, glossary, model$)
2: $I \leftarrow D$ ▷ initialize chase facts to D
3: **for each** $\sigma \in \Sigma$ and $\mathbf{i} \in I$ **do**
4: $\sigma_{nl} \leftarrow$ verbalize($\sigma.body, glossary$) ▷ verbalize rule and fact with glossary
5: $\mathbf{i}_{nl} \leftarrow$ verbalize($\mathbf{i}, glossary$)
6: $\mathbf{i}_{\mathbf{mappings}} \leftarrow \emptyset$ ▷ initialize mappings to empty set
7: **if** LINEAR(σ) **then**
8: $\mathbf{i}_{\mathbf{mappings}} \leftarrow$ *model*.bindLinear($\sigma_{nl}, \mathbf{i}_{\mathbf{nl}}$) ▷ get mappings via LLM
9: **else**
10: **if** JOIN(σ) **then**
11: $\mathbf{i}_{\mathbf{mappings}} \leftarrow$ *model*.bindAndMatchJoin($\sigma_{nl}, \mathbf{i}_{\mathbf{nl}}$) ▷ also check join via LLM
12: **if** $\mathbf{i}_{\mathbf{mappings}} \neq \emptyset$ **then**
13: $\mathbf{i}' \leftarrow$ VADALOG.apply($\sigma, \mathbf{i}_{\mathbf{mappings}}$) ▷ activate rule via VADALOG
14: $\mathbf{i}'_{\mathbf{nl}} \leftarrow$ verbalize($\mathbf{i}', glossary$)
15: **if** *model*.check_termination(I, $\mathbf{i}'_{\mathbf{nl}}$) **then** ▷ check termination via LLM
16: $I = I \cup \mathbf{i}'$ ▷ add newly generated fact
17: **return** $I.output$

sets of mappings. For instance, the NL fact "*EGTech also bought a high-risk asset of size 0.5 at time 1*" maps to the verbalized form of atom *Open(x,y,t)*, that is, "*$< x >$ is a trader sending an order to open a position of size $< y >$ at time $< t >$*". In this case, the LLM generates a set of mappings from the atom to the fact, e.g., $\{x \rightarrow EGTech, y \rightarrow 0.5, t \rightarrow 1\}$. The verification is performed by the LLM itself, which in our case is a LLAMA 3 model fine-tuned to find the bindings by matching the semantic content of the fact to the structure of the rule, while filtering out additional information such as that the asset was a high-risk one.

If the rule involves a *join*, it further processes the mappings to check whether the values corresponding to the join variables match semantically (line 11). For instance, the fact *The price of positions at time 1 is 124$*" (the NL version of *Price(124, 1)*) and the NL one above match on the join argument $\langle time\ 1, 1 \rangle$.

Now, if the set i_{mappings} of mappings resulting from the above steps is not empty, the original logic rule is deterministically activated via the VADALOG reasoner over it (line 13). The resulting logic fact i' undergoes a *termination check* to ensure that it is not already present in the CHASE instance I, essential to prevent loops in recursive settings. To achieve this, the LLM is employed once again and the verbalized version of i' is semantically compared with the ones of the facts in I (line 15).

To further specialize the LLM into the domain of interest for the reasoning task, thus enabling a more accurate semantic unification throughout the procedure, we can also make available additional knowledge and terminology via RAG mechanisms. As further discussed in Section 5, RAG enhances the model's contextual understanding by retrieving relevant documents or data points that contain specific information related to the concepts (i.e., the atoms and the facts) involved in the binding at hand.

Figure 7 illustrates the CHASE graph augmented with the results of the soft CHASE approach to our running example. Indeed, we believe that this approach paves the way to addressing the inherent rigidity of traditional ontological reasoning systems, employing

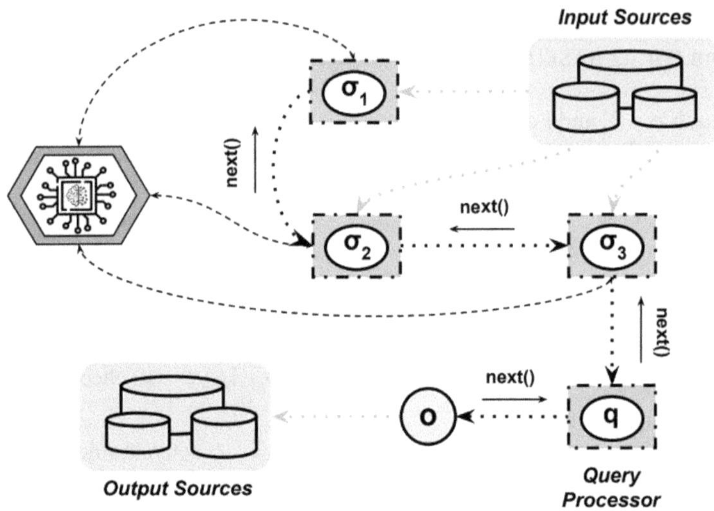

Figure 6. Processing pipeline of soft CHASE in VADALOG for Example 1. Dashed edges denote an interaction with the semantic unifier.

Large Language Models as semantic unifiers to enhance the flexibility and semantic understanding of rule activations over unstructured and natural language data.

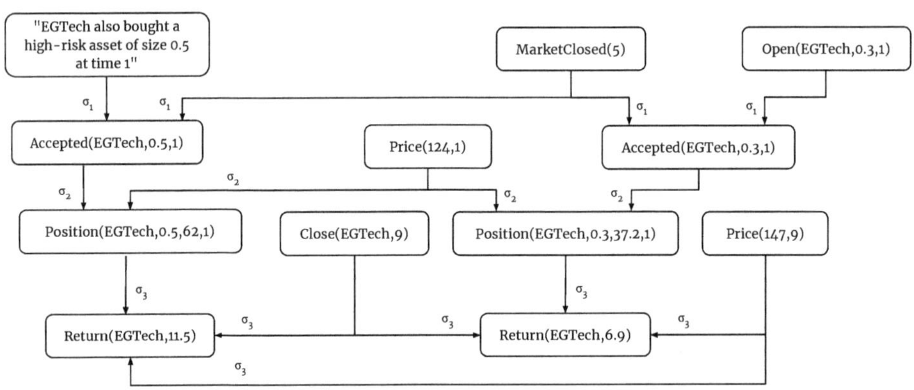

Figure 7. Instance of soft CHASE graph for Example 1.

4.3. Chase-based Graph Retrieval-Augmented Generation

The third KGLM task consists in employing the domain-expert LLM, fine-tuned in the first task, to act as NL-based interface to the KG. To achieve this, we leverage the CHASE and make available to the model the full knowledge around the KG, that is, the extensional data, the derived one from the reasoning process, as well as the full CHASE graph, injecting the capability of answering *explanatory questions* of how each reasoning output is inferred. To address this, we extended KGLM with a dedicated module that supports the LLM in correctly handling such questions by retrieving the CHASE-based explanations from a *graph database* such as Neo4j, leveraging the recently proposed GraphRAG mechanism [62]. Algorithm 4 and Algorithm 5 provide the pseudo-code describing the task, corresponding to the right path of the pipeline in Figure 3.

Algorithm 4 Chase embedding and knowledge graph construction in graph database.

```
1: function CHASEFACTEMBEDDING(chase, model, glossary, graphDB)
2:   for each fact in chase.facts do
3:     nlFact ← verbalize(fact, glossary)                          ▷ verbalize fact
4:     embeddedFact ← model.embed(nlFact)
5:     addNode(graphDB, {fact, nlFact, embeddedFact})             ▷ add fact as node
6:     for i ← 1 to arity(fact) do                       ▷ iterate over fact arguments
7:       predicate ← getPredicate(fact)
8:       argument ← getArgument(fact, i)
9:       if isEntity(predicate, i, glossary) then    ▷ check if argument is an entity
10:        if argument not in graphDB.nodes then
11:          addNode(graphDB, argument)                        ▷ add entity as node
12:        addRelatedToEdge(graphDB, fact, argument)                  ▷ add relation
13:  for each rule in chase.rules do
14:    for each inferredFact in rule.inferredFacts do
15:      for each sourceFact in rule.sourceFacts do
16:        addDerivesEdge(graphDB, sourceFact, inferredFact, rule) ▷ add derivation
```

After a reasoning task is completed, the process begins by iterating over each fact in the *chase*. For each fact, it verbalizes it into natural language via the verbalizer (line 3 Algorithm 4) and then creates an embedding of this natural language fact using an embedder LLM like GPT (line 4 Algorithm 4). The *chase* fact properties—logical form, natural language form, and embedded form—are added together as a node to the graph database (line 5 Algorithm 4). Next, the algorithm iterates over each argument of the fact (line 6 Algorithm 4). For each argument, if it is identified as an entity (line 9 Algorithm 4), it checks whether this entity already exists in the graph. If not, it creates a new node for this entity (lines 10, 11 Algorithm 4). Subsequently, it adds a "*related to*" edge between the fact node and the entity node to represent the relationship (line 12 Algorithm 4). Following this, the algorithm iterates over each rule in the *chase*. For each inferred fact from these rules, it processes each source fact that contributed to the inference and adds a "*derives*" edge in the graph database, linking the source facts to the inferred facts and annotating it with the corresponding rule details (line 16 Algorithm 4). Figure 8 illustrates an excerpt of the resulting knowledge graph structure for Example 1.

Let us now assume that a users asks the LLM to answer an explanatory question. It is at this point that the actual retrieval process begins. First, the input request is embedded and a vector search is performed to identify the corresponding CHASE node in the graph database (line 2 Algorithm 5). Then, as we are interested in the full explanation of the fact referred to in the request, we perform a deterministic *back-composition* along the derivation edges, from the fact of interest up to the extensional ones that began such sequences of rule activations during the reasoning process. The result is an *explanation subgraph* of the CHASE graph, featuring both the facts and the activated rules in the paths.

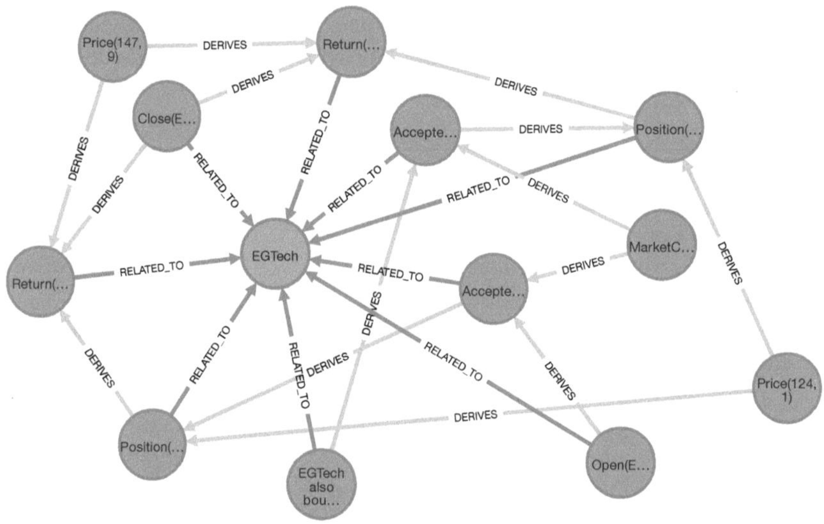

Figure 8. Excerpt of KG augmented with soft CHASE from Figure 7. Blue nodes are CHASE facts, green nodes are entities. Red edges show "*related to*" relationships, yellow edges show "*derives*" relationships.

By concatenating the resulting verbalized CHASE steps, we obtain the deterministic NL explanation of the fact of interest as a sequence of *"Since* $\{body\}$*, then* $\{head\}$*"* sentences (line 14 Algorithm 5). Note that the final order of the verbalizations reflects the breadth-first traversal of the graph and thus respects logical dependency. Finally, the explanation is passed to our LLM, acting as KG interface, to answer the original user question (line 15 Algorithm 5).

Algorithm 5 Chase-based LLM explanation retrieval via GraphRAG.

1: **function** GRAPHRAGEXPLANATION(*chase*, *model*, *query*, *graphDB*)
2:   *embeddedQuery* ← *model*.embed(*query*) ▷ embed the input request
3:   *fact* ← vectorSearch(*embeddedQuery*, *graphDB*) ▷ perform vector search
4:   *factStep* ← extractStep(*chase*, *fact*)
5:   *explanationSubgraph* ← {*factStep*}
6:   *predecessors* ← {*factStep*}
7:   **while** not *predecessors.isEmpty*() **do** ▷ explanation subgraph creation
8:     *currentStep* ← *predecessors.dequeue*()
9:     *currentPreds* ← getPredecessors(*currentStep*, *chase*)
10:     **for each** *predStep* in *currentPreds* **do**
11:       **if** not *predStep* in *explanationSubgraph* **then**
12:         *explanationSubgraph* ← *explanationSubgraph* ∪ {*predStep*}
13:         *predecessors.enqueue*(*predStep*)
14:   *detExplanation* ← concatenate(*explanationSubgraph*)
15:   **return** *model*.answer(*query*, *detExplanation*)

5. KGLM Integration for Financial Applications

The KGLM system can seamlessly be integrated into enterprise environments and business applications to enhance data processing and KG navigation tasks. In this section, we illustrate an example of such an integration to support business analysts addressing complex real-world tasks in the financial and corporate economics realm.

The KG-Roar environment. We recently introduced KG-ROAR [39], a web-based environment designed for the interactive development and navigation of logical KGs derived from augmenting an input graph database with intensional definitions of new nodes and edges in the form of VADALOG programs. Such programs are user-defined or pre-built code snippets encapsulated in *reasoning widgets* (as illustrated in Figure 9), and act as a metaphor for capturing and integrating business-specific knowledge into the KG, thus enriching its representational power. Indeed, KG-Roar offers a productivity toolkit where the user can select widgets of interest and augment the KG interactively at runtime with new knowledge thanks to the scalability and responsiveness of the underlying VADALOG reasoning engine. A *virtual* representation of the KG is provided in an interactive visualization window within the environment. The goal of KG-ROAR is to enable users to perform complex analyses, seamlessly building, browsing, and querying even complex and large enterprise knowledge graphs.

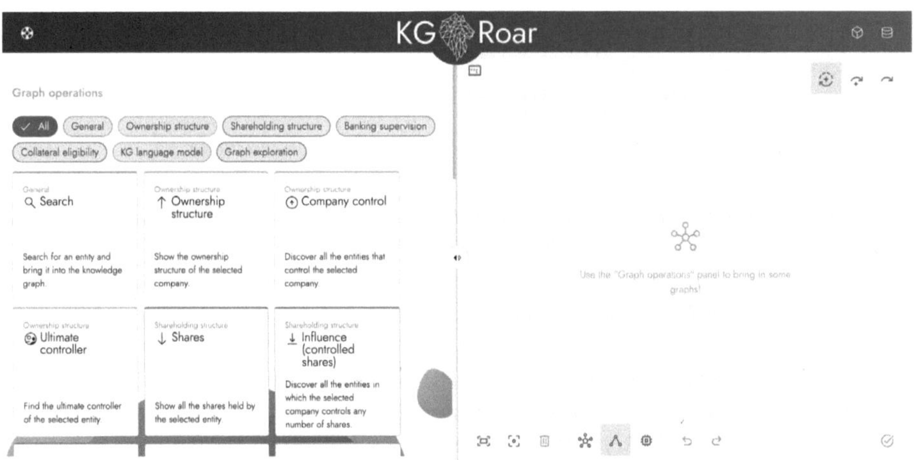

Figure 9. Financial use cases in the form of executable widgets.

Financial use cases. Before delving into the application of KGLM within KG-ROAR, let us consider two scenarios involving a financial KG. Specifically, we refer to an excerpt of European Ownership KG managed by the Central Bank of Italy [33], where the extensional component consists of *Owns* relationships, as depicted in Figure 10.

On top of the KG, we can formalize an intensional component into VADALOG rules, which augment the graph with new knowledge in the form of novel edges.

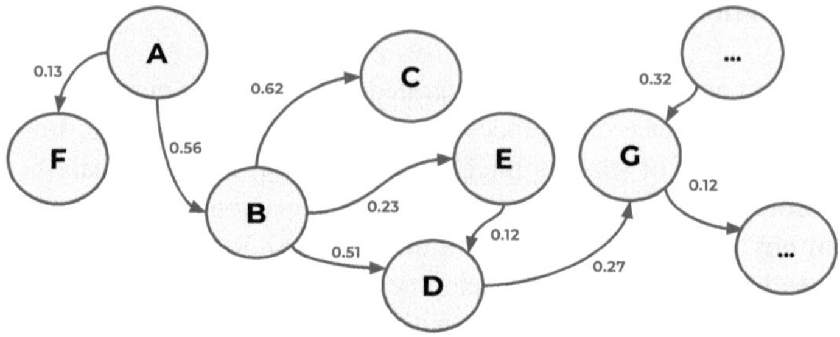

Figure 10. Portion of ownership knowledge graph. Nodes are companies. Solid edges are *owns* relationships with the shares of the target node owned by the source node.

Example 2 *(Company Control) This scenario allows analysts to understand who has decision power in companies, based on who controls the majority of votes, in a "one-share one-vote" assumption. To this end, the task augments the ownership graph with "control" edges, as follows [63]: A company x directly owning s shares of a company y, controls such shares via y itself (rule σ_4). If x controls a company z and z owns s shares of y, then x controls s shares of y via z (rule σ_5). Finally, if x controls the majority of the shares of y, directly or indirectly, then x controls y (rule σ_6).*

$$Owns(x,y,s) \rightarrow ControlledShares(x,y,y,s) \quad (\sigma_4)$$

$$Controls(x,z), Owns(z,y,s) \rightarrow ControlledShares(x,z,y,s) \quad (\sigma_5)$$

$$ControlledShares(x,\_,y,s), ts = sum(s), ts > 0.5 \rightarrow Controls(x,y) \quad (\sigma_6)$$

Example 3 *(Collateral Eligibility). Integrated ownership refers to the total stake a single entity holds in another entity, considering both direct and indirect ownership throughout the graph, with finite or infinite paths [64]. The value of integrated ownership I is calculated as* $lim_{\varepsilon \to 0} \sum_{P_i \in B_\varepsilon} w_\varepsilon(P_i)$, *where* B_ε *is the set of all paths* $P = [x, p_1, \ldots, p_k, y]$ *in the ownership graph such that* $x \neq p_i$ *for* $i = 1, \ldots, k$, *and where* $w_\varepsilon(P) = \Pi_{(p_i,p_j) \in P} w(p_i,p_j) > \varepsilon$, *with* $w(p_i,p_j)$ *representing the direct ownership of* p_i *on* p_j, $\varepsilon \in \mathbb{R}^+$, *and* $0 < \varepsilon \leq 1$. *Note that integrated ownership differs from simple ownership used in Example 2. Applying this formulation to the regulation of the European Central Bank [65], we can say that x is in close link with y if: (i) the integrated ownership of x on y is at least 20% (rule* σ_7*); (ii) y is in close link with x (rule* σ_8*); (iii) there is a third company z, whose integrated ownership on x and y is at least 20% (rule* σ_9*). Companies involved in close links cannot act as collateral for each other's loans.*

$$IntOwns(x,y,s), s > 0.2 \rightarrow CloseLink(x,y) \quad (\sigma_7)$$

$$CloseLink(x,y) \rightarrow CloseLink(y,x) \quad (\sigma_8)$$

$$IntOwns(x,y,s_1), IntOwns(x,z,s_2), s_1 > 0.2, s_2 > 0.2, \\ x \neq y, x \neq z, y \neq z \rightarrow CloseLink(y,z) \quad (\sigma_9)$$

The result of the application of the above VADALOG rules to the excerpt of the ownership knowledge graph is shown in Figure 11.

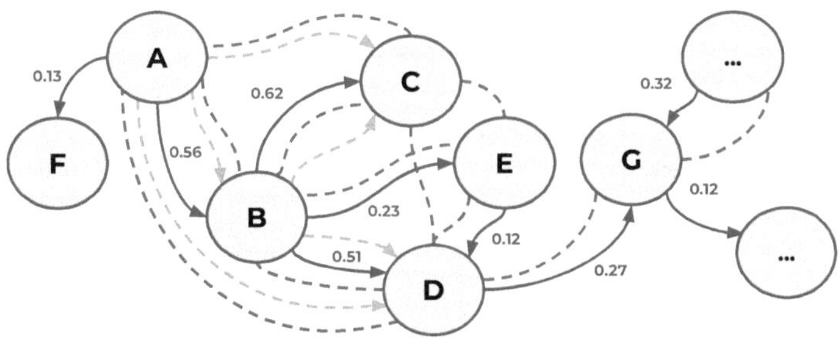

Figure 11. Portion of ownership knowledge graph from Figure 10 augmented with new edges by reasoning on the scenarios from Example 2 and 3. Nodes are companies. Solid edges are *owns* relationships with their shares (*int owns* omitted to avoid clutter). Dashed edges respectively denote *control* relationships (orange, directed) and *close links* (purple, undirected).

Integrating KGLM into KG-Roar. To support financial data analysts and enable a more human-like interaction with KG-ROAR [47,58], we integrate the environment with the KGLM framework presented in the previous section. Specifically, we provide users with a *knowledge pal* that enables natural language-based interactions with KG-ROAR. Such an agent acts as a chatbot, standing upon a LLAMA 3-70B model specialized in the domain of interest by leveraging KGLM's CHASE-based fine-tuning corpora. By interacting with KGLM via the knowledge pal, users are able to:

- perform reasoning tasks over the connected data, extending the original KG with the result of the inference process. Tasks can be directly selected from the available widgets or they can be described to the knowledge pal, which will launch the widget or the sequence of widgets required to address them in a CoT-like fashion by interacting with the VADALOG reasoner. The augmented graph is stored into a Neo4j instance and can be visualized in a dedicated window of KG-ROAR. Additionally, the KG can be further processed by dynamically injecting temporary knowledge for *what-if* analysis tasks, even in natural language by leveraging the soft CHASE mechanism [39].
- go beyond the visual representation of the derived edges in the KG, less intuitive in the presence of highly connected graphs, by asking more complex questions that are focused on determining why a certain fact exists. As summarized in Figure 12, facts of interest can be selected from the corresponding edge in the knowledge graph or by directly prompting the request in NL to the knowledge pal. Leveraging KGLM's GraphRAG mechanism previously introduced, the full CHASE-based explanation of the fact is retrieved, further enhancing its readability and providing it to the user as an accurate business report.

Application flow. With respect to the financial use cases introduced above, and leveraging the KGLM overview in the previous section, we outline an example of interaction with the environment performed by a financial analyst.

First, the user requests KG-ROAR to execute the *company control* reasoning task by clicking on the corresponding widget. The reasoning is performed via KGLM by leveraging VADALOG and the internal LLAMA 3 model to soften rule activation. The results are embedded and pushed to the Neo4j instance and the resulting KG, derived from augmenting the input ownerships with the new *controls* edges, is visualized in the framework. From the graph, the user requests the explanation for a result of interest by

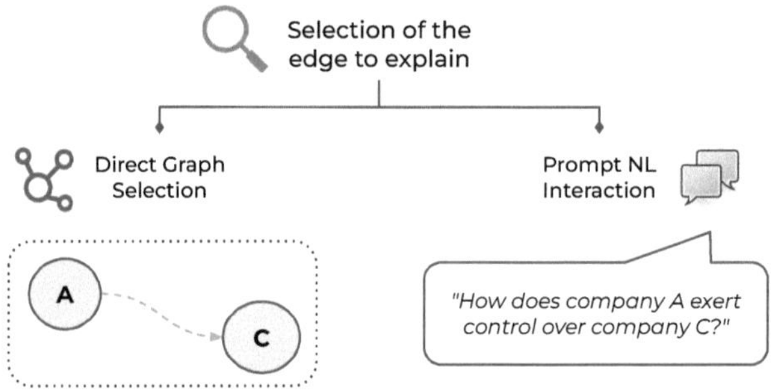

Figure 12. Possible interactions with KGLM within KG-ROAR to select facts to explain.

clicking on the corresponding edge, namely *controls(Darrows, DunkelMeier)*, representing the fact that the company *Darrows* owns, directly or indirectly, more than 50% of the company *DunkelMeier*. KGLM deterministically fetches the fact in Neo4j and retrieves the corresponding explanation by composing back along the stored CHASE sequences. The textual explanation is passed to the knowledge pal, which improves it fluency and clarity, whereas the excerpt of the KG with the involved nodes and edges is visualized on the right. The generated report can be interactively explored by highlighting tagged entities, as illustrated in Figure 13.

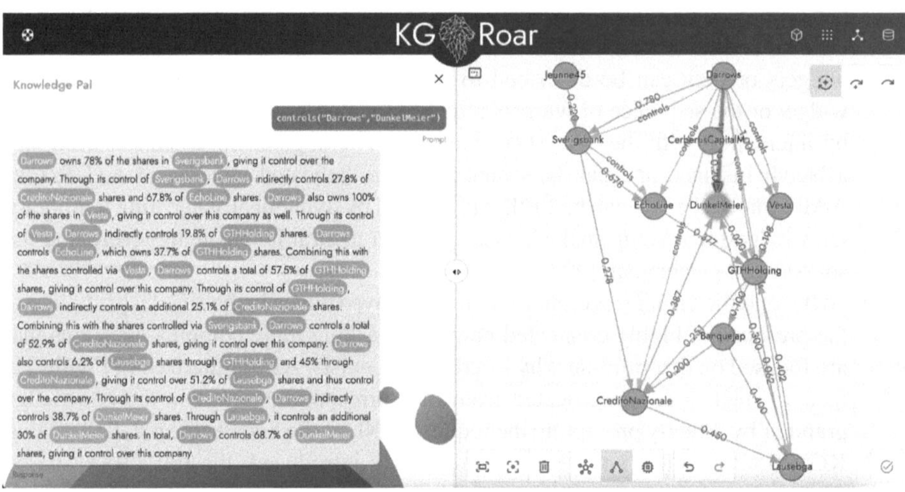

Figure 13. Instance of explanation panel for *company control* use case via visual edge selection.

Then, the financial analyst further explores the *DunkelMeier* entity, asking in natural language to the knowledge pal whether it is involved in a *close link* relationship with a known bank of interest called *IberianBank*. The user request is processed by the LLAMA 3 70B model, which leverages its knowledge of the financial domain to determine that the reasoning task required to answer the request is *collateral eligibility*. Thus, it performs the new reasoning task over the pre-existing KG and it stores the new edges into the Neo4j instance. Finally, via embedding similarity the fact *close_link(DunkelMeier,*

IberianBank) is identified and, as before, its explanation is deterministically retrieved and passed to the knowledge pal, as illustrated in Figure 14.

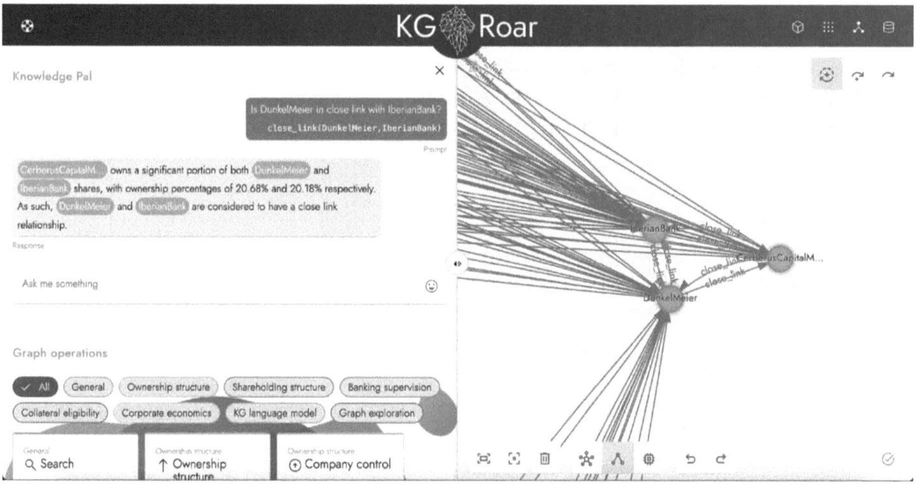

Figure 14. Instance of explanation panel for *collateral eligibility* use case via knowledge pal interaction.

Soft CHASE evaluation. The primary goal of this evaluation is to assess the extent to which the injection of "softness" enhances the standard CHASE by recognizing similar entities and relationships according to real-world semantics. This enables augmenting the inference capabilities of the traditional approach while also preventing the generation of redundant data that represents the same knowledge in different syntactic forms. We conducted the experiments on an instance of the *company control* scenario, both before and after integrating the LLM with detailed knowledge of the domain of interest via RAG. We compared the three distinct approaches (standard CHASE, soft CHASE, soft CHASE with RAG) according to the following metrics:

- *precision*, i.e., the fraction of inferred controlled shares that are correct;
- *recall*, i.e., the fraction of correct controlled shares that are inferred;
- *F1 score*, i.e., the harmonic mean of precision and recall;
- *false positive (FP) shares*, i.e., the fraction of incorrect controlled shares inferred.

For this evaluation, the correct instances of controlled shares were determined through a golden set, manually curated by domain experts.

Results are illustrated in Figure 15. The standard CHASE featured full precision by definition, as it derived controlled shares solely through strict logical binding with structured facts. However, this precision came at the cost of recall, as the standard CHASE was unable to bind rules to unstructured input, leading to missed inferences throughout the reasoning process. On the other hand, the soft CHASE demonstrated lower precision but higher recall, as it leveraged the LLM to recognize and semantically unify unstructured concepts with structured relationships. Furthermore, the introduction of RAG significantly improved both precision and recall. Indeed, the domain-specific knowledge retrieved effectively mitigated LLM hallucinations, reducing false positive bindings and consequently the incorrect inference of controlled shares in the soft CHASE approach.

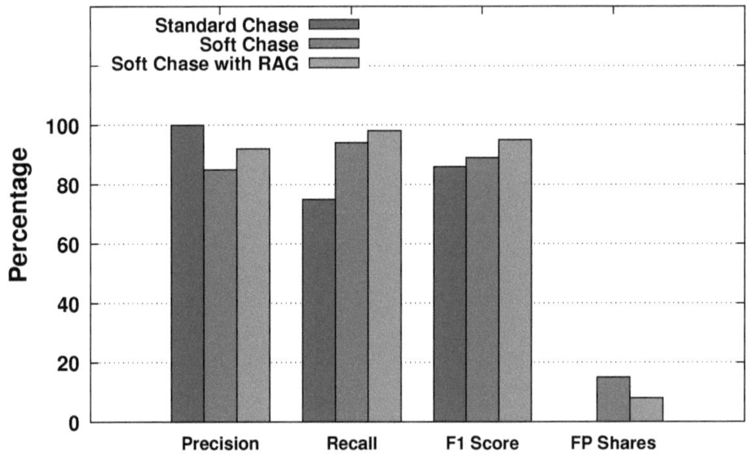

Figure 15. Comparison of precision, recall, F1 score, and FP shares for standard CHASE, soft CHASE, and soft CHASE with RAG, evaluated on an instance of Example 2.

6. Conclusion

The rising demand for AI solutions to enable scalable and accountable decision-making over complex domains is acting as catalyst for the research and development of novel neurosymbolic solutions that go beyond the inherent lack of factuality and explainability of ML-based technologies such as LLMs by combining them with logic-based KGs and ontological reasoning methodologies. With the goal of contributing to such a pivotal challenge, in this chapter we addressed such limitations and presented KGLM, the first, to the best of our knowledge, hybrid framework that enables performing complex inference tasks by combining the human-like understanding and flexibility of LLMs with the robustness and domain-awareness of KRR methodologies at the foundation of our VADALOG system. Capitalizing on our experience in the field, we also illustrated the integration of our framework into KG-ROAR, a well-established KG environment for financial tasks, empowering business analysts to conduct interactive graph-based data analysis in natural language. By continuing to expand and refine KGLM, we strive to make it a significant neurosymbolic asset for organizations, driving innovation and fostering trust in AI-driven decisions across high-stakes domains.

Acknowledgements

The work on this chapter was supported by the Vienna Science and Technology Fund (WWTF) [10.47379/VRG18013, 10.47379/NXT22018, 10.47379/ICT2201]. This research was funded in whole or in part by the Austrian Science Fund (FWF) 10.55776/COE12.

References

[1] Kanbach DK, Heiduk L, Blueher G, Schreiter M, Lahmann A. The GenAI is out of the bottle: generative artificial intelligence from a business model innovation perspective. Review of Managerial Science. 2023:1-32.

[2] Radford A, Narasimhan K, Salimans T, Sutskever I, et al. Improving language understanding by generative pre-training. 2018.

[3] Touvron H, Martin L, Stone K, Albert P, Almahairi A, Babaei Y, et al. Llama 2: Open foundation and fine-tuned chat models. arXiv preprint arXiv:230709288. 2023.

[4] Chang Y, Wang X, Wang J, Wu Y, Yang L, Zhu K, et al. A survey on evaluation of large language models. ACM Transactions on Intelligent Systems and Technology. 2024;15(3):1-45.

[5] Kocmi T, Federmann C. Large language models are state-of-the-art evaluators of translation quality. arXiv preprint arXiv:230214520. 2023.

[6] Koh JY, Fried D, Salakhutdinov RR. Generating images with multimodal language models. NIPS. 2024;36.

[7] Shu D, Chen T, Jin M, Zhang Y, Du M, Zhang Y. Knowledge Graph Large Language Model (KG-LLM) for Link Prediction. arXiv preprint arXiv:240307311. 2024.

[8] Wei J, Wang X, Schuurmans D, Bosma M, Xia F, Chi E, et al. Chain-of-thought prompting elicits reasoning in large language models. NIPS. 2022;35:24824-37.

[9] Kojima T, Gu SS, Reid M, Matsuo Y, Iwasawa Y. Large language models are zero-shot reasoners. NIPS. 2022;35:22199-213.

[10] Zhao H, Chen H, Yang F, Liu N, Deng H, Cai H, et al. Explainability for large language models: A survey. arXiv preprint arXiv:230901029. 2023.

[11] Fandinno J, Schulz C. Answering the "why" in answer set programming–A survey of explanation approaches. Theory and Practice of Logic Programming. 2019;19(2):114-203.

[12] Hong JI. Teaching the FATE Community about Privacy. Commun ACM. 2023 jul;66(8):10–11.

[13] Baldazzi T, Bellomarini L, Ceri S, Colombo A, Gentili A, Sallinger E. Fine-tuning large enterprise language models via ontological reasoning. In: International Joint Conference on Rules and Reasoning. Springer; 2023. p. 86-94.

[14] Wu K, Wu E, Zou J. How faithful are RAG models? Quantifying the tug-of-war between RAG and LLMs' internal prior. arXiv preprint arXiv:240410198. 2024.

[15] Lewis P, Perez E, Piktus A, Petroni F, Karpukhin V, Goyal N, et al. Retrieval-augmented generation for knowledge-intensive nlp tasks. Advances in Neural Information Processing Systems. 2020;33:9459-74.

[16] Krötzsch M, Thost V. Ontologies for knowledge graphs: Breaking the rules. In: International Semantic Web Conference. Springer; 2016. p. 376-92.

[17] Calì A, Gottlob G, Pieris A. Towards more expressive ontology languages: The query answering problem. Artificial Intelligence. 2012;193:87-128.

[18] Ceri S, Gottlob G, Tanca L, et al. What you always wanted to know about Datalog(and never dared to ask). IEEE transactions on knowledge and data engineering. 1989;1(1):146-66.

[19] Caroprese L, Vocaturo E, Zumpano E. Argumentation approaches for explanaible AI in medical informatics. Intelligent Systems with Applications. 2022;16:200109. Available from: https://www.sciencedirect.com/science/article/pii/S2667305322000473.

[20] Abiteboul S, Hull R, Vianu V. Foundations of databases. vol. 8. Addison-Wesley Reading; 1995.

[21] Calì A, Gottlob G, Lukasiewicz T. A general Datalog-based framework for tractable query answering over ontologies. J Web Semant. 2012;14:57-83. Available from: https://doi.org/10.1016/j.websem.2012.03.001.

[22] Calì A, Gottlob G, Lukasiewicz T, Marnette B, Pieris A. Datalog+/-: A family of logical knowledge representation and query languages for new applications. In: 2010 25th annual IEEE symposium on logic in computer science. IEEE; 2010. p. 228-42.

[23] Bellomarini L, Fakhoury D, Gottlob G, Sallinger E. Knowledge Graphs and Enterprise AI: The Promise of an Enabling Technology. In: ICDE; 2019. p. 26-37.

[24] Barceló P, Pichler R. Datalog in Academia and Industry: Second International Workshop, Datalog 2.0, Vienna, Austria, September 11-13, 2012, Proceedings. vol. 7494. Springer; 2012.

[25] Dantsin E, Eiter T, Gottlob G, Voronkov A. Complexity and Expressive Power of Logic Programming. ACM Comput Surv. 2001 sep;33(3):374–425. Available from: https://doi.org/10.1145/502807.502810.

[26] Bellomarini L, Gottlob G, Pieris A, Sallinger E. Swift Logic for Big Data and Knowledge Graphs. In: Proceedings of the Twenty-Sixth International Joint Conference on Artificial Intelligence, IJCAI-17; 2017. p. 2-10. Available from: https://doi.org/10.24963/ijcai.2017/1.

[27] Baldazzi T, Bellomarini L, Benedetto D, Sallinger E, Vlad A. Softening Ontological Reasoning with Large Language Models. In: RuleML+ RR (Companion); 2024. .

[28] Pan S, Luo L, Wang Y, Chen C, Wang J, Wu X. Unifying Large Language Models and Knowledge Graphs: A Roadmap. arXiv preprint arXiv:230608302. 2023.

[29] Bellomarini L, Benedetto D, Gottlob G, Sallinger E. Vadalog: A modern architecture for automated reasoning with large knowledge graphs. Inf Syst. 2022;105:101528. Available from: https://doi.org/10.1016/j.is.2020.101528.

[30] Baldazzi T, Bellomarini L, Gerschberger M, Jami A, Magnanimi D, Nissl M, et al. Vadalog: Overview, Extensions and Business Applications. Reasoning Web Causality, Explanations and Declarative Knowledge: 18th International Summer School 2022, Berlin, Germany, September 27–30, 2022, Tutorial Lectures. 2023:161-98.

[31] Bellomarini L, Bencivelli L, Biancotti C, Blasi L, Conteduca FP, Gentili A, et al. Reasoning on company takeovers: From tactic to strategy. Data Knowl Eng. 2022;141:102073.

[32] Baldazzi T, Benedetto D, Brandetti M, Vlad A, Bellomarini L, Sallinger E. Datalog-based Reasoning with Heuristics over Knowledge Graphs. In: Datalog. vol. 3203 of CEUR Workshop Proceedings. CEUR-WS.org; 2022. p. 114-26.

[33] Atzeni P, Bellomarini L, Iezzi M, Sallinger E, Vlad A. Weaving Enterprise Knowledge Graphs: The Case of Company Ownership Graphs. In: EDBT. OpenProceedings.org; 2020. p. 555-66.

[34] Atzeni P, Bellomarini L, Iezzi M, Sallinger E, Vlad A. Augmenting Logic-based Knowledge Graphs: The Case of Company Graphs. In: KR4L@ECAI. vol. 3020. CEUR-WS.org; 2020. p. 22-7.

[35] Dwyer OP, Baldazzi T, Davies J, Sallinger E, Vlad A. Reasoning over Health Records with Vadalog: a Rule-based Approach to Patient Pathways. In: Vanthienen J, Kliegr T, Fodor P, Lanti D, Arndt D, Kostylev EV, et al., editors. Proceedings of the 17th International Rule Challenge and 7th Doctoral Consortium @ RuleML+RR 2023 co-located with 19th Reasoning Web Summer School (RW 2023) and 15th DecisionCAMP 2023 as part of Declarative AI 2023, Oslo, Norway, 18 - 20 September, 2023. vol. 3485 of CEUR Workshop Proceedings. CEUR-WS.org; 2023. Available from: https://ceur-ws.org/Vol-3485/paper9111.pdf.

[36] Vlad A, Vahdati S, Nayyeri M, Bellomarini L, Sallinger E. Towards Hybrid Logic-based and Embedding-based Reasoning on Financial Knowledge Graphs. In: EDBT/ICDT Workshops. vol. 3135; 2022. .

[37] Dwyer OP, Baldazzi T, Davies J, Sallinger E, Vlad A. Reasoning over Health Records with Vadalog: a Rule-based Approach to Patient Pathways. 2023.

[38] Beeri C, Vardi MY. A proof procedure for data dependencies. Journal of the ACM (JACM). 1984;31(4):718-41.

[39] Bellomarini L, Benedetti M, Gentili A, Magnanimi D, Sallinger E. KG-Roar: Interactive Datalog-Based Reasoning on Virtual Knowledge Graphs. Proc VLDB Endow. 2023 aug;16(12):4014–4017.

[40] Liu Z, Huang D, Huang K, Li Z, Zhao J. Finbert: A pre-trained financial language representation model for financial text mining. In: IJCAI 2020; 2021. .

[41] Wu S, Irsoy O, Lu S, Dabravolski V, Dredze M, Gehrmann S, et al. BloombergGPT: A Large Language Model for Finance. CoRR. 2023;abs/2303.17564.

[42] Garcez Ad, Lamb LC. Neurosymbolic AI: The 3 rd wave. Artificial Intelligence Review. 2023;56(11):12387-406.

[43] Dong XL. Generations of Knowledge Graphs: The Crazy Ideas and the Business Impact. arXiv preprint arXiv:230814217. 2023.

[44] Hamilton K, Nayak A, Bozic B, Longo L. Is Neuro-Symbolic AI Meeting its Promise in Natural Language Processing? A Structured Review. CoRR. 2022;abs/2202.12205. Available from: https://arxiv.org/abs/2202.12205.

[45] Wang S, Wei Z, Xu J, Li T, Fan Z. Unifying structure reasoning and language model pre-training for complex reasoning. arXiv preprint arXiv:230108913. 2023.

[46] Trajanoska M, Stojanov R, Trajanov D. Enhancing knowledge graph construction using large language models. arXiv preprint arXiv:230504676. 2023.

[47] Baldazzi T, Bellomarini L, Ceri S, Colombo A, Gentili A, Sallinger E. "Please, Vadalog, tell me why": Interactive Explanation of Datalog-based Reasoning. In: Tanca L, Luo Q, Polese G, Caruccio L, Oriol

X, Firmani D, editors. Proceedings 27th International Conference on Extending Database Technology, EDBT 2024, Paestum, Italy, March 25 - March 28. OpenProceedings.org; 2024. p. 834-7. Available from: https://doi.org/10.48786/edbt.2024.82.

[48] Shen S, Logeswaran L, Lee M, Lee H, Poria S, Mihalcea R. Understanding the Capabilities and Limitations of Large Language Models for Cultural Commonsense. arXiv preprint arXiv:240504655. 2024.

[49] Bender EM, Gebru T, McMillan-Major A, Shmitchell S. On the dangers of stochastic parrots: Can language models be too big? In: Proceedings of the 2021 ACM conference on fairness, accountability, and transparency; 2021. p. 610-23.

[50] Kaddour J, Harris J, Mozes M, Bradley H, Raileanu R, McHardy R. Challenges and applications of large language models. arXiv preprint arXiv:230710169. 2023.

[51] Gottlob G, Pieris A. Beyond SPARQL under OWL 2 QL entailment regime: Rules to the rescue. In: Twenty-Fourth International Joint Conference on Artificial Intelligence; 2015. .

[52] Shkapsky A, Yang M, Zaniolo C. Optimizing recursive queries with monotonic aggregates in DeALS. In: 2015 IEEE 31st International Conference on Data Engineering. IEEE; 2015. p. 867-78.

[53] Johnson DS, Klug AC. Testing Containment of Conjunctive Queries under Functional and Inclusion Dependencies. J Comput Syst Sci. 1984;28(1):167-89.

[54] Bellomarini L, Sallinger E, Gottlob G. The Vadalog System: Datalog-Based Reasoning for Knowledge Graphs. Proc VLDB Endow. 2018 may;11(9):975–987. Available from: https://doi.org/10.14778/3213880.3213888.

[55] Baldazzi T, Bellomarini L, Sallinger E, Atzeni P. Eliminating Harmful Joins in Warded Datalog+/-. In: RuleML+RR. vol. 12851 of Lecture Notes in Computer Science. Springer; 2021. p. 267-75.

[56] Baldazzi T, Bellomarini L, Favorito M, Sallinger E. Ontological Reasoning over Shy and Warded Datalog+/–for Streaming-Based Architectures. In: International Symposium on Practical Aspects of Declarative Languages. Springer; 2024. p. 169-85.

[57] Graefe G, McKenna WJ. The Volcano Optimizer Generator: Extensibility and Efficient Search. In: ICDE. IEEE Computer Society; 1993. p. 209-18.

[58] Baldazzi T, Bellomarini L, Ceri S, Colombo A, Gentili A, Sallinger E, et al. Explaining Enterprise Knowledge Graphs with Large Language Models and Ontological Reasoning. In: The Provenance of Elegance in Computation-Essays Dedicated to Val Tannen (2024). Schloss Dagstuhl–Leibniz-Zentrum für Informatik; 2024. .

[59] Afrati FN, Gergatsoulis M, Toni F. Linearisability on datalog programs. Theor Comput Sci. 2003;308(1-3):199-226.

[60] Brown T, et al. Language Models are Few-Shot Learners. In: NeurIPS. vol. 33. Curran Associates, Inc.; 2020. p. 1877-901.

[61] Zhang* T, Kishore* V, Wu* F, Weinberger KQ, Artzi Y. BERTScore: Evaluating Text Generation with BERT. In: International Conference on Learning Representations; 2020. Available from: https://openreview.net/forum?id=SkeHuCVFDr.

[62] Edge D, Trinh H, Cheng N, Bradley J, Chao A, Mody A, et al. From local to global: A graph rag approach to query-focused summarization. arXiv preprint arXiv:240416130. 2024.

[63] Gulino A, Ceri S, Gottlob G, Sallinger E, Bellomarini L. Distributed Company Control in Company Shareholding Graphs. In: IEEE 37th International Conference on Data Engineering (ICDE). Los Alamitos, CA, USA; 2021. p. 2637-48.

[64] Magnanimi D, Iezzi M. Ownership Graphs and Reasoning in Corporate Economics. In: EDBT/ICDT Workshops. vol. 3135 of CEUR Workshop Proceedings. CEUR-WS.org; 2022. .

[65] European Central Bank. GUIDELINE (EU) 2011/14 of the ECB Guideline; 2011.

Handbook on Neurosymbolic AI and Knowledge Graphs
P. Hitzler et al. (Eds.)
IOS Press, 2025

doi:10.3233/FAIA250220

Knowledge Graph Question Answering and Large Language Models

Debayan BANERJEE[a,1], Nan HU[b], Yimin TAN[b], Dehai MIN[b], Yike WU[b], Ricardo USBECK[a], Guilin QI[b]

[a]*Leuphana Universität, Lüneburg, Germany*
[b]*Southeast University, China*

ORCID IDs:
Debayan Banerjee: https://orcid.org/0000-0001-7626-8888
Ricardo Usbeck: https://orcid.org/0000-0002-0191-7211
Nan Hu: https://orcid.org/0009-0001-4062-3515
Yimin Tan: https://orcid.org/0000-0002-2431-7809
Dehai Min: https://orcid.org/0009-0003-8528-6916
Yike Wu: https://orcid.org/0009-0000-7963-1021
Guilin Qi: https://orcid.org/0000-0003-0150-7236

Abstract. Knowledge Graph Question Answering (KGQA) is an evolving field that aims to leverage structured knowledge graphs to provide precise answers to user queries. As Knowledge Graphs continue to expand in complexity and size, efficiently navigating and extracting relevant information from these vast datasets has become increasingly challenging. Recent advancements in Large Language Models (LLMs), offer promising capabilities in understanding and processing natural language. By integrating LLMs with KGQA systems, it is possible to enhance the accuracy and contextual relevance of answers generated. In this chapter, we explore the intersection of KGQA and LLMs, evaluating their combined potential to fetch information from knowledge graphs.

Keywords. Knowledge Graphs, Question Answering, Large Language Models

1. Introduction

In this chapter, we address the role of Large Language Models (LLMs) in the task of Knowledge Graph Question Answering (KGQA). In the following sections, we first describe popular techniques used in KGQA, and then describe different kind of LLMs found useful for KGQA. Subsequently, we describe two working KGQA systems which employ LLMs. Additionally, we describe specific cases of how LLMs can be used to evaluate KGQA better. At the end, we present our view of the current limitations of LLMs for KGQA, and future directions of research.

[1]All authors contributed equally to this work.

In the larger context of this book, which is neuro-symbolic AI, we shall appropriately highlight those approaches, which adhere more strongly to the neuro-symbolic approach. The neuro-symbolic approach signifies the combination of neural networks and symbolic reasoning. Typically in KGQA, this combination is achieved when a neural network is used to produce a query, or a logical form for a given input question. The queries allow symbolic reasoning over the KG, through the manipulation of the query constituents and grammar.

1.1. Knowledge Graph Question Answering (KGQA)

A Knowledge Graph (KG) is an information store that represents knowledge as node-edge-node triples. Nodes, referred to as entities, are connected by edges, known as properties or relations. In a general-purpose KG, entities often include persons, places, and objects of interest, while the properties define the relationships between these entities, as illustrated in Figure 1. KGs are usually curated by humans, ensuring the accuracy of the information they contain. Examples of well-known general-purpose KGs include Wikidata [92], DBpedia [93], Freebase [94], and Yago [95].

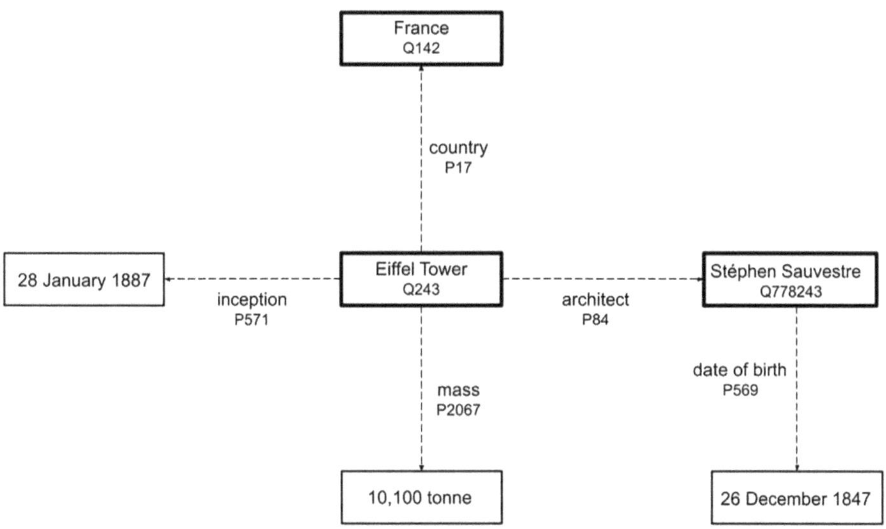

Figure 1. A sub-graph sample from Wikidata KG for the entity `Eiffel Tower`. Bold boxes represent entities, while light boxes represent literals.

In addition to general-purpose knowledge graphs, there are also domain-specific knowledge graphs. These include knowledge graphs in fields such as medicine [97], finance [98], academia [99], and music [100]. Recently, the concept of personal knowledge graphs [101] has emerged, designed to store details of our everyday activities on a personal server. For a comprehensive history of the development of Knowledge Graphs, readers can refer to Gutierrez et al. [106].

The goal of Knowledge Graph Question Answering (KGQA) [102,103] is to retrieve answers from a knowledge graph based on a natural language question. The questions may be divided into two categories, simple and complex. In a *simple question*,

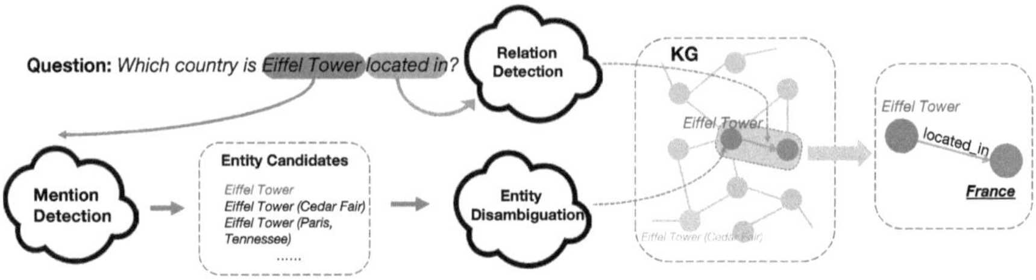

Figure 2. The general structure of KGQA.

only one triple is involved in forming the content, for example, Which country is Eiffel Tower located in?. To answer this question, the triple <Q243> <P17> <Q142> is sufficient (see Figure 1). In the case of *complex questions*, information from more than one triple is required to successfully answer a question. For example, What is the date of birth of the architect of the Eiffel Tower?. This requires the two triples: <Q243><P84><Q778243> and <Q778243><P569><26 December 1847>.

Normally, as shown in Figure 2, the process starts with Entity Linking, which includes Mention Detection (identifying potential entities in the question) and Entity Disambiguation (linking these mentions to the correct entities in the knowledge graph). Next is Relation Detection, where relationships or predicates connecting the identified entities are determined. Finally, a structured query, typically in a language like SPARQL, is constructed using these entities and relationships to extract the answer from the knowledge graph. This multi-step process enables accurate extraction of information from vast and complex data structures.

1.2. Large Language Models

In the year 2017, Vaswani et al. developed the Transformer architecture [69], that showed remarkable performance in a variety of Natural Language Processing (NLP) tasks, eg: the Glue benchmark [166]. The Transformer architecture's parallel encoder design allows efficient training over a large corpus of text, and this feature has led to the arrival of the pre-trained Transformer-based models which may have billions of trainable parameters. Due to the large number of trainable parameters, such models are also called Large Language Models.

GPT-1 [49] was the first LLM architecture, developed by the enterprise OpenAI and released in 2018. In 2020, Google and Facebook almost simultaneously released T5 [128] and BART [77], generative models everyone could download, use, fine-tune, and adapt to individual use cases. Since then, a large number of LLMs have arrived, which we describe later in Section 3.

Due to the impressive abilities of LLMs in NLP tasks, it is natural to utilise them in the KGQA pipeline. Especially in the first part of the pipeline, which requires language understanding, or understanding the semantics of the input question, LLMs may be applied. LLMs may also be used to highlight the important parts of an input questions, such as entities and relations, and may also be used to produce output queries, which can then be executed on a KG to retrieve the final answer. In Section 4, we describe in detail some practical implementations of the combination of LLMs and KGQA.

2. Knowledge Graph Question Answering

A common first step in KGQA is identifying spans of entities in the given text, a process known as Named Entity Recognition (NER). Entities are distinct and identifiable objects or concepts, often nouns, such as people, places, and things. In the sample question, `What is the date of birth of the architect of the Eiffel Tower?`, the entity would be `Eiffel Tower`, identified by the entity ID `Q243` in the Wikidata KG. The next step is to locate the corresponding node for this entity in the KG. This can be challenging due to the possibility of multiple people sharing the same name, necessitating further *disambiguation*. This process is known as Entity Linking (EL). For a detailed overview of the challenges associated with this task, we refer the reader to the surveys by Sevgili et al. [104] and Möller et al. [105].

Once the correct entity node is identified in the KG, the neighboring edges and nodes must be analyzed to answer the question. For instance, in the given question, the edges of interest are `architect` and `date of birth`. As seen in Figure 1, these relations are assigned unique relation IDs in Wikidata starting with the letter `P`. Identifying the correct edges is referred to as Relation Linking (RL).

At this stage, some systems fetch the answer by further exploring the discovered neighborhood, especially when the answer is another node in the graph. This method is known as the *retrieval-based approach*.

However, for more complex or multi-hop questions, such as queries requiring a count or aggregation (e.g., `What is the total number of visitors to the Eiffel Tower in the last 5 years?`), the answer may not be found directly in a node or edge in the graph. Instead, a formal query must be generated to compute the total. Generating logical forms offers the added benefit of *explainability*, allowing users to read and understand how the final answer was derived.

The task of generating a formal query is known as *semantic parsing*, and when the generation of the query involves a neural network, it corresponds closely to the *neuro-symbolic approach*. Earlier systems using semantic parsing relied on *rule-based approaches* to match questions to query templates, which could then be executed on a KG to fetch the answer. Modern systems, however, use generative models, such as LLMs, to produce logical forms instead of relying on templates.

2.1. Rule-based Approach

In the early days, researchers relied on pre-defined rules or templates to understand questions and convert them into a format the KG could understand. One basic approach for using template-based question answering, is to map a question template to a corresponding SPARQL query. For example:

```
Potential Question: Who directed Inception?

Corresponding Template: Who directed [MOVIE]?

SPARQL Template:

SELECT ?director WHERE {
    ?movie rdf:type :Movie .
```

```
        ?movie :name [MOVIE] .
        ?movie :directed_by ?director .
    }
```

In template-based systems, there is a basic assumption, that the test questions will belong to a pre-defined set of template questions. This also exposes the limitation of such systems, that they fail to handle completely new category of questions.

More advanced approaches involved a step-by-step parser as in Berant at al. [134]. This parser first linked words and phrases in the question to entities or relationships in the KG using a large text corpus. Then, for a given question, it built the answer step-by-step, relying on a dictionary, that mapped question phrases to KG elements and a set of defined operations, such as join, aggregate, bridge and intersection. To avoid exploring irrelevant options, the parser used a model that scored different parsing paths based on handcrafted features.

Another method that used templates was Aqqu [135]. This system, could only handle questions that fit into three predefined formats. Aqqu would first find entities in the KG that matched parts of the question, including synonyms. Then, it would try to fit the question into one of the templates, using the KG information around the matched entities. Finally, it would pick the best fit based on handcrafted features and use that to query the KG for the answer.

However, these template approaches struggled with complex questions. To address this, some researchers explored ways to automatically learn templates from data . Their system, called QUINT [136], used two types of templates: one based on the KG structure and another based on the question's grammar. During testing, QUINT would first match the question to relevant question templates, then use those templates to generate candidate queries for the KG. Finally, it would use a ranking model to select the most promising query and retrieve the answer from the KG.

2.2. *Retrieval-based Approach*

In the retrieval-based approach, the entities of interest in the text are first determined and then linked to the KG. Then, relevant sub-graphs from the neighbourhood of these entities are extracted from the KG. The nodes and edges in the sub-graphs are treated as candidate answers. Based on the features extracted from the questions and candidate answers, a scoring function is used to model their semantic relevance and predicts the final answers. Based on the feature representation technology, retrieval-based methods can be classified into those based on feature engineering and those based on representation learning.

With respect to feature engineering, Yao et al. [137] analyzed the question syntax information and extracted four types of features from each questions dependency parse result, i.e., the question word, question focus word, topic word , and central verb. All the four features are combined to form a question graph, and a KG sub-graph is extracted according to the topic word. All the nodes in the KG sub-graph are treated as candidate answers, then question features from the question graph and candidate answers features form the KG sub-graph are combined with pairwise concatenation to capture the semantic association. Whether a node is a corresponding answer or not is determined by a classification model based on the above features.

Compared to feature engineering-based methods, representation learning-based methods convert questions and candidate answers into vectors in the common vector space, and treat KGQA as semantic matching calculation between distributed representations of questions and candidate answers. Bordes at al. [138] first introduced the representation learning-based method. Embeddings of question words are summed as the question representation. Each candidate answer entity is represented by summing vectors from three aspects: the answer entity, the relationship path between the answer entity and the topic entity, and the sub-graph related to the answer entity. The semantic relevance is calculated by dot product, and a margin ranking loss between positive and negative examples is used to train the model parameters.

Retrieval-based methods get rid of a large number of manually defined templates, and can be trained in an end-to-end manner. However, it may have difficulty handling complex questions, because the fetching of candidates across multiple connected triples (also called as multi-hop) may lead to combinatorial explosion of candidate answers. Additionally, retrieval-based methods are generally weaker than rule-based or semantic parsing-based methods in interpretability. It is difficult for a human to understand precisely which criterion resulted in a higher ranking for a candidate answer. Because of the lack of symbolic generation of logical forms or queries, retrieval-based approaches lie outside the category of *neuro-symbolic* approaches.

2.3. Semantic Parsing Techniques

We briefly visited template-based semantic parsing in Section 2.1, hence, we now address modern methods employed for the task of semantic parsing. In the semantic parsing approach, as opposed to retrieval-based approach, the output of the system is a query or a logical form (eg: λ-DCS, SPARQL), which can be executed to retrieve the results from a KG. The primary advantage of such systems is that they are *explainable*, because an inspection of the query leads to precise identification of the cause of the retrieved results. Additionally, a system that generates queries can potentially answer every possible question that can be translated to a valid query. This alleviates the limitations of rule-based systems, which are limited to pre-defined templates, and retrieval-based systems, which only produce a winning candidate node or edge as answer.

Gu et al. [53] outline three main approaches widely adopted in neural semantic parsing for KGQA: *ranking methods, coarse-to-fine methods, and generative methods*. Ranking methods [118,119,120,121] initially generate a list of candidate paths, spanning entities and relations from the KG and rely on computing the matching score for each candidate-path and question pair. Coarse-to-fine methods [122,123,124,125] first create query skeletons and then connect these skeletons to the KG using permissible schema items. The discovery of permissible schema may be made by exploring the KG nodes and their neighbourhoods, or in cases where an ontology is available, following the rules specified in the ontology. For example, an invalid schema item would be a case where we try to connect an edge of type `spouse` to a node of type `place`. Generative methods typically employ models such as LSTMs [126] or GRUs [127] which can produce the query as output via step-by-step decoding.

Despite this categorization by Gu et al. [117], an end-to-end KGQA system may fall into multiple categories. For example, GETT-QA [133] first generates a skeleton query which falls under the *coarse-to-fine* method. In a subsequent step, candidate entities and relations are re-ranked, which may fall in the *re-ranking approach*. Additionally, since the initial coarse query is generated by a generative LM, namely T5, this system also belongs to the *generative approach*. Largely, modern semantic parsing-based KGQA systems firmly lie in the *neuro-symbolic* category.

2.4. Retrieval Augmented Generation

Very recently, since the inception of instruction-tuned LLMs, a new class of approaches has gained popularity, namely Retrieval Augmented Generation (RAG) [165]. In this approach, a question is first parsed and the relevant entities are linked to a KG. Then, similar to the retrieval approach in Section 2.2, relevant neighbouring sub-graphs are fetched and ranked as candidate answers. Subsequently, the question, the candidate answers and an instruction prompt are passed to an instruction-tuned LLM, which produces the final answer. The addition of an LLM to the standard *retrieval approach* allows the handling of an unlimited variety of questions, including comparison and aggregation, which generally retrieval-based systems are unable to handle. Moreover, RAG-based systems can also handle subjective questions, such as `Which brand is better for TVs, Sony or Panasonic?`, which may lie beyond the scope of semantic parsing-based systems which produce a query. The reason is that an LLM may take into account a summary of multiple factors, including its own pre-trained knowledge, when producing the final answer. This makes the RAG-based method a powerful approach the most powerful approach, although it can not be said to belong to the neuro-symbolic approach, as the LLM output is not a formal query. Instead, the LLM directly generates the final answer.

3. Introduction to Large Language Models (LLMs)

3.1. Early Pre-trained models

In the rapidly evolving field of artificial intelligence, the introduction of pre-trained models marked a significant turning point. These models, which are trained on large volumes of data before being fine-tuned for specific tasks, have dramatically improved the efficiency and effectiveness of machine learning systems. Among the earliest and most influential of these models are BERT [67] (Bidirectional Encoder Representations from Transformers) and GPT [68] (Generative Pre-trained Transformer). These two PTMs respectively use auto-regressive language modeling and auto-encoding language modeling as pre-training objectives. This section explores their development and architecture.

3.1.1. Transformer

Before Transformer [69], RNNs [66] have long been a typical tool for processing sequential data, especially for processing natural languages. As RNNs are equipped with sequential nature, they read a word at each time step in order. For each word, RNNs refer to all hidden states of its previous words to process it. Such a mechanism is considered to be difficult to take advantage of the parallel capabilities of high-performance computing devices such as GPUs and TPUs.

As shown in Figure 3, Transformer is a non-recurrent sequence-to-sequence (seq2seq) architecture consisting of an encoder and a decoder. The encoder and decoder of a Transformer are both stacked by several identical blocks. Each encoder block is composed of a multi-head self-attention layer and a position-wise feed-forward layer. Compared with the encoder block, each decoder block has an additional cross-attention layer since the decoder requires to consider the output of the encoder as a context for generation. Between neural layers, residual connection and layer normalization are employed, making it possible to train a deep Transformer.

Input Embedding (1) Embedding. Both the encoder and decoder begin with embedding layers. These convert input tokens (words, characters, or subwords) into vectors of a specified size, typically denoted as d_{model}. The embedding layers transform discrete input tokens into continuous vectors that are fed into subsequent layers. (2) Positional Encodings. Since transformers do not have recurrent or convolutional layers, they lack a mechanism to account for the order of tokens. Positional encodings are added to the embeddings to provide some information about the relative or absolute position of the tokens in the sequence. These encodings have the same dimension d_{model} as the embeddings, allowing the two to be summed. The sinusoidal patterns (sine and cosine functions of different frequencies) help the model to distinguish positions, as each position will have a unique encoding. The positional encoding formula is as follow:

$$PE(pos,2i) = \sin\left(\frac{pos}{10000^{2i/d_{\text{model}}}}\right) \tag{1}$$

$$PE(pos,2i+1) = \cos\left(\frac{pos}{10000^{2i/d_{\text{model}}}}\right) \tag{2}$$

where pos is the position, i is the dimension index, and d_{model} is the dimension of the output of the embeddings.

Encoder Layer (1) Multi-Head Self-Attention Mechanism. The purpose of multi-head attention is to run the attention mechanism several times in parallel. The attention mechanism itself is used to draw global dependencies between input and output. The inputs consist of queries, keys, and values, which are usually linear transformations of the embeddings. By projecting the queries, keys, and values multiple times with different, learned linear transformations, the model can attend to information from different representation sub-spaces at different positions, providing a richer representation of the data. This mechanism allows the model to attend to different parts of the input sequence. It is composed of multiple attention heads, each performing scaled dot-product attention:

$$\text{Attention}(Q,K,V) = \text{softmax}\left(\frac{QK^T}{\sqrt{d_k}}\right)V \tag{3}$$

Here, Q, K, and V represent queries, keys, and values, respectively, and d_k is the dimensionality of the keys. Each head in multi-head attention generates different attention scores, and their outputs are combined:

$$\text{MultiHead}(Q,K,V) = \text{Concat}(\text{head}_1,...,\text{head}_h)W^O \tag{4}$$

$$\text{head}_i = \text{Attention}(QW_i^Q, KW_i^K, VW_i^V) \tag{5}$$

(2) Position-wise Feed-Forward Neural Networks. Each position in the encoder's output passes through the same feed-forward neural network, which consists of two linear transformations with a ReLU activation in between.

$$\text{FFN}(x) = \max(0, xW_1 + b_1)W_2 + b_2 \tag{6}$$

This layer applies the same transformation to each position separately and identically. This is useful for interpreting the representations from the attention layer, adding another level of transformation and abstraction.

Decoder Layer (1) Masked Multi-Head Self-Attention. The decoder is also composed of layers that include multi-head self-attention mechanisms. However, the self-attention layers in the decoder are masked to ensure that the predictions for a certain position can only depend on the known outputs at positions before it. This masking, combined with subsequent layers that attend to the encoder's output, allows each position in the decoder to attend to all positions in the previous layer of the decoder and all positions in the encoder. (2) Encoder-Decoder Attention. After the masked multi-head attention, the decoder applies a multi-head attention over the encoder's output. Here, the queries come from the previous decoder layer, and the memory keys and values come from the encoder's output. This allows every position in the decoder to attend to all positions in the input sequence—crucial for tasks like machine translation.

Layer Normalization and Residual Connections (1) Normalization and Residuals. Each sub-layer in both the encoder and decoder (including attention and feed-forward layers) has a residual connection around it followed by layer normalization: $\text{LayerNorm}(x + \text{Sublayer}(x))$. This setup helps in training deeper models by allowing gradients to flow through the networks directly (via residual connections) and stabilizing the learning process.

Output (1) Output Projection and Softmax. The decoder outputs a vector at each position which is transformed into a predicted next token. A linear layer projects each vector to a much larger vocabulary size, and the softmax layer converts these logits to probabilities of each vocabulary token: $\text{softmax}(z_i) = \frac{e^{z_i}}{\sum_j e^{z_j}}$. This step determines the final output sequence probability distribution, allowing the model to make predictions for the next token in the sequence.

Owing to its significant impact, the Transformer has become a fundamental architecture for natural language understanding and generation. It also forms the core structure for the subsequent development of Pre-trained Models (PTMs). In the following sections, we will explore two pivotal developments—GPT and BERT—that have ushered in the era of large-scale, self-supervised PTMs. Generally, GPT excels in generating natural language, whereas BERT is better suited for understanding it

3.1.2. BERT

BERT (Bidirectional Encoder Representations from Transformers) represents a pivotal point in the evolution of machine learning models for natural language processing (NLP). Developed by researchers at Google AI, BERT's introduction in 2018 shifted the land-

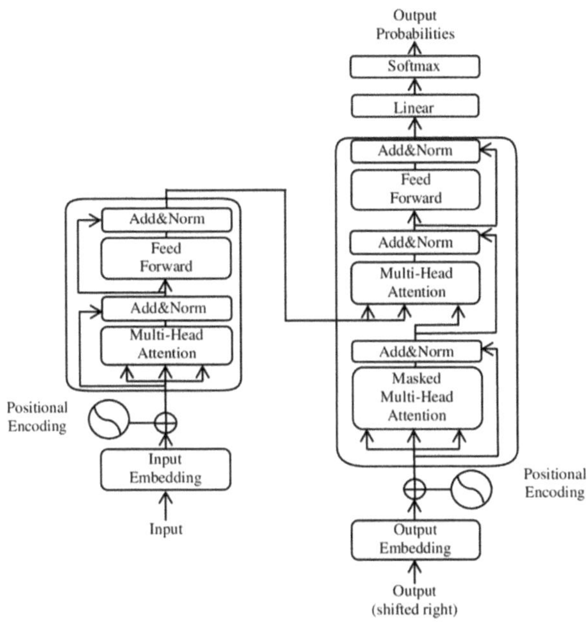

Figure 3. The architecture of transformer.

scape of NLP applications, establishing new benchmarks across a wide array of tasks such as sentiment analysis, question answering, and language inference. This chapter aims to elucidate the architecture, workings, and theoretical foundations of BERT, providing readers with a comprehensive understanding of its mechanisms and applications.

BERT's architecture is a multi-layer bidirectional transformer encoder. Based on the Transformer model, it adapts the encoder stacks to create a deep bidirectional representation. Commonly, BERT is available in two configurations: (1) BERT_BASE: Consisting of 12 layers (transformer blocks), 768 hidden units (dimensions of the hidden layers), 12 attention heads, and a total of 110 million parameters. (2) BERT_LARGE: Encompassing 24 layers, 1024 hidden units, 16 attention heads, and 340 million parameters. The formula for the transformer's attention mechanism, which BERT uses extensively, is given by:

$$\text{Attention}(Q,K,V) = \text{softmax}\left(\frac{QK^T}{\sqrt{d_k}}\right)V \tag{7}$$

where Q, K, and V represent the queries, keys, and values, respectively, and d_k is the dimension of the keys.

Pre-training BERT BERT is pre-trained using two innovative strategies: (1) Masked Language Model (MLM): This task randomly masks some of the tokens from the input, and the objective is to predict the original vocabulary id of the masked word based only on its context. Approximately 15(2)Next Sentence Prediction (NSP): In this task, BERT learns to model relationships between sentences, which is particularly useful for tasks like question answering. During pre-training, when given two sentences A and B, the model predicts whether B is the actual next sentence that follows A in the corpus or a randomly sampled sentence.

Fine-Tuning BERT After pre-training on large corpora, BERT can be fine-tuned with additional output layers for a wide array of specific tasks. This involves simply adding a small number of task-specific parameters and training all the parameters on the downstream tasks by simply minimizing the loss on the task-specific data. This process adapts BERT to specific tasks without substantial modifications to the underlying model.

BERT's introduction has not only advanced the state of NLP but also opened new avenues for exploring how deep learning models can be designed and applied. Its ability to integrate context from both directions makes it a powerful model for understanding language nuances, thereby reshaping how machines understand human language.

3.1.3. GPT

GPT represents the first iteration in the series of generative pre-trained transformers. Its primary innovation lies in the application of a transformer-based model pre-trained on a diverse corpus of text and then fine-tuned for specific tasks. This approach differed significantly from previous models, which often relied on task-specific architectures or extensive hand-engineering.

GPT is based on the transformer architecture, predominantly utilizing the decoder component of the Transformer model. The model is characterized by the following: (1) Model Configuration: GPT comprises 12 layers (transformer blocks), with each layer having 12 attention heads and a hidden layer size of 768, culminating in a total of 117 million parameters. (2) Decoder-Based Architecture: Unlike BERT, which utilizes the encoder component, GPT uses a stack of transformer decoders, where each block performs masked self-attention, allowing it to process information from previous tokens but not future ones during training.

The core attention mechanism in GPT-1 is described by:

$$\text{Attention}(Q,K,V) = \text{softmax}\left(\frac{QK^T}{\sqrt{d_k}}\right)V \tag{8}$$

where Q, K, and V. stand for queries, keys, and values, respectively, with d_k representing the dimensionality of the keys.

Pre-training GPT GPT is pre-trained on a corpus of books combined with other diverse datasets available on the internet. The pre-training is unsupervised and uses the following objective: The model is trained to predict the next word in a sentence, given the previous words, effectively learning the probability distribution of a word sequence. The objective function maximizes the likelihood of predicting the next word:

$$L(\theta) = \sum_i \log P(w_i|w_{i-1}, \ldots, w_1; \theta) \tag{9}$$

where θ represents the model parameters.

Fine-Tuning GPT After the unsupervised pre-training, GPT can be fine-tuned on specific tasks such as text classification, sentiment analysis, or question answering. During fine-tuning, all the parameters of GPT are updated to minimize the loss on the task-specific dataset, adapting the general language model to particular needs.

GPT not only showcased the effectiveness of transformer models in handling language but also set a new direction for future explorations in generative models. By efficiently leveraging unsupervised pre-training followed by supervised fine-tuning, GPT has become a cornerstone model that exemplifies the power of modern NLP techniques. This approach has broad implications, influencing both academic research and practical applications in generating human-like text across various domains.

3.1.4. Distilled Pretrained Language Models

Despite the remarkable capabilities demonstrated by early pre-trained language models such as BERT and RoBERTa across multiple natural language processing tasks, they possess significantly larger parameter sizes compared to traditional neural network models, thereby consuming more computational resources and increasing time costs. Lightweight Pre-trained Language Models (PLMs) such as ALBERT [22], DistilBERT [48], and DistilRoBERTa are designed to offer a balance between performance and efficiency, making them suitable for environments with limited computational resources. These models are derived by distilling the knowledge of larger, more complex models into smaller, faster versions that retain a significant portion of the original model's language understanding capabilities. These lightweight models are particularly valuable for applications requiring fast processing times and reduced model size without a substantial drop in accuracy.

ALBERT (A Lite BERT) is a model developed for optimizing the architecture of BERT to improve memory efficiency and training speed. Introduced by Google researchers, ALBERT refines BERT by sharing parameters across all layers, which drastically reduces the model's size without significantly impacting performance. It also introduces two additional modifications: factorized embedding parameterization, which separates the size of the hidden layers from that of the vocabulary embeddings, and a self-supervised loss for sentence order prediction, which helps the model understand text sequence better. These innovations enable ALBERT to achieve similar or even superior performance on various natural language processing tasks while utilizing fewer parameters compared to its predecessors.

Architecture ALBERT's fundamental architecture is similar to that of BERT. Relative to BERT, ALBERT's model architecture exhibits two modifications. One of the core techniques employed in ALBERT is factorized embedding parameterization. This approach tackles the problem of large-scale embeddings by decomposing the vocabulary embedding matrix into two smaller matrices. The technique separates the embedding size from the hidden layers, effectively reducing the parameter count. In traditional models like BERT, the embedding matrix size is the product of vocabulary size and the hidden layer dimension, which can be quite large. Factorized embedding parameterization instead uses a low-dimensional embedding that projects into the higher-dimensional hidden space, thus maintaining expressive power while significantly reducing the number of parameters. This not only decreases the model's memory footprint but also aids in faster training and scaling.

Another pivotal innovation in ALBERT is cross-layer parameter sharing. This technique involves sharing the same set of parameters across all the layers of the model rather than having separate parameters for each layer. By doing so, ALBERT minimizes redundancy and further reduces the total number of parameters needed for training. This parameter sharing extends across all components of a layer — attention and feed-forward networks — ensuring that the learning capacity is preserved while the memory cost is cut down. This approach not only helps in combating overfitting by regularizing the model but also enhances the model's ability to generalize across different tasks, making it efficient yet powerful in handling complex language understanding tasks.

Pre-Training Objective In addition to the traditional pre-training objective of next-sentence prediction (NSP), ALBERT introduces a unique pre-training objective called Sentence Order Prediction (SOP), which is a departure from BERT's Next Sentence Prediction (NSP). SOP is designed to improve the model's understanding of the coherence and flow of ideas in texts. In this task, the model is trained to determine whether two segments follow each other in the original text or if their order has been swapped. This objective focuses specifically on modeling inter-sentence coherence, making it more effective in understanding the logical flow of discourse compared to NSP, which often conflated topic prediction with coherence. The SOP task encourages ALBERT to develop a deeper contextual comprehension, leading to better performance on downstream tasks involving complex reasoning and text structuring.

ALBERT is a streamlined version of BERT designed to provide a more efficient framework for natural language processing. It introduces two main innovations: factorized embedding parameterization, which reduces the size of the model by decomposing large embedding matrices into smaller, more manageable components, and cross-layer parameter sharing, which minimizes the number of parameters by reusing the same weights across all layers of the model. These techniques significantly reduce the memory requirements and increase the training speed without compromising performance. ALBERT's design allows it to perform at par or better on various language understanding benchmarks, making it a valuable tool for handling complex NLP tasks with greater efficiency.

DistilBERT, developed by researchers at Hugging Face, is a streamlined version of the popular BERT model designed for natural language processing tasks. It achieves a balance between performance and resource efficiency by retaining 97% of BERT's language understanding capabilities while being 40% smaller and 60% faster. This reduction is achieved through a technique known as knowledge distillation, where the smaller model, DistilBERT, is trained to replicate the behavior of the larger BERT model. It is particularly useful in environments where computing power is limited, such as on mobile devices or in client-side applications, making advanced NLP more accessible and practical for widespread use.

Architecture DistilBERT's architecture is a simplified adaptation of the original BERT model, designed to maintain substantial performance while reducing the model size and computational requirements. DistilBERT consists of a multi-layer transformer architecture, with each layer comprising two primary subcomponents: a multi-head self-attention mechanism and a feed-forward neural network. While BERT typically has 12 transformer blocks, DistilBERT uses only 6, effectively halving the depth of the model. Each transformer block in DistilBERT also integrates layer normalization and a residual connection, similar to BERT.

Pre-Training Objective DistilBERT is initialized from its teacher model, BERT, by retaining every alternate layer. DistilBERT employs gradient accumulation to handle large batches, processing up to 4,000 examples per batch. It uses dynamic masking and omits the next sentence prediction objective, operating on a combined dataset of English Wikipedia and the Toronto Book Corpus. The pre-training objective of DistilBERT is centered around a process called knowledge distillation, which is conducted during the training phase. This involves a teacher-student learning setup where DistilBERT, the student, learns from BERT, the teacher model. DistilBERT is trained to mimic the output distributions of BERT by aligning its own predictions with those of the fully-trained BERT model. Specifically, the training objective combines a distillation loss over the soft target probabilities of the teacher, which makes DistilBERT's output probabilities close to those of BERT, with a supervised training loss on the masked language modeling task, similar to BERT. This dual approach allows DistilBERT to effectively retain a significant portion of BERT's language understanding capabilities despite its reduced size.

DistilBERT is a compact derivative of the BERT model, optimized for faster performance and reduced size while maintaining most of BERT's language processing capabilities. This model employs knowledge distillation, where a smaller model is trained to mimic a larger one, to effectively reduce its size by 40% and increase processing speed by 60%. Despite its smaller footprint, DistilBERT preserves approximately 97% of BERT's effectiveness in language understanding tasks. It is particularly suited for applications where computational resources are limited, such as mobile devices, making it a practical choice for deploying advanced natural language processing in resource-constrained environments.

DistilRoBERTa is a distilled version of the RoBERTa model. DistilRoBERTa is designed to provide a more efficient alternative to RoBERTa, retain a significant portion of RoBERTa's language understanding capabilities while being smaller and faster. This efficiency is achieved through a process known as knowledge distillation, where the larger model (RoBERTa) teaches the distilled model to replicate its behavior. DistilRoBERTa is particularly useful in resource-limited environments, as it requires significantly less computational power and memory, making it ideal for deploying NLP applications on edge devices or in scenarios where quick response times are crucial.

Architecture DistilRoBERTa is a lightweight version of RoBERTa, characterized by a reduction in layers and parameters, meticulously designed to preserve the maximum extent of its original performance capabilities. Specifically, it utilizes a transformer-based architecture similar to RoBERTa but with half the number of layers. The model comprises 6 layers, 768 dimension and 12 heads, totaling 82 million parameters, in contrast to the 125 million parameters of RoBERTa-base. On average, DistilRoBERTa operates at twice the speed of RoBERTa-base.

Pre-Training Objective Similar to DistilBERT, DistilRoBERTa incorporates the original RoBERTa's Masked Language Model (MLM) pre-training objective with an additional focus on knowledge distillation. In the MLM pre-training objective, a certain percentage of the input tokens are randomly masked, and the model is trained to predict these masked tokens based solely on their context. Furthermore, DistilRoBERTa incorporates an additional training technique known as "distillation" during the pre-training phase. This involves the model learning from a larger, already trained RoBERTa model, essentially mimicking its predictions on a given set of training data. In summary, the training objective of DistilRoBERTa integrates a distillation loss based on the soft target probabilities provided by the teacher model and a supervised training loss for the MLM task. This pre-training process enables DistilRoBERTa to retain a significant portion of RoBERTa's language understanding capabilities, while being more computationally efficient due to its smaller size and fewer parameters.

DistilRoBERTa is a compact and efficient version of RoBERTa. It utilizes knowledge distillation, a technique where the distilled model learns from a pre-trained larger model, to retain much of the original's capabilities while significantly reducing its size and computational requirements. This makes DistilRoBERTa an ideal choice for applications needing a balance between performance and efficiency, such as mobile apps, edge devices, or any environment where computational resources are limited.

3.1.5. Knowledge-enhanced Pretrained Language Models

Despite extensive pre-training on large-scale text corpora, pre-trained language models continue to struggle with issues such as factual inaccuracy and outdated knowledge. To mitigate these deficiencies, a line of work has focused on enhancing these models' capabilities for downstream tasks through the integration of external knowledge. These studies involve augmenting pre-trained language models by retrieving pertinent information from external knowledge bases, consequently elevating their performance in downstream applications. They typically involve modifying the pre-training objective or model architecture to inject external knowledge into the models. Through this integration, pretrained language models are better equipped to manage knowledge intensive tasks, such as question answering, document summarization, and complex decision-making. This enhances their applicability across various industries including healthcare, finance, and legal.

LUKE (Language Understanding with Knowledge-based Embeddings) is a state-of-the-art pretrained language model that leverages entity-aware self-attention to enhance natural language understanding. Developed by Studio Ousia, LUKE extends the transformer-based architecture, incorporating both word and entity embeddings to better understand the nuances and relations inherent in text. By integrating information from large-scale knowledge graphs like Wikipedia, LUKE achieves superior performance on a variety of natural language processing tasks, including named entity recognition, entity typing, and relation extraction. Its design allows it to contextually understand entities and their relationships, making it highly effective in tasks requiring deep semantic understanding.

Architecture LUKE employs RoBERTa as its foundational architecture. In contrast to the original RoBERTa, LUKE has expanded its vocabulary by adding entity vocabulary. Consequently, LUKE's parameters total approximately 483M, comprising 355M from RoBERTa and 128M from entity vector representations. To enhance computational efficiency, our entity vocabulary does not encompass all entities but is restricted to the 500K entities most frequently appearing in entity annotations. The input vector representation for tokens and entities includes three types: token embedding, position embedding, and entity type embedding. Token embedding consists of word token embedding and entity token embedding. Position embedding indicates the position of the token within a sequence of words. Entity type embedding signifies that the token is an entity. Given that LUKE processes two types of token, word tokens and entity tokens, it extends the traditional self-attention mechanism to incorporate entity-aware self-attention. Specifically, the attention score e_{ij} is computed as follows:

$$e_{ij} = \begin{cases} \mathbf{K}_{x_j}^{\top}\mathbf{Q}_{x_i}, & \text{if both } x_i \text{ and } x_j \text{ are words} \\ \mathbf{K}_{x_j}^{\top}\mathbf{Q}_{w2e}x_i, & \text{if } x_i \text{ is word and } x_j \text{ is entity} \\ \mathbf{K}_{x_j}^{\top}\mathbf{Q}_{e2w}x_i, & \text{if } x_i \text{ is entity and } x_j \text{ is word} \\ \mathbf{K}_{x_j}^{\top}\mathbf{Q}_{e2e}x_i, & \text{if both } x_i \text{ and } x_j \text{ are entities} \end{cases} \quad (10)$$

Among them, $\mathbf{Q}_{w2e}, \mathbf{Q}_{e2w}, \mathbf{Q}_{e2e} \in \mathbb{R}^{L\times D}$ are query matrices. Through this entity-aware self-attention mechanism, LUKE effectively integrates and leverages both linguistic context and structured entity knowledge, allowing it to perform better on tasks that require understanding of complex relationships and entities in text.

Pre-Training Objective For the initialization of LUKE, a traditional Masked Language Model (MLM) approach is employed, alongside a novel pretraining task devised to enhance entity recognition capabilities. This task extends the traditional MLM process by leveraging Wikipedia hyperlinks as entity annotations. The training involves utilizing a substantial corpus from Wikipedia, which has been annotated with these entities. During the pretraining phase, a predefined proportion of these entities are obscured by replacing them with designated [MASK] tokens. The primary objective of this training is to enable the model to accurately identify and predict these masked entities. The final loss function is the sum of MLM loss and cross-entropy loss on predicting the masked entities.

LUKE is a knowledge-enhanced pretrained language model that improves the performances of pretrained language model on a wide range of natural language processing tasks by integrating knowledge from Wikipedia. LUKE employs a unique approach by considering both words and entities as distinct tokens. It processes these tokens through the transformer architecture to generate both intermediate and final representations for each token. This methodology allow LUKE to excel in tasks that require deep semantic comprehension such as named entity recognition and relation extraction. Built on a transformer-based architecture, LUKE uses entity-aware self-attention mechanisms to effectively understand and utilize the relationships between entities within texts. This approach not only improves the model's performance on standard benchmarks but also broadens its applicability in extracting and leveraging nuanced information from complex language data. As for the pretraining task, besides the traditional MLM, LUKE utilizes an extension of MLM to learn entity representations. Through these techniques, LUKE enhances the performance of its backbone model, RoBERTa by a large margin.

KEPLER is a knowledge-enhanced pretrained language model that integrates structured knowledge from knowledge graphs directly into the training process of transformer-based language models. It encodes the texts and entities into a unified semantic space with the same PLM as the encoder, and jointly optimize the KE and the masked language modeling (MLM) objectives. By incorporating entities and their relations during pretraining, KEPLER aims to improve the model's understanding of real-world facts and relations, thereby enhancing its ability to handle knowledge-driven tasks. The inclusion of structured knowledge enables KEPLER to demonstrate superior performance in tasks requiring deep understanding and reasoning, making it a valuable tool for applications in question answering, information retrieval, and beyond.

3.2. Early text-to-text models like T5 and BART

Both encoder structures (e.g., BERT) and decoder structures (e.g., GPT) face a significant challenge when it comes to filling in blanks with variable lengths [73,74]. Decoder-based models struggle because they can only generate text at the end of the sequence, making it difficult to fill in gaps within the sequence. Encoder-based models encounter problems because using a fixed number of [MASK] tokens can inadvertently leak information about the sequence length. A natural solution to this problem is to leverage encoder-decoder architectures, originally designed for machine translation, which can generate variable lengths of target sequences conditioned on the input sources. This approach allows for more flexible and contextually appropriate filling of blanks.

The pioneer in this genre is the MASS [75], which introduces a masked-prediction strategy into the encoder-decoder structure. However, MASS does not fully address the problem of filling variable-length blanks. We next describe how T5 [76] and BART [77] address this problem. T5 masks variable-length spans in the text with only one masking token and asks the decoder to recover the entire masking sequence. BART, on the other hand, introduces the interesting idea of destroying the source sequence with a variety of operations such as truncation, deletion, substitution, shuffling, and masking, rather than just masking.

3.2.1. T5

T5, the Text-To-Text Transfer Transformer, is a highly versatile model introduced by Google Research. It reimagines all natural language processing (NLP) tasks as text-to-text problems, allowing a single model to be fine-tuned on a variety of tasks without any task-specific modifications. This unified approach simplifies the process of handling different NLP tasks, making T5 a powerful and flexible tool in the field.

The key innovation of T5 is its unified text-to-text framework. This framework converts every task into a text-to-text format, where both the input and output are text strings. For example:

1. Translation: "translate English to German: That is good." -> "Das ist gut."
2. Summarization: "summarize: The quick brown fox jumps over the lazy dog." -> "Fox jumps over dog."
3. Sentiment Analysis: "classify sentiment: This movie is great!" -> "positive"

This approach allows T5 to leverage the same model architecture and training procedure across various tasks, simplifying the learning process and improving the model's adaptability.

Architecture T5 employs a standard encoder-decoder transformer architecture, with both components consisting of multiple layers of attention mechanisms and feed-forward neural networks. The encoder processes the input text, while the decoder generates the output text.

The encoder takes the input text and converts it into a sequence of continuous representations. It consists of several layers, each with two sub-layers: (1) Self-Attention Mechanism: Allows each token to attend to all other tokens in the input sequence, capturing contextual information. (2) Feed-Forward Neural Network: Applies a point-wise transformation to each token representation.

Formally, the output of the encoder at layer l can be expressed as:

$$\text{EncoderOutput}_l = \text{FFN}(\text{SelfAttention}(\text{EncoderOutput}_{l-1})) \tag{11}$$

where FFN denotes the feed-forward network, and SelfAttention represents the self-attention mechanism.

The decoder generates the target sequence by attending to both its previous outputs and the encoder's output. It also consists of multiple layers, each with three sub-layers: (1) Self-Attention Mechanism: Allows each token to attend to previous tokens in the target sequence. (2) Encoder-Decoder Attention Mechanism: Allows each token to attend to all tokens in the encoder's output, providing contextual information from the input sequence. (3) Feed-Forward Neural Network: Applies a point-wise transformation to each token representation.

Pre-Training Objective T5's pre-training objective is designed to enable the model to handle variable-length gaps in the text. The pre-training process involves the following steps: (1) Span Corruption: Random spans of text in the input sequence are replaced with a single unique mask token (e.g., "<extra_id_0>"). (2) Reconstruction: The model is trained to reconstruct the original text by predicting the masked spans in the output sequence.

For example, given the input sequence: Input = *"The quick brown <extra_id_0> over the lazy dog."* The target sequence would be: Target = *"fox jumps"*.

The pre-training objective is to minimize the negative log-likelihood of the target sequence given the encoder's output:

$$L = -\sum_{t=1}^{T} \log P(y_t | y_{<t}, \text{EncoderOutput}) \tag{12}$$

where y_t represents the tokens in the target sequence.

After pre-training, T5 can be fine-tuned on a specific downstream task by training it on a labeled dataset for that task. The text-to-text format ensures that fine-tuning is straightforward and consistent across different tasks.

T5 enhances efficiency and adaptability in handling natural language processing tasks by treating them uniformly as text-to-text problems. This unified approach minimizes the necessity for task-specific modifications, streamlining the training process. Moreover, T5's adaptability is evidenced by its proficiency in managing a diverse range of NLP tasks using a singular architectural framework. Additionally, the model employs a novel approach by using a single mask token to represent variable-length spans, which enhances its capability to accurately fill in the blanks in text, effectively preventing information leakage. This feature improves the model's generative and interpretative abilities, making it a robust solution for complex language understanding and generation tasks.

3.2.2. BART

BART, or Bidirectional and Auto-Regressive Transformers, is a powerful sequence-to-sequence model introduced by Facebook AI. BART's core innovation lies in its unique pre-training strategy, which involves corrupting text and then training the model to reconstruct the original text. This approach makes BART robust and versatile, capable of handling tasks such as text summarization, translation, and question answering.

Architecture BART employs a standard transformer-based encoder-decoder architecture. The encoder is responsible for understanding the input text, while the decoder generates the target text.

The encoder processes the input text, converting it into a sequence of continuous representations. It uses multiple layers of self-attention and feed-forward neural networks to capture contextual information from the entire input sequence.

The decoder generates the target text by attending to both its previous outputs and the encoder's output. It consists of multiple layers, each with three sub-layers:

1. Self-Attention Mechanism: Allows each token to attend to previous tokens in the target sequence.
2. Encoder-Decoder Attention Mechanism: Allows each token to attend to all tokens in the encoder's output, providing contextual information from the input sequence.
3. Feed-Forward Neural Network: Applies a point-wise transformation to each token representation.

Pre-Training Objective BART's pre-training involves corrupting the input text in various ways and then training the model to reconstruct the original text. This corruption can include:

1. Token Masking: Randomly masking some tokens in the input sequence.
2. Token Deletion: Randomly deleting some tokens.
3. Token Shuffling: Randomly shuffling the order of tokens.
4. Token Replacement: Randomly replacing some tokens with incorrect ones.
5. Sentence Permutation: Shuffling the order of sentences in the input text.
6. Document Rotation: Rotating the document by randomly choosing a token and making it the start of the sequence.

For example, given the original text:

$$\text{Original} = \text{"The quick brown fox jumps over the lazy dog."}$$

A corrupted version might be:

$$\text{Corrupted} = \text{"The quick <mask> fox jumps over the lazy <mask>."}$$

The model is trained to minimize the negative log-likelihood of the original sequence given the corrupted input:

$$L = -\sum_{t=1}^{T} \log P(y_t | y_{<t}, \text{EncoderOutput})$$

where y_t represents the tokens in the original text.

After pre-training, BART can be fine-tuned on a specific downstream task by training it on a labeled dataset for that task. The encoder-decoder architecture allows BART to handle a wide range of tasks by generating the appropriate output text based on the input text.

BART's innovative pre-training strategy, which involves corrupting text and then learning to reconstruct it, significantly enhances its robustness to noisy inputs. This method not only allows BART to adeptly manage different types of textual corruption—such as missing words, rephrased sentences, or shuffled paragraphs—but also equips it with a nuanced understanding of language structure and context. Furthermore, BART combines the strengths of both bidirectional and autoregressive transformers. The bidirectional component comprehensively analyzes input texts from both directions, ensuring a deep contextual understanding. The autoregressive component, on the other hand, focuses on predicting the next token in the sequence, which is crucial for generating coherent and contextually relevant text. Together, these features make BART particularly effective across a wide range of Natural Language Processing tasks, including text generation, translation, and summarization. By leveraging this dual approach, BART not only performs with high accuracy but also maintains consistency in generating readable and contextually appropriate outputs.

3.2.3. After T5 and BART

The introduction of encoder-decoder architectures like T5 and BART has provided significant advancements in handling variable-length blank filling in text sequences. T5's approach of masking spans and requiring the decoder to predict the entire sequence, along with BART's diverse corruption techniques, have proven to be effective strategies for improving the flexibility and robustness of sequence-to-sequence models. Subsequent works, such as PEGASUS [78] and PALM [79], continue to build on these foundations, further refining and specializing in specific seq2seq tasks.

3.3. Open-source Large Language Models

The landscape of language models has undergone a significant transformation with the advent of Large Language Models (LLMs), distinguished from their predecessors, Pretrained Language Models (PLMs), by their sheer scale and advanced capabilities. While PLMs like BERT and GPT-2 had hundreds of millions to a few billion parameters, LLMs have escalated to tens and even hundreds of billions of parameters, enabling unprecedented advancements in natural language understanding and generation. This chapter delves into the key features, innovations, and impacts of these colossal models, showcasing their evolution and differentiating factors.

3.3.1. FlanT5

FlanT5 represents a significant stride in the domain of language model instruction finetuning. The model, which is an evolution of the T5 (Text-to-Text Transfer Transformer) architecture, has been enhanced through a process known as instruction finetuning. This process involves further training the model on a diverse array of tasks, all framed as instructions, thereby bolstering the model's proficiency in handling a multitude of language understanding and generation tasks.

Flan-T5 has a suite of models with varying sizes to cater to different computational needs and applications. The models range from smaller, more efficient sizes up to larger models that offer increased capabilities. Here are the model scales available in the Flan-T5 family: Flan-T5-Small(80M), Flan-T5-Base(250M), Flan-T5-Large(780M), Flan-T5-XL(3B) and Flan-T5-XXL(11B).

At the core of FlanT5's capabilities is its training regimen, which includes a substantial scaling up in three pivotal dimensions: the number of finetuning tasks, the size of the model, and the incorporation of chain-of-thought data. This comprehensive approach has yielded remarkable improvements across various model classes, prompting setups, and evaluation benchmarks. One of the most notable outcomes of FlanT5's instruction finetuning is the substantial leap in performance on benchmarks such as MMLU (Massive Multi-task Language Understanding), BBH, TyDiQA, and MGSM. FlanT5's adeptness at generalizing to unseen tasks is exemplified by its state-of-the-art results, such as achieving 75.2% on five-shot MMLU evaluation.

Architecture Flan-T5 models are based on the dense encoder-decoder structure of the original T5 model. This architecture consists of a stack of transformer layers that process input sequences and generate output sequences. Each model within the Flan-T5 series, regardless of its size, inherits this core structure, ensuring consistency in how they interpret and generate text. (1) The encoder part of the model is designed to read and understand the input text. It employs self-attention mechanisms that allow it to capture relationships within the input sequence and build a contextual representation of the text. (2) The decoder generates the output text based on the encoder's representations and its own previous outputs. It also uses self-attention to focus on the generated sequence progressively building towards the final output.

Pre-training Objective Flan-T5 models are pre-trained using a span corruption objective, which involves masking parts of the input text and training the model to predict the original span. This process enhances the model's ability to understand and reconstruct text, which is crucial for its strong performance on a variety of tasks.

Training Corpora The training data for Flan-T5 models is a blend of diverse sources that provide a broad and comprehensive coverage of language patterns and structures. The training data includes a wide array of text types, ranging from news articles and books to scientific papers and websites. This diversity ensures that the models are exposed to a rich tapestry of language uses and styles. In addition to general language data, Flan-T5 models are finetuned on task-oriented datasets that are phrased as instructions. These datasets cover a spectrum of tasks such as question answering, translation, summarization, and more, which are crucial for evaluating and improving the model's performance on specific language understanding and generation tasks. To enhance the model's reasoning capabilities, Flan-T5 incorporates chain-of-thought (CoT) data in its finetuning process. CoT data includes examples that demonstrate step-by-step reasoning, which is particularly beneficial for complex tasks that require multi-step logical inference.

3.3.2. LLaMA Model Family

As of the writing of this article, Meta AI's LLaMA model family has released several versions: LLaMA-1 and LLaMA-2. These models have set new standards in instruction following and have been extensively fine-tuned or pretrained for various applications. Their open-source nature and exceptional benchmark performance have made them extremely popular in both research and industry settings.

LLaMA-1 LLaMA-1 marked a significant milestone in the development of large language models, introducing a robust architecture that set the stage for future advancements. With a focus on transformer-based mechanisms, it incorporated several key innovations to enhance training stability and performance.

The model's architecture was built upon the transformer framework, with the addition of pre-normalization to stabilize training dynamics. It also adopted the SwiGLU activation function for improved non-linear transformations and rotary positional embeddings for better handling of sequential data. LLaMA-1 was trained on a rich mixture of data sources, including CommonCrawl, C4, Github, Wikipedia, Books, ArXiv, and Stack Exchange. Each source contributed to the model's broad understanding of various domains and languages.

Recognizing the potential for further enhancement, a significant number of researchers have sought to extend the capabilities of the LLaMA models. This has been achieved primarily through instruction tuning or continual pretraining, with instruction tuning emerging as a particularly popular method. This approach is favored due to its relatively lower computational costs compared to other methods. Among the extensions of the LLaMA models, Stanford Alpaca [142] stands out as the first open instruct-following model fine-tuned from LLaMA (7B). It was trained using 52K instruction-following demonstrations generated through self-instruct [143] with text-davinci-003.

LLaMA-2 LLaMA-2 expanded upon the initial design with critical enhancements. The context length was increased to 4096 tokens, allowing the model to process more extensive information and maintain coherence over longer sequences. Additionally, the introduction of Group Query Attention (GQA) improved inference scalability, making the model more efficient without compromising performance. The training data for LLaMA 2 was carefully curated to include a larger volume of factual content, helping to mitigate the risk of hallucinatory responses. The data mixture was expanded by 40%, doubling the context length and further enriching the model's knowledge base.

A significant advancement in LLaMA 2 was the integration of supervised fine-tuning and reinforcement learning with human feedback (RLHF). In comparison to LLaMA 1, the development of LLaMA 2 stands out due to the incorporation of an extensive dataset for fine-tuning purposes. For SFT, LLaMA 2 leveraged a substantial collection of 100k human-annotated examples. Furthermore, to refine the model's alignment with human preferences even more, LLaMA 2 employed RLHF using an impressive 1 million instances of human preference data. This data was gathered to train a reward model that captures the nuances of human feedback on model outputs. By using these preferences, the model was iteratively adjusted to prioritize the generation of responses that are not only helpful but also safe and appropriate.

LLaMA 2 builds upon the strengths of its predecessor, addressing its limitations with architectural improvements and a more nuanced approach to training data. The increased context length and GQA are particularly noteworthy, as they enhance the model's ability to handle long-range dependencies and improve computational efficiency. This GQA addresses the computational efficiency of the auto-regressive models by optimizing the way attention mechanisms handle memory usage during the generation of responses.

3.4. Closed-source Large Language Models

There are many types of closed-source LLMs, and we choose the most popular and powerful models from the GPT family as representatives to introduce.

3.4.1. GPT-3

The GPT-3 model, developed by a team at OpenAI, is an autoregressive language model that boasts 175 billion parameters, marking a significant leap from its predecessors. This model has been designed to demonstrate impressive task-agnostic, few-shot performance, often rivaling or exceeding the capabilities of previously established fine-tuning approaches. GPT-3's training and application do not require gradient updates or fine-tuning; instead, it leverages text interaction for task specification and demonstration.

Architecture GPT-3 employs the same model architecture as its predecessor, GPT-2, with certain enhancements. It utilizes a modified initialization, pre-normalization, and reversible tokenization. A distinguishing feature of GPT-3 is its use of alternating dense and locally banded sparse attention patterns within the transformer layers, akin to the Sparse Transformer model. This architectural choice allows GPT-3 to manage its vast parameter space efficiently.

Training The primary objective of GPT-3's pre-training is to create a task-agnostic model that can be applied broadly across various language tasks. The model is trained to predict the next token in a sequence, a process that relies on a large and diverse dataset. This approach enables GPT-3 to develop a deep understanding of language structure and usage, which is foundational for its few-shot learning capabilities. After pre-training, GPT-3 does not undergo fine-tuning for specific tasks. Instead, it is applied directly to tasks in a few-shot setting, where it is provided with a small number of examples. This method contrasts with traditional approaches that require large datasets for supervised learning.

Version Differences and Improvements GPT-3 represents a significant scaling up from GPT-2, not just in terms of parameter count but also in its capabilities. The newer version demonstrates smoother scaling trends across most tasks, with the performance gap between zero-shot, one-shot, and few-shot settings often increasing with model capacity. This suggests that larger models, like GPT-3, are more proficient as meta-learners. The improvements in GPT-3 are not just quantitative but also qualitative. It shows a better understanding of context and can generate more coherent and relevant responses, even when prompted with very few examples.

3.4.2. InstructGPT

The InstructGPT model is based on the GPT-3 architecture, utilizing a deep transformer network with attention mechanisms that allow it to process and generate text effectively. To align the LM with user intent, the authors employed a two-step fine-tuning process. Initially, they used supervised learning with a dataset of labeler demonstrations to fine-tune GPT-3. This was followed by reinforcement learning from human feedback (RLHF), using a reward model trained on human-labeled comparisons of model outputs to further refine the model's behavior. The InstructGPT model represents a significant step towards creating AI systems that are better aligned with human values and intentions.

3.4.3. GPT-3.5 Series

GPT-3.5 Series are one of the most famous series among commercial LLMs. They appear on the OpenAI platform under the name "davinci" and include: 1) text-davinci-002, an

SFT model with the FeedME technique built on top of code-davinci-002; 2) text-davinci-003, a refined model using PPO built on top of text-davinci-002; 3) gpt-3.5-turbo, a chat-optimized model built on top of text-davinci-003, which is also widely known for serving ChatGPT on OpenAI's website; 4) gpt-3.5-turbo-instruct, a completion model trained similarly to the previous InstructGPT models such as the text-davinci series.

3.4.4. GPT-4

The GPT-4 model represents a significant leap in the field of large-scale multimodal AI, showcasing human-level performance across a spectrum of professional and academic benchmarks. Although it still has limitations, such as the potential for "hallucinations" and a limited context window, GPT-4 demonstrates remarkable capabilities in understanding and generating natural language, especially in complex scenarios.

Architecture GPT-4 is a Transformer-based model that follows the architectural blueprint established by its predecessors but is enhanced to handle both image and text inputs. The model's architecture is designed to predict the next token in a sequence, leveraging the vast amounts of data available on the internet and from third-party providers.

Training The pre-training objective of GPT-4 is to forecast the next token in a document, a task that is achieved through the consumption of a diverse range of text data. This process lays the foundation for the model's understanding of language structure and semantics. After pre-training, GPT-4 undergoes a fine-tuning phase using Reinforcement Learning from Human Feedback (RLHF). This stage aligns the model's outputs more closely with desired behaviors, enhancing its performance on tasks that require adherence to factuality and specific guidelines.

Differences Between Versions and Improvements Compared to its predecessor GPT-3.5, GPT-4 exhibits substantial improvements in performance, particularly in its ability to generate accurate and reliable responses. The latest version GPT-4 also includes several enhancements over the early version, such as a reduction in the generation of harmful content, improved adherence to content policies, and better alignment with user intent. The model has been fine-tuned to refuse certain types of requests that could lead to unsafe outputs, and it has been calibrated to provide more accurate and safer responses.

4. LLMs for KGQA

4.1. PLMs in Simple KGQA

Pre-trained language models (PLMs), the progenitors of today's extensive language models, typically feature millions of parameters. As landmark developments in natural language processing (NLP), PLMs employ self-supervised learning on vast text corpora to capture rich semantic knowledge, enhancing a range of NLP tasks [54]. Manning [1] explains that PLMs learn the meaning of words because meaning can be considered as a connection of linguistic forms, and PLMs have seen many connections of words to understand the meaning of words. For example, PLMs understand the word "Washington, D.C." by these two sentences "Washington, D.C. is the capital city and federal district of the United States" and "Washington, D.C. is located on the east bank of the Potomac

River". As a result, PLMs significantly improve the performance of most NLP tasks through such learning.

The adoption of PLMs, whether through fine-tuning or prompting, has become standard practice for NLP tasks. The introduction of initial models like BERT [20] and GPT [49] sparked a surge in PLM development. Innovations such as DistilBERT [48] and TinyBERT [47] aimed to streamline models by reducing parameter counts, thus speeding up training and inference times. Others, like ERNIE [35] and KEPLER [36], have integrated structured knowledge to better handle knowledge-driven tasks. Despite these advancements, the application of PLMs to KGQA, a critical NLP sub-task, remains underexplored.

KGQA leverages structured knowledge from knowledge graphs (KGs), typically organized as triples (*subject*, *relation*, *object*), to answer natural language questions. The strategic application of various PLMs to KGQA warrants exploration due to:

1. **Efficiency Concerns**: The vastness of general domain KGs—such as Freebase [38] with over 3 billion triples—poses significant challenges in terms of training and inference time. Some studies have sought to mitigate these issues by restricting the search space within KGs, albeit at the expense of extended training durations [40,41,42]. Efforts to optimize KGQA approaches often sacrifice performance for speed [43,44,45]. Given the considerable performance benefits PLMs offer, their integration into KGQA systems necessitates a careful consideration of the trade-off between performance and operational efficiency.
2. **Complexity of Task**: KGQA involves numerous NLP subtasks such as mention detection, entity disambiguation, and relation detection. There is extensive research using PLMs to successfully tackle these subtasks [28,29,30,31,32]. Additionally, structured knowledge has significantly improved PLM capabilities beyond mere large-scale corpus training, especially in tasks like mention detection [33] and relation detection [34,35,36,37]. However, comprehensive comparisons of PLMs' effectiveness across these specific subtasks are lacking. Exploring PLMs' utility in KGQA could also yield insights for these related areas.

This section aims to thoroughly evaluate the performance of various PLMs in KGQA, assessing metrics of accuracy, efficiency, and scalability. We explore these aspects using four incrementally sized KGs and test three categories of nine PLMs, including mainstream models like BERT [20] and GPT2 [49], lightweight alternatives like ALbert [22], and knowledge-enhanced variants such as Luke [33]. These evaluations consider different pre-trained task categories and employ basic KGQA frameworks involving PLMs and simple linear layers, allowing for focused comparisons of model effectiveness without the interference of complex neural architectures. Further, we extend our description to include experiments comparing the fine-tuned performance of these PLMs against zero-shot applications using ChatGPT on KGQA tasks.

4.1.1. Two Basic KGQA Frameworks

Summary of the Framework To evaluate the practical application of PLMs in KGQA, we describe two fundamental frameworks based on common approaches in the field: a classification-based KGQA framework (KGQAcl) and a retrieval and ranking-based KGQA framework (KGQArr). These frameworks are designed to assess the performance of various PLMs without the influence of complex KG embedding methods, which are reserved for future studies [23].

KGQAcl approaches, referenced in prior studies [2,3,4,5,6], typically employ deep neural networks to encode questions and map them to a KG relational dictionary. KGQArr approaches [7,8,9,10,11,12,13,14,15,16], on the other hand, start by retrieving one-hop adjacent relations of linked entities, then use newly designed network architectures or contextual information to rank these relations. Some studies within this framework also incorporate relation detection models to reorder entities [7] and adopt joint training strategies to enhance performance [10,13].

Both basic frameworks consist of four modules, including (1) **Mention Detection**, (2) **Entity Disambiguation**, (3) **Relation Detection** and (4) **Answer Query**. The primary distinction between the two lies in their approach to relation detection: KGQArr focuses on ranking candidate relations through information retrieval, while KGQAcl is geared towards mapping the question's intent directly to KG relations via semantic parsing. Mention detection and entity disambiguation are also integrated as part of the entity linking task, treated in sequence under KGQArr and as separate modules under KGQAcl.

Mention Detection This involves identifying the named entity within a question, traditionally handled as a named entity recognition task. Various models such as RNNs, CNNs, and their variants [2,5,6,12], or BERT [14] have been employed, with some approaches treating it as a span detection task [3] or using CNN-LSTM as an encoder-decoder to generate entity mentions directly [4].

Entity Disambiguation Once mentions are detected, candidate entities are collected and ranked. Techniques like n-gram heuristics [2,3,6], character similarity [2,3,4], and TF-IDF scoring [6] are used to refine the selection. Our frameworks adopt these simple yet effective methodologies.

Relation Detection This module differentiates the two frameworks. KGQAcl classifies the encoded question into KG relational categories independently of other modules using models like RNN, LSTM [2,4,5], and BERT [3]. KGQArr, resembling a similarity matching task, uses linked entities to retrieve and select candidate relations based on their alignment with the question content, enhanced by attention mechanisms [11,12] and external contextual features [16].

Answer Query This involves combining candidate entities and relations, scored and queried against the KG to identify the correct answers. The highest total scores from entity-relation pairings determine the correct answers [2,3,4,5,6]. Joint training of entity disambiguation and relation detection has been explored [9,10,12,13], though it is not feasible in our PLM-based frameworks due to GPU constraints.

Both frameworks are designed to be minimalistic, incorporating only PLMs and simple linear layers, allowing for a focused comparison of PLM capabilities across different KGQA tasks. Next, we will detail these two PLM-based KGQA frameworks, highlighting how each manages the integration and functionality of these modules.

4.1.2. The Basic Classification-based KGQA Framework

The basic Classification-based KGQA framework (KGQAcl) as depicted in Figure 4 is composed of four modules outlined in Section 4.1.1: Mention Detection, Entity Disambiguation, Relation Detection, and Answer Query.

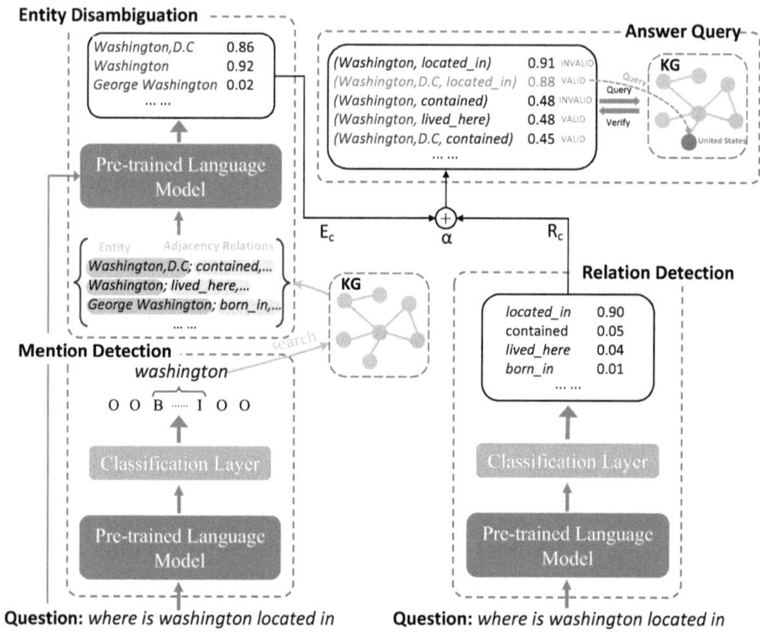

Figure 4. The basic classification-based KGQA framework.

Mention Detection In this module, given a question Q the objective is to identify the subject mention m. For instance, in the question shown in Figure 4, the subject mention is "*washington*". We approach this task as a named entity recognition problem, utilizing PLMs to encode the question sequence. A linear classification layer then assigns a label to each token in the sequence: B for the beginning of mention, I for intermediate, and O for non-mention. Due to varied tokenization methods by different PLMs, only the first token of each word is annotated, and subsequent tokens are filled with the special character $\langle pad \rangle$.

Entity Disambiguation The detected mention m is used to link to corresponding entities in the KG. An inverted index dictionary pre-maps mentions to potential KG entities, aiding in the retrieval of candidate entities E_c based on the mention "*washington*". For example, this could yield entities such as "*Washington, D.C.*", the state "*Washington*" or "*George Washington*". Besides, the adjacent relations r_{e_i} for each $e_i \in E_c$ retrieved from KG will be used for disambiguation. Using a PLM-based approach, entities are scored by $S_{e_i} = g_{\text{PLM}}(Q|e_i|r_{e_i})$, where $|$ refers to the connection symbol, $g_{\text{PLM}}()$ represents an PLM encoder. The loss function of the entity disambiguation model based on PLM is:

$$\mathcal{L}_{ED} = -logP(y = e_k), \tag{13}$$

$$P(y = e_k) = \frac{e^{S_{e_k}}}{e^{S_{e_k}} + \sum_{j=1}^{N} e^{S_{e_j}}}, \tag{14}$$

where e_k denotes the gold entity, N indicates the number of negative samples, e_j represents negative entities and $P(y{=}e_k)$ is the probability of e_k. To refine the model, initial entity ranking employs fuzzy string matching based on Levenshtein Distance between the entity names and the mention m.

Relation Detection This task within the KGQAcl framework classifies the relation for a given question Q. The process involves encoding the question using PLMs to produce a vector h, which is then processed through a linear layer to classify the KG relation r as per the probability distribution over possible relations:

$$\mathscr{L}_{RD} = -logP(y = \hat{r}|Q), \tag{15}$$

$$P(y = \hat{r}|Q) = \frac{e^{h_{\hat{r}}}}{\sum_{j=1}^{M} e^{h_{r_j}}}, \tag{16}$$

where $\hat{r}$ refers to the correct relation, M is to the number of relation categories, and $P(y = \hat{r}|Q)$ is the probability that$\hat{r}$ is the relation corresponding to the question.

Answer Query This final module combines the candidate entities E_c and relations R_c into pairs (e, r) to query the KG. Each pair is scored based on a weighted sum of entity and relation scores:

$$S_{(e,r)} = \lambda S_e + (1 - \lambda) S_r, \tag{17}$$

The weight λ is tuned on a validation set. Invalid (e, r) pairs that do not exist in the KG are filtered out during querying. Popularity metrics from sources like FACC1[1] are used to further refine the selection process based on the frequency and connectivity of entities.

4.1.3. The Basic Retrieval and Ranking-based KGQA Framework

The Retrieval and Ranking-based KGQA framework (KGQArr), illustrated in Figure 5, adopts a pipeline structure similar to the KGQAcl framework but differs primarily in the relation detection module. This framework maintains identical modules for mention detection, entity disambiguation, and answer query as in KGQAcl.

Different from KGQACL, the aim of relation detection in KGQARR is to select the relation in candidate relations R_c that has the highest semantic similarity score to the question pattern p. R_c consists of all adjacent relations searched by candidate entity E_c in KG. The question pattern p is obtained by using a special token $\langle e \rangle$ by mention m to replace the mention m in the question q,

Adopting a dual PLM encoding strategy inspired by Sentience-Bert [27], both the question pattern and relations are encoded separately using parameter-sharing PLMs, enhancing encoding efficiency compared to cross-encoding methods. For each relation

[1] http://lemurproject.org/clueweb12/FACC1/

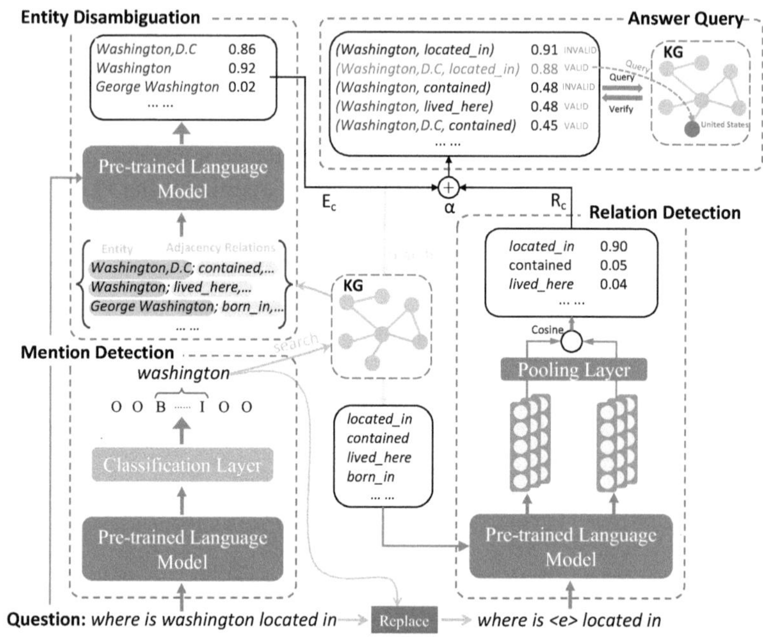

Figure 5. The basic retrieval and ranking-based KGQA framework.

$r_i \in R_c$, we compute their similar score $Score(p, r_i)$. The final predicted relation $\hat{r}$ is computed as follows:

$$\hat{r} = \text{argmax}_{r_i \in R_c} Score(p, r_i), \tag{18}$$

$$Score(q, r_i) = \cos(Pool(h_p), Pool(h_{r_i})), \tag{19}$$

where h_p and h_{r_i} are both obtained by PLMs, $Pool()$ refers to the pooling layer. During training, we adopt the hinge loss to maximize the margin between the gold relation r^+ and the negative relation r^- in E_c.

$$\mathscr{L}_{RD} = \sum_{i=1}^{k} \mathtt{max} \left\{0, \gamma - Score(p, r^+) + Score(p, r_i^-)\right\}, \tag{20}$$

where γ is a constant parameter, where k is the number of negative relations. As with the KGQACL framework, the candidate relations R_c with scores and the candidate entities E_c with scores will be fed into the answer query module together.

This retrieval and ranking approach within KGQArr allows for a nuanced handling of relation semantics relative to the query context, optimizing the framework's effectiveness in interpreting and responding to complex question patterns within KGQA tasks.

Table 1. The overall comparison of the KG for the four benchmarks. Average Degree represents the average number of adjacent relations of the entities appearing in the dataset.

	Entities	Relations	Triples	Average Degree
SQS	1,951,909	6,701	7,188,636	88
SQM-A	61,558,084	11,127	105,003,132	176
SQM-B	90,282,560	12,227	202,002,048	293
SQL	108,183,882	12,794	292,088,464	407

4.1.4. Benchmarks

This section outlines the four benchmarks used in our experiments, the method for constructing these benchmarks (section 4.1.4), and introduces the evaluation metrics for accuracy, efficiency, and scalability of the KGQA systems based on PLMs (section 4.1.4).

Construction of the benchmarks For our experiments, we use four benchmarks. The well-known SimpleQuestions benchmark [24] is supplemented by three additional benchmarks designed to assess the scalability of PLMs on KGQA tasks. These benchmarks progressively increase in scale from the original SimpleQuestions' knowledge graph, and they share the same question-answering dataset.

(a) SimpleQuestions with small-scale KG (SQS) [24]: This original benchmark comprises over 100,000 questions split into training, validation, and testing sets with a 7/1/2 ratio. The associated KG, denoted as $\mathbb{G}_S$, includes 2M entities and 6.7K relations. Unlike some prior studies, we do not prune the KG to fit specific methodologies, ensuring a fair comparison across all models.

(b) SimpleQuestions with large-scale KG (SQL): To construct $\mathbb{G}_L$, we include all one-hop triples from entities in the FACC1 subset of the Freebase dump[2], which lists common names and popularity. The resulting KG, $\mathbb{G}_L = \mathbb{G}_{FACC1} \bigcup \mathbb{G}_S$, contains 108M entities, 12.7K relations, and 292M triples, encompassing $\mathbb{G}_S$.

(c) SimpleQuestions with medium-scale KG_A (SQM-A). The KG $\mathbb{G}_{M-A}$ of SQM-A includes 61M entities, 11.1K relations and 105M triples, which completely covers $\mathbb{G}_S$.

(d) SimpleQuestions with medium-scale KG_B (SQM-B). The KG $\mathbb{G}_{M-B}$ of SQM-B includes 90M entities, 12.2K relations and 202M triples, which completely covers $\mathbb{G}_S$.

A comparison of the four benchmarks, including the number of entities, relations, and triples, as well as the average degree of entities (reflecting benchmark complexity), is provided in Table 1.

Evaluation Metrics We evaluate the **accuracy**, **efficiency** and **scalability** of KGQA systems. The accuracy metric measures the correctness the correctness of inferred (s,r) pairs against the ground truth, where both subject $\hat{s}$ and predicate $\hat{r}$ must match:

$$accuracy = \frac{\sum_{i=1}^{N} 1_{[(\hat{s}_i,\hat{r}_i)=(s_i,r_i)]}}{N}, \tag{21}$$

where N is the number of questions.

We assess the average training and testing time of all KGQA systems, maintaining consistent batch sizes and negative sampling rates across different PLMs. To evalu-

[2]https://developers.google.com/freebase

ate **scalability**, we introduce two metrics: Variation in Accuracy (VA) and Variation in average test Time (VT).

Definition 1 (VA). *VA of a KGQA system in a benchmark KG_x represents the gap between the accuracy of the system on KG_x and the accuracy of the system on small-scale KG benchmarks* KGS. VA $= accuracy_{\text{KGS}} - accuracy_{KG_x}$, *where KG_x represents one of our four benchmarks. A **higher** VA means that the system performs worse in terms of scalability.*

Definition 2 (VT). *VT of a KGQA system on a benchmark KG_x represents the change in the average test time of the system on KG_x compared to the average test time of the system on small-scale KG benchmarks* KGS. VT $= time_{KGx} - time_{\text{KGS}}$, *where KG_x represents one of our four benchmarks. A **higher** VT means that the system performs worse in terms of scalability.*

These metrics help us understand the trade-offs between accuracy, efficiency, and scalability across different scales of KGs when deploying PLMs for KGQA tasks.

4.1.5. Experiments

In this section, we first present all the PLMs-based KGQA systems (Section 4.1.5) and the experimental setup (Section 4.1.5). We then show the overall experimental results and discuss the results in light of the three research questions (section 4.1.5). We further explore the sub-modules of KGQA and discuss them according to the three new research questions (Section 4.1.6). Besides, we also evaluate all systems on two other KGQA datasets apart from the SimpleQuestions family (Section 4.1.7). Finally, we compare the performance between ChatGPT and other PLMs on datasets SimpleQuestions, WebQuestionSP and FreebaseQA (Section 4.1.8).

All KGQA Systems Based on PLMs In this work, 18 KGQA systems (9 PLMs * 2 basic KGQA frameworks) were implemented for evaluation. **Three** classes of **nine** PLMs were used for evaluation, including the common large-scale PLMs BERT, ROBERTA, XLNET and GPT2, the lightweight PLMs ALBERT, DISTILBERT and DISTILROBERTA, and the knowledge-enhanced PLMs LUKE and KEPLER. As common models serve as the backbone models for lightweight PLMs and knowledge-enhanced PLMs, we follow [54] to further classify the common PLMs according to pre-trained task categories, namely, Masked Language Modeling (MLM, i.e., BERT and ROBERTA), Language Modeling (LM, i.e., GPT2), and Permuted Language Modeling (PeLM, i.e., XLNET).

Experimental Setup Experiments were conducted using an NVIDIA GeForce RTX 2080 TI GPU. We utilized a grid search to select optimal hyperparameters based on the highest accuracy achieved. An early stop strategy with a patience setting of 3 was used during training. Due to the large size of PLM-based entity disambiguation models, batch sizes were set to 1, supplemented by gradient accumulation to manage convergence challenges. This approach ensured consistency in the effective batch size across different PLMs within the same task, allowing for a fair comparison of training times. KGQA systems were configured to output Top-50 results for entity disambiguation and Top-5 for relation detection, enabling the combination of (subject, relation) pairs for final output.

Overall Results and Discussions In this section, we present the results of 18 KGQA systems using various PLMs and discuss their performance in terms of accuracy and efficiency. The key points of discussion are: (1) Which PLMs show the best performance in accuracy or efficiency? (2) How do the two KGQA frameworks differ in their performance? (3) How do the scalability of PLMs vary with the size of the KG?

Discussion on the Accuracy of KGQA systems The accuracy results for all PLM-based KGQA systems across different benchmarks are summarized in Table 2. The highest accuracy for each benchmark are highlighted in bold.

RoBERTa, LUKE, and KEPLER generally achieve the best accuracy results. Both LUKE and KEPLER, which are knowledge-enhanced and based on RoBERTa, excel in knowledge-intensive KGQA tasks, performing optimally on smaller-scale KGs. Conversely, RoBERTa performs better on larger-scale KGs, suggesting that the addition of knowledge-enhancement objectives may impact model robustness. The KGQArr framework outperforms KGQAcl on the small-scale KG (SQs), but this trend reverses as KG size increases, indicating that KGQArr may struggle with scalability. XLnet and GPT2 exhibit lower accuracy across most benchmarks. This may be due to their modeling approaches: XLnet uses a permutation-based language model and GPT2 an autoregressive model, both less suited for the NLU tasks typical of KGQA.

Table 2. Overall accuracy (%) of different PLMs-based KGQA systems on four benchmarks. Bolded numbers indicate the highest accuracy.

Frameworks	KGQACL				KGQARR			
PLMs \ **Benckmarks**	SQs	SQM-A	SQM-B	SQL	SQs	SQM-A	SQM-B	SQL
Common PLMs								
BERT (*MLM*)	74.79	68.02	66.03	64.81	76.76	67.75	66.54	65.39
ROBERTA (*MLM*)	75.32	68.97	**66.33**	**65.63**	77.12	68.20	**66.81**	**65.66**
XLNET (*PeLM*)	74.30	66.47	65.31	59.92	76.26	66.41	65.40	58.55
GPT2 (*LM*)	73.39	66.52	64.53	64.30	23.18	20.04	19.88	19.75
Lightweight PLMs								
ALBERT	74.26	67.01	65.37	64.66	76.20	66.80	65.60	65.10
DISTILBERT	74.29	67.87	65.45	64.36	75.11	68.07	65.55	64.46
DISTILROBERTA	74.04	67.32	64.67	64.39	73.24	67.37	65.48	64.00
Knowledge-enhanced PLMs								
LUKE	**75.67**	**69.25**	65.26	64.86	77.00	67.97	65.11	64.26
KEPLER	74.87	68.41	65.23	65.15	**77.41**	**68.41**	66.20	64.94

The scalability of the systems, analyzed using the VA and VT metrics (defined in Section 4.1.4), generally decreases as KG size increases. This is depicted in Figure 6. Notably: XLnet shows particularly poor scalability, especially in the largest KG (SQL). The knowledge-enhanced PLMs, LUKE and KEPLER, perform worse on larger KGs

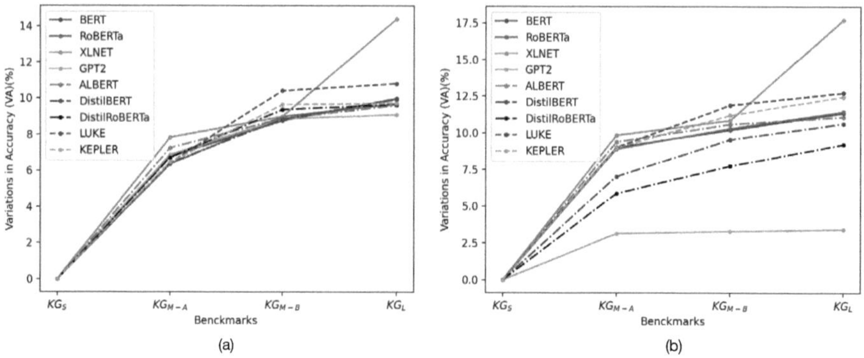

Figure 6. Scalability of all KGQACL frameworks (a) and KGQARR frameworks (b) in terms of accuracy variation.

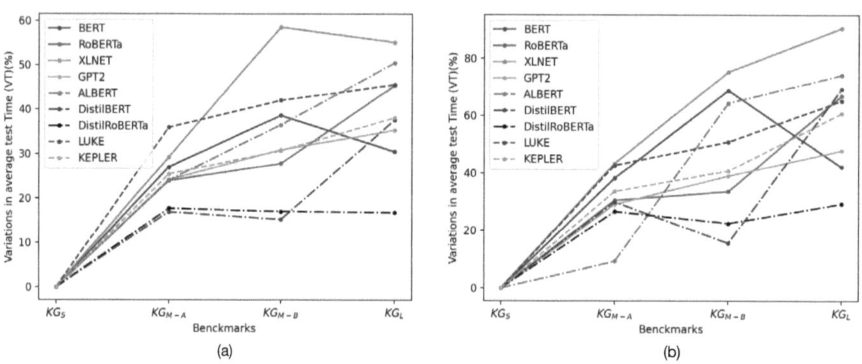

Figure 7. Scalability of all KGQACL frameworks (a) and KGQARR frameworks (b) in terms of average test time variation.

compared to other PLMs. In contrast, the lightweight models like DistilBERT and DistilRoBERTa exhibit better scalability and robustness to KG size variations.

Discussion on the Efficiency of KGQA Systems Efficiency results are detailed in Table 3, indicating the training and testing times for each system. Consistently: DistilBERT and DistilRoBERTa offer the best efficiency, significantly faster than other models like XLnet in both training and testing phases. The efficiency of all PLMs worsens as the KG size increases. The KGQArr framework consistently takes longer than KGQAcl, particularly as KG scale increases, suggesting a better efficiency profile for KGQAcl in larger KGs.

The efficiency scalability of all PLMs based on both frameworks is shown in Figure 7. All PLMs show an increasing trend in VT as the KG size increases. Among them, DISTILROBERTA has the best scalability as it has the smallest VT on all benchmarks. Another lightweight PLM, DITILBERT, also shows good scalability. Section 4.1.5 also demonstrates DISTILROBERTA and DITILBERT have the equivalent accuracy performance as the other PLMs on large-scale KG. These findings indicate that the two knowledge distillation PLMs have excellent scalability. The knowledge distillation is a promising approach for PLMs applied to KGQA.

Table 3. Efficiency of all PLMs-based KGQA frameworks on four benchmarks. Tr denotes average training time (ms) and Te denotes average test time (ms). Underlined ones indicate the shortest time spent.

Frameworks		KGQACL				KGQARR			
PLMs \ Benckmarks		SQS	SQM-A	SQM-B	SQL	SQS	SQM-A	SQM-B	SQL
Common PLMs									
BERT (*MLM*)	Tr	489.1	492.5	1042.8	584.5	1296.8	1190.4	2538.0	1563.7
	Te	45.9	72.9	84.5	76.4	70.4	108.6	139.2	112.6
ROBERTA (*MLM*)	Tr	523.6	782.8	701.0	772.6	1450.1	1341.8	1470.2	1906.1
	Te	45.8	69.7	73.6	91.2	70.0	100.5	103.6	136.9
XLNET (*PeLM*)	Tr	850.4	602.7	631.3	655.6	2325.5	2500.7	2308.9	1685.3
	Te	85.3	114.5	143.8	140.4	117.5	160.9	192.8	208.0
GPT2 (*LM*)	Tr	467.2	879.6	484.9	502.1	854.2	1341.1	1078.0	1076.9
	Te	48.4	72.5	79.3	83.7	75.6	104.7	114.6	123.5
Lightweight PLMs									
ALBERT	Tr	661.8	709.2	581.8	896.6	2679.6	1609.0	1500.8	1969.8
	Te	54.9	78.9	91.4	105.4	105.6	114.8	170.0	179.8
DISTILBERT	Tr	452.3	521.6	553.2	463.3	749.7	970.7	1169.4	1120.8
	Te	26.3	43.2	41.5	63.9	48.4	78.3	64.0	117.7
DISTILROBERTA	Tr	477.5	902.6	871.4	901.0	801.7	1422.6	1504.1	1290.6
	Te	28.0	45.7	45.0	44.8	42.9	69.5	65.4	72.2
Knowledge-enhanced PLMs									
LUKE	Tr	462.7	1227.3	590.5	634.1	1738.6	2430.3	2213.9	1609.2
	Te	41.5	77.4	83.5	87.1	67.9	110.6	118.8	133.1
KEPLER	Tr	960.5	1299.1	753.4	1130.7	2164.4	2522.4	2100.8	2011.5
	Te	48.4	73.8	79.1	86.5	69.0	102.6	109.8	129.8

New Research Questions From these observations, we formulate several new research questions: (1) What sub-modules of the KGQA system are primarily responsible for the differences in accuracy and efficiency? (2) What sub-modules in the KGQA system are most susceptible to the variation in the size of KG? (3) Why does the KGQARR framework have worse scalability? We explore these three questions by examining the performance of the submodules of all KGQA systems.

4.1.6. Study of the KGQA Sub-modules

Results and Discussion on KGQA Sub-modules We further compared the sub-module performance of each KGQA system in this section to explore the primary influencers of accuracy and efficiency for each PLMs. Additionally, we compared the two KGQA base frameworks to explore the reasons for their large variability.

We analyzed the results for Mention Detection (MD), Entity Disambiguation (ED), and Relation Detection (RD) across all systems. **Mention Detection (MD)**: All PLMs, except for GPT2, performed similarly in MD tasks. GPT2 struggled, likely due to its auto-regressive modeling approach, which is less suited for NER tasks. BERT achieved the highest F1 score but at a cost to efficiency, whereas its distilled counterpart, DistilBERT, nearly doubled the efficiency with only a minor drop in performance. **Entity Disambiguation (ED)**: RoBERTa had the best accuracy, while DistilBERT and DistilRoBERTa were the most efficient. The size of the KG significantly impacts the performance of ED tasks, with larger KGs leading to more candidate entities and connections, thereby affecting accuracy and test times. XLnet exhibited the largest accuracy decline, while ALbert saw the most significant increase in test times. **Relation Detection (RD)**: Significant performance differences were observed between the two frameworks. The KGQAcl framework was generally more efficient than KGQArr, which requires encoding all candidate relations for similarity calculations, making it more sensitive to increases in KG size. KGQArr demonstrated higher accuracy for smaller-scale KGs but did not scale as well with larger KGs.

4.1.7. Validation Beyond the SimpleQuestions Benchmarks

Beyond the SimpleQuestions dataset, we evaluated system performance on the WebQuestionSP and FreebaseQA datasets, both of which utilize the extensive Freebase KG and feature a high proportion of straightforward questions suitable for single-triple answers. After preprocessing to focus on simple questions amenable to our benchmarks, we observed consistent performance trends with our initial findings:

RoBERTa and Luke outperformed other models in accuracy, while GPT2 lagged, particularly under the KGQArr framework. DistilBERT and DistilRoBERTa showcased superior efficiency. Notably, all models underperformed on FreebaseQA, with Luke achieving the highest accuracy. An error analysis revealed substantial issues with question labeling and answerability within FreebaseQA.

These additional validations underscore the robustness of our findings across different datasets and highlight the critical balance between model complexity, efficiency, and accuracy in KGQA systems.

4.1.8. ChatGPT for Zero-Shot KGQA

We conducted experiments to evaluate the performance of ChatGPT[3] in comparison with other PLMs on a set of 300 questions sampled from the SimpleQuestions, WebQuestionSP, and FreebaseQA datasets. Notably, ChatGPT operated in a zero-shot KGQA setting, whereas the other PLMs were fine-tuned using training sets within their respective optimal frameworks (GPT2 in KGQACL and other PLMs in KGQARR). ChatGPT received the questions alongside a standard instruction to ensure consistency in response generation. Despite this, the responses generated by ChatGPT were evaluated against gold standard answers by two professionals to ensure accuracy and reliability.

Table 4 demonstrates that ChatGPT significantly outperformed other PLMs on WebQuestionSP by up to 12% and on FreebaseQA by up to 54%. However, its performance

[3]The version of ChatGPT is Jau 30, 2023.

Table 4. Accuracy (%) of ChatGPT, KGQACL framework with GPT2 and KGQARR frameworks with the other PLMs on SimpleQuestions (SQ), WebQuestionSP (WB) and FreebaseQA (FBQ). Bolded numbers indicate the highest accuracy.

PLMs	Benckmarks		
	SQ	WQ	FBQ
BERT	76.7	68.7	41.7
ROBERTA	**77.7**	69.0	42.0
XLNET	75.7	68.0	41.0
GPT2	72.7	64.3	39.0
ALBERT	76.3	66.7	41.3
DISTILBERT	76.7	67.7	41.3
DISTILROBERTA	76.0	67.0	40.3
LUKE	78.0	68.3	42.0
KEPLER	77.3	68.7	41.7
CHATGPT	29.3	**76.3**	**93.7**

on SimpleQuestions was notably poor, with an accuracy of only 29.3%. This variance in performance is likely due to the origins of the datasets: WebQuestionSP and FreebaseQA questions are derived from web sources, which may be represented in ChatGPT's training data, whereas SimpleQuestions' human-crafted items based on Freebase triples might not be as well represented.

We further categorized the error cases of ChatGPT on SimpleQuestions. Further analysis revealed that 38.2% of errors on SimpleQuestions were due to enumeration issues, where ChatGPT failed to include all correct items in its responses. Additionally, 26.9% of errors were categorized as wrong answers, where ChatGPT's responses did not match the gold answers. Notably, there was evidence of factual inaccuracies, or "hallucinations", where ChatGPT provided factually incorrect information. Issues of ambiguity and lack of necessary knowledge were evident in 22.6% of errors, and misunderstandings of question semantics constituted 1.4% of errors.

4.1.9. Conclusion

Due to the improved performance of PLMs on most NLP tasks, it has become a consensus to use PLMs as a skeleton to solve NLP tasks. In this chapter, we describe the application of PLMs to solve a knowledge-intensive task, namely knowledge graph question answering. We conduct comprehensive experiments to explore the accuracy and efficiency performance of PLMs on KGQA, as well as the scalability of PLMs as KG size increases. In addition, we compare the performance between ChatGPT and other PLMs on three KGQA datasets. We present a detailed analysis of these experimental results and draw some important conclusions regarding the use of PLMs in KGQA.

1. **Performance by PLM Type**: ROBERTA, LUKE, and KEPLER consistently showed superior accuracy across different KG scales. However, LUKE and KEPLER performed best on smaller-scale KGs, while ROBERTA excelled on larger ones.

2. **Efficiency and Scalability**: Lightweight PLMs like DistilBert and DistilRoBERTa demonstrated high efficiency and scalability, performing comparably to heavier models on larger KGs despite their simplified architecture.
3. **Modeling Approach**: The performance of XLNet and Gpt2 lagged, particularly in scenarios that favored masked language modeling over their respective permuted and autoregressive approaches.
4. **Comparison with Traditional Methods**: Despite advancements, PLMs did not significantly outperform a traditional fuzzy matching method in entity disambiguation within the broader context of KGQA, suggesting that the final answer accuracy was minimally impacted by the sophisticated capabilities of PLMs.
5. **ChatGPT's Zero-Shot Performance**: While ChatGPT excelled in zero-shot settings on WebQuestions and FreebaseQA, its performance dipped on the manually curated SimpleQuestions. This highlights potential limitations in its training corpus and the impact of dataset construction on model efficacy.

These findings enrich our understanding of PLM capabilities and limitations in KGQA tasks, highlighting the need for careful consideration of the dataset characteristics and the specific capabilities of each model type. Future research will continue to refine these approaches and explore more neuro-symbolic systems to enhance the scalability and accuracy of PLMs in diverse NLP tasks.

4.2. End-to-End KGQA

In this section, we present a complex end-to-end KGQA system named GETT-QA [133]. GETT-QA produces SPARQL quries for given questions, and hence is a semantic parsing-based system, and belongs to the *neuro-symbolic* family.

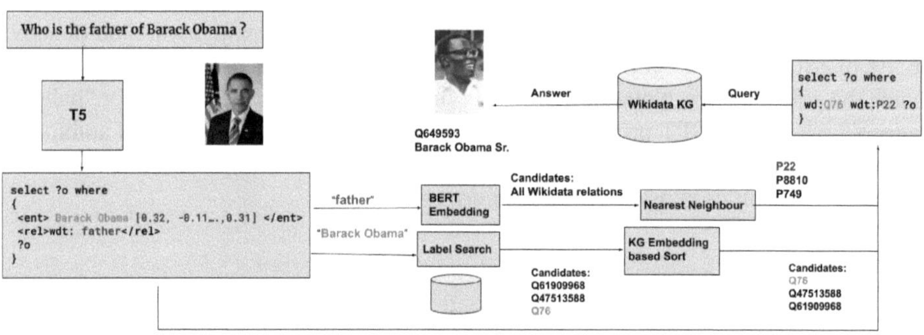

Figure 8. Architecture of GETT-QA: T5 generates a skeleton SPARQL query with entity and relation labels and a truncated KG embedding string. The entity labels are grounded using label based search and embedding based sorting, while the relations are grounded using BERT embedding based sorting. The final query is executed against a KG to fetch the answer. Source [133]

As shown in Figure 8, the system consists of five major steps:

- T5 generates a skeleton SPARQL query from input natural language question.
- The entity labels and truncated KG embeddings are extracted. A label search is performed to fetch entity candidates.

- The entity candidates are re-ranked using an embedding similarity metric.
- In parallel, the relation label is extracted and matched against Wikidata relations based on BERT embeddings.
- The final query is grounded to KG nodes and executed to receive the answer.

4.2.1. Truncated KG Embeddings

T5 is trained to generate truncated vector strings of KG embeddings. We use TransE [163] embeddings for Wikidata entities that were provided by Pytorch-BigGraph[4] [164]. These are 200-dimensional vectors of floats. The truncated KG embeddings used are a shorter version of the same embeddings. For most experiments, the first 10 dimensions of these embeddings are used, and the precision of the floats are further reduced to 3 digits after the decimal. This is done since T5 is expected to produce these truncated KG embeddings while still in the text-to-text mode. In other words, T5 produces these vectors of floats considering them as a string. Truncated KG embeddings are used instead of original embeddings to reduce the decoding load of T5. The aim is not to learn the entire embedding space. Instead, the aim is to learn identifiers that can aid the entity disambiguation phase. We produce these truncated KG embeddings only for entities, not for relations.

4.2.2. Intuition

The initial idea behind the approach is to allow T5 to use its significant linguistic capability derived from pre-training over a large corpus for the task of semantic parsing. As a result, T5 is used to produce SPARQL tokens and entity and relation labels.

At first glance, it may appear that the production of entity labels is sufficient for grounding to KG entity nodes. However, in most KGs, several entities share the same labels. For example in Wikidata KG, the entity IDs `Q76` and `Q47513588` both share the label `Barack Obama`. In reality, `Q76` represents the President while `Q47513588` is the entity ID for a painting of the President. As a result of such collision of labels, a further step called *disambiguation* is required.

The next idea is to not just rely on T5's linguistic abilities but also to try and teach the model how to generate identifiers for the entities, which can aid the grounding and disambiguation process in a subsequent step. One way could be to generate the Wikidata IDs directly. However, the IDs do not correspond in any hierarchical way to the underlying entities. For example, while `Q76` is `Barack Obama`, `Q77` is `Uruguay`. Although the IDs are close to each other, the categories are completely different. Models cannot be expected to produce accurate IDs of this nature, especially on unseen input questions. As a result, other schemes of entity identifiers are considered that exhibit some hierarchical properties.

It turns out KG embeddings fulfill these requirements handsomely, and hence it is decided to use truncated KG embeddings as the "soft" identifier of choice. Another possibility would be to generate entity descriptions instead of truncated KG embeddings, however, roughly 50% of entities in Wikidata do not have corresponding descriptions (eg: Q67395985[5]), hence the focus on generating truncated KG embeddings instead.

[4] `https://github.com/facebookresearch/PyTorch-BigGraph`
[5] `https://www.wikidata.org/wiki/Q67395985`

While the production of such truncated embeddings may also aid the grounding of relations, this is not attempted, since Wikidata only contains a few thousand relations, while the number of entities run into several millions. For the grounding of relations, a simpler text embedding based method is used, as described later in Section 4.2.7.

4.2.3. Models

We experiment with fine-tuning two variants of the T5 model: `T5-Small` with 60 million parameters and `T5-Base` with 220 million parameters. For the GETT-QA system results reported in Tables 7 and 8 the `T5-Base` based model is used, whereas in the analysis Section 4.2.11 a comparative study against `T5-Small` is presented.

4.2.4. Skeleton SPARQL

As shown in Figure 8, the first step of the KGQA system is to generate a skeleton SPARQL query from the given natural language question. The skeleton query consists of SPARQL tokens such as `SELECT, WHERE, {}`, entity and relation labels, and truncated KG embeddings, which are an array of `floats`. Some additional tokens are used to surround the entity and relation labels, such as `<ent>, </ent>,<rel>,</rel>` so that in a later step their extraction can be performed using regular-expression operations. The extraction of the labels and the truncated KG embedding are essential for the subsequent grounding step. Notably, entity and relation IDs are not a part of a skeleton SPARQL query.

During training via fine-tuning, pairs of questions and skeleton SPARQL queries are presented to T5. For this purpose, the original dataset is pre-processed, which contains gold SPARQL queries for each question. The SPARQL query is converted to a skeleton SPARQL query by replacing the entity and relation IDs with their gold labels while appending the entity labels with a truncated KG embedding. Hence, the following gold SPARQL query:

```
select ?o where {  wd:Q76 wdt:P22 ?o }
```

is converted to:

```
select ?o where
{
 <ent>Barack Obama [...] </ent>
 <rel>father</rel>
 ?o
}
```

for the purposes of training T5, where the truncated KG embedding is represented by `[...]`.

4.2.5. Entity Candidates

During inference, when T5 generates a skeleton query, all entity and relation labels, as well as truncated KG embeddings, are extracted using regular expressions. For the entity labels, a BM-25-based [154] label search is performed on a database of all Wikidata entity labels, out of which top-k candidates are retrieved per entity label. For this text search we use the Elasticsearch database[6]. For the experiments, k is fixed at 100.

4.2.6. *Entity Candidates Re-ranking and Ordering*

The top-3 entity candidates based on label matching are retained. For the next 3 candidates, truncated KG embedding-based sorting is used. For each item in the list of 100 entity candidates fetched, their gold KG embeddings are also fetched, and converted to truncated KG embeddings. For the truncated KG embedding generated by T5, its dot product is computed against the gold truncated KG embeddings fetched and re-rank them in descending order. The dot product is used as a comparator because this was the same function that was used during the production of the TransE embeddings. From this re-ranked list based on truncated KG embedding similarity, top-3 candidates are retained.

These `top-3` truncated KG embedding-sorted candidates are appended to the `top-3` label-sorted candidates, and proceed to the subsequent steps with a list of 6 candidate entities for each entity label.

4.2.7. *Relation Candidates*

No truncated KG embeddings for relation IDs are generated, as their numbers are orders of magnitudes smaller when compared to entities in Wikidata. From the relation labels generated by T5, compute their BERT embeddings are computed and the cosine similarity against the BERT embeddings are found for all Wikidata properties. The list of properties is sorted based on this similarity score, and the top-3 matches are considered for the subsequent steps.

4.2.8. *Candidate Combinations*

For a generated query, each entity label and each relation label has 6 and 3 candidates each, respectively. The serial order of the entities is preserved and relations as produced in the query, and generated all possible combinations of the entities and relations, which generates several queries of the same structure but different entity and relation IDs. For example, if the query contains just one entity and one relation, the number of possible SPARQL queries generated would be $6 \times 3 = 18$. Each query is excecuted on the KG in sorted order of entity and relation IDs received in previous steps. The execution is stopped when the KG returns a non-empty response. This response is considered the output of our KGQA system. The top 3 beams produced by T5 decoder are considered as probable queries. The first beam producing a valid response from the KG is considered the output of our KGQA system.

4.2.9. *Dataset*

The authors evaluate their approach on the LC-QuAD 2.0 [155] dataset, which consists of approximately 30,000 questions based on the Wikidata KG. Each question contains the corresponding SPARQL query as gold annotation. The dataset consists of a wide variety of questions, such as simple, complex, multi-hop, count, min/max, dual and boolean types. This dataset also uses the recently introduced hyper-relational [156] structure of the Wikidata KG.

[6] `https://www.elastic.co/`

Table 5. Sample question from LC-QuAD 2.0

Question	SPARQL
Tell me the female beauty pageant that operates in all countries and contains the word model in it's name?	`SELECT DISTINCT ?sbj ?sbj_label WHERE { ?sbj wdt:P31 wd:Q58863414 . ?sbj wdt:P2541 wd:Q62900839 . ?sbj rdfs:label ?sbj_label . FILTER(CONTAINS(lcase(?sbj_label), "model")) . FILTER (lang(?sbj_label) = "en") } LIMIT 25`

Table 6. Sample question from SimpleQuestions-Wikidata

Question	SPARQL
What type of music does David Ruffin play ?	`SELECT ?x WHERE { wd:Q1176417 wdt:P136 ?x }`

Table 7. Results on LC-QuAD 2.0

	P@1
UNIK-QA	0.005
Pullnet	0.011
Platypus	0.036
QAnswer	0.308
UNIQORN	0.331
GETT-QA without truncated embeddings	0.327 ± 0.002
GETT-QA (with truncated embeddings)	$\mathbf{0.403} \pm 0.0$

Table 8. Results on SimpleQuestions-Wikidata

	F1
KEQA	0.405
Text2Graph	0.618
GETT-QA without truncated embeddings	0.752 ± 0.004
GETT-QA (with truncated embeddings)	$\mathbf{0.761} \pm 0.002$

Additionally, they evaluate their approach on the SimpleQuestions-Wikidata [157][7] dataset, which consists of 34,374 train questions and 9,961 test questions. This dataset is derived from the original SimpleQuestions dataset [132], which was later aligned with the Wikidata KG. A sample question from each dataset can be seen in Tables 5 and 6.

4.2.10. Results

In Table 7, the bottom two rows contain the results of GETT-QA system in two different settings for LC-QuAD 2.0. In the first case, GETT-QA uses the top-6 entity candidates based on label match, without the use of truncated KG embeddings for re-ranking. In the

[7] `https://github.com/askplatypus/wikidata-simplequestions`

second case, the top-3 entity candidates are retained based on label match and appended to the top-3 candidates based on truncated KG embedding match.

The key finding in Table 7 is that when compared to the last two rows, GETT-QA system performs better with an absolute gain of approximately 8% when truncated KG embeddings are used.

In Table 8, for SimpleQuestions-Wikidata the method without truncated KG embeddings already outperforms the nearest competitor by an absolute margin of 13%. This demonstrates the natural ability of T5 to predict the correct entity and relation labels given a question. Since the query structure of all the questions in this dataset is the same, no challenge is posed to T5 in trying to learn the query itself. It is noteworthy however, that after the inclusion of truncated KG embedding re-ranking, the performance remains similar. An insignificant margin of absolute improvement of 0.9% is seen.

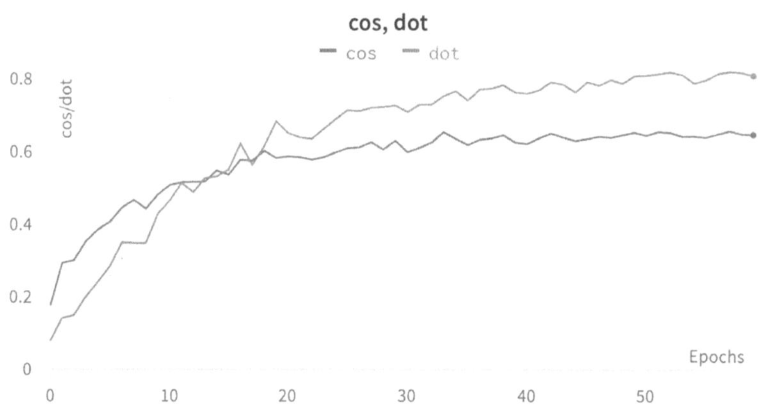

Figure 9. Cosine and Dot Product based similarities of truncated KG embeddings

4.2.11. Truncated KG Embedding Learning

It is discovered that T5 is able to produce a vector of floats while still in the text-to-text mode of decoding. For this functionality, no change of loss function or decoding scheme is made in the experiments. It effectively learns a simplified embedding space, but with certain limitations. To further explore this ability of T5, the authors performed some additional experiments on the 200 questions dev set of LC-QuAD 2.0 with `T5-Small`.

In Figure 9, the authors compare how the model learns the embedding space with each epoch of training. The TransE embeddings have an angular component and a magnitude component. Since the dot operation was used to train the original embeddings, the magnitude of each embedding may be greater than 1. It appears in Figure 9 that around step 20 the angular component of the embeddings has been learned by T5 to the best of its abilities, and it proceeds to learn the magnitude component (denoted by the orange line) further.

In Figure 10 the authors chart the LC-QuAD 2.0 dev set performance of `T5-Small` and `T5-Base` in varying truncated KG embedding lengths. For `T5-Small` (pink line) they set the truncated KG embedding length at 30, so this should only directly be com-

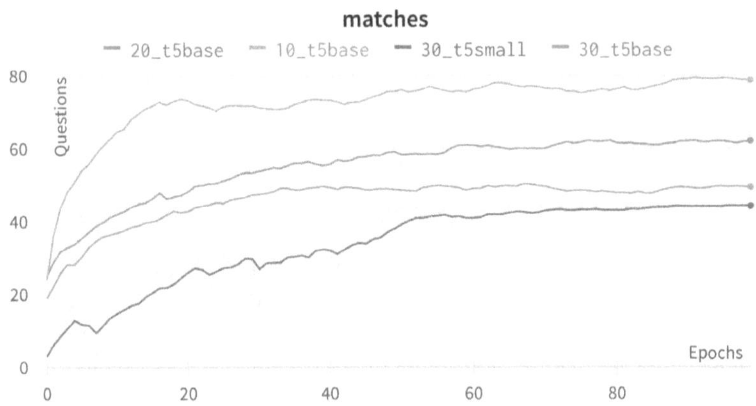

Figure 10. Dev Set matches for varying truncated KG embedding lengths

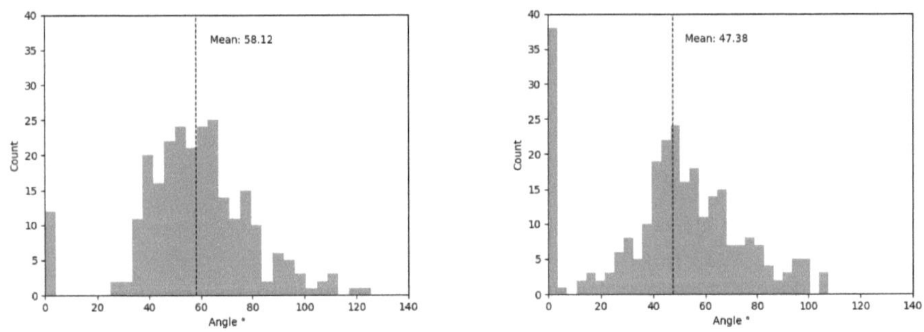

(a) 10 epochs (b) 40 epochs

Figure 11. Distribution of angular difference between gold and predicted truncated KG embeddings on LC-QuAD 2.0 dev set. The mean angular difference can be seen reducing as the epochs progress, suggesting that the model is learning the embedding space.

pared against `T5-Base` with truncated KG embedding length 30 (green line). In the matches metric, which only looks at the keywords and labels produced in the skeleton SPARQL query (truncated KG embeddings have been removed from the generated query), the two reach similar performance. This suggests that a larger number of parameters helps learn the embedding space better, but for the textual component the extra number of parameters of `T5-Base` remain unused.

With a truncated KG embedding length of 10 (yellow line), we see the best label match accuracy and hence we persist with this family of models for reporting results in Table 7.

In Figure 11, they plot the distribution of the angular difference between the gold and predicted truncated embeddings on the LC-QuAD 2.0 dev set. The model seems to learn the embedding space in two distinctly different manners: firstly, for several entities it is able to print the exact embedding, with an angular difference of $0°$. Secondly, for the entities which it is unable to learn the embedding of exactly, it produces a more familiar distribution, where the mean shifts every few epochs, reducing the angular difference. This suggests that the model is learning the embedding space effectively.

4.3. Evaluation of LLMs for KGQA

In this section, we delve into the evaluation of the current open-domain LLM in the context of the KGQA task, discussing three research questions:

RQ1:Can LLM directly serve as a support for natural language question-answering within an open-domain KB? Specifically, this section necessitates a discussion on the question-answering performance and robustness of LLM KGQA, comparing it with existing robust traditional models.

RQ2: Can LLM address diverse types of complex questions? In this segment, we analyze the strengths and weaknesses of LLM across two dimensions: the factual nature of the questions and the composite reasoning required to answer them.

RQ3: What does In-context learning contribute to LLM KGQA? In-Context Learning (ICL) has been demonstrated as a highly effective approach to enhancing LLM's performance in downstream tasks. When considering LLM as a KB or KGQA model, the focus of this segment lies in determining the form of human thought guidance or constraints that are most acceptable to LLM.

Evaluation Framework The evaluation framework for LLM KGQA is illustrated in Figure 12, consists of four primary modules. The Question Type Labeling module assigns predefined type labels to each question. The QA Prompt Construction module generates four QA prompts with ICL strategy for each question. The Answer Checking module assesses the correctness of LLMs' responses In the Performance Evaluation part, three evaluation objectives are established. The Overall Evaluation focuses on the overall QA performance of the LLMs. The Question-type Focused Evaluation concentrates on identifying the types of questions that the LLM excels at or struggles with. Lastly, the CheckList-based evaluation aims to assess the LLM's robustness such as basic reasoning abilities, output consistency, and controllability.

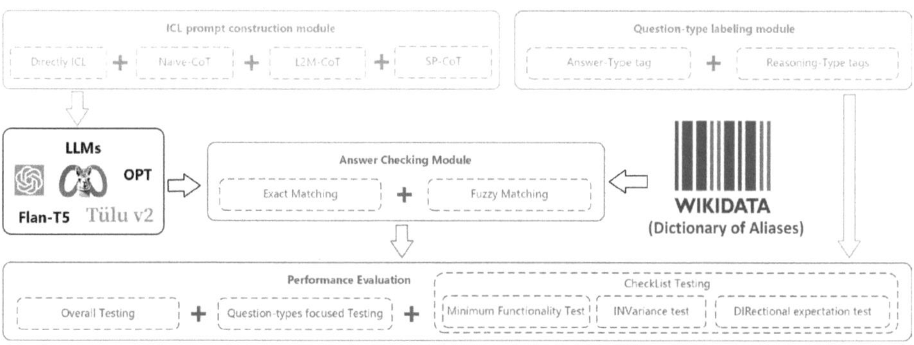

Figure 12. The framework for LLM KGQA evaluation

In the Question Type Labeling module, complex inquiries are categorized based on both the types of answers required to address the questions and the composite reasoning types needed to do so. Table 9 enumerates the definitions of each type accordingly.

There are eight answer types, namely Person (PER), Location (LOC), Reason (WHY), Date (DATE), Organization (ORG), Yes/No (Boolean), Number (NUM), and Miscellaneous fact (MISC), as well as seven types of reasoning: set operations (SetOperation), conditional filtering (Filter), numerical computation (Counting), comparative (Comparative), single-hop reasoning (Single-hop), chained multi-hop reasoning (Multi-hop), and multi-hop reasoning with a star-shaped query subgraph (Star-shape). I have refined this passage to make it more coherent and fluid.

Table 9. The feature-driven question tags defined in this paper.

Answer type	Description
MISC	The answer to the question is the miscellaneous fact defined by the named entity recognition task.
PER	The answer to the question is the name of a person.
LOC	The answer to the question is a location.
WHY	The answer explains the reasons for the facts mentioned in the question.
DATE	The answer to the question is a date or time.
NUM	The answer to the question is a number.
Boolean	The answer to the question is yes or no.
ORG	The answer to the question is the name of a organization.
UNA	The input question is unable to answer.
Reasoning type	**Description**
SetOperation	The process of obtaining answers involves set operations.
Filter	The answer is obtained through condition filtering.
Counting	The process of obtaining an answer involves counting operations.
Comparative	The answer needs to be obtained by comparing or sorting numerical values.
Single-hop	Answering questions requires a single-hop Reasoning.
Multi-hop	Answering questions requires multi-hop Reasoning.
Star-shape	The reasoning graph corresponding to inputting question is star-shape.

In the QA prompt construction module, we not only consider non-ICL and Directly ICL, but also draw from previous multi-step prompt KGQA works to establish three CoTs, all of which are founded on the core strategy of 'complex question decomposition'. These include:

(a) Naive-CoT, as shown in Table 10, a demonstration is provided to guide LLMs in decomposing the original question into 3-5 sub-questions and prompting the LLMs to answer each of these sub-questions. Subsequently, these sub-questions, along with the corresponding LLMs' answers, are concatenated with the original questions and used to prompt the LLMs for a final response;

(b) SP-CoT, as shown in Table 11, Inspired by [81], a CoT is constructed based on semantic parsing for question decomposition. The original query is designed to align with three clauses within the structured query. The 'From' clause specifies the entity type related to the query, the 'SELECT' clause corresponds to the reasoning operation necessary for deriving the response, and the 'WHERE' clause denotes the constraint conditions. A predefined process is established for handling queries, requiring sequential responses from the LLM to these three inquiries. Each subsequent response builds upon

Table 10. Demonstration of CoT-Naive

Instruction	**<Instruction>** Answer the input question. You can generate any intermediate lists and states, but the final output should only contain the exact answer(s): {'Answer(s) to the input question...'} **</Instruction>**
Approach	**<Approach>** To answer the input question follow these steps: 1. Generate 5 sub-questions based on the input question. 2. Answer the generated sub-questions. 3. Answer the input question. **</Approach>**

Examples	**<Examples>**
	Input: For what was John Houseman (who is in the Jewish ethnic group) nominated for an Academy Award for Best Picture ?
	Sub questions:
	['Who is John Houseman?','What is the Jewish ethnic group?','Was John Houseman nominated for an Academy Award','In which category was John Houseman nominated?','What was the film John Houseman was nominated for in the category of Best Picture at the Academy Awards?']
	Answers to Sub-questions:
	['Who is John Houseman?','What is the Jewish ethnic group?','Was John Houseman nominated for an Academy Award','In which category was John Houseman nominated?','What was the film John Houseman was nominated for in the category of Best Picture at the Academy Awards?']
	Output:
	{
	'John Houseman, being a prominent figure in the film industry, was nominated for an Academy Award for Best Picture as a producer. His nomination was for the film "Julius Caesar.," which was released in 1973.'
	SPARQL: SELECT count(*) FROM city WHERE city.population > 150,000
	}
	</Examples>

the context provided by the previous one. Upon completion of all three responses, the structured query associated with the original question is considered resolved;

(c) L2M-CoT, taking inspiration from the research of [82], as shown in Table 12, the process of addressing complex questions is divided into two stages: i. Decomposition: This stage involves a prompt that includes an example demonstrating the decomposition process, followed by the presentation of the specific question to be decomposed; ii. Sub-question solving: The prompt for this stage comprises three components: (1) an example illustrating the resolution of sub-questions; (2) a potentially empty list of previously addressed sub-questions and their resultant solutions, and (3) the question awaiting an answer. These two stages are carried out iteratively for the input question, with the LLM independently determining the termination condition, indicating whether sufficient information has been gathered from the sub-questions to answer the original input question. Ultimately, the LLM produces the final answer.

For the assessment of LLMs' performance in Knowledge Graph Question Answering (KGQA) tasks, an expanded answer matching approach is proposed. As figure 13

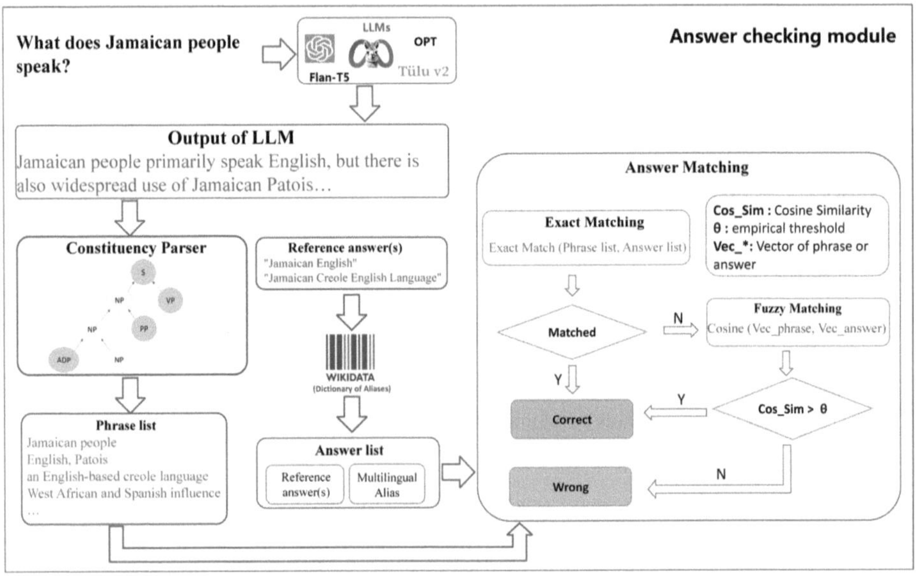

Figure 13. The Answer Checking Module first parses the output from the LLMs into candidate answers(or a list of candidate answers) using a constituent tree. Subsequently, the gold answer is expanded into a list of gold answers, leveraging the multilingual aliases provided by Wikidata. The Module performs an exact match between the candidate answer list and the gold answer list. If the exact match fails and the answer type meets the conditions for fuzzy matching, we employ fuzzy matching based on vector similarity and an empirical threshold.

shows, it comprises three primary components: The parsing of LLMs' output involves the use of constituent trees [83] to extract NP or VP root node phrases, establishing the candidate answer pool. Each reference answer is enriched with multilingual alias lists sourced from WikiData, encompassing a range of names and aliases. These broadened reference answers are subsequently utilized for exact matching with the candidate answers. In cases where an exact match falls short, m-BERT [84] is employed to calculate the maximum Cosine similarity between the reference and candidate answers to facilitate fuzzy matching. This fuzzy matching strategy is applied exclusively for answer types that are not 'NUM', 'DATE', or 'Boolean'. The experience threshold, as per our prior work [85], is set at 0.78 to minimize the occurrence of false positives and false negatives.

In the Performance Evaluation phase, we take a different approach compared to the Overall and Question-Type focused evaluations, which assess QA accuracy based on sample division. For the CheckList-based evaluation, we need to design specific evaluation metrics for each of the three testing objectives: MFT, INV, and DIR, within the context of KGQA.

MFT is designed to evaluate the basic functionalities of a model. In the context of KGQA, we identify the core functionality of a model as its capacity to perform various types of reasoning. Thus, we focus on assessing the QA performance of LLMs by limiting the scope to questions that involve only a single type of reasoning operation. Following this, we compare and analyze how the models perform when tasked with questions that require a single reasoning operation versus those require multiple reasoning operations.

Table 11. Demonstration of CoT-SP

Instruction	**<Instruction>** Answer the input question. You can generate any intermedate lists and states, but the final output should only contain the exact answer(s): {'Answer(s) to the input question...'} **</Instruction>**
Approach	**<Approach>** To answer the input question follow these steps: 1. Determine the topic entity type of the input question. 2. Determine the reasoning operation in the input question. 3. Determine the conditional constraints in the input question. 4. Generate the SPARQL query for input question. 5. Answer the input question based on the SPARQL query. **</Approach>**

Examples	**<Examples>**
	Input: how many major cities are there ?
	From_QA:
	('Question: 'how many major cities are there ?', what is the sentence talks about?','Answer: city')
	SELECT_QA:
	('Question: 'how many major cities are there? ' from city, what is the sentence asks to select?','Answer: count(*)')
	WHERE_QA:
	('Question: 'how many major cities are there?' from city select count(*), what is the sentence requires ?','Answer: city.population > 150,000')
	SPARQL: SELECT count(*) FROM city WHERE city.population > 150,000
	Output:
	{
	The number of major cities can vary depending on the criteria used to define a "major" city. Generally, major cities are often determined based on factors such as population, economic significance, cultural importance, infrastructure, and political influence. Different sources may provide different lists of major cities. For example, some common lists include the Global Cities Index, Megacity classification, or simply cities with high population numbers. According to the United Nations, as of 2021, there are more than 30 megacities (cities with a population of over 10 million) worldwide, and numerous other cities with populations ranging from millions to several hundred thousand.It's important to note that the exact number of major cities can change over time due to urbanization, population growth, and other factors.
	}
	</Examples>

The INV test is designed to assess the model's capability to generate similar or identical responses to multiple similar or identical queries, thereby evaluating the consistency of the model's output. Following the methodology outlined in [86], we record instances where the LLM receives five identical or similar inputs for the same question across 'Non-ICL input', 'Directly-ICL input', and the three 'CoT-ICL inputs'. We then tally the accuracy of the answers provided. If the output accuracy remains consistent across all five instances, it suggests that the LLM exhibits consistency for that test sample. We calculate the model's consistency ratio across the entire dataset, which serves as the evaluation metric for the INV test.

Table 12. Demonstration of CoT-L2M

Instruction	**<Instruction>** Answer the input question. You can generate any intermediate lists and states, but the final output should only contain the exact answer(s): {'Answer(s) to the input question...'} **</Instruction>**
Approach	**<Approach>** To answer the input question follow these steps: 1. Find the current first sub-question need to solve. 2. Answer the generated sub-question, and find the current first sub-question need to solve. 3. Answer the input question. **</Approach>**

Examples	**<Examples>**
	Input: For what was John Houseman (who is in the Jewish ethnic group) nominated for an Academy Award for Best Picture?
	Iteration question and answering:
	{
	Iteration 1
	Q1: To solve "For what was John Houseman (who is in the Jewish ethnic group) nominated for an Academy Award for Best Picture ?", what we need to solve first?
	A1: Has John Houseman ever been nominated for an Academy Award for Best Picture?
	Q2: Has John Houseman ever been nominated for an Academy Award for Best Picture?
	A2: Yes
	Iteration 2
	Q1: To solve "For what was John Houseman (who is in the Jewish ethnic group) nominated for an Academy Award for Best Picture ?", we know that John Houseman have been nominated for an Academy Award for Best Picture.Then, what we need to solve next?
	A1: Which specific movie was John Houseman nominated for Best Picture ?
	Q2: Which specific movie was John Houseman nominated for Best Picture ?
	A2: Julius Caesar
	Iteration End
	Q: We know that John Houseman have been nominated for an Academy Award for Best Picture. we know that the John Houseman's movie Julius Caesar win an Academy Award for Best Picture. So, For what was John Houseman (who is in the Jewish ethnic group) nominated for an Academy Award for Best Picture ?
	A: Julius Caesar
	}
	Output:
	{
	'John Houseman, being a prominent figure in the film industry, was nominated for an Academy Award for Best Picture as a producer. His nomination was for the film "Julius Caesar.," which was released in 1973.'
	}
	</Examples>

The DIR test aims to evaluate whether LLMs can produce outputs that meet expectations when the inputs are modified, thus reflecting the controllability of the model's output. In our evaluation, we utilize the success rate of LLMs in generating complete intermediate results and final answers in a format that align with CoT prompts during the

QA process. This success rate serves as the evaluation metric for DIR test.

Datasets Five representative Knowledge Graph Question Answering (KGQA) datasets were chosen for this endeavor. Upon sampling, the answer types and reasoning types for the question set were uniformly annotated, thus creating the evaluation test data for this chapter. The statistical details are presented in Table 14.

Comparison of the LLMs with Traditional KGQA Models (RQ1) The overall results displayed in Table 13 indicate a significant shortfall of LLMs when compared to traditional KGQA models across four datasets: KQApro, LC-Quad2.0, CWQ, and GrailQA. Interestingly, LLMs show superior performance in two datasets, GraphQuestions (surpassing the best traditional models by 29.21%) and WQSP (surpassing the best traditional models by 3.71%). Notably, no new state-of-the-art models have been proposed for the GraphQuestions dataset since 2022. Among the datasets where traditional KGQA models perform better, the least margin by which a traditional model surpasses the highest-scoring LLM is on CWQ (3.89%), and the most is on KQAPro (43.5%).

On the other hand, the CheckList test results further highlight the gap between current LLMs and becoming reliable knowledge bases and question-answering models. Table 14 reflects the consistency (or stability) of LLMs when given 5 identical inputs. 'CCCCC' indicates all outputs provide correct answers, while 'WWWWW' indicates all outputs provide wrong answers. The sum of the proportions of these two results reflects the model's consistency performance. It can be observed that the model with the best consistency performance is GPT-4, which also has the highest "CCCCC" proportion. LLaMA2-7B achieves a level close to the GPT-3.5-turbo series. Moreover, by observing the consistency scores of LLaMA2-7B and Vicuna-7B-v1.5, it can be seen that the fine-tuning carried out by Vicuna has harmed the consistency of the model. It's worth noting that, compared to the 100% consistency of traditional KGQA models, a significant gap still exists in LLMs, which severely limits their potential to become reliable knowledge graphs and QA systems. When LLMs use ICL strategies, besides focusing on the accuracy of the final output of the model, it is also crucial to pay attention to whether the LLMs can follow the question decomposition process prescribed by ICL prompts, which reflects the controllability of the LLMs. As shown in Table 15, the open-source LLMs represented by OPT, LLaMA2, and Vicuna perform poorly in terms of controllability, especially the combination of the OPT model with SP-CoT and LLaMA2 with Naive-COT. In stark contrast, the controllability of the GPT series is all above 92%, with GPT4 performing the best at 98%. This indicates that there is still considerable room for improvement in the controllability of the output of current open-source LLMs.

In summary of the aforementioned evaluation results, although current LLMs can superficially perform the function of answering open-domain questions using their own knowledge, their question-answering performance, consistency as answering models, and the lower adherence to user instructions exhibited by open-source LLMs restrict them from directly becoming reliable knowledge bases and question-answering models.

Table 13. The overall QA results on each dataset are presented, where 'SOTA' signifies the best-performing traditional models (non-LLM-based KGQA models, encompassing both supervised and unsupervised models) on the datasets. The LLM and its variants from the same series, along with versions implementing ICL strategies, are grouped together. The top five scores on each dataset are highlighted, with darker shades representing higher scores. Among the datasets, LC-quad2.0 and GraphQuestions are evaluated using the F1 metric, while the remaining datasets employ Accuracy (Hits@1) as the evaluation metric. '↑' indicates that ICL strategy improves the model's score, while '↓' indicates that ICL strategy decreases the model's score.

Datasets	KQApro	LC-quad2.0	WQSP	CWQ	GrailQA	GraphQuestions
	Acc	F1	Acc	Acc	Acc	F1
SOTA(supervised)	95.32 [8]	83.45 [9]	82.10 [90]	72.20 [88]	76.31	31.8 [89]
SOTA(unsupervised)	94.20 [87]	-	62.98 [91]	-	-	-
FLAN-T5-XXL	37.27	30.14	59.87	46.69	29.02	32.27
LLaMA2-7B	49.78	50.85	82.39	63.04	46.74	61.01
LLaMA2-7B-Direct	44.79 ↓	44.88 ↓	69.16 ↓	55.49 ↓	38.46 ↓	45.92 ↓
LLaMA2-7B-Naive	50.59 ↑	44.86 ↓	73.36 ↓	58.24 ↓	40.47 ↓	50.98 ↓
LLaMA2-7B-L2M	47.59 ↓	40.17 ↓	64.39 ↓	54.27 ↓	35.25 ↓	43.91 ↓
LLaMA2-7B-SP	45.53 ↓	41.22 ↓	58.18 ↓	53.98 ↓	33.79 ↓	40.70 ↓
LLaMA2-13B	48.42	48.92	80.66	59.14	45.22	61.18
LLaMA2-70B	51.82	51.83	85.81	63.85	48.88	63.15
OPT-30B	30.61	30.01	43.74	45.52	23.76	27.44
OPT-30B-Direct	28.21 ↓	29.62 ↓	49.34 ↑	41.04 ↓	22.08 ↓	28.87 ↑
OPT-30B-Naive	34.53 ↑	33.77 ↑	52.45 ↑	44.81 ↓	26.42 ↑	31.51 ↑
OPT-30B-L2M	3.58 ↓	8.96 ↓	34.15 ↓	24.53 ↓	15.00 ↓	21.60 ↓
OPT-30B-SP	2.17 ↓	0.75 ↓	1.98 ↓	3.11 ↓	2.17 ↓	4.81 ↓
OPT-iml-30B	23.76	22.61	73.30	38.66	15.75	25.96
OPT-iml-max-30B	23.10	22.75	73.68	37.24	15.11	26.74
TULU-2-7B	36.11	34.19	62.91	47.17	29.54	39.36
TULU-2-dpo-7B	42.47	48.59	79.65	55.12	36.05	45.25
TULU-2-qlora-7B	34.61	35.03	58.62	46.55	27.68	35.97
Vicuna-7B-v1.5	38.67	39.92	67.89	49.06	33.40	49.06
Vicuna-7B-v1.5-Direct	29.52 ↓	32.17 ↓	64.15 ↓	43.90 ↓	24.94 ↓	36.79 ↓
Vicuna-7B-v1.5-Naive	38.43 ↓	36.28 ↓	50.50 ↓	46.95 ↓	32.25 ↓	37.25 ↓
Vicuna-7B-v1.5-L2M	25.22 ↓	22.82 ↓	43.97 ↓	25.21 ↓	24.74 ↓	29.96 ↓
Vicuna-7B-v1.5-SP	27.33 ↓	22.97 ↓	37.60 ↓	28.75 ↓	20.83 ↓	22.40 ↓
Vicuna-13B-v1.5	39.81	40.85	74.75	51.11	35.10	35.12
Alpaca-7B	35.01	34.98	67.09	46.37	29.13	34.72
text-davinci-001	38.28	33.04	67.68	51.77	27.58	38.32
text-davinci-002	38.01	33.77	72.34	53.96	30.50	40.85
text-davinci-003	40.35	39.04	79.60	57.54	35.43	47.95
GPT-3.5-turbo	48.76	50.03	83.70	62.94	43.28	58.19
GPT-3.5-turbo-Direct	30.73 ↓	39.05 ↓	78.21 ↓	50.67 ↓	34.02 ↓	44.51 ↓
GPT-3.5-turbo-Naive	46.44 ↓	48.43 ↓	83.24 ↓	61.32 ↓	29.56 ↓	42.73 ↓
GPT-3.5-turbo-L2M	43.82 ↓	45.01 ↓	76.69 ↓	60.49 ↓	38.73 ↓	49.35 ↓
GPT-3.5-turbo-SP	42.68 ↓	42.68 ↓	77.01 ↓	54.10 ↓	37.93 ↓	48.83 ↓
GPT-3.5-turbo-instruct	47.59	47.94	82.71	59.85	39.30	53.50
GPT-3.5-turbo-instruct-Direct	31.50 ↓	40.39 ↓	78.32 ↓	54.55 ↓	32.07 ↓	44.51 ↓
GPT-3.5-turbo-instruct-Naive	51.49 ↑	54.21 ↑	85.67 ↑	68.31 ↑	30.30 ↓	41.50 ↓
GPT-3.5-turbo-instruct-L2M	46.72 ↓	49.00 ↑	82.92 ↑	67.09 ↑	40.93	52.45 ↓
GPT-3.5-turbo-instruct-SP	47.35 ↓	49.03 ↑	81.32 ↓	61.97 ↑	41.08 ↑	53.12 ↓
GPT-4	50.19	54.53	83.49	65.57	43.96	60.38
GPT-4-Direct	41.60 ↓	43.58 ↓	77.74 ↓	54.06 ↓	35.28 ↓	48.49 ↓
GPT-4-Naive	46.42 ↓	49.72 ↓	74.15 ↓	60.57 ↓	37.26 ↓	49.53 ↓
GPT-4-L2M	50.09 ↓	51.32 ↓	77.74 ↓	64.34 ↓	42.92 ↓	51.51 ↓
GPT-4-SP	50.00 ↓	49.91 ↓	78.30 ↓	62.17 ↓	42.08 ↓	52.55 ↓

Table 14. The INV results, **C** represents instances where the LLMs produce the correct answer to a specific question, while **W** denotes instances of wrong answers. A sequence formed by **C** and **W** represents the number of correct and wrong responses from a model over five attempts at the same question. For example, **CCCCC** means that LLMs answers some questions correctly 5 times. We use the sum of the proportions of **CCCCC** and **WWWWW** to represent the Stability Rate of the LLMs.

LLM	CCCCC	CCCCW	CCCWW	CCWWW	CWWWW	WWWWW	Consistency
OPT-30B	1.23%	5.98%	12.51%	10.94%	12.45%	56.89%	58.12%
Vicuna-7B-v1.5	5.65%	9.37%	10.95%	10.45%	12.14%	51.44%	57.09%
LLaMA2-7B	30.32%	8.78%	6.45%	7.15%	9.67%	37.64%	67.96%
GPT-3.5-turbo	27.15%	9.44%	6.14%	6.90%	9.14%	41.24%	68.39%
GPT-3.5-turbo-instruct	28.73%	9.83%	6.96%	6.60%	8.77%	39.10%	67.83%
GPT-4	37.43%	8.83%	5.87%	6.32%	6.96%	34.58%	**72.01%**

Table 15. The DIR results reflect the proportion of intermediate steps that large models can generate gradually according to the given CoT. This includes the success rate of generating specific CoT and the overall success rate on all CoTs.

	Naive	L2M	SP	Overall
OPT-30B	94.69%	38.22%	0.02%	44.31%
Vicuna-7B-v1.5	23.21%	15.05%	12.75%	17.0%
LLaMA2-7B	0.83%	38.22%	69.88%	37.06%
GPT-3.5-turbo	79.21%	97.97%	99.87%	92.35%
GPT-3.5-turbo-instruct	87.85%	99.37%	99.89%	95.7%
GPT-4	94.54%	99.67%	99.89%	98.03%

The performance of LLMs in answering various types of questions (RQ2) Based on the previously defined question types, we will analyze the ability of LLMs to answer various categories of questions from the perspectives of answer types and reasoning types.

As shown in Table 16, among different answer types of questions, LLMs perform better in answering Location and Boolean types of questions, with the best performances being 72.64% and 87.16% respectively. However, when the answer involves NUM, Dates, and Persons, the best model's accuracy is still below 62%. Specific to the models: The LLaMA2 series generally outperforms GPT series in Boolean and NUM categories, GPT-3.5-turbo-instruct with Naive-CoT excels when the answer is a Location or Organization, and GPT-4 is superior in answering MISC, WHY, PER, and Dates type questions. Moreover, different models exhibit significant variations in strengths and weaknesses across different types of questions. For instance in the NUM category, LLaMA2 performs 16% better than GPT-4, and in the date type, GPT-4 surpasses LLaMA2 by about 20%. Next, we explore the effects of various ICL strategies on LLMs across different types of answers. Our analysis reveals that among the four ICL strategies examined, Directly-ICL notably enhances the performance of the OPT-30B model, achieving a 9% improvement for numerical (NUM) questions and a 2% increase for person(PER) questions. The SP-COT strategy results in a least enhancement of approximately 1.1% for GPT-3.5-turbo-instruct in PER questions. Furthermore, the L2M-COT strategy significantly boosts GPT-3.5-turbo-instruct's performance across a variety of question types, with improvements of 2% for miscellaneous (MISC), 4.8% for location (LOC), 5% for date-related questions, 6% for PER, and 5% for organization (ORG) questions. Among the strategies, Naive-COT stands out as the most impactful, particularly for GPT-3.5, where it leads to a 7.9% improvement in WHY questions, and for the OPT model, where it enhances performance by 2.48% in NUM questions. This strategy also benefits both the OPT model and GPT-3.5 across multiple question types (MISC, LOC, DATE, PER, NUM, and ORG). In Boolean questions, Naive-COT significantly improves the performance of several models, including GPT-3.5-turbo, GPT-3.5-turbo-instruct, LLaMA2-7B, and GPT-4, with an average increase of 4.3%.

Table 17 shows the performance comparison of LLMs from the perspective of reasoning types. We can see that LLMs perform well in Set Operation, Comparison, and Single-Hop Reasoning. However, they show poorer performance in multi-hop reasoning and counting types, with the best model's accuracy still falling short of 60.0%. In terms of comparisons between models, LLaMA-7B clearly outperforms other models in the counting type, being approximately 26% higher than GPT-4, while the GPT family performs better in other types. It is noteworthy that in the comparison-type questions, the early GPT-3.5 model achieves a performance noticeably higher than later models such as GPT-4 and GPT-3.5-turbo. With respect to different ICL strategies, Naive-COT significantly improves the performance of the GPT-3.5-turbo-instruct model across all reasoning types. The most substantial improvement is in set operations, with an increase of about 28%, followed by filtering operations, with an increase of over 10.8%. Among other ICL strategies, only Directly-ICL improves OPT-30B's performance in counting types, with an enhancement of around 8%.

The Impact of ICL strategies for LLMs (RQ3) We apply ICL strategies to evaluate some LLMs. Based on their representativeness and ability to follow instructions, we choose the following models for evaluation: OPT-30B, LLAMA2-7B, Vicuna-7B-V1.5, GPT-3.5-turbo, GPT-3.5-turbo-instruct, and GPT-4. Among the four ICL strategies used in the experiments, Directly-ICL provides only a few samples in the prompt for in-context few-shot learning. Meanwhile, Naive-COT, L2M-COT, and SP-COT progressively increase the specificity of the question decomposition process. From the results in Table 13, it can be observed that the four ICL strategies have a negative impact on the LLMs' QA performance of Vicuna-7B-V1.5, GPT-3.5-turbo, and GPT-4. On LLAMA-7B, only the Naive-COT achieves less than 1% improvement on the KQAPro dataset. Contrary to this, OPT-30B and GPT-3.5-turbo-instruct show some improvement after using ICL strategies. Among them, the Naive-COT strategy performs best, leading to an approximate 4.31% increase in the average score of OPT-30B across five datasets, with less than a 1% decrease on the CWQ dataset. For GPT-3.5-turbo-instruct, Naive-COT leads to an average improvement of about 5.74% across four datasets, but also shows a decline of over 10% on the GrailQA and GraphQuestions datasets.

Further comparing these six LLMs and different ICL strategy combinations, the results show that among the models scoring lowest on each dataset, 34.28% use Directly-ICL, 37.14% use SP-COT, and L2M-COT and Naive-COT each account for 14.29%. This result suggests that in handling KGQA tasks representing the use of LLM internal knowledge to respond to natural language query tasks, simply providing QA pairs for few-shot learning is not helpful. On the other hand, overly detailed process prompts also have a negative impact on LLMs.

Table 16. The accuracy (Hits@1) of LLMs in answering various types of questions is presented. The top five scores on each dataset are highlighted, with darker shades representing higher scores. '↑' indicates that ICL strategy improves the model's score, while '↓' indicates that ICL strategy decreases the model's score.

	MISC	WHY	LOC	DATE	PER	Boolean	NUM	ORG
FLAN-T5-XXL	35.67	27.69	52.91	24.81	30.84	62.43	16.08	41.62
LLaMA2-7B	55.41	44.21	70.87	36.03	49.49	69.52	46.56	60.65
LLaMA2-7B-Direct	46.56 ↓	30.53 ↓	64.37 ↓	26.12 ↓	40.08 ↓	87.16 ↑	39.34 ↓	50.76 ↓
LLaMA2-7B-Naive	50.28 ↓	34.74 ↓	64.52 ↓	32.15 ↓	41.25 ↓	74.12 ↑	43.25 ↓	52.80 ↓
LLaMA2-7B-L2M	45.56 ↓	32.63 ↓	61.79 ↓	30.92 ↓	37.24 ↓	68.04 ↓	37.35 ↓	49.33 ↓
LLaMA2-7B-SP	44.48 ↓	33.68 ↓	60.96 ↓	23.05 ↓	36.78 ↓	74.14 ↑	39.07 ↓	47.11 ↓
LLaMA2-13B	39.12	18.95	56.35	14.65	33.03	34.71	43.51	37.83
LLaMA2-70B	54.80	43.16	67.32	31.59	49.06	71.37	39.14	63.87
OPT-30B	32.98	23.16	44.92	12.59	29.65	49.32	10.45	41.62
OPT-30B-Direct	32.91 ↓	10.00 ↓	44.22 ↓	26.92 ↑	31.62 ↑	27.69 ↓	19.01 ↑	40.46 ↓
OPT-30B-Naive	38.80 ↑	16.67 ↓	48.74 ↑	30.57 ↑	33.70 ↑	39.67 ↓	12.48 ↑	45.94 ↑
OPT-30B-L2M	15.90 ↓	3.33 ↓	24.93 ↓	15.38 ↑	15.21 ↓	23.97 ↓	8.71 ↓	26.20 ↓
OPT-30B-SP	1.76 ↓	0.00 ↓	3.48 ↓	0.61 ↓	0.22 ↓	22.31 ↓	2.18 ↓	1.16 ↓
OPT-iml-30B	27.07	16.84	33.38	14.24	24.06	46.27	11.16	32.44
OPT-iml-max-30B	25.96	15.79	32.12	13.39	22.87	47.89	10.41	31.81
TULU-2-7B	40.48	29.47	52.13	27.00	33.56	47.84	16.38	45.94
TULU-2-dpo-7B	50.11	43.16	61.30	33.24	42.26	62.55	26.47	57.40
TULU-2-qlora-7B	38.06	32.63	49.81	25.81	34.16	53.65	17.37	44.25
Vicuna-7B-v1.5	42.73	30.53	57.08	26.19	36.38	62.35	31.96	45.86
Vicuna-7B-v1.5-Direct	34.76 ↓	22.11 ↓	50.98 ↓	23.32 ↓	31.52 ↓	54.14 ↓	22.32 ↓	41.04 ↓
Vicuna-7B-v1.5-Naive	39.97 ↓	30.53 -	54.60 ↓	21.42 ↓	33.28 ↓	53.35 ↓	32.30 ↑	43.34 ↓
Vicuna-7B-v1.5-L2M	25.43 ↓	16.84 ↓	28.80 ↓	12.23 ↓	24.42 ↓	37.07 ↓	22.33 ↓	25.86 ↓
Vicuna-7B-v1.5-SP	25.98 ↓	18.95 ↓	36.30 ↓	9.65 ↓	19.67 ↓	35.87 ↓	23.03 ↓	24.64 ↓
Vicuna-13B-v1.5	43.95	32.63	59.00	31.74	39.43	64.47	31.81	48.76
Alpaca-7B	39.66	33.68	53.18	24.17	33.66	44.57	30.14	44.47
text-davinci-001	40.79	32.31	56.92	37.07	37.53	39.96	19.66	50.01
text-davinci-002	42.35	27.69	58.93	36.15	41.36	42.56	21.01	50.58
text-davinci-003	46.42	49.23	62.71	42.54	45.10	53.23	20.31	54.62
GPT-3.5-turbo	55.05	45.26	68.14	43.95	51.45	63.50	26.57	61.61
GPT-3.5-turbo-Direct	43.72 ↓	30.53 ↓	56.04 ↓	34.33 ↓	40.13 ↓	32.66 ↓	14.92 ↓	48.79 ↓
GPT-3.5-turbo-Naive	51.77 ↓	42.39 ↓	67.29 ↓	43.45 ↓	49.12 ↓	71.26 ↑	14.77 ↓	60.59 ↓
GPT-3.5-turbo-L2M	49.49 ↓	33.68 ↓	64.09 ↓	42.82 ↓	48.95 ↓	64.10 ↑	15.47 ↓	57.90 ↓
GPT-3.5-turbo-SP	48.24 ↓	31.58 ↓	59.92 ↓	28.60 ↓	42.78 ↓	60.82 ↓	17.98 ↓	55.81 ↓
GPT-3.5-turbo-instruct	52.51	42.11	64.58	44.34	48.85	67.15	20.32	59.22
GPT-3.5-turbo-instruct-Direct	44.74 ↓	35.79 ↓	57.79 ↓	39.22 ↓	42.91 ↓	33.09 ↓	15.98 ↓	51.64 ↓
GPT-3.5-turbo-instruct-Naive	59.12 ↑	50.00 ↑	72.64 ↑	51.19 ↑	55.42 ↑	79.13 ↑	19.13 ↓	67.53 ↑
GPT-3.5-turbo-instruct-L2M	54.59 ↑	38.95 ↓	69.45 ↑	49.31 ↑	54.44 ↑	60.41 ↓	16.89 ↓	64.49 ↑
GPT-3.5-turbo-instruct-SP	53.18 ↑	41.05 ↓	65.92 ↑	44.75 ↑	50.11 ↑	69.45 ↑	19.54 ↓	62.24 ↑
GPT-4	61.11	66.67	69.94	56.88	61.82	60.33	30.69	65.34
GPT-4-Direct	51.24 ↓	56.67 ↓	59.77 ↓	49.60 ↓	52.63 ↓	34.71 ↓	27.72 ↓	55.39 ↓
GPT-4-Naive	53.46 ↓	63.33 ↓	63.86 ↓	55.47 ↓	56.13 ↓	62.81 ↑	18.22 ↓	59.37 ↓
GPT-4-L2M	57.35 ↓	53.33 ↓	67.07 ↓	53.04 ↓	56.46 ↓	63.22 ↑	26.73 ↓	64.01 ↓
GPT-4-SP	56.88 ↓	53.33 ↓	66.64 ↓	52.63 ↓	57.44 ↓	57.85 ↓	30.30 ↓	63.02 ↓

Table 17. From the viewpoint of reasoning types, the accuracy of various LLMs' responses is compared. The five highest scores on each dataset are highlighted, with darker shades signifying superior performance. '↑"' indicates that ICL strategy improves the model's score, while '↓' indicates that ICL strategy decreases the model's score.

	SetOperation	Filtering	Counting	Comparison	Single-hop	Multi-hop	Star-shape
FLAN-T5-XXL	60.11	45.01	10.68	72.13	41.00	35.68	37.23
LLaMA2-7B	63.16	63.22	56.24	65.71	58.26	53.21	53.73
LLaMA2-7B-Direct	54.27 ↓	55.51 ↓	45.98 ↓	60.14 ↓	58.61 ↑	44.91 ↓	46.82 ↓
LLaMA2-7B-Naive	57.40 ↓	57.55 ↓	51.94 ↓	63.64 ↓	50.38 ↓	47.87 ↓	49.21 ↓
LLaMA2-7B-L2M	52.00 ↓	53.19 ↓	43.40 ↓	60.34 ↓	49.39 ↓	42.77 ↓	44.56 ↓
LLaMA2-7B-SP	50.55 ↓	52.17 ↓	46.63 ↓	57.91 ↓	50.32 ↓	42.32 ↓	43.97 ↓
LLaMA2-13B	62.15	58.06	36.69	61.84	27.41	41.22	42.80
LLaMA2-70B	77.51	66.61	50.55	77.40	59.05	49.71	49.71
OPT-30B	46.94	42.95	13.65	54.67	31.67	28.84	28.53
OPT-30B-Direct	29.16 ↓	35.14 ↓	22.50 ↑	33.33 ↑	49.45 ↑	29.81 ↑	29.70 ↑
OPT-30B-Naive	34.44 ↓	39.65 ↓	16.11 ↑	42.73 ↑	50.83 ↑	33.22 ↑	33.30 ↑
OPT-30B-L2M	16.25 ↓	17.51 ↓	9.72 ↓	23.94 ↓	12.29 ↓	15.61 ↓	17.45 ↓
OPT-30B-SP	0.64 ↓	1.71 ↓	0.56 ↓	0.71 ↓	4.28 ↓	2.28 ↓	2.54 ↓
OPT-iml-30B	36.54	36.99	14.93	39.62	37.30	24.25	24.32
OPT-iml-max-30B	35.68	35.99	14.47	38.01	40.31	23.39	23.52
TULU-2-7B	44.17	46.13	24.33	49.05	38.68	38.17	39.10
TULU-2-dpo-7B	51.51	54.52	42.09	56.58	56.56	46.43	46.74
TULU-2-qlora-7B	40.52	44.63	26.34	44.74	40.05	36.76	38.36
Vicuna-7B-v1.5	48.62	49.39	24.29	53.26	48.35	40.85	42.01
Vicuna-7B-v1.5-Direct	37.69 ↓	42.63 ↓	17.21 ↓	41.55 ↓	41.87 ↓	34.60 ↓	35.56 ↓
Vicuna-7B-v1.5-Naive	46.10 ↓	45.94 ↓	28.93 ↑	53.96 ↑	38.66 ↓	38.21 ↓	38.68 ↓
Vicuna-7B-v1.5-L2M	34.42 ↓	29.13 ↓	28.77 ↑	37.38 ↓	30.67 ↓	23.14 ↓	22.75 ↓
Vicuna-7B-v1.5-SP	34.98 ↓	30.88 ↓	14.10 ↓	45.83 ↓	27.99 ↓	22.80 ↓	23.99 ↓
Vicuna-13B-v1.5	48.71	51.24	23.99	51.53	50.70	42.93	44.40
Alpaca-7B	44.41	46.39	18.77	55.99	42.06	36.67	37.53
text-davinci-001	60.12	49.06	17.56	72.44	38.72	41.09	42.28
text-davinci-002	62.03	51.24	20.83	74.00	42.54	42.98	43.96
text-davinci-003	66.86	55.43	20.83	80.00	49.22	47.06	48.17
GPT-3.5-turbo	60.11	61.92	35.76	61.64	56.42	53.77	55.38
GPT-3.5-turbo-Direct	44.20 ↓	49.23 ↓	19.15 ↓	41.96 ↓	46.38 ↓	41.44 ↓	42.60 ↓
GPT-3.5-turbo-Naive	57.77 ↓	60.87 ↓	23.05 ↓	60.68 ↓	56.80 ↑	51.16 ↓	53.22 ↓
GPT-3.5-turbo-L2M	53.98 ↓	58.15 ↓	17.52 ↓	61.96 ↑	52.20 ↓	48.93 ↓	51.54 ↓
GPT-3.5-turbo-SP	54.40 ↓	54.84 ↓	24.81 ↓	57.84 ↓	51.05 ↓	45.10 ↓	46.13 ↓
GPT-3.5-turbo-instruct	54.80	58.85	26.90	56.95	56.02	51.49	52.78
GPT-3.5-turbo-instruct-Direct	42.76 ↓	50.97 ↓	19.23 ↓	42.34 ↓	48.28 ↓	43.51 ↓	44.23 ↓
GPT-3.5-turbo-instruct-Naive	82.08 ↑	69.89 ↑	27.30 ↑	64.31 ↑	60.49 ↑	59.41 ↑	61.27 ↑
GPT-3.5-turbo-instruct-L2M	56.33 ↑	62.99 ↑	20.59 ↓	63.91 ↑	53.65 ↓	54.74 ↑	55.84 ↑
GPT-3.5-turbo-instruct-SP	56.71 ↑	60.78 ↑	25.96 ↓	61.25 ↑	55.84 ↓	52.09 ↑	53.21 ↑
GPT-4	56.93	62.85	29.17	55.67	78.59	57.52	57.59
GPT-4-Direct	46.51 ↓	53.35 ↓	23.33 ↓	45.39 ↓	70.99 ↓	47.17 ↓	47.50 ↓
GPT-4-naive	48.12 ↓	56.38 ↓	14.17 ↓	49.82 ↓	75.00 ↓	50.25 ↓	50.26 ↓
GPT-4-L2M	52.16 ↓	59.27 ↓	21.67 ↓	52.84 ↓	77.21 ↓	53.28 ↓	53.39 ↓
GPT-4-SP	52.57 ↓	59.01 ↓	26.11 ↓	53.72 ↓	75.00 ↓	52.38 ↓	53.10 ↓

5. Summary and Current Limitations

We summarize findings from recent studies involving modern Large Language Models (LLMs) in Knowledge Graph Question Answering (KGQA) tasks. In Faria et al. [139], GPT-3 was evaluated on KGQA using the QALD-9 dataset. The study found that GPT-3 struggled with SPARQL generation, even in few-shot and zero-shot scenarios. Surprisingly, fine-tuning GPT-3 with 340 sample queries using the API did not significantly improve performance beyond the few-shot setting. However, due to GPT-3's closed nature, details on the fine-tuning process remain unclear. Interestingly, when GPT-3 directly provided answers without generating SPARQL queries, its performance doubled.

Similarly, in Klager at al. [140], GPT-3 and ChatGPT also showed subpar performance in KGQA semantic parsing tasks. The authors highlighted differences between DBpedia and Wikidata KGs, noting that DBpedia's language-based URIs were easier to handle than Wikidata's numeric identifiers. Generally, LLMs struggle with entity linking tasks, often necessitating external entity linkers in semantic parsing-based KGQA systems.

Contrasting these findings, Xu et al. [141] and Shu et al. [142] demonstrated that fine-tuned models outperform prompted LLMs in KGQA semantic parsing tasks. However, the high cost associated with fine-tuning LLMs due to their extensive parameter count raises concerns about practicality. Moreover, Shu et al. [142] experimented with data augmentation techniques to facilitate transfer learning across different KGs but achieved limited success, underscoring challenges in generalization across KGs.

A critical challenge in semantic parsing, termed compositional generalization, remains unresolved for LLMs in default settings [143]. Notably, advanced prompting techniques like least-to-most prompting [144] and chain-of-thought prompting [145] show promise by breaking tasks into simpler sub-tasks and iteratively processing through the LLM, yielding improved results. However, the effectiveness of these methods heavily depends on prompt design, exemplar selection, and dataset-specific nuances.

In summary, while LLMs present significant potential for KGQA tasks, their effective deployment requires overcoming substantial challenges such as SPARQL generation, entity linking, and compositional generalization.

6. Conclusion and Future Directions

In this chapter, we visited the topic of LLMs and their utility in the task of KGQA. We first learnt about various techniques used in KGQA, and some techniques, such as semantic parsing, which are particularly relevant from the perspective of *neuro-symbolic* AI. We learnt about the various LLMs in existence, and how they can be leveraged for the task of KGQA. As exemplars, we described two KGQA systems, one that can handle simple questions, and another that handles complex questions. Additionally, we presented how LLMs can be useful in the evaluation of KGQA systems.

Looking ahead in the direction of future research on KGQA, significant challenges remain, particularly when considering LLMs. While LLMs demonstrate exceptional performance in tasks such as text generation, they also have a tendency to generate incorrect facts. Since KGs contain meticulously curated information, there is a strong desire to connect the answers generated by LLMs to these KGs. Integrating LLMs with KGs remains an open question in the field, explored in Pan et al. [146], which outlines several potential avenues for future research.

One approach involves enriching the LLM pre-training corpus with KG triples [147,148]. Another direction focuses on grounding LLM-generated answers to KGs during inference [165,150]. Recent advancements in attention mechanisms within Transformers, as discussed in Bertsch et al. [151], suggest modifying the decoder to directly access external KGs during inference.

A different approach suggests adapting KGs themselves to better align with LLMs by replacing current identifiers with equivalents in a "word space". For example, in Zhao et al. [152], encoding sub-graphs as text yields performance comparable to Graph Neural Network embeddings, with the added benefit of interpretability. Additionally, renaming KG nodes in word-space, as explored in Fatemi et al. [153], facilitates easier referencing by pre-trained models during inference.

Regarding the relevance of KGs in contemporary contexts, LLMs often excel in QA tasks without referencing KGs or generating queries, prompting questions about the necessity of KGQA. However, domain-specific KGs, such as industrial or proprietary, contain crucial out-of-distribution information not covered in general pre-training data used by LLMs. Neuro-symbolic approaches such as semantic parsing produce logical queries executable on KGs, offers advantages in explainability compared to LLMs, which operate more opaquely despite controlled prompting.

Given these limitations of LLMs, we argue that KGs retain relevance and require further exploration for effective integration with LLMs. This integration aims to comprehensively address the diverse needs of KGQA sub-domains, ensuring robust performance and interpretability in future applications.

In terms of the evaluation of the performance of LLMs on KGQA, the future research will focus on addressing several identified deficiencies and expanding our inquiry into new directions. Despite extensive testing across multiple models and datasets, our findings highlighted critical areas where LLMs fail to meet the performance standards of traditional KGQA systems, primarily due to inconsistencies in QA performance and a lack of output reliability. Key focus areas include optimizing in-context learning strategies to better utilize LLMs' internal knowledge, enhancing output consistency by addressing decoding randomness and conflicting training data, integrating LLMs with traditional Knowledge Graphs to handle numerical answers, and exploring domain-specific question answering to leverage LLMs' knowledge effectively while managing costs and computational demands. These efforts aim to refine LLM capabilities in KGQA and broaden their applicability across various domains.

References

[1] Manning, C.D.: Human Language Understanding & Reasoning. In: Daedalus, pp. 127-138 (2022). https://doi.org/10.1162/daed_a_01905

[2] Mohammed, S., Shi, P., Lin, J.J.: Strong Baselines for Simple Question Answering over Knowledge Graphs with and without Neural Networks. In: Proceedings of the 2018 Conference of the North American Chapter of the Association for Computational Linguistics, pp. 291–296 (2018). https://doi.org/10.18653/v1/n18-2047

[3] Lukovnikov, D., Fischer, A., Lehmann, J.: Pretrained Transformers for Simple Question Answering over Knowledge Graphs. In: 18th International Semantic Web Conference, pp. 470-486 (2019). https://doi.org/10.1007/978-3-030-30793-6_27

[4] Golub, D., He, X.: Character-Level Question Answering with Attention. In: Proceedings of the 2016 Conference on Empirical Methods in Natural Language Processing, pp. 1598-1607 (2016). https://doi.org/10.18653/v1/d16-1166

[5] Petrochuk, M., Zettlemoyer, L.: SimpleQuestions Nearly Solved: A New Upperbound and Baseline Approach. In: Proceedings of the 2018 Conference on Empirical Methods in Natural Language Processing, pp. 554-558 (2018). https://doi.org/10.18653/v1/d18-1051

[6] Türe, F., Jojic, O.: No Need to Pay Attention: Simple Recurrent Neural Networks Work! In: Proceedings of the 2017 Conference on Empirical Methods in Natural Language Processing, pp. 2866-2872 (2017). https://doi.org/10.18653/v1/d17-1307

[7] Yu, M., Yin, W., Hasan, K.S., Santos, C.N., Xiang, B., Zhou, B.: Improved Neural Relation Detection for Knowledge Base Question Answering. In: Proceedings of the 55th Annual Meeting of the Association for Computational Linguistics, pp. 571-581 (2017). https://doi.org/10.18653/v1/P17-1053

[8] Cui, H., Peng, T., Feng, L., Bao, T., Liu, L.: Simple Question Answering over Knowledge Graph Enhanced by Question Pattern Classification. In: Knowl. Inf. Syst., pp. 2741-2761 (2021). https://doi.org/10.1007/s10115-021-01609-w

[9] Lukovnikov, D., Fischer, A., Lehmann, J., Auer, S.: Neural Network-based Question Answering over Knowledge Graphs on Word and Character Level. In: Proceedings of the 26th International Conference on World Wide Web, pp. 1211-1220 (2017). https://doi.org/10.1145/3038912.3052675

[10] Hao, Y., Liu, H., He, S., Liu, K., Zhao, J.: Pattern-revising Enhanced Simple Question Answering over Knowledge Bases. In: Proceedings of the 27th International Conference on Computational Linguistics, pp. 3272-3282 (2018). https://aclanthology.org/C18-1277/

[11] Yin, W., Yu, M., Xiang, B., Zhou, B., Schütze, H.: Simple Question Answering by Attentive Convolutional Neural Network. In: Proceedings of the 26th International Conference on Computational Linguistics, pp. 1746-1756 (2016). https://aclanthology.org/C16-1164/

[12] Zhao W., Chung T., Goyal AK., Metallinou A.: Simple question answering with subgraph ranking and joint-scoring. In: Proceedings of the 2019 Conference of the North American Chapter of the Association for Computational Linguistics, pp. 324–334 (2019). https://doi.org/10.18653/v1/n19-1029

[13] Hao, Y., Zhang, Y., Liu, K., He, S., Liu, Z., Wu, H., Zhao, J.: An End-to-End Model for Question Answering over Knowledge Base with Cross-Attention Combining Global Knowledge. In: Proceedings of the 55th Annual Meeting of the Association for Computational Linguistics, pp. 221–231 (2017). https://doi.org/10.18653/v1/P17-1021

[14] Luo, D., Su, J., Yu, S.: A BERT-based Approach with Relation-aware Attention for Knowledge Base Question Answering. In: 2020 International Joint Conference on Neural Networks, pp. 1-8 (2020). https://doi.org/10.1109/IJCNN48605.2020.9207186

[15] Dai, Z., Li, L., Xu, W.: CFO: Conditional Focused Neural Question Answering with Large-scale Knowledge Bases. In: Proceedings of the 54th Annual Meeting of the Association for Computational Linguistics, pp. 800–810 (2016). https://doi.org/10.18653/v1/p16-1076

[16] Lan, Y., Wang, S., Jiang, J.: Knowledge Base Question Answering With a Matching-Aggregation Model and Question-Specific Contextual Relations. In: IEEE ACM Trans. Audio Speech Lang. Process., pp. 1629-1638 (2019). https://doi.org/10.1109/TASLP.2019.2926125

[17] Vaswani, A., Shazeer, N.M., Parmar, N., Uszkoreit, J., Jones, L., Gomez, A.N., Kaiser, L., Polosukhin, I.: Attention is All you Need. In: Advances in Neural Information Processing Systems, pp. 5998-6008 (2017)

[18] Hochreiter, S., Schmidhuber, J.: Long Short-Term Memory. In: Neural Computation, pp. 1735-1780 (1997)

[19] Krizhevsky, A., Sutskever, I., Hinton, G.E.: ImageNet classification with deep convolutional neural networks. In: Communications of the ACM, pp. 84 - 90 (2017). http://doi.org/10.1145/3065386

[20] Devlin, J., Chang, M., Lee, K., Toutanova, K.: BERT: Pre-training of Deep Bidirectional Transformers for Language Understanding. In: Proceedings of the 2019 Conference of the North American Chapter of the Association for Computational Linguistics, pp. 4171-4186 (2019). https://doi.org/10.18653/v1/n19-1423

[21] Liu, Y., Ott, M., Goyal, N., Du, J., Joshi, M., Chen, D., Levy, O., Lewis, M., Zettlemoyer, L., Stoyanov, V.: RoBERTa: A Robustly Optimized BERT Pretraining Approach. In: ArXiv, 1907.11692 (2019)

[22] Lan, Z., Chen, M., Goodman, S., Gimpel, K., Sharma, P., Soricut, R.: ALBERT: A Lite BERT for Self-supervised Learning of Language Representations. In: 8th International Conference on Learning Representations (2020)

[23] Huang, X., Zhang, J., Li, D., Li, P.: Knowledge Graph Embedding Based Question Answering. In: Proceedings of the Twelfth ACM International Conference on Web Search and Data Mining, pp. 105-113 (2019). https://doi.org/10.1145/3289600.3290956

[24] Bordes, A., Usunier, N., Chopra, S., Weston, J.: Large-scale Simple Question Answering with Memory Networks. In: ArXiv, 1506.02075 (2015)

[25] Mikolov, T., Sutskever, I., Chen, K., Corrado, G.S., Dean, J.: Distributed Representations of Words and Phrases and their Compositionality. In: Advances in Neural Information Processing Systems, pp. 3111-3119 (2013)

[26] Pennington, J., Socher, R., Manning, C.D.: GloVe: Global Vectors for Word Representation. In: Proceedings of the 2014 Conference on Empirical Methods in Natural Language Processing, pp. 1532-1543 (2014). https://doi.org/10.3115/v1/d14-1162

[27] Reimers N. , Gurevych I.: Sentence-BERT: Sentence Embeddings using Siamese BERT-Networks. In: Proceedings of the 2019 Conference on Empirical Methods in Natural Language Processing, pp. 3980-3990 (2019). https://doi.org/10.18653/v1/D19-1410

[28] Li, B.Z., Min, S., Iyer, S., Mehdad, Y., Yih, W.: Efficient One-Pass End-to-End Entity Linking for Questions. In: Proceedings of the 2020 Conference on Empirical Methods in Natural Language Processing, pp. 6433-6441 (2020). https://doi.org/10.18653/v1/2020.emnlp-main.522

[29] Wu, L.Y., Petroni, F., Josifoski, M., Riedel, S., Zettlemoyer, L.: Scalable Zero-shot Entity Linking with Dense Entity Retrieval. In: Proceedings of the 2020 Conference on Empirical Methods in Natural Language Processing, pp. 6397-6407 (2020). https://doi.org/10.18653/v1/2020.emnlp-main.519

[30] Chen, S., Wang, J., Jiang, F., Lin, C.: Improving Entity Linking by Modeling Latent Entity Type Information. In: The Thirty-Fourth AAAI Conference on Artificial Intelligence, pp. 7529-7537 (2020)

[31] Oliya, A., Saffari, A., Sen, P., Ayoola, T.: End-to-End Entity Resolution and Question Answering Using Differentiable Knowledge Graphs. In: Proceedings of the 2021 Conference on Empirical Methods in Natural Language Processing, pp. 4193-4200 (2021). https://doi.org/10.18653/v1/2021.emnlp-main.345

[32] Wang, Z., Ng, P.K., Nallapati, R., Xiang, B.: Retrieval, Re-ranking and Multi-task Learning for Knowledge-Base Question Answering. In: Proceedings of the 16th Conference of the European Chapter of the Association for Computational Linguistics, pp. 347-357 (2021). https://doi.org/10.18653/v1/2021.eacl-main.26

[33] Yamada, I., Asai, A., Shindo, H., Takeda, H., Matsumoto, Y.: LUKE: Deep Contextualized Entity Representations with Entity-aware Self-attention. In: Proceedings of the 2020 Conference on Empirical Methods in Natural Language Processing, pp. 6442-6454 (2020). https://doi.org/10.18653/v1/2020.emnlp-main.523

[34] Zhang, T., Wang, C., Hu, N., Qiu, M., Tang, C., He, X., Huang, J.: DKPLM: Decomposable Knowledge-enhanced Pre-trained Language Model for Natural Language Understanding. In: Thirty-Sixth AAAI Conference on Artificial Intelligence, pp. 11703-11711 (2022)

[35] Zhang, Z., Han, X., Liu, Z., Jiang, X., Sun, M., Liu, Q.: ERNIE: Enhanced Language Representation with Informative Entities. In: Proceedings of the 57th Conference of the Association for Computational Linguistics, pp. 1441-1451 (2019). https://doi.org/10.18653/v1/p19-1139

[36] Wang, X., Gao, T., Zhu, Z., Liu, Z., Li, J., Tang, J.: KEPLER: A Unified Model for Knowledge Embedding and Pre-trained Language Representation. In: Transactions of the Association for Computational Linguistics, 9, pp. 176-194. (2021). https://doi.org/10.1162/tacl_a_00360

[37] Peters, M.E., Neumann, M., RobertL.Logan, I., Schwartz, R., Joshi, V., Singh, S., Smith, N.A.: Knowledge Enhanced Contextual Word Representations. In: Proceedings of the 2019 Conference on Empirical Methods in Natural Language Processing, pp. 43-54 (2019). https://doi.org/10.18653/v1/D19-1005

[38] Bollacker, K.D., Evans, C., Paritosh, P.K., Sturge, T., Taylor, J.: Freebase: a collaboratively created graph database for structuring human knowledge. In: Proceedings of the ACM SIGMOD International Conference on Management of Data, pp. 1247-1250 (2008). https://doi.org/10.1145/1376616.1376746

[39] Danny Sullivan.: A reintroduction to our Knowledge Graph and knowledge panels. https://blog.google/products/search/about-knowledge-graph-and-knowledge-panels/ (2020). Accessed 3 October 2022

[40] Lan, Y., Jiang, J.: Query Graph Generation for Answering Multi-hop Complex Questions from Knowledge Bases. In: Proceedings of the 58th Annual Meeting of the Association for Computational Linguistics, pp. 969-974 (2020). https://doi.org/10.18653/v1/2020.acl-main.91

[41] Gu, Y., Kase, S.E., Vanni, M.T., Sadler, B.M., Liang, P., Yan, X., Su, Y.: Beyond I.I.D.: Three Levels of Generalization for Question Answering on Knowledge Bases. In: Proceedings of the Web Conference,

pp. 3477-3488 (2021). https://doi.org/10.1145/3442381.3449992
[42] Ye, X., Yavuz, S., Hashimoto, K., Zhou, Y., Xiong, C.: RNG-KBQA: Generation Augmented Iterative Ranking for Knowledge Base Question Answering. In: Proceedings of the 60th Annual Meeting of the Association for Computational Linguistics, pp. 6032-6043 (2022). https://doi.org/10.18653/v1/2022.acl-long.417
[43] Gu, Y., Su, Y.: ArcaneQA: Dynamic Program Induction and Contextualized Encoding for Knowledge Base Question Answering. In: Proceedings of the 29th International Conference on Computational Linguistics, pp. 1718-1731 (2022)
[44] Chen, S., Liu, Q., Yu, Z., Lin, C., Lou, J., Jiang, F.: ReTraCk: A Flexible and Efficient Framework for Knowledge Base Question Answering. In: Proceedings of the 59th Annual Meeting of the Association for Computational Linguistics, pp. 325-336 (2021). https://doi.org/10.18653/v1/2021.acl-demo.39
[45] Qin, K., Li, C., Pavlu, V., Aslam, J.A.: Improving Query Graph Generation for Complex Question Answering over Knowledge Base. In: Proceedings of the 2021 Conference on Empirical Methods in Natural Language Processing, pp. 4201-4207 (2021). https://doi.org/10.18653/v1/2021.emnlp-main.346
[46] Xie, T., Wu, C., Shi, P., Zhong, R., Scholak, T., Yasunaga, M., Wu, C., Zhong, M., Yin, P., Wang, S.I., Zhong, V., Wang, B., Li, C., Boyle, C., Ni, A., Yao, Z., Radev, D., Xiong, C., Kong, L., Zhang, R., Smith, N.A., Zettlemoyer, L., Yu, T.: UnifiedSKG: Unifying and Multi-Tasking Structured Knowledge Grounding with Text-to-Text Language Models. In: ArXiv, 2201.05966 (2022)
[47] Jiao, X., Yin, Y., Shang, L., Jiang, X., Chen, X., Li, L., Wang, F., Liu, Q.: TinyBERT: Distilling BERT for Natural Language Understanding. In: Findings of the Association for Computational Linguistics, pp. 4163-4174 (2020). https://doi.org/10.18653/v1/2020.findings-emnlp.372
[48] Sanh, V., Debut, L., Chaumond, J., Wolf, T.: DistilBERT, a distilled version of BERT: smaller, faster, cheaper and lighter. In: ArXiv, 1910.01108 (2019)
[49] Radford, A., Narasimhan, K., Salimans, T., Sutskever, I.: Improving language understanding by generative pre-training. https://s3-us-west-2.amazonaws.com/openai-assets/research-covers/language-unsupervised/language_understanding_paper.pdf (2018). Accessed 4 October 2022
[50] Yang, Z., Dai, Z., Yang, Y., Carbonell, J.G., Salakhutdinov, R., Le, Q.V.: XLNet: Generalized Autoregressive Pretraining for Language Understanding. In: Advances in Neural Information Processing Systems, pp. 5754-5764 (2019)
[51] Zhang, C., Lai, Y., Feng, Y., Zhao, D.: A review of deep learning in question answering over knowledge bases. In: AI Open, pp. 205-215 (2021)
[52] Lan, Y., He, G., Jiang, J., Jiang, J., Zhao, W.X., Wen, J.: Complex Knowledge Base Question Answering: A Survey. In: IEEE TKDE (2021)
[53] Gu, Y., Pahuja, V., Cheng, G., Su, Y.: Knowledge Base Question Answering: A Semantic Parsing Perspective. ArXiv, In: ArXiv, 2209.04994 (2022)
[54] Qiu, X., Sun, T., Xu, Y., Shao, Y., Dai, N., Huang, X.: Pre-trained models for natural language processing: A survey. In: Science China Technological Sciences, pp. 1872 - 1897 (2020)
[55] Han, N., Topic, G., Noji, H., Takamura, H., Miyao, Y.: An empirical analysis of existing systems and datasets toward general simple question answering. In: COLING, pp. 5321-5334 (2020)
[56] Jiang, K., Wu, D., Jiang, H.: FreebaseQA: A New Factoid QA Data Set Matching Trivia-Style Question-Answer Pairs with Freebase. In: North American Chapter of the Association for Computational Linguistics, pp. 318-323 (2019)
[57] Yih, W., Richardson, M., Meek, C., Chang, M., Suh, J.: The Value of Semantic Parse Labeling for Knowledge Base Question Answering. In: Annual Meeting of the Association for Computational Linguistics (2016)
[58] Hu, N., Bi, S., Qi, G., Wang, M., Hua, Y., Shen, S.: Improving Core Path Reasoning for the Weakly Supervised Knowledge Base Question Answering. In: DASFAA, pp. 162-170 (2022)
[59] Zhang, J., Zhang, X., Yu, J., Tang, J., Tang, J., Li, C., Chen, H.: Subgraph Retrieval Enhanced Model for Multi-hop Knowledge Base Question Answering. In: Annual Meeting of the Association for Computational Linguistics, pp. 5773-5784 (2022)
[60] Das, R., Zaheer, M., Thai, D.N., Godbole, A., Perez, E., Lee, J., Tan, L., Polymenakos, L., McCallum, A.: Case-based Reasoning for Natural Language Queries over Knowledge Bases. In: Conference on Empirical Methods in Natural Language Processing, pp. 9594-9611 (2021)
[61] Ye, X., Yavuz, S., Hashimoto, K., Zhou, Y., Xiong, C.: RNG-KBQA: Generation Augmented Iterative Ranking for Knowledge Base Question Answering. In: Annual Meeting of the Association for Computational Linguistics, pp. 6032-6043 (2021)

[62] Qin, C., Zhang, A., Zhang, Z., Chen, J., Yasunaga, M., Yang, D.: Is ChatGPT a General-Purpose Natural Language Processing Task Solver? In: ArXiv, 2302.06476 (2023)

[63] Bang, Y., Cahyawijaya, S., Lee, N., Dai, W., Su, D., Wilie, B., Lovenia, H., Ji, Z., Yu, T., Chung, W., Do, Q.V., Xu, Y., Fung, P.: A Multitask, Multilingual, Multimodal Evaluation of ChatGPT on Reasoning, Hallucination, and Interactivity. In: ArXiv, 2302.04023 (2023)

[64] Guo, B., Zhang, X., Wang, Z., Jiang, M., Nie, J., Ding, Y., Yue, J., Wu, Y.: How Close is ChatGPT to Human Experts? Comparison Corpus, Evaluation, and Detection. In: ArXiv, 2301.07597 (2023)

[65] Christiano, P.F., Leike, J., Brown, T.B., Martic, M., Legg, S., Amodei, D.: Deep Reinforcement Learning from Human Preferences. In: Neural Information Processing Systems, pp. 4299-4307 (2017)

[66] Sutskever, Ilya, Oriol Vinyals, Quoc, V Le, 2014. Sequence to sequence learning with neural networks. In: Proceedings of NeurIPS, pp. 3104–3112.

[67] J. Devlin, M. Chang, K. Lee, and K. Toutanova, "BERT: pre-training of deep bidirectional transformers for language understanding," in Proceedings of the 2019 Conference of the North American Chapter of the Association for Computational Linguistics: Human Language Technologies, NAACL-HLT 2019, Minneapolis, MN, USA, June 2-7, 2019, Volume 1 (Long and Short Papers), J. Burstein, C. Doran, and T. Solorio, Eds. Association for Computational Linguistics, 2019, pp. 4171–4186.

[68] A. Radford, K. Narasimhan, T. Salimans, I. Sutskever et al., "Improving language understanding by generative pre-training," 2018.

[69] Vaswani, Ashish, Shazeer, Noam, Parmar, Niki, Uszkoreit, Jakob, Jones, Llion, Gomez, Aidan N., Kaiser, Łukasz, Polosukhin, Illia, 2017. Attention is all you need. In: Proceedings of NeurIPS, pp. 5998–6008.

[70] Dong, Li, Yang, Nan, Wang, Wenhui, Wei, Furu, Liu, Xiaodong, Wang, Yu, Gao, Jianfeng, Zhou, Ming, Hon, Hsiao-Wuen, 2019. Unified language model pre-training for natural language understanding and generation. In: Proceedings of NeurIPS.

[71] Joshi, Mandar, Chen, Danqi, Liu, Yinhan, Daniel, S Weld, Zettlemoyer, Luke, Levy, Omer, 2020. Spanbert: improving pre-training by representing and predicting spans. TACL 8, 64–77.

[72] Clark, Kevin, Luong, Minh-Thang, Quoc, V Le, Manning, Christopher D., 2020. Electra: pre-training text encoders as discriminators rather than generators. In: Proceedings of ICLR.

[73] Du, Zhengxiao, Qian, Yujie, Liu, Xiao, Ding, Ming, Qiu, Jiezhong, Yang, Zhilin, Tang, Jie, 2021. All Nlp Tasks Are Generation Tasks: A General Pretraining Framework arXiv preprint arXiv:2103.10360.

[74] Shen, Tianxiao, Quach, Victor, Barzilay, Regina, Jaakkola, Tommi, 2020b. Blank language models. In: Proceedings of EMNLP, pp. 5186–5198.

[75] Song, Kaitao, Tan, Xu, Qin, Tao, Lu, Jianfeng, Liu, Tie-Yan, 2019. Mass: masked sequence to sequence pre-training for language generation. In: Proceedings of ICML, pp. 5926–5936.

[76] Raffel, Colin, Shazeer, Noam, Roberts, Adam, Lee, Katherine, Narang, Sharan, Matena, Michael, Zhou, Yanqi, Li, Wei, Liu, Peter J., 2020. Exploring the limits of transfer learning with a unified text-to-text transformer. JMLR 21, 1–67.

[77] Lewis, Mike, Liu, Yinhan, Goyal, Naman, Ghazvininejad, Marjan, Mohamed, Abdelrahman, Levy, Omer, Veselin Stoyanov, Zettlemoyer, Luke, 2020a. BART: denoising sequence-to-sequence pre-training for natural language generation, translation, and comprehension. In: Proceedings of ACL, pp. 7871–7880.

[78] Zhang, Jingqing, Zhao, Yao, Saleh, Mohammad, Liu, Peter, 2020a. Pegasus: pre-training with extracted gap-sentences for abstractive summarization. In: Proceedings of ICML, pp. 11328–11339.

[79] Bi, Bin, Li, Chenliang, Wu, Chen, Yan, Ming, Wang, Wei, 2020. Palm: pre-training an autoencoding&autoregressive language model for context-conditioned generation. In: Proceedings of EMNLP, pp. 8681–8691.

[80] Srinivasan Iyer, Xi Victoria Lin, Ramakanth Pasunuru,Todor Mihaylov, Daniel Simig, Ping Yu, Kurt Shuster, Tianlu Wang, Qing Liu, Punit Singh Koura, Xian Li, Brian O'Horo, Gabriel Pereyra, Jeff Wang, Christopher Dewan, Asli Celikyilmaz, Luke Zettlemoyer, Ves Stoyanov, 2022. Opt-iml: Scaling language model instruction meta learning through the lens of generalization. In: arXiv 2212.12017.

[81] Jingfeng Yang, Haoming Jiang, Qingyu Yin, Danqing Zhang, Bing Yin, Diyi Yang, 2022. SEQZERO: Few-shot Compositional Semantic Parsing with Sequential Prompts and Zero-shot Models. In: Proceedings of NAACL-HLT, pp. 49-60.

[82] Denny Zhou, Nathanael Schärli, Le Hou, Jason Wei, Nathan Scales, Xuezhi Wang, Dale Schuurmans, Claire Cui, Olivier Bousquet, Quoc V. Le, Ed H. Chi, 2023. Least-to-most prompting enables complex reasoning in large language models. In: Proceedings of ICLR.

[83] Han He, Jinho D. Choi, 2021. The Stem Cell Hypothesis: Dilemma behind Multi-Task Learning with Transformer Encoders. In Proceedings of EMNLP, pp, 5555-5577.
[84] Jacob Devlin, Ming-Wei Chang, Kenton Lee, Kristina Toutanova, 2019. BERT: Pre-training of Deep Bidirectional Transformers for Language Understanding. In: Proceedings of NAACL, pp, 4171-4186.
[85] Yiming Tan, Dehai Min, Yu Li, Wenbo Li, Nan Hu, Yongrui Chen, Guilin Qi, 2023. Can ChatGPT replace traditional KBQA models? An in-depth analysis of the question answering performance of the GPT LLM family. In: Proceedings of ISWC, pp, 348-367.
[86] Reham Omar, Omij Mangukiya, Panos Kalnis, Essam Mansour, 2023. ChatGPT versus Traditional Question Answering for Knowledge Graphs: Current Status and Future Directions Towards Knowledge Graph Chatbots. In: arXiv 2302.06466.
[87] Lunyiu Nie, Shulin Cao, Jiaxin Shi, Jiuding Sun, Qi Tian, Lei Hou, Juanzi Li, Jidong Zhai, 2022. GraphQ IR: Unifying the Semantic Parsing of Graph Query Languages with One Intermediate Representation. In: Proceedings of EMNLP, pp, 5848-5865.
[88] Xixin Hu, Xuan Wu, Yiheng Shu, Yuzhong Qu, 2022. Logical form generation via multi-task learning for complex question answering over knowledge bases. In: Proceedings of ICCL, pp, 1687-1696.
[89] Yu Gu, Yu Su, 2022. ArcaneQA: Dynamic Program Induction and Contextualized Encoding for Knowledge Base Question Answering. In: Proceedings of COLING, pp, 1718-1731.
[90] Donghan Yu, Sheng Zhang, Patrick Ng, Henghui Zhu, Alexander Hanbo Li, Jun Wang, Yiqun Hu, William Yang Wang, Zhiguo Wang, Bing Xiang, 2023. Decaf: Joint decoding of answers and logical forms for question answering over knowledge bases. In: Proceedings of COLING.
[91] Xi Ye, Semih Yavuz, Kazuma Hashimoto, Yingbo Zhou, Caiming Xiong, 2022. RNG-KBQA: Generation Augmented Iterative Ranking for Knowledge Base Question Answering. In: Proceedings of ACL, pp, 6032-6043.
[92] Vrandečić, Denny, Krötzsch, Markus, 2014. Wikidata: A Free Collaborative Knowledgebase. In: Communications of the ACM, vol. 57, no. 10, pp. 78–85.
[93] Lehmann, Jens, Isele, Robert, Jakob, Max, Jentzsch, Anja, Kontokostas, Dimitris, Mendes, Pablo N., Hellmann, Sebastian, Morsey, Mohamed, van Kleef, Patrick, Auer, Sören, Bizer, Christian, 2015. DBpedia - A Large-scale, Multilingual Knowledge Base Extracted from Wikipedia. In: Semantic Web Journal, vol. 6, no. 2, pp. 167–195. Available at: https://content.iospress.com/articles/semantic-web/sw134.
[94] Bollacker, Kurt, Evans, Colin, Paritosh, Praveen, Sturge, Tim, Taylor, Jamie, 2008. Freebase: A Collaboratively Created Graph Database for Structuring Human Knowledge. In: Proceedings of the 2008 ACM SIGMOD international conference on Management of data (SIGMOD '08), Vancouver, Canada, pp. 1247–1250. Available at: http://portal.acm.org/citation.cfm?id=1376746.
[95] Suchanek, Fabian M., Kasneci, Gjergji, Weikum, Gerhard, 2007. Yago: A Core of Semantic Knowledge. In: Proceedings of the 16th International Conference on World Wide Web, Banff, Alberta, Canada, pp. 697–706. Available at: https://doi.org/10.1145/1242572.1242667.
[96] Wikidata, 2012. A sample sub-graph from Wikidata KG. Available at: https://upload.wikimedia.org/wikipedia/commons/6/60/Linked_Data_-_San_Francisco.svg. An image. Last accessed on 23.04.2024.
[97] Cui, Hejie, Lu, Jiaying, Wang, Shiyu, Xu, Ran, Ma, Wenjing, Yu, Shaojun, Yu, Yue, Kan, Xuan, Ling, Chen, Zhao, Liang, Ho, Joyce, Wang, Fei, Yang, Carl, 2023. A Survey on Knowledge Graphs for Healthcare: Resources, Applications, and Promises. Available at: https://arxiv.org/abs/2306.04802. arxiv.org eprint.
[98] Wang, Shuai, 2022. On the Analysis of Large Integrated Knowledge Graphs for Economics, Banking, and Finance. In: EDBT/ICDT Workshops, CEUR Workshop Proceedings, pp. 1–6. Available at: https://ceur-ws.org/Vol-3135/EcoFinKG_2022_paper2.pdf.
[99] Färber, Michael, Lamprecht, David, Krause, Johan, Aung, Linn, Haase, Peter, 2023. SemOpenAlex: The Scientific Landscape in 26 Billion RDF Triples. In: The Semantic Web, Part II, Athens, Greece, pp. 94–112. Available at: https://link.springer.com/chapter/10.1007/978-3-031-47243-5_6.
[100] Rashid, Sabbir M., De Roure, David, McGuinness, Deborah L., 2018. A Music Theory Ontology. In: Proceedings of the 1st International Workshop on Semantic Applications for Audio and Music, Monterey, CA, USA, pp. 6–14. Available at: https://doi.org/10.1145/3243907.3243913.
[101] Balog, Krisztian, Kenter, Tom, 2019. Personal Knowledge Graphs: A Research Agenda. In: Proceedings of the 2019 ACM SIGIR International Conference on Theory of Information Retrieval, Santa Clara, CA, USA, pp. 217–220. Available at: https://doi.org/10.1145/3341981.3344241.
[102] Höffner, K., Walter, S., Marx, E., Usbeck, R., Lehmann, J., Ngonga Ngomo, A.-C. (2017). Sur-

vey on challenges of question answering in the semantic web. Semantic Web, 8(6), 895-920. https://www.semantic-web-journal.net/system/files/swj1375.pdf

[103] Lan, Y., He, G., Jiang, J., Jiang, J., Zhao, W. X., Wen, J.-R. (2021). A survey on complex knowledge base question answering: Methods, challenges and solutions. In Proceedings of the Thirtieth International Joint Conference on Artificial Intelligence (pp. 4483-4491). Retrieved from https://doi.org/10.24963/ijcai.2021/611

[104] Sevgili, Ö., Shelmanov, A., Arkhipov, M., Panchenko, A., Biemann, C. (2022). Neural entity linking: A survey of models based on deep learning. Semantic Web, 13, 527-570. https://doi.org/10.3233/SW-222986

[105] Möller, C., Lehmann, J., Usbeck, R. (2022). Survey on English entity linking on Wikidata: Datasets and approaches. Semantic Web, 13(6), 925-966. Retrieved from https://content.iospress.com/articles/semantic-web/sw212865

[106] Gutierrez, C., Sequeda, J. F. (2021). Knowledge graphs. Communications of the ACM, 64(3), 96-104. https://doi.org/10.1145/3418294

[107] Zettlemoyer, L., Collins, M. (2007). Online learning of relaxed CCG grammars for parsing to logical form. In Proceedings of the 2007 Joint Conference on Empirical Methods in Natural Language Processing and Computational Natural Language Learning (EMNLP-CoNLL) (pp. 678-687). Prague, Czech Republic. Retrieved from https://aclanthology.org/D07-1071

[108] Zettlemoyer, L. S., Collins, M. (2005). Learning to map sentences to logical form: Structured classification with probabilistic categorical grammars. In Proceedings of the Twenty-First Conference on Uncertainty in Artificial Intelligence (pp. 658-666). Edinburgh, Scotland. Retrieved from https://dl.acm.org/doi/10.5555/3020336.3020416

[109] Berant, J., Chou, A., Frostig, R., Liang, P. (2013). Semantic parsing on Freebase from question-answer pairs. In Proceedings of the 2013 Conference on Empirical Methods in Natural Language Processing (pp. 1533-1544). Seattle, Washington, USA. Retrieved from https://aclanthology.org/D13-1160

[110] Reddy, S., Lapata, M., Steedman, M. (2014). Large-scale semantic parsing without question-answer pairs. Transactions of the Association for Computational Linguistics, 2, 377-392. Retrieved from https://aclanthology.org/Q14-1030

[111] Artzi, Y., Zettlemoyer, L. (2013). Weakly supervised learning of semantic parsers for mapping instructions to actions. Transactions of the Association for Computational Linguistics, 1, 49-62. Retrieved from https://aclanthology.org/Q13-1005

[112] Unger, C., Bühmann, L., Lehmann, J., Ngonga Ngomo, A.-C., Gerber, D., Cimiano, P. (2012). Template-based question answering over RDF data. In Proceedings of the 21st International Conference on World Wide Web (pp. 639-648). Lyon, France. https://doi.org/10.1145/2187836.2187923

[113] Bar-Hillel, Y. (1953). A quasi-arithmetical notation for syntactic description. Language, 29(1), 47-58. Retrieved from http://www.jstor.org/stable/410452

[114] Kamath, A., Das, R. (2018). A survey on semantic parsing. Retrieved from http://arxiv.org/abs/1812.00978

[115] Kumar, P., Bedathur, S. (2020). A survey on semantic parsing from the perspective of compositionality. Retrieved from https://arxiv.org/abs/2009.14116

[116] Zhu, Q., Ma, X., Li, X. (2019). Statistical learning for semantic parsing: A survey. Big Data Mining and Analytics, 2(4), 217-239. Retrieved from https://ieeexplore.ieee.org/document/8787228/

[117] Gu, Y., Kase, S., Vanni, M., Sadler, B., Liang, P., Yan, X., Su, Y. (2021). Beyond I.I.D.: Three levels of generalization for question answering on knowledge bases. In Proceedings of the Web Conference (pp. 3477-3488). Ljubljana, Slovenia. https://doi.org/10.1145/3442381.3449992

[118] Abujabal, A., Yahya, M., Riedewald, M., Weikum, G. (2017). Automated template generation for question answering over knowledge graphs. In Proceedings of the 26th International Conference on World Wide Web (pp. 1191-1200). Perth, Australia. https://doi.org/10.1145/3038912.3052583

[119] Berant, J., Liang, P. (2014). Semantic parsing via paraphrasing. In Proceedings of the 52nd Annual Meeting of the Association for Computational Linguistics (Volume 1: Long Papers) (pp. 1415-1425). Baltimore, Maryland. Retrieved from https://aclanthology.org/P14-1133

[120] Ye, X., Yavuz, S., Hashimoto, K., Zhou, Y., Xiong, C. (2022). RNG-KBQA: Generation augmented iterative ranking for knowledge base question answering. In Proceedings of the 60th Annual Meeting of the Association for Computational Linguistics (Volume 1: Long Papers) (pp. 6032-6043). Dublin, Ireland. Retrieved from https://aclanthology.org/2022.acl-long.417

[121] Zafar, H., Napolitano, G., Lehmann, J. (2018). Formal query generation for question answering over

knowledge bases. In *The Semantic Web - ESWC* (pp. 714-728). Hersonissos, Greece: Springer International Publishing. Retrieved from https://link.springer.com/chapter/10.1007/978-3-319-93417-4_46
[122] Bhutani, N., Zheng, X., Jagadish, H. V. (2019). Learning to answer complex questions over knowledge bases with query composition. In *Proceedings of the 28th ACM International Conference on Information and Knowledge Management* (pp. 739-748). Beijing, China. https://doi.org/10.1145/3357384.3358033
[123] Das, R., Zaheer, M., Thai, D., Godbole, A., Perez, E., Lee, J. Y., Tan, L., Polymenakos, L., McCallum, A. (2021). Case-based reasoning for natural language queries over knowledge bases. In *Proceedings of the 2021 Conference on Empirical Methods in Natural Language Processing* (pp. 9594-9611). Online and Punta Cana, Dominican Republic. Retrieved from https://aclanthology.org/2021.emnlp-main.755
[124] Sun, Y., Zhang, L., Cheng, G., Qu, Y. (2020). SPARQA: Skeleton-based semantic parsing for complex questions over knowledge bases. *Proceedings of the AAAI Conference on Artificial Intelligence, 34*, 8952-8959. Retrieved from https://cdn.aaai.org/ojs/6426/6426-13-9651-1-10-20200517.pdf
[125] Zhang, H., Cai, J., Xu, J., Wang, J. (2019). Complex question decomposition for semantic parsing. In *Proceedings of the 57th Annual Meeting of the Association for Computational Linguistics* (pp. 4477-4486). Florence, Italy. Retrieved from https://aclanthology.org/P19-1440
[126] Hochreiter, S., Schmidhuber, J. (1997). Long short-term memory. *Neural Computation, 9*(8), 1735-1780. Retrieved from https://www.bioinf.jku.at/publications/older/2604.pdf
[127] Cho, K., van Merriënboer, B., Gulcehre, C., Bahdanau, D., Bougares, F., Schwenk, H., Bengio, Y. (2014). Learning phrase representations using RNN encoder-decoder for statistical machine translation. In *Proceedings of the 2014 Conference on Empirical Methods in Natural Language Processing (EMNLP)* (pp. 1724-1734). Doha, Qatar. Retrieved from https://aclanthology.org/D14-1179
[128] Raffel, C., Shazeer, N., Roberts, A., Lee, K., Narang, S., Matena, M., Zhou, Y., Li, W.,Liu, P. J. (2020). Exploring the limits of transfer learning with a unified text-to-text transformer. *Journal of Machine Learning Research, 21*(140), 1-67. Retrieved from http://jmlr.org/papers/v21/20-074.html
[129] Vaswani, A., Shazeer, N., Parmar, N., Uszkoreit, J., Jones, L., Gomez, A. N., Kaiser, Ł., Polosukhin, I. (2017). Attention is all you need. In *Proceedings of the 31st International Conference on Neural Information Processing Systems* (pp. 6000-6010). Long Beach, California, USA. Retrieved from https://proceedings.neurips.cc/paper_files/paper/2017/file/3f5ee243547dee91fbd053c1c4a845aa-Paper.pdf
[130] Ravishankar, S., Thai, J., Abdelaziz, I., Mihindukulasooriya, N., Naseem, T., Kapanipathi, P., Rossillo, G., Fokoue, A. (2021). A two-stage approach towards generalization in knowledge base question answering. arXiv. Retrieved from https://arxiv.org/abs/2111.05825
[131] Diomedi, D., Hogan, A. (2021). Question answering over knowledge graphs with neural machine translation and entity linking. arXiv. Retrieved from https://arxiv.org/abs/2107.02865
[132] Bordes, A., Usunier, N., Chopra, S., Weston, J. (2015). Large-scale simple question answering with memory networks. arXiv. Retrieved from https://arxiv.org/abs/1506.02075
[133] Banerjee, D., Nair, P. A., Usbeck, R., Biemann, C. (2023). GETT-QA: Graph embedding based T2T transformer for knowledge graph question answering. In *The Semantic Web: 20th International Conference, ESWC 2023, Hersonissos, Crete, Greece, May 28–June 1, 2023, Proceedings* (pp. 279-297). Retrieved from https://doi.org/10.1007/978-3-031-33455-9_17
[134] Berant, J., Chou, A., Frostig, R., Liang, P. (2013). Semantic parsing on Freebase from question-answer pairs. In D. Yarowsky, T. Baldwin, A. Korhonen, K. Livescu, S. Bethard (Eds.), *Proceedings of the 2013 Conference on Empirical Methods in Natural Language Processing* (pp. 1533-1544). Seattle, Washington, USA: Association for Computational Linguistics. Retrieved from https://aclanthology.org/D13-1160
[135] Bast, H., Haussmann, E. (2015). More accurate question answering on Freebase. In *Proceedings of the 24th ACM International on Conference on Information and Knowledge Management* (pp. 1431-1440). New York, NY, USA: Association for Computing Machinery. https://doi.org/10.1145/2806416.2806472
[136] Abujabal, A., Yahya, M., Riedewald, M., Weikum, G. (2017). Automated template generation for question answering over knowledge graphs. In *Proceedings of the 26th International Conference on World Wide Web* (pp. 1191-1200). Republic and Canton of Geneva, CHE: International World Wide Web Conferences Steering Committee. https://doi.org/10.1145/3038912.3052583
[137] Yao, X., Van Durme, B. (2014). Information extraction over structured data: Question answering with Freebase. In K. Toutanova H. Wu (Eds.), *Proceedings of the 52nd Annual Meeting of the Association for Computational Linguistics (Volume 1: Long Papers)* (pp. 956-966). Baltimore, Maryland: Associ-

ation for Computational Linguistics. https://doi.org/10.3115/v1/P14-1090

[138] Bordes, A., Chopra, S., Weston, J. (2014). Question answering with subgraph embeddings. In A. Moschitti, B. Pang, W. Daelemans (Eds.), *Proceedings of the 2014 Conference on Empirical Methods in Natural Language Processing (EMNLP)* (pp. 615-620). Doha, Qatar: Association for Computational Linguistics. https://doi.org/10.3115/v1/D14-1067

[139] Faria, B., Perdigão, D., Gonçalo Oliveira, H. (2023). Question answering over linked data with GPT-3. In *12th Symposium on Languages, Applications and Technologies* (Vol. 113, pp. 1:1-1:15). Dublin, Ireland. https://drops.dagstuhl.de/entities/document/10.4230/OASIcs.SLATE.2023.1

[140] Klager, G. G., Polleres, A. (2023). Is GPT fit for KGQA? In *Proceedings of the International Workshop on Knowledge Graph Generation from Text, co-located with Extended Semantic Web Conference 2023*. Hersonissos, Greece. https://ceur-ws.org/Vol-3447/Text2KG_Paper_11.pdf

[141] Xu, S., Liu, S., Culhane, T., Pertseva, E., Wu, M.-H., Semnani, S., Lam, M. (2023). Fine-tuned LLMs know more, hallucinate less with few-shot sequence-to-sequence semantic parsing over Wikidata. In *Proceedings of the 2023 Conference on Empirical Methods in Natural Language Processing* (pp. 5778-5791). Singapore. https://aclanthology.org/2023.emnlp-main.353

[142] Shu, Y., Yu, Z. (2023). Data distribution bottlenecks in grounding language models to knowledge bases. arxiv.org eprint. https://arxiv.org/abs/2309.08345

[143] Drozdov, A., Schärli, N., Akyürek, E., Scales, N., Song, X., Chen, X., Bousquet, O., Zhou, D. (2022). Compositional semantic parsing with large language models. arxiv.org eprint. https://arxiv.org/abs/2209.15003

[144] Zhou, D., Schärli, N., Hou, L., Wei, J., Scales, N., Wang, X., Schuurmans, D., Cui, C., Bousquet, O., Le, Q. V., Chi, E. H. (2023). Least-to-most prompting enables complex reasoning in large language models. In The Eleventh International Conference on Learning Representations (ICLR 2023), Kigali, Rwanda. https://openreview.net/forum?id=WZH7099tgfM

[145] Wei, J., Wang, X., Schuurmans, D., Bosma, M., Ichter, B., Xia, F., Chi, E., Le, Q., Zhou, D. (2023). Chain-of-thought prompting elicits reasoning in large language models. arxiv.org eprint. https://arxiv.org/abs/2201.11903

[146] Pan, S., Luo, L., Wang, Y., Chen, C., Wang, J., Wu, X. (2023). Unifying large language models and knowledge graphs: A roadmap. arxiv.org eprint. https://arxiv.org/abs/2306.08302

[147] Kang, M., Baek, J., Hwang, S. J. (2022). KALA: Knowledge-Augmented Language Model Adaptation. In Proceedings of the 2022 Conference of the North American Chapter of the Association for Computational Linguistics: Human Language Technologies (pp. 5144-5167). Seattle, United States. https://aclanthology.org/2022.naacl-main.379

[148] Xiong, W., Du, J., Wang, W. Y., Stoyanov, V. (2019). Pretrained Encyclopedia: Weakly Supervised Knowledge-Pretrained Language Model. Retrieved from `https://arxiv.org/abs/1912.09637`

[149] Lewis, P., Perez, E., Piktus, A., Petroni, F., Karpukhin, V., Goyal, N., Küttler, H., Lewis, M., Yih, W.-t., Rocktäschel, T., Riedel, S., Kiela, D. (2020). Retrieval-Augmented Generation for Knowledge-Intensive NLP Tasks. In *Proceedings of the 34th International Conference on Neural Information Processing Systems* (pp. 9459-9474). Vancouver, BC, Canada. https://dl.acm.org/doi/abs/10.5555/3495724.3496517

[150] Wu, Y., Zhao, Y., Hu, B., Minervini, P., Stenetorp, P., Riedel, S. (2022). An Efficient Memory-Augmented Transformer for Knowledge-Intensive NLP Tasks. In *Proceedings of the 2022 Conference on Empirical Methods in Natural Language Processing* (pp. 5184-5196). Abu Dhabi, United Arab Emirates. https://aclanthology.org/2022.emnlp-main.346

[151] Bertsch, A., Alon, U., Neubig, G., Gormley, M. R. (2023). Unlimiformer: Long-Range Transformers with Unlimited Length Input. In *Conference on Neural Information Processing Systems (NeurIPS)*. New Orleans, USA. Retrieved from https://arxiv.org/abs/2305.01625

[152] Zhao, J., Zhuo, L., Shen, Y., Qu, M., Liu, K., Bronstein, M., Zhu, Z., Tang, J. (2023). GraphText: Graph reasoning in text space. *arXiv preprint arXiv:2310.01089*. Retrieved from `https://arxiv.org/abs/2310.01089`

[153] Fatemi, B., Halcrow, J., Perozzi, B. (2023). Talk like a Graph: Encoding Graphs for Large Language Models. *arXiv preprint arXiv:2310.04560*. Retrieved from `https://arxiv.org/abs/2310.04560`

[154] Robertson, S. E., Walker, S. (1994). Some simple effective approximations to the 2-Poisson model for probabilistic weighted retrieval. In *SIGIR* (pp. 232-241). Dublin, Ireland. Retrieved from `https://link.springer.com/chapter/10.1007/978-1-4471-2099-5_24`

[155] Dubey, M., Banerjee, D., Abdelkawi, A., Lehmann, J. (2019). LC-QuAD 2.0: A large dataset for complex question answering over Wikidata and DBpedia. In *The Semantic Web – ISWC* (pp. 69-78). Auckland, New Zealand. Retrieved from https://link.springer.com/chapter/10.1007/978-3-030-30796-7_5

[156] Galkin, M., Trivedi, P., Maheshwari, G., Usbeck, R., Lehmann, J. (2020). Message passing for hyper-relational knowledge graphs. In *Proceedings of the 2020 Conference on Empirical Methods in Natural Language Processing* (pp. 7346-7359). Online. Retrieved from https://aclanthology.org/2020.emnlp-main.596

[157] Diefenbach, D., Pellissier Tanon, T., Singh, K. D., Maret, P. (2017). Question answering benchmarks for Wikidata. In *Proceedings of the ISWC Posters & Demonstrations and Industry Tracks co-located with 16th International Semantic Web Conference*. Vienna, Austria. Retrieved from https://hal.science/hal-01637141

[158] Pramanik, S., Alabi, J., Saha Roy, R., Weikum, G. (2021). UNIQORN: Unified Question Answering over RDF Knowledge Graphs and Natural Language Text. *arXiv preprint arXiv:2108.08614*. Retrieved from https://arxiv.org/abs/2108.08614

[159] Diefenbach, D., Both, A., Singh, K. D., Maret, P. (Year). Towards a Question Answering System over the Semantic Web. *Semantic Web – Interoperability, Usability, Applicability, 11*(3), 421-439. Retrieved from https://hal.archives-ouvertes.fr/hal-02013956

[160] Oguz, B., Chen, X., Karpukhin, V., Peshterliev, S., Okhonko, D., Schlichtkrull, M., Gupta, S., Mehdad, Y., Yih, S. (2022). UniK-QA: Unified Representations of Structured and Unstructured Knowledge for Open-Domain Question Answering.

[161] Sun, H., Bedrax-Weiss, T., Cohen, W. (2019). PullNet: Open Domain Question Answering with Iterative Retrieval on Knowledge Bases and Text. In *Proceedings of the Conference on Empirical Methods in Natural Language Processing and the 9th International Joint Conference on Natural Language Processing* (pp. 2380-2390). Hong Kong, China. Retrieved from https://aclanthology.org/D19-1242

[162] Pellissier Tanon, T., Dias de Assunção, M., Caron, E., Suchanek, F. M. (2018). Demoing Platypus - A Multilingual Question Answering Platform for Wikidata. In *The Semantic Web: ESWC* (Vol. 11155, pp. 111-116). Heraklion, Crete, Greece. Retrieved from https://doi.org/10.1007/978-3-319-98192-5_21

[163] Bordes, A., Usunier, N., Garcia-Duran, A., Weston, J., Yakhnenko, O. (2013). Translating Embeddings for Modeling Multi-relational Data. In *27th Annual Conference on Neural Information Processing Systems* (pp. 2787-2795). Retrieved from https://proceedings.neurips.cc/paper_files/paper/2013/file/1cecc7a77928ca8133fa24680a88d2f9-Paper.pdf

[164] Lerer, A., Wu, L., Shen, J., Lacroix, T., Wehrstedt, L., Bose, A., Peysakhovich, A. (2019). Pytorch-BigGraph: A Large Scale Graph Embedding System. In *Proceedings of Machine Learning and Systems* (Vol. 1, pp. 120-131). Retrieved from https://proceedings.mlsys.org/paper_files/paper/2019/file/1eb34d662b67a14e3511d0dfd78669be-Paper.pdf

[165] Lewis, P., Perez, E., Piktus, A., Petroni, F., Karpukhin, V., Goyal, N., Küttler, H., Lewis, M., Yih, W.-t., Rocktäschel, T., Riedel, S., Kiela, D. (2020). Retrieval-Augmented Generation for Knowledge-Intensive NLP Tasks. In *Proceedings of the 34th International Conference on Neural Information Processing Systems* (pp. 9459-9474). Vancouver, BC, Canada. https://dl.acm.org/doi/abs/10.5555/3495724.3496517

[166] Wang, A., Singh, A., Michael, J., Hill, F., Levy, O., Bowman, S. (2018). GLUE: A multi-task benchmark and analysis platform for natural language understanding. In T. Linzen, G. Chrupała, A. Alishahi (Eds.), Proceedings of the 2018 EMNLP Workshop BlackboxNLP: Analyzing and Interpreting Neural Networks for NLP (pp. 353–355). Association for Computational Linguistics. https://doi.org/10.18653/v1/W18-5446

Handbook on Neurosymbolic AI and Knowledge Graphs
P. Hitzler et al. (Eds.)
IOS Press, 2025

doi:10.3233/FAIA250221

Neurosymbolic Program Synthesis

Swarat CHAUDHURI
The University of Texas at Austin

Abstract. We survey *neurosymbolic program synthesis*, an emerging research area at the interface of deep learning and symbolic artificial intelligence. As in classical machine learning, the goal in neurosymbolic program synthesis is to learn functions from data. However, these functions are represented as *programs* that use symbolic primitives, often in conjunction with neural network components, and must, in some cases, satisfy certain additional behavioral constraints. The programs are induced using a combination of symbolic search and gradient-based optimization. In this survey, we categorize the main ways in which symbolic and neural learning techniques come together in this area. We also showcase the key advantages of the approach — specifically, greater reliability, interpretability, verifiability, and compositionality — over end-to-end deep learning.

Keywords. Neurosymbolic AI, Program Synthesis, Machine Learning

1. Introduction

Research on artificial intelligence (AI) has, for a long time, been split between the symbolists and the connectionists. The older symbolic agenda sought to describe the world using logic-based rules. In contrast, the machine learning (ML) perspective posited that patterns can be learned purely from data. In recent years, the ML perspective has tended to win out — in particular, thanks to breathtaking progress in the field of deep learning.

At the same time, concerns remain about the use of deep learning in real-world problems [1]. As opaque black boxes, deep neural networks are hard to trust and interpret. They cannot be easily taught to conform to commonsense knowledge that humans have. They cannot reuse components in the way traditional software can. Their training can be unreliable and fail in data-poor environments.

Neurosymbolic machine learning [1,2,3] is an increasingly prominent response to these concerns. The idea here is to inject human-held symbolic knowledge into a deep learning process. This knowledge can constrain the learned functions to use certain algorithmic abstractions, and can also serve as a *regularizer*, allowing more reliable learning.

In particular, this paper focuses on an emerging form of neurosymbolic learning called *neurosymbolic program synthesis* (NSP). NSP generalizes classical program synthesis [4], where the goal is to automatically discover programs that are written in a domain-specific language (DSL) and satisfy a logical specification. These programs are obtained through the composition of a set of symbolic modules with well-specified interpretations, using combinators that enforce natural requirements at the interface of different components. The program synthesis problem is solved using symbolic methods, e.g., discrete search and logic-based pruning.

NSP broadens both the problem statement and the solution space of program synthesis. The programs in NSP can be built entirely from symbolic primitives. Often, however, they use a mix of symbolic code and neural modules. The synthesis problem in NSP is to induce a program — including the program's discrete structure, or *architecture*, as well as the parameters of its neural components, if any — that minimizes a cost function. In some cases, the synthesized program is also required to satisfy a set of additional behavioral constraints like in classical program synthesis. This synthesis problem is solved using a variety of strategies that bring together deep learning (including the use of large language models [5,6]) and symbolic search and reasoning techniques.

2. Motivating Goals

Now we elaborate on the main technical goals of NSP.

Generalization. Generalization is a foundational concept in machine learning. A learner *generalizes* if it can predict well on new test cases outside of its training set, ideally after training with a relatively small number of training samples. A key benefit of NSP is that neurosymbolic models can potentially generalize better than fully neural models.

For example, one way to improve the learner's ability to generalize is through *regularization*, which is a way of supplying an *inductive bias* — a preference order among hypotheses. Over the years, many regularization schemes for deep learning have been proposed. NSP introduces a new form of regularization by constraining the syntax and semantics of hypotheses using specifications (DSLs and behavioral constraints). This kind of *programmatic regularization* facilitates the use of domain knowledge. That is, a human user can encode insights about true solutions to the task in the language specification, biasing the learner towards hypotheses that are more likely to generalize.

Programmatic regularization is especially beneficial for procedural tasks, in which an agent performs sequences of actions realizing complex objectives, and for learning over structured data types like sequences and trees. In these settings, neural networks often fail to generalize from a modest number of examples. In contrast, one can often represent solutions to these tasks as programs that use high-level data and control abstractions. Such a task representation inductively generalizes *by construction*, for example, using looping primitives that operate over data of unbounded length or branching primitives that can break up a task into subtasks.

The PROPEL [7] approach to reinforcement learning (RL) is an example of this kind of regularization. The goal in RL is to learn a *policy* — a function mapping environment states to actions — for an agent exploring an unknown environment. In contrast to standard deep RL, a policy in PROPEL is a neurosymbolic program that additively combines a neural network and a symbolic program. The symbolic program is a composition of traditional control primitives (e.g., PID controllers) and thus captures expert knowledge. The neural net gives this program data-derived flexibility. PROPEL's learning algorithm simultaneously induces the neural and symbolic parts of the policy from data gathered via exploration. Compared to using a purely neural policy, this approach has provably lower variance (and is thus more sample-efficient) [7]. Empirically, policies learned through PROPEL tend to memorize fewer low-level details of the training environment (compared to neural policies), and thus generalize better to changes in the environment.

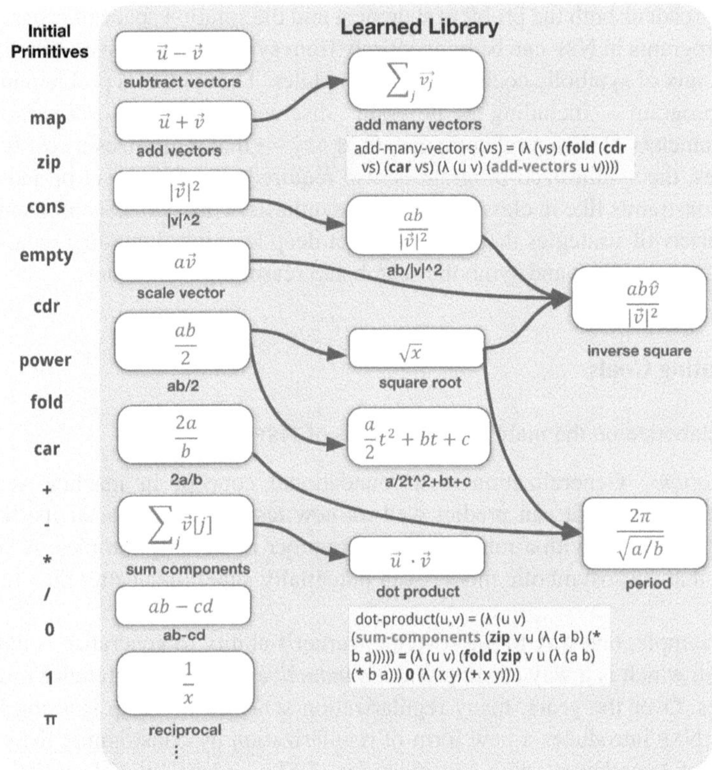

Figure 1. A sample output of DREAMCODER [8]. The system is tasked with synthesizing programs, written in a basic functional language, that fit random data simulated from physics equations. In synthesizing these programs it assembles a library of reusable procedures, including basic vector algebra and common patterns found in physics equations, which can be *transferred* to future synthesis tasks.

Modular Learning. Modern high-level programming is inherently modular. Programmers commonly break down complex coding tasks into subtasks that are solved using pre-existing library modules. An important promise of NSP is that it enables such modularity in learning using high-level programming primitives.

Specifically, NSP can use symbolic primitives to decompose a learning task into a composition of simpler tasks. These simpler tasks can be represented by either symbolic or neural modules. The modules can be learned afresh on a new task, or drawn from a "library" learned on previous tasks.

HOUDINI [9] and DREAMCODER [8] are two well-known frameworks for modular NSP. Both approaches exploit modularity to *transfer* knowledge across tasks. Specifically, HOUDINI is trained on a curriculum of tasks and iteratively grows a library of neural modules during this training. The synthesis algorithm in HOUDINI searches over programs that compose library modules, functional combinators such as **map** and **fold**, and fresh neural modules, and finds a program that solves the task. After outputting this program, the newly trained modules are added to the library for use in future tasks. On a set of tasks involving algorithmic computation over images, this approach outperforms neural approaches to transfer learning.

(a)

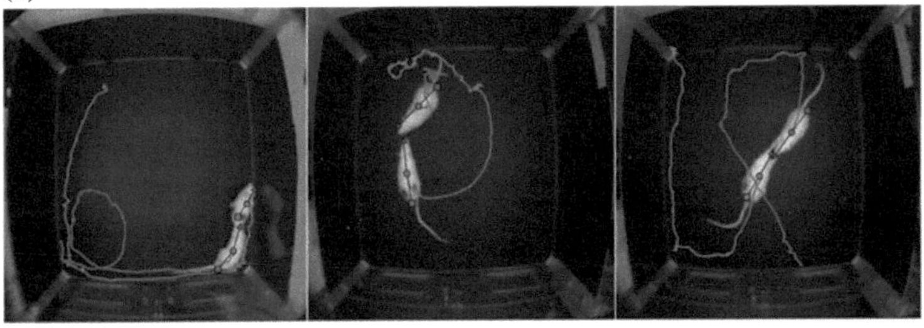

(b)

map (**lambda** x_t.**if** $DistAffine_{[.0217];-.2785}(x_t)$
then $AccAffine_{[-.0007,.0055,.0051,-.0025];3.7426}(x_t)$
else $DistAffine_{[-.2143];1.822)}(x_t)$) x

Figure 2. (a) Stills from the CRIM13 behavior-tracking dataset for mice. (b) Programmatic classifier for a "sniff" action, learned using NEAR [10]. *DistAffine* and *AccAffine* are functions that first select the parts of the input that represent distance and acceleration measurements, respectively (the subscripts represent numerical parameters). The program has an accuracy of 0.87 (vs. 0.89 for a recurrent neural network baseline) and can be interpreted as: if the distance between two mice is small, they are doing a "sniff". Otherwise, they are doing a "sniff" if the difference between their accelerations is small.

DREAMCODER [8] (Figure 1) exploits modularity for transfer learning using symbolic modules. Starting with a set of first- and higher-order symbolic primitives and a corpus of training problems, DREAMCODER iteratively synthesizes code satisfying each training specification and mines this code for symbolic "templates" that can be reused in future tasks. The method is shown to solve a range of problems, including classic inductive programming, symbolic regression, and the design of complex scenes, that are beyond the scope of purely neural approaches.

Interpretability. *Interpretability* is an important consideration in many machine learning applications. However, interpretability is often at odds with learning performance. Deep neural networks are performant but not interpretable. On the other hand, linear models and shallow decision trees are interpretable but lack performance on complex tasks.

The representation of machine learning models as programs is an alternative path to interpretability. Interpreting a model's functionality now amounts to reading its code step by step and understanding the semantics of the underlying language primitives. Symbolic program analysis techniques can also now be used to algorithmically discover the model's properties. At the same time, assuming a suitably sophisticated DSL, even short programs can express complex computations and perform tasks beyond the reach of shallow learning models.

For example, the NEAR [10] approach, which we will describe in more detail in Section 5, was used to discover interpretable models of animal behavior. Figure 2-(a) shows stills from a video of such behavior for laboratory mice. Figure 2-(b) illustrates a sample program that describes when two mice are doing a "sniff" action.

Safety Verification. Safety is increasingly a central concern in deep learning research. It is well-known that deep networks can fail badly on adversarial or unexpected inputs. At the same time, it is impossible to reason about their correctness using traditional manual techniques. This makes the deployment of deep networks in safety-critical applications a fraught endeavor.

Automatic verification of neural networks, using formal methods such as abstract interpretation and SMT-solving, is an increasingly popular response to this challenge. Unfortunately, formal methods tend to only be efficient for programs that are small or have an architecture that enables compositional verification of subproblems. Neural networks do not satisfy either property. As a result, verification of neural networks has so far only scaled to fairly small models.

In contrast, approaches based on NSP can use high-level abstractions to facilitate verification. So far, these methods have been primarily used to learn programmatic policies for RL agents that provably satisfy invariants such as smoothness [11,7] and stability [12], and in some cases, more comprehensive functional correctness requirements [12].

Some of these methods, such as PIRL [11] and Viper [12], learn fully symbolic programs that can be verified using classical formal methods. However, even when learned programs have neural modules, they can sometimes be soundly approximated by symbolic programs. For example, Zhu et al. [13] and Anderson et al. [14] consider neurosymbolic policies of the form "**if** $(\psi(x, f(x))$ **then** $f(x)$ **else** $g(x)$", where g is a neural network and f and ψ are short symbolic expressions. To verify such programs, they abstract the neural component g with a nondeterministic choice, then automatically verify that the resulting symbolic program is safe under all instantiations of this choice. If it is, then the original neurosymbolic program is safe as well.

3. Applications

The technical goals described in Section 2 cut across many real-world applications. Now we present an incomplete list of some of these applications.

Scientific Discovery. Building learning algorithms that discover new scientific hypotheses and guide experiments is a grand challenge in AI. Such algorithms must respect constraints known to hold in the world and produce outputs that scientists can interpret. This makes NSP a natural fit to this space.

For example, Cranmer et al. [15] proposed a method for *symbolic regression* — the automatic discovery of symbolic equations from data — and apply it to a task in cosmology (dark matter prediction). Also, some of the NSP efforts mentioned in this survey were applied in the behavior analysis of laboratory animals. Specifically, NEAR [10], described in Section 5, was used to classify sequential animal behaviors. The NSP-based representation learning method [16] we describe in Section 4 as an exemplar of "symbolically guided deep learning" was used for interpretable clustering of such behaviors. FunSearch [5], an NSP method that uses large language models to direct evolutionary searches over programs, was utilized to discover witnesses to mathematical statements. LaSR [6], which augments a FunSearch-like method with a form of LLM-directed concept learning, was used to solve symbolic regression tasks, and in particular, discovered a new scaling law for LLMs.

Programming Systems. Over the last few years, code generation has emerged as one of the most successful applications of deep learning. Most approaches here generate programs token by token using a neural language model. While this strategy has worked remarkably well for high-level, API-manipulating code that follows idioms well-represented in publicly available code. However, generating code with novel structure, interpreting and satisfying sophisticated requirements, and maintaining consistency within large amounts of generated code remain challenges. Given that symbolic methods have long been used successfully to rigorously analyze programs and requirements and verify programs, NSP is a natural way to overcome some of these issues.

Recent work on code generation systems has begun to capitalize on some of this promise. Specifically, the emerging body of work on language-model *agents* for programming [17,18] and mathematical reasoning [19] do not just generate programs using a language model, but execute and analyze the resulting code and use the feedback from these processes to influence generation. As such, they can be seen as an instance of NSP.

Dialog Systems. Task-oriented dialog systems assist users with specific goals through a natural language interface. As digital assistants, they facilitate travel booking, database question answering, scheduling, and much more. The key challenge of task-oriented dialog is *state tracking* – identifying the user's intent and parameters in each dialog act, and using them to drive the system's actions. Fundamentally, dialog state is an intermediate symbolic representation that depends on complex, high-dimensional semantic context, namely dialog history and the underlying knowledge base or API. Thereby, NSP is a natural choice for modeling dialog state, successfully applied in many domains. For example, Andreas et al. [20] design a calendar assistant in which scheduling actions, dialog corrections, and exceptions are represented as compositional programs, synthesized by neurosymbolic models in context.

Process Automation. The field of *robotic process automation (RPA)* aims to automate procedural GUI workflows to facilitate business digitization and software testing. RPA agents interact with Web browsers, GUI applications, and APIs to accomplish the user's parameterized tasks. They are typically pretrained for each task using natural language commands, UI-grounded demonstrations, task completion rewards, or some combination thereof.

In RPA, the agent's state and action spaces are enormous – the current screen or Web page defines the state and the action space includes all possible interactions with its elements. Learning a robust and interpretable RPA agent is challenging even from grounded demonstrations as supervision. Instead, recent approaches leverage NSP ideas and model the agent as a neurosymbolic task program. For example, Srivastava et al. [21] combine neural language modeling with inductive program synthesis [4] to learn a generative model of programs that both guarantees consistency with the demonstrations and optimizes natural language alignment.

Robotics and Control. When designing policies or controllers for autonomous embodied systems, factors such as safety and data efficiency become paramount. For both low-level control and high-level planning problems, the standard practice has been to leverage symbolic domain knowledge (e.g., the governing equations of motion for the system, or an automaton representation of the high-level states) to design structured models that have certifiable guarantees, good generalization, or both (*e.g.*, Verma et al. [7]). An emerging research direction is to automatically learn or discover the structure of the symbolic knowledge (*e.g.*, Xu et al. [22]), which can be viewed as an instance of NSP.

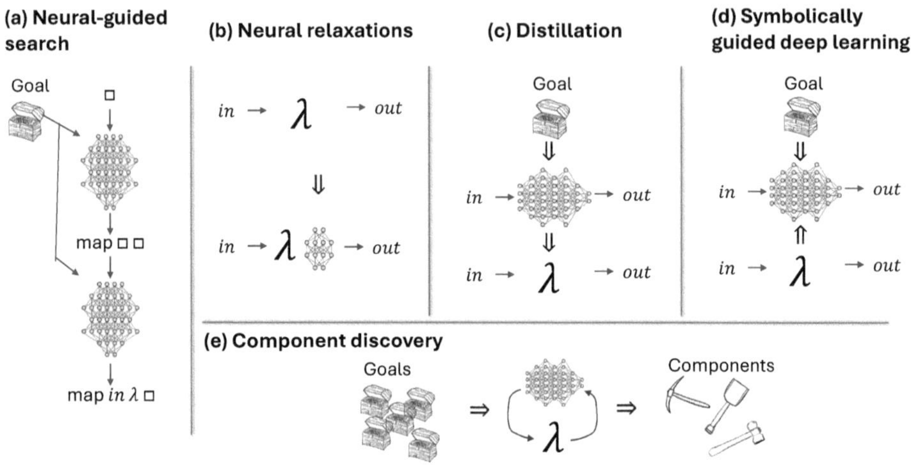

Figure 3. A taxonomy of learning algorithms in NSP. (a) shows neural-guided search algorithms, in which a neural network, trained using a corpus of programming tasks, is used to guide a search over programs. (b) illustrates *neural relaxation* methods, which approximate programs by differentiable neural functions. (c) depicts the dual distillation paradigm, in which neural functions are approximated by programs. (d) shows symbolically-guided deep learning, where a deep learning process incorporates synthesized symbolic information. (e) shows techniques for discovering new DSL components from synthesized programs.

4. Learning Algorithms

Now we sketch the main categories of learning algorithms used to synthesize programs in NSP. A high-level overview of these approaches is shown in Figure 3.

4.1. Starting Point: Search and Train

Algorithms in NSP build on a substantial prior literature on search-based program synthesis [4]. Common algorithmic strategies in that literature include enumeration, sampling, version-space techniques, and the use of solvers. In *top-down* enumerative search [23,24], one repeatedly applies the rules of a DSL's grammar, starting with the initial nonterminal, until complete programs are generated. On the way, automatic deduction is used to recursively decompose the task specification into subgoals, as well as to rule out choices that provably fail to guarantee the specification. In *genetic programming* approaches [25], one maintains a pool of candidate programs and progressively modifies the pool using crossover and mutation operations. Bottom-up enumeration techniques [26] also maintain pools of candidates, updating the pool by composing simple programs into more complex ones.

There is also a body of methods that use stochastic methods, for example, Metropolis-Hastings sampling [27] and Sequential Monte Carlo, to effectively sample desirable programs from a space defined by a DSL. Version space methods use a specialized data structure to represent exponentially sized sets of programs. *Solver-driven* search [28] translates the space of programs and the specification into a joint constraint that is solved using a satisfiability solver.

The simplest learning methods in NSP use these search methods to generate program architectures and then train the resulting architectures using gradient descent. For such *search-and-train* methods to work, the programs must be *differentiable* in their parameters. This assumption does not hold in general but can be realized either by restricting the DSL or through the continuous relaxation techniques discussed in Section 4.3.

For example, the HOUDINI system [9] uses a search-and-train approach. HOUDINI uses top-down enumerative search to iterate over strongly-typed, differentiable program architectures, using a type system to significantly prune the search space on the way. For each architecture that is fully generated, the parameters of these modules are learned using gradient descent.

4.2. Neural-Guided Search

The main challenge with search-and-train approaches is scalability. Symbolic methods can rule out untenable programs using logical techniques. However, they do not give a way to find optimal architectures and are of limited value when the synthesis problem is not tightly constrained by logical requirements. As a result, recent research has studied ways to accelerate the search over programs using neural techniques. Collectively, these algorithmic techniques form the core of the area of NSP.

The most well-established of these methods are naturally described as *neural-guided search*. Here, one learns, from data, neural *policies* that generate probability distributions over the space of program architectures. These distributions can then be used to guide a combinatorial search over programs.

ROBUSTFILL [29], a neural-guided method for programming by example, was an early exemplar of such a method. ROBUSTFILL uses an encoder-decoder model with an attention mechanism to learn a distribution over programs conditioned on input-outputs. Next, it uses a beam search to generate programs from the learned distribution.

The neural models used in ROBUSTFILL were relatively small. Over the last few years, much larger transformer models trained on large code corpora have been used to guide program generation. There are many such methods; here we mention one, Alphacode [30]. This method solves programming problems using an encoder-decoder neural network that is pretrained on open-source code corpora available on the internet, then finetuned on programming competition problems. In addition to the basic neural-guided program generation strategy, the method uses additional innovations, such as the use of a neural network to generate candidate inputs for synthesized programs. Programs that exhibit the same behavior on these generated inputs are clustered into equivalence classes; from each equivalence class, a single member is selected for final use.

Later efforts have used more sophisticated stochastic search methods — in particular, reinforcement learning (RL) — to discover policies for program synthesis [31,32]. The challenge here is that sampling over programs is difficult, as "bad" programs vastly outnumber the "good" ones — which means stochastic methods may need massive numbers of samples to learn to find good programs. To overcome this problem, Bunel et al. [31] first train a supervised model for program generation. Then they use the REINFORCE algorithm to fine-tune the model by sampling programs from the distribution and giving a positive reward for a program that produces the desired output. Chen et al. [32] use automated deduction to use automated deduction to prune out subspaces of undesirable programs as the search progresses, and also to give the learner a signal regarding the kind of programs to avoid exploring.

Such RL methods have been recently scaled in efforts such as AlphaTensor [33] and AlphaDev [34]. In particular, AlphaDev studies the problem of discovering, given an assembly-language program, a *low-latency* equivalent program. This problem is framed as an RL task in which the reward depends on both correctness and latency. Innovations include the use of separate encoders for program and memory, and a "two-headed" RL value function in which one head is used for latency and the other for correctness.

Recent approaches to program synthesis and mathematical reasoning that combine language modeling, tool use, and search can also be seen to follow the general paradigm of neural-guided search. For example, SWE-agent [17] repeatedly invokes a large language model (LLM) that is allowed to use symbolic software tools, such as those for creating and editing code files, navigating software repositories, and executing tests and other programs. It is shown that this approach substantially exceeds the performance achieved via state-of-the-art non-interactive language models. Thakur et al. [19] use an LLM-guided search for formal theorem-proving in frameworks like Lean [35]. The FunSearch [5] and LaSR [6] approaches use LLMs to direct an evolutionary search over programs in the application context of mathematical and scientific discovery.

4.3. Neural Relaxations

A different category of methods *relaxes* the program learning problem into a smooth optimization problem, then solves using gradient descent. Such a strategy can be valuable for two reasons. First, the DSL may permit architectures that use non-differentiable constructs (*e.g.*, branching or sampling operations). Relaxations allow the parameters of such programs to be learned using gradient-based methods. Second, in some cases, one can use smooth relaxations of the discrete landscape of program architectures into a continuous landscape that allows easier optimization.

Smooth interpretation [36,37] was an early example of program relaxations in parameter learning. This method defines a *smooth operational semantics* of programs that amounts to stochastically perturbing the program's input and taking the expectation of the (probabilistic) output on this input. This semantics is now used to produce a signal for a continuous optimizer.

NEAR [10] points to a different way of using neural relaxations. The goal here is to find a program that optimally fits a labeled dataset. To meet this goal, NEAR derives programs top-down. Incomplete programs encountered during this derivation process are approximated by differentiable neurosymbolic functions that are trained end to end, and the training loss is used as a *heuristic function* that can guide informed searches (such as A^*) over programs. We describe this method in more depth in Section 5.

Cui et al. [38] have extended NEAR into an end-to-end differentiable method for program synthesis. Building on prior work on differentiable architecture search, this methods models the entire DSL as a differentiable program. That is, at each node in the search graph, the categorical choice between different edges out of the node is relaxed into a trainable softmax. The gradient updates for these softmax weights are guided by a lower-level signal from neural relaxations.

4.4. Distillation

In the related *distillation* paradigm [11,7,12,14,13], one starts by relaxing the set of all programs in the DSL into a differentiable, overparameterized space of functions represented by a neural network. Because the neural network can be assumed to be more

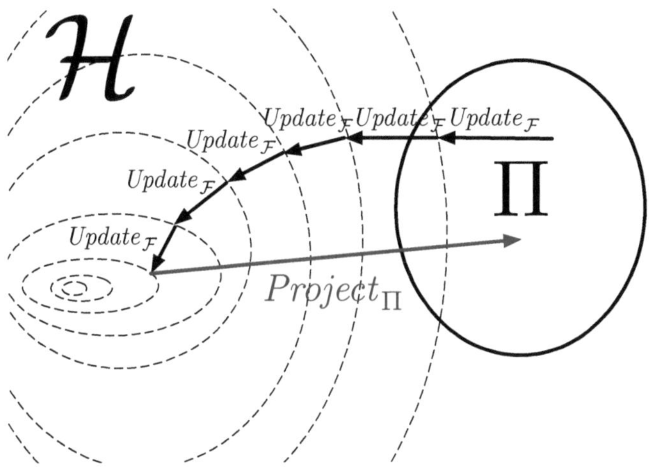

Figure 4. The PROPEL algorithm [7]. $\mathscr{H}$ is the relaxed space; Π is the space of DSL programs. *Update*$_{\mathscr{F}}$ represents gradient updates; *Project*$_{\Pi}$ is the distillation operation.

expressive than the DSL, every program in the DSL has a representation as a parameterization of the network. At the same time, the neural representation can be optimized using gradient-based methods. The learning algorithm uses this fact to learn an optimal function g in the relaxed space. This function may not have a symbolic representation in the DSL, hence it is *distilled* into a DSL program whose behavior is as close as possible to g.

The PIRL [11] and VIPER [12] methods for "programmatic" reinforcement learning (RL) were the first distillation approaches to NSP. The goal in both methods is to learn a policy, expressed in a symbolic DSL, that maximizes an RL agent's long-term reward. Solving this problem requires program synthesis as well as computationally complex planning over a long time horizon. PIRL and VIPER first eliminate the program synthesis dimension of the problem by learning a relaxed neural policy using a standard deep RL algorithm. Distilling this policy into a symbolic one is now framed as *imitation learning* problem, which does not require planning and can be reduced to a supervised learning task. This supervised learning problem is solved using an extension of classic program synthesis techniques.

PROPEL [7] (Figure 4) repeatedly performs distillation and relaxation during training. The method considers two policy classes: the class of policies representable as programs in the DSL, and the relaxed class of policies of the form $f(x)+g(x)$, where $f(x)$ is a neural network and $g(x)$ is a program in the DSL. The discovery of an optimal programmatic policy is framed as a form of mirror descent. In every learning step, the algorithm first applies a series of gradient updates to the neural component of the current neurosymbolic policy. Next, using distillation techniques like in PIRL, the algorithm distills this neurosymbolic policy into a program from the DSL. This program is then lifted back into the relaxed policy representation by adding a neural term.

Recent work has extended these ideas to the setting of formally verified learning. Specifically, Zhu et al. [13] give a method similar to PIRL but uses a distillation step that is guaranteed to produce a formally verified program. Anderson et al. [14] extend PROPEL so that distillation, relaxation, and gradient updates in the relaxed policy space all preserve the invariant of provable safety. While these methods learn using neurosymbolic representations, they only verify the distilled purely symbolic programs.

4.5. Symbolically Guided Deep Learning

A fourth category of methods uses synthesized programs to inject human-held knowledge into a deep learning process. In particular, such programs can be used to: (i) augment latent vector representations learned through neural methods, and (ii) to automatically construct loss functions used to train deep networks.

The *neurosymbolic encoders* presented by Zhan et al. [16] exemplify the former strategy. The approach modifies the variational autoencoder (VAE) framework, where a model comprises an encoder that compresses inputs into latent vectors and a decoder that decompresses these vectors back. It replaces the neural encoder with a "parallel composition" of a neural encoder and a symbolic program — i.e., the latent encoding now also includes some "bits" computed using the program. The neural and symbolic encoders and trained jointly with the neural decoder in an alternating optimization scheme that builds on NEAR. The method is shown to build representations that are significantly more well-factorized than those from standard VAEs, and demonstrated to lead to practical gains on downstream analysis tasks, such as for behavior classification.

AUTOSWAP, by Tseng et al. [39], is an instance of the second strategy. This method falls in the paradigm of weakly supervised learning, where *labeling functions* are used to automatically annotate data. While labeling functions are traditionally hand-written, AUTOSWAP uses the NEAR method to automatically discover task-level labeling functions from a small labeled dataset. A key technical idea is the use of a novel structural diversity cost that allows for the synthesis of *diverse* sets of LFs. The paper shows that AUTOSWAP outperforms existing approaches to behavior analysis using only a fraction of the data.

4.6. Component Discovery

So far, we have discussed methods for learning programs for a predefined language. Now we proceed to neurosymbolic methods for learning DSLs. In general, a DSL consists of some universal combinators (*e.g.*, constructs for looping, branching, or processing basic data structures) and a "library" of reusable modules. These methods induce these reusable modules — either neural, symbolic, or both — and reuse them in new program learning tasks.

Learning neural modules. Methods for transferring neural modules start with a "pre-training" phase in which the module library is constructed, followed by a "deployment" or test-time phase when this library is used to solve new problems. During the "pre-training" phase, an inventory of small neural networks are composed to solve training synthesis tasks in tandem with training the weights of each network. The size of this bank of neural modules can either be fixed ahead of time — such as in modular meta-learning [40] and memoised wake-sleep [41] — or grow in size after each training experience, such as in HOUDINI [9]. At the test time or "deployment" phase, these neural modules can be used wholesale, with frozen weights [9]. Alternatively, their pretrained weights can be adapted to to each new task [40]. In either case, they do not need massive amounts of data to learn at test time.

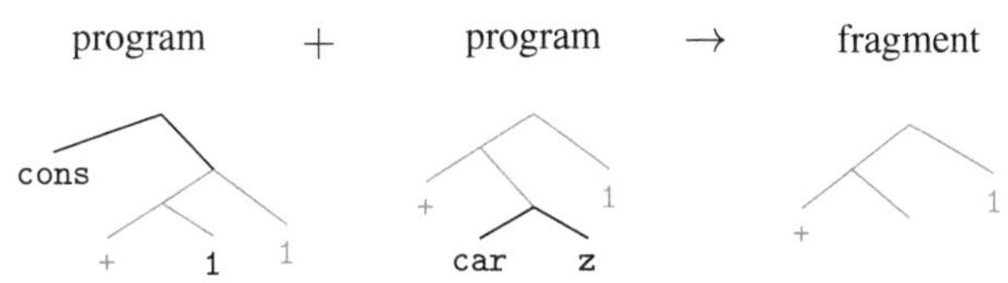

Example synthesized programs	Proposed library expression

`(λ (s) (map (λ (x)`
`(if (= x '.') '-' x))) s)`
`(λ (s) (map (λ (x)`
`(if (= x '-') ',' x))) s)`
	`(λ (s) (map (λ (x)`
	`(if (= x α) β x))) s)`

Figure 5. Top: syntax trees of two programs sharing common structure, highlighted in orange, from which DREAMCODER [8] can extract a reused fragment (bottom). The programs may be constructed through the *refactoring* of known programs using a set of rewrite rules. **Bottom:** two actual programs, and the generalized library abstraction created from their shared fragment.

Learning Symbolic Modules. There are also methods for inducing a library of reusable symbolic code. The most popular strategy is to compress out reused syntax trees across a training corpus of programs. DREAMCODER [42] is a canonical example of such an approach. As outlined before, it is initialized with a set of basic primitives and a corpus of training tasks. It tackles these training tasks by jointly learning a neural network that can guide the synthesis of programs that perform these tasks, while also building a library of reused symbolic functions by mining synthesized programs for templates. The latter task is performed via a deductive method that uses a set of semantics-preserving rewrite rules refactor a set of existing programs and identify shared structure. Figure 5 illustrates a special case.

The subsequent STITCH approach [43] takes on the same problem as DREAMCODER, but discovers abstractions via a top-down search rather than a deductive refactoring-based method. It is shown to be several orders of magnitude faster than DREAMCODER.

5. A Deeper Dive: NEAR

Now we do a deeper dive into a specific NSP approach, NEAR [10]. Here, we spell out the problem that the method targets as well as its algorithmic approach. Figure 2 illustrates a sample problem solved using NEAR. See the original paper for more detailed experimental results.

Problem Statement. NEAR takes on a supervised learning task: given a dataset of labeled examples and a cost function, it seeks to find a program in a given DSL that minimizes the cost function.

Let us view a program abstractly as a pair (α, θ), where α is a discrete *program structure* (or *architecture*) and θ is a vector of real-valued parameters. It is assumed that the architecture α is generated using a *context-free grammar* [44]. The grammar starts with an initial nonterminal, then iteratively applies the rules to produce a series of *partial architectures*: sentences made from one or more nonterminals and zero or more terminals. The process continues until there are no nonterminals left, i.e., we have a complete architecture.

The *semantics* of the architecture α is given by a function $[\![\alpha]\!](x,\theta)$, defined by rules that are fixed for the DSL. This function is required to be differentiable in θ. Also, a *structural cost* is defined for architectures. Let each rule r in the DSL grammar have a non-negative real cost $s(r)$. The structural cost of α is defined us $s(\alpha) = \sum_{r \in \mathscr{R}(\alpha)} s(r)$, where $\mathscr{R}(\alpha)$ is the multiset of rules used to create α. Intuitively, architectures with lower structural costs are simpler are more human-interpretable.

Now we formalize the learning problem in NEAR. Let us assume an unknown distribution $D(x,y)$ over inputs x and labels y, and consider the prediction error function $\zeta(\alpha,\theta) = \mathbf{E}_{(x,y)\sim D}[\mathbf{1}([\![\alpha]\!](x,\theta) \neq y)]$, where $\mathbf{1}$ is the indicator function. The learning problem, then, is to find an architecturally simple program with low prediction error, i.e., to solve the optimization problem:

$$(\alpha^*,\theta^*) = \arg\min_{(\alpha,\theta)}(s(\alpha) + \zeta(\alpha,\theta)). \tag{1}$$

Program synthesis as Graph Search. NEAR piggybacks an informed search on a *program derivation graph* that models the top-down construction of program architectures. The nodes in this graph are incomplete architectures; at a node u, the heuristic $h(u)$ approximates the *cost to go*, i.e., the additional cost incurred by the best sequence of program derivation actions that can be taken from this point on.

More precisely, NEAR considers a graph $\mathscr{G}$ in which:

- The node set consists of all partial and complete architectures permissible in the DSL.
- The *source node* u_0 is the empty architecture. Each complete architecture α is a *goal node*.
- Edges are directed and capture single-step applications of rules of the DSL. Edges can be divided into: (i) *internal edges* (u,u') between partial architectures u and u', and (ii) *goal edges* (u,α) between partial architecture u and complete architecture α. An internal edge (u,u') exists if one can obtain u' by substituting a nonterminal in u following a rule of the DSL. A goal edge (u,α) exists if we can complete u into α by applying a rule of the DSL.
- The cost of an internal edge (u,u') is given by the structural cost $s(r)$, where r is the rule used to construct u' from u. The cost of a goal edge (u,α) is $s(r) + \zeta(\alpha,\theta^*)$, where $\theta^* = \arg\min_\theta \zeta(\alpha,\theta)$ and r is the rule used to construct α from u.

An example of such a graph appears in Figure 6.

Let a *completion* of a partial architecture u be a (complete) architecture $u[\alpha_1,\ldots,\alpha_k]$ obtained by replacing the nonterminals in u by suitably typed architectures α_i. Let θ_u be the parameters of u and θ be parameters of the α_i-s. The *cost-to-go* at u is now given by:

$$J(u) = \min_{\alpha_1,\ldots,\alpha_k,\theta_u,\theta}((s(u[\alpha_1,\ldots,\alpha_k] - s(u)) + \zeta(u[\alpha_1,\ldots,\alpha_k],(\theta_u,\theta)) \tag{2}$$

where the structural cost $s(u)$ is the sum of the costs of the grammatical rules used to construct u.

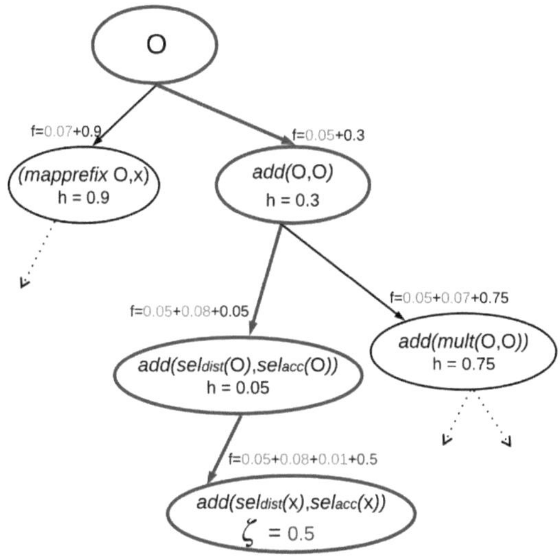

Figure 6. An example of program synthesis formulated as graph search [10]. Structural costs are in red, heuristic values in black, prediction errors ζ in blue, O refers to a nonterminal in a partial architecture, and the path to a goal node returned by A* search with NEAR heuristics is in teal.

Neural Heuristics. To compute a heuristic cost $h(u)$ for a partial architecture u encountered during search, NEAR substitutes the nonterminals in u with neural networks parameterized by ω. These networks are *type-correct* — for example, if a nonterminal is supposed to generate subexpressions whose inputs are sequences, then the neural network used in its place is recurrent.

Let us view the neurosymbolic programs resulting from this substitution as tuples $(u,(\theta_u,\omega))$. One can define a semantics for such programs by extending our DSL's semantics, and lift the function ζ to assign costs $\zeta(u,(\theta_u,\omega))$ to such programs. The heuristic cost for u is now given by:

$$h(u) = \min_{w,\theta} \zeta(u,(\theta_u,\omega)). \tag{3}$$

As $\zeta(u,(\theta_u,\omega))$ is differentiable in ω and θ_u, $h(u)$ can be computed using gradient descent.

ε-Admissibility. The neural networks used to guide the search may only form an approximate relaxation of the space of programs; also, the training of these networks may not reach global optima. To account for these errors, NEAR considers an approximate notion of admissibility [45]. For a fixed constant $\varepsilon > 0$, let an *ε-admissible heuristic* be a function $h^*(u)$ over architectures such that $h^*(u) \leq J(u) + \varepsilon$ for all u. Now consider any completion $u[\alpha_1,\ldots,\alpha_k]$ of an architecture u. As neural networks with adequate capacity are universal function approximators, there exist parameters ω^* for the neurosymbolic program such that for all $u, \alpha_1,\ldots,\alpha_k$, θ_u, and θ:

$$\zeta(u,(\theta_u,\omega^*)) \leq \zeta(u[\alpha_1,\ldots,\alpha_k],(\theta_u,\theta)) + \varepsilon. \tag{4}$$

Because edges in the search graph have non-negative costs, $s(u) \leq s(u[\alpha_1, \ldots, \alpha_k])$, implying:

$$\begin{aligned} h(u) &\leq \min_{\alpha_1,\ldots,\alpha_k,\theta_u,\theta} \zeta(u[\alpha_1,\ldots,\alpha_k],(\theta_u,\theta)) + \varepsilon \\ &\leq \min_{\alpha_1,\ldots,\alpha_k,\theta_u,\theta} \zeta(u[\alpha_1,\ldots,\alpha_k],(\theta_u,\theta)) + (s(u[\alpha_1,\ldots,\alpha_k]) - s(u)) + \varepsilon \\ &= J(u) + \varepsilon. \end{aligned} \tag{5}$$

In other words, $h(u)$ is ε-admissible.

6. Conclusion

We have given an overview of NSP, an emerging field at the intersection of deep learning and program synthesis. We have sketched the main technical goals of the area and listed some of its applications. We have described a taxonomy of algorithmic approaches in the area and described NEAR as an exemplar of such approaches.

Limitations and Challenges. NSP-based approaches face two broad challenges. The first challenge is *scalability*. Searching over program architectures is a combinatorially hard problem. When the architectures follow broadly known idioms, neural language models trained on large code corpora can effectively guide this search. However, the generation of entirely novel program architectures remains a hard open problem.

The second challenge is *specification*. NSP assumes that humans can specify domain knowledge effectively via DSLs and behavioral constraints. While these specifications can help with generalization, constructing the "right" specification for a domain is nontrivial, and unnecessarily restrictive specifications can impede learning performance.

LLMs form a powerful response to both challenges. In the best case, an LLM can generate entire program architectures step by step, eliminating the need for explicit search. However, many applications of neurosymbolic programming require the creation of *novel* programs, rather than programs well-represented in the pretraining corpus. However, methods such as Funsearch [5] and LaSR [6] illustrate that the priors and abstraction capabilities of LLMs can prove useful even when novelty is desirable. As for specification, LLMs have been successfully used in the *autoformalization* of informal mathematical statements [46]. One can imagine such autoformalization techniques being more generally used to construct specifications for NSP.

Collectively, these two limitations imply that there are many tasks — for example, answering complex, non-synthetic questions over open-domain text, or the discovery of programmatic policies for real-world, learning-enabled robots — in which NSP is applicable in principle but not yet in practice. For NSP to reach its full potential, there needs to be progress on both fronts. Specifically, algorithmic innovations that enable the generation of more complex program structures are required. Also, more research must be done on systematizing the inductive bias that different kinds of specifications introduce, precisely evaluating their benefits with respect to goals such as interpretability and safety verification, and simplifying or automating the design of such specifications.

Future Horizons. Overall, we are excited about the trajectory of NSP. Data-efficiency, safety, and interpretability are increasingly salient issues in ML, and these issues open up a window of opportunity for fresh learning approaches like NSP. As the field further develops methods to address the aforementioned limitations, another opportunity is creating software frameworks — equivalents of Pytorch [47] or Keras [48] for NSP— that can accelerate the adoption of these methods. Standardized benchmarks and competitions that showcase the value of neurosymbolic methods and are also of interest to the broader AI community would also be of great value. ARC [49], the AI Math Olympiad, and Natural Plan [50] are three examples of such challenges. Finally, NSP researchers should prioritize the development of algorithms and infrastructures that enable their methods to scale. Of particular interest are new methods to parallelize search over program architectures and parameters and new interfaces for interacting between neural models (in particular, large language models) and symbolic tools.

References

[1] Marcus G, Davis E. Rebooting AI: Building artificial intelligence we can trust. Pantheon; 2019.

[2] Garcez Ad, Lamb LC. Neurosymbolic AI: The 3rd Wave. arXiv preprint arXiv:201205876. 2020.

[3] Chaudhuri S, Ellis K, Polozov O, Singh R, Solar-Lezama A, Yue Y, et al. Neurosymbolic programming. Foundations and Trends® in Programming Languages. 2021;7(3):158-243.

[4] Gulwani S, Polozov O, Singh R. Program synthesis. Foundations and Trends in Programming Languages. 2017;4(1-2):1-119.

[5] Romera-Paredes B, Barekatain M, Novikov A, Balog M, Kumar MP, Dupont E, et al. Mathematical discoveries from program search with large language models. Nature. 2024;625(7995):468-75.

[6] Grayeli A, Sehgal A, Costilla-Reyes O, Cranmer M, Chaudhuri S. Symbolic regression with a learned concept library. In: Neural Information Processing Systems; 2024. .

[7] Verma A, Le HM, Yue Y, Chaudhuri S. Imitation-Projected Programmatic Reinforcement Learning. In: Neural Information Processing Systems (NeurIPS); 2019. .

[8] Ellis K, Wong C, Nye MI, Sablé-Meyer M, Morales L, Hewitt LB, et al. DreamCoder: bootstrapping inductive program synthesis with wake-sleep library learning. In: PLDI '21. ACM; 2021. p. 835-50.

[9] Valkov L, Chaudhari D, Srivastava A, Sutton C, Chaudhuri S. HOUDINI: Lifelong Learning as Program Synthesis. In: Neural Information Processing Systems (NeurIPS); 2018. p. 8701-12.

[10] Shah A, Zhan E, Sun JJ, Verma A, Yue Y, Chaudhuri S. Learning Differentiable Programs with Admissible Neural Heuristics. In: Advances in Neural Information Processing Systems; 2020. .

[11] Verma A, Murali V, Singh R, Kohli P, Chaudhuri S. Programmatically Interpretable Reinforcement Learning. In: ICML; 2018. p. 5052-61.

[12] Bastani O, Pu Y, Solar-Lezama A. Verifiable Reinforcement Learning via Policy Extraction. In: Neural Information Processing Systems (NeurIPS); 2018. p. 2499-509.

[13] Zhu H, Xiong Z, Magill S, Jagannathan S. An Inductive Synthesis Framework for Verifiable Reinforcement Learning. In: PLDI; 2019. .

[14] Anderson G, Verma A, Dillig I, Chaudhuri S. Neurosymbolic Reinforcement Learning with Formally Verified Exploration. In: Neural Information Processesing Systems (NeurIPS); 2020. .

[15] Cranmer M, Sanchez-Gonzalez A, Battaglia P, Xu R, Cranmer K, Spergel D, et al. Discovering symbolic models from deep learning with inductive biases. In: Neural Information Processing Systems (NeurIPS); 2020. .

[16] Zhan E, Sun JJ, Kennedy A, Yue Y, Chaudhuri S. Unsupervised Learning of Neurosymbolic Encoders; 2021.

[17] Yang J, Jimenez CE, Wettig A, Lieret K, Yao S, Narasimhan K, et al. Swe-agent: Agent-computer interfaces enable automated software engineering. arXiv preprint arXiv:240515793. 2024.

[18] Zhang Y, Ruan H, Fan Z, Roychoudhury A. Autocoderover: Autonomous program improvement. arXiv preprint arXiv:240405427. 2024.

[19] Thakur A, Tsoukalas G, Wen Y, Xin J, Chaudhuri S. An In-Context Learning Agent for Formal Theorem-Proving; 2024. Available from: `https://arxiv.org/abs/2310.04353`.

[20] Andreas J, Bufe J, Burkett D, Chen C, Clausman J, Crawford J, et al. Task-Oriented Dialogue as Dataflow Synthesis. Transactions of the Association for Computational Linguistics. 2020 Dec;8:556–571.
[21] Srivastava S, Polozov O, Jojic N, Meek C. Learning Web-based Procedures by Reasoning over Explanations and Demonstrations in Context. In: Proceedings of the 58th Annual Meeting of the Association for Computational Linguistics; 2020. p. 7652-62.
[22] Xu D, Nair S, Zhu Y, Gao J, Garg A, Fei-Fei L, et al. Neural task programming: Learning to generalize across hierarchical tasks. In: 2018 IEEE International Conference on Robotics and Automation (ICRA). IEEE; 2018. p. 3795-802.
[23] Feser JK, Chaudhuri S, Dillig I. Synthesizing data structure transformations from input-output examples. In: ACM SIGPLAN Notices. vol. 50. ACM; 2015. p. 229-39.
[24] Albarghouthi A, Gulwani S, Kincaid Z. Recursive program synthesis. In: International conference on computer aided verification. Springer; 2013. p. 934-50.
[25] Langdon WB, Poli R. Foundations of genetic programming. Springer Science & Business Media; 2013.
[26] Udupa A, Raghavan A, Deshmukh JV, Mador-Haim S, Martin MM, Alur R. TRANSIT: specifying protocols with concolic snippets. ACM SIGPLAN Notices. 2013;48(6):287-96.
[27] Schkufza E, Sharma R, Aiken A. Stochastic superoptimization. In: ACM SIGARCH Computer Architecture News. vol. 41. ACM; 2013. p. 305-16.
[28] Solar-Lezama A, Jones C, Arnold G, Bodík R. Sketching Concurrent Datastructures. In: PLDI 08; 2008. .
[29] Devlin J, Uesato J, Bhupatiraju S, Singh R, Mohamed A, Kohli P. RobustFill: Neural Program Learning under Noisy I/O. In: ICML; 2017. .
[30] Li Y, Choi D, Chung J, Kushman N, Schrittwieser J, Leblond R, et al. Competition-level code generation with alphacode. Science. 2022;378(6624):1092-7.
[31] Bunel R, Hausknecht MJ, Devlin J, Singh R, Kohli P. Leveraging Grammar and Reinforcement Learning for Neural Program Synthesis. In: 6th International Conference on Learning Representations, ICLR 2018, Vancouver, BC, Canada, April 30 - May 3, 2018, Conference Track Proceedings. OpenReview.net; 2018. .
[32] Chen Y, Wang C, Bastani O, Dillig I, Feng Y. Program Synthesis Using Deduction-Guided Reinforcement Learning. In: International Conference on Computer Aided Verification. Springer; 2020. p. 587-610.
[33] Fawzi A, Balog M, Huang A, Hubert T, Romera-Paredes B, Barekatain M, et al. Discovering faster matrix multiplication algorithms with reinforcement learning. Nature. 2022;610(7930):47-53.
[34] Mankowitz DJ, Michi A, Zhernov A, Gelmi M, Selvi M, Paduraru C, et al. Faster sorting algorithms discovered using deep reinforcement learning. Nature. 2023;618(7964):257-63.
[35] Moura Ld, Ullrich S. The Lean 4 theorem prover and programming language. In: Automated Deduction–CADE 28: 28th International Conference on Automated Deduction, Virtual Event, July 12–15, 2021, Proceedings 28. Springer; 2021. p. 625-35.
[36] Chaudhuri S, Solar-Lezama A. Smooth interpretation. In: PLDI; 2010. p. 279-91.
[37] Chaudhuri S, Solar-Lezama A. Smoothing a Program Soundly and Robustly. In: CAV; 2011. p. 277-92.
[38] Cui G, Zhu H. Differentiable Synthesis of Program Architectures. Advances in Neural Information Processing Systems. 2021;34.
[39] Tseng A, Sun JJ, Yue Y. Automatic synthesis of diverse weak supervision sources for behavior analysis. In: Proceedings of the IEEE/CVF Conference on Computer Vision and Pattern Recognition; 2022. p. 2211-20.
[40] Alet F, Lozano-Pérez T, Kaelbling LP. Modular meta-learning. Conference on Robot Learning (CoRL). 2018.
[41] Hewitt LB, Le TA, Tenenbaum JB. Learning to learn generative programs with Memoised Wake-Sleep. UAI. 2020.
[42] Ellis K, Wong C, Nye M, Sable-Meyer M, Cary L, Morales L, et al. Dreamcoder: Growing generalizable, interpretable knowledge with wake-sleep Bayesian program learning. arXiv preprint arXiv:200608381. 2020.
[43] Bowers M, Olausson TX, Wong L, Grand G, Tenenbaum JB, Ellis K, et al. Top-down synthesis for library learning. Proceedings of the ACM on Programming Languages. 2023;7(POPL):1182-213.
[44] Hopcroft JE, Motwani R, Ullman JD. Introduction to automata theory, languages, and computation, 3rd Edition. Pearson international edition. Addison-Wesley; 2007.

[45] Harris LR. The heuristic search under conditions of error. Artificial Intelligence. 1974;5(3):217-34.
[46] Wu Y, Jiang AQ, Li W, Rabe M, Staats C, Jamnik M, et al. Autoformalization with large language models. Advances in Neural Information Processing Systems. 2022;35:32353-68.
[47] Paszke A, Gross S, Massa F, Lerer A, Bradbury J, Chanan G, et al. Pytorch: An imperative style, high-performance deep learning library. Advances in neural information processing systems. 2019;32.
[48] Chollet F. Deep learning with Python. Simon and Schuster; 2021.
[49] Chollet F. On the measure of intelligence. arXiv preprint arXiv:191101547. 2019.
[50] Zheng HS, Mishra S, Zhang H, Chen X, Chen M, Nova A, et al. NATURAL PLAN: Benchmarking LLMs on Natural Language Planning. arXiv preprint arXiv:240604520. 2024.

Handbook on Neurosymbolic AI and Knowledge Graphs
P. Hitzler et al. (Eds.)
IOS Press, 2025

doi:10.3233/FAIA250222

Neuro-Symbolic Relation Extraction

Xi YAN [a], Aida USMANOVA [b] Cedric MÖLLER [a,1] Patrick WESTPHAL [a] and Ricardo USBECK [b]

[a] *University of Hamburg, Department of Informatics, Semantic Systems, Germany*
[b] *Leuphana University Lüneburg, Institute for Information Systems, Artificial Intelligence and Explainability, Germany*
ORCiD ID: Xi Yan https://orcid.org/0009-0004-7379-4080, Aida Usmanova https://orcid.org/0009-0000-0124-8727, Cedric Möller https://orcid.org/0000-0001-6700-3482, Patrick Westphal https://orcid.org/0000-0002-3855-4485, Ricardo Usbeck https://orcid.org/0000-0002-0191-7211

Abstract. Neuro-symbolic relation extraction lies at the intersection of neural networks and symbolic reasoning, presenting promising opportunities to enhance the capabilities of natural language processing (NLP) systems. Despite its potential, a comprehensive review of how these systems are developed and applied to the task of relation extraction has been lacking. This chapter addresses this gap by offering an in-depth overview of the current landscape in neuro-symbolic relation extraction, focusing on key methodologies and the datasets utilized in this field. We systematically categorize existing approaches, emphasizing how they integrate neural and symbolic components to tackle various challenges and the types of information they incorporate. Additionally, we review the datasets used to evaluate neuro-symbolic relation extraction systems, detailing their statistics, creation processes, and underlying domains. Furthermore, we discuss future research directions and challenges, such as the analysis of symbolic information and the integration of datasets with existing knowledge graphs. By synthesizing these findings, this chapter aims to provide researchers and practitioners with a clear understanding of the state of neuro-symbolic relation extraction and to inspire further innovations in this rapidly evolving field.

Keywords. Relation Extraction, Neural Symbolic Systems, Hybrid AI, Information Extraction

1. Introduction

Relation Extraction (RE) is a fundamental problem in the area of Natural Language Processing (NLP). The goal is to classify the *relation* expressed between two *entities* in unstructured texts. An entity represents a notion of a "thing" and a relation is an association between two entities. Entities could be words, phrases or other syntactic units. Together, two entities and one relation form a *triple* [1], formally defined as (e_1, r, e_2). For example, in the following sentence, we can identify two entities "Barack Obama" and "Michele Obama" and multiple potential relations to be extracted:

[1]Corresponding Author: Cedric Möller, cedric.moeller@uni-hamburg.de

Barack Obama married Michele in 1992.

One could extract that the relation `spouse` holds between Barack Obama and Michele. Here, we denote `spouse` as an identifier for the actual relation defined as "significant other in a marriage". Other human-readable identifiers such as `married_to` or non-human-readable identifiers such as `P26` (the identifier given to the relation in Wikidata [2]) are possible as well.

Another potential relation occurring in the sentence is that the `wedding_year` of the marriage was 1992. In this case, the two entities between the relation holds are actually the statement "Barack Obama married Michele" on the one hand and the year "1992" on the other. Such a statement is also called a hyper-relational statement, essentially a statement on a statement [3]. These can be arbitrarily complex.

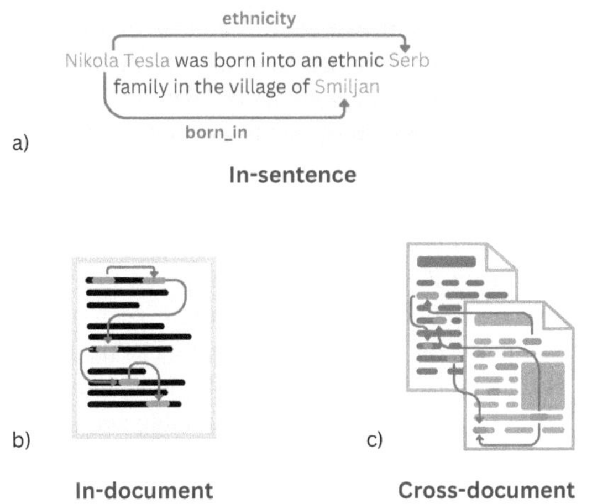

Figure 1. Different Relation Extraction types: a) in-sentence, b) in-document, c) cross-document.

Relation Extraction for such arbitrary complex relations can be applied to different types of texts: in-sentence, in-document, or cross-document [4] as illustrated in a, b and c in Figure 1. In-sentence relation extraction focuses on entities occurring only in a single sentence. In-document relation extraction is occupied with a single document on a certain topic containing multiple sentences. Especially, are of interest relations holding between entities occurring in different sentences. This usually makes some type of more complex reasoning necessary. Finally, cross-document relation extraction extends this not only to a single document but also to several documents with relations holding between entities that are occurring in separate documents. Additionally, many works focus on only identifying which relations hold between two entities, ignoring to cases where no relation holds. Predicting the non-existence of a relation is especially important when confronted with an in-document or cross-document relation, as the number of potential relations increases quadratically with an increasing number of occurring entities in the text.

Notably, some other tasks in NLP, such as event extraction [5] and syntactic parsing [6], fall within this definition. Both tasks aim to extract relationships (syntactic or event-related) between entities in unstructured texts. However, we do not include them here for two reasons. First, research in syntactic parsing and event extraction often does not label itself as relation extraction, making it difficult to gather relevant studies. Second, the extensive body of work in these areas makes it impractical to cover all the research within this chapter. For the same reason, we do not consider work which contains multimodal relation extraction, but rather focus on the text. Multimodal relation extraction is a process that involves extracting meaningful relationships from multiple types of data sources, such as text, images, and videos.

Also, the task of Relation Extraction is closely related to other tasks such as Named Entity Recognition (NER), knowledge graph population or knowledge graph question answering. NER [7] extracts entity mentions from text for further processing and is a prerequisite to relation extraction. In contrast to NER, Knowledge graph population and knowledge graph question answering [8] are tasks where Relation Extraction is necessary. In knowledge graph population [9], new triples need to be extracted from given text, where each triple usually consists of two entities connected by a relation. In knowledge graph question answering, especially when focusing on semantic parsing, extracting relations is essential for constructing a correct query [10].

While machine learning models have achieved high performance on Relation Extraction from pure text, they face robustness problems. These methods rely on large-scale training data and complex feature engineering, which limit the model's capacity to generalize to new entities and domain-specific texts. Introducing symbolic information is a crucial step in addressing these problems. Compared to machine learning models, which produce unstable results, symbolic information, such as Knowledge Graphs or logic, offers clear reasoning paths and robustness but lacks the flexibility and scalability of neural networks. By integrating neural and symbolic techniques, neuro-symbolic relation extraction methods aim to create more interpretable and generalizable models that can effectively understand and process complex relationships within text. In the sections below, we categorize and define common relation extraction methods, which are based on machine learning models, and neuro-symbolic relation extraction methods, which add symbolic information on top.

1.1. Common Relation Extraction

Today, Relation Extraction is commonly solved by applying a Pre-trained Language Model (PLM) [11] to the input. This means either encoding the input via an encoder-only model such as BERT [11] and then applying a classification head on top of it, or, alternatively, (encoder-decoder or decoder-only) generative models [12,13] are used to directly generate the relation label. Generative models are especially suitable if the goal is not only to classify a relation, but to extract full triples [14].

Beyond the standard definition and methodologies, Relation Extraction can also be approached in few-shot or zero-shot settings [15]. In these scenarios, the relations encountered during training are different from those encountered during inference. Thus, the model must generalize to new, unseen relations with either a few examples (few-shot) or no examples (zero-shot) provided during training. These settings challenge the model to leverage its learned knowledge to make accurate predictions for novel relations.

1.2. Neuro-symbolic Relation Extraction

While PLM-based Relation Extraction methods are powerful and efficient in extracting information, they suffer from problems such as hallucination due to instability and weak reasoning capacity [16]. Therefore, researchers attempt to add further concrete and verified information to address the lack of contextual information and to deepen the reasoning capacity of these models.

We define Neuro-Symbolic Relation Extraction as any relation extraction method that relies not only on the textual information at hand, but also on additional symbolic information related to the entities or relations in context. This information can either be explicitly defined for the task at hand or gathered from sources such as a Knowledge Graph (KG). Among various types of symbolic information added to existing neuro-symbolic RE models, we categorize them into KG, linguistic, prior meta-information and logical rules. A more detailed definition can be found in section 2.2. In the next chapters, we systemically categorize and list all neuro-symbolic methods from published papers after 2021 and the datasets used by them.

2. Methods

Neuro-symbolic relation extraction represents a trend in the field of natural language processing of combining the strengths of neural networks and symbolic reasoning to enhance the generalizability and interpretability of information extraction. This section enumerates an exhaustive list of recent neuro-symbolic relation extraction, categorizes them systemically, and summarizes the methods with a focus on how incorporation of symbolic data improves the former methods in terms of reasoning capabilities and advantages.

Existing methods can be separated into two categories, each representing a different way of incorporating symbolic information. First, symbolic information can be utilised to **improve distant supervision** by using ontological information to mine or refine labels of textual data. Second, symbolic information is used during training and inference as additional information to **improve the relation extraction** performance directly. Through a detailed examination of recent advancements, we will illustrate how neuro-symbolic techniques are paving the way for more robust and reliable relation extraction systems. The papers are listed in chronological order in the improving distant supervision section and we categorize the works in the improving relation extraction section by the types of the symbolic information.

2.1. Improving Distant Supervision

Distant supervision is the idea of taking unlabeled data and labeling it via heuristics or an existing method. In the realm of Relation Extraction, this means identifying *entities* and the *relations* between them.

The *distant supervision assumption* implies that any sentence, containing two entities that participate in a relation, will express that relation [17]. Such an approach is a common way to identify entities and the relations between them by using the wealth of information available in a Knowledge Graph. Given an unlabeled sentence/document(s),

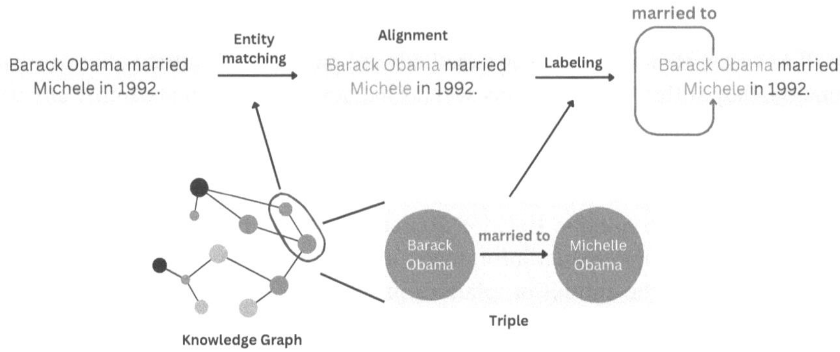

Figure 2. Alignment of entities from the sentence with the triple information from the KG. First, entities are matched and aligned with nodes from KG. Then, the relation between entities is labeled based on the edge between the matched nodes in KG.

it is checked whether two mentioned entities in the sentence/document(s) are connected by a triple (see Figure 2). If they are, it is assumed that the relation expressed by the triple is also expressed in the sentence.

This approach presents several difficulties. First, the entities need to be connected to the actual correct entities in the Knowledge Graph, this is a challenging research problem known as entity linking [18]. Second, the mere co-occurrence of two entities within the same sentence does not necessarily indicate that the relation of a connecting triple is being expressed. Third, in connection to that, there might exist multiple relations between entities, which are usually not expressed at the same time in a single sentence. Lastly, most Knowledge Graphs are extremely sparse and incomplete, not covering everything expressed in an actual sentence. This leads to a lot of false negatives [19]. Nevertheless, pre-training on distantly supervised data leads to an improvement in performance when combined with fine-tuning on manually annotated data [20]. While there exist some approaches like bagging [21] to reduce the influence of the noisy distantly supervised labels, utilising symbolic information such as n-hop paths in a Knowledge Graph or actual ontological information can improve the quality of distantly supervised labels as well.

The work by Dai et al. [22] utilises an universal graph, here denoted as the combination of a KG and a large-scale text collection. The idea is that the sparse information in the KG is compensated by the additional textual documents, and together they act as distantly-supervised information. For each of the sources, textual and KG, multi-hop paths are computed and encoded. This gives textual, KG and hybrid (combining both text and KG) paths. An attention mechanism is used to combine the different sources of information. The authors suggest that pre-training the model sequentially on the different sources of information is crucial. Otherwise, the information in the KG has an excessive impact and the model is biased towards the information in it. After pre-training the model sequentially, they finally train on all sources together. This procedure is demonstrated to alleviate the problem of the bias. They show that the combination of the two sources leads to an increase in performance.

The *ASP-enhanced Entity-Relation extraction (ASPER)* framework, developed by Le et al. [23] refines distantly-supervised labels by applying Answer Set Programming (ASP). They start with labeling an unlabeled dataset using an already trained model. Then they translate the underlying rules of a KG into ASP atoms. Those encompass type declarations targeting the domain and range of a relation, inference rules targeting relationships between relations, and optional rules that are dataset-specific. Given the atoms, the answer set with the highest score is computed using an ASP solver. Then, the answer sets which contain new pseudo-labels are used for retraining. Importantly, the retraining starts with a high confidence answer and progressively proceeds to train on lower-confidence answers as well. The inclusion of labels gathered in such a way significantly increases the performance. The downside is the additional effort for identifying and formulating the underlying rules describing a KG. However, in comparison to manually labeling such a large amount of data, this is often the preferred option. The quality of the distantly-labeled data increases and leads to superior performance of the RE model.

Table 1. A table for different types of symbolic information used in distant supervision model.

Source	Paper	Info
KG	Dai et al. [22]	KG path
KG	ASPER [23]	Type declaration

To sum up, there exist only a few works using symbolic information to improve distant-supervision, marking a significant research gap. The existing methodologies leverage external sources, such as subgraph paths and entity types, necessitating entity linking due to the extensive information available in KGs. Following the alignment of text to the KG, the methods for integrating KG information vary. Some approaches directly enhance the text with KG-derived information, while others utilize KG embeddings or generate constraints to incorporate the knowledge. However, none of the papers investigate whether the additional information introduced is noisy or biased, given the overwhelming amount of data typically contained in KGs. This issue is addressed by incorporating an attention mechanism, allowing the model to maintain a strong focus on the text. Nevertheless, it was shown by the existing works that refining distantly-supervised data using ontological information can lead to an increase in quality. Examining the impact of ontological information together with the generative power of PLM might be a direction to pursue in the future. Additionally, the optimal methods for aligning and filtering information from KGs with PLMs are still to be explored and examined. An overview of all systems in this category with their source and the detailed information can be found in Table 1.

2.2. *Improving Relation Extraction*

Symbolic information is believed to improve the performance of RE during inference as well. The key concept is that providing additional symbolic information on the included relations or entities will help identify the correct relation for the statement at hand (see Figure 3). In this section, we focus on methods in which the integration of neural and symbolic information extends beyond distant supervision. External information is not only concatenated with text, but is also used to generate constraints, which are applied during both the training and inference stages. Among the papers we reviewed, symbolic information can be categorized into several types: KGs, prior meta-information, inferred logical rules, linguistic information, temporal information and commonsense rules.

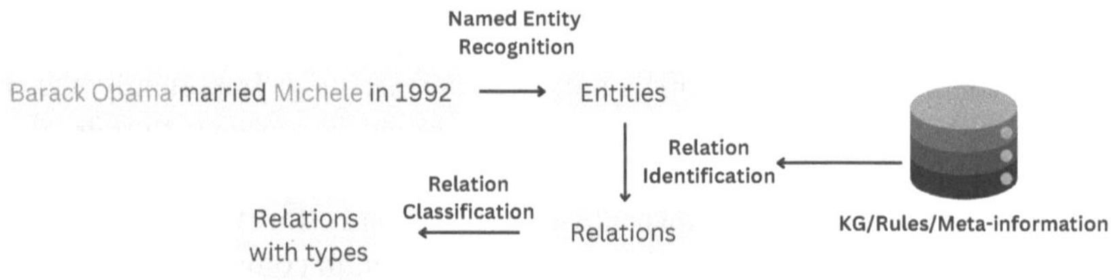

Figure 3. RE enhanced with external information from KG/logical rules/meta-information.

2.2.1. Knowledge Graphs

KGs are naturally discrete symbolic representations of information. Symbolic information in KG includes entities, relations, attributes, labels, hierarchies, temporal information, classes, etc. Such information originating from a KG can be used during inference or training to enhance the contextual information and reasoning capacity of the Pre-trained Language Model [24].

Entity attributes, like labels, descriptions and type information can be included as a first step of RE. For instance, the *Relation Extraction using Knowledge Graph Context in a Graph Neural Network (RECON)* [24] approach automatically identifies relations in a sentence by encoding the sentence and incorporating additional entity-related information from a KG. Information from the KG is included in two ways. First, **Entity Attribute Context** are encoded via a word embedding method and combined using a Convolutional Neural Network (CNN). Second, **Triple Context** is incorporated by encoding each entity and relation by an initial vector. Each triple is represented by a projected concatenation of subject, object and relation. To gather a contextual representation, neighbouring triples are aggregated using an architecture resembling a Graph Attention Network (GAN). Finally, for a pair of entities where a relation is to be predicted, the entities are mapped to a relation-aware representation and a score is calculated using the translational equation $e_1 + r = e_2$. The Triple Context representation is combined with the Entity Attribute Context representation and a text representation to predict the final relation. Especially, the Entity Attribute Context has a large impact.

Knowledge Enhanced Few-shot RC model for the Domain Adaptation (KEFDA) [25] uses the same entity information as additional features for few-shot RE. By incorporating general and domain-specific Knowledge Graphss they address the problem of few-shot RE. The method consists of two elements, first, a **knowledge-enhanced prototypical network** that combines the representations of the support set. The enhanced representations are computed from the contextual representation of the input sentence, the entity descriptions and a learned representation of the concept. The matching degree between instances is calculated by a distance based scoring function. Second, they use a **relation-meta learning network**, to identify meta-relations between the involved concepts. For that, they solely rely on the learned concept representation and the contextual representation of the concept description. They create each possible concept pair, calculate a pair-wise representation and finally a weighted average over all such pair-wise representations to get the plausibility that such relation exists. The entity description and concept representations had the largest impact on performance and led to superior performance compared to past methods, while the influence of the meta-relations was less significant.

The *Discriminative Rule-based Knowledge (DRK)* approach [26] introduces a external KG and logic rules in the encoding and inference stage of relation extraction model. This work adopts a few shot learning setting, in which each sample includes a support set (labeled sentences) and the query set (unlabeled sentences). Both sets are linked to an external KG to extract the related information of the entity and relation (e.g., entity types and relation description). The entities, text and relation representation would then be encoded separately before fed to the logic aware inference module. Based on the relation information, some logic rules can be inferred, for instance, the relation "Mother" implies that the type of the head and tail entity should be "Person" and the relation description is semantically equivalent to "Mother". Based on the inferred rules, the authors propose a hierarchical contrastive learning optimized against the probability distribution of the relations. The model is tested on one RE dataset and outperform former baselines.

The work by Liu et al. [27] focuses on few-shot relation extraction. They combine a contrastive-learning-based fine-tuning approach with knowledge enhancement. To enhance the stability and learning ability of contrastive learning-based fine-tuning, the authors use a data augmentation mechanism and type-aware networks to enrich the instances and incorporate class-sensitive features. Knowledge enhancement is achieved by incorporating type information and by including pre-trained entity node representations. Especially the knowledge enhancement leads to a significant improvement in performance.

ReOnto [28] is an approach incorporating a KG to improve RE in the biomedical domain. Here, KG paths between mentioned entities are extracted and used in parallel to the text-only method to improve the accuracy of the relation extractor. Furthermore, they not only extract n-hop paths but also include ontological information expressing, for example, class subsumption. However, the ontological information is included by encoding them through a PLM, no formal logic is actually used. The additional information has a significant impact and surpasses the performance of the same model which only relies on the textual data.

The work by Aghaebrahimian et al. [29] introduces ontological information into the task of biomedical relation extraction. They accomplish this through two perspectives: 1) they enrich the encoded input text with type embedding of the entity, and 2) they include ontology graph embedding. The ontology graph embedding are here node embedding of specific concepts, such as genes or diseases. The node embedding is learned by first generating paths using random walks and encoding them using Skip-Gram [30]. They show that the inclusion of those two types of information has a positive effect on performance. They either use an ontology available with the dataset or the Unified Medical Language System (UMLS) [31] (an unified biomedical database for terminology).

2.2.2. Linguistics

Pre-trained language models (PLMs) typically project words into embeddings. Beyond this, the integration of linguistic and lexical knowledge associated with entities allows PLMs to effectively tackle fine-grained tasks such as named entity recognition [32], relation extraction [33], etc.

The *Sememe Knowledge-enhanced Abstract Meaning Representation and Reasoning (SKAMRR)* [34] approach introduces sememe knowledge from HowNet [35] (a sememe Knowledge Graph) to enhance entity representation. A sememe is the minimum semantic unit in linguistics, and HowNet proposes that annotated sememes can represent senses and words well in a real-world scenario. Therefore, the authors extract the word senses and sememes from the OpenHowNet API [36] and combine this linguistic information with the textual feature of the input text for extracting an Abstract Meaning Representation (AMR) graph. An AMR graph, on the other hand, models the relations between entity pairs. The AMR graph is then sent to a reasoning module that builds an entity-pair graph, which is used for relation classification with a Global Adaptive Loss (GAL) to alleviate imbalances of the data. SKAMRR is tested on four document-level relation extraction datasets, including texts from Wikipedia and biomedical documents. The model shows competitive performance across all datasets which demonstrates its capacity to explore feature information within and across sentences, and infer classes of relations between entities.

Jain et al. [37] focuses on the task of document-relation-extraction. The model consists of two submodules, first a document based encoding, combining two elements: 1) a graph consisting of mention and sentence nodes, and 2) attention-based pooling of the contextual encoding of the input document. Second, external KG information is incorporated by learning entity node representations through a relational graph convolutional network (RGCN). Both types of information are combined and used in the final prediction. The method uses information about existing triples as well as WordNet(an English lexical database) [38] entity synonyms and types. They use Wikidata as the background KG. Especially, the inclusion of the Wikidata information leads to a large increase in performance on three different datasets.

Jain et al. [39] develop a cross-document relation extraction method, relying on two types of information: the type information of the source and target entities, and the paths connecting both entities in the KG, specifically Wikidata. These paths are transformed into textual paths and concatenated with the textualized entity types to create a context, which is used to filter relevant sentences in the documents. The selected sentences are then concatenated with the context and further filtered based on their relevance to the entity path. Finally, the sentences and context are encoded using a specialized attention module generated from the text path for the final classification of the relation between entity pairs. This framework demonstrates improvement over baseline models on one benchmark dataset and also provides explainability for deep learning models.

2.2.3. Prior Meta-information

Prior meta-information refers to any pre-existing, heuristic or statistical, information about the entities and relations between them. Systematic incorporation of prior meta-information is also among popular approaches within RE. Using meta-information provides a context to the text, guiding the RE process. Examples include, entity co-occurrence, precomputed entity similarity scores, etc. Such information can help to disambiguate entities and reduce noise.

The *RAtionale Graph* (RAG) [40] assumes that global co-occurrence statistics among relations, entity types and trigger words are known. Using those, they build a *rationale graph.* This graph contains nodes corresponding to relations, trigger words or entity-type-pairs. Then, directed edges are introduced between trigger words and entity-type-pairs (in both directions) and from triggers words/entity-type-pairs to the relations. The edge weights correspond to the co-occurrence probability between the respective elements. During each inference step, the type-pair is predicted, and its representation is merged with the type-pair representation in the graph. The same happens for the trigger words. The whole graph is updated using a graph neural network. Lastly, using the co-occurrence probabilities, the relation representations are updated each and combined with the textual encoding to predict the final relation. This leads to a strong improvement over a model not using the co-occurrence statistics.

Specifically for extracting the relation from news articles, Zhang et al. [41] model the inter-document casual relations by generating the storytrees. The authors firstly extract the keywords from the articles, to feed to EventX [42], a clustering algorithm which outputs events by gathering the stories. Those event clusters are converted into storytrees with nodes being the articles with high semantic similarity scores. Based on the generated trees, two basic constraints (discouragement of causal relations between two news articles occurring at the same time and with very low similarity) and five types of constraints generated accordingly are generated based on the information of nodes and links. The constraints are utilized by Integer Linear Programming (ILP) [43] methods to perform global inference for classification of the relations with added information based on the articles' textual features. The model is tested on three datasets crawled from news articles and outperformed the extensively used classifiers and a state-of-the-art deep learning models.

Xu et al. [44] focus on document relation extraction. They encode the input text via an encoder-only model, then construct a graph consisting of mention and entity nodes, and compute a structural embedding using a Graph Neural Network (GNN). Furthermore, they construct the shortest possible paths between two entities in a document and encode them using a Long Short-term Memory (LSTM) network. All such path representations are pooled while using the attention mechanism. The pooled representation is used together with the structural embedding to classify the final relation. Incorporating the path-based representations helps to interpret long-range dependencies between entities and leads to an increase in the model performance.

The *Graph-based Model Generation (GM_GEN)* framework [45] includes relation description as part of the few shot examples for the few shot relation extraction task. A PLM-based encoder firstly takes query samples (10 unlabeled sentences), relation description and support samples (10×5 labeled sentences) as input. The encoded information is then sent to a graph-based generation module, which aims to combine the topology information with the attributes of samples and the relation descriptions. This module forms a graph matrix, with the nodes being the samples from query, relations or support samples and calculate the edges between them using a bilinear transformation based on the embedding from the PLM encoder. This matrix is then passed to each few shot learning relation extraction task for offering knowledge background. This framework is then applied to a CNN and a Bidirectional Encoder Representations from Transformers (BERT) model on two benchmark datasets while being compared to other CNN and BERT-based models. GM_GEN performs the best among all methods using the same encoder.

2.2.4. Logical Rules

In some cases, employing a pre-defined set of rules could enhance the performance of RE, particularly within well-defined domains, like medical reports or financial statements. Rule-based approaches are exceptionally effective when dealing with legal documents, templates and forms, where patterns and specific phrases are prevailing. Such domains benefit from consistency and precision that rule-based approach methods offer, ensuring reliable and accurate results. Many studies also favour this approach when dealing with limited or small labeled datasets, as it does not require large amounts of training data.

The Knowledge-evolving Framework by Iterative Consolidation and Expansion (KICE) model, developed by Lu et al. [46], employs the Masked Language Modeling (MLM) paradigm to generate rules for each relation. Initially, a rule-generator is trained with a few training examples. The generator generates an entity pattern, assigning to each entity a type, based on the input. Secondly, it generates a relation pattern, assigning to each entity-pattern combination a relation. Both such patterns together give a rule. Using such a trained rule-generator, rules are created for a larger set of unlabeled data. From this point on, the model is trained repeatedly on the same data using the soft-labels from previous iterations. At each iteration, human-annotators are included, for example where the most-matching rule has high ambiguity. A rule matches if the cosine similarity of the encodings surpasses some threshold. The approach achieves competitive results while needing a much smaller number of training examples than traditional approaches.

A study by Fan et al. [35] deals with documents, it presents a logic enhanced framework that boosts *Document-level Relation Extraction (DocRE)* by *Mining and Injecting Logical Rules (MILR)*. Upon the other DocRE models which optimize the logit towards prediction of correct relation type, MILR has modules which optimize the model towards logical consistency during training and inference. The logical consistency is referring to the logical rules, which are mined based on frequency from the annotated relations, with a confidence score estimated by the conditional probability of the co-occurrence of the relations. In the training phase, the authors combine the loss function from relation classification with the consistency regularization loss for predicting the logical rules. The trained model is then used to perform inference which aligns with the logical rules. The predicted logit over relation classification is taken as silver label, combined with rules and become a new objective to optimize against, which result in a set of logical constraints. The MILR is then applied on top of four established DocRE systems and tested on two datasets. It turns out that MILR is model agnostic and consistently improves the performance of other models.

The *weighted multi-channel transformer* (WMCT) [47] focuses on the task of document-relation-extraction. It is noted that useful information about an entity in the context of a document, like its pronoun and keywords, are neglected. Authors advocate that such information should be involved in the graph as new types of nodes. The entity-level graphs are constructed based on several rules, and eventually consists of mention, pronoun, evidence word and dependency nodes of a given entity. The GAN, applied on each graph, aggregates the node representations of each mention node in the end. Then the pairwise concatenated representation of the mention nodes predicts the relation. Interestingly, the multi-view processing via the different graphs have a positive impact on the overall performance.

In conclusion, numerous neural-symbolic methods enhancing relation extraction models during both the training and inference stages. Unlike distant supervision, these methods incorporate a greater variety of symbolic information types. Some methods use the information directly, such as adding entity descriptions to textual representations, while others use encoded information, such as integrating structural KG ontology em-

Table 2. A table for different types of symbolic information used in improving relation extraction.

Source	Paper	Info
KG	RECON [24]	KG path
KG	KEFDA [25]	Entity Description, Concept description
KG	DRK [26]	Entity types, relation description
KG	Liu et al. [27]	Type information
KG	ReOnto [28]	Class subsumption, KG paths
KG	Aghaebrahimian [29]	Entity type, ontology graph
Linguistics	SKAMRR [34]	Word sense, sememe
KG + Linguistics	Jain et al. [37]	WordNet entity synonyms and types
Prior meta-information	RAG [40]	Co-occurrence statistics
Prior meta-information	Zhang et al. [41]	Generated constraints
Prior meta-information	Xu et al. [44]	Shortest possible paths
Prior meta-information	GM_GEN [45]	Relation description
Logical rules	KICE [46]	Entity and relation pattern
Logical rules	MILR [35]	Logical consistency
Logical rules	WMCT [47]	Entity-level graph with pronoun and mention

bedding into sentence representations. Additionally, some approaches transform this information into constraints for training, like contrastive learning. These advancements highlight the potential and effectiveness of combining statistical PLMs with more definitive symbolic information, thereby improving the robustness and generalizability of the models. We summarize the systems discussed in this section in Table 2.

The integration of neural-symbolic methods in Relation Extraction has shown significant promise, leveraging symbolic reasoning to enhance the performance of deep learning-based language models. Despite progress in data-efficient few-shot and zero-shot learning, these methods still rely heavily on diverse and robust datasets that can be effectively combined with external information. Therefore, the choice and quality of datasets are pivotal in advancing neural-symbolic models, enabling them to learn intricate patterns and relationships more effectively.

3. Datasets

There exist various datasets focusing on the problem of Relation Extraction. These datasets exhibit considerable variation in the type of input texts across multiple dimensions.

Firstly, they can be differentiated by the specific relation extraction task they are designed to address, which could be at the sentence level, document level, or even across multiple documents.

Secondly, the datasets can be categorized based on their domains. These domains include, but are not limited to, legal texts, biomedical literature, biological studies, wikis, news articles, dialogues, and more. Each domain presents its unique challenges and nuances, which can significantly influence the complexity and nature of the relation extraction task. For instance, biomedical datasets often contain highly specialized terminology and require an understanding of complex scientific concepts, whereas news datasets might involve more general language but require handling a broader range of topics and events.

Lastly, datasets can also be distinguished by the number of relations they encompass. Datasets with a higher number of relations generally pose a more challenging relation extraction problem. This is because an increase in the number of possible relations typically leads to greater ambiguity and complexity. The more relations there are, the harder it becomes to accurately identify and classify the correct relation, as there are more possibilities to consider and distinguish between.

As far as we are aware, there exists no dataset with a dedicated focus on neuro-symbolic relation extraction. Despite this, to thoroughly investigate the impact of incorporating symbolic information into relation extraction tasks, it is crucial to determine whether such symbolic information is available within the existing datasets.

In the following sections, we will provide a comprehensive overview of all the different Relation Extraction datasets used in the aforementioned works. We will specify the type of each dataset, detailing the nature of the texts and the specific relation extraction tasks they are designed to address. Furthermore, we will examine whether symbolic information, which can include structured data, ontologies, or other forms of symbolic representations, is readily available within these datasets. This information is essential for researchers who aim to leverage symbolic approaches in their work, as it can guide the selection of appropriate datasets and inform the design of experiments and models.

3.1. Sentence Relation Extraction

As sentence-based Relation Extraction is the earliest existing type of Relation Extraction, the majority of existing datasets belong to this category. The majority of the datasets either belong to the news [48,49,50,51,49] or biomedical domain [52,53,54,55,56,57] with some recent datasets focusing more on wikis [58,59] or even dialogs [60]. Possible reasons for that are on one hand the large interest in an working relation extraction in biomedicine on the one hand the abundance of news articles on the other.

In the following, we shortly summarise each sentence-based relation extraction dataset used in the previously presented works. Furthermore, an overview of the datasets can be found in Table 3.

ADE [53] is a biomedical relation extraction dataset, usually used by either classifying whether an adverse drug effect exists or whether none is expressed. Therefore, it only contains two relations. The entities in the dataset are not explicitly linked to an external KG, making separate linking necessary to introduce symbolic knowledge into the task.

AGAC [61] is a relation extraction dataset with a focus on relations between genes. It contains two different relations and the mentioned entities are matched to DrugBank entries [62].

BioRel [63] is a large-scale biomedical relation extraction dataset encompassing over 500k sentences with overall 125 different relations. The advantage of this dataset is the availability of the concept unique identifier (CUI) for each entity occurring in the text. Concept unique identifiers are assigned to different concepts in the UMLS which is used throughout several different available ontologies. This allows the examination of the impact of various ontologies on the relation extraction task.

ChemProt [57] is a relation extraction dataset with a focus on Chemical-Protein-interactions. The mentioned entities are not linked to a background KG or ontology.

DDI [64] is a dataset used to investigate the extraction of drug-drug-interactions. It contains entity annotations to the MedLine[2] and DrugBank ontologies. This simplifies research conducted in the realm of neuro-symbolic research. The only relation expressed in the dataset is whether there is an interaction.

i2b2 [65] is a relation extraction dataset with a focus on the relations between medical problems and their treatments. It contains eight different relations. It is unclear whether the mentioned entities are linked to a background KG or ontology.

CoNLL04 [48] is a relation extraction dataset annotated on the news domain. It is not directly connected to any background KG or ontology, making an additional linking step necessary. It contains only five different relations.

NYT10 [68] is a relation extraction dataset containing annotated New York Times articles. The entity mentions in the dataset were matched against entities in the Freebase KG. Furthermore, they use distant-supervision to assign Freebase [69] relations to the entity pairs mentioned in the dataset. The authors note that the dataset suffers from false negatives which means that some actual expressed relations are not annotated as such. The Freebase identifiers of the entities are available for the dataset.

Re-TACRED [66] is an improved version of the TACRED [70] dataset. It resolves several labelling errors by analysing the original dataset and re-annotating it using crowdsourcing. The entity mentions are not linked to a background KG or ontology.

FewRel 2.0 [58] is a relation extraction dataset with a focus on few-shot relation extraction. it is based on the first FewRel dataset [71], which manually annotates a distantly-supervised subset of Wikipedia articles. Additionally, FewRel 2.0 provides a new test set, which consists of PubMed[3] articles aligned with the UMLS KG. This allows to study the generalization abilities of few-shot methods between different domains. It is a valuable resource as it contains examples from two sources aligned with two different KGs.

Wikidata dataset [67] is a distantly-supervised annotated dataset over Wikipedia using the Wikidata. It contains a large number of 353 different relations. Each entity mentioned is linked to Wikidata, facilitating the research on the impact of symbolic information.

DialogRE [60] is a human-annotated dialog-focused relation extraction dataset. It annotates the original script of the TV-show Friends with 36 relations and is available in Chinese and English. It is not connected to an ontology or KG.

In summary, the availability of background KG greatly influences the ease of integrating neuro-symbolic methods into relation extraction tasks. Biomedical and Wiki datasets often benefit from existing links to KG, such as UMLS for biomedical data and Wikidata for Wiki-based data. In contrast, the news datasets and the dialog dataset lack such direct connections, necessitating additional linking steps to incorporate symbolic information effectively.

[2]https://www.nlm.nih.gov/medline/medline_overview.html
[3]https://pubmed.ncbi.nlm.nih.gov

Table 3. All sentence relation extraction datasets. #R stands for the number of relations, #D for the number of documents, #S for the number of sentences, Linked denotes whether the entities are linked to a KG or ontology

Corpus	Desc.	#R	#D	#S	Text Type	Linked
ADE [53]	Biomedical Data (Adverse Drug Event)	1	3000	20,967	Biological	✗
AGAC [61]	Biomedical data (Genes)	2	-	5,080	Biological Abstracts	✗
BioRel [63]	Biomedical Data (Adverse Drug Event)	125	-	533,560	Biological	✓
ChemProt [57]	BioCreative VI chemical-protein interaction Track 5	14	-	36,400	Biological Abstracts	✗
DDI [64]	Drug-drug interactions from biomedical texts	1	-	33,553	Biological	✓
i2b2 [65]	Biomedical data (Medical problems and treatment relations)	8	1,371	-	Biological Abstracts	✗
CoNLL04 [48]	Newspaper	5	-	1,441	News	✗
NYT10 [50]	New York Times newspaper	52	-	627,827	News	✓
Re-TACRED [66]	Revised version of TACRED	40	-	91,467	News	✗
FewRel 2.0 [58]	Wikipedia articles	125	-	70,000	Wiki	✓
Wikidata dataset [67]	Wikipedia articles	353	-	732,393	Wiki	✓
DialogRE [60]	Dialog-based datasets focusing on the Friends TV-Show	37	-	7900	Dialog	✗

3.2. Document Relation Extraction

Document-wide relation extraction (DocRE) emerged as a distinct task with datasets introduced between 2016 and 2017 [72,73,74], primarily focusing on the biomedical domain or suffering from limited scope and quality. The release of the DocRED dataset [20]

in 2019 marked a significant advancement by offering a large-scale, open-domain dataset with comprehensive manually annotated train, development, and test sets, thereby driving increased research into this domain of RE. An overview of all datasets used in the methods gathered in the previous section can be found in Table 4.

SciERC [75] is a document-wide Relation Extraction dataset containing 500 fully annotated paper abstracts. The papers encompass the topics of general AI, speech, machine learning and computer vision. The dataset is manually annotated and contains seven different relations. The entity mentions are not linked to a background KG.

DocRED [20] is large-scale document-wide RE dataset. It contains 96 different relations, making it one of the dataset with most-diverse relation set. It consists of a manually-annotated training, development and test set. Additionally, another large distantly-supervised dataset training dataset is offered as well. While the dataset was created by first linking the entity mentions to Wikipedia entities, the actual dataset does not provide the links. Furthermore, a later work [19] points out that the manually-annotated part contains a larger number of false-negatives.

Re-DocRED [19] revised the previously mentioned DocRED dataset to improve upon three problems: False Negatives, logical inconsistencies and coreferential errors. They accomplished this by iteratively improving the quality through a human-in-the-loop method. This leads to nearly two to three times as many triples annotated in the revised dataset. Similar to DocRED, Re-DocRED is not linked to an existing KG.

CDR [76] is a document-wide Relation Extraction dataset consisting of annotated PubMed abstracts created for the Fifth BioCreative Challenge Evaluation Workshop [77]. It contains only a single relation, whether a chemical-disease interaction holds. Each entity is equipped with Medical Subject Headings (MeSH) [78] allowing the connection to background KGs or ontologies.

GDA [79] is a gene-disease association dataset containing distantly-labeled MEDLINE abstracts. It contains UniProt [80] or CTD [81] gene ids for each gene and MeSH ids or CUIs for each mentioned disease allowing the study of the impact of an external KG. It again contains a single relation, whether an association holds or not.

DWIE [82] is a corpus of annotated English "Deutsche Welle" [4] news articles. It contains annotations of entity mentions, entity links, coreferences and relations. Due to the inclusion of entity linking, this makes this dataset very suitable to explore neuro-symbolic relation extraction. The annotated entity links point to Wikidata.

HacRED [83] is a dataset similar to DocRED focusing on Chinese documents while also constructing the dataset in such a way to include harder examples. Plain texts in the Chinese DBpedia [88] are annotated using entity reocgnition and entity linking. This leads to a distantly-supervised dataset from which hard cases are sampled based on some heuristics. These are then manually-annotated and a model is trained to identify further hard cases in the full dataset. Finally, crowdsourcing was used to exhaustively annotate all identified hard cases. The actual dataset does not contain the original links to DBpedia.

[4] `https://www.dw.com/`

Table 4. All document relation extraction datasets. #R stands for the number of relations, #D for the number of documents, #S for the number of sentences, Linked denotes whether the entities are linked to a KG or ontology

Corpus	Desc.	#R	#D	#S	Text Type	Linked
SciERC [75]	Abstract of computer science research papers	7	500	2,700	Paper abstract	✗
DocRED [20]	Wikipedia and Wikidata	96	5,053	-	Wiki	✗
Re-DocRED [19]	Revised DocRED by correcting false negatives	96	5,053	-	Wiki	✗
CDR [76]	PubMed biomedical documents	1	1500	-	Biomedical papers	✓
GDA [79]	MEDLINE abstracts	1	30192	-	Biomedical Abstracts	✓
DWIE [82]	News Articles	65	802	-	News	✓
HacRED [83]	Documents from Chinese DBpedia	26	9231	-	Wiki	✗
HiEve [84]	Event-Event Hierarchies	2	100	-	News articles	✗
MATRES [85]	Event-Event temporal relations	4	-	-	News articles	✗
Event StoryLine [86]	Event-Event temporal and causal relations	4	258	-	News articles	✗
APTERDOC [87]	Threat-intelligence field	9	124	12,906	Reports	✗

HiEve [84] is a Relation Extraction dataset focusing on events and their spatio-temporal relations. Of interest are here two relations, whether an event spatio-temporally contains another event or whether it they are coreferences of each other. The event mentions are not linked to any background KG.

MATRES [85] is a temporal Relation Extraction dataset. It contains four relations: "before", "after", "vague" and "equal" and focuses on news articles. Events are expressed verb instead of a noun. The events are not linked to a background KG or ontology.

Event StoryLine [86] is a Relation Extraction dataset with a focus temporal or causal relations between events. Four different relations “contains”, “before”, “after” and “overlap" are annotated. The focus is on news articles. The mentioned events are not linked to a background KG or ontology.

APTER-DOC [87] is a document-wide Relation Extraction dataset in the threat-intelligence field. It consists of annotated advanced persistent threats reports. Nine different relations are annotated specific to the threat-intelligence field. The annotated entities are not connected to a background Knowledge Graph or ontology.

Many datasets, such as SciERC and Re-DocRED, despite their substantial annotations, do not link entities to background KGs, necessitating additional linking efforts. Conversely, datasets like CDR and GDA benefit from built-in connections to biomedical ontologies, simplifying the integration of external knowledge. Datasets from other domains, including news articles (MATRES, Event StoryLine) and threat intelligence (APTER-DOC), lack such connections as well, reflecting the ongoing challenge of integrating symbolic knowledge across different fields.

3.3. Cross-document Relation Extraction

Cross-document relation extraction datasets are a fairly recent introduction to the problem area. Here, one is confronted with multiple documents each containing multiple sentences with again multiple entities inside. Relations can hold between entities inside the documents but also between them. Constructing datasets for this relation extraction category is more complex, hence why much fewer datasets are published for that.

See Table 5 for an overview of all the cross-document relation extraction datasets.

CodRED [89] is a cross-document relation extraction dataset annotated over Wikipedia while using Wikidata. It was annotated in three stages: 1) distant supervision, 2) manual annotation and 3) generating hard negative examples. It contains a large number of 276 different relations. As each entity mention is linked to Wikidata, studying the impact of symbolic data is significantly simplified.

Yahoo/Reuters/CNN [41] are cross-document relation extraction datasets focusing on causal relations between events. It contains only a single relation. The mentioned events are not linked to a background KG or ontology.

CodRED stands out with its comprehensive approach, utilizing Wikidata to simplify the integration of symbolic data and covering an extensive range of 276 relations. In contrast, the Yahoo/Reuters/CNN datasets focus on causal relations between events but lack connections to background KGs, posing additional challenges for incorporating external knowledge.

Table 5. All cross-document relation extraction datasets. #R stands for the number of relations, #D for the number of documents, #S for the number of sentences, Linked denotes whether the entities are linked to a KG or ontology

Corpus	Desc.	#R	#D	#S	Text Type	Linked
CodRED [89]	Wikipedia articles	276	-	30,504 [5]	Paper abstract	✓
Yahoo [41]	News Articles	1	1046	-	News	✗
Reuters [41]	News Articles	1	1212	-	News	✗
CNN [41]	News Articles	1	1190	-	News	✗

4. Challenges

Despite the numerous methods developed in neural-symbolic relation extraction, several challenges persist in this domain. One significant issue is the sheer volume of symbolic information, which, if fully utilized in neural models, might introduce bias or noise. There has been limited research on identifying which sources of symbolic information are most valuable for information extraction and on strategies to mitigate bias. Another challenge is aligning symbolic information with neural models. Neural models typically process text input to generate high-dimensional embeddings, whereas symbolic information can take various forms, including text and rules, with dimensions ranging from low to high. Some approaches use linear transformation or concatenation to align the dimensionality of the representations, while others integrate rules into the neural model training process, such as through the loss function or constrained generation. Successfully integrating these diverse types of information into a cohesive model remains a complex and ongoing task.

As for the datasets, it is evident that many datasets do not contain links to an existing KG or ontology. While this often is the case for datasets in the biomedical domain and to some extent for those which were initially annotated by distant-supervision, the majority are lacking such links. This is problematic due to several reasons. First, the linking needs to be done by an entity linker. However, the performance of different entity linkers vary vastly. Therefore, the actual linked entities might be different from method to method, introducing a variability in the starting conditions. Therefore, not only the developed method but also the quality of the entity linker has an impact on the results. While summarising the presented methods, it becomes evident that many papers did not state how the entity links were gathered. Second, the linking might be done against different versions of a KG. This again introduces more uncertainty in regard to differences between reported results. In the future, to better study the interaction between symbolic and neural relation extractions method, constructing datasets containing such links is vital. Furthermore, specifying against which KG the entities were annotated is very important as well.

5. Conclusion

In summary, RE is a pivotal task in NLP that focuses on identifying and classifying relationships between entities within text. The versatility of RE spans various types of text, including in-sentence, in-document, and cross-document contexts, making it a critical component in constructing KGs and answering complex queries. The advancement of machine learning models, particularly Pre-trained Language Models, has significantly enhanced the performance of RE by enabling efficient extraction of relations from unstructured text. However, these models often grapple with issues of robustness and generalization, especially when dealing with unseen entities and domain-specific texts.

To address these challenges, the integration of symbolic information, such as KGs and logical rules, has emerged as a promising approach. Neuro-symbolic RE methods aim to combine the interpretability and reasoning capabilities of symbolic systems with the flexibility and scalability of neural networks. Despite their potential, these methods face several challenges, including the effective alignment of symbolic and neural representations and the mitigation of bias introduced by symbolic information.

The current landscape of RE research highlights the necessity for improved datasets that include explicit links to existing KGs or ontologies. Such datasets would enable more consistent and comparable evaluations of RE methods. Additionally, further research is needed to identify the most valuable sources of symbolic information and develop robust strategies for integrating them into neural models.

Looking forward, the continued exploration of neuro-symbolic approaches holds promise for developing more robust, interpretable, and generalizable RE models. By addressing the existing challenges and leveraging both neural and symbolic techniques, future work can significantly advance the state of relation extraction, ultimately contributing to more sophisticated and accurate NLP systems.

Abbreviations used in this chapter

AMR Abstract Meaning Representation
ASP Answer Set Programming
ASPER ASP-enhanced Entity-Relation extraction
BERT Bidirectional Encoder Representations from Transformers
CNN Convolutional Neural Network
DocRE Document-level Relation Extraction
DRK Discriminative Rule-based Knowledge
GAL Global Adaptive Loss
GNN Graph Neural Network
GM_GEN Graph-based Model Generation
ILP Integer Linear Programming
KG Knowledge Graph
KICE Knowledge-evolving Framework by Iterative Consolidation and Expansion
LSTM Long Short-term Memory
MILR Mining and Injecting Logical Rules
NER Named Entity Recognition
NLP Natural Language Processing
PLM Pre-trained Language Model
RE Relation Extraction
RECON Relation Extraction using Knowledge Graph Context in a Graph Neural Network
SKAMRR Sememe Knowledge-enhanced Abstract Meaning Representation and Reasoning
GAN Graph Attention Network
UMLS Unified Medical Language System

References

[1] Chen Z, Wang Y, Zhao B, Cheng J, Zhao X, Duan Z. Knowledge Graph Completion: A Review. IEEE Access. 2020;8:192435-56.
[2] Pellissier Tanon T, Vrandečić D, Schaffert S, Steiner T, Pintscher L. From Freebase to Wikidata: The great migration. In: Proceedings of the 25th International Conference on World Wide Web; 2016. p. 1419-28.
[3] Galkin M, Trivedi P, Maheshwari G, Usbeck R, Lehmann J. Message Passing for Hyper-Relational Knowledge Graphs. In: Webber B, Cohn T, He Y, Liu Y, editors. Proceedings of the 2020 Conference on Empirical Methods in Natural Language Processing, EMNLP 2020, Online, November 16-20, 2020. Association for Computational Linguistics; 2020. p. 7346-59. Available from: `https://doi.org/10.18653/v1/2020.emnlp-main.596`.
[4] Han X, Gao T, Lin Y, Peng H, Yang Y, Xiao C, et al. More Data, More Relations, More Context and More Openness: A Review and Outlook for Relation Extraction. arXiv preprint arXiv:200403186. 2020.
[5] Ahn D. The stages of event extraction. In: Proceedings of the Workshop on Annotating and Reasoning about Time and Events; 2006. p. 1-8.
[6] Gorrell P, et al. Syntax and parsing. vol. 76. Cambridge University Press Cambridge; 1995.
[7] Yadav V, Bethard S. A Survey on Recent Advances in Named Entity Recognition from Deep Learning models. In: Bender EM, Derczynski L, Isabelle P, editors. Proceedings of the 27th International Conference on Computational Linguistics. Santa Fe, New Mexico, USA: Association for Computational Linguistics; 2018. p. 2145-58. Available from: `https://aclanthology.org/C18-1182`.

[8] Pereira A, Trifan A, Lopes RP, Oliveira JL. Systematic review of question answering over knowledge bases. IET Software. 2022;16(1):1-13.
[9] Ye H, Zhang N, Chen H, Chen H. Generative Knowledge Graph Construction: A Review. In: Goldberg Y, Kozareva Z, Zhang Y, editors. Proceedings of the 2022 Conference on Empirical Methods in Natural Language Processing, EMNLP 2022, Abu Dhabi, United Arab Emirates, December 7-11, 2022. Association for Computational Linguistics; 2022. p. 1-17. Available from: https://doi.org/10.18653/v1/2022.emnlp-main.1.
[10] Galstyan A. A systematic survey of relation extraction for knowledge graph question answering; 2022.
[11] Devlin J, Chang M, Lee K, Toutanova K. BERT: Pre-training of Deep Bidirectional Transformers for Language Understanding. In: Burstein J, Doran C, Solorio T, editors. Proceedings of the 2019 Conference of the North American Chapter of the Association for Computational Linguistics: Human Language Technologies, NAACL-HLT 2019, Minneapolis, MN, USA, June 2-7, 2019, Volume 1 (Long and Short Papers). Association for Computational Linguistics; 2019. p. 4171-86. Available from: https://doi.org/10.18653/v1/n19-1423.
[12] Raffel C, Shazeer N, Roberts A, Lee K, Narang S, Matena M, et al. Exploring the Limits of Transfer Learning with a Unified Text-to-Text Transformer. J Mach Learn Res. 2020;21:140:1-140:67. Available from: http://jmlr.org/papers/v21/20-074.html.
[13] Touvron H, Lavril T, Izacard G, Martinet X, Lachaux M, Lacroix T, et al. LLaMA: Open and Efficient Foundation Language Models. CoRR. 2023;abs/2302.13971. Available from: https://doi.org/10.48550/arXiv.2302.13971.
[14] Josifoski M, Cao ND, Peyrard M, Petroni F, West R. GenIE: Generative Information Extraction. In: Carpuat M, de Marneffe M, Ruíz IVM, editors. Proceedings of the 2022 Conference of the North American Chapter of the Association for Computational Linguistics: Human Language Technologies, NAACL 2022, Seattle, WA, United States, July 10-15, 2022. Association for Computational Linguistics; 2022. p. 4626-43. Available from: https://doi.org/10.18653/v1/2022.naacl-main.342.
[15] Qu M, Gao T, Xhonneux LP, Tang J. Few-shot Relation Extraction via Bayesian Meta-learning on Relation Graphs. In: III HD, Singh A, editors. Proceedings of the 37th International Conference on Machine Learning. vol. 119 of Proceedings of Machine Learning Research. PMLR; 2020. p. 7867-76. Available from: https://proceedings.mlr.press/v119/qu20a.html.
[16] Rawte V, Sheth A, Das A. A survey of hallucination in large foundation models. arXiv preprint arXiv:230905922. 2023.
[17] Mintz M, Bills S, Snow R, Jurafsky D. Distant supervision for relation extraction without labeled data. In: Su K, Su J, Wiebe J, editors. ACL 2009, Proceedings of the 47th Annual Meeting of the Association for Computational Linguistics and the 4th International Joint Conference on Natural Language Processing of the AFNLP, 2-7 August 2009, Singapore. The Association for Computer Linguistics; 2009. p. 1003-11. Available from: https://aclanthology.org/P09-1113/.
[18] Sevgili Ö, Shelmanov A, Arkhipov M, Panchenko A, Biemann C. Neural entity linking: A survey of models based on deep learning. Semantic Web. 2022;13(3):527-70.
[19] Tan Q, Xu L, Bing L, Ng HT, Aljunied SM. Revisiting DocRED - Addressing the False Negative Problem in Relation Extraction. In: Goldberg Y, Kozareva Z, Zhang Y, editors. Proceedings of the 2022 Conference on Empirical Methods in Natural Language Processing, EMNLP 2022, Abu Dhabi, United Arab Emirates, December 7-11, 2022. Association for Computational Linguistics; 2022. p. 8472-87. Available from: https://doi.org/10.18653/v1/2022.emnlp-main.580.
[20] Yao Y, Ye D, Li P, Han X, Lin Y, Liu Z, et al. DocRED: A Large-Scale Document-Level Relation Extraction Dataset. In: Korhonen A, Traum DR, Màrquez L, editors. Proceedings of the 57th Conference of the Association for Computational Linguistics, ACL 2019, Florence, Italy, July 28- August 2, 2019, Volume 1: Long Papers. Association for Computational Linguistics; 2019. p. 764-77. Available from: https://doi.org/10.18653/v1/p19-1074.
[21] Ye Z, Ling Z. Distant Supervision Relation Extraction with Intra-Bag and Inter-Bag Attentions. In: Burstein J, Doran C, Solorio T, editors. Proceedings of the 2019 Conference of the North American Chapter of the Association for Computational Linguistics: Human Language Technologies, NAACL-HLT 2019, Minneapolis, MN, USA, June 2-7, 2019, Volume 1 (Long and Short Papers). Association for Computational Linguistics; 2019. p. 2810-9. Available from: https://doi.org/10.18653/v1/n19-1288.
[22] Dai Q, Heinzerling B, Inui K. Universal Graph based Relation Extraction.
[23] Le TH, Cao H, Cao Son T. ASPER: Answer Set Programming Enhanced Neural Network Models for

Joint Entity-Relation Extraction. Theory and Practice of Logic Programming. 2023 Jul;23(4):765-81.

[24] Bastos A, Nadgeri A, Singh K, Mulang' IO, Shekarpour S, Hoffart J, et al. RECON: Relation Extraction using Knowledge Graph Context in a Graph Neural Network. In: Leskovec J, Grobelnik M, Najork M, Tang J, Zia L, editors. WWW '21: The Web Conference 2021, Virtual Event / Ljubljana, Slovenia, April 19-23, 2021. ACM / IW3C2; 2021. p. 1673-85. Available from: https://doi.org/10.1145/3442381.3449917.

[25] Zhang J, Zhu J, Yang Y, Shi W, Zhang C, Wang H. Knowledge-Enhanced Domain Adaptation in Few-Shot Relation Classification. In: Zhu F, Ooi BC, Miao C, editors. KDD '21: The 27th ACM SIGKDD Conference on Knowledge Discovery and Data Mining, Virtual Event, Singapore, August 14-18, 2021. ACM; 2021. p. 2183-91. Available from: https://doi.org/10.1145/3447548.3467438.

[26] Wang M, Zheng J, Cai F, Shao T, Chen H. DRK: Discriminative Rule-based Knowledge for Relieving Prediction Confusions in Few-shot Relation Extraction. In: Calzolari N, Huang CR, Kim H, Pustejovsky J, Wanner L, Choi KS, et al., editors. Proceedings of the 29th International Conference on Computational Linguistics. Gyeongju, Republic of Korea: International Committee on Computational Linguistics; 2022. p. 2129-40. Available from: https://aclanthology.org/2022.coling-1.186.

[27] Liu Y, Dai F, Gu X, Fan H, Liu D, Li B, et al. Powering Fine-Tuning: Learning Compatible and Class-Sensitive Representations for Domain Adaption Few-shot Relation Extraction. In: Wang X, Sapino ML, Han W, Abbadi AE, Dobbie G, Feng Z, et al., editors. Database Systems for Advanced Applications - 28th International Conference, DASFAA 2023, Tianjin, China, April 17-20, 2023, Proceedings, Part IV. vol. 13946 of Lecture Notes in Computer Science. Springer; 2023. p. 121-31. Available from: https://doi.org/10.1007/978-3-031-30678-5_10.

[28] Jain M, Singh K, Mutharaju R. ReOnto: A Neuro-Symbolic Approach for Biomedical Relation Extraction. In: Joint European Conference on Machine Learning and Knowledge Discovery in Databases. Springer; 2023. p. 230-47.

[29] Aghaebrahimian A, Anisimova M, Gil M. Ontology-Aware Biomedical Relation Extraction.

[30] Mikolov T, Sutskever I, Chen K, Corrado GS, Dean J. Distributed representations of words and phrases and their compositionality. Advances in neural information processing systems. 2013;26.

[31] Bodenreider O. The Unified Medical Language System (UMLS): integrating biomedical terminology. Nucleic Acids Res. 2004;32(Database-Issue):267-70. Available from: https://doi.org/10.1093/nar/gkh061.

[32] Li Y, Yu B, Mengge X, Liu T. Enhancing Pre-trained Chinese Character Representation with Word-aligned Attention. In: Jurafsky D, Chai J, Schluter N, Tetreault J, editors. Proceedings of the 58th Annual Meeting of the Association for Computational Linguistics. Online: Association for Computational Linguistics; 2020. p. 3442-8. Available from: https://aclanthology.org/2020.acl-main.315.

[33] Tuo M, Yang W. Review of entity relation extraction. Journal of Intelligent & Fuzzy Systems. 2023;44(5):7391-405.

[34] Zhao Q, Gao T, Guo N. Document-level relation extraction based on sememe knowledge-enhanced abstract meaning representation and reasoning. Complex & Intelligent Systems. 2023;9(6):6553-66.

[35] Fan S, Mo S, Niu J. Boosting Document-Level Relation Extraction by Mining and Injecting Logical Rules. In: Proceedings of the 2022 Conference on Empirical Methods in Natural Language Processing; 2022. p. 10311-23.

[36] Qi F, Yang C, Liu Z, Dong Q, Sun M, Dong Z. OpenHowNet: An Open Sememe-based Lexical Knowledge Base. arXiv preprint arXiv:190109957. 2019.

[37] Jain M, Mutharaju R, Kavuluru R, Singh K. Revisiting Document-Level Relation Extraction with Context-Guided Link Prediction. In: Wooldridge MJ, Dy JG, Natarajan S, editors. Thirty-Eighth AAAI Conference on Artificial Intelligence, AAAI 2024, Thirty-Sixth Conference on Innovative Applications of Artificial Intelligence, IAAI 2024, Fourteenth Symposium on Educational Advances in Artificial Intelligence, EAAI 2014, February 20-27, 2024, Vancouver, Canada. AAAI Press; 2024. p. 18327-35. Available from: https://doi.org/10.1609/aaai.v38i16.29792.

[38] Miller GA. WordNet: A Lexical Database for English. Commun ACM. 1995;38(11):39-41. Available from: https://doi.org/10.1145/219717.219748.

[39] Jain M, Mutharaju R, Singh K, Kavuluru R. Knowledge-Driven Cross-Document Relation Extraction. CoRR. 2024;abs/2405.13546. Available from: https://doi.org/10.48550/arXiv.2405.13546.

[40] Zhang Z, Yu B, Shu X, Mengge X, Liu T, Guo L. From What to Why: Improving Relation Extraction with Rationale Graph. In: Findings of the Association for Computational Linguistics: ACL-IJCNLP 2021. Online: Association for Computational Linguistics; 2021. p. 86-95.

[41] Zhang C, Lyu J, Xu K. A storytree-based model for inter-document causal relation extraction from news articles. Knowledge and Information Systems. 2023;65(2):827-53.

[42] Liu B, Han FX, Niu D, Kong L, Lai K, Xu Y. Story Forest: Extracting Events and Telling Stories from Breaking News. ACM Transactions on Knowledge Discovery from Data (TKDD). 2020;14(3):1-28.

[43] Gao L, Choubey PK, Huang R. Modeling Document-level Causal Structures for Event Causal Relation Identification. In: Proceedings of the 2019 Conference of the North American Chapter of the Association for Computational Linguistics: Human Language Technologies, Volume 1 (Long and Short Papers); 2019. p. 1808-17.

[44] Xu W, Chen K, Zhao T. Document-Level Relation Extraction with Path Reasoning. ACM Transactions on Asian and Low-Resource Language Information Processing. 2023;22(4):1-14.

[45] Li W, Qian T. Graph-based Model Generation for Few-Shot Relation Extraction. In: Goldberg Y, Kozareva Z, Zhang Y, editors. Proceedings of the 2022 Conference on Empirical Methods in Natural Language Processing. Abu Dhabi, United Arab Emirates: Association for Computational Linguistics; 2022. p. 62-71. Available from: https://aclanthology.org/2022.emnlp-main.5.

[46] Lu Y, Wang X, Yang H, Tang S. KICE: A Knowledge Consolidation and Expansion Framework for Relation Extraction. In: Proceedings of the AAAI Conference on Artificial Intelligence. vol. 37; 2023. p. 13336-43.

[47] Haotian C, Yijiang C, Xiangdong Z. Understanding More Knowledge Makes the Transformer Perform Better in Document-level Relation Extraction. In: Asian Conference on Machine Learning. PMLR; 2024. p. 231-46.

[48] Roth D, Yih W. A Linear Programming Formulation for Global Inference in Natural Language Tasks. In: Ng HT, Riloff E, editors. Proceedings of the Eighth Conference on Computational Natural Language Learning, CoNLL 2004, Held in cooperation with HLT-NAACL 2004, Boston, Massachusetts, USA, May 6-7, 2004. ACL; 2004. p. 1-8. Available from: https://aclanthology.org/W04-2401/.

[49] Doddington GR, Mitchell A, Przybocki MA, Ramshaw LA, Strassel SM, Weischedel RM. The Automatic Content Extraction (ACE) Program - Tasks, Data, and Evaluation. In: Proceedings of the Fourth International Conference on Language Resources and Evaluation, LREC 2004, May 26-28, 2004, Lisbon, Portugal. European Language Resources Association; 2004. Available from: http://www.lrec-conf.org/proceedings/lrec2004/summaries/5.htm.

[50] Riedel S, Yao L, McCallum A. Modeling Relations and Their Mentions without Labeled Text. In: Balcázar JL, Bonchi F, Gionis A, Sebag M, editors. Machine Learning and Knowledge Discovery in Databases, European Conference, ECML PKDD 2010, Barcelona, Spain, September 20-24, 2010, Proceedings, Part III. vol. 6323 of Lecture Notes in Computer Science. Springer; 2010. p. 148-63. Available from: https://doi.org/10.1007/978-3-642-15939-8_10.

[51] Yan J, He L, Huang R, Li J, Liu Y. Relation Extraction with Temporal Reasoning Based on Memory Augmented Distant Supervision. In: Burstein J, Doran C, Solorio T, editors. Proceedings of the 2019 Conference of the North American Chapter of the Association for Computational Linguistics: Human Language Technologies, NAACL-HLT 2019, Minneapolis, MN, USA, June 2-7, 2019, Volume 1 (Long and Short Papers). Association for Computational Linguistics; 2019. p. 1019-30. Available from: https://doi.org/10.18653/v1/n19-1107.

[52] Pyysalo S, Ginter F, Heimonen J, Björne J, Boberg J, Järvinen J, et al. BioInfer: a corpus for information extraction in the biomedical domain. BMC Bioinform. 2007;8. Available from: https://doi.org/10.1186/1471-2105-8-50.

[53] Gurulingappa H, Rajput AM, Roberts A, Fluck J, Hofmann-Apitius M, Toldo L. Development of a benchmark corpus to support the automatic extraction of drug-related adverse effects from medical case reports. J Biomed Informatics. 2012;45(5):885-92. Available from: https://doi.org/10.1016/j.jbi.2012.04.008.

[54] Zhao Z, Yang Z, Luo L, Lin H, Wang J. Drug drug interaction extraction from biomedical literature using syntax convolutional neural network. Bioinform. 2016;32(22):3444-53. Available from: https://doi.org/10.1093/bioinformatics/btw486.

[55] Kulkarni C, Xu W, Ritter A, Machiraju R. An Annotated Corpus for Machine Reading of Instructions in Wet Lab Protocols. In: Walker MA, Ji H, Stent A, editors. Proceedings of the 2018 Conference of the North American Chapter of the Association for Computational Linguistics: Human Language Technologies, NAACL-HLT, New Orleans, Louisiana, USA, June 1-6, 2018, Volume 2 (Short Papers). Association for Computational Linguistics; 2018. p. 97-106. Available from: https://doi.org/10.18653/v1/n18-2016.

[56] Kruiper R, Vincent JFV, Chen-Burger J, Desmulliez MPY, Konstas I. In Layman's Terms: Semi-Open Relation Extraction from Scientific Texts. In: Jurafsky D, Chai J, Schluter N, Tetreault JR, editors. Proceedings of the 58th Annual Meeting of the Association for Computational Linguistics, ACL 2020, Online, July 5-10, 2020. Association for Computational Linguistics; 2020. p. 1489-500. Available from: https://doi.org/10.18653/v1/2020.acl-main.137.

[57] Hailu N, Hunter L, Cohen KB. UColorado_SOM: extraction of drug-drug interactions from biomedical text using knowledge-rich and knowledge-poor features. In: Second Joint Conference on Lexical and Computational Semantics (* SEM), Volume 2: Proceedings of the Seventh International Workshop on Semantic Evaluation (SemEval 2013); 2013. p. 684-8.

[58] Gao T, Han X, Zhu H, Liu Z, Li P, Sun M, et al. FewRel 2.0: Towards More Challenging Few-Shot Relation Classification. In: Inui K, Jiang J, Ng V, Wan X, editors. Proceedings of the 2019 Conference on Empirical Methods in Natural Language Processing and the 9th International Joint Conference on Natural Language Processing, EMNLP-IJCNLP 2019, Hong Kong, China, November 3-7, 2019. Association for Computational Linguistics; 2019. p. 6249-54. Available from: https://doi.org/10.18653/v1/D19-1649.

[59] Ellis J, Getman J, Mott J, Li X, Griffitt K, Strassel SM, et al. Linguistic Resources for 2013 Knowledge Base Population Evaluations. In: Proceedings of the Sixth Text Analysis Conference, TAC 2013, Gaithersburg, Maryland, USA, November 18-19, 2013. NIST; 2013. Available from: https://tac.nist.gov/publications/2013/additional.papers/KBP2013_annotation_overview.TAC2013.proceedings.pdf.

[60] Yu D, Sun K, Cardie C, Yu D. Dialogue-Based Relation Extraction. In: Jurafsky D, Chai J, Schluter N, Tetreault JR, editors. Proceedings of the 58th Annual Meeting of the Association for Computational Linguistics, ACL 2020, Online, July 5-10, 2020. Association for Computational Linguistics; 2020. p. 4927-40. Available from: https://doi.org/10.18653/v1/2020.acl-main.444.

[61] Wang Y, Zhou K, Gachloo M, Xia J. An Overview of the Active Gene Annotation Corpus and the BioNLP OST 2019 AGAC Track Tasks. In: Kim J, Nédellec C, Bossy R, Deléger L, editors. Proceedings of The 5th Workshop on BioNLP Open Shared Tasks, BioNLP-OST@EMNLP-IJNCLP 2019, Hong Kong, China, November 4, 2019. Association for Computational Linguistics; 2019. p. 62-71. Available from: https://doi.org/10.18653/v1/D19-5710.

[62] Knox C, Wilson M, Klinger CM, Franklin M, Oler E, Wilson A, et al. DrugBank 6.0: the DrugBank knowledgebase for 2024. Nucleic acids research. 2024;52(D1):D1265-75.

[63] Xing R, Luo J, Song T. BioRel: towards large-scale biomedical relation extraction. BMC bioinformatics. 2020;21:1-13.

[64] Herrero-Zazo M, Segura-Bedmar I, Martínez P, Declerck T. The DDI corpus: An annotated corpus with pharmacological substances and drug-drug interactions. J Biomed Informatics. 2013;46(5):914-20. Available from: https://doi.org/10.1016/j.jbi.2013.07.011.

[65] Uzuner Ö, South BR, Shen S, DuVall SL. 2010 i2b2/VA challenge on concepts, assertions, and relations in clinical text. J Am Medical Informatics Assoc. 2011;18(5):552-6. Available from: https://doi.org/10.1136/amiajnl-2011-000203.

[66] Stoica G, Platanios EA, Póczos B. Re-TACRED: Addressing Shortcomings of the TACRED Dataset. In: Thirty-Fifth AAAI Conference on Artificial Intelligence, AAAI 2021, Thirty-Third Conference on Innovative Applications of Artificial Intelligence, IAAI 2021, The Eleventh Symposium on Educational Advances in Artificial Intelligence, EAAI 2021, Virtual Event, February 2-9, 2021. AAAI Press; 2021. p. 13843-50. Available from: https://doi.org/10.1609/aaai.v35i15.17631.

[67] Sorokin D, Gurevych I. Context-Aware Representations for Knowledge Base Relation Extraction. In: Palmer M, Hwa R, Riedel S, editors. Proceedings of the 2017 Conference on Empirical Methods in Natural Language Processing, EMNLP 2017, Copenhagen, Denmark, September 9-11, 2017. Association for Computational Linguistics; 2017. p. 1784-9. Available from: https://doi.org/10.18653/v1/d17-1188.

[68] Riedel S, Yao L, McCallum A. Modeling Relations and Their Mentions without Labeled Text. In: Balcázar JL, Bonchi F, Gionis A, Sebag M, editors. Machine Learning and Knowledge Discovery in Databases, European Conference, ECML PKDD 2010, Barcelona, Spain, September 20-24, 2010, Proceedings, Part III. vol. 6323 of Lecture Notes in Computer Science. Springer; 2010. p. 148-63. Available from: https://doi.org/10.1007/978-3-642-15939-8_10.

[69] Bollacker K, Evans C, Paritosh P, Sturge T, Taylor J. Freebase: a collaboratively created graph database for structuring human knowledge. In: Proceedings of the 2008 ACM SIGMOD International Conference

on Management of Data. SIGMOD '08. New York, NY, USA: Association for Computing Machinery; 2008. p. 1247–1250. Available from: https://doi.org/10.1145/1376616.1376746.

[70] Zhang Y, Zhong V, Chen D, Angeli G, Manning CD. Position-aware Attention and Supervised Data Improve Slot Filling. In: Palmer M, Hwa R, Riedel S, editors. Proceedings of the 2017 Conference on Empirical Methods in Natural Language Processing, EMNLP 2017, Copenhagen, Denmark, September 9-11, 2017. Association for Computational Linguistics; 2017. p. 35-45. Available from: https://doi.org/10.18653/v1/d17-1004.

[71] Han X, Zhu H, Yu P, Wang Z, Yao Y, Liu Z, et al. FewRel: A Large-Scale Supervised Few-Shot Relation Classification Dataset with State-of-the-Art Evaluation. In: Riloff E, Chiang D, Hockenmaier J, Tsujii J, editors. Proceedings of the 2018 Conference on Empirical Methods in Natural Language Processing. Brussels, Belgium: Association for Computational Linguistics; 2018. p. 4803-9. Available from: https://aclanthology.org/D18-1514.

[72] Quirk C, Poon H. Distant Supervision for Relation Extraction beyond the Sentence Boundary. In: Lapata M, Blunsom P, Koller A, editors. Proceedings of the 15th Conference of the European Chapter of the Association for Computational Linguistics, EACL 2017, Valencia, Spain, April 3-7, 2017, Volume 1: Long Papers. Association for Computational Linguistics; 2017. p. 1171-82. Available from: https://doi.org/10.18653/v1/e17-1110.

[73] Li J, Sun Y, Johnson RJ, Sciaky D, Wei C, Leaman R, et al. BioCreative V CDR task corpus: a resource for chemical disease relation extraction. Database J Biol Databases Curation. 2016;2016. Available from: https://doi.org/10.1093/database/baw068.

[74] Peng N, Poon H, Quirk C, Toutanova K, Yih W. Cross-Sentence N-ary Relation Extraction with Graph LSTMs. Trans Assoc Comput Linguistics. 2017;5:101-15. Available from: https://doi.org/10.1162/tacl_a_00049.

[75] Luan Y, He L, Ostendorf M, Hajishirzi H. Multi-task identification of entities, relations, and coreference for scientific knowledge graph construction. arXiv preprint arXiv:180809602. 2018.

[76] Zhang T, Lin H, Tadesse MM, Ren Y, Duan X, Xu B. Chinese medical relation extraction based on multi-hop self-attention mechanism. International Journal of Machine Learning and Cybernetics. 2021;12:355-63.

[77] Kim S, Dogan RI, Chatr-Aryamontri A, Tyers M, Wilbur WJ, Comeau DC. Overview of biocreative v bioc track. In: Proceedings of the Fifth BioCreative Challenge Evaluation Workshop, Sevilla, Spain; 2015. p. 1-9.

[78] Lipscomb CE. Medical subject headings (MeSH). Bulletin of the Medical Library Association. 2000;88(3):265.

[79] Li J, Sun Y, Johnson RJ, Sciaky D, Wei CH, Leaman R, et al. BioCreative V CDR task corpus: a resource for chemical disease relation extraction. Database. 2016;2016.

[80] Consortium U. UniProt: a hub for protein information. Nucleic acids research. 2015;43(D1):D204-12.

[81] Mattingly CJ, Colby GT, Forrest JN, Boyer JL. The comparative toxicogenomics database (CTD). Environmental health perspectives. 2003;111(6):793-5.

[82] Zaporojets K, Deleu J, Develder C, Demeester T. DWIE: An entity-centric dataset for multi-task document-level information extraction. Inf Process Manag. 2021;58(4):102563. Available from: https://doi.org/10.1016/j.ipm.2021.102563.

[83] Cheng Q, Liu J, Qu X, Zhao J, Liang J, Wang Z, et al. HacRED: A Large-Scale Relation Extraction Dataset Toward Hard Cases in Practical Applications. In: Zong C, Xia F, Li W, Navigli R, editors. Findings of the Association for Computational Linguistics: ACL/IJCNLP 2021, Online Event, August 1-6, 2021. vol. ACL/IJCNLP 2021 of Findings of ACL. Association for Computational Linguistics; 2021. p. 2819-31. Available from: https://doi.org/10.18653/v1/2021.findings-acl.249.

[84] Glavas G, Snajder J, Moens M, Kordjamshidi P. HiEve: A Corpus for Extracting Event Hierarchies from News Stories. In: Calzolari N, Choukri K, Declerck T, Loftsson H, Maegaard B, Mariani J, et al., editors. Proceedings of the Ninth International Conference on Language Resources and Evaluation, LREC 2014, Reykjavik, Iceland, May 26-31, 2014. European Language Resources Association (ELRA); 2014. p. 3678-83. Available from: http://www.lrec-conf.org/proceedings/lrec2014/summaries/1023.html.

[85] Ning Q, Wu H, Roth D. A Multi-Axis Annotation Scheme for Event Temporal Relations. In: Gurevych I, Miyao Y, editors. Proceedings of the 56th Annual Meeting of the Association for Computational Linguistics, ACL 2018, Melbourne, Australia, July 15-20, 2018, Volume 1: Long Papers. Association for Computational Linguistics; 2018. p. 1318-28. Available from: https://aclanthology.org/

P18-1122/.

[86] Caselli T, Vossen P. The Event StoryLine Corpus: A New Benchmark for Causal and Temporal Relation Extraction. In: Caselli T, Miller B, van Erp M, Vossen P, Palmer M, Hovy EH, et al., editors. Proceedings of the Events and Stories in the News Workshop@ACL 2017, Vancouver, Canada, August 4, 2017. Association for Computational Linguistics; 2017. p. 77-86. Available from: https://doi.org/10.18653/v1/w17-2711.

[87] Wang X, Xiong M, Luo Y, Li N, Jiang Z, Xiong Z. Joint Learning for Document-Level Threat Intelligence Relation Extraction and Coreference Resolution Based on GCN. In: 2020 IEEE 19th International Conference on Trust, Security and Privacy in Computing and Communications (TrustCom). IEEE; 2020. p. 584-91.

[88] Auer S, Bizer C, Kobilarov G, Lehmann J, Cyganiak R, Ives ZG. DBpedia: A Nucleus for a Web of Open Data. In: Aberer K, Choi K, Noy NF, Allemang D, Lee K, Nixon LJB, et al., editors. The Semantic Web, 6th International Semantic Web Conference, 2nd Asian Semantic Web Conference, ISWC 2007 + ASWC 2007, Busan, Korea, November 11-15, 2007. vol. 4825 of Lecture Notes in Computer Science. Springer; 2007. p. 722-35. Available from: https://doi.org/10.1007/978-3-540-76298-0_52.

[89] Yao Y, Du J, Lin Y, Li P, Liu Z, Zhou J, et al. CodRED: A Cross-Document Relation Extraction Dataset for Acquiring Knowledge in the Wild. In: Moens MF, Huang X, Specia L, Yih SWt, editors. Proceedings of the 2021 Conference on Empirical Methods in Natural Language Processing. Online and Punta Cana, Dominican Republic: Association for Computational Linguistics; 2021. p. 4452-72. Available from: https://aclanthology.org/2021.emnlp-main.366.

Handbook on Neurosymbolic AI and Knowledge Graphs
P. Hitzler et al. (Eds.)
IOS Press, 2025

doi:10.3233/FAIA250223

Neurosymbolic Methods for Dynamic Knowledge Graphs

Mehwish ALAM [a,1] , Genet Asefa GESESE [b] and Pierre-Henri PARIS [c]
[a] *Télécom Paris, Institut Polytechnique de Paris, France*
[b] *FIZ Karlsruhe, Karlsruhe Institute of Technology, Germany*
[c] *University of Paris Saclay, France*

Abstract. Knowledge graphs (KGs) have recently been used for many tools and applications, making them rich resources in structured format. However, in the real world, KGs grow due to the additions of new knowledge in the form of entities and relations, making these KGs dynamic. This chapter formally defines several types of dynamic KGs and summarizes how these KGs can be represented. Additionally, many neurosymbolic methods have been proposed for learning representations over static KGs for several tasks such as KG completion and entity alignment. This chapter further focuses on neurosymbolic methods for dynamic KGs with or without temporal information. More specifically, it provides an insight into neurosymbolic methods for dynamic (temporal or non-temporal) KG completion and entity alignment tasks. It further discusses the challenges of current approaches and provides some future directions.

Keywords. Dynamic Knowledge Graphs, Temporal Knowledge Graphs, Dynamic Entity Alignment, Dynamic Knowledge Graph Completion

1. Introduction

Knowledge Graphs (KGs) [1] have gained attention in the past few years for representing information in a structured way, i.e., entities and relations. It has been used for various applications and domains from search engines and recommendation systems [2] to bio-informatics [3] and social sciences [4]. They capture relationships between entities in a way that is both human-readable and machine-processable, enabling advanced reasoning and inference capabilities. The significance of KGs lies in their ability to integrate vast amounts of heterogeneous data, providing a unified framework that supports comprehensive querying and analysis.

However, the real world is dynamic, with changes happening continuously—new entities emerge, existing relationships evolve, and facts that were once true may become outdated. In such scenarios, traditional static KGs fall short as they cannot accommodate these changes in real-time. This limitation has led to the development of *Dynamic Knowledge Graphs (DKGs)*, which can evolve by incorporating temporal information. Dynamic KGs update the data and track changes, enabling temporal queries and historical analysis.

[1]Corresponding Author: mehwish.alam@telecom-paris.fr.

The inclusion of temporality in KGs poses significant challenges. Firstly, the representation of time-sensitive data requires precise modeling to capture the validity period of facts. For example, without temporal information, a query asking about the president of the United States might return multiple results, leading to ambiguity. Temporal dynamics are crucial in contexts like legal documents, medical records, and financial transactions, where the timing of events plays a pivotal role in decision-making. Thus, preserving temporality in KGs is beneficial and necessary for ensuring the accuracy and relevance of the information.

Furthermore, learning representations over DKGs is essential for several reasons. It enables the development of models that can predict future changes, discover hidden patterns, and provide insights based on the temporal evolution of data. This is particularly valuable in predictive analytics, trend analysis, and anomaly detection, where understanding the temporal context can significantly enhance the accuracy of the results.

Entity alignment, the task of identifying equivalent entities across different datasets or KGs, becomes increasingly complex in dynamic settings. As entities and their attributes change over time, ensuring they are correctly matched requires sophisticated techniques that can handle temporal variations. This is crucial for maintaining data integrity, improving the accuracy of merged datasets, and enhancing the overall quality of the KG.

In summary, the dynamic and temporal dimensions of KGs are critical for accurately reflecting the complexity of real-world data. Addressing the challenges associated with these aspects can significantly advance the field of KG research and its applications, paving the way for more intelligent and responsive information systems.

This book chapter is structured as follows: Section 2 reviews related work and positions this chapter within the broader context. Section 3 provides fundamental definitions of the DKGs. Section 4 details how the dynamic information can be represented in the form of a KG. Following the discussion on representation techniques, the book chapter then moves on to explaining how neurosymbolic methods have been utilized for learning representations over DKGs for KG Completion (Section 5) and dynamic entity alignment (Section 6).

2. Related Work

One of the very recent studies provides an overview of the DKGs [5]. However, this chapter mostly focuses on providing a formal definition of different categories of DKGs along with neurosymbolic methods for DKGs, such as learning representations over such symbolic representations using methods based on neural networks along with the downstream tasks such as KG completion and entity alignment.

Several studies have been conducted on learning representations over KGs. For instance, various techniques for refining KGs are summarized in [6], including methods for KG completion. A categorization of static KG completion algorithms is given in [7]. In contrast, an exhaustive survey on multimodal KG embedding algorithms that utilize literal (text, numeric, image) information within the static KGs are presented in [8] along with an experimental comparison of these algorithms. Furthermore, a recent article [9] provides an overview of various KG completion tasks, such as transductive and inductive link prediction. It details methods incorporating background information from large language models and discusses embeddings considering description logic axioms. However, all these studies are limited to static KGs and do not consider the dynamic aspects in a KG. In contrast, [10] surveys the methods for Temporal Knowledge Graph (TKG) completion. This book chapter builds on this by formally defining the fundamental differences between DKGs and TKGs. It provides a comprehensive overview of representation learning for these types of KGs, highlighting their unique characteristics and challenges. Additionally, the chapter discusses various downstream tasks associated with these graphs, such as KG completion and entity alignment, offering insights into the methodologies and applications tailored to DKGs and TKGs.

3. Preliminaries

This section formally defines static, temporal, and dynamic KGs with examples.

Definition 1 (Static Knowledge Graph) *Let* $G = (E, R, L, F)$ *be a directed labeled graph, where E, R, and L are the sets of entities, relations, and literals, respectively.* $F \subseteq E \times R \times (E \cup L)$ *represents a set of facts such that* $f = (h, r, t)$ *or* $f = (h, r, l)$ *represent one triple where* $f \in F$, $h, t \in E$, $r \in R$, *and* $l \in L$.

Example 1 *Consider a simple knowledge graph* $G = (E, R, L, F)$ *where:*

- ***Entities (E)***: *{Barack_Obama, USA}*
- ***Relations (R)***: *{president_of}*
- ***Literals (L)***: $\emptyset$
- ***Facts (F)***: *{(Barack_Obama, president_of, USA)}*

The example shows that Barack Obama is the president of the USA. Now, suppose we update the graph with the following:

- $E = E \cup \{Donald\_Trump\}$
- $R = R$
- $L = \emptyset$
- $F = F \cup (Donald\_Trump, president\_of, USA)$

In this static representation, the knowledge graph indicates that both Barack Obama and Donald Trump have been (or are) presidents of the USA. However, without temporal information, it is unclear when each individual held office.

The definition of a static KG can further be extended to a temporal KG, where each triple can have a time interval representing its temporal validity:

Definition 2 (Temporal Knowledge Graph) *Let* $G = (E, R, L, T, Q)$ *be a directed labeled graph, where E, R, L, and T represent the set of entities, relations, literals, and timestamps, respectively.* $Q \subseteq E \times R \times (E \cup L) \times (T \cup \{\emptyset\})$ *represents a set of facts such that* $q = (h, r, t, [\tau_s, \tau_e])$ *or* $q = (h, r, l, [\tau_s, \tau_e])$ *represent one quadruple where* $q \in Q$, $h, t \in E$, $r \in R$, $l \in L$, *and* $\tau_s, \tau_e \in T \cup \{\emptyset\}$ *and* τ_s *and* τ_e *represent the start and end time, i.e.,* $\tau_s \leq \tau_e$ *. If* $\tau_s = \tau_e$ *then it represents a point in time* $\tau \in T$.

Example 2 *Consider a simple knowledge graph* $G = (E, R, L, F)$ *where:*

- ***Entities (E)**: {Barack_Obama, USA}*
- ***Relations (R)**: {president_of}*
- ***Literals (L)**: {2009, 2017} (representing years)*
- ***Quadruples (Q)**: {(Barack_Obama, president_of, USA, [2009, 2017])}*

The example shows when the fact that Barack Obama held office is a valid fact, i.e., from 2009 to 2017.

Definition 3 (Dynamic Knowledge Graph) *A dynamic knowledge graph G is a sequence of knowledge graphs* $\{G_{t_0}, G_{t_1}, \ldots, G_{t_n}\}$ *indexed by time steps* $t_0, t_1, \ldots, t_n$ *such that* $t_0 < t_1 < \cdots < t_n$ *and* $\forall t_i, t_i \in T$*, where T is the set of all timestamps. Each graph* G_{t_i}*, at time step* t_i*, can be either a static knowledge graph (see Definition 1) or a temporal knowledge graph (see Definition 2).*

The graph G_{t_i} *represents a snapshot of the dynamic graph G at time* t_i*. The transition between two consecutive snapshots* $G_{t_{i-1}}$ *and* G_{t_i} *can be characterized by changes in entities, relations, literals, and facts. Formally:*

$$E_{t_i} = E_{t_{i-1}} \cup E^+_{t_i} \setminus E^-_{t_{i-1}} \quad \text{where } E^+_{t_i} \text{ and } E^-_{t_{i-1}} \text{ represent the additions and removals of entities,}$$

$$R_{t_i} = R_{t_{i-1}} \cup R^+_{t_i} \setminus R^-_{t_{i-1}} \quad \text{where } R^+_{t_i} \text{ and } R^-_{t_{i-1}} \text{ represent the additions and removals of relations,}$$

$$L_{t_i} = L_{t_{i-1}} \cup L^+_{t_i} \setminus L^-_{t_{i-1}} \quad \text{where } L^+_{t_i} \text{ and } L^-_{t_{i-1}} \text{ represent the additions and removals of literals,}$$

$$G_{t_i} = G_{t_{i-1}} \cup G^+_{t_i} \setminus G^-_{t_{i-1}} \quad \text{where } G^+_{t_i} \text{ and } G^-_{t_{i-1}} \text{ represent the additions and removals of facts.}$$

Additionally, if G_{t_i} *is a temporal knowledge graph, it can include changes in the temporal intervals of the quadruples.*

Example 3 *Consider the first snapshot of a simple knowledge graph* $G_0 = (E_0, R_0, L_0, F_0)$ *where:*

- ***Entities** (E_0): {Barack_Obama, USA}*
- ***Relations** (R_0): {president_of}*
- ***Literals** (L_0): $\emptyset$*
- ***Facts** (F_0): {(Barack_Obama, president_of, USA)}*

We can see that Barack Obama is the president of the USA as in the first example. Now, suppose we update the graph with the following new snapshot $G_1 = (E_1, R_1, L_1, F_1)$*:*

- ***Entities** (E_1): $E_0 \setminus$ {Barack_Obama} $\cup$ {Donald_Trump}*
- ***Relations** (R_1): R_0*
- ***Literals** (L_1): $L_0 = \emptyset$*
- ***Facts** (F_1): {(Donald_Trump, president_of, USA)}*

Now, Donald Trump is the president of the USA in the last snapshot G_1*, which no longer contains information about Barack Obama.*

Finally, consider the temporal KG of Example 2 as the first snapshot G_0 *of a simple knowledge graph. It can be updated with the following new snapshot* $G_1 = (E_1, R_1, L_1, F_1)$*:*

- ***Entities** (E_1): $E_0 \cup$ {Donald_Trump}*
- ***Relations** (R_1): R_0*

- ***Literals*** *(L_1):* $L_0 \cup \{2021\}$
- ***Quadruples*** *(Q_1):* $Q_0 \cup \{(Donald\_Trump, president\_of, USA, [2017, 2021])\}$

This example is more complete because it keeps both facts with their respective time validity.

4. Representing Dynamic and Temporal Knowledge Graphs

This section presents the different techniques to represent temporal information in knowledge graphs and that can be used for temporal KGs or dynamic KGs.

4.1. Techniques to Represent Temporal Information in Knowledge Graphs

The first nucleus to represent time is the use of various XML Schema Definition [11] (XSD) datatypes, such as `xsd:dateTime`, `xsd:duration`, `xsd:date`, and others, that allows for precise representation of temporal data, including specific moments, durations, calendar dates, and individual time components, in KGs. These datatypes have been designed to facilitate the accurate and standardized encoding of temporal information, enabling robust temporal querying and reasoning.

4.1.1. Temporal Properties

Temporal properties directly incorporate time into relationships within a KG. These properties provide inherent temporal aspects to the entities and relationships they describe. For example (please note that all examples are provided in the Turtle syntax[2]):

```
:Alice :birthDate "1990-01-01"^^xsd:date .
:Alice :employedAt :CompanyX .
:Alice :employmentStart "2020-01-01"^^xsd:date .
:Alice :employmentEnd "2022-01-01"^^xsd:date .
```

In this example, a simple temporal relation is represented using a time interval: Alice's employment relationship with CompanyX includes specific start and end dates, enabling queries about her employment duration. The advantage of this approach is its straightforwardness and direct annotation of temporal data within the relationships themselves. However, it may lack flexibility for more complex temporal scenarios because one need to know that "*employmentStart*" is related to "*employedAt*". Additionally, if one wants to keep track of Alice's employment history, this became more complex to represent. Temporal attributes can also be represented, e.g., we also know her birth date, which is a fixed point in time.

All cross-domain general-purpose KGs have some form of temporal information, e.g., Wikidata [12], DBpedia [13], YAGO [14,15], etc.

---

[2] `https://www.w3.org/TR/rdf12-turtle/`

4.1.2. Reification

Reification allows a triple to be treated as a subject of another triple, thereby attaching metadata such as temporal information. There are several ways to reify a triple.

The standard reification [16] is a built-in functionality in RDF, i.e., a resource is used to denote the fact and additional information about the statement can be added using the RDF vocabulary (the properties "*rdf:subject*", "*rdf:predicate*", and "*rdf:object*"). For instance:

```
_:statement rdf:type rdf:Statement .
_:statement rdf:subject :Alice .
_:statement rdf:predicate :knows .
_:statement rdf:object :Bob .
_:statement :since "2022-01-01"^^xsd:date .
```

Through reification, the relationship between Alice and Bob can be annotated with the date they became acquainted. This approach offers flexibility in adding metadata to existing triples but can lead to increased data redundancy and complexity.

Other possibilities to reify a fact are to use n-ary relations [17] or to use singleton properties [18]. The interested reader can refer to Hernández et al. [19] for more details and an in depth comparison of these approaches.

4.1.3. Time Ontology in OWL

The Time Ontology in OWL[3] provides a comprehensive framework for representing temporal concepts. This ontology includes classes and properties for describing instants, intervals, and durations. Thus, the ontology is designed to support complex temporal reasoning and querying following Allen's interval algebra [20]. For example:

```
@prefix ex: <http://example.org/ns#> .
@prefix time: <http://www.w3.org/2006/time#> .

# Define Alice as a person
ex:Alice a ex:Person ;
    ex:worksSince ex:JobStart .

# Define the job start time
ex:JobStart a time:Instant ;
    time:inXSDDateTime "2020-01-01T00:00:00Z"^^xsd:dateTime .

# Define a class for persons who have been working for more
# than 3 years
ex:LongTermEmployee a owl:Class ;
    owl:equivalentClass [
        owl:intersectionOf (
            ex:Person
            [
```

[3]https://www.w3.org/TR/owl-time/

```
                owl:onProperty ex:worksSince ;
                owl:someValuesFrom [
                    owl:restriction [
                        owl:onProperty time:before ;
                        owl:hasValue
                            "2021-01-01T00:00:00Z"^^xsd:dateTime
                    ]
                ]
            ]
        )
    ] .

# Reasoning
ex:Alice a ex:LongTermEmployee .
```

In this example, we use the OWL Time ontology to describe the start date of Alice's employment and perform basic reasoning to determine if she qualifies as a long-term employee.

The interesting definition is the class ex:LongTermEmployee used to represent individuals who have been working for more than three years. This class is specified using owl:equivalentClass to intersect ex:Person and a restriction on the ex:worksSince property. The restriction requires that the ex:worksSince property has a value indicating a work start date before January 1, 2021.

The reasoner determines that since Alice's work start date is "2020-01-01," which is before the cutoff date "2021-01-01," she meets the criteria for long-term employment.

4.1.4. Named Graphs and Quadruples

Named graphs [21] group triples into a single graph that can have metadata associated with it. This allows for temporal information to be added at the graph level. For example:

```
GRAPH <http://example.org/graph/2022-01-01> {
    :Alice :knows :Bob .
}
```

This structure facilitates temporal data management by associating entire sets of triples with specific temporal contexts. Named graphs are advantageous for segmenting data into manageable subgraphs but can introduce overhead in graph management and querying.

Quadruples[4] extend RDF triples by adding a fourth element, often used to represent the context or the named graph, which can include temporal information. Contrary to named graphs, quadruples are not a separate graph but a part of the RDF data model, thus, informations can be attached to the fact level instead of the whole graph. For example:

```
:Alice :knows :Bob "2022-01-01"^^xsd:date .
```

[4] https://www.w3.org/TR/rdf12-n-quads/

This quadruple includes a timestamp indicating when Alice and Bob's acquaintance began. The use of quadruples simplifies the representation of contextual information but requires a data store that supports quad storage and querying.

4.1.5. RDF-star

RDF-star[5] is an extension of the RDF data model that offers a more compact and intuitive way to represent complex statements, including those involving temporal information. Examples include:

```
<< :Alice :knows :Bob >> :since "2022-01-01"^^xsd:date .
<< :Alice :worksAt :CompanyX >> :startDate "2020-01-01"^^xsd:date ;
       :endDate "2022-01-01" .
<< :Alice :attended :ConferenceX >> :onDate "2023-06-15"^^xsd:date .
<< :Document123 :hasVersion :Version1 >> :timestamp
       "2024-01-01T10:00:00Z" .
<< :DataItem :createdBy :User123 >> :creationTime
       "2024-07-01T09:00:00Z" .
```

RDF-star enables a streamlined representation of temporal information, simplifying the construction and querying of knowledge graphs. Its compactness reduces data redundancy and complexity but requires support for RDF-star syntax and semantics in RDF processors.

4.1.6. Versioning

Maintaining historical data with timestamps is crucial for tracking changes over time. Versioning techniques ensure that the evolution of data is documented, enabling temporal queries and historical analysis. One can use simple approaches, such as adding a timestamp to each triple, or more complex methods, such as reification or named graphs. For example, using versioning:

```
:Document123 :hasVersion :Version1 .
:Version1 :timestamp "2024-01-01T10:00:00Z" .
```

More complex versioning systems have been proposed over time: Frommhold et al. [22] developed a Version Control System for KGs, emphasizing the need for efficient change detection across graphs, including handling blank nodes. Their system uses invertible patches to manage changes, supporting operations like revert and merge, and ensuring data integrity through secure hashing of patches. This approach is foundational, particularly in tracking changes in complex datasets and ensuring reliable data history.

Pelgrin et al. [23] provided a comprehensive survey and analysis of KG archiving systems, highlighting the lack of standardization and scalability in existing solutions. They introduced RDFev, a framework for studying the dynamicity of RDF data, which offers insights into dataset evolution at both low and high levels. Their work outlines the essential features of a fully-fledged RDF archiving system, emphasizing the need for robust support for concurrent updates, efficient query processing and comprehensive version control features like branching and tagging.

---

[5] https://w3c.github.io/rdf-star/cg-spec/editors_draft.html

Table 1. Comparison of Temporal and Dynamic Capabilities Across Various RDF Techniques. The presence of a feature is indicated by an 'X'. The asterisk under Named Graphs & Quadruples denotes that a choice must be made between temporal and dynamic, depending on the semantics intended by the graph owner.

	Properties	Reification	Time Ontology	Named Graphs & Quadruples	RDF-star	Versioning
Temporal	X	X	X	X*	X	
Dynamic		X		X*	X	X

Table 1 provides a summary of the temporal and dynamic capabilities of the various RDF techniques presented in this section For instance, temporal properties give a straightforward way to annotate data with time, but they may not offer the flexibility needed for complex scenarios where relationships between different temporal attributes must be explicitly defined. Reification and Named Graphs/Quadruples allow for more detailed metadata, such as temporal context, versioning, or provenance, which can be crucial for historical analyses or data integrity. However, these methods can introduce data redundancy and increase the complexity of queries. Additionally, only one value can be used as a fourth value or as the name of the named graph.

The Time Ontology in OWL is particularly useful for those needing to model complex temporal relations, such as intervals and durations, and supports reasoning over these data types. This makes it ideal for applications requiring detailed temporal reasoning, such as historical data analysis or event tracking.

RDF-star offers a more compact and intuitive representation, which reduces data redundancy and simplifies the data structure. This can be particularly advantageous when dealing with large datasets or when the overhead of traditional reification methods becomes a concern. However, RDF processors must support RDF-star syntax and semantics, which might not be universally available.

Versioning techniques are essential for tracking changes over time, ensuring that a KG can evolve while maintaining a record of past states. This is particularly relevant in domains where data history is as important as the data itself, such as legal or historical research, or dynamic KG completion.

When choosing a method for representing temporal information in KGs, researchers and practitioners should consider the specific requirements of their application, including the complexity of the temporal relationships, the need for metadata, the size of the dataset, and the capabilities of the RDF processors they are using.

4.2. Prominent Knowledge Graphs

We now describe some of the most prominent general-purpose KGs and how they represent temporal information.

4.2.1. DBpedia

DBpedia [13] incorporates temporal aspects into its dataset through properties that denote specific time-related data. For example, temporal properties such as *dbo:birthDate* and *dbo:deathDate* indicate birth and death dates for people, while other properties capture periods of activity or events, such as *dbo:productionStartDate* and *dbo:productionEndDate* for manufacturing or production events. This inclusion of temporal data allows for queries about the duration of events or the temporal relationships between entities. However, representing complex temporal scenarios might require additional context or metadata, as basic temporal properties might not inherently indicate their relation to other properties without such context.

DBpedia handles versioning primarily by maintaining historical data, which allows tracking changes over time. The DBpedia Live system plays a crucial role in this aspect, as it continuously synchronizes with Wikipedia to update the dataset with the latest information. This system utilizes a stream of updates from Wikipedia, enabling DBpedia to reflect recent edits with minimal delay, typically within a few minutes. Versioning also exists in DBpedia through snapshots, ensuring that historical changes are documented, which is essential for conducting temporal queries and historical analyses.

4.2.2. YAGO

The second iteration of YAGO [14] incorporates temporal dimensions into its KG by assigning existence times to entities and facts. This is achieved using specific relations such as *wasBornOnDate*, *diedOnDate*, *wasCreatedOnDate*, and *wasDestroyedOnDate*, which are standardized under generic entity-time relations like *startsExistingOnDate* and *endsExistingOnDate*. For events lasting a single day, YAGO2 uses *happenedOnDate*, which is a sub-property of both *startsExistingOnDate* and *endsExistingOnDate*. Facts are assigned a time point if they are instantaneous events or a time span if they have an extended duration with known beginning and end. This approach allows the system to deduce the temporal scope of entities and events, providing a comprehensive temporal annotation across the dataset.

For example, entities such as people are assigned birth and death dates, while artifacts and groups have creation and potential destruction dates. In cases where the data is incomplete or not applicable (e.g., abstract concepts or mythological entities), no temporal data is assigned, adhering to a conservative approach. This temporal framework is essential for enabling time-based queries and analyses, such as determining the lifespan of individuals or the duration of historical events.

YAGO 4.5 [15] builds upon the temporal framework of previous versions by enhancing its capacity to handle temporal information more flexibly and in more detail. The integration of temporal data into YAGO 4.5 utilizes the RDF-star model, allowing for more intricate annotations of facts. This temporal tagging is crucial for representing the evolving nature of the KG, allowing for dynamic queries that reflect changes over time. All YAGO versions are accessible only as archives, as the live version is not publicly available.

4.2.3. Wikidata

Wikidata [12] utilizes a system of qualifiers to provide additional context to statements, including temporal information. Qualifiers in Wikidata are versatile and can specify details such as the period during which a statement is valid. For instance, in the following example, Douglas Adams's education at St John's College is annotated with start and end dates, providing a temporal dimension to his academic history:

```
wd:Q42 wdt:P69 wd:Q3918 .
wd:Q42 p:P69 _:statement .
_:statement ps:P69 wd:Q3918 .
_:statement pq:P580 "1971-10-01T00:00:00Z"^^xsd:dateTime .
```

```
_:statement pq:P582 "1974-06-01T00:00:00Z"^^xsd:dateTime .
```

In this data snippet, '*wd:Q42*' represents Douglas Adams, '*wd:Q3918*' represents St John's College, '*p:P69*' and '*ps:P69*' denote the property for educational institutions attended, and '*pq:P580*' and '*pq:P582*' provide the start and end times of the education period, respectively.

Qualifiers in Wikidata allow for highly detailed annotations of statements, including dates, locations, and other contextual information. This feature supports complex data representation but requires sophisticated data parsing and querying mechanisms to retrieve and interpret the full context of the data.

Wikidata's approach to versioning involves maintaining a complete history of all edits, thus allowing for comprehensive tracking of changes over time. This version history is essential for verifying data provenance and understanding the evolution of knowledge within the graph. Unlike other KGs, Wikidata's version history is openly accessible, providing a transparent view of the data's editorial process.

Furthermore, Wikidata is a DKG, continuously updated by a large community of contributors. This live updating system ensures that Wikidata remains current, reflecting the latest information and corrections as they become available. The dynamic nature of Wikidata, combined with its detailed versioning and temporal annotations, supports both real-time applications and historical research, making it a versatile tool for a wide range of uses.

4.2.4. EventGraph

EventKG [24,25], a multilingual event-centric TKG, focuses heavily on capturing and representing temporal relations and events. The system models events using a canonical representation that incorporates both the start and end times of events, leveraging a variety of data sources, including Wikidata, DBpedia, and YAGO. Temporal information in EventKG is linked to entities and events, allowing for detailed historical analysis and event tracking. The model uses properties such as *sem:hasBeginTimeStamp* and *sem:hasEndTimeStamp* to define the temporal span of events and entities' involvement in those events.

Additionally, EventKG employs the Simple Event Model (SEM) as its foundational schema, which it extends to represent temporal relations better. This includes modeling not only event-entity relationships but also complex temporal relations between multiple entities or events, such as sequences of events and their hierarchical relationships. This comprehensive temporal modeling enables sophisticated queries and analyses concerning the temporal dynamics of historical and contemporary events.

Using named graphs and quadruples, EventKG also addresses versioning indirectly by maintaining a provenance framework that tracks the sources and version history of the data it integrates. Provenance information is critical in EventKG, as it helps verify the accuracy and credibility of the temporal data. Each piece of information, including temporal annotations, is associated with metadata that details its origin, the specific version of the source data, and the extraction date.

5. Dynamic Knowledge Graph Completion

In the existing literature [26], TKGC methods are generally classified into two categories: interpolation-based and extrapolation-based. Interpolation-based methods aim to predict missing knowledge by leveraging existing quadruplets. In contrast, extrapolation-based methods are designed for continuous TKGs, enabling prediction of future events by learning embeddings from previous or historical snapshots of entities and relations. This work treats interpolation methods as TKGC for TKGs, while extrapolation-based methods are applied to dynamic KGs, as defined in Section 3.

5.1. Temporal Knowledge Graph Completion (TKGC)

Temporal Knowledge Graphs (TKGs) often contain millions or billions of quadruplets, but they are typically incomplete for several reasons. First, extracting information from unstructured text sources can be error-prone, resulting in incomplete data. Second, capturing or integrating all available information, particularly from diverse or complex sources, is challenging. Third, the sources themselves may lack comprehensiveness or be biased, leading to selective inclusion of information and omission of other relevant facts. Lastly, the dynamic nature of information, with knowledge continuously evolving, contributes to these gaps.

The KGC task – commonly known as link prediction (LP) – aims to predict missing links by utilizing existing information. Various techniques have been developed for this task. However, a significant limitation of these methods is their difficulty in capturing the temporal dynamics of facts. They are typically designed for static knowledge graphs (KGs) that assume facts do not change over time. Therefore, these methods are ineffective when applied to TKGs, as they overlook the crucial temporal information inherent in TKGs. Temporal KGC (TKGC) methods have emerged to enhance LP accuracy by addressing the limitations of traditional KGC methods. TKGC methods improve upon these by incorporating timestamps of facts into the learning process in addition to the facts themselves. For instance, with TKGC, it is possible to infer the fact `(Gerhard Schröder, succeeded, Angela Merkel, 2005)` using the existing quadruplets `(Angela Merkel, Chancelor of, Germany, [2005 to 2021])` and `(Gerhard Schröder, Chancelor of, Germany, [1998 - 2005])`.

TKGC aims to predict possible links between two entities at a specific time. This can be accomplished in different ways: i) *tail prediction* - given the head and relation at a certain time, predicting the tail entity ($< h, r, ? >$), ii) *head prediction* - given the tail and relation at a particular time, predicting the head entity ($<?, r, t >$), iii) *relation prediction* - given the head and tail at a certain time, predicting the relation ($< h, ?, t >$). Inspired by the survey in [27], TKGC methods could be categorized into timestamps-dependent-based TKGC, timestamps-specific functions-based TKGC, and deep learning-based TKGC methods. A summary of these TKGC methods is provided in Table 2. Timestamps dependent-based TKGC methods such as TuckERTNT [28], TTransE [29], ST-TransE [30], T-SimplE [31], Canonical Polyadic (CP) [32], TKGFrame [33], TBDRI [34] associate timestamps to corresponding entities and relations to capture their evolution without directly manipulating the timestamps.

Timestamps-specific Functions-based TKGC methods use specialized functions, such as diachronic embedding, Gaussian, and transformation function, to learn embeddings for timestamps. Transformation functions-based TKGC methods include BoxTE [35], SPLIME [36], TARGCN [37], TASTER [38], Time-LowFER [39], Goel et al. [40], and DEGAT [41]. Complex embedding functions-based TKGC methods include ChronoR [42], TComplEx and TNTComplEx [43], TeRo [44], TGeomE [45], TeLM [46], RotateQVS [47], ST-NewDE [48], BiQCap [49],HA-TKGE [50], STKE [51], and HTKE [52]. Non-linear embedding functions-based TKGC methods iclude DyERNIE [53], ATiSE [54], HERCULES [55], and TKGC-AGP [56].

Deep learning-based TKGC methods capture the evolution of entities and relations by encoding timestamps using deep learning algorithms. These methods can be further grouped into i) Timestamps-Specific Space such as HyTE [57], HTKE [52], TRHyTE [58], BTHyTE [59], ToKEi [60], SANe [61], and QDN [62], ii) Long Short-Term Memory (LSTM)-based TKGC methods such as TA-TransE and TA-DistMult [63], TDG2E [64], Ma et al [65], CTRIEJ [66], and TeCre [67], and iii) Temporal constraint-based TKGC methods such as Chekol et al. [68], Kgedl [69], T-GAP [70], TempCaps [71], RoAN [72], and TAL-TKGC [73].

Training procedure: Given a TKG G and a set of facts Q in G, a scoring function $g(q)$ is defined to assign a factual score for a fact or a true quadruplet $q \in Q$. A negative sampling strategy [74] is employed to create a set of negative samples, i.e., factually incorrect quadruplets Q', to enhance the expressiveness of learned representations for the entities and relations in G.

Loss function: A loss function L aims at maximizing $g(q)$ for all $q \in Q$ and minimizing $g(q')$ for their negative samples $q' \in Q$. The following are the commonly used loss functions by TKGC approaches.

- **Margin-based ranking loss (MRL)** [75] enforces that the confidence in the corrupted quadruplet is lower than in the true quadruplet by a certain margin. MRL is computed as

$$L_{MRL} = \sum_{q \in Q} \left[\lambda + g(q) - \sum_{q' \in Q'} g(q')\right]_+, \tag{1}$$

  where $[x]_+ = max(x,0)$ and $\lambda > 0$ is a margin hyperparameter.
- **Cross-entropy loss (CEL)** [76] also aims at obtaining a large gap between true quadruplets and the negative samples but without enforcing a fixed margin for all facts.

$$L_{CEL} = \sum_{q \in Q} \frac{exp(g(q))}{\sum_{q' \in Q'} exp(g(q'))} \tag{2}$$

- **Binary cross-entropy loss (BCEL)** [77] emphasizes the score of individual true quadruplets and negative samples as follows:

$$L_{BCEL} = \sum_{q \in Q \cup Q'} yg(q) + (1-y)g(q'), \tag{3}$$

  where $y = 1$ if $q \in Q$ and $y = 0$ otherwise.

Table 2. Comparative Analysis of the TKGC methods presented in Section 5.1. ILP, CS, and SKGC stand for Integer Linear Programming, Coordinate System, and Static Knowledge Graph Completion, respectively.

Technique	TKGC Methods	Remarks
Translation	TTransE [29], ST-TransE [30], BoxTE [35]	TTransE and ST-TransE struggle with handling temporally evolving facts. All are SKGC methods.
Tensor Decomp.	TuckERTNT [28], T-SimplE [31], Time-LowFER [39], QDN [62]	Time-LowFER ignores the rich contextual information in the graph structure. All except QDN are SKGC methods
ILP	TKGFrame [33]	TKGFrame can not handle complex scenarios like path queries.
Manifold	HERCULES [55], DyERNIE [53]	Both are SKGC methods. HERCULES does not show significant differences over benchmarks due to its limited use of temporal information.
Block Decomp.	TBDRI [34]	TBDRI is an SKGC method.
GCN	TARGCN [37]	TARGCN is an SKGC method.
GAT	DEGAT [41]	
Transformation	SPLIME [36]	SPLIME is an SKGC method.
Sparse Matrix	TASTER [38]	TASTER is an SKGC method.
Gaussian	ATiSE [54]	
Gaussian/Markov	TKGC-AGP [56]	
Polar CS	HA-TKGE [50], HTKE [52]	Both are SKGC methods.
Spherical CS	STKE [51]	
Complex Space	TNTComplEx [43], TeRo [44], ChronoR [42]	All are SKGC methods.
Quaternion Space	TeLM [46], RotateQVS [47], TGeomE [45]	All are SKGC methods. TeLM ignores the rich contextual information in the graph structure.
Dihedron Algebra	ST-NewDE [48]	ST-NewDE is an SKGC method.
Biquaternions/Manifold	BiQCap [49]	BiQCap is an SKGC method.
Time-Encoding	TA-DistMult [63], ToKEi [60]	Both are SKGC methods.
Time-Encoding/LSTM	TeCre [67]	TeCre is an SKGC method.
Temporal-Hyperp	HyTE [57], BTHyTE [59]	Both are SKGC methods.
Temporal-Hyperp/GRU	TRHyTE [58]	TRHyTE is an SKGC method.
Multi-semantic Space	SANe [61]	
GRU	TDG2E [64]	
GRU/Negative Sampling	CTRIEJ [66]	CTRIEJ is an SKGC method.
Path Reasoning	Kgedl [69]	
GNN	T-GAP [70]	
Capsule Network	TempCaps [71]	
Attention	RoAN [72], TAL-TKGC [73]	Both are SKGC methods.

Evaluation techniques: Typically, evaluating TKGC methods involves performing both head and tail predictions for each test quadruple q. For head prediction, the head entity in q is replaced with every possible entity in the TKG. Similarly, the tail entity is replaced with every possible entity for tail prediction. The scores generated by the scoring function for these modified quadruples are then ranked. Commonly used accuracy metrics for this evaluation include Mean Rank (MR), Mean Reciprocal Rank (MRR), and Hits@k.

Benchmark datasets: The commonly used benchmark datasets for TKGC can be categorized into those used for interpolation methods, such as ICEWS14 [63], ICEWS05-15 [63], GDELT [78], YAGO11k [57], YAGO15k [63], and Wikidata12k [57], and those used for extrapolation methods, including ICEWS14 [63], ICEWS18 [79], GDELT [78], WIKI [29], and YAGO [80].

5.2. Non-Temporal Dynamic KG Completion

Traditional methods for generating KG embeddings do not consider the evolving nature of a KG where new entities and relations are constantly being added to the KG. This requires training the embeddings over the new KG from scratch even if the changes are minimal which can lead to increased computational costs. Various attempts have been made to deal with this challenge. One of the first attempts to address this issue is online learning, which learns incrementally as new information arrives. However, one of the drawbacks of these methods of KG embedding is that they do not consider the problem of catastrophic forgetting. To mitigate this issue, continual or lifelong learning [81] methods were proposed, alleviating the problem of catastrophic forgetting in various tasks. In catastrophic forgetting, adaptation to a new distribution generally results in a largely reduced ability to capture the old ones.

Continual KG Embedding methods (CKGE) has recently received growing attention which perform fine-tuning with only new knowledge, leading to reduced training costs. These methods effectively alleviate the problem of catastrophic forgetting while learning the representations of the newly added knowledge. Continual Learning-based methods further target two kinds of solutions. First, the full-parameter fine-tuning paradigm which memorizes old knowledge by replaying a core old dataset or introducing additional regularization constraints. Although this paradigm effectively mitigates catastrophic forgetting, it significantly increases training costs, especially when handling large-scale KGs. Second, it adopts the incremental-parameter fine-tuning paradigm, with only a few parameters to learn emerging knowledge. This strategy may still lead to an increase in parameters and training time.

Recently, low-rank adapters such as LoRA have enabled efficient parameter fine-tuning and are used to reduce the training time in Large Language Models (LLMs). One of the very recent studies, FastKGE, introduces incremental low-rank adaptation mechanisms, IncLoRAs, to reduce training costs for continual learning for KG embeddings. The rest of the section discusses and compares these methods in detail.

5.2.1. Online Learning Based Methods

puTransE [82]. The current translational models (KG embedding models using translation-based scoring functions) for static KG embeddings have three significant shortcomings. First, translational models are highly sensitive to hyperparameters such as margin and learning rate [83]. Second, for one triple, there is only one representation if the translation principle is followed, leading to low precision due to the congestion of entities and relations in vector space. Last but not least, new unseen entities or relations are not handled. One of the first methods to deal with the drawbacks mentioned above is Parallel Universe TransE (puTransE) – an extension of TransE – which learns multiple embeddings.

puTransE follows three steps: (i) triple selection (structurally and semantically aware triple selection), (ii) generation of random configurations, and (iii) learning embeddings.

Triple Selection Triple Selection includes semantically and structurally aware triple selection. To select semantically relevant entities, the puTransE samples a relation $r \in R$ and generates a set of entities $\{e_1, e_2, \ldots, e_n\} \in E$ of all entities containing r as either an outgoing or incoming edge. For structurally aware triple selection, the authors adopt the bidirectional random walk model using the entities selected as starting nodes. puTransE creates multiple embedding spaces each time new entities or relations arrive, and for each embedding, it defines a triple constraint both in count and diversity.

Generate Random Configurations Instead of defining a global configuration, puTransE generates different hyperparameter configurations for each embedding space. It randomly generates the value of the original TransE hyperparameters, i.e., margin and learning rate but also the values of triple constraint and number of training epochs.

Learning Embeddings puTransE uses a margin-based loss function.

puTransE, however, learns embeddings from the local parts of the KG, avoiding the retraining of the whole embedding space, which leads to the loss of global structural information in the learned embedding space. Additionally, since puTransE is an increment over TransE, it uses the scoring function of TransE, which does not work well for 1-to-N, N-to-1, and N-to-N relations.

DKGE [84] learns joint embedding for each entity and relation by considering their contextual information leading to an improvement over puTransE which only considers local information. The context of an entity e_1 is the one-hop neighborhood subgraph of the entity represented as $sg(e_1) \in E$. The context of a relation r_1 is represented by the relation path $p_1 = (r_1, r_2)$. The first step is to encode the contextual information of entity and relation as vector representations, which is then combined with the entity and relation embeddings (referred to as knowledge embeddings). After that, a scoring function and a loss function based on translation operations for parameter training are defined.

The algorithm uses Attentive GCN (AGCN) Model to effectively take into account the neighborhood information (modeled by GCN) and only use the information that may be important (modeled by the attention mechanism). Given x where $x \in EorR$ and its context, i.e., a subgraph with n vertices $\{v_i\}_{i=1}^{n}$, DKGE builds the adjacency matrix $A \in \mathbb{R}^{n \times n}$ and initializes the vertex feature matrix $H^{(0)} \in \mathbb{R}^{n \times d^0}$ where d^0 is the number of the initialized features for each vertex. Each row in $H^{(0)}$ is denoted as v_i. If x is an entity, then v_i is an entity and $\mathbf{v_i}$ is its contextual element embedding. When x is a relation, if v_i is a relation path consisting of two relations, then $\mathbf{v_i}$ is the sum of the contextual element embeddings of these two relations.

The final contextual subgraph embedding $\mathbf{sg}(x)$ of the subgraph $sg(x)$ is given by a weighted sum of the vectors of all vertices $\{v_i\}_{i=1}^{n}$ as follows:

$$\mathbf{sg}(x) = \sum_{i=n}^{n} \alpha_{i(x)} \mathbf{v_i} \tag{4}$$

The scoring function is given as follows:

$$f(h,r,t) = \parallel \mathbf{h^*} + \mathbf{r^*} - \mathbf{t^*} \parallel_{l_1} \tag{5}$$

where **h***, **r*** and **t*** are computed by Eq. (4), and $\parallel \odot \parallel_{l_1}$ denotes the l_1 norm. A margin-based loss function is utilized for training. During online learning, at time step $T+1$, the knowledge embeddings and contextual element embeddings for new entities (relations) are randomly initialized according to a uniform distribution. For existing entities (relations), their knowledge embeddings and contextual element embeddings are carried over from the embedding results at time step T. These methods, however, do not consider literal information along with the structural information of a KG.

DKGC-JSTD [85] proposes a DKG completion model that jointly learns the structural and textual information of entities and relations based on a deep RNN. This model learns the embedding of an entity's name and parts of its text description to connect unseen entities to KGs. Deep memory network and association matching mechanism are used to extract semantic feature information and establish relevance between entity and relations from entity text-description. It then uses Recurrent Neural Networks to model the dependency between topology-structure and text description.

5.2.2. Continual Learning Based Methods

Various methods based on continual learning have been proposed. In this chapter, we discuss some of the fundamental algorithms.

Lifelong Knowledge Graph Embedding (LKGE) [86] learns the embedding of an entity or relation based on its masked first-order subgraph given as follows:

$$\bar{x}_i = MAE\left(\bigcup_{j=1}^{i} N_j(x)\right) \tag{6}$$

where $x \in E$ *or* R, and $N_j \subseteq D_j$ denotes the involved facts of x in the j-th snapshot and D represents the training set. $MAE()$ is an encoder that represents the input subgraph. The objective of the KG encoder is to align the entity or relation embedding with the reconstructed representation as follows:

$$L_{MAE} = \sum_{e \in E_i} \parallel e_i - \bar{e}_i \parallel_2^2 + \sum_{r} \in R_i \parallel r_i - \bar{r}_i \parallel_2^2 \tag{7}$$

Graph Convolution Networks (GCN) and Transformer are two common encoders. If they are updated for lifelong learning, the changed model parameters will affect the embedding generation of all old entities, including the involved old entities in new facts. This can lead to catastrophic forgetting of the previous snapshots. For this reason, the entity and relation embedding transition functions are used as encoders by LKGE, which do not introduce additional parameters and use TransE. TransE is leveraged to train the embeddings from the new data and update the knowledge transfer for each snapshot.

$$L_{new} = \sum_{(h,r,t)\in D_i} max(0, \gamma + f(h,r,t) - f(h',r,t')) \tag{8}$$

where γ is the margin. (h',r,t') is the embedding of a negative fact. The subject or object is randomly replaced with a random entity $e' \in E_i$ for each positive fact. The embeddings of unseen entities **e** and relations **r** are randomly initialized. To avoid catastrophic forgetting, regularization methods constrain the updates of the parameters. Accordingly, the loss function of regularization methods is given as:

$$L_{old} = \sum_{e\in E_{i-1}} w(e) \parallel e_i - e_{i-1} \parallel_2^2 + \sum_{r} \in R_{i-1} w(r) \parallel r_i - r_{i-1} \parallel_2^2 \tag{9}$$

where $w(x)$ is the regularization weight for x. The regularization weight is only computed once per snapshot. The overall learning objective is as follows:

$$L = L_{new} + \alpha L_{old} + \beta L_{MAE} \tag{10}$$

where α, β are hyperparameters for balancing the objectives.

One of the recent approaches uses low-rank adaptation for learning dynamic KG embeddings. Incremental Low-Rank Adaptation (IncLoRA) [87] operated in three stages. During the first graph layering stage, new entities and relations are divided into several layers based on the distance from the old graph and node degrees. The second stage involves IncLoRA learning, in which incremental LoRAs with adaptive rank allocation represent the embeddings of entities and relations in each layer. In the final stage, link prediction is performed, which composes all new LoRAs into a LoRA group and concat all LoRA groups and initial embeddings for inference.

Several previous studies have proposed using different mechanisms to learn the representations of the initial state of KGs and then incrementally learning the representations upon the arrival of new entities and relations. Some continual learning based algorithms use translational embeddings [88], progressive neural networks [89], incremental knowledge distillation [90], and graph attention networks [91].

6. Dynamic Entity Alignment

This section provides an overview of the temporal entity alignment methods between two KGs. In addition to TKG alignment, a few methods have been proposed considering new data while performing entity alignment.

6.1. Temporal Entity Alignment Methods

Most of the methods for temporal entity alignment use GCNs or GNNs to learn the representations of the entities alongside the temporal attention mechanism. In the following, we briefly overview the methods proposed so far.

In [92], the authors exploit both relation and temporal information for entity alignment by first creating a reverse link, i.e., introducing the inverse of the relations to handle the beginning and end of the relation. The method utilizes a time-aware attention mechanism with GCN to assign different weights to entities according to their relation and temporal information. On the other hand, TKG Entity Alignment via Representation Learning (Tem-EA) [93] incorporates temporal information with the help of Recurrent Neural Networks to learn temporal sequence representations. GCN and translation-based embedding models are used for learning representations over structural and attribute information for computing entity similarity separately on the two KGs to be aligned. These representations are combined using linear weighting. The concept of nearest-neighbor matching is performed to find the most similar entity pair based on the distance matrix.

A recent study [94] proposes a simple temporal information matching mechanism for entity alignment between TKGs. Most of the methods proposed prior to this use a time-aware attention mechanism to incorporate relational and temporal information into entity embeddings. This study assumes that learning the representations from the temporal information is unnecessary since a temporal matching mechanism, in addition to the GNN-based model, achieves better results. In [95], the authors perform entity alignment for TKGs via adaptive graph networks. More specifically, a time-aware graph attention network model is used as an encoder to aggregate the features and temporal relationships of neighboring nodes. DualMatch [96] is an unsupervised method that fuses the relational and temporal information for EA by encoding temporal and relational information into embeddings using a dual-encoder and combining both the information and transforming it into alignment using a novel graph-matching-based decoder called GM-Decoder.

6.2. Temporal and Evolving Entity Alignment Methods

Temporal Relational Entity Alignment (TREA) [97] learns alignment-oriented TKG embeddings and represents new emerging entities. The first step is to map entities, relations, and timestamps into an embedding space, and the initial feature of each entity is represented by fusing the embeddings of its connected relations and timestamps as well as its neighboring entities. A Graph Neural Network (GNN) is employed to capture intra-graph information, and a temporal relational attention mechanism is utilized to integrate relation and time features of links between nodes. Finally, a margin-based full multi-class log-loss is used for efficient training, and a sequential time regularizer is used to model unobserved timestamps.

Incremental Temporal Entity Alignment (ITEA) [98] targets the problem of temporality as well as evolving KGs. It uses a combination of knowledge distillation with the Graph Attention Network (GAT) and the GCN acting as the teacher and student models, respectively. The proposed model transfers knowledge from a complex model, the teacher, whose output (in terms of probabilities) is used to train a simpler model, the student. The teacher Model within knowledge distillation provides instructional guidance to the student model during its training phase.

As a first stage, entity embeddings are generated from the entity labels obtained using GloVe. For preserving structural information in the teacher model, a masked attention mechanism over the neighboring entities of the entity e_i. Time-aware structure embedding is obtained using a multi-head attention-based GNN. This allows the teacher model to not only learn the node features and time-aware structural information but also adjust their contributions adaptively based on the requirements of the specific task. The student model uses an importance-sampling strategy to select a small subset of nodes or neighbors in each layer, and the model is trained on mini-batches of nodes.

Entity alignment module aligns the newly incoming entities with the existing ones, and these alignments are achieved through string matching, structural similarity, etc. The margin-based logistic loss function measures the dissimilarity between the embeddings of aligned entities. The output from the teacher model is collected by passing the new data through the teacher model to compute its output probabilities, P_t. Then, the output of the student model is collected by passing the same data through the student model to compute its output probabilities, P_s. The total loss L can be written as:

$$L = \alpha_1 \times L_{standard} + \alpha_2 \times L_{distillation}$$

where α_1 and α_2 are weights that determine the relative importance of the standard loss and the distillation. Grid search is used to define possible values for α_1 and α_2. The standard loss compares the student's outputs P_s with the true labels y. $L_{standard}$ for a classification task is typically the cross-entropy loss given as:

$$L_{standard} = -\sum y \times log(P_s)$$

where the sum is over all classes, and y is a one-hot encoded vector of the true labels. The distillation loss that compares the student's outputs P_s with the teacher's outputs P_t. $L_{distillation}$ is the Kullback-Leibler divergence between the teacher's outputs and the student's outputs and is given as:

$$L_{distillation} = \sum P_t \times log(\frac{P_t}{P_s})$$

7. Discussion & Future Directions

This chapter formally defines various types of DKGs and explores how this knowledge can be represented within KGs. It then delves into different representation learning techniques for both non-temporal and temporal DKGs, focusing on tasks related to KG completion. Additionally, it covers methods for aligning temporal and dynamic KGs. The studies discussed in this chapter primarily rely on the triple structure or treat the KG as a graph by incorporating the contextual information of entities and relationships while largely overlooking schematic or ontological information [9]. Furthermore, the adaptability of these algorithms to domain-specific and real-world applications is limited, especially as KGs can expand to contain billions or even trillions of triples. Many of these algorithms also fail to utilize the literal information within KGs. Only one of the recent studies has attempted to use Large Language Models (LLMs) as background information for TKGC [99] based on few-shot learning and concluded that LLMs do not bring significant increases in performance. However, the study misses the analysis of the results in the sense of how many predictions were hallucinations or overgenerations of LLMs for the specific task.

References

[1] Hogan A, Blomqvist E, Cochez M, d'Amato C, de Melo G, Gutierrez C, et al. Knowledge Graphs. ACM Comput Surv. 2022;54(4):71:1-71:37. Available from: https://doi.org/10.1145/3447772.

[2] Iana A, Alam M, Paulheim H. A survey on knowledge-aware news recommender systems. Semantic Web. 2024;15(1):21-82. Available from: https://doi.org/10.3233/SW-222991.

[3] Jonquet C, LePendu P, Falconer SM, Coulet A, Noy NF, Musen MA, et al. NCBO Resource Index: Ontology-based search and mining of biomedical resources. J Web Semant. 2011;9(3):316-24.

[4] Chen Y, Sack H, Alam M. Analyzing social media for measuring public attitudes toward controversies and their driving factors: a case study of migration. Soc Netw Anal Min. 2022;12(1):135. Available from: https://doi.org/10.1007/s13278-022-00915-7.

[5] Polleres A, Pernisch R, Bonifati A, Dell'Aglio D, Dobriy D, Dumbrava S, et al. How Does Knowledge Evolve in Open Knowledge Graphs? TGDK. 2023;1(1):11:1-11:59.

[6] Paulheim H. Knowledge graph refinement: A survey of approaches and evaluation methods. Semantic Web. 2017;8(3):489-508.

[7] Wang Q, Mao Z, Wang B, Guo L. Knowledge Graph Embedding: A Survey of Approaches and Applications. IEEE Trans Knowl Data Eng. 2017;29(12):2724-43.

[8] Gesese GA, Biswas R, Alam M, Sack H. A survey on knowledge graph embeddings with literals: Which model links better literal-ly? Semantic Web. 2021;12(4):617-47.

[9] Alam M, van Harmelen F, Acosta M. Towards Semantically Enriched Embeddings for Knowledge Graph Completion. CoRR. 2023;abs/2308.00081.

[10] Cai B, Xiang Y, Gao L, Zhang H, Li Y, Li J. Temporal Knowledge Graph Completion: A Survey. In: Proceedings of the Thirty-Second International Joint Conference on Artificial Intelligence, IJCAI 2023, 19th-25th August 2023, Macao, SAR, China. ijcai.org; 2023. p. 6545-53.

[11] Thompson HS, Beech D, Maloney M, Mendelsohn N, et al. XML schema part 1: structures second edition. W3C recommendation. 2004;39.

[12] Vrandecic D. Wikidata: a new platform for collaborative data collection. In: Mille A, Gandon F, Misselis J, Rabinovich M, Staab S, editors. Proceedings of the 21st World Wide Web Conference, WWW 2012, Lyon, France, April 16-20, 2012 (Companion Volume). ACM; 2012. p. 1063-4.

[13] Lehmann J, Isele R, Jakob M, Jentzsch A, Kontokostas D, Mendes PN, et al. DBpedia - A large-scale, multilingual knowledge base extracted from Wikipedia. Semantic Web. 2015;6(2):167-95.

[14] Hoffart J, Suchanek FM, Berberich K, Weikum G. YAGO2: A spatially and temporally enhanced knowledge base from Wikipedia. Artif Intell. 2013;194:28-61.

[15] Suchanek FM, Alam M, Bonald T, Chen L, Paris PH, Soria J. YAGO 4.5: A Large and Clean Knowledge Base with a Rich Taxonomy. In: Proceedings of the 47th International ACM SIGIR Conference on Research and Development in Information Retrieval. New York, NY, USA: Association for Computing Machinery; 2024. p. 131–140. Available from: https://doi.org/10.1145/3626772.3657876.

[16] McBride B. The Resource Description Framework (RDF) and its Vocabulary Description Language RDFS. In: Staab S, Studer R, editors. Handbook on Ontologies. International Handbooks on Information Systems. Springer; 2004. p. 51-66.

[17] Erxleben F, Günther M, Krötzsch M, Mendez J, Vrandecic D. Introducing Wikidata to the Linked Data Web. In: The Semantic Web - ISWC 2014 - 13th International Semantic Web Conference, Riva del Garda, Italy, October 19-23, 2014. Proceedings, Part I. vol. 8796 of Lecture Notes in Computer Science. Springer; 2014. p. 50-65.

[18] Nguyen V, Bodenreider O, Sheth AP. Don't like RDF reification?: making statements about statements using singleton property. In: Chung C, Broder AZ, Shim K, Suel T, editors. 23rd International World Wide Web Conference, WWW '14, Seoul, Republic of Korea, April 7-11, 2014. ACM; 2014. p. 759-70.

[19] Hernández D, Hogan A, Krötzsch M. Reifying RDF: What Works Well With Wikidata? In: Proceedings of the 11th International Workshop on Scalable Semantic Web Knowledge Base Systems co-located with 14th International Semantic Web Conference (ISWC 2015), Bethlehem, PA, USA, October 11, 2015. vol. 1457 of CEUR Workshop Proceedings. CEUR-WS.org; 2015. p. 32-47.
[20] Allen JF, Ferguson G. Actions and Events in Interval Temporal Logic. J Log Comput. 1994;4(5):531-79.
[21] Carroll JJ, Bizer C, Hayes PJ, Stickler P. Named graphs. J Web Semant. 2005;3(4):247-67.
[22] Frommhold M, Piris RN, Arndt N, Tramp S, Petersen N, Martin M. Towards Versioning of Arbitrary RDF Data. In: Proceedings of the 12th International Conference on Semantic Systems; 2016. .
[23] Pelgrin O, Galárraga L, Hose K. Towards fully-fledged archiving for RDF datasets. Semantic Web. 2021;12(6):903-25.
[24] Gottschalk S, Demidova E. EventKG: A Multilingual Event-Centric Temporal Knowledge Graph. In: Gangemi A, Navigli R, Vidal M, Hitzler P, Troncy R, Hollink L, et al., editors. The Semantic Web - 15th International Conference, ESWC 2018, Heraklion, Crete, Greece, June 3-7, 2018, Proceedings. vol. 10843 of Lecture Notes in Computer Science. Springer; 2018. p. 272-87.
[25] Gottschalk S, Demidova E. EventKG+TL: Creating Cross-Lingual Timelines from an Event-Centric Knowledge Graph. In: Gangemi A, Gentile AL, Nuzzolese AG, Rudolph S, Maleshkova M, Paulheim H, et al., editors. The Semantic Web: ESWC 2018 Satellite Events - ESWC 2018 Satellite Events, Heraklion, Crete, Greece, June 3-7, 2018, Revised Selected Papers. vol. 11155 of Lecture Notes in Computer Science. Springer; 2018. p. 164-9.
[26] Wang J, Wang B, Qiu M, Pan S, Xiong B, Liu H, et al. A survey on temporal knowledge graph completion: Taxonomy, progress, and prospects. arXiv preprint arXiv:230802457. 2023.
[27] Cai B, Xiang Y, Gao L, Zhang H, Li Y, Li J. Temporal knowledge graph completion: A survey. arXiv preprint arXiv:220108236. 2022.
[28] Shao P, Zhang D, Yang G, Tao J, Che F, Liu T. Tucker decomposition-based temporal knowledge graph completion. Knowledge-Based Systems. 2022;238:107841.
[29] Leblay J, Chekol MW. Deriving validity time in knowledge graph. In: Companion proceedings of the the web conference 2018; 2018. p. 1771-6.
[30] Ni R, Ma Z, Yu K, Xu X. Specific Time Embedding for Temporal Knowledge Graph Completion. In: 2020 IEEE 19th International Conference on Cognitive Informatics & Cognitive Computing (ICCI* CC); 2020. p. 105-10.
[31] Lin L, She K. Tensor decomposition-based temporal knowledge graph embedding. In: 2020 IEEE 32nd International Conference on Tools with Artificial Intelligence (ICTAI); 2020. p. 969-75.
[32] He P, Zhou G, Zhang M, Wei J, Chen J. Improving temporal knowledge graph embedding using tensor factorization. Applied Intelligence. 2023;53(8):8746-60.
[33] Zhang J, Sheng Y, Wang Z, Shao J. TKGFrame: a two-phase framework for temporal-aware knowledge graph completion. In: Web and Big Data: 4th International Joint Conference, APWeb-WAIM 2020, Tianjin, China, September 18-20, 2020, Proceedings, Part I 4; 2020. p. 196-211.
[34] Yu M, Guo J, Yu J, Xu T, Zhao M, Liu H, et al. TBDRI: block decomposition based on relational interaction for temporal knowledge graph completion. Applied Intelligence. 2023;53(5):5072-84.
[35] Messner J, Abboud R, Ceylan II. Temporal knowledge graph completion using box embeddings. In: Proceedings of the AAAI Conference on Artificial Intelligence. vol. 36; 2022. p. 7779-87.
[36] Radstok W, Chekol M, Velegrakis Y. Leveraging static models for link prediction in temporal knowledge graphs. In: 2021 IEEE 33rd International Conference on Tools with Artificial Intelligence (ICTAI). IEEE; 2021. p. 1034-41.
[37] Ding Z, Ma Y, He B, Tresp V. A simple but powerful graph encoder for temporal knowledge graph completion. arXiv 2022. arXiv preprint arXiv:211207791.
[38] Wang X, Lyu S, Wang X, Wu X, Chen H. Temporal knowledge graph embedding via sparse transfer matrix. Information Sciences. 2023;623:56-69.
[39] Dikeoulias I, Amin S, Neumann G. Temporal knowledge graph reasoning with low-rank and model-agnostic representations. arXiv preprint arXiv:220404783. 2022.
[40] Goel R, Kazemi SM, Brubaker M, Poupart P. Diachronic embedding for temporal knowledge graph completion. In: Proceedings of the AAAI conference on artificial intelligence. vol. 34; 2020. p. 3988-95.
[41] Wang J, Zhu C, Zhu W. Dynamic embedding graph attention networks for temporal knowledge graph completion. In: International Conference on Knowledge Science, Engineering and Management. Springer; 2022. p. 722-34.
[42] Sadeghian A, Armandpour M, Colas A, Wang DZ. Chronor: Rotation based temporal knowledge graph

embedding. In: Proceedings of the AAAI conference on artificial intelligence. vol. 35; 2021. p. 6471-9.
[43] Lacroix T, Obozinski G, Usunier N. Tensor decompositions for temporal knowledge base completion. arXiv preprint arXiv:200404926. 2020.
[44] Xu C, Nayyeri M, Alkhoury F, Yazdi HS, Lehmann J. TeRo: A time-aware knowledge graph embedding via temporal rotation. arXiv preprint arXiv:201001029. 2020.
[45] Xu C, Nayyeri M, Chen YY, Lehmann J. Geometric algebra based embeddings for static and temporal knowledge graph completion. IEEE Transactions on Knowledge and Data Engineering. 2022;35(5):4838-51.
[46] Xu C, Chen YY, Nayyeri M, Lehmann J. Temporal knowledge graph completion using a linear temporal regularizer and multivector embeddings. In: Proceedings of the 2021 Conference of the North American Chapter of the Association for Computational Linguistics: Human Language Technologies; 2021. p. 2569-78.
[47] Chen K, Wang Y, Li Y, Li A. Rotateqvs: Representing temporal information as rotations in quaternion vector space for temporal knowledge graph completion. arXiv preprint arXiv:220307993. 2022.
[48] Nayyeri M, Vahdati S, Khan MT, Alam MM, Wenige L, Behrend A, et al. Dihedron algebraic embeddings for spatio-temporal knowledge graph completion. In: European Semantic Web Conference. Springer; 2022. p. 253-69.
[49] Zhang S, Liang X, Li Z, Feng J, Zheng X, Wu B. Biqcap: A biquaternion and capsule network-based embedding model for temporal knowledge graph completion. In: International Conference on Database Systems for Advanced Applications. Springer; 2023. p. 673-88.
[50] Zhang J, Yu H. Hierarchy-Aware Temporal Knowledge Graph Embedding. In: 2022 IEEE International Conference on Knowledge Graph (ICKG). IEEE; 2022. p. 373-80.
[51] Wang S, Liu R, Shen L, Khattak AM. Stke: Temporal knowledge graph embedding in the spherical coordinate system. In: International Conference on Artificial Intelligence and Security. Springer; 2022. p. 292-305.
[52] He P, Zhou G, Liu H, Xia Y, Wang L. Hyperplane-based time-aware knowledge graph embedding for temporal knowledge graph completion. Journal of Intelligent & Fuzzy Systems. 2022;42(6):5457-69.
[53] Han Z, Ma Y, Chen P, Tresp V. Dyernie: Dynamic evolution of riemannian manifold embeddings for temporal knowledge graph completion. arXiv preprint arXiv:201103984. 2020.
[54] Xu C, Nayyeri M, Alkhoury F, Yazdi H, Lehmann J. Temporal knowledge graph completion based on time series gaussian embedding. In: The Semantic Web–ISWC 2020: 19th International Semantic Web Conference, Athens, Greece, November 2–6, 2020, Proceedings, Part I 19. Springer; 2020. p. 654-71.
[55] Montella S, Rojas-Barahona L, Heinecke J. Hyperbolic temporal knowledge graph embeddings with relational and time curvatures. arXiv preprint arXiv:210604311. 2021.
[56] Zhang L, Zhou D. Temporal knowledge graph completion with approximated Gaussian process embedding. In: Proceedings of the 29th International Conference on Computational Linguistics; 2022. p. 4697-706.
[57] Dasgupta SS, Ray SN, Talukdar P. Hyte: Hyperplane-based temporally aware knowledge graph embedding. In: Proceedings of the 2018 conference on empirical methods in natural language processing; 2018. p. 2001-11.
[58] Yuan L, Li Z, Qu J, Zhang T, Liu A, Zhao L, et al. Trhyte: Temporal knowledge graph embedding based on temporal-relational hyperplanes. In: International Conference on Database Systems for Advanced Applications. Springer; 2022. p. 137-52.
[59] Liu K, Zhang Y. A Temporal Knowledge Graph Completion Method Based on Balanced Timestamp Distribution. arXiv preprint arXiv:210813024. 2021.
[60] Leblay J, Chekol MW, Liu X. Towards temporal knowledge graph embeddings with arbitrary time precision. In: proceedings of the 29th acm international conference on information & knowledge management; 2020. p. 685-94.
[61] Li Y, Zhang X, Zhang B, Ren H. Each snapshot to each space: Space adaptation for temporal knowledge graph completion. In: International Semantic Web Conference. Springer; 2022. p. 248-66.
[62] Wang J, Wang B, Gao J, Li X, Hu Y, Yin B. QDN: A quadruplet distributor network for temporal knowledge graph completion. IEEE Transactions on Neural Networks and Learning Systems. 2023.
[63] García-Durán A, Dumančić S, Niepert M. Learning sequence encoders for temporal knowledge graph completion. arXiv preprint arXiv:180903202. 2018.
[64] Tang X, Yuan R, Li Q, Wang T, Yang H, Cai Y, et al. Timespan-aware dynamic knowledge graph embedding by incorporating temporal evolution. IEEE Access. 2020;8:6849-60.

[65] Ma S, Li A, Zhao X, Song Y. Learning BiLSTM-based embeddings for relation prediction in temporal knowledge graph. In: Journal of Physics: Conference Series. vol. 1871. IOP Publishing; 2021. p. 012050.
[66] Li T, Wang W, Li X, Wang T, Zhou X, Huang M. Embedding uncertain temporal knowledge graphs. Mathematics. 2023;11(3):775.
[67] Ma J, Zhou C, Chen Y, Wang Y, Hu G, Qiao Y. Tecre: A novel temporal conflict resolution method based on temporal knowledge graph embedding. Information. 2023;14(3):155.
[68] Chekol M, Pirrò G, Schoenfisch J, Stuckenschmidt H. Marrying uncertainty and time in knowledge graphs. In: Proceedings of the AAAI Conference on Artificial Intelligence. vol. 31; 2017. .
[69] Wang Y, Qiao Y, Ma J, Hu G, Zhang C, Sangaiah AK, et al. A novel time constraint-based approach for knowledge graph conflict resolution. Applied Sciences. 2019;9(20):4399.
[70] Jung J, Jung J, Kang U. Learning to walk across time for interpretable temporal knowledge graph completion. In: Proceedings of the 27th ACM SIGKDD Conference on Knowledge Discovery & Data Mining; 2021. p. 786-95.
[71] Fu G, Meng Z, Han Z, Ding Z, Ma Y, Schubert M, et al. TempCaps: a capsule network-based embedding model for temporal knowledge graph completion. In: Proceedings of the Sixth Workshop on Structured Prediction for NLP. Association for Computational Linguistics; 2022. p. 22-31.
[72] Bai L, Ma X, Meng X, Ren X, Ke Y. RoAN: A relation-oriented attention network for temporal knowledge graph completion. Engineering Applications of Artificial Intelligence. 2023;123:106308.
[73] Nie H, Zhao X, Yao X, Jiang Q, Bi X, Ma Y, et al. Temporal-structural importance weighted graph convolutional network for temporal knowledge graph completion. Future Generation Computer Systems. 2023;143:30-9.
[74] Yang Z, Ding M, Zhou C, Yang H, Zhou J, Tang J. Understanding negative sampling in graph representation learning. In: Proceedings of the 26th ACM SIGKDD international conference on knowledge discovery & data mining; 2020. p. 1666-76.
[75] Bordes A, Usunier N, Garcia-Duran A, Weston J, Yakhnenko O. Translating embeddings for modeling multi-relational data. Advances in neural information processing systems. 2013;26.
[76] Li Z, Jin X, Guan S, Li W, Guo J, Wang Y, et al. Search from history and reason for future: Two-stage reasoning on temporal knowledge graphs. arXiv preprint arXiv:210600327. 2021.
[77] Liu Y, Hua W, Xin K, Zhou X. Context-aware temporal knowledge graph embedding. In: Web Information Systems Engineering–WISE 2019: 20th International Conference, Hong Kong, China, November 26–30, 2019, Proceedings 20; 2019. p. 583-98.
[78] Leetaru K, Schrodt PA. Gdelt: Global data on events, location, and tone, 1979–2012. In: ISA annual convention. vol. 2; 2013. p. 1-49.
[79] Jin W, Qu M, Jin X, Ren X. Recurrent event network: Autoregressive structure inference over temporal knowledge graphs. arXiv preprint arXiv:190405530. 2019.
[80] Mahdisoltani F, Biega J, Suchanek FM. Yago3: A knowledge base from multilingual wikipedias. In: CIDR; 2013. .
[81] Wang L, Zhang X, Su H, Zhu J. A Comprehensive Survey of Continual Learning: Theory, Method and Application. IEEE Trans Pattern Anal Mach Intell. 2024;46(8):5362-83.
[82] Tay Y, Luu AT, Hui SC. Non-Parametric Estimation of Multiple Embeddings for Link Prediction on Dynamic Knowledge Graphs. In: Proceedings of the Thirty-First AAAI Conference on Artificial Intelligence, February 4-9, 2017, San Francisco, California, USA. AAAI Press; 2017. p. 1243-9.
[83] Ali M, Berrendorf M, Hoyt CT, Vermue L, Galkin M, Sharifzadeh S, et al. Bringing Light Into the Dark: A Large-Scale Evaluation of Knowledge Graph Embedding Models Under a Unified Framework. IEEE Trans Pattern Anal Mach Intell. 2022;44(12):8825-45.
[84] Wu T, Khan A, Yong M, Qi G, Wang M. Efficiently embedding dynamic knowledge graphs. Knowl Based Syst. 2022;250:109124.
[85] Xie W, Wang S, Wei Y, Zhao Y, Fu X. Dynamic Knowledge Graph Completion with Jointly Structural and Textual Dependency. In: Qiu M, editor. Algorithms and Architectures for Parallel Processing - 20th International Conference, ICA3PP 2020, New York City, NY, USA, October 2-4, 2020, Proceedings, Part II. vol. 12453 of Lecture Notes in Computer Science. Springer; 2020. p. 432-48.
[86] Cui Y, Wang Y, Sun Z, Liu W, Jiang Y, Han K, et al. Lifelong Embedding Learning and Transfer for Growing Knowledge Graphs. In: Thirty-Seventh AAAI Conference on Artificial Intelligence, AAAI 2023, Thirty-Fifth Conference on Innovative Applications of Artificial Intelligence, IAAI 2023, Thirteenth Symposium on Educational Advances in Artificial Intelligence, EAAI 2023, Washington, DC, USA, February 7-14, 2023. AAAI Press; 2023. p. 4217-24.

[87] Liu J, Ke W, Wang P, Wang J, Gao J, Shang Z, et al.. Fast and Continual Knowledge Graph Embedding via Incremental LoRA; 2024. Available from: https://arxiv.org/abs/2407.05705.

[88] Song H, Park S. Enriching Translation-Based Knowledge Graph Embeddings Through Continual Learning. IEEE Access. 2018;6:60489-97.

[89] Daruna AA, Gupta M, Sridharan M, Chernova S. Continual Learning of Knowledge Graph Embeddings. IEEE Robotics Autom Lett. 2021;6(2):1128-35. Available from: https://doi.org/10.1109/LRA.2021.3056071.

[90] Liu J, Ke W, Wang P, Shang Z, Gao J, Li G, et al. Towards Continual Knowledge Graph Embedding via Incremental Distillation. In: Thirty-Eighth AAAI Conference on Artificial Intelligence, AAAI 2024, Thirty-Sixth Conference on Innovative Applications of Artificial Intelligence, IAAI 2024, Fourteenth Symposium on Educational Advances in Artificial Intelligence, EAAI 2014, February 20-27, 2024, Vancouver, Canada. AAAI Press; 2024. p. 8759-68.

[91] Kou X, Lin Y, Liu S, Li P, Zhou J, Zhang Y. Disentangle-based Continual Graph Representation Learning. In: Proceedings of the 2020 Conference on Empirical Methods in Natural Language Processing, EMNLP 2020, Online, November 16-20, 2020. Association for Computational Linguistics; 2020. p. 2961-72. Available from: https://doi.org/10.18653/v1/2020.emnlp-main.237.

[92] Xu C, Su F, Lehmann J. Time-aware Graph Neural Networks for Entity Alignment between Temporal Knowledge Graphs. CoRR. 2022;abs/2203.02150.

[93] Song X, Bai L, Liu R, Zhang H. Temporal Knowledge Graph Entity Alignment via Representation Learning. In: Database Systems for Advanced Applications - 27th International Conference, DASFAA 2022, Virtual Event, April 11-14, 2022, Proceedings, Part II. vol. 13246 of Lecture Notes in Computer Science. Springer; 2022. p. 391-406.

[94] Cai L, Mao X, Ma M, Yuan H, Zhu J, Lan M. A Simple Temporal Information Matching Mechanism for Entity Alignment between Temporal Knowledge Graphs. In: Proceedings of the 29th International Conference on Computational Linguistics, COLING 2022, Gyeongju, Republic of Korea, October 12-17, 2022. International Committee on Computational Linguistics; 2022. p. 2075-86.

[95] Li J, Song D, Wang H, Wu Z, Zhou C, Zhou Y. Entity alignment for temporal knowledge graphs via adaptive graph networks. Knowl Based Syst. 2023;274:110631.

[96] Liu X, Wu J, Li T, Chen L, Gao Y. Unsupervised Entity Alignment for Temporal Knowledge Graphs. In: Proceedings of the ACM Web Conference 2023, WWW 2023, Austin, TX, USA, 30 April 2023 - 4 May 2023. ACM; 2023. p. 2528-38.

[97] Xu C, Su F, Xiong B, Lehmann J. Time-aware Entity Alignment using Temporal Relational Attention. In: Laforest F, Troncy R, Simperl E, Agarwal D, Gionis A, Herman I, et al., editors. WWW '22: The ACM Web Conference 2022, Virtual Event, Lyon, France, April 25 - 29, 2022. ACM; 2022. p. 788-97.

[98] Li Y, Chen L, Liu C, Zhou R, Li J. Efficient and Effective Entity Alignment for Evolving Temporal Knowledge Graphs. In: Chen G, Khan L, Gao X, Qiu M, Pedrycz W, Wu X, editors. IEEE International Conference on Data Mining, ICDM 2023, Shanghai, China, December 1-4, 2023. IEEE; 2023. p. 349-58.

[99] Luo R, Gu T, Li H, Li J, Lin Z, Li J, et al. Chain of History: Learning and Forecasting with LLMs for Temporal Knowledge Graph Completion. CoRR. 2024;abs/2401.06072. Available from: https://doi.org/10.48550/arXiv.2401.06072.

Handbook on Neurosymbolic AI and Knowledge Graphs
P. Hitzler et al. (Eds.)
IOS Press, 2025

doi:10.3233/FAIA250224

Neurosymbolic Methods for Rule Mining

Agnieszka ŁAWRYNOWICZ [a,1], Luis GALÁRRAGA [b] Mehwish ALAM [c]
Bérénice JAULMES [c] Václav ZEMAN [d] and Tomáš KLIEGR [d]
[a] *Poznan University of Technology, Poland*
[b] *INRIA/IRISA, Rennes, France*
[c] *Télécom Paris, Institut Polytechnique de Paris, France*
[d] *Prague University of Economics and Business, Czech Republic*
ORCiD ID: Agnieszka Ławrynowicz https://orcid.org/0000-0002-2442-345X, Luis Galárraga https://orcid.org/0000-0002-0241-5379, Mehwish Alam https://orcid.org/0000-0002-7867-6612, Tomáš Kliegr https://orcid.org/0000-0002-7261-0380

Abstract. In this chapter, we address the problem of rule mining, beginning with essential background information, including measures of rule quality. We then explore various rule mining methodologies, categorized into three groups: inductive logic programming, path sampling and generalization, and linear programming. Following this, we delve into neurosymbolic methods, covering topics such as the integration of deep learning with rules, the use of embeddings for rule learning, and the application of large language models in rule learning.

Keywords. rule mining, rule learning, representation learning

1. Introduction

The schema of knowledge graphs (KGs) can be represented using ontological axioms and/or rules. Rules can be used for explainable inference for tasks such as link prediction or fact checking [1].

Hovewer, formulating rules manually is demanding in practice. For that reason, automatic rule learning approaches have attracted attention.

Wu et al. in their survey [2] distinguish three major groups of rule learning methods: Inductive Logic Programming-based, statistical path generalisation and neuro-symbolic. In this chapter, to introduce the topic of rule mining and provide the necessary background, we discuss each of these groups and give a more detailed example of algorithms within each group, paying the most attention to neuro-symbolic ones. We also discuss the topic of using Large Language Models (LLMs) for rule mining.

2. Background

Rules A (Horn) rule is an expression of the form

[1] Corresponding Author.

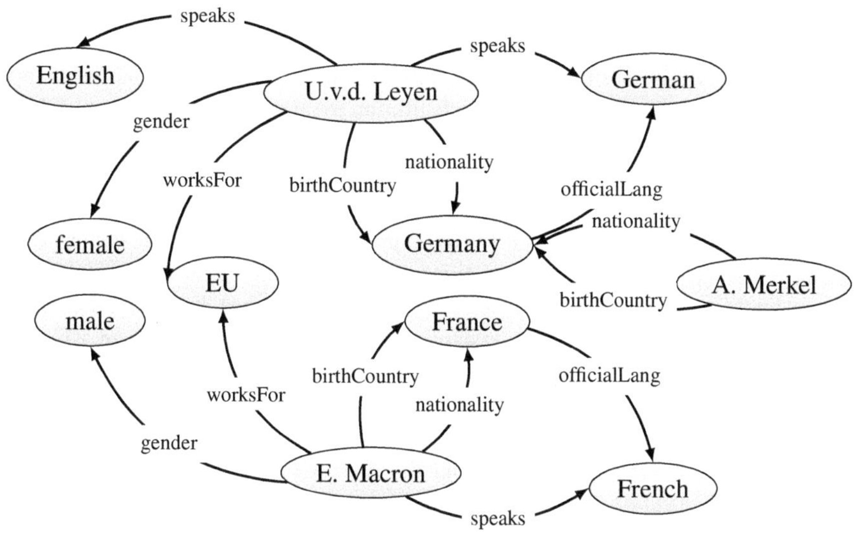

Figure 1. Sample knowledge graph.

$$q_1(z_0,z_1) \wedge \ldots \wedge q_n(z_{n-1},z_n) \Rightarrow p(x,y) \tag{1}$$

where $p(z,y)$ and each term $q_i(z_{i-1},z_i)$ is an atom, that is, a KG fact such that at least one of its terms is a variable $v \in \mathcal{V}$. In the remainder of this chapter we denote variables $v \in \mathcal{V}$ by lowercase letters, and constants by capitalized names, e.g., *Germany* $\in \mathcal{E}$, where $\mathcal{E}$ is a set of entities. The left-hand side part of the rule is a logical conjunction of atoms that we call the *body* or *antecedent* of the rule, denoted by **B**, whereas the right-hand side atom is called the *head* or the *succedent* of the rule, denoted by H. We say two atoms are connected if they share at least one argument. A conjunction of atoms or a rule is connected if every atom is transitively connected to every other atom. For instance the rule $\mathit{nationality}(x,z_1) \wedge \mathit{officialLang}(z_1,y) \Rightarrow \mathit{nationality}(x,y)$ is connected, whereas the rule $\mathit{speaks}(x,z_1) \wedge \mathit{officialLang}(z_2,z_3) \Rightarrow \mathit{speaks}(x,y)$ is not because the second atom is not reachable from any other atom. Applications on KGs usually require connected rules.

We say a rule is *safe* if the head variables are present in the rule's body. For example, the rule $\mathit{birthCountry}(x,z_1) \wedge \mathit{nationality}(x,z_2) \wedge \mathit{officialLang}(z_2,z_3) \Rightarrow \mathit{speaks}(x,y)$ is not safe because variable y is absent in the antecedent, which actually means that y is existentially quantified. In other words, this rule could be interpreted as $\forall x\, \exists y,z_1,z_2,z_3 : \mathit{birthCountry}(x,z_1) \wedge \mathit{nationality}(x,z_2) \wedge \mathit{officialLang}(z_2,z_3) \Rightarrow \mathit{speaks}(x,y)$. Safeness ensures that the rule makes concrete predictions. In our example, the rule states that if someone with the known birth country is a citizen of a country with an official language, that person speaks some language – we still do not know which. If we instead consider a safe version of this rule, i.e., $\forall x,y\, \exists y,z_1,z_2 : \mathit{birthCountry}(x,z_1) \wedge \mathit{nationality}(x,z_2) \wedge \mathit{officialLang}(z_2,y) \Rightarrow \mathit{speaks}(x,y)$, we can now predict the person speaks the official language of their country of citizenship. If no variable is existentially quantified, i.e., each variable appears in at least two different atoms, we say the rule is *closed*. Most applications relying on rules resort to safe rules, or more frequently to closed rules such as $\forall x,y,z_2\ : \mathit{birthCountry}(x,z_2) \wedge \mathit{nationality}(x,z_2) \wedge \mathit{officialLang}(z_2,y) \Rightarrow \mathit{speaks}(x,y)$.

As mentioned before, safe rules can be used to draw specific conclusions, e.g., deduce the nationality of a person from known information in a KG $\mathcal{K}$. To do so, we need to introduce the notion of substitution. A *substitution* $\sigma : \mathcal{V} \to \mathcal{E}$ is a partial mapping from variables to constants. Applying a substitution to an atom replaces the variables of the rule by the constants associated with those variables in the substitution. We call the result of this operation an *instantiation*. This operation can be naturally ported to conjunctions of atoms, which returns a set of instantiations. If we apply the substitution $\sigma = \{x \to E.Macron, z_1 \to France, y \to French\}$ to the conjunction $\mathbf{B} : birthCountry(x,z_1) \wedge officialLang(z_1,y)$, we obtain instantiations that are actual facts (no variables left) $\sigma(\mathbf{B}) = \{birthCountry(E.Macron,France), officialLang(France,French)\}$. Let R be a rule of the form $\mathbf{B} \Rightarrow H$ and σ an instantiation. We say R and σ *fire* in KG $\mathcal{K}$, if $\sigma(\mathbf{B}) \subseteq \mathcal{K}$, denoted by $\sigma(\mathbf{B}) \Vdash \mathcal{K}$. Put differently, an instantiated rule fires in a KG if all the instantiated body atoms are facts from the KG. If additionally $\sigma(H) \in \mathcal{K}$, we say the rule *predicts* the fact obtained by instantiating H, which we denote by $\sigma(R) \Vdash \mathcal{K}$. That is the case for our example rule and the KG in Figure 1 since both $\sigma(\mathbf{B})$ and $\sigma(H) = speaks(E.\ Macron, French)$ are in the KG.

Logical rules in KGs are unlikely to make correct predictions every time they fire. That is why we usually talk about *soft rules*, that is, rules with exceptions. Take as an example the rule $birthCountry(x,z_1) \wedge officialLang(z_1,y) \Rightarrow speaks(x,y)$. It is easy to see that such a rule is overall accurate but may have exceptions, e.g., people born in a country but raised elsewhere. On a related note, we should be sceptical about rules that fire or hold in very few cases. It follows from these observations that we need metrics to quantify the predictive power of rules before using them in applications. A popular score to quantify the significance of a rule $\mathbf{B} \Rightarrow H$ in a KG $\mathcal{K}$ is the *support*, defined as:

$$supp_{\mathcal{K}}(\mathbf{B} \Rightarrow H) = \#\sigma_H : \sigma_H(\mathbf{B} \Rightarrow H) \Vdash \mathcal{K}. \tag{2}$$

In this equation $\#\sigma_H$ is the number of unique instantiations $\sigma_H : vars(H) \to \mathcal{E}$, that is, instantiations that map the rule head variables to constants in the KG. Intuitively the support is the number of observed predictions of the rule in the KG. Those predictions are the *positive examples* of the rule. The higher the support, the more evidence about the soundness of the rule we have. If we take as an example the rule

$$R : birthCountry(x,z_1) \wedge officialLang(z_1,y) \Rightarrow speaks(x,y), \tag{3}$$

we can see that its support is

$$supp_{\mathcal{K}}(R) = \#(x,y) : \exists z_1 : birthCountry(x,z_1) \wedge officialLang(z_1,y) \wedge speaks(x,y).$$

In our example graph of Figure 1, this value is 2 because of the substitutions $\{x \to E.Macron, y \to French\}$ and $\{x \to U.v.d.Leyen, y \to German\}$. A popular variant of the support normalizes Eq. (2) by the number of facts in the head relation. This is called the *head coverage*:

$$hc_{\mathcal{K}}(\mathbf{B} \Rightarrow H) = \frac{supp(\mathbf{B} \Rightarrow H)}{\#r(x,y) : r(x,y) \in \mathcal{K}}. \tag{4}$$

Our example rule has a head coverage of $\frac{2}{3}$ in Figure 1 since it predicts 2 out of the 3 facts of the relation *speaks*. The support and head coverage are anti-monotonic scores. This means that adding atoms to an existing rule cannot increase its support. This property is crucial when designing efficient algorithms that learn those rules automatically.

But even if a rule has many supporting positive examples, it may also have many counter-examples, to put it another way, instantiations for which the rule fires but its predictions are false. If those false predictions outnumber the correct predictions, then we should take the rule's predictions with a grain of salt. This illustrates the risk of learning only from positive examples. The *confidence* score solves this issue by normalizing the support by the total number of examples of the rule, both positive and negative:

$$conf_{\mathcal{K}}(\mathbf{B} \Rightarrow H) = \frac{supp(\mathbf{B} \Rightarrow H)}{supp(\mathbf{B} \Rightarrow H) + (\#\sigma_H : \sigma_H(\mathbf{B}) \Vdash \mathcal{K} \wedge \sigma_H(H) \nVdash \mathcal{K})}. \quad (5)$$

The expression on the right-hand side of the denominator describes the number of examples that make the rule fire but whose predictions, represented by $\sigma_H(H)$, are not entailed by the KG. By "not entailed" we mean they contradict what is stated in the data. Bear in mind, however, that KGs do not store negative information. They cannot state things like "Emanuel Macron does not speak English". One could argue that the absence of such fact in our example graph (Figure 1) entails that Macron does not speak English. Unfortunately, most KGs, and most particularly Web-based KGs, are inherently incomplete: the absence of evidence is not evidence of absence. This means that if the KG does not say anything about Macron speaking English, we cannot conclude he does not speak English. This information is unknown. Take as an example the rule $worksFor(x, EU) \Rightarrow speaks(x, English)$. Since E. Macron works for the EU, this rule predicts he speaks English. We, therefore, have a problem when computing the confidence of this rule because we do not have a way to say whether this prediction is an example or a counter-example. As we will see in the next paragraph, one needs to make some assumptions about the completeness of KGs in order to evaluate the accuracy of logical rules and their inferences.

Closed World vs Open World Assumption The Closed World Assumption (CWA), commonly applied in database systems and logic programming, is the assumption that KGs are complete. This means that any statement not explicitly present in the KG is assumed false. This applies for *speaks*(*E. Macron*, *English*) in our example graph from Figure 1. It follows that this fact would be considered as a counter-example for the rule $worksFor(x, EU) \Rightarrow speaks(x, English)$. The CWA allow us to devise a confidence metric for rules, hence Eq. (5) becomes:

$$std\text{-}conf_{\mathcal{K}}(\mathbf{B} \Rightarrow H) = \frac{supp(\mathbf{B} \Rightarrow H)}{\#\sigma_H : \sigma_H(\mathbf{B}) \Vdash \mathcal{K}}. \quad (6)$$

The CWA confidence, also called *standard confidence* normalizes the support of the rule by the number of examples that make the rule fire. This denominator term includes both the positive examples and the predictions that are not present in the KG, which are now assumed to be negative examples. In our example KG of Figure 1, the rule $birthCountry(x, EU) \Rightarrow speaks(x, English)$ has a confidence of $\frac{2}{3}$ because Angela Merkel

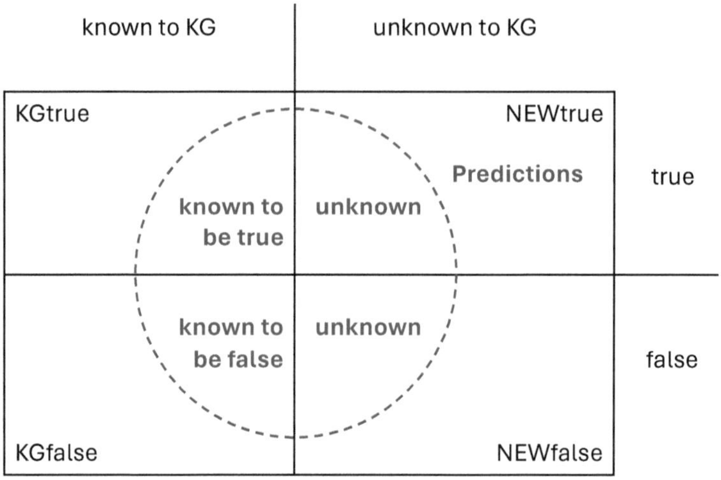

Figure 2. The classification of predictions made by a rule $B_1 \wedge B_2 \wedge \ldots \wedge B_n \implies p(x,y)$ pertains to a fact in the rule head. This fact can be either true or false in the real world and can be known or unknown to the KG. This results in four possible situations regarding the KG and the real world. Predictions made by the rule with respect to the KG are represented inside the circle.

satisfies the conditions of the rule but the conclusion is not in the KG. Albeit sensible for databases and classical association rule mining, the CWA is problematic for KGs because they are inherently incomplete and operate under the *Open World Assumption* that says nothing about absent statements: they are unknown.

In contrast, the OWA does not offer a solution to the problem of determining whether a prediction should be counted as a counter-example or not (see Figure 2). A way to deal with this issue is the *partial completeness assumption* [3], also called the *local closed world assumption* [4]. The PCA assumes that information in KGs is added in "batches". If the KG constructor included one language for, let us say, U.v.d. Leyen, then it included *all* her languages in the KG. This assumption allows us to devise a new criterion to define counter-examples for rules: if a rule such as $worksFor(x, EU) \Rightarrow speaks(x, English)$ predicts a new language for a person, and that language is different from the languages stated in the KG, then that prediction must be a counter-example. An important corollary of this assumption is that if the KG does not know any language for that person, then the OWA applies, and that example is labeled unknown and therefore excluded both as a positive example or as a counter-example. This assumption can be therefore used to devise a new confidence score, the *PCA confidence* [3]:

$$pca\text{-}conf_{\mathscr{K}}(\mathbf{B} \Rightarrow H) = \frac{supp(\mathbf{B} \Rightarrow H)}{\#\sigma_H : \sigma_H(\mathbf{B} \wedge H') \Vdash \mathscr{K}}, \quad H' = r(x, y') \text{ or } H' = r(x', y). \quad (7)$$

Eq. (7) normalizes the support by the number of head substitutions that make the rule fire and for which there is a known head fact. This fact can be the rule's prediction but can be different since the new variables x', y' in the formula are existentially quantified. In our example from Figure 1, the PCA confidence of the rule $speaks(E.\ Macron, English)$ is $\frac{2}{2}$. Differently from the standard confidence, Angela Merkel is not used as a counter-example because the KG does not know anything about the languages she speaks, i.e., there is no match for the head atom. Furthermore, the PCA confidence assumes the prediction is made in one direction, usually the more functional direction: we predict the language of a person instead of predicting all the speakers of a language. Therefore the choice of the atom H' depends on the nature of the head relation.

As shown by Galárraga et al. [5], the PCA is a sensible assumption for many relations, specially functional (1-1) or quasi-functional (almost 1-1) relations such as place of birth or nationality. The PCA is clearly less sound for n-to-n relations such as friendships or co-authorships and can make mistakes for quasi-functions. In our example graph (Figure 1), the PCA is right about the nationalities, birth countries and genders of our example entities, but it is false for the languages they speak since it would assume E. Macron does not speak English and U.v.d. Leyen does not speak any other languages besides English and German – which is actually not true.

3. Rule Mining

Rule mining is the task of learning logical rules from a knowledge graph fully automatically. This problem is challenging for two main reasons. First, it is computationally expensive, especially for large KGs, because it requires the exploration of a very large search space. Second, it requires to make assumptions about what constitutes a counter-example in order to evaluate the quality of the rules. Since those rules are usually used for inference tasks, it is common to focus on closed rules, which, as a side effect, also reduces the space of rules to explore. There are different approaches to rule mining that we will describe in the following.

3.1. Inductive Logic Programming

The study of learning Horn clauses has been a significant focus in the inductive logic programming (ILP) field [6,7,8]. ILP methods are based on search of the space of possible patterns or rules. To systematically explore the space during the learning process, ILP methods usually use *refinement operators*. A refinement operator defines a way to move from one candidate rule to another, more specific or more general. In rule mining, particularly within ILP, refinement operators help navigate the pattern or rule space in a structured manner. Refinement operators usually add/remove atoms or specialize/generalize predicates. We will see example refinement operator in Section 3.1.1 where the algorithm AMIE is discussed.

3.1.1. AMIE

AMIE [3] is a top-down closed rule mining algorithm designed for large KGs under the OWA. AMIE constructs new rules by adding atoms to already discovered rules. This process is called refinement. Some of those rules will be intermediate non-closed rules that AMIE refines but does not output. By default, the algorithm starts with all the rules of the form $\emptyset \Rightarrow r(x,y)$ that are iteratively refined via three mining operators:

Add dangling atom refines a rule with a new atom containing a fresh variable. For rule $\emptyset \Rightarrow speaks(x,y)$, this operator could produce rules such as $hasOfficialLang(z_1,y) \Rightarrow speaks(x,y)$ or $nationality(x,z_1) \Rightarrow speaks(x,y)$.

Add closing atom adds a new atom without fresh variables. In our previous example, this operator could lead to the rule $likes(x,y) \Rightarrow speaks(x,y)$. Similarly, the rule $hasOfficialLang(z_1,y) \Rightarrow speaks(x,y)$ could be closed by adding the atom $nationality(x,z_1)$ to the body.

Add instantiated atom refines the rule with an instantiated atom, that is, an atom where one of the arguments is a constant, e.g., the rule $likes(x,y) \Rightarrow speaks(x,y)$ could become $is(x,Linguist) \wedge likes(x,y) \Rightarrow speaks(x,y)$. By default, this operator is disabled, but can be turned on by the user. This also allows the system to start with rules of the form $\emptyset \Rightarrow r(x,C)$ or $\emptyset \Rightarrow r(C,y)$ for constants C from the KG.

These mining operators allow AMIE to explore the space of closed Horn rules. AMIE imposes a user-defined minimum threshold on support and a maximum rule length (also configurable by the user) to keep the search space under control. By default, AMIE finds rules up to 3 atoms and stops the refinement as soon as head coverage drops below 1%. This policy, based on the anti-monotonicity of the head coverage, speeds up the mining by avoiding noisy rules that cover too few positive examples. AMIE can also enforce user-defined thresholds on standard and PCA confidence (set by default to 10%).

All these considerations made AMIE the fastest rule mining algorithm on KGs at its time of publication, achieving a speed up of at least 3 orders of magnitude w.r.t. classical inductive logic programming approaches such as WARMR [9] and ALEPH [10] on modern KGs such as YAGO2 [11] (approx. 1M facts) – previous approaches could not handle larger datasets such as DBpedia. Moreover, and in contrast to its competitors, its reliance on the PCA confidence to quantify the quality of rules made it produce more and more precise predictions than its competitors. On YAGO2, for instance, the rules had a precision in the range of 30%-40% and the PCA confidence proved more suitable than the standard confidence at ranking best the rules that inferred good new predictions – predictions beyond the KG.

AMIE+ [5] improves over AMIE with the help of various algorithmic optimizations to speed up rule mining. This included changes in the rule refinement procedure as well as some heuristics to discard potentially noisy rules. AMIE+ avoids refining rules when the resulting refinement cannot lead to a closed rule given the maximal length constraint. It also implements some query simplification for recursive rules, i.e., rules where a predicate appears more than once. It also implements a skyline technique that stops refining closed rules that have already attained 100% confidence and propose lower bounds and confidence estimations that prune noisy rules, i.e., rules of very low confidence, before computing their actual confidence scores – a computationally expensive task. All these optimizations allowed AMIE+ to run on larger datasets such as DBpedia 3.8 and Wikidata 2014 and achieve a speed up of at least one order of magnitude w.r.t. AMIE.

AMIE 3 Lajus et al. [12] introduced the latest version of AMIE, called as AMIE3, that features several query processing and data representation improvements. For example, the *existential variable detection* heuristic optimizes the queries required to compute the rule confidence scores by properly identifying variables with existential semantics whose instantiations do not need to be fully enumerated. AMIE3 also proposes a lazy evaluation criterion for the confidence scores. This strategy stops the enumeration of the solutions of the normalization term (denominator) of the confidence scores as soon as it is clear that the resulting confidence will be below the minimum confidence threshold. Other optimizations include the parallelization of the construction of some indexes and the use of an integer-based representation for the entities and triples of the KG. AMIE3 is then further compared with modern rule miners such as Rudik [13] and ScaleKB [14] on YAGO2, DBPedia, and Wikidata and find that AMIE3 is one order of magnitude faster.

3.2. Path Sampling and Generalization

RuDiK [13] is an algorithm that discovers both positive and negative rules. Mining negative rules helps to detect erroneous facts, which can be common in knowledge bases, due to errors being propagated. RuDiK consists of three modules: the first module generates negative examples, the second one is an incremental rule miner and the last module executes rules, to generate new facts and find inconsistencies.

Negative example generator creates negative examples, given a knowledge base and a target predicate. It does this by leveraging the Local Closed-World Assumption (LCWA) [15]. Under this assumption, if a triple $q(s,o)$ does not occur in a knowledge base, but $q(s,x)$ is present, then $q(s,o)$ is false. Similarly, if $q(s,o)$ is present but $q'(s,o)$ is not, then $q'(s,o)$ is false. RuDiK finds entities whose information is more likely to be complete, to generate good negative examples.

Incremental rule miner discovers Horn Rules. Here, the atoms are of the form $q(s,o)$. The algorithm uses a set of positive examples G and a set of negative examples V. The ideal solution is the minimal set of rules for which all the examples in G are valid and none of those in V are. The goal of this rule miner is to find the optimal set of weighted rules. The weight of a rule has two components. The first is the ratio between the coverage of this rule over G and G itself. The second component measures the same thing over V. Parameter α is set to define the weight of the first component. There is also β, defined as 1-α. β defines the importance of the second component. This definition of weight is extended to define a marginal weight as follows. If R is a set of rules and r is a rule :

$$w_m(r) = w(R \cup r) - w(R) \tag{8}$$

A rule will not be added to the solution if its marginal weight is at or below 0. A valid rule r(x,y) can be represented as a path between x and y in the knowledge base, which is represented as a directed graph. Another type of atoms can be included in the rules : literal comparison. For example, the rule
$bornIn(a,x) \wedge \mathrm{x} \neq \mathrm{U.S.A.} \implies \neg\, president(a, U.S.A.)$.

The algorithm starts with an entity x and keeps a set of candidate paths. At each step, the path with the smallest marginal weight is expended. Once a path is considered valid, it is added to the solution, and it stops being expended.

Rule execution Once a rule has been discovered, RuDiK can run it in the knowledge base, as a SPARQL query. This enables it to deduce new facts, or to detect erroneous ones that are in the knowledge base. The accuracy for new facts is 85%, and 97% for inconsistencies. When running RuDiK over Wikidata, DBpedia and YAGO 3, the proportion of erroneous triples was respectively 0.23%, 0.26% and 0.6%.

Different parameters impact on the performance of RuDiK. Turning off literal comparison visibly degrades accuracy for both positive and negative rules. The level of noise in the database also affects the performance, though RuDiK is rather robust in this regard. Another important parameter is the maximum path length. When it is set at 2, precision for positive rules drops to 49%. When it is set at 4, RuDiK does not finish after 24 hours, and the precision is not notably better than when it is set at 3. Therefore, 3 is used as the maximum path length. The last parameter is α and β, the weight parameters. There are different optimal values for positive and negative rules, however the algorithm is robust and the variation in performance are limited as long as α (and β) is in the [0.1,0.9] range.

AnyBURL [16] is a bottom-up algorithm inspired by Golem [17] and Aleph [10]. The algorithm chooses random paths of a set path profile, and generalizes them to rules. A path profile "describes path length and whether the path is cyclic or acyclic". The support and confidence of these rules are then computed, and the rules that fulfil a given criteria, usually minimum support or confidence, are stored. Given a completion task, the candidates are ranked by the maximum confidence of the rules that have generated them, then by the second best one, and so on, until one rule stands out. There is more than one round of mining and selection of rules. Each round lasts a set amount of time. At the end, the length of possible paths can be increased if the set of results reaches *saturation*, i.e. if the number of new rules being discovered is too low.

AnyBURL also uses reinforcement learning to determine how much effort should be dedicated for each path profile. It also uses *Object Identity*, which assumes that when two variables appear in a rule, they designate different entities. This is made to avoid redundant rules. There is a new version of AnyBURL [18], which introduces four major modifications. The first modification is object identity as described in [19], to avoid learning redundant rules, which would skew the confidence score. The second modification is confidence sampling, which serves to avoid a depth-first search when computing the confidence of a rule in a very large dataset. The third modification is reinforcement learning-based sampling which makes the path sampling more robust, and especially less sensitive to change in parameter settings. The fourth modification is multi-threading which enhances the performance of AnyBURL on very large graphs and makes it 20 times faster than SOTA.

RARL [20] uses rule relatedness (or TBox relatedness) to rank candidate rules. The authors define two boxes. The ABox contains the facts, while the TBox contains the underlying schema of the knowledge base. Rules are considered related when they often link the same subjects and objects in the ABox. The confidence of these rules is computed under the Partial Completeness Assumption [5], which allows the creation of negative examples.

3.3. Linear Programming

A recent paper [21] presents LPRules, an algorithm for rule mining that uses linear programming to mine rules inside a knowledge graph. It creates a weighted linear combination of FOL rules that are then used as a scoring function for knowledge graph completion. It also limits the size of the rules, to increase human interpretability.

4. Neurosymbolic Methods

4.1. Deep Learning and Rules

We now introduce end-to-end approaches that utilize deep neural networks (DNNs) to learn rules by optimizing objective functions approximating path patterns.

4.1.1. Neural Logic Programming

Neural LP [22] is one of the pioneering efforts to integrate rule structure learning with parameter learning in an end-to-end differentiable model. It draws inspiration from the *TensorLog* [23] differentiable probabilistic logic framework. The TensorLog framework compiles rule inference into a series of differentiable operations by linking rule application to sparse matrix multiplications. The method thus simplifies the rule learning problem to algebraic operations on neural embedding-based representations of a given knowledge graph.

The reasoning task the NeuralLP addresses involves three components: *query*, an entity *tail* about which the query is made, and an entity *head* that serves as the query's answer. The objective is to generate a ranked list of entities in response to the query, aiming to position the correct answer (i.e., the head) as high as possible on this list. We can formalize the query as a rule

$$q_1(x,z_1) \wedge \ldots \wedge q_n(x,z_n) \Rightarrow p(x,y) \tag{9}$$

with associated confidence $\alpha \in [0,1]$, where $p(x,y)$ is the query, and $q_1,\ldots,q_n$ are relations in the knowledge base. During inference, given an entity x, the score for each entity y is calculated as the sum of the confidence scores of rules that imply $p(x,y)$. A ranked list of entities is then returned, where a higher score corresponds to a higher ranking.

TensorLog TensorLog maps each entity $e_i \in \mathscr{E}$ to a one-hot vector $\mathbf{v}_i \in \{0,1\}^{|\mathscr{E}|}$ where only the i-th entry is 1, and it defines an operator M_q for each relation q by mapping each relation $q \in \mathscr{R}$ to a matrix $\mathbf{M}_q \in \{0,1\}^{|\mathscr{E}|\times|\mathscr{E}|}$ such that its (i,j) entry is 1 iff $q(e_i,e_j)$ is a fact in the KG, where $e_i,e_j \in \mathscr{E}$. So $\mathbf{M}_q$ is essentially an adjacency matrix.

For instance, considering a subgraph of the *KG* presented in Figure 1 consisting of 5 entities, every entity is encoded as a one-hot vector of length 5, corresponding to the number of the entities in the subgraph, so, for relations q_1 = birthCountry, q_2 = officialLang we have the following adjacency matrices:

$$\mathbf{M}_{q_1} = \begin{array}{c} \begin{array}{ccccc} \text{E. Macron} & \text{U.v. Leyen} & \text{EU} & \text{French} & \text{France} \end{array} \\ \left[\begin{array}{ccccc} 0 & 0 & 0 & 0 & 1 \\ 0 & 0 & 0 & 0 & 0 \\ 0 & 0 & 0 & 0 & 0 \\ 0 & 0 & 0 & 0 & 0 \\ 0 & 0 & 0 & 0 & 0 \end{array}\right] \end{array} \begin{array}{c} \\ \textbf{E. Macron} \\ \text{U.v. Leyen} \\ \text{EU} \\ \text{French} \\ \text{France} \end{array}$$

$$\mathbf{M}_{q_2} = \begin{array}{c} \\ \left[\begin{array}{ccccc} 0 & 0 & 0 & 0 & 0 \\ 0 & 0 & 0 & 0 & 0 \\ 0 & 0 & 0 & 0 & 0 \\ 0 & 0 & 0 & 0 & 0 \\ 0 & 0 & 0 & 1 & 0 \end{array}\right] \end{array} \begin{array}{c} \\ \text{E. Macron} \\ \text{U.v. Leyen} \\ \text{EU} \\ \text{French} \\ \text{France} \end{array}$$

(columns: E. Macron, U.v. Leyen, EU, French, France)

We now establish the connection between TensorLog operations and logical rule inference, where the goal is to imitate logical rule inference for some entity e_i. The application of the rule on an entity e_i can be represented by performing matrix multiplications

$$\mathbf{M}_{q_1} \cdot \mathbf{M}_{q_2} \cdot \ldots \cdot \mathbf{M}_{q_n} \cdot \mathbf{v}_i = \mathbf{s} \tag{10}$$

For example, consider the rule

$$birthCountry(x,z), officialLang(z,y) \Rightarrow speaks(x,y) \tag{11}$$

which we can translate, for the sake of inference, to:

$$\mathbf{M}_{birthCountry}\ \mathbf{M}_{officialLang}\ \mathbf{v}_y = \mathbf{s} \tag{12}$$

The non-zero entries in the vector $\mathbf{s}$ point to the entities for which $p(x,y)$ (in this case, $speaks(x,y)$) is derived. These non-zero entries of the vector $\mathbf{s}$ equals the set of y such that there exists z that $birthCountry(x,z)$ and $officialLang(z,y)$ are in the KG.

$$\mathbf{M}_{q_1 \times q_2} = \left[\begin{array}{ccccc} 0 & 0 & 0 & 1 & 0 \\ 0 & 0 & 0 & 0 & 0 \\ 0 & 0 & 0 & 0 & 0 \\ 0 & 0 & 0 & 0 & 0 \\ 0 & 0 & 0 & 0 & 0 \end{array}\right] \begin{array}{c} \text{E. Macron} \\ \text{U.v. Leyen} \\ \text{EU} \\ \text{French} \\ \text{France} \end{array}$$

(columns: E. Macron, U.v. Leyen, EU, **French**, France)

By assigning $\mathbf{v}_x = [1,0,0,0,0]^\top$ to point to E. Macron and performing the matrix multiplications, we obtain $\mathbf{s} = [0,0,0,1,0]^\top$, which points to French.

Let β_i denote an ordered list of all relations appearing in the rules. Following [22], the inference for each query is defined, more generally, as:

$$\sum_l \alpha_l \prod_{k \in \beta_l} \mathbf{M_{q_k}} \tag{13}$$

$$\mathbf{s} = \sum_l (\alpha_l (\prod_{k \in \beta_l} \mathbf{M_{q_k}} \mathbf{v_y})), \ \ score(x|y) = \mathbf{v_x}^\top \mathbf{s} \tag{14}$$

In summary, the learning problem for each query becomes:

$$\max_{\{\alpha_l,\beta_l\}} \sum_{\{x,y\}} score(x|y) = \max_{\{\alpha_l,\beta_l\}} \sum_{\{x,y\}} \mathbf{v}_x^\top \left(\sum_l (\alpha_l (\prod_{k \in \beta_l} \mathbf{M}_{q_k} \mathbf{v}_y)) \right) \tag{15}$$

The goal is to extract the rules from the solution of the above optimization problem by using the defined operators.

Learning rules The set of rules that imply each query and the confidences associated with these rules need to be learnt, that is $\{\alpha_l, \beta_l\}$ are to be learnt. To facilitate this by addressing the problem of enumerating rules, Yang et al. [22] propose to rewrite Eq. (13) in the following way:

$$\prod_{t=1}^{T} \sum_{k}^{|\mathscr{R}|} \alpha_t^k \mathbf{M}_{q_k} \tag{16}$$

where T denotes the maximum length of rules and $|\mathscr{R}|$ the number of relations in the knowledge graph. In order to combine the enumeration of the rules and confidence assignment, the key difference in this new formulation is that each relation in the rules is associated with a weight.

Since rules may be of different lengths, Yang et al. [22] introduced a recurrent formulation that resembles this in Eq. (14). This version uses auxiliary memory vectors $\mathbf{u}_t$, which are at the beginning set to the given entity $\mathbf{v}_y$:

$$\mathbf{u_0} = v_y \tag{17}$$

Then, at each step, the model first computes a weighted average of the previous memory vectors using the memory attention vector $\mathbf{b}_t$, and secondly, it applies the TensorLog operators using the operator attention vector $\mathbf{a}_t$:

$$\mathbf{u_t} = \sum_{k}^{|\mathscr{R}|} a_t^k \mathbf{M}_{q_k} \left(\sum_{\tau=0}^{t-1} b_t^\tau \mathbf{u}_\tau \right) \text{ for } 1 \leq t \leq T \tag{18}$$

In the last step, the model computes a weighted average of the memory vectors. In order to choose a proper rule length, attention is used in this step:

$$\mathbf{u_{T+1}} = \sum_{\tau=0}^{T} b_{T+1}^\tau \mathbf{u}_\tau \tag{19}$$

The learnable parameters are the memory and operator attention vectors. Recurrent neural networks can now be used that fit this recurrent formulation, and the authors of [22] used LSTM for this purpose.

Neural-Num-LP [24] enhances Neural-LP by incorporating the ability to learn rules with negations and numeric values. Additionally, it improves on Neural-LP through an implicit representation of essential matrix operations. These improvements include the use of dynamic programming, cumulative sums for numerical comparison features, and low-rank factorisations for negated atoms.

DRUM [25] was introduced to mitigate a tendency of Neural-LP to learn meaningless rules with high confidence that share atoms with valid rules. To mitigate this issue, DRUM employs bidirectional RNNs to prune potentially incorrect rules as well as low-rank decompositions of matrix M_p.

4.1.2. Decoupling Models

To address the challenges of optimization in joint learning of rule structures and confidence, several methods have been proposed that separate these two tasks.

RNNLogic [26] addresses the challenges in existing methods that struggle with navigating a large search space (as in neural logic programming). RNNLogic is composed of a rule generator and a reasoning predictor. The rule generator is responsible for structure learning and a reasoning predictor for confidence learning. The rule generator produces logic rules for the reasoning predictor for a given query. The reasoning predictor uses the generated rules as input to reason over a knowledge graph and predict the answer. In each iteration, the rule generator produces a set of logic rules. Moreover, in each iteration, the reasoning predictor is updated to explore these rules for reasoning. In the next step, a set of high-quality rules is identified from the generated rules via posterior inference. In the final step, the rule generator is updated to align with the high-quality rules identified in the previous step.

RNNLogic is optimized using an Expectation-Maximization (EM) algorithm.

RLogic [27] is a method for mining chain-like rules. The authors highlight two limitations of other algorithms: their dependence on observed rule instances to define the score function for rule evaluation, and their inability to mine rules that lack support from rule instances. To address these challenges, RLogic operates by sampling closed paths within a knowledge graph and proposes a sequential rule learning algorithm that decomposes a sequential model into smaller atomic models in a recursive manner. For example, the relation path $[birthCountry, officialLang]$ existing in our sample KG (Figure 1) can be replaced by a single relation *nativeLang*. To address cases when the relation to replace with might not be present in the knowledge graph, a "null" predicate is also introduced into the relations set.

The authors introduce a *relation path encoder* and a *close ratio predictor*. The goal of the relation path encoder is to find a head relation p_h to replace an entire relation path. The relation path encoder reduces the rule body $[q_1, ..., q_n]$ to a head p_h by recursively merging relation pairs using a greedy algorithm. The close ratio predictor is based on the observation that, even after logically deducing a reduction of the relation path to a single relation head, this head relation may not always be present in the knowledge graph. Therefore, the task of the close ratio predictor is to estimate the ratio that a path will close and the probability of replacing a relation pair with a single relation. A two-layer, fully connected neural network (MLP) is used for this purpose.

4.2. Embeddings and Rule Learning

Among other things, the previously mentioned algorithms have been designed to provide a rule-based approach for solving predictive tasks, e.g. the KG completion, with a set of mined rules. The main feature of rule-based systems is the need to first obtain rules whose relevance is then computed based on the coverage of a given rule by some examples occurring in the input KG. Hence, the rules searching process and their relevance determination often require storing the entire KG in the memory to allow for fast exploration of the search space or walking through the graph. This may be a problem for large KGs since they have high resource requirements, and the existing systems are not able to effectively scale input data and the mining process.

Graph embeddings are often regarded as an alternative to rule-based approaches for solving specific prediction tasks over graph data, e.g. for link prediction. The graph-embeddings prediction model is composed of a nodes/relations representation (e.g. vectors, matrices) and a scoring function (to calculate the reliability of a predicted entity). The popularity of these kinds of models is given by a simple vector or matrix representation of the entire graph where fast and scalable vector operations can be performed, e.g., to determine similarities among nodes within Euclidean space. Recent studies have also shown that some techniques using graph embeddings outperform convenient rule-based approaches, like AnyBURL [28,29]. Some well-known methods to transform a KG or its individual components (nodes and edges) into vectors are, e.g. RESCAL [30], HolE [31] and TransE [32]. Besides pure graph embedding models, some algorithms even combine the rule-based with the graph embedding approach.

An early approach combining embeddings and rule-based systems was called EmbedRULES [33]. The RLvLR algorithm [34] uses low-dimension embeddings of RDF KG resources and predicates for fast search of Horn rules. This algorithm, which according to the authors' benchmark, outperforms EmbedRULES, focuses on a specific predicate p at the head position. For each p, it creates a sample of an input KG with such facts that are connected to p up to the maximum length of the rule. This operation is required for a large KG since RLvLR uses the RESCAL factorization to create embeddings by default, which can be slow for large data sets. Most of the mining sub-processes, such as pathfinding, support and confidence computations, are performed by matrix operations from embeddings and adjacency matrices. Although this method can be faster than state-of-the-art approaches, such as AMIE, it is limited only to learning rules for a specific predicate and is not designed to discover rules with constants. The main use case of this algorithm is traceable KG completion with a given predicate.

Another rule mining system using embeddings is RuLES[2] [35]. It uses the AMIE approach to generate rules (with or without constants) and an embedding pre-trained model by TransE, HolE, or SSP [36] for computing measures of significance.

While learning rules from embeddings has certain advantages, it is also known to have multiple weaknesses.

Differences in predictive performance between rule-based, rule embedding and pure embedding models There is a paucity of research showing better performance of embeddings-based rule approaches over pure rule learning approaches. Compared with the state-of-the-art RLvLR algorithm, the pure rule-learning approaches AnyBURL and its enhanced version SAFRAN [37] are reported to perform better [37]. However, this benchmark is based only on one dataset (FB15K-237). The same paper [37] also shows that SAFRAN generally performs on part with the best embedding-based (latent) approaches, but unlike them, it is rule-based and thus inherently interpretable. It should be noted the evaluation in [37] is limited by possibly different evaluation conditions between RLvLR and SAFRAN and may not be free of bias, as the evaluation was done by the author of some of the compared methods.

Explainability With the growing emphasis on explainability in machine learning, a major limitation is that the predictions generated by graph embedding models are not traceable. Thus, the reliability of the prediction is given by the scoring function, which, how-

[2]https://github.com/hovinhthinh/RuLES

ever, does not explain to us what parameters lead to a given score. This contrasts rule-based models, where a specific score (confidence) value can be traced back to individual paths in the training data. For example, the RDFRules system offers a graphical interface to easily trace predictions based on AMIE-like rule-based models [38].

4.3. RLvLR: Rule Learning via Learning Representations

The Rule Learning via Learning Representations (RLvLR) algorithm is inspired by NeuralLP. It mines *closed* rules introduced in section 2, that have the form shown in Eq. (1).

$$p_1(x,z_1) \wedge p_2(z_1,z_2) \ldots \wedge p_n(z_n - 1, y) \Rightarrow p(x,y). \tag{20}$$

RLvLR uses the Standard confidence (Eq. (6)) and Head Coverage (Eq. (4)) to evaluate the quality of rules. RLvLR authors state three main improvements compared to previous approaches, such as NeuralLP described earlier:

- removing data not relevant for computation,
- argument embeddings: new rule quality measure through,
- rule quality computed through matrix operations.

Removing data not relevant for computation This operation takes advantage of the problem formulation, where for a given head predicate p and maximum rule length l, only entities that are directly or indirectly related to p and are relevant to mining.

For each head predicate p, this procedure creates a subset of the input KG containing facts that are connected to p up to the maximum length of the rule $l (l \geq 2)$. The fact and entity selection is done so that the subset contains all information relevant for learning rules of length l with a given head predicate p. The algorithm first identifies the sets $e_0 \ldots e_i \ldots e_{l-2}$, which contain entities in facts directly (for $i = 0$) or indirectly (for $i > 0$) related to p. Consequently a subset of the original KG is generated, referred to as KG'. KG' contains only those facts from the original KG, where both entities in the fact (subject and object) are present among the previously identified entities (those in $E' = \bigcup_i^{l-2} e_i$).

Referring to the sample knowledge graph in Figure 1, consider this procedure for *speaks* as the head predicate p and $l = 2$. The algorithm first identifies the set e_0, which contains entities in facts directly related to p. In this case, the directly related facts are $\{speaks(UvdLeyen, English), speaks(Macron, French)\}$, hence the set $e_0 = \{Macron, French, UvdLeyen, English\}$. Since $l = 2$, the set $e'_{l=2} = e_0$ and $KG'_2 = speaks(EMacron, French), speaks(U.v.d.Leyen, English)$. However, there is no non-trivial rule of length 2 that can be extracted from $KG'_{l=2}$. We need to, therefore, increase the value of l to $l = 3$. Now, we additionally need to compute the set e_1, which will contain those entities that are linked to any of the entities in e_0 by any predicate. We get $e_1 = \{English, German, Germany, EU, female, France, male\}$. Consequently, $e_{l=3}$ will contain all entities from the original KG except *A. Merkel*. Based on $e_{l=3}$, we will get $KG'_{l=3}$, which will contain all statements in the original KG in Figure 1 except for *nationality(A. Merkel, Germany)* and *birthCountry(A. Merkel, Germany)*. From this KG, the algorithm can extract rules such as the one in Eq. (3) and the absence of some facts (in this case, two facts with A Merkel), will make this process faster.

Note that while this step was originally called 'sampling' by RLvLR authors, it does not, in our opinion, correspond to the probabilistic implementation of sampling, which is typically understood as a random process affecting a user-set percentage of data samples. As the example shows, in RLvLR, this step can be variously effective based on the rule length (l parameter) and the graph's overall characteristics.

Argument embedding KG embeddings, as implemented by, e.g., the RESCAL algorithm, apply to entities and relations. RLvLR uses both synonymy and the newly introduced co-occurrence scoring functions.

Using the notation we introduced in section 4.1.1, predicates in a body of a RLvLR rule are represented using adjacency matrices $\mathbf{P}_1, \ldots, \mathbf{P}_n$ and the head predicate using embedding matrix $\mathbf{P}$, the product $\mathbf{P}_1 \cdot \mathbf{P}_2 \cdot \ldots \cdot \mathbf{P}_n$ should, according to the authors, capture pairs of entities connected by the body of the rule. As the body should be predictive of the head, the more this product is similar to the matrix $\mathbf{P}$, the better. In addition to the synonymy scoring function, the RLvLR algorithm uses the *co-occurrence scoring function*. To compute this, the RLvLR authors introduced the concept of argument embeddings, which are averages of the "embedding vectors" in the subject and object positions of the given predicate. Details on how these two scoring functions are computed can be found in [39,40].

Matrix computation of rule evaluation measures The RLvLR algorithm uses adjacency matrices to obtain rule support, which is required to compute additional measures such as head coverage or rule confidence.

Let us use the sample knowledge graph in Figure 1, and the following rule shown earlier in Eq. (3): $birthCountry(x, z_1) \wedge officialLang(z_1, y) \Rightarrow speaks(x, y)$ as an example. In the following, there are adjacency matrices for the two predicates in the body of the rule.

$$
\mathbf{M}_{\text{birthCountry}} = \begin{array}{l} \\ \text{U.v.d. Leyen} \\ \text{A. Merkel} \\ \text{E. Macron} \\ \text{Germany} \\ \text{France} \\ \text{EU} \\ \text{English} \\ \text{German} \\ \text{French} \\ \text{male} \\ \text{female} \end{array}
\begin{array}{c} \begin{array}{ccccccccccc} \text{UvL} & \text{AM} & \text{EM} & \text{Gy} & \text{Fr} & \text{EU} & \text{En} & \text{Ge} & \text{Fr} & \text{ma} & \text{fe} \end{array} \\
\begin{bmatrix}
0 & 0 & 0 & 1 & 0 & 0 & 0 & 0 & 0 & 0 & 0 \\
0 & 0 & 0 & 1 & 0 & 0 & 0 & 0 & 0 & 0 & 0 \\
0 & 0 & 0 & 0 & 1 & 0 & 0 & 0 & 0 & 0 & 0 \\
0 & 0 & 0 & 0 & 0 & 0 & 0 & 0 & 0 & 0 & 0 \\
0 & 0 & 0 & 0 & 0 & 0 & 0 & 0 & 0 & 0 & 0 \\
0 & 0 & 0 & 0 & 0 & 0 & 0 & 0 & 0 & 0 & 0 \\
0 & 0 & 0 & 0 & 0 & 0 & 0 & 0 & 0 & 0 & 0 \\
0 & 0 & 0 & 0 & 0 & 0 & 0 & 0 & 0 & 0 & 0 \\
0 & 0 & 0 & 0 & 0 & 0 & 0 & 0 & 0 & 0 & 0 \\
0 & 0 & 0 & 0 & 0 & 0 & 0 & 0 & 0 & 0 & 0 \\
0 & 0 & 0 & 0 & 0 & 0 & 0 & 0 & 0 & 0 & 0
\end{bmatrix} \end{array}
$$

$$
\mathbf{M}_{officialLang} = \begin{array}{l|ccccccccccc|}
 & \text{UvL} & \text{AM} & \text{EM} & \text{Gy} & \text{Fr} & \text{EU} & \text{En} & \text{Ge} & \text{Fr} & \text{ma} & \text{fe} \\
\text{U.v.d. Leyen} & 0 & 0 & 0 & 0 & 0 & 0 & 0 & 0 & 0 & 0 & 0 \\
\text{A. Merkel} & 0 & 0 & 0 & 0 & 0 & 0 & 0 & 0 & 0 & 0 & 0 \\
\text{E. Macron} & 0 & 0 & 0 & 0 & 0 & 0 & 0 & 0 & 0 & 0 & 0 \\
\text{Germany} & 0 & 0 & 0 & 0 & 0 & 0 & 0 & 1 & 0 & 0 & 0 \\
\text{France} & 0 & 0 & 0 & 0 & 0 & 0 & 0 & 0 & 1 & 0 & 0 \\
\text{EU} & 0 & 0 & 0 & 0 & 0 & 0 & 0 & 0 & 0 & 0 & 0 \\
\text{English} & 0 & 0 & 0 & 0 & 0 & 0 & 0 & 0 & 0 & 0 & 0 \\
\text{German} & 0 & 0 & 0 & 0 & 0 & 0 & 0 & 0 & 0 & 0 & 0 \\
\text{French} & 0 & 0 & 0 & 0 & 0 & 0 & 0 & 0 & 0 & 0 & 0 \\
\text{male} & 0 & 0 & 0 & 0 & 0 & 0 & 0 & 0 & 0 & 0 & 0 \\
\text{female} & 0 & 0 & 0 & 0 & 0 & 0 & 0 & 0 & 0 & 0 & 0
\end{array}
$$

The product of these matrices is:

$$
\mathbf{M}_{\text{body}} = \begin{array}{l|ccccccccccc|}
 & \text{UvL} & \text{AM} & \text{EM} & \text{Gy} & \text{Fr} & \text{EU} & \text{En} & \text{Ge} & \text{Fr} & \text{ma} & \text{fe} \\
\text{U.v.d. Leyen} & 0 & 0 & 0 & 0 & 0 & 0 & 0 & 1 & 0 & 0 & 0 \\
\text{A. Merkel} & 0 & 0 & 0 & 0 & 0 & 0 & 0 & 1 & 0 & 0 & 0 \\
\text{E. Macron} & 0 & 0 & 0 & 0 & 0 & 0 & 0 & 0 & 1 & 0 & 0 \\
\text{Germany} & 0 & 0 & 0 & 0 & 0 & 0 & 0 & 0 & 0 & 0 & 0 \\
\text{France} & 0 & 0 & 0 & 0 & 0 & 0 & 0 & 0 & 0 & 0 & 0 \\
\text{EU} & 0 & 0 & 0 & 0 & 0 & 0 & 0 & 0 & 0 & 0 & 0 \\
\text{English} & 0 & 0 & 0 & 0 & 0 & 0 & 0 & 0 & 0 & 0 & 0 \\
\text{German} & 0 & 0 & 0 & 0 & 0 & 0 & 0 & 0 & 0 & 0 & 0 \\
\text{French} & 0 & 0 & 0 & 0 & 0 & 0 & 0 & 0 & 0 & 0 & 0 \\
\text{male} & 0 & 0 & 0 & 0 & 0 & 0 & 0 & 0 & 0 & 0 & 0 \\
\text{female} & 0 & 0 & 0 & 0 & 0 & 0 & 0 & 0 & 0 & 0 & 0
\end{array}
$$

The matrix $\mathbf{M}_{\text{body}}$ shows which entities satisfy the body of the rule. Note that in our example, all elements are 0 or 1. If any matrix element would be greater than 1, such value would be replaced by 1. Comparing this matrix with Figure 1, we see that the body of the rule is matched by $path_1$=*{birthCountry(U.v.d. Leyen, Germany), officialLang(Germany, German)}*, $path_2$=*{birthCountry(Merkel, Germany), officialLang(Germany, German)}* and $path_3$=*{birthCountry(E. Macron, France), officialLang(France, French)}* corresponding to the instantiations of $\#\sigma_H : \sigma_H(\mathbf{B}) \Vdash \mathscr{K}$ from Eq. (6).

Now, we want to compare how this connects with the adjacency matrix for the head relation *speaks*:

$$
\mathbf{M}_{head} = \begin{array}{l} \\ \text{U.v.d. Leyen} \\ \text{A. Merkel} \\ \text{E. Macron} \\ \text{Germany} \\ \text{France} \\ \text{EU} \\ \text{English} \\ \text{German} \\ \text{French} \\ \text{male} \\ \text{female} \end{array}
\begin{array}{c} \begin{array}{ccccccccccc} \text{UvL} & \text{AM} & \text{EM} & \text{Gy} & \text{Fr} & \text{EU} & \text{En} & \text{Ge} & \text{Fr} & \text{ma} & \text{fe} \end{array} \\
\begin{bmatrix}
0 & 0 & 0 & 0 & 0 & 0 & 1 & 1 & 0 & 0 & 0 \\
0 & 0 & 0 & 0 & 0 & 0 & 0 & 0 & 0 & 0 & 0 \\
0 & 0 & 0 & 0 & 0 & 0 & 0 & 0 & 1 & 0 & 0 \\
0 & 0 & 0 & 0 & 0 & 0 & 0 & 0 & 0 & 0 & 0 \\
0 & 0 & 0 & 0 & 0 & 0 & 0 & 0 & 0 & 0 & 0 \\
0 & 0 & 0 & 0 & 0 & 0 & 0 & 0 & 0 & 0 & 0 \\
0 & 0 & 0 & 0 & 0 & 0 & 0 & 0 & 0 & 0 & 0 \\
0 & 0 & 0 & 0 & 0 & 0 & 0 & 0 & 0 & 0 & 0 \\
0 & 0 & 0 & 0 & 0 & 0 & 0 & 0 & 0 & 0 & 0 \\
0 & 0 & 0 & 0 & 0 & 0 & 0 & 0 & 0 & 0 & 0 \\
0 & 0 & 0 & 0 & 0 & 0 & 0 & 0 & 0 & 0 & 0
\end{bmatrix} \end{array}
$$

Here, we can see that $\mathbf{M}_{head}$ and $\mathbf{M}_{body}$ overlap in two facts that relate to the head predicate: *speaks(U.v.d Leyen, German)*, which connects to body $path_1$ and *speaks(Macron, French)*, which connects to body $path_3$. Hence, we got two complete instantiations for rule $birthCountry(x, z_1) \wedge officialLang(z_1, y) \Rightarrow speaks(x, y)$. According to Eq. (2), the value of support is 2.

4.4. Large Language Models for Learning Rules

This section discusses some of the recent studies using Large Language Models for learning rules.

4.4.1. Hypotheses-to-Theories

One of the recent frameworks, Hypotheses-to-Theories (HtT) [41] is designed to learn a set of rules from training examples, which is then used for reasoning over test samples using Large Language Models (LLMs). The framework is designed with the objective to target the issue of incorrect rule generation by LLMs which is often the case when LLMs rely on their implicit knowledge for rule creation instead of taking into account the problem at hand or the data provided. The framework employs both inductive and deductive reasoning through few-shot prompting. Inductive reasoning involves deriving general rules from specific observations, while deductive reasoning involves deriving new facts based on the existing ones.

Induction Stage: Learning a Rule Library. The induction stage aims to learn rules from training examples without explicit rule annotations. For each training example (a question-answer pair), HtT prompts an LLM to generate rules for answering the question. Regular expressions are then used to extract rules from the LLM's output. Given the noisy nature of LLM reasoning, rules and accuracy metrics are collected from a sufficient number of training examples. The rules are filtered based on criteria from [3], considering both coverage and confidence. Coverage indicates how likely a rule is to be reused, while confidence indicates how likely it is to be correct.

Deduction Stage: Reasoning using the Rule Library. The rule library generated in the induction phase is used for deductive reasoning prompts based on Chain-of-Thought prompting. The examples are modified to teach the LLM to retrieve rules from the library whenever it needs to generate a rule. If all the rules required by a question are present in the library, the LLM should generate correct rules for each step without errors. In order to facilitate the rule retrieval process, the rule library is organized into a hierarchy using XML, where each tag refers to a cluster.

4.4.2. ChatRule

ChatRule [42] is a framework designed for mining logical rules for Knowledge Graph (KG) reasoning tasks. The initial step involves an LLM-based rule generator that leverages both the semantic and structural information of KGs to prompt LLMs to create logical rules. To achieve this, the **rule sampler** conducts a Breadth-First Search (BFS) to sample several closed paths from KGs.

For instance, given a triple (h_1, r_j, t_1), the closed-path is defined as a sequence of relations $r_1, \ldots, r_n$ that connects h_1 and t_1 in KGs, i.e., $h_1 \xrightarrow{r_1} h_2 \xrightarrow{r_2} \ldots \xrightarrow{r_j} e_L$. For example, given a triple (Alice, GrandMother, Charlie), a closed-path p can be found as:

$$p := Alice \overset{Mother}{\longrightarrow} Bob \overset{Father}{\longrightarrow} Charlie,$$

which completes the triple (Alice, GrandMother, Charlie) in KGs. For a given target relation, a set of seed triples is selected from KGs, and BFS is conducted to sample a set of closed paths with lengths less than L, forming a set of rule instances. The actual entities in these rule instances are then replaced with variables to create rule samples. Each generated rule is verbalized into a natural language sentence, which is then incorporated into the prompt template.

To refine the generated rules, a rule ranking module assesses their quality by integrating facts from existing KGs. This ranking process utilizes support, coverage, confidence, and PCA confidence, as inspired by [3]. The ranked rules are then used for reasoning over KGs, addressing downstream tasks such as knowledge graph completion. In these tasks, candidate answers are ranked based on scores derived from coverage, confidence, or PCA confidence.

5. Conclusions

In this chapter, we described rule learning algorithms for knowledge graphs. We began with a comprehensive overview of the rule mining problem, followed by a discussion of popular rule mining algorithms to establish a foundation. Finally, we explored state-of-the-art neuro-symbolic rule learning approaches.

Acknowledgments

Part of section 4.2 is adapted from the dissertation thesis of VZ [43].

References

[1] Boschin A, Jain N, Keretchashvili G, Suchanek F. Combining Embeddings and Rules for Fact Prediction (Invited Paper). In: DROPS-IDN/v2/document/10.4230/OASIcs.AIB.2022.4. Schloss Dagstuhl – Leibniz-Zentrum für Informatik; 2022. Available from: https://drops.dagstuhl.de/entities/document/10.4230/OASIcs.AIB.2022.4.

[2] Wu H, Wang Z, Wang K, Omran PG, Li J. Rule Learning over Knowledge Graphs: A Review. DROPS-IDN/v2/document/104230/TGDK117. 2023. Available from: https://drops.dagstuhl.de/entities/document/10.4230/TGDK.1.1.7.

[3] Galárraga LA, Teflioudi C, Hose K, Suchanek F. AMIE: association rule mining under incomplete evidence in ontological knowledge bases. In: Proceedings of the 22nd international conference on World Wide Web. WWW '13. New York, NY, USA: Association for Computing Machinery; 2013. p. 413-22. Available from: https://doi.org/10.1145/2488388.2488425.

[4] Dong XL, Gabrilovich E, Heitz G, Horn W, Lao N, Murphy K, et al. Knowledge Vault: A Web-Scale Approach to Probabilistic Knowledge Fusion. In: The 20th ACM SIGKDD International Conference on Knowledge Discovery and Data Mining, KDD; 2014. p. 601-10. Available from: http://www.cs.cmu.edu/~nlao/publication/2014.kdd.pdf.

[5] Galárraga L, Teflioudi C, Hose K, Suchanek FM. Fast rule mining in ontological knowledge bases with AMIE$$+$$. The VLDB Journal. 2015 Dec;24(6):707-30. Available from: https://doi.org/10.1007/s00778-015-0394-1.

[6] Muggleton S, de Raedt L. Inductive Logic Programming: Theory and methods. The Journal of Logic Programming. 1994 May;19-20:629-79. Available from: https://www.sciencedirect.com/science/article/pii/0743106694900353.

[7] Nienhuys-Cheng S, de Wolf R. Foundations of Inductive Logic Programming. vol. 1228 of Lecture Notes in Computer Science. Springer; 1997. Available from: https://doi.org/10.1007/3-540-62927-0.

[8] Raedt LD. Inductive Logic Programming. In: Sammut C, Webb GI, editors. Encyclopedia of Machine Learning and Data Mining. Boston, MA: Springer US; 2017. p. 648-56. Available from: https://doi.org/10.1007/978-1-4899-7687-1_135.

[9] Goethals B, Van den Bussche J. Relational Association Rules: Getting Warmer. In: Hand DJ, Adams NM, Bolton RJ, editors. Pattern Detection and Discovery. Berlin, Heidelberg: Springer Berlin Heidelberg; 2002. p. 125-39.

[10] Muggleton S. Learning from positive data. In: Muggleton S, editor. Inductive Logic Programming. Berlin, Heidelberg: Springer Berlin Heidelberg; 1997. p. 358-76.

[11] Suchanek FM, Kasneci G, Weikum G. Yago: a core of semantic knowledge. In: Proceedings of the 16th International Conference on World Wide Web. WWW '07. New York, NY, USA: Association for Computing Machinery; 2007. p. 697–706. Available from: https://doi.org/10.1145/1242572.1242667.

[12] Lajus J, Galárraga L, Suchanek F. Fast and exact rule mining with AMIE 3. In: The Semantic Web: 17th International Conference, ESWC 2020, Heraklion, Crete, Greece, May 31–June 4, 2020, Proceedings 17. Springer; 2020. p. 36-52.

[13] Ortona S, Meduri VV, Papotti P. Robust Discovery of Positive and Negative Rules in Knowledge Bases. In: 2018 IEEE 34th International Conference on Data Engineering (ICDE); 2018. p. 1168-79. ISSN: 2375-026X. Available from: https://ieeexplore.ieee.org/document/8509329.

[14] Chen Y, Wang DZ, Goldberg S. ScaLeKB: scalable learning and inference over large knowledge bases. The VLDB Journal. 2016 dec;25(6):893–918. Available from: https://doi.org/10.1007/s00778-016-0444-3.

[15] Dong XL, Gabrilovich E, Heitz G, Horn W, Murphy K, Sun S, et al. From data fusion to knowledge fusion. arXiv preprint arXiv:150300302. 2015.

[16] Meilicke C, Chekol MW, Ruffinelli D, Stuckenschmidt H. An introduction to AnyBURL. In: KI 2019: Advances in Artificial Intelligence: 42nd German Conference on AI, Kassel, Germany, September 23–26, 2019, Proceedings 42. Springer; 2019. p. 244-8.

[17] Muggleton SH, Feng C, et al. Efficient induction of logic programs. Turing Institute London, UK; 1990.

[18] Meilicke C, Chekol MW, Betz P, Fink M, Stuckeschmidt H. Anytime bottom-up rule learning for large-scale knowledge graph completion. The VLDB Journal. 2024 Jan;33(1):131-61. Available from: https://doi.org/10.1007/s00778-023-00800-5.

[19] Semeraro G, Esposito F, Malerba D, Brunk C, Pazzani M. Avoiding non-termination when learning logic programs: A case study with FOIL and FOCL. In: Logic Program Synthesis and Transformation—Meta-Programming in Logic: 4th International Workshops, LOPSTR'94 and META'94 Pisa, Italy, June 20–21, 1994 Proceedings. Springer; 1994. p. 183-98.

[20] Pirrò G. Relatedness and TBox-Driven Rule Learning in Large Knowledge Bases. Proceedings of the AAAI Conference on Artificial Intelligence. 2020 Apr;34(03):2975-82. Available from: https:

//ojs.aaai.org/index.php/AAAI/article/view/5690.

[21] Dash S, Goncalves J. Rule induction in knowledge graphs using linear programming. In: Proceedings of the AAAI Conference on Artificial Intelligence. vol. 37; 2023. p. 4233-41.

[22] Yang F, Yang Z, Cohen WW. Differentiable learning of logical rules for knowledge base reasoning. In: Proceedings of the 31st International Conference on Neural Information Processing Systems. NIPS'17. Red Hook, NY, USA: Curran Associates Inc.; 2017. p. 2316-25.

[23] Cohen WW. TensorLog: A Differentiable Deductive Database. CoRR. 2016;abs/1605.06523. Available from: http://arxiv.org/abs/1605.06523.

[24] Wang PW, Stepanova D, Domokos C, Kolter JZ. Differentiable learning of numerical rules in knowledge graphs; 2020. Available from: https://iclr.cc/virtual_2020/poster_rJleKgrKwS.html.

[25] Sadeghian A, Armandpour M, Ding P, Wang DZ. DRUM: End-To-End Differentiable Rule Mining On Knowledge Graphs. In: Advances in Neural Information Processing Systems. vol. 32. Curran Associates, Inc.; 2019. Available from: https://proceedings.neurips.cc/paper/2019/hash/0c72cb7ee1512f800abe27823a792d03-Abstract.html.

[26] Qu M, Chen J, Xhonneux LP, Bengio Y, Tang J. RNNLogic: Learning Logic Rules for Reasoning on Knowledge Graphs; 2020. Available from: https://openreview.net/forum?id=tGZu6DlbreV.

[27] Cheng K, Liu J, Wang W, Sun Y. RLogic: Recursive Logical Rule Learning from Knowledge Graphs. In: Proceedings of the 28th ACM SIGKDD Conference on Knowledge Discovery and Data Mining. KDD '22. New York, NY, USA: Association for Computing Machinery; 2022. p. 179-89. Available from: https://dl.acm.org/doi/10.1145/3534678.3539421.

[28] Rossi A, Barbosa D, Firmani D, Matinata A, Merialdo P. Knowledge graph embedding for link prediction: A comparative analysis. ACM Transactions on Knowledge Discovery from Data (TKDD). 2021;15(2):1-49. https://doi.org/10.1145/3424672.

[29] Meilicke C, Fink M, Wang Y, Ruffinelli D, Gemulla R, Stuckenschmidt H. Fine-Grained Evaluation of Rule and Embedding-Based Systems for Knowledge Graph Completion. In: International Semantic Web Conference. Springer; 2018. p. 3-20. https://doi.org/10.1007/978-3-030-00671-6_1.

[30] Nickel M, Tresp V, Kriegel HP. A Three-Way Model for Collective Learning on Multi-Relational Data. In: ICML. vol. 11; 2011. p. 809-16. https://dl.acm.org/doi/10.5555/3104482.3104584.

[31] Nickel M, Rosasco L, Poggio T. Holographic Embeddings of Knowledge Graphs. In: Proceedings of the Thirtieth AAAI Conference on Artificial Intelligence. AAAI'16. AAAI Press; 2016. p. 1955–1961. https://dl.acm.org/doi/10.5555/3016100.3016172.

[32] Bordes A, Usunier N, Garcia-Duran A, Weston J, Yakhnenko O. Translating embeddings for modeling multi-relational data. In: Advances in neural information processing systems. NIPS'13. Red Hook, NY, USA: Curran Associates Inc.; 2013. p. 2787-95. https://dl.acm.org/doi/10.5555/2999792.2999923.

[33] Yang B, Yih W, He X, Gao J, Deng L. Embedding Entities and Relations for Learning and Inference in Knowledge Bases. In: Bengio Y, LeCun Y, editors. 3rd International Conference on Learning Representations, ICLR 2015, San Diego, CA, USA, May 7-9, 2015, Conference Track Proceedings; 2015. Available from: http://arxiv.org/abs/1412.6575.

[34] Omran PG, Wang K, Wang Z. Scalable Rule Learning via Learning Representation. In: Proceedings of the 27th International Joint Conference on Artificial Intelligence. IJCAI'18. AAAI Press; 2018. p. 2149-55. https://dl.acm.org/doi/10.5555/3304889.3304958.

[35] Ho VT, Stepanova D, Gad-Elrab MH, Kharlamov E, Weikum G. Rule Learning from Knowledge Graphs Guided by Embedding Models. In: International Semantic Web Conference. Springer; 2018. p. 72-90. https://doi.org/10.1007/978-3-030-00671-6_5.

[36] Xiao H, Huang M, Meng L, Zhu X. SSP: Semantic Space Projection for Knowledge Graph Embedding with Text Descriptions. In: Thirty-First AAAI Conference on Artificial Intelligence; 2017. .

[37] Ott S, Meilicke C, Samwald M. SAFRAN: An interpretable, rule-based link prediction method outperforming embedding models. arXiv preprint arXiv:210908002. 2021.

[38] Zeman V, Kliegr T, Svátek V. RDFRules: Making RDF rule mining easier and even more efficient. Semantic web. 2021;12(4):569-602.

[39] Omran PG, Wang K, Wang Z. An embedding-based approach to rule learning in knowledge graphs. IEEE Transactions on Knowledge and Data Engineering. 2019;33(4):1348-59.

[40] Yang B, Yih SWt, He X, Gao J, Deng L. Embedding Entities and Relations for Learning and Inference in Knowledge Bases. In: Proceedings of the International Conference on Learning Representations (ICLR) 2015; 2015. .

[41] Zhu Z, Xue Y, Chen X, Zhou D, Tang J, Schuurmans D, et al. Large Language Models can Learn Rules. CoRR. 2023;abs/2310.07064.
[42] Luo L, Ju J, Xiong B, Li Y, Haffari G, Pan S. ChatRule: Mining Logical Rules with Large Language Models for Knowledge Graph Reasoning. CoRR. 2023;abs/2309.01538.
[43] Zeman V. Rule mining over linked data. Prague University of Economics and Business; 2023. Dissertation thesis.

Handbook on Neurosymbolic AI and Knowledge Graphs
P. Hitzler et al. (Eds.)
IOS Press, 2025

doi:10.3233/FAIA250225

Neuro-Symbolic Query Optimization in Knowledge Graphs

Maribel ACOSTA [a,1], Chang QIN [a,b] and Tim SCHWABE [a]
[a] *Technical University of Munich*
[b] *Fraunhofer-Institut für Intelligente Analyse- und Informationssysteme IAIS*
ORCiD ID: Maribel Acosta https://orcid.org/0000-0002-1209-2868, Chang Qin https://orcid.org/0009-0002-4781-2391, Tim Schwabe https://orcid.org/0009-0009-7957-603X

Abstract. This chapter delves into the emerging field of neuro-symbolic query optimization for knowledge graphs (KGs), presenting a comprehensive exploration of how neural and symbolic techniques can be integrated to enhance query processing. Traditional query optimizers in knowledge graphs rely heavily on symbolic methods, utilizing dataset summaries, statistics, and cost models to select efficient execution plans. However, these approaches often suffer from misestimations and inaccuracies, particularly when dealing with complex queries or large-scale datasets. Recent advancements have introduced neural models, which capture non-linear aspects of query optimization, offering promising alternatives to purely symbolic methods. In this chapter, we introduce neuro-symbolic query optimizers, a novel approach that combines the strengths of symbolic reasoning with the adaptability of neural computation. We discuss the architecture of these hybrid systems, highlighting the interplay between neural and symbolic components to improve the optimizer's ability to navigate the search space and produce efficient execution plans. Additionally, the chapter reviews existing neural components tailored for optimizing queries over knowledge graphs and examines the limitations and challenges in deploying neuro-symbolic query optimizers in real-world environments.

Keywords. Query Optimization, Machine Learning, Neuro-Symbolic AI, Relational Database, Knowledge Graph, Cardinality Estimation, Cost Models, Plan Traversal

1. Introduction

Knowledge graphs (KGs) and other data models can be interrogated using queries formulated in a query language. For example, for knowledge graphs modeled with the Resource Description Framework (RDF), queries are formulated using the SPARQL query language. To compute the answer for a given query, a query processor comprises different components that implement strategies to speed up the query execution while producing correct results. Such strategies include resorting to access methods to retrieve portions of the stored dataset efficiently, re-ordering the operators that occur in the query to minimize the number of intermediate results, or implementing specific algorithms to implement operators that produce intermediate results quickly.

[1]Corresponding Author: Maribel Acosta, maribel.acosta@tum.de

In query processing, the optimizer is the component that selects the strategies to execute a given query over a dataset. These strategies are encoded in a query plan, which is represented as a tree. The leaves of this tree correspond to access methods to retrieve relevant data from the dataset, while the internal nodes are operators to combine intermediate results and produce the final query answer. Formally, the query optimization problem can be defined as a search problem [1] whose goal is to identify a plan from the space of possible plans that minimizes some objective function, e.g., the query runtime or latency. Ibaraki and Kameda [2] formally demonstrated that identifying the optimal plan is an NP-complete problem. To explore the search space and identify efficient plans, traditional query optimizers implement symbolic components based on dataset summaries, statistics, cost models, (algebraic) rules, or heuristics.

However, even with detailed statistics and advanced techniques, symbolic query optimizers are prone to errors due to misestimations or inaccurate models. Producing suboptimal plans has tremendous effects on query latency, where execution times can be affected by orders of magnitude or even prevent a query from being answered in a reasonable amount of time. This problem is exacerbated when evaluating complex queries or dealing with very large KG. To overcome these limitations, neural models for query optimization have been proposed for query engines over relational databases and knowledge graphs. Most of these solutions focus on replacing a specific component in the query optimizer by using machine learning models based on neural networks or deep learning, as they are able to capture complex relationships of the factors that affect the query performance, e.g., data correlations, complexity of the query operators, and (hardware) resource usage. This chapter goes a step beyond the literature and introduces the notion of neuro-symbolic query optimizers, where we discuss the integration of neural and symbolic components during query optimization. Furthermore, this chapter provides details of existing solutions for neural components to optimize queries over knowledge graphs. We finally present a discussion of existing limitations and future directions of neuro-symbolic query optimizers.

The remainder of this chapter is structured as follows. §2 introduces the preliminaries, including symbolic methods for query optimization and the general architecture of query optimizers. §3 briefly presents existing neural and neuro-symbolic methods for relational databases. §4 describes the architecture of neuro-symbolic optimizers for knowledge graphs. §5 discusses challenges and future directions for deploying neuro-symbolic optimizers in real-world systems. §6 concludes this chapter.

2. Preliminaries

2.1. Symbolic Methods for Query Optimization

Symbolic query optimization typically refers to a type of optimization that involves manipulating and reasoning about the symbolic representation of queries and their plans. This approach focuses on theoretical and logical transformations. The database literature distinguishes three types of optimizers related to symbolic query optimization: heuristics-based, rule-based, and cost-based optimization.

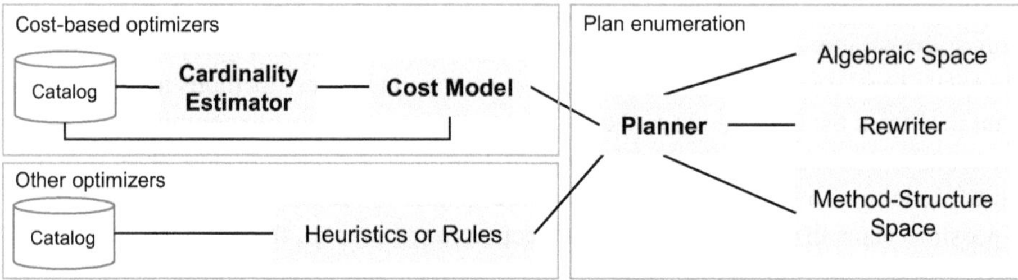

Figure 1. Simplified architecture of query optimizers

Heuristic-based Optimization These optimizers use heuristics and 'rules of thumb' to make decisions about query plans. They rely on strategies or heuristics to simplify and speed up the optimization process. For example, a heuristic might dictate that certain subplans should always be preferred. These optimizers are generally fast (i.e., polynomial time), but they do not always find the optimal plan.

Rule-based Optimization These optimizers use predefined rules to devise plans. In contrast to heuristics, these rules are typically based on the properties of the query workload and the schema of the database at hand. For instance, a rule might specify that using a specific access method is preferable for certain query types. Rule-based optimizers are straightforward to implement, are predictable, and can generate plans fast. Yet, they suffer from similar limitations as heuristics-based optimizers.

Cost-based Optimization These optimizers explore a larger space of possible plans for a query while estimating the cost of each plan. The optimizer then selects the plan with the lowest estimated cost. Cost-based optimizers are generally more accurate in finding the optimal plan because they assess more plans and consider their execution costs, though they can be more computationally expensive than other optimizers.

From these methods, rule-based optimizers are most directly related to symbolic query optimization due to their reliance on symbolic transformation rules. Heuristics-based optimizers also use symbolic reasoning but in a more practical way. Lastly, cost-based optimizers focus more on empirical cost analysis, yet they still perform some symbolic manipulations by exploiting algebraic transformations over query expressions to preserve the equivalence of plans.

2.2. General Architecture of Query Optimizers

Figure 1 outlines the components of query optimizers. The cost-based optimizer components include the cardinality estimator (§2.2.1) and the cost model (§2.2.2). The planner (§2.2.3) explores potential plans to identify the optimal execution strategy using the cost model (in the case of cost-based optimizers) or pre-defined strategies encoded as heuristics or rules (in the case of other symbolic optimization techniques).

2.2.1. Cardinality Estimator

This component determines the cardinality or number of results produced by a subplan. In query optimization, the cardinality of a subplan is typically assumed to be directly related to the cost of executing such subplan. Essentially, the more results there are to process, the more expensive the execution of the subplan is in terms of time and space.

To perform cardinality estimation, the optimizer relies on statistical summaries of the dataset stored in the catalog. These summaries typically include relation cardinalities, data distributions, and other relevant statistics captured in histograms, data samples, and even pre-computed results for frequent query patterns. However, even with detailed statistics, cost-based optimizers can produce inaccurate estimations. This is because they often assume that attribute values are independent and uniformly distributed, which allows for simplifying the process of computing the statistics, performing fast cardinality estimations, updating the summaries, and generalizing the optimization techniques to several datasets. However, these assumptions do not always hold in practice [3], thus, requiring advanced techniques such as multivariate statistics, enhanced histograms, and even machine learning. The latter will be the focus of this chapter.

In some scenarios, accurate statistical summaries of the dataset are not available. For example, in query processing over remote data sources, it may not be possible to gather sufficient statistics. Another example is in query processing over dynamic data, where the dataset changes frequently, making it nearly impossible for the optimizer to maintain up-to-date statistics. For cases like this, the optimization process needs to be complemented with adaptive query processing techniques [3–5] to adjust the plan execution based on the performance observed during runtime.

2.2.2. Cost Model

In cost-based optimization, the cost model is used to estimate the resources required to execute query plans. In this context, the cost is a numerical value which is associated with each plan. Although this cost does not necessarily represent the exact runtime of a query, it is correlated with it: a higher cost indicates a longer query runtime.

Different database systems implement different models or formulas to estimate the cost of a plan. Still, a typical cost model formula considers several factors, such as I/O cost, CPU cost, and sometimes memory usage. For example, for a plan that involves scanning a table and applying a filter, the cost might be estimated as the linear combination of number of sequential pages read from disk plus the number of tuples processed. The following is an example of such a cost model implemented in PostgreSQL [6]:

$$Cost(P) = \overbrace{(C_{seq\_page} \cdot \underbrace{\#disk\_pages\_read}_{\textit{Catalog}})}^{\textbf{I/O Cost}} + \overbrace{(C_{cpu\_tuple} \cdot \underbrace{\#tuples\_scanned}_{\textit{Cardinality estimator}})}^{\textbf{CPU Cost}} \quad (1)$$

As shown in Figure 1 and Eq. (1), the cost model relies on the dataset statistics stored in the catalog and the cardinality estimator to compute the efficiency of a plan.

In practice, developing a cost model that accurately reflects the true execution cost of different query plans can be complex. Finding suitable values for the constants C used in a cost model is not straightforward as these are coupled to the database configuration, the query workload diversity, and even the hardware where the database is deployed. Furthermore, all of these factors can change over time due to changes in the dataset, queries, and technical infrastructure. Therefore, finding optimal values for constants and other parameters in a cost model requires a combination of theoretical knowledge, empirical analysis, and continuous tuning to ensure the cost model remains accurate over time.

2.2.3. Planner

For a given query, the planner traverses the search space of possible plans by comparing *equivalent plans*, i.e., plans whose executions produce the same results. The space of equivalent plans is given by [7]: (i) the *algebraic space*, which is the set of rules that preserve plan equivalence [36] (e.g, operator commutativity and associativity), (ii) the *rewriter* applies simple transformations to the query to produce more efficient plans, e.g., by using views, flattening out subqueries, redundant subexpression elimination, etc. and (iii) the *method-structure space* that contains the available implementations of access methods and logical operations specified in the query.

During the plan traversal, the planner compares equivalent plans to find an optimal plan. For this, planners may implement different search strategies [86, 96], including exhaustive search using Dynamic Programming [144], greedy algorithms that prune large sub-spaces of plans and typically run in polynomial time, randomized algorithms that generate an initial plan randomly which is later refined, and hybrid search strategies such as Iterative Dynamic Programming (IDP) [96] combining DP with greedy steps.

In cost-based optimization, the planner relies on the cost model to guide the exploration of plans and identify the best ones. Similarly, optimizers with different architectures may also implement search strategies like the ones discussed here, but they use heuristics or rules to enumerate and compare equivalent plans.

3. Literature in Neural Components in Relational Databases

In the context of neural approaches for relational databases, the cardinality estimators, cost models, and plan traversal components are enhanced with learned models. Each of these components benefits from learning different aspects of query processing via machine learning and neural networks. In the following sections, we will explore how the learned models are integrated into optimizers to improve the query performance.

3.1. Learned Cardinality Estimation

Cardinality estimators that rely on machine learning may follow two paradigms: the query modeling (§3.1.1) and the data modeling (§3.1.2). Query modeling approaches learn a mapping function between a query or a plan and its cardinality, treating cardinality estimation as a regression problem. Instead, data modeling treats cardinality estimation as a density estimation problem by focusing on learning joint data distributions [8]. An overview of existing solutions for learned cardinality estimations is shown in Table 1.

3.1.1. Query-Driven Models

Query-driven models are applied when the full dataset is unavailable or too large to learn from. These approaches use query logs to predict the cardinality of the new queries with similar patterns and, therefore, it is regarded as a supervised learning process.

Query-driven modeling approaches perform (1) a *sampling phase* to extract information related to schema and attribute values tables, columns from the schema, values from each column for predicates [8], or the physical plans generated by the optimizer [10] are gathered. To pass this information to a neural network, the approaches build a (2) *query featurization* where the operations included in the query are transformed into numerical

Table 1. Overview of learned cardinality estimation techniques for databases. Adapted from [9]

Category	Learning Method	Techniques
Query-Driven	Statistical Model	Linear Model; Tree-based Ensemble; XGBoost; Mixture Model
	NN-Based	Fully Connected Neural Network; Multi-set Convolutional Network; Adding Pooling Layers; Adding Containment Rate; Query Masking; Segmentation; Ensemble of Deep Models; Bayesian Deep Learning; Query Re-optimization
Data-Driven	Kernel-Based	Kernel Density Function
	Auto-Regressive Model	Adding Gaussian Mixture Models; Single Table; Multi-Table
	Probabilistic Graphic Model	Bayesian Network; Revitalized Bayesian Network; Sum-Product Network; FSPN, Factor Graph and Join Histogram
	Others	Normalizing Flow; Summarization Models
Hybrid	Others	Deep Auto-Regressive Models; Attention on Transformer Models

vectors, e.g., binary or one-hot encoding vectors. Based on the query features, the approaches learn (3) a *regression model* to predict the cardinality. As for model selection, neural approaches are preferred because the data can have non-linear, complex distributions in general [11]. Many customized models based on neural networks have been investigated and proven to outperform traditional cardinality estimators. These models include Multi-set Convolutional Networks (MSCNs) [12], Recurrent Neural Networks (RNNs) [13], and Fully Connected Networks (FCNs) [14].

Query-driven methods are proven to accurately predicate cardinalities, but only when the distributions of training and test queries are similar [14]. Besides, collecting queries for the training data and executing them on real databases is also expensive. Given these limitations, data-driven approaches for learning cardinality estimation are widely investigated.

3.1.2. Data-Driven Models

These models learn to predict the query cardinality from data distributions by learning a joint data distribution of each data point in the dataset [8]. Existing modeling approaches greatly differ in the model selection, as shown in Table 1.

In the following, we briefly discuss unsupervised methods for data-driven modeling that are neural-based. Prominent approaches based on neural networks are Sum-Product Networks (SPNs) and autoregressive models. SPNs [15] split data into clusters and groups based on similarity and correlation, respectively, using SUM and PRODUCT operators to efficiently compute joint data distributions and cardinalities. Autoregressive models treat each tuple or row as a sequence [16, 17]. To predict the value of the next attribute in the tuple, it factorizes the joint distribution and computes conditional distributions based on the preceding attributes. It then aggregates these probabilities for data samples matching a query to estimate the query's cardinality [8].

Although these approaches can achieve high accuracy, their inference time is much longer because of the adoption of more specialized models. For example, the total time of

Naru [16] is sensitive to the running device, which needs 5ms to 15ms on GPU, whereas CPU can be up to 20× slower, which will be a blocking issue of bringing these accurate data-driven unsupervised learned estimators into production [18].

3.2. Learned Cost Models

Learned cost models based on neural (§3.2.1) and neuro-symbolic (§3.2.2) approaches have been widely investigated and proven to outperform traditional methods [8, 19–23].

3.2.1. Neural Cost Models

Neural–based approaches to learned cost models are mainly supervised methods and are applied to replace cost models by predicting performance metrics. The input is generally presentations of queries, operators or other required characteristics which are fed into the neural networks. NN-based [19], tree convolution [20, 22] and tree-structured deep neural network [10] are used to capture the complex relationships and patterns in query plans. As for output, various performance metrics, such as latency, are predicted [20,22].

3.2.2. Neuro-symbolic Cost Models

Although learning-based approaches with neural networks for cost estimation have been intensively studied these years, the inherent limitations, such as training overhead, poor generalization among databases as well as the lack of explainability for end-to-end predictions, are unavoidable [23]. Therefore, traditional formula-based cost models –as the example from Eq. (1)– have now improved with advanced learning-based models [23].

Instead of manually setting the values for constants and parameters in formula-based cost models, the neuro-symbolic cost models learn optimal settings offline. As new data and query workloads come into the system, parameters are further refined and adjusted dynamically with online learning to adapt to changing conditions or configurations. In this way, transferability can also be achieved by a lightweight learning scheme. Besides, inherent advantages of formula-based cost models are utilized, such as training is based on the existing knowledge of the cost model and the interpretability of the cost model, which makes the training process more efficient and interpretable [23].

3.3. Learned Plan Traversal

One of the main challenges in cost-based query optimization is that the plan enumeration phase is sensitive to errors in the cardinality estimations and the cost model. To avoid this, learned plan traversal approaches skip these aspects, and learn a model to effciently identify the subspace of plans where optimal plans may reside.

Current learned planners are neural-based using deep reinforcement learning (DRL) [21]. With DRL, an agent learns to chose the policy which make the cumulative rewards maximun. In the context of query optimization, the state and action of reinforcement learning are the current subplans and the combination of two subplans into a new plan. In this way, the planner learns a decision policy to map states to actions, with the maximum expected reward [24]. Depending on learning from past queries or during the execution of the current query, learned plan travesal can be categorized into offline-learning and online-learning methods.

Offline Learning Methods like Q-learning [24, 25], Deep Q-Network [26], and policy gradient methods [27] are implemented to develop policies based on prior experiences, which include actions, states, and rewards derived from previous queries. The query plans (trees), as states, can include information about tables and operation selections [24, 27] as well as the structure plan's with tree-structured long short-term memory [28].

While offline learning can predict better operation orders, they also exist inherent limitations. The main shortcoming of these methods is that new queries must be similar to prior queries to make the prediction effective, and this similarity must be recognizable [29]. In contrast, online learning offer adaptive strategies that continuously update their models based on new queries, as explained in the following.

Online Learning With online-learning methods, the query optimizer learns to find optimal operator orders at runtime. This approach was first investigated through an adaptive query processing mechanism known as Eddies. While Eddies are not neural-base, it inspires the subsequent work to improve adaptive query processing using Reinforcement Learning [30]. The fundamental idea treats the query execution process as a training episode, whereas a more advanced approach [29] splits the execution into many small time slices, during each of which it executes a selected subplan, trains the Upper Confidence Bounds to Trees based on the subplan's real-time performance, and finally, merges the intermediate results produced in each time slice to generate the final result [31].

Fully online-learning and adaptive approaches introduces overhead, which may increase the runtime of individual queries [24]. Besides, the complexity of fully online-learning query optimizer makes its integration into production systems difficult [29].

4. Towards Neuro-Symbolic Optimizers for Knowledge Graphs

The problem of query optimization and solutions for knowledge graphs (KGs) takes a lot of inspiration from the ones developed for relational databases. However, existing data models for KGs present fundamental properties that greatly differ from the relational model. This hinders the direct application of database techniques to KGs. In the context of query optimization, three of these **fundamental properties of KGs** are:

1. Connectedness: KGs are graph-based structures where entities are represented as nodes, which are interconnected via edges that represent relationships between them. In graph models such as RDF, where the atomic data structure is a triple, the relationships or connections in the KG are considered first-class citizens.
2. Semi-structuredness: KGs follow a schema-less paradigm without imposing the same structures or restrictions over the entire datasets. Due to their schema-less nature, KGs often present irregular data structures where some nodes are over-specified with multiple attributes or predicates while others are highly incomplete.
3. Unexpected data correlations: The data distributions in real-world KGs follow a power law, e.g., a small number of nodes have a high degree of connections, while most nodes have a few connections. This is very common in RDF graphs [32] due to the presence of frequent properties defined in RDF/S and OWL.

The properties (1), (2), and (3) make the process of learning patterns and joint data distributions from the KG very challenging. In particular, property (3) impedes applying techniques from relational databases, where data is typically more uniformly distributed.

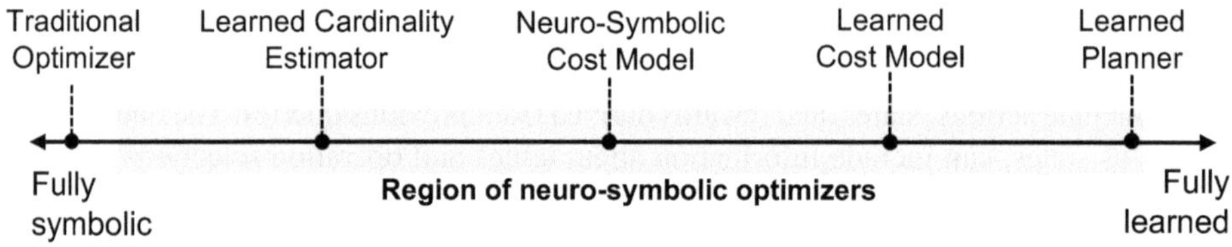

Figure 2. Spectrum of integrating learned components into a query optimizer

Due to these fundamental differences, neural and neuro-symbolic methods for query optimization have been proposed for KGs. In this chapter, first, we present a characterization of neuro-symbolic architectures for query optimizers (§4.1). Then, we describe how the components of a KG query optimizer can implement learned cardinality estimation (§4.2), learned cost models (§4.3), and learned planned traversal (§4.4).

4.1. Architecture of a Neuro-Symbolic Query Optimizer

Query optimizers can integrate learned or neural components in different ways. To characterize this, we present in Figure 2 a spectrum comprising a progression from traditional, fully symbolic query optimizers to fully learned, neural network-based optimizers, with various hybrid neuro-symbolic approaches in between.

Fully Symbolic or Traditional Optimizer This represents the classic, rule-based query optimizer found in most systems (cf. §2). It relies entirely on symbolic methods, such as dataset statistics, predefined rules, and heuristics to make optimization decisions.

Fully Learned Optimizer At the far end of the spectrum, this represents a fully learned query optimizer that relies entirely on neural networks or other machine learning models to perform all aspects of query optimization, from cost estimation to plan selection.

Region of Neuro-Symbolic Optimizers This middle area represents a blend of symbolic and neural approaches. It includes optimizers that combine learned models with traditional symbolic components, including:

- Learned Cardinality Estimator: A neural model is used to estimate the cardinalities of intermediate query results.
- Neuro-Symbolic Cost Model: Integrates a learned model into the cost estimation process, either by learning the weights of the factors in the cost model or by combining neural estimates with traditional cost models. Currently, there are no approaches for neuro-symbolic cost models over KGs.
- Learned Cost Model: The entire cost model is replaced by a learned model, which predicts the cost of executing query plans using machine learning techniques.
- Learned Planner: The planning process itself is guided by a learned model, which suggests query plans based on data obtained from estimates or performance measurements obtained online or from past executions.

The following sections focus on the architecture of components to build neuro-symbolic optimizers and discuss limitations and open challenges of existing solutions.

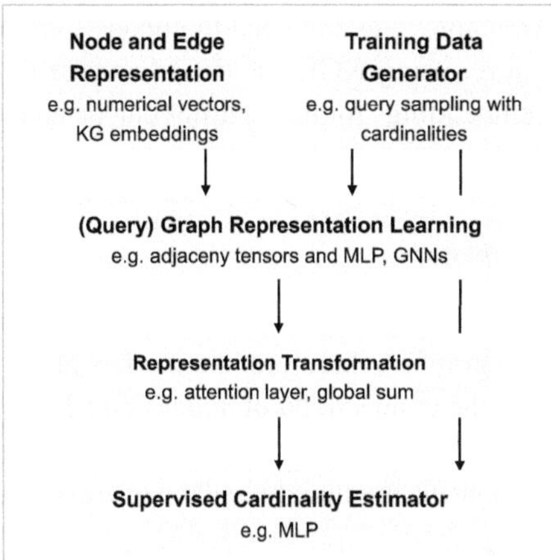

(a) Query-driven models

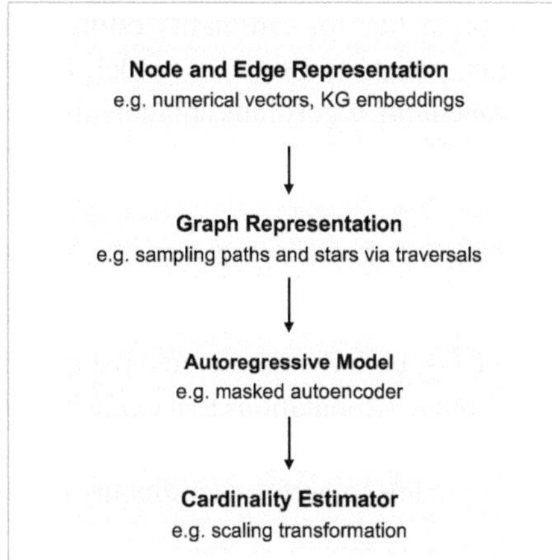

(b) Data-driven models

Figure 3. Neural architectures of learned cardinality estimators for knowledge graphs

4.2. Learned Cardinality Estimation

Different architectures can be applied to learn cardinality estimations over KGs as shown in Figure 3. In query-driven architectures (cf. Figure 3a), the model is trained in a supervised way using labeled training data, i.e., queries and their corresponding cardinalities. For this, the approaches first obtain a representation of the terms (nodes and edges) that occur in the queries and learn a representation for the queries themselves. These representations can be transformed, e.g., into a vector, and then passed to a supervised model to predict query cardinalities. In data-driven architectures (cf. Figure 3b), the model can be trained in an unsupervised way by learning the latent probability distributions of the nodes and edges in the KG. For this, the approaches traverse the KG to perform subgraph sampling. The sampled subgraphs are then used in an autoregressive model to learn the probabilities of the KG terms (nodes and edges); these probabilities are finally transformed into cardinality values by performing some scaling transformation.

4.2.1. Node and Edges Representation

The first step is to represent the entities (nodes) and predicates (edges) that occur in the input data (i.e., queries or the KG itself) in a suitable way for neural models. This is done by transforming the nodes and edges into vector-based representations.

Numerical Vector Encoding A simple approach to represent entities and predicates is to assign them a numerical ID, and then represent these IDs with binary or one-hot encoding vectors. This representation is simple but does not include any information about the meaning or interconnections of entities or predicates in the KG, forcing the subsequent model to learn the semantics of these.

Embedding-enhanced Representation To represent the individual entities and predicates that occur in the query, it is possible to use Knowledge Graph Embeddings (KGE), instead of assigning them arbitrary numerical IDs. KGE can be trained from parts of the entire KG, and capture rich information about the entities and predicates, which can thus be predictive for cardinality estimation. This alleviates the need to encode this information into the subsequent model. Furthermore, using KGE has the advantage that some embedding algorithms are inductive, i.e., embeddings for new entities can be added incrementally without requiring retraining of the existing ones.

4.2.2. Graph Representation and Cardinality Estimation

Performing cardinality estimation over KGs is inherently different from the relational case. In KGs, both the dataset and the queries are graphs[2], therefore, the models greatly benefit from representations that explicitly encode the connectivity of nodes and edges in the dataset. Multiple ways exist of encoding KGs and queries to suitably represent them to neural models to perform cardinality estimation, differing mainly in their expressivity.

Adjacency Tensors with Multilayer Perceptrons This is a rather simple encoding to represent the input data using an adjacency matrix. This representation can only be used in query modeling approaches, as the adjacency matrix of the entire KG is typically a very large and sparse structure. To represent a query, it is sufficient to use three matrices [33]. One is an adjacency tensor, to represent the graph structure of the query. The size of this tensor is fixed a priori with the maximum number of edges allowed by the model in any query. The other two matrices are also of fixed size to encode the entities and predicates that occur in a query, respectively, using vectors or embeddings as detailed in §4.2.1. These three matrices can be flattened into vectors and processed using Multilayer-Perceptrons (MLP), combined, and transformed into a cardinality estimate using another MLP [33]. This is a simple and efficient architecture, yet it has several drawbacks. First, the fixed dimensions of the MLPs implicate only queries with a (maximum) fixed number of nodes and edges can be processed by a given model, requiring training multiple models. Second, processing the adjacency tensor as a flattened vector using an MLP does not account for the permutation invariance of (query) graphs. That is, a permutation of the entities in the adjacency will still represent the same query graph but will look vastly different to the model. This requires the model to have more training data to learn this invariance, or to compute query canonical representations where permutations of the same query always produce the same representation.

Graph Neural Networks Instead of representing the KG or the graph queries using matrices, a fitting approach is to compute a representation using a Graph Neural Network (GNN). While this approach can also be applied to the entire KG, it can be challenging to scale up to very large KGs. Therefore, existing approaches instead apply it to query graphs [34, 35]. Using GNNs to represent graph structures and their connectedness has two main advantages. First, a single GNN model can process arbitrary query shapes and sizes by default, so there is no need for multiple models. Second, GNNs are permutation-invariant and thus capture commutative of joins or AND operations in query graphs, which makes these models more data efficient. The learned node representation with the GNN can then be combined, e.g., with a global sum to perform cardinality estimations using directly an MLP [34] or an attention layer followed by an MLP [35].

[2]Basic Graph Patterns in SPARQL correspond to subgraph patterns.

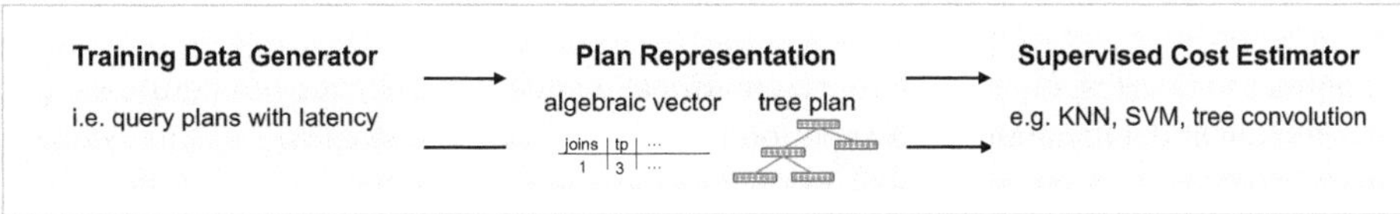

Figure 4. Architecture of learned cost models for KGs

Autoregressive Models In the context of cardinality estimation, autoregressive models learn the correlation between the nodes and edges in the KG in an unsupervised way. For this, the models perform random walks over the KG while traversing sub-structures with different shapes, e.g., stars that comprise several edges with the same subject or paths that are sequences of edges. One option is to use a masked autoencoder that predicts the probability of each term in the representation [33]. This architecture is efficient since, by masking, all probabilities can be calculated in a single model, instead of relying on sequential processing. The estimated probability of the represented data can then be turned into a cardinality, e.g., by multiplying it by the size of the KG. Nonetheless, the main limitation of this approach is that this architecture is tightly coupled to the sampled structures. In practice, autoregressive models can capture paths or stars for cardinality estimation, yet it is difficult to implement them for more complex subgraphs [33].

4.2.3. Limitations and Open Challenges

Current neural models for cardinality estimation show impressive results in terms of accuracy, but they still present several limitations. First, while the studied models are rather small in terms of parameters, training on large corpora still requires extensive time and computational resources. In particular, supervised approaches require a representative and diverse query workload to be able to generalize to new queries. Still, real-world query workloads are not always accessible, and generating diverse queries is not necessarily straightforward and can also be challenging in terms of time and resource consumption. Second, while many methods show degraded yet acceptable performance in dynamic KGs, i.e., new entities are added to the KG, substantial changes to the KG – i.e., large amounts of added entities, schema changes – require retraining the models, which hinders scalability. Hence, future work needs to develop more efficient models for rapid adaptability to dynamic data changes, e.g., embeddings or representations that are easily updatable and tailored to cardinality estimation as a downstream task.

4.3. Learned Cost Models

Current learned cost models for KGs aim to directly predict the latency or runtime of a plan before execution. These models can be directly used by the query optimizer to aid the search for plans with minimal query latency. Compared to the relational case, models for KGs face the challenges of a possibly large number of operations in the query, resulting in a larger plan to be processed and difficulty in gathering concise statistics due to the semi-structuredness and unexpected data correlations that occur in KGs. Figure 4 shows the general architecture of learned cost models for KGs.

4.3.1. Query Plan Representation

In contrast to queries, query plan representations include the sequence of operations and other technical details about the execution strategies that the system will use to evaluate a query. To enable a trained model to predict the latency of a specific query plan, it is necessary to encode the plan into a format that the model can process, as discussed below.

Algebraic and Graph Similarity Vectors Query plans can be represented using fixed vectors that encode their characteristics. Algebraic features, including the number of triple patterns, operators and their order occurring in the plan, and depth of the query tree, can be used to coarsely characterize the plan [36]. The structure of a query graph can be coarsely encoded by calculating its graph edit distances to a set of representative queries and using those distances as features [36].

Query Tree Representation Apart from these coarse representations, a plan can also be represented directly as a tree. The structure then explicitly encodes the operators and their order, and the nodes can be encoded as vectors that hold information such as the cardinality of the subtree, as well as nodes and edges instantiated in the query, etc.

4.3.2. Cost Model Predictors

Various machine learning architectures leverage the representation of query plans to estimate their latency accurately. Some architectures include simple models like k-nearest neighbors and support vector machines. More advanced methods, such as tree convolution, utilize the structural information inherent in query trees. These methods demonstrate the evolution from coarse representations to more sophisticated techniques that better capture the complexities of query execution plans.

K-Nearest Neighbors and Support Vector Machines Based on the algebraic and graph similarity vectors, various simple models like k-nearest neighbors or support vector machines can be trained to predict the latency of the represented plan [36].

Tree Convolution As the fixed-size algebraic and graph similarity vectors only encode the plan coarsely, the explicit query tree representation is a more powerful approach. For this, approaches like tree convolution can be used to process tree-structured data and, thus, capture all information in the representation [37]. Such a model can also be trained in a supervised way using the tree representations of queries and the corresponding latency. In experiments, using a tree convolution with algebraic and graph-similarity features leads to a three-fold improvement over just using the coarse features.

4.3.3. Limitations and Open Challenges

Compared to approaches for relational databases, fewer approaches exist for learned cost estimation over KGs. While existing approaches already display good results in terms of latency prediction accuracy, they can be further enhanced in terms of explicit and fine-grained representation of the query tree regarding operators and statistics about involved nodes and edges (e.g., using KG embeddings). The existing approaches also do not treat the problem of dynamic data or changes in the underlying hardware where the KG is stored, which can lead to significant changes in latency. For the latter, devising neuro-symbolic cardinality estimators is a promising direction, as they allow for decoupling the impact on the cost of the algebraic aspects of the query plan and the technical characteristics of the hardware used to store and manage the KG.

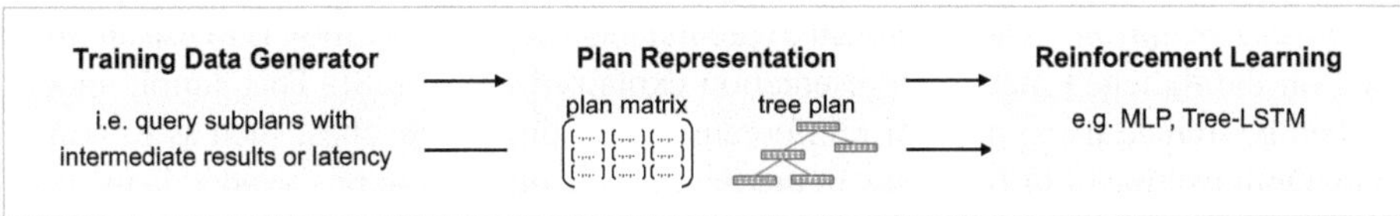

Figure 5. Architecture of learned plan traversal models for KG

4.4. Learned Plan Traversal

Learned end-to-end models for plan traversal in KG aim to learn a greedy heuristic for operator ordering that minimizes the query execution latency. Similar to relational databases, existing works in KG also frame this task as a reinforcement learning (RL) problem. Figure 5 shows the general architecture of a learned planner. In the RL models, the current *state* of the environment is a partially completed plan, and the model can choose as *actions* viable query operators that have not yet been included in the plan. The model is trained to optimize for a reward that correlates with the cost of the produced query plans, e.g., the number of intermediate results or the plan latency.

Unlike the relational case, the heterogeneity of KGs prevents encoding the complete database into the query plan representation, as done in the work by Marcus et al. [27]. Furthermore, queries in KGs usually contain a significantly larger number of operations (especially joins) than queries over relational databases, making them harder to optimize.

4.4.1. Plan Representation

Learned plan traversal models for KGs need to represent (sub)plans in a suitable way for reinforcement learning (RL) models. The following paragraphs discuss two common methods for encoding plans: matrix representation and query tree representation.

Matrix Representation One way to encode a (sub)plan is using a square matrix, where each entry encodes an atomic operator [38], e.g., a triple pattern for SPARQL queries or a subgraph pattern for other KG data models. Entries on the diagonal represent operators still missing in the plan, while entries on the off-diagonal either represent performed operators or placeholders indicating that the operator can or cannot be performed. In the case of triples, they can be encoded using IDs for the nodes, edges, and variables. While simple, this representation does not explicitly model the query tree and has no semantic information about the KG terms.

Query Tree Representation Like learned cost models, another way is to explicitly represent the plan as a tree, where the nodes can be enhanced with nodes and edges that occur in the query, potential KG embeddings thereof [39], and subplan cardinalities.

4.4.2. Neural Architectures

Learned planners leverage reinforcement learning to enhance and devise efficient query plans. The following paragraphs describe two specific neural network approaches – Multilayer Perceptrons (MLPs) and Tree-LSTMs – employed to predict the next operation in a query plan, each with unique capabilities and advantages.

Multilayer Perceptron One approach to predict the next join operation is to use an MLP based on the flattened matrix representation explained above [38]. This simple model can then be trained using popular reinforcement learning approaches, such as Proximal Policy Optimization or Q-Learning, to predict the next operator to be included in the plan such that the overall number of results or the query latency is minimized.

Tree-LSTM As in learned cost models, another approach is to use an architecture that can directly process a tree structure. Apart from the already introduced tree convolution is to use a Tree-LSTM that can similarly process an explicit tree structure to derive an output, in this case, the next join operation to be performed [39]. This model can be trained equally to the MLP but has a higher expressive power.

4.4.3. Limitations and Open Challenges

While current approaches for learned plan traversal show results comparable to dynamic programming while attaining a linear runtime, issues similar to learned cardinality and cost methods remain. Reinforcement learning is typically sample inefficient, and thus, a large set of query plans and their corresponding runtime is needed. Furthermore, changes to the data or the database setup make resampling the dataset and retraining the models necessary. Future approaches thus need to enhance how such models are optimized, e.g., by using fast and efficient representation learning and incorporating fast-to-obtain statistics to enable faster and less frequent learning of the models themselves. In this regard, approaches not based on reinforcement learning are also a promising avenue.

5. Challenges and Future Directions for Neuro-Symbolic Query Optimization

This chapter has presented the architecture of neuro-symbolic optimizers, where one or several symbolic components of the optimizer are entirely replaced by neural components. Another paradigm of using neural models during query optimization is to build a hybrid architecture where neural networks have a supporting role while the decision-making process is still delegated to the symbolic components. For instance, neural networks could be used to estimate the cost of a plan, which is then validated or adjusted using traditional rule-based or statistical methods. This hybrid approach can offer the benefits of neural models (e.g., learning from data) while maintaining the interpretability of symbolic methods. This hybrid architecture, however, introduces overhead during query optimization as it requires executing additional components, which hinders the overall query performance. For this reason, the goal is then to build neuro-symbolic optimizers where the neural components are first-class citizens. Besides the technical challenges already discussed in §4, in the following, we discuss further challenges and future directions to deploy neuro-symbolic query optimizers in real-world systems.

Generalization One of the key challenges in neuro-symbolic query optimization is ensuring that the models generalize well across different types of queries, dataset structures, and data distributions. A model that performs well on one type of workload may not necessarily generalize to others, particularly in the presence of novel query patterns or changes in the underlying dataset.

Future Directions:

- Hybrid data-query neural architectures: Data- and query-driven models for query optimization present inherent strengths and limitations. In particular, data-driven models can be challenging to scale up to large datasets, while query-driven models may overfit the training workload. Hence, hybrid data-query architectures can help the query-driven model generalize beyond the specific queries seen during training.
- Robust feature extraction: Improving the feature extraction process to ensure that the neural network can capture the most relevant and generalizable information of the query and database, which will reduce overfitting to specific types of queries.
- Meta-learning: Explore meta-learning approaches that enable the neural components in the query optimizer to learn how to learn. This enables quick adaption to new scenarios with minimal retraining.

Training Overhead and Scalability to Large Datasets Compared to traditional optimizer components that compute summaries or statistics, training neural components often requires a large amount of input data and significant computational resources. The training process can be time-consuming, especially for large datasets and complex queries. In particular, data-driven neural architectures may suffer from scalability over large datasets, as learning from KGs with billions of statements is currently impractical. Furthermore, especially in the case of query-driven neural architectures, training data (i.e., a query workload) that is representative and diverse is not always available.

Future Directions:

- Training data generators: Develop advanced data generators to efficiently produce large training data, e.g., KG with certain structures or queries and their costs, that is diverse and representative of various dataset states and query patterns. Furthermore, these data generators should be able to resemble realistic query workloads, incorporating common query patterns, edge cases, and noise that the optimizer might encounter in production environments.
- Hybrid data-query neural architectures: Hybrid architectures can incorporate query-level or other statistics during learning. This relieves the data-driven model from learning from large datasets and increases training efficiency.
- Efficient training algorithms: Research on more efficient training algorithms tailored to (knowledge graph) databases. For example, leveraging few-shot or transfer learning would reduce the overhead associated with training.
- Incremental learning: Focus on developing incremental learning methods that allow the optimizer to adapt and update its knowledge without retraining the neural components whenever new data or queries are introduced.

Interpretability In traditional query optimizers, the (symbolic) components are inherently interpretable. This is an important feature for database administrators who need to understand the system's decision-making process to perform fine-tuning or correcting actions. Yet, neural components often function as opaque boxes. This lack of interpretability makes it difficult for users to understand, trust, and diagnose the optimizer's behavior, particularly when it makes unexpected or suboptimal decisions.

Future Directions:

- Hybrid explainability techniques: Develop methods to provide explanations for the neural components' decision-making processes during query optimization. These methods may translate neural predictions into symbolic rules or use attention mechanisms that highlight important features of the queries or the dataset that impacted the component's output.
- User-centric tools: Build tools that allow users to query the decision process of neuro-symbolic components, thus improving trust and transparency.

Uncertainty Traditional optimizers are sensitive to misestimations and other errors that introduce uncertainty along the query optimization process and lead to suboptimal plans. Besides these inaccuracies, neuro-symbolic optimizers can also be sensitive to noise, variations in the input, or biases introduced during learning, e.g., underrepresented query types in the training workload. This uncertainty can degrade the query performance, making it crucial to ensure that these systems are robust and can quantify their own uncertainty in decision-making.

Future Directions:

- Uncertainty quantification: Develop techniques to quantify and communicate the uncertainty in the neural predictions, which could be used to trigger fallbacks to symbolic, reliable methods when uncertainty is high.
- Neuro-symbolic robust query optimization: Robust query optimization for relational databases [40] and KGs [41, 42] aims at identifying alternative, potentially non-optimal plans that are less sensitive or "robust" to optimization errors or unexpected adverse runtime conditions. Implementing neural-symbolic robust techniques requires incorporating adversarial examples during training to understand the vulnerabilities of the neural components and devise efficient plans.
- Neuro-symbolic adaptive query processing: Adaptive query processing (AQP) [3] goes beyond query optimization. AQP adjusts the behavior of the query execution schedulers when they are affected by unexpected conditions (i.e., uncertainty at runtime), e.g., suboptimal plans due to unexpected data correlations or environment unpredictability. For this, AQP implements monitoring mechanisms that collect performance feedback at runtime and take corrective actions, e.g., by changing the plan on the fly. Existing adaptive learning-based approaches [5, 43] implement simple techniques that do not scale well to different uncertainty types. Therefore, novel neuro-symbolic AQP architectures that can learn adaptivity policies are required to cope with runtime uncertainty during query processing.

6. Conclusion

In this chapter, we explored neuro-symbolic architectures for query optimization in knowledge graphs. As a relatively novel research area within database management and knowledge graph querying, this topic presents a unique intersection of symbolic reasoning and neural computation. As the literature shows, recent query optimization solutions have focused on replacing symbolic components, e.g., a cardinality estimator, with neural ones. Yet, this chapter highlighted the potential benefits of integrating symbolic and neural elements within a query optimizer. This interplay allows the optimizer to more effectively navigate the search space and devise efficient execution plans.

However, despite these promising advancements, several significant challenges remain in deploying neuro-symbolic query optimizers in real-world systems. Among these challenges are the difficulties in generalizing the neural models to handle new query workloads and dynamic updates to the dataset, which are common requirements in real-world knowledge graphs. Furthermore, when applied to large datasets, the training overhead and scalability issues of machine learning models pose substantial obstacles. Lastly, incorporating neural components into query optimizers introduces issues of interpretability and uncertainty, which hamper the tasks related to database administration and must be managed to ensure reliable and predictable query optimization and execution.

References

[1] Chaudhuri S. An overview of query optimization in relational systems. In: Proceedings of the seventeenth ACM SIGACT-SIGMOD-SIGART symposium on Principles of database systems; 1998. p. 34-43.
[2] Ibaraki T, Kameda T. On the optimal nesting order for computing n-relational joins. ACM Transactions on Database Systems (TODS). 1984;9(3):482-502.
[3] Deshpande A, Ives Z, Raman V, et al. Adaptive query processing. Foundations and Trends® in Databases. 2007;1(1):1-140.
[4] Acosta M, Vidal ME, Lampo T, Castillo J, Ruckhaus E. ANAPSID: an adaptive query processing engine for SPARQL endpoints. In: The Semantic Web–ISWC 2011: 10th International Semantic Web Conference, Bonn, Germany, October 23-27, 2011, Proceedings, Part I 10. Springer; 2011. p. 18-34.
[5] Acosta M, Vidal ME. Networks of linked data eddies: An adaptive web query processing engine for RDF data. In: The Semantic Web-ISWC 2015: 14th International Semantic Web Conference, Bethlehem, PA, USA, October 11-15, 2015, Proceedings, Part I 14. Springer; 2015. p. 111-27.
[6] Documentation P. Using EXPLAIN; 2024. Accessed: 2024-08-12. Available from: https://www.postgresql.org/docs/current/using-explain.html.
[7] Ioannidis YE. Query optimization. ACM Computing Surveys (CSUR). 1996;28(1):121-3.
[8] Sun J, Zhang J, Sun Z, Li G, Tang N. Learned cardinality estimation: a design space exploration and a comparative evaluation. Proc VLDB Endow. 2021 sep;15(1):85–97. Available from: https://doi.org/10.14778/3485450.3485459.
[9] Zhu R, Weng L, Ding B, Zhou J. Learned Query Optimizer: What is New and What is Next. In: Companion of the 2024 International Conference on Management of Data; 2024. p. 561-9.
[10] Sun J, Li G. An end-to-end learning-based cost estimator. arXiv preprint arXiv:190602560. 2019.
[11] Dutt A, Wang C, Nazi A, Kandula S, Narasayya V, Chaudhuri S. Selectivity estimation for range predicates using lightweight models. Proceedings of the VLDB Endowment. 2019;12(9):1044-57.
[12] Kipf A, Kipf T, Radke B, Leis V, Boncz P, Kemper A. Learned cardinalities: Estimating correlated joins with deep learning. arXiv preprint arXiv:180900677. 2018.
[13] Ortiz J, Balazinska M, Gehrke J, Keerthi SS. An empirical analysis of deep learning for cardinality estimation. arXiv preprint arXiv:190506425. 2019.
[14] Kim K, Jung J, Seo I, Han WS, Choi K, Chong J. Learned cardinality estimation: An in-depth study. In: Proceedings of the 2022 international conference on management of data; 2022. p. 1214-27.
[15] Hilprecht B, Schmidt A, Kulessa M, Molina A, Kersting K, Binnig C. Deepdb: Learn from data, not from queries! arXiv preprint arXiv:190900607. 2019.
[16] Yang Z, Liang E, Kamsetty A, Wu C, Duan Y, Chen X, et al. Deep unsupervised cardinality estimation. arXiv preprint arXiv:190504278. 2019.
[17] Hasan S, Thirumuruganathan S, Augustine J, Koudas N, Das G. Deep learning models for selectivity estimation of multi-attribute queries. In: Proceedings of the 2020 ACM SIGMOD International Conference on Management of Data; 2020. p. 1035-50.

[18] Wang X, Qu C, Wu W, Wang J, Zhou Q. Are we ready for learned cardinality estimation? arXiv preprint arXiv:201206743. 2020.

[19] Boulos J, Viemont Y, Ono K. A neural networks approach for query cost evaluation. Transaction of Information Processing Society of Japan. 1997;38(12):2566-75.

[20] Marcus R, Negi P, Mao H, Zhang C, Alizadeh M, Kraska T, et al. Neo: A learned query optimizer. arXiv preprint arXiv:190403711. 2019.

[21] Lan H, Bao Z, Peng Y. A survey on advancing the dbms query optimizer: Cardinality estimation, cost model, and plan enumeration. Data Science and Engineering. 2021;6:86-101.

[22] Marcus R, Papaemmanouil O. Plan-structured deep neural network models for query performance prediction. arXiv preprint arXiv:190200132. 2019.

[23] Yang J, Wu S, Zhang D, Dai J, Li F, Chen G. Rethinking Learned Cost Models: Why Start from Scratch? Proceedings of the ACM on Management of Data. 2023;1(4):1-27.

[24] Krishnan S, Yang Z, Goldberg K, Hellerstein J, Stoica I. Learning to optimize join queries with deep reinforcement learning. arXiv preprint arXiv:180803196. 2018.

[25] Ramadan M, El-Kilany A, Mokhtar HM, Sobh I. RL_QOptimizer: A Reinforcement Learning Based Query Optimizer. IEEE Access. 2022;10:70502-15.

[26] Heitz J, Stockinger K. Join query optimization with deep reinforcement learning algorithms. arXiv preprint arXiv:191111689. 2019.

[27] Marcus R, Papaemmanouil O. Deep reinforcement learning for join order enumeration. In: Proceedings of the First International Workshop on Exploiting Artificial Intelligence Techniques for Data Management; 2018. p. 1-4.

[28] Yu X, Li G, Chai C, Tang N. Reinforcement Learning with Tree-LSTM for Join Order Selection. In: 36th IEEE International Conference on Data Engineering, ICDE 2020, Dallas, TX, USA, April 20-24, 2020. IEEE; 2020. p. 1297-308. Available from: https://doi.org/10.1109/ICDE48307.2020.00116.

[29] Trummer I, Wang J, Wei Z, Maram D, Moseley S, Jo S, et al. Skinnerdb: Regret-bounded query evaluation via reinforcement learning. ACM Transactions on Database Systems (TODS). 2021;46(3):1-45.

[30] Tzoumas K, Sellis T, Jensen CS. A reinforcement learning approach for adaptive query processing. History. 2008:1-25.

[31] Zhou X, Chai C, Li G, Sun J. Database meets artificial intelligence: A survey. IEEE Transactions on Knowledge and Data Engineering. 2020;34(3):1096-116.

[32] Zloch M, Acosta M, Hienert D, Conrad S, Dietze S. Charaterizing RDF graphs through graph-based measures - framework and assessment. Semantic Web. 2021;12(5):789-812. Available from: https://doi.org/10.3233/SW-200409.

[33] Davitkova A, Gjurovski D, Michel S. LMKG: Learned Models for Cardinality Estimation in Knowledge Graphs. In: Stoyanovich J, Teubner J, Guagliardo P, Nikolic M, Pieris A, Mühlig J, et al., editors. Proceedings of the 25th International Conference on Extending Database Technology, EDBT 2022, Edinburgh, UK, March 29 - April 1, 2022. OpenProceedings.org; 2022. p. 2:169-2:182. Available from: https://doi.org/10.48786/edbt.2022.07.

[34] Schwabe T, Acosta M. Cardinality Estimation over Knowledge Graphs with Embeddings and Graph Neural Networks. Proc ACM Manag Data. 2024;2(1):44:1-44:26. Available from: https://doi.org/10.1145/3639299.

[35] Zhao K, Yu JX, Li Q, Zhang H, Rong Y. Learned sketch for subgraph counting: a holistic approach. VLDB J. 2023;32(5):937-62. Available from: https://doi.org/10.1007/s00778-023-00781-5.

[36] Zhang WE, Sheng QZ, Qin Y, Taylor K, Yao L. Learning-based SPARQL query performance modeling and prediction. World Wide Web. 2018;21(4):1015-35. Available from: https://doi.org/10.1007/s11280-017-0498-1.

[37] Casals D, Buil-Aranda C, Valle C. SPARQL query execution time prediction using Deep Learning. 2023.

[38] Warnke B, Martens K, Winker T, Groppe S, Groppe J, Adhiyaman P, et al. ReJOOSp: Reinforcement Learning for Join Order Optimization in SPARQL. Big Data and Cognitive Computing. 2024;8(7). Available from: https://www.mdpi.com/2504-2289/8/7/71.

[39] Eschauzier R, Taelman R, Morren M, Verborgh R. Reinforcement Learning-Based SPARQL Join Ordering Optimizer. In: Pesquita C, Skaf-Molli H, Efthymiou V, Kirrane S, Ngonga A, Collarana D, et al., editors. The Semantic Web: ESWC 2023 Satellite Events - Hersonissos, Crete, Greece, May 28 - June 1, 2023, Proceedings. vol. 13998 of Lecture Notes in Computer Science. Springer; 2023. p. 43-7. Available from: https://doi.org/10.1007/978-3-031-43458-7_8.

[40] Markl V, Raman V, Simmen D, Lohman G, Pirahesh H, Cilimdzic M. Robust query processing through progressive optimization. In: Proceedings of the 2004 ACM SIGMOD international conference on Management of data; 2004. p. 659-70.

[41] Heling L, Acosta M. Cost- and Robustness-Based Query Optimization for Linked Data Fragments. In: Pan JZ, Tamma VAM, d'Amato C, Janowicz K, Fu B, Polleres A, et al., editors. The Semantic Web - ISWC 2020 - 19th International Semantic Web Conference, Athens, Greece, November 2-6, 2020, Proceedings, Part I. vol. 12506 of Lecture Notes in Computer Science. Springer; 2020. p. 238-57. Available from: https://doi.org/10.1007/978-3-030-62419-4_14.

[42] Heling L, Acosta M. Robust query processing for linked data fragments. Semantic Web. 2022;13(4):623-57. Available from: https://doi.org/10.3233/SW-212888.

[43] Avnur R, Hellerstein JM. Eddies: Continuously adaptive query processing. In: Proceedings of the 2000 ACM SIGMOD international conference on Management of data; 2000. p. 261-72.

Handbook on Neurosymbolic AI and Knowledge Graphs
P. Hitzler et al. (Eds.)
IOS Press, 2025

doi:10.3233/FAIA250226

Visual Transfer Learning Using Knowledge Graphs

Sebastian MONKA [a,1], and Achim RETTINGER [b]
[a] *Bosch Center for Artificial Intelligence, Renningen, Germany*
sebastian.monka@de.bosch.com
[b] *Trier University, Trier, Germany*
rettinger@uni-trier.de
ORCiD ID: Sebastian Monka https://orcid.org/0009-0006-7983-1625, Achim Rettinger https://orcid.org/0000-0003-4950-1167

Abstract. While humans find it easy to process visual information from the real world, machines struggle with this task due to the unstructured and complex nature of the information. *Computer vision* (CV) is the approach of artificial intelligence that attempts to automatically analyze, interpret, and extract such information. Recent CV approaches mainly use *deep learning* (DL) due to its very high accuracy. DL extracts useful features from unstructured images in a training dataset to use them for specific real-world tasks. However, DL requires a large number of parameters, computational power, and meaningful training data, which can be noisy, sparse, and incomplete for specific domains. Furthermore, DL tends to learn correlations from the training data that do not occur in reality, making DNNs poorly generalizable and error-prone. Therefore, the field of visual transfer learning is seeking methods that are less dependent on training data and are thus more applicable in the constantly changing world. One idea is to enrich DL with prior knowledge. *Knowledge graphs* (KG) serve as a powerful tool for this purpose because they can formalize and organize prior knowledge based on an underlying ontological schema. They contain symbolic operations such as logic, rules, and reasoning, and can be created, adapted, and interpreted by domain experts. Due to the abstraction potential of symbols, KGs provide good prerequisites for generalizing their knowledge. To take advantage of the generalization properties of KG and the ability of DL to learn from large-scale unstructured data, attempts have long been made to combine explicit graph and implicit vector representations. However, with the recent development of knowledge graph embedding methods, where a graph is transferred into a vector space, new perspectives for a combination in vector space are opening up. This work introduces visual transfer learning using KG, with the goal of making DL approaches more generalizable, more efficient, and more interpretable through prior knowledge.

Keywords. Neuro-symbolic AI, Knowledge Graph, Deep Learning

1. Introduction

Artificial intelligence (AI) can be defined as the theory and development of computer systems capable of performing tasks that normally require human intelligence, such as visual

[1]Corresponding Author: Sebastian Monka, sebastian.monka@de.bosch.com

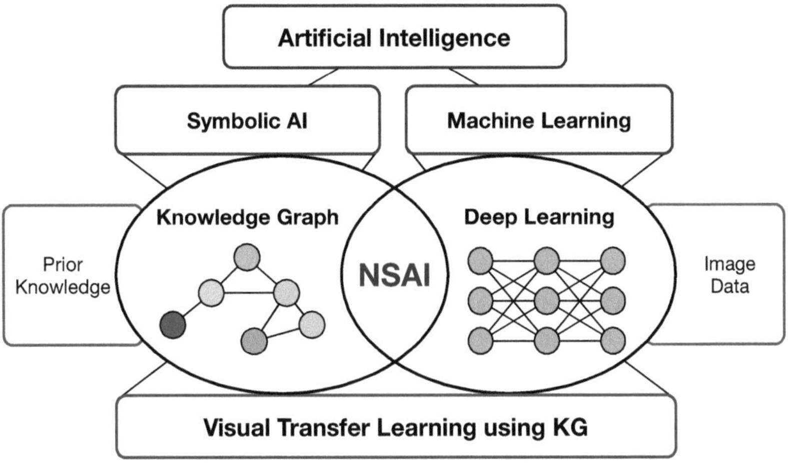

Figure 1. Visual transfer learning using KG is part of *neuro-symbolic AI* (NSAI) and combines prior knowledge with image data. While a *knowledge graph* (KG) as a representative of symbolic AI is well suited to store and process explicit prior knowledge, *deep learning* (DL) as a representative of machine learning can handle unstructured data, such as images, well.

perception, speech recognition, decision-making, and language translation [1]. While the topic of AI used to be only part of research, it has recently attracted a lot of interest from general public. From self-driving cars to virtual assistants, AI is becoming an integral part of daily lives, and its impact is expected to continue to grow in the coming years. *Computer vision* (CV) is the research area of AI that deals with the visual perception of the environment and visual transfer learning is the subfield that focuses on improving the robustness of current CV approaches to naturally occurring visual changes.

On the one hand, *deep learning* (DL), as representative of *machine learning* (ML), has gained popularity in recent years due to its very high accuracy on CV tasks. Its main strength lies in the large-scale statistical exploitation of huge amounts of unstructured data and the availability of high computational power. For this purpose, DL models, i.e. *deep neural networks* (DNN), implicitly learn highly detailed features of images based on correlations in a training dataset and use them to recognize objects in the real world. On the other hand, symbolic AI was the main driver of AI before DL gained prominence. There was a general belief that symbols are the root of intelligent action and therefore symbols should be the main topic of AI [2].

In Figure 1, we provide an overview of visual transfer learning using *knowledge graphs* (KG), which combines prior knowledge of a KG with unstructured image data encoded by DL to improve the generalization of DL. KG, as an emerging technology of symbolic AI, provide a way to encode prior knowledge about entities, including objects, events, situations, or concepts, and their various relationships in a structured way. Due to their underlying ontological schema, they use symbolic operations such as logic, rules, and reasoning, and can be created, adapted, and interpreted by human experts. A KG as a large-scale semantic network of real-world entities is therefore well suited as additional and controlled input for unstructured image data. The research area of AI that combines symbolic AI and ML is referred to as *neuro-symbolic AI* (NSAI) [3] and includes the idea of combining prior knowledge of a KG with unstructured image data encoded by DL.

1.1. Motivation

DL approaches achieve very high accuracy for a number of tasks and outperform traditional CV approaches by a large margin. Despite their widespread successes in AI-based applications like autonomous driving, they face a number of weaknesses. First, DL approaches are resource hungry. They require a large number of parameters, computational power, and expressive training data to perform well. In addition, the training data must be balanced, as well as carefully selected and labeled. Second, DL approaches have a poor ability to generalize. They tend to overfit the training data, learning spurious correlations which are not present when applying these models in the real world. Therefore, they require a training dataset that fully corresponds to the environment in which the model is used. If reality differs from the training data, DL can lead to unpredictable errors.

Visual transfer learning is the research area of CV with the goal of making DL approaches more robust to these failures and thus generalizable or transferable to related domains. Aiming to address the drawbacks of data-driven DL approaches, we consider another dimension and therefore propose to introduce prior knowledge about relevant correlations into the learning process. Prior knowledge of a domain, such as higher-level class relationships, should support DL to learn faster from the given training data but also to learn more robust features that generalize to related domains. Explicit prior knowledge is best encoded with symbolic approaches such as KGs. They can be constructed, customized, or interpreted by domain experts. Moreover, KGs are a promising technology to unify prior knowledge about domains using ubiquitous concepts and an underlying ontological schema.

Therefore, we aim to combine a KG with DL to learn meaningful representations of large-scale unstructured image data using prior knowledge. However, the combination of symbolic, i.e. KG, and subsymbolic knowledge, i.e. DL, still poses a number of serious challenges, which will be discussed in the following.

1.2. Problem Definition

DL and KG are coexisting technologies of AI that are commonly used for different problems due to their distinct strengths and weaknesses. DL, as part of ML, can make sense of highly unstructured data such as images or text using high-dimensional vector representations in a parallel manner. KGs, as part of symbolic AI, sequentially operate on symbol representations, use logic and rules, are explainable, and therefore well suited as an interface to human knowledge and experts. Due to their complementary strengths and weaknesses, the field of NSAI attempts to combine ML and symbolic AI, as illustrated in Figure 1.

However, the combination of explicit graph representations of symbolic AI and implicit vector representations of ML proves to be challenging. Therefore, most approaches to NSAI consider both fields independently. ML is responsible for extracting vector-based features from unstructured image data and transferring them into symbolic output representations, e.g. recognized entities. Symbolic AI then uses these extracted symbols to apply graph-based post-processing based on prior knowledge to improve the results. However, traditional NSAI approaches do not consider the fact that features learned by ML are highly dependent on the training data. If the domain changes, these features of the images are not recognized by DL, and symbolic post-processing no longer works. Therefore, to solve transfer learning problems other approaches need to be explored.

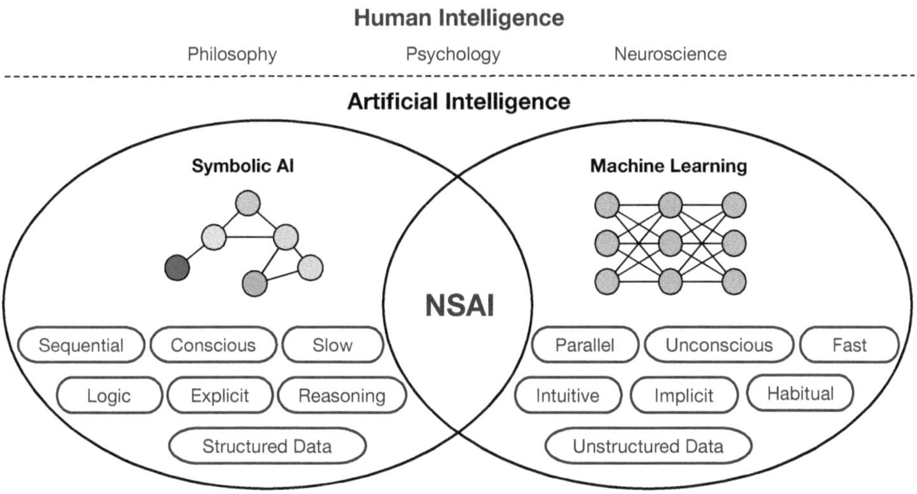

Figure 2. Prerequisites for artificial intelligence can be derived from theories of human intelligence, based on research in philosophy, psychology, and neuroscience. Human intelligence is comprised of two working processes: a sequential, conscious, and slow part, based on logic and reasoning, forming explicit representations of structured data, akin to the principles of symbolic AI. The parallel, unconscious, and fast part, based on habitual and intuitive processing, forms implicit representations of unstructured data, akin to the principles of machine learning.

With the recent development of KGE methods, where a graph is transferred into a vector space, new possibilities have emerged to combine symbolic representations, e.g. KGs, with subsymbolic ones, e.g. DL. In the context of this work, we therefore provide insights into visual transfer learning using KG.

2. Neuro-Symbolic AI

Enabling machines to behave intelligently like humans is one of the main challenges of AI. Human intelligence is often defined as the ability to achieve goals in a wide range of environments [4]. Whereas ML approaches achieve impressive results on several tasks, they can only solve problems in their specific training domains. With the goal of improving ML, other approaches to AI, like symbolic AI, came back into focus. Symbolic AI and ML have evolved separately over the years.

A KG is part of the symbolic AI, hence they make use of structured data, logic, and reasoning, and operate in an explicit and sequential manner. DL, however, is part of the ML approaches. It can leverage knowledge from unstructured data, is fast, intuitive, and operates in an implicit and parallel manner. Because of their complementary properties, recent efforts have been made to combine the two fields into one called NSAI. In this new form of AI, ML is used to develop a deep understanding of unstructured data, and symbolic AI is used to provide structure, causality, and interpretability.

Figure 2 illustrates the relation between symbolic AI and ML and their relationship to human intelligence and AI. Nowadays, NSAI mainly uses symbolic AI and ML as sequential and independent modules. However, cognitive science presumes that both fields should be connected in a hybrid and interactive manner [5]. Therefore, NSAI needs to draw inspiration from cognitive theories of human decision making [6], by enriching DL approaches with well-founded knowledge representations and reasoning capabilities [7].

In this section, we shed light on why a combination of both fields seems promising. Therefore, we introduce theories of human intelligence from philosophy, psychology, and neuroscience and link them to the properties of symbolic AI and ML. Further, we introduce the combination of KG and DL as a promising step to build NSAI models that suit the complexity of the real world.

2.1. Human Intelligence

Defining human intelligence is a widely discussed and controversial topic [8]. There are efforts from philosophy, psychology, and neuroscience to better understand the fundamentals of intelligence. These disciplines differ in their focus and approach to understanding the human mind and behavior. Whereas philosophy uses a more abstract and theoretical approach, psychology and neuroscience are empirical and data-driven. Psychology focuses on the study of behavior and mental processes, while neuroscience focuses on the biological origin of these processes.

2.1.1. Philosophy

Philosophers in ancient Greece already started to think about human intelligence. Due to Plato, intelligence is the perceptible part of the soul, and knowledge is justified true belief. He separated intelligence into discursive reason and intuitive reason [9]. The discursive reason is based on explicit steps, it is slow and based on logic and rules. Intuitive reason is a fast use of reason, drawing conclusions without going through the whole deductive process [10]. Aristotle distinguished between three types of souls, where the intellectual soul corresponds to humans and their ability to think [11]. Later, Descartes, Félix Ravaisson, and Henri Bergson defined intuition.

In general, philosophers described the brain as a system that uses symbolic logic to reason about the world [12]. If the mind goes beyond the data given, another source of information must make up the difference [13].

2.1.2. Psychology

In the 20th century, intelligence became an object of study in psychology. Jean Piaget studies the development of intelligence in children. Howard Gardner proposes a popular but controversial theory of multiple intelligences. Catell introduced 1971 the theory of fluid and crystallized intelligence [14,15].

Aligned with assumptions from philosophy [9], Kahneman [5] introduced a framework about human intelligence. He distinguished between two working principles, a *system 1* type and a *system 2* type. *System 1* is relatively slow, uses logic and reasoning, and operates in an explicit and sequential manner. *System 2* is fast, intuitive, and operates in an implicit and parallel manner. Moreover, *system 1* and *system 2* work in tandem, not as separate entities.

In psychology, it is assumed that the large majority of the skills and knowledge is learned, rather than innate [16]. However, some kind of core knowledge seems to be built into the structure of the brain, since human knowledge comes with priors [4].

2.1.3. Neuroscience

Neuroscience, as a descendant of philosophy and psychology, became an independent research field in the 20th century. In 1952 the first version of a biological *spiking neural network* (SNN), the Hodgkin–Huxley model, was introduced to explain the working principles of a network of neurons in the brain [17]. Whereas an SNN differs from the traditional artificial NN from computer science in many ways, their abstract working principles are comparable. Referring to the findings of psychology [5], neuroscientists claim that the brain is not literally divided into two systems. Moreover, these systems evolve based on higher-level abstractions. *System 1* and *system 2* work in tandem, not as separate entities, such that a single reasoning process always involves both systems. It is shown that there is no better system, both systems can be biased and make mistakes.

However, we do not yet know enough about neuroscience to literally reverse engineer the brain. AI can help to decipher the brain, rather than the other way around [18]. Since most findings are based on models comparing the brain with artificial NNs, these findings need to be taken with caution.

2.2. Artificial Intelligence

One of the ultimate goals of AI is to develop systems that possess intelligence similar to that of humans. Therefore, most AI methods draw inspiration from theories of human intelligence. While symbolic AI is oriented to the brain's sophisticated reasoning capabilities that use symbolic processing, ML focuses on the unconscious and intuitive part, where information is extracted from a variety of unstructured data. In the history of AI, there have been many debates about which AI approach is the most promising.

2.2.1. Symbolic AI

Symbolic AI focuses on human reasoning capabilities. Symbolic logic can be traced back to the rhetoric of ancient Greece, which was later developed into formal logic. The goal of formal logic was to provide a complete and rigorous foundation for mathematics, but also to produce logical representations of everyday knowledge. Nowadays, instead of the strings or trees of classical logic, graphs are increasingly used to represent knowledge. These KGs are vast graph networks that are increasingly finding applications in web search and product recommendation [12].

In general, symbolic AI is based on logic and declarative knowledge representation. It mimics human reasoning, which is why the methods are explicit and understandable to humans. Moreover, these methods thus provide an interface to the representation of expert knowledge. The approaches work with symbols, which are high-level abstractions of real-world information and are therefore able to generalize to unknown domains.

However, reasoning on symbols also has some drawbacks. For example, symbolic AI approaches are quite slow because they are sequential in nature. They require symbols based on structured data as input, which are very difficult to determine in unstructured data such as images or texts. Symbolic AI methods are therefore mostly used in controlled environments and include logic, planning, search, and optimization.

2.2.2. Machine Learning

ML is based on the idea of developing systems that, like humans, learn from observations and can thus draw conclusions about their environment. In the course of research into the learning behavior of living things, biological learning theories were formulated as early as around 1940 [19,20]. These mathematical principles were later first implemented in the perceptron [21] algorithm, in which a single neuron is trained. With the invention of the backpropagation [22] algorithm, it was possible to train deeper neural networks with one or two hidden layers, which were able to solve more complex tasks because of their higher capacity. With the further increase of neurons in additional hidden layers, data, and computational power, DL approaches [23,24,25] have been able to provide significant results for a range of tasks. Moreover, the wide application of DL in various areas of AI has earned ML a high reputation in society.

ML approaches can work with unstructured data, such as text and images. Based on raw data, they can extract recurring patterns and classify or predict them. Their strength is that they learn a model that works well in the complexity of the real world. However, they lack interpretability and explainability. They require large and well-curated datasets and have limited generalizability and robustness.

2.3. Combining Knowledge Graph and Deep Learning

Based on theories of human intelligence, as well as the complementary strengths and weaknesses of symbolic AI and ML, there is a recent trend toward NSAI. In particular, the combination of KGs, as a method of symbolic AI, and DL, as a method of ML, led to promising results.

First, the symbolic principle of the human mind, a sequential, slow, and deliberate processing of explicit, structured knowledge involving logic and reasoning, can be related to the properties of a KG. KGs work with structured data and symbolic representations, use sequential processing, and are relatively slow. They use rules, reasoning, and compositionality based on and driven by general human knowledge, resulting in general knowledge modules that can be reused for related domains.

Second, the subsymbolic principle is a parallel, rapid, and unconscious processing of implicit, unstructured knowledge that is intuitive and habitual. This principle can be associated with DL, which extracts information from unstructured data, such as text or images, and is highly parallel and fast. However, they are implicit and therefore not understandable and interactable by humans.

Although all fields of research agree that human intelligent behavior is reflected in a synergy of symbolic and subsymbolic behavior, it is still not clear whether the symbolic structure is innate or evolves from the implicit knowledge of a densely interconnected biological NN. This debate can be directly applied to the combination of KG and DL. While some argue that symbolic behavior should be explicitly modeled [26], others think that symbolic structures evolve from the DL itself [27]. These discussions raise further questions, e.g. how a future NSAI architecture should look such that the explicit knowledge in the KG can be used efficiently with DL.

3. Modalities of Data, Information, and Knowledge

The goal of AI is to enable machines to interpret and understand the world in the same way that humans do. This includes the ability to automatically analyze raw data, convert it into information about objects, and make predictions about the world.

The terms data, information, and knowledge are closely related but also have significant differences. A widely accepted definition for data, information, and knowledge is that data are character sets representing empirical stimuli or perceptions, information is a character set representing empirical knowledge, and knowledge is a character set representing the meaning of thoughts that the individual reasonably believes to be true [28]. In short, data is the raw material, information is the processed material, and knowledge is the understanding that results from processing the information.

Implicit knowledge is the form of knowledge that is gathered through experience and repetition and is hard to articulate or transfer to others. Explicit knowledge is the type of knowledge that is conscious. It can be formalized, interpreted, managed, and transmitted to others.

Moreover, data, information, and knowledge can occur in different modalities, i.e. specific forms of representation. For instance, humans work with modalities such as vision, audition, touch, etc. In the scope of this work, we focus on a more fine-grained concept of modality. Hereby, the modality of vision relates to visual representations, the modality of language to language representations, and the modality of KGs to KG representations. For the task of visual transfer learning, we further define the sources of prior knowledge, i.e. language and knowledge graph, as semantic modalities.

3.1. Vision

The modality of vision refers to data, information, and knowledge that is based on images. The generation of images or digital images is based on the fundamentals of the human visual system. The human visual system processes the light information in the eye and encodes the visual signal into electrical stimuli using neurons on the retina. Likewise, camera sensors record the visual information of the world in digital images. Most sensors transform the visual signal of the world into a continuous voltage waveform. This waveform is then converted into a digital image by sampling and quantization. Therefore, an image is not only defined by the visual input but also by the sensor and its digitization procedure.

A digital image is composed of picture elements, also called pixels. Each pixel has a finite, discrete set of numerical representations for its intensity or gray level, which is an output of its two-dimensional functions input by its spatial coordinates denoted by x, y, respectively [29]. Since images exist in a fixed-size grid structure in Euclidean space, images can be seen as a particular case of graphs with special adjacency [30].

In addition to grayscale information, images can also encode color information. Color images can be represented using various color models, e.g., RGB, CMYK, or HSI. In Figure 3 we show the discrete nature of an RGB image. An RGB image consists of discrete pixels with three channels each for the colors red, green, and blue.

Besides the structure of an image, it is also relevant what kind of information is contained in an image. The information of an image is defined by regions or parts of the image. These regions are called features and describe, among other things, color, shape,

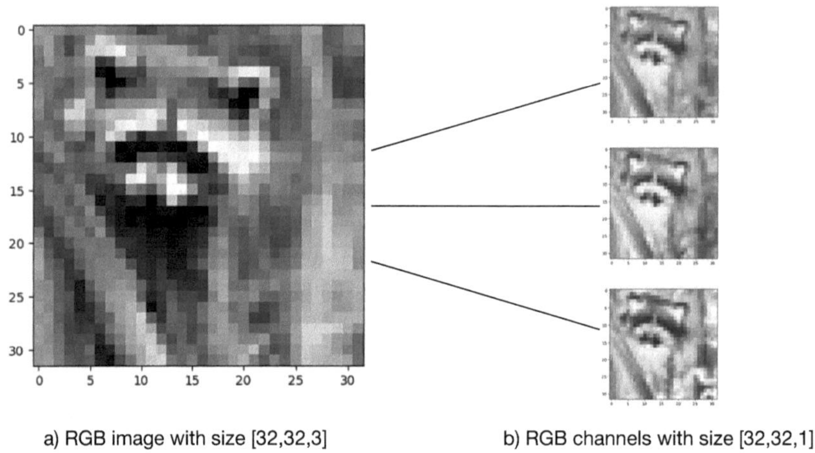

Figure 3. The modality of vision is an encoded version of the visual signal based on the light information in the real world. An RGB image is a digitized version of the visual signal and consists of pixels, here 32x32, and three RGB channels, i.e. red, green, and blue. The information in the image is comprised of the individual pixels of the channels and their correlations.

and texture [31]. Based on these features, humans, but also machines, are able to derive higher-level semantic information, e.g. objects or classes, from an image.

3.2. Language

The modality of language includes data, information, and knowledge that is based on texts. In the scope of visual transfer learning, we refer to the modality of language as a semantic modality. Humans use language data as a medium for communication and knowledge transfer.

Linguistics is the scientific study of human language and text, that investigates the structure of sentences (syntax), their meaning (semantics), the structure of words (morphology), speech sounds and equivalent gestures in sign languages (phonetics), the abstract sound system of a particular language (phonology), and how social context contributes to meaning (pragmatics) [32]. Text linguistics is a subfield of linguistics that studies language used in written or spoken texts [33]. It provides linguistic theories, concepts, and frameworks that are used to analyze text data. The subfield of computational linguistics deals with the use of computer technology to analyze and generate natural language. It provides the technical tools and methods to apply linguistic theories and concepts to large-scale text data.

As illustrated in Figure 4, text data is an extended structure of syntactic units such as words, groups, and clauses and textual units that is marked by both coherence among the elements and completion. A non-text consists of random sequences of linguistic units such as sentences, paragraphs, or sections in any temporal and spatial extension. [34] Practically, text data is a sequence of discrete tokens [35] and can be seen as a one-dimensional grid or ring graph [30]. Language is therefore a finite collection with its complexity limited by the number of letters, tokens, and words that can be represented.

To extract information from text data, rules or statistical methods are applied to extract text features. These features are, for instance, the grammatical structure, the used

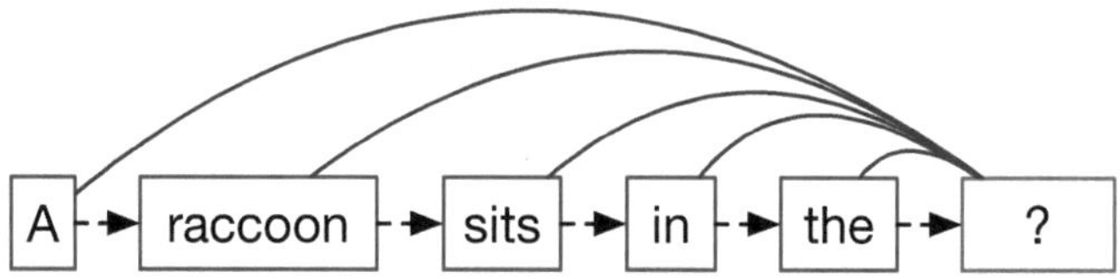

Figure 4. The modality of language has a rich underlying structure based on syntax, semantics, morphology, etc. A sentence is an extended structure of syntactic units. It consists of many features interlinking the statistical probability of a word (?) occurrence to the previous words and their order.

characters and their frequency, and co-occurrences. Based on these features, humans, as well as machines, can derive higher-level sets of information, such as meaning.

3.3. Knowledge Graph

The modality of KG describes data, information, and knowledge that is based on KGs. In the scope of visual transfer learning, we refer to the modality of KG as a semantic modality [36]. A KG is a form of a semantic network, that stores explicit knowledge in a graphical format [37]. KGs are a structured representation of facts, consisting of entities, relationships, and semantic descriptions. A comprehensive definition is given by the authors of [38] where a KG is defined as *a graph of data with the objective of accumulating and conveying real-world knowledge, where entities are represented by nodes and relationships between entities are represented by edges.* Entities can be real-world objects and abstract concepts, relationships represent the relation between entities, and semantic descriptions of entities and their relationships contain types and properties with well-defined meanings.

Knowledge can be expressed in a factual triple in the form of (head, relation, tail) or (subject, predicate, object) under the Resource Description Framework (RDF), for example, (Albert Einstein, WinnerOf, Nobel Prize). In its most basic form, we see a KG as a set of triples $G = H, R, T$, where H is a set of entities, $T \subseteq E \times L$, is a set of entities and literal values and R, set of relationships which connects H and R.

A graph model is a model which structures the data, including its schema and/or instances in form of graphs, and the data manipulation is realized by graph-based operations and adequate integrity constraints [39]. Each graph model has its formal definition based on the mathematical foundation, which can vary according to different characteristics, for instance, directed vs. undirected, labeled vs. unlabeled, etc. The most basic model is composed of labeled nodes and edges, easy to comprehend but inappropriate to encapsulate multidimensional information. Other graph models allow for the representation of information utilizing complex relationships in the form of hypernodes or hyperedges.

Table 1 illustrates three graph models, namely directed labeled graphs, hypergraphs, or hyper-relational graphs, a KG can be constructed. A KG can be based on any such graph model utilizing nodes and edges as a fundamental modeling form. To extract information or knowledge from the raw graph data, methods operate on symbolic rules or ML. Both approaches extract features in the graph data, based on regions or pieces. Such features can be for example specific combinations of nodes and relations, frequencies of their occurrences, or distinct graph structures. In the following, we discuss in detail the three common graph models used in practice to represent data graphs:

Table 1. A KG can be constructed using various graph models. The following three common graph models can be used as an underlying structure for knowledge representation in KGs: 1) Directed Labeled Graphs; 2) Hypergraphs; and 3) Hyper-relational Graphs [36].

	Directed Labeled Graphs	**Hypergraphs**	**Hyper-Relational Graphs**
Nodes and Literals	- Real-world and abstract entities - Entity's attribute value	- Real-world and abstract entities - Entity's attribute value	- Real-world and abstract entities - Entity's attribute value
Relationships	- Binary relations between entities - Relations between an entity and its attribute's values	- Binary relations between entities - Relations between an entity and its attribute's values - Many-to-many relations between entities (Hyperedge)	- Binary relations between entities - Relations between an entity and its attribute's values - Additional information encoded in a relationship (Hyper-relation)
Semantics	Connect two nodes	Connect an arbitrary set of nodes	Connect two nodes with additional contextual information
Example	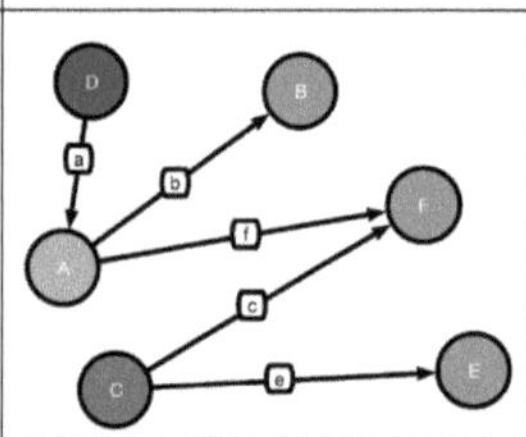	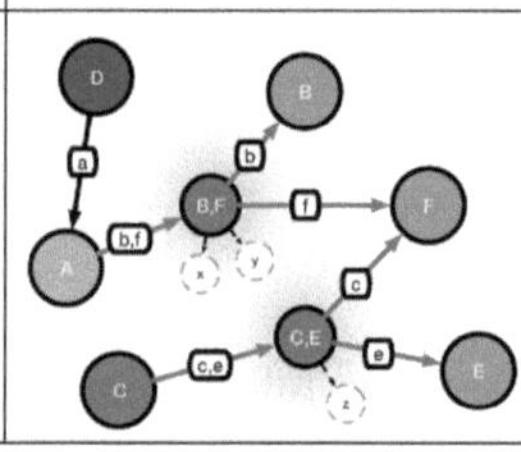	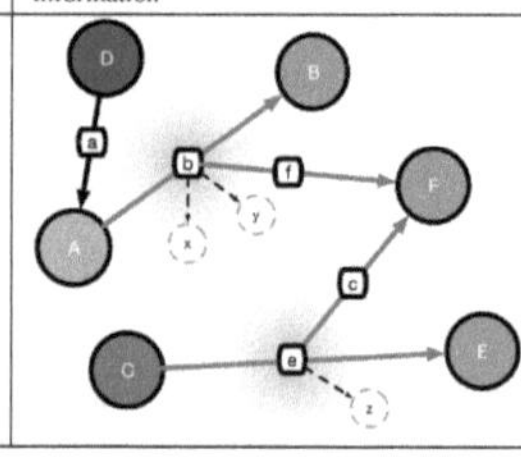

3.3.1. *Directed Labeled Graphs*

A directed labeled graph is comprised of a set of nodes and a set of edges connecting those nodes, labeled based on a specific vocabulary [39]. The direction of the edge of two paired nodes is important, which clearly distinguishes between the start node and the end node. This intuitively enables the organization of information via the utilization of binary relationships.

3.3.2. *Hypergraphs*

Hypergraphs extend the definition of binary edges by allowing the modeling of multiple and complex relationships [39]. On the other hand, hypernodes modularize the notion of a node, by allowing nesting graphs inside nodes. In addition, the notion of a hyperedge enables the definition of n-ary relations between different concepts.

3.3.3. *Hyper-Relational Graphs*

A hyper-relational graph is also a labeled directed multigraph where each node and edge might have several associated key-value pairs [40]. Internally, nodes and edges are annotated according to a chosen vocabulary and have unique identifiers, making them a flexible and powerful form of modeling for graph analysis with weighted edges.

4. Feature Extraction

A feature extractor is a transformation function from higher dimensional into lower dimensional vector space [41,42]. Since it has been shown that most downstream tasks can be solved better on a reduced dimensionality, feature extractors are also a fundamental building block of modern systems working on visual and semantic data.

However, more and more conventional feature extraction methods have been replaced with DNNs. A DNN is an artificial *neural network* (NN) with multiple layers between the input and output layers, having the ability to automatically extract lower

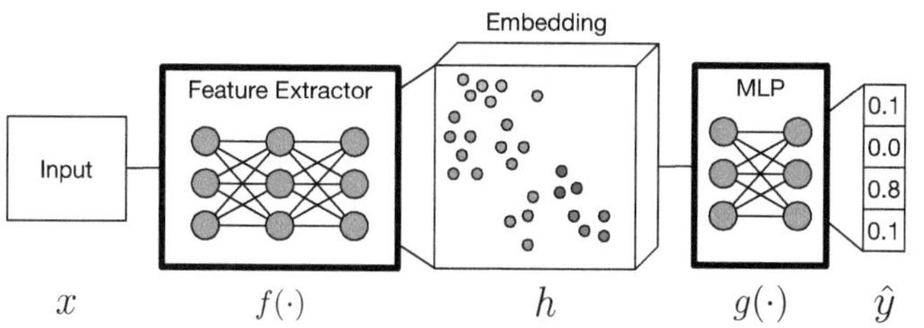

Figure 5. A DNN that takes $\vec{x}$ as input and predicts $\hat{\vec{y}}$ can be decoupled into a feature extractor $f(\cdot)$ with its embedding space $\vec{h}$ and a projection head $g(\cdot)$ [36].

dimensional features from the input data [43,44]. As depicted in Figure 5, a DNN can be decoupled in a feature extractor $f(\cdot)$, with its embedding $\vec{h}$ and a projection head $g(\cdot)$, expressing the function

$$\hat{\vec{y}} = g(f(\vec{x})). \tag{1}$$

There are different architectures of DNNs, but they always consist of the same components: neurons, synapses, weights, biases, and functions [45].

The basic architecture that builds a DNN is a *multilayer perceptron* (MLP). An MLP can be extended by modules using convolutions, recurrences, or attention. Whereas DNNs are usually trained end-to-end resulting in a task-dependent embedding space $\vec{h}$, more recently, attempts have been made to independently pre-train the feature extractor and their embedding space, such that it can be applied to several visual transfer learning downstream tasks [46].

4.1. Embedding

When referring to an embedding or embedding space we address a vector-based representation of input data. A feature extractor maps input data $\vec{x}$ to an embedding $\vec{h} = f(\vec{x}) \in \mathbb{R}^{d_E}$, where the activations of the final pooling layer and thus the representation layer have a dimensionality d_E, where d_E depends on the architecture of the feature extractor that is used. Ideally, an embedding captures the semantics of the input by placing semantically similar inputs close together in the vector space.

4.2. Projection

A projection or projection space is a transformation from the embedding to a different dimensional vector space. This transformation is done in DNNs using a projection head $g(\vec{h})$, e.g. MLP. A *projection head* $g(\cdot)$ maps the embedding $\vec{h}$ into a projection $\vec{z} = g(\vec{h}) \in \mathbb{R}^{d_P}$. For the projection network $g(\cdot)$, often a multi-layer perceptron [47] with an input dimensionality d_E, and output vector of size d_P is used. In standard end-to-end DNN training for classification, d_P is the number of predicted classes and $\vec{z} = \hat{\vec{y}}$.

4.3. Visual Features Extractor

As shown in Figure 6, feature extractors can extract different types of information and therefore occur in different forms. A visual features extractor $f_v(\cdot)$, shown in Figure 6a, is

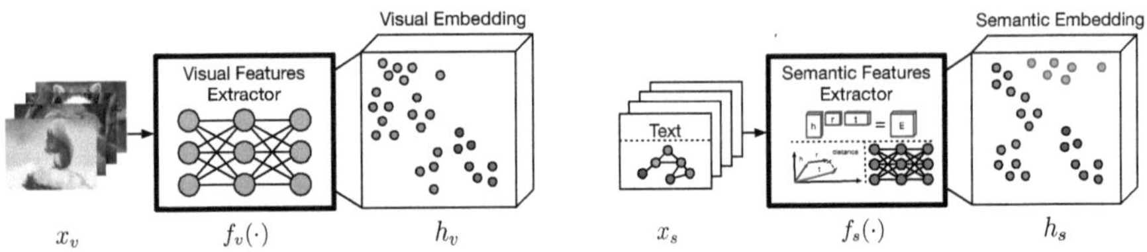

(a) Visual features extractor (b) Semantic features extractor

Figure 6. A Feature extractor transforms input data into embedding space: a) a visual features extractor transforms visual input data, i.e. images, into visual embedding space; and b) a semantic features extractor transforms semantic input data, e.g. text or graphs, into semantic embedding space [36].

a transformation function that transforms visual input data $\vec{x}_v$ from a higher-dimensional image space into a lower dimensional visual embedding space $\vec{h}_v$. A formal definition is given by

$$\vec{h}_v = f_v(\vec{x}_v), \tag{2}$$

where the final dimensionality of $\vec{h}_v$ is determined by the architecture.

Whereas early approaches used traditional visual features extractors as *scale-invariant feature transform* (SIFT)[48] or *histogram of oriented gradients* (HOG) [49], modern CV methods use almost only DNN-based approaches. Architectures of DNNs to process images are MLPs, *convolutional neural networks* (CNN), *recurrent neural networks* (RNN), and *transformers*.

Each architecture has its advantages and is therefore preferred for a particular type of input data and particular task [45]. MLPs use fully connected neurons between each layer of the network, CNNs move filter kernels over grid-structured input data to learn recurrent features and thus scale to large and computationally intensive images, RNNs use recurrent connections to process temporal information of the input data [45], and transformer models use a multi-headed attention mechanism to learn rich information of the underlying iNeunput data [50].

4.3.1. Visual Embedding

A visual embedding contains low-dimensional representations of images. Each image is therefore associated with a particular vector in the visual embedding. It has been shown that the embedding encapsulates relevant information about the images in a dense format. Therefore, the similarity of images is encoded by distances in the embedding. In a visual embedding learned from data, visually similar images are more likely to be encoded near, while visually dissimilar images are more likely to be encoded far. It is quite common to use pre-trained visual feature extractors for large image datasets and use them for related tasks.

4.4. Semantic Features Extractor

A semantic features extractor $f_s(\cdot)$, shown in Figure 6b, is a transformation function that transforms semantic input data $\vec{x}_s$ from a higher dimensional image space into a lower dimensional semantic embedding space $\vec{h}_s$ [36]. A formal definition is given by

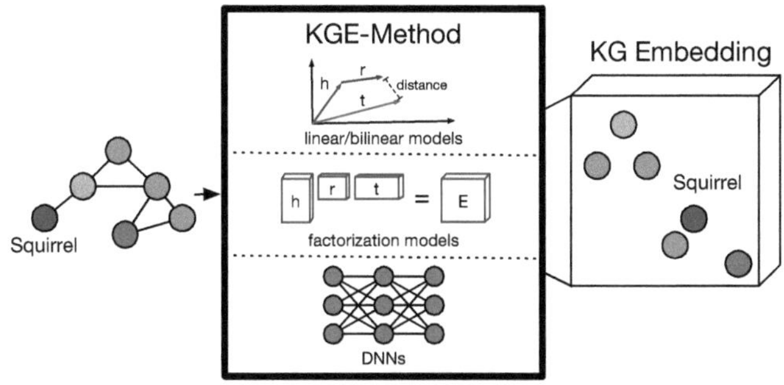

Figure 7. A KGE method transforms a *knowledge graph* (KG) into a vector-based KG embedding $\vec{h}_s$ such that each node is assigned to a position in vector space. There are many different types of KGE methods, e.g. linear/bilinear models, factorization models, or DNNs [36].

$$\vec{h}_s = f_s(\vec{x}_s), \tag{3}$$

where the final dimensionality of $\vec{h}_s$ is determined by the architecture.

The term semantic data is here used for both, unstructured data from language and structured data from a KG. Although the input data structure differs in its original format, the output of the semantic features extractor is always a low-dimensional and vector-based semantic embedding space. This similarity enables a seamless transfer from hybrid approaches of vision and language to hybrid approaches of vision and KGs.

4.4.1. Knowledge Graph Embedding

A knowledge graph embedding $\vec{h}_s$ is a representation of a KG in vector space, where close relationships between entities in a KG are reflected by local neighborhoods. KGE is generated by a KGE method $KGE(\cdot)$, which maps the entities and relations of a KG into low-dimensional vectors while capturing their semantic meanings and relations [51]. Therefore, a KGE method is a special case of the semantic features extractors $f_s(\cdot)$ that works on graph data.

In Figure 7, the general pipeline of KGE methods which transform a KG into $\vec{h}_s$ is illustrated. KGE methods can be categorized based on their learning mode and their used input format. Since most graph embedding algorithms are originally developed on tripled-based entity relations before being extended to n-ary relational data, we further divide the KGE methods into KGE methods that work on directed labeled graphs, hyper-relational graphs, and hypergraphs as introduced in Section 3.3.

4.4.2. KGE Methods - Learning Mode

Originally, KGE methods were developed to solve graph-based tasks such as node classification or link prediction. However, there is an increasing interest to apply KGE methods for visual tasks, such as classification, detection, or segmentation. We briefly categorize KGE methods therefore into unsupervised and supervised KGE methods, as Chami et al. [52] recently proposed for graph embedding algorithms.

Unsupervised KGE methods form $\vec{h}_s$ based on the inherent graph structure and the node features, without considering additional task-specific labels for the graph or its nodes. An overview of unsupervised KGE methods is given by Ji et al. [53], who categorized KGE methods based on their *representation space* (vector, matrix, and tensor space), the *scoring function* (distance-based, similarity-based), the *encoding model* (linear/bilinear models, factorization models, neural networks), and the *prior information* (text descriptions, type constraints).

In contrast, supervised KGE methods learn $\vec{h}_s$ to best predict node or graph labels. Forming $\vec{h}_s$ by using task-specific labels for the node features, $\vec{h}_s$ can be optimized for a particular task while retaining the full expressiveness of the graph. The most common supervised KGE methods are *graph neural networks* (GNN) [54]. GNNs are extensions of standard DNNs that can directly work on a graph structure as provided by a KG. For scalability reasons and to overcome challenges that arise from graph irregularities various adaptations have emerged, such as *graph convolutional networks* (GCN) [55] or *graph attention networks* (GAT) [56]. Furthermore, non-Euclidean graph convolutional methods, such as *hyperbolic graph convolutional neural networks* (HGCN) [57] are used to deal with a hierarchical structure of the input data.

4.4.3. KGE Methods - Input Type

The majority of existing KGE methods only work on directed labeled graphs, expecting binary relations in a tripled-based format [58,59,60]. However, as shown in Section 3.3, a basic triplet representation oversimplifies the complex nature of the information that can be stored in hypergraphs and hyper-relational graphs [61].

A hypergraph or hyper-relational graph can be transformed into directed labeled graphs, either by *reification* [62], that converts the graphs into binary-relation graphs, by creating additional triplets from a hyper-relational fact or by the *star-to-clique* [63] technique, that converts a tuple defined on k entities into $\binom{k}{2}$ tuples. However, these conversions lead to suboptimal and incomplete models as well as information loss. They only convert a set of key-value pairs, that are unaware of the triplet structure [61,62]. To preserve the whole expressiveness of the KG, a set of new KGE methods are developed to directly operate on hypergraphs and hyper-relational graphs.

Methods that are extended to deal with hypergraphs are HEBE [64], HGE [65], Hyper2vec [66], HNN [67], HCN [68], DHNE [69], HHNE [70], Hyper-SAGNN [71], HypE [62]. HEBE [64] aims to learn the embedding for each object in a specific heterogeneous event by representing it as a hyperedge and HGE [65] incorporates multi-way relations using Laplacian tensors. Hyper2vec [66], hypergraph neural networks [67] and hypergraph convolution networks [68] are used for hypergraph embedding, however, cannot be directly used for predicting hyperedges. In addition, DHNE [69] and HHNE [70] use an MLP as their encoding model and therefore are limited to a fixed type and size of heterogeneous hyperedges. Hyper-SAGNN [71] is based on a self-attention-based graph neural network that can predict hyperedges and deal with variable hyperedge size and HypE [62] learns positional convolutional embeddings for each entity.

Methods that embed hyper-relational graphs are m-TransH [63], HypE, HSimple [62], RAE [72], GETD [73], TuckER [74], NaLP [75], HINGE [61], StarE [76]. m-TransH [63] that uses the star-to-clique method to convert the graph to binary relations. HypE, HSimple [62] and RAE [72] convert the hyper-relational facts into n-ary facts with one abstract relation that represents all relations of the original fact. GETD [73] and TuckER [74] are tensor factorization approaches for n-ary relational facts. NaLP [75] and HINGE [61] are convolutional models that support multiple entities and relations in one fact. Recently, GNNs have been demonstrated to be capable of encoding also multi-relational KGs [77], such as StarE [76] that can encode the structure of hyper-relational graphs.

5. Inductive Biases in Deep Learning

When data and computation increase a definition of heuristic specifications becomes harder and training learning systems become more effective [78]. However, all data-driven methods such as DL use inductive biases or prior assumptions to learn a model from data, as depicted in Figure 8. For instance, they assume the smoothness of the hidden function, the translation invariance for CNNs, and a hierarchical organization principle of concepts. The no-free-lunch theorem for ML [79] basically says that some set of priors over the space of all functions is necessary to obtain generalization.

However, priors can be imperfect and therefore they needed to be collected with care [80]. KGs and other structures such as probabilistic variants of those are only one way to inject human knowledge into a model [81]. Therefore, we list inductive biases that influence intentionally and unintentionally the learning of the model. Previous work [82] describe levels of knowledge integration, based on the training data, the hypothesis set, the learning algorithm, and the final hypothesis. We explain how the labels, the data augmentation, the network architecture, and the loss function influence the learned DNN.

5.1. Dataset

The dataset on which the DNN is trained can be seen as an inductive bias. It provides the model with a set of examples to learn from, and these examples shape the model's internal representation of the problem domain. The specific patterns and regularities that are present in the dataset influence how the DNN learns from data and therefore how it generalizes to new data.

DNNs are data-driven approaches, which means that they adapt highly to the image data distribution of the training dataset. Therefore, the underlying independent and identically distributed (i.i.d.) assumptions of machine learning require the training domain to perfectly reflect the test domain. However, this strong assumption does not hold for real-world scenarios, where the test domain always differs from the training domain. Features that do occur in the training data but are not present in future testing domains are called spurious correlations.

DNNs are known to learn many spurious correlations of a training dataset, such as camera metadata or background information affecting the specific task [83]. For example, if a dataset contains a lot of images of dogs in a forest, a DNN that is trained on this dataset may learn to associate dogs with forests, rather than learning the higher-level semantics of what a dog is.

Learning spurious correlations of the dataset limits the applicability of DNNs because they do not reflect the higher-level semantics of the images. To avoid learning spurious correlations, it is important to have a balanced dataset. We further argue that a dataset needs to have a balanced distribution of samples and a balanced distribution of style to learn generalizable features that can be applied in reality.

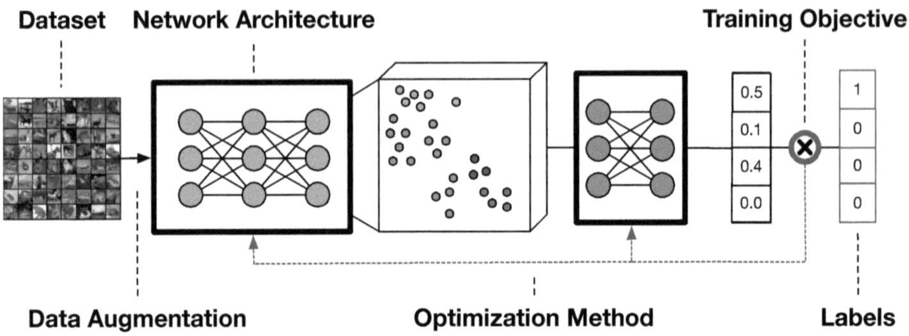

Figure 8. Inductive biases in deep learning. How a *deep neural network* (DNN) learns from data heavily depends on several inductive biases, such as the dataset, the data augmentation, the labels, the network architecture, the training objective, and the optimization method. Therefore, the combination of these inductive biases determines the performance of a DNN.

5.1.1. Distribution of Samples

Statistical learning methods, e.g. DL approaches, highly depend on the number of training samples for individual classes. Having a balanced dataset ensures prediction fairness. If the dataset is not balanced, low frequent classes will not be learned since their occurrence probability is too low. However, often low-frequent classes are important to be detected. For instance in autonomous driving, corner case scenarios contain safety-relevant information, such as dangerous traffic situations. Therefore, corner case scenarios are artificially collected or re-weighted to ensure their detection even if the data is underrepresented.

5.1.2. Distribution of Style

The style of available image datasets varies greatly. Most image datasets are collected from a variety of publicly available sources on the Internet [84]. Therefore, they contain many different styles of images, e.g. different color distributions, lighting, resolution, etc. This enables large image datasets to regularize their models in some sense. However, in autonomous driving, most datasets are collected through driving scenarios with a similar camera setup. For example, a DNN that was trained on a fisheye camera will fail if applied to a linear camera, or a model trained on grayscale images will lose performance if applied to color images.

5.2. Data Augmentation

Data augmentation is the process of changing the distribution of the input data. It is a method to artificially increase the number of data samples, but also a way to regularize a model by inducing some prior knowledge about the test domain. The goal is to avoid overfitting and to increase the performance on a target domain However, the right composition of data augmentation operations is crucial for learning good representations [85] for multiple domains.

5.2.1. Image Data Augmentation

Image data augmentation is a widely used technique in the field, where the goal is to increase the size and diversity of a training dataset in order to improve the robustness and generalization of DNNs. The process involves applying various transformations to the original images, such as color jittering, random grayscaling, rotation, flipping, and cropping, in order to simulate different real-world conditions. The survey [86] summarizes used data augmentation strategies for image data. Further authors show that the individual image augmentations are class dependent [87]. Whereas some augmentations increase the performance of some classes of a dataset, they harm the performance of others.

5.2.2. Knowledge Graph Data Augmentation

Graph augmentation refers to the process of adding new nodes, edges, or attributes to a graph representation, in order to improve its representational power or generalizability. There are various graph augmentation strategies that have been proposed in the literature, each with its own advantages and limitations. Some of these strategies include node splitting, graph addition, node embedding, and graph convolution. These methods can be used individually or in combination, depending on the specific task and the desired outcome. The survey [88] provides an overview of graph augmentation strategies.

5.3. Labels

In DL, i.e. supervise learning, the labeling of data samples plays an important role in the training of ML models. These labels describe how the DNN should interpret the individual image based on the task. For instance, in classification, the label provides the name of the object in the image. Labels can be either hard or soft, and the choice of labeling method affects the performance and interpretability of the model. Hard labels are binary or categorical representations that assign a unique class to each data sample, while soft labels are continuous or probabilistic representations that assign a probability distribution over the classes for each sample.

5.3.1. Hard-Labels

The common approach in supervised learning is to assign a hard-labels to an image. A hard label is used as one-hot encoding to a data sample, e.g. an image is a "cat". Hard labels provide a clear and decisive assignment of class membership, which makes them simple and straightforward to use in the training process. However, a hard label treats all instances of a class in a similar way and does not take into account the fact that instances of one class may be more similar to some other classes than to others.

5.3.2. Soft-Labels

Soft labels are continuous or probabilistic representations of class labels in DL [89]. Soft labels induce additional knowledge about the similarity of the image to other classes. Soft labeling comes with the assumption that assigning a discrete class to an image can be a hard task in the real world. In this labeling method, each data sample is assigned a probability distribution over the classes. For instance, if the task is image classification, a sample may be assigned a probability distribution such as [0.6, 0.3] over the classes "cat" and "dog", respectively. This means the sample is 60% likely a cat and 40% likely a dog. However, the use of soft labels can also introduce additional uncertainty and noise into the training process.

5.4. Network Architecture

Network architectures define or constrain the interaction between specific parameters in the DNN. Therefore, DNN architectures can be seen as hard constraints to the learning problem, such that specific architectures are only suited for specific tasks.

5.4.1. Spatial Dependency

Object recognition tasks rely on a strong inductive bias of spatial localization and translation invariance, such that an object is to be recognized without considering its localization in the image. For instance, CNNs make use of spatial dependency. These networks assume that important features are based on local neighborhoods. Therefore, they learn filter kernels of small size, e.g. 5x5 or 3x3, and slide them over the whole image. By sharing learned kernels they can save parameters and avoid learning correlations of unrelated far regions in the image.

5.4.2. Sequential Dependency

Sequential data in texts, or temporal data in videos, need to take previous data into consideration. These temporal dependencies can be modeled by recurrent neural networks. Typical representatives are RNNs, LSTMs, and GRUs. Their main principle is to aggregate a state over several timestamps in a dynamic environment. Hereby, it is assumed that every timestep representation is dependent on an aggregation of previous timestep representations.

5.4.3. Structural Dependency

In graph neural networks the architecture is defined by the underlying graph structure. A graphical neighborhood is defined by relationships rather than spatial distances. Every node is dependent on its connected neighbors through its relationships. Especially, for molecule synthesis or social network prediction the provided graph structure helps to constrain the problem space.

5.5. Training Objective

The training objective is also known as loss function in DL. Loss functions are mathematical functions that measure the difference between the predicted output of a model and the true output, i.e. label. The choice of a suitable loss function depends on the task at hand, as well as the type of data being used. For image-only methods, the *mean squared error* (MSE) is commonly used for regression problems, while the cross-entropy loss is used for classification problems. There are several derivatives of both basic loss functions. Since the applicable loss function depends on the task and on the modality being compared, we focus on loss functions being applied for joint embedding spaces of semantic and visual embeddings.

Aligning latent samples in high-dimensional space often leads to problems, as distances are not well defined. Therefore, a common idea is to reduce dimensionality before comparison. A projection head is a linear layer or a few-layer NN that learns to convert a higher-dimensional output into a lower-dimensional output. To use various dimensional KGE with the visual embedding space of the neural network a projection head can be integrated into the training pipeline of the DNN. Since visual and semantic information can be encoded in a vector-based embedding space forming $\vec{h}_v$ and $\vec{h}_s$, there are several training objectives to learn a joint embedding. The objectives and also DNNs are optimized using an optimization method. The optimization method minimizes an objective, that measures how far apart the ground truth from the predicted probability distribution or value is. The most common principle to derive specific objectives that are good estimators for different models is the maximum likelihood principle. These objectives can be seen as cross entropy between the empirical distribution of the training set and the probability distribution defined by model [45].

Here we present some of the basic objectives used in visual transfer learning using KG, which can be augmented with additional regularization terms or hyperparameters. There are configurations of visual and semantic embedding space that only allow certain objectives to be applied. We define $\vec{l} \in \mathbb{R}^K$ as the network's output vector (logits), and $\vec{t} \in 0,1^K$ as the one-hot encoded vector of targets, where $\|t\|_1 = 1$. We refer to visual data as x_v and semantic data as x_s, and equally to visual embedding as $\vec{h}_v$ and semantic embedding as $\vec{h}_s$.

5.5.1. The Effect on Network Layers

Recently there was the idea that a loss function can influence how the DNN learns from data. However, work [90,91] showed that the objectives have a smaller impact on the learned DNN than suspected. A loss function only influences the penultimate layers of a DNN [92]. Using centered kernel alignment to measure similarity between hidden representations of networks, they find that differences between loss functions are only visible in the last layers of the network. They look more closely at the penultimate layer representations and find that different objectives and hyperparameter combinations lead to dramatically different levels of class separation.

5.6. Pointwise Objectives

In pointwise objectives the loss function is computed for each individual data point and then aggregated to form the overall objective.

5.6.1. Softmax Cross-Entropy (CE) [93]

CE is the most common objective to learn multi-class classification tasks. The softmax represents a probability distribution over a discrete variable with K possible values, i.e. classes. CE learns the DNN end-to-end by comparing the logits $\vec{l}$ with the target vector $\vec{t}$ and is given by

$$L_{CE}(\vec{l},\vec{t}) = -\sum_{k=1}^{K} t_k \log\left(\frac{\exp(l_k)}{\sum_{j=1}^{K}\exp(l_j)}\right) \tag{4}$$

$$= -\sum_{k=1}^{K} t_k l_k + \log\sum_{k=1}^{K}\exp(l_k). \tag{5}$$

5.6.2. Mean Squared Error (MSE)

MSE is the most intuitive way of attracting two vectors and is given by

$$L_{MSE} = \frac{1}{K}\sum_{k=1}^{K}\left\|\vec{h}_{s,k} - \vec{h}_{v,k})\right\|^2. \tag{6}$$

The MSE loss calculates the Euclidean distance and maps a training image $x_{v,k}$ and its visual feature vector $h_{v,k)}$ to a semantic embedding vector $h_{s,k}$, corresponding to the same class k [94].

However, using the Euclidean distance as a metric fails in high-dimensional space [95]. An alternative metric in high dimensions is the cosine distance, which is given by $sim(\vec{u},\vec{v}) = \vec{u}^{\top}\vec{v}/\,\|\vec{u}\|\,\|\vec{v}\|$.

5.7. Pairwise Objectives

Pairwise objectives [96] always rely on the information of positive and negative samples. They have the goal to pull positive visual embedding vectors $\vec{h}_{v,p}$ to its corresponding semantic embedding anchor vector $\vec{h}_{s,a}$ and push negatives $\vec{h}_{v,n}$ away [97].

Triplet and Hinge Rank Loss [98]: The triplet and hinge rank loss requires explicit negative sampling. It uses a margin α as a regularization term and it is given by

$$L_{tri} = \sum_{n \neq p} max[0, \alpha - sim(\vec{h}_{s,a},\vec{h}_{v,p}) + sim(\vec{h}_{s,a}),\vec{h}_{v,n}]. \tag{7}$$

5.7.1. Contrastive Loss

The contrastive loss extends the triplet loss by a version of the softmax and handles multiple positives and negatives at a time and is given by

$$L_{con} = -\log\frac{\exp(sim(\vec{h}_{s,a},\vec{h}_{v,p})/\tau)}{\sum_{n=1}^{2N}\mathbb{1}_{n\neq a}\exp(sim(\vec{h}_{s,a},\vec{h}_{v,n})/\tau)}. \tag{8}$$

where, $\mathbb{1}_{n\neq a} \in \{0,1\}$ is an indicator function that returns 1 iff $n \neq a$, and $\tau > 0$ denotes a temperature parameter.

5.8. Optimization Method

The basic principle of a DNN is to adjust many parameters to map an input, i.e. image pixels, to a desired output. The process of finding the optimal set of parameters that satisfy the mapping task is called optimization. Optimization involves searching through a high-dimensional space of possible parameters, e.g. weights of the DNN, to find the optimal set that produces the lowest loss between the output of the DNN and the labels. In the context of DNNs, gradient-based methods are typically used for optimization, where each model parameter is assigned a gradient with respect to the gradient of the loss function. The individual parameter gradient provides information on how to update the parameter efficiently to minimize the overall loss.

One of the most widely used gradient-based optimization methods for DNNs is *stochastic gradient descent* (SGD) [99]. SGD is a version of gradient descent that computes the gradient of the loss function on a small batch of data at a time, rather than the entire dataset. This approach is computationally more efficient and allows for fast convergence to a good solution. However, SGD has some limitations such as the tendency to get stuck in local minima. In recent years, several extensions to SGD have been developed to improve the learning of DNNs. Some of these methods include AdaGrad, Adam, and RMSProp [100]. These optimization methods incorporate adaptive learning rates, momentum, and other advanced techniques to help the model to converge to an optimal solution. However, the choice of an appropriate optimization method depends on the characteristics of the problem being solved, as well as on other inductive biases of the DNN, such as the architecture or the distribution of the dataset.

Nearly all variants of SGD rely on back-propagation [101] as a learning algorithm to distribute the gradient of the loss to the individual parameters of the DNN, based on their influence on the final outcome. Iteratively, every parameter is assigned with a gradient and then updated in the direction to minimize the final error. It is worth noting that the optimization method heavily influences the way a DNN learns from data and that there are more and more conjectures that the human brain learns differently from data than DNNs. For example, the brain can learn from a few training examples with many neurons, while DNNs learn dense representations into a few neurons from many training examples. Moreover, there is no convincing evidence that the cortex explicitly propagates error derivatives or stores neural activities for use in a subsequent backward pass [102]. However, research on alternative learning algorithms is still in its early stages and there are not many viable alternatives that scale yet. Alternative learning algorithms are for example the Boltzmann Learning Algorithm [103] or the Forward-Forward Algorithm [102].

However, not only the optimization method itself but also the choice of hyperparameters and the initialization of the weights can have a significant impact on the performance of DNNs. Therefore, it is important to tune these parameters carefully to achieve the best possible performance.

5.8.1. Hyperparameter Selection

Hyperparameters are parameters that are set before training and are not learned during training. These include variables such as the number of layers, the number of neurons in each layer, the learning rate, and the stack size. Choosing appropriate hyperparameters is critical for a good performance of DNNs. For example, if the learning rate is set too high, the model may overshoot the optimal solution and oscillate, causing it to miss the optimal solution. On the other hand, if the learning rate is set too low, the training process may get stuck in local minima and is relatively slow. Similarly, if the DNN is too small, the DNN may not be able to capture complex patterns in the data, while if it is too large, the DNN may overfit.

However, selecting the right hyperparameters remains a challenge, and most approaches use heuristics that try different hyperparameter configurations and select the best one. A common approach to hyperparameter selection is grid search, where the user specifies a range of values for each hyperparameter and the system trains the model for each combination of values in that range. Grid search is excellent for randomly testing combinations that are known to generally perform well. Another approach is random search [104], in which the system randomly selects values from a given range for each hyperparameter and trains the model for each combination of values. Random search is excellent for discovering hyperparameter combinations that would not have been thought of intuitively, although it often takes more time to execute. Sometimes more advanced methods are used, such as Bayesian optimization and evolutionary optimization.

5.8.2. Weight Initialization

Weights are usually initialized randomly before the training process begins. The initial values of the weights can affect how fast the model converges and whether it gets stuck at a local minimum. If the initial weights are too large, the model can go into saturation and produce very small gradients, slowing down the learning process. On the other hand, if the initial weights are too small, it may take a long time for the model to converge or get stuck in local minima.

Therefore, choosing the right method to initialize the weights is important to achieve fast convergence of the model and better performance. A common approach for initializing the weights is to take the initial values from a normal distribution with a mean of 0 and a standard deviation of 1. However, this approach can lead to slow convergence and poor performance in some cases.

A better approach is to use initialization techniques specific to the activation function used in each layer. For example, the Xavier initialization method [105] scales the weights by the square root of the number of inputs to the layer, which has been shown to improve convergence and reduce the likelihood of disappearing or exploding gradients. However, the Xavier initialization method has been found to cause problems when initializing DNNs that use the *rectified linear unit* (ReLU) activation function. Another popular initialization method that can handle ReLU activations is the He initialization method [106], which scales the weights using the square root of the number of neurons in the previous layer.

6. Transfer Learning using Prior Knowledge

Transfer learning is a powerful approach to learning that enables the application of knowledge gained from one domain to another. The concept of transfer learning may have originated in educational psychology. Psychology assumes that people frequently engage in transfer learning in everyday life. They may reuse learned knowledge to better interpret new things or to learn them more quickly.

Therefore, there are also attempts to use the theory of transfer learning for DL. Since training DNNs is a rather tedious task and requires a lot of data and computational power, the idea of training a model on a source domain and reusing it for related target domains with sparse data is quite prominent in DL. Moreover, the principle of DL, where features are learned in a training domain to be applied in a test domain, implicitly requires transfer learning skills since reality is always different from the training data [107].

While DNNs tend to be highly specialized in the domain on which they were trained, this specialization may come at the cost of poor generalization to new and unknown domains [108]. Therefore, to achieve optimal performance in transfer learning for DL, it is important to strike a balance between specialization and generalization. To this end, DL approaches either try to avoid transfer learning by increasing the source domain size or focus on inducing additional biases in the learning process. The main goal is always to relax the strong training data dependency and provide additional knowledge that is valid for both source and associated target domains.

However, finding the right inductive bias for a transfer learning task is not straightforward, as the choice hardly depends on the setting, e.g. the data, the domain shift, or the model. Moreover, these inductive biases are inflexible, limited, and do not correspond to the way humans think about domains. Since humans are well suited to provide additional high-level knowledge about the relationship between the source and target domains, there is an urgent need to find such an interface that can better utilize human prior knowledge.

We hypothesize that symbolic prior knowledge about a domain is much more flexible and better suited to describe human prior knowledge and thus provide DL with additional knowledge. In this context, we introduce the notion of transfer learning using prior knowledge, where DNNs are supported with prior knowledge to decide what distinguishes a good feature from an incorrect one. Additionally, we argue that such prior knowledge can be well encoded and formalized with KGs since KGs provide the necessary tools to encode such knowledge in an explicit and implicit format. Therefore, transfer learning using KG can help to learn better-generalized DNNs and transfer knowledge across different domains and tasks. It has the potential to enable more effective and robust use of DL for many real-world applications.

6.1. Fundamentals of Transfer Learning

Transfer learning is a phenomenon that can be observed when humans interpret or learn new things, e.g. languages, music instruments, or sports. If the new task is related to a task that has been already acquired in the past, learned knowledge can be reused. However, transfer learning is not always beneficial and can be separated into positive and negative transfer. Positive transfer refers to a scenario where acquired knowledge of a source domain can be leveraged to better understand a novel target domain. Negative transfer refers to a scenario where acquired knowledge of a source domain hinders understanding a novel target domain [109]. Whether positive or negative transfer will occur may depend on several factors, such as the relevance between the source and the target domains and the learner's capacity of finding the transferable and beneficial part of the knowledge across domains. [110]. The main goal of transfer learning can be directly transferred to DL and is therefore to enable positive and avoid negative transfer.

A theoretical framework for transfer learning is presented as follows [111,112]:

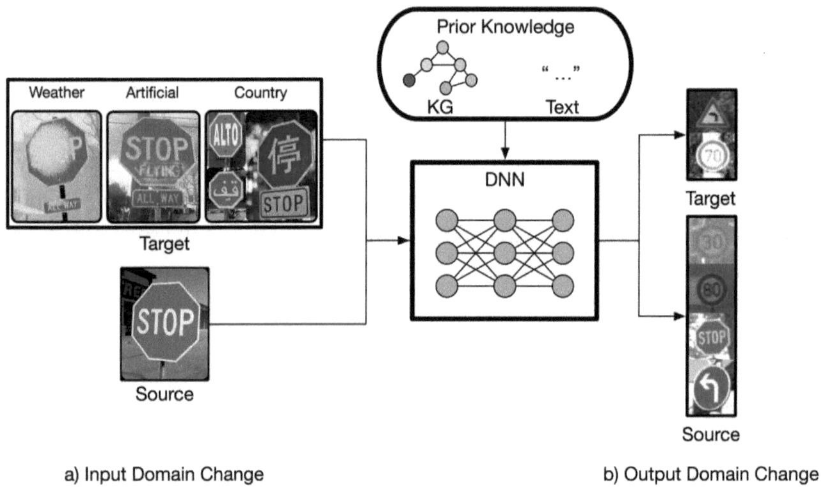

Figure 9. Transfer learning can be divided into two distinct scenarios: a) input domain change, where a distribution shift is happening in the input, and b) output domain change, where a distribution shift is happening in the output. Prior knowledge, such as knowledge graphs or textual descriptions, can help a DNN deal with these scenarios.

Given a source domain D_S with input data X_S, a corresponding source task T_S with labels Y_S, as well as a target domain D_T with input data X_T and a target task T_T with labels Y_T, the objective of transfer learning is to learn the target conditional probability distribution $P_T(Y_T|X_T)$ with the information gained from D_S and T_S where $D_S \neq D_T$ or $T_S \neq T_T$.

6.1.1. Transfer Learning Scenarios

Transfer learning can occur in two distinct scenarios, either input domain change or output domain change. Input domain change refers to scenarios, where the same type of object is represented using different but related types of input. Output domain change happens if a new type of object that is related to the initial type of object is added to the possible outputs.

Figure 9 describes both transfer learning scenarios: a) input domain change, where a distribution shift is happening in the input, and b) output domain change, where a distribution shift is happening in the output.

Input Domain Change: Input domain change refers to scenarios where the initial input changes from source to target domain. For instance, the source domain, on which the DNN was trained, contains images of road signs, and the target domain, to which the DNN is applied, contains the same road sign images deviating in terms of weather, artificial changes, or country.

The scenario of input domain change includes two distinct tasks, domain generalization, and domain adaptation. *Domain generalization* is a transfer learning task with access to labeled source domain data and unlabeled target domain data. Domain generalization aims to extract implicit knowledge of the source domain D_S and transfer this knowledge to an unknown target domain D_T [113,114]. If domain generalization has ac-

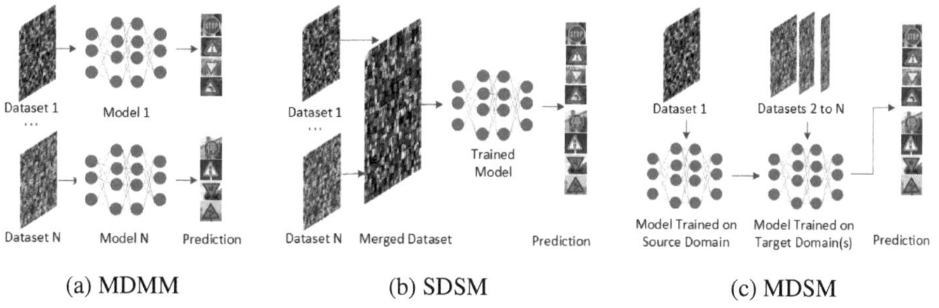

Figure 10. Strategies for handling transfer learning scenarios in DL. Approaches of DL that deal with multiple domains can be categorized into a) *Multiple Domains Multiple Models* (MDMM); b) *Single Domain Single Model* (SDSM); and c) *Multiple Domains Single Model* (MDSM).

cess to an additional set of labeled target data X_T, the task is called *domain adaptation*. Figure 9 a) shows a *stop* road sign of a source domain and various variations of the *stop* road sign of the target domain. Examples of the target domains are the same road signs with deviating weather, artificial changes, or different countries.

Output Domain Change: Output domain change refers to scenarios where the initial output changes from the source to the target domain. For example, the DNN was trained on road signs, including *speed limit 30*. When applied to a target domain, the model must also predict a *speed limit 70* that was not present in the initial domain and therefore not present at training time.

The scenario of output domain change includes two tasks, zero-shot learning, and few-shot learning. *Zero-shot learning* is a transfer learning task with labeled source domain data and unlabeled target domain data. Zero-shot learning aims to extract implicit knowledge of the classes in the source domain task T_S and transfers this knowledge to unknown classes of the target domain task T_T [111]. If zero-shot learning has access to an additional set of labeled target data X_T, the task is called *few-shot learning*. Figure 9 b) depicts road signs of a source domain and additional road signs of a target domain. The goal of the tasks is to leverage the knowledge of the source domain road signs and transfer it to the ones from the target domain.

6.1.2. Strategies in Transfer Learning

It is an open question of how to effectively deal with transfer learning scenarios in DL. Since the strong dependency on the training data is a fundamental problem of DL, there is no satisfactory solution to deal with distribution shifts so far.

DL pipelines that deal with distribution shifts can be grouped into three main categories as depicted in Figure 10: a) *Multiple Domains Multiple Models* (MDMM); b) *Single Domain Single Model* (SDSM); and c) *Multiple Domains Single Model* (MDSM). MDMM approaches treat all datasets as independent and train a respective model for each of them. Therefore, these approaches are very costly to train, and learned knowledge cannot be transferred between datasets. SDSM approaches train a single model on a large dataset merged from many smaller ones. However, it is difficult to create a balanced dataset required by the DNN to learn a general representation suitable for all domains. MDSM approaches train a single model on various datasets at different stages, and can therefore transfer learned knowledge to new domains. However, if trained with the standard cross entropy these models suffer from an unpredictable and error-prone knowledge transfer and catastrophic forgetting, where learned knowledge from previous datasets tends to be forgotten after training on the current dataset.

All approaches deal with the transfer learning problem in different ways. MDMM avoids the transfer learning problem by design, SDSM increases the source domain to also include the target domain, and MDSM needs to find relevant features that also suit the source domain. In the context of this work, transfer learning methods that need to generalize and learn transferable features are methods that belong to MDSM.

6.2. Domain Change in Deep Learning

DL as an ML technique is broadly used to successfully solve CV tasks. Its main strength lies in its ability to find complex underlying features in a given set of images. A common method for training a DNN is to minimize the *cross-entropy* (CE) loss on a training domain, which is equivalent to maximizing the negative log-likelihood between the empirical distribution of the training set and the probability distribution defined by the model. This idea relies on the *independent and identically distributed* (i.i.d.) assumptions as underlying rules of basic ML. This assumption states that the examples in each dataset are independent of each other, that train and test sets are identically distributed, and that they are drawn from the same probability distribution [45]. However, if the train and test domains follow different distributions, which means that there is a domain change, the i.i.d. assumptions are violated, and DL leads to unpredictable and poor results [115]. This has been demonstrated by using adversarially constructed examples [116] or variations in the test images such as noise, blur, and JPEG compression [117]. Moreover, it is shown [118] that the real world also contains unpredictable distribution shifts to a training and testing dataset, which can lead to critical errors in standard DNNs.

6.2.1. Specialization-Generalization Trade-off in DL

DNNs are designed to learn complex features from large datasets. This is achieved by learning complex patterns and relationships between the input and output data. The main assumption in learning from data is that any learning algorithm will generalize better on some distributions and worse on others [79]. Therefore, every learning process involves a delicate trade-off between specialization and generalization [119].

Specialization refers to the model's ability to fit the training data accurately. Therefore the model is trained to learn every individual feature that maximizes the prediction accuracy of a model on a specific task. However, if a model is too specialized, it can overfit the training data, capturing noise and random fluctuations in the data instead of the underlying patterns. Such features are also called spurious correlations of the training data. When learning these spurious correlations the model will perform well on the training dataset but poorly on the target data. The model memorized the training dataset rather than learning generalizable features. Moreover, If the model can only fit the training data, it will not be useful in real-world applications, since the real world will always deviate slightly from the training data.

Generalization is the ability of a DNN to perform well on new and unseen data. Generalization is critical because it allows the model to be useful in real-world applications. The ability to generalize well is achieved by learning the underlying patterns and relationships that are common across the training data. However, if a model is too generalized, it underfits the training data and does not capture the relevant features in the data. This results in a model that performs poorly on both source and target data, as it is unable to learn the relevant features and relationships in the data.

Therefore, the specialization-generalization trade-off is a fundamental concept in DL and also known as optimization-generalization dilemma [119]. DNNs can either specialize in fitting to the training data, leading to high accuracy on the training data but poor generalization to new data, or generalize better to new data but sacrifice accuracy on the training data. The goal of DL is to find a balance between specialization and generalization that maximizes performance on both the source and target domains. Achieving this balance is critical for the success of DNNs, as it determines their ability to learn from data and make accurate predictions in real-world applications.

6.2.2. Enabling Deep Learning to Generalize

The use of DL to handle dynamic, and changing conditions of the real world has limitations. To enable a DNN to handle such conditions it needs to be able to generalize or transfer to novel domains. Therefore, most approaches either increase the source domain to avoid transfer learning or incorporate inductive biases, such as those introduced in Section 5, into a DNN to handle the specialization-generalization trade-off.

Scaling the Source Domain: Enabling DL to generalize to novel domains is a quite challenging task due to the specialization-generalization trade-off. Therefore, one approach to make DNNs generalizable is scaling the source domain, such that a target domain will already be inside the source domain and therefore be seen at training time. As described in Section 6.1.2, we assign such models to the category SDSM. Having such a huge source domain avoids the difficult task of transfer learning in some sense. Recent methods that use that trick are for example foundation models [120] of language and vision. Through a self-supervised training task, they enable large-scale training on a huge amount of data from the Internet.

However, whereas this approach seems to provide good transfer learning results, it is quite debated if such models are leading to better transferable features. One assumption is that these models learn better-generalized features through a self-regularization due to a large amount of training data and its large variability. Another assumption is that these large models just remember the training data and that the huge domain is just a way to avoid the transfer learning problem of DL since the model has already seen data from the target domain. Therefore, it needs to be further investigated if scale can improve the transfer learning capabilities of DL.

Usage of Inductive Biases: To enable models of the category MDSM, as described in Section 6.1.2, to transfer, the learning process from unstructured data needs to be influenced. Consistent with the specialization-generalization trade-off, there are many possible solutions to a learning problem that exhibit equally performance on the training data. Given a finite training set, the only way to generalize to new input configurations is then to rely on some assumptions about the preferred solution [80]. These assumptions that guide the learning process are called inductive biases.

Inductive biases are non-learnable parts of the DNN that cause the learning algorithm to favor solutions with certain properties. In Section 5 we provided an overview of the inductive biases of DL. Inductive biases occur in various parts of the DNN, such as in the input data, augmentation methods, architecture, training objectives, labels, and optimization methods. They include assumptions such as function smoothness, translation invariance for CNNs, and a hierarchical organization of concepts as a general assumption of DL [81].

Inductive biases are mostly chosen by human intuition. For instance, if the target domain consists of just grayscale images, it is helpful to provide grayscale data augmentation to the source domain data when learning the DNN that should be applied to the target domain. Another strong inductive bias for vision is the usage of convolutional layers in CNNs, which assume for instance translation invariance such that objects and features retain their semantic meaning no matter in which part of the image they appear. Using such inductive biases DL can learn more efficient and more robust models in the real world. An important question for AI research aiming at human-level performance then is to identify relevant inductive biases for the real world. However, there is still much work to be done to improve our understanding of inductive biases and how to incorporate them into DL [80].

In summary, incorporating inductive biases into DL can help to enable transferability and generalizability. Inductive biases are parts of DNNs that are human-defined and not learned. They are highly dependent on human experts and their prior knowledge and can be seen as constraints on how DL learns from unstructured data. However, there is still much work to be done to improve our understanding and incorporate these biases effectively. Achieving a balance between specialization and generalization requires careful consideration of inductive biases and is essential for the success of DNNs in real-world applications.

6.3. Transfer Learning using Knowledge Graphs

Transfer learning using KG relates to the task of improving the transfer learning capabilities of DL using prior knowledge encoded in a KG. We introduce the effect of prior knowledge on human cognition and relate important concepts to the development of AI systems and transfer learning. Further, we show that prior knowledge can be divided into explicit and implicit knowledge and explain the different types in detail.

To use prior knowledge in combination with DL we suggest using KGs as a representation format and describe why KGs are well suited to encode prior knowledge for transfer learning. Hereby, we argue that KGs are ideal for representing prior knowledge since they are able to encode both, explicit and implicit knowledge. Therefore KGs can suit as an interface to explicit human knowledge, as well as to implicit embeddings learned from data through a KGE.

The theoretical framework for transfer learning using KG can be defined as follows:

> *Given a source domain D_S, a target domain D_T, and their corresponding tasks T_S and T_T as well as the prior knowledge represented by a KG and embedded into a latent space $\mathbf{h}_s$, the objective of a transfer learning task using a KG is to learn a probability distribution $P_{KG}(Y_T|X_T, KG)$ with the information gained from D_S and T_S where $D_S \neq D_T$ or $T_S \neq T_T$ and the prior knowledge given by KG.*

6.3.1. Types of Prior Knowledge

The concept of prior knowledge in human cognition has been used in various fields of study, such as psychology, education, and cognitive science, among others. Prior knowledge refers to knowledge that an individual has acquired before encountering a new problem or situation. It is the knowledge and experience that a person brings to a new situation that can be used to aid in learning or problem-solving. Prior knowledge has typically been shown to facilitate learning [121], increase the rate at which novel categories are learned [122], decrease prediction errors during learning, and make it possible for learners to acquire categories with a complex relational structure [123]. Prior knowledge can play an important role in learning and problem-solving by providing a foundation on which new knowledge can be built [123,124] It is assumed that prior knowledge interacts with other variables to influence learning outcomes [125].

In the context of AI and DL, prior knowledge also refers to any knowledge that exists about the problem domain before the learning process begins [81]. In this context, the term prior knowledge is also commonly used to refer to knowledge that can be leveraged to improve the performance of DL. Consistent with theories of human cognition, prior knowledge is not only important to solve transfer learning problems, but also a way to influence the way a DNN learns from unstructured data [126].

As seen in Section 6.2, most transfer learning approaches from DL address the domain shift problem by reducing dependence on source domain data through inductive biases. As shown in Section 6.2.2 inductive biases can be seen as a specific type of prior knowledge, since they influence what kind of features are learned on the training data. However, choosing the right inductive bias for a problem is a complicated and error-prone process [80]. Therefore, DL approaches also incorporate other types of prior knowledge to solve the transfer learning issue of DL. Prior knowledge can be divided into explicit and implicit knowledge [127].

Explicit Knowledge: Explicit knowledge refers to knowledge that is codified, recorded, or otherwise formalized in some tangible form that can be easily transmitted and communicated to others. It is the knowledge that can be articulated and expressed through language or other symbols, and is often easily documented, stored, and shared. We refer to explicit knowledge as a form of symbolic knowledge, that is represented and processed using symbols, such as words, numbers, or other abstractions. Explicit knowledge can be constructed, is intuitive, compositional, and controllable by human experts. Examples of explicit knowledge include information from textbooks, technical specifications, scientific articles, and other written or visual materials that convey information in a structured and systematic way often represented in graphs.

Implicit Knowledge: Implicit or tacit knowledge is often deeply ingrained in an individual's cognitive and experiential background and can be difficult to communicate to others through formal means. It is difficult to articulate or codify and is often based on personal experience, intuition, and informal interactions. Implicit knowledge is therefore embedded knowledge based on a specific context. As shown in Section 4 it can be extracted from data and stored using feature extractors, forming embeddings of different modalities using specific contexts. These embeddings are a dense representation of contextual knowledge illustrated through vectors in high-dimensional space. Therefore, implicit knowledge can encode a large amount of information efficiently.

6.3.2. Knowledge Graph as a Representation Format

As introduced in Section 3.3, KGs are an effective representation format for capturing prior knowledge. Through the development of KGE methods, they can represent both

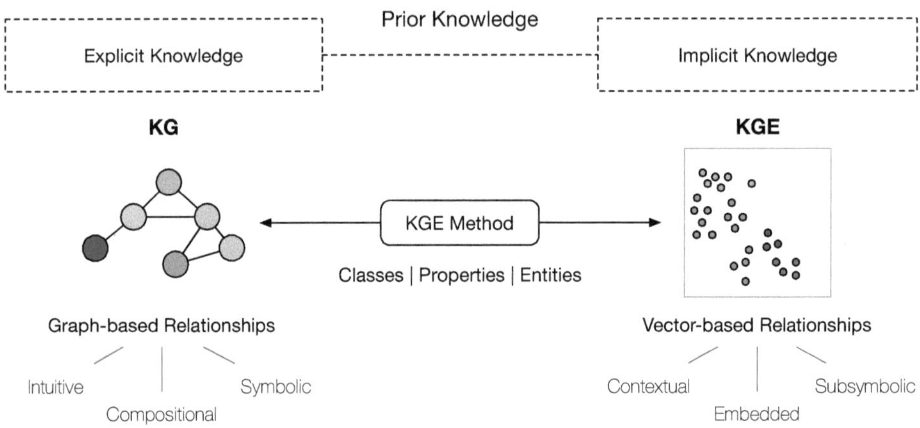

Figure 11. A *knowledge graph* (KG) can represent prior knowledge explicitly and implicitly. This makes a KG an ideal representation format for prior knowledge, as it interfaces with explicit human knowledge through its *knowledge graph embedding* (KGE) and connects to implicit embeddings of data from other modalities, such as vision or language.

implicit and explicit types of knowledge as depicted in Figure 11. To encode explicit prior knowledge, KGs use a graph-based representation format, where classes, properties, and entities are represented through nodes and their relationships through edges. These graphs allow for interaction with human experts and include underlying concepts to unify data. Due to their established tool set, KGs provide excellent preconditions for modeling, reusing, reasoning, and interlinking heterogeneous knowledge. KGs can include domain knowledge, from human experts, taxonomies, books, or other sources of data, which can be used to model classes, entities, their properties, and relationships. Since KGs offer a natural interface for encoding, modifying, and using explicit prior knowledge, they allow for a more comprehensive understanding of the domain and enable effective knowledge management.

Moreover, KGs are also able to represent their knowledge using an implicit format. With the recent development of KGE methods that transform KGs into vector spaces, the symbolic encoded prior knowledge of a KG can be transformed into an implicit representation. Therefore KGEs can be linked to implicit embeddings of data from other modalities, such as vision or language. In contrast to visual or language embeddings that are based on the collection of the underlying training data, KGE methods provide more flexibility to manually influence how the training data, i.e., the KG, is built and how the implicit knowledge is formed. As shown in Section 4.4.1, there are many different KGE methods that influence how knowledge is represented in its implicit form. Implicit knowledge of a KG, i.e. KGE, is therefore a form of knowledge represented in vector space that reflects similarities between different entities and classes based on their positions in an embedding space. Hereby, KGEs encode the knowledge about relationships of objects due to the similarities and distances in the embedding space.

In summary, A KG can represent prior knowledge explicitly and implicitly. This makes a KG an ideal representation format for prior knowledge, as it interfaces with explicit human knowledge through the KG and connects to implicit embeddings of data from other modalities, such as vision or language, through its KGE. KGs are flexible, in-

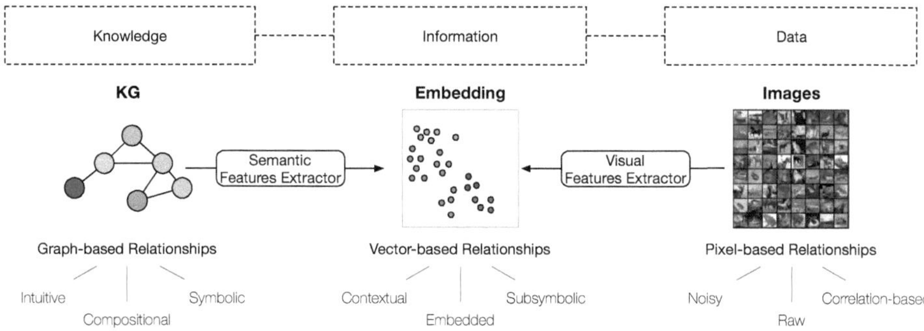

Figure 12. Combining KG and DL

terpretable, and modifiable, and come with an established toolset to build, reason, interact, and embedding heterogeneous sources of information. Therefore, KGs can be considered an ideal representational format for encoding prior knowledge for visual transfer learning.

6.4. KG and DL Combinations

The combination of KG and DL is rooted on the idea of having a joint representation in an embedding space.

As illustrated in Figure 12 we see this pipeline as the unification of data and knowledge. Therefore, data and knowledge are transferred into a joint embedding using the respective semantic or visual features extractors. Based on our definition in Section 3 we use the term information when referring to the generated embedding. As introduced in Section 4, these features extractors translate either graph-based relationships or pixel-based relationships into vector-based relationships. A joint learning process ensures that only relevant features in both modalities are used to form a joint embedding. In contrast to a DL pipeline that only relies on image data, we assume that a joint embedding of data and knowledge is based on less spurious correlations than an embedding based on data only.

As depicted in Figure 13 there are various ways how a KG can be combined with DL [36], namely *Knowledge Graph as a Reviewer*, *Knowledge Graph as a Trainee*, *Knowledge Graph as a Trainer*, and *Knowledge Graph as a Peer*.

6.4.1. Knowledge Graph as a Reviewer

Approaches of the category *Knowledge Graph as a Reviewer* arrange the visual model and the KG in sequential order. The visual output of a pre-trained DNN or its intermediate feature layers suit as an input to a graph or graph-based network. Unlike the other categories, the *KG as a Reviewer* does not learn a joint embedding space, instead, it uses the KG to reason over the independent output of a visual model [128,129,130,131].

6.4.2. Knowledge Graph as a Trainee

The *KG as a Trainee* describes a join embedding learning where the visual information is used as a supervision signal. This means that only the semantic features extractor is influenced using the unchanged visual information. The semantic-visual features ex-

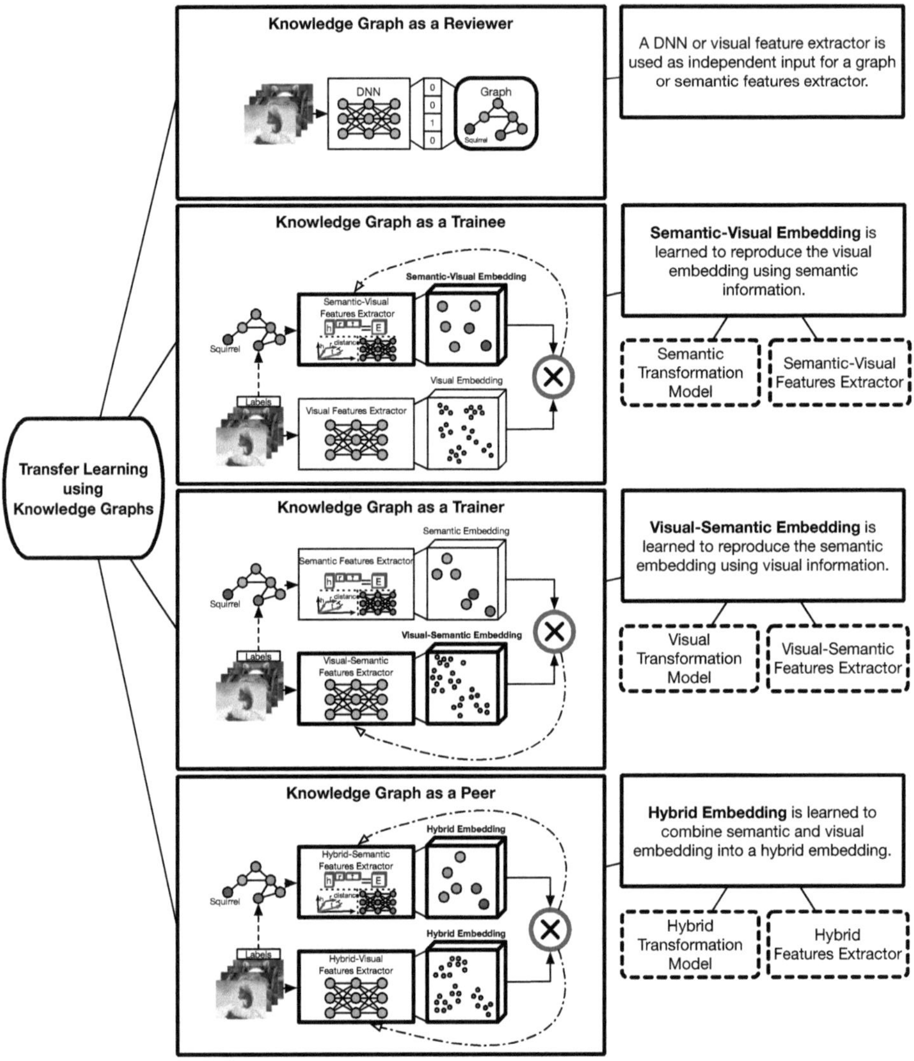

Figure 13. Visual transfer learning using KG is divided into four categories based on the role of the KG: 1) *Knowledge Graph as a Reviewer*; 2) *Knowledge Graph as a Trainee*; 3) *Knowledge Graph as a Trainer*; and 4) *Knowledge Graph as a Peer*. Each of the categories can be further separated into transformation models or feature extractors[36].

tractor learns to directly transform the KG into a semantic-visual embedding using the supervision of the visual embedding space [132,133,134,135,136,132,137,138].

6.4.3. Knowledge Graph as a Trainer

The *KG as a Trainer* describes an architecture to combine a KG and visual information. It describes a joint embedding learning where the visual features extractor is influenced by the information from the KG, whereas the semantic features extractor remains unchanged. The KG acts as a trainer and supervises the training of the DNN using, rather than letting the DNN learn a solely depending on the data distribution of the images.

We refer to such an embedding of visual information learned under the supervision of a semantic embedding as a visual-semantic embedding. To combine semantic and visual information, some approaches either learn a transformation function, e.g. MLP, on a pre-trained and fixed visual embedding or learn a visual-semantic features extractor directly [139,140,141].

6.4.4. Knowledge Graph as a Peer

The "KG as a Peer" is a joint embedding framework where both the semantic and the visual features extractor influence each other. This ensures that both modality embeddings come to an agreement which fits both best. The final hybrid embedding space is either a combination of pre-trained visual embedding and semantic embedding, using a transformation function, e.g. MLP, or a combination of hybrid-visual and hybrid-semantic features extractors. [142,143]

7. Conclusion

The combination of KG with DL is based on the discussion of combining symbolic AI with ML, and the deeper-rooted question of how to achieve artificial human intelligence. We hope that this work will help the reader to systematically combine the technology of KG with DL for developing models that benefit from the appropriate combination of semantic prior knowledge with visual information. In this work, we have shown that a KG is able to influence the behavior of a DNN. If we further learn how to fully control how the DNN learns from unstructured data, there is an opportunity to overcome the drawbacks of DL and improve future AI.

To achieve the goal of effectively using KG with DL, it will be important to further investigate the impact of knowledge structures, the relevance of KGE methods, and the role of inductive biases in the learning process. If KG-DL is supposed to be used for better and safer products, extensions to our method need to be developed that leverage data at scale, include sample-based in addition to the class-based context in the KG, fully constrain the DNN, induce explicit rules, use temporal knowledge, deal with evolving knowledge, and leverage the KG in combination with the DNN at inference time.

Scaling Models: Humans have been shown to be significantly intellectually superior to apes, yet cognitive scientists assume that the human brain may just be a scaled-up version of the primate brain [144]. The fact that scale is essential for the development of intelligent systems is also evident in recent applications of AI, such as foundation models. Foundation models are huge DNNs trained on large and diverse datasets, outperforming more specialized and optimized, but also smaller, models in most downstream NLP and CV tasks [120]. However, obtaining labeled training data can be a rather tedious, error-prone, and sometimes impossible process.

Therefore, foundation models use various tricks to train without the need for additional expensive labels, enabling them to leverage information from vast amounts of data. Foundation models for CV, e.g. CLIP [84], use the fact that most images on the Internet co-occur with additional text descriptions. CLIP uses these noisy text annotations as labels, assuming that the content of the image is at least partially described by the noisy text annotation. To relate all the heterogeneous text descriptions based on their underlying meaning, an LLM is used to transform the text description into a lower-dimensional semantic embedding. Similar to the category *KG as a Trainer*, CLIP then uses the semantic embedding to train the visual DNN. Since the major difference between CLIP and KG-NN, is the availability of large amounts of free image-text pairs, one future direction is to explore where prior KG-image pairs are already available or how they could be collected automatically.

In particular, areas such as autonomous driving, the production line, or the *Internet of things* (IoT) are promising, since huge amounts of graph-based metadata could be automatically collected with images. Moreover, we assume that a foundation model of KG-DL would lead to even more generalized features and higher accuracy, especially in visual transfer learning tasks.

Unifying Sample-based and Class-based Context: In the scope of this work, KG-NN is only trained with class-based context, i.e. each image of a class has the same representation in KGE due to its properties and its relationship to other classes in the KG. More specifically, the KG contains class-based context due to higher-level class properties, e.g., *stop sign - has shape - octagon*, *stop sign - has background color - red*, etc. However, class-based context needs expensive data labeling to define the relevant class for the images and the assumption that the information in the image is just defined by the class does not fully reflect the real world.

In reality, images of different classes can also be similar due to other visual properties. We refer to such visual properties of images as sample-based context, that describe the properties of an individual image and therefore its relationship to other images, e.g., *has camera*, *has environment*, *has location*, etc.

Moreover, Sample-based context could be manually annotated or automatically collected in many real-world applications of CV. The KG can include higher-level concepts, relating the class-based context with the sample-based context, to provide further meaning to noisy collected data. When using the *KG as a Trainer*, each image will be assigned to a specific contextual position in the semantic embedding space based on its sample and class-based context. Furthermore, we argue that unifying class-based context and sample-based context in a KG will help KG-DL models to further improve accuracy and generalization.

Constraining Models and Inducing Explicit Rules: If models should be deployed into safety-relevant products, such as autonomous driving, they should be able to follow certain constraints and obey certain rules. One of the main goals of NSAI is to enable DL to operate on fixed structures where constraints, rules, and reasoning can be applied. We argue that inducing such a structure, e.g. an ontology or a KG, into the learning process will enable DL to learn more efficiently and constrained from data. Rules, as abstractions derived from general experience, generalize well to related domains. KG-NN uses the KG to induce additional prior knowledge into DL-based learning from unstructured data. However, when transferring the KG to a vector-based KGE, the explicit rules and constraints of the KG are omitted and, if present, are only implicit.

Therefore, methods should be explored that can constrain the huge hypothesis space using structured and robust KGs in combination with unstructured text and images. Methods that can learn implicit representations from data based on explicit rules and semantic structures, will pave the way for future machine intelligence.

Using Temporal Knowledge: Temporal data provides valuable information about the motion and acceleration of objects, essential for object detection and tracking. However, temporal data also provide important information about the relationship between images, objects, and features that cannot be described without temporal dependency. Shuffling data and pretending that the image frames are i.i.d. is a false assumption and a loss of information [78]. Therefore, acquiring the temporal information is important to identify relevant correlations and avoid learning spurious correlations from the data [83]. However, video data is very complex, and DL methods can only effectively analyze single frames due to computational limitations.

We argue that KGs can serve as temporal memories that store contextual information about images, such as metadata features or objects, across multiple timestamps. If KG-DL would be able to reuse the information from a temporal KG memory during training, important correlations in single image frames could be identified, even after shuffling the data. In a temporal KG-DL, metadata for the images can be transferred to a KG that links and stores temporal information. When training the DNN, this KG metadata can be reused to allow the DNN to extract temporally relevant features and avoid learning spurious correlations.

In summary, such a method combining a temporal KG and DL can leverage temporal information to distinguish between relevant and spurious features in image data. Having such a system would enable DL to be more accurate and more robust when predicting in the real world.

Evolving Knowledge: Knowledge of the real world or specific knowledge of a domain can evolve rapidly. The main problem of DNNs is that they require a time-consuming and resource-intensive re-training process when updated with new data. For KG-NN, where the KG influences how a DNN learns, the same problem applies.

However, there are ideas on how KG-DL can deal with evolving knowledge. One possibility to deal with evolving knowledge is to extract implicit knowledge from the DNN [13] or heterogeneous knowledge from external sources and integrate it into a KG that can be updated, managed, and refined by humans. Progress has already been made in the area of KG construction by embedding and information extraction methods [145, 146,147]. This would allow the application of rules and reusable knowledge structures over detected visual features in the images.

If the goal is to process evolving unstructured data, methods must be developed to extract implicit features from DNNs, integrate these features into KGs, and either induce the evolved knowledge of the KG back into the DNN during inference or use the knowledge of the KG directly for prediction.

Using the Knowledge Graph at Inference: DNNs struggle or behave unpredictably when presented with noisy visual data during inference. In contrast, humans are able to make robust and accurate predictions by leveraging multiple sources of information at inference. For example, when driving at night on a highway, humans can predict the presence of a car by simply seeing two lights in front of them, using commonsense to fill in the gaps in their visual input.

However, DL systems rely solely on visual input and therefore fail if that input is noisy or degraded. To address this challenge, it is important to explore ways to incorporate additional knowledge into the system at inference time, especially in situations where training data is scarce.

We propose three different ideas to leverage a KG to improve the performance of DNNs during inference. The first idea involves using the *KG as a Reviewer*, where the plausibility of the output of the DNN is evaluated and constrained by the KG. The second idea involves model-agnostic fusion of modalities, in which the DNN stacks image data with vector-based prior knowledge of the KG and automatically learns how best to combine the two to solve the task. Finally, the third idea involves infusing the prior knowledge directly into the embedding space, allowing the two modalities to be combined in a way that optimizes the performance of the DNN. However, whether these methods will be helpful to improve KG-DL performance at inference needs further investigation.

Although incorporating prior knowledge from a KG into a DL system at inference is not straightforward, it will be essential to improve KG-DL performance in situations where visual data is noisy or scarce, and where humans are able to make accurate predictions by leveraging multiple sources of information.

References

[1] OED Online. *artificial intelligence, n.* Oxford University Press, 2022.
[2] Allen Newell and Herbert A. Simon. Computer science as empirical inquiry: Symbols and search. *Commun. ACM*, 19(3):113–126, mar 1976.
[3] Brenden M. Lake, Tomer D. Ullman, Joshua B. Tenenbaum, and Samuel J. Gershman. Building machines that learn and think like people. *CoRR*, abs/1604.00289, 2016.
[4] François Chollet. On the measure of intelligence. *CoRR*, abs/1911.01547, 2019.
[5] Daniel Kahneman. *Thinking, fast and slow*. Farrar, Straus and Giroux, New York, 2011.
[6] Grady Booch, Francesco Fabiano, Lior Horesh, Kiran Kate, Jonathan Lenchner, Nick Linck, Andrea Loreggia, Keerthiram Murugesan, Nicholas Mattei, Francesca Rossi, and Biplav Srivastava. Thinking fast and slow in AI. In *Thirty-Fifth AAAI Conference on Artificial Intelligence, AAAI 2021, Thirty-Third Conference on Innovative Applications of Artificial Intelligence, IAAI 2021, The Eleventh Symposium on Educational Advances in Artificial Intelligence, EAAI 2021, Virtual Event, February 2-9, 2021*, pages 15042–15046. AAAI Press, 2021.
[7] Artur S. d'Avila Garcez and Luís C. Lamb. Neurosymbolic AI: the 3rd wave. *CoRR*, abs/2012.05876, 2020.
[8] Nicolas Palanca-Castan, Beatriz Sánchez Tajadura, and Rodrigo Cofré. Towards an interdisciplinary framework about intelligence. *Heliyon*, 7(2):e06268, 2021.
[9] Plato. Diálogos iv. *Republica (Republic), Gredos*, 1988.
[10] Plato. Phaedrus. *Gredos*, 2011.
[11] Aristotele. De anima. 350 BC.
[12] Henry A. Kautz. The third AI summer: AAAI robert s. engelmore memorial lecture. *AI Mag.*, 43(1):93–104, 2022.
[13] Joshua B. Tenenbaum, Charles Kemp, Thomas L. Griffiths, and Noah D. Goodman. How to grow a mind: Statistics, structure, and abstraction. *Science*, 331(6022):1279–1285, 2011.
[14] Raymond B Cattell. Raymond b. cattell. In *A history of psychology in autobiography, Vol VI*, pages 61–100. Prentice-Hall, Inc, Englewood Cliffs, 2007.
[15] K S Mcgrew. The Cattell-Horn-Carroll theory of cognitive abilities: Past, present, and future. In D P L Flanagan & P, editor, *Contemporary Intellectual Assessment: Theories, Tests, and Issues*, pages 136–181. The Guilford Press, 2005.
[16] Elizabeth S. Spelke and Katherine D. Kinzler. Core knowledge. *Developmental Science*, 10(1):89–96, January 2007.
[17] A.L. Hodgkin and A.F. Huxley. A quantitative description of membrane current and its application to conduction and excitation in nerve. *Journal of Physiology*, 117:500–544, 1952.
[18] Gary Marcus. Deep learning: A critical appraisal. *CoRR*, abs/1801.00631, 2018.
[19] Warren S McCulloch and Walter Pitts. A logical calculus of the ideas immanent in nervous activity. *The bulletin of mathematical biophysics*, 5(4):115–133, December 1943.

[20] G L Shaw. Donald hebb: The organization of behavior. In *Brain Theory*, pages 231–233. Springer Berlin Heidelberg, 1986.
[21] F Rosenblatt. The perceptron: a probabilistic model for information storage and organization in the brain. *Psychol. Rev.*, 65(6):386–408, November 1958.
[22] David E Rumelhart, Geoffrey E Hinton, and Ronald J Williams. Learning representations by back-propagating errors. *Nature*, 323(6088):533–536, October 1986.
[23] Geoffrey E. Hinton, Simon Osindero, and Yee Whye Teh. A fast learning algorithm for deep belief nets. *Neural Comput.*, 18(7):1527–1554, 2006.
[24] Yoshua Bengio, Pascal Lamblin, Dan Popovici, and Hugo Larochelle. Greedy layer-wise training of deep networks. In Bernhard Schölkopf, John C. Platt, and Thomas Hofmann, editors, *Advances in Neural Information Processing Systems 19, Proceedings of the Twentieth Annual Conference on Neural Information Processing Systems, Vancouver, British Columbia, Canada, December 4-7, 2006*, pages 153–160. MIT Press, 2006.
[25] Marc'Aurelio Ranzato, Christopher S. Poultney, Sumit Chopra, and Yann LeCun. Efficient learning of sparse representations with an energy-based model. In Bernhard Schölkopf, John C. Platt, and Thomas Hofmann, editors, *Advances in Neural Information Processing Systems 19, Proceedings of the Twentieth Annual Conference on Neural Information Processing Systems, Vancouver, British Columbia, Canada, December 4-7, 2006*, pages 1137–1144. MIT Press, 2006.
[26] Gary Marcus and Ernest Davis. Insights for AI from the human mind. *Commun. ACM*, 64(1):38–41, 2021.
[27] Geoffrey E. Hinton. How to represent part-whole hierarchies in a neural network. *Neural Comput.*, 35(3):413–452, 2023.
[28] Chaim Zins. Conceptual approaches for defining data, information, and knowledge. *J. Assoc. Inf. Sci. Technol.*, 58(4):479–493, 2007.
[29] Rafael C. Gonzalez and Richard E. Woods. *Digital image processing*. Prentice Hall, Upper Saddle River, N.J., 2008.
[30] Michael M. Bronstein, Joan Bruna, Taco Cohen, and Petar Veličković. Geometric Deep Learning: Grids, Groups, Graphs, Geodesics, and Gauges. 2021.
[31] Robert Geirhos, Patricia Rubisch, Claudio Michaelis, Matthias Bethge, Felix A. Wichmann, and Wieland Brendel. Imagenet-trained cnns are biased towards texture; increasing shape bias improves accuracy and robustness. In *7th International Conference on Learning Representations, ICLR 2019, New Orleans, LA, USA, May 6-9, 2019*. OpenReview.net, 2019.
[32] Adrian Akmajian. *Linguistics - An Introduction to Language and Communication*. MIT Press, Cambridge, 2010.
[33] Tom B. Brown, Benjamin Mann, Nick Ryder, Melanie Subbiah, Jared Kaplan, Prafulla Dhariwal, Arvind Neelakantan, Pranav Shyam, Girish Sastry, Amanda Askell, Sandhini Agarwal, Ariel Herbert-Voss, Gretchen Krueger, Tom Henighan, Rewon Child, Aditya Ramesh, Daniel M. Ziegler, Jeffrey Wu, Clemens Winter, Christopher Hesse, Mark Chen, Eric Sigler, Mateusz Litwin, Scott Gray, Benjamin Chess, Jack Clark, Christopher Berner, Sam McCandlish, Alec Radford, Ilya Sutskever, and Dario Amodei. Language models are few-shot learners. In Hugo Larochelle, Marc'Aurelio Ranzato, Raia Hadsell, Maria-Florina Balcan, and Hsuan-Tien Lin, editors, *Advances in Neural Information Processing Systems 33: Annual Conference on Neural Information Processing Systems 2020, NeurIPS 2020, December 6-12, 2020, virtual*, 2020.
[34] Egon Werlich. A text grammar of english. 1976.
[35] Yann LeCun. A Path Towards Autonomous Machine Intelligence Version 0.9.2, 2022-06-27.
[36] Sebastian Monka, Lavdim Halilaj, and Achim Rettinger. A survey on visual transfer learning using knowledge graphs. *Semantic Web*, 13(3):477–510, 2022.
[37] John F. Sowa. Semantic Networks. 1987.
[38] Aidan Hogan, Eva Blomqvist, Michael Cochez, Claudia d'Amato, Gerard de Melo, Claudio Gutierrez, José Emilio Labra Gayo, Sabrina Kirrane, Sebastian Neumaier, Axel Polleres, Roberto Navigli, Axel-Cyrille Ngonga Ngomo, Sabbir M. Rashid, Anisa Rula, Lukas Schmelzeisen, Juan F. Sequeda, Steffen Staab, and Antoine Zimmermann. Knowledge graphs. *CoRR*, abs/2003.02320, 2020.
[39] Renzo Angles and Claudio Gutierrez. An introduction to graph data management. In George H. L. Fletcher, Jan Hidders, and Josep-Lluís Larriba-Pey, editors, *Graph Data Management, Fundamental Issues and Recent Developments*, Data-Centric Systems and Applications, pages 1–32. Springer, 2018.
[40] Renzo Angles, Harsh Thakkar, and Dominik Tomaszuk. Mapping RDF databases to property graph

databases. *IEEE Access*, 8:86091–86110, 2020.

[41] Christopher M. Bishop. *Pattern recognition and machine learning, 5th Edition*. Information science and statistics. Springer, 2007.

[42] Xuechuan Wang and Kuldip K. Paliwal. Feature extraction and dimensionality reduction algorithms and their applications in vowel recognition. *Pattern Recognit.*, 36(10):2429–2439, 2003.

[43] Geoffrey E Hinton and Ruslan R Salakhutdinov. Reducing the dimensionality of data with neural networks. *science*, 313(5786):504–507, 2006.

[44] Koray Kavukcuoglu, Marc'Aurelio Ranzato, Rob Fergus, and Yann LeCun. Learning invariant features through topographic filter maps. In *2009 IEEE Computer Society Conference on Computer Vision and Pattern Recognition (CVPR 2009), 20-25 June 2009, Miami, Florida, USA*, pages 1605–1612. IEEE Computer Society, 2009.

[45] Ian J. Goodfellow, Yoshua Bengio, and Aaron C. Courville. *Deep Learning*. Adaptive computation and machine learning. MIT Press, 2016.

[46] Ting Chen, Simon Kornblith, Kevin Swersky, Mohammad Norouzi, and Geoffrey E. Hinton. Big self-supervised models are strong semi-supervised learners. In *NeurIPS*, 2020.

[47] Trevor Hastie, Jerome H. Friedman, and Robert Tibshirani. *The Elements of Statistical Learning: Data Mining, Inference, and Prediction*. 2001.

[48] David G. Lowe. Distinctive image features from scale-invariant keypoints. *Int. J. Comput. Vis.*, 60(2):91–110, 2004.

[49] Navneet Dalal and Bill Triggs. Histograms of oriented gradients for human detection. In *2005 IEEE Computer Society Conference on Computer Vision and Pattern Recognition (CVPR 2005), 20-26 June 2005, San Diego, CA, USA*, pages 886–893. IEEE Computer Society, 2005.

[50] Ashish Vaswani, Noam Shazeer, Niki Parmar, Jakob Uszkoreit, Llion Jones, Aidan N. Gomez, Lukasz Kaiser, and Illia Polosukhin. Attention is all you need. In Isabelle Guyon, Ulrike von Luxburg, Samy Bengio, Hanna M. Wallach, Rob Fergus, S. V. N. Vishwanathan, and Roman Garnett, editors, *Advances in Neural Information Processing Systems 30: Annual Conference on Neural Information Processing Systems 2017, December 4-9, 2017, Long Beach, CA, USA*, pages 5998–6008, 2017.

[51] Quan Wang, Zhendong Mao, Bin Wang, and Li Guo. Knowledge graph embedding: A survey of approaches and applications. *IEEE Trans. Knowl. Data Eng.*, 29(12):2724–2743, 2017.

[52] Ines Chami, Sami Abu-El-Haija, Bryan Perozzi, Christopher Ré, and Kevin Murphy. Machine learning on graphs: A model and comprehensive taxonomy. *CoRR*, abs/2005.03675, 2020.

[53] Shaoxiong Ji, Shirui Pan, Erik Cambria, Pekka Marttinen, and Philip S. Yu. A survey on knowledge graphs: Representation, acquisition and applications. *CoRR*, abs/2002.00388, 2020.

[54] M. Gori, G. Monfardini, and F. Scarselli. A new model for learning in graph domains. In *Proceedings. 2005 IEEE International Joint Conference on Neural Networks, 2005.*, volume 2, pages 729–734 vol. 2, 2005.

[55] Thomas N. Kipf and Max Welling. Semi-supervised classification with graph convolutional networks. In *5th International Conference on Learning Representations, ICLR 2017, Toulon, France, April 24-26, 2017, Conference Track Proceedings*. OpenReview.net, 2017.

[56] Petar Velickovic, Guillem Cucurull, Arantxa Casanova, Adriana Romero, Pietro Liò, and Yoshua Bengio. Graph attention networks. In *6th International Conference on Learning Representations, ICLR 2018, Vancouver, BC, Canada, April 30 - May 3, 2018, Conference Track Proceedings*. OpenReview.net, 2018.

[57] Ines Chami, Zhitao Ying, Christopher Ré, and Jure Leskovec. Hyperbolic graph convolutional neural networks. In Hanna M. Wallach, Hugo Larochelle, Alina Beygelzimer, Florence d'Alché-Buc, Emily B. Fox, and Roman Garnett, editors, *Advances in Neural Information Processing Systems 32: Annual Conference on Neural Information Processing Systems 2019, NeurIPS 2019, December 8-14, 2019, Vancouver, BC, Canada*, pages 4869–4880, 2019.

[58] Antoine Bordes, Nicolas Usunier, Alberto García-Durán, Jason Weston, and Oksana Yakhnenko. Translating embeddings for modeling multi-relational data. In Christopher J. C. Burges, Léon Bottou, Zoubin Ghahramani, and Kilian Q. Weinberger, editors, *Advances in Neural Information Processing Systems 26: 27th Annual Conference on Neural Information Processing Systems 2013. Proceedings of a meeting held December 5-8, 2013, Lake Tahoe, Nevada, United States*, pages 2787–2795, 2013.

[59] Maximilian Nickel, Kevin Murphy, Volker Tresp, and Evgeniy Gabrilovich. A review of relational machine learning for knowledge graphs. *Proceedings of the IEEE*, 104(1):11–33, 2016.

[60] Mikhail Galkin, Etienne G. Denis, Jiapeng Wu, and William L. Hamilton. Nodepiece: Compositional

and parameter-efficient representations of large knowledge graphs. In *The Tenth International Conference on Learning Representations, ICLR 2022, Virtual Event, April 25-29, 2022*. OpenReview.net, 2022.

[61] Paolo Rosso, Dingqi Yang, and Philippe Cudré-Mauroux. Beyond triplets: Hyper-relational knowledge graph embedding for link prediction. In Yennun Huang, Irwin King, Tie-Yan Liu, and Maarten van Steen, editors, *WWW '20: The Web Conference 2020, Taipei, Taiwan, April 20-24, 2020*, pages 1885–1896. ACM / IW3C2, 2020.

[62] Bahare Fatemi, Perouz Taslakian, David Vázquez, and David Poole. Knowledge hypergraphs: Prediction beyond binary relations. In Christian Bessiere, editor, *Proceedings of the Twenty-Ninth International Joint Conference on Artificial Intelligence, IJCAI 2020*, pages 2191–2197. ijcai.org, 2020.

[63] Jianfeng Wen, Jianxin Li, Yongyi Mao, Shini Chen, and Richong Zhang. On the representation and embedding of knowledge bases beyond binary relations. In Subbarao Kambhampati, editor, *Proceedings of the Twenty-Fifth International Joint Conference on Artificial Intelligence, IJCAI 2016, New York, NY, USA, 9-15 July 2016*, pages 1300–1307. IJCAI/AAAI Press, 2016.

[64] Huan Gui, Jialu Liu, Fangbo Tao, Meng Jiang, Brandon Norick, and Jiawei Han. Large-scale embedding learning in heterogeneous event data. In Francesco Bonchi, Josep Domingo-Ferrer, Ricardo Baeza-Yates, Zhi-Hua Zhou, and Xindong Wu, editors, *IEEE 16th International Conference on Data Mining, ICDM 2016, December 12-15, 2016, Barcelona, Spain*, pages 907–912. IEEE Computer Society, 2016.

[65] Chia-An Yu, Ching-Lun Tai, Tak-Shing Chan, and Yi-Hsuan Yang. Modeling multi-way relations with hypergraph embedding. In Alfredo Cuzzocrea, James Allan, Norman W. Paton, Divesh Srivastava, Rakesh Agrawal, Andrei Z. Broder, Mohammed J. Zaki, K. Selçuk Candan, Alexandros Labrinidis, Assaf Schuster, and Haixun Wang, editors, *Proceedings of the 27th ACM International Conference on Information and Knowledge Management, CIKM 2018, Torino, Italy, October 22-26, 2018*, pages 1707–1710. ACM, 2018.

[66] Jie Huang, Chuan Chen, Fanghua Ye, Jiajing Wu, Zibin Zheng, and Guohui Ling. Hyper2vec: Biased random walk for hyper-network embedding. In Guoliang Li, Jun Yang, João Gama, Juggapong Natwichai, and Yongxin Tong, editors, *Database Systems for Advanced Applications - 24th International Conference, DASFAA 2019, Chiang Mai, Thailand, April 22-25, 2019, Proceedings, Part III, and DASFAA 2019 International Workshops: BDMS, BDQM, and GDMA, Chiang Mai, Thailand, April 22-25, 2019, Proceedings*, volume 11448 of *Lecture Notes in Computer Science*, pages 273–277. Springer, 2019.

[67] Yifan Feng, Haoxuan You, Zizhao Zhang, Rongrong Ji, and Yue Gao. Hypergraph neural networks. In *The Thirty-Third AAAI Conference on Artificial Intelligence, AAAI 2019, The Thirty-First Innovative Applications of Artificial Intelligence Conference, IAAI 2019, The Ninth AAAI Symposium on Educational Advances in Artificial Intelligence, EAAI 2019, Honolulu, Hawaii, USA, January 27 - February 1, 2019*, pages 3558–3565. AAAI Press, 2019.

[68] Naganand Yadati, Madhav Nimishakavi, Prateek Yadav, Vikram Nitin, Anand Louis, and Partha P. Talukdar. Hypergcn: A new method for training graph convolutional networks on hypergraphs. In Hanna M. Wallach, Hugo Larochelle, Alina Beygelzimer, Florence d'Alché-Buc, Emily B. Fox, and Roman Garnett, editors, *Advances in Neural Information Processing Systems 32: Annual Conference on Neural Information Processing Systems 2019, NeurIPS 2019, December 8-14, 2019, Vancouver, BC, Canada*, pages 1509–1520, 2019.

[69] Ke Tu, Peng Cui, Xiao Wang, Fei Wang, and Wenwu Zhu. Structural deep embedding for hyper-networks. In Sheila A. McIlraith and Kilian Q. Weinberger, editors, *Proceedings of the Thirty-Second AAAI Conference on Artificial Intelligence, (AAAI-18), the 30th innovative Applications of Artificial Intelligence (IAAI-18), and the 8th AAAI Symposium on Educational Advances in Artificial Intelligence (EAAI-18), New Orleans, Louisiana, USA, February 2-7, 2018*, pages 426–433. AAAI Press, 2018.

[70] Inci M. Baytas, Cao Xiao, Fei Wang, Anil K. Jain, and Jiayu Zhou. Heterogeneous hyper-network embedding. In *IEEE International Conference on Data Mining, ICDM 2018, Singapore, November 17-20, 2018*, pages 875–880. IEEE Computer Society, 2018.

[71] Ruochi Zhang, Yuesong Zou, and Jian Ma. Hyper-sagnn: a self-attention based graph neural network for hypergraphs. In *8th International Conference on Learning Representations, ICLR 2020, Addis Ababa, Ethiopia, April 26-30, 2020*. OpenReview.net, 2020.

[72] Richong Zhang, Junpeng Li, Jiajie Mei, and Yongyi Mao. Scalable instance reconstruction in knowledge bases via relatedness affiliated embedding. In Pierre-Antoine Champin, Fabien L. Gandon, Mou-

nia Lalmas, and Panagiotis G. Ipeirotis, editors, *Proceedings of the 2018 World Wide Web Conference on World Wide Web, WWW 2018, Lyon, France, April 23-27, 2018*, pages 1185–1194. ACM, 2018.

[73] Yu Liu, Quanming Yao, and Yong Li. Generalizing tensor decomposition for n-ary relational knowledge bases. In Yennun Huang, Irwin King, Tie-Yan Liu, and Maarten van Steen, editors, *WWW '20: The Web Conference 2020, Taipei, Taiwan, April 20-24, 2020*, pages 1104–1114. ACM / IW3C2, 2020.

[74] Ivana Balazevic, Carl Allen, and Timothy M. Hospedales. Tucker: Tensor factorization for knowledge graph completion. In Kentaro Inui, Jing Jiang, Vincent Ng, and Xiaojun Wan, editors, *Proceedings of the 2019 Conference on Empirical Methods in Natural Language Processing and the 9th International Joint Conference on Natural Language Processing, EMNLP-IJCNLP 2019, Hong Kong, China, November 3-7, 2019*, pages 5184–5193. Association for Computational Linguistics, 2019.

[75] Saiping Guan, Xiaolong Jin, Yuanzhuo Wang, and Xueqi Cheng. Link prediction on n-ary relational data. In Ling Liu, Ryen W. White, Amin Mantrach, Fabrizio Silvestri, Julian J. McAuley, Ricardo Baeza-Yates, and Leila Zia, editors, *The World Wide Web Conference, WWW 2019, San Francisco, CA, USA, May 13-17, 2019*, pages 583–593. ACM, 2019.

[76] Mikhail Galkin, Priyansh Trivedi, Gaurav Maheshwari, Ricardo Usbeck, and Jens Lehmann. Message passing for hyper-relational knowledge graphs. In Bonnie Webber, Trevor Cohn, Yulan He, and Yang Liu, editors, *Proceedings of the 2020 Conference on Empirical Methods in Natural Language Processing, EMNLP 2020, Online, November 16-20, 2020*, pages 7346–7359. Association for Computational Linguistics, 2020.

[77] Shikhar Vashishth, Soumya Sanyal, Vikram Nitin, and Partha P. Talukdar. Composition-based multi-relational graph convolutional networks. In *8th International Conference on Learning Representations, ICLR 2020, Addis Ababa, Ethiopia, April 26-30, 2020*. OpenReview.net, 2020.

[78] Leon Bottou. Learning Representation with Causal Invariance (ICLR 2019). https://leon.bottou.org/talks/invariances.

[79] D.H. Wolpert and W.G. Macready. No free lunch theorems for optimization. *IEEE Transactions on Evolutionary Computation*, 1(1):67–82, April 1997.

[80] Anirudh Goyal and Yoshua Bengio. Inductive biases for deep learning of higher-level cognition. *CoRR*, abs/2011.15091, 2020.

[81] Max Welling. Do we still need models or just more data and compute? *University of Amsterdam*, 2019.

[82] Laura von Rüden, Sebastian Mayer, Jochen Garcke, Christian Bauckhage, and Jannis Schücker. Informed machine learning - towards a taxonomy of explicit integration of knowledge into machine learning. *CoRR*, abs/1903.12394, 2019.

[83] Martin Arjovsky, Léon Bottou, Ishaan Gulrajani, and David Lopez-Paz. Invariant risk minimization. Technical report, arXiv:1907.02893, 2019.

[84] Alec Radford, Jong Wook Kim, Chris Hallacy, Aditya Ramesh, Gabriel Goh, Sandhini Agarwal, Girish Sastry, Amanda Askell, Pamela Mishkin, Jack Clark, et al. Learning transferable visual models from natural language supervision. *Image*, 2:T2, 2021.

[85] Ting Chen, Simon Kornblith, Mohammad Norouzi, and Geoffrey E. Hinton. A simple framework for contrastive learning of visual representations. In *ICML*, 2020.

[86] Connor Shorten and Taghi M. Khoshgoftaar. A survey on image data augmentation for deep learning. *J. Big Data*, 6:60, 2019.

[87] Randall Balestriero, Léon Bottou, and Yann LeCun. The effects of regularization and data augmentation are class dependent. *CoRR*, abs/2204.03632, 2022.

[88] Kaize Ding, Zhe Xu, Hanghang Tong, and Huan Liu. Data augmentation for deep graph learning: A survey. *CoRR*, abs/2202.08235, 2022.

[89] Geoffrey E. Hinton, Oriol Vinyals, and Jeffrey Dean. Distilling the knowledge in a neural network. *CoRR*, 2015.

[90] Malik Boudiaf, Jérôme Rony, Imtiaz Masud Ziko, Eric Granger, Marco Pedersoli, Pablo Piantanida, and Ismail Ben Ayed. A unifying mutual information view of metric learning: Cross-entropy vs. pairwise losses. In Andrea Vedaldi, Horst Bischof, Thomas Brox, and Jan-Michael Frahm, editors, *Computer Vision - ECCV 2020 - 16th European Conference, Glasgow, UK, August 23-28, 2020, Proceedings, Part VI*, volume 12351 of *Lecture Notes in Computer Science*, pages 548–564. Springer, 2020.

[91] Simon Kornblith, Honglak Lee, Ting Chen, and Mohammad Norouzi. What's in a loss function for image classification? *CoRR*, abs/2010.16402, 2020.

[92] Simon Kornblith, Ting Chen, Honglak Lee, and Mohammad Norouzi. Why do better loss functions lead to less transferable features? In Marc'Aurelio Ranzato, Alina Beygelzimer, Yann N. Dauphin, Percy

Liang, and Jennifer Wortman Vaughan, editors, *Advances in Neural Information Processing Systems 34: Annual Conference on Neural Information Processing Systems 2021, NeurIPS 2021, December 6-14, 2021, virtual*, pages 28648–28662, 2021.

[93] John S. Bridle. Probabilistic interpretation of feedforward classification network outputs, with relationships to statistical pattern recognition. In Françoise Fogelman-Soulié and Jeanny Hérault, editors, *Neurocomputing - Algorithms, Architectures and Applications, Proceedings of the NATO Advanced Research Workshop on Neurocomputing Algorithms, Architectures and Applications, Les Arcs, France, February 27 - March 3, 1989*, volume 68 of *NATO ASI Series*, pages 227–236. Springer, 1989.

[94] Richard Socher, Milind Ganjoo, Christopher D. Manning, and Andrew Y. Ng. Zero-shot learning through cross-modal transfer. In Christopher J. C. Burges, Léon Bottou, Zoubin Ghahramani, and Kilian Q. Weinberger, editors, *Advances in Neural Information Processing Systems 26: 27th Annual Conference on Neural Information Processing Systems 2013. Proceedings of a meeting held December 5-8, 2013, Lake Tahoe, Nevada, United States*, pages 935–943, 2013.

[95] L. V. D. Maaten and Geoffrey E. Hinton. Visualizing data using t-sne. *Journal of Machine Learning Research*, 9:2579–2605, 2008.

[96] Raia Hadsell, Sumit Chopra, and Yann LeCun. Dimensionality reduction by learning an invariant mapping. In *2006 IEEE Computer Society Conference on Computer Vision and Pattern Recognition (CVPR 2006), 17-22 June 2006, New York, NY, USA*, pages 1735–1742. IEEE Computer Society, 2006.

[97] Andrea Frome, Gregory S. Corrado, Jonathon Shlens, Samy Bengio, Jeffrey Dean, Marc'Aurelio Ranzato, and Tomás Mikolov. Devise: A deep visual-semantic embedding model. In Christopher J. C. Burges, Léon Bottou, Zoubin Ghahramani, and Kilian Q. Weinberger, editors, *Advances in Neural Information Processing Systems 26: 27th Annual Conference on Neural Information Processing Systems 2013. Proceedings of a meeting held December 5-8, 2013, Lake Tahoe, Nevada, United States*, pages 2121–2129, 2013.

[98] Jiang Wang, Yang Song, Thomas Leung, Chuck Rosenberg, Jingbin Wang, James Philbin, Bo Chen, and Ying Wu. Learning fine-grained image similarity with deep ranking. In *2014 IEEE Conference on Computer Vision and Pattern Recognition, CVPR 2014, Columbus, OH, USA, June 23-28, 2014*, pages 1386–1393. IEEE Computer Society, 2014.

[99] Herbert E. Robbins. A stochastic approximation method. *Annals of Mathematical Statistics*, 22:400–407, 1951.

[100] Diederik P. Kingma and Jimmy Ba. Adam: A method for stochastic optimization. In Yoshua Bengio and Yann LeCun, editors, *3rd International Conference on Learning Representations, ICLR 2015, San Diego, CA, USA, May 7-9, 2015, Conference Track Proceedings*, 2015.

[101] D. Rumelhart, Geoffrey E. Hinton, and R. J. Williams. Learning representations by back-propagating errors. *Nature*, 323:533–536, 1986.

[102] Geoffrey E. Hinton. The forward-forward algorithm: Some preliminary investigations. *CoRR*, abs/2212.13345, 2022.

[103] David H. Ackley, Geoffrey E. Hinton, and Terrence J. Sejnowski. A learning algorithm for boltzmann machines. *Cogn. Sci.*, 9(1):147–169, 1985.

[104] James Bergstra and Yoshua Bengio. Random search for hyper-parameter optimization. *J. Mach. Learn. Res.*, 13:281–305, 2012.

[105] Xavier Glorot and Yoshua Bengio. Understanding the difficulty of training deep feedforward neural networks. In Yee Whye Teh and D. Mike Titterington, editors, *Proceedings of the Thirteenth International Conference on Artificial Intelligence and Statistics, AISTATS 2010, Chia Laguna Resort, Sardinia, Italy, May 13-15, 2010*, volume 9 of *JMLR Proceedings*, pages 249–256. JMLR.org, 2010.

[106] Kaiming He, Xiangyu Zhang, Shaoqing Ren, and Jian Sun. Delving deep into rectifiers: Surpassing human-level performance on imagenet classification. In *2015 IEEE International Conference on Computer Vision, ICCV 2015, Santiago, Chile, December 7-13, 2015*, pages 1026–1034. IEEE Computer Society, 2015.

[107] Alexander D'Amour, Katherine A. Heller, Dan Moldovan, Ben Adlam, Babak Alipanahi, Alex Beutel, Christina Chen, and Jonathan Deaton. Underspecification presents challenges for credibility in modern machine learning. *CoRR*, 2020.

[108] Chuanqi Tan, Fuchun Sun, Tao Kong, Wenchang Zhang, Chao Yang, and Chunfang Liu. A survey on deep transfer learning. In *ICANN*, 2018.

[109] David Perkins and Gavriel Salomon. Transfer of learning. 11, 07 1999.

[110] Fuzhen Zhuang, Zhiyuan Qi, Keyu Duan, Dongbo Xi, Yongchun Zhu, Hengshu Zhu, Hui Xiong, and

Qing He. A comprehensive survey on transfer learning. *Proc. IEEE*, 109(1):43–76, 2021.

[111] Sinno Jialin Pan and Qiang Yang. A survey on transfer learning. *IEEE Trans. Knowl. Data Eng.*, 22(10):1345–1359, 2010.

[112] Sebastian Ruder and Barbara Plank. Learning to select data for transfer learning with bayesian optimization. In *EMNLP*, 2017.

[113] Gilles Blanchard, Gyemin Lee, and Clayton Scott. Generalizing from several related classification tasks to a new unlabeled sample. In John Shawe-Taylor, Richard S. Zemel, Peter L. Bartlett, Fernando C. N. Pereira, and Kilian Q. Weinberger, editors, *Advances in Neural Information Processing Systems 24: 25th Annual Conference on Neural Information Processing Systems 2011. Proceedings of a meeting held 12-14 December 2011, Granada, Spain*, pages 2178–2186, 2011.

[114] Krikamol Muandet, David Balduzzi, and Bernhard Schölkopf. Domain generalization via invariant feature representation. In *Proceedings of the 30th International Conference on Machine Learning, ICML 2013, Atlanta, GA, USA, 16-21 June 2013*, volume 28 of *JMLR Workshop and Conference Proceedings*, pages 10–18. JMLR.org, 2013.

[115] Chuanqi Tan, Fuchun Sun, Tao Kong, Wenchang Zhang, Chao Yang, and Chunfang Liu. A survey on deep transfer learning. In Vera Kurková, Yannis Manolopoulos, Barbara Hammer, Lazaros S. Iliadis, and Ilias Maglogiannis, editors, *Artificial Neural Networks and Machine Learning - ICANN 2018 - 27th International Conference on Artificial Neural Networks, Rhodes, Greece, October 4-7, 2018, Proceedings, Part III*, volume 11141 of *Lecture Notes in Computer Science*, pages 270–279. Springer, 2018.

[116] Ian J. Goodfellow, Jonathon Shlens, and Christian Szegedy. Explaining and harnessing adversarial examples. In Yoshua Bengio and Yann LeCun, editors, *3rd International Conference on Learning Representations, ICLR 2015, San Diego, CA, USA, May 7-9, 2015, Conference Track Proceedings*, 2015.

[117] Dan Hendrycks and Thomas G. Dietterich. Benchmarking neural network robustness to common corruptions and perturbations. In *7th International Conference on Learning Representations, ICLR 2019, New Orleans, LA, USA, May 6-9, 2019*. OpenReview.net, 2019.

[118] Alexander D'Amour, Katherine A. Heller, Dan Moldovan, Ben Adlam, and et. al. Underspecification presents challenges for credibility in modern machine learning. *CoRR*, abs/2011.03395, 2020.

[119] Jianyu Zhang, David Lopez-Paz, and Léon Bottou. Rich feature construction for the optimization-generalization dilemma. In Kamalika Chaudhuri, Stefanie Jegelka, Le Song, Csaba Szepesvári, Gang Niu, and Sivan Sabato, editors, *International Conference on Machine Learning, ICML 2022, 17-23 July 2022, Baltimore, Maryland, USA*, volume 162 of *Proceedings of Machine Learning Research*, pages 26397–26411. PMLR, 2022.

[120] Rishi Bommasani, Drew A. Hudson, Ehsan Adeli, and et al. On the Opportunities and Risks of Foundation Models, July 2022.

[121] Gregory Murphy and E.J. Winiewski. Feature correlations in conceptual representations. In G Tiberghien, editor, *Advances in Cognitive Science*, volume 2, pages 23–45. Ellis Horwood, Chichester, 1989.

[122] A. S. Kaplan and G. L. Murphy. Category learning with minimal prior knowledge. *Journal of Experimental Psychology. Learning, Memory, and Cognition*, 26(4):829–846, July 2000.

[123] Joseph J. Williams and Tania Lombrozo. Explanation and prior knowledge interact to guide learning. *Cognitive Psychology*, 66(1):55–84, February 2013.

[124] Anmei Dong, Morris Siu-Yung Jong, and Ronnel B. King. How Does Prior Knowledge Influence Learning Engagement? The Mediating Roles of Cognitive Load and Help-Seeking. *Frontiers in Psychology*, 11, 2020.

[125] Edward S. Shapiro. *Academic Skills Problems: Direct Assessment and Intervention, 4th Ed.* Academic Skills Problems: Direct Assessment and Intervention, 4th Ed. Guilford Press, New York, NY, US, 2011.

[126] Hugo Larochelle, Dumitru Erhan, and Yoshua Bengio. Zero-data learning of new tasks. In Dieter Fox and Carla P. Gomes, editors, *Proceedings of the Twenty-Third AAAI Conference on Artificial Intelligence, AAAI 2008, Chicago, Illinois, USA, July 13-17, 2008*, pages 646–651. AAAI Press, 2008.

[127] Michael Polanyi. Personal Knowledge: Towards a Post-Critical Philosophy.

[128] Christoph H. Lampert, Hannes Nickisch, and Stefan Harmeling. Learning to detect unseen object classes by between-class attribute transfer. In *2009 IEEE Computer Society Conference on Computer Vision and Pattern Recognition (CVPR 2009), 20-25 June 2009, Miami, Florida, USA*, pages 951–958. IEEE Computer Society, 2009.

[129] Ruotian Luo, Ning Zhang, Bohyung Han, and Linjie Yang. Context-aware zero-shot recognition. In *The Thirty-Fourth AAAI Conference on Artificial Intelligence, AAAI 2020, The Thirty-Second Innovative Applications of Artificial Intelligence Conference, IAAI 2020, The Tenth AAAI Symposium on Educational Advances in Artificial Intelligence, EAAI 2020, New York, NY, USA, February 7-12, 2020*, pages 11709–11716. AAAI Press, 2020.

[130] Ke Gong, Yiming Gao, Xiaodan Liang, Xiaohui Shen, Meng Wang, and Liang Lin. Graphonomy: Universal human parsing via graph transfer learning. In *IEEE Conference on Computer Vision and Pattern Recognition, CVPR 2019, Long Beach, CA, USA, June 16-20, 2019*, pages 7450–7459. Computer Vision Foundation / IEEE, 2019.

[131] Xiaodan Liang, Zhiting Hu, Hao Zhang, Liang Lin, and Eric P. Xing. Symbolic graph reasoning meets convolutions. In Samy Bengio, Hanna M. Wallach, Hugo Larochelle, Kristen Grauman, Nicolò Cesa-Bianchi, and Roman Garnett, editors, *Advances in Neural Information Processing Systems 31: Annual Conference on Neural Information Processing Systems 2018, NeurIPS 2018, December 3-8, 2018, Montréal, Canada*, pages 1858–1868, 2018.

[132] Xiaolong Wang, Yufei Ye, and Abhinav Gupta. Zero-shot recognition via semantic embeddings and knowledge graphs. In *2018 IEEE Conference on Computer Vision and Pattern Recognition, CVPR 2018, Salt Lake City, UT, USA, June 18-22, 2018*, pages 6857–6866. IEEE Computer Society, 2018.

[133] Zhao-Min Chen, Xiu-Shen Wei, Peng Wang, and Yanwen Guo. Multi-label image recognition with graph convolutional networks. In *IEEE Conference on Computer Vision and Pattern Recognition, CVPR 2019, Long Beach, CA, USA, June 16-20, 2019*, pages 5177–5186. Computer Vision Foundation / IEEE, 2019.

[134] Michael Kampffmeyer, Yinbo Chen, Xiaodan Liang, Hao Wang, Yujia Zhang, and Eric P. Xing. Rethinking knowledge graph propagation for zero-shot learning. In *IEEE Conference on Computer Vision and Pattern Recognition, CVPR 2019, Long Beach, CA, USA, June 16-20, 2019*, pages 11487–11496. Computer Vision Foundation / IEEE, 2019.

[135] Junyu Gao, Tianzhu Zhang, and Changsheng Xu. I know the relationships: Zero-shot action recognition via two-stream graph convolutional networks and knowledge graphs. In *The Thirty-Third AAAI Conference on Artificial Intelligence, AAAI 2019, The Thirty-First Innovative Applications of Artificial Intelligence Conference, IAAI 2019, The Ninth AAAI Symposium on Educational Advances in Artificial Intelligence, EAAI 2019, Honolulu, Hawaii, USA, January 27 - February 1, 2019*, pages 8303–8311. AAAI Press, 2019.

[136] Zhimao Peng, Zechao Li, Junge Zhang, Yan Li, Guo-Jun Qi, and Jinhui Tang. Few-shot image recognition with knowledge transfer. In *2019 IEEE/CVF International Conference on Computer Vision, ICCV 2019, Seoul, Korea (South), October 27 - November 2, 2019*, pages 441–449. IEEE, 2019.

[137] Riquan Chen, Tianshui Chen, Xiaolu Hui, Hefeng Wu, Guanbin Li, and Liang Lin. Knowledge graph transfer network for few-shot recognition. In *The Thirty-Fourth AAAI Conference on Artificial Intelligence, AAAI 2020, The Thirty-Second Innovative Applications of Artificial Intelligence Conference, IAAI 2020, The Tenth AAAI Symposium on Educational Advances in Artificial Intelligence, EAAI 2020, New York, NY, USA, February 7-12, 2020*, pages 10575–10582. AAAI Press, 2020.

[138] Yuxia Geng, Jiaoyan Chen, Zhuo Chen, Jeff Z. Pan, Zhiquan Ye, Zonggang Yuan, Yantao Jia, and Huajun Chen. Ontozsl: Ontology-enhanced zero-shot learning. In Jure Leskovec, Marko Grobelnik, Marc Najork, Jie Tang, and Leila Zia, editors, *WWW '21: The Web Conference 2021, Virtual Event / Ljubljana, Slovenia, April 19-23, 2021*, pages 3325–3336. ACM / IW3C2, 2021.

[139] Sebastian Monka, Lavdim Halilaj, Stefan Schmid, and Achim Rettinger. Learning visual models using a knowledge graph as a trainer. In Andreas Hotho, Eva Blomqvist, Stefan Dietze, Achille Fokoue, Ying Ding, Payam M. Barnaghi, Armin Haller, Mauro Dragoni, and Harith Alani, editors, *The Semantic Web - ISWC 2021 - 20th International Semantic Web Conference, ISWC 2021, Virtual Event, October 24-28, 2021, Proceedings*, volume 12922 of *Lecture Notes in Computer Science*, pages 357–373. Springer, 2021.

[140] Mirantha Jayathilaka, Tingting Mu, and Uli Sattler. Ontology-based n-ball concept embeddings informing few-shot image classification. In Mehwish Alam, Mehdi Ali, Paul Groth, Pascal Hitzler, Jens Lehmann, Heiko Paulheim, Achim Rettinger, Harald Sack, Afshin Sadeghi, and Volker Tresp, editors, *Machine Learning with Symbolic Methods and Knowledge Graphs co-located with European Conference on Machine Learning and Principles and Practice of Knowledge Discovery in Databases (ECML PKDD 2021), Virtual, September 17, 2021*, volume 2997 of *CEUR Workshop Proceedings*. CEUR-WS.org, 2021.

[141] Paul Hager, Martin J. Menten, and Daniel Rueckert. Best of both worlds: Multimodal contrastive learning with tabular and imaging data. In *IEEE/CVF Conference on Computer Vision and Pattern Recognition, CVPR 2023, Vancouver, BC, Canada, June 17-24, 2023*, pages 23924–23935. IEEE, 2023.

[142] Muhammad Ferjad Naeem, Yongqin Xian, Federico Tombari, and Zeynep Akata. Learning graph embeddings for compositional zero-shot learning. In *IEEE Conference on Computer Vision and Pattern Recognition, CVPR 2021, virtual, June 19-25, 2021*, pages 953–962. Computer Vision Foundation / IEEE, 2021.

[143] Sebastian Monka, Lavdim Halilaj, and Achim Rettinger. Context-driven visual object recognition based on knowledge graphs. In Ulrike Sattler, Aidan Hogan, C. Maria Keet, Valentina Presutti, João Paulo A. Almeida, Hideaki Takeda, Pierre Monnin, Giuseppe Pirrò, and Claudia d'Amato, editors, *The Semantic Web - ISWC 2022 - 21st International Semantic Web Conference, Virtual Event, October 23-27, 2022, Proceedings*, volume 13489 of *Lecture Notes in Computer Science*, pages 142–160. Springer, 2022.

[144] Suzana Herculano-Houzel. The remarkable, yet not extraordinary, human brain as a scaled-up primate brain and its associated cost. *Proceedings of the National Academy of Sciences*, 109(supplement_1):10661–10668, June 2012.

[145] Anastasia Dimou, Miel Vander Sande, Pieter Colpaert, Ruben Verborgh, Erik Mannens, and Rik Van de Walle. RML: A generic language for integrated RDF mappings of heterogeneous data. In Christian Bizer, Tom Heath, Sören Auer, and Tim Berners-Lee, editors, *Proceedings of the Workshop on Linked Data on the Web co-located with the 23rd International World Wide Web Conference (WWW 2014), Seoul, Korea, April 8, 2014*, volume 1184 of *CEUR Workshop Proceedings*. CEUR-WS.org, 2014.

[146] Natthawut Kertkeidkachorn and Ryutaro Ichise. An automatic knowledge graph creation framework from natural language text. *IEICE Trans. Inf. Syst.*, 101-D(1):90–98, 2018.

[147] Danilo Dessì, Francesco Osborne, Diego Reforgiato Recupero, Davide Buscaldi, and Enrico Motta. Generating knowledge graphs by employing natural language processing and machine learning techniques within the scholarly domain. *Future Gener. Comput. Syst.*, 116:253–264, 2021.

Handbook on Neurosymbolic AI and Knowledge Graphs
P. Hitzler et al. (Eds.)
IOS Press, 2025

doi:10.3233/FAIA250227

Neurosymbolic Visual Reasoning with Scene Graphs and Multimodal LLMs

M. Jaleed KHAN [a,c,1] Filip ILIEVSKI [b] Edward CURRY [c]
[a] *Medical Sciences Division, University of Oxford, UK*
[b] *Department of Computer Science, Vrije Universiteit Amsterdam, The Netherlands*
[c] *Insight Research Ireland Centre for Data Analytics, University of Galway, Ireland*

Abstract. This chapter explores the advancements and challenges in achieving comprehensive scene understanding and visual reasoning through neurosymbolic integration and Multimodal Large Language Models (MLLMs). It begins by highlighting the limitations of basic vision tasks in extracting contextual and relational information from scenes, introducing scene graphs as a structured representation to bridge this gap. The chapter delves into Scene Graph Generation (SGG) methods, emphasising the importance of incorporating common sense knowledge from knowledge graphs to enhance the accuracy and expressiveness of scene graphs. The NeuSyRE framework is presented as a neurosymbolic approach for enriched scene graph generation and reasoning, demonstrating its effectiveness in downstream tasks such as image captioning and visual question answering. The chapter also examines the role of MLLMs in visual reasoning, discussing their architectures, performance on zero-shot tasks and challenges in handling fine-grained visual details. MARVEL, a novel benchmark for abstract visual reasoning, is introduced to evaluate the perceptual and reasoning capabilities of MLLMs. Insights from MARVEL highlight the limitations of current MLLMs in solving complex reasoning tasks and underscore the potential of neurosymbolic systems to address these challenges. The chapter concludes by emphasising the synergy between neurosymbolic approaches and MLLMs in advancing visual intelligence and achieving robust and explainable AI systems.

Keywords. neurosymbolic integration, visual reasoning, scene graph, common sense knowledge, multimodal large language models, knowledge graphs, multimodal deep learning

1. Introduction

The past decade has witnessed significant advancements in visual intelligence, driven by the synergy of deep learning and multimodal techniques. These technological strides have transformed basic vision tasks, achieving remarkable accuracy and versatility. For instance, image classification systems now excel at distinguishing fine-grained categories, and object detection algorithms can identify specific models of cars and estimate their speed and trajectory in real-time video streams. Image segmentation has progressed to accurately delineate individual objects in crowded scenes, from identifying spectators

[1]Corresponding author. M. J. Khan (jaleed.khan@wrh.ox.ac.uk)

in stadiums to distinguishing different coral types in underwater photographs [1]. Despite these advancements, basic vision tasks fail to achieve comprehensive scene understanding and visual reasoning. For example, while basic vision systems can identify people and objects in a family picnic scene, they often miss deeper contextual insights, such as interactions between individuals or the anticipation of a dog eyeing a sandwich. Achieving such high-level understanding necessitates a deeper dive into semantic and relational information, focusing on the dynamics and interactions of the objects within the scene. Figure 1 shows some examples of low-level vision tasks and high-level visual reasoning tasks.

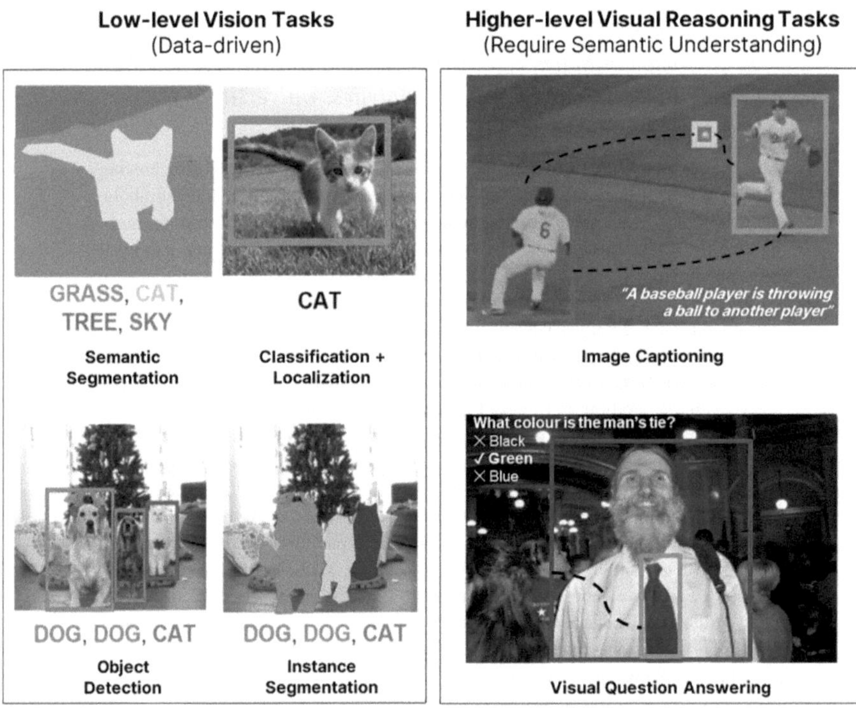

Figure 1. Examples of low-level vision tasks and high-level visual reasoning tasks (Adapted from `http://cs231n.stanford.edu/slides/2017/cs231n_2017_lecture11.pdf` and [2])

Neurosymbolic visual reasoning has emerged as a promising approach to bridge the gap between basic vision tasks and comprehensive scene understanding. By combining the learning capabilities of neural networks with the reasoning power of symbolic approaches, neurosymbolic integration aims to achieve more expressive and accurate scene representations. This integration is crucial for understanding beyond mere object recognition, capturing the intricate relationships and contexts in real-world scenes. Central to this approach is the concept of scene graphs, which model objects and their relationships in a structured manner [3]. Scene Graph Generation (SGG) involves detecting and analyzing objects, attributes, and relationships to construct a symbolic representation of a scene. Deep learning architectures, such as Convolutional Neural Networks (CNNs) and Graph Neural Networks (GNNs), play a crucial role by extracting complex visual features and capturing relationships between objects. Incorporating common sense knowledge enhances scene graphs' quality and expressiveness. This knowledge fills informational gaps, facilitating the prediction and interpretation of complex interactions and relationships [4]. Infusing this knowledge into SGG narrows the gap between limited training data and the vast semantic space, improving accuracy and generalizability [5].

Section 2 introduces various approaches to integrating scene graphs and common sense knowledge [5], highlighting techniques, datasets, evaluation metrics and current challenges. We discuss methods for enhancing scene graph generation using common sense knowledge [6], utilizing heterogeneous knowledge sources to enrich scene graphs. We present NeuSyRE [7], a neurosymbolic scene understanding and visual reasoning framework extending enriched scene graphs for downstream reasoning tasks. We also present use cases and applications including image captioning [7], multimedia event processing [8], the Internet of Multimedia Things (IoMT) [9], image colourization [10] and decentralized data management systems [11].

Building on the foundation laid in the previous sections, Section 3 explores the integration of Multimodal Large Language Models (MLLMs) for visual reasoning. While Section 2 focuses on scene graphs and common sense knowledge for visual reasoning, Section 3 focuses on the application of MLLMs to visual reasoning tasks like Visual Question Answering (VQA) and Abstract Visual Reasoning (AVR). This transition highlights the complementary nature of neurosymbolic approaches and advanced MLLMs in achieving robust visual reasoning. By examining the VQA datasets and zero-shot evaluation capabilities of MLLMs [12,13,14], the architecture of state-of-the-art MLLMs, emphasizing their vision encoders, bridge modules, and LLM backbones [15], we provide a comprehensive view of how these models can leverage neurosymbolic approaches and extend their capabilities. Additionally, we discuss AVR using benchmarks like MARVEL [16] that assess the perception and reasoning capabilities of MLLMs through complex puzzles. This comprehensive examination of MLLMs provides insights into their current performance, challenges and future directions in visual reasoning.

2. Visual Reasoning with Enriched Scene Graphs

Scene understanding and visual reasoning are fundamental components of artificial intelligence that enable systems to interpret and interact with visual data meaningfully. This involves identifying objects and their attributes in images, understanding the relationships and contexts that link these objects together, and reasoning over this information to perform complex tasks. Deep learning, mainly through Convolutional Neural Networks (CNNs), has revolutionized how AI systems process visual data. These models excel at detecting objects and recognizing image patterns by learning hierarchical representations from raw data. However, deep learning models often operate as "black boxes," lacking transparency in their decision-making processes. This opaqueness is particularly problematic in applications requiring interpretability and trust, such as autonomous driving and medical diagnostics.

A scene graph is a graph-based structure where nodes represent objects, and edges denote relationships between these objects. Scene Graph Generation (SGG) involves detecting oir attributes and the relationships between them to construct these graphs, as illustrated in Figure 2. The generation of scene graphs poses several challenges, including the need for high-quality annotated data and the ability to generalize to new and unseen relationships. The quality of annotations is crucial, as the accuracy of the generated scene graphs depends heavily on the precision of the detected objects and relationships [17]. Additionally, the skewed distribution of relationship predicates in crowd-sourced datasets, such as Visual Genome, can lead to biases in the scene graphs. For instance, common predicates like "on" and "has" dominate the dataset, while more nuanced relationships are underrepresented. This imbalance affects the system's ability to predict less frequent but semantically rich relationships accurately. Another challenge is the ability to generalize to new and unseen relationships. The vast semantic space of possible relationships in a scene makes it nearly impossible to capture all of them within a finite training dataset [5].

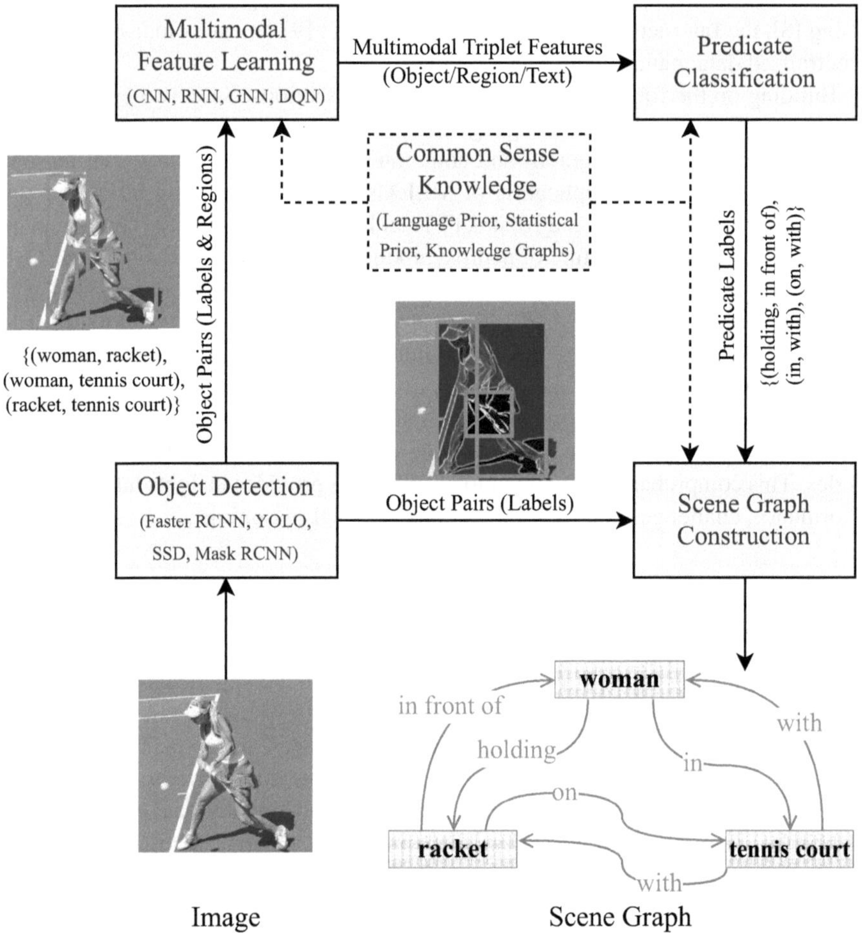

Figure 2. A schematic representation of the typical scene graph generation process (beginning at the bottom left and concluding at the bottom right) that comprises object detection, multimodal feature learning, common sense knowledge infusion, relationship predicate classification, and scene graph construction

Interpretable models are essential in applications where understanding the rationale behind a system's decisions is critical [18]. For instance, it is crucial to understand why a

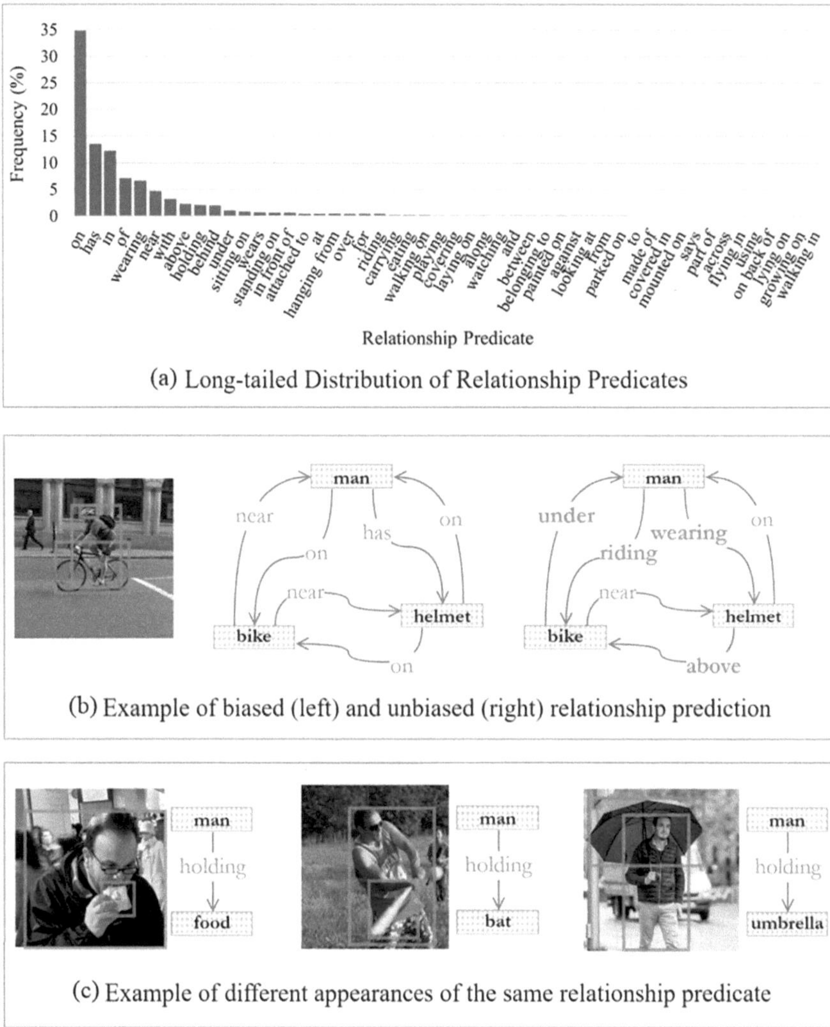

(a) Long-tailed Distribution of Relationship Predicates

(b) Example of biased (left) and unbiased (right) relationship prediction

(c) Example of different appearances of the same relationship predicate

Figure 3. Common challenges in scene graph generation

system chose a particular action in response to a given visual scene in autonomous driving. Scene graphs play a vital role in this context by providing a structured and human-readable representation of the visual data. This structure allows the system to explain its reasoning process, linking its decisions to specific objects and relationships within the scene. Using scene graphs in interpretable visual reasoning involves generating them from images and leveraging them for various tasks. For example, in visual question answering, the system can use the scene graph to find relevant objects and relationships that answer a given question. However, the limited expressiveness of scene graphs hinders the ability to answer questions accurately and provide a clear rationale for the system's decisions. The lack of transparency in the decision-making processes of data-centric approaches is particularly problematic in applications where understanding the rationale behind the system's decisions is critical [19]. The ability to trace the reasoning process

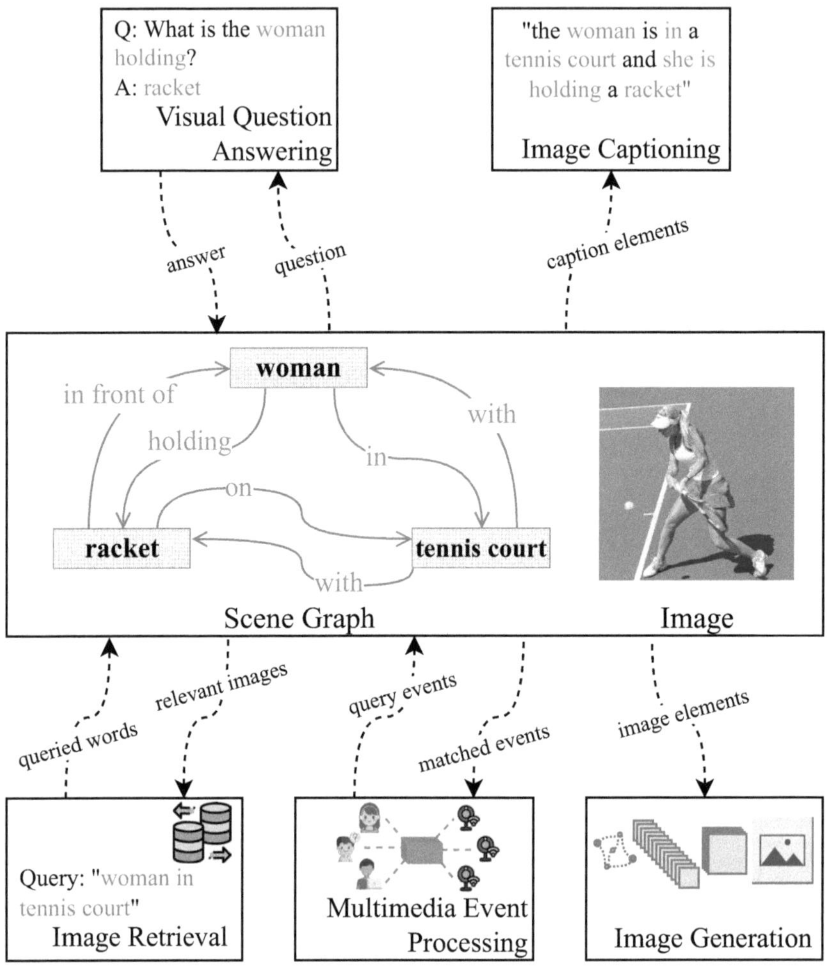

Figure 4. Scene graph-based visual reasoning tasks

through the scene graph is essential for the transparency and trustworthiness of the AI system. Some of the key challenges in SGG are illustrated in Figure 3.

To address these challenges, researchers have explored various techniques for enhancing the robustness and expressiveness of scene graphs. One approach uses statistical and language priors to capture structural regularities and semantic information. Statistical priors leverage the observed correlations between objects and relationships in the training data, providing a probabilistic framework for predicting relationships. Language priors, on the other hand, use semantic embeddings of words to infer relationships based on their meanings. For instance, even if the training data does not contain many examples of "a child holding a kite," the language prior helps infer this relationship by understanding the semantic similarity between "kite" and more common objects that children hold, like "toy" [5].

Knowledge graphs provide another powerful tool for enhancing scene graphs. Knowledge graphs are structured databases that store information about entities and their relationships. They offer a rich source of common sense knowledge, which includes background information about the world humans typically know. For example, knowledge graphs provide information that "birds are likely to be found in trees," allowing the system to infer this relationship even if it is not explicitly present in the training data. By leveraging knowledge graphs such as ConceptNet [20], CSKG [21] and others, AI systems improve accuracy and contextual understanding of scene representations. Data-driven SGG approaches struggle with scene understanding and visual reasoning tasks that require high-level reasoning or the integration of contextual knowledge not present in the training data. By integrating knowledge graphs with scene graphs, visual AI systems leverage this background knowledge to improve the accuracy and contextual understanding of visual scenes. This is achieved by enriching scene graphs with common sense knowledge to provide structured and expressive representations of visual scenes that allow for an intuitive understanding of the scene [17]. This facilitates higher-level visual reasoning tasks such as Visual Question Answering (VQA), image captioning, image retrieval, event processing and image generation, as shown in Figure 4).

Neurosymbolic approaches combine the strengths of neural networks and symbolic reasoning to address the limitations of purely data-driven methods. Neural networks, particularly deep learning models, excel at recognizing patterns and making predictions based on large amounts of data. However, they cannot often incorporate explicit knowledge and logical reasoning. Symbolic AI, on the other hand, focuses on knowledge representation and reasoning using formal languages and rules. By integrating these two paradigms, neurosymbolic AI seeks to create systems that are both data-efficient and capable of high-level reasoning [22]. In loosely coupled neurosymbolic systems, neural and symbolic components operate relatively independently, interacting as needed to complete specific tasks. This approach allows each component to leverage its strengths while retaining the flexibility to operate independently. For example, a neural network might detect objects and relationships in an image, while a symbolic reasoning system uses this information to infer higher-level insights and make decisions. Tightly coupled systems, in contrast, integrate symbolic knowledge directly into neural network architectures. This deep integration allows seamless interaction between the components, enabling the system to perform complex reasoning tasks more effectively. Tightly coupled systems often encode symbolic knowledge into the neural network's distributed representation, enhancing its ability to reason about the data [5].

The neurosymbolic integration of common sense knowledge helps visual AI systems to generalize better to new and unseen scenarios. Neurosymbolic AI approaches enhance scene understanding and visual reasoning by integrating deep learning with formal knowledge representation and reasoning techniques. This integration allows AI systems to perform complex reasoning tasks that require both pattern recognition and logical inference. For example, neurosymbolic systems use a neural network to detect objects and relationships in an image and then use a symbolic reasoning component to infer higher-level insights, such as the likely actions or intentions of the detected entities. This combination of neural and symbolic methods provides a more robust and flexible framework for scene understanding and visual reasoning. One of the key benefits of neurosymbolic AI is its ability to provide explainable and interpretable results. By integrating symbolic reasoning capabilities, these systems can generate explanations for their decisions, linking them to specific objects, relationships, and background knowledge. This transparency is essential in applications where understanding the rationale behind the system's decisions is critical, such as in healthcare and autonomous driving. Moreover, the use of formal knowledge representation allows the system to incorporate expert knowledge and ensure consistency and coherence in its reasoning process [19].

2.1. The NeuSyRE Framework

Scene Graph Generation (SGG) involves detecting objects, attributes and relationships within an image to create a structured representation known as a scene graph. This graph includes nodes representing objects and edges denoting relationships between these objects, providing a detailed and semantically rich representation of the visual scene. Scene graph enrichment enhances these graphs by incorporating common sense knowledge from external sources, such as knowledge graphs, to fill informational gaps and correct inaccuracies, thus making the scene graph more expressive and contextually aware. Scene graph reasoning utilizes these enriched graphs for high-level visual reasoning tasks, such as image captioning and visual question answering. Khan et al. [7] proposed the NeuSyRE framework that integrates neural and symbolic approaches to improve SGG. The framework, shown in 5, comprises three main tasks: SGG, scene graph enrichment, and downstream reasoning. Neurosymbolic integration plays a crucial role in this process by combining the learning capabilities of deep neural networks with the reasoning power of symbolic methods. Knowledge graphs, such as the Common Sense Knowledge Graph (CSKG), are leveraged to provide background information and context, enhancing the accuracy and expressiveness of the generated scene graphs.

2.2. Methodology

The NeuSyRE framework involved a multimodal DNN-based approach for scene graph generation, followed by a rule-based enrichment process utilizing common sense knowledge from CSKG, as illustrated in Figure 5. The scene graph generation process began with object detection using a Faster R-CNN, which employed a ResNeXt-101-FPN architecture to extract feature maps and predict object bounding boxes and class labels. These features were then encoded using Bi-directional Long Short Term Memory (Bi-LSTM) layers to capture long-term dependencies and contextual information about objects in the image. Pairwise visual relationships were predicted by combining individual visual context features, language priors and contextual union features. These features were fused using a summation function and fed into a softmax classifier to predict relationship labels and confidence scores. The resulting scene graph, comprising detected objects and their relationships, was then refined and enriched using common sense knowledge from CSKG. Graph embeddings were employed to compute the similarity between nodes during the refinement and enrichment stages. Irrelevant or redundant predictions were eliminated based on the similarity of labels and overlapping bounding boxes. New triplets from CSKG were integrated into the scene graph by querying the knowledge graph for related facts and background information, which were then filtered and connected to existing nodes based on structural similarity.

2.3. Evaluation and Findings

The experimental setup for evaluating the NeuSyRE framework involves using well-established datasets and metrics to assess the performance of scene graph generation and

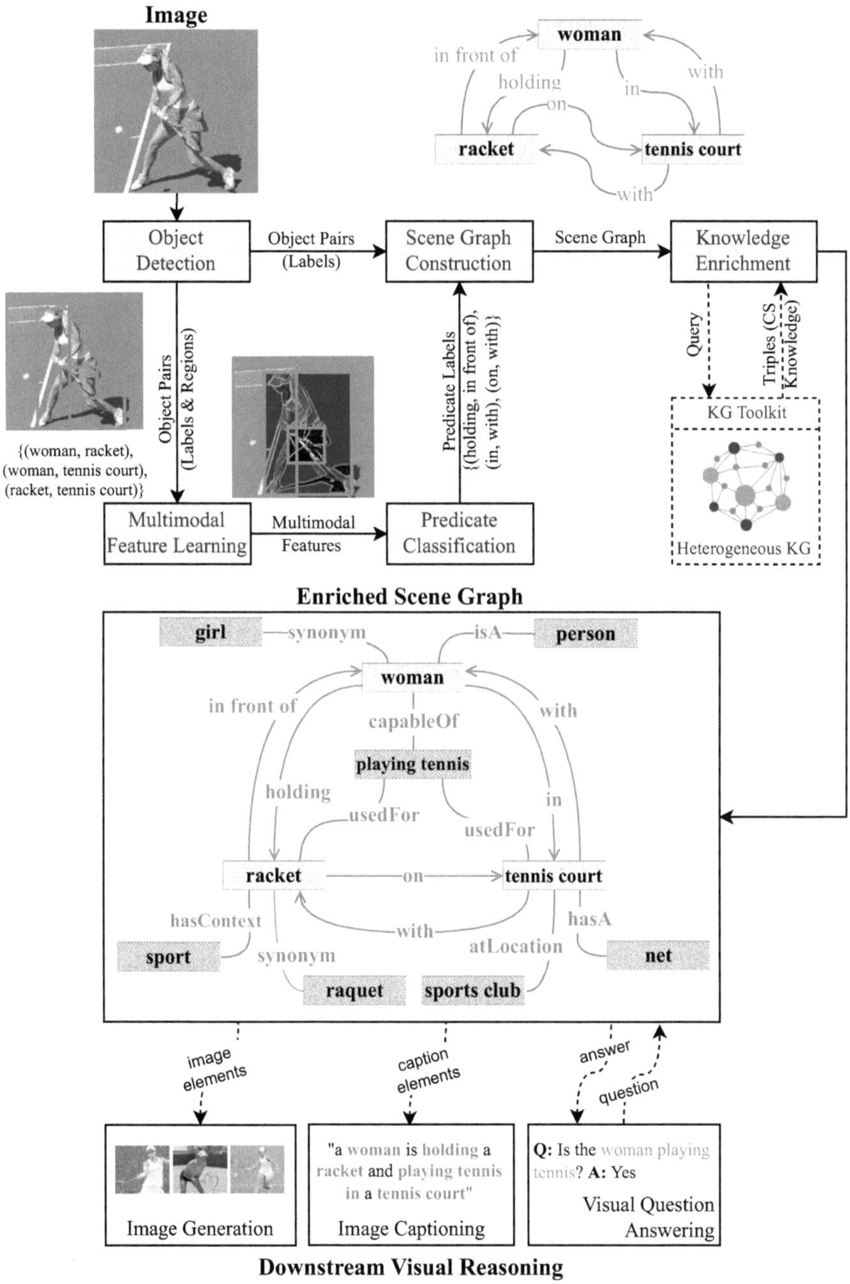

Figure 5. NeuSyRE: Neurosymbolic Visual Reasoning Framework based on Enriched Scene Graphs

enrichment. The primary datasets used are Visual Genome (VG) and Microsoft COCO, which provide extensive annotations for objects and relationships within images. The VG dataset contains 108,000 labelled images with 150 object classes and 50 predicate classes, while the COCO dataset offers 132,000 labelled images with detailed annotations for objects and captions. The evaluation metrics employed include Recall@K (R@K) and mean Recall@K (mR@K) for relationship prediction performance. R@K measures the fraction of correct relationships predicted within the top K confident predictions, while mR@K provides an average recall score across all relationship categories, minimizing bias towards frequently occurring relationships. For object detection, mean Average Precision (mAP) is used, which calculates the precision-recall curve's area for detecting objects. Additionally, cross-entropy loss is used to evaluate the training performance of the Faster R-CNN and SGG models, providing insights into how well the models learn to predict object classes and relationships.

The NeuSyRE framework demonstrated significant improvements in scene graph generation and enrichment, as evidenced by experimental results on the VG and COCO datasets. The proposed method achieved higher recall rates for relationship prediction than conventional SGG methods. Specifically, the recall scores R@20, R@50 and R@100 increased from 26.1, 32.7 and 36.5 to 29.9, 35.5 and 39.1, respectively, on the VG test set. A similar trend was observed for the COCO dataset, with R@K values increasing significantly after knowledge enrichment. The enriched scene graphs resulted in more accurate and expressive representations, reducing the number of missed or incorrect predictions. The qualitative analysis showed that the enriched scene graphs contained valuable background facts and contextual information, improving the expressiveness and meaningfulness of the generated captions. The recall rates for various relationship predicates improved, indicating that knowledge enrichment effectively mitigates bias towards frequent relationships and enhances the overall robustness of scene graph generation.

2.4. Downstream Reasoning

2.4.1. Image Captioning

The NeuSyRE framework [7] incorporated scene graph-based image captioning as a downstream task to evaluate the effectiveness of enriched scene graphs in generating meaningful and accurate captions. The enriched scene graphs were first decomposed into sub-graphs and then sampled using neighbour sampling techniques. This process involved selecting a random set of seed nodes and extracting their immediate neighbours to form sampled sub-graphs. Redundant sub-graphs were removed using greedy non-maximal suppression, ensuring the selection of the most relevant and meaningful sub-graphs. The nodes and edges of the scene graph were augmented with their visual features and text embeddings using a Graph Convolutional Network (GCN). The GCN aggregated contextual information from neighbouring nodes through multiple graph convolutions and ReLU layers. The relationship information was integrated into the GCN, and the features of nodes obtained from the GCN were used for sub-graph scoring. A two-layer Multi-Layer Perceptron (MLP) with a sub-graph readout function ranked the sub-graphs, followed by sigmoid normalization. An attention-based LSTM assigned importance scores to the sub-graph nodes, which were used by a language LSTM to generate sentences corresponding to each sub-graph. The results demonstrated that using enriched scene graphs significantly improved the performance of the image captioning model. The SPICE and CIDEr scores increased from 20.7 and 115.3 to 23.8 and 131.4, respectively. Improving SPICE and CIDEr scores was significant because SPICE prioritizes semantic content over textual fluency, making it highly correlated with human judgment. At the same time, CIDEr focuses on the cosine similarity between TF-IDF weighted n-grams, ensuring precision and recall of visually informative terms. These improvements indicated that enriched scene graphs provided more contextually rich and semantically meaningful captions, enhancing the overall expressiveness and accuracy of visual reasoning. The qualitative analysis further supported these findings, showing that enriched scene graphs resulted in more intuitive and contextually appropriate captions than conventional ones. This demonstrated the potential of neurosymbolic integration in advancing the capabilities of visual reasoning systems by leveraging common sense knowledge to enrich scene representations.

2.4.2. Image Generation

The NeuSyRE framework [7] extended its capabilities to image generation as a downstream task [6], aiming to evaluate how enriched scene graphs could improve the quality and realism of generated images. The approach employed an existing image generation method [23], specifically tailored to work with scene graphs, to create images that reflect the semantic content encoded within the graphs. The process began with the generation of enriched scene graphs using the proposed neurosymbolic integration method. These enriched graphs incorporated common sense knowledge from the CommonSense Knowledge Graph (CSKG), which provided additional contextual information and relationships not explicitly present in the initial scene graphs. This enrichment aimed to enhance the expressiveness and accuracy of the scene representations. For the image generation task, the framework used a neural network model trained on the Visual Genome dataset. This model took the enriched scene graphs as input and generated images that visually represented the scenes described by the graphs. The integration of common sense knowledge was crucial in improving the coherence and contextual relevance of the generated images. The results demonstrated significant improvements in the quality of the generated images when using enriched scene graphs compared to those generated from non-enriched graphs. The enriched graphs enabled the generation of more realistic and contextually appropriate images, capturing intricate details and relationships between objects that were often missed by conventional methods. For instance, images generated from enriched graphs displayed better object positioning, more accurate spatial relationships and higher overall visual fidelity than those generated from conventional scene graphs.

2.4.3. Other Tasks

A neurosymbolic approach for scene graph-based *Visual Question Answering (VQA)*, akin to NeuSyRE, enhances scene graphs with knowledge enrichment, adding semantic and relational context. This enrichment improves the understanding of complex questions, allowing for more accurate and contextually aware answers. By leveraging the structured representation of scene graphs combined with extensive common sense knowledge, the model performs high-level semantic reasoning. This leads to significant improvements in VQA performance, particularly in achieving higher accuracy on open-ended questions, which are challenging for data-centric methods, and higher validity, consistency, and plausibility scores compared to approaches without knowledge enrichment. The enriched scene graphs provide a deeper semantic understanding, enabling the model to handle diverse and complex questions better, resulting in more precise and contextually relevant answers [5]. Ward et al. [10] presented a neurosymbolic approach combining deep learning-based colourization with knowledge graphs to improve the accuracy and realism of automatic *image colourization*. This method used KGs to provide contextual information about the probable colours of objects and scenes, which the colourization model then applied to grayscale images. By leveraging structured knowledge from sources like ConceptNet and the Common Sense Knowledge Graph (CSKG) [21], the system could make more informed colour predictions, resulting in more contextually appropriate and visually accurate colourizations. In *event processing*, especially for the Internet of Multimedia Things (IoMT) and smart cities, neurosymbolic models effectively address the complexities of multimodal event streams. Traditional systems often struggle with unstructured data and multimodal analysis, but integrating deep neural networks for feature extraction with symbolic reasoning for event pattern detection allows these models to process and analyze diverse data streams more effectively. This hybrid approach creates high-level knowledge representations, enhancing the detection of complex event patterns across various modalities, including spatial and temporal constraints [9]. Such advancements enable more accurate and context-aware event processing, crucial for real-time applications in smart city environments. For *image retrieval*, scene graphs offer explicit semantic structures, detailing objects and their relationships within images, which enables efficient querying and retrieval from large databases. The neurosymbolic, scene graph-based methods provide a more organized and semantically rich alternative to traditional textual descriptions, improving retrieval accuracy and relevance [5]. For *data spaces*, multimodal knowledge graphs offer a unified and semantically grounded representation of data from multiple sources, facilitating real-time analysis and integration. These graphs enhance data sharing and management by providing detailed insights into complex patterns and relationships within the data, enabling better decision-making. In smart cities, they support applications such as traffic monitoring and public safety by combining structured data from sensors and GPS with unstructured data from cameras and social media [11].

3. Visual Reasoning with Multimodal LLMs

3.1. Visual Question Answering (VQA)

Visual Question Answering (VQA) is a fundamental task with a broad range of downstream applications in many critical domains, from biomedicine [24,25,26] to traffic monitoring [27,28] and remote sensing [29,30]. As annotating reliable answers for a large number of question-image pairs is expensive and time-consuming, and thus impractical, it has become common to answer visual questions in a domain without having access to annotated data from that specific task and domain. This evaluation paradigm is known as *zero-shot* evaluation.

Various VQA datasets have been introduced. **TextVQA** [31] contains 5,000 questions about textual sequences that appear in 3,166 images, where more than half of the answers require perceiving texts that occupy less than 0.005 of the total image area. Therefore, TextVQA emphasizes how well a model can read small text, which can serve as a surrogate for how well a model can perceive fine visual details. TextVQA provides Optical Character Recognition (OCR) annotations [32] which we use to approximate the ground-truth answer bounding box for each question by selecting the OCR bound-

Table 1. Architectural overview of seven MLLMs evaluated in [41].

Model	Vision Encoder	Bridge Module	LLM Backbone
BLIP-2	ViT-g	Q-Former	Flan-$T5_{XXL}$
InstructBLIP	ViT-g	Q-Former	Vicuna-13B
LLaVA-1.5	ViT-l	Linear	Vicuna-13B
Qwen-VL-Chat	ViT-bigG	Resampler	Qwen-7B
Fuyu-8B	-	-	Persimmon-8B
GPT-4V		Not released	
Gemini-Pro-Vision		Not released	

ing box containing the text with the highest string similarity with the human-provided answer. This bounding box is used for cropping in `human-CROP`. **GQA** [33] contains 12,578 questions paired with 398 images, using the scene graphs of Visual Genome [34] to construct highly compositional questions requiring spatial, logical, relational, and comparative reasoning, and explicitly controlling the answer distribution for different groups of questions in order to prevent educated guesses using language and world priors. **AOKVQA** [35] contains 1,145 questions about 1,122 images, where the questions require additional knowledge and cannot be answered from the image-question pair alone. **VQAv2** [36] is a large-scale dataset, a subset of COCO [37], containing 214,354 questions paired with 40,504 images from various objects and settings.

Multimodal Large Language Models (MLLMs) [12,13,14] have shown promising accuracy in zero-shot VQA, commonly attributed to their pretraining on terabytes of image and language data with billion-parameter Transformer-based neural networks. MLLMs typically have three primary components: a vision encoder, a bridge module, and an LLM backbone [15]. Commonly, MLLMs utilize CLIP-ViT [38] as the vision encoder, which divides the input image into patches and feeds them into Transformer blocks sequentially in a raster-scan order. The resulting visual features from the vision encoder are then either linearly projected [39] or condensed into a fixed-sized representation [40] to align with the textual representation space, using a bridge module. The transformed visual features are then prepended to the text embedding within the LLM.

State-of-the-art MLLMs follow different choices for these three components, as shown in Table 1. Both BLIP-2 [40] and InstructBLIP [42] utilize the Q-Former as a bridge module, while InstructBLIP integrates instructions into the Q-Former for an instruction-awarding visual feature. LLaVA-1.5 [43] projects the visual feature from ViT into the LLM space with an MLP layer. Qwen-VL-Chat [44] chooses a larger vision encoder ViT-bigG and a one-layer cross-attention module to perceive visual features. Fuyu-8B [45] uniquely removes the external vision encoder, directly incorporating pixel information into the language decoder. The training of MLLMs typically undergoes an initial pre-training on extensive image-text datasets such as LAION [46], followed by specialized multimodal instruction tuning [39]. Enhancements in MLLMs have been pursued through various means, including increasing image resolution [15], scaling data and model size [47], extending to multilingual context [48], and introducing interleaved data formats [49].

Given the potentially broad adoption of MLLMs in downstream tasks, we have recently analyzed their robustness and limitations in dealing with phenomena such as object sizes, distractors, and image quality. In [50], we analyzed the ability of MLLMs to

Table 2. Sensitivity of zero-shot accuracy of VQA models to the size of visual concepts in TextVQA.

BLIP2 Model	Crop Method	Answer Bbox Size (S) small	medium	large
FlanT5$_{XL}$	w/o cropping	19.91	29.07	36.81
	`human-CROP`	32.06	41.31	38.84
OPT$_{2.3B}$	w/o cropping	19.38	26.09	33.28
	`human-CROP`	27.19	34.36	33.25

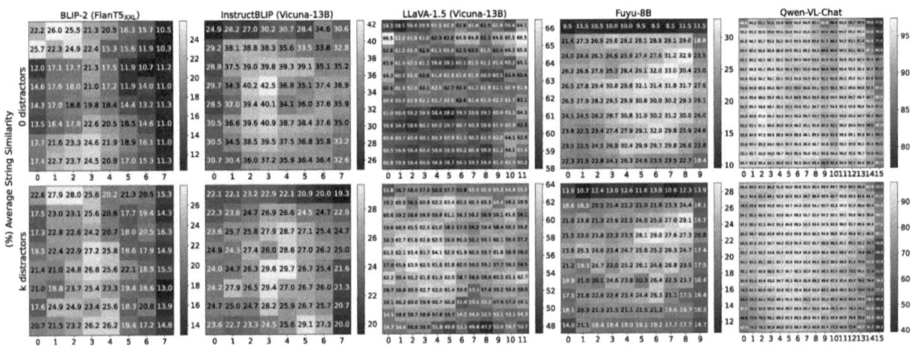

Figure 6. The effect text (number) location in the image on MLLMs' ability to read the text correctly, with and without distractors (bottom and top, respectively). Higher values are presented in lighter colors.

answer questions about visual objects of different sizes. The results of this analysis (Table 2) show that as the relative visual size of the answer decreases (right to left in each row), there is a significant decline in the accuracy of the original models. Meanwhile, human-based visual cropping reduces this accuracy gap. These observations are somewhat surprising since the visual encoding in BLIP2 is theoretically not restricted in its visual resolution and, therefore, should be able to perceive objects regardless of their visual sizes. In follow-up work, we generalized this finding to seven open- and closed-source models, showing that this is a general limitation of MLLMs. Inspired by the positive impact of human visual cropping on answering fine-visual detail questions, we devised a framework with automatic visual cropping methods called ViCrop, achieving accuracy gains both when using external localization models and especially when using the attention maps of the MLLM itself. These results suggest that the model attention can be leveraged to partially approximate human cropping. We further investigated how visual cropping affects different question types, and observed a consistently positive effect on questions regarding text reading, object attributes, and categorization, and a detrimental impact on localization and counting questions.

Moreover, object size is not the only factor that impacts the performance of MLLMs. In [41], we also investigated the impact of the object quality, object position, and object distractors, using a text reading objective. We opted for text reading as a task because manipulating text is easier than manipulating complex objects, while still allowing for evaluation of recognition of object shapes and their spatial relationships. To evaluate the effect of distractors, we placed k distractor numbers beside the correct number, each associated with a variable, and asked the MLLM to provide the number associated with a

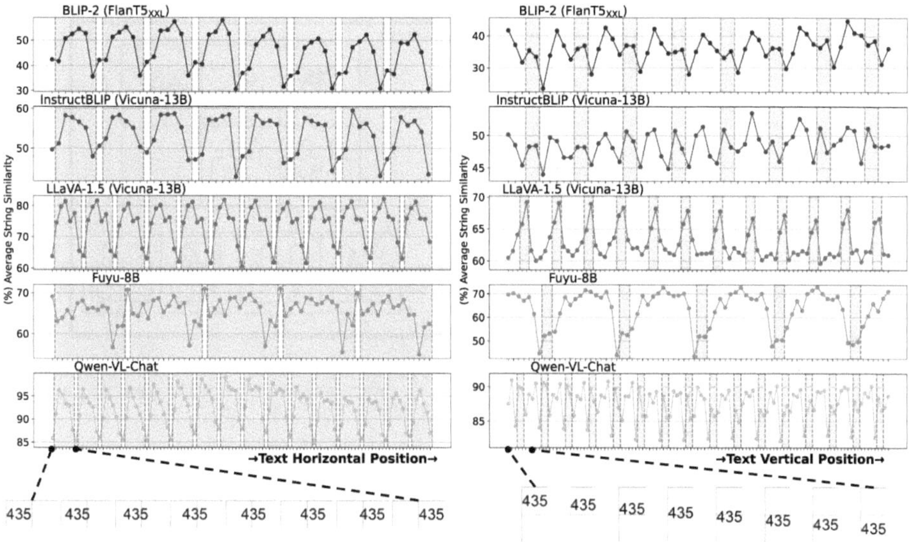

Figure 7. The performance of MLLMs in text recognition tasks demonstrates notable variability when textual content is vertically (left) and horizontally (right) cut by image patch boundaries. Gray area indicates that the target texts are cut by a patch boundary. We provide two local illustrations below showing that a text is shifted between two adjacent image patches.

certain variable. In this experiment, with fonts of sizes 8 and 12, we observed a constant decline in performance for all models as more distractors were added. The only exception was Qwen-VL-Chat, which reaches and preserves a perfect score for font-12 questions while suffering a strong decline for font-8 questions. The experiments with object quality revealed trends well-aligned with human performance, and that the model performance is relatively high as long as the quality is above a certain threshold.

In terms of object location, we analyzed two settings: sensitivity to global positioning and to local cutting boundaries. Namely, in the global positioning experiment (Figure 6), we placed a number centrally into each image patch, once at a time, and asked the model to read out the number. The results indicate that most MLLMs struggle to recognize the text when it is placed on the right side of the image, and some MLLMs struggle with text placed on the left side of the image, or in the first row. This indicates the positional bias of MLLMs. Curiously, our local cut experiment (Figure 7) shows that contrary to one's intuition, the text is easier to recognize by MLLMs when it is divided across multiple patches. Therefore, even with the same size and quality, small objects seem to be more recognizable by MLLMs when they are divided into different image patches. Conversely, all models have a decline when the number is placed in the center of a single patch. When performing horizontal cuts, we observe that the model performance declines more, but the performance is not higher at the cut boundaries.

In the next section, we proceed with further analysis of the ability of MLLMs to perform abstract visual reasoning, together with a discussion of the role of neurosymbolic systems in circumventing the challenges with perception and reasoning.

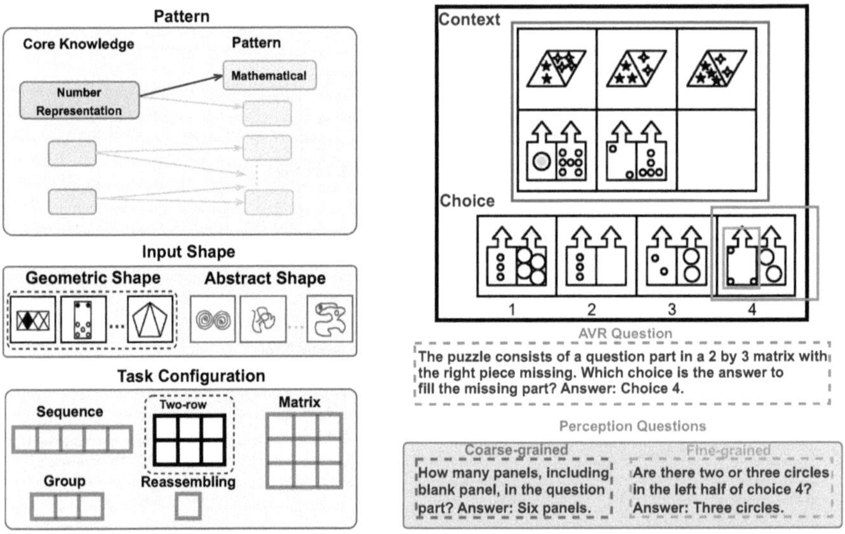

Figure 8. An abstract visual reasoning puzzle in **MARVEL**. The puzzle contains **mathematical** pattern governing the element number in **geometric shapes** with **two-row** task configuration. The AVR question focuses on the final answer for the puzzle, while the perception questions focus on the fine-grained detail about one choice or coarse-grained detail over the whole puzzle.

3.2. Abstract Visual Reasoning

Abstract visual reasoning (AVR) puzzles [51,52], a common component in human intelligence tests, test the ability of models to recognize abstract patterns in sequences of two-dimensional figures. An example of a 2×3 matrix configuration is shown in Figure 8 (top-right). To solve this AVR puzzle, we need to identify the addition and subtraction patterns that govern the sequence of input shapes and their attribute (number of stars/circles) in the first row. Then, the identified pattern must be applied to the second row, to reason about the optimal figure that coherently completes the row with the first row. Thus, the guiding logic of AVR puzzles is that each row represents a progression with a different surface structure, yet guided by the same principles of abstraction. These principles rely on preserving relational regularities, and can thus be seen as analogical abstractions.

There is a wide variety of AVR benchmarks [53], typically relying on a discriminatory cognitive process. Problems such as Raven's Progressive Matrices [54,55,56] and Visual Analogy Problems [57] involve completing sequences of panels with abstracts shapes selected from a predefined set of options. Another popular format are the Bongard problems [58,59], which require discovering the rules that govern abstract shapes across sets of panels, where the result must be described in natural language. A popular generative task is the Abstraction and Reasoning Corpus (ARC) [60], which tests the ability to recreate missing panels without choosing from predefined options. A comprehensive overview of AVR problems is given in [53].

Recently, we developed MARVEL [16]: a novel benchmark that is designed to cover a comprehensive set of patterns, input shapes, and configurations, along with rigorous

Table 3. Comparing MARVEL to related benchmarks: RAVEN [52], G-set [61], VAP [51], Bongard-LOGO [62], SVRT [63], ARC [64], DOPT [65]. *ARC puzzles are provided in a generative format.

Dimension		RAVEN	G-set	VAP	Bongard-LOGO	SVRT	DOPT	ARC*	**MARVEL**
Shape	Geometric	✓	✓	✓			✓	✓	✓
	Abstract				✓	✓			✓
Pattern	Temporal	✓	✓				✓	✓	✓
	Spatial					✓		✓	✓
	Quantities	✓	✓	✓	✓	✓	✓	✓	✓
	Mathematical	✓	✓	✓				✓	✓
	2D-Geometry				✓	✓			✓
	3D-Geometry								✓
Config.	Sequence						✓		✓
	Two-row			✓					✓
	Matrix	✓	✓						✓
	Group				✓	✓			✓
	Reassembling								✓
Perception Question									✓

checks to assess that model answers are grounded in both perception and reasoning. As such, MARVEL addresses two challenges in evaluating MLLMs comprehensively. 1) Prior AVR benchmarks cover a subset of the overall spectrum, which hinders comprehensive evaluation of MLLMs [66] (see Table 3). Without theoretical foundations, existing benchmarks lack diverse reasoning patterns in real-world tasks and fail to provide a holistic evaluation of MLLM's ability [64], which can not be solved by simple joint evaluations[67]. In contrast, MARVEL not only includes geometric and abstract shapes and five different task configurations but also builds its reasoning patterns based on the core knowledge system in cognitive science, enriching abstract reasoning that exists in the real world. 2) Prior studies [68,69] employ an end-to-end evaluation framework, leaving it unclear whether the model's performance is attributed to perception or reasoning [70]. Inspired by prior analysis of visual details and perceptual bias, MARVEL introduces perception questions to ensure the MLLMs correctly perceive the presented visual patterns.

The design of MARVEL combines three dimensions. First, MARVEL supports five complementary task configurations: sequence, two-row, matrix, group, and reassembling. Each of these configurations organizes the input context into a different layout structure. Second, MARVEL supports both geometric and abstract shapes. Its geometric shapes consist of more than two different elementary geometric shapes to mitigate potential biases and increase complexity, while its abstract shapes have a much more significant variance. Third, MARVEL's patterns are derived from core knowledge theory [71], which dictates that human infants with no real-world knowledge and limited experience represent their environment using abstraction patterns. These patterns can be categorized into four types of core knowledge, which is the foundation for inference and reasoning [72] in real-world scenarios. MARVEL supports three of these four patterns (object, number, and geometry knowledge) and expands each into two patterns for a fine-grained assessment of abstract reasoning. MARVEL's data is sourced from public

Table 4. Main zero-shot accuracy over MARVEL across all MLLMs in two accuracy metrics: $Prec^C$ = group-based accuracy over all coarse-grained perception questions (model must answer all three questions correctly), $Perc^{C\&F}$ = group-based accuracy combining all perception questions (coarse/fine-grained), AVR = AVR Question. The best performance among all models is in **bold**, and the best result in two MLLMs categories is underlined. *Gemini refuses to answer the puzzle due to safety problems in 7% cases so the performance is computed based on the left set. † notes the result is attributed to inductive bias.

Category	Model	AVR Question	Fine-grained Perception	$Perc^C$	$Perc^{C\&F}$	$Perc^{C\&F}$ & AVR
	Random	25.00	50.00	-	-	-
Open-source MLLMs	Qwen-VL (7B)	19.61	37.27	0.52	0.39	0.00
	Fuyu (8B)	24.29†	34.94	0.00	0.00	0.00
	BLIP-2 (FlanT5$_{XXL}$-11B)	24.81†	53.38	1.04	0.52	0.26
	InstructBLIP (Vicuna-13B)	24.68†	49.48	0.00	0.00	0.00
	LLaVA-1.5 (Vicuna-13B)	26.36	51.43	1.14	0.52	0.13
Closed-source MLLMs	GPT-4V	22.34	51.56	18.31	9.22	2.73
	GPT-4o	27.79	**68.44**	**62.73**	**43.77**	**12.21**
	Gemini-pro-vision*	25.06†	44.42	15.19	6.75	1.69
	Claude3 (Sonnet)	26.49†	50.91	38.70	19.87	5.06
	Claude3 (Opus)	**28.83**	47.27	44.94	20.13	5.97
	Human	68.86 ± 9.74	98.67	-	-	-

websites and enhanced by manual annotation to ensure that each subcategory has at least 45 puzzles. Ultimately, MARVEL includes 770 high-quality puzzles over six high-level patterns across five distinct task configurations.

Moreover, MARVEL adds a follow-up step to distinguish between the perception and reasoning skills of models (and avoid shortcut learning and inductive biases [67]), making it a hierarchical evaluation framework. For this purpose, MARVEL is enriched with perception questions [70] designed to test models' perception ability on visual details (Figure 8). For each puzzle, MARVEL provides three coarse-grained questions and one pattern-related fine-grained question. The coarse-grained question aims to test if models can understand the task configuration correctly by directly asking about the number of panels in puzzles. The fine-grained question in binary-choice format examines models' understanding of input shapes, which focus on the visual details categorized by Tong et al. [73] such as shape attributes (number of edges) and spatial relationship (left, right) based on the pattern contained in the puzzle. For example, in Figure 8, the fine-grained perception question tests whether models can understand the number of circles because the puzzle is based on *Mathematical Pattern*.

MARVEL evaluates closed-source MLLMs: GPT-4 [14], Gemini [74] and Claude3 [75], in both zero-shot and few-shot [76] settings. It also tests MLLMs smaller than 13B: InstructBLIP [77], BLIP-2 [12], Fuyu [78], Qwen-VL [79] and LLaVA [80]. These MLLMs are only evaluated in a zero-shot setting due to their single-image input settings [81]. The results (Table 4) show that human performance is relatively high, whereas all models perform close to random. This leaves a 40% accuracy gap, which is a significant difference between humans and MLLMs. The performance of the closed-source models is slightly higher than the open-source ones, though they perform comparably overall. Few-shot demonstrations have a marginal impact, bringing improvement for GPT-4V and a decline for Claude3 (Opus). Further analysis shows that, among the six patterns, *3D-Geomertry* pattern is the most challenging for humans and MLLMs.

Closed-source MLLMs demonstrate more robust performance on coarse-grained perception group accuracy compared to open-sourced MLLMs, with a performance gap ranging from 14.05% to 61.59%. However, even the best model fails to reach an acceptable accuracy (<65%). Fine-grained perception questions further confirm this argument, with all models except GPT-4o showing near-random performance. Models perform relatively better at color perception but have difficulty recognizing location (e.g., ‘a’ is on the left of ‘b’). Finally, analysis through group-based metrics shows that no model can solve the AVR puzzles with consistent reasoning, with the best model reaching only 12.21% group accuracy. To further delineate perceptual and reasoning skills, Jiang et al. tested models with the same puzzle but asked for possible underlying patterns in a multiple-choice setting instead of the whole AVR reasoning question. Closed-source models show non-random results when reasoning about the underlying pattern, while nearly all open-source models struggle to outperform random baselines. This gap indicates that closed-source models partially understand the patterns, but more accurate visual perception is needed to complete the entire task. Similarly, adding accurate text descriptions of the puzzle to the input enables GPT-4V to reach human-level accuracy (65%), while open-source models still significantly lag behind. This shows that closed-source models possess partial problem-solving abilities, but these are often overshadowed by visual perception.

How can future AI systems address AVR problems? One possibility is to pursue tailored neural architectures that can solve a variety of AVR tasks through a dynamic weighting of their parameters [82]. However, a robust abstraction method likely needs to enhance neural networks with a symbolic component. Such a method called AlphaGeometry has recently been proposed for the related task of solving geometry problems [83]. AlphaGeometry uses a neural language model, trained from scratch on large scale synthetic data, to guide a symbolic deduction engine based on infinite branching points. Other neuro-symbolic methods, e.g., based on belief graphs [84] or Python code generation [85], also hold a promise to be applied for AVR tasks. At the moment of writing, these pursuits represent exciting future research directions, and have not been explored in depth.

4. Conclusion

Neurosymbolic visual reasoning represents a significant advancement in achieving expressive and intuitive scene understanding beyond basic vision tasks. By integrating deep learning with symbolic reasoning, neurosymbolic approaches enhance scene graph generation, enabling detailed and contextually rich representations of visual data. This integration addresses the limitations of traditional deep learning methods, which often struggle with high-level reasoning. Scene graphs, enriched with common sense knowledge from knowledge graphs, provide a robust framework for interpreting and interacting with visual scenes, improving visual reasoning tasks like image captioning, event processing and visual question answering. The NeuSyRE framework exemplifies the benefits of this integration, demonstrating improved accuracy and expressiveness in scene graph generation and downstream reasoning tasks. The incorporation of Multimodal Large Language Models (MLLMs) further enhances visual reasoning capabilities, leveraging extensive pretraining to achieve zero-shot performance in complex tasks. However, challenges remain, particularly in accurately perceiving and reasoning about fine-grained visual details. The MARVEL benchmark highlights these challenges, emphasizing the need for better integration of perceptual and reasoning skills. Future advancements in neurosymbolic approaches and tailored neural architectures promise to address these challenges, paving the way for more robust and explainable AI systems in visual reasoning.

Acknowledgments

This publication has emanated from research conducted with the financial support of Taighde Éireann – Research Ireland under Grant number SFI/12/RC/2289 P2.

References

[1] Hassaballah M, Awad AI. Deep learning in computer vision: principles and applications. CRC Press; 2020.
[2] Krishna R, Zhu Y, Groth O, Johnson J, Hata K, Kravitz J, et al. Visual genome: Connecting language and vision using crowdsourced dense image annotations. International Journal of Computer Vision. 2017;123(1):32-73.
[3] Chang X, Ren P, Xu P, Li Z, Chen X, Hauptmann A. Scene Graphs: A Survey of Generations and Applications. arXiv preprint arXiv:210401111. 2021.
[4] Zhu G, Zhang L, Jiang Y, Dang Y, Hou H, Shen P, et al. Scene graph generation: A comprehensive survey. arXiv preprint arXiv:220100443. 2022.
[5] Khan MJ, Ilievski F, Breslin JG, Curry E. A survey of neurosymbolic visual reasoning with scene graphs and common sense knowledge. Neurosymbolic Artificial Intelligence. 2024;(Preprint):1-24.
[6] Khan MJ, Breslin JG, Curry E. Expressive Scene Graph Generation Using Commonsense Knowledge Infusion for Visual Understanding and Reasoning. In: European Semantic Web Conference. Springer; 2022. p. 93-112.
[7] Khan MJ, Breslin J, Curry E. NeuSyRE: Neuro-Symbolic Visual Understanding and Reasoning Framework based on Scene Graph Enrichment. Semantic Web. 2023.
[8] Khan MJ, Curry E. Neuro-symbolic Visual Reasoning for Multimedia Event Processing: Overview, Prospects and Challenges. In: Proceedings of the 29th ACM International Conference on Information and Knowledge Management (CIKM'2020) Workshops; 2020. .
[9] Curry E, Salwala D, Dhingra P, Pontes FA, Yadav P. Multimodal Event Processing: A Neural-Symbolic Paradigm for the Internet of Multimedia Things. IEEE Internet of Things Journal. 2022.
[10] Ward R, Khan MJ, Breslin JG, Curry E. Knowledge-Guided Colorization: Overview, Prospects and Challenges. In: 17th International Workshop on Neural-Symbolic Learning and Reasoning; 2023. .
[11] Usmani A, Khan MJ, G Breslin J, Curry E. Towards Multimodal Knowledge Graphs for Data Spaces. In: Companion Proceedings of the ACM Web Conference 2023; 2023. p. 1494-9.
[12] Li J, Li D, Savarese S, Hoi S. Blip-2: Bootstrapping language-image pre-training with frozen image encoders and large language models. In: International conference on machine learning. PMLR; 2023. p. 19730-42.
[13] Alayrac JB, Donahue J, Luc P, Miech A, Barr I, Hasson Y, et al. Flamingo: a visual language model for few-shot learning. Advances in Neural Information Processing Systems. 2022;35:23716-36.
[14] OpenAI. GPT-4 Technical Report; 2023.
[15] Yu T, Hu J, Yao Y, Zhang H, Zhao Y, Wang C, et al. Reformulating vision-language foundation models and datasets towards universal multimodal assistants. arXiv preprint arXiv:231000653. 2023.
[16] Jiang Y, Zhang J, Sun K, Sourati Z, Ahrabian K, Ma K, et al.. MARVEL: Multidimensional Abstraction and Reasoning through Visual Evaluation and Learning; 2024.
[17] Khan MJ, Breslin JG, Curry E. Common Sense Knowledge Infusion for Visual Understanding and Reasoning: Approaches, Challenges, and Applications. IEEE Internet Computing. 2022;26(4):21-7.
[18] He F, Wang Y, Miao X, Sun X. Interpretable visual reasoning: A survey. Image and Vision Computing. 2021;112:104194.
[19] Hitzler P, Eberhart A, Ebrahimi M, Sarker MK, Zhou L. Neuro-symbolic approaches in artificial intelligence. National Science Review. 2022;9(6):nwac035.

[20] Speer R, Chin J, Havasi C. Conceptnet 5.5: An open multilingual graph of general knowledge. In: Thirty-first AAAI conference on artificial intelligence; 2017. p. 4444-51.
[21] Ilievski F, Szekely P, Zhang B. Cskg: The commonsense knowledge graph. In: European Semantic Web Conference. Springer; 2021. p. 680-96.
[22] Garcez Ad, Lamb LC. Neurosymbolic AI: The 3rd wave. Artificial Intelligence Review. 2023:1-20.
[23] Johnson J, Gupta A, Fei-Fei L. Image generation from scene graphs. In: Proceedings of the IEEE Conference on Computer Vision and Pattern Recognition; 2018. p. 1219-28.
[24] Seenivasan L, Islam M, Krishna AK, Ren H. Surgical-vqa: Visual question answering in surgical scenes using transformer. In: International Conference on Medical Image Computing and Computer-Assisted Intervention. Springer; 2022. p. 33-43.
[25] Naseem U, Khushi M, Kim J. Vision-language transformer for interpretable pathology visual question answering. IEEE Journal of Biomedical and Health Informatics. 2022;27(4):1681-90.
[26] Lau JJ, Gayen S, Ben Abacha A, Demner-Fushman D. A dataset of clinically generated visual questions and answers about radiology images. Scientific data. 2018;5(1):1-10.
[27] Xu L, Huang H, Liu J. Sutd-trafficqa: A question answering benchmark and an efficient network for video reasoning over traffic events. In: Proceedings of the IEEE/CVF Conference on Computer Vision and Pattern Recognition; 2021. p. 9878-88.
[28] Zhang J, Ilievski F, Ma K, Kollaa A, Francis J, Oltramari A. A Study of Situational Reasoning for Traffic Understanding. KDD. 2023.
[29] Sarkar A, Rahnemoonfar M. Vqa-aid: Visual question answering for post-disaster damage assessment and analysis. In: 2021 IEEE International Geoscience and Remote Sensing Symposium IGARSS. IEEE; 2021. p. 8660-3.
[30] Lobry S, Marcos D, Murray J, Tuia D. RSVQA: Visual question answering for remote sensing data. IEEE Transactions on Geoscience and Remote Sensing. 2020;58(12):8555-66.
[31] Singh A, Natarajan V, Shah M, Jiang Y, Chen X, Batra D, et al. Towards vqa models that can read. In: Proceedings of the IEEE/CVF conference on computer vision and pattern recognition; 2019. p. 8317-26.
[32] Borisyuk F, Gordo A, Sivakumar V. Rosetta: Large scale system for text detection and recognition in images. In: Proceedings of the 24th ACM SIGKDD international conference on knowledge discovery & data mining; 2018. p. 71-9.
[33] Hudson DA, Manning CD. Gqa: A new dataset for real-world visual reasoning and compositional question answering. In: Proceedings of the IEEE/CVF conference on computer vision and pattern recognition; 2019. p. 6700-9.
[34] Krishna R, Zhu Y, Groth O, Johnson J, Hata K, Kravitz J, et al. Visual genome: Connecting language and vision using crowdsourced dense image annotations. International journal of computer vision. 2017;123:32-73.
[35] Schwenk D, Khandelwal A, Clark C, Marino K, Mottaghi R. A-okvqa: A benchmark for visual question answering using world knowledge. In: Computer Vision–ECCV 2022: 17th European Conference, Tel Aviv, Israel, October 23–27, 2022, Proceedings, Part VIII. Springer; 2022. p. 146-62.
[36] Goyal Y, Khot T, Summers-Stay D, Batra D, Parikh D. Making the v in vqa matter: Elevating the role of image understanding in visual question answering. In: Proceedings of the IEEE conference on computer vision and pattern recognition; 2017. p. 6904-13.
[37] Lin TY, Maire M, Belongie S, Hays J, Perona P, Ramanan D, et al. Microsoft coco: Common objects in context. In: Computer Vision–ECCV 2014: 13th European Conference, Zurich, Switzerland, September 6-12, 2014, Proceedings, Part V 13. Springer; 2014. p. 740-55.
[38] Radford A, Kim JW, Hallacy C, Ramesh A, Goh G, Agarwal S, et al. Learning transferable visual models from natural language supervision. In: International conference on machine learning. PMLR; 2021. p. 8748-63.
[39] Liu H, Li C, Wu Q, Lee YJ. Visual instruction tuning. Advances in neural information processing systems. 2024;36.
[40] Li J, Li D, Savarese S, Hoi S. BLIP-2: Bootstrapping Language-Image Pre-training with Frozen Image Encoders and Large Language Models. In: Krause A, Brunskill E, Cho K, Engelhardt B, Sabato S, Scarlett J, editors. Proceedings of ICML. vol. 202. PMLR; 2023. p. 19730-42.
[41] Zhang J, Hu J, Khayatkhoei M, Ilievski F, Sun M. Exploring perceptual limitation of multimodal large language models. arXiv preprint arXiv:240207384. 2024.
[42] Dai W, Li J, Li D, Tiong AMH, Zhao J, Wang W, et al.. InstructBLIP: Towards General-purpose Vision-Language Models with Instruction Tuning; 2023.

[43] Lin B, Zhu B, Ye Y, Ning M, Jin P, Yuan L. Video-LLaVA: Learning United Visual Representation by Alignment Before Projection. arXiv preprint arXiv:231110122. 2023.

[44] Bai J, Bai S, Yang S, Wang S, Tan S, Wang P, et al. Qwen-VL: A Versatile Vision-Language Model for Understanding, Localization, Text Reading, and Beyond. arXiv preprint arXiv:230812966. 2023.

[45] Bavishi R, Elsen E, Hawthorne C, Nye M, Odena A, Somani A, et al.. Introducing our Multimodal Models; 2023. Available from: https://www.adept.ai/blog/fuyu-8b.

[46] Schuhmann C, Beaumont R, Vencu R, Gordon C, Wightman R, Cherti M, et al. LAION-5b: An open large-scale dataset for training next generation image-text models. Advances in Neural Information Processing Systems. 2022;35:25278-94.

[47] Wang W, Lv Q, Yu W, Hong W, Qi J, Wang Y, et al.. CogVLM: Visual Expert for Pretrained Language Models; 2023.

[48] Hu J, Yao Y, Wang C, Wang S, Pan Y, Chen Q, et al. Large Multilingual Models Pivot Zero-Shot Multimodal Learning across Languages. arXiv preprint arXiv:230812038. 2023.

[49] Lin J, Yin H, Ping W, Lu Y, Molchanov P, Tao A, et al. Vila: On pre-training for visual language models. arXiv preprint arXiv:231207533. 2023.

[50] Zhang J, Khayatkhoei M, Chhikara P, Ilievski F. Visual cropping improves zero-shot question answering of multimodal large language models. arXiv preprint arXiv:231016033. 2023.

[51] Hill F, Santoro A, Barrett DG, Morcos AS, Lillicrap T. Learning to make analogies by contrasting abstract relational structure. arXiv preprint arXiv:190200120. 2019.

[52] Zhang C, Gao F, Jia B, Zhu Y, Zhu SC. Raven: A dataset for relational and analogical visual reasoning. In: Proceedings of the IEEE/CVF conference on computer vision and pattern recognition; 2019. p. 5317-27.

[53] Małkiński M, Mańdziuk J. A review of emerging research directions in Abstract Visual Reasoning. Information Fusion. 2023;91:713-36. Available from: https://www.sciencedirect.com/science/article/pii/S1566253522002214.

[54] Raven JC. STANDARDIZATION OF PROGRESSIVE MATRICES, 1938. British Journal of Medical Psychology. 1941;19(1):137-50.

[55] Barrett DGT, Hill F, Santoro A, Morcos AS, Lillicrap T. Measuring abstract reasoning in neural networks; 2018.

[56] Zhang C, Gao F, Jia B, Zhu Y, Zhu SC. RAVEN: A Dataset for Relational and Analogical Visual rEasoNing. In: Proceedings of the IEEE Conference on Computer Vision and Pattern Recognition (CVPR); 2019. .

[57] Webb TW, Dulberg Z, Frankland SM, Petrov AA, O'Reilly RC, Cohen JD. Learning representations that support extrapolation. In: Proceedings of the 37th International Conference on Machine Learning. ICML'20. JMLR.org; 2020. .

[58] Bongard MM. The Recognition Problem. Foreign Technology Div Wright-Patterson AFB Ohio, Tech. Rep.; 1968.

[59] Nie W, Yu Z, Mao L, Patel AB, Zhu Y, Anandkumar A. BONGARD-LOGO: a new benchmark for human-level concept learning and reasoning. In: Proceedings of the 34th International Conference on Neural Information Processing Systems. NIPS '20. Red Hook, NY, USA: Curran Associates Inc.; 2020. .

[60] Chollet F. On the Measure of Intelligence; 2019.

[61] Mańdziuk J, Żychowski A. DeepIQ: A human-inspired AI system for solving IQ test problems. In: 2019 International Joint Conference on Neural Networks (IJCNN). IEEE; 2019. p. 1-8.

[62] Nie W, Yu Z, Mao L, Patel AB, Zhu Y, Anandkumar A. Bongard-logo: A new benchmark for human-level concept learning and reasoning. Advances in Neural Information Processing Systems. 2020;33:16468-80.

[63] Fleuret F, Li T, Dubout C, Wampler EK, Yantis S, Geman D. Comparing machines and humans on a visual categorization test. Proceedings of the National Academy of Sciences. 2011;108(43):17621-5.

[64] Chollet F. On the measure of intelligence. arXiv preprint arXiv:191101547. 2019.

[65] Webb T, Dulberg Z, Frankland S, Petrov A, O'Reilly R, Cohen J. Learning representations that support extrapolation. In: International conference on machine learning. PMLR; 2020. p. 10136-46.

[66] van der Maas HL, Snoek L, Stevenson CE. How much intelligence is there in artificial intelligence? A 2020 update. Intelligence. 2021;87:101548.

[67] Małkiński M, Mańdziuk J. A review of emerging research directions in abstract visual reasoning. Information Fusion. 2023;91:713-36.

[68] Benny Y, Pekar N, Wolf L. Scale-localized abstract reasoning. In: Proceedings of the IEEE/CVF Conference on Computer Vision and Pattern Recognition; 2021. p. 12557-65.
[69] Hu S, Ma Y, Liu X, Wei Y, Bai S. Stratified rule-aware network for abstract visual reasoning. In: Proceedings of the AAAI Conference on Artificial Intelligence. vol. 35; 2021. p. 1567-74.
[70] Selvaraju RR, Tendulkar P, Parikh D, Horvitz E, Ribeiro MT, Nushi B, et al. Squinting at vqa models: Introspecting vqa models with sub-questions. In: Proceedings of the IEEE/CVF Conference on Computer Vision and Pattern Recognition; 2020. p. 10003-11.
[71] Spelke ES, Kinzler KD. Core knowledge. Developmental science. 2007;10(1):89-96.
[72] Lipton JS, Spelke ES. Discrimination of large and small numerosities by human infants. Infancy. 2004;5(3):271-90.
[73] Tong S, Liu Z, Zhai Y, Ma Y, LeCun Y, Xie S. Eyes wide shut? exploring the visual shortcomings of multimodal llms. arXiv preprint arXiv:240106209. 2024.
[74] Google GT. Gemini: A Family of Highly Capable Multimodal Models; 2023.
[75] Anthropic. Claude 3; 2024. Available from: `https://www.anthropic.com/news/claude-3-family`.
[76] Brown T, Mann B, Ryder N, Subbiah M, Kaplan JD, Dhariwal P, et al. Language models are few-shot learners. Advances in neural information processing systems. 2020;33:1877-901.
[77] Dai W, Li J, Li D, Tiong AMH, Zhao J, Wang W, et al. Instructblip: Towards general-purpose vision-language models with instruction tuning. Advances in Neural Information Processing Systems. 2024;36.
[78] Bavishi R, Elsen E, Hawthorne C, Nye M, Odena A, Somani A, et al.. Introducing our Multimodal Models; 2023. Available from: `https://www.adept.ai/blog/fuyu-8b`.
[79] Bai J, Bai S, Yang S, Wang S, Tan S, Wang P, et al. Qwen-vl: A frontier large vision-language model with versatile abilities. arXiv preprint arXiv:230812966. 2023.
[80] Liu H, Li C, Wu Q, Lee YJ. Visual instruction tuning. arXiv preprint arXiv:230408485. 2023.
[81] Zhao H, Cai Z, Si S, Ma X, An K, Chen L, et al. Mmicl: Empowering vision-language model with multi-modal in-context learning. arXiv preprint arXiv:230907915. 2023.
[82] Małkiński M, Mańdziuk J. One self-configurable model to solve many abstract visual reasoning problems. In: Proceedings of the AAAI Conference on Artificial Intelligence. vol. 38; 2024. p. 14297-305.
[83] Trinh TH, Wu Y, Le QV, He H, Luong T. Solving olympiad geometry without human demonstrations. Nature. 2024;625(7995):476-82.
[84] Kassner N, Tafjord O, Sabharwal A, Richardson K, Schuetze H, Clark P. Language models with rationality. arXiv preprint arXiv:230514250. 2023.
[85] Li C, Liang J, Zeng A, Chen X, Hausman K, Sadigh D, et al. Chain of code: Reasoning with a language model-augmented code emulator. arXiv preprint arXiv:231204474. 2023.

Handbook on Neurosymbolic AI and Knowledge Graphs
P. Hitzler et al. (Eds.)
IOS Press, 2025

doi:10.3233/FAIA250228

Enhancing Foundation Model-Based Reasoning with Neuro-Symbolic Cognitive Methods

Kaushik ROY [a,1], Siyu WU [b] and Alessandro OLTRAMARI [c]

[a] *Artificial Intelligence Institute South Carolina*
[b] *College of Information Sciences and Technology, the Pennsylvania State University*
[c] *Bosch Center for Artificial Intelligence*

ORCiD ID: Kaushik Roy https://orcid.org/0000-0001-6610-7845, Siyu Wu https://orcid.org/0009-0007-5903-4909, Alessandro Oltramari https://orcid.org/0000-0003-1559-4852

Abstract. Foundation models have emerged as powerful tools, exhibiting extraordinary performance across various tasks, such as language processing, visual recognition, code generation, and human-centered engagement. However, recent studies have highlighted their limitations when grounded, abstract, and generalized reasoning capabilities are required. Complex tasks often involve multiple hierarchical reasoning steps, which are typical features of human thinking processes. In fact, in this chapter we claim that cognitively-inspired computational models, such as the so-called Common Model of Cognition, are key to enable complex reasoning within foundation model-based artificial intelligence (AI) systems. We investigate neurosymbolic approaches for mapping AI system components to those of the Common Model of Cognition, either fully or partially. Specifically, two pathways are explored: (i) Given a task and its solution, we explore the effect of fine-tuning foundation models on the output traces obtained through a cognitive architecture such as ACT-R. The hypothesis is that, after fine-tuning, the foundation model will more closely emulate the cognitive reasoning processes necessary to solve the specific task. (ii) In the second approach, given a task, we explore mapping the solution requirements to various components of the common model of cognition and invoke a combination of foundation model-based pattern recognition, external knowledge augmentation and control flow planning to facilitate cognitive reasoning for the task. The chapter covers the background of foundation models and the common model of cognition, a survey of the existing landscape in integrating foundation models and cognitive architectures, and a discussion of insights from preliminary implementations of the two neurosymbolic pathways across real-world and synthetic tasks.

Keywords. Foundation Models, Common Model of Cognition, Neurosymbolic AI

[1]Corresponding Author: Kaushik Roy, kaushikr@email.sc.edu

1. An Introduction to Foundation Models

Foundation models are large-scale machine learning models, typically based on deep learning architectures, that are trained on vast amounts of data and designed to be adaptable to a wide range of downstream tasks. These models are termed "foundation models" because they serve as a basis from which more specialized models can be derived or fine-tuned for specific applications [1].

Perception Key features of foundation models include (i) Scale: They are often extremely large, with billions or even trillions of parameters, enabling them to capture complex patterns and knowledge from the training data. (ii) Pre-training and Fine-tuning: Foundation models are usually pre-trained on a large and diverse dataset in a self-supervised or unsupervised manner. After pre-training, they can be fine-tuned on smaller, domain-specific datasets to perform particular tasks, such as natural language understanding, image recognition, etc. (iii) Versatility: Due to their broad training, foundation models can be adapted to perform a wide range of tasks, often with little modification. For example, a foundation model trained on general text data might be fine-tuned for tasks like sentiment analysis, translation, or question answering [2]. Foundation models span multiple modalities, for example, GPT (Generative Pre-trained Transformer) text models like GPT-3 and vision models like CLIP (Contrastive Language-Image Pre-training) [3]. Foundation Models represent a significant and disruptive advancement in AI, providing a great starting point for a wide range of AI applications such as natural language and vision processing tasks. We refer to such tasks as *perception* tasks [4].

Reasoning Despite their capabilities, foundation models can struggle with tasks involving complex reasoning, often requiring the ability to "understand" abstract concepts, draw connections between disparate pieces of information, and engage in multi-step, hierarchical "thinking" or "cognition", which we refer to as cognitive reasoning. Recent work has exposed the lack of structured and logical reasoning capabilities in foundation models [5,6]. For example, solving a complex mathematical problem often requires multiple reasoning steps, each building on the previous one. Foundation models have been shown to struggle with basic arithmetic and simple algebraic operations [7]. Recent progress towards such reasoning has been demonstrated by augmenting foundation models with external procedures such as policy search to enable multi-step problems, especially those involving abstract concepts like proofs or applying theorems (e.g., Deepmind's AlphaGeometry and AlphaProof) [8].

Fundamentally, the limitations of foundation models lie in their inherent design. These systems are statistical learners, optimized for pattern recognition rather than logical deduction or abstract thought [9]. While they can mimic certain aspects of reasoning through pattern-based learning, they often lack the deeper, structured understanding required for cognitive reasoning. Figure 1 illustrates a scenario where the GPT-3.5 model engages in problematic reasoning.

Grounding and Verifiability As mentioned, foundation models are statistical learners that rely on patterns in the data they are trained on. However, they don't inherently include any mechanism to verify whether those patterns are grounded in real-world facts or reflect human-like commonsense and reasoning. As a result, they can produce logically flawed or nonsensical outputs [11]. This behavior manifests in many concerning ways ranging from seemingly innocuous adverse outcomes such as *hallucinations* – generat-

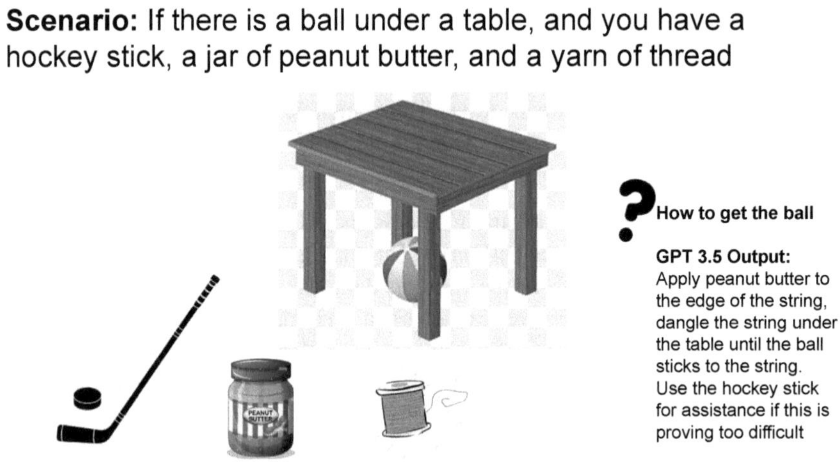

Figure 1. An example of problematic cognitive reasoning by GPT-3.5. The correct reasoning would result in simply poking the ball from under the table using the hockey stick, however, GPT-3.5 insists on using all three objects in a strange way to retrieve the ball from under the table (Example inspired from Joshua B. Tenenbaum's AAAI 2023 Keynote Address[2])[10].

ing information that appears coherent and plausible but is entirely fabricated or incorrect, to more harmful outcomes such as *regurgitating harmful biases* – generating biased or discriminatory content, reflecting stereotypes and prejudices present in the training data [12]. For instance, they might associate certain professions with a particular gender or make assumptions based on race [13]. Fundamentally, foundation models generate content based on probabilities derived from training data, which can result in the confident assertion of falsehoods.

2. An Introduction to The Common Model of Cognition

The Common Model of Cognition (CMC) is a theoretical framework that presents a model of human cognition codified as a computational architecture [14]. The CMC is a brain-inspired framework validated by large-scale neuroscience data [15]: it identifies core components and processes fundamental to human cognition, including memory, perception, motor actions, and decision-making. The model assumes a cyclical process where these components interact to produce intelligent behavior.

Key components of the CMC*:*

1. **Perception:** The process of acquiring and transforming raw inputs from the environment into a representation useful for solving a given task.
2. **Working Memory:** A temporary storage system where task-relevant information is actively held and manipulated.
3. **Long-term Memory:** A more permanent storage system where factual syntactic and semantic knowledge is maintained.

4. **Procedural Memory:** Stores the necessary skills and procedures, formatted as rules (e.g., if-then rules) that can be applied for solving a given task.
5. **Motor or Action:** Executes solutions to the given task by applying the relevant rules from the procedural memory to the contents of the working memory.

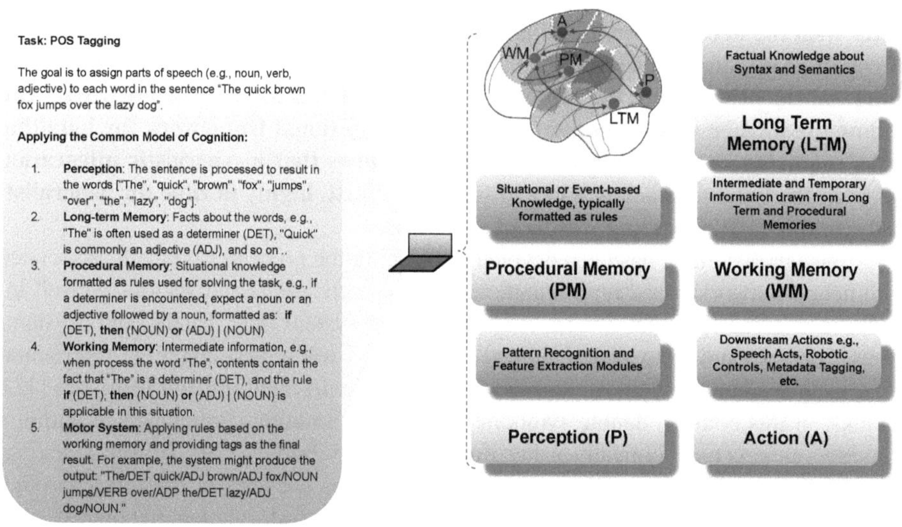

Figure 2. The Common Model of Cognition with an Illustration of Applying it to Solve Part-of-Speech Tagging on the Example Sentence "The quick brown fox jumps over the lazy dog".

The CMC provides a cognitively-grounded structured approach to problem-solving by breaking down the reasoning process into perceiving input, storing and manipulating information in working memory, reasoning based on available knowledge applied to the contents of the working memory, and manifesting responses by means of motor actions or speech acts. CMC-based reasoning processes aim to mirror how humans think about and understand the physical and social worlds, making it an attractive framework for building cognitively-inspired artificial intelligent systems. Figure 2 illustrates the CMC and how it maps to the human brain. The figure also provides an example of how the CMC is applied to solve a part-of-speech tagging task.

3. The Current Landscape of Methods for Integrating Foundation Models and Cognitively-Inspired Systems in AI Systems

The importance of integrating cognitively-inspired mechanisms into large scale machine learning models has been recently acknowledged by one of the key figures in deep learning, Yann LeCun: in a position paper published in 2022 [16], he described a biologically-inspired cognitive architecture, where a so-called *configurator* orchestrates information provided by different modules, such as the *perception module* and the *world model module*, which replicate the functions emerging from prefrontal-cortical processes. Furthermore, a *motivation model* – designed to mimic the role of the amygdala in producing basic emotional states like pain and pleasure – is used to compute intrinsic costs associated with current and future actions, a mechanism that is instrumental to inform predictive capabilities. In line with the current trend of investigating computational models of cognition in the context of large-scale neural networks, a recent blog [17] provides an overview of how large language models (LLMs) could be used to control autonomous agents. **In general, the mutual benefits of integrating foundation models and cognitively-inspired systems are clear: on one hand, the former can provide the latter with the necessary scaffolding to solve tasks at scale, a well-known limitation of cognitive systems, which are heavily dependent on manual design and programming; on the other hand, the latter - especially through the CMC framework - can endow the former with a human-inspired computational framework for handling tasks requiring cognitive reasoning. Thus, it follows that a synergistic integration between the two approaches is key to support robust, highly flexible (or generalist) and scalable task reasoning within AI systems.**

Considerable effort has been devoted to bridging the processes typically associated with neural network-based representations, such as activations and vectors. Newell introduced a framework that divides a computational system into "bands" and "system-levels," corresponding to neural representations and traditional cognitive representations, such as chunks, symbols, high-level algorithmic descriptions, and heuristics [18]. Chunks, in this context, denote symbolic units of information communicated within a cognitive architecture, typically using limited-capacity buffers [19]. Newell's distinction is based on the premise that neural representations are learned from data through prediction-focused objectives, thus representing *stochastic* information. In contrast, cognitive representations are typically *declared* as production rules (which can be likened to if-else rules) and propositional statements (chunks), representing deterministic information. The fundamental difference between these representations—*stochastic* versus *declarative*—presents a significant challenge in integrating neural network-based and cognitive reasoning-based approaches [20].

Sumers et al. adopt a contemporary perspective based on LLMs, utilizing cognitive architecture-inspired task pipelines with *language agents*. This approach involves multiple language models, referred to as language agents, executing tasks through operations guided by language model-driven control logic (e.g., vector similarity-based external knowledge retrieval, function calling, or prompt-chaining) [21]. However, since contemporary LLMs fundamentally operate through predictive mechanisms, this approach assumes implicitly that all cognition is achieved through an auto-regressive predictive process. It has been demonstrated categorically that cognitive reasoning cannot be attained solely through predictive mechanisms [22]. Kelly and Reitter explore an integrated approach to bridging cognitive and neural representations using holographic declarative memories, wherein the declarative memory (long-term memory) module of the CMC is replaced with a distributional semantics model, such as an autoregressive language model. They argue that tokenization, encoding, and decoding operations provide effective translations between cognitive declarative information and neural stochastic information [23].

While we recognize the promise of the approaches discussed so far, as evidenced by experimental data, we propose that an *abstraction* layer should serve as an intermediate representation between neural and cognitive representations, rather than relying on direct translation between the two [24]. Recent work supports this notion, showing the emergence of "meta-optimizers" within LLMs and analyzing how these models operate when provided with instructions [25]. Simply put, a LLM executes instructions in a manner akin to executing learned "metacognitive" rules, which follow a globally-contextualized meta-optimization step, as opposed to a locally-contextualized optimization step conveyed by gradients. More precisely, this type of instruction-following procedure operates through an intermediate *abstraction* layer that is distinct from predictions based on gradient information in neural representation spaces and from cognitive reasoning based on the symbolic information contained in cognitive representations. For example, the part-of-speech tagging task illustrated in Figure 2 provides an example of task-specific metacognitive rules-of-thumb.

Hypothesis Statement

In this chapter, we hypothesize that cognitive reasoning can be achieved using mechanisms similar to executing metacognitive rules-of-thumb, similar to instruction prompts in modern LLMs. This approach would allow us to leverage foundation models within the CMC framework to effectively bridge neural and cognitive representations, thereby enabling cognitive reasoning in AI systems.

In the following sections, we refine these ideas and propose a neurosymbolic framework for integrating foundation models with the CMC. Specifically, we suggest leveraging neurosymbolic mechanisms to implement semantic reasoning processes using metacognitive instruction-based reasoning, thereby facilitating the integration of foundation models (e.g., prompts) and the CMC (e.g., procedural memory) for enabling cognitive reasoning [26,27].

4. CMC-scaffolded Neurosymbolic AI for Cognitive Reasoning

Neurosymbolic AI has been conceptualized in various ways, with detailed categorizations of available implementation methods [28]. To ensure clarity, this work adopts a categorization similar to that proposed by Sheth et al., which includes: **(i) Compressing cognitive representations for integration with neural representations**, followed by neural pattern recognition; and **(ii) Mapping neural representations to cognitive representations, followed by instruction-based reasoning** [29]. The subsequent sections analyze specific implementations of these approaches within the CMC framework, applied to particular tasks, and evaluate them in relation to the **hypothesis statement** introduced in Section 3.

4.1. Compressing Cognitive Representations for Integration with Neural Representations

In this experiment, we utilize the LLAMA architecture for neural representations and the ACT-R cognitive architecture for a system based on the CMC. This section first addresses the preliminary concepts, followed by a detailed description of our experiment and the conclusions related to the hypothesis, as presented in Section 3.

4.1.1. The ACT-R Cognitive Architecture in Decision Making

The CMC integrates essential features from various cognitive architectures, which are computational frameworks designed to capture the invariant mechanisms of human cognition (for an introduction on cognitive architectures, see [30]). These mechanisms include functions related to attention, control, learning, memory, adaptivity, perception, and action. Cognitive architectures propose a set of fixed mechanisms to model human behavior, functioning akin to agents and aiming for a unified representation of the mind. By utilizing task-specific knowledge, these architectures not only simulate but also explain behavior through direct examination and real-time reasoning tracing. One representative cognitive architectures is ACT-R [31].

ACT-R encompasses perception, memory, goal-setting, and action. It uses two primary types of knowledge representations: declarative and procedural. Declarative knowledge comprises chunks of information, stored in declarative memory. Procedural knowledge, on the other hand, involves performing basic operations, moving data among buffers, and executing instructions. Over the years, ACT-R has accounted for a broad range of tasks at a high level of fidelity, reproducing aspects of complex human behavior, from everyday activities like event planning [32] and car driving [33], to highly technical tasks such as piloting an airplane [34], and monitoring a network to prevent cyberattacks [35]. The modeling approaches used include: *strategy or rule-based*, where different problem-solving strategies are implemented through various production rules, and successful strategies emerge on the basis of suitable reward functions [36,37]; *exemplar or instance-based*, an approach that relies on past experiences stored in declarative memory to solve problems [38]; *hybrid*, which combine rule-based and instance-based approaches [39]. ACT-R was chosen for this study to provide the intermediate representations of cognitive reasoning steps. Three key features distinguish the use of ACT-R in creating models for decision-making tasks that involve learning:

- *Self-configuration*: ACT-R efficiently translates instructions into structured rules, forming the basis for task-specific production rules that enhance the efficiency of task execution.
- *Modular design mirroring human cognition*: ACT-R's modules emulate human cognitive functions - perceptual modules update the system's view of the environment, a goal module tracks progress towards objectives, a declarative module uses past experiences for contextual understanding, and a central buffer system enables communication between modules. Additionally, the central production system recognizes patterns to initiate coordinated actions.
- *Subsymbolic processes for decision-making*: ACT-R excels in its ability to reliably retrieve relevant memories and activate appropriate rules, ensuring both efficient and adaptive performance in decision-making tasks, such as skills training. It does so at a pace that mirrors human performance and offers the opportunity to model learning during this process.

4.1.2. Problem Definition: Design for Manufacturing

We define the terminology that constitutes our problem. The problem setting is a prototypical manufacturing production-line workflow, from supplier to customer, for which there exists a Value Stream Map (VSM; see Figure 3), which allows for tracking the efficiency at different sectors of the process and abstracts the overall problem for mathematical modeling and optimization. Key sectors include: Body Production, Pre-Assembly, Assembly, Honing, Washing, Testing, and Packaging. Early sectors pose potential efficiency problems in the workflow and may warrant optimization (triangles), while later stages are governed by *First-In-First-Out* (FIFO) processes. The metrics at each stage include Cycle Time (CT), Overall Equipment Effectiveness (OEE), and Mean Absolute Error (MAE); the flow progresses through each stage, aiming for efficient operation, performance monitoring, and error minimization to ensure high-quality production output and timely customer delivery.

Focused on maintaining stable output for manufacturing plants, we consider plant managers' feedback alongside the VSM structure to define two decision-making problems that aim to reduce Total Assembly Time (TAT) while minimizing Total Defect Rate (TDR). An agent $\mathscr{G}$ is a predictive model that takes a natural language question $\mathscr{Q}$ as a prompt, along with N snapshots of the sector-wise production flow data $\{$CT, OEE, MAE$\}$. In a *single-facet decision-making problem*, $\mathscr{G}$ outputs a binary decision (0 or 1) on which of two sectors, pre-assembly or assembly, requires a time reduction. In a more-challenging *multi-faceted decision-making problem*, $\mathscr{G}$ should output the same binary decision as before, about which sector should be the optimization target, along with an optimization *strategy* S. Here, S is a strategy defined by one of several decision-making personas that govern manufacturing process management, which we refer to in the manuscript as 'novice', 'intermediate', and 'expert'.

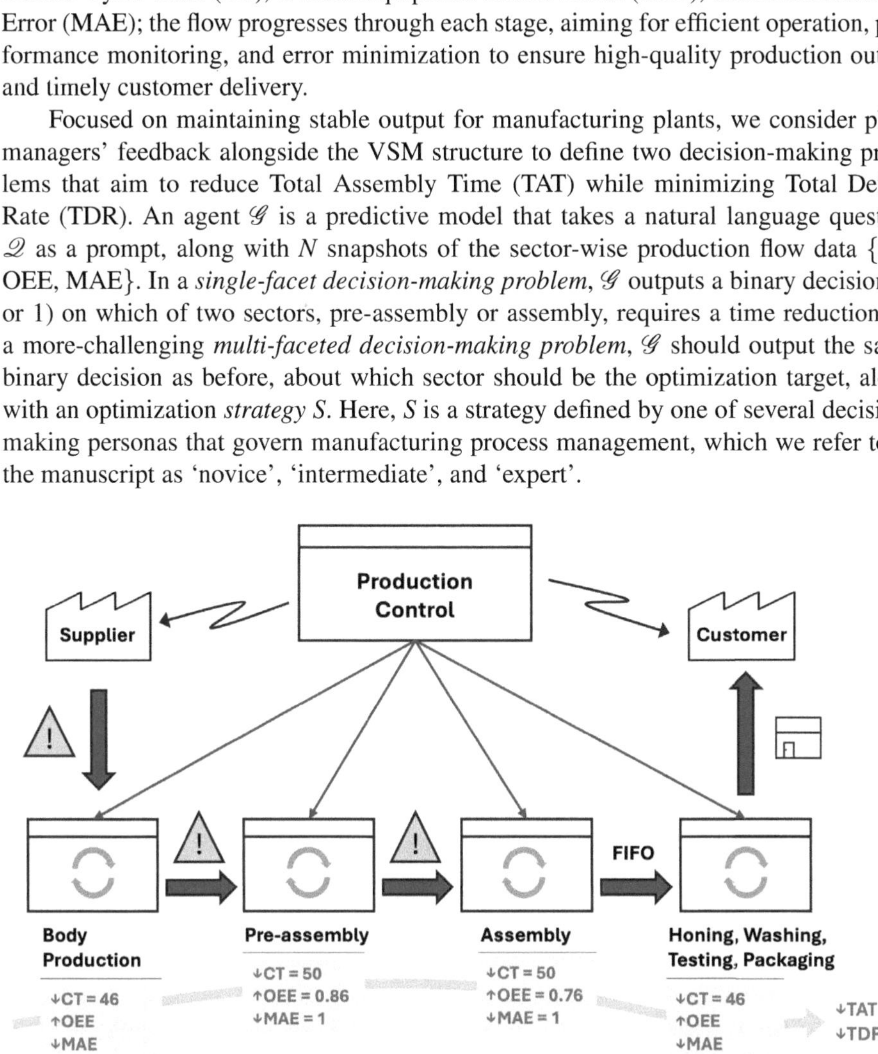

Figure 3. A *Value Stream Map* of manufacturing process.

4.1.3. A Cognitive Model for the Manufacturing Domain

In recent work, we released VSM-ACTR 2.0 (hereafter referred to as VSM-ACTR), a rule-based ACT-R cognitive model for decision support in manufacturing. VSM-ACTR has incorporated the meta-cognitive processes that reflect on and evaluate the progress of chosen strategies—with an emphasis on headcount cost evaluation, through a reward structure that enables a process akin to reinforcement learning. This system allows the model to dynamically assess the impact of headcount costs on decision-making outcomes, computing a reward or penalty for each decision cycle. These rewards or penalties then propagate back to the initial production rule that initiated the decision cycle, thereby dynamically adjusting the utility of each decision-making strategy. VSM-ACTR integrates the prototypical decision process with insights into how cognitive models represent different levels of expertise [40,41], categorizing users into three levels of expertise: novices, intermediates, and experts. Novices engage in decision-making using intuitive deliberative chunks. Intermediates can manage key metrics such as CT and OEE but struggle with the systematic analysis of intertwined variables. Experts, on the other hand, make judgments systematically. The cognitive model employs three types of knowledge chunks: decisions, decision merits, and goals. The 'decision chunk' encodes eight slots including reduction time (goal), decision-making state (novice, intermediate, expert), and related variables. The 'decision merits chunk' holds information on sector weights, defect increases by sector, and comparative defect rate increases. The 'goal chunk' captures the initial production conditions and the ultimate goal of achieving the optimal decision. In addition, the model uses 18 procedural rules driven by goal-focused objectives across 20 states, covering actions such as choosing strategies, actions, working memory management, decisions, and evaluations.

Production Rule Sets Three sets of production rules represent the decision-making behaviors of novice, intermediate, and expert decision-makers. We use the expert production rule set as an example, once the decision-choice center decides to activate a set of expert decision productions, the process begins by perceiving the problem and retrieving related decision-making metrics from chunks. The imaginal buffer then acts as a working memory platform, holding and manipulating relevant information during the decision-making process. It allows the model to construct new mental representations or modify existing ones based on incoming data or problem-solving needs. This involves using the imaginal buffer to assess the relationships between the decision target and decision metrics, particularly considering the impact of each sector's weight on the defect rate change, and determining the final defect rate increase for each sector. These results are stored in the imaginal buffer and later retrieved for comparison. This enables the model to select the sector with the lowest defect increase. After one decision-making cycle, the model evaluates the headcount cost, rewarding or penalizing the entire process based on the evaluation results and decision strategy used before looping back to the next decision-making round.

Level of Expertise Mechanism The model can learn while performing tasks through two mechanisms leading to varying levels of expertise through differentiating knowledge representations, as shown in figure 4. **Declarative Memories**: These memories store knowledge that aligns with human intuition and expertise gained from the VSM. For example, the green triangles in the figure represents a portion of the intuition used by novice decision-makers. **Production Rules**: These rules capture the rational decision-making processes observed in human subjects. The green lines illustrate how the imaginal buffer retrieves relevant portions of the novice declarative memory and feeds them to the novice production rule set. Intermediate and expert decision-making levels follow the same principle. Red and blue shapes represent their respective declarative memory chunks, and the corresponding colored arrows show the flow of information through

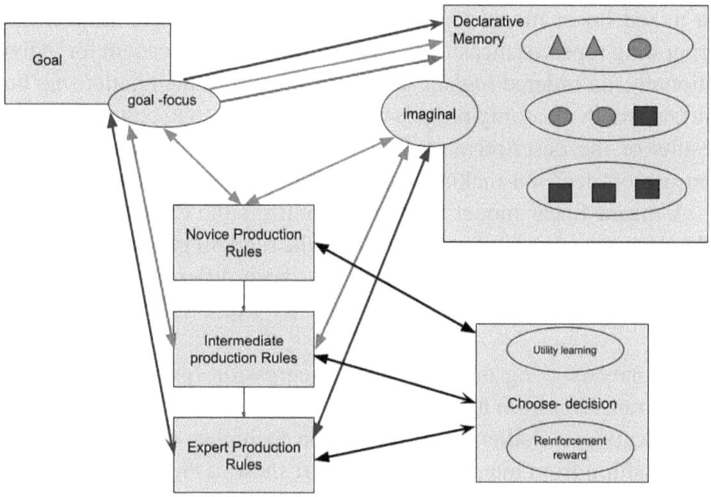

Figure 4. Level of expertise mechanism in VSM-ACT-R

their production rule sets. Finally, the goal buffer utilizes the "goal focus" command to manipulate the different phases of the task.

Beyond mimicking human behavior, the model also simulates the learning progress achieved by the **Decision-Choice Control**, which manages errors, learning, and memory through utility learning and reinforcement rewards. Novice decision-making starts with a utility base and includes a noise setting. The intermediate and expert production rules receive rewards when the corresponding decision-making results are achieved. The utility of these production rules updates is based on the rewards received and the retention of memory, which depends on the time passed since the rule last fired.

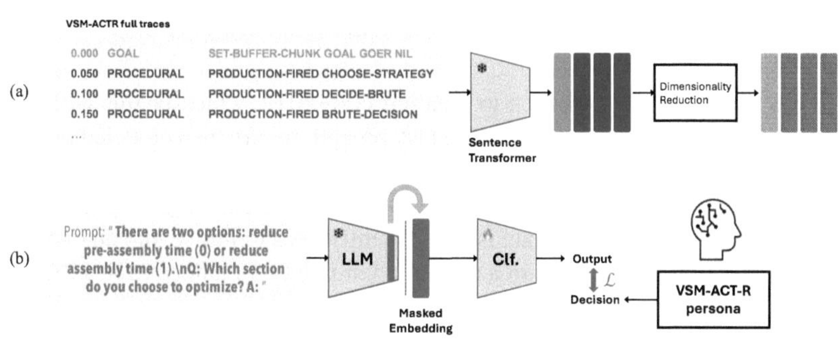

Figure 5. (a) Obtaining decision representations from VSM-ACT-R. (b) LLM feature extraction for behavior prediction.

VSM-ACTR model evaluation We ran the VSM-ACTR model across 2012 decision-making trials and 32 problem sets to analyze its behavior [42]. Each model run comprised 15-16 trials until reach a more stable expert behavior. We encoded decision types as 0, 1, and 2 for novice, intermediate, and expert strategies, respectively.

To assess learning, individual differences, and progression, we initially used descriptive statistics to chart the average progression of decision types over 16 trials. We then employed a mixed linear model to evaluate the influence of trial numbers on decision types, incorporating repeated measures and random effects to account for individual variance. Additionally, an ordered logistic regression analyzed the relationship between the number of trials and the learning progression from novice to expert.

The results of the descriptive statistics demonstrate a significant positive impact of trial exposure on decision-making progression, evidenced by a coefficient of 0.086 ($P < 0.05$). A mixed linear model regression confirms the effect of trials on decision-making and further reveals a variance of 0.007 in the random group effects. This indicates that while there are differences between groups, these differences are relatively small, suggesting that the trials themselves predominantly explain the variability in decision type.

Threshold analysis using ordered logistic regression reveals significant transition thresholds. The transition from novice to intermediate has a significant threshold of 0.88 ($P < 0.05$), indicating a challenging progression to higher decision-making skills. In contrast, the transition from intermediate to expert shows a significantly lower threshold of 0.1 (P = 0.021), suggesting it is easier to progress from intermediate to expert than from novice to intermediate.

4.1.4. The LLM-ACTR *Framework*

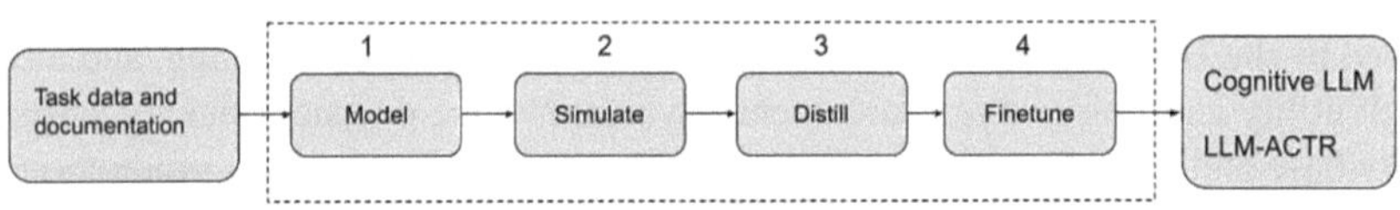

Figure 6. Decision augmentation using a neural-symbolic cognitive architecture approach. (1) Tasks are modeled with cognitive architecture. (2) Cognitive model used to run stochastic simulation of task at scale. (3) Synthetic data are distilled from simulation and combined with prompt requests. (4) A fine tuning pipeline is used to calibrate open source LLM to perform decision augmentation for task in exercise.

Figure 6 illustrates the approach to creating LLM-ACTR, which begins with the collection of task data and documentation. The task procedures are then modeled using ACT-R, employing stochastic simulations to analyze these tasks on a large scale. After the simulation phase, the generated synthetic data is semi-automatically distilled and combined with prompt requests. This data is subsequently used to infuse into an open source LLM through fine-tuning, resulting in a type of cognitive LLM, named LLM-ACTR.

Selecting Salient Decision Information ACT-R traces capture cognitive reasoning steps in real-time. These traces log the operations executed by various modules at each discrete decision point, including the activation of the goal module, the use of the imaginal buffer for accessing working memory, procedural memory matching and firing, utility updating driven by reinforcement learning, etc.

Preserving information from ACT-R model's decision-making traces poses challenges. A single decision-making round can generate a vast number of traces, each timestamped as frequently as every 5 milliseconds. Deciding which lines to select—or whether to preserve all lines—requires a balance between minimizing information loss and balancing computational costs. The rationale for choosing outputs from specific modules as reliable sources within the decision representation lies in their clear correspondence to deterministic cognitive processes. The rationale for preserving all traces involves processes of semantic embedding extraction and dimensional reduction.

The information used to augment decision-making in this study focuses on distilling macro-level cognitive processes related to executive function[43], capturing the evolution of decision-making results across trials and how decisions adapt through learning and experience. Furthermore, the decision actions are categorized into strategy levels (novice, intermediate, expert), reflecting the learning phases.

Learning an Embedding Space of Decision Traces The next step involves converting the traces into tensors that the LLM can process. This study explores two approaches: one uses selected traces, and another uses full traces.

The selected traces are components distilled from macro-level cognitive processes related to executive function. This process requires human involvement to log decision results and strategy traces, which are then numerically encoded. For instance, '0' represents a decision for reduced time in pre-assembly section, and '1' for assembly. These data are subsequently fed into the neural network as single vectors.

In contrast, the holistic traces approach (see Figure 5a) retains both macro- and micro-level cognitive processes, with the latter including meta-cognition [44]. Metacognition involves an awareness and understanding of one's own cognitive processes, as exhibited through model traces that demonstrate the use of the imaginal buffer for accessing working memory, procedural memory matching and firing, headcount cost analysis, and the assessment of strategy effectiveness.

The investigation begins with the transformation of full traces from VSM-ACTR, representing both cognitive and metacognitive processes, into a format that balances information retention with computational efficiency. Cognitive reasoning traces for each task are processed through a sentence transformer to obtain semantic embeddings for each time stamp. A Sum of Ranked Explanatory Effects (SREE) analysis is then applied to determine the number (N) of principal components that account for at least 70% of the variance. Finally, these embeddings are reduced to N dimensions using Principal Components Analysis (PCA)[45].

Injecting Decision Information into LLMs With the VSM-ACTR model, which represents human-like cognitive reasoning in repeated decision-making tasks, this section outlines the experimental settings for fine-tuning of the LLM-ACTR framework. Fine-tuning, sometimes referred to as transfer learning, involves optimizing all model weights for the given task. The process includes parsing consistent template prompts that reflect the decision making task into an open-source LLM, aligning the task for the cognitive model using the LLM as the base model to access the last hidden layer and obtain masked embeddings, constructing a classification layer with softmax activation on top of the base model, using targets containing the salient decision representations of the cognitive model and features from the masked embeddings of the base LLM, and fine-tuning the LLM for classification using the LORA method. The key points are: (1) The targets decode the salient decision information from the cognitive model. (2) Use the final layer of contextualized embeddings in transformer-based LLMs, generated through the attention block mechanism. The attention block, a key feature of transformers, distinguishes them from other architectures like recurrent neural networks [46]. It creates embeddings that capture the in-context meaning of tokens by recombining them with other tokens' embeddings. Successive attention blocks further refine these embeddings, producing multiple layers of abstraction. The final layer, a blend of these refined embeddings, is used in this pipeline because it offers the richest semantic information while balancing minimal information loss and reduced computational costs for fine-tuning. (3) Use Low-Rank Adaptation (LoRa) for its efficiency in fine-tuning, reducing the computational resources and time required while maintaining high model performance [47].

4.1.5. Experiments

Problem Setting As an instantiation of the problem definition, above, our manufacturing line has two sections with potential defect sources: pre-assembly and assembly. Pre-assembly takes 40 seconds with an OEE rate of 88%, while assembly takes 44 seconds with an OEE rate of 80.1%. To reduce total assembly time by 4, we must identify which section can be shortened with minimal defect increase. We note that reducing cycle time will also lead to an increase in headcount costs.

Implementation Details The LLAMA-2 13B model was chosen as the foundation for this research because of its demonstrated effectiveness and efficiency in NLP tasks (Huang et al., 2024). As a state-of-the-art large language model, LLAMA has been trained on trillions of tokens from publicly available datasets. Unlike other transformer-based models such as the GPT family, which can only be accessed at the user's end, LLAMA 's architecture, including its pre-trained weights, is fully accessible. Furthermore, its proven capability to extract the last hidden layer for predicting behavioral discrepancies has been provided[48]. These attributes collectively establish LLAMA -2 13B as an optimal choice for this study.

To determine the dataset size that can effectively perform the task while balancing efficacy and resource limitations, we referred to [49], who showed evidence that LLAMA -2 13B achieves F1 scores above 0.9 in resource-limited text classification tasks, with datasets as 1,000 rows per class. Based on this, we developed the dataset size for fine-tuning as *N* (number of classes) * 1,000. The ACT-R dataset for binary decision-making classification contains 2,012 decision-making trials, Obtained by running the developed ACT-R model across 32 problem sets, each ACT-R persona was run for 15-16 trials until more stable expert behavior was achieved [42].

Baseline Models This study compared the goodness-of-fit and prediction accuracy of the resulting models using holdout data against two baselines: a random guess model and LLAMA without fine-tuning, obtained by reading out log-probabilities of the pre-trained LLAMA .

A random guess model serves as the most basic form of chance level baseline and represents the simplest hypothesis for model comparison. In psychological interdisciplinary experiments, control conditions often employ random responses to distinguish the effects of treatment from chance [50]. This approach allows assessing the extent to which decisions are influenced by knowledge versus being purely stochastic.

On the other hand, using LLAMA without fine-tuning as a baseline provides a reference point to measure the impact of fine-tuning on the model's performance. This comparison reveals how much the model 'learns' from the fine-tuning process compared to its generic, pre-trained state.

Research Questions Based on our framework's components, we identify a set of research questions that we answer through experiments.

1. *What are the properties of a useful neural network representation of the decision-making process in Cognitive Architectures?*

Answering this question sets the groundwork for developing a context-aware domain knowledge base for augmenting decision-making in LLMs.

2. *What level of complexity in behavior representation can* LLMs *effectively capture?*

Previous research has used LLM conceptual embeddings to predict human behavior based on past behavioral studies [51], confirming LLMs' ability to replicate known human patterns. However, high costs and extensive data collection efforts limit this method. By incorporating cognitive model simulations, the study seeks to address these limitations and broaden the investigation to determine the extent to which LLMs can reproduce decision-making knowledge. This will, in turn, help define the depth of decision-making domain knowledge that can be effectively integrated with the innate learning capabilities of LLMs.

3. *Can we inform the* LLM *with knowledge about the reasoning process of the cognitive architecture?*

Inspired by previous works on knowledge-injection [52,53], answering this question offers insights into knowledge transfer from domain-specific bases to LLMs and evaluates its impact on performance in holdout tasks. The method for addressing RQ1 was introduced in the first two sections of our approach framework.

Feature Extraction for Behavior Prediction To answer RQ2: What level of complexity in behavior representation can LLMs effectively capture? Building on previous research that used conceptual embeddings from LLMs to predict human behavior with historical behavioral data [51], we adopted the same method of LLM feature extraction for behavior prediction [54]. We created datasets consisting of last contextual embeddings as features and the corresponding different levels of VSM-ACTR decision actions representations as targets. We obtained embeddings by passing prompts that included all the information that VSM-ACTR had access to on a given trial through LLAMA and then extracting the hidden activations of the final layer, as shown in Figure 5b.

The first dataset used features extracted from prompts identical to the VSM-ACTR task, with targets being the VSM-ACTR decision-making results, where '0' indicates reduced time in preassembly and '1' indicates assembly. The second dataset's prompt template added an explanation of the strategy adopted by VSM-ACTR and used compound targets comprising both the decision-making results and the strategies reflecting the learning trajectory (novice, intermediate, and expert). The targets were encoded as follows: 0, 1, and 2 for preassembly choices using novice, intermediate, and expert strategies, respectively, and 3, 4, and 5 for assembly choices following the same pattern. With these two datasets, we fitted a regularized logistic regression model using 10-fold cross-validation for dataset 1 and multinomial regression using 10-fold cross-validation with L2 regularization for dataset 2. Model performance was assessed by measuring the goodness of fit through negative log-likelihood (NLL) and the predictive accuracy of hold-out data.

Fine Tuning for Knowledge Transfer To answer RQ3: whether LLMs can be informed with knowledge about the reasoning processes of cognitive architecture—we use the fine-tuning approach of `LLM-ACTR` Framework. The fine-tuning process employs Cross-

Entropy as the loss function and uses Adam optimization. Training involves a train test split of 0.2 and uses a batch size of 5 for both training and validation phases. The learning rate is set to 1e-5, with the training spanning across 10 epochs. To ensure regularization and prevent overfitting, a weight decay of 0.01, and a dropout of 0.5 are applied, and gradient accumulation is set to 2. Last but not least, gradient clipping is employed to maintain a maximum gradient norm of 1.0 for gradient explosion control. We evaluate the model fitting and generalization quality using training loss and validation loss across epochs, then compare the goodness of fit and prediction accuracy of the hold-out data against the baseline models.

4.1.6. Results

Finding Useful Decision Process Embeddings The approach of distilling macro-level cognitive processes related to executive function captures the evolution of decision-making results across trials and how decisions adapt through learning and experience, all represented as a sequential single vector. This format facilitates ease of use for down-stream tasks involving knowledge transfer. However, this method retains only partial cognitive decision-making knowledge.

In contrast, the holistic semantic preservation approach encompasses both macro and micro-level cognition processes. However, the embeddings produced vary in shape due to the individual differences in traces originating from stochastic simulations. They cannot be directly fed into neural networks for downstream tasks. Nevertheless, the first two principal components of the reduced embeddings, which correspond to the semantic mapping of ACT-R's components—including procedural, imaginal, goal knowledge, utility updating, and decision-making—are detailed in Figure 6.

The MANOVA analysis was conducted to assess the overall effect of the independent variables, which include label categories or ACT-R components, on the combined dependent variables—components of reduced embeddings. This analysis reveals a significant relationship with the semantic mapping of ACT-R's components. For instance, the extremely low Wilks' lambda value (0.0004) suggests that the label or ACT-R component categories explain nearly all the variance in the dependent variables, indicative of a strong group effect. The statistical tests applied—Wilks' lambda, Pillai's trace, Hotelling-Lawley trace, and Roy's greatest root—all demonstrate strong significance, as evidenced by the extremely low p-values across all tests. These findings highlight that the principal components retained in the PCA successfully capture the essential variance related to these cognitive processes.

This result validates that our semantic abstraction method has the potential to retain the maximum semantics of neural symbolic representations at a minimal computational cost. However, further work is required to address the issue of ragged tensors for downstream tasks.

In a preliminary experiment, we addressed the issue of ragged tensors by employing padding with value imputation. We then integrated the 240 full cognitive reasoning traces from the VSM-ACTR model with LLM using embedding concatenation and conducted feature extraction for behavior prediction. Specifically, we transposed the reduced embeddings from each cognitive model run into a (1, X) dimension tensor and subsequently concatenated this with the LLM's last contextual embedding from the same prompt. These concatenated embeddings served as resources for predicting decision-making within the VSM-ACTR model. The prediction targets were multifaceted, including both the decision-making results and the strategies used. The results showed no significant improvement in prediction accuracy with concatenated embeddings compared to using LLM embeddings alone.

One possible explanation is the relative scale of the VSM-ACTR reduced embeddings compared to those of LLaMA , which is disproportionately small (1:10). Consequently, the LLaMA embeddings may dominated the decision-making process within the model due to their larger scale. A potential solution could be to generate longer VSM-ACTR model traces, including tenfold more decision-making trials, thereby enhancing the scale and variability of its features.

Also, the method we use to handle ragged tensors—padding followed by value imputation—could potentially dilute the VSM-ACTR embeddings and reduce their accuracy. Finding an alternative method to preserve the full embeddings from VSM-ACTR may potentially improve the results.

Lastly, the limited dataset size could be influencing the results. The preliminary test used only 240 complete traces. Expanding the dataset may provide more insights into the performance of the proposed approach.

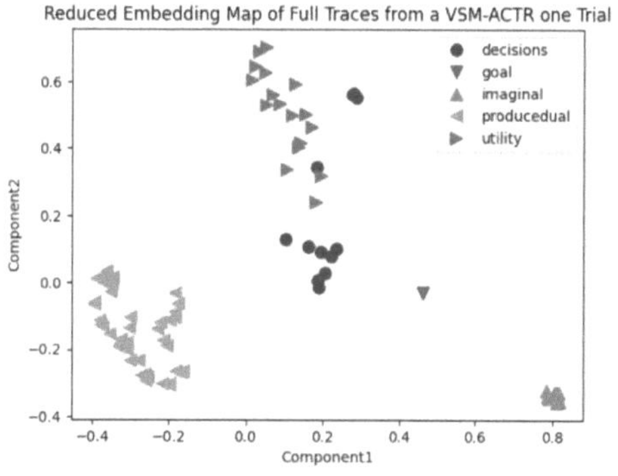

Figure 7. ACTR embedding mapping

Assessing Behavior Complexity Captured by LLMs Table 1 shows that LLM-ACTR captures a single facet of decision-making, achieving an average accuracy of 0.64 across 10 validation folds in the holdout task. When decision-making targets involve multiple facets—encompassing both choices and strategies that shape the learning trajectory—the accuracy decreases to 0.42. While this reduction suggests that capturing complex decision-making processes is less accurate, the results still show promise in handling these complexities. However, the Negative Log-Likelihood (NLL) reveals greater predictive uncertainty for multifaceted decision-making processes, as evidenced by a significantly higher NLL of 1.18 compared to 0.65 in single-facet scenarios.

Injecting LLMs *with CA Decision Process* We first report training and validation losses, across 10 epochs, to reveal the fine-tuned model's learning and generalization behavior. Initially, the training loss begins at approximately 0.73, with a slight fluctuation observed in subsequent epochs, peaking around epoch 2 and showing a notable dip at epoch 7. In contrast, the validation loss starts at around 0.64 and remains remarkably stable throughout the epochs. This consistency in validation loss, coupled with a generally downward trend in training loss after its initial variations, suggests that the model is learning ef-

Table 1. Evaluation for Single and Multi Facets Targets.

Target Type	NLL	Accuracy
Single Facet Target	0.63	0.64
Multi Facets Target	1.18	0.42

Table 2. Comparison of VSM-ACTR with baselines.

Model	NLL	Accuracy
Chance-level	0.6931	0.4826
LLAMA	1.1330	0.3564
LLM-ACTR(ours)	**0.6534**	**0.6576**

fectively. The overall trend indicates an improvement in model performance over time, reflecting its capability to generalize well on unseen data.

We then report the comparison of the LLM-ACTR with the baseline models on goodness of fit using negative log likelihood (NLL) and accuracy score for hold-out data. Table 2 shows the LLM-ACTR model demonstrates significantly better performance across all metrics compared to the LLAMA -only model, highlighting its effectiveness in decision-making tasks involving sequential cognitive reasoning. Additionally, the LLAMA -only model performs worse than the chance-level model. This underscores the necessity of fine-tuning pre-trained language models like LLAMA to adapt them to specific human-aligned repeated decision-making tasks.

4.1.7. Discussion

The results shown in the previous section support our hypothesis that task-specific semantic interpretation enables cognitive reasoning mechanisms in AI. Our experiments demonstrate the benefits of using neuro-symbolic architectures to bridge the gap between neural pattern recognition and cognitive reasoning in AI. By leveraging task-specific semantic interpretations through cognitive model integration, we enable enhanced decision-making capabilities. The results validate the hypothesis that cognitive reasoning can be achieved using mechanisms similar to executing metacognitive rules captured within the parametric memory of foundation models, providing a plausible pathway for future developments in cognitively-inspired AI.

4.2. Mapping Neural Representations to Cognitive Representations and Instruction-Based Reasoning

In the previous experiment, we adopted a design inspired by the CMC by compressing cognitive reasoning traces into neural representations. In this section, we explore an alternative approach, utilizing various neural network foundation models enhanced with external knowledge sources for perception and grounding. This is followed by a cognitive reasoning framework, also inspired by the CMC.

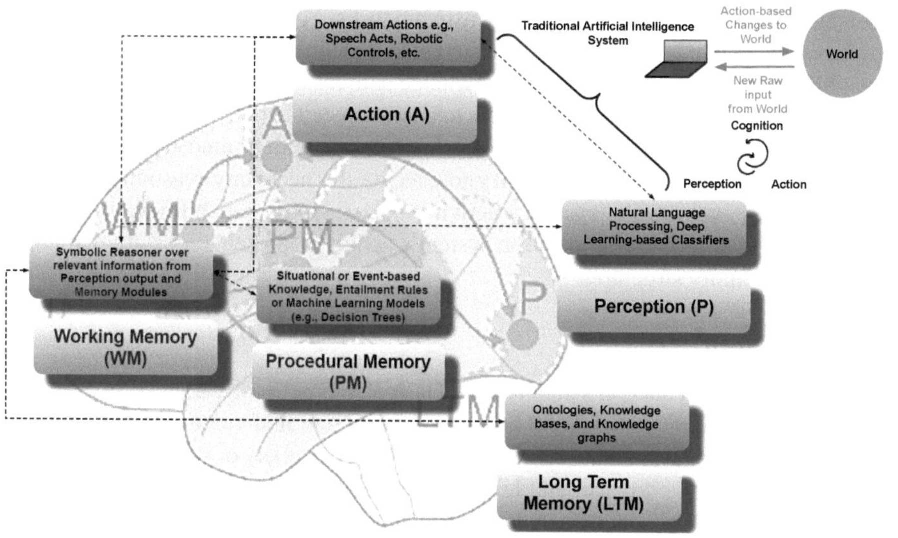

Figure 8. The common model of cognition [14]. The figure shows how traditional components of an AI system map to the various components of the CMC.

4.2.1. *Preliminaries - Traditional AI Components and the* CMC

Figure 8 illustrates how traditional AI components correspond to the CMC components introduced in Section 2. Neural network-based processing methods are typically employed for perception, transforming raw data into abstractions that can be utilized by other CMC components (e.g., converting raw text in documents into noun phrases and other grammatical or syntactic structures).

The long-term memory stores "rules," which can be understood as sets of abstractions that, when evaluated, lead to other abstractions (e.g., if a text chunk is identified as a noun phrase, the next chunk is likely to be a verb phrase). Declarative knowledge refers to the semantics assigned to these abstractions in the procedural memory, often derived from curated knowledge bases, graphs, and ontologies (e.g., a noun phrase is composed of parts-of-speech such as nouns, adjectives, etc.). The working memory integrates the outputs of perception, procedural knowledge, and declarative knowledge to perform reasoning. For instance, if the current input is classified as a noun phrase, a rule in the procedural memory may suggest that the next chunk is likely to be a verb phrase.

4.2.2. *Experimental Setup*

The experimental setup focuses on activity recognition in egocentric scenes, which involves understanding specific actions within first-person perspectives. These scenes present a significant challenge due to the unpredictable behaviors often observed. For instance, during a cooking task, an individual may switch to unrelated activities, such as checking emails while waiting for food to boil. This introduces added complexity to the activity distribution within the scene.

Motivation As illustrated in Figure 8, the perception and cognition stages of the perception-cognition-action cycle involve an interplay between declarative, procedural, and working memory. This interaction builds a comprehensive representation of activity understanding, which is essential for downstream tasks. For example, in cooking-related activities, declarative memory may store factual knowledge, such as "foods contain salt," potentially supplemented by external knowledge sources. Procedural memory, typically a set of reasoning rules, could include how to answer specific video-related queries based on facts stored in declarative memory. Working memory, with limited capacity, draws on both declarative and procedural memory to execute the necessary reasoning steps during runtime. To evaluate the system's activity understanding capabilities, we designed two tasks aimed at monitoring how the system's activity representations are maintained across these memory structures.

4.2.3. Dataset-EGO4D

The dataset utilized in our experiments is EGO4D, a comprehensive collection of egocentric videos [55]. It consists of 3,600 hours of densely narrated video content, accompanied by detailed human annotations. The dataset covers a variety of scenarios—including household, outdoor, workplace, and leisure settings—recorded across 74 locations in 9 different countries. The video segments include supplementary data such as audio, 3D environmental meshes, eye gaze tracking, stereo video, and synchronized footage from multiple egocentric cameras capturing the same event. Additionally, this dataset includes challenges related to episodic memory recall and future event forecasting, with ground truth annotations provided. In the context of EGO4D, the queries often focus on atypical activity patterns. For example, a query related to "headphones" may need to be inferred by identifying appropriate video frames, such as those depicting a person multitasking by answering emails while cooking.

4.2.4. Methodology - Simulating the Perception-Cognition-Action Cycle in Egocentric Activity Recognition

To simulate the perception-cognition-action cycle in our experiment, we iterate between two tasks:

Task 1 - Episodic Memory Recall In this task, a video scene and a natural language query are provided as inputs. The system is expected to output a sequence of frames from the video that likely contain the answer to the query, effectively "recalling" specific segments or "episodes" of the video. This process requires the system to establish and retrieve memory representations of the query and the video scene, particularly their relationship in the context of the video's activity patterns. Figure 9 illustrates the inputs and outputs expected for a system performing this task. Notably, the query may involve complex associations, such as asking about headphones in relation to an unusual activity, like answering emails while boiling water. This presents a significant challenge for an AI system to interpret and infer.

Task 2 - Forecasting In this task, a partial sequence of frames from a video is given as input, and the system must predict the action category for the next frame. Solving this task requires the system to make informed and constrained predictions about the possible upcoming actions, despite the potentially large number of possibilities. The quality of the memory structures, particularly in capturing activity patterns, is critical to the success of the prediction. Figure 10 illustrates this challenge, showing how the space of potential next actions can quickly become overwhelming. Typically, some external con-

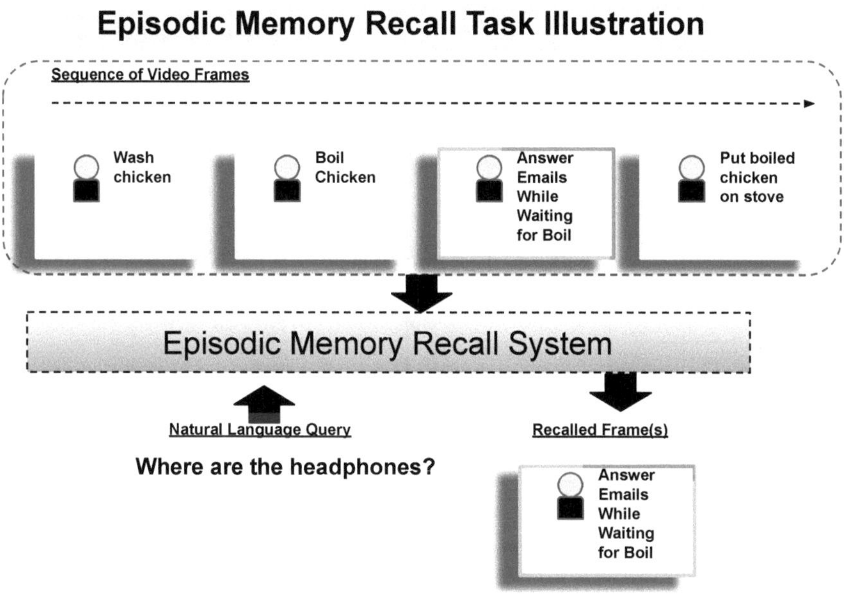

Figure 9. Task 1 - Episodic Memory Recall.

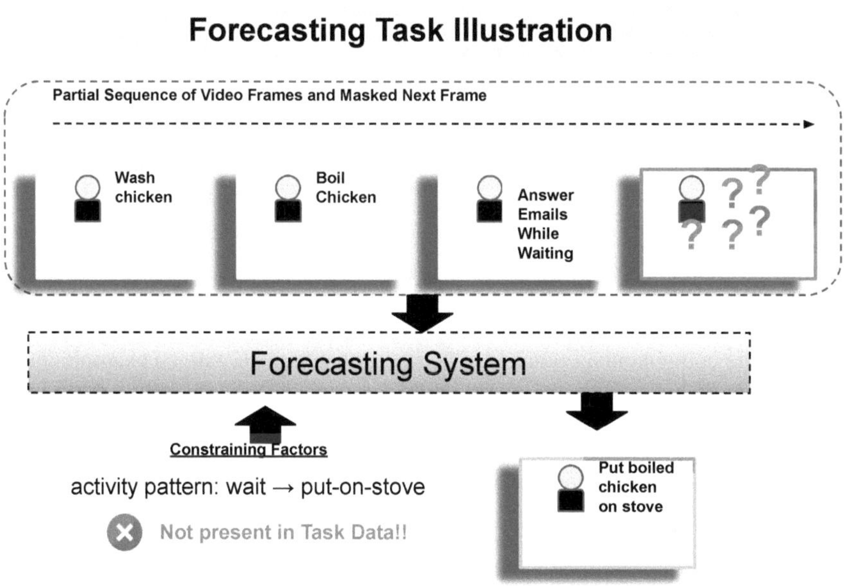

Figure 10. Task 2 - Forecasting.

straint—beyond the task dataset—is required to manage this complexity, and memory structures play a key role in applying these constraints.

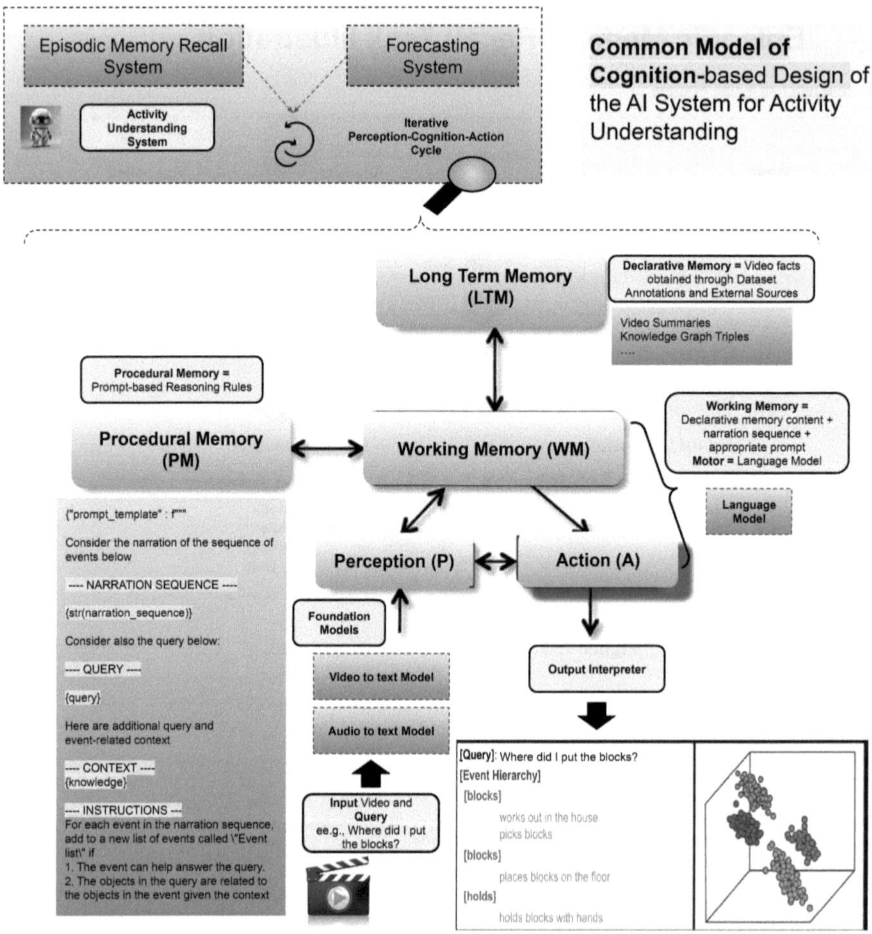

Figure 11. CMC-inspired solution approach and system design.

The Perception-Cognition-Action Cycle for Activity Understanding Our proposed approach uses the CMC and components as scaffolding and maps foundation models as needed across the components. Figure 11 illustrates the approach with an example query and video (inputs do not contain the query in the forecasting task and only a partial clip of the video). We note that the system is *language-centric*, i.e., the task execution takes language-based inputs and produces language-based outputs. All other modalities of information are, therefore, first converted to natural language (text) before processing by the system.

Why a language-centric approach? We choose a language-based core (representation and reasoning) for our approach for three reasons: (a) Language models are the most extensively studied foundation model, leading to better ease of access, software availability, and widespread methods for achieving relatively lower computation footprints, a key consideration for developing solutions to resource-bounded tasks. (b) Multimodal foundation models are still in their nascent stages. Therefore, multimodal model pipelines typically consist of projection to common representation spaces, and for reasons mentioned in (a), we choose language to be such a representation space. (c) Foundation models are prone to generating erroneous outputs, e.g., hallucinations, and augmenting the model with common sense knowledge is often beneficial in mitigating such errors. Most large-scale and publicly available knowledge bases are based on language, making language an attractive representation choice for augmenting language models with information from knowledge bases. The details of the individual CMC components are:

1. **Perception** The perception module takes the raw input, in this case, the video and the query, and transforms the information in the video, both the visual information and audio modalities, into text that consists of obtaining a "narration sequence" – a frame-by-frame narration of the video. The task Figures 9 and 10 show examples of such a narration sequence, i.e., the list [*Wash chicken, boil chicken, answer emails while waiting, and put boiled chicken on stove, ...*].
2. **Procedural Memory** In prototypical cognitive systems, procedural memory essentially consists of a set of rules or instructions that tell the system how to reason given an objective and the contents of the working memory. In this work, since the reasoner is language-based, the procedural memory contains prompts that guide or *instruct* the language model's reasoning.
3. **Declarative Memory** The declarative memory consists of language-based video annotations, such as video summaries and information sourced in knowledge graphs (verbalized using a verbalizer prompt). This information is meant to augment the narration sequence information and provide additional context to the reasoner.
4. **Working Memory** The working memory relies on outputs from the perception component, and the procedural and declarative memories. It is instantiated during reasoning to process the narration sequence, extracting task-related outputs by using relevant declarative memory content and procedural memory prompts. Importantly, the working memory is limited by the context window size of the reasoning LLM, a critical resource constraint. This CMC-inspired design emphasizes creating efficient representations and instructions in declarative and procedural memories to optimize reasoning within these constraints.
5. **Motor Module** The motor module consists of the language model that reasons about the task output given the contents of the working memory: in this regard, such module is responsible for speech acts. Accordingly, we augment the motor component with an output interpreter module that constructs a mapping of the combined contents of the working memory and predicted task outputs to an embedding space for visualizing task-related activity patterns.

4.2.5. Experimental Configuration

In this section, we describe the experimental configuration in detail. The CMC components are standard across the episodic memory recall and forecasting tasks, with only the input and output capture being slightly different (as shown in figures 9 and 10). The episodic memory recall task uses a video sequence as input and expects a video frame as a response to a natural language query, whereas in the forecasting task, the input is a partial sequence of contiguous frames, and the output is predicted action categories for the next frame. We now describe the details of the CMC components.

1. **Perception** The ground-truth annotations for the EGO4D dataset already consist of narration sequences obtained using model-based translations from visual and audio inputs. These annotations also contain the video clip time slice corresponding to each narration segment.
2. **Procedural Memory** The procedural memory consists of prompts (such as the one shown in Figure 11) for reasoning about events and actions in the video given narration sequences and declarative memory information.
3. **Declarative Memory** For declarative memory, the EGO4D dataset includes annotations for video summaries. Additionally, we utilize triples from the Common Sense Knowledge Graph (CSKG) [56]. The triple extraction process generally follows a three-stage pipeline: (i) Identifying action phrases in the input query and narration sequences using the syntax parser from the Flair library [57]. (ii) Performing keyword-based triple extraction by matching individual words in the action phrases (using the word tokenizer from nltk) [58]. (iii) Verbalizing only the relevant subset of triples through a language model based on a given prompt. We also employ a third type of declarative memory, referred to as "internal" knowledge. This is derived by querying the language model to further analyze the input query and narration sequences, with the aim of retrieving relevant information embedded within its parametric knowledge. The various prompts used are available at this Github repository[3].
   Note: During the execution of the forecasting task pipeline, we also maintain a memory bank of videos in declarative memory – This bank is updated when the episodic memory pipeline successfully identifies the correct video frame associated with the query, with high accuracy. Figure 10 shows how a constraint specification is essential to assist the system with predicting plausible next-action categories. This memory bank (i.e., the action distributions across the videos in this bank) acts as such a constraint specification.
   Metacognitive Instruction-based Prompting *The steps involving procedural memory construction from declarative memory elements, mainly the various types of knowledge sources, denote the core of the metacognitive rule construction, where we aim to accurately specify a robust semantic interpretation of the task in the prompt (seen as a rule) to engender cognitive reasoning by the foundation model during prompt execution.*
4. **Working Memory** The working memory is simply a *text string* that is a combination of the query (the input), the narration sequence (from the perception component), the context (from the declarative memory), and the appropriate prompt (from the procedural memory). The size of the *text string* is limited by the context-window lengths of the language models used in the motor component. In the forecasting task, the working memory involves an information retrieval mechanism to retrieve a set of top-k similar videos from the memory bank in the declarative memory to constrain the set of possible next-action categories (k is set to 3 in our experiments, and the retrieval method used is RAPTOR [59]).
5. **Motor** The language models that we experiment with are LLaMA 3-8b-8192, mixtral-8x7b-32768, and gemma-7b-it, accessed using the GROQ API[4]. The 'x'b part of the name denotes the number of parameters in billions, and the third part

[3]https://github.com/kauroy1994/Bosch_Research_Summer_2024
[4]https://groq.com/

of the name after the '-' denotes the context window lengths in terms of no. of tokens (each token is roughly equal to a word).

4.2.6. Results and Discussion

Episodic Memory Task Tables 3, 4, and 5 present performance across different declarative memory options. Due to the complex action distributions in EGO4D, such as "answering emails while wearing headphones during cooking," the internal knowledge within the LLM is less effective for inference. In contrast, human-annotated video summaries perform best, with CSKG triples nearly matching their accuracy. Additionally, models with larger context windows tend to perform better overall.

Table 3. Evaluation of Episodic Memory Task with Internal Knowledge.

LLM	Accuracy	Precision	Recall	F1-score
gemma-7b-it	0.3962	0.4999	0.3962	0.4363
LLaMA 3.1-8b	0.5869	0.6749	0.5869	0.6203
mixtral-8x7b	**0.6291**	**0.7444**	**0.6291**	**0.6736**

Table 4. Evaluation of Episodic Memory Task with Video Summary Knowledge.

LLM	Accuracy	Precision	Recall	F1-score
gemma-7b-it	0.5999	0.6999	0.5999	0.6444
LLaMA 3.1-8b	0.7962	0.8999	0.7962	0.8363
mixtral-8x7b	**0.7999**	**0.9999**	**0.7999**	**0.8888**

Table 5. Evaluation of Episodic Memory Task with CSKG Knowledge.

LLM	Accuracy	Precision	Recall	F1-score
gemma-7b-it	0.5749	0.5493	0.5899	0.6076
LLaMA 3.1-8b	**0.7523**	0.7886	**0.8274**	0.7000
mixtral-8x7b	0.7269	**0.8666**	0.7799	**0.8133**

Forecasting Task - In the forecasting task, Tables 6-8 demonstrate that, without clarity on plausible next-action distributions as constraints, the performance of the declarative knowledge sources is quite poor. An exception to this is the summary knowledge, which performs better as it is annotated by humans. However, when information about similar videos is retrieved from the memory bank, the results are notably improved, as evidenced by Table 9.

5. Conclusion and Validity of the Hypothesis Statement

This chapter introduces a novel CMC-inspired approach to foundation model-based neurosymbolic cognitive AI systems with improved cognitive reasoning. The experiments conducted show that either strategy—compressing cognitive representations for inte-

Table 6. Evaluation of Forecasting Task with Internal Knowledge.

LLM	Accuracy	Precision	Recall	F1-score
gemma-7b-it	0.21	0.23	0.2899	0.30
LLAMA 3.1-8b	0.223	0.26	0.265	**0.3**
mixtral-8x7b	**0.286**	**0.3**	**0.33**	0.21

Table 7. Evaluation of Forecasting Task with Video Summary Knowledge.

LLM	Accuracy	Precision	Recall	F1-score
gemma-7b-it	0.66	0.7333	0.78	0.69
LLAMA 3.1-8b	0.63	0.78	0.779	0.78
mixtral-8x7b	**0.75**	**0.93**	**0.81**	**0.87**

Table 8. Evaluation of Forecasting Task with CSKG Knowledge.

LLM	Accuracy	Precision	Recall	F1-score
gemma-7b-it	0.13	0.14	0.20	0.33
LLAMA 3.1-8b	0.23	0.27	**0.30**	0.23
mixtral-8x7b	**0.28**	**0.29**	0.258	**0.29**

Table 9. Evaluation of Forecasting Task with Information Retrieval

LLM	Accuracy	Precision	Recall	F1-score
gemma-7b-it	0.52	0.6212	0.55	0.49
LLAMA 3.1-8b	0.65	0.71	0.633	0.69
mixtral-8x7b	**0.68**	**0.733**	**0.6412**	**0.7111**

gration with neural networks or mapping neural to cognitive representations followed by instruction-based reasoning—yield promising results. A CMC-based framework improves cognitive reasoning in foundation models, particularly by enabling metacognitive instruction-following behavior, supporting the main hypothesis.

References

[1] Ce Zhou, Qian Li, Chen Li, Jun Yu, Yixin Liu, Guangjing Wang, Kai Zhang, Cheng Ji, Qiben Yan, Lifang He, et al. A comprehensive survey on pretrained foundation models: A history from bert to chatgpt. *arXiv preprint arXiv:2302.09419*, 2023.

[2] Devon Myers, Rami Mohawesh, Venkata Ishwarya Chellaboina, Anantha Lakshmi Sathvik, Praveen Venkatesh, Yi-Hui Ho, Hanna Henshaw, Muna Alhawawreh, David Berdik, and Yaser Jararweh. Foundation and large language models: fundamentals, challenges, opportunities, and social impacts. *Cluster Computing*, 27(1):1–26, 2024.

[3] Nanyi Fei, Zhiwu Lu, Yizhao Gao, Guoxing Yang, Yuqi Huo, Jingyuan Wen, Haoyu Lu, Ruihua Song, Xin Gao, Tao Xiang, et al. Towards artificial general intelligence via a multimodal foundation model. *Nature Communications*, 13(1):3094, 2022.

[4] Sébastien Bubeck, Varun Chandrasekaran, Ronen Eldan, Johannes Gehrke, Eric Horvitz, Ece Kamar, Peter Lee, Yin Tat Lee, Yuanzhi Li, Scott Lundberg, et al. Sparks of artificial general intelligence: Early experiments with gpt-4. *arXiv preprint arXiv:2303.12712*, 2023.

[5] Marianna Nezhurina, Lucia Cipolina-Kun, Mehdi Cherti, and Jenia Jitsev. Alice in wonderland: Simple tasks showing complete reasoning breakdown in state-of-the-art large language models. *arXiv preprint arXiv:2406.02061*, 2024.

[6] Subbarao Kambhampati. Can large language models reason and plan? *Annals of the New York Academy of Sciences*, 1534(1):15–18, 2024.

[7] Ruoqi Shen, Sébastien Bubeck, Ronen Eldan, Yin Tat Lee, Yuanzhi Li, and Yi Zhang. Positional description matters for transformers arithmetic. *arXiv preprint arXiv:2311.14737*, 2023.

[8] Trieu H Trinh, Yuhuai Wu, Quoc V Le, He He, and Thang Luong. Solving olympiad geometry without human demonstrations. *Nature*, 625(7995):476–482, 2024.

[9] Emily M Bender, Timnit Gebru, Angelina McMillan-Major, and Shmargaret Shmitchell. On the dangers of stochastic parrots: Can language models be too big? In *Proceedings of the 2021 ACM conference on fairness, accountability, and transparency*, pages 610–623, 2021.

[10] Joshua Tennenbaum. AAAI-23 Invited Speaker Series. `https://aaai-23.aaai.org/invited-speakers/`, 2023. [Online; accessed 9-Sep-2024].

[11] Goonmeet Bajaj, Valerie L Shalin, Srinivasan Parthasarathy, and Amit Sheth. Grounding from an ai and cognitive science lens. *IEEE Intelligent Systems*, 39(2):66–71, 2024.

[12] Vipula Rawte, Swagata Chakraborty, Agnibh Pathak, Anubhav Sarkar, SM Towhidul Islam Tonmoy, Aman Chadha, Amit Sheth, and Amitava Das. The troubling emergence of hallucination in large language models-an extensive definition, quantification, and prescriptive remediations. In *Proceedings of the 2023 Conference on Empirical Methods in Natural Language Processing*, pages 2541–2573, 2023.

[13] Ameet Deshpande, Vishvak Murahari, Tanmay Rajpurohit, Ashwin Kalyan, and Karthik Narasimhan. Toxicity in chatgpt: Analyzing persona-assigned language models. In *Findings of the Association for Computational Linguistics: EMNLP 2023*, pages 1236–1270, 2023.

[14] John E Laird, Christian Lebiere, and Paul S Rosenbloom. A standard model of the mind: Toward a common computational framework across artificial intelligence, cognitive science, neuroscience, and robotics. *Ai Magazine*, 38(4):13–26, 2017.

[15] Andrea Stocco, Catherine Sibert, Zoe Steine-Hanson, Natalie Koh, John E Laird, Christian J Lebiere, and Paul Rosenbloom. Analysis of the human connectome data supports the notion of a "common model of cognition" for human and human-like intelligence across domains. *NeuroImage*, 235:118035, 2021.

[16] Yann LeCun. A path towards autonomous machine intelligence version 0.9. 2, 2022-06-27. *Open Review*, 62, 2022.

[17] Lilian Weng. Llm-powered autonomous agents. *lilianweng.github.io*, Jun 2023.

[18] Allen Newell. *Unified theories of cognition.* Harvard University Press, 1994.

[19] Terrence C Stewart. *A methodology for computational cognitive modelling.* PhD thesis, Carleton University, 2007.

[20] J Cliff Shaw, Allen Newell, Herbert A Simon, and TO Ellis. A command structure for complex information processing. In *Proceedings of the May 6-8, 1958, western joint computer conference: contrasts in computers*, pages 119–128, 1958.

[21] Theodore Sumers, Shunyu Yao, Karthik Narasimhan, and Thomas Griffiths. Cognitive architectures for language agents. *Transactions on Machine Learning Research.*

[22] Mudit Verma, Siddhant Bhambri, and Subbarao Kambhampati. Theory of mind abilities of large language models in human-robot interaction: An illusion? In *Companion of the 2024 ACM/IEEE Interna-*

tional Conference on Human-Robot Interaction, pages 36–45, 2024.
[23] Matthew A Kelly and David Reitter. Holographic declarative memory: Using distributional semantics within act-r. In *2017 AAAI Fall Symposium Series*, 2017.
[24] Amit Sheth and Kaushik Roy. Neurosymbolic value-inspired artificial intelligence (why, what, and how). *IEEE Intelligent Systems*, 39(1):5–11, 2024.
[25] Yanda Chen, Ruiqi Zhong, Sheng Zha, George Karypis, and He He. Meta-learning via language model in-context tuning. In *Proceedings of the 60th Annual Meeting of the Association for Computational Linguistics (Volume 1: Long Papers)*, pages 719–730, 2022.
[26] Pascal Hitzler and Md Kamruzzaman Sarker. Neuro-symbolic artificial intelligence: The state of the art. 2022.
[27] Alessandro Oltramari. Enabling high-level machine reasoning with cognitive neuro-symbolic systems. In *Proceedings of the AAAI Symposium Series*, volume 2, pages 360–368, 2023.
[28] Artur d'Avila Garcez and Luis C Lamb. Neurosymbolic ai: The 3 rd wave. *Artificial Intelligence Review*, 56(11):12387–12406, 2023.
[29] Amit Sheth, Kaushik Roy, and Manas Gaur. Neurosymbolic artificial intelligence (why, what, and how). *IEEE Intelligent Systems*, 38(3):56–62, 2023.
[30] Iuliia Kotseruba and John K Tsotsos. 40 years of cognitive architectures: core cognitive abilities and practical applications. *Artificial Intelligence Review*, 53(1):17–94, 2020.
[31] John R Anderson. Act: A simple theory of complex cognition. *American psychologist*, 51(4):355, 1996.
[32] Sterling Somers, Alessandro Oltramari, and Christian Lebiere. Cognitive twin: A cognitive approach to personalized assistants. In *AAAI Spring Symposium: Combining Machine Learning with Knowledge Engineering (1)*, 2020.
[33] Mehdi Cina and Ahmad B Rad. Categorized review of drive simulators and driver behavior analysis focusing on act-r architecture in autonomous vehicles. *Sustainable Energy Technologies and Assessments*, 56:103044, 2023.
[34] Hao Chen, Shuang Liu, Liping Pang, Xiaoru Wanyan, and Yufeng Fang. Developing an improved act-r model for pilot situation awareness measurement. *IEEE Access*, 9:122113–122124, 2021.
[35] Noam Ben-Asher, Alessandro Oltramari, Robert F Erbacher, and Cleotilde Gonzalez. Ontology-based adaptive systems of cyber defense. In *STIDS*, pages 34–41, 2015.
[36] S. Wu, R. Ferreira, F. E. Ritter, and L. Walter. Comparing llms for prompt-enhanced act-r and soar model development: A case study in cognitive simulation. In *Proceedings of the 38th Annual Association for the Advancement of Artificial Intelligence (AAAI) Conference on Artificial Intelligence, Fall Symposium Series on Integrating Cognitive Architecture and Generative Models*, Arlington, Virginia, USA, 2023.
[37] B. J. Best and C. Lebiere. Teamwork, communication, and planning in act-r agents engaging in urban combat in virtual environments. In *Proceedings of the 2003 IJCAI Workshop on Cognitive Modeling of Agents and Multi-Agent Interactions*, pages 64–72, 2003.
[38] C. Gonzalez, J. F. Lerch, and C. Lebiere. Instance-based learning in dynamic decision making. *Cognitive Science*, 27:591–635, 2003.
[39] Sabine Prezenski, André Brechmann, Susann Wolff, and Nele Russwinkel. A cognitive modeling approach to strategy formation in dynamic decision making. *Frontiers in Psychology*, 8:1335, 2017.
[40] S. B. Blessing and J. R. Anderson. How people learn to skip steps. *Journal of Experimental Psychology: Learning, Memory, and Cognition*, 22(3):576, 1996.
[41] M. K. Martin, C. Gonzalez, and C. Lebiere. Learning to make decisions in dynamic environments: Act-r plays the beer game. In *Proceedings of the Sixth International Conference on Cognitive Modeling*, Pittsburgh, PA, 2004. Carnegie Mellon University/University of Pittsburgh.
[42] F. E. Ritter, M. J. Schoelles, K. S. Quigley, and L. C. Klein. *Determining the number of model runs: Treating cognitive models as theories by not sampling their behavior*, pages 97–116. Springer-Verlag, London, 2011.
[43] S. J. Gilbert and P. W. Burgess. Executive function. *Current Biology*, 18(3):R110–R114, 2008.
[44] T. O. Nelson and L. Narens. Why investigate metacognition? *Journal Name Here*, Volume Here(Issue Number Here):Page Numbers Here, 1994.
[45] H. Abdi and L. J. Williams. Principal component analysis. *Wiley Interdisciplinary Reviews: Computational Statistics*, 2(4):433–459, 2010.
[46] Alex Graves. Sequence transduction with recurrent neural networks. *arXiv preprint arXiv:1211.3711*, 2012.
[47] Edward J Hu, Yelong Shen, Phillip Wallis, Zeyuan Allen-Zhu, Yuanzhi Li, Shean Wang, Lu Wang, and

Weizhu Chen. LoRA: Low-rank adaptation of large language models. In *International Conference on Learning Representations*, 2022.

[48] M. Binz and E. Schulz. Using cognitive psychology to understand gpt-3. *Proceedings of the National Academy of Sciences*, 120(6):e2218523120, 2023.

[49] Amit Kumar, Rakesh Sharma, and Punam Bedi. Towards optimal nlp solutions: Analyzing gpt and llama-2 models across model scale, dataset size, and task diversity. *Engineering, Technology & Applied Science Research*, 14(3):14219–14224, 2024.

[50] Jens Gaab, Joe Kossowsky, Ulrike Ehlert, and Cosima Locher. Effects and components of placebos with a psychological treatment rationale—three randomized-controlled studies. *Scientific Reports*, 9(1):1421, 2019.

[51] M. Binz and E. Schulz. Turning large language models into cognitive models. In *Proceedings of the International Conference on Learning Representations (ICLR)*, 2024. In press.

[52] Alessandro Oltramari, Jonathan Francis, Filip Ilievski, Kaixin Ma, and Roshanak Mirzaee. Generalizable neuro-symbolic systems for commonsense question answering. In *Neuro-Symbolic Artificial Intelligence: The State of the Art*, pages 294–310. IOS Press, 2021.

[53] Kaixin Ma, Jonathan Francis, Quanyang Lu, Eric Nyberg, and Alessandro Oltramari. Towards generalizable neuro-symbolic systems for commonsense question answering. *arXiv preprint arXiv:1910.14087*, 2019.

[54] Z. Hussain, M. Binz, R. Mata, and D. U. Wulff. A tutorial on open-source large language models for behavioral science. *PsyArXiv preprint*, 2023.

[55] Kristen Grauman, Andrew Westbury, Eugene Byrne, Zachary Chavis, Antonino Furnari, Rohit Girdhar, Jackson Hamburger, Hao Jiang, Miao Liu, Xingyu Liu, et al. Ego4d: Around the world in 3,000 hours of egocentric video. In *2022 IEEE/CVF Conference on Computer Vision and Pattern Recognition (CVPR)*, pages 18973–18990. IEEE Computer Society, 2022.

[56] Filip Ilievski, Pedro Szekely, and Bin Zhang. Cskg: The commonsense knowledge graph. In *The Semantic Web: 18th International Conference, ESWC 2021, Virtual Event, June 6–10, 2021, Proceedings 18*, pages 680–696. Springer, 2021.

[57] Alan Akbik, Tanja Bergmann, Duncan Blythe, Kashif Rasul, Stefan Schweter, and Roland Vollgraf. Flair: An easy-to-use framework for state-of-the-art nlp. In *Proceedings of the 2019 conference of the North American chapter of the association for computational linguistics (demonstrations)*, pages 54–59, 2019.

[58] Edward Loper and Steven Bird. Nltk: The natural language toolkit. In *Proceedings of the ACL-02 Workshop on Effective Tools and Methodologies for Teaching Natural Language Processing and Computational Linguistics*, pages 63–70, 2002.

[59] Parth Sarthi, Salman Abdullah, Aditi Tuli, Shubh Khanna, Anna Goldie, and Christopher D Manning. Raptor: Recursive abstractive processing for tree-organized retrieval. In *The Twelfth International Conference on Learning Representations*.

Handbook on Neurosymbolic AI and Knowledge Graphs
P. Hitzler et al. (Eds.)
IOS Press, 2025

doi:10.3233/FAIA250229

Knowledge Enhanced Neural Networks

Alessandro DANIELE [a,1] and Luciano SERAFINI [a]
[a] *Fondazione Bruno Kessler, Trento, Italy*
ORCiD ID: Alessandro Daniele https://orcid.org/0000-0001-9441-0729, Luciano Serafini https://orcid.org/0000-0003-4812-1031

Abstract. In the recent past, there has been a growing interest in Neural-Symbolic Integration frameworks, i.e., hybrid systems that integrate connectionist (neural networks) and symbolic approaches: on the one hand, connectionist approaches show remarkable abilities to learn from a large amount of data in presence of noise, on the other, pure symbolic methods can perform reasoning as well as learning from few samples. In theory, by combining the two paradigms, it could be possible to obtain a system that can both learn from data and apply inference over some background knowledge. This chapter introduces KENN (Knowledge Enhanced Neural Networks), a Neural-Symbolic architecture that injects prior knowledge, codified in a set of universally quantified FOL clauses, into a neural network model. In KENN, clauses are used to generate a new final layer of the neural network which modifies the initial predictions based on the knowledge. Among the advantages of this strategy, there is the possibility to include additional learnable parameters, the *clause weights*, each of which represents the strength of a specific clause, meaning that the model can learn the impact of the clause on the final predictions. As a special case, if the training data contradicts a constraint, KENN learns to ignore it, making the system robust to the presence of wrong knowledge. Another advantage of KENN resides in its scalability, thanks to a flexible treatment of dependencies between the rules obtained by stacking multiple logical layers.

Keywords. Neural-Symbolic Integration, Fuzzy Logic, Learning with constraints

1. Introduction

In the last decade, deep learning approaches gained a lot of interest in the AI community, becoming the state of the art on many fields, such as Computer Vision [1], Machine Translation [2], Speech Recognition [3], etc. Indeed, Neural networks (NNs) are suited for pattern recognition, even in the presence of noisy data. They are particularly good at mapping low-level perceptions to more abstract concepts (for instance, going from images to classes). However, it is hard for a NN to reason with these high-level abstractions. Furthermore, NNs are demanding in terms of training data. On the other hand, pure logical approaches are not suited for learning from low-level perceptions and they struggle in the presence of noise. Nevertheless, they perform well in reasoning with highly abstract concepts and learning from a small number of samples. Given these opposite strengths and weaknesses, it is not a surprise that a lot of interest has been drawn toward Neural-Symbolic (NeSy) systems. Indeed, the goal is to combine these two paradigms to obtain the best of the two worlds.

[1] Corresponding Author: Alessandro Daniele, e-mail: daniele@fbk.eu.

1.1. KENN

Among NeSy methods there is KENN (*Knowledge Enhanced Neural Network*) [4,5], a model composed of a Neural Network enhanced with additional layers which codify logical knowledge. KENN has multiple advantages over other NeSy methods, such as its capacity to learn *clause weights* and the ability to impose the knowledge not only during training but even at inference time.

Suppose we have a Neural Network for a classification task, which is called *base NN*, that takes in input the feature vector $\mathbf{x} \in \mathbb{R}^n$ and returns an output $\mathbf{y} \in [0,1]^m$ which contains the predictions for m classes. A background knowledge $\mathscr{K}$ is also provided. $\mathscr{K}$ is defined as a set of clauses, i.e. disjunctions of literals, that represent constraints on the m classes to be predicted. For instance, in an image classification task, the clause $\forall x\ \neg Dog(x) \vee Animal(x)$, stating that dogs are animals, can be used by KENN, in conjunction with the base NN, to predict the two labels *Dog* and *Animal*. Figure 1 shows a high-level overview of KENN.

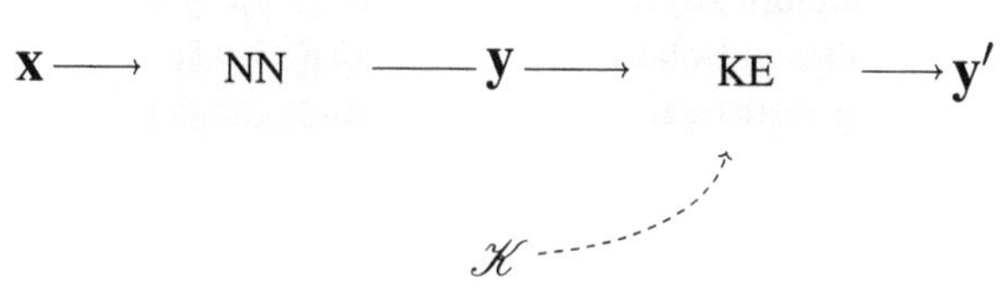

Figure 1. KENN model: features are given as input to a neural network (NN) and predictions on predicates values are returned. Knowledge Enhancer (KE) modifies the predictions based on logical constraints ($\mathscr{K}$)

Predictions $\mathbf{y}$ are revised by a differentiable function, called *Knowledge Enhancer* (KE), which corresponds to a new layer on top of the base NN. Its role is to update the predictions $\mathbf{y}$ of the base NN into $\mathbf{y}'$ to increase the truth value of each clause $c \in \mathscr{K}$. Since both base NN and KE are differentiable, the entire architecture is differentiable end-to-end, making it possible to apply back-propagation algorithm directly on the whole model.

KE increases the satisfaction of each clause c separately obtaining $|\mathscr{K}|$ different vectors, each of which represents the changes to be applied on $\mathbf{y}$ to obtain the improvement of satisfaction of c. These changes are combined linearly to obtain the final change to be applied on the base NN's predictions.

An important question arises: what does it mean to increase the satisfaction of a clause? KENN use fuzzy semantic, where the satisfaction of a clause is given by applying a t-conorm function $\perp$ on the truth values of the literals of the clause. Therefore, the objective of the final layer should be increasing the value of the chosen t-conorm. However, we are not relying on an optimization process to add knowledge, so it is not possible to just optimize the value of the t-conorm at run time. On the contrary, we want to inject the knowledge as a differentiable layer on top of a neural network: the optimization must be done analytically!

To do so, [4] proposes the concept of *t-conorm boost functions* (TBFs). Intuitively, a TBF is a function $\delta : [0,1]^n \to [0,1]^n$ that proposes the changes to be applied on a set of n truth values to increase the value of the t-conorm applied on them: $\perp(\mathbf{t}+\delta(\mathbf{t})) \geq \perp(\mathbf{t})$. KENN include a soft differentiable approximation of a TBF in its last layer and it uses it to enhance the prediction of the base NN.

Moreover, KE contains additional parameters that can be learned as well: for each clause $c \in \mathcal{K}$ there is an associated *clause weight* w_c which determines the strength of c, i.e., it defines the influence that the clause has on the final predictions. Differently from other Neural-Symbolic integration approaches, clauses weights are not given, but they are learned. Moreover, by changing the weight of clause, KENN can learn to ignore clauses in the Prior Knowledge that are not fully satisfied inside training data by assigning zero to the weight.

KENN has been evaluated on multiple aspects, showing remarkable results on the Predicate Detection task of Visual Relationship Detection Dataset (VRD Dataset) [4], on collective classification on citation graphs [5], and on Point Cloud Semantic Segmentation [6].

2. Related Work

Many previous works attempt to combine learning models with logical knowledge. Among them there is Statistical Relational Learning (SRL), a subfield of Machine Learning that aims at applying statistical methods in domains that exhibit both uncertainty and relational structure [7]. Generally speaking, SRL deals with the knowledge either by combining logic rules with probabilistic graphical models (e.g., Markov Logic Networks [8], and *Probabilistic Soft Logic* (PSL) [9]) or by extending logic programming languages to handle uncertainty (e.g., ProbLog [10]).

The recent achievements of deep learning methods lead to a renewed interest in another line of research, called Neural-Symbolic Integration, which focuses on combining neural network architectures with logical knowledge [11]. This can be achieved in multiple ways depending on the role of the knowledge. For instance, works like TensorLog [12], Neural Theorem Prover (NTP) [13,14], DeepProbLog [15], Neural Logic Machines [16], and NeuralLog [17] focus on the development of differentiable approaches for reasoning, which can be used in combination with neural networks. Another line of research comes from methods like ∂ILP [18], [19], and Neural Logic Rule Layer (NLRL) [20]. In these cases, the goal is to learn general knowledge from the data, either from scratch or by refining an initial knowledge. Finally, more related to our purposes, some methods focus on learning in the presence of prior knowledge, which acts as additional supervision. In this section, we are going to focus on these types of methods, since KENN falls in this category.

There are mainly two approaches for learning in the presence of prior knowledge: the first consists of treating logical rules as constraints on the predictions of the neural network. The problem is reduced to maximize the satisfiability of the constraints and can be efficiently tackled by adding a regularization term in the Loss function. The second approach is to modify the neural network by injecting the knowledge into its structure.

Two notable examples of regularization approaches are *Logic Tensor Network* (LTN) [21] and *Semantic Based Regularization* (SBR) [22]. Both methods maximize the satisfaction of the constraints, expressed as FOL formulas, under a fuzzy logic semantic. A similar strategy is employed also by *Semantic Loss Function* [23], but instead of relying on fuzzy logic, it optimizes the probability of the rules being true. Nevertheless, this approach is restricted to propositional logic. [24] introduces DL2. Nonetheless, it can be used only in the context of regression tasks, where the predicates correspond to comparison constraints (e.g. $=$, $\neq$, $\leq$). [25] also proposes a method that regularizes the Loss, but they focus on a specific task of Natural Language Processing. Their approach differs from the others because it makes use of adversarial examples to calculate the regularization term. Finally, in [26], a distillation mechanism is used to inject FOL rules: here a teacher network (which encodes the rules) is used to regularize the Loss applied to a student network.

Approaches based on regularization force the constraints satisfaction solely at training time. As a consequence, there are no guarantees that they will be satisfied at inference time as well. Instead, model-based methods inject knowledge directly into the model structure, and they are naturally capable of enforcing the knowledge at inference time. Another advantage is the possibility to learn a weight that codifies the importance of a logical rule directly from the data. This is no possible at all with methods based on regularization, since the logical formulas are directly codified inside the Loss function.

Among the model-based approaches there is KENN, a framework that injects knowledge on top of the NN model through an additional layer which increases the satisfaction of the constraints in a fuzzy logic semantic. Another approach is provided by Li and Srikumar who recently proposed a method that codifies the logical constraints directly into the neural network model [27]. However, they restrict the rules to implications with exactly one consequent and they do not provide the possibility to learn clause weights, which in their system are added as hyper-parameters. Going in the same direction, [28] proposed Relational Neural Networks (RNM). RNM can be also inserted in the set of approaches that add the logic directly into the model and, like KENN, is capable of learning the clause weights. RNM integrates a neural network model with a FOL reasoner. This is done in two stages: in the first one, the NN is used to calculate initial predictions for the atomic formulas; in the second stage a graphical model is used to represent a probability distribution over the set of atomic formulas. To obtain the final predictions a Maximum a Posteriori (MAP) estimation is performed, finding the most probable assignment to the grounded atoms given the output of the NN and the set of constraints. At a high-level RNM approach is similar to KENN, since in both cases a NN makes initial predictions and a post elaboration step is applied to such predictions to provide the final classification. However, RNM requires to solve an optimization problem at inference time and after each training step. This has the advantage of considering all the logical rules together at the same time at the expense of an increased computational effort. Contrary, in KENN each rule is considered separately from the others, and the second stage is directly integrated inside the model as a differentiable function that can be trained end-to-end with the NN.

3. Prior Knowledge

KENN defines the Prior Knowledge in terms of formulas of a function-free first order language $\mathscr{L}$. Its signature is defined with a set of constants $\mathscr{C} \triangleq \{a_1, a_2, ...a_l\}$ and a set of predicates $\mathscr{P} \triangleq \{P_1, P_2...P_q\}$.

Unary predicates can be used to express properties of singular objects. For instance, to represents that a person $a \in \mathscr{C}$ is a smoker, we can use $Smoker(a)$, where $Smoker \in \mathscr{P}$ is a predicate with arity one. Predicates with higher arity can express relations among multiple objects in the domain, e.g. $Friends(a,b)$ states that person a is a friend of b.

The Prior Knowledge is defined as a set of clauses: $\mathscr{K} \triangleq \{c_1, c_2, ... c_r\}$. A clause is a disjunction of literals, each of which is a possibly negated atom:

$$c \triangleq \bigvee_{i=1}^{m} l_i \tag{1}$$

where m is the number of literals in c and l_i is the ith literal. We assume that there are no repeated literals.

As an example, the clause $\neg Smoker(x) \vee \neg Friends(x,y) \vee Smoker(y)$ states that if a person x is a smoker and he is a friend of another person y, then y is also a smoker.

Notice that the previous clause has no constants and the two variables x and y in it are assumed to be universally quantified. This is because we are interested in representing general knowledge, and in the following, we will always apply this assumption implicitly to each clause in our knowledge.

We define the grounding of a clause c, denoted by $c[x/a, y/b...]$, as the clause obtained by substituting all of its free variables with the corresponding constant symbol. For instance, if we take into consideration two specific persons a and b, then

$$(\neg Smoker(x) \vee \neg Friends(x,y) \vee Smoker(y))[x/a, y/b] \tag{2}$$

is equivalent to

$$\neg Smoker(a) \vee \neg Friends(a,b) \vee Smoker(b) \tag{3}$$

We will denote with $\mathscr{G}(c, \mathscr{C})$ the set of all the groundings of a clause c and with $\mathscr{G}(\mathscr{K}, \mathscr{C})$ the set of all the grounded clauses.

3.1. Semantic of $\mathscr{L}$

The semantic of $\mathscr{L}$ is defined in terms of an intepretation $\mathscr{I}$, which is a function that maps terms and grounded atoms to real values. More in details, constant symbols $o \in \mathscr{C}$ of $\mathscr{L}$ are interpreted as real-valued vectors and atoms as values in $[0,1]$.

Intuitively, the vectors associated to constants represent the features of the corresponding objects in the real world, and they are given as input, while the truth values of atomic formulas are provided by a neural network. Since we are dealing with neural network predictions, which returns continuos values, we can not make use of classic logic. For this reason KENN relies on fuzzy logic, where the truth values of atoms are mapped to values in the range $[0,1]$.

Formally, given a list of constants $o_i \in \mathscr{C}$, and a predicate $P \in \mathscr{P}$ with ariety n, an intepretation $\mathscr{I}$ is a function that satisfies the following properties:

- $\mathscr{I}(o_i) = \mathbf{x}_i$, with $\mathbf{x}_i \in \mathbb{R}^l$
- $\mathscr{I}(P) = \mathbb{R}^{nl} \rightarrow [0,1]$, where $\mathscr{I}(P)$ is a function which takes as input the interpretation (features) $\mathscr{I}(o_1), \mathscr{I}(o_2) \dots \mathscr{I}(o_n)$ of n constant symbols and returns the truth value of $P(o_1, o_2 \dots o_n)$.

3.2. T-conorm Functions

Previous definition of interpretation provides the semantic for terms and atoms. We need to specify how to interpret clauses, i.e., define the interpretation of negation and disjunction operators.

In fuzzy logic, a standard way to calculate the truth value of a negated atom is the Lukasiewicz negation: $\mathscr{I}(\neg A) = 1 - \mathscr{I}(A)$. On the other hand, the satisfaction of a disjunction of literals is represented with a t-conorm function, which maps the truth values (expressed in the range $[0,1]$) of two literals to the truth value of their disjunction.

Definition 1. *A t-conorm $\bot : [0,1] \times [0,1] \rightarrow [0,1]$ is a binary function which satisfies the following properties:*

1. $\bot(a,b) = \bot(b,a)$
2. $\bot(a,b) \leq \bot(c,d)$ *if* $a \leq c$ *and* $b \leq d$
3. $\bot(a,\bot(b,c)) = \bot(\bot(a,b),c)$
4. $\bot(a,0) = a$

We represent a t-conorm as a unary function over vectors ($\mathbf{t} = \langle t_1, t_2 ... t_n \rangle$):

$$\bot(\mathbf{t}) = \bot(t_1, \bot(t_2, \bot(t_3 ... \bot(t_{n-1}, t_n)))) \tag{4}$$

Given a clause c composed of n literals, if the ith component of $\mathbf{t}$ is the truth value of the ith literal of c, then $\bot(\mathbf{t})$ is the truth value of c. In the following, we will use the vector $\mathbf{t}$ to represent the predictions of the literals' truth values and vector $\mathbf{y}$ for the predictions of all the grounded atoms.

We have now all the elements to intepret all the sentences in $\mathscr{L}$: the intepretation $\mathscr{I}$ defined in Section 3.1 is implicitly extended to the clauses by inductively applying the following rules:

- $\mathscr{I}(\neg A) = 1 - \mathscr{I}(A)$
- $\mathscr{I}(c) = \bot(\mathscr{I}(l_1), \mathscr{I}(l_2), \ldots, \mathscr{I}(l_m))$

where A is an atomic formula and c is a clause.

4. Clause Enhancement

Intuitively, given the interpretation of the constant symbols, the base NN returns the interpetation for the atomic formulas. The KE should take as input the intepretation provided by the neural network and return a new interpretation with increased satisfaction of the contraints, i.e., with higher truth values of the grounded clauses, which in turns corresponds to increase the t-conorm value.

In this section, we will focus on the enhancment of a single clause: given the truth values $\mathbf{t}$ of the clause's literals, we want to produce a new assignment for $\mathbf{t}$ that increase the t-conorm value. In order to achieve this goal, we will define a new class of functions, called *t-conorm boost functions*. Later, we will extend the results of this section with the enhancement of the entire knowledge.

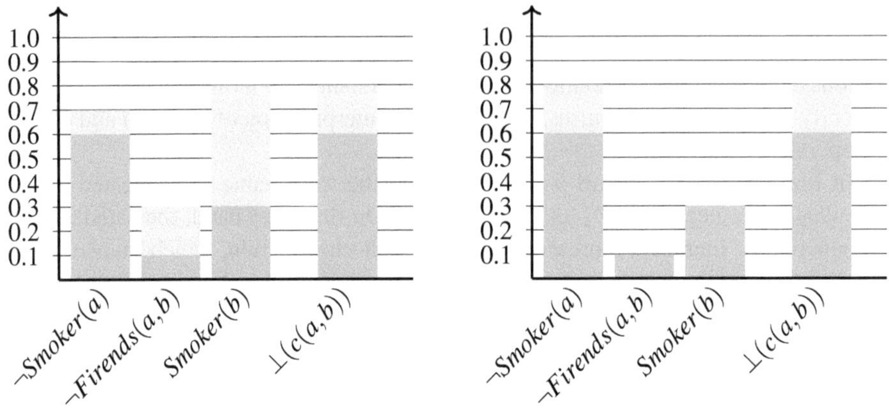

Figure 2. Effect of TBFs on base NN predictions for the grounded clause $c(a,b) : \neg Smoker(a) \vee \neg Friends(a,b) \vee Smoker(b)$, where predicate *Friends* is true when the two persons are friends. The gray areas represent the original predictions of the base NN while the green ones the changes applied by the TBF. The last bar represents the truth value of c under the Gödel t-conorm, which is increased in both cases. Indeed, both graphs shows a TBF. The improvements on the left are not minimal, since it is possible to reach the same improvement with smaller changes. On the contrary, the TBF on the right is minimal for the Gödel t-conorm.

4.1. T-conorm Boost Functions

Definition 2. *A function* $\delta : [0,1]^n \to [0,1]^n$ *is a* t-conorm boost function *(TBF) if:*

$$\forall n \in \mathbb{N} \ \ \forall \mathbf{t} \in [0,1]^n \ \ 0 \leq t_i + \delta(\mathbf{t})_i \leq 1 \tag{5}$$

Let Δ denote the set of all TBFs.

Proposition 1. *For every t-conorm* $\perp$ *and every TBF* δ, $\perp(\mathbf{t}) \leq \perp(\mathbf{t} + \delta(\mathbf{t}))$

Proof. By definition of TBF, $\forall i \in [1,n]$, $t_i \leq t_i + \delta(\mathbf{t})_i$; the conclusion directly follows from Property 2. of t-conorms. □

TBFs are used in the KE to update the initial predictions $\mathbf{y}$ done by the base NN. While there are infinite many TBFs, not all of them can be used for our purposes. Consider for example the function $\delta(\mathbf{t}) = \mathbf{1} - \mathbf{t}$: this of course is a TBF and it makes the t-conorm completely true for every possible initial predictions:

$$\perp(\mathbf{t} + \delta(\mathbf{t})) = \perp(\mathbf{t} + \mathbf{1} - \mathbf{t}) = \perp(\mathbf{1}) \tag{6}$$

Although the constraint reaches its maximum satisfaction, such a function returns a constant value for each literal ($\forall i \ t_i = 1$) which is useless for our purposes since the NN's predictions are not taken into account. We want to find a balance between the NN's predictions and the satisfaction of the clause: the TBF should keep the change on the initial predictions as minimal as possible. Therefore we look at TBF's that improve the t-conorm value *in a minimal way* so that it is not possible to obtain a higher improvement with smaller modifications on literals values. An example of this idea can be seen in Figure 2. We now define the concept of minimality for a TBFs.

Definition 3. *A function $\delta \in \Delta$ is minimal with respect to a norm $\|\cdot\|$ and a t-conorm $\perp$ iff:*

$$\begin{aligned}&\forall \delta' \in \Delta \;\; \forall n \in \mathbb{N} \;\; \forall \mathbf{t} \in [0,1]^n \\ &\|\delta'(\mathbf{t})\| < \|\delta(\mathbf{t})\| \to \perp(\mathbf{t}+\delta'(\mathbf{t})) < \perp(\mathbf{t}+\delta(\mathbf{t}))\end{aligned} \tag{7}$$

Minimal TBF is defined with respect to a given norm $\|\cdot\|$ and a t-conorm $\perp$. KENN uses the Gödel t-conorm, which is defined as

$$\perp(\mathbf{t}) = \max_{i=1}^{n}(t_i) \tag{8}$$

and l_p-norm:

$$\|\mathbf{t}\|_p = \left(\sum_{k=1}^{n} |t_k|^p\right)^{1/p} \tag{9}$$

Notice that Gödel t-conorm value depends only on the highest literal in the clause. Since we are interested in the minimal change in the predictions it seems reasonable to increase only the highest truth value.

For any function $f : \mathbb{R}^n \to \mathbb{R}$ we define $\delta^f : \mathbb{R}^n \to \mathbb{R}^n$ as

$$\delta^f(\mathbf{t})_i = \begin{cases} f(\mathbf{t}) & \text{if } i = \text{argmax}_{j=1}^{n} t_j \\ 0 & \text{otherwise} \end{cases} \tag{10}$$

Theorem 1. *If we choose function f such that $0 \leq f(\mathbf{t}) \leq 1 - \max_{j=1}^{n} t_j$, then δ^f function is minimal TBFs for the Gödel t-conorm and l_p-norm.*

Figure 3 shows a geometric interpretation for Theorem 1. In the example, it is shown a specific case: the initial truth values for the two literals $\neg$*Smoker*(x) and *Cancer*(x) are 0.5 and 0.3 respectively. The Gödel t-conorm value is 0.5, since it is the highest value. To be minimal, a TBF must increase the value of the t-conorm with the smallest possible change, meaning that it is not possible to reach the same improvement on the t-conorm with smaller changes. The blue circle contains the set of points that apply a smaller change to $\mathbf{t}$ than δ^f (in this case, we consider the l_2-norm). The picture shows that for all those points the Gödel t-conorm is smaller than 0.65, the value obtained by using δ^f.

Of course, this does not represent a proof for the minimality of δ^f, since it is applied to a specific set of truth values and it considers only l_2-norm. We need to prove it formally.

Proof. It is easy to see that $\delta(\mathbf{t})$ is a TBF: the function always returns values inside the range $[0,1]$ and even the final predictions are in this range. We need to prove that it is minimal. Suppose that $\delta \in \Delta$ is such that

$$\|\delta(\mathbf{t})\|_p < \|\delta^f(\mathbf{t})\|_p \tag{11}$$

If $j = \text{argmax}_{k=1}^{n}(t_k + \delta(\mathbf{t})_k)$, we can derive:

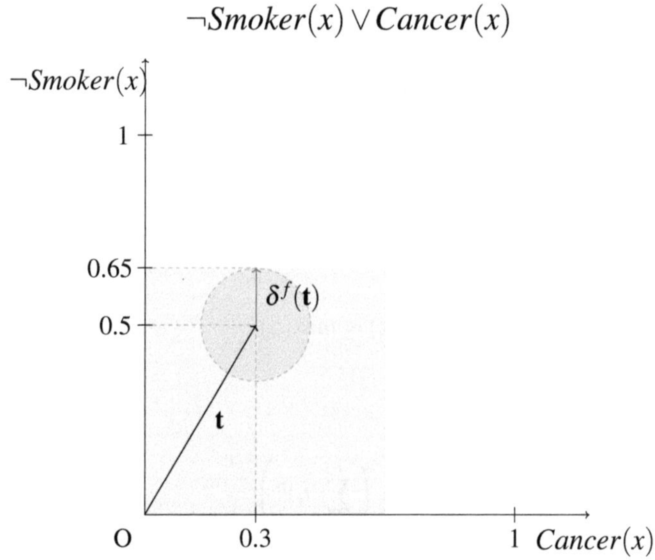

Figure 3. Geometric intuition for minimality of δ^f: an example with $\mathbf{t} = [0.3, 0.5]$ (black line). The blue circle represents the set of points $\mathbf{t}+\mathbf{k}$ with $\|\mathbf{k}\|_2 < \|\delta^f(\mathbf{t})\|_2$. The green area is the set of all point $\mathbf{t}+\mathbf{k}$ with $\perp(\mathbf{t}+\mathbf{k}) < \perp(\mathbf{t}+\delta^f(\mathbf{t}))$. The blue area is completely inside the green square, i.e. $\delta^f(\mathbf{t})$ (blue line) is the minimal change we could apply for incrementing the t-conorm of 0.15.

$$\perp(\mathbf{t}+\delta(\mathbf{t})) = t_j + \delta(\mathbf{t})_j \tag{12}$$

and, if $i = \operatorname{argmax}_{k=1}^{n} t_k$, we have that

$$\perp(\mathbf{t}+\delta^f(\mathbf{t})) = t_i + f(\mathbf{t}) \tag{13}$$

Since $t_i \geq t_j$, we just need to demonstrate that $\delta(\mathbf{t})_j < f(\mathbf{t})$. Notice that:

$$\delta(\mathbf{t})_j = (|\delta(\mathbf{t})_j|^p)^{1/p} \leq \left(\sum_{k=1}^{n} |\delta(\mathbf{t})_k|^p\right)^{1/p} = \|\delta(\mathbf{t})\|_p < \|\delta^f(\mathbf{t})\|_p \tag{14}$$

Since $\delta^f(\mathbf{t})$ changes only the value of the ith component of $\mathbf{t}$, $\|\delta^f(\mathbf{t})\|_p = f(\mathbf{t})$. □

5. Boosting Preactivations

In previous sections, we proved that, with an appropriate choice of function f, δ^f is a TBF. However, we still need to choose a function f suitable for our purposes. Notice that we have to respect the constraint that the final predictions remain in $[0,1]$. Indeed, Theorem 1 states that $0 \leq f(\mathbf{t}) \leq 1 - \max_{j=1}^{n} t_j$. This limits the possible functions f that can be used. For instance, f cannot be a linear function. In this section, we will extend the results obtained so far, showing that such a constraint does not have to be respected when applying δ^f directly on the preactivations of the NN's last layer.

More in details, the outputs $\mathbf{y}$ of the base NN are calculated by applying an activation function over the preactivations $\mathbf{z}$ generated in the last layer. We assume the activation function to be the logistic function, i.e.:

$$y_i = \sigma(z_i) = \frac{1}{1+e^{-z_i}} \tag{15}$$

where y_i is the activation of the ith predicate and z_i the corresponding preactivation. As with the activations, we distinguish between preactivations of the grounded atoms and the ones of the literals of a grounded clause by using $\mathbf{z}$ and $\mathbf{v}$ respectively. More precisely:

$$\mathbf{v} = \sigma^{-1}(\mathbf{t}) \tag{16}$$

In section 4.1 we showed that if we increase only the value of the highest literal (highest activation), such a change is minimal for Gödel t-conorm. We can apply the same strategy to preactivations and still have a minimal change that increases the t-conorm. In other words, we can increase v_i instead of t_i, when $i = \mathrm{argmax}_{j=1}^{n} v_j$ and the previously proven properties still hold.

The initial predictions are $\mathbf{t} = \sigma(\mathbf{v})$ and the final ones are $\mathbf{t}' = \sigma(\mathbf{v} + \delta^f(\mathbf{v}))$.

Proposition 2. *For any function $f : \mathbb{R}^n \to \mathbb{R}^+$, the function*

$$\delta^g(\mathbf{t}) = \sigma(\mathbf{v} + \delta^f(\mathbf{v})) - \sigma(\mathbf{v}) \tag{17}$$

is a minimal TBF for Gödel t-conorm and l_p-norm.

Proof. Notice that final predictions $\mathbf{t}' = \sigma(\mathbf{v} + \delta^f(\mathbf{v}))$ are in $[0,1]$ since this range is the image of logistic function. Furthermore, σ is monotonic increasing, which means that the highest preactivation corresponds to the highest activation:

$$\underset{j=1}{\overset{n}{\mathrm{argmax}}}\, \sigma(v_j) = \underset{j=1}{\overset{n}{\mathrm{argmax}}}\, v_j \tag{18}$$

Another implication of the monotonicity of σ is that increasing a preactivation produces also an increase of the corresponding activation:

$$f(\mathbf{v}) \geq 0 \to \sigma(v_i + f(\mathbf{v})) \geq \sigma(v_i) \tag{19}$$

Putting the previous two together we obtain that increasing the highest preactivation does indeed imply an increase of the highest activation, meaning that δ^g is a minimal TBF.

More formally, lets define function $g(\mathbf{t}) = \sigma(v_i + f(\mathbf{v})) - \sigma(v_i)$. We obtain:

$$\begin{aligned} \delta^g(\mathbf{t})_i &= \sigma(\mathbf{v} + \delta^f(\mathbf{v}))_i - \sigma(\mathbf{v})_i \\ &= \begin{cases} g(\mathbf{t}) & \text{if } i = \mathrm{argmax}_{j=1}^{n} t_j \\ 0 & \text{otherwise} \end{cases} \end{aligned} \tag{20}$$

Theorem 1 guarantees that δ^g is a minimal TBF for Gödel t-conorm and l_p-norm □

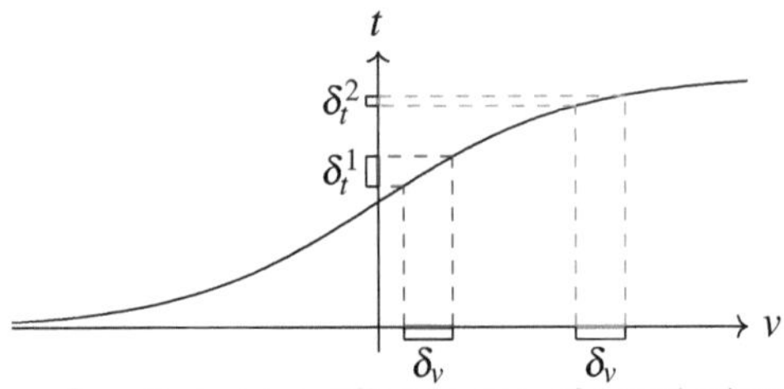

Figure 4. The same change δ_v applied on two different values of preactivations results in different changes on activations: the more close the preactivation to zero (maximum uncertainty) the highest the modification on final predictions

The function δ^g is not directly used by KENN; it is implicitly induced by the application of δ^f on $\mathbf{v}$. Therefore, by showing that it is a minimal TBF, we prove that applying δ^f on $\mathbf{v}$ is indeed equivalent to apply a minimal TBF on the NN predictions.

Until now we have seen that we can modify the preactivations $\mathbf{v}$ instead of changing directly the final truth values ($\mathbf{t}$), but we haven't justified why it is better to do this. The first reason is that applying changes on $\mathbf{v}$ has the advantage of guaranteeing the final predictions to be in $[0,1]$ which means that we don't have any constraint on the choice of function f. Moreover, we could interpret the results of the Neural Network as levels of confidence in its predictions. According to this view, an initial value close to one (or zero) of the activation means high confidence in the prediction and we would like f to apply a small change in such cases. On the other hand, if the initial prediction is close to 0.5 (preactivation close to 0) then we have the maximum uncertainty. Figure 4 shows how the same change on two different preactivation values results in different changes on the activations: the closer the initial value is to zero (maximum uncertainty), the higher the change on final truth values.

Summarizing, to increase c satisfaction we increase the preactivation of its highest literal. The extent of the change depends on the function f. KENN uses a distinct f_c function for every clause c. This is motivated by the fact that we want δ^{f_c} to be proportional to *clause weight* w_c (learnable parameter) which expresses the strength of the clause. The simplest function that conforms to this property is the constant function w_c (with $w_c \in [0,\infty]$). The function applied to $\mathbf{v}$ to increase c satisfaction is therefore δ^{w_c} defined as in 10:

$$\delta^{w_c}(\mathbf{v})_i = \begin{cases} w_c & \text{if } i = \text{argmax}_{j=1}^{n} v_j \\ 0 & \text{otherwise} \end{cases} \tag{21}$$

Notice that, although δ^{w_c} respects our minimality property, there are two problems when using it inside a neural network: first, it is not differentiable; second, it is too strict when multiple literals have close values. In those cases, it increases just one of the values even if the difference is minimal. To obviate these problems, in our implementation we substitute δ^{w_c} with the softmax function multiplied by w_c, that can be seen as a soft differentiable approximation of δ^{w_c}:

$$\delta_s^{w_c}(\mathbf{v})_i = w_c \cdot \delta_s(\mathbf{v}) = w_c \cdot \text{softmax}(\mathbf{v})_i = w_c \cdot \frac{e^{v_i}}{\sum_{j=1}^{n} e^{v_j}} \tag{22}$$

where δ_s is the approximation of δ^{w_c} for the unitary weight $w_c = 1$.

6. Handling Negations

Until now we assumed the literals truth values to be provided inside vector **t**, and their preactivations on vector **v**. However, note that the base NN returns truth values only for atomic formulas (positive), which means that we need to define the preactivations of a negated atom.

As seen in Section 3.2, the negation is interpreted as:

$$\mathscr{I}_N(\neg A) = 1 - \mathscr{I}_N(A) \tag{23}$$

Logistic function has the following property:

$$1 - \sigma(x) = \sigma(-x) \tag{24}$$

and given that we work with preactivations:

$$\mathscr{I}_N(\neg A) = 1 - \mathscr{I}_N(A) = 1 - \sigma(z_A) = \sigma(-z_A) \tag{25}$$

where z_A is the preactivation of grounded atom A.

Therefore, the preactivation of a negated atom is equal to the one of the not negated atom multiplied by -1:

$$z_{\neg A} = -z_A \tag{26}$$

7. Increasing the Satisfaction of the Entire Knowledge

Until now we considered only the changes to be applied to increase a single clause, while in the general case $\mathscr{K}$ will be composed of multiple clauses. We need a way to aggregate the multiple changes proposed by each clause to obtain the final changes to be applied on all the predictions based on the entire knowledge.

Given a grounded clause $c = \bigvee_{i=1}^{m} l_i$ we define $\mathbf{z}_c$ as the vector containing preactivations of its literals:

$$\mathbf{z}_c = \langle z_{l_1}, z_{l_2}, \ldots z_{l_m} \rangle \tag{27}$$

From $\mathbf{z}_c$, we define $\delta_{c[a],P(a)}$ as the change applied to $P(a)$ based on the grounded clause $c[a]$:

$$\delta_{c[a],P(a)} = \begin{cases} \delta_s(\mathbf{z}_c)_{P(a)} & \text{if } P(a) \in c[a] \\ -\delta_s(\mathbf{z}_c)_{\neg P(a)} & \text{if } \neg P(a) \in c[a] \end{cases} \tag{28}$$

where δ_s is the approximated TBF with weight 1 of Equation 22. Finally, the $\boldsymbol{\delta}_c$ matrices are combined linearly inside the KE to obtain the final change $\boldsymbol{\delta}$ to be applied on the NN's predictions, and the $\boldsymbol{\delta}$ is summed to the initial pre-activations $\mathbf{z}$ and passed to the activation function:

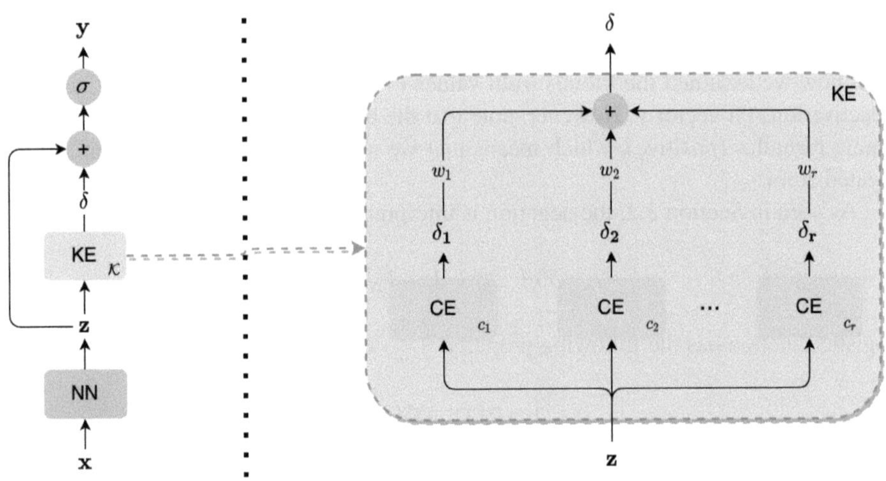

Figure 5. Model architecture. Left: KENN model overview. Right: Knowledge Enhancer.

$$y_{P(a)} = \sigma\Big(z_{P(a)} + \sum_{\substack{c \in \mathcal{K} \\ P(x) \in c}} w_c \cdot \delta_{c[a],P(a)}\Big) \tag{29}$$

where w_c is the *clause weight*, $P(a)$ a grounded atom, $y_{P(a)}$ its final prediction, and $z_{P(a)}$ its pre-activations.

8. KENN Architecture

Figure 5(left) shows a high-level overview of KENN architecture, where a residual layer, called *Knowledge Enhancer* (KE), is inserted between the NN and the final activation function. The role of KE is to revise the final predictions returned by the NN in order to increase the truth value of each clause $c \in \mathcal{K}$.

Since both NN and KE are differentiable, the entire architecture is differentiable end-to-end, making it possible to apply back-propagation algorithm on the whole model. Figure 5(right) shows the architecture of KE, which computes the summation of Equation 29.

More in details, for each clause $c \in \mathcal{K}$, the KE contains a submodule, the *Clause Enhancer* (CE), which proposes the changes $\boldsymbol{\delta}_c = \delta_s(\mathbf{z}_c)$ to be applied on the NN's preactivations in order to increase the satisfaction of c.

Note that the KE applies a linear combination of the $\boldsymbol{\delta}_c$ matrices, which can be done under the assumption of independence between the clauses. When multiple clauses share common predicates, the assumption is violated. As a consequence, in such scenarios, the changes proposed by KENN could only partially improve the satisfaction of the knowledge. We will further analyze this problem in Section 10. Finally, note that, when the NN predictions satisfy the constraints, the effect of the KE is to increase the confidence of the current predictions. Therefore, if the NN predictions are correct with respect to the ground truth, the clause weights tend to increase during learning.

8.1. Extending KENN for Relational Domains

In the architecture defined so far, the groundings involve a single object and $\mathbf{z}$ is defined as a matrix, where columns represent predicates and rows constants. Figure 6(left) introduces the representation of $\mathbf{z}$: it is defined as a matrix such that the element z_{ij} contains the pre-activation of $P_j(a_i)$, with P_j the jth predicate and a_i the ith constant.

Note that this kind of representation is common when working with neural networks since the columns (predicates) correspond to the labels and the rows (groundings) to the samples. An important aspect of this representation lies in the fact that each grounded atom can be found in the matrix exactly one time. This allows to parallelize computations of Equation 29 since a grounded clause involves only atoms in the same row, and each row can be managed in parallel inside a GPU. This can be done only if the same atom does not appear in multiple rows, since the changes are applied independently to each row and are not aggregated together. This property always holds with unary clauses.

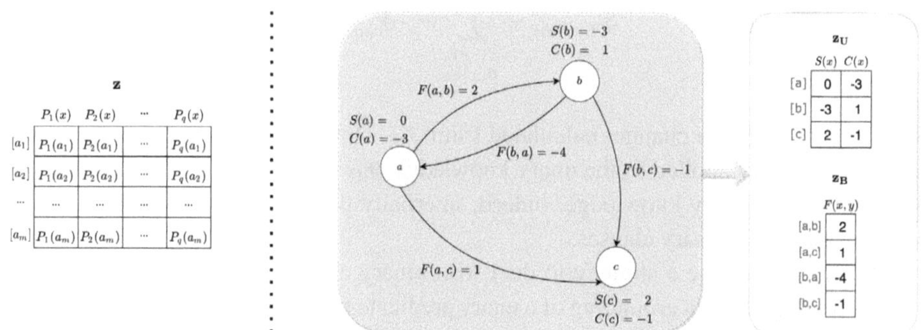

Figure 6. The representation of NN's final pre-activations. Left: unary case. Right: representation of relational data. Pre-activations are represented as integers instead of reals to simplify the figure.

To represent relational data, KENN has been extended with an extra matrix $\mathbf{z}_B$, which contains the binary predicates' pre-activations. For uniformity of notation we use $\mathbf{z}_U$ to denote the unary matrix $\mathbf{z}$ of the not relational KENN. Matrix $\mathbf{z}_B$ contains one row for every pair of objects we are interested in and a column for each binary predicate. Figure 6(right) shows this representation using the classical Smoker-Friends-Cancer example, where the domain is composed of three constants (persons) $\mathscr{C} = \{a,b,c\}$, the unary predicates are S and C (for *Smoker* and *Cancer*), and a binary predicate F (for *Friends*). The blue box shows the graph representation with nodes and edges labelled with pre-activation of unary and binary predicates respectively. The grey box shows the corresponding matrix representation used by KENN.

The architecture of KENN for relational domains is very similar to the architecture of traditional KENN of Figure 5, with KE substituted by a *Relational KE* (RKE). From a high level perspective, the RKE differs from the traditional KE on the amount of inputs and outputs. As seen before, in the relational case the pre-activations are divided in two different matrices ($\mathbf{z}_U$ and $\mathbf{z}_B$) and, as a consequence, also the $\boldsymbol{\delta}$ matrix and predictions $\mathbf{y}$ are now splitted in unary and binary matrices ($\boldsymbol{\delta}_U$ and $\boldsymbol{\delta}_B$ for the residues, $\mathbf{y}_U$ and $\mathbf{y}_B$ for the final predictions).

The RKE has the same role as the KE in the unary case. However, it is capable to consider also binary predicates. When binary knowledge is available, additional steps are required since the independence between object can not be assumed anymore.

Let $\mathscr{K}_U$ be the set of unary clauses and $\mathscr{K}_B$ the set of binary clauses. The prior knowledge is now defined as $\mathscr{K} = \mathscr{K}_U \cup \mathscr{K}_B$. The idea is to apply the KE to these two sets separately. Equation 29 can be decomposed using the new defined partition of the knowledge:

$$y_A = \sigma\left(z_A + \sum_{c \in \mathscr{K}_U[\mathscr{C}]} w_c \cdot \delta_{c,A} + \sum_{c \in \mathscr{K}_B[\mathscr{C}]} w_c \cdot \delta_{c,A} \right) \tag{30}$$

where A is a grounded atom (i.e. $P(a)$ or $P(a,b)$, depending on the arity of P). We define $\boldsymbol{\delta}_{\mathscr{K}_U}$ as the changes deriving from unary clauses:

$$\delta_{\mathscr{K}_U,P(a)} = \sum_{\substack{c \in \mathscr{K}_U \\ P(x) \in c}} w_c \cdot \delta_{c[a],P(a)} \tag{31}$$

Similarly, $\boldsymbol{\delta}_{\mathscr{K}_B}$ are the changes calculated from $\mathscr{K}_B$. Notice that the approach defined so far can be directly applied to the unary knowledge $\mathscr{K}_U$ to calculate $\boldsymbol{\delta}_U$ since traditional KE can manage unary knowledge. Indeed, internally the RKE contains a standard KE which manages the unary clauses.

We need to define a strategy to deal with binary clauses. Indeed, when a clause c contain two variables, a grounding of a unary predicate may occur in multiple groundings of c. For instance, consider the clause $\neg Smoker(x) \vee \neg Friends(x,y) \vee Smoker(y)$. The two groundings $c_{SF}[a,b]$ and $c_{SF}[b,c]$ share a common grounded atom: $Smoker(b)$. For this reason, when dealing with the predictions of a unary predicate in a relational domain, we need to account for such repetitions:

$$\delta_{\mathscr{K}_B,P(a)} = \sum_{b \neq a} \Big(\sum_{\substack{c \in \mathscr{K}_B \\ P(x) \in c}} w_c \cdot \delta_{c[a,b],P(a)} + \sum_{\substack{c \in \mathscr{K}_B \\ P(y) \in c}} w_c \cdot \delta_{c[b,a],P(a)} \Big) \tag{32}$$

Putting all together, the predictions $y_{P(a)}$ for a grounded unary predicate P are:

$$y_{P(a)} = \sigma(z_{P(a)} + \delta_{\mathscr{K}_U,P(a)} + \delta_{\mathscr{K}_B,P(a)}) \tag{33}$$

The predictions for a binary predicate R can be found only in binary clauses and any possible grounding of R can be found in only one corresponding grounding of each clause $y_{R(a,b)} = \sigma(z_{R(a,b)} + \delta_{\mathscr{K}_B,R(a,b)})$, with

$$\delta_{\mathscr{K}_B,R(a,b)} = \sum_{\substack{c \in \mathscr{K}_B \\ R(x,y) \in c}} w_c \cdot \delta_{c[a,b],R(a,b)} \tag{34}$$

Figure 7 shows the entire architecture of KENN for relational data.

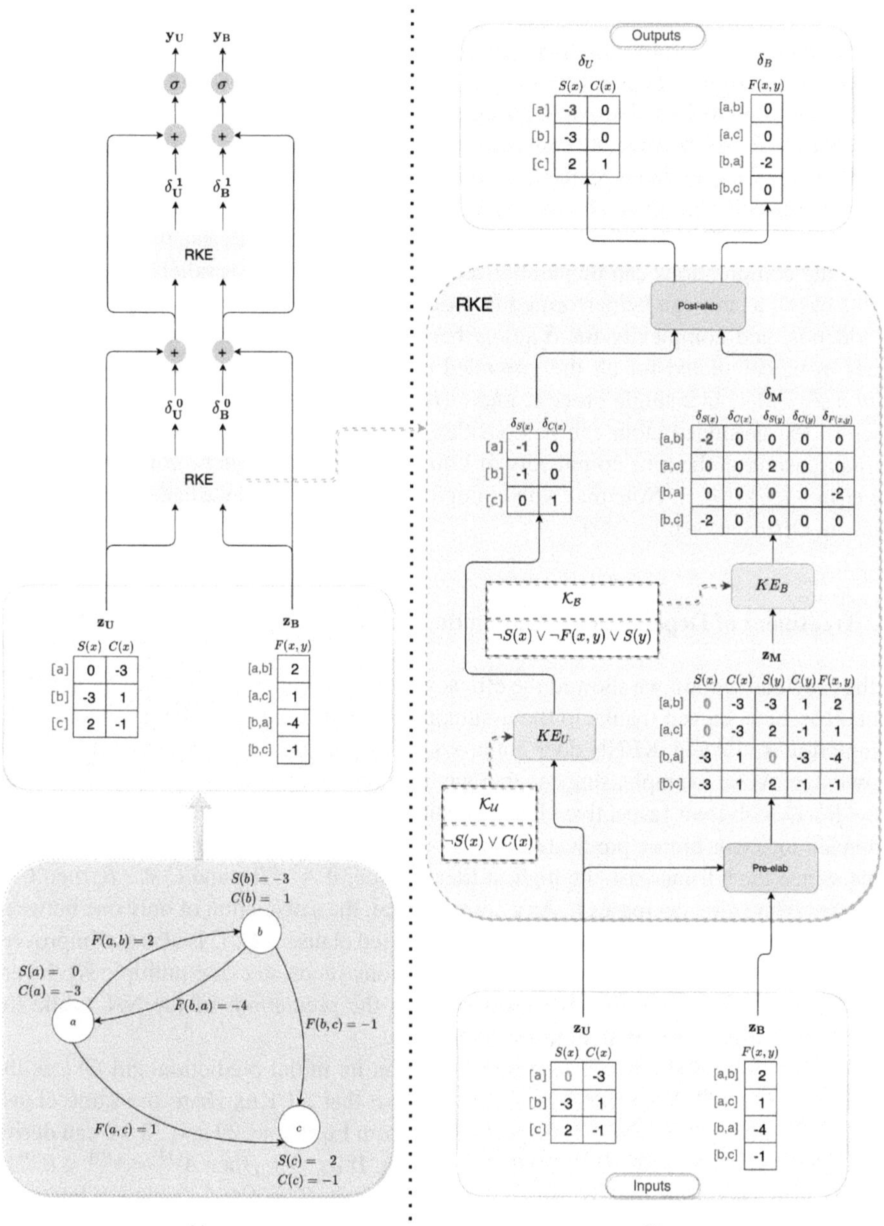

Figure 7. KENN for relational domains: (a) the architecture of KENN. A graph (blue box) is represented in terms of the two matrices $\mathbf{z}_U$ and $\mathbf{z}_B$ and given as input to the Relational KE (RKE). Multiple RKEs are stacked together and the activation function is called; (b) the architecture of the RKE module: the unary knowledge is enforced directly by the KE_U; the binary knowledge is enforced by the KE_B on matrix $\mathbf{z}_M$, which is created by joining $\mathbf{z}_U$ with $\mathbf{z}_B$ on the pre-elab step. $\mathbf{z}_M$ contains multiple instances of the same atoms, for instance $S[a]$ (red cells). As a consequence, multiple residues are returned for a single atom, and such values are summed in the post-elab (blue cells).

9. Time Complexity

Here we analyze the time complexity of an RKE layer with respect to domain size m, number of predicates $|\mathscr{P}|$, and number of rules $|\mathscr{K}|$. We also assume the maximum number L of literals in a clause to be a small constant.

Let us first analyze the time complexity for calculating the $\delta_{c[a]}$ used in Equations 31, and 32. Each $\delta_{c[a],P(a)}$ can be calculated in time $O(1)$ (see Equation 28). Computing $\delta_{c[a]}$ also requires constant time. The sum of Equation 31 require time $O(|\mathscr{K}|)$, which is the time necessary to compute $\delta_{\mathscr{K}_U,P(a)}$. Note that neural networks are usually run on GPUs, where the computations can be parallelized. Assuming enough parallel processes ($|\mathscr{K}|$ in this case), a sum can be performed in a time logarithmic with respect to the number of addends, and complexity for $\delta_{\mathscr{K}_U,P(a)}$ becomes $O(log(|\mathscr{K}|))$. Finally, Equation 31 needs to be calculated for all the grounded unary predicates $P(a)$, for a total time of $O(m \cdot |\mathscr{P}| \cdot |\mathscr{K}|)$ in a single process, and $O(log(|\mathscr{K}|))$ with multiple parallel processes (each of the grounded atom can be considered independently from the others). With a similar reasoning, the time complexity of Equations 32 and 34 can be computed, obtaining $O(m^2 \cdot |\mathscr{P}| \cdot |\mathscr{K}|)$. Note that with enough parallel processes we can compute all the deltas in $O(log(m) + log(|\mathscr{K}|))$.

10. Treatment of Dependencies Among the Rules

In the previous section we showed the efficacy of the method in terms of execution time, which can be achieved thanks to the assumption of independence. However, when this assumption is violated, KENN does not provide any guarantees on the satisfaction of the knowledge. As an example, suppose that we have two grounded clauses $c_1 : \neg A \vee B$ and $c_2 : \neg B \vee C$ with their respective clause enhancers CE_1 and CE_2, where A, B and C are grounded unary or binary predicates. The atom B appears in both clauses with opposite signs. Since the CE increase the highest literal value, if $A < B$ [2] and $C < \neg B$, then CE_1 increases B and CE_2 decreases it. As a consequence, the satisfaction of only one between c_1 and c_2 is increased. The satisfaction of the entailed clause $\neg A \vee C$ is also not improved.

A solution has been proposed in [5], which consists on stacking multiple KE layers on top of each other: the first KE layer corrects the predictions of the NN, while the second one corrects the predictions of the first, etc.

For any grounded atom G, lets define $G^{(0)}$ as its initial prediction and $G^{(i)}$ as the prediction of the ith KE layer. Moreover, suppose that all KEs share the same clause weights w_1 and w_2 (for c_1 and c_2 respectively). From Equations 29 and 28 we can derive $B^{(1)} = B^{(0)} + w_1 - w_2$, and $\neg B^{(1)} = \neg B^{(0)} + w_2 - w_1$. If $w_1 \geq w_2$, then $A^{(1)} = A^{(0)} < B^{(0)} \leq B^{(1)}$. As a consequence, the first rule will increase again B even at the next KE layer. On the other hand, the value of $\neg B$ is reduced, which means that there is an increased chance for $C^{(1)} > \neg B^{(1)}$, which would solve the problem since CE_2 would increase C instead of $\neg B$. Notice that, since the weights are the same at each level, it is always true that $\neg B^{(i+1)} \leq \neg B^{(i)}$, meaning that with enough KE layers both clauses' satisfaction will be increased (and as a consequence, also their entailments).

The problem analyzed in this section becomes even more relevant in relational domains since in these contexts an atom can be shared not only by multiple clauses but

[2]With an abuse of notation, we use atoms symbols to refer also to their truth value

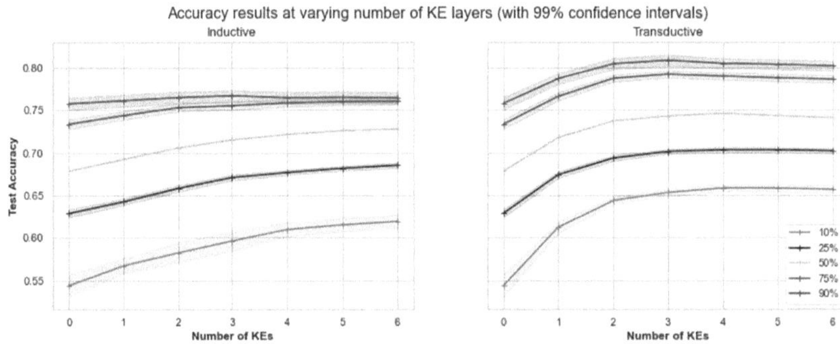

Figure 8. Accuracies of KENN on CiteSeer dataset at the varying number of KEs layers. Zero layers corresponds to the accuracies obtained by the base NN, with no knowledge. Each line is associated with a different percentage of training samples and it is surrounded by a 99% confidence interval.

also by different groundings of the same clause (for instance, in $c_{SF}[a,b]$ and $c_{SF}[b,c]$). For this reason, in these contexts stacking multiple RKEs is recommended. An empirical demonstration of the advantage of this strategy as been introduced in [5] and summarized in Figure 8, where the accuracy on the Citeseer dataset [29] is shown at varying number of KEs layers. Indeed, the performances increase after each KE layer is added, in particular in contexts where the training data is scarse. Moreover, the Figure provide also a measure of the amount of information carried out by the knowledge. For instance, consider blue and yellow lines, corresponding to a training set with 25% and 50% of the samples, respectively. In the inductive scenario, the accuracy obtained with 25% with the addition of the knowledge is almost the same as the standard NN with 50% of the data (even higher in the transductive scenario). In this case, adding the knowledge has the same effect of doubling up the training data! Indeed, one of the main motivations behind Neural-Symbolic Integration consists in reducing the required amount of training samples since collecting labeled data is costly in practice.

11. Conclusions

KENN is a method for injecting Prior Knowledge expressed as logical clauses into a neural network model, merging in this way the learning capabilities of Neural Networks with the expressivity of First Order Logic. KENN can be used in combination with many different types of neural networks and differs from other methods on the way logic is injected, that is by adding a new differentiable layer (the Knowledge Enhancer) at the top of a NN which provides predictions for the atomic formulas of the logic clauses.

KENN relies on the concept of minimal t-conorm boost function (minimal TBF), which is a function that modifies minimally the truth values of the literals of a clause to increase its satisfaction in terms of a fuzzy logic t-conorm.

In addition, the KE contains clause weights, which are learnable parameters that represent the strength of the clauses. The ability to learn clause weights makes KENN suitable for tasks where the provided knowledge is not totally reliable or when some of the clauses are not hard constraints and it is not known a priori the strength of the constraints encoded in the clauses. This has proven to be a major advantage in the experiments with

VRD Dataset [30], where the results obtained by KENN outperform SOTA methods [4]. Indeed, in those experiments, multiple clause weights have been set to zero by the learning process, meaning that KENN learned to ignore the corresponding clauses [4].

References

[1] Alex Krizhevsky, Ilya Sutskever, and Geoffrey E. Hinton. Imagenet classification with deep convolutional neural networks. In *Proceedings of the 25th International Conference on Neural Information Processing Systems - Volume 1*, NIPS'12, pages 1097–1105, USA, 2012. Curran Associates Inc.

[2] Dzmitry Bahdanau, Kyunghyun Cho, and Yoshua Bengio. Neural machine translation by jointly learning to align and translate. *arXiv preprint arXiv:1409.0473*, 2014.

[3] Geoffrey Hinton, Li Deng, Dong Yu, George Dahl, Abdel-rahman Mohamed, Navdeep Jaitly, Andrew Senior, Vincent Vanhoucke, Patrick Nguyen, Brian Kingsbury, et al. Deep neural networks for acoustic modeling in speech recognition. *IEEE Signal processing magazine*, 29, 2012.

[4] Alessandro Daniele and Luciano Serafini. Knowledge enhanced neural networks. In Abhaya C. Nayak and Alok Sharma, editors, *PRICAI 2019: Trends in Artificial Intelligence*, pages 542–554, Cham, 2019. Springer International Publishing.

[5] Alessandro Daniele and Luciano Serafini. Knowledge enhanced neural networks for relational domains. In *International Conference of the Italian Association for Artificial Intelligence*, pages 91–109. Springer, 2022.

[6] Eleonora Grilli, Alessandro Daniele, Maarten Bassier, Fabio Remondino, and Luciano Serafini. Knowledge enhanced neural networks for point cloud semantic segmentation. *Remote Sensing*, 15(10):2590, 2023.

[7] Daphne Koller, Nir Friedman, Sašo Džeroski, Charles Sutton, Andrew McCallum, Avi Pfeffer, Pieter Abbeel, Ming-Fai Wong, David Heckerman, Chris Meek, et al. *Introduction to statistical relational learning*. MIT press, 2007.

[8] Matthew Richardson and Pedro Domingos. Markov logic networks. *Mach. Learn.*, 62(1-2):107–136, February 2006.

[9] Stephen H. Bach, Matthias Broecheler, Bert Huang, and Lise Getoor. Hinge-loss Markov random fields and probabilistic soft logic. *Journal of Machine Learning Research*, 18(109):1–67, 2017.

[10] Luc De Raedt, Angelika Kimmig, and Hannu Toivonen. Problog: A probabilistic prolog and its application in link discovery. In *IJCAI*, volume 7, pages 2462–2467. Hyderabad, 2007.

[11] Tarek R. Besold, Artur S. d'Avila Garcez, Sebastian Bader, Howard Bowman, Pedro M. Domingos, Pascal Hitzler, Kai-Uwe Kühnberger, Luís C. Lamb, Daniel Lowd, Priscila Machado Vieira Lima, Leo de Penning, Gadi Pinkas, Hoifung Poon, and Gerson Zaverucha. Neural-symbolic learning and reasoning: A survey and interpretation. *CoRR*, abs/1711.03902, 2017.

[12] William W Cohen. Tensorlog: A differentiable deductive database. *arXiv preprint arXiv:1605.06523*, 2016.

[13] Tim Rocktäschel and Sebastian Riedel. Learning knowledge base inference with neural theorem provers. In *Proceedings of the 5th Workshop on Automated Knowledge Base Construction*, pages 45–50, 2016.

[14] Tim Rocktäschel and Sebastian Riedel. End-to-end differentiable proving. In *Advances in Neural Information Processing Systems*, pages 3788–3800, 2017.

[15] Robin Manhaeve, Sebastijan Dumancic, Angelika Kimmig, Thomas Demeester, and Luc De Raedt. Deepproblog: Neural probabilistic logic programming. In *Advances in Neural Information Processing Systems*, pages 3749–3759, 2018.

[16] Honghua Dong, Jiayuan Mao, Tian Lin, Chong Wang, Lihong Li, and Denny Zhou. Neural logic machines. *arXiv preprint arXiv:1904.11694*, 2019.

[17] Victor Guimarães and Vítor Santos Costa. Neurallog: a neural logic language. *CoRR*, abs/2105.01442, 2021.

[18] Richard Evans and Edward Grefenstette. Learning explanatory rules from noisy data. *Journal of Artificial Intelligence Research*, 61:1–64, 2018.

[19] Andres Campero, Aldo Pareja, Tim Klinger, Josh Tenenbaum, and Sebastian Riedel. Logical rule induction and theory learning using neural theorem proving. *arXiv preprint arXiv:1809.02193*, 2018.

[20] Jan Niclas Reimann and Andreas Schwung. Neural logic rule layers. *arXiv preprint arXiv:1907.00878*, 2019.

[21] Luciano Serafini and Artur S. d'Avila Garcez. Logic tensor networks: Deep learning and logical reasoning from data and knowledge. *CoRR*, abs/1606.04422, 2016.

[22] Michelangelo Diligenti, Marco Gori, and Claudio Saccà. Semantic-based regularization for learning and inference. *Artif. Intell.*, 244:143–165, 2017.

[23] Jingyi Xu, Zilu Zhang, Tal Friedman, Yitao Liang, and Guy Van den Broeck. A semantic loss function for deep learning with symbolic knowledge. In Jennifer Dy and Andreas Krause, editors, *Proceedings of the 35th International Conference on Machine Learning*, volume 80 of *Proceedings of Machine Learning Research*, pages 5502–5511, Stockholmsmässan, Stockholm Sweden, 10–15 Jul 2018. PMLR.

[24] Marc Fischer, Mislav Balunovic, Dana Drachsler-Cohen, Timon Gehr, Ce Zhang, and Martin Vechev. Dl2: Training and querying neural networks with logic. In *International Conference on Machine Learning*, pages 1931–1941, 2019.

[25] Pasquale Minervini and Sebastian Riedel. Adversarially regularising neural nli models to integrate logical background knowledge. *arXiv preprint arXiv:1808.08609*, 2018.

[26] Zhiting Hu, Xuezhe Ma, Zhengzhong Liu, Eduard H. Hovy, and Eric P. Xing. Harnessing deep neural networks with logic rules. In *Proceedings of the 54th Annual Meeting of the Association for Computational Linguistics, ACL 2016, August 7-12, 2016, Berlin, Germany, Volume 1: Long Papers*. The Association for Computer Linguistics, 2016.

[27] Tao Li and Vivek Srikumar. Augmenting neural networks with first-order logic. In *Proceedings of the 57th Annual Meeting of the Association for Computational Linguistics*, pages 292–302, Florence, Italy, July 2019. Association for Computational Linguistics.

[28] Giuseppe Marra, Michelangelo Diligenti, Francesco Giannini, Marco Gori, and Marco Maggini. Relational neural machines. *arXiv preprint arXiv:2002.02193*, 2020.

[29] Qing Lu and Lise Getoor. Link-based classification. In *Proceedings of the Twentieth International Conference on International Conference on Machine Learning*, ICML'03, page 496–503. AAAI Press, 2003.

[30] Cewu Lu, Ranjay Krishna, Michael S. Bernstein, and Fei-Fei Li. Visual relationship detection with language priors. In *ECCV (1)*, volume 9905 of *Lecture Notes in Computer Science*, pages 852–869. Springer, 2016.

Part V

Explainable and Interpretable AI

Handbook on Neurosymbolic AI and Knowledge Graphs
P. Hitzler et al. (Eds.)
IOS Press, 2025

doi:10.3233/FAIA250231

Empowering Mechanistic Interpretability of Deep Neural Networks with Knowledge Graphs

Yong GUAN [a,b], Freddy LÉCUÉ [c], Jiaoyan CHEN [d], Ru LI [b], and Jeff Z. PAN [e]
[a] *Department of Computer Science and Technology, Tsinghua University, China*
[b] *School of Computer & Information Technology, Shanxi University, China*
[c] *Inria, France*
[d] *Department of Computer Science, The University of Manchester, UK*
[e] *School of Informatics, The University of Edinburgh, UK*

Abstract. Although neural models have achieved remarkable performance, they still encounter doubts due to the intransparency. To this end, model prediction explanation is attracting more and more attentions. However, current methods rarely incorporate external knowledge and still suffer from three limitations: (1) **Neglecting concept completeness**. Merely selecting concepts may not sufficient for prediction. (2) **Lacking concept fusion**. Failure to merge semantically-equivalent concepts. (3) **Difficult in manipulating model behavior**. Lack of verification for explanation on original model. To address these issues, we propose a novel knowledge-aware neuron interpretation framework to explain model predictions for image scene classification. Specifically, for concept completeness, we present core concepts of a scene based on knowledge graph, ConceptNet, to gauge the completeness of concepts. Our method, incorporating complete concepts, effectively provides better prediction explanations compared to baselines. Furthermore, for concept fusion, we introduce a knowledge graph-based method known as Concept Filtering, which produces over 23% point gain on neuron behaviors for neuron interpretation. At last, we propose Model Manipulation, which aims to study whether the core concepts based on ConceptNet could be employed to manipulate model behavior. The results show that core concepts can effectively improve the performance of original model by over 26%.

Keywords. Neurosymbolic AI, Knowledge Graphs

1. Introduction

Deep neural network (DNN) architectures are designed to be increasingly sophisticated, with scaled up the model size, and have been achieving unprecedented advancements in various areas of artificial intelligence [1,2]. Despite their strengths, DNNs are not fully transparent and often perceived as "black-box" algorithms, which can impair users' trust and hence diminish usability of such systems [3]. As shown in Figure 1(a), the model predicts the image as `utility room`, which is different from the ground truth (target label) `bedroom`. However, it is unclear why the model predicts this label, making it hard to understand, debug and improve.

There has been a growing interest in exploring explanations of model predictions [4,5], which, generally speaking, could be categorized into two methods: functional analysis and decision analysis [6]. Functional analysis methods try to capture overall behavior by investigating the relations between the decision and the image, using saliency map [7], occlusion techniques [8], and rationale [9]. Such methods typically lack in-depth understanding of internal modules of the model, often failing to provide comprehensive insights into the decision-making process. The decision analysis methods explore explanation by analyzing the internal components' behavior, such as decomposing the network classification decision into contributions of input elements [10,11]. Furthermore, studying neuron-level explanation enables more accurate orientation and editing of the decision-making process [12]. However, they do not offer the most intuitive explanations that are easily understandable to humans, and the link between the decision and internal components is not obvious.

Some studies attempt to utilize concepts to enhance the interpretation of model decisions, establishing relations between the decision and the input image through a selected number of concepts, such as ACE [13], ConceptSHAP [14], and VRX [15]. Although the decision is explained by presenting a set of concepts found within image, these methods still exhibit certain three key limitations. (1) **Neglecting concept completeness**. These methods select a set of concepts salient to the corresponding scene, but they do not guarantee that these concepts are sufficient to explain the prediction. As shown in Figure 1(a), the model selects a set of salient concepts, including *armchair*, *floor*, *wall*, and more. However, their prediction mislabels scene as `utility room` instead of `bedroom`, due to an incomplete concept set [16] that overlooks the *bed* concept. (2) **Lacking concept fusion**. These methods merely group segments based on resemblance, but they do not merge semantically-equivalent concepts. As depicted in Figure 1(b), concepts *armchair* and *chair* can be fused [17], as they convey identical meanings. (3) **Hard to manipulate model behavior**. These methods mainly focus on explanation, but they do not provide guidance on how to rectify mistakes made by the original model.

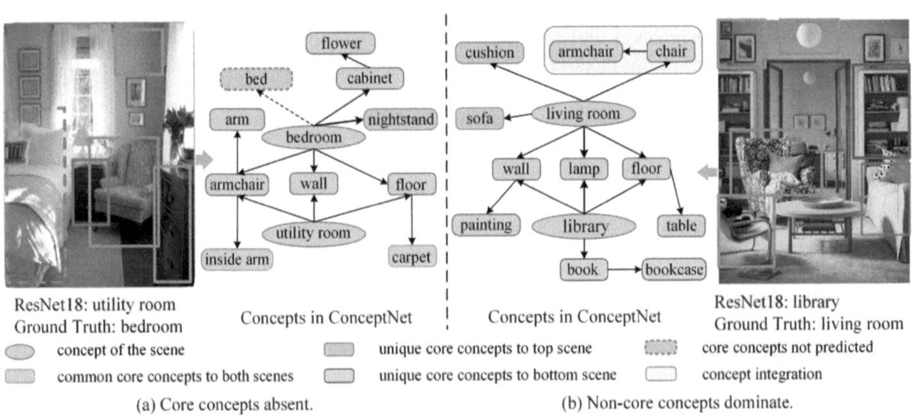

Figure 1. Example of false prediction explanations[1]. Concepts that are essential to the meaning of a scene are called core concepts, such as *bed* in scene `bedroom`. Concepts that are not necessary for understanding the scene and can be omitted or ignored are called non-core concepts, such as *book* and *bookcase* in `living room`.

To address the above problems, we propose a novel knowledge-aware neuron interpretation framework for scene classification. As well-defined knowledge will help to further enhance the model explanation and facilitate human understanding. Specifically, for **concept completeness**, we present core concepts (CC) of a scene to gauge the completeness of concepts. CC refers to the fundamental elements that collectively constitute the scene [18]; e.g., *bed*, *cabinet*, *armchair*, *floor*, *wall*, *nightstand* and *lamp* are the CC of scene `bedroom`. To formulate the CC, we leverage knowledge graphs (KG) [19,20], such as ConceptNet. Additionally, we introduce the MinMax-based NetDissect method to establish links between neuron behavior and concepts at the neuron level. As for **concept fusion**, we introduce a Concept Filtering method, which effectively merge semantically-equivalent concepts based on ConceptNet in order to enhance the existing neuron interpretation. Furthermore, for **manipulate model behavior**, we propose Model Manipulation, which aims to study whether the CC obtained from ConceptNet could be employed to manipulate model behavior, such as identifying the positive/negative neurons in model, integrating CC into original model design phase. At last, our method, integrating CC, will help to answer a variety of interpretability questions across different datasets, such as ADE20k and Opensurfaces, and multiple models, such as ResNet, DenseNet, AlexNet and MobileNet.

- Do complete concepts base on core concepts provide benefit to model prediction explanation? We propose core concepts of scene derived from ConceptNet, along with three evaluation metrics, to establish the link between decisions and concepts in image. The experimental results show that our method, integrating complete concepts, achieves better results than the existing methods.
- Furthermore, do external knowledge through concept fusion improve existing neuron interpretation? We propose *Concept Filtering* method, which produces over 23% point gain on neuron behaviors for neuron interpretation.
- In addition, do explanations based on core concepts contribute to model performance? We propose both unsupervised and supervised methods based on core concepts extracted from ConceptNet to manipulate model behavior. The overall results prove that core concepts and related explanation metrics can help optimise the original model, leading to 26.7% of performance improvement[2].

2. Preliminaries

2.1. Neuron Interpretation

Neuron interpretation aims to improve the interpretability of models by understanding the neuron behavior. Observations of neurons (a.k.a hidden units) in neural networks have revealed that human-interpretable concepts sometimes emerge as individual latent variables. Thus, a pioneer work on interpreting neurons [21] designed a network dis-

[1](a) The model does not predict the CC *bed* of `bedroom`, and thus mistakenly predicts the scene to be `utility room`. (b) The model mainly focuses on non-core concepts, including *book* and *bookcase*, which are CC of scene `library`.

[2]Code and data are available at: https://github.com/neuroninter
pretation/EIIC

(a) Input Image x. (b) Activation $F_{483}(x)$.

(c) Activation over T_{483} (d) Concept water.

Figure 2. Unit 483 of layer 4 in ResNet-18, as a `water` detector (d) with a IoU score of .14 for pixelwise annotated input images x in (a) wrt. the upscaled unit activation map (b), determined by areas of significative activation (c).

section (*NetDissect*) tool to quantify the interpretability of a model and particularly its neurons.

Given a neural network f trained and used for prediction, f maps an image x_i to a latent representation that is also known as neuron features or units (e.g., unit 483 of ResNet-18 layer 4 in Figure 2), denoted as $\{f_1, f_2, ..., f_n\}$, where n denotes the dimension and f_t $(1 \leq t \leq n)$ is known as t-th neuron features. Given C the set of concepts of a given dataset, $L: (x_i, c) \mapsto \{0,1\}$ is a concept function which indicates whether an image (region) x_i is an instance of a concept $c \in C$; e.g., $L(x_i, water) = 1$ means x_i is an image (region) containing water. *NetDissect* computes the most relevant concepts from C to the neuron feature f_t over the set of images x:

$$NWD(f_t, x, C) = argmax\{\sigma(A_t(x_i), L(x_i, c))\} \tag{1}$$

where σ is a measure function, such as intersection over union (IoU) and Jaccard index, while $A_t(x_i)$ is the activation of f_t for x_i, and can be scaled up to the mask resolution using bilinear interpolation. The unit f_t is regarded as a detector which selects the highest scoring concept. For example, unit 483 in Figure 2 is regarded as a `water` descriptor (d) for images (a) wrt. activation (b) using threshold (c).

2.2. Problem Statement

Let $\mathcal{D} = \{x_1, x_2, ..., x_{|\mathcal{D}|}\}$ be a set of images, C be the overall concept set, and $Y = \{y_1, y_2, ..., y_{|Y|}\}$ be a set of scenes. Each image $x_i \in \mathcal{D}$ belongs to a scene $y_j \in Y$ and contains multiple concepts representing the scene in x_i; e.g., the image of Figure 1(a) is labelled as scene `bedroom` and contains concepts such as *wall, lamp, armchair*. For each scene y_j, it has multiple images in $\mathcal{D}$, denoted as $\mathcal{D}_{y_j} \subseteq \mathcal{D}$. $C_{y_j} \subseteq C$ refers to the set of associated concepts of y_j. $LC(x_i)$ is the set of learning concepts of neuron features f_t by computing the correlation between f_t and the corresponding concept set. In the rest of paper, assumed that the KG contains all concepts in C.[3]

[3] In practice, if some concepts in C are not in the KG, we could align them to similar concepts in the KG.

For each image x_i, it has a label y_p predicted by f and a target (ground truth) label y_j. In this paper, we consider three tasks: *(T1)* model prediction explanation: explaining why f predicts x_i as y_p, and why the prediction is correct (i.e., $y_p = y_j$) or wrong (i.e., $y_p \neq y_j$); *(T2)* neuron interpretation: studying the effectiveness of external knowledge used in *T1* on existing neuron interpretation; *(T3)* model manipulation: exploiting CC used in *T1 and T2* to optimise model performance.

3. Approach

In this section, we present the knowledge-aware framework to address the three tasks mentioned above. Task *T1*, corresponding to the limitation of concept completeness, contains three sections: MinMax-based NetDissect, Core Concepts, and Model Prediction Explanations. Task *T2*, corresponding to the limitation of concept fusion, is detailed in Concept Filtering. Task *T3*, corresponding to the limitation of manipulate model behavior, is detailed in Model Manipulation.

3.1. MinMax-based NetDissect

MinMax-based NetDissect aims to learn which concepts are closest to the neuron. Following existing work [21,22], we use NetDissect to evaluate the alignment between each hidden unit and a set of concepts. Note that the original NetDissect method computes the general neuron behavior on the dataset level while ignoring features that are unique and useful for an individual image prediction. In contrast, we aim to learn the neuron behavior for individual scene, e.g., `bedroom`, to see whether concepts in scene can help explain model prediction. To achieve this, we propose a new variant MinMax-based NetDissect method to learn the neuron behavior for individual image. Formally, given f a neural network, f_t the t-th neuron in intermediate layer, C_{y_j} the associated concepts of y_j, x_i the target image, σ measure function, and A_t the activated neuron features of the t-th neuron, $L(x_i, c)$ the concept function where c is a concept in C_{y_j}, we have:

$$MM\text{-}NWD\ (f_t, x_i, C_{y_j}) = Ths\{\sigma(A_t(x_i), L(x_i, c))\} \tag{2}$$

We use IoU as the measure function σ. Thus, the concepts $LC(x_i)$ learned by a target neuron can be obtained from concept selection strategy[4] $Ths\{\cdot\}$. We consider three ways of selecting concepts that neuron learns.

(1) *Whole layer*: all concepts with IoU scores larger than 0 are regarded as valid concepts;

(2) *Highest IoU*: only select the concept with the highest IoU score, treating the neuron as a concept detector.

(3) *Threshold*: only utilize the concepts with IoU scores higher than a MinMax-based threshold that we compute as follows: (a) select the concept with the highest IoU for each neuron; (b) use the lowest IoU value among the IoU values of the selected concepts as the threshold.

[4] In NetDissect, they directly use the concept with highest score of neuron. However, neurons do not express a single concept, but make predictions from multiple concepts [23].

3.2. Core Concepts

Core concepts (CC) are the fundamental elements that are strong candidates for scene concepts introduced in [18]; e.g., *bed, cabinet, armchair, floor, wall, nightstand* and *lamp* are the CC of scene `bedroom`. A well-defined KG, such as ConceptNet, contains essential concepts in the scene and facilitates human understanding. Therefore, we leverage ConceptNet to help to define two types of CC to address the challenge of concept completeness, including scoping core concepts (SCC) and identifier core concepts (ICC). Informally speaking, the SCC for a scene involves concepts that are shared between the scene-related concepts within the dataset and the scene-related concepts within the KG. On the other hand, the ICC for a scene involves concepts that are uniquely suited to a particular scene, such as *bed, nightstand* for `bedroom`. Between SCC and ICC, SCC takes into account concept coverage for the scene, while ICC considers the concepts specific to the scene. Next, two types of CC are defined as follows.

Definition. (Scoping Core Concepts) *Given a scene $y_j \in Y$ ($j \in \{1,...,|Y|\}$), its associated concepts in whole dataset $\mathscr{D}$ are denoted as C_{y_j}, and $RC(y_j,\mathscr{G})$ is the concepts from KG $\mathscr{G}$ that are related to y_j. We define the* **scoping core concepts** *for scene y_j as follows: $SCC(y_j,\mathscr{G}) = RC(y_j,\mathscr{G}) \cap C_{y_j}$.*

Definition. (Identifier Core Concepts) *Given a scene $y_j \in Y$ ($j \in \{1,...,|Y|\}$), its associated images and concepts in whole dataset $\mathscr{D}$ are $\mathscr{D}_{y_j}$ and C_{y_j}, respectively.*

- *Concepts of a scene that obtained form dataset. $Count(y_j,p) \subseteq C_{y_j}$ is the set of overlapping ground truth concepts, from C_{y_j}, over at least $p\%$ of the images in $\mathscr{D}_{y_j}$,*
- *Specificity concepts for a scene obtained form dataset. P_c is the highest percentage such that, for any i, j, $i \neq j$, $Count(y_i,P_c) \neq Count(y_j,P_c)$.*
- *Concepts of a scene obtained form dataset and KG. $SCount(y_j,\mathscr{G},p)$ is the set of overlapping ground truth concepts, from $(RC(y_j,\mathscr{G}) \cap C_{y_j}) \cup TopkOfCount(y_j)$, over at least $p\%$ of the images in $\mathscr{D}_{y_j}$, where $TopkOfCount(y_j)$ is the set of the top k concepts of $Count(y_j, P_c)$ and $\mathscr{G}$ is Knowledge Graph,*
- *Specificity concepts of a scene obtained form dataset and KG. P_{sc} is the highest percentage such that, for any i, j, $i \neq j$, $SCount(y_i,\mathscr{G},P_{sc}) \neq SCount(y_j,\mathscr{G},P_{sc})$).*

We define the **identifier core concepts** *for scene y_j as follows:*

$$ICC(y_j,\mathscr{G}) = SCount(y_j,\mathscr{G},P_{sc}) \tag{3}$$

We consider the balance between concepts in the KG and annotated concepts of y_j, by including the top k (in our experiments, $k = 2$) most popular concepts, no matter whether they are in the KG or not. As ICC is more specific, it often has a smaller size than SCC.

3.3. Model Prediction Explanations

Model Prediction Explanations aims to utilize CC to establish the link between decisions and concepts in image. For this purpose, we propose the following metrics accordingly.

Prediction explanations (PE) are explanations provided together with predictions, with ground truth (target) scene unknown. Given an image x_i, concepts $LC(x_i)$ learned by neurons, scene y_j, and its core concepts $CC_l(y_j)$, where $CC_l \in \{SCC, ICC\}$. We propose the consistency metric (similarity metric, difference metric) for measuring the consistency (similarity, difference, resp.):

$$CM(x_i, y_j) = \frac{|LC(x_i) \cap CC_l(y_j)|}{|CC_l(y_j)|} \tag{4}$$

$$SM(x_i, y_j) = \frac{|LC(x_i) \cap CC_l(y_j)|}{|LC(x_i) \cup CC_l(y_j)|} \tag{5}$$

$$DM(x_i, y_j) = \frac{|LC(x_i) \setminus CC_l(y_j)|}{|CC_l(y_j)|} \tag{6}$$

Note y_j is the predicted scene. The larger (smaller) the *CM* and *SM* (*DM*) scores become, the smaller the gap between the learned concepts and scene.

Post-prediction explanations (PPE) are explanations when both predicted and target scene are known. Given an image x_i of scene y_t, and the scene y_p predicted by model, the first task here is to explain why the prediction is wrong, i.e., why $y_t \neq y_p$. One would expect that the LC should be closer to the predicted scene (i.e., $CM(x_i, y_p) > CM(x_i, y_t)$ and $SM(x_i, y_p) > SM(x_i, y_t)$) and be more different from the target scene (i.e., $DM(x_i, y_p) > DM(x_i, y_t)$). The consistency metric for set D_f of false predictions (as scene y_p) CM^{FP} can be defined as follows:

$$CM^{FP} = \frac{|\{x_i \in D_f | CM(x_i, y_p) > CM(x_i, y_t)\}|}{|D_f|} \tag{7}$$

The difference and similarity metrics, denoted as DM^{FP} and SM^{FP} can be defined respectively.

Given an image x_i of scene y_t, the second task here is to explain why the prediction is correct. We propose to compare the set of images with true prediction (D_t) against those with false prediction (D_f), with the expectation that the consistency metric over the correctly predicted images CM^{TP} of D_t should be larger than that over the falsely predicted images CM^{T_FP}: $CM^{TP} > CM^{T\_FP}$.[5] Thus, the consistency metric for the set D_t of correctly predicted images and that for the set D_f of falsely predicted images in scene y_t can be defined as follows :

$$CM^{TP} = \frac{\Sigma_{x_i \in D_t} CM(x_i, y_t)}{|D_t|} \tag{8}$$

$$CM^{T\_FP} = \frac{\Sigma_{x_i \in D_f} CM(x_i, y_t)}{|D_f|} \tag{9}$$

[5]The symbol T refers to calculating true prediction explanation.

Table 1. Results of false and true prediction explanation. Top_10 means the top 10 concepts of scene as CC.

LC	CC	False Prediction Explanation (%)			True Prediction Explanation (%)			
		CM^{FP}	DM^{FP}	SM^{FP}	CM^{TP}	CM^{T_FP}	SM^{TP}	SM^{T_FP}
ConceptSHAP	–	51.93	43.24	50.87	21.04	18.51	19.68	17.32
CLIP-Dissect	SCC	53.31	86.57	33.45	12.64	11.78	13.72	13.16
	ICC	46.94	67.06	38.94	33.31	32.44	21.76	21.17
Whole Layer	Top_10	43.04	19.13	42.77	11.29	6.12	4.38	2.49
	SCC	**78.51**	87.30	69.85	12.95	9.94	8.17	6.85
	ICC	51.43	69.32	29.58	**53.73**	**47.33**	22.76	22.13
Highest IoU	Top_10	34.61	19.12	34.56	9.20	5.18	7.51	4.03
	SCC	65.77	85.76	64.07	6.52	5.04	5.91	4.64
	ICC	49.42	67.76	42.24	26.32	21.86	21.27	18.11
Threshold	Top_10	42.52	18,69	42.42	11.17	6.07	7.48	4.12
	SCC	78.03	**87.38**	**72.13**	11.83	9.22	10.09	8.07
	ICC	50.32	69.81	34.11	49.60	44.13	**34.97**	**32.34**

Similarly, we can define similarity metric for D_t and D_f, denoted as SM^{TP} and SM^{T_FP}, respectively, with the expectation that $SM^{TP} > SM^{T\_FP}$.

3.4. Neuron Interpretation via Concept Filtering

This section aims to optimize neuron interpretation by merging semantically-equivalent concepts based on ConceptNet. In context of image classification and object detection, there could be a large number of concepts and many of which might have similar semantics, e.g. *armchair* and *chair*. This could lead to misleading or even wrong explanations for predictions. To address this challenge, given each set of scene associated concepts C_{y_j}, we compute the embeddings of the concepts in C_{y_j} and align them to concepts in a KG like ConceptNet, using classic KG embeddings techniques, such as TransE, Dismult and TransD, then group them w.r.t. their distances, into clusters $Cl_1(C_{y_j}),...,Cl_r(C_{y_j})$. One can transform C_{y_j} into $CF(C_{y_j})$ by selecting one representative concept in each cluster $Cl_i(C_{y_j})(1 \leq i \leq r)$ to represent all concepts in $Cl_i(C_{y_j})$. Our *hypothesis* is that replacing C_{y_j} with $CF(C_{y_j})$ could help optimise model prediction explanation and existing neuron interpretation.

3.5. Model Manipulation

Model Manipulation aims to study whether the CC could help to manipulate model behavior, including Neuron Identifying via CC and Re-training via CC. In addition, we propose using PE metrics for re-training.

Neuron Identification via CC aims to identify the positive and negative neurons by calculating contribution score to see the model behavior. The contribution score for the neurons f_t, over images x_i in y_j with true prediction, can be calculated as follows:

$$Con\_Score(f_t) = \sum_{x_i \in D^T_{y_j}} (P(x_i, CC_l) - N(x_i, CC_l)) \tag{10}$$

where $P(x_i, CC_l)$ and $N(x_i, CC_l)$ are the number of LC in and not in CC_l, respectively.

For true prediction, we disable top-k positive neurons (by setting the neuron features to 0 [23]) for the scene and see whether the model still correctly predicts the scene. For false prediction, we disable top-k (in our evaluation, $k = 20$) negative neurons for the scene and see whether the model can make better prediction.

Re-training via CC aims to integrate CC into original model design phase to further improve its performance. In the original models, the training objective is scene loss $\mathscr{L}_s$. We add another core concept loss:

$$\mathscr{L}_c = -\sum \log \mathscr{P}(c^*|\theta) \tag{11}$$

where $c^* \in C$ is the golden concept. For example, given scene `bedroom` with concepts *bed, armchair and fridge*, the new overall objective will let model pay more attention to the CC, such as *bed* and *armchair*.

Re-training via PE aims to utilize the explanation metrics as features to optimise the original model. We use a classical classifier SVM [24], but not an arbitrary neural network, as it will not introduce unexplained factors. For training the classifier, we utilize three types of features: (1) the features of metrics CM, SM and DM; (2) the MRR (mean reciprocal rank) feature which integrates the three metrics over all scenes; (3) the hidden states which learned by the original model.

4. Experiments

4.1. Datasets

For testing, we use two scene datasets ADE20k [25] and Opensurfaces [26]. ADE20k is a challenging scene parsing benchmark with pixel-level annotations, which contains 22,210 images. There are 1,105 unique concepts in ADE20k, categorized by scene, object, part, and color, and each image belongs to a scene. We utilize the version from existing work CEN [23]. Opensurfaces is a large database created from real-world consumer photographs with pixel-level annotations. It contains 25,329 images which are annotated with surface properties, including material, color and scene.

4.2. Do Completing Concepts Based on Core Concepts Provide Benefit to Model Prediction Explanation?

Yes. The overall results show that our method, integrating complete concepts, achieves better results than existing methods across false and true prediction. In details, we first report the results of false/true prediction explanation, and then enhance the model prediction explanation by integrating concept filtering. Furthermore, we conduct experiments on different models.

Results of False Prediction Explanation For false prediction explanation, we expect to have higher scores on the three metrics (*CM*, *DM*, *SM*). The higher the score, which means the better the explanations. The results are reported in Table 1, and we have the following three observations.

(1) When compared to the results of the baseline method Top_10, both SCC and ICC achieve significant better results, indicating our proposed method is effective and reasonable.

Table 2. Integrating concept filtering for false prediction.

Neurons' concepts: whole layer (%)			
Methods	CM^{FP}	DM^{FP}	SM^{FP}
Top_10	58.76	26.14	58.82
SCC	**81.17**	**85.97**	**74.74**
ICC	55.73	69.85	37.39

Table 3. Integrating concept filtering for true prediction.

Neurons' concepts: whole layer (%)				
Methods	Consistency Metrics		Similarity Metrics	
	CM^{TP}	CM^{T_FP}	SM^{TP}	SM^{T_FP}
Top_10	15.79	9.88	6.23	3.59
SCC	25.31	19.69	18.23	15.01
ICC	**66.60**	**59.78**	**41.19**	**38.16**

(2) All the best scores for false prediction explanation (across CM^{FP}, DM^{FP} and SM^{FP}) come from SCC. The reason is that SCC has broader coverage than ICC: if some concepts are not in SCC, then they are most likely to be incorrect. On the other hand, ICC is more specific, thus it might exclude some (partially) correct concepts.

(3) Among the three methods to represent neurons' learned concepts in section MinMax-based NetDissect, the threshold-based method achieves better results, demonstrating that our method can explain false predictions well.

(4) The results from ConceptSHAP [14] and CLIP-Dissect [27] are in line with the trends observed in NetDissect, and all satisfy our assumptions.

Results of True Prediction Explanation For true prediction explanation, we expect to observe that CM^{TP} and SM^{TP} are larger than CM^{T_FP} and SM^{T_FP} respectively. The bigger the scores as well as the gap between CM^{TP} and CM^{T_FP} and between SM^{TP} and SM^{T_FP}, the better the results are. As a whole, the results in Table 1, ICC achieves the better results. Although the gap between SM^{TP} and SM^{T_FP} for top 10 (Highest IoU) is bigger, these SM^{TP} and SM^{T_FP} scores are very low.

Integrating Concept Filtering for Model Prediction Explanation Tables 2 and 3 show the results for false prediction explanation and true prediction explanation when using concept filtering to simplify the concept sets. For false prediction, SCC achieves the best performance compared to ICC and Top_10. For true prediction, once again the results of CM^{TP} and SM^{TP} are larger than CM^{T_FP} and SM^{T_FP} respectively. In addition, results are better than that without concept filtering in Table 1.

Model Prediction Explanation on Different Models We further implement our method on different architectures to verify the generalization. We randomly select 1000 samples from the ADE20k data for the experiment by considering the effect of time efficiency.

The results of false prediction explanation are shown in Table 4. From the CC perspective, SCC has better results than ICC over every model, which is similar to the ob-

Table 4. Results of false prediction explanation on different models and utilize the MinMax-based threshold to learn the neurons' concepts.

Models	CC	CM^{FP}	DM^{FP}	SM^{FP}
ResNet-50	SCC	**80.85**	**89.36**	**74.46**
	ICC	53.19	69.15	36.17
DenseNet-161	SCC	**78.63**	**81.32**	**45.65**
	ICC	55.47	57.54	21.29
AlexNet	SCC	**76.58**	**83.26**	**71.34**
	ICC	60.23	68.33	31.57

Table 5. IoU gain (%) of different clusters.

Cluster Nb.	TransD	Dismult	ProjE	TransE
160	+17.01	+22.20	+19.94	+20.11
165	+18.11	+22.84	+17.48	+25.77
167	+18.44	+23.42	+18.03	+26.05
168	+21.78	+23.15	+17.80	**+26.31**
169	+20.72	+22.84	**+23.86**	+26.01
170	+20.90	+23.22	+22.35	+25.36
175	+21.27	**+23.88**	+21.74	+22.47
180	**+25.29**	+23.07	+23.04	+22.63
185	+24.10	+23.34	+22.49	+22.32

servation over ResNet-18 from Table 1. The results of SCC on ResNet-50 achieve the best performance across all models.

4.3. Do External Knowledge with Concept Fusion Improve Existing Neuron Interpretation?

Yes. Our method, Concept Filtering, merges semantically-equivalent concepts based on ConceptNet, which effectively produces over 23% point gain on neuron behaviors for neuron interpretation. As KG embedding techniques could have an impact on the number of optimal clusters, as well as on the interpretability of neurons, we ran some experiments with ResNet-18 over the ADE20k dataset to evaluate their impact. In particular we evaluated the impact of TransE [28], Dismult [29], ProjE [30] and TransD [31] on the (1) optimal number of clusters, and (2) quality of interpretability, measured using IoU similarly described as in CEN. The final number of cluster also captures the final number of core concepts to be considered for explanation, as a cluster is described by a unique concept in ConceptNet. The knowledge graph used for computing the embeddings is a subset of ConceptNet. In particular, we extracted all concepts in ADE20k, as well as direct 1-hop and 2-hop neighbors of ADE20k concepts in ConceptNet. We applied fuzzy matching for 0.1% of ADE20k concepts due to some misalignment between concepts in ADE20k and ConceptNet.

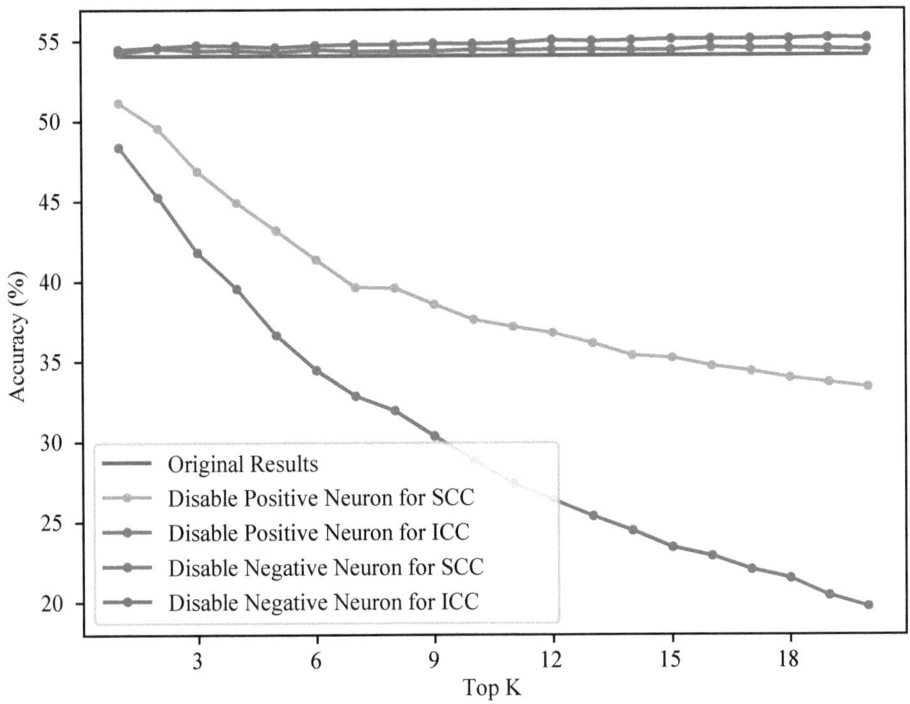

Figure 3. Neuron contribution on ADE20k.

The IoU gain is measured by capturing the interpretability improvement from (A) concept with no clustering strategy to (B) concept with a k-clustering strategy with (k: Cluster Nb.) using Embeddings. The IoU gain is defined as $^{(B-A)}/_{A}$. Table 5 captures the main results. We can see that: (1) Fusing of semantically-equivalent concepts leads to significant performance enhancement across all methods. In essence, reducing cluster number exposes more interpretable units in the neural model. (2) Among various embedding techniques, TransE outperforms others, achieving a remarkable 26.3% improvement with 168 clusters compared to the non-clustering strategy, i.e., 512 neurons in the context of ResNet-18. (3) From a clustering perspective, optimal performance arises within the 168-180 class range. Fewer than 168 clusters imply fusion of less semantically related concepts, while over 180 clusters suggest the disregard of partially semantically-equivalent concepts.

4.4. Do Explanations based on Core Concepts Contribute to Model Performance?

Yes. We show that core concepts and related explanation metrics can help optimise the model, leading to 26.7% of performance improvement. After verifying the effectiveness of CC on explanations, a natural question is whether CC can be further used to help manipulate model behavior.

Results of Neuron Identification via CC Figure 3 shows the model performance when we disable the positive neurons or negative neurons. We have the following three observations: (1) when negative (resp. positive) neurons are disabled, the model performance is improved (resp. decreases), proving that the CC facilitates identifying impor-

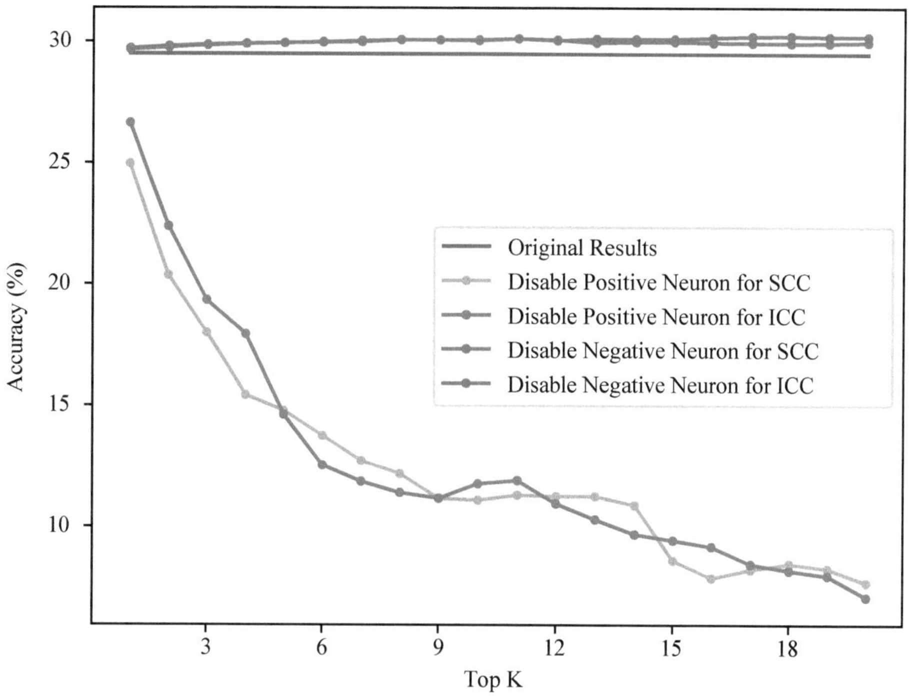

Figure 4. Neuron contribution on Opensurface.

tant neurons during decision-making of the model; (2) model accuracy tends to decrease as the number of inhibitory positive neurons increases; (3) compared to SCC, ICC can better identify both the positive and negative neurons. As shown in Figure 4, we can also see that the model performance decreases when we disable the positive neurons. Note that the accuracy on ADE20k decreases more, indicating that more positive neurons could be detected on ADE20k.

When inhibiting negative neurons, the model performance is improved on both ADE20k and Opensurfaces. The results on Opensurfaces do not show as much growth as the results on ADE20k. This is probably because Opensurfaces mainly focuses on annotating the surface property, such as material, which makes the core concept of different scenes with limited differentiation. For example, concepts *painted*, *wood* will be core concepts for most scenes, such as `living room`, `family room`, `office` and `staircase`. From the overall experimental results, with the help of core concepts, our method can effectively identify the positive and negative neurons, and then augment the model performance.

Results of Re-training via CC From Figures 3 and 4, we can see that the performance change of disabling negative neurons is not as large as disabling positive neurons on both datasets. This is reasonable, since the model we explain is trained with its parameters fixed and it is difficult to correct false predictions by only removing some negative neurons. However, the improvements on different datasets still indicate that our method is effective to retrieve negative neurons.

To address this challenge, we re-train the initial models with the help of CC, and the results are shown in Figure 5. In Figure 3 and 4, the experiments are based on the model

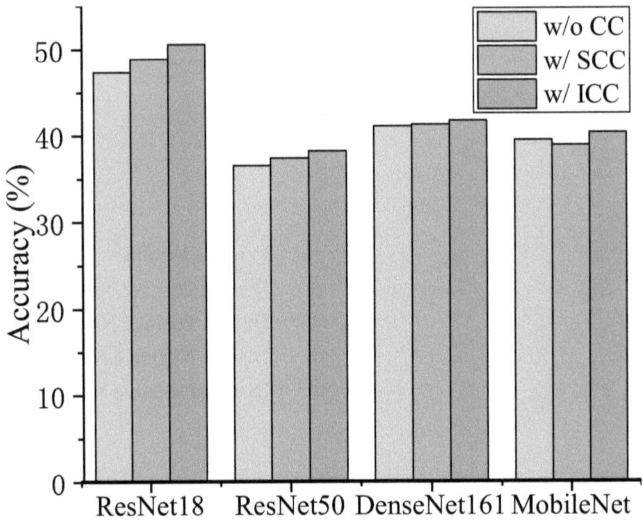

Figure 5. The results of model re-training via CC.

Table 6. Results of PE.

Method	Acc. (%)	
	ADE20k	Opensurfaces
ResNet18	52.96	29.26
SVM (SCC)	66.54	31.62
SVM (ICC)	**67.11**	**32.27**

ResNet18, and the results have improved about 1.3% by removing the negative neurons. However, in Figure 5, the corresponding performance of ResNet18 has improved 3.27%. On the other models, the results by adding ICC are all improved. Compared to SCC, utilizing the ICC for re-training model is more effective.

The above two parts mainly focus on manipulating the model behavior, such as identifying the positive/negative neurons and re-training from scratch. In the following part, we further verify the effectiveness of explanation metrics CM, SM and DM; cf., Eqs. (4), (5) and (6).

Results of Re-training via PE The results are shown in Table 6, and ResNet18 is the fundamental model. The results are improved for SCC and ICC on both datasets. ICC-based SVM on ADE20k achieves the best performance with 67.11, and outperforms the basic ResNet18 by a large margin of 14.15, which amouts to 26.7% improvement.

5. Conclusion

In this study, we investigated knowledge-aware neuron interpretation for image scenes classification. To address the concept completeness, we proposed two types of core concepts (i.e., SCC and ICC) based on KGs. We show that SCC is effective on explaining false predictions, while ICC excels in neuron identification and model optimisation with concept loss. Our results also show that concept fusion and CC based metrics are effective for neuron interpretation and model optimisation, respectively, significantly outperforming state of the art approaches by over 20%. As for future work, we consider using concept fusion methods involving uncertainty [32,33] and datatype [34] reasoning.

Acknowledgments

We would like to thank the anonymous reviewers for their constructive comments and suggestions. This work is supported by a grant from the Institute for Tsinghua University Initiative Scientific Research Program, by the Science and Technology Cooperation and Exchange Special Program of Shanxi Province (No.202204041101016), by the Institute for Guo Qiang, Tsinghua University (2019GQB0003), by the Chang Jiang Scholars Program (J2019032), and the EPSRC project ConCur (EP/V050869/1).

References

[1] Thoppilan R, Freitas DD, Hall J, Shazeer N, Kulshreshtha A, Cheng H, et al.. LaMDA: Language Models for Dialog Applications; 2022. Available from: https://arxiv.org/abs/2201.08239.

[2] OpenAI. GPT-4 Technical Report; 2023. Available from: https://doi.org/10.48550/arXiv.2303.08774.

[3] Brik B, Chergui H, Zanzi L, Devoti F, Ksentini A, Siddiqui MS, et al.. A Survey on Explainable AI for 6G O-RAN: Architecture, Use Cases, Challenges and Research Directions; 2023. Available from: https://doi.org/10.48550/arXiv.2307.00319.

[4] Chen J, Lecue F, Pan JZ, Horrocks I, Chen H. Knowledge-based Transfer Learning Explanation. In: Proc. of the International Conference on Principles of Knowledge Representation and Reasoning (KR2018); 2018. p. 349-58.

[5] Deng S, Zhang N, Zhang W, Chen J, Pan JZ, Chen H. Knowledge-Driven Stock Trend Prediction and Explanation via Temporal Convolutional Network. In: Proc. of the World Wide Web Conference (WWW 2019); 2019. p. 678-85.

[6] Shahroudnejad A. A Survey on Understanding, Visualizations, and Explanation of Deep Neural Networks; 2021. Available from: https://arxiv.org/abs/2102.01792.

[7] Akhtar N, Jalwana MAAK. Rethinking Interpretation: Input-Agnostic Saliency Mapping of Deep Visual Classifiers. In: Proceedings of the AAAI Conference on Artificial Intelligence. AAAI Press; 2023. p. 178-86. Available from: https://ojs.aaai.org/index.php/AAAI/article/view/25089.

[8] Kortylewski A, Liu Q, Wang A, Sun Y, Yuille AL. Compositional Convolutional Neural Networks: A Robust and Interpretable Model for Object Recognition Under Occlusion. Int J Comput Vis. 2021;129(3):736-60. Available from: https://doi.org/10.1007/s11263-020-01401-3.

[9] Jiang Z, Zhang Y, Yang Z, Zhao J, Liu K. Alignment Rationale for Natural Language Inference. In: Proceedings of the 59th Annual Meeting of the Association for Computational Linguistics and the 11th International Joint Conference on Natural Language Processing, ACL/IJCNLP. Association for Computational Linguistics; 2021. p. 5372-87. Available from: https://doi.org/10.18653/v1/2021.acl-long.417.

[10] Montavon G, Lapuschkin S, Binder A, Samek W, Müller K. Explaining nonlinear classification decisions with deep Taylor decomposition. Pattern Recognit. 2017;65:211-22. Available from: https://doi.org/10.1016/j.patcog.2016.11.008.

[11] Tian Y, Liu G. MANE: Model-Agnostic Non-linear Explanations for Deep Learning Model. In: 2020 IEEE World Congress on Services, SERVICES 2020, Beijing, China, October 18-23, 2020. IEEE; 2020. p. 33-6. Available from: https://doi.org/10.1109/SERVICES48979.2020.00021.

[12] Teotia D, Lapedriza À, Ostadabbas S. Interpreting Face Inference Models Using Hierarchical Network Dissection. Int J Comput Vis. 2022;130(5):1277-92. Available from: https://doi.org/10.1007/s11263-022-01603-x.

[13] Ghorbani A, Wexler J, Zou JY, Kim B. Towards Automatic Concept-based Explanations. In: Advances in Neural Information Processing Systems 32: Annual Conference on Neural Information Processing Systems, NeurIPS; 2019. p. 9273-82. Available from: https://proceedings.neurips.cc/paper/2019/hash/77d2afcb31f6493e350fca61764efb9a-Abstract.html.

[14] Yeh C, Kim B, Arik SÖ, Li C, Pfister T, Ravikumar P. On Completeness-aware Concept-Based Explanations in Deep Neural Networks. In: Advances in Neural Information Processing Systems 33: Annual Conference on Neural Information Processing Systems, NeurIPS. Red Hook, NY, USA: Curran Associates Inc.; 2020. p. 12. Available from: https://proceedings.neurips.cc/paper/2020/hash/ecb287ff763c169694f682af52c1f309-Abstract.html.

[15] Ge Y, Xiao Y, Xu Z, Zheng M, Karanam S, Chen T, et al. A Peek Into the Reasoning of Neural Networks: Interpreting With Structural Visual Concepts. In: IEEE Conference on Computer Vision and Pattern Recognition, CVPR. Computer Vision Foundation / IEEE; 2021. p. 2195-204. Available from: https://openaccess.thecvf.com/content/CVPR2021/html/Ge_A_Peek_Into_the_Reasoning_of_Neural_Networks_Interpreting_With_CVPR_2021_paper.html.

[16] Zhu M, Gao Z, Pan JZ, Zhao Y, Xu Y, Quan Z. TBox Learning from Incomplete Data by Inference in BelNet+. Knowledge Based Systems. 2015:30-40.

[17] Wang H, Fang Z, Zhang L, Pan JZ, Ruan T. Towards Effective Online Knowledge Graph Fusion. In: Proc. of 14th International Semantic Web Conference (ISWC 2015); 2015. .

[18] Kozorog M, Stanojević D. Towards a definition of the concept of scene: Communicating on the basis of things that matter. Sociologija. 2013;55(3):353-74. Available from: http://scindeks-clanci.ceon.rs/data/pdf/0038-0318/2013/0038-03181303353K.pdf.

[19] Pan JZ, Vetere G, Gomez-Perez JM, Wu H, editors. Exploiting Linked Data and Knowledge Graphs for Large Organisations. Springer; 2017.

[20] Pan JZ, Calvanese D, Eiter T, Horrocks I, Kifer M, Lin F, et al. Reasoning Web: Logical Foundation of Knowledge Graph Construction and Querying Answering. Springer; 2017.

[21] Bau D, Zhou B, Khosla A, Oliva A, Torralba A. Network Dissection: Quantifying Interpretability of Deep Visual Representations. In: IEEE Conference on Computer Vision and Pattern Recognition,CVPR. IEEE Computer Society; 2017. p. 3319-27. Available from: https://doi.org/10.1109/CVPR.2017.354.

[22] Guan Y, Chen J, Lecue F, Pan J, Li J, Li R. Trigger-Argument based Explanation for Event Detection. In: Findings of the Association for Computational Linguistics: ACL 2023. Toronto, Canada: Association for Computational Linguistics; 2023. p. 5046-58.

[23] Mu J, Andreas J. Compositional Explanations of Neurons. In: Advances in Neural Information Processing Systems 33: Annual Conference on Neural Information Processing Systems, NeurIPS; 2020. p. 11. Available from: https://proceedings.neurips.cc/paper/2020/hash/c74956ffb38ba48ed6ce977af6727275-Abstract.html.

[24] Cesa-Bianchi N, Gentile C, Zaniboni L. Hierarchical classification: combining Bayes with SVM. In: Cohen WW, Moore AW, editors. Machine Learning, Proceedings of the Twenty-Third International Conference, ICML. vol. 148. ACM; 2006. p. 177-84. Available from: https://doi.org/10.1145/1143844.1143867.

[25] Zhou B, Zhao H, Puig X, Fidler S, Barriuso A, Torralba A. Scene Parsing through ADE20K Dataset. In: 2017 IEEE Conference on Computer Vision and Pattern Recognition, CVPR. IEEE Computer Society; 2017. p. 5122-30. Available from: https://doi.org/10.1109/CVPR.2017.544.

[26] Bell S, Bala K, Snavely N. Intrinsic images in the wild. ACM Trans Graph. 2014;33(4):159:1-159:12. Available from: https://doi.org/10.1145/2601097.2601206.

[27] Oikarinen T, Weng TW. CLIP-Dissect: Automatic Description of Neuron Representations in Deep Vision Networks; 2023.

[28] Bordes A, Usunier N, García-Durán A, Weston J, Yakhnenko O. Translating Embeddings for Modeling Multi-relational Data. Curran Associates Inc. 2013:2787-95. Available from: https://proceedings.neurips.cc/paper/2013/hash/1cecc7a77928ca8133fa24680a88d2f9-Abstract.html.

[29] Yang B, tau Yih W, He X, Gao J, Deng L. Embedding Entities and Relations for Learning and Inference in Knowledge Bases; 2015.

[30] Shi B, Weninger T. ProjE: Embedding Projection for Knowledge Graph Completion. In: Proceedings of the Thirty-First AAAI Conference on Artificial Intelligence, AAAI. AAAI Press; 2017. p. 1236-42. Available from: http://aaai.org/ocs/index.php/AAAI/AAAI17/paper/view/14279.

[31] Ji G, He S, Xu L, Liu K, Zhao J. Knowledge Graph Embedding via Dynamic Mapping Matrix. In:

Proceedings of the 53rd Annual Meeting of the Association for Computational Linguistics and the 7th International Joint Conference on Natural Language Processing of the Asian Federation of Natural Language Processing, ACL. The Association for Computer Linguistics; 2015. p. 687-96. Available from: https://doi.org/10.3115/v1/p15-1067.

[32] Pan JZ, Stamou G, Tzouvaras V, Horrocks I. f-SWRL: A Fuzzy Extension of SWRL. In: Proc. of the International Conference on Artificial Neural Networks (ICANN 2005), Special section on "Intelligent multimedia and semantics"; 2005. .

[33] Qi G, Pan JZ, Ji Q. A Possibilistic Extension of Description Logics. In: Proc. of 2007 International Workshop on Description Logics (DL2007); 2007. .

[34] Pan JZ, Horrocks I. Web Ontology Reasoning with Datatype Groups. In: Fensel D, Sycara K, Mylopoulos J, editors. Proc. of the 2nd International Semantic Web Conference (ISWC2003); 2003. .

Handbook on Neurosymbolic AI and Knowledge Graphs
P. Hitzler et al. (Eds.)
IOS Press, 2025

doi:10.3233/FAIA250232

Expressive Power of Monotonic Graph Neural Networks via Datalog

David J. TENA CUCALA [a,b,1], Bernardo CUENCA GRAU [a], Boris MOTIK [a], and Egor V. KOSTYLEV [c]

[a] *Dept. of Computer Science, University of Oxford*
[b] *Dept. of Computer Science, Royal Holloway, University of London*
[c] *Dept. of Informatics, University of Oslo*

Abstract. Graph Neural Networks (GNNs) are often used to learn transformations of graph data. While effective in practice, GNN-based approaches make predictions via numeric manipulations, and so their expressive power (i.e., a logical description of what they can do) is difficult to understand. In this chapter, we describe our recent research into *monotonic max GNNs*, a sub-family of GNNs that correspond to a class of programs expressed in Datalog, a well-known rule-based formalism. These GNNs are subject to restrictions ensuring that no prediction made by them is lost when extending or renaming their input. As a result, each monotonic max GNN is equivalent to a round of application of a finite and computable set of tree-shaped Datalog rules. Furthermore, these GNNs can be effectively trained in practice for tasks such as knowledge graph completion, achieving performance similar or superior to other state-of-the-art rule-learning systems.

Keywords. graph neural networks, Datalog, monotonicity, expressive power, explainability, neurosymbolic

1. Introduction

Numerous tasks over knowledge graphs (KGs), such as KG completion [1], node classification [2], question answering [3], and recommendation [4] can be conceptualised as a problem of finding a suitable transformation of datasets consisting of relational facts [5]. For example, in a recommender system, we can represent a KG with user–item interactions and background knowledge as a dataset, and the system must transform it into another dataset containing recommendations. Figure 1 shows an example where the input dataset includes the bibliographic facts *Author*(*Dostoevsky*, *Crime_and_Punishment*) and *Author*(*Dostoevsky*, *The_Idiot*), and a user's past interactions with the system, using the fact *Likes*(*Crime_and_Punishment*). The output dataset contains a fact *Recommend*(*The_Idiot*) representing a recommendation for the user.

Graph Neural Networks (GNNs)—models specifically developed for processing graph data [6]—are increasingly being used to learn transformations between datasets automatically [7,8,9,10,11,12,13,14,15,16]. The key advantage of GNNs is that their output is resilient to the renaming of vertices (i.e., applying a GNN to isomorphic graphs

[1]Corresponding Author: david.tenacucala@rhul.ac.uk

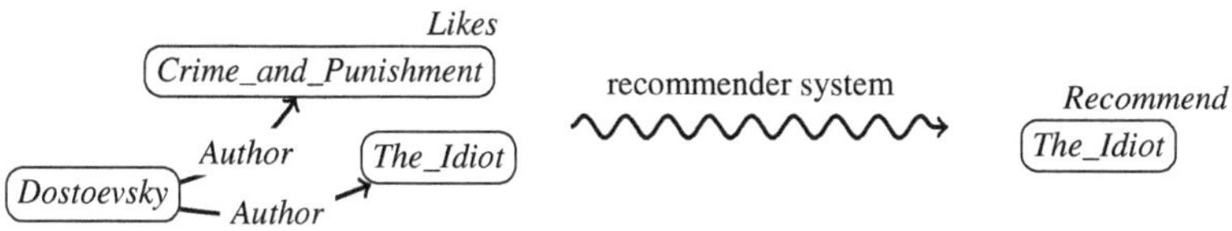

Figure 1. Graphical representation of a recommender system as a transformation of datasets

produces isomorphic outputs). Dataset transformations are often expected to exhibit analogous properties; for example, we would expect distinct users interacting with sets of items in exactly the same way to receive the same recommendations.

An important question in such applications is understanding the *expressive power* of the class of GNNs used—that is, giving a logical characterisation of the transformations that such GNNs can compute. This can be achieved by identifying a logic-based language that can express these transformations and developing algorithmic means to find a logical theory in this language that is equivalent to a given GNN within the relevant class. Such correspondences allow for a rigorous understanding and comparison of different families of GNN-based models. Furthermore, they facilitate practical applications such as the formal verification of model properties and the explanation of their predictions. For instance, a property of interest can be expressed as a logical formula, and logical methods can then be used to determine if it is a consequence of the logical theory characterising the model. This is especially important in safety-critical domains. Additionally, an output fact of the ML-based transformation can be explained by generating a proof that shows how the fact logically follows from the theory describing the transformation. These rigorous yet human-readable explanations can enhance trust in the system's predictions and ensure compliance with explainability policies [17].

The study of the expressive power of GNNs has steadily garnered attention in recent years. In a pioneering work, Barceló et al. [18] showed that each GNN-induced transformation expressible in first-order logic is equivalent to a concept query of the $\mathscr{ALCQ}$ description logic [19]. Huang et al. [20] proved an analogous result for a slightly different class of GNNs. Grohe [21] generalised these results by showing that GNN-induced transformations can, under mild restrictions, be captured by the guarded fragment of FOL with counting terms GFO+C. Logic-based approaches for formal verification problems over GNNs have also been independently developed [22,23,24].

In this chapter, we describe a recent line of research [25,26] identifying conditions for a GNN-based transformation to be equivalent to a set of rules expressed in Datalog [5], a well-known declarative language primarily used for deductive databases and knowledge representation. Datalog uses 'if-then' rules, which can be applied to a set of facts to derive new facts. Datalog is theoretically well-understood and it is also widely used in practice. Therefore, extracting equivalent Datalog programs from GNN-based transformations enables the application of a powerful suite of symbolic reasoning techniques to verification and explanation problems of GNN-based models. For example, the following Datalog rule could be used to explain the prediction in Figure 1:

$$Author(x,y_1) \wedge Author(x,y_2) \wedge Likes(y_1) \rightarrow Recommend(y_2); \tag{1}$$

this rule states that a book should be recommended to a user if they previously liked a book by the same author. It explains why the user was recommended *The_Idiot*: they read *Crime_and_ Punishment* by the same author, *Dostoevsky*.

In Section 2 we recapitulate the definition of Datalog; then, in Section 3, we introduce a general GNN-based transformation of datasets which encodes a dataset as a vector-labelled graph, applies the GNN to this graph, and then decodes the GNN's output into a dataset. We use a *canonical* encoding/decoding scheme that neither introduces nor omits information. We also describe several key relationships between GNNs and Datalog rules, including the notion of *equivalence*, which holds when both realise the same transformation; this notion is the basis for our analysis of the expressive power of GNNs.

In Section 4, we introduce *monotonic max* GNNs, a sub-class of GNNs with several important restrictions: first, the transformation matrices in these models are non-negative; second, they aggregate information using the max function; and third, their activation and output classification functions are monotonic and have a non-negative range. Under these restrictions, we show that a GNN is *monotonic under homomorphisms*: extending or renaming the input does not remove any prediction in the output. We then show that each monotonic max GNN is equivalent to a computable Datalog program where each rule is *tree-like*, in the sense that its *primal graph*—a description of the structure of the rule's body—is a tree. Finally, we conclude by showing the converse result: for each tree-like Datalog program, we can construct an equivalent monotonic max GNN. Consequently, the class of tree-like Datalog programs fully characterises monotonic max GNNs.

In Section 5, we define a more powerful GNN-based transformation based on a more expressive encoding/decoding scheme, which allows us to tackle problems such as link prediction in knowledge graphs. Furthermore, we show how to exploit our previous results to compute an equivalent Datalog program for each such transformation.

In Section 6, we present an empirical evaluation of monotonic max GNNs on the task of knowledge graph completion. We show that monotonic max GNNs can be successfully trained and their performance is comparable and often superior to other state-of-the-art models based on rule extraction. We also show that the restrictions of monotonic max GNNs do not necessarily affect negatively their performance; in fact, in some cases, they improve their performance, which suggests that they function as a useful inductive bias.

Finally, in Section 7, we compare our approach with other existing techniques for studying the expressive power of neural networks and related areas such as rule learning, formal verification over GNNs, and explanation of predictions by GNNs.

This chapter overviews results reported in two conference publications [25,26].

2. Datalog

We recapitulate the standard definition of Datalog [5]. We assume a signature of disjoint, countable sets of *predicates* and *constants*. Each predicate is associated with a non-negative integer arity. A predicate is *unary* if its arity is 1, and *binary* if it is 2. We also consider a countably infinite set of *variables* disjoint with the sets of predicates and constants. A *term* is a variable or a constant. An *atom* is an expression of the form $P(t_1, \ldots, t_n)$, where P is a predicate of arity n and $t_1, \ldots, t_n$ are terms. A *fact* is a variable-free atom, and a *dataset* is a finite set of facts. In this chapter, we see *knowledge graphs* as datasets where each fact is either unary or binary.

A (Datalog) *rule* is an expression of form $B_1 \wedge \cdots \wedge B_n \rightarrow H$ where $n \geq 0$, $B_1, \ldots, B_n$ are *body* atoms and H is the *head* atom. A rule is *safe* if each variable occurring in H also occurs in a body atom. A (Datalog) *program* is a finite set of rules. Note that we do not require rules to be safe and allow rules with an empty body (denoted as $\top$).

A *substitution* μ is a mapping of variables to constants. For α an atom or a conjunction of atoms, $\alpha\mu$ is the result of replacing in α each variable in the domain of μ with $\mu(x)$. A rule $r = B_1 \wedge \cdots \wedge B_n \to H$ defines the *immediate consequence* operator T_r on datasets as follows: for D a dataset, $T_r(D)$ is the dataset that contains the fact $H\mu$ for each substitution μ mapping all variables of r to constants of D such that $B_i\mu \in D$ for each $i \in \{1,\ldots,n\}$. Observe that T_r always derives a finite number of facts, even if r is unsafe. For example, for rule $r = \top \to R(x,y)$, $T_r(D)$ is the set of all facts $R(a,b)$ where a and b are constants occurring in D. For P a program, we let $T_P(D) = \bigcup_{r\in P} T_r(D)$.

Conjunctions α and β of atoms are *equal up to variable renaming* if there exists a bijective mapping μ from the set of all variables of α to those of β such that the result of replacing each variable x in α by $\mu(x)$ contains exactly the same conjuncts as β; this notion is extended to rules in the obvious way. Moreover, a set S *contains* a conjunction or rule α *up to variable renaming* if there exists $\beta \in S$ such that α and β are equal up to variable renaming. We sometimes abuse our notation by treating conjunctions as sets of conjuncts; for example, $\alpha \subseteq \beta$ means that each conjunct of α is a conjunct of β. Rule $r = B_1 \wedge \cdots \wedge B_n \to H$ *subsumes* rule $r' = B'_1 \wedge \cdots \wedge B'_m \to H'$ if there exists a mapping μ of variables to terms such that $H\mu = H'$ and $\{B_1\mu,\ldots,B_n\mu\} \subseteq \{B'_1,\ldots,B'_m\}$. If r subsumes r', then $T_{r'}(D) \subseteq T_r(D)$ for each dataset D.

A *homomorphism* from a dataset D to a dataset D' is a mapping h of constants to constants that is defined on the set of all constants of D and satisfies $h(D) \subseteq D'$, where $h(D)$ is obtained by replacing each constant a in D with $h(a)$ and removing all duplicate facts. An operator T from datasets to datasets over the same constants is *monotonic under homomorphisms* if, for all datasets D and D' to which T is applicable, each homomorphism from D to D' is also a homomorphism from $T(D)$ to $T(D')$. It is well-known that T_P is monotonic under homomorphisms for each constant-free program P [5].

3. Graph Neural Network-Based Transformations

In this section, we define a transformation of datasets based on a general GNN model. In Section 3.1, we introduce the model, which has a fixed number of layers, an arbitrary aggregation function, and operates on graphs with coloured edges and vertices labelled with real-valued vectors. In Section 3.2, we show how to encode a dataset into a suitable input for the model and how to decode the model's output into a dataset; we then use this encoding/decoding scheme to formally define our transformation. In Section 3.3, we show how to compare GNNs and Datalog programs based on the transformations that they realise. Here and elsewhere in the chapter, vectors and matrices are over the reals $\mathbb{R}$. For a vector $\mathbf{v}$, we let $(\mathbf{v})_i$ be its i-th element; similarly, for a matrix $\mathbf{A}$, we let $(\mathbf{A})_{i,j}$ be the element in row i, column j. We apply scalar functions to vectors element-wise.

3.1. Graph Neural Networks

We consider a GNN model that is applied to graphs of a form given by Definition 1. Intuitively, these are directed graphs where each vertex is labelled with a numeric *feature vector* of a given dimension, and where each edge has a *colour* from a given finite set. These graphs can have self-loops (i.e., edges with the same beginning and end) but they only allow at most one edge of each colour c from one vertex to another (multiple edges from one vertex to another are allowed if each edge has a different colour).

Definition 1. *Let* Col *be a finite, nonempty set of* colours *and let* δ *be a positive integer. A* (Col,δ)*-graph* $\mathcal{G}$ *is a tuple* $\langle \mathcal{V}, \{\mathcal{E}^c\}_{c\in\mathsf{Col}}, \lambda\rangle$ *where* $\mathcal{V}$ *is a finite set of* vertices*;* $\mathcal{E}^c \subseteq \mathcal{V}\times\mathcal{V}$ *is a set of directed* edges *for each colour* $c \in \mathsf{Col}$*; and* labelling λ *assigns to each* $v \in \mathcal{V}$ *a vector* $\lambda(v)$ *of dimension* δ*. Furthermore,* $\mathcal{G}$ *is* Boolean *if* $\lambda(v) \in \{0,1\}^\delta$ *for each* $v \in \mathcal{V}$*. Finally, if* $\langle v,w\rangle \in \mathcal{E}^c$*, then* w *is a* c-neighbour *of* v*.*

Our GNN model has finitely many layers and is parameterised by a finite nonempty colour set Col and a positive integer δ; the inputs and outputs of a (Col,δ)-GNN are (Col,δ)-graphs. Given an input graph, the GNN updates each vertex's feature vector once per layer; to do so, it aggregates (using a fixed but arbitrary function) the feature vectors of its c-neighbours separately for each colour c; then, it applies a linear transformation to each aggregate and to the current feature vector for the vertex; finally, it sums all results and applies a (typically non-linear) activation function. This is a non-recursive variant of the original GNN model described by Scarselli et al. [27], and it is expressive enough to capture many GNN models used in practice, including, for example, the data-independent variant of the well-known Relational Graph Convolutional Network (R-GCN) [7]. This intuition is formalised in Definition 2. Note that the aggregation and activation functions are the same in all layers; this is a non-fundamental requirement that we have included for the sake of simplicity. In practice, the transformation matrices and the bias vectors are typically learnable parameters, whereas the aggregation, activation, and classification functions are hyper-parameters fixed prior to training.

Definition 2. *Given a finite, nonempty set* Col *of colours and positive integers* δ *and* L*, a* (Col,δ)*-GNN of* L layers *is a tuple*

$$\langle\, \{\mathbf{A}_\ell\}_{1\le\ell\le L},\ \{\mathbf{B}_\ell^c\}_{c\in\mathsf{Col}\text{ and }1\le\ell\le L},\ \{\mathbf{b}_\ell\}_{1\le\ell\le L},\ \mathsf{agg},\ \sigma,\ \mathsf{cls}\,\rangle, \tag{2}$$

where, for each $\ell \in \{1,\dots,L\}$ *and* $c \in \mathsf{Col}$*,* $\mathbf{A}_\ell$ *and* $\mathbf{B}_\ell^c$ *are* transformation *matrices of dimension* $\delta_\ell \times \delta_{\ell-1}$*, where* $\delta_0 = \delta_L = \delta$ *and each* δ_ℓ *is a fixed but arbitrary positive integer,* $\mathbf{b}_\ell$ *is a* bias *vector of dimension* δ_ℓ*,* agg *is an* aggregation *function mapping each finite multi-set of real numbers into a single real number,* σ *is an* activation *function from* $\mathbb{R}$ *to* $\mathbb{R}$*, and* cls *is a* classification *function from* $\mathbb{R}$ *to* $\{0,1\}$*.*

Applying a (Col,δ)*-GNN* $\mathcal{N}$ *of form* (2) *to a* (Col,δ)*-graph* $\mathcal{G} = \langle \mathcal{V}, \{\mathcal{E}^c\}_{c\in\mathsf{Col}}, \lambda\rangle$ *induces a sequence* $\lambda_0,\dots,\lambda_L$ *of vertex labelling functions such that* $\lambda_0 = \lambda$ *and, for each* $\ell \in \{1,\dots,L\}$ *and* $v \in \mathcal{V}$*, the value* $\lambda_\ell(v)$ *is given by*

$$\sigma\Big(\mathbf{A}_\ell\lambda_{\ell-1}(v) + \sum_{c\in\mathsf{Col}} \mathbf{B}_\ell^c\,\mathsf{agg}_\ell(\{\{\,\lambda_{\ell-1}(w) \mid \langle v,w\rangle \in \mathcal{E}^c\,\}\}) + \mathbf{b}_\ell\Big). \tag{3}$$

The result $\mathcal{N}(\mathcal{G})$ *of applying* $\mathcal{N}$ *to* $\mathcal{G}$ *is the Boolean* (Col,δ)*-graph with the same vertices and edges as* $\mathcal{G}$*, but where each vertex* v *is labelled by* $\mathsf{cls}(\lambda_L(v))$*.*

3.2. Canonical Transformation

We next define a transformation of datasets induced by a (Col,δ)-GNN, which we will call its *canonical transformation.* We concentrate on datasets over a signature with only unary and binary predicates (i.e., knowledge graphs) such that each colour corresponds to a unique binary predicate and there are δ unary predicates. To this end, we need to be able to encode such datasets into (Col, δ)-graphs; furthermore, we also need to decode the (Col, δ)-graph output by the GNN into a dataset. Here we use a straightforward encoding and decoding which neither introduce nor omit any information. This ensures that our study of the expressive power of canonical transformations can also be seen as a study of the expressive power of GNNs over a class of graphs representing knowledge graphs.

We assume that constants occurring in datasets correspond one-to-one to vertices of labelled graphs—that is, each term a is paired with a unique vertex v^a; this is without loss of generality since the result of applying a GNN to a coloured graph does not depend on the identity of vertices, but only on the graph structure and the feature vectors. The encoding maps constants to vertices and uses vertex connectivity to describe binary facts, and Boolean feature vectors to encode the presence of unary facts. Our decoding works in the exact opposite way: vertices are transformed into constants, edges into binary facts, and Boolean feature vectors into sets of unary facts. This *canonical* encoding/decoding scheme is commonly used in the literature with minor variations [7,8,18].

Formally, given a finite, nonempty set Col of colours and a positive integer δ, we consider a signature with δ distinct unary predicates $U_1, \dots, U_\delta$ and a distinct binary predicate E^c for each $c \in \mathsf{Col}$, which we call the (Col, δ)-*signature*, and we let (Col, δ)-*datasets* be those that contain only facts over predicates in the (Col, δ)-signature. Any such dataset can be easily transformed into a Boolean (Col, δ)-graph using the so-called canonical encoding formalised in the following definition; conversely, any Boolean (Col, δ)-graph can be easily transformed into a (Col, δ)-dataset using the canonical decoding also formalised there. Therefore, with this encoding/decoding scheme, a (Col, δ)-GNN induces a transformation over (Col, δ)-datasets where we first apply the canonical encoding to obtain a (Col, δ)-graph, then we apply the GNN to update its feature vectors, and finally we apply the canonical decoding to obtain a new (Col, δ)-dataset.

Definition 3. *The* canonical encoding $\mathsf{enc}(D)$ *of a* (Col, δ)*-dataset D is the Boolean* (Col, δ)*-graph* $\mathcal{G} = \langle \mathcal{V}, \{\mathcal{E}^c\}_{c \in \mathsf{Col}}, \lambda \rangle$ *with a vertex* $v^a \in \mathcal{V}$ *for each constant a occurring in D, an edge* $\langle v^a, v^b \rangle \in \mathcal{E}^c$ *for each fact* $E^c(a,b) \in D$*, and where the i-th element of* $\mathbf{v}^a$ *is* 1 *if and only if* $U_i(a) \in D$*.*

The canonical decoding $\mathsf{dec}(\mathcal{G})$ *of a Boolean* (Col, δ)*-graph* $\mathcal{G} = \langle \mathcal{V}, \{\mathcal{E}^c\}_{c \in \mathsf{Col}}, \lambda \rangle$ *is the dataset that contains the fact* $E^c(a,b)$ *for each* $\langle v^a, v^b \rangle \in \mathcal{E}^c$ *and* $c \in \mathsf{Col}$*, and the fact* $U_i(a)$ *for each* $v^a \in \mathcal{V}$ *and* $i \in \{1, \dots, \delta\}$ *such that the i-th element of* $\lambda(v^a)$ *is* 1*.*

Each (Col, δ)*-GNN* $\mathcal{N}$ *induces the* canonical *transformation* $T_\mathcal{N}$ *on* (Col, δ)*-datasets defined by* $T_\mathcal{N}(D) = \mathsf{dec}(\mathcal{N}(\mathsf{enc}(D)))$ *for each* (Col, δ)*-dataset D.*

Figure 2 shows the canonical encoding of a book recommendation dataset that extends that in Section 1. Colours c_A and c_L correspond to binary predicates *Author* and *Likes*, respectively; moreover, we identify unary predicates *User* and *Novel* with unary predicates U_1, and U_2, respectively. Thus, can see the dataset as a (Col, δ)-dataset where $\mathsf{Col} = \{c_A, c_L\}$ and $\delta = 2$. We then introduce vertices v^D, v^{CP}, v^{TI}, and v^B in $\mathsf{enc}(D)$ for the constants *Dostoevsky*, *Crime_and_Punishment*, *The_Idiot*, and *Bob*, respectively. Next, we introduce a c_L-coloured edge $\langle v^B, v^{CP} \rangle$ for the fact *Likes*(*Bob*, *Crime_and_Punishment*), and c_A-coloured edges $\langle v^D, v^{TI} \rangle$ and $\langle v^D, v^{CP} \rangle$ for facts *Author*(*Dostoevsky*, *The_Idiot*) and *Author*(*Dostoevsky*, *Crime_and_Punishment*), respectively. Finally, we set to one the first element of the feature vector of v^B to represent the fact *User*(*Bob*), and the second element of the feature vectors of v^{TI} and v^{CP} to represent facts *Novel*(*The_Idiot*) and *Novel*(*Crime_and_Punishment*), respectively.

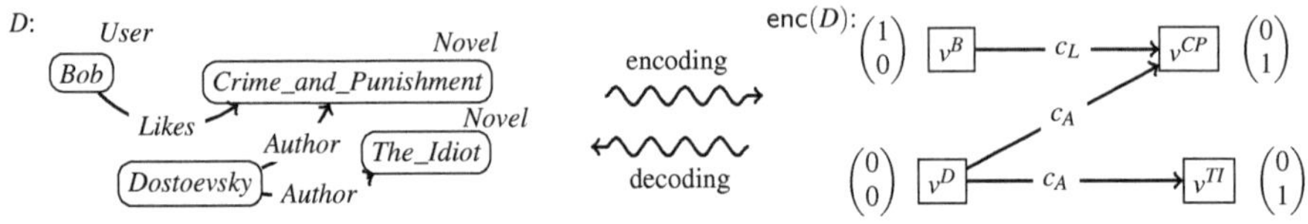

Figure 2. A dataset D for a book recommendation system and its canonical encoding $\mathsf{enc}(D)$

The parameters Col and δ of the GNN determine the datasets that a canonical transformation can be applied to. For example, the transformation induced by a (Col, δ)-GNN cannot be applied to datasets with more than δ unary predicates. In practical applications, the relevant set of unary and binary predicates is known before training, so a user should select and train a GNN model with appropriate Col and δ.

The canonical transformation is clearly invariant under renamings—that is, renaming each constant in the input to a different constant and then applying the transformation produces the same result as applying the transformation and then renaming the constants. This is because the canonical encoding and decoding do not depend on the constant names, and the application of $\mathcal{N}$ does not depend on the identity of the vertices.

We also observe that a (Col, δ)-transformation cannot introduce new binary facts, since the GNN does not introduce new edges. This can be a limitation in applications such as knowledge graph completion, which often requires the derivation of new links between entities. In Section 5, we will describe a variant of the canonical transformation that can derive new binary facts, and we will show how our expressivity results for canonical transformations can be extended to cover such transformations.

3.3. Connections to Datalog Rules

Our encoding/decoding scheme bridges the gap between GNNs and (sets of) rules, as both now can be seen as transformations of datasets. This allows us to formally compare a program P and a GNN $\mathcal{N}$ based on the transformations that they respectively induce.

Definition 4. *A Datalog program P is* sound *for a (Col, δ)-GNN $\mathcal{N}$ if $T_P(D) \subseteq T_{\mathcal{N}}(D)$ for each (Col, δ)-dataset D; it is* complete *for $\mathcal{N}$ if $T_{\mathcal{N}}(D) \subseteq T_P(D)$ for each (Col, δ)-dataset D, and it is* equivalent *to $\mathcal{N}$ if it is both sound and complete for $\mathcal{N}$.*

In other words, if a program is sound or complete for a GNN, then the results obtained by applying the GNN to any given dataset always contain or are contained in, respectively, the results obtained by applying the rules to the same dataset. If a program is equivalent to a GNN, then both implement the same (canonical) transformation over datasets. The central problem in the next section consists in identifying conditions ensuring that a given (Col, δ)-GNN $\mathcal{N}$ is equivalent to a Datalog program, and ascertaining whether such program can be computed from $\mathcal{N}$.

4. Monotonic Max GNNs

In this section, we study the expressive power of canonical transformations induced by *monotonic max GNNs*, a sub-class of GNN that imposes restrictions on the general GNN model from Section 3 to ensure monotonicity under homomorphisms, thus capturing the essence of Datalog rule application. In Section 4.1, we define monotonic max GNNs and show that their canonical transformations are monotonic under homomorphisms. In Section 4.2, we show how to exploit the property of monotonicity under homomorphisms to check if a Datalog rule is sound for a given monotonic max GNN; this method will later be crucial for computing an equivalent Datalog program for a monotonic max GNN. In Section 4.3, we show that each fact predicted by a monotonic max GNN can be explained by a sound Datalog rule from a finite class of *tree-like* rules. In Section 4.4, we show how to compute an equivalent set of tree-like rules for a given monotonic max GNN. Finally, in Section 4.5, we provide the converse result and show how to compute an equivalent monotonic max GNN for a given tree-like Datalog program.

4.1. Definition and Properties of Monotonic Max GNNs

For an arbitrary (Col, δ)-GNN $\mathcal{N}$, there is no guarantee that its canonical transformation will be monotonic under homomorphisms. For example, a trivial way to produce a non-monotonic transformation is to use a GNN with an activation or classification function that is not *monotonically increasing*, a property that holds if $f(x) \leq f(y)$ for each pair of inputs x and y such that $x < y$. However, even if we require that both these functions are monotonically increasing, the presence of negative weights in the matrices of $\mathcal{N}$ can easily cause non-monotonic behaviour, as shown in the following example.

Example 5. *Let $\mathcal{N}$ be a $(\{c\},1)$-GNN of form* (2) *with $L = 1$ where $\mathbf{A}_1 = (0)$, $\mathbf{B}_1^c = (-1)$, and $\mathbf{b}_1 = (1)$,* agg *is* sum*, σ is ReLU—that is, $\sigma(x) = x$ if $x \geq 0$ and $\sigma(x) = 0$ otherwise—and* cls *is the step function with threshold* 1*—that is, $\mathsf{cls}(x) = 0$ if $x < 1$ and $\mathsf{cls}(x) = 1$ otherwise. Note that both σ and* cls *are monotonically increasing.*

Consider the result of applying $T_{\mathcal{N}}$ to the dataset $D = \{E^c(a,b)\}$. The canonical encoding of D is a graph with vertices v^a and v^b labelled with vector (0) and a c-coloured edge from v^a to v^b. The output for v^a computed by $\mathcal{N}$ when applied to the encoding of D is given by $\mathsf{cls}(ReLU(0 \cdot 0 - 1 \cdot 0 + 1)) = 1$, and so $T_{\mathcal{N}}(D) = \{U_1(a)\}$.

However, if we extend D with fact $U_1(b)$, the canonical encoding of the extended dataset $D' = \{U_1(b), E^c(a,b)\}$ is as above, except that the feature vector for v^b is (1). This time, the output for v^a is given by $\mathsf{cls}(ReLU(0 \cdot 0 - 1 \cdot 1 + 1)) = 0$, and so $T_{\mathcal{N}}(D') = \emptyset$.

More generally, having negative elements in the products in Eq. (3)—due to negative matrix weights or to negative elements of feature vectors—can easily lead to non-monotonic behaviour. To prevent this, monotonic max GNNs will require that all the elements of the transformation matrices are non-negative, and that the range of the activation function does not include negative numbers, thus ensuring that all feature vectors generated by the GNN are non-negative. If a GNN satisfies these requirements, then its canonical transformation is monotonic, in the sense that none of the facts obtained when applying it to a dataset are lost by extending the dataset with additional facts. This, combined with invariance under (injective) renamings, ensures that the transformation is monotonic under *injective* homomorphisms—that is, homomorphisms that send different constants to different constants. However, the transformation may not yet be monotonic under all homomorphisms, as the following example shows.

Example 6. *Consider a* $(\{c\},2)$*-GNN* $\mathcal{N}$ *of* 1 *layer of form* (2) *where the element in the second row, first column of* $\mathbf{B}_1^c$ *is* 1, *and all other elements of matrices and the bias of* $\mathcal{N}$ *are* 0; *let the aggregation function be* sum, *the activation function be ReLU, and the classification function be a step function with threshold* 2.

Consider the dataset $D = \{E^c(a,b), U_1(b), E^c(a,d), U_1(d)\}$. *Its encoding is a graph with vertices* v^a, v^b, *and* v^d; *the first vertex is labelled by a* 2*-dimensional vector where both components are* 0, *and the last two vertices are labelled by a* 2*-dimensional vector whose first element is* 1 *and the second is* 0; *furthermore, there are c-coloured edges from* v^a *to both* v^b *and* v^d. *Eq.* (4) *shows the feature vector for* v^a *obtained after applying* $\mathcal{N}$ *to the encoding of D, and so* $T_{\mathcal{N}}(D) = \{U_2(a)\}$.

$$\mathsf{cls}\left(ReLU\left(\begin{pmatrix} 0 & 0 \\ 1 & 0 \end{pmatrix} \cdot \left(\begin{pmatrix} 1 \\ 0 \end{pmatrix} + \begin{pmatrix} 1 \\ 0 \end{pmatrix} \right) \right) \right) = \mathsf{cls}\left(\begin{pmatrix} 0 \\ 2 \end{pmatrix} \right) = \begin{pmatrix} 0 \\ 1 \end{pmatrix} \tag{4}$$

Consider now the dataset $D' = \{E^c(a,e), U_1(e)\}$ *obtained by (non-injectively) renaming both b and d to a new constant e, which directly induces a non-injective homomorphism from D to D'. Its encoding has only two vertices* v^a *and* v^e, *labelled as* v^a *and* v^b *above, respectively, and a c-coloured edge from* v^a *to* v^e. *Eq.* (5) *shows the feature vector for* v^a *obtained after applying* $\mathcal{N}$ *to the encoding of* D', *and so* $T_{\mathcal{N}}(D') = \emptyset$.

$$\mathsf{cls}\left(ReLU\left(\begin{pmatrix} 0 & 0 \\ 1 & 0 \end{pmatrix} \cdot \left(\begin{pmatrix} 1 \\ 0 \end{pmatrix} \right) \right) \right) = \mathsf{cls}\left(\begin{pmatrix} 0 \\ 1 \end{pmatrix} \right) = \begin{pmatrix} 0 \\ 0 \end{pmatrix} \tag{5}$$

A similar behaviour can be observed for GNNs with other aggregation functions such as average, min, or softmax. Recall, however, that Datalog transformations are always monotonic under *all* homomorphisms, not just injective ones. Thus, to ensure that $T_{\mathcal{N}}$ can be expressed in Datalog, we need to choose another aggregation function: max.

Using max aggregation helps us address the potential problems caused by two or more constants being renamed into a single one because, whenever two or more vertices are combined into a single vertex due to a constant renaming, each element in the label of the new vertex is 1 if and only if *at least one* of the original vertices had a feature vector with a 1 in the same position. Hence, using max ensures that the output of the aggregation does not decrease if multiple c-neighbours of a vertex are combined.

In summary, our discussion suggests that we need to impose four restrictions on the general GNN model from Section 3 to ensure monotonicity under homomorphisms: first, the weights of the matrices of the GNN must be non-negative; second, the aggregation function must be max; third, the activation function must be monotonically increasing and its range must not contain any negative number; fourth, the classification function must also be monotonically increasing.

Definition 7. *Given a finite nonempty set* Col *of colours and a positive integer* δ, *a* monotonic max (Col,δ)*-GNN is a GNN of form* (2) *satisfying the following:*

1. *for each* $\ell \in \{1,\ldots,L\}$ *and* $c \in \mathsf{Col}$, *matrices* $\mathbf{A}_\ell$ *and* $\mathbf{B}_\ell^c$ *are non-negative;*
2. *for each* $\ell \in \{1,\ldots,L\}$, *aggregation* agg_ℓ *is* max *(assuming that* $\max\{\} = 0$*);*
3. σ *is monotonically increasing and its range is non-negative, and*
4. cls *is monotonically increasing.*

The conditions of Definition 7 ensure that if $\mathcal{N}$ is a monotonic max (Col, δ)-GNN $\mathcal{N}$, then operator $T_{\mathcal{N}}$ is monotonic under homomorphisms.

Theorem 8. *If $\mathcal{N}$ is a monotonic max (Col, δ)-GNN, then its canonical transformation $T_{\mathcal{N}}$ is monotonic under homomorphisms.*

We have already illustrated why the restrictions from Definition 4.1 ensure that Theorem 8 holds. Please, see our paper [25] for a proof of Theorem 8. Although these restrictions ensure monotonicity under homomorphisms, this is merely a *necessary* condition to ensure that we can find an equivalent Datalog program. Our next two sections show that the restrictions are also *sufficient* to ensure the existence of such a program.

4.2. Checking Rule Soundness

In this section, we show how to check whether an arbitrary Datalog rule over the (Col, δ)-signature is sound for a given monotonic max (Col, δ)-GNN $\mathcal{N}$. Attempting to do this directly using Definition 4 would involve applying T_r and $T_{\mathcal{N}}$ to infinitely many (Col, δ)-datasets, which is clearly infeasible in practice. However, we will take advantage of the fact that $T_{\mathcal{N}}$ is monotonic under homomorphisms to design a simple rule soundness test.

Before presenting our soundness check, we rule out some edge cases. First, applying $T_{\mathcal{N}}$ to a dataset does not change the set of binary facts, so checking the soundness of a rule with a binary head atom is clearly not interesting. Second, the result of applying $T_{\mathcal{N}}$ to any dataset does not depend on the identity of constants in the dataset; hence, if a rule with constants is sound for $\mathcal{N}$, this rule is implied by another constant-free rule that is also sound for $\mathcal{N}$. Thus, we restrict our attention to checking soundness of an arbitrary constant-free rule r with a head atom $U_i(x)$.

Our method for checking soundness depends on whether the rule r is safe or not. If r is safe, then we consider the set B_r of all body atoms of r, and a substitution μ that maps each variable in r to a different constant. To check whether r is sound for $\mathcal{N}$, we simply need to check whether $U_i(\mu(x))$ is in $T_{\mathcal{N}}(B_r\mu)$. To see this, observe that since $B_r\mu$ uses a different constant for each variable in r, then for each match of the body of r to a (Col, δ)-dataset D, there is a homomorphism from $B_r\mu$ to D that specifically maps $\mu(x)$ to the constant corresponding to x in this match. Thus, if $U_i(\mu(x)) \in T_{\mathcal{N}}(B_r\mu)$, then monotonicity under homomorphisms ensures that the above homomorphism is also a homomorphism from $\{U_i(\mu(x))\}$ to $T_{\mathcal{N}}(D)$, and so the head corresponding to this match of r's body in D is in $T_{\mathcal{N}}(D)$. Hence, $T_r(D) \subseteq T_{\mathcal{N}}(D)$. On the other hand, if $U_i(\mu(x)) \notin T_{\mathcal{N}}(B_r\mu)$, then dataset $B_r\mu$ is a counterexample disproving r's soundness.

If r is unsafe, then x does not appear in the body of r, and so r is sound if and only if $T_{\mathcal{N}}$ derives $U_i(a)$ for each constant a of each (Col, δ)-dataset D that matches the body of r. However, GNNs operate independently on each connected component of the input graph, and so whether $T_{\mathcal{N}}$ derives $U_i(a)$ for each constant a in a dataset cannot depend on whether the dataset matches r's body; thus, r is sound if and only if $T_{\mathcal{N}}$ derives $U_i(a)$ for each constant a of each (Col, δ)-dataset D. To check if this is the case, we apply $\mathcal{N}$ to a (Col, δ)-graph consisting of a single vertex v^d labelled with a vector where all elements are 0, letting $\mathbf{d}$ be the output vector for v^d computed by $\mathcal{N}$ on this graph. Since $\mathcal{N}$ is monotonic max, $\mathbf{d}$ is a lower bound on any vector obtained by applying $\mathcal{N}$ to any Boolean (Col, δ)-graph and so, if the i-th element of $\mathbf{d}$ (which corresponds to predicate U_i, as per the canonical decoding) is 1, then $T_{\mathcal{N}}$ will derive $U_i(a)$ for each constant a

in each (Col,δ)-dataset. If it is 0, however, then we can construct a counterexample to soundness using a dataset where the vector output by $\mathcal{N}$ for some vertex of its encoding coincides with $\mathbf{d}$. For example, we can consider dataset $D = \{E^c(b,a)\}$: in its encoding, v^a is labelled with a vector of zeros and it has no c-neighbours (since it has no outgoing edges), and so its output vector clearly coincides with $\mathbf{d}$, which ensures $U_i(a) \notin T_{\mathcal{N}}(D)$.

Proposition 9. *Let $\mathcal{N}$ be a monotonic max (Col,δ)-GNN of L layers, and let r be a constant-free Datalog rule over the (Col,δ)-signature with a unary head atom U_i.*

- *If r is safe, then r is sound for $\mathcal{N}$ if and only if $U_i\mu \in T_{\mathcal{N}}(B_r\mu)$, for B_r the body atoms of r and μ a substitution mapping each variable in B_r to a different constant.*
- *If r is unsafe, then r is sound for $\mathcal{N}$ if and only if the i-th element of the vector obtained by applying $\mathcal{N}$ to a (Col,δ)-graph consisting of a single vertex labelled with a vector of zeroes is* 1.

We are now able to check whether a Datalog rule is sound for a given (Col,δ)-GNN. Our approach allows for practical checks that can be used to formally verify properties of a GNN; for example, we can verify whether the recommender system mentioned in Section 1 always recommends books written by authors whose other books have been liked by the user—a property expressed by rule (1). Moreover, in Section 4.4, we will present a method for extracting an equivalent program from a monotonic max GNN that operates by applying the soundness check to certain candidate rules.

4.3. Explaining Predictions Using Tree-Like Rules

In this section, given a monotonic max (Col,δ)-GNN $\mathcal{N}$, we define a special, finite class of *tree-like* Datalog rules for it, and then we provide an algorithm that takes as input $\mathcal{N}$, an arbitrary (Col,δ)-dataset D, and a fact α in $T_{\mathcal{N}}(D)$, and extracts a rule that: (1) belongs in the aforementioned special class, (2) derives α from D, and (3) is sound for $\mathcal{N}$. The latter property is particularly important, because it shows that the extracted rule is a *data-independent* property of $\mathcal{N}$ justifying the derivation of α by $T_{\mathcal{N}}$ from D.

Tree-like rules are of the form $\varphi \rightarrow U(x)$, where φ is a tree-like conjunction for x (intuitively, φ forms a directed tree rooted at x). Definition 10 formalises this notion and classifies tree-like rules according to the maximum *fan-out* and *depth* of its variables.

Definition 10. *A conjunction φ is* tree-like for a variable x *if its* primal (multi)graph, *i.e. the directed unlabelled graph whose vertices are the variables of φ and which has a directed edge from y to z for each atom $E^c(y,z)$ in φ, is a tree rooted at x.*

The fan-out *of a variable y in a tree-like conjunction φ is the number of distinct variables z_i with a colour c such that $E^c(y,z_i)$ is a conjunct in φ. The* depth *of y is the maximal n for which there exist variables $y_0,\ldots,y_n$ and predicates $E^{c_1},\ldots,E^{c_n}$ such that $y_0 = x$, atom $E^{c_i}(y_{i-1},y_i)$ is a conjunct of φ for each $i \in \{1,\ldots,n\}$, and $y_n = y$. The* depth *of the conjunction φ is the maximum depth of a variable in φ.*

For d and f non-negative integers, a tree-like conjunction φ is (d,f)-tree-like *if, for each variable y in φ, the depth i of y is at most d and the fan-out of y is at most $f(d-i)$. Moreover, a Datalog rule is* (d,f)-tree-like *if it is of form $\varphi \rightarrow U(x)$, where φ is a (d,f)-tree-like conjunction for x.*

Algorithm 1 Rule extraction algorithm

Inputs:
$\mathcal{N}$: a monotonic max (Col, δ)-GNN with L layers and dimensions $\delta_0, \ldots, \delta_L$
D : a (Col, δ)-dataset
$U_i(a)$: a fact in $T_{\mathcal{N}}(D)$

1: Let $\langle \mathcal{V}, \{\mathcal{E}^c\}_{c \in \mathsf{Col}}, \lambda \rangle$ be the graph $\mathsf{enc}(D)$
2: Let $\lambda_0, \ldots, \lambda_L$ be the labellings of the vertices $\mathcal{V}$ when $\mathcal{N}$ is applied to $\mathsf{enc}(D)$
3: $r := \top \rightarrow U_i(x)$
4: $\theta := \theta' := \{x \mapsto a\}$
5: **for** ℓ **from** L **down to** 1 **do**
6: **for each** $y \mapsto b$ in θ, **each** $c \in \mathsf{Col}$, and **each** $j \in \{1, \ldots, \delta_{\ell-1}\}$ **do**
7: $V := \{v \in \mathcal{V} \mid \langle v^b, v \rangle \in \mathcal{E}^c \text{ and } (\lambda_{\ell-1}(v))_j \neq 0\}$
8: **if** $V \neq \emptyset$ **then**
9: Choose a vertex $v \in V$ with highest $(\lambda_{\ell-1}(v))_j$
10: Let e be the constant such that $v = v^e$, and let z be a fresh variable
11: Add $E^c(y, z)$ to the body of r
12: $\theta' := \theta' \cup \{z \mapsto e\}$
13: $\theta := \theta'$
14: Add $U_j(y)$ to the body of r for each y in r such that $U_j(\theta(y)) \in D$
15: **return** r

For example, the primal graph of conjunction $A(x) \wedge R(x,y) \wedge S(x,z)$ is a tree with root x and children y and z; thus, it is (1,2)-tree like for x, but it is not (1,1)-tree-like for x because x is at distance 0 from itself and so, to belong in this class, it should have no more than one child. In contrast, the primal graph of $A(x) \wedge R(x,y) \wedge S(x,z) \wedge T(y,z)$ is a triangle with nodes x, y, and z, so it is not (d, f)-tree-like for x for any d and f. Note that the body of a tree-like rule can be $\top$; for example, $\top \rightarrow U(x)$ is a valid $(0,0)$-tree-like rule. We also observe that for each two non-negative integers d and f, there exists a finite set containing all (d, f)-tree-like rules up to variable renaming.

For a (Col, δ)-GNN $\mathcal{N}$, let $\delta_{\mathcal{N}}$ be the maximum of the dimensions $\delta_0, \delta_1 \ldots, \delta_L$ of its layers. Algorithm 1 takes as input a monotonic max (Col, δ)-GNN $\mathcal{N}$, a (Col, δ)-dataset D, and a fact $U_i(a) \in T_{\mathcal{N}}(D)$, and extracts a sound $(L, |\mathsf{Col}| \cdot \delta_{\mathcal{N}})$-tree-like rule r for $\mathcal{N}$ such that $U_i(a) \in T_r(D)$. The algorithm computes the canonical encoding of D (line 1), and then applies $\mathcal{N}$ to it, extracting also the induced vertex labellings (line 2). Rule r uses the predicate U_i in the head, and it starts with an empty body (line 3). The algorithm then extends the body of this rule by intuitively 'unfolding' the sub-graph in the encoding of D that $\mathcal{N}$ uses to compute the output feature vector for vertex v^a (i.e., $\mathsf{cls}(\lambda_L(v^a))$). Each variable mentioned in r will represent a vertex in the encoding of D (two or more variables might representing the same vertex); the algorithm also maintains a substitution θ that associates each variable in r to the vertex it represents. Variable x always represents vertex v^a, so θ is initialised as $\{x \mapsto a\}$ (line 4); so is θ', an auxiliary variable that will be used to update θ.

After the initialisation is complete, the algorithm iterates over each layer ℓ of the GNN from the last layer L to the first layer 1 (line 5). Intuitively, at the start of the iteration for layer ℓ, each variable y currently in r represents a vertex v^b (with $b = \theta(y)$) in the encoding of D whose feature vector in layer ℓ is used by $\mathcal{N}$ to compute the output feature vector for v^a. Then, for each such variable y, colour $c \in \mathsf{Col}$, and position $j \in \{1, \ldots, \delta_{\ell-1}\}$ (line 6), the algorithm finds the c-neighbour v^e of vertex v^b that contributes with the maximum non-zero value in position j in the aggregation of vectors of c-neighbours of v^b in layer $\ell - 1$ (lines 7 to 9); if it exists, it introduces a new variable z to represent this vertex (line 10), extending the body of r with an atom $E^c(y,z)$ (line 11), and defining $\theta(z) = e$ (line 12). In this way, at the end of the loop from line 6, all the variables in the body of r represent vertices in the encoding of D whose feature vectors in layer $\ell - 1$ are used by $\mathcal{N}$ to compute the output feature vector of v^a.

When the loop from line 5 is complete, the variables in r represent all vertices in the encoding of D that $\mathcal{N}$ uses to compute the output feature vector for v^a. The algorithm then extends the body of r with unary atoms representing the initial feature vectors of such vertices (line 14), and returns the resulting r (line 15).

Algorithm 1 is clearly terminating. Moreover, its output rule r satisfies the three key properties mentioned at the beginning of the section: (1) it is a $(L, |\mathsf{Col}| \cdot \delta_{\mathcal{N}})$-tree-like rule, (2) $U_i(a) \in T_r(D)$, and (3) it is sound for $\mathcal{N}$. The following theorem captures this.

Theorem 11. *For each monotonic max (Col, δ)-GNN, each (Col, δ)-dataset D, and each fact $U_i(a) \in T_{\mathcal{N}}(D)$, Algorithm 1 computes a $(L, |\mathsf{Col}| \cdot \delta_{\mathcal{N}})$-tree-like rule r that satisfies $U_i(a) \in T_r(D)$ and is sound for $\mathcal{N}$.*

We next give a brief summary of why each of the three properties holds; see our paper [26] for a full proof of the theorem.

Property (1) Rule r is trivially a $(L, |\mathsf{Col}| \cdot \delta_{\mathcal{N}})$-tree-like if its body is empty. Otherwise, Algorithm 1 ensures that x must appear in its body. The depth of the primal graph of the body of r rooted at x is at most L since the loop in line 5 runs a total of L times. Furthermore, the depth of a variable y introduced in the ℓ-th iteration of this loop cannot be more than ℓ, and so it is present in at most $L - \ell$ iterations of the loop. In each such iteration, at most $\delta_{\mathcal{N}}$ new atoms of the form $E^c(y,z)$ for each colour c are added to the body of r, and so y will have at most $(L - \ell) \cdot |\mathsf{Col}| \cdot \delta_{\mathcal{N}}$ children in the primal graph.

Property (2) $U_i(a) \in T_r(D)$ follows as Algorithm 1 ensures that for each $E^c(y,z)$ and $U_j(y)$ in the body of r, $E^c(\theta(y), \theta(z)) \in D$ and $U_j(\theta(y)) \in D$, respectively, and $\theta(x) = a$.

Property (3) If r is unsafe, then Algorithm 1 ensures that it can only be of form $\top \to U_i(x)$; furthermore, the i-th value of the output feature vector for v^a is always 1 even when no neighbour of v^a contributes to the aggregation function in any layer and all elements in its initial feature vector are 0. Under such circumstances, $T_{\mathcal{N}}$ derives $U_i(a)$ for each constant a in the input dataset, and so $r = \top \to U_i(x)$ is sound for $\mathcal{N}$. If r is safe, then we use Proposition 9 to verify its soundness. We consider a substitution μ mapping each variable to a different constant; then, the construction of the body B_r of r in Algorithm 1 ensures that the computation of the output feature vector for $v^{\mu(x)}$ by $\mathcal{N}$ on the encoding of $B_r\mu$ mimics the computation of the output feature vector for v^a by $\mathcal{N}$ on the encoding of D. Thus, $U_i(\mu(x))$ is derived in the former case since $U_i(a)$ is derived in the latter. Then, from Proposition 9, it follows that r is sound.

An important consequence of Theorem 11 is that a set that contains up to variable renaming all $(L, |\mathsf{Col}| \cdot \delta_{\mathcal{N}})$-tree-like rules sound for the GNN will suffice to derive all unary facts produced by the GNN. In the next section, we will show how this allows us to compute an equivalent Datalog program for the GNN.

We conclude this section with an example of the application of Algorithm 1.

Example 12. *Let* $\mathsf{Col} = \{c\}$, *let* $\delta = 1$, *and let* $\mathcal{N}$ *be a monotonic max* (Col, δ)*-GNN with two layers with the following transformation matrices and bias vectors:*

$$\mathbf{A}_1 = (0), \mathbf{B}_c^1 = (1), \mathbf{b}_1 = (0), \mathbf{A}_2 = (1), \mathbf{B}_2^c = (1), \text{ and } \mathbf{b}_2 = (-1). \tag{6}$$

Moreover, let the activation function be ReLU, and let the classification function be a step function with a threshold of 1. *Finally, let D be the* (Col, δ)*-dataset*

$$\{E^c(a,b), E^c(b,a), E^c(a,e), E^c(b,e), U_1(e), E^c(g,b)\} \cup D_g, \tag{7}$$

where D_g *is a* (Col, δ)*-dataset that does not mention a, b, or e. The canonical encoding of D is a* $(\{c\}, 1)$*-graph given on the left in Figure 3. It includes vertices* v^a, v^b, v^e, *and* v^g *and edges between them, as well as a sub-graph* $\mathcal{G}_g$ *encoding* D_g *represented by a dashed line; note that the only connection between* $\mathcal{G}_g$ *and the vertices* v^a, v^b, *and* v^e, *is an edge from* v^g *to* v^b. *Applying* $\mathcal{N}$ *to the encoding of D induces the labellings* λ_0, λ_1, *and* λ_2, *which take the following values for vertices* v^a, v^b, *and* v^e*:*

$$\lambda_0(v^a) = \lambda_0(v^b) = \lambda_1(v^e) = \lambda_2(v^e) = (0), \tag{8}$$

$$\lambda_0(v^e) = \lambda_1(v^a) = \lambda_1(v^b) = \lambda_2(v^a) = \lambda_2(v^b) = (1). \tag{9}$$

Note that $\mathcal{G}_g$ *has no effect on the labellings of* v^a, v^b, *and* v^e, *because there is no outgoing edge from any of these three vertices to a vertex of* $\mathcal{G}_g$. *It follows that* $U_1(a) \in T_{\mathcal{N}}(D)$.

We now apply Algorithm 1 to $\mathcal{N}$, *D, and the fact* $U_1(a)$ *to obtain a* $(2,1)$*-tree-like rule r that satisfies* $U_1(a) \in T_r(D)$ *and is sound for* $\mathcal{N}$. *The algorithm initialises r as* $\top \rightarrow U_1(x)$ *and* θ *as* $\{x \mapsto a\}$. *For* $\ell = 1$, *the loop in line 6 runs a single time, for variable x, colour c, and position* $j = 1$. *The set V of vertices v such that there is an edge* $\langle v^a, v \rangle$ *in the encoding of D and the first element of its feature vector in layer* 1 *is positive is just* $\{v^b\}$, *and so the algorithm introduces a fresh variable y, updates r to* $E^c(x,y) \rightarrow U_1(x)$, *and extends* θ *with* $\{y \mapsto b\}$. *For* $\ell = 0$, *the loop in line 6 runs twice: the first time it runs for variable x, colour c, and position* $j = 1$. *In this case, the set V is just* $\{v^e\}$, *and so the algorithm introduces a fresh variable* z_1, *extends r to* $E^c(x,y) \wedge E^c(x,z_1) \rightarrow U_1(x)$, *and extends* θ *with* $\{z_1 \mapsto e\}$. *The second iteration of the loop considers variable y, colour c, and position* $j = 1$. *The set V is now again* $\{v^e\}$, *and so the algorithm introduces a fresh variable* z_2 *and extends r to* $E^c(x,y) \wedge E^c(x,z_1) \wedge E^c(y,z_2) \rightarrow U_1(x)$, *and* θ *with* $\{z_2 \mapsto e\}$. *Finally, the algorithm extends r with body unary atoms corresponding to unary facts in the dataset for the relevant variables, so r becomes*

$$E^c(x,y) \wedge E^c(x,z_1) \wedge E^c(y,z_2) \wedge U_1(z_1) \wedge U_1(z_2) \rightarrow U_1(x). \tag{10}$$

The primal graph of the body of this rule is shown on the right in Figure 3; note that r is $(2,1)$*-tree-like. Furthermore,* θ *witnesses that* $U_1(a) \in T_r(D)$. *Finally, the method from Section 4.2 easily shows that r is sound for* $\mathcal{N}$.

Algorithm 1 not only plays an instrumental role in the proof of Theorem 11, but it also has an important practical use. If we wish to explain a fact predicted by a monotonic max GNN on a given dataset, we can run the algorithm directly so that the extracted rule provides a justification for the prediction. However, we can exploit some properties of

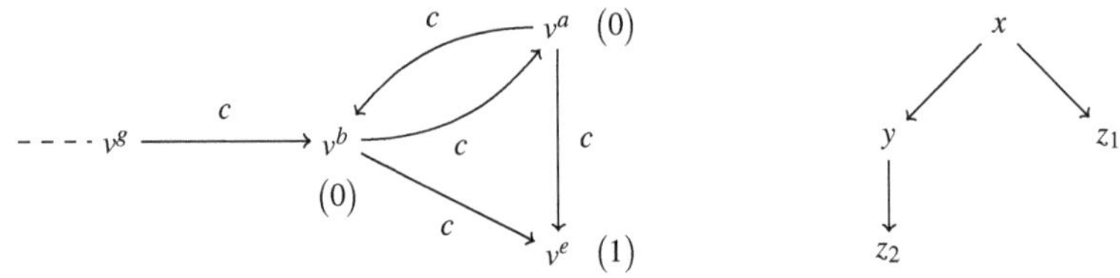

Figure 3. Canonical encoding of D in Example 12 and primal graph of the rule extracted by Algorithm 1.

the model (such as matrix sparsity) to optimise the algorithm and produce a rule with as few body atoms as possible, resulting in a simple and highly readable explanation. For further details on such techniques, please see our paper [28].

4.4. Equivalent Program

We have already established that each unary fact derived by a monotonic max (Col, δ)-GNN can be explained by a sound $(L, |\mathsf{Col}| \cdot \delta_{\mathcal{N}})$-tree-like rule. It then follows that the subset of all sound rules in this finite (modulo variable renaming) set, combined with rules for edge preservation, yields a program equivalent to $\mathcal{N}$.

Theorem 13. *For a monotonic max (Col, δ)-GNN $\mathcal{N}$, the program $P_{\mathcal{N}}$ containing up to variable renaming each $(L, |\mathsf{Col}| \cdot \delta_{\mathcal{N}})$-tree-like rule r sound for $\mathcal{N}$ and the rule $E^c(x,y) \rightarrow E^c(x,y)$ for each $c \in \mathsf{Col}$ is equivalent to $\mathcal{N}$.*

To compute this program, we can enumerate all $(L, |\mathsf{Col}| \cdot \delta_{\mathcal{N}})$-tree-like rules and then apply our test from Section 4.2 to each rule to check if it is sound. This procedure is unlikely to be practical, since the number of $(L, |\mathsf{Col}| \cdot \delta_{\mathcal{N}})$-tree-like rules is usually very large in practice. However, we can optimise our search by exploiting relations between rules so as to reduce the number of soundness checks that need to be carried out. For example, if we find that a rule r is sound for the GNN, then we do not need to test any rule r' that is subsumed by r, since $T_{r'}(D) \subseteq T_r(D)$ and so r' is also sound for the GNN. In our paper [28], we show that this and other optimisations allow us to extract equivalent Datalog programs from monotonic max GNNs in several practical cases.

The next section concludes our study of monotonic max GNNs by showing the converse of Theorem 13: each Datalog program that consists of tree-like rules can be expressed by a monotonic max GNN. Together, these results imply that the class of such Datalog programs exactly characterises the expressive power of monotonic max GNNs.

4.5. From Tree-Like Programs to GNNs

Let d and f be non-negative integers, and let P be a Datalog program consisting of (d, f)-tree-like rules over a (Col, δ)-signature. To ensure that the program can be equivalent to the canonical transformation induced by a GNN, which neither introduces nor removes any binary atom, we assume that it additionally contains the rule $E^c(x,y) \rightarrow E^c(x,y)$ for each $c \in \mathsf{Col}$. Furthermore, for simplicity, we assume, without loss of generality, that no two rules in P have any variables in common. We show how to construct a monotonic max (Col, δ)-GNN $\mathcal{N}_P$ equivalent to P.

Let the *depth* of a variable in P be its depth in the primal graph of the body of the rule where it appears. We define $\mathcal{N}_P$ to be a monotonic max (Col, δ)-GNN of form

(2) where the number of layers is $L = d+2$, the activation function is ReLU, and the classification function cls is the step function with threshold 1. To specify the weights of $\mathcal{N}_P$, we first define a sequence of tree-like conjunctions for each layer; intuitively, these are the 'features' that each layer recognises. For each $\ell \in \{1,\ldots,d+1\}$, let $\tau_{\ell,1},\ldots,\tau_{\ell,\delta_\ell}$ be an arbitrary (but fixed) enumeration of the smallest set of (d,f)-tree-like conjunctions for x that satisfy the following properties for each variable y in a rule $r \in P$:

(C1) if the depth of y is less than $d-(\ell-1)$, then there is $i \in \{1,\ldots,\delta_\ell\}$ such that $\tau_{\ell,i}\{x \mapsto y\}$ is the conjunction of all unary atoms in the body of r that mention y;

(C2) if the depth of y is $d-(\ell-1)$, then there is $i \in \{1,\ldots,\delta_\ell\}$ and a variable renaming μ such that $\tau_{\ell,i}\mu$ is the unique tree-like conjunction for y in the body of r that is *maximal*, i.e. no tree-like conjunction for y in the body of r strictly contains it.

Intuitively, the $\tau_{\ell,i}$ represent important tree-like sub-conjunctions of bodies of rules of P; the sequences are defined in a way that allows us to build the conjunctions $\tau_{\ell+1,i}$ in layer $\ell+1$ inductively from the conjunctions $\tau_{\ell,j}$ in layer ℓ while keeping the total number of conjunctions per layer to a minimum.

The transformation matrices $\mathbf{A}_\ell$ and $\mathbf{B}_\ell^c$, and the bias vectors $\mathbf{b}_\ell$ are defined as follows for each $c \in \mathsf{Col}$, $\ell \in \{1,\ldots,L\}$, $i \in \{1,\ldots,\delta_\ell\}$, and $j \in \{1,\ldots,\delta_{\ell-1}\}$:

$$(\mathbf{A}_\ell)_{i,j} = \begin{cases} 1 \text{ if one of the following holds:} \\ \quad \bullet\ \ell = 1 \text{ and } \tau_{1,i} \text{ contains } U_j(x); \\ \quad \bullet\ \ell \in \{2,\ldots,L-1\} \text{ and } \tau_{\ell-1,j} \text{ is the conjunction of all unary atoms in} \\ \quad\quad \tau_{\ell,i} \text{ that mention } x; \\ \quad \bullet\ \ell = L \text{ and } P \text{ contains rule } \tau_{L-1,j} \to U_i(x) \text{ up to variable renaming;} \\ 0 \text{ otherwise;} \end{cases}$$

$$(\mathbf{B}_\ell^c)_{i,j} = \begin{cases} 1 \text{ if } \ell \in \{2,\ldots,L-1\} \text{ and there is a variable renaming } \mu \text{ such that } \tau_{\ell-1,j}\mu \\ \quad \text{is the maximal tree-like conjunction for } x\mu \text{ in } \tau_{\ell,i} \text{ and } E^c(x,x\mu) \in \tau_{\ell,i}; \\ 0 \text{ otherwise;} \end{cases}$$

$$(\mathbf{b}_\ell)_i = \begin{cases} 1 - \sum_{j=1}^{\delta_{\ell-1}} \left((\mathbf{A}_\ell)_{i,j} + \sum_{c \in \mathsf{Col}} (\mathbf{B}_\ell^c)_{i,j} \right) & \text{if } \ell \in \{1,\ldots,L-1\}; \\ 0 & \text{otherwise.} \end{cases}$$

To understand the intuition behind the choice of weights for $\mathcal{N}_P$, assume that $\mathcal{N}_P$ is applied to $\mathsf{enc}(D)$, and consider a vector $\lambda_\ell(v^a)$ labelling in layer ℓ a vertex v^a for some constant a of D. Then, the i-th element of $\lambda_\ell(v^a)$ is paired with a tree-like conjunction $\tau_{\ell,i}$; this element is always Boolean, and it indicates whether it is possible to evaluate $\tau_{\ell,i}$ over D by mapping variable x to a. Formally, this is captured by the following statement.

Lemma 14. *For each* (Col,δ)*-dataset* D*, layer* $\ell \in \{1,\ldots,L-1\}$ *of* $\mathcal{N}_P$*, position* $i \in \{1,\ldots,\delta_\ell\}$*, and constant* a *in* D*, and for* $\lambda_\ell(v^a)$ *the labelling in layer* ℓ *of the vertex corresponding to* a *when* $\mathcal{N}_P$ *is applied to* $\mathsf{enc}(D)$*,* $(\lambda_\ell(v^a))_i = 1$ *if there exists a substitution* θ *mapping* x *to* a *such that* $\tau_{\ell,i}\theta \in D$*, and* $(\lambda_\ell(v^a))_i = 0$ *otherwise.*

A simple inductive argument proves the lemma; we refer the reader to our paper [26] for details. Eventually, when $\ell = d+1$, the conjunctions $\tau_{d+1,i}$ correspond to the bodies of the rules in P, and layer $d+2$ simply connects them to the corresponding heads.

To further illustrate the intuition behind the definition of the weights of $\mathcal{N}_P$, we next provide an example showing how $\mathcal{N}_P$ is computed for a simple program P.

Example 15. *Let* $\mathsf{Col} = \{c\}$, $\delta = 2$, *and* P *consist of the following* $(1,1)$*-tree-like rule* r

$$U_1(x) \wedge E^c(x,y) \wedge U_1(y) \wedge U_2(y) \rightarrow U_2(x). \tag{11}$$

The GNN $\mathcal{N}_P$ *will have* $d+2 = 3$ *layers. We next define the conjunctions* $\tau_{\ell,i}$, *as well as the transformation matrices and bias vectors of the model for each layer.*

The primal graph for the body of r *consists of two vertices* x *and* y, *and an edge from* x *to* y. *In layer* $\ell = 1$, *the only variable in this graph with depth smaller than* $(d-(\ell-1)) = 1-(1-1) = 1$ *is* x, *and so we let* $\tau_{1,1}$ *be* $U_1(x)$, *the conjunction of all unary atoms for* x *in the body of rule* r. *Moreover, the only variable of depth exactly* $(d-(\ell-1)) = 1$ *is* y, *and so we let* $\tau_{1,2}$ *be* $U_1(x) \wedge U_2(x)$, *which is equal (up to variable renaming) to the maximal tree-like conjunction for* y *in the body of* r. *We then define*

$$\mathbf{A}_1 = \begin{pmatrix} 1 & 0 \\ 1 & 1 \end{pmatrix}, \qquad \mathbf{B}_1^c = \begin{pmatrix} 0 & 0 \\ 0 & 0 \end{pmatrix}, \qquad \mathbf{b}_1 = \begin{pmatrix} 0 \\ -1 \end{pmatrix}. \tag{12}$$

Clearly, if $\mathcal{N}_P$ *is applied to the encoding* $\mathsf{enc}(D)$ *of a dataset* D, *the feature vector* $\lambda_1(v^a)$ *for an arbitrary constant* a *is a Boolean vector whose first element is* 1 *if and only if* $U_1(a) \in D$, *and its second element is* 1 *if and only if* $\{U_1(a), U_2(a)\} \subseteq D$.

In layer $\ell = 2$, *there are no variables of depth smaller than* $d-(\ell-1) = 1-(2-1) = 0$, *and the only variable of this depth is* x; *so we define* $\tau_{2,1}$ *as* $U_1(x) \wedge E^c(x,y) \wedge U_1(y) \wedge U_2(y)$, *the maximal tree-like conjunction for* x *in the body of* r. *We then define*

$$\mathbf{A}_2 = \begin{pmatrix} 1 & 0 \end{pmatrix}, \qquad \mathbf{B}_2^c = \begin{pmatrix} 0 & 1 \end{pmatrix}, \qquad \mathbf{b}_2 = \begin{pmatrix} -1 \end{pmatrix}. \tag{13}$$

Now $(\lambda_2(v^a))_1 = 1$ *for a constant* a *if and only if* $U_1(a) \in D$ *(recognised by the first element of* $\mathbf{A}_2$*), and* a *is connected by predicate* E^c *to a constant* b *such that* $\{U_1(b), U_2(b)\} \subseteq D$ *(recognised by the second element of* $\mathbf{B}_2^c$*), with the negative bias element* $\mathbf{b}_2$ *testing that both conditions are present.*

In the final layer $\ell = 3$, *we relate the body of the rule with its head* U_2, *and so*

$$\mathbf{A}_3 = \begin{pmatrix} 0 \\ 1 \end{pmatrix}, \qquad \mathbf{B}_3^c = \begin{pmatrix} 0 \\ 0 \end{pmatrix}, \qquad \mathbf{b}_3 = \begin{pmatrix} 0 \\ 0 \end{pmatrix}. \tag{14}$$

Note that in $\mathcal{N}_P$ the maximum possible value of δ_ℓ for each $\ell \in \{1,\dots,L-1\}$ is determined by the number of (d,f)-tree-like formulas of depth up to $\ell-1$ which are distinct up to variable renaming, and so δ_{L-1} can be the largest such number. We next establish an upper bound on δ_{L-1}. By Definition 10, the fan-out of a variable of depth i is at most $f(d-i)$. The number of variables of depth i is at most the number of variables of depth $i-1$ times the fan-out of each variable, which is $f^i \cdot d \cdot \ldots \cdot (d-i+1)$ and is bounded by $f^i \cdot d!$. By adding up the contribution for each depth, there are at most $f^d \cdot (d+1)!$ variables. Each variable is labelled by one of the 2^δ conjunctions of depth zero, and each non-root variable is connected by one of the $|\mathsf{Col}|$ predicates to its parent. Hence, there are at most $(|\mathsf{Col}| \cdot 2^{\delta})^{f^d \cdot (d+1)!}$ tree-like formulas.

Theorem 16. *Program P and GNN $\mathcal{N}_P$ are equivalent, and $\delta_{L-1} \leq (|\mathsf{Col}| \cdot 2^{\delta})^{f^d \cdot (d+1)!}$.*

In general, the values δ_ℓ are much smaller than this; in particular, it follows from our definition of $\mathcal{N}_P$ that δ_ℓ is bounded by the number of distinct variables in the program.

5. Non-Canonical Encoding/Decoding Schemes

As we observed in Section 3.2, the canonical encoding/decoding scheme makes the canonical transformation unable to derive new binary facts. There exist other schemes [25,29,10] which overcome this limitation by introducing vertices representing combinations of constants, so that facts of higher arity can be encoded in feature vectors. Our analysis can be extended to transformations based on such a scheme if the latter can be expressed as the composition of the canonical encoding/decoding scheme with a pair of programs P_{enc} and P_{dec} expressed in Datalog or some extension of it.

Consider an encoding/decoding scheme where the encoder maps each dataset D over some fixed signature Σ into a Boolean (Col, δ)-graph $\mathcal{G}_D$, for fixed parameters Col and δ (which may depend on Σ), and the decoder maps each Boolean (Col, δ)-graph $\mathcal{G}$ into a dataset $D_{\mathcal{G}}$ over Σ. The corresponding end-to-end transformation induced by a (Col, δ)-GNN $\mathcal{N}$ first applies the encoding, then $\mathcal{N}$, and then the decoding. Now, suppose that there exist programs P_{enc} and P_{dec}, expressed in Datalog or in some extension of it, such that applying $T_{P_{\mathsf{enc}}}$ to each dataset D over Σ produces a (Col, δ)-dataset whose canonical encoding is $\mathcal{G}_D$, and applying $T_{P_{\mathsf{dec}}}$ to the canonical decoding of a Boolean (Col, δ)-graph $\mathcal{G}$ produces $D_{\mathcal{G}}$. Then, the corresponding end-to-end transformation maps each dataset D over Σ to $T_{P_{\mathsf{dec}}}(T_{\mathcal{N}}(T_{P_{\mathsf{enc}}}(D)))$. Now, if $\mathcal{N}$ is equivalent to a Datalog program $P_{\mathcal{N}}$, then the composition of P_{enc}, $P_{\mathcal{N}}$, and P_{dec} characterises the end-to-end transformation. Furthermore, the programs P_{enc}, $P_{\mathcal{N}}$, and P_{dec} can usually be combined by applying the standard *unfolding* technique [5] where, starting with the rules of P_{dec}, we apply hyperresolution steps with rules of P_{enc} and $P_{\mathcal{N}}$ until the rules only mention predicates in Σ remain. Then, the transformation T_P induced by the unfolded program P is equivalent to the end-to-end transformation.

In the remainder of this section, we illustrate this approach for a (non-canonical) encoding/decoding scheme that we introduce in a previous paper [25]. In Section 6, we will use the end-to-end transformation induced by this encoding to tackle knowledge graph completion tasks. Further examples of this approach can be found in our paper [26].

The encoding from [25] is applicable to a dataset D over unary predicates $A_1, \ldots, A_\varepsilon$ and binary predicates $R_{\varepsilon+1}, \ldots, R_\delta$, for ε a non-negative integer, and δ a positive integer. It transforms D into a (Col, δ)-graph over colours $\mathsf{Col} = \{c_1, c_2, c_3, c_4\}$ that is *symmetric*, i.e. if there is a c-coloured edge from a vertex v to a vertex w, then there is also a c-coloured edge from w to v. The encoding introduces a vertex v^a for each constant a in D as well as vertices $v^{a,b}$ and $v^{b,a}$ for each pair of constants a, b occurring together in a binary fact in D. All (unary and binary) predicates are assigned fixed positions in labelling vectors so that the value of each element in a feature vector indicates the presence or absence of a specific fact in D. For example, if $A_i(a) \in D$, then the i-th element in the labelling of v^a in the encoding graph is set to 1; analogously, if $R_j(a,b) \in D$, then the j-th

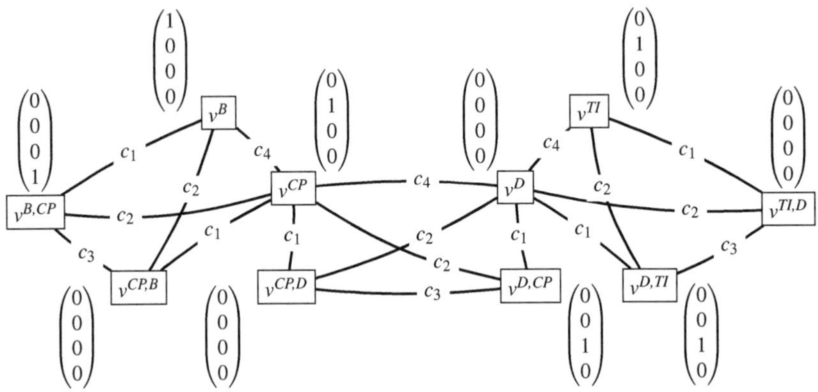

Figure 4. Dataset D from Figure 2 encoded as in our paper [25]; each c-coloured edge and its inverse are jointly represented as a single, undirected, c-coloured edge

element of the labelling of $v^{a,b}$ is set to 1. Edges indicate different types of 'connections' between constants. In particular, vertices v^a (resp. v^b) and $v^{a,b}$ are connected by edges of colour c_1 (resp. c_2) to indicate that constant a (resp. b) occurs first (resp. second) in the constant pair. Vertices $v^{a,b}$ and $v^{b,a}$ are connected by edges of colour c_3 to represent that the corresponding pairs of constants are inverses of each other, and vertices v^a and v^b are connected by edges of colour c_4 if a and b appear together in a fact.

Example 17. *Figure 4 shows the encoding of the dataset D from Figure 2. As in the canonical encoding, we introduce vertices* v^B, v^{CP}, v^D, *and* v^{TI} *to represent the constants of D; however, we additionally introduce vertices* $v^{D,CP}$, $v^{CP,D}$, $v^{D,TI}$, $v^{TI,D}$, $v^{B,CP}$, *and* $v^{CP,B}$. *We do not introduce vertices such as* $v^{CP,TI}$ *and* $v^{TI,CP}$ *because constants Crime_And_Punishment and The_Idiot do not occur together in a fact of D. We then encode unary and binary predicates in the feature vectors labelling the graph's vertices. In our example, User, Novel, Author, and Likes replace* A_1, A_2, R_3, *and* R_4, *respectively, and so we assign to these predicates positions 1, 2, 3, and 4, respectively. For example, we represent fact* $Novel(The\_Idiot)$ *by setting to one the second element of the feature vector of* v^{TI}, *and we represent fact* $Likes(Bob, Crime\_and\_Punishment)$ *by setting to one the fourth element of the feature vector of* $v^{B,CP}$. *Finally, we connect with coloured edges all pairs of vertices that refer to related constants. For example, we connect vertices* v^D *and* $v^{D,CP}$ *by edges of colour* c_1 *to indicate that Dostoevsky occurs first in the first position of the constant pair of* $v^{D,CP}$, *and we connect* $v^{CP,D}$ *and* $v^{D,CP}$ *by edges of colour* c_3 *to indicate that the constant pairs of the two vertices are inverses of each other.*

We next show how to capture this encoding using rules. Note that the encoder introduces vertices of the form $v^{a,b}$ for pairs of constants a and b, so the encoding program P_{enc} requires value invention. This can be conveniently realised using functional terms. For example, we can represent the pair (a,b) using term $f(a,b)$, so vertex $v^{a,b}$ in the original encoding can be now represented by vertex $v^{f(a,b)}$. Thus, applying the encoding program P_{enc} to a dataset produces a (Col, δ)-dataset with functional terms, which, however, can be processed by the GNN as if these terms were constants; for example, the canonical encoding transforms $f(a,b)$ into vertex $v^{f(a,b)}$. Based on this idea, the encoding program P_{enc} contains the following rules instantiated for each $i \in \{1,\ldots,\varepsilon\}$ and each $j \in \{\varepsilon+1,\ldots,\delta\}$, expressed in an extension of Datalog with function symbols.

$$A_i(x) \to U_i(x) \qquad R_j(x,y) \to U_j(f(x,y)) \tag{15}$$

$$R_j(x,y) \to E^{c_1}(x,f(x,y)) \qquad R_j(x,y) \to E^{c_1}(f(x,y),x) \tag{16}$$

$$R_j(x,y) \to E^{c_1}(y,f(y,x)) \qquad R_j(x,y) \to E^{c_1}(f(y,x),y) \tag{17}$$

$$R_j(x,y) \to E^{c_2}(y,f(x,y)) \qquad R_j(x,y) \to E^{c_2}(f(x,y),y) \tag{18}$$

$$R_j(x,y) \to E^{c_2}(x,f(y,x)) \qquad R_j(x,y) \to E^{c_2}(f(y,x),x) \tag{19}$$

$$R_j(x,y) \to E^{c_3}(f(x,y),f(y,x)) \qquad R_j(x,y) \to E^{c_3}(f(y,x),f(x,y)) \tag{20}$$

$$R_j(x,y) \to E^{c_4}(x,y) \qquad R_j(x,y) \to E^{c_4}(y,x) \tag{21}$$

The two rules in line (11) ensure that all unary and binary facts in the input dataset are encoded as facts of the form $U_i(a)$ and $U_j(f(a,b))$; thus, when these are further transformed into a (Col,δ)-graph, the vectors labelling vertices v^a and $v^{f(a,b)}$ encode all input facts of the form $A_i(a)$ and $R_j(a,b)$ for $i \in \{1,\ldots,\varepsilon\}$ and $j \in \{\varepsilon+1,\ldots,\delta\}$, respectively. The remaining rules encode the adjacency relationships between terms: colour c_1 connects terms of the form $f(a,b)$ and a, colour c_2 connects terms of the form $f(a,b)$ and b, colour c_3 connects terms of the form $f(a,b)$ and $f(b,a)$, and colour c_4 connects terms of the form a and b that occur jointly in a binary fact.

Program P_{dec} capturing the decoder contains the following rules instantiated for each $i \in \{1,\ldots,\varepsilon\}$ and each $j \in \{\varepsilon+1,\ldots,\delta\}$. Intuitively, these rules just 'read off' the facts from the labels of vertices of the form v^a and $v^{f(a,b)}$.

$$U_i(x) \to A_i(x) \qquad U_j(f(x,y)) \to R_j(x,y) \tag{22}$$

Clearly, for each dataset D, the graph obtained by applying the encoding from our paper [25] outlined above is isomorphic to the graph obtained by applying the canonical encoding from Definition 3 to $T_{P_{\mathsf{enc}}}(D)$; moreover, the same can be said about the decoder. Thus, for each monotonic max GNN $\mathcal{N}$, the composition $T_{P_{\mathsf{dec}}}(T_{\mathcal{N}}(T_{P_{\mathsf{enc}}}(D)))$ coincides with applying to D the end-to-end transformation induced by $\mathcal{N}$ and the (non-canonical) encoding/decoding scheme from [25]. Furthermore, we can unfold P_{dec} with the rules of the program equivalent to $\mathcal{N}$ and P_{enc}, and the result is a Datalog program where rules are of the form $C_x \to A(x)$ or $C_x \wedge B_{x,y} \wedge C_y \to R(x,y)$, where C_x and C_y are $(L,|\mathsf{Col}|\cdot\delta_{\mathcal{N}})$-tree-like conjunctions for x and y, respectively, with no variables in common, and $B_{x,y}$ is a nonempty constant-free conjunction of binary atoms of the form $R_i(x,y)$ or $R_i(y,x)$ [25]. These rules describe the expressive power of the transformation.

6. Evaluation

We have implemented our monotonic max GNN model using Python 3.8.5 and Pytorch Geometric v1.7.1. Our implementation supports the canonical encoding/decoding scheme as well as that from Section 5. We next describe our empirical evaluation of the

Table 1. Number of facts for each benchmark and phase (training, validation, and testing)

	FB15K-237				NELL-995				WN18RR			
	v1	v2	v3	v4	v1	v2	v3	v4	v1	v2	v3	v4
Training	4,245	9,739	17,986	27,203	4,687	8,219	16,393	7,546	5,410	15,262	25,901	7,940
Validation	489	1,166	2,194	3,352	414	922	1,851	876	630	1,838	3,097	934
Testing	2,198	4,623	8,271	13,138	933	5,062	8,857	7,804	1,806	4,452	6,932	13,763

monotonic max GNN model using benchmarks for knowledge graph completion, where we have compared its classification performance with that of other models. All experiments discussed in this section have been performed on a MacBook Pro equipped with the M2 processor and 8GB of RAM, running macOS Ventura 13.3.

Benchmarks Our evaluation is focused on the task of knowledge graph (KG) completion: the problem of extending a dataset D over unary and binary predicates (i.e., a KG) to its complete version D' by adding missing facts. As a classification problem, the aim of KG completion is to learn a Boolean function $f(\cdot,\cdot)$ that takes a dataset D and a fact α over a fixed set of unary and binary predicates such that $f(D,\alpha)$ returns *true* if and only if $\alpha \in D'$. We focus on the *inductive* variant of this problem, where the test dataset may mention constants not occurring in the training or validation datasets (but all predicates in the test dataset are the same as in the training dataset). Inductive KG completion is more challenging than its *transductive* variant [30], where all constants mentioned in the test dataset also occur in the training dataset.

We used the 12 inductive KG completion benchmarks by Teru et al. [16], which are based on the FB15K-237 [30], NELL-995 [31], and WN18RR [32] datasets; each of the datasets are used in 4 benchmarks, and we refer to them by XXX.vi, where XXX is the dataset name, and $i \in \{1,\ldots,4\}$. Each benchmark provides disjoint datasets $\mathcal{T}$, $\mathcal{V}$, and $\mathcal{S}$ for training, validation, and testing, respectively. The benchmarks' statistics are presented in Table 1. Each benchmark provides a method for randomly splitting its testing dataset $\mathcal{S}$ into the incomplete dataset $\mathcal{S}_I$ and the set $\mathcal{S}_C$ of additional facts that should hold in the completion of $\mathcal{S}_I$. For each fact $\alpha \in \mathcal{S}_C$, we used $(\mathcal{S}_I,\alpha)$ as a positive example for testing. Additionally, we randomly constructed $|\mathcal{S}_C|$ distinct facts $\beta_1,\ldots,\beta_n$ using the predicates of $\mathcal{S}_I$ satisfying $\beta_i \notin \mathcal{S}$, and we used each $(\mathcal{S}_I,\beta_i)$ as a negative example for testing. Sampling of negative test examples was necessary due to the large number of possible facts that are not present in $\mathcal{S}_C$, and random sampling ensures that our evaluation does not favour any specific method of constructing negative examples during training. We maintained an equal number of positive and negative examples to ensure a balance between precision and recall.

Evaluated Systems We considered both monotonic max GNNs, which we abbreviate as M-MGNNs in this section, and instances of the general GNN model described in Section 3.1 using sum aggregation with no other restrictions; these are a data-independent variant of the well-known R-GCN model [7]. We also considered two state-of-the-art rule-based approaches to KG completion.

- M-MGNN implements the dataset transformation induced by a monotonic max GNN with the encoding/decoding scheme described in Section 5. This scheme allows us to derive binary facts that are not in the input dataset, which is crucial for KG completion. Each GNN uses two layers, where the dimension of the middle layer is twice the size of the input layer, and the activation function is ReLU.

- R-GCN [7] is defined as M-MGNN, but using summation as aggregation function and imposing no restrictions on the sign of the weights in matrices $\mathbf{A}_\ell$ and $\mathbf{B}_\ell^c$. We use this model as a baseline to investigate whether the monotonicity requirements impact the performance of monotonic max GNNs on KG completion tasks.
- DRUM [33] learns an end-to-end differentiable model that, given a dataset D and a fact α, returns a score representing the likelihood of α belonging to the completion of D; predictions are then computed by applying a threshold to the score. Additionally, DRUM can also produce *chain rules* of the form $B_1(x_0,x_1) \wedge B_2(x_1,x_2) \wedge \cdots \wedge B_n(x_{n-1},x_n) \rightarrow H(x_0,x_n)$, each associated with a confidence score. These rules aim to explain the model's predictions symbolically; however, Wang et al. [34] showed that the produced rules are neither sound nor complete with respect to the model. Hence, the rules produced by DRUM generate only approximate explanations of the model's predictions.
- AnyBURL [35] uses path sampling to produce chain rules of a slightly more general form, where variables can be replaced with constants. As in DRUM, each produced rule is associated with a confidence score. To determine whether fact α belongs to the completion of D, AnyBURL applies all rules to D once, combines the confidence score of all rules that derive α, and applies a threshold to the result.

Training For each KG completion benchmark, we trained an instance of each of the four systems described above. All GNN models, including R-GCN, were trained as denoising autoencoders [36]. The training dataset $\mathcal{T}$ was first split randomly with a 9:1 ratio into an incomplete dataset $\mathcal{T}_I$ and a set $\mathcal{T}_C$ of facts that should hold in the completion of $\mathcal{T}_I$. To train GNN models, we used $(\mathcal{T}_I,\alpha)$ for each fact $\alpha \in \mathcal{T}_C$ as a positive example, and we obtained negative examples $(\mathcal{T}_I,\beta)$ by replacing the predicates of positive examples α to obtain new facts β not in $\mathcal{T}$. We used cross-entropy loss, and we trained our models using Adam optimisation with the standard learning rate (0.01) and weight decay (5×10^{-4}), and a maximum of $50,000$ epochs for training. We trained DRUM and AnyBURL using their (publicly available) code with their default configurations. To choose classification thresholds for the testing phase, we classified the negative and positive examples in the validation dataset using a range of thresholds ranging from 0.01 to 0.99, and we selected the threshold that maximised accuracy. Training times for all models were similar.

Evaluation Results For each system, we classified the positive and negative testing examples and calculated the precision, recall, accuracy, and F1 score using standard methods. Additionally, we computed the area under the precision–recall curve (AUC) by considering various classification thresholds. Table 2 shows the results of our evaluation. The performance of monotonic max GNNs is competitive with that of the baselines for most benchmarks. For example, M-MGNN provides the best accuracy and F1 score on eight and nine out of our 12 benchmarks, respectively. Interestingly, on 11 benchmarks, M-MGNN achieves a better F1 score than R-GCN, although the difference is typically small. This suggests that the monotonicity requirement does not negatively impact the performance of KG completion and can, in fact, function as a useful inductive bias.

Rule Extraction Experiments For each benchmark, we extracted the subset $P'_{\mathcal{N}} \subseteq P_{\mathcal{N}}$ of all non-redundant rules of $P_{\mathcal{N}}$ with at most two body atoms. The first two columns of Table 3 show the number of rules with 1 and 2 body atoms in each such $P'_{\mathcal{N}}$. We

Table 2. Results for M-MGNN (M), R-GCN (R), DRUM (D), and AnyBURL (A)

		Precision (%)				Recall (%)				Accuracy (%)				F1 Score				AUC			
		M	R	D	A	M	R	D	A	M	R	D	A	M	R	D	A	M	R	D	A
FB15K-237	v1	95.1	98.8	82.2	**100.0**	**58.0**	41.0	40.5	25.6	**77.5**	70.3	65.9	62.9	**72.0**	58.0	54.2	41.1	**75.4**	65.5	68.6	62.0
	v2	93.6	**100.0**	85.3	**100.0**	**66.5**	48.7	48.5	47.9	**81.0**	74.3	70.0	74.0	**77.8**	65.5	61.9	64.5	**79.8**	75.5	76.0	73.8
	v3	98.2	99.4	85.6	**100.0**	58.2	**71.4**	45.2	43.6	78.6	**85.6**	68.8	71.2	73.1	**83.1**	59.2	60.7	78.0	**87.5**	73.3	71.7
	v4	94.7	98.6	88.8	**100.0**	**70.3**	48.3	41.6	46.0	**83.2**	73.8	68.2	73.0	**80.7**	64.8	56.7	63.0	**81.0**	75.7	73.7	73.0
NELL-995	v1	87.6	**100.0**	94.7	97.5	**91.2**	17.6	18.0	77.0	**89.4**	58.9	58.5	87.5	**89.7**	30.0	30.3	86.0	**91.6**	59.9	52.6	85.7
	v2	**100.0**	99.0	80.7	**100.0**	42.1	41.4	41.2	**53.1**	71.0	70.5	65.7	**76.6**	59.2	58.4	54.5	**69.4**	65.2	69.4	74.6	**76.3**
	v3	47.8	80.0	85.8	**100.0**	**87.4**	42.1	45.6	47.3	46.0	65.8	69.0	**73.7**	61.8	55.1	59.6	**64.2**	**85.6**	64.3	75.3	69.3
	v4	89.7	97.3	80.3	**100.0**	**68.6**	46.3	26.8	44.3	**80.4**	72.5	60.1	72.2	**77.7**	62.8	40.2	61.4	81.3	**72.8**	67.1	71.6
WN18RR	v1	93.3	97.8	97.9	**99.1**	**92.1**	82.4	73.4	58.5	92.7	90.3	85.9	79.0	**92.7**	89.5	83.4	73.6	**93.9**	90.7	92.5	78.8
	v2	99.4	**100.0**	96.3	**100.0**	**84.4**	81.7	69.8	75.7	**92.0**	90.9	83.6	87.9	**91.3**	89.9	80.9	86.2	88.2	**90.0**	87.4	59.8
	v3	**99.7**	98.4	91.3	**99.7**	**59.9**	58.3	59.7	48.4	**79.9**	78.7	77.0	74.1	**74.9**	73.2	72.2	65.2	69.3	73.2	**85.2**	60.6
	v4	97.9	98.6	98.3	**99.9**	**84.7**	81.9	65.6	71.6	**91.5**	90.3	82.2	85.8	**90.8**	89.4	78.7	83.4	88.3	88.4	**93.9**	59.0

Table 3. Rules of $P'_{\mathcal{N}}$ extracted with 1 atom, 2 atoms, and to explain 10 arbitrary facts

Benchmark		# Rules in $P'_{\mathcal{N}}$ with 1 body atom	# Rules in $P'_{\mathcal{N}}$ with 2 body atoms	# Body atoms per explanatory rule (median)
FB15K-237	v1	2,102	41,341	7
	v2	3,370	27,900	4
	v3	3,199	42,590	6
	v4	8,464	82,003	12
NELL-995	v1	149	215	1
	v2	1,784	3,087	4
	v3	2,308	5,085	4
	v4	1,308	4,348	4
WN18RR	v1	19	3	1
	v2	22	35	1
	v3	23	19	1
	v4	20	54	1

analysed $P'_{\mathcal{N}}$ manually and noticed that our transformation was able to learn numerous sound rules such as symmetry (e.g., $\mathit{sibling}(x,y) \rightarrow \mathit{sibling}(y,x)$ on FB15K-237), inverse relations (e.g., $\mathit{capitalOfArea}(x,y) \rightarrow \mathit{areaHasCapital}(y,x)$ on FB15K-237), and relationship subsumption (e.g., $\mathit{athleteLedSportsTeam}(x,y) \rightarrow \mathit{athletePlayedForTeam}(x,y)$ on NELL-995).

Furthermore, for each of the benchmarks, we sampled ten derived facts, and for each one we produced a rule that explained the derivation using an optimised version of Algorithm 1. The last column of Table 3 shows the median of the lengths of the ten rules extracted to justify the ten facts from each benchmark. Rules with a single body atom were common and corresponded to symmetry rules, such as the rules $\mathit{collaboratesWith}(x,y) \rightarrow \mathit{collaboratesWith}(y,x)$ and $\mathit{seeAlso}(x,y) \rightarrow \mathit{seeAlso}(y,x)$ produced on NELL-995 and WN18RR, respectively. The low median values for rule length offer evidence that we can extract simple and understandable rules in practice.

7. Related Work

Rule Extraction from Neural Networks There are two types of techniques for extracting rules from neural models that operate on relational data. Systems in the first category learn a neural model using training data, and then extract rules from the learned model. Early systems of this kind focused on extracting propositional (i.e., variable-free) rules from feed-forward neural networks [37]. Neural-LP [38] is a prominent example of a modern system of this kind, and it is a precursor of DRUM [33]. In Neural-LP, DRUM, and several recent approaches [39,40], the weights of the model are learned using Recurrent Neural Networks, and the extracted rules are chain rules as outlined in Section 6. Neural-LP has also been extended to learn rules with counting [41]. Other approaches in this first category extract Datalog rules (typically chain rules) from models based on reinforcement learning [31,42], dynamic neural module networks [43,44], or graph embeddings [45,46]. Beyond chain rules, Ferreira et al. [47] extract rules expressed as axioms in *description logics*—a popular KR formalism—from feed-forward neural networks for image classification. A limitation of these approaches is that the formal relationship between a model and the rules extracted from it is usually left unspecified. As a result, the predictions made by the model can differ in principle (and often in practice, as shown by Tena Cucala et al. [48] and Wang et al. [34]) from the result of applying the rules.

Systems in the second category, often called *rule-mining* systems, represent training data as a graph and identify frequent patterns of paths that are represented as rules. They use heuristics to estimate the quality of the extracted rules, but they do not train a neural model and they provide no formal guarantees about their output. AMIE+ [49] and AnyBURL [35] are prominent examples of this approach, and many similar approaches have been proposed recently [50,51].

Similarly to our work, techniques for neural learning of monotonic functions on the ordering of real numbers [52,53,54] also rely on nonnegative matrices and monotonic activation functions. We, however, focus on learning monotonic functions on the ordering induced by the existence of homomorphisms between datasets.

Inductive Logic Programming The techniques listed above can be used to automatically learn logical rules from training data. *Inductive Logic Programming (ILP)* is an alternative approach to rule learning, where rules are generated from a dataset and a set of examples of positive and negative inferences so that the application of the generated rules produces all positive and no negative examples [55,56]. Standard ILP techniques satisfy all examples *exactly* and, as a result, are intolerant to noise: small inconsistencies in the input examples can significantly affect the quality of the produced rules [57]. This limitation also applies to more recent rule learning approaches [58,59,60]. Other recent ILP systems, such as ∂ILP [57], achieve robustness to noise by interpreting the ILP task as a binary classification problem and providing a differentiable implementation of deduction. Traditionally, these techniques focus on learning very expressive rules from small datasets, but their application to large datasets such as those involved in KG completion has not been thoroughly studied.

Explanation and Formal Verification for GNNs Existing methods for explaining the predictions of a GNN focus on identifying parts of the input graph that are most relevant to a given prediction [61,62,63]. These techniques are largely independent from the specifics of the model used. In contrast, we focus on a specific type of GNN; moreover, our explanations do not only identify a part of the input dataset that is relevant for a particular prediction, but also a sound rule responsible for making this prediction. Salzer and Lange [22] provide a method to verify well-known properties such as output reachability and adversarial robustness on GNNs where the maximum degree of input graphs is bounded. Wu et al. [64] translate parts of a GNN and the formal property to be verified into a system of linear equations and equations with ReLU, and then process them with highly optimised solvers, with no guarantee of completeness.

Expressive Power of GNNs Characterising the expressivity of ML models for data management has steadily gained importance, and computational logic has been widely used to this end. In a pioneering study, Barceló et al. [18] showed that each GNN-induced transformation expressible in first-order logic is equivalent to a concept query of the $\mathcal{ALCQ}$ description logic [19]. Huang et al. [20] proved an analogous result for a class of GNNs with a dedicated vertex and colour, Pflueger et al. [9] did so for a class of recurrent GNNs, as well as demonstrated that functions realised by all (non-recurrent) GNNs are precisely the functions invariant under partial counting bisimulations. Grohe [21] has recently shown that a graph query can be realised by a GNN from a class with mild restrictions if and only if it can be expressed in the guarded fragment of first-order logic with two variables and counting terms for the number of assignments satisfying a formula; Benedikt et al. [23] have shown that transformations realised by GNNs with bounded piece-wise linear activation functions correspond to formulas expressed in *Presburguer logic*, a language that is decidable but not comparable with first-order logic. Our Theorem 13 provides a tighter upper bound on the expressive power of monotonic max GNNs. Morris et al. [29] and Xu et al. [65] independently showed that GNNs can distinguish nodes distinguishable by a certain partial graph isomorphism test, while Sourek et al. [66] characterised the expressivity of GNNs using a hybrid language of Datalog rules annotated with tensors. Finally, Wang et al. [34] characterised the expressive power of DRUM models.

Encoding Logic Programs into Neural Networks Early approaches to neuro-symbolic reasoning focused on identifying classes of first-order rules for which the immediate consequence operator can be simulated by recurrent [67], fibring [68], or feed-forward networks [69]. However, their embedding methods are very different from ours: they transform a dataset into a vector of real numbers by encoding groups of facts as components of the vector. Certain neural-symbolic architectures can simulate the intuition of forward [70,44] and backwards chaining [43] of Horn clauses. Sadeghian et al. [33] show how programs of chain-like Datalog rules can be encoded into DRUM models. Recently, Dong et al. [70] presented a network architecture that simulates the application of arbitrary function-free first-order rules to a dataset; to this end, they use multilayer perceptrons to learn Boolean operations between ground atoms and combinatorial tensor calculus to simulate quantification. Although these approaches construct a model equivalent to a given program, they do not address the converse problem of extracting an equivalent program from a given model.

8. Conclusion and Future Work

We introduced a class of GNN-based transformations of datasets that mimic a round of application of Datalog rules. The predictions made by our transformations can be explained symbolically, and they can be successfully trained in practice. We see many avenues for future work. On the theoretical side, we shall develop extensions that capture more complex rules (e.g., transitivity), as well as non-monotonic extensions with negation or aggregation (including attention mechanisms). On the practical side, our current results show that, although extracting simple rules to explain single facts is practically feasible, extracting a full equivalent program from a GNN is not always so. We will approach this challenge by developing three different lines of research. First, we will study further optimisations of our rule extraction algorithms, for example, by introducing a heuristic-based exploration of the search space and by parallelising our implementation. Second, we will study mechanisms for simplifying a model that facilitate rule extraction and have minimal effect on its predictive accuracy. Third, we will produce new algorithms where the extracted rules *approximate* the model under some suitable and formally-defined notion of approximation, instead of being strictly equivalent to it.

References

[1] Lin Y, Liu Z, Sun M, Liu Y, Zhu X. Learning Entity and Relation Embeddings for Knowledge Graph Completion. In: Proc. AAAI. AAAI Press; 2015. p. 2181–2187.

[2] Portisch J, Paulheim H. The DLCC Node Classification Benchmark for Analyzing Knowledge Graph Embeddings. In: Proc. ISWC. Springer International Publishing; 2022. p. 592-609.

[3] Lukovnikov D, Fischer A, Lehmann J, Auer S. Neural Network-based Question Answering over Knowledge Graphs on Word and Character Level. In: Proc. WWW. International World Wide Web Conferences Steering Committee; 2017. p. 1211–1220.

[4] Wang X, He X, Cao Y, Liu M, Chua TS. KGAT: Knowledge Graph Attention Network for Recommendation. In: Proc. ACM SIGKDD. Association for Computing Machinery; 2019. p. 950–958.

[5] Abiteboul S, Hull R, Vianu V. Foundations of Databases. Reading, MA: Addison-Wesley; 1995.

[6] Wu L, Cui P, Pei J, Zhao L. Graph Neural Networks: Foundations, Frontiers, and Applications. Singapore: Springer; 2023.

[7] Schlichtkrull MS, Kipf TN, Bloem P, van den Berg R, Titov I, Welling M. Modeling Relational Data with Graph Convolutional Networks. In: Proc. ESWC. vol. 10843 of LNCS. Springer; 2018. p. 593-607.

[8] Pflueger M, Tena Cucala DJ, Kostylev EV. GNNQ: A Neuro-Symbolic Approach to Query Answering over Incomplete Knowledge Graphs. In: Proc. ISWC. vol. 13489 of Lecture Notes in Computer Science. Springer; 2022. p. 481-97.

[9] Pflueger M, Tena Cucala D, Kostylev EV. Recurrent Graph Neural Networks and Their Connections to Bisimulation and Logic. In: Proc. AAAI. AAAI Press; 2024. p. 14608-16.

[10] Liu S, Cuenca Grau B, Horrocks I, Kostylev EV. INDIGO: GNN-Based Inductive Knowledge Graph Completion Using Pair-Wise Encoding. In: Proc. NeurIPS; 2021. p. 2034-45.

[11] Ioannidis VN, Marques AG, Giannakis GB. A Recurrent Graph Neural Network for Multi-relational Data. In: Proc. ICASSP. IEEE; 2019. p. 8157-61.

[12] Qu M, Bengio Y, Tang J. GMNN: Graph Markov Neural Networks. In: Proc. ICML. vol. 97; 2019. p. 5241-50.

[13] Yang Z, Cohen WW, Salakhutdinov R. Revisiting Semi-Supervised Learning with Graph Embeddings. In: Proc. ICML. vol. 48 of JMLR Workshop and Conference Proceedings; 2016. p. 40-8.

[14] Kipf TN, Welling M. Semi-Supervised Classification with Graph Convolutional Networks. In: Proc. ICLR. OpenReview.net; 2017. .

[15] Zhang M, Chen Y. Link Prediction Based on Graph Neural Networks. In: Proc. NeurIPS; 2018. p. 5171-81.

[16] Teru KK, Denis E, Hamilton W. Inductive Relation Prediction by Subgraph Reasoning. In: Proc. ICML. vol. 119. PMLR; 2020. p. 9448-57.

[17] Tzimas T. Algorithmic Transparency and Explainability under EU Law. European Public Law. 2023;29(4):385-411.

[18] Barceló P, Kostylev EV, Monet M, Pérez J, Reutter JL, Silva JP. The Logical Expressiveness of Graph Neural Networks. In: Proc. ICLR. OpenReview.net; 2020. .

[19] Baader F, Calvanese D, McGuinness D, Nardi D, Patel-Schneider PF, editors. The Description Logic Handbook: Theory, Implementation and Applications. 2nd ed. Cambridge University Press; 2007.

[20] Huang X, Orth MAR, Ceylan İİ, Barceló P. A Theory of Link Prediction via Relational Weisfeiler-Leman. CoRR. 2023;abs/2302.02209.

[21] Grohe M. The Descriptive Complexity of Graph Neural Networks. In: Proc. LICS. IEEE; 2023. p. 1-14.
[22] Sälzer M, Lange M. Fundamental Limits in Formal Verification of Message-Passing Neural Networks. In: Proc. ICLR. OpenReview.net; 2023. .
[23] Benedikt M, Lu C, Motik B, Tan T. Decidability of Graph Neural Networks via Logical Characterizations. In: Proc. ICALP. vol. 297 of LIPIcs. Schloss Dagstuhl - Leibniz-Zentrum für Informatik; 2024. p. 127:1-127:20. Available from: https://doi.org/10.4230/LIPIcs.ICALP.2024.127.
[24] Nunn P, Sälzer M, Schwarzentruber F, Troquard N. A Logic for Reasoning About Aggregate-Combine Graph Neural Networks. CoRR. 2024;abs/2405.00205. Available from: https://doi.org/10.48550/arXiv.2405.00205.
[25] Tena Cucala D, Cuenca Grau B, Kostylev EV, Motik B. Explainable GNN-Based Models over Knowledge Graphs. In: Proc. ICLR; 2022. .
[26] Tena Cucala D, Cuenca Grau B, Motik B, Kostylev EV. On the Correspondence Between Monotonic Max-Sum GNNs and Datalog. In: Proc. KR; 2023. p. 658-67.
[27] Scarselli F, Gori M, Tsoi AC, Hagenbuchner M, Monfardini G. The Graph Neural Network Model. IEEE Transactions on Neural Networks. 2009;20:61-80.
[28] Tena Cucala D, Cuenca Grau B, Motik B, Kostylev EV. From Monotonic Graph Neural Networks to Datalog and Back: Expressive Power and Practical Applications. Currently under review.
[29] Morris C, Ritzert M, Fey M, Hamilton WL, Lenssen JE, Rattan G, et al. Weisfeiler and Leman Go Neural: Higher-Order Graph Neural Networks. In: Proc. AAAI. AAAI Press; 2019. p. 4602-9.
[30] Bordes A, Usunier N, García-Durán A, Weston J, Yakhnenko O. Translating Embeddings for Modeling Multi-relational Data. In: Proc. NeurIPS; 2013. p. 2787-95.
[31] Xiong W, Hoang T, Wang WY. DeepPath: A Reinforcement Learning Method for Knowledge Graph Reasoning. In: Proc. EMNLP. Association for Computational Linguistics; 2017. p. 564-73.
[32] Dettmers T, Minervini P, Stenetorp P, Riedel S. Convolutional 2D Knowledge Graph Embeddings. In: Proc. AAAI. AAAI Press; 2018. p. 1811-8.
[33] Sadeghian A, Armandpour M, Ding P, Wang DZ. DRUM: End-To-End Differentiable Rule Mining On Knowledge Graphs. In: Proc. NeurIPS; 2019. p. 15321-31.
[34] Wang X, Cucala DJT, Grau BC, Horrocks I. Faithful Rule Extraction for Differentiable Rule Learning Models. In: Proc. ICLR; 2024. .
[35] Meilicke C, Chekol MW, Ruffinelli D, Stuckenschmidt H. Anytime Bottom-Up Rule Learning for Knowledge Graph Completion. In: Proc. IJCAI. AAAI Press; 2019. p. 3137-43.
[36] Vincent P, Larochelle H, Lajoie I, Bengio Y, Manzagol PA, Bottou L. Stacked denoising autoencoders: Learning useful representations in a deep network with a local denoising criterion. J of Machine Learning Res. 2010;11(12).
[37] Andrews R, Diederich J, Tickle AB. Survey and Critique of Techniques for Extracting Rules from Trained Artificial Neural Networks. Knowl Based Syst. 1995;8(6):373-89.
[38] Yang F, Yang Z, Cohen WW. Differentiable Learning of Logical Rules for Knowledge Base Reasoning. In: Proc. NeurIPS; 2017. p. 2319-28.
[39] Liu T, Lv Q, Wang J, Yang S, Chen H. Learning Rule-Induced Subgraph Representations for Inductive Relation Prediction. In: Proc. NeurIPS. vol. 36. Curran Associates, Inc.; 2023. p. 3517-35.
[40] Qu M, Chen J, Xhonneux LPAC, Bengio Y, Tang J. RNNLogic: Learning Logic Rules for Reasoning on Knowledge Graphs. In: Proc. ICLR. Virtual Event, Austria; 2021. .
[41] Wang P, Stepanova D, Domokos C, Kolter JZ. Differentiable learning of numerical rules in knowledge graphs. In: Proc. ICLR. OpenReview.net; 2020. .
[42] Das R, Dhuliawala S, Zaheer M, Vilnis L, Durugkar I, Krishnamurthy A, et al. Go for a Walk and Arrive at the Answer: Reasoning Over Paths in Knowledge Bases using Reinforcement Learning. In: Proc. ICLR. OpenReview.net; 2018. .
[43] Rocktäschel T, Riedel S. End-to-end Differentiable Proving. In: Proc. NeurIPS; 2017. p. 3788-800.
[44] Campero A, Pareja A, Klinger T, Tenenbaum J, Riedel S. Logical Rule Induction and Theory Learning Using Neural Theorem Proving. CoRR. 2018;abs/1809.02193.
[45] Omran PG, Wang K, Wang Z. Scalable Rule Learning via Learning Representation. In: Proc. IJCAI; 2018. p. 2149-55.
[46] Zhang W, Paudel B, Wang L, Chen J, Zhu H, Zhang W, et al. Iteratively Learning Embeddings and Rules for Knowledge Graph Reasoning. In: Proc. WWW; 2019. p. 2366-77.
[47] Ferreira J, de Sousa Ribeiro M, Gonçalves R, Leite J. Looking Inside the Black-Box: Logic-based Explanations for Neural Networks. In: Kern-Isberner G, Lakemeyer G, Meyer T, editors. Proc. KR;

2022. .
[48] Tena Cucala D, Cuenca Grau B, Motik B. Faithful Approaches to Rule Learning. In: Proc. KR; 2022. p. 484-93.
[49] Galárraga L, Teflioudi C, Hose K, Suchanek FM. Fast Rule Mining in Ontological Knowledge Bases with AMIE+. VLDB J. 2015;24(6):707-30.
[50] Ahmadi N, Huynh V, Meduri VV, Ortona S, Papotti P. Mining Expressive Rules in Knowledge Graphs. ACM J Data Inf Qual. 2020;12(2):8:1-8:27.
[51] Gu Y, Guan Y, Missier P. Efficient Rule Learning with Template Saturation for Knowledge Graph Completion. CoRR. 2020;abs/2003.06071.
[52] You S, Ding D, Canini KR, Pfeifer J, Gupta MR. Deep Lattice Networks and Partial Monotonic Functions. In: Proc. NeurIPS; 2017. p. 2981-9.
[53] Gupta MR, Cotter A, Pfeifer J, Voevodski K, Canini KR, Mangylov A, et al. Monotonic Calibrated Interpolated Look-Up Tables. Journal of Machine Learning Research. 2016;17:109:1-109:47.
[54] Wehenkel A, Louppe G. Unconstrained Monotonic Neural Networks. CoRR. 2019;abs/1908.05164.
[55] Muggleton S. Inductive Logic Programming. New Gener Comput. 1991;8(4):295-318.
[56] Cropper A, Dumancic S. Inductive Logic Programming At 30: A New Introduction. J Artif Intell Res. 2022;74:765-850.
[57] Evans R, Grefenstette E. Learning Explanatory Rules from Noisy Data. JAIR. 2018;61:1-64.
[58] Cropper A, Muggleton SH. Logical Minimisation of Meta-Rules Within Meta-Interpretive Learning. In: Proc. ILP. vol. 9046 of LNCS. Springer; 2014. p. 62-75.
[59] Si X, Raghothaman M, Heo K, Naik M. Synthesizing Datalog Programs using Numerical Relaxation. In: Proc. IJCAI. AAAI Press; 2019. p. 6117-24.
[60] Raghothaman M, Mendelson J, Zhao D, Naik M, Scholz B. Provenance-Guided Synthesis of Datalog Programs. Proc ACM Program Lang. 2020;4(62):1-27.
[61] Ying Z, Bourgeois D, You J, Zitnik M, Leskovec J. GNNExplainer: Generating Explanations for Graph Neural Networks. In: Proc. NeurIPS; 2019. p. 9240-51.
[62] Luo D, Cheng W, Xu D, Yu W, Zong B, Chen H, et al. Parameterized Explainer for Graph Neural Network. In: Proc. NeurIPS; 2020. .
[63] Lin W, Lan H, Li B. Generative Causal Explanations for Graph Neural Networks. In: Proc. ICML. vol. 139; 2021. p. 6666-79.
[64] Wu H, Ozdemir A, Zeljić A, Irfan A, Julian KD, Gopinath D, et al. Parallelization Techniques for Verifying Neural Networks. 2020 Formal Methods in Computer Aided Design (FMCAD). 2020:128-37.
[65] Xu K, Hu W, Leskovec J, Jegelka S. How Powerful are Graph Neural Networks? In: Proc. ICLR. OpenReview.net; 2019. .
[66] Sourek G, Zelezný F, Kuzelka O. Beyond Graph Neural Networks with Lifted Relational Neural Networks. Mach Learn. 2021;110(7):1695-738.
[67] Hölldobler S, Kalinke Y, Störr HP. Approximating the Semantics of Logic Programs by Recurrent Neural Networks. Appl Intell. 1999;11(1):45-58.
[68] Bader S, d'Avila Garcez AS, Hitzler P. Computing First-Order Logic Programs by Fibring Artificial Neural Networks. In: Proc. FLAIRS; 2005. p. 314-9.
[69] Bader S, Hitzler P, Hölldobler S, Witzel A. A Fully Connectionist Model Generator for Covered First-Order Logic Programs. In: Proc. IJCAI; 2007. p. 666-71.
[70] Dong H, Mao J, Lin T, Wang C, Li L, Zhou D. Neural Logic Machines. In: Proc. ICLR. OpenReview.net; 2019. .

Handbook on Neurosymbolic AI and Knowledge Graphs
P. Hitzler et al. (Eds.)
IOS Press, 2025

doi:10.3233/FAIA250233

Individual CNN Hidden-Layer Neurons Are Good Concept Encoders

Abhilekha DALAL, [a] Rushrukh RAYAN, [a] Adrita BARUA, [a]
Samatha Ereshi AKKAMAHADEVI, [a] Md Kamruzzaman SARKER, [b]
Cara WIDMER, [c] and Pascal HITZLER, [a] and Eugene Y. VASSERMAN [a,1]
[a] *Kansas State University, Manhattan, KS, USA*
[b] *Bowie State University, Prince George's County, MD, USA*
[c] *Kairos Research, LLC, Dayton, OH, USA*

Abstract.
This work discusses some recent advances and continued limitations in explainable deep learning, leveraging neurosymbolic methods to identify human-understandable concepts which are "recognized" by machine models and drive their behaviors. Results suggest that models' hidden layers do encode information as discrete human-understandable concepts, and that the information is meaningful not just from the point of view of the model output, or even groups of hidden-layer neurons, but even down to individual neurons.

Keywords. Explainable AI, Concept Induction, Deep Learning, Convolutional Neural Network, Knowledge Graph, Large Language Model

1. Introduction

Explainable AI (XAI) is a crucial area of research and development in artificial intelligence that aims to make AI systems more transparent, understandable, and trustworthy [1]. As AI increasingly influences critical decisions in fields directly impacting human lives, the need for systems that can explain their reasoning becomes paramount. XAI provides insights into how AI models arrive at their predictions or decisions, enabling users to comprehend, trust, and verify the results. Explainable models help bridge the gap between complex neural network models (which often function as "black boxes") by providing human-understandable explanations of their internal behavior.

Researchers are exploring ways to make neural networks more explainable, either by designing models that generate explanations or by employing post-hoc explanation methods that analyze a trained network's behavior. A significant portion of current XAI research focuses on model-agnostic post-hoc algorithms [2]. These methods seek to provide insights into how pre-existing models generate predictions for any given input, without compromising accuracy. Techniques such as gradient-based saliency maps and perturbation-based methods have been widely adopted to identify key input features through explanation maps [3, 4]. However, the challenges associated with visualizing

[1] Corresponding Author

these maps and their susceptibility to adversarial attacks have prompted a shift toward alternative models [5].

2. Neuron Concept Labels

One promising direction within XAI involves the use of concept-based models [6], particularly within the framework of neurosymbolic AI [7]. *Concept induction* [8, 9, 10] focuses on identifying the concepts used by a neural network for a given input, as these can provide valuable insights into the network's decision-making process. By extracting relevant concepts and their correlations with respective individual neurons' activation, it is possible to generate explanations in logical or natural language that accurately reflect the network's "reasoning". These explicit representations of concepts or knowledge units not only make the models more interpretable but also enable symbolic reasoners to intervene and debug the network by modifying these concepts [11]. Despite advances in XAI, generating meaningful and context-specific concepts from input data remains a significant challenge. This process requires explanations that accurately depict a model's behavior while remaining comprehensible to humans [5, 6, 12].

2.1. Neuron Label Generation

Concept induction [8, 9, 10] is a model-agnostic, zero-shot technique meant to add explainability to arbitrary "black-box" deep neural network models. The approach automatically generates concepts from input data using a symbolic approach and assigns explanatory labels (or label conjunctions) to individual hidden-layer neurons by drawing upon a knowledge graph (e.g., an extract from Wikipedia [13]). Previous work by Sarker et al. proposed a post-hoc explainability strategy using publicly available structured knowledge to "bootstrap" concept induction [8]. Subsequently, Widmer et al. explored whether the resulting explanations "make sense" to humans [14] and found that they can indeed be used to explain data differentials in machine learning classifications, though human-generated explanations still tend to be superior.

While neurons could be labeled from a manually-compiled list of concepts that may be expected to appear in the input image set, using a general knowledge base saves us from many implicit assumptions that human annotators would make in generating concepts, such as excessive or insufficient label precision, incomplete concept coverage, and many other unknown and unknowable issues inherent in manual labeling. (Such issues may still occur due to the content of the background knowledge base, but a large and general knowledge corpus composed by many users should be more resilient than a small set of people creating non-reusable lists for the purpose of individual explainability experiments.) In general, concept induction can be performed using either provably correct [9] or heuristic [15] deduction.

More precisely, the ECII concept induction tool [15] was used to generate "label hypotheses" for hidden-layer neurons (the last dense layer) in a convolutional neural network (CNN) using an annotated image data set as input (ADE20K [16]), and those hypotheses were then tested using images retrieved from Google Images results for the concept label. (For example, a neuron with the label hypothesis "building" was tested on the images returned when searching for "building".) Neurons were only considered to have labels when their label hypotheses were confirmed [17, 18]. Occasionally, ECII would generate logical conjunctions of concepts, such as "edifice and skyscraper"; when this occurred, both concepts together (but not individually) were treated as that neuron's concept label, and hypothesis confirmation was performed by searching for both concepts together.

Large language models are an alternative method for generating label hypotheses, drawing upon their "common sense knowledge". A number of research efforts have compared concept induction-generated labels to those generated by LLMs [17, 19, 20]. Dalal et al. compared concept induction-generated neuron label hypotheses to those generated by GPT-4 [17]. The LLM was prompted to "Generate the top three classes of objects or general scenario that better represent what images in the positive set (P) have but the images in the negative set (N) do not" where P and N were object tags from the image sets — GPT-4 did not directly analyze any images. (Note that while the prompt asked for the top three, only one concept was selected to preserve consistency with the use of the ECII tool [15], where only the top concept or concept conjunction was used. Additional experiments may be required to resolve this ambiguity.)

2.2. *Explainable Explainability*

While human-generated explanations — manual annotations of images in the input set — remain superior for the purpose of human understanding, concepts derived from Large Language Models (LLMs) are more comprehensible to humans compared to those generated by ECII [14, 19], even while concept induction showed superior *accuracy* in labeling hidden neurons when compared to the GPT-4 LLM [17]. These results suggest that LLMs could be used in place of concept induction for identifying the high-level concepts to which hidden-layer neurons respond. The reasons for this are unclear; it may be due to the "common sense" knowledge which is captured by LLMs, or possibly because the background knowledge graph available for use with concept induction is more limited compared to LLM training sets. There is ongoing research on the feasibility of merging the best features of neurosymbolic reasoning and of LLMs for the purpose of generating high-quality explanations [19].

The use of LLMs to explain other black-box models comes with an interesting conundrum: how can we trust one "black-box" model to explain another? In other words, while the method may work from the point of view of providing reasonable and human-understandable explanations, we do not know whether it is reliable. Concept induction, on the other hand, is a formal process, with every explanation traceable to the background knowledge. Using concept induction for hidden neuron labeling implies that the system as a whole not only "bootstraps" explainability for arbitrary deep neural network (DNN) from a knowledge graph, but also that *the explainability system is itself explainable* and explanations are fully traceable to their original sources.

3. Mind the (Precision) Gap

The accuracy ("appropriateness") of neuron labels is confirmed via extensive statistical analysis, demonstrating that neurons were consistently activated when concepts in the input image matched the neurons' label(s) [17, 18]. This hypothesis confirmation step used the *extent* to which a neuron was activated, i.e., its activation value: neurons activated beyond a particular threshold were considered "sufficiently" activated for confirmation. The authors arbitrarily set the hypothesis acceptance threshold to a neuron activation of at least 80% [17, 18] and non-target activation of at most 20%. Labeled neurons were not activated (above an 80% threshold) by any other (non-label) concept in the knowledge graph. Under this constraint, neuron concept labels were found to exhibit consistently high recall (between 0.81 and 1) but their precision was highly variable (between 0.15 and 0.85) [17, 18] — while neurons were very likely to be activated if their labeled concept was present in the input, neurons were also frequently activated even if their label was absent from the input.

Concept induction itself is a separate process from the pre-trained model's inference process (hence its ability to explain models which have already been trained). It uses a set of images activating a neuron, and another set of images not activating the same neuron, to identify relevant concepts for the respective neuron but does not use neuron's activation values as inputs. The non-overlapping nature with respect to neurons' activation between the explainer and the explainee processes require verification of presence of the concepts in the hidden layer neurons' activation space. To that extent, Concept Activation Vector (CAV) [21] and Concept Activation Region (CAR) [22] were used to measure presence of concepts in the hidden layer activation space in [18] and results indicate that indeed concepts identified using concept induction were adequately present in hidden layer activation space.

3.1. Concept Ranking and Partial Activation

The findings above demonstrate that neuron labels do serve as useful tools to explain the behavior of the overall model in terms of final classification results. When we ask the two questions: 1. To what extent a neuron activates when target label is present? and 2. To what extent a neuron unit activates when target label is not present? we see that a higher value of the former and considerably lower value of the latter indicate that neurons are *useful* as concept encoders.

A more detailed look at "spurious" neuron activation reveals an incomplete, but still interesting insight: a number of images retrieved from Google Images that were responsible for spurious activation were indirect indicators of concept relevance to the source image while the concept itself was not present [17]. For example, the "crosswalk" concept was activated by an image that shows a traffic sign indicated a crosswalk, without the crosswalk itself appearing in the image. We can interpret this as an ambiguity in both human image annotation and human intention when searching Google Images (and this how Google Images treats such ambiguity): it is a reasonable assumption that a human searching for images of a crosswalk may in fact be looking for images that show crosswalk signage, but this assumption does not hold for concept identification. This finding further suggests that Google Images, a human-targeted search engine, may not be a completely appropriate source of test images for concept identification especially if the deep learning model's use case necessitates a crisp separation of concepts as explanations across its neurons. Concept induction's concept labeling to neurons is rather introduced as a promising white-box XAI method and is not to be considered *complete*. To further examine the possible reasons for non-target/spurious neuron activation, manual inspection into non-target activation at extreme low thresholds (any non-zero activation) may reveal additional insights.

The extent of uncertainty regarding the explanatory power of each neuron's activation can be conveyed directly to the system user: the *measured difference* between how frequently a neuron activates for target images (consistent with its label) versus non-target images (not expressed by the label) can be directly shown to the system user. A straight-forward way is to show the labels of all neurons (that were activated beyond a certain threshold), ranked by their measured uncertainty [23, 24, 25]. While this allows the user to make an informed final choice of whether or not to believe a given explanation, given a large amount of information that would normally be hidden inside the system, it is overall an unsatisfying solution, as it appears to provide possible, but not definitive, explanations.

In follow-up work, the authors considered a 60% threshold (i.e., achieving 60% of the max activation value for a given neuron unit), very few images not containing the target label activated the respective neuron [23]. For example, only 3.8% of all images which do not contain "central reservation" activated the neuron which was labeled with "central reservation". When the threshold is 0%, which is a very lenient definition of activation, allowing even infinitesimal activation of a neuron with respect to the max activation it can achieve, more non-target concepts were "purposefully" allowed to activate the neuron (which is similar to performing a stress test). With this low threshold, non-label concepts activate labeled neurons, but as the threshold was increased, the degree of non-label concepts activating the neurons decreased rapidly were almost absent above 60% [23].

3.2. Surprising Findings

Information in a neural network is, intuitively, collectively encoded by the entire machine model, so examining the behavior of individual neurons in depth does not initially appear as a promising investigative avenue. *Counter-intuitively*, the behavior of individual hidden-layer neurons plays an important role in explaining the behavior of the deep neural network as a whole. While not captured in model output, the *level of activation* of individual neurons may shed light on more precise explanations. Dalal et al. had previously examined whether or not neurons had been activated beyond a particular but arbitrarily-chosen threshold (specifically 80%) [17, 18], but alternative choices, derived by studying the *extent* to which a neuron is activated for particular inputs, may conceal the key to improved explainability [23]. Setting neuron activation thresholds at 60% dramatically shrinks the perception-recall gap, now achieving ≥ 0.80 recall with precision of ≥ 0.85 [23]. This implies that individual neurons at the hidden layer are excellent "concept encoders" — not only does a neuron respond to the "appropriate" concept in the input more than 80% of the time, but also that *there is no concept in the background knowledge graph* that reliably activates the neuron.

Similar to issues with training versus testing images for "crosswalk" (see Section 3.1) is the inconsistent labeling of "skyscraper", "edifice", and "building". One might assume that every skyscraper is a building, and some skyscrapers are edifices, and yet "edifice and skyscraper" appears as neuron labels but there are no instances of "building and skyscraper" [17, 18]. It is not possible to determine the reason without reexamining the annotations of the training set; perhaps human annotators assumed that the fact that every skyscraper is a building to be obvious.

Another counter-intuitive finding is that identifying concepts in an image via the behavior of multiple hidden-layer neurons, i.e., *neuron ensembles*, does not always yield better results than that of individual neurons [23, 26]. Neurons activated by the same concept were analyzed as all possible combinations (i.e., every pair, every triplet, etc.), and while some combinations (taken together) yield better precision and recall for the presence of a concept in the input image, some combinations performed worse than other combinations, and even *worse than some individual neurons within those combinations* on either precision or recall, but rarely both. This finding raises a question for future work: if individual neurons are used to identify concepts in the input, could neuron ensembles be used to improve their the precision or the recall of individual neurons?

4. Discussion and Limitations

When using background knowledge to generate concepts, the source of that background knowledge has historically been one of convenience as suitable (large-scale) datasets are not available [13, 27, 28]. It is conceivable, though unlikely, that there exist significant gaps in the background knowledge, leading to incomplete, imprecise, or otherwise biased explanations which are based on concept induction. Moreover, individual neuron activations may be the result of even less clearly-understood processes, encoding more holistic combinations of elements found within images, so much so that the data sets of convenience are limited not by their captured concepts but by the lack of clear *expressibility* of certain concepts in some (or all) human languages. Lacking a way to communicate these concepts ourselves may render the answers to such questions unknowable.

Concluding that individual neurons may respond to specific concepts is consistent with the behavior of high-level neurons in the visual cortex [29, 30, 31]. If we continue to expect analogous behavior, then it is conceivable — if not likely — that neuron activations are caused not (only) by the positioning of (types of) objects, but also by other image features such as prevalence, (relative) positioning of lines or round shapes [32], contrasts across the image, colors, object distribution and positioning, and almost any other conceivable relationship(s). Much additional work is needed on various scales of neural networks (the work referenced above is limited to CNNs with only 64 neurons in the final dense layer [17, 18, 23, 26]). The results are theoretically applicable to other DNNs but this would need to be experimentally confirmed, especially in natural language processing (NLP) systems.

Despite extensive past and ongoing work, our knowledge of the behavior of even simple neural networks is dwarfed by what we do not yet know. As we work toward XAI, we run into fundamental limits of explainability in a way that eludes our current concept encoding capabilities (e.g., natural language). Emerging large language models offer additional challenges due to their massive scale and more complex architectures; existing explainability solutions will need to grow and evolve to catch up to large language models, and significant efficiency gains will be required [15] if current approaches are to scale to even small modern language models.

Acknowledgments The authors acknowledge partial funding under National Science Foundation grants 2119753 and 2333782, and by the Kansas State University Game-changing Research Initiative Program (GRIP).

References

[1] Angelov PP, Soares EA, Jiang R, Arnold NI, Atkinson PM. Explainable artificial intelligence: an analytical review. Wiley Interdisciplinary Reviews: Data Mining and Knowledge Discovery. 2021;11(5):e1424.

[2] Slack D, Hilgard A, Singh S, Lakkaraju H. Reliable post hoc explanations: Modeling uncertainty in explainability. Advances in neural information processing systems. 2021;34:9391-404.

[3] Simonyan K, Vedaldi A, Zisserman A. Deep inside convolutional networks: visualising image classification models and saliency maps. In: Proceedings of the International Conference on Learning Representations (ICLR). ICLR; 2014. .

[4] Ivanovs M, Kadikis R, Ozols K. Perturbation-based methods for explaining deep neural networks: A survey. Pattern Recognition Letters. 2021;150:228-34.

[5] Das A, Rad P. Opportunities and challenges in explainable artificial intelligence (XAI): A survey. arXiv preprint arXiv:200611371. 2020.

[6] Gupta A, Narayanan P. A survey on Concept-based Approaches For Model Improvement. arXiv preprint arXiv:240314566. 2024.

[7] Campagner A, Cabitza F. Back to the feature: A neural-symbolic perspective on explainable AI. In: Machine Learning and Knowledge Extraction: International Cross-Domain Conference (CD-MAKE). Springer; 2020. p. 39-55.

[8] Sarker MK, Xie N, Doran D, Raymer ML, Hitzler P. Explaining Trained Neural Networks with Semantic Web Technologies: First Steps. In: Besold TR, d'Avila Garcez AS, Noble I, editors. Proceedings of the Twelfth International Workshop on Neural-Symbolic Learning and Reasoning (NeSy). vol. 2003 of CEUR Workshop Proceedings. CEUR-WS.org; 2017. Available from: https://ceur-ws.org/Vol-2003/NeSy17_paper4.pdf.

[9] Lehmann J, Hitzler P. Concept learning in description logics using refinement operators. Mach Learn. 2010;78(1-2):203-50.

[10] Lehmann J, Völker J. Perspectives on Ontology Learning. vol. 18 of Studies on the Semantic Web. IOS Press; 2014. Available from: https://doi.org/10.3233/978-1-61499-379-7-i.

[11] Koh PW, Nguyen T, Tang YS, Mussmann S, Pierson E, Kim B, et al. Concept bottleneck models. In: International conference on machine learning. PMLR; 2020. p. 5338-48.

[12] Adadi A, Berrada M. Peeking inside the black-box: A survey on explainable artificial intelligence (XAI). IEEE Access. 2018;6:52138-60.

[13] Sarker MK, Schwartz J, Hitzler P, Zhou L, Nadella S, Minnery BS, et al. Wikipedia Knowledge Graph for Explainable AI. In: Iberoamerican Conference on Knowledge Graphs and Semantic Web; 2020. p. 72-87. Available from: https://api.semanticscholar.org/CorpusID:225081087.

[14] Widmer CL, Sarker MK, Nadella S, Fiechter J, Juvina I, Minnery B, et al. Towards human-compatible XAI: Explaining data differentials with concept induction over background knowledge. Journal of Web Semantics. 2023;79.

[15] Sarker MK, Hitzler P. Efficient Concept Induction for Description Logics. In: The Thirty-Third AAAI Conference on Artificial Intelligence (AAAI) The Thirty-First Innovative Applications of Artificial Intelligence Conference (IAAI), The Ninth AAAI Symposium on Educational Advances in Artificial Intelligence (EAAI). AAAI Press; 2019. p. 3036-43.

[16] Zhou B, Zhao H, Puig X, Xiao T, Fidler S, Barriuso A, et al. Semantic understanding of scenes through the ADE20K dataset. International Journal of Computer Vision. 2019;127(3):302-21.

[17] Dalal A, Rayan R, Barua A, Vasserman EY, Sarker MK, Hitzler P. On the Value of Labeled Data and Symbolic Methods for Hidden Neuron Activation Analysis. In: Proceedings of the International Workshop on Neural-Symbolic Learning and Reasoning (NeSy); 2024. To appear.

[18] Dalal A, Rayan R, Barua A, Vasserman EY, Sarker MK, Hitzler P. On the Value of Labeled Data and Symbolic Methods for Hidden Neuron Activation Analysis. arXiv preprint arXiv:240413567. 2024.

[19] Barua A, Widmer C, Hitzler P. Concept Induction using LLMs: A user experiment for assessment. In: Proceedings of the International Workshop on Neural-Symbolic Learning and Reasoning (NeSy); 2024. To appear.

[20] Achiam J, Adler S, Agarwal S, Ahmad L, Akkaya I, Aleman FL, et al. GPT-4 technical report. arXiv preprint arXiv:230308774. 2023.

[21] Kim B, Wattenberg M, Gilmer J, Cai CJ, Wexler J, Viégas FB, et al. Interpretability Beyond Feature Attribution: Quantitative Testing with Concept Activation Vectors (TCAV). In: Dy JG, Krause A, editors. Proceedings of the International Conference on Machine Learning (ICML). vol. 80 of Proceedings of Machine Learning Research. PMLR; 2018. p. 2673-82. Available from: http://proceedings.mlr.press/v80/kim18d.html.

[22] Crabbé J, van der Schaar M. Concept Activation Regions: A Generalized Framework For Concept-Based Explanations. In: Koyejo S, Mohamed S, Agarwal A, Belgrave D, Cho K, Oh A, editors. Advances in Neural Information Processing Systems. vol. 35. Curran Associates, Inc.; 2022. p. 2590-607.

[23] Dalal A, Rayan R, Hitzler P. Error-margin Analysis for Hidden Neuron Activation Labels. In: Proceedings of the International Workshop on Neural-Symbolic Learning and Reasoning (NeSy); 2024. To appear.

[24] Dalal A, Hitzler P. ConceptLens: from Pixels to Understanding;. Accessed: 2024-08-20. https://conceptlens.streamlit.app/Explore_ConceptLens.

[25] Akkamahadevi SE, Dalal A, Hitzler P. Automating CNN Neuron Interpretation using Concept Induction. In: International Semantic Web Conference (ISWC) Posters and Demos. CEUR Workshop Proceedings. CEUR-WS.org; 2024. To appear.

[26] Dalal A, Rayan R, Hitzler P. Error-margin Analysis for Hidden Neuron Activation Labels. arXiv preprint arXiv:240509580. 2024.

[27] Widmer CL, Sarker MK, Nadella S, Fiechter J, Juvina I, Minnery B, et al. Towards human-compatible XAI: Explaining data differentials with concept induction over background knowledge. Journal of Web Semantics. 2023;79:100807. Available from: https://www.sciencedirect.com/science/article/pii/S1570826823000367.

[28] Sarker MK, Schwartz J, Hitzler P, Zhou L, Nadella S, Minnery BS, et al. Wikipedia Knowledge Graph for Explainable AI. In: Villazón-Terrazas B, Ortiz-Rodríguez F, Tiwari SM, Shandilya SK, editors. Proceedings of the Knowledge Graphs and Semantic Web Second Iberoamerican Conference and First Indo-American Conference (KGSWC). vol. 1232 of Communications in Computer and Information Science. Springer; 2020. p. 72-87.

[29] Grill-Spector K, Malach R. The human visual cortex. Annual Review of Neuroscience. 2004;27(Volume 27, 2004):649-77. Available from: https://www.annualreviews.org/content/journals/10.1146/annurev.neuro.27.070203.144220.

[30] Perrett DI, Mistlin AJ, Chitty AJ. Visual neurones responsive to faces. Trends in Neurosciences. 1987;10(9):358-64. Available from: https://doi.org/10.1016/0166-2236(87)90071-3.

[31] Rolls ET, Burton MJ, Mora F. Hypothalamic neuronal responses associated with the sight of food. Brain Research. 1976;111(1):53-66. Available from: https://www.sciencedirect.com/science/article/pii/0006899376910489.

[32] de Haas B, Schwarzkopf DS, Alvarez I, Lawson RP, Henriksson L, Kriegeskorte N, et al. Perception and Processing of Faces in the Human Brain Is Tuned to Typical Feature Locations. The Journal of neuroscience: The official journal of the Society for Neuroscience. 2016;36(36):9289-302.

Handbook on Neurosymbolic AI and Knowledge Graphs
P. Hitzler et al. (Eds.)
IOS Press, 2025

doi:10.3233/FAIA250234

Knowledge-Augmented Explainable and Interpretable Learning for Anomaly Detection and Diagnosis

Martin ATZMUELLER [a,b], Tim BOHNE [b] Patricia WINDLER [b]
[a] *Semantic Information Systems Group, Osnabrück University, Wachsbleiche 27, 49090 Osnabrück, Germany*
[b] *German Research Center for Artificial Intelligence (DFKI), Hamburger Str. 24, 49084 Osnabrück, Germany*

Abstract. Knowledge-augmented learning enables the combination of knowledge-based and data-driven approaches. For anomaly detection and diagnosis, understandability is typically an important factor, especially in high-risk areas. Therefore, explainability and interpretability are also major criteria in such contexts. This chapter focuses on knowledge-augmented explainable and interpretable learning to enhance understandability, transparency and ultimately computational sensemaking. We exemplify different approaches and methods in the domains of anomaly detection and diagnosis – from comparatively simple interpretable methods towards more advanced neuro-symbolic approaches.

Keywords. Explainable Learning, Interpretable Modeling, Pattern Mining, Domain Knowledge, Neuro-Symbolic Learning, Hybrid Models

1. Introduction

In the context of complex systems, anomaly detection [1, 2] and diagnosis [3–7] are important tasks for gaining insight into the behavior of a system, for example to prevent critical situations or to address specific problems like faults or failures in technical systems. However, this does not only apply to technical systems [8–11], but also to biological systems [12–14] or the medical domain [15–17]. Here, with the ever-growing amount of collected data, we can investigate, analyze and interpret observed phenomena at considerably larger scale and in much more detail.

Particularly in prominent areas of artificial intelligence and machine learning, such as anomaly detection and diagnosis, there usually exists some knowledge which can be exploited for guiding and/or augmenting specific learning methods. Augmentation can take place at different levels, e. g., serving as a starting point for these models, providing constraints for them, or integrating specific hybrid models consisting of both data-driven as well as knowledge-based components. However, with the constantly growing amount of available data and accordingly refined models, e. g., from the field of machine learning, gaining insights into a system, model – or a decision made by those – becomes much more difficult due to its inherent complexity [18].

Hence, in many domains and applications an important goal is to enable human insight into the methods and/or models in order to ultimately allow for computational sensemaking [19]. In such cases, explainability and interpretability play a major role for making sense of the according systems, models and methods. In general, explainability and specifically the term explanation [20, 21] have been widely investigated in different disciplines. Providing answers to questions, it should support humans in their decision-making [22]. This is particularly relevant for complicated black box models being applied in sensitive application contexts like medicine, Industry 4.0, etc. (cf. [18]). While interpretability [23–27] and explainability [28–30] are often used synonymously, they can be distinguished in the following way: "Systems are interpretable if their operations can be understood by a human, either through introspection or through a produced explanation" [23], whereas "explainability is viewed as an active characteristic of a model or method generating an explanation" [29]. Thus, while interpretable methods are always explainable, explainable methods are not always interpretable, specifically if the inner mechanics of the system are not understandable by a human. In particular, rule-based and pattern-based methods, e. g., [24,31–34], have shown considerable impact and promise in this respect, since such models are directly interpretable and thus also explainable. In contrast, black box methods such as deep learning approaches typically require post-hoc methods, e. g., [35–38], for generating explanations, e. g., [39–41]. For the knowledge-augmented interpretable and explainable dimensions, there are a variety of methods that can be applied, e. g., ranging from simple (linear) models to more complex but interpretable pattern-based methods, and finally to deep-learning-based approaches. In the latter case, this specifically refers to neuro-symbolic approaches [42,42–44] whenever advanced deep learning methods are complemented by symbolic components, e. g., domain knowledge. This knowledge is typically provided via ontologies or knowledge graphs [45, 46], but can also refer to other forms. Thus, with such neuro-symbolic approaches it is possible to integrate rich data-driven methods with according knowledge-based representations, e. g., applying domain knowledge.

This chapter aims to provide a focused view on these topics by reviewing and discussing exemplary methods in this domain, specifically considering the articles [47, 48] for a targeted view on pattern mining in the context of anomaly detection, as well as [49–51] for learning scoring systems in the form of diagnostic scores, and a significantly adapted summary of the article [52], covering a neuro-symbolic approach for anomaly detection and diagnosis. Thus, we review simple knowledge representations such as diagnostic scores as well as interpretable pattern-based methods in combination with different forms of symbolic knowledge. Furthermore, we also look into a hybrid neuro-symbolic method integrating deep learning with symbolic knowledge.

The remainder of this chapter is structured as follows: Section 2 summarizes knowledge-augmented pattern mining and its application for anomaly detection. Next, Section 3 briefly reviews scoring systems, how to learn and refine them in a knowledge-augmented way, as well as an exemplary application in the medical domain. After that, Section 4 summarizes a neuro-symbolic approach for explainable diagnosis, exemplified in a technical diagnosis domain. Finally, Section 5 concludes with a summary and presents interesting directions for future research.

2. Knowledge-Augmented Pattern Mining for Anomaly Detection

In general, pattern mining provides a broadly applicable and powerful set of methods for exploratory data analysis, knowledge discovery, and computational sensemaking on complex data [19, 31, 51, 53, 54]. Exemplary methods include association rule mining [55], subgroup discovery [31, 56], exceptional model mining [31, 57, 58] as well as graph (pattern) mining [59–61]. In particular, whenever semi-automatic and interactive approaches can be provided, constraints and user interests can often be directly integrated [62–64]. An alternative and/or complementary approach is to inject domain knowledge into the pattern mining process. Here, first approaches for such an integration utilizing knowledge graphs – exploiting information formalized in ontologies and a set of instance data – have been proposed in the area of semantic data mining [65–68]. Furthermore, [47] presents a mixed-initiative approach for semantic feature engineering using a knowledge graph, which is constructed in a semi-automatic process. Here, the resulting features are then provided for data analysis. A similar approach is applied in [69]. Here, data from heterogeneous data sources is integrated into a knowledge graph, which then provides the basis for knowledge discovery.

In this chapter, we review and discuss approaches and an application use case for knowledge-augmented pattern mining [31,47,48], specifically focusing on subgroup discovery connected to domain knowledge formalized in knowledge graphs. Hence, we focus on an integrated approach, exploiting knowledge-based semantic structures, i. e., sets of knowledge components connected to a local pattern mining method. Exceptions and anomalies can then be detected via appropriate measures of interestingness.

2.1. Pattern Mining Using Subgroup Discovery

Subgroup discovery is a flexible approach for exploratory data analysis and knowledge discovery, enabling computational sensemaking on complex data. In its simplest form, subgroup discovery aims to detect relations between dependent (characterizing) variables and an independent target concept, e. g., comparing the share or the mean of a nominal/numeric target variable in the subgroup vs. the share or mean in the total population, respectively [31, 56, 70]. Thus, in the simplest case, a binary target variable is considered, where the share in a subgroup can be compared to the share in the dataset in order to detect (exceptional) deviations. In the most general formalization, however, the interestingness of a pattern is flexibly defined by a specific interestingness measure. For example, the so-called target concept can then also relate to a complex model, e. g., a linear regression model or Bayesian network induced on the subgroup vs. one such model learned from the total dataset, where significant deviations can be estimated. The latter case is the focus of exceptional model mining [31, 57, 58] as a specialization of the general subgroup discovery approach. The patterns are typically described by a description language using conjunctions of attribute-value restrictions, i. e., referring to value constraints on features, similar to simple rules [31]. In contrast to typical machine learning approaches, subgroup discovery aims at discovering local patterns, e. g., "nuggets" in the data [71, 72]. Due to their simple conjunctive structure, subgroup patterns are typically interpretable, relating to interpretable machine learning [23] which is particularly important when the discovered patterns need to be actionable [73–75].

2.2. Subgroup Discovery Basics

For a more formal view on subgroup discovery, we adapt the presentation in [31], to which we refer to for a detailed discussion. Basically, we distinguish between *patterns* – which are typically provided in conjunctive form – and *subgroups* as extensions of such descriptive patterns. The patterns cover specific subsets of a dataset (or database). Then, an *interestingness measure* (also called *quality function*) formalizes which patterns are considered interesting for ranking patterns (and subgroups). For the interestingness measure, this typically includes the concept of interest, as already sketched above. As we will see below, such an interestingness measure can also capture a typical *key performance indicator* (KPI), e. g., for process analysis, which formalizes the specific constraints of the user relating to discovering interesting subgroups for the analysis task at hand.

More formally, we consider a database $DB = (I,A)$, which is given by a set of individuals I (often called instances) and a set of attributes A. In the following, we restrict our focus to nominal attributes, where numeric attributes can be handled via discretization, e. g., [70, 76]. For nominal attributes, a selection descriptor $(a = v)$ is a Boolean function $I \rightarrow \{0,1\}$ that is true if the value of attribute $a \in A$ is equal to v for the respective individual. Δ denotes the set of all selection descriptors. As basic elements in subgroup discovery, we consider patterns, i. e., subgroup descriptions and subgroups. A subgroup description p is given by a set of selection descriptors $p = \{d_1, \ldots, d_l\}, d_i \in \Delta, i = 1, \ldots, l$, i. e., having length l, which is being interpreted as a conjunction of the contained descriptors. We also call p a (complex) pattern. In principle, such a pattern can be interpreted as the body of a conjunctive rule. Furthermore, we distinguish between the pattern – as an intensional description – and the extent of the pattern, i. e., the respective subgroup described by the pattern. A subgroup $s = \{i \in I \,|\, p(i) = true\}$, is the set of all individuals that are covered by the subgroup description p.

In a top-k setting, a subgroup discovery algorithm returns the top-k subgroups according to a given quality function $q\colon 2^{\Delta} \rightarrow \mathbb{R}$, cf. [31]. The applied quality function thus estimates the interestingness of a pattern. For example, for a binary target concept, a standard quality function combines the size $n_p = |s|$ of a subgroup s described by pattern p, i. e., its support, and the share t_p of the target concept t in s, i. e., its confidence as follows: $q^e(p) = n_p^e \cdot (t_p - t_0)$, where t_0 denotes the (default) share of the target concept in the database DB, and $e \in \mathbb{R}$. Standard quality functions include the so-called *Piatetsky-Shapiro* quality function q^1, the binomial test quality function $q^{0.5}$, and the gain quality function q^0. The latter focuses on improving the target share and thus can be applied for finding patterns with a high confidence, however, it then requires a minimal size threshold ensuring sufficient support. While a quality function provides a ranking of the discovered subgroup patterns, often also a statistical assessment of the patterns is useful in data exploration and knowledge discovery. Quality functions that directly apply a statistical test, for example the *Chi-square* quality function, e. g., [31], provide a p-value for simple interpretation.

Using a given subgroup discovery algorithm, e. g., [31] the result of top-k subgroup discovery is then the set of the k patterns $p_1, \ldots, p_k$, where $p_i \in 2^{\Delta}$, with the highest interestingness value according to the applied quality function.

2.3. Use Case: Anomaly Detection in Industrial Logistics Data

In the following, we summarize an application use case of knowledge-augmented pattern mining for anomaly detection in the domain of industrial logistics, adapting the presentation in [48]. Here, the goal for anomaly detection is to identify exceptional patterns in the context of inventory differences. More specifically, the major goal of the analysis was to identify specific logistic processes in a larger production context which could potentially indicate erroneous financial assessments. These are called inventory differences in this context, cf. [48]. Overall, the whole process was considerably assisted by domain specialists, where large-scale data as well as domain dependencies were integrated into a knowledge graph representation. A further important goal was to provide interpretable representations in order to enable explanation and transparency, which was addressed via a knowledge-augmented pattern mining approach using subgroup discovery.

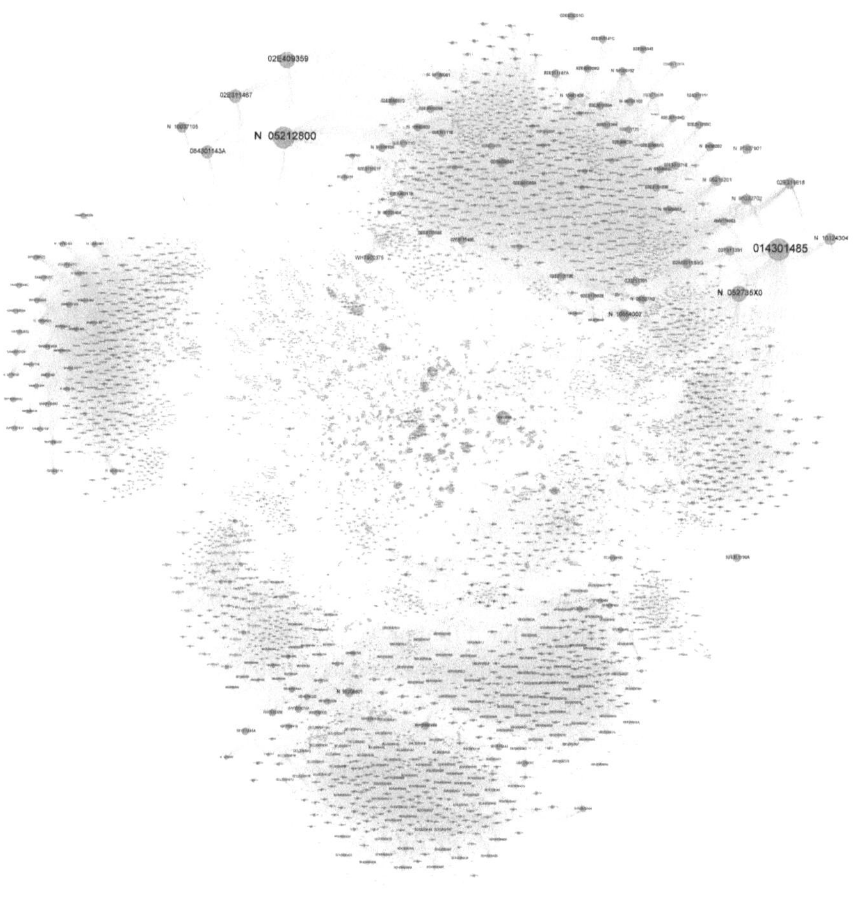

Figure 1. Visualization [48] of the structure data graph (bill of materials information). Each node represents some material, with a node's size proportional to its degree. The color of a node tends to indicate its price in a traffic light scheme from green to yellow and red, where more inexpensive (basic) materials are colored in green and more expensive materials range from yellow to red. We refer to [48] for a more detailed discussion.

Initially, business and data understanding as in the CRISP-DM model [77] for data mining was applied in order to determine the most relevant data sources for the targeted inventory difference problem. This resulted in a rather complex structure of different databases and further process information (see [48] for more details) as the basis for building the knowledge graphs. Here, two graphs were considered: the so-called *structure data graph* (see Figure 1 for a visualization) that represents information and dependencies of the specific bills of materials, and the *accounting data graph* which captures dependencies of material flow information within the respective production processes.

For anomaly detection and identifying relevant patterns, a key challenge was to assess the relevant bookings of a material and its dependent materials. Given the complexity and volume of data, manual analysis was only feasible for small cases. Therefore, for pattern mining, a specific *key performance indicator* (KPI) was developed as a complex interestingness measure. This KPI was applied as a data analytics feature for each material node in the structure data graph. Essentially, this KPI operates across both graphs: The structure data graph, which represents the bill of materials (i. e., the part–part structure), and the accounting data graph, which records bookings (i. e., information about movements of parts). Basically, the KPI traces the construction dependencies within the structure data graph, from basic materials (e. g., screws, aluminum) to final products (e. g., gears, exhaust systems, etc.) that incorporate those materials. For each material node, the accounting data graph provides the corresponding booking information and effective quantities. The domain specialists expected that the aggregated amounts from the two graphs would cancel each other out if the booking calculations and movements were correct. This method essentially provided a kind of logistical balance for each material node of the graph. If the respective balance aligned with the expectations of the domain specialists, i. e., that the data, calculations and expected movement information was correct and reflected their understanding of the respective processes, then the KPI would be close to zero. Any deviation from zero would therefore indicate potential issues in the data, i. e., a divergence from zero would indicate either data discrepancies or issues in the domain model. Consequently, anomalous subgroups exhibiting such deviations were identified and investigated.

The analysis revealed significant deviations from the experts' expectations. For example, when analyzing subgroups for different work shifts, it was discovered that specific types of logistic bookings were strongly correlated with particular shifts. Additionally, when focusing on material application and price fluctuations, technical issues were identified in a data import process. This problem was flagged by patterns showing bookings with empty storage groups, which conflicted with the experts' expectations. Furthermore, subgroup analyses targeting the fluctuations of component prices revealed incomplete price data for a large group of parts. In subsequent iterations, another systematic issue was uncovered, for example, where cost center IDs for the same physical cost center were inconsistent across different but interrelated logistic systems. We refer to [48] for a more detailed discussion. Potential extensions of such knowledge-augmented analysis method can consider the graph structures directly, for detecting according graph patterns, e. g., [59, 78, 79], also when integrating domain knowledge, e. g., [69].

3. Knowledge-Augmented Interpretable Learning of Diagnostic Scoring Systems

Knowledge-based diagnosis is a prominent area of research, including early approaches in the field of expert systems and knowledge systems. These often use explicitly formalized knowledge, often complemented by ontology-based approaches [4, 80–84, 84–88] as well as more recent data-driven learning methods [49, 89–94]. These become more and more important in the context of the diagnosis of complex systems that generate large amounts of data, e. g., in medical [17, 89, 95] or industrial [69, 84, 96] domains. In general, the automated diagnosis of such complex systems is a challenging task. To successfully apply either approach, adequate knowledge and data is required, while the connection between the systems, e. g., for handling different types of information in respective abstractions, is not automatically provided. Furthermore, knowledge acquisition is often costly, while purely data-driven techniques require large amounts of data of sufficient quality. Therefore, hybrid knowledge-augmented approaches can combine the advantages of both purely knowledge-based and solely data-driven approaches, i. e., an initial set of high-quality knowledge, which can be extended, refined and fine-tuned by data-driven learning. In this section, we summarize such an approach [49–51] based on scoring systems [93,97], namely diagnostic scores [15,97]. We discuss initial knowledge-augmented learning as well as knowledge refinement, and present an exemplary use case in the medical domain.

3.1. An Overview on Scoring Systems

For diagnosis, *diagnostic scores* are a widely used formalism for medical decision-making, e. g., [15,16,98,99]. We follow the presentation in [49] for such *scoring systems*, also including refinement and adaptation methods described in [50,51]. In particular, below, the term *scoring system* denotes a set of diagnostic scores in the form of *scoring rules*, i. e., the resulting *(scoring) rule base*.

Essentially, scoring systems as linear models are a relatively simple and lightweight knowledge representation. For a diagnostic application, we distinguish inputs (*features*) and outputs as *concepts* (*diagnoses*) of a model. In order to derive a concept (e. g., a diagnosis), a limited number of features is utilized in a regular and easy-to-interpret manner. Then, in its simplest form, each observed feature contributes a single point to a *score*. If the score exceeds a predetermined threshold, then the diagnostic concept is considered as established. There are variations where multiple categories are used instead of just using one point, where both negative and positive contributions are considered, and where multiple thresholds are employed to express varying degrees, such as distinguishing between "possible" and "probable" in the derivation of a concept. Furthermore, we can also generalize categories to arbitrary points (natural numbers) or real values for general scoring systems. For diagnostic scores, however, simple to interpret *(symbolic) categories* are often preferred for their improved understandability. Diagnostic scores are typically implemented using scoring rules, which assign specific points to a diagnosis as defined in the rule action. Unlike general rules, scoring rules usually do not involve logical combinations in their preconditions. However, they can be arranged hierarchically such that a concept inferred through a score can be used to infer another concept, enabling more complex (hierarchical) models.

3.2. Diagnostic Scores

In the following, we provide a more formal view on diagnostic scores, summarizing the presentation and definitions given in [49]. For a diagnostic model implemented as a knowledge system, we consider attributes respectively attribute values (or findings) as inputs, and diagnoses as its outputs. We define Ω_A as the universal set of all attributes available in the problem domain. Then, a value $v \in dom(a)$ assigned to an attribute $a \in \Omega_A$ is called an *attribute value* or *finding*. Furthermore, let $\Omega_{\mathscr{F}}$ denote the set of all possible attribute values in the given problem domain. An attribute value $f \in \Omega_{\mathscr{F}}$ is denoted by $a{:}v$ for $a \in \Omega_A$ and $v \in dom(a)$. The set $F_a \subseteq \Omega_{\mathscr{F}}$ of possible attribute values for a given attribute a is defined as $F_a := \{f \in \Omega_{\mathscr{F}} \,|\, f = a{:}v \wedge v \in dom(a)\}$. Each attribute value $f \in \Omega_{\mathscr{F}}$ is defined as a possible input of the model, e. g., a diagnostic knowledge system. We denote a *diagnosis* d as a possible output of the respective model. $\Omega_{\mathscr{D}}$ is defined as the universe of all possible diagnoses for a given problem domain.

For modeling scoring systems (or diagnostic scores) we consider simple scoring rules. A *simple scoring rule* r is denoted as $r := f \xrightarrow{s} d$, where $f \in \Omega_{\mathscr{F}}$ is an attribute value, $d \in \Omega_{\mathscr{D}}$ is the targeted diagnosis, and $s \in \Omega_S$ denotes a symbolic confirmation category. Ω_S denotes the full set of symbolic confirmation categories. Basically, enlarging this set enables a more fine-grained approach for learning and fine-tuning, while a coarser approach facilitates manual specification, fine-tuning and adaptation, since the choice of the specific categories is restricted. In general, the category s reflects the concept of the points in a scoring system in a symbolic and thus more interpretable form for the given rule r. Diagnostic scores are then used to represent a qualitative approach for deriving diagnoses with symbolic confirmation categories. These categories state the degree of confirmation or disconfirmation of a particular diagnosis. Categories can be aggregated according to some suitable aggregation scheme, e. g., such that four equal categories together result in the next higher category. Then, according to the obtained confirmation categories (the symbolic score), the respective concept (diagnosis) is established.

3.3. Learning Diagnostic Scores

The approach described in [49] aims to learn diagnostic scoring rules in a data-driven way by estimating the association strength between all findings $f \in \Omega_{\mathscr{F}}$ and all diagnoses $d \in \Omega_{\mathscr{D}}$, basically relying on statistical tests. In principle, first so-called diagnostic profiles are constructed for each diagnosis $d \in \Omega_{\mathscr{D}}$ for which all contributing findings $f \in \Omega_{\mathscr{F}}$ having a positive or negative association with the diagnosis above a certain user-specified threshold are considered. Then, the respective score of the rule, i. e., the symbolic scoring confirmation category is estimated based on the predictive performance of the finding with respect to the diagnosis. For this, standard measures [100, 101] like precision and the false positive rate are applied, cf. [49] for details. The direction of the statistical association is used for inferring positive or negative scores (points), i. e., for a positive association a positive score is applied, and for a negative association a negative score likewise. Finally, the derivation of the symbolic confirmation categories is obtained via a mapping table, which is predefined according to domain knowledge and user requirements, e. g., regarding the applied thresholds for determining the categories as well as the number of categories. If being integrated with other optimization/refinement approaches (e. g., as discussed below), then this mapping can also be applied at a later stage, for example, when optimization/refinement has been finalized.

Since usually a large number of (statistical) associations are derived, it is important to prune the resulting score rule base. This can be done via domain knowledge, e. g., such that only associations between *abnormal* findings and diagnoses are considered. Also, in the medical domain it is often possible to partition the set of findings and diagnoses into partially disjunct subsets, i. e., *partition classes*, corresponding to specific problem areas of the application domain, cf. [102]. In the medical domain of sonography, e. g., these subsets can correspond to problem areas like *liver*, *pancreas*, *kidney*, *stomach* and *intestine*. Then, for learning associations between findings and diagnoses, these associations can be restricted to certain of these subsets, such that only rules based on associations within a specific subset are derived. Furthermore, we can apply heuristic pruning, e. g., to remove rules if they contribute only negative but no positive scores for a diagnosis, taking into account whether a diagnosis can be (de-)established or not based on the available rules. For more details, we refer to [49]. We briefly revisit the results of [49] as an example enabling the bootstrapping of diagnosis systems below.

In addition to the simple scheme outlined above, there are also extensions of such a simple rule-based diagnostic score scheme so that more complex rules can be learned, e. g., using subgroup discovery, cf. [103, 104]. Then, either the simple learning approach or the more complex one – for obtaining more complex rules, i. e., rules with more than one element in the precondition – can be applied for rapid knowledge capture. In particular, these can be applied in a knowledge-augmented way, e. g., incorporating domain knowledge for learning the rules as well as extending a given model (in the form of a rule base) with new rules.

3.4. Refining Scoring Rules

Whenever an initial scoring rule base has been provided, either manually or using a learning approach, its optimization and maintenance are important for the further development of the according scoring system [50, 51, 92, 93, 103]. For example, in the medical domain, scoring systems are often constructed manually by domain specialists first. Here, a domain specialist typically assigns ratings to all correlations between findings and solutions, estimating the respective point score based on the domain specialist's expertise. However, if the impact of a combination of attribute values is not proportionately strong compared to the effect of individual attribute observations, for example, then this knowledge representation becomes inadequate. This is because the contribution of attribute values to the diagnostic score is strictly linear. Then, refinement and adaptation of the scoring rules contributions becomes necessary, which can be supported by automatic methods. This includes semi-automatic methods [50, 51, 103] as well as optimization-based approaches [92, 93].

For refinements of scoring systems, providing control during the modification and refinement process is usually important. This is enabled, for example, via interactive approaches, e. g., [103], based on pattern mining methods using subgroup discovery for detecting patterns that cause incorrect behavior of the scoring rule base such that errors in the predictions are identified. For example, rules can be adapted and/or extended, e. g., by adding conditions to the rule, by modifying the respective action, or by tweaking the assigned confirmation category. Using visualization, the respective analytical elements uncovered by the pattern mining approach can be interactively checked, and according modifications can be performed, cf. [103] for further details.

Furthermore, we can apply semi-automatic optimization methods [50, 51] for getting proposals for adapting the respective confirmation categories based on ideas of perceptron learning. Given suitable test cases for the scoring systems, adaptations of the points / confirmation categories can then be proposed – similar to adapting the perceptron weights during its training phase, cf. [104]. There are also further optimization approaches [92, 93] both for learning and refining scoring systems. Combinations of the aforementioned techniques are also possible so that interactive approaches can be linked with advanced optimization and refinement techniques, as well as integrated with other diagnosis formalisms, e. g., [105].

3.5. Use Case: Bootstrapping Diagnostic Knowledge Systems

A prominent use case is to bootstrap diagnostic knowledge systems, that is, to support the domain specialists when building such a diagnostic knowledge system from scratch. Applying the learning method, an initial set of scoring rules can be obtained, which can be adapted and refined in a second step.

Table 1. Exemplary evaluation results [103]: Options for including domain knowledge (partition class information, abnormality information) and heuristic pruning (cf. [103] for details). ∅Rules indicates the average number of rules per diagnosis, ∅AV the average number of attribute values used, ∅SC the average number of score categories, and ∅ACC the mean accuracy.

Partition Class / Abnormality / Pruning	∅Rules	∅Size	∅AV	∅SC	∅ACC
– / – / –	10.93±5.18	786.80	245.80	2.69	0.90
+ / + / –	3.37±1.45	242.90	112.60	1.77	0.85
+ / + / +	2.12±0.96	152.70	82.50	0.92	0.85

In [103], the presented method was evaluated in such a context for learning an initial scoring system in the domain of medical diagnosis, using a case base collected by the fielded knowledge system SonoConsult [17, 106]: It targets the field of abdominal ultrasound (liver, portal tract, gallbladder, spleen, kidneys, adrenal glands, pancreas, stomach, intestine, lymph nodes, abdominal aorta, cava inferior, prostate, and urinary bladder) mainly for structured documentation and diagnosis. In the evaluation, 1340 instances from SonoConsult were applied, with an average number of 4.32 ± 2.79 diagnoses and an average number of 76.89 ± 20.59 relevant attribute values per instance, cf. [103]. For the experiments, the presented method for learning diagnostic scores was applied in a standard 10-fold cross-validation evaluation setting. Table 1 summarizes the main results for the correlation threshold of 0.5. Specifically, we observe that applying domain knowledge can significantly reduce the number of learned rules, so that the understandability of the rule base is improved. However, the accuracy is also reduced slightly when rules are pruned via applying domain knowledge. With additional heuristic pruning of the scoring rules – e. g., by removing non-contributing rules as discussed above – the rule base is further reduced so that only the "more meaningful" rules remain. Thus, the presented method allows for a fine-grained approach for learning scoring systems, where a knowledge-augmented approach can remove potential spurious associations which can cause overfitting of the learned scoring rule base, while also reducing the total number of learned rules. The latter then improves interpretability and understandability of the resulting scoring system, which can then be extended and refined further.

4. Explainable Neuro-Symbolic Anomaly Detection and Diagnosis

For the explainable neuro-symbolic approach to anomaly detection and diagnosis described in [52], the overall idea is to utilize a *knowledge graph* (KG) that guides the diagnostic process, combined with *neural networks* that enable the interpretation of sensor signals suggested by the KG for investigation. Essentially, this integrates knowledge- and machine-learning-based fault diagnosis, combining both paradigms. A key element is an iterative diagnosis cycle in which rough hypotheses are refined using both knowledge-based and data-driven methods. Explainability is essential for diagnosis and is enabled via the hybrid approach. The advantage of the neuro-symbolic approach to the problem of automated diagnosis compared to previous methods is that it is designed in a way that both paradigms are mutually beneficial. Thus, it is motivated by the previous lack of explainability and exploitation of available domain knowledge in data-driven methods, and the extensive manual effort and shortcomings with respect to sensor signal evaluation in expert systems. Ultimately, a comprehensive explanation is constructed by contextualizing all diagnostic artifacts with symbolic state transitions as an explanatory report. Additionally, they augment the KG and enable to learn the most significant aspects of the signal types over time.

Below, we first summarize how to generate explanations for time series predictions using saliency maps [107, 108]. After that, we review neuro-symbolic fault diagnosis as presented in [52] before we summarize and discuss an exemplary application use case in the automotive domain.

4.1. Saliency Map Generation for Time Series & Explanatory Reports

Despite the commonplace of a black box nature of deep learning approaches, CNNs, among other architectures, offer the advantage of explainability, e. g., through *Class Activation Mapping* techniques [108, 109], providing explanatory insights into the temporal / spatial segments that are important for a network's prediction, cf. [107, 108]. A crucial idea of the overall approach in [52] is to close the loop and feed this information back into the KG. In case of an anomaly, it is the information where the error is located in the signal, i. e., generally where the system tells us to look to identify the problem under consideration, the region of interest (ROI). This is very valuable knowledge that is unavailable a priori. Moreover, it is a very useful debugging resource, highlighting issues such as overfitting and deviation from expert judgements. Thus, subsequent to the classification of a signal, the explanation of the decision proceeds on the basis of *Class Activation Maps* (CAMs). This is to ensure that not only accurate predictions are obtained, but also predictions that are comprehensible for users, which should reduce the proneness to errors, and can further enable computational sensemaking [19, 110].

There are several techniques used in deep learning to visualize areas of an image that are most relevant to predicting a certain class, e. g., *Grad-CAM* [109], *HiResCAM* [111], *Grad-CAM++* [112], *Score-CAM* [113], *SmoothGrad* [114], and *LayerCAM* [115]. They provide a way to interpret the decision made by an ANN model (with compatible architecture, unless model-agnostic) by highlighting the regions of the input image that contribute the most to the classification result. Then, this can then provide important information for human interpretation of the model and according explainability for a prediction, towards computational sensemaking [116, 117].

The basic idea behind vanilla *Grad-CAM* is to use the gradients of the output class with respect to the feature maps of the last convolutional layer in the network [109]. The result is a set of gradient feature maps with the same dimensions as the feature maps of the last convolutional layer. Each element represents the sensitivity of the output score with respect to the corresponding element in the feature map, i. e., how much the output would change if the corresponding element in the feature map were to change. The gradient feature maps are used to compute an importance weight for each feature map in the final convolutional layer w.r.t. the considered prediction. This is done via *Global Average Pooling* (GAP). Finally, the feature maps are weighted with these values and then added up to generate a heatmap that can be overlaid on top of the original image to provide a visual explanation. The regions with higher values in the heatmap correspond to the regions of the image that had the greatest impact on the model's prediction. Based on the considered architecture, the heatmap may need to be rescaled to match the original dimensions of the input, which may impair its accuracy.

Grad-CAM is primarily designed to work with CNNs, since it relies on the feature maps of the last convolutional layer. However, the general idea of using gradients to visualize the importance of input features can be applied to other architectures as well. The technique is based on the idea of a hierarchy of feature representations, as in CNNs, where the output of each layer can be interpreted as a set of learned features that capture increasingly complex aspects of the input. The choice of the heatmap generation technique depends on the specific application and requirements of the task. Open source implementations of some of these techniques are available as part of the *tf-keras-vis*[1] library, which is primarily intended to be applied to image data. With time series data, the input features are arranged sequentially over time rather than like pixels in an image. The *tf-keras-vis* implementations can also be used for time series data, assuming the input data has the appropriate format. The gradient-based approaches also work with $1D$ convolutional layers along the temporal dimension of the input. Thus, saliency maps can be generated for a time series classification model analogous to the standard case with image data. Finally, each of the methods receives the normalized time series values $V' \in \mathbb{R}^n$, the trained model M, and an optional prediction y (default is the "best guess", i. e., $y = \text{argmax}_i P(i|V') \forall i \in \{0,1\}$) as input, and outputs a heatmap $H \in [0,1]^n$ highlighting the parts that are most relevant for the classification. We are interested in values $h \in H$ close to 1, these are the most important parts of the signal V'. Each value $h_i \in H$ rates the importance of a corresponding input value $v_i \in V', \forall i \in \{1,\dots n\}$.

Since the respective methods have different advantages and weaknesses, the best-suited one depends on the considered task. Probably most important is accuracy, i. e., how well the heatmap reflects the significant regions. Interpretability is also a relevant criterion, as is computational efficiency and flexibility. The latter refers to the applicability to different types of model architectures. Figure 2 shows a side-by-side plot of all generated heatmaps. In this example, the different methods agree very well on the relevant regions for the prediction. In the end, it enables domain experts to assess whether these areas are plausible bases for decision making and allows for knowledge discovery through the resulting KG entries. Since plausibility may also depend on the context of the classification, the interpretable symbolic state transitions etc. are crucial for the assessment.

[1] https://keisen.github.io/tf-keras-vis-docs/

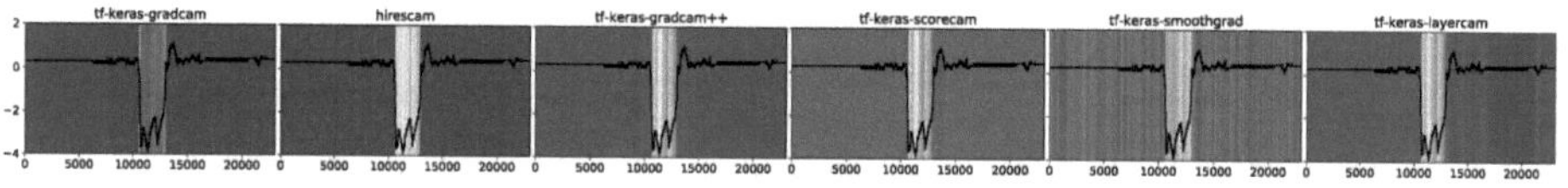

Figure 2. Visualization [52]: Heatmap generation methods, cf. [52] for a more detailed discussion; the x-axis shows the respective sampling points, the y-axis the normalized voltage, see Figure 6.

If the classification of a whole range of signals reveals that, for instance, certain highlighted segments correlate with certain errors, this is again very valuable knowledge that is unavailable a priori. For experts, it is often particularly difficult to precisely specify the properties of an ROI. It is often a very intuitive, experience-based and hard to grasp process, so it could be very valuable to simply learn the ROIs in this way and then compare them to the intuitive notions of human experts. There may also be patterns that are very subtle and difficult for humans to recognize. Thus, the classification, i. e., the neural part of the neuro-symbolic system, benefits from the KG, which essentially narrows down the search space, and the KG in turn benefits from the neural part, namely from the results and explanation of the ANN-based classification. In the end, if a threshold is exceeded for an error, i. e., a certain number of roughly agreeing heatmaps has been gathered for it, one could crop this sub-ROI and train a classification model for it. Once this error occurs, the sub-ROI is cropped and the more specialized model is applied, resulting in a sub-ROI patch classification. In conclusion, the system theoretically gets better at diagnosing errors that it has seen frequently in the past. A further option is to cluster all recorded heatmaps, irrespective of the particular fault, in order to find patterns. This is only one illustration of the opportunities for knowledge discovery.

4.2. Neuro-Symbolic Fault Diagnosis

The neuro-symbolic fault diagnosis system proposed in [52] makes use of both KGs and their reasoning capabilities as well as explainable learning through CNNs. It thus combines the advantages of KGs, which incorporate human expertise into the diagnostic process, with the advantages of deep neural networks, which excel at recognizing patterns in complex signals.

The fault diagnosis system is applicable in a variety of domains in which the following conditions are met: The system to be diagnosed consists of multiple components with causal relationships between one another, i. e., an anomaly in one component can transfer to another component, and these causal relationships can be formally described in a KG. Moreover, each component can be inspected individually, and checking all components would not be an efficient solution, i. e., it is desired to minimize the number of inspections. Lastly, it is expected that (sensor) data like time series or images can be recorded at the components and classified by a neural network.[2]

According to the taxonomy in [118] that categorizes neuro-symbolic systems based on the integration of the neural and symbolic components, this approach belongs to the *Symbolic[Neuro]* category. The KG initiates the anomaly classification networks as needed and uses the classification result to guide the subsequent diagnostic step(s).

[2]Recording tabular data would also be an option, but the chosen neural network architecture and XAI techniques would have to be adapted accordingly.

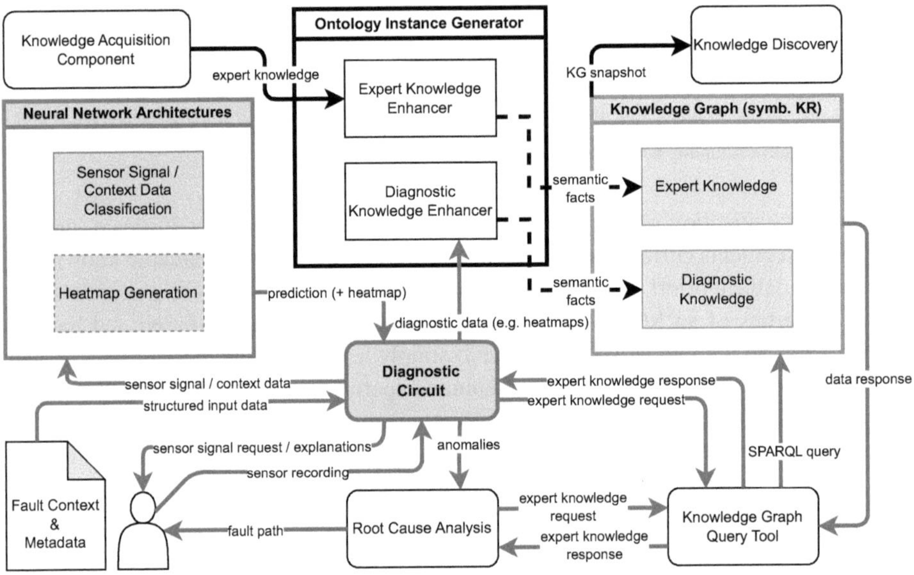

Figure 3. Overview (adapted from [52]) of the NEURO-SYMBOLIC architecture.

The architecture of the diagnosis system with its various elements and their connections is shown in Figure 3. A central element of the diagnosis process is the diagnostic circuit. It connects the symbolic and neural parts of the system and navigates the diagnostic process. Note that the system is not a continuous monitoring system, but is only applied on demand if there are indications of an error, e. g., through the occurrence of symptoms. Hence, the diagnosis process is started by supplying a fault context and metadata (e. g., error codes or observed symptoms, depending on the domain). Via the *Knowledge Graph Query Tool*, which is a library of predefined SPARQL queries that allow for the retrieval of relevant knowledge from the KG, the diagnostic circuit accesses expert knowledge that instructs the user to take measurements at a certain component. This instruction is transferred to the user via the diagnostic circuit, who then performs measurements, sensor recordings or inspections according to the instruction. The measurement is transferred to the neural component of the system, which then classifies it (e. g., using a CNN), leading to a binary classification result and optionally to a heatmap generated through CAM methods, highlighting the most relevant segments of the time series or image for the classification. If the classification result is an anomaly, a *Root Cause Analysis* (RCA) is performed. An anomaly does not mean that the respective component is defective, as errors can propagate through a chain of components that are causally related. The first component in the chain from which the error originates is expected to be the root cause. In order to find the root cause, a request is sent via the *Knowledge Graph Query Tool* to the KG, which returns a list of all components that affect the identified anomalous component. The classification process is repeated recursively until one or more anomalous components are found that are not affected by any other anomalous component, i. e., that are root causes. The resulting fault path, which represents the chain of anomalous components through which the error propagated, is generated and presented to the user, as are the heatmaps at each classification step. This demonstrates the interpretability and transparency of the diagnosis system which, combined with the explainability of the neural classification methods achieved through CAM approaches, enhances the trustworthiness of the system by allowing the user to understand and verify the results as well as each step of the process. At the end of the process, all steps and artifacts (measurements, classification predictions, heatmaps, fault paths, etc.) of the diagnosis process are automatically saved in the KG via the *Diagnostic Knowledge Enhancer*. The diagnostic knowledge that accumulates over time enables *Knowledge Discovery*, i. e., the discovery of previously unknown statistical relationships between certain error patterns and root causes, thus offering the opportunity of improving the RCA process and making it even more efficient in the future.

The expert knowledge that is a prerequisite for the process needs to be made available by domain experts. This is facilitated by a *Knowledge Acquisition Component*, e. g., in the form of a web interface, in order to ensure that the knowledge can be entered in a structured way before it is added to the KG via the *Expert Knowledge Enhancer*. Crucial knowledge for the functioning of the system are the causal connections between components and the connections between fault contexts and the suspected components. The ontology can be adapted to contain many additional domain-specific concepts and relations that are helpful for diagnosis within the respective domain. The following section illustrates an adaptation to the automotive domain.

4.3. Use Case: Neuro-Symbolic Fault Diagnosis in the Automotive Domain

Neuro-symbolic fault diagnosis for automobiles, instantiating the approach described in Section 4.2, has the potential to relieve mechatronics engineers of many time-consuming and error-prone tasks. The practical motivation of [52] is to tackle the increasing complexity and diversity of modern vehicles, which pose a major challenge for their diagnosis, i. e., to extract meaning from multimodal data that is unmanageable for humans, and to recognize complex patterns.

Symbolic Knowledge Representation To capture and structure diagnosis-relevant knowledge, an ontology[3] was defined (cf. Figure 4), which leads to a KG by populating it with large amounts of instance data, e. g., through expert interviews, supplemented with industry partner data. Essentially, there are three levels of abstraction: The raw definition of the ontology, vehicle-agnostic *expert knowledge* regarding on-board diagnostics (OBD, ISO 15031-6[4]), and vehicle-specific *diagnostic knowledge* automatically generated based on OBD logs read in workshops and acquired as part of the diagnostic process (recorded sensor data, interpretations, etc.). However, as illustrated in Figure 3, the two types of knowledge are not isolated from each other, but connected by meaningful links (e. g., connecting classification instances to the diagnostic associations that led to them) to learn from previous diagnostic runs. All three levels combined constitute the KG. The acquisition of expert knowledge is accomplished via a web interface (collaborative *knowledge acquisition component*) through which the knowledge is entered, stored in the *Resource Description Framework* (RDF) format, and hosted on an *Apache Jena Fuseki*[5] server. In addition, this knowledge is retrievable in the diagnostic process via predefined SPARQL queries (*KG query tool*), as well as making the KG expandable and editable in general (*ontology instance generator*).

[3] https://github.com/tbohne/obd_ontology/releases/tag/v0.1.1
[4] https://www.iso.org/standard/66369.html
[5] https://jena.apache.org/documentation/fuseki2/

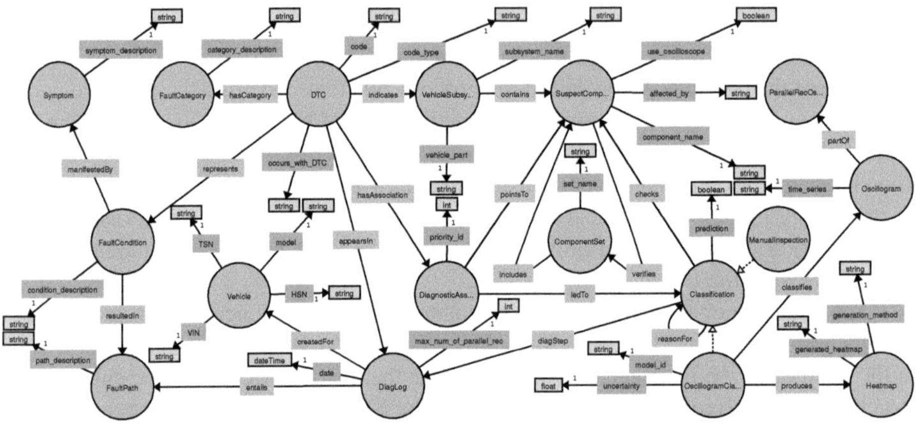

Figure 4. Ontology [52] for capturing knowledge about On-Board Diagnostics (OBD).

Expert Knowledge Modeled in the Ontology At the core of the knowledge captured in the ontology are the standardized *Diagnostic Trouble Codes* (DTCs), which are a perfect example of what is meant by *fault context* in the neuro-symbolic architecture visualization in Figure 3. In order to efficiently handle the occurrence of DTCs in a vehicle's electronic control unit (ECU), a DTC parser[6] has been developed that is capable of resolving all digits of the read code and outputting the resulting error information. A `DTC` can have `DiagnosticAssociations` with physical components in a car (`SuspectComponent`). A crucial aspect of such an association is the `priority_id`, based on which components are suggested to be examined in a certain order in the presence of a given DTC. In addition, `affected_by` represents a list of other components whose malfunction could affect the correct functionality of the considered component (dependencies can be conceived as a tree, cf. Figure 7). Experts can define a `ComponentSet` to reduce the number of redundant diagnostic steps in case there is a specific component that can be leveraged to verify the correct functioning of a whole set of components. Furthermore, each component is contained in a `VehicleSubsystem`, which is associated with a specific part of the vehicle. Moreover, each DTC represents a `FaultCondition` manifested by one or more `Symptoms`.

Diagnosis Knowledge Modeled in the Ontology There is another theme to the ontology, which is the acquisition and reasonable arrangement of diagnostic data. For each `Vehicle` instance that is entered into the KG, i. e., for each vehicle that is diagnosed with the system, a `DiagLog` is created that provides the KG with a kind of explanatory summary of the entire diagnostic process. However, this is not a mere summary, but each entry is automatically sorted into the existing web of expert knowledge and past diagnostic data by instantiating the concepts of the ontology. Initially, any recorded DTC appears in this log, as this is always the starting point for a diagnosis. Perhaps most significant are the diagnostic steps, which are also part of the log in the form of `Classification` instances that store their reason, either another classification that detected an anomaly (`reasonFor`) or a diagnostic association with a DTC recorded in the vehicle (`ledTo`). Each classification has a binary result (`prediction`) that indicates

[6] https://github.com/tbohne/dtc_parser/releases/tag/v0.1

whether the checked component has an anomaly or not. The concept `Classification` has two sub-concepts: `ManualInspection` is a classification performed manually by a mechanic. This is necessary in cases where oscilloscope-based analysis is not reasonable for a component, i. e., `use_oscilloscope` := `false`, or when we simply cannot provide a classification model for the specific component yet. The other sub-concept is `OscillogramClassification`, which classifies an oscilloscope signal using a classification model. In this case, we specify an uncertainty value and an ID of the model that produced the classification. The subject of an oscillogram classification are the `Oscillograms` (time series), which are also stored in the KG and possibly grouped as an instance of a `ParallelRecOscillogramSet`. Finally, we also provide heatmaps for the classification of the oscillograms, which allow an interpretation of the predictions (cf. Sec. 4.1). `Heatmaps` are stored in the KG along with their generation method. The final diagnosis takes the form of a series of `FaultPaths` that start with one component (root cause) and subsequently cascade to others. These fault paths are not only stored in the diagnostic log, but also associated with the fault conditions, which offers interesting potential for future analysis.

Enhancement of Expert Knowledge The *expert knowledge enhancer* can be used to augment the KG hosted by the *Fuseki* server with vehicle-agnostic OBD knowledge. In particular, it generates semantic facts based on the information entered through a web interface and connects these facts in a meaningful way to what is already available in the KG, i. e., it serves as a backend for the *knowledge acquisition component.* There are three general types of instance data that can be entered along with their specific associated information: *DTCs*, *vehicle components*, and semantically meaningful *sets of components* grouped together. Alternatively, it is possible to select an existing instance, view the currently available data, and refine it. Entering a new instance leads to a series of operations in the backend. Quite a number of semantic facts have to be generated when an expert enters few information. Thus, it is always expert knowledge input via the web interface and corresponding generation of semantic facts in the backend. All of this is accompanied by a series of input validation mechanisms. This way, a simple KG extension for the expert goes hand in hand with an automatic proper "wiring" of semantic facts in the background.

Enhancement of Vehicle-Specific Diagnosis Knowledge As a further element, the *diagnostic knowledge enhancer*, on the other hand, enhances the KG with diagnosis-specific instance data, i. e., it connects the OBD data recorded in a particular vehicle, as well as sensor readings, classifications, etc. generated during the diagnostic process, with corresponding background knowledge stored in the KG. The process typically starts by creating an instance of the vehicle to be diagnosed, e. g., through `extend_kg_with_vehicle("DummyVehicle", "ID2342713")`. Likewise, it typically ends with a call to `extend_kg_with_diag_log`, which takes numerous arguments, including the DTC instances that are part of the diagnosis and the vehicle identification number (VIN), e. g., `["P2563"]` and `"ID2342713"`. This leads, for instance, to `FaultCondition` "*Boost Control Position Sensor Circuit: Implausible Signal*", represented by `"P2563"`, `resultedIn` a `FaultPath`, entailed by a `DiagLog` instance, `createdFor` the `Vehicle` instance with `VIN` `"ID2342713"`. Moreover, `"P2563"` `appearsIn` this particular instance of `DiagLog`. These are only a few examples of the information collected during diagnosis and its interrelationships. The full set of concepts and relations can be seen in the visualization of the ontology (cf. Figure 4), for all of which automatic semantic fact generation and thus KG extension is implemented.

Knowledge Graph Query Tool There is a library of predefined SPARQL queries and response processing to access information stored in the KG that is used in the diagnostic process, such as `query_vehicle_instance_by_vin(vin)`, `query_symptoms_by_dtc(dtc)` and `query_suspect_components_by_dtc(dtc)`. The latter, for instance, automatically sends and processes the query for a given DTC , e. g.,"`P2563`" in the example [52] shown in Figure 5:

```
/OBD/sparql                                    JSON
PREFIX do: <http://www.semanticweb.org/diag_ontology#>
SELECT ?comp_name WHERE {
    ?comp a do:SuspectComponent; do:component_name ?comp_name .
    ?dtc a do:DTC; do:code "P2563"; do:hasAssociation/do:pointsTo ?comp .
}
```

Figure 5. Example [52]: SPARQL query to retrieve components for DTC "P2563".

ANN-Based Oscillogram Classification A key idea of the developed diagnosis system revolves around sensor information of a certain type. Oscilloscope recordings are performed on specific physical components in the vehicle to detect indications of problems (anomalies). The recorded oscillograms are fed into a classification model previously trained on a large dataset, which evaluates whether each recording contains anomalies.[7] The task comes down to binary univariate time series classification. In the following example, we consider the battery voltage during the engine starting process. For battery voltage records $V \in \mathbb{R}^n$, performance was best when z-normalization was applied to the raw time series data, i. e., $V' := \{\frac{x_i - \mu V}{\sigma V} \,|\, x_i \in V\}$. Figure 6a shows a regular (1) and an anomalous (0) z-normalized voltage sample.

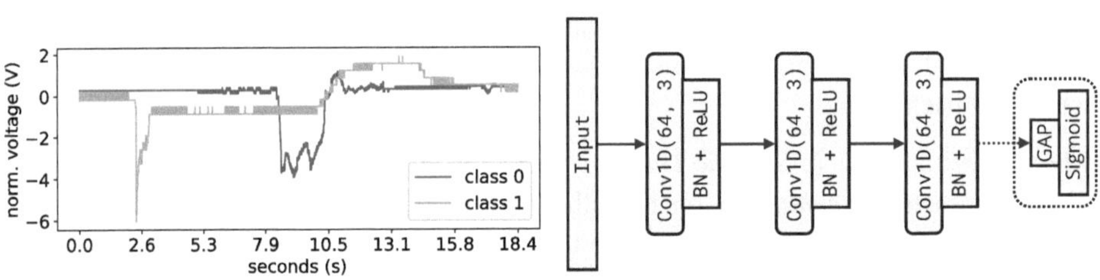

(a) Normalized Battery Voltage [52]. (b) FCN Architecture [52].

Figure 6. Time series classification and the applied ANN architecture, cf. [52] for more details.

Since the main focus of [52] is not to propose a novel ANN architecture for binary classification (anomaly detection) of time series data, we compared several standard architectures from the literature, made slight adjustments, and selected the best performing one for our purposes, which was a *Fully Convolutional Network* (FCN). The FCN model (vis. in Figure 6b) is based on [119], in which the authors propose a strong baseline architecture for time series classification.

[7] https://github.com/tbohne/oscillogram_classification/releases/tag/v0.1.1

Neuro-Symbolic Anomaly Detection and Fault Diagnosis As the previous sections have shown, knowledge- and machine-learning-based vehicle diagnosis requires the integration of various components. For the prototypical overall process (*diag. circuit* in Figure 3) and to integrate all developed modules, a hierarchical state machine was defined.[8], see [52] for a detailed discussion.

Initially, there is meta and context data processing. Based on the read information, the vehicle-specific instance data is entered into the KG. If DTC data is available, the KG is extended with the processed OBD data, i. e., the information that the fault conditions represented by the individual DTCs occurred in the respective vehicle, etc. If the vehicle instance already exists in the KG, it is extended, otherwise it is newly created. Based on the acquired fault context, the actual diagnostic process is initiated via the embedded state machine `DIAGNOSIS`.

This state machine starts with a state in which a best-suited DTC instance is selected for further processing. There is a number of possible transitions. If an instance is selected or generated, the process continues with suggesting suspect components. Otherwise, no anomaly was detected and the indirect conclusion of a potential sensor malfunction is provided. This conclusion should be verified or refuted by the mechanic. Then, either the sensor works, which means that the diagnosis was unsuccessful (only the disproved initial hypothesis and the context are provided due to unmanageable uncertainty), or there is a diagnosis of a defective sensor. The more interesting case: Certain components in the vehicle are recommended to be investigated in light of the available information (fault context). Based on the selected DTC instance, the *KG query tool* is used to query the corresponding suspect components, and for each, whether it can be reasonably diagnosed with an oscilloscope. Afterwards, we first distinguish between the subset of suspect components for which oscilloscope diagnosis is appropriate and those that must be verified manually. Then, synchronized *sensor recordings* are performed at the proposed components of the respective subset, and the resulting *oscillograms are classified* using trained ANN models. The prediction can be interpreted by *overlaid heatmaps* (cf. Sec. 4.1). Subsequently, the subset of recordings to be inspected manually is handed over to the mechanic. In the end, there is a set of anomalous components identified by the trained models and the mechanic. If this set is empty, i. e., no anomaly has been detected, then the next iteration of suggestions follows. However, if no anomaly is detected and there are no remaining components to suggest, then the next DTC instance is selected. If anomalies are found, though, the *root cause analysis* in Figure 3 follows. For further details on the diagnostic procedure, we refer to [52].

Root Cause Analysis to Determine the Source of the Defect Once an anomaly is identified in the described manner, the fault is isolated by recursively inspecting the cause-effect relationships in the vehicle, which are part of the KG (cf. Figure 4), i. e., graph traversal coupled with anomaly detection. This basically creates a causal sub-graph for each anomalous component from which the root cause can be derived. After all, in technological systems errors are rarely encountered that are entirely independent of other components in the system. Typically, there are cascading paths where a problem starts at one component and then spreads to others. The actual interest is directed at the root cause instead of mere side conditions. The termination criterion is that there are no further known components that have not yet been examined and that could directly affect

[8] https://github.com/tbohne/vehicle_diag_smach/releases/tag/v0.1.1

an anomalous component. During the recursive procedure, the fault path, explicitly considered links, etc. are tracked. The result is visualized dynamically for each diagnosis, e. g., Figure 7. The recursive and dynamic sub-graph construction is based on KG queries

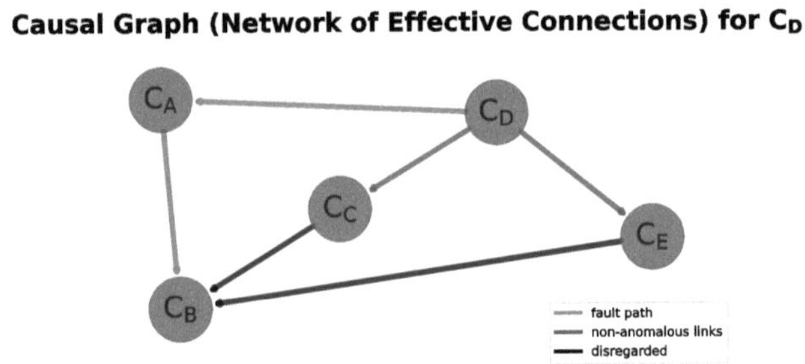

Figure 7. Example [52]: Fault Isolation Result using the Causal Graph.

using the initial anomalous component C_D. After isolating the problem, the diagnosis is entered into the KG, along with a detailed record of all relevant information that led to it, in order to learn from it and facilitate future diagnoses.

Ultimately, the diagnosis is presented in the form of the inverted fault path in Figure 7 as this was the *affected-by*-direction, not the direction starting from the probable root cause of the fault. For the example in Figure 7, this would be $\{C_B \rightarrow C_A \rightarrow C_D\}$. So the problem probably started at C_B, cascaded through C_A, and finally to C_D. Although it is not guaranteed to be the actual root cause, it should provide an experienced mechanic with a fairly strong understanding of the problem prevailing in the vehicle in question.

5. Conclusions

In this chapter, we provided an overview on knowledge-augmented, explainable and interpretable learning in the context of anomaly detection and diagnosis. For this, we have outlined the general context and discussed exemplary methods in this domain, specifically considering the articles [47, 48] for discussing pattern mining in the context of anomaly detection as well as [49–51] on learning scoring systems. Furthermore, we provided a significantly adapted summary of the article [52] – on a neuro-symbolic approach for anomaly detection and diagnosis. Thus, we covered simple knowledge representations such as diagnostic scores, pattern-based methods in combination with various forms of symbolic knowledge, as well as a hybrid neuro-symbolic method integrating deep learning with symbolic knowledge.

For future work, further extending knowledge-augmented approaches, particularly regarding advanced neuro-symbolic approaches, is a major interesting research direction. Here, directly integrating interpretability and explainability in the methodology is an interesting option to consider. Specifically, this also relates to different types of complex data, e. g., graphs, images, etc. Moreover, we are planning to work on a further generalization of the neuro-symbolic diagnosis framework presented in [52] as well as a systematic evaluation of its architecture using randomized, parameterized and domain-agnostic synthetic problem instances and corresponding ground truth solutions generated based on the abstract formulation of the general problem of diagnosing systems with interconnected components based on sensor signal assessment.

References

[1] Chandola V, Banerjee A, Kumar V. Anomaly Detection: A Survey. ACM computing surveys (CSUR). 2009;41:1-58.
[2] Pang G, Shen C, Cao L, Hengel AVD. Deep Learning for Anomaly Detection: A Review. ACM Computing Surveys (CSUR). 2021;54:1-38.
[3] Szolovits P, Patil RS, Schwartz WB. Artificial Intelligence in Medical Diagnosis. Annals of internal medicine. 1988;108(1):80-7.
[4] Puppe F. Systematic Introduction to Expert Systems. Heidelberg: Springer; 1993.
[5] Travé-Massuyès L. Bridging Control and Artificial Intelligence Theories for Diagnosis: A Survey. Engineering Applications of Artificial Intelligence. 2014;27:1-16.
[6] Liu R, Yang B, Zio E, Chen X. Artificial Intelligence for Fault Diagnosis of Rotating Machinery: A Review. Mechanical Systems and Signal Processing. 2018;108:33-47.
[7] Su H, Lee J. Machine Learning Approaches for Diagnostics and Prognostics of Industrial Systems Using Industrial Open Source Data: A Review. International Journal of Prognostics and Health Management. 2024;15(2).
[8] Majstorović V. Expert Systems for Diagnosis and Maintenance: The State-of-the-Art. Computers in Industry. 1990;15(1-2):43-68.
[9] Reinertsen R. Residual Life of Technical Systems; Diagnosis, Prediction and Life Extension. Reliability Engineering & System Safety. 1996;54(1):23-34.
[10] Lei Y, Yang B, Jiang X, Jia F, Li N, Nandi AK. Applications of Machine Learning to Machine Fault Diagnosis: A Review and Roadmap. Mechanical Systems and Signal Processing. 2020;138:106587.
[11] Chen Z, Yang Y, Hu Z. A Technical Framework and Roadmap of Embedded Diagnostics and Prognostics for Complex Mechanical Systems in Prognostics and Health Management Systems. IEEE Transactions on Reliability. 2012;61(2):314-22.
[12] Ishiguro A, Watanabe Y, Uchikawa Y. Fault Diagnosis of Plant Systems using Immune Networks. In: Proceedings of 1994 IEEE International Conference on MFI'94. Multisensor Fusion and Integration for Intelligent Systems. IEEE; 1994. p. 34-42.
[13] Alcaraz-González V, López-Bañuelos RH, Steyer JP, Méndez-Acosta HO, González-Álvarez V, Pelayo-Ortiz C. Interval-Based Diagnosis of Biological Systems – a Powerful Tool for Highly Uncertain Anaerobic Digestion Processes. CLEAN–Soil, Air, Water. 2012;40(9):941-9.
[14] Fezai R, Abodayeh K, Mansouri M, Nounou H, Nounou M. Fault Diagnosis of Biological Systems Using Improved Machine Learning Technique. International Journal of Machine Learning and Cybernetics. 2021;12(2):515-28.
[15] Eich HP, Ohmann C. Internet-Based Decision-Support Server for Acute Abdominal Pain. Artificial Intelligence in Medicine. 2000;20(1):23-36.
[16] Buscher HP, Engler C, Führer A, Kirschke S, Puppe F. HepatoConsult: A Knowledge-Based Second Opinion and Documentation System. Artif Intell Med. 2002;24(3):205-16.
[17] Puppe F, Atzmueller M, Buscher G, Huettig M, Lührs H, Buscher HP. Application and Evaluation of a Medical Knowledge-System in Sonography (SonoConsult). In: Proc. ECAI. IOS; 2008. p. 683-7.
[18] Rudin C. Stop Explaining Black Box Machine Learning Models for High Stakes Decisions and Use Interpretable Models Instead. Nature Machine Intelligence. 2019;1(5):206-15.
[19] Atzmueller M. Declarative Aspects in Explicative Data Mining for Computational Sensemaking. In: Proc. International Conference on Declarative Programming (DECLARE). Springer; 2018. p. 97-114.
[20] Roth-Berghofer TR, Richter MM. On Explanation. Künstliche Intelligenz. 2008 May;22(2):5-7.
[21] Atzmueller M, Roth-Berghofer T. The Mining and Analysis Continuum of Explaining Uncovered. In: Proc. Research and Development in Intelligent Systems XXVII. SGAI 2010. Springer; 2010. p. 273-8.
[22] Schank RC. Explanation: A First Pass. In: Kolodner JL, Riesbeck CK, editors. Experience, Memory, and Reasoning. Hillsdale, NJ: Lawrence Erlbaum Associates; 1986. p. 139-65.
[23] Biran O, Cotton C. Explanation and Justification in Machine Learning: A Survey. In: Proc. IJCAI Workshop on XAI; 2017. p. 8-13.
[24] Molnar C, Casalicchio G, Bischl B. Interpretable Machine Learning – A Brief History, State-of-the-Art and Challenges. In: Proc. Joint European Conference on Machine Learning and Knowledge Discovery in Databases. Springer; 2020. p. 417-31.
[25] Das S, Agarwal N, Venugopal D, Sheldon FT, Shiva S. Taxonomy and Survey of Interpretable Machine Learning Method. In: Proc. IEEE Symposium Series on Computational Intelligence (SSCI). IEEE; 2020. p. 670-7.

[26] Vollert S, Atzmueller M, Theissler A. Interpretable Machine Learning: A Brief Survey From the Predictive Maintenance Perspective. In: Proc. IEEE International Conference on Emerging Technologies and Factory Automation (ETFA 2021). IEEE; 2021. p. 1-8.
[27] Rudin C, Chen C, Chen Z, Huang H, Semenova L, Zhong C. Interpretable Machine Learning: Fundamental Principles and 10 Grand Challenges. Stat Surveys. 2022;16:1-85.
[28] Gunning D, Stefik M, Choi J, Miller T, Stumpf S, Yang GZ. XAI - Explainable Artificial Intelligence. Science Robotics. 2019;4:eaay7120.
[29] Barredo Arrieta A, Díaz-Rodríguez N, Del Ser J, Bennetot A, Tabik S, Barbado A, et al. Explainable Artificial Intelligence (XAI): Concepts, Taxonomies, Opportunities and Challenges Toward Responsible AI. Information Fusion. 2020;58:82-115.
[30] Burkart N, Huber MF. A Survey on the Explainability of Supervised Machine Learning. Journal of Artificial Intelligence Research. 2021;70:245-317.
[31] Atzmueller M. Subgroup Discovery. WIREs Data Mining and Knowledge Discovery. 2015;5(1):35-49.
[32] Fürnkranz J, Kliegr T, Paulheim H. On Cognitive Preferences and the Plausibility of Rule-Based Models. Machine Learning. 2020;109(4):853-98.
[33] Fürnkranz J, Kliegr T. A Brief Overview of Rule Learning. In: International Symposium on Rules and Rule Markup Languages for the Semantic Web. Springer; 2015. p. 54-69.
[34] Roscher R, Bohn B, Duarte MF, Garcke J. Explainable Machine Learning for Scientific Insights and Discoveries. IEEE Access. 2020;8:42200-16.
[35] Ribeiro MT, Singh S, Guestrin C. Why Should I Trust You?: Explaining the Predictions of Any Classifier. In: Proc. ACM SIGKDD. ACM; 2016. p. 1135-44.
[36] Lundberg SM, Lee SI. A Unified Approach to Interpreting Model Predictions. In: Proc. International Conference on Neural Information Processing Systems. NIPS'17. Curran Associates Inc.; 2017. p. 4768–4777.
[37] Ribeiro MT, Singh S; Guestrin C. Anchors: High-Precision Model-Agnostic Explanations. In: Proc. AAAI Conference on Artificial Intelligence. AAAI; 2018. p. 1527-35.
[38] Selvaraju RR, Das A, Vedantam R, Cogswell M, Parikh D, Batra D. Grad-CAM: Why Did You Say That? Visual Explanations from Deep Networks via Gradient-based Localization. CoRR. 2016;abs/1610.02391.
[39] Han T, Srinivas S, Lakkaraju H. Which Explanation Should I Choose? A Function Approximation Perspective to Characterizing Post Hoc Explanations. Advances in Neural Information Processing Systems. 2022;35:5256-68.
[40] Iferroudjene M, Lonjarret C, Robardet C, Plantevit M, Atzmueller M. Methods for Explaining Top-N Recommendations Through Subgroup Discovery. Data Mining and Knowledge Discovery. 2023;37(2):833-72.
[41] Atzmueller M, Fürnkranz J, Kliegr T, Schmid U. Explainable and Interpretable Machine Learning and Data Mining. Data Mining and Knowledge Discovery. 2024.
[42] Besold TR, d'Avila Garcez AS, Bader S, Bowman H, Domingos PM, Hitzler P, et al. Neural-Symbolic Learning and Reasoning: A Survey and Interpretation. In: Neuro-Symbolic Artificial Intelligence: The State of the Art. vol. 342 of Frontiers in Artificial Intelligence and Applications. IOS Press; 2021. p. 1-51.
[43] Hitzler P, Eberhart A, Ebrahimi M, Sarker MK, Zhou L. Neuro-Symbolic Approaches in Artificial Intelligence. National Science Review. 2022;9(6):nwac035.
[44] Liu H, Ma R, Li D, Yan L, Ma Z. Machinery Fault Diagnosis Based on Deep Learning for Time Series Analysis and Knowledge Graphs. J Signal Process Syst. 2021;93:1433-55.
[45] Hogan A, Blomqvist E, Cochez M, d'Amato C, Melo GD, Gutierrez C, et al. Knowledge Graphs. ACM Computing Surveys (CSUR). 2021;54:1-37.
[46] Ji S, Pan S, Cambria E, Marttinen P, Yu PS. A Survey on Knowledge Graphs: Representation, Acquisition, and Applications. IEEE Transactions on Neural Networks and Learning Systems. 2021;33:494-514.
[47] Atzmueller M, Sternberg E. Mixed-Initiative Feature Engineering Using Knowledge Graphs. In: Proc. International Conference on Knowledge Capture. ACM; 2017. p. 1-4.
[48] Sternberg E, Atzmueller M. Knowledge-Based Mining of Exceptional Patterns in Logistics Data: Approaches and Experiences in an Industry 4.0 Context. In: Proc. International Symposium on Methodologies for Intelligent Systems. LNCS. Heidelberg: Springer; 2018. p. 67-77. Available from: https://doi.org/10.1007/978-3-030-01851-1_7.

[49] Atzmueller M, Baumeister J, Puppe F. Semi-Automatic Learning of Simple Diagnostic Scores Utilizing Complexity Measures. Artificial Intelligence in Medicine. 2006;37:19-30.

[50] Baumeister J, Atzmueller M, Kluegl P, Puppe F. Conservative and Creative Strategies for the Refinement of Scoring Rules. In: Proc. International Florida Artificial Intelligence Research Society Conference. Palo Alto, CA, USA: AAAI Press; 2006. p. 408-13.

[51] Atzmueller M, Baumeister J, Puppe F. Introspective Subgroup Analysis for Interactive Knowledge Refinement. In: Proc. International Florida Artificial Intelligence Research Society Conference (FLAIRS). AAAI; 2006. p. 402-7.

[52] Bohne T, Windler AKP, Atzmueller M. A Neuro-Symbolic Approach for Anomaly Detection and Complex Fault Diagnosis Exemplified in the Automotive Domain. In: Proceedings of the 12th Knowledge Capture Conference 2023. K-CAP '23. New York, NY, USA: Association for Computing Machinery; 2023. p. 35–43. Available from: `https://doi.org/10.1145/3587259.3627546`.

[53] Atzmueller M, Puppe F. Semi-Automatic Visual Subgroup Mining using VIKAMINE. Journal of Universal Computer Science. 2005;11(11):1752-65.

[54] Fournier-Viger P, Gan W, Wu Y, Nouioua M, Song W, Truong T, et al. Pattern Mining: Current Challenges and Opportunities. In: International Conference on Database Systems for Advanced Applications. Springer; 2022. p. 34-49.

[55] Agrawal R, Srikant R. Fast Algorithms for Mining Association Rules. In: Proc. VLDB. Morgan Kaufmann; 1994. p. 487-99.

[56] Wrobel S. An Algorithm for Multi-Relational Discovery of Subgroups. In: Proc. European Conference on Principles of Data Mining and Knowledge Discovery (PKDD). Springer; 1997. p. 78-87.

[57] Lemmerich F, Becker M, Atzmueller M. Generic Pattern Trees for Exhaustive Exceptional Model Mining. In: Proc. Proc. Joint European Conference on Machine Learning and Knowledge Discovery in Databases (ECML/PKDD). Springer; 2012. p. 277-92.

[58] Duivesteijn W, Feelders AJ, Knobbe A. Exceptional Model Mining. Data Mining and Knowledge Discovery. 2016;30(1):47-98.

[59] Kaytoue M, Plantevit M, Zimmermann A, Bendimerad A, Robardet C. Exceptional Contextual Subgraph Mining. Machine Learning. 2017;106(8):1171-211.

[60] Atzmueller M, Soldano H, Santini G, Bouthinon D. MinerLSD: Efficient Mining of Local Patterns on Attributed Networks. Applied Network Science. 2019;4(43).

[61] Atzmueller M, Günnemann S, Zimmermann A. Mining Communities and Their Descriptions on Attributed Graphs: A Survey. Data Mining and Knowledge Discovery. 2021;35(3):661-87.

[62] Atzmueller M, Puppe F. A Case-Based Approach for Characterization and Analysis of Subgroup Patterns. Journal of Applied Intelligence. 2008;28(3):210-21.

[63] Atzmueller M, Lemmerich F. VIKAMINE - Open-Source Subgroup Discovery, Pattern Mining, and Analytics. In: Proc. Joint European Conference on Machine Learning and Knowledge Discovery in Databases (ECML/PKDD). vol. 7524 of LNCS. Springer; 2012. p. 842-5.

[64] Dzyuba V, van Leeuwen M. Interactive Discovery of Interesting Subgroup Sets. In: Proc. International Symposium on Intelligent Data Analysis. Springer; 2013. p. 150-61.

[65] Vavpetic A, Podpecan V, Lavrac N. Semantic Subgroup Explanations. Journal of Intelligent Information Systems. 2014;42(2):233-54.

[66] Rauch J, Simunek M. Learning Association Rules from Data through Domain Knowledge and Automation. In: Proc. RuleML. Springer; 2014. p. 266-80.

[67] Dou D, Wang H, Liu H. Semantic Data Mining: A Survey of Ontology-based Approaches. In: Proc. IEEE International Conference on Semantic Computing. IEEE; 2015. p. 244-51.

[68] Nalepa GJ, Bobek S, Kutt K, Atzmueller M. Semantic Data Mining in Ubiquitous Sensing: A Survey. Sensors. 2021;21(13):4322.

[69] Atzmueller M, Kloepper B, Mawla HA, Jäschke B, Hollender M, Graube M, et al. Big Data Analytics for Proactive Industrial Decision Support. atp edition. 2016;58:62.

[70] Lemmerich F, Atzmueller M, Puppe F. Fast Exhaustive Subgroup Discovery with Numerical Target Concepts. Data Mining and Knowledge Discovery. 2016;30:711-62.

[71] Klösgen W. 16.3: Subgroup Discovery. In: Handbook of Data Mining and Knowledge Discovery. Oxford University Press, New York; 2002. p. 354-61.

[72] Knobbe A, Crémilleux B, Fürnkranz J, Scholz M. From Local Patterns to Global Models: the LeGo Approach to Data Mining. From Local Patterns to Global Models: Proc ECML/PKDD LeGo Workshop. 2008;8:1-16.

[73] Lavrac N, Cestnik B, Gamberger D, Flach P. Decision Support Through Subgroup Discovery: Three Case Studies and the Lessons Learned. Machine Learning. 2004 October;57(1-2):115-43.
[74] Atzmueller M, Puppe F, Buscher HP. Profiling Examiners using Intelligent Subgroup Mining. In: Proc. 10th International Workshop on Intelligent Data Analysis in Medicine and Pharmacology (IDAMAP-2005). Aberdeen, Scotland; 2005. p. 46-51.
[75] Antonacopoulou EP. Actionable Knowledge. International Encyclopaedia of Organization Studies. 2007.
[76] Fayyad UM, Irani KB. Multi-Interval Discretization of Continuous-Valued Attributes for Classification Learning. In: Proceedings of the International Joint Conference on Uncertainty in AI. Morgan Kaufmann; 1993. p. 1022-7.
[77] Chapman P, Clinton J, Kerber R, Khabaza T, Reinartz T, Shearer C, et al.. CRISP-DM 1.0. CRISP-DM Consortium; 2000.
[78] Atzmueller M, Kloepper B. Mining Attributed Interaction Networks on Industrial Event Logs. In: Proc. International Conference on Intelligent Data Engineering and Automated Learning. Heidelberg: Springer; 2018. p. 94-102.
[79] Atzmueller M, Bloemheuvel S, Kloepper B. A Framework for Human-Centered Exploration of Complex Event Log Graphs. In: Proc. International Conference on Discovery Science (DS 2019). Heidelberg: Springer; 2019. p. 335-50).
[80] Hayes-Roth F, Waterman DA, Lenat DB. Building Expert Systems. London: Addison-Wesley; 1983.
[81] Puppe F. Knowledge Reuse Among Diagnostic Problem-Solving Methods in the Shell-Kit D3. International Journal of Human-Computer Studies. 1998;49:627-49.
[82] Studer R, Fensel D, Decker S, Benjamins VR. Knowledge Engineering: Survey and Future Directions. In: XPS-99: Knowledge-Based Systems – Survey and Future Directions. Proc. Biannual German Conference on Knowledge-Based Systems; 1999. p. 1-23.
[83] Baumeister J, Striffler A. Knowledge-Driven Systems for Episodic Decision Support. Knowledge-Based Systems. 2015;88:45-56.
[84] Chi Y, Dong Y, Wang ZJ, Yu FR, Leung VC. Knowledge-Based Fault Diagnosis in Industrial Internet of Things: A Survey. IEEE Internet of Things Journal. 2022;9:12886-900.
[85] Nan C, Khan F, Iqbal MT. Real-Time Fault Diagnosis Using Knowledge-Based Expert System. Process Safety and Environmental Protection. 2008;86:55-71.
[86] Li W, Li H, Gu S, Chen T. Process Fault Diagnosis with Model- and Knowledge-Based Approaches: Advances and Opportunities. Control Engineering Practice. 2020;105:104637.
[87] Stefik M. Introduction to Knowledge Systems. Morgan Kaufmann Publishers; 1995.
[88] Steenwinckel B, Heyvaert P, De Paepe D, Janssens O, Vanden Hautte S, Dimou A, et al. Towards Adaptive Anomaly Detection and Root Cause Analysis by Automated Extraction of Knowledge from Risk Analyses. In: Proc. International Semantic Sensor Networks Workshop. CEUR; 2018. p. 17-31.
[89] Kononenko I. Machine Learning for Medical Diagnosis: History, State of the Art and Perspective. Artificial Intelligence in Medicine. 2001;23:89-109.
[90] Klemettinen M, Mannila H, Toivonen H. A Data Mining Methodology and its Application to Semi-Automatic Knowledge Acquisition. In: Proc. International Conference on Database and Expert Systems Applications (DEXA). IEEE; 1997. p. 670-7.
[91] Leitich H, Adlassnig KP, Kolarz G. Evaluation of Two Different Models of Semi-Automatic Knowledge Acquisition for the Medical Consultant System CADIAG-II/RHEUMA. Artificial Intelligence in Medicine. 2002;25:215-25.
[92] Ustun B, Rudin C. Supersparse Linear Integer Models for Optimized Medical Scoring Systems. Machine Learning. 2016;102:349-91.
[93] Ustun B, Rudin C. Learning Optimized Risk Scores. Journal of Machine Learning Research. 2019;20(150):1-75.
[94] Yun W, Zhang X, Li Z, Liu H, Han M. Knowledge Modeling: A Survey of Processes and Techniques. International Journal of Intelligent Systems. 2021;36:1686-720.
[95] Puppe F, Buscher G, Atzmueller M, Huettig M, Buscher HP. Clinical Experiences with a Knowledge-Based System in Sonography (SonoConsult). In: Professional Knowledge Management. No. 3782 in LNAI; 2005. p. 319—329.
[96] Gao Z, Cecati C, Ding SX. A Survey of Fault Diagnosis and Fault-Tolerant Techniques—Part I: Fault Diagnosis with Model-Based and Signal-Based Approaches. IEEE Transactions on Industrial Electronics. 2015;62:3757-67.

[97] Puppe F. Knowledge Formalization Patterns. In: Proc. Pacific Knowledge Acquisition Workshop (PKAW). Sydney, Australia; 2000. p. 1-10.

[98] Harry E Pople J. 5. In: Heuristic Methods for Imposing Structure on Ill-Structured Problems: The Structuring of Medical Diagnostics. Routledge; 1982. p. 119-90.

[99] Miller RA, Pople HE, Myers J. INTERNIST-1, an Experimental Computer-Based Diagnostic Consultant for General Internal Medicine. New England Journal of Medicine. 1982;307:468-76.

[100] Naidu G, Zuva T, Sibanda EM. A Review of Evaluation Metrics in Machine Learning Algorithms. In: Silhavy R, Silhavy P, editors. Artificial Intelligence Application in Networks and Systems. Cham: Springer; 2023. p. 15-25.

[101] Rainio O, Teuho J, Klén R. Evaluation Metrics and Statistical Tests for Machine Learning. Scientific Reports. 2024;14(1):6086.

[102] Atzmueller M, Baumeister J, Puppe F. Evaluation of two Strategies for Case-Based Diagnosis handling Multiple Faults. In: Proc. Conference on Professional Knowledge Management (WM2003). vol. P-28 of LNI. Luzern, Switzerland: GI; 2003. p. 275-6.

[103] Atzmueller M, Baumeister J, Hemsing A, Richter EJ, Puppe F. Subgroup Mining for Interactive Knowledge Refinement. In: Proc. 10th Conference on Artificial Intelligence in Medicine (AIME 05). LNAI 3581. Heidelberg: Springer; 2005. p. 453-62.

[104] Atzmueller M, Baumeister J, Klügl P, Puppe F. Rapid Knowledge Capture Using Subgroup Discovery with Incremental Refinement. In: Proc. International Conference on Knowledge Capture (K-CAP). New York, NY, USA: ACM Press; 2007. p. 31-8.

[105] Papakonstantinou A, Kondylakis H, Marakakis E. INTEGRA: A Web-based Differential Diagnosis System Combining Multiple Knowledge Bases. In: Proc. International Conference on Pervasive Technologies Related to Assistive Environments. ACM; 2020. p. 1-6.

[106] Huettig M, Buscher G, Menzel T, Scheppach W, Puppe F, Buscher HP. A Diagnostic Expert System for Structured Reports, Quality Assessment, and Training of Residents in Sonography. Medizinische Klinik. 2004;99(3):117-22.

[107] Ullah I, Jian M, Hussain S, Guo J, Yu H, Wang X, et al. A Brief Survey of Visual Saliency Detection. Multimedia Tools and Applications. 2020;79:34605-45.

[108] He M, Li B, Sun S. A Survey of Class Activation Mapping for the Interpretability of Convolution Neural Networks. In: Proc. ICSINC. Springer; 2022. p. 399-407.

[109] Selvaraju RR, Cogswell M, Das A, Vedantam R, Parikh D, Batra D. Grad-CAM: Visual Explanations from Deep Networks via Gradient-Based Localization. In: Proc. IEEE International Conference on Computer Vision (ICCV). IEEE; 2017. p. 618-26.

[110] Holzinger A. Human-Computer Interaction and Knowledge Discovery (HCI-KDD): What is the Benefit of Bringing Those Two Fields to Work Together? In: Proc. CD-ARES. Springer; 2013. p. 319-28.

[111] Draelos RL, Carin L. Use HiResCAM Instead of Grad-CAM for Faithful Explanations of Convolutional Neural Networks. arXiv preprint arXiv:201108891. 2020.

[112] Chattopadhay A, Sarkar A, Howlader P, Balasubramanian VN. Grad-CAM++: Generalized Gradient-Based Visual Explanations for Deep Convolutional Networks. In: Proc. WACV. IEEE; 2018. p. 839-47.

[113] Wang H, Wang Z, Du M, Yang F, Zhang Z, Ding S, et al. Score-CAM: Score-Weighted Visual Explanations for Convolutional Neural Networks. In: Proc. IEEE/CVF Conference on Computer Vision and Pattern Recognition Workshops. IEEE; 2020. p. 24-5.

[114] Smilkov D, Thorat N, Kim B, Viégas F, Wattenberg M. SmoothGrad: Removing Noise by Adding Noise. arXiv preprint arXiv:170603825. 2017.

[115] Jiang P, Zhang C, Hou Q, Cheng M, Wei Y. LayerCAM: Exploring Hierarchical Class Activation Maps for Localization. IEEE Trans Image Process. 2021;30:5875-88.

[116] Lin YS, Lee WC, Celik ZB. What Do You See? Evaluation of Explainable Artificial Intelligence (XAI) Interpretability Through Neural Backdoors. In: Proc. ACM SIGKDD Conference on Knowledge Discovery and Data Mining. ACM; 2021. p. 1027-35.

[117] Kaur H, Adar E, Gilbert E, Lampe C. Sensible AI: Re-imagining Interpretability and Explainability Using Sensemaking Theory. In: Proc. ACM Conference on Fairness, Accountability, and Transparency. ACM; 2022. p. 702-14.

[118] Kautz HA. The Third AI Summer: AAAI Robert S. Engelmore Memorial Lecture. AI Magazine. 2022;43:93-104.

[119] Wang Z, Yan W, Oates T. Time Series Classification from Scratch with Deep Neural Networks: A Strong Baseline. In: Proc. IJCNN. IEEE; 2017. p. 1578-85.

Part VI

Interdisciplinary Perspectives and Real-World Applications

Handbook on Neurosymbolic AI and Knowledge Graphs
P. Hitzler et al. (Eds.)
IOS Press, 2025

doi:10.3233/FAIA250236

Knowledge-Based News Event Analysis and Forecasting

Oktie HASSANZADEH [1], Sola S. SHIRAI
IBM Research, USA

Abstract. This chapter explores a framework for knowledge-based news event analysis and forecasting. Central to our approach is a Knowledge Graph (KG) that aggregates event-related information from both structured and unstructured sources. The research presented in this chapter delves into the development and capabilities of a versatile toolkit built upon this KG. Key functionalities of the toolkit include: 1) mapping current news headlines to relevant concepts within the KG, 2) facilitating retrieval, reasoning, and visualization to support causal analysis and forecasting, and 3) extracting causal knowledge from textual documents to enrich the KG with additional domain-specific insights. Each function leverages state-of-the-art neurosymbolic techniques, enabling a robust and explainable solution for event analysis and forecasting. Through this chapter, we demonstrate how the integration of these components can assist in building a human-in-the-loop system that enhances the interpretability and effectiveness of event forecasting methodologies.

Keywords. Event Prediction, News Event Analysis, Causal Knowledge, Knowledge Graphs

1. Introduction

Enterprises of varying sizes, as well as government organizations, can significantly benefit from monitoring ongoing global and local news events and analyzing how these developments might affect their operations. One effective method for such analysis involves curating a comprehensive structured knowledge base of past events and their outcomes. This allows for the mapping of current events to similar past occurrences within the knowledge base, enabling reasoning about their causes and potential consequences. For instance, on January 8, 2020, when news outlets began reporting on the World Health Organization's (WHO) announcement of a new virus causing a pneumonia outbreak in Wuhan, China, it became possible to quickly identify similar historical events, such as WHO's March 2003 announcement during the 2002–2004 SARS outbreak. Organizations in industries like tourism or oil and gas could then promptly take steps to mitigate the potential impact of a major disease outbreak on their operations.

Building such a solution, however, presents a range of significant research challenges. Constructing and maintaining an accurate and up-to-date knowledge base neces-

[1]Corresponding Author: Oktie Hassanzadeh, IBM Research, 1101 Kitchawan Rd, Yorktown Heights, NY, 10598, USA; E-mail: hassanzadeh@us.ibm.com. Parts of this chapter are based on work previously published and presented in other venues [1,2,3]

sitates the continuous integration of vast amounts of data from diverse and heterogeneous sources, such as news articles, social media, and official reports. Advanced natural language processing (NLP) and information extraction techniques are crucial for accurately identifying and categorizing relevant information. Additionally, dealing with noisy or incomplete data is a persistent issue, as not all sources provide reliable or complete information.

Another challenge lies in developing effective algorithms for mapping current events to historical ones within the knowledge base. This task requires sophisticated methods for similarity detection and matching, considering not only surface-level details but also the underlying context and causal relationships. Furthermore, enabling reasoning over the knowledge base to derive meaningful insights about potential future outcomes involves integrating symbolic reasoning with data-driven approaches, such as machine learning and statistical modeling, to account for the complexity and uncertainty inherent in real-world events.

Finally, ensuring the explainability and interpretability of the predictions and recommendations generated by the system is crucial, especially when end-users include decision-makers in sensitive sectors like government and healthcare. The implementation must also address ethical considerations, such as avoiding biases that could arise from the data or the models used. Addressing these challenges requires interdisciplinary research efforts, combining expertise from artificial intelligence, data science, linguistics, human-computer interaction, ethics, and possibly other areas of science such as political science and social science.

In this chapter, we first present a vision for a framework for neurosymbolic event prediction. This framework integrates knowledge representation, natural language processing, and machine learning to enable the mapping of current events to similar historical occurrences, facilitating causal analysis and forecasting. The framework comprises several key components, including a neurosymbolic knowledge base constructed using causal knowledge extraction, algorithms for event similarity detection, and tools for reasoning and visualization. In the subsequent sections, we discuss a prototype news event analysis toolkit implemented based on this framework [1]. We will explore each component of the toolkit in detail, including the methodologies employed and the research challenges associated with them. Specifically, we will cover the processes of knowledge extraction and integration, the development of neurosymbolic reasoning algorithms, and the techniques used to ensure the system's interpretability and explainability. By examining these elements, we aim to provide insights into the application of neurosymbolic techniques in event prediction and outline future directions for research.

2. Knowledge-Based News Event Analysis Framework

Monitoring and analyzing ongoing news events and predicting their consequences have long been challenging in political science, intelligence, and finance communities [4,5,6]. Traditionally, most event analysis and forecasting efforts have relied on structured data inputs, such as time series data and event databases [7,8]. In this section, we introduce a framework for event analysis and forecasting that focuses on understanding natural language descriptions of events from text documents. Our approach leverages a symbolic knowledge graph, curated using generic neural knowledge extraction methods applied

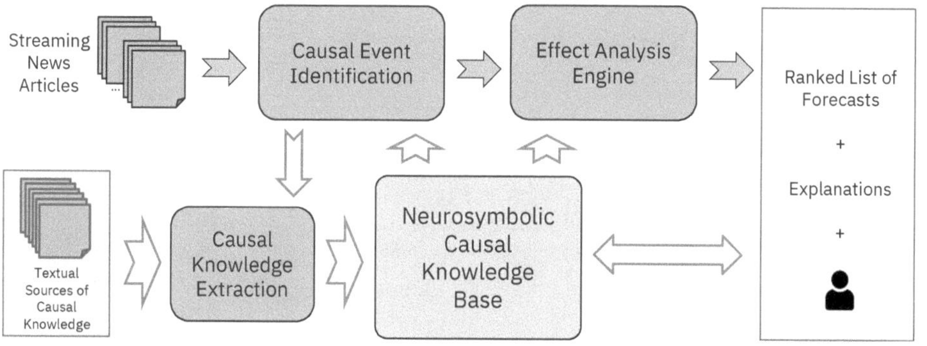

Figure 1. Framework for Knowledge-Based News Event Analysis System

to publicly available text documents, to develop a robust AI agent for event analysis and forecasting. While our proposed framework provides versatile functions that can be applied to a variety of domains, including scientific discovery, finance, and risk management, our primary focus is on analyzing significant societal events, such as disease outbreaks, natural disasters, and protests.

Figure 1 presents a high-level architecture of the envisioned framework. The architecture consists of several key components, and continuously monitors news sources to detect significant events or early indicators of potential major occurrences. This module serves as the first layer of the system, providing real-time situational awareness. The framework also includes components dedicated to the extraction of causal knowledge from text. This involves identifying and modeling the causal relationships between different types of events, which are subsequently stored in a neuro-symbolic knowledge base. This knowledge base comprises both symbolic representations of the extracted knowledge and vectorized encodings, facilitating deep retrieval and analysis tasks.

Central to the framework is the reasoning component, designed to infer potential outcomes based on current conditions. This component could employ computational creativity techniques [9,10] to not only predict futures that align with historical data but also generate novel and high-impact scenarios. The output of the system is a ranked list of forecasts, each accompanied by confidence scores and detailed explanations. The framework also supports additional functionalities, such as the capability to further analyze and debate potential forecasts, incorporating user input to refine predictions. Moreover, the system can integrate other forecasting methods, particularly those leveraging structured data sources, to validate and enhance the accuracy of the generated forecasts. This comprehensive approach aims to provide a robust and flexible tool for event analysis and forecasting.

3. News Event Analysis Toolkit

Building on our envisioned framework, we developed a comprehensive toolkit for knowledge-based news event analysis and forecasting. Figure 2 illustrates the components of this toolkit, with a central feature being a knowledge graph (KG) of events that links event types to their causes and consequences [1]. The nodes in the KG represent

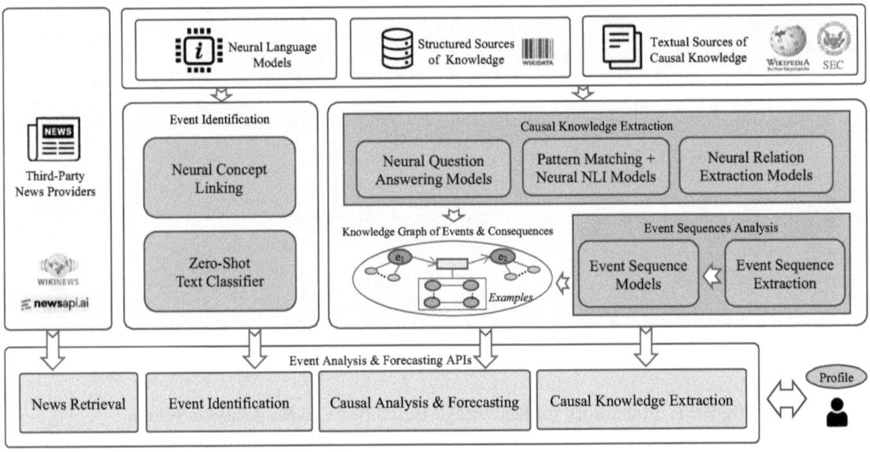

Figure 2. News Event Analysis Toolkit Components and APIs [1]

various event types, connected by edges that denote causal relationships. Each edge is supported by evidence, which may include instances of past events and their outcomes, or textual descriptions explaining how one event could lead to another. The KG is curated using publicly available sources of knowledge and is further augmented through different causal knowledge extraction pipelines, as well as event sequence analysis.

The toolkit offers several functions for conducting a range of analytical tasks on events identified from current and trending news headlines. The primary method of analysis involves matching these events to similar ones in the KG. The toolkit's functions can be integrated into an end-to-end event forecasting solution, enabling the monitoring of ongoing news events, mapping them to historical analogs, and reasoning about their potential consequences. Additionally, the toolkit can be applied across various domains, providing valuable support for knowledge-based decision-making, risk management, and comprehensive event analysis. In the following sections, we describe each component of the toolkit in more detail and highlight some of the challenges encountered in implementing these components in our solution.

4. Knowledge Graph of Events and Consequences

For the version of the toolkit presented in this chapter, the primary sources of knowledge used to curate the toolkit's KG are Wikipedia and Wikidata [11]. Wikipedia offers a comprehensive repository of information about major events and their consequences, with many pages dedicated to detailing various aspects of significant newsworthy events. These pages often contain explicit descriptions of the causes and effects of events, as well as implicit information embedded in statements, sections, or timelines. Wikidata complements this by providing a structured representation of most events described in Wikipedia, along with a rich set of event-related facts. Figure 3 shows examples of causal knowledge available in Wikidata, alongside causal statements from Wikipedia—some of which are already present in Wikidata, while others are not but can be extracted from the text. For domain-specific use cases, the toolkit can support other sources of knowledge. For example, public financial statements from the U.S. Securities and Exchange Com-

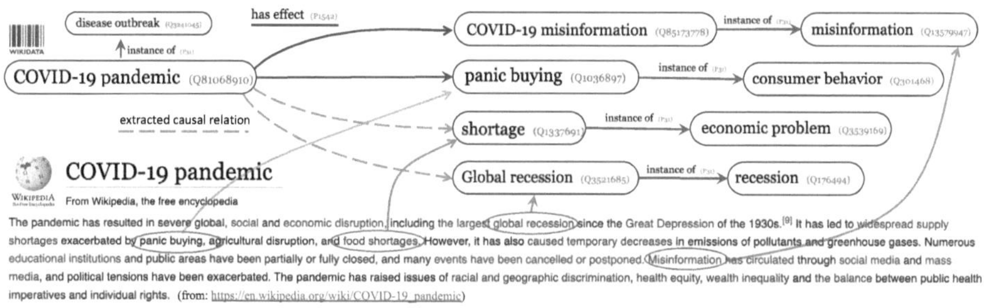

Figure 3. Examples of Event-Related Causal Knowledge in Wikipedia and Wikidata [12]

```
conflict  theft  massacre  mass_shooting  aviation_accident  earthquake
economic_crisis  aircraft_crash  statutory_law  impeachment  infectious_disease
fraud  protest  arson  civil_disorder  school_shooting  social_issue
natural_disaster  risk_factor  work_accident  scandal  bomb_attack  shortage
accident  tsunami  procession  hazard  disaster  coup_d'état  attack
armed_conflict  emerging_communicable_disease  mass_murder  war
impeachment_in_the_United_States  riot  demonstration  crime  regime_change
volcanic_eruption  murder  explosion  financial_crisis  looting  suicide
disease_outbreak  epidemic  homicide  energy_crisis  industrial_disaster
```

Figure 4. Select Top-Level News Event Classes in our KG [12]

mission (SEC) portal can offer valuable event-related causal knowledge for applications in finance.

The KG is constructed first by curating a base KG from existing concepts and links in Wikidata. For our current focus on analyzing major newsworthy events, we include a select set of event types that have at least one instance linked to a Wikinews article in the base KG, as shown in Figure 4. We then query Wikidata for existing causal relations using properties such as `has effect (P1542)`, `contributing factor of (P1537)`, `immediate cause of (P1536)`, and their inverse properties. Event types connected either directly or through their instances are grouped accordingly. Each link between event types is annotated with base scores derived from simple frequency analyses, such as the number of example pairs of instances, the number of triples associated with the event type and its instances, and the number of Wikipedia pages linked to instances of that type. The result is a collection of event types and their consequences, supplemented with examples for each cause-effect pair and scores that can be used to rank potential consequences for a given event. The KG is further augmented by extracting knowledge from Wikipedia articles using the functions described in Section 8. Figure 6 provides a visualization of the toolkit KG around the “Disease Outbreak” event.

5. News Retrieval: Gathering News Headlines and Articles

To facilitate the monitoring of the latest news and the identification of major events or their early indicators, it is essential to have mechanisms for retrieving news headlines from various reliable third-party sources, ensuring a comprehensive and timely collection of event data. In our toolkit, we explored an integration with two primary sources:

Wikinews and EventRegistry [13], also known as newsapi.ai. It is also possible to retrieve news from proprietary sources such as news agencies that may include all the required news for a given end application.

Wikinews, while not always as comprehensive or timely as some other news outlets, offers unrestricted access for both research and commercial use, making it an ideal source for academic and commercial projects. Additionally, Wikinews articles are often categorized using Wikimedia categories, which facilitates seamless integration with knowledge derived from other Wikimedia-based sources, such as Wikipedia. This consistency in categorization enhances the toolkit's ability to cross-reference and enrich the knowledge graph with related information from the broader Wikimedia ecosystem.

EventRegistry [13], also known as newsapi.ai, provides a robust source of high-quality text about ongoing news events, enriched with detailed metadata. This metadata includes information such as event timelines, involved entities, and geolocation, which adds valuable context to the retrieved news data. EventRegistry's free tier plan allows for cost-effective access to a wealth of information, making it accessible for a wide range of users. The inclusion of these interfaces in our toolkit ensures that users have access to diverse and reliable news sources, enabling them to perform thorough and accurate event analysis and forecasting.

There is potential to expand the monitoring capabilities by integrating additional news data providers. Platforms like webz.io offer access to a wide array of news articles, blogs, and forums in real-time, aggregating data from thousands of sources and providing it in a structured format. This could enhance the ability to filter content based on specific parameters such as language, country, and publication date. Similarly, News API offers access to news articles from a diverse range of sources, allowing for a comprehensive view of global news coverage. Another potential addition is Media Cloud, an open-source platform that provides tools for analyzing media coverage, which could offer valuable insights into the framing and dissemination of news stories. By incorporating these additional sources, the solution could offer an even more extensive and nuanced understanding of global events, further enhancing its utility for event analysis and forecasting.

6. Event Identification: Mapping News Headlines to Event Classes

Event identification functions in our toolkit not only associate ongoing news with an event type in the knowledge graph (KG) but also capture the context of these events, such as locations, people, and organizations involved, using standard entity linking methods. This context enriches the knowledge base, allowing for a more comprehensive analysis of events. In this section, we specifically address the task of mapping ongoing news to event-related classes within a knowledge base. While entity linking has been widely studied and implemented, the task of mapping news headlines to event classes, which involves categorizing events based on their nature and impact, has received comparatively less attention in the literature. Addressing this gap is crucial for creating a knowledge-driven event analysis system.

One approach to this task is to treat event classes as a set of categories (or topics) and classify news headlines accordingly. Previous research has examined various methods for classifying news headlines (e.g., see [14,15] and references therein). The majority

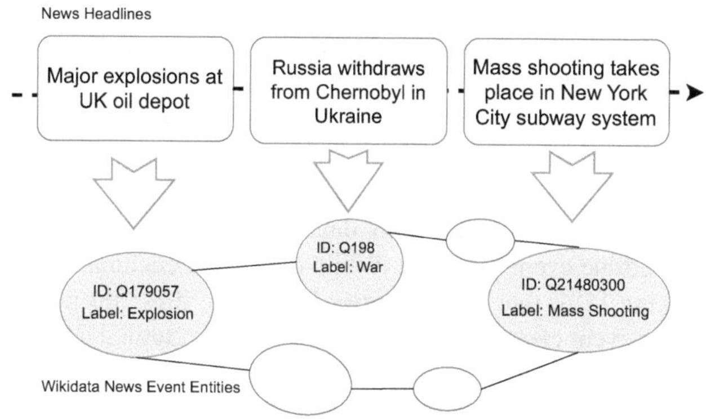

Figure 5. Example of News Headlines and Event Classes in Our Benchmark [2]

of these methods rely on supervised learning techniques, which necessitate a training dataset. However, for a solution that needs to adapt to evolving event classes or be easily customized for different domains, relying on the availability of sufficiently large training corpora is impractical for achieving accurate classification.

When training data is unavailable, an alternative approach is to use unsupervised or weakly supervised classification methods that require minimal or no training data. These methods often depend on rule-based systems or pre-trained generic models. Recently, pre-trained language models, particularly large language models, have demonstrated superior performance in such scenarios. This has led to a proliferation of models, each varying in architecture, parameters, pre-training datasets, and fine-tuning techniques. Selecting the appropriate model for a specific task necessitates an evaluation framework to assess the models' accuracy in relation to the target task.

In this section, we first define the event identification task and then introduce an evaluation framework for the unsupervised mapping of news headlines to event classes within a knowledge graph. We then outline our methodology for constructing the benchmark dataset. Following this, we present the evaluation results of several methods, focusing on two distinct categories of unsupervised techniques. We conclude with a discussion of the key insights gained and explore potential directions for future research. The datasets used in our experiments, along with the evaluation framework, are publicly accessible [16].

6.1. Task Definition

The objective of our task is as follows: Given a news headline and a set of event classes from a knowledge graph, identify the most relevant event class that corresponds to the news headline. A news headline is a brief text (typically a single sentence) that summarizes the content of a news article, providing an overview of its key points. The knowledge graph contains various event-related classes, each associated with one or more labels, a description, and, in some cases, a class hierarchy and additional attributes. Figure 5 illustrates examples of news headlines, event classes, and their corresponding mappings. We term this task as *News Headline Event Mapping*. It is distinct from the event linking task as defined by [17], which involves identifying a specific Wikipedia article for an event mention (a phrase) given a surrounding context. Despite the differences, as discussed in Section 6.3.1, methods developed for event linking can be adapted to address our task.

6.2. Benchmark Dataset

When we began our research, no benchmark dataset was available, to our knowledge, for the task of news headline event mapping. While there are benchmarks for related tasks, such as entity linking [18], that include news headlines, these do not provide ground truth annotations for event classes. To address this gap, we curated a new dataset specifically designed for the news headline event mapping task using data from Wikidata and Wikinews. We first utilized the links to Wikinews articles available in Wikidata to compile a collection of event-related instances. To ensure a focus on event classes, we filtered out instances that were not subclasses of `occurrence (Q1190554)` and removed classes with very short labels, as some non-event entities were also linked to Wikinews. Finally, we manually reviewed these articles to verify their relevance to news headlines and events. This process resulted in 105 Wikinews headlines mapped to corresponding Wikidata event classes. We supplemented this by manually adding five additional headlines from other sources, resulting in a final dataset of 110 headline-to-event class mappings. The labels of the Wikidata classes included in our benchmark are a subset of those displayed in Figure 4. The examples shown in Figure 5 were drawn from this dataset.

Several other benchmark datasets exist in the literature for tasks related to ours. The task most similar to ours is zero-shot sentence classification. Yin et al. [19] provide a comprehensive review of benchmarks for this area. Many of these benchmarks focus on binary classification tasks, such as detecting emotions, sentiment, or clickbait, or cover only a small set of topics. The closest benchmark to ours is the Yahoo! dataset [20], which includes 10 different topics. However, to our knowledge, there are no other benchmarks designed specifically for the task of mapping news headlines to event classes in a knowledge graph or for handling a large number of well-defined topics.

6.3. Evaluation

We leverage our benchmark and evaluation framework to assess the effectiveness of various methods for news headline event mapping. First, we provide a detailed description of each approach, including the implementation specifics. Following this, we present the evaluation results, accompanied by a discussion of the key insights gained and potential directions for future research.

6.3.1. Methods

We explore a range of methods for news headline event mapping, from a simple similarity-based baseline to adaptations of traditional entity linking tools and advanced generative language models.

6.3.2. Zero-Shot Classifiers

We evaluate two zero-shot text classification approaches. The first is a basic baseline based on textual similarity, and the second employs state-of-the-art pre-trained language models for classification.

Similarity-Based Baseline (`Fuzzy`) This approach extracts a substring from a headline that suggests an event occurrence and identifies the most similar event class label in the knowledge graph for that substring. The substring is determined using a sliding window technique with bigrams and trigrams of word tokens from the input. The method then matches these substrings to target event class labels using Levenshtein distance [21]. The event class with the smallest distance is returned as the most similar match to the headline.

Zero-Shot Text Classifier using Natrual Language Inference (`ZSTC`) This classifier is based on the "MNLI" model, which is a pre-trained language model fine-tuned on the Multi-Genre Natural Language Inference (NLI) corpus from the RepEval workshop [22]. The MNLI corpus contains sentence pairs labeled as either "Entailment", "Contradiction", or "Neutral", indicating whether the first sentence entails the second, contradicts it, or is independent of it. MNLI models can be adapted for zero-shot text classification by using the text to be classified as the first sentence (sentence1) and a textual representation of a target class as the second sentence (sentence2). In our experiments, the textual representation of each class (sentence2) is the English label of the class from Wikidata, while sentence1 is the headline to be classified. The class label with the highest Entailment score is selected as the predicted class for the headline. Our zero-shot text classifier utilizes the RoBERTa-large [23] language model fine-tuned on MNLI.

6.3.3. Classic Entity Linkers & Adaptations

We evaluated several state-of-the-art open-source entity linking (EL) systems for potential adaptation in our experiments. Most existing EL solutions are specifically trained to identify named entities (e.g., people, locations, organizations) and typically struggle when applied to events. Therefore, we focused on EL systems that could be more readily adapted for mapping news headlines to event classes. The systems we considered included BLINK [24], OpenTapioca [25], Falcon [26], and Wikifier [27]. Among these, our adaptation of BLINK did not yield satisfactory performance, and OpenTapioca required a training corpus. Although training OpenTapioca with our dataset showed promising results—highlighting another potential application of our dataset—we excluded these results from this paper to maintain a focus on fully unsupervised (zero-shot) methods.

Falcon 2.0 (`Falcon EM`) Falcon 2.0 [26] utilizes natural language processing (NLP) techniques to achieve state-of-the-art entity linking performance across various EL datasets, particularly for question-based prompts [26]. Given a prompt, Falcon 2.0 generates a list of entity surface forms, similar to event mentions. After identifying these surface forms or tokens, it retrieves candidate entities by searching an information retrieval (IR) index, powered by Elasticsearch), within a Wikidata data dump. To adapt Falcon 2.0 for our task, we included only those Wikidata concepts that are recursively instances or subclasses of event classes in the dump, ensuring relevance to event-based queries.

In our evaluation, we used Falcon to match news headlines to Wikidata concept labels. If Falcon did not initially generate at least one candidate concept, we progressively removed tokens from the end of the headline, creating increasingly generalized phrases. This process was repeated until either a candidate concept was identified or the phrase was reduced to an empty string. Once candidate concepts were generated, they were ranked using SPARQL ASK queries to measure the taxonomic distance between each candidate concept and our predefined set of news event classes. The event class with the shortest distance from a Falcon-generated candidate concept was selected as the predicted class for the headline.

Wikifier (`Wikifier`) Wikifier [27] is a tool designed for "wikification," which involves taking an input text and annotating phrases within it with links to corresponding Wikipedia URLs. Wikifier uses the surface forms of hyperlinks found throughout Wikipedia to link phrases in the text to Wikipedia entities. For example, the Wikipedia page for earthquakes may include a hyperlink to the tsunami page, indicating a relationship between these entities. When a surface form appearing in Wikipedia matches a phrase in the input text, Wikifier generates a candidate entity based on the underlying Wikipedia entity. It then builds a directed mention-concept graph that connects these surface forms to their candidate entities. Wikifier performs a global disambiguation using a metric based on the hyperlink distance between entities, which is the number of hyperlink hops required to navigate from one page to another. The shorter the distance, the more related the entities are considered to be. This relatedness metric is used to rank and score candidate entities, and Wikifier returns these entities as predictions along with their scores. For our evaluation, we mapped Wikipedia hyperlinks to corresponding Wikidata concepts using a simple lookup query. We then selected the top prediction that matched one of our target event classes as the predicted event class for the headline.

6.3.4. Large Generative Language Models

Another approach for zero-shot classification is to use generative large language models (LLMs) with prompts. A variety of LLMs are available, differing in architecture, parameter size, and resource requirements. For this study, we chose to use GPT-J 6B [28], a well-known LLM with manageable resource demands, ensuring that our experiments are reproducible without relying on commercial APIs or high-cost GPUs. In this paper, we present results using two different prompting strategies with GPT-J 6B. Experiments involving a broader range of LLMs and more extensive prompt engineering are left for future exploration.

GPT-J Event Mapping (`GPT-J EM`) The objective here is to craft a prompt that enables the LLM to generate the relevant event class. One approach is to use a "few-shot" strategy, where we provide several examples formatted as headline + delimiter + known event class label, followed by the headline to be classified and the same delimiter, prompting the model to generate the appropriate completion text. After experimenting with various prompting techniques, we adopted a co-training approach [29].

In the co-training approach, each headline is initially mapped using GPT-J in a zero-shot manner. The best-performing headlines are then selected to construct a few-shot prompt, which helps guide the model more effectively. The output is an event label, which we subsequently map to the corresponding concept in Wikidata.

GPT-J Event Mapping with Types (`GPT-J EMT`) We extended our experiments with GPT-J by incorporating all event classes directly into the prompt along with the pre-training examples. The set of labels from our news event classes was listed separately and prefixed with "types:" to indicate the available categories. This list was added at the beginning of the prompt to guide the model in selecting from these predefined options. Each annotation in the pre-training examples was also prefixed with "type:" to reinforce this association. Additionally, we implemented a fallback mechanism for cases where the

Table 1. Accuracy Results

	Fuzzy	ZSTC	Falcon EM	Wikifier	GPT-J EM	GPT-J EMT
Correct @1	22	23	33	49	65	74
Accuracy	0.2	0.209	0.3	0.445	0.591	0.673

model's prediction did not match any event class label. In such instances, we performed a textual similarity match between the prediction and our target event labels to identify and return the closest event class as the output.

6.4. Results

For our evaluation, we applied each system described in Section 6.3.1 to the headlines in our news event corpus, generating each system's top predicted event class. We then calculated the accuracy of each system as the percentage of top-ranked predictions that matched the gold-standard event class. The results are presented in Table 1. Alongside the benchmark datasets, all our output data and the evaluation script are available in our GitHub repository [16].

The zero-shot classifier methods (`Fuzzy` and `ZSTC`) showed comparable performance. Both methods performed well on headlines that exhibited linguistic overlap with a target class label. `Fuzzy` excels when there is direct surface or lexical overlap, while `ZSTC` leverages semantic similarity. Examples of headlines with such overlap include: "*Major explosions at UK oil depot*," "*Mass shooting takes place in New York City subway system*," and "*Myanmar military vows to abide by constitution amid coup fears*." In the first two examples, the target event classes are *explosion* and *mass shooting*, and the labels for these classes appear verbatim in the headlines.

Linguistic overlap can also lead to frequent false positives, especially for very general target classes. For instance, in the headline "*More than 80 people killed in Nice, France attack on Bastille Day*," both methods linked "killed" to the `killing` event class and "attack" to the `attack` class. Ideally, both classes would be included among the gold-standard classes, and a ranking metric could be applied to credit multiple (ranked) system predictions. However, for simplicity and to ensure a fair comparison with systems that do not produce ranked or scored outputs, we report only the accuracy (correct @1).

Among the classic entity linking methods, `Wikifier` outperformed `Falcon EM`. It was generally more effective at mapping challenging headlines that lacked obvious linguistic overlap with class labels. For example, it successfully mapped the headline "*Russia withdraws from Chernobyl in Ukraine*" to the `war` event class.

The LLM-based methods also demonstrated the capability to map news headlines to event classes when the labels did not explicitly appear in the headline. Examples include: "*Nine firefighters killed in South Carolina blaze*" (mapped to the event class `fire`), and "*Attack at Texas elementary school kills at least 19, including 18 children*" (mapped to the event class `school shooting`). The second example is particularly notable because the LLM-based methods favored the more specific `school shooting` class over the more general `killing` class, despite the overlap in terminology. Furthermore, the LLM-based methods (`GPT-J EM` and `GPT-J EMT`) consistently demonstrated an ability to map headlines to event classes that were generalizations of terms in the headlines, such as `violence` and `natural disasters`.

6.5. Lessons Learned and Future Work

An Ensemble Approach Although the classifier and entity linking methods did not perform as well as the LLM-based methods, they are complementary. Combining their successful mappings across the dataset yields an overall accuracy of 95%. When comparing their coverage, these methods tend to succeed and fail on different types of headlines. The classic entity linking adaptations are more effective for headlines with single-word event mentions that directly match event classes. In contrast, the LLM-based mappers perform well with multi-word event mentions that are not necessarily substrings of the event class labels, as well as headlines without explicit event mentions. They are able to associate these more ambiguous mentions with relevant event entities, likely due to their exposure to large amounts of text during training. This is further evidenced by the fact that, among the 33% of headlines the LLM-based methods failed to map correctly, 87% contained clear event mentions closely matching the event class labels. Despite some overlap between the two approaches, there is a significant portion of headlines that can be mapped by one method but not the other, which suggests that an ensemble approach—strategically combining classic entity linking techniques with LLMs and deciding when to apply each—could further enhance performance on this task.

A Larger Dataset Despite the relatively small size of our current dataset, we believe the results are informative and effectively showcase the strengths and limitations of different types of methods. The limited size of the data also aligns with the real-world scenario of building a generic and adaptable event monitoring system, where obtaining ground truth data for supervised approaches may be prohibitively costly. Nevertheless, the methodology outlined in Section 6.2 can be expanded to compile a larger and more diverse collection of news headlines mapped to event classes. One approach would be employing a similar approach, targeting news headlines referenced within Wikipedia's event-related articles, to curate a second, significantly larger version of our dataset.

More Experiments on LLMs With the increasing availability of publicly accessible LLMs, as well as commercial APIs that provide access to these models and support more extensive prompt engineering efforts, our dataset and its larger extensions offer a valuable resource for studying a wide range of LLM-based methods for news headline event mapping.

7. Causal Analysis & Forecasting.

Given an event of interest, such as a news event identified through the event identification functions, the causal analysis and forecasting functions in our toolkit are designed to examine its potential causes and consequences. Additionally, these functions facilitate the exploration of relationships between multiple events, offering a comprehensive view of their interconnected dynamics. This section provides an overview of these functions and the methods used to implement them.

7.1. Analyzing Causes & Consequences.

A core mechanism for causal analysis in our toolkit is based on understanding the causes and consequences of past similar events, as represented in the knowledge graph

(KG) curated through text-based knowledge extraction. The toolkit offers two functions, `get_causes` and `get_consequences`, which take an event of interest (e.g., one identified through the event identification functions) as input, along with optional parameters that define the event's context and the user profile. These functions generate a ranked list of potential causes and consequences, with the ranking determined by one or more scores calculated based on the characteristics of the input event and the user profile. Our current implementation includes two primary scores: 1) **impact**, which measures the potential significance of an event, and 2) **surprise**, which evaluates how unexpected the event's occurrence might be. These scores can be computed using a combination of statistical analysis of past events, along with their causes and consequences in the KG, and reasoning about the event's context and the user profile, if available. A simple realization of the impact measure in the toolkit KG is to use the number of effects for a given event as an indication of how impactful that event could be. The surprise measure can be based on the frequency of a consequence given the context. For example, a landslide resulting from an earthquake event would be less surprising if it has occurred many times in the past for that specific event context (e.g., location).

7.2. Sequence-Based Analysis.

Another mechanism of understanding the causes of an event and its potential consequences is through an analysis of historical sequences of events involving the same type of event. This function of our toolkit is implemented by analyzing pre-built event models that are learned using sequences of event types extracted from textual descriptions of events [30], as well as event sequences generated by LLMs [31]. The temporal event models are based on a variation of the work of [32] around graphical event models, and allow for retrieval of a set of *influencers* for a given event type, i.e., those event types that most affect its probability of occurrence. Our toolkit APIs include capabilities for identifying sets of event types that are amplifiers or inhibitors for a user-specifed event type, i.e. make it more or less likely to happen, respectively.

7.3. Case-based Reasoning for Event Prediction

We describe in Section 9 a mechanism of using the toolkit knowledge graph to perform event prediction through inductive link prediction.

7.4. Visualization.

We also provide a visualization function for the KG to support effective causal analysis. This function displays an interactive directed node-edge network graph, as shown in Figure 6, with options for adjusting node and edge sizes based on impact and other frequency-based measures.

8. Causal Knowledge Extraction

As previously mentioned, our toolkit features a comprehensive knowledge graph (KG) curated from publicly available sources using advanced causal knowledge extraction

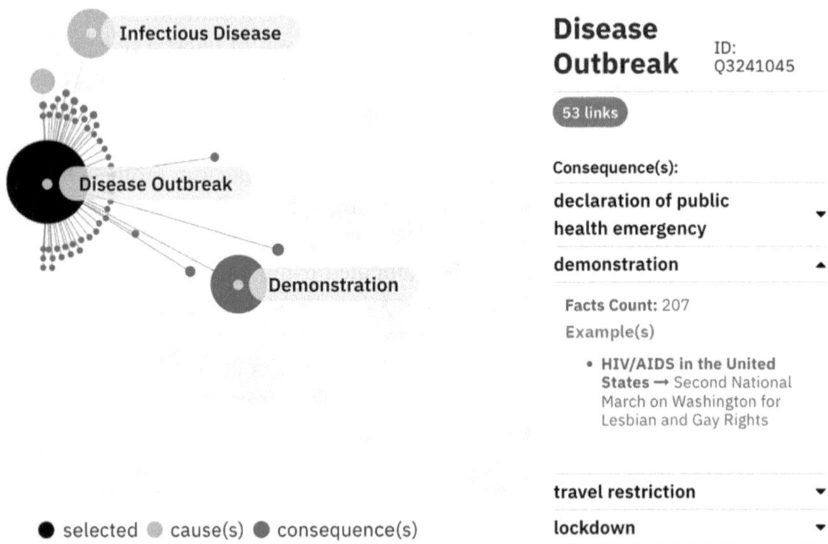

Figure 6. Visualization Function Showing A Portion of our Toolkit KG around Disease Outbreak Events [1]

techniques. These extraction methods are also accessible as functions within the toolkit, enabling users to augment or modify the existing KG with knowledge from user-provided sources specific to their domain. Augmentation can take various forms: a) identifying new consequences for a given event of interest, b) discovering new cause-effect instance pairs for a pair of event types, and c) calculating scores that reflect the likelihood or significance of a causal relationship between two events. Given the diverse ways causal knowledge can be expressed in text, our toolkit includes multiple knowledge extraction approaches, encompassing three classes of solutions for extracting causal knowledge.

8.1. Unsupervised Causal Knowledge Extraction.

This causal extraction pipeline used in our toolkit builds upon our previous work [33,12], which divides the causal extraction process into two steps: 1) extracting pairs of cause-effect phrases, and 2) linking each cause and effect to event concepts. The pipeline is illustrated in Figure 7. As mentioned earlier, various methods are available for extracting cause-effect pairs, including supervised sequence tagging approaches (e.g., [34]) as well as weakly-supervised and unsupervised techniques (e.g., [35,36] and references therein). Our toolkit includes different versions of knowledge graphs, with the option to select a preferred KG for different experiments. In one version, we use causal pairs from CauseNet [37], which applies several state-of-the-art extraction methods, including a supervised sequence tagger. Another version of the KG is curated using a question-answering approach over the associated Wikidata concept labels in a Wikipedia corpus as seed terms to extract causal relations. We refer to these as QAL (Question Answering & Linking) KGs. These are constructed by using the seed terms to generate open-ended causal questions. For example, a seed term like `event` might generate questions such as “What does `event` lead to?” or “What causes `event`?” These questions are then posed to either the opening paragraph or all paragraphs in the associated articles. The resulting

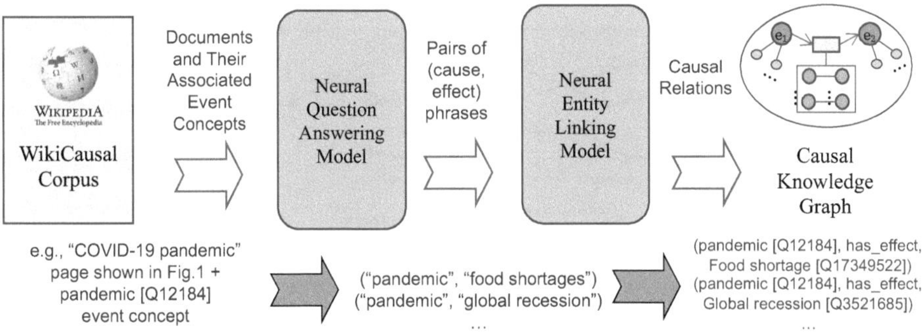

Figure 7. Question Answering and Linking (QAL) Pipeline for Causal Knowledge Extraction [12]

answer span, along with the input label, forms a cause-effect pair, with one side already linked to an event concept from the seed set.

Once we have a collection of cause-effect phrase pairs, the next step is to link them to event concepts. While this task is similar to the classic entity linking tasks extensively studied in the literature, most existing solutions are designed for named entities (e.g., persons, organizations) rather than event concepts. What is required is a generic event disambiguation method that takes a mention and its context as input and outputs the identified event concepts. For the results presented in this paper, we utilize the entity disambiguation function of BLINK [38], using the cause or effect phrase as the span and the phrase used during the extraction of the pair as the context for disambiguation. In the future, we plan to explore other alternatives, such as an adaptation of BLINK called EVELINK [17], which is specifically tuned to achieve better performance than BLINK when linking event mentions.

8.2. Supervised Models for Causal Knowledge Extraction.

In this pipeline, we frame causal knowledge extraction as a sequence labeling task, where each token in an input sequence is assigned one of the following labels: B-Cause, I-Cause, B-Effect, I-Effect, O. Here, "B" denotes the "Beginning" of a cause or effect, "I" indicates "Inside," and "O" represents "Outside" (tokens not part of a causal phrase). We use a state-of-the-art Transformer-based sequence labeling model [14] to extract causal phrases from a corpus of event-related Wikipedia articles. The model employs XLM-RoBERTa [39] as the input sequence encoder and is fine-tuned with the BECAUSE (Bank of Effects and Causes Stated Explicitly) dataset [40]. The extracted causal phrases are then linked to concepts in the knowledge graph (KG).

8.3. Event Sequence Analysis

This pipeline begins by extracting event sequences from textual descriptions or timelines of events. The extracted sequences are then mapped to event types within the knowledge graph (KG). Next, temporal event models [32,41,42] are applied to these sequences, enabling a more detailed analysis of potential temporal and causal relationships between event types. These models also generate likelihood scores, which aid in ranking potential consequences for a given event and context more effectively.

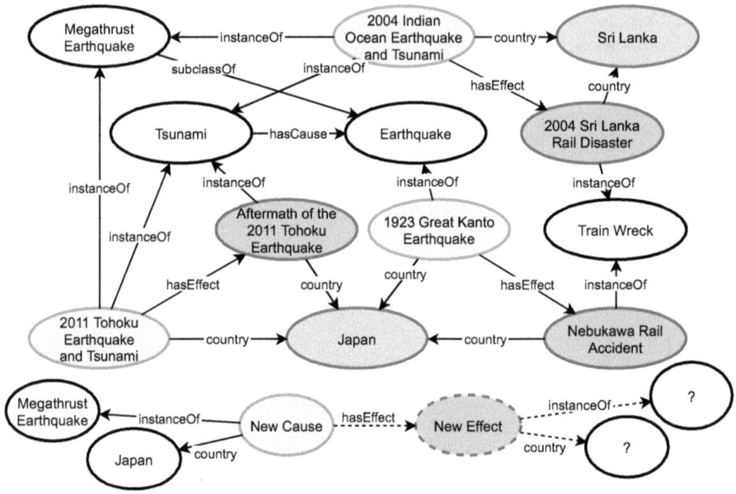

Figure 8. A running example depicting a snippet of Wikidata containing causal events as well as a new cause event and effect event for which we wish to make predictions.

9. Case-based Reasoning for Event Prediction

In this section we describe a KG-driven approach to the task of event prediction for news events [3]. This approach serves to demonstrate how extracting, generating, and curating knowledge about events in a KG can used to support forecasting of future events.

Figure 8 shows a snippet of our KG surrounding a number of events, together with a running example for forecasting the effects that a new event will cause. Suppose that we would like to forecast the effect of a new major earthquake which will occur in Japan – in our example, we depict this as some New Cause event entity together with its properties. The goal of our forecast is then to predict properties of some yet-unseen New Effect event entity.

An important aspect to consider for this problem is that both the new causal event for which we want to perform forecasting and its effect will be entities that do not actually exist within the KG. In such an inductive link prediction paradigm, we turn out sights to knowledge about past events to inform our forecasts of future events.

In the example KG snippet, we can see several examples of events that are somehow similar to our new event, such as past Megathrust Earthquakes and other events that have occurred in Japan. The main idea of our approach, EvCBR, is to leverage such past *cases* of cause-effect event pairs to predict properties about new cause-effect pairs. EvCBR is a case-based reasoning approach which frames the forecasting of effect events as a 2-hop link prediction task – starting from a cause event, for which properties are known, we aim to predict the properties of a future effect event which it may cause. EvCBR also makes use of non-parametric measures for similarity and prediction confidences, making it well suited to a KG about events which may see frequent additions or changes to its contents.

9.1. Problem Formalization

To perform event forecasting using link prediction methods, our goal is to make predictions about new events based on a causal relation between two events. Given our KG $G = (E, R, T)$, consisting of a set of entities E, relation R, and triples T, we represent the cause-effect event pair using the triple (c, r, e), where c, r, and e denote the cause event, causal relation, and effect event, respectively. The properties of the effect event which we aim to forecast are then a set of triples of the form $(e, r_e, ?z) \in Out_e$, where $r_e \in R$ and $?z \in E$. In the remainder of this section, we treat c as if it has already been added to our event KG, for the sake of simplicity. In practice, c may be a real event that occurred for which we wish to make new forecasts, in which case it would actually reside within the KG – we treat this similarly as if we are performing a prediction for some c that does not actually exist. We also focus on the case where r is a causal relation between events, like `has_effect`.

Example. In Figure 8, our task is to perform predictions for New Effect based on the triple (New Cause, `hasEffect`, New Effect). Further, we make predictions about each of New Effect's properties, as (New Effect, `instanceOf`, $?z$) and (New Effect, `country`, $?z$).

The challenge of event forecasting, then, is that we must predict links connected to the effect event e when the only available information about e is that it is caused by c. EvCBR frames this problem as a 2-hop LP task starting from c – that is, predicting the tail entity for the 2-hop link (c, r, r_e, $?z$) for each triple in Out_e.

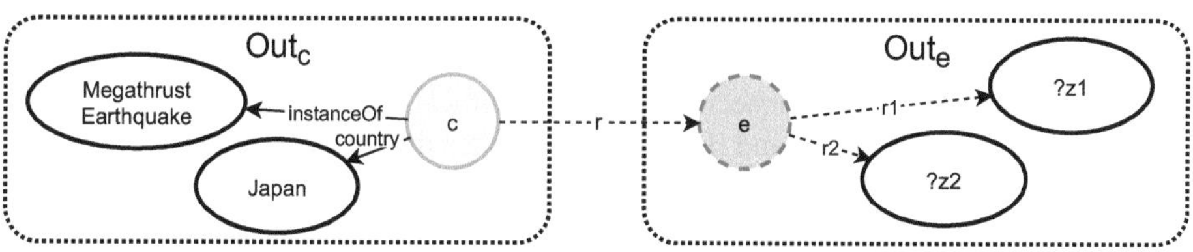

Figure 9. The task setup for our running example.

We additionally denote the set of outgoing triples from c as Out_c – we assume that outgoing properties of the cause event c are provided or already present in the KG, and our method only makes use of such outgoing triples[2] from c. A graphical depiction of this problem setup for our running example is shown in Figure 9.

9.2. EvCBR Method Details

EvCBR is a case-based reasoning approach which aims to make predictions about new events based on background knowledge about similar cause-effect events. The core idea of case-based reasoning is to solve new *problems* based on past experiences, or *cases*, that have been seen by a system. In the context of an event KG, these past cases refer to past cause-effect events which we can draw upon to inform forecasting of future events.

[2]We are motivated to only consider outgoing edges because we can expect a new event entered into the KG to have little to no incoming relations present.

This approach can then be broken down into 3 main steps: (1) retrieve relevant past events, which are similar to the new cause event; (2) identify reasoning paths through the KG which can be used to make predictions; and (3) apply the reasoning paths to make predictions about our new cause-effect event pair.

9.2.1. Case Retrieval

To select cases of cause-effect events that will be useful to inform our new event forecast, we aim to identify other similar events in the KG. Of course, how to determine "similarity" can be challenging in itself. Here, we can make use of the rich semantics which are encoded within KGs to more effectively identify similar types of entities without the need to perform training, and these similar entities in turn can inform whether events are similar to our new cause event.

We first compute entity-level similarity among entities in the KG. Intuitively, this similarity is computed by initializing a vector for each entity representing its connections to other entities. This vector's length is equal to the number of entities in the KG, and each index corresponds to an entity – the index is set to 1 if the entity has any relation connecting to that index's corresponding entity, or if the entity is a subclass of the index's corresponding entity. This essentially gives us a 1-hot encoding of entities which are connected to each other, capturing the idea that similar entities are likely to be connected to the same entities. We also apply inverse document frequency (IDF) weighting to the vector, to make less common entities apply more importance.

Example. The Kanto Earthquake and Tohoku Earthquake both have an outgoing connection to Japan, which might indicate that they are more similar than other earthquake events that occurred in different countries. Additionally, while these two earthquakes do not have any other outgoing connections that are identical, the `subclassOf` relation between Megathrust Earthquake and Earthquake indicates that both the Kanto and Tohoku Earthquakes are a type of Earthquake.

The entity-level similarity is then used to inform event-level similarity. As we only know information about the cause event in our forecast, we mainly aim to determine similarity of the cause events in cause-effect pairs, and compute this similarity based on the set of c's outgoing triples, denoted as $(c, r_c, t_c) \in Out_c$.

For each triple in Out_c, we define the importance of that triple based on (1) the probability that any triple in T containing the tail entity t_c also contains the relation r_c, denoted $P(r_c|t_c)$, and (2) the probability that the tail entity t_c occurs in any triple in T, denoted $P(t_c)$. We posit that triples containing uncommon relations or that lead to uncommon entities should be considered more important when performing our forecasting.

The importance I of a triple is then computed as shown in Eq. (1):

$$I(c, r_c, t_c) = \log\left(\frac{P(r_c|t_c)}{P(t_c)}\right) \tag{1}$$

Example. The importance of (c, instanceOf, Megathrust Earthquake) will be greater than the importance of (c, country, Japan). The $P(r_c|t_c)$ terms for both triples will be equal to 1 in our KG snippet, while the $P(\text{Japan})$ is greater than $P(\text{Megathrust Earthquake})$.

After computing the importance of each triple in Out_c, we then compute the similarity of a past cause event c_s to our new event c as the weighted sum of similarities between each outgoing triple from c_s (denoted $cOut_s$) and Out_c, using the most similar triple from each set for each unique relation. Denoting $ROut_c$ as the set of relations that occur in Out_c, we compute the case head similarity CS_h as in Eq. (2):

$$CS_h(c, c_s) = \sum_{r_c \in ROut_c} \max_{\substack{(c_s, r_c, t_s) \in cOut_s \\ (c, r_c, t_c) \in Out_c}} (nI(c, r_c, t_c) * ES(t_c, t_s)) \tag{2}$$

where nI is the normalized importance of the triple and ES is the entity-level similarity between entities.

Example. Tohoku Earthquake has the greatest CS_h to our cause c, given that both the `instanceOf` and `country` have an exact match. Kanto Earthquake has the second highest CS_h, because it has an exact match with c for the `country` relation leading to Japan and in its `instanceOf` relation, the entity similarity ES between Earthquake and Megathrust earthquake is high.

To select cases, lastly, we also wish to ensure that we can produce useful predictions by selecting past cases where the effect event had the same kinds of properties as those we wish to predict. For each case, we incorporate the jaccard similarity of the effect event's outgoing properties with the properties of the new event that we wish to forecast. The final similarity scores of past cases are used to select some number of cases which will be used in subsequent steps of EvCBR.

We denote the set of cases selected through this procedure as S.

9.2.2. Prediction Path Enumeration and Scoring

The next step is to use our retrieved cases of similar cause-effect events to identify useful reasoning paths through the KG to make new predictions.

We first enumerate a set of paths which connect cause events to their effect event's properties. We define a path as a sequence of triples through the KG that can connect two entities. Given a start entity x and end entity y, we can express a path of length n connecting them as a sequence of triples, $p = [(x, r_1, e_1), ..., (e_{n-1}, r_n, y)]$. We define the *relation path* as the sequence of relations used in each triple of a path, denoted $rel(p) = (r_1, ..., r_n)$. We denote the list of entities that can be reached starting from entity x following the relation path $rel(p)$ as $\mathbb{E}_{p,x}$. Note that $\mathbb{E}_{p,x}$ is not a set, and may contain repeated entries of an entity that can be reached by different paths through the KG.

For each case (c_s, r, e_s) in our set of retrieved cases S and relation $r_e \in ROut_e$, let E_{r_e,e_s} denote the set of entities connected to e_s by the outgoing relation r_e, i.e., $(e_s, r_e, t) \in T$ for all $t \in E_{r_e,e_s}$. We then randomly sample up to N_p unique paths of length ≤ 3 connecting c_s to any entity in E_{r_e,e_s}.

Example. Figure 10 shows two example paths, highlighted in red (light) and blue (dark), connecting the Tohoku Earthquake event to its effect's `instanceOf` property. $rel(p_{red})$ consists of the three relations [instanceOf, subclassOf, hasCause^{-1}] while $rel(p_{blue})$ is the single relation [instanceOf]. We do not sample paths that traverse through the Aftermath event.

The path sampling steps are repeated for each case in S, and the set of all paths sampled from each case, connecting the case's cause to its effect's r_e properties, is denoted as $\mathscr{P}_{S,r_e}$.

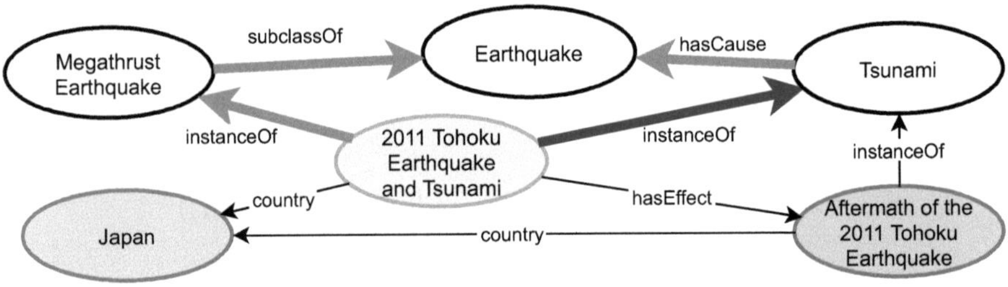

Figure 10. Example paths for the Tohoku Earthquake case.

We then compute confidence scores for each path. Intuitively, this score aims to indicate how accurately we can use each path to perform predictions *based on our set of similar event cases* – if a reasoning path is effective at performing forecasts for past events, we expect it to also be reliable when applied to forecast for a new event.

We base our confidence scoring on a simple precision measure, aiming to score how well a given relation path leads to the correct entities for the target relation. We also weight paths which lead to correct predictions for more cases of cause-effect events as more confidence. Note that it is possible for some reasoning paths to not be relevant to a case if there is not a valid path that can be followed from the cause event to some terminal node – in this case, we do not penalize the path as being incorrect, but it is weighted lower than other paths which have high accuracy and occur more frequently. This path score is denoted as *PScore*.

Example. To make a prediction about the effect's `country` in our three cases, we can sample the relation path $rel(p)$ = [country]. For all three of our cases, following the relation path [country] from the cause leads to the correct country property of its effect. On the other hand, for a relation path like $rel(p)$ = [instanceOf] from our example in Figure 10, which aims to predict the `instanceOf` relation of the effect, the correct entity is only reached in 1 out of 2 results for the Tohoku Earthquake, and 0 out of 3 total results for the other two cases.

9.2.3. Applying Prediction Paths

Our last step is to apply the prediction paths to our new event in order to forecast its effect's properties. Formally, for our query event (c, r, e) and a single property for which we want to predict $(e, r_e, ?z)$, we score each candidate prediction entity z as follows:

$$EScore(c, r, r_e, z) = \sum_{\substack{rel(p) \in \mathscr{P}_{r_e} \\ z' \in \mathbb{E}_{p,c}}} PScore(r_e, rel(p))[z' = z] \tag{3}$$

In Eq. (3), we choose to calculate the score for a prediction z as a summation of path *PScore*s so that the score is increased for (1) entities that are frequently reached by a given relation path, and (2) entities that are reached by a variety of different relation paths.

For the target relation r_e we compute all $EScore$ values for all entities for which a path $rel(p) \in \mathscr{P}_{r_e}$ exists between it and c, denoted $E_{\mathscr{P}_{r_e},c}$. We use these scores to sort and rank our predictions for the given 2-hop link. To make predictions for all properties Out_e

of that we wish to predict, we repeat the procedures in Section 9.2.2 for each $r_e \in ROut_e$ and the aforementioned scoring procedure.

Example. Let us consider applying paths to make predictions for e's `instanceOf` relation. There are only two valid paths that may be sampled to make this prediction, $rel(p_1)$ = [instanceOf] and $rel(p_2)$ = [instanceOf, subclassOf, hasCause^{-1}], both coming from the Tohoku Earthquake case. Using a simplified *PScore* calculation for this example, the *PScore* for these two path are $PScore(p_1) = 1/5$ and $PScore(p_2) = 1$. Applying these two paths to our cause event c results in predicting e to be an instance of $MegathrustEarthquake$ with a score of $1/5$ and $Tsunami$ with a score of 1. The best prediction in our minimal running example is that the new effect event will be a tsunami.

Algorithm 1 provides a high-level overview of our model's inputs and the steps that are performed to produce predictions for each property of the unseen effect event up to this point.

Algorithm 1 EvCBR Event Prediction Overview

Inputs: $(c,r,e), ROut_e, N_h, N_t, N_p$
$(c,r,e) \leftarrow$ the cause c, causal relation r, and unseen effect e
$ROut_e \leftarrow$ the set of relations about the effect to predict
$N_p \leftarrow$ number of paths to sample

```
1: Retrieve cases from the KG
2: for r_e ∈ ROut_e do                          ▷ Repeat for each prediction relation
3:     Sample N_p paths from each case
4:     Compute each path's score using PScore
5:     Follow each path starting from c to generate predictions
6:     Score each prediction using EScore
7:     Rank and report top predictions for r_e
```

9.2.4. Prediction Score Refinement

Optionally, after making predictions for all of our event prediction relations $ROut_e$, we introduce an additional step to refine our forecasting results. Intuitively, the idea of our refinement is to repeat the same process but *in reverse*. Since EvCBR does not inherently rely on special properties about causal relations, it would work similarly if we started from an effect event and try to predict its cause – therefore, in the refinement phase, if predictions about the effect event are accurate, we expect to be able to also accurately "predict" the cause event.

9.3. Experimental Validation

We validate the effectiveness of our method to support KG-driven event forecasting using a KG of cause-effect events curated from Wikidata. We use an approach similar to [43] to identify 307 event-related classes based on links between entries in Wikidata and news articles in Wikinews, and select 6 causal relations[3] to collect event pairs. Our Wikidata-based event KG encompassed 157 unique event classes, connecting 284 cause events and 311 effect events.

[3] `https://www.wikidata.org/wiki/Wikidata:List_of_properties/causality`

9.3.1. Baseline Models

We compare EvCBR's performance against a set of proven link prediction baselines, with modifications made where needed to support the 2-hop link prediction task setup. The main baselines used were TransE [44], ComplEx [45], RotatE [46], NoGE [47], ProbCBR [48], and AnyBURL [49]. We also investigate the effectiveness of EvCBR on its own, indicated as EvCBR_{base}, the use of the optional prediction refinement, as EvCBR_{re}, and a combination of the base and refinement scores, as, $\text{EvCBR}_{re+base}$.

We apply each model to rank predictions for each tail entity in the test set of 2-hop links and report the mean reciprocal rank (MRR) and Hits@K metrics for each model. Experimental results are shown in Table 2; the best performing model for each dataset is highlighted in bold and the second best is underlined (for EvCBR's results we only highlight the best performance of any one variation).

Table 2. Experimental results.

Dataset: Wikidata Causal Events			
Model	MRR	Hits@1	Hits@10
TransE	0.139	0.096	0.207
ComplEx	0.030	0.024	0.050
RotatE	0.097	0.081	0.125
NoGE	<u>0.149</u>	0.118	<u>0.210</u>
AnyBURL	<u>0.149</u>	<u>0.121</u>	0.202
ProbCBR	0.122	0.107	0.154
EvCBR_{base}	0.156	0.118	0.222
EvCBR_{re}	0.158	**0.130**	0.212
$\text{EvCBR}_{re+base}$	**0.159**	0.125	**0.227**

For our causal event dataset we can see that our approach showed strong performance over the baselines. We also can see how our approach to refine forecasting predictions can lead to a higher Hits@1 score, while the refinement and baseline scores together had a higher overall MRR and Hits@10 – this demonstrates a valuable tradeoff of precision at high-ranks versus recall, which may be a relevant consideration for event forecasting use cases.

The fact that EvCBR does not require training also makes it even more applicable to ever-expanding event KGs, where we might see frequent additions or changes of event knowledge. Such a situation can be seen in pipelines such as our News Event Analysis Toolkit, which would continuously ingest and process new event information.

As an example of applying EvCBR to ongoing events, we performed a prediction for the effect of a Protest event in Iran. Similar cases retrieved from the KG included the Bahraini Protests of 2011, the Iranian Revolution, and the 2019-21 Chilean Protests. The top `instanceOf` predictions for the effect were Resignation, Demonstration, and Civil Resistance, while the top `country` predictions were Iran, Iraq, and Azerbaijan. We find that EvCBR shows promise in terms of factors such as predicting the possibility of events in Iraq and Azerbaijan, which both are geographically and politically intertwined with Iran, and are already dealing with consequences of the events in Iran. The method also performs well in retrieving cases of past events that have similar causes and likely similar consequences. This sort of interpretability of EvCBR's case-based reasoning approach also may be of great value in event forecasting use cases, where it is important to both produce predictions and understand why or how a system output certain results.

10. Conclusion

In this chapter, we presented an exploration of our work towards a vision of a framework for knowledge-based news event analysis and forecasting. Performing analysis and forecasting in this domain is highly challenging, owing to factors such as the ambiguity of natural language making it difficult to produce structured factual knowledge about them, the need for varying levels of context to understand and compare historic versus novel events, and the need to generate interpretable and explainable results for end-users to have trust in forecasted outcomes. To demonstrate how such challenges may be overcome, we discuss our development of a framework for neurosymbolic event prediction and its components which serve to curate news articles, identify and extract useful causal information, and perform analyses and predictions using a variety of neurosymbolic approaches.

Throughout the toolkit components and prediction methods, we can observe many instances where different types of models – neural, neurosymbolic, and symbolic – present tradeoffs and benefits. For example, generative LLMs were highly capable at using context clues to map events to headlines. On the other hand, symbolic methods such as EvCBR demonstrated how we can utilize light-weight approaches to operate over continuously-changing KGs and provide explainability through its use of prediction paths. By integrating such a variety of methods into a holistic framework, we can get the best of both neural and symbolic worlds.

Acknowledgements

The contents of this chapter is based on work done by several researchers at IBM Research as well as interns and collaborators: Parul Awasthy, Ken Barker, Onkar Bhardwaj, Debarun Bhattacharjya, Mark Feblowitz, Aamod Khatiwada, Lee Martie, Steve Fonin Mbouadeu, Jian Ni, Anik Saha, Sola Shirai, Kavitha Srinivas, Lucy Yip. Portions of this chapter are based on work that is published and presented in other venues [1,2,3]. This document has been proof-read and edited with the assistance of AI tools. The authors take full responsibility for the accuracy, integrity, and content of the text.

References

[1] Oktie Hassanzadeh, Parul Awasthy, Ken Barker, Onkar Bhardwaj, Debarun Bhattacharjya, Mark Feblowitz, Lee Martie, Jian Ni, Kavitha Srinivas, and Lucy Yip. Knowledge-based news event analysis and forecasting toolkit. In *Proceedings of the Thirty-First International Joint Conference on Artificial Intelligence, IJCAI 2022, Vienna, Austria, 23-29 July 2022*, pages 5904–5907. ijcai.org, 2022.

[2] Steve Fonin Mbouadeu, Martin Lorenzo, Ken Barker, and Oktie Hassanzadeh. An evaluation framework for mapping news headlines to event classes in a knowledge graph. In *Proceedings of the 6th Workshop on Challenges and Applications of Automated Extraction of Socio-political Events from Text*, pages 44–52, Varna, Bulgaria, September 2023. INCOMA Ltd., Shoumen, Bulgaria.

[3] Sola Shirai, Debarun Bhattacharjya, and Oktie Hassanzadeh. Event prediction using case-based reasoning over knowledge graphs. In *Proceedings of the ACM Web Conference 2023, WWW 2023, Austin, TX, USA, 30 April 2023 - 4 May 2023*, pages 2383–2391. ACM, 2023.

[4] Graham Elliott and Allan Timmermann. Forecasting in economics and finance. *Annual Review of Economics*, 8(1):81–110, 2016.

[5] Sathappan Muthiah, Patrick Butler, Rupinder Paul Khandpur, Parang Saraf, Nathan Self, Alla Rozovskaya, Liang Zhao, Jose Cadena, Chang-Tien Lu, Anil Vullikanti, Achla Marathe, Kristen Summers, Graham Katz, Andy Doyle, Jaime Arredondo, Dipak K. Gupta, David Mares, and Naren Ramakrishnan. EMBERS at 4 years: Experiences operating an open source indicators forecasting system. In *Proceedings of the 22nd ACM SIGKDD International Conference on Knowledge Discovery and Data Mining*, KDD '16, page 205–214, New York, NY, USA, 2016. Association for Computing Machinery.

[6] S. Sohrabi, M. Katz, O. Hassanzadeh, O. Udrea, and M. D. Feblowitz. IBM scenario planning advisor: Plan recognition as AI planning in practice. In *Proceedings of the Twenty-Seventh International Joint Conference on Artificial Intelligence, IJCAI 2018, July 13-19, 2018, Stockholm, Sweden*, pages 5865–5867, 2018.

[7] Fatma Ezzahra Gmati, Salem Chakhar, Wided Lejouad Chaari, and Mark Xu. A taxonomy of event prediction methods. In Franz Wotawa, Gerhard Friedrich, Ingo Pill, Roxane Koitz-Hristov, and Moonis Ali, editors, *Advances and Trends in Artificial Intelligence. From Theory to Practice*, pages 12–26, Cham, 2019. Springer International Publishing.

[8] Liang Zhao. Event prediction in the big data era: A systematic survey. *ACM Comput. Surv.*, 54(5), May 2021.

[9] Dharmashankar Subramanian, Debarun Bhattacharjya, and Lav R. Varshney. Generalization across contexts in unsupervised computational creativity. In François Pachet, Anna Jordanous, and Carlos León, editors, *Proceedings of the Ninth International Conference on Computational Creativity, ICCC 2018, Salamanca, Spain, June 25-29, 2018*, pages 40–47. Association for Computational Creativity (ACC), 2018.

[10] Lav R. Varshney, Florian Pinel, Kush R. Varshney, Debarun Bhattacharjya, Angela Schörgendorfer, and Yi-Min Chee. A big data approach to computational creativity: The curious case of chef watson. *IBM J. Res. Dev.*, 63(1):7:1–7:18, 2019.

[11] Denny Vrandecic and Markus Krötzsch. Wikidata: a free collaborative knowledgebase. *Commun. ACM*, 57(10):78–85, 2014.

[12] Oktie Hassanzadeh. Wikicausal: Corpus and evaluation framework for causal knowledge graph construction, 2024.

[13] Gregor Leban, Blaz Fortuna, Janez Brank, and Marko Grobelnik. Event registry: Learning about world events from news. In *Proceedings of the 23rd International Conference on World Wide Web*, WWW '14 Companion, page 107–110, New York, NY, USA, 2014. Association for Computing Machinery.

[14] Parul Awasthy, Jian Ni, Ken Barker, and Radu Florian. IBM MNLP IE at CASE 2021 task 1: Multigranular and multilingual event detection on protest news. In *Proceedings of the 4th Workshop on Challenges and Applications of Automated Extraction of Socio-political Events from Text (CASE 2021)*, pages 138–146, Online, August 2021. Association for Computational Linguistics.

[15] Mazhar Iqbal Rana, Shehzad Khalid, and Muhammad Usman Akbar. News classification based on their headlines: A review. In *17th IEEE International Multi Topic Conference 2014*, pages 211–216, December 2014.

[16] Steve Mbouadeu, Ken Barker, and Oktie Hassanzadeh. An Evaluation Framework for Mapping News Headlines to Event Classes in a Knowledge Graph. `https://github.com/mbouadeus/news-headline-event-linking`, May 2023.

[17] Xiaodong Yu, Wenpeng Yin, Nitish Gupta, and Dan Roth. Event linking: Grounding event mentions to Wikipedia. In *Proceedings of the 17th Conference of the European Chapter of the Association for Computational Linguistics*, pages 2679–2688, Dubrovnik, Croatia, May 2023. Association for Computational Linguistics.

[18] Marieke van Erp, Pablo Mendes, Heiko Paulheim, Filip Ilievski, Julien Plu, Giuseppe Rizzo, and Joerg Waitelonis. Evaluating entity linking: An analysis of current benchmark datasets and a roadmap for doing a better job. In *Proceedings of the Tenth International Conference on Language Resources and Evaluation (LREC'16)*, pages 4373–4379, Portorož, Slovenia, May 2016. European Language Resources Association (ELRA).

[19] Wenpeng Yin, Jamaal Hay, and Dan Roth. Benchmarking zero-shot text classification: Datasets, evalu-

ation and entailment approach. In *Proceedings of the 2019 Conference on Empirical Methods in Natural Language Processing and the 9th International Joint Conference on Natural Language Processing (EMNLP-IJCNLP)*, pages 3914–3923, Hong Kong, China, November 2019. Association for Computational Linguistics.

[20] Xiang Zhang, Junbo Zhao, and Yann LeCun. Character-level convolutional networks for text classification. In C. Cortes, N. Lawrence, D. Lee, M. Sugiyama, and R. Garnett, editors, *Advances in Neural Information Processing Systems*, volume 28. Curran Associates, Inc., 2015.

[21] B. Chandrasekar, Bharath Ramesh, Vishalakshi Prabhu, S. Sajeev, Pratik K. Mohanty, and G. Shobha. Development of intelligent digital certificate fuzzer tool. In *Proceedings of the 2017 International Conference on Cryptography, Security and Privacy*, ICCSP '17, page 126–130, New York, NY, USA, 2017. Association for Computing Machinery.

[22] Adina Williams, Nikita Nangia, and Samuel Bowman. A broad-coverage challenge corpus for sentence understanding through inference. In *Proceedings of the 2018 Conference of the North American Chapter of the Association for Computational Linguistics: Human Language Technologies, Volume 1 (Long Papers)*, pages 1112–1122, New Orleans, Louisiana, June 2018. Association for Computational Linguistics.

[23] Yinhan Liu, Myle Ott, Naman Goyal, Jingfei Du, Mandar Joshi, Danqi Chen, Omer Levy, Mike Lewis, Luke Zettlemoyer, and Veselin Stoyanov. Roberta: A robustly optimized bert pretraining approach, 2019.

[24] Ledell Wu, Fabio Petroni, Martin Josifoski, Sebastian Riedel, and Luke Zettlemoyer. Scalable zero-shot entity linking with dense entity retrieval. In *Proceedings of the 2020 Conference on Empirical Methods in Natural Language Processing (EMNLP)*, pages 6397–6407, Online, November 2020. Association for Computational Linguistics.

[25] Antonin Delpeuch. OpenTapioca: Lightweight entity linking for Wikidata. *CoRR*, abs/1904.09131, 2019.

[26] Ahmad Sakor, Kuldeep Singh, Anery Patel, and Maria-Esther Vidal. Falcon 2.0: An entity and relation linking tool over wikidata. In *Proceedings of the 29th ACM International Conference on Information & Knowledge Management*, CIKM '20, page 3141–3148, New York, NY, USA, 2020. Association for Computing Machinery.

[27] Janez Brank, Gregor Leban, and Marko Grobelnik. Annotating documents with relevant wikipedia concepts. *Proceedings of the Slovenian Conference on Data Mining and Data Warehouses (SiKDD 2017)*, 472, 2017.

[28] Ben Wang and Aran Komatsuzaki. GPT-J-6B: A 6 Billion Parameter Autoregressive Language Model. `https://github.com/kingoflolz/mesh-transformer-jax`, May 2021.

[29] Hunter Lang, Monica N Agrawal, Yoon Kim, and David Sontag. Co-training improves prompt-based learning for large language models. In Kamalika Chaudhuri, Stefanie Jegelka, Le Song, Csaba Szepesvari, Gang Niu, and Sivan Sabato, editors, *Proceedings of the 39th International Conference on Machine Learning*, volume 162 of *Proceedings of Machine Learning Research*, pages 11985–12003. PMLR, 17–23 Jul 2022.

[30] Maria Chang, Achille Fokoue, Rosario Uceda-Sosa, Parul Awasthy, Ken Barker, Sadhana Kumaravel, Oktie Hassanzadeh, Elton F. S. Soares, Tian Gao, Debarun Bhattacharjya, Radu Florian, and Salim Roukos. CHRONOS: A schema-based event understanding and prediction system. In *Thirty-Eighth AAAI Conference on Artificial Intelligence, AAAI 2024, Thirty-Sixth Conference on Innovative Applications of Artificial Intelligence, IAAI 2024, Fourteenth Symposium on Educational Advances in Artificial Intelligence, EAAI 2014, February 20-27, 2024, Vancouver, Canada*, pages 22871–22877. AAAI Press, 2024.

[31] Somin Wadhwa, Oktie Hassanzadeh, Debarun Bhattacharjya, Ken Barker, and Jian Ni. Distilling event sequence knowledge from large language models. In *The Semantic Web - ISWC 2024 - 23rd International Semantic Web Conference*, 2024.

[32] Debarun Bhattacharjya, Dharmashankar Subramanian, and Tian Gao. Proximal graphical event models. In *Advances in Neural Information Processing Systems 31: Annual Conference on Neural Information Processing Systems 2018, NeurIPS 2018, December 3-8, 2018, Montréal, Canada*, pages 8147–8156, 2018.

[33] Oktie Hassanzadeh. Building a knowledge graph of events and consequences using wikidata. In *Proceedings of the 2nd Wikidata Workshop (Wikidata 2021) co-located with the 20th International Semantic Web Conference (ISWC 2021), Virtual Conference, October 24, 2021*, volume 2982 of *CEUR Workshop*

Proceedings. CEUR-WS.org, 2021.

[34] Jesse Dunietz, Lori S. Levin, and Jaime G. Carbonell. Automatically tagging constructions of causation and their slot-fillers. *Trans. Assoc. Comput. Linguistics*, 5:117–133, 2017.

[35] Manik Bhandari, Mark Feblowitz, Oktie Hassanzadeh, Kavitha Srinivas, and Shirin Sohrabi. Unsupervised causal knowledge extraction from text using natural language inference (student abstract). In *Thirty-Fifth AAAI Conference on Artificial Intelligence, AAAI 2021, Thirty-Third Conference on Innovative Applications of Artificial Intelligence, IAAI 2021, The Eleventh Symposium on Educational Advances in Artificial Intelligence, EAAI 2021, Virtual Event, February 2-9, 2021*, pages 15759–15760. AAAI Press, 2021.

[36] Anik Saha, Alex Gittens, Jian Ni, Oktie Hassanzadeh, Bülent Yener, and Kavitha Srinivas. SPOCK @ causal news corpus 2022: Cause-effect-signal span detection using span-based and sequence tagging models. In Ali Hürriyetoglu, Hristo Tanev, Vanni Zavarella, and Erdem Yörük, editors, *Proceedings of the 5th Workshop on Challenges and Applications of Automated Extraction of Socio-political Events from Text, CASE@EMNLP 2022, Abu Dhabi, United Arab Emirates (Hybrid), December 7-8, 2022*, pages 133–137. Association for Computational Linguistics, 2022.

[37] Stefan Heindorf, Yan Scholten, Henning Wachsmuth, Axel-Cyrille Ngonga Ngomo, and Martin Potthast. Causenet: Towards a causality graph extracted from the web. In *CIKM '20: The 29th ACM International Conference on Information and Knowledge Management, Virtual Event, Ireland, October 19-23, 2020*, pages 3023–3030. ACM, 2020.

[38] Ledell Wu, Fabio Petroni, Martin Josifoski, Sebastian Riedel, and Luke Zettlemoyer. Scalable zero-shot entity linking with dense entity retrieval. In *Proceedings of the 2020 Conference on Empirical Methods in Natural Language Processing, EMNLP 2020, Online, November 16-20, 2020*, pages 6397–6407. Association for Computational Linguistics, 2020.

[39] Alexis Conneau, Kartikay Khandelwal, Naman Goyal, Vishrav Chaudhary, Guillaume Wenzek, Francisco Guzmán, Edouard Grave, Myle Ott, Luke Zettlemoyer, and Veselin Stoyanov. Unsupervised cross-lingual representation learning at scale. In *Proceedings of the 58th Annual Meeting of the Association for Computational Linguistics*, pages 8440–8451, Online, July 2020. Association for Computational Linguistics.

[40] Jesse Dunietz, Lori Levin, and Jaime Carbonell. The BECauSE corpus 2.0: Annotating causality and overlapping relations. In *Proceedings of the 11th Linguistic Annotation Workshop*, pages 95–104, Valencia, Spain, April 2017. Association for Computational Linguistics.

[41] Debarun Bhattacharjya, Tian Gao, and Dharmashankar Subramanian. Order-dependent event models for agent interactions. In Christian Bessiere, editor, *Proceedings of the Twenty-Ninth International Joint Conference on Artificial Intelligence, IJCAI 2020*, pages 1977–1983. ijcai.org, 2020.

[42] Debarun Bhattacharjya, Saurabh Sihag, Oktie Hassanzadeh, and Liza Bialik. Summary markov models for event sequences. In *Proceedings of the Thirty-First International Joint Conference on Artificial Intelligence, IJCAI 2022, Vienna, Austria, 23-29 July 2022*, pages 4836–4842. ijcai.org, 2022.

[43] Oktie Hassanzadeh. Building a knowledge graph of events and consequences using wikidata. In *Proceedings of the 2nd Wikidata Workshop (Wikidata 2021) co-located with the 20th International Semantic Web Conference (ISWC 2021), Virtual Conference, October 24, 2021*, volume 2982 of *CEUR Workshop Proceedings*. CEUR-WS.org, 2021.

[44] Antoine Bordes, Nicolas Usunier, Alberto Garcia-Durán, Jason Weston, and Oksana Yakhnenko. Translating embeddings for modeling multi-relational data. In *Proceedings of the 26th International Conference on Neural Information Processing Systems - Volume 2*, NIPS'13, page 2787–2795, Red Hook, NY, USA, 2013. Curran Associates Inc.

[45] Théo Trouillon, Johannes Welbl, Sebastian Riedel, Éric Gaussier, and Guillaume Bouchard. Complex embeddings for simple link prediction. In *Proceedings of the 33nd International Conference on Machine Learning, ICML 2016, New York City, NY, USA, June 19-24, 2016*, volume 48 of *JMLR Workshop and Conference Proceedings*, pages 2071–2080. JMLR.org, 2016.

[46] Zhiqing Sun, Zhi-Hong Deng, Jian-Yun Nie, and Jian Tang. Rotate: Knowledge graph embedding by relational rotation in complex space. In *International Conference on Learning Representations*, 2019.

[47] Dai Quoc Nguyen, Vinh Tong, Dinh Phung, and Dat Quoc Nguyen. Node co-occurrence based graph neural networks for knowledge graph link prediction. In *Proceedings of the Fifteenth ACM International Conference on Web Search and Data Mining*, WSDM '22, page 1589–1592, New York, NY, USA, 2022. Association for Computing Machinery.

[48] Rajarshi Das, Ameya Godbole, Nicholas Monath, Manzil Zaheer, and Andrew McCallum. Probabilistic

case-based reasoning for open-world knowledge graph completion. In *Findings of the Association for Computational Linguistics: EMNLP 2020*, November 2020.

[49] Christian Meilicke, Melisachew Wudage Chekol, Daniel Ruffinelli, and Heiner Stuckenschmidt. Anytime bottom-up rule learning for knowledge graph completion. In *Proceedings of the Twenty-Eighth International Joint Conference on Artificial Intelligence, IJCAI-19*, pages 3137–3143. International Joint Conferences on Artificial Intelligence Organization, 7 2019.

Handbook on Neurosymbolic AI and Knowledge Graphs
P. Hitzler et al. (Eds.)
IOS Press, 2025

doi:10.3233/FAIA250237

SmartBook: AI-Assisted Situation Report Generation for Intelligence Analysts

Revanth GANGI REDDY [a,1], Daniel LEE [b], Yi Ren FUNG [a], Khanh DUY NGUYEN [a], Qi ZENG [a], Manling LI [c], Ziqi WANG [a], Clare VOSS [d] and Heng JI [a]

[a] *University of Illinois Urbana-Champaign*
[b] *University of Calgary*
[c] *Northwestern University*
[d] *Army Research Laboratory*

Abstract. Timely and comprehensive understanding of emerging events is crucial for effective decision-making; automating situation report generation can significantly reduce the time, effort, and cost for intelligence analysts. In this chapter, we introduce SMARTBOOK, an automated framework designed to generate situation reports from large volumes of news data, creating structured reports by automatically discovering event-related strategic questions. These reports include multiple hypotheses (claims), summarized and grounded to sources with factual evidence, to promote in-depth situation understanding. Our comprehensive evaluation of SMARTBOOK, encompassing a user study alongside a content review with an editing study, reveals SMARTBOOK's effectiveness in generating accurate and relevant situation reports. Qualitative evaluations indicate over 80% of questions probe for strategic information, and over 90% of summaries produce tactically useful content, being consistently favored over summaries from a large language model integrated with web search. The editing study reveals that minimal information is removed from the generated text (under 2.5%), suggesting that SMARTBOOK provides analysts with a valuable foundation for situation reports.

Keywords. Intelligence Analysis, News Summarization, Knowledge Extraction

1. Introduction

In today's rapidly changing world, intelligence analysts face the constant challenge of staying informed amidst an overwhelming influx of news, rumors, and evolving narratives. To understand unfolding events, it is essential to extract common truths from heterogeneous data sources. Currently, intelligence analysts prepare *situation reports* that provide an overview of the state of affairs, potential risks or threats, and perspectives, along with recommended actions to guide action planning and strategic development [1,2]. Situation reports are expected to present salient information about key events and trends with a clear logical structure to facilitate understanding, tracking, and easy access to information. The downstream consumers of these reports (general public, decision-makers, and stakeholders) are not just looking for raw information; they are

[1]Corresponding Authors: {revanth3,hengji}@illinois.edu

Table 1. Example of situation understanding for the Ukraine-Russia crisis. GPT-4 is incapable of generating situation reports because it has limited knowledge of up-to-date events, while Smartbook is able to generate timely, multi-source, and trustworthy answers.

Question: Is Russian positioning forces for possible follow-on actions into Ukraine after the initial invasion?
GPT-4: As an AI language model, I cannot provide real-time information on current events. However, it is essential for intelligence analysts to monitor the activities of various countries, including troop movements and military exercises,to assess potential threats and anticipate future actions. To determine if Russia is positioning forces for possible actions into Ukraine, one must analyze the latest intelligence reports, satellite imagery, and open-source information. Additionally, understanding the political and historical context of the region can provide valuable insight into the intentions of the countries involved.
SmartBook: The arrival of Russian forces in Slavutych came after several days of shelling against the city, which is strategically located close to the Dnieper River, about 95 miles (150 kilometers) north of Kyiv and close to the border with Belarus. Russia has been using Belarus as a springboard for many of its air operations in Ukraine, according to intelligence collected by NATO surveillance planes flying over the Polish-Ukrainian border and radar seen by CNN. So far, however, US officials have not seen Belarusian troops "being readied to move into Ukraine" or "that they are moving or are in Ukraine", a senior US defense official said Monday, adding that the forces inside Ukraine are Russian.

seeking clarity, context, and actionable insights. However, these reports, being manually crafted, come with limitations: they are time-consuming to produce [3], might exhibit biases [4,5], factual errors [6], and may be restricted due to the large volume of information they must process [7,8]. Intelligence analysts spend a lot of time sifting through vast and complex data sources [9,10] (*e.g.,* social media rumor propagation, news outbreak, background statistics, domain expert opinions, etc.), and readers often grapple with information that's either too dense or not sufficiently comprehensive. Given the sheer volume of information, it is challenging for analysts to do deep analysis and critical thinking, to be able to formulate strategic questions and generate insights. We hypothesize that automatic situation report generation can bridge the gap between reading and writing intelligence information. However, existing summarization approaches [11,12,13] generate plain-form text and do not yield the details, structures, and high-level strategic information to support decision-making for the downstream consumer. In particular, current large language model-based approaches such as GPT-4/ChatGPT [14] may return no answers or incorrect answers to user questions as they do not update information in real-time and lack fact-checking mechanisms (e.g., Table 1).

In this chapter, we present **SMARTBOOK**, a framework designed to assist human analysts who author situation reports. SmartBook ingests data from multiple sources to generate a comprehensive report with information updated regularly. Human analysts typically source information by asking questions based on their own understanding of the situation. However, these questions can be static or too vague, and become outdated as the situation evolves rapidly. In contrast, SMARTBOOK automatically discovers questions important for situation analysis and gathers salient information for generating the report. For all questions about a major event, the report contains summaries with tactical information coming from relevant claims, presented with local context and links to source news articles. SMARTBOOK structures data in a manner that mirrors current intelligence analyst workflows–breaking down events into timelines, chapters, and question-

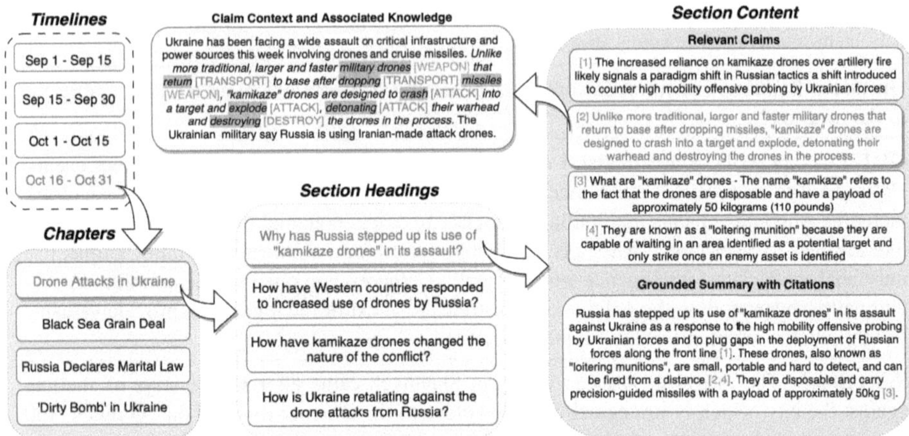

Figure 1. Figure showing an example from SmartBoook for the Ukraine-Russia Crisis. SMARTBOOK is organized on a timeline, with 2-week time spans containing chapters and corresponding sections. The section headings are strategic questions and each section content consists of a grounded summary with links to relevant claims, each highlighted for factual evidence and knowledge elements. The italicized entities and events, which comprise the associated knowledge elements, are highlighted in red and blue respectively.

based sections. Each section contains a grounded query-focused summary with its relevant claims. This intuitive structure facilitates easier assimilation of information for both reading and writing. Designed with a human-centered approach, our goal is to augment the capabilities of human analysts rather than replace them. Figure 1 shows an example from SMARTBOOK for the Ukraine-Russia crisis, with the structured hierarchy of timespans, chapters, and corresponding sections.

In our comprehensive evaluation of SMARTBOOK, we conducted two complementary studies: a utility study (in §5.1) for assessing usability and interaction, and a content review (in §5.2) for examining the quality of text summaries. The user study, involving intelligence analysts and decision-makers, focused on key research questions to explore SMARTBOOK's usability, intuitiveness, and effectiveness in situation report generation. Participants engaged in semi-structured interviews and post-study questionnaires, reflecting on their experience with the system. The content review complemented this by assessing the readability, coherence, and relevance of SMARTBOOK-generated reports, including an editing study where an expert analyst revised the summaries to meet their standards of acceptability. The primary goal of this process was to evaluate the viability of using SMARTBOOK as a tool for creating preliminary drafts of situation reports. The findings indicate that the content generated by SMARTBOOK was mostly accurate, requiring minimal edits to correct a few factual errors. However, most of the effort in the editing process was focused on adding evidence to support the summaries. The results of the editing study suggest that while SMARTBOOK provides a solid foundation, it significantly benefits from human refinement.

The contributions of this work are as follows:

- **SMARTBOOK**, an automated framework that generates comprehensive, up-to-date situation reports from various sources and presents them in an intuitive and user-friendly manner. It identifies critical strategic questions, ensuring that down-

stream readers receive targeted, relevant, and evidence-grounded information to aid their decision-making processes.
- A thorough utility evaluation involving intelligence analysts and decision-makers investigating the usability of the system.
- A content review to grade the quality of the information generated, along with an editing study to understand how viable SMARTBOOK is for producing preliminary first drafts of situation reports.

2. Related Work

2.1. *AI for Intelligence Analysis*

AI has ushered in a new era for intelligence analysis, as traditional methods can be often tedious and time-consuming. AI, however, can manage vast data sets and swiftly analyze information, ensuring accurate and timely insights. The intelligence analysis begins with data collection and ingestion, where automated tools play a pivotal role in efficient categorization and storage as highlighted by studies [15,16,17]. These tools gather data from diverse sources, simplifying access for further analysis. In the domain of data visualization and examination [18], AI significantly enhances the ability to discern complex data patterns, aiding analysts in drawing meaningful inferences. Furthermore, the assessment of evidence reliability is crucial. AI-driven tools can systematically evaluate information credibility, ensuring the use of verified data [19,20]. Further, they can examine the depth and accuracy of insights, verifying the validity of intelligence reports [21]. AI innovations, such as those exemplified by HITIQA [22], have facilitated scenario-based question answering, essential for dissecting specific situations and deriving precise insights. This approach is crucial in intelligence analysis, where generating potential hypotheses is a key aspect [23,24]. While these developments represent significant progress, challenges persist. Studies [25,26,27,28,29] point out that current tools often require extensive crowdsourcing or necessitate human-machine collaboration for report drafting, highlighting the need for further improvement in this area.

SmartBook brings in a significant advancement in automated situation report generation. SmartBook aims to produce initial report drafts, allowing analysts to channel their energies on critical thinking and comprehensive assessments. Additionally, the system's integration of a large language model aids in topic discovery, navigating the longstanding issue of analysts being unaware of unknown factors. By generating strategic questions for varying events, it guides analysts towards previously unseen patterns, prompting the exploration of new hypotheses, even when confronted with contradictory information. In an age where data inundation is a constant challenge for intelligence analysts, tools like SmartBook offer not just relief, but a pathway to enhanced efficiency and deeper insights. This research underscores the promise of SmartBook, positioning it as a significant milestone in AI-assisted intelligence analysis.

2.2. *Multi-Document Summarization*

Multi-document summarization aims to extract critical information across multiple documents into a few-sentence summary [11,12,13,30,31,32,33]. Large Language Models

(LLMs) have also shown unprecedented ability to generate summaries [34,35,36,37,38, 39]. SmartBook differs from these summarization tools with its structural narratives, its focus on situational intelligence, and its automatic event-related question discovery. First, the current summarization methods lack the organizational structure needed for intelligence situation reports, which require synthesizing diverse data points into a coherent narrative. SmartBook, by contrast, generates inherently structured reports that are broken down into time spans, major events, strategic questions, and their grounded summaries. This layered structure, reminiscent of a book, provides a comprehensive view and intuitive navigation through the complex scenario being analyzed. Second, while news summarization aims to provide a condensed version of events, SmartBook not only states what happened but also explores multiple aspects including implications, potential trajectories, and strategic importance of these events. Third, previous query-based methods rely on human effort to identify important events as guidance or prompts, while SmartBook introduces an innovative mechanism to discover pertinent event-related questions automatically, allowing the system to probe deeper into events to offer users richer insights.

2.3. AI-Assisted Writing

AI-assisted writing [40,41,42,43] is a rapidly growing field in human-computer interaction research. In recent years, researchers have explored various approaches to develop AI systems that can assist users in writing tasks. AI-assisted writing tools have demonstrated benefits to a variety of end-users, like academics [44], screenwriters [45] and developers [46]. CoAuthor [47] crafts a dataset that encapsulates the rich interactions observed between multiple writers and instances of GPT-3 over numerous writing sessions, thereby highlighting the efficacy of AI in fostering collaborative writing endeavors. In the area of automated story-writing [48], attempts such as Creative Help [49], Writing Buddy [50] and WordCraft [51] aid the user in producing full stories with creative control throughout the process. More recently, with humans struggling to identify text as being machine generated [52], concerns have been raised about academic integrity [53] and plagiarism[54] when using AI-assisted writing tools. In light of the ongoing developments in the AI-assisted writing, SmartBook introduces a unique automated framework designed specifically for generating situation reports for intelligence analysts. While the existing body of work predominantly focuses on augmenting creative and collaborative writing, SmartBook seamlessly integrates with analysts' workflows, emphasizing efficiency, analytical depth, and breadth.

2.4. Structured Report Generation in Other Domains

Structured report generation has become pivotal across a multitude of domains, driven by the quest to extract meaningful insights from vast datasets. Medicine is one of the domains where structured report generation has gained significant traction. Natural language processing (NLP) and computer vision algorithms have been used to generate radiology reports by analyzing medical images [55,56]. In the finance sector, firms leverage machine learning and AI models to sift through vast amounts of financial data to produce concise, structured quarterly or yearly financial reports [57].

In the domain of meteorological reporting, AI's application spans from predicting weather patterns to offering detailed narratives [58,59]. Sports analytics, on the backdrop of rising demand, has moved towards converting raw match data into post-match summaries, aiding analysts and enthusiasts alike in deciphering game dynamics [60,61]. Similarly, the urgency of environmental concerns has spurred the use of satellite data integrated with machine learning algorithms, producing environmental reports on critical subjects such as deforestation and urbanization [62,63].

Lastly, the corporate sector, especially e-commerce, has not remained untouched. Businesses, overwhelmed with vast pools of data, employ AI-driven tools to decode this data and produce structured reports. These reports offer pivotal insights into sales trends, customer behaviors, and market dynamics, thus aiding decision-making processes [64]. Such extensive applications across various sectors underscore the potential of AI-driven tools, with SmartBook aiming to assist intelligence analysts by presenting them with thorough situation reports.

3. Situation Reports

A situation report is a document that an intelligence analyst produces as part of their work as a product of collecting, analyzing, and disseminating critical information. The report typically focuses on a specific issue or topic and provides a comprehensive overview of the information available on that topic. Intelligence analysts draft situation reports through a meticulous and systematic approach that begins with the collection of information from diverse sources, such as news articles, broadcasts, and potentially classified intelligence feeds. Once gathered, they prioritize the verification of this data, cross-referencing against various sources to ascertain accuracy. The subsequent analysis phase involves delving deep into the raw data to discern patterns, motivations, and implications, often requiring specialized knowledge or technical expertise. Post-analysis, the synthesized information is integrated into a cohesive narrative, emphasizing relevance and urgency, resulting in a clear, concise, and actionable report that communicates the prevailing situation to stakeholders.

The ultimate goal of such reports from intelligence analysts is to support downstream users (ex. policy-makers, government officials, and other experts) in keeping track of developments and provide them with the necessary information to make informed decisions and take appropriate actions.

3.1. Challenges

Writing situation reports is an inherently challenging task. In an era characterized by rapid information dissemination and a constantly shifting geopolitical landscape, intelligence analysts are tasked with the effort of sifting through this vast sea of information, discerning fact from fiction, and then distilling their findings into actionable insights. This must be done often under tight time constraints and the knowledge that the stakes are high; an inaccurate report could have significant ramifications. Given this backdrop, some of the core challenges they face include:

- *Information Overload*: Analysts are often swamped with more data than they can efficiently process. [7] discusses how excessive information collection leads to information overload on both the individual and institutional levels, impairing the US intelligence community's ability to do its job. [8] highlights how the amount

of data and information that intelligence analysts must process, exploit, and disseminate has drastically increased over the past 30 years.
- *Disinformation and Misinformation*: Not all information sources are reliable. [9] discuss how analysts must remain vigilant against fabricated evidence and learn to identify relevant, credible information.
- *Cognitive Biases*: Analysts, like all humans, are susceptible to cognitive biases. These biases can affect the interpretation of information, potentially leading to inaccurate assessments. [4] posits that biases in military intelligence analysis are significant as they are pervasive and cannot be eradicated. [5] identifies eight biases that may manifest at various stages of intelligence analysis include confirmation bias, anchoring bias, availability bias, representativeness bias, hindsight bias, framing effect bias, overconfidence bias, and groupthink bias.
- *Time Restrictions*: Especially in crisis situations, there's pressure to produce reports quickly, which can lead to oversights. [3] highlights how analysts must work under substantial time pressure, often with mental fatigue, while making decisions that have life-and-death implications.
- *Complexity and Ambiguity*: Real-world situations can be complex, with many interconnected factors. [10] highlights how sometimes the information available is ambiguous or contradictory, making it challenging to arrive at definitive conclusions.

Each of the above challenges, whether faced individually or collectively, can significantly impede the effective generation of situation reports, underscoring the need for assistance and sophisticated tools in the intelligence domain. With this in mind, we aim to generate a situation report, given a collection of documents from a variety of sources, that embodies characteristics such as containing salient information that is presented with a logical structure and organized chronologically as timelines, while being grounded to factual content. In the following, we expand our design choices, emphasizing their advantages for both users (i.e. intelligence analysts) and downstream readers (i.e. policy makers).

4. SmartBook Framework

SmartBook is an AI-assisted system for situation report generation that provides analysts with a first-draft report to work from as they respond to time-critical information requirements on emerging events. SmartBook consists of: 1) An intuitive user interface (shown in Figure 2), and 2) a back-end framework (shown in Figure 3) that, when given a collection of documents from a variety of news sources, automatically generates a situation report.

Our automatic situation report is organized into coherent, chronological timelines spanning two weeks each, enhancing the tracking and comprehension of events' developments. Within these timelines, major events are identified by clustering news articles, forming the basis for subsequent chapters (see §4.1). To guide detailed chapter analysis, we incorporate a logical structure with automatically generated section headings in the form of strategic questions covering various aspects of each major event (details in §4.2). SmartBook generates content addressing these questions from a strategic perspective, by pinpointing relevant claims in news articles (see §4.3). Further, the extracted claims

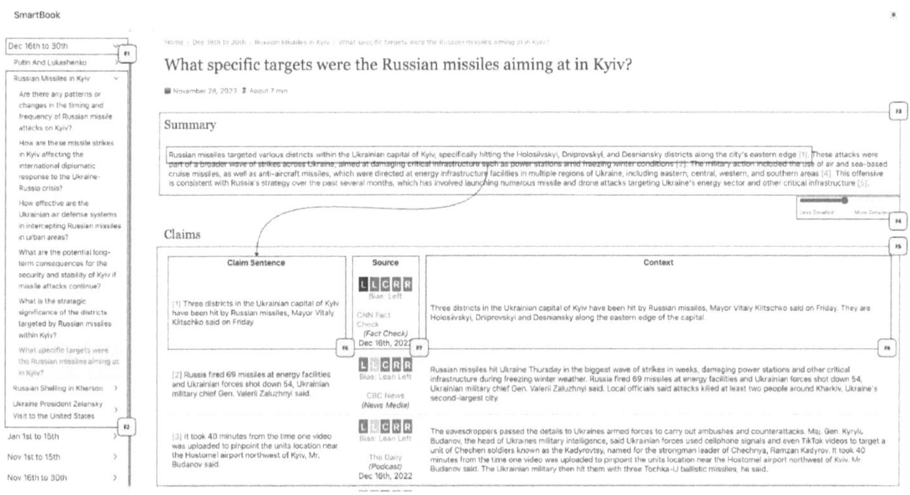

Figure 2. A screenshot of SMARTBOOK's front-end interface. Within the given situation, the user can navigate timelines (F1), explore strategic questions related to an event (F2), read the overarching summary on a given strategic question (F3), control the depth and length of information (F4), investigate all the claims in the summary (F5), trace each claim to corresponding summary fragment (F6), investigate the source metadata (F7) and read the context from which the claims were extracted (F8).

are enriched with a structured view of corresponding attributes, knowledge elements and inter-claim relations to provide analysts with a comprehensive perspective (see §4.4). Each section contains query-focused summaries that answer the strategic questions, providing a comprehensive view of the event's contexts and implications (see §4.5). These summaries include citation links that allow for factual verification and cross-checking by experts.

SMARTBOOK is designed for efficiency, utilizing smaller models [65,66] for tasks that have training data available, such as event headline generation, duplicate question detection, and claim extraction. Conversely, for more complex tasks—such as generating long-form summaries with citations or identifying strategic questions, we employ large language models [14,67].

In this section, we describe the various components within SMARTBOOK, along with emphasizing the advantages of each aspect of SMARTBOOK's design for users (i.e., intelligence analysts) and for recipients of the final situation report (i.e., decision-makers), who both initiate information requirements and are downstream readers.

4.1. Major Events within Timespans as Chapters

Situation reports cover event progressions over considerably long periods. Hence, it is beneficial to organize such reports in the form of timelines (F1 in Figure 2), which enables seamless report updates [68] with new events and helps facilitate [69] users tracking and understanding of situation context. Timelines aid intelligence analysts in understanding event progression and predicting future trends by organizing events chronologically and highlighting cause-and-effect relationships. For readers, especially those less familiar with the subject, timelines provide a visual guide to easily grasp the sequence

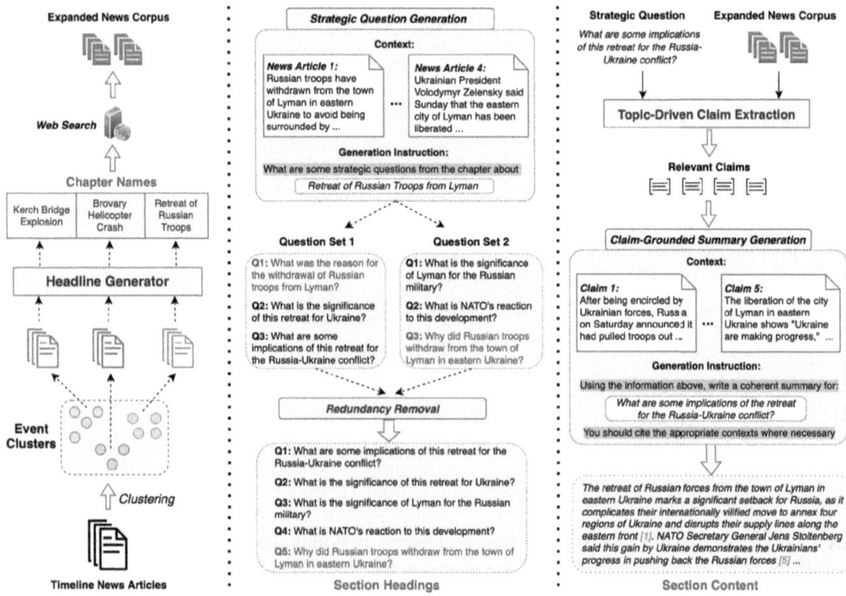

Figure 3. Backend workflow for constructing SMARTBOOK. Given the articles corresponding to a specific timeline, the figure shows the process for obtaining the chapters, their section headings, and the corresponding section content.

and significance of events in a scenario. Our automatic situation report has timelines to provide a coherent, chronological representation of event developments.

In each timespan, we first identify major events by clustering daily news summaries from the period into major event groups using an agglomerative hierarchical clustering algorithm [70] based on term frequency-inverse document frequency (TF-IDF) scores [71]. Finally, we are left with clusters of news snippets, each providing a focused view of a major event. However, since news summary snippets are condensed in detail, we improve the comprehensiveness of each event cluster by expanding the news corpus, as described next. First, to create a chapter name for SMARTBOOK and also use it for additional news article retrieval, we generate a concise headline for each event cluster. To achieve this, we utilize a sequence-to-sequence transformer-based [72] language model, BART [66], that takes the concatenated title and text from all the news snippets within the event cluster as input and generates a short event heading. We made use of the model trained on the NewsHead dataset [73] for generating multi-document headlines. In that dataset, each cluster contained up to five news articles, and a crowd-sourced headline of up to 35 characters described the major information in that cluster. We then use these chapter names as the query to retrieve additional relevant news articles via Google News.

4.2. Strategic Questions as Section Headings

A situation report should have a logical structure and descriptive section titles (F2 in Figure 2) for clarity and easy access to information for intelligence analysts. SMARTBOOK not only describes event details in each chapter but also aims to present strategic insights that support decision-making and policy planning. To guide such detailed analysis, we incorporate a logical structure by automatically generating section headings in the form of strategic questions relating to each major event. These questions cover insightful details such as the motivations behind actions in an event and its potential future consequences.

Recent work [74,75] has shown that LLMs are capable of generating comprehensive, natural questions that require long-form and informative answers, in comparison to existing approaches [76,77] that mainly generate questions designed for short and specific answers. In this work, we direct the LLM (GPT-4) to generate strategic questions about specific events, using news articles from the event cluster to anchor the context and reduce model-generated hallucinations [78,79]. To ensure diversity in the generated questions, we sample multiple question sets using nucleus sampling [80].

Our analysis reveals that questions may occasionally be repeated across different sets, as depicted in Figure 3 where duplicates are highlighted in blue. To address this, we perform question de-duplication using a RoBERTa-large [65] model trained on the Quora Duplicate Question Pairs dataset, thereby consolidating the sets into a singular, diverse collection of strategic questions relevant to the event.

4.3. Extraction of Claims and Hypotheses

Intelligence analysts, given the high stakes nature of their work but limited time, need systems that quickly identify key information in documents. This enables them to focus on urgent matters without sorting through irrelevant data. Hence, automated situation report generation should be able to identify and extract the most scenario-relevant and crucial information across multiple documents (F5 in Figure 2). Readers of the situation report benefit from information salience because they are presented with a concise, relevant overview of a situation. Essential points need to be highlighted, to enhance readability and clarity. Moreover, we also present the bias of each news source (taken from AllSides) to help analysts consider information presented from different perspectives.

Providing readers with a comprehensive understanding of event context requires foraging for different claims and hypotheses from the source documents (i.e., news articles) that help explain a situation [29]. We adopt a Question Answering (QA) formulation to identify claims relevant to a given strategic question, driven by the ability of directed queries to systematically extract relevant claims from news articles, as demonstrated in recent research [81,82]. Our QA pipeline utilizes a transformer-based RoBERTa-large encoder model [65] that has been trained on SQuAD 2.0 [83] and Natural Questions [84]. The model takes as input the news corpus split into snippets along with the strategic question, and outputs answer extractions to these questions. The corresponding sentences that contain these answers are considered as the extracted claims. However, the risk of high-confidence false positives [85] necessitates validation [86,87] of these answers. To address this, we utilize an answer sentence selection model [88] that verifies each context against the strategic question. The model is a binary classifier with a RoBERTa-large backbone trained on datasets such as Natural Questions [84] and WikiQA [89], and outputs a validation score ranging from 0 (incorrect) to 1 (correct), which is used to select the top-5 relevant contexts for summarization.

4.4. Claim Network and Knowledge Graph Construction

Automatic claim detection approaches [90,91,92] usually simply mine arguments from the provided corpora. Instead of identifying claims in isolation, structured claim extrac-

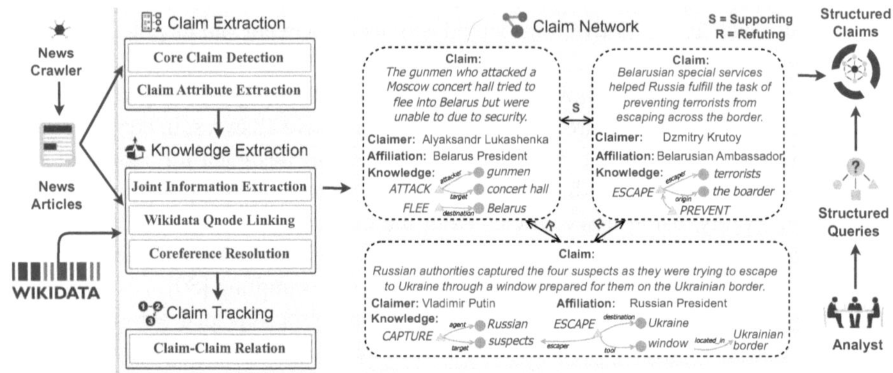

Figure 4. Architecture of the structured claim attribute and knowledge extraction system.

tion [93] considers claim attributes [81] along with their associated knowledge elements. This provides a structured perspective of claim semantics and enables the discovery of semantic relatedness across multiple claims via knowledge elements. The semantic relations are in the form of inter-claim connections, for identifying supporting, refuting and equivalent claims. Figure 4 illustrates the claim network and knowledge graph construction framework based on [93], for which a brief overview is provided below.

For each extracted claim, we aim to extract the knowledge elements that correspond to the entities, relations, and events extracted from the claim span and within the sentences before and after the claim span. For knowledge extraction we apply a joint neural information extraction framework [94] first to identify entities, events, and corresponding relations. Further, we apply entity linking [95] and coreference resolution [96] to map the extracted entities to Wikidata and consolidate them at a corpus level. Finally, the claim-claim relations are determined based on the Wikidata linking results and claim attributes. Claims that share similar attributes, such as sub-topic, claim-object, and stance (see Figure 4) are considered equivalent. Determining claims as supporting or refuting each other is treated as a natural language inference task [97], where the claims are considered as a premise-hypothesis pair. High entailment or contradiction scores are used as an indication of whether two claims support or refute each other.

4.5. Grounded Summaries as Section Content

Considering the issue of hallucination in LLM-based summarization [98,99,100], factuality is far more important than creativity for situation report generation. A reliable situation report must be anchored in verifiable sources to ensure credibility. This supports analysts in drawing robust, evidence-based conclusions, and the embedded links act as a springboard to more extensive research for readers wanting to dive deeper (F6, F7, F8 in Figure 2).

Using strategic questions obtained for each chapter as section *headings*, we incorporate query-focused summarization to generate each section's *content*. A concise summary is generated for each section in SMARTBOOK based on the relevant claim contexts. Recent work [101,102,103] has shown that humans overwhelmingly prefer summaries from prompt-based LLMs [104,105] over models fine-tuned on article-summary pairs [66,106,107], due to better controllability and easier extension to novel scenarios. For summary generation, we feed the LLM (GPT-4) with the top-5 most relevant contexts (from §4.3) and instructions to summarize with respect to the given strategic question and include citations. This approach not only aids in maintaining accuracy by grounding on claim contexts but also enhances the trustworthiness of the summaries by allowing verification against the cited sources.

5. Results

To comprehensively evaluate SMARTBOOK and its efficacy in aiding intelligence analysis, we performed three distinct but interrelated studies: a utility evaluation, a content review and an editing study. The utility evaluation (in (§5.1) aimed to answer three research questions concerning SMARTBOOK's usability, focusing on its effectiveness for intelligence analysts and decision-makers in generating and interacting with situation reports. Complementing this, the content review (in §5.2) assessed the quality of SMARTBOOK's automatically generated questions and summaries, focusing on readability, coherence, and relevance. Finally, the editing study (in §5.3) involved an expert analyst editing the generated reports to assess their value as a preliminary first draft.

5.1. Utility Study: Evaluating the System

During this user study, we conducted an interview with semi-structured questions and a post-study questionnaire on the usability of the SMARTBOOK. Each user study session was structured in four segments: (i) an introductory overview, (ii) a free-form investigation, (iii) a guided exploration, and (iv) a concluding reflective discussion. The participants were ten intelligence analysts with experience in government and military roles, and two decision-makers from Canadian government boards. These decision-makers engaged in the initial qualitative study but did not answer subsequent post-study questionnaires, due to time constraints. The study investigated the following research questions:

- **RQ1:** How do intelligence analysts interact and leverage the features within SMARTBOOK?
- **RQ2:** Do intelligence analysts find SMARTBOOK intuitive, usable, trustable and useful?
- **RQ3:** How do decision-makers interact, perceive and use SMARTBOOK?

Participants and Recruitment: For our studies, we targeted individuals with experience in government and military roles. We distributed a pre-screening survey to ascertain their background in creating situation reports. Participants qualifying for the study were either experienced intelligence analysts or had a minimum of one year of equivalent experience. The final group comprised 10 military personnel from different branches, as shown in Table 2. Their experience in intelligence report writing varied between 1 and 10 years. Compensation ranged from $25 to $35 per hour, reflecting participants' levels of experience.

We implemented a targeted outreach strategy to recruit decision-makers for our study. These participants, identified through email addresses sourced from government boards and social media profiles (e.g., LinkedIn, Twitter), were self-identified professionals who make decisions based on prepared reports in their official capacity. Our group comprised of individuals with current or past experience on Canadian government boards. Unlike intelligence analysts, these participants did not receive compensation due to their government affiliation.

Table 2. Demographic info. of study participants along with experience in intelligence report generation.

PID	Age	Education	Intelligence Exp.	AI Knowledge	LLM Usage
IA1	25 - 34	Bachelor's	5 - 10 years	2 - Intermediate	Rarely
IA2	25 - 34	High School Diploma	2 - 5 years	3 - Proficient	Rarely
IA3	18 - 24	High School Diploma	1 - 2 years	2 - Intermediate	Daily
IA4	25 - 34	Bachelor's	2 - 5 years	2 - Intermediate	Rarely
IA5	45 - 54	Bachelor's	2 - 5 years	1 - Basic	Rarely
IA6	45 - 54	Master's	1 - 2 years	1 - Basic	Rarely
IA7	35 - 44	High School Diploma	5 - 10 years	1 - Basic	Weekly
IA8	45 - 54	Master's	1 - 2 years	2 - Intermediate	Rarely
IA9	35 - 44	Bachelor's	2 - 5 years	2 - Intermediate	Rarely
IA10	25 - 34	Bachelor	2 - 5 years	4 - Advanced	Weekly

Study Procedure: Upon commencement of the study, (i) participants received a concise introduction to SMARTBOOK, outlining its core premise. This orientation was designed to acquaint them with the system without biasing their exploration. Subsequently, (ii) participants were invited to freely investigate SMARTBOOK, with the specific task of exploring a minimum of three questions across five chapters of their choosing. This approach afforded substantial freedom, enabling interactions with the user interface that reflected their natural inclinations and interests. Following the free-form investigation, participants were systematically introduced (iii) to the SMARTBOOK framework. This process involved tracing the journey from a chosen question related to a specific event within a designated timespan, to the corresponding claims, contexts, and sources, resulting in a summarized answer. Subsequently, a semi-structured interview (iv) was conducted to gather reflective feedback on the participants' experience with SMARTBOOK, focusing on its efficacy and potential areas of enhancement. Finally, to conclude the session, participants were asked to complete a post-study questionnaire. This questionnaire was focused on assessing the usability of SMARTBOOK, gathering quantitative data to complement the qualitative insights gained from the semi-structured interviews. Upon collecting, discussing and iterating on the data, behaviors and insights were merged into the following themes:

5.1.1. UI Understandability and Interaction

The structured layout of the user interface (UI) was notably effective, as seen in the free-form investigation (ii) with a 100% feature discovery rate (10 out of 10 participants). All participants successfully engaged with key features, underscoring the UI's design intuitiveness. This high feature discovery rate indicates that the UI aligns with users' cognitive patterns, facilitating intuitive interaction without extensive training, providing us with a positive response to **RQ1**. This sentiment was further emphasized in the post-study questionnaire. As seen in the results in Figure 5, 70% of participants strongly agreed that most intelligence analysts would learn to use the system very quickly, while 80% strongly disagreed that the system was difficult to navigate and use. However, we

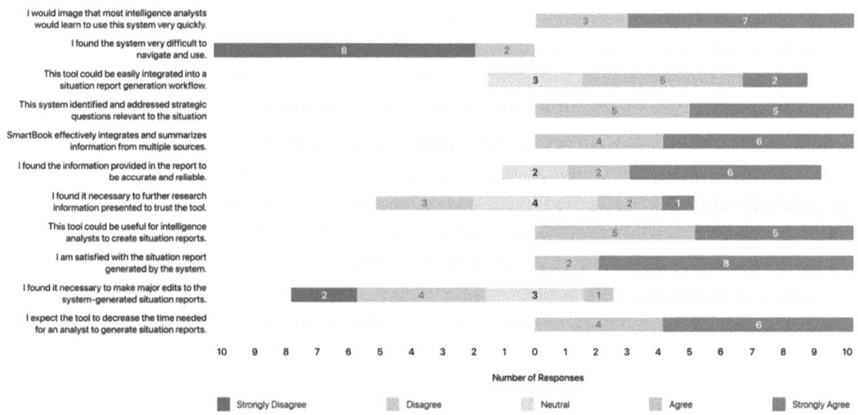

Figure 5. Quantitative results from the post-study questionnaire in the utility evaluation.

observed mixed views on UI flexibility, specifically in personalization and customization. While most found the tool easily integrateable into their workflow, a minority (30%) remained neutral. When further prompted, two participants described the UI as a "one size fits all" solution, lacking personalization.

5.1.2. Building Trust on SMARTBOOK

In the study, trust in the SMARTBOOK system developed progressively, resembling the formation of trust in a human analyst. Initially, users exhibited skepticism, thoroughly scrutinizing the system's sources and assertions. This included validating the authenticity of sources, the accuracy and pertinence of ratings, and the correct representation of context. As users became more acquainted with SMARTBOOK and evaluated its reliability, their dependence on extensive source verification lessened. As can be seen in Figure 5, three out of ten participants did not feel the need to conduct additional research beyond the presented information to trust the tool, while another three felt additional research was necessary. This trust was found to be context-dependent, with two participants noting that their trust varied based on the "impact severity" or the potential negative consequences of disseminating incorrect information. Nonetheless, a majority (eight out of ten) concurred that the information provided was accurate and reliable, a positive answer to **RQ2**.

5.1.3. Perceived Benefits for Intelligence Analysts

The primary benefit identified was the substantial reduction in time and effort required for compiling and analyzing complex data. SMARTBOOK's automation of initial report generation processes, such as data collection and summarization, was highly valued by analysts as it allowed more focus on thorough analysis and strategic planning. As seen in Figure 5, all participants agreed on the tool's utility in assisting intelligence analysts in creating situation reports, expressing satisfaction with the system-generated reports, thereby providing a positive response to **RQ2**. Regarding the necessity of significant edits to the system-generated reports, half participants suggested that this need was not inherently due to report deficiencies but varied based on the report's intended purpose or audience. We later conducted a study (described in §5.3) to understand the extent of edits needed.

5.1.4. SmartBook *as a Learning Tool for Decision-Makers*

Decision-makers highly valued SmartBook's ability to rapidly deliver accurate and easily digestible information. Their primary engagement with the interface centered around utilizing the summaries, to learn about different topics in various degrees. The system's effectiveness in simplifying complex data into structured, clear formats was particularly appreciated, to help aid in swift understanding and decision-making processes. Although data lineage and source transparency were recognized as important, these were considered secondary to the primary need for timely and format-specific information delivery. While SmartBook's target users are intelligence analysts, the decision-makers' view highlights SmartBook's dual functionality as both an analytical tool and a decision-support system, providing a key capability for the high-paced and information-intensive needs of decision-makers, addressing **RQ3**.

5.2. Content Review: Evaluating the Generated Content

Our content review study primarily involves evaluation of the quality of automatically generated strategic questions and summaries within SmartBook. The studies involved two participant groups: one senior expert intelligence analyst and six text evaluators. The expert analyst, affiliated with a US national defense and security firm, possessed a decade of experience in intelligence analysis, training, and AI-based tool assessment. The text evaluators, all fluent in English and US-based, involved undergraduate and graduate students with experience in Natural Language Processing.

5.2.1. Evaluation of Strategic Questions

Evaluation of the quality of strategic questions, which are used as section headings in SmartBook, is done by drawing parallels to the traditional construction process of a situation report, which involves the participation of both senior and junior analysts. A senior analyst's role is usually to come up with strategic questions, which are then passed onto a junior analyst. The junior analyst then gathers tactical information that can help answer or provide more background to the strategic questions. Our human evaluation of the questions within SmartBook measures the following aspects, based on guidelines defined by the expert intelligence analyst:

- **Strategic Importance**: Evaluating the strategic importance of a question requires introspection on whether the question provided within SmartBook probes for an insightful aspect of the event. The scoring rubric involves marking the question as one of three categories, namely, 'Not Strategic', 'Some Strategic Value', and 'Definitely Strategic'. This metric is based on the level of speculative nature, such as questioning the background/motives/reasons behind actions taken by actors (governments/military, etc) involved in the event.
- **Tactical Information**: Another dimension of evaluating the quality of a question is how much relevant tactical information can be gathered using that question. In this case, the question is evaluated based on its corresponding SmartBook summary, in terms of whether the question-relevant tactical information in the sum-

Table 3. Table showing summaries for two strategic questions corresponding to a SMARTBOOK chapter on Russian missile attacks. The tactically useful and relevant information has been highlighted in blue. Tactically useful but irrelevant information has been highlighted in red.

Question: What were the motives behind the attack on Russian missile in Dnipro?	**Question:** What is the capability of Ukraine's air defense systems in repelling the missile attacks from Russian missiles
Summary: The Russian missile attack on the city of Dnipro on Saturday was part of the Kremlin's efforts to limit Ukraine's ability to heat and power itself in the middle of winter. The attack was reportedly carried out with a Kh-22 missile, an older and less accurate weapon than most modern missiles. It is believed that the attack was part of the Kremlin's attempts to retake a town, Soledar, and the nearby city of Bakhmut, as a way to grind down the best Ukrainian forces and prevent them from launching counterattacks elsewhere. Nine people were killed, including a 15-year old girl, Kyrylo Tymoshenko, and Russia denied responsibility for the attack, claiming it was caused by Ukrainian air defences.	**Summary:** Ukraine's air defense systems have demonstrated their capability in repelling the missile attacks from Russian forces in Kyiv. [1] reported that Ukrainian air defense forces shot down 37 of "about 40" rockets that entered the city's airspace, with one person injured. [2] revealed that a commander, who asked to be identified only by the call sign "Hera" for security reasons, stated that a cruise missile was shot down by a machine gun from the city's territorial defense mobile group. [3] mentioned that U.S. President Joe Biden had pledged to deliver one Patriot surface-to-air missile battery system to Ukraine, which is one of the most advanced U.S. air defense systems and is capable of intercepting threats such as aircraft and ballistic missiles.

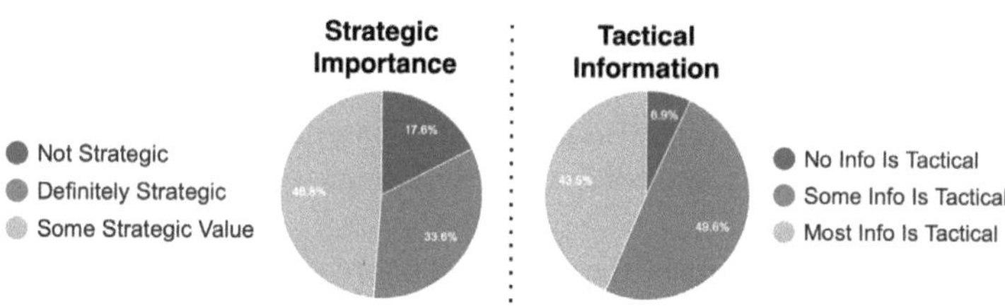

Figure 6. Results from the human evaluation of the strategic questions (section headings) in SMARTBOOK. Judgments are based on the strategic importance of the question and tactical information that can be gathered using the question.

mary is helpful for an analyst to gain deeper insights into the situation. Tactical information is defined as content that is neither obvious nor trivially obtained (e.g. cannot be obtained from a news header). The scoring rubric is categorized as 'No information is tactical', 'Some information is tactical', and 'Most information is tactical'. Table 3 shows examples for summaries with corresponding tactical information.

We randomly selected 25 chapters from SMARTBOOK, comprising 125 strategic questions, with each question evaluated by three annotators. Results show that most questions are strategic (detailed split in Figure 6), with at least 82% having some strategic value. Further, we see that these questions can help gather relevant tactical information in roughly 93% of the cases, as judged by the annotators that most summaries to these questions have tactically relevant information. When assessing the diversity of strategic questions within each chapter, evaluators noted that 64% of chapters contained questions

Table 4. Results of human evaluation comparing the summaries within SmartBook (3) against those either generated directly from news articles via query-focused summarization (1) or obtained from the internet by web search combined with generation from a large language model (2). Results are on a 1-5 scale (worst to best). 50 summaries were evaluated with a text evaluator coverage of 3.

Summary-Type	*Background*	*Coherence*	*Relevance*	*Usefulness*
(1) Query-Focused	News	4.39	3.85	3.77
(2) Web Search + LLM	Web	4.44	4.07	3.83
(3) SmartBook	News	**4.56**	**4.23**	**4.17**

addressing different aspects, 28% had up to two questions on similar aspects, and 8% included more than two questions on similar aspects.

5.2.2. *Evaluation of* SMARTBOOK *Summaries*

Next, we assess the quality of text summaries generated by SMARTBOOK, which uses question-driven claim extraction to identify and summarize relevant information. For baseline comparisons, we utilize two methods: firstly, a *query-focused summarization* baseline that processes entire news articles directly with an LLM to generate summaries for the strategic question as the query. This approach uses the same LLM and prompt as in SMARTBOOK, except the entire news article texts are passed as input context without an explicit claim extraction step. Secondly, we compare against a web search + LLM baseline, where relevant web pages sourced from the internet serve as the input context, which are then summarized by an LLM. This method simulates using an LLM-enabled web search engine (like perplexity.ai), incorporating the strategic question as the query along with a phrase "*concerning the Ukraine-Russia crisis between <timeline>*". Since the LLM-enabled web search was using GPT-3.5 [14] at the time of experiments, we used GPT-3.5 as the LLM in SmartBook and other baselines for a fair comparison. We randomly select summaries corresponding to 50 strategic questions from SMARTBOOK to perform the evaluation.

For each generated summary, three evaluators are asked to assess the coherence, relevance, and usefulness with scores ranging from 1 (worst) to 5 (best). Simply, *coherence* measures the quality of all summary sentences collectively regardless of the question. *Relevance* quantifies whether the summary contains key points that answer the given question. We define *usefulness* as an indication of whether the summary provides non-trivial and insightful information for analysts, and suggests the breadth and depth of the provided key points. Table 4 shows results from the evaluation study. We observe that SMARTBOOK outperforms alternative competitive strategies in coherence, relevance, and usefulness. The advantage of the question-driven claim extraction in SMARTBOOK is evident, yielding significantly more relevant summaries compared to the direct query-focused summarization without such a step (row (3) vs (1)). Additionally, summaries generated using information sourced from the Web are less useful than those generated through SMARTBOOK's news-driven approach (row (2) vs (3)). Table 5 displays an example showing the difference in outputs. Overall, the evaluation demonstrates that across the metrics, SMARTBOOK excels over the baselines in providing high-quality summaries.

We also evaluated the citation quality in SMARTBOOK's summaries using metrics for citation precision and recall as defined by gao2023enabling. Citation recall assesses whether the output sentence is fully supported by the cited context, whereas citation pre-

Table 5. An example comparing the summaries produced by different approaches evaluated in Table 4. It can be seen that the SmartBook summary contains considerably more question-relevant information (highlighted in blue). The *Web Search + LLM* baseline output contains hallucinated content (highlighted in red) that suggests *both* Russia and Ukraine have been using the drones.

Question: How have kamikaze drones changed the nature of the Russia-Ukraine conflict?

Query-Focused	Web Search + LLM	SmartBook
Kamikaze drones, or suicide drones, have been used by Russia in its attacks on Ukrainian cities such as Kyiv, Vinnytsia and Odesa. They are known as a "loitering munition" because they are capable of waiting in an area identified as a potential target and only strike once an enemy asset is identified. Russia is using Iranian-made Shahed-136 drones, which have a payload of approximately 50 kilograms and are hard to detect due to their small size. Ukraine has responded by developing an app that civilians can use to report sightings of incoming drones and missiles, and increasing the proportion shot down before they hit the ground.	Russia and Ukraine have been using Iranian-made Shahed-136 drones in the conflict. These drones are known as 'kamikaze' drones due to their ability to self-destruct on impact. The use of these drones has been highlighted by Russia's growing reliance on them and their use as both military weapons and psychological weapons. On October 13, 2022, kamikaze drones and missiles hit north and south Ukraine, though the Kremlin denied any involvement from President Putin in talks between Russia and the West.	The Russia-Ukraine conflict has seen a paradigm shift in the nature of Russian tactics, with the increased reliance of kamikaze drones over artillery fire. These drones, which are designed to crash into a target and explode, can spray potentially deadly debris and are being used to plug gaps in the deployment of Russian forces along the front line. Russia is reportedly using Iranian-made Shahed series drones, which are showcased at Kashan Airfield south of Tehran. This shift in tactics has seen an escalation in the aerial bombardment of densely populated urban areas and an attack on critical infrastructure and power sources.

cision identifies any irrelevant citations. These metrics were calculated using the 11B-parameter TRUE model [108], which is trained on a collection of natural language inference datasets, and is frequently employed to evaluate attribution accuracy [109,110]. Overall, 97% of the sentences in SmartBook's summaries included citations, while 29.5% had multiple citations. We observed a citation precision and recall of 64.7% and 69.2%, respectively.

5.3. Editing Study: Evaluation as a Preliminary Draft

SmartBook serves as an initial draft for intelligence analysts to refine or adapt to their specific needs. We evaluate SmartBook's effectiveness in producing situation reports through an editing study with an expert analyst, by measuring how much of the content the analyst directly accepts or further edits. The analyst actively explored SmartBook's features and subsequently edited 94 randomly selected summaries from SmartBook-generated situation reports, until they met professional intelligence reporting standards.

Based on the revised summaries by the expert analyst, we assessed the alterations made to the original content. We quantified these changes using token-overlap metrics like BLEU [111] and ROUGE [112] scores, and Levenshtein edit distance, which cal-

Table 6. Example showing expert analyst edits for an automatic machine generated SmartBook summary on the use of 'kamikaze' drones in the Ukraine-Russia crisis. Text that has been added by the expert is colored, with blue corresponding to additional tactical information, whereas green corresponds to insights/conclusions added by the analyst.

SmartBook Summary: Russia has reportedly stepped up its use of kamikaze drones in its assault against Ukraine. The increased reliance on kamikaze drones over artillery fire likely signals a paradigm shift in Russian tactics a shift introduced to counter high mobility offensive probing by Ukrainian forces.
Analyst-edited Summary: Russia has reportedly stepped up its use of kamikaze drones in its assault against Ukraine. The aircraft are called kamikaze drones because they attack once and don't come back. The increased reliance on kamikaze drones over artillery fire likely signals a paradigm shift in Russian tactics - a shift introduced to counter high mobility offensive probing by Ukrainian forces. Their low price means the drones can be deployed in large numbers and they hover before they strike, so they have a psychological effect on civilians as they watch and wait for them to strike. These drones allow Russia to target Ukrainians far away from the front line, away from the primary battle space. The emergence of swarms of drones in Ukraine is part of a shift in the nature of the Russian offensive, which some speculate indicates that Moscow may be running low on long-range missiles.

culates character-level modifications needed to transform the original into the revised summary.

Empirical results show high token overlap between the generated and post-edited texts, with BLEU and ROUGE-L scores respectively at 59.0% and 74.1%, indicating that the SMARTBOOK-generated reports are of sufficiently good quality and extensive human expert revision may not be necessary. However, we acknowledge that a gap still exists between the automatically generated summaries and human expert curation, as the Levenshtein edit distance computed at the character level is 34.4%. Notably, 15% of the generated summaries had no edits made by the expert analyst.

Further analysis revealed that the analyst predominantly added rather than removed content, with insertions at 49.6% and deletions at 2.3%. This suggests that automated summary generation may generally need to be more detailed.

Table 6 shows an example of edits (in color) made by an expert analyst for a machine-generated summary in SMARTBOOK. We can see here that the human analyst added additional tactical information (in blue) to elaborate on certain aspects (e.g. what is special about the "kamikaze" type of drone). Further, the analystalso added some interesting insights (in green) based on the information in the summary. Overall, this shows that SMARTBOOK provides a good starting point for analysts to expand upon for the generation of situation reports.

It is noteworthy that 15% of summaries produced by SMARTBOOK needed no modifications, highlighting its proficiency in creating acceptable reports in some scenarios without human intervention. This suggests that as technology advances and iterative refinements are applied, this rate will likely improve, reducing the workload for analysts in the future. To gain a better understanding of the different types of errors in the remaining summaries, we asked the expert analyst to categorize the errors within them. The analyst was also shown the strategic question and the corresponding extracted contexts that were used to automatically generate the summary. The summary errors were categorized as follows:

- *No relevant contexts:* None of the extracted contexts are relevant to the question (and thereby the summary is expected to be irrelevant too).
- *Inaccurate information in summary:* Summary has incorrect information, that is not reflective of the underlying input contexts.
- *Incoherent summary:* Summary is incomprehensible and unclear.
- *Incomplete summary:* Important information in the input contexts is missing in the summary.
- *Irrelevant information in summary:* Summary has material that is not relevant to the question, despite some extracted contexts being relevant.

We see that incompleteness of summaries (55.2%) is a predominant error, primarily due to missing important information or not being sufficiently complete. While the predominance of incomplete summaries could be a concern, this can also be framed positively: it represents a conservative approach ensuring that SMARTBOOK does not overextend based on limited data, and instead offers a foundational understanding. Other errors corresponded to summaries with inaccurate (18.6%) or irrelevant (14.6%) information. Directing the LLMs to reference input documents while generating summaries does improve factuality, aligning with recent findings [113]. Nevertheless, LLMs' tendency to hallucinate [78,114], calls for validation and cross-referencing techniques (discussed in §6.2) to address these issues. Finally, we see that very few summaries (3.1%) were judged incoherent, as expected given that large language models have been shown [101,35] to generate fluent and easy-to-read output.

6. Discussion

SMARTBOOK, with its modular design, automates the generation of situation reports efficiently across various contexts, including geopolitical, environmental, or humanitarian situations. Unlike traditional approaches that require substantial research and domain-specific expertise, SMARTBOOK can adapt to new domains with minimal configuration, thereby delivering accurate reports in diverse and rapidly changing global contexts. SMARTBOOK's efficacy was primarily evaluated on news from the Ukraine-Russia military conflict. Here, we briefly explore SMARTBOOK's applicability in a humanitarian scenario–the Turkey-Syria earthquake. By modifying the input data to identify key events in the specified time window (February 6-13, 2023), SMARTBOOK produced relevant reports detailing the earthquake's aftermath (link), international aid (link), rising casualties (link), and notable incidents like the disappearance of a Ghanaian soccer star (link). This adaptability from military to humanitarian crises highlights SMARTBOOK's robustness and versatility. It also emphasizes the importance of the source articles and suggests that, with mission-relevant data input, SMARTBOOK has the potential to be an invaluable tool for analysts across diverse scenarios.

6.1. Outlook

The SMARTBOOK developed is an innovative framework that generates situation reports with comprehensive, current, and factually-grounded information extracted from diverse sources. SMARTBOOK goes beyond mere information aggregation; it presents chronologically ordered sequences of topically summarized events extracted from news sources and placed into a UI layout structure that aligns with the workflow of intelligence analysis. SMARTBOOK establishes a foundation for situation understanding in a variety of scenarios. However, history repeats itself, sometimes in a bad way. Historical patterns, particularly those leading to natural or man-made disasters, can be a useful signal to trigger proactive measures for crisis mitigation. Building on prior research in event prediction [115,116,117], SMARTBOOK can guide the development of a news simulator that forecasts event outcomes in crisis situations. This tool would be invaluable for humanitarian workers and policymakers to exercise reality checks, enhancing their capacity to prevent and respond to disasters effectively. Moreover, through its capabilities to analyze textual nuances and discrepancies in reported information, SMARTBOOK's reasoning framework can be leveraged to benefit downstream applications centered on identifying false narratives, detecting misinformation, understanding propaganda, and mitigating data contamination in model pretraining corpus. The broader impacts of SMARTBOOK are significant in helping maintain the integrity and reliability of information communication in critical situations, safeguarding societal trust and decision-making processes.

6.2. Limitations and Future Extensions

While SMARTBOOK represents a significant advancement in the automated generation of situation reports, it is essential to acknowledge certain limitations that stem from both the technical aspects of the system and the scope of its application. These include (i) unverified news source credibility, (ii) potential inaccuracies in reflecting source material despite citations, and (iii) user studies focused mainly on military intelligence analysts, which may not represent the needs of a wider analytical audience. Recognizing these limitations is crucial for guiding future improvements and ensuring the framework's applicability across diverse intelligence analysis sectors. We elaborate on the limitations in more detail in the supplementary material. Here, we provide key future extensions designed to elevate SMARTBOOK's utility as a comprehensive, unbiased, and reliable tool for situation report generation in intelligence analysis:

- *Incorporating Multimodal, Multilingual Information*: Intelligence analysis increasingly relies on integrating diverse data types such as text, images, videos, and audio to understand global events comprehensively. We aim to enhance SMARTBOOK's situation reports by correlating textual claims with corresponding multimedia, utilizing advanced systems like GAIA [118] for multimedia knowledge extraction. Furthermore, global events' reach necessitates multilingual intelligence analysis to capture local nuances missed by solely using English. Employing cross-lingual techniques [94] allows for the inclusion of multiple languages, thereby enhancing understanding of local dynamics and cultural subtleties that influence global situations. Thereby, integrating multilingual sources democratizes intelligence analysis, shifting away from a predominantly English-centric perspective. Ultimately, SMARTBOOK aims to set new standards in intelligence reporting, fostering a more inclusive and globally informed approach.

- *Controlling the Bias of News Sources*: News sources carry inherent biases influenced by editorial policies, audience demographics, and geographical locations. Dominance of a single perspective may obscure crucial details or alternative viewpoints. In developing the next version of SMARTBOOK, we seek to mitigate these biases by incorporating a diverse spectrum of news outlets representing various political stances. This approach aims to diminish informational blind spots and expand the scope of scenarios available to intelligence analysts, thereby enhancing SMARTBOOK's utility.

- *Co-Authoring with Iterative Refinement*: Authoring situation reports is an iterative process, where analysts continuously refine and update the reports. In the next iteration, we aim to provide a dynamic multi-turn editing process with SMARTBOOK, by leveraging analyst feedback for self-improvement. Techniques like Reinforcement Learning with Human Feedback [119,120] and other personalization algorithms [121,122] will further enhance the system's capability to integrate human feedback, and progressively adapt to the preferences and decision-making styles of analysts. This strategy will align SMARTBOOK more closely with human analysts, leading to tailored situation reports that meet the specific requirements of intelligence analysis workflows. Ultimately, SMARTBOOK will evolve from a preliminary drafting tool to a comprehensive AI co-author for generating situation reports.

- *Improving Reliability of the Generated Reports*: The integrity of data and claims in situation reports is crucial for strategic decision-making. A key challenge in automating these reports is guaranteeing the accuracy and reliability of data from diverse sources. To address this, we propose introducing a 'verification score' for each claim, which evaluates the reliability of information based on source credibility, corroborative data, historical accuracy of similar claims, and multi-agent role-playing debate. This mechanism provides intelligence analysts with a confidence metric to quickly assess data reliability. Higher scores indicate greater confidence and facilitate rapid integration into reports, whereas lower scores necessitate comprehensive review and possibly further verification. While the claims with lower verification score can also be considered for inclusion in SMARTBOOK to enhance diverse multi-view perspectives, the content should be summarized in wording that reflects the uncertainty level properly for transparency and trustworthiness.

Acknowledgement

We would like to acknowledge the invaluable contributions of Paul Sullivan, who passed away before the publication of this paper. His enduring commitment to knowledge is greatly missed and deeply appreciated. We are grateful to Lisa Ferro and Brad Goodman from MITRE for their valuable comments and help with expert evaluation. This research is based upon work supported by U.S. DARPA AIDA Program No. FA8750-18-2-0014, DARPA KAIROS Program No. FA8750-19-2-1004, DARPA SemaFor Program No. HR001120C0123, DARPA INCAS Program No. HR001121C0165 and DARPA MIPS Program No. HR00112290105. The views and conclusions contained herein are those of the authors and should not be interpreted as necessarily representing the official policies, either expressed or implied, of DARPA, or the U.S. Government. The U.S. Government is authorized to reproduce and distribute reprints for governmental purposes notwithstanding any copyright annotation therein.

References

[1] Organization WH, et al. Coronavirus disease 2019 (COVID-19): situation report, 73. 2020.

[2] Organization WH, et al. Emergency in Ukraine: external situation report# 13, published 26 May 2022: reporting period: 19–25 May 2022. World Health Organization. Regional Office for Europe; 2022.

[3] National Academies of Sciences E, Medicine, et al. A decadal survey of the social and behavioral sciences: A research agenda for advancing intelligence analysis. 2019.

[4] Castonguay MJRP. INTELLIGENCE ANALYSIS: FLAWED WITH BIASES; 2013. CANADIAN FORCES COLLEGE. https://www.cfc.forces.gc.ca/259/290/301/305/castonguay.pdf.

[5] Belton IK, Dhami MK. Cognitive biases and debiasing in intelligence analysis. In: Routledge Handbook of Bounded Rationality. Routledge; 2020. p. 548-60.

[6] Sun L, Huang Y, Wang H, Wu S, Zhang Q, Gao C, et al. TrustLLM: Trustworthiness in Large Language Models. In: Proc. The Forty-first International Conference on Machine Learning (ICML2024); 2024. .

[7] Doggette BD, Command UA, College GS. Information overload: impacts on brigade combat team S-2 current operations intelligence analysts. Fort Leavenworth, KS: US Army Command and General Staff College; 2020.

[8] Young A. Too Much Information: Ineffective Intelligence Collection; 2019. Harvard International Review. https://hir.harvard.edu/too-much-information/.

[9] Golson P, Ferraro MF. To Resist Disinformation, Learn to Think Like an Intelligence Analyst. CIA Studies in Intelligence. 2018;62(1):31-2.

[10] Council NR, et al. Intelligence analysis for tomorrow: Advances from the behavioral and social sciences. National Academies Press; 2011.

[11] Fabbri A, Li I, She T, Li S, Radev D. Multi-News: A Large-Scale Multi-Document Summarization Dataset and Abstractive Hierarchical Model. In: Proceedings of the 57th Annual Meeting of the Association for Computational Linguistics. Florence, Italy: Association for Computational Linguistics; 2019. p. 1074-84. Available from: https://aclanthology.org/P19-1102.

[12] Abdi A, Idris N, Alguliyev RM, Aliguliyev RM. Query-based multi-documents summarization using linguistic knowledge and content word expansion. Soft Computing. 2017;21(7):1785-801.

[13] Li C, Liu Y, Liu F, Zhao L, Weng F. Improving multi-documents summarization by sentence compression based on expanded constituent parse trees. In: Proceedings of the 2014 Conference on Empirical Methods in Natural Language Processing (EMNLP); 2014. p. 691-701.

[14] OpenAI. GPT-3.5; 2021. Computer software. Available from: https://openai.com/research/.

[15] Stottlemyre SA. HUMINT, OSINT, or something new? Defining crowdsourced intelligence. International Journal of Intelligence and CounterIntelligence. 2015;28(3):578-89.

[16] Billman D, Convertino G, Shrager J, Pirolli P, Massar J. Collaborative intelligence analysis with CACHE and its effects on information gathering and cognitive bias. In: Human Computer Interaction Consortium Workshop. vol. 35. Citeseer; 2006. .

[17] Pohl D, Bouchachia A, Hellwagner H. Automatic sub-event detection in emergency management using social media. In: Proceedings of the 21st international conference on world wide web; 2012. p. 683-6.

[18] Prunckun H. Handbook of scientific methods of inquiry for intelligence analysis. 2010;11.

[19] Barnes A. Making intelligence analysis more intelligent: Using numeric probabilities. Intelligence and National Security. 2016;31(3):327-44.

[20] Toniolo A, Cerutti F, Oren N, Norman TJ, Sycara K. Making informed decisions with provenance and argumentation schemes. In: Proceedings of the Eleventh International Workshop on Argumentation in Multi-Agent Systems. vol. 2014; 2014. .

[21] Brody S, Kantor P. Automatic assessment of coverage quality in intelligence reports. In: Proceedings of the 49th Annual Meeting of the Association for Computational Linguistics: Human Language Technologies; 2011. p. 491-5.

[22] Small S, Strzalkowski T, Liu T, Ryan S, Salkin R, Shimizu N, et al. HITIQA: Scenario Based Question Answering. In: Proceedings of the Workshop on Pragmatics of Question Answering at HLT-NAACL 2004. Boston, Massachusetts, USA: Association for Computational Linguistics; 2004. p. 52-9. Available from: https://aclanthology.org/W04-2507.

[23] Heuer RJ. Psychology of intelligence analysis. 1999.

[24] Cerutti F, Norman TJ, Toniolo A, Middleton SE. CISpaces. org: From Fact Extraction to Report Generation. COMMA. 2018;2018:269-80.

[25] van Gelder T, Kruger A, Thomman S, de Rozario R, Silver E, Saletta M, et al. Improving analytic reasoning via crowdsourcing and structured analytic techniques. Journal of Cognitive Engineering and

Decision Making. 2020;14(3):195-217.
[26] Xia H, Osterlund C, McKernan B, Folkestad J, Rossini P, Boichak O, et al. TRACE: A stigmergic crowdsourcing platform for intelligence analysis. 2019.
[27] Pirolli P, Card S. The sensemaking process and leverage points for analyst technology as identified through cognitive task analysis. In: Proceedings of international conference on intelligence analysis. vol. 5. McLean, VA, USA; 2005. p. 2-4.
[28] Pioch NJ, Everett JO. POLESTAR: collaborative knowledge management and sensemaking tools for intelligence analysts. In: Proceedings of the 15th ACM international conference on Information and knowledge management; 2006. p. 513-21.
[29] Toniolo A, Cerutti F, Norman TJ, Oren N, Allen JA, Srivastava M, et al. Human-machine collaboration in intelligence analysis: An expert evaluation. Intelligent Systems with Applications. 2023;17:200151.
[30] Xiong C, Li X, Li Y, Liu G. Multi-documents summarization based on TextRank and its application in online argumentation platform. International Journal of Data Warehousing and Mining (IJDWM). 2018;14(3):69-89.
[31] Abdi A, Shamsuddin SM, Aliguliyev RM. QMOS: Query-based multi-documents opinion-oriented summarization. Information Processing & Management. 2018;54(2):318-38.
[32] Abdi A, Shamsuddin SM, Hasan S, Piran J. Machine learning-based multi-documents sentiment-oriented summarization using linguistic treatment. Expert Systems with Applications. 2018;109:66-85.
[33] DeYoung J, Beltagy I, van Zuylen M, Kuehl B, Wang LL. Ms2: Multi-document summarization of medical studies. arXiv preprint arXiv:210406486. 2021.
[34] Zhang H, Liu X, Zhang J. Extractive summarization via chatgpt for faithful summary generation. arXiv preprint arXiv:230404193. 2023.
[35] Zhang T, Ladhak F, Durmus E, Liang P, McKeown K, Hashimoto TB. Benchmarking Large Language Models for News Summarization. arXiv preprint arXiv:230113848. 2023.
[36] Yang X, Li Y, Zhang X, Chen H, Cheng W. Exploring the limits of chatgpt for query or aspect-based text summarization. arXiv preprint arXiv:230208081. 2023.
[37] Zhang Z, Elfardy H, Dreyer M, Small K, Ji H, Bansal M. Enhancing Multi-Document Summarization with Cross-Document Graph-based Information Extraction. In: Proceedings of the 17th Conference of the European Chapter of the Association for Computational Linguistics; 2023. p. 1688-99.
[38] Wang J, Liang Y, Meng F, Zou B, Li Z, Qu J, et al.. Zero-Shot cross-lingual summarization via large language models. Apr; 2023.
[39] Zeng Q, Sidhu M, Chan HP, Wang L, Ji H. Meta-review Generation with Checklist-guided Iterative Introspection. arXiv preprint arXiv:230514647. 2023.
[40] Wang Q, Huang L, Jiang Z, Knight K, Ji H, Bansal M, et al. PaperRobot: Incremental Draft Generation of Scientific Ideas. In: Proc. The 57th Annual Meeting of the Association for Computational Linguistics (ACL2019); 2019. .
[41] Wang Q, Zeng Q, Huang L, Knight K, Ji H, Rajani NF. ReviewRobot: Explainable Paper Review Generation based on Knowledge Synthesis. In: Proc. The 13th International Conference on Natural Language Generation (INLG2020); 2020. .
[42] Wang Z, Mao S, Wu W, Ge T, Wei F, Ji H. Unleashing Cognitive Synergy in Large Language Models: A Task-Solving Agent through Multi-Persona Self-Collaboration. In: arxiv; 2023. .
[43] Cardon P, Fleischmann C, Aritz J, Logemann M, Heidewald J. The Challenges and Opportunities of AI-Assisted Writing: Developing AI Literacy for the AI Age. Business and Professional Communication Quarterly. 2023:23294906231176517.
[44] Gero KI, Liu V, Chilton L. Sparks: Inspiration for science writing using language models. In: Designing interactive systems conference; 2022. p. 1002-19.
[45] Mirowski P, Mathewson KW, Pittman J, Evans R. Co-Writing Screenplays and Theatre Scripts with Language Models: Evaluation by Industry Professionals. In: Proceedings of the 2023 CHI Conference on Human Factors in Computing Systems; 2023. p. 1-34.
[46] Chen M, Tworek J, Jun H, Yuan Q, Pinto HPdO, Kaplan J, et al. Evaluating large language models trained on code. arXiv preprint arXiv:210703374. 2021.
[47] Lee M, Liang P, Yang Q. Coauthor: Designing a human-ai collaborative writing dataset for exploring language model capabilities. In: Proceedings of the 2022 CHI conference on human factors in computing systems; 2022. p. 1-19.
[48] Klein S, Aeschlimann JF, Balsiger DF, Converse SL, Foster M, Lao R, et al. Automatic novel writing: A status report. University of Wisconsin-Madison Department of Computer Sciences; 1973.

[49] Roemmele M, Gordon AS. Creative help: A story writing assistant. In: Interactive Storytelling: 8th International Conference on Interactive Digital Storytelling, ICIDS 2015, Copenhagen, Denmark, November 30-December 4, 2015, Proceedings 8. Springer; 2015. p. 81-92.
[50] Samuel B, Mateas M, Wardrip-Fruin N. The design of Writing Buddy: a mixed-initiative approach towards computational story collaboration. In: Interactive Storytelling: 9th International Conference on Interactive Digital Storytelling, ICIDS 2016, Los Angeles, CA, USA, November 15–18, 2016, Proceedings 9. Springer; 2016. p. 388-96.
[51] Yuan A, Coenen A, Reif E, Ippolito D. Wordcraft: story writing with large language models. In: 27th International Conference on Intelligent User Interfaces; 2022. p. 841-52.
[52] Wahle JP, Ruas T, Kirstein F, Gipp B. How Large Language Models are Transforming Machine-Paraphrase Plagiarism. In: Proceedings of the 2022 Conference on Empirical Methods in Natural Language Processing; 2022. p. 952-63.
[53] Perkins M. Academic Integrity considerations of AI Large Language Models in the post-pandemic era: ChatGPT and beyond. Journal of University Teaching & Learning Practice. 2023;20(2):07.
[54] Wahle JP, Ruas T, Foltýnek T, Meuschke N, Gipp B. Identifying machine-paraphrased plagiarism. In: International Conference on Information. Springer; 2022. p. 393-413.
[55] Kisilev P, Walach E, Barkan E, Ophir B, Alpert S, Hashoul SY. From medical image to automatic medical report generation. IBM Journal of Research and Development. 2015;59(2/3):2-1.
[56] Monshi MMA, Poon J, Chung V. Deep learning in generating radiology reports: A survey. Artificial Intelligence in Medicine. 2020;106:101878.
[57] Antwi BO, Adelakun BO, Eziefule AO. Transforming Financial Reporting with AI: Enhancing Accuracy and Timeliness. International Journal of Advanced Economics. 2024;6(6):205-23.
[58] Leon DN, Talbert ML. An intelligent user interface to support weather report generation. Weather and forecasting. 2002;17(1):115-23.
[59] Sripada S, Burnett N, Turner R, Mastin J, Evans D. A case study: NLG meeting weather industry demand for quality and quantity of textual weather forecasts. In: Proceedings of the 8th International Natural Language Generation Conference (INLG); 2014. p. 1-5.
[60] Araújo D, Couceiro M, Seifert L, Sarmento H, Davids K. Artificial intelligence in sport performance analysis. Routledge; 2021.
[61] Bhatnagar R, Babbar M. A systematic review of sports analytics. International Journal of Technology Transfer and Commercialisation. 2022;19(4):393-406.
[62] Van Dijk A, Mount R, Gibbons P, Vardon M, Canadell P. Environmental reporting and accounting in Australia: progress, prospects and research priorities. Science of the Total Environment. 2014;473:338-49.
[63] Piedelobo L, Ortega-Terol D, Del Pozo S, Hernández-López D, Ballesteros R, Moreno MA, et al. HidroMap: A new tool for irrigation monitoring and management using free satellite imagery. ISPRS international journal of geo-information. 2018;7(6):220.
[64] Negash S. Business intelligence. Communications of the association for information systems. 2004;13(1):15.
[65] Liu Y, Ott M, Goyal N, Du J, Joshi M, Chen D, et al. Roberta: A robustly optimized bert pretraining approach. arXiv preprint arXiv:190711692. 2019.
[66] Lewis M, Liu Y, Goyal N, Ghazvininejad M, Mohamed A, Levy O, et al. BART: Denoising Sequence-to-Sequence Pre-training for Natural Language Generation, Translation, and Comprehension. In: Proceedings of the 58th Annual Meeting of the Association for Computational Linguistics; 2020. p. 7871-80.
[67] Achiam J, Adler S, Agarwal S, Ahmad L, Akkaya I, Aleman FL, et al. Gpt-4 technical report. arXiv preprint arXiv:230308774. 2023.
[68] Ma Y, Ye C, Wu Z, Wang X, Cao Y, Pang L, et al. Structured, Complex and Time-complete Temporal Event Forecasting. arXiv preprint arXiv:231201052. 2023.
[69] Singh J, Nejdl W, Anand A. Expedition: a time-aware exploratory search system designed for scholars. In: Proceedings of the 39th International ACM SIGIR conference on Research and Development in Information Retrieval; 2016. p. 1105-8.
[70] Jain AK, Dubes RC. Algorithms for clustering data. 1988.
[71] Sparck Jones K. A statistical interpretation of term specificity and its application in retrieval. Journal of documentation. 1972;28(1):11-21.
[72] Vaswani A, Shazeer N, Parmar N, Uszkoreit J, Jones L, Gomez AN, et al. Attention is all you need.

Advances in neural information processing systems. 2017;30.

[73] Gu X, Mao Y, Han J, Liu J, Yu H, Wu Y, et al. Generating Representative Headlines for News Stories. In: Proc. of the the Web Conf. 2020; 2020. .

[74] Sharma S. Generative Models for Question Generation. Available at SSRN 3970263. 2021.

[75] Wang Z, Valdez J, Basu Mallick D, Baraniuk RG. Towards Human-Like Educational Question Generation with Large Language Models. In: International Conference on Artificial Intelligence in Education. Springer; 2022. p. 153-66.

[76] Murakhovs'ka L, Wu CS, Laban P, Niu T, Liu W, Xiong C. MixQG: Neural Question Generation with Mixed Answer Types. In: Findings of the Association for Computational Linguistics: NAACL 2022. Seattle, United States: Association for Computational Linguistics; 2022. p. 1486-97. Available from: https://aclanthology.org/2022.findings-naacl.111.

[77] Du X, Shao J, Cardie C. Learning to Ask: Neural Question Generation for Reading Comprehension. In: Proceedings of the 55th Annual Meeting of the Association for Computational Linguistics (Volume 1: Long Papers). Vancouver, Canada: Association for Computational Linguistics; 2017. p. 1342-52. Available from: https://aclanthology.org/P17-1123.

[78] Ji Z, Lee N, Frieske R, Yu T, Su D, Xu Y, et al. Survey of hallucination in natural language generation. ACM Computing Surveys.

[79] Maynez J, Narayan S, Bohnet B, McDonald R. On Faithfulness and Factuality in Abstractive Summarization. In: Proceedings of the 58th Annual Meeting of the Association for Computational Linguistics; 2020. p. 1906-19.

[80] Holtzman A, Buys J, Du L, Forbes M, Choi Y. The Curious Case of Neural Text Degeneration. In: International Conference on Learning Representations; 2019. .

[81] Reddy RG, Chinthakindi SC, Wang Z, Fung Y, Conger K, Elsayed A, et al. Newsclaims: A new benchmark for claim detection from news with attribute knowledge. In: Proceedings of the 2022 Conference on Empirical Methods in Natural Language Processing; 2022. p. 6002-18.

[82] Reddy RG, Chinthakindi SC, Fung YR, Small K, Ji H. A Zero-Shot Claim Detection Framework using Question Answering. In: Proceedings of the 29th International Conference on Computational Linguistics; 2022. p. 6927-33.

[83] Rajpurkar P, Jia R, Liang P. Know What You Don't Know: Unanswerable Questions for SQuAD. In: Proceedings of the 56th Annual Meeting of the Association for Computational Linguistics (Volume 2: Short Papers); 2018. p. 784-9.

[84] Kwiatkowski T, Palomaki J, Redfield O, Collins M, Parikh A, Alberti C, et al. Natural Questions: A Benchmark for Question Answering Research. Transactions of the Association for Computational Linguistics. 2019;7:452-66.

[85] Chakravarti R, Sil A. Towards confident machine reading comprehension. arXiv preprint arXiv:210107942. 2021.

[86] Reddy RG, Sultan MA, Kayi ES, Zhang R, Castelli V, Sil A. Answer Span Correction in Machine Reading Comprehension. In: Findings of the Association for Computational Linguistics: EMNLP 2020; 2020. p. 2496-501.

[87] Zhang Z, Vu T, Moschitti A. Joint Models for Answer Verification in Question Answering Systems. In: Proceedings of the 59th Annual Meeting of the Association for Computational Linguistics and the 11th International Joint Conference on Natural Language Processing (Volume 1: Long Papers); 2021. p. 3252-62.

[88] Garg S, Vu T, Moschitti A. TANDA: Transfer and Adapt Pre-Trained Transformer Models for Answer Sentence Selection. Proceedings of the AAAI Conference on Artificial Intelligence. 2020 Apr;34(05):7780–7788. Available from: http://dx.doi.org/10.1609/AAAI.V34I05.6282.

[89] Yang Y, Yih Wt, Meek C. WikiQA: A Challenge Dataset for Open-Domain Question Answering. In: Proceedings of the 2015 Conference on Empirical Methods in Natural Language Processing. Lisbon, Portugal: Association for Computational Linguistics; 2015. p. 2013-8. Available from: https://aclanthology.org/D15-1237.

[90] Stab C, Miller T, Schiller B, Rai P, Gurevych I. Cross-topic Argument Mining from Heterogeneous Sources. In: Proceedings of the 2018 Conference on Empirical Methods in Natural Language Processing; 2018. p. 3664-74.

[91] Levy R, Bilu Y, Hershcovich D, Aharoni E, Slonim N. Context dependent claim detection. In: Proceedings of COLING 2014, the 25th International Conference on Computational Linguistics: Technical Papers; 2014. p. 1489-500.

[92] Levy R, Gretz S, Sznajder B, Hummel S, Aharonov R, Slonim N. Unsupervised corpus–wide claim detection. In: Proceedings of the 4th Workshop on Argument Mining; 2017. p. 79-84.

[93] Li M, Reddy RG, Wang Z, Chiang YS, Lai T, Yu P, et al. Covid-19 claim radar: A structured claim extraction and tracking system. In: Proceedings of the 60th annual meeting of the association for computational linguistics: system demonstrations; 2022. p. 135-44.

[94] Du X, Zhang Z, Li S, Yu P, Wang H, Lai T, et al. RESIN-11: Schema-guided event prediction for 11 newsworthy scenarios. In: Proceedings of the 2022 Conference of the North American Chapter of the Association for Computational Linguistics: Human Language Technologies: System Demonstrations; 2022. p. 54-63.

[95] Lai T, Ji H, Zhai C. Improving Candidate Retrieval with Entity Profile Generation for Wikidata Entity Linking. In: Findings of the Association for Computational Linguistics: ACL 2022; 2022. p. 3696-711.

[96] Lai TM, Bui T, Kim DS. End-to-end neural coreference resolution revisited: A simple yet effective baseline. In: ICASSP 2022-2022 IEEE International Conference on Acoustics, Speech and Signal Processing (ICASSP). IEEE; 2022. p. 8147-51.

[97] Williams A, Nangia N, Bowman S. A Broad-Coverage Challenge Corpus for Sentence Understanding through Inference. In: Proceedings of the 2018 Conference of the North American Chapter of the Association for Computational Linguistics: Human Language Technologies, Volume 1 (Long Papers). Association for Computational Linguistics; 2018. .

[98] Ji Z, Lee N, Frieske R, Yu T, Su D, Xu Y, et al. Survey of hallucination in natural language generation. ACM Computing Surveys. 2023;55(12):1-38.

[99] Li J, Cheng X, Zhao WX, Nie JY, Wen JR. Halueval: A large-scale hallucination evaluation benchmark for large language models. In: Proceedings of the 2023 Conference on Empirical Methods in Natural Language Processing; 2023. p. 6449-64.

[100] Bang Y, Cahyawijaya S, Lee N, Dai W, Su D, Wilie B, et al. A Multitask, Multilingual, Multimodal Evaluation of ChatGPT on Reasoning, Hallucination, and Interactivity. In: Proceedings of the 13th International Joint Conference on Natural Language Processing and the 3rd Conference of the Asia-Pacific Chapter of the Association for Computational Linguistics (Volume 1: Long Papers); 2023. p. 675-718.

[101] Goyal T, Li JJ, Durrett G. News Summarization and Evaluation in the Era of GPT-3. arXiv preprint arXiv:220912356. 2022.

[102] Bhaskar A, Fabbri AR, Durrett G. Zero-Shot Opinion Summarization with GPT-3. arXiv preprint arXiv:221115914. 2022.

[103] Reddy RG, Elfardy H, Chan HP, Small K, Ji H. SumREN: Summarizing Reported Speech about Events in News. arXiv preprint arXiv:221201146. 2022.

[104] Brown T, Mann B, Ryder N, Subbiah M, Kaplan JD, Dhariwal P, et al. Language models are few-shot learners. Advances in neural information processing systems. 2020;33:1877-901.

[105] Chowdhery A, Narang S, Devlin J, Bosma M, Mishra G, Roberts A, et al. Palm: Scaling language modeling with pathways. arXiv preprint arXiv:220402311. 2022.

[106] Zhang J, Zhao Y, Saleh M, Liu P. Pegasus: Pre-training with extracted gap-sentences for abstractive summarization. In: International Conference on Machine Learning. PMLR; 2020. p. 11328-39.

[107] Liu Y, Liu P, Radev D, Neubig G. BRIO: Bringing Order to Abstractive Summarization. In: Proceedings of the 60th Annual Meeting of the Association for Computational Linguistics (Volume 1: Long Papers); 2022. p. 2890-903.

[108] Honovich O, Aharoni R, Herzig J, Taitelbaum H, Kukliansy D, Cohen V, et al. TRUE: Re-evaluating Factual Consistency Evaluation. In: Carpuat M, de Marneffe MC, Meza Ruiz IV, editors. Proceedings of the 2022 Conference of the North American Chapter of the Association for Computational Linguistics: Human Language Technologies. Seattle, United States: Association for Computational Linguistics; 2022. p. 3905-20. Available from: `https://aclanthology.org/2022.naacl-main.287`.

[109] Bohnet B, Tran VQ, Verga P, Aharoni R, Andor D, Soares LB, et al. Attributed question answering: Evaluation and modeling for attributed large language models. arXiv preprint arXiv:221208037. 2022.

[110] Gao L, Dai Z, Pasupat P, Chen A, Chaganty AT, Fan Y, et al. RARR: Researching and Revising What Language Models Say, Using Language Models. In: Proceedings of the 61st Annual Meeting of the Association for Computational Linguistics (Volume 1: Long Papers); 2023. p. 16477-508.

[111] Papineni K, Roukos S, Ward T, Zhu WJ. Bleu: a method for automatic evaluation of machine translation. In: Proceedings of the 40th annual meeting of the Association for Computational Linguistics; 2002. p. 311-8.

[112] Lin CY. Rouge: A package for automatic evaluation of summaries. In: Text summarization branches out; 2004. p. 74-81.

[113] Gao T, Yen H, Yu J, Chen D. Enabling Large Language Models to Generate Text with Citations. In: Bouamor H, Pino J, Bali K, editors. Proceedings of the 2023 Conference on Empirical Methods in Natural Language Processing. Singapore: Association for Computational Linguistics; 2023. p. 6465-88. Available from: https://aclanthology.org/2023.emnlp-main.398.

[114] Tam D, Mascarenhas A, Zhang S, Kwan S, Bansal M, Raffel C. Evaluating the Factual Consistency of Large Language Models Through Summarization. arXiv preprint arXiv:221108412. 2022.

[115] Li M, Li S, Wang Z, Huang L, Cho K, Ji H, et al. The Future is not One-dimensional: Complex Event Schema Induction by Graph Modeling for Event Prediction. In: Proceedings of the 2021 Conference on Empirical Methods in Natural Language Processing; 2021. p. 5203-15.

[116] Wang H, Zhang Z, Li S, Han J, Sun Y, Tong H, et al. Schema-guided event graph completion. arXiv preprint arXiv:220602921. 2022.

[117] Li S, Zhao R, Li M, Ji H, Callison-Burch C, Han J. Open-Domain Hierarchical Event Schema Induction by Incremental Prompting and Verification. In: Proceedings of the 61st Annual Meeting of the Association for Computational Linguistics (Volume 1: Long Papers); 2023. p. 5677-97.

[118] Li M, Zareian A, Lin Y, Pan X, Whitehead S, Chen B, et al. Gaia: A fine-grained multimedia knowledge extraction system. In: Proceedings of the 58th Annual Meeting of the Association for Computational Linguistics: System Demonstrations; 2020. p. 77-86.

[119] Stiennon N, Ouyang L, Wu J, Ziegler D, Lowe R, Voss C, et al. Learning to summarize with human feedback. Advances in Neural Information Processing Systems. 2020;33:3008-21.

[120] Bai Y, Jones A, Ndousse K, Askell A, Chen A, DasSarma N, et al. Training a helpful and harmless assistant with reinforcement learning from human feedback. arXiv preprint arXiv:220405862. 2022.

[121] Wu C, Wu F, An M, Huang J, Huang Y, Xie X. NPA: neural news recommendation with personalized attention. In: Proceedings of the 25th ACM SIGKDD international conference on knowledge discovery & data mining; 2019. p. 2576-84.

[122] Monzer C, Moeller J, Helberger N, Eskens S. User perspectives on the news personalisation process: Agency, trust and utility as building blocks. Digital Journalism. 2020;8(9):1142-62.

Handbook on Neurosymbolic AI and Knowledge Graphs
P. Hitzler et al. (Eds.)
IOS Press, 2025

doi:10.3233/FAIA250238

Analysing Objectives of Auxiliary Inputs in Semantic Web Machine Learning Systems

Anna BREIT [a,1], Artem REVENKO [a], Victor MIRELES [e], Majlinda LLUGIQI [b]
Fajar J. EKAPUTRA [b,c], Laura WALTERSDORFER [b,c], Heiko PAULHEIM [d] and Marta SABOU [b]

[a] *Semantic Web Company, Austria*
[b] *Vienna University of Economics and Business (WU Wien), Austria*
[c] *Vienna University of Technology (TU Wien), Austria*
[d] *University of Mannheim, Germany*
[e] *National Autonomous University of Mexico, Mexico City, Mexico*

ORCiD ID: Anna Breit https://orcid.org/0000-0001-6553-4175, Artem Revenko https://orcid.org/0000-0001-6681-3328, Victor Mireles https://orcid.org/0000-0003-3264-3687, Majlinda Llugiqi https://orcid.org/0000-0002-5008-6856, Fajar J. Ekaputra https://orcid.org/0000-0003-4569-2496, Laura Waltersdorfer https://orcid.org/0000-0002-6932-5036, Heiko Paulheim https://orcid.org/0000-0003-4386-8195, Marta Sabou https://orcid.org/0000-0001-9301-8418

Abstract. With the increasing popularity of neuro-symbolic systems, the number of systems incorporating both symbolic knowledge and statistical machine learning models is on the rise, leading to a wide variety of system architectures. Authors have different rationales behind their architectural decisions to include certain components into their processing flows, however, these *objectives* have not been thoroughly investigated. In this chapter, we examine the objectives targeting quality attributes of systems that combine symbolic knowledge represented by Semantic Web Technologies with machine learning approaches, known as SWeML systems. Building on top of the previously introduced SWeML classification system, we conduct a comprehensive analysis of the objectives for adding *auxiliary inputs* to these systems, i.e., inputs that are not needed to fulfil the system's primary purpose, but to enhance its capabilities. Specifically, we manually analyze 293 research papers that integrate multiple inputs, exploring the various objectives behind the inclusion of additional symbolic knowledge or sub-symbolic inputs, such as improving performance, reducing response times, and enhancing interpretability. Additionally, we relate the objectives to system characteristics, such as system architecture, targeted task, or application domain, uncovering trends and correlations that can provide deeper insights into the design choices and priorities of SWeML systems.

Keywords. semantic web, machine learning, knowledge graph, neuro-symbolic integration, system design, auxiliary inputs

[1]Corresponding Author. e-mail: anna.breit@semantic-web.com

1. Introduction

There has been long-standing interest in combining symbolic and sub-symbolic paradigms as complementary techniques to mitigate weaknesses and boost advantages of each other: symbolic approaches are said to provide human-readable knowledge representation and reasoning capabilities, but require experts and suffer from knowledge acquisition problems [20]. On the other hand, sub-symbolic approaches such as traditional machine learning (ML) and more recently deep learning (DL) approaches can detect patterns from unstructured data, but are intransparent [23]. Neuro-symbolic AI has seen a surge in interest over the last years, covered in various surveys from different perspectives [18,29,20]. Semantic Web Machine Learning (SWeML) systems [10], which specifically exploit Semantic Web (SW) structures, such as vocabularies, ontologies, taxonomies, or knowledge graphs, have also seen high interest [10].

To further define SWeML systems, Figure 1 provides an overview of interconnected fields: symbolic approaches include knowledge representation and reasoning while sub-symbolic approaches involve different machine learning methods.

By combining these two paradigms, SWeML systems are used to solve tasks in various applications areas, ranging from text processing [24] to graph- [12] or image-related [16] tasks. In order to do so, a wide variety of different system architectures can be applied, which vary in the models and resources used, as well as in processing flows. These system architectures, can be described in terms of processing patterns [8,19], which describe the different components of the system, i.e.,inputs, outputs, and processing units, in addition to the flow of information through the systems.

In a SWeML system, each system design decision is subject to a certain motivation or *objective*. While the *primary objective* of each system component is usually to fulfil the task at hand, the rationale for including some components may go beyond the primary task the system is intended to tackle. This also holds for inputs, which may be *primary inputs* essential to make the system work (i.e., the system could not fulfil its purpose without it), or *auxiliary inputs*, which may enhance the system's capabilities (the system could fulfil its purpose also without it, albeit inferior). In particular, authors may integrate (additional) resources or components into an existing approach to achieve certain desirable, externally defined qualities such as good performance, quick response time, or interpretability. We refer to these rationales for the usage of specific system components as *supplementary objectives*. For example, a given system might be designed to answer questions in natural language from a set of documents (primary objective), and an author might choose to expand the query with concepts retrieved via entity linking (auxiliary input) in order to enrich it and thus attain higher recall (supplementary objective) than with a purely text-based ML method.

These supplementary goals have not yet been thoroughly researched, however, their analysis can lead to many advances. Since supplementary goals reflect the aspects that SWeML developers and architects want to improve, studying them helps to paint a picture of the current landscape of SWeML systems and to identify research trends and gaps. By analysing how, why, and when different resources and components are used in SWeML systems, we can identify exploitation patterns, as well as desired characteristics of these technologies, and provide guidance to developers on how to build more effective resources, especially in the Semantic Web domain. Finally, a deeper understanding of the problems that authors are trying to solve with the use of particular resources and compo-

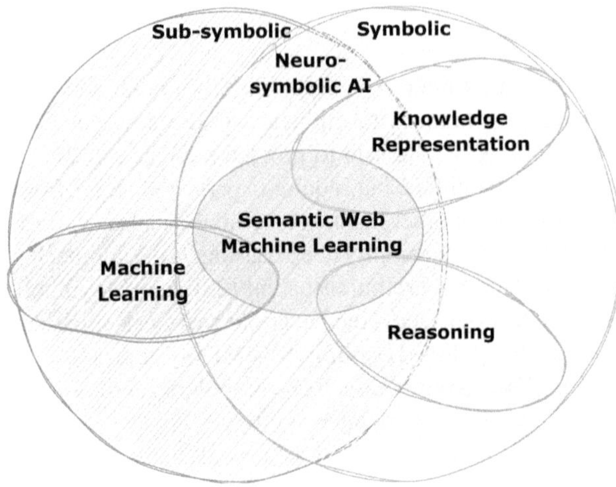

Figure 1. Overview of different research areas surrounding Semantic Web Machine Learning

nents forms the basis for an empirical evaluation of the effectiveness of their integration into SWeML systems in achieving their goals.

In this chapter, we conduct a detailed examination of auxiliary inputs and their objectives in SWeML systems. The questions we aim to answer are:

- Which objectives exist that can be addressed by auxiliary inputs?
- Which architectural patterns exist to add those auxiliary inputs? Do some of those patterns correlate with particular objectives?
- Are there differences by primary task, application domain, or machine learning component?

To answer these questions, we reuse an annotated corpus of 476 papers describing SWeML systems [10]. From that corpus, we extract a subset of 178 papers describing systems with auxiliary inputs, and distill insights and answers to the above papers. The results can be seen as recipes for building SWeML systems fulfilling particular primary and supplementary objectives.

2. Background

In this section, we give an introduction to *objectives of system design decisions* (Section 2.1), and related work on *neuro-symbolic AI*, specifically *SWeML systems* and *neuro-symbolic objectives* (Section 2.2).

2.1. Objectives of System Design Decisions

Software system architects and engineers–of SWeML or any other systems–have different rationales, or *objectives*, behind their architectural decisions [4] and thus, these design decisions should be carefully selected [14].

These rationales are ideally grounded in the system-specific requirements which are connected to certain externally defined desirable factors. We can follow [7,17] and classify software system requirements into three categories: (1) functional requirements, (2) quality attribute requirements, and (3) constraints.

Functional requirements define what the system should do, outlining specific behaviors and functionalities. These are the essential tasks and operations that the system must perform to fulfil its purpose. *Quality attribute requirements*, on the other hand, specify the system's desired properties such as performance, security, and usability. They address how well the system performs its functions under varying conditions and how users interact with it. *Constraints* impose limitations or restrictions on the design choices, often due to technological, economic, or regulatory factors.

While requirements vary greatly from system to system and must be determined individually, for quality attributes, several standards aim to provide comprehensive frameworks. One prominent example is the `ISO/IEC 25010: Product Quality Model` [21], which groups the product quality into nine characteristics, namely functional suitability, performance efficiency, compatibility, interaction capabilities, reliability, security, maintainability, flexibility, and safety. These characteristics are further refined in sub-characteristics (see Figure 2).

SOFTWARE PRODUCT QUALITY								
FUNCTIONAL SUITABILITY	PERFORMANCE EFFICIENCY	COMPATIBILITY	INTERACTION CAPABILITY	RELIABILITY	SECURITY	MAINTAINABILITY	FLEXIBILITY	SAFETY
FUNCTIONAL COMPLETENESS	TIME BEHAVIOUR	CO-EXISTENCE	APPROPRIATENESS RECOGNIZABILITY	FAULTLESSNESS	CONFIDENTIALITY	MODULARITY	ADAPTABILITY	OPERATIONAL CONSTRAINT
FUNCTIONAL CORRECTNESS	RESOURCE UTILIZATION	INTEROPERABILITY	LEARNABILITY	AVAILABILITY	INTEGRITY	REUSABILITY	SCALABILITY	RISK IDENTIFICATION
FUNCTIONAL APPROPRIATENESS	CAPACITY		OPERABILITY	FAULT TOLERANCE	NON-REPUDIATION	ANALYSABILITY	INSTALLABILITY	FAIL SAFE
			USER ERROR PROTECTION	RECOVERABILITY	ACCOUNTABILITY	MODIFIABILITY	REPLACEABILITY	HAZARD WARNING
			USER ENGAGEMENT		AUTHENTICITY	TESTABILITY		SAFE INTEGRATION
			INCLUSIVITY		RESISTANCE			
			USER ASSISTANCE					
			SELF-DESCRIPTIVENESS					

iso25000.com

Figure 2. The Product Quality Model defined in ISO/IEC 25010[2]

In the context of SWeML systems, we categorize objectives targeting functional requirements as *primary objectives*, while objectives targeting quality attributes as *supplementary objectives* [3].

The primary objective of a SWeML system refers to the main purpose or goal that the system is designed to achieve. It is the overarching reason for the system's existence, guiding its development, deployment, and usage. The primary objective serves as the foundation upon which functional requirements of SWeML system are built, ensuring that the software system delivers the intended value. For instance, a wildlife organisation might deploy a SWeML system with the primary objective of recognising animals from video footage, while other functional requirements might include user management to ensure only authorised persons can access the system.

In contrast, *supplementary objectives* aim at quality attributes exceeding primary system functionalities and entail design choices. For instance, the primary objective of an ML-based recommendation system is to suggest relevant items to users, while the integration of a Knowledge Graph into the system could aim to improve the interpretabil-

---

[2] `https://iso25000.com/images/figures/iso_25010_en.png`

[3] As constraints represent fixed limitations opposed to goals, we consider them out of scope when investigating objectives.

ity of the recommendations. In this example, the Knowledge Graph serves as *auxiliary input*, i.e., a resource or data ingested into the system not to fulfill a primary objective, but rather to support a supplementary objective[4]. We will explore auxiliary inputs and other type of system modifications in greater detail in section 3.2.

To describe these supplementary objectives, SWeML system architects can build upon established requirement frameworks, but they also have unique objectives that classical software engineering does not typically address. Specifically, machine learning [5], and Semantic Web [28] have additional complexities, for instance, considerations around the training data of a machine learning model, such as data volume, quality, and ethical sourcing, are critical to and distinct in AI these systems.

2.2. Related Work

Neuro-symbolic AI. Neuro-symbolic AI, which combines symbolic and sub-symbolic AI paradigms, has a longstanding history [6,15] and has seen a surge in interest over the last years [9]. Despite this growing interest, the impact of architectural patterns and quality attributes when integrating these paradigms has not been thoroughly examined.

Over time, different taxonomies have been defined for describing systems incorporating both types of AI: In 2005, Bader and Hitzler proposed eight dimensions along three groups, namely, interrelation, language, and usage [6]. Kautz introduced six top-level types of neuro-symbolic AI, ranging from symbolic knowledge being transformed into vectors (which he called *symbolic Neuro symbolic)* to approaches where a reasoner and a neural network solve complementary tasks (*Neuro: Symbolic → Neuro)* or logic being used as constraint for neural networks *(Neuro_Symbolic)* [22]. Another notable work by van Harmelen and ten Teije proposes 15 design patterns to describe the data and processing flows of neuro-symbolic systems [19], which is extended with additional elements in another work [8].

Semantic Web Machine Learning Systems. SWeML can be considered a subset of neuro-symbolic AI systems (see Figure 1). A recent survey characterizes SWeML systems into workflow patterns in a large-scale study of over 400 papers [10]. As an extension a knowledge graph was constructed to make these investigated works available [13]. Another survey focusing on knowledge graph reasoning, specifically the tasks knowledge graph completion, and question answering, provides an overview of common models and their mechanisms [29]. Von Rueden provides a general taxonomy of how knowledge can be used in machine learning with examples [26].

Neuro-symbolic Objectives. Few works have investigated supplementary objectives for neuro-symbolic AI [2,18,27] (cf. Table 1):

Sarker et al. [27] reuse two taxonomies [6,22] to classify surveyed papers and also check whether *desirable neuro-symbolic features* such as interpretability (most papers fell into this category), out of distribution handling, learning from small data and error recovery apply. Another recent survey from Hamilton et al. on neuro-symbolic AI focusing on natural language processing reuses the former list of features from Sarker et al. and synthesizes them to the following *goals*: out-of distribution generalisation, transferability, interpretability, reduced data and reasoning [18].

[4]It is important to note that supplementary objectives are not inherently optional but, analogous to quality attributes, may be necessary for a system to be useful in practice

Hamilton et al. also mention the difficulty to assess and evaluate different works due to inconsistencies in terminology, namely in regards to reasoning (e.g. human-level, common-sense, etc.).

Recently, Allen and Ilievski have reported an early work on identifying reference architectures for neuro-symbolic approaches for Knowledge Engineering [2]. Their work shows empirical evidence of more than twenty quality attributes of these systems, including accessibility, affordability, comprehensiveness, among others, which are derived from their prior analysis of Knowledge Engineering requirements over the years [3].

These works [2,3,18,27] represent first attempts to identify and describe supplementary objectives of neuro-symbolic AI systems. However, except for the survey on neuro-symbolic approaches for knowledge engineering [2], which maps SWeML system patterns to quality attributes for knowledge engineering, the other surveys only map objectives in relation to high-level patterns (e.g [22]). Furthermore, these works do not relate objectives in terms of more detailed system characteristics, such as their architectural make-ups (i.e., system components), used ML/KR models, tasks, or domains. Consequently, there is only limited systematised knowledge about the links between neurosymbolic AI systems patterns/components and relevant supplementary objectives.

To fill this gap, we obtain an extended list of supplementary objectives by analysing a set of annotated papers to extend the current understanding of such objectives. Furthermore, we empirically investigate the role of auxiliary inputs in SWeML systems in terms of different characteristics (e.g. tasks, application domain, pattern type).

Table 1. Related surveys investigating supplementary objectives of neuro-symbolic AI.

Ref	Description	Identified Supplementary Objectives
[27]	43 conference papers grouped to *desirable neuro-symbolic features*	out-of- distribution handling, interpretability, error recovery, learning from small data
[18]	181 works (journal & conference articles), former *desirable features* [27] are reused, extended and synthesized to *goals*	out-of- distribution generalisation, transferability interpretability, reduced data, reasoning.
[2]	139 papers on Neuro-symbolic approaches for Knowledge Engineering annotated with quality attribute requirements described in [3]	interoperability, curatability, scalability, modularity, customizability.

3. Methods

To investigate the relation between the theoretical objectives of SWeML system design decisions, and their real-world usage and application, we performed an empirical literature study, analysing the authors' rationales behind adding additional inputs to their systems. To this end, we start from an existing Systematic Mapping Study [10][5] on SWeML

[5]Data publicly accessible at `https://semantic-systems.org/sites/swemls-kg/`.

systems, and then manually expand and analyze this dataset. Figure 3 provides a visual overview over the main steps of this study; they can be summarized as follows:

- *Data Collection*: Starting from 476 SWeML systems that were annotated with foundational information, including SWeML processing flows.
- *Scoping*. Refining the types of system changes attributable to supplementary objectives that we want to consider in this study, including a corresponding pre-selection of relevant systems. 293 papers left after scoping.
- *Auxiliary Input Identification*. Annotating the components which are deemed relevant with respect to the supplementary objective. 176 papers with auxiliary inputs.
- *Supplementary Objective Classification*. Extracting and categorizing the supplementary objectives of the identified components.

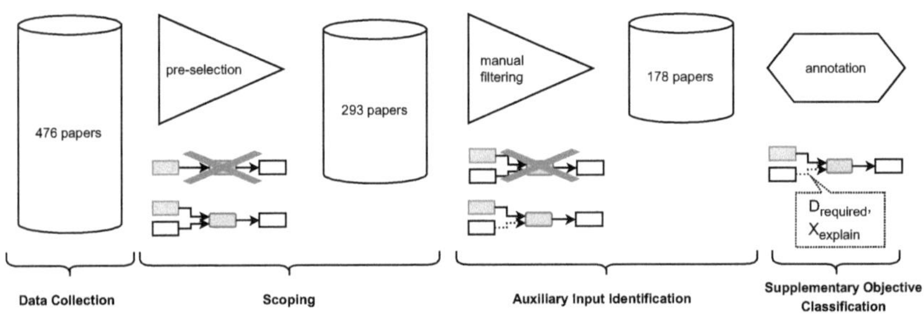

Figure 3. Overview over the paper selection and annotation process.

3.1. Data Collection

An in-depth characterisation of SWeML systems has been performed as part of a large Systematic Mapping Study (SMS) [10]. During the SMS, major digital libraries (WebOfScience, ACM Digital Library, IEEE Xplore, Scopus)[6] were queried for papers published during the 2010-2020 period that, in their abstract and keywords, mention terms related to the Semantic Web (e.g., *knowledge graph, linked data, semantic web, ontolog**, etc.) and to Machine Learning (e.g., *deep learning, neural network, embedding, representation learning, feature learning, language model*, etc.). Furthermore, since the focus was on concrete systems that fulfil a given task, paper abstracts also needed to mention typical application areas (e.g., *Natural Language Processing, Computer Vision, Information Retrieval, Data Mining, Information integration, Knowledge management, Pattern recognition, Speech recognition*, etc.).

The original search lead to 1,986 papers. Subsequently, two cycles of selection followed in which the authors of [10] systematically applied a number of selection criteria to identify the most suitable papers. For further in-depth methodological information about the paper selection process the interested reader is referred to [10] and its accompanying protocol document.

[6] http://www.webofknowledge.com/, https://dl.acm.org/, https://ieeexplore.ieee.org/, https://www.scopus.com/

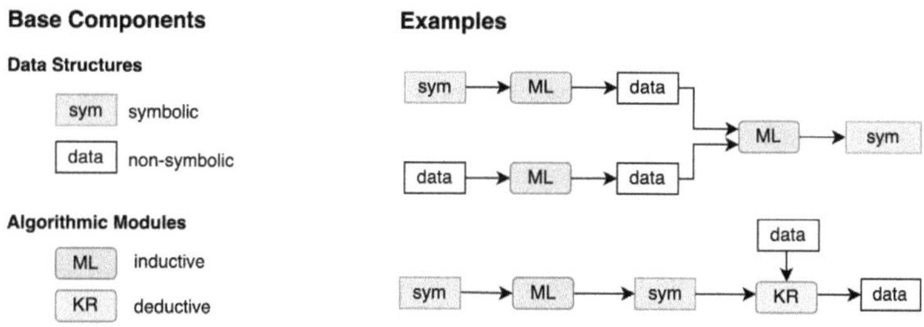

Figure 4. Boxology-based notation of system patterns. Left: legend, i.e., components of the boxology; Right: two concrete system patterns based on this boxology.

SWeML systems can be described from different angles. In particular, during the SMS, key data was extracted, related to:

1. *Bibliographic information* such as authors, their institutions, publication year and venue.
2. The *domain of application* (e.g., life sciences) and the *task solved* by the system (e.g., text analysis). SWeML systems can be built for a specific application domain, from *Natural Sciences*, *Culture & Education*, to *Software & Tech*, or be domain-independent (*General Domain*). SWeML systems are designed to fulfil one main task, such as question answering or relation extraction. These can be grouped into four main task categories: (1) *Natural Language Processing (NLP)*, (2) *Graph*, (3) *Image*, and (4) *Other*.
3. *System architecture* in terms of their inputs/outputs and the order of their processing units.
4. Characteristics of the *Machine Learning* modules such as the *type* (e.g., attention) and *training* (e.g., supervised) approach. Each SWeML system has one or more atomic components implementing an ML model. We differentiate between three types of models (*ML Types*): *Classical ML*, which are not neural-network-based, *Deep Learning* (DL), which are neural-network-based, and *Graph Deep Learning* (Graph DL), exploiting graph structures with neural networks.
5. Characteristics of the *Semantic Web modules* used as input to the system, such as their *type* (e.g., taxonomy, ontology, knowledge graphs), *size*, *formalisation language*, etc.
6. The level of *maturity of the systems* (e.g., prototype, industrial strength application), *system transparency* in terms of code availability, details of infrastructure, and evaluation setup as well as the existence of *provenance capturing mechanisms*.

Pattern Notation. To describe internal processing flows and organise the data extracted under point 3 above (*system architecture*), we rely on the boxology for neuro-symbolic systems introduced by [19]. This boxology consistes of two base elements or *components*: algorithmic modules (i.e., objects that perform some computation) that can be of type *inductive (ML)* or *deductive (KR)*, and data structures, which are the input and output to such modules that can be of *symbolic (sym)* (such as semantic entities or relations) or *non-symbolic (data)* nature (such as text, images, or embeddings). Note that the distinction between *symbolic* and *non-symbolic* representations is a reflection of "model-based" vs. "model-free" representations as explained in detail in [19]. Figure 4 depicts both the components of the boxology (left) as well as two concrete system patterns based on this boxology (right). The boxology has both a graphical notation and a corresponding textual notation.From the 15 system patterns introduced in [19], we could identify 11 patterns in use in the surveyed systems. Additionally, 33 new systems patterns were discovered, thus resulting in a total of 44 known patterns as a key output of the SMS.

Pattern Type. Depending on the way the atomic components of a system are connected, SWeML patterns can be classified into the following *pattern types*:

- A- and I-Patterns - single (A) or chain of (I) data-processing modules each with a single data input. *(Note: these patterns types are out of scope for the current work, since with a single (mandatory) data input, they cannot have a auxiliary input.).*
- F-Patterns - a single data-processing module (i.e., ML) that consumes more than one data input component;
- T-Patterns - a chain of A-Patterns and F-Patterns;
- Y-Patterns - the combination of two (or more) A-Patterns via an F-Pattern;
- O-Patterns - patterns that do not fall in any of the previous types, typically quite complex workflows;

3.2. Scoping

Due to the complexity of the relations between system components and objectives, and to ensure the feasibility of the study, we decided to limit our investigation with respect to the types of system modifications we include in this study. In the following section, we give a short overview over different types of system modifications, followed by a description of the modification type we consider, i.e., the addition of auxiliary input.

3.2.1. Types of System Modifications

As supplementary objectives stand in contrast to previous or minimal systems, they can be defined for actions that modify the system in some way. When analysing these modifications of SWeML systems, supplementary objectives can be targeted on different levels and through various strategies.

At the *component level*, different aspects of individual components within the system are altered to pursue certain supplementary objectives (cf. Figure 5). One aspect is the choice of model or algorithm which is being used in a certain component. For example, replacing a deep learning network with a decision tree classifier might make the model's output more interpretable to human users, thereby improving explainability. Another aspect is the decision on how data sources are utilized within a component, e.g., changing the exploitation level of a Knowledge Graph resource, by not only taking label data, but also definitions or neighbouring labels into account, to better support the generalisation capabilities of the downstream classifier.

At the *pattern level*, modifications involve changes to the overall architecture or processing flow of the SWeML system (cf. Figure 6). These adaptations might include the addition, or removal of system components (both data input and data-processing), for example, to provide additional background information as an input in order to improve the accuracy and reliability of subsequent ML models, or removing redundant components

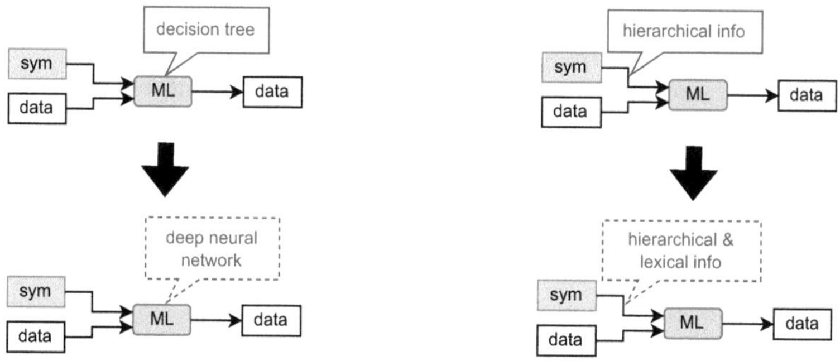

Figure 5. Examples of system modifications on component level. Left: modifying algorithm of component. Right: modifying utilisation of resource

to streamline the system, enhancing performance and reducing complexity. Another type of adaptation might target the substitution of certain components, e.g., replacing an ML component with a KR component could improve the system's ability to incorporate expert knowledge and provide more predictable and explainable results.

Figure 6. Examples of system modifications on pattern level. Left: addition of auxiliary input resource. Right: exchange of algorithmic module

In practice, the modifications applied to SWeML systems in order to pursue a certain supplementary objective might be quite complex, and consist of a set of the above mentioned aspects. Moreover, exchanging one component can create dependencies that require adjustments in others. For example, adding new input sources may necessitate adapting subsequent processing modules to accommodate the new input.

3.2.2. *Modification via Addition of Auxiliary Inputs*

As changes from one system to another can be manifold, subdividing the specific modifications can be hard. This poses a challenge for their systematic investigation, e.g., to analyse which changes pursue which objectives.

To facilitate this analysis, we use the system architecture patterns as a level of abstraction, which reduces the scope to *pattern-level* changes: only modifications in the system's overall structure are reflected, while component level changes are disregarded. This allows for a more focused and efficient analysis of the modifications and their underlying objectives. Moreover, we will focus on one specific example of pattern-level alterations of SWeML systems, i.e., the addition of *auxiliary input* sources. An auxiliary input is defined as a resource which is consumed by the system, not necessary to fulfil the targeted task, but to improve the system otherwise.

Following this scoping, in a pre-selection step, we discard those papers where only one input is being used, i.e., systems that implement A- and I-patterns are filtered out.

3.3. Auxiliary Input Identification

Since we focus on supplementary objectives which are attained by adding input components to a system, for the pre-selected systems, we manually verify that any of the inputs of the system at hand can be considered auxiliary, and identify the inputs which fall under this category.

In order to be included in this study, systems need to have at least one auxiliary input, though multiple auxiliary inputs–serving the same or different objectives–are also permissible. Additionally, we identify systems where multiple–or all–inputs can be considered auxiliary, albeit not simultaneously. This means that while each input might be auxiliary individually, their classification as such is mutually exclusive. We call such systems *flexible systems*. It shall be noted, that the addition of an auxiliary input may require additional processing steps before it can be fed in the original system. In this case, we identify the entire new sub-process as auxiliary part.

Out of the 476 papers initially identified in the SWeMLS SMS study, we found that 178 papers (approximately 37%) incorporated auxiliary input. Notably, this proportion—over one-third of the total—was higher than anticipated given the applied scoping, providing a robust basis for a comprehensive analysis of the subject. For the subsequent analysis, we include all 176 of these papers, with no subsampling applied.

In the pattern diagram, the auxiliary inputs are highlighted using dashed lines to clearly distinguish them from the original inputs (see Figure 6, left). This visual distinction helps in understanding how the system's architecture evolves with the addition of new inputs and aids in identifying which supplementary objectives these changes aim to address.

3.4. Supplementary Objective Classification

In this study, we focus on the question of *Which supplementary objective were the authors pursuing when they decided to include this particular input component into their system?*. To this end, we rely on the authors' stated rationale, without necessarily evaluating the actual impact or effectiveness of the modifications.

Our initial step of the supplementary objective classification involved identifying and extracting the objectives mentioned by the authors. This process allowed us to iteratively classify the objectives into fine-grained categories, providing a detailed view of the various goals pursued. To ensure consistent annotations and alignment among annotators, we conducted a piloting phase prior to the main annotation process. In this phase, all annotators were given the same five diverse papers to annotate, followed by a series of discussions to resolve discrepancies and establish consensus. During the annotation phase, regular meetings were held to discuss challenging papers until a common agreement was reached.

[7] including understandability and/or interpretability

Table 2. Broad and fine-grained objectives, and their mapping to quality attributes of the ISO/IEC 25010: Product Quality Model. Additionally,–where applicable–mappings to objectives from previous work [2,18,27].

Broad Objective	Fine-grained Objective	ISO/IEC 25010
P Performance	$\mathbf{P_{general}}$ in general $\mathbf{P_{coverage}}$ coverage (e.g., recall, diversity) $\mathbf{P_{correct}}$ correctness (e.g., precision, specificity) $\mathbf{P_{rare\_cls}}$ on rare classes $\mathbf{P_{fine\_cls}}$ on close fine-grained classes	Functional suitability
D Data	$\mathbf{D_{required}}$ reduce size of required training data [18,27] $\mathbf{D_{available}}$ increase size of available training data $\mathbf{D_{effort}}$ reduce effort in training data creation $\mathbf{D_{sparsity}}$ overcome data sparsity $\mathbf{D_{noise}}$ better handle noise in data $\mathbf{D_{bg\_know}}$ use background knowledge as training constraints [27]	Maintainability/ Reliability
X Explainability	$\mathbf{X_{explain}}$ improve explainability[7] [2,18,27] $\mathbf{X_{log\_cons}}$ improve logical consistency of results	Security / Interaction capabilities
T Transfer	$\mathbf{T_{cls}}$ to new classes [2] $\mathbf{T_{domain}}$ to new domains/contexts [2,18] $\mathbf{T_{task}}$ to new tasks [2]	Flexibility
U Usability	$\mathbf{U_{usability}}$ improve usability	Interaction capabilities
M Model Tuning	$\mathbf{M_{robust}}$ facilitate model tuning for more robustness $\mathbf{M_{feat\_select}}$ improve feature selection	Reliability
E Execution Time	$\mathbf{E_{process}}$ decrease processing time $\mathbf{E_{train}}$ decrease training time	Performance efficiency

To structure our findings, we subsequently organized these fine-grained objectives inspired by the `ISO/IEC 25010: Product Quality Model` into broader, coarse-grained categories, enabling a clearer comparison and analysis of the different aims highlighted across the papers. We also map objectives from other surveys [2,18,27], where applicable. The final list of fine-grained and coarse-grained objectives that we extracted from our analysis, as well as their mapping to the quality attributes from `ISO/IEC 25010` can be seen in Table 2.

Interestingly, our analysis revealed that the papers we examined encompassed 7 out of the 9 quality attributes from `ISO/IEC 25010`. The attributes addressed included functional suitability, performance efficiency, security, interaction capabilities, reliability, maintainability, and flexibility. However, notably absent were objectives related to safety, and compatibility. None of the papers explicitly mentioned these categories as their goals, suggesting a potential gap in the current research focus or perhaps an implicit assumption that these aspects are either already integrated into the system design or are outside the scope of the improvements being reported. We further acknowledge that future research may identify additional objectives being reported.

It must be noted that authors may not always explicitly state their objective for including optional inputs–especially, in case of short papers and/or papers originating from outside of the computer science domain. In such cases we defaulted to the most general objective P / $P_{general}$.

4. Examples

To clarify the annotation process, we provide detailed examples from three diverse papers included in our study to illustrate how we classify and annotate supplementary objectives. By showcasing these examples, we aim to make the annotation process more transparent and comprehensible, highlighting how we translate author statements into our objectives. The selection of these papers was solely based on their representative characteristics, without considering other factors.

Ex1 – Ontology-Guided Data Augmentation for Medical Document Classification [1] The task of this work is medical document classification. The authors write "*As the medical input data is often not enough in the real world, in this work a novel ontology-guided method is proposed for data augmentation to enrich input data.*", i.e., for the sake of data augmentation, new documents are created via 1) linking Unified Medical Language System (UMLS) entities to existing documents and 2) replacing occurrences of the linked entities with their scientific name. The new documents are considered the auxiliary input, which is assigned with the supplementary objective $D_{available}$ – increase size of available training data.

The authors combine UMLS and documents in the first step of their processing flow to produce new features, which are processed together with documents using different neural networks, hence the system is of T-pattern-type.

A graphical visualisation of Ex1 can be found in (Figure 7).

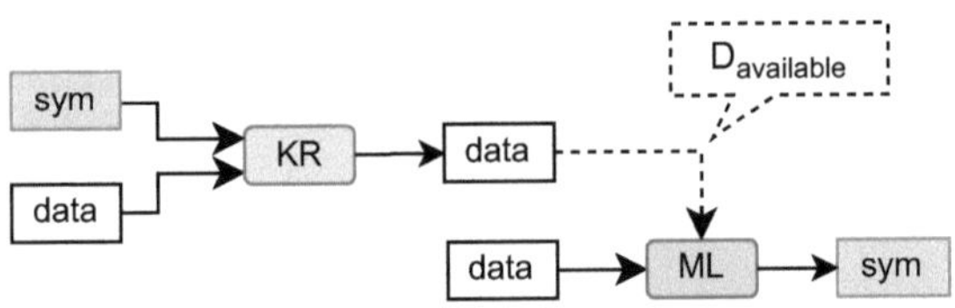

Figure 7. Visual representation of Ex1 – Ontology-Guided Data Augmentation for Medical Document Classification [1]

Ex2 – Next News Recommendation via Knowledge-Aware Sequential Model [11] The task of this work is news recommendation based on sequences from the interaction histories of users. "*3) We leverage the knowledge graph as side information to mine deep connections between news, thus improving reasonable diversity and extensibility of recommendation.*", therefore, we classify the objective as $P_{coverage}$. However, authors also provide an example of interpreting the results: "*Figure 4(c) visualizes the weight matrix of the vanilla-attention module in the reference-interpreting decoder. It shows the attention weight of 3 target news articles towards the contextual-entities of the input sequence, which intuitively present how much a contextual-entity contributes to the recommendation score of the knowledge-aware modelling.*", therefore aiming at $X_{explain}$ – improve explainability. As a consequence, we identify two supplementary objectives in this paper.

For the auxiliary input authors state "*A Chinese news-specific knowledge graph G is proposed for the recommendation task. It contains fruitful facts and connections among entities, which provides us a wider perspective to explore uses' preferences in the field of news.*"

A graphical visualisation of Ex2 can be found in (Figure 8).

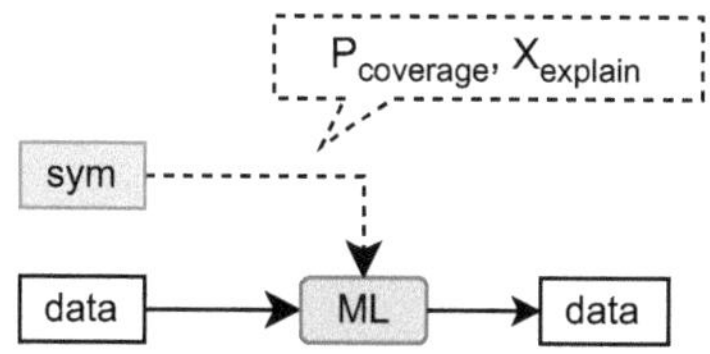

Figure 8. Visual representation of Ex2 – Next News Recommendation via Knowledge-Aware Sequential Model [11]

Ex3 – Revisiting Text and Knowledge Graph Joint Embeddings: The Amount of Shared Information Matters! [25] This work focuses on the creation of potent latent representations by combining text and graph inputs as "*jointly learning embeddings from text and a Knowledge Graph benefits both word and entity/relation embeddings by taking advantage of both large-scale unstructured content (text) and high-quality structured data (the Knowledge Graph)*". The authors demonstrate the flexibility of their embeddings by employing them in different downstream systems, e.g., to extract relations from text, or to perform link prediction on a knowledge graph. Therefore, depending on the viewpoint, either the knowledge graph or text can be considered auxiliary input, i.e., we classify the system as *flexible system.*

With respect to the objective behind the combination of these two inputs, authors stay rather vague, solely stating that with their new approach they are "aiming at releasing the power of such joint embeddings", thus we conclude their objective to be $P_{general}$.

A graphical visualisation of Ex3 can be found in Figure 9.

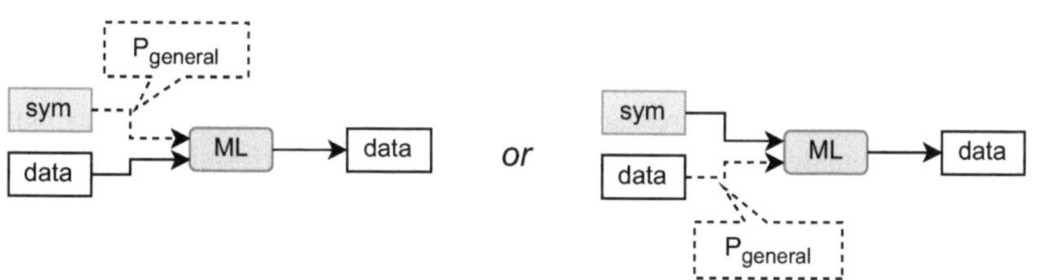

Figure 9. Visual representation of Ex3 – Revisiting Text and Knowledge Graph Joint Embeddings: The Amount of Shared Information Matters! [25]

5. Results

Out of 293 research papers describing systems with several inputs we identified 178 systems as having at least one auxiliary input and, therefore, supplementary objectives. A number of works in our analysis pursued more than one supplementary objective. In this case all identified supplementary objectives were annotated and participated in further analysis. Therefore, the total count of objectives (218) is higher than the total number of papers with supplementary objectives (178) [8].

[8]Unless stated otherwise, the following analysis is based on the count of objectives, not systems.

5.1. Supplementary Objectives

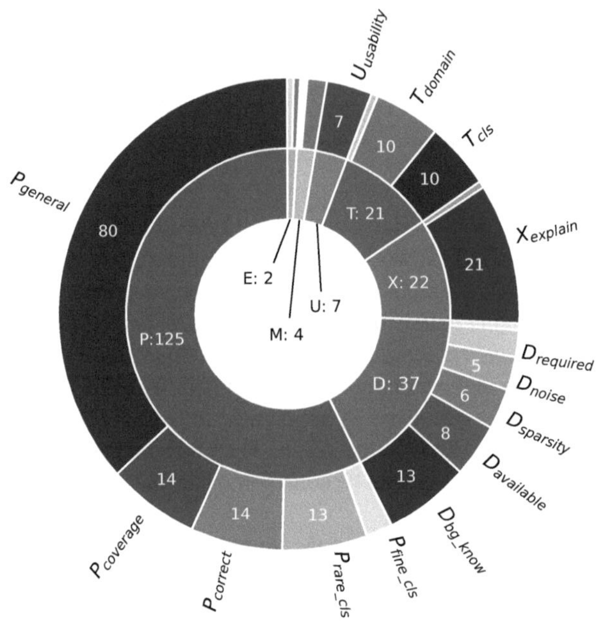

Figure 10. Distribution of broader and fine-grained supplementary objectives.

Distribution of Objectives. To provide a comprehensive understanding of the supplementary objectives pursued by researchers, we analyzed their distribution as depicted in Figure 10. The analysis reveals a predominant focus on Performance (P) objectives addressed by 125 works.

This stands in comparison to 80 objectives covered by the broader objectives Data (D), Explainability (X) and Transfer (T). The remaining broader objectives Usability (U), Model Tuning (M) and Execution Time (E) make only up a small portion of the systems (in total 13 papers).

This focus on performance likely reflects the rapid development and early stage of maturity in the field of modern day machine learning approaches and applications, where performance optimization is often prioritized before addressing other objectives like explainability. This is also underlined when analysing the finer-grained objectives of P: in 80 cases–almost two thirds–authors reported their aim to improve the general performance of their system, or do not specifically name any particular performance metric ($P_{general}$). Metrics such as recall ($P_{coverage}$), precision ($P_{correct}$), or the performance on rare (P_{rare_cls}) or similar classes (P_{fine_cls}) are only optimized in 45 cases in total.

Among the papers focusing on Explainability (X), only one paper improves logical consistency of results (X_{log_cons}), the rest aims to improve explainability in general ($X_{explain}$). For Transfer, the majority of works are split between transfer to new classes (T_{cls}) and to new domains (T_{domain}), while the transfer to new tasks T_{task} is only addressed by a single work.

Multiple Objectives. It is noteworthy that the total number of papers where authors would tackle more than one objective is growing over the years, as shown in Figure 11. This might indicate a growing complexity of SWeML systems allowing authors to pursue diverse improvements simultaneously. In total, 37 papers mentioned more than one supplementary objective.

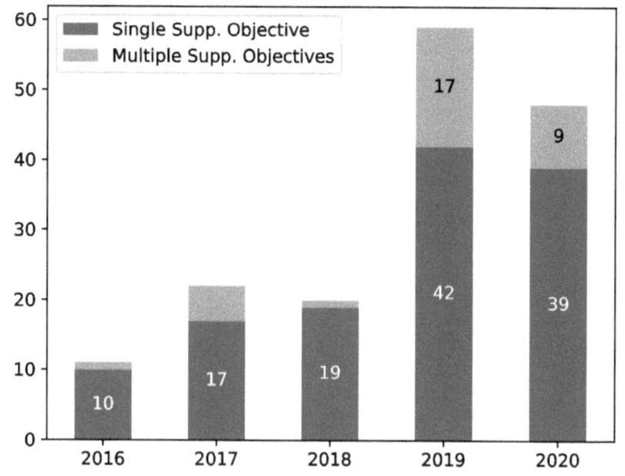

Figure 11. Systems with multiple objectives over years. Years with less than 10 papers are omitted. Counts represent analysed systems, not objectives.

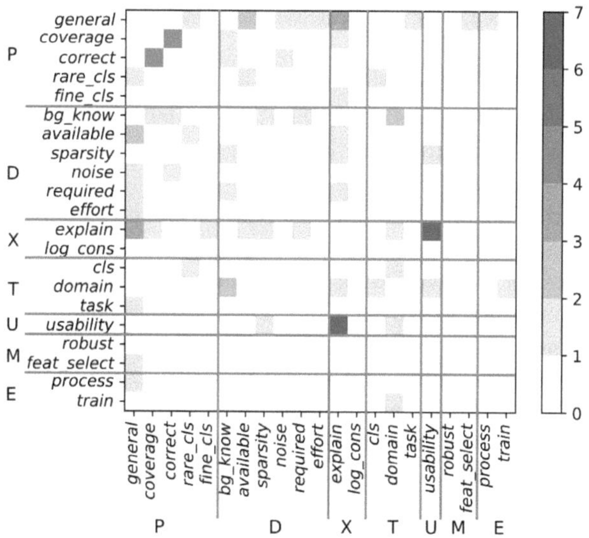

Figure 12. Co-occurrence of supplementary objectives within systems.

Figure 12 shows the co-occurrence of supplementary objectives.

The objective pair $U_{usability}$ and $X_{explain}$, which seeks to enhance both explainability and usability, has the highest co-occurrence value of 7. Interestingly, this pair encompasses all the papers that mention improving usability ($U_{usability}$), indicating that every work aiming to improve usability also aims to improve explainability. This interdependence suggests that a more understandable system inherently supports better user interactions.

Furthermore, authors frequently pair the improvement of $P_{coverage}$ with $P_{correct}$, trying to minimize the trade-off between these two aspects.

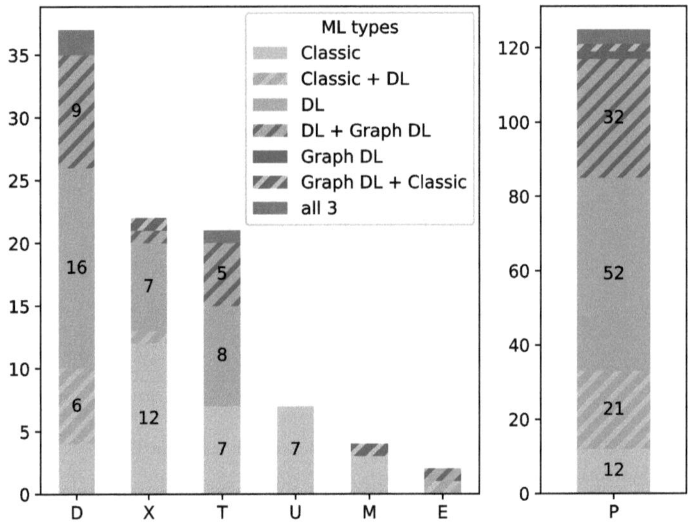

Figure 13. ML types per broader supplementary objectives.

Objective vs ML Types In Figure 13 concerning the machine learning types per objective, we can identify that Deep Learning (DL) models are overall most often used, followed by Classic ML models. Last in line are Graph DL models, which are almost always combined with other ML types.

When comparing the different objective types, it can be seen that data-focused objectives (D) are mainly a concern when working with data-intensive DL and Graph DL models. Similar results are revealed for Performance and Transfer objectives. For these objectives, the combination of DL and Graph DL is also frequent.

In contrast, objectives focusing on Explainability (X), Usability (U), and Model Tuning (M), are often addressed in systems where Classical ML models are in use. This trend may be attributed to the lower complexity of these models, potentially facilitating the generation of corresponding explanations, or, the longer research history of Classical ML models may have shifted the focus of researchers toward objectives beyond performance and data optimisation.

Objective vs Task Category The tasks most commonly targeted in the analysed works were in the area of NLP, followed by Graph, and Image-related tasks, where the task distribution within the P objective resembles the overall distribution of tasks (cf. Figure 14).

Interestingly, Image tasks are very rarely accompanied by non-performance-related objectives, even though these tasks have significant potential for objectives in the area of e.g., explainability or usability. When Performance objectives (P) are not being pursued, authors typically focus on improving transferability (T objectives). A similar case can be observed for NLP tasks, where no works aimed at Usability or Model Tuning objectives,

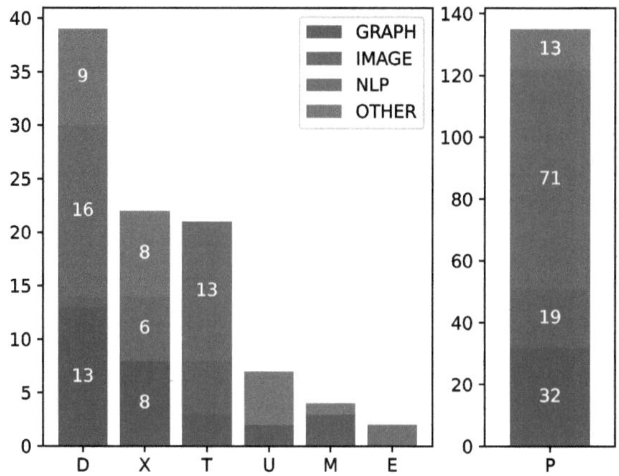

Figure 14. Targeted tasks per broader supplementary objectives.

and which are underrepresented in Explainability (X) objectives, meaning the underlying systems are mostly altered to optimize their Performance, Data-, or Transfer-capabilities.

Graph tasks are distributed among many objectives, while Model Tuning objective is mostly combined with Graph tasks.

Objective vs Application Domain Overall, General Domain and Natural Sciences are the most targeted domains with a total of 97 and 63 objectives, respectively. As it can be seen in Figure 15, the two domains have a similar distribution and absolute numbers for supplementary objectives excluding P objectives. The number of P objectives used in Natural Science papers is significantly lower than in the General Domain. This might indicate a higher demand for data enhancement (D), transferability (T) and explainability (X) in Natural Sciences than for performance improvement (P). Two other domains with an overrepresentation of explainability are News & Social Media and Software & Tech.

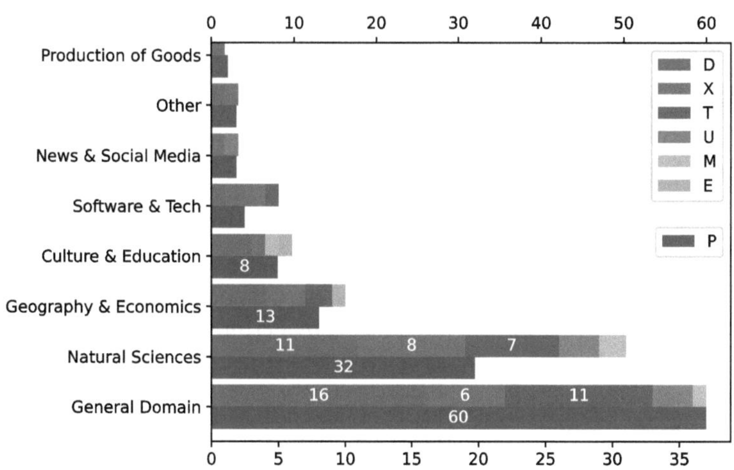

Figure 15. Broader objectives per application domain.

Objective vs Pattern Type The distribution of pattern types is analogous to their simplicity in terms of processing units, with F-patterns being the simplest and most frequent one, followed by T- and Y-, and O-patterns being the most complex and least present ones. We observe in Figure 16 that about 50% of F-patterns do not have any supplementary objectives, meaning that both inputs are needed to fulfil the task whereas only 25-30% of more complex systems do not have supplementary objectives, suggesting that as complexity increases, there is a greater degree of flexibility regarding auxiliary inputs.

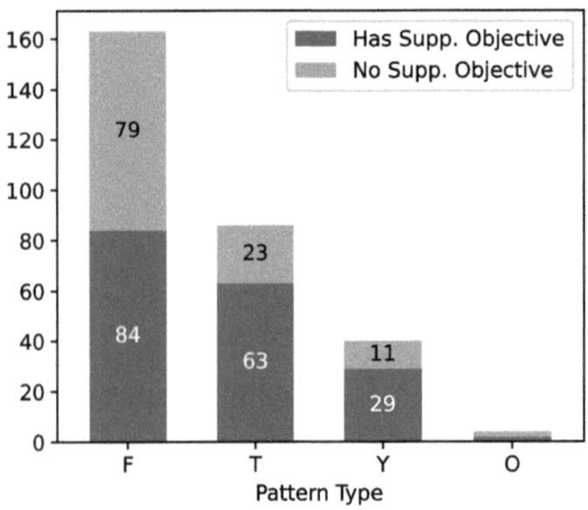

Figure 16. Presence of auxiliary input / supplementary objective per pattern type. Counts represent analysed systems, not objectives.

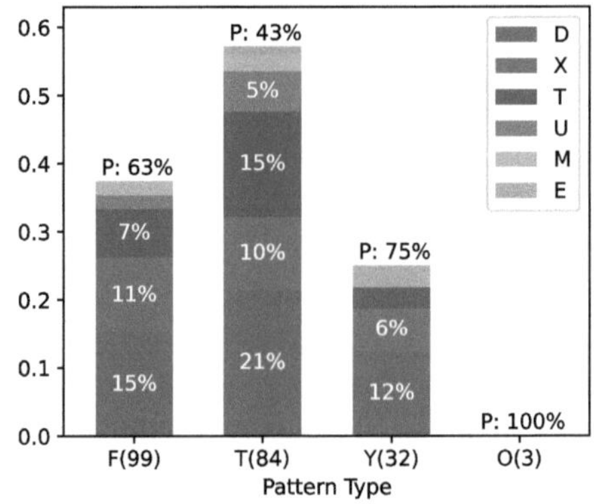

Figure 17. Distribution of broader supplementary objectives per pattern type. P objectives are shown as numbers only due to their over-representation.

Figure 17 shows the relative distribution of broader supplementary objectives within pattern types. As expected, performance-related objectives (P) make up the highest share in all pattern types although their prevalence varies significantly between them: while systems which follow a Y-pattern try to optimize towards performance in 75% of the cases, T-pattern-based systems only do so in approximately 43% of the cases. As a result, T-pattern systems target a high diversity of non-performance objectives, led by data-related (21%), transferability (15%), and explainability (10%). Furthermore, T-patterns are a favourite choice when pursuing transferability or usability objectives.

Remarkably, T-patterns are also the only pattern type where non-performance objectives are in total more frequent than Performance objectives. However, it should be noted that SWeML systems employing T-patterns target more than one supplementary objective in about one-third of the cases (compared to 18% for F-patterns and 10% for Y-patterns). Consequently, around 57% of T-pattern systems include a performance (P) objective among their targets.

In comparison to T-patterns, F-patterns have a similar share of Explainability objectives (11%), but lower shares of data-related (D), transferability (T), and usability-related (U) objectives. Y-patterns are clearly dominated by Performance objectives, while 50% of non-performance objectives are data-related (D).

5.2. Type of Auxiliary Input

Machine learning research has traditionally focused on processing non-symbolic inputs, such as numeric, textual, or image data. Therefore, it is no surprise that the auxiliary inputs used in SWeML systems are predominantly symbolic (152 versus 37 non-symbolic[9]). This trend reflects a broader movement towards enhancing existing ML approaches by creating neuro-symbolic systems.

Notably, this distribution of auxiliary inputs remains consistent across various ML types, including Graph DL (cf. Figure 18): even though these ML models per se use symbolic data as main, non-auxiliary input, the authors still show a high (i.e, 75%) tendency to use symbolic data also as auxiliary input. This finding is consistent when looking at the tasks targeted: 70% of systems targeting GRAPH tasks add auxiliary symbolic inputs, which stands in comparison to 80% of systems aiming to solve tasks of type NLP, Image and Other with this kind of input.

On the one hand, this can be attributed to the fact that about 20% of the systems used for Graph tasks employ patterns that use two (or more) symbolic inputs, hence both the main and the optional input are of symbolic nature. Additionally, various systems exploit additional symbolic inputs for Graph tasks that focus on the creation of resources (e.g., Knowledge Graph creation). On the other hand, this originates from the framing of the targeted task, i.e., tasks, that are not inherently bound to Semantic Web input structures are formulated as Graph tasks in order to exploit Semantic Web resources as additional input, which in turn often goes hand in hand with the usage of Graph DL models. Examples for this would be Patient Diagnosis or Outcome Prediction in the medical domain.

While the difference of optional input type across different ML types remains rather small, differences are more pronounced across the objectives to be achieved by introducing the auxiliary inputs. Figure 19 shows the relative distribution of optional input types among supplementary broader objectives. To achieve Performance (P), Data (D), and Explainability (X) objectives, the majority of systems, i.e., 11-21% use symbolic data as auxiliary input–for both Model Tuning (M) and Execution Time (E) improvements, symbolic is even exclusively used. However, Usability (U) and also Transfer (T) objectives are comparatively often addressed by the addition of non-symbolic input, specifically, in 43% and 33% of the cases, respectively. This trend suggests that while symbolic data enhances explainability, non-symbolic data is better suited for improving usability in aspects and user experience. For transferability, non-symbolic data might capture more hidden connections and patterns or benefit from the greater availability of unstructured data resources, facilitating adaptation to diverse contexts.

5.3. Flexible Systems

From the total of 178 systems with supplementary objectives, 11 can be classified as flexible systems as defined in Section 3.3, i.e., either input could be the non-optional input in a minimal or previous system. Despite the relative minority of flexible systems, their count is on a rising trend. Over the years, there has been a modest yet steady increase in the count of flexible systems. Beginning with a single such system in 2014, two flexible systems in 2018 and then increased to three flexible systems introduced each in 2019 and 2020.

Figure 20 illustrates that flexible systems aim to improve Performance (P), Data (D) and Transfer (T) as supplementary objectives. Out of the 11 flexible systems analysed, performance improvement emerged as a prominent supplementary objective for 9 systems. More precisely, 8 systems aim to improve performance in general ($P_{general}$), while

[9]Note that *flexible systems* are counted twice in this analysis

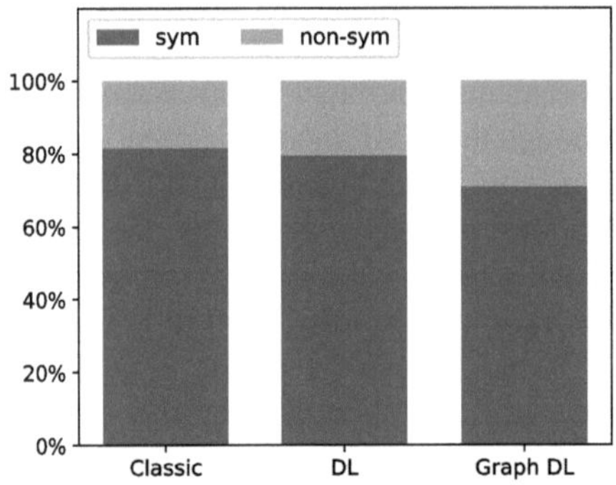

Figure 18. Type of auxiliary input per ML type

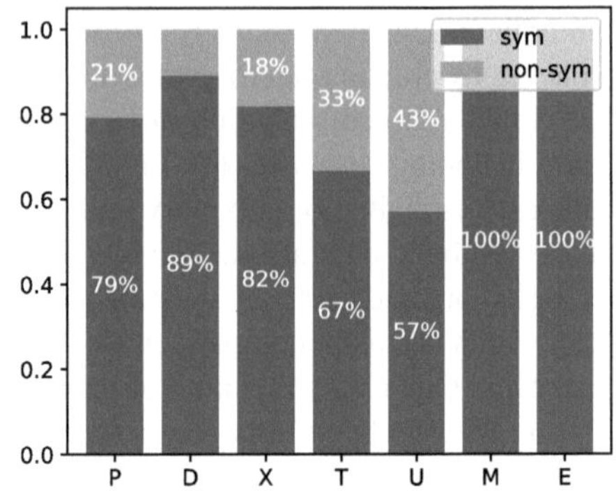

Figure 19. Distribution of auxiliary input type per supplementary objectives

one system specifically aims to increase $P_{correct}$. Further, one flexible system exhibited efforts towards enhancing transferability, specifically aiming to enable transfer to new domains or contexts (T_{domain}), while another system seeks to "improve" data, specifically by employing background knowledge as additional training constraints (D_{bg_know}).

Interestingly, all of these flexible systems consume one symbolic, and one non-symbolic input. A common strategy for utilising these inputs is the employment of *joint embeddings*, i.e., the computation of vector representations for entities that are learned jointly from text and semantic resources. Different approaches can be observed: (1) embedding the semantic resource and the text in isolation and later joining/aligning the two embedding spaces, or (2) using a joint loss function for text and semantic resource, where the latter is more prominent. Mixed approaches are also occasional, e.g., using the loss of a pre-trained text or semantic resource embedding within a joint loss function.

In the papers reviewed for this study, the authors often claim a performance gain of joint embeddings over the use of embeddings only learned from structured (semantic) or unstructured (text) data alone. However, many papers do not really prove this claim, e.g., using an ablation study. In cases where ablation studies are present, they usually compare text only to joint embeddings, whereas the comparison of semantic resource only to joint embeddings is rarely observed.

6. Conclusion

In this work, we have investigated the supplementary objectives that authors pursue by adding auxiliary inputs to their SWeML systems.Following the `ISO/IEC 25010` standard, we have identified seven out of nine high-level objectives, which can be divided into 21 fine-grained objectives. While including auxiliary inputs into a system is not the only way to achieve these objectives, we found that 178 of the 293 analysed papers opted for this route. Most of the auxiliary inputs were of symbolic nature, but there was still over 20% of the papers which opted for adding non-symbolic inputs, mostly when applying graph based deep learning methods, or when striving to increase transferability (T) or usability (U).

Interestingly, two of the quality attributes described in `ISO/IEC 25010`, namely compatibility and security, have not been encountered as supplemental objectives in our

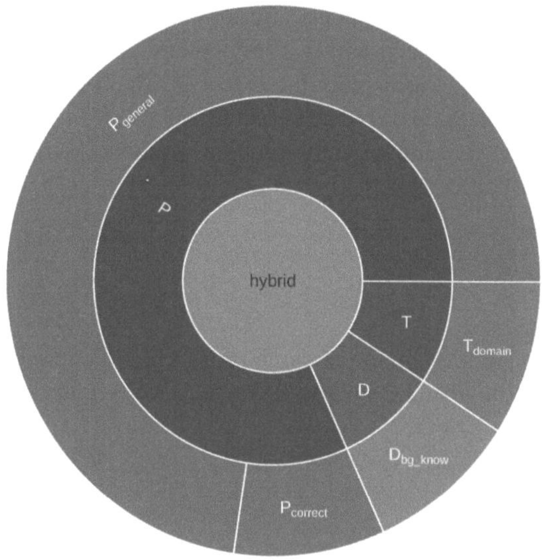

Figure 20. Distribution of broader and fine-grained supplementary objectives in flexible systems

study. Especially for compatibility, this is surprising, since ontologies and semantic models can be a key enabler for interoperability, and interoperability of AI systems may become an important topic in the near future. Moreover, with the amount of resources available on the Web growing, and there standardization being pushed forward, we expect to see more of such systems and SWeMLS being built rather in a plug-and-play fashion than by manual engineering.

Not all systems make a clear cut between primary and auxiliary inputs. We have found a category which we later coined *flexible systems*, which are systems with multiple inputs, where a functioning system can be built with each subset of those inputs. Though in our survey, we only encountered 11 such systems, their number is steadily increasing over the recent years as systems get more complex.

We observe a rise in the number of systems pursuing supplementary objectives over the years, specially those related to transferability (T), explainability (X) and data enhancement (D). The analysis performed reveals patterns in co-occurrences of the objectives, remarkably, explainability (X) and usability (U) are found together in many systems.

Overall, it can be seen that while objectives related to performance (P)–i.e., result quality–are most dominant, there is a diverse field of objectives, and the number of systems pursuing multiple objectives is increasing. This is in line with the maturing world of AI, resulting in growing number of requirements that an AI system is expected to fulfil. To effectively support authors in their design decisions, they need to understand the implications of these decisions for their systems.

As a first step, with this survey, we provide the axes of objectives as well as an overview of the characteristics of a currently used strategy to satisfy these objectives. As a next step, we will integrate this information into the existing SWeML classification system and KG, to facilitate querying and exploitation. This will allow authors of

SWeML systems to query the knowledge base for examples, such as "which additional inputs could I use to improve the usability of my system".

Future work would need to explore the extent to which these objectives are being met given the design choices made by the authors. This would be the basis for guidelines to develop customised AI solutions that combine symbolic knowledge and statistical approaches in the most efficient way.

Acknowledgement

This work has been supported by the research project SENSE (project number 894802) and FAIR-AI (project number FO999904624) which were funded by the Austrian Research Promotion Agency FFG.

Supplemental Material Statement

We provide a SPARQL query that retrieves all papers that participated in this survey from the SWeMLS KG[10] under the following link: `https://api.triplydb.com/s/pR0xV1v90`.

The results are returned in a user-friendly representation utilizing YASGUI[11]. Additionally, the annotations of supplementary objectives can be found here: `https://bit.ly/supp_obj_papers`

References

[1] Abdollahi, M., Gao, X., Mei, Y., Ghosh, S., Li, J.: Ontology-guided data augmentation for medical document classification. In: Michalowski, M., Moskovitch, R. (eds.) Artificial Intelligence in Medicine. pp. 78–88. Springer International Publishing, Cham (2020)

[2] Allen, B.P., Ilievski, F.: Standardizing Knowledge Engineering Practices with a Reference Architecture. Transactions on Graph Data and Knowledge **2**(1), 5:1–5:23 (2024). , `https://drops.dagstuhl.de/entities/document/10.4230/TGDK.2.1.5`

[3] Allen, B.P., Ilievski, F., Joshi, S.: Identifying and consolidating knowledge engineering requirements (2023), `https://arxiv.org/abs/2306.15124`

[4] Ameller, D., Galster, M., Avgeriou, P., Franch, X.: A survey on quality attributes in service-based systems. Software quality journal **24**, 271–299 (2016)

[5] Amershi, S., Begel, A., Bird, C., DeLine, R., Gall, H., Kamar, E., Nagappan, N., Nushi, B., Zimmermann, T.: Software engineering for machine learning: A case study. In: 2019 IEEE/ACM 41st International Conference on Software Engineering: Software Engineering in Practice (ICSE-SEIP). pp. 291–300. IEEE (2019)

[6] Bader, S., Hitzler, P.: Dimensions of neural-symbolic integration-a structured survey. arXiv preprint cs/0511042 (2005)

[7] Bass, L., Clements, P., Kazman, R.: Software Architecture in Practice. SEI series in software engineering, Addison-Wesley (2003), `https://books.google.at/books?id=mdiIu8Kk1WMC`

[8] van Bekkum, M., de Boer, M., van Harmelen, F., Meyer-Vitali, A., ten Teije, A.: Modular design patterns for hybrid learning and reasoning systems. Applied Intelligence **51**(9), 6528–6546 (2021)

[10] `https://semantic-systems.org/sites/swemls-kg/`

[11] `https://github.com/TriplyDB/Yasgui`

[9] Besold, T.R., d'Avila Garcez, A., Bader, S., Bowman, H., Domingos, P., Hitzler, P., Kühnberger, K.U., Lamb, L.C., Lima, P.M.V., de Penning, L., et al.: Neural-symbolic learning and reasoning: A survey and interpretation 1. In: Neuro-Symbolic Artificial Intelligence: The State of the Art, pp. 1–51. IOS Press (2021)

[10] Breit, A., Waltersdorfer, L., Ekaputra, F.J., Sabou, M., Ekelhart, A., Iana, A., Paulheim, H., Portisch, J., Revenko, A., Teije, A.t., van Harmelen, F.: Combining machine learning and semantic web: A systematic mapping study. ACM Comput. Surv. (mar 2023). , `https://doi.org/10.1145/3586163`, just Accepted

[11] Chu, Q., Liu, G., Sun, H., Zhou, C.: Next news recommendation via knowledge-aware sequential model. In: Sun, M., Huang, X., Ji, H., Liu, Z., Liu, Y. (eds.) Chinese Computational Linguistics. pp. 221–232. Springer International Publishing, Cham (2019)

[12] Dandala, B., Joopudi, V., Tsou, C.H., Liang, J., Suryanarayanan, P.: Extraction of Information Related to Drug Safety Surveillance From Electronic Health Record Notes: Joint Modeling of Entities and Relations Using Knowledge-Aware Neural Attentive Models. JMIR medical informatics **8**(7) (2020)

[13] Ekaputra, F.J., Llugiqi, M., Sabou, M., Ekelhart, A., Paulheim, H., Breit, A., Revenko, A., Waltersdorfer, L., Farfar, K.E., Auer, S.: Describing and organizing semantic web and machine learning systems in the swemls-kg (2023)

[14] Falessi, D., Cantone, G., Kazman, R., Kruchten, P.: Decision-making techniques for software architecture design: A comparative survey. ACM Computing Surveys (CSUR) **43**(4), 1–28 (2011)

[15] Garcez, A., Broda, K., Gabbay, D., et al.: Neural-symbolic learning systems: foundations and applications. Springer (2002)

[16] Garcia, N., Renoust, B., Nakashima, Y.: Context-aware embeddings for automatic art analysis. In: Proceedings of the 2019 on International Conference on Multimedia Retrieval. pp. 25–33 (2019)

[17] Glinz, M.: On non-functional requirements. In: 15th IEEE international requirements engineering conference (RE 2007). pp. 21–26. IEEE (2007)

[18] Hamilton, K., Nayak, A., Božić, B., Longo, L.: Is neuro-symbolic ai meeting its promises in natural language processing? a structured review. Semantic Web **Preprint**, 1–42 (2022)

[19] van Harmelen, F., ten Teije, A.: A boxology of design patterns for hybrid learning and reasoning systems. Journal of Web Engineering (2019)

[20] Hitzler, P., Bianchi, F., Ebrahimi, M., Sarker, M.: Neural-symbolic integration and the Semantic Web. Semantic Web **11**(1) (2020)

[21] Systems and software engineering — Systems and software Quality Requirements and Evaluation (SQuaRE) — Product quality model. Standard, ISO/IEC JTC 1/SC 7 (11 2023)

[22] Kautz, H.: The Third AI Summer, AAAI Robert S. Engelmore Memorial Lecture, 34th AAAI, 2020

[23] Marcus, G.: Deep learning: A critical appraisal. arXiv preprint arXiv:1801.00631 (2018)

[24] Qiu, Q., Xie, Z., Wu, L., Tao, L.: Dictionary-Based Automated Information Extraction From Geological Documents Using a Deep Learning Algorithm. Earth and Space Science **7**(3) (2020)

[25] Rosso, P., Yang, D., Cudré-Mauroux, P.: Revisiting text and knowledge graph joint embeddings: The amount of shared information matters! In: 2019 IEEE International Conference on Big Data (Big Data). pp. 2465–2473 (2019).

[26] von Rueden, L., Mayer, S., Beckh, K., Georgiev, B., Giesselbach, S., Heese, R., Kirsch, B., Walczak, M., Pfrommer, J., Pick, A., et al.: Informed machine learning-a taxonomy and survey of integrating prior knowledge into learning systems. IEEE Transactions on Knowledge & Data Engineering **01**, 1–1 (2021)

[27] Sarker, M., Zhou, L., Eberhart, A., Hitzler, P.: Neuro-symbolic artificial intelligence current trends. arXiv:2105.05330 (2021)

[28] Tamašauskaitė, G., Groth, P.: Defining a knowledge graph development process through a systematic review. ACM Transactions on Software Engineering and Methodology **32**(1), 1–40 (2023)

[29] Zhang, J., Chen, B., Zhang, L., Ke, X., Ding, H.: Neural, symbolic and neural-symbolic reasoning on knowledge graphs. AI Open **2**, 14–35 (2021)

Handbook on Neurosymbolic AI and Knowledge Graphs
P. Hitzler et al. (Eds.)
IOS Press, 2025

doi:10.3233/FAIA250239

Neuro-Symbolic AI in Life Sciences

Robert HOEHNDORF [a,1], Catia PESQUITA [b], and Fernando ZHAPA-CAMACHO [a]
[a] *Computer Science Program, Computer, Electrical and Mathematical Sciences & Engineering Division (CEMSE), King Abdullah University of Science and Technology, 4700 KAUST, Thuwal 23955, Saudi Arabia*
[b] *LASIGE, Faculdade de Ciências da Universidade de Lisboa, Portugal*
ORCiD ID: Robert Hoehndorf https://orcid.org/0000-0001-8149-5890, Catia Pesquita https://orcid.org/0000-0002-1847-9393, Fernando Zhapa-Camacho https://orcid.org/0000-0002-0710-2259

Abstract. Life sciences have a long history of driving advancements in various disciplines, including mathematics, philosophy, and logic. In recent years, life sciences have also become a significant application area for Artificial Intelligence (AI) technologies, including for neuro-symbolic AI methods. The life sciences knowledge infrastructure, characterized by its widespread use of ontologies, complex annotation models, large size, and community standards, presents unique challenges and opportunities for neuro-symbolic AI. We outline how neuro-symbolic methods have been applied and developed to address these challenges. We describe semantic similarity measures, knowledge graph embeddings, ontology embeddings, and knowledge-enhanced learning in the context of formalized life science knowledge. While there has been significant progress, we also outline multiple remaining challenges that provide opportunities for future research.

Keywords. neuro-symbolic AI, biomedicine, bio-ontologies, knowledge-enhanced learning

1. Introduction

Life sciences have a long history of being the driver behind development of novel methods in different disciplines, in particular in mathematics, philosophy, and logic. Aristotle's work on anatomy, physiology, and zoology influenced his advances in logic, in particular the development of syllogism, inductive reasoning, and his work on genus-differentia definitions. For example, Aristotle provided one of the first classifications of animals in his "History of Animals", a description of anatomy in "Parts of Animals", and an analysis of physiological functions in "On the Movement of Animals". His work on classifying living beings helped him develop a logical framework for categorizing information, including genus–differentia definitions and syllogisms [1].

Galen is maybe the best-known example among the Greek scholars who used medical research to develop methods in logic and philosophy. In his essay "That the Best Physician Is Also a Philosopher" [2], Galen outlined the necessity of logical reasoning for diagnosis, for determining adequate treatments, and for predicting the course of a

[1]Corresponding Author: Robert Hoehndorf, robert.hoehndorf@kaust.edu.sa

disease. Galen developed Aristotle's syllogism further and applied it to medical reasoning; he combined syllogisms with forms of abductive reasoning (reasoning to the best explanation) to infer the diagnosis from a set of observed symptoms, and inductive reasoning to determine which treatments are effective. In a way, his emphasis on combining empirical evidence (data or observation) with general principles (knowledge) and Aristotelian syllogisms (deduction) relates not only to more recent developments in empirical medicine, but also integrated inductive learning with logical deduction, similar to some aims of neuro-symbolic methods today.

The influence of medical and biological research on logic, mathematics and philosophy was not limited to Ancient Greece or Europe, but a large body of work was produced by Islamic scholars in the Middle East, which led to many modern advances. Abu Bakr Muhammad ibn Zakariyya al-Razi (Rhazes in Latin) built on Galen's work [3], both by providing an elaborate classification of diseases, and by describing in detail in his medical treatises, Kitab al-Mansuri and Al-Shukuk 'ala Jalinus, how logic should be used to interpret empirical observations. Ibn Sina's work in classifying diseases (Qanun dar Teb) distinguished between necessary and possible symptoms for diseases and medical conditions leading to his development of modal logic (in Kitab al-Shifa') and its application to (differential) diagnosis.

There are many other famous examples where scholars who studied medicine influenced and developed novel methods in mathematics, ontology, and logic, including Hippocrates, Moses ben Maimon, Abu Nasr Muhammad al-Farabi, or Roger Bacon. It is therefore not surprising that life sciences are now also driving the development of novel methods in Artificial Intelligence (AI). Indeed, life sciences have been one of the earliest and most impactful application areas for AI technologies, with expert systems like Dendral [4] and MYCIN [5] being some of the earliest examples where biological, chemical, or biomedical problems have driven methods development in AI, in particular, the development of expert systems. The Generalised Architecture for Languages, Encyclopedias and Nomenclatures in Medicine project, adequately abbreviated GALEN [6], has resulted in developments for representing large amounts of data as graphs, in some of the first uses of ontology for classification in life sciences [7], development of standards for expressing Description Logics [8], and the development of modern Description Logic reasoners [9, 10]; many of these technologies have influenced the Semantic Web.

Today, life sciences continue to foster developments in multiple AI fields, including large language models, reinforcement learning, and neuro-symbolic AI. Undoubtedly, one of the reasons for this driving force is that applications in life sciences have a clear impact with a straightforward motivation. At the same time, life sciences provide unique challenges and features that are rarely found in other domains. Life sciences are heavily invested in building an infrastructure for storing and managing not only data but also knowledge, and consequently there are not only large databases used but also several large knowledge bases and ontologies; and these knowledge bases require deductive inference to be explored.

In fact, both symbolic and neuro-symbolic AI methods have been used for a long time in life sciences, with notable examples in Markov Logic Networks [11, 12], probabilistic logic programming [13, 14], and inductive logic programming [15]. The life sciences domain is also on of the main application settings for knowledge graph embedding methods for knowledge-enhanced learning [16], as well as of ontology embedding methods [17]. Nevertheless, several challenges remain for applying neuro-symbolic AI in life sciences. In particular, the enormous size of the data and knowledge used in life sciences requires efficient and scalable methods. Furthermore, in life sciences, just as in other empirical sciences, there is a strong focus on prioritizing novel discoveries that are, to some degree, "surprising", and AI systems that identify novel and surprising scientific knowledge need to follow, in some form, the scientific method. There is also a strong focus on explainability, in particular in medical and biomedical applications.

Here, we outline how life sciences have led to the advancement of methods in neuro-symbolic AI, and where and how neuro-symbolic methods are currently applied in life sciences. We focus primarily on ontology-based methods that make use of life science data and knowledge infrastructure due to the central role that ontologies play. Section 2 provides an overview of this infrastructure, its size, and unique features. Section 3 describes different forms of semantic similarity measures which are used widely in life sciences as well as the task of knowledge base completion as an extension of semantic similarity. Section 4 focuses on knowledge-enhanced learning and describes how the methods for computing semantic similarity and knowledge base completion are used in combination with other biological data to inject background knowledge in machine learning models. In Section 5, we describe and evaluate different neuro-symbolic methods on the task of predicting gene–disease associations using different types of background knowledge, and Section 6 lists open challenges and provides a conclusion.

2. Life Science Knowledge Infrastructure

Biological laws and models are often derived from the systematic comparison of entities — such as genes, cells, organisms, populations, and species — to discern their similarities and differences. Comparison and classification are the foundation of Linnaeus' system of taxonomy and Darwin's theory of natural selection. Consequently, life sciences have a long history of organizing knowledge using structured, symbolic representations. The approaches include the use of classification systems, taxonomies, knowledge graphs, and ontologies to systematically categorize and describe biological phenomena. Due to the requirements for knowledge representation in the life sciences, life science knowledge infrastructure has several unique characteristics that are not commonly found in other domains. These include the widespread use of ontologies, complex "annotation" models used to capture metadata, evidence, and provenance about assertions, large size, often the absence of named individuals, and several community standards.

2.1. Ontologies

An ontology is the explicit, shared representation of a conceptualization of a domain [18]. In life sciences, and in particular in molecular biology, ontologies emerged as a consequence of technological and scientific progress. The Gene Ontology (GO), the first bio-ontology that was and still is widely used, emerged as a consequence of breakthroughs in gene and genome sequencing and the resulting understanding of how many genes are conserved and have the same functions in different organisms [19]. This novel understanding, combined with the rapid change of knowledge in the field of molecular biology, necessitated the development of the GO, to keep track of the changing knowledge in the field and simultaneously provide a means to describe the knowledge of gene and protein functions obtained through comparative and functional genomics. Using an ontology for describing protein functions solved many challenges. A form of deductive inference ("true path rule") allowed capturing the most specific information about a protein as possible while still allowing inference of more general information (and thereby the combination of knowledge in related domains, such as in other organisms, where functions are either different due to biological differences between the organisms, or where the state of knowledge has not yet revealed specific functions), and use of a taxonomy allowed knowledge to evolve by gradually adding more specific functions to a protein without invalidating previous assertions.

There are now hundreds [20] of ontologies available in all areas of biology. Many bio-ontologies are part of a set of community-developed ontologies called the OBO Foundry [21]. The OBO Foundry provides guidelines and standards for ontology development. These standards include the use of a common identifier scheme, i.e., use of identifiers that are numerical and semantics-free, shared use of relations from the OBO Relationship Ontology [22], inclusion of natural language definitions, and several metadata and reporting standards [21].

There are different types of ontologies in life sciences. In particular in the OBO Foundry, *reference* ontologies for biological domains and sub-domains are developed and maintained; a reference ontology is a general knowledge base for a domain and reference ontologies include ontologies for the anatomy of specific species such as the Mouse Anatomy Ontology [23], ontologies for the structure and functions of chemicals [24], the Gene Ontology [19], or phenotype ontologies [25]. Reference ontologies are intended to be widely used for data integration across databases. A second type of ontology are specific to particular tasks or applications, i.e., they are *application* ontologies; for example, the Uberon ontology [26] is designed to integrate anatomical entities across multiple species by explicitly representing mappings between anatomical entities; similarly, the Monarch [27] ontologies serve to integrate phenotypes and diseases, and consist mainly of mappings between different ontologies.

One feature that stands out in life science ontologies is that they rarely contain any instances [28]; instead, they consist almost entirely of names classes and axioms that constrain them. In Description Logic terminology [29], they consist only of a TBox; alternatively formulated, they consist of universally quantified statements without constant or function symbols. For example, an anatomy ontology will contain named classes for classes of anatomical entities (such as "arm", "hand", "liver"), and axioms that constrain the use of these classes (e.g., every hand is a part of some arm, or every arm has a hand as part). The ontology will then be able to resolve questions such as what parts an arm has, etc. There are no instances as the ontology is usually not used to classify or catalog individual body parts; instead, the ontology may be used as a knowledge base for answering anatomical queries, or as a way to integrate data that is linked to anatomical parts (such as the anatomical site of gene expression).

As a consequence of ontologies not having any instances, they cannot become inconsistent. There is also no simple way to perform "grounding" for these ontologies, i.e., use the named instances to generate variable-free theories. This is an important limitation because many neuro-symbolic methods rely on some form of grounding [30, 31, 32].

Instead of "instances", ontologies are used in databases to "annotate" entities with ontology classes [33]. An "annotation" links a biological entity (such as a gene, protein, or chemical) with an ontology class and metadata; for example, a protein p can be an-

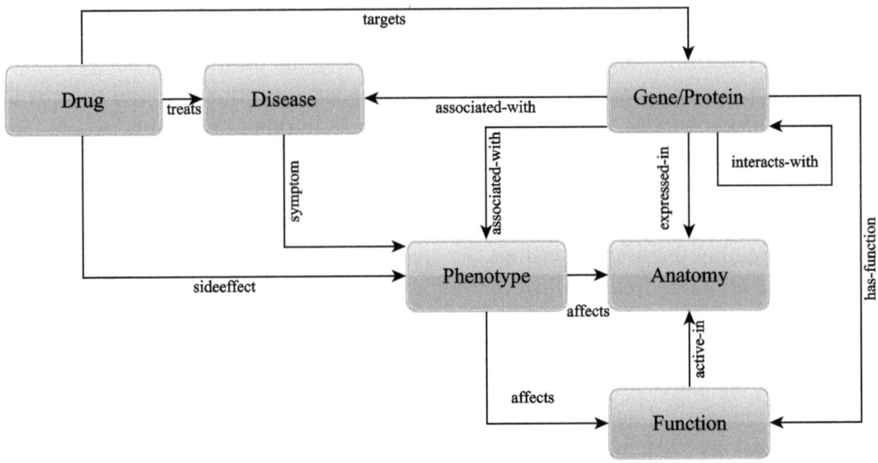

Figure 1. The schema for a knowledge graph in the biomedical domain.

notated with the class "liver" from an anatomy ontology to indicate that p is expressed in the liver (potentially under some conditions, or in a specific experiment). However, proteins themselves are not necessarily instances but may be better represented as classes [34].

2.2. Knowledge Graphs, and Interaction with Ontologies

Entities such as genes or proteins with these annotations are often included in knowledge graphs. Knowledge graphs represent, for example, interaction networks between genes or proteins, or different types of interactions between entities. A schema of a prototypical knowledge graph for knowledge about human diseases and used in biomedical research is shown in Figure 1; many knowledge graphs in life sciences will cover parts of the graph shown in Figure 1. A selection of life science knowledge graphs that have been maintained over longer periods of time and are widely used are shown in Table 1. These knowledge graphs include the "annotations" of biological entities with ontology classes, such as annotations with Gene Ontology classes, anatomy ontology classes, or phenotype ontology classes. Importantly, the size of the knowledge graphs used in life sciences is large; often, these knowledge graphs contain billion of triples and millions of entities. Furthermore, due to the widespread use of ontologies in life sciences, many knowledge graphs contain OWL axioms and rely at least partially on deductive inference for query answering.

Bio-ontologies interact with knowledge graphs in different ways. Historically, starting with the Gene Ontology [19], bio-ontologies were developed in a graph-based form, with dedicated graph-based ontology editors [43] such as DAGEdit, OilEd [44], or OBOEdit [45]. The graph-based language used to develop biomedical ontologies (the OBO Format [46]) was later replaced with OWL as main way to formalize bio-ontologies.

For integrating OWL ontologies with knowledge graphs, there are several options. The OWL axioms can be encoded as a graph directly, using the OWL RDF syntax; how-

Table 1. Summary of Biomedical Knowledge Resources

Resource	Description	Triples	Nodes	Expressivity
UniProtKB [35]	Comprehensive information about proteins, their domains, structure, and function	161,612,947,128	41 million	RDF, lightweight ontology (RDFS)
DisGeNET [36]	Gene disease associations	99,057,987 (1,134,942 gene-disease associations, 369,554 variant-disease associations)	21,671 genes, 30,170 diseases, traits, phenotypes	RDF, lightweight ontology (RDFS)
STRING [37] and STITCH [38]	Functional interactions between proteins (STRING), and interactions between proteins and chemicals (STITCH)	27 billion (STRING), 1.6 billion (STITCH)	60 million proteins (STRING), 9.6 million proteins and 0.5 million chemicals (STITCH)	RDF
Monarch Knowledge Graph [39]	Genes and phenotypes across different model organism species	11 million	571k genes, 124k phenotypes, 28k diseases, 1 million total nodes	RDF, OWL 2 DL ontology axioms
Hetionet [40]	Interactions between diseases, drugs, genes, and pathways	2,250,197 triples	47,031 nodes	RDF, lightweight ontology (RDFS)
PheKnowLator [41]	Interactions between diseases, drugs, genes, and pathways	41 million triples	13.8 million nodes	RDF, OWL 2 DL
NBDC RDF Portal [42]	Various biomedical and life sciences data in RDF format	160,307,491,527 triples	330,745 classes and 21,959,099,840 instances	RDF, OWL Full

Table 2. Transformation rules to convert OWL axioms into a graph.

Condition 1	Condition 2	Triple(s)
$A \sqsubseteq QR_0 \dots QR_m D$ $A \equiv QR_0 \dots QR_m D$	$D := B_1 \sqcup \dots \sqcup B_n \mid B_1 \sqcap \dots \sqcap B_n$	$\langle A, (R_0 ... R_m), B_i \rangle$ for $i \in 1 \dots n$
$A \sqsubseteq B$	–	$\langle A, SubClassOf, B \rangle$
$A \equiv B$	–	$\langle A, EquivalentTo, B \rangle$

ever, a purely syntactic representation of the axioms is not usually desirable for interacting with knowledge graphs where it is usually assumed that relations have a biological interpretation. Therefore, the OWL axioms in an ontology can also be converted into graphs using a set of relational patterns [47]; these patterns "project" one or more axioms into edges that form the knowledge graph. The patterns can either be defined using only the logical syntax of OWL, or they can be domain-specific. OWL2Vec* [48] is an ontology embedding method that includes a graph projection using static projection rules based only on syntactic patterns of the axioms. For example, OWL2Vec* projects axioms of the type $A \sqsubseteq \exists R.B$ or $A \sqsubseteq \forall R.B$ onto the edge $A \xrightarrow{R} B$. Table 2 shows a subset of the transformation rules employed by OWL2Vec*. Alternatively, the projection rules can be domain-specific. A number of domain-specific projection rules are defined in the OBO Relationship Ontology [22], which maintains relational patterns to be used across different bio-ontologies. Some of the relational patterns in the RO are used to generate OBO Graphs as a uniform way to create graphs from OWL-based bio-ontologies [49, 47, 50].

Knowledge graphs can also be used to generate ontology axioms. One option is to utilize the projection patterns as in OWL2Vec* "backwards", generating axioms from edges in a graph. For example, the knowledge graph triple (p_1, interacts-with, p_2) could be expressed as the axiom $p_1 \sqsubseteq \exists \text{interacts-with}.p_2$. Here p_1 and p_2 may be proteins (or genes) that interact, and in the axiom they would be treated as classes (and potentially subclasses of a *Protein* class). Ideally, the graph projections are injective so that each edge corresponds to exactly one axiom [51]. Alternatively, the triple can also be used directly as an ABox statement, $\text{interacts-with}(p_1, p_2)$ where p_1 and p_2 are individuals (and potentially instances of a *Protein* class).

2.3. Annotations beyond Knowledge Graphs: Metadata, Provenance, and Evidence

An "annotation" of a biological entity with an ontology class goes beyond what is usually represented in a knowledge graph and will, at the minimum, include metadata such as provenance (a reference from which the association between the biological entity and ontology class was derived) and the evidence provided within the publication for the assertion. This annotation model was first introduced and explored in depth in the context of GO annotations [33]. An annotation may also include "qualifiers", the most important of which includes "NOT" [52] which negates an association between a biological entity and the ontology class. It is used only when there is explicit evidence (usually, by experiment) that the biological entity is not associated with the ontology class; representing these negations requires a semantics beyond knowledge graphs, or a translation pattern that includes the negations [53].

Annotations are further extended with other types of qualifiers [52] that usually specify the type of association between the biological entity and ontology class. For example, the association could be a mereological relation, or a regulatory relation to a biological process. However, despite some ontological and formal analyses for specific databases [54], the semantics of an annotation and the qualifiers used in them are database- or context-specific, and there is no standard semantics for annotation models across databases.

2.4. Tasks for Ontologies and Knowledge Graphs

Ontologies and knowledge graphs support several critical tasks in the life science data infrastructure. The first task is querying. Ontologies provide standard identifiers across databases and knowledge graphs, enabling querying across different databases. In the context of knowledge graphs, SPARQL (SPARQL Protocol and RDF Query Language) [55] is commonly used for querying, and some of the largest bioinformatics database providers, most notably the Japanese DBCLS and NDBC [56] and, in the past, the European Bioinformatics Institute (EBI) [57], provide access to their database content through SPARQL. Interaction with the axioms in ontologies is done through the SPARQL reasoning capabilities, or using hybrid systems that perform OWL reasoning outside the SPARQL query and combine it with SPARQL query results [58]. The reason for using hybrid systems is that the majority of axioms in bio-ontologies are TBox axioms, and TBox reasoning is not as well supported by SPARQL query engines as reasoning over RDF graphs.

Ontologies and knowledge graphs are also used for predictive methods. Prediction tasks can be divided into two categories. The first are tasks such as knowledge graph completion or knowledge base completion that use *only* symbolically represented information to infer new knowledge; examples for this task includes the prediction of gene–disease associations from other knowledge about genes and diseases, prediction of protein–protein interactions based on the functions of the proteins, or prediction of drug–target interactions based on knowledge about their side effects [59]; essentially, every relation in the knowledge graph schema shown in Figure 1 can be predicted given the other relations. The second type of prediction tasks in which knowledge graphs or ontologies are involved are hybrid and involve both symbolic and subsymbolic representations; an example of such a task is the prediction of gene–disease association from both phenotypes (represented symbolically using a phenotype ontology) and facial images [60], or the prediction of protein functions from symbolically represented knowledge of protein–protein interactions and subsymbolic representations of a protein sequence (although protein sequences are arguably symbol structures on their own, although their composition rules are not known or well understood and still subject to research in genome biology).

Due to the widespread use of ontologies instead of or in addition to knowledge graphs, it is also important to distinguish between knowledge graph completion and knowledge base completion. Knowledge graph completion is the task of predicting "missing" edges from a knowledge graph, and knowledge base completion is the task of predicting "missing" axioms from a knowledge base; both tasks commonly use only information in the knowledge graph or knowledge base as input. However, the nature of "missing" is different between the two tasks. In a knowledge graph, "missing" usually refers to edges that are not there and are also not inferrable from the edges in the graph; in a knowledge base (or ontology), axioms can be semantically entailed and "missing" can either mean that the axioms are not explicitly stated but could be entailed, or that the axioms cannot be entailed but may be added [61].

There is another distinction in the different tasks and that is whether the predictions are based on a supervised signal (where a relation is being learned) or whether the predictions are entirely based on a notion of similarity. For similarity-based predictions, the "guilt by association" principle is exploited. "Guilt by association" [62] is the principle that if entity a is related to phenomenon P, and b is somehow associated with (or similar to) a, then b is also likely related to P. This logical fallacy (*argumentum ad odium*) is widely employed in life sciences despite serious concerns about its applicability [62]. The principle is used, for instance, to identify candidate disease genes. Different approaches use different types of "association" or "similarity". For example, disease genes can be identified using random walks on interaction networks [63]; in this case, "association" is the presence of an edge in the interaction network. They can also be identified through "similarity" to known disease genes, where "association" is implemented through a similarity measure; if the similarity measure exploits knowledge graphs or ontologies, we consider it a "semantic similarity" measure.

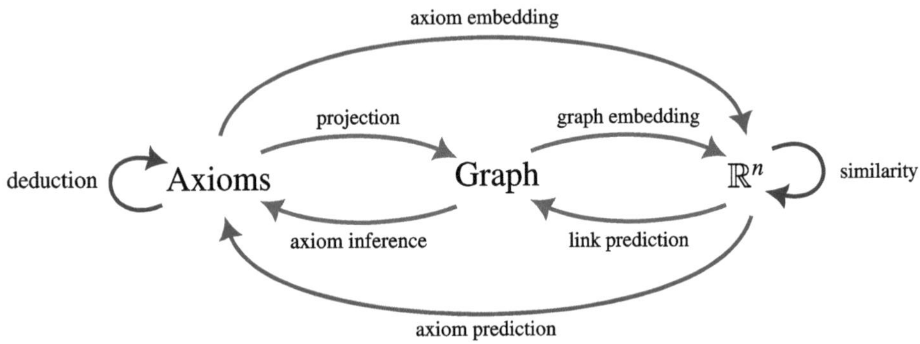

Figure 2. Overall: Ontology embedding (left to right) and axiom inference/prediction (right to left) processes. Blue arrows describe the ontology embedding as a two-step process involving transforming the ontology into a graph. Axiom inference involves performing link prediction on the graph. Green arrows describe ontology embedding process where axioms are embedded directly. Axiom prediction requires a truth value function from the embedding space $\mathbb{R}^n$. The *deduction* loop represent deductive reasoning processes in the axiom space. The *similarity* loop represent similarity computation between embeddings.

3. Similarity and Embeddings

3.1. From Axioms to an Embedding Space

Ontology and knowledge graph embeddings are latent representations of entities and relationships in an ontology or knowledge graph, that aim to capture the semantic information and structural patterns of the knowledge graph in a continuous vector space. Knowledge graph embeddings facilitate various tasks, such as link prediction, entity classification, and similarity computation, by enabling the application of algebraic operations and distance metrics in the vector space.

Methods for learning knowledge graph or ontology embeddings can be categorized under three broad approaches according to the properties they aim to preserve: (i) relational structure preserving; (ii) model structure preserving; and (iii) subgraph similarity preserving. While relational and model structure preserving methods are trained (i.e., use a supervised signal) to achieve knowledge graph or ontology completion (typically by predicting a triple or axiom), methods that preserve subgraph similarity aim to capture the similarity between entities in the knowledge graph. This difference influences the type of downstream applications that are suitable for each KG embedding type.

A common first step in generating ontology embeddings is to derive new axioms from existing ones using logical inference rules, enabling the extraction of implicit knowledge from explicitly stated information (see Figure 2). Many ontology embedding methods and also classical semantic similarity measures include the computation of the deductive closure of the ontology as an initial step. Both the embedding approaches OPA2Vec [64] and Onto2Vec [65] and the classical semantic similarity measure SimGIC [66] adopt the deductive closure of an ontology with entailment reasoning, effectively enriching the graph representation of the ontology.

Relational structure-preserving methods and many similarity-preserving ones are designed to work with graph data structures, where nodes represent KG entities and edges represent the relations between them. While the taxonomical component of an ontology can be directly inferred from its axioms as one of the standard OWL reasoning tasks, creating general graph structures that better capture the ontologies' semantic content is more challenging, requiring the identification of existential patterns in the deductive closure of ontologies [67].

However, OWL ontologies include rich, logical constructs like property restrictions and logical assertions, that require the application of projection techniques to be transformed into a graph. Therefore, many approaches require a graph projection step before embeddings can be learned.

Following [51], a graph projection for $\mathcal{O}$ is a function p that maps an ontology into a relational graph $G = (V, E, L)$ such that $C \cup R \cup I \subseteq V \cup L$ (i.e., each class, role name and individual is represented as a node or edge label in G) and for each axiom $a \in \mathbb{A}x$ (the set axioms in $\mathcal{O}$), $p(a) \subseteq E$ (i.e., p maps an axiom onto a subgraph of G).

Most approaches employ the OWL to RDF Graph Mapping guidelines[2] defined by the W3C. Simple axioms, such as membership and subsumption axioms for atomic entities and relational assertions between atomic instances, can be directly transformed into RDF triples, while axioms involving complex class expressions require multiple triples and often rely on blank nodes. More sophisticated methods, such as OWL2Vec* [68] employ specific projection rules that minimize the use of blank nodes — which may introduce noise into the embedding learning process — but sacrifice an exact representation of the axioms in the graph. The output of these techniques ensures that every triple in the graph is justified by one or more axioms entailed by the ontology, with classes being represented as nodes while edges represent relations among them.

Once a graph structure is created, both relational structure and subgraph similarity-preserving embedding methods can be applied. Relational structure-preserving methods encompass methods that aim to capture the triple-based structure of the graph. Both geometric models and semantic matching approaches can fall under this category. Geometric models that preserve the relation structure interpret relations as geometric operations in the latent space, typically formulated as translation operations. This includes popular methods such as TransE [69] or RotatE [70]. The head embedding undergoes a spatial transformation modulated by the relation embedding and the triple score is given by the distance between the resulting vector and the tail vector. Semantic Matching models employ a similarity-based scoring function to evaluate triples. Semantic matching models are also referred to as matrix factorization models or tensor decomposition models, because they interpret the KG as a three-dimensional adjacency matrix, which can be decomposed into into a combination of low-dimensional vectors that represent the entity and relation embeddings. Popular approaches include DistMult, ComplEx and HolE [71].

Similarity-preserving methods aim to be partially faithful to correlations and co-occurrences of symbols in the axioms of the ontology or in graph paths. These methods are typically based on sequence modelling obtained over sequences extracted from single ontology axioms (e.g., Onto2Vec, OPA2Vec) or random walks on the projected graph (e.g., RDF2Vec, OWL2Vec*, DL2Vec). One of the first KG embedding methods based on graph walks was RDF2Vec [72]. It uses random walks over RDF graphs to generate a corpus of sequences of entities and relations. A neural language model — Word2Vec [73] — is then applied to the corpus to learn vector representations of entities. More sophisticated methods have extended this basic notion by employing more com-

[2]https://www.w3.org/TR/owl2-mapping-to-rdf/

plex graph projection approaches that better capture OWL semantics (e.g., DL2Vec [74], OWL2Vec* [68]), and by also embedding the literals in data and annotation properties (e.g. OPA2Vec, OWL2Vec*).

Model-structure-preserving methods aim to capture the semantics of ontologies based on models. An interpretation $\mathcal{I}$ for an ontology consists of a domain $\Delta^{\mathcal{I}}$ and a function $\cdot^{\mathcal{I}}$ that maps ontology individuals into elements of $\Delta^{\mathcal{I}}$, ontology classes into subsets of $\Delta^{\mathcal{I}}$, ontology roles into subsets of $\Delta^{\mathcal{I}} \times \Delta^{\mathcal{I}}$. If the interpretation $\mathcal{I}$ satisfies all axioms in the ontology, then it is a *model*.

Model-structure-preserving methods usually define the interpretation domain as $\mathbb{R}^n$ and the interpretation function is learned under the appropriate set of constraints. For example, geometric model-generating methods [75, 76] constrain the interpretation of an ontology class as a convex region in $\mathbb{R}^n$, which can be a n-dimensional ball as in ELEmbeddings [75] or n-dimensional box [76] as in Box^{2}EL. Furthermore, interpretation of operations such as intersection or existential restricion is defined geometrically. For example, intersection of classes is defined as the intersection of convex regions, and in EL-Embeddings, existential restrictions are defined as ball translations. Embedding methods based on fuzzy logic, such as Logic Tensor Networks [30], represent ontology classes as fuzzy sets, and logical connectives as fuzzy operators [31].

The learning process generates embeddings for individuals, classes and roles by optimizing an axiom scoring function $\phi : Ax \mapsto [0,1]$ which is applied to every axiom in the ontology. The idea is that when the function ϕ reaches its optimal state, the generated embeddings preserve the model structure of the ontology. Ideally, this would mean that $\phi(ax) = 1$ for every axiom existing in the ontology as well as every axiom in the deductive closure of the ontology, therefore preserving the model structure.

Geometric methods do not require the existence of individuals because the model interpretation of a class is given by a convex region in $\mathbb{R}^n$, however, geometric methods usually target the $\mathcal{EL}^{++}$ language, which does not include operations such as full negations, union or universal quantification. On the other hand, LTN based methods can target more expressive languages such as $\mathcal{ALC}$ with the condition that instances exist in order to perform existential or universal quantification.

3.2. Similarity

There are two popular approaches to measure semantic similarity within ontologies and KGs: classical semantic similarity measures and embedding-based similarity. While "classical" measures are based on expert-crafted algorithms that aim to directly capture the properties of ontology entities that influence their similarity according to the expert's definition of similarity, the embedding-based similarity is based on learning representations of ontology entities using self-supervised approaches that are then comparable in a vector space.

Following [77], we establish that a function $sim : D \times D$ is a similarity function on a domain D if it fulfils the following requirements: (1) it is non-negative: $(sim(x,y) \geq 0)$; (2) it is symmetric $(sim(x,y) = sim(y,x))$; and (3) if self-similarity yields the highest similarity values within the domain $(sim(x,x) = max_D)$, or if self-similarity is higher than similarity to any other domain entity $(sim(x,x) \geq sim(x,y))$.

Classical methods for semantic similarity rely on first determining the graph structure of the ontology, followed by the application of graph-based algorithms that aim to capture some aspects of similarity. In its simplest form, the semantic similarity between two ontology classes can be straightforwardly computed from their distance as measured by counting the number of edges in the path connecting them. When multiple paths exist, the shortest path or the average distance of all possible paths can be considered. Semantic similarity can then be defined as the inverse of the semantic distance score. Distance-based methods typically assume that all edges carry the same weight. Although this edge-counting method is intuitive and simple, it overlooks the nodes' depth, treating paths of equal length as having the same degree of similarity, regardless of their degree of specificity within the ontology.

Formally, class specificity is a function $\sigma : C \mapsto \mathbb{R}$ which meets the condition that for all $x, y \in C$, if $x \sqsubseteq y$ then $\sigma(x) \geq \sigma(y)$ [78]. To measure the specificity of a class, we can take structure-based approaches, such as the distance to the root or number of subclasses, or explore information-theoretic principles. The information content of a class c measures its likelihood of occurrence, quantified as the negative log-likelihood, $-\log p(c)$, where $p(c)$ is the probability of c occurring in a specific corpus, typically estimated by how frequently the class is used to describe biomedical entities (e.g., how many genes are assigned a specific Gene Ontology class). To measure the similarity between ontology classes, we can then quantify the information the two classes share, exploring the IC of their common ancestors. Two principal approaches exist for this purpose: the Most Informative Common Ancestor (MICA) technique, which considers only the common ancestor with the highest IC, and the Disjoint Common Ancestors (DCA) technique, which includes all disjoint common ancestors—those that do not subsume any other common ancestor. Several measures have been used to quantify the information shared by two GO terms. The simplest of these is Resnik's measure, which takes the IC of the MICA as the similarity between two terms and was among the first to be applied to biomedical ontologies:

$$\mathrm{Sim}_{\mathrm{Resnik}}(a,b) = \max_{c \in \mathrm{SCA}(a,b)} \mathrm{IC}(c) \tag{1}$$

where a and b are classes in an ontology, $\mathrm{SCA}(a,b)$ represents the set of shared common ancestors of a and b, and $\mathrm{IC}(c)$ is the information content of concept c.

Many biomedical applications require computing the similarity between ontology individuals or entities annotated to ontology classes, which consist of comparing sets of classes. For instance, to measure the similarity between two proteins, it is common to measure the similarity between the sets of Gene Ontology annotations they have [79]. There are two primary methods for determining the similarity between sets of classes A and B. The first method involves computing the pairwise similarities between all class pairs (a,b) where $a \in A$ and $b \in B$, and then aggregating these similarity values using a combination strategy, such as averaging or maximum [80]. The second method defines a similarity measure directly between the two sets A and B using a set similarity measure, such as the Jaccard index:

$$\mathrm{Jaccard}(A,B) = \frac{|A \cap B|}{|A \cup B|} \tag{2}$$

Using set similarity measures to capture semantic similarity requires a preprocessing step that extends each set with respect to the transitive closure of hierarchical relations in the ontology. This allows set similarity measures to capture similarities at different levels in the ontology hierarchy. For example, if $a \in A$ and a' is a superclass of a, then a' should also be included in A. Set similarity can account for class specificity, such as using the weighted Jaccard index in the SimGIC measure.

While more classical semantic similarity measures rely on handcrafted algorithms to capture aspects of the ontology which are relevant for similarity computation, such as specificity or shared ancestors, it is also possible to compute semantic similarity based on knowledge graph embeddings. Operations such as cosine similarity are routinely applied to KG embeddings.

3.3. From an Embedding Space to Axioms

Embedding spaces created by relational and model structure-preserving methods can be explored to predict links in a KG or axioms in an ontology. For relational structure-preserving models, the model can be used to predict missing links by evaluating the scoring function for potential triples. Typically, given a head entity h and a relation r, the model predicts the tail entity t by solving:

$$\hat{t} = \arg\max_{t' \in \mathscr{E}} f(h, r, t') \tag{3}$$

The newly predicted links can then be added to the graph where inference techniques can be applied to derive novel axioms. Some works explore the relational embedding space directly for axiom induction. This includes first generating a pool of possible axioms and then predicting the score of each axiom based on estimating their truth value using the embedding space [81].

Model-structure-preserving methods optimize a set of embeddings together with a function $\phi : Ax \mapsto [0,1]$. Once the optimization process is finished, the function ϕ can be used to query for the truth value of a novel axiom ax. If $\phi(ax) > k$ for some threshold $k \in [0,1]$, the axiom ax is evaluated as true in the learned geometric model. Since the model structure of the ontology is preserved, it is expected that $\phi(ax) > k$ for every axiom ax in the deductive closure of the ontology. Furthermore, regularities from the data (the set of axioms) that are captured during the training enable the query of novel axioms that are not in the deductive closure but are probable to be true. In this way, model-structure-preserving methods allow framing the knowledge base completion problem as the computation of truth in the learned model.

Beyond the computation of truth of axioms, model-structure-preserving methods also enable *approximate semantic entailment*. For an axiom ax, classical semantic entailment means that the axiom is true in all (potentially infinite) models of the ontology. In practice it is not possible to generate all possible geometric or fuzzy-logic-based models. However, by sampling a finite number k of models, it is possible to approximate semantic entailment for the axioms ax by aggregating the truth values of ax over all k models.

4. Knowledge-Enhanced Learning

Knowledge-enhanced learning relies on machine learning models being able to access some form of prior knowledge. This knowledge can be presented as a knowledge graph or knowledge base, and may also include ontologies. In recent years, owing in large parts to the well-developed knowledge infrastructure in the life sciences, structured and formalized knowledge has been incorporated into predictive models in many life science domains; the majority of methods relies on knowledge graph embeddings, but some other approaches also emerged.

4.1. Based on Knowledge Graphs

A common use is to use embeddings generated from biological knowledge graphs as features to more complex prediction models. This approach is relatively mature and has been used in many domains and applications, exploiting almost every relation in Figure 1.

For example, DeepGO [82] is a function prediction model that used pre-generated knowledge graph embeddings as features. The knowledge graph used by DeepGO encodes for interactions between proteins and orthology (i.e., an evolutionary relationship) between proteins, and the embeddings of proteins in this knowledge graph encode for similarity, thereby implementing the "guilt-by-association" principle for function prediction. OntoProtein [83] and KeAP [84] are protein representation learning methods that combine a protein language model with a knowledge graph encoding for protein functions (based on the Gene Ontology).

The embeddings can also be multi-modal and include structured knowledge and text. DTiGEMS+ [85] and DTI-Voodoo [86] use a knowledge graph with information about drug side effects, drug targets, and protein–protein interactions to predict drug targets. The knowledge graph is used as pre-trained embedding or using a relational graph convolutional neural network (R-GCN) [87]. Otter Knowledge [88] is an approach for drug discovery that combines multiple different representation learning methods to generate embeddings (for chemicals, proteins, diseases, or similar) and combines this with a knowledge graph embedding objective. KANO [89] uses a knowledge graph about properties of chemical elements and their relation to functional groups of molecules to improve representation learning for molecular properties.

The common principle underlying all of these methods is that a traditional prediction model for a relation r between entities a and b of types A and B can be enriched by including, as a feature, embeddings that also encode for knowledge of a and b. Using the graph in Figure 1 as example, any prediction model that uses a sub-symbolic representation of entities a and b in the graph as input can be enriched (and usually improved) by adding an embedding of the entities (based on their knowledge graph embeddings) as additional feature; or, in classification problems where entity a is classified, adding the knowledge graph embedding of a as feature; and similarly in regression problems.

4.2. Based on Ontologies

While the application of knowledge graph and ontology embeddings is the most common way in which knowledge-enhanced learning is implemented, there are also some other approaches. For example, in chemistry, ontology-based loss functions have been applied [90] to exploit prior knowledge contained in the ChEBI ontology [91, 92]. A semantic loss functions [93] imposes logical constraints as part of the loss and usually ensures that the loss is zero if all constraints are satisfied.

DeepGOZero [94] and DeepGO-SE [95] predict protein functions using geometric, model-preserving ontology embeddings. DeepGOZero formulates the protein function prediction problem as a problem of finding a logical geometric model $\mathscr{M}$ of the Gene Ontology, learning a projection function of a protein p into this geometric model, and then testing the truth value of a statement asserting that the protein has a function F in the model $\mathscr{M}$; i.e., DeepGOZero tests for $\mathscr{M} \models (\exists \text{has-function}.F)(p)$. The model $\mathscr{M}$ is an approximate model of the Gene Ontology where classes (unary predicates) correspond to n-dimensional balls; the truth value of statements in this model can range from 0 to 1. Knowledge-enhanced learning in DeepGOZero can be used to predict a function of a protein even if, during training, not a single protein has been observed with that function (knowledge-enhanced zero-shot predictions). DeepGO-SE extends DeepGOZero by generating multiple approximate models $\mathscr{M}_1, ..., \mathscr{M}_n$ and aggregating the truth values across $\mathscr{M}_1, ..., \mathscr{M}_n$ using an aggregation function (e.g., the mean, the maximum, or the minimum) to compute an approximate value of semantic entailment for the statement $(\exists \text{has-function}.F)(p)$. Similarly to DeepGOZero, it can perform zero-shot predictions and is generally more robust than DeepGOZero.

Another use of ontologies in knowledge-enhanced learning is for analyzing phenotype data and predicting gene–disease associations. Mantis-ML [96] is a machine learning framework that uses a biomedical knowledge graph similar to the one outlined in Figure 1 to assess gene–disease probabilities; the graph is constructed, among others, from ontologies, including the Gene Ontology and the Human Phenotype Ontology. The resulting graph is then exploited by a graph convolutional neural network.

5. Use Case: Phenotype-Based Candidate Gene Prediction

The phenotype-based prioritization of candidate genes for diseases is a major use-case for neuro-symbolic methods in life sciences, and this use-case has led to the development of several neuro-symbolic methods. The simplest formulation of the task is this: given a set of phenotypes Q (the query), rank a set of genes based on the likelihood that a variant or mutation in these genes caused the set of phenotypes. The task assumes that there is a database of gene-to-phenotype associations and the genes are ranked by a measure of semantic similarity to the query phenotypes Q. The task can come in several facets; if the gene-to-phenotype associations are from a database of human diseases such as the Online Mendelian Inheritance in Men (OMIM) [97] database or the Human Phenotype Ontology database, the specific application of the task is to provide a candidate diagnosis given the query Q; if the gene-to-disease associations come from another database such as phenotypes observed in knockout mouse models, the task is to find either animal models of a human disease [98] or to suggest hypotheses about human disease genes [99].

Often, the prediction of gene–disease associations is not used on its own but combined with other biological features to predict, for example, genomic variants associated with a set of observed phenotypes. This approach was first used in the Exomiser tool [100] that takes as input the whole genome or whole exome of a patient together with a set of phenotypes, and outputs a ranked list of genomic variants based on the likelihood the variant causes the set of phenotypes. Exomiser is used widely to provide molecular diagnoses for rare genetic (Mendelian) diseases [101]. Several similar tools have been developed and applied to more complex diseases.

In all these tasks or sub-tasks, phenotypes are encoded using a phenotype ontology and a neuro-symbolic method is used to implement the semantic similarity between phenotypes or to directly predict gene–disease associations. When gene–disease associations are predicted by similarity, the query Q is a set of phenotypes and each gene g is represented by a set of phenotypes $P(g)$; the semantic similarity then computes similarity between Q and $P(g)$, $sim(Q, P(g))$. Computing this similarity for genes from a list of genes (either all genes, or a selected list) results in a ranked list of genes which is then used for evaluation.

This "guilt by association" method does not use any supervised signal to predict gene–disease associations; while it may result in a method that is less prone to biases (e.g., degree biases), its performance may not be sufficient for some tasks. Therefore, other methods use a supervised signal; these methods include link prediction methods. These methods have another advantage over methods that rely only on semantic similarity, as they can integrate and utilize different types of information that are not "similar" to the query but otherwise related. In particular, since the query Q consists of a set of phenotypes, genes must also be represented by phenotypes and related through a phenotype ontology; however, there are other properties of genes, in particular their functions expressed through the GO, that can be used to relate genes and diseases, and these properties are harder to exploit using approaches that rely entirely on similarity.

We showcase the performance of different methods on the candidate gene prediction problem, specifically the task of finding candidate human disease genes using the phenotypes associated with mouse models [98]. We use the integrated phenotype ontology UPheno [27], which contains phenotype information across several species including human and mouse. Since genes and diseases are expected to be associated by phenotype similarity, we add three types of annotations to UPheno: (1) gene–phenotype from the mouse organism, mouse genes are mapped to human genes and phenotypes belong to the Mammalian Phenotype Ontology. (2) disease–phenotype, where diseases are in the OMIM database and phenotypes are in the Human Phenotype ontology and (3) gene–disease, which are associations between human genes and OMIM diseases. The extended UPheno ontology is used to train a neuro-symbolic method to generate ontology embeddings. Finally, the generated embeddings are used to predict candidate genes for a disease: the query is a disease entity and the prediction is a ranked list of candidate genes (Figure 3).

Table 3 shows the performance of the different types of methods: semantic similarity measures, semantic preserving embeddings, relational-structure-preserving and model-structure-preserving [3]. Semantic similarity measures can be considered purely symbolic methods. To generate a prediction, a gene and a disease are represented as sets of phenotypes and the gene-disease score is given by semantic similarity score of their phenotype sets. We show two examples of similarity measures: SimGIC [66] with Resnik's term specificity measure [102] and Resnik's similarity measure [103] with Resnik's term specificity and the best-match-average (BMA) [78] aggregation strategy. SimGIC is a groupwise measure between sets of phenotypes and Resnik+BMA uses the Resnik pairwise measure and aggregates pairwise similarities with the best match average. Methods in the other categories are neuro-symbolic and rely on the generation of embeddings of genes and diseases to generate predictions. In terms of training procedure, all the neuro-symbolic methods support only transductive learning, therefore being unable to generate a prediction for new diseases or add new genes to the ranking.

[3]Source code for experiments on the candidate gene prediction task can be found at `https://github.com/bio-ontology-research-group/gda_analysis`.

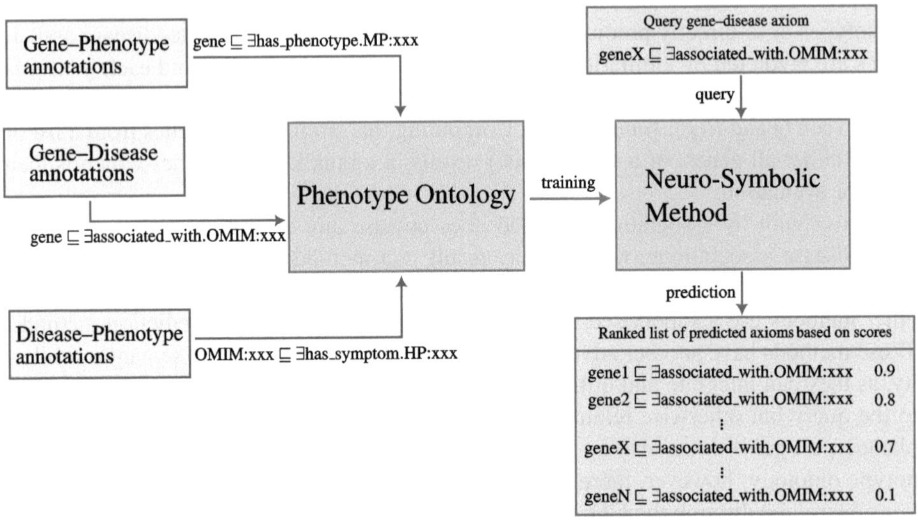

Figure 3. Example of training a candidate gene prediction system. A phenotype ontology integrates phenotype information about human and model organisms. The phenotype ontology is extended with annotations between (1) genes and phenotypes, (2) genes and diseases and (3) diseases and phenotypes. The extended ontology is used to generate embeddings using a neuro-symbolic method. The prediction is a list of axioms relating *n* genes with the disease of interest (the query disease). Finally, the list is sorted based on prediction scores (assigned to axioms), and genes are ranked for the query disease based on the scores the axioms receive.

All the methods are evaluated as ranking systems with metrics such as Mean Rank (MR), Mean Reciprocal Rank (MRR), Hits@10, and Rank AUC. The evaluation procedure involves two settings: averaging the metrics per testing gene-disease pair and averaging the metrics per disease. When averaging by gene–disease pair, most neuro-symbolic methods obtain a better performance than semantic similarity measures. However, when averaging by disease the tendency is inverted and semantic similarity measures are performing better than semantic similarity measures. This phenomenon might suggest that neuro-symbolic methods are affected by biases of the phenotype annotations [104]; since the "query" is usually the set of phenotypes associated with the disease, the disease-based evaluation is the more important one.

The generation of candidate genes for a given disease is framed differently by every type of method. Similarity preserving embeddings, which generate a corpus, use a vector simlarity score function to rank genes for a disease. The corpus can be generated by rendering ontology axioms and annotations as text (OPA2Vec) or through random walks across an intermediate graph structure (OWL2Vec*). The graph structure, generated for example by OWL2Vec*, can also be used to train a knowledge graph embedding method (such as TransE or DistMult). In this case, the prediction of gene–disease association is addressed as a link prediction problem. Finally, model structure preserving methods model the ontology semantics in a geometric space (ELEmbeddings) or fuzzy logic space (FALCON) and score gene–disease associations as computation of truth of axioms or approximate semantic entailment, respectively.

Table 3. Evaluation of different neuro-symbolic methods on a gene–disease association benchmark. We list the graph projection (OWL2Vec*) used in graph-based methods. OWL2Vec* is also a similarity-preserving embedding method based on the OWL2Vec* graph projection and using node2vec for the graph embedding. We trained ELEmbeddings with 1 generated model and FALCON with 5 generated models.

Type of Method	Method	Graph Projection	MR	MRR	H@10	AUC
	Metrics averaged per gene-disease pair					
Semantic Similarity Measures	SimGIC	–	4989	0.012	0.024	0.625
	Resnik-BMA	–	3457	0.012	0.024	0.741
Similarity Preserving Embeddings	OPA2Vec	–	2969	0.014	0.028	0.777
	OWL2Vec*	OWL2Vec*	3958	0.002	0.002	0.703
Relational Structure Preserving Embeddings	Graph+TransE	OWL2Vec*	3194	0.008	0.011	0.760
	Graph+DistMult	OWL2Vec*	3103	0.014	0.025	0.767
Model Structure Preserving Embeddings	ELEmbeddings	–	2982	0.010	0.017	0.776
	FALCON	–	4044	0.002	0.001	0.696
	Metrics averaged per disease					
Semantic Similarity Measures	SimGIC	–	3450	0.019	0.039	0.749
	Resnik-BMA	–	3130	0.020	0.041	0.772
Similarity Preserving Embeddings	OPA2Vec	–	3452	0.015	0.028	0.748
	OWL2Vec*	OWL2Vec*	4549	0.002	0.002	0.667
Relational Structure Preserving Embeddings	Graph+TransE	OWL2Vec*	4191	0.002	0.002	0.692
	Graph+DistMult	OWL2Vec*	3563	0.009	0.015	0.738
Model Structure Preserving Embeddings	ELEmbeddings	–	3764	0.007	0.009	0.724
	FALCON	–	4569	0.002	0.002	0.665

6. Conclusions

Life sciences are unique in that they have a rich and complex infrastructure for symbolic representations that are tied directly into data analysis methods underlying biological discovery. Over the past decades, life sciences have provided the problems through which methods in AI, including in neuro-symbolic AI, have advanced substantially, and we expect this trend to continue in the coming years. In fact, there is still an outstanding challenge to design an AI system that can win the Nobel prize in Physiology by 2050 [105], and such a system will, at the very least, have to be able to formulate goals or hypothesis, generate and collect data, interpret and reason over the collected data, and formulate a coherent manuscript to publish. Many of these steps, and the entire process of scientific discovery, need to inherently combine neural and symbolic methods.

Here, we have investigated parts of the life sciences knowledge infrastructure and how neuro-symbolic methods are applied in them. There are several key challenges remaining that need to be addressed in the future. One of the main challenges is the size of knowledge bases (ontologies and knowledge graph) as well as the size of the data that is being generated in life sciences. Scalability is still a major problem for some neuro-symbolic methods, in particular for those that can handle complex axioms in expressive Description Logics or in first order logic, such as Logic Tensor Networks [30]. Scalability is therefore still a problem and makes many neuro-symbolic methods challenging to apply to impactful problems in the life sciences.

A second challenge is that a large number of neuro-symbolic methods that are applicable to complex axioms require some form of grounding, or at least the presence of constant symbols in the knowledge base. However, constant symbols (or individual names) are commonly absent from life science knowledge bases, and it is unclear how they can be created *ad hoc*. Methods based on logic programming or on explicitly creating (finite) models that enumerate individuals and provide (fuzzy) interpretations for these individuals in predicates are not easily applicable. This limitation has led to the development of geometric methods that preserve model structures which overcomes the limitation of requiring grounding for application of neuro-symbolic methods; however, these methods are only applicable for variants of the Description Logic EL and not for more expressive logics; they are therefore only applicable to a subset of life science knowledge bases.

A third challenge in applying any AI model in life sciences, or in applying AI in empirical sciences, is that the interesting applications usually involve "novel", and surprising, findings. Here, "novel" refers to novelty with respect to total knowledge (e.g., a novel function of a gene product, or a surprising association between a gene and a disease) not just to the input of the model. There is also a long history of predictive methods (neuro-symbolic or not) that overfit to biases in data (with clinical decision support for COVID 19 [106] being just some recent examples); explainability, and consistency with background knowledge, are two properties that can be used to address these.

A fourth challenge is related to the explainability of these methods. For AI to effectively serve as a scientific tool, it must be capable of providing scientific explanations [107]. Although there is a general consensus that computational models can help explain real-world phenomena, the relationship between explaining natural phenomena and explaining algorithmic outputs that aim to capture them is still very much an open question. Recent works have aimed to explore KG embeddings [108] and semantic similarity to predict and explain biological phenomena such as protein–protein interactions or gene–disease associations [109]. These works have demonstrated that the intepretability of features — something most methods sacrifice when learning subsymbolic representations in an embedding space — is key to support explainability. Addressing this challenge will be fundamental to design AI methods that can function as true epistemic tools.

Life sciences offer unique opportunities to drive the development of novel neuro-symbolic AI approaches. The coexistance of large datasets and rich ontologies to describe them opens challenges related to both scalability and handling axiom complexity that few domains can offer. Moreover, the requirements for scientific discovery and explainability provide a solid motivation for the use of neuro-symbolic methods. Historically, the life sciences have spurred other scientific disciplines towards increased maturity, and this may very well be the case for neuro-symbolic AI.

Acknowledgements

CP was partially supported by Fundação para a Ciência e Tecnologia through the LASIGE Research Unit, ref. UIDB/00408/2020 (https://doi.org/10.54499/UIDB/00408/2020) and ref. UIDP/00408/2020 (https://doi.org/10.54499/UIDP/00408/2020). CP work was also partially supported by the KATY project, which has received funding from the European Union's Horizon 2020 research and innovation programme under grant agreement No 101017453, and in part by project 41, HfPT: Health from Portugal, funded by the Portuguese Plano de Recuperação e Resiliência. RH and FZC were supported by funding from King Abdullah University of Science and Technology (KAUST) Office of Sponsored Research (OSR) under Award No. URF/1/4355-01-01, URF/1/4675-01-01, URF/1/4697-01-01, URF/1/5041-01-01, REI/1/5334-01-01; the KAUST Center of Excellence for Smart Health (KCSH), under award number 5932; and the SDAIA-KAUST Center of Excellence in Data Science and Artificial Intelligence (SDAIA-KAUST AI).

References

[1] Aristotle. Complete Works of Aristotle, Volume 1: The Revised Oxford Translation. Barnes J, editor. Princeton University Press; 2014. Available from: http://dx.doi.org/10.2307/j.ctt5vjv4w.

[2] Galen. In: Singer PN, editor. That the Best Physician is Also a Philosopher. World's Classics S.. Oxford, England: Oxford University Press; 1997. .

[3] Tibi S. Al-Razi and Islamic Medicine in the 9th Century. Journal of the Royal Society of Medicine. 2006 Apr;99(4):206–207. Available from: http://dx.doi.org/10.1177/014107680609900425.

[4] Feigenbaum EA, Buchanan BG, Lederberg J. Applications of artificial intelligence for chemical inference. I. The DENDRAL project. Journal of the American Chemical Society. 1971;94(20):6821-30.

[5] Shortliffe EH, Davis R, Axline SG, Buchanan BG, Green CC, Cohen SN. MYCIN–A Knowledge-Based Computer Program Applied to Infectious Diseases. Proceedings of the 1974 ACM Annual Conference. 1974:306-20.

[6] Rector AL, Nowlan WA, Consortium G. The GALEN project. Computer Methods and Programs in Biomedicine. 1994 Oct;45(1–2):75–78. Available from: http://dx.doi.org/10.1016/0169-2607(94)90020-5.

[7] Rector AL, Rogers JE, Pole P. The GALEN High Level Ontology. In: Brender J, Christensen JP, Scherrer JR, McNair P, editors. Studies in Health Technology and Informatics. vol. Volume 34: Medical Informatics Europe '96. Amsterdam, The Netherlands: IOS Press; 1996. p. 174 178.

[8] Fensel D, van Harmelen F, Horrocks I, McGuinness DL, Patel-Schneider PF. OIL: an ontology infrastructure for the Semantic Web. IEEE Intelligent Systems. 2001 Mar;16(2):38–45. Available from: http://dx.doi.org/10.1109/5254.920598.

[9] Horrocks I. Using an Expressive Description Logic: FaCT or Fiction? In: International Conference on Principles of Knowledge Representation and Reasoning; 1998. p. 636-45. Available from: https://api.semanticscholar.org/CorpusID:16798388.

[10] Dentler K, Cornet R, ten Teije A, de Keizer N. Comparison of reasoners for large ontologies in the OWL 2 EL profile. Semant Web. 2011 apr;2(2):71–87.

[11] Lippi M, Frasconi P. Prediction of protein β-residue contacts by Markov logic networks with grounding-specific weights. Bioinformatics. 2009 Jul;25(18):2326–2333. Available from: http://dx.doi.org/10.1093/bioinformatics/btp421.

[12] Dai HJ, Chang YC, Tsai RTH, Hsu WL. Integration of gene normalization stages and co-reference resolution using a Markov logic network. Bioinformatics. 2011 Jun;27(18):2586–2594. Available from: http://dx.doi.org/10.1093/bioinformatics/btr358.

[13] Mørk S, Holmes I. Evaluating bacterial gene-finding HMM structures as probabilistic logic programs. Bioinformatics. 2012 Jan;28(5):636–642. Available from: http://dx.doi.org/10.1093/bioinformatics/btr698.

[14] Merrell D, Gitter A. Inferring signaling pathways with probabilistic programming. Bioinformatics. 2020 Dec;36(Supplement_2):i822–i830. Available from: http://dx.doi.org/10.1093/bioinformatics/btaa861.

[15] King RD, Whelan KE, Jones FM, Reiser PGK, Bryant CH, Muggleton SH, et al. Functional genomic hypothesis generation and experimentation by a robot scientist. Nature. 2004 Jan;427(6971):247–252. Available from: http://dx.doi.org/10.1038/nature02236.

[16] Mohamed SK, Nounu A, Nováček V. Biological applications of knowledge graph embedding models. Briefings in Bioinformatics. 2020 Feb;22(2):1679–1693. Available from: http://dx.doi.org/10.1093/bib/bbaa012.

[17] Chen J, Mashkova O, Zhapa-Camacho F, Hoehndorf R, He Y, Horrocks I. Ontology Embedding: A Survey of Methods, Applications and Resources; 2024. Available from: https://arxiv.org/abs/2406.10964.

[18] Gruber TR. Toward principles for the design of ontologies used for knowledge sharing? International Journal of Human-Computer Studies. 1995 Nov;43(5–6):907–928. Available from: http://dx.doi.org/10.1006/ijhc.1995.1081.

[19] Ashburner M, Ball CA, Blake JA, Botstein D, Butler H, Cherry JM, et al. Gene Ontology: tool for the unification of biology. Nature Genetics. 2000 May;25(1):25–29. Available from: http://dx.doi.org/10.1038/75556.

[20] Salvadores M, Alexander PR, Musen MA, Noy NF. BioPortal as a dataset of linked biomedical ontologies and terminologies in RDF. Semantic Web. 2013;4(3):277–284. Available from: http://dx.doi.org/10.3233/SW-2012-0086.

[21] Smith B, Ashburner M, Rosse C, Bard J, Bug W, Ceusters W, et al. The OBO Foundry: coordinated evolution of ontologies to support biomedical data integration. Nature Biotechnology. 2007 Nov;25(11):1251–1255. Available from: http://dx.doi.org/10.1038/nbt1346.

[22] Smith B, Ceusters W, Klagges B, Köhler J, Kumar A, Lomax J, et al. Relations in biomedical ontologies. Genome Biology. 2005;6(5):R46. Available from: http://dx.doi.org/10.1186/gb-2005-6-5-r46.

[23] Hayamizu TF, Baldock RA, Ringwald M. Mouse anatomy ontologies: enhancements and tools for exploring and integrating biomedical data. Mammalian Genome. 2015 Jul;26(9–10):422–430. Available from: http://dx.doi.org/10.1007/s00335-015-9584-9.

[24] Hastings J, de Matos P, Dekker A, Ennis M, Harsha B, Kale N, et al. The ChEBI reference database and ontology for biologically relevant chemistry: enhancements for 2013. Nucleic Acids Research. 2012 Nov;41(D1):D456–D463. Available from: http://dx.doi.org/10.1093/nar/gks1146.

[25] Gkoutos GV, Schofield PN, Hoehndorf R. The anatomy of phenotype ontologies: principles, properties and applications. Briefings in Bioinformatics. 2017 Apr;19(5):1008–1021. Available from: http://dx.doi.org/10.1093/bib/bbx035.

[26] Mungall CJ, Torniai C, Gkoutos GV, Lewis SE, Haendel MA. Uberon, an integrative multi-species anatomy ontology. Genome Biology. 2012;13(1):R5. Available from: http://dx.doi.org/10.1186/gb-2012-13-1-r5.

[27] Shefchek KA, Harris NL, Gargano M, Matentzoglu N, Unni D, Brush M, et al. The Monarch Initiative in 2019: an integrative data and analytic platform connecting phenotypes to genotypes across species. Nucleic Acids Research. 2019 Nov;48(D1):D704–D715. Available from: http://dx.doi.org/10.1093/nar/gkz997.

[28] Hoehndorf R, Schofield PN, Gkoutos GV. The role of ontologies in biological and biomedical research: a functional perspective. Briefings in Bioinformatics. 2015 Apr;16(6):1069–1080. Available from: http://dx.doi.org/10.1093/bib/bbv011.

[29] Baader F, Calvanese D, McGuinness DL, Nardi D, Patel-Schneider PF, editors. The Description Logic Handbook: Theory, Implementation and Applications. Cambridge, UK: Cambridge University Press; 2007. Available from: http://dx.doi.org/10.1017/CBO9780511711787.

[30] Badreddine S, d'Avila Garcez A, Serafini L, Spranger M. Logic Tensor Networks. Artificial Intelligence. 2022 Feb;303:103649. Available from: http://dx.doi.org/10.1016/j.artint.2021.103649.

[31] van Krieken E, Acar E, van Harmelen F. Analyzing Differentiable Fuzzy Logic Operators. Artificial Intelligence. 2022 Jan;302:103602. Available from: http://dx.doi.org/10.1016/j.artint.2021.103602.

[32] Yang Z, Ishay A, Lee J. NeurASP: Embracing Neural Networks into Answer Set Programming. In: Proceedings of the Twenty-Ninth International Joint Conference on Artificial Intelligence. IJCAI-PRICAI-2020. International Joint Conferences on Artificial Intelligence Organization; 2020. p. 1755-62. Available from: http://dx.doi.org/10.24963/ijcai.2020/243.

[33] Hill DP, Smith B, McAndrews-Hill MS, Blake JA. Gene Ontology annotations: what they mean and where they come from. BMC Bioinformatics. 2008 Apr;9(S5). Available from: http://dx.doi.org/10.1186/1471-2105-9-S5-S2.

[34] Natale DA, Arighi CN, Blake JA, Bult CJ, Christie KR, Cowart J, et al. Protein Ontology: a controlled structured network of protein entities. Nucleic Acids Research. 2013 Nov;42(D1):D415–D421. Available from: http://dx.doi.org/10.1093/nar/gkt1173.

[35] Bateman A, Martin MJ, Orchard S, Magrane M, Ahmad S, Alpi E, et al. UniProt: the Universal Protein Knowledgebase in 2023. Nucleic Acids Research. 2022 Nov;51(D1):D523–D531. Available from: http://dx.doi.org/10.1093/nar/gkac1052.

[36] Piñero J, Saüch J, Sanz F, Furlong LI. The DisGeNET cytoscape app: Exploring and visualizing disease genomics data. Computational and Structural Biotechnology Journal. 2021;19:2960–2967. Available from: http://dx.doi.org/10.1016/j.csbj.2021.05.015.

[37] Szklarczyk D, Kirsch R, Koutrouli M, Nastou K, Mehryary F, Hachilif R, et al. The STRING database in 2023: protein–protein association networks and functional enrichment analyses for any sequenced genome of interest. Nucleic Acids Research. 2022 Nov;51(D1):D638–D646. Available from: http://dx.doi.org/10.1093/nar/gkac1000.

[38] Szklarczyk D, Santos A, von Mering C, Jensen LJ, Bork P, Kuhn M. STITCH 5: augmenting protein–chemical interaction networks with tissue and affinity data. Nucleic Acids Research. 2015 Nov;44(D1):D380–D384. Available from: http://dx.doi.org/10.1093/nar/gkv1277.

[39] Putman TE, Schaper K, Matentzoglu N, Rubinetti V, Alquaddoomi F, Cox C, et al. The Monarch Initiative in 2024: an analytic platform integrating phenotypes, genes and diseases across species. Nucleic Acids Research. 2023 Nov;52(D1):D938–D949. Available from: http://dx.doi.org/10.1093/nar/gkad1082.

[40] Himmelstein DS, Lizee A, Hessler C, Brueggeman L, Chen SL, Hadley D, et al. Systematic integration of biomedical knowledge prioritizes drugs for repurposing. eLife. 2017 Sep;6. Available from: http://dx.doi.org/10.7554/eLife.26726.

[41] Callahan TJ, Tripodi IJ, Stefanski AL, Cappelletti L, Taneja SB, Wyrwa JM, et al. An open source knowledge graph ecosystem for the life sciences. Scientific Data. 2024 Apr;11(1). Available from: http://dx.doi.org/10.1038/s41597-024-03171-w.

[42] Kawashima S, Katayama T, Hatanaka H, Kushida T, Takagi T. NBDC RDF portal: a comprehensive repository for semantic data in life sciences. Database. 2018 Jan;2018. Available from: http://dx.doi.org/10.1093/database/bay123.

[43] Lambrix P, Habbouche M, Pérez M. Evaluation of ontology development tools for bioinformatics. Bioinformatics. 2003 Aug;19(12):1564–1571. Available from: http://dx.doi.org/10.1093/bioinformatics/btg194.

[44] Bechhofer S, Horrocks I, Goble C, Stevens R. In: OilEd: A Reason-able Ontology Editor for the Semantic Web. Springer Berlin Heidelberg; 2001. p. 396–408. Available from: http://dx.doi.org/10.1007/3-540-45422-5_28.

[45] Day-Richter J, Harris MA, Haendel M, Lewis S. OBO-Edit—an ontology editor for biologists. Bioinformatics. 2007 Jun;23(16):2198–2200. Available from: http://dx.doi.org/10.1093/bioinformatics/btm112.

[46] Tirmizi S, Aitken S, Moreira DA, Mungall C, Sequeda J, Shah NH, et al. Mapping between the OBO and OWL ontology languages. Journal of Biomedical Semantics. 2011;2(Suppl 1):S3. Available from: http://dx.doi.org/10.1186/2041-1480-2-S1-S3.

[47] Hoehndorf R, Oellrich A, Dumontier M, Kelso J, Rebholz-Schuhmann D, Herre H. Relations as patterns: bridging the gap between OBO and OWL. BMC Bioinformatics. 2010 Aug;11(1). Available from: http://dx.doi.org/10.1186/1471-2105-11-441.

[48] Chen J, Hu P, Jimenez-Ruiz E, Holter OM, Antonyrajah D, Horrocks I. OWL2Vec*: embedding of OWL ontologies. Machine Learning. 2021 Jun. Available from: http://dx.doi.org/10.1007/s10994-021-05997-6.

[49] Caufield JH, Putman T, Schaper K, Unni DR, Hegde H, Callahan TJ, et al. KG-Hub—building and exchanging biological knowledge graphs. Bioinformatics. 2023 Jun;39(7). Available from: http://dx.doi.org/10.1093/bioinformatics/btad418.

[50] Tirmizi S, Aitken S, Moreira DA, Mungall C, Sequeda J, Shah NH, et al. Mapping between the OBO and OWL ontology languages. Journal of Biomedical Semantics. 2011;2(Suppl 1):S3. Available from: http://dx.doi.org/10.1186/2041-1480-2-S1-S3.

[51] Zhapa-Camacho F, Hoehndorf R. From axioms over graphs to vectors, and back again: evaluating the properties of graph-based ontology embeddings; 2023. Available from: https://arxiv.org/abs/2303.16519.

[52] Huntley RP, Lovering RC. In: Annotation Extensions. Springer New York; 2016. p. 233–243. Available from: http://dx.doi.org/10.1007/978-1-4939-3743-1_17.

[53] Ceusters W, Elkin P, Smith B. Negative findings in electronic health records and biomedical ontologies: A realist approach. International Journal of Medical Informatics. 2007 Dec;76:S326–S333. Available from: http://dx.doi.org/10.1016/j.ijmedinf.2007.02.003.

[54] Santana da Silva F, Jansen L, Freitas F, Schulz S. Ontological interpretation of biomedical database content. Journal of Biomedical Semantics. 2017 Jun;8(1). Available from: http://dx.doi.org/10.1186/s13326-017-0127-z.

[55] SPARQL 1.1 Query Language. W3C; 2013. Available from: http://www.w3.org/TR/sparql11-query.

[56] Kawashima S, Katayama T, Hatanaka H, Kushida T, Takagi T. NBDC RDF portal: a comprehensive repository for semantic data in life sciences. Database. 2018 Jan;2018. Available from: http://dx.doi.org/10.1093/database/bay123.

[57] Jupp S, Malone J, Bolleman J, Brandizi M, Davies M, Garcia L, et al. The EBI RDF platform: linked open data for the life sciences. Bioinformatics. 2014 Jan;30(9):1338–1339. Available from: http://dx.doi.org/10.1093/bioinformatics/btt765.

[58] Hoehndorf R, Slater L, Schofield PN, Gkoutos GV. Aber-OWL: a framework for ontology-based data access in biology. BMC Bioinformatics. 2015 Jan;16(1). Available from: http://dx.doi.org/10.1186/s12859-015-0456-9.

[59] Campillos M, Kuhn M, Gavin AC, Jensen LJ, Bork P. Drug Target Identification Using Side-Effect Similarity. Science. 2008 Jul;321(5886):263–266. Available from: http://dx.doi.org/10.1126/science.1158140.

[60] Gurovich Y, Hanani Y, Bar O, Nadav G, Fleischer N, Gelbman D, et al. Identifying facial phenotypes of genetic disorders using deep learning. Nature Medicine. 2019 Jan;25(1):60–64. Available from: http://dx.doi.org/10.1038/s41591-018-0279-0.

[61] Mashkova O, Zhapa-Camacho F, Hoehndorf R. Enhancing Geometric Ontology Embeddings for $\mathscr{EL}^{++}$ with Negative Sampling and Deductive Closure Filtering; 2024. Available from: https://arxiv.org/abs/2405.04868.

[62] Gillis J, Pavlidis P. "Guilt by Association" Is the Exception Rather Than the Rule in Gene Networks. PLoS Computational Biology. 2012 Mar;8(3):e1002444. Available from: http://dx.doi.org/10.1371/journal.pcbi.1002444.

[63] Köhler S, Bauer S, Horn D, Robinson PN. Walking the Interactome for Prioritization of Candidate Disease Genes. The American Journal of Human Genetics. 2008 Apr;82(4):949–958. Available from: http://dx.doi.org/10.1016/j.ajhg.2008.02.013.

[64] Smaili FZ, Gao X, Hoehndorf R. OPA2Vec: combining formal and informal content of biomedical ontologies to improve similarity-based prediction. Bioinformatics. 2019 Jun;35(12):2133–2140.

[65] Smaili FZ, Gao X, Hoehndorf R. Onto2Vec: joint vector-based representation of biological entities and their ontology-based annotations. Bioinformatics. 2018 Jul;34(13):i52–i60.

[66] Pesquita C, Faria D, Bastos H, Ferreira AE, Falcão AO, Couto FM. Metrics for GO based protein semantic similarity: a systematic evaluation. In: BMC bioinformatics. vol. 9. Springer; 2008. p. 1-16.

[67] Rodríguez-García MA, Hoehndorf R. Inferring ontology graph structures using OWL reasoning. BMC Bioinformatics. 2018 Jan;19(1). Available from: http://dx.doi.org/10.1186/s12859-017-1999-8.

[68] Chen J, Hu P, Jimenez-Ruiz E, Holter OM, Antonyrajah D, Horrocks I. OWL2Vec*: embedding of OWL ontologies. Machine Learning. 2021 Jul;110(7):1813–1845.

[69] Bordes A, Usunier N, Garcia-Durán A, Weston J, Yakhnenko O. Translating embeddings for modeling multi-relational data. In: Proceedings of the 26th International Conference on Neural Information Processing Systems - Volume 2. NIPS'13. Red Hook, NY, USA: Curran Associates Inc.; 2013. p. 2787–2795.

[70] Sun Z, Deng ZH, Nie JY, Tang J. RotatE: Knowledge Graph Embedding by Relational Rotation in Complex Space. CoRR. 2019;abs/1902.10197. Available from: http://dblp.uni-trier.de/db/journals/corr/corr1902.html#abs-1902-10197.

[71] Wang Q, Mao Z, Wang B, Guo L. Knowledge Graph Embedding: A Survey of Approaches and Applications. IEEE Transactions on Knowledge and Data Engineering. 2017;29(12):2724-43.

[72] Ristoski P, Paulheim H. RDF2Vec: RDF Graph Embeddings for Data Mining. In: Groth P, Simperl E, Gray A, Sabou M, Krötzsch M, Lecue F, et al., editors. The Semantic Web – ISWC 2016. Cham: Springer International Publishing; 2016. p. 498–514.

[73] Mikolov T, Sutskever I, Chen K, Corrado GS, Dean J. Distributed Representations of Words and Phrases and their Compositionality. In: Advances in Neural Information Processing Systems. vol. 26. Curran Associates, Inc.; 2013. p. 3111-9. Available from: https://proceedings.neurips.cc/paper/2013/hash/9aa42b31882ec039965f3c4923ce901b-Abstract.html.

[74] Chen J, Althagafi A, Hoehndorf R. Predicting candidate genes from phenotypes, functions and anatomical site of expression. Bioinformatics. 2021;37(6):853-60.

[75] Kulmanov M, Liu-Wei W, Yan Y, Hoehndorf R. EL Embeddings: Geometric Construction of Models for the Description Logic EL++. In: Proceedings of the Twenty-Eighth International Joint Conference on Artificial Intelligence, IJCAI-19. International Joint Conferences on Artificial Intelligence Organization; 2019. p. 6103-9. Available from: https://doi.org/10.24963/ijcai.2019/845.

[76] Jackermeier M, Chen J, Horrocks I. Dual Box Embeddings for the Description Logic EL++. In: Proceedings of the ACM on Web Conference 2024. WWW '24. ACM; 2024. p. 2250 2258. Available from: http://dx.doi.org/10.1145/3589334.3645648.

[77] Kulmanov M, Smaili FZ, Gao X, Hoehndorf R. Semantic similarity and machine learning with ontologies. Briefings in Bioinformatics. 2021 Jul;22(44):bbaa199.

[78] Harispe S, Ranwez S, Janaqi S, Montmain J. Semantic Similarity from Natural Language and Ontology Analysis. Synthesis Lectures on Human Language Technologies. 2015 May;8(1):1–254. Available from: http://dx.doi.org/10.2200/S00639ED1V01Y201504HLT027.

[79] Lord PW, Stevens RD, Brass A, Goble CA. Investigating semantic similarity measures across the Gene Ontology: the relationship between sequence and annotation. Bioinformatics. 2003 Jul;19(10):1275–1283. Available from: http://dx.doi.org/10.1093/bioinformatics/btg153.

[80] Schlicker A, Domingues FS, Rahnenführer J, Lengauer T. A new measure for functional similarity of gene products based on Gene Ontology. BMC Bioinformatics. 2006 Jun;7(1). Available from: http://dx.doi.org/10.1186/1471-2105-7-302.

[81] Zhang W, Paudel B, Wang L, Chen J, Zhu H, Zhang W, et al. Iteratively Learning Embeddings and Rules for Knowledge Graph Reasoning. In: The World Wide Web Conference. WWW '19. ACM; 2019. p. 2366 2377. Available from: http://dx.doi.org/10.1145/3308558.3313612.

[82] Kulmanov M, Khan MA, Hoehndorf R. DeepGO: predicting protein functions from sequence and interactions using a deep ontology-aware classifier. Bioinformatics. 2017 Oct;34(4):660–668. Available from: http://dx.doi.org/10.1093/bioinformatics/btx624.

[83] Zhang N, Bi Z, Liang X, Cheng S, Hong H, Deng S, et al. OntoProtein: Protein Pretraining With Gene Ontology Embedding. In: International Conference on Learning Representations; 2022. Available from: https://openreview.net/forum?id=yfe1VMYAXa4.

[84] Zhou HY, Fu Y, Zhang Z, Cheng B, Yu Y. Protein Representation Learning via Knowledge Enhanced Primary Structure Reasoning. In: The Eleventh International Conference on Learning Representations; 2023. Available from: https://openreview.net/forum?id=VbCMhg7MRmj.

[85] Thafar MA, Olayan RS, Ashoor H, Albaradei S, Bajic VB, Gao X, et al. DTiGEMS+: drug–target interaction prediction using graph embedding, graph mining, and similarity-based techniques. Journal of Cheminformatics. 2020 Jun;12(1). Available from: http://dx.doi.org/10.1186/s13321-020-00447-2.

[86] Hinnerichs T, Hoehndorf R. DTI-Voodoo: machine learning over interaction networks and ontology-based background knowledge predicts drug–target interactions. Bioinformatics. 2021 Jul;37(24):4835–4843. Available from: http://dx.doi.org/10.1093/bioinformatics/btab548.

[87] Schlichtkrull M, Kipf TN, Bloem P, van den Berg R, Titov I, Welling M. In: Modeling Relational Data with Graph Convolutional Networks. Springer International Publishing; 2018. p. 593–607. Available from: http://dx.doi.org/10.1007/978-3-319-93417-4_38.

[88] Lam HT, Sbodio ML, Galindo MM, Zayats M, Fernández-Díaz R, Valls V, et al.. Otter-Knowledge: benchmarks of multimodal knowledge graph representation learning from different sources for drug discovery; 2023. Available from: https://arxiv.org/abs/2306.12802.

[89] Fang Y, Zhang Q, Zhang N, Chen Z, Zhuang X, Shao X, et al. Knowledge graph-enhanced molecular contrastive learning with functional prompt. Nature Machine Intelligence. 2023 May;5(5):542–553. Available from: http://dx.doi.org/10.1038/s42256-023-00654-0.

[90] Glauer M, Mossakowski T, Neuhaus F, Memariani A, Hastings J. Neuro-Symbolic Semantic Learning for Chemistry. In: Hitzler P, Sarker MK, Eberhart A, editors. Compendium of Neurosymbolic Artificial Intelligence. vol. 369 of Frontiers in Artificial Intelligence and Applications. IOS Press; 2023. p. 460-84. Available from: https://doi.org/10.3233/FAIA230153.

[91] Hastings J, Owen G, Dekker A, Ennis M, Kale N, Muthukrishnan V, et al. ChEBI in 2016: Improved services and an expanding collection of metabolites. Nucleic Acids Research. 2015 Oct;44(D1):D1214–D1219. Available from: http://dx.doi.org/10.1093/nar/gkv1031.

[92] Flügel S, Glauer M, Mossakowski T, Neuhaus F. A semantic loss for ontology classification; 2024. Available from: https://arxiv.org/abs/2405.02083.

[93] Xu J, Zhang Z, Friedman T, Liang Y, Van den Broeck G. A Semantic Loss Function for Deep Learning with Symbolic Knowledge. In: Dy J, Krause A, editors. Proceedings of the 35th International Conference on Machine Learning. vol. 80 of Proceedings of Machine Learning Research. PMLR; 2018. p. 5502-11. Available from: https://proceedings.mlr.press/v80/xu18h.html.

[94] Kulmanov M, Hoehndorf R. DeepGOZero: improving protein function prediction from sequence and zero-shot learning based on ontology axioms. Bioinformatics. 2022 Jun;38(Supplement 1):i238–i245. Available from: http://dx.doi.org/10.1093/bioinformatics/btac256.

[95] Kulmanov M, Guzmán-Vega FJ, Duek Roggli P, Lane L, Arold ST, Hoehndorf R. Protein function prediction as approximate semantic entailment. Nature Machine Intelligence. 2024 Feb;6(2):220–228. Available from: http://dx.doi.org/10.1038/s42256-024-00795-w.

[96] Middleton L, Melas I, Vasavda C, Raies A, Rozemberczki B, Dhindsa RS, et al. Phenome-wide identification of therapeutic genetic targets, leveraging knowledge graphs, graph neural networks, and UK Biobank data. Science Advances. 2024 May;10(19). Available from: http://dx.doi.org/10.1126/sciadv.adj1424.

[97] Amberger JS, Bocchini CA, Schiettecatte F, Scott AF, Hamosh A. OMIM.org: Online Mendelian Inheritance in Man (OMIM®), an online catalog of human genes and genetic disorders. Nucleic Acids Research. 2014 Nov;43(D1):D789–D798. Available from: http://dx.doi.org/10.1093/nar/gku1205.

[98] Hoehndorf R, Schofield PN, Gkoutos GV. PhenomeNET: a whole-phenome approach to disease gene discovery. Nucleic Acids Research. 2011 Jul;39(18):e119–e119. Available from: http://dx.doi.org/10.1093/nar/gkr538.

[99] Chen CK, Mungall CJ, Gkoutos GV, Doelken SC, Köhler S, Ruef BJ, et al. MouseFinder: Candidate disease genes from mouse phenotype data. Human Mutation. 2012 Mar;33(5):858–866. Available from: http://dx.doi.org/10.1002/humu.22051.

[100] Smedley D, Jacobsen JOB, Jäger M, Köhler S, Holtgrewe M, Schubach M, et al. Next-generation diagnostics and disease-gene discovery with the Exomiser. Nature Protocols. 2015 Nov;10(12):2004–2015. Available from: http://dx.doi.org/10.1038/nprot.2015.124.

[101] The 100,000 Genomes Project Pilot Investigators. 100,000 Genomes Pilot on Rare-Disease Diagnosis in Health Care — Preliminary Report. New England Journal of Medicine. 2021 Nov;385(20):1868–1880. Available from: http://dx.doi.org/10.1056/NEJMoa2035790.

[102] Resnik P. Semantic classes and syntactic ambiguity. In: Proceedings of the Workshop on Human Language Technology. HLT '93. USA: Association for Computational Linguistics; 1993. p. 278–283. Available from: https://doi.org/10.3115/1075671.1075733.

[103] Resnik P. Using information content to evaluate semantic similarity in a taxonomy. In: Proceedings of the 14th International Joint Conference on Artificial Intelligence - Volume 1. IJCAI'95. San Francisco, CA, USA: Morgan Kaufmann Publishers Inc.; 1995. p. 448–453.

[104] Alghamdi SM, Schofield PN, Hoehndorf R. Contribution of model organism phenotypes to the computational identification of human disease genes. Disease Models & Mechanisms. 2022 Jul;15(7). Available from: http://dx.doi.org/10.1242/dmm.049441.

[105] Kitano H. Nobel Turing Challenge: creating the engine for scientific discovery. npj Systems Biology and Applications. 2021 Jun;7(1). Available from: http://dx.doi.org/10.1038/s41540-021-00189-3.

[106] Leeuwenberg AM, Schuit E. Prediction models for COVID-19 clinical decision making. The Lancet Digital Health. 2020 Oct;2(10):e496–e497. Available from: http://dx.doi.org/10.1016/S2589-7500(20)30226-0.

[107] Durán JM. Dissecting scientific explanation in AI (sXAI): A case for medicine and healthcare. Artificial Intelligence. 2021 Aug;297:103498. Available from: http://dx.doi.org/10.1016/j.artint.2021.103498.

[108] Sousa RT, Silva S, Pesquita C. Explainable Representations for Relation Prediction in Knowledge Graphs. In: Proceedings of the Twentieth International Conference on Principles of Knowledge Representation and Reasoning. KR-2023. International Joint Conferences on Artificial Intelligence Organization; 2023. p. 635 646. Available from: http://dx.doi.org/10.24963/kr.2023/62.

[109] Sousa RT, Silva S, Pesquita C. Explaining protein–protein interactions with knowledge graph-based semantic similarity. Computers in Biology and Medicine. 2024 Mar;170:108076. Available from: http://dx.doi.org/10.1016/j.compbiomed.2024.108076.

Handbook on Neurosymbolic AI and Knowledge Graphs
P. Hitzler et al. (Eds.)
IOS Press, 2025

doi:10.3233/FAIA250240

Enriching Large Language Models with Knowledge Graphs for Computational Literary Studies

Thora HAGEN [*,1], Janna OMELIYANENKO [*], Anton EHRMANNTRAUT, Andreas HOTHO, Albin ZEHE and Fotis JANNIDIS

Center for Artificial Intelligence and Data Science (CAIDAS), Julius-Maximilians-Universität Würzburg

ORCiD ID: Thora Hagen https://orcid.org/0000-0002-3731-6397, Janna Omeliyanenko https://orcid.org/0009-0006-2159-9413, Anton Ehrmanntraut https://orcid.org/0000-0001-6677-586X, Andreas Hotho https://orcid.org/0000-0002-0483-5772, Albin Zehe https://orcid.org/0000-0002-9472-0783, Fotis Jannidis https://orcid.org/0000-0001-6944-6113

Abstract. In this chapter, we explore the integration of knowledge graphs into large language models (LLMs) to enhance computational literary studies, a key subfield of computational humanities. Computational humanities have evolved significantly over the past decades, driven by the increasing digitization of cultural heritage data, advancements in computing power, and the development of advanced analytical methods. This digitization progress has particularly enabled the creation of knowledge graphs that capture the semantic relationships embedded in humanities data, including texts. These graphs represent structured knowledge that can enrich LLMs, enabling them to generate semantically rich representations even in domains with limited computational resources. We explore how integrating knowledge graphs can enhance natural language processing (NLP) applications, specifically for the analysis of literary texts. To benefit the humanities and support the integration of KGs with LLMs for computational humanities, we discuss the specific content new KGs should ideally encompass. This necessitates a broader conceptualization of knowledge graphs, and supplies novel challenges for the field of knowledge graph creation, including for example diachronic concept alignment. Alongside this new perspective, we also propose the automatic creation of knowledge graphs from literary texts, such as graph-based plot representation, to allow for graph-based text analyses but also, again, create literary-informed LLMs through the integration of such graphs. By demonstrating these techniques through the lens of computational literary studies, we illustrate the significant impact that knowledge graphs can have on enriching LLMs and advancing the humanities.

Keywords. knowledge graphs, natural language processing, computational humanities, computational literary studies

[*] Equal Contribution.
[1] Corresponding Author: Thora Hagen, `thora.hagen@uni-wuerzburg.de`.

1. Introduction

Since the availability of computers there has been research focusing on cultural heritage data: novels and other texts, paintings and other images, music and other audio data, feature films and other movies, excavation sites and other 3-dimensional objects. Though the digital humanities exist now for more than 60 years, only in the last 10–15 years enough material was digitized, enough computing power was available to process it, and methods sophisticated enough to analyze it had been developed. This confluence was the basis for a new sub-field: computational humanities (CH) [1]. CH are challenging because the humanities encompass numerous different disciplines that specialize in very different times and cultures. In each of these disciplines, cultural artifacts cannot be adequately studied without the relevant linguistic and cultural knowledge. A considerable amount of this knowledge has long been processed in dictionaries, lexicons, encyclopedias and other reference works. The comparatively small amount of surviving material further exacerbates the problem. In this situation, the possibility of significantly improving very modern research tools such as language models by means of knowledge graphs, into which dictionaries etc. have been transferred, represents an important opportunity to create semantically rich representations even for areas in which the prerequisites for modern computational access are not actually given.

In this chapter, we will use the example of computational literary studies, a sub-field of computational humanities, to show how these techniques are applied. In the first section we will clarify the notion of knowledge graphs and discuss what the term knowledge graphs means in the context of humanities data and the historical encyclopedia we study and use. In the second section, we will examine different ways of modeling texts as graphs, such as character networks, feature-based text similarity graphs, and plot structures. We argue that this kind of text modeling provides a novel perspective on literary text analysis, while also bearing the potential for language model integration. In the third section, we will review how knowledge graphs may be used in tandem with large language models. On the one hand, knowledge graphs can function as a resource to aid in language modeling. On the other hand, language models can also be employed for knowledge graph completion. Both techniques combined may for example aid in knowledge transfer from parameter-heavy LLMs to other models.

2. Knowledge Graphs in the Humanities

2.1. Definition

Definitions of what the term “knowledge graph” (KG) entails vary, not only across but within areas of research as well. Generally speaking, knowledge graphs are directed graphs with labeled nodes and edges. These are usually encoded as sets of triples, where head, relation, and tail of each triple correspond to human knowledge (often also referred to subject, predicate, and object). The nodes of the graph are also often referred to as entities, however the interpretation of what the term "entity" entails can be different. As per Hogan et al. [2], "nodes represent entities of interest and [...] edges represent relations between these entities." The authors also add that a knowledge graph is "intended to accumulate and convey knowledge of the real world," meaning entities in a knowledge graphs are supposed to represent real world objects, and typically not concepts. As the term "knowledge graph" was first popularized by Google with the integration of multiple knowledge bases into their search engine ("things, not strings" [3]), it is predominantly understood that the knowledge contained in KGs corresponds to this kind of factual, real world knowledge (traditional definition, see e.g. [2,4,5,6]). However, another modernized definition of knowledge graphs has emerged over time, which strives to push the boundaries of KGs to also encompass any kind of human knowledge [7,8,9]. Knowledge graphs are accompanied by ontologies, which contain such formal constraints of the graph, for example which relations are allowed between which classes of entities. Crucial to any knowledge graph is also the disambiguation of subjects in the graph via unique identifiers, so that multiple subjects bearing the same name can be distinguished from each other. For machine readability, triples are typically represented in RDF format [10].

The definition provided by Hogan et al. [2] indicates that existing KGs and the methods associated with them in the computer science domain are still predominantly centered on real world objects. In the humanities, this practice is useful for museums, libraries, etc., where the main purpose of linked open data is to link cultural objects, however a broader approach is necessary to cover other aspects of the humanities as well. In this section, we explain why this modern approach to knowledge graphs is essential for creating new knowledge graphs tailored to the humanities. Across this chapter, we will highlight two specific approaches to knowledge graph creation which are based on our wider definition of the term: constructing a semantic network from encyclopedias to link concepts across time (Section 2.3), and generating graphs from text using a variety of inherent text characteristics (Section 3).

Broadly speaking, knowledge may be separated into the following two categories: factual knowledge (entity or world knowledge) and commonsense knowledge (e.g. agent-based knowledge or basic word meanings). Additionally, there is a domain-specific dimension to factual knowledge: some facts are general knowledge, such as *Berlin is the capital of Germany*, and other facts are native to a thematic domain, for example biomedical knowledge about drugs and diseases. Usually, language models capture human understanding through processing vast amounts of text. However, not all that humans know about the world is captured in this way, such as historical knowledge about people, concepts, customs, etc., that became less important or replaced over time. Knowledge graphs may be used to infuse additional knowledge into language models, as knowledge is expressed differently than through text (see Section 4, Adaptation). The humanities in particular have access to a multitude of semi-structured resources (*lexical-semantic resources* or *LSR*), such as dictionaries, encyclopedias, glossaries, which already convey knowledge in a similar fashion. These resources can further be refined into knowledge graphs.

Most experiments and benchmarks in NLP research concentrate on contemporary English. Here, research is often concerned with devising or refining methods, where input and evaluation data often play a secondary role. Because of that, KGs that are already available are often re-used across studies, because on the one hand it saves time and on the other hand, comparing methodological research becomes easier. Almost always, research concentrates on the KGs Wikidata (or subgraphs of it), ConceptNet, or WordNet (see Table 2 by Wei et al. [11] for an overview of data used). With that however, NLP sometimes overlooks historical varieties, other languages or textual specificities, all of which lie at the core of humanities research. But leveraging resources of cultural heritage, which are often available to humanities researchers, can be an important step to fill these knowledge gaps for computationally processing and analyzing texts from resource-poor domains. These gaps are most mainly 1) time-specific or historical knowledge 2) language specific knowledge (endangered languages, dialects) and, for CLS in particular, 3) text domain knowledge. The humanities therefore care about all three knowledge types mentioned above, specific examples including:

- historical representation of facts and common sense, as they may change over time
- comprehensive vocabulary and word meaning representation for low-resource languages
- domain specific text knowledge about, for example, fictional worlds

This is why LSR are of special importance: They provide a thorough and oftentimes historical snapshot of knowledge about a language (dictionaries) or topics and facts (encyclopedias), and they can potentially function as KGs in the computational humanities. However, this means that humanities researchers need to create their own KGs from these sources to adopt the methods devised in NLP.

Because of the traditional KG definition, KG creation often relies on standard methods centered around named entities (NE recognition, NE linking, see [12,13,14]). KG creation for the humanities implies a slight shift towards concepts rather than entities, which is just one challenge that the field poses. In the following, we will outline the two main challenges of KG creation for the humanities [15]:

- diachronic data diversity (historicity and semantic change)
- synchronic data diversity (interdisciplinary knowledge).

2.2. *Short Survey of Knowledge Graph Applications in the Humanities*

2.2.1. *From Structured Data to Knowledge Graphs*

The topic of linked open data (LOD) in the humanities has actually been a long standing tradition beyond the usage of knowledge graphs. Especially in libraries, museums and archives, LOD catalogs have been a staple technology stack for the last decades, along with controlled vocabularies (such as VIAF[2]) and metadata sets (e.g. Dublin Core [16]). The overarching goal of LOD in the humanities is to promote accessibility and interoperability across diverse cultural domains and sources.[3] In humanities scholarship, traditionally, much research in the area has therefore been concerned with creating controlled vocabularies, classification schemes, or establishing cross-domain links [17,18].

Knowledge graphs and linked open data have now emerged as a new way to study and analyse cultural artifacts on a larger scale beyond simply digitally publishing data in LOD form [19]. Prominent application examples from the humanities are: character networks [20], correspondence networks and geospatial analysis [21,22], linked document collections through external or internal features [23,24,25], and metadata networks in general [26,27].

These examples demonstrate that the origin of knowledge graphs in the humanities can be very different: They may be built upon pre-structured knowledge as provided

[2]`https://viaf.org/`
[3]`https://lod-cloud.net/`

by libraries for example, or they may be built from the ground up from the basis of unstructured text. When building a knowledge graph from text, it depends on the use case of the resulting knowledge graph what kind of creation or knowledge extraction methods can be applied. Named entities and artifact metadata are also a staple of the humanities, where many pre-existing extraction methods and ontologies (most notably CIDOC CRM [28]) can be reused. But the use cases extend beyond that, such as building semantic networks like WordNet (which was manually created) or identifying specific inter-textual dependencies. Building a graph from text, be it to connect concepts across multiple texts (Section 2.3) or to better understand and analyze whole texts or their relationship with each other (Section 3) is where the most challenges arise for the field of knowledge graph creation in the humanities. We will discuss these challenges as well as opportunities in Section 2.3 on the basis of EncycNet.[4]

2.2.2. Interplay with the Computational Humanities

Structured data can take on different functions in the workflow of the computational humanities. On the one hand, as we already alluded to and which we will further discuss in Section 4, we may use knowledge graphs to enhance our computational model. On the other hand, we want to argue that structured data can also benefit the collection of other data and also allow model evaluation. Concepts in the humanities are less clear cut – for example the definition of a genre, the boundaries of a lexical field, or word meaning – in comparison to the tasks and interests that NLP prioritizes. As such, the subject of study may be harder to define in terms of representative data, which makes data collection or the establishment of a ground truth difficult. The same applies to model evaluation, where the (often manual and time consuming) creation of appropriate original datasets, is an indispensable step in every workflow.

This is where previous work on controlled vocabularies, taxonomies, schemas, etc., by humanists can also be exceptionally useful to the computational humanities. Thus, speaking from a broader point of view, we argue that all kinds of newly developed structured knowledge that pertain to the humanities can be profitable for symbolic representation in AI, and not just KGs. For instance, concerning the data collection, in a separate project we turned to a manually curated, digital dictionary of keywords in order to extract the lexical field of *privacy*, to be able to analyze how the whole field has semantically changed over time [29]. Concerning the model evaluation, we also developed new datasets for evaluating lexical semantics in LMs by harvesting word relations from other LSR and linked data sources – the German dictionary *Duden* and German Wiktionary – to aid in evaluating German pre-trained language models and word embeddings [30].

2.3. EncycNet: A Case Study for Knowledge Graph Creation

2.3.1. Challenges of EncycNet Knowledge Graph Creation

EncycNet aims to construct a historical German knowledge graph from nineteenth-century encyclopedias by computational means. The project offers one of the first openly accessible linked semantic data resources specifically for historical German. It is one of multiple projects within humanities research that uses LSR to create linked data. Among

[4] `https://encycnet.github.io/`

Table 1. Overview of the conversational encyclopedias in the EncycNet corpus.

Editor	Year	Description	# Entries	# Tokens
Brockhaus	1809–1811	Conversational encyclopedia	6 960	1 186 000
Herloßsohn	1834–1838	*Damen Conversations Lexikon*, specifically aimed at women	7 099	1 461 000
Brockhaus	1837–1841	Illustrated conversational encyclopedia	7 049	2 604 000
Herder	1854–1857	Conversational encyclopedia	39 755	2 256 000
Meyer	1905–1909	Comprehensive conversational encyclopedia	156 264	17 437 000
Brockhaus	1911	Conversational encyclopedia, paperback edition	82 780	2 434 000

other projects are, for example, LiLa[5] and PURA[6], which both aim to create diachronic linguistic knowledge graphs from historical thesauri for Latin and Greek, respectively. In comparison, EncycNet is focused on word meaning and semantics rather than word formation and linguistics, which is due to the nature of encyclopedias compared to thesauri or dictionaries. Common relations in semantic graphs include synonym and antonym word pairs for example, similar to some of the edges that can be found in ConceptNet or WordNet. An impression of the contents of EncycNet can be found in Figure 1, and an overview of the encyclopedias used can be seen in Table 1.

All these projects, which facilitate digital access to LSR, emphasize the importance of these cultural resources for the computational humanities. This also includes projects that make LSR digitally accessible in the first place, such as the *Nineteenth-Century Knowledge Project*[7] indexing the entries of the *Encyclopedia Britannica*, and the corpus curation for EncycNet [31]. These examples show that, even though LSR are analogue knowledge bases, they bear great potential for KG transformation, partly already due to their semi-structured nature.

The KG creation process can be separated into three steps: 1) ontology creation, that is, devising a conceptual schema that guides the design of the KG, 2) concept identification, and 3) relation extraction. In the particular case of EncycNet, broadly speaking, the encyclopedia entries function as subjects in the graph, while literals from the entries' texts and other entries function as objects. Concept identification in EncycNet thus also consists of alignment and disambiguation across encyclopedias. The challenges mentioned influence all steps of the KG creation process.

2.3.2. *Diachronic Perspective: Historicity and Semantic Change*

Most of the data within the humanities are time-sensitive, as simply most of human society and culture lie in the past. As already mentioned, NLP is mostly concerned with contemporary data, not only because KGs are more readily available, but evaluation data as well. In EncycNet, historicity plays a challenging part for KG creation, firstly, because the historical nature adds to data heterogeneity, and secondly because the semantic change of word meanings makes concept definition more difficult.

The genre of the encyclopedia has undergone a significant amount of change over the last few centuries. While striving to be a source of unbiased information today, ency-

[5] `https://lila-erc.eu`

[6] `https://pric.unive.it/projects/pura/home`

[7] `https://tu-plogan.github.io/`

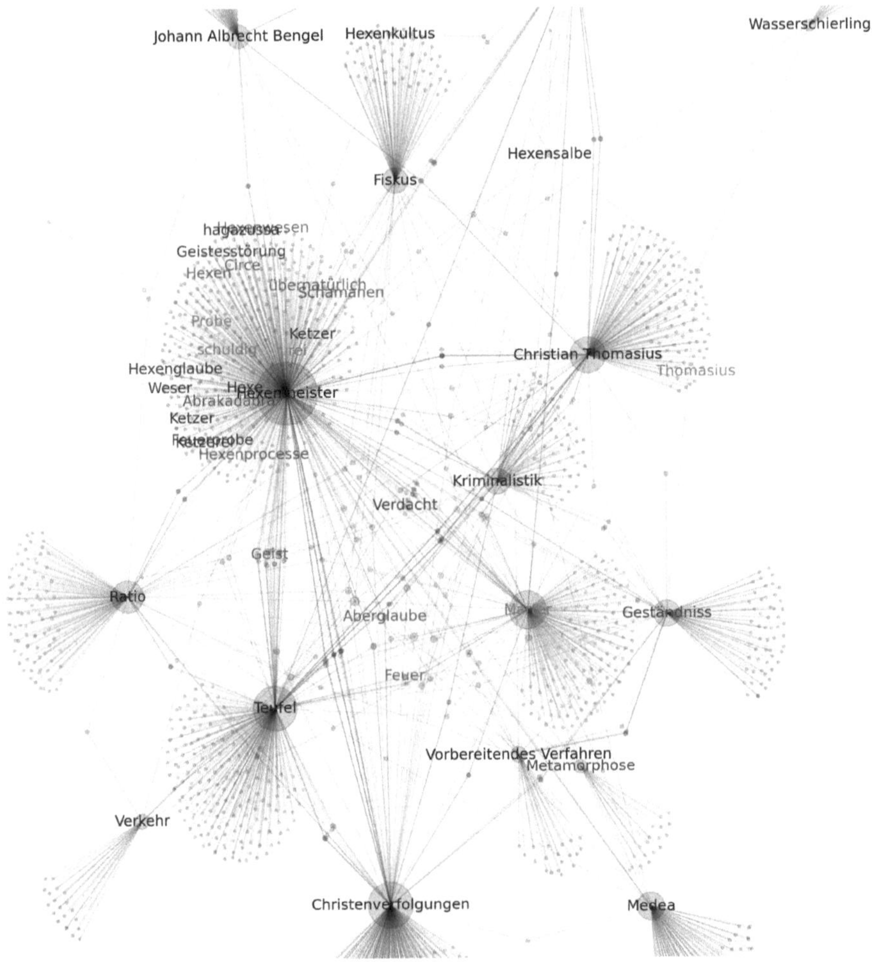

Figure 1. EncycNet subgraph representation of selected outgoing edges of central node *Hexe* (*witch*). Includes all neighbors of depth 1 and up to 30 more neighbors of depth 2 (for visibility purposes). Colors indicate different encyclopedias, i.e. where the edge or node was extracted from (green: Brockhaus 1837, red: Herder 1854, blue: Meyers 1905).

clopedias in the 19th century were highly diverse, even when discussing the same general concepts. This concerns the selection and organization of concepts, as well as the structure, scope, style and interpretation of individual concepts. Due to the fact that none of the encyclopedias can serve as an objective baseline, the alignment procedure would need to turn to another comprehensive and objective source. This is why in EncycNet, we chose to solve this step by aligning to Wikipedia/Wikidata as an intermediate step.

Entries of encyclopedias are made up of more than just named entities. This is why KG creation cannot turn to the method of entity linking in order to align concepts across sources. Rather, the procedure would need to adapt methods from word sense alignment (WSA) and word sense disambiguation (WSD) [32,33,34]. Here, three types can be distinguished: text-to-text, text-to-graph, and graph-to-graph. Therefore, alignment procedures are often either based on text or graph similarity measures. We modeled the alignment as a text-to-text similarity problem: concepts sharing the most similar definitions, given either by the entries gloss or the summary part of Wikipedia, would be aligned. We first selected candidates for alignment through Wikipedia's search function, targeting Wikipedia's disambiguation pages in particular. For our model, we performed continued training on TSDAE [35], a LM trained specifically to produce sentence or paragraph embeddings, using Wikipedia and encyclopedia entries to adapt to the text genre. We then generated gloss embeddings for each concept and its corresponding candidates with TSDAE. Using cosine distance, we aligned concepts with its most similar candidate. We manually annotated a balanced evaluation dataset of ambiguous entries in the encyclopedias with their ground truth Wikipedia pages, which then, for our automated retrieval, resulted in a quite high median number of candidates (10.5). We achieved an overall F1 of 0.66 on our testset, where we found that disambiguation is generally harder for named entities (0.47 for people, 0.58 for locations) than for abstract concepts (0.66) and objects (0.70) [36].

The concept alignment across multiple encyclopedias – spanning now two centuries when including Wikipedia – bears significant challenges. First, as concepts have undergone semantic change, it becomes difficult to assess whether a concept should actually be aligned with its counterpart from a different time period. Definitions could have become broader or narrower, now perhaps even merging two previously different concepts (sometimes resulting in archaic words) or splitting into two entirely. In the *witch* example from Figure 1 for instance, both *Hexenmeister* and *Hexe* were aligned to the same Wikidata entry, one being the male and one being the female version of a witch. It remains to be discussed how to asses concept boundaries and their shifts computationally, and where the semantic threshold for cross-temporal alignment lies.

Historical variation is additionally noticeable in terms of orthography. For instance, the contemporary word form *Freiheit* appears as historical orthographic variant *Freyheit*, similarly *Tier* vs. *Thier*, *Konzert* vs. *Concert*, etc. In EncycNet, we performed orthographic normalization using the rule-based tool CAB, developed and maintained by the DTA (*Deutsches Textarchiv*). In fact, orthographic text normalization remains an open problem. An evaluation on parallel data between historical literary texts (c. 1750–1900) and their normalized editions shows that even sequence-to-sequence Transformer-based normalizers still make about one error per one hundred words [37].[8] In fact, the impact of orthographic varieties on downstream NLP/CLS tasks is largely unknown, and further investigations in this area are required.

2.3.3. Synchronic Perspective: Cross-Domain Knowledge

The encyclopedias in the EncycNet corpus are so-called "conversational" encyclopedias (*Konversationslexika*), which means that they encompass any kind of knowledge. Consequently, facts, common sense and certain domain-specific aspects must be taken into account simultaneously when creating the KG, at least when following a holistic approach. To make such knowledge extraction feasible, generic classes of entries need to be identified as a first step. The classes of EncycNet consist of two types of entities (people, locations) and three types of concepts (objects, abstract concepts, fictional concepts), which were retrieved after the Wikidata alignment from Wikidata's taxonomy.

[8] https://github.com/aehrm/hybrid_textnorm

In a second step, the most important relations for each class may be selected for knowledge extraction. This ensures not giving preferential treatment to some (at times highly specific) knowledge domains, simply because they seem easy to extract. Even if knowledge graphs are not manually curated, the choice of computational methods or knowledge to extract can lead to biased data, especially when handling nearly all human knowledge at the same time. To give some examples, this applies to chemical notations, currency exchanges, weight conversions, or highly nested hierarchies, which can be found for languages for example.

The interdisciplinary approach for knowledge graph creation also influences the choice of the underlying ontology. There exist multiple ontologies already which aim to support linked data from cultural heritage sources. The ontology CIDOC CRM [28] is the most prominent one and is often referenced in the digital humanities. The data model is extremely vast, however the focus lies on the traditional KG definition, meaning on entities and events. To add lexemes to KG ontologies (in contrast to focusing on named entities only) has just recently been a point of interest in the community, such as the lexical import of WordNet into Wikidata. Other ontologies such as OntoLex aim to support the exact representation of LSR to KG (e.g. one entry references another), however this data model does not take semantic relationships between lexemes into account. Overall, these standards are well suited for sub-areas of encyclopedias, but the complete representation of all content that EncycNet strives for, including mainly lexical properties, is not entirely possible. Besides the advantages for alignment, this is also why we chose the most extensive data model, Wikidata, where we only included properties relevant to EncycNet.

2.3.4. Outlook and Discussion

EncycNet is one of the first openly available historical German knowledge graphs,[9] striving to be a new data source for DH and NLP alike. In future work, we will further analyze how the data can impact LM integration, in particular when it comes to the detection of semantic change for historical German LMs.

To summarize, it can be said that the field of knowledge graphs is already making a stronger impact in favour of the humanities, but there is still room for improvement in many areas. For one, there is a greater need in terms of a machine-readable data representation for time-sensitive data. Even though RDF* and many other projects exist to adapt RDF (reification in particular) to allow for time annotations, many of the ideas are still preliminary or are not consistently supported formats throughout libraries or applications. Second, the de-facto standard for cultural heritage modeling, CIDOC CRM, is extremely complex and vast. Currently, this is why it is necessary to build domain specific extensions of the ontology [38], meaning it is not suited for a cross-domain knowledge approach. Wikidata on the other hand provides an easy-to-use and extensive data model, where projects can rather select properties and concepts of interest instead of extending the model, however it lacks standardization. Compromising between standardization and generalization when developing ontologies in cultural heritage therefore remains to be a challenge in the field. Third, development of methods surrounding concepts and disambiguation of word senses will have to move into the foreground, not just for the sake of

---

[9] `https://encycnet.github.io/`; RDF knowledge graph available at `http://dx.doi.org/10.5281/zenodo.10219192`

KG creation. Many WSD techniques rely on linked data resources as "sense inventories" [39]. To create a historical linked data source with sense disambiguated concepts at this point in time means relying on contemporary data, and in turn integrating potentially false assumptions. Especially for resources like encyclopedias, where every sense of a word is listed and in turn is a highly ambiguous resource, we need to refine methods that do not rely on external data. This entails for example, as stated in Section 2.3.2, a clear cut model of when a word sense changes meaning.

3. Text as Graphs

In the previous section, we have discussed the challenges and chances in creation of KGs from existing semantic resources for CLS and provided a specific example, with the knowledge graph EncycNet. In addition to this semi-manual creation from existing resources, it is also feasible – and in many cases very promising – to extract graph representations from the texts themselves. On the one hand, this enables the use of graph-based methods to further process the extracted information. On the other hand, it also gives us the chance to directly feed the information we have extracted so far back into our models using, among others, the methods we will describe in Section 4 – leading to a kind of feedback loop, where the model can iteratively gain a better understanding of the texts by reading through them multiple times and re-using the knowledge the model has gained in previous passes. One example where graph representations are directly suitable for literature are character networks. These networks can serve as a kind of condensed representation of a text. A very simple character network could show which characters interact in the text, while more sophisticated versions could include information about friendship or family relations. This is also a prime example for the feedback loop: A model can extract information about the characters in a text to a character graph and then directly incorporate this graph to gain a better understanding of the text.

In the remainder of this section, we will describe existing experiments towards the use of graph representations for the processing of literary texts. We start by introducing research on representing characters and static character networks using graph neural networks, before introducing an approach to provide a temporal partitioning of the texts in scenes and finally working towards combining these two approaches to represent texts as a sequence of scenes represented by character networks, among other features. Our intended next step in future work is to finalize this combination by applying temporal graph neural networks to the sequence of character networks, building a more comprehensive representation of the plot of a novel.

3.1. Character Networks as a Representation for Literary Characters

In previous work [40], we have extracted character networks from different texts in Tolkien's Legendarium in a semi-automated way, creating a joint character network over all texts. We have shown that applying graph neural networks to this representation leads to better representations of the characters than just using word embeddings based on the texts.

We use the English full text of The Lord of the Rings (consisting of three volumes: The Fellowship of the Ring, The Two Towers and The Return of the King), The Hobbit and The Silmarillion. The texts are pre-processed using BookNLP[10] and co-references are resolved in a semi-automatic way, only resolving explicit named mentions (e.g., "Peregrin Took", "Sam Gamgee") due to the difficulty of full co-reference resolution on literary texts, especially due to its long document length [41]. A joint character network for all texts is then constructed from co-occurrences of characters in the same sentence.

We evaluate the suitability of Graph Neural Networks for the representation of the character network in two downstream tasks: character classification and link prediction. In the first task, we aim to build a classifier that is able to detect which book (Hobbit, Silmarillion or Lord of the Rings) a character is most strongly affiliated with. This shows the model's ability to represent the structure of the character networks. The same approach can also be used to classify characters with regard to their role in a text, for example main character, mentor or antagonist, when a larger collection of texts is available with these roles annotated. In the second task, we want to build a model that is able to infer whether a link (i.e., an interaction) between two characters is missing from the network. This can be used to reconstruct co-occurrences in the texts that have been missed due to errors in the co-reference resolution.

For both of these tasks, we compare character embeddings created using different types of graph neural networks with Word2Vec embeddings of the character names. These word embeddings are trained on Tolkien's novels, but lack the structural information from the character networks. We show that Graph Convolutional Networks using Word2Vec embeddings as additional node features outperform pure Word2Vec embeddings in both tasks, raising the F1-score for node classification from 79.45 % to 92.32 % and the ROC/AUC score for link prediction from 78.16 % to 81.67 %. This proves that the structural information encoded in the character networks is indeed useful for representing the characters in the texts.

In addition to these quantitative evaluations, we also use both Word2Vec embeddings and embeddings produced from graph neural networks to build visualizations of the character networks. Figure 2 shows the resulting visualizations. We can see that the GNN-based visualization provides a clear separation between the three books, while the Word2Vec-based visualization mixes characters from all books.

Overall, our experiments in this paper show that NLP methods and graph based methods can be combined very effectively: We can use NLP methods to extract graphs from texts and then use these graphs to build better representations of the entities in the text.

3.2. Segmentation of Novels into Scenes

While the static representations used above [40] can provide a good overview of the story's structure and characters, they ignore one of the most important aspects of literature: the development of the story over time. In order to model this development, a segmentation of the text into coherent parts is necessary. This may be done on a purely structural level, for example by using paragraphs or pages as a unit for segmentation. However, we argue that a segmentation strategy grounded in literary theory is desirable. Therefore, we have proposed the task of scene segmentation, where a text is to be split into segments that are coherent across four dimensions: time, space, action and character constellation [43]. In short, this means that a scene should not contain major jumps in

[10]`https://github.com/booknlp/booknlp`.

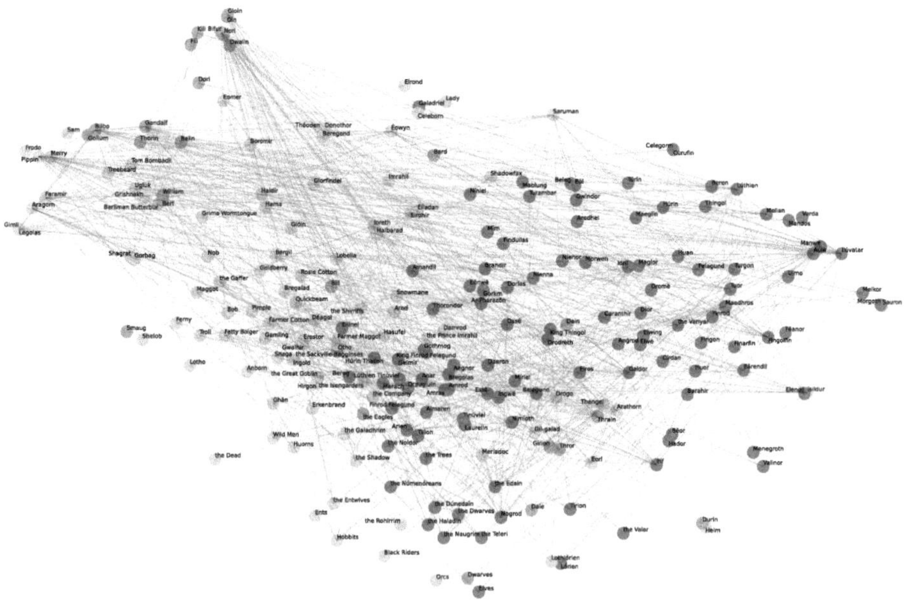

(a) Latent space embedding of characters obtained by applying the word embedding Word2Vec to the whole text corpus

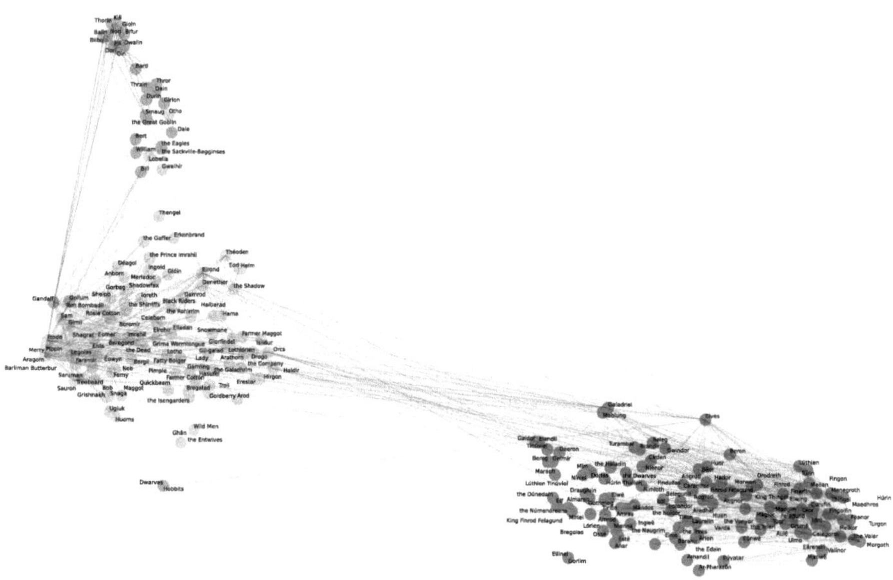

(b) Latent space embeddings obtained by the Graph Convolutional Network using Word2Vec character embeddings as additional node features

Figure 2. Comparison of two latent space embeddings of characters in Tolkien's Legendarium using (a) Word2Vec and (b) the hidden layer activations of a Graph Convolutional Network, where nodes carry additional features that correspond to Word2Vec embeddings. Node colors indicate the work in which characters appear most frequently (red: The Hobbit, green: The Lord of the Rings, blue: The Silmarillion). Edges represent character co-occurrences in the text. Two-dimensional visualizations were generated using the dimensionality reduction technique t-SNE [42].

time, should take place in a single location, contain a fixed set of characters and narrate one main course of action.

After initially discussing the task [44], we have formally introduced it along with an annotated dataset [43] and organized a shared task to collect new approaches [45]. The most successful approach so far was one of the contributions to the shared task, introduced by Kurfalı and Wirén [46]. It models the problem as a sequential sentence classification task, where each sentence is classified as either a scene border or no scene border. The model takes as input a piece of text consisting of multiple sentences, which are interleaved by SEP tokens between the sentences, and the resulting representation is passed through a pre-trained encoder model, for example BERT. The resulting contextualized representations of the SEP tokens are then used as input to a multi-layer perceptron, which classifies each SEP token independently as either a scene border or no scene border.

We were able to slightly improve the performance of this model by using a BERT-model with additional domain-adaptation on literary texts, as described in Sec. 4.1 [47]. While this approach constitutes the current state of the art in scene segmentation, the performance still leaves room for improvements: The model is evaluated on two different test sets, one constructed from the same type of texts as the training data (i.e., dime novels) and one from high-brow literature texts that are expected to be more challenging to understand and therefore segment. The model reaches F1-scores of 0.40 and 0.35 on the in- and out of-domain data, respectively.

3.3. Plot as Temporal Graphs

In [48], we made a step towards combining these two approaches to generate a computational representation of the abstract concept of the *plot* of a novel. We applied a scene segmentation algorithm to a set of dime novels from the genres horror and romance to partition each of them as a sequence of scenes. We then extracted, for each scene, a set of features to form an explicit representation of the scene and compile these scene representations to a time series representing a novel. This representation is comprised of several factors:

- the characters that are present in the scene;
- triples of (subject, verb, object) representing the action in the scene;
- valence and arousal values extracted using a sentiment lexicon;
- association with a few simple types of interactions: fighting, erotic actions and talking;
- character-level values for valence and arousal; and
- a distribution over topics in the scene extracted using topic modeling.

We evaluate the suitability of this time series representation to capture the plot of a novel via three proxy tasks: First, we compare the similarity of novels from different genres. We find that our representation is able to capture the difference between horror and romance novels well, assigning a higher distance between novels of different genres on average. However, we show that this simple task can also be solved by static representations of the texts, as for example tf-idf-representations.

To further validate our approach, we construct synthetic evaluation datasets by permuting the order of scenes in the novels. If our representation is capable of capturing the usual structure of the plot, the similarity between the unmodified novels should be higher than between the shuffled novels. Our experiments show that this is indeed the case, indicating that the model takes into account the order of scenes.

3.4. Open Challenges

Throughout our experiments towards the conversion of novels into structured representations, we have identified several research challenges that need to be addressed in order to improve the suitability of these representations.

Co-Reference Resolution The most obvious use case for graph representations in CLS is the creation of character networks. However, these can only be accurately extracted when character references can be detected and resolved reliably. High-quality co-reference resolution is therefore an extremely important prerequisite for these character network-based representations of novels. So far, we have relied either on the performance of existing co-reference resolution algorithms being sufficient [48] or fallen back to semi-automatic resolution [40]. However, this is one of the points where our previously mentioned feedback loop is promising: We can collect knowledge about characters in a graph representation and then use this information to improve the performance of co-reference resolution. For example, since the model has access to the information which characters are friends or enemies, it can therefore better reason about the likelihood of interactions between the characters. We are currently actively working towards the development of models implementing this feedback loop.

Detecting Present Characters Another challenge for the extraction of character networks is the detection of which characters are present in the current scene. While a good enough co-reference resolution can tell us which characters are mentioned, it is still necessary to determine whether a character is actually present in the scene or not (e.g., is only mentioned in conversation or even just used as a reference, or if the character is not mentioned at all). This can be partially addressed by considering only characters that are referenced outside of direct speeches, but a more comprehensive detection is still an open research question.

Temporal Graph Models While the use of graph neural networks (GNNs) has seen great development in the last couple of years, most of these GNNs are still focused on representing static graphs. While implementations for temporal graph neural networks are also available [49], these have so far not shown good results in our experiments. We are on collaboration with researchers from the field of graph learning to develop approaches that are better suited for the representation of literary texts.

Temporal Order of Scenes The order of scenes in a text in many cases does not follow the chronological order within the narration – flashbacks or parallel narrations are very common tools. For a more accurate representation of novels as a sequence of scenes, we are currently working towards automatically detecting the chronological ordering of scenes.

4. Improving NLP Models with Knowledge Graph Data

Pre-trained language models (LMs) trained on vast amounts of textual data – broadly understood here to include both contextualized models such as BERT, and also decontextualized ones such as word embeddings – have demonstrated powerful abilities in modeling language semantics and achieving state-of-the-art performance on most natural language processing downstream tasks. The effectiveness of a pre-trained LM for the CLS task depends heavily on its ability to capture not only contemporary language semantics and knowledge but also historical and time-specific contexts. Tasks such as the automated creation of social networks of characters from a specific book depend on the performance of named entity recognition (NER) and named entity linking (NEL) techniques, which, in turn, rely on the quality of the model's language representation of the book's time period. Due to the limitation of low-resource data, domain-specific language models trained on domain-specific text corpora often struggle to accurately capture the semantics of the domain-specific language. Consequently, they perform significantly worse on downstream tasks than models trained on large, general language corpora.

Literary studies in general have only a small amount of training text data available, making it challenging to train LM or static word embeddings with a good language representation of a given domain or time period. Therefore, there is a need for solutions that enable learning a good semantic language representation under the constraints of a small training dataset.

Recent research has shown the effectiveness of adaptation of pre-trained language models, initially trained on large general language corpora, to domain-specific language by further pre-training them on smaller, domain-specific text corpora [50,51,52]. Complementing the work on domain adaptation through pre-training on domain-specific text corpora, a number of research works have shown the potential of integrating knowledge graphs that explicitly model semantic relations, into pre-trained language model to improve its domain semantics and performance on domain-specific tasks [53,54,55,56,57].

In this chapter, we will present our work on investigating the potential of integrating knowledge graphs into language models to improve their semantics and performance on downstream tasks within the field of CLS. First, we will review the applicability of domain adaption to the CLS domain by continuing the pre-training the model on small CLS relevant historical domain corpora to improve performance on downstream tasks of named entity recognition and the detection of speech rendition. Secondly, we will demonstrate the potential of applying knowledge graph information to adjust non-contextualized word embeddings trained in low-resource settings using retrofitting and fusion methods to improve their semantic representation. Next, we will show how pre-trained language models, trained on vast amounts of textual data, can enrich the knowledge graph with information on the semantic relation strength between concepts. We will use this weighted knowledge graph to adjust non-contextualized embeddings through retrofitting, further enhancing their semantic representations. Finally, we will propose an approach for continually integrating newly occurring knowledge graphs into pre-trained language models, while avoiding catastrophic forgetting.

To demonstrate these approaches, we apply them in this chapter to the well-established BERT language model [58], as this model has been extensively used in knowledge graph research [59,60]. Nevertheless, we note that the methods themselves are model-agnostic and discuss strategies to apply them to alternative language models in Sec. 5.

4.1. Language Model Adaptation to Historical Domains

Inspired by [51], we investigate the applicability of further pre-training on (unlabeled) domain-specific datasets to the low-resource CLS domains of interest, prior to fine-tuning the language model to CLS-specific tasks. This adjustment aims to improve the quality of the model language representation and the performance of CLS tasks in domain-specific contexts.

4.1.1. Methodology

In our work, we utilized a German BERT model [58] pre-trained on German texts from heterogeneous domains and a DistilBERT [61] model based on German BERT. To adapt the generally pre-trained models to the desired domain or temporal language, we employed a two-step procedure. In the first step, we followed the methodology from [51], where the model is continuously trained further on domain-specific text data, task-specific (unlabeled) text data, or a combination of both. In the second step, the models pre-trained in step one are fine-tuned on two downstream tasks: named entity recognition (NER) and detection of speech rendition. Additionally, we alternatively pre-trained an ELECTRA [62] model from scratch on domain-specific textual data and downstream task data. We chose this model because it requires less training data and time while providing a performance similar to that of BERT. The pre-training parameters for the models, as well as further details on the experimental setup, can be found in [63].

4.1.2. Named Entity Recognition

Named entity recognition is an information extraction downstream task that aims to extract and classify the named entities mentioned in unstructured textual data. In our experiments, we have used the German Corpus of Novels (DROC) [64], which brings together 90 annotated fragments of German language novels.

4.1.3. Detection of Speech Rendition

Detection of speech rendition is a classification task that aims to identify and classify types of speech within unstructured textual data. For our experiments, we used the labeled dataset "Redewiedergabe" [65], which categorizes speech into four possible classes: direct, indirect, free indirect, and reported. Detailed information on the dataset and the task can be found in [63].

4.1.4. Results

We compared our models to those without further fine-tuning on domain-specific datasets. The results of our experiments are presented in Table 2. As expected, due to low-resource constraints, the ELECTRA baseline trained from scratch showed low performance. The results indicate that continued pre-training on domain-specific textual data and downstream task textual data consistently improves performance over models directly trained on downstream tasks. While using textual data and downstream task data separately enhances performance, the combination of both further boosts the performance of the models. We hypothesize [63] that precisely this pre-training on the (unlabeled) task test data may allow the language model to build a better representation of the test data, helping in accurately solving the downstream task. This is particularly useful in the context of CLS, where the datasets we are interested in are often very small and closed. In summary, the results demonstrate the potential of applying continued pre-training for domain adaptation to improve language representations for domains of interest in CLS.

Table 2. Results of 10-fold cross-validation on the DROC NER and speech rendition tasks per model. Reported numbers are F1 scores. *Base* refers to models fine-tuned without additional pre-training steps. *Domain* models are pre-trained on the domain corpus and *Task* models on the downstream task text corpus. *Task+Domain* refers to the combination of both. [63]

	DROC NER			Speech Rendition		
Model	**BERT**	**DistilBERT**	**ELECTRA**	**BERT**	**DistilBERT**	**ELECTRA**
Base	.859 (.032)	.838 (.32)	.791 (0.03)	.538 (.086)	.455 (.04)	.373 (.057)
Domain	.863 (.041)	.854 (.028)	n.a.	.637 (.234)	.557 (.356)	n.a.
Task	.882 (.039)	.853 (.031)	n.a.	.587 (.403)	.568 (.18)	n.a.
Task+Domain	**.927 (.029)**	.893 (.043)	n.a.	**.691 (.136)**	.655 (.132)	n.a.

4.2. KGs for Word Embeddings for Lexical Semantics

In the previous section, we demonstrated that continued pre-training on small domain-specific textual data has the potential to improve language representation in CLS domains. Complementary to continued fine-tuning on textual data, many research works have shown that pre-training on structured knowledge such as KGs can be used to further improve the performance of static and contextual language representation [66,57,53,56,54,55]. Some semantic word relations occur infrequently in text data and are even more rare in domains with limited textual data sources such as CLS. This makes learning a good semantic word representation even more challenging. KGs on the other hand, as described in Sec. 2, models these semantic relations explicitly. By integrating this information into static or contextualized word representations, the semantic relations that are difficult to capture directly from the text data can be represented.

As discussed in 2.1, CLS studies focus on cultural heritage, which encompasses structured information sources such as encyclopedias and dictionaries. These sources contain historical and time-specific knowledge and information about word semantics and semantic relations between these words. These structured information sources can be used to create historical KGs such as EncycNet (Sec. 2.3). This makes it attractive to apply these solutions to these high quality CLS data to learn better semantic word representation in low resource scenario of CLS.

In our work, we propose to integrate structured semantic information from dictionaries into static word embeddings by using established applications of 1) retrofitting and 2) fusion to improve the semantic representation of words when data resources are limited.

4.2.1. Methodology

In this section, we describe in detail the approaches we propose to apply.

Retrofitting Retrofitting [67] proposes to utilize the relational information KGs to refine existing word embeddings by forcing the words that are connected to each other in KG to have a similar representation. The main idea is to re-adjust the embedding vector of each word so that it is both close to its original embedding vector and close to the embeddings of all connected words in the KG.

Formally, the retrofitting refinement objective can be formulated to minimize

$$\Psi(Q) = \sum_{i \in V} \left[\alpha_i ||q_i - \hat{q}_i||^2 + \sum_{(i,j) \in E} \beta_{i,j} ||q_i - q_j||^2 \right] \quad (1)$$

where q_i and $\hat{q}_i$ denote the adjusted and original embeddings vectors of word or entity i from a set of entities V of a KG respectively, and $\beta_{i,j}$ represents the weight of the edge (i, j) connecting word i with word j in the KG. The hyper-parameter α_i determines how close q_i should stay to its original vector $\hat{q}_i$. In our work, an optimized version [68] of the retrofitting algorithm was used.

Fusion The fusion approach [69] proposes an alternative solution for adjusting word representation embeddings using semantics represented in KGs. This solution trains two types of embeddings. KG embeddings for given KGs using established approaches such as TransE [70], RotatE [71] on the one hand, and word embeddings on text data such as Word2Vec [72], FastText [73] on the other hand. The embedding of the word is concatenated with the respective embedding of the entity on the KG and then reduced to the desired dimensionality using methods such as PCA, AVG, SVD [69]. In our work, we used RotatE to train KG embeddings and FastText for word embeddings. PCA was used for dimensionality reduction.

4.2.2. Datasets

To train the FastText word embedding, we used a sample of German OSCAR [74] dataset. German is not a low-resource language, but to simulate a low resource setting, we randomly selected a small subset of sentences from OSCAR, resulting in a dataset of about 20MB (about 3.6M tokens, 47,000 types). Since we evaluated general linguistic performance in terms of word meaning representation, rather than performance for a specific thematic domain, we proceeded with this type of corpus creation to represent a low-resource language. We used GermaNet [75] as a KG source to train RotatE embeddings. GermaNet describes semantic relations between words and is therefore suitable for our study. In [76], we have described detailed information on data pre-processing and the resulting data statistics.

4.2.3. Evaluation Setup

We evaluated the resulting KG adjusted word embeddings on the established tasks of word similarity and word relatedness by using multiple German datasets: Schm280 [77] (translated WordSim-353 [78]), SimLex999 [79] (translated from [80]), ZG222 [81] as well as Gur65 (translated RG-65 [82]) and Gur350 [83]. The datasets contain word pairs with annotated human ratings indicating how similar or related these words are. In our experiments, we used the cosine similarity of the resulting word embeddings to calculate the similarity/relatedness score, and computed correlation to gold human scores. We compared the results of KG-adapted word embeddings with FastText embeddings without KG integration.

Table 3. Performance of the adapted word embeddings on the selected data sets (Spearman correlations between the cosine similarities of the word vector pairs and the human ratings). For the FastText model, the standard deviations of 15 runs are also given. Retro+Fusion averages the cosine similarities of both models.

	SimLex-999	**Schm280**	**ZG222**	**Gur65**	**Gur350**
# instances	825	242	120	49	237
FastText	0.224 (0.004)	0.495 (0.01)	0.299 (0.01)	0.320 (0.03)	0.653 (0.01)
Retro	0.267	0.512	0.291	0.490	0.607
Retro (only synsets)	0.253	0.487	0.273	0.374	0.652
Fusion	0.250	0.484	**0.347**	0.426	**0.666**
Retro+Fusion	**0.278**	**0.537**	0.337	**0.497**	0.660

4.2.4. Results

In Table 3, it can be seen that the KG-adapted embeddings consistently perform better than the word embeddings without KG integration, emphasizing the applicability and potential of using KG for CLS studies with low resource constraints.

4.3. LM4KG

The information represented in KGs can be used to adapt language representations of word embeddings and LMs to new domains or to understand new knowledge [66,54,53,55]. As shown in the previous section, this information is very useful when learning word representations under the constraint of limited training data. An important aspect of this type of adaptation is understanding the reasonability and strength of relations between concepts in these KGs. As specified in Eq. (1) the retrofitting approach uses weight information of edges $\beta_{i,j}$ that connects two entities i and j in a KG, when adjusting respective word embedding representation. Therefore, the quality of the adjusted word embeddings when using these approaches strongly depends on the quality of the information about the relation weights. Not all relations in KGs are equally strong, some are more meaningful and relevant than others. For example, in ConceptNet [66], a common sense KG that contains general world knowledge, considering the entity "word" would return "God" and "language" as related entities. In most contexts, however, the term “language” is more appropriate therefore this information should be represented accordingly as a weight in the KG [84]. In addition to factual and common sense KGs, character graphs [40] also describe relations between characters in a book that vary greatly in strength and meaningfulness. However, most of available KGs lack explicit information about the strength or weights of relations, so that each relation is considered equally important. Therefore, an automatic solution for assessing the strength of relations in KGs is of high interest.

It has been shown that pre-trained LMs contain a certain amount of factual knowledge [85] and are even able to perform question answering to a certain extent without being explicitly trained on this task [86].

In this section, we present our *REWEIGHT* [84] approach, which leverages this inherent knowledge available in a pre-trained LMs to assess the strength of the relations in KGs. This LM enriched KG is then utilized to generate more accurate word embeddings, demonstrating the potential of both utilizing LM to improve KGs and applying these enhanced KGs to better model language semantics. The *REWEIGHT* methodology consists of several steps. For each relation (edge) between two words in a given KG, we construct a natural language sentence representation using a manually defined set of templates and automated grammar correction. These generated sentences are then fed into a pre-trained LM, and the output perplexity of the model is estimated. To map the estimated perplexity to the weight range of the original graph, we apply a transformation where a high edge weight represents a strong semantic relation between two words. Finally, the estimated weights are inserted into the original KG, resulting in an enriched knowledge resource that reflects the strength of its relations. By applying retrofitting to this enriched KG, we obtained static word embeddings with improved semantic representations.

4.3.1. Methodology

In this section, we describe in detail the methodology of our proposed *REWEIGHT* solution for the automatic weighting of relations in KGs, and application of the enhanced KG to produce word embeddings with improved semantic representation. In addition, we describe the datasets used as well as the evaluation setup.

Sentence Generation We aim to evaluate the weight of relations in a knowledge graph (KG) using a pre-trained language model (LM). To do this, we first need to represent the KG's relations as natural language sentences. We have manually defined a set of templates to map the relations between graph entities to sentences. For example, a "DefinedAs" relation between words A and B in the ConceptNet KG is converted to the sentence *"A is defined as B."* The complete list of templates is provided in [84]. This simple template-based solution can produce grammatically poor sentences for some relations. Since LMs have been shown to encode both syntactic and semantic information, and we want to use the LM to assess only the semantics, it is important to mitigate the influence of poor grammar. To achieve this, we applied a grammar correction model to all generated sentences, resulting in equivalent sentences with improved syntax.

Weight Generation After constructing a sentence representation for each relation in the KG, we use a LM to assess the strength of these relations. To achieve this, we evaluate the meaningfulness of the generated sentences using perplexity. We assume that a pre-trained LM will assign high perplexity to sentences describing questionable or uncommon relations. In our work, we used the bidirectional language model BERT [58]. It has been shown that the common definition of perplexity is not applicable to bidirectional LMs [87]. Therefore, in our experiments, we used their perplexity approximation to calculate the score for each sentence.

Weight Transformation To convert the estimated weights to the weight range of the original graph, where a high weight represents a strong relation between two words, we propose two approaches: $REWEIGHT_{\mathrm{light}}$ and $REWEIGHT_{\mathrm{mod}}$. Here, we only provide a description of $REWEIGHT_{\mathrm{light}}$ and refer to [84] for the alternative approach.

$REWEIGHT_{light}$ This variant of the perplexities transformation, calculates the weight in the range of the original KG for a relation r as follows

$$\beta_{\mathrm{RWL}}(r) := \frac{\gamma_{\max}}{pp(r)} \tag{2}$$

Figure 3. Sankey diagram showing the change of ConceptNet weights before and after REWEIGHTing. The blocks on the left resp. right side represent sets of ConceptNet relations, clustered by their respective weights, before and after REWEIGHTing, into interval. The streams between the blocks represent the changes in the compositions of the clusters.

where γ_{max} denotes the maximum weight in the original KG and $pp(r)$ the perplexity assigned to a sentence describing relation r by an LM. The resulting weights are then used to replace the edge weights of the KG.

4.3.2. Experiments

We applied our methodology to the ConceptNet KG. Although KG relations have weights, these weights reflect the trustworthiness of the source from which the relation was extracted rather than the semantic strength of the relationship between two words. The changes in weight distribution before and after applying our method are illustrated in Figure 3.

To evaluate the quality of the new LM-generated weights, we used the ConceptNet KG in a retrofitting process similar to Sec. 4.2 to adjust word embeddings semantics, following the experiments proposed by Speer et al. [66].

We take the word embeddings retrofitted from the original ConceptNet weights (*NumberBatch*) as baseline, and then compare them to retrofitted word embeddings which have been obtained from our LM-based reweighting approach $REWEIGHT_{\text{light}}$ and $REWEIGHT_{\text{mod}}$. The quality of the adjusted embeddings was evaluated on word similarity and relatedness tasks using multiple established datasets: MEN3000 [88], Rare Words [89], MTurk-771 [90], WS353 [78], SimLex999 [80], and Semeval17-2a [91]. Unlike the experiment from previous Section 4.2, these datasets are in English.

4.3.3. Results

The results of our experiments can be found in Table 4. The results demonstrate that embeddings adjusted using ConceptNet with weights from our method perform consistently better than the baseline. This highlights the potential synergy between KGs and LMs in refining semantic representations, which is crucial for the CLS tasks.

Table 4. Spearman correlation of embeddings generated through retrofitting with different KGs on multiple word similarity datasets. Significant difference to baseline through Fischer's z-transformation with $^{\dagger}p < 0.01$, $^{\S}p < 0.05$.

Group	Embedding	MEN3000	RW	MTurk	WS353	SemEval	SimLex	Average
Baseline	*Numberbatch*	0.872	0.630	0.822	0.833	0.779	**0.633**	0.762
Ours	$REWEIGHT_{\text{light}}$	0.877	†**0.663**	0.827	0.840	**0.783**	**0.633**	**0.770**
	$REWEIGHT_{\text{mod}}$	†**0.881**	§0.651	**0.828**	**0.845**	0.780	0.618	0.767

4.4. CapsKG

The knowledge landscape is constantly evolving, with new information emerging regularly in the form of new facts, KGs, genres, books, and character graphs. CLS studies on cultural heritage focus on structured knowledge sources, such as encyclopedias and dictionaries that are specific to various domains or time periods. These studies consistently provide high-quality information sources, such as historical KG EncycNet (Section 2.3). Consequently, language models need to be able to seamlessly integrate and update to accommodate this new knowledge input to better represent the semantics of a particular domain, time, genre, or even book character networks.

However, previous solutions for iterative fine-tuning often face the major obstacle of catastrophic forgetting [92]. This phenomenon refers to the tendency of models to forget previously learned information when they are updated with new data. Although there are solutions that aim to prevent catastrophic forgetting, they often have the disadvantage that they cannot effectively transfer the knowledge previously learned by the model, which is crucial in a low-resource domain such as CLS. As CLS studies continuously create new knowledge sources like EncycNet, it is important to have solutions that integrate new knowledge into language models without causing catastrophic forgetting. Such solutions should also enable access to previously learned information, which is especially beneficial for low-resource domains. In our CapsKG study, we propose the use of capsule architecture to address these problems. CapsKG enables the continual integration of new knowledge into LMs while simultaneously overcoming the problem of catastrophic forgetting.

4.4.1. Methodology

In this section, we describe the details of our proposed solution CapsKG [93] for the continual integration of newly occurring knowledge into a language model. The main goal of CapsKG is the continuous integration of knowledge into an LM when new knowledge sources become available. As such, CapsKG faces two main challenges. On the one hand, the model needs to make knowledge from previously integrated sources available when integrating new information, to prevent learning of redundancies and enable knowledge transfer. On the other hand, previously integrated knowledge also needs to be protected from catastrophic forgetting during the continual integration of new information sources. To address these challenges, CapsKG uses two main components. A source-specific feature extractor module extracts relevant information for the currently integrated knowledge source and leverages a routing mechanism to make the relevant information from previously integrated sources available. Additionally, a shared adapter module provides joint access of model parameters to all sources while preventing catastrophic forgetting of previously learned sources through a gating mechanism.

To introduce CapsKG in detail, we will first discuss the input representation and the training objective for integrating knowledge sources into the LM. Next, we will explore both the source-specific feature extractor module with routing mechanism that enables the reuse of information and the shared adapter module.

Input Representation and Training Strategy To integrate new knowledge into a language model l, we employed a well-established approach. This method entails training the model on the link prediction task using the prompting method [94,59], which involves converting knowledge triples t of a KG into natural language sentences, referred to as prompts. Although automated methods for this conversion exist, e.g. [95], we chose to use the method from Sec. 4.3.1, which relies on manually created sentence templates for simplicity. For example, given the triple *"Alexandria _location_location_containedby Egypt"*, the generated sentence is *"Alexandria is located in Egypt"*. To train the model on this knowledge, we applied a masking training strategy similar to Bosselut et al. [94] and Fichtel et al. [59]. We masked the object or subject in each sentence, resulting in the prompt p *"Alexandria is located in [MASK]"* and trained the model to predict the missing entity *"[MASK]"*. The model was trained using cross-entropy loss. Given a conversion function *prompt* that transforms an incomplete knowledge graph triple (e,r) with kept entity e into a prompt p with a masked entity e', and a pre-trained LM l, the link prediction using LM can be formally defined as follows:

$$prom(e,r) \rightarrow p, \qquad l(p) \rightarrow e' \tag{3}$$

where r is the relation type and e' is predicted by the LM.

Source-Specific Feature Extractor with Routing Mechanism The task of the source-specific feature extractor with routing mechanism is to extract features relevant to each knowledge source and enable knowledge transfer between similar sources to complement each other. To achieve this, the module contains knowledge source-specific extractor capsules, which are a set of small fully connected layers that extract relevant low-level features. A transfer capsule layer represents the transferable features extracted by the extractor capsules. A special similarity based routing mechanism, consisting of several steps, is used to transfer features between lower-layer extractor capsules and higher-layer transfer capsules. This mechanism enables knowledge exchange between similar sources while avoiding exchanges between dissimilar sources, thus preventing the introduction of noise that could negatively influence representations. The detailed mathematical definition of this module can be found in [93].

Shared Adapter Module To address the problem of catastrophic forgetting when continually learning new knowledge, the capsule architecture proposes utilizing an adapter solution [96] within the shared adapter module. Adapters consist of small trainable neural layers inserted into the layers of a pre-trained language models l. They are trained to learn relevant features for a new task, such as link prediction [97] for a particular KG with ID k, while the base language model l remains frozen. This solution allows the language model l to learn new knowledge while preserving its original language representations. Formally, the adapter can be defined as follows:

$$h'^{(k)} = f_c(f_d(h^{(k)}))) + h^{(k)}. \tag{4}$$

where $h^{(k)} \in \mathbb{R}^{d_s \times d_e}$ denotes the output of an intermediate layer of the language model l, where d_s represents the sequence length and d_e represents the dimension of the base model's hidden state output. This output serves as the input to the adapter. f_c and f_d define the fully connected layers of the adapter. Adapter layers map the input to an intermediate adapter dimensionality, which can be freely chosen, and then back to the hidden dimensionality space of the model. Finally, the intermediate output of the original base model is added via skip connections. To facilitate further knowledge transfer, the capsule architecture utilizes a single adapter for all knowledge sources. To prevent catastrophic forgetting in the adapter when training with a new knowledge source, a masking strategy is applied. For each KG' ID k and each adapter layer, a mask $m^{(k)}$ is calculated from the knowledge graph embedding $e^{(k)}$ based on the KG's ID. The masks have the same dimensionality as the respective adapter layer. The KG embeddings $e^{(k)}$ are learned during training. The mask is calculated by converting the knowledge graph embedding into a pseudo-gating function, applying the Sigmoid activation function σ and a scale hyper-parameter s. Formally, this is defined as follows:

$$m^{(k)} = \sigma(se^{(k)}) \tag{5}$$

The scale hyper-parameter s is a positive scalar that is gradually increased during the training procedure, forcing the learned mask to contain values closer to 0 or 1. The obtained pseudo-binary masks $m_d^{(k)}$ and $m_c^{(k)}$ for the respective adapter layers f_c and f_d are multiplied element-wise with these adapter layers, calculating the output of the shared adapter module as follows:

$$h'^{(k)} = f_c(f_d(h^{(k)}) \otimes m_d^{(k)}) \otimes m_c^{(k)} + h^{(k)} \tag{6}$$

Applying masks of previously learned knowledge sources to the gradients during training on new one, preserves the information learned from previous KGs, thus preventing catastrophic forgetting of already learned knowledge. Additionally, other KGs can reuse already reserved neurons in the forward path, further facilitating knowledge sharing between different KGs.

4.4.2. Experiments and Datasets

Since CLS studies focus on cultural heritage including structured information sources and analyses of the social network of characters, the task of link prediction is highly relevant in CLS domain. We trained and evaluated our solution on the link prediction task using three established English KG datasets: YAGO [98,99], WN18 [70], and FreeBase [100]. The preprocessing steps and resulting dataset statistics for the three English KG datasets can be found in [93]. To also show the potential of the proposed solution for CLS, we conducted experiments with a German historical knowledge graph, EncycNet [36].

For the German historical EncycNet dataset, we split the graph into 19 sub-KGs, each containing triples of a specific relation type. Each subgraph represents a distinct knowledge source that is newly introduced and needs to be integrated into the LM. This

Table 5. Dataset characteristics of the used EncycNet dataset after preprocessing according to [93].

dataset	relation types	entities	train triples	dev triples	test triples	total
EncycNet	19	671341	275680	59263	58843	393786

allowed us to integrate these KGs into the LM separately and demonstrate the benefits of reusing previously learned knowledge when learning new knowledge. The resulting subgraphs were then randomly split into training, validation, and test datasets with a ratio of 70 %, 15 %, and 15 %, respectively. Following this, all preprocessing steps from [93] were applied to the resulting subgraph splits. Statistics for the EncycNet dataset after preprocessing are provided in Table 5.

We evaluated the following models in our experiments:

BERT$_{\text{frozen}}$ A BERT base model that is prompted without any fine tuning.

BERT An independent BERT base model is trained and evaluated for each relation type [59].

BERT-CL A single BERT base model is iteratively trained for all relation types and evaluated once at the end.

Adapter An independent BERT base model with frozen parameters and one trainable Adapter is trained and evaluated for each relation type [101].

Adapter-CL A frozen BERT base model with a single trainable Adapter is iteratively trained for all relation types and evaluated once at the end.

CapsKG The CapsKG model [93] is iteratively trained for all relation types and evaluated once at the end.

4.4.3. Results

The experimental results are presented in Table 6. Next to the general common sense knowledge graphs of WN18, YAGO, and FB15k, our proposed solution for continual knowledge integration also consistently outperforms all baselines on the EncycNet dataset. This demonstrates its potential for effectively integrating new knowledge into LM in the CLS domain.

For a closer interpretation of CapsKG's performance on the EncycNet dataset, we report the model's performance on the individual relation types contained in EncycNet in Table 7. Since our goal is to integrate newly acquired knowledge into the LM, we

Table 6. Results for link prediction on WN18, YAGO, FB15k with 5 random seeds, and EncycNet with 10 random seeds, reporting mean and standard deviation of Hits@1 performance.

Model/Dataset	WN18	YAGO	FB15k	EncycNet
BERT$_{\text{frozen}}$	10.7 (0.0)	27.0 (0.0)	5.5 (0.0)	7.4 (0.0)
BERT	25.8 (0.5)	48.0 (0.1)	34.7 (0.7)	38.93 (0.5)
Adapter	26.4 (0.5)	48.7 (0.4)	35.6 (0.2)	39.93 (0.3)
BERT-CL	20.2 (1.2)	40.4 (4.0)	11.4 (3.2)	23.6 (5.9)
Adapter-CL	18.4 (1.2)	41.5 (0.7)	16.3 (1.4)	25.0 (5.6)
CapsKG	**27.4 (0.4)**	**49.4 (0.3)**	**36.1 (0.3)**	**40.7 (0.3)**

Table 7. Results for link prediction on EncycNet on individual relation types for a frozen BERT model and the full CapsKG method, reporting mean and standard deviation of Hits@1 performance for CapsKG over 10 random seeds.

Relation Name	**BERT$_{frozen}$**		**CapsKG**	
	train	test	train	test
Komposition	1.90	0.60	86.89 (7.30)	26.40 (0.49)
Nomenklatorischer Typ	0.00	0.00	95.97 (1.33)	93.89 (0.76)
Relevante Person	3.60	3.60	28.27 (1.16)	24.98 (0.25)
Alternativer Name	2.30	3.20	49.86 (4.45)	39.82 (2.27)
Etymon	6.60	6.20	62.62 (5.94)	38.61 (2.78)
Beschrieben-in	0.00	0.00	51.01 (10.66)	45.73 (1.86)
Wörtliche Übersetzung	3.90	4.20	32.27 (5.61)	16.16 (1.14)
Synonym	4.40	4.60	59.73 (8.15)	49.67 (1.98)
Affiliation	0.40	0.40	31.54 (3.43)	27.63 (0.86)
Ist-eine	4.20	4.00	54.79 (5.27)	48.66 (0.41)
Taxon Hypernym	76.10	76.90	94.35 (1.06)	93.26 (0.52)
Klasse	0.00	0.00	75.56 (0.70)	75.07 (0.45)
Übersetzung	0.50	0.30	19.15 (6.38)	11.80 (0.48)
Definition	4.50	4.20	41.20 (2.82)	39.30 (0.82)
Sprache	21.30	22.70	77.77 (0.46)	75.31 (0.43)
Aspekt-von	0.50	1.30	27.43 (5.30)	13.93 (1.44)
Bedeutender Autor	0.60	0.70	9.69 (0.16)	10.36 (0.23)
Verwandter Begriff	0.50	0.60	20.58 (2.26)	17.36 (0.27)
Bedeutender Ort	7.50	7.90	29.51 (1.15)	25.58 (0.41)

also report the model's performance on the training split to assess how well it accommodates new information. The results show that some relation types can be learned better by the model than others. Specifically, general concepts related to common sense abstractions such as hypernyms (Taxon Hypernym), the language of a concept (Sprache), or the biological nomenclatural type (Nomenklatorischer Typ) appear to be well represented within the model. Conversely, highly specific knowledge related to specific persons (Relevante Person) or public literary figures (Bedeutender Autor) appears to result in lower accuracies. Some relation types, such as compounds (Komposition), are challenging for the LM to generalize but can be effectively accommodated by the model. Still, the proposed approach is able to learn a large variety of historical knowledge, as evidenced by the comparison to the standard BERT$_{frozen}$ model. This regular pre-trained BERT model that was not fine-tuned on the knowledge graph performs exceptionally poorly on most relation types, indicating that integrating available knowledge from knowledge graphs provides significant benefits to language models.

5. Outlook: Applications of Neurosymbolic Systems and Knowledge Graphs

Enhancing LLMs with structured knowledge is only one step towards creating more stable knowledge representations within LLMs. On the one hand, LLMs such as Llama or GPT possess quite an extensive and thorough repository of knowledge. On the other hand, significant drawbacks of LLMs are their unpredictability when prompted as well as a lack of transparency, not only when it comes to the data that is actually contained in them, but also potentially additional knowledge filtering steps the user might not know about. In comparison, KGs offer a straight-forward knowledge representation, however they only cover a fraction of how humans actually store and process knowledge. To integrate KGs and LLMs means seeking to remedy the drawbacks of one another to some extent: transparent (but shallow) knowledge from KGs with vast (but unpredictable) knowledge from LLMs.

In this chapter, we demonstrated multiple strategies for integrating information from knowledge graphs into language models. We showed how existing word embeddings may be updated according to a knowledge graph through retrofitting and fusion. Additionally, we demonstrated CapsKG, an approach for continuously integrating knowledge graphs into language models through parameter-efficient fine-tuning. Lastly, we also showcased the LM4KG method for extracting information contained in a language model and integrating it into an existing knowledge graph. While our demonstrations of these approaches rely on established encoder-based language models, we note that these approaches can also be adapted to currently popular large decoder-based language models. As the intuition behind the LM4KG method is directly reliant on a generative intuition of model perplexity, decoder-based language models are directly applicable and may even be better suitable for assessing viable candidate concepts as they enable a direct perplexity calculation due to their unidirectional nature. Additionally, current LLMs can be prompted to focus on specific historical periods or domains, facilitating a more detailed assessment of triple strength based on the given context. As these models can process longer input texts, prompts can be extended with relevant documents, such as books, enabling the model to evaluate triple strength based on information specific to those documents. For CapsKG, the adapter-based methodology used for fine-tuning the model to the knowledge graph closely corresponds to current parameter-efficient fine-tuning strategies of large decoder-based language models and is directly transferable to these architectures.

Overall, in this chapter, we argued that LLMs can benefit from knowledge graphs representing historical and cultural heritage as well as literary text characteristics, thus advancing the field of computational literary studies. Conversely, knowledge graph creation and completion can also benefit from the latest advancements in LLMs.

However, the research area of KG and LLM integration can only advance state-of-the-art language modeling up to a certain degree, as the grounding problem stretches far wider than what KGs can actually provide. As Mollo and Millière argue, the key to to creating a LM that is better connected to the real world may not necessarily lie in the kind of data provided, but rather in the nature of the model's learning process [102]. Future work in the field will need to focus on integrating novel data and data structures with appropriate and innovative learning procedures.

Acknowledgements

This publication was partially funded by the Deutsche Forschungsgemeinschaft (DFG, German Research Foundation) under the project LitBERT, project no. 529659926.[11]

[11] `https://gepris.dfg.de/gepris/projekt/529659926`.

References

[1] Biemann C, Crane GR, Fellbaum CD, Mehler A. Computational Humanities. Bridging the gap between Computer Science and Digital Humanities (Dagstuhl Seminar 14301). Dagstuhl Reports. 2014;4(7):80-111. doi:10.4230/DAGREP.4.7.80.

[2] Hogan A, Blomqvist E, Cochez M, D'amato C, Melo GD, Gutierrez C, et al. Knowledge Graphs. ACM Computing Survey. 2021;54(4):71:1-71:37. doi:10.1145/3447772.

[3] Singhal A. Introducing the knowledge graph: Things, not strings; 2012. Google Blog. Available from: `https://blog.google/products/search/introducing-knowledge-graph-things-not`.

[4] Nickel M, Murphy K, Tresp V, Gabrilovich E. A review of relational machine learning for knowledge graphs. Proceedings of the IEEE. 2015;104(1):11-33. doi:10.1109/JPROC.2015.2483592.

[5] Cimiano P, Paulheim H. Knowledge graph refinement: A survey of approaches and evaluation methods. Semantic Web. 2017;8(3):489-508. doi:10.3233/SW-160218.

[6] Abu-Salih B. Domain-specific knowledge graphs: A survey. Journal of Network and Computer Applications. 2021;185. Article 103076. doi:10.1016/j.jnca.2021.103076.

[7] Peng C, Xia F, Naseriparsa M, Osborne F. Knowledge graphs: Opportunities and challenges. Artificial Intelligence Review. 2023;56(11):13071-102. doi:10.1007/s10462-023-10465-9.

[8] Ji S, Pan S, Cambria E, Marttinen P, Philip SY. A survey on knowledge graphs: Representation, acquisition, and applications. IEEE transactions on neural networks and learning systems. 2021;33(2):494-514. doi:10.1109/TNNLS.2021.3070843.

[9] Zhang H, Liu X, Pan H, Song Y, Leung CWK. ASER: A Large-scale Eventuality Knowledge Graph. In: Proceedings of The Web Conference 2020. Association for Computing Machinery; 2020. p. 201–211. doi:10.1145/3366423.3380107.

[10] Cyganiak R, Wood D, Lanthaler M. RDF 1.1 Concepts and Abstract Syntax; 2014. World Wide Web Consortium (W3C) Recommendation. Available from: `https://www.w3.org/TR/rdf11-concepts/`.

[11] Wei X, Wang S, Zhang D, Bhatia P, Arnold A. Knowledge enhanced pretrained language models: A compreshensive survey; 2021. ArXiv preprint. doi:10.48550/arXiv.2110.08455.

[12] Kejriwal M. Domain-specific Knowledge Graph Construction. Springer; 2019. doi:10.1007/978-3-030-12375-8.

[13] Zhong L, Wu J, Li Q, Peng H, Wu X. A comprehensive survey on automatic knowledge graph construction. ACM Computing Surveys. 2023;56(4):1-62. doi:10.1145/3618295.

[14] Zeng K, Li C, Hou L, Li J, Feng L. A comprehensive survey of entity alignment for knowledge graphs. AI Open. 2021;2:1-13. doi:10.1016/j.aiopen.2021.02.002.

[15] Hagen T. Von A bis Z: Überlegungen zur Erstellung eines Wissensgraphen aus historischen Enzyklopädien. In: Busch A, Trilcke P, editors. Abstracts zur 9. Jahrestagung des Verbands Digital Humanities im deutschsprachigen Raum e.V. (DHd2023); 2023. doi:10.5281/zenodo.7688632.

[16] Apps A. Guidelines for encoding bibliographic citation information in dublin core metadata; 2005. Dublin Core Metadata Initiative.

[17] Haslhofer B, Isaac A, Simon R. Knowledge graphs in the libraries and digital humanities domain; 2018. ArXiv preprint. doi:10.48550/arXiv.1803.03198.

[18] Hawkins A. Archives, Linked Data and the Digital Humanities: Increasing Access to Digitised and Born-digital Archives via the Semantic Web. Archival Science. 2022;22(3):319-44. doi:10.1007/s10502-021-09381-0.

[19] Hyvönen E. Using the Semantic Web in digital humanities: Shift from data publishing to data-analysis and serendipitous knowledge discovery. Semantic Web. 2020;11(1):187-93. doi:10.3233/SW-190386.

[20] Labatut V, Bost X. Extraction and analysis of fictional character networks: A survey. ACM Computing Surveys. 2019;52(5):1-40. doi:10.1145/3344548.

[21] Ryan YC, Ahnert SE. The measure of the archive: The robustness of network analysis in early modern correspondence. Journal of Cultural Analytics. 2021;6(3):57-88. doi:10.22148/001c.25943.

[22] Windhager F, Salisu S, Liem J, Mayr E. In: Dammann F, Kremer D, editors. The Knowledge Graph as a Data Sculpture: Visualising Arts and Humanities Data with Maps, Graphs, and Sets over Time. Bielefeld University Press; 2024. p. 113-34. doi:10.1515/9783839469187-007.

[23] Schöch C, Hinzmann M, Röttgermann J, Dietz K, Klee A. Smart Modelling for Literary History. International Journal of Humanities and Arts Computing. 2022;16(1):78-93. doi:10.3366/ijhac.2022.0278.

[24] Zamani M, Tejedor A, Vogl M, Kräutli F, Valleriani M, Kantz H. Evolution and transformation of early modern cosmological knowledge: A network study. Scientific Reports. 2020;10(1):article 19822.

doi:doi.org/10.1038/s41598-020-76916-3.

[25] Barber M. Reading and understanding text reuse data through graphs: a case study on pre-modern Arabic book history and historiography. In: Andrews T, Diehr F, Efer T, Kuczera A, van Zundert J, editors. Proceedings of the 6th International Conference on Graphs and Networks in the Humanities; 2022. Available from: https://graphentechnologien.hypotheses.org/files/2022/01/Reading_and_understanding_text_reuse_data_through_graphs_etc-Barber.pdf.

[26] Jain N, Múnera AS, Lomaeva M, Streit J, Thormeyer S, Schmidt P, et al. Generating Domain-Specific Knowledge Graphs: Challenges with Open Information Extraction. In: Tiwari S, Mihindukulasooriya N, Osborne F, Kontokostas D, D'Souza J, Kejriwal M, editors. Proceedings of the 1st International Workshop on Knowledge Graph Generation From Text and the 1st International Workshop on Modular Knowledge (TEXT2KG/MK @ ESWC). vol. 3184 of CEUR Workshop Proceedings; 2022. p. 52-69. Available from: https://ceur-ws.org/Vol-3184/TEXT2KG_Paper_4.pdf.

[27] Verhoeven D, Burrows T. Building the Australian Knowledge Graph: HuNI (Humanities Networked Infrastructure). In: Andrews T, Diehr F, Efer T, Kuczera A, van Zundert J, editors. Proceedings of the 6th International Conference on Graphs and Networks in the Humanities; 2022. Available from: https://graphentechnologien.hypotheses.org/files/2022/01/Building_the_Australian_Knowledge_Graph_HuNI_Humanities_Networked_etc-Verhoeven_Burrows.pdf.

[28] Doerr M. The CIDOC CRM, an Ontological Approach to Schema Heterogeneity. In: Kalfoglou Y, Schorlemmer M, Sheth A, Staab S, Uschold M, editors. Semantic Interoperability and Integration. vol. 4391 of Dagstuhl Seminar Proceedings. Leibniz-Zentrum für Informatik; 2005. p. 1-5. doi:10.4230/DagSemProc.04391.22.

[29] Hagen T, Ketzan E. Introducing Traveling Word Pairs in Historical Semantic Change: A Case Study of Privacy Words in 18th and 19th Century English. In: Šeļa A, Jannidis F, Romanowska I, editors. Proceedings of the Computational Humanities Research Conference 2023 (CHR2023). vol. 1613 of CEUR Workshop Proceedings; 2023. p. 461-74. Available from: https://ceur-ws.org/Vol-3558/paper5360.pdf.

[30] Ehrmanntraut A, Hagen T, Konle L, Jannidis F. Type-and Token-based Word Embeddings in the Digital Humanities. In: Ehrmann M, Karsdorp F, Wevers M, Andrews TL, Burghardt M, Kestemont M, et al., editors. Proceedings of the Computational Humanities Research Conference 2023 (CHR2023). vol. 2989 of CEUR Workshop Proceedings. CEUR; 2021. p. 16-38. Available from: https://ceur-ws.org/Vol-2989/long_paper35.pdf.

[31] Hagen T, Ketzan E, Jannidis F, Witt A. Twenty-two Historical Encyclopedias Encoded in TEI: a New Resource for the Digital Humanities. In: DeGaetano S, Kazantseva A, Reiter N, Szpakowicz S, editors. Proceedings of the 4th Joint SIGHUM Workshop on Computational Linguistics for Cultural Heritage, Social Sciences, Humanities and Literature (LaTeCH-CLfL 2020). International Committee on Computational Linguistics; 2020. p. 112-20. Available from: https://aclanthology.org/2020.latechclfl-1.13.

[32] Matuschek M. Word Sense Alignment of Lexical Resources; 2015. PhD Thesis, Technische Universität Darmstadt. Available from: https://tuprints.ulb.tu-darmstadt.de/id/eprint/4355.

[33] Pais V, Tufiș D, Ion R. MWSA Task at GlobaLex 2020: RACAI's Word Sense Alignment System using a Similarity Measurement of Dictionary Definitions. In: Kernerman I, Krek S, McCrae JP, Gracia J, Ahmadi S, Kabashi B, editors. Proceedings of the 2020 Globalex Workshop on Linked Lexicography. European Language Resources Association; 2020. p. 69-75. Available from: https://aclanthology.org/2020.globalex-1.12.

[34] Loureiro D, Rezaee K, Pilehvar MT, Camacho-Collados J. Analysis and Evaluation of Language Models for Word Sense Disambiguation. Computational Linguistics. 2021;47(2):387-443. doi:10.1162/coli_a_00405.

[35] Wang K, Reimers N, Gurevych I. TSDAE: Using Transformer-based Sequential Denoising Auto-Encoder for Unsupervised Sentence Embedding Learning. In: Moens MF, Huang X, Specia L, Yih SW, editors. Findings of the Association for Computational Linguistics: EMNLP 2021. Association for Computational Linguistics; 2021. p. 671-88. Available from: https://aclanthology.org/2021.findings-emnlp.59.

[36] Hagen T, Jannidis F, Witt A. Word Sense Alignment and Disambiguation for Historical Encyclopedias. In: Andrews T, Diehr F, Efer T, Kuczera A, van Zundert J, editors. Proceedings of the 6th International Conference on Graphs and Networks in the Humanities. Leibniz-Institut für Deutsche Sprache (IDS); 2022. Available from: https://nbn-resolving.org/urn:nbn:de:bsz:mh39-109834.

[37] Ehrmanntraut A. Historical German Text Normalization Using Type- and Token-Based Language Modeling; 2024. ArXiv preprint. doi:10.48550/arXiv.2409.02841.

[38] Hiebel G, Doerr M, Eide Ø. CRMgeo: A spatiotemporal extension of CIDOC-CRM. International Journal on Digital Libraries. 2017;18:271-9. doi:10.1007/s00799-016-0192-4.

[39] Loureiro D, Rezaee K, Pilehvar MT, Camacho-Collados J. Language models and word sense disambiguation: An overview and analysis; 2020. ArXiv preprint. doi:10.48550/arXiv.2008.11608.

[40] Perri V, Qarkaxhija L, Zehe A, Hotho A, Scholtes I. One Graph to Rule them All: Using NLP and Graph Neural Networks to analyse Tolkien's Legendarium. In: Karsdorp F, Nielbo KL, editors. Proceedings of the Computational Humanities Research Conference 2022 (CHR 2022). vol. 3290 of CEUR Workshop Proceedings; 2022. p. 291-317. Available from: https://ceur-ws.org/Vol-3290/long_paper2171.pdf.

[41] Gupta T, Hatzel HO, Biemann C. Coreference in Long Documents using Hierarchical Entity Merging. In: Bizzoni Y, Degaetano-Ortlieb S, Kazantseva A, Szpakowicz S, editors. Proceedings of the 8th Joint SIGHUM Workshop on Computational Linguistics for Cultural Heritage, Social Sciences, Humanities and Literature (LaTeCH-CLfL 2024). Association for Computational Linguistics; 2024. p. 11-7. Available from: https://aclanthology.org/2024.latechclfl-1.2.

[42] Maaten Lvd, Hinton G. Visualizing Data using t-SNE. Journal of Machine Learning Research. 2008;9(86):2579-605. Available from: http://jmlr.org/papers/v9/vandermaaten08a.html.

[43] Zehe A, Konle L, Dümpelmann LK, Gius E, Hotho A, Jannidis F, et al. Detecting scenes in fiction: A new segmentation task. In: Merlo P, Tiedemann J, Tsarfaty R, editors. Proceedings of the 16th conference of the European chapter of the Association for Computational Linguistics (EACL 2021). Main volume. Association for Computational Linguistics; 2021. p. 3167-77. doi:10.18653/v1/2021.eacl-main.276.

[44] Gius E, Jannidis F, Krug M, Zehe A, Hotho A, Puppe F, et al. Detection of Scenes in Fiction. In: Book of Abstracts of the Digital Humanities 2019 (DH2019); 2019. doi:10.34894/OOY9CE.

[45] Zehe A, Konle L, Guhr S, Dümpelmann L, Gius E, Hotho A, et al. Shared Task on Scene Segmentation @ KONVENS 2021. In: Proceedings of the Shared Task on Scene Segmentation. vol. 3001 of CEUR Workshop Proceedings; 2021. p. 1-21. Available from: http://ceur-ws.org/Vol-3001/paper1.pdf.

[46] Kurfalı M, Wirén M. Breaking the narrative: Scene segmentation through sequential sentence classification. In: Zehe A, Konle L, Guhr S, Dümpelmann L, Gius E, Hotho A, et al., editors. Proceedings of the Shared Task on Scene Segmentation. vol. 3001; 2021. p. 49-53. Available from: http://ceur-ws.org/Vol-3001/paper6.pdf.

[47] Ehrmanntraut A, Konle L, Jannidis F. LLpro: A Literary Language Processing Pipeline for German Narrative Texts. In: Georges M, Herygers A, Friedrich A, Roth B, editors. Proceedings of the 19th Conference on Natural Language Processing (KONVENS 2023). Association for Computational Lingustics; 2023. p. 28-39. Available from: https://aclanthology.org/2023.konvens-main.3.

[48] Konle L, Jannidis F. Modeling Plots of Narrative Texts as Temporal Graphs. In: Karsdorp F, Nielbo KL, editors. Proceedings of the Computational Humanities Research Conference 2022 (CHR 2022). CEUR Workshop Proceedings. CEUR; 2022. p. 318-36. Available from: https://ceur-ws.org/Vol-3290/long_paper2313.pdf.

[49] Rozemberczki B, Scherer P, He Y, Panagopoulos G, Riedel A, Astefanoaei M, et al. PyTorch Geometric Temporal: Spatiotemporal Signal Processing with Neural Machine Learning Models. In: Proceedings of the 30th ACM International Conference on Information and Knowledge Management. Association for Computing Machinery; 2021. p. 4564–4573. doi:10.1145/3459637.3482014.

[50] Zhang R, Reddy RG, Sultan MA, Castelli V, Ferritto A, Florian R, et al. Multi-Stage Pre-training for Low-Resource Domain Adaptation. In: Webber B, Cohn T, He Y, Liu Y, editors. Proceedings of the 2020 Conference on Empirical Methods in Natural Language Processing (EMNLP). Association for Computational Linguistics; 2020. p. 5461-8. Available from: https://aclanthology.org/2020.emnlp-main.440/.

[51] Gururangan S, Marasović A, Swayamdipta S, Lo K, Beltagy I, Downey D, et al. Don't Stop Pretraining: Adapt Language Models to Domains and Tasks. In: Jurafsky D, Chai J, Schluter N, Tetreault J, editors. Proceedings of the 58th Annual Meeting of the Association for Computational Linguistics. Association for Computational Linguistics; 2020. p. 8342-60. doi:10.18653/v1/2020.acl-main.740.

[52] Diao S, Xu T, Xu R, Wang J, Zhang T. Mixture-of-Domain-Adapters: Decoupling and Injecting Domain Knowledge to Pre-trained Language Models' Memories. In: Rogers A, Boyd-Graber J, Okazaki

N, editors. Proceedings of the 61st Annual Meeting of the Association for Computational Linguistics (Volume 1: Long Papers). Association for Computational Linguistics; 2023. p. 5113-29. Available from: https://aclanthology.org/2023.acl-long.280.

[53] Zhang Z, Han X, Liu Z, Jiang X, Sun M, Liu Q. ERNIE: Enhanced Language Representation with Informative Entities. In: Korhonen A, Traum D, Màrquez L, editors. Proceedings of the 57th Annual Meeting of the Association for Computational Linguistics. Association for Computational Linguistics; 2019. p. 1441-51. doi:10.18653/v1/P19-1139.

[54] Wang X, Gao T, Zhu Z, Zhang Z, Liu Z, Li J, et al. KEPLER: A Unified Model for Knowledge Embedding and Pre-trained Language Representation. Transactions of the Association for Computational Linguistics. 2021;9:176-94. doi:10.1162/tacl_a_00360.

[55] Moiseev F, Dong Z, Alfonseca E, Jaggi M. SKILL: Structured Knowledge Infusion for Large Language Models. In: Carpuat M, de Marneffe MC, Meza Ruiz IV, editors. Proceedings of the 2022 Conference of the North American Chapter of the Association for Computational Linguistics: Human Language Technologies. Association for Computational Linguistics; 2022. p. 1581-8. doi:10.18653/v1/2022.naacl-main.113.

[56] Liu W, Zhou P, Zhao Z, Wang Z, Ju Q, Deng H, et al. K-bert: Enabling language representation with knowledge graph. In: Proceedings of the AAAI Conference on Artificial Intelligence: Technical Tracks 3. AAAI Conference and Symposium Proceedings. Association for the Advancement of Artificial Intelligence; 2020. p. 2901-8. doi:10.1609/aaai.v34i03.5681.

[57] Beltagy I, Lo K, Cohan A. SciBERT: A pretrained language model for scientific text; 2019. ArXiv preprint. doi:10.48550/arXiv.1903.10676.

[58] Devlin J, Chang MW, Lee K, Toutanova K. BERT: Pre-training of deep bidirectional transformers for language understanding; 2018. ArXiv preprint. doi:10.48550/arXiv.1810.04805.

[59] Fichtel L, Kalo JC, Balke WT. Prompt tuning or fine-tuning-investigating relational knowledge in pre-trained language models. In: Proceedings of the 3rd Conference on Automated Knowledge Base Construction (AKBC 2021); 2021. Available from: https://openreview.net/forum?id=o7sMlpr9yBW.

[60] Yao L, Mao C, Luo Y. KG-BERT: BERT for knowledge graph completion; 2019. ArXiv preprint. doi:10.48550/arXiv.1909.03193.

[61] Sanh V, Debut L, Chaumond J, Wolf T. DistilBERT, a distilled version of BERT: smaller, faster, cheaper and lighter; 2019. ArXiv preprint. doi:10.48550/arXiv.1910.01108.

[62] Clark K, Luong MT, Le QV, Manning CD. ELECTRA: Pre-training Text Encoders as Discriminators Rather Than Generators; 2020. ArXiv preprint. doi:10.48550/arXiv.2003.10555.

[63] Konle L, Jannidis F. Domain and Task Adaptive Pretraining for Language Models. In: Karsdorp F, McGillivray B, Nerghes A, Wevers M, editors. Proceedings of the Workshop on Computational Humanities Research (CHR 2020). vol. 2723 of CEUR Workshop Proceedings; 2020. p. 248-56. Available from: https://ceur-ws.org/Vol-2723/short33.pdf.

[64] Krug M, Weimer L, Reger I, Macharowsky L, Feldhaus S, Puppe F, et al.. Description of a Corpus of Character References in German Novels: DROC [Deutsches ROman Corpus]; 2017. Nr. 27 in DARIAH-DE Working Papers. Available from: https://resolver.sub.uni-goettingen.de/purl?gro-2/108301.

[65] Brunner A, Engelberg S, Jannidis F, Tu NDT, Weimer L. Corpus REDEWIEDERGABE. In: Calzolari N, Béchet F, Blache P, Choukri K, Cieri C, Declerck T, et al., editors. Proceedings of the 12th Language Resources and Evaluation Conference (LREC 2020). European Language Resources Association; 2020. p. 803-12. Available from: https://www.aclweb.org/anthology/2020.lrec-1.100.

[66] Speer R, Chin J, Havasi C. ConceptNet 5.5: an open multilingual graph of general knowledge. In: Proceedings of the Thirty-First AAAI Conference on Artificial Intelligence (AAAI 2017). AAAI Press; 2017. p. 4444-51. doi:10.1609/aaai.v31i1.11164.

[67] Faruqui M, Dodge J, Jauhar SK, Dyer C, Hovy E, Smith NA. Retrofitting Word Vectors to Semantic Lexicons. In: Mihalcea R, Chai J, Sarkar A, editors. Proceedings of the 2015 Conference of the North American Chapter of the Association for Computational Linguistics: Human Language Technologies. Association for Computational Linguistics; 2015. p. 1606-15. doi:10.3115/v1/N15-1184.

[68] Lengerich B, Maas A, Potts C. Retrofitting Distributional Embeddings to Knowledge Graphs with Functional Relations. In: Bender EM, Derczynski L, Isabelle P, editors. Proceedings of the 27th International Conference on Computational Linguistics. Association for Computational Linguistics; 2018. p. 2423-36. Available from: https://aclanthology.org/C18-1205.

[69] Thoma S, Rettinger A, Both F. Towards holistic concept representations: Embedding relational knowledge, visual attributes, and distributional word semantics. In: d'Amato C, Fernandez M, Tamma V, Lecue F, Cudré-Mauroux P, Sequeda J, et al., editors. Proceedings of the 16th International Semantic Web Conference (IWSC 2017). No. 10587 in Lecture Notes in Computer Science. Springer; 2017. p. 694-710. doi:10.1007/978-3-319-68288-4_41.
[70] Bordes A, Usunier N, Garcia-Duran A, Weston J, Yakhnenko O. Translating Embeddings for Modeling Multi-relational Data. In: Burges CJ, Bottou L, Welling M, Ghahramani Z, Weinberger KQ, editors. Advances in Neural Information Processing Systems (NIPS 2013). vol. 26. Curran Associates; 2013. Available from: https://proceedings.neurips.cc/paper_files/paper/2013/file/1cecc7a77928ca8133fa24680a88d2f9-Abstract.pdf.
[71] Sun Z, Deng ZH, Nie JY, Tang J. RotatE: Knowledge Graph Embedding by Relational Rotation in Complex Space. In: The Seventh International Conference on Learning Representations (ICLR 2019); 2019. Available from: https://openreview.net/pdf?id=HkgEQnRqYQ.
[72] Mikolov T, Chen K, Corrado G, Dean J. Efficient estimation of word representations in vector space; 2013. ArXiv preprint. doi:10.48550/arXiv.1301.3781.
[73] Bojanowski P, Grave E, Joulin A, Mikolov T. Enriching Word Vectors with Subword Information. Transactions of the Association for Computational Linguistics. 2017;5:135-46. doi:10.1162/tacl_a_00051.
[74] Ortiz Suárez PJ, Romary L, Sagot B. A Monolingual Approach to Contextualized Word Embeddings for Mid-Resource Languages. In: Jurafsky D, Chai J, Schluter N, Tetreault J, editors. Proceedings of the 58th Annual Meeting of the Association for Computational Linguistics. Association for Computational Linguistics; 2020. p. 1703-14. doi:10.18653/v1/2020.acl-main.156.
[75] Hamp B, Feldweg H. GermaNet. A Lexical-Semantic Net for German. In: Vossen P, Adriaens G, Calzolari N, Sanfilippo A, Wilks Y, editors. Proceeedings of the ACL/EACL Workshop on Automatic Information Extraction and Building of Lexical Semantic Resources for NLP Applications. Association for Computational Linguistics; 1997. Available from: https://aclanthology.org/W97-0802.
[76] Hagen T. Verwendung von Wissensgraphen zur inhaltlichen Ergänzung kleinerer Textkorpora. In: Geierhos M, editor. Abstracts zur 8. Jahrestagung des Verbands Digital Humanities im deutschsprachigen Raum e.V. (DHd2022); 2022. doi:10.5281/zenodo.6328009.
[77] Köper M, Scheible C, Schulte im Walde S. Multilingual Reliability and "Semantic" Structure of Continuous Word Spaces. In: Purver M, Sadrzadeh M, Stone M, editors. Proceedings of the 11th International Conference on Computational Semantics (IWCS 2015). Association for Computational Linguistics; 2015. p. 40-5. Available from: https://aclanthology.org/W15-0105.
[78] Finkelstein L, Gabrilovich E, Matias Y, Rivlin E, Solan Z, Wolfman G, et al. Placing search in context: The concept revisited. In: Proceedings of the 10th International Conference on World Wide Web (WWW10); 2001. p. 406-14. Available from: https://www.ra.ethz.ch/CDstore/www10/papers/pdf/p431.pdf.
[79] Leviant I, Reichart R. Separated by an un-common language: Towards judgment language informed vector space modeling; 2015. ArXiv preprint. doi:10.48550/arXiv.1508.00106.
[80] Hill F, Reichart R, Korhonen A. SimLex-999: Evaluating Semantic Models With (Genuine) Similarity Estimation. Computational Linguistics. 2015;41(4):665-95. doi:10.1162/COLI_a_00237.
[81] Zesch T, Gurevych I, Mühlhäuser M. Comparing Wikipedia and German Wordnet by Evaluating Semantic Relatedness on Multiple Datasets. In: Sidner C, Schultz T, Stone M, Zhai C, editors. Human Language Technologies 2007: The Conference of the North American Chapter of the Association for Computational Linguistics. Association for Computational Linguistics; 2007. p. 205-8. Available from: https://aclanthology.org/N07-2052.
[82] Rubenstein H, Goodenough JB. Contextual correlates of synonymy. Communications of the ACM. 1965;8(10):627-33. doi:10.1145/365628.365657.
[83] Gurevych I. Using the Structure of a Conceptual Network in Computing Semantic Relatedness. In: Dale R, Wong KF, Su J, Kwong OY, editors. Proceedings of the Second International Joint Conference on Natural Language Processing (IJCNLP 2005). No. 3651 in Lecture Notes in Computer Science. Springer; 2005. doi:10.1007/11562214_67.
[84] Omeliyanenko J, Zehe A, Hettinger L, Hotho A. LM4KG: Improving common sense knowledge graphs with language models. In: Pan JZ, Tamma V, d'Amato C, Janowicz K, Fu B, Polleres A, et al., editors. Proceedings of the 19th International Semantic Web Conference (IWSC 2020). No. 12506 in Lecture Notes in Computer Science. Springer; 2020. p. 456-73. doi:10.1007/978-3-030-62419-4_26.

[85] Petroni F, Rocktäschel T, Riedel S, Lewis P, Bakhtin A, Wu Y, et al. Language Models as Knowledge Bases? In: Inui K, Jiang J, Ng V, Wan X, editors. Proceedings of the 2019 Conference on Empirical Methods in Natural Language Processing and the 9th International Joint Conference on Natural Language Processing (EMNLP-IJCNLP 2019). Association for Computational Linguistics; 2019. p. 2463-73. doi:10.18653/v1/D19-1250.

[86] Radford A, Wu J, Child R, Luan D, Amodei D, Sutskever I. Language models are unsupervised multitask learners; 2019. Available from: `https://openai.com/index/better-language-models/`.

[87] Chen X, Liu X, Ragni A, Wang Y, Gales MJ. Future word contexts in neural network language models. In: Proceedings of the 2017 IEEE Automatic Speech Recognition and Understanding Workshop (ASRU). IEEE; 2017. p. 97-103. doi:10.1109/ASRU.2017.8268922.

[88] Bruni E, Tran NK, Baroni M. Multimodal distributional semantics. Journal of Artificial Intelligence Research. 2014;49:1-47. doi:10.1613/jair.4135.

[89] Luong T, Socher R, Manning C. Better Word Representations with Recursive Neural Networks for Morphology. In: Hockenmaier J, Riedel S, editors. Proceedings of the Seventeenth Conference on Computational Natural Language Learning (CoNLL 2013). Association for Computational Linguistics; 2013. p. 104-13. Available from: `https://aclanthology.org/W13-3512`.

[90] Halawi G, Dror G, Gabrilovich E, Koren Y. Large-scale learning of word relatedness with constraints. In: Proceedings of the 18th ACM SIGKDD International Conference on Knowledge Discovery and Data Mining (KDD 2012). Association for Computing Machinery; 2012. p. 1406-14. doi:10.1145/2339530.2339751.

[91] Camacho-Collados J, Pilehvar MT, Collier N, Navigli R. SemEval-2017 Task 2: Multilingual and Cross-lingual Semantic Word Similarity. In: Bethard S, Carpuat M, Apidianaki M, Mohammad SM, Cer D, Jurgens D, editors. Proceedings of the 11th International Workshop on Semantic Evaluation (SemEval-2017). Association for Computational Linguistics; 2017. p. 15-26. doi:10.18653/v1/S17-2002.

[92] Kirkpatrick J, Pascanu R, Rabinowitz N, Veness J, Desjardins G, Rusu AA, et al. Overcoming catastrophic forgetting in neural networks. Proceedings of the National Academy of Sciences. 2017;114(13):3521-6. doi:10.1073/pnas.1611835114.

[93] Omeliyanenko J, Zehe A, Hotho A, Schlör D. CapsKG: Enabling Continual Knowledge Integration in Language Models for Automatic Knowledge Graph Completion. In: Payne TR, Presutti V, Qi G, Poveda-Villalón M, Stoilos G, Hollink L, et al., editors. Proceedings of the 22th International Semantic Web Conference (ISWC 2023). No. 14266 in Lecture Notes in Computer Science. Springer Nature; 2023. p. 618-36. doi:10.1007/978-3-031-47240-4_33.

[94] Bosselut A, Rashkin H, Sap M, Malaviya C, Celikyilmaz A, Choi Y. COMET: Commonsense Transformers for Automatic Knowledge Graph Construction. In: Korhonen A, Traum D, Màrquez L, editors. Proceedings of the 57th Annual Meeting of the Association for Computational Linguistics. Association for Computational Linguistics; 2019. p. 4762-79. doi:10.18653/v1/P19-1470.

[95] Agarwal O, Ge H, Shakeri S, Al-Rfou R. Knowledge Graph Based Synthetic Corpus Generation for Knowledge-Enhanced Language Model Pre-training. In: Toutanova K, Rumshisky A, Zettlemoyer L, Hakkani-Tur D, Beltagy I, Bethard S, et al., editors. Proceedings of the 2021 Conference of the North American Chapter of the Association for Computational Linguistics: Human Language Technologies. Association for Computational Linguistics; 2021. p. 3554-65. doi:10.18653/v1/2021.naacl-main.278.

[96] Houlsby N, Giurgiu A, Jastrzebski S, Morrone B, De Laroussilhe Q, Gesmundo A, et al. Parameter-Efficient Transfer Learning for NLP. In: Chaudhuri K, Salakhutdinov R, editors. Proceedings of the 36th International Conference on Machine Learning. vol. 97 of Proceedings of Machine Learning Research; 2019. p. 2790-9. Available from: `http://proceedings.mlr.press/v97/houlsby19a/houlsby19a.pdf`.

[97] Kumar A, Singh SS, Singh K, Biswas B. Link prediction techniques, applications, and performance: A survey. Physica A: Statistical Mechanics and its Applications. 2020;553. Article 124289. doi:10.1016/j.physa.2020.124289.

[98] Mahdisoltani F, Biega J, Suchanek FM. YAGO3: A Knowledge Base from Multilingual Wikipedias. In: Proceedings of the 7th Biennial Conference on Innovative Data Systems Research (CIDR 2015); 2015. Available from: `http://www.cidrdb.org/cidr2015/Papers/CIDR15_Paper1.pdf`.

[99] Tran HN, Takasu A. Raedt LD, editor. MEIM: Multi-partition Embedding Interaction Beyond Block Term Format for Efficient and Expressive Link Prediction. International Joint Conferences on Artificial Intelligence; 2022. doi:10.24963/ijcai.2022/314.

[100] Toutanova K, Chen D. Observed versus latent features for knowledge base and text inference. In: Allauzen A, Grefenstette E, Hermann KM, Larochelle H, Yih SWt, editors. Proceedings of the 3rd Workshop on Continuous Vector Space Models and their Compositionality. Association for Computational Linguistics; 2015. p. 57-66. doi:10.18653/v1/W15-4007.

[101] Lauscher A, Majewska O, Ribeiro LF, Gurevych I, Rozanov N, Glavaš G. Common Sense or World Knowledge? Investigating adapter-based Knowledge Injection into Pretrained Transformers; 2020. ArXiv preprint. doi:10.48550/arXiv.2005.11787.

[102] Mollo DC, Millière R. The vector grounding problem; 2023. ArXiv preprint. doi:10.48550/arXiv.2304.01481.

Handbook on Neurosymbolic AI and Knowledge Graphs
P. Hitzler et al. (Eds.)
IOS Press, 2025

doi:10.3233/FAIA250241

Mutual Understanding Between People and Systems via Neurosymbolic AI and Knowledge Graphs

Irene CELINO [a,1], Mario SCROCCA [a] and Agnese CHIATTI [b]
[a] *Cefriel, viale Sarca 226, 20126 Milano, Italy*
[b] *Politecnico di Milano, Piazza Leonardo da Vinci 32, 20133, Milano, Italy*
ORCiD ID: Irene Celino https://orcid.org/0000-0001-9962-7193, Mario Scrocca https://orcid.org/0000-0002-8235-7331, Agnese Chiatti https://orcid.org/0000-0003-3594-731X

Abstract. This chapter investigates the concept of mutual understanding between humans and systems, positing that Neuro-symbolic Artificial Intelligence (NeSy AI) methods can significantly enhance this mutual understanding by leveraging explicit symbolic knowledge representations with data-driven learning models. We start by introducing three critical dimensions to characterize mutual understanding: sharing knowledge, exchanging knowledge, and governing knowledge. Sharing knowledge involves aligning the conceptual models of different agents to enable a shared understanding of the domain of interest. Exchanging knowledge relates to ensuring the effective and accurate communication between agents. Governing knowledge concerns establishing rules and processes to regulate the interaction between agents. Then, we present several different use case scenarios that demonstrate the application of NeSy AI and Knowledge Graphs to aid meaningful exchanges between human, artificial, and robotic agents. These scenarios highlight both the potential and the challenges of combining top-down symbolic reasoning with bottom-up neural learning, guiding the discussion of the coverage provided by current solutions along the dimensions of sharing, exchanging, and governing knowledge. Concurrently, this analysis facilitates the identification of gaps and less developed aspects in mutual understanding to address in future research.

Keywords. mutual understanding, knowledge sharing, knowledge exchange, knowledge governance, human agents, artificial agents, robotic agents, neuro-symbolic AI, knowledge graphs

1. Introduction

In his popular book "Thinking, fast and slow" [1], Daniel Kahneman proposed his cognitive theory of human decision-making with a differentiation between two modes of thought – a fast, instinctive and emotional system and a slower, more deliberative, and more logical one. The former is more unconscious and less explainable, showing some characteristics that resemble those of machine learning systems; the latter is more ex-

[1] Corresponding Author: Irene Celino, irene.celino@cefriel.com.

plicit and reasonable, displaying traits that are common in knowledge representation and reasoning systems.

When designing artificial intelligence systems, therefore, we can think of Neuro-symbolic AI [2] as the combination of "System 1" neural, connectionist approaches with "System 2" symbolic intelligent systems, to build hybrid solutions that take the best out of the two worlds [3]. Broadly speaking, Neuro-symbolic systems combine methods based on Artificial Neural Networks (i.e., the *neural* component) with methods based on the explicit manipulation of *symbols*. Although the distinction between symbols and non-symbols is a subject of active debate, we follow [4] in using the term symbol to refer to semantic descriptions of objects, classes and relations in the world (e.g., labels, relations, other explanations of historical data records). This hybrid learning process can also be seen as one that combines patterns extracted intuitively via bottom-up observation with top-down cognitive expectations about the environment [5].

With reference to human decision-making and inter-personal relationships, we are used to think that clear and meaningful conversations between people are needed to produce and achieve *mutual understanding* and successful outcomes. If we refer to classical definitions like Wittgenstein's, we also know that such achievement is oftentimes hard to reach: "We speak of understanding a sentence in the sense in which it can be replaced by another which says the same; but also in the sense in which it cannot be replaced by any other" [6], which challenges the very notion of understanding.

How can we promote achieve *mutual understanding between people* when their interaction is mediated by a digital artificial system? Can we also foster *mutual understanding between machines*, supporting interoperability and meaningful exchange? What are successful cases of employment of symbolic approaches (e.g., knowledge graphs and semantic web solutions), neural approaches (e.g., machine learning, generative AI, robotics) and a mix of them to achieve mutual understanding?

In this chapter, we aim at providing some answers to those questions, by proposing a set of dimensions to characterise mutual understanding (Section 2), by illustrating and analysing different use case scenarios that adopt Neuro-symbolic AI and Knowledge Graphs (Sections 3-8), and by providing a synthesis and challenges for future work (Section 9).

2. Dimensions of Mutual Understanding

Mutual understanding (between people) happens "when different minds mutually infer they agree on an understanding of an object, person, place, event, or idea" and this is usually supported by **conceptual alignment**, which is the "condition in which individuals' mental representations have become aligned, or sufficiently compatible, despite those individuals' idiosyncratic experiences and knowledge structures" [7].

A classic study [8] on communication behaviours of human agents during analyst-client interviews highlighted that there are three key processes that affect mutual understanding between people: *shifting perspective* (the process of tuning into the interlocutor's frame of reference [9] or the individual's capacity to relate in a manner most appropriate to the particular communication situation [10]), *managing transactions* (the ability to handle the procedural aspects of structuring, controlling, and maintaining a conversation [11]), and *establishing rapport* (an aspect of an interpersonal relationships that may be defined as creating a state of harmony, accordance, and congruity developed in a relationship [12]). Therefore, in the context of our investigation, we contextualise those three key processes in the area of mutual understanding between people and system, mediated by digital artificial systems, as follows:

Sharing knowledge (corresponding to *shifting perspective*) defined as the ability of the involved agents to share a common conceptual model about the domain of interest (e.g., an ontology to represent knowledge in a given domain);

Exchanging knowledge (corresponding to *managing transactions*) defined as the ability to meaningfully exchange information between two or more agents;

Governing knowledge (corresponding to *establishing rapport*) defined as the set of processes, roles and rules to regulate the sharing and exchange of knowledge between the involved actors.

In this chapter, we intend to analyse various scenarios of mutual understanding between people and systems supported by Neurosymbolic AI, highlighting how they potentially require solving issues in the three key processes of sharing, exchanging and governing knowledge.

Finally, we will characterise each described scenario, by identifying the involved agents (both human users and artificial systems, whether they are based on symbolic, sub-symbolic and neurosymbolic AI or on any other technology), the role they play in the scenario and the sources of knowledge they access to (e.g. data, schema, documents, machine learning models or even tacit knowledge).

3. Case 1: Human Data Collection and Processing

In this section, we address the problem of easing the collection, interpretation and analysis of structured data from people through dedicated applications and questionnaires, in order to facilitate automation of data analysis and reuse as well as longitudinal and comparative studies, by enabling *mutual understanding between researchers who want to exchange and reuse data collected from human respondents.*

3.1. Problem Scenario

Jaime launched a citizen science project to involve people around all over the world to collect data about environmental pollution. He employed a gamified application to engage people to classify pictures that can be used to improve the understanding of the pollution issue. Through a dedicated campaign, he managed to engage a few hundred people in all five continents, who helped classifying some tens of thousands pictures; however, he noticed a varying level of quality and participation between the contributors, with some of them very active and others who seemed to lose interest over time.

Jaime wants to understand if it is worth continuing involving people to perform the classification task – which indirectly contributes to raising awareness about environmental challenges – or if he should use the classified pictures as a training set for a machine learning classifier. Moreover, he wants to understand what are the factors that influence their motivation to participate to his citizen science initiative and decides to run a survey, asking all the participants in his network to compile a structured questionnaire.

Since he is a scientist, he performs a comparative study to contrast people and machine classification and he adopts questionnaire design best practices and reuse a motivation analysis framework from literature, because he want to compare his findings with the previous works. However, he knows from experience that, once he collects people responses, he will end up doing a lot of data cleaning and preparation before running his analyses. Jaime would love to find a solution to simplify the design, collection and analysis of his questionnaire data, also enabling other citizen science researchers to potentially repeat his investigation and compare their findings.

3.2. Technical Solution

Games with a purpose to engage people in collecting data

Human Computation [13] is the research area devoted to harnessing human intelligence to solve computational problems that machines find hard to solve; Games with a Purpose (or GWAP) [14] are a Human Computation approach that, in order to solicit people participation in solving computational problems, adopts gaming applications to provide an intrinsic incentive.

In the context of the collection and sense-making of structured data (linked data, knowledge graphs), GWAPs proved to be a suitable solution to engage people and we built a framework [15] to ease the setup of gamified applications for data linking, specifically for link creation, link ranking and link validation; moreover, we showed how to dynamically compute the "mutual understanding" between human contributors with an incremental truth inference algorithm [16].

We adopted the GWAP approach to build Night Knights [17], a gamified application to classify pictures in the area of light pollution (cf. also Figure 1) and we managed to involve ~1.000 players to classify ~40.000 pictures over a couple of months.

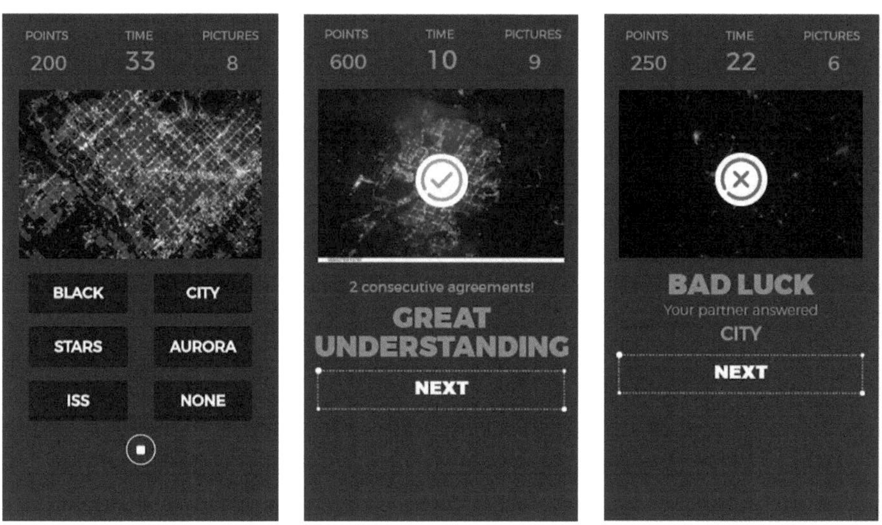

(a) Classify an image (b) Agreement (c) Disagreement

Figure 1. Game with a Purpose for data linking and image classification

Patterns in human and machine learning involvement for classification

When involving people in human computation effort to solve computational problem, the analysis of their behaviour reveals several interesting characteristics to investigate their role and the relevance of their contributions. We studied the participation data of the already mentioned Night Knights game to uncover the relationship between game incentives, player profiles and task difficulty [18]; some example findings are displayed in Figure 2.

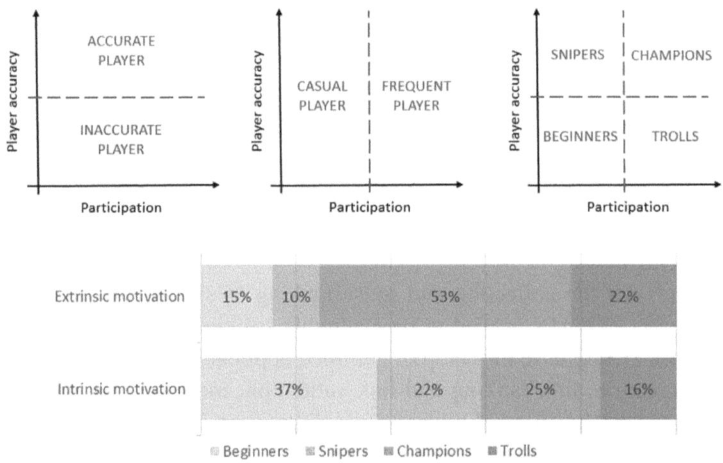

Figure 2. Definition of GWAP player profiles and their distribution with different incentive mechanisms

Such analysis also serves to the purpose of understanding how to build hybrid human-machine data processing pipelines, to make the best out of both worlds [17]. Is it better to rely on human capabilities, asking people to perform tasks, or to train a machine learning system to automatically solve the problem? The answer largely depends on the specific case and the required accuracy: humans may be more reliable – especially if they are domain experts – but automatic processing can be cheaper. We performed an experimental comparison of different Human Computation and Machine Learning approaches to solve the same image classification task: we compared and contrasted them in order to come up with a long term combined strategy to address the specific issue at scale. While it is hard to ensure a long-term engagement of users to exclusively rely on Human Computation, manual classification is indispensable to overcome the "cold start" problem of automated data modelling (cf. hybrid human-machine workflow in Figure 3).

Survey research as research objects

Another way to study people participation to collaborative efforts is to directly ask them about their subjective perception through a quantitative research survey. That is what we did to analyse the factors that influence active participation to citizen science and crowdsourcing [19]. In order to do so, we designed a survey to investigate different factors, we implemented it in a conversational survey tool [20] that allows for semantically tagging of questions and answers and for collecting structured data described with respect to a survey ontology [21] out of it.

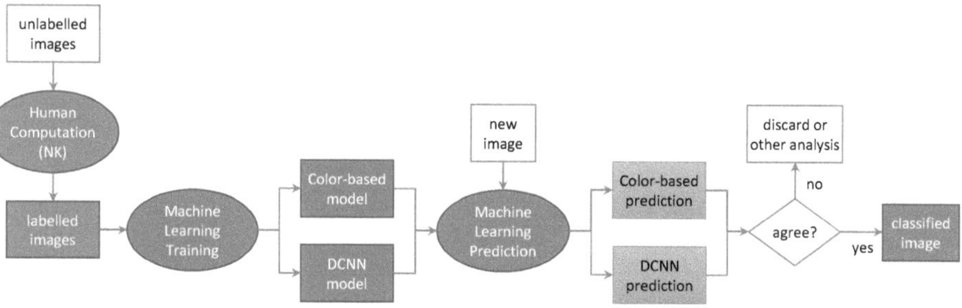

Figure 3. A possible combination of human and machine processing in a hybrid classification solution

The Survey Ontology[2] satisfies different requirements that often emerge when designing a questionnaire to collect quantitative data: (1) making the survey structure available as structured data, to make its knowledge explicit; (2) annotating questions with the respective investigated variables and (3) annotating answers with their numerical coding, to ease data analysis; (4) making the collected answers available as structure data, to enable comparisons and longitudinal studies; (5) keeping provenance of answers, to trace back in case of need; and (6) sharing the survey methodology, to foster repeatability and reproducibility of research. The ontology reuses concepts and relations from PROV-O and the Research Object suite of ontologies [22]: this allows to package a composite artifact that represents, annotates, and shares a representation of both the questionnaire structure and the gathered survey responses.

3.3. Positioning w.r.t. Mutual Understanding Framework

The main source of knowledge in this scenario is constituted by *people*, because they provide their expertise or their ability to recuperate important information. People's knowledge is then collected, saved and managed in various *information systems* (e.g. the GWAP application, the survey platform, the data analysis tool), which may support the long-term preservation of such knowledge.

The main mutual understanding problem addressed in this section is related to *sharing knowledge*: involving people in a data collection and processing pipeline through a Human Computation approach means that we leverage their ability to provide their expertise and knowledge in solving a computational task, paving also the way to a hybrid human-machine processing (potentially also human-neurosymbolic); moreover, the goal of adopting a survey conceptual model to describe a questionnaire, a knowledge graph to collect respondent data and a research object to pack together methodology, data and analysis, is to facilitate and standardize the reuse of investigation approaches across different studies. The research object artifact also supports the *governing knowledge* challenge, in that it provides a way to keep track of the entire survey campaign and to make its analyses reproducible, and partially also the *exchanging knowledge* challenge, in that it allows the exchange of survey methodology and results between researchers, to perform comparative or longitudinal studies.

[2]Cf. `https://w3id.org/survey-ontology`.

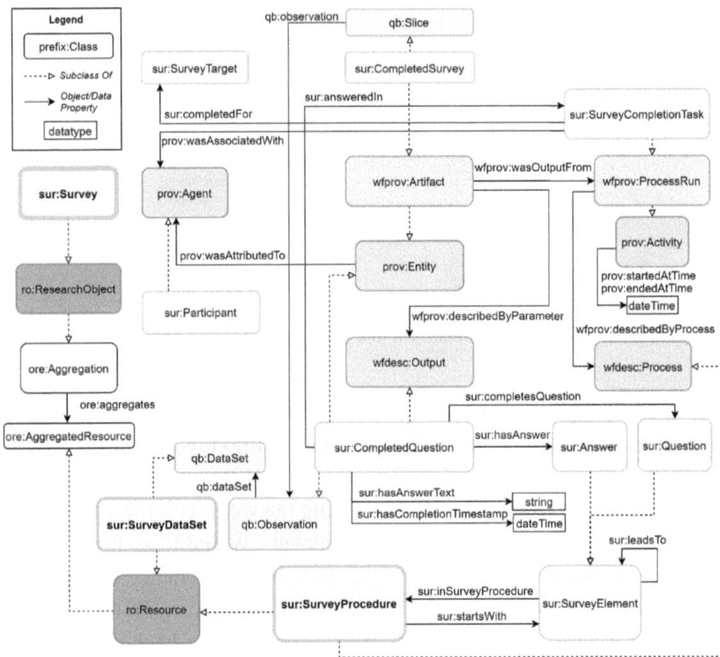

Figure 4. Overview of the Survey Ontology

3.4. Open Challenges and Possible Extensions

Combining symbolic and sub-symbolic approaches to build composite patterns of data processing is the focus of the well-known "boxology" of design patterns for hybrid learning and reasoning systems [23], as well as the topic of the analysis of mixed machine learning-semantic web systems [24]. Further extending those works to take into account also the *human component* would lead to the definition of hybrid human-neurosymbolic design patterns for intelligent systems that bring together artificial and human intelligence; in this respect, the recent wave of Generative AI solutions, with their human-like capabilities, seems to suggest that this combination will lead to a *new generation of hybrid systems* to solve complex challenges in a more effective way.

With respect to questionnaires to collect and analyse quantitative data, our conversational survey tool [20] was designed to provide respondents with a chat-like interactive experience to improve their engagement. The current and constant improvements to Conversational AI systems due to the advent of large language models are very likely to bring new forms of interactive survey systems. While in literature several works highlight the ability of chatbots to administer interviews and to increase participant engagement [25], trust [26] and self-disclosure [27], a significant improvement could come from successfully mixing those neural approaches with symbolic ones to achieve structured data collection and answers' classification and coding.

4. Case 2: Knowledge Extraction and Acquisition

In this section, we address the problem of extracting knowledge from unstructured data sources and of making tacit knowledge explicit by involving people in knowledge acquisition by enabling *mutual understanding between people who need to transfer/acquire knowledge, possibly supported by digital systems.*

4.1. Problem Scenario

Jenny is a product manager of a manufacturing company. She is responsible to ensure that the supporting documentation for the use, repair and troubleshooting of her products is available, clear and up-to-date. Her team always makes an effort to build manuals containing all the relevant information.

However, Jenny realises that, even if her team always makes an effort to build manuals containing all the relevant information, two problems often arise: (1) this information is not easily accessible, as manuals are often very long; for example, a maintainer who is asked to repair a product upon customer request may need to find the right document and, within the document, to find the relevant information among a lot of other less useful detail for the problem at hand; (2) a part of the knowledge remains tacit in the head of people; for example, a novice or less experienced employee may often need to ask for advice to senior experts, because not all the relevant information can always be documented, some knowledge remains implicit or is acquired only through direct experience. Jenny would love to find a solution to extract relevant knowledge from documents and to facilitate the explicitation of the tacit knowledge of experienced colleagues.

4.2. Technical Solution

Information retrieval and structured knowledge

The desire to find the relevant information for the task at hand is a common challenge in the industrial sector [28]. Finding the right piece of knowledge or the right answer is the main basis and motivation for any information retrieval and question answering approach. More recently, the advent of Generative AI led to the rise of Retrieval-Augmented Generation approaches (RAG [29]), which combine vector indexes with pre-trained parametric models. Among different RAG approaches, Knowledge Graph-based RAG architectures are emerging, exploiting the power of structured information – also described with respect to an ontological conceptual model – together with neural approaches.

It is indeed well-known that structured data makes it easier to find relevant information, and that knowledge graphs are a powerful solution to model, share, and preserve structured descriptions of relevant entities and relationships. For this reason, we have been working on building a modular ontology to facilitate document retrieval and knowledge extraction in industrial settings [30]. The proposed ontology can be used at different stages of annotation, storage/indexing, search and query answering (cf. Figure 5).

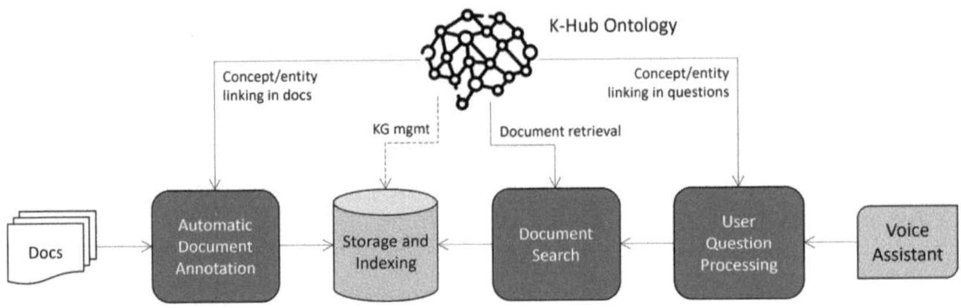

Figure 5. Use of the K-Hub ontology [30] in a document processing and search pipeline

Knowledge extraction from unstructured information

Traditional and emerging NLP techniques can be used to extract relevant information form text and other kinds of unstructured sources: when knowledge is embedded in documents (but also pictures and other multimedia formats), it is common to perform (named) entity recognition, relation extraction and entity linking. The goal is to turn unstructured information into structured descriptions, often in the form of a knowledge graph, according to a predefined ontology and possibly linking to pre-existing knowledge bases.

In the area of process and procedural knowledge, some work exists to automatically or semi-automatically extract relevant information from textual descriptions, also leveraging LLM capabilities [31,32]. Still, a holistic solution to this challenge is still missing, as documents may be incomplete (e.g., information given for granted, background knowledge, common sense, contextual data) or they may require specialised expertise to be interpreted and understood. Furthermore, the same piece of information sometimes can be made explicit in similar but different ways, making it difficult to completely automate the knowledge extraction task [33].

Knowledge acquisition from people

In order to correctly extract relevant information from unstructured sources, it is of course also possible to ask knowledgeable people to manually annotate documents, especially when the user is guided in identifying and tagging with an explicit semantics [34]; however, this kind of manual task is known to be a tedious and expensive work, and also very error-prone.

Moreover, when knowledge is not documented at all, because it remains tacit, i.e. "in the head" of the human expert, no kind of manual or automatic annotation can be adopted. In this case, the need to make tacit knowledge explicit calls for acquisition solutions that guide the user to collect and structure their specialised information, in order to facilitate transfer and preservation of such knowledge. Whether knowledge is (semi-)automatically extracted from documents or acquired from people, it is very common to adopt *human-in-the-loop* approaches for knowledge validation, as in [35]: building hybrid information processing pipelines that combine human and machine intelligence can help finding the best trade-off between quality and cost.

4.3. Positioning w.r.t. Mutual Understanding Framework

The main sources of knowledge in this scenario are *unstructured information* (especially documents) and again *people* (for tacit knowledge); the challenge is to populate and maintain up-to-date structured sources for long-term preservation and access.

The main mutual understanding problem addressed in this section is related to *sharing knowledge*, in that the goal of collecting information from documents or people is to facilitate its later reuse by other (artificial or human) users. When made explicit and structured, the elicited information could also support *exchanging knowledge* between different actors. Finally, a holistic neurosymbolic solution to the extraction/acquisition challenge would also need to address the *governing knowledge* dimension, in that it would help in the long-term management of domain knowledge.

4.4. Open Challenges and Possible Extensions

Regarding the knowledge extraction from text, there are currently different generative AI-based approaches to support tasks like entity recognition and relation extraction [36,37,38]; however, the precision and reliability of such extraction is still far from ideal, especially when the documents does not contain the entire contextual knowledge, because it is implicit or common sense.

Regarding the knowledge acquisition from people, as discussed, involving domain expert is a very expensive task and it is not even always possible. To this end, neurosymbolic approaches for semi-automatic annotation/collection with human-in-the-loop seem to be a suitable research direction, especially adopting mixed and iterative strategies: people could be supported or guided in the process, either by leveraging a conceptual domain model (e.g. to give the expert a "structure" to follow to make their knowledge explicit) or by providing an interactive solution to ease the acquisition (e.g. using conversational AI to facilitate knowledge disclosure [27]).

5. Case 3: Interoperability between Information Systems

In this section, we address the problem of enabling data interoperability among information systems. Interoperability means reconciling heterogeneous data sources, so to facilitate integration and reuse, i.e. to enable *mutual understanding between different information systems that need to meaningfully exchange information.*

5.1. Problem Scenario

Tiago works for a company that realises digital solutions for traffic management in urban environments. In particular, his team develops a decision support system (DSS) for city mobility officers that includes near real-time and forecast information about city traffic. This system gathers data from multiple information sources (e.g., public transport vehicle tracking, traffic lights configuration, video cameras monitoring car flows, etc.), processes incoming data through machine learning solutions, and displays the current and forecast status on an interactive dashboard.

Every time a new city approaches Tiago to customize the DSS solution, he faces significant challenges. Despite the existence of (open) data platforms collecting potential input data sources, Tiago often has to deal with disparate metadata schemas and custom APIs, which further complicate data integration. He needs to identify and understand every available information source, decode their often undocumented data formats and conventions, and perform extensive data pre-processing and transformation to integrate this data into the DSS.

Additionally, Tiago's team requires historical datasets to support the development of tailored machine-learning systems for the DSS. These datasets are often unavailable and should be collected from real-time data sources. Also in this case, harmonising data according to a common data format is crucial to facilitate the training of models considering different information sources from several cities.

These tasks are tedious and expensive, yet essential for ensuring compatibility between the information sources and the DSS solution. Tiago is seeking a way to simplify the process of achieving mutual understanding between the diverse information sources of each city and his DSS.

5.2. Technical Solution

In the generic scenario depicted in Figure 6, open and private data catalogues describe and host data from different information systems. Each data catalogue may contain: (i) datasets in different formats and/or using different data models (A, B, C); (ii) data services relying on heterogeneous specifications and technologies (I, II); (iii) data sources described according to different metadata specifications (d,e).

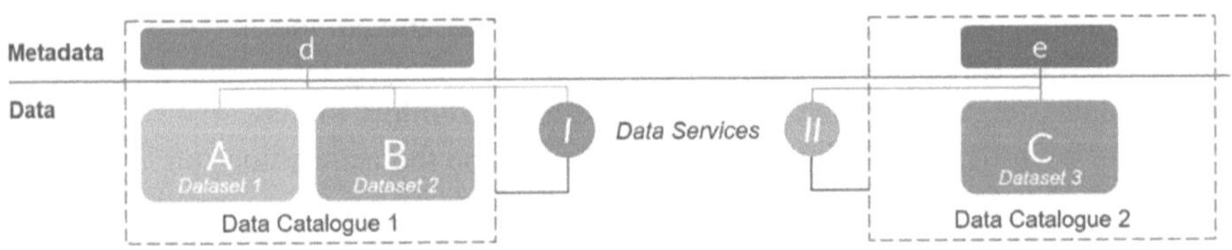

Figure 6. Generic scenario requiring interoperability across information systems.

The definition of a proper solution to this heterogeneity is not straightforward and should face five challenges (Locate, Access, Harmonise, Integrate, Extract).

Identifying a single solution to the abovementioned challenges is impossible since a single interoperability problem cannot be formulated [39]. Indeed, the identified data interoperability issues are widely heterogeneous and pose various requirements that can be possibly faced only by considering a set of tools appropriately configured.

We developed an end-to-end solution for data interoperability based on Knowledge Graph technologies to solve the heterogeneity issue in traffic management highlighted above in four different European cities [40]. The proposed solution, represented in Figure 7, deals with the mentioned challenges and proposes an integrated set of components that can be configured and extended to address interoperability issues in a generic domain.

The first challenge is the findability and discoverability of data. Data cannot be re-used and (made) interoperable if they cannot be found. For this reason, data catalogues/portals are implemented to describe data sources through a set of metadata. The challenge is associated with the need for a proper, structured and machine-readable de-

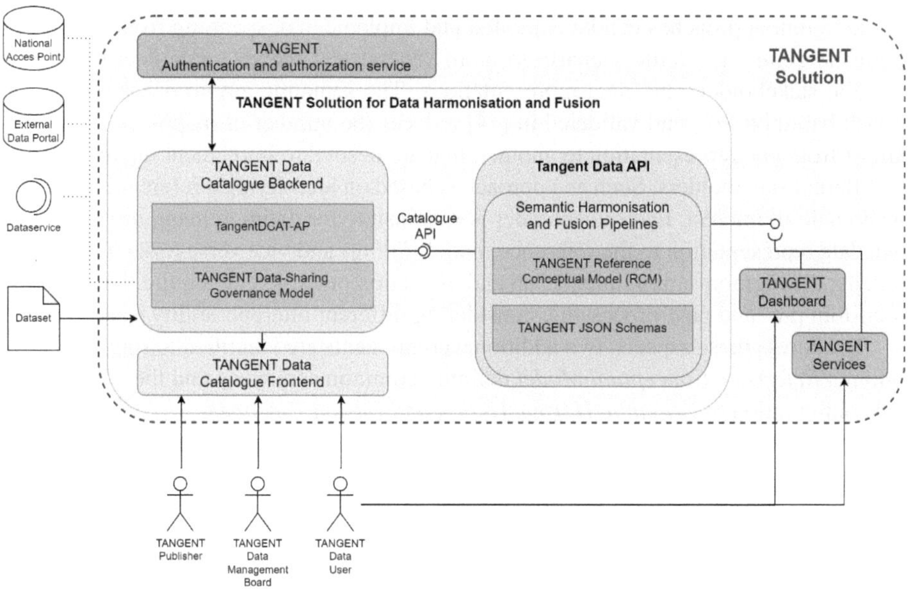

Figure 7. End-to-end solution for data interoperability in the TANGENT project.

scription of data sources that could also support interoperability across different data catalogues. Once data sources are located, the second challenge is related to data accessibility. Data catalogues adopt different strategies for data access mainly associated with the architectural choices for the hosting and storing of static and dynamic data sources. The challenge is to enable uniform access to heterogeneous data sources by external information stystem.

For these reasons, the first two core components of the proposed solution are a shared *Data Catalogue* to enable the findability of data sources and a uniform *Data API* for accessibility. The *Data Catalogue* provides a user interface and an API to discover all the relevant data sources harvested by other data portals and or directly described and published by users. Data interoperability is guaranteed by adopting a common metadata specification based on well-known vocabularies such as DCAT-AP [41] that may be extended to support the specific requirements of a domain or customer scenario. Moreover, being the point of access for users interacting with data sources, the *Data Catalogue* also enables the enforcement of processes and rules according to a common data-sharing governance model [42]. The *Data API* provides uniform access to data sources collected through the Data Catalogue and represents the integration point for the downstream information systems accessing the data sources.

The remaining three data interoperability challenges (harmonise, integrate, and extract) are related to the processing of (meta)data to enable their integration and exploitation according to common semantics. A flexible solution is required to address heterogeneous requirements in terms of: (a) schema and data transformation: information manipulation to obtain syntactic (structural) and semantic interoperability of (meta)data; (b) integration with existing information systems as data sources (i.e., components generating or storing the data) and/or data sinks (i.e., components consuming or archiving data).

Different approaches can be exploited and implemented, spanning from ad-hoc solutions targeting a specific scenario to more general and scalable solutions supporting multiple stakeholders and data representations. The semantic any-to-one mapping approach based on [43] and validated in [44] reduces the number of mappings, i.e., translations from one representation to another, that are needed to implement interoperability by different stakeholders. Such an approach is based on identifying a reference model for the domain of interest. Each stakeholder is responsible for defining mappings from their own data representation to the reference model (*lifting*) and vice versa (*lowering*). Additionally, the harmonisation, integration and extraction process may require the definition of custom pre- and post-processing, considering different interoperability issues.

To address these aspects, two additional components are identified to support the solution: a *Reference Conceptual Model* defining common semantics and the composition and configuration of *Semantic Harmonisation and Fusion Pipelines*.

The *Reference Conceptual Model* supports representing heterogeneous information from different data sources through a common ontological model to enable shared semantics and interoperability. The model is based on existing data standards to adopt the correct domain terminology and covers the representation of all the entities and properties required to implement meaningful data exchanges among the involved stakeholders.

A flexible and scalable technology for the implementation of the pipelines should provide (i) a set of reusable building blocks that can be configured according to specific requirements, and (ii) a declarative approach to configure the lifting and lowering transformations without developing ad-hoc and hard-to-maintain solutions. Chimera[3] [45] is an open-source solution based on Apache Camel to enable the definition of semantic data transformation pipelines with different components for knowledge graph construction, transformation, validation, and exploitation. The advantage of Chimera is its integration with Apache Camel, providing off-the-shelf and production-ready components to implement Enterprise Integration Patterns and to integrate pipelines with heterogeneous systems (e.g., HTTP API, WebSocket, MQTT).

The implemented pipelines are documented within the *Data Catalogue* to publish the description of newly generated data sources or to describe the availability of a data source according to a specific format. The *Data API* integrates the integration and execution of the pipelines to provide access to data sources according to the requested format. Such an approach can be applied for the harmonisation of heterogeneous metadata to enable the federation of existing data portals [46] or directly for the integration and fusion of data sources [47]. Moreover, the application of pipelines over time to collect, harmonise and store data can be leveraged to generate historical datasets for the training of machine learning models.

5.3. Positioning w.r.t. Mutual Understanding Framework

The main source of knowledge associated with this scenario is related to the structured *metadata and data managed by information systems*; the challenge is to enable easy discoverability, access and exchange of such knowledge. The problem presented in this section is mainly related to the *exchanging knowledge* challenge, as the mutual understanding issue is mainly related to the possibility of enabling a meaningful exchange of data between the information systems. However, the adoption of a shared conceptual model

[3]`https://github.com/cefriel/chimera`

also addresses the *sharing knowledge* dimension while the catalogue, as well as the API layer, are meant to support the *governing knowledge* aspect.

5.4. Open Challenges and Possible Extensions

The semantic interoperability solution described above contributes to the mutual understanding between the systems that need to meaningfully exchange information by means of two important types of artifacts: (1) data and metadata models, expressed as ontologies, vocabularies and metadata profiles, and (2) mappings that encode the correspondences between the conceptual model and the data formats adopted by the different sources and systems. Considering the first artifact, while the proposed technical solution mainly leverage symbolic approaches, the interoperability of data and metadata is essential to support the retrieval and exploitation of data sources for machine learning [48].

With respect to the latter, several approaches exist to define those mappings. Declarative approaches for knowledge graph construction can effectively support lifting transformations to RDF, while a standardised lowering solution to convert RDF to any format using a generic declarative language is currently missing [49]. Despite the encoding and execution of the mapping, a well-known challenge is related to the identification of the conceptual mappings, which is a very expensive and intensive activity. Some recent approaches aim at adopting neurosymbolic approaches, by exploiting language models to identify similarities among concepts and generate the mappings [50,51,52]. While a complete automation of the mapping generation is not yet achievable, the current ability of Generative AI solution seems promising to support a domain expert in the semi-automatic definition of mappings. Future research directions may also investigate the potentiality of leveraging non-symbolic models to transform data directly from one format to another. A multi-agent approach may support data harmonisation through the cooperation of not-symbolic transformations and iterative corrections based on the symbolic validation of results according to the target data schema (e.g., ontology).

On the other side, open challenges are also related to the configuration of pipelines for data exchanges. Low-code and no-code solutions are proposed to facilitate these tasks and the integration with code generation techniques from natural language can further facilitate the user in this task [53].

6. Case 4: Reproducibility and Trustability between Stakeholders

In this section, we address the problem of guaranteeing reproducibility and trustability in a digital environment involving different stakeholders, i.e., to enable *mutual understanding of operations executed by users with different roles and responsibilities through digital artefacts*.

6.1. Problem Scenario

We present two scenarios where multiple stakeholders should cooperate and act together within a digital environment. The first scenario focuses on monitoring the deployment, execution and use of intelligent asset management systems relying on AI-based approaches for prescriptive maintenance. This scenario involves the integration and reuse of components developed by different stakeholders requiring *mutual understanding be-*

tween people and data pipelines. The second scenario addresses the challenge of defining, applying and exchanging business agreements between different actors that should cooperate and trust each other. The objective is to enable *mutual understanding of the terms and conditions of a business agreement* between the stakeholders involved.

Intelligent asset management system (IAMS)

Renzo is an infrastructure manager, responsible for the maintenance of a complex railway network. To ensure the proper operations of the railway, Renzo coordinates a group of different stakeholders with challenges about data management, runtime interactions and trust among the parties. They have different digital systems, including predictive and prescriptive machine learning models that are used to manage the maintenance activities, by foreseeing the need for an intervention on the network (e.g. the need for a future repair work on the trails) and by scheduling the actual work of the operators (e.g. the planning of employees turns).

If something does not go as planned (e.g., failure of the network due to maintenance issue), it is of utmost importance for Renzo to audit the operations executed by people and systems, to safely reproduce what happened to identify the root cause, and to inject the new knowledge in the system so to ensure that future planning avoids repeating mistakes and learn for the past experience. Renzo would love to find a solution to reliably execute and monitor machine learning pipelines and to create a trusted environment for governing and coordinating the different systems and people, thus enabling mutual understanding between all the involved stakeholders.

Business agreements for multimodal transportation

The new ride-sharing service RideWithMe would like to provide drivers and passengers with a trusted service to organize shared rides and to cooperate with other transport operators to promote multimodal journeys. A shared ride booked via RideWithMe can be seen as a business agreement between the user offering a shared ride with her/his car and the passengers. Each driver can be considered a private transport service provider (TSP) offering transportation services on a specific route. The passenger accepts to pay a certain price in exchange for a shared ride from a certain location to a specific destination. Such information should be shared in a trusted way so that RideWithMe can ensure dispute resolution mechanisms among the driver and the passengers. RideWithMe leverages the blockchain and smart contracts to guarantee trust among the parties. Similarly, RideWithMe and other transport service providers agreed to use smart contracts to support the definition of multimodal packages for travellers. In both cases, even if a shared data model ensures interoperability in data exchanges among information systems, the implementation-dependent nature of smart contracts makes it difficult to represent univocally the terms and conditions of the agreements using the proper domain terminology. Indeed, while the adoption of blockchain technology ensures trustability, it affects the mutual understanding of the implemented business agreements.

6.2. Technical Solution

The technical solutions proposed leverage Knowledge Graphs to support the reproducibility of data-driven solutions and trustability over blockchain architectures in the multi-stakeholder environment.

IAMS integration support framework

The adoption of intelligent maintenance solutions requires collecting data from different sources, implementing specific software components for data analytics and visualisation, and integrating them to support data pipelines. A significant challenge lies in the variety of stakeholders involved in deploying such solutions and executing the target maintenance processes.

To support these challenges, we proposed the IAMS Integration Support Framework [54] based on three macro-functionalities: (i) a shared catalogue to enhance the findability and reusability of digital artifacts (IAMS Shared Catalogue); (ii) a runtime area for the integrated deployment and execution of artifacts associated with intelligent maintenance scenarios (IAMS Runtime Area); and (iii) a blockchain-based system to handle the monitoring and tracking of artifacts, processes and operations performed by users (IAMS Process Tracking).

Figure 8 provides an overview of the main components for an intelligent maintenance solution and their dependencies. We identified four basic digital artifact types: Dataset, Software Components, Machine Learning Model, and Maintenance Plan. For each of them, we defined a metadata schema relying on well-known vocabularies.

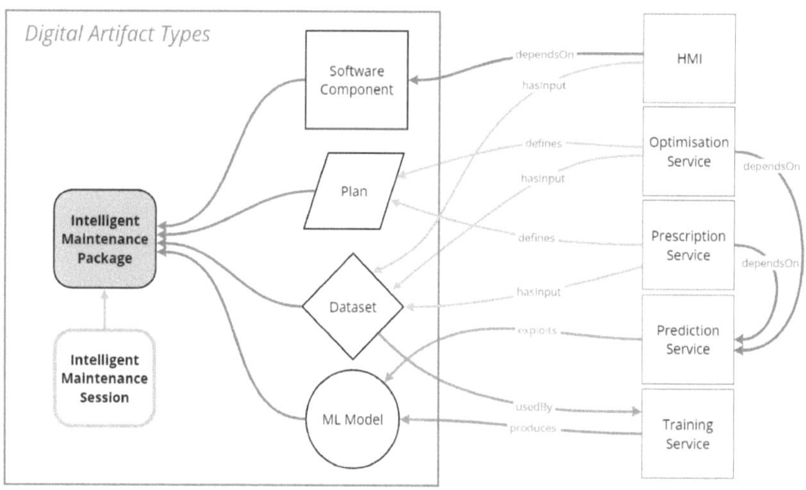

Figure 8. IAMS Shared Catalogue: artifact types and their dependencies.

Under the overall maintenance scenario, describing and tracking each digital artifact individually is not enough to foster reproducibility. For this reason, two additional digital artifact types are defined to fully describe the dependencies and usage of digital artifacts:

- an **Intelligent maintenance package** (IAM Package) describes a maintenance scenario that leverages different digital artifacts and can be executed in an integrated runtime environment (e.g., the datasets supporting the training of a certain machine learning model, the training software component and the predict/prescribe components exploiting such model);
- an **Intelligent maintenance session** (IAM Session) describes the information about operations made by a user in the interaction with digital artifacts composing an *Intelligent maintenance package* (e.g., a certain user requested the re-training

of a machine learning model with different hyper-parameters and then generated a maintenance plan relying on the trained model).

A *package* resembles the concept of a Research Object, mentioned in Section 3. It contains static information on *digital artifacts* used for a particular scenario and the configuration for their integration. A *session* contains provenance information obtained at runtime on the usage of a *package*, e.g. the software component used to generate a machine learning model, and traced on the blockchain. The *RO-Crate* specifications can support the serialization of such information. Each digital artifact can be seen as a resource in a *RO-Crate* [55] using a specific set of metadata.

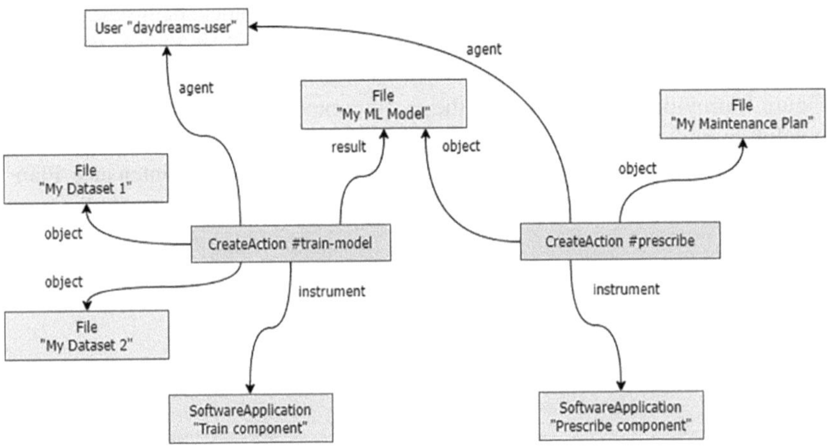

Figure 9. Example of Process RO-Crate in the context of an intelligent maintenance scenario in the DAYDREAMS project.

Considering an intelligent maintenance session, the *Process RO-Crate* profile [56] can be used to represent all the lifecycle operations performed on the digital artifacts of the package, and all the runtime operations executed within an IAM Session. Figure 9 represents an example Process RO-Crate describing two operations (*CreateAction* entities in purple), their connection with specific digital artifacts (*File* enties in blue, *SoftwareApplication* entities in green) and the identification of the user (*User* entity in yellow) that performed them. A *train-model* operation is described by identifying the user requesting the training, the datasets used, the software component executed and the produced machine learning model. Similarly, a *prescribe* operation can be described by identifying the user requesting the prescription process, the machine learning model used, the software component executed and the produced maintenance plan

The integration of such information as digital artifacts in the shared catalogue supports reproducibility and trustability for intelligent maintenance scenarios implemented through the *IAMS Integration Support Framework.*

Ontological smart contracts for multimodal transportation

In an ecosystem with various stakeholders, the implementation of business agreements through a distributed ledger provides several benefits regarding information trust and the automatic execution of the agreed terms modelled as smart contracts. This approach, however, doesn't provide any guarantee about the interoperability of the defined agreements from a technological and semantic perspective. On one hand, the domain terminology shared among the involved stakeholders should be referenced by the modelled entities, on the other hand, other software systems can benefit from a machine-readable representation of the agreements.

We proposed a solution to describe smart contracts implemented on the blockchain using an ontology [57]. The concept of *Ontological Smart Contract* [58] can be leveraged to model the semantic of business agreements. The following steps should be performed: (i) investigation of the business agreements to be modelled in the considered scenario (use cases and user stories), (ii) analysis of the domain terminology covered by the business agreements (facts and competency questions), (iii) identification of existing vocabularies covering the relevant domain entities and relationships, and/or implementation of an ontology supporting their representation, (iv) modelling of each business agreement as an ontological smart contract identifying the involved entities and the terms of the agreement, and, optionally, (v) representation of specific instances of the business agreement stored on the ledger using the ontology. In this way, different stakeholders are able to access through uniform terminology a description of the smart contracts and, possibly, their instances.

The *Ride2Rail Ontology for Agreements* (`https://w3id.org/ride2rail/terms#`) enables the application of this concept to support the interoperability of business agreements in the multimodal transportation scenario detailed above. The ride-sharing booking is modelled as an agreement between the driver and the passengers for dispute resolution, and the definition of multimodal packages as agreements between different transport service providers. The RDF dataset with the modelled agreements is published at `https://w3id.org/ride2rail/agreements#` and the agreement for a ridesharing booking is reported in Figure 10.

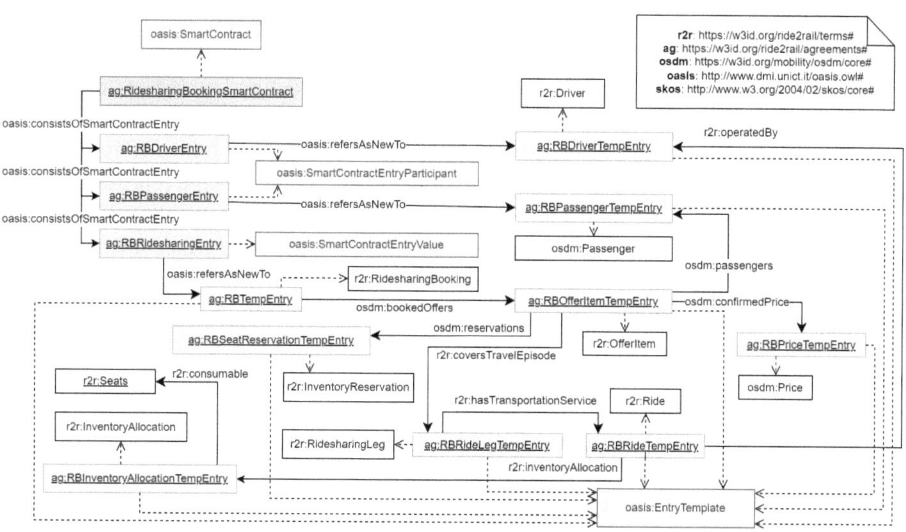

Figure 10. Diagram describing the *RidesharingBookingSmartContract* agreement

This approach addresses two needs of mutual understanding: (i) the description in an implementation-independent way of the smart contracts defined according to a specific blockchain-based solution, and (ii) the adoption of proper and shared terminology to describe domain entities and their relationships.

6.3. Positioning w.r.t. Mutual Understanding Framework

The main sources of knowledge in this scenario are *provenance information* to guarantee reproducibility and auditing of operations performed by users and software components. The challenge is to trace and collect the relevant information while guaranteeing trust between the stakeholders. The main mutual understanding problem addressed in this section is related to the *governing knowledge* aspect, in that the final goal is to allow different stakeholders to correctly operate and to trust each other: the proposed solutions allow for monitoring and auditing the interconnected systems in a trustworthy way. The discussed IAMS solution highlights how symbolic approaches can support the governance of neural ones, enabling the reproducibility of pipelines and the auditing of performed operations.

In solving the governance aspect, the catalogue also provides an environment to share and access the relevant artefacts (datasets, software components, machine learning models, etc.) and their respective dependencies, also in accordance with the FAIR principles, thus directly addressing also the *sharing knowledge* aspect. This is also enhanced by the adoption of the Research Object approach, to enable reproducibility and understanding of what happened in previous sessions. In solving the *governing knowledge* aspect, the blockchain provides a mechanism for trust that should be complemented via a shared conceptual model (*sharing knowledge*) to ensure mutual understanding among the involved parties.

6.4. Open Challenges and Possible Extensions

The main open challenge discussed in this section is related to the integration of neurosymbolic approaches not only as part of hybrid algorithms but also to support the sharing and governance of digital artefacts. The adoption of a structured metadata description can facilitate their findability and reuse, as discussed also in Section 5, but should not be limited to isolated and static information. Additional metadata on how different digital artefacts are combined together and runtime information on their usage represents a key element for reproducibility. In this direction, additional information may be retrieved not only by tracing the interaction among the components but also by further instrumenting neuro-symbolic components for more granular auditing [59].

An additional challenge is related to the difficulties of encoding and communicating all the relevant details of business agreements by adopting a fully symbolical approach. Indeed, often agreements leverage the blurred boundaries of legal terminology that can hardly be represented using a logical encoding. In this context, the adoption of LLMs can be leveraged to combine business agreement terms in structured and unstructured formats and provide natural language explanations and answers to the users involved.

7. Case 5: Building Shared Spatio-Temporal Understanding

In this section, we address the problem of building reliable world models to support robots and autonomous agents in making sense of complex deployment environments.

This model building process was originally introduced by Lake et al. [60] as one of the essential requirements for achieving human-like intelligence in machines. However, building and maintaining accurate world models is also crucial to achieve a *mutual understanding whenever robots are expected to be of service to people [61], as well as in the case of mixed teams where robots and humans co-operate towards shared goals* [62].

In this context, the model building problem can be seen as one of devising a unified representation of the environment that is both machine-readable and human-understandable. Thus, the concept of model building is highly interlinked with the long-standing issue of grounding observations and raw sensory information to symbols [63,64]. In Robotics, efforts towards tackling this issue have consolidated the proposal of semantic maps, world models that contain "in addition to spatial information about the environment, assignments of mapped features to entities of known classes" [65]. As such, semantic maps provide an intermediate representation between sub-symbolic features learned directly from the environment and semantic symbols that can be mapped to natural language. Hence, as argued in [66], semantic maps are a prime example of Neuro-symbolic system, which synthesises the inputs of different data-driven and knowledge-driven components. Ideally, semantic maps should not only be spatially contextualised but also reflect the evolution of the target environment, providing a spatio-temporal record of the robot's observations and activities (e.g., the set of waypoints and objects encountered along the robot's navigation route).

In the remainder of this section, we explore a model building method based on semantic maps and instantiate this general method in assistive robotics scenarios to discuss the potential of this solution from the standpoint of mutual understanding.

7.1. Problem Scenario

Brian is the primary caregiver for John, who is starting to show mild dementia symptoms. John often misplaces his copy of the house keys, and forgets where he has put his belongings, like his walking stick, or glasses. Brian decides to join a pilot study where commercial humanoid robots are deployed in selected households to help assisting elderly patients at home while their caregivers are away. Thus, this scenario concerns the interaction between human and robotic agents.

On the day the robot is delivered to the house, the team of researchers running the study sets up the platform to map the entire layout of Brian's house. This 2D map will provide a basis for the robot to localise itself during future monitoring rounds.

The researchers would like to test how often the robot can accurately retrieve John's personal items when instructed to. During an initial setup phase, the user selects a few objects that the robot must learn to recognize. While patrolling, the robot identifies and records the locations of these items. Subsequently, the user can request the robot's assistance to retrieve a specific object. Since the tested solution is still under development, the robot simply locates the items and notifies the users without actually grasping any of the objects, to avoid damaging equipment and causing incidents. A sample visualization of the object retrieval routine is provided in Figure 11.

7.2. Technical Solution

To fit the requirements of a mobile robot that monitors the environment while navigating it, we developed a solution that comprises object recognition and spatial reasoning capa-

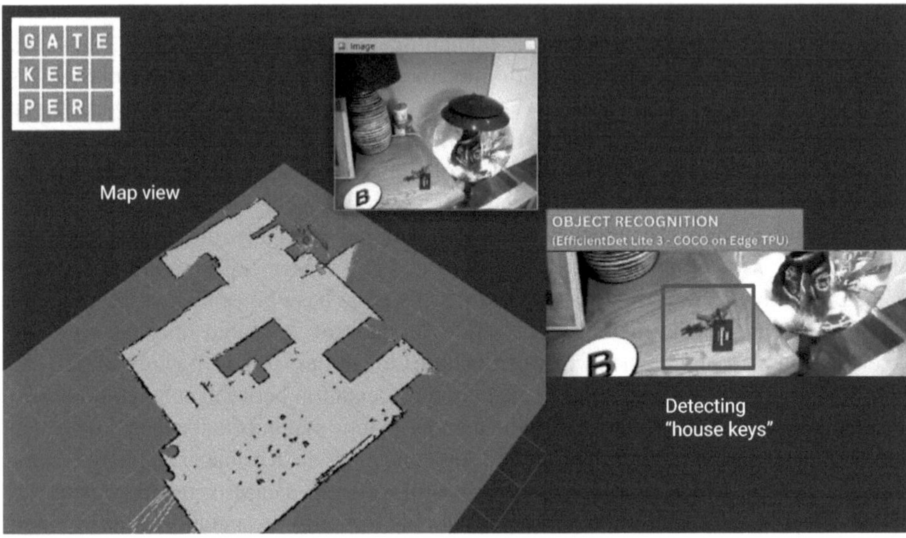

Figure 11. Visualization of the object retrieval routine. Picture courtesy of the Gatekeeper EU project consortium. On the left: the depth measurements collected through the robot camera (multi-color) are projected on the 2D house floorplan. On the right: the RGB image stream is fed to the object recognition module to detect the presence of personal items.

bilities. Importantly, the proposed framework is robust to variations in the robot's viewpoint and object orientation. Indeed, as the robot moves, its viewpoint changes over time. Moreover, the objects observed may follow different spatial orientations. Therefore, we introduce a *contextualised frame of reference* [67], which allows to interpret the configuration of spatial objects with respect to both the robot's viewpoint and the location of nearby objects (e.g., "car keys on the left of a potted plant"). In the proposed framework, geometric spatial operators are also mapped to common spatial predicates in natural language, to ensure that users' instructions (e.g., "bring me the cup that is on the kitchen table") can be opportunely parsed and linked to the relevant geometric operations.

At the core of this solution is the construction of a semantic map. That is, the 2D layout map acquired in the robot setup phase is enhanced with semantic information about the nature of the objects (e.g., a chair, a table), labels representing the different rooms (e.g., a kitchen, a bedroom), and the relationships between objects (e.g., a chair near the table, cable in the corridor). In practice, we represent object instances recognised through the robot's RGB-Depth (RGB-D) camera as anchors stored in a spatial database. Anchors serve as 3D abstractions of physical objects, formed by aggregating multiple measurements returned by the object recognition module.

At each time frame, the distance between the robot's pose and the surfaces detected by the laser in the depth sensor is measured. These data, referred to as *depth images*, can be converted into collections of 3D geometrical points within the given frame of reference, known as *PointClouds*. Having access to Pointcloud measurements allows us to transform the 2D bounding boxes that represent object regions as minimum oriented 3D boxes, by applying the Convex Hull algorithm to the segmented PointCloud. We store the resulting spatial anchors in a PostgreSQL database, to capitalise on the availability of 3D spatial operators provided with the PostGIS engine and the SFCGAL backend. Thanks to these spatial operators, we can compute spatial relations between the detected

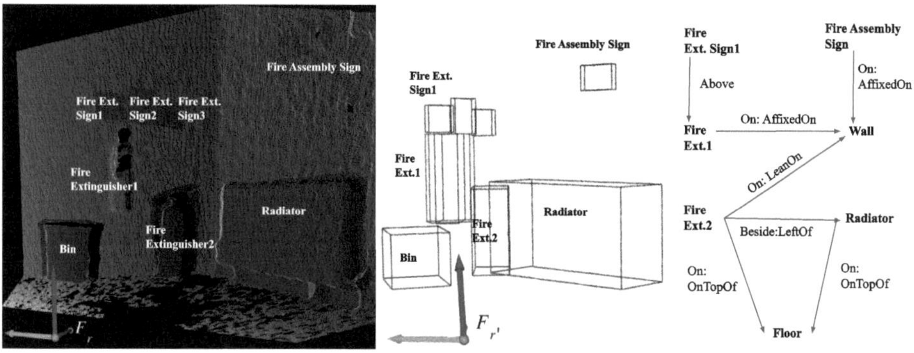

(a) (b) (c)

Figure 12. Example of operational workflow, taken from [67]: (a) the PointCloud of the observed scene is segmented and annotated with object categories. Then, (b) the minimum oriented bounding boxes and contextualised bounding boxes (in blue) are constructed. Lastly, (c) a set of qualitative spatial relations is derived.

objects. A concrete example of the operational steps followed to extract spatial relations from raw RGB-D data is showcased in Figure 12. Further details on the qualification process we followed to map PostGIS operators to spatial predicates expressed in natural language (e.g., *onTopOf*, *near*, *affixedTo*, *LeftOf*, etc.) can be found in [67].

Anchors are intrinsically linked to the robot's perception. Thus, an anchor for a specific object does not exist unless the robot has detected that object. Similarly, an anchor must be removed from the semantic map if no new perceptions confirm its current location. The anchor life cycle is handled through automatic triggers in the PostgreSQL database. Namely, existing anchors are kept updated with the latest measurements that match the centroid location of the 3D bounding box. Whenever a new measurement is received that cannot be matched to any existing anchor, a new anchor is generated.

For the object recognition module, we relied on Few-Shot Learning (FSL) methods that can learn from limited training examples, i.e., only the few pictures of the target personal items collected during the robot setup phase. Moreover, we prioritised lightweight models that could be fine-tuned on device via an Edge TPU USB-powered device, directly installed on the robot.

The implemented solution provides a common world model that can be further extended even when the robot assistant is not the only device used for collecting environmental data. Smart Home sensors, for instance, can usefully complement the robot's observations [61], e.g., enabling to infer the patient's location through a smart watch or fitness tracker. In this context, the semantic map provides a unified model to reconcile data collected from multiple sources and modalities.

7.3. Positioning w.r.t. Mutual Understanding Framework

The model building problem is mainly aligned with the *sharing knowledge* dimension of mutual understanding. Indeed, the semantic map introduced in this section acts as a common conceptual model that mediates between the robot's sensemaking, the data collection via external environmental sensors, and the users' requests. Through the semantic map, the robot and human operators can access the perceptual predictions produced by object detection models based on Deep Learning, as well as semantic relations between objects computed by the spatial engine.

Two specific interventions have been explored to achieve a common ground between the human and artificial actors involved in this scenario. First, we adopted a frame of reference that more clearly expresses the robot's viewpoint from which the relative positioning of objects is inferred ("keys on coffee table"). This configuration provides an alternative to directly relying on the coordinate system of the map ("keys North of main door"), which is not adequately intelligible to users. Second, we mapped the geometric spatial operators used to extract spatial relations from sensory data (e.g., *3DIntersection*, *Rotation*) to linguistic predicates commonly used in natural language to describe spatial relations between objects (e.g., *near*, *rightOf*).

In sum, the proposed representational model provides a more transparent, easier-to-understand interface for: i) patients and caregivers interacting directly with the robot, ii) researchers assessing the robot's capability to comprehend the environment.

7.4. Open Challenges and Possible Extensions

Accurate and reliable model building remains an open challenge and the aforementioned solution opens up many opportunities of extension. In the following, we focus primarily on those directions of improvement that directly impact the goal of achieving a mutual understanding between robots and users.

The solution described in the previous section implies that whenever the user asks the robot to retrieve a specific object, only the last known location of the object is visited. If the object is not found, the full space is scouted to update the semantic map. This approach is sub-optimal from the standpoint of navigation, and it overlooks key information priors that can be derived from previous interactions with the user. For instance, users may repeatedly leave certain items at typical locations, which the robot could visit before scouting other areas of the house. This extension would help making more explicit the implicit user patterns and norms that contribute to mutual understanding. It would also offer an alternative direction of exploration to the increasing number of works focusing on goal-based navigation from a single image example [68]. These fully neural pipelines jointly learn map construction and symbol grounding via end-to-end optimisation. Hence, they limit feature reuse under changing environmental conditions [69] and do not take advantage of previous knowledge of the monitored environment.

Moreover, the proposed solution does not discriminate between object classes when handling anchor updates. However, objects like furniture and large appliances (sofa, fridge, TV stand) are less likely to change their location over time, while movable objects like personal items, chairs and utensils ought to be re-mapped more frequently. This is implicitly understood by us humans as we process the world visually. In fact, our assessment of previously-constructed mental models is only triggered in the presence of change, making our information processing most efficient [70]. Another key extension contributing to building a common cognitive ground between robot assistants and humans may thus concern eliciting and integrating relevant commonsense knowledge representing the spatio-temporal trajectories of objects [71].

The extensions discussed above concern knowledge sharing in mutual understanding. From the standpoint of exchanging knowledge, the discussed solution provides a very limited coverage. In this configuration, the robot receives the user instructions and starts searching for a target object, without communicating its plans and activities back to the user. However, establishing a two-way interaction would significantly contribute to the mutual understanding of both involved actors, especially in cases where an adaptive switching between different tasks is required. The most recent advancement of solutions based on Large Language Models (LLMs) can significantly facilitate the integration of this missing link. Despite the limited ability of state-of-the-art LLMs to effectively manage robot planning tasks [72,73], they are undoubtedly powerful tools for translating and summarising programmed actions (i.e., code) to natural language.

This improvement could be further extended by equipping assistive robots with the capability to infer patients' requests from implicit feedback. For example, in the motivating scenario of this section, the patient's expressed intention of "going out for a walk" could trigger the robot's search for the walking stick. These implicit user preferences and patterns can be learned by directly interacting with the user and observing the environment, overcoming the burden of modelling explicitly user-specific constraints. Thus, this function is best supported by neural methods, such as Reinforcement Learning solutions [74]. Learning adaptive robot behaviors, in tandem with the extraction of typical object locations, directly contributes to consolidating the user's trust and acceptance of the system, and to the dimension of governing knowledge.

8. Case 6: Hybrid Reasoning for Robot Deliberation

To operate reliably in real-world environments, autonomous robots ought to be equipped with advanced reasoning and decision-making capabilities. Having access to accurate world models, as discussed in the previous section, is only part of the equation: methods for advanced robot deliberation are also required [75]. Specifically, to ensure that a *mutual understanding is reached between the autonomous agent and the users and personnel interacting with the robot, it is essential to ensure that these deliberation processes are handled in a controlled and transparent way.*

This requirement is especially crucial in the case of safety-critical applications, such as in search and rescue operations, transportation, and medicine. In these challenging settings, the ability to learn and reason *bottom-up* directly from the environment through information acquired at the sensory level needs to be opportunistically coupled with *top-down* cognitive expectations about the environment [5]. Namely, observations collected bottom-up via sub-symbolic learning ought to be combined with top-down symbolic knowledge modelling the environment, in line with the definition of Neuro-symbolic AI (NeSy) [2]. Indeed, as the complexity of the environment increases and in the presence of uncertainty, i.e., incomplete and conflicting information, lower-level pattern recognition and sensory-motor skills are insufficient for successful problem solving. Knowledge-based behaviors ought to emerge, where mental models built over time support the formulation and selection of specific plans [5].

In the remainder of this section, we use the case of a robot assistant that monitors the Health and Safety of office environments as a running example to discuss the potential and open challenges of building Neuro-symbolic systems to support hybrid (top-down and bottom-up) reasoning.

8.1. Problem Scenario

The Health and Safety Robot Inspector (HanS) is expected to periodically patrol an office environment to spot any potential causes of harms to the Health and Safety of employees. Thus, similarly to the previous scenario, this use case involves the interaction between human and robotic agents to achieve shared goals.

HanS ought to interpret the current state of the environment to identify any potential risks. First and foremost, this task entails robustly recognising objects. It also requires for HanS to be capable of considering the different properties that characterise the observed objects. Additionally, the robot should be aware of any constraints that govern the safety of the environment.

Ultimately, given a set of observed objects with their related properties and a set of constraints, the robot must select the Health and Safety rules that are most relevant to the observed situation. If any violation to these rules is detected, HanS must promptly notify the designated fire wardens.

8.2. Technical Solution

To address the problem of autonomously assessing the risk of an observed situation through a mobile robot, we developed the following modules.

Semantic mapping As in the previous use case, a semantic map is autonomously built representing the robot's operational environment. In this case, we extend the interface presented in the previous section to allow users to annotate Areas of Interest (AoI) on the map. For the HanS case study, we defined three types of AoI: (i) fire escape routes, (ii) waste collection areas, and (iii) areas representing the fire call points. Nonetheless, the same interface could be seamlessly applied to define other types of AoI, such as rooms, product-specific stocking spaces, or other landmarks relevant to the end application. The map (and associated spatial database) is populated with anchors generated via the following module.

3D object anchoring. Object predictions (i.e., their class and 2D bounding boxes) are predicted via Deep Learning from the RGB image stream collected through the robot camera (Figure13a). The generated bounding boxes are used to segment the raw PointClouds, yielding 3D object regions that can be stored in the spatial database, to compute the size and spatial relations of each object. Different observations are linked to the same object (i.e., anchor) if the distance between the centroids of their 3D boxes is lower than a pre-defined threshold, in terms of Euclidean distance.

Size and spatial reasoning. Based on the estimated size and spatial relations of each anchor, Deep Learning (DL) predictions selected as "potentially incorrect" are autonomously corrected by relying on a supporting knowledge base. Specifically, we consider prior knowledge of the typical size and spatial relations of objects, repurposed from external knowledge bases (e.g., mugs are typically smaller than armchairs; fire extinguishers are usually affixed to the wall) to modify the ranking of predictions returned by the DL algorithm. Namely, we sourced typical sizes from ShapeNet [76], Amazon and manually-collected measurements, while typical spatial relations were extracted from Visual Genome [77]. Further details on this phase can be found in [78].

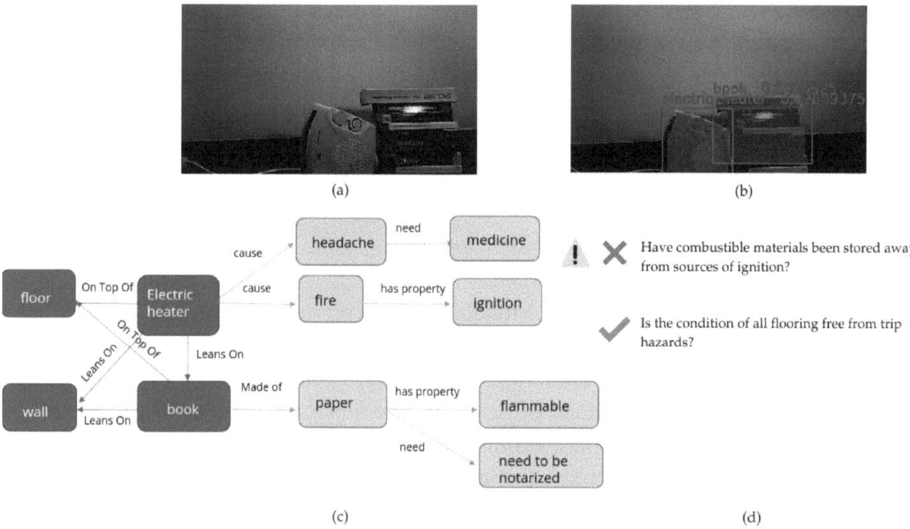

Figure 13. An electric heater is spotted near a pile of books. Because a flammable object is in contact with an ignition source, this scenario represents a potential fire hazard.

Scene graph generation. The consolidated object anchors and extracted spatial relations are used to construct a scene graph, i.e., a graph were nodes represent the objects in a scene and edges symbolise relationships between different objects. Relying on this representation allowed us to autonomously enrich the graph with additional symbolic knowledge expressing object properties as triplets (subject, predicate, object: e.g., *paper is flammable*, Figure 13c). Specifically, we retrieved the object fabrication materials (e.g., *book made of paper*) from ShapeNet and other causal and material properties relevant to HanS' use-case from Quasimodo [79]. Crucially, the scene graph format enables the application of rule-based inference techniques, to verify any violations to the Health and Safety rules, as exemplified in Figure 13d. To this aim, we formally express rules from the fire wardens' checklists and internal documents as First Order Logic (FOL) axioms.

8.3. Positioning w.r.t. Mutual Understanding Framework

Similarly to the previous section, this case is rooted in the robot's model building capability and is thus closely linked with the dimension of *sharing knowledge*. In addition to the semantic map, which acts as an overarching world model, scene graphs are also introduced as another key representation to describe successive fram sequences. However, the HanS use-case also makes an initial contribution to the two remaining ingredients of mutual understanding.

Regarding the *exchanging knowledge* dimension, the proposed NeSy framework capitalises on collective knowledge previously curated as large-scale knowledge repositories to: i) autonomously verify and correct the robot's predictions, generated via Deep Learning, ii) enrich the produced scene graphs with relevant contextual knowledge of the object properties and fabrication materials.

Ultimately, the robot's risk assessment is regulated by a set of reference rules. We elicited these rules from standard practices followed by security officers and expressed them in a format that enables direct testing against the scene graphs. This step contributes to the challenge of *governing knowledge* in mutual understanding.

Overall, the type of knowledge sources exchanged and accessed in this use case scenario range from latent representations used for classifying objects through Deep Learning methods to structured Knowledge Bases (like Quasimodo, Visual Genome, and ShapeNet) and formal logic constraints describing safety rules.

8.4. Open Challenges and Possible Extensions

The recent rise of Vision Language Models (VLMs) pre-trained on large-scale collections of images and text has expedited the progress on scene understanding and scene graph generation tasks [80,81]. Therefore, the discussed solution can be significantly updated by querying a VLM, instead of devoting two separate modules to object recognition and scene graph generation. From the standpoint of mutual understanding, dialoguing with a VLM would increase the users' participation in the robot's activities. For instance, Computer Vision tasks would be expressed in a conversational format (e.g., "which objects do you see in this scene and what is their location?"). However, in this context, scene graphs remain an important representational tool to complement textual prompts. First, scene graphs embedded in prompts have been found to augment the compositional reasoning capabilities of VLMs on visual tasks [82]. Moreover, scene graphs can provide a graphical aid for users interacting with the robot to comprehend and verify the model responses, making the robot's deliberation functions more transparent.

The Neuro-symbolic reasoning pipeline presented in the previous section, albeit leveraging top-down and bottom-up reasoning to infer object classes from images, operates only in one direction: background knowledge modelling the robot's environment guides the correction of the sub-symbolic predictions. However, a valuable feedback loop could be established, where the robot's bottom-up observation of the environment informs the generation of new knowledge, yielding a fully bi-directional NeSy pipeline. This improvement can especially facilitate the extraction of tacit knowledge. Indeed, tacit knowledge is often taken for granted as we reach mutual understanding in everyday interactions, because it is mainly learned through experience and inherently difficult to express and formalise [83].

9. Synthesis and Open Challenges for Mutual Understanding

In this chapter, we summarised a series of efforts in knowledge graph and neurosymbolic AI and we analysed them with the lens of mutual understanding dimensions. The surveyed works touch very different aspects: the involved agents (human, digital and robotic), the types of knowledge (tacit vs. explicit, declarative vs. procedural vs. causal), the varying sources of such knowledge (people, data, documents, media), the type of AI techniques adopted (symbolic, neural, neurosymbolic). While we don't claim our analysis to be exhaustive, we covered a wide range of real-world cases, with their respective requirements and challenges, and our aspiration is that those concrete and pragmatic examples can be used as incentives for research directions and applied system designs to provide impact to a large set of stakeholders [84].

Table 1. Summary of symbolic and neural approaches to solve the mutual understanding challenges (in the cells, darker color and H means higher coverage, lighter color and L means lower coverage).

Use Case Scenario	Sharing		Exchanging		Governing	
	Symb	Neur	Symb	Neur	Symb	Neur
Human Data Collection and Analysis	H	L	L	L	L	
Knowledge Extraction and Acquisition	H	H	L	L	L	
Interoperability between Information Systems	L		H	H	L	
Reproducibility and Trustability	H	L			H	L
Building Shared Spatio-Temporal Understanding	H	H		L		L
Hybrid Reasoning for Robot Deliberation	H	H	H	H	L	

Table 1 graphically summarises the level of achievement of the three main dimensions of mutual understanding – sharing, exchange and governance of knowledge – across the presented scenarios.

Regarding the *sharing knowledge dimension*, it is clear that existing solutions, especially in the symbolic AI area already well cover this challenge: conceptual models and structured data, especially when enriched with clear semantics, are the basis for a true mutual understanding between different agents. In this regards, neural approaches are already adopted for knowledge extraction, scene understanding and sense-making. There is still a clear potential for future evolution of knowledge sharing with mixed neurosymbolic AI solutions, which mix and match bottom-up with top-down semantic models of the domain and context to provide richer and more useful representations of the world.

We highlighted also several contributions of both symbolic and neural approaches to address the *exchanging knowledge* challenge: while the interaction between different agents will always include some custom configuration and agreement to enable exchange, several directions are already visible. Data interoperability is a central ingredient to enable meaningful exchanges between systems and neurosymbolic approaches can definitely help in reducing the human costs by automating some steps. In particular, the advent of large-scale generative AI systems can support a new generation of conversational agents that enrich and support the communication between agents and, as such, the knowledge exchange.

The challenge that may require further attention and research is related to the *governing knowledge dimension*: it has become mandatory to find solutions to the delicate task of managing processes, roles and rules to regulate the interactions between agents, especially in the era of the AI Act [85]. A number of symbolic approaches to address governance exist, especially by providing explicit representations of artifacts, business agreements and constraints; a few approaches also address the elicitation of implicit norms and patterns from data and background knowledge. We believe that the application of neurosymbolic AI to the governance challenge will result in further solutions to iteratively and collaboratively involve different stakeholders and agents in finding a mutual understanding on processes and rules to regulate their relationships and interactions.

Acknowledgments

The authors would like to thank Antonia Azzini, Ilaria Baroni, Alessio Carenini, Valentina Carriero, Marco Comerio, Marco Grassi, Gloria Re Calegari, Enrico Motta, Gianluca Bardaro, Alessio Antonini, Enrico Daga for their precious collaboration in the research efforts summarised in this chapter. This work is partially supported by the PERKS project (Grant agreement ID: 101120323), co-funded by the European Commission under the Horizon Europe Framework Programme.

References

[1] Kahneman D. Thinking, fast and slow. Farrar, Straus and Giroux; 2011.

[2] Sarker MK, Zhou L, Eberhart A, Hitzler P. Neuro-symbolic artificial intelligence. AI Communications. 2021;34(3):197-209.

[3] Booch G, Fabiano F, Horesh L, Kate K, Lenchner J, Linck N, et al. Thinking fast and slow in AI. In: Proceedings of the AAAI Conference on Artificial Intelligence. vol. 35; 2021. p. 15042-6.

[4] van Bekkum M, de Boer M, van Harmelen F, Meyer-Vitali A, Teije At. Modular design patterns for hybrid learning and reasoning systems: a taxonomy, patterns and use cases. Applied Intelligence. 2021;51(9):6528-46.

[5] Cummings M. Rethinking the maturity of artificial intelligence in safety-critical settings. AI Magazine. 2021;42(1):6-15.

[6] Wittgenstein L. Philosophical investigations. John Wiley & Sons; 2009.

[7] Stolk A, Verhagen L, Toni I. Conceptual alignment: How brains achieve mutual understanding. Trends in cognitive sciences. 2016;20(3):180-91.

[8] Tan M. Establishing mutual understanding in systems design: An empirical study. Journal of Management Information Systems. 1994;10(4):159-82.

[9] Tan MJ. An investigation of the communication behaviors of systems analysts. School of Business, The University of Queensland. 1989.

[10] Montgomery BM. The form and function of quality communication in marriage. Family Relations. 1981:21-30.

[11] Wiemann JM. Explication and test of a model of communicative competence. Human communication research. 1977;3(3):195-213.

[12] Guinan P, Bostrom RP. Development of computer-based information systems: A communication framework. ACM SIGMIS Database: the DATABASE for Advances in Information Systems. 1986;17(3):3-16.

[13] Law E, Von Ahn L. Human computation. Morgan & Claypool Publishers; 2011.

[14] Von Ahn L. Games with a purpose. Computer. 2006;39(6):92-4.

[15] Re Calegari G, Fiano A, Celino I. A framework to build games with a purpose for linked data refinement. In: The Semantic Web–ISWC 2018: 17th International Semantic Web Conference, Monterey, CA, USA, October 8–12, 2018, Proceedings, Part II 17. Springer; 2018. p. 154-69.

[16] Celino I, Re Calegari G, Fiano A. Refining linked data with games with a purpose. Data Intelligence. 2020;2(3):417-42.

[17] Re Calegari G, Nasi G, Celino I. Human computation vs. machine learning: an experimental comparison for image classification. Human Computation. 2018;5:13-30.

[18] Re Calegari G, Celino I. Interplay of game incentives, player profiles and task difficulty in games with a purpose. In: Knowledge Engineering and Knowledge Management: 21st International Conference, EKAW 2018, Nancy, France, November 12-16, 2018, Proceedings 21. Springer; 2018. p. 306-21.

[19] Celino I, Re Calegari G, Scrocca M, Zamorano J, Gonzalez Guardia E. Participant motivation to engage in a citizen science campaign: the case of the TESS network. Journal of Science Communication. 2021;20(6):A03.

[20] Celino I, Re Calegari G. Submitting surveys via a conversational interface: An evaluation of user acceptance and approach effectiveness. International Journal of Human-Computer Studies. 2020;139:102410.

[21] Scrocca M, Scandolari D, Re Calegari G, Baroni I, Celino I. The Survey Ontology: Packaging Survey Research as Research Objects. In: Proceedings of the 2nd Workshop on Data and Research Objects Management for Linked Open Science (DaMaLOS), co-located with ISWC 2021; 2021. .

[22] Belhajjame K, Zhao J, Garijo D, Gamble M, Hettne K, Palma R, et al. Using a suite of ontologies for preserving workflow-centric research objects. Journal of Web Semantics. 2015;32:16-42.

[23] Van Harmelen F, Ten Teije A. A boxology of design patterns for hybrid learning and reasoning systems. Journal of Web Engineering. 2019;18(1-3):97-123.

[24] Breit A, Waltersdorfer L, Ekaputra FJ, Sabou M, Ekelhart A, Iana A, et al. Combining machine learning and semantic web: A systematic mapping study. ACM Computing Surveys. 2023;55(14s):1-41.

[25] Xiao Z, Zhou MX, Liao QV, Mark G, Chi C, Chen W, et al. Tell Me About Yourself: Using an AI-Powered Chatbot to Conduct Conversational Surveys. arXiv preprint arXiv:190510700. 2019.

[26] Akbar F, Grover T, Mark G, Zhou MX. The Effects of Virtual Agents' Characteristics on User Impressions and Language Use. In: Proceedings of the 23rd International Conference on Intelligent User Interfaces Companion. ACM; 2018. p. 56.

[27] Zhou MX, Mark G, Li J, Yang H. Trusting Virtual Agents: The Effect of Personality. ACM Transactions on Interactive Intelligent Systems (TiiS). 2019;9(2-3):10.

[28] Rula A, Re Calegari G, Azzini A, Bucci D, Baroni I, Celino I. Eliciting and Curating Procedural Knowledge in Industry: Challenges and Opportunities. Qurator. 2022.

[29] Lewis P, Perez E, Piktus A, Petroni F, Karpukhin V, Goyal N, et al. Retrieval-augmented generation for knowledge-intensive nlp tasks. Advances in Neural Information Processing Systems. 2020;33:9459-74.

[30] Rula A, Re Calegari G, Azzini A, Bucci D, Carenini A, Baroni I, et al. K-Hub: a modular ontology to support document retrieval and knowledge extraction in Industry 5.0. In: European Semantic Web Conference. Springer; 2023. p. 454-70.

[31] Bellan P, Dragoni M, Ghidini C. Extracting business process entities and relations from text using pre-trained language models and in-context learning. In: International Conference on Enterprise Design, Operations, and Computing. Springer; 2022. p. 182-99.

[32] Rula A, D'Souza J. Procedural Text Mining with Large Language Models. In: Proceedings of the 12th Knowledge Capture Conference 2023; 2023. p. 9-16.

[33] Carriero VA, Azzini A, Baroni I, Scrocca M, Celino I. Human Evaluation of Procedural Knowledge Graph Extraction from Text with Large Language Models. In: under review; 2024. .

[34] Rula A, Re Calegari G, Azzini A, Baroni I, Celino I. Annotation and Extraction of Industrial Procedural Knowledge from Textual Documents. In: Proceedings of the 12th Knowledge Capture Conference 2023; 2023. p. 1-8.

[35] Tsaneva S, Sabou M. Enhancing Human-in-the-Loop Ontology Curation Results through Task Design. ACM Journal of Data and Information Quality. 2024;16(1):1-25.

[36] Kumar A, Pandey A, Gadia R, Mishra M. Building Knowledge Graph using Pre-trained Language Model for Learning Entity-aware Relationships. In: 2020 IEEE International Conference on Computing, Power and Communication Technologies (GUCON); 2020. p. 310-5.

[37] Ding N, Xu G, Chen Y, Wang X, Han X, Xie P, et al. Few-nerd: A few-shot named entity recognition dataset. arXiv preprint arXiv:210507464. 2021.

[38] Shi S, Xu Z, Hu B, Zhang M. Generative Multimodal Entity Linking. In: Proceedings of the 2024 Joint International Conference on Computational Linguistics, Language Resources and Evaluation (LREC-COLING 2024); 2024. p. 7654-65.

[39] Sadeghi M, Carenini A, Corcho O, Rossi M, Santoro R, Vogelsang A. Interoperability of heterogeneous Systems of Systems: from requirements to a reference architecture. The Journal of Supercomputing. 2024 May;80(7):8954-87. Available from: https://doi.org/10.1007/s11227-023-05774-3.

[40] Scrocca M, Grassi M, Comerio M, Carriero VA, Delgado Dias T, Vieira Da Silva A, et al. Intelligent Urban Traffic Management via Semantic Interoperability. In: Proceedings of the 23rd International Semantic Web Conference (ISWC2024); 2024. .

[41] Van Nuffelen B. DCAT Application profile for data portals in Europe (DCAT-AP);. [Online; accessed 2024-07-16]. Available from: https://joinup.ec.europa.eu/collection/semantic-interoperability-community-semic/solution/dcat-application-profile-data-portals-europe/release/211.

[42] Azzini A, Comerio M, Metta S, Scrocca M. The TANGENT Governance Model for Mobility Data Sharing. In: Transport Transitions: Advancing Sustainable and Inclusive Mobility - Proceedings of the 10th TRA Conference. Lecture Notes in Mobility. Springer; 2024. (to appear).

[43] Vetere G, Lenzerini M. Models for semantic interoperability in service-oriented architectures. IBM Systems Journal. 2005;44(4):887-903.

[44] Scrocca M, Comerio M, Carenini A, Celino I. Turning Transport Data to Comply with EU Standards While Enabling a Multimodal Transport Knowledge Graph. In: Proceedings of the 19th International Semantic Web Conference. vol. 12507. Springer; 2020. p. 411–429.

[45] Grassi M, Scrocca M, Carenini A, Comerio M, Celino I. Composable Semantic Data Transformation Pipelines with Chimera. In: Proceedings of the 4th International Workshop on Knowledge Graph Construction co-located with 20th Extended Semantic Web Conference. vol. 3471 of CEUR Workshop Proceedings. Hersonissos, Greece: CEUR; 2023. ISSN: 1613-0073. Available from: https://ceur-ws.org/Vol-3471/paper9.pdf.

[46] Carenini A, Fiano A, Scrocca M, Comerio M, Celino I. Enabling Cross-Border Travel Offers Through National Access Point Federation via Metadata Harmonisation. In: Chaves-Fraga D, Colpaert P, Sadeghi M, Scrocca M, Comerio M, editors. Proceedings of the 3rd International Workshop Semantics And The Web For Transport. vol. 2939 of CEUR Workshop Proceedings. Online, September: CEUR; 2021. ISSN:

1613-0073. Available from: http://ceur-ws.org/Vol-2939/paper6.pdf.

[47] Comerio M, Fiano A, Grassi M, Scrocca M. Mobility data harmonisation: the TANGENT solution. In: Transport Transitions: Advancing Sustainable and Inclusive Mobility - Proceedings of the 10th TRA Conference. Lecture Notes in Mobility. Springer; 2024. (to appear).

[48] Akhtar M, Benjelloun O, Conforti C, Gijsbers P, Giner-Miguelez J, Jain N, et al. Croissant: A Metadata Format for ML-Ready Datasets. In: Proceedings of the Eighth Workshop on Data Management for End-to-End Machine Learning. DEEM '24. New York, NY, USA: Association for Computing Machinery; 2024. p. 1–6. Available from: https://doi.org/10.1145/3650203.3663326.

[49] Scrocca M, Carenini A, Grassi M, Comerio M, Celino I. Not Everybody Speaks RDF: Knowledge Conversion between Different Data Representations. In: Fifth International Workshop on Knowledge Graph Construction@ ESWC2024; 2024..

[50] Randles A, O'Sullivan D. R2[RML]-ChatGPT Framework. In: Chaves-Fraga D, Dimou A, Iglesias-Molina A, Serles U, Assche DV, editors. Proceedings of the 5th International Workshop on Knowledge Graph Construction. vol. 3718 of CEUR Workshop Proceedings. Hersonissos, Greece: CEUR; 2024. ISSN: 1613-0073. Available from: https://ceur-ws.org/Vol-3718/paper5.pdf.

[51] Hosseini M, Kalwar S, Rossi M, Sadeghi M. Automated Mapping for Semantic-based Conversion of Transportation Data Formats. In: Kaffee LA, Endris KM, Vidal ME, Comerio M, Sadeghi M, Chaves-Fraga D, et al., editors. Joint Proceedings of the 1st International Workshop On Semantics For Transport and the 1st International Workshop on Approaches for Making Data Interoperable. vol. 2447 of CEUR Workshop Proceedings. Karlsruhe, Germany: CEUR; 2019. ISSN: 1613-0073. Available from: https://ceur-ws.org/Vol-2447/paper7.pdf.

[52] Hofer M, Frey J, Rahm E. Towards self-configuring Knowledge Graph Construction Pipelines using LLMs - A Case Study with RML. In: Chaves-Fraga D, Dimou A, Iglesias-Molina A, Serles U, Assche DV, editors. Proceedings of the 5th International Workshop on Knowledge Graph Construction. vol. 3718 of CEUR Workshop Proceedings. Hersonissos, Greece: CEUR; 2024. ISSN: 1613-0073. Available from: https://ceur-ws.org/Vol-3718/paper6.pdf.

[53] Rao N, Tsay J, Kate K, Hellendoorn V, Hirzel M. AI for Low-Code for AI. In: Proceedings of the 29th International Conference on Intelligent User Interfaces. IUI '24. New York, NY, USA: Association for Computing Machinery; 2024. p. 837–852. Available from: https://doi.org/10.1145/3640543.3645203.

[54] Scrocca M, Baroni I, Carenini A, Comerio M, Celino I. An Integration Framework to Support Data Sharing and Process Tracking in Intelligent Asset Management Systems. In: Proceedings of the 10th Transport Research Arena. Lecture Notes in Mobility. Springer; 2024. (to be published).

[55] Soiland-Reyes S, et al. Packaging research artefacts with RO-Crate. Data Science. 2022 Jan;5(2):97-138. Publisher: IOS Press.

[56] Workflow Run RO-Crate Working Group. Workflow Run RO-Crate Profiles - Process Run Crate;. Available from: https://www.researchobject.org/workflow-run-crate/profiles/process_run_crate.html.

[57] Scrocca M, Comerio M, Carenini A, Celino I. Modelling Business Agreements in the Multimodal Transportation Domain Through Ontological Smart Contracts. In: Towards a Knowledge-Aware AI. IOS Press; 2022. p. 137-51. Available from: https://ebooks.iospress.nl/doi/10.3233/SSW220016.

[58] Cantone D, Longo CF, Nicolosi Asmundo M, Santamaria DF, Santoro C. Ontological Smart Contracts in OASIS: Ontology for Agents, Systems, and Integration of Services. In: Intelligent Distributed Computing XIV. Studies in Computational Intelligence. Cham: Springer International Publishing; 2022. p. 237-47.

[59] Breit A, Waltersdorfer L, Ekaputra FJ, Karampatakis S, Miksa T, Käfer G. Combining Semantic Web and Machine Learning for Auditable Legal Key Element Extraction. In: Pesquita C, Jimenez-Ruiz E, McCusker J, Faria D, Dragoni M, Dimou A, et al., editors. The Semantic Web. Cham: Springer Nature Switzerland; 2023. p. 609-24.

[60] Lake BM, Ullman TD, Tenenbaum JB, Gershman SJ. Building machines that learn and think like people. Behavioral and Brain Sciences. 2017;40.

[61] Bardaro G, Antonini A, Motta E. Robots for elderly care in the home: A landscape analysis and co-design toolkit. International Journal of Social Robotics. 2022;14(3):657-81.

[62] Tiddi I, De Boer V, Schlobach S, Meyer-Vitali A. Knowledge engineering for hybrid intelligence. In: Proceedings of the 12th Knowledge Capture Conference 2023; 2023. p. 75-82.

[63] Coradeschi S, Saffiotti A. An introduction to the anchoring problem. Robotics and autonomous systems. 2003;43(2-3):85-96.

[64] Bonarini A, Matteucci M, Restelli M. Anchoring: do we need new solutions to an old problem or do we have old solutions for a new problem. In: Proceedings of the AAAI Symposium on Anchoring Symbols to Sensor Data in Single and Multiple Robot Systems; 2001. p. 79-86.

[65] Nüchter A, Hertzberg J. Towards semantic maps for mobile robots. Robotics and Autonomous Systems. 2008;56(11):915-26.

[66] Chiatti A, Bardaro G, Matteucci M, Motta E. Visual Model Building for Robot Sensemaking: Perspectives, Challenges, and Opportunities. In: Proceedings of the Bridge Session on AI and Robotics of the thirty-seventh AAAI conference on Artificial Intelligence (AAAI-23), Washington, WA, USA; 2023. p. 7-14.

[67] Chiatti A, Bardaro G, Motta E, Daga E. A Spatial Reasoning Framework for Commonsense Reasoning in Visually Intelligent Agents. In: Proceedings of the 8th International workshop on Artificial Intelligence and Cognition (AIC 2022). CEUR; 2022. .

[68] Li B, Han J, Cheng Y, Tan C, Qi P, Zhang J, et al. Object goal navigation in eobodied AI: A survey. In: Proceedings of the 2022 4th International Conference on Video, Signal and Image Processing; 2022. p. 87-92.

[69] Hu J, Cao L, Tong T, Ye Q, Zhang S, Li K, et al. Architecture disentanglement for deep neural networks. In: Proceedings of the IEEE/CVF international conference on computer vision; 2021. p. 672-81.

[70] Snowden R, Snowden RJ, Thompson P, Troscianko T. Basic vision: an introduction to visual perception. Oxford University Press; 2012.

[71] Chiatti A, Motta E, Daga E. Towards a framework for Visual Intelligence in Service Robotics: epistemic requirements and gap analysis. In: Proceedings of the International Conference on Principles of Knowldge Representation and Reasoning (KR) -Special session on KR & Robotics. IJCAI; 2020. p. 905-16.

[72] Kambhampati S. Can large language models reason and plan? Annals of the New York Academy of Sciences. 2024;1534(1):15-8.

[73] Kambhampati S, Valmeekam K, Guan L, Verma M, Stechly K, Bhambri S, et al. Position: LLMs Can't Plan, But Can Help Planning in LLM-Modulo Frameworks. In: Forty-first International Conference on Machine Learning; 2024. .

[74] Maroto-Gómez M, Malfaz M, Castillo JC, Castro-González Á, Salichs MÁ. Personalizing Activity Selection in Assistive Social Robots from Explicit and Implicit User Feedback. International Journal of Social Robotics. 2024:1-19.

[75] Ingrand F, Ghallab M. Deliberation for autonomous robots: A survey. Artificial Intelligence. 2017;247:10-44.

[76] Savva M, Chang AX, Hanrahan P. Semantically enriched 3D models for common-sense knowledge. In: Proceedings of the IEEE Conference on Computer Vision and Pattern Recognition Workshops (CVPRW). IEEE; 2015. p. 24-31.

[77] Krishna R, Zhu Y, Groth O, Johnson J, et al. Visual genome: Connecting language and vision using crowdsourced dense image annotations. International Journal of Computer Vision. 2017;123(1):32-73.

[78] Chiatti A, Motta E, Daga E. Robots with Commonsense: Improving Object Recognition through Size and Spatial Awareness. In: Proceedings of the AAAI Symposium on Machine Learning and Knowledge Engineering for Hybrid Intelligence (AAAI-MAKE). CEUR; 2022. .

[79] Romero J, Razniewski S. Inside quasimodo: Exploring construction and usage of commonsense knowledge. In: Proceedings of the 29th ACM International Conference on Information & Knowledge Management; 2020. p. 3445-8.

[80] Wang W, Lv Q, Yu W, Hong W, Qi J, Wang Y, et al. Cogvlm: Visual expert for pretrained language models. arXiv preprint arXiv:231103079. 2023.

[81] Chen B, Xu Z, Kirmani S, Ichter B, Sadigh D, Guibas L, et al. Spatialvlm: Endowing vision-language models with spatial reasoning capabilities. In: Proceedings of the IEEE/CVF Conference on Computer Vision and Pattern Recognition; 2024. p. 14455-65.

[82] Mitra C, Huang B, Darrell T, Herzig R. Compositional chain-of-thought prompting for large multimodal models. In: Proceedings of the IEEE/CVF Conference on Computer Vision and Pattern Recognition; 2024. p. 14420-31.

[83] Davis E, Marcus G. Commonsense reasoning and commonsense knowledge in artificial intelligence. Communications of the ACM. 2015;58(9):92-103.

[84] Chaves-Fraga D, Corcho O, Dimou A, Vidal ME, Iglesias-Molina A, Van Assche D. Are Knowledge Graphs Ready for the Real World? Challenges and Perspective (Dagstuhl Seminar 24061). Dagstuhl Reports. 2024;14(2):1-70. Available from: https://drops.dagstuhl.de/entities/document/10.4230/DagRep.14.2.1.

[85] European Parliament, Council of the European Union. Regulation (EU) 2024/1689 of the European Parliament and of the Council of 13 June 2024 laying down harmonised rules on artificial intelligence; 2024. Available from: http://data.europa.eu/eli/reg/2024/1689/oj.

Handbook on Neurosymbolic AI and Knowledge Graphs
P. Hitzler et al. (Eds.)
IOS Press, 2025

doi:10.3233/FAIA250242

Neurosymbolic Methods for Food Computing

Gjorgjina CENIKJ [a] Mauro DRAGONI [b] Tome EFTIMOV [a]
Barbara KOROUŠIĆ SELJAK [a] Agnieszka ŁAWRYNOWICZ [c] Fnu MOHBAT [d]
Oshani SENEVIRATNE [d] Yoko YAMAKATA [e] Mohammed J. ZAKI [d]

[a] *Computer Systems Department, Jožef Stefan Institute, Ljubljana, Slovenia*
[b] *Fondazione Bruno Kessler, Trento, Italy*
[c] *Poznan University of Technology, Poland*
[d] *Rensselaer Polytechnic Institute, Troy, NY, USA*
[e] *The University of Tokyo, Japan*

ORCiD ID: Gjorgjina Cenikj https://orcid.org/0000-0002-2723-0821, Mauro Dragoni https://orcid.org/0000-0003-0380-6571, Tome Eftimov https://orcid.org/0000-0001-7330-1902, Barbara Koroušić Seljak https://orcid.org/0000-0001-7597-2590, Agnieszka Ławrynowicz https://orcid.org/0000-0002-2442-345X, Fnu Mohbat https://orcid.org/0000-0001-9204-6812, Oshani Seneviratne https://orcid.org/0000-0001-8518-917X, Yoko Yamakata https://orcid.org/0000-0003-2752-6179, Mohammed J. Zaki https://orcid.org/0000-0003-4711-0234

Abstract. In this chapter, we explore the integration of symbolic reasoning and neural network-based methods within the domain of food science. We provide a comprehensive overview of symbolic methods such as food ontologies, knowledge graphs, and their construction, emphasizing their role in enhancing data interoperability and supporting complex food computing tasks. We then discuss neural network-based techniques for extracting food information from textual and image data, food representation learning through embeddings, and present various methodologies for food category classification, nutrition estimation, and ingredient substitution. Practical applications such as personalized nutrition, dietary management, food logging, and recipe creation using generative AI are also discussed, showcasing the transformative impact of neurosymbolic methods in food computing.

Keywords. Food Computing, Neurosymbolic Methods, Food Ontologies, Knowledge Graphs, Named Entity Recognition, Information Extraction, Personalized Nutrition, Food Recommendation Systems, Food Representation Learning, Ingredient Substitution, Recipe Generation

1. Introduction

Food computing leverages computer science methods for food-related topics [1]. It is an interdisciplinary field that merges principles and technologies from computer science, data science, and food science to address a wide range of issues related to food production, distribution, and consumption.

At the core of food computing is data collection and analysis. Food computing uses computational approaches to acquire heterogeneous food data such as food logs, food images, and recipes. Data analytics and machine learning (ML) algorithms are then employed to process and interpret vast amounts of data related to food production, supply chains, and consumer preferences. Food computing leverages computational techniques to analyze and model various aspects of the food ecosystem, enabling innovations that can enhance food quality, safety, sustainability, and accessibility. It intersects with agronomy, gastronomy, and health, among other things. Consumer health and nutrition benefit from food computing through personalized nutrition and food recommendation systems. Data analytics is used to develop personalized dietary recommendations based on individual health profiles and preferences. ML creates intelligent systems that suggest recipes and food products tailored to consumers' tastes and nutritional needs.

Food computing continues to expand its scope as an evolving field, driven by technological advancements and a growing recognition of the need for smarter food systems. To support complex food computing tasks like retrieval or question answering, an effective approach is to build ontologies and knowledge graphs (KGs) focused on food [2].

1.1. The Utility of Neurosymbolic Methods in Food Computing

Symbolic reasoning, through the use of ontologies and KGs, provides a structured framework for representing food-related knowledge. This structure facilitates data interoperability, allowing diverse datasets and systems to communicate effectively. Neural network-based methods, such as deep learning, on the other hand, can process vast amounts of unstructured data, extracting valuable insights that can be integrated into the structured knowledge base. They also excel at extracting information from unstructured data sources like text and images. When combined with symbolic reasoning, which provides context and relationships between entities, the accuracy and comprehensiveness of information extraction in food science can be significantly improved.

Neural networks are also adept at handling image and text data, making them ideal for tasks such as food recognition, classification, and nutritional estimation from images. Symbolic reasoning can then be used to interpret these results within a broader context, such as linking recognized food items to nutritional databases and dietary guidelines. Understanding and influencing human behavior is crucial in health applications. Symbolic reasoning can model behavior change theories and health guidelines, while neural networks can analyze individual behavior data to provide personalized interventions that promote healthier lifestyles and tailored advice. Therefore, by integrating symbolic reasoning with neural networks, it becomes possible to create highly personalized nutrition and dietary recommendations.

Many problems in food science require the integration of diverse data sources and complex reasoning. Examples include predicting the impact of dietary changes on health or optimizing food supply chains. Neural networks can identify patterns and trends in the data, while symbolic reasoning can ensure that solutions adhere to logical constraints and domain-specific knowledge. Additionally, neural networks can scale to handle large datasets, while symbolic reasoning can provide flexible frameworks for incorporating new knowledge. This combination allows for the continuous improvement and expansion of food computing systems as new data and research become available.

2. Food Data Structures and Semantic Frameworks

The vast amount of food-related information readily available online has opened up exciting possibilities for structuring this knowledge through food ontologies and KGs.

2.1. Food Data Sources

Food data encompasses a wide array of information related to various aspects of food, including its composition, production, distribution, consumption, and impact on health and the environment. This data can be categorized into aspects such as:

- *Nutritional Data:* Information on the nutritional content of food items, including macronutrients (e.g., proteins, carbohydrates, fats), micronutrients (e.g., vitamins, minerals), and other bioactive compounds.
- *Sensory Data:* Data related to the sensory attributes of food such as taste, texture, aroma, and appearance.
- *Consumption Data:* Patterns and trends in food consumption, including dietary habits and preferences.
- *Production Data:* Data from food production processes, including agricultural practices, food manufacturing, and supply chain information.
- *Environmental Data:* Data on the environmental impact of food production and consumption, such as carbon footprint, water usage, and sustainability metrics.
- *Regulatory Data:* Information on food safety standards, regulations, and compliance requirements.

In the context of food computing, acquiring comprehensive and high-quality data is crucial for developing accurate and effective models and solutions. The primary sources of food data include databases and repositories such as the USDA National Nutrient Database [3], which offers detailed nutritional information for a wide range of food items, including macronutrients, micronutrients, and other bioactive compounds. Managed by the USDA, FoodData Central [4] provides comprehensive data on food composition, including nutrient and food component values, food item metadata, and links to external data sources [5]. Additionally, various international databases, such as the Food and Agriculture Organization (FAO) databases [4], offer data on food production, consumption, and trade at a global scale.

The integration of sensors and IoT in food production and consumption environments generates real-time data that is valuable for monitoring and optimizing various processes related to food data. For instance, sensors deployed in agricultural settings collect data on soil moisture, temperature, humidity, and other environmental factors that influence crop growth and yield [6]. Similarly, IoT (Internet of Things) devices are used to monitor the safety and quality of food during production, transportation, and storage. These sensors can detect spoilage, contamination, and other hazards [7]. IoT-enabled kitchen appliances, such as smart refrigerators and cooking devices, track food inventory, usage patterns, and expiration dates, providing valuable data on food consumption and waste [8].

Furthermore, crowd-sourcing leverages the collective intelligence and contributions of individuals to gather data on food-related topics. Online surveys and questionnaires collect data on dietary habits, food preferences, and consumption patterns from a broad

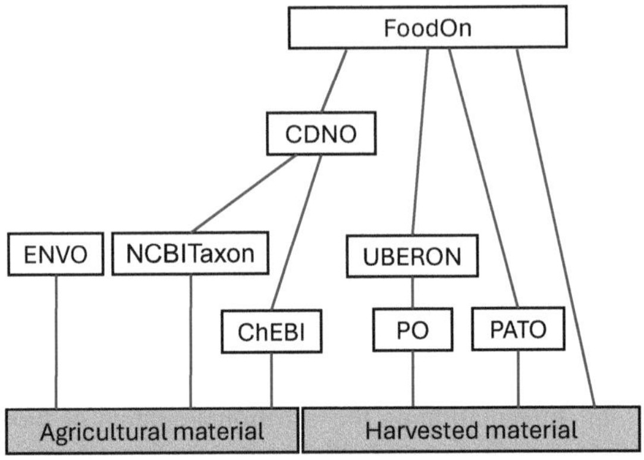

Figure 1. FoodOn [12,13] incorporates terms from various OBO Foundry [13] and other ontologies, including environmental terms from ENVO [14], organisms from NCBITaxon [15], chemical entities of biological interest from ChEBI [16], plant and animal anatomy terms from PO [17] and UBERON [18], phenotype and traits from PATO [19], and nutritional components from CDNO [20].

audience [9]. Nutrition and diet-tracking apps gather detailed information on users' food intake, physical activity, and health metrics [10]. Social media platforms like Twitter/X, Instagram, Reddit, and Facebook contain vast amounts of user-generated content related to food, including recipes, reviews, recommendations, and food-related queries [11].

2.2. Food Ontologies

Several notable ontologies exist to represent food knowledge, with the primary one being FoodOn [12]. FoodOn encompasses extensive information on food categorization and processing and integrates knowledge from various ontologies related to food safety, agricultural and animal husbandry practices, culinary arts, nutrition, and chemical ingredients and processes. It also incorporates information on raw materials that cover anatomy, taxonomy, geography, and cultural heritage. FoodOn is part of the Open Biological and Biomedical Ontology Foundry (OBO) consortium [13], which consists of interoperable, life science-oriented ontologies. It serves as a central point for gathering information on food from several other ontologies (Figure 1). On the other hand, a growing list of ontologies, including ontologies on the environment, crop dietary nutrition, nutritional studies, food interactions with drugs, food biomarkers, and others, are reusing FoodOn terms.

SNOMED CT [21] is a multilingual clinical terminology standard used in electronic health records by healthcare professionals. Beyond its primary focus on medical concepts, it includes a category for Food, aiding in the normalization of food-related terms. The Hansard taxonomy [22], developed through the SAMUELS project (2014-2016), organizes concepts into 37 high-level semantic groups, including 'Food and Drink,' enabling semantic searches of its data. FoodEx2 [23], created by the European Food Safety Agency, is a standardized system for classifying and describing foods. It uses various facets to detail food properties and aspects, improving the comparability of food consumption data across different sources and enhancing data analysis.

The Personalized Information Platform for Health and Life Services (PIPS) ontology [24] focuses on healthcare applications. The Healthy Life Style (HeLiS) Ontology

[25] includes food concepts like 'BasicFood' and 'Recipe.' The Food Product Ontology [26] prioritizes business-oriented information like price and brand, making it suitable for industry applications. FoodOntoMap [27] is a resource containing food concepts extracted from recipes and annotated with semantic tags from eight different food ontologies. This resource aids in normalizing food concepts across different ontologies and supports applications that explore the relationships between food systems, human health, and the environment.

2.3. Food Knowledge Graphs and Data Stores

KGs can offer a comprehensive and interconnected representation of food data, encompassing recipe details, nutritional information, health benefits, ingredient substitutions, and even personal preferences. One research direction on Food KGs studies the molecular composition and its impact on food and health [28,29,30] while another research direction studies the relationship between different foods, ingredients, and nutritional values [31,32].

Considering the utility of flavor molecules for ingredients, foods, and fragrances and regulating the metabolism, FlavorDB [28] compiled a repository of 25,595 flavor molecules representing a number of tastes and odors. FlavorDB could be used to study the properties and pairing of ingredients and foods. To study the relations between ingredients and their chemical compounds [29] introduced Flavor-Graph, a large-scale food graph created from millions of food recipes and flavor molecules. The resulting graph improves the prediction of relations between foods and compounds and helps to analyze food pairing and recommendations. Due to the impact of diet and lifestyle on preventing chronic diseases, specifically 30-40% of all cancers, Veselkov et al. [30] processed 1962 drugs to generate a gene-gene graph, which is then used to profile bio-active molecules within 7962 foods. The gene-gene connection network is then fed to a classifier to detect anti-cancer food molecules. Despite the creation of many domain ontologies and web applications, ProductKG [33] addresses the lack of connection between knowledge and environment by integrating modular product information from the Web as well as environmental information from a semantic digital twin. Thus, a KG could assist users in daily activities through custom applications such as an augmented reality shopping assistant or a dietary recommender.

Despite the presence of several food ontologies, there is a lack of a unified KG that is oriented towards healthiness, and integrated food suggestion services that encompass food and recipes are needed. The first extensive FoodKG [31] stands out, containing over a million recipes and 67 million triples that connect recipes, ingredients, and nutritional data. Another notable KG, RecipeKG [32], leverages the RecipeON [34] to build a KG on a massive scale, featuring 56 million instances, 209 million facts, and data from 0.8 million recipes. This KG further categorizes ingredients into three groups (main, side, and flavor) and assigns action properties to each ingredient. Additionally, RecipeKG utilizes OpenAI's GPT API[1] to convert sampled subgraphs into natural language recipe text. This annotation of ingredient types proves particularly valuable for exploring ingredient substitutions by narrowing down the potential replacements.

Methods have also been developed to analyze recipe texts using natural language processing (NLP) techniques to obtain the structure of their cooking procedures. Ya-

[1]https://openai.com/api

makata et al. proposed a method to convert the instructional text of a web-based recipe into a flow graph structure by utilizing named entity recognition (NER) and dependency parsing techniques [35,36].

3. Food Knowledge Extraction and Representation

3.1. Knowledge Graph Construction

The first step in constructing a KG is collecting data from diverse sources (e.g., those outlined in Section 2.1). These sources can include structured databases, unstructured text, and semi-structured documents. Structured data sources include databases and APIs like USDA's National Nutrient Database [3] and FoodData Central [5], whereas unstructured and/or semi-structured data sources can be recipe websites, blogs, and social media posts that could be parsed into XML/JSON files. Once the data has been collected, the next steps involve entity and relationship extraction.

Entity extraction involves identifying and classifying key entities within the collected data. Entities in the food domain can include food items, nutrients, recipes, and health effects. NER techniques are used to automatically detect and classify entities in text. Popular NER tools like spaCy [37] and Stanford NER [38] can be leveraged for this purpose augmented with advanced ML models, such as bidirectional long short-term memory (LSTM) and conditional random fields (CRF), or transformer-based models, to improve the accuracy of entity extraction. Additionally, dictionary-based methods, such as the semantic data dictionary [39], leverage predefined dictionaries of food-related terms to identify entities in structured and semi-structured data.

Relationship extraction aims to identify and categorize the connections between extracted entities, which is crucial for creating a meaningful and interconnected KG. There are several approaches for relationship extraction: Pattern-based methods use predefined linguistic patterns to identify relationships in text [40]. Supervised learning techniques may also be used for training models on labeled data to recognize relationships between entities [41,42,43]. Dependency parsing analyzes the grammatical structure of sentences to extract relationships based on syntactic dependencies [44,45].

Once entities and relationships are extracted, the next step is to construct the KG and enrich it with additional information by linking the extracted entities to authoritative knowledge sources such as FoodOn [12,13]. Such ontology mapping helps define the structure and semantics of the KG, including entity types, relationships, and constraints, and improves its comprehensiveness and utility.

3.2. Information and Knowledge Extraction

In this section, we discuss the processes and methodologies for extracting relevant information and knowledge from textual and image data in the food domain. We explore various techniques, such as NER, NEL, and relation extraction, along with the creation of annotated corpora and the application of advanced ML models. Additionally, we highlight the challenges and advancements in food image recognition, focusing on the use of datasets and models to improve accuracy and applicability in real-world scenarios.

3.2.1. Food Information Extraction from Textual Data

Information extraction (IE) from unstructured text facilitates the detection and identification of entities, along with their classification and semantic annotation. This process involves enhancing the text by adding descriptors (metadata) from selected vocabularies and standards (i.e., semantic resources), which supports further knowledge discovery. Although bioinformaticians have developed various methodologies for IE, there is a lack of approaches and semantic resources (vocabularies and standards) tailored to the specific needs of the food domain.

NER is a subset of IE that identifies words or phrases in the text and classifies them into predefined labels or classes relevant to a specific domain. Various NER methods include:

- Terminology-driven NER (Dictionary-based NER): Matches text phrases with concept synonyms in terminological resources, often combined with heuristics to improve performance. However, it only recognizes entities present in the resources.
- Rule-based NER: Utilizes regular expressions informed by terminological resources and entity characteristics. Its main drawback is the time-consuming manual construction of rules.
- Corpus-based NER: Uses annotated corpora and ML algorithms to predict entity labels, requiring extensive human effort to create annotated datasets for new domains.

Active learning can significantly improve the efficiency of NLP models by prioritizing the most informative data points for annotation [46]. It reduces the need for large labeled datasets, enabling models to achieve high performance with fewer annotated examples. In addition, recent advancements have used deep neural networks (especially transformer [47] and LSTM [48] architectures for corpus-based NER to provide the best results on the NER task.

When the food entities are recognized, the next step is named entity linking (NEL), which connects entities in the text to their unique identifiers within a knowledge base, typically a semantic model or ontology. Ontologies structure domain-specific knowledge by defining entities, their attributes, relationships, and constraints. This organization aids in knowledge sharing, reasoning, and system interoperability. Using unique identifiers allows for aggregating information about the same entity from various sources, even if different terms are used. This step is essential for effective data interoperability, aligning with the findable, accessible, interoperable, and reusable, i.e., FAIR principles [49].

Rule-based NER. DrNER [50] is a rule-based system focused on extracting information from evidence-based dietary recommendations, with a scope that extends beyond nutritional details to encompass various food concepts. However, it identifies phrases mentioning food entities rather than individual food items. FoodIE [51] has been developed to solve this identification issue, which introduces a rule-based method designed for extracting food-related information from recipes.

Creation of gold text food corpora. Rule-based approaches enable the automated creation of a silver annotated corpus, which initially includes both false negatives and false positives. Domain experts can utilize human-computer interaction (HCI) tools to correct these automatic annotations, thereby incorporating missed instances (false negatives) and eliminating incorrect ones (false positives). This process transforms the corpus into a gold-standard annotated corpus suitable for training corpus-based NERs. Below, we will describe several annotated food corpora together with an HCI tool developed for food annotations where applicable.

- FoodBase [52] is an annotated dataset comprising 1000 recipes sourced from Allrecipes, the largest social network dedicated to food enthusiasts. These recipes were chosen from five distinct categories: 'Appetizers and Snacks,' 'Breakfast and Lunch,' 'Dessert,' 'Dinner,' and 'Drinks.' Semantic tags derived from the Hansard corpus [22] were employed to annotate the names of food entities within the dataset.
- CafeteriaFCD [53] is created by utilizing the curated FoodBase [52] and employing two annotation methods: the National Center for Biomedical Ontology (NCBO) annotator [54] (for FoodOn and SNOMED CT annotations) and the semi-automatic StandFood method [55] (for FoodEx2 [23] annotations). CafeteriaFCD corpus is a revised golden standard of FoodBase. It includes annotated recipes with semantic tags from FoodOn, SNOMED CT, Hansard, and FoodEx2 resources, promoting interoperability across four semantic domains.
- CafeteriaSA [56] is the first annotated corpus that comprises 500 scientific abstracts, containing 6,407 annotated food entities categorized according to Hansard taxonomy, with 4,299 annotated for FoodOn and 3,623 for SNOMED CT.
- FoodOntoMap [27] comprises food entities extracted from recipes and annotated using semantic tags from eight distinct food ontologies. This resource serves to standardize food concepts across ontologies and support the development of applications aimed at exploring the relationships between food systems, human health, and the environment.
- FoodViz [57] is proposed as an HCI tool implemented as a web-based framework aimed at making the links between different food semantic resources understandable by food subject matter experts. It is used to present food annotation results from existing NLP and ML pipelines in combination with different food semantic data models, allowing users to become more familiar with the links between different food semantic data models and also allowing opportunities to correct false positives and negatives.
- The recipe flow graph (r-FG) [35] dataset contains 266 Japanese recipes annotated with eight tags: food, tool, duration, quantity, chef's action, action by foods, food state, and tool state.
- CURD [58] includes 300 annotated and 350 unannotated recipes using the Minimal Instruction Language for the Kitchen (MILK) [59].
- TASTEset [60] comprises 1,000 sets of ingredients manually annotated with several tags.

Corpus-based NER. Once a gold standard is established, corpus-based NERs can be developed. These systems leverage information from annotated corpora created by domain experts in the relevant field, employing ML algorithms to predict entity labels. We will now discuss different corpus-based NERs developed for food entity recognition, utilizing recent advancements in NLP.

- BuTTER [48] leverages the newly introduced FoodBase corpus and represents the pioneering corpus-based method for food NER. This approach integrates bidirectional long short-term memory (BiLSTM) with CRF and representation learning, utilizing textual representations such as GloVe [61], Word2Vec [62], and FastText [63]. BuTTER's NER models are trained using two distinct architectures: a BiLSTM-CRF model with word embeddings and another BiLSTM-CRF model integrating both word and character embeddings. Despite the limited amount of annotated data, experiments demonstrate BuTTER's capability to effectively distinguish food entities (food vs. non-food) from raw text, achieving an impressive average macro F1 score of 94.6% [48].

- FoodNER [47] encompasses a suite of corpus-based methods for NER related to food items. It comprises 15 distinct models derived from fine-tuning three pre-trained bidirectional encoder representations from transformers (BERT [64]) models across five semantic categories: distinguishing food versus non-food entities, two subsets of Hansard food semantic tags, FoodOn semantic tags, and SNOMED CT food semantic tags. This exploration demonstrates how BERT can be effectively adapted for extracting food-related information, achieving state-of-the-art results. The BERT models consistently achieved high macro F1 scores, ranging from 93.30% to 94.31%, in discerning food versus non-food entities. Moreover, in tasks predicting semantic tags, these models also performed strongly, with macro F1 scores ranging from 73.39% to 78.96%.
- Food Voting NER [65] is a voting strategy proposed to enhance the precision of existing food NER models by combining their predictions with rule-based models, which are unaffected by the training corpus. It utilizes a voting strategy to aggregate predictions from BuTTER, FoodNER, and two rule-based models utilizing dictionaries containing common or scientific names of foods extracted from FooDB[2]. A token extracted by any of these models is deemed a valid food entity if it has been extracted by at least two of BuTTER, FoodNER, or the non-scientific FooDB model or if the FoodNER method successfully links it to an external resource. Further post-processing steps can eliminate entities deemed too general to be useful or entities lacking nouns, which are likely false positives.
- SciFoodNER [65] is a scientific food NER and NEL model derived by fine-tuning transformer models on a corpus of scientific abstracts annotated with food entities. This model identifies mentions of food entities in raw text and links them to the Hansard Taxonomy, FoodOn, and SNOMED CT. Among the evaluated models, the best results are achieved by the BioBERT model [66], with median macro-averaged F1 scores of 0.90 for the NER task, 0.66 for linking to the Hansard Taxonomy, 0.43 for linking to the FoodOn ontology, and 0.58 for linking to the SNOMED CT ontology.

Relation extraction. FooDis [67] is a relation extraction pipeline that utilizes state-of-the-art approaches in NLP to mine abstracts of biomedical scientific papers and automatically suggests potential 'cause' or 'treat' relations between food and disease entities in various existing semantic resources. When compared with already known relations, it is observed that the relations predicted by FooDis match for 90% of the food-disease pairs that are common with the NutriChem [68,69] database and 93% of the common pairs

[2]https://www.foodb.ca/

in the DietRx[3] platform. Additionally, it is demonstrated that relations suggested by the FooDis pipeline [67] exhibit high precision.

The performance of three state-of-the-art relation-mining pipelines (FooDis, FoodChem [70], and ChemDis [71]) was evaluated [72], which extract relations between food, chemical, and disease entities from textual data. In two case studies, relations were automatically extracted by the pipelines, organized in a KG, and validated by domain experts. The results show that relations can be extracted with an average precision of around 70%, making new discoveries available to domain experts with reduced human effort, as they need only evaluate the results rather than find and read all new scientific papers.

3.2.2. Food Information Extraction from Images

The task of food IE from images involves identifying and classifying food items in various contexts using advanced machine-learning models. In this section, we focus on the capabilities and challenges associated with the food recognition model and provide an overview of established models like NutriNet [73], which has demonstrated proficiency in identifying a wide range of food and drink items. Additionally, we discuss various datasets used for training these models, the limitations faced in real-world applications, and recent advancements aimed at improving food image recognition accuracy and applicability.

An established model like NutriNet [73] exemplifies current capabilities in food recognition, which can identify 520 distinct food and drink items. NutriNet was trained on a dataset of 130,517 images, with careful curation, including 100 images per label. The dataset underwent rigorous post-processing for accurate annotations.

Additional datasets such as UEC-FOOD101 [74], UEC-FOOD256 [75], UEC-FoodPix [76], and UEC-FoodPixComplete [77] offer varying compositions: single food items per image in the former two and multiple items in the latter pair. The UNIMID2016 dataset [78] extends this scope with images of multiple food items in a controlled lab setting.

Despite these advancements, models trained on such datasets often struggle with real-world applications. A recent benchmark dataset sourced from MyFoodRepo [79] attempts to bridge this gap, containing 24,119 food images and 39,325 segmented polygons across 273 food classes. However, standardized labeling for nutritional quality and other food attributes remains a significant challenge in food image recognition.

The YOLOv5 segmentation model [80] was fine-tuned on the NutriGreen dataset [81] to detect food labels, which consist of 10,472 images depicting branded food products. Each image includes annotations for three distinct labels: nutritional quality assessed by Nutri-Score [82], vegan or vegetarian status indicated by V-label [83], and the EU organic certification logo [84]. The Nutri-Score spans grades A to E, with varying image counts per grade. The impressive accuracy of 94.0% [81] highlights the dataset's potential to train advanced systems capable of recognizing food labels, positioning it as a valuable benchmark for future developments in CV applications.

3.3. Multi-Modal Food Knowledge Graphs

KGs about food provide abstract symbols describing food entities that can be used for several purposes, ranging from supporting the tasks described later in Section 4 to the

[3] http://cosylab.iiitd.edu.in/dietrx/

creation of applications like the ones described in Section 5. The creation of applications is exactly the aspect requiring KGs to support the representation of different perceptions of the same entity. If we consider the food domain, this means that a KG must include, for each food-related entity, e.g., a recipe, its abstract symbolic definition together with further equivalent representations of the same entity, e.g., its picture or video showing how to create it. To address this challenge, the creation of Multi-Modal Knowledge Graphs (MMKG) can be a solution to equipping KGs with such a multi-perception capability. We briefly recap the most recent MMKGs to give a general overview of the state-of-the-art in this field. Then, we focus on the nutrition domain by reporting the most available knowledge resources, and we present an ontology modeling pattern to support the integration of multi-modal information into KGs.

Within the literature, two main methodologies to build MMKGs are described: (i) image-based visual knowledge extraction and (ii) symbolic grounding.

The first methodology comes from the computer vision (CV) community, and it is focused on building knowledge artifacts by starting from the labels provided by CV systems [85,86]. The NEIL system [87] implements a pre-trained classifier to annotate images with a single label, and it applies heuristic rules about the locations of extracted objects to extract visual relations. Differently, the GAIA system [88] focuses on news documents by extracting both fine-grained concepts together with their fine-grained relationships. Similarly, the RESIN solution [89], which is based on the GAIA framework, aims to extract events from news documents and to identify related visual entities and concepts. Finally, the MMEKG system [90] aims to optimize some modules of the GAIA framework to increase its scalability to work on billion-scale universal events extraction.

The second methodology refers to the process of finding appropriate multi-modal items (e.g., images) to describe the knowledge (e.g., entity, concept, or a relational triple) in a given KG [91]. IMGpedia [92] links images from Wikimedia Commons[4] to DBpedia[5] via the structured Wikipedia data in RDF format already extracted in DBpedia Commons [93], which additionally adds the similarity relations between images. ImageGraph [94] uses entities in KGs as queries to search images from search engines. Similarly, MMKG [95] introduces the alignment operation between entities to support multiple KGs. It is important to highlight that these systems focus only on images' representativeness without considering their diversity, which is an important dimension for enabling the differentiation of contexts and views. This issue has been partially addressed by the Richpedia system [96] that aims to train an additional diversity retrieval model to select diverse images. However, the categories of entities in Richpedia are limited to cities, sights, and persons.

Despite the wealth of information on food recipes on the Web, only one KG focusing on recipes, namely FoodKG [97], exists to date. FoodKG uses the Foodon Ontology [98] to categorize food, combined with nutritional data about food from the US Department of Agriculture's (USDA) National Nutrient Database for Standard Reference[6], and chemical and other components of foods. In general, an MMKG can reuse the basic structure of different food-related ontologies like the HeLiS ontology [99]. However, unlike RecipeKG, FoodKG is oriented towards consumers who wish to determine what recipe to make based on the ingredients at hand while accounting for constraints, such

[4]https://wikimediafoundation.org/our-work/commons

[5]https://www.dbpedia.org/resources/knowledge-graphs

[6]https://catalog.data.gov/dataset/food-and-nutrient-databasefor-dietary-studies-fndds

as allergies. Finally, Open Food Facts[7] is an open platform that allows individuals to add and edit information about packaged foods worldwide. Open Food Facts uses a scoring system similar to the FSA score from UK's Food Standards Agency nutrient profiling system[8].

Besides KGs, several food ontologies have become available over the years [100], and some of them incorporate nutritional information. The ONS [101] ontology models nutritional concepts commonly encountered in intervention and observational studies, while FOBI [102] primarily focuses on metabolic data. HeLiS [99] models food concepts and their relation to physical activities. NAct [103] also models food concepts but from a medical perspective. Unlike existing ontologies and vocabularies that focus on nutritional information modeling, an effective MMKG should focus on recipes and their ingredients and reuse existing ingredients defined within a food-related ontology, as well as its concepts related to nutrition, to calculate recipes' healthiness.

As mentioned above, the construction of an MMKG should follow a symbolic grounding methodology. Within this context and according to [104], two ways have been adopted in the MMKGs literature to represent multi-modal resources: (i) as an attribute or (ii) as an entity. In the former, the multi-modal resource is associated with an entity through an attribute value, typically an Internationalized Resource Identifier (IRI). Instead, in the latter, the multi-modal resource is modeled as a new entity within the KG. Concerning the construction of an MMKG, we suggest modeling a multi-modal resource as a new entity, given our intent of providing fine-grained information about the multi-modal aspects associated with the entities contained within the KG. Despite multimodality not being a completely novel aspect of KG, an ontology design pattern supporting the modeling of multimodal resources is still missing. Below, we propose a novel pattern to fill this gap.

Multi-Modal Design Pattern The main principle we adopted to model the multi-modality of recipes consists of decoupling the conceptualization of a recipe from the multi-modal resource associated with it. Figure 2 shows the pattern we propose to support the modeling of a multi-modal resource that is then associated with an entity already defined within a KG. For instance, a recipe may be associated with different types of multi-modal resources, e.g., a video describing how to prepare the recipe or a picture showing what the recipe looks like when it is served. We define two main concepts: *Modality* and *ModalDescriptor*. The *Modality* concept is the most abstract concept subsuming most specific concepts specifying the different modalities, like *Image* and *Video*. The rationale behind creating a specific concept for each type of modality is to enable the possibility of modeling individuals instantiating such concepts with the purpose of sharing common attributes. For example, an item *Image_jpeg_430x320* instantiating the concept *Image* defines an image characterized by a width of 430 pixels (datatype property *width*), a height of 320 pixels (datatype property *height*), and encoded in the jpeg format (annotation *dcterms:format*[9]).

The *ModalDescriptor* concept has been modeled as a subclass of *dcat:Resource* from the Data Catalog Vocabulary[10] (DCAT). It is defined as a resource published or cu-

[7] https://world.openfoodfacts.org/
[8] https://www.gov.uk/government/publications/the-nutrient-profiling-model
[9] https://www.dublincore.org/specifications/dublin-core/dcmi-terms/terms/format
[10] https://www.w3.org/TR/vocab-dcat-3/#Class:Resource

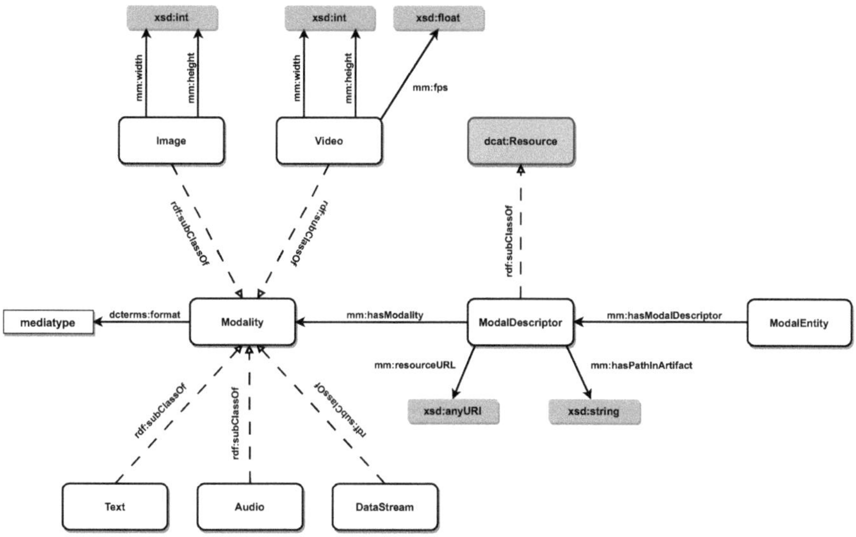

Figure 2. Design pattern of a multi-modal resource. White boxes refer to the concepts modeled within an MMKG, while grey boxes represent concepts imported from external resources. Solid and dashed lines are used to represent objects/data and RDF core properties.

rated by a single agent, encompassing properties such as title and creators. The *ModalDescriptor* concept works as the reification of the relationships between the *ModalEntity*, representing the entity having a modal resource associated with it, the associated resources themselves, and their modalities. These relationships are defined through the *hasModality* object property having *ModalDescriptor* as domain and *ModalEntity* as range. Additionally, as shown in Figure 2, the *ModalDescriptor* has two datatype properties: *resourceURL* and *hasPathInArtifact*. The *resourceURL* datatype property aims to provide a pointer to a multi-modal resource available on the Web, e.g., the URL of an image. Differently, the *hasPathInArtifact* datatype property is used when the multi-modal resource is contained within host packages, e.g., a Zip archive. In such cases, the *resourceURL* contains the URL of the Zip archive, while the *hasPathInArtifact* contains the specific path within the multi-modal resource within the Zip archive.

MMKG Running Example To show how an MMKG can be populated and, in particular, how the design pattern proposed above has been implemented, we describe in Figure 3 an example of a recipe for which we provided both the associated multi-modal resources and the description of the preparation process. The recipe shown in Figure 3 refers to the instance named *Recipe1m-60* (namely, Crock Pot Caramelized Onion). This recipe is associated with two instances of type *ModalDescriptor*, i.e., *Recipe1m-60-image_jpeg_480x320-1* and *Recipe1m-60-image_jpeg_550x826-1*[11], each one pointing to different *Image* modalities. It is important to notice that the nomenclature of a *ModalDescriptor* instance includes the recipe name, the modality metadata (e.g., image, video), and a progressive number. This number aims to disambiguate multiple instances asso-

[11]Due to space limitations, we reported only two of the modal descriptors associated with this recipe. To access the complete list of *ModalDescriptor* associated with this recipe, the reader may refer to the content of MMKG.

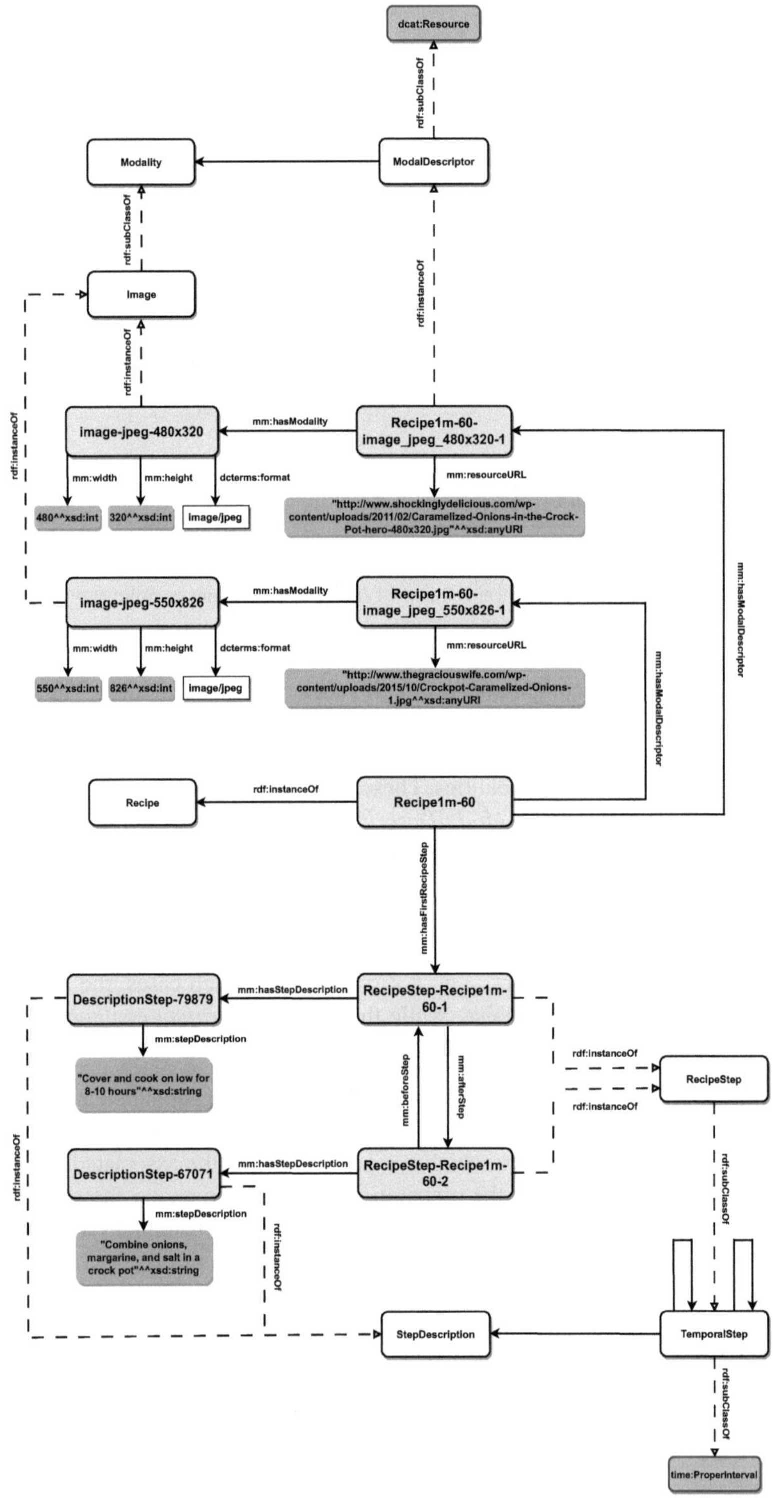

Figure 3. Excerpt of an MMKG for the instance Recipe1m-60.

ciated with the same modality within a recipe. Indeed, a recipe may have multiple images that share image modalities. For example, *Recipe1m-60* may have multiple images of the same format and size, leading to sequentially numbered modal descriptors (e.g., *Recipe1m-60-image_jpeg_480x320-2*) sharing the *image-jpeg_480x320* modality.

Then, the bottom part of Figure 3 shows the individuals of type *RecipeStep*: *RecipeStep-Recipe1m-60-1* and *RecipeStep-Recipe1m-60-2*. Each step has a different *StepDescription*, namely, *DescriptionStep-79879* and *DescriptionStep-67071*, respectively. The connection between *Recipe1m-60* and its first step *RecipeStep-Recipe1m-60-1* is modeled through the *hasFirstRecipeStep* object property. The temporal relations between *RecipeStep-Recipe1m-60-1* and *RecipeStep-Recipe1m-60-2* are modeled by the object properties *afterStep* and *beforeStep* (with step *RecipeStep-Recipe1m-60-1* preceding step *RecipeStep-Recipe1m-60-2*).

4. Tasks

The importance of food for promoting well-being and the abundance of food data, coupled with modern ML techniques, opens multiple avenues of innovation in food research, from representation learning to recipe generation and even the recommendation of foods or ingredients based on health guidelines and personal preferences. Numerous datasets were curated to study these food tasks, each dataset aiming to advance one or more tasks. Some of the key datasets used for food representation learning, classification, and recipe generation are listed in Table 1. We can see that the size and complexity of these datasets have increased over time, enabling more comprehensive studies across multiple food-related tasks.

4.1. Food Representation Learning

Learning effective recipe representations is fundamental to food studies. Reciptor [105] is a transformer-based model that learns recipe representations using ingredients and instructions. It uses the KG triplet sampling approach to optimize learned embeddings so that related recipes are closer to the embedding space. To do so, they used a FoodKG [31] based triplet loss during training that forces similar recipes closer and dissimilar recipes farther in the embedding space.

Tian et al. introduced RecipeRec [106], a heterogeneous graph learning model designed for recipe recommendations. RecipeRec leverages a heterogeneous graph neural network with hierarchical attention and an ingredient set transformer to effectively capture recipe content. Additionally, they introduced a graph contrastive augmentation strategy to extract graph knowledge in a self-supervised manner. They also designed a joint objective function that integrates recommendation and contrastive learning to optimize the model.

Additionally, Tian et al. introduced Recipe2Vec [107], a multi-modal recipe representation learning model with graph neural networks. They also introduced an adversarial attack strategy to enhance stability and performance during learning and designed a joint objective function that combines node classification and adversarial learning to optimize the model. They presented experimental results on the tasks of cuisine category classification and region prediction.

Table 1. Food Datasets for ML Tasks: The number of the images to classes and attributes per recipe evolved over the years.

Dataset	Year	Class/Tags	Images	Recipes	Type
UEC Food100 [110]	2012	100	9132	-	Japanese
UEC Food256 [75]	2014	256	25,088	-	Japanese
ETH Food-101 [111]	2014	101	101,000	-	Western
Food500 [112]	2016	508	148,408	-	Misc
ChineseFoodNet [113]	2017	208	192,000	-	Chinese
ISIA Food-200 [114]	2019	200	197,323	-	Misc
FoodAI-756 [115]	2019	756	400,000	-	Misc
ISA Food-500 [116]	2020	500	399,726	-	Misc
Food2k [117]	2021	2,000	1,036,564	-	Misc
Recipe1M [118]	2017	497	0.8 Million	1 Million	Misc
Recipe1M+ [119]	2019	497	13 Million	1 Million	Misc
RecipeNLG [120]	2020	-	-	2.2 Million	Misc
Nutrition5k [121]	2021	5,006	5,006	5,006	Video/Depth

Food representation learning was also used to populate an ontology. Youn et al. [108] introduced a semi-supervised approach for automating the population of the FoodOn ontology by employing word embeddings (Word2vec). To train the food word embeddings, they used all class and instance labels to query the Wikipedia corpus. They used a mapping function using the embeddings to assign candidate instances to the appropriate target classes. All relationships between instances and classes were defined as "is a" in their approach. The predicted ontology, compared to the ground truth ontology, performs better using precision metrics.

Another goal of food representation learning was tackled in the FlavorGraph [29], which addressed the challenge of learning representations of food and food chemical compounds for the purpose of food pairing.

An ML pipeline was developed to predict nutrient content based on vector representations of recipe names [109]. This study compared the effectiveness of using embeddings from ingredient lists instead of recipe descriptions. Since nutrient content is tied to ingredients, a domain-specific heuristic was introduced to merge these embeddings by incorporating ingredient quantities. Results showed improved accuracy, particularly in protein prediction, achieving up to 97.98% accuracy. The domain-specific approach outperformed conventional methods, enhancing accuracy by up to 60% in some cases.

4.2. Food Category Classification and Nutrition Estimation

The Food Category Classification Task was initiated for the purpose of dietary assessment; Kitamura et al. developed the first application to analyze nutritional balance from food images [122]. Instead of estimating nutrition, they classified dishes into five categories (grains, vegetables, meals/legumes, milk, and fruits) and visualized how many items were included in each category [123]. Chen et al. collected data on 101 different meals from 11 popular fast food chains and built a classification model with a bag of scale-invariant feature transform (SIFT) features and scalable vector machines (SVMs) [124]. Matsuda and Yanai published UEC Food100, a dataset consisting of 100 different images of Japanese meals [110]. Kawano and Yanai published UEC Food256, which increased the number of categories to 256 [75]. Deep learning has been extensively investigated and has advanced the field of food image recognition [125], and the purpose of food image recognition has also become more refined where the task has evolved from simply classifying categories to estimating their volume, ingredients, and nutritional value.

There are three primary methods for estimating nutritional values from food images: food category classification, ingredient estimation, and direct estimation of nutritional values.

- *Food Category Classification*: This method involves predefining nutritional data for each food category (typically identified by the name of the dish). When a food image is input, the system identifies the category and outputs the associated nutritional data. For example, if an image is recognized as "Carbonara Spaghetti," it will display nutritional values such as 433kcal of energy, 18g of protein, 23g of fat, and 54g of carbohydrates. These values are derived from typical recipes for that category. This method is widely used in many food logging applications, including commercial ones, and the accuracy of categorizing food images has reached a practical level. However, a significant limitation is that dishes identified under the same category are always assigned the same nutritional values, regardless of actual portion sizes and ingredient variations. Many applications address this issue by introducing more detailed food categories or allowing users to adjust portion sizes (e.g., "0.5 servings"). Some combine depth images acquired by depth sensors or stereo images and semantic segmentation to estimate the volume of each food item.
  Im2Calories, developed by Myers et al. [126], estimated the calories in a meal by analyzing meal images with a CNN-based image recognition model to identify meal items and then estimating the size of each item through semantic segmentation. Mezgec and Koroušić Seljak [73] introduced NutriNet, a food and beverage recognition system based on the AlexNet architecture. Ma et al. [127] fine-tuned four deep architectures pre-trained on the ImageNet dataset. These authors relied on the classification results to estimate nutritional values since food categories are predefined and have fixed nutritional configurations (e.g., calories, carbohydrates, proteins).
- *Direct Nutritional Value Estimation*: This method involves constructing a regression model to directly estimate major nutrients from a food image. While this approach can provide direct nutritional estimations, it lacks transparency regarding the basis for the calculated nutritional values, leading to potential reliability issues. Thames et al. [121] first trained a portion-independent regression model to predict calories and macronutrients per gram in food from a single RGB image. This network achieves a mean absolute error (MAE) of 9.5% when predicting calories per gram and an average MAE of 14.7% when predicting macronutrients per gram. They also apply the same architecture to directly regress these absolute values and total mass. Reinforcing the accuracy of portion estimation with a depth image of the food, they achieved a calorie MAE of 16.5% and a macronutrient MAE of 26.2%.
- *Ingredient Estimation*: In this method, a food image is used to estimate ingredients as a list of food items with associated nutritional values and their respective weights. This approach closely resembles the method used by nutritionists to evaluate food, thus providing high explanatory power. However, it has not yet achieved

practical accuracy due to difficulties in recognizing ingredients like sugar and oil that significantly impact nutritional value but do not have distinct visual characteristics. Additionally, accurately estimating the weight of each ingredient presents a significant challenge.

Chen et al. [128] built a model that estimates the visible ingredients used in a recipe from its food image. They trained the model to not only estimate ingredients but also to classify food categories at the same time, thereby improving the accuracy of ingredient estimation by leveraging the co-occurrence relationship between categories and ingredients. For example, if a dish is identified as "Carbonara Spaghetti", it is naturally expected to contain pasta as an ingredient. Furthermore, Wang et al. constructed a model that estimates the list of ingredients from a food image not by ingredient name but by food item number, which is a unique identifier assigned in the Japan Standard Food Composition Table [129], used to link each ingredient to its corresponding nutritional information [130].

Since most meal images contain multiple food items, nutritional estimation is a multi-stage process that first detects each of these areas and then performs nutritional estimation of each area. In the first stage, in cultures where each food item is served on a different plate, such as Japanese cuisine, food region detection is performed using a bounding box [123,110,75], while semantic segmentation is used when multiple meals are served on a single plate [126]. Food semantic segmentation using U-Net [131] was utilized in DepthCalorieCam [132], and the model by Ege et al. [76]. In the work of Lu et al. [133], they developed goFOOD, which included Mask-RCNN [134] for automatic food segmentation. The volume of food has the greatest impact on its nutritional content, but this is difficult to estimate from images. Dehais et al. estimated the volume of a meal by reconstructing a 3D model from two images [135]. Special instrumentation is an option in cases where more precise nutritional calculations are required, such as in medical practice diet management applications. Joshua et al. [136] developed "Smart Plate Health to Eat" for patients with type 2 diabetes mellitus. They used a plate stand with a built-in weight sensor to achieve more precise nutritional values.

There are a variety of datasets and complex multi-task networks that help achieve superior performance. Ege and Yanai [137] built a CNN-based model that simultaneously performs food dish detection and food calorie estimation by multi-task learning using two different datasets: UEC Food-100 [74] that includes multiple-dish food photos attached with bounding boxes, and a calorie-annotated food photo dataset [138] that contains single-dish food photos with food calories. Lu et al. [139] introduced a multi-task learning-based vision-based dietary assessment (VBDA) network that incorporates food recognition, segmentation, and volume estimation simultaneously. The network utilized a feature extraction module consisting of ResNet-50 [140] and a feature pyramid network (FPN) [141], with a region proposal net (RPN) [142] for bounding box generation.

A series of VBDA experiments were conducted by Thames et al. [121] using their proposed Nutrition5k dataset. The authors utilized an Inception V2 [143] backbone to extract feature maps, followed by average-pooling and two fully connected (FC) layers. Each regression task (calorie, mass, and macronutrients) had its separate multi-task head, consisting of two FC layers with different sizes. The experiments encompassed several scenarios, including estimating nutrients per gram from RGB images and estimating total nutrients from RGB images with depth information (RGB-D). The findings revealed that depth information was crucial for accurately estimating nutrients for images with different portion sizes.

With the Nutrition5k RGB-D images dataset, Shao et al. [144] used a ResNet backbone and included multi-scale fusion and multimodal feature fusion (MMFF) modules. For the multi-scale fusion stage, embeddings are passed into FPN to extract data from different stages of the model backbone. MMFF modules consist of the balanced feature pyramid (BFP) and the convolutional block attention module (CBAM), aiming to refine the output feature map with more details and semantics [144]. With a different approach, Shao et al. [145] introduced Swin-Nutrition, a Swin Transformer [146] backbone to improve the performance of nutrition estimation.

4.3. Recommendation

As the internet has made food recipes increasingly accessible and globalization has facilitated the exchange of culinary traditions, culinary practices have evolved beyond geographical boundaries, adapting to local customs, tastes, and ingredient availability. This shift has piqued researchers' interest in exploring food recommendation systems that offer personalized experiences. These systems typically draw on a variety of factors to suggest relevant recipes. These factors include the recipe content itself, such as its ingredients [147,148], the user's past interactions and behavior [148,149], and their expressed dietary preferences [150]. By considering these elements comprehensively, food recommendation systems aim to tailor suggestions to individual tastes and needs, enhancing the overall user experience.

Researchers have approached the scientific exploration of food recommendation by framing it as a retrieval problem [151,152], where the goal is to identify recipes that align with specific user requirements. Others have formulated it as a constraint question answering task [150], seeking solutions that satisfy both user preferences and dietary restrictions. Recognizing the importance of personalized and healthy recipe creation, a significant body of research has focused on ingredient substitution [153,154,155,156] as a sub-task within food recommendation. This line of research delves into suggesting suitable alternatives based on individual preferences and dietary constraints, enhancing the adaptability of culinary recommendations.

Retrieval-based methods learn embeddings for both recipe text attributes (title, ingredients, cooking steps) and visual attributes of food images. These embeddings essentially represent the information contained in each modality in a lower-dimensional space, allowing for efficient comparison and retrieval tasks. For instance, [157] curated a substantial corpus comprising over a million recipes and 800,000 food images, known as Recipe1M, and then explored cross-modal embeddings of recipes (ingredients and cooking steps) and food images. They learned cross-modal embeddings using triplet loss. In comparison, [158] considered cross-modal translation consistency along with triplet loss via an Adversarial Cross-Modal Embedding framework. Both of these works assessed the effectiveness of the learned embeddings and their approaches through image-to-recipe and recipe-to-image retrieval tasks. To expand the Recipe1M dataset, a subsequent effort [119] gathered additional images, resulting in the Recipe1M+ dataset containing approximately 13 million food images, with several recipes having multiple associated images. These datasets proved instrumental in advancing research on multi-modal food recipe comprehension, food recommendation systems, and ingredient substitution tasks.

Inspired by the sequential nature of recipe cooking instructions, [159] conceptualized cooking steps as a sequence of actions represented in the form of a graph. Subsequently, they established joint embeddings between food images and recipes, which exhibited improved performance in cross-modal retrieval tasks. Notably, the enhanced recognition capabilities of visual embeddings and recipe embeddings also facilitated the generation of food images using generative adversarial networks (GANs).

Moving beyond retrieval tasks, [147] leveraged a predefined list of ingredients to estimate quantities and identify suitable substitutes, thereby generating healthier pseudo-recipes. Their system additionally recommends recipes similar to the generated pseudo-recipe, offering a wider range of options tailored to the user's needs. Similarly, [149] factored in user-specific data such as body mass index (BMI), food calorie intake, and past dietary habits to recommend personalized nutritious recipes. The pFoodREQ work [150] presented a unique approach by formulating food recommendations as a constraint question-answering framework within a large-scale food knowledge base (KBQA). By structuring queries around user preferences, dietary constraints, and health guidelines, the framework orchestrated a unified approach to tailor recommendations. Subsequently, they mapped both questions and recipes into the same embedding space, allowing it to retrieve recipes most closely aligned with the user's specific requirements during the inference stage.

Building upon the successful application of KGs in food recommendation systems, recent research [160,151] has delved into KG representation learning methods for healthy food recommendation. Li et al. [160] proposed a method for fine-tuning a pre-trained BERT model to learn KG embeddings. This approach involved predicting masked ingredients and triplet plausibility within the KG. Additionally, the authors explored adversarial attacks on KG embeddings for ingredient substitution, considering the context of both ingredients and recipes. In contrast, [151] focused on employing graph neural networks (GNNs) over two separate graphs: one representing food preferences and another representing healthiness. By processing these interconnected graphs, the GNN learns recipe embeddings that simultaneously capture both user preferences and health considerations.

With the increased use of AI methods to provide recommendations in the health and dietary recommendation space, there is also an increased need for the explainability of those recommendations. Such explanations benefit users of recommendation systems by empowering them with justifications for following the system's suggestions. To address this need, the food explanation ontology (FEO) [161] provides a formalism for modeling explanations to users for food-related recommendations. The motivation behind using FEO is to empower users to make informed decisions about their health by providing reasoning behind AI-generated recommendations, ensuring transparency and trust in personalized dietary suggestions. FEO models food recommendations using concepts from the explanation domain to create responses to user questions about the food recommendations they receive from AI systems, such as personalized knowledge-based question-answering systems. FEO employs a modular, extensible structure that lends itself to a variety of explanations while preserving important semantic details to accurately represent explanations of food recommendations. The FEO was evaluated using a set of competency questions derived from explanation types present in literature that are relevant to food recommendations.

5. Applications

5.1. Food Logging

Traditionally, dietary assessment is performed by nutritionists and usually requires users to remember their diets over a period of time, e.g., 24-h-dietary recall (24-HDR) [162], food frequency questionnaire (FFQ) [163,164], dietary record (DR) [165], and brief dietary assessment instruments or screeners [166]. Although these manual recordings have contributed to the development of nutrition research, they are time-consuming, inaccurate, labor-intensive, and highly demanding for a certain level of communication skills [167]. Many methods to decrease labor-intensiveness and cognitive load have been explored.

The easiest way to record a meal is to take a photo just before eating it. It is now possible to automatically analyze these photos to estimate when and how much of what food the user ate. Many food management applications utilize image recognition technology. Kitamura et al. developed the first application to analyze nutritional balance from meal images [122]. Instead of estimating nutrition, they classified dishes into five categories (grains, vegetables, meals and beans, milk, and fruits) and visualized how many dishes they contained [123]. Since then, with the advent of deep learning, it has become possible to predict nutritional values more accurately, and many applications are now API services. MyFitnessPal [168], which is currently the most widely used food management application, incorporates a function called "Meal Scan" that allows users to recognize a meal image, identify the category of that meal, and record the nutritional information associated with it. Applications with similar nutrition estimation capabilities based on meal image classification include Carorie Mama [169], FoodVisor [170], LogMeal [171], FoodAI [172], goFOOD [173] and FoodLog Athl [174]. In addition, many companies, such as LogMeal, FoodAI, Foodvisor, and Calorie Mama, provide web APIs that take a food image and return its name and nutritional intake. As discussed in Section 4.2, the performance of the AI built into these applications depends on how similar the meals to be understood are to the dataset used to train their models. They are particularly sensitive to food culture, with Carorie Mama and goFOOD, developed in Europe, and FoodAI and FoodLog Athl, developed in Asia, tending to interpret the same meal based on their respective cultural knowledge. In more precise food logging, the fact that different people may use different recipes for the same category of meals and, therefore, have different compositions also makes the understanding of food by AI more difficult. Yamakata et al. [175] proposed a recipe-based food logging technique that captures food consumption with recipe information. They are able to track nutrition consumption by linking ingredients to a nutrition facts table, allowing a traceable nutrition estimation.

5.2. Dietary Management

Recent advances in technology and data analytics enable innovative approaches to promote healthier and more sustainable food choices among consumers [176]. Data-evidence-driven behavior change, leveraging personalized feedback, gamification, and interactive education, has demonstrated promising results in shifting food consumption patterns towards healthier and environmentally friendly options [177,178]. Mobile applications have been at the forefront of this revolution. They analyze personal dietary habits and offer recommendations, empowering consumers to make informed decisions [179]. MyFitnessPal[12] tracks food intake and exercise, driving insights and suggestions for a balanced diet. Fooducate[13] grades foods based on nutritional value, suggesting healthier options. Meanwhile, GreenChoice[14] focuses on the environmental impact, educating users on how their food choices affect the planet, while OpenFoodFacts[15] and Yuka[16] provide detailed information about food products, including their ingredients and nutritional value. Similarly, Myrealfood[17] and Ekilu[18] help users adopt healthier habits, including nutritional information and recipes. Others, such as FoodPrint[19], aid chefs in sustainability by calculating the environmental impact of their recipes. Research reveals that those apps can significantly improve dietary behavior [180] and contribute to a more significant societal shift towards more responsible and health-conscious food consumption patterns [181]. Nevertheless, literature also shows that, beyond providing seamless access to comprehensive food databases, they should enhance user satisfaction and engagement and ensure the reliability of nutritional analysis and suggestions. Future research should refine these technologies by integrating social, regional, and cultural factors into personalized recommendations [182,183] while ensuring the quality of dietary suggestions through validation processes, expert knowledge, and authoritative sources [184].

5.3. Substitution

The objective behind ingredient substitution relies on individual preferences, dietary restrictions, and potential alterations in dish flavor. For example, the substitution might entail replacing meat-based components with vegan alternatives or swapping high-carb ingredients for low-carb options. A suitable substitute should possess similar flavors, textures, and classification (e.g., various types of onions) or serve a comparable purpose (e.g., as a protein source). A successful substitution should achieve the intended goal while preserving the essence of the recipe.

Early investigations relied on hand-crafted features grounded in semantic similarity to identify feasible substitutions [153,154]. However, due to the scarcity of substitution data, these approaches lacked formal evaluations. Subsequent methods employed techniques such as food ontology [32,185] or parsing user comments to get ingredient substitutions [160,155]. Li et al. [160] leveraged KGs and adversarial attacks on language models to learn embeddings for ingredient substitutions within a given context. A recent approach [186] curated the Recipe1MSub dataset for ingredient substitution by extracting and analyzing user comments from a subset of the Recipe1M dataset. They then developed a graph-based ingredient substitution module to recommend ingredient substitutes.

Most of these do not directly consider the impact on food or the reasoning behind suggesting the substitutes. Addressing this gap, [185] proposes an ontology-based model that employs both similarities and reasoning about ingredient substitution in food recipes.

[12]`https://www.myfitnesspal.com`
[13]`https://www.fooducate.com/`
[14]`https://about.greenchoicenow.com/`
[15]`https://world.openfoodfacts.org/`
[16]`https://yuka.io/en/`
[17]`https://www.myrealfood.app/es`
[18]`https://ekilu.com/`
[19]`https://foodprint.org/`

The proposed system consists of an ML-based component for suggesting candidate ingredient substitutes and a logical program based on answer set programming (ASP) to identify unacceptable ingredients in a recipe and remove inappropriate substitute suggestions.

Substituting ingredients not only requires considering user constraints and the impact on the outcome of food, but it also is important to consider if substitution requires any modification in the cooking steps. Thus, considering the entities as nodes and actions as edges from parsed cooking instructions, [187] converts food recipes to a flow graph for identifying viable substitutes. They then propose a novel graph embedding method to learn embeddings for entities (nodes) and actions (edges) of the flow graph, which outperforms the base graph models.

5.4. Recipe Creation and Generative AI

The process of food recipe generation encompasses the creation of various elements of a recipe, such as its title, list of ingredients, and cooking steps. This can be achieved either directly from a food image or by leveraging additional information like the title or ingredients provided alongside the image. Initial work on recipe generation explored the applications of LSTM and recurrent neural networks for cooking step generation [188]. Later, the success of generative models for language tasks motivated researchers to apply them for generating ingredients for cooking steps from recipe titles [189,190, 191,192]. More recently, the emergence of multi-modal models (MMMs) has garnered attention owing to their capability to handle diverse data types. Consequently, a series of studies have endeavored to generate recipes from food images, either independently or in conjunction with recipe titles or ingredients [193,194].

Various endeavors have been made in the domain of recipe generation, showcasing diverse methodologies. For instance, Chef Watson [188] adopted a Bayesian network approach over a knowledge representation schema. Another notable contribution by Wang et al. [195] introduced a novel structure-aware generation technique tailored specifically for deriving recipes from food images. Expanding upon the Recipe1M+ recipe dataset [119], RecipeNLG [120] proposed a clean and large-scale recipe dataset that contains over 2 million recipes. They showcase the effectiveness of their dataset for recipe generation by fine-tuning and evaluating the GPT-2 model [196] on their dataset.

Inverse cooking [197] is an innovative image-to-recipe generation framework employing ResNet [140] to extract image features and Set Transformer [198] to translate these features into recipes. Enhancing this concept, [186] integrated a Graph-based Ingredient Substitution Module (GISMo) into inverse cooking, thereby devising a framework for ingredient substitution that enhances recipe personalization, albeit limited to substituting one ingredient at a time. Another notable approach, RecipeGM [191], utilizes a hierarchical convolutional neural network, while Chef Transformer [192] employs the T5 generative model [199] to generate recipes from predetermined ingredient lists. Recognizing recipes as sequences of actions, Carvalho et al. [158] proposed modeling recipe learning as a sequence of actions from food images or existing recipes, thus improving cross-modal representations.

RecipeGPT [189] leveraged the GPT-2 [196] architecture for recipe generation by defining two tasks: cooking instruction generation from recipe title and list of ingredients and ingredients estimation from recipe title and cooking instructions. With the aim to eliminate the irregularities in generated recipes, RecipeMC [190] employed Monte Carlo Tree Search (MCTS) on top of GPT-2. They studied the generation of ingredients from the recipe titles and the generation of cooking steps from the recipe titles and ingredients. When generated ingredients combined with the recipe title are used to generate cooking steps, the error in ingredient identification propagates, and as a result, the performance on cooking step generation becomes sub-optimal compared to when ground truth ingredients are input along with the recipe title. RecipeGPT and RecipeMC both introduced special tokens for the start and end of recipe titles and ingredients, which helped the models understand different parts of the recipe; it limits their use for natural language question-answer applications.

FIRE [193] used the BLIP model [200] for food title generation and a vision transformer (ViT) [201] based multi-class classifier to extract ingredients from food images. Subsequently, they merged both outputs as a unified input for the T5 model [199] to generate recipes. Although this methodology achieves recipe generation from images alone, the reliance on three separate models introduces complexity and error propagation from the earlier two models to the final stage. Therefore, a shift towards employing a single MMM could offer a more streamlined solution. A notable advancement, FoodLMM [194], adapted LISA [202], a MMM for various food-related tasks such as classification, ingredient detection, segmentation, and recipe generation. However, the multitasking nature of FoodLMM slightly compromises its performance, specifically in recipe generation. While FoodLMM exhibits enhanced performance in multiple tasks compared to baseline models, it shows sub-optimal performance in recipe generation. LLaVA-Chef [203], evaluated several large language models (LLMs) and MMMs for food recipe generation where the authors showed pre-trained LLaVA [204] has more food domain knowledge compared to other models. Subsequently, LLaVA was fine-tuned on food data by formulating a multi-stage training scheme and penalizing it with a custom loss that gradually improved the quality of generated recipes. A sample recipe generated by various open source LLMs and LLaVA-Chef are shown in Figure 4. Compared to the pre-trained LLMs (GPT2, Mistral, LLaMA, LLaVA) and one open-source recipe generation model (Chef Transformer), LLaVA-Chef generates better recipes.

5.5. Health

There is a growing trend of developing virtual health and well-being assistants to support lifestyle and disease management, partly due to the growing societal need for managing health and preventing illness. A change of behavior is typically necessary to improve an individual's situation, which emphasizes how AI-based solutions can collaborate with the individual to support the individual's ambition to improve their health through behavior change, e.g., by adhering to medical guidelines or treatment protocols, increasing physical activity, changing nutrition habits, reducing stress, or reducing the intake of toxic substances. As a basis for deciding how to act, such solutions may explore the functional status information (FSI) of monitored individuals through the application of neuro-symbolic techniques, enabling the integration of medical knowledge with the data collected from citizens.

A necessary foundation for a medical and health-related system's reasoning, decision-making, and acting is (i) the medical knowledge that the AI system utilizes, (ii) the theories and knowledge about how humans form motivation and change behavior

	**Prompt:** Generate a comprehensive recipe for crafting **Thai-Style Radish and Watermelon Salad** with the listed ingredients: *1/4 cup plus 2 tablespoons fresh lime juice, 1 tablespoon Asian fish sauce, 1 tablespoon sambal oelek or other Asian chile sauce, 2 teaspoons finely grated fresh ginger, Kosher salt, Freshly ground pepper, One 5-pound watermelon rind and seeds removed, flesh cut into 1 1/2-inch chunks (8 cups), 12 radishes, very thinly sliced, n 8 scallions, thinly sliced, 2 fresh hot red chiles, such as Holland or cayenne, thinly sliced crosswise, 3/4 cup lightly packed mint leaves, coarsely chopped, 3/4 cup lightly packed Thai basil leaves, torn.*
Ground Truth	1. In a large bowl, whisk the lime juice, fish sauce, sambal oelek, and ginger. 2. Season with salt and pepper. 3. Add the watermelon, radishes, scallions, and red chiles and toss. 4. Fold in the mint and basil, season with salt and pepper, and serve right away
LLaVA-Chef	1. In a large bowl, whisk together the lime juice, fish sauce, sambal oelek, ginger, and salt and pepper to taste.2. Add the watermelon, radishes, scallions, and chiles.3. Toss to combine.4. Add the mint and basil.5. Toss again.6. Serve immediately.
LLaVA	1. In a large bowl, whisk together the lime juice, fish sauce, sambal oelek, and ginger. Season the mixture with salt and pepper to taste.2. Add the watermelon, radishes, scallions, chiles, and mint leaves to the bowl. Toss everything together until the ingredients are evenly coated with the dressing.3. Transfer the salad to a serving bowl and garnish with the torn Thai basil leaves.4. Serve the Thai-style radish and Watermelon Salad immediately or refrigerate it for a few hours before serving. This Thai-style radish and Watermelon Salad is a refreshing and flavorful dish that combines the sweetness of watermelon with the crunch of radishes and the spiciness of chiles. The combination of lime juice, fish sauce, and sambal oelek creates a tangy and savory dressing that complements the natural flavors of the ingredients. The mint and basil add a burst of freshness and aroma, while the chiles provide a spicy kick that balances the overall taste. This salad is perfect for a light and healthy meal or as a side dish to accompany other dishes during a gathering or party.
Chef Transformer	Combine the lime juice, sesamms, fish sauce, sate olek, ginger, salt, and pepper in the jar of a blender. Process until smooth. Pour into a large bowl. Add all of the remaining ingredients and toss well. Refrigerate the soup for at least 8 hours to let the flavors blend before serving.
GPT2	1/4 cup finely chopped fresh ginger, 1/4 cup finely chopped fresh ginger, 1/4 cup finely chopped fresh ginger
Mistral	Per Serving:31 calories; 0.2 g total fat; 0 mg cholesterol; 173 mg sodium. 7.5 g carbohydrates; 1.1 g protein; Full Nutrition
LLaMA	Cook the radishes and watermelon in a large saucepan of boiling salted water until tender, about 5 minutes. Drain and rinse under cold water. Drain again and pat dry. In a large bowl, whisk together the lime juice, fish sauce, sambal oelek, ginger, salt, and pepper. Add the watermelon and radishes and toss to coat it. Add the scallions, chiles, mint, and basil and toss to combine. Serve at once. This salad can be made one day ahead. Cover and chill. This salad can be made one day ahead. Cover and chill. This salad can be made one day ahead. Cover and chill. This salad can be made one day ahead. Cover and chill. This salad can be made one day ahead. Cover and chill. This salad can be made one day ahead. Cover and chill. This salad can be made one day ahead. Cover and chill. This salad can be made one day ahead. Cover and chill.

Figure 4. Comparison between recipes generated by various open-source pre-trained LLMs and the proposed LLaVA-Chef model.

as well as manage physical, social, and psychological barriers; and, (iii) the FSI (data) about the individual as well as the individuals' narrative about their behavior change journey, information that needs to be treated following ethical guidelines and regulations. Moreover, the realization of such systems relies on the integration of effective, efficient, and ethical strategies for adapting behavior in a situation depending on the individual's context, personal preferences, and needs (e.g., displaying motivational messages that are tailored to each individual's resources and current situation).

Understanding a person's functional status (FS) is a key step toward tailoring precise interventions and providing services to improve an individual's health status and maximize functional independence in daily activities. However, managing health often poses different challenges related to healthcare systems being unable to provide adequate support to individuals with chronic illnesses or disabilities due to the scarcity of resources. The National Committee on Vital and Health Statistics (NVHCS)[20] states that understanding the FS is necessary to achieve optimal health outcomes. The evaluation of the FS is characterized by a clinician-patient interaction to get insights into patients' lifestyles, together with standardized tests. Nevertheless, these assessments provide merely a snapshot of an individual's health status, while effective behavior change for health improvements is a long-term process. Consequently, a gap exists between an individual's health objectives and the "infrequent" health assessments conducted in healthcare settings, which may prevent the delivery of high-quality care. Therefore, frequent data collection is required to bridge this gap and ensure continual support.

Physicians and researchers have conducted a few studies on elderly people that led to the identification of the risk factors able to detect those most susceptible to functional decline [205,206,207]. Nonetheless, FSI is underutilized, limiting its potential impact [208]. One of the reasons may be that many physicians do not fully recognize the significance of this information [209,210,211,212]. Indeed, even when informed about a patient's health status, only a minority alter patient management accordingly.

Studies based on self-reports of functional performance and early decline show successful prediction of actual performance and decline [213,214]. However, researchers note these reports capture only a fraction of the problems [207]. Consequently, innovative methods to assess FS are needed, including nonintrusive approaches that evaluate the patient's functional performance in both normal and abnormal conditions without relying solely on physician-patient interaction. For example, in [215], sensor-based systems can detect a decline in daily activities, thus facilitating tailored interventions. Given the increasing elderly population, such systems are crucial for early detection and intervention to prevent functional deterioration and reduce the decline of functional ability.

The FoodKG [31], a comprehensive food KG designed to assist in food recommendation that brings together recipes, nutrition data, food taxonomies, and links to existing ontologies, is leveraged in a cognitive agent that performs knowledge-base question answering to improve people's diets [216]. The system demonstration involves three categories of questions: simple queries for nutritional information, comparisons of nutrients between different foods, and constraint-based queries to find recipes matching certain criteria. By leveraging FoodKG, the cognitive agent can provide accurate and relevant dietary guidance, helping users make better food choices and improving their overall health outcomes. FoodKG thus enables the investigation of this research field, aiming to facilitate the development of AI-powered systems capable of helping individuals monitor their FS and prevent function decline. The adoption of FoodKG in real-world scenarios is strongly connected to the design of behavior change solutions since, given the detection of declining FS, the knowledge modeled within FoodKG can be exploited to perform reasoning operations to discover possible behavior change trajectories aimed at improving a person's overall FS. Concerning this point, FoodKG fills a gap in the state-of-the-art since, to our knowledge, KGs covering the whole FS landscape have not been proposed yet.

An example of a recent collaborative effort to develop observable and replicable interventions for influencing behavior and health can be found in the behavioral change techniques taxonomy outlined by [217]. This taxonomy facilitates the consolidation of knowledge regarding behavior and behavior change, promoting the sharing and reuse

[20]https://ncvhs.hhs.gov/

of useful sources of behavior knowledge. Additionally, we note that, as far as we are aware, no publicly accessible conceptual classification exists that conceptualizes barriers to behavior change.

An important taxonomy to mention is the human behavior taxonomy developed by the World Health Organization (WHO) [218][21]. This taxonomy, rooted in the WHO's expertise and the International Classification of Functioning (ICF), Disability, and Health, provides detailed class definitions based heavily on the U.S. National Cancer Institute (NCI) Thesaurus, as well as the Oxford English Dictionary [219]. Another important effort aimed at understanding human behavior is the Semantic Mining of Activity, Social, and Health Data (SMASH) [220], which focuses on predicting human behavior and providing explanations for these predictions. Additionally, the Health Behavior Change Ontology (HBCO) was developed for a project to establish automated dialogues between a psychologist and a user to provide behavioral counseling [221].

6. Conclusion

The field of food computing represents a transformative approach to addressing the multifaceted challenges associated with food production, distribution, and consumption. By integrating symbolic reasoning with neural network-based methods, neurosymbolic approaches provide powerful tools for enhancing food data acquisition, analysis, and interpretation. This chapter has detailed the construction and application of food ontologies and KGs, underscoring their importance in supporting complex food computing tasks. Advanced techniques in information extraction from textual and image data have the potential to improve data interoperability and create intelligent food systems. We have explored the significance of food representation learning through embeddings and presented various methodologies for food category classification, nutrition estimation, and ingredient substitution. Practical applications such as personalized nutrition, dietary management, food logging, and recipe creation using generative AI highlight the substantial impact of food computing on consumer health and well-being. The application of AI-powered systems in health and nutrition showcases the potential for behavior change and lifestyle management, aiming to improve overall health outcomes. As technology continues to advance, the integration of neurosymbolic methods will undoubtedly play a crucial role in shaping the future of food computing. These innovations are expected to drive improvements in food quality, safety, sustainability, and accessibility.

References

[1] Min W, Jiang S, Liu L, Rui Y, Jain R. A Survey on Food Computing. ACM Computing Surveys. 2019 Sep;52(5):92:1-92:36. Available from: https://doi.org/10.1145/3329168.

[2] Min W, Liu C, Xu L, Jiang S. Applications of knowledge graphs for food science and industry. Patterns. 2022 May;3(5):100484. Available from: https://www.sciencedirect.com/science/article/pii/S2666389922000691.

[3] USDA National Nutrient Database;. Accessed: 2024-06-29. https://agdatacommons.nal.usda.gov/articles/dataset/USDA_National_Nutrient_Database_for_Standard_Reference_Legacy_Release/24661818.

[21] https://www.who.int/classifications/drafticfpracticalmanual.pdf

[4] FAO Databases;. Accessed: 2024-06-29. http://www.fao.org/faostat/en/#data.

[5] FoodData Central;. Accessed: 2024-06-29. https://fdc.nal.usda.gov/.

[6] Kayad A, Paraforos DS, Marinello F, Fountas S. Latest advances in sensor applications in agriculture. Agriculture. 2020;10(8):362.

[7] Bouzembrak Y, Klüche M, Gavai A, Marvin HJ. Internet of Things in food safety: Literature review and a bibliometric analysis. Trends in Food Science & Technology. 2019;94:54-64.

[8] Green K, Harvey M, McMeekin A. Transformations in food consumption and production systems. Journal of Environmental Policy & Planning. 2003;5(2):145-63.

[9] Noronha J, Hysen E, Zhang H, Gajos KZ. Platemate: crowdsourcing nutritional analysis from food photographs. In: Proceedings of the 24th annual ACM symposium on User interface software and technology; 2011. p. 1-12.

[10] Franco RZ, Fallaize R, Lovegrove JA, Hwang F. Popular nutrition-related mobile apps: a feature assessment. JMIR mHealth and uHealth. 2016;4(3):e5846.

[11] Lewis T. Digital food: from paddock to platform. Communication Research and Practice. 2018;4(3):212-28.

[12] Dooley DM, Griffiths EJ, Gosal GS, Buttigieg PL, Hoehndorf R, Lange MC, et al. FoodOn: a harmonized food ontology to increase global food traceability, quality control and data integration. npj Science of Food. 2018 Dec;2(1):23. Available from: https://www.nature.com/articles/s41538-018-0032-6.

[13] Dooley DM, Andrés-Hernández L, Bordea G, Carmody L, Cavalieri D, Chan LE, et al. OBO Foundry Food Ontology Interconnectivity. In: Sanfilippo EM, Kutz O, Troquard N, Hahmann T, Masolo C, Hoehndorf R, et al., editors. Proceedings of the Joint Ontology Workshops 2021 Episode VII: The Bolzano Summer of Knowledge co-located with the 12th International Conference on Formal Ontology in Information Systems (FOIS 2021), and the 12th International Conference on Biomedical Ontologies (ICBO 2021), Bolzano, Italy, September 11-18, 2021. vol. 2969 of CEUR Workshop Proceedings. CEUR-WS.org; 2021. Available from: http://ceur-ws.org/Vol-2969/paper13-IFOW.pdf.

[14] Buttigieg P, Morrison N, Smith B, Mungall CJ, Lewis SE, the ENVO Consortium. The environment ontology: contextualising biological and biomedical entities. Journal of Biomedical Semantics. 2013;4(1):43. Available from: http://jbiomedsem.biomedcentral.com/articles/10.1186/2041-1480-4-43.

[15] Federhen S. The NCBI Taxonomy database. Nucleic Acids Research. 2012 Jan;40(D1):D136-43. Available from: https://academic.oup.com/nar/article-lookup/doi/10.1093/nar/gkr1178.

[16] De Matos P, Alcántara R, Dekker A, Ennis M, Hastings J, Haug K, et al. Chemical Entities of Biological Interest: an update. Nucleic Acids Research. 2010 Jan;38(suppl_1):D249-54. Available from: https://academic.oup.com/nar/article-lookup/doi/10.1093/nar/gkp886.

[17] Walls RL, Cooper L, Elser J, Gandolfo MA, Mungall CJ, Smith B, et al. The Plant Ontology Facilitates Comparisons of Plant Development Stages Across Species. Frontiers in Plant Science. 2019 Jun;10:631. Available from: https://www.frontiersin.org/article/10.3389/fpls.2019.00631/full.

[18] Mungall CJ, Torniai C, Gkoutos GV, Lewis SE, Haendel MA. Uberon, an integrative multi-species anatomy ontology. Genome Biology. 2012;13(1):R5. Available from: http://genomebiology.biomedcentral.com/articles/10.1186/gb-2012-13-1-r5.

[19] Gkoutos GV, Schofield PN, Hoehndorf R. The anatomy of phenotype ontologies: principles, properties and applications. Briefings in Bioinformatics. 2017 Apr;19(5):1008-21. Available from: https://www.ncbi.nlm.nih.gov/pmc/articles/PMC6169674/.

[20] Azman Halimi R, Barkla BJ, Andrés-Hernandéz L, Mayes S, King GJ. Bridging the food security gap: an information-led approach to connect dietary nutrition, food composition and crop production. Journal of the Science of Food and Agriculture. 2020 Mar;100(4):1495-504. Available from: https://onlinelibrary.wiley.com/doi/10.1002/jsfa.10157.

[21] SNOMED CT;. Accessed: 2024-07-15. https://www.nlm.nih.gov/healthit/snomedct/index.html.

[22] The SAMUELS Project. The Hansard Corpus - (British Parliament); 2016. Accessed: 2024-07-29. Available from: https://www.english-corpora.org/hansard/.

[23] EFSA. Food classification standardisation – The FoodEx2 system;. Accessed: 2024-07-15. https://www.efsa.europa.eu/en/data/data-standardisation.

[24] Cantais J, Dominguez D, Gigante V, Laera L, Tamma V. An example of food ontology for diabetes control. In: Proceedings of the International Semantic Web Conference 2005 workshop on Ontology Patterns for the Semantic Web; 2005. p. 1-9.

[25] Dragoni M, Bailoni T, Maimone R, Eccher C. Helis: An ontology for supporting healthy lifestyles. In: The Semantic Web–ISWC 2018: 17th International Semantic Web Conference, Monterey, CA, USA, October 8–12, 2018, Proceedings, Part II 17. Springer; 2018. p. 53-69.

[26] Kolchin M, Zamula D. Food product ontology: initial implementation of a vocabulary for describing food products. In: Proceeding of the 14th conference of open innovations association FRUCT, Helsinki, Finland; 2013. p. 11-5.

[27] Popovski G, Korousic-Seljak B, Eftimov T. FoodOntoMap: Linking Food Concepts across Different Food Ontologies. In: International Conference on Knowledge Engineering and Ontology Development; 2019. Available from: https://api.semanticscholar.org/CorpusID:204754826.

[28] Garg N, Sethupathy A, Tuwani R, NK R, Dokania S, Iyer A, et al. FlavorDB: a database of flavor molecules. Nucleic Acids Research. 2018 Jan;46(D1):D1210-6. Available from: https://doi.org/10.1093/nar/gkx957.

[29] Park D, Kim K, Kim S, Spranger M, Kang J. FlavorGraph: a large-scale food-chemical graph for generating food representations and recommending food pairings. Scientific Reports. 2021 Jan;11(1):931. Available from: https://www.nature.com/articles/s41598-020-79422-8.

[30] Veselkov K, Gonzalez G, Aljifri S, Galea D, Mirnezami R, Youssef J, et al. HyperFoods: Machine intelligent mapping of cancer-beating molecules in foods. Scientific Reports. 2019 Jul;9(1):9237.

[31] Haussmann S, Seneviratne O, Chen Y, Ne'eman Y, Codella J, Chen CH, et al. FoodKG: a semantics-driven knowledge graph for food recommendation. In: The Semantic Web–ISWC 2019: 18th International Semantic Web Conference, Auckland, New Zealand, October 26–30, 2019, Proceedings, Part II 18. Springer; 2019. p. 146-62.

[32] Razzaq MS, Maqbool F, Ilyas M, Jabeen H. EvoRecipes: A Generative Approach for Evolving Context-Aware Recipes. IEEE Access. 2023.

[33] Kümpel M, Beetz M. ProductKG: A Product Knowledge Graph for User Assistance in Daily Activities. In: JOWO; 2023. .

[34] GESIS - Leibniz-Institute for the Social Sciences. Recipes Ontology; 2024. Accessed: 2024-08-17. https://hajirajabeen.github.io/EvoRecipesOntology.

[35] Mori S, Maeta H, Yamakata Y, Sasada T. Flow Graph Corpus from Recipe Texts. In: Calzolari N, Choukri K, Declerck T, Loftsson H, Maegaard B, Mariani J, et al., editors. Proceedings of the Ninth International Conference on Language Resources and Evaluation (LREC'14). Reykjavik, Iceland: European Language Resources Association (ELRA); 2014. p. 2370-7. Available from: http://www.lrec-conf.org/proceedings/lrec2014/pdf/763_Paper.pdf.

[36] Yamakata Y, Mori S, Carroll J. English Recipe Flow Graph Corpus. In: Calzolari N, Béchet F, Blache P, Choukri K, Cieri C, Declerck T, et al., editors. Proceedings of the Twelfth Language Resources and Evaluation Conference. Marseille, France: European Language Resources Association; 2020. p. 5187-94. Available from: https://aclanthology.org/2020.lrec-1.638.

[37] Honnibal M, Montani I. spaCy 2: Natural language understanding with Bloom embeddings, convolutional neural networks and incremental parsing. To appear. 2017;7(1):411-20.

[38] Finkel JR, Grenager T, Manning CD. Incorporating non-local information into information extraction systems by gibbs sampling. In: Proceedings of the 43rd annual meeting of the association for computational linguistics (ACL'05); 2005. p. 363-70.

[39] Rashid SM, McCusker JP, Pinheiro P, Bax MP, Santos HO, Stingone JA, et al. The semantic data dictionary–an approach for describing and annotating data. Data intelligence. 2020;2(4):443-86.

[40] Hearst MA. Automatic acquisition of hyponyms from large text corpora. In: COLING 1992 volume 2: The 14th international conference on computational linguistics; 1992. .

[41] Gharibi M, Zachariah A, Rao P. Foodkg: A tool to enrich knowledge graphs using machine learning techniques. Frontiers in big Data. 2020;3:12.

[42] Tonda A, Boukhelifa N, Chabin T, Barnabé M, Génot B, Lutton E, et al. Interactive machine learning for applications in food Science. Human and Machine Learning: Visible, Explainable, Trustworthy and Transparent. 2018:459-77.

[43] Halac D, Sokic E, Turajlic E. Almonds classification using supervised learning methods. In: 2017 XXVI International Conference on Information, Communication and Automation Technologies (ICAT). IEEE; 2017. p. 1-6.

[44] Qiao L, Li H, Wang W, Wang D. A Knowledge Graph Construction Method for Food Nutrition. In: 2022 IEEE/WIC/ACM International Joint Conference on Web Intelligence and Intelligent Agent Technology (WI-IAT). IEEE; 2022. p. 577-81.

[45] Pan LM, Chen J, Wu J, Liu S, Ngo CW, Kan MY, et al. Multi-modal cooking workflow construction for food recipes. In: Proceedings of the 28th ACM International Conference on Multimedia; 2020. p. 1132-41.

[46] Zhang Z, Strubell E, Hovy E. A survey of active learning for natural language processing. arXiv preprint arXiv:221010109. 2022.

[47] Stojanov R, Popovski G, Cenikj G, Seljak BK, Eftimov T. A Fine-Tuned Bidirectional Encoder Representations From Transformers Model for Food Named-Entity Recognition: Algorithm Development and Validation. Journal of medical Internet research. 2021 8;23,8 e28229.

[48] Cenikj G, Popovski G, Stojanov R, Seljak BK, Eftimov T. BuTTER: BidirecTional LSTM for Food Named-Entity Recognition. In: 2020 IEEE International Conference on Big Data (Big Data); 2020. p. 3550-6.

[49] Wilkinson MD, Dumontier M, Aalbersberg IJ, Appleton G, Axton M, Baak A, et al. The FAIR Guiding Principles for scientific data management and stewardship. Scientific data. 2016;3(1):1-9.

[50] Eftimov T, Koroušić Seljak B, Korošec P. A rule-based named-entity recognition method for knowledge extraction of evidence-based dietary recommendations. PloS one. 2017;12,6 e0179488.

[51] Popovski G, Kochev S, Korousic-Seljak B, Eftimov T. FoodIE: A Rule-based Named-entity Recognition Method for Food Information Extraction. In: International Conference on Pattern Recognition Applications and Methods; 2019. Available from: `https://api.semanticscholar.org/CorpusID:88488573`.

[52] Popovski G, Seljak BK, Eftimov T. FoodBase corpus: a new resource of annotated food entities. Database: The Journal of Biological Databases and Curation. 2019 Nov;2019:baz121. Available from: `https://www.ncbi.nlm.nih.gov/pmc/articles/PMC6827550/`.

[53] Ispirova G, Cenikj G, Ogrinc M, Valenčič E, Stojanov R, Korošec P, et al. CafeteriaFCD Corpus: Food Consumption Data Annotated with Regard to Different Food Semantic Resources. Foods. 2022;11(17). Available from: `https://www.mdpi.com/2304-8158/11/17/2684`.

[54] Jonquet C, Shah NH, Youn CH, Musen MA, Callendar C, Storey MA. NCBO annotator: semantic annotation of biomedical data. In: ISWC 2009-8th International Semantic Web Conference, Poster and Demo Session. 171; 2009. .

[55] Eftimov T, Korošec P, Koroušić Seljak B. StandFood: standardization of foods using a semi-automatic system for classifying and describing foods according to FoodEx2. Nutrients. 2017;9(6):542.

[56] Cenikj G, Valenčič E, Ispirova G, Ogrinc M, Stojanov R, Korošec P, et al. CafeteriaSA corpus: scientific abstracts annotated across different food semantic resources. Database. 2022 12;2022:baac107.

[57] Stojanov R, Popovski G, Jofce N, Trajanov D, Seljak BK, Eftimov T. FoodViz;. Accessed: 2024-07-15. `http://foodviz.env4health.finki.ukim.mk/#/recipes`.

[58] la Torre FD, Hodgins JK, Bargteil AW, Martin X, Macey JR, Collado AT, et al. Guide to the Carnegie Mellon University Multimodal Activity (CMU-MMAC) Database; 2008. Available from: `https://api.semanticscholar.org/CorpusID:16721121`.

[59] Tasse D, Smith NA. SOUR CREAM: Toward semantic processing of recipes. Carnegie Mellon University, Pittsburgh, Tech Rep CMU-LTI-08-005. 2008.

[60] Lawrynowicz A, Wróblewska A, Kaliska A, Pawlowski M, Wiśniewski D, Sosnowski W, et al. Fine-Grained and Complex Food Entity Recognition Benchmark for Ingredient Substitution. In: Proceedings of the 12th Knowledge Capture Conference 2023. K-CAP '23. New York, NY, USA: Association for Computing Machinery; 2023. p. 25-9. Available from: `https://doi.org/10.1145/3587259.3627543`.

[61] Pennington J, Socher R, Manning CD. Glove: Global vectors for word representation. In: Proceedings of the 2014 conference on empirical methods in natural language processing (EMNLP); 2014. p. 1532-43.

[62] Mikolov T, Chen K, Corrado G, Dean J. Efficient estimation of word representations in vector space. arXiv preprint arXiv:13013781. 2013.

[63] Bojanowski P, Grave E, Joulin A, Mikolov T. Enriching word vectors with subword information. Transactions of the association for computational linguistics. 2017;5:135-46.

[64] Devlin J, Chang MW, Lee K, Toutanova K. BERT: Pre-training of Deep Bidirectional Transformers for Language Understanding. In: Burstein J, Doran C, Solorio T, editors. Proceedings of the 2019

Conference of the North American Chapter of the Association for Computational Linguistics: Human Language Technologies, Volume 1 (Long and Short Papers); 2019. p. 4171-86.

[65] Cenikj G, Petelin G, Koroušić Seljak B, Eftimov T. SciFoodNER: Food Named Entity Recognition for Scientific Text. In: 2022 IEEE International Conference on Big Data (Big Data); 2022. p. 4065-73.

[66] Lee J, Yoon W, Kim S, Kim D, Kim S, So CH, et al. BioBERT: a pre-trained biomedical language representation model for biomedical text mining. Bioinformatics. 2020;36(4):1234-40.

[67] Cenikj G, Eftimov T, Koroušić Seljak B. FooDis: A food-disease relation mining pipeline. Artificial Intelligence in Medicine. 2023;142:102586. Available from: https://www.sciencedirect.com/science/article/pii/S0933365723001008.

[68] Jensen K, Panagiotou G, Kouskoumvekaki I. NutriChem: a systems chemical biology resource to explore the medicinal value of plant-based foods. Nucleic acids research. 2015;43(D1):D940-5.

[69] Ni Y, Jensen K, Kouskoumvekaki I, Panagiotou G. NutriChem 2.0: exploring the effect of plant-based foods on human health and drug efficacy. Database. 2017;2017:bax044.

[70] Cenikj G, Korousic-Seljak B, Eftimov T. FoodChem: A food-chemical relation extraction model. CoRR. 2021;abs/2110.02019. Available from: https://arxiv.org/abs/2110.02019.

[71] Tung CW, Wang CC, Wang SS, Lin P. ChemDIS-Mixture: an online tool for analyzing potential interaction effects of chemical mixtures. Scientific reports. 2018;8(1):10047.

[72] Cenikj G, Strojnik L, Angelski R, Ogrinc N, Koroušić Seljak B, Eftimov T. From language models to large-scale food and biomedical knowledge graphs. Scientific reports. 2023;13(1):7815.

[73] Mezgec S, Koroušić Seljak B. NutriNet: a deep learning food and drink image recognition system for dietary assessment. Nutrients. 2017;9(7):657.

[74] Matsuda Y, Hoashi H, Yanai K. Recognition of multiple-food images by detecting candidate regions. In: 2012 IEEE international conference on multimedia and expo. IEEE; 2012. p. 25-30.

[75] Kawano Y, Yanai K. Automatic expansion of a food image dataset leveraging existing categories with domain adaptation. In: Computer Vision-ECCV 2014 Workshops: Zurich, Switzerland, September 6-7 and 12, 2014, Proceedings, Part III 13. Springer; 2015. p. 3-17.

[76] Ege T, Shimoda W, Yanai K. A new large-scale food image segmentation dataset and its application to food calorie estimation based on grains of rice. In: Proceedings of the 5th International Workshop on Multimedia Assisted Dietary Management; 2019. p. 82-7.

[77] Okamoto K, Yanai K. UEC-FoodPIX Complete: A large-scale food image segmentation dataset. In: Pattern Recognition. ICPR International Workshops and Challenges: Virtual Event, January 10–15, 2021, Proceedings, Part V. Springer; 2021. p. 647-59.

[78] Ciocca G, Napoletano P, Schettini R. Food recognition: a new dataset, experiments, and results. IEEE journal of biomedical and health informatics. 2016;21(3):588-98.

[79] Mohanty SP, Singhal G, Scuccimarra EA, Kebaili D, Héritier H, Boulanger V, et al. The food recognition benchmark: Using deep learning to recognize food in images. Frontiers in Nutrition. 2022;9:875143.

[80] Ultralytics. ultralytics/yolov5: v7.0 - YOLOv5 SOTA Realtime Instance Segmentation; 2022. Accessed: 7th May, 2023. https://github.com/ultralytics/yolov5.com. Available from: https://doi.org/10.5281/zenodo.7347926.

[81] Drole J, Pravst I, Eftimov T, Koroušić Seljak B. NutriGreen image dataset: a collection of annotated nutrition, organic, and vegan food products. Frontiers in nutrition. 2024;11:1342823.

[82] Romero Ferreiro C, Lora Pablos D, Gómez de la Cámara A. Two dimensions of nutritional value: Nutri-Score and NOVA. Nutrients. 2021;13(8):2783.

[83] V-Label International. V-Label: World's Leading Vegan & Vegetarian Trademark; 2024. Accessed: 2024-07-28. Available from: https://www.v-label.com.

[84] European Commission. The Organic Logo - European Commission; 2024. Accessed: 2024-07-28. Available from: https://agriculture.ec.europa.eu/farming/organic-farming/organic-logo_en.

[85] Chen K, Gao J, Nevatia R. Knowledge Aided Consistency for Weakly Supervised Phrase Grounding. In: 2018 IEEE Conference on Computer Vision and Pattern Recognition, CVPR 2018, Salt Lake City, UT, USA, June 18-22, 2018. Computer Vision Foundation / IEEE Computer Society; 2018. p. 4042-50. Available from: http://openaccess.thecvf.com/content_cvpr_2018/html/Chen_Knowledge_Aided_Consistency_CVPR_2018_paper.html.

[86] Ramanishka V, Das A, Zhang J, Saenko K. Top-Down Visual Saliency Guided by Captions. In: 2017 IEEE Conference on Computer Vision and Pattern Recognition, CVPR 2017, Honolulu, HI, USA, July

21-26, 2017. IEEE Computer Society; 2017. p. 3135-44. Available from: https://doi.org/10.1109/CVPR.2017.334.

[87] Chen X, Shrivastava A, Gupta A. NEIL: Extracting Visual Knowledge from Web Data. In: IEEE International Conference on Computer Vision, ICCV 2013, Sydney, Australia, December 1-8, 2013. IEEE Computer Society; 2013. p. 1409-16. Available from: https://doi.org/10.1109/ICCV.2013.178.

[88] Li M, Zareian A, Lin Y, Pan X, Whitehead S, Chen B, et al. GAIA: A Fine-grained Multimedia Knowledge Extraction System. In: Celikyilmaz A, Wen T, editors. Proceedings of the 58th Annual Meeting of the Association for Computational Linguistics: System Demonstrations, ACL 2020, Online, July 5-10, 2020. Association for Computational Linguistics; 2020. p. 77-86. Available from: https://doi.org/10.18653/v1/2020.acl-demos.11.

[89] Wen H, Lin Y, Lai TM, Pan X, Li S, Lin X, et al. RESIN: A Dockerized Schema-Guided Cross-document Cross-lingual Cross-media Information Extraction and Event Tracking System. In: Sil A, Lin XV, editors. Proceedings of the 2021 Conference of the North American Chapter of the Association for Computational Linguistics: Human Language Technologies: Demonstrations, NAACL-HLT 2021, Online, June 6-11, 2021. Association for Computational Linguistics; 2021. p. 133-43. Available from: https://doi.org/10.18653/v1/2021.naacl-demos.16.

[90] Ma Y, Wang Z, Li M, Cao Y, Chen M, Li X, et al. MMEKG: Multi-modal Event Knowledge Graph towards Universal Representation across Modalities. In: Basile V, Kozareva Z, Stajner S, editors. Proceedings of the 60th Annual Meeting of the Association for Computational Linguistics, ACL 2022 - System Demonstrations, Dublin, Ireland, May 22-27, 2022. Association for Computational Linguistics; 2022. p. 231-9. Available from: https://doi.org/10.18653/v1/2022.acl-demo.23.

[91] Taddeo M, Floridi L. Solving the symbol grounding problem: a critical review of fifteen years of research. J Exp Theor Artif Intell. 2005;17(4):419-45. Available from: https://doi.org/10.1080/09528130500284053.

[92] Ferrada S, Bustos B, Hogan A. IMGpedia: A Linked Dataset with Content-Based Analysis of Wikimedia Images. In: d'Amato C, Fernández M, Tamma VAM, Lécué F, Cudré-Mauroux P, Sequeda JF, et al., editors. The Semantic Web - ISWC 2017 - 16th International Semantic Web Conference, Vienna, Austria, October 21-25, 2017, Proceedings, Part II. vol. 10588 of Lecture Notes in Computer Science. Springer; 2017. p. 84-93. Available from: https://doi.org/10.1007/978-3-319-68204-4_8.

[93] Vaidya G, Kontokostas D, Knuth M, Lehmann J, Hellmann S. DBpedia Commons: Structured Multimedia Metadata from the Wikimedia Commons. In: Arenas M, Corcho Ó, Simperl E, Strohmaier M, d'Aquin M, Srinivas K, et al., editors. The Semantic Web - ISWC 2015 - 14th International Semantic Web Conference, Bethlehem, PA, USA, October 11-15, 2015, Proceedings, Part II. vol. 9367 of Lecture Notes in Computer Science. Springer; 2015. p. 281-9. Available from: https://doi.org/10.1007/978-3-319-25010-6_17.

[94] Oñoro-Rubio D, Niepert M, García-Durán A, Gonzalez-Sanchez R, López-Sastre RJ. Answering Visual-Relational Queries in Web-Extracted Knowledge Graphs. In: 1st Conference on Automated Knowledge Base Construction, AKBC 2019, Amherst, MA, USA, May 20-22, 2019; 2019. Available from: https://doi.org/10.24432/C56P45.

[95] Liu Y, Li H, García-Durán A, Niepert M, Oñoro-Rubio D, Rosenblum DS. MMKG: Multi-modal Knowledge Graphs. In: Hitzler P, Fernández M, Janowicz K, Zaveri A, Gray AJG, López V, et al., editors. The Semantic Web - 16th International Conference, ESWC 2019, Portorož, Slovenia, June 2-6, 2019, Proceedings. vol. 11503 of Lecture Notes in Computer Science. Springer; 2019. p. 459-74. Available from: https://doi.org/10.1007/978-3-030-21348-0_30.

[96] Wang M, Wang H, Qi G, Zheng Q. Richpedia: A Large-Scale, Comprehensive Multi-Modal Knowledge Graph. Big Data Res. 2020;22:100159. Available from: https://doi.org/10.1016/j.bdr.2020.100159.

[97] Haussmann S, Seneviratne O, Chen Y, Ne'eman Y, Codella JV, Chen C, et al. FoodKG: A Semantics-Driven Knowledge Graph for Food Recommendation. In: Ghidini C, Hartig O, Maleshkova M, Svátek V, Cruz IF, Hogan A, et al., editors. The Semantic Web - ISWC 2019 - 18th International Semantic Web Conference, Auckland, New Zealand, October 26-30, 2019, Proceedings, Part II. vol. 11779 of Lecture Notes in Computer Science. Springer; 2019. p. 146-62. Available from: https://doi.org/10.1007/978-3-030-30796-7_10.

[98] Dooley DM, Griffiths EJ, Gosal GS, Buttigieg PL, Hoehndorf R, Lange MC, et al. FoodOn: a harmonized food ontology to increase global food traceability, quality control and data integration. npj

Science of Food. 2018;2(1):23.

[99] Dragoni M, Bailoni T, Maimone R, Eccher C. HeLiS: An Ontology for Supporting Healthy Lifestyles. In: Vrandecic D, Bontcheva K, Suárez-Figueroa MC, Presutti V, Celino I, Sabou M, et al., editors. The Semantic Web - ISWC 2018 - 17th International Semantic Web Conference, Monterey, CA, USA, October 8-12, 2018, Proceedings, Part II. vol. 11137 of Lecture Notes in Computer Science. Springer; 2018. p. 53-69. Available from: https://doi.org/10.1007/978-3-030-00668-6_4.

[100] Boulos MNK, Yassine A, Shirmohammadi S, Namahoot CS, Brückner M. Towards an "Internet of Food": Food Ontologies for the Internet of Things. Future Internet. 2015;7(4):372-92. Available from: https://doi.org/10.3390/fi7040372.

[101] Vitali F, Lombardo R, Rivero D, Mattivi F, Franceschi P, Bordoni A, et al. ONS: an ontology for a standardized description of interventions and observational studies in nutrition. Genes & nutrition. 2018;13:1-9.

[102] Castellano-Escuder P, González-Domínguez R, Wishart DS, Andres-Lacueva C, Sánchez-Pla A. FOBI: an ontology to represent food intake data and associate it with metabolomic data. Database J Biol Databases Curation. 2020;2020. Available from: https://doi.org/10.1093/databa/baaa033.

[103] Tsatsou D, Lalama E, Wilson-Barnes SL, Hart K, Cornelissen VA, Buys R, et al. NAct: The Nutrition & Activity Ontology for Healthy Living. In: Neuhaus F, Brodaric B, editors. Formal Ontology in Information Systems - Proceedings of the Twelfth International Conference, FOIS 2021, Bozen-Bolzano, Italy, September 11-18, 2021. vol. 344 of Frontiers in Artificial Intelligence and Applications. IOS Press; 2021. p. 129-43. Available from: https://doi.org/10.3233/FAIA210377.

[104] Zhu X, Li Z, Wang X, Jiang X, Sun P, Wang X, et al. Multi-Modal Knowledge Graph Construction and Application: A Survey. CoRR. 2022;abs/2202.05786. Available from: https://arxiv.org/abs/2202.05786.

[105] Li D, Zaki MJ. RECIPTOR: An Effective Pretrained Model for Recipe Representation Learning. In: Proceedings of the 26th ACM SIGKDD International Conference on Knowledge Discovery & Data Mining. New York, NY, USA: Association for Computing Machinery; 2020. p. 1719-27. Available from: https://doi.org/10.1145/3394486.3403223.

[106] Tian Y, Zhang C, Guo Z, Huang C, Metoyer R, Chawla NV. RecipeRec: A Heterogeneous Graph Learning Model for Recipe Recommendation. vol. 4; 2022. p. 3466-72. Available from: https://www.ijcai.org/proceedings/2022/481.

[107] Tian Y, Zhang C, Guo Z, Ma Y, Metoyer R, Chawla NV. Recipe2Vec: Multi-modal Recipe Representation Learning with Graph Neural Networks. vol. 4; 2022. p. 3473-9. Available from: https://www.ijcai.org/proceedings/2022/482.

[108] Youn J, Naravane T, Tagkopoulos I. Using Word Embeddings to Learn a Better Food Ontology. Frontiers in Artificial Intelligence. 2020;3:93. Available from: https://www.frontiersin.org/article/10.3389/frai.2020.584784.

[109] Ispirova G, Eftimov T, Koroušić Seljak B. Domain heuristic fusion of multi-word embeddings for nutrient value prediction. Mathematics. 2021;9(16):1941.

[110] Matsuda Y, Yanai K. Multiple-food recognition considering co-occurrence employing manifold ranking. In: Proceedings of the 21st International Conference on Pattern Recognition (ICPR2012); 2012. p. 2017-20.

[111] Bossard L, Guillaumin M, Van Gool L. Food-101–mining discriminative components with random forests. In: Computer Vision–ECCV 2014: 13th European Conference, Zurich, Switzerland, September 6-12, 2014, Proceedings, Part VI 13. Springer; 2014. p. 446-61.

[112] Merler M, Wu H, Uceda-Sosa R, Nguyen QB, Smith JR. Snap, Eat, RepEat: A food recognition engine for dietary logging. In: Proceedings of the 2nd international workshop on multimedia assisted dietary management; 2016. p. 31-40.

[113] Chen X, Zhu Y, Zhou H, Diao L, Wang D. Chinesefoodnet: A large-scale image dataset for chinese food recognition. arXiv preprint arXiv:170502743. 2017.

[114] Min W, Liu L, Luo Z, Jiang S. Ingredient-guided cascaded multi-attention network for food recognition. In: Proceedings of the 27th ACM International Conference on Multimedia; 2019. p. 1331-9.

[115] Sahoo D, Hao W, Ke S, Xiongwei W, Le H, Achananuparp P, et al. FoodAI: Food image recognition via deep learning for smart food logging. In: Proceedings of the 25th ACM SIGKDD International Conference on Knowledge Discovery & Data Mining; 2019. p. 2260-8.

[116] Min W, Liu L, Wang Z, Luo Z, Wei X, Wei X, et al. Isia food-500: A dataset for large-scale food recognition via stacked global-local attention network. In: Proceedings of the 28th ACM International

Conference on Multimedia; 2020. p. 393-401.

[117] Min W, Wang Z, Liu Y, Luo M, Kang L, Wei X, et al. Large scale visual food recognition. Transactions on Pattern Analysis and Machine Intelligence. 2023.

[118] Marin J, Biswas A, Ofli F, Hynes N, Salvador A, Aytar Y, et al. Recipe1M+: A Dataset for Learning Cross-Modal Embeddings for Cooking Recipes and Food Images. arXiv:181006553 [cs]. 2019 Jul. ArXiv: 1810.06553. Available from: http://arxiv.org/abs/1810.06553.

[119] Marin J, Biswas A, Ofli F, Hynes N, Salvador A, Aytar Y, et al. Recipe1M+: A Dataset for Learning Cross-Modal Embeddings for Cooking Recipes and Food Images. IEEE Trans Pattern Anal Mach Intell. 2019.

[120] Bień M, Gilski M, Maciejewska M, Taisner W, Wisniewski D, Lawrynowicz A. RecipeNLG: A cooking recipes dataset for semi-structured text generation. In: Proceedings of the 13th International Conference on Natural Language Generation; 2020. .

[121] Thames Q, Karpur A, Norris W, Xia F, Panait L, Weyand T, et al. Nutrition5k: Towards automatic nutritional understanding of generic food. In: Proceedings of the IEEE/CVF Conference on Computer Vision and Pattern Recognition; 2021. p. 8903-11.

[122] Kitamura K, Yamasaki T, Aizawa K. Food log by analyzing food images. In: Proceedings of the 16th ACM International Conference on Multimedia. MM '08. New York, NY, USA: Association for Computing Machinery; 2008. p. 999–1000. Available from: https://doi.org/10.1145/1459359.1459548.

[123] Kitamura K, Yamasaki T, Aizawa K. FoodLog: capture, analysis and retrieval of personal food images via web. In: Proceedings of the ACM Multimedia 2009 Workshop on Multimedia for Cooking and Eating Activities. CEA '09. New York, NY, USA: Association for Computing Machinery; 2009. p. 23–30. Available from: https://doi.org/10.1145/1630995.1631001.

[124] Chen M, Dhingra K, Wu W, Yang L, Sukthankar R, Yang J. PFID: Pittsburgh fast-food image dataset. In: 2009 16th IEEE International Conference on Image Processing (ICIP); 2009. p. 289-92.

[125] Wang W, Min W, Li T, Dong X, Li H, Jiang S. A review on vision-based analysis for automatic dietary assessment. Trends in Food Science & Technology. 2022;122:223-37.

[126] Meyers A, Johnston N, Rathod V, Korattikara A, Gorban A, Silberman N, et al. Im2Calories: towards an automated mobile vision food diary. In: Proceedings of the IEEE International Conference on Computer Vision; 2015. p. 1233-41.

[127] Ma P, Lau CP, Yu N, Li A, Liu P, Wang Q, et al. Image-based nutrient estimation for Chinese dishes using deep learning. Food Research International. 2021;147:110437.

[128] Chen J, Zhu B, Ngo CW, Chua TS, Jiang YG. A Study of Multi-Task and Region-Wise Deep Learning for Food Ingredient Recognition. IEEE Transactions on Image Processing. 2021;30:1514-26.

[129] Office for Resources, Policy Division Science and Technology Policy Bureau. STANDARD TABLES OF FOOD COMPOSITION IN JAPAN - 2015 - (Seventh Revised Version);. Accessed: 2024-08-14. https://www.mext.go.jp/en/policy/science_technology/policy/title01/detail01/1374030.htm.

[130] Wang L, Yamakata Y, Aizawa K. Automatic Dataset Creation from User-generated Recipes for Ingredient-centric Food Image Analysis. In: Proceedings of the 5th ACM International Conference on Multimedia in Asia. MMAsia '23. New York, NY, USA: Association for Computing Machinery; 2024. Available from: https://doi.org/10.1145/3595916.3626748.

[131] Ronneberger O, Fischer P, Brox T. U-net: Convolutional networks for biomedical image segmentation. In: Proceedings of the 18th International Conference on Medical Image Computing and Computer-Assisted Intervention; 2015. p. 234-41.

[132] Ando Y, Ege T, Cho J, Yanai K. Depthcaloriecam: A mobile application for volume-based foodcalorie estimation using depth cameras. In: Proceedings of the 5th International Workshop on Multimedia Assisted Dietary Management; 2019. p. 76-81.

[133] Lu Y, Stathopoulou T, Vasiloglou MF, Pinault LF, Kiley C, Spanakis EK, et al. goFOODTM: an artificial intelligence system for dietary assessment. Sensors. 2020;20(15):4283.

[134] He K, Gkioxari G, Dollár P, Girshick R. Mask r-cnn. In: Proceedings of the IEEE International Conference on Computer Vision; 2017. p. 2961-9.

[135] Dehais J, Anthimopoulos M, Shevchik S, Mougiakakou S. Two-View 3D Reconstruction for Food Volume Estimation. IEEE Transactions on Multimedia. 2017;19(5):1090-9.

[136] Joshua SR, Shin S, Lee JH, Kim SK. Health to Eat: A Smart Plate with Food Recognition, Classification, and Weight Measurement for Type-2 Diabetic Mellitus Patients' Nutrition Control. Sensors.

2023;23(3):1656.
[137] Ege T, Yanai K. Simultaneous estimation of dish locations and calories with multi-task learning. IEICE TRANSACTIONS on Information and Systems. 2019;102(7):1240-6.
[138] EGE T, YANAI K. Image-Based Food Calorie Estimation Using Recipe Information. IEICE Transactions on Information and Systems. 2018;E101.D(5):1333-41.
[139] Lu Y, Allegra D, Anthimopoulos M, Stanco F, Farinella GM, Mougiakakou S. A multi-task learning approach for meal assessment. In: Proceedings of the Joint Workshop on Multimedia for Cooking and Eating Activities and Multimedia Assisted Dietary Management; 2018. p. 46-52.
[140] He K, Zhang X, Ren S, Sun J. Deep residual learning for image recognition. In: Proceedings of the IEEE Conference on Computer Vision and Pattern Recognition; 2016. p. 770-8.
[141] Lin TY, Dollár P, Girshick R, He K, Hariharan B, Belongie S. Feature pyramid networks for object detection. In: Proceedings of the IEEE Conference on Computer Vision and Pattern Recognition; 2017. p. 2117-25.
[142] Ren S, He K, Girshick R, Sun J. Faster r-cnn: Towards real-time object detection with region proposal networks. Advances in Neural Information Processing Systems. 2015;28.
[143] Szegedy C, Vanhoucke V, Ioffe S, Shlens J, Wojna Z. Rethinking the inception architecture for computer vision. In: Proceedings of the IEEE Conference on Computer Vision and Pattern Recognition; 2016. p. 2818-26.
[144] Shao W, Min W, Hou S, Luo M, Li T, Zheng Y, et al. Vision-based food nutrition estimation via RGB-D fusion network. Food Chemistry. 2023;424:136309.
[145] Shao W, Hou S, Jia W, Zheng Y. Rapid Non-Destructive Analysis of Food Nutrient Content Using Swin-Nutrition. Foods. 2022;11(21):3429.
[146] Liu Z, Lin Y, Cao Y, Hu H, Wei Y, Zhang Z, et al. Swin transformer: Hierarchical vision transformer using shifted windows. In: Proceedings of the IEEE/CVF International Conference on Computer Vision; 2021. p. 10012-22.
[147] Chen M, Jia X, Gorbonos E, Hoang CT, Yu X, Liu Y. Eating healthier: Exploring nutrition information for healthier recipe recommendation. Information Processing & Management. 2020;57(6):102051.
[148] Forbes P, Zhu M. Content-boosted matrix factorization for recommender systems: experiments with recipe recommendation. In: Proceedings of the fifth ACM conference on Recommender systems; 2011. p. 261-4.
[149] Ling Y, Nie JY, Nielsen D, Knäuper B, Yang N, Dubé L. Following good examples-health goal-oriented food recommendation based on behavior data. In: Proceedings of the ACM Web Conference 2022; 2022. p. 3745-54.
[150] Chen Y, Subburathinam A, Chen CH, Zaki MJ. Personalized food recommendation as constrained question answering over a large-scale food knowledge graph. In: Proceedings of the 14th ACM international conference on web search and data mining; 2021. p. 544-52.
[151] Li D, Zaki MJ, Chen Ch. Health-guided recipe recommendation over knowledge graphs. Journal of Web Semantics. 2023;75:100743.
[152] Kobayashi A, Mori S, Hashimoto A, Katsuragi T, Kawamura T. Functional Food Knowledge Graph-based Recipe Recommendation System Focused on Lifestyle-Related Diseases. In: 2024 IEEE 18th International Conference on Semantic Computing (ICSC). IEEE; 2024. p. 261-8.
[153] Akkoyunlu S, Manfredotti C, Cornuéjols A, Darcel N, Delaere F. Investigating substitutability of food items in consumption data. In: Second International Workshop on Health Recommender Systems co-located with ACM RecSys. vol. 5; 2017. .
[154] Pan Y, Xu Q, Li Y. Food recipe alternation and generation with natural language processing techniques. In: 2020 IEEE 36th international conference on data engineering workshops (ICDEW). IEEE; 2020. p. 94-7.
[155] Shirai SS, Seneviratne O, Gordon ME, Chen CH, McGuinness DL. Identifying ingredient substitutions using a knowledge graph of food. Frontiers in Artificial Intelligence. 2021;3:621766.
[156] Shirai SS, Seneviratne O, Gordon ME, Chen CH, McGuinness DL. Semantics-Driven ingredient substitution in the foodKG? In: International Semantic Web Conference: Posters, Demos, and Industry Tracks. CEUR-WS; 2020. .
[157] Salvador A, Hynes N, Aytar Y, Marin J, Ofli F, Weber I, et al. Learning Cross-modal Embeddings for Cooking Recipes and Food Images. In: Proceedings of the IEEE Conference on Computer Vision and Pattern Recognition; 2017. .
[158] Carvalho M, Cadène R, Picard D, Soulier L, Thome N, Cord M. Cross-modal retrieval in the cooking

context: Learning semantic text-image embeddings. In: The 41st International ACM SIGIR Conference on Research & Development in Information Retrieval; 2018. p. 35-44.
[159] Papadopoulos DP, Mora E, Chepurko N, Huang KW, Ofli F, Torralba A. Learning program representations for food images and cooking recipes. In: Proceedings of the IEEE/CVF Conference on Computer Vision and Pattern Recognition; 2022. p. 16559-69.
[160] Li D, Zaki MJ. Food Knowledge Representation Learning with Adversarial Substitution. In: Proceedings of the 2nd Conference of the Asia-Pacific Chapter of the Association for Computational Linguistics and the 12th International Joint Conference on Natural Language Processing; 2022. .
[161] Padhiar I, Seneviratne O, Chari S, Gruen D, McGuinness DL. Semantic modeling for food recommendation explanations. In: 2021 IEEE 37th International Conference on Data Engineering Workshops (ICDEW). IEEE; 2021. p. 13-9.
[162] Kirkpatrick SI, Subar AF, Douglass D, Zimmerman TP, Thompson FE, Kahle LL, et al. Performance of the Automated Self-Administered 24-hour Recall relative to a measure of true intakes and to an interviewer-administered 24-h recall. The American Journal of Clinical Nutrition. 2014;100(1):233-40.
[163] Forster H, Fallaize R, Gallagher C, O'Donovan CB, Woolhead C, Walsh MC, et al. Online dietary intake estimation: the Food4Me food frequency questionnaire. Journal of Medical Internet Research. 2014;16(6):e3105.
[164] Kristal AR, Kolar AS, Fisher JL, Plascak JJ, Stumbo PJ, Weiss R, et al. Evaluation of web-based, self-administered, graphical food frequency questionnaire. Journal of the Academy of Nutrition and Dietetics. 2014;114(4):613-21.
[165] Gersovitz M, Madden JP, Smiciklas-Wright H. Validity of the 24-hr. dietary recall and seven-day record for group comparisons. Journal of the American Dietetic Association. 1978;73(1):48-55.
[166] Illner A, Freisling H, Boeing H, Huybrechts I, Crispim S, Slimani N. Review and evaluation of innovative technologies for measuring diet in nutritional epidemiology. International Journal of Epidemiology. 2012;41(4):1187-203.
[167] Gibney M, Allison D, Bier D, Dwyer J. Uncertainty in human nutrition research. Nature Food. 2020;1(5):247-9.
[168] MyFitnessPal, Inc . MyFitnessPal;. Accessed: 2024-08-14. `https://www.myfitnesspal.com/`.
[169] Azumio Inc . Carorie Mama Food AI;. Accessed: 2024-08-14. `https://caloriemama.ai/`.
[170] foodvisor io. Foodvisor App;. Accessed: 2024-08-14. `https://www.foodvisor.io/en/`.
[171] Bolaños M, Valdivia M, Radeva P. Where and What Am I Eating? Image-Based Food Menu Recognition. In: Leal-Taixé L, Roth S, editors. Computer Vision – ECCV 2018 Workshops. Cham: Springer International Publishing; 2019. p. 590-605.
[172] Sahoo D, Hao W, Ke S, Xiongwei W, Le H, Achananuparp P, et al. FoodAI: Food Image Recognition via Deep Learning for Smart Food Logging. In: Proceedings of the 25th ACM SIGKDD International Conference on Knowledge Discovery and Data Mining. KDD '19. New York, NY, USA: Association for Computing Machinery; 2019. p. 2260–2268. Available from: `https://doi.org/10.1145/3292500.3330734`.
[173] GoFood;. Accessed: 2024-08-14. `https://go-food.tech/`.
[174] Nakamoto K, Kumazawa K, Karasawa H, Amano S, Yamakata Y, Aizawa K. FoodLog Athl: Multimedia Food Recording Platform for Dietary Guidance and Food Monitoring. In: Proceedings of the 4th ACM International Conference on Multimedia in Asia. MMAsia '22. New York, NY, USA: Association for Computing Machinery; 2022. Available from: `https://doi.org/10.1145/3551626.3564978`.
[175] Yamakata Y, Ishino A, Sunto A, Amano S, Aizawa K. Recipe-oriented Food Logging for Nutritional Management. In: Proceedings of the 30th ACM International Conference on Multimedia; 2022. p. 6898-904.
[176] Herrero M, Thornton PK, Mason-D'Croz D, Palmer J, Benton TG, Bodirsky BL, et al. Innovation can accelerate the transition towards a sustainable food system. Nature Food. 2020;1(5):266-72.
[177] Ögel Aydın S, Argan M. Understanding how gamification influences consumers' dietary preferences. Journal of Social Marketing. 2021;11(2):82-123.
[178] Reinders MJ, Starke AD, Fischer AR, Verain MC, Doets EL, Van Loo EJ. Determinants of consumer acceptance and use of personalized dietary advice: A systematic review. Trends in Food Science & Technology. 2023;131:277-94.
[179] Samoggia A, Riedel B. Assessment of nutrition-focused mobile apps' influence on consumers' healthy food behaviour and nutrition knowledge. Food Research International. 2020;128:108766.
[180] Scarry A, Rice J, O'Connor EM, Tierney AC. Usage of mobile applications or mobile health technol-

ogy to improve diet quality in adults. Nutrients. 2022;14(12):2437.

[181] Seid A, Fufa DD, Bitew ZW. The use of internet-based smartphone apps consistently improved consumers' healthy eating behaviors: a systematic review of randomized controlled trials. Frontiers in Digital Health. 2024;6:1282570.

[182] Stancu V, Frank DA, Lähteenmäki L, Grunert KG. Motivating consumers for health and fitness: The role of app features. Journal of Consumer Behaviour. 2022;21(6):1506-21.

[183] Reščič N, Mayora O, Eccher C, Luštrek M. Food frequency questionnaire personalisation using multi-target regression. Nutrients. 2022;14(19):3943.

[184] Samad S, Ahmed F, Naher S, Kabir MA, Das A, Amin S, et al. Smartphone apps for tracking food consumption and recommendations: Evaluating artificial intelligence-based functionalities, features and quality of current apps. Intelligent Systems with Applications. 2022;15:200103.

[185] Adrian WT, Kutyla M, Potoniec J, Lawrynowicz A. Reasoning about Ingredient Substitutions with Ontologies and Rules. In: Vanthienen J, Kliegr T, Fodor P, Lanti D, Arndt D, Kostylev EV, et al., editors. Proceedings of the 17th International Rule Challenge and 7th Doctoral Consortium @ RuleML+RR 2023 co-located with 19th Reasoning Web Summer School (RW 2023) and 15th DecisionCAMP 2023 as part of Declarative AI 2023, Oslo, Norway, 18 - 20 September, 2023. vol. 3485 of CEUR Workshop Proceedings. CEUR-WS.org; 2023. Available from: `https://ceur-ws.org/Vol-3485/paper8961.pdf`.

[186] Fatemi B, Duval Q, Girdhar R, Drozdzal M, Romero-Soriano A. Learning to Substitute Ingredients in Recipes. arXiv preprint arXiv:230207960. 2023.

[187] Shirai SS, Kim H. EaT-PIM: Substituting Entities in Procedural Instructions Using Flow Graphs and Embeddings. In: Sattler U, Hogan A, Keet M, Presutti V, Almeida JPA, Takeda H, et al., editors. The Semantic Web – ISWC 2022. vol. 13489. Cham: Springer International Publishing; 2022. p. 161-78. Available from: `https://link.springer.com/10.1007/978-3-031-19433-7_10`.

[188] Varshney LR, Pinel F, Varshney KR, Bhattacharjya D, Schörgendorfer A, Chee YM. A big data approach to computational creativity. IBM Journal of Research and Development. 2019.

[189] H Lee H, Shu K, Achananuparp P, Prasetyo PK, Liu Y, Lim EP, et al. RecipeGPT: Generative pre-training based cooking recipe generation and evaluation system. In: Companion Proceedings of the Web Conference; 2020. .

[190] Taneja K, Segal R, Goodwin R. Monte Carlo tree search for recipe generation using GPT-2. arXiv preprint arXiv:240105199. 2024.

[191] Reusch A, Weber A, Thiele M, Lehner W. RecipeGM: A Hierarchical Recipe Generation Model. In: 2021 IEEE 37th International Conference on Data Engineering Workshops (ICDEW). IEEE; 2021. p. 24-9.

[192] Farahani M, Godawat K, Aekula H, Pandian D, Broad N. Chef Transformer. URL: https://huggingfaceco/flax-community/t5-recipe-generation (accessed 16 Dec 2023). 2023.

[193] Chhikara P, Chaurasia D, Jiang Y, Masur O, Ilievski F. FIRE: Food Image to REcipe generation. arXiv preprint arXiv:230814391. 2023.

[194] Yin Y, Qi H, Zhu B, Chen J, Jiang YG, Ngo CW. FoodLMM: A Versatile Food Assistant using Large Multi-modal Model. arXiv preprint arXiv:231214991. 2023.

[195] Wang H, Lin G, Hoi SC, Miao C. In: Structure-aware generation network for recipe generation from images. Springer; 2020. .

[196] Radford A, Wu J, Child R, Luan D, Amodei D, Sutskever I, et al. Language models are unsupervised multitask learners. OpenAI blog. 2019.

[197] Salvador A, Drozdzal M, Giró-i Nieto X, Romero A. Inverse cooking: Recipe generation from food images. In: Proceedings of the IEEE/CVF Conference on Computer Vision and Pattern Recognition; 2019. .

[198] Vaswani A, Shazeer N, Parmar N, Uszkoreit J, Jones L, Gomez AN, et al. Attention is all you need. Advances in Neural Information Processing Systems. 2017;30.

[199] Raffel C, Shazeer N, Roberts A, Lee K, Narang S, Matena M, et al. Exploring the limits of transfer learning with a unified text-to-text transformer. The Journal of Machine Learning Research. 2020.

[200] Li J, Li D, Xiong C, Hoi S. Blip: Bootstrapping language-image pre-training for unified vision-language understanding and generation. In: International conference on machine learning. PMLR; 2022. p. 12888-900.

[201] Dosovitskiy A, Beyer L, Kolesnikov A, Weissenborn D, Zhai X, Unterthiner T, et al. An image is worth 16x16 words: Transformers for image recognition at scale. arXiv preprint arXiv:201011929. 2020.

[202] Lai X, Tian Z, Chen Y, Li Y, Yuan Y, Liu S, et al. Lisa: Reasoning segmentation via large language model. arXiv preprint arXiv:230800692. 2023.
[203] Mohbat F, Zaki MJ. LLaVA-Chef: A Multi-modal Generative Model for Food Recipes. In: Proceedings of the 33rd ACM International Conference on Information and Knowledge Management (CIKM). ACM; 2024. Available from: https://doi.org/10.1145/3627673.3679562.
[204] Liu H, Li C, Wu Q, Lee YJ. Visual instruction tuning. arXiv preprint arXiv:230408485. 2023.
[205] Fried LP, Bandeen-Roche K, Chaves P, Johnson BA, et al. Preclinical mobility disability predicts incident mobility disability in older women. Journals of Gerontology-Biological Sciences and Medical Sciences. 2000;55(1):M43.
[206] Onder G, Penninx BW, Ferrucci L, Fried LP, Guralnik JM, Pahor M. Measures of physical performance and risk for progressive and catastrophic disability: results from the Women's Health and Aging Study. The Journals of Gerontology Series A: Biological Sciences and Medical Sciences. 2005;60(1):74-9.
[207] Wolinsky FD, Miller DK, Andresen EM, Malmstrom TK, Miller JP. Further evidence for the importance of subclinical functional limitation and subclinical disability assessment in gerontology and geriatrics. The Journals of Gerontology Series B: Psychological Sciences and Social Sciences. 2005;60(3):S146-51.
[208] LI I, MS G. Capturing and classifying functional status information in administrative databases. Health Care Financ Rev. 2003;3(24):61-76. Available from: https://pubmed.ncbi.nlm.nih.gov/12894635/.
[209] Nelson E, Conger B, Douglass R, Gephart D, Kirk J, Page R, et al. Functional health status levels of primary care patients. Jama. 1983;249(24):3331-8.
[210] Calkins DR, Rubenstein LV, Cleary PD, Davies AR, Jette AM, Fink A, et al. Failure of physicians to recognize functional disability in ambulatory patients. Annals of internal medicine. 1991;114(6):451-4.
[211] Calkins DR, Rubenstein LV, Cleary PD, Davies AR, Jette AM, Fink A, et al. Functional disability screening of ambulatory patients. Journal of General Internal Medicine. 1994;9(10):590-2.
[212] Cassell EJ. Doctoring: The nature of primary care medicine. Oxford University Press, USA; 2002.
[213] Fried LP, Young Y, Rubin G, Bandeen-Roche K, Group WICR, et al. Self-reported preclinical disability identifies older women with early declines in performance and early disease. Journal of clinical epidemiology. 2001;54(9):889-901.
[214] Wakefield BJ, Holman JE. Functional trajectories associated with hospitalization in older adults. Western Journal of Nursing Research. 2007;29(2):161-77.
[215] Alexander GL, Rantz M, Skubic M, Aud MA, Wakefield B, Florea E, et al. Sensor Systems for Monitoring Functional Status in Assisted Living Facility Residents. Research in Gerontological Nursing. 2008;1(4):238-44. Available from: https://journals.healio.com/doi/abs/10.3928/19404921-20081001-01.
[216] Haussmann S, Chen Y, Seneviratne O, Rastogi N, Codella J, Chen CH, et al. Foodkg enabled q&a application. In: ISWC Satellite Tracks. CEUR-WS; 2019. .
[217] Michie S, Carey RN, Johnston M, Rothman AJ, de Bruin M, Kelly MP, et al. From Theory-Inspired to Theory-Based Interventions: A Protocol for Developing and Testing a Methodology for Linking Behaviour Change Techniques to Theoretical Mechanisms of Action. Annals of Behavioral Medicine. 2017 12;52(6):501-12. Available from: https://doi.org/10.1007/s12160-016-9816-6.
[218] Larsen KRT, Michie S, Hekler E, Gibson B, Spruijt-Metz D, Ahern D, et al. Behavior change interventions: the potential of ontologies for advancing science and practice. Journal of Behavioral Medicine. 2016;40:6-22.
[219] Weisz J, Ng MY, Bearman S. Odd Couple? Reenvisioning the Relation Between Science and Practice in the Dissemination-Implementation Era. Clinical Psychological Science. 2014;2:58 74.
[220] Phan N, Dou D, Wang H, Kil D, Piniewski B. Ontology-based deep learning for human behavior prediction with explanations in health social networks. Information Sciences. 2017;384:298-313. Available from: https://www.sciencedirect.com/science/article/pii/S0020025516306090.
[221] Bickmore TW, Schulman D, Sidner CL. A reusable framework for health counseling dialogue systems based on a behavioral medicine ontology. Journal of biomedical informatics. 2011;44(2):183-97.

Handbook on Neurosymbolic AI and Knowledge Graphs
P. Hitzler et al. (Eds.)
IOS Press, 2025

doi:10.3233/FAIA250243

Capturing the Semantics of Internet Memes

Filip ILIEVSKI [a] Riccardo TOMMASINI [b]
[a] *Department of Computer Science, Vrije Universiteit Amsterdam, The Netherlands*
[b] *INSA Lyon, France*

Abstract. Internet memes have emerged as a novel format for expressing ideas on the web. They have evolved from a simple form of entertainment to a sophisticated medium of communication that reflects societal sentiments, values, trends, and occasionally unethical and harmful behavior. Internet memes are multimodal, succinct, relatable, and fluid, making them challenging and inspiring for many stakeholders, including content moderators, marketing strategists, and social science researchers. Interpreting internet memes is also a challenging objective for (neurosymbolic) AI, requiring knowledge about memes to be collected, curated, enriched, and integrated with multimodal processing models. This chapter provides background on internet memes and discusses key considerations in machines' interpretation of memes towards developing robust and explainable methods that can estimate meme similarity, detect toxic memes at scale, and reason about the impact of cultural and personal values. We discuss challenges for meme knowledge collection and curation and describe our approach to generating the Internet Meme Knowledge Graph. We describe methods for estimating meme similarity to ground memes from the web, designed to capture content, form, identity, and stance. We review ongoing efforts to develop explainable hate speech detection methods in memes. Finally, we list open challenges and promising future directions for reliable AI reasoning over internet memes.

Keywords. internet memes, semantics, visual language models, knowledge graphs

1. Introduction

Internet memes have emerged as a novel format for expressing ideas on the web, evolving from a simple form of entertainment to a sophisticated medium of communication that reflects societal sentiments, values, and trends, and occasionally unethical and harmful behavior. An internet meme (IM) can be defined as a piece of culture, typically a joke, which gains influence through online transmission [1]. Internet memes are based on a medium, typically an image representing a well-understood reference (e.g., to a movie scene), signifying a prototypical situation or a viewpoint recognized by a certain community [2]. Internet memes are multimodal, concise, relatable, and fluid, which makes them challenging and inspiring for a broad set of stakeholders, from content moderators to marketing strategists to social science researchers. Namely, social scientists study how memes spread and what personal or cultural aspects influence their relatability [3,4]. Marketing strategists must monitor the sentiment and stances expressed in memes about their brand [5]. Content moderators seeking to detect toxic content online promptly and fairly need mechanisms for interpreting and classifying memes [6].

Given the scale and complexity of IMs, it is not feasible to achieve such goals solely based on manual effort, motivating the use of AI to assist human experts. However, while today's AI can deal with scale, the multifaceted semantics of memes represent a notable challenge, requiring significant advances at the intersection of multimodal processing, knowledge representation, and neuro-symbolic AI. While multimodal models have reported sizable increases in performance on many tasks, their perceptual robustness, abstraction, and common sense remain challenging [7,8,9,10], perhaps best illustrated by abstract visual reasoning studies [11]. Knowledge representation faces challenges in terms of how to best connect the dots between information on a different time scale (e.g., recent and historical events), how to incorporate personal and cultural values, and how to enable effective retrieval of knowledge in context [12]. Finally, neuro-symbolic AI can contribute methods to align language and vision with background knowledge and cultural considerations, built to provide robustness and explainability. Neuro-symbolic AI methods hold the promise to estimate meme similarity in a controlled manner, detect harmful memes in an explainable way, and reason about the impact of cultural and personal values; however, achieving these goals requires further research to improve their accuracy, generalizability, and scale.

This chapter provides an overview of recent work on capturing the semantics of IMs from a perspective of neuro-symbolic AI and knowledge graphs (KGs). It aims to critically describe the state of the art and reflect on open issues. Section 2 provides background on internet memes and discusses key considerations in interpreting them by machines. In Section 3, we discuss challenges for meme knowledge collection and curation and describe our approach to generating the Internet Meme Knowledge Graph. We then describe methods for estimating meme similarity to ground memes online, designed to capture content, form, identity, and stance in Section 4. In Section 5, we review ongoing efforts to develop explainable hate speech detection methods in memes. Finally, Section 6 lists open challenges and future directions for reliable AI reasoning over IMs.

2. Internet Memes

2.1. Definitions and Key Concepts

As initially defined by Richard Dawkins in 1976, memes are a "unit of cultural transmission or a unit of imitation" [13]. In different terms, memes are concepts and customs, patterns and behaviors, attitudes and habits - the building blocks of culture, science, religion, and even society itself. In the loosest definition, the term indicates everything that can be transmitted between individuals through imitation. Dawkins elaborates upon this further by drawing an analogy to genes - both being, in a sense, self-replicating entities that propagate themselves through people and, thus, through time. Understandably, this definition has been a source of much controversy. In "The Meme Machine" [14], Susan Blackmoore discusses three problems with the memes/gene analogy: the unit of a meme cannot be specified, the mechanism for copying and storing memes is unknown, and memetic evolution is "Lamarckian" (i.e., an organism can acquire characteristics for its offspring). Such critics highlight the limits of a quantitative study on memes [15] as cultural transmitters [16] that builds on the analogy with genes. Nevertheless, the study of memes in social sciences, philosophy, and cognitive psychology has progressed, particularly with the rise of internet phenomena and culture.

IMs can be seen as parallels to the original biological memes. An IM is a piece of culture, typically a joke, which gains influence through online transmission [1]. The term was invented by Mike Godwin in 1993[1], to describe the "recent" diffusion of the meme phenomenon in digital channels: initially usenet groups and email, and then, social media platforms. While IMs are often associated with parody, Patrick Davison reinforces that humor is not part of the definition of IMs, as apparent also from their use as a vehicle for political propaganda [17], hate speech [18], and traumatic confessions [19]. In Dawkins' terms, the most significant part of this definition is *online transmission*, which requires the meme to be encoded into an internet-viable medium, be it image, text, or video. This additional property of "readable data" now allows us to discern discrete units and observe the mechanisms of replication and storage in action, at least within the online environment - providing an opportunity for quantitative analysis.[2]

A singular format for internet memes does not exist. Shifman provides a small taxonomy in her book [20], which has grown further over the years. In general, most IMs share the property of intertextuality (i.e., is the shaping of a text's meaning by another text) and are multimodal constructions of text and image [21,22] (we discuss other properties below). Our chapter focuses on *Image Macros*, which are perhaps the most representative subgenre of IMs, often regarded as the classic IMs [21,22].

Definition 1. *Image Macros are internet memes consisting of:*

1. *A background image that is chosen such that it is immediately recognizable by the intended audience and provides them with context;*
2. *Superimposed text as a caption containing the message and sometimes additional contextual information.*

The caption in an Image Macro may take the form of a catchphrase or a snowclone (i.e., a phrasal template that can be recognized in multiple variants) and contain additional context. Therefore, we make the following distinction of a template (Figure 1a):

Definition 2. *Templates are multimedia structures, typically consisting of an image and a placeholder for caption text.*

While a given meme is generated by precisely one template, multiple templates can be associated with a given instance. Indeed, templates are user-proposed and can be duplicated or adapted over time, i.e., a template can be a variant of another template, as illustrated by "One Does Not Simply Spiderman".[3]

Definition 3. *Meme instances are multimedia structures that specify a template for one or more domains.*

---

[1] `https://en.wikipedia.org/wiki/Internet_meme`

[2] Studies on IMs in sociology and psychology provide complementary insights. Limor Shifman's book "Memes in Digital Culture" [20] builds on Blackmoore's observation reported above. Shifman suggests reassessing the meme definition by looking at those aspects that people may imitate (memetic dimensions) and looking at them not as single entities but as groups of content units with common characteristics [20].

[3] `https://imgflip.com/memetemplate/20502958/one-does-not-simply-Spider-Man`

Figure 1. The "One does not simply" template and several instances.

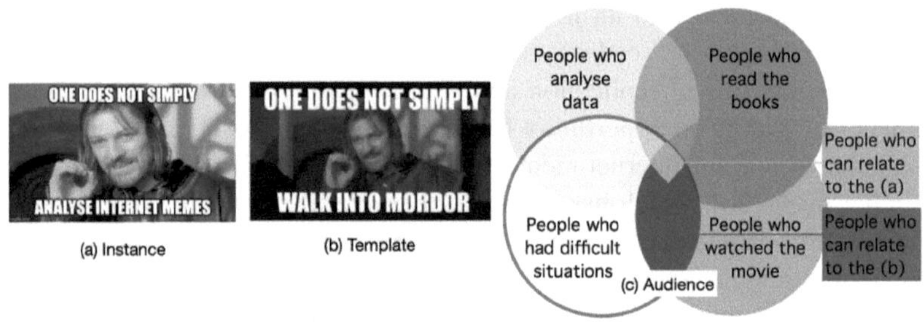

Figure 2. Examples of meme multimodality and relatability for an audience.

In Figure 1b, respectively, the domains for the four instances are internet memes, bullying, news,[4] and popular culture.[5]

2.2. Characteristics of IMs

This section delves into the defining characteristics of IMs that contribute to their unique nature and widespread appeal. Understanding these attributes is essential for analyzing how memes function, spread, and impact digital culture.

C1 Multimodality: Internet memes come in various formats, typically involving visuals and text, but they can also include GIFs and sounds. Figure 2a and 2b illustrate multimodality with the template and an example of the meme "One does not simply walk into Mordor," featuring a frame from Peter Jackson's 2002 film adaptation showing Sean Bean. Combining visual and textual elements allows for creative expression, including humor and political commentary, and relies significantly on background knowledge [2].

C2 Succinctness: Internet memes convey complex messages with simple language. The IM conciseness owes to the stratified semantics that include the original media frame, the template, a meme adaptation, and the background knowledge that constitutes the IMs' lore. According to [23], memes should be considered as examples of multimodal similes, not multimodal metaphors, since the source and the target domain are not blended but continue to be available as dissimilar, yet corresponding, domains.

C3 Relatability: Internet memes are recognizable by the members of a certain community. Figure 2c exemplifies the community associated with the IM "One does not simply

[4] https://edition.cnn.com/2024/05/30/europe/schiphol-airport-engine-death-scli-intl/index.html

[5] In Western culture, grandmas stereotypically overfeed their grandchildren.

walk into Mordor" as we used in our example "One does not simply analyse internet memes". The target audience of our IM is those who normally analyze data used for difficult tasks. Nonetheless, the IM results are clearer to those who have read the book and/or watched the movie.

Relatability is responsible for IMs fecundity [13], i.e., the ability of IMs to be reproduced in big numbers. Indeed, the IMs seem to trigger a sense of sympathy in the viewer, especially those who understand the lore. Thus, IMs can be powerful tools for social good, such as traumatic confessions [19] and coping mechanisms [24], but also vehicles for political propaganda [25] and hate speech [26]. A humorous and lightweight tone often supports relatability, but many other emotions can be involved. For instance, while Figure 2 does not pass a positive message, the expected reaction from a target viewer is positive and empathetic.

C4 Fluidity: IMs evolve rapidly as they circulate across various platforms and contexts. A study by Meta identified 121,605 different variants of a particular meme shared in 1.14 million status updates. A prominent example is the meme "One does not simply walk into Mordor," which demonstrates several variations in Figure 3. As they travel across communities, IMs mutate carrying (i) *community-specific slang*: the text and image are modified to include terminology or references unique to specific communities, making the meme more relatable and engaging for those groups. (ii) *extended lore*: the meme's setting or characters are reimagined or combined with elements from other fictional universes, such as placing the characters in a "Doctor Who" setting; (iii) *contextual visual changes*: modifications to the image or text align more closely with the context in which the meme is used, often enhancing its relevance or humor; (iv) *crossover revisions*: the meme is altered to include elements from entirely different sources, such as integrating Disney's logo, creating a new layer of meaning or humor.

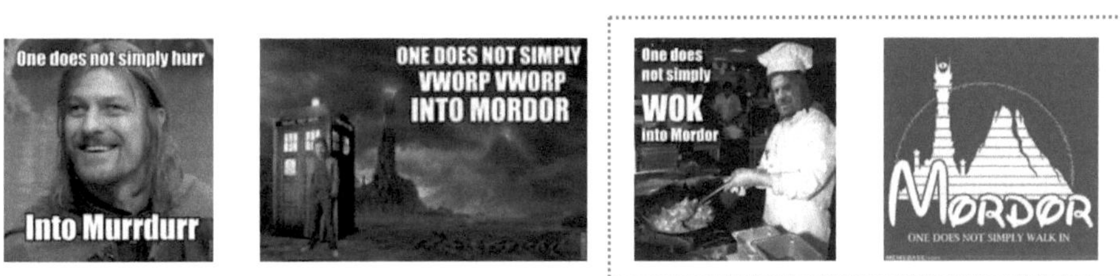

(i) (ii) (iii) (iv)

Figure 3. Examples of Variations and Succinctness (in red).

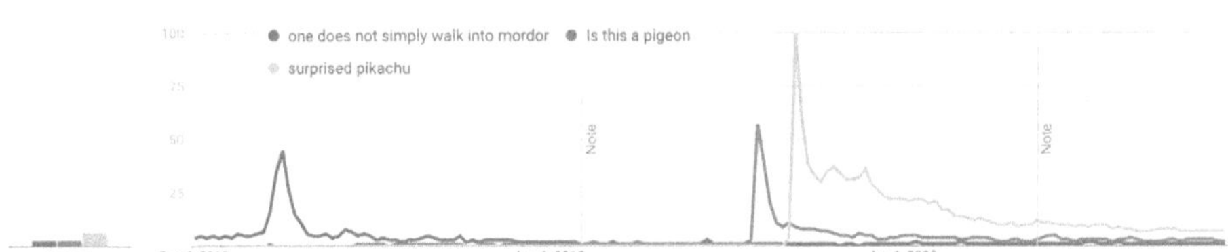

Figure 4. Popularity of three memes (search) in Google trends: One Does Not Simply Walk into Mordor (blue); Is this a pigeon (red); Surprised Pikachu (yellow).

C5 Virality: IMs, like any other content on the Web, follow a popularity lifecycle. What is peculiar about IMs is their spread and obsolescence velocity, contrasting the long-lasting nature of general memes theorized by Dawkins [13]. The challenge of virality for internet memes involves understanding what features contribute to their spread. Factors such as intended audience, specific tones (hateful, racist, political), emotions portrayed, presence of characters, and image scale can impact the virality of a meme [27]. Online communities may differ in their culture-specific indicators that influence IM virality. Figure 4 shows the popularity trends of three memes over time, highlighting their limited period of peak popularity.

Notably, these five IM characteristics are tightly connected: for example, fluidity combines with reliability, making IMs attractive for spreading across online communities. Relatability can impact multimodality because some communities are more present on social media networks with more video content than images.

2.3. Memes for Machines

The discussed properties of memes (multimodality, relatability, succinctness, fluidity, and virality; C1-C5) can be translated into research challenges for AI systems.

The *multimodality (**C1**)* of memes stems from the complex interplay between text and visual elements. While in some cases, the interplay relies on a mere surface connection between the two (Figure 5a), in other cases, this may depend on background knowledge (Figure 5b) or even a specific cultural perspective (Figure 5c). The different aspects of meaning captured between the meme modalities are probably most apparent from prior work on meme clustering, which deals with notions of identity, co-occurring events, and meme template similarity [28]. Meanwhile, recent research has shown that visual-language models (VLMs) show biases that affect their perception of small objects [8] and in the presence of more challenging distractors [9]. The challenges of multimodal models with reasoning over complex media are also apparent from abstract reasoning challenges. A recent study [11] has shown that the performance of VLMs on various abstract visual reasoning problems is consistently close to random. The underlying cause for such poor results lies in both weaknesses in perception and reasoning. Our ongoing research notes similar weaknesses for multimodal lateral thinking puzzles.

While human communication is broadly governed by pragmatic laws of providing the least possible amount of information [29], memes are remarkably *succinct* (**C2**) pack-

Figure 5. Example mysoginous memes. Meme a. can be interpreted as harmful based on surface cues, meme b. requires background knowledge about the identity of Anna Frank, and meme c.'s interpretation as hateful depends on knowledge about current events (e.g., the banning of burkas in Western Europe) and background knowledge about cultural perspectives and customs.

ages. Their interpretation relies heavily on background knowledge about identity (e.g., famous people depicted in a meme), current or historical events (e.g., the ongoing invasion in Gaza), figures of speech (e.g., structures of a typical dad joke), and recognizable media (e.g., movie scenes). Prior work has attempted to aggregate information about memes into comprehensive knowledge resources to bridge such gaps. One example is IMKG [12], which connects visual, textual, and meta-information extracted from meme templates with background knowledge about concepts and events from Wikidata, and with meme instances from a generation site. KnowMeme [30] builds a KG with external facts geared towards reasoning about hate speech. One can employ ConceptNet [31] instead, as done by the KERMIT method [32] to incorporate commonsense knowledge.

The *relatability (C3)* of memes is a critical factor that makes certain memes more appealing to a person than others. Can AI extract and connect meme information to people's personal and cultural values? As user profiles are challenging to study at scale, such research has typically been undertaken by researchers who connect AI with social and communication science techniques and theories. Shifman [3] discusses the role of memes as tools for expressing political commentary, social activism, and collective identity. Memes' relatability has been employed for toxic use cases targeting individuals, communities, and societies, employing misinformation, stereotyping, and cyberbullying [33]. The Hateful Meme Challenge [34] dataset has inspired a sizeable line of work in AI that attempts to design systems for detecting hateful memes. The systems adapted for this purpose range from neural [35,36] to neuro-symbolic [30,37] methods, and their focus includes both accuracy and explainability. A notable challenge with this task, owing to relatability, is the objective judgment of whether a meme is toxic [37,38]. This is illustrated by the memes on Figure 5, which become more dependent on knowledge and values when moving from left to right.

The meme *fluidity* (**C4**) is tightly connected to their relatable nature, but it also shows their potential as media for creative expression. As discussed before, meme variations may or may not follow the stance, content, form, or identities depicted in the original template. They may remix existing meme templates by combining any subset of these elements. Consequently, the fluidity of memes makes it challenging to connect meme instances to their template, to link novel templates to their origins, and to cluster meme instances based on their similarity [39].

AI can be designed to study how memes differ in terms of *virality* (**C5**), why some memes are more viral than others, and how this varies across time and locations. Virality refers to the phenomenon of gaining widespread popularity and extensive dissemination and can be measured in terms of speed of dissemination and breadth of audience reach [40]. Prior work has found that content evoking high-arousal emotions and personal relevance is a key factor for meme virality [41,42]. Moreover, memes that are humorous, simpler, and culturally aligned with their audience tend to have a better reach [3,43,44]. Data mining techniques inspired by epidemiological disease models can be used to trace the spread of popular memes [45]. Such studies have emphasized the importance of the network structure - namely, networks with high interconnectedness, activity levels, and presence of influencers tend to make memes more viral [46,47].

2.4. Layers of Meme Knowledge

According to Shifman, IMs have multiple memetic dimensions and should be group content units with common characteristics [20]. Such intuition suggested layered semantics

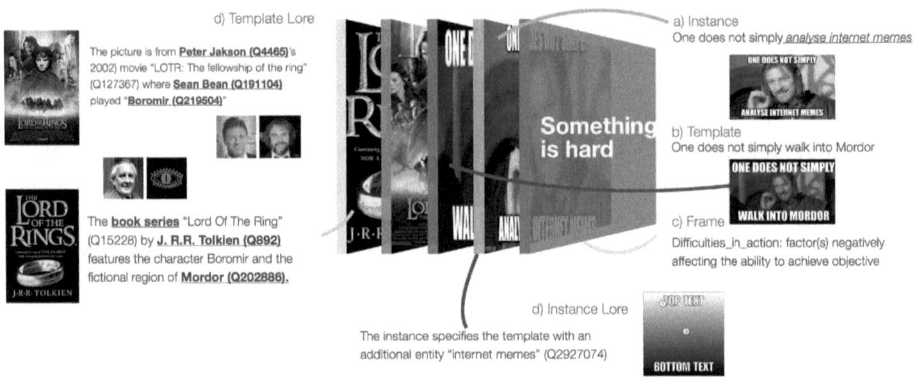

Figure 6. Dissection of an IM.

that span across the text (cf. intertextuality of the caption), the cultural background (lore), the semantic entities that populate it, the social context (online community) where the IMs are used, and the reference frames (as defined below).

Definition 4. *A frame is a schematic representation of a situation involving various participants, props, and other conceptual roles [48].*

Figure 6 shows such a stratification into four layers for the "One does not simply walk into Mordor" example. Intuitively, the extraction starts from the instance (a) "One does not simply *analyze internet memes*" that we introduced before. A first level of decomposition separates the template (b) from the snowclone. The application domain is *recursive* and concerns internet memes represented by the Wikidata entity (Q2927074). On the lore expansion, which can leverage visual and textual aspects, we can see entities from Peter Jackson (Q4465)'s 2002 Movie (Q127367), as pointed out in Section 2. The analysis of the snowclone and the characters also link to Sean Bean (Q191104) portraying Boromir (Q219504). Also, the book source of the book and related entities are listed respectively: the book series (Q15228), J. R.R. Tolkien (Q892), and Mordor (Q202886). Last, the stratification identified a reference frame *Difficulty in Action*. Namely, one can reuse the Lord of the Rings frame that symbolizes a futile undertaking [21] to express their perspective that analyzing memes is more complex than expected.

2.5. Sources of Internet Memes

Table 1 summarises the characteristics of different IM sources. It shows that open and high-quality information about IMs is available in IM encyclopedias and large KGs, while the information type varies across sources. For instance, lore is described in encyclopedias, and usage information is found in generators in social media.

Social Media. Large social content-sharing platforms, such as Reddit, 4chan, Instagram, Twitter, and Facebook, are the natural habitat for IMs and thus provide the largest sample. However, they are often restricted in their access, and they provide a platform not just for IMs, increasing required data curation efforts. Given the phenomenon's immense variety and velocity, obtaining metrics for precisely what fraction of the circulated content comprises IMs is challenging. Furthermore, these platforms seldom provide mean-

Table 1. Summary of Internet Meme Sources.

	Example	Open	Data Quality	Virality	Lore	Usage
Social Media	Reddit, Twitter	partially	low	yes	no	yes
Generators	ImgFlip	partially	medium	partially	no	yes
Encyclopedias	KYM	yes	high	yes	yes	partially
Large KGs	Wikidata	yes	high	no	partially	no

ingful information alongside the IM itself. These issues cumulatively render social media platforms insufficient for a comprehensive analysis.

Meme Generators. An essential aspect of IMs' virality is their accessibility to the general public: anybody is a content creator on the Web. Meme generators, e.g., ImgFlip, provide IM templates for users without requiring editing skills. *ImgFlip* is one of the most popular sites for meme generation, allowing users to quickly personalize one of the available meme templates using a custom caption. Moreover, registered users can vote and comment on the quality of the instantiated memes. ImgFlip organizes memes around templates, a blank version of the IM to be captioned. Users can also propose templates that others can adopt. Multiple templates may be derived from any original template, and many memes may be created based on each template.

Meme Encyclopedias are non-academic efforts dedicated to collecting and cataloging IMs. Analogous to how Wikipedia serves as a reference source for general world knowledge, these encyclopedias serve as references for memes. Meme encyclopedias aim to explain the underlying lore, identifying their origins, variations, usage, and sometimes even interpretations of their meaning. Like Wikipedia, IM encyclopedias are collaborative, relying on volunteers to provide information as unstructured and semi-structured text. *KnowYourMeme* (KYM) is a well-known collaborative encyclopedia with information about IMs and people and events relevant to IM understanding. KYM provides the most extensive and structured catalog of IMs and their lore, origin, and meaning.

Knowledge Graphs. The popularity of IMs has reached a level that KGs like Wikidata [49], DBpedia [50], and Freebase [51] provide a wealth of background knowledge about IMs and their described concepts. As such, these sources promise to provide implicit knowledge not offered in IMs or their metadata. Among the listed sources, Wikidata has been found to have the highest quality [52], owing to its crowd-sourcing approach, semantic validation mechanisms, and active contributor pool. Wikidata has nearly 1.5 billion statements about almost 100 million entities, with reliable links to thousands of other sources, including KYM. *Wikidata* is an open knowledge graph maintained by the Wikimedia Foundation. It includes the item internet memes (`Q2927074`), with a conceptualization that is sufficiently similar to ours, i.e., *concept that spreads from person to person via the Internet.* At the time of writing of [12], Wikidata included 556 instances of such classes, characterized by *977* unique properties, including both object properties (that connect a given IM to other entities) and datatype properties.

3. Meme Knowledge Curation

Several ontological and epistemological works have further debated the ultimate nature of IMs [53]. This section presents the first attempt to collect and curate meme knowledge systematically and semantically. The Internet Meme Knowledge Graph [12] is the first of

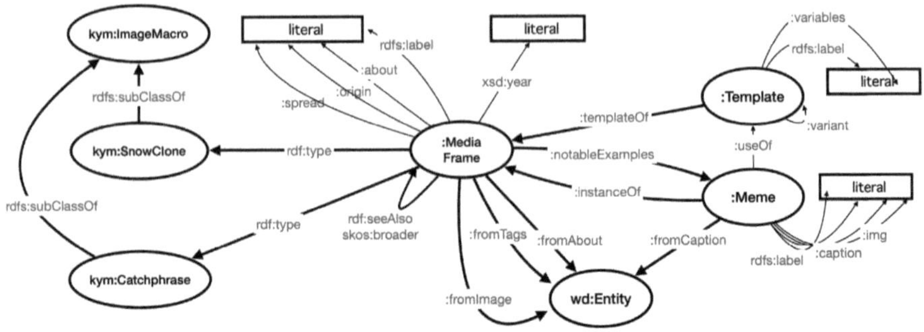

Figure 7. Data Model of IMKG from [12].

its genre as it links memes templates, instances, and related entities extracted from text and media. The resulting KG consists of over 2 million edges describing over 600K nodes collected from a popular meme encyclopedia (KnowYourMeme), a generation website (ImgFlip), and an open KG (Wikidata). This section provides information about IMKG's data model and construction.

3.1. Data Model

Following the principles for data integration [54], we designed a conceptual model to facilitate the lightweight compilation of IMs collected from the selected sources. Figure 7 shows the conceptual model of IMKG. At the heart of IMKG's model is the class `Media Frame`, defined as follows:

Definition 5. *A media frame is a multimedia object representing a "memeable" situation, i.e., one familiar to the creator and a broader community.*

For instance, the quote "One does not simply walk into Mordor" is a Media Frame that comes directly from the movie Lord of the Rings. Media Frames are instances of specific subclasses of Image macro, such as `kym:Catchphrase`, thus allowing the organization of IMs into a hierarchy. Media Frames are described in terms of their origin, spread, about, label, and year, and have connections to other media frames that are similar (`rdf:seeAlso`) or broader (`skos:broader`). Media Frames may refer to entities in their tags, about sections, or images.

Media frames can be adapted numerous times by a `Meme`. A Meme is, therefore, a notable example of a Media Frame. A Meme inherits the "about" section, tags, and the image but builds on top of them by adding a new caption. The entities associated with a Meme are those present in the caption. We also store a Meme's textual label, caption, and image URI as strings.

3.2. Construction

The construction of IMKG consists of four steps, as shown in Figure 8. We design a KG model that captures the semantics of internet memes, encompassing their multimodality, intended succinctness, relatability, fluidity, and virality. Next, we collect data from representative sources of internet memes, including encyclopedias, meme generation sites, and open large KGs. We then enrich the collected information using textual processing,

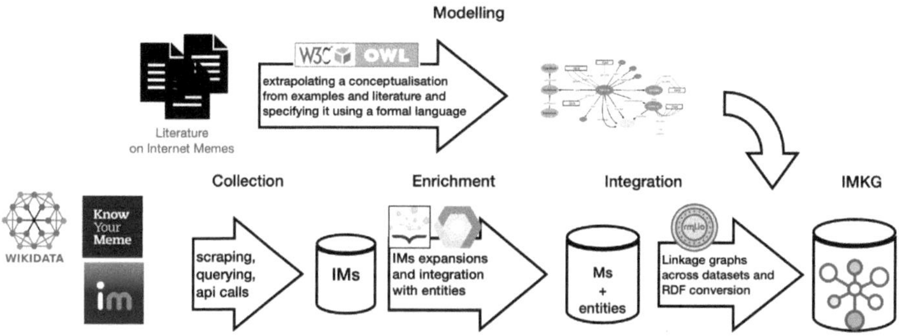

Figure 8. IMKG Construction Logical Pipeline.

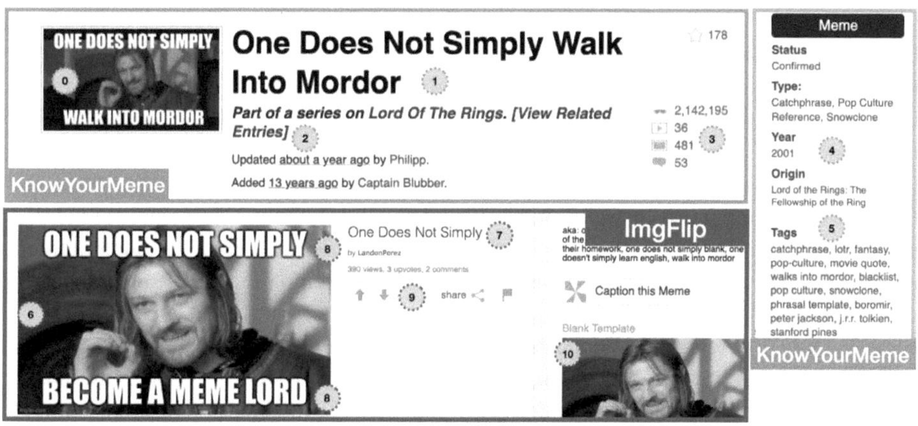

Figure 9. Snippet of information on KYM (red box) and ImgFlip (green box).

visual processing, and background knowledge. Finally, we integrate the extracted data according to the developed model using a schema mapping language, and we publish IMKG in both RDF and labeled property graph (LPG) formats.

Step 1: Data Modelling. We design an integrated conceptual model that can express key properties of IMs following data integration principles [54]. We scope the coverage of IMKG to **Image macros** (see Definition 1). The IMKG associates a Template with two literals: its label and the default number of captions (variable). For a Media Frame to be used, IM generators publish a captionable blank image to generate a Meme. In ImgFlip, the template base structure is set but modifiable, e.g., the On Does Not Simply[6] Template starts with two text boxes.

Step 2: Data Collection. We bootstrap the construction of IMKG starting from open large KGs like Wikidata and expanding onto IM generators (ImgFlip) and encyclopedias (KYM). We prioritize these sources over social media platforms since such platforms seldom provide meaningful information alongside the IMs. We denote the initial Wikidata IMs as *seeds* in the IMKG. As KYM lacks an API or a similar method for programmatically querying this data, we crawl the entire KYM website, starting from a particular

[6]https://imgflip.com/meme/One-Does-Not-Simply

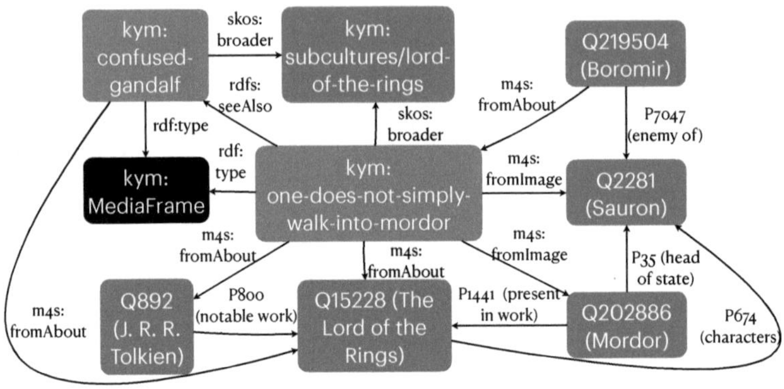

Figure 10. Enrichment example for *kym:one-does-not-simply-walk-into-mordor*.

IM page and following the links to other pages describing related memes. The scraping focuses on collecting the following information: media frame (note 0 in Figure 9), meme label (1), links to broader ("Part of a series on" section) and related ("View Related Entries") memes (2), popularity statistics (3), an infobox containing information about status, type, year, and origin of the meme (4), and the set of tags (5). Not shown in this figure, we also obtain the paragraphs describing a meme's about, origin, and spread. For each Meme from ImgFlip, we recorded the media (6), title, author, views, and comment counts (7), the captioning text (8), upvotes (9), and the Template ID (10), which can be used to reconstruct the template URI.

Step 3: Data Enrichment. We perform three different types of enrichment: 1. textual enrichment, by extracting and linking entities from media frame; 2. visual enrichment, by extracting entities from IM images by object detection; and 3. knowledge enrichment, by iteratively enriching information about memes and their entities with existing KGs.

We perform *textual enrichment* using DBpedia Spotlight [55]. Specifically, we extract entities from the paragraphs scraped from KYM, i.e., about, origin, and spread, and from the textual captions from ImgFlip. We filter out entities with confidence below 0.5. We map the resulting entities and entity types from DBpedia to Wikidata entities via the site links mapping file to maintain the usage of Wikidata as a central background resource. We also convert KYM tags to Wikidata entities following the same method.

We perform *visual enrichment* using the Google Vision API.[7] Given the cost of the service, we limit the extraction of objects to only the Media Frame image. The vision extraction tool detects objects and links them to Freebase. We map these entities to Wikidata by using the identifier property *P646*.

We perform two forms of *knowledge enrichment* using Wikidata. First, we obtain all information directly associated with the seed memes in Wikidata, i.e., we collect statements whose subject is one of the 556 seed memes. Second, we extract all Wikidata statements connecting two nodes (entities or memes) from the former enrichment steps. We use the Knowledge Graph Toolkit [56] to extract background knowledge about the meme seeds and entities from Wikidata.

An example snippet of an enriched graph for the media frame *kym:one-does-not-simply-walk-into-mordor* is shown in Figure 10. The figure shows that this enrichment

[7]`https://cloud.google.com/vision`

includes key entities such as Lord of the Rings, J.R.R. Tolkien, Mordor, Sauron, and Boromir, extracted from images or the About section in KnowYourMeme. The entities are tightly connected based on numerous Wikidata links, indicating, for instance, that Mordor is present in the work Lord of the Rings, created by Tolkien, that Boromir is the enemy of Sauron, and that Sauron is a character in Lord of the Rings. The figure also shows the effect of the data modeling, which allows us to connect similar media frames based on their broader subculture or explicit "rdfs:seeAlso" links in KnowYourMeme.

Step 4: Data Integration. We integrate the various datasets by establishing links across their entities. Specifically, we connect 276 memes in Wikidata and KYM via the property *P6760*. On the other hand, the linkage between KYM and ImgFlip, however, involves three steps. First, we extract all direct ImgFlip links mentioned within our KYM crawled data and manually select the most reliable connections. Next, we perform a string match between meme titles in both datasets, identifying about 60 matches with a similarity threshold of 85%. Finally, for the 276 seed IMs identified above, we manually map the Templates (from ImgFlip) to the corresponding Media Frame (from KYM). Notably, given the user-based nature of ImgFlip templates, this relationship is one-to-many; that is, a given Media Frame has many Templates, while a Template is assigned to one and only one Media Frame, e.g., *One does not simply Spiderman.*

Given that the data comes in various formats (e.g., crawled data in JSON, Wikidata in the KGTK TSV format [56]), we include a *data conversion* step using RML [57], a mapping language for KG construction. To support FAIR data management [58], we choose RDF as our data model and N-Triples as the data format. We implement a parallel conversion pipeline from various sources for scalability. For maintainability, we put significant effort into defining identifiers: whenever possible, we reuse those from Wikidata, ImgFlip, and KYM, and we avoid using blank nodes. In addition to RDF, we provide a property graph version of IMKG in the KGTK format for scalable analytics.

Pipeline Implementation. The IMKG pipeline depicted in Figure 11 is implemented using Apache Airflow and Docker. This pipeline facilitates data retrieval and quickly updates the Internet Meme Knowledge Graph. The pipeline consists of three parts: an ingestion area (blue) where ImgFlip and KYM scraping occur. Data is saved in files loaded in Postgres and mapped to RDF following the data model specification.

Enrichment and integration occur in the staging/wrangling area (red). Firstly, we conduct textual enrichment using DBpedia Spotlight by extracting entities from paragraphs obtained from KnowYourMeme and ImgFlip, such as the origin or description of memes. Subsequently, we associate the resulting entities and entity types from DBpedia with Wikidata entities using a link mapping file. Finally, we do visual enrichment using the Google Vision API. The vision extraction tool detects objects, people, or animals in images, and we link these entities to Wikidata using the identification property P646. Finally, the IMKG is served for queries using Virtuoso as a SPARQL endpoint (green).

4. Meme Similarity

4.1. Grounding Memes from the Web

As IMs permeate almost every corner of our online world, there is a need to understand the depth and breadth of their influence [59,2]. IMs' fluid and relatable nature are re-

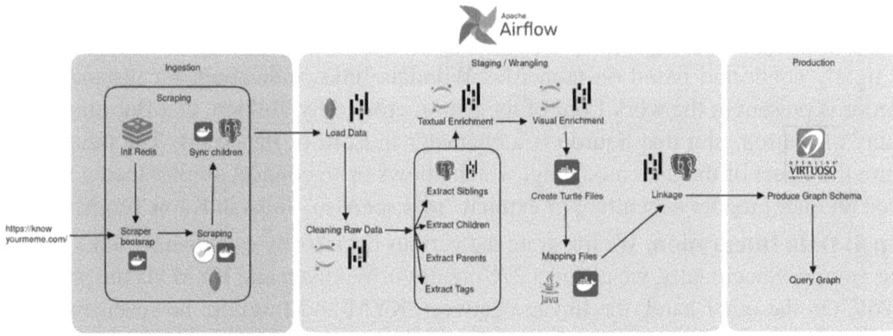

Figure 11. IMKG Construction Physical Pipeline.

flected in their widespread use across both mainstream and fringe platforms [60]. At the same time, their succinctness and multimodality make memes a challenging puzzle for state-of-the-art computational systems [12]. Can IMs across social media platforms be contextualized using a semantic knowledge repository, i.e., a knowledge graph?

In [28], we collected thousands of potential IM posts from two popular social media platforms, Reddit and Discord. These platforms were primarily chosen for their popularity: Reddit, with its vast user-generated content, serves as a primary hub for emerging memes [61], while Discord, accommodating millions of global users, offers unrestricted access to meme-rich interactions within its diverse while goal-driven community servers [62,63]. Another criterion for prioritizing these two platforms was their data accessibility via APIs and established libraries. Then, we performed an extract-transform-load procedure to create a data lake with candidate memes. After preliminary analysis, we identified five subreddits - `r/memes`, `r/meme`, `r/HistoryMemes`, `r/PoliticalMemes`, and `r/ProgrammerHumor`, as well as five Discord channels - `auto_memes_2`, `TheDungeon`, `meme_shitposting`, `MemeStash`, and `meme_stealing`, with the highest volume of shared meme content. We analyzed the media from these ten communities over one month (July 1 - 31, 2023).

At the same time, we leveraged IMKG's organization into Media Frames, Templates, and Meme Instances and their semantic relationships to systematically identify meme candidates from images sourced from Reddit and Discord. Specifically, we selected three instances of each template from IMKG as a representative sample. We encoded candidate memes from the social media platforms and the IMKG instances with a Vision Transformer (ViT) [64]. We opted for ViT because of its state-of-the-art performance in encoding images for various tasks. We leveraged FAISS for vector similarity search against the instances from IMKG. The encoded images from Discord and Reddit were used as queries against the FAISS index to determine whether they were memes or not. Namely, the images from Reddit and Discord that had a match in IMKG with sufficiently high visual similarity were considered to be memes, whereas the rest were classified as non-memes.

Our analysis revolved around four questions. First, can memes be effectively identified by mapping them to IMKG? Distinguishing memes from non-memes is often a subtle goal, mainly when the image contains a textual caption [65]. In practice, we evaluated several similarity thresholds to strike an optimal tradeoff between precision and recall. Due to the nature of the task, we favored high precision (over 0.9), which yielded a recall

Table 2. Distribution of **P**osts, **I**mage **P**osts, **M**eme **P**osts, and **M**eme to **I**mage **R**atio in Reddit subreddits and Discord channels.

Reddit					**Discord**				
Subreddit	**#P**	**#IP**	**#MP**	**#MIR**	**Channel**	**#P**	**#IP**	**#MP**	**#MIR**
r/meme	2794	2243	392	0.17	auto_memes_2	1679	1341	252	0.18
r/PoliticalMemes	716	653	53	0.08	meme_shitposting	926	611	22	0.03
r/HistoryMemes	1635	1414	237	0.16	TheDungeon	12044	6624	1184	0.17
r/ProgrammerHumor	901	626	151	0.24	meme_stealing	205	177	3	0.01
r/memes	7129	6561	1120	0.17	MemeStash	1131	1072	33	0.03
Total	**13175**	**11497**	**1953**	**0.16**	**Total**	**15985**	**9825**	**1494**	**0.15**

of between 0.6 and 0.7 for both platforms. Using the relatively simple procedure, we can detect two out of every three memes with nearly perfect precision.

Second, how prevalent are IMKG memes on Reddit and Discord, and which communities are most populated with memes? With the plethora of IMs distributed across these platforms, it is crucial to identify subreddits and channels that are richest in terms of memes. The distribution of the selected subreddit and Discord channel posts, as well as those with an image (i.e., *image posts*), is presented in Table 2. Overall, we note that the number of identified memes is comparable over the two platforms. Discord has a higher number of overall posts, but the number of image posts within those is lower. Regarding specific communities, over half of the memes in the Reddit collection came from the subreddit `r/memes`, and over half of the Discord memes came from the channel `TheDungeon`. The highest relative yield of memes was observed for the `r/ProgrammerHumor` subreddit, for which 24% of the images are identified as memes. This quick investigation showcased how IMKG can quickly identify thousands of memes with high precision.

Third, which memes are most popular on Reddit and Discord? Popular memes can illuminate topics and themes that resonate within online user communities, enabling us to decode their shared interests and sentiments. Interestingly, we noticed that 4 of the top 5 memes, namely *Drake-Hotline-Bling*, *Afraid-To-Ask-Andy*, *Press-button-hard-choice*, and *undertaker*, were shared on both platforms. These popular memes show what has been trending in the digital meme world in July 2023, which can be helpful for marketers, researchers, and regular users, and it demonstrates the high overlap between the trends on these two platforms. For three of these memes, Figure 12 provides examples of two of their instances from both Reddit and Discord, as well as an example corresponding meme found in IMKG, showing high relatability through the width of situations expressing the same idea. Our choice to match memes based on visual features was underpinned by the objective of bridging the gap between different instances of the same meme template, highlighting these visual media's universal appeal and adaptability.

Fourth, we investigated how IMKG could aid a more refined comprehension of meme culture. We examined the "Disloyal Boyfriend" memes sourced from platforms such as Reddit and Discord utilizing IMKG, emphasizing its utility in structuring and understanding these memes (see Figure 13). The media frame in IMKG enables access to encyclopedic information from KYM, such as a general "about" description, "origin" as an exhaustive chronicle of the meme's inception and evolution, and tags like "disloyal man with his girlfriend looking at another girl". The integration of this data into IMKG, from sources like KnowYourMeme and ImgFlip, along with Wikidata entities extracted from the image (`m4s:fromImage`), from the instance captions (`m4s:fromCaption`), and

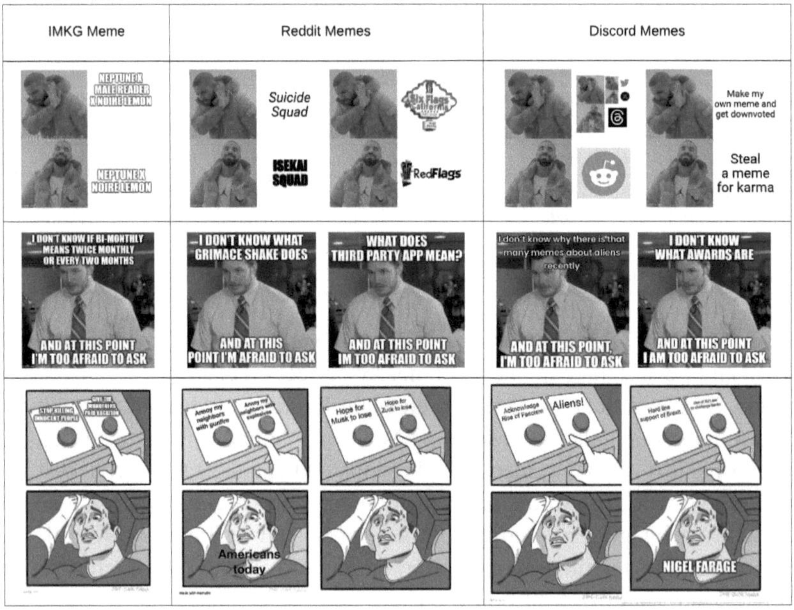

Figure 12. Mapping between IMKG, Reddit, and Discord for three popular memes: *Drake-Hotline-Bling*, *Afraid-To-Ask-Andy*, and *Press-button-hard-choice*.

from the description (`m4s:fromAbout`), demonstrates the structured approach of IMKG in connecting memes to a broad spectrum of world knowledge. The meme instances are associated with several pieces of information, including their alternative text, for easy access to the caption. This direct linkage between meme templates, their originating contexts, and subsequent variations underscores IMKG's comprehensive framework for IM analysis.

Next to IMKG's promise to contextualize social media memes in terms of existing memes and world knowledge, we also noted three drawbacks of its current version. First, the figure's dotted line connecting the template and the media frame underscores a standing challenge of entity resolution in IMKG, where specific templates are not formally linked to their media frame. Second, while we note that IMKG provides useful information highlighted through our manual summary in the yellow box for supporting social media meme interpretation, this detailed interpretation emerges from our focused examination of IMKG's structure rather than being an inherent feature of the graph. Specifically, this involves selectively examining relevant subgraphs within IMKG to facilitate a more manageable and insightful analysis. This approach underscores the necessity of navigating IMKG's complexity through targeted knowledge selection, which is critical for distilling meaningful insights from the vast array of data. Such a targeted exploration is essential for effectively utilizing IMKG to comprehend memes' multifaceted nature, cultural significance, and evolution over time. Third, the dynamic nature of meme culture, with new memes emerging daily, presents an additional challenge, as these will not be immediately present in IMKG, potentially limiting the methodology's ability to capture the most recent trends. Future work must address these challenges to make IMKG and related resources more effective for meme contextualization.

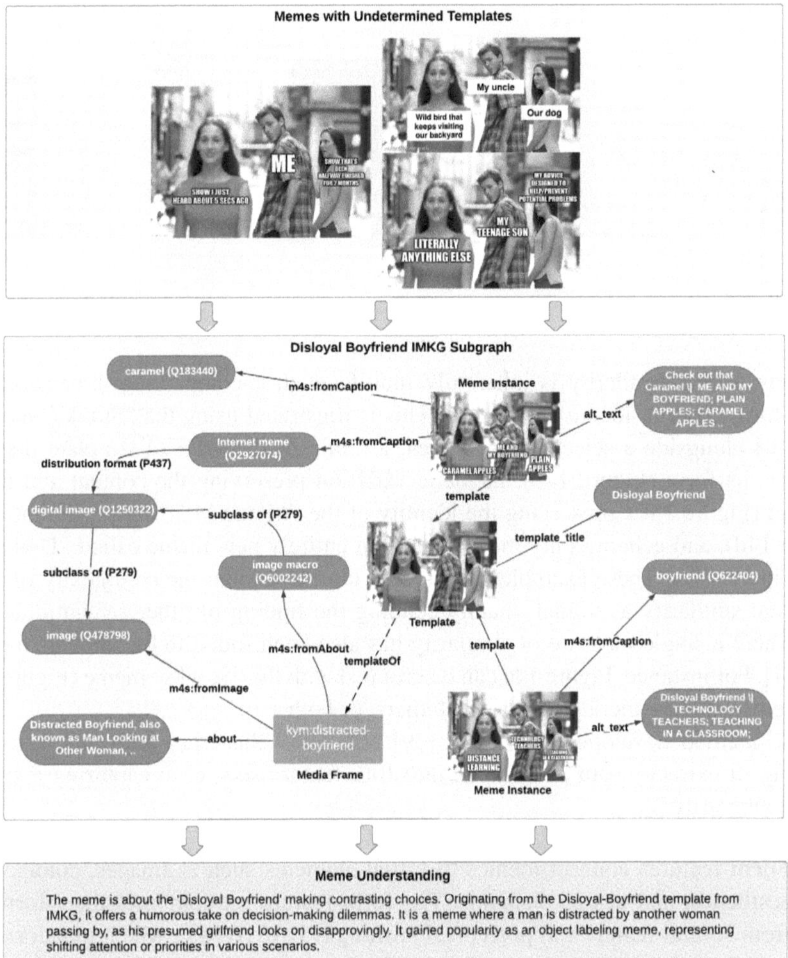

Figure 13. IM contextualization using the IMKG knowledge, illustrated on the Disloyal Boyfriend meme.

4.2. *Dimensional Similarity of Memes*

The previous section assumed that memes can be matched to other memes based on visual appearance. This similarity measure based on visual correspondence is typically considered the single goal behind the similarity matching of memes. Such an assumption is inherent to both template-based matching (such as the one in the previous section) and bottom-up clustering methods (using feature extraction) [66,60], which assume a single decision on whether two memes are matched. Recent work by Bloem [39] challenges this assumption, starting from the observation that, in practice, memes frequently defy strict template boundaries. New variants regularly emerge, which may borrow elements from other memes, mimic them, remix multiple memes, or repurpose images in a novel context. This requires novel evaluation and solution methods to deal with heterogeneity beyond near-duplicates.

(a) Original (b) Form (c) Content (d) Identity (e) Stance

Figure 14. The "Stonks" meme and four variations of it related via form, content, identity, and stance.

Thus, meme similarity is inherently multifaceted, encompassing dimensions like shared form content, identity, or stance. This is illustrated using the "Stonks" meme in Figure 14 alongside a selection of memes: a remix of the original template that only preserves its form (Figure 14b), memetic variation preserving the content and mostly the form (Figure 14c), preserving the identity of the "Meme Man" in a different meme (Figure 14d), and echoing only the stance in an entirely new meme called "Drakeposting" (Figure 14e). These examples provide an intuition about the complexity of defining meme similarity as a goal, mainly echoing the finding of other semantic analysis areas where a single measure of similarity has also been found to be an oversimplified goal [67]. For instance, Figure 14c can be grouped with the "Stonks" meme (Figure 14a), with memes about America's founding fathers, or both.

The method developed by Bloem [39] combines clustering with template-based matching. It extracts features grouped into four feature sets, each capturing a specific facet of similarity:

1. **Form** features connect memes to visual elements such as images, colors, fonts, aesthetics, and design elements. The form feature set combines the information from several features: a) perceptual hashing (PHASH) [68], which transforms images into 8x8 grayscale matrices to focus on the visual structure of an image quickly; b) color histograms, capturing color density in the HSV space, thus complementing the PHASH grayscale information; and c) speeded-up robust features (SURF) [69], which uses Hessian matrix detector to identify points of interest with significant intensity variations, such as corners, blobs, or edges. SURF is particularly effective for small and distinctive elements such as specific characters, gestures, or logos.
2. **Visual** content features capture the overall image by segmenting it into patches and applying the ViT method.
3. **Textual** features aim to capture similar captions, such as catchphrases and snowcones. To embed textual features, Bloem leverages BERT [70] to embed the captions but assigns greater weight to bigrams that occur at least twice in the meme dataset.
4. **Identity** features aim to capture similarity in terms of memes using the same real individuals or fictional characters. For this purpose, the face landmark features are being used, implemented using a ResNet-based deep convolutional neural network.

Bloem constructs adjacency matrices per feature set and a combined adjacency matrix that combines the information from all feature sets to assess similarity. Aligning these matrices enables targeted analysis of specific similarity dimensions and the forming of robust clusters that simultaneously encompass multiple dimensions. The combined feature set is used to identify near-duplicates. To do so, the combined matrix is filtered and translated into a graph structure, after which a Louvain clustering method for community detection is applied. The identified clusters act as templates. The available memes are matched against these templates using the desired (combination of) feature sets. Each meme image is allocated to the most similar cluster iteratively and receives a similarity rank, thus enabling a tradeoff between cluster coherence and the number of memes clustered.

To evaluate the developed modular method, this paper relies on carefully designed human evaluation studies featuring two tasks: imposter identification among clustered images and assessing the quality of the clusters directly as a function of the clustering ranks. The human annotators are also randomly prompted to indicate how the memes are related: by form, visual content, text, or identity. Moreover, KnowYourMeme provides a set of clusters that can be evaluated against the proposed method, with the caveat that the motivations behind which memes are clustered are opaque.

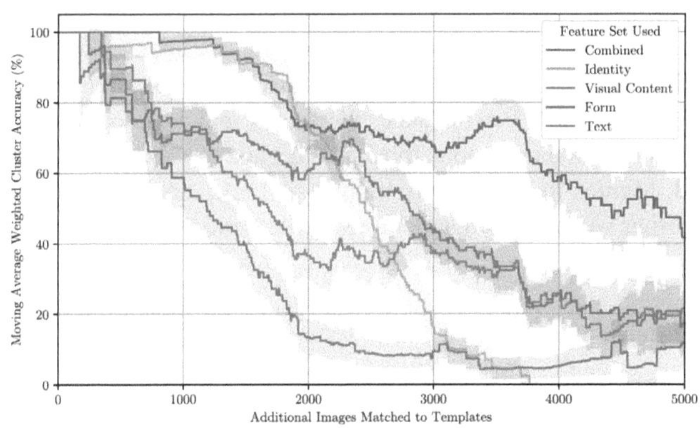

Figure 15. Moving average accuracy of image matching using various feature sets. At each increment of images, the average is estimated over all clusters with that many images matched or fewer, using a rolling window of 1500.

As anticipated, the clustering accuracy is the highest for the images with lower ranks (higher overall similarity) and declines gradually as the cluster memberships grow. The coherence results are better than those of standard clustering; compared to ViT, they are higher for mid-range similarities but lower for low-range similarities. However, comparing the derived clusters to those from KnowYourMeme shows that the combined method outperforms the ViT method, which only produces visual features. This difference is especially notable when clusters are more extensive, contrary to the previous result.

The evaluation of different feature sets (Figure 15) shows that combining the features consistently yields the best or second-best accuracy, confirming the benefits of multi-faceted similarity integration. Clustering based on identity only performs well for the first 2000 (out of 11000) memes. This finding results from the binary nature of identity, where the only exceptions are group photos where the identity matching can be partial. The

Figure 16. Identified template for "WAT Grandma" and matches through the four feature dimensions.

impact of form features is also curious, with the performance dropping quickly before stabilizing somewhat and then declining again. Such trends highlight the limitations of matching memes solely on form. As can be expected, the least effective features are the textual ones, as only a small portion of the dataset relies on textual elements like catchphrases.

Conversely, a benefit of this method is that it can retrieve similar memes based on particular dimensions. This is illustrated in Figure 16 for the "WAT Grandma" meme. Here, the visual features retrieve memes that mostly look similar but do not capture the core semantics of the template. The identity feature set retrieves other memes that depict the same woman, even if they deviate from the original meme form. Textual features link this meme to others that use the "what" caption. Besides tailoring the retrieval to the similarity dimension of interest, this analysis also shows how combining features can bring the best of all worlds. For instance, the fourth match based on the form features will be prioritized over the erroneous third match once the text and identity features are also considered. Memes that only rank high in a single dimension remain challenging and motivate further work, likely using more explicit and elaborate reasoning.

5. Detecting Hateful Memes

While IMs are often perceived as mere entertainment, internet memes have also been a critical "weapon" in the digital debates. Namely, due to their scale and relatability, they can be used to express concise messages about various geo-political events and social issues [6,71,72,73]. In such a context, toxic memes may harm individuals, organizations, or entire communities, raising the importance of detecting harmful and hateful memes. Harm is a broad category that includes mental abuse, defamation, psycho-physiological injury, proprietary damage, emotional disturbance, and compromised public image [74].

Risks associated with toxic memes include violence in the public discourse, public manipulation, psychological impacts, and material-world effects [38]. Detecting toxic content is traditionally done by content moderators, who may decide to remove, flag, or demote offensive content to a particular target. Inaccurate classification of memes by moderators may lead to inadequate interventions (e.g., removal), which may cause a further decrease in public trust in social media platforms and moderation policies. On the one hand, moderators may react late, inconsistently, or unfairly, thus angering users [75] and potentially reinforcing conspiratorial narratives [76,72]. On the other hand, minimal moderation may permit coordinated influence operations [77] or enable the formation of toxic communities, such as the Manosphere [78].

Considering the scale and complexity of internet memes, their moderation requires machine-augmented methods for tracking and toxicity classification. Consequently, automated approaches for meme toxicity classification have been gaining popularity [38]. This has been driven by the recent introduction of over 30 popular tasks for meme toxicity, the most popular ones being the Hateful Memes Challenge [18], the Misogyny Identification task (MAMI) [79], and HatReD [80]. Enabled by parallel advancements in multimodal representation learning, various methods have been developed based on neural networks and later using Transformer models [81]. Recent advances in large language and vision models have inspired researchers to consider applying these models to interpreting internet memes. The original benchmark paper of the Hateful Memes Challenge reported that the multimodal models ViLBERT [82] and VisualBERT [83] performed highly competitively on this task. More recently, prompting approaches were introduced, with the general idea of performing this task without adaptation or retraining of the models. For example, PromptHate [84] combines prompts with a pre-trained RoBERTa language model, whereas Ji et al. [85] demonstrate how using a prompt-based model on its own can achieve state-of-the-art performance.

These methods show promising performance, but their black-box design hinders end users' trust. Considering the complex interplay between text, vision, background knowledge, and culture in memes, it is important to develop methods with a native ability to explain or justify their decisions. This section provides a deep dive into two methods for explainable classification of hate speech in memes: a case-based reasoning method representing interpretable machine learning and a modular VLM approach. For both methods, we describe their motivation, design, and experimental results, highlighting their strengths and weaknesses. Then, we provide further analysis of the models' granular performance on different partitions of the hate speech task, split based on the meme target and whether the meme contains political content. The section concludes with a discussion of existing gaps and open research directions.

5.1. Case-based Reasoning over Internet Memes

In Thakur et al. [2], we designed a modular framework for the interpretable classification of IMs (Figure 17). This framework supports two case-based reasoning (CBR) methods: example- and prototype-based. Example-based classification [86] retrieves training examples that have a similar representation to the test example from the model's point of view, thus providing a proxy for the model behavior. Conversely, prototype-based classification is based on the prototype theory [87], which dictates that any concept has a real-world example that best represents it (*prototype*). The other concepts belong to a conceptual category to some extent, some closer to the prototype than others. The prototype-based classification relies on learning label-wise prototypes from the training dataset followed by a rule-based decision algorithm for the classification, which makes these models inherently interpretable. Specifically, we adopted the xDNN method, which learns classwise prototypes, formalized as local peaks for class distribution representing the data points near the prototype. The decision-making consists of two steps: *(i) local (per class) decision making:* finding the classwise prototype with the highest similarity, *(ii) global decision making:* comparing the best prototypes across all the classes and choosing the one with the highest similarity to decide the final label. Notably, the explanations of the example-based method are extracted post hoc, whereas the explanations of the

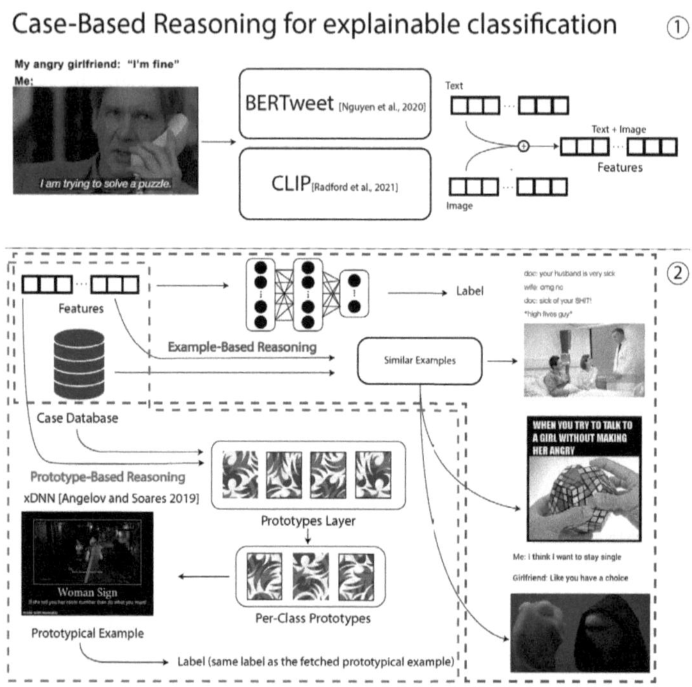

Figure 17. Interpretable framework from [2] with two steps: feature extraction (1) and case-based reasoning (2). The framework supports two CBR variants: example-based (shown in blue) and prototype-based (in red).

prototype-based method are inherent to the decision-making model. We compare these two methods because there is some controversy over the superiority of one over the other, with claims that prototypical examples are more effective [88] and vice versa [89].

Both CBR methods utilize a frozen pre-trained model to extract features from a meme in a transfer learning setup. In [2], we experimented with textual models (BERT and BERTweet [90]), multimodal models (CLIP [91]), and their combination. We included BERTTweet because we hypothesize that it will enable understanding of slang, which is prominent in meme captions. CLIP was chosen because of its reported high performance on various tasks in a zero-shot setting. The final step of the framework is a classification model (feed-forward neural network), which makes the ultimate decision.

The evaluation of this framework on the tasks of hateful memes and misogyny detection reveals the following findings: 1) misogyny detection is an easier task for all of the models, likely because it is more constrained and easier to specialize than the more general challenge of hateful memes; 2) example-based methods, albeit simpler, generally perform better than their prototype-based counterparts, which may be because prototype-based methods are generally challenging to optimize [92]; 3) the best combination of feature extractors is the one combining CLIP and BERTTweet, which is intuitive, because this model covers both the visual and the textual modality, while also accounting for slang. To analyze the model behavior in more detail, we designed a user interface that visualizes the three closest examples according to each model. Figure 18 visualizes nearest neighbors for a meme according to example-based classification with various feature extractors. The meme to be classified is misogynous, indicating a stereotype against women of being unnecessarily complex. The combined model and CLIP can combine

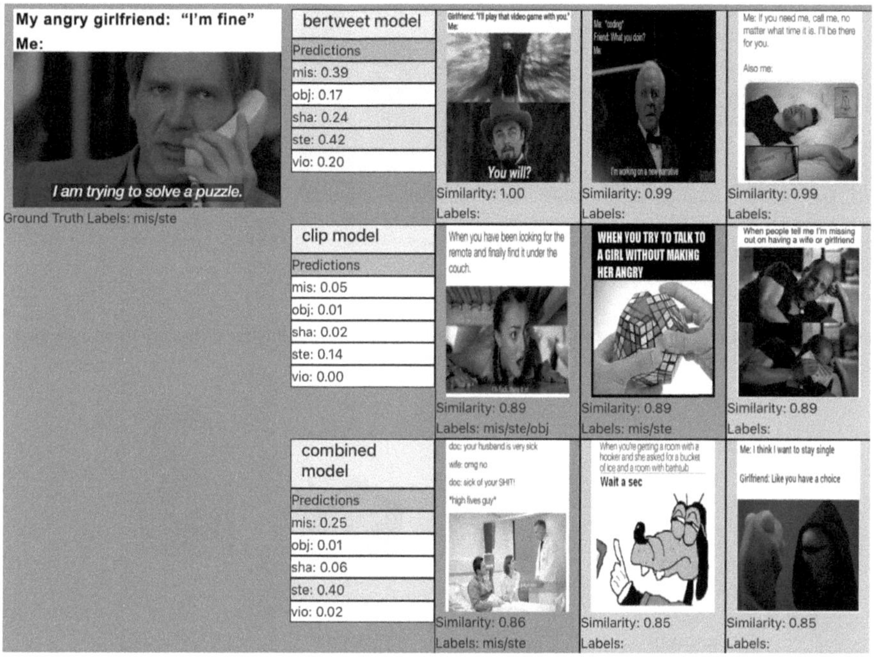

Figure 18. User interface visualizing the nearest neighbors for a meme according to example-based classification with various feature extractors. Green stands for a non-misogynous meme, and red stands for a misogynous meme. The other labels refer to objectification (obj), shaming (sha), stereotyping (set), and violence (vio).

textual and visual information and retrieve memes that have a similar stance. However, the predictions are more aligned with the ground truth labels in the case of the combined model. The BERTTweet model retrieves three non-misogynous memes that refer to similar topics (e.g., a game) but miss the essence of the meme. Looking closer into the prototype-based classification, we observed that this model learned a prototype for every meme in the training set. This confirms that further engineering work is needed to optimize this IM method.

5.2. Hate Detection using Explicit Descriptions

As discussed before, a downside of end-to-end neural methods is that their classification outcomes are challenging to interpret. In a typical architecture, the image and meme text are embedded separately and fed into a classification model. In recent work, Kaya [93] investigated the impact of describing the image with a separate model (BLIP-2) on the final classification. In this approach, the extracted description is embedded as part of the textual features and only then combined with the visual features. While this is a relatively minor change in the models, it provides an entrance to analyze model performance as a function of the description (caption) quality. The intuition of this method is shown in Figure 19.

The results of this initial evaluation indicate no noticeable differences between the test accuracy with and without using descriptions. Namely, the test accuracy and AUROC scores increase for the BERT-based text encoder and decrease for the RoBERTa-based encoder. To analyze the relation between the caption quality and the downstream

Figure 19. Intuition of adding explicit descriptions of meme images, illustrated through three examples.

	1	2	3
Image:			
Text	"Alabama sperm react to new anti-abortion law"	"c-c-c mon Morty ! we g- got to *burp* we have to solve income inequality ! Wubbaluba dubdub ! feel the Bern ! "	"you can't hate jews if there's no more jews"
Dataset:	Harm-P	MultiOFF	Hateful Memes
Ground truth label:	Harmful	Harmful	Harmful
CLIP label:	Non-Harmful	Non-Harmful	Harmful
Gemini label:	Non-Harmful	Non-Harmful	Harmful

Figure 20. Three examples of hateful memes: two political and one non-political one.

performance trends, Kaya uses a Likert scale, concluding a nearly balanced split between the labels: not useful at all, moderately useful, and very useful. A particularly misleading aspect is identity: a meme with Angela Merkel is merely captioned with "a woman with a funny expression on her face," thus hindering the model from reaching the correct interpretation. Conversely, a meme described as "a woman holding a monkey on a chain" enables the classification model to reason over the meme text "Mr. Obama, it is an honor" and classify it as hateful. Thus, while adding high-quality descriptions can be expected to improve model performance, state-of-the-art descriptions often lack essential details, which may not help and possibly may mislead the downstream decision-making method.

5.3. Granular Model Performance

Existing datasets for hateful meme classification provide further opportunities to analyze model performance. Szumski [94] samples two partitions from the existing datasets: political and non-political memes. The assumption in this work is that political memes will be more challenging for VLMs than non-political memes, which is evaluated for the CLIP [95] encoder model and the Gemini 1.5 [96] decoder model. In the CLIP pipeline, the text and the visual inputs are encoded separately and then combined into a 2x2 matrix, ultimately fed into a Softmax layer. The Gemini pipeline is more straightforward:

the image and the text are used to construct a prompt, which is used to generate an output by the Gemini model using the Open AI API. Both models were tested in a zero-shot setting to address the dynamic nature of internet memes. The Gemini model was tested in two settings: with and without providing an explicit definition of hatefulness.

The results show that CLIP and the two versions of Gemini perform significantly better on non-political memes than on political memes. Furthermore, Gemini's performance increases when the definition of hatefulness is explicitly stated. Examples of these phenomena for three hateful memes are provided in Figure 20. The first two memes are political and incorrectly classified as non-hateful, presumably because their interpretation requires a greater nuance. The first meme, for instance, shows President Trump celebrating, which is hateful in the context of him securing a majority in the Supreme Court through three of his nominees to overturn the Roe v. Wade decision. In contrast, the third meme is already strongly suggested to be hateful through its inclusion of words like 'hate' and 'Jews' next to each other, together with suggestions of elimination of this demographic. These examples illustrate that political memes often require more subtle reasoning to be classified as hateful or non-hateful.

Szumski further analyzed the model performance on four target granularities: individuals (e.g., Joe Biden), organizations (e.g., the U.S. federal government), communities (e.g., the republican party), and societies (e.g., police). Here, CLIP's performance has a clear trend: it encounters the greatest difficulty in identifying hateful content of individuals (29% accuracy), whereas its performance grows steadily for broader societal groups, reaching up to 55% accuracy for the society target. The trends for Gemini are nearly identical, with the organizations and community targets being progressively more challenging than individuals, except that the largest group (society) performs similarly to the individual targets. The explanation for these observations is that reasoning about individuals or smaller groups requires more precise information, possibly including a specific context or personal details. Broader targets may be attacked based on stereotypes, which may be more generalizable. Further analysis of these labels supports these hypotheses. Still, it also reveals a limitation in the annotation of ground truth data, where many of the hatefulness labels may be subjective, echoing the challenge raised by Thakur et al. [2].

6. Open Challenges

This chapter reviewed state-of-the-art methods for knowledge engineering, similarity estimation, and hate speech classification of IMs. The chapter shows that the goal of capturing meme semantics has been receiving increasing attention, resulting in valuable benchmarks, knowledge resources, and methods. At the same time, achieving reliable performance towards these goals remains well beyond state-of-the-art ability. We list three critical challenges for future work on capturing the semantics of memes by AI, ideally in collaboration with experts in social science, linguistics, and philosophy:

1. **Systematic Evaluation.** Benchmarks that evaluate meme classification have been instrumental in developing methods. These benchmarks have been initially designed to perform end-to-end toxicity classification using 2-5 labels. However, these benchmarks report low inter-annotator agreements, suggesting that the end-to-end task is largely subjective. Recent benchmarks address this by including finer-grained objectives, such as specific targets [74] and rationales [80]. We en-

vision this trend will continue and result in comprehensive benchmarks for systematically evaluating meme methods. Such benchmarks should distinguish, for example, between a) cases where harmfulness can be deduced from the surface form of the image or the text, b) cases where the textual and vision modality need to be connected with common knowledge, and c) cases where the classification of the meme depends strongly on personal or cultural values. The analysis should capture the dimensions of intent, tactic, and target beyond the toxic meme. Finally, it is important to generalize such a systematic evaluation across many other meme toxicity tasks organized in [38], including disinformation, exploitation, and propaganda.

2. **Comprehensive Knowledge.** Existing knowledge sources that describe internet memes, including IMKG [12] and KYMKB [97], cover a relatively large collection of memes. However, their knowledge focuses on surface features (e.g., entities extracted from text, vision, and metadata), lacking information about concurrent events, common sense, and stance considerations. More broadly, existing work in AI rarely considers harmful speech about moral values and culture [98]. Going beyond the state-of-the-art, we plan to develop resources that connect these dots. Building on the data and leveraging the experience from IMKG, future work will create new resources that can suit hateful meme classification. Such resources must qualify knowledge of cultural tendencies and personal moral values, following existing theories such as the Moral Foundation Theory [99] and frameworks such as Social Chemistry 101 [100]. Moreover, the knowledge representation must be grounded in cognitive theories about framing, analogies, and metaphors [101,102, 103].
3. **Effective and Expressive Reasoning.** Existing benchmarks focus on end-to-end meme classification into coarse labels and have thus inspired black-box methods whose comprehension of internet memes is hard to estimate. A crucial future direction is to devise neuro-symbolic methods that leverage the latest advances in neural processing of perceptual multimodal media but enrich them with reasoning components to enable consistency, explainability, and abstraction. Recent surveys on neuro-symbolic reasoning in the visual domain [7] and neuro-symbolic methods such as Alpha Geometry [104], the LLM sandwich [105], Logic-LM [106], and belief graphs [107] provide an opening for novel and integrated architectures for multimodal and granular reasoning over internet memes. A recent method by Grasso et al. [32] provides an initial attempt to include commonsense knowledge from ConceptNet [31] into internet memes, aiming to capture broad cultural expectations. Integrated architectures that combine state-of-the-art knowledge engineering, reasoning methods, and multimodal representation learning may bridge the gaps between these promising methods.

References

[1] Davison P. In: The Language of Internet Memes. New York University Press; 2012. p. 120–134.
[2] Thakur AK, Ilievski F, Sandlin HÂ, Mermoud A, Sourati Z, Luceri L, et al. Multimodal and explainable internet meme classification. NeSy. 2023.
[3] Shifman L. Memes in a digital world: Reconciling with a conceptual troublemaker. Journal of computer-mediated communication. 2013;18(3):362-77.

[4] Shifman L. Internet memes and the twofold articulation of values. Society and the internet: How networks of information and communication are changing our lives. 2019:43-57.
[5] Teng H, Lo CF, Lee HH. How do internet memes affect brand image? Online Information Review. 2022;46(2):304-18.
[6] Pierri F, Luceri L, Ferrara E. How Does Twitter Account Moderation Work? Dynamics of Account Creation and Suspension During Major Geopolitical Events. arXiv preprint arXiv:220907614. 2022.
[7] Khan MJ, Ilievski F, Breslin JG, Curry E. A survey of neurosymbolic visual reasoning with scene graphs and common sense knowledge. Neurosymbolic Artificial Intelligence. 2024;(Preprint):1-24.
[8] Zhang J, Khayatkhoei M, Chhikara P, Ilievski F. Visual cropping improves zero-shot question answering of multimodal large language models. arXiv preprint arXiv:231016033. 2023.
[9] Zhang J, Hu J, Khayatkhoei M, Ilievski F, Sun M. Exploring perceptual limitation of multimodal large language models. arXiv preprint arXiv:240207384. 2024.
[10] Liang PP, Zadeh A, Morency L. Foundations and Recent Trends in Multimodal Machine Learning: Principles, Challenges, and Open Questions. CoRR. 2022;abs/2209.03430. Available from: `https://doi.org/10.48550/arXiv.2209.03430`.
[11] Jiang Y, Zhang J, Sun K, Sourati Z, Ahrabian K, Ma K, et al. MARVEL: Multidimensional Abstraction and Reasoning through Visual Evaluation and Learning. arXiv preprint arXiv:240413591. 2024.
[12] Tommasini R, Ilievski F, Wijesiriwardene T. IMKG: The internet meme knowledge graph. In: European Semantic Web Conference. Springer; 2023. p. 354-71.
[13] Dawkins R. The Selfish Gene. Oxford University Press; 1976.
[14] Blackmore SJ. The Meme Machine. Oxford University Press; 1999.
[15] McNamara A. Can we measure memes? Frontiers in evolutionary neuroscience. 2011;3:1.
[16] Cavalli-Sforza LL, Feldman MW. Cultural transmission and evolution: A quantitative approach. 16. Princeton University Press; 1981.
[17] Nieubuurt JT. Internet Memes: Leaflet Propaganda of the Digital Age. Frontiers in Communication. 2021;5:116. Available from: `https://www.frontiersin.org/article/10.3389/fcomm.2020.547065`.
[18] Kiela D, Firooz H, Mohan A, Goswami V, Singh A, Ringshia P, et al.. The Hateful Memes Challenge: Detecting Hate Speech in Multimodal Memes; 2021.
[19] Vickery JR. The curious case of Confession Bear: the reappropriation of online macro-image memes. Information, Communication & Society. 2014;17(3):301-25. Available from: `https://doi.org/10.1080/1369118X.2013.871056`.
[20] Shifman L. Memes in a digital world: Reconciling with a conceptual troublemaker. Journal of computer-mediated communication: JCMC. 2013;18(3):362–377.
[21] Dancygier B, Vandelanotte L. Internet memes as multimodal constructions. Cognitive Linguistics. 2017;28(3):1515 –2017–0074.
[22] Zenner E, Geeraerts D. In: Winter-Froemel E, Thaler V, editors. One does not simply process memes: Image macros as multimodal constructions. De Gruyter; 2018. p. 167–194.
[23] Lou A. Multimodal simile: The "when" meme in social media discourse. English Text Construction. 2017;10(1):106-31.
[24] Akram U, Irvine K, Allen SF, Stevenson JC, Ellis JG, Drabble J. Internet memes related to the COVID-19 pandemic as a potential coping mechanism for anxiety. Scientific Reports. 2021;11(1):22305.
[25] Nieubuurt JT. Internet Memes: Leaflet Propaganda of the Digital Age. In: Frontiers in Communication; 2021. Available from: `https://api.semanticscholar.org/CorpusID:231607158`.
[26] Kiela D, Firooz H, Mohan A, Goswami V, Singh A, Ringshia P, et al.. The Hateful Memes Challenge: Detecting Hate Speech in Multimodal Memes. arXiv; 2020. Available from: `https://arxiv.org/abs/2005.04790`.
[27] Ling C, AbuHilal I, Blackburn J, De Cristofaro E, Zannettou S, Stringhini G. Dissecting the meme magic: Understanding indicators of virality in image memes. Proceedings of the ACM on Human-Computer Interaction. 2021;(CSCW).
[28] Joshi S, Ilievski F, Luceri L. Contextualizing Internet Memes Across Social Media Platforms. In: Companion Proceedings of the ACM on Web Conference 2024; 2024. p. 1831-40.
[29] Grice HP. Logic and conversation. In: Speech acts. Brill; 1975. p. 41-58.
[30] Shang L, Youn C, Zha Y, Zhang Y, Wang D. KnowMeme: A knowledge-enriched graph neural network solution to offensive meme detection. In: 2021 IEEE 17th International Conference on eScience (eScience). IEEE; 2021. p. 186-95.

[31] Speer R, Chin J, Havasi C. Conceptnet 5.5: An open multilingual graph of general knowledge. In: Proceedings of the AAAI conference on artificial intelligence. vol. 31; 2017. .

[32] Grasso B, La Gatta V, Moscato V, Sperlì G. KERMIT: Knowledge-EmpoweRed Model In harmful meme deTection. Information Fusion. 2024;106:102269.

[33] Phillips W. This is why we can't have nice things: Mapping the relationship between online trolling and mainstream culture. Mit Press; 2015.

[34] Kiela D, Firooz H, Mohan A, Goswami V, Singh A, Ringshia P, et al. The hateful memes challenge: Detecting hate speech in multimodal memes. Advances in neural information processing systems. 2020;33:2611-24.

[35] Zhu R. Enhance multimodal transformer with external label and in-domain pretrain: Hateful meme challenge winning solution. arXiv preprint arXiv:201208290. 2020.

[36] Gan Z, Chen YC, Li L, Zhu C, Cheng Y, Liu J. Large-scale adversarial training for vision-and-language representation learning. Advances in Neural Information Processing Systems. 2020;33:6616-28.

[37] Thakur AK, Ilievski F, Sandlin HÂ, Sourati Z, Luceri L, Tommasini R, et al. Explainable Classification of Internet Memes. In: NeSy; 2023. p. 395-409.

[38] Pandiani DSM, Sang ETK, Ceolin D. Toxic Memes: A Survey of Computational Perspectives on the Detection and Explanation of Meme Toxicities. arXiv preprint arXiv:240607353. 2024.

[39] Bloem T. Beyond Visual Similarity: Clustering Internet Memes Across Similarity Dimensions; 2024.

[40] Nahon K, Hemsley J. Going viral. Polity; 2013.

[41] Berger J, Milkman KL. What makes online content viral? Journal of marketing research. 2012;49(2):192-205.

[42] Heath C, Bell C, Sternberg E. Emotional selection in memes: the case of urban legends. Journal of personality and social psychology. 2001;81(6):1028.

[43] Dynel M. "I has seen image macros!" Advice animals memes as visual-verbal jokes. International Journal of Communication. 2016;10:29.

[44] Weng L, Flammini A, Vespignani A, Menczer F. Competition among memes in a world with limited attention. Scientific reports. 2012;2(1):335.

[45] Boyd DM, Ellison NB. Social network sites: Definition, history, and scholarship. Journal of computer-mediated Communication. 2007;13(1):210-30.

[46] Bauckhage C. Insights into internet memes. In: Proceedings of the International AAAI Conference on Web and Social Media. vol. 5; 2011. p. 42-9.

[47] Goel S, Anderson A, Hofman J, Watts DJ. The structural virality of online diffusion. Management science. 2016;62(1):180-96.

[48] Fillmore CJ, et al. Frame semantics. Cognitive linguistics: Basic readings. 2006;34:373-400.

[49] Vrandečić D, Krötzsch M. Wikidata: a free collaborative knowledgebase. Communications of the ACM. 2014;57(10):78-85.

[50] Auer S, Bizer C, Kobilarov G, Lehmann J, Cyganiak R, Ives Z. Dbpedia: A nucleus for a web of open data. In: The semantic web. Springer; 2007. p. 722-35.

[51] Bollacker K, Evans C, Paritosh P, Sturge T, Taylor J. Freebase: a collaboratively created graph database for structuring human knowledge. In: Proceedings of the 2008 ACM SIGMOD international conference on Management of data; 2008. p. 1247-50.

[52] Färber M, Bartscherer F, Menne C, Rettinger A. Linked data quality of dbpedia, freebase, opencyc, wikidata, and yago. Semantic Web. 2018;9(1):77-129.

[53] Castaño Díaz CM. Defining and characterizing the concept of Internet Meme. Ces Psicología. 2013;6(2):82-104.

[54] Lenzerini M. Data Integration: A Theoretical Perspective. In: Popa L, Abiteboul S, Kolaitis PG, editors. Proceedings of the Twenty-first ACM SIGACT-SIGMOD-SIGART Symposium on Principles of Database Systems, June 3-5, Madison, Wisconsin, USA. ACM; 2002. p. 233-46.

[55] Mendes PN, Jakob M, García-Silva A, Bizer C. DBpedia spotlight: shedding light on the web of documents. In: Proceedings of the 7th international conference on semantic systems; 2011. p. 1-8.

[56] Ilievski F, Garijo D, Chalupsky H, Divvala NT, Yao Y, Rogers C, et al. KGTK: A Toolkit for Large Knowledge Graph Manipulation and Analysis. In: International Semantic Web Conference. Springer; 2020. p. 278-93. Available from: https://arxiv.org/pdf/2006.00088.pdf.

[57] Dimou A, Sande MV, Colpaert P, Verborgh R, Mannens E, de Walle RV. RML: A Generic Language for Integrated RDF Mappings of Heterogeneous Data. In: Bizer C, Heath T, Auer S, Berners-Lee T, editors. Proceedings of the Workshop on Linked Data on the Web co-located with the 23rd International

World Wide Web Conference (WWW 2014), Seoul, Korea, April 8, 2014; 2014. .
[58] Wilkinson MD, Dumontier M, Aalbersberg IJ, Appleton G, Axton M, Baak A, et al. The FAIR Guiding Principles for scientific data management and stewardship. Scientific data. 2016;3(1):1-9.
[59] Luceri L, Braun T, Giordano S. Social influence (deep) learning for human behavior prediction. In: Complex Networks IX: Proceedings of the 9th Conference on Complex Networks CompleNet 2018 9. Springer; 2018. p. 261-9.
[60] Zannettou S, Caulfield T, Blackburn J, De Cristofaro E, Sirivianos M, Stringhini G, et al. On the origins of memes by means of fringe web communities. In: Proceedings of the internet measurement conference 2018; 2018. p. 188-202.
[61] Singer P, Flöck F, Meinhart C, Zeitfogel E, Strohmaier M. Evolution of reddit: from the front page of the internet to a self-referential community? In: Proceedings of the 23rd international conference on world wide web; 2014. p. 517-22.
[62] Fairchild T. It's funny because it's true: The transmission of explicit and implicit racism in internet memes. 2020.
[63] Kamenetz A. Right-Wing Hate Groups Are Recruiting Video Gamers; 2018. Accessed: 2023-08-16. Available from: `https://www.npr.org/2018/11/05/660642531/right-wing-hate-groups-are-recruiting-video-gamers`.
[64] Dosovitskiy A, Beyer L, Kolesnikov A, Weissenborn D, Zhai X, Unterthiner T, et al.. An Image is Worth 16x16 Words: Transformers for Image Recognition at Scale; 2021.
[65] Sherratt V. Towards Contextually Sensitive Analysis of Memes: Meme Genealogy and Knowledge Base. In: Proceedings of the Thirty-First International Joint Conference on Artificial Intelligence (IJCAI-22), Vienna, Austria; 2022. p. 5871-2.
[66] Theisen W, Cedre DG, Carmichael Z, Moreira D, Weninger T, Scheirer W. Motif mining: Finding and summarizing remixed image content. In: Proceedings of the IEEE/CVF Winter Conference on Applications of Computer Vision; 2023. p. 1319-28.
[67] Girju R, Moldovan D, Tatu M, Antohe D. On the semantics of noun compounds. Computer speech & language. 2005;19(4):479-96.
[68] Klinger E, Starkweather D. pHash: The open source perceptual hash library. accessed 2016-05-19.[Online]. Available: http://www. phash. org/apps; 2013.
[69] Bay H, Ess A, Tuytelaars T, Van Gool L. Speeded-up robust features (SURF). Computer vision and image understanding. 2008;110(3):346-59.
[70] Devlin J, Chang MW, Lee K, Toutanova K. Bert: Pre-training of deep bidirectional transformers for language understanding. arXiv preprint arXiv:181004805. 2018.
[71] Nogara G, Vishnuprasad PS, Cardoso F, Ayoub O, Giordano S, Luceri L. The Disinformation Dozen: An Exploratory Analysis of Covid-19 Disinformation Proliferation on Twitter. In: 14th ACM Web Science Conference 2022; 2022. p. 348-58.
[72] Chen E, Jiang J, Chang HCH, Muric G, Ferrara E, et al. Charting the information and misinformation landscape to characterize misinfodemics on social media: COVID-19 infodemiology study at a planetary scale. Jmir Infodemiology. 2022;2(1):e32378.
[73] Pierri F, Perry BL, DeVerna MR, Yang KC, Flammini A, Menczer F, et al. Online misinformation is linked to early COVID-19 vaccination hesitancy and refusal. Scientific reports. 2022;12(1):1-7.
[74] Pramanick S, Dimitrov D, Mukherjee R, Sharma S, Akhtar MS, Nakov P, et al. Detecting harmful memes and their targets. arXiv preprint arXiv:211000413. 2021.
[75] Habib H, Nithyanand R. Exploring the Magnitude and Effects of Media Influence on Reddit Moderation. Proceedings of the International AAAI Conference on Web and Social Media. 2022 May;16(1):275-86. Available from: `https://ojs.aaai.org/index.php/ICWSM/article/view/19291`.
[76] Luceri L, Cresci S, Giordano S. Social media against society. The Internet and the 2020 Campaign. 2021;2021:1.
[77] DiResta R, Grossman S. Potemkin pages & personas: Assessing GRU online operations, 2014-2019. White Paper https://fsi-live s3 us-west-1 amazonaws com/s3fs-public/potemkin-pagespersonas-sio-wp pdf. 2019.
[78] Mamié R, Horta Ribeiro M, West R. Are anti-feminist communities gateways to the far right? evidence from reddit and youtube. In: 13th ACM Web Science Conference 2021; 2021. p. 139-47.
[79] Fersini E, Gasparini F, Rizzi G, Saibene A, Chulvi B, Rosso P, et al. SemEval-2022 Task 5: Multimedia automatic misogyny identification. In: Proceedings of the 16th International Workshop on Semantic

Evaluation (SemEval-2022); 2022. p. 533-49.
[80] Hee MS, Chong WH, Lee RKW. Decoding the underlying meaning of multimodal hateful memes. arXiv preprint arXiv:230517678. 2023.
[81] Hermida PCdQ, Santos EMd. Detecting hate speech in memes: a review. Artificial Intelligence Review. 2023:1-19.
[82] Lu J, Batra D, Parikh D, Lee S. Vilbert: Pretraining task-agnostic visiolinguistic representations for vision-and-language tasks. Advances in neural information processing systems. 2019;32.
[83] Li LH, Yatskar M, Yin D, Hsieh CJ, Chang KW. Visualbert: A simple and performant baseline for vision and language. arXiv preprint arXiv:190803557. 2019.
[84] Cao R, Lee RKW, Chong WH, Jiang J. Prompting for Multimodal Hateful Meme Classification. arXiv preprint arXiv:230204156. 2023.
[85] Ji J, Ren W, Naseem U. Identifying creative harmful memes via prompt based approach. In: Proceedings of the ACM Web Conference 2023; 2023. p. 3868-72.
[86] Renkl A. Toward an Instructionally Oriented Theory of Example-Based Learning. Cognitive Science. 2014;38(1):1-37. Available from: `https://onlinelibrary.wiley.com/doi/abs/10.1111/cogs.12086`.
[87] Rosch EH. Natural categories. Cognitive Psychology. 1973;4(3):328-50. Available from: `https://www.sciencedirect.com/science/article/pii/0010028573900170`.
[88] Johansen MK, Kruschke JK. Category representation for classification and feature inference. J Exp Psychol Learn Mem Cogn. 2005 Nov;31(6):1433-58.
[89] Medin DL, Schaffer MM. Context theory of classification learning. Psychol Rev. 1978 May;85(3):207-38.
[90] Nguyen DQ, Vu T, Tuan Nguyen A. BERTweet: A pre-trained language model for English Tweets. In: Proceedings of the 2020 Conference on Empirical Methods in Natural Language Processing: System Demonstrations. Online: Association for Computational Linguistics; 2020. p. 9-14. Available from: `https://aclanthology.org/2020.emnlp-demos.2`.
[91] Radford A, Kim JW, Hallacy C, Ramesh A, Goh G, Agarwal S, et al.. Learning Transferable Visual Models From Natural Language Supervision. arXiv; 2021. Available from: `https://arxiv.org/abs/2103.00020`.
[92] Sourati Z, Deshpande D, Ilievski F, Gashteovski K, Saralajew S. Robust Text Classification: Analyzing Prototype-Based Networks. arXiv preprint arXiv:231106647. 2023.
[93] Kaya A. Caption-augmented Multimodal Classification of Hateful Memes; 2024.
[94] Szumski J. From Satire To Severity: Classifying Hate in Political and Non-Political Memes; 2024.
[95] Radford A, Kim JW, Hallacy C, Ramesh A, Goh G, Agarwal S, et al. Learning transferable visual models from natural language supervision. In: International Conference on Machine Learning. PMLR; 2021. p. 8748-63.
[96] Reid M, Savinov N, Teplyashin D, Lepikhin D, Lillicrap T, Alayrac Jb, et al. Gemini 1.5: Unlocking multimodal understanding across millions of tokens of context. arXiv preprint arXiv:240305530. 2024.
[97] Bates L, Christensen PE, Nakov P, Gurevych I. A Template Is All You Meme. arXiv preprint arXiv:231106649. 2023.
[98] Stranisci MA, et al. Semantic-Aware Methods for the Analysis of Bias and Underrepresentation in Language Resources. 2024.
[99] Graham J, Haidt J, Koleva S, Motyl M, Iyer R, Wojcik SP, et al. Moral foundations theory: The pragmatic validity of moral pluralism. In: Advances in experimental social psychology. vol. 47. Elsevier; 2013. p. 55-130.
[100] Forbes M, Hwang JD, Shwartz V, Sap M, Choi Y. Social chemistry 101: Learning to reason about social and moral norms. arXiv preprint arXiv:201100620. 2020.
[101] Gentner D. Structure-mapping: A theoretical framework for analogy. Cognitive science. 1983;7(2):155-70.
[102] MacLachlan GL, Reid I. Framing and interpretation. (No Title). 1994.
[103] Lakoff G, Johnson M. Metaphors we live by. University of Chicago press; 2008.
[104] Trinh TH, Wu Y, Le QV, He H, Luong T. Solving olympiad geometry without human demonstrations. Nature. 2024;625(7995):476-82.
[105] Chu-Carroll J, Beck A, Burnham G, Melville DO, Nachman D, Özcan AE, et al. Beyond LLMs: Advancing the Landscape of Complex Reasoning. arXiv preprint arXiv:240208064. 2024.
[106] Pan L, Albalak A, Wang X, Wang WY. Logic-lm: Empowering large language models with symbolic

solvers for faithful logical reasoning. arXiv preprint arXiv:230512295. 2023.
[107] Kassner N, Tafjord O, Sabharwal A, Richardson K, Schuetze H, Clark P. Language models with rationality. arXiv preprint arXiv:230514250. 2023.

Handbook on Neurosymbolic AI and Knowledge Graphs
P. Hitzler et al. (Eds.)
IOS Press, 2025

doi:10.3233/FAIA250244

Neurosymbolic AI for Healthcare

Mohan TIMILSINA [a,1] M. Jaleed KHAN [b] Samuele BUOSI [a] Conor JUDGE [c] Gabriel DAVIS JONES [b] Edward CURRY [a]

[a] *Insight SFI Research Centre for Data Analytics, University of Galway, Ireland*
[b] *Nuffield Department of Women's & Reproductive Health, University of Oxford, UK*
[c] *College of Medicine Nursing Health Sciences, University of Galway, Ireland*

Abstract. The recent developments in Neurso-Symbolic AI (NESyAI) for healthcare predictive models and explainable techniques have demonstrated immense potential in transforming medical diagnostics and treatment. This chapter dives into the integration of neural networks with symbolic reasoning to enhance both the precision and interpretability of AI systems in healthcare. By harmonising the strength of these approaches, NeSY AI can analyse complex medical data, make accurate diagnoses, and develop effective treatment plans personalised to patients. Applications such as drug repurposing, lung cancer tumour recurrence prediction, and the classification of chronic kidney disease caused from clinical notes exemplify the practical benefits of this hybrid AI approach. Detailed case studies and the methodologies illustrate how NeSY can create more accurate, interpretable and trustworthy examination systems. This dual potential not only boosts patient outcomes but also encourages clinician acceptance, accelerating the integration of AI into mainstream medical fields. Because of these advancements, NeSY holds the promise of significantly enhancing healthcare delivery and patient care.

Keywords. Neuro-Symbolic AI, Explainable AI, Healthcare, Predictive Models, Machine Learning, Lung Cancer, Chronic Kidney Disease, LLM, Knowledge Graphs.

1. Introduction

Background on NeSyAI in Healthcare: Neuro symbolic (NeSY) artificial intelligence (AI) means to AI systems that search for integrating neural network based methods with symbolic knowledge -based approaches. The term "neural" is derived from the neural networks and "symbolic" which are based on clear symbol manipulation such as network or graph algorithms and natural language questions , symbol manipulation and knowledge reasoning [1]. NeSy AI, which integrates symbolic reasoning with connectionist learning, holds significant potential in the healthcare industry. It can analyse medical data, make accurate diagnoses, and develop effective treatment plans. By leveraging this hybrid approach, NeSy AI enhances the precision and efficiency of medical decision-making processes. This technology can be utilised to create more accurate and interpretable medical diagnostic systems by merging symbolic reasoning with clinical data. Applications include drug discovery, personalised medicine, and predicting patient outcomes, ultimately improving healthcare delivery and patient care. A key limitation in the

[1]Corresponding author. M. Timilsina (mohan.timilsina@insight-centre.org)

health domain is developing transparent and interpretable AI systems. One area where AI techniques are particularly valuable is drug repurposing (DR), which involves identifying new uses for existing drugs. In this line of work, the authors describe the use of a NeSY algorithm [2] to explain the process of link prediction in knowledge graph-based computational drug repurposing. Link prediction involves generating hypotheses about the relationships between known molecules and specific targets, thereby facilitating the discovery of new drug indications. Similarly, Lavin et. al [3] introduces a novel probabilistic programmed deep kernel learning approach that effectively predicts cognitive decline in Alzheimer's disease. The authors demonstrate that this method is a powerful tool for diagnosing neuro-degenerative diseases and prognostic modelling, suggesting its potential efficacy in other disease areas as well.

Evolution and Importance of NeSyAI in Medical Diagnostics and Treatment: Neuro-Symbolic AI represents a major leap forward in medical diagnostics and treatment. By merging the learning capabilities of neural networks with the interpretability and reasoning strengths of symbolic AI, this hybrid approach overcomes the limitations of using each method in isolation. In medical diagnostics, NeSyAI enhances accuracy by integrating extensive data with established medical knowledge, leading to more precise and interpretable diagnostic results. For example, it can simultaneously analyse complex patterns in medical images and apply logical rules based on medical guidelines, thereby improving diagnostic reliability [4,5]. In treatment, NeSyAI can facilitate personalised medicine by synthesising patient data and medical literature to recommend tailored treatment plans. The evolution of NeSyAI is crucial in bridging the gap between data-driven insights and actionable medical knowledge, ensuring that AI systems deliver high-performance diagnostics while also generating explanations that clinicians can trust and act upon. This dual capability of NeSyAI is pivotal in fostering clinician acceptance and accelerating the integration of AI into mainstream medical practice, ultimately enhancing patient outcomes through more informed and transparent decision-making processes.

Overview of Key AI Techniques Used in Healthcare: AI techniques have significantly transformed healthcare by enhancing diagnostics, treatment planning, and patient care. Machine learning, particularly deep learning, is extensively used for analysing medical images and detecting abnormalities with high accuracy. Convolutional neural networks (CNNs) have shown remarkable success in identifying diseases such as cancer from radiological images [6]. Natural language processing (NLP) extracts valuable information from unstructured medical records, supporting clinical decision-making and improving patient management [7]. Furthermore, reinforcement learning optimises treatment protocols by leveraging patient data and clinical outcomes, thereby advancing personalised medicine [8]. Incorporating these AI techniques into healthcare enhances not only diagnostic accuracy but also improves the efficiency of treatment plans and overall patient care.

Scope of the Chapter: This chapter explores the advancements in Neuro-Symbolic AI (NeSyAI) within healthcare, focusing on predictive models and explainable techniques. NeSyAI combines the learning capabilities of neural networks with the reasoning strengths of symbolic AI, enhancing precision and interpretability in medical diagnostics and treatment planning. Specific areas of focus include lung cancer tumor recurrence prediction and automated concept extraction from clinical notes, showcasing how NeSyAI can analyze complex medical data to make accurate diagnoses and develop personalized treatment plans.

In discussing lung cancer tumor recurrence prediction, the chapter examines the use of knowledge graphs to model clinical data from Electronic Health Records (EHRs). This method integrates diverse data sources, enabling complex relationship analysis and improving predictive accuracy. Graph-based machine learning techniques like ComplEx-N3 leverage these structured relationships, while explainable AI methods provide transparency and build clinician trust by clarifying the factors behind predictions.

The chapter also investigates advanced natural language processing (NLP) techniques for classifying chronic kidney disease (CKD) causes from clinical notes. By employing models such as DistilBERT, high precision and recall in categorizing conditions like IgA Nephropathy, Diabetes, and Hypertension are achieved. This enhances the accuracy and efficiency of disease classification, reducing human error and improving patient outcomes.

Furthermore, the integration of these AI techniques into clinical workflows demonstrates the transformative potential of NeSyAI in healthcare, leading to better patient care and resource utilization. The chapter underscores the significant potential of NeSyAI in improving clinical decision-making in Obstetrics and Gynecology, where traditional deep learning models often face challenges like lack of interpretability and data inefficiency. By combining the data-driven capabilities of neural networks with structured symbolic reasoning and healthcare knowledge graphs, NeSyAI can enhance the accuracy, reliability, and interpretability of AI systems, thereby improving patient care and outcomes in women's health.

2. Knowledge Graphs and Explainable AI for Lung Cancer Tumor Recurrence Prediction

Motivation: Predicting lung cancer relapse using Neuro-Symbolic AI and Explainable AI is crucial as it significantly enhances predictive accuracy and personalised patient care by leveraging the strengths of both neural networks and symbolic reasoning. Explainable AI methods ensure transparency, enabling clinicians to understand the contributing factors behind each prediction, thereby increasing trust and clinical acceptance. This approach facilitates better risk stratification, tailored treatment decisions, and evidence-based insights, ultimately improving decision support in clinical settings. Furthermore, the methodologies used are adaptable and scalable, potentially applicable to other diseases, making this a significant advancement in medical AI for cancer prognosis.

2.1. Case Study: Early-Stage Lung Cancer Recurrence Prediction Using Graph-Based Technique

Data Representation: Electronic Health Records (EHRs), which are clinical data, can be represented as a knowledge graph. This involves representing patients, diseases, treatments, and other clinical entities as nodes, with the relationships between them as edges. This structured representation is a key aspect of symbolic reasoning, allowing the system to encode domain knowledge and logical relationships. Knowledge graphs facilitate the integration of various data sources, including clinical records, genetic information, and literature. This symbolic structure enables the system to reason about complex relationships and dependencies within the data. Compared to modelling data in tables, knowledge graphs offer significant advantages for incorporating heterogeneous data sources. Graph datasets are highly compatible with various reasoning approaches, including logical, machine learning-based, and hybrid methods. This compatibility allows for inferences over long-range dependencies between concepts such as patients, diseases, biomarkers, genes, and drugs. Additionally, knowledge graphs facilitate the seamless integration of core clinical data with population-level genetics, pharmaceutical information, disease data, and relevant scientific literature.

Dataset: Table 1 is the summarised table that includes the major characteristics of the dataset. The detailed description of the datasets can be found in our work [9,10]

Table 1. A summarised cohort of the early stage patients which were used to create the knowledge graph.

Characteristics	Relapse	No Relapse	Total
Total Patients	517	870	1387
Age (mean, range)	65.7 (33 - 88)	65.6 (31 - 118)	65.7 (31 - 118)
Gender (Male)	407	636	1043
Gender (Female)	110	234	344
Smoking History (Current/Previous)	460	750	1210
Smoking History (Non-Smoker)	57	120	177
Surgery	459	848	1307
Chemotherapy	379	318	697

Knowledge Graph Creation: The creation of the knowledge graph involves modeling the clinical data of 1,387 early-stage NSCLC patients into a structured graph format. In this graph, various clinical entities such as patients, diseases, treatments, tumor characteristics, and biomarkers are represented as nodes, while the relationships between these entities are depicted as edges. This structured representation allows for the integration of heterogeneous data sources, including electronic health records (EHRs), genetic information, and treatment histories. By capturing complex relationships and dependencies between different clinical entities, the knowledge graph provides a comprehensive and holistic view of each patient's medical profile. The detailed discussion of the creation of the knowledge graph can be found in our work [11]. Figure 1 demonstrates the clinical data modeled as a knowledge graph.

Graph-Based Machine Learning: The graph machine learning techniques leverage the structured relationships within the knowledge graph. ComplEx-N3 [12] is a state-of-the-art knowledge graph embedding model that captures complex relationships between entities in the graph, enabling the system to make accurate predictions based on the patterns and connections within the data.

Model Training and Validation: The graph machine learning model is trained on a dataset of 1,387 early-stage NSCLC patients, including clinical features such as tumor characteristics, treatment details, and patient demographics. Embeddings for entities and relationships within the graph are created to predict cancer recurrence likelihood. The model's performance is evaluated using binary classification metrics such as accuracy, precision, recall, F1 score, area under the PR curve (AUC-PR), and area under the ROC curve (AUC-ROC). A specific train/validation/test split protocol is employed for robust evaluation: 200 patients (14.8%) are allocated to the test set, and 100 patients (7.4%) to

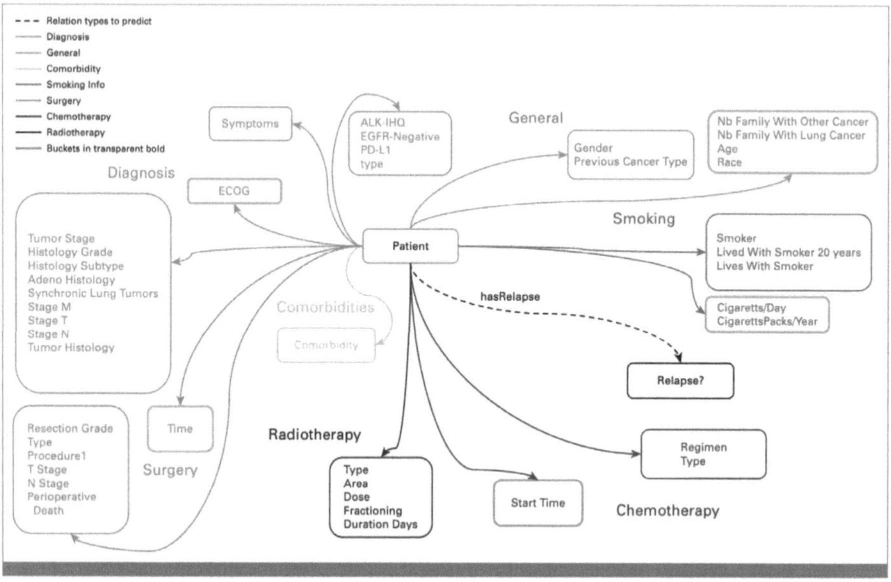

Figure 1. Diagram of the clinical data modelled as a knowledge graph.

the validation set. This ensures balanced class distribution, reliable performance metrics, and an unbiased estimate of predictive performance on unseen data.

Model Selection, Hyperparameter Values: We have adopted the ComplEX-N3 algorithms which achieves the state-of-the-art results. The hyperparameters are selected with a grid search across the following values: embedding size(50/100/200), number of negative triples are generated at runtime during training for each positive (5/25), and initializer (Xavier/uniform). For each parameter configuration, we select the best model according to accuracy score on the weight lambda = 1e-4 training epochs = 400 with batches count = 5, early stopping. Embedding dimension is fixed to k = 100, synthetic negative ratio eta = 25 and uniform initializer. Random seed is set to default value.

Implementation:[2] All the experiments are implemented using Python 3.7, with the Knowledge Graph Embedding Library called Ampligraph.

Explanation System: The explainable AI techniques are used to provide context for the predictions. In this context, we employed an example-based approach . This method highlights similar past patients in the model space to the current patient being predicted, offering a comparison that aids the prediction. Along with the prediction score for the relapse, the model returns an accompanying textual description to support the evidence of the prediction, enhancing interpretability and providing the clear explanation of the results.

Results: The results of the classical machine learning algorithms along with graph-based approach is displayed in the Table 2:

The graph-based machine learning model ComplEx-N3 demonstrates notable performance, particularly in terms of F1 score and recall. With an F1 score of 0.7176 and a recall of 0.6594, ComplEx-N3 effectively balances the trade-off between precision and

[2]L. Costabello, N. McCarthy, P. Tabacof, R. McGrath, C. L. Van, A. Janik, C. Clauss, and A. Alto, "Accenture/AmpliGraph: AmpliGraph 1.4.0." [Online]. Available: https://zenodo.org/record/2595043

Table 2. Result of the binary classification evaluation for three classical machine learning classifiers and one graph-based model.

Models	Accuracy	Precision	Recall	F1	AUC-PR	AUC-ROC
Random Baseline	0.512 ± 0.031	0.384 ± 0.028	0.507 ± 0.043	0.436 ± 0.030	0.373 ± 0.002	0.500 ± 0.000
Gradient Boosting	0.746 ± 0.026	0.667 ± 0.052	0.649 ± 0.088	0.653 ± 0.044	0.765 ± 0.032	0.807 ± 0.035
Logistic Regression	0.735 ± 0.039	0.632 ± 0.049	0.692 ± 0.074	0.660 ± 0.054	0.708 ± 0.052	0.787 ± 0.041
Random Forest	0.761 ± 0.030	0.701 ± 0.049	0.632 ± 0.074	0.662 ± 0.049	0.762 ± 0.035	0.813 ± 0.031
ComplEx-N3	0.685	0.718	0.610	0.659	0.633	0.685

recall, indicating its capability in identifying relevant instances of the target class, which is crucial in medical diagnoses such as predicting relapse in lung cancer patients. This model's performance suggests that it is particularly adept at capturing complex relationships and dependencies in the data, which might be overlooked by traditional tabular models.

Explanation: Figure 2 demonstrates the explanation provided by the system. The AI model predicts a 31% relapse chance for patient ID 514293 by leveraging a knowledge graph-based approach, drawing on data from 1,048 patients. Key influential examples, including patients 513642, 513853, and 906926, were analysed. Patient 514293 shares attributes with these examples, such as tumour stage, histology subtype, and surgical history. Specifically, patient 906926's relapse case, characterised by adenocarcinoma histology-acinar and specific comorbidities, aligns closely with patient 514293's profile, highlighting the risk factors contributing to the AI's relapse prediction. This transparent analysis helps in understanding the critical factors influencing the prediction.

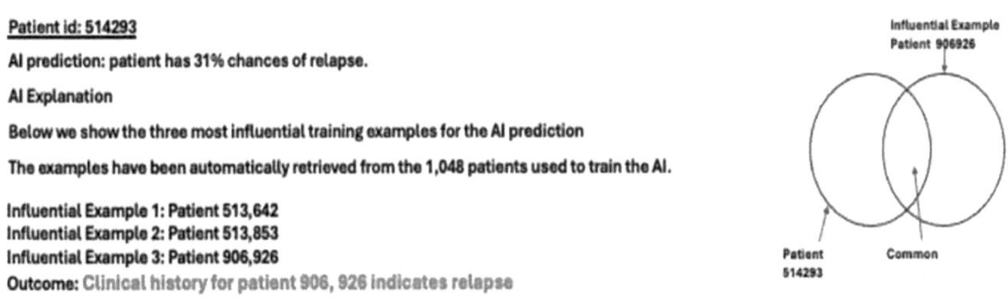

Name	Attributes only in predicted 514,293	Attributes in common	Attributes only in example 906926
Diagnosis	Histology subtype:adeno histology-Papilary	Stage T: T2a, Stage N: N0, Stage M: M0, Tumor Stage: IB, Histology Grade: Moderately differentiated, Histology Subtype: adeno histology, Tumor Histology: Adenocarcinoma, ECOG: ≤ 0	Histology subtype: adeno histology—Acinar
General	No. of family members with other cancer: 3-5, Gender: Female	Age: 60-65, Race: Caucasian, No. of family members with lung cancer: <= 0	Previous cancer type: Colorectal, No. of family members with other cancer: ≤ 0, Gender: Male
Comorbities	Cardiopathy	Dyslipidemia, HTA, Others	COPD, Hypercholesterolemia
Smoking	No. of cigarettes/day: 5-10	Smoker	None
Surgery	Procedure 1: Right inferior	lobectomy Time: 0-10, Type: Curative, Resection Grade: R0, Stage T: T2a, Stage N: N0	Procedure 1: Typical segmentectomy

Figure 2. Example-Based Explanation of Graph Model for Lung Cancer Relapse Prediction.

2.2. *Discussion on the Impact and Implications of Clinical Practice*

Knowledge graphs enable the modelling of complex dependencies between various clinical data points, such as patient characteristics, treatments, and outcomes, facilitating a more understanding of relapse risk. Explainable AI further enhances this approach by providing transparent, interpretable predictions that allow clinicians to understand the underlying factors driving the model's assessments. For instance, example-based explanations in graph models highlight influential past patients with similar profiles. This dual approach not only enhances the accuracy of relapse predictions but also ensures that clinicians can trust and act on these insights, leading to more personalised and effective patient care. By leveraging these advanced AI techniques, healthcare providers can optimise monitoring and treatment strategies, improve patient outcomes, and ultimately, offer more targeted and efficient care for NSCLC patients.

3. Large Language Models in Clinical Text Processing

3.1. *Case Study: BERT-Based Deep Learning for Accurate Classification of IgA Nephropathy, Diabetes, and Hypertension from Clinical Notes*

Overview: This work explores the application of advanced natural language processing techniques to enhance the classification of chronic kidney disease (CKD) causes using unstructured clinical notes. The study utilised a dataset from the Kidney Disease Clinical Patient Management System (KDCPMS), which contains clinical notes from haemodialysis and transplant centres within the Health Service Executive (HSE) in Ireland. The core idea focuses on developing and evaluating machine learning models based on the DistilBERT[3] a large language model architecture to categorise clinical notes into three specific classes: IgA Nephropathy, Diabetes, and Hypertension. The results highlight the varying performance metrics of the models, with the IgA Nephropathy classifier demonstrating high precision and recall, whereas the Diabetes and Hypertension classifiers show notable, though comparatively lower, effectiveness. The study underscores the potential of BERT-based approaches in clinical note classification, advocating for ongoing model refinement and collaboration with medical experts to improve clinical applicability and accuracy.
Dataset: The dataset comprises clinical notes from haemodialysis and transplant centres across Ireland, collected since 2007. Initially, 45,645 clinical notes were extracted, of which 43,500 were deemed usable after filtering out entries with fewer than 50 words. These notes were further anonymized to protect patient privacy, and a subset of 2,972 notes was meticulously annotated by a team of five physicians using the Prodigy[4] tool, labelling the data for IgA Nephropathy, Diabetes, and Hypertension. To address class imbalances, undersampling and oversampling techniques were employed, ensuring a balanced representation for effective machine learning model training.
Methodology: Figure 3 illustrates the methodology used in the study for classifying clinical notes from the KDCPMS dataset into categories of **"IgA Nephropathy"**, **"Diabetes"**, and **"Hypertension"**. The process begins with the extraction of raw clinical

[3] https://huggingface.co/docs/transformers/en/model_doc/distilbert
[4] https://prodi.gy/

notes and involves several key steps: data anonymization using the TextWash tool, data preprocessing (including cleaning, scaling, and encoding), and data annotation by physicians using the Prodigy tool. The annotated and preprocessed data are then split into training, validation, and test sets. The training data is used to train the DistilBERT model, while the validation data helps fine-tune the model. New clinical notes, along with the test data, are processed through an inference pipeline to generate predictions. These predictions are evaluated using metrics such as precision, recall, F1 score, and accuracy, with the results analysed through confusion matrices.

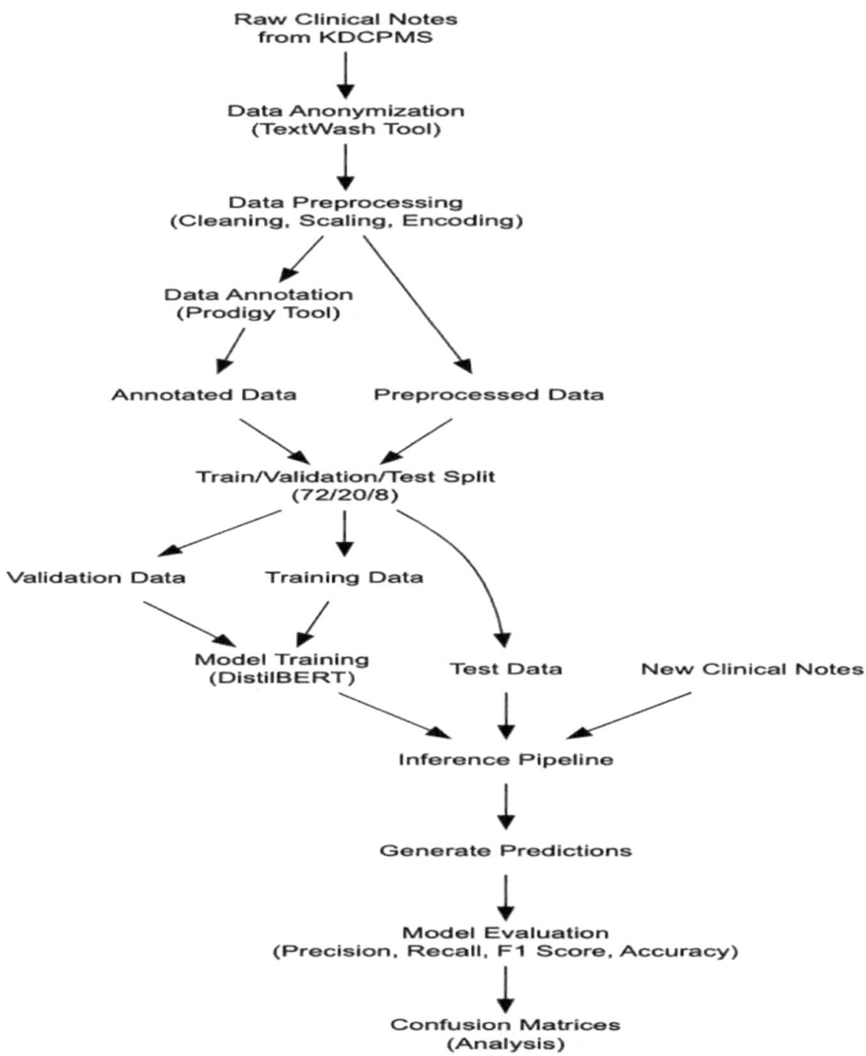

Figure 3. Methodology Flowchart for the Classification of Clinical Notes.

Results: The results of the BERT models for classifying clinical notes into IgA Nephropathy, Diabetes, and Hypertension categories reveal varying levels of performance across the three conditions as shown in Table 3. The IgA Nephropathy classifier demonstrated the highest effectiveness, with impressive metrics including 99.38% precision, 99.37% recall, 99.37% F1 score, and 99.37% accuracy, indicating robust identification of positive instances with minimal false positives and negatives. The Diabetes classifier, while showing commendable precision at 81.74% and recall at 80.62%, achieved a slightly lower F1 score of 80.45%, highlighting challenges in balancing precision and recall. For the Hypertension classifier, competitive performance metrics were observed with an 82.95% precision, 82.29% recall, 81.59% F1 score, and 81.63% accuracy, indicating balanced identification of positive cases with a relatively low false negative rate. These findings underscore the classifiers' varying strengths and weaknesses, suggesting that while the models are effective in identifying certain conditions, further refinement is necessary to enhance their overall accuracy and applicability in clinical settings.

Table 3. Performance Metrics for Different Labels.

Labels	Precision	Recall	F1 Score
IgA Neuropathy	0.993	0.993	0.993
Diabetes	0.817	0.806	0.804
Hypertension	0.829	0.822	0.815

The BERT-based classifiers for IgA Nephropathy, Diabetes, and Hypertension demonstrated notable performance in categorising clinical notes. The IgA Nephropathy classifier achieved exceptionally high precision and recall , indicating robust and reliable detection of true positive cases with minimal false positives and negatives. The Hypertension classifier also showed balanced performance, resulting in a strong F1 score and accuracy. While the Diabetes classifier exhibited good precision and recall, it faced challenges in balancing these metrics, leading to a higher false negative rate (25%). Overall, the results underscore BERT's effectiveness in understanding context in clinical notes, significantly enhancing the accuracy and efficiency of disease classification in medical settings.

3.2. Discussion on the Impact and Implications of Clinical Practice

The results of this study have significant implications for clinical practice, particularly in the management and diagnosis of chronic kidney disease (CKD). The high precision and recall achieved by the IgA Nephropathy classifier demonstrate that advanced machine learning models, like BERT, can accurately identify specific diseases from unstructured clinical notes. This capability can enhance the accuracy of diagnoses and ensure that patients receive timely and appropriate treatment. By integrating these models into clinical workflows, healthcare providers can leverage automated systems to assist in the classification and documentation of complex cases, reducing the burden on medical professionals and minimising the risk of human error. Consequently, this could lead to improved patient outcomes and more efficient use of healthcare resources. Furthermore, the balanced performance of the Hypertension classifier and the good performance of the Diabetes classifier suggest that BERT-based models can be generalised to various conditions, making them valuable tools for a wide range of clinical applications. However, the challenges observed in balancing precision and recall for the Diabetes classifier highlight the need for ongoing refinement and adaptation of these models. Collaboration between data scientists and clinical experts is crucial to ensure that the models are continuously updated and aligned with clinical realities.

4. Neurosymbolic AI for Women's Health

Neurosymbolic AI, which combines neural networks and symbolic reasoning, aims to enhance the robustness, explainability, and efficiency of AI systems by integrating the data-driven learning capabilities of neural networks with the structured reasoning of symbolic AI [13]. In healthcare, including women's health, this approach holds substantial potential for improving clinical decision making and overcoming the limitations of traditional deep learning models. Clinical decision making in Obstetrics and Gynaecology (O&G) is particularly challenging due to the complexity and variability of clinical scenarios. Accurate diagnosis and timely interventions are crucial for managing high-risk pregnancies and improving outcomes. Traditional deep learning models, while powerful, often suffer from issues such as lack of interpretability, data inefficiency, and brittleness when faced with rare or complex cases [14]. These challenges are amplified in the context of high-risk pre-term pregnancies, where subtle and complex patterns in Fetal Heart Rate (FHR) data need to be identified and interpreted accurately.

Large Language Models (LLMs) like ChatGPT have demonstrated significant potential in processing and generating human-like text, which can be invaluable in medical contexts by analyzing vast amounts of data, providing insights, and supporting clinical decision-making [14]. However, LLMs face challenges such as brittleness, lack of explainability, and the need for extensive data. Neurosymbolic AI can mitigate these issues by incorporating structured symbolic reasoning. This approach enhances the interpretability of AI systems and leverages the structured knowledge contained in healthcare knowledge graphs [15]. Healthcare knowledge graphs represent entities and their relationships in a structured form and can be integrated with deep learning to enhance AI performance and interpretability in clinical settings. These knowledge graphs facilitate comprehensive data analytics and support advanced clinical decision-making processes by leveraging vast medical knowledge. They can integrate diverse data sources to support clinical decision-making, drug discovery, and public health surveillance. In visual reasoning, neurosymbolic AI can use scene graphs to represent visual elements and their relationships [16], improving the interpretability and accuracy of diagnostic tools in women's health.

Neurosymbolic AI and knowledge graphs offer promising solutions to the limitations of deep learning and LLMs in healthcare. These technologies can significantly improve medical diagnosis and clinical decision-making processes by enhancing interpretability, data integration, and reasoning capabilities. This is useful for identifying high-risk pre-term pregnancies, where accurate and timely diagnosis is critical. Integrating knowledge graphs with deep learning models and LLMs provides a structured and comprehensive framework for analyzing complex medical data, thereby improving the accuracy and reliability of clinical predictions and recommendations. Leveraging both neural networks and symbolic reasoning, neurosymbolic AI can address the challenges of clinical decision making in women's health, providing more accurate, interpretable, and trustworthy AI-driven insights, ultimately enhancing patient care and outcomes.

4.1. Clinical Decision Making

4.1.1. Case Study Overview

We present our study [17] that examines the capabilities of ChatGPT in interpreting and responding to international gold standard benchmark assessments in O&G, specifically

MRCOG Part One and Two examinations of the Royal College of Obstetricians and Gynaecologists (RCOG). The study evaluates ChatGPT's domain-specific accuracy, the influence of linguistic complexity on performance, and its self-assessment confidence and uncertainty, which are essential for safe clinical decision-making. The MRCOG examinations are designed to assess the clinical knowledge and reasoning of candidates in O&G. The Part One exam focuses on foundational scientific knowledge, while the Part Two exam tests the application of this knowledge in clinical scenarios through single best answer (SBA) and extended matching questions (EMQ).

4.1.2. Dataset and Experimental Setup

A dataset of MRCOG examination questions was developed from sources beyond the reach of LLMs to mitigate the risk of prior exposure. A dual-review process validated the technical and clinical accuracy of the questions, omitting those dependent on previous content, duplicates, or requiring image interpretation. Questions were converted to JSON format to facilitate ChatGPT's interpretation, incorporating question types and background information. Interactions with ChatGPT were conducted via OpenAI's API, ensuring consistent and contextually informed responses. Linguistic complexity was evaluated using unique token counts and type-token ratios (TTR) to explore their influence on performance. ChatGPT was instructed to assign confidence scores to its answers, reflecting its self-perceived accuracy. Responses were categorized by correctness and statistically analyzed through entropy calculation to assess ChatGPT's capacity for self-evaluating certainty and knowledge boundaries.

4.1.3. Methodology

The methodology involved extracting SBA and EMQ questions from the MRCOG Part One and Two examinations from online sources not available to LLMs. The questions underwent a dual-review process for validation and were converted into JSON format for ChatGPT's interpretation. Interaction with ChatGPT was structured to mirror the interactive nature of the ChatGPT interface, including the provision of context where necessary. Linguistic complexity was analyzed by tokenizing each question and computing unique token counts and TTR. ChatGPT's self-assessed confidence and uncertainty were evaluated by instructing it to assign probabilistic confidence scores to each answer option. Entropy was calculated to measure the model's uncertainty, providing a statistical layer to the confidence scores and enriching the understanding of the model's performance.

4.1.4. Results and Findings

ChatGPT demonstrated commendable accuracy on the MRCOG Part One exam, achieving 72.2% accuracy. However, its performance was significantly reduced on the more clinically demanding Part Two exam, with an overall accuracy of 50.4%. ChatGPT performed better on SBA questions than on EMQs. Domain-specific performance varied, with the highest accuracy in Biochemistry and the lowest in Biophysics for Part One. In Part Two, the highest accuracy was in Urogynaecology, and the lowest was in Management of Labour. Linguistic complexity analysis revealed a marginal increase in unique token count for correct answers in Part One compared to incorrect ones. TTR analysis showed higher medians for correct answers, with negligible effect sizes. Regarding self-assessed confidence, ChatGPT exhibited high confidence in both correct and incorrect responses, indicating a lack of reliable self-assessment mechanisms. Entropy values were identical for correct and incorrect responses, suggesting no discernible distinction in ChatGPT's prediction certainty.

4.1.5. Discussion

The case study shows that while ChatGPT is promising for basic medical queries, its performance significantly declines in complex clinical scenarios, highlighting limitations in its clinical reasoning and self-assessment capabilities [17]. The hybrid neurosymbolic approach can enhance robustness, interpretability, and efficiency of AI systems in women's health by providing human-readable explanations of AI predictions and decisions, increasing trust and adoption in clinical settings [13]. Knowledge graphs provide a structured way to integrate clinical knowledge into AI systems, aligning AI-driven recommendations with established medical practices and guidelines, thus improving the reliability and acceptance of AI systems [15]. By leveraging knowledge graphs, AI systems can utilize vast amounts of biomedical knowledge to enhance data efficiency and reduce dependency on large datasets. The limitations of ChatGPT, such as its high confidence in incorrect responses and lack of reliable self-assessment mechanisms, highlight the need for a more structured approach to AI in healthcare. Integrating carefully curated and clinically verified knowledge graphs can serve as a safety and guidance layer for AI systems, enhancing their diagnostic efficacy and clinical workflow in women's health. This integration ensures AI systems provide accurate and reliable recommendations, ultimately improving patient outcomes [17]. Future research should focus on developing scalable algorithms and architectures that can seamlessly integrate neural and symbolic components. Efficient training and inference mechanisms are essential for deploying neurosymbolic AI systems in real-time clinical settings. Additionally, developing standardized frameworks and protocols for integrating neurosymbolic AI with electronic health records (EHRs) and other clinical systems is crucial for widespread adoption [13].

4.2. Identifying High-Risk Pre-Term Pregnancies

4.2.1. Case Study Overview

We present a study [18] in which we developed a machine learning algorithm to identify high-risk pre-term pregnancies with adverse outcomes using Fetal Heart Rate (FHR) monitoring. FHR monitoring is a common and affordable test performed during pregnancy to evaluate fetal health. It provides real-time insights into fetal physiology, helping to identify patterns associated with adverse pregnancy outcomes such as asphyxia, growth restriction, and stillbirth. However, human identification of these complex patterns is often sub-optimal. This is particularly relevant in low- and middle-income countries where most perinatal deaths occur. Pre-term birth complications are the leading cause of death in children under five, with a significant portion being preventable. In this study, we sourced antepartum FHR traces from high-risk pre-term pregnancies, which were matched with normal pregnancies delivered at term. Seven distinct FHR patterns were extracted and used to train six machine learning algorithms. The best-performing algorithm was then evaluated using a validation dataset based on metrics such as AUC, sensitivity, and specificity. We analyzed FHR recordings from 4,867 high-risk pre-term pregnancies and 4,014 normal pregnancies. The random forest classifier was the most effective model, achieving an AUC of 0.88. The model consistently exceeded an AUC of 0.80 across all gestational ages, demonstrating robustness and high discriminative ability between pregnancy outcomes.

4.2.2. Dataset and Experimental Setup

Data were extracted from the Oxford University Hospitals maternity database, comprising singleton pregnancies between 27^{+0} and 36^{+6} gestational weeks. The normal cohort included healthy pregnancies delivered at term, while the high-risk cohort included pre-term deliveries with adverse outcomes. Seven FHR features were extracted: basal FHR, accelerations, decelerations, most lost beats, short-term variation (STV), and time spent in episodes of high and low variation. Six machine learning algorithms (decision tree, Gaussian naïve Bayes, logistic regression, random forest, support vector machine, and XGBoost) were trained using 10-fold cross-validation. The random forest classifier showed the best performance and was selected for further analysis. The model was evaluated on the validation dataset using metrics such as AUC, sensitivity, specificity, F1 score, and Cohen's Kappa.

4.2.3. Methodology

Normal and high-risk pre-term adverse outcome cohorts were developed based on specific inclusion and exclusion criteria. High-risk pregnancies were those with adverse outcomes such as low acidaemia, stillbirth, asphyxia, low birthweight, extended special care admission, hypoxaemic ischaemic encephalopathy, low Apgar scores, neonatal sepsis, perinatal infections, or respiratory conditions. The extracted FHR features were transformed and normalized. Machine learning algorithms were trained to predict whether a trace belonged to a normal or high-risk pre-term pregnancy. Hyperparameters were optimized using Bayesian optimization, and the models were evaluated based on AUC and other performance metrics.

4.2.4. Results and Findings

The random forest classifier achieved the highest AUC of 0.88, with a sensitivity of 76.2% and specificity of 87.5% at the Youden index threshold. The model showed robust performance across different gestational ages and specific adverse outcomes, with a median AUC of 0.85 for individual outcomes. Decision curve analysis indicated that the model outperformed both the treat-all and treat-none strategies across most probability thresholds, demonstrating its potential clinical utility in identifying high-risk pre-term pregnancies.

4.2.5. Discussion

The results of the case study demonstrate that machine learning algorithms can effectively identify high-risk pre-term pregnancies using FHR monitoring. However, the study also highlights several limitations, such as the potential for model overfitting and the need for large, diverse datasets to ensure generalizability. Neurosymbolic AI can address these challenges by enhancing the interpretability and reliability of machine learning models in O&G. By integrating symbolic reasoning with neural networks, neurosymbolic AI systems can provide clear and understandable explanations for their decisions, increasing trust in their use for clinical decision-making. Additionally, neurosymbolic

AI can help to identify and mitigate biases inherent in data-driven models, further improving their accuracy and fairness [13]. Knowledge graphs can serve as a safety layer, scrutinizing model outputs and providing contextually relevant information, which can improve diagnostic efficacy and clinical workflow, particularly in identifying high-risk pre-term pregnancies. Knowledge graphs can also enhance ML models by incorporating structured background knowledge, improving their generalizability and interpretability [15]. The integration of Knowledge graphs can address several limitations of current ML approaches in O&G. By combining data-driven learning with symbolic reasoning, these technologies can mitigate biases, enhance data integration, and support comprehensive reasoning, ultimately leading to more accurate and trustworthy clinical decisions [16]. Future research should focus on further developing and validating neurosymbolic AI models and knowledge graphs for O&G applications. This includes expanding the scope of data sources, improving algorithms for better performance, and ensuring seamless integration into clinical practice. Such advancements will contribute to more effective identification and management of high-risk pre-term pregnancies and other critical challenges.

5. Conclusion

Neuro-Symbolic AI (NeSyAI) represents a significant advancement in AI technology by integrating neural networks with symbolic reasoning. This hybrid approach enhances the precision, interpretability, robustness, and efficiency of AI systems, particularly in healthcare. NeSyAI improves medical diagnostics and treatment planning by leveraging the strengths of data-driven learning and structured reasoning. Practical applications of NeSyAI include drug repurposing, lung cancer tumor recurrence prediction, and the classification of chronic kidney disease (CKD) from clinical notes, demonstrating substantial benefits across various medical fields.

In healthcare, including women's health, NeSyAI holds substantial potential for improving clinical decision-making and overcoming the limitations of traditional deep learning models. Clinical decision-making in Obstetrics and Gynaecology (O&G) is particularly challenging due to the complexity and variability of clinical scenarios. Accurate diagnosis and timely interventions are crucial for managing high-risk pregnancies and improving outcomes. Traditional deep learning models, while powerful, often suffer from issues such as lack of interpretability, data inefficiency, and brittleness when faced with rare or complex cases. NeSyAI addresses these challenges by providing more accurate, interpretable, and trustworthy AI-driven insights, ultimately enhancing patient care and outcomes.

In lung cancer tumor recurrence prediction, clinical data from Electronic Health Records (EHRs) is modeled into knowledge graphs to integrate heterogeneous data sources and facilitate complex relationship analysis. Techniques like ComplEx-N3 leverage these knowledge graphs to capture intricate data relationships, enhancing predictive capabilities. Example-based explanations provide transparency, helping clinicians understand the factors behind predictions and fostering trust in AI systems. This approach not only improves the accuracy of predictions but also ensures that clinicians can confidently rely on AI-driven insights for making informed decisions.

Similarly, the classification of CKD causes using BERT-based models, such as DistilBERT, highlights the potential of natural language processing (NLP) in healthcare. By categorizing clinical notes into conditions like IgA Nephropathy, Diabetes, and Hypertension, these models achieve high precision and recall, particularly for IgA Nephropathy. This enhances the accuracy and efficiency of disease classification, reducing human error and improving patient outcomes. The integration of BERT-based models into clinical workflows can assist healthcare providers in managing and diagnosing chronic kidney disease more effectively, ultimately leading to better patient care and resource utilization.

Furthermore, Large Language Models (LLMs) like ChatGPT have demonstrated significant potential in processing and generating human-like text, which can be invaluable in medical contexts by analyzing vast amounts of data, providing insights, and supporting clinical decision-making. However, LLMs face challenges such as brittleness, lack of explainability, and the need for extensive data. Neurosymbolic AI can mitigate these issues by incorporating structured symbolic reasoning. This approach enhances the interpretability of AI systems and leverages the structured knowledge contained in healthcare knowledge graphs, representing entities and their relationships in a structured form. These knowledge graphs facilitate comprehensive data analytics and support advanced clinical decision-making processes by integrating diverse data sources, supporting clinical decision-making, drug discovery, and public health surveillance.

The use of NeSyAI and knowledge graphs offers promising solutions to the limitations of deep learning and LLMs in healthcare. These technologies can significantly improve medical diagnosis and clinical decision-making processes by enhancing interpretability, data integration, and reasoning capabilities. This is particularly useful for identifying high-risk pre-term pregnancies, where accurate and timely diagnosis is critical. By leveraging both neural networks and symbolic reasoning, NeSyAI addresses the challenges of clinical decision-making in women's health, providing more accurate, interpretable, and trustworthy AI-driven insights, ultimately enhancing patient care and outcomes.

Acknowledgement

This publication has emanated from research conducted with the financial support of Science Foundation Ireland (SFI) under Grant Number SFI/12/RC/2289_P2, co-funded by the European Regional Development Fund.

References

[1] Parveen A, Kannan G. Healthcare transformed: a comprehensive survey of artificial intelligence trends in healthcare industries. Digital Healthcare in Asia and Gulf Region for Healthy Aging and More Inclusive Societies. 2024:395-424.

[2] Drancé M. Neuro-symbolic XAI: Application to drug repurposing for rare diseases. In: International Conference on Database Systems for Advanced Applications. Springer; 2022. p. 539-43.

[3] Lavin A. Neuro-symbolic neurodegenerative disease modeling as probabilistic programmed deep kernels. In: International Workshop on Health Intelligence. Springer; 2021. p. 49-64.

[4] Garcez Ad, Besold TR, De Raedt L, Földiak P, Hitzler P, Icard T, et al. Neural-symbolic learning and reasoning: contributions and challenges. In: 2015 AAAI Spring Symposium Series; 2015. .

[5] Timilsina M, Alsamhi S, Haque R, Judge C, Curry E. Knowledge Graphs, Clinical Trials, Dataspace, and AI: Uniting for Progressive Healthcare Innovation. In: 2023 IEEE International Conference on Big Data (BigData). IEEE; 2023. p. 4997-5006.

[6] Esteva A, Kuprel B, Novoa RA, Ko J, Swetter SM, Blau HM, et al. Dermatologist-level classification of skin cancer with deep neural networks. nature. 2017;542(7639):115-8.
[7] Topol EJ. High-performance medicine: the convergence of human and artificial intelligence. Nature medicine. 2019;25(1):44-56.
[8] Yu C, Liu J, Nemati S, Yin G. Reinforcement learning in healthcare: A survey. ACM Computing Surveys (CSUR). 2021;55(1):1-36.
[9] Timilsina M, Buosi S, Janik A, Minervini P, Costabello L, Torrente M, et al. Machine Learning Survival Models for Relapse Prediction in a Early Stage Lung Cancer Patient. In: 2023 International Joint Conference on Neural Networks (IJCNN). IEEE; 2023. p. 1-8.
[10] Timilsina M, Fey D, Buosi S, Janik A, Costabello L, Carcereny E, et al. Synergy between imputed genetic pathway and clinical information for predicting recurrence in early stage non-small cell lung cancer. Journal of Biomedical Informatics. 2023;144:104424.
[11] Janik A, Torrente M, Costabello L, Calvo V, Walsh B, Camps C, et al. Machine learning–assisted recurrence prediction for patients with early-stage non–small-cell lung cancer. JCO Clinical Cancer Informatics. 2023;7:e2200062.
[12] Trouillon T, Welbl J, Riedel S, Gaussier É, Bouchard G. Complex embeddings for simple link prediction. In: International Conference on Machine Learning (ICML). PMLR; 2016. p. 2071-80.
[13] Garcez Ad, Lamb LC. Neurosymbolic AI: The 3rd wave. Artificial Intelligence Review. 2023:1-20.
[14] Thirunavukarasu AJ, Ting DSJ, Elangovan K, Gutierrez L, Tan TF, Ting DSW. Large language models in medicine. Nature medicine. 2023;29(8):1930-40.
[15] Abu-Salih B, Al-Qurishi M, Alweshah M, Al-Smadi M, Alfayez R, Saadeh H. Healthcare knowledge graph construction: A systematic review of the state-of-the-art, open issues, and opportunities. Journal of Big Data. 2023;10(1):81.
[16] Khan MJ, Ilievski F, Breslin JG, Curry E. A survey of neurosymbolic visual reasoning with scene graphs and common sense knowledge. Neurosymbolic Artificial Intelligence. 2024;(Preprint):1-24.
[17] Bachmann ME, Duta I, Mazey E, Cooke W, Vatish M, Davis Jones G. Exploring the Capabilities of ChatGPT in Women's Health. medRxiv. 2024:2024-02.
[18] Davis Jones G, Cooke W, Vatish M. Identifying high-risk pre-term pregnancies using the fetal heart rate and machine learning. medRxiv. 2024:2024-02.

Subject Index

P. Hitzler et al. (Eds.)
IOS Press, 2025

Author Index

If you are based in the European Union and have safety concerns related to physical Sage products, in compliance with GPSR, please contact our Authorized Representative:

EC REP

International Associates Auditing & Certification Limited
The Black Church, St Mary's Place,
Dublin 7, D07 P4AX Ireland
EUAR@ie.ia-net.com